SECOND EDITION, 2017 UPDATE

INTERMEDIATE ACCOUNTING

REPORTING AND ANALYSIS

James M. Wahlen
Professor of Accounting, James R. Hodge Chair of Excellence
Kelley School of Business, Indiana University

Jefferson P. Jones
Associate Professor
School of Accountancy, Auburn University

Donald P. Pagach
Professor of Accounting
Poole College of Management, North Carolina State University

australia • brazil • japan • korea • mexico • singapore • spain • united kingdom • united states

Intermediate Accounting: Reporting and Analysis, 2E, 2017 update

James M. Wahlen, Jefferson P. Jones and Donald P. Pagach

Vice President, General Manager, Science, Math & Quantitative Business: Balraj Kalsi

Product Director: Mike Schenk

Content Development Manager: Daniel Celenza

Senior Marketing Manager: Robin LeFevre

Production Management, Cover Design update, and Composition: Cenveo Publisher Services

Media Developer: Jessica Robbe

Intellectual Property Analyst: Brittani Morgan

Manufacturing Planner: Doug Wilke

Senior Art Director, 2016 edition: Stacy Shirley

Internal Designer, 2016 edition: Mike Stratton

Cover Image: © Donald McCullough

© 2017, 2016 Cengage Learning®

ALL RIGHTS RESERVED. No part of this work covered by the copyright herein may be reproduced or distributed in any form or by any means, except as permitted by U.S. copyright law, without the prior written permission of the copyright owner.

> For product information and technology assistance, contact us at **Cengage Learning Customer & Sales Support, 1-800-354-9706**
>
> For permission to use material from this text or product, submit all requests online at **www.cengage.com/permissions**
> Further permissions questions can be emailed to
> **permissionrequest@cengage.com**

The authors have drawn on public filings of numerous public companies in developing the materials included in this book. Except as expressly noted by the authors, if at all, no public companies have participated in the development of this book and the inclusion of any company's financial information herein should not be construed as an endorsement of this book by that, or any other, company.

Library of Congress Control Number: 2016938104

Student Edition ISBN: 978-1-337-11661-9

Student LLF Edition ISBN: 978-1-337-11668-8

Cengage Learning
20 Channel Center Street
Boston, MA 02210
USA

Cengage Learning is a leading provider of customized learning solutions with office locations around the globe, including Singapore, the United Kingdom, Australia, Mexico, Brazil, and Japan. Locate your local office at: **www.cengage.com/global**

Cengage Learning products are represented in Canada by Nelson Education, Ltd.

To learn more about Cengage Learning Solutions, visit **www.cengage.com**

Purchase any of our products at your local college store or at our preferred online store **www.cengagebrain.com**

Printed in the United States of America
Print Number: 04   Print Year: 2018

For our students,
With thanks for permitting us to take the journey with you

For Loren Nikolai and John Bazley,
With thanks for allowing us the privilege to carry on their legacy of teaching through this book

For our families, with love,
Debbie, Jessica, Jaymie, Melaney, Parker, Morgan, Elisabeth, Graham, Olivia, and Luke

Jim   Jeff   Don

SET COURSE EXPECTATIONS AND GUIDE STUDENTS TO SUCCESS!

MOTIVATION

Many students come to intermediate accounting with an unrealistic idea of what the course entails. Students are often surprised by both the brisk pace of the course and the necessary amount of time they need to spend outside of class working through homework assignments.

CengageNOWv2 Start-Up Center *NEW!*

The CengageNOWv2 **Start-Up Center** will help students identify what they need to do and where they need to focus in order to be successful with a variety of brand new resources.

What Is Accounting, this section includes an:

- Introduction to Accounting
- Success Strategies

Accounting Review Module, designed to help students refresh their understanding of basic accounting skills, including:

- Accounting equation
- Rules of debits and credits
- Journal entries and posting
- Adjusting entries—accruals and deferrals
- Financial statements
- Time value of money
- And more

NEW **How to Use CengageNOWv2 Module** allows students to focus on learning accounting, not on a particular software system. Quickly familiarize your students with CengageNOWv2 and direct them to all of its built-in student resources.

SEE WHY IT MATTERS!

MOTIVATION

Positive Business-Focused Context

Intermediate Accounting 2e infuses context by using Starbucks as a running case and draws on other identifiable companies to help students understand why accounting information is important to a company and what implications this information will have for financial statement users. Other, highly recognizable companies provide additional context.

A Risky Proposition

In order to determine if they should provide resources to a company, investors and creditors analyze the risk involved. Financial statement information relating to current liabilities and contingent obligations is particularly useful in the analysis of a company's liquidity, financial flexibility, and credit risk. To assess a company's liquidity, which represents the company's ability to meet its short-term obligations, financial statement users will examine the relationship between a company's current assets and its current liabilities. Starbucks's current liabilities, which represent obligations to employees, suppliers, and other short-term creditors, make up approximately 76% of the company's total liabilities as of the end of fiscal year 2013, as shown below.

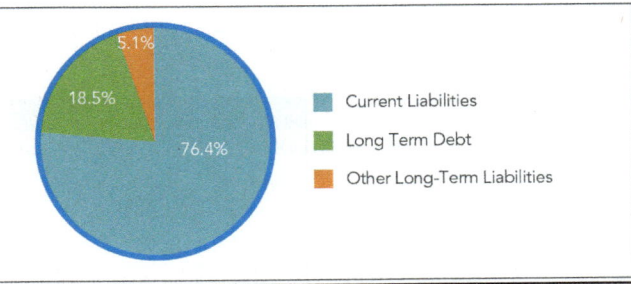

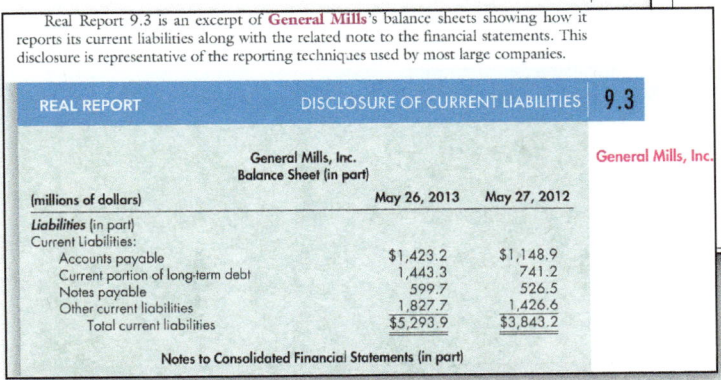

Real Reports

Real Reports allow students to interact with actual annual report excerpts, analyze them, and apply what they have learned by answering the corresponding questions. Students have the ability to practice activities they will encounter in the real world as they sharpen analytical skills.

EXPOSE STUDENTS TO CONCEPTS BEFORE CLASS BEGINS!

MOTIVATION

Students don't want to waste time going over concepts that they have already mastered. With the NEW Adaptive Study Plan, they can focus on learning new topics and fully understanding difficult concepts.

Adaptive Study Plan

The Adaptive Study Plan in CengageNOWv2 is an assignable/gradable study center that adapts to each student's unique needs and provides a remediation pathway to keep students progressing.

The Adaptive Study Plan is assignable/gradable in CengageNOWv2 and available for self-study and review.

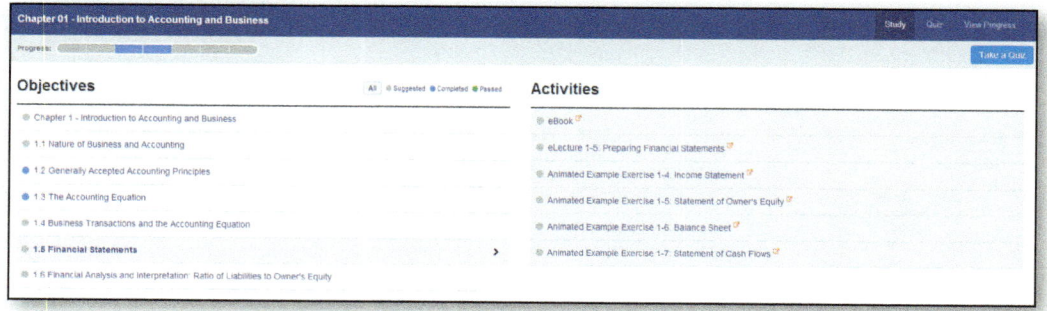

How does it work?

Step 1: Students take a chapter-level quiz consisting of questions that cover both conceptual and procedural aspects of the chapter.

Step 2: Students receive feedback for each answer option explaining why the answer is right or wrong.

Step 3: Based on the quiz results, students are provided a remediation path that includes media assets and algorithmic practice problems to help them improve their understanding of the course material.

Instructors may use prerequisites that require students to achieve mastery in the Adaptive Study Plan before moving on to new material.

> *The new Adaptive Study Plan offers the benefit of customization coupled with remediation.*
> — Jennifer Schneider, professor at University of North Georgia

NEW FEATURES SHOW STUDENTS HOW TO APPLY WHAT THEY LEARN!

MOTIVATION

Video: Tell Me More

Tell Me More activities explain the core concepts of the chapter through an assignable/gradable presentation that is ideal for all class formats—flipped model, online, hybrid, face-to-face.

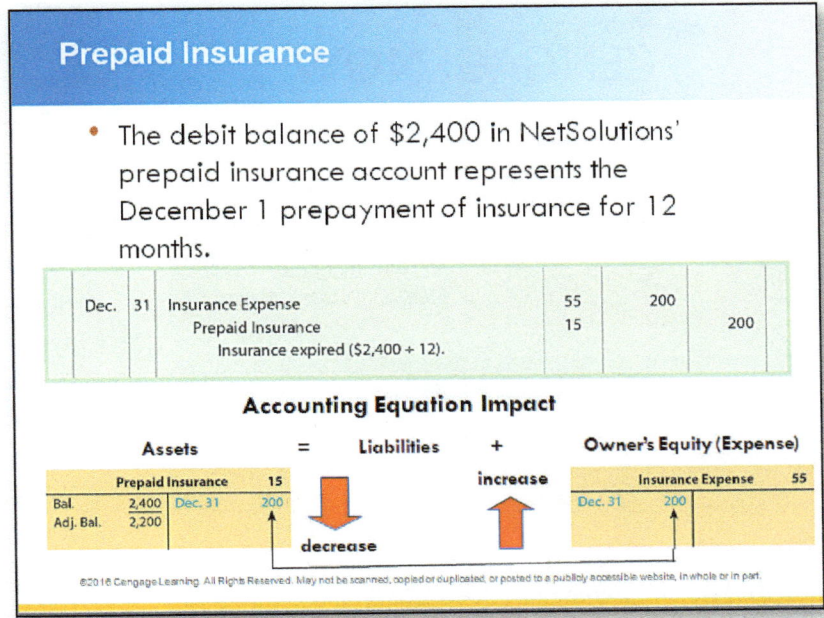

Tell Me More activities for every Learning Objective are assignable/gradable in CengageNOWv2 and available for self-study and review.

The best way to learn accounting is through practice, but students often get stuck when attempting homework assignments on their own.

Video: Show Me How

Created for the most frequently assigned end-of-chapter items, NEW Show Me How problem demonstration videos provide a step-by-step model of a similar problem. Embedded tips and warnings help students avoid common mistakes and pitfalls.

Show Me How videos are linked to assignments in CengageNOWv2 and available for self-study and review.

vii

CLOSE THE GAP BETWEEN HOMEWORK AND EXAM PERFORMANCE!

APPLICATION

> Good tool to make students understand concepts without overly relying on technology's help.
> — Ramesh Narasimhan, professor at Montclair State University

> I like it because it appears to bridge the gap between the homework and my exam.
> — Lawrence Chui, professor at University of St. Thomas

> This will minimize students' complaints about how the exam looks different from the homework format.
> — Rama Ramamurthy, professor at Georgetown University

Many students perform well on homework but struggle when it comes to exams. Now, with the new Blank Sheet of Paper Experience, students must problem-solve on their own, just as they would if taking a test on a blank sheet of paper.

Blank Sheet of Paper Experience

A less-leading Blank Sheet of Paper Experience discourages overreliance on the system.

- The use of drop-down menus and Smart Entry (type-ahead) has been eliminated.
- Students must refer to the Chart of Accounts and decide for themselves what account is impacted.
- The number of accounts in each transaction is not given away.
- Whether the account should be debited or credited is not given away.
- Transactions may be entered in any order (as long as the entries are correct).
- Check My Work Feedback only reports on what students have actually attempted, which prevents students from "guessing" their way through the assignment.

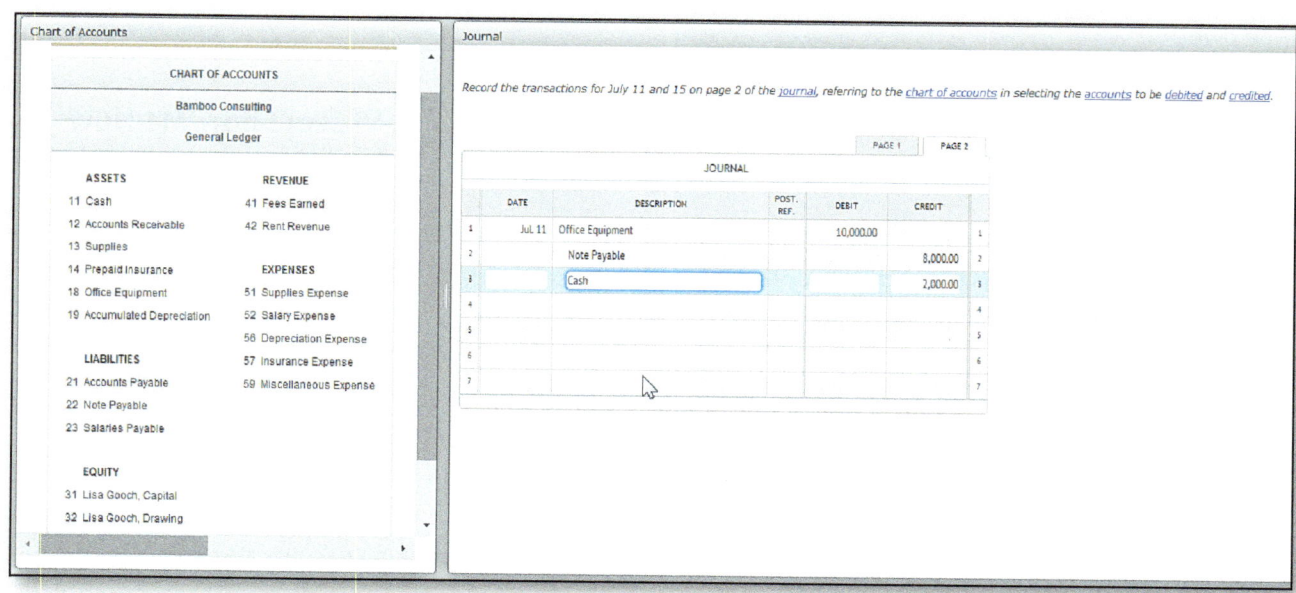

Check it out! Visit **cnowv2demo.cengage.com** for an interactive demo.

HELP STUDENTS MAKE CONNECTIONS AND SEE THE BIG PICTURE!

Homework software should not get in the way of learning. One of the biggest complaints students have about online homework is the scrolling, which prevents students from seeing the big picture and understanding the accounting system. The new Multi-Panel View addresses this issue and enhances student learning.

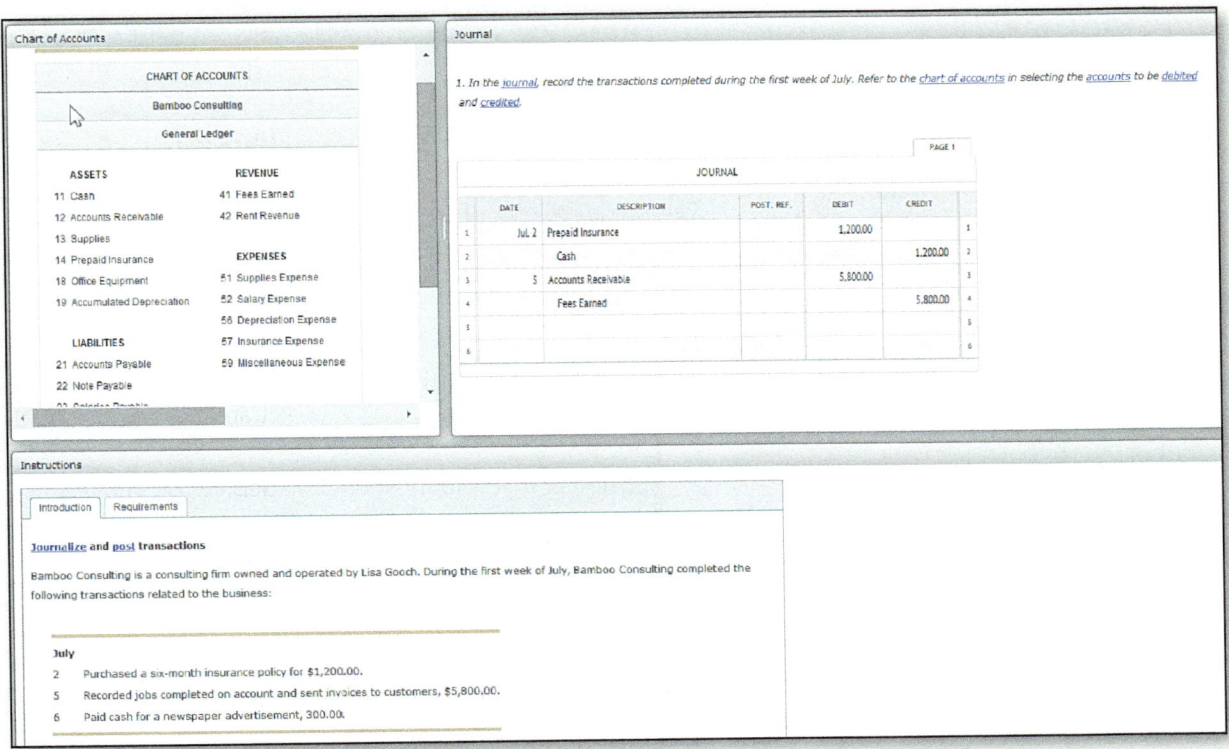

Multi-Panel View NEW!

The NEW Multi-Panel View in CengageNOWv2 enables students to see all the elements of a problem on one screen.

- Students make connections and see the tasks as connected components in the accounting process.
- Dramatically reduced scrolling eliminates student frustration.

With the ability to move and resize journals, ledgers, forms, and financial statements, it is easier to navigate the problem and understand the accounting system.

> *This is just a lot better and less confusing than scrolling up and down. . . . Having it like that would make it much easier—not so much scrolling and it wouldn't be so confusing.*
>
> — Tyler Mason, student at Northern Essex Community College

> *Multi-Panel View makes it much easier for students to see how each piece of the accounting cycle impacts the other pieces. Having it all in one view reduces student frustration and gives them a clearer picture of the complete accounting cycle.*
>
> — Kristen Quinn, professor at Northern Essex Community College

APPLICATION

CLOSE THE GAP BETWEEN HOMEWORK AND EXAM PERFORMANCE!

APPLICATION

Students often complete homework at odd times. And when they use CengageNOWv2, they get help right when they need it.

Adaptive Feedback

Adaptive Feedback in CengageNOWv2 responds to students based upon their unique answers and alerts them to the type of error they have made without giving away the answer.

In addition to groundbreaking, adaptive feedback, CengageNOWv2 continues to provide multiple layers of guidance to keep students on track and progressing.

- **Check My Work Feedback** provides general guidance and hints as students work through homework assignments.
- NEW **Check My Work Feedback** in CengageNOWv2 now only reports on what students have actually attempted, which prevents them from "guessing" their way through assignments.
- **Explanations** are available after the assignment has been submitted and provide a detailed description of how to arrive at the solution.

I like the adaptive feedback. It will reduce a number of errors that cause students to give up.

— Kevin Jones, professor at Drexel University

Excellent! Often learning from feedback is more powerful than learning from the instructor, text, etc.

— Lisa Brown, professor at Indiana Institute of Technology

Check it out! Visit **cnowv2demo.cengage.com** for an interactive demo.

KEEP STUDENTS ON TRACK AND PROGRESSING!

APPLICATION

The best way to learn accounting is through practice, but students often get stuck when attempting homework assignments on their own.

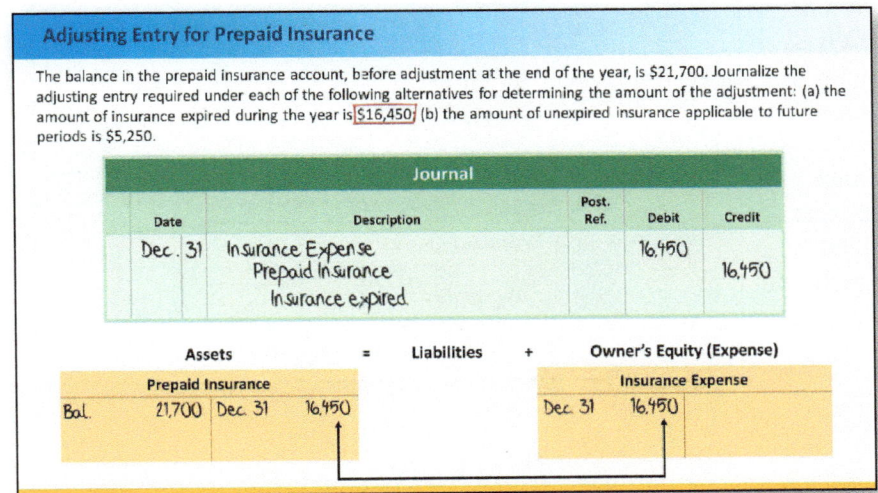

Video: Show Me How *NEW!*

Created for the most frequently assigned end-of-chapter items, NEW Show Me How problem demonstration videos provide a step-by-step model of a similar problem. Embedded tips and warnings help students avoid common mistakes and pitfalls.

Show Me How videos are linked to assignments in CengageNOWv2 and available for self-study and review.

Got It?

A helpful "Got It?" series of questions appears after coverage of each Learning Objectives to confirm students understand the material presented and are ready to continue in the chapter. Students have the opportunity to spend additional time reviewing and mastering a concept before moving ahead. In addition, these questions can now be assigned within CNOWv2 and provide instructors with open ended questions that will allow their students an opportunity to dive deeper into various concepts and topics associated with their Intermediate Accounting course.

GOT IT?

8-10 What is the necessary condition for the retail inventory method to provide valid results?

8-11 Explain the meaning of the following terms: markup, additional markup, markup cancellation, net additional markup, markdown, markdown cancellation, and net markdown.

8-12 Describe how a company computes the cost-to-retail ratio for the following cost flow assumptions: FIFO, average cost, LIFO, and lower of average cost or market. Why do the different methods approximate each cost flow assumption?

8-13 What assumptions are necessary for the lower of cost or market retail inventory method to actually produce an inventory value equal to the lower of average cost or market?

8-14 The retail inventory method indicated an inventory value of $80,000. A physical inventory indicated a value of $70,000. Suggest possible causes of this discrepancy.

Roger CPA Review

Student Access to CPA Exam Questions. With the purchase of this textbook, students receive exclusive access to Roger CPA Review (rogerCPAreview.com). Roger CPA review questions are also available in the Instructor's Resource Center, as well as assignable content in CengageNOW.

HELP STUDENTS GO BEYOND MEMORIZATION TO TRUE UNDERSTANDING!

MASTERY

Review Center

An all-new Review Center at the end of each chapter summarize all major concepts from the chapter at a glance. These timely Review Centers condense and summarize review material for each Learning Objective. These review features also present Key Terms and Key Calculations grouped by Learning Objective for quick review. This at-a-glance resource saves students time and allows them to find chapter highlights in one consistent, easy-to-locate place in each chapter.

Next Level

Next Level requirements encourage students to master advanced thinking skills. These requirements within select end-of-chapter questions require students to go beyond the basic understanding of accounting rules and procedures and develop critical-thinking and decision-making skills. Specific open-ended requirements are now converted into fill-in-the-blank questions in CengageNOW™ and are automatically gradable assignments.

Starbucks Annual Report

The Starbucks continuing thread case integrates actual financial information throughout the book. Students are motivated and engaged by the integration of the real financial information and business strategy of Starbucks in discussions and examples throughout this edition. Specific end-of-chapter applications demonstrate how a wide variety of accounting concepts apply to a single company. In addition, excerpts from their annual report can be found as Appendix A in the back of the text.

ONLINE SOLUTIONS

CengageNOWv2 is a powerful course management and online homework resource that provides control and customization to optimize the student learning experience. Included are many proven resources such as algorithmic activities, test bank, course management tools, reporting and assessment options, and much more.

Recent CengageNOW Enhancements

- **Refreshed Design:** This refreshed look will help you and your students focus easily and quickly on what is important, while maintaining the same functionality that CengageNOW users know and love.
- **Integration with Popular Learning Management Systems:** Single login, deep linking, and grade return! (Check with your local Learning Consultant for more details!)
- **Upload Files Capability:** You can now upload files in CengageNOW for student use—including videos, Excel files, Word files, and more.
- **Email Instructor Feature:** Students can now send you a screenshot of the question they are working on directly through CengageNOW and ask specific questions about where they are stuck.
- **Better Date Management:** When modifying assignment due dates for a whole course, the system will now automatically adjust due dates based on a new start date, making it easier to reuse a course from one term to the next and adjust for snow days.
- **Streamlined Assignment Creation Process:** A simplified and streamlined Assignment Creation process allows instructors to quickly set up and manage assignments from a single page!
- **New Report Options:** New reporting options allow you to get better reports on your students' progress.
- **New Student Registration Process:** When you create a course, a URL will be generated that will automatically take students right into the instructor's course without them having to enter the course key!

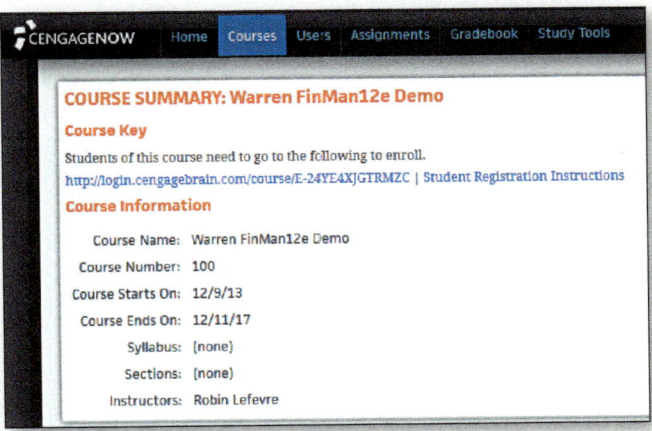
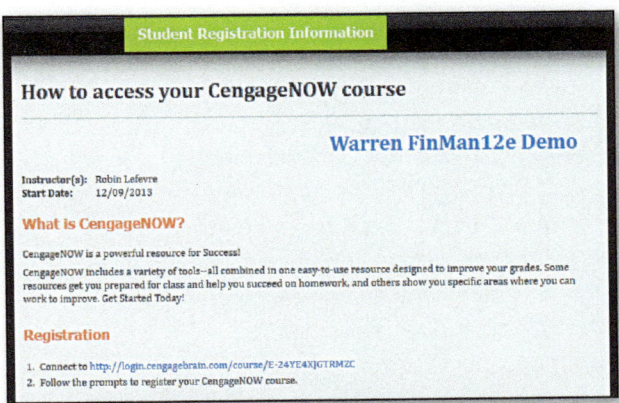

MindTap eReader

The MindTap eReader for Wahlen/Jones/Pagach's *Intermediate Accounting* 2e is the most robust digital reading experience available. Hallmark features include:

- Fully optimized for the iPad.
- Note taking, highlighting, and more.
- Embedded digital media such as Dynamic Exhibits.

The MindTap eReader also features ReadSpeaker®, an online text-to-speech application that vocalizes, or "speech-enables," online educational content. This feature is ideally suited for both instructors and learners who would like to listen to content instead of (or in addition to) reading it.

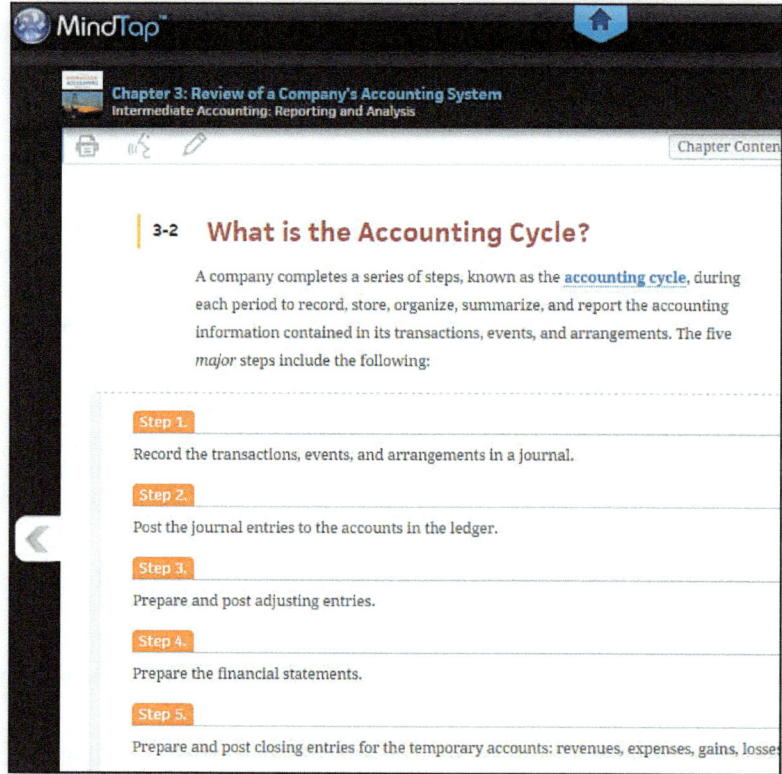

NEW TO THIS EDITION

New! Updated Coverage of Revenue Recognition and Investments, and Starbucks' 2015 Financial Statements

Intermediate Accounting 2e Update is completely updated to address both the new standard for recognizing revenue and the new investments standard. The revenue standard provides a robust framework for addressing revenue recognition issues and will replace almost all existing revenue recognition guidance. The authors have updated and revised all of the material that is impacted by this important new standard. While the most significant changes are seen throughout Chapter 17, Advanced Issues in Revenue Recognition, the authors have updated almost every chapter to incorporate the new standard. The investment standard primarily affects the classification and measurement of minority passive investments in equity securities. Under this standard, all equity investments will generally be measured at fair value with changes in fair value reported through earnings. The effects of this standard have the greatest impact in Chapter 13.

The authors have also updated all of the discussion in each Chapter to include Starbucks' 2015 financial statements, to make accounting come to life for students. In addition to the many new digital assets created for this edition of *Intermediate Accounting*, the textbook content itself has also been thoroughly revised.

In all chapters, the following improvements have been made:

- The new "Got It?" feature is a quick check at the end of each section that allows students to immediately check their comprehension of a topic before moving on.
- At the end of each chapter, a new "Review Center" collects the most important highlights from the chapter in one place, letting students see at a glance the key takeaways, terms, and formulas for each learning objective.

Chapter 1
- Updated discussion of the FASB and IASB efforts toward convergence, including the completed projects and the projects that may not achieve convergence

Chapter 2
- Updated discussion of the FASB's Conceptual Framework

Chapter 3
- More effective presentation of the accounting equation and the double-entry system of accounting
- A more streamlined presentation of the accounting cycle

Chapter 4
- Updated presentation of Starbucks's most recent balance sheets, including balance-sheet-based ratios analysis

Chapter 5
- Updated discussion of the new revenue recognition principles
- Updated discussion of the statement of comprehensive income
- Updated presentation of Starbucks's most recent income statements, including ratios analysis
- Removed discussion of extraordinary items due to its elimination from GAAP as part of the FASB's Simplification Initiative.

Chapter 6
- Updated the sales discounts, trade discounts, and sales returns and allowances discussion (as well as any related end-of-chapter material) for accuracy with the new revenue recognition standard

Chapter 7
- Added new example journal entries for alternative inventory systems (Example 7.1)

Chapter 8
- Updated coverage of the lower of cost or market rule to reflect changes as part of the FASB's Simplification Initiative.

Chapter 9
- New example for recording deposits (as well as additional end-of-chapter material)
- Updated warranty discussion (as well as any related end-of-chapter material) for accuracy with the revenue recognition standard
- New example for recording coupons and cash rebates

Chapter 10
- New Why It Matters feature that compares Verizon with AT&T
- Added new end-of-chapter material related to asset retirement obligations

Chapter 13
- Updated coverage reflect current FASB decisions regarding the classification, measurement, and impairment of investments

Chapter 14
- Updated coverage of debt issuance costs to reflect changes made as part of the FASB's Simplification Initiative.

Chapter 16
- Additional discussion of noncontrolling interests

Chapter 17
- Entirely new coverage of revenue from contracts with customers
- Multiple examples related to each step of revenue recognition
- New end-of-chapter multiple-choice, review exercises, exercises, problems, and cases

Chapter 18
- New chapter organization to better focus on interperiod income tax allocation
- Improved discussion of permanent differences
- Updated coverage of classification of deferred taxes to reflect changes made as part of the FASB's Simplification Initiative.

Chapter 19
- Revised organization to aid understanding of defined benefit pension plans

Chapter 20
- Updated discussion of current FASB lease exposure draft
- Improved organization of chapter examples to improve student learning

Chapter 21
- Revised and improved opening vignette and improved chapter examples
- New organization to improve discussion of the direct and indirect methods

ABOUT THE AUTHORS

**James M. Wahlen,
Indiana University**

James M. Wahlen is the James R. Hodge Chair, Professor of Accounting, Chairman of the Accounting Department, and the former Chairman of the MBA Program at the Kelley School of Business at Indiana University. He received his Ph.D. from the University of Michigan and has served on the faculties of the University of North Carolina at Chapel Hill, the University of Chicago, INSEAD, the University of Washington, and Pacific Lutheran University. Professor Wahlen's teaching and research interests focus on financial accounting, financial statement analysis, and the capital markets. His research investigates earnings quality and earnings management, earnings volatility as an indicator of risk, fair value accounting for financial instruments, accounting for loss reserve estimates by banks and insurers, stock market efficiency with respect to accounting information, and testing the extent to which future stock returns can be predicted with earnings and other financial statement information. His research has been published in a wide array of academic and practitioner journals in accounting and finance. He has had public accounting experience in both Milwaukee and Seattle and is a member of the American Accounting Association. He has received numerous teaching awards during his career. Professor Wahlen is also a coauthor of *Financial Reporting, Financial Statement Analysis, and Valuation: A Strategic Perspective*. In his free time, he loves outdoor sports (biking, hiking, skiing, golf), spending time with his adorable granddaughter, Ailsa, cooking (and, of course, eating), and listening to rock music (especially if it is loud and live).

**Jefferson P. Jones,
Auburn University**

Jefferson P. Jones is an Associate Professor of Accounting in the School of Accountancy at Auburn University. He received his Bachelors in Accounting and Master of Accountancy degrees from Auburn University and his Ph.D. from Florida State University. His research interests focus on financial accounting, specifically investigating the quality of reported accounting information and accounting education. He has published articles in numerous journals, including *Advances in Accounting, Review of Quantitative Finance and Accounting, Issues in Accounting Education, International Journal of Forecasting*, and *The CPA Journal*. Professor Jones has received numerous teaching awards, including the Auburn University Beta Alpha Psi Outstanding Teaching Award (seven times); the Auburn University Outstanding Master of Accountancy Professor Teaching Award (five times), the Auburn University Outstanding Distance Master of Accountancy Teaching Award (two times); and the Auburn University College of Business McCartney Teaching Award. In addition, he has made numerous presentations around the country on research and pedagogical issues. He holds a CPA certificate in the state of Alabama (inactive) and is a member of the American Accounting Association, the American Institute of Certified Public Accountants (AICPA), and the Alabama Society of CPAs (ASCPA). He has had public accounting experience as an auditor for Deloitte & Touche. Professor Jones is also a coauthor of *Cornerstones of Financial Accounting*. He is married, has two children, and enjoys playing golf and watching college football.

**Donald P. Pagach,
North Carolina State University**

Donald P. Pagach is a Professor of Accounting at the Poole College of Management at North Carolina State University. He received his Bachelors in Accounting and Masters of Accountancy degrees from the University of Wisconsin–Madison and his Ph.D. from Florida State University. His research interests focus on financial accounting and enterprise risk management, with a specific focus on forecasting and financial statement analysis. He has published articles in numerous journals, including *Journal of Accounting Research, Contemporary Accounting Research, Journal of Accounting, Auditing and Finance*, and *The CPA Journal*. Professor Pagach has been named a University Outstanding Teacher and has received research awards for his work on Enterprise Risk Management. Previously, Professor Pagach taught at Louisiana State University and has had public accounting experience working for Coopers & Lybrand as an auditor. He holds a CPA certificate in the state of North Carolina and is a member of the American Accounting Association, the American Institute of Certified Public Accountants (AICPA), and the International Accounting Section. Professor Pagach is married, has three children, and enjoys traveling, especially if the trip includes a beach.

ACKNOWLEDGEMENTS

Many individuals provided invaluable assistance in the preparation of this book and we would like to acknowledge their help here.

We would like to thank all of the reviewers and focus group participants whose insights and thoughtful comments helped to shape this and past editions.

Daniel Bayak, *Lehigh University*
Brian Bratten, *University of Kentucky*
Robert Braun, *Southeastern Louisiana University*
Mary Ellen Carter, *Boston College*
Kimberly Charland, *Kansas State University*
Bryan Church, *Georgia Tech*
Janice Cobb, *Texas Christian University*
W. Terry Dancer, *Arkansas State University*
Araya Debessay, *University of Delaware*
Joan DiSalvio, *Fairleigh Dickinson University*
Dana Hollie, *Louisiana State University*
Travis Holt, *University of Tennessee at Chattanooga*
Bambi Hora, *University of Central Oklahoma*
Adam Koch, *University of Virginia*
Jo Lynne Koehn, *University of Central Missouri*
Lisa Koonce, *The University of Texas at Austin*
Joseph Krupka, *Georgia Southwestern State University*
Yvette J. Lazdowski, *Plymouth State University*
Byunghwan Lee, *California State Polytechnic University, Pomona*
Mostafa Maksy, *Kutztown University of Pennsylvania*
Katie Maxwell, *University of Arizona*
Lakshmana Krishna Moorthy, *Rutgers University*
Barbara J. Muller, *Arizona State University*
Ramesh Narasimhan, *Montclair State University*
Derek Oler, *Texas Tech University*
Shailendra Pandit, *University of Illinois at Chicago*
Jeff Paterson, *Florida State University*
Alee Phillips, *University of Kansas*
Catherine Plante, *University of New Hampshire*
Cheryl Prachyl, *University of North Texas at Dallas*
Nathan Slavin, *Hofstra University*
John Smigla, *University of Kentucky*
Greg Sommers, *Southern Methodist University*
Charles Stanley, *Baylor University*
Margaret M. Tanner, *University of Arkansas*
Bruce Wampler, *University of Tennessee at Chattanooga*
Janis Weber, *University of Louisiana at Monroe*
Peter Westort, *University of Wisconsin Oshkosh*
Gail E. Wright, *Stevenson University*
Xiaoli Yuan, *Elizabeth City State University*

We are also indebted to our supplement preparers, whose efforts have contributed to enhancing the overall experience of the instructors and students using this book, and our verifiers, whose work has helped ensure the utmost quality and accuracy of this edition.

David S. Baglia, *Grove City College*
Beth S. Blankers, *Buena Vista University*
Gary R. Bower, *Community College of Rhode Island*
Melodi Bunting, *Edgewood College*
Bruce Caster, *Utica College*
Amy Crouch, *International Business College*
David T. Dearman, *University of Arkansas at Little Rock*
Bruce England, *Massasoit C College and Bridgewater State University*
Drew M. Goodson, *Central Carolina Community College*
Jana Wilson Hosmer, *Blue Ridge Community College*
David M. Karn, *Howard Community College*
Yvette J. Lazdowski, *Plymouth State University*
Patti Little, *Henry Ford Community College*
Steve Ludwig, *Northwest Missouri State University*
Kenneth H. Martin, *Martinique Development Services*
Katie Maxwell, *University of Arizona*
Michelle McFeaters, *Grove City College*
Dr. Rodney R. Michael
Linda D. Miller, *Northeast Community College*
Barbara J. Muller, *Arizona State University*
Kristine N. Palmer
Kristen P. Quinn, *Northern Essex Community College*
Vernon J. Richardson, *University of Arkansas*
Fernando Rodriguez
John J. Sabbagh, *Northern Essex Community College*
Angela H. Sandberg, *Shorter University*
Paul Schloemer, *Ashland University*
Stacie A. Surowiec, *Harford Community College*
Diane L. Tanner, *University of North Florida*
Arthur Wharton, *Towson University*
Amanda Wilson Beck
Alexander Woloszyn Jr., *Binghamton University*

INSTRUCTOR RESOURCES

Solutions Manual

Author-written and carefully verified multiple times to ensure accuracy and consistency with the text, the Solutions Manual contains answers to the Got It? questions, Multiple-Choice questions, Review Exercises, Exercises, Problems, Cases, and Using Codification questions that appear in the text. These solutions help you easily plan, assign, and efficiently grade assignments.

Test Bank *NEW!*

NEW for this edition, Test Bank content is now delivered in an online platform. Cengage Learning Testing Powered by Cognero is a flexible, online system that allows you to:

- Author, edit, and manage test bank content from multiple Cengage Learning solutions
- Create multiple test versions in an instant
- Deliver tests from your LMS, your classroom, or wherever you want

The second edition tests have been completely reviewed, revised, and verified to ensure accuracy.

Companion Website

This robust companion website provides immediate access to a rich array of teaching and learning resources—including PowerPoint slides and Excel Template Solutions. Easily download the instructor resources you need from the password-protected, instructor-only section of the site.

Instructor's Manual Discover new ways to engage your students by utilizing the Instructor's Manual ideas for class discussion, group learning activities, writing exercises, and Internet activities. Moreover, simplify class preparation by reviewing each chapter's Learning Objectives, a detailed Lecture Outline teaching tips regarding a suggested approach to the material, questions students frequently ask in the classroom, lecture aids, and demonstration problems in the Instructor's Manual. Quickly identify the assignments that best align with your course with the called out Relevant Examples and Exhibits.

PowerPoint Slides Bring your lectures to life with slides designed to clarify difficult concepts for your students. The lecture PowerPoints include key terms and definitions, equations, examples, exhibits, and all Example Exercises (with solutions) from the textbook.

Excel Template Solutions Excel Templates are provided for selected long or complicated end-of-chapter exercises and problems to assist the student as they set up and work the problem. Certain cells are coded to display a tip or guidance about what should be entered, which helps students stay on track. Selected problems that can be solved using these templates are designated by an icon in the textbook and are listed in the assignment preparation grid in the Instructor's Manual. The Excel Template Solutions provide answers to these templates.

STUDENT RESOURCES

Roger CPA Review

Student Access to CPA Exam Questions. With the purchase of this textbook, students receive exclusive access to Roger CPA Review (rogerCPAreview.com). Roger CPA review questions are also available in the Instructor's Resource Center, as well as assignable content in CengageNOW.

Website

Designed specifically for your students' accounting needs, this website features Excel Templates, learning games, and flashcards.

- **Excel Templates:** These Excel Templates help students stay on track. If students enter an incorrect answer in certain cells, a red asterisk will appear to let them know something is wrong. Problems that can be solved using these templates are designated by an icon.
- **Crossword Puzzles:** Students can focus on learning the key terms and definitions for each chapter in a different way by completing these crossword puzzles.
- **Flashcards:** Students can prepare with these flashcards, which cover the key terms and definitions they need to know for each chapter.
- **Beat the Clock and Quiz Bowl:** These interactive games are a fun way for students to strengthen their understanding of the key terms used throughout the book.

BRIEF CONTENTS

PART 1 **FINANCIAL REPORTING & STATEMENTS: OBJECTIVES, CONCEPTS, & ANALYSIS**
1. THE DEMAND FOR AND SUPPLY OF FINANCIAL ACCOUNTING INFORMATION 1-1
2. FINANCIAL REPORTING: ITS CONCEPTUAL FRAMEWORK 2-1
3. REVIEW OF A COMPANY'S ACCOUNTING SYSTEM 3-1
4. THE BALANCE SHEET AND THE STATEMENT OF SHAREHOLDERS' EQUITY 4-1
5. THE INCOME STATEMENT AND THE STATEMENT OF CASH FLOWS 5-1

TIME VALUE OF MONEY MODULE M-1

PART 2 **BUSINESS OPERATING ACTIVITIES**
6. CASH AND RECEIVABLES 6-1
7. INVENTORIES: COST MEASUREMENT AND FLOW ASSUMPTIONS 7-1
8. INVENTORIES: SPECIAL VALUATION ISSUES 8-1
9. CURRENT LIABILITIES AND CONTINGENT OBLIGATIONS 9-1

PART 3 **INVESTING ACTIVITIES**
10. PROPERTY, PLANT, AND EQUIPMENT: ACQUISITION AND SUBSEQUENT INVESTMENTS 10-1
11. DEPRECIATION, DEPLETION, IMPAIRMENT, AND DISPOSAL 11-1
12. INTANGIBLES 12-1
13. INVESTMENTS AND LONG-TERM RECEIVABLES 13-1

PART 4 **FINANCING ACTIVITIES**
14. FINANCING LIABILITIES: BONDS AND LONG-TERM NOTES PAYABLE 14-1
15. CONTRIBUTED CAPITAL 15-1
16. RETAINED EARNINGS AND EARNINGS PER SHARE 16-1

PART 5 **SPECIAL TOPICS IN FINANCIAL REPORTING**
17. ADVANCED ISSUES IN REVENUE RECOGNITION 17-1
18. ACCOUNTING FOR INCOME TAXES 18-1
19. ACCOUNTING FOR POSTRETIREMENT BENEFITS 19-1
20. ACCOUNTING FOR LEASES 20-1
21. THE STATEMENT OF CASH FLOWS 21-1
22. ACCOUNTING FOR CHANGES AND ERRORS 22-1

APPENDIX A	Starbucks Corporation's Annual Report (Excerpts)	A-1
APPENDIX B	List of the Official Pronouncements of the AICPA and FASB	B-1
APPENDIX C	List of the Official Pronouncements of the IASB	C-1
APPENDIX D	Brief Guide to Key Differences between IFRS and U.S. GAAP by Chapter	D-1
INDEX		I-1

CONTENTS

PART 1
FINANCIAL REPORTING & STATEMENTS: OBJECTIVES, CONCEPTS, & ANALYSIS

1 THE DEMAND FOR AND SUPPLY OF FINANCIAL ACCOUNTING INFORMATION — 1-1

Introduction — 1-2

Why Does the World Need Financial Accounting Information? — 1-4
- *Business Activities* — 1-4
- *Who Are the Stakeholders? What Do They Need to Know?* — 1-5
- *What Drives Stakeholders' Demand for Accounting Information?* — 1-6
- *What Drives the Demand for Accounting Standards and Independent Audits?* — 1-7

The Supply of Financial Accounting Information — 1-9
- *The Role of the Securities and Exchange Commission (SEC)* — 1-9

The FASB — 1-11
- *The Structure of the FASB* — 1-11
- *FASB Emerging Issues Task Force (EITF)* — 1-11

FASB Accounting Standards Codification — 1-12
- *FASB Pronouncements* — 1-12
- *Codification* — 1-13
- *The FASB's Process and Operating Procedures* — 1-16

The IASB and IFRS — 1-17
- *Convergence of FASB and IASB Accounting Standards* — 1-18
- *The SEC and International Convergence* — 1-19
- *Standard Setting in a Political Environment* — 1-20

What Is the Product? Financial Reporting and the Financial Statements — 1-21
- *Brief Introduction: Starbucks's Business* — 1-22
- *The Balance Sheet: Measuring Financial Position* — 1-22
- *Income Statement: Measuring and Reporting Performance* — 1-25
- *Statement of Cash Flows* — 1-28
- *Statement of Shareholders' Equity* — 1-28
- *Important Information with the Financial Statements* — 1-30

Why Is Accounting Important? The Economic Consequences of Financial Reporting — 1-33
- *Ethics and Integrity in the Accounting Profession* — 1-34

2 FINANCIAL REPORTING: ITS CONCEPTUAL FRAMEWORK — 2-1

What Is the FASB's Conceptual Framework? — 2-2
- *How Do Principles, Concepts, Standards, and Rules Differ?* — 2-3
- *Conceptual Framework: Brief History and Current Status* — 2-5

What Are the Objectives of Financial Reporting? — 2-6
- *Information Useful in Decision Making* — 2-8
- *Types of Useful Information for Investors, Lenders, and Other Creditors* — 2-9

What Qualities Make Accounting Information Useful? — 2-11
- *Qualitative Characteristics* — 2-11
- *Decision Usefulness* — 2-12
- *Enhancing Characteristics* — 2-14

What Are the Most Important Assumptions in Accounting? — 2-16
- *Reporting Entity* — 2-16
- *Going Concern* — 2-18
- *Period of Time* — 2-18
- *Monetary Unit* — 2-19
- *Mixed Attribute Measurement* — 2-19
- *Recognition* — 2-20
- *Accrual Accounting* — 2-20
- *Conservatism* — 2-21

What Is the Financial Reporting Model in the Conceptual Framework? — 2-22

3 REVIEW OF A COMPANY'S ACCOUNTING SYSTEM — 3-1

What Are the Components of an Accounting System? — 3-2
- *Accounting Equation* — 3-3
- *How Business Activities Impact the Accounting Equation* — 3-4
- *Transactions, Events, Arrangements, and Supporting Documents* — 3-5
- *Accounts* — 3-5
- *Financial Statements* — 3-7

What Is the Accounting Cycle? — 3-8

How Do We Record Entries in the General Journal (Step 1)? — 3-9

Illustrating the Accounting Cycle	3-9
How Do We Post to the General Ledger (Step 2)?	**3-13**
Trial Balance	3-14
How Do We Prepare Adjusting Entries (Step 3)?	**3-15**
Deferrals	3-15
Accruals	3-18
Accounting Estimates	3-19
Periodic Inventory	3-21
How Do We Prepare Financial Statements (Step 4)?	**3-23**
Income Statement	3-24
Statement of Shareholders' Equity	3-25
Balance Sheet	3-25
Statement of Cash Flows	3-26
How Do We Prepare Closing Entries (Step 5)?	**3-27**
How Do We Use a Worksheet to Prepare Financial Statements?	**3-29**
What Is the Purpose of Reversing Entries?	**3-31**
Alternative Procedures	3-32
How Do We Use Subsidiary Ledgers and Special Journals?	**3-34**
Subsidiary Ledgers	3-34
Special Journals	3-35
Appendix 3.1: What Is Cash-Basis Accounting?	**3-35**

4 THE BALANCE SHEET AND THE STATEMENT OF SHAREHOLDERS' EQUITY — 4-1

What Is the Purpose of the Balance Sheet?	**4-2**
What Elements Are Recognized on the Balance Sheet?	**4-4**
Assets	4-4
Liabilities	4-5
Shareholders' Equity	4-6
How Are the Elements of a Balance Sheet Measured?	**4-7**
Historical Cost and Adjusted Historical Cost	4-8
Present Value and Adjusted Present Value	4-9
Fair Value	4-10
Current Replacement Cost	4-12
Net Realizable Value	4-13
How Are Items Classified and Reported on the Balance Sheet?	**4-14**
Current Assets	4-16
Long-Term Investments	4-17
Property, Plant, and Equipment	4-17
Intangible Assets	4-18
Other Assets	4-19
Current Liabilities	4-19
Long-Term Liabilities	4-20
Shareholders' Equity	4-21
Contributed Capital	4-22
Earned Capital	4-23
Noncontrolling Interests	4-24
What Is the Statement of Shareholders' Equity?	**4-25**
Additional Balance Sheet Disclosures	**4-26**
Summary of Accounting Policies	4-26
Fair Value and Risk of Financial Instruments	4-27
Loss and Gain Contingencies	4-27
Subsequent Events	4-29
Related Party Transactions	4-31
Comparative Financial Statements	4-31
How Do We Analyze Balance Sheet Information?	**4-32**
Intracompany and Intercompany Comparisons	4-32
Common-Size Analysis	4-33
Rate of Change Analysis	4-33
Ratio Analysis	4-35
Return on Investment	4-36
Return on Common Equity	4-38
Risk and Financial Flexibility Ratios	4-38
Leverage	4-39
Liquidity	4-39
Operating Capability Ratios	4-41
How Does Balance Sheet Classification and Presentation Differ under IFRS versus U.S. GAAP?	**4-45**

5 THE INCOME STATEMENT AND THE STATEMENT OF CASH FLOWS — 5-1

What Are the Purposes of the Income Statement?	**5-2**
What Is Income?	**5-4**
Capital Maintenance Concept	5-4
Comprehensive Income and Net Income	5-5
What Are the Elements of the Income Statement?	**5-6**
Revenues	5-6
Expenses	5-10
Gains and Losses	5-11
What Are the Major Components of the Income Statement?	**5-12**
Single-Step and Multiple-Step Formats	5-13
Sales Revenue	5-15

Cost of Goods Sold	5-15
Operating Expenses	5-16
Other Operating Income Items	5-16
Operating Income (Loss)	5-17
Items Resulting from Financing and Investing Activities	5-17
Unusual and Nonrecurring Gains and Losses	5-17
Pretax Income from Continuing Operations	5-18
Income Tax Expense Related to Continuing Operations	5-18
Income from Continuing Operations	5-19
Net Income Attributable to Noncontrolling Interests	5-19
How Does Net Income Affect Retained Earnings?	5-20
How Do Income Statements Report Results from Discontinued Operations?	**5-21**
Reporting Results of Discontinued Operations	5-21
Determining a Discontinued Operation	5-23
Operating Income (or Loss) of a Discontinued Operation	5-23
Gain or Loss on Sale	5-24
Disclosures	5-26
How Do We Compute and Report Earnings Per Share?	**5-26**
Basic Earnings per Share	5-26
Diluted Earnings per Share	5-27
Disclosures	5-27
How Do Companies Report Comprehensive Income?	**5-28**
U.S. GAAP versus IFRS: Similarities and Differences in Reporting Income	**5-30**
How Do Companies Report the Statement of Cash Flows?	**5-34**
Overview and Uses of the Statement of Cash Flows	5-34
Reporting the Statement of Cash Flows	5-34
Operating Activities: Direct Method	5-37
How Do We Analyze the Information in Income Statements and Cash Flow Statements?	**5-38**
Common-Size and Profit Margin Analysis	5-38
Rate of Change Analysis	5-39
Ratio Analysis	5-40
Earnings Quality and Earnings Management	5-42
Appendix 5.1: Segment and Interim Reporting	**5-43**
Segment Reporting	5-43
Interim Financial Reports	5-47
Preparation and Disclosure of Summarized Interim Financial Data	5-50
TIME VALUE OF MONEY MODULE	**M-1**
What Is the Time Value of Money?	**M-3**
Simple Interest versus Compound Interest	M-4

How Do We Compute the Future Value of a Single Sum?	**M-5**
The Idea	M-5
Formula Approach	M-6
Table Approach	M-7
Application	M-7
How Do We Compute the Present Value of a Single Sum?	**M-9**
The Idea	M-9
Formula and Table Approaches	M-9
Application	M-10
What Are Annuities?	**M-11**
How Do We Compute the Future Value of an Ordinary Annuity?	**M-12**
Formula Approach	M-12
Table Approach	M-13
Applications	M-14
How Do We Compute the Future Value of an Annuity Due?	**M-15**
Table Approach	M-15
How Do We Compute the Present Value of an Ordinary Annuity?	**M-16**
How Do We Compute the Present Value of an Annuity Due?	**M-20**
Formula Approach	M-20
Table Approach	M-22
Application	M-23
How Do We Compute the Present Value of a Deferred Annuity?	**M-24**
Application	M-25
Summary of Present and Future Value Calculations	**M-26**
How Do We Use Present Value Techniques in Financial Reporting?	**M-27**

PART 2
BUSINESS OPERATING ACTIVITIES

6	CASH AND RECEIVABLES	6-1
	What Is Cash?	**6-3**
	Cash and Cash Equivalents	6-4
	Why Do Businesses Need Cash Controls?	**6-5**
	Cash Control Procedures	6-5
	Electronic Payments	6-6
	What Are the Different Types of Receivables?	**6-7**
	Overview of Accounting for Trade Receivables	6-8
	How Are Accounts Receivable Recorded?	**6-8**

Revenue Recognition and Valuation	6-8
Trade Discounts	6-9
Cash (Sales) Discounts	6-9
Sales Returns and Allowances	6-11
How Are Uncollectible Accounts Receivable Estimated?	**6-12**
Allowance Method	6-13
Direct Write-Off Method	6-18
How Do Companies Account for the Financing of Accounts Receivable	**6-20**
Secured Borrowing	6-21
Sale of Accounts Receivable	6-23
Recording the Sale of Accounts Receivable	6-24
Disclosure of Financing Agreements of Accounts Receivable	6-26
How Do Companies Account for Notes Receivable?	**6-27**
Short-Term Interest-Bearing Notes Receivable	6-27
Short-Term Non-Interest-Bearing Notes Receivable	6-28
Sales or Assignments of Notes Receivable	6-28
Notes Receivable Reported at Fair Value	6-30
How Are Receivables Disclosed?	**6-30**
Appendix 6.1: Internal Controls for Cash	**6-34**
Petty Cash	6-34
Bank Reconciliation	6-35

7 INVENTORIES: COST MEASUREMENT AND FLOW ASSUMPTIONS   7-1

How Do Companies Classify Inventory?	**7-3**
Raw Materials Inventory	7-3
Work-in-Process Inventory	7-3
Finished Goods Inventory	7-3
Flow of Inventory Costs	7-3
How Do Companies Report Inventory in Their Financial Statements?	7-5
How Do Companies Keep Track of Inventory?	**7-6**
Perpetual Inventory System	7-6
Periodic Inventory System	7-6
Comparison of Perpetual and Periodic Inventory Systems	7-8
How Do Companies Determine Inventory Quantities?	**7-9**
Goods in Transit	7-9
Consigned Goods	7-9
Product Financing Arrangements	7-9
Bill and Hold Sales	7-11
Purchase Obligations	7-11
How Do Companies Determine Inventory Costs?	**7-12**
Purchase Discounts	7-13

What Are the Different Cost Flow Assumptions?	**7-14**
Specific Identification	7-15
First-In, First-Out (FIFO)	7-16
Average Cost	7-18
Last-In, First-Out (LIFO)	7-19
Comparison of Inventory Cost Flow Assumptions	7-21
What Are the Consequences of Using Alternative Inventory Cost Flow Assumptions?	**7-22**
Income Measurement	7-22
Income Tax Effects	7-23
Liquidation of LIFO Layers	7-24
Earnings Management	7-24
Inventory Valuation	7-26
What Does Management Need to Consider in Selecting an Inventory Cost Flow Assumption?	7-26
What Is the Dollar-Value LIFO Method?	**7-30**
Cost Indexes	7-30
Inventory Pools	7-31
Application of Dollar-Value LIFO	7-31
How Do Companies Disclose Inventory Values and Methods?	**7-33**
LIFO Valuation Allowance (LIFO Reserve)	7-34
Interim Statements Using LIFO	7-35
Inventory Disclosure	7-35

8 INVENTORIES: SPECIAL VALUATION ISSUES   8-1

What Is the Lower of Cost or Market Rule?	**8-2**
Determining Market Value	8-3
Application of the Lower of Cost or Market Rule	8-4
Approaches to Implementing the Lower of Cost or Market Rule	8-6
Recording the Reduction of Inventory to Market	8-7
Reporting Lower of Cost or Market	8-8
Conceptual Evaluation of Lower of Cost or Market	8-9
Can Inventory Be Valued Above Cost?	**8-11**
How Is Inventory Estimated Using the Gross Profit Method?	**8-12**
Evaluation of the Gross Profit Method	8-13
How Is Inventory Estimated Using the Retail Inventory Method?	**8-14**
Retail Inventory Method Terminology	8-15
Application of the Retail Inventory Method	8-16
Additional Adjustments under the Retail Method	8-19
Conceptual Evaluation of the Retail Inventory Method	8-20
What Is the Dollar-Value Retail Method?	**8-21**
What Are the Effects of Inventory Errors?	**8-24**
Appendix 8.1: Application of Lower of Cost or Market in a Periodic Inventory System	**8-25**

9 CURRENT LIABILITIES AND CONTINGENT OBLIGATIONS — 9-1

What Are Liabilities? — 9-3

What Is a Current Liability? — 9-4
Classification and the Operating Cycle or Year — 9-4
Liquidity, Financial Flexibility, and Current Liabilities — 9-5
Classification of Current Liabilities — 9-6
How Are Current Liabilities Valued? — 9-7

How Do You Account for Current Liabilities Based on a Contractual Amount? — 9-8
Trade Accounts Payable — 9-8
Notes Payable — 9-8
Currently Maturing Portion of Long-Term Debt — 9-10
Dividends Payable — 9-12
Refundable Deposits — 9-12
Property Taxes — 9-13

How Do We Account for Current Liabilities with Amounts Determined by Operating Activities? — 9-14
Unearned (Deferred) Revenues — 9-15
Accrued Liabilities — 9-15
Liabilities Related to Compensation — 9-15
Sales and Use Taxes — 9-21
Income Taxes — 9-21

How Do We Account for Contingent Obligations? — 9-22
Loss Contingencies — 9-22
Warranty Obligations — 9-27
Premium, Coupon, and Cash Rebate Obligations — 9-29
Gain Contingencies — 9-31

How Are Current Liabilities and Contingencies Presented in the Financial Statements? — 9-32

PART 3
INVESTING ACTIVITIES

10 PROPERTY, PLANT, AND EQUIPMENT: ACQUISITION AND SUBSEQUENT INVESTMENTS — 10-1

What Are the Characteristics of Property, Plant, and Equipment? — 10-3

How Do We Account for the Acquisition of Property, Plant, and Equipment? — 10-5
Determination of Cost — 10-5
Asset Retirement Obligations — 10-8
Lump-Sum Purchase — 10-9
Deferred (Future) Payments — 10-9
Issuance of Securities — 10-10
Assets Acquired by Donation — 10-10

How Do We Account for Nonmonetary Asset Exchanges? — 10-13
Exception to the General Rule to Use Fair Value for Nonmonetary Exchanges — 10-15

What Is the Cost of Self-Constructed Assets? — 10-16
Overhead Costs — 10-16
Interest during Construction — 10-17

How Do We Account for Expenditures Subsequent to Acquisition? — 10-24
Additions — 10-25
Improvements and Replacements — 10-25
Rearrangement and Moving — 10-26
Repairs and Maintenance — 10-26

Appendix 10.1: Oil and Gas Properties — 10-27

11 DEPRECIATION, DEPLETION, IMPAIRMENT, AND DISPOSAL — 11-1

What Are the Factors Involved in Depreciation? — 11-2
Asset Cost — 11-3
Service Life — 11-3
Residual Value — 11-3
Methods of Cost Allocation — 11-4

What Are the Methods of Cost Allocation? — 11-4
Time-Based Methods — 11-5
Activity Methods — 11-8
Recording Depreciation — 11-9

Conceptual Evaluation of Depreciation Methods — 11-10
Financial Statement Effects — 11-10
Other Factors — 11-11

What Additional Depreciation Methods Exist? — 11-14
Group Depreciation — 11-14
Composite Depreciation — 11-16

How Are Depreciable Assets Disclosed? — 11-18

What Are Some Additional Issues Related to Depreciation? — 11-19
Depreciation for Partial Periods — 11-19
Changes and Corrections of Depreciation — 11-21
Depreciation and Accretion Related to Asset Retirement Obligations — 11-22

How Do We Account for the Impairment of Property, Plant, and Equipment? — 11-23
Impairment of Assets to Be Held and Used — 11-24
Impairment of Assets Held for Sale — 11-26

Conceptual Evaluation of Asset Impairment	11-26
How Do We Account for the Disposal of Property, Plant, and Equipment?	**11-29**
How Is Depletion Recorded?	**11-31**
Appendix 11.1: How Is Depreciation Calculated for Income Tax Purposes?	**11-33**
MACRS Principles	11-34

12 INTANGIBLES — 12-1

How Do We Account for Intangible Assets?	**12-3**
Initial Valuation of Intangible Assets	12-3
Amortization and Impairment of Intangible Assets	12-4
How Do We Account for Research and Development Costs?	**12-7**
In-Process R&D	12-10
Start-Up Costs	12-10
How Are Intangible Assets Disclosed?	**12-11**
Identifiable Intangible Assets	**12-13**
Marketing-Related Intangible Assets	12-14
Customer-Related Intangible Assets	12-14
Artistic-Related Intangible Assets	12-15
Contract-Based Intangible Assets	12-15
Technology-Based Intangible Assets	12-16
How Do We Account For Unidentifiable Intangibles?	**12-19**
Internally Developed Goodwill	12-19
Purchased Goodwill	12-19
Impairment of Goodwill	12-20
Bargain Purchase	12-22

13 INVESTMENTS AND LONG-TERM RECEIVABLES — 13-1

How Are Investments Classified and Reported?	**13-3**
Fair Value Option	13-5
How Are Investments in Held-to-Maturity Securities Measured and Reported?	**13-6**
Recording Initial Cost	13-6
Recognition of Interest Income and Amortization of Bond Premiums and Discounts	13-6
Amortization for Bonds Acquired between Interest Dates	13-9
Sale of a Held-to-Maturity Investment Prior to Maturity	13-9
How Are Investments in Trading Securities Measured and Reported?	**13-10**
Recording the Initial Cost of Trading Securities	13-11
Recording Interest and Dividend Income	13-11
Recognition of Unrealized Holding Gains and Losses	13-12
Realized Gains and Losses on Sales of Trading Securities	13-13
How Are Investments in Available-for-Sale Securities Measured and Reported?	**13-14**
Recording the Initial Cost of Available-for-Sale Securities	13-14
Recording Interest and Dividend Income	13-14
Recognition of Unrealized Holding Gains and Losses	13-15
Realized Gains and Losses on Sales of Available-for-Sale Securities	13-16
Summary and Conceptual Discussion	13-17
How Do We Account for Transfers and Impairments?	**13-19**
Transfers of Investments between Categories	13-19
Impairments	13-21
How Do You Account for Minority Active Investments?	**13-23**
Accounting Procedures	13-24
Special Issues	13-27
How Are Investments Disclosed in the Financial Statements?	**13-29**
What Is the Accounting for Other Types of Investments?	**13-33**
Long-Term Notes Receivable	13-33
Cash Surrender Value of Life Insurance	13-36
Investments in Funds	13-36
Appendix 13.1: Derivative Financial Instruments	**13-37**
Fair Value Hedge	13-38
Cash Flow Hedge	13-42

PART 4
FINANCING ACTIVITIES

14 FINANCING LIABILITIES: BONDS AND LONG-TERM NOTES PAYABLE — 14-1

Why Do Companies Issue Long-Term Financing Liabilities?	**14-2**
What Are the Characteristics of Bonds Payable?	**14-3**
Characteristics of Bonds	14-3
The Bond Issue Process	14-4
How Is the Issue Price of Bonds Payable Computed?	**14-5**
Face Value and Price	14-6
How Is the Issuance of Bonds Payable Recorded?	**14-7**
Bonds Issued between Interest Payment Dates	14-8
How To Amortize Discounts and Premiums	**14-10**
Effective Interest Method	14-10
Bond Interest Schedules—Effective Interest Method	14-12
Straight-Line Method	14-14
Accruing Bond Interest	14-15
Zero-Coupon Bonds	14-16

Debt Issuance Costs	14-16	*Stock Warrants*		15-14
Fair Value Option	14-17	**How Do Companies Account for Noncompensatory Share Purchase Plans?**		**15-17**
How Do We Account for the Extinguishment of Liabilities?	**14-18**	**What Are Share-Based Compensation Plans?**		**15-18**
Bonds Retired at Maturity	14-19	*Overview of Compensatory Share Option Plans*		15-18
Bonds Retired Prior to Maturity	14-19	*How Do We Account for Compensatory Share Option Plans?*		15-19
How Do We Account for Bonds with Equity Characteristics?	**14-20**	*Restricted Share Unit Plans and Share Appreciation Rights*		15-26
Bonds Issued with Detachable Stock Warrants	14-20	*Additional Disclosures*		15-30
Convertible Bonds	14-22	*Conceptual Evaluation*		15-33
How Do We Account for Long-Term Notes Payable?	**14-28**	**What Characteristics Describe Preferred Stock?**		**15-33**
Notes Payable Issued for Cash	14-28	*Preference as to Dividends*		15-34
Notes Payable Exchanged for Cash and Rights or Privileges	14-30	*Cumulative Preferred Stock*		15-34
Notes Payable Exchanged for Property, Goods, or Services	14-31	*Participating Preferred Stock*		15-34
		Convertible Preferred Stock		15-35
Guarantees	14-32	*Preferred Stock with Stock Warrants*		15-36
What Should Be Disclosed for Long-Term Liabilities?	**14-33**	*Callable Preferred Stock*		15-37
		Redeemable Preferred Stock		15-37
Appendix 14.1: Troubled Debt Restructurings	**14-35**	*Preference in Liquidation*		15-38
		Voting Rights		15-38
How Does a Debtor Account for Troubled Debt Restructuring?	14-36	**What Is Treasury Stock and How Is It Accounted For?**		**15-38**
How Does a Creditor Account for Troubled Debt Restructuring?	14-40	*Cost Method*		15-39
Conceptual Evaluation of Accounting for Troubled Debt Restructurings	14-42	**How Is the Contributed Capital Section Structured?**		**15-43**
15 CONTRIBUTED CAPITAL	**15-1**	**16 RETAINED EARNINGS AND EARNINGS PER SHARE**		**16-1**
What Information Does Shareholders' Equity Provide?	**15-2**	**What Comprises Retained Earnings?**		**16-2**
How Are Corporations Organized?	**15-4**	**How Do We Account for Dividends?**		**16-2**
How Are Corporations Classified?	15-4	*Requirements to Distribute Dividends*		16-3
How Are Corporations Formed?	15-4	**What Are the Different Types of Dividends?**		**16-3**
How Is the Capital Structure of a Corporation Defined?	**15-5**	*Cash Dividends*		16-3
		Property Dividends		16-7
Capital Stock and Shareholders' Rights	15-5	*Scrip Dividends*		16-8
Basic Terminology	15-6	*Stock Dividends*		16-9
Legal Capital	15-7	*Stock Splits*		16-12
Additional Paid-in Capital	15-8	*Liquidating Dividends*		16-12
How Do We Account for the Issuance of Capital Stock?	**15-10**	**How Do We Account for Prior Period Adjustments (Restatements)?**		**16-13**
Authorization	15-10	*Restrictions (Appropriations) of Retained Earnings*		16-14
Issuance for Cash	15-10	**How Do Companies Report Changes in Shareholders' Equity?**		**16-15**
Stock Issuance Costs	15-11			
Stock Subscriptions	15-11	*Accumulated Other Comprehensive Income*		16-16
Combined Sales of Stock	15-12	*Statement of Retained Earnings*		16-16
Nonmonetary Issuance of Stock	15-13	*Miscellaneous Changes in Shareholders' Equity*		16-17
Stock Splits	15-13	*Noncontrolling Interest*		16-17

Earnings Per Share	16-20		Disclosure	17-25
How Are Basic Earnings per Share (EPS) Computed?	16-20		What Are the Methods to Account for Long-Term Contracts?	17-26
Numerator Calculations	16-21		Long-Term Contracts	17-26
Denominator Calculations	16-21		How Do We Account for Long-Term	
Components of Earnings per Share	16-24		Contracts over Time?	17-27
When Do Companies Report Diluted Earnings per Share?	16-26	18	ACCOUNTING FOR INCOME TAXES	18-1
			What Are the Accounting Issues Related to Income Taxes?	18-3
Computing Diluted Earnings per Share	16-26		What Are the Basic Issues for Interperiod	
Share Options and Warrants	16-27		Income Tax Allocation?	18-4
Convertible Securities	16-29		Temporary Differences	18-4
Computation of Tentative and Final Diluted Earnings per Share	16-31		Interperiod Income Tax Allocation: Conceptual Issues	18-6
Special Issues Related to Diluted Earnings per Share	16-32		How Are Current and Deferred Taxes Recorded and Reported Under Interperiod Income Tax Allocation?	18-9
Additional Considerations	16-34		Basic Entries	18-9
EPS Disclosure Illustration	16-35		Change in Income Tax Laws or Rates	18-15

PART 5
SPECIAL TOPICS IN FINANCIAL REPORTING

17 ADVANCED ISSUES IN REVENUE RECOGNITION	17-1		How Do We Account for Permanent Differences?	18-16
When Can Companies Recognize Revenue?	17-2		How Do We Account for Operating Loss Carrybacks and Carryforwards?	18-19
The 5-Step Revenue Recognition Model	17-3		Conceptual Issues	18-20
How Do You Identify a Contract with a Customer?	17-5		How Does Intraperiod Income Tax Allocation Affect the Income Statement?	18-27
What Are the Issues in Identifying a Contract?	17-5		How Are Income Tax Items Presented and Disclosed in the Financial Statements?	18-30
How Do You Identify Performance Obligations in a Contract?	17-10		Balance Sheet Presentation	18-30
Upfront Payments	17-11		Financial Statement Disclosures	18-31
Licensing	17-12		What Are Accounting Issues Related to Uncertain Tax Positions?	18-34
Principal—Agent Contract Consideration	17-14			
How Do You Determine the Transaction Price?	17-15	19	ACCOUNTING FOR POSTRETIREMENT BENEFITS	19-1
Time Value of Money	17-15		What Are the Characteristics of Pension Plans?	19-2
Variable Consideration	17-16		What Types of Pensions Plans Are There?	19-3
Noncash Consideration	17-18		How Do Companies Account for Pension Plans?	19-5
Consideration Payable to a Customer	17-18		Accounting for Defined Contribution Plans	19-5
How Do You Allocate the Transaction Price to the Performance Obligations in the Contract?	17-19		How Do Companies Account for Defined Benefit Plans?	19-7
			What Are the Components of Pension Expense?	19-7
			Pension Obligation	19-10
Changes in Transaction Price	17-21		Pension Assets	19-10
When Should You Recognize Revenue?	17-21		Demonstrating Accounting for Defined Benefit Pension Plans	19-19
Methods for Revenue Recognition When Performance Obligations are Satisfied Over Time	17-23		Disclosure	19-26
Contract Costs	17-24		Pension Spreadsheet	19-32
What Are the Required Disclosures for Revenue Recognition?	17-25		What Are the Additional Issues Related to Accounting for Pensions?	19-35
Presentation	17-25			

Conceptual Issues	19-35	
Reporting Issues	19-37	
Technical Issues	19-37	
How Do You Account for Other Postretirement Benefits?	**19-40**	
Conceptual Overview of Other Postretirement Benefits	19-41	
Accounting Principles	19-42	
Net Postretirement Benefit Expense	19-42	
OPRB Liability	19-44	
Attribution Period	19-44	
Differences from Accounting for Pensions	19-44	
OPRB Disclosure	19-45	

20 ACCOUNTING FOR LEASES — 20-1

How Are Leases Classified?	**20-2**
What Are the Advantages of Leasing?	**20-4**
What Are the Advantages and Disadvantages to the Lessee?	20-5
What Are the Advantages and Disadvantages to the Lessor?	20-7
Understanding Leasing	20-7
How Does a Lessee Account for and Report Its Leases?	**20-11**
Contingent Rental Payments by the Lessee—Operating Lease	20-12
Capital Lease Accounting by a Lessee	20-12
Other Lessee Capitalization Issues	20-20
How Does the Lessee Present Lease Cash Flows and Disclose Leases?	**20-22**
Lessee Statement of Cash Flows Presentation	20-22
Disclosure Requirements	20-22
How Does a Lessor Account for and Report a Lease?	**20-23**
Lessor Accounting for an Operating Lease	20-24
Direct Financing Leases (Lessor)	20-25
Initial Direct Costs Involved in a Direct Financing Lease	20-31
Sales-Type Leases (Lessor)	20-31
Initial Direct Costs Involved in a Sales-Type Lease	20-34
Unguaranteed and Guaranteed Residual Values	20-34
How Does the Lessor Present Lease Cash Flows and Disclose Leases?	**20-34**
Lessor Statement of Cash Flow Presentation	20-34
Disclosure Requirements	20-35
Appendix 20.1: Specialized Lease Issues and Changes in Lease Provisions	**20-35**
Sale-Leaseback Transactions	20-35
Real Estate Leases	20-38
Changes in Lease Provisions	20-41

21 THE STATEMENT OF CASH FLOWS — 21-1

What Information Does the Statement of Cash Flows Provide, and How Is It Reported?	**21-2**
What Classifications Are Used in the Statement of Cash Flows?	21-3
Presentation and Content of the Statement of Cash Flows	21-5
What Information Does the Statement of Cash Flows Help Financial Statement Users Understand?	21-6
Cash Inflows and Outflows	21-8
How Are Cash Flows for Operating Activities Reported?	**21-9**
Direct Method	21-10
Indirect Method	21-14
How Is a Statement of Cash Flows Prepared under the Visual Inspection Method?	**21-18**
How Is the Statement of Cash Flows Prepared Using the Spreadsheet Method?	**21-23**
The Spreadsheet Method: A Four-Step Process	21-24
How Are Special Items Accounted for in the Statement of Cash Flows?	**21-33**
Sale of Depreciable Asset	21-33
Retirement of Bonds	21-33
Interest Paid and Income Taxes Paid	21-34
Short- and Long-Term Investments	21-35
Cash Dividends Declared	21-37
Cash Flows for Compensatory Share Option Plans	21-37
Changes in Foreign Currency Exchange Rates	21-39
Appendix 21.1: Prepare the Operating Activities Section under the Direct Method	**21-39**
Visual Inspection—Direct Method	21-40
Spreadsheet Method	21-42

22 ACCOUNTING FOR CHANGES AND ERRORS — 22-1

What Are the Types of Accounting Changes, and How Are They Reported?	**22-3**
Method of Reporting Accounting Changes and Errors	22-3
How Do We Account for a Change in Accounting Principle?	**22-4**
Retrospective Adjustment Method	22-5
Direct and Indirect Effects	22-11
Impracticability of Retrospective Adjustment	22-11
Accounting Changes in Interim Financial Statements	22-12
How Do We Account for a Change in an Accounting Estimate?	**22-12**
A Change in Principle Distinguished from a Change in an Estimate	22-13

How Do We Account for a Change in a Reporting Entity?	**22-15**	APPENDIX B List of the Official Pronouncements of the AICPA and FASB	B-1
How Do We Account for a Correction of an Error?	**22-15**	APPENDIX C List of the Official Pronouncements of the IASB	C-1
Error Analysis	22-19	APPENDIX D Brief Guide to Key Differences between IFRS and U.S. GAAP by Chapter	D-1
Error Correction	22-21		
APPENDIX A Starbucks Corporation's Annual Report (Excerpts)	A-1	INDEX	I-1

PART 1

FINANCIAL REPORTING & STATEMENTS:
Objectives, Concepts, & Analysis

CHAPTER 1
The Demand for and Supply of Financial Accounting Information

CHAPTER 2
Financial Reporting: Its Conceptual Framework

CHAPTER 3
Review of a Company's Accounting System

CHAPTER 4
The Balance Sheet and the Statement of Shareholders' Equity

CHAPTER 5
The Income Statement and the Statement of Cash Flows

Time Value of Money Module

CHAPTER 1

THE DEMAND FOR AND SUPPLY OF FINANCIAL ACCOUNTING INFORMATION

Your Future Is Bright!

As the world of business becomes increasingly international and technologically advanced, you might wonder what the future has in store for the accounting profession. More importantly, as you consider accounting as a major, you might ask what the future holds for **you** upon graduation. Recent evidence suggests that a very exciting future awaits!

Accounting is a profession devoted to helping people by creating and reporting the financial information they need to make good business decisions. Investors and creditors are becoming increasingly sophisticated and global, demanding more relevant and reliable information from companies all over the world. All indications are that future years will present great opportunities for the accounting profession to continue to create tremendous value in the world economy and in local economies. In a recent survey of small business owners, accountants were viewed as among the most trusted business advisers. In addition, many companies are placing increasing importance on accounting skills in their executive training programs, and emphasizing the certified public accountant (CPA) credential in their executive searches.

The ongoing growth in hiring individuals with strong accounting skills is expected to continue. According to data from the Bureau of Labor Statistics,[1] accountants and auditors are expected to experience faster than average

[1] See http://www.bls.gov/ooh/business-and-financial/accountants-and-auditors.htm.

LEARNING OBJECTIVES

After reading this chapter you will be able to

LO 1.1 Understand the forces that drive the demand for financial accounting information in the world economy.

LO 1.2 Understand the forces that determine the supply of accounting information, including the role of the Securities and Exchange Commission (SEC).

LO 1.3 Explain the role of the Financial Accounting Standards Board (FASB) for establishing U.S. generally accepted accounting principles (U.S. GAAP).

LO 1.4 Explain and use the FASB Accounting Standards Codification system, and understand the standard-setting process.

LO 1.5 Explain the role of the International Accounting Standards Board (IASB) in establishing International Financial Reporting Standards (IFRS) and the efforts to try to converge accounting standards between the FASB and the IASB.

LO 1.6 Understand the output of the financial reporting process and the four primary financial statements, as well as the important information reported with financial statements.

LO 1.7 Understand that, because financial accounting information triggers important economic consequences, integrity, and the ability to resolve ethical dilemmas is essential to the accounting profession.

employment growth through 2022, and CPAs should have the best prospects. Employment of accountants and auditors is expected to grow by 13% by 2022, faster than the average for all occupations. This occupation will see a large increase in the number of new jobs, about 166,700 over the decade, and a total of over 500,000 job openings. The overall health of the economy and business growth, changing financial laws and corporate governance regulations, and increased accountability for protecting an organization's stakeholders will drive job growth.

To further support this exciting potential, a recent survey by the American Institute of Certified Public Accountants (AICPA)[2] noted that hiring of accounting graduates by public accounting firms increased by over 40,000 new jobs in 2012 alone. When asked about projections of hiring trends, 89% of all of the firms surveyed expect to hire the same number or more accounting graduates. Further, 97% of the firms surveyed expected to need the same number or more CPAs on staff. These accountants are going to need skills to understand business and accounting in a global context, with expertise in U.S. and international accounting methods.

Various surveys commonly rank public accounting among the top five careers for people who want more pay, more upside career growth potential, and more control over where they are going. Finally, accounting is traditionally one of the top majors on college campuses, in part because accounting is a service profession devoted to helping people. By all indications, accounting skills are very valuable and in high demand, and your future professional career in accounting appears bright!

INTRODUCTION

The accounting profession creates one of the most valuable and essential resources in the world economy—relevant and reliable financial information that people use to make informed decisions about companies. The world economy, which allocates scarce resources and enables productive investments, creates the standard of living that people enjoy. The world economy cannot function effectively or efficiently without useful and credible financial information. Corporations, governments, the capital markets, investors, creditors, banks, suppliers, customers, employees, labor unions, pension funds, regulatory authorities, academic institutions, individuals, and many others rely on financial information to make important economic decisions.

> The role of financial accounting is to identify, measure, record, and report financial information that is relevant and faithfully represents companies to present and potential future stakeholders.

As such, accounting is the "language of business." The objective of this text is to prepare you to be a successful professional accountant with the knowledge and skills necessary to produce this valuable information.

The prior paragraph may sound like it is overstating the importance of accounting—but that is not the case. Every day, around the world, investors, bankers and other lenders, financial analysts, corporate managers, and many others pore through financial accounting information to analyze the profitability, risk, and growth of companies and make informed investing, financing, operating, strategic, and other decisions. The parties that depend on financial accounting information to make important decisions include:

- Investors and analysts commonly use the information to value companies and shares of stock and make buy and sell decisions every day.

[2] See http://www.aicpa.org/InterestAreas/AccountingEducation/NewsAndPublications/Documents/2013-TrendsReport.pdf.

- Bankers and other lenders use the information to assess credit risk and make lending decisions.
- Corporate boards and executives use the information to evaluate the performance of their company and its strategy and the executive management team's success (or lack thereof) in executing the strategy.
- Compensation committees within boards of directors use this information to determine whether corporate managers have achieved certain goals and objectives measured with accounting information (such as sales growth or earnings targets), and then determine whether managers have earned bonuses that depend on achieving those goals.
- Companies evaluate this information to assess the strategies and performance of competitors, to evaluate potential acquisitions of other companies, to evaluate investment opportunities in other countries, and to assess prospective customers, suppliers, and partners.
- Individuals use this information to evaluate companies as potential employers or investment opportunities.
- Because of this widespread interest, the financial media (print, broadcast, and online) provides daily news coverage about companies based on newly released accounting information, such as quarterly or annual earnings announcements.

For these important decisions and many more in the world economy, accounting information plays an essential role.

This text will help you learn the principles, concepts, standards, and methods that the accounting profession uses to produce financial accounting information that is relevant and faithfully represents companies to decision makers. The text will help you understand:

- the conceptual framework of financial reporting;
- the financial reporting process and the financial statements—balance sheets, income statements, statements of cash flows, and statements of shareholders' equity;
- the key elements of financial statements as well as the methods and practices for measuring and reporting them.

The text also prepares you to account for a wide array of very different business activities using U.S. Generally Accepted Accounting Principles (U.S. GAAP) as well as International Financial Reporting Standards (IFRS), which are used in roughly 130 countries. This text will illustrate these methods and principles for you using a variety of real company examples from around the world. In particular, each chapter of the text uses the financial statements of **Starbucks** and various other companies as illustrative cases to help you understand financial statement information and accounting principles and methods under U.S. GAAP. In addition, the text also uses the financial statements of **Nestlé**, **LVMH**, and other international companies to help you understand similarities and differences between IFRS and U.S. GAAP. The text will deepen your understanding of why accounting information is relevant and representationally faithful to many different stakeholders by illustrating how financial statement users use the information you will produce as an accountant. The text will also make you aware of the types of ethical issues you may face as a professional accountant.

The first chapter in the text describes and motivates what we do as accountants, why we do what we do, the financial statement information we produce, and who cares about that information. By focusing on demand for, supply of, content, and economic consequences of accounting information, this chapter gives you an important frame of reference as we work together through all the later chapters of the book. Specifically, this chapter will help you:

- Understand the forces that drive the demand for accounting information. Why does the world need accounting information?
- Introduce the supply of accounting information. How do accountants produce useful information for decision makers?

- Review the information content of the financial statements. What is the output of the accounting production process?
- Appreciate the economic consequences of financial reporting. In what ways does accounting information make a positive difference in the world?

WHY DOES THE WORLD NEED FINANCIAL ACCOUNTING INFORMATION?

LEARNING OBJECTIVE 1.1
Understand the forces that drive the demand for financial accounting information in the world economy.

Companies compete for a wide variety of resources—financial capital, physical and natural resources, intellectual property and technology, new product and service ideas, skilled employees and executives, customers and new sales channels and markets to reach more customers, suppliers that can provide essential production resources, and many others. To compete successfully, companies first develop a business plan, with broad strategic objectives as well as specific tactics. To be profitable, a company's business model should guide its strategy and business activities to be different from that of its rivals, utilizing whatever competitive advantages it might have.

Business Activities

After formulating a strategic plan, the company will typically engage in three sets of activities: *financing*, *investing*, and *operating*. Companies will engage in these activities regularly, some of them daily, throughout the life of the firm.

Financing Activities A company must first engage in **financing activities** to raise the capital it will need to run its operations. The first step in financing is to raise equity capital by attracting investments from business owners, such as common shareholders. These owners invest capital, with no guarantee of repayment or return on their investment. If the company is not profitable, the common shareholders could lose their entire investment. However, if the company is profitable, the common shareholders enjoy dividends and increases in the value of their shares. As owners, common shareholders also typically have control of the company. With votes associated with each common equity share, the shareholders can vote to determine the direction and actions the company will take.

Once equity capital is in place, companies sometimes seek additional financial capital from lenders by issuing bonds in the capital market or taking loans from banks or other credit institutions. Credit capital obligates the company to repay the borrowed funds at some future date and to pay periodic interest payments as a return on the borrowed funds. As such, creditors take less downside risk but enjoy less upside potential than common shareholders. On the upside, profitable companies will simply pay interest and principal as required by the lending agreement. On the downside, an unsuccessful company may default on the loan and perhaps declare bankruptcy. In that unfortunate outcome, the creditors might receive only a partial (or zero) repayment of the loans, depending on the liquidation value (if any) of the company's assets.

Investing Activities Once a company has financial capital, it typically engages in **investing activities** to invest that capital in productive resources that are necessary to operate the business. These resources can include property, plant, and equipment; technology (software and information systems); intellectual property (such as patents or copyrights); legal rights (such as licenses, franchises, or other legal rights); and operating agreements (such as leases, distributorships, or partnerships).

Operating Activities With necessary resources in place, the company can commence day-to-day **operating activities**, producing goods and/or services and selling them to customers. The company will likely hire employees and managers to run the business. It will also likely have to acquire raw materials, supplies, and inventory to produce goods for customers. It may need to establish agreements with suppliers of key materials for production. The company will also need to establish a customer base, sales channels, and markets. The company will have to comply with all applicable laws and regulations governing the business, including paying payroll taxes, property taxes, sales or value-added taxes, import or export duties, and, of course, income taxes.

Who Are the Stakeholders? What Do They Need to Know?

Most companies have many different **stakeholders** (parties with some type of interest in the company): common equity shareholders, banks, creditors, managers and employees, suppliers, customers, labor unions, pension funds, government authorities (tax, regulatory, and legal), local communities, and others. In fact, it is helpful to think of the firm as a legal entity (such as a corporation) that engages in a wide array of explicit and implicit contracts, agreements, arrangements, and transactions with various stakeholders, as illustrated in Exhibit 1.1.

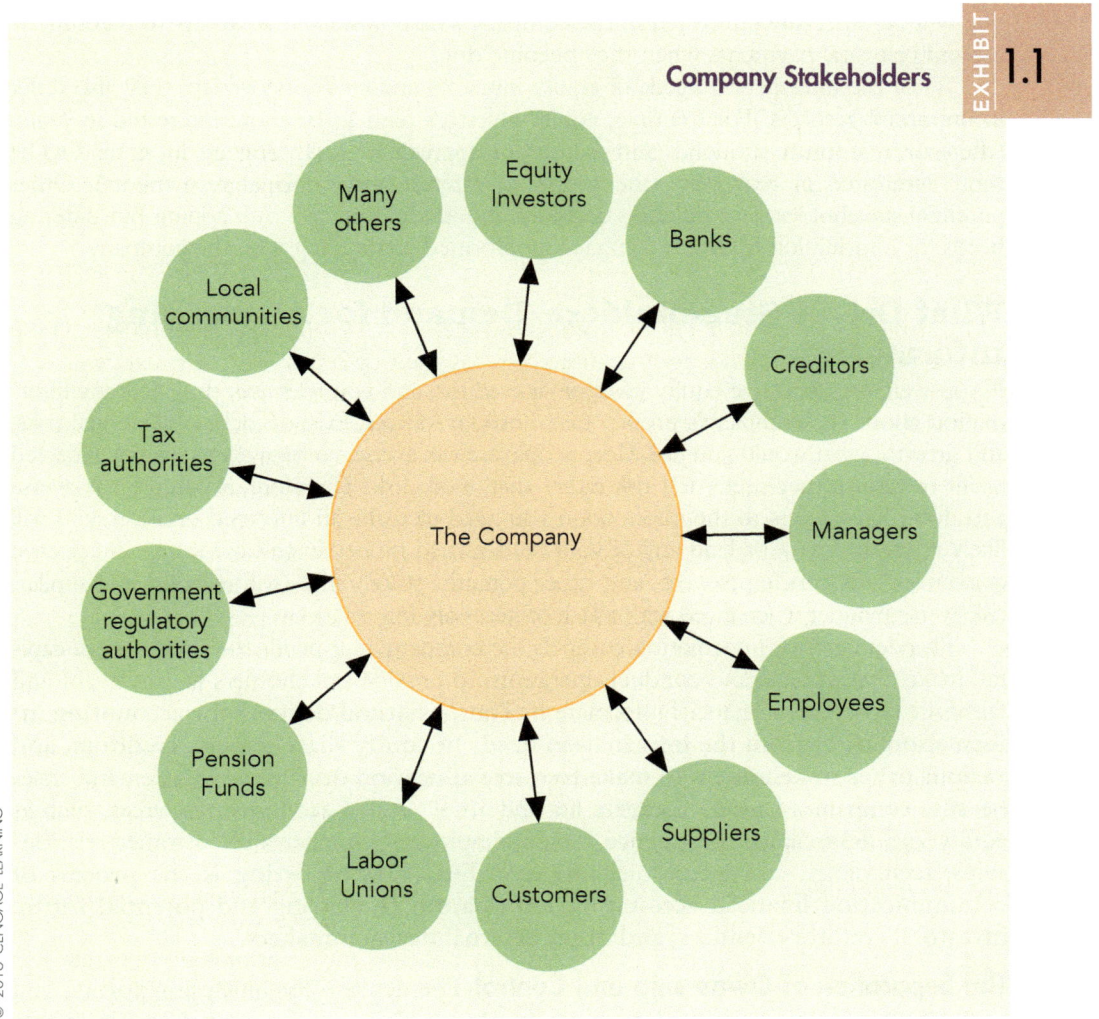

EXHIBIT 1.1 Company Stakeholders

What information does each type of stakeholder need about the company?

Investors Equity investors enjoy the upside profits if the company is successful, but they also bear the bottom-line risk if the company is not successful. As a potential equity investor, what would you like to know about the company in order to make an informed investment decision (e.g., whether or not to invest, how many shares of stock to purchase, and what price to pay)? In addition to knowing about the business model, strategies, and competitive advantages of the company, you might be interested to know what resources the company owns and uses in conducting its operations, right? You may also be very interested to know if the company is generating a profit and positive cash flows, and whether profits and cash flows are growing over time. You should also find out how much debt the company owes, so you can assess the riskiness of the business.

Creditors Creditors face less risk of loss of their investments because they have superior claim in bankruptcy over equity investors, but creditors do not share in the same upside potential as equity investors. If you are a potential creditor, what information will you need to know about the company before you can make an informed decision about whether or not to lend to this company? For example, you will probably want to know how much equity capital the company has in place, so you know how much capital the owners are willing to risk before you will be willing to risk any of your own capital, right? You may also be interested in the resources the company owns to conduct business, as well as any outstanding loans and obligations the company may already have. Finally, you will be especially interested in the company's cash flows and its ability to meet interest and principal payments when they become due.

While the information needs of equity investors and creditors overlap, they also differ in important respects. For example, equity investors tend to be more interested in *profits* (the source of future dividends and share value appreciation), whereas creditors tend to be more interested in *cash flows* (the source of interest and principal repayments). Other potential stakeholders face differing decisions and, therefore, have overlapping but differing needs for information in order to engage in informed contracting with the company.

What Drives Stakeholders' Demand for Accounting Information?

If you were a prospective equity investor or creditor, and you were *not* provided any information about the company's profits, cash flows, resources, existing debt obligations, risks, and growth, what would you do? Most people are risk averse, so for a given level of expected profit or return, they prefer less risk rather than more risk. Therefore, if you are risk averse and don't have access to the information you need to make an informed decision, you will likely refuse to invest or lend any of your hard-earned money in this company. Prospective customers, suppliers, employees, and other potential stakeholders will respond in a similar, risk averse manner when faced with a lack of necessary information.

This demand for information compels the company that needs to raise financial capital, make investments, and conduct operations to provide stakeholders with relevant and faithfully represented financial information. Thus, a **natural demand for accounting information arises from the information needs of equity shareholders, creditors, and various other stakeholders to make resource allocation decisions.** This demand arises because companies have to compete for and attract scarce economic resources, such as equity and debt capital, productive capital, employees, supplier and customer relationships, technology, and intellectual property. **Financial reporting is the process of communicating financial accounting information to existing and potential future investors, creditors, lenders, and other external decision makers.**

The Separation of Ownership and Control The demand for financial reporting and accounting information is further driven by the need to avoid potential problems that can arise because of the separation of ownership and control of a company's resources. In a typical corporation, for example, common equity shareholders and creditors (the principals) provide financial resources by investing in and lending to the company. The company executives, managers, and employees (the **agents**) have been hired to invest those financial resources and run the company's daily business activities on behalf of the investors and creditors. Problems can arise because of the **separation of ownership and control**. The investors and creditors (the **principals**) who have provided financial capital *own* the resources but *are separate from* the executives, managers, and employees (the agents) who have day-to-day *control* of those resources. Exhibit 1.2 illustrates the separation of ownership and control.

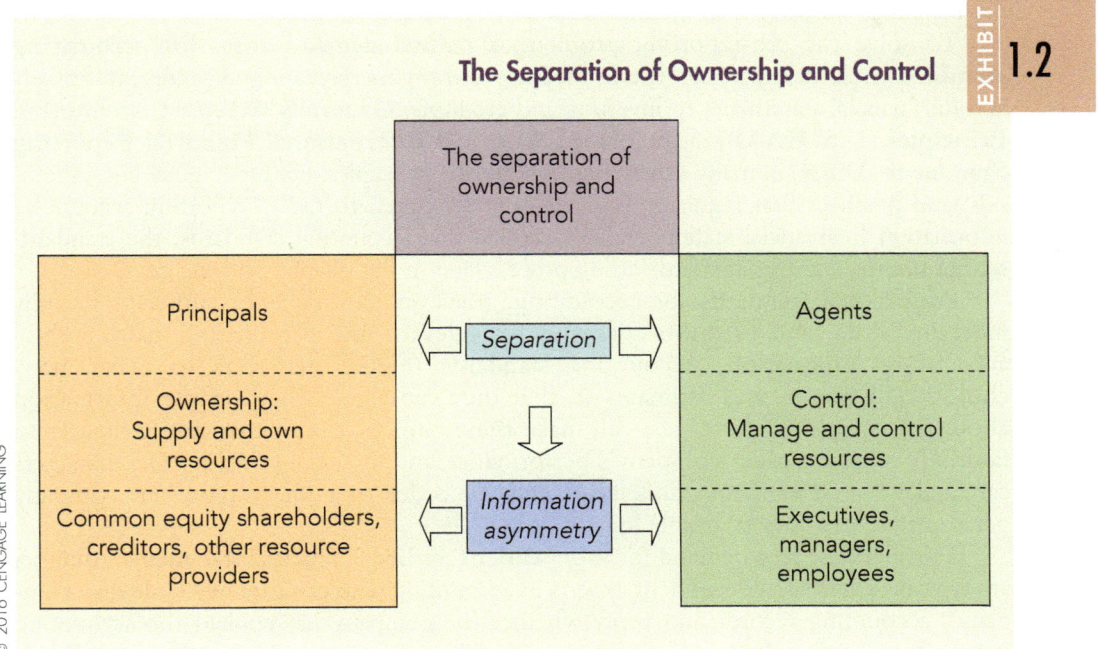

The separation of ownership and control gives rise to **information asymmetry problems**, which simply means problems arising from parties not having the same information. A company's managers usually have a wealth of inside information about the company—what resources the company has invested in; how the sales, profits, and cash flows are shaping up for the year; how the company is spending cash; strategic directions; new products; and so forth. The investors and creditors need but might not have the detailed information the managers have. If investors and creditors do not have the information they need, they might refuse to provide the financial capital the company requires.

How do you bridge this information gap? **The need to bridge the information gap created by the separation of ownership and control also creates the demand for financial accounting information.** Periodic reporting of relevant and representationally faithful financial statement information helps mitigate information asymmetry problems. Financial reporting enables company managers to provide investors and creditors with necessary information to value the company, monitor the company's actions, and enter contracts with many other potential stakeholders. Quarterly and annual reporting of sales and profits, cash flows, financial position, and other relevant financial information provides periodic reports that investors and creditors can use to make resource allocation decisions.

Periodic reporting of financial statements also helps inform investors and creditors about the stewardship of the managers. Financial statements reveal how the managers are using company resources, spending cash, creating revenue growth, controlling expenses, and generating profits. Not surprisingly, company managers can often earn bonuses if they meet certain goals, such as revenue growth targets or earnings targets, in order to align managers' incentives and actions with those preferred by the investors and creditors.

What Drives the Demand for Accounting Standards and Independent Audits?

Investors' and creditors' demands for information will not be entirely satisfied, and problems arising from the separation of ownership and control will not be completely eliminated, based solely on a system of companies self-reporting financial information.

If managers self-report their performance, measuring sales and profits and recognizing assets and liabilities as they wish, the demand for faithfully represented information will not be met because the managers will have incentives to provide biased reports of their performance, showing their actions in the most favorable light.

To solve the self-reporting problem, a natural demand arises for **accounting standards** that managers can use to measure and report relevant and representationally faithful financial statements to investors and creditors. **Generally Accepted Accounting Principles** (**U.S. GAAP**) in the United States and **International Financial Reporting Standards** (**IFRS**) in many other countries are the principles, concepts, guidelines, methods, and practices that regulated companies are required to use in reporting accounting information in financial statements. We discuss the accounting standards, the standard-setting bodies, and the standard-setting process later in this chapter and the next.

Professional standards for accounting, however, are also not sufficient to fully meet investors' and creditors' demand for relevant and representationally faithful accounting information. Accounting standards require managers to make many choices, judgments, and estimates so that they can report their private information about the company.[3] Managers can make these choices, judgments, and estimates to faithfully represent their company's performance and financial position. Or, managers can make biased estimates and judgments, in order to unfairly represent company performance in a very favorable light.

This gives rise to a demand for **independent audits** of financial statements. Auditors are typically external, independent experts in accounting who can carefully evaluate a company's accounting records and verify whether the company has applied the accounting standards and principles fairly and consistently. The auditors provide a statement of their opinion, attesting to whether a set of financial statements has been prepared in accordance with U.S. GAAP or IFRS and whether the statements fairly represent the company. To be useful, auditors must be independent of the company, they must be experts in accounting and auditing methods, and they must tell the truth. As such, if the auditor provides an opinion that the financial statements are fairly presented in accordance with professional standards, then it is a good indication that users can rely on those financial statements. Only then can financial statements meet the demands for useful financial information.

GOT IT?

1-1 What is the role of financial *accounting*? What is the role of financial *reporting*? How do they relate?

1-2 What are the major categories of stakeholders in companies that need financial information?

1-3 Distinguish between investors and creditors as users of financial statements. Why might their decision-making differ? How will those differences affect their information needs?

1-4 What causes problems of information asymmetry? How does financial reporting help solve problems of information asymmetry?

1-5 What drives the demand for financial reporting and financial accounting information?

1-6 What creates the demand for accounting standards and independent audits?

1-7 What are generally accepted accounting principles (GAAP)?

---

[3] For example, company managers are required to determine the company's resources (assets) and obligations (liabilities). Managers must also estimate the useful lives of property and equipment, the collectible value of receivables from customers, the present value of future pension obligations, and many other accounting amounts. Accounting freedom allows managers to share their private information about these elements of the company.

THE SUPPLY OF FINANCIAL ACCOUNTING INFORMATION

LEARNING OBJECTIVE 1.2
Understand the forces that determine the supply of accounting information, including the role of the Securities and Exchange Commission (SEC).

What factors determine the supply of accounting information that companies provide to investors, creditors, and other stakeholders? How do companies choose what to report in their financial statements; how to measure their operating, investing, and financing activities; and what information stakeholders need? The supply of accounting information that companies report is determined primarily by the interactions between two forces:

- authoritative professional accounting standards, such as U.S. GAAP or IFRS, that govern in the company's country of incorporation
- choices, methods, estimates, and judgments that the company must make in order to apply those accounting standards to measure and report their financial statements

In this chapter, we consider the first of these two forces—the accounting standards companies must follow in supplying accounting information to external stakeholders. The remaining chapters present the latter force by describing and demonstrating the many choices, methods, estimates, and judgments that companies must use to apply U.S. GAAP or IFRS to prepare and report financial statements.

As we examine the supply of accounting information, we first describe the role of the Securities and Exchange Commission, the body within the U.S. government with the authority and responsibility to determine acceptable financial accounting standards. We then describe the FASB as the standard-setting body for U.S. companies and the IASB for non-U.S. companies. We also discuss U.S. GAAP and IFRS, the efforts to converge the two sets of standards, and the important influence of social and political forces.

The Role of the Securities and Exchange Commission (SEC)

In most countries, the formal authority to regulate financial reporting and to establish and enforce accounting standards usually rests with the government body responsible for the capital markets and securities trading. The capital markets regulator has governmental authority over accounting standards and financial reporting because of the essential importance of financial accounting information to the protection of investors and the effective and efficient functioning of capital markets. In the United States, this authority rests with the **Securities and Exchange Commission** (**SEC**).[4] **The stated mission of the U.S. Securities and Exchange Commission is to "protect investors, maintain fair, orderly, and efficient markets, and facilitate capital formation."**

The U.S. Congress created the SEC to administer the Securities Act of 1933 and the Securities Exchange Act of 1934. Under these Acts, **the SEC has the legal authority to prescribe accounting principles and reporting practices for all corporations issuing publicly traded securities within the U.S. capital markets**. Roughly 17,000 corporations are subject to the SEC's authority. This authority is very broad, encompassing *all* companies that publicly issue and list their securities (such as stocks or bonds) on the U.S. capital markets, whether the companies are U.S. corporations (such as **The Coca-Cola Company**, **Microsoft**, and **Google**) or corporations of other countries (such as **Nestlé** and **Toyota**).

The U.S. capital markets, such as the New York Stock Exchange (NYSE) and the NASDAQ Stock Market, comprise the largest, most active, and most efficient markets for financial securities in the world. As such, these markets enable companies from around the world to raise capital at a relatively low cost and attract investors and creditors from all over the globe. Literally, millions of trades occur and trillions of dollars of capital change hands through these markets each day. Therefore, the SEC's authority

---
[4] See http://www.sec.gov for more information about the SEC.

and impact within the global capital markets is huge, extending far beyond the U.S. borders. The SEC has, by far, the largest regulatory authority and responsibility for companies, investors, creditors, and capital markets in the world.

The SEC has mandated that the information communicated to external users in financial reporting must be based on professionally established accounting principles, such as GAAP for U.S companies and IFRS for non-U.S. companies. **Professionally established accounting principles and standards, such as U.S. GAAP and IFRS, establish the rules, guidelines, procedures, and practices that listed companies are required to use in recording and reporting the accounting information in audited financial statements.**

The SEC's Reporting Requirements The Securities Act of 1933 requires each company offering securities (shares of stock, bonds, or other securities) for sale to the public in the primary and secondary markets to file a registration statement (known as Form S-1).[5] The Securities Exchange Act of 1934 established extensive reporting requirements for listed companies.[6] Among the most commonly required reports are:

- **Form 10-K.** An extensive annual report, including financial statements
- **Form 10-Q.** An extensive quarterly report, including financial statements
- **Form 20-F.** An extensive annual report, including financial statements, from non-U.S. companies
- **Form 8-K.** A report used to describe significant events that have affected or may affect the company
- **Proxy Statement.** A report used when management requests the right to vote through proxies for shareholders at shareholders' meetings

The SEC requires registered companies to file these forms electronically. These forms can be downloaded from the SEC's Electronic Data Gathering Analysis and Retrieval System (known as EDGAR).[7]

The SEC's Authority over Accounting Standards and Financial Reporting Although the SEC frequently enforces its regulations on companies, exchanges, and investors, the SEC seldom uses its authority to establish accounting standards. Instead, the SEC delegates that authority to private standard-setting bodies within the accounting profession, such as the **Financial Accounting Standards Board (FASB)** for establishing GAAP for U.S. companies and the **International Accounting Standards Board (IASB)** for establishing IFRS for companies from other countries. The SEC monitors closely the standards being developed by these standard setters.

The SEC exercises its most direct impact on accounting standards through its input and informal approval (or rejection) of standards that have been proposed but not yet issued. While the SEC has the authority to decide what constitutes "generally accepted accounting principles," it commonly exercises this authority through persuasion rather than edict. The SEC has endorsed the concept of "substantial authoritative support" by asserting that "principles, standards, and practices promulgated by the FASB will be considered by the Commission as having substantial authoritative support, and those contrary to such FASB promulgations will be considered to have no such support." The result of this position has been to allow accounting principles to be formulated in the private sector rather than by the government.

---

[5] Corporations can raise capital by issuing common stock or bonds, either through public offerings or through private placements. Public offerings involve the sale of securities to the general public through capital markets such as the NYSE. Private placements involve the direct sale of securities to a few private investors. After the initial public offering of securities in the capital markets, these corporations are called *publicly held* (or *publicly traded* or *listed*) companies.

[6] The SEC establishes the specific requirements for the information contained within these required reports. It issues reporting guidelines in its *Regulation S-X, Financial Reporting Releases,* and *Staff Accounting Bulletins* for companies that file with the SEC.

[7] See http://www.sec.gov/edgar.shtml.

> **GOT IT?**
>
> **1-8** What are the two primary forces determining the supply of accounting information?
>
> **1-9** What is the role of the SEC in financial reporting?

THE FASB

> **LEARNING OBJECTIVE 1.3**
>
> Explain the role of the Financial Accounting Standards Board (FASB) for establishing U.S. generally accepted accounting principles (U.S. GAAP).

Accounting standard setting began in the United States in 1938 when the AICPA formed the Committee on Accounting Procedure (CAP), which issued Accounting Research Bulletins (ARBs) to establish acceptable accounting procedures. In 1959, the AICPA replaced the CAP by forming the Accounting Principles Board (APB), which issued pronouncements called Accounting Principles Board Opinions. In 1973, the AICPA phased out the APB and replaced it with the **Financial Accounting Standards Board** (**FASB**). However, the *ARBs* and *APB Opinions* remain sources of GAAP unless they have been specifically superseded or amended by the FASB.

The Structure of the FASB

There are seven board members of the FASB. Board members are full-time employees with no other organizational ties. They represent a wide cross-section of interests (financial statement preparers, auditors, users, and academics). Each Board member is required to have a knowledge of and experience in accounting, finance, business, and accounting education and research; high intelligence, integrity, and discipline; and a concern for the public interest regarding investing, financial accounting, and financial reporting. The FASB is responsible for identifying financial accounting issues, conducting research to address these issues, and resolving them by issuing new accounting standards. The FASB is supported by a full-time professional research and technical staff that conducts research, communicates with constituents, and drafts preliminary findings. The full-time administrative staff assists the FASB by handling library, publications, personnel, and other activities. Exhibit 1.3 shows the current structure of the FASB.

The Financial Accounting Foundation (FAF) is the parent organization of the FASB. It is governed by a 14- to 18-member Board of Trustees appointed from the memberships of eight organizations interested in the establishment of accounting principles.[8] The primary responsibilities of the FAF are to oversee the effectiveness and efficiency of the standard-setting process and to appoint the members of the FASB. The FAF also appoints and oversees the Financial Accounting Standards Advisory Council as well as the Private Company Council, both of which provide advisory input to the FASB on standard-setting issues.

FASB Emerging Issues Task Force (EITF)

The FASB established the **Emerging Issues Task Force** (**EITF**) in 1984 as a response to the need for timely guidance on new, specific accounting issues. Members of the EITF include technical experts from all the major CPA firms and representatives from smaller CPA firms and from industry. These individuals are knowledgeable in accounting and financial reporting and are in positions to be aware of emerging problems. The Chief Accountant of the SEC also participates in EITF meetings. The primary objectives of the EITF are:

- to identify significant emerging accounting issues (i.e., unique transactions and accounting problems) that it feels the FASB should address.
- to develop *consensus positions* on the implementation issues involving the application of standards. In some cases, these consensus positions may be viewed as the "best available guidance" on GAAP, particularly as they relate to new accounting issues.

---

[8] These organizations are the AICPA, Financial Executives International, Institute of Management Accountants, CFA Institute, American Accounting Association, Securities Industry and Financial Markets Association, Government Finance Officers Association, and National Association of State Auditors, Comptrollers, and Treasurers.

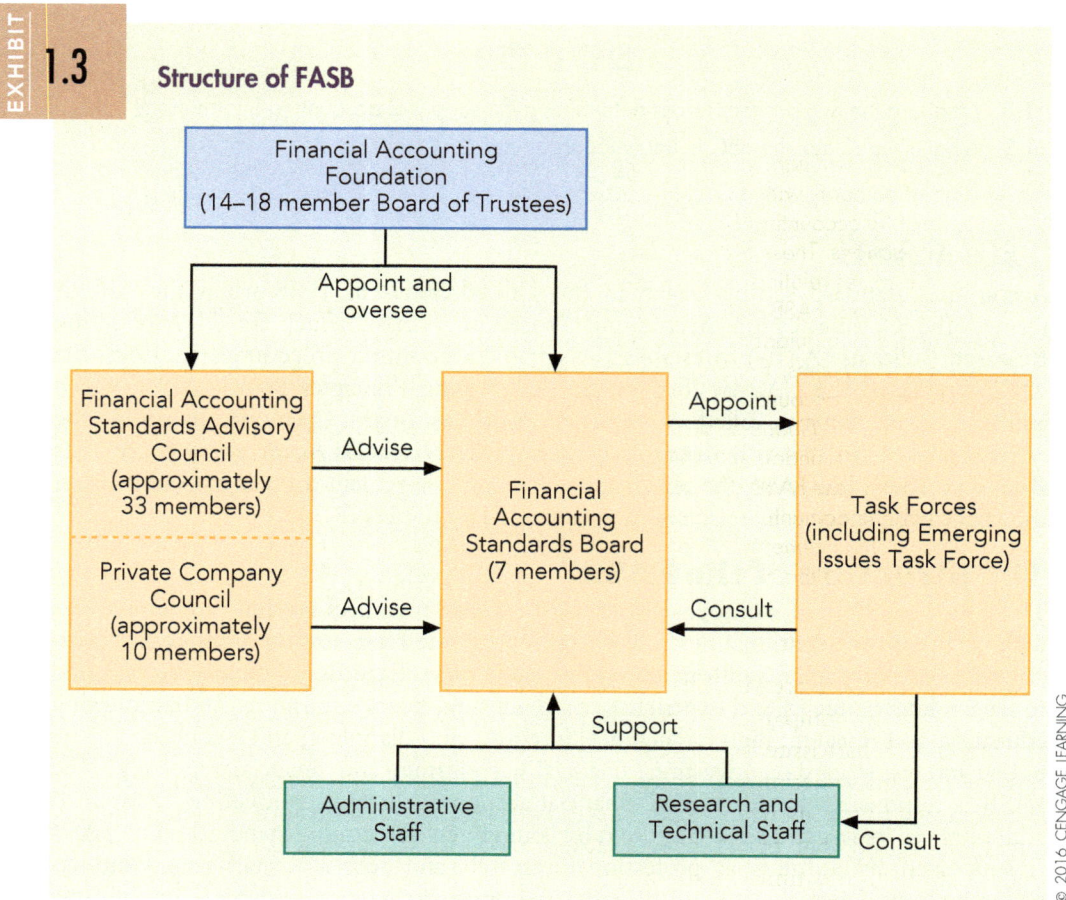

EXHIBIT 1.3 Structure of FASB

GOT IT?

1-10 What is the role of the FASB in financial reporting?

1-11 What role does the ETF play in assisting the FASB with standard setting?

LEARNING OBJECTIVE 1.4

Explain and use the FASB Accounting Standards Codification system, and understand the standard-setting process.

FASB ACCOUNTING STANDARDS CODIFICATION

GAAP has been formed over many years and contains standards developed by many different accounting policy-making bodies, particularly the FASB and the SEC. Until mid-2009, the accounting standards issued by these organizations were located in hundreds of different documents (called "pronouncements").

FASB Pronouncements

Prior to 2009, the FASB issued several types of pronouncements which had different levels of authority. Exhibit 1.4 provides a list of the types of pronouncements by the FASB that comprised GAAP.[9] The types of pronouncements are listed in descending order of the relative weight of authority they had within GAAP. For example, Statements of Financial Accounting Standards had the highest-level authority, followed by Interpretations, and so on. Although the FASB no longer issues these types of pronouncements, it

---

[9] "The Hierarchy of Generally Accepted Accounting Principles," *FASB Statement of Financial Accounting Standards 162* (Norwalk, CT: FASB, 2008).

> **EXHIBIT 1.4 Historical Types of FASB Pronouncements**
>
> 1. *Statements of Financial Accounting Standards.* These pronouncements carried the highest authority within GAAP, establishing the methods and procedures required on specific accounting issues.
> 2. *Interpretations.* These pronouncements refined GAAP by clarifying conflicting or unclear issues relating to previously issued standards.
> 3. *Staff Positions.* FASB staff issued pronouncements to provide more timely and consistent application guidance and to make narrow and limited revisions of standards.
> 4. *Technical Bulletins.* FASB staff issued these pronouncements to clarify, explain, or elaborate on accounting and reporting problems related to specific standards.
> 5. *Statements of Financial Accounting Concepts.* These pronouncements establish a theoretical foundation for financial accounting and reporting standards. They are the output of the FASB's "Conceptual Framework" project (discussed in Chapter 2). They are fundamental principles that guide the development of GAAP.
> 6. *Other Pronouncements.* On a major topic, the FASB staff also may issue a *Guide for Implementation,* in the form of questions and answers.

is important that you are familiar with them because they are still cited in accounting literature and many companies still refer to them to explain how they applied GAAP.

The FASB had issued over 2,000 pronouncements, many of which were lengthy, hard to use, and sometimes conflicting. Even though the FASB established an authoritative hierarchy to specify which types of standards had the greatest authority, accountants sometimes found that the standards lacked a consistent and logical structure, which made it difficult and time-consuming for them to determine the "right" answer to an accounting issue. To rectify these problems, the FASB conducted a major project that resulted in the *FASB Accounting Standards Codification*™.

Codification

The **FASB Accounting Standards Codification** (or, simply, the **Codification**) is an electronic database that integrates and topically organizes U.S. GAAP into one coherent body of literature.[10] Over 200 people worked on the project team from 2004 through mid-2009 to incorporate the more than 2,000 original pronouncements into this database. The Codification became effective on July 1, 2009. The FASB developed the Codification to achieve three goals:

- Simplify user access by organizing and categorizing (codifying) all authoritative U.S. GAAP in one database.
- Ensure the codified content accurately represented all authoritative U.S. GAAP.
- Create a codification research system that is up to date, including the most recently updated standards.

The FASB Accounting Standards Codification is now the *only* source of authoritative GAAP for U.S. companies to determine how to record their transactions, events, or circumstances, and how to report the results in their financial statements.[11] The Codification does not change GAAP. However, in contrast to the hierarchy of GAAP that preceded the Codification, all GAAP in the Codification has an equal level of authority.

---

[10] The Codification is at https://asc.fasb.org. You may also access the Codification at http://aaahq.org/asclogin.cfm if your institution participates in the American Accounting Association's academic access initiative. Many FASB documents may be downloaded for free from the FASB web site (Http://www.fasb.org).

[11] FASB ASC 105-10-05: Generally Accepted Accounting Principles: Overall: Overview and Background. Exceptions are the rules and interpretive releases of the SEC, which are sources of authoritative GAAP for publicly traded companies that are required to file their financial statements with the SEC. For convenience, the Codification includes selected portions of GAAP issued by the SEC for publicly traded companies. The Codification does not contain all the SEC's rules and regulations that constitute GAAP.

The framework of the Codification contains six levels, which are increasingly more specific: (1) Areas, (2) Topics, (3) Subtopics, (4) Sections, (5) Subsections, and (6) Paragraphs.[12] The **Areas** are listed on the left side of the home page and are links to nine broad and general accounting subjects: *General Principles, Presentation, Assets, Liabilities, Equity, Revenue, Expenses, Broad Transactions,* and *Industry,* along with a *Master Glossary* link and a "*Go To*" box for users familiar with the Codification numbering system, as shown in Exhibit 1.5. The home page also has a "*Search*" box at the top.

EXHIBIT 1.5 **FASB Accounting Standards Codification Web Page**

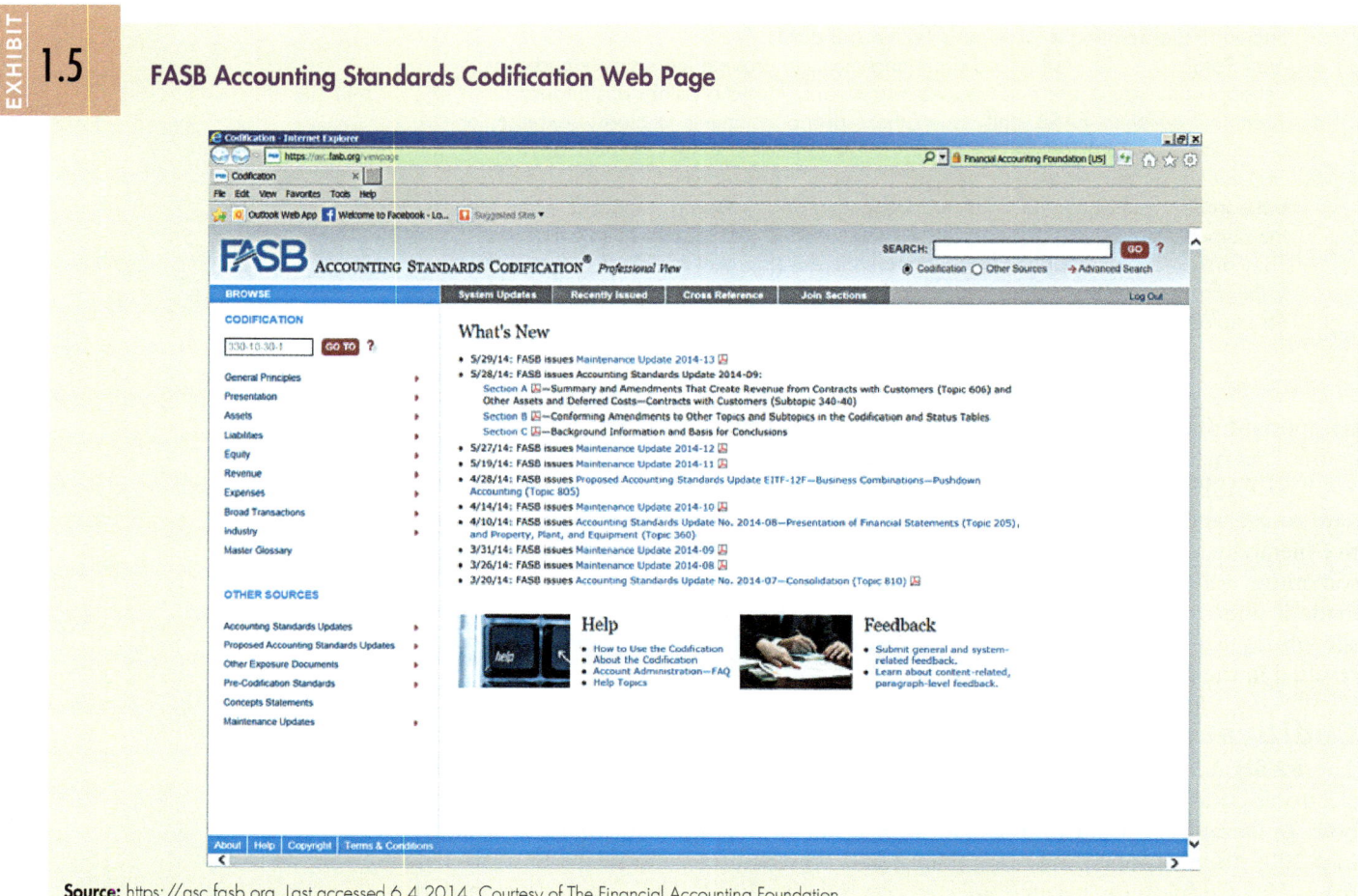

Source: https://asc.fasb.org. Last accessed 6.4.2014. Courtesy of The Financial Accounting Foundation.

The Topics, Subtopics, Sections, Subsections, and Paragraphs are descending levels within the Codification, and each item in each level is numbered for reference and search purposes.[13]

- **Topics** involve a collection of related guidance on a particular subject area (e.g., Cash and Cash Equivalents, Receivables, Investments, Inventory, and various others within the Assets area).
- **Subtopics** are subsets of a Topic and generally are distinguished by type or by scope (e.g., under the Investments Topic, there are Subtopics for different types of investments).
- **Sections** characterize the nature of the content in a Subtopic (e.g., Scope, Recognition, Measurement, and Disclosure).

---

[12] This section assumes that users have access to the professional version. Users of the basic version will note some differences in functionality and presentation.
[13] The following discussion is a summary of the FASB's document, "About the Codification" (version 4.9).

- **Subsections**, if necessary, refine and break down Sections into narrower and more specific items. If a Subsection is necessary, it is *not* numbered but does include the Paragraphs that contain the guidance that constitutes GAAP.
- **Paragraphs** contain the specific guidance that constitutes GAAP.

Exhibit 1.6 illustrates the hierarchical relationships between Topics, Subtopics, Sections, and Subsections.

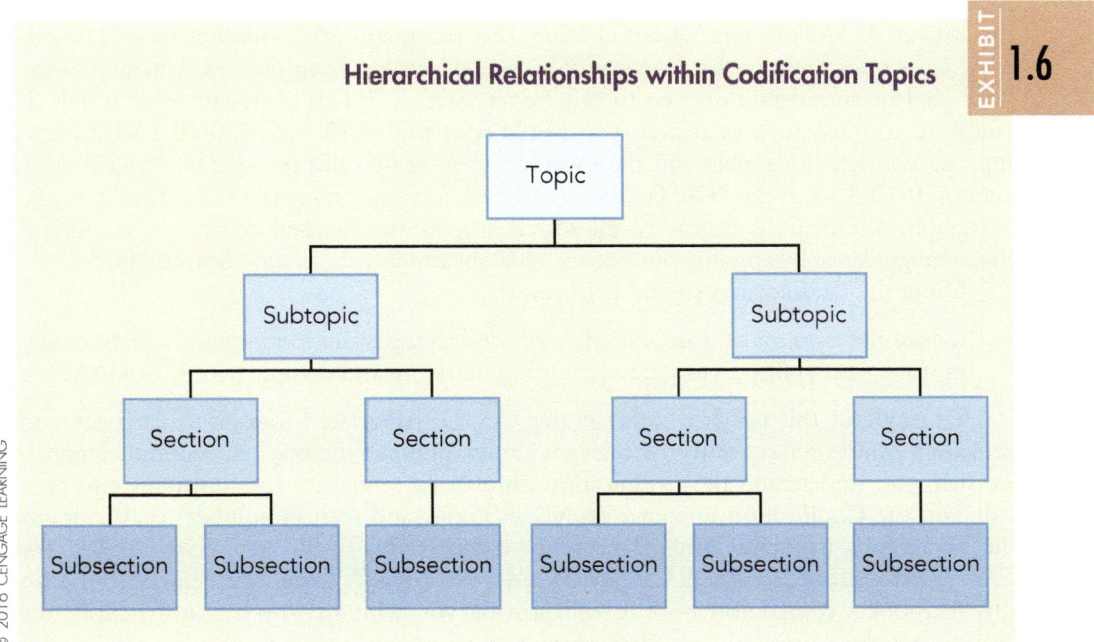

Using the Codification Suppose you need to determine how a company should measure the value of inventory. Exhibit 1.7 shows the steps to find the answer in the Codification, as well as the reference numbers. You may want to go to the Codification web site and complete the steps as we discuss them.

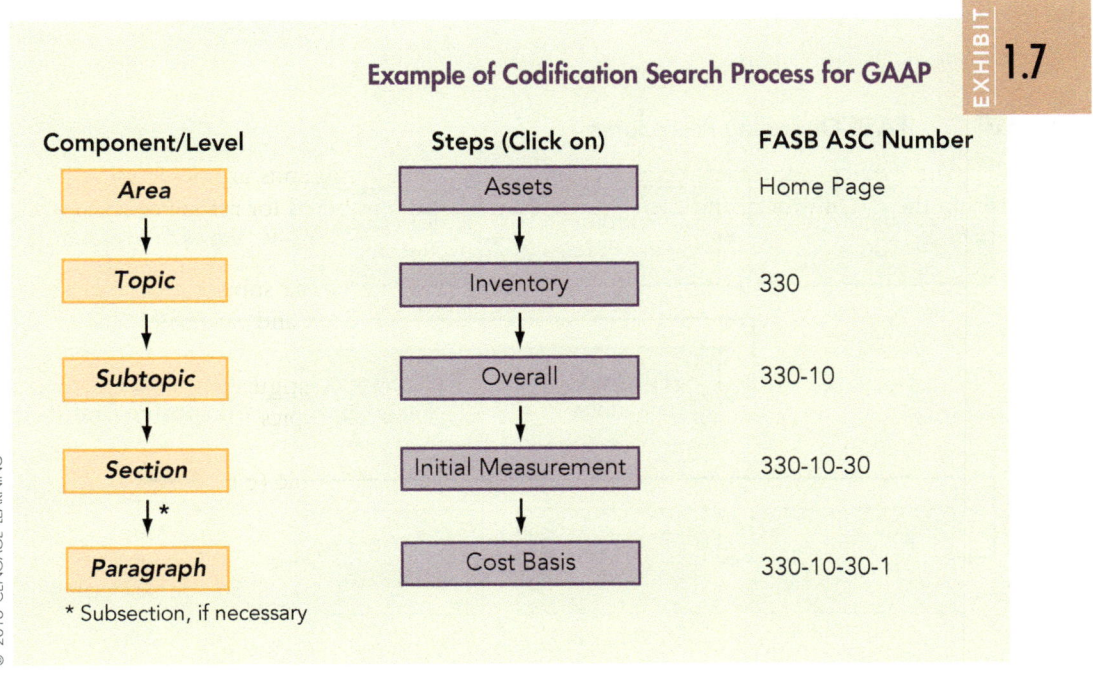

After logging in, go to the Area links in the left column of the home page and click on *Assets*. This brings you to a menu of seven Topics of assets. Click on *Inventory* (note that its Codification number is 330). This brings you to a menu containing one Subtopic, *Overall* (note that it is number 10, so that the combined Topic/Subtopic Codification number is 330-10), along with numerous links relating to various industries. Click on *Overall*, for a menu containing more than a dozen *Sections*. Here, you decide which Section is most likely to contain the answer to your question. In this case, click on *Initial Measurement* (note that it is number 30), which brings you to the paragraphs containing the answer (GAAP) to your question. Note that paragraph 30-1 indicates that "The primary basis of accounting for inventories is cost, which has been defined generally as the price paid or consideration given to acquire an asset. ..." This completes your search. If you want to reference this answer, you would refer to "FASB ASC 330-10-30-1." Now, suppose you left this screen and then wanted to return to this paragraph. To save time, enter 330-10-30-1 in the "**Go To**" box on the home page, and it takes you directly to the paragraph. Alternatively, instead of the search process we discussed above, you could find the same guidance by entering "inventory initial measurement" in the "**Search**" box.

Using the Codification should help you to:

- Reduce the amount of time and effort needed to solve an accounting research issue.
- Improve your ability to use the accounting literature and comply with U.S. GAAP.

Throughout this book, we discuss the U.S. GAAP related to a particular issue and provide footnote reference to the relevant paragraph(s) of the original pronouncements. To help you understand the Codification numbering structure, the footnotes also provide you the Codification reference (topic, subtopic, and section number) that contains the paragraphs from the original pronouncement (e.g., FASB ASC 850-10-50). *The FASB's Accounting Standards Codification: A User-Friendly Guide* supplement found on this textbook's companion website will provide you with step-by-step instructions for how to use the Codification to determine how to properly record and report particular transactions, events, and commercial arrangements in accordance with U.S. GAAP.

The FASB's Process and Operating Procedures

When the FASB issues a new standard it is referred to as an *Accounting Standards Update*. Before issuing a new standard, the FASB generally completes a multistage process as outlined in Exhibit 1.8. Initially, a topic or project is identified and placed on the

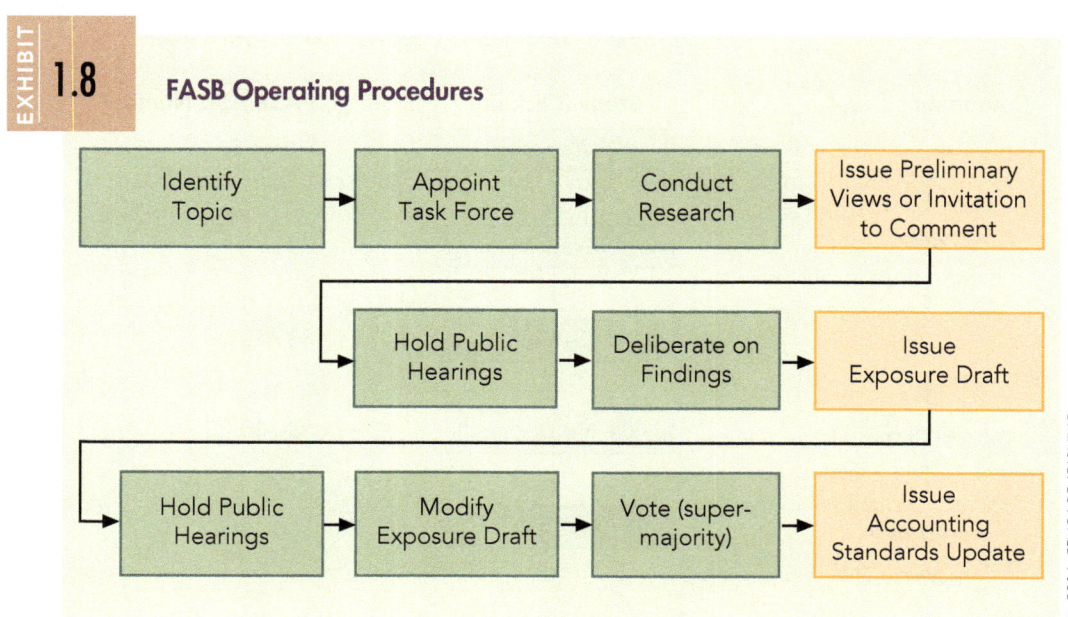

EXHIBIT 1.8 FASB Operating Procedures

FASB's agenda. On major issues, a Task Force may be appointed to advise and consult with the FASB's Research and Technical Staff. The Staff conducts any research specifically related to the project.

Then the FASB usually publishes a Preliminary Views document or Invitation to Comment (which outlines the research related to the issues) and sets a public comment period. During this period, the FASB holds public hearings similar to those conducted by Congress. Many interested parties submit written comment letters and position papers or make oral presentations. These parties include preparers and auditors of corporate financial statements, security analysts, members of professional accounting associations, and academics. After deliberating on the views expressed and the information collected, the FASB issues an Exposure Draft of the proposed *Accounting Standards Update*. Interested parties generally have 30 to 90 days to provide written comments. On major issues, the FASB may hold more public hearings or conduct "field tests" of the proposed standards. Once the FASB has concluded the public comment and research process, it will draft the proposed standard for a final vote. The FASB will issue an *Accounting Standards Update* only if it passes with a *super-majority* (five of seven Board members vote in favor).

An *Accounting Standards Update* typically describes how the Update changes U.S. GAAP, including specific amendments to the FASB Codification as well as when the changes become effective. In addition, an Update contains a section entitled "Basis for Conclusions" which explains the Board's reasoning and motivation for the new accounting standard. In addition, if certain Board members dissent and vote (in the minority) against an *Accounting Standards Update*, that *Update* will include a section in which those Board members explain why they dissented.[14]

GOT IT?

1-12 What is the FASB Accounting Standards Codification? Why did the FASB undertake this project? How did it change GAAP? Prior to the Codification, what types of pronouncements comprised GAAP?

1-13 Briefly describe the process followed by the FASB for issuing an Accounting Standard Update.

THE IASB AND IFRS

LEARNING OBJECTIVE 1.5
Explain the role of the International Accounting Standards Board (IASB) in establishing International Financial Reporting Standards (IFRS) and the efforts to try to converge accounting standards between the FASB and the IASB.

Virtually all large companies, and the majority of medium and small companies, conduct international operations by producing, selling, and buying products and services in other countries. In addition, many investors and creditors search for attractive investments in the world's major capital markets. The globalization of operating, investing, and financing activities has led to increased demand for accounting information and financial statements from companies all over the world. Companies, securities regulators, investors, and creditors in international markets, in turn, prefer that the financial statement information they use for business and investment decisions be comparable from company to company across countries. The IASB is the international accounting standard setter, establishing IFRS which are required or permitted in roughly 130 countries. As noted earlier, the SEC accepts reports filed by non-U.S. companies with financial statements prepared according to IFRS.

The structure of the IASB is similar to that of the FASB. The IFRS Foundation is the parent organization of the IASB. The IFRS Foundation consists of a group of *Trustees* that is responsible for fund-raising, appointing IASB members, and overseeing the

---
[14] The time to complete steps in the standard-setting process varies depending on the complexity of the topic and the magnitude of the impact of the new standard. For complex topics, it takes several years; for less complex topics the process may take only a few months.

effectiveness of the IASB. The IASB, which issues International Financial Reporting Standards (IFRS), includes 16 members from various countries.[15] In addition, the *IFRS Interpretations Committee* provides authoritative interpretive guidance (IFRICs) on how to apply IFRS to various accounting issues. In setting new IFRSs, the IASB follows a thorough, open, and transparent due process. The process is similar to that of the FASB and includes studying the topic, issuing a discussion paper, issuing an Exposure Draft, evaluating comments, and drafting the proposed standard. If approved by at least 10 of the 16 members of the IASB (or 9 if there are fewer than 16 members), the proposed standard becomes an *International Financial Reporting Standard*. At the time of this writing, the IASB has issued 13 IFRSs, in addition to the 41 *International Accounting Standards* (*IASs*) that were issued by its predecessor the International Accounting Standards Committee, and that are still applicable unless they have been amended or withdrawn. In addition, the IFRS Interpretations Committee has issued 21 IFRICs to date. A list of these documents is provided in Appendix C at the end of this book, and all of these documents can be viewed online and downloaded from the IFRS Foundation web site.[16]

Convergence of FASB and IASB Accounting Standards

The ongoing globalization of business activities creates an increasing demand for consistent and comparable financial statements for companies from different countries. Because of the increasing importance of international operating, investing, and financing activities, professional accountants must be bilingual—able to speak U.S. GAAP and IFRS. Even though they are headquartered in the United States, companies like **The Coca-Cola Company** and **McDonald's Corporation** make more than 70% and 65% of their sales, respectively, in countries other than the United States. Similarly, **Toyota Corporation** makes more than 64% of its sales in countries other than Japan. Companies that are large or small, whether headquartered in major cities or in small towns, conduct business with companies from other countries. Hundreds of companies from outside the United States list their securities on U.S. capital markets like the NYSE, and hundreds of U.S. companies list their securities on capital markets outside the United States, including the London Stock Exchange and the Tokyo Stock Exchange.

Currently, for companies that list their securities on U.S. capital markets, the SEC mandates that U.S. corporations are subject to the accounting standards established by the FASB, while foreign corporations are subject to IFRS or accounting standards set by their national accounting standards boards. These differences in accounting standards have led to differences among U.S. and non-U.S. corporations' financial statements. These differences, in turn, have made it difficult for investors and creditors to make valid comparisons across corporations and to make effective investment and credit decisions in the U.S. and foreign capital markets. There is demand for international convergence of accounting standards driven by investors' and creditors' needs for high-quality, internationally comparable financial information that is useful for decision-making in our increasingly global capital markets.

International convergence of accounting standards refers to both a goal and the path taken to reach it. The FASB states:[17]

> "The FASB believes that the ultimate **goal** of convergence is the development of a unified set of high-quality, international accounting standards that companies worldwide would use for both domestic and cross-border financial reporting. From 2002 to 2013, the **path** toward that goal has been the collaborative efforts of the FASB and the IASB to both *improve* U.S. GAAP and IFRS *and*

---

[15] The IFRS Foundation Constitution stipulates that the IASB should be comprised of four members each from Asia/Oceania, Europe, and North America; one member each from Africa and South America; and two members from any other area.
[16] See http://www.ifrs.org.
[17] See http://www.fasb.org/jsp/FASB/Page/SectionPage&cid=1176156245663.

eliminate or minimize the differences between them. Moving forward, the FASB will continue to work on global accounting issues with the IASB through its members in the Accounting Standards Advisory Forum (ASAF), a newly established advisory body comprising 12 standards setters from across the globe."

The FASB and the IASB have been working together toward convergence since 2002. At that time, the two Boards entered into the "Norwalk Agreement" for the development of high-quality, compatible accounting standards that could be used for both domestic and cross-border financial reporting. In 2009 and 2010 the Boards identified a number of major projects to undertake jointly as well as short-term projects (in which convergence occurred fairly quickly). Because the short-term convergence projects are less complex than the major projects, the two Boards have already made substantial progress in converging a number of standards.

The Boards have completed most of their major project milestones. The major projects the Boards have completed have achieved convergence of accounting standards for:

- consolidated financial statements (converged standards issued in 2011)
- fair value measurement (coverged standards issued in 2011)
- financial statement presentation (amendments to reporting comprehensive income completed in 2011; other joint work discontinued)
- revenue recognition (converged standards issued in 2014)

Moving forward, the FASB will continue to work on global accounting issues with the IASB through its membership in the Accounting Standards Advisory Forum (ASAF). Both Boards provide quarterly progress reports which can be downloaded from their web sites.[18]

The SEC and International Convergence

In 2007 the SEC decided to allow foreign companies to use IFRS rather than U.S. GAAP to prepare the financial statements that those companies report in their *Forms 20-F*.[19] Many countries, including all member countries in the European Union, Canada, China, Japan, India, Brazil, and Australia, have adopted IFRS (or are in the process of transitioning to IFRS) as the required accounting standards for companies that are publicly traded.[20] The SEC agreed to accept IFRS-based filings from non-U.S. companies, and it decided that these companies do not need to reconcile how differences between IFRS and U.S. GAAP affect their reported financial statements.[21]

Professional accountants must be fluent in U.S. GAAP and IFRS. Therefore, in this book we will discuss U.S. GAAP and IFRS. For each major topic where there are differences between U.S. GAAP and IFRS, we will describe those differences in an International Dimension feature as well as Appendix D at the end of the book. We also will indicate how accounting by U.S. companies would have to change to be in compliance with IFRS and potential consequences. Under this approach, you will be well informed about both U.S. GAAP and IFRS when you enter the accounting profession.[22]

---

[18] See FASB at http://www.fasb.org or IASB at http://www.ifrs.org.

[19] For more discussion, see "Concept Release on Allowing U.S. Issuers to Prepare Financial Statements in Accordance with International Financial Reporting Standards," *SEC Concepts Release 33-8831* (August 7, 2007 at http://sec.gov/.

[20] Many countries adopt IFRS as the required accounting principles for listed companies but still maintain their own country-specific accounting standards for non-listed companies.

[21] The SEC accepts filings from companies with financial statements prepared with home-country standards; however, the SEC requires the companies to reconcile their financial statements to U.S. GAAP. Therefore, such companies must file *Form 20-F* to show how critical accounting amounts such as net income, total assets, and total common shareholders' equity differ between the amounts reported using home-country standards and the amounts that would be reported under U.S. GAAP.

[22] The AICPA as well as the "Big 4" accounting firms also have portions of their web sites devoted to IFRS issues. For more information about IFRS, visit the AICPA web site http://www.ifrs.com, as well as the accounting firm web sites http://www.deloitte.com, http://www.ey.com, http://www.kpmg.com, and http://www.pwc.com.

LOOKING AHEAD

In July 2012, the SEC staff issued its final report considering incorporating IFRS into the financial reporting system for U.S. companies. The report was the final phase of a work plan, initiated in February 2010, to consider specific issues relevant to the SEC's determination as to where, when, and how the current financial reporting system for U.S. issuers should be transitioned to a system incorporating IFRS.

The 2012 report summarized the staff's findings regarding key issues surrounding the potential incorporation of IFRS into U.S. financial reporting, but did not make any recommendation to the Commission. "Additional analysis and consideration of this threshold policy question is necessary before any decision by the Commission concerning the incorporation of IFRS into the financial reporting system for the U.S. issuers can occur," the report said.

In the report, the staff identified a number of unresolved issues relating to the potential incorporation of IFRS into the U.S. financial reporting system. These issues include the diversity in how IFRS are interpreted, applied, and enforced in various jurisdictions around the world; the potential cost to U.S issuers of adopting or incorporating IFRS; investor education; and governance.

Potential Problems with International Convergence

The use of IFRS by non-U.S. companies filing with the SEC has created two potential problems for U.S. companies that use U.S. GAAP. First, U.S. companies' financial statements are different from those of the foreign companies they compete with for capital, creating difficulties for investors and creditors in comparing companies. Second, if U.S. companies have subsidiaries operating in foreign countries, they may be required to prepare their subsidiaries' financial statements according to IFRS for local filings. Because these companies still have to prepare their consolidated financial statements using U.S. GAAP to file with the SEC, this creates costly inefficiencies.

Other potential issues include the following:[23]

- Many U.S. companies (particularly smaller ones) filing with the SEC do not operate globally so they would obtain little benefit from using IFRS rather than U.S. GAAP.
- Most U.S. corporations are small companies and do *not* issue publicly traded securities and therefore are not regulated by the SEC. These corporations would likely continue to use U.S. GAAP in preparing their financial statements. A switch to IFRS for regulated U.S. companies would create a "dual-GAAP" system in the United States.
- Accountants, auditors, and financial statement users would have to be trained to understand the impact of IFRS on the preparation of financial statements of companies using IFRS.
- Many companies have entered into contracts based on U.S. GAAP. (For example, companies may have borrowed money with debt covenants based on U.S. GAAP that restrict their financing activities.) A shift to IFRS may require renegotiating these contracts.

The SEC must consider these and many other issues as it deliberates whether it should continue to require the use of U.S. GAAP or whether it should require the use of IFRS. The FASB and the IASB remain committed to improving U.S. GAAP and IFRS.

Standard Setting in a Political Environment

The accounting standards established by the FASB and IASB have significant economic consequences because they determine the information companies provide to external stakeholders, and that information, of course, influences stakeholders' decisions and wealth. Because of the importance of accounting standards, the FASB and the IASB operate so that they develop new accounting standards in a thorough, thoughtful, and

---

[23] The following discussion is a summary of the key issues identified in "Concept Release on Allowing U.S. Issues to Prepare Financial Statements in Accordance with International Financial Reporting Standards," *SEC Concepts Release 33-8831* (August 7, 2007). For more details, see the *Concepts Release* link at http://sec.gov/.

efficient manner, with due process, and in open public forums. Both Boards consider all related research on a particular topic, as well as the (often conflicting) views and opinions of all interested parties, before coming to a logical conclusion about the appropriate accounting standard that will provide users with useful information.

However, because of the substantial economic consequences, key constituents often disagree about the objectives for new standards. Because the Boards hold public hearings and open meetings, various external user groups (e.g., investors and creditors) and other interested parties (e.g., affected corporations and CPA firms) exert pressure to influence the new standards, continue existing standards, or change existing standards in their own best interests. In addition, research results about the likely effects of new standards are sometimes conflicting, and only "best guesses" can be made of the future consequences of current standards.

A contentious example occurred in the 1990s when the FASB proposed a new accounting standard for measuring and expensing stock options granted to employees as compensation. The proposal received strong opposition from certain companies (particularly high-tech firms), and the FASB received pressure from the U.S. Congress to rescind the proposal. Therefore, it issued in 1995 a standard that effectively allowed companies to choose whether or not to recognize stock option expenses. In 2004, after the IASB adopted a standard that required expensing stock options, the FASB revised its standard and required expensing of share-based compensation payments, including stock options. More recently, during the financial crisis, both the FASB and the IASB came under significant political pressure from governments and banking regulators in the United States and Europe to relax the accounting standards requiring recognition of fair value losses on loans and investment securities.

Because of the important economic and political consequences associated with accounting information, the FASB and the IASB often make decisions about new accounting standards that require compromise between conflicting views and interests. Compromise is inevitable as the FASB and the IASB respond to the globalization of capital markets.

GOT IT?

1-14 How are the FASB and IASB different, and how are they similar?

1-15 What are International Financial Reporting Standards (IFRS)?

1-16 How are U.S. GAAP and IFRS changing over time?

1-17 Are accounting standards established by the FASB and the IASB according to objective standards of "pure" conceptually and theoretically correct accounting? If not, why not?

WHAT IS THE PRODUCT? FINANCIAL REPORTING AND THE FINANCIAL STATEMENTS

LEARNING OBJECTIVE 1.6
Understand the output of the financial reporting process and the four primary financial statements, as well as the important information reported with financial statements.

We have described the demand for accounting information, which is driven by competition for scarce economic resources, particularly financial capital. We have also described the supply of accounting information, in which generally accepted accounting principles are developed by standard setters like the FASB and the IASB and are then applied by managers to measure, summarize, and report their company's financial performance and position. We next turn to the output of this production process: the financial reports and financial statements that companies provide to external stakeholders. In the following sections, we describe the primary financial statements—balance sheet, income statement, statement of cash flows, and statement of shareholders' equity—as well as the notes and other items that typically accompany these statements.[24]

---
[24] We provide more detailed discussions of these statements in Chapters 4 and 5.

In each chapter, we make accounting information and methods come to life by using real company examples. In particular, we use **Starbucks**, which is widely admired for being a well-run company, an excellent employer, and a mindful corporate citizen, to illustrate numerous financial accounting issues. To begin, it is important to understand Starbucks's business model and strategy as a context for understanding its accounting.

Brief Introduction: Starbucks's Business

Starbucks grew from a single coffee shop near Pike's Place Market in Seattle to a multinational chain and a worldwide brand name through what it refers to as the "*Starbucks Experience.*" The *Starbucks Experience* is how Starbucks differentiates its customers' experiences in their coffee shops from other chains and fast-food restaurants such as **McDonald's**. The *Starbucks Experience* involves many things, including high-quality products, friendly and competent service enabling customers to specify their beverages exactly to their tastes, relaxed and inviting shop environments, and convenient locations.

At the end of fiscal 2015, Starbucks had 23,043 coffee shops worldwide. Of that total, Starbucks owns and operates 12,235 shops (53.1%) and licensees own and operate 10,808 shops (46.9%). *Licensees* are individuals or companies that pay Starbucks a license fee and a royalty (a percentage of their coffee shop sales) in exchange for the rights to use Starbucks's name, trademarks, logos, products, and methods. Although 14,803 (64.2%) of Starbucks's owned and licensed shops are located in the Americas, 8,240 (35.8%) are in other countries around the world, including the United Kingdom, Canada, China, and Japan. In addition to operating coffee shops, Starbucks also sells coffee beans, tea, and instant coffee to foodservice distributors who supply institutional food servers (such as dormitory cafeterias). In addition, Starbucks sells packaged coffee and tea in grocery stores and warehouse club chains. Starbucks is also a partner in several joint ventures to develop and sell coffee-based products, such as the North American Coffee Partnership with **PepsiCo** to make and sell ready-to-drink beverages such as the Frappuccino (a creamy iced-coffee beverage).

The Balance Sheet: Measuring Financial Position

According to the FASB and the IASB, the balance sheet is the cornerstone of financial reporting. The **balance sheet**, or **statement of financial position**, presents a snapshot of the resources of a firm (assets) and the claims on the firm (liabilities and shareholders' equity) as of a specific date (usually the last day of the fiscal quarter or the fiscal year). The balance sheet reports the following equality:

Assets = Liabilities + Shareholders' Equity

That is, a firm's assets are in balance with, or equal to, the claims on the company by creditors (liabilities) and owners (shareholders' equity). The balance sheet views resources from two perspectives:

- specific resources the firm holds (e.g., cash, inventory, and equipment)
- the claims on the firm by the persons or entities that provided the resources (e.g., investors, creditors, lenders, suppliers, employees, and other stakeholders)

Exhibit 1.9 presents **Starbucks**'s balance sheet as of fiscal year-end, September 27, 2015, which reports total assets of $12,446.1 million. The claims on the company include total liabilities of $6,626.3 million and total equity of $5,819.8 million.

EXHIBIT 1.9

STARBUCKS CORPORATION
CONSOLIDATED BALANCE SHEETS
(in millions, except per share data)

	Sep 27, 2015	Sep 28, 2014
ASSETS		
Current assets:		
Cash and cash equivalents	$ 1,530.1	$ 1,708.4
Short-term investments	81.3	135.4
Accounts receivable, net	719.0	631.0
Inventories	1,306.4	1,090.9
Prepaid expenses and other current assets	334.2	285.6
Deferred income taxes, net	381.7	317.4
Total current assets	4,352.7	4,168.7
Long-term investments	312.5	318.4
Equity and cost investments	352.0	514.9
Property, plant and equipment, net	4,088.3	3,519.0
Deferred income taxes, net	828.9	903.3
Other long-term assets	415.9	198.9
Other intangible assets	520.4	273.5
Goodwill	1,575.4	856.2
TOTAL ASSETS	$12,446.1	$10,752.9
LIABILITIES AND EQUITY		
Current liabilities:		
Accounts payable	$ 684.2	$ 533.7
Accrued liabilities	1,760.7	1,514.4
Insurance reserves	224.8	196.1
Stored value card liability	983.8	794.5
Total current liabilities	3,653.5	3,038.7
Long-term debt	2,347.5	2,048.3
Other long-term liabilities	625.3	392.2
Total liabilities	6,626.3	5,479.2
Shareholders' equity:		
Common stock ($0.001 par value) — authorized, 2,400.0 shares; issued and outstanding, 1,485.1 and 1,499.1 shares, respectively	1.5	0.7
Additional paid-in capital	41.1	39.4
Retained earnings	5,974.8	5,206.6
Accumulated other comprehensive income/(loss)	(199.4)	25.3
Total shareholders' equity	5,818.0	5,272.0
Noncontrolling interest	1.8	1.7
Total equity	5,819.8	5,273.7
TOTAL LIABILITIES AND EQUITY	$12,446.1	$10,752.9

Assets Assets are probable future economic benefits obtained or controlled by a company as a result of past transactions or events. The assets portion of the balance sheet reports the effects of the following decisions:

- *Operating* decisions: Principally involving assets used in day-to-day activities to produce and deliver products and services to customers
- *Investing* decisions: Principally involving investments in long-lived tangible and intangible productive resources, as well as financial assets to generate interest income, dividends, and other returns on investment

For Starbucks, these decisions can be seen in the following assets:

Operating Activities	Investing Activities
Assets used in day-to-day activities to produce and deliver products and services to customers: • Cash and cash equivalents • Accounts receivable • Inventories • Prepaid expenses	Long-lived tangible resources, intangible resources, and financial resources: • Property, plant, and equipment • Goodwill and other intangible assets • Short-term investment securities • Long-term investment securities • Investments in the equity securities of noncontrolled affiliates (joint-venture partnerships)

Starbucks's largest assets (in dollar amounts) on the 2015 balance sheet are $4,088.3 million in property, plant, and equipment (furniture, equipment, and leasehold improvements in coffee shops, coffee roasting plants, and warehouses), $1,575.4 million in goodwill, and $1,530.1 million in cash and cash equivalents.

Liabilities Liabilities are the probable future sacrifices of economic benefits arising from present obligations of a company to transfer assets or provide services in the future to other entities as a result of past transactions or events. The liabilities portion of the balance sheet reports obligations that arise from the following decisions:

- *Operating* decisions: Involving obligations to pay employees and suppliers as well as obligations to deliver goods and services to customers
- *Financing* decisions: Raising financial capital from banks and other lenders

For Starbucks, these decisions can be seen in the following liabilities:

Operating Activities	Financing Activities
Obligations to pay employees and suppliers of goods and services: • Accounts payable • Accrued liabilities • Insurance reserves • Other long-term liabilities Obligations to deliver products to customers: • Stored value card liability	Financial capital from loans from banks and other lenders: • Long-term debt

As of the 2015 balance sheet date, Starbucks's liabilities primarily arise from obligations from operating activities. Of the total $6,626.3 million in liabilities, only $2,347.5 million involves capital from long-term debt. Therefore, Starbucks owes employees, suppliers, customers, and other creditors related to operating activities a total of $4,278.8 million ($6,626.3 million − $2,347.5 million).

Shareholders' Equity The shareholders' equity in a firm is a residual interest claim. That is, the owners have a claim on all assets not required to meet the claims of creditors. Therefore, the valuation of assets minus the valuation of liabilities in the balance sheet determines the valuation of total shareholders' equity.

Balance sheets separate total shareholders' equity into the following two general categories, both of which reflect financing and operating activities:

- Contributed capital accounts: Amounts initially contributed by shareholders for an ownership interest in a firm
- Earned capital accounts: Cumulative amounts of profits that have been earned by the firm, net of the amounts of profits that have been paid out to shareholders through dividends and share repurchases

For Starbucks, these accounts break down as follows:

Paid-In Capital Accounts	Earned Capital Accounts
Capital contributed by shareholders for an ownership interest in the firm: • Common stock • Additional paid-in capital • Noncontrolling interest	Cumulative amounts of profits that have been earned by the firm, net of the amounts of profits that have been paid out to shareholders: • Retained earnings • Accumulated other comprehensive income (loss)

The 2015 balance sheet reports that Starbucks's retained earnings represents the majority of its equity capital, comprising $5,974.8 million of a total of $5,819.8 million in equity capital.

Chapter 4 describes the many principles and techniques under U.S. GAAP and IFRS that accountants use to measure and report balance sheets, including how to define and recognize assets, liabilities, and equity accounts; how they are measured and classified; and how balance sheets are typically reported.

Income Statement: Measuring and Reporting Performance

The **income statement** measures and reports the financial results of a firm's performance for a period of time, usually a quarter or a year. The income statement provides information about the profits or losses the company has generated during the period by conducting operating, investing, and financing activities. We use the terms **net income** (**or net loss**) and **earnings** interchangeably when referring to the bottom-line amount in the income statement. Later in this chapter, we provide some striking evidence on the relationship between changes in accounting earnings and changes in stock prices in the capital markets.[25] Exhibit 1.10 presents **Starbucks**'s income statements for 2013 through 2015.

Operating Activities The majority of a company's income arises from the revenues generated minus expenses incurred in the operating activities of the business. **Revenues** measure the inflows of assets and the settlements of obligations from selling goods and providing services to customers. **Expenses** measure the outflows of assets that a company consumes and the obligations it incurs in the process of operating the business to generate revenues. As a measure of performance, revenues report the resources generated by a company and expenses report the resources consumed.

Revenue and expense accounts associated with Starbucks's operating activities include the following:

Operating Revenues	Operating Expenses
• Company-operated store revenues • Licensed store revenues • CPG, foodservice and other revenues • Income from equity investees	• Cost of sales and occupancy costs • Store operating expenses • Other operating expenses • Depreciation and amortization expenses • General and administrative expenses • Litigation charge/(credit)

Starbucks generates revenues primarily from owning and operating coffee shops. Revenues from company-operated retail stores amounted to $15,197.3 million, which accounted for roughly 79.3% of its total revenues of $19,162.7 million in fiscal 2015.

---

[25] Chapter 5 describes revenue recognition, expense measurement, and income measurement. Later chapters describe the techniques for accounting for various revenues, expenses, gains, and losses on income statements.

EXHIBIT 1.10

STARBUCKS CORPORATION
CONSOLIDATED STATEMENTS OF EARNINGS
(in millions, except per share data)

Fiscal Year Ended	Sep 27, 2015	Sep 28, 2014	Sep 29, 2013
Net revenues:			
Company-operated stores	$15,197.3	$12,977.9	$11,793.2
Licensed stores	1,861.9	1,588.6	1,360.5
CPG, foodservice and other	2,103.5	1,881.3	1,713.1
Total net revenues	19,162.7	16,447.8	14,866.8
Cost of sales including occupancy costs	7,787.5	6,858.8	6,382.3
Store operating expenses	5,411.1	4,638.2	4,286.1
Other operating expenses	522.4	457.3	431.8
Depreciation and amortization expenses	893.9	709.6	621.4
General and administrative expenses	1,196.7	991.3	937.9
Litigation charge/(credit)	—	(20.2)	2,784.1
Total operating expenses	15,811.6	13,635.0	15,443.6
Income from equity investees	249.9	268.3	251.4
Operating income/(loss)	3,601.0	3,081.1	(325.4)
Gain resulting from acquisition of joint venture	390.6	—	—
Loss on extinguishment of debt	(61.1)	—	—
Interest income and other, net	43.0	142.7	123.6
Interest expense	(70.5)	(64.1)	(28.1)
Earnings/(loss) before income taxes	3,903.0	3,159.7	(229.9)
Income tax expense/(benefit)	1,143.7	1,092.0	(238.7)
Net earnings including noncontrolling interests	2,759.3	2,067.7	8.8
Net earnings/(loss) attributable to noncontrolling interests	1.9	(0.4)	0.5
Net earnings attributable to Starbucks	$ 2,757.4	$ 2,068.1	$ 8.3
Earnings per share — basic	$ 1.84	$ 1.37	$ 0.01
Earnings per share — diluted	$ 1.82	$ 1.35	$ 0.01
Weighted average shares outstanding:			
Basic	1,495.9	1,506.3	1,498.5
Diluted	1,513.4	1,526.3	1,524.5

STARBUCKS CORPORATION
CONSOLIDATED STATEMENTS OF COMPREHENSIVE INCOME
(in millions)

	Sep 27, 2015	Sep 28, 2014	Sep 29, 2013
Net earnings including noncontrolling interests	$2,759.3	$2,067.7	$ 8.8
Other comprehensive income/(loss), net of tax:			
Unrealized holding gains/(losses) on available-for-sale securities	1.4	1.6	(0.6)
Tax (expense)/benefit	(0.5)	(0.6)	0.2
Unrealized gains/(losses) on cash flow hedging instruments	47.6	24.1	47.1
Tax (expense)/benefit	(16.8)	(7.8)	(24.6)
Unrealized gains/(losses) on net investment hedging instruments	4.3	25.5	32.8
Tax (expense)/benefit	(1.6)	(9.4)	(12.1)
Translation adjustment	(222.7)	(75.8)	(41.6)
Tax (expense)/benefit	6.0	(1.6)	0.3
Reclassification adjustment for net (gains)/losses realized in net earnings for available-for-sale securities, hedging instruments, and translation adjustment	(65.9)	(1.5)	46.3
Tax expense/(benefit)	23.5	3.8	(3.5)
Other comprehensive income/(loss)	(224.7)	(41.7)	44.3
Comprehensive income including noncontrolling interests	2,534.6	2,026.0	53.1
Comprehensive income/(loss) attributable to noncontrolling interests	(29.2)	(0.4)	0.5
Comprehensive income attributable to Starbucks	$2,563.8	$2,026.4	$ 52.6

Not surprisingly, expenses associated with operating activities represent the primary costs of Starbucks's operating activities. Overall, 2015 was a very profitable year for Starbucks's operations, generating operating income of $3,601.0 million.[26]

Investing and Financing Activities Companies also generate income and incur expenses arising from the investing and financing activities of the business. Investing activities, such as holding stock or bonds in an investment portfolio, will generate interest and dividend income and gains or losses from the sales of investment securities. Investing activities can also generate income if companies hold partial ownership interests in other companies through joint ventures or partnerships. Financing activities generally incur expenses, such as interest expense, for the costs associated with borrowed capital.

Income statement accounts associated with Starbucks's investing and financing activities include the following:

Investing Activities	Financing Activities
• Interest income	• Interest expense

Starbucks's income from investing activities primarily arises in the form of interest income that it earns on the cash, short-term, and long-term investment securities it holds. Starbucks's financing activities triggered interest expenses on the long-term debt outstanding. During 2015, Starbucks earned $43.0 million in interest income and incurred $70.5 million in interest expense.

Net Income Net income (or net loss) measures the bottom-line profit (or loss) of a company for the period. Net income (or loss) represents the wealth gained (or lost) by the company for the common shareholders during the period:

$$\text{Net Income} = \text{Revenues} - \text{Expenses} + \text{Gains} - \text{Losses}$$

Income statements commonly report gains and losses that arise from selling assets or settling liabilities for more or less than their book values. Such gains and losses are normally reported separately on income statements to distinguish them from the results of normal, ongoing, and recurring activities. For example, in fiscal 2015, Starbucks recognized a $390.6 million gain resulting from the acquisition of a joint venture, as well as a $61.1 million loss on the early extinguishment of debt. Income statements also report the effects of income taxes, as firms commonly have to pay income taxes on their profits. In 2015, Starbucks recognized an income tax expense amounting to $1,143.7 million. During fiscal 2015, Starbucks was very profitable, generating net earnings of $2,757.4 million for its common equity shareholders.[27]

Comprehensive Income Comprehensive income is the change in equity of a company during a period from transactions, events, and circumstances relating to nonowner sources. It includes all changes in equity during a period except those resulting from investments by owners or distributions to owners. Comprehensive income includes net income, plus (or minus) certain other types of gains (or losses) that are recognized in comprehensive income (and not in net income until they are realized in a cash flow). U.S. GAAP requires four types of gains and losses be recognized in comprehensive income, all of which will be discussed in subsequent chapters. For fiscal 2015, comprehensive income attributable to Starbucks amounted to $2,563.8 million. The primary items causing Starbucks's comprehensive income to differ from net income in 2015 were foreign currency translation adjustments (a topic covered in advanced financial accounting textbooks).

---

[26] Note that Starbucks also includes $249.9 million in income from equity investees in operating income. Equity investees are joint ventures and partnerships in which Starbucks generally holds a 50% ownership stake. This amount of income represents Starbucks's proportionate share of the income of those joint ventures and partnerships. Starbucks could classify these investments as either operating activities or as investing activities, depending on whether it has an active role or a passive role (primarily as an investor) in managing them. Starbucks has chosen to report income from equity investees as part of income from operating activities rather than as an investing activity which indicates that it takes a more active role.

[27] Starbucks also reports net earnings attributable to noncontrolling interests. Chapter 5 discusses noncontrolling interests in detail.

Statement of Cash Flows

The **statement of cash flows** reports for a period of time the net cash flows (inflows minus outflows) from operating, investing, and financing activities. The purpose of the statement of cash flows is simple but important: to provide useful information about how a firm is generating and using cash. The statement of cash flows provides information to complement the income statement, demonstrating how cash flows differ from accrual-based income. It is particularly useful to creditors and other stakeholders to help them evaluate the company's cash-generating ability and to give them information about the likelihood of future cash flows for future payments of obligations.[28] Exhibit 1.11 presents the statement of cash flows for **Starbucks** for the years 2013 through 2015.

Operating Activities Selling goods and providing services are among the most important ways a financially healthy company generates cash. Companies generate operating cash flows by collecting revenues in cash from customers, and they use operating cash flows to pay expenses, pay obligations to suppliers, and acquire operating assets such as inventory. Assessing cash flow from operations over several years indicates the extent to which operating activities have provided the necessary cash to maintain operating capabilities. Starbucks's statement of cash flows reveals that cash flows from operating activities were substantial during this period, generating over $3.7 billion in 2015, over $600 million in 2014, and more than $2.9 billion in 2013.

Investing Activities The acquisition of long-lived productive assets, particularly property, plant, and equipment, usually represents major ongoing uses of cash. If companies want to sustain operations, they must replace such long-lived assets as they wear out. If companies are to grow and increase the scale of their operations, they must acquire additional long-lived productive assets. Sometimes companies obtain cash from sales of existing assets. Starbucks's statement of cash flows reveals that one of the major uses of cash flows for investing activities involved additions to property, plant, and equipment, ranging from $1,303.7 million in 2015 to $1,151.2 million in 2013.

Financing Activities A company obtains cash from short- and long-term borrowing and from issuing preferred and common stock. It uses cash to repay short- and long-term borrowing, to pay dividends, and to reacquire shares of outstanding preferred and common stock. In 2015, Starbucks raised $848.5 million by issuing long-term debt and made repayments of $610.1 million on long-term debt. In 2015, Starbucks also used $928.6 million of cash to pay dividends to common equity shareholders and $1,436.1 million to repurchase outstanding shares of common stock.

Statement of Shareholders' Equity

The **statement of shareholders' equity** (sometimes called the **statement of changes in shareholders' equity**) provides information about the common shareholders' equity claims on the company and how those claims changed during the period. The year-end amounts reported in this statement equal the amounts reported in the shareholders' equity section of the balance sheet. Similar to the balance sheet, the statement of shareholders' equity will report the following:

- amounts initially contributed by shareholders for an interest in a company (Common Stock, Additional Paid-In Capital, and Other Additional Paid-In Capital)
- cumulative net income in excess of dividends declared (Retained Earnings)
- shareholders' equity effects from the recognition or valuation of certain assets or liabilities (Accumulated Other Comprehensive Income)
- cumulative amounts of cash distributed to shareholders to repurchase shares (Treasury Stock; sometimes these amounts are subtracted from Retained Earnings, like dividends; Starbucks is an example)

---

[28] Chapter 5 provides an introduction to preparing a statement of cash flows. Chapter 21 provides a more detailed demonstration of techniques for preparing statements of cash flows.

STARBUCKS CORPORATION
CONSOLIDATED STATEMENTS OF CASH FLOWS
(in millions)

Fiscal Year Ended	Sep 27, 2015	Sep 28, 2014	Sep 29, 2013
OPERATING ACTIVITIES:			
Net earnings including noncontrolling interests	$ 2,759.3	$ 2,067.7	$ 8.8
Adjustments to reconcile net earnings to net cash provided by operating activities:			
Depreciation and amortization	933.8	748.4	655.6
Litigation charge	—	—	2,784.1
Deferred income taxes, net	21.2	10.2	(1,045.9)
Income earned from equity method investees	(190.2)	(182.7)	(171.8)
Distributions received from equity method investees	148.2	139.2	115.6
Gain resulting from acquisition/sale of equity in joint ventures and certain retail operations	(394.3)	(70.2)	(80.1)
Loss on extinguishment of debt	61.1	—	—
Stock-based compensation	209.8	183.2	142.3
Excess tax benefit on share-based awards	(132.4)	(114.4)	(258.1)
Other	53.8	36.2	23.0
Cash provided/(used) by changes in operating assets and liabilities:			
Accounts receivable	(82.8)	(79.7)	(68.3)
Inventories	(207.9)	14.3	152.5
Accounts payable	137.7	60.4	88.7
Accrued litigation charge	—	(2,763.9)	—
Income taxes payable, net	87.6	309.8	298.4
Accrued liabilities and insurance reserves	124.4	103.9	47.3
Stored value card liability	170.3	140.8	139.9
Prepaid expenses, other current assets and other long-term assets	49.5	4.6	76.3
Net cash provided by operating activities	3,749.1	607.8	2,908.3
INVESTING ACTIVITIES:			
Purchases of investments	(567.4)	(1,652.5)	(785.9)
Sales of investments	600.6	1,454.8	60.2
Maturities and calls of investments	18.8	456.1	980.0
Acquisitions, net of cash acquired	(284.3)	—	(610.4)
Additions to property, plant and equipment	(1,303.7)	(1,160.9)	(1,151.2)
Proceeds from sale of equity in joint ventures and certain retail operations	8.9	103.9	108.0
Other	6.8	(19.1)	(11.9)
Net cash used by investing activities	(1,520.3)	(817.7)	(1,411.2)
FINANCING ACTIVITIES:			
Proceeds from issuance of long-term debt	848.5	748.5	749.7
Repayments of long-term debt	(610.1)	—	(35.2)
Cash used for purchase of non-controlling interest	(360.8)	—	—
Proceeds from issuance of common stock	191.8	139.7	247.2
Excess tax benefit on share-based awards	132.4	114.4	258.1
Cash dividends paid	(928.6)	(783.1)	(628.9)
Repurchase of common stock	(1,436.1)	(758.6)	(588.1)
Minimum tax withholdings on share-based awards	(75.5)	(77.3)	(121.4)
Other	(18.1)	(6.9)	10.4
Net cash used by financing activities	(2,256.5)	(623.3)	(108.2)
Effect of exchange rate changes on cash and cash equivalents	(150.6)	(34.1)	(1.8)
Net (decrease)/increase in cash and cash equivalents	(178.3)	(867.3)	1,387.1
CASH AND CASH EQUIVALENTS:			
Beginning of period	1,708.4	2,575.7	1,188.6
End of period	$1,530.1	$1,708.4	$2,575.7
SUPPLEMENTAL DISCLOSURE OF CASH FLOW INFORMATION:			
Cash paid during the period for:			
Interest, net of capitalized interest	$ 69.5	$ 56.2	$ 34.4
Income taxes, net of refunds	$ 1,072.2	$ 766.3	$ 539.1

See Notes to Consolidated Financial Statements

The new information in this statement arises because the statement provides detail about how each of those accounts changed during the year. Changes in shareholders' equity accounts can result from operating, investing, and financing activities. Although the statement of shareholders' equity is not required by U.S. GAAP, most large firms report it. This statement is required by IFRS.

Exhibit 1.12 presents the statement of shareholders' equity for **Starbucks** for the years 2013 through 2015. The statement reveals that, in fiscal 2015 for example (the bottom panel of information), Starbucks's total shareholders' equity increased from $5,273.7 million to $5,819.8 million. The increase was largely attributable net earnings ($2,759.3 million), minus dividends declared ($1,016.2 million) and repurchases of common stock ($1,431.8 million).

Important Information with the Financial Statements

To provide more relevant and representationally faithful information for financial statement users, companies typically provide additional information with the financial statements, including the Notes, Management Discussion and Analysis, and Managers' and Independent Auditors' Attestations.

Notes The **notes** to the financial statements explain how the accounts and amounts have been determined. These notes provide important details about the accounting principles, methods, and estimates the company has used to measure assets, liabilities, equity, revenues, expenses, gains, and losses. For example, the notes explain how the company accounts for inventory and what cost methods the company uses to value inventory and the cost of goods sold. The notes explain how the company values property, plant, and equipment, how it is being depreciated, how much depreciation has been accumulated to date, and the expected useful lives of the assets. Notes also provide important details about financial statement estimates such as fair values of investment securities, pension and postemployment liabilities, income taxes, and intangible assets.

In its 2015 10-K (Appendix A), Starbucks provides a total of 18 notes (a total of 36 pages) to explain the accounting principles, methods, and estimates used to prepare the financial statements. These notes provide important information to help financial statement users understand the firm's accounting.

Management Discussion and Analysis Many companies accompany the financial statements and notes with extensive narrative discussion and quantitative analysis from the company managers. The **management discussion and analysis (MD&A)** section provides managers' insights into their strategies and their evaluation of their performance. In addition, managers typically provide some discussion and analysis of the company's exposure to business risk factors (a required disclosure in Form 10-K filed with the SEC). In some cases, MD&A discussions provide glimpses into managers' expectations about the future of the company.

In its 2015 10-K, Starbucks provides roughly 23 pages of MD&A (excerpts of which are presented in Appendix A). In the MD&A, Starbucks describes the business as a whole, as well as each of the operating segments. The MD&A section reports the financial performance of each segment, with managers' analysis comparing results of 2015 to 2014 and 2014 to 2013. In addition, Starbucks's MD&A section provides important insights into the company's business risks and the way it is managing them, critical accounting policies it has applied, and its liquidity and capital resource situation. The MD&A section also provides plans for the future, such as the plan in 2016 to open roughly 1,800 new stores and spend $1.4 billion of capital expenditures on store renovations and new stores. Because the MD&A section provides insight into the company from the managers' point of view, financial statement users should read it carefully to obtain all of the information available.

EXHIBIT 1.12

STARBUCKS CORPORATION
CONSOLIDATED STATEMENTS OF EQUITY
(in millions)

	Common Stock Shares	Common Stock Amount	Additional Paid-In Capital	Retained Earnings	Accumulated Other Comprehensive Income/(Loss)	Shareholders' Equity	Noncontrolling Interest	Total
Balance, September 30, 2012	749.3	$0.7	$39.4	$5,046.2	$22.7	$5,109.0	$5.5	$5,114.5
Net earnings	—	—	—	8.3	—	8.3	0.5	8.8
Other comprehensive income/(loss)	—	—	—	—	44.3	44.3	—	44.3
Stock-based compensation expense	—	—	144.1	—	—	144.1	—	144.1
Exercise of stock options/vesting of RSUs, including tax benefit of $259.9	14.4	0.1	366.7	—	—	366.8	—	366.8
Sale of common stock, including tax benefit of $0.2	0.3	—	20.4	—	—	20.4	—	20.4
Repurchase of common stock	(10.8)	—	(288.5)	(255.6)	—	(544.1)	—	(544.1)
Cash dividends declared, $0.445 per share	—	—	—	(668.6)	—	(668.6)	—	(668.6)
Noncontrolling interest resulting from divestiture	—	—	—	—	—	—	(3.9)	(3.9)
Balance, September 29, 2013	753.2	$0.8	$282.1	$4,130.3	$67.0	$4,480.2	$2.1	$4,482.3
Net earnings	—	—	—	2,068.1	—	2,068.1	—	2,067.7
Other comprehensive income/(loss)	—	—	—	—	(41.7)	(41.7)	(0.4)	(41.7)
Stock-based compensation expense	—	—	185.1	—	—	185.1	—	185.1
Exercise of stock options/vesting of RSUs, including tax benefit of $114.8	6.5	—	154.8	—	—	154.8	—	154.8
Sale of common stock, including tax benefit of $0.2	0.3	—	22.3	—	—	22.3	—	22.3
Repurchase of common stock	(10.5)	(0.1)	(604.9)	(164.8)	—	(769.8)	—	(769.8)
Cash dividends declared, $0.550 per share	—	—	—	(827.0)	—	(827.0)	—	(827.0)
Balance, September 28, 2014	749.5	$0.7	$39.4	$5,206.6	$25.3	$5,272.0	$1.7	$5,273.7
Net earnings	—	—	—	2,757.4	—	2,757.4	1.9	2,759.3
Other comprehensive income/(loss)	—	—	—	—	(193.6)	(193.6)	(31.1)	(224.7)
Stock-based compensation expense	—	—	211.7	—	—	211.7	—	211.7
Exercise of stock options/vesting of RSUs, including tax benefit of $131.3	14.6	—	224.4	—	—	224.4	—	224.4
Sale of common stock, including tax benefit of $0.2	0.6	—	23.5	—	—	23.5	—	23.5
Repurchase of common stock	(29.0)	—	(459.6)	(972.2)	—	(1,431.8)	—	(1,431.8)
Cash dividends declared, $0.680 per share	—	—	—	(1,016.2)	—	(1,016.2)	—	(1,016.2)
Two-for-one stock split	749.4	0.8	—	(0.8)	—	—	—	—
Noncontrolling interest resulting from acquisition	—	—	1.7	—	—	1.7	411.1	411.1
Purchase of noncontrolling interest	—	—	—	—	(31.1)	(29.4)	(381.7)	(411.1)
Balance, September 27, 2015	1,485.1	$1.5	$41.1	$5,974.8	$(199.4)	$5,818.0	$1.8	$5,819.8

Managers' and Independent Auditors' Attestations The financial statements and financial reports are the responsibility of a company's managers. In response to managers' misrepresenting their financial statements in now infamous cases involving **Enron**, **Global Crossing**, **Qwest Communications**, and other firms, Congress passed the **Sarbanes-Oxley Act of 2002**, which explicitly defines the responsibility of managers for financial statements. This requirement states management's responsibility not only for the financial statements, but also for the underlying accounting and control system that generates the financial statements. The Chief Executive Officer and the Chief Financial Officer must sign this management report. Starbucks's management report appears in Appendix A after Note 18.

Although the financial statements are the responsibility of the company managers, the SEC and most stock exchanges require listed companies to have their accounting records and financial statements audited by independent auditors. The independent auditor assesses a company's internal control system, designs its audit tests in light of the quality of these internal controls, and then forms an opinion about the fairness of the amounts reported in the financial statements. The independent auditor must provide dual opinions on the effectiveness of the internal control system (referred to as the **Assurance Opinion**) and the fairness of the amounts reported in the financial statement (referred to as the **Audit Opinion**). The independent auditor's attestation as to the fairness of a company's financial statements relative to U.S. GAAP or IFRS is an essential element for the reliability of financial statements in the capital markets. Investors and other users of the financial statements can rely on a firm's financial statements *only* after an independent auditor has examined the accounting records and has concluded that the financial statements are fair and reliable according to U.S. GAAP or IFRS.

The report of **Starbucks**'s independent auditor (**Deloitte & Touche LLP**) appears in Appendix A after Note 18. Note that the second to last paragraph includes the opinion on the financial statements and reads as follows:

> "In our opinion, such consolidated financial statements present fairly, in all material respects, the financial position of Starbucks Corporation and subsidiaries as of September 27, 2015 and September 28, 2014, and the results of their operations and their cash flows for each of the three years in the period ended September 27, 2015, in conformity with accounting principles generally accepted in the United States of America."

GOT IT?

1-18 What is the purpose of a balance sheet? What information does it provide? Identify at least one type of stakeholder that would be interested in the information on a company's balance sheet.

1-19 What is the purpose of an income statement? What information does it provide? Identify at least one type of stakeholder that would be interested in the information on a company's income statement.

1-20 What is the purpose of a statement of cash flows? What information does it provide? Identify at least one type of stakeholder that would be interested in the information on a company's statement of cash flows.

1-21 What is the purpose of the statement of shareholders' equity? What information does it provide? Identify at least one type of stakeholder that would be interested in the information on a company's statement of shareholders' equity.

1-22 Why do companies provide so much additional information with financial statements? What is the purpose of the notes to the statements?

WHY IS ACCOUNTING IMPORTANT? THE ECONOMIC CONSEQUENCES OF FINANCIAL REPORTING

LEARNING OBJECTIVE 1.7
Understand that, because financial accounting information triggers important economic consequences, integrity and the ability to resolve ethical dilemmas is essential to the accounting profession.

Financial reporting provides external stakeholders, such as common equity shareholders, with valuable information that helps them evaluate the profitability, risk, and growth of the company, which is information they can use to value the company's shares. The striking link between accounting earnings and stock returns has been demonstrated in many empirical accounting research studies, beginning with Ball and Brown (1968).[29] For recent evidence showing that changes in earnings are strongly associated with changes in share prices, consider the results from a study by D. Craig Nichols and James Wahlen.[30] They studied the average cumulative market-adjusted stock returns generated by companies during the 12 months leading up to and including the month in which each company announced annual earnings numbers. For a sample of 31,923 company-years between 1988 and 2001, they found that the average firm that announced an increase in earnings (over the prior year's earnings) experienced stock returns that beat market average returns by roughly 19.2%. On the other hand, the average company that announced a decrease in earnings experienced stock returns that were roughly 16.4% lower than the market average. Their results suggest that merely the sign of the change in earnings (increase versus decrease) was associated with a 35.6% stock return differential in one year, on average, over their sample period. Exhibit 1.13 presents a graph of these results.

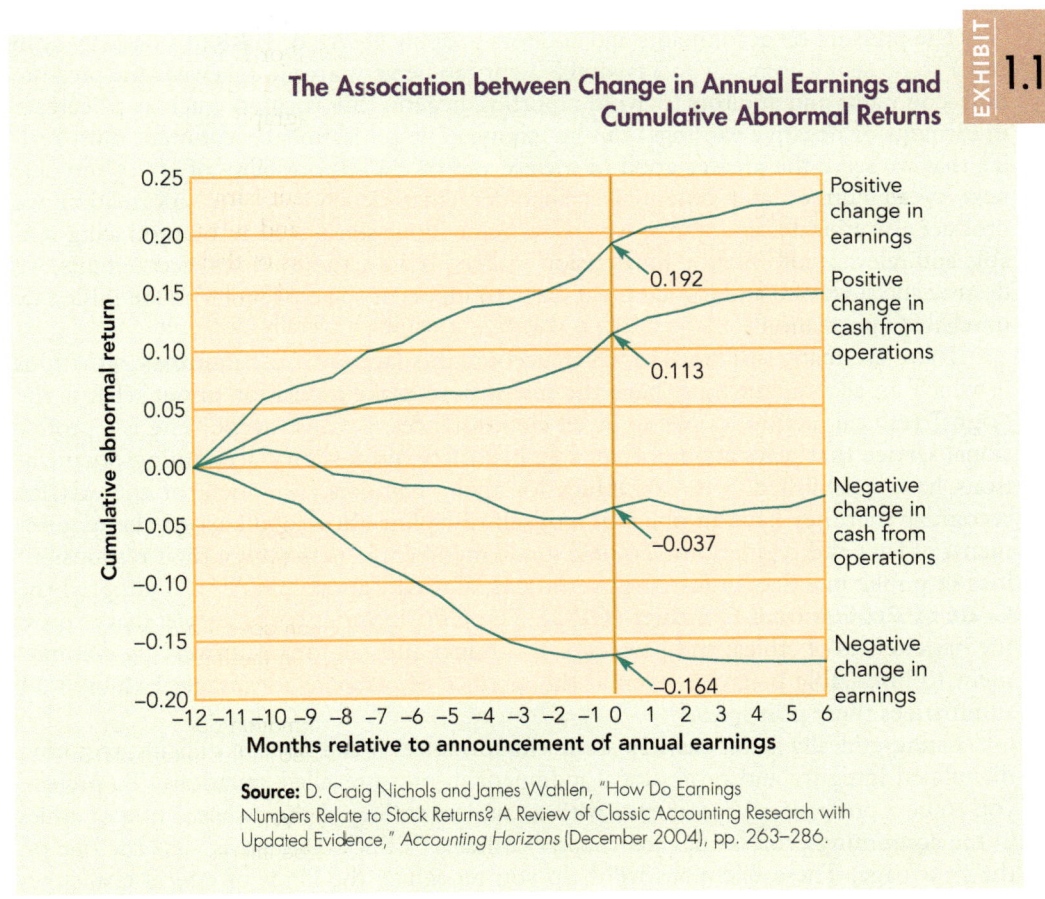

EXHIBIT 1.13 The Association between Change in Annual Earnings and Cumulative Abnormal Returns

Source: D. Craig Nichols and James Wahlen, "How Do Earnings Numbers Relate to Stock Returns? A Review of Classic Accounting Research with Updated Evidence," *Accounting Horizons* (December 2004), pp. 263–286.

---

[29] R. Ball and P. Brown, "An Empirical Evaluation of Accounting Income Numbers," *Journal of Accounting Research*, Vol. 6, No. 2, Autumn, 1968, pp. 159–178.

[30] D. Craig Nichols and James Wahlen, "How Do Earnings Numbers Relate to Stock Returns? A Review of Classic Accounting Research with Updated Evidence," *Accounting Horizons* (December 2004), pp. 263–286.

To an accountant, the results of this study confirm that accounting earnings are very informative to the capital markets. For nonaccountants, the results underscore why company managers, equity investors, analysts, and fund managers pay so much attention to earnings numbers. The results also reveal why analysts and investors spend enormous amounts of time and energy developing forecasts of earnings changes and making investment decisions in stocks on the basis of their earnings expectations.

Empirical research in accounting has deepened our understanding of the many dimensions of the role of accounting numbers and financial statement information in the capital markets and other stakeholder settings. We will refer to important research results such as these throughout this book.

Ethics and Integrity in the Accounting Profession

The evidence in the preceding section shows that earnings numbers are associated with important economic consequences for share prices in the capital markets. In addition, financial statement information has a number of additional economic consequences. For example, financial statement information commonly affects a company's ability to borrow, enabling a financially healthy company to raise capital from creditors or pushing a distressed company into bankruptcy. In addition, the financial performance of a company, particularly in generating revenues and earnings, will impact employees' compensation and bonuses. Because of these consequences, accountants face intense pressure to behave with the highest level of professional ethics and integrity.

The pressure on accountants and auditors to apply GAAP or IFRS in a biased way in order to present a company in a favorable light can be very strong. Likewise, the pressure on accountants and auditors to avoid reporting negative information (such as a decrease in earnings or negative earnings) can be intense. The professional accountant must realize that we serve the greater good of society and owe a responsibility of ethics and fairness to all current and potential stakeholders that depend on the information we produce. As ethical accountants, we create tremendous social welfare by producing reliable and relevant information for decision makers. If we act as unethical accountants, we destroy social welfare and can do great harm to innocent stakeholders who are misled by unreliable information.

There are many situations in which accountants face **ethical dilemmas**, situations in which an accountant must have the integrity to make a decision about what is the "right" (ethical) action to take in given circumstances. Because accounting is a professional service that plays an important role in society, professional accounting organizations have established codes of ethics for their members. Members of the AICPA recognize that they have an obligation of self-discipline above and beyond the requirements of laws and regulations. To help guide members in performing their responsibilities in public practice, industry, government, and education, the AICPA adopted the **Code of Professional Conduct** (**CPC**). The CPC includes six *principles* that express the basic tenets of ethical and professional conduct and call for an unswerving commitment to honorable behavior, even at the sacrifice of personal advantage. Exhibit 1.14 summarizes these principles.[31]

Acting ethically is not easy. In some circumstances it can be very difficult, requiring disciplined integrity and professional judgment in pressure-filled situations. To prepare you to be a professional accountant with an understanding of the essential role of ethics in the accounting profession, each chapter contains "Ethical Dilemmas" like the one on the next page. These dilemmas will help you recognize the kinds of ethical challenges you may face in your career as an accountant, and they will help prepare you to deal with them with integrity.

---

[31] See *AICPA Code of Professional Conduct*, AICPA, http://www.aicpa.org.

> **Principles of the AICPA Code of Professional Conduct** — EXHIBIT 1.14
>
> I. **Responsibilities:** In carrying out their responsibilities as professionals, members should exercise sensitive professional and moral judgments in all their activities.
> II. **The Public Interest:** Members should act in a way that will serve the public interest, honor the public trust, and demonstrate commitment to professionalism.
> III. **Integrity:** To maintain and broaden public confidence, members should perform all professional responsibilities with the highest sense of integrity.
> IV. **Objectivity and Independence:** A member should be objective and free from conflicts of interest in discharging professional responsibilities. A member in public practice should be independent in fact and appearance when providing auditing and other attestation services.
> V. **Due Care:** A member should observe the profession's technical and ethical standards, strive continually to improve competence and the quality of services, and discharge professional responsibility to the best of the member's ability.
> VI. **Scope and Nature of Services:** A member in public practice should observe the Principles of the CPC in determining the scope and nature of services to be provided.

ETHICAL DILEMMA

Suppose an accountant discovers that the company holds substantial amounts of inventory that are now obsolete and worthless. Should the accountant report the truth, write off the inventory as an asset, and take a loss on obsolete inventory in earnings? Suppose the accountant also knows that the company is already in distress. Should the accountant seek ways to avoid or delay recognizing inventory losses that will cause the company to report lower earnings and thereby experience a drop in stock price and potential bankruptcy? What if the accountant knows the company is growing quickly and generating healthy profits?

GOT IT?

1-23 How are changes in stock prices associated with changes in earnings? What does research evidence indicate about the economic consequences of earnings information?

1-24 Why do accountants have to be ethical in their duties and responsibilities?

1-25 What are the six principles of the AICPA Code of Professional Conduct?

REVIEW CENTER

At the beginning of this chapter, we discussed the important roles financial accounting and financial reporting play in the world economy. In addition, we identified a number of objectives you would accomplish after reading the chapter. These objectives are listed below and followed with a brief review of the key takeaways.

LEARNING OBJECTIVE 1.1

Understand the forces that drive the demand for financial accounting information in the world economy.

KEY TAKEAWAYS

- The objective of financial reporting and financial accounting is to provide relevant and representationally faithful information to a variety of stakeholders (equity investors, creditors, managers, suppliers, customers, employees, and many others) so they can make rational and intelligent resource allocation decisions about companies.
- The demand for accounting information arises because companies need to compete for scarce resources.
- The demand for accounting information also arises to bridge the information gap between company managers (agents) and investors, creditors, and other stakeholders (principals) that provide scarce resources. This demand for information arises because the investors and creditors who own resources are separate from the managers who manage and control those resources.
- The demand for accounting information also drives the demand for professionally established accounting standards (U.S. GAAP and IFRS) that provide authoritative guidance on how to measure and report economic activities in financial statements, as well as the demand for independent auditing.

KEY TERMS

accounting standards, p. 1-8
agents, p. 1-6
financial reporting, p. 1-6
financing activities, p. 1-4
Generally Accepted Accounting Principles (U.S. GAAP), p. 1-8
independent audits, p. 1-8
information asymmetry problems, p. 1-7

International Financial Reporting Standards (IFRS), p. 1-8
investing activities, p. 1-4
operating activities, p. 1-4
principals, p. 1-6
separation of ownership and control, p. 1-6
stakeholders, p. 1-5

LEARNING OBJECTIVE 1.2

Understand the forces that determine the supply of accounting information, including the role of the Securities and Exchange Commission (SEC).

KEY TAKEAWAYS

- The supply of accounting information that companies report to external stakeholders is determined primarily by the interactions between two forces:
  - the authoritative professional accounting standards that govern in the company's country of incorporation (e.g., U.S. GAAP or IFRS), and
  - the many choices, methods, estimates, and judgments that the company must make in order to apply those accounting standards to measure and report their financial statements.
- The government body with the responsibility and authority over financial reporting in the United States is the Securities and Exchange Commission (SEC).

KEY TERMS

Financial Accounting Standards Board (FASB), p. 1-10
Form 10-K, p. 1-10
Form 10-Q, p. 1-10
Form 20-F, p. 1-10
Form 8-K, p. 1-10

International Accounting Standards Board (IASB), p. 1-10
Proxy Statement, p. 1-10
Securities and Exchange Commission (SEC), p. 1-9

LEARNING OBJECTIVE 1.3

Explain the role of the Financial Accounting Standards Board (FASB) for establishing U.S. generally accepted accounting principles (U.S. GAAP).

KEY TAKEAWAYS

- U.S. GAAP is established in the private sector by the Financial Accounting Standards Board (FASB) for U.S. companies, and IFRS are established by the International Accounting Standards Board (IASB) for non-U.S. companies.
- The FASB is a seven-member board representing a wide cross-section of interests in accounting (financial statement preparers, auditors, users, and academics).

KEY TERM
Emerging Issues Task Force (EITF), p. 1-11

KEY TAKEAWAYS
- The FASB organized and categorized U.S. GAAP into one structured, comprehensive body of literature known as the FASB Accounting Standards Codification system. The objective of the Codification is to simplify user access by organizing all authoritative U.S. GAAP in one comprehensive and up-to-date searchable database.
- The Codification is organized into a six-tiered hierarchical structure: (1) Areas, (2) Topics, (3) Subtopics, (4) Sections, (5) Subsections, and (6) Paragraphs.
- Before the FASB or the IASB issue an accounting standard update, a proposed topic undergoes an extensive due process that includes considerable research, preliminary views documents, numerous public hearings, exposure drafts, and frequent deliberations.

LEARNING OBJECTIVE 1.4
Explain and use the FASB Accounting Standards Codification system, and understand the standard-setting process.

KEY TERMS
Accounting Standards Update, p. 1-16   FASB Accounting Standards Codification, p. 1-13

KEY TAKEAWAYS
- International Financial Reporting Standards (IFRS) are established by the International Accounting Standards Board (IASB) for non-U.S. companies.
- The IASB is a sixteen-member board representing a wide cross-section of interests in accounting (financial statement preparers, auditors, users, and academics) from around the world.
- The FASB and the IASB are continuing to work together to converge U.S. GAAP and IFRS into a harmonized, consistent set of high-quality accounting principles.
- While accounting standards are intended to provide users with relevant and representationally faithful information for their decision-making needs, the FASB and IASB face intense social and political pressures, leading to final standards that can be a result of compromise.

LEARNING OBJECTIVE 1.5
Explain the role of the International Accounting Standards Board (IASB) in establishing International Financial Reporting Standards (IFRS) and the efforts to try to converge accounting standards between the FASB and the IASB.

KEY TERM
International convergence of accounting standards, p. 1-18

KEY TAKEAWAYS
- The balance sheet is the cornerstone of financial reporting. The balance sheet reports the assets, liabilities, and shareholders' equity which comprise the financial position of a company at a point in time, resulting from the company's operating, investing, and financing activities.
  - Assets represent probable future economic benefits obtained or controlled by the company as a result of past transactions and events.
  - Liabilities are obligations of the company to transfer assets or provide services to other entities in the future. Liabilities result from operating activities and from the company's use of short- and long-term borrowing to finance assets.
  - Shareholders' equity is the residual interest in the assets of the company, after satisfying the liabilities.
- The income statement reports the profitability of a company over a period of time. The income statement reports the financial performance of the company's operating activities, particularly revenues generated by selling goods and delivering services to customers, as well as the expenses incurred to operate the business.

LEARNING OBJECTIVE 1.6
Understand the output of the financial reporting process and the four primary financial statements, as well as the important information reported with financial statements.

- Revenues measure the inflows of assets and the settlements of obligations from selling goods and providing services to customers.
- Expenses represent resources consumed (or obligations incurred) for the costs of operating the company and generating revenues during a period of time.
- The income statement also reports income amounts related to investing activities (e.g., interest and dividend income) and financing activities (e.g., interest expense).
- The income statement also reports gains and losses from peripheral activities as well as income taxes.
- Net income reports the bottom-line profit or loss for the period for common equity shareholders.
- Comprehensive income is the change in equity of a company during a period from transactions, events, and circumstances relating to nonowner sources. Comprehensive income includes net income, plus (or minus) certain other types of gains (or losses) that are recognized in comprehensive income (and not in net income until they are realized in a cash flow).

- The statement of cash flows reflects the sources and uses of cash during a period. The statement classifies cash flows into operating, investing, and financing categories.
- The statement of shareholders' equity reports the amounts of shareholders' equity at the end of a period and how those amounts changed during the period.
- The notes to the financial statements explain the accounting methods, assumptions, estimates, and judgments used to prepare the statements.
- The MD&A section provides managers' insights and evaluation of the company's performance and risks.
- The managers' attestation and the independent auditor's attestation provide statements about and take responsibility for the quality and effectiveness of the company's internal control system and the fairness of its financial statements and notes in reporting a company's financial position, performance, and cash flows. The independent audit adds credibility and reliability to the financial statements and notes prepared by management.

KEY TERMS

assets, p. 1-24
assurance opinion, p. 1-32
audit opinion, p. 1-32
balance sheet, p. 1-22
comprehensive income, p. 1-27
earnings, p. 1-25
expenses, p. 1-25
income statement, p. 1-25
liabilities, p. 1-24
management discussion and analysis (MD&A), p. 1-30

net income (or net loss), p. 1-25
notes, p. 1-30
revenues, p. 1-25
Sarbanes-Oxley Act of 2002, p. 1-32
shareholders' equity, p. 1-24
statement of cash flows, p. 1-28
statement of changes in shareholders' equity, p. 1-28
statement of financial position, p. 1-22
statement of shareholders' equity, p. 1-28

KEY CALCULATIONS

$$\text{Assets} = \text{Liabilities} + \text{Shareholders' Equity}$$

$$\text{Net Income} = \text{Revenues} - \text{Expenses} + \text{Gains} - \text{Losses}$$

LEARNING OBJECTIVE 1.7
Understand that, because financial accounting information triggers important economic consequences, integrity and the ability to resolve ethical dilemmas is essential to the accounting profession.

KEY TAKEAWAYS

- Accounting information triggers important economic consequences about companies. For example, research evidence shows that firms that report earnings increases enjoy stock returns that are much higher than market-average returns, whereas firms that report earnings decreases experience stock returns that are much lower than the market average.

- Because accounting information triggers important economic consequences, accountants must act with integrity and exercise ethical professional judgment, especially in pressure-filled situations.
- The AICPA has adopted a Code of Professional Conduct that sets forth six principles for ethical and professional behavior.

KEY TERMS

Code of Professional Conduct (CPC), p. 1-34

ethical dilemmas, p. 1-34

EXERCISE

E1-1
LO 1.4

Pronouncements Although U.S. GAAP is now organized in the FASB Accounting Standards Codification, GAAP was initially created by many different types of pronouncements. The following is a list of seven types of pronouncements as well as a list of statements describing each pronouncement.

A. Statements of Financial Accounting Standards
B. Opinions
C. Technical Bulletins
D. Statements of Financial Accounting Concepts
E. Interpretations
F. Staff Positions
G. Accounting Research Bulletins

_____ 1. Pronouncements that provide clarification of conflicting or unclear issues relating to previously issued FASB *Statements of Standards*, APB *Opinions*, or *Accounting Research Bulletins*.

_____ 2. Issued by the FASB to provide guidance on accounting and reporting problems related to *Statements of Standards* or *Interpretations*.

_____ 3. Pronouncements of the APB that constitute generally accepted accounting principles unless specifically amended or rescinded.

_____ 4. Issued by the FASB as a series establishing a theoretical foundation upon which to base financial accounting and reporting standards.

_____ 5. Pronouncements of the Committee on Accounting Procedure (CAP) that constitute generally accepted accounting principles unless superceded or amended by the FASB.

_____ 6. Pronouncements issued by the FASB that establish generally accepted accounting principles and indicate the methods and procedures required on specific accounting issues.

_____ 7. Pronouncements issued to provide more timely and consistent application guidance in regard to FASB literature.

Required:
Place the appropriate letter (A–G) identifying each pronouncement on the line in front of the statement describing the pronouncement.

CASES

COMMUNICATION

C1-1
LO 1.3
AICPA Adapted

Accounting Principles
At the completion of the Darby Department Store audit, the president asks about the meaning of the phrase "in conformity with generally accepted accounting principles" that appears in your audit report on the management's financial statements. He observes that the meaning of the phrase must include more than what he thinks of as "principles."

(continued)

Required:
1. Explain the meaning of the term "accounting principles" as used in the audit report. (Do not discuss in this part the significance of "generally accepted.")
2. The president wants to know how an accounting principle becomes "generally accepted." Prepare a brief memo that provides an answer to the president's question.

C1-2
LO 1.3
CMA Adapted

Standard Setting

Considerable political and social influence is wielded by financial statement preparers and users—those parties who are most interested in or affected by accounting standards.

A premise of the FASB's standard-setting process is that it should operate in full view of the public, affording interested parties ample opportunity to make their views known. The extensive procedural steps employed by the FASB in the standard-setting process supports this premise.

Required:
Write a brief report that describes why financial accounting standards inspire or encourage political action and involvement during the standard-setting process.

C1-3
LO 1.3

Organization of the FASB

The FASB is organized to establish generally accepted accounting principles. It is assisted by various groups and operates under a set of procedures.

Required:
Prepare a short written report that summarizes the structure, operating procedures, and pronouncements of the FASB.

C1-4
LO 1.7

Code of Professional Conduct

In a few years, you may become a member of the AICPA and be subject to its *Code of Professional Conduct (CPC)*.

Required:
Identify and briefly discuss the first five principles of the CPC. Provide examples that illustrate each principle.

CREATIVE AND CRITICAL THINKING

C1-5
LO 1.3

Lobbying the FASB

One of your friends remarks, "I understand that before voting on an Update to Accounting Standards, the FASB allows written comments and oral presentations in which interested parties can lobby for a particular ruling. Do you think this is a good idea?"

Required:
Prepare a written response that discusses the advantages and disadvantages of the FASB's allowing interested parties to provide input to its deliberative process.

C1-6
LO 1.5

International Convergence

Your friend who is taking his first accounting course says to you, "We live in the United States. I thought that companies in the United States would follow U.S. accounting rules for preparing their financial statements. I also thought that foreign companies would follow international accounting rules. Now I hear something about the "convergence" of U.S. accounting rules and international accounting rules. And, I hear that the SEC is thinking about requiring U.S. companies to use international accounting rules for financial statements filed with it. What is going on and how will it be resolved?"

Required:
Prepare a memo that provides an in-depth answer to your friend's question.

C1-7
LO 1.6

Starbucks's Financial Statements

A friend is very interested in **Starbucks** as a company. Your friend is not a business major and has asked for your help to learn more about Starbucks. Refer to the financial statements and supplementary data for Starbucks in Appendix A.

Required:
Read through Appendix A, including the financial statements, the notes, managers' discussion and analysis, the managers' attestation statement, and the audit opinion. Prepare a brief written report for your friend that (in your opinion) provides two interesting and important pieces of information about Starbucks from the:

- Balance Sheet
- Income Statement
- Statement of Cash Flows
- Statement of Shareholders' Equity
- Management Discussion and Analysis

C1-8
LO 1.6

Nestlé's Financial Statements

You have just become friends with an exchange student from Switzerland. Your friend is very interested in **Nestlé** as a company. Your friend is not a business major and has asked for your help to learn more about Nestlé. Obtain Nestlé's 2013 annual report using the "Investor Relations" portion of its web site (do a Web search for Nestlé investor relations).

Required:
Read carefully through Nestlé's financial statements. Prepare a brief written report for your friend that (in your opinion) provides two interesting and important pieces of information about Nestlé from the:

- Balance Sheet
- Income Statement
- Statement of Cash Flows

C1-9
LO 1.6

Coca-Cola's Financial Statements

You are preparing to visit a friend who now lives in Atlanta. Your friend is very interested in **The Coca-Cola Company**. Your friend is not a business major and has asked for your help to learn more about Coca-Cola. Obtain The Coca-Cola Company's 2013 annual report either using the "Investor Relations" portion of its web site (do a Web search for Coca-Cola investor relations) or go to http://www.sec.gov and click "Search for company filings" under "Filings and Forms (EDGAR)."

Required:
Read carefully through Coca-Cola's financial statements. Prepare a brief written report for your friend that (in your opinion) provides two interesting and important pieces of information about Coca-Cola from the:

- Balance Sheet
- Income Statement
- Statement of Cash Flows

C1-10
LO 1.7

Ethical Responsibilities

Each person in one of your accounting classes is required to write a report on an accounting topic. Included in the report must be a discussion from a specific library book. When you go to the library, you find that the only copy of the book is missing. While sitting at a study desk, you overhear one of your classmates say that he has "misfiled" the book in the library so he can use it again later without having to wait for other students to finish using it.

Required:
Discuss the steps you would take to address this ethical dilemma. It is not necessary to state what ethical action you would take, but be prepared to discuss your reasoning for each step.

C1-11
LO 1.7

Ethical Responsibilities

You and a friend are in the same accounting class. During the first test, you observe your friend cheating by copying one of her answers from another student (who was unaware of the copying). When the exams are returned, your grade is a B, while your friend's grade is an A.

Required:
Discuss the steps you would take to address this ethical dilemma. It is not necessary to state what ethical action you would take, but be prepared to discuss your reasoning for each step.

USING CODIFICATION

C1-12 Codification

Situation

You are working as a teaching assistant for an accounting professor. The professor is preparing a new introductory accounting course for college-level students. In preparing the course, the professor has asked for your help in developing materials to introduce students to the FASB Accounting Standards Codification system. The professor is planning to have the Codification discussion toward the end of the course, after students have been introduced to the financial statements and what they report, and the major accounts and what they represent.

Directions

Write a memo that can be used as a handout in class for college students in an introductory course in accounting. The memo should explain:

a. What the FASB Accounting Standards Codification system is
b. How it is structured
c. Step-by-step instructions for how students should use it

C1-13 Codification

Situation

You are conducting an accounting research project for your manager. Your manager has asked you to determine the appropriate U.S. GAAP that specifies how your company should recognize and value a newly purchased piece of equipment on the company's balance sheet. Your manager also wants you to determine the GAAP guidance for how the equipment should be depreciated. Your manager has a lot of knowledge and experience in accounting, and has heard about, but has never used, the FASB Accounting Standards Codification system.

Directions

Use the FASB Accounting Standards Codification system to conduct the research your manager has assigned to you. Use the Codification to determine how to recognize, value, and depreciate a piece of equipment. Be prepared to show your manager the specific FASB ASC references that provide the appropriate guidance. Also prepare a brief memo explaining to your manager the different levels of the Codification and how to use the Codification system.

C1-14 Codification

Situation

You are conducting an accounting research project for your boss. Your boss has asked you to determine the appropriate U.S. GAAP that specifies how your company should recognize revenues from the sales of products in a retail store. Your boss is confused because most customers pay cash, but some customers purchase on credit terms, and pay in cash 30 days later. Your manager also wants you to determine the GAAP guidance for how revenue should be recognized in income. Your manager has a lot of knowledge and experience in accounting and has heard about, but has never used, the FASB Accounting Standards Codification system.

Directions

Use the FASB Accounting Standards Codification system to conduct the research your manager has assigned to you. Use the Codification to determine how to recognize revenue from retail sales, including the right to return. Be prepared to show your manager the specific FASB ASC references that provide the appropriate guidance. Also prepare a brief memo explaining to your manager the different levels of the Codification and how to use the Codification system.

CHAPTER 2

FINANCIAL REPORTING: ITS CONCEPTUAL FRAMEWORK

The Constitution of Financial Accounting ... The Conceptual Framework

When lawmakers and legislators in the United States propose new laws to govern the country, how do they know whether or not the proposed laws are consistent with the country's basic objectives for governing its people? What basis do proponents and opponents of the proposal have to assess the potential fairness of a new law? Often, they will evaluate whether or not the proposed law is consistent with the U.S. Constitution, which establishes the fundamental objectives and structure of government and the rights of freedom, justice, and equality for the people of the United States.

Within the accounting profession, the role of the Conceptual Framework is similar to the role of the Constitution because it sets forth the fundamental objectives, principles, and concepts that guide accounting standard setters, preparers, auditors, and users of financial statements. New accounting standards proposed by the FASB are evaluated relative to the Conceptual Framework. Existing standards that may need to be updated to improve financial reporting are also evaluated for their consistency with the Conceptual Framework.

LEARNING OBJECTIVES

After reading this chapter you will be able to

LO 2.1 Explain the FASB's Conceptual Framework.

LO 2.2 Explain the general and specific objectives of general purpose financial reporting.

LO 2.3 Explain the qualitative characteristics of decision-useful information as identified in the FASB and IASB Joint Conceptual Framework project.

LO 2.4 Understand and apply the major assumptions of financial reporting and U.S. GAAP.

LO 2.5 Describe the financial reporting model in the FASB's Conceptual Framework.

The Conceptual Framework sets forth essential components that are the foundation of financial reporting, including:

- the objectives of financial reporting
- the qualities of useful financial accounting information
- the definitions of basic elements like assets and liabilities
- the types of transactions, events, and arrangements that should be recognized in financial statements
- the measurement attributes to use to measure and report transactions, events, and arrangements
- how financial information should be presented and classified in financial statements

The Financial Accounting Standards Board (FASB) and the International Accounting Standards Board (IASB) worked together for several years to develop a common Conceptual Framework that would help standard setters achieve the goal of uniform, consistent, high-quality financial reporting standards. The joint efforts of the two Boards have concluded, and each Board is now working independently on further improvements to their own Conceptual Framework. The SEC has recommended that future accounting standards should not follow a rules-based nor principles-only approach, but should be "objectives-oriented." This objectives-oriented approach to standard setting must be built on an improved and consistently applied Conceptual Framework. New standards should state the accounting objective of the standard, provide sufficient detail and structure so that the standard can be applied consistently, and minimize exceptions to the standards. The development of conceptually sound, objectives-oriented standards should improve the usefulness of financial statement information, allowing investors, creditors, and other financial statement users to make more efficient and effective resource allocation decisions.

In this chapter, we describe three of the most fundamental aspects of the FASB's Conceptual Framework:

- objectives of financial reporting
- qualitative characteristics of useful accounting information
- fundamental principles and assumptions that guide financial accounting and reporting

In Chapters 4 and 5, we describe measurement and reporting in the balance sheet, income statement, statement of cash flows, and statement of shareholders' equity. In those chapters, we also describe the remaining fundamental components of the Conceptual Framework that apply directly to the financial statements:

- ten elements that comprise accounting information presented in financial statements
- measurement attributes used to measure and report economic transactions, events, and arrangements in financial statements
- accounting principles that guide recognition, derecognition, and disclosure, as well as the classification and presentation of information in financial statements

LEARNING OBJECTIVE 2.1
Explain the FASB's Conceptual Framework.

WHAT IS THE FASB'S CONCEPTUAL FRAMEWORK?

The FASB states the intent of the **Conceptual Framework** is to establish objectives and fundamental concepts that are the basis for development of financial accounting and reporting guidance. The objectives identify the goals and purposes of financial reporting. The fundamental underlying concepts of financial accounting guide the selection of transactions and events to be accounted for, their recognition and measurement, and the means of summarizing and communicating them to interested parties.

According to the FASB,

> "The Conceptual Framework is a coherent system of interrelated objectives and fundamental concepts that prescribes the nature, function, and limits of financial accounting and reporting and that is expected to lead to consistent guidance. It is intended to serve the public interest by providing structure and direction to financial accounting and reporting to facilitate the provision of unbiased financial and related information. That information helps capital and other markets to function efficiently in allocating scarce resources in the economy and society. Establishment of objectives and identification of fundamental concepts will not directly solve financial accounting and reporting problems. Rather, objectives give direction, and concepts are tools for solving problems."[1]

The Conceptual Framework therefore establishes a foundation of objectives, concepts, principles, and definitions that leads to high-quality financial accounting standards and the appropriate application of those standards in accounting practice. The Conceptual Framework is intended to:

- guide the FASB in establishing accounting standards
- establish objectives and concepts to guide financial statement preparers and auditors to resolve questions and make appropriate judgments in the preparation of financial statements, even in situations where a standard does not exist
- increase users' understanding of and confidence in financial reporting
- enhance financial statement comparability across companies and over time

To establish the Conceptual Framework, the FASB has issued a number of ***Statements of Financial Accounting Concepts (Concepts Statements)***. Concepts Statements are general proclamations that establish:

- fundamental principles of accounting
- objectives of financial reporting
- qualities of useful financial accounting information
- definitions of basic elements like assets and liabilities
- types of economic transactions, events, and arrangements to be recognized in financial statements
- measurement attributes to use to measure and report these transactions, events, and arrangements
- how transactions, events, and arrangements should be presented and classified in financial statements

How Do Principles, Concepts, Standards, and Rules Differ?

What are the differences between principles, concepts, standards, and rules? In the broadest sense, **accounting principles** are fundamental theories, truths, and propositions that serve as the practical foundation for financial accounting and financial reporting. The most fundamental statements of these principles come from the FASB's Concepts Statements.

The Concepts Statements and fundamental principles form the basis and the objectives of **generally accepted accounting principles (GAAP)**, which are the specific methods and practices that U.S. companies are required to use in preparing and reporting specific items of accounting information in financial statements for use by external stakeholders and decision makers. GAAP consists of the full set of formal statements, known as **accounting standards**, that establish the authoritative guidance on how companies should account for and report specific transactions, events, and arrangements in their financial statements. In the United States, GAAP is established by the FASB and is

---

[1] FASB, "Conceptual Framework for Financial Reporting," (Norwalk, CT, September 2010).

organized in the **Accounting Standards Codification**. The FASB establishes new GAAP through **Accounting Standards Updates** to the Codification. While the Concepts Statements themselves are not considered GAAP, they establish the objectives, concepts, definitions, and principles of accounting that GAAP applies to specific areas and topics. For example, Concepts Statements define assets, liabilities, revenues, expenses, and other elements. Specific accounting standards in GAAP provide guidance on when and how to recognize and measure these elements in financial statements. Exhibit 2.1 shows the relationship among the objectives, concepts, principles, and definitions in the Conceptual Framework and the standards issued by the FASB that comprise GAAP.

EXHIBIT 2.1 Relationship of the FASB's Conceptual Framework to the Standard-Setting Process

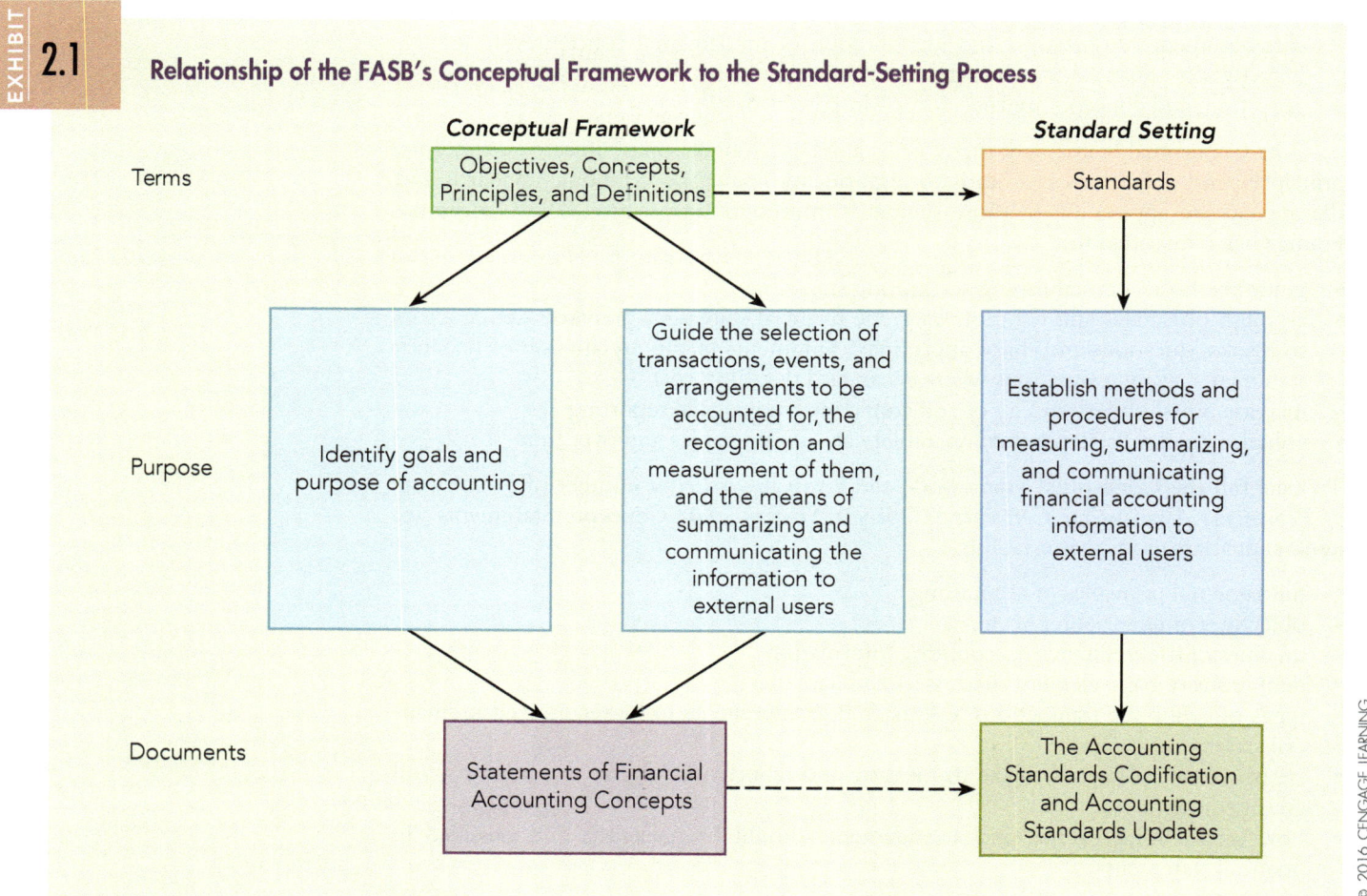

Rules represent specific implementation guidelines through which financial statement preparers apply accounting standards to measure and report a company's financial statements. Rules are typically written within standards. Rules differ from standards in that rules set forth specific methods and guidance for applying accounting standards. For example, a company might determine that its inventory should be recognized on the balance sheet as an asset if the inventory is consistent with the Conceptual Framework's definition of an asset. Specific standards will provide the company guidance on when to recognize inventory, what methods to use to account for inventory (such as LIFO, FIFO, or weighted average), and when to derecognize the inventory once it is sold to a customer. Specific rules exist for inventory accounting, such as the rule that the company must report the inventory value at the lower of the cost or market value. To compare:

- **Concepts Statements and principles are broad and definitional.**
- **Standards are authoritative statements that comprise GAAP and are applications of concepts and principles to different types of transactions, events, and arrangements.**
- **Rules are specific implementation procedures within accounting standards.**

Recent debate in the accounting profession has been devoted to whether accounting standards should be principles-based or rules-based. Some assert that IFRS are principles-based whereas U.S. GAAP is rules-based. However, both U.S. GAAP and IFRS are based on concepts, principles, and rules. Therefore, standards should be evaluated based on how well they meet the objectives established in the Conceptual Framework. Rules should be evaluated by whether they enable practitioners to implement the standards in order to provide relevant and representationally faithful information to financial statement users, or whether they enable practitioners to manipulate reported financial statement amounts.

Conceptual Framework: Brief History and Current Status

In establishing the Conceptual Framework, the FASB divided its initial activities into several projects, as shown in Exhibit 2.2. The first project resulted in *Statement of Financial Accounting Concepts No. 1*, "Objectives of Financial Reporting by Business

EXHIBIT 2.2 Conceptual Framework Projects for Financial Accounting and Reporting

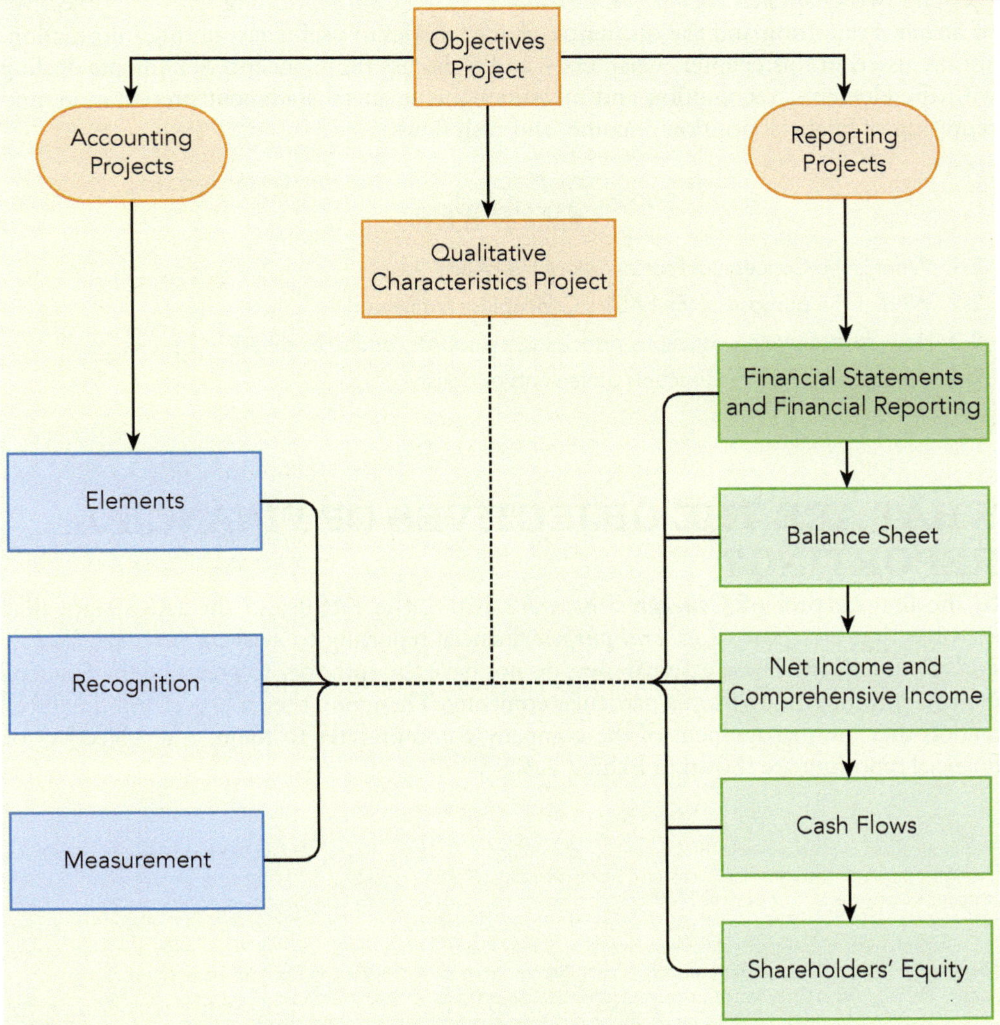

Source: Adapted from Figure 1 in "The Conceptual Framework Project," Financial Accounting Standards Board (Stamford, CT, 1980).

Enterprises," issued in 1978. This document established the primary objectives of financial accounting and established the focus of the remaining projects, which were divided into two groups, accounting and reporting. The Qualitative Characteristics Project linked together the accounting and reporting projects. It resulted in *Statement of Financial Accounting Concepts No. 2*, "Qualitative Characteristics of Accounting Information," issued in 1980.

The accounting projects define the accounting elements (such as assets, liabilities, revenues, expenses) and identify which elements should be recognized in financial statements, when they should be reported, and how they should be measured.[2] The reporting projects deal with how the elements of financial reports are classified and presented in financial statements, what information should be provided, and where the information should be presented.[3]

The FASB and the IASB worked closely together on a Joint Conceptual Framework. As a result of their collaboration, the FASB and the IASB released a joint Concepts Statement in September 2010.[4] *Statement of Financial Accounting Concepts No. 8*, "Conceptual Framework for Financial Reporting," contains two chapters. Chapter 1 is titled "The Objective of General Purpose Financial Reporting," and Chapter 3 is titled "Qualitative Characteristics of Useful Financial Information." These chapters supersede FASB *Concepts Statements No. 1* and *No. 2*.

The two chapters of *Concepts Statement No. 8 (Con 8)*, dealing with the objectives of financial reporting and the qualitative characteristics of useful accounting information, are discussed in this chapter. Chapters 4 and 5 discuss the Concepts Statements dealing with the elements, recognition and measurement, financial statement presentation, and reporting of financial position, income, and cash flows.

GOT IT?

2-1 What is the Conceptual Framework of the FASB?
2-2 What is the purpose of the FASB's Conceptual Framework?
2-3 How do accounting concepts, principles, standards, and rules differ?
2-4 What do the FASB's Concepts Statements establish?

LEARNING OBJECTIVE 2.2
Explain the general and specific objectives of general purpose financial reporting.

WHAT ARE THE OBJECTIVES OF FINANCIAL REPORTING?

In the first chapter of *Concepts Statement No. 8*, the FASB and the IASB state that the objectives are those of *general purpose* financial reporting to *external investors, lenders, and other creditors*. These external users do not have the authority to prescribe the financial information they desire from a particular company. Therefore, they must rely on the information that the management of the company communicates to them. The objectives of financial reporting are shown in Exhibit 2.3.

---

[2] For a discussion of these and other issues, see L. T. Johnson and R. K. Storey, 'Recognition in Financial Statements: Underlying Concepts and Practical Conventions,' *Research Report* (Stamford, CT: FASB, 1982).

[3] Appendix B provides a list of all of the FASB Concepts Statements. The FASB defined the financial reporting elements in *Statement of Financial Accounting Concepts No. 6*, "Elements of Financial Statements" (issued in 1986 to replace *Concepts No. 3*, titled "Elements of Financial Statements of Business Enterprises"). The FASB addresses recognition and measurement and other issues in *Statement of Financial Accounting Concepts No. 5*, "Recognition and Measurement in Financial Statements of Business Enterprises" (1984), and in *Statement of Financial Accounting Concepts No. 7*, "Using Cash Flow Information and Present Value in Accounting Measurements" (2000. The FASB also addresses conceptual issues for nonbusiness organizations in *Statement of Financial Accounting Concepts No. 4*, "Objectives of Financial Reporting by Nonbusiness Organizations," which we do not discuss in this text.

[4] The FASB and IASB have concluded their joint efforts, and each Board is proceeding independently on further developments to their respective Conceptual Frameworks. This chapter focuses on the FASB's Conceptual Framework.

Objectives of Financial Reporting

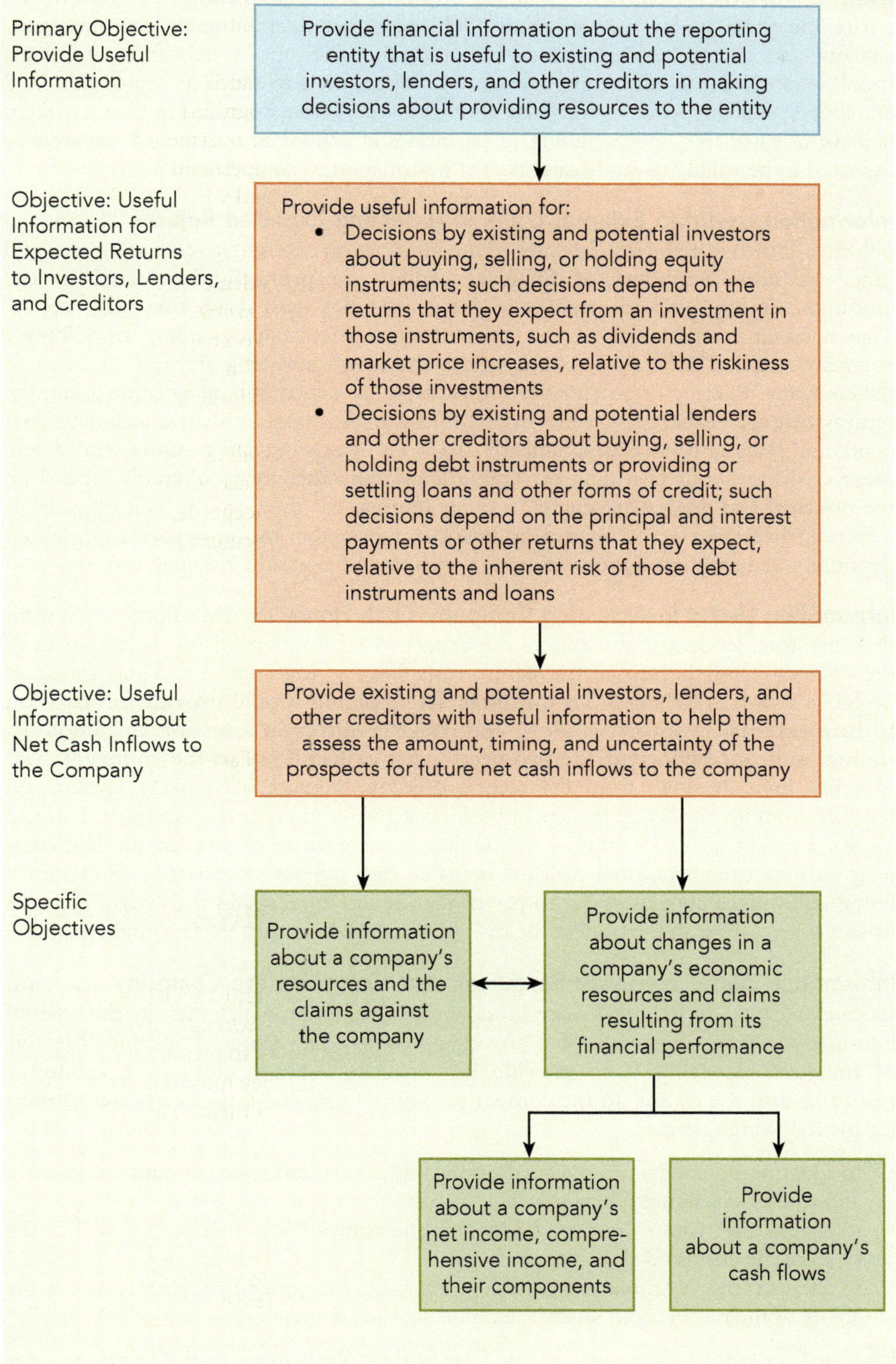

EXHIBIT 2.3

Primary Objective: Provide Useful Information
> Provide financial information about the reporting entity that is useful to existing and potential investors, lenders, and other creditors in making decisions about providing resources to the entity

Objective: Useful Information for Expected Returns to Investors, Lenders, and Creditors
> Provide useful information for:
> - Decisions by existing and potential investors about buying, selling, or holding equity instruments; such decisions depend on the returns that they expect from an investment in those instruments, such as dividends and market price increases, relative to the riskiness of those investments
> - Decisions by existing and potential lenders and other creditors about buying, selling, or holding debt instruments or providing or settling loans and other forms of credit; such decisions depend on the principal and interest payments or other returns that they expect, relative to the inherent risk of those debt instruments and loans

Objective: Useful Information about Net Cash Inflows to the Company
> Provide existing and potential investors, lenders, and other creditors with useful information to help them assess the amount, timing, and uncertainty of the prospects for future net cash inflows to the company

Specific Objectives
- Provide information about a company's resources and the claims against the company ↔ Provide information about changes in a company's economic resources and claims resulting from its financial performance
  - Provide information about a company's net income, comprehensive income, and their components
  - Provide information about a company's cash flows

Information Useful in Decision Making

The primary objective in Exhibit 2.3 states that **financial reporting should provide useful information about the reporting entity for existing and potential investors, lenders, and other creditors in making decisions about providing resources to the entity**. Investors are the equity security holders (shareholders), equity fund managers, analysts, and others. Lenders include banks, lending institutions, debt security holders (bondholders), and credit rating agencies. Creditors include suppliers, customers, and employees, and other parties with claims on the firm. These external users are expected to have a reasonable understanding of business and economic activities. They are also expected to be willing to study carefully the information to comprehend it.

Information Useful to External Users in Assessing Expected Returns The second objective shown in Exhibit 2.3 relates to the information needs of investors, lenders, and other creditors. **Suppliers of financial capital are primarily interested in the amounts, timing, and uncertainty of the prospective cash flows they will receive.** They need information to assess the expected returns from buying, selling, or holding a company's equity, debt, or other financial instruments or issuing and settling loans to the company. Existing or potential investors' decisions depend on information about the returns that they expect to receive from an investment in equity shares, including dividends and share price increases. Similarly, decisions by existing and potential lenders and other creditors about providing or settling loans and other forms of credit depend on the principal and interest payments or other returns that they expect. This objective is important because external users need financial information to form expectations about the timing and amount of prospective cash receipts and assess the risk involved.

Information Useful in Assessing Company Cash Flows The cash flows and returns that investors, lenders, and creditors can expect to receive depend on the resources of the company and the prospective future cash flows of the company. Thus, the third objective shown in Exhibit 2.3 is that **financial reporting should provide information to help external investors, lenders, and other creditors in assessing the amounts, timing, and uncertainty of the prospective net cash inflows to the company**. This objective logically flows from the second objective because a company invests cash received from investors and lenders in business activities in order to earn more cash and receive a return *on* its investment in addition to a return *of* its investment. The company's ability to generate net cash inflows (i.e., cash inflows greater than its cash outflows) determines both its ability to pay dividends and interest and the market prices of its securities. These, in turn, affect the cash flows to the investors, lenders, and creditors.

Information about Economic Resources and Claims on the Company The most specific objectives in Exhibit 2.3 are those in the bottom tier, which indicate the types of information that a company should provide in its financial reports. **A specific objective of financial reporting is to provide information about a company's economic resources and the claims on the company.**[5] This information is useful to external users for the following reasons:

- to identify the company's resources, obligations, financial strengths and weaknesses, and to assess its liquidity and solvency
- to specify the types of resources in which the company has invested, as well as the types of the claims on the company
- to indicate the potential future cash flows from the company's resources and the ability of the resources to satisfy the claims on the company

Information about Changes in the Company's Resources and Claims Another specific objective of financial reporting is to **provide information about the financial**

---

[5] We discuss measuring and reporting financial position in Chapter 4.

performance, as well as other transactions and events, which cause the company's resources and the claims on the company to change during the period. Information about a company's financial performance helps external users assess the return a company has earned on its economic resources and form expectations about its future performance. In particular, information concerning the company's net income, comprehensive income, and their components is useful to external users in:

- evaluating management's performance
- estimating the company's "earning power" or other amounts that are representative of persistent long-term income-producing ability
- predicting future income and net cash inflows
- assessing the risk of investing in or lending to the company

Net income and comprehensive income should measure and report the economic resources the company has generated and consumed during the period. Accrual accounting measures and reports the economic effects of a company's transactions, events, and circumstances on a company's economic resources and claims in the periods in which those effects occur, even if the related cash receipts and payments occur in a different period. This is important because information about a company's economic resources and claims, as well as the changes in these resources and claims, provides a better basis for assessing the company's past and future financial performance than information solely about cash receipts and payments.

Another specific objective of financial reporting is to **provide information about how a company's cash flows cause changes in the company's resources and claims**. Cash flow information shows how a company obtains and spends cash for its operating, investing, and financing activities, including cash dividends and other distributions of company resources to owners.[6] Investors, lenders, and other creditors use cash flow information about a company to:

- help understand its operations and cash-generating ability
- evaluate its strategic sourcing and use of cash for financing and investing activities
- assess its liquidity and solvency
- interpret other information about financial performance

Concepts Statement No. 8 also notes another important objective implicit in assessing a company's prospects for future cash inflows. **Financial reporting should provide information about how efficiently and effectively the company's management and governing board have discharged their responsibilities to use the company's resources.** This is commonly referred to as management's stewardship responsibility. Management is responsible to the owners for the custody and safekeeping of the resources, their efficient and profitable use, and their protection against unfavorable economic impacts, technological developments, and social changes.

Information about a company's financial performance helps users to understand how well management has discharged its responsibilities to make efficient and effective use of those resources. Information about the variability and components of financial performance also is important, especially in assessing the uncertainty of future cash flows. Information about a company's past financial performance and how its management discharged its responsibilities is useful for decisions by existing investors, lenders, and other creditors who have the right to vote on or otherwise influence management's actions.

Types of Useful Information for Investors, Lenders, and Other Creditors

Investors, lenders, and other creditors have different needs for information to assess their potential future cash receipts. In general, the following types of information are

---

[6] We discuss performance reporting, comprehensive income, and the statement of cash flows in Chapter 5.

helpful in assessing the amounts, timing, and uncertainty of expected future cash flows to a company:

- return on investment
- risk
- financial flexibility
- liquidity
- operating capability

Return on investment provides a measure of overall company performance for equity shareholders. Shareholders invest capital for a share of the equity of a company, giving them a claim on the company and its future comprehensive income. These investors are primarily concerned with the expected return *on* capital relative to the level of risk. Shareholders receive a return on capital from the dividends they receive as well as the appreciation in the value of their shares, which are determined by the company's profitability.

Risk is the uncertainty or unpredictability of the future profitability of a company. The greater the variability and uncertainty in a company's future financial performance, the greater the risk of an investment in or extension of credit to the company. Risk is caused by numerous factors including high rates of technological change, uncertainty about demand, exposure to the effects of unexpected price changes, unexpected changes in the economy, and political changes. The greater the risk of a particular company, the higher the rate of return expected by investors and lenders.

Financial flexibility is the ability of a company to use its financial resources to adapt to change and to take advantage of opportunities when they arise. Financial flexibility is important because it enables a company to respond to unexpected needs and opportunities. Financial flexibility comes from a company's ability to:

- adapt operations to increase net operating cash inflows
- raise new capital through, for instance, issuing debt or stock securities
- obtain cash by selling assets without disrupting ongoing operations

Financial flexibility affects risk as well as cash flows. Greater financial flexibility reduces the risk of failure in the event of an unexpected shortage in net cash flows from operations.

Liquidity of a company refers to how quickly a company can convert its assets into cash to meet short-term obligations and cover operating costs. The liquidity of an asset depends on the company's ability to quickly turn the asset into cash.

- For current operating assets, such as receivables and inventory, liquidity arises from cash inflows in the normal course of business operations.
- For noncurrent operating assets, such as property, plant, and equipment, liquidity refers to marketability. General purpose assets like land or an office building will have greater marketability than a unique asset such as a customized production plant.
- For financial assets, such as investment securities, liquidity depends on how efficiently the securities can be sold and converted into cash.

Liquidity is positively related to financial flexibility but negatively related to both risk and return on investment. A more liquid company is likely to have a lower risk of failure as well as a superior ability to adapt to unexpected opportunities and meet obligations as they become due. On the other hand, liquid assets often generate lower rates of return than illiquid assets.

Operating capability refers to the ability of a company to efficiently produce goods and services for customers. Operating capability may be indicated by:

- the quantity of goods (inventory) or services produced in a given period
- the productive capacity of the long-lived assets (e.g., property, plant, and equipment and intangibles)
- the efficiency of the production process

Information about operating capability is helpful in understanding a company's past performance and in predicting future changes in its volume of activities. Operating capability may be affected by changes in methods of operations, changes in product or service lines, and the timing of the replacement of the service potential used up in operations.

> ### GOT IT?
>
> **2-5** What is the most general objective of financial reporting? Who are investors, lenders, and other creditors?
>
> **2-6** What is the Objective: Useful Information for Expected Returns to Investors, Lenders, and Other Creditors, and why is it important?
>
> **2-7** What is the Objective: Useful Information about Net Cash Inflows to the Company, and why is it important?
>
> **2-8** List the reasons why external stakeholders use information about a company's (a) economic resources and claims to these resources, (b) comprehensive income and its components, and (c) cash flows.
>
> **2-9** Why should financial reporting provide useful information about the stewardship of company management?
>
> **2-10** Define (a) return on investment, (b) risk, (c) financial flexibility, (d) liquidity, and (e) operating capability.

WHAT QUALITIES MAKE ACCOUNTING INFORMATION USEFUL?

LEARNING OBJECTIVE 2.3
Explain the qualitative characteristics of decision-useful information as identified in the FASB and IASB Joint Conceptual Framework project.

In the previous sections, we discussed the objectives of financial reporting and the types of information that are helpful in investment and credit decision making. But what are the *qualities* of useful information? The purpose of Chapter 3 in the joint FASB and IASB *Concepts Statement No. 8* is to specify the qualitative characteristics that make information most useful to existing and potential investors, lenders, and other creditors.[7] The Joint Conceptual Framework identifies and defines decision-useful information in terms of fundamental (necessary) characteristics and enhancing characteristics. These characteristics guide standard setters and financial statement preparers when choosing among accounting alternatives because these qualities distinguish more-useful from less-useful information.

Each accounting alternative, however, may possess a greater degree of one quality and less of another. Although there is much agreement about the qualitative characteristics that useful accounting information should possess, there exists no consensus about the best combination of qualitative characteristics for every financial statement user's decision-making purposes.

Qualitative Characteristics

Exhibit 2.4 illustrates the relations between the qualitative characteristics of useful accounting information, including the fundamental characteristics, enhancing characteristics, and constraints on decision-useful information as described in the joint FASB and IASB *Concepts Statement No. 8.*

---

[7] The discussion in this section is primarily a summary of the discussion in Chapter 3, "Qualitative Characteristics of Useful Financial Information" in FASB *Statement of Financial Accounting Concepts No. 8*, "Conceptual Framework for Financial Reporting," (Norwalk, CT, 2010).

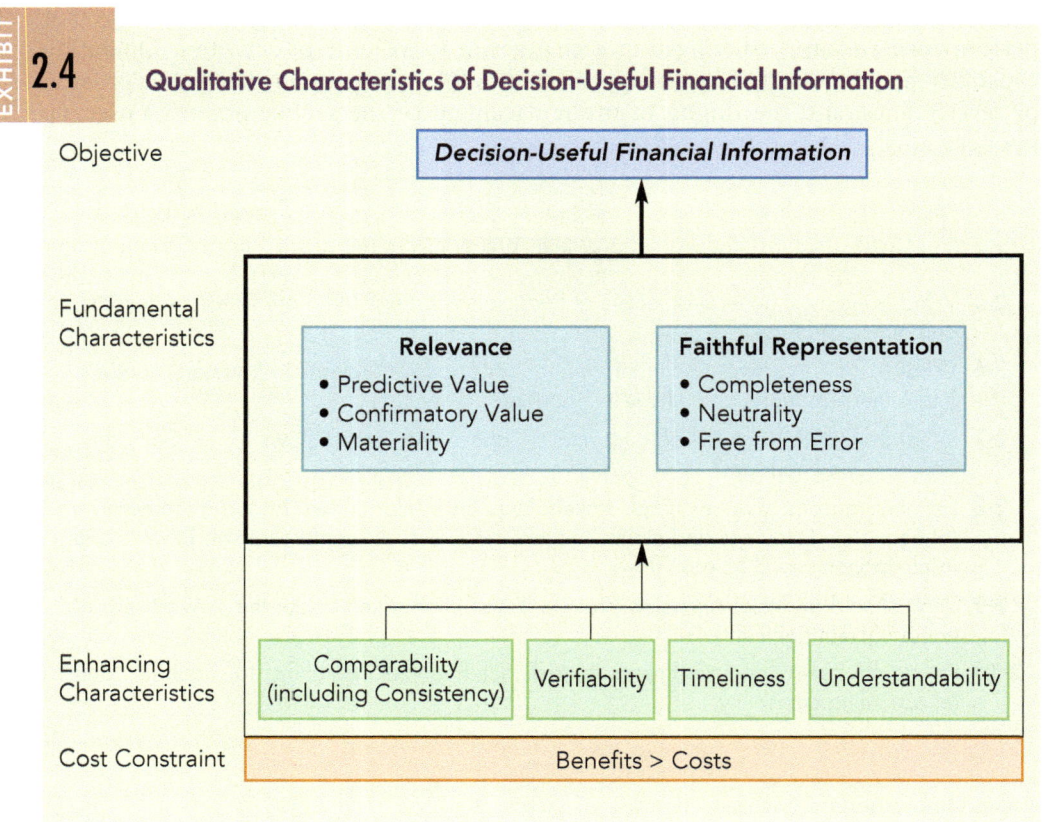

EXHIBIT 2.4 Qualitative Characteristics of Decision-Useful Financial Information

Decision Usefulness

Decision usefulness is the ultimate objective of accounting information. The FASB and the IASB state that the objective of financial reporting is decision usefulness for investors, lenders, and other creditors. This overall goal of decision usefulness can be achieved if the accounting information has a sufficient degree of the fundamental characteristics of relevance and faithful representation.

Relevance Accounting information has **relevance** if it is capable of making a difference in decisions made by financial statement users. Information can make a difference if it helps users predict future outcomes and/or confirm or correct prior expectations, and if it is material in nature and amount.

Predictive Value and Confirmatory Value To have **predictive value**, accounting information should help users form expectations about the future. The information itself does not have to be expressed as a prediction. Information about a company's current resources or obligations or about its past performance can provide a useful basis for expectations for the future. Financial information has predictive value if it can be used as an input to a process to predict future outcomes (such as an analyst's forecast).

Financial information has **confirmatory value** if it provides feedback to confirm or correct prior predictions and expectations. Often, relevant information will have both predictive and confirmatory value. Information about outcomes from a company's previous actions (i.e., feedback) generally will improve a decision maker's ability to predict the future outcomes from similar actions. For example, current period revenue is relevant if it helps users confirm (or correct) their revenue expectations for the current period, which will help users predict future revenues.

Materiality Materiality is an entity-specific aspect of relevance. **Materiality** refers to the nature and magnitude of an omission or misstatement of accounting information that would influence the judgment of a reasonable person relying on that information.

A company may make a decision to disclose certain information because users need that information (it is relevant) *and* because the amount is large enough to make a difference (it is material). Alternatively, a decision not to disclose certain information may be made because the user has no need for the information (it is not relevant) *or* because the amount is too small to make a difference (it is not material).

Because materiality depends on entity-specific circumstances, the FASB did not set quantitative guidelines for materiality in the Statements of Concepts. Instead, materiality requires judgment to determine whether an item would influence users' decisions. To assist in the evaluation of materiality, the FASB suggested that companies should consider:

- the *nature* of the item (i.e., minor items that result from routine transactions; for example, it might not be material to report liabilities for wages payable separately from the accrued payroll taxes on those wages)
- the *relative size* rather than absolute size of an item (i.e., a $10,000 error in inventory of a large company may be insignificant while a similar $10,000 error by a small company may be material)

Several groups (such as the SEC, the AICPA, and the PCAOB) have also provided guidance in assessing the materiality of a misstated item for a company.[8] These include, for instance, whether the misstatement:

- has an effect on trends (particularly trends in profitability)
- masks a change in earnings and earnings per share
- is currently immaterial but may have a material impact in future periods because of a cumulative effect
- changes a net loss into net income (or vice versa)
- misrepresents the company's compliance with loan agreements
- relates to a segment of the company that is particularly important to the company's long-run profitability
- increases management's compensation

Thus, companies may use a quantitative threshold as an initial step in assessing materiality, but need to consider qualitative factors in determining the materiality of an item.

Faithful Representation Financial reports represent economic transactions, events, and arrangements with words and numbers. Accounting information is a **faithful representation** of the underlying economic transactions, events, and arrangements when the words and numbers accurately depict the economic substance of what they purport to represent. To be a faithful representation, the information must be complete, neutral, and free from error.[9]

- A **complete representation** provides a user with full disclosure of all the information necessary to understand the information being reported, with all necessary facts, descriptions, and explanations.
- A **neutral representation** is not biased, slanted, emphasized, or otherwise manipulated to achieve a predetermined result or to influence users' behavior in a *particular* direction. However, neutral does not mean that accounting information does not influence human behavior. Indeed, accounting information is intended to be useful in decision making, thereby influencing the decision makers' behavior but not in a predetermined or manipulated direction.

---

[8] For more extensive discussions of materiality, see "Materiality," *SEC Staff Accounting Bulletin No. 99* (Washington, D.C.: SEC, 1999); "Audit Risk and Materiality in Conducting an Audit," *AICPA Professional Standards, Volume 1* (New York: AICPA, 2007), section 312; and "Consideration of Materiality in Panning and Performing an Audit," *PCAOB Auditing Standards No. 11.*

[9] Sometimes, in conjunction with faithful representation, you will hear that accounting information needs to be *transparent* (rather than opaque). Transparent accounting information is clear and not distorted, which allows external users to clearly see through the information in order to understand the underlying transactions, events, and arrangements the information represents.

- **Free from error** means the information is measured and described as accurately as possible, using a process that reflects the best available inputs. Free from error does not imply certainty or precision. For instance, many of the amounts reported on financial statements are estimates based on expectations of future outcomes. Nevertheless, estimates may be faithful representations if they are described as estimates, they are depicted in a way to provide users with a complete understanding of the inputs to the estimates, the inputs are unbiased, and the estimates are based on a reasonably accurate estimation process.

The Relation between Relevance and Faithful Representation Accounting information is most useful to decision makers when it is both relevant and faithfully represented. Accounting does not help users make good decisions when it provides a faithful representation of a piece of irrelevant information, or an unfaithful representation of relevant information.

Relevance and faithful representation are not necessarily tradeoffs—one may not have to be sacrificed for the other. Accounting standards and accounting practitioners must strive to maximize both characteristics to provide users with the most decision-useful information possible. For example, one company might report on its balance sheet the fair value of an investment in a share of common equity of another firm (an investment security), and that value might be very relevant and faithfully represented if the fair value is determined using market prices for identical or similar securities that are readily traded. On the other hand, if the security was purchased many years ago, the amount of initial investment in that security may be a very faithful representation of the historical cost, but might not be very relevant to financial statement users today. Similarly, suppose that the share of stock is in a private company that is not traded, and that company provides its own estimate of the fair value of its own shares. That fair value is relevant but might not be a faithful representation of value.

The most efficient and effective process for applying the fundamental qualitative characteristics is as follows:

- *Step 1.* Identify an economic transaction, event, or arrangement that needs to be recognized in the financial statements.
- *Step 2.* Identify the type of information that would be most relevant—material and capable of making a difference in decision makers' predictions of future outcomes and/or confirmations of past predictions.
- *Step 3.* Determine whether that information can be faithfully represented in a manner that is complete, neutral, and free from error.
- *Step 4.* Assess whether the benefits of that information are likely to exceed its cost. If so, that information has the fundamental characteristics that are necessary to be useful. If not, repeat the process with the next-most-relevant type of information.

Enhancing Characteristics

The FASB and IASB also describe four characteristics that enhance the decision usefulness of information that is relevant and faithfully represented:

- comparability
- verifiability
- timeliness
- understandability

Because these characteristics improve the usefulness of financial information, they should be maximized to the extent possible. However, they cannot, either individually or in combination with each other, make irrelevant or unfaithfully represented information useful for decision making.

Comparability Information about a company is more useful if it can be compared with similar information from other companies (*intercompany* comparison) or from past periods within the company (*intracompany* comparison). Because investors, lenders, and creditors often compare different companies or assess how certain companies change over time, comparability enhances the usefulness of relevant and faithfully represented information. It is an *interactive quality* of the relationship between two or more items of information. **Comparability** of accounting information enables users to identify and explain similarities and differences between two or more sets of economic facts. Note that comparability does not mean uniformity. Comparability means similar things look similar and different things look different.

Although related to comparability, **consistency** means that accounting methods and procedures are applied in the same manner from period to period. Consistency is a quality of the accounting process rather than a quality of the accounts and amounts themselves. Consistency helps to achieve the goal of comparability across periods, but only if the underlying phenomena being reported remain the same. If the economic circumstances change, or preferable new accounting standards become available, a company will have to sacrifice consistency to improve the usefulness of its accounting information.

Comparability ensures that investors, lenders, and creditors have useful accounting information when comparing different companies or the same company for different periods.

Verifiability Accounting information is **verifiable** when different knowledgeable and independent observers can reach consensus (but not necessarily complete agreement) that a particular representation is faithful. Verification means that other accountants would agree that the words to describe an account or an activity represent fairly what they purport to represent and that the amount or value used to depict that account or activity is measured without error or bias (although they may not necessarily agree on the exact amount). That is, the measurement results can be independently duplicated. Verification mitigates financial statement users' skepticism about potential bias, because by using the same method to repeat measurements, both unintentional and intentional errors are reduced. When auditors issue an opinion verifying that financial statements have been prepared by the company fairly according to GAAP, it enhances users' confidence that the financial statements faithfully represent the company's economic resources, claims, and financial performance.

Timeliness Accounting information is **timely** when it is available to decision makers in time to influence their decisions. If information is not available when it is needed, it lacks relevance and is not useful. Timeliness alone cannot make information relevant, but a lack of timeliness reduces its potential relevance. However, increasing relevance by increasing timeliness may require the sacrifice of other desirable qualitative characteristics (e.g., verifiability). The SEC has established minimum requirements for timeliness, requiring that each large company under its jurisdiction file a Form 10-K annual report within 60 days of its fiscal year-end and a Form 10-Q quarterly report within 40 days of the end of each quarter.

Understandability **Understandability** means that accounting information should be comprehensible to users who have a reasonable knowledge of business and economic activities and who are willing to study the information carefully. Although financial accounting measures and reports business activities and events that can be very complex, the objective is to provide relevant and representationally faithful information about those activities and events that conscientious financial statement users can understand.

The Cost Constraint To identify what financial information should be disclosed in financial reports, the qualitative characteristics are bounded by a single, pervasive constraint—the **cost constraint**. While accounting information is very beneficial to decision makers, it is also costly to prepare and use. The preparer (the company) initially incurs the costs of collecting, processing, auditing, and communicating the information.

The costs might also include the risk of losing a competitive advantage by disclosing the information. The benefits from the information are enjoyed by a diverse group of investors and creditors and by the company itself because, by providing the information, it can compete for and attract scarce economic resources (recall the discussion in Chapter 1). To be reported, accounting information not only must be relevant and faithfully represented but it also must pass an economic test by satisfying the benefit/cost constraint. In adopting new accounting standards, the FASB must have reasonable assurance that the costs of implementing a standard will not exceed the benefits. The determination of whether the benefits of providing (and receiving) financial information justify the related costs is usually more of a qualitative assessment than a quantitative one.

GOT IT?

2-11 What are the two primary qualities of useful accounting information?

2-12 What is relevant accounting information? Identify and define the characteristics of relevant accounting information.

2-13 What is materiality, and how does it relate to relevance?

2-14 What is faithfully represented accounting information? Identify and define the characteristics of faithful representation of accounting information.

2-15 Identify the enhancing characteristics of useful accounting information. Why is each one important, and how do they enhance information usefulness?

2-16 Compare and contrast comparability and consistency.

2-17 What is the cost constraint, and how does it affect financial reporting?

LEARNING OBJECTIVE 2.4
Understand and apply the major assumptions of financial reporting and U.S. GAAP.

WHAT ARE THE MOST IMPORTANT ASSUMPTIONS IN ACCOUNTING?

Certain assumptions have had an important impact on the development of accounting and U.S. GAAP. Exhibit 2.5 is useful for understanding the relationship among the objectives, types of useful information, qualitative characteristics, accounting assumptions, generally accepted accounting principles, financial reports, and elements of financial statements. We discuss the accounting assumptions listed in Exhibit 2.5 in this section. We will discuss the others later in the book as they apply to specific accounting standards.

Reporting Entity

The **reporting entity assumption** (**economic entity assumption**) states that a business enterprise is a legally and economically distinct entity, so that financial statements can be prepared and reported specifically for that entity. Business entities vary in size from small, one-owner proprietorships such as hair salons or restaurants, to partnerships such as law or accounting firms, to large multinational corporations such as **Starbucks**. Financial accounting is useful for measuring and reporting the economic activity of each of these entities, regardless of size.

In accounting, we assume the reporting entity is distinct from its owners. Each separate reporting entity prepares its own financial records and reports. For companies that are legally distinct entities, such as *corporations*, the reporting entity is distinct from the common equity shareholders who own the company. In *sole proprietorships*, in which an individual may both own and operate the business, the accounting system serves to record and report the transactions and events of the business separately from the proprietor's personal transactions. Accounting views a *transaction* as an exchange of items of value between the reporting entity and another party (e.g., another company, an employee, a lender, or an investor).

Framework of Financial Reporting

EXHIBIT 2.5

Framework	Content
Objectives	• Provide financial information about the reporting entity that is useful to existing and potential investors, lenders, and other creditors in making decisions about providing resources to the entity • Provide useful information for decisions by existing and potential investors about buying, selling, or holding equity instruments; such decisions depend on the returns that they expect from an investment in those instruments, such as dividends and market price increases, relative to the riskiness of those investments • Provide useful information for decisions by existing and potential lenders and other creditors about buying, selling, or holding debt instruments or providing or settling loans and other forms of credit; such decisions depend on the principal and interest payments or other returns that they expect, relative to the inherent risk of those debt instruments and loans • Provide existing and potential investors, lenders, and other creditors with useful information to help them assess the amount, timing, and uncertainty of the prospects for future net cash inflows to the company • Provide information about a company's economic resources and the claims against the company • Provide information about changes in a company's economic resources and claims resulting from its financial performance
Types of Useful Information	• Return on investment • Risk • Financial flexibility • Liquidity • Operating capability
Qualitative Characteristics of Useful Accounting Information	• Decision Usefulness • Relevance (predictive value, confirmatory value, materiality) • Faithful Representation (complete, neutral, free from error) • Enhancing Characteristics: Comparability, Verifiability, Timeliness, Understandability • Cost Constraint: Benefits > Costs
Accounting Assumptions	• Reporting Entity • Mixed-Attribute Measurement • Going Concern • Recognition • Period of Time • Accrual Accounting • Monetary Unit • Conservatism
Generally Accepted Accounting Principles	• The guidelines, procedures, and practices that a company is required to use in recording and reporting its accounting information in its audited financial statements • The Accounting Standards Codification: A single body of authoritative literature for U.S. GAAP
Financial Reports	• Balance sheet • Income statement and comprehensive income statement • Statement of cash flows • Statement of shareholders' equity • Notes to financial statements • Management's discussion and analysis and supplementary information
Elements of Financial Statements	• Assets, liabilities, and equity • Revenues, expenses, gains, and losses • Operating, investing, and financing cash flows • Comprehensive income, investments by and distributions to owners

Some (usually large) reporting entities may own multiple *subsidiary* companies, each of which may be a separate legal entity. Each subsidiary company will keep separate sets of financial records and produce financial statements. The reporting entity (the *parent* company) will consolidate (combine) those separate financial statements into a *consolidated set of financial statements* to report more completely the resources, obligations, and financial performance of the entire reporting entity.

Going Concern

The **going-concern assumption** (**continuity assumption**) is that the company will continue to operate in the foreseeable future. It does not imply permanence. It simply indicates that, without substantial evidence to the contrary, the company can be reasonably expected to operate long enough to realize economic benefits from its assets and satisfy its existing obligations. If a company appears to be going bankrupt, it cannot meet the going-concern assumption. The company then reports its financial statements on a liquidation basis, with all assets and liabilities valued at the amounts estimated to be collected or paid when they are sold or liquidated.

Period of Time

Financial statement users need timely information to evaluate a company's financial position, profitability, and cash flows on an ongoing basis. In accordance with the **period-of-time assumption**, companies prepare and report financial statements at the end of each year and include them in an annual report and in annual filings with the SEC. The annual reporting period is sometimes called the **accounting period** (or **fiscal year**).

Most companies adopt the calendar year as the accounting period. However, many companies choose a fiscal year that more closely approximates their annual **business cycle**, which is the yearly period from lowest sales through highest sales and back to lowest sales. For example, a company that owns and operates ski resorts would generate peak sales each year in the winter months, while the lowest sales volume occurs in the summer months. If that company reported on a calendar-year basis, its financial reports would be prepared during the midpoint of the business cycle and would not represent a full cycle. Alternatively, if that company reported using a fiscal year that ended on June 30, the financial statements would represent a complete annual business cycle.

Many large retail chains have a fiscal year-end that follows the peak Christmas selling season. For example, **Wal-Mart**'s fiscal year-end is January 31, which enables Wal-Mart to report financial performance immediately after its biggest selling season. Fiscal-year reports that include an annual business cycle contain information that is more comparable to past and future periods because annual sales patterns are not broken by the reporting period. In the same vein, some companies, including **Starbucks**, choose a 52-week fiscal year that spans the business cycle in order to provide financial reports measured over comparable length periods.[10]

In addition to annual reports, publicly traded companies issue financial statements for interim (quarterly) periods. These interim periods are integral parts of the annual period, and interim reports disclose summary information to provide investors, lenders, and other creditors with a steady flow of timely information.

Reporting on a periodic basis requires the accountant to measure the assets, liabilities, and owners' equity as of the last day of each period. In addition, the accountant must measure the financial performance during each period, including the income generated during the period as well as the cash inflows and outflows. As mentioned earlier (and discussed in more detail shortly), the purpose of the accrual accounting process is to measure the economic effects of transactions, events, and arrangements in each period,

---

[10] Ironically, if a company uses a 52-week fiscal year for financial reporting, and if the company wants the fiscal year to end around the same calendar date each year, then once every six or seven years the company will have to report based on a 53-week fiscal year. This obviously reduces comparability from year to year. As an example, Starbucks's fiscal 2010 was a 53-week year, while fiscal years 2011 through 2015 were all 52-week fiscal years, and 2016 will be a 53-week fiscal year.

even though the related cash receipts or payments may occur in different periods. The objectives of accrual accounting and the period-of-time assumption create the need to make adjusting entries at the end of each accounting period in order to correctly measure the balance sheet and income statement amounts for that period. This process is described in Chapter 3.

Monetary Unit

Under the **monetary unit assumption**, accountants generally use the national currency of the reporting entity as the monetary unit of measure in preparing financial statements. In using the dollar, the euro, or any other currency, accountants traditionally assume that it is stable over time; but that assumption is not necessarily valid.[11] Currently, in the United States the dollar is considered to be a stable monetary unit for preparing a company's financial statements.

Although the value of the monetary unit may be stable, the values of the assets and liabilities being measured and reported on the balance sheet can change with time. Consider the building you are now in. An accurate measurement of the physical size of that building would yield the same results each year. In contrast, the monetary value of the same building has probably changed over time and will continue to change.

Mixed Attribute Measurement

In order to provide financial statement users with the most relevant and representationally faithful measures of companies' resources, obligations, and financial performance, accounting uses a mixture of measurement attributes. The **mixed attribute measurement model** seeks to measure assets, liabilities, revenues, expenses, and other elements of the financial statements with the most relevant and faithful measurement available. The types of measurement attributes used include historical costs, allocated historical costs, fair values, present values of future cash flows, net realizable values, and others.[12]

The economic activities and resources of a company initially are measured using the exchange price at the time each transaction occurs. At the time of most transactions, the **historical cost** (the **exchange price**) is the most relevant and faithful representation of the value of the exchange. Historical cost provides evidence that independent parties have willingly agreed on the value of the items exchanged at the time of the transaction. Thus, historical cost has the qualities of relevance, representational faithfulness (neutrality), and verifiability.

Accountants understand that historical cost information can lose *relevance* for financial decisions if the economic value of the resource or obligation has changed since the time of the original transaction. For example, the historical cost of a piece of land will still be a faithful representation of cost, but will lose relevance as land values change over time.

For certain types of assets and liabilities, accounting standards *require* the use of valuation methods other than historical cost to report more relevant values to financial statement users.

- The FASB and IASB increasingly require measurement using the *fair value* of selected items in the financial statements. These methods are required when fair values provide more relevant information and can be faithfully represented.
- For long-term assets and liabilities that represent claims to receive or obligations to pay cash flows in the future, the accounting standards require the use of *present value* measures.
- When assets may have declined in value, accounting standards require the use of *net realizable value* (such as the value of accounts receivable, net of the allowance for uncollectible accounts).

---

[11] In developing economies that may be subject to hyperinflation, the monetary unit may lose purchasing power over time.
[12] In Chapter 4, we discuss the various methods used in the mixed attribute measurement model.

ETHICAL DILEMMA

You have been hired as an accounting consultant to review the financial reporting policies of Parker Company as it enters merger negotiations with an interested buyer. Of particular interest is the way in which Parker accounts for its property, plant, and equipment. When rumors of possible mergers began several years ago, the company's management periodically began using independent valuation experts to appraise fair market values for the company's net assets. As a result of these analyses, management determined that its long-term productive assets had appraised market values that were significantly higher than their book values. Citing these appraisals, management increased the company's assets up to appraised values in order "to provide investors and creditors with the most relevant information possible and to be consistent with the FASB's increasing use of fair value measurements." How does this decision create the potential for unethical reporting by Parker?

Recognition

Recognition is the process of formally recording and reporting an item in the financial statements of a company. A recognized item is shown in both words and numbers, with the amount included in the financial statement totals. The FASB has identified four fundamental recognition criteria.[13] To be recognized, an item must:

- meet the definition of an element (such as an asset, liability, revenue, expense, etc.)
- be measurable
- be relevant
- be representationally faithful

In Chapter 4, we explain the elements that are recognized on the balance sheet (assets, liabilities, owners' equity), and when they trigger recognition and derecognition. In Chapters 5 and 17, we explain the elements that are recognized on the income statement, particularly the revenue recognition and expense recognition criteria.

Accrual Accounting

As described earlier, **accrual accounting** is the process of measuring and reporting the economic effects of transactions, events, and arrangements on a company's economic resources and claims in the period when those effects occur, even though the cash flows may occur in a different period. If a company creates economic resources by selling products to customers in a particular period, accrual accounting will recognize the revenues in that period, even though the customers may have paid cash for the products in an earlier period or will pay cash in a future period. Likewise, when a company consumes resources during a period, accrual accounting measures the economic effects of the resources consumed in that period, even though the company may have paid cash for those resources in a prior period or will pay for them in a future period. The objectives of accrual accounting are to appropriately measure financial position and financial performance each period.

When economic effects are recognized in the current period, even though the cash flows will occur in a later period, they are usually referred to as **accruals** (e.g., an accrued expense and an accrued liability for wages). When cash flows occur in the current period but the economic effects will be recognized in a later period, they are usually referred to as **deferrals** (e.g., recognizing an asset for a prepaid expense, such as prepaid rent, deferring the rent expense to the future period when it is used).[14]

The Revenue Recognition Principle The revenue recognition principle is an application of accrual accounting. The **revenue recognition principle** determines the

---

[13] "Recognition and Measurement in Financial Statements of Business Enterprises," *FASB Statement of Financial Accounting Concepts No. 5* (Stamford, CT: FASB, 1984), par. 63 and 83.

[14] Accruals and deferrals are discussed in Chapter 3.

appropriate period in which a company creates economic benefits and can recognize revenues in income. Companies should recognize revenue to depict the transfer of goods or services that reflects the consideration to which the entity expects to be entitled. This occurs when a company satisfies its performance obligations, or promises within the contract with a customer.[15] For example, **Starbucks** recognizes revenues from credit sales, even though they have not yet been collected (accounts receivable), because it has satisfied its performance obligation to the customer and expects to collect the amount due. Similarly in the period when Starbucks sells a gift card to a customer, it does not recognize revenue until the future period when the customer redeems the card because that is when the company will satisify its obligation to the customer.[16]

The Expense Recognition Principle The **expense recognition principle** determines the appropriate period in which a company has consumed economic resources in conducting business operations. Companies typically recognize expenses in a particular period on the basis of three methods, all of which apply accrual accounting principles:

- cause and effect
- immediate consumption
- systematic and rational allocation over time

Cause and effect recognition occurs when some expenses are caused directly in the course of generating revenues, such as the costs of the goods sold to customers or the commissions paid to the sales force on the basis of sales revenues. Cause and effect recognition, which is often termed the matching principle, matches the expense to the period in which the economic benefits are consumed by generating revenues. Many expenses represent economic benefits that are immediately consumed and recognized entirely within one accounting period, such as expenses for wages and salaries. Other expenses are recognized on the basis of systematic and rational allocation of the consumption of long-lived resources over time, such as the periodic depreciation of property and equipment and the amortization of intangibles over their useful lives.[17]

Conservatism

Conservatism is an approach that accountants use to avoid overstating net assets and net income when these amounts are uncertain. When accounting valuations are uncertain and alternative accounting valuations for assets or liabilities are equally possible, the accountant should select the one that is least likely to overstate the company's assets and income in the current period. The application of conservatism results in the reporting of lower asset values or higher liability values when those values are uncertain. In addition, accountants typically use a lower threshold for the recognition of losses than for gains. For example, the lower of cost of market rule for inventory recognizes declines in the value of inventory but not gains, as will be discussed in detail in Chapter 8.

Conservatism is not desirable, nor is it a principle of accounting; instead, it is a practical approach accountants take to avoid misleading investors, lenders, and other creditors when valuations are uncertain. Conservatism is sometimes described as **prudence**. That is, conservatism is a prudent reaction to uncertainty to ensure, to the extent possible, that the uncertainties and risks inherent in business situations are adequately considered. These uncertainties and risks should be reflected in accounting information to improve its predictive value and neutrality. While the FASB does not advocate conservatism, accountants will most likely continue to exercise conservatism when they are faced with uncertainties.[18]

---

[15] FASB ASC 606-10-05-4: Revenue from Contracts with Customers.
[16] Revenue recognition principles are discussed in Chapters 5 and 17.
[17] Expense recognition is also discussed in Chapter 5.
[18] FASB Statement of Financial Accounting Concepts No. 2, op. cit., par. 95–97.

Over the years, conservatism gained prominence as a counterweight to balance the optimism of company managers. Unfortunately, conservatism in current-year measurements can trigger "anticonservative" measures in the years following. That is, a conservative asset valuation (say, a write-down of inventory) with a corresponding loss in net income in one year might result in higher reported income in a later year when the asset is sold because of the lower recorded value of the asset. Furthermore, conservatism can conflict with qualitative characteristics such as neutrality. While conservatism is typically not established in generally accepted accounting principles, it can and often does affect accounting practice.

GOT IT?

2-18 What is the reporting entity assumption? How does it affect the scope of financial reporting?

2-19 What is the going-concern assumption, and why is it important in financial reporting?

2-20 What is the period-of-time assumption, and why is it important in financial reporting?

2-21 Why does financial reporting utilize a mixed set of measurement attributes?

2-22 Discuss the relationship among historical cost, relevance, and faithful representation.

2-23 What is recognition in accounting?

2-24 Describe accrual accounting. What are the objectives of accrual accounting?

2-25 What drives the timing of revenue recognition? When should revenue be recognized?

2-26 What drives expense recognition? When should expenses be recognized?

2-27 What is conservatism? Why do accountants sometimes find it necessary to be conservative in financial reporting?

LEARNING OBJECTIVE 2.5
Describe the financial reporting model in the FASB's Conceptual Framework.

WHAT IS THE FINANCIAL REPORTING MODEL IN THE CONCEPTUAL FRAMEWORK?

In its Conceptual Framework, the FASB has identified various sources from which investors, lenders, and other creditors might obtain useful information for decision making, as shown in Exhibit 2.6.

Conceptually, the FASB's financial reporting model identifies the five specific financial statements listed in Exhibit 2.6. As described in Chapter 1, they are the:

- balance sheet (statement of financial position)
- income statement
- comprehensive income statement
- statement of cash flows
- statement of shareholders' equity

Under GAAP, the financial statements should also include the notes to explain the policies, methods, and estimates the company used to measure and report the financial statement elements, as well as any required supplementary information. These three primary sources of useful information are represented in the first three boxes in the financial reporting model in Exhibit 2.6. In addition, the model suggests that investors, lenders and other creditors can obtain useful information from many other sources, including management's discussion and analysis, other disclosures the company may provide, analysts' reports, financial and economic news, and many other sources.[19]

---

[19] We discuss the financial statements and their elements in later chapters of this book, particularly Chapters 4, 5, and 21. In addition, we discuss supplementary schedules and notes to the financial statements.

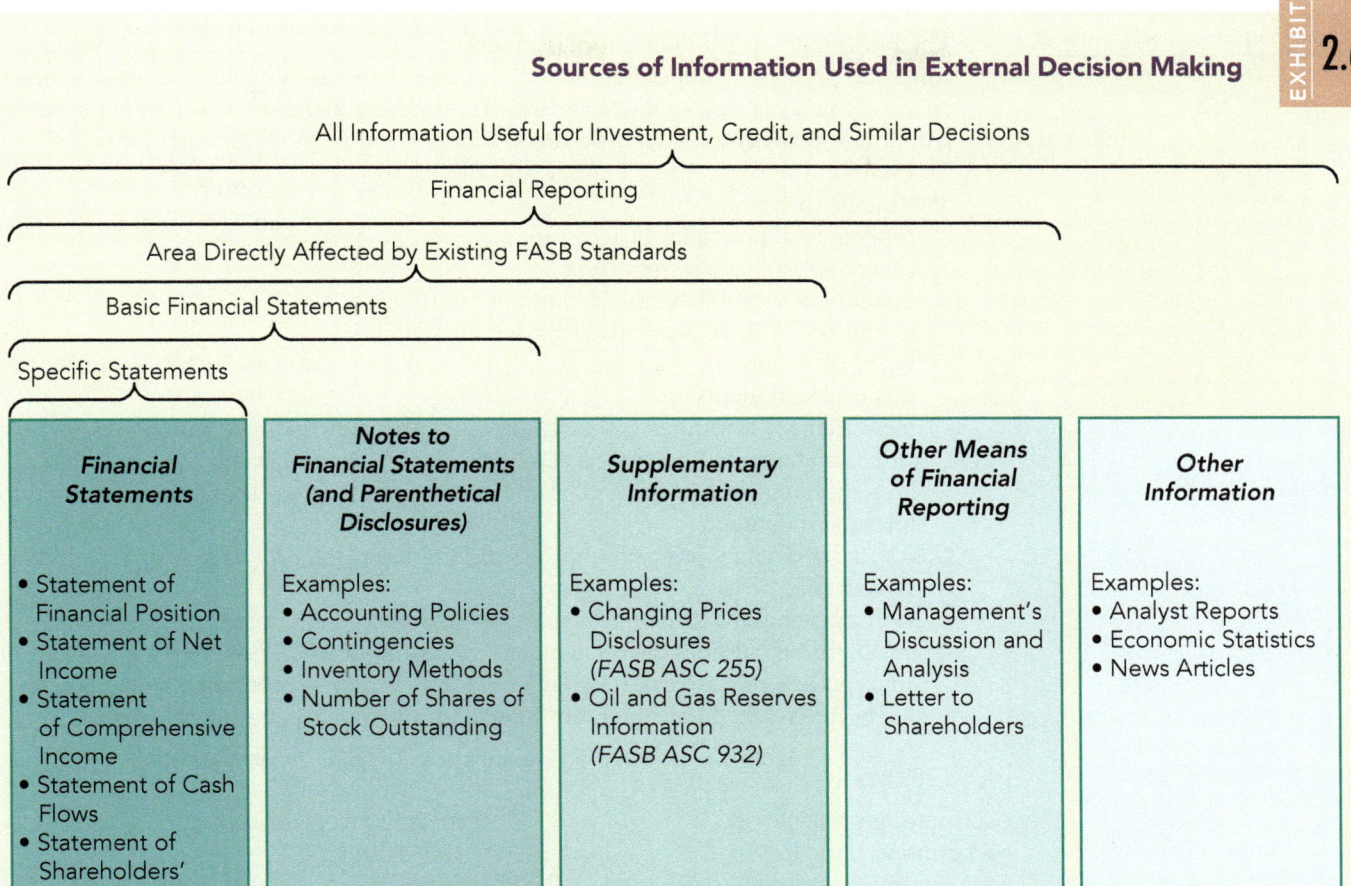

Source: Adapted from diagram in "Recognition and Measurement in Financial Statements of Business Enterprises," *FASB Statement of Financial Accounting Concepts No. 5* (Stamford, CT: FASB, 1985), p. 5.

GOT IT?

2-28 Describe the financial reporting model within the FASB Conceptual Framework.

2-29 What are the primary sources of useful information identified in the model?

REVIEW CENTER

At the beginning of the chapter, we made a grandiose comparison, noting the Conceptual Framework for Financial Reporting was similar in purpose (but not in significance or profoundness) to the U.S. Constitution. The Constitution sets forth the basic objectives and principles of government and the fundamental rights of the people of the United States. The Conceptual Framework for Financial Reporting sets forth the fundamental objectives, concepts, principles, and definitions of accounting and financial reporting. We also identified several objectives you would accomplish after reading the chapter. The objectives are listed below and followed by a brief summary of the key points.

Chapter 2 Financial Reporting: Its Conceptual Framework

LEARNING OBJECTIVE 2.1

Explain the FASB's Conceptual Framework.

KEY TAKEAWAYS

- The FASB Conceptual Framework is a theoretical foundation of interrelated objectives, concepts, principles, and definitions that enable the establishment and application of consistent financial accounting standards. It provides a logical structure to guide standard setters, financial statement preparers, auditors, and financial statement users.
- To establish the Conceptual Framework, the FASB has issued a number of Concepts Statements that establish:
  - fundamental principles of accounting
  - objectives of financial reporting
  - qualities of useful financial accounting information
  - definitions of basic elements like assets and liabilities
  - types of economic transactions, events, and arrangements to be recognized in financial statements
  - measurement attributes to use to measure and report these transactions, events, and arrangements
  - how transactions, events, and arrangements should be presented and classified in financial statements
- Concepts statements, principles, standards, and rules differ because they serve different purposes.
  - Concepts Statements and principles are broad and definitional.
  - Standards are authoritative statements that comprise GAAP and are applications of concepts and principles to different types of transactions, events, and arrangements.
  - Rules are specific implementation procedures within accounting standards.

KEY TERMS

accounting principles, p. 2-3
accounting standards, p. 2-3
Accounting Standards Codification, p. 2-4
Accounting Standards Updates, p. 2-4
Conceptual Framework, p. 2-2

generally accepted accounting principles (GAAP), p. 2-3
rules, p. 2-4
Statements of Financial Accounting Concepts (Concepts Statements), p. 2-3

LEARNING OBJECTIVE 2.2

Explain the general and specific objectives of general purpose financial reporting.

KEY TAKEAWAYS

- The FASB Conceptual Framework consists of four levels of objectives. The most general and primary objective is to provide financial information about the reporting entity that is useful to existing and potential investors, lenders, and other creditors in making decisions about providing resources to the entity. Those decisions involve buying, selling, or holding equity and debt instruments and providing or settling loans and other forms of credit.
- Decisions by existing and potential investors depend on the investment returns that they should expect, such as dividends and market price increases, relative to the investment risk. Decisions by existing and potential lenders and other creditors depend on the principal and interest payments or other returns that they expect, relative to the credit risk they face.
- In order to determine what returns and risks they should expect, existing and potential investors, lenders, and other creditors need information to help them assess the amount, timing, and uncertainty of the prospects for future net cash inflows to the company.
- Financial reporting should provide information about:
  - economic resources and the claims on the company
  - changes in the company's economic resources and claims resulting from the company's financial performance and cash flows during a specified period of time
  - how the management of a company has discharged its stewardship responsibility
- Information relating to return on investment, risk, financial flexibility, liquidity, and operating capability is considered to be useful in assessing the amounts, timing, and uncertainty of a company's future net cash flows.

KEY TERMS

financial flexibility, p. 2-10
liquidity, p. 2-10
operating capability, p. 2-10
return on investment, p. 2-10
risk, p. 2-10
stewardship, p. 2-9

KEY TAKEAWAYS

LEARNING OBJECTIVE 2.3
Explain the qualitative characteristics of decision-useful information as identified in the FASB and IASB Joint Conceptual Framework project.

- The fundamental characteristics that make accounting information useful for decision making are relevance and faithful representation.
- Accounting information is relevant if it is capable of making a difference in decisions made by financial statement users. Financial information is capable of making a difference if it is material in nature and magnitude and helps users predict future outcomes and/or confirm or correct prior expectations.
- Accounting information is a reliable depiction of the underlying economic transactions, events, and arrangements when the words and numbers faithfully represent what they purport to represent. That is, the information must be complete, neutral, and free from error.
- Accounting information is most useful to decision makers when it is both relevant and faithfully represented. Accounting standards and accounting practitioners must strive to maximize both characteristics to provide users with the most decision-useful information possible.
- Four characteristics can enhance the decision usefulness of relevant and faithfully represented information: comparability, verifiability, timeliness, and understandability.
- The cost constraint states that the costs of providing financial information should not exceed the benefits received from using the information.

KEY TERMS

comparability, p. 2-15
complete representation, p. 2-13
confirmatory value, p. 2-12
consistency, p. 2-15
cost constraint, p. 2-15
decision usefulness, p. 2-12
faithful representation, p. 2-13
free from error, p. 2-14
materiality, p. 2-12
neutral representation, p. 2-13
predictive value, p. 2-12
relevance, p. 2-12
timely, p. 2-15
understandability, p. 2-15
verifiable, p. 2-15

KEY TAKEAWAYS

LEARNING OBJECTIVE 2.4
Understand and apply the major assumptions of financial reporting and U.S. GAAP.

- Various assumptions greatly influence the development of GAAP and its practical application:
  - *Reporting entity assumption*: Accounting measures and reports economic activities for a particular economic entity, which is distinct from the owners of the entity.
  - *Going-concern assumption (continuity assumption)*: It is assumed that a company will continue to operate in the foreseeable future unless substantial evidence to the contrary exists.
  - *Period-of-time assumption*: Financial statement users need timely information to evaluate a company's financial position, profitability, and cash flows on an ongoing basis; accordingly, companies prepare and report periodic financial statements, usually each year (and some firms report each quarter).
  - *Monetary unit assumption*: Financial statement elements can be expressed in terms of the national currency of the reporting entity, like the dollar for U.S. companies.
  - *Mixed attribute measurement model*: Accounting strives to measure assets, liabilities, revenues, expenses, and other elements of the financial statements with the most relevant and faithful measurement available; therefore, financial statement elements are measured and reported using a mixture of measurement attributes.

- *Recognition*: Recognition is the process of formally recording and reporting an item in the financial statements of a company. To be recognized, an item must meet the definition of an element (such as an asset, liability, revenue, expense, etc.), be measurable, be relevant, and be faithfully represented.
- *Accrual accounting*: Accruals and deferrals measure and report the economic effects of transactions, events, and circumstances on a company's economic resources and claims in the period when those effects occur, even though the cash consequences may occur in a different period. This involves the application of both revenue and expense recognition principles.
- *Conservatism*: When accounting valuations are uncertain and alternative accounting valuations for assets or liabilities are equally possible, the accountant should select the one that is least likely to overstate the company's assets and income in the current period.

KEY TERMS

accounting period, p. 2-18
accrual accounting, p. 2-20
accruals, p. 2-20
business cycle, p. 2-18
conservatism, p. 2-21
continuity assumption, p. 2-18
deferrals, p. 2-20
economic entity assumption, p. 2-16
exchange price, p. 2-19
expense recognition principle, p. 2-21
fiscal year, p. 2-18

going-concern assumption, p. 2-18
historical cost, p. 2-19
mixed attribute measurement model, p. 2-19
monetary unit assumption, p. 2-19
period-of-time assumption, p. 2-18
prudence, p. 2-21
recognition, p. 2-20
reporting entity assumption, p. 2-16
revenue recognition principle, p. 2-20

LEARNING OBJECTIVE 2.5
Describe the financial reporting model in the FASB's Conceptual Framework.

KEY TAKEAWAYS

- The FASB's Conceptual Framework outlined the financial reporting model, identifying five basic financial statements as core sources of useful information:
  - balance sheet
  - income statement
  - comprehensive income statement
  - statement of cash flows
  - statement of shareholders' equity
- Under GAAP, the financial statements should also include the notes to explain the policies, methods, and estimates the company used to measure and report the financial statement elements, as well as any required supplementary information.

MULTIPLE-CHOICE (AICPA ADAPTED)

Select the best answer for each of the following.

M2-1 **LO 2.1** The information provided by financial reporting pertains to:
a. individual companies, rather than to industries or the economy as a whole or to members of society as consumers
b. individual companies and industries, rather than to the economy as a whole or to members of society as consumers
c. individual companies and the economy as a whole, rather than to industries or to members of society as consumers
d. individual companies, industries, and the economy as a whole, rather than to members of society as consumers

M2-2 **LO 2.3** Which of the following is considered a constraint on useful information by *Statement of Financial Accounting Concepts No. 8*?
a. benefits > costs
b. conservatism
c. timeliness
d. verifiability

M2-3
LO 2.3
According to *Statement of Financial Accounting Concepts No. 8*, to be relevant an earnings report is expected to have which of the following?

	Predictive Value	Confirmatory Value
a.	No	No
b.	Yes	Yes
c.	Yes	No
d.	No	Yes

M2-4
LO 2.3
Which characteristic states that accounting information should be supported by sufficient evidence to allow two or more qualified individuals to arrive at similar measures and conclusions?

a. matching
b. verifiability
c. periodicity
d. monetary unit

M2-5
LO 2.3
Under *Statement of Financial Accounting Concepts No. 8*, which of the following enhances decision-useful information?

a. timeliness
b. neutrality
c. confirmatory value
d. materiality

M2-6
LO 2.4
Under *Statement of Financial Accounting Concepts No. 6*, which of the following means the process of formally recording and reporting an item in the financial statements of a company?

a. allocation
b. verification
c. recognition
d. realization

M2-7
LO 2.4
Accruing net losses on obsolete inventory is an example of the accounting concept of:

a. conservatism
b. historical cost
c. consistency
d. materiality

M2-8
LO 2.4
The valuation of a promise to receive cash in the future at present value on the financial statements of a company is valid because of the accounting concept of:

a. entity
b. materiality
c. going concern
d. neutrality

M2-9
LO 2.4
An accrued expense is an expense:

a. incurred but not paid
b. incurred and paid
c. paid but not incurred
d. not reasonably estimable

M2-10
LO 2.4
A patent purchased in 2016 and being amortized over a 10-year life was determined to be worthless in 2019. The write-off of the asset in 2019 is an example of which of the following expense recognition principles?

a. associating cause and effect
b. immediate consumption
c. systematic and rational allocation
d. objectivity

EXERCISES

E2-1
LO 2.3
Qualitative Characteristics The following is a list of qualitative characteristics of useful accounting information identified in the FASB's and the IASB's *Statement of Financial Accounting Concepts No. 8* and statements describing the qualities.

A. Comparability
B. Decision usefulness
C. Relevance
D. Faithful representation
E. Predictive value
F. Confirmatory value
G. Verifiability
H. Neutrality
I. Free from error
J. Consistency

(continued)

K. Materiality
L. Timeliness
M. Understandability
N. Completeness

_____ 1. Different knowledgeable and independent observers can reach consensus that a particular representation is faithful.
_____ 2. Making information available to decision makers before it loses its capacity to influence decisions.
_____ 3. Capacity to make a difference in a decision, enabling users to predict future outcomes and/or confirm prior expectations.
_____ 4. Overall objective of financial information.
_____ 5. Absence of bias intended to influence financial statement users' behavior in a particular direction.
_____ 6. Presented as accurately as possible, using a process that reflects the best available inputs.
_____ 7. Helps decision makers form expectations about the future.
_____ 8. Full disclosure of all the information necessary to understand the information being reported.
_____ 9. Enables users to identify and explain similarities and differences between two or more sets of economic facts.
_____ 10. The nature and magnitude of an omission or misstatement that would influence the judgment of reasonable users of that information.
_____ 11. Accounting methods and procedures applied in the same manner from period to period.
_____ 12. Helps decision makers confirm or correct prior predictions or expectations
_____ 13. When the words and amounts accurately depict the economic substance of what they purport to depict.
_____ 14. Comprehensible to users.

Required:
Place the appropriate letter identifying each quality on the line in front of the statement describing the quality.

E2-2
LO 2.4
Accounting Assumptions The following is a list of accounting assumptions that have had an important impact on the development of generally accepted accounting principles and statements describing certain accounting practices.

A. Reporting entity
B. Going concern
C. Period of time
D. Historical cost
E. Monetary unit
F. Recognition
G. Accrual accounting
H. Revenue recognition
I. Expense recognition
J. Conservatism

_____ 1. To provide timely information, companies prepare and report financial statements at the end of each year.
_____ 2. Appropriate recognition when a company consumes economic resources in conducting business operations.
_____ 3. Accounting measurements for U.S. companies are reported in dollars.
_____ 4. The financial statements represent the business, rather than its owners.
_____ 5. In the absence of evidence to the contrary, the business can be reasonably expected to operate long enough to carry out its existing commitments.
_____ 6. Appropriate recognition when a company creates economic benefits (inflows of assets or settlements of obligations) by providing goods or services to customers.
_____ 7. Transactions and events are recognized initially at the exchange price to provide relevant and reliable information.
_____ 8. An accounting alternative is selected that is least likely to overstate assets and income.
_____ 9. The process of formally recording and reporting an item in the financial statements of a company.
_____ 10. The process of measuring and reporting the economic effects of transactions, events, and circumstances in the appropriate period when those effects occur, even though the cash consequences may occur in a different period.

Required:
Select the accounting assumption that justifies each accounting practice and place the appropriate letter on the line preceding the statement.

CASES

COMMUNICATION

C2-1 **Objectives of Financial Reporting**
LO 2.2 The FASB has identified several objectives of financial reporting. These objectives proceed from the more general to the more specific and are intended to act as guidelines for providing accounting information in financial reports.

Required:
Starting with the most general objective, prepare a written report that identifies and briefly explains the objectives of financial reporting.

C2-2 **Useful Accounting Information**
LO 2.3 A friend, who is not an accounting major, is not familiar with the *usefulness* of accounting information. The friend states, "I've seen you prepare financial statements for homework, but how is the information in these statements useful? What is useful accounting information?"

Required:
Prepare a written response for your friend that identifies and explains useful accounting information.

C2-3 **Characteristics of Useful Accounting**
LO 2.3 **Information**
A friend, who is not an accounting major, is interested in what makes accounting useful to decision makers. The friend asks, "I have a gut feel for what makes information useful to me, but how do you know what makes accounting information useful to users of financial statements? What qualities does useful accounting information have?"

Required:
Prepare a written response for your friend that identifies and explains the qualitative characteristics of useful accounting information.

C2-4 **Characteristics of Useful Accounting**
LO 2.3 **Information**
CMA Adapted Financial accounting and reporting provide information that is useful for resource allocation decisions. In *Statement of Financial Accounting Concepts No. 8*, Chapter 1, "The Objective of General Purpose Financial Reporting," the FASB and the IASB defined the following basic objectives of financial reporting:
Financial reporting should provide understandable information to present and potential investors, lenders, and other creditors:

- that is useful in making rational capital allocation decisions
- that facilitates assessing the amounts, timing, and uncertainty related to the company's cash flows
- that is informative about the company's economic resources, its claims to those resources, and the changes in its resources and obligations occurring from earnings and other operating activities

The qualitative characteristics of useful accounting information were identified in the FASB's and the IASB's *Statement of Financial Accounting Concepts No. 8*, Chapter 3, "Qualitative Characteristics of Useful Accounting Information". These characteristics distinguish better information (more useful) from inferior information (less useful).

Required:
1. For the primary quality *relevance*, (a) define relevance and (b) explain the meaning and importance of each of the three ingredients of relevance.
2. For the primary quality *faithful representation*, (a) define faithful representation and (b) explain the meaning and importance of each of the three ingredients of faithful representation.
3. Describe how relevance and faithful representation should be applied to determine useful accounting information.
4. Explain the following enhancing characteristics:
    a. comparability (including consistency)
    b. verifiability
    c. timeliness
    d. understandability
5. Explain the cost constraint.

C2-5 **Cost and Expense Recognition**
LO 2.4 An accountant must be familiar with the concepts involved in determining earnings of a company.
AICPA Adapted The amount of earnings reported for a company is dependent on the proper recognition, in general, of revenue and expense for a given time period. In some situations, costs are recognized as expenses at the time of product sale; in other situations, costs are recognized as expenses or losses based on other criteria.

(continued)

Required:
1. Explain the rationale for recognizing costs as expenses at the time of product sale.
2. What is the rationale underlying the appropriateness of treating costs as expenses of a period instead of assigning the costs to an asset? Explain.
3. Some expenses are assigned to specific accounting periods on the basis of systematic and rational allocation of asset cost. Explain the underlying rationale for recognizing expenses on this basis.

CREATIVE AND CRITICAL THINKING

C2-6 **Relevance versus Faithful Representation**
LO 2.3
CMA Adapted

You are listening to two accounting majors, both of whom are seniors. They are debating the merits of having relevant versus faithfully represented accounting information for external decision making. One student states, "In my decision making, if given a choice between relevant and representationally faithful accounting information, I would prefer to have relevant information." The other student replies, "Nonsense! If you cannot rely on the information, then of what use is it?"

Required:
Based on your knowledge of the FASB's Conceptual Framework, define the qualitative characteristics of relevance and faithful representation. Include definitions of the ingredients of each. Which do you think is more important?

C2-7 **Conceptual Framework**
LO 2.3

The FASB's Conceptual Framework for Financial Reporting states the objectives of financial reporting. It also identifies two fundamental qualitative characteristics and several enhancing qualitative characteristics of decision-useful financial reporting information, as well as a constraint on financial accounting information.

Required:
Define the objectives of general purpose external financial reporting. Then discuss each of the fundamental and enhancing qualitative characteristics of decision-useful financial reporting information. Finish by discussing the constraint.

C2-8 **Objectives, Users, and Stewardship**
LO 2.4
CMA Adapted

The owners of CSC Inc., a privately held company, are considering a public offering of the company's common stock as a means of acquiring additional funds. Prior to making a decision about a public offering, the owners want to have a lengthy conversation with you, CSC's chief financial officer. You have already informed the owners of the reporting requirements of the Securities and Exchange Commission, including the necessity for audited financial statements. Now the owners wish to discuss with you the objectives of financial reporting, the sophistication of users of financial information, and the stewardship responsibilities of management, all of which are addressed in *Statement of Financial Accounting Concepts No. 8*, Chapter 1, "The Objective of General Purpose Financial Reporting."

Required:
1. How will you discuss the primary objectives of financial reporting?
2. How will you describe the level of sophistication that can be expected of the users of financial information?
3. How will you explain the stewardship responsibilities of management? What role does financial reporting play with respect to stewardship?

C2-9 **Reporting Entity**
LO 2.4
AICPA Adapted

The concept of the reporting entity is a fundamental accounting concept, one that pervades all of accounting.

Required:
1. What is a reporting entity? Explain why the reporting entity concept is so fundamental that it pervades all of accounting.
2. For each of the following, indicate whether the accounting concept of reporting entity can be applied. Discuss and give illustrations.
   a. a unit created by or under law
   b. the product-line operating segment of an enterprise
   c. a combination of legal units and/or product-line operating segments
   d. all of the activities of an owner of a company
   e. an industry
   f. the economy of the United States

C2-10 **Accruals and Deferrals**
LO 2.4
AICPA Adapted

Generally accepted accounting principles require the use of accruals and deferrals in the determination of income.

Required:
How does accrual accounting affect the determination of income? Include in your discussion what constitutes an accrual and a deferral and give appropriate examples of each.

C2-11 Revenue Recognition
LO 2.4

The following are brief descriptions of two companies in different lines of business.

A. Company A is a retailer. It makes sales on a daily basis for cash and on credit cards.
B. Company B is a health spa. It has recently signed contracts with numerous individuals to use its facilities over a two-year period. The contract price was collected in advance.

Required:
Describe when revenue should be recognized by each company. If revenue should not be recognized at the time of sale, indicate what method should be used to recognize the revenue. Justify your decision.

C2-12 Violations of Assumptions and Principles
LO 2.4

The following are accounting procedures and practices used by several companies.

A. As soon as it purchases inventory, Sokolich Company records the purchase price as cost of goods sold to simplify its accounting procedures.
B. At the end of each year, Sloan Company records and reports the value of its land based on appraisal values.
C. Ebert Company prepares financial statements only every two years to reduce its costs of preparing the statements.
D. Guthrie Company receives orders from customers and records revenue at that time, even though it has not yet delivered products or services to the customers.
E. Because of inflation, Cross Company adjusts its financial statements each year to show the current purchasing power for all items.
F. David Thomas combines his personal transactions and business transactions when he prepares his company's financial statements so that he can tell how well he is doing on an "overall" basis.
G. At the end of each year, Vann Company reports its economic resources on a liquidation basis even though it is likely to operate in the future.

Required:
Identify what accounting assumption or principle each procedure or practice violates, and indicate what should be done to rectify the violation.

C2-13 Ethics and Income Reporting

You have been hired as an "accounting consultant" by Watson Company to evaluate its financial reporting policies. Watson is a small corporation with a few shareholders owning stock that is not publicly traded. In a discussion with you, Chris Watson, the company president, says, "For Watson Company's annual income statement, it is our policy to always record and report revenues when we collect the cash and to record and report expenses when we pay the cash. I like this approach, and I think our shareholders and creditors do too. This policy results in income that is reliable and conservative, which is the way accounting should be. Besides, it is easy to keep track of our income. All I need are the receipts and payments recorded in the company's checkbook."

Required:
From financial reporting and ethical perspectives, how would you reply to Chris?

C2-14 Inconsistent Statements on Accounting
LO 2.2 **Principles**
LO 2.5

AICPA Adapted

The following two statements have been taken directly or with some modification from the accounting literature. Each of them is either taken out of context, involves circular reasoning, and/or contains one or more fallacies, half-truths, erroneous comments, conclusions, or inconsistencies (internally or with generally accepted principles or practices).

Statement 1 Accounting is a service activity. Its function is to provide quantitative financial information that is intended to be useful in making economic decisions about and for companies. Thus, the accounting function might be viewed primarily as being a tool or device for providing quantitative financial information to management to facilitate decision making.

Statement 2 Financial statements that were developed in accordance with generally accepted accounting principles should be conservative.

Required:
Evaluate each of the preceding numbered statements as follows:
1. List the fallacies, half-truths, circular reasoning, erroneous comments or conclusions, and/or inconsistencies.
2. Explain by what authority and/or on what basis each item listed can be considered to be fallacious, circular, inconsistent, a half-truth, or an erroneous comment or conclusion. If the statement or a portion of it is merely out of context, indicate the context(s) in which the statement would be correct.

CHAPTER 3

REVIEW OF A COMPANY'S ACCOUNTING SYSTEM

Double-Entry Accounting: The Modern Is Ancient

Double-entry accounting systems have been in use for over 500 years. The Middle Ages in Europe marked a turning point in the history of the world, in part because of the explosion of international trade. Fueled by merchants in Florence and Venice, silks, spices, gold, and other items were being traded between countries. However, these medieval merchants needed information systems to keep track of their capital—how much they owned (assets), who owed them and how much (receivables), how much they owed others (liabilities), the amounts they had received for the items they sold (receipts), and the amounts they had paid for the goods they purchased (payments). Not surprisingly, these enterprising minds developed simple but effective systems for keeping track of assets, liabilities, receipts, and payments.

These early accounting systems were first described in Luca Pacioli's *Summa de Arithmetica, Geometria, Proportioni et Proportionalita*, (Everything About Arithmetic, Geometry, Proportion and Proportionality), which was published in Venice in 1494—only 2 years after Columbus discovered the New World. Pacioli, an Italian mathematician and Franciscan friar, was a friend and collaborator of Leonardo da Vinci, and his book was a synthesis of algebra and the mathematical knowledge of his time.

Notably, it included the first published description of the method of accounting that Venetian merchants used during the Italian Renaissance, the double-entry accounting system. Pacioli did not invent double-entry bookkeeping, but his text

LEARNING OBJECTIVES

After reading this chapter you will be able to

- **LO 3.1** Understand the components of an accounting system.
- **LO 3.2** Know the five major steps in the accounting cycle.
- **LO 3.3** Record transactions, events, and arrangements using journal entries in the general journal.
- **LO 3.4** Post to the general ledger and prepare a trial balance.
- **LO 3.5** Prepare adjusting entries.
- **LO 3.6** Prepare financial statements.
- **LO 3.7** Prepare closing entries.
- **LO 3.8** Prepare financial statements using a worksheet (spreadsheet).
- **LO 3.9** Prepare reversing entries.
- **LO 3.10** Use subsidiary ledgers and special journals.
- **LO 3.11** *(Appendix 3.1)* Convert cash-basis financial statements to accrual-basis.

described it in detail as the accounting system that had been in use in Renaissance Italy for many years. This system included the accounting cycle as we know it today. He also described the use of journals and ledgers and warned that a person should not go to sleep at night until the debits equaled the credits. His ledger had accounts for assets (including receivables and inventories), liabilities, capital (equity), income, and expenses—the same types of accounts that are reported on balance sheets and income statements today. He demonstrated year-end closing entries and proposed that a trial balance be used to prove a balanced ledger. As we still do today, Pacioli described that debit amounts from the ledger are listed on the left side of the balance sheet and credits on the right. The two totals must equal in order for the ledger to be balanced. If not, says Pacioli, "that would indicate a mistake in your ledger, which mistake you will have to look for diligently with the industry and intelligence God gave you."

Like Pacioli's ancient text, this chapter describes how to maintain an accounting system that is essential to ensuring that a company's economic transactions and financial information are properly entered into the accounting records so that financial reports can be prepared in an accurate and timely fashion. While the trial balance was the end of Pacioli's accounting cycle, modern accounting extends this cycle to report a company's financial information in its financial statements.

A company's financial statements are the result of the financial accounting process. **Starbucks**'s 2015 financial statements, for example, summarize and report the effects of literally millions of separate transactions around the world during fiscal 2015, through which Starbucks generated $19,162.7 million in revenues and held $12,446.1 million in assets at fiscal year-end. To understand financial accounting, you need to be familiar with the accounting system that companies such as Starbucks use to accumulate and report the information in financial statements.

LEARNING OBJECTIVE 3.1
Understand the components of an accounting system.

WHAT ARE THE COMPONENTS OF AN ACCOUNTING SYSTEM?

The primary purpose of a company's **accounting system** is to record, organize, summarize, and report useful information to external financial statement users and stakeholders, as well as to the company's managers for making operating, investing, and financing decisions. All companies have accounting systems, ranging from the simple to the complex. Around the world, whether the companies use U.S. GAAP, IFRS, or home-country standards, accounting systems are based on the concepts and methods we describe in this chapter. A company can use this system in either a computer or manual accounting process. Although accounting systems will differ in how information is processed, the basic components are the same. They include the:

- accounting equation, which is the framework of the system
- source documents used to generate accounting information
- records used to organize and store accounting information
- outputs—the financial statements

Accounting Equation

The **accounting equation** provides the framework for the accounting system and is the structure in which companies record transactions, events, and arrangements. This equation is usually expressed as follows:

$$\text{Assets} = \text{Liabilities} + \text{Shareholders' Equity}$$

In the accounting equation, **assets** are the company's economic resources, **liabilities** are its obligations owed to creditors, and **shareholders' equity** is the shareholders' residual interest in the company's assets after the liabilities have been satisfied. This equation must remain in balance at all times because the left side summarizes the company's economic resources, while the right side summarizes the claims to those economic resources. This fundamental accounting equation, which represents the balance sheet, is the foundation of the accounting system. Other useful equations can be derived from this basic one, as shown in Exhibit 3.1.

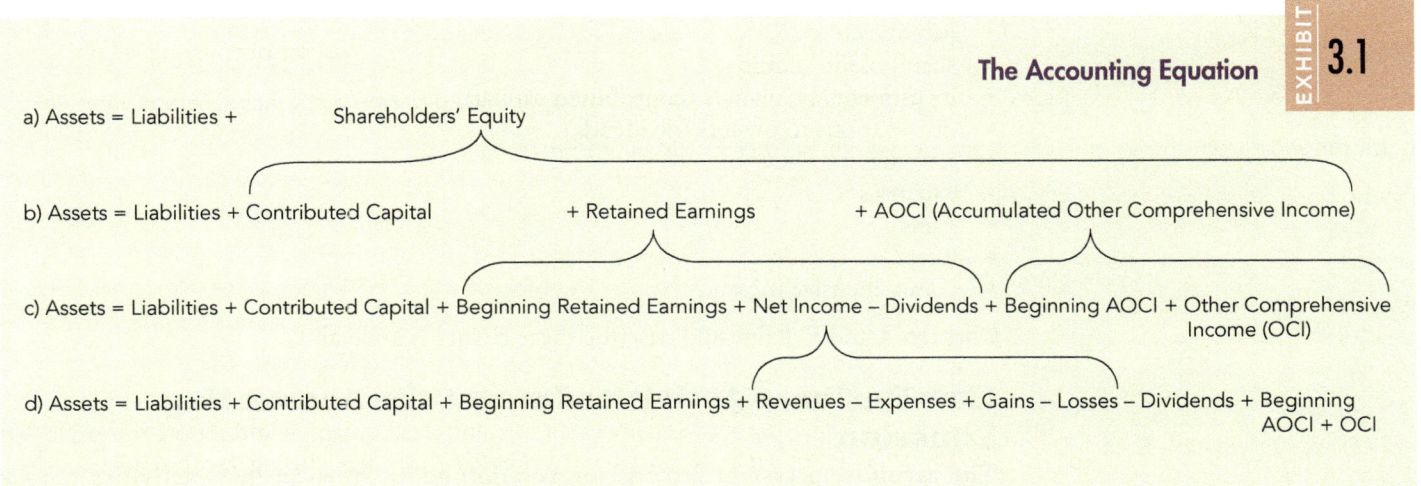

EXHIBIT 3.1 The Accounting Equation

In expanding from Equation a to Equation b in Exhibit 3.1, you can see that Shareholders' Equity consists of three parts:

- **Contributed capital** includes the amount of capital invested by owners.[1]
- **Retained earnings** is the cumulative amount of **net income** generated by the company minus the **dividends** distributed to owners.
- **Accumulated other comprehensive income (AOCI)** measures and reports the total amount of **other comprehensive income (OCI)** items, which consist of a few specific income items that the FASB has designated to be recognized in AOCI until they are realized, at which time they are recognized in net income. For simplicity, we will save further discussion of AOCI and OCI until Chapters 4 and 5.

Equation c shows that:

$$\text{Ending Balance in Retained Earnings} = \text{Beginning Balance in Retained Earnings} + \text{Net Income} - \text{Dividends}$$

Equation d, also called the expanded accounting equation, simply breaks net income into four components:

$$\text{Net Income} = \text{Revenues} - \text{Expenses} + \text{Gains} - \text{Losses}$$

---

[1] Shareholders invest by purchasing shares from the corporation when it issues them. Contributed capital in a partnership or a proprietorship arises when the partners or the proprietor make direct investments of capital in the company.

- **Revenues** measure the inflows of assets and the settlements of obligations from selling goods and providing services to customers.
- **Expenses** measure the outflows of assets that a company consumes and the obligations a company incurs in the process of operating the business.
- **Gains** or **losses** result from transactions in which the company sells assets or settles liabilities for more or less than their book values.
- In measuring net income, revenues and gains recognize the resources generated by a company during the period, whereas expenses and losses recognize the resources consumed during the period.

The expanded accounting equation at the bottom of Exhibit 3.1 only differs from Equation a by presenting the components of shareholders' equity in greater detail. The expanded accounting equation shows how all 10 elements of financial accounting impact the balance sheet, which include:

- assets
- liabilities
- shareholders' equity
- investments by owners (contributed capital)
- distributions to owners (dividends)
- revenues
- expenses
- gains
- losses
- comprehensive income

Chapters 4 and 5 define and describe these elements in detail.

How Business Activities Impact the Accounting Equation

The accounting system records information about how business activities *change* the company's balance sheet. Exhibit 3.2 uses the fundamental accounting equation to provide a framework for how a company's primary business activities change the balance

EXHIBIT 3.2 How Business Activities Change the Accounting Equation

Beginning of Period	Assets	= Liabilities + Contributed Capital	+ Retained Earnings + AOCI
Acquiring Assets by Issuing Equity	+ Assets	= + Contributed Capital	
Acquiring Assets by Issuing Debt	+ Assets	= + Liabilities	
Using Assets to Retire Equity	– Assets	= – Contributed Capital	
Using Assets to Retire Debt	– Assets	= – Liabilities	
Generating Net Income:			
Revenues Create Assets	+ Assets	=	+ Retained Earnings (Revenues)
Revenues Satisfy Obligations	No Change in Assets	= – Liabilities	+ Retained Earnings (Revenues)
Expenses Consume Assets	– Assets	=	– Retained Earnings (Expenses)
Expenses Incur Obligations	No Change in Assets	= + Liabilities	– Retained Earnings (Expenses)
Gains Create Assets	+ Assets	=	+ Retained Earnings (Gains)
Losses Consume Assets	– Assets	=	– Retained Earnings (Losses)
Paying Dividends	– Assets	=	– Retained Earnings (Dividends)
End of Period	Assets	= Liabilities + Contributed Capital	+ Retained Earnings + AOCI

sheet and should be recorded in the accounting system. For example, when a company engages in transactions that change assets, liabilities, and contributed capital, those transactions are recorded directly in the affected accounts, keeping the equation in balance. When a company raises cash by issuing common stock, it records that transaction by increasing the cash (assets) and common stock (shareholders' equity) accounts. If a company borrows money from a bank and uses the money to acquire assets, it records that transaction by increasing the affected liability and asset accounts. If a company uses cash to pay off a liability, it records that transaction by decreasing directly the cash and related liability account.

Net income and dividends also represent *changes* in assets and liabilities and are reflected in retained earnings. For example, when a company recognizes revenues (or gains), it either receives assets from customers (usually consideration in the form of cash or receivables) or reduces liabilities by satisfying performance obligations to customers (unearned or deferred revenue). Therefore, the company records the revenue transaction by increasing assets (or decreasing liabilities) and increasing revenues, which increases retained earnings. In contrast, when the company incurs expenses (or losses), it uses up assets or incurs obligations. The company then records the expense by decreasing assets (or increasing liabilities) and increasing an expense account, which decreases retained earnings. Dividends are distributions of assets to owners, which reduce retained earnings.

Transactions, Events, Arrangements, and Supporting Documents

For financial accounting purposes, the operating, investing, and financing activities that change a company's economic resources (assets), obligations (liabilities), or residual interest (shareholders' equity) can arise through transactions, events, or arrangements.

- A **transaction** involves the transfer or exchange of resources between the company and another party, such as the purchase of inventory from a supplier or the sale of a product or service to a customer.
- An **event** is an occurrence that affects the company. The event may be *internal*, such as using equipment in operations, or *external*, such as a gain in the fair value of an investment security.
- An **arrangement** is an agreement or a promise by the company with another party or entity. For example, a company may have arrangements such as warranties to repair defective products sold to customers or promises to pay pension and other retirement benefits to employees.

The company records the transactions, events, and arrangements in its accounting system using business documents, or **source documents**, as initial information for the recording process. These documents (such as sales invoices, checks, freight bills, and contracts) include the monetary amount, parties involved, terms and conditions, and other relevant information.

Accounts

A company uses **accounts** to store the recorded monetary information from its transactions, events, and arrangements. Examples of these accounts include Cash, Accounts Receivable, Buildings, Accounts Payable, Wages Payable, Sales Revenue, Cost of Goods Sold, Salaries Expense, Common Stock, Retained Earnings, and Dividends. The company assigns each account a number in its **chart of accounts**. This numbering system organizes the accounts efficiently and minimizes errors in the recording process.[2] Complex accounting systems for large organizations can involve thousands of accounts.

The **T-account** format is used for all accounts. Each T-account has a **debit** (left) and a **credit** (right) side. Because each account accumulates information about both

---

[2] To find the chart of accounts that we use throughout this book, go to www.cengagebrain.com and search for this book by its title.

increases and decreases resulting from various transactions, events, and arrangements, there is a "double-entry" rule for recording these changes. In the **double-entry accounting system**, **for each transaction, event, or arrangement that a company records, the total dollar amount of the debits must be equal to the total dollar amount of the credits.**

In the double-entry system, all accounts on the left side of the accounting equation (assets) are increased by debits (entries on the left side of the T-account) and decreased by credits (entries on the right side of the T-account). All accounts on the right side of the equation (liabilities and shareholders' equity) are increased by credits (entries on the right side of the T-account) and decreased by debits (entries on the left side of the T-account). Exhibit 3.3 shows these relationships.

EXHIBIT 3.3 Accounting Equation and Double-Entry System

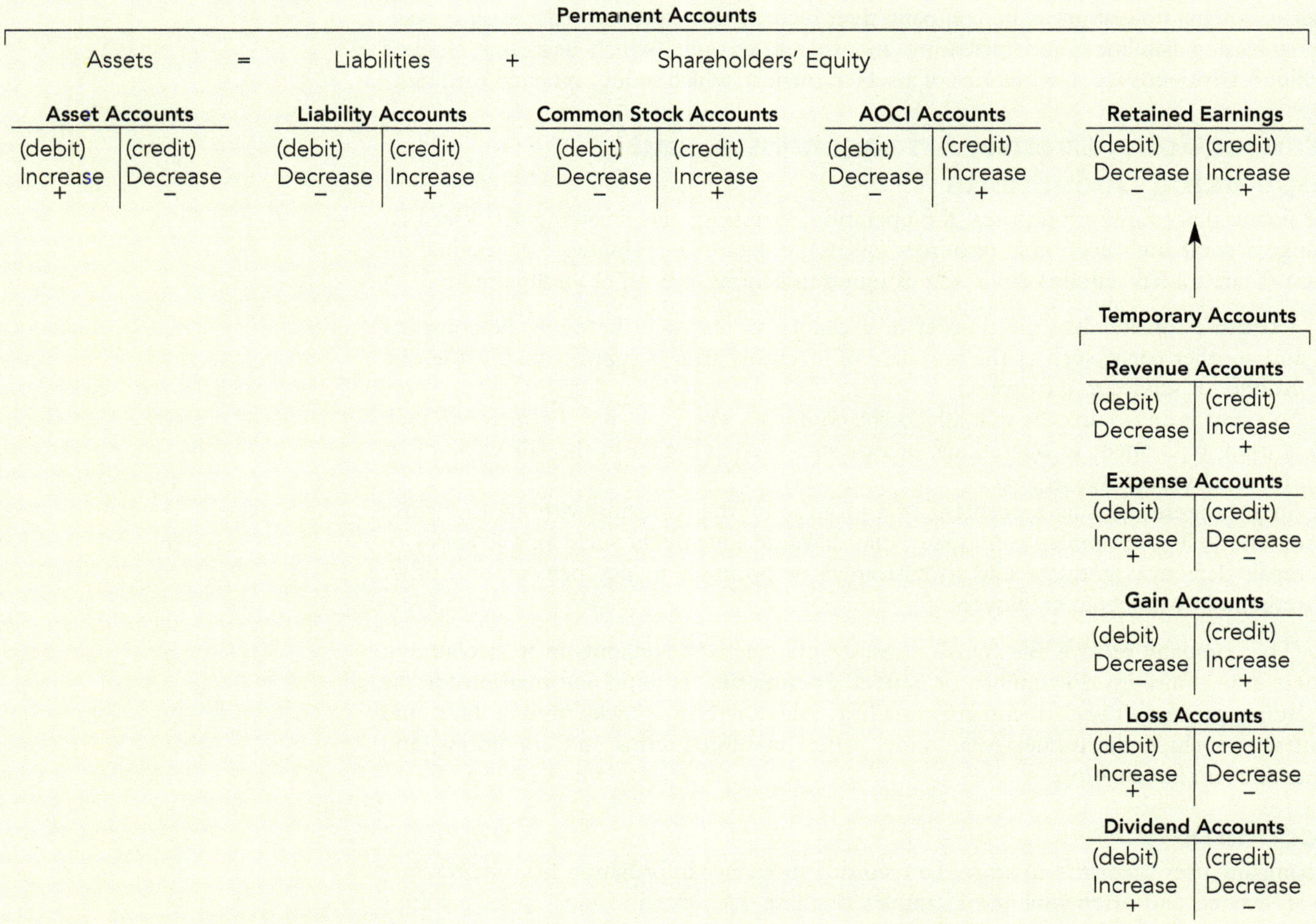

Permanent Accounts

Assets = Liabilities + Shareholders' Equity

Asset Accounts
(debit) | (credit)
Increase | Decrease
+ | −

Liability Accounts
(debit) | (credit)
Decrease | Increase
− | +

Common Stock Accounts
(debit) | (credit)
Decrease | Increase
− | +

AOCI Accounts
(debit) | (credit)
Decrease | Increase
− | +

Retained Earnings
(debit) | (credit)
Decrease | Increase
− | +

Temporary Accounts

Revenue Accounts
(debit) | (credit)
Decrease | Increase
− | +

Expense Accounts
(debit) | (credit)
Increase | Decrease
+ | −

Gain Accounts
(debit) | (credit)
Decrease | Increase
− | +

Loss Accounts
(debit) | (credit)
Increase | Decrease
+ | −

Dividend Accounts
(debit) | (credit)
Increase | Decrease
+ | −

Suppose that shareholders invest $20,000 in a corporation by purchasing 2,000 shares of stock at $10 per share. The corporation records this transaction with a debit (increase) of $20,000 in an asset account, Cash, and with a $20,000 credit (increase) to a contributed capital account in shareholders' equity, Common Stock. Note that the accounting equation remains in balance (both sides increase by $20,000) and that the total debits equal the total credits.

Accounts are classified as permanent or temporary accounts:

- The **permanent accounts** are the asset, liability, and shareholders' equity accounts whose balances at the *end* of the period are carried forward to the next period.
- The **temporary accounts** (**periodic accounts**) are used to determine the changes in retained earnings that occur *during a period*, and their account balances are *not* carried forward. These accounts are the revenue, expense, gain, loss, and dividend accounts, shown on the far right of Exhibit 3.3.

At the end of each period, temporary accounts are closed, and their amounts are included in retained earnings. Because an increase in revenues causes an increase in retained earnings, it is recorded as a credit. Because a gain increases retained earnings, it also is recorded as a credit. In contrast, recording increases in expenses, losses, and dividends is the *opposite* of those for revenues. For instance, because it reduces retained earnings, an increase in an expense (or dividend or loss) account is recorded as a debit.

Sometimes a company will use a **contra account** to show a reduction in a related account. The rules for increasing or decreasing a contra account are exactly the *opposite* of those for the related account it is intended to reduce. For instance, Accumulated Depreciation is a contra account used to accumulate the depreciation recorded for Property, Plant, and Equipment. We illustrate contra accounts in a later section.

The **balance** of an account is the difference between the total debits and credits recorded in that account. A company uses these balances to prepare its financial statements.

Financial Statements

Financial statements are summary reports prepared at the end of each accounting period, typically a fiscal year. These statements are based on the interrelated equations presented in Exhibit 3.1 (p. 3-3). A company's **annual report** usually contains the financial statements for the company's fiscal year, along with the accompanying supporting schedules and notes, management's discussion and analysis, and other information disclosed to the various external users. Companies often also prepare financial statements for shorter time periods. These are called **interim statements** (or **quarterly statements**).

As described in Chapter 1, **the balance sheet summarizes the amounts of the assets, liabilities, and shareholders' equity at the end of the period.** The balance sheet reports the company's financial position at a point in time. In contrast, the other primary financial statements—the income statement, statement of cash flows, and statement of shareholders' equity—explain *changes* in the company's financial position.

The income statement summarizes the results of the income-producing activities for the period. Net income is determined by subtracting the total expenses from the total revenues and adding any gains or subtracting any losses.

The statement of cash flows summarizes the cash receipts and cash payments during the period. The statement of cash flows reports for a period of time the net cash flows (inflows minus outflows) from operating, investing, and financing activities. The statement of cash flows reconciles the beginning cash balance with the ending cash balance.

The statement of shareholders' equity provides information about the common shareholders' equity claims and how those claims changed during the period. For example, it will show how retained earnings changed during the period by adding the net income to the beginning balance in the Retained Earnings account and subtracting the dividends declared.

The balance sheet shows the financial position at the end of the period, and the income statement, statement of cash flows, and statement of shareholders equity report

Example Suppose that Jaymie returned $300 of inventory that it had purchased on credit from its supplier. Jaymie could record the return in one of two ways:

Using Contra Account			Reducing Inventory Account		
Accounts Payable	300		Accounts Payable	300	
Purchase Returns & Allowances		300	Inventory		300

Some suppliers offer a discount on credit sales for prompt payment within a discount period. To the purchasing company, this is a **purchase discount**. A purchase discount is also a reduction in the cost of the inventory.[5]

During 2016, Jaymie engages in various transactions. **Example 3.1** lists these transactions and provides an analysis of the accounts and amounts to be debited and credited. This analysis is based on a review of the related source documents.

EXAMPLE 3.1 — 2016 Transactions and Analyses (Jaymie Corporation)

Date	Transaction	Analysis
1/1	Various shareholders invest in Jaymie by purchasing 2,000 shares of no-par stock at $10 per share.	Asset account Cash increased (debited) by $20,000; shareholders' equity account Common Stock increased (credited) by $20,000.
1/16	Jaymie purchases 2 acres of land as a building site, paying $1,500 an acre.	Asset account Land increased (debited) by $3,000; Cash decreased (credited) by $3,000.
3/30	Jaymie purchases a building and equipment for $15,320 and $2,120, respectively. Jaymie pays $10,840 and signs a 12% note (interest and principal to be paid after 2 years) for the $6,600 balance.	Asset accounts Building and Equipment increased (debited) by $15,320 and $2,120, respectively; Cash decreased (credited) by $10,840; liability account Notes Payable increased (credited) by $6,600.
3/30	Jaymie purchases a 1-year comprehensive insurance policy for $360.	Asset account Prepaid Insurance increased (debited) by $360; Cash decreased (credited) by $360.
3/31	Jaymie purchases $7,300 of inventory on credit from Bark Company.	Asset account Inventory increased (debited) by $7,300; liability account Accounts Payable increased (credited) by $7,300.
4/2	Jaymie sells inventory to customers for $8,000 cash. The cost of the inventory was $5,090.	Cash increased (debited) by $8,000; revenue account Sales Revenue increased (credited) by $8,000. Expense account Cost of Goods Sold increased (debited) by $5,090; Inventory decreased (credited) by $5,090.
4/8	Jaymie pays $7,300 to Bark for inventory purchased on 3/31.	Accounts Payable decreased (debited) by $7,300; Cash decreased (credited) by $7,300.
7/15	Jaymie purchases inventory for $3,300 cash.	Inventory increased (debited) by $3,300; Cash decreased (credited) by $3,300.
9/1	Jaymie sells 1 acre of land (original cost $1,500) and receives a $1,320, 6-month, 15% note from buyer.	Asset account Notes Receivable increased (debited) by $1,320; Loss on Sale of Land increased (debited) by $180; Land decreased (credited) by $1,500.
10/1	Jaymie pays the first 6 months' salaries (April–September) totaling $1,800 to employees.	Expense account Salaries Expense increased (debited) by $1,800; Cash decreased (credited) by $1,800.
11/23	Jaymie makes sales on credit of $5,000 to Frank Company and $4,000 to Knox Company. The cost of the inventory was $5,400.	Accounts Receivable increased (debited) by $9,000; Sales Revenue increased (credited) by $9,000. Cost of Goods Sold increased (debited) by $5,400; Inventory decreased (credited) by $5,400.
12/1	Jaymie rents part of its building to Fritz Company, receiving 3 months' rent in advance at $150 per month.	Cash increased (debited) by $450; liability account Unearned Rent increased (credited) by $450.

(continued)

---

[5] We show how to record purchase discounts in Chapter 7.

Date	Transaction	Analysis
12/2	Jaymie collects $2,000 of accounts receivable from Frank Company.	Cash increased (debited) by $2,000; Accounts Receivable decreased (credited) by $2,000.
12/27	Jaymie purchases $1,900 of inventory on credit from Ajax Company.	Inventory increased (debited) by $1,900; Accounts Payable increased (credited) by $1,900.
12/28	Jaymie pays $428 of miscellaneous operating expenses.	Other Expenses increased (debited) by $428; Cash decreased (credited) by $428.
12/29	Jaymie distributes dividends of $500 ($0.25 per share for 2,000 shares) to shareholders.	Dividends account increased (debited) by $500; Cash decreased (credited) by $500.

Based on the transaction analysis listed in **Example 3.1**, Jaymie prepares the general journal entries shown in **Example 3.2**. Traditionally, journal entries first list the accounts being debited and then list and indent the accounts being credited, followed by a brief explanation.

EXAMPLE 3.2

General Journal Entries (Jaymie Corporation)

Date		Account Titles and Explanations	Debit	Credit
2016				
Jan.	1	Cash	20,000	
		Common Stock		20,000
		Issued 2,000 shares of no-par stock at $10 per share.		
	16	Land	3,000	
		Cash		3,000
		Purchased 2 acres of land at $1,500 per acre.		
Mar.	30	Building	15,320	
		Equipment	2,120	
		Cash		10,840
		Notes Payable		6,600
		Purchased a building and equipment for cash and a note payable.		
	30	Prepaid Insurance	360	
		Cash		360
		Purchased a 1-year comprehensive insurance policy.		
	31	Inventory	7,300	
		Accounts Payable		7,300
		Purchased inventory on credit from Bark Company.		
Apr.	2	Cash	8,000	
		Sales Revenue		8,000
		To record cash sales.		
	2	Cost of Goods Sold	5,090	
		Inventory		5,090
		To record cost of sales.		
	8	Accounts Payable	7,300	
		Cash		7,300
		Paid Bark Company for purchases made on credit on March 31.		
July	15	Inventory	3,300	
		Cash		3,300
		Purchased inventory for cash.		

(continued)

EXAMPLE 3.2 (Continued)

Date	Account Titles and Explanations	Debit	Credit
Sept. 1	Notes Receivable	1,320	
	Loss on Sale of Land	180	
	Land		1,500
	Sold 1 acre of land, incurring a loss; received a note due in 6 months bearing 15% annual interest.		
Oct. 1	Salaries Expense	1,800	
	Cash		1,800
	Paid 6 months' of employees' salaries.		
Nov. 23	Accounts Receivable	9,000	
	Sales Revenue		9,000
	To record sales on credit to Frank Company ($5,000) and Knox Company ($4,000).		
23	Cost of Goods Sold	5,400	
	Inventory		5,400
	To record cost of sales.		
Dec. 1	Cash	450	
	Unearned Rent		450
	Received 3 months' rent in advance at $150 per month from Fritz Company.		
2	Cash	2,000	
	Accounts Receivable		2,000
	Frank Company paid a portion of its accounts receivable.		
27	Inventory	1,900	
	Accounts Payable		1,900
	Purchased inventory on credit from Ajax Company.		
28	Other Expenses	428	
	Cash		428
	Paid miscellaneous operating expenses.		
29	Dividends	500	
	Cash		500
	Distributed dividends of $0.25 per share to shareholders.		

GOT IT?

3-8 Why is it advantageous to a company to initially record each of its transactions in a journal?

3-9 What is a perpetual inventory accounting system? What journal entries are involved?

3-10 Give examples of transactions that:
   a. Increase an asset and a liability
   b. Increase an asset and shareholders' equity
   c. Increase an asset and decrease a different asset
   d. Decrease an asset and a liability
   e. Decrease an asset and shareholders' equity

3-11 Give examples of transactions that:
   a. Increase inventory and a liability
   b. Decrease inventory and a liability
   c. Increase inventory and decrease an asset
   d. Decrease inventory and increase an asset

HOW DO WE POST TO THE GENERAL LEDGER (STEP 2)?

LEARNING OBJECTIVE 3.4
Post to the general ledger and prepare a trial balance.

A **general ledger** is the entire set of accounts for a company. After a company records its transactions, events, and arrangements in a general journal, it updates each account in the general ledger by **posting** (transferring) the date and debit and credit amounts from the journal entries to the accounts in the general ledger. Thus, **after posting, the *general journal* contains the journal entry information in chronological order, whereas the *general ledger* includes the journal entry information within all of the accounts.** **Example 3.3** shows all the accounts in Jaymie Corporation's general ledger. To conserve space, these accounts include the postings not only for the journal entries shown in

EXAMPLE 3.3

General Ledger (Jaymie Corporation)

Cash			
1/1	20,000	1/16	3,000
4/2	8,000	3/30	10,840
12/1	450	3/30	360
12/2	2,000	4/8	7,300
		7/15	3,300
		10/1	1,800
		12/28	428
		12/29	500
Balance	2,922		

Accounts Receivable			
11/23	9,000	12/2	2,000
Balance	7,000		

Allowance for Doubtful Accounts			
		12/31 Adj	170

Notes Receivable			
9/1	1,320		

Interest Receivable			
12/31 Adj	66		

Inventory			
3/31	7,300	4/2	5,090
7/15	3,300	11/23	5,400
12/27	1,900		
Balance	2,010		

Prepaid Insurance			
3/30	360	12/31 Adj	270
Balance	90		

Land			
1/16	3,000	9/1	1,500
Balance	1,500		

Building			
3/30	15,320		

Accumulated Depreciation: Building			
		12/31 Adj	264

Equipment			
3/30	2,120		

Accumulated Depreciation: Equipment			
		12/31 Adj	120

Accounts Payable			
4/8	7,300	3/31	7,300
		12/27	1,900
		Balance	1,900

Notes Payable			
		3/30	6,600

Salaries Payable			
		12/31 Adj	900

Interest Payable			
		12/31 Adj	594

Income Taxes Payable			
		12/31 Adj	600

Unearned Rent			
12/31 Adj	150	12/1	450
		Balance	300

Common Stock			
		1/1	20,000

Retained Earnings			
12/31 Cl	500	12/31 Cl	1,400
		Balance	900

Sales Revenue			
12/31 Cl	17,000	4/2	8,000
		11/23	9,000

Interest Income			
12/31 Cl	66	12/31 Adj	66

Rent Income			
12/31 Cl	150	12/31 Adj	150

Cost of Goods Sold			
4/2	5,090	12/31 Cl	10,490
11/23	5,400		

Salaries Expense			
10/1	1,800	12/31 Cl	2,700
12/31 Adj	900		

Other Expenses			
12/28	428	12/31 Cl	428

Loss on Sale of Land			
9/1	180	12/31 Cl	180

Depreciation Expense: Building			
12/31 Adj	264	12/31 Cl	264

Depreciation Expense: Equipment			
12/31 Adj	120	12/31 Cl	120

Bad Debts Expense			
12/31 Adj	170	12/31 Cl	170

Insurance Expense			
12/31 Adj	270	12/31 Cl	270

Interest Expense			
12/31 Adj	594	12/31 Cl	594

Income Tax Expense			
12/31 Adj	600	12/31 Cl	600

Income Summary			
12/31 Cl	15,816	12/31 Cl	17,216
12/31 Cl	1,400		

Dividends			
12/29	500	12/31 Cl	500

Example 3.2, but also for the *adjusting* entries (*Adj* is shown in the account) and the *closing* entries (*Cl*), which are discussed later in Examples 3.4 and 3.10.[6]

Trial Balance

After a company prepares and posts its journal entries for the accounting period, the balance in each account is the difference between the total debit entries and the total credit entries to the account. A **trial balance** is prepared, which is a worksheet that lists all the general ledger accounts and their balances. It is used to verify that the total of the debit balances is equal to the total of the credit balances. A trial balance is included on the worksheet in Example 3.11.

If a trial balance does not balance, there is an error. To find errors, add the debit and credit columns again. If the column totals do not agree, check the amounts in the debit and credit columns to be sure that an account balance was not mistakenly listed in the wrong column. If still in error, compute the difference between the debit and credit column totals and divide by 9. When the difference is evenly divisible by 9, a *transposition* or a *slide* may have occurred. A *transposition* is when two digits in a number are mistakenly reversed. For instance, suppose an asset account in the general ledger has a $1,500 balance but is mistakenly listed as $5,100 on the trial balance. On the trial balance, the debit column total would exceed the credit column total by the amount of the error, $3,600, which is evenly divisible by 9. A *slide* is when the digits are listed in the correct order but are mistakenly moved one decimal place to the left or right. For instance, suppose a liability account in the general ledger with a $1,900 balance is listed on the trial balance as $190. In the trial balance, the credit column total would exceed the debit column total by the amount of the error, $1,710, which is evenly divisible by 9.

A transposition or a slide may have occurred when the account balances were computed initially or transferred to the trial balance. To find the error, compare the balances listed on the trial balance with the balances in the ledger. Then recompute the ledger account balances, and if no error is found, double-check the postings. Finally, review the journal entries for accuracy.

The equality of the debit and credit totals in the trial balance, however, does not necessarily mean that the information in the accounting system is error-free. A trial balance does not identify several types of errors, including the following:

- An entire transaction may not have been recorded, or may have been accidentally recorded twice.
- An entire transaction may not have been posted to the accounts, or may have been posted twice.
- Equal dollar amounts of debits and credits, but the wrong amounts, may have been recorded for a transaction.
- A journal entry may have recorded a transaction using a wrong account.
- A journal entry may have been posted to a wrong account.

Even when the trial balance is in balance, it is worthwhile to double-check all of the journal entries, postings, and account totals to make sure they are correct.

GOT IT?

3-12 What different purposes do the general journal and the general ledger serve?

3-13 What is the purpose of a trial balance?

3-14 Define the following:
   a. account
   b. contra account
   c. general ledger
   d. journal
   e. posting

---

[6] A company may also use subsidiary ledgers, such as an accounts receivable subsidiary ledger and an accounts payable subsidiary ledger. We discuss subsidiary ledgers later in this chapter.

HOW DO WE PREPARE ADJUSTING ENTRIES (STEP 3)?

LEARNING OBJECTIVE 3.5
Prepare adjusting entries.

Both U.S. GAAP and IFRS require the accrual method of accounting. Under **accrual accounting**, a company recognizes revenues in the period in which it satisfies performance obligations to customers, even though the cash flows from customers may occur in a different period. The company also records expenses in the period in which assets have been consumed (or liabilities incurred) during the course of business operations, even though the cash outflow might occur in a different period. Although the initial trial balance will reflect all of the journal entries recorded during the period, many of the asset, liability, revenue, and expense accounts may not be completely up to date at the end of the accounting period. A company must record **adjusting entries** so that all revenues and expenses are recorded in the appropriate period and all assets and liabilities have correct ending balances.

Adjusting entries always affect both a permanent (balance sheet) and a temporary (income statement) account. Adjusting entries may be classified into four broad categories: deferrals, accruals, estimates, and periodic inventory.

- *Deferrals*: Arise when cash flows occur prior to recognition of an item in income (for example, prepaid expenses and deferred revenues).
- *Accruals*: Arise when cash flows occur after recognition of an item in income (for example, wages payable and accounts receivable).
- *Estimates*: Recognized amounts on the balance sheet and income statement that are not known with certainty and must be estimated (for example, depreciation expense and bad debt expense).
- *Periodic Inventory*: Some firms use periodic inventory systems that require adjusting entries each period.

Deferrals

Deferrals are transactions, events, or arrangements in which the cash flows occur *before* the related expenses are incurred or revenues are recognized. Adjusting entries for deferrals, therefore, allocate items such as prepaid expenses and unearned revenues across periods so that the income statement for each period reports the appropriate amounts of revenue and expense and the balance sheet each period reports the appropriate amounts of assets and liabilities. Deferred expenses on the balance sheet represent economic benefits that are not completely used up by the end of the period, which the company can consume in operations in future periods. Deferred revenues on the balance sheet represent unsatisfied performance obligations when customers prepay for goods and services, which the company will satisfy in future periods when it delivers the goods or services.

Prepaid Expenses A **prepaid expense** is a good or service purchased but not fully used up by the end of the period. Examples of expenses that are often prepaid include rent, office supplies, insurance, advertising, and licenses. **Starbucks**'s 2015 balance sheet, for example, recognizes $334.2 million in Prepaid Expenses and Other Current Assets, which primarily represents prepaid rent for stores. When the company initially purchases the good or service, it records the *cost* as an asset (prepaid expense) and reduces cash for the amount paid. The company uses some of these goods or services during the period. The adjusting entry should reduce the amount of the prepaid expense asset for the portion consumed, and that amount should be recognized as an expense. The unused portion of the prepaid expense should be recognized as an asset. Exhibit 3.5 shows the effect of a prepaid expense adjusting entry on a company's accounts.

EXHIBIT 3.5 — Effects of Adjusting Entries for Prepaid Expenses

Effect on Accounts: Decrease Asset → Increase Expense

Example: Adjusting Entries for Prepaid Expenses

In the Jaymie Corporation example, Jaymie purchased a 1-year comprehensive insurance policy on March 30, 2016. It recorded an asset, Prepaid Insurance, for $360. At the end of the year, 9 months of insurance coverage has expired, while 3 months of coverage remains in force. Insurance Expense is increased (debited) by $270 ($30 per month for 9 months), and Prepaid Insurance is decreased (credited) by $270. The result is a $270 increase in expenses and a $90 remaining balance in the asset Prepaid Insurance. This adjusting entry is shown in **Example 3.4**, and it is posted to the ledger accounts shown in **Example 3.3** (p. 3-13).[7]

EXAMPLE 3.4 Adjusting Entries for 2016 (Jaymie Corporation)

Date	Account Titles and Explanations	Debit	Credit
2016	*Adjusting Entries*		
Dec. 31	Insurance Expense	270	
	Prepaid Insurance		270
	To record expiration of 9 months of insurance coverage purchased on March 30.		
31	Unearned Rent	150	
	Rent Income		150
	To record earning 1 month of rent income from receipt collected in advance on December 1.		
31	Salaries Expense	900	
	Salaries Payable		900
	To record 3 months' salaries earned by employees but not yet paid.		
31	Interest Expense	594	
	Interest Payable		594
	To record interest accumulated on the note payable issued on March 30 and due March 30, 2018.		
31	Interest Receivable	66	
	Interest Income		66
	To record interest income earned on the note receivable from September 1 to December 31.		
31	Depreciation Expense: Building	264	
	Accumulated Depreciation: Building		264
	To record 9 months' depreciation on building acquired March 30.		
31	Depreciation Expense: Equipment	120	
	Accumulated Depreciation: Equipment		120
	To record 9 months' depreciation on equipment acquired March 30.		
31	Bad Debts Expense	170	
	Allowance for Doubtful Accounts		170
	To record estimated uncollectible accounts receivable.		
31	Income Tax Expense	600	
	Income Taxes Payable		600
	To record income taxes for the period.		

[7] Each adjusting entry date in the ledger is followed by the abbreviation Adj to distinguish adjusting entries from closing entries (denoted Cl), which are described later in **Example 3.10**.

Deferred Revenues **Deferred revenue** (also called **unearned revenue**) arises when customers pay in advance for the future delivery of goods or performance of services. Customers pay in advance for such items as subscriptions, memberships, airfares, tickets to concerts or sporting events, and gift cards. Some of the examples used to illustrate prepaid expenses in the prior subsection, such as rent and insurance, would trigger deferred revenues for the sellers of these services. At the time of the transaction, the company selling prepaid goods or services records an increase in an asset (usually cash) and an increase in a liability for deferred (or unearned) revenue. **Starbucks**'s 2015 balance sheet, for example, recognizes $983.8 million in deferred revenue as a current liability in the Stored Value Card Liability, which primarily represents unsatisfied performance obligations to customers related to Starbucks's Stored Value Cards (gift cards). In some cases, the company delivers the goods or services at a particular point in time, satisfying its performance obligation to the customer. The company then recognizes revenue and reduces the liability. For example, when a customer redeems a gift card in exchange for a cup of coffee, Starbucks recognizes revenue and reduces the obligation for deferred revenues. As another example, on the day a passenger takes a flight or a fan attends a sporting event for which the ticket was prepaid, the company recognizes revenue and eliminates the corresponding liability. However, in some cases, the company satisfies the performance obligation to the customer over a period of time, for example, deferred rent revenues or deferred insurance premiums. In such cases, the company should recognize an adjusting entry at the end of the period to recognize the portion of revenue related to the performance obligations that have been satisfied and to reduce the deferred revenue liability to reflect the remaining amount of performance obligations to customers at year-end. Exhibit 3.6 shows the effect of a deferred revenue adjusting entry on a company's accounts.

EXHIBIT 3.6 Effects of Adjusting Entries for Deferred Revenues

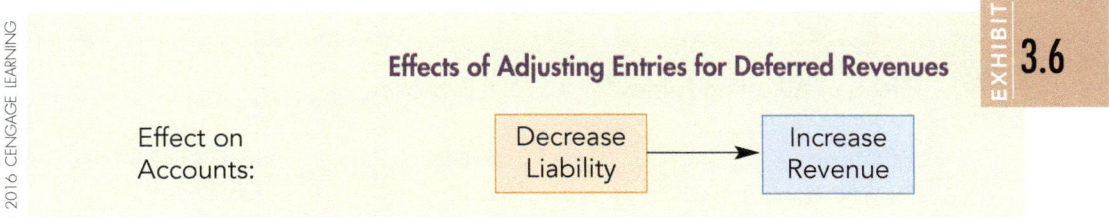

Effect on Accounts: Decrease Liability → Increase Revenue

Example: Adjusting Entries for Deferred Revenues

On December 1, Jaymie Corporation received $450 for 3 months' rent in advance. It recorded the cash and the liability (Unearned Rent) to provide the use of a portion of the building. By December 31, it has earned 1 month of rent. The adjusting entry is a debit (decrease) of $150 to the Unearned Rent liability and a credit (increase) of $150 to Rent Income. The result is a $150 increase in revenues and a $300 remaining balance in the Unearned Rent liability. This adjusting entry is the second entry presented in **Example 3.4**.

A company might *initially* record the entire prepayment as an expense (instead of as an asset) or the entire receipt in advance as a revenue (instead of a liability). For example, Jaymie Corporation *could* have recorded the March 30 payment as a $360 debit to Insurance Expense (instead of Prepaid Insurance), and it *could* have recorded the December 1 receipt of $450 as a credit to Rent Revenue (instead of Unearned Rent). In cases like these, the adjusting procedure calculates the appropriate ending balances in the permanent accounts and adjusts the balance sheet and income statement accounts accordingly. For instance, the Prepaid Insurance asset should have an ending balance of $90. The adjusting

When customers pay in advance for goods or services to be delivered in the future, like buying tickets to concerts prior to the show, the company must record an increase in both assets and liabilities (because it has a performance obligation to provide goods or services).

entry would debit (increase) Prepaid Insurance for $90 and credit (decrease) Insurance Expense for $90. Similarly, the Unearned Rent liability should have an ending balance of $300. The year-end adjusting entry must *reduce* the revenue and *increase* the Unearned Rent liability account by this amount. The adjusting entry would debit (decrease) Rent Revenue for $300 and credit (increase) the Unearned Rent liability account for $300. The results of these adjusting entries are the *same* balances in the respective accounts as we show in the comprehensive illustration. ∎

Accruals

Accruals represent transactions, events, or arrangements in which the cash flows occur *after* the related expenses are incurred or revenues are recognized. Like deferrals, the adjusting entries for accruals measure the appropriate amount of revenue or expense for that particular accounting period, as well as the appropriate amounts of assets and liabilities for the balance sheet. Accrued expenses, such as wages payable or income taxes payable, are obligations to make future payments for expenses or benefits the company consumed in the current period. Accrued revenues, such as accounts receivable, are assets that represent amounts the company is entitled to receive because it has satisfied performance obligations to customers, but has not yet collected from them.

Accrued Expenses An **accrued expense** is an expense that has been incurred but has not yet been paid. **Starbucks**'s 2015 balance sheet, for example, recognizes $1,760.7 million in accrued expenses as current liabilities in the Accrued Liabilities account. To appropriately measure expenses and liabilities, a company must make an adjusting entry for each accrued expense. Exhibit 3.7 shows the effect of such an adjusting entry.

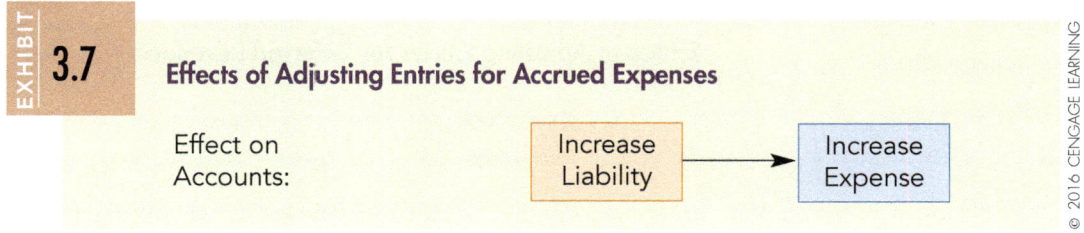

EXHIBIT 3.7 Effects of Adjusting Entries for Accrued Expenses

Example: Accrued Salaries

Jaymie Corporation pays employees' salaries every 6 months, making the last $1,800 payment on October 1. At the end of December, its employees have earned salaries for 3 months (October through December), but they have not been paid. The adjusting entry is a debit (increase) to Salaries Expense for $900 and a credit (increase) to Salaries Payable for $900. The result is a $900 increase in expenses and a $900 ending balance in Salaries Payable. **Example 3.4** (p. 3-16) shows this adjusting entry. ∎

Example: Accrued Interest

On March 30, Jaymie Corporation issued a $6,600, 12% note payable due at the end of 2 years. Although it will not pay the principal and interest until 2018, 9 months of interest expense has accumulated and is a liability at the end of 2016. The interest is computed as follows:

$$\text{Interest} = \text{Principal} \times \text{Rate} \times \text{Time}$$
$$= \$6{,}600 \times 0.12 \times 9/12$$
$$= \$594$$

The adjusting entry involves a debit (increase) to Interest Expense for $594 and a credit (increase) to Interest Payable for $594, as shown in **Example 3.4** (p. 3-16). ∎

Accrued Income Taxes Corporations are subject to a federal (and often state) income tax. Although a corporation may not pay its income taxes until the following period, they are an expense and a year-end obligation of the period in which the corporation earned the income. The adjusting entry for income taxes is prepared *after* all the other adjusting entries because the amount is computed by multiplying the current-period income before income taxes by the applicable income tax rate.

Example: Accrued Income Taxes
Based on its current income before income taxes and assuming a 30% tax rate,[8] Jaymie Corporation calculates that its 2016 income taxes are $600, with the entire amount payable in 2017. The adjusting entry is a debit (increase) to Income Tax Expense for $600 and a credit (increase) to Income Taxes Payable for $600, and is shown as the last item in **Example 3.4** (p. 3-16). ■

Accrued Revenues Accrued revenues are assets that represent amounts that a company is entitled to receive because it has satisfied performance obligations to customers, but has not yet received. The company must make an adjusting entry to increase its assets and revenues at the end of the period. The most common form of accrued revenues arises when a company sells goods or services to customers on credit, debiting Accounts Receivable and crediting Sales Revenues. Exhibit 3.8 shows the effect of an accrued revenue adjusting entry on a company's accounts.

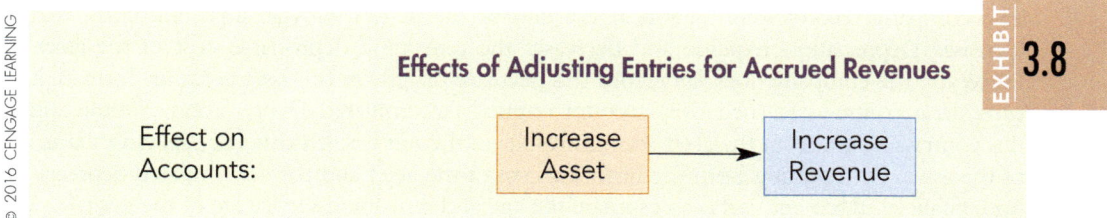

EXHIBIT 3.8 Effects of Adjusting Entries for Accrued Revenues

Example: Accrued Interest Income
On September 1, Jaymie Corporation accepted a $1,320, 15% note as payment when it sold an acre of land. Although it will not collect the note and interest until 2017, Jaymie has earned 4 months of interest in 2016. The company records the $66 of interest ($1,320 × 0.15 × 4/12) as a debit (increase) to Interest Receivable and a credit (increase) to Interest Income. The result is a $66 increase in Interest Income and a $66 increase in Interest Receivable. **Example 3.4** (p. 3-16) shows this adjusting entry. ■

Accounting Estimates
Certain types of adjusting entries are based on **accounting estimates**, which are amounts that are not known with certainty and must be estimated at the end of each period. In some instances, the estimated amounts relate to past expenditures that are expected to affect multiple periods, such as depreciation on property, plant, and equipment. In other instances, the accounting amounts must be estimated because they relate, at least in part, to expected future events. Adjustments for estimates involving future events might include the uncollectibility of some accounts receivable, estimated amounts of warranty expense and liability, and estimates for obligations to pay future pension and retirement benefits to employees. Typically, accounting estimates involve adjusting entries to recognize an expense and either decrease an asset or increase a liability. Exhibit 3.9 shows the effect of such an adjusting entry.

---

[8] As shown in **Example 3.6** (p. 3-24), Jaymie Corporation's income before income taxes is $2,000. Multiplying this amount by an assumed tax rate of 30% yields income taxes of $600.

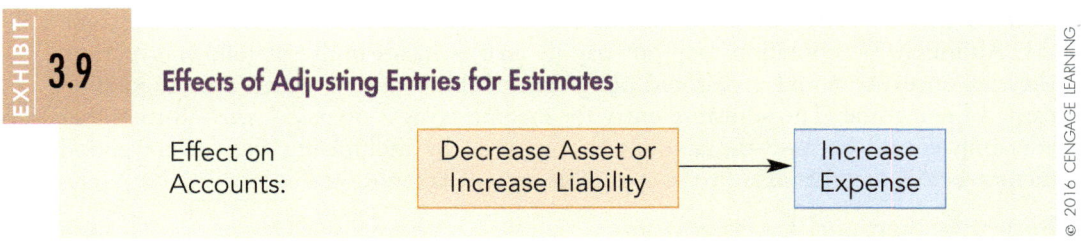

Exhibit 3.9 Effects of Adjusting Entries for Estimates

Accumulated Depreciation and Depreciation Expense When a company acquires a long-lived asset to use in its operations, the company records the cost as an economic resource (asset). Once the company has completed its use of the asset, the company will dispose of it at a value much less than its original cost. The difference between the original cost and an estimate of this later value (called *residual value* or *salvage value*) is the asset's **depreciable cost**. This depreciable cost is allocated as an expense to each period in which the asset is used. This cost allocation process is referred to as **depreciation**. One depreciation method is **straight-line depreciation**, which allocates a proportionate amount as an expense to each period and is computed as follows:

$$\text{Annual Depreciation Expense} = \frac{\text{Cost} - \text{Estimated Residual Value}}{\text{Estimated Service Life}}$$

The company records depreciation at the end of the period with an adjusting entry that increases Depreciation Expense and decreases the remaining depreciable cost of the asset. However, the company does *not* record this decrease directly in the asset account. Instead, it *increases* a contra-asset (negative) account entitled Accumulated Depreciation. Subtracting this contra account from the asset account results in the **net book value** (or **carrying value**) of the asset. By reporting both the historical cost of the asset and the accumulated depreciation, financial statement users can estimate the age and remaining service life of the asset.[9]

Example: Accumulated Depreciation and Depreciation Expense

Jaymie Corporation has two depreciable assets, the building and the equipment acquired on March 30, 2016. These assets have estimated lives of 35 years and 12 years, respectively. Jaymie estimates that the residual value of the building will be $3,000 and the residual value of the equipment will be $200 at the end of these lives. Because it used the building and equipment for only 9 months during 2016, the depreciation expense amounts are computed as follows:

Depreciation Expense: Building: $264 = [($15,320 − $3,000) ÷ 35] × 9/12
Depreciation Expense: Equipment: $120 = [($2,120 − $200) ÷ 12] × 9/12

The adjusting entry for the building is a debit (increase) to Depreciation Expense: Building for $264 and a credit (increase) to Accumulated Depreciation: Building for $264. The adjusting entry for the equipment is a debit to Depreciation Expense: Equipment for $120 and a credit to Accumulated Depreciation: Equipment for $120. The result is an increase in expenses and a *decrease* in the book value that the company reports on its balance sheet for the building and the equipment. **Example 3.4** (p. 3-16) shows these adjusting entries. ■

Allowance for Uncollectible Accounts and Bad Debt Expense
Many companies make large amounts of sales to customers on credit. Regardless of a company's collection efforts, it is likely to have a certain amount of **bad debts**—customer accounts that will not be collected. Although a company does not know which specific customers will not pay their accounts until a later period, it must estimate bad debt expense in the *period of the sale*. Furthermore, the company must reduce its assets so that at the end of the period

---

[9] Chapter 11 provides more discussion of various depreciation methods.

its accounting records show the amount of accounts receivable that it expects to collect. The adjusting entry to record the increase in expenses and the decrease in assets requires an estimate of future uncollectible accounts. However, because the company does not know in the period of sale which specific customers will default on their accounts, it does not directly reduce Accounts Receivable. Instead, it *increases* a contra-asset account, Allowance for Doubtful Accounts. This account is deducted from Accounts Receivable on the balance sheet to report the estimated collectible amount.

Example: Bad Debts Expense

Jaymie Corporation estimates its bad debts to be 1% of total sales. Sales revenues total $17,000, so the adjusting entry is a debit (increase) to Bad Debts Expense for $170 and a credit (increase) to Allowance for Doubtful Accounts for $170. The result is an increase in expenses and a *decrease* in the accounts receivable shown on the company's balance sheet. **Example 3.4** (p. 3-16) shows this adjusting entry.

Periodic Inventory

Some small companies use a **periodic inventory system** to record inventory purchases in a Purchases account, so that the Inventory account balance does not change during the period. Also, at the time of sale, the company does not make a second journal entry to record the increase in the cost of goods sold and the decrease in inventory. Instead, it takes a physical inventory at the end of the accounting period. The company then *derives* its **cost of goods sold** by first computing its **cost of goods available for sale** as follows:

Cost of Goods Available for Sale = Beginning Inventory + Net Purchases

*Net purchases are purchases minus returns, allowances, and discounts.

Cost of Goods Sold = Cost of Goods Available for Sale − Ending Inventory

The company then makes adjusting entries to close the Purchases account into the Inventory account, and to reduce the Inventory account for the Cost of Goods Sold.

Example Assume that Jaymie Corporation uses a periodic inventory system. Jaymie made purchases of $12,600, had purchases returns and allowances of $300, and had taken purchases discounts of $100. Jaymie takes a physical inventory at the end of 2016 to determine that its ending inventory is $2,140. It would compute the cost of goods sold of $10,060 and report this computation on the income statement for 2016, as follows:

Inventory, 1/1/2016	$ 0
Purchases	12,600
Purchases returns and allowances	(300)
Purchases discounts	(100)
Cost of goods available for sale	$12,200
Less: Inventory, 12/31/2016	(2,140)
Cost of goods sold	$10,060

Jaymie would record adjusting entries at the end of 2016 for purchases and the costs of goods sold as follows:

Inventory	12,200	
Purchase Returns and Allowances	300	
Purchase Discounts	100	
Purchases		12,600
To close the Purchases accounts into Inventory.		
Cost of Goods Sold	10,060	
Inventory		10,060
To adjust Inventory for the Cost of Goods Sold.		

Summary The basic framework for common adjusting entries is illustrated in Exhibit 3.10. This framework will help you visualize the appropriate debit and credit entry for the most common types of adjusting entries. However, you must be careful to identify the proper accounts to use in each adjusting entry.

EXHIBIT 3.10 Framework for Common Adjusting Entries

Type of Adjusting Entry	Accounts Debited	Accounts Credited
Deferrals:		
Prepaid Expenses	Expense (Increase)	Asset (Decrease)
Deferred Revenues	Liability (Decrease)	Revenue (Increase)
Accruals:		
Accrued Expenses	Expense (Increase)	Payables (Increase)
Accrued Revenues	Receivables (Increase)	Revenue (Increase)
Estimates:		
Use of Long-Lived Assets	Expense (Increase)	Asset (Decrease by Increasing a Contra Account)
Future Events	Expense (Increase)	Asset (Decrease) or Liability (Increase)
Periodic Inventory:		
Close purchases	Inventory (increase)	Purchases (decrease)
Cost of sales	Cost of good sold (increase)	Inventory (decrease)

GOT IT?

3-15 What are adjusting entries, and why are they necessary?

3-16 Explain and provide examples of deferrals, accruals, and estimates.

3-17 Explain why companies sometimes recognize deferrals for prepaid expenses and deferred revenues. Give an example of an adjusting entry to update each of these items at year-end.

3-18 Explain why companies sometimes recognize accruals for accrued expenses and accrued revenues. Give an example of an adjusting entry to record each of these items.

3-19 Give two examples of adjusting entries to record estimated items. Include in one example a discussion of how straight-line depreciation expense is computed.

3-20 What is a periodic inventory system? How is cost of goods sold computed when a company uses a periodic inventory system?

ETHICAL DILEMMA

As a newly hired accountant at a Fortune 500 company, you were responsible for making many of the routine adjusting entries related to the preparation of the year-end financial statements. The controller was pleased with your diligence and assured you that he would increase your responsibilities in the financial reporting department. However, 3 months later, as you prepare the adjusting entries for the next fiscal quarter, you realize that you overlooked several adjustments that you should have recorded at year-end. While the overlooked adjustments would most likely not be considered material to last year's financial statements, you are certain that your boss would lose confidence in your abilities. Realizing that you can easily fix the mistake by incorporating the overlooked adjustments into the first quarter adjusting entries for this year, what course of action should you take?

HOW DO WE PREPARE FINANCIAL STATEMENTS (STEP 4)?

LEARNING OBJECTIVE 3.6
Prepare financial statements.

After a company prepares and posts the adjusting entries to the general ledger accounts, it prepares its financial statements as follows:

- *Step 1.* The balance of each account in the ledger is recomputed if necessary to reflect the effects of the adjusting entries.
- *Step 2.* An **adjusted trial balance** is prepared, listing all the accounts and account balances *after* adjustments (but *before* closing) in either a debit or a credit column. The adjusted trial balance is used to verify that the debit balances total is equal to the credit balances total. **Example 3.5** shows Jaymie Corporation's adjusted trial balance.
- *Step 3.* The income statement and balance sheet are prepared in sequential order directly from the information in the adjusted trial balance.

EXAMPLE 3.5

Adjusted Trial Balance

JAYMIE CORPORATION
Adjusted Trial Balance
December 31, 2016

	Debit	Credit
Cash	$ 2,922	
Accounts Receivable	7,000	
Allowance for Doubtful Accounts		$ 170
Notes Receivable	1,320	
Interest Receivable	66	
Inventory	2,010	
Prepaid Insurance	90	
Land	1,500	
Building	15,320	
Accumulated Depreciation: Building		264
Equipment	2,120	
Accumulated Depreciation: Equipment		120
Accounts Payable		1,900
Notes Payable		6,600
Salaries Payable		900
Interest Payable		594
Income Taxes Payable		600
Unearned Rent		300
Common Stock		20,000
Retained Earnings		0
Dividends	500	
Sales Revenue		17,000
Interest Income		66
Rent Income		150
Cost of Goods Sold	10,490	
Salaries Expense	2,700	
Other Expenses	428	
Loss on Sale of Land	180	
Depreciation Expense: Building	264	

(continued)

EXAMPLE 3.5 (Continued)

	Debit	Credit
Depreciation Expense: Equipment	$ 120	
Bad Debts Expense	170	
Insurance Expense	270	
Interest Expense	594	
Income Tax Expense	600	
Totals	$48,664	$48,664

Income Statement

Example 3.6 shows Jaymie Corporation's income statement for 2016. Sales revenue is listed first. The cost of goods sold is deducted from sales revenue to determine the gross profit. The various operating expenses are deducted next to determine the income from operations. The other items section typically reports nonrecurring items (such as the loss on the sale of land) and recurring income items that are related to investing and financing activities (such as interest income, interest expense, and rent income). The total amount of

EXAMPLE 3.6 Income Statement

JAYMIE CORPORATION
Income Statement
For Year Ended December 31, 2016

Sales revenue		$ 17,000
Cost of goods sold		(10,490)
Gross profit		$ 6,510
Operating expenses:		
Salaries expense	$2,700	
Other expenses	428	
Depreciation expense: Building	264	
Depreciation expense: Equipment	120	
Bad debts expense	170	
Insurance expense	270	
Total operating expenses		(3,952)
Income from operations		$ 2,558
Other items:		
Interest income	$ 66	
Rent income	150	
Interest expense	(594)	
Loss on sale of land	(180)	(558)
Income before income taxes		$ 2,000
Income tax expense		(600)
Net income		$ 1,400
Earnings per share (2,000 shares)		$ 0.70

the other items is deducted to determine the income before income taxes. Finally, the income tax expense is deducted to determine the net income ($1,400). The $0.70 earnings per share is computed by dividing the $1,400 net income by the 2,000 shares owned by the shareholders.[10]

Statement of Shareholders' Equity

After preparing the income statement, and before preparing the balance sheet, the ending balances in the shareholders' equity accounts, including retained earnings, must be computed so that they can be included in the balance sheet. **Example 3.7** shows Jaymie Corporation's statement of shareholders' equity for 2016. Because 2016 is its first year of operations, the beginning balances in the Common Stock and Retained Earnings accounts were zero. Jaymie generated net income of $1,400 and distributed dividends of $500, resulting in ending retained earnings of $900. Some companies do not report the statement of shareholders' equity and instead only report the changes that affect retained earnings (particularly net income and dividends) within a retained earnings statement.

EXAMPLE 3.7

Statement of Shareholders' Equity

JAYMIE CORPORATION
Statement of Shareholders' Equity
For Year Ended December 31, 2016

	Common Stock	Retained Earnings	Total
Balances, January 1, 2016	$ 0	$ 0	$ 0
Issue of common shares, 2,000 shares of no-par stock	20,000		20,000
Net income		1,400	1,400
Cash dividends		(500)	(500)
Balances, December 31, 2016	$20,000	$ 900	$20,900

Balance Sheet

Example 3.8 shows Jaymie Corporation's balance sheet at the end of 2016. The assets are divided into current assets and noncurrent assets.

- **Current assets** are cash and those assets that are expected to be converted into cash or consumed within one year or the operating cycle, whichever is longer. Current assets generally include cash, receivables, investments in marketable securities, inventories, and prepaid items.
- **Noncurrent assets** are those assets that are expected to be consumed over more than one year or one operating cycle. This section includes noncurrent assets that are tangible (such as property, plant, and equipment), intangible (such as licenses, patents, copyrights, goodwill), financial (investments), and natural resources (such as timber and timberlands and oil and gas reserves).

Liabilities are divided into current liabilities and noncurrent liabilities.

- **Current liabilities** are those obligations that will become due within one year or the operating cycle, whichever is longer.
- **Noncurrent liabilities** are obligations that will become due after one year or one operating cycle.

---

[10] Chapter 5 will discuss income statement presentation in detail.

Shareholders' equity includes contributed capital (Common Stock) and retained earnings. Total assets amount to $31,794 and equal total liabilities plus shareholders' equity.[11]

EXAMPLE 3.8 Balance Sheet

JAYMIE CORPORATION
Balance Sheet
December 31, 2016

Assets			Liabilities		
Current Assets:			Current Liabilities:		
Cash		$ 2,922	Accounts payable		$ 1,900
Accounts receivable	$ 7,000		Salaries payable		900
Less: Allowance for doubtful accounts	(170)	6,830	Income taxes payable		600
Notes receivable			Unearned rent		300
(due March 1, 2017)		1,320	Total current liabilities		$ 3,700
Interest receivable		66	Noncurrent Liabilities:		
Inventory		2,010	Notes payable (due March 30, 2018)		$ 6,600
Prepaid insurance		90	Interest payable (due March 30, 2018)		594
Total current assets		$13,238	Total long-term liabilities		$ 7,194
Noncurrent Assets:			Total Liabilities		$10,894
Property, Plant, and Equipment:					
Land		$ 1,500	**Shareholders' Equity**		
Building	$15,320		Contributed Capital:		
Less: Accumulated depreciation	(264)	15,056	Common stock, no par (2,000 shares)	$20,000	
			Retained earnings	900	
Equipment	$ 2,120		Total Shareholders' Equity		20,900
Less: Accumulated depreciation	(120)	2,000			
Total property, plant, and equipment		$18,556			
Total Assets		$31,794	Total Liabilities and Shareholders' Equity		$31,794

Statement of Cash Flows

Example 3.9 shows Jaymie Corporation's statement of cash flows for fiscal year 2016. The statement of cash flows reports for a period of time the net cash flows (inflows minus outflows) from operating, investing, and financing activities.[12]

EXAMPLE 3.9 Statement of Cash Flows

JAYMIE CORPORATION
Statement of Cash Flows
For the Year Ended December 31, 2016

Operating Activities:	
Net income	$ 1,400
Adjustments to reconcile net income with cash from operations:	
Depreciation expense: Building	264
Depreciation expense: Equipment	120
Bad debts expense	170
Loss on sale of land	180
	(continued)

---

[11] Chapter 4 will discuss presentation of the balance sheet and the statement of shareholders' equity in detail.
[12] Chapters 5 and 21 will provide a more complete discussion of the presentation of the statement of cash flows.

Cash provided (used) by changes in operating assets and liabilities:		
Accounts receivable	$ (7,000)	
Interest receivable	(66)	
Inventory	(2,010)	
Prepaid insurance	(90)	
Accounts payable	1,900	
Salaries payable	900	
Income taxes payable	600	
Unearned rent	300	
Interest payable	594	
Net cash used by operating activities		$ (2,738)
Investing Activities:		
Purchase of land	$ (3,000)	
Purchase of building	(15,320)	
Purchase of equipment	(2,120)	
Net cash used by investing activities		(20,440)
Financing Activities:		
Issue of notes payable	$ 6,600	
Issue of common shares	20,000	
Cash dividends paid	(500)	
Net cash provided by financing activities		26,100
Net change in cash		$ 2,922
Beginning cash balance		0
Ending cash balance		$ 2,922

GOT IT?

3-21 What is the difference between a trial balance and an adjusted trial balance? Why are both useful?

3-22 What are the major financial statements of a company, and what information does each summarize?

HOW DO WE PREPARE CLOSING ENTRIES (STEP 5)?

LEARNING OBJECTIVE 3.7
Prepare closing entries.

The final step in the accounting process involves preparing and posting closing entries. **Closing entries** are journal entries that a company makes at the end of the period to:

- reduce the balance in each temporary (periodic) account to zero
- update the Retained Earnings account

A company uses the temporary accounts (namely, all the revenue, expense, gain, loss, and dividend accounts) during each accounting period to accumulate and summarize information for its net income and dividends *for that period*. After the period is over and the company's financial statements are prepared, the balances in these accounts are no longer needed. Furthermore, these accounts must begin the *next* period with a zero balance to collect and summarize the company's net income and dividend information for that period. Also, Retained Earnings must be updated for the net income and dividend information contained in the temporary accounts.

In closing, temporary income statement accounts with credit balances (such as revenues) are debited and the total of the debits is credited to a temporary closing account titled **Income Summary**. Similarly, accounts with debit balances (such as expenses) are credited and the total of the credits to these accounts is debited to Income Summary. A resulting *credit* balance in the Income Summary account is the net income for the period. This credit balance is closed to zero with a debit to Income Summary and a credit to Retained Earnings. If there is a *debit* balance in Income Summary, there is a net loss for the period. This debit balance is closed to zero with a credit to Income Summary and a debit to Retained Earnings. Finally, the Dividends account is credited, and Retained Earnings is debited.[13]

Example 3.10 shows the closing entries for Jaymie Corporation, which are posted to the ledger accounts shown in **Example 3.3** (p. 3-13).[14] The total credit to Income Summary is $17,216, and the total debit to Income Summary is $15,816.

EXAMPLE 3.10 Closing Entries for 2016 (Jaymie Corporation)

Date	Account Titles and Explanations	Debit	Credit
2016	*Closing Entries*		
Dec. 31	Sales Revenue	17,000	
	Interest Income	66	
	Rent Income	150	
	Income Summary		17,216
	To close the temporary accounts with credit balances.		
31	Income Summary	15,816	
	Cost of Goods Sold		10,490
	Salaries Expense		2,700
	Other Expenses		428
	Loss on Sale of Land		180
	Depreciation Expense: Building		264
	Depreciation Expense: Equipment		120
	Bad Debts Expense		170
	Insurance Expense		270
	Interest Expense		594
	Income Tax Expense		600
	To close the temporary accounts with debit balances.		
31	Income Summary	1,400	
	Retained Earnings		1,400
	To close the Income Summary balance (net income) to Retained Earnings.		
31	Retained Earnings	500	
	Dividends		500
	To close the Dividends to Retained Earnings.		

The Income Summary account now has a credit balance of $1,400. This amount, the net income (**Example 3.6**) (p. 3-24), is transferred to Retained Earnings by a debit to Income Summary for $1,400 (which creates a zero balance in this account) and a credit to Retained Earnings for $1,400. Finally, the debit balance in the Dividends account is reduced to zero by a debit to Retained Earnings for $500 and a credit to Dividends for $500.

The result of the closing entries is that:

- all of the company's revenue, expense, gain, loss, and dividend accounts are closed (have zero balances) and are ready to accumulate the revenue, expense, gain, loss, and dividend information for the next accounting period
- the ending balance in the Retained Earnings account is increased by $900 because of the excess of net income over dividends
- only the permanent balance sheet accounts have nonzero balances

After companies prepare and post the closing entries, they prepare a **post-closing trial balance** to verify that the debit balances total is equal to the credit balances total in

---

[13] If a firm has temporary accounts for gains or losses that are included in Other Comprehensive Income, then those temporary accounts are closed through the same process, with the balances being closed to the Accumulated Other Comprehensive Income/(Loss) account.
[14] The abbreviation Cl is used to identify each December 31 closing entry in the ledger accounts.

the permanent accounts. The accounting cycle is now complete and a new cycle for the next accounting period begins.

> **GOT IT?**
>
> **3-23** What are closing entries, and what is their purpose?
>
> **3-24** What is the purpose of the Income Summary account in closing?

HOW DO WE USE A WORKSHEET TO PREPARE FINANCIAL STATEMENTS?

LEARNING OBJECTIVE 3.8
Prepare financial statements using a worksheet (spreadsheet).

A company often prepares a **worksheet** (**spreadsheet**) to minimize errors, simplify recording of adjusting and closing entries in the general journal, and make it easier to prepare the financial statements. A worksheet is *not* a substitute for any accounting records or financial statements; it is merely a working paper designed to facilitate preparing financial statements.

A worksheet may be a large sheet of multicolumn accounting paper or an electronic spreadsheet, such as Microsoft Excel®. **Example 3.11** (p. 3-30) shows a worksheet for Jaymie Corporation using information presented earlier in the chapter. It has a column listing all the ledger accounts, plus debit and credit columns for the trial balance, adjustments, adjusted trial balance, income statement, retained earnings, and balance sheet.

There are five steps in completing a worksheet.

- *Step 1.* Prepare the trial balance. List all of the company's accounts and account balances (prior to adjustments) and total the debit and credit columns of the trial balance to verify the equality of the debits and credits. Because this is the first year of operations for Jaymie Corporation, the Accumulated Depreciation: Building, Accumulated Depreciation: Equipment, and Retained Earnings accounts have zero balances, prior to adjustments. Normally, these accounts have nonzero balances in the trial balance.
- *Step 2.* Enter adjusting entries. Analyze each of the accounts to determine the necessary adjustments and enter these as adjusting entries in the general journal and in the adjustments columns on the worksheet. As you can see, the adjusting journal entries for Jaymie in **Example 3.4** are now entered in the adjustments column of the worksheet. If an adjustment involves an account that does not currently have a balance, enter the account title on the first available row below the other account titles. Note also that we code the accounts in each adjusting entry with the same letter to reduce the likelihood of error. Explanations to these entries appear at the bottom of the worksheet, which are similar to the adjusting entry explanations included in **Example 3.4**. After entering all of the adjustments, total the adjustments columns to verify the equality of the debits and credits.
- *Step 3.* Determine the adjusted amount for each account. Combine the trial balance amount of each account with the adjustments to that account to determine the correct, adjusted balance. At this point, some companies prepare an adjusted trial balance in the next set of columns in the worksheet. In the worksheet for Jaymie, we have omitted the adjusted trial balance to save space, but if shown, it would look like **Example 3.5** (p. 3-23). Then carry the adjusted total for each account over to the proper column of the financial statement on which the item will be reported. For example, for Jaymie, we combine the $360 debit balance in Prepaid Insurance with the $270 credit adjustment and carry the new balance of $90 over to the debit column of the balance sheet.
- *Step 4.* Total the income statement debit and credit columns. Ordinarily the debit column total differs from the credit column total, the difference being the income (or loss) before income taxes. For Jaymie, the $17,216 credit total exceeds the $15,216 debit total, indicating income before income taxes equals $2,000. At this point, multiply the income before income taxes by the applicable tax rate (30% in this case) to determine the income tax ($600) and then record the adjusting entry for income taxes, and carry the amounts to the proper columns of the financial statements.

EXAMPLE 3.11

Worksheet (Jaymie Corporation)

	A	B	C	D	E	F	G	H	I	J	K	L	M
1	Jaymie Corporation												
2	Worksheet												
3	For the Year Ended Dec. 31, 2016												
4													
5		Trial Balance		Adjustments				Income Statement		Retained Earnings		Balance Sheet	
6	Account Titles	Debit	Credit	Debit		Credit		Debit	Credit	Debit	Credit	Debit	Credit
7	Cash	2,922										2,922	
8	Accounts Receivable	7,000										7,000	
9	Notes Receivable	1,320										1,320	
10	Inventory	2,010										2,010	
11	Prepaid Insurance	360				(a)	270					90	
12	Land	1,500										1,500	
13	Building	15,320										15,320	
14	Acc. Depreciation: Building		0			(f)	264						264
15	Equipment	2,120										2,120	
16	Acc. Depreciation: Equipment		0			(g)	120						120
17	Accounts Payable		1,900										1,900
18	Notes Payable		6,600										6,600
19	Unearned Rent		450	(b)	150								300
20	Common Stock		20,000										20,000
21	Retained Earnings (1/1/16)		0								0		
22	Dividends	500								500			
23	Sales Revenue		17,000						17,000				
24	Cost of Goods Sold	10,490						10,490					
25	Salaries Expense	1,800		(c)	900			2,700					
26	Other Expenses	428						428					
27	Loss on Sale of Land	180						180					
28		45,950	45,950										
29	Insurance Expense			(a)	270			270					
30	Rent Income					(b)	150		150				
31	Salaries Payable					(c)	900						900
32	Interest Expense			(d)	594			594					
33	Interest Payable					(d)	594						594
34	Interest Receivable			(e)	66							66	
35	Interest Income					(e)	66		66				
36	Depreciation Expense: Bldg.			(f)	264			264					
37	Depreciation Expense: Equip.			(g)	120			120					
38	Bad Debts Expense			(h)	170			170					
39	Allow. for Doubtful Accounts					(h)	170						170
40					2,534		2,534	15,216	17,216				
41	Income Tax Expense			(i)	600			600					
42	Income Taxes Payable					(i)	600						600
43								15,816	17,216				
44	Net Income							1,400			1,400		
45					3,134		3,134	17,216	17,216	500	1,400		
46	Retained Earnings, 12/31/16									900			900
47										1,400	1,400	32,348	32,348
48													
49													
50	(a) To record 9 months of insurance expense												
51	(b) To record 1 month of rent revenue												
52	(c) To record 3 months of accrued salaries expense												
53	(d) To record 9 months of accrued interest expense												
54	(e) To record 4 months of accrued interest revenue												
55	(f) To record 9 months depr. expense on building												
56	(g) To record 9 months depr. expense on equipment												
57	(h) To record estimated bad debts expense												
58	(i) To record income tax expense												

- *Step 5.* Total the income statement columns again. The difference between the debit and credit totals is the net income or loss. For Jaymie, the net income is $1,400. We use this amount to balance the income statement columns and enter it in the retained earnings credit column.[15] Combine the beginning retained earnings balance ($0 in

---

[15] The arrows in **Example 3.11** are for illustrative purposes; they ordinarily are not included on the worksheet.

this case) with the net income to determine the $1,400 credit total. The $500 debit total represents the dividends distributed. The $900 difference is the ending balance in retained earnings. We use it to balance the retained earnings columns and transfer it to the balance sheet credit column. Finally, total the balance sheet debit and credit columns. The $32,348 total of the debit and credit columns indicates that our accounting system is in balance and the worksheet is complete.

The worksheet trial balance helps identify the necessary adjusting entries, which we enter in the worksheet and record in the general journal. The worksheet also helps simplify the closing entries and shows that we need to:

- Credit the $17,216 total of the income statement credit column to the Income Summary account.
- Debit the individual temporary accounts with credit balances.
- Debit the $15,816 subtotal of the income statement debit column to the Income Summary account.
- Credit the individual temporary accounts with debit balances.

The remaining closing entries involve closing both net income and dividends to Retained Earnings.

Finally, the worksheet helps prepare the financial statements. We report the amounts from the worksheet columns for each financial statement in the proper order on that financial statement. For instance, note that we can easily prepare the income statement, the balance sheet, and the retained earnings portion of the statement of shareholders' equity shown in **Examples 3.6, 3.7,** and **3.8** from the respective worksheet columns. The worksheet is very useful in preparing interim (such as quarterly) financial statements when a company does not actually adjust or close its accounts. The adjusting entries needed to update the financial statements may be made on the worksheet only, thereby enabling the company to keep its accounts on an annual basis.

GOT IT?

3-25 What is a worksheet? How does the use of a worksheet facilitate the completion of the accounting cycle?

WHAT IS THE PURPOSE OF REVERSING ENTRIES?

LEARNING OBJECTIVE 3.9

Prepare reversing entries.

Prior to recording journal entries for the transactions of a new period, some companies prepare reversing entries. A **reversing entry** is the exact reverse (accounts and amounts) of an adjusting entry. A company usually makes reversing entries immediately following recording the closing entries or on the first day of the *next* period. A reversing entry is *optional* and has one purpose: to simplify the recording of subsequent transactions related to the adjusting entry. A reversing entry enables a company to routinely record the subsequent transactions without having to consider the possible impact of the prior adjusting entry.

As a general guideline, reversing entries are made for adjusting entries that *create a new balance sheet account* at the end of the accounting period for transactions that will be completed during the next accounting period, as follows:

- adjusting entries that accrue revenues to be collected in the next accounting period
- adjusting entries that accrue expenses to be paid in the next accounting period
- adjusting entries that defer costs by recording them as prepaid expenses, which will be consumed in the next accounting period
- adjusting entries that defer revenues for prepayments from customers by recording them as unearned or deferred revenues, which will be recognized in the next accounting period

Reversing entries *should not* be made for any adjusting entry that adjusts the ending balance of an *existing balance sheet account* for transactions that will not be completed during the next accounting period, as follows:

- adjusting entries that deferred expenses by recording them initially as assets that will not be completely consumed in the next accounting period
- adjusting entries that deferred revenues by recording them initially as liabilities that will not be completely recognized in the next accounting period
- adjusting entries related to estimated items such as depreciation or bad debts

Example: Reversing Entry

Jaymie Corporation should consider reversing two of the adjusting entries recorded in **Example 3.4** (p. 3-16): the entries to record accrued interest revenue and accrued salaries expense. Each of these relates to a transaction that will be completed in the *next* accounting period (when Jaymie receives the interest revenues and pays the salaries).[16] Although the adjusting entry for interest expense created an accrued expense, Interest Payable, this entry is not reversed because the subsequent transaction will not be completed until 2018, when the interest will be paid. **Example 3.12** (p. 3-33) illustrates reversing entries and how they simplify the recording of subsequent transactions for Interest Revenue and Salaries Expense. The entries in the left column assume a reversing entry is *not* made so you can see the complex subsequent journal entry and analysis that is needed. The entries in the right column assume a reversing entry is made so you can see the much simpler subsequent journal entry and analysis.

Whether or not it makes reversing entries, Jaymie Corporation will collect $1,419 on March 1, 2017, for the 15%, 6-month note receivable accepted on September 1, 2016. The $1,419 includes the $1,320 note and $99 of interest ($1,320 × 0.15 × 6/12). If it does not make a reversing entry, when Jaymie records this collection it must determine what portion of the interest relates to 2016 ($66 of Interest Receivable) and what portion is Interest Revenue for 2017 ($33 for 2 months). The use of a reversing entry eliminates this analysis. The entire amount of the $99 received in excess of the face value of the note is credited to Interest Revenue. Because the reversing entry created a $66 *debit* balance in Interest Revenue, the $99 credit results in a $33 *credit* balance, the 2 months of interest for 2017, in the Interest Revenue account.

Similarly, on April 1, 2017, Jaymie will pay its employees another 6 months of salaries, or $1,800. If Jaymie does not make a reversing entry, when it pays the salaries it must determine what portion of the salary payment relates to 2016 ($900 of Salaries Payable) and what portion is Salaries Expense for 2017 ($900 for 3 months). The use of a reversing entry eliminates this analysis. The entire $1,800 payment is debited to Salaries Expense. When combined with the $900 *credit* balance in Salaries Expense established by the reversing entry, the result is a $900 *debit* balance, the amount representing 3 months of salaries expense for 2017. ■

Alternative Procedures

As we indicated in the discussion of the adjusting entry for deferred revenues, some companies initially record the receipt of revenues in advance of being recognized as a revenue instead of a liability. As shown, Jaymie *could* have recorded the December 1 receipt of 3 months' advance rent as a credit to Rent Income for $450. In this case, the adjusting entry is a debit to Rent Income for $300 and a credit to Unearned Rent for $300. This adjusting entry creates a balance sheet account and should be reversed. On January 1, 2017, a reversing entry should be made debiting Unearned Rent for $300 and crediting Rent Income for $300. This entry eliminates the Unearned Rent account balance and creates a $300 credit balance in Rent Income for the 2 months of rent recognized during 2017. No further adjusting entry is needed in 2017.

---

[16] The entry to record income taxes is generally not reversed because the income taxes payable will be paid during the next year, and the subsequent income tax expense will depend on income before taxes for 2017.

EXAMPLE 3.12

Reversing Entries (Jaymie Corporation)

Accrued Revenue
Adjusting Entry

12/31/16	Interest Receivable	66	
	Interest Revenue		66
12/31/16	Revenues and expenses are CLOSED.		

If reversing entry is not made:

Reversing Entry
1/1/17 None

Subsequent Entry
3/1/17	Cash	1,419	
	Notes Receivable		1,320
	Interest Receivable		66
	Interest Revenue		33

If reversing entry is made:

Reversing Entry
| 1/1/17 | Interest Revenue | 66 | |
| | Interest Receivable | | 66 |

Subsequent Entry
3/1/17	Cash	1,419	
	Notes Receivable		1,320
	Interest Revenue		99

Analysis of Subsequent Entry
Interest of $99 is collected, but $66 was recorded in Interest Receivable at end of last period. Consequently, Interest Receivable must be credited for $66, and Interest Revenue credited for $33.

Analysis of Subsequent Entry
Interest of $99 is collected and credited to Interest Revenue. The net result in Interest Revenue is a $33 credit balance.

Accrued Expense
Adjusting Entry

12/31/16	Salaries Expense	900	
	Salaries Payable		900
12/31/16	Revenues and expenses are CLOSED.		

If reversing entry is not made:

Reversing Entry
1/1/17 None

Subsequent Entry
4/1/17	Salaries Expense	900	
	Salaries Payable	900	
	Cash		1,800

If reversing entry is made:

Reversing Entry
| 1/1/17 | Salaries Payable | 900 | |
| | Salaries Expense | | 900 |

Subsequent Entry
| 4/1/17 | Salaries Expense | 1,800 | |
| | Cash | | 1,800 |

Analysis of Subsequent Entry
Salaries of $1,800 for 6 months are paid, but $900 was recorded in Salaries Payable at end of last period. Consequently, Salaries Payable must be debited for $900, and Salaries Expense must be debited for $900.

Analysis of Subsequent Entry
Salaries of $1,800 for 6 months are paid and debited to Salaries Expense. Because reversing entry was made for $900, the net result in Salaries Expense is a $900 debit balance.

> **GOT IT?**
>
> **3-26** What are reversing entries, and why are they used?
>
> **3-27** Give an example of an adjusting entry and a reversing entry for salaries payable, and the later entry to pay the salaries.

LEARNING OBJECTIVE 3.10

Use subsidiary ledgers and special journals.

HOW DO WE USE SUBSIDIARY LEDGERS AND SPECIAL JOURNALS?

Most companies engage in many transactions that must be recorded in the accounting system each period. Subsidiary ledgers and special journals create efficiencies in recording and organizing similar types of transactions that occur frequently.

Subsidiary Ledgers

A **subsidiary ledger** is a group of accounts, all of which relate to one specific company activity. A company creates subsidiary ledgers that supplement the general ledger to:

- reduce the size of the general ledger
- minimize errors
- divide the accounting tasks
- keep up-to-date records of its credit customers and suppliers

Most companies have separate subsidiary ledgers for accounts receivable and accounts payable. These ledgers enable a company to focus specifically on the collection and payment process for the receivables and payables.[17] For example, the *accounts receivable* subsidiary ledger contains the individual accounts of all the company's credit customers. Because the individual customer accounts have debit balances, this subsidiary ledger has a *total* debit balance (computed by preparing a schedule of the individual customer account balances).

When a company uses this subsidiary ledger, it still keeps an Accounts Receivable account in the general ledger. This account is referred to as a **control account** because its debit balance must be equal to that of the subsidiary ledger. In a computerized accounting system, each posting to the Accounts Receivable control account is also automatically posted to the applicable subsidiary ledger account. Similarly, the *accounts payable* subsidiary ledger contains the individual accounts of all the company's credit suppliers. Because these accounts have credit balances, the credit total of this subsidiary ledger must agree with the credit total of the Accounts Payable control account in the general ledger. If Jaymie Corporation used a subsidiary ledger for the accounts receivable, the ledger and control account balances at the end of 2016 would appear as shown in **Example 3.13**.

EXAMPLE 3.13 Accounts Receivable Control Account and Subsidiary Ledger

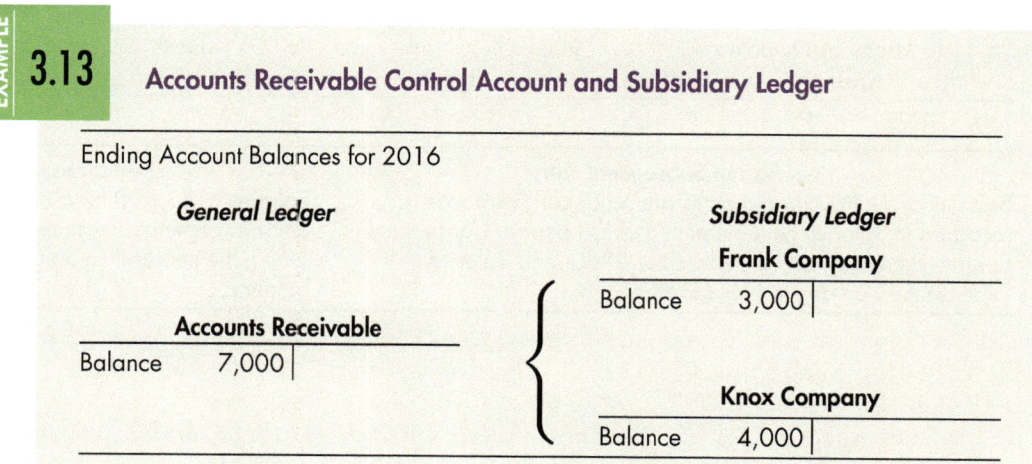

[17] Many companies also use subsidiary ledgers for major categories of accounts, such as property, plant, and equipment, selling expenses, and administrative expenses.

Special Journals

A **special journal** enables a company to record specific types of frequent, similar transactions. When a company increases in size and complexity, it needs to efficiently record and summarize many daily transactions. Special journals are used to:

- divide the accounting tasks
- reduce the time needed to complete the various accounting activities
- create a chronological listing of similar transactions

The four most common types of special journals are:

- **Sales Journal.** Record all (and only) sales of merchandise on credit.
- **Purchases Journal.** Record all (and only) purchases of merchandise on credit.
- **Cash Receipts Journal.** Record all cash receipts.
- **Cash Payments Journal.** Record all cash payments.

Because operating procedures and transactions vary across companies, each company organizes its special journals in a way best suited to its operations.

Most companies use computer software to process their accounting information. Software has been developed for the subsidiary ledgers and special journals, as well as other financial accounting functions relating to accounts receivable, accounts payable, inventory, payroll, and the general ledger.

GOT IT?

3-28 What are subsidiary ledgers and control accounts, and why are they used? Describe how they work.

3-29 What are special journals, and why are they used? What are the major special journals? Give an example of transactions that would be recorded in each journal.

APPENDIX 3.1: WHAT IS CASH-BASIS ACCOUNTING?

LEARNING OBJECTIVE 3.11
Convert cash-basis financial statements to accrual-basis.

Under *accrual accounting*, a company recognizes revenues in the accounting period in which performance obligations to customers are satisfied, and it records expenses in the accounting period in which they are incurred, even though the related cash flows occur in a different period. Under **cash-basis accounting**, a company records revenues when it collects cash from sales and records expenses when it pays cash for its operations. Under cash-basis accounting, net income is the same as the net operating cash flow for the period. The company may choose not to prepare a balance sheet. However, it frequently keeps track of certain assets such as amounts owed by customers (accounts receivable), amounts paid in advance (prepaid expenses), and any property and equipment it owns. It also frequently keeps track of certain liabilities such as amounts owed to suppliers (accounts payable) and amounts owed to employees (accrued expenses). Cash-basis accounting, however, is not allowed under GAAP or IFRS.

Sometimes a company that is using cash-basis accounting must prepare its financial statements based on accrual accounting. This might happen, for instance, if it applies for a bank loan and the bank requires financial statements prepared using generally accepted accounting principles. In this case, the company must convert its cash-basis income statement to an accrual-basis income statement and must prepare a balance sheet. This involves making adjustments to the cash receipts to convert them to sales revenues and making adjustments to the cash payments to convert them to the cost of goods sold and operating expenses. It also involves combining the information it has about its assets and liabilities into a formal balance sheet.

Exhibit 3.11 shows the basic adjustments that a company must make to convert its cash receipts and cash payments into accrual-based revenues, cost of goods sold, and operating expenses. In addition, the company must include depreciation expense on its property and equipment in the operating expenses.

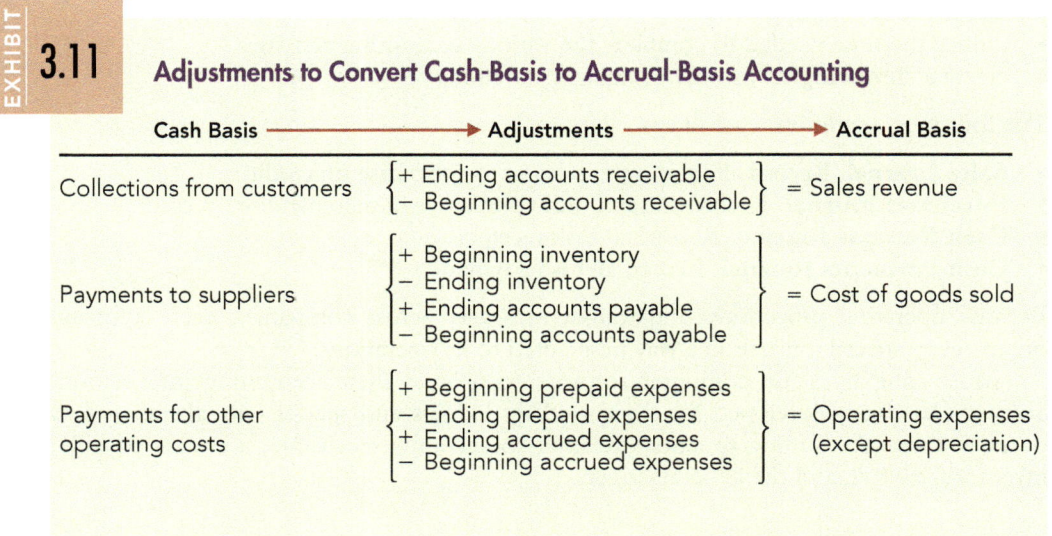

EXHIBIT 3.11 Adjustments to Convert Cash-Basis to Accrual-Basis Accounting

Example: Cash-Basis Accounting

Assume that your friend starts Jessica Company (a small landscaping service company organized as a sole proprietorship) on January 1, 2016, by investing cash of $20,000. Jessica uses cash-basis accounting but wants to prepare its financial statements on an accrual basis. At the end of the year, Jessica's checkbook shows cash receipts from customers of $95,000, cash payments of $106,000, and an ending cash balance of $9,000. Based on a physical inventory, Jessica determined that its inventory at the end of 2016 was $7,200. It also determined that, at the end of 2016, customers owed it $4,300 and that it owed suppliers $5,100 and employees $500. Jessica examined its checkbook and found that during 2016:

1. It paid suppliers $54,000 and paid other operating costs of $29,000. Included in the other operating costs was $6,000 that it paid on January 1 for 2 years of rent.
2. It paid $8,000 for equipment on January 1. It planned to use straight-line depreciation and expected to use the equipment for 5 years, after which the equipment would have a zero residual value.
3. Jessica withdrew $15,000 during the year.

Using accrual accounting, Jessica prepared its income statement for 2016, shown in **Example 3.14**, and its balance sheet at the end of 2016, shown in **Example 3.15**.

In **Example 3.14**, Jessica computed its $99,300 in sales revenues by adding the $4,300 ending accounts receivable to the $95,000 it collected from customers. The company computed its $51,900 cost of goods sold by beginning with the $54,000 it paid to suppliers and then subtracting the $7,200 ending inventory and adding the $5,100 ending accounts payable. It computed the $26,500 other operating expenses by beginning with the $29,000 it paid for operating costs and then subtracting the $3,000 prepaid rent (the cost of the remaining year of rent it had paid for in advance) and adding the $500 ending salaries payable. It computed the $1,600 depreciation expense by dividing the $8,000 cost of the equipment by the 5-year estimated life.

> **EXAMPLE 3.14**

Income Statement

JESSICA COMPANY
Income Statement
For Year Ended December 31, 2016

Sales revenue		$99,300[a]
Cost of goods sold		(51,900)[b]
Gross profit		$47,400
Operating expenses:		
Depreciation expenses	$1,600[c]	
Other operating expenses	26,500[d]	
Total expenses		(28,100)
Net income		$19,300

[a] $95,000 collections from customers + $4,300 ending accounts receivable
[b] $54,000 payments to suppliers − $7,200 ending inventory + $5,100 ending accounts payable
[c] $29,000 payments for other operating costs + $500 ending salaries payable − $3,000 ending prepaid rent ($6,000 × 1/2)
[d] $8,000 equipment ÷ 5 years

> **EXAMPLE 3.15**

Balance Sheet

JESSICA COMPANY
Balance Sheet
December 31, 2016

Assets			Liabilities		
Current Assets:			Current Liabilities:		
Cash	$9,000		Accounts payable	$5,100	
Accounts receivable	4,300		Salaries payable	500	
Inventory	7,200		Total Liabilities		$5,600
Prepaid rent	3,000				
Total current assets		$23,500			
			Owner's Equity		
Property, Plant, and Equipment:			Jessica, capital		24,300
Equipment	$8,000				
Less: Accumulated depreciation	(1,600)				
Total property, plant, and equipment		6,400			
Total Assets		$29,900	Total Liabilities and Equity		$29,900

In **Example 3.15**, most of the amounts come from the initial information presented for Jessica. The $1,600 accumulated depreciation is the depreciation to date (1 year, in this example). The company computed the $24,300 amount of the Jessica capital account by beginning with the $20,000 initial investment, adding the $19,300 net income, and subtracting the $15,000 withdrawals. ∎

In more complex situations, a company may have items such as deferred revenues and accrued revenues, purchases returns and allowances, and interest revenue and expense, as well as gains or losses on sales of equipment. In these cases, the company may make additional adjustments to determine its revenues and expenses and may provide more detail in the revenues, cost of goods sold, and operating expenses sections of its income statement.

> ### GOT IT?
>
> **3-30** What is cash-basis accounting? What must a company do to convert its cash-basis accounting records to an accrual-based income statement?

REVIEW CENTER

At the beginning of the chapter, we described how double-entry accounting systems have been used to organize and create helpful business information for well over 500 years, being first described in a book by Luca Pacioli in 1494. Double-entry accounting systems, journal entries, and trial balances are still being used today. We also identified several objectives you would accomplish after reading the chapter. The objectives are listed below and followed by a brief summary of the key takeaways.

LEARNING OBJECTIVE 3.1
Understand the components of an accounting system.

KEY TAKEAWAYS

- The framework of the accounting system is the fundamental accounting equation, which measures the equality between the company's resources (assets) and the claims on those resources (liabilities and shareholders' equity). The accounting equation is: Assets = Liabilities + Shareholders' Equity.
- The inputs to this accounting system are source documents that contain information about transactions, events, and arrangements that affect a company's economic resources, obligations, and equity.
- The monetary information from every transaction, event, and arrangement is recorded and stored in the accounts.
- Each transaction, event, and arrangement has a dual effect on the accounting system (debits equal credits), so they are recorded in the accounts using the double-entry accounting system.
- The information in the accounting system enables preparation of the financial statements: the balance sheet, the income statement, the statement of cash flows, and the statement of shareholders' equity.

KEY TERMS

accounting equation, p. 3-3
accounting system, p. 3-2
accounts, p. 3-5
accumulated other comprehensive income (AOCI), p. 3-3
annual report, p. 3-7
arrangement, p. 3-5
assets, p. 3-3
balance, p. 3-7
chart of accounts, p. 3-5
contra account, p. 3-7
contributed capital, p. 3-3
credit, p. 3-5

debit, p. 3-5
dividends, p. 3-3
double-entry accounting system, p. 3-6
event, p. 3-5
expenses, p. 3-4
gains, p. 3-4
interim statements, p. 3-7
liabilities, p. 3-3
losses, p. 3-4
net income, p. 3-3
other comprehensive income (OCI), p. 3-3
periodic accounts, p. 3-7

permanent accounts, p. 3-7
quarterly statements, p. 3-7
retained earnings, p. 3-3
revenues, p. 3-4
shareholders' equity, p. 3-3

source documents, p. 3-5
T-account, p. 3-5
temporary accounts, p. 3-7
transaction, p. 3-5

KEY TAKEAWAYS

- The five major steps in the accounting cycle are:
  - *Step 1.* Record transactions, events, and arrangements in a journal.
  - *Step 2.* Post the journal entries to the accounts in the general ledger.
  - *Step 3.* Prepare and post adjusting entries.
  - *Step 4.* Prepare the financial statements.
  - *Step 5.* Prepare and post closing entries for the temporary accounts: revenues, expenses, gains, losses, and dividends accounts.

KEY TERM

accounting cycle, p. 3-8

LEARNING OBJECTIVE 3.2
Know the five major steps of the accounting cycle.

KEY TAKEAWAYS

- To record a journal entry, enter the date in the date column. Next, enter the title of the account and amount to be debited in the account titles column and debit column, respectively. Then, enter the title of the account and amount to be credited in the account titles column and credit column, respectively. Finally, write a short explanation of the transaction in the account titles column.
- It is advantageous to use a general journal because:
  - It helps prevent errors. Because the accounts and debit and credit amounts for each transaction are initially recorded on a single journal page, rather than directly in the numerous accounts, it is easier to verify the equality of the debits and credits.
  - All the journal entry information (including the explanation) is recorded in chronological order in one place, which is especially useful during the auditing process or if an error is discovered later in the accounting cycle.

LEARNING OBJECTIVE 3.3
Record transactions, events, and arrangements using journal entries in the general journal.

KEY TERMS

general journal, p. 3-9
journal entry, p. 3-9
perpetual inventory system, p. 3-9

purchase allowance, p. 3-9
purchase discount, p. 3-10
purchase return, p. 3-9

KEY TAKEAWAYS

- To post to the general ledger, for each journal entry, first transfer from the general journal the date and the amount debited to the account in the general ledger. Next, transfer the date and the amount credited to the account in the general ledger.
- To prepare a trial balance at the end of the accounting period, first compute the balance in each account. Then, list each account and its balance in the debit or credit column of the trial balance. Finally, total the debit and credit columns to verify that the totals are equal.

LEARNING OBJECTIVE 3.4
Post to the general ledger and prepare a trial balance.

KEY TERMS

general ledger, p. 3-13
posting, p. 3-13

trial balance, p. 3-14

LEARNING OBJECTIVE 3.5
Prepare adjusting entries.

KEY TAKEAWAYS
- Adjusting entries apply accrual accounting concepts to ensure that all revenues earned and all expenses incurred during a period are recorded and net income is measured correctly, even though the inflow or outflow of cash might occur in a different period, and to ensure that assets, liabilities, and shareholders' equity are appropriately measured and reported.
- Adjusting entries are journal entries made at the end of the accounting period to record:
    - deferrals, which arise when cash flows occur prior to recognition of an item in income
    - accruals, which arise when cash flows occur after an item is recognized in income
    - estimated items, which are accounting amounts that are not known with certainty and must be estimated
    - inventory and cost of goods sold for companies using periodic inventory systems

KEY TERMS
accounting estimates, p. 3-19
accrual accounting, p. 3-15
accruals, p. 3-18
accrued expenses, p. 3-18
accrued revenues, p. 3-19
adjusting entries, p. 3-15
bad debts, p. 3-20
carrying value, p. 3-20
cost of goods available for sale, p. 3-21
cost of goods sold, p. 3-21
deferrals, p. 3-15

deferred revenue, p. 3-17
depreciable cost, p. 3-20
depreciation, p. 3-20
net book value, p. 3-20
periodic inventory system, p. 3-21
prepaid expense, p. 3-15
residual value, p. 3-20
salvage value, p. 3-20
straight-line depreciation, p. 3-20
unearned revenue, p. 3-17

KEY CALCULATIONS
Accrued Interest = Principal × Rate × Time

Annual Depreciation Expense = (Cost − Estimated Residual Value)/Estimated Service Life

Cost of Goods Available for Sale = Beginning Inventory + Net Purchases
(Net purchases equal purchases minus purchase returns, allowances, and discounts.)

Cost of Goods Sold = Cost of Goods Available for Sale − Ending Inventory

LEARNING OBJECTIVE 3.6
Prepare financial statements.

KEY TAKEAWAYS
- To prepare a company's financial statements, first prepare an adjusted trial balance to verify that the total of the debit balances is equal to the total of the credit balances in the company's accounts.
    - Then, prepare the income statement, which includes the company's revenues, expenses, and net income.
    - Next, compute the ending retained earnings by adjusting the beginning retained earnings for the net income and dividends.
    - Next, prepare the balance sheet, which includes the company's assets, liabilities, and shareholders' equity.
    - Next, prepare the statement of cash flows, which reports cash inflows and cash outflows for operating, investing, and financing activities.
    - Finally, prepare the statement of shareholders' equity.

KEY TERMS

adjusted trial balance, p. 3-23
current assets, p. 3-25
current liabilities, p. 3-25
noncurrent assets, p. 3-25
noncurrent liabilities, p. 3-25

KEY TAKEAWAYS

LEARNING OBJECTIVE 3.7
Prepare closing entries.

- Closing entries are journal entries of a company made at the end of the accounting period to:
  - reduce the balance in each temporary account (revenue, expense, gain, loss, and dividend accounts) to zero
  - update the Retained Earnings account

KEY TERMS

closing entries, p. 3-27
Income Summary, p. 3-27
post-closing trial balance, p. 3-28

KEY TAKEAWAYS

LEARNING OBJECTIVE 3.8
Prepare financial statements using a worksheet (spreadsheet).

- A worksheet is a tool designed to minimize errors, simplify the recording of adjusting and closing entries in the general journal, and help in preparing financial statements.
- To prepare financial statements using a worksheet, take the following steps:
  - *Step 1.* List each account and its balance in the debit or credit column of the trial balance.
  - *Step 2.* Enter the adjusting entries as debits or credits in the adjustments columns.
  - *Step 3.* Combine the trial balance amount of each account with the adjustments to that account and carry over the resulting amount to the proper column of the financial statement in which the account is included.
  - *Step 4.* Subtotal the income statement debit and credit columns, make an adjusting entry for any income taxes on the difference between the columns (the pretax income), and carry the adjustment amounts to the appropriate financial statement columns.
  - *Step 5.* Subtotal the income statement columns. List the difference as net income (or net loss), write the amount in the debit (credit) column, and balance the income statement columns. Transfer the net income (net loss) amount to the retained earnings columns and balance these columns. Then transfer the retained earnings balance to the balance sheet credit column and balance these columns.

KEY TERMS

spreadsheet, p. 3-29
worksheet, p. 3-29

KEY TAKEAWAYS

LEARNING OBJECTIVE 3.9
Prepare reversing entries.

- A reversing entry is the exact reverse (accounts and amounts) of an adjusting entry. Reversing entries are made at the end of a period (after the financial statements have been prepared) to enable a company to record the later transaction without having to consider the possible impact of the prior adjusting entry.
- As a general guideline, reversing entries are made for adjusting entries that create a new balance sheet account at the end of the accounting period for transactions that will be completed during the next accounting period. Reversing entries should not be made for any adjusting entry that adjusts the ending balance of an existing balance sheet account for transactions that will not be completed during the next accounting period.

KEY TERM

reversing entry, p. 3-31

LEARNING OBJECTIVE 3.10
Use subsidiary ledgers and special journals.

KEY TAKEAWAYS

- A subsidiary ledger is a group of accounts, all of which pertain to one type of activity. Most companies have subsidiary ledgers for accounts receivable and accounts payable to better focus on collections from customers and payments to suppliers.
- When a company uses a subsidiary ledger, it still maintains a control account in its general ledger. The balance of the control account must equal the total of the balances of all the individual accounts in the subsidiary ledger.
- Special journals increase the efficiency and effectiveness of the accounting cycle because they are used to efficiently record frequent, similar types of transactions. The most common special journals are the:
  - sales journal (for sales on credit)
  - purchases journal (for purchases on credit)
  - cash receipts journal
  - cash payments journal
- The general journal is used with these for all other (miscellaneous) transactions.

KEY TERMS

control account, p. 3-34
cash payments journal, p. 3-35
cash receipts journal, p. 3-35
sales journal, p. 3-35

special journal, p. 3-35
subsidiary ledger, p. 3-34
purchases journal, p. 3-35

LEARNING OBJECTIVE 3.11
(Appendix 3.1) Convert cash-basis financial statements to accrual-basis.

KEY TAKEAWAY

- First, start with the income statement. Make adjustments to the collections from customers for any changes in accounts receivable. Make adjustments to the payments to suppliers for any changes in inventory and accounts payable. Make adjustments to the payments for other operating costs for any changes in prepaid expenses or accrued expenses, and for depreciation expense. Complete the accrual-basis income statement and balance sheet using the resulting amounts.

KEY TERM

cash-basis accounting, p. 3-35

REVIEW EXERCISES

RE3-1
LO 3.3
On May 1, Johnson Corporation purchased inventory for $40,000 on credit. On May 15, Johnson sold inventory with a cost of $10,000 for $25,000 on credit. Prepare journal entries to record these transactions.

RE3-2
LO 3.3
On January 1, Tolson Company purchased a building by paying $85,000. The building has an estimated life of 40 years and an estimated residual value of $5,000. Prepare journal entries to record the purchase and the related year-end adjusting entry.

RE3-3
LO 3.3
LO 3.5
On July 1, Friler Company purchased a 1-year insurance policy by paying $5,400. Prepare journal entries to record the purchase and the related year-end adjusting entry.

RE3-4
LO 3.3
LO 3.5
On October 1, Bandor Company sold land (that cost $30,000) on credit for $35,000. The buyer issued an 8%, 12-month note for this amount, with the interest to be paid on the maturity date. Prepare journal entries to record the sale of the land and the related year-end adjusting entry.

RE3-5 Garcia Company rents out a portion of its building to Jerry Company for $1,000 per month. On August 1, 2016,
LO 3.3 Jerry paid Garcia $12,000 for 1 year of rent in advance. Prepare journal entries for Garcia to record the collection
LO 3.5 of rent and the related year-end adjusting entry.

RE3-6 On April 1, 2016, Ringo Company borrowed $20,000 from its bank by issuing a 9%, 12-month note, with the in-
LO 3.3 terest to be paid on the maturity date. Prepare journal entries to record the issuance of the note and the related
LO 3.5 year-end adjusting entry.

RE3-7 Goldfinger Corporation had account balances at the end of the current year as follows: sales revenue, $29,000; cost of
LO 3.6 goods sold, $12,000; operating expenses, $6,200; and income tax expense, $4,320. Assume shareholders owned 4,000
shares of Goldfinger's common stock during the year. Prepare Goldfinger's income statement for the current year.

RE3-8 Using the information from **RE3-7**, prepare Goldfinger's closing entries for the current year.
LO 3.7

RE3-9 For the current year, Vidalia Company reported revenues of $250,000 and expenses of $225,000. At the beginning
LO 3.1 of the year, its retained earnings had a balance of $95,000. During the year, Vidalia paid $11,000 dividends to
LO 3.3 shareholders. Its contributed capital was $56,000 at the beginning of the year, and it did not issue any new stock
LO 3.7 during the year. Vidalia's assets total $237,500 on December 31 of the current year. What are Vidalia's total liabil-
ities on December 31 of the current year?

RE3-10 Use the information in **RE3-6**, (a) assuming Ringo Company makes reversing entries, prepare the reversing entry on
LO 3.9 January 1, 2017, and the journal entry to record the payment of the note on April 1, 2017; and (b) assuming Ringo
does not make reversing entries, prepare the journal entry to record the payment of the note on April 1, 2017.

RE3-11 *(Appendix 3.1)* Vickelly Company uses cash-basis accounting. At the end of the current year, Vickelly's checkbook
LO 3.11 shows cash receipts from customers of $112,000 and cash payments for operating expenses of $48,000 for the year.
At the end of the year, Vickelly determined that customers owed it $12,000, and it owed creditors $10,000. Com-
pute Vickelly's sales revenue, operating expenses, and net income on an accrual basis.

EXERCISES

E3-1 **Financial Statement Interrelationship** Draw a diagram that shows the interrelationship between the beginning
LO 3.1 balance sheet, income statement, retained earnings statement, and the ending balance sheet.

E3-2 **Journal Entries** Mead Company uses a perpetual inventory system and engaged in the following transactions
LO 3.3 during the month of May:

SHOW
ME HOW

Date		Transaction
May	1	Made cash sales of $6,300; the cost of the inventory was $3,700.
	5	Purchased $2,000 of inventory on credit.
	9	Made credit sales of $3,300; the cost of the inventory sold was $1,900.
	13	Paid sales salaries of $900 and office salaries of $600.
	14	Paid for the May 5 purchases.
	18	Purchased sales equipment costing $8,000; made a down payment of $2,000 and agreed to pay the balance in 60 days.
	21	Purchased $600 of inventory for cash.
	27	Sold land that had originally cost $1,900 for $2,600.

Required:
Record the preceding transactions in a general journal.

E3-3 **Journal Entries** The following are selected accounts and account balances of Sawyer Company on May 31:
LO 3.3
LO 3.4

	Debit	Credit
Cash	$12,523	
Accounts Receivable	23,052	
Inventory	16,300	
Office Equipment	35,860	

SHOW
ME HOW

(continued)

	Debit	Credit
Accumulated Depreciation		$10,540
Notes Payable		3,400
Accounts Payable		3,500
Sales Revenue		47,872
Gain on Sale of Office Equipment		400
Cost of Goods Sold	$22,354	
Utilities Expense	1,124	

Sawyer entered into the following transactions during June:

Date	Transaction
June 3	Sold for $700 office equipment that had cost $2,000 and has associated accumulated depreciation of $1,500.
7	Made sales of $2,000 on credit; the cost of the inventory sold was $1,200.
10	Purchased $1,000 of inventory for cash.
15	Purchased new office equipment costing $4,000, paying $1,500, and signing a 90-day note for the balance.
16	Received check for June 7 credit sale.
17	Made cash sales of $4,200; the cost of the inventory sold was $2,300.
20	Purchased $2,600 of inventory on credit.
24	Returned $200 of defective inventory from the June 20 purchase for a credit to its account.
29	Paid for the June 20 purchase minus the return.
30	Paid the June utility bill, $210.

Required:
1. Record the preceding transactions in a general journal.
2. Post to general ledger T-accounts.

E3-4
LO 3.5

SHOW ME HOW

Adjusting Entries Your examination of Sullivan Company's records provides the following information for the December 31, year-end adjustments:
1. Bad debts are to be recorded at 2% of sales. Sales made on credit totaled $25,000 for the year.
2. Salaries at year-end that have accumulated but have not been paid total $1,400.
3. Annual straight-line depreciation for the company's equipment is based on a cost of $30,000, an estimated life of 8 years, and an estimated residual value of $2,000.
4. Prepaid insurance in the amount of $800 has expired.
5. Interest that has been earned but not collected totals $500.
6. The company has satisfied performance obligations entitling it to rent in the amount of $1,000.
7. Interest on a note payable that has accumulated but has not been paid totals $600.
8. The income tax rate is 30% on current income and is payable in the first quarter of the next year. The pretax income before the preceding adjusting entries is $6,800.

Required:
Prepare the adjusting entries to record the preceding information.

E3-5
LO 3.5

Adjusting Entries The following are several transactions of Ardery Company that occurred during the current year and were recorded in *permanent* (that is, balance sheet) accounts unless indicated otherwise:

Date	Transaction
Apr. 1	Purchased a delivery van for $10,000, paying $1,000 down, and issuing a 1-year, 12% note payable for the $9,000 balance. It is estimated that the van has a 4-year life and an $800 residual value; the company uses straight-line depreciation. The interest on the note will be paid on the maturity date.
May 15	Purchased $830 of office supplies.
June 2	Purchased a 2-year comprehensive insurance policy for $960.
Aug. 1	Received 6 months' rent in advance at $260 per month and recorded the $1,560 receipt as Rent Revenue.
Sept. 15	Advanced $600 to sales personnel to cover their future travel costs.
Nov. 1	Accepted a $6,000, 6-month, 12% (annual rate) note receivable from a customer, the interest to be collected when the note is collected.

The following information also is available:
1. On January 1, the Office Supplies account had a $250 balance. On December 31, an inventory count showed $190 of office supplies on hand.

2. The weekly (5-day) payroll of Ardery Company amounts to $2,000. All employees are paid at the close of business each Wednesday. A 2-day accrual is required for the current year.
3. Sales personnel travel cost reports indicate that $490 of advances had been used to pay travel expenses.
4. The income tax rate is 30% on current income and is payable in the first quarter of next year. The pretax income before the adjusting entries is $8,655.

Required:
On the basis of the above information, prepare journal entries to record whatever adjustments are necessary to bring the accounts up to date on December 31. Each journal entry explanation should show any related computations.

E3-6 **Adjusting Entries** The following partial list of accounts and account balances has been taken from the trial balance
LO 3.5 and the adjusted trial balance of Baye Company:

	Trial Balance		Adjusted Trial Balance	
	Debit	Credit	Debit	Credit
Accumulated Depreciation		$5,200		$6,600
Allowance for Doubtful Accounts		380		650
Income Taxes Payable		0		2,250
Interest Payable		0		320
Prepaid Insurance	$350		$90	
Salaries Payable		0		720
Unearned Rent		900		300

Required:
Next Level Prepare the adjusting entry that caused the change in each account balance.

E3-7 **Basic Income Statement** The following are selected account balances of Rule Corporation at the end of 2016:
LO 3.6

SHOW ME HOW

	Debit	Credit
Operating Expenses	$3,800	
Sales Revenue		$15,600
Cost of Goods Sold	8,300	
Interest Expense	800	
Gain on Sale of Land		500

Rule is subject to a 30% income tax rate, and shareholders own 800 shares of its capital stock.

Required:
Prepare a 2016 income statement for Rule.

E3-8 **Periodic Inventory System** Raynolde Company uses a periodic inventory system. At the end of 2016, the follow-
LO 3.7 ing information is available:

SHOW ME HOW

Purchase returns and allowances	$ 1,400
Inventory, 12/31/2016	11,900
Purchases	21,200
Inventory, 1/1/2016	10,800
Purchase discounts	600

Required:
Prepare a schedule to compute Raynolde's cost of goods sold for 2016.

E3-9 **Closing Entries** Lloyd Bookstore shows the following dividends, revenue, and expense account balances before closing:
LO 3.7

	Debit	Credit		Debit	Credit
Dividends	$ 250		Gain on Sale of Land		$300
Sales Revenue		$2,200	Salaries Expense	$300	
Cost of Goods Sold	1,350		Utilities Expense	130	
			Miscellaneous Expenses	120	
			Income Tax Expense	180	

Required:
Prepare closing entries.

E3-10 **Financial Statements** Turtle Company has prepared the following adjusted trial balance for the year ended December 31, 2016:

LO 3.6
LO 3.7

	Debit	Credit
Cash	$ 1,700	
Accounts Receivable (net)	2,100	
Inventory	1,800	
Equipment	5,400	
Accumulated Depreciation		$ 1,700
Accounts Payable		2,300
Salaries Payable		300
Income Taxes Payable		360
Common Stock (400 shares)		3,200
Retained Earnings		2,500
Dividends	200	
Sales Revenue		7,900
Cost of Goods Sold	4,300	
Selling Expenses	1,800	
Administrative Expenses	600	
Income Tax Expense	360	
Totals	$18,260	$18,260

Required:
For 2016, prepare in proper form: (1) an income statement, (2) a retained earnings statement, (3) an ending balance sheet, and (4) closing entries.

E3-11 **Worksheet for Service Company** Whitaker Consulting Company has prepared a trial balance on the following partially completed worksheet for the year ended December 31, 2016:

LO 3.6
LO 3.8

	A	B	C	D	E	F	G	H	I	J	K
1									Retained		
2						Income		Earnings		Balance	
3		Trial Balance		Adjustments		Statement		Statement		Sheet	
4	Accounts	Debit	Credit	Debit	Credit	Debit	Credit	Debit	Credit	Debit	Credit
5	Cash	3,800									
6	Prepaid Rent	2,400									
7	Office Equipment	7,000									
8	Accumulated Depreciation		1,400								
9	Note Payable (due 7/1/17)		2,000								
10	Common Stock (200 shares)		4,000								
11	Retained Earnings (1/1/16)		3,200								
12	Dividends	200									
13	Consulting Revenues		6,100								
14	Salaries Expense	2,500									
15	Miscellaneous Expenses	800									
16	Totals	16,700	16,700								
17											

Additional information: (a) On January 1, 2016, the company had paid 2 years' rent in advance at $100 a month for office space, (b) the office equipment is being depreciated on a straight-line basis over a 10-year life, and no residual value is expected, (c) interest of $150 has accrued on the note payable but has not been paid, and (d) the income tax rate is 30% on current income and will be paid in the first quarter of 2017.

Required:
1. Complete the worksheet.
2. Prepare financial statements for 2016.

E3-12 **Worksheet, Including Inventory** Surian Motors Company prepared a trial balance on the following partially completed worksheet for the year ended December 31, 2016:

LO 3.6
LO 3.7
LO 3.8

	A	B	C	D	E	F	G	H	I	J	K
1									Retained		
2						Income		Earnings		Balance	
3		Trial Balance		Adjustments		Statement		Statement		Sheet	
4	Accounts	Debit	Credit	Debit	Credit	Debit	Credit	Debit	Credit	Debit	Credit
5	Cash	2,500									
6	Accounts Receivable	4,000									
7	Allowance for Doubtful Accounts		300								
8	Inventory	8,200									
9	Prepaid Rent	3,600									
10	Equipment	30,000									
11	Accumulated Depreciation		12,000								
12	Accounts Payable		3,700								
13	Note Payable (due 7/1/17)		5,000								
14	Common Stock (1,000 shares)		8,900								
15	Retained Earnings (1/1/16)		10,200								
16	Dividends	1,000									
17	Sales Revenues		45,000								
18	Cost of Goods Sold	21,000									
19	Salaries Expense	7,100									
20	Utilities Expense	3,300									
21	Advertising Expense	4,400									
22	Totals	85,100	85,100								
23											

Additional information: (a) The equipment is being depreciated on a straight-line basis over a 10-year life, with no residual value; (b) salaries accrued but not recorded total $500; (c) on January 1, 2016, the company had paid 3 years' rent in advance at $100 per month; (d) bad debts are expected to be 1% of total sales; (e) interest of $400 has accrued on the note payable; and (f) the income tax rate is 40% on current income and will be paid in the first quarter of 2017.

Required:
1. Complete the worksheet.
2. Prepare financial statements for 2016.
3. Prepare closing entries in the general journal.

E3-13 **Reversing Entries** On December 31, 2016, Kellams Company made the following adjusting entries for its annual accounting period:

LO 3.9

SHOW ME HOW

Depreciation Expense	2,400	
Accumulated Depreciation		2,400
To record depreciation on buildings.		
Interest Receivable	500	
Interest Revenue		500
To record interest on note receivable due January 28, 2017.		
Rent Expense	400	
Prepaid Rent		400
To record expired prepaid rent.		
Interest Expense	620	
Interest Payable		620
To record interest on note payable due March 16, 2017.		

Required:
Prepare whatever reversing entries are appropriate.

E3-14 Special Journals
LO 3.10

The following are several transactions of a company that uses special journals:

Transaction	Journal
1. Purchase of inventory for cash.	-----
2. Sale of inventory on credit.	-----
3. Payment of sales salaries.	-----
4. Purchase of inventory on credit.	-----
5. Sale of merchandise for cash.	-----
6. Purchase of land by issuing note payable.	-----
7. Collection of short-term note receivable and related interest.	-----
8. Return of defective inventory to supplier for credit to account.	-----
9. Preparation of adjusting entries.	-----
10. Purchase of equipment for cash.	-----

Required:
Indicate in which journal the transaction would be recorded using the codes: *G* for general journal, *S* for sales journal, *P* for purchases journal, *CR* for cash receipts journal, and *CP* for cash payments journal.

E3-15 (Appendix 3.1) Cash-Basis Accounting
LO 3.11

Puntarelli Contracting keeps its accounting records on a cash basis during the year. At year-end, it adjusts its books to the accrual basis for preparing its financial statements. At the end of 2015, Puntarelli reported the following balance sheet items:

	Debit	Credit
Cash	$ 2,700	
Accounts receivable	4,200	
Inventory	5,600	
Equipment	12,000	
Accumulated depreciation		$ 4,800
Accounts payable		6,100
T. Puntarelli, capital		13,600
Totals	$24,500	$24,500

It is now the end of 2016. The company's checkbook shows a balance of $4,700, which includes cash receipts from customers of $51,300 and cash payments of $49,300.

An examination of the cash payments shows that: (1) $30,600 was paid to suppliers, (2) $12,700 was paid for other operating costs (including $7,200 paid on January 1 for 2 years' annual rent), and (3) $6,000 was withdrawn by T. Puntarelli.

On December 31, 2016, (1) customers owed Puntarelli Contracting $5,900, (2) Puntarelli owed suppliers and employees $7,000 and $900, respectively, and (3) the ending inventory was $6,300. Puntarelli is depreciating the equipment using straight-line depreciation over a 10-year life (no residual value).

Required:
1. Using accrual-based accounting, prepare a 2016 income statement (show supporting calculations).
2. Using accrual-based accounting, prepare a December 31, 2016, balance sheet (show supporting calculations).

PROBLEMS

P3-1 Adjusting Entries
LO 3.5

The following information for Drake Company, which adjusts and closes its accounts every December 31, is available for 2016:
1. Salaries accrued but unpaid total $2,840 on December 31, 2016.
2. The $247 December utility bill arrived on December 31 and has not been paid or recorded.
3. Buildings with a cost of $78,000, 25-year life, and $9,000 residual value are to be depreciated; equipment with a cost of $44,000, 8-year life, and $2,000 residual value is also to be depreciated. The straight-line method is to be used.

4. A count of supplies indicates that the Store Supplies account should be reduced by $128 and the Office Supplies account reduced by $397 for supplies used during the year.
5. The company holds a $6,000, 12% (annual rate), 6-month note receivable dated September 30, 2016, from a customer. The interest is to be collected on the maturity date.
6. Bad debts expense is estimated to be 1% of annual sales. Sales for 2016 total $65,000.
7. An analysis of the company insurance policies indicates that the Prepaid Insurance account is to be reduced for $528 of expired insurance.
8. A review of travel expense reports indicates that $310 has been paid for airfare for a salesperson (and recorded as Travel Expenses), but has not yet been used.
9. The income tax rate is 30% on current income and will be paid in the first quarter of 2017. The pretax income of the company before adjustments is $18,270.

Required:
Journalize the necessary adjusting entries for Drake at the end of 2016. Show supporting calculations in your journal entry explanations.

P3-2
LO 3.5

Adjusting Entries Clapton Guitar Company entered into the following transactions during 2016. [The transactions were properly recorded in *permanent* (balance sheet) accounts unless otherwise indicated.]

Date		Transaction
Jan.	25	Purchased $480 of office supplies.
Feb.	1	Rented a warehouse from Hendrix Company, paying 1 year's rent of $3,600 in advance. Recorded the $3,600 payment as rent expense.
Mar.	1	Borrowed $10,000 from the bank, signing a 1-year note at an annual interest rate of 12%. The bank insisted on collecting the interest in advance, so it withheld the interest amount from the funds disbursed to Clapton. The company recorded the transaction as a debit to Cash, $8,800, a debit to Interest Expense, $1,200, and a credit to Notes Payable, $10,000.
May	1	Purchased office equipment for $15,000, paying $3,000 down and signing a 2-year, 12% (annual rate) note payable for the balance. The office equipment is expected to have a useful life of 10 years and a residual value of $1,500. Straight-line depreciation is appropriate.
May	31	Purchased a 3-year comprehensive insurance policy for $720.
Aug.	1	Sold land for $9,000. The purchaser made a $2,000 down payment and signed a 1-year, 10% note for the balance. The interest and principal will be collected on the maturity date.
Oct.	1	Rented a portion of the retail floor space to Harrison Inc. for $120 per month, collecting 8 months' rent in advance. Recorded the $960 receipt as rent revenue.
Nov.	13	Issued checks to sales personnel totaling $900. The checks are advances for expected travel costs during the remainder of the year.

On December 31, 2016, the following additional information is available:
1. Property taxes for 2016 are due to be paid by April 1, 2017. The company has not paid or recorded its $2,300 property taxes for 2016.
2. The $302 December utility bill has not been recorded or paid.
3. Salaries accrued but not paid total $927.
4. Travel cost reports indicate that $787 of the $900 advanced has been used to pay for travel expenses by company personnel.
5. The Office Supplies account had a balance of $129 on January 1, 2016. A physical count on December 31, 2016, showed $174 of office supplies on hand.
6. On January 1, 2016, the Buildings account and the Store Equipment account had balances of $100,000 and $65,000, respectively. The buildings are expected to have a 20-year useful life and an $8,000 residual value, while the store equipment is expected to have a 10-year life and a $2,000 residual value. They are being depreciated using the straight-line method.
7. The income tax rate is 30% on current income and is payable in the first quarter of 2017. The pretax income of the company before adjustments is $27,749.

Required:
On the basis of the preceding information, prepare journal entries to adjust Clapton's books as of December 31, 2016. Each entry explanation should include supporting computations. (Round to the nearest dollar.)

P3-3
LO 3.5

Adjusting Entries Sarah Company's trial balance on December 31, 2016 (the end of its annual accounting period), included the following account balances *before* adjustments:

	Debit	Credit
Notes Receivable	$10,000	
Insurance Expense	3,000	
Delivery Equipment	14,000	
Building	60,000	
Unearned Rent		$4,320
Notes Payable		7,200
Office Supplies Expense	1,000	

Reviewing the company's recorded transactions and accounting records for 2016, you find the following data pertaining to the December 31, 2016, adjustments:

1. On July 2, the company had accepted a $10,000, 9-month, 10% (annual rate) note receivable from a customer. The interest is to be collected when the note is collected.
2. On August 2, the company had paid $3,000 for a 2-year insurance policy.
3. The building was acquired in 1998 and is being depreciated using the straight-line method over a 25-year life. It has an estimated residual value of $8,000.
4. The delivery equipment was purchased on April 2, 2016. It is to be depreciated using the straight-line method over a 10-year life, with an estimated residual value of $2,000.
5. On September 1, the company had received 2 years' rent in advance ($4,320) for a portion of a building it is renting to Victoria Company.
6. On December 1, the company had issued a $7,200, 3-month, 12% (annual rate) note payable to a supplier. The interest is to be paid when the note is paid.
7. On January 2, the company purchased $1,000 of office supplies. A physical count on December 31 revealed that there are $400 of office supplies still on hand. No supplies were on hand at the beginning of the year.

Required:
Prepare the adjusting entries that are necessary to bring Sarah's accounts up to date on December 31, 2016. Each journal entry explanation should summarize your calculations.

P3-4
LO 3.6

Income Statement Calculations Taylor Company uses a periodic inventory system. The following is partial information from its income statements for 2016 and 2017:

	2016	2017
Beginning inventory	$ (b)	$ (d)
Sales	220,000	(f)
Purchases	118,000	140,000
Purchase returns	2,000	3,000
Ending inventory	48,000	74,000
Gross profit	(a)	77,000
Cost of goods sold	106,000	(e)
Expenses	65,000	62,000
Net income	(c)	15,000

Required:
Next Level Fill in the blanks lettered a through f. (*Hint:* It probably is easiest to work through the blanks according to the sequential letters.)

P3-5
LO 3.5
LO 3.6

Errors in Financial Statements At the end of the current year, Jodi Corporation's controller discovers the following items of information:

1. Salaries are paid every Friday for a 5-day work week. The normal weekly payroll is $40,000. The year-end falls on a Tuesday this year.
2. The company has a $20,000, 9-month, 12% (annual rate) note payable outstanding at the end of the year. The note was issued on October 1; the interest is due when the note is paid.
3. Examining the Rent Expense account, the controller finds that it includes a $4,800 advance payment for 3 months' rent. The payment was made on November 1.

4. The storeroom contains $500 of office supplies. At the beginning of the year, there were no office supplies. During a year, the company purchased $3,500 of office supplies which were debited to the Office Supplies account.
5. The company received a large order in May with a $13,000 advance payment. The advance payment was credited to Unearned Revenue. In November, the order was delivered to the customer.

Required:

For each of the preceding items, indicate the effect on net income, assets, liabilities, and shareholders' equity in the financial statements of the company for the year if the controller fails to make an adjusting entry for the item (ignore income taxes). (*Contributed by Paula L. Koch*)

P3-6 **Journal Entries, Posting, and Trial Balance** Luke Unlimited Company's account balances on November 1 are as follows:
LO 3.3
LO 3.4
LO 3.6

	Debit	Credit		Debit	Credit
Cash	$ 7,800		Patents	$25,000	
Accounts Receivable	12,530		Accounts Payable		$ 38,750
Allowance for Doubtful Accounts		$ 740	Notes Payable		2,400
Notes Receivable	6,000		Common Stock, no par		165,000
Inventory	25,121		Retained Earnings, January 1		24,958
Prepaid Insurance	840		Sales Revenue		36,833
Office Supplies	465		Cost of Goods Sold	32,000	
Land	74,350		Sales Salaries Expense	6,200	
Buildings	66,580		Office Salaries Expense	4,300	
Accumulated Depreciation:			Advertising Expense	1,250	
Buildings		21,400	Utilities Expense	1,845	
Equipment	37,620		Interest Revenue		550
Accumulated Depreciation:			Interest Expense	210	
Equipment		11,480			

During the month of November, the following transactions took place:

Date	Transaction
Nov. 2	Made cash sales of $3,400; the cost of the inventory sold was $2,040.
3	Purchased $900 of inventory for cash.
5	Sold an unused 1/2 acre of land for $4,000; the land had originally cost $3,650.
8	Purchased a 2-year comprehensive insurance policy for $528.
12	Leased an unused portion of its building to WebbCo, collecting 6 months' rent in advance at $220 per month.
13	Made $2,300 of sales on credit to Lauren Company; the cost of the inventory sold was $1,400.
16	Collected the $200 monthly payment plus $30 interest on a customer's note receivable.
17	Purchased $1,600 of inventory on credit from Katy Company.
20	Purchased land for a future building site. Made a $2,000 down payment and signed a 12%, 90-day, $6,000 note payable for the balance.
23	Collected the Lauren Company account for the November 13 sale.
26	Paid for the November 17 purchase of inventory.
27	Paid the city newspaper $420 for advertising that had appeared during November.
30	Paid $520 of sales salaries and $390 of office salaries.

Required:
1. Prepare general journal entries to record the preceding transactions.
2. Post to general ledger T-accounts.
3. Prepare a trial balance on November 30.

P3-7
LO 3.3
LO 3.5
LO 3.6

Effects of Errors During the current accounting period, Page Company makes the following errors. The company uses a perpetual inventory system.

Error	Net Income	Total Assets	Total Liabilities	Total Shareholders' Equity
Example: Failed to record a cash sale:	U	U	N	U
1. The purchase of equipment for cash is recorded as a debit to Equipment and a credit to Accounts Payable.				
2. Failed to record the purchase of inventory on credit.				
3. Cash received from a customer in payment of its account is recorded as if the receipt were for a current period sale.				
4. Failed to record a credit sale.				
5. At the end of the year, the receipt of money from a 60-day, 12% bank loan is recorded as a debit to Cash and a credit to Sales Revenue.				
6. Failed to record depreciation at the end of the current period.				

Required:
Indicate the effect of each error on the net income, total assets, total liabilities, and total shareholders' equity at the end of the accounting period by using the following code: O = overstated, U = understated, N = no effect. Disregard income taxes.

P3-8
LO 3.6
LO 3.7

SHOW ME HOW

Financial Statements Mackenzie Inc. uses a perpetual inventory system and has prepared the following *adjusted trial balance* on December 31, 2016:

	Debit	Credit
Cash	$ 2,000	
Accounts Receivable	2,700	
Allowance for Doubtful Accounts		$ 250
Inventory	6,500	
Prepaid Insurance	800	
Land	5,200	
Buildings and Equipment	31,000	
Accumulated Depreciation		15,000
Accounts Payable		3,100
Salaries Payable		420
Unearned Rent		360
Income Taxes Payable		2,625
Note Payable (due July 1, 2020)		5,000
Interest Payable (due July 1, 2020)		750
Common Stock (1,500 shares)		9,000
Retained Earnings, January 1, 2016		6,770
Dividends	1,200	
Sales Revenue		30,900
Rent Revenue		1,440
Cost of Goods Sold	15,040	
Selling Expenses	4,800	
Administrative Expenses	3,000	
Interest Expense	750	
Income Tax Expense	2,625	
Totals	$75,615	$75,615

Required:
Prepare in proper form for 2016 the company's: (1) income statement, (2) retained earnings statement, (3) ending balance sheet, and (4) closing entries in its general journal.

P3-9
LO 3.6
LO 3.7

Financial Statements Carolyn Company has prepared the following alphabetical adjusted trial balance on December 31, 2016:

	Debit	Credit
Accounts Payable		$ 6,400
Accounts Receivable	$ 5,700	
Accumulated Depreciation: Buildings		19,000
Accumulated Depreciation: Equipment		11,000
Additional Paid-in Capital		15,000
Administrative Expenses	6,500	
Allowance for Doubtful Accounts		600
Buildings	42,000	
Common Stock, $1 par (4,000 shares)		4,000
Cash	5,000	
Cost of Goods Sold	27,400	
Current Income Taxes Payable		4,035
Dividends	2,400	
Equipment	22,000	
Income Tax Expense	4,035	
Interest Expense	650	
Interest Payable (due July 1, 2017)		650
Inventory	10,800	
Land	6,800	
Notes Payable (due July 1, 2020)		10,000
Prepaid Insurance	1,600	
Rent Revenue		2,800
Retained Earnings, January 1, 2016		14,500
Sales Revenue		54,900
Selling Expenses	9,700	
Unearned Rent		700
Wages Payable		1,000
	$144,585	$144,585

Required:
Prepare the following 2016 items in proper form for Carolyn:
1. the income statement
2. the retained earnings statement
3. the ending balance sheet (*Hint:* The Common Stock, Additional Paid-in Capital, and Retained Earnings accounts are summed to determine the total shareholders' equity.)
4. the closing entries in the general journal

P3-10
LO 3.5
LO 3.6
LO 3.7
LO 3.8

Worksheet Victoria Company has the following account balances on December 31, 2016, prior to any adjustments:

	Debit	Credit		Debit	Credit
Cash	$ 1,900		Unearned Rent		$ 1,200
Accounts Receivable	4,700		Mortgage Payable (due		
Allowance for Doubtful Accounts		$ 60	January 1, 2018)		7,300
Inventory	8,700		Common Stock (2,000 shares)		10,000
Prepaid Insurance	600		Retained Earnings (January 1, 2016)		18,075
Land	4,100		Dividends	$ 1,300	
Buildings	38,000		Sales Revenue		49,355
Accumulated Depreciation:			Cost of Goods Sold	27,185	
Buildings		11,500	Salaries Expense	4,080	
Equipment	10,700		Utilities Expense	2,000	
Accumulated Depreciation:			Office Supplies Expense	770	
Equipment		3,100	Delivery Expense	1,275	
Accounts Payable		4,300	Other Expenses	980	
Notes Payable (due March 1, 2017)		1,400			

(*continued*)

Additional adjustment information: (a) depreciation on buildings, $1,100; on equipment, $600; (b) bad debts expense, $240; (c) interest accumulated but not paid: on note payable, $50; on mortgage payable, $530 (this interest is due during the next accounting period); (d) insurance expired, $175; (e) salaries accrued but not paid $370; (f) rent was collected in advance and the performance obligation is now satisfied, $800; (g) office supplies on hand at year-end, $230 (expensed when originally purchased earlier in the year); and (h) the income tax rate is 30% on current income and is payable in the first quarter of 2017.

Required:
1. Transfer the account balances to a 10-column worksheet and prepare a trial balance.
2. Prepare the adjusting entries in the general journal and complete the worksheet.
3. Prepare the company's income statement, retained earnings statement, and balance sheet.
4. Prepare closing entries in the general journal.

P3-11 **Worksheet** Devlin Company has prepared the following partially completed worksheet for the year ended December 31, 2016:

LO 3.5
LO 3.6
LO 3.7
LO 3.8

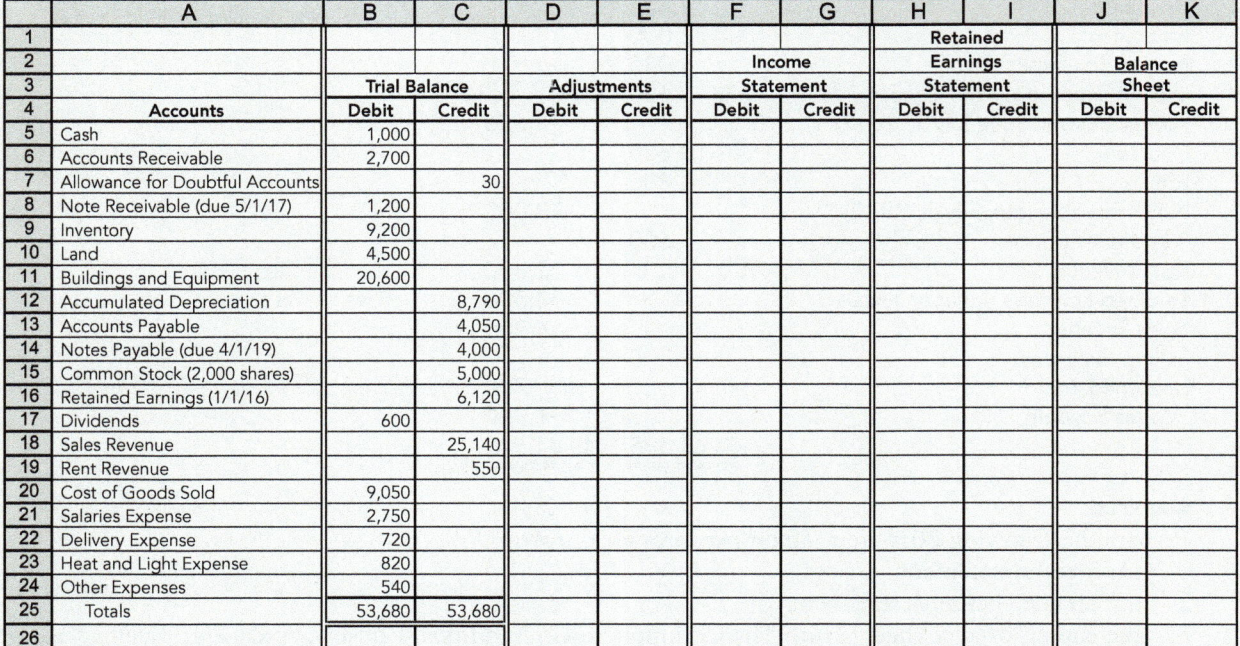

	A	B	C	D	E	F	G	H	I	J	K
1								Retained			
2						Income		Earnings		Balance	
3		Trial Balance		Adjustments		Statement		Statement		Sheet	
4	Accounts	Debit	Credit	Debit	Credit	Debit	Credit	Debit	Credit	Debit	Credit
5	Cash	1,000									
6	Accounts Receivable	2,700									
7	Allowance for Doubtful Accounts		30								
8	Note Receivable (due 5/1/17)	1,200									
9	Inventory	9,200									
10	Land	4,500									
11	Buildings and Equipment	20,600									
12	Accumulated Depreciation		8,790								
13	Accounts Payable		4,050								
14	Notes Payable (due 4/1/19)		4,000								
15	Common Stock (2,000 shares)		5,000								
16	Retained Earnings (1/1/16)		6,120								
17	Dividends	600									
18	Sales Revenue		25,140								
19	Rent Revenue		550								
20	Cost of Goods Sold	9,050									
21	Salaries Expense	2,750									
22	Delivery Expense	720									
23	Heat and Light Expense	820									
24	Other Expenses	540									
25	Totals	53,680	53,680								
26											

The following additional information is available: (a) salaries accrued but unpaid total $250; (b) the $80 heat and light bill for December has not been recorded or paid; (c) depreciation expense totals $810 on the buildings and equipment; (d) interest accrued on the note payable totals $380 (this will be paid when the note is repaid); (e) the company leases a portion of its floor space to KT & Daniel Specialty Company for $50 per month, and KT & Daniel has not yet paid its December rent; (f) interest accrued on the note receivable totals $80; (g) bad debts expense is $70; and (h) the income tax rate is 30% on current income and is payable in the first quarter of 2017.

Required:
1. Complete the worksheet. (Round to the nearest dollar.)
2. Prepare the company's financial statements.
3. Prepare (a) adjusting and (b) closing entries in the general journal.

P3-12 **Comprehensive** On November 30, 2016, Davis Company had the following account balances:

LO 3.3
LO 3.4
LO 3.5
LO 3.6
LO 3.7
LO 3.8

	Debit	Credit		Debit	Credit
Cash	$ 3,090		Common Stock, no par (2,000 shares)		$20,000
Accounts Receivable	9,900		Retained Earnings (1/1/2016)		42,400
Allowance for Doubtful Accounts		$ 100	Dividends	$ 2,000	
Inventory	17,750		Sales Revenue		69,700
Supplies	1,400		Cost of Goods Sold	36,860	
Land	9,000		Salaries Expense	12,500	
Buildings and Equipment	42,000		Advertising Expense	8,100	
Accumulated Depreciation		4,200	Other Expenses	4,500	
Accounts Payable		10,700			

During the month of December, Davis entered into the following transactions:

Date	Transaction
Dec. 4	Made cash sales of $3,000; the cost of the inventory sold was $1,800.
7	Purchased $2,400 of inventory on credit.
14	Collected $900 of accounts receivable.
18	Sold land for $7,800; the land originally cost $5,000.
20	Made credit sales of $4,000; the cost of the inventory sold was $2,400.
21	Returned $360 of defective inventory to supplier for credit to the Davis Company's account.
27	Purchased $1,250 of inventory for cash.
28	Paid $1,100 of accounts payable.
31	Purchased land at a cost of $6,000; made a $1,000 down payment and signed a 12%, 2-year note for the balance.

Required:
1. Prepare general journal entries to record the preceding transactions.
2. Post to general ledger T-accounts.
3. Prepare a year-end trial balance on a worksheet and complete the worksheet using the following information: (a) accrued salaries at year-end total $1,200; (b) for simplicity, the building and equipment are being depreciated using the straight-line method over an estimated life of 20 years with no residual value; (c) supplies on hand at the end of the year total $630; (d) bad debts expense for the year totals $830; and (e) the income tax rate is 30%; income taxes are payable in the first quarter of 2017.
4. Prepare the company's financial statements for 2016.
5. Prepare the 2016 (a) adjusting and (b) closing entries in the general journal.

P3-13 **Reversing Entries** During 2016, Thomas Company entered into two transactions involving promissory notes and properly recorded each transaction.

LO 3.9

1. On November 1, 2016, it purchased land at a cost of $8,000. It made a $2,000 down payment and signed a note payable agreeing to pay the $6,000 balance in 6 months plus interest at an *annual* rate of 10%.
2. On December 1, 2016, it accepted a $4,200, 3-month, 12% (*annual* interest rate) note receivable from a customer for the sale of merchandise. On December 31, 2016, Thomas made the following related adjustments:

Interest Expense	100	
Interest Payable		100
Interest Receivable	42	
Interest Revenue		42

Required:
1. Assuming that Thomas uses reversing entries, prepare journal entries to record:
   a. the January 1, 2017, reversing entries
   b. the March 1, 2017, $4,326 collection of the note receivable
   c. the May 1, 2017, $6,300 payment of the note payable
2. Assuming instead that Thomas does *not* use reversing entries, prepare journal entries to record the collection of the note receivable and the payment of the note payable.

P3-14 Reversing Entries
LO 3.9

On December 31, 2016, Mason Company made the following proper year-end adjusting entries:

Date	Account Titles	Debit	Credit
Dec. 31	Bad Debts Expense	530	
	Allowance for Doubtful Accounts		530
31	Salaries Expense	940	
	Salaries Payable		940
31	Unearned Rent	1,230	
	Rent Revenue		1,230
31	Interest Expense	220	
	Interest Payable (due July 1, 2017)		220
31	Rent Receivable	310	
	Rent Revenue		310
31	Depreciation Expense	5,100	
	Accumulated Depreciation		5,100
31	Insurance Expense	312	
	Prepaid Insurance		312
31	Interest Receivable (due February 1, 2018)	225	
	Interest Revenue		225
31	Office Supplies	100	
	Office Supplies Expense		100
31	Advances to Salespersons	300	
	Salaries Expense		300
31	Income Tax Expense	4,300	
	Income Taxes Payable		4,300

Required:
1. Prepare journal entries to record whatever reversing entries you think are appropriate.
2. Explain your reasoning for each reversing entry.

P3-15 Adjusting Entries
LO 3.5
LO 3.9

At the end of 2016, Richards Company prepared a trial balance, recorded and posted its adjusting entries, and then prepared an adjusted trial balance. Selected accounts and account balances from the trial balance and adjusted trial balance are as follows:

	Partial Trial Balance		Partial Adjusted Trial Balance	
	Debit	Credit	Debit	Credit
Depreciation Expense	$ 0		$3,960	
Interest Payable (due May 14, 2018)		$ 0		$ 810
Bad Debts Expense	0		410	
Utilities Expense	1,480		1,682	
Rental Revenue		1,650		2,635
Income Tax Expense	0		2,740	
Prepaid Insurance	1,742		1,380	
Office Salaries Payable		0		540
Rent Expense	0		800	
Accumulated Depreciation		14,820		18,780
Interest Receivable (due March 1, 2017)	0		320	
Prepaid Rent	1,600		800	
Office Salaries Expense	5,600		6,140	
Income Taxes Payable		0		2,740
Insurance Expense	300		662	
Allowance for Doubtful Accounts		130		540
Interest Expense	0		810	
Unearned Rent		600		0

	Partial Trial Balance		Partial Adjusted Trial Balance	
	Debit	Credit	Debit	Credit
Utilities Payable		$ 0		$ 202
Interest Revenue		620		940
Sales Salaries Expense	$7,300		$7,850	
Office Supplies	1,150		700	
Rent Receivable	0		385	
Advances to Salespersons	770		220	
Office Supplies Expense	0		450	

Required:

1. **Next Level** By comparing the partial trial balance to the partial adjusted trial balance, determine the adjusting entries that the company made on December 31, 2016. Prepare your answers in general journal form.
2. Assuming that the company uses reversing entries, indicate which adjusting entries should be reversed.

P3-16 **Comprehensive** *(Appendix 3.1)* Presented below is information pertaining to Delsnyder Specialty Foods, a calendar-year sole proprietorship, maintaining its books on the cash basis during the year. At year-end, however, A. J. Delsnyder's accountant adjusts the books to the accrual basis only for sales, purchases, and cost of sales, and records depreciation to more clearly reflect the business income.

LO 3.11

AICPA Adapted

Trial Balance
December 31, 2016

	Debit	Credit
Cash	$ 18,500	
Accounts Receivable, 12/31/15	4,500	
Inventory, 12/31/15	20,000	
Equipment	35,000	
Accumulated Depreciation, 12/31/15		$ 9,000
Accounts Payable, 12/31/15		4,800
Payroll Taxes Withheld		850
A. J. Delsnyder, Withdrawals	24,000	
A. J. Delsnyder, Capital, 12/31/15		33,650
Sales		187,000
Purchases	82,700	
Salaries	29,500	
Payroll Taxes	2,900	
Rent	8,400	
Miscellaneous Expense	3,900	
Insurance	2,400	
Utilities	3,500	
	$235,300	$235,300

During 2016, Delsnyder signed a new 8-year lease for the store premises and is in the process of negotiating a loan for remodeling purposes. The bank requires Delsnyder to present financial statements for 2016 prepared on the accrual basis. To do so, Delsnyder's accountant obtained the following additional information for 2016:

1. Amounts due from customers totaled $7,900 at December 31.
2. A review of the receivables at December 31, disclosed that an allowance for doubtful accounts of $1,100 should be provided. Delsnyder had recorded no bad debt losses from the inception of the company through December 31.
3. The inventory amounted to $23,000 at December 31, based on a physical count of goods priced at cost. No reduction to market was required.
4. On signing the new lease on October 1, 2016, Delsnyder paid $8,400, representing 1 year's rent in advance for the lease year ending October 1, 2017. The $7,500 annual rental under the old lease was paid on October 1, 2015, for the lease year ended October 1, 2016.

(continued)

5. On April 1, 2016, Delsnyder paid $2,400 to renew the comprehensive insurance coverage for 1 year. The premium was $2,160 on the old policy, which expired on April 1, 2016.
6. Depreciation on the equipment was computed at $5,800 for 2016.
7. Unpaid vendors' invoices for food purchases totaled $8,800 at December 31.
8. Accrued expenses at December 31, 2015 and December 31, 2016, were as follows:

	12/31/15	12/31/16
Payroll taxes	$250	$400
Salaries	375	510
Utilities	275	450

After obtaining the preceding information, Delsnyder's accountant prepared the following partially completed worksheet:

	A	B	C	D	E	F	G
1		Cash Basis		Adjustments		Accrual Basis	
2	Accounts	Debit	Credit	Debit	Credit	Debit	Credit
3	Cash	18,500					
4	Accounts Receivable	4,500					
5	Allowance for Doubtful Accounts						
6	Inventory	20,000					
7	Equipment	35,000					
8	Accumulated Depreciation		9,000				
9	Prepaid Rent						
10	Prepaid Insurance						
11	Accounts Payable		4,800				
12	Accrued Expenses						
13	Payroll Taxes Withheld		850				
14	A. J. Delsnyder, Withdrawals	24,000					
15	A. J. Delsnyder, Capital		33,650				
16							
17	Sales		187,000				
18	Purchases	82,700					
19	Income Summary—Inventory						
20	Salaries	29,500					
21	Payroll Taxes	2,900					
22	Rent	8,400					
23	Miscellaneous Expenses	3,900					
24	Insurance	2,400					
25	Utilities	3,500					
26	Depreciation						
27	Bad Debts						
28	Totals	235,300	235,300				
29							

Required:
1. Complete the preceding worksheet to convert Delsnyder Specialty Foods's trial balance to the accrual basis for the year ended December 31, 2016.
2. Prepare a statement showing the changes in A. J. Delsnyder, Capital, for the year ended December 31, 2016.

P3-17 **Comprehensive** *(Appendix 3.1)* Dawson O'Connor is the owner of Miller Island Sales, a distributor of fishing supplies. The following is the balance sheet of the company as of December 31, 2015:

LO 3.6
LO 3.8
LO 3.11

Cash	$ 2,300	Accounts payable	$ 6,400
Accounts receivable	10,400	Salaries payable	1,200
Inventory	12,500		
Equipment	8,000		
Less: Accumulated depreciation	(6,500)	D. O'Connor, capital	19,100
	$26,700		$26,700

Dawson keeps very few records and has asked you to help him prepare the 2016 financial statements for Miller Island Sales. An analysis of the 2016 cash transactions recorded in the company's checkbook indicates deposits and checks as follows:

Total deposits: $173,200; all were collections from customers except for a long-term $10,000 bank loan.
Checks written: $169,800 summarized as follows:

Inventory	$123,100
Salaries	4,250
Rent	4,800
Equipment	4,000
Note payments (including interest of $650)	2,650
Office expense	3,400
Auto expense	4,100
Withdrawals	23,500
	$169,800

Other information about the company is as follows:
1. Accounts receivable at December 31, 2016: $9,200.
2. Accounts payable at December 31:

2015: Inventory	$6,100	2016: Inventory	$8,500
Office expense	300	Auto expense	200
	$6,400		$8,700

3. Salaries payable at December 31, 2016, $1,800.
4. Equipment is depreciated by the straight-line method over a 10-year life. The equipment purchased in 2016 was acquired on July 1. All of the equipment will have zero salvage value at the end of its useful life.
5. Interest payable at December 31, 2016: $140.
6. The company uses a periodic inventory system. Inventory at December 31, 2016: $17,400.

Required:
1. Prepare a worksheet to summarize the transactions and adjustments of Miller Island Sales for 2016.
   (*Hint:* Include debit and credit columns for both transactions and adjustments.)
2. Prepare a 2016 income statement and a balance sheet as of December 31, 2016.
   (*Contributed by Walter A. Parker*)

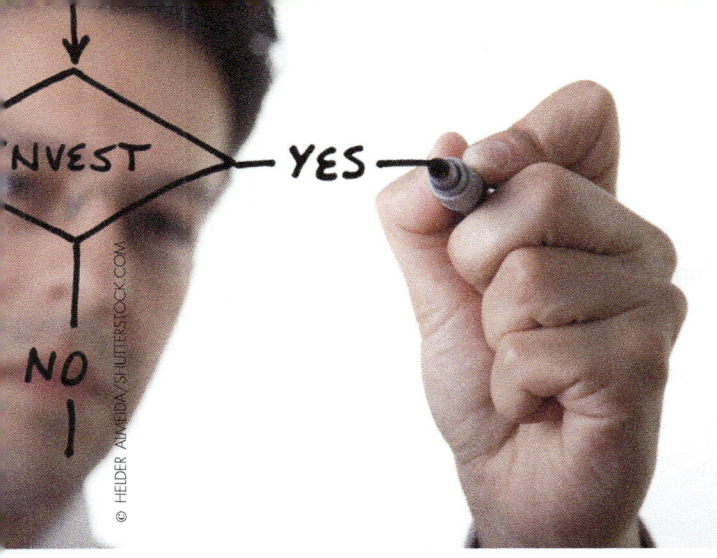

CHAPTER 4

THE BALANCE SHEET AND THE STATEMENT OF SHAREHOLDERS' EQUITY

Using Balance Sheet Information

As described in Chapter 2, the FASB's and IASB's Joint Conceptual Framework states that the primary objective of financial reporting is to provide useful information about the reporting entity for existing and potential investors, lenders, and other creditors in making decisions about providing resources to the entity. One of the FASB's and IASB's specific objectives of financial reporting is to provide information about the company's economic resources and claims against those resources. The balance sheet provides this important information. On its 2015 year-end balance sheet, **Starbucks** reports total assets of $12,446.1 million (Appendix A). The claims on those assets include total liabilities of $6,626.3 million and total shareholders' equity of $5,819.8 million. How does this information help financial statement users, such as investors, lenders, and other creditors?

Balance sheet information, together with information from the income statement and the statement of cash flows, helps users assess a company's profitability, risk, liquidity, financial flexibility, and operating capability. To illustrate, Starbucks's balance sheet provides useful information about the company's financial health. Investors, lenders, and other creditors can see that Starbucks is very profitable (discussed in Chapter 5), with relatively low risk, substantial liquidity, considerable financial flexibility, and solid operating capability.

LEARNING OBJECTIVES

After reading this chapter, you will be able to

LO 4.1 Understand the purpose and the elements of the balance sheet.

LO 4.2 Explain how to measure the elements of a balance sheet.

LO 4.3 Classify the assets, liabilities, and shareholders' equity of a balance sheet.

LO 4.4 Prepare a statement of shareholders' equity.

LO 4.5 Understand balance sheet disclosure issues.

LO 4.6 Apply financial statement analysis techniques to analyze balance sheet information.

LO 4.7 Understand the similarities and differences in how balance sheets are presented under IFRS versus U.S. GAAP.

A key element of *risk* is financial leverage—the total amount of liabilities used to finance the company's assets. Starbucks's balance sheet reveals that it has a moderate degree of financial leverage at the end of fiscal 2015, because total liabilities ($6,626.3 million) are only 53.2% of total assets ($12,446.1 million) and shareholders' equity ($5,819.8 million) is 46.8% of total assets.

Starbucks's 2015 balance sheet also indicates that it has a reasonable amount of *liquidity* because it has $1.19 in current assets ($4,352.7 million) for every $1.00 in current liabilities ($3,653.5 million). The balance sheet also suggests Starbucks has considerable *financial flexibility*, with $1,530.1 million in cash and cash equivalents, as well as $81.3 million in short-term investments classified as current assets. In addition, Starbucks's balance sheet reveals it has no short-term borrowings from lenders, and only $2,347.5 million in long-term borrowings, so presumably Starbucks could borrow additional capital if necessary. With financial flexibility in cash, investment securities, and borrowing capacity, Starbucks has financial resources it can use to adapt to change or to take advantage of business opportunities.

Operating capability is the ability of a company to produce goods and services for customers. It is indicated by the quantity of goods or services produced in a given period, and by the productive capacity of a company's operating assets (i.e., inventory and property, plant, and equipment). Starbucks's 2015 balance sheet reports solid operating capability, with $1,306.4 million in inventory and $4,088.3 million in property, plant, and equipment.

As described in Chapter 1, *annual reports* contain five major financial statements together with supporting notes, management's discussion and analysis, and managers' and independent auditors' attestations. A company's five major financial statements are the:

- *balance sheet*, which reports the financial position at the end of the accounting period
- *income statement*, which reports the results of the income-producing activities for the accounting period
- *comprehensive income statement*, which reports the comprehensive income for the accounting period, including net income and various other comprehensive income items
- *statement of cash flows*, which shows the cash inflows and cash outflows from operating, investing, and financing activities for the accounting period
- *statement of shareholders' equity*, which reports the ending amounts and changes in each item of shareholders' equity for the accounting period

In this chapter, we focus primarily on the balance sheet, and briefly discuss the statement of shareholders' equity. In Chapter 5, we focus on the income statement, the comprehensive income statement, and the statement of cash flows.

LEARNING OBJECTIVE 4.1
Understand the purpose and the elements of the balance sheet.

WHAT IS THE PURPOSE OF THE BALANCE SHEET?

The FASB and the IASB have established the balance sheet as the cornerstone of financial reporting because it reports the **financial position** of the company using the accounting equation:

Assets = Liabilities + Shareholders' Equity

The purpose of the **balance sheet** (also called the **statement of financial position**) is to report the resources of a company (assets) and the claims on the company (liabilities and shareholders' equity) as of a specific date, usually the last day of the fiscal quarter or the fiscal year. The balance sheet reports the financial position from two perspectives:

- specific resources the company controls
- claims on the company by the persons or entities that provided the resources, including the creditors and lenders (liabilities) and investors (shareholders' equity)

The other four financial statements report *changes in the financial position* of the company during the period:

- The elements of the income statement—revenues, expenses, gains and losses, and net income—are measured in terms of *changes* in assets and liabilities.
- The elements of the comprehensive income statement—primarily unrealized gains and losses—are measured in terms of *changes* in the values of certain types of assets and liabilities.
- The statement of cash flows explains *changes* in financial position in terms of cash inflows and outflows during the period.
- The statement of shareholders' equity reports owners' claims on the company and how those claims changed during the period.

Consequently, you need to know the purpose, content, format, and measurement of the balance sheet to understand the more complex issues involving recognition and measurement of assets, liabilities, equities, income, and cash flows that we discuss throughout this book.

Exhibit 4.1 illustrates the articulation (the relationships) between the financial statements. The solid lines indicate the major flows of accounting information between the financial statements. These flows are triggered by transactions, events, and arrangements during the period. Beginning with the assets, liabilities, and shareholders' equity

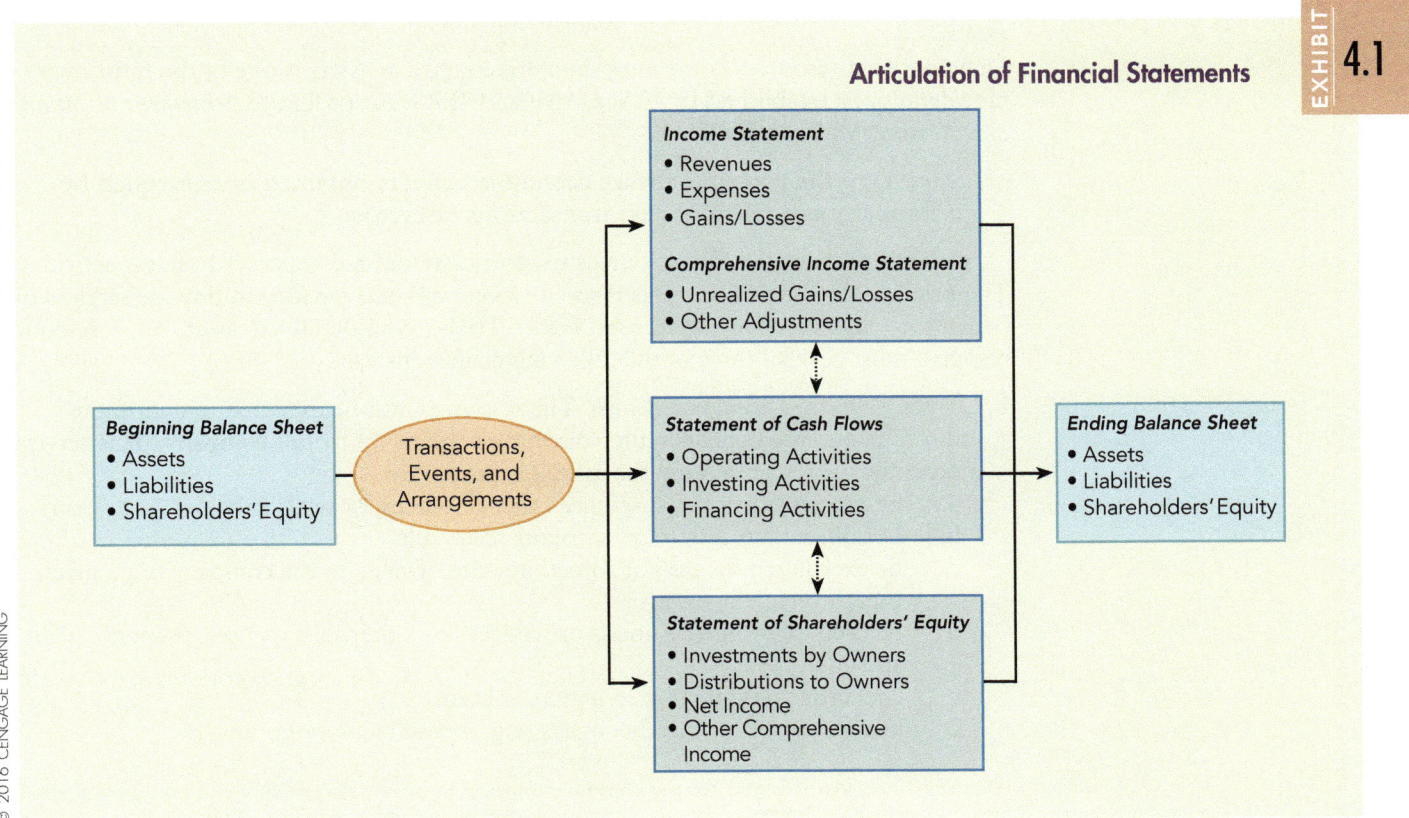

EXHIBIT 4.1 Articulation of Financial Statements

at the start of the period, the income-producing activities reported on the income statement and comprehensive income statement, the cash inflows and outflows shown on the statement of cash flows, and the changes in equity claims determine the assets, liabilities, and equity reported on the ending balance sheet. The dashed lines indicate the relationships between the four statements that report changes in financial position. We further explain the relationships between each of the financial statements in the remaining sections of this chapter and in later chapters of this book.

To provide relevant and faithfully represented information about assets, liabilities, and shareholders' equity to investors, lenders, and other creditors, the company must determine:

- *What* elements are recognized on the balance sheet
- *How* the elements are measured (valued)
- *Where* to classify and report the elements on the balance sheet.

U.S. GAAP and IFRS establish the principles and standards that companies must use to determine what to recognize on balance sheets.

WHAT ELEMENTS ARE RECOGNIZED ON THE BALANCE SHEET?

Recall from Chapter 2 that **recognition is the process of formally recording and reporting an element in the financial statements**. It includes depiction of an element in both words and numbers, with the amount included in the totals. For an item of information to be recognized on a balance sheet, it must meet the definition of a balance sheet element, it must be measurable, and it must be relevant and faithfully represented. The elements of financial statements are defined in *FASB Statement of Financial Accounting Concepts No. 6*. The elements of the balance sheet are the assets, liabilities, and shareholders' equity.[1]

Assets

Defining what resources companies should recognize as assets is one of the most important definitions established by U.S. GAAP and IFRS. According to *Statement of Financial Accounting Concepts No. 6*:

> **Assets** are the probable future economic benefits obtained or controlled by a company as a result of past transactions or events.

Assets are the economic resources used to carry out a company's business activities. The primary attribute of all assets is *service potential*—the capacity to provide services or benefits to the company that uses them. To be considered an asset, an economic resource must have all three of the following characteristics:

1. *Probable Future Economic Benefit.* The resource must be expected to contribute future economic benefits either directly or indirectly to the company. This service potential may exist because the asset is expected to:
    a. be used to cover costs, acquire other resources, or settle liabilities (e.g., cash)
    b. be collected in cash (e.g., accounts receivable)
    c. be exchanged for cash or something else of value to the company (e.g., inventory, investment securities)
    d. be used in producing goods or services (e.g., prepaid expenses, property, plant, and equipment)
    e. convey legal rights (e.g., a patent or license)
    f. increase the value of other assets (e.g., brand name or goodwill)

---

[1] The discussion of the elements in the following sections is a summary of that presented in "Elements of Financial Statements of Business Enterprises," *FASB Statement of Financial Accounting Concepts No. 6* (Stamford, CT: FASB, 1985).

2. *Control*. The company must be able to obtain the future benefit and control others' access to it. Control means that the company can deny or restrict the ability of others to use the asset.
3. *Acquisition*. The transaction or event giving the company the right to or control over the benefit must have occurred. Stated negatively, a company cannot recognize an asset if the transaction or event has not yet occurred. Once an asset is acquired by a company, it continues to be an asset until it is exchanged or used up, or until some other event destroys the future benefits or removes the company's ability to obtain or control the future benefits.

These three criteria clearly require that asset recognition depends on a company's expectations for future economic benefits. A company can recognize as assets *only* those resources for which it controls the rights to future economic benefits and can faithfully represent these benefits. If a company has assets on the balance sheet that no longer represent future economic benefits, it must remove those assets from the balance sheet (e.g., write off uncollectible receivables, unsalable inventory, or useless equipment).

A resource that *does not meet all three criteria* cannot be capitalized as an asset and must be expensed. When a resource does not meet the definition of an asset or cannot be measured reliably, then GAAP and IFRS do not permit recognition of the resource as an asset. Examples of resources that companies do not normally recognize as assets because they fail to meet one or more of the criteria include the following:

- employees—not obtained or controlled by the company (e.g., they can quit)
- unfilled purchase orders placed with suppliers—not fulfilled with a past transaction
- a high-quality reputation with employees, customers, or the community—not reliably measurable

One of **Starbucks**'s most valuable resources is its brand name. Starbucks developed its brand name through many years of running a successful company. However, without an external purchase transaction, it is very difficult for Starbucks to objectively measure the value of its brand name. Even if it could hire reputable brand name valuation experts, each expert would likely use a different valuation approach and measure a different value for its brand name. Therefore, because internally developed intangible assets like brand names are difficult to measure faithfully, U.S. GAAP and IFRS do not permit companies such as Starbucks to recognize a brand name as an asset on its balance sheet unless it was purchased from a third party in an external transaction (and is therefore objectively measurable).

Assets on the balance sheet can be viewed as either *monetary* or *nonmonetary* (*financial* or *nonfinancial*).

- **Monetary assets** (or **financial assets**) include cash and claims to cash receivable in the future. Starbucks's monetary assets include cash, accounts and notes receivable, and investments in debt and equity securities issued by other companies.
- **Nonmonetary assets** (or **nonfinancial assets**) represent future service potential from resources used by the company to produce goods and services for customers. In contrast to monetary assets, nonmonetary assets do not represent claims to future cash flows. Nonmonetary assets include assets that are *tangible* (e.g., have a physical substance) such as inventories, land, buildings, equipment, and vehicles, as well as assets that are *intangible* (e.g., usually legal substance or reputation) including patents, trademarks, licenses, and goodwill.

Liabilities

Under U.S. GAAP and IFRS, companies must recognize obligations as liabilities if they meet the definition of a liability. According to *Statement of Financial Accounting Concepts No. 6*:

> **Liabilities** are the probable future sacrifices of economic benefits arising from present obligations of a company to transfer assets or provide services in the future to other entities as a result of past transactions or events.

Under this definition, an obligation of a company must have three characteristics to be recognized as a liability:

1. *Transfer.* It must involve a responsibility that will be settled by a sacrifice involving the transfer of assets, provision of services, or other use of assets at a specified or determinable date, on occurrence of a specified event, or on demand. The company does not need to know the specific identity of the creditor for a liability to exist.
2. *Nonavoidable.* The responsibility must obligate the company so that it has little or no discretion to avoid the future sacrifice. Although most liabilities involve legal rights and duties, some are the result of equitable (ethical or moral) obligations or constructive (inferred from the facts) obligations. Thus, the company must be bound by a legal, equitable, or constructive responsibility to transfer assets or provide services.
3. *Incurred.* An obligating transaction, event, or arrangement must have occurred. Once a liability has been incurred, it continues to be a liability until the company settles it or another event eliminates the company's obligation.

Most troublesome questions regarding liability recognition relate to **executory contracts** (contracts in the process of being fulfilled, such as a purchase order) and **contingent obligations** (obligations that arise conditional on something else occurring, such as a performance-based bonus). Under U.S. GAAP and IFRS, companies do not recognize executory contracts until the company receives the benefits and becomes obligated to pay for them. For example, a company should not recognize a liability when it places an order to purchase inventory.[2] The obligation arises when the company receives the inventory. Likewise, the company should not recognize a liability for future wages to employees. Instead, it should recognize the liability once the employees have earned the wages.

Most liabilities are monetary (requiring future payments of cash) and arise primarily from purchasing goods or services on credit and from borrowing funds. Other liabilities create performance obligations, resulting from customers prepaying for future delivery of goods or services. Liabilities also arise from selling products subject to warranties, and from taxes and regulations imposed by government units. Liabilities reflect managers' expectations of the future sacrifices of resources required to satisfy existing obligations.

Appendix A includes **Starbucks**'s balance sheet at September 27, 2015. Liabilities for Starbucks include obligations to deliver products to customers (the stored value card liability) as well as obligations to pay cash to:

- employees and suppliers (accounts payable; accrued liabilities for operating expenses including compensation and related costs and accrued occupancy costs; and other long-term liabilities)
- governments (accrued taxes)
- banks and other lenders (long-term debt)

Shareholders' Equity

Under U.S. GAAP and IFRS, shareholders' equity represents the ownership interest in a company. *FASB Statement of Financial Accounting Concepts No. 6* defines equity as a residual claim:

> **Equity** is the residual interest in the assets of a company after deducting its liabilities.

The owners have a claim on all assets that are not required to meet the claims of lenders and creditors. Therefore, the value of assets minus the value of liabilities on the

---

[2] Upon placing an order to purchase inventory, the company should not recognize the inventory as an asset or recognize a liability to pay for the inventory until it receives the inventory. Subsequent chapters discuss accounting for liabilities and contingent claims more fully.

balance sheet determines the value of equity. For a corporation, shareholders' equity represents the interest of the shareholders, who bear the risks involved in the company's operations and activities and who obtain the resulting rewards. It is created by shareholders' investments of economic resources and later is modified by additional investments, net income, dividends and other distributions to owners, and other changes in assets and liabilities. Because it is a residual interest, shareholders' equity does not exist apart from the company assets and liabilities.

Balance sheets separate total shareholders' equity into three general categories:

- **Contributed capital**—amounts invested by shareholders for an ownership interest in a company
- **Earned capital**—the cumulative amounts of profits that have been earned by the company, plus (minus) any net unrealized gains (losses), minus the amounts of profit that have been paid out to shareholders through dividends (or in some cases, share repurchases)
- **Noncontrolling interests**—equity capital amounts invested by minority shareholders in consolidated subsidiaries

For the contributed capital category, **Starbucks** uses two accounts: Common Stock and Additional Paid-in Capital. For the earned capital accounts category, Starbucks uses two accounts: Retained Earnings and Accumulated Other Comprehensive Income/(Loss). Retained Earnings represents Starbucks's cumulative net income minus the dividends that Starbucks has declared and minus the amounts that Starbucks has paid to repurchase shares. Accumulated Other Comprehensive Income/(Loss) represents cumulative unrealized gains and losses from the recognition and valuation of certain assets or liabilities. Starbucks also recognizes a small amount of equity capital in Noncontrolling Interests.

GOT IT?

4-1 What is the accounting equation? The balance sheet reports financial position from which two perspectives?

4-2 What is the purpose of a company's balance sheet?

4-3 How does the balance sheet at the end of an accounting period relate to the other four financial statements?

4-4 What does *recognition* mean in accounting?

4-5 Define an *asset*. What are the three characteristics of an asset?

4-6 Define a *liability*. What are the three characteristics of a liability?

4-7 What is *equity*? How is equity determined?

HOW ARE THE ELEMENTS OF A BALANCE SHEET MEASURED?

LEARNING OBJECTIVE 4.2

Explain how to measure the elements of a balance sheet.

As the definitions above establish, **assets and liabilities represent expectations for the future.** Assets are expected to provide future economic benefits, and liabilities represent obligations to sacrifice economic resources in the future. However, as described in Chapter 2, measuring assets and liabilities under U.S. GAAP and IFRS follows a **mixed attribute measurement model**. Under this model, different types of assets and liabilities are valued using different measurement bases, including historical costs, fair values, present values, net realizable values, and others. Accounting follows a mixed attribute model because the objective of U.S. GAAP and IFRS is to provide the most *relevant* information that can be *faithfully represented* in the financial statements.

Measurement methods that reflect *historical values* include the following:

- historical cost or acquisition cost (assets) and historical proceeds or originally incurred obligation amounts (liabilities)
- allocated historical amounts (for assets and liabilities allocated over time)
- initial present value and adjusted present value (assets and liabilities that represent future cash flows)

At the time a company acquires an asset or incurs a liability, historical measures are timely and objective, so are both representationally faithful and relevant to financial statement users.

As time passes, however, historical measures can lose relevance if they do not reflect current values. Current values update historical values with relevant information about the fair value of assets and liabilities as of the balance sheet date. Measurement methods that reflect *current values* or a *combination of historical and current values* include the following:

- fair value (assets and liabilities)
- present value (assets and liabilities)
- current replacement cost (assets)
- net realizable value (assets)

The remainder of this section provides brief descriptions and examples of the primary valuation alternatives that are most common for balance sheet accounts. Keep in mind that, although the discussion focuses on asset and liability measurement, because of the articulation of the income statement with the balance sheet, the measurements of assets and liabilities also determine the measurement of income. This discussion sets the stage for a more detailed understanding of accounting for balance sheet elements and income measurement in later chapters.

Historical Cost and Adjusted Historical Cost

The **historical cost** (or **acquisition cost**) of an asset is the amount paid initially to acquire the asset. The cost of an asset is measured initially by the cash paid for the asset or by the estimated cash equivalent in a noncash asset exchange. Acquisition cost includes all costs required to prepare the asset for its intended use, including shipping, installation, setup, and testing. For liabilities, historical measurement is the amount of the originally incurred obligation. At the time assets are obtained or liabilities are incurred, historical cost measurements are ideal because they are both relevant and faithful representations of the amounts that companies actually paid to acquire resources and the amounts of the obligations incurred.

Example Suppose **Starbucks** paid $1,500,000 to acquire a tract of land for a coffee bean roasting plant. It also paid $75,000 in commissions to the real estate agent, $10,000 to attorneys for a title search and to prepare the required legal documents for the purchase, and a $3,000 real estate transfer tax. To finance the land acquisition, Starbucks borrowed $1,300,000 with a 5-year note payable from a local bank and paid cash for the remainder. Starbucks would record the acquisition cost of the land at $1,588,000 ($1,500,000 + $75,000 + $10,000 + $3,000). It would record the note payable at the originally incurred obligation, $1,300,000. ■

The economic benefits of some assets (e.g., property, plant, and equipment, prepaid insurance, and rent) are consumed gradually over their service life. As the company receives benefits, it must recognize an expense for the portion of the asset used up each period and decrease the balance sheet value of the asset to reflect the benefits that have been consumed. As a result, the asset is recognized at its **adjusted historical cost**.

For property, plant, and equipment, the use of the asset is recognized through depreciation expense, and the acquisition cost is adjusted through the contra-asset account, Accumulated Depreciation. For intangible assets, the use of the asset is recognized through amortization expense, and the acquisition cost is adjusted through the contra-asset account, Accumulated Amortization. For prepaid assets like insurance and rent, the acquisition cost of the asset is reduced ratably for the amount consumed and expensed each period.

Example Assume **JetBlue Airways** acquires from a regional airline the landing rights at various airports for $150 million. The landing rights expire in 5 years. JetBlue initially recognizes the landing rights as an intangible asset of $150 million, and then it amortizes the $150 million acquisition cost over the 5 years of use. Accordingly, the cost of the landing rights ratably declines $30 million each year, to an adjusted cost of zero at the end of 5 years.

Example Suppose **PepsiCo** prepays in July for five 30-second spots for commercial airtime during the next Super Bowl, the following February. It pays $15 million to the network broadcasting the game and recognizes a prepaid advertising asset of $15 million on its balance sheet. On the day of the Super Bowl, the economic benefits of the advertising time are consumed. PepsiCo then reduces the asset value to zero and recognizes $15 million in advertising expense.

To measure adjusted historical cost, managers must exercise considerable judgment, estimating the expected useful life and salvage value of productive assets as well as selecting a depreciation or amortization method. In some cases, like the two previous examples, estimating useful life and salvage value are straightforward because the useful life is specified, after which the asset value will be zero. In other cases, a plant or a building could provide many years of service potential, and it is difficult to directly measure or verify the consumption of service potential each period.

Present Value and Adjusted Present Value

Monetary assets and liabilities represent amounts of cash the company expects to receive or is obligated to pay in the future. Examples of monetary assets include cash, accounts receivable, and notes receivable. Monetary liabilities include accounts payable, accrued expenses, notes payable, mortgages, and bonds payable. Companies typically recognize monetary assets and liabilities using **present values**.[3] By discounting the expected future cash flows to a present value, the monetary assets and liabilities are reported in terms of current cash equivalent values.[4] When the monetary asset or liability is initially recognized in the financial statements, the present value computation uses interest rates appropriate for the particular financing arrangement at that time. For monetary assets and liabilities due within 1 year, U.S. GAAP and IFRS permit companies to ignore discounting for the time value of money.

For certain types of monetary assets and liabilities, the present value of the cash flows will change because of the passage of time. For example, zero-coupon notes receivable or notes payable do not trigger interest cash flows until the notes mature, at which time all of the accumulated interest is paid, along with the principal of the note. Companies typically recognize these types of monetary assets and liabilities using **adjusted present values** to reflect the passage of time.

Example Suppose **Cisco** sells computer equipment to **Netflix**, and Netflix agrees to pay Cisco $1,000,000 3 years from now. The note agreement reflects an implicit 8% interest rate. The present value of $1,000,000, when discounted at 8% for 3 years, is

---

[3] *FASB Statement of Financial Accounting Concepts No. 5, op. cit.,* par. 67, "Conceptual Framework for Financial Accounting and Reporting: Elements of Financial Statements and Their Measurement," *FASB Discussion Memorandum, op. cit.,* pp. 196–206. "Using Cash Flow Information and Present Value in Accounting Measurements," *FASB Statement of Financial Accounting Concepts No. 7* (Norwalk, CT: FASB, 2000), p. 1. *FASB Statement of Financial Accounting Standards No. 157, op. cit.,* par. B12–B15 (FASB ASC 820-10-55).

[4] Time value of money techniques are explained and demonstrated in the Time Value of Money Module.

$793,832. Cisco records a note receivable and sale, while Netflix records a purchase of equipment and note payable. In both cases, the transactions are recorded at the initial present value of $793,832. During the first year, interest of $63,507 (0.08 × $793,832) accumulates on the note, which increases the book value of the note to $857,339 ($793,832 + $63,507). The note receivable on Cisco's balance sheet and the note payable on Netflix's balance sheet at the end of the first year will be recognized at $857,339. This amount equals the adjusted present value of $1,000,000 discounted at the historical interest rate of 8% for the 2 remaining years. ■

Fair Value

The relevance of historical cost-based measures for assets and liabilities may diminish over time if they do not reflect current economic conditions. As a consequence, to provide more decision-useful information, the FASB and the IASB have adopted numerous accounting standards that value assets and liabilities using fair value approaches. For instance, U.S. GAAP and IFRS require that certain types of assets and liabilities (such as trading securities and investment securities available for sale) be measured at fair values.

The FASB and the IASB define **fair value** as "the price that would be received to sell an asset or paid to transfer a liability in an orderly transaction between market participants at the measurement date."[5] This definition explicitly characterizes fair value as a measure of market-based exit value, which is the amount for which a company could sell an asset or pay to settle or transfer a liability. In so doing, the Boards rejected alternative notions for fair value, including entry value (price that would be paid to acquire an asset or the obligation that would be incurred to issue a liability on the balance sheet date) and value in use (value of an asset or liability to the company using it).[6]

On the date a company acquires an asset by paying cash, the fair value is known and is equal to the historical cost of the asset recorded for the transaction (assuming an independent buyer and seller). Similarly, upon the inception of a financial liability, the fair value and the original incurred obligation amount are the same. So the initial recognition of financial assets and liabilities at historical costs, which are equivalent to fair values, achieves optimal levels of relevance and representational faithfulness. However, on a subsequent measurement date (i.e., the end of a company's accounting period), the fair value of the financial asset and liability may have changed.

Both the FASB and the IASB allow companies a **fair value option** for financial instruments (such as loans, notes receivable or payable, and bonds receivable or payable). Upon acquisition of a financial asset or inception of a financial liability, companies can elect to report the financial instrument at fair value (with subsequent changes in fair values to flow through earnings). Once elected, the company must remain on that measurement basis for the life of that financial asset or liability. While the fair value option can be used by all types of companies, it is most useful for financial institutions (e.g., banks and insurers) because the majority of their assets and liabilities are financial in nature.[7]

How Is Fair Value Measured? Fair value measurement assumes that the asset could be sold or the liability could be settled in a hypothetical transaction on the measurement date. The transaction is hypothetical because the company does not actually sell the asset or settle the liability. Instead, the question is: What price *could* the company get for the asset *if* it was sold on the balance sheet date in an orderly market? Or: How much *would* the company have to pay *if* it were to settle the financial liability on the balance sheet date? In determining fair value, a company should consider the specific attributes of the asset or liability that independent, informed market participants would consider in the transaction.

---

[5] Financial Accounting Standards Board, *FASB Codification Topic 820*, "Fair Value Measurements and Disclosures" and International Accounting Standards Board, *IFRS 13*, "Fair Value Measurement."

[6] For a conceptual discussion of present value approaches, see Financial Accounting Standards Board, *Statement of Financial Accounting Concepts No. 7*, "Using Cash Flow Information and Present Value Accounting Measurement," (February 2000).

[7] Financial Accounting Standards Board, *FASB Codification Topic 825*, "The Fair Value Option for Financial Assets and Financial Liabilities." International Accounting Standards Board, *IFRS 9*, "Financial Instruments," (revised July 2014).

Fair value measurements can be extremely relevant and representationally faithful when they are based on observable prices in orderly liquid markets for stocks, bonds, securities, commodities, derivatives, and other items. However, a potential measurement issue arises: How should a company determine fair value when there is no quoted price in an active market? There is a three-tiered hierarchy within U.S. GAAP and IFRS that distinguishes among different inputs for determining fair values.[8]

- **Level 1**. Level 1 inputs are quoted prices in active markets for identical assets or liabilities on the measurement date. A quoted market price provides the most representationally faithful evidence of fair value and is to be used whenever available. For example, a company holding shares of stock as investment securities would measure the fair value of those shares using the closing selling prices in the stock market on the balance sheet date.
- **Level 2**. Level 2 inputs are observable market prices for similar assets or liabilities in active markets, or other observable inputs, such as interest rates, for the asset or liability. Level 2 inputs are to be used when Level 1 inputs are not readily available. For example, suppose a company holds a bond that is not actively traded. The company could determine fair value for the bond using Level 2 inputs by obtaining quoted market prices for similar bonds and then adjusting those prices for any differences in maturity, interest rates, and credit risk.
- **Level 3**. Level 3 inputs are the company's estimates and assumptions used to calculate fair value for an asset or a liability. Level 3 inputs should be used to measure fair value only when Level 1 or Level 2 inputs are not available, or the costs of obtaining them exceed the benefits. Level 3 inputs reflect the company's assumptions and estimates about how market participants would price the asset or liability. These inputs should be developed based on the best information available, which might include the company's own data about the expected cash flows and the appropriate discount rate. For example, a company may estimate the fair value of its investment in shares of common stock in a private company based on a model of the present value of the expected future cash flows associated with the shares, discounted at a rate appropriate to reflect the risk of that investment.

Fair value accounting (also known as "mark-to-market" accounting) for financial assets and liabilities is becoming increasingly common within U.S. GAAP and IFRS. Although the relevance of fair values is obvious, given the subjective nature of fair value estimates using Level 2 and Level 3 inputs, the representational faithfulness of fair values is sometimes questioned.

Example **SunTrust Bank** is the 13th largest bank in the United States, with its headquarters in Atlanta. Until September 2012, SunTrust Bank held roughly 30 million shares of **Coca-Cola** common stock. SunTrust had held those shares since 1919, when it participated in Coca-Cola's initial public offering of shares and accepted shares of stock in lieu of underwriting fees. The historical cost basis of those shares was only $69,295. Coca-Cola shares are actively traded on the New York Stock Exchange, so SunTrust used Level 1 inputs (the market price for Coca-Cola shares as of December 31, 2011) to recognize the investment at a fair value of roughly $2.1 billion. In September 2012, SunTrust divested its ownership of those shares through stock sales and a charitable contribution, at which time it realized a pretax gain of roughly $1.9 billion in net income. ∎

Example After **Cisco** sells networking equipment to **Google** in exchange for a note, Cisco reports a note receivable, and Google reports a note payable at a book value of $828,032 (which equals the present value of four payments of $250,000 discounted at the historical interest rate of 8%). Assume that the market interest rate appropriate for

---

[8] FASB ASC 820-10-35: Fair Value Measurement, Overall, Subsequent Measurement. IFRS incorporate the same Level 1, Level 2, and Level 3 hierarchy.

this note declines from 8% to 6%. The present value of these payments at 6% is then $866,276. If Cisco and/or Google elected the fair value option at the inception of this note, the note would be revalued to $866,276 to reflect the change in fair value caused by the change in the discount rate. If notes very similar to this are traded on active markets and yield a 6% interest rate, using that market-determined rate to estimate the fair value would be considered a Level 2 input. If there are no similar notes traded in active markets, and if Google or Cisco determined that 6% is the appropriate interest rate based on their own estimates (without reference to market-based interest rates), it would be considered a Level 3 input. ■

In some cases, it becomes necessary to value nonmonetary assets at fair value. If nonmonetary assets are traded on active exchanges, such as commodity markets, determining fair value can be accomplished using Level 1 or Level 2 inputs. Most commonly, however, nonmonetary assets are not traded on active exchanges. Because the cash flows for a nonmonetary asset are not predetermined, valuation requires forecasts of the timing and amount of the expected cash flows, as well as the appropriate discount rates. Revaluations of the asset each period reflect changes in expected cash flows, changes in the discount rate, or both. Thus, the representational faithfulness of such estimates depends on the method of forecasting cash flows and estimating discount rates, which entail considerable subjectivity.

Example Note 5 to **Starbucks**'s 2015 annual report discloses that $809.1 million (more than half) of its inventory is unroasted and roasted coffee beans. There is an actively traded commodities market for coffee on the New York Board of Trade. If it were necessary for Starbucks to measure the coffee bean portion of its inventory at fair value, it could do so using commodity market prices for coffee beans as Level 1 inputs. ■

Example **Kimpton Hotels** owns numerous boutique hotels throughout North America. It reports these hotels at acquisition cost, adjusted for accumulated depreciation. If Kimpton were to measure the hotels at fair value, it would be difficult because there is no actively traded market in individual hotels upon which to determine the fair value of each property (no Level 1 or Level 2 inputs). Instead, one alternative for determining fair value would require Kimpton to forecast the net cash flows it would reasonably expect to receive from selling each hotel and discount them to a present value using current interest rates (Level 3 inputs). ■

Fair Value Disclosures U.S. GAAP and IFRS require extensive disclosures for reporting the fair values of assets and liabilities. The intent is to enable external users to assess the reliability of the inputs used to develop fair value measurements. For instance, the company must segregate its fair value measurements into those based on Level 1, 2, and 3 inputs. Also, for any fair values measured using Level 3 inputs, the company must include the valuation technique used to measure the fair value, a reconciliation of the changes in fair value during the period (known as a "rollforward" that reconciles the beginning and ending balances), and related discussion.

Current Replacement Cost

Current replacement cost is the amount a company would have to pay currently to acquire an asset it now holds, either through purchase or production. The most common use of current replacement cost is through application of lower of cost or market valuation of inventories. Current replacement cost should reflect normal purchases and sales between unrelated parties, not distressed purchases and sales in which one party holds a major advantage in setting prices. Whereas the FASB advocates exit prices for fair valuation in general, current replacement cost relies on the entry value. Current replacement cost valuations generally involve greater subjectivity than acquisition cost valuations, but they are less subjective when based on observable prices for similar assets or liabilities in active markets, such as spot prices in commodities markets.

Example As noted earlier, **Starbucks** holds $809.1 million in coffee bean inventory at the end of fiscal 2015. Suppose that perfect conditions in major coffee growing regions triggered a surge in the available supply of coffee beans, driving down the spot price of coffee beans on the commodity exchanges. Suppose that, if Starbucks were to replace its existing inventory of coffee beans, it could do so for only $667.0 million. As such, Starbucks would have an unrealized holding loss for this inventory of $142.1 million ($667.0 million − $809.1 million) and so must reduce the value of the coffee bean portion of inventory to the current replacement cost of $667.0 million.[9] ■

Net Realizable Value

Net realizable value is the net amount a company would receive if it sold an asset, or the present value of cash flows it expects to realize from an asset. Net realizable valuation is usually triggered by a decline in the expected economic benefits of an asset to a value less than historical cost. Examples include uncollectible accounts receivable, a decline in the salable value of inventory (part of the lower of cost or market rule), or the impairment of the value of tangible or intangible assets. Thus, historical cost provides a reference point to determine whether net realizable value measurements are necessary.

Net realizable value is a hybrid measurement approach involving both historical cost and fair value. Like fair value, it refers to exit values. It focuses on the amount a company is likely to realize given prevailing market conditions, minus any pertinent selling costs. Measuring assets using net realizable values has the same advantages and disadvantages as using current replacement costs. Net realizable values may provide more relevant information to financial statements users but require greater subjectivity when active markets for the assets do not exist.

Example Inventory for **Pulte Homes** is approximately two-thirds of total assets and reflects primarily house and land inventory. The credit crisis and recession caused a reduction in the demand for new homes and land, which resulted in the net realizable value of Pulte's inventory being below acquisition cost. Certain land and homes held by Pulte were written down to net realizable value, reflecting estimated fair value minus costs to sell. ■

Example **SunTrust Bank** manages large portfolios of loans to commercial, residential, and consumer borrowers. At the end of 2013, the present value of its loan portfolio was over $127.8 billion. Based on the age of the various loans, historical credit risk experience, and recent economic activity, SunTrust estimates that roughly $2.0 billion will ultimately become uncollectible. The initial present value of the loans receivable is offset by a $2.0 billion allowance for loan losses, to recognize the net realizable value on the balance sheet, which the bank reports at roughly $125.8 billion. ■

Not Strictly Separate Categories Note that, although we have used distinct categories to describe the various historical cost-based and fair value-based approaches, these categories overlap and are not mutually exclusive. Many practical applications often involve a hybrid approach. The main point to understand is that there are numerous approaches to asset and liability measurement.

For instance, **SunTrust**'s loan portfolio represents monetary assets. At the time new loans are made and recognized as assets, the initial valuation of the loans simply reflects the historical cost. At this point, the historical cost equals the present value of future cash flows from the loans. Subsequently, SunTrust estimates uncollectible loans and records a valuation allowance. This is similar to using an adjusted historical cost valuation for the loans. Moreover, you also could view the reduction in the value of the loans resulting from the valuation allowance as reporting the loans at their net realizable value.

[9] Chapter 8 describes the application of current replacement cost and the lower of cost or market rule in detail.

GOT IT?

4-8 What is a mixed attribute measurement model? Why is it used in accounting?

4-9 Identify at least five alternatives for measuring assets.

4-10 Identify at least three alternatives for measuring liabilities.

4-11 How are the measurement attributes *historical cost* and *fair value* defined? When are they the same?

ETHICAL DILEMMA

As the controller for a struggling manufacturing company, you are in the process of closing the books for the year and notice that the company is going to be in technical violation of its debt covenants. Such a violation could result in bankruptcy, which would result in the loss of hundreds of jobs, including your own. You quickly analyze the financial statements and realize that, by decreasing the allowance for uncollectible accounts, the estimated value for accounts receivable will increase, and the company will be able to avoid a violation of its debt covenants. While you don't believe the revised estimate would best represent the economic reality of your company's collectible receivables, you also don't believe the estimate is unreasonably aggressive. Do you revise the estimate?

LEARNING OBJECTIVE 4.3
Classify the assets, liabilities, and shareholders' equity of a balance sheet.

HOW ARE ITEMS CLASSIFIED AND REPORTED ON THE BALANCE SHEET?

Financial statement classifications are designed to help financial statement users' analysis and decision-making by grouping items with similar characteristics. The intent is to improve the predictive value and, hence, the usefulness, of the financial information for assessing the amounts, timing, and uncertainty of future cash flows.[10] We describe here the general classification scheme that captures the majority of items reported by most companies, but we emphasize that actual classifications reflect differences in companies, industries, and economic conditions.

A corporation usually divides its balance sheet into three sections for assets, liabilities, and shareholders' equity, reporting similar items within each section. A common classification would be:

1. *Assets*
    a. Current assets
    b. Long-term investments
    c. Property, plant, and equipment
    d. Intangible assets
    e. Other assets
2. *Liabilities*
    a. Current liabilities
    b. Long-term liabilities
    c. Other liabilities
3. *Shareholders' Equity*
    a. Contributed capital
        (1) Common stock
        (2) Additional paid-in capital
    b. Retained earnings
    c. Accumulated other comprehensive income
    d. Noncontrolling interests

[10] *FASB Statement of Financial Accounting Concepts No. 5*, par. 20–22.

We discuss each category in the following sections. We show a comprehensive illustration of a balance sheet at December 31, 2016, for Caron Manufacturing Company in **Example 4.1**. Appendix A includes **Starbucks**'s balance sheet at September 27, 2015.

EXAMPLE 4.1

Balance Sheet

CARON MANUFACTURING COMPANY
Balance Sheet
December 31, 2016

Assets
Current Assets:
Cash and cash equivalents		$ 14,300	
Investments in available-for-sale securities		19,700	
Accounts receivable	$68,200		
Less: Allowance for doubtful accounts	(3,200)	65,000	
Inventories:			
Raw materials	$32,000		
Work in process	49,500		
Finished goods	66,100	147,600	
Prepaid items:			
Insurance	$ 4,800		
Office supplies	2,200	7,000	
Total current assets			$253,600

Long-Term Investments:
Investment in held-to-maturity bonds		$ 17,000	
Fund to retire long-term bonds payable		17,400	
Total long-term investments			34,400

Property, Plant, and Equipment:

	Cost	Accumulated Depreciation	Book Value
Land	$ 36,000	—	$ 36,000
Buildings	428,000	$207,000	221,000
Equipment	192,000	63,700	128,300
Totals	$656,000	$270,700	$385,300

Total property, plant, and equipment			385,300
Intangible Assets:			
Trademarks		$ 12,600	
Patents (net)		16,900	
Total intangible assets			29,500
Total Assets			**$702,800**

Liabilities
Current Liabilities:
Accounts payable		$ 87,100	
Salaries payable		3,300	
Income taxes payable		27,400	
Advances from customers		19,600	
Current portion of mortgage payable		8,400	
Total current liabilities			$145,800

(continued)

EXAMPLE 4.1 (Continued)

Long-Term Liabilities:		
Bonds payable (10%, due 2026)	$90,000	
Less: Unamortized bond discount	(8,200)	$ 81,800
Mortgage payable (12%, due 2018–2021)		52,600
Accrued pension cost		34,700
Deferred income taxes		14,300
Total long-term liabilities		183,400
Total Liabilities		**$329,200**
Shareholders' Equity		
Contributed Capital:		
Common stock, $5 par (20,000 shares authorized, 14,300 shares issued and outstanding)	$ 71,500	
Additional paid-in capital	173,900	
Total contributed capital		$245,400
Retained earnings		116,200
Accumulated Other Comprehensive Income:		
Unrealized fair value gain on available-for-sale securities		12,000
Total Shareholders' Equity		**$373,600**
Total Liabilities and Shareholders' Equity		**$702,800**

Current Assets

Current assets are cash and other assets that a company expects to convert into cash, sell, or consume within 1 year or the normal operating cycle, whichever is longer. An **operating cycle** is the average length of time taken by a company to spend cash to purchase or produce inventory, sell the inventory, and collect the receivables, converting them back into cash. Most companies have operating cycles of a year or less. A few, such as large-project construction, lumber, and distillery companies, have operating cycles that are longer than 1 year. In that case, the longer time period can be used to determine the current assets.[11]

Companies commonly report the following types of current assets:

- *Cash and Cash Equivalents.* **Cash** includes cash on hand and readily available in checking and savings accounts. Many companies also include **cash equivalents**, which are highly liquid, low-risk securities, such as money market funds and treasury bills that will mature in 3 months or less from the date acquired by the holder. Cash and cash equivalents are measured and reported at present value, which is equal to fair value.
- *Short-Term Investments.* **Investments in marketable securities** include debt and equity securities that are classified as trading securities, and debt securities that are classified as available-for-sale, which are reported at fair value, as well as held-to-maturity securities that will mature within a year, which are reported at historical cost.
- *Receivables.* Receivables include **accounts receivable** and **notes receivable** with short-term maturity dates, reported at their estimated collectible amounts (net realizable values).
- *Inventories.* **Inventories** include goods held for resale in the normal course of business, as well as **raw materials** (items to be converted into **finished goods** for sale to customers) and **work in process** (partially completed goods) inventories. They are measured at the lower of historical cost or market value (either replacement cost or net realizable value). The inventory costing method (LIFO, FIFO, average cost,

[11] FASB ASC 210-10-45: Balance Sheet, Overall, Other Presentation Matters.

specific identification) is disclosed in the related notes. To reduce balance sheet detail, companies often report a total inventory amount in current assets and include a schedule of the components in the notes to the financial statements. **Starbucks** uses this procedure, as shown in Note 5 to its 2015 annual report, in Appendix A.
- *Other Current Assets.* **Prepaid items** such as insurance, rent, office supplies, and advertising will not be converted into cash but will be consumed. If a company prepays for multiple years of expenses (such as prepaying 3 years of insurance or rent), the portion of the prepayment that will be consumed in the next year or operating cycle should be classified as a current asset, with the remainder classified as a noncurrent asset. Prepaid items are listed at the historical cost of the remaining amounts.

Office supplies are typically considered current assets. They are prepaid items that will provide future economic benefits to the company.

These titles are general and many companies use synonymous or more specific titles. Under U.S. GAAP, these items usually are presented in the current assets section in order of liquidity, as shown in **Example 4.1**.

Long-Term Investments

Companies invest for a variety of reasons. They may be interested in appreciation of the market value of the investment; in income from interest or dividends; in exercising influence over other companies (such as a major supplier); or in saving cash for specific future purposes such as the acquisition of property, plant, and equipment or the retirement of long-term debt. If the company expects to hold the investment for more than 1 year or the operating cycle, whichever is longer, it is classified as a **long-term investment**.

Long-term investments include:

- investments in available-for-sale debt securities, as well as investments in equity securities, that the company does not intend to convert into cash within 1 year or the operating cycle
- investments in debt securities (e.g., bonds) expected to be held to maturity when maturity is beyond 1 year
- investments in affiliated companies
- notes receivable, advances to customers or suppliers, and other financial instruments that are noncurrent
- property being held for investment purposes (such as a building held for rental activities rather than operating activities) or future operations (such as land being held for a future building site)
- special funds established to retire bonds payable or preferred stock (often called sinking funds) or to acquire future facilities
- miscellaneous long-term investments (such as the cash surrender value of life insurance policies)

Long-term investments are listed at their fair value, historical cost, or present value, depending on the type of investment. The method of valuation for each long-term investment should be disclosed either parenthetically or in the notes to the financial statements. **Example 4.1** shows the long-term investments section of Caron Manufacturing Company's balance sheet (p. 4-15). **Starbucks**'s balance sheet in Appendix A reports two types of long-term investments: Long-Term Investments and Equity and Cost Investments (which represent investments in affiliated companies).

Property, Plant, and Equipment

The **property, plant, and equipment** section of a company's balance sheet includes the long-lived tangible assets used in its operations. Often these are called **fixed assets** because of their relative permanency in the company's operations. This category typically includes long-lived assets that have a physical existence, such as land, buildings, equipment, machinery, furniture, and natural resources, as well as property, plant, and equipment held under certain long-term lease contracts. Because the lease allows the lessee company rights to the use of the asset for an extended period, the rights are economic resources to the company, even though the company does not legally own the asset.[12] In addition, companies that have made substantial improvements to assets held under lease will also report **leasehold improvements** in this category. For example, leasehold improvements total $5,409.6 million for **Starbucks**, comprising the largest category of property, plant, and equipment, as disclosed in Note 7 of the 2015 annual report in Appendix A. Finally, companies that are building new productive facilities will report the costs incurred to date as **construction in progress**.

As described in Chapter 3, the depreciable costs of all the fixed assets are allocated to expense over the expected service life of the asset (applicable terms are **depreciation** for tangible assets, **depletion** for natural resources, or **amortization** for intangibles), except for construction in progress (which will become depreciable once it is completed and put into service) and land. Land is listed at its historical cost, while the remaining fixed assets are listed at their adjusted historical cost (which is historical cost minus accumulated depreciation; this is sometimes called **net book value**). The contra-asset account Accumulated Depreciation reports the amount of the depreciable assets used up already. Book values of depreciable assets reflect the remaining amount of asset value expected to provide future economic benefits. Companies are required to disclose the method of depreciating fixed assets and the expected useful lives in the notes to the financial statements. If the expected economic benefits of a fixed asset have been impaired, the fixed asset is reported at fair value or net realizable value. **Example 4.1** shows the property, plant, and equipment section of Caron Manufacturing Company's balance sheet (p. 4-15).

Some companies report net property, plant, and equipment on their balance sheets and disclose the historical costs of individual asset categories and accumulated depreciation in the related notes. **Starbucks** uses this procedure for its property, plant, and equipment in Note 7 to the 2015 financial statements in Appendix A.

Intangible Assets

Intangible assets are noncurrent economic resources that have no physical or financial nature. They generally derive their value from the legal, intellectual, and intangible benefits they convey to the company. Companies may acquire intangibles by purchasing them from an external third party and by developing them *internally* through research and development, marketing and advertising, training of executives and personnel, developing production processes, and similar activities. Intangible resources are normally recognized as assets only when they have been acquired by a company in an external transaction. When intangible resources are developed internally, it is very difficult to measure and value them faithfully because of the lack of an exchange price. Many companies have developed valuable intangible resources, such as their human resources and intellectual capital, but these resources are not reported on the balance sheet as assets because of the difficulty in faithfully measuring their value.

The following three categories of intangible assets that have been acquired in external market transactions are commonly recognized on balance sheets:

- *Intangible Assets with Finite Useful Lives.* **Intangible assets with finite useful lives** (such as patents, franchises, licenses, and computer software) are amortized over their useful lives and reported on the balance sheet at their adjusted historical cost (historical cost minus accumulated amortization). The accumulated amortization of these intangibles is disclosed in the notes to the financial statements.
- *Intangible Assets with Indefinite Lives.* **Intangible assets with indefinite useful lives** (such as trademarks or acquired brand names) are not amortized because their potential services are indefinitely long; however, they are reviewed for impairment

[12] We discuss the accounting for leases in Chapter 20.

annually. Impairment arises when the earning power of an intangible asset has been reduced to the point where its fair value is less than its historical cost. These intangible assets are reported on the balance sheet at their historical cost or, if impaired, at their fair value, whichever is lower.

- *Goodwill.* **Goodwill** represents the purchase premium paid when one company acquires another company. In an acquisition, the acquiring company might pay a price that is greater than the fair value of the net assets acquired because the target company has valuable intangible resources (such as popular and profitable products, a good reputation with customers and employees, a skilled workforce, access to key channels of distribution for supplies or products, or other arrangements). When a company acquires goodwill through a merger or acquisition transaction, it is recognized as an asset but it is not amortized. It is reviewed for impairment annually. Goodwill is also reported on the balance sheet at its historical cost or, if impaired, at its lower fair value. **Example 4.1** shows the intangibles section of Caron Manufacturing Company's balance sheet (p. 4-15).[13]

On its 2015 balance sheet, Starbucks recognizes $1,575.4 million in Goodwill and $520.4 million in Other Intangible Assets, which primarily consist of trade names, trademarks, patents, and acquired rights. Starbucks discloses more detailed information about these intangible assets in Note 8 to the 2015 financial statements in Appendix A.

Other Assets

Other assets include miscellaneous assets that do not fit in one of the previous categories. Examples of items that are sometimes classified in this section include long-term prepayments (such as for rent, insurance, or licenses), deferred tax assets (net), assets of a component of the company that is being discontinued, advances to officers, security deposits paid by the company, and assets temporarily restricted by foreign countries.

Current Liabilities

Current liabilities are obligations that the company expects to settle or satisfy within 1 year or the normal operating cycle, whichever is longer. Companies commonly report the following types of current liabilities:

- *Payables and Accrued Expenses.* **Payables** and **accrued expenses** include accruals for obligations for items (goods or services) that have been received but not yet paid. These include, for instance, accounts payable and salaries payable. In addition, payables usually include accrued liabilities for expenses that have been incurred and will be paid in the next year or operating cycle, such as interest payable, taxes payable, and the current portion of product warranty liabilities.
- *Deferred Revenues.* **Deferred revenues** (**unearned revenues**) are performance obligations from advance payments from customers for the future delivery of goods or services. They include unearned rent and insurance premiums, prepaid tickets or airfares, and deferred revenues for gift cards (such as **Starbucks**'s stored value cards).
- *Short-Term Debt.* **Short-term debt** represents short-term financing instruments that will be paid within 1 year or the operating cycle, such as short-term borrowing from banks and commercial paper. **Current maturities of long-term debt** reflect the portions of long-term financing instruments that mature during the next year. A short-term debt obligation for which the company has both the intent and the ability to refinance by issuing new long-term debt is not classified as a current liability and instead will be classified with long-term debt.

These obligations are listed on the balance sheet at the amount owed (historical proceeds) or estimated to be owed. **Example 4.1** shows the current liabilities section of Caron Manufacturing Company's balance sheet.

---

[13] We discuss the accounting for intangible assets in Chapter 12.

Long-Term Liabilities

Long-term liabilities (**noncurrent liabilities**) are obligations that a company does not expect to settle within 1 year or the normal operating cycle (whichever is longer). Companies commonly report three types of long-term liabilities:

- *Long-Term Accruals.* Long-term accruals include accrued expenses for obligations that may be outstanding for many years. They include obligations for pension and other postemployment benefits, estimated liabilities from long-term warranties, and deferred tax liabilities.
- *Long-Term Financing Instruments.* Long-term financing instruments are formal borrowings to finance the assets and operations of the company, including long-term notes payable, capital lease obligations, mortgages payable, bonds payable, and other noncurrent financing instruments.
- *Other Liabilities.* Some companies may also report other liabilities, which include miscellaneous long-term liabilities.

Most long-term liabilities are reported at their present value, but some long-term financing instruments are reported at fair value if the company elects the fair value option. Any applicable interest rates, maturity dates, principal amounts, and other provisions are disclosed parenthetically on the balance sheet or in the notes to the financial statements. Some companies show a total amount of long-term liabilities on their balance sheets and a schedule of the individual amounts in the related notes. **Kimberly-Clark Corporation** uses this procedure for its long-term debt, as shown in Real Report 4.1.

4.1 LONG-TERM DEBT — REAL REPORT

Kimberly-Clark Corporation

Kimberly-Clark Corporation
Liabilities (in part):

(in millions)	December 31 2013	December 31 2012
Current portion of long-term debt	$ 312	$ 756
Long-term debt	5,386	5,070

Notes to Consolidated Financial Statements (in part)

Note 7. Debt
Long-term debt is comprised of the following:

	Weighted-Average Interest Rate	Maturities	December 31 2013	December 31 2012
			(in millions)	
Notes and debentures	5.2%	2014–2043	$5,163	$4,857
Dealer remarketable securities	4.2%	2014–2016	200	200
Industrial development revenue bonds	0.2%	2015–2034	261	261
Bank loans and other financings in various currencies	5.6%	2014–2025	74	508
Total long-term debt			5,698	5,826
Less current portion			312	756
Long-term portion			$5,386	$5,070

Fair value of total long-term debt at December 31, 2013 and 2012 was $6,271 million and $6,527 million, respectively. Fair values were estimated based on quoted prices for financial instruments for which all significant inputs were observable, either directly or indirectly.

Scheduled maturities of long-term debt for the next five years are $312 million in 2014, $353 million in 2015, $302 million in 2016, $962 million in 2017 and $902 million in 2018.

In May 2013, we issued $250 million aggregate principal amount of floating rate notes due May 15, 2016, $350 million aggregate principal amount of 2.4% notes due June 1, 2023, and $250 million aggregate principal amount of 3.7% notes due June 1, 2043. Proceeds from the offering were used to repay our $500 million aggregate principal amount of 5.0% notes due August 15, 2013, to fund investment in our business and for general corporate purposes.

We maintain a $1.5 billion revolving credit facility, scheduled to expire in October 2016, as well as the option to increase this facility by an additional $500 million. This facility, currently unused, supports our commercial paper program and would provide liquidity in the event our access to the commercial paper market is unavailable for any reason.

Questions:

1. What is the book value of Kimberly-Clark's total long-term debt on the 2013 balance sheet? What is the fair value? Why might book value and fair value differ?
2. What amounts of debt are scheduled to mature in each of the next 5 years?
3. How much additional debt did Kimberly-Clark issue in 2013 and for what purposes?
4. If the weighted average interest rates do not change, and the total long-term debt remains outstanding for all of 2014, how much will Kimberly-Clark incur in interest expense on that debt?

Suggested answers to these questions are found at the end of the chapter.

Conceptual Guidelines for Classifying Assets and Liabilities In the previous sections, we discussed the typical classifications of assets and liabilities in a balance sheet. A company, however, should classify its assets and liabilities in the most informative manner for its financial statement users. In addition to the current/noncurrent classifications we discussed earlier, the FASB has suggested several guidelines for developing *homogeneous classes* of assets and liabilities. These guidelines include separately reporting:

- assets and liabilities that serve different functions in the operations of the company or are subject to restrictions that affect the financial flexibility of the company (e.g., assets used in operations, assets held for investment, assets subject to restrictions, and assets intended for sale outside of the normal course of operating activities, such as assets of a segment being discontinued)
- assets and liabilities according to the method used to value the items (e.g., assets and liabilities measured at fair value versus historical cost)

These general guidelines are intended to result in asset and liability classifications that help users assess the nature, amounts, and liquidity of available resources and obligations.

Shareholders' Equity

Shareholders' equity is the residual interest of the shareholders in the assets of the corporation, after deducting the liabilities. The corporation is a separate legal entity.[14] As described in Chapter 1, usually there is separation of ownership and control, where most of the shareholders are not involved in managing the day-to-day activities of the

---

[14] A company can also be organized as a sole proprietorship or a partnership. A sole proprietorship is a single-owner company. This is usually a small company where the owner acts as manager and has direct access to the accounting records. Total owner's equity is usually summarized in a single *capital account*. A partnership involves two or more persons who have agreed to combine their capital and efforts in the operations of a company. The partnership agreement usually specifies the investment requirements, allocation of income, and withdrawal provisions for each partner. Separate capital accounts summarize each partner's equity.

corporation. To protect these owners, state laws have been established, many of which relate to the accounting for shareholders' equity. Shareholders' equity most commonly consists of two components: contributed capital and earned capital.[15] A third component can arise when equity capital is invested by noncontrolling interests.

Contributed Capital

Contributed capital is recognized when the corporation raises capital by issuing shares directly to shareholders. When the investor purchases shares on the stock market or from another investor, it does not give rise to contributed capital for the corporation. Accounting for contributed capital can involve as many as four (and sometimes more) components:

- common stock
- additional paid-in capital
- treasury stock
- preferred stock

Common Stock and Additional Paid-in Capital **Common stock** carries the right to vote (giving common shareholders control over the corporation) and to share in residual profits. The corporate charter includes the number of shares that a corporation is legally authorized to issue, as well as the types and characteristics of its common stock. Common stock is the most prevalent type of stock, and large corporations typically list their common shares for exchange on a stock market, and trading among investors establishes the market value of the shares.

Depending on state laws, a corporation may issue common stock with (1) par or stated value or (2) no-par value. Legally, some states require common stock to carry a **par value** (or **stated value**), which refers to the minimum dollar amount per share that investors are required to invest and is printed on the stock certificate.[16] Often, this par value is a very small amount because states generally do not allow a corporation to issue stock at less than par. For instance, the par value of **Starbucks**'s common stock is $0.001 per share. The par value of a share of stock has no direct relationship to the share's market value. Nonetheless, the legal (par) value must be accounted for separately, apart from other contributed capital.

When a corporation issues par value common stock, it must allocate the proceeds (market price per share times the number of shares issued) between a Common Stock at Par Value account and an Additional Paid-in Capital account for the difference between the par and the market value. This latter account can also be called Paid-in Capital in Excess of Par, or Premium on Common Stock.

Example Crosley Corporation sold 100 shares of its $5 par common stock for $30 per share. The journal entry to record the transaction is as follows:

Cash	3,000	
Common Stock, $5 par		500
Additional Paid-in Capital on Common Stock		2,500

When a corporation issues common stock with no par or stated value, the corporation records the entire amount it receives in the Common Stock account. Because of various other stock transactions, it is possible for a corporation to have multiple accounts for additional paid-in capital from differing sources, even if it issues no-par stock.

---

[15] In rare instances, a company may receive donated assets from a governmental unit or it may discover previously unrecorded assets. In either case, when the company records the asset's fair value, it also increases shareholders' equity. These items are listed separately in shareholders' equity.

[16] There are certain legal differences between par value and stated value. We discuss these in Chapter 15. Because the accounting for stated value stock generally is identical to that for par value stock, we focus here on par value stock.

Treasury Stock A corporation sometimes will repurchase some of its own common shares. When it does, the number of shares outstanding is reduced. The corporation usually records the cost to reacquire shares in a contra shareholders' equity account entitled **Treasury Stock**. This account has a debit balance, and the corporation deducts the amount from the total of contributed capital, retained earnings, and accumulated other comprehensive income to determine its total shareholders' equity.

However, be aware that some companies that repurchase common shares will not recognize a treasury stock contra account, and they will instead reduce common stock, additional paid-in capital, and retained earnings for the amount used to repurchase shares. Companies use this approach if incorporated in states that require accounting for treasury share repurchases as if the shares have been retired.

Preferred Stock Corporations may issue preferred stock in addition to common stock. **Preferred stock** has different ownership features from common stock, including the first right to a specified dividend, if one is paid. In bankruptcy, preferred stock typically has a lower priority to debt capital but a higher priority to common equity. Preferred stock is usually reported on the balance sheet in the shareholders' equity section and valued at the amount of capital raised from the preferred stock issue. In some instances, preferred shares may have a par or stated value, in which case the preferred share issue proceeds would be reported in two accounts, Preferred Stock and Additional Paid-in Capital (similar to the accounting treatment for common share issues).

Total Contributed Capital The sum of the balances in the Preferred Stock, Common Stock, and Additional Paid-in Capital accounts, minus the amount in the Treasury Stock contra account, determines the total amount of contributed capital. The par value or stated value per share, as well as the number of shares authorized, issued, and outstanding, should be disclosed either parenthetically in the contributed capital section, on the statement of shareholders' equity, or in the notes to the financial statements.

Example Starbucks reports 2.4 billion shares authorized and 1,485.1 million shares issued and outstanding at the end of fiscal 2015. Starbucks's 2015 balance sheet reports $1.5 million in Common Stock at par, plus $41.1 million in Additional Paid-in Capital. Starbucks has issued no preferred shares. When Starbucks repurchases common shares, it accounts for the repurchases as if the shares are being retired (required under Washington state law) and reduces contributed capital and retained earnings for the amount of the purchase, rather than recognizing a treasury stock account. ■

Example 4.1 shows the contributed capital section of Caron Manufacturing Company's balance sheet (p. 4-16).

Earned Capital

Earned capital always consists of retained earnings and, for some companies, accumulated other comprehensive income.

Retained Earnings **Retained earnings** is the total amount of corporate net income that has been earned but has not been distributed to shareholders as dividends. At the end of the closing process described in Chapter 3, a corporation closes its temporary accounts, adds its total net income for the period to retained earnings, and subtracts from retained earnings the dividends declared during the period. A corporation may retain the assets generated from this net income to use in its daily operations, to maintain its productive facilities, or for growth. In any event, a retained earnings balance has no relationship to the cash that is available for dividends. The resources generated by net income are invested in all assets. The Retained Earnings account balance is an addition in shareholders' equity. A negative (debit) retained earnings balance (due to cumulative net losses and/or dividends exceeding cumulative net income), called a **deficit**, is subtracted in shareholders' equity.

Sometimes a company *restricts* or *appropriates* a portion of retained earnings to indicate that it cannot be reduced by the distribution of dividends. This may occur as a result of a legal or contractual requirement. Usually, a company discloses such a restriction in the notes to its financial statements.

Example In its shareholders' equity, **Starbucks** reports retained earnings of $5,974.8 million at the end of fiscal 2015. The beginning balance in retained earnings at the start of 2015 was $5,206.6 million. It increased because of Starbucks's $2,757.4 million in net earnings, and it decreased due to $1,016.2 million in cash dividends declared, $972.2 million paid for repurchases of common stock, and a $0.8 million adjustment for a two-for-one stock split. ∎

Accumulated Other Comprehensive Income (Loss) The second component of earned capital, **accumulated other comprehensive income (loss)**, is the cumulative amount of other comprehensive income (or loss) items. As we discuss in Chapter 5, comprehensive income includes both net income and other comprehensive income items. Under U.S. GAAP, other comprehensive income items for a given period may include:

- unrealized fair value gains or losses on investments in available-for-sale securities
- translation adjustments from converting the financial statements of a company's foreign operations into U.S. dollars
- certain gains and losses on derivative financial instruments designated as cash flow hedges
- certain pension plan gains, losses, and prior service cost adjustments

Some companies may not experience any of these items. In that case, net income and comprehensive income are the same, and accumulated other comprehensive income is zero. On the other hand, larger companies may experience significant effects from all four items and may over time compile a large amount of accumulated other comprehensive income. Each of these four items will be discussed in later chapters.

The corporation accumulates the other comprehensive income (or loss) items in its Accumulated Other Comprehensive Income (Loss) account reported in shareholders' equity. If a corporation has more than one item of other comprehensive income, it may report the amount of accumulated other comprehensive income for each item in shareholders' equity separately, or it may report the total amount of accumulated other comprehensive income for all the items and then disclose the amounts for each of the items in the notes to its financial statements.[17]

Example **Starbucks**'s accumulated other comprehensive loss amounted to $-199.4 million at the end of fiscal 2015. Caron Manufacturing Company has one item of accumulated other comprehensive income, as shown in **Example 4.1** (p. 4-16). ∎

Noncontrolling Interests

Some companies will recognize a third component of shareholders' equity, known as **noncontrolling interests**. This component of equity only arises when one company (known as a *parent company*) owns a majority of the common shares of another company (known as a *subsidiary company*) but does not own 100% of the shares. In a situation like this, the parent company will consolidate 100% of the subsidiary company's financial statements with its own financial statements. In consolidating the financial statements, the parent company includes all of the assets, liabilities, and equity of the subsidiary company. However, the parent company does not own all of the equity of the subsidiary. The noncontrolling shareholders own a minority proportion of the subsidiary shares. For this reason, the parent corporation includes the Noncontrolling Interests account to recognize the amount of equity capital attributable to minority investors.

---

[17] FASB ASC 220-10-45: Comprehensive Income, Overall, Other Presentation Matters.

Example ParentCo is a large corporation that owns 77% of the shares of SubCo, a small company. Other investors own the other 23% of SubCo's shares. ParentCo's consolidated balance sheet will report all of its assets, liabilities, and equities combined with those of SubCo. The Noncontrolling Interests account recognizes that 23% of the equity invested in SubCo is attributable to other investors and is not owned by ParentCo. ∎

Example Note that in the shareholders' equity section of its 2015 balance sheet, **Starbucks** reports noncontrolling interests of $1.8 million. Accounting for intercompany investments and noncontrolling interests will be described in more depth in Chapter 13. ∎

GOT IT?

4-12 List the major sections (and the typical components of each section) of a company's balance sheet.

4-13 How are *current assets* defined, and what are the major items that may be included in current assets? How are *current liabilities* defined? Give three examples of such liabilities.

4-14 What items are classified as noncurrent assets in the following categories: (a) long-term investments; (b) property, plant, and equipment; and (c) intangible assets?

4-15 What items are classified as long-term liabilities?

4-16 What are the two most common components of shareholders' equity? How do they differ?

4-17 Define (a) *common stock*, (b) *additional paid-in capital*, (c) *treasury stock*, (d) *retained earnings*, and (e) *accumulated other comprehensive income*.

4-18 What are *noncontrolling interests*?

WHAT IS THE STATEMENT OF SHAREHOLDERS' EQUITY?

LEARNING OBJECTIVE 4.4
Prepare a statement of shareholders' equity.

When a corporation issues financial statements, it must disclose the ending balances and the changes in its shareholders' equity accounts. The SEC requires this disclosure as a separate financial statement for listed companies, but smaller companies may report it in a supporting schedule or a note to the financial statements.[18] This reporting is consistent with the FASB's suggestion that a full set of financial statements should show, among other information, investments by and distributions to owners during the period. The intent is to report on the changes in a company's financial structure to help users in assessing its financial flexibility and risk.

FASB Statement of Financial Accounting Concepts No. 6 defines investments by owners and distributions to owners as follows:

- **Investments by owners** are increases in the equity of a company resulting from transfers of something valuable to the company from other entities to obtain or increase ownership interests.
- **Distributions to owners** are decreases in the equity of a company caused by transferring assets, rendering services, or incurring liabilities to owners.

Investments by owners typically involve owners contributing assets (commonly cash) in exchange for a share of ownership in the company. However, investments by owners may include transfers of assets other than cash, services, or the conversion of liabilities of the company. Distributions by a company to its owners (such as paying cash dividends

---

[18] FASB ASC 505-10-50: Equity, Overall, Disclosure.

or repurchasing common shares) decrease its net assets and decrease or terminate ownership interests of those who receive them.[19]

To report investments by and distributions to owners, many companies prepare a **statement of shareholders' equity** (or **statement of changes in shareholders' equity**), which reports the changes in the contributed capital, treasury stock, retained earnings, accumulated other comprehensive income, noncontrolling interests (if any), as well as the ending balances. **Example 4.2** illustrates this statement for Caron Manufacturing Company. Also note that **Starbucks** reports the statement of shareholders equity in its 2015 annual report, which is in Appendix A. Note that the totals of the columns in the statements of shareholders' equity are the same as those shown in the shareholders' equity section of the balance sheet.

EXAMPLE 4.2

Statement of Shareholders' Equity

Schedule A
Caron Manufacturing Company
Statement of Shareholders' Equity
For Year Ended December 31, 2016

	Common Stock, $5 par	Additional Paid-In Capital	Retained Earnings	Accumulated Other Comprehensive Income	Total
Balance, January 1, 2016	$65,000	$143,400	$ 64,900	$10,000	$283,300
Unrealized gain in fair value of available-for-sale securities				2,000	2,000
Net income			62,500		62,500
Cash dividends paid			(11,200)		(11,200)
Common stock issued	6,500	30,500			37,000
Balance, December 31, 2016	$71,500	$173,900	$116,200	$12,000	$373,600

GOT IT?

4-19 What is the purpose of the statement of shareholders' equity?

4-20 What are *investments by owners*? *Distributions to owners*?

LEARNING OBJECTIVE 4.5
Understand balance sheet disclosure issues.

ADDITIONAL BALANCE SHEET DISCLOSURES

A company cannot report all the relevant financial information about its financial position and activities directly in the body of the financial statements because some items do not meet the recognition criteria discussed earlier in the chapter. As indicated throughout the balance sheet discussion, a company may make many disclosures in the notes accompanying its financial statements.

Summary of Accounting Policies

To understand a company's financial statements, external users need to know the company's accounting policies, practices, and methods. For this reason, GAAP requires the company to disclose in the notes to the annual report a description of all its significant

---

[19] *FASB Statement of Financial Accounting Concepts No. 6, op. cit.*, par. 66–69.

accounting policies. The disclosure should include principles relating to revenue recognition and asset allocation, particularly when these principles and methods are:

- choices from existing acceptable alternatives
- peculiar to the industry in which the company operates
- unusual or innovative applications of GAAP

Notes to the financial statements usually disclose accounting policies related to the basis of presentation, revenue recognition, depreciation methods, amortization of intangibles, inventory, recognition of profits on long-term contracts, and many others. These disclosures are particularly useful, so companies often disclose a note titled *Summary of Significant Accounting Policies* as the very first note to the financial statements.[20] Appendix A contains the notes to **Starbucks**'s 2015 financial statements, including Note 1, *Summary of Significant Accounting Policies*.

Fair Value and Risk of Financial Instruments

Some companies, particularly financial services firms like banks, insurers, and brokerage firms, deal in financial instruments. These **financial instruments** include plain vanilla items such as stocks, bonds, and notes payable and receivable, but they may also include more exotic instruments such as contracts for loan commitments, collateralized mortgages, interest-rate swaps, and put and call options on stocks. Because of the prevalence and variety of the types and uses of financial instruments, U.S. GAAP requires companies to disclose in the notes the fair values of all financial instruments (assets and liabilities), whether or not they are measured at fair value on its balance sheet. Companies are also required to disclose all significant concentrations of credit risk due to its financial instruments.

GAAP also requires companies to report all derivative financial instruments as either assets or liabilities on its balance sheet and to measure these items at their fair value. A **derivative financial instrument** derives its value from changes in the price of the underlying resource to which it is linked. For example, a stock option gives the holder the right to buy stock at a specified price, so the value of the stock option depends on (is derived from) the market price of the underlying stock. Companies are also required to disclose information such as the types of derivative instruments held, objectives in holding the instruments, and strategies for achieving these objectives. The description must indicate the company's risk management policy in regard to each type of instrument. These disclosures are designed to improve the reporting of a company's risk, liquidity, and financial flexibility.

As mentioned earlier, GAAP provides companies the option to report certain financial assets and financial liabilities at fair value on its balance sheet. If a company elects this option, it must separate them from those similar financial assets and liabilities that are reported using another measurement attribute (e.g., historical cost). Also, the company must report any unrealized gains or losses resulting from changes in the fair value of these items in earnings on its income statement.[21]

Loss and Gain Contingencies

On the balance sheet date, certain situations may exist that create uncertainty as to possible losses or gains that the company may incur if some future event occurs or fails to occur. These are known as **loss contingencies** or **gain contingencies**, and they may need to be recognized directly in the company's financial statements or disclosed in an accompanying note.[22]

---

[20] FASB ASC 235-10-50: Notes to Financial Statements, Overall, Disclosure.

[21] FASB ASC 825-10-50: Financial Instruments, Overall, Disclosure. We discuss required and elected fair value reporting and disclosures more fully in Chapters 6, 13, and 14.

[22] We discuss loss and gain contingencies further in Chapter 9. FASB ASC 450-10-50: Contingencies, Overall, Overview and Background.

A contingent gain could arise, for example, if a company entered into a contract to sell a piece of land (which would trigger a gain) in which the buyer will only purchase the land if the buyer receives a change in municipal zoning restrictions. Because of the uncertainty about whether they will be realized, gain contingencies are not recognized in a company's financial statements until they are realized. If contingent gains are disclosed in a note, they should be carefully explained to avoid misleading implications as to the likelihood of future revenues or gains.

Loss contingencies are much more common, including examples such as product warranties, uncollectible accounts receivable, guarantees of another company's debt, and pending litigation against the company. Companies must accrue a loss and a liability (or an asset impairment) from a loss contingency if:

- it is *probable* that a liability has been incurred (or an asset impaired) and
- the amount of the loss can be *reasonably estimated*

If either of these conditions is *not* met, the company must disclose the loss contingency in the notes to its financial statements. Exhibit 4.2 illustrates the alternative ways of accounting for loss contingencies.

EXHIBIT 4.2 Recognize or Disclose Loss Contingencies

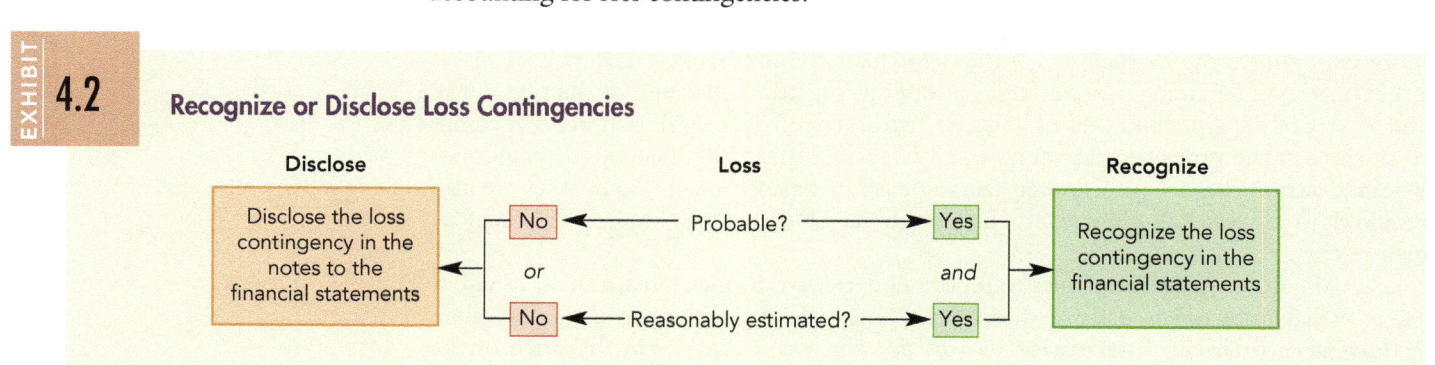

Recognition and disclosure of loss contingencies helps external users predict the company's future use of its financial resources. Quantitative information disclosed would include the amount of any claims against the company, the company's best estimate of the maximum exposure to losses, and a tabulation of its recognized loss contingencies. Qualitative disclosures would include a description of the contingency, factors that are likely to affect the ultimate outcome, an assessment of the most likely outcome, and the terms of relevant insurance.[23] Examples of a loss contingency that are commonly disclosed in the notes to the financial statements include guarantees of the debts of others and pending litigation against the company, when either the outcome of the litigation or the amount of possible loss is uncertain. An illustration of this type of contingency for **Apple Inc.** is shown in Real Report 4.2.

REAL REPORT 4.2 CONTINGENCY

Apple Inc.

Notes to Financial Statements (in part)

Note 10. Commitments and Contingencies
The Company is subject to various legal proceedings and claims that have arisen in the ordinary course of business and that have not been fully adjudicated. In the opinion of management, there was not at least a reasonable possibility the Company may have

---

[23] FASB ASC 450-10-50: Contingencies, Overall, Overview and Background and FASB ASC 450-10-20: Contingencies, Overall, Disclosure.

incurred a material loss, or a material loss in excess of a recorded accrual, with respect to loss contingencies. However, the outcome of litigation is inherently uncertain. Therefore, although management considers the likelihood of such an outcome to be remote, if one or more of these legal matters were resolved against the Company in a reporting period for amounts in excess of management's expectations, the Company's consolidated financial statements for that reporting period could be materially adversely affected.

Apple Inc. v. Samsung Electronics Co., Ltd, et al.
On August 24, 2012, a jury returned a verdict awarding the Company $1.05 billion in its lawsuit against Samsung Electronics Co., Ltd and affiliated parties in the United States District Court, Northern District of California, San Jose Division. On March 1, 2013, the District Court upheld $599 million of the jury's award and ordered a new trial as to the remainder. Because the award is subject to entry of final judgment, partial re-trial and appeal, the Company has not recognized the award in its results of operations.

VirnetX, Inc. v. Apple Inc., et al.
On August 11, 2010, VirnetX, Inc. filed an action against the Company alleging that certain of its products infringed on four patents relating to network communications technology. On November 6, 2012, a jury returned a verdict against the Company, and awarded damages of $368 million. The Company is challenging the verdict, believes it has valid defenses and has not recorded a loss accrual at this time.

Questions:

1. The contingency involves two legal cases involving Apple Inc. In the first case, a jury awarded Apple $599 million in its lawsuit against Samsung. In the second case, the jury ruled against Apple, awarding $368 million in damages to VirnetX, Inc. As of the end of fiscal 2013, Apple has recognized neither a contingent gain for the Samsung award, nor a contingent loss for the VirnetX case. How does Apple explain the lack of recognition for the contingent loss?
2. Does Apple explain the lack of recognition for the contingent gain? If not, why has Apple not recognized this gain as of the end of fiscal 2013?

Suggested answers to these questions are found at the end of the chapter.

Subsequent Events

A company usually does not issue its annual report for several weeks or months after the end of the accounting period because of the time needed for adjusting and closing the books and auditing the financial statements. During this time, it is possible for significant business events and transactions to occur that, if not disclosed in the company's annual report, would cause this report to be misleading.

A **subsequent event** is one that occurs between a company's balance sheet date and the date when it issues its annual report, as shown below.

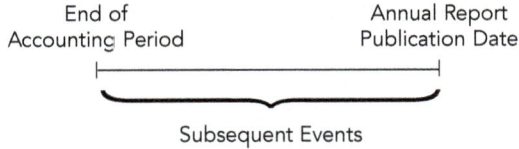

The company must make an adjustment to the financial statements if a subsequent event occurs that:

- provides additional evidence about conditions that *existed* on the balance sheet date
- significantly affects the estimate(s) used in preparing the company's financial statements

For instance, if a company obtains new information indicating that a major customer's account receivable is unlikely to be collected, it makes an adjustment to the allowance for doubtful accounts and the bad debt expense.

When a subsequent event occurs that provides evidence concerning conditions that did *not* exist on the company's balance sheet date but instead occurred after that date, the company does *not* adjust its financial statements. Instead, the information is disclosed in a note, in a pro forma ("as if") statement, or in an explanatory paragraph in the audit report, depending upon the materiality of the financial impact. Examples of these events include a fire or flood loss, a litigation settlement, and the sale of a bond or stock issue after the balance sheet date.

Real Report 4.3 presents an excerpt from **Starbucks**'s 2013 Annual Report, including discussion of a contingent loss that triggered a subsequent event for the fiscal year 2013.

4.3 | CONTINGENT LOSS AND SUBSEQUENT EVENT | REAL REPORT

Starbucks

Notes to Financial Statements (in part)

Note 15. Commitments and Contingencies

Legal Proceedings

In the first quarter of fiscal 2011, Starbucks notified Kraft Foods Group, Inc. ("Kraft") that we were discontinuing our distribution arrangement with Kraft on March 1, 2011 due to material breaches by Kraft of its obligations under the Supply and License Agreement between the Company and Kraft, dated March 29, 2004 (the "Agreement"), which defined the main distribution arrangement between the parties. Through our arrangement with Kraft, Starbucks sold a selection of Starbucks and Seattle's Best Coffee branded packaged coffees in grocery and warehouse club stores throughout the US, and to grocery stores in Canada, the UK and other European countries. Kraft managed the distribution, marketing, advertising and promotion of these products.

Kraft denied it had materially breached the Agreement. On November 29, 2010, Starbucks received a notice of arbitration from Kraft putting the commercial dispute between the parties into binding arbitration pursuant to the terms of the Agreement. In addition to denying it materially breached the Agreement, Kraft further alleged that if Starbucks wished to terminate the Agreement it must compensate Kraft as provided in the Agreement in an amount equal to the fair value of the Agreement, with an additional premium of up to 35% under certain circumstances.

We believe we had valid claims of material breach by Kraft under the Agreement that allowed us to terminate the Agreement and certain other relationships with Kraft without compensation to Kraft. Although Kraft disclosed to the press and in federal court filings a $750 million offer Starbucks made to Kraft in August 2010 to avoid litigation and ensure a smooth transition of the business, the figure was not a proper basis upon which to estimate a possible outcome of the arbitration but was based upon facts and circumstances at the time. Kraft rejected the offer immediately and did not provide a counter-offer, effectively ending the discussions between the parties with regard to any payment. Moreover, the offer was made prior to our investigation of Kraft's breaches and without consideration of Kraft's continuing failure to comply with material terms of the agreements. As a result, prior to receiving the arbitrator's ruling we could not reasonably estimate the possible loss. Accordingly, no loss contingency was recorded for this matter.

On November 12, 2013, the arbitrator ordered Starbucks to pay Kraft $2,227.5 million in damages plus prejudgment interest and attorneys' fees. We have estimated prejudgment interest, which includes an accrual through the estimated payment date, and attorneys' fees to be approximately $556.6 million. As a result, we recorded a litigation charge of $2,784.1 million in our fiscal 2013 operating results.

Questions:
1. What is the basis for the dispute between Kraft and Starbucks?
2. Why did Starbucks not recognize a loss for this litigation dispute prior to the arbitrator's ruling?
3. How much did the arbitrator order Starbucks to pay Kraft?
4. The arbitrator ruled on November 12, 2013, and Starbucks's fiscal year ended on September 29, 2013. Starbucks recognized the loss from the litigation charge and the related liability in its 2013 financial statements. By treating this as a subsequent event, are Starbucks's 2013 financial statements more or less representationally faithful than if Starbucks had merely disclosed the litigation charge in the notes?

Suggested answers to these questions are found at the end of the chapter.

Related Party Transactions

Related party transactions frequently occur in the normal course of business. Related parties of a company include affiliated entities such as subsidiaries, trusts for the benefit of employees, its management and board of directors, and its principal owners or immediate families. Relationships between related parties may enable one of the parties to influence the other so that it is given preferential treatment. To provide sufficient information for external users to understand a company's financial statements, GAAP requires certain disclosures by the company. For related party transactions, these include the following:

- nature of the relationship involved
- description of the transactions
- dollar amounts of the transactions
- any amounts due to or from the related parties on the balance sheet date[24]

Comparative Financial Statements

Many external users are interested in comparing the current financial statements with those of prior years in order to identify trends in the company's financial position and performance. For this reason, nearly all companies present **comparative financial statements** for the current and preceding accounting periods. The annual report for Starbucks in Appendix A provides comparative financial statements, including the balance sheets for 2 years, and the income statements, statements of cash flows, and statements of shareholders' equity for 3 years.

Selected Financial Data In addition to comparative financial statements, many companies will present a supplemental schedule with a summary of key accounting information for, say, the past 5 to 10 years. The SEC requires *specific* disclosures for a *5-year period*. These include net sales or operating revenues, income (loss) from continuing operations and related earnings per share, total assets, long-term obligations and redeemable stock, and cash dividends declared per share. The SEC encourages the inclusion of other information that will help users understand and highlight trends. Appendix A also contains Starbucks's disclosure of a 5-year history of Selected Financial Data, which includes the items required by the SEC as well as other information about the numbers and types of coffee shops and comparable store growth rates.

Common Stock Market Prices and Dividends The SEC also requires several disclosures about company stock prices and dividends. These include the principal trading markets for the company's common stock, high and low market prices for each quarter in the last 2 years, approximate number of shareholders, the dividends paid in the last 2 years, and any dividend restrictions.

---

[24] FASB ASC 850-10-50: Related Party Disclosures, Overall, Disclosure.

> ### GOT IT?
>
> **4-21** What accounting policies are disclosed in the notes accompanying a company's financial statements? Why is this disclosure important?
>
> **4-22** Give several examples of financial instruments and identify the required disclosures for a company's financial instruments.
>
> **4-23** What is a loss *contingency*? What criteria have to be met for a company to accrue a loss contingency? If these criteria are not met, how does a company disclose a loss contingency?
>
> **4-24** Why is it necessary for a company to disclose subsequent events? What kinds of subsequent events are recognized in the company's financial statements, and what kinds are disclosed in a note?
>
> **4-25** What must a company disclose for related party transactions?
>
> **4-26** Why are comparative financial statements important?

LEARNING OBJECTIVE 4.6

Apply financial statement analysis techniques to analyze balance sheet information.

HOW DO WE ANALYZE BALANCE SHEET INFORMATION?

As an accounting professional, it is important to have a good understanding of how users analyze and interpret financial statement information. This section describes various tools of financial analysis using balance sheet information. In Chapter 5, we describe analysis techniques using information from income statements and statements of cash flows. Exhibit 4.3 depicts several financial statement analysis approaches.

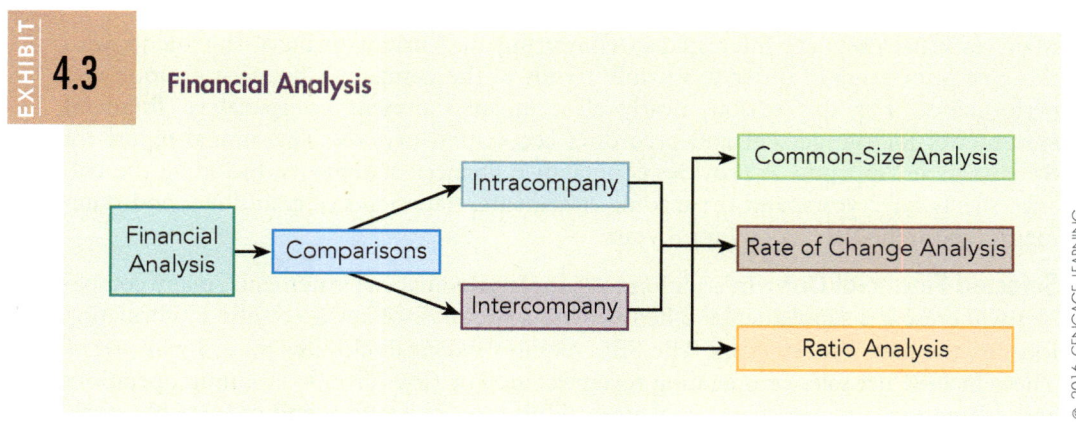

EXHIBIT 4.3 Financial Analysis

After carefully reading a company's financial statements, users typically conduct further analyses using the techniques we describe in this chapter and the next. Financial statement analysis techniques help users identify relationships between and among financial statements, reveal trends over time, and make comparisons between companies. With these analyses, financial statements users can gain very useful information for investing and lending decisions and for assessing the amounts, timing, and uncertainty of a company's future cash flows. Financial statement analysis helps users assess a company's return on investment, risk, liquidity, financial flexibility, and operating capabilities.

Intracompany and Intercompany Comparisons

One method of evaluating a company's current financial performance and condition is to analyze the company over time, sometimes called **time-series analysis**. This analysis involves **intracompany comparisons** because the company today is compared to itself in prior periods. This type of comparison reveals trends—indications of whether a company's financial position and performance are stable, improving, or deteriorating, not only in recent periods but also over the longer run. A critical point when conducting financial statement analysis for intracompany comparisons is the need for *consistency* in accounting methods and principles over time, so that valid comparisons can be made.

A second method of evaluation is to compare a company's performance with that of key competitors, with the industry averages, or with the results in related industries. This is known as **cross-sectional analysis**, and it involves **intercompany comparisons**, which may be made for a single period or for several periods. A competitor's financial information may be obtained from its respective financial statements. Information on the financial position and performance of the industry as a whole or of related industries may be based on compilations of financial information by such companies as **Moody's**, **Standard and Poor's**, and **Dun & Bradstreet**.

A financial statement analyst is concerned not only with consistency over time, but also with *comparability* of data across companies. No two companies are exactly alike, and perfect apples-to-apples comparisons do not exist. Differences in business strategies, product mix, markets and customers, and many other factors make intercompany comparisons interesting and challenging. It is also essential for users to read the financial statement notes to understand the similarities and differences in the accounting methods used by the companies being compared. Different accounting practices (such as LIFO versus FIFO for inventory costing or accelerated versus straight-line depreciation) can trigger very different results across companies. When analyzing financial statement data across companies, users must take into account differences in business strategies and accounting practices in order to draw correct inferences from *common-size analysis*, *rate of change analysis*, and *ratio analysis*.

Common-Size Analysis

In **common-size analysis**, financial statement users compute the percentage amounts of each item on the financial statement relative to the relevant total for that statement. Common-size analysis of balance sheet information expresses the asset, liability, and equity amounts as percentages of total assets. A common-size balance sheet reveals the proportions each asset represents of total assets and the proportions of financing provided by each type of liability and equity account. Common-size analysis of income statement information expresses all of the amounts as percentages of total revenues. Common-size income statements reveal profit margins as a percentage of total revenues. For example, net income as a percent of total revenues is the net profit margin. When analysts use common-size analysis for comparisons of financial statements over several periods, they can easily identify trends or changes in the relationships between items.

Example: Analyzing Starbucks's Balance Sheets: Common-Size Analysis

Exhibit 4.4 presents **Starbucks**'s balance sheet information for the fiscal year-ends 2013, 2014, and 2015 in amounts in millions of dollars and in common-size percentages. These common-size percentages reveal that cash decreased from 22.4% of total assets in 2013 to 12.3% in 2015. During the same period, property and equipment (net of accumulated depreciation) increased from 27.8% of total assets in 2013 to 32.8% in 2015. The common-size percentages also reveal a change in Starbucks's capital structure, with total liabilities declining from 61.1% of total assets in 2013 to 53.2% in 2015, whereas total equity increased from 38.9% to 46.8% over the same period. ■

Rate of Change Analysis

In **rate of change analysis**, a financial statement user computes the percentage rates of change in a company's financial position and performance *over time*. This method is frequently used to compute growth rates in items reported on the balance sheet and on the income statement. Rate of change analysis enables users to identify which items on the balance sheet and income statement are growing quickly or slowly.

EXHIBIT 4.4 Starbucks's Consolidated Balance Sheets: Common-Size Analyses

	Dollar Amounts in Millions			Common-Sized		
	2013	2014	2015	2013	2014	2015
Assets						
Current Assets						
Cash and Cash Equivalents	$ 2,575.7	$ 1,708.4	$ 1,530.1	22.4%	15.9%	12.3%
Short-Term Investments	658.1	135.4	81.3	5.7%	1.3%	0.7%
Accounts Receivable, net	561.4	631.0	719.0	4.9%	5.9%	5.8%
Inventories	1,111.2	1,090.9	1,306.4	9.6%	10.1%	10.5%
Prepaid Expenses and Other Current Assets	287.7	285.6	334.2	2.5%	2.7%	2.7%
Deferred Income Taxes, net	277.3	317.4	381.7	2.4%	3.0%	3.1%
Total Current Assets	$ 5,471.4	$ 4,168.7	$ 4,352.7	47.5%	38.8%	35.0%
Long-Term Investments	58.3	318.4	312.5	0.5%	3.0%	2.5%
Equity and Cost Investments	496.5	514.9	352.0	4.3%	4.8%	2.8%
Property, Plant and Equipment, Gross	7,782.1	8,581.1	9,641.8	67.6%	79.8%	77.5%
Accumulated Depreciation	(4,581.6)	(5,062.1)	(5,553.5)	−39.8%	−47.1%	−44.6%
Property, Plant and Equipment, net	3,200.5	3,519.0	4,088.3	27.8%	32.7%	32.8%
Deferred Income Taxes, net	967.0	903.3	828.9	8.4%	8.4%	6.7%
Other Long-Term Assets	185.3	198.9	415.9	1.6%	1.8%	3.3%
Other Intangible Assets	274.8	273.5	520.4	2.4%	2.5%	4.2%
Goodwill	862.9	856.2	1,575.4	7.5%	8.0%	12.7%
Total Assets	$ 11,516.7	$ 10,752.9	$ 12,446.1	100.0%	100.0%	100.0%
Liabilities and Shareholders' Equity						
Current Liabilities						
Accounts Payable	$ 491.7	$ 533.7	$ 684.2	4.3%	5.0%	5.5%
Accrued Litigation Charge	2,784.1	—	—	24.2%	0.0%	0.0%
Accrued Liabilities	1,269.3	1,514.4	1,760.7	11.0%	14.1%	14.1%
Insurance Reserves	178.5	196.1	224.8	1.5%	1.8%	1.8%
Stored Value Card Liability	653.7	794.5	983.8	5.7%	7.4%	7.9%
Total Current Liabilities	$ 5,377.3	$ 3,038.7	$ 3,653.5	46.7%	28.3%	29.4%
Long-Term Debt	1,299.4	2,048.3	2,347.5	11.3%	19.0%	18.9%
Other Long-Term Liabilities	357.7	392.2	625.3	3.1%	3.6%	5.0%
Total Liabilities	$ 7,034.4	$ 5,479.2	$ 6,626.3	61.1%	51.0%	53.2%
Shareholders' Equity						
Common Stock	0.8	0.7	1.5	0.0%	0.0%	0.0%
Additional Paid-In Capital	282.1	39.4	41.1	2.4%	0.4%	0.3%
Retained Earnings	4,130.3	5,206.6	5,974.8	35.9%	48.4%	48.0%
Accumulated Other Comprehensive Income/(Loss)	67.0	25.3	(199.4)	0.6%	0.2%	−1.6%
Total Shareholders' Equity	$ 4,480.2	$ 5,272.0	$ 5,818.0	38.9%	49.0%	46.7%
Noncontrolling Interest	2.1	1.7	1.8	0.0%	0.0%	0.0%
Total Equity	$ 4,482.3	$ 5,273.7	$ 5,819.8	38.9%	49.0%	46.8%
Total Liabilities and Equity	$ 11,516.7	$ 10,752.9	$ 12,446.1	100.0%	100.0%	100.0%

To compute rates of change, the current year amount for each financial statement item is computed as a percentage rate of change from the prior year amount. When analyzing data for multiple years, the percentage rate of change from year to year is computed for each year.

Example Starbucks's total assets were $11,516.7 million, $10,752.9 million, and $12,446.1 million in 2013, 2014, and 2015, respectively. This implies Starbucks's total assets shrunk by −6.6% from 2013 to 2014 [($10,752.9 million − $11,516.7 million) ÷ $11,516.7 million] and then grew at a rate of 15.7% from 2014 to 2015 [($12,446.1 million − $10,752.9 million) ÷ $10,752.9 million]. ∎

To compute a compound annual rate of growth over a 3-year period, divide the most recent year amount (say, 2015) by the base year amount (say, 2013). Take the square root of the result. From that result, subtract 1 and then multiply by 100 to convert it to the compound percentage rate of growth over that period.[25]

Example To illustrate, we compute the compound rate of change in **Starbucks**'s total assets from 2013 to 2015. For Starbucks, total assets amounted to $11,516.7 million at the end of fiscal 2013 and $12,446.1 million at the end of 2015. Dividing produces the following result: $12,446.1 million ÷ $11,516.7 million = 1.081. Taking the square root of this result, $\sqrt[0.5]{1.081} = 1.040$. After converting to a percentage, Starbucks generated a 4.0% compounded annual growth in total assets from 2013 to 2015. This is computed as $1.040 - 1 = 0.040$; $0.040 \times 100 = 4.0\%$ growth. ∎

When computing and analyzing rates of change, users must interpret them carefully. If a base figure is zero or negative, although an *amount* of change can be determined, it cannot be expressed as a valid percentage change because dividing by zero or a negative number is meaningless. Also, it is not meaningful to add or subtract percentage growth rates for different financial statement items because the percentage growth rates result from the use of different bases. Finally, for items with small base amounts, a relatively small dollar change may result in a very high percentage rate of change, thus potentially making the item appear more significant than may be warranted.

Example: Analyzing Starbucks's Balance Sheet: Rates of Change

Exhibit 4.5 presents **Starbucks**'s balance sheet information for the fiscal year-ends 2013, 2014, and 2015 in amounts in millions of dollars and rates of change. For the rates of change, we present the year-to-year rates of change for 2013 to 2014, and 2014 to 2015, as well as the compound rates of change from 2013 to 2015. Notice how total assets grew at a compound rate of 4.0% from 2013 to 2015, with the fastest growth occurring in long-term investments and goodwill. These growth rates also confirm the change in Starbucks's capital structure during this period, with total liabilities shrinking at a compound rate of −2.9% and total equity growing at a compound rate of 13.9%. ∎

Ratio Analysis

Analysts also compute and interpret **financial statement analysis ratios**. Ratios represent relationships between and among items on financial statements. They are useful indicators of financial position and performance, serving as benchmarks against which to compare a company's results over time and against its competitors to evaluate its effectiveness. Financial statement analysis ratios are used by many different external users in intracompany and intercompany comparisons for many economic decisions.

Ratios are computed by dividing one or more items on the financial statements by another related item or items. Many different ratios exist.[26] In this discussion, however, we focus on the most frequently used ratios to evaluate a company's:

- return on investment
- risk
- liquidity
- financial flexibility
- operating capability

In this chapter, we discuss ratios that primarily (but not exclusively) utilize balance sheet data. In the next chapter, we discuss ratios that primarily use income statement data.

---

[25] To compute a compound rate of change over a 5-year period (say, from 2011 to 2015), follow the same procedures, but take the fourth root of the result rather than the square root (because a 5-year period spans 4 years of change).

[26] In addition to the standard ratios described in this chapter, financial statement users compute many other ratios to capture unique aspects of different industries or individual companies.

EXHIBIT 4.5 Starbucks's Consolidated Balance Sheets: Rate of Change Analyses

	Dollar Amounts in Millions			Rates of Change		
	2013	2014	2015	2014	2015	Compound
Assets						
Current Assets						
Cash and Cash Equivalents	$ 2,575.7	$ 1,708.4	$ 1,530.1	−33.7%	−10.4%	−22.9%
Short-Term Investments	658.1	135.4	81.3	−79.4%	−40.0%	−64.9%
Accounts Receivable, net	561.4	631.0	719.0	12.4%	13.9%	13.2%
Inventories	1,111.2	1,090.9	1,306.4	−1.8%	19.8%	8.4%
Prepaid Expenses and Other Current Assets	287.7	285.6	334.2	−0.7%	17.0%	7.8%
Deferred Income Taxes, net	277.3	317.4	381.7	14.5%	20.3%	17.3%
Total Current Assets	$ 5,471.4	$ 4,168.7	$ 4,352.7	−23.8%	4.4%	−10.8%
Long-Term Investments	58.3	318.4	312.5	446.1%	−1.9%	131.5%
Equity and Cost Investments	496.5	514.9	352.0	3.7%	−31.6%	−15.8%
Property, Plant and Equipment, Gross	7,782.1	8,581.1	9,641.8	10.3%	12.4%	11.3%
Accumulated Depreciation	(4,581.6)	(5,062.1)	(5,553.5)	10.5%	9.7%	10.1%
Property, Plant and Equipment, net	3,200.5	3,519.0	4,088.3	10.0%	16.2%	13.0%
Deferred Income Taxes, net	967.0	903.3	828.9	−6.6%	−8.2%	−7.4%
Other Long-Term Assets	185.3	198.9	415.9	7.3%	109.1%	49.8%
Other Intangible Assets	274.8	273.5	520.4	−0.5%	90.3%	37.6%
Goodwill	862.9	856.2	1,575.4	−0.8%	84.0%	35.1%
Total Assets	$ 11,516.7	$ 10,752.9	$ 12,446.1	−6.6%	15.7%	4.0%
Liabilities and Shareholders' Equity						
Current Liabilities						
Accounts Payable	$ 491.7	$ 533.7	$ 684.2	8.5%	28.2%	18.0%
Accrued Litigation Charge	2,784.1	–	–	−100.0%	na	na
Accrued Liabilities	1,269.3	1,514.4	1,760.7	19.3%	16.3%	17.8%
Insurance Reserves	178.5	196.1	224.8	9.9%	14.6%	12.2%
Stored Value Card Liability	653.7	794.5	983.8	21.5%	23.8%	22.7%
Total Current Liabilities	$ 5,377.3	$ 3,038.7	$ 3,653.5	−43.5%	20.2%	−17.6%
Long-Term Debt	1,299.4	2,048.3	2,347.5	57.6%	14.6%	34.4%
Other Long-Term Liabilities	357.7	392.2	625.3	9.6%	59.4%	32.2%
Total Liabilities	$ 7,034.4	$ 5,479.2	$ 6,626.3	−22.1%	20.9%	−2.9%
Shareholders' Equity						
Common Stock	0.8	0.7	1.5	−12.5%	114.3%	36.9%
Additional Paid-In Capital	282.1	39.4	41.1	−86.0%	4.3%	−61.8%
Retained Earnings	4,130.3	5,206.6	5,974.8	26.1%	14.8%	20.3%
Accumulated Other Comprehensive Income/(Loss)	67.0	25.3	(199.4)	−62.2%	−888.1%	na
Total Shareholders' Equity	$ 4,480.2	$ 5,272.0	$ 5,818.0	17.7%	10.4%	14.0%
Noncontrolling Interest	2.1	1.7	1.8	−19.0%	5.9%	−7.4%
Total Equity	$ 4,482.3	$ 5,273.7	$ 5,819.8	17.7%	10.4%	13.9%
Total Liabilities and Equity	$ 11,516.7	$ 10,752.9	$ 12,446.1	−6.6%	15.7%	4.0%

Return on Investment

The **rate of return on investment** measures how profitably a company uses its resources. Commonly computed ratios that measure return on investment include the *return on assets* and *return on common equity*. **Example 4.3** includes the return on investment formulas and ratios for **Starbucks** for 2014 and 2015. Refer to this information for the calculations that follow.

EXAMPLE 4.3

Starbucks Financial Statement Analysis: Return on Investment Ratios

Ratio	Formula	2014	2015
Return on Assets	$\dfrac{\text{Net Income (including income attributable to noncontrolling interests)} + [\text{Interest Expense} \times (1 - \text{Tax Rate})]}{\text{Average Total Assets}}$	$= \dfrac{\$2{,}067.7 + \left[\$64.1 \times \left(1 - \dfrac{\$1{,}092.0}{\$3{,}159.7}\right)\right]}{(\$11{,}516.7 + \$10{,}752.9)/2}$ $= 18.9\%$	$= \dfrac{\$2{,}759.3 + \left[\$70.5 \times \left(1 - \dfrac{\$1{,}143.7}{\$3{,}903.0}\right)\right]}{(\$10{,}752.9 + \$12{,}446.1)/2}$ $= 24.2\%$
Return on Common Equity	$\dfrac{\text{Net Income}}{\text{Average Total Common Equity}}$	$= \dfrac{\$2{,}068.1}{(\$4{,}480.2 + \$5{,}272.0)/2}$ $= 42.4\%$	$= \dfrac{\$2{,}757.4}{(\$5{,}272.0 + \$5{,}818.0)/2}$ $= 49.7\%$

Return on Assets **Return on assets** measures how profitably a company uses its assets and is computed as follows:

$$\text{Return on Assets} = \frac{\text{Net Income (including income attributable to noncontrolling interests)} + [\text{Interest Expense} \times (1 - \text{Tax Rate})]}{\text{Average Total Assets}}$$

Because net income is earned over the entire period, we use the *average* total assets [(Beginning + Ending Total Assets) ÷ 2] as the denominator. To measure net income generated by asset utilization, we adjust *total* net income (net income before subtracting any income attributable to noncontrolling interests) by adding back interest expense, after the income tax savings associated with interest expense.[27]

We add back after-tax interest expense [Interest Expense × (1 − Tax Rate)] to net income because interest expense is a cost of financing, rather than a cost of using assets to operate the business. Average total assets in the denominator include all of the resources of the company (whether financed with equity, debt, or noncontrolling interests). To be consistent, net income in the numerator should include all of the income generated by those assets, before considering the effects of any financing costs (such as interest expense on debt or earnings attributable to noncontrolling interests).

Example Refer to **Example 4.3**. For 2014, **Starbucks** generated net income (before deducting income attributable to noncontrolling interests) of $2,067.7 million. It incurred $64.1 million in interest expense before tax effects. Starbucks experienced an effective tax rate of 34.6% in 2014 (computed as the tax provision of $1,092.0 million ÷ $3,159.7 million of income before tax). The after-tax interest expense is therefore $41.9 million [$64.1 million × (1 − 0.346 tax rate)]. Adding this amount back to net income indicates Starbucks generated $2,109.6 million ($2,067.7 million + $41.9 million) in income before financing expenses. Dividing that amount by the average total assets of $11,134.8 million [($11,516.7 million + $10,752.9 million) ÷ 2] yields a return on assets in 2014 of 18.9%. This ratio reveals that in 2014 Starbucks was very profitable, generating 18.9 cents in profits (before financing charges) for every average dollar of assets it used during 2014. ■

---

[27] After-tax interest expense is usually computed by multiplying the pretax interest expense by 1 minus the effective income tax rate. The effective tax rate is computed by dividing the income tax provision by income before taxes.

Example 4.3 also shows that in 2015, using the same formula, Starbucks generated an impressive 24.2% return on assets—even more profitable than in 2014. Starbucks clearly used its assets very profitably in 2014 and 2015. ∎

Return on Common Equity

Another insightful measure of return on investment is the return on common equity. **Return on common equity** measures the profitability of the company relative to the amount of equity capital invested by the common shareholders. It is computed as follows:

$$\text{Return on Common Equity} = \frac{\text{Net Income}}{\text{Average Total Common Shareholders' Equity}}$$

When this return is higher than the return on total assets, the company is effectively using financial leverage to generate higher returns for shareholders. As with the computation of return on assets, we use *average* shareholders' equity in the denominator. The return on common equity is informative because it relates the bottom line of the income statement (net income) to the bottom line of the balance sheet—the amount of equity capital invested by the common shareholders.

Example Refer to Example 4.3. As noted, for 2014, **Starbucks** generated net income of $2,068.1 million. Note that in computing the return on common equity we use the net income figure that excludes the income attributable to noncontrolling interests, in order to include only the income attributable to Starbucks's shareholders. Dividing that amount by the average total common shareholders' equity (excluding noncontrolling interests) of $4,876.1 million [($4,480.2 million + $5,272.0 million) ÷ 2] yields a return on common equity in 2014 of 42.4%. Interpreting this result, for every dollar of equity capital invested by common shareholders during 2014, Starbucks generated $0.424 of profits—an impressive rate of return. ∎

Example 4.3 also shows that in 2015, Starbucks generated an even more impressive 49.7% return on common equity. Starbucks's shareholders are likely very pleased with this very profitable performance. ∎

Risk and Financial Flexibility Ratios

Financial statement users evaluate risk and financial flexibility ratios to assess the leverage and long-run solvency of a company. These ratios are complementary: greater risk usually implies less financial flexibility, and vice versa. These ratios provide evidence of the risk of the capital invested in the company by financial stakeholders, including lenders, preferred shareholders, and common shareholders. Example 4.4 shows the risk and financial flexibility ratios for **Starbucks**. We discuss each ratio in the following sections.

EXAMPLE 4.4

Starbucks Financial Statement Analysis: Risk and Financial Flexibility Ratios

Ratio	Formula	2014	2015
Debt-to-Assets	$\dfrac{\text{Total Liabilities}}{\text{Total Assets}}$	$= \dfrac{\$5{,}479.2}{\$10{,}752.9}$ $= 0.51$	$= \dfrac{\$6{,}626.3}{\$12{,}446.1}$ $= 0.53$
Debt-to-Equity	$\dfrac{\text{Total Liabilities}}{\text{Total Common Equity}}$	$= \dfrac{\$5{,}479.2}{\$5{,}273.7}$ $= 1.04$	$= \dfrac{\$6{,}626.3}{\$5{,}819.8}$ $= 1.14$

Leverage

Financial leverage refers to the amount of debt financing, relative to the equity and total assets of the company. Greater leverage typically is a key indicator of greater financial risk. Standard ratios that measure the leverage include the debt-to-assets ratio and the debt-to-equity ratio. The **debt-to-assets ratio** measures the percentage of total assets financed by creditors and is computed as follows:

$$\text{Debt-to-Assets} = \text{Total Liabilities} \div \text{Total Assets}$$

The **debt-to-equity ratio** measures the number of dollars of debt financing per dollar of financing from total common shareholders' equity and is computed as follows:

$$\text{Debt-to-Equity} = \text{Total Liabilities} \div \text{Total Common Shareholders' Equity}$$

While it is common to measure debt for these ratios as total liabilities, sometimes the ratios will include only formal debt financing instruments, including short-term borrowings and long-term bonds, notes, mortgages, and lease obligations. In our examples and in the exercises and problems, we use total liabilities.

The appropriate level of debt-to-assets or debt-to-equity depends on the company's strategy and industry. In general, shareholders prefer a higher debt ratio if the company is generating profits and cash flows that enable it to easily cover the costs of debt, which is known as favorable financial leverage. This occurs when the company borrows money from creditors at an interest rate (net of income taxes) that is lower than the return the company can earn by using that capital in its operations. However, as the financial leverage ratio increases, there is a trade-off in that the company becomes riskier. An extremely high debt ratio is likely to be a disadvantage because it limits the company's financial flexibility when it needs to attract additional external capital. More importantly, high leverage creates risk, such that if a company's profits and cash flows suddenly fall, the company may face difficulty in making interest and principal payments and could face bankruptcy.

Example Example 4.4 shows the debt ratios for **Starbucks**, which are measured using total liabilities. At the end of 2015, Starbucks had total liabilities of $6,626.3 million and total assets of $12,446.1 million, producing a debt-to-assets ratio of 0.53. At the same time, Starbucks had total common shareholders' equity of $5,819.8 million, resulting in a debt-to-equity ratio of 1.14. These ratios suggest that, in 2015, Starbucks relied on total liabilities to finance 53% of its assets and that for every $1 in common shareholders' equity Starbucks has borrowed $1.14. Evaluating them over time, these ratios indicate that from 2014 to 2015 Starbucks increased its leverage slightly. The debt-to-assets ratio increased a bit from 0.51 to 0.53, and the debt-to-equity ratio climbed from 1.04 to 1.14. Note that, although Starbucks's assets increased by over $1.6 billion (a 15.7% increase) from 2014 to 2015, Starbucks's total liabilities increased by over $1.1 billion (an increase of 20.9%). At the same time, common shareholders' equity increased from $5,273.7 million to $5,819.8 million during 2015 (an increase of 10.4%). These ratios reveal that total liabilities increased relatively more quickly than total assets and common equity, thereby increasing Starbucks's leverage.

Liquidity

Liquidity ratios indicate a company's ability to meet its currently maturing financial obligations. These ratios generally involve all or most of the components of a company's **working capital**—current assets minus current liabilities. **Example 4.5** includes the liquidity ratios and formulas for **Starbucks** for 2014 and 2015. We discuss each ratio in the following sections.

EXAMPLE 4.5 Starbucks Financial Statement Analysis: Liquidity Ratios

Ratio	Formula	2014	2015
Current	$\dfrac{\text{Current Assets}}{\text{Current Liabilities}}$	$= \dfrac{\$4,168.7}{\$3,038.7} = 1.37$	$= \dfrac{\$4,352.7}{\$3,653.5} = 1.19$
Quick	$\dfrac{\text{Quick Assets}}{\text{Current Liabilities}}$	$= \dfrac{(\$1,708.4 + \$135.4 + \$631.0)}{\$3,038.7}$ $= 0.81$	$= \dfrac{(\$1,530.1 + \$81.3 + \$719.0)}{\$3,653.5}$ $= 0.64$

Current Ratio The **current ratio** is the most commonly used ratio to evaluate liquidity. The current ratio indicates the number of dollars in current assets for each dollar in current liabilities and is computed as follows:

$$\text{Current Ratio} = \text{Current Assets} \div \text{Current Liabilities}$$

The current ratio indicates the *relative* relationship between the current assets and current liabilities, allowing comparisons of liquidity across different sized companies. Interpreting the current ratio involves assessing whether a company's liquidity is adequate to cover future obligations as they mature next period. A current ratio that is *too high* relative to the company's strategy and similar companies within the same industry may indicate inefficient management of current assets. Conversely, a current ratio that is *too low* may indicate liquidity problems and difficulty in paying current liabilities when they come due.

In analyzing the current ratio, keep in mind that some types of current assets can be converted into cash more quickly than others. Cash and cash equivalents and investments in marketable securities are highly liquid, whereas other assets such as prepaid expenses likely cannot be converted into cash. For current liabilities, analysts should distinguish those that require cash payments, such as wages payable and short-term debt, from those that do not but instead involve performance obligations, such as deferred revenues.

Quick Ratio The mix of a company's current assets and the impact on its liquidity are considered in the quick ratio. The **quick ratio** is a tougher test of a company's liquidity because it includes only the current assets that may be easily converted into cash. The quick ratio includes the **quick assets** that can be converted into cash within 90 days (typically including cash and cash equivalents, short-term investment securities, and receivables). Inventories are excluded because their ability to be sold quickly is uncertain, and they frequently are sold on credit. Prepaid items are excluded because they are not convertible into cash. The quick ratio is computed as follows:

$$\text{Quick Ratio} = \text{Quick Assets} \div \text{Current Liabilities}$$

The quick ratio highlights potential liquidity problems because of an illiquid mix of current assets. For instance, the use of this ratio can reveal potential liquidity problems facing a company with very low amounts of assets that can be easily converted into cash in order to pay current liabilities.

Example Refer to **Example 4.5** (p. 4-40). At the end of 2015, **Starbucks** had current assets of $4,352.7 million and current liabilities of $3,653.5 million, producing a current ratio of 1.19. At the same time, Starbucks had quick assets of $2,330.4 million (cash of $1,530.1 million + short-term investment securities of $81.3 million + accounts receivable of $719.0 million), resulting in a quick ratio of 0.64. These ratios suggest that, at the end of 2015, Starbucks was reasonably liquid, with $1.19 in current assets and $0.64 in quick assets for every $1 in current liabilities.

The data in **Example 4.5** also show that Starbucks's current ratio and quick ratio dropped from 2014 to 2015, indicating a reduction in liquidity. In 2014, Starbucks had $1.37 in current assets and $0.81 in quick assets for every $1 in current liabilities. Current liabilities increased considerably (20.2%) during 2015 while current assets grew more slowly (4.4%). Given that Starbucks has $1,530.1 million in cash, and generates strong cash flows from operations, investors and creditors can expect that Starbucks will have sufficient liquidity and financial flexibility to be able to meet its current obligations without risk of bankruptcy. ∎

Operating Capability Ratios

Financial statements users examine **operating capability ratios** (also called **efficiency ratios** or **activity ratios**) to evaluate the efficiency with which the company uses its economic resources to generate revenues. These ratios are often measured in terms of the number of days of activity that operating assets like inventory or receivables represent. These ratios also reveal the length of a company's **operating cycle**, which is the length of time it takes to produce and sell inventory and then collect the receivables in cash, minus the number of days of it takes to pay accounts payable. **Example 4.6** shows the operating capability ratios for **Starbucks**. We discuss each ratio in the following sections.

EXAMPLE 4.6

Starbucks Financial Statement Analysis: Operating Capability Ratios

Ratio	Formula	2014	2015
Inventory Turnover	$\dfrac{\text{Cost of Goods Sold}}{\text{Average Inventory}}$	$= \dfrac{\$6{,}858.8}{[(\$1{,}090.9 + \$1{,}111.2)/2]}$ $= 6.2$	$= \dfrac{\$7{,}787.5}{[(\$1{,}306.4 + \$1{,}090.9)/2]}$ $= 6.5$
Inventory Turnover in Days	(a) $\dfrac{365 \text{ Days}}{\text{Inventory Turnover}}$	$= 58.6$ days	$= 56.2$ days
Accounts Receivable Turnover	$\dfrac{\text{Total Credit Sales}}{\text{Average Accounts Receivable*}}$	$= \dfrac{(\$1{,}588.6 + \$1{,}881.3)}{[(\$631.0 + \$561.4)/2]}$ $= 5.8$	$= \dfrac{(\$1{,}861.9 + \$2{,}103.5)}{[(\$719.0 + \$631.0)/2]}$ $= 5.9$
Accounts Receivable Turnover in Days	(b) $\dfrac{365 \text{ Days}}{\text{Accounts Receivable Turnover}}$	$= 62.7$ days*	$= 62.1$ days*
Accounts Payable Turnover	$\dfrac{\text{Inventory Purchases**}}{\text{Average Accounts Payable}}$	$= \dfrac{[\$6{,}858.8 + (\$1{,}090.9 - \$1{,}111.2)]}{[(\$533.7 + \$491.7)/2]}$ $= 13.3$	$= \dfrac{[\$7{,}787.5 + (\$1{,}306.4 - \$1{,}090.9)]}{[(\$684.2 + \$533.7)/2]}$ $= 13.1$
Accounts Payable Turnover in Days	(c) $\dfrac{365}{\text{Accounts Payable Turnover}}$	$= 27.4$ days**	$= 27.8$ days**
Operating Cycle (in days)	$a + b - c$	$58.6 + 62.7 - 27.4 = 93.9$ days	$56.2 + 62.1 - 27.8 = 90.5$ days

(continued)

EXAMPLE 4.6 (Continued)

Ratio	Formula	2014	2015
Fixed Asset Turnover	$\dfrac{\text{Total Revenues}}{\text{Average Net Fixed Assets}}$	$= \dfrac{\$16{,}447.8}{[(\$3{,}519.0 + \$3{,}200.5)/2]} = 4.90$	$= \dfrac{\$19{,}162.7}{[(\$4{,}088.3 + \$3{,}519.0)/2]} = 5.04$
Total Asset Turnover	$\dfrac{\text{Total Revenues}}{\text{Average Total Assets}}$	$= \dfrac{\$16{,}447.8}{[(\$10{,}752.9 + \$11{,}516.7)/2]} = 1.48$	$= \dfrac{\$19{,}162.7}{[(\$10{,}752.9 + \$12{,}446.1)/2]} = 1.65$

*Computation for Starbucks includes Licensed Store Revenues and CPG, Foodservice, and Other Revenues only because Company Operated Store Revenues are primarily cash sales.
**Inventory purchases equals cost of goods sold plus the change in inventory.

Inventory Turnover The **inventory turnover ratio** indicates the average number of times the inventory "turned over" or sold during that period and is computed as follows:

$$\text{Inventory Turnover} = \text{Cost of Goods Sold} \div \text{Average Inventory}$$

As a general rule, higher inventory turnover indicates the company (1) was more effective in managing production and supply chain operations, (2) tied up a lower amount of cash in inventory, and (3) had a shorter operating cycle to replenish cash. A company with a higher inventory turnover is usually more efficient, and it is also minimizing the chance of having obsolete inventory. However, *too* high an inventory turnover may indicate lost sales opportunities as a result of insufficient inventory.

Dividing the inventory turnover rate into the number of operating days in a fiscal year (usually 365) reveals the average number of days it takes to convert inventory into sales in the operating cycle, computed as follows:

$$\text{Inventory Turnover in Days} = 365 \text{ Days} \div \text{Inventory Turnover}$$

Example As shown in **Example 4.6**, **Starbucks**'s inventory turnover for 2015 is 6.5 times, computed by dividing cost of goods sold of $7,787.5 million by the average balance in inventory of $1,198.65 million [($1,306.4 million + $1,090.9 million) ÷ 2]. Dividing 365 days by 6.5 turns indicates Starbucks turned over inventory on average approximately every 56.2 days in 2015. These ratios also show that Starbucks's inventory management became slightly more efficient in 2015 compared to 2014, when Starbucks held inventory for an average of 58.6 days. ∎

Accounts Receivable Turnover If a company sells its inventory on credit, the company then collects the receivables to complete its operating cycle. The **accounts receivable turnover ratio** indicates how efficiently the company collects its receivables and is computed as follows:

$$\text{Accounts Receivable Turnover} = \text{Total Credit Sales} \div \text{Average Accounts Receivable}$$

As a general rule, the higher the turnover the better, because the company has less cash tied up in receivables, collects this cash at a faster pace, and usually has fewer uncollectible accounts. When net credit sales information is not available, net sales are used in the calculations.

The accounts receivable turnover can also be divided into the number of days in the year to show the average collection period in days, computed as follows:

$$\text{Accounts Receivable Turnover in Days} = 365 \text{ Days} \div \text{Accounts Receivable Turnover}$$

If the number of days to collect grows unusually long, it often indicates the company is experiencing credit quality problems.

Example To compute accounts receivable turnover for **Starbucks**, we include only credit sales from the licensed store, CPG, foodservice, and other revenues because these revenues generate accounts receivable. Revenues from company-operated retail coffee shops are primarily cash sales, which would not affect accounts receivable. As shown in **Example 4.6** (p. 4-41), the accounts receivable turnover for 2015 is 5.9 times, computed by dividing credit sales of $3,965.4 million [$1,861.9 million + $2,103.5 million] by the average balance in accounts receivable of $675.0 million [($719.0 million + $631.0 million) ÷ 2]. Dividing 365 days by 5.9 turns indicates that it took Starbucks roughly 62.1 days on average to collect accounts receivable during 2015. These ratios also show that Starbucks's receivable collection efficiency improved slightly from 2014, when Starbucks took on average roughly 62.7 days to collect. ■

Accounts Payable Turnover The **accounts payable turnover ratio** measures the number of times accounts payable turn over during the year and is computed as follows:

$$\text{Accounts Payable Turnover} = \text{Inventory Purchases}^* \div \text{Average Accounts Payable}$$
$$^*\text{Inventory Purchases} = \text{Cost of Goods Sold} + \text{Change in Inventory}$$

The accounts payable turnover ratio also may be divided into the number of days in the year to show the average payment period in days, computed as follows:

$$\text{Accounts Payable Turnover in Days} = 365 \div \text{Accounts Payable Turnover}$$

The shorter the number of payables days, the shorter the time between the purchase of inventory and the cash payment. If a company's payables turn over more slowly than the average for its industry, it may indicate that either the company has purchasing power and is able to negotiate longer payment terms from its suppliers, or that the company is having financial difficulty.

Example Refer to **Example 4.6** (p. 4-41). For 2015, **Starbucks**'s accounts payable turnover is 13.1 times, computed by dividing inventory purchases of $8,003.0 million [cost of goods sold of $7,787.5 million plus the growth in the inventory balance of $215.5 million ($1,306.4 million − $1,090.9 million)] by the average balance in accounts payable of $608.95 million [($684.2 million + $533.7 million) ÷ 2]. Dividing 365 days by 13.1 turns indicates that Starbucks took an average of roughly 27.8 days to pay suppliers during 2015. These ratios also show that Starbucks paid suppliers quite promptly in 2014, taking an average of 27.4 days. ■

Days in Operating Cycle Together, the three turnover ratios indicate the total number of days in the company's operating cycle from the payment of cash to purchase inventory to the collection of cash from sales, minus the number of days of financing from payables, computed as follows:

$$\text{Days in Operating Cycle} = \text{Inventory Turnover in Days} + \text{Accounts Receivable Turnover in Days} - \text{Accounts Payable Turnover in Days}$$

Example Refer to **Example 4.6** (p. 4-41). **Starbucks** took an average of 56.2 days to produce and sell inventory in 2015, an average of 62.1 days to collect accounts receivable, and 27.8 days to pay its suppliers. Starbucks's operating cycle was an average of 90.5 days in 2015. This cycle was 3.4 days more efficient than in 2014, when it was 93.9 days. ■

Fixed Asset Turnover and Total Asset Turnover Other operating capability ratios include the fixed asset turnover ratio and the total asset turnover ratio. The **fixed asset turnover ratio** indicates the average number of sales dollars the company generated per average dollar invested in net fixed assets and is computed as follows:[28]

$$\text{Fixed Asset Turnover} = \text{Total Revenues} \div \text{Average Net Fixed Assets}$$

This is an important ratio, particularly for fixed-asset intensive companies, such as manufacturers or airlines, because the efficient utilization of their fixed assets is a key determinant of profitability. More broadly, the **total asset turnover ratio** indicates how efficiently a company generates sales relative to its total asset base and is computed as follows:

$$\text{Total Asset Turnover} = \text{Total Revenues} \div \text{Average Total Assets}$$

Example Refer to **Example 4.6** (p. 4-41). In 2015, **Starbucks** generated total revenues of $19,162.7 million with an average of $3,803.7 million in property and equipment [($4,088.3 million + $3,519.0 million) ÷ 2], resulting in $5.04 in revenues for every $1 in property, plant, and equipment. Starbucks's fixed asset efficiency improved in 2015 compared to 2014, when it generated $4.90 in sales for every $1 in fixed assets.

The total asset turnover in 2015 is computed by dividing total revenues of $19,162.7 million with average total assets of $11,599.5 million [($12,446.1 million + $10,752.9 million) ÷ 2], resulting in $1.65 in revenues in 2015 for every dollar in total assets. These ratios also indicate significant improvement in operating capability in 2015 relative to 2014, when an average $1 of total assets generated only $1.48 in revenues. ■

> ### GOT IT?
> **4-27** What are *intracompany comparisons*? What are *intercompany comparisons*? How do they differ?
>
> **4-28** What is *common-size analysis*? What is *rate of change analysis*? How do they differ?

---

[28] Net fixed assets is the balance in property, plant, and equipment, net of accumulated depreciation.

4-29 What are two frequently used ratios measuring return on investment? How are they computed, and what do they mean?

4-30 What are two frequently used ratios measuring leverage? How are they computed, and what do they mean?

4-31 What are two frequently used ratios measuring liquidity? How are they computed, and what do they mean?

4-32 Which two ratios indicate a company's efficiency in managing inventory and accounts receivable? How are they computed, and what do they mean?

4-33 Define a company's *operating cycle*. How do you compute the length of a company's operating cycle? What does it mean?

HOW DOES BALANCE SHEET CLASSIFICATION AND PRESENTATION DIFFER UNDER IFRS VERSUS U.S. GAAP?

LEARNING OBJECTIVE 4.7

Understand the similarities and differences in how balance sheets are presented under IFRS versus U.S. GAAP.

The financial statements required under IFRS are similar to those required under U.S. GAAP. They include a balance sheet, income statement, statement of comprehensive income, statement of cash flows, and statement of shareholders' equity, as well as related notes and other explanatory material. IFRS require that companies classify assets on the balance sheet as either noncurrent or current. Noncurrent assets include property, plant, and equipment, as well as other items such as investments, long-term receivables, and intangibles. Current assets are defined similarly to those under U.S. GAAP. However, assets are often presented in a different order under IFRS, with noncurrent assets presented first, followed by current assets.

The ordering of the liabilities and shareholders' equity sections is also usually different than under U.S. GAAP. "Capital and reserves," which includes issued capital (capital stock and additional paid-in capital), reserves, and accumulated profits or losses (retained earnings), is usually listed first. A company is required to disclose the par value, as well as the number of shares authorized, issued and fully paid, and issued but not fully paid. It must also disclose dividends that have been proposed but not formally approved for payment. Reserves may result from upward revaluations of properties and investments, as well as currency translation differences (similar to the U.S. GAAP classification of accumulated other comprehensive income). A company must provide a description of the nature and purpose of each reserve. Liabilities are generally similar to those under U.S. GAAP. However, noncurrent liabilities are usually listed next, and current liabilities are listed last.

A company's statement of shareholders' equity includes the company's comprehensive income for the period, the changes in contributed capital, and dividends. A company must also disclose any changes in accumulated profits (losses) due to changes in accounting policies, corrections of errors, and dividends.

In the notes to the financial statements, IFRS requires companies to disclose items similar to those under U.S. GAAP. These disclosures include its accounting policies, narrative descriptions of financial statement items, and contingencies. For revaluations allowed under IFRS (e.g., the upward revaluation of property, plant, and equipment from cost to fair value), a company also includes the measurement basis used. In the following chapters, we will discuss the major differences between U.S. GAAP and IFRS as they apply to specific assets, liabilities, and income.

INTERNATIONAL DIMENSION

DIFFERENCES IN BALANCE SHEET PRESENTATION

Example 4.7 shows comparative balance sheets for **LVMH Group** (**Moet Hennessy – Louis Vuitton**), which manages a portfolio of over 60 of the world's leading brands in luxury goods. LVMH actively manages branded products in five different sectors: (1) Wine and Spirits, (2) Fashion and Leather Goods, (3) Perfumes and Cosmetics, (4) Watches and Jewelry, and (5) Selective Retailing. Headquartered in France, LVMH Group prepares its balance sheet and other financial statements following IFRS.

EXAMPLE 4.7

International Comparative Balance Sheets: LVMH

CONSOLIDATED BALANCE SHEET

ASSETS (EUR Millions)	Notes	2013	2012[a]	2011[a]
Brands and other intangible assets	3	11,458	11,510	11,482
Goodwill	4	9,959	7,806	6,957
Property, plant and equipment	6	9,602	8,769	8,017
Investments in associates	7	152	163	170
Non-current available for sale financial assets	8	7,080	6,004	5,982
Other non-current assets	9	432	519	478
Deferred tax	27	909	954	760
Non-current assets		**39,592**	**35,725**	**33,846**
Inventories and work in progress	10	8,586	8,080	7,510
Trade accounts receivable	11	2,189	1,985	1,878
Income taxes		235	201	121
Other current assets	12	1,851	1,811	1,455
Cash and cash equivalents	14	3,221	2,196	2,303
Current assets		**16,082**	**14,273**	**13,267**
Total assets		**55,674**	**49,998**	**47,113**

LIABILITIES AND EQUITY (EUR millions)	Notes	2013	2012[a]	2011[a]
Share capital	15.1	152	152	152
Share premium account	15.1	3,849	3,848	3,801
Treasury shares and LVMH-share settled derivatives	15.2	(451)	(414)	(485)
Cumulative translation adjustment	15.4	(8)	342	431
Revaluation reserves		3,900	2,731	2,637
Other reserves		15,817	14,341	12,770
Net profit, Group share		3,436	3,424	3,065
Equity, Group share		26,695	24,424	22,371
Minority interests	17	1,028	1,084	1,055
Total equity		**27,723**	**25,508**	**23,426**
Long-term borrowings	18	4,159	3,836	4,132
Non-current provisions	19	1,755	1,756	1,530
Deferred tax	27	3,934	3,960	3,925
Other non-current liabilities	20	6,403	5,456	4,506
Non-current Liabilities		**16,251**	**15,008**	**14,093**

LIABILITIES AND EQUITY (EUR millions)	Notes	2013	2012[a]	2011[a]
Short-term borrowings	18	4,688	2,976	3,134
Trade accounts payable		3,308	3,134	2,952
Income taxes		382	442	443
Current provisions	19	322	335	349
Other current liabilities	21	3,000	2,595	2,716
Current liabilities		**11,700**	**9,482**	**9,594**
Tool Liabilities and equity		**55,674**	**49,998**	**47,113**

(a) The balance sheets as of December 31, 2012 and 2011 have been restated to reflect the retrospective application as of January 1, 2011 of IAS 19 Employee Benefits as amended. See Note 1.2.

Note that there are a number of differences in LVMH Group's balance sheets compared to those prepared under U.S. GAAP.

- LVMH Group's balance sheets have two categories of assets, noncurrent assets and current assets, with the noncurrent assets listed first.
- LVMH presents the assets in ascending order of liquidity, with the least liquid assets (brands and goodwill) listed first and the most liquid asset (cash) listed last, which is opposite the order in which they would be presented under U.S. GAAP.
- After total assets, the equity category is listed next, followed by the noncurrent liabilities and current liabilities.
- There are a number of differences in account titles such as "Revaluation Reserves" and "Current Provisions," which are not allowed under U.S. GAAP.
- The equity section of the balance sheet does not contain a Retained Earnings account, as would be the case under U.S. GAAP, but instead LVMH Group reports "Other Reserves," which is similar to beginning retained earnings adjusted for dividends during the period, and "Net Profit, Group Share," which is analogous to net income for the period.

Source: IAS 1 (See Appendix C at the end of this book.)

GOT IT?

4-34 Briefly list the format of a company's balance sheet under IFRS.

REVIEW CENTER

At the beginning of the chapter, we described how balance sheet information is useful to investors, lenders, and other creditors. We described how financial statement users examine balance sheet information to evaluate return on investment, risk, liquidity, financial flexibility, and operating capability. We also identified several objectives you would accomplish after reading the chapter. The objectives are listed below and followed by a brief summary of the key takeaways.

LEARNING OBJECTIVE 4.1

Understand the purpose and the elements of the balance sheet.

KEY TAKEAWAYS

- A balance sheet summarizes the *financial position* of a corporation on a specific date by reporting its assets, liabilities, and shareholders' equity. The balance sheet reports a corporation's *resource structure* and its *financial structure*.
- By providing information about a company's resources and claims on the company, the balance sheet helps users assess a company's return on investment, risk, liquidity, financial flexibility, and operating capability.
- The elements of a balance sheet that should be recognized are assets, liabilities, and shareholders' equity.
- Assets are the probable future economic benefits obtained or controlled by a company as a result of past transactions or events.
- Liabilities are the probable future sacrifices of economic benefits arising from present obligations of a company to transfer assets or provide services in the future to other entities as a result of past transactions or events.
- Equity is the residual interest in the assets of a company after deducting its liabilities. Shareholders' equity consists of three general categories: (1) contributed capital, (2) earned capital, and (3) noncontrolling interests.

KEY TERMS

assets, p. 4-4
balance sheet, p. 4-3
contingent obligations, p. 4-6
contributed capital, p. 4-22
earned capital, p. 4-7
equity, p. 4-6
executory contracts, p. 4-6
financial assets, p. 4-5

financial position, p. 4-2
liabilities, p. 4-5
monetary assets, p. 4-5
noncontrolling interests, p. 4-7
nonfinancial assets, p. 4-5
nonmonetary assets, p. 4-5
recognition, p. 4-4
statement of financial position, p. 4-3

KEY CALCULATION

Assets = Liabilities + Shareholders' Equity

LEARNING OBJECTIVE 4.2

Explain how to measure the elements of a balance sheet.

KEY TAKEAWAYS

- U.S. GAAP and IFRS measure the values of assets and liabilities using the mixed attribute measurement model to provide the most relevant and representationally faithful information. Some asset and liability values are measured based on historical values: historical cost, adjusted historical cost, or present values. Other asset and liability values are measured based on current values: fair value, replacement cost, or net realizable value.
- Fair values should be measured as exit values, with the most representationally faithful inputs being Level 1—observable market prices for identical assets or liabilities. If Level 1 inputs are not available, the fair value should be measured with Level 2 inputs—observable market prices for similar assets or liabilities. If Level 2 inputs are not available, then fair value should be estimated with Level 3 inputs—present value models discounting the expected future cash flows of the assets and liabilities.
- Accounting Standards Updates to U.S. GAAP and new standards within IFRS increasingly require the use of fair values in the valuation of certain assets and liabilities. Additionally, U.S. GAAP gives companies the option to use fair value measurement for financial assets and liabilities for transactions in which they are not required to use fair values.

KEY TERMS

acquisition cost, p. 4-8
adjusted historical cost, p. 4-8

adjusted present values, p. 4-9
current replacement cost, p. 4-12

fair value, p. 4-10
fair value option, p. 4-10
historical cost, p. 4-8
Level 1, p. 4-11
Level 2, p. 4-11

Level 3, p. 4-11
mixed attribute measurement model, p. 4-7
net realizable value, p. 4-13
present values, p. 4-9

KEY TAKEAWAYS

- When presenting a balance sheet, a company will classify the elements in order to improve the usefulness of the information for the external users.
- The assets of a balance sheet may be classified into five groups: (1) current assets; (2) long-term investments; (3) property, plant, and equipment; (4) intangible assets; and (5) other assets.
- The classification of assets and liabilities as current and noncurrent is a key distinction made on a company's balance sheet that allows users to more easily assess its liquidity and financial flexibility.
- Assets that are expected to provide economic benefits within 1 year or one operating cycle, whichever is longer, are classified as current assets. Assets that are expected to provide economic benefits for more than 1 year or the operating cycle are classified as noncurrent assets and include long-term investments; property, plant, and equipment; and intangible assets.
- Obligations that will be satisfied within 1 year or the operating cycle are classified as current liabilities. Obligations that will not be satisfied within 1 year or the operating cycle are classified as noncurrent liabilities.
- Shareholders' equity is the residual interest in the net assets of the corporation, after the liabilities have been deducted. Equity consists of contributed capital, retained earnings, accumulated other comprehensive income, and, for some companies, noncontrolling interests.

LEARNING OBJECTIVE 4.3
Classify the assets, liabilities, and shareholders' equity of a balance sheet.

KEY TERMS

accounts receivable, p. 4-16
accrued expenses, p. 4-19
accumulated other comprehensive income (loss), p. 4-24
amortization, p. 4-18
cash, p. 4-16
cash equivalents, p. 4-16
common stock, p. 4-22
construction in progress, p. 4-18
current assets, p. 4-16
current liabilities, p. 4-19
current maturities of long-term debt, p. 4-19
deferred revenues, p. 4-19
deficit, p. 4-23
depletion, p. 4-18
depreciation, p. 4-18
finished goods, p. 4-16
fixed assets, p. 4-17
goodwill, p. 4-19
intangible assets, p. 4-18
intangible assets with finite useful lives, p. 4-18
intangible assets with indefinite useful lives, p. 4-18

inventories, p. 4-16
investments in marketable securities, p. 4-16
leasehold improvements, p. 4-18
long-term investment, p. 4-17
long-term liabilities, p. 4-20
net book value, p. 4-18
noncontrolling interests, p. 4-24
noncurrent liabilities, p. 4-20
notes receivable, p. 4-16
operating cycle, p. 4-16
other assets, p. 4-19
par valuer, p. 4-22
payables, p. 4-19
preferred stock, p. 4-23
prepaid items, p. 4-17
property, plant, and equipment, p. 4-17
raw materials, p. 4-16
retained earnings, p. 4-23
shareholders' equity, p. 4-21
short-term debt, p. 4-19
stated value, p. 4-22
treasury stock, p. 4-23
unearned revenues, p. 4-19
work in process, p. 4-16

LEARNING OBJECTIVE 4.4
Prepare a statement of shareholders' equity.

KEY TAKEAWAYS
- A statement of shareholders' equity reports the changes and the ending balances in all of the shareholders' equity accounts, including investments by and distributions to owners.
- A statement of shareholders' equity starts with the beginning balances of Common Stock, Additional Paid-In Capital, Treasury Stock, Retained Earnings, Accumulated Other Comprehensive Income, and Noncontrolling Interests (if any). It then reconciles these beginning balances to the ending balances by showing the changes (and reasons for the changes) in each of these items.

KEY TERMS
distributions to owners, p. 4-25
investments by owners, p. 4-25
statement of changes in shareholders' equity, p. 4-26
statement of shareholders' equity, p. 4-26

LEARNING OBJECTIVE 4.5
Understand balance sheet disclosure issues.

KEY TAKEAWAYS
- The notes accompanying the financial statements contain relevant information about a company's significant accounting policies, financial position, and activities that supplements the information reported in the body of the financial statements. These disclosures help users understand the elements of the balance sheet and other financial statements. This information includes:
  - a summary of the company's accounting policies,
  - the fair value and risk of its financial instruments,
  - any contingent liabilities and assets,
  - any subsequent events,
  - any related party transactions, and
  - comparative financial statements, all of which must be audited.

KEY TERMS
comparative financial statements, p. 4-31
derivative financial instrument, p. 4-27
financial instruments, p. 4-27
gain contingencies, p. 4-27
loss contingencies, p. 4-27
related party transactions, p. 4-31
subsequent event, p. 4-29

LEARNING OBJECTIVE 4.6
Apply financial statement analysis techniques to analyze balance sheet information.

KEY TAKEAWAYS
- Financial statement users apply various analytical tools to use balance sheet information to make intracompany and intercompany comparisons.
- Users can evaluate return on investment, risk, liquidity, financial flexibility, and operating capability using common-size financial statements, rate of change analyses, and various financial ratios.

KEY TERMS
accounts payable turnover ratio, p. 4-43
accounts receivable turnover ratio, p. 4-42
activity ratios, p. 4-41
common-size analysis, p. 4-33
cross-sectional analysis, p. 4-33
current ratio, p. 4-40
debt-to-assets ratio, p. 4-39
debt-to-equity ratio, p. 4-39
efficiency ratios, p. 4-41
financial leverage, p. 4-39
financial statement analysis ratios, p. 4-35
fixed asset turnover ratio, p. 4-44
intercompany comparison, p. 4-33
intracompany comparison, p. 4-32
inventory turnover ratio, p. 4-42
operating capability ratios, p. 4-41
operating cycle, p. 4-41
quick assets, p. 4-40
quick ratio, p. 4-40
rate of change analysis, p. 4-33
rate of return on investment, p. 4-36
return on assets, p. 4-37

return on common equity, p. 4-38
time-series analysis, p. 4-32

total asset turnover ratio, p. 4-44
working capital, p. 4-39

KEY CALCULATIONS

$$\text{Return on Assets} = \frac{\text{Net Income (including income attributable to noncontrolling interests)} + [\text{Interest Expense} \times (1 - \text{Tax Rate})]}{\text{Average Total Assets}}$$

$$\text{Return on Common Equity} = \frac{\text{Net Income}}{\text{Average Total Common Shareholders' Equity}}$$

Debt-to-Assets = Total Liabilities ÷ Total Assets

Debt-to-Equity = Total Liabilities ÷ Total Common Shareholders' Equity

Current Ratio = Current Assets ÷ Current Liabilities

Quick Ratio = Quick Assets ÷ Current Liabilities

Inventory Turnover = Cost of Goods Sold ÷ Average Inventory

Inventory Turnover in Days = 365 Days ÷ Inventory Turnover

Accounts Receivable Turnover = Total Credit Sales ÷ Average Accounts Receivable

Accounts Receivable Turnover in Days = 365 Days ÷ Accounts Receivable Turnover

Accounts Payable Turnover = Inventory Purchases* ÷ Average Accounts Payable
*Inventory Purchases = Cost of Goods Sold + Change in Inventory

Accounts Payable Turnover in Days = 365 ÷ Accounts Payable Turnover

Days in Operating Cycle = Inventory Turnover in Days + Accounts Receivable Turnover in Days − Accounts Payable Turnover in Days

Fixed Asset Turnover = Total Revenues ÷ Average Net Fixed Assets

Total Asset Turnover = Total Revenues ÷ Average Total Assets

KEY TAKEAWAYS

- The financial statements required by the IASB are similar to those required by U.S. GAAP. Differences in balance sheet presentation can involve the order in which assets and liabilities are presented, as well as the account titles used.

LEARNING OBJECTIVE 4.7
Understand the similarities and differences in how balance sheets are presented under IFRS versus U.S. GAAP.

ANSWERS TO REAL REPORT QUESTIONS

Real Report 4.1 Answers Kimberly-Clark Corporation—Long-Term Debt

1. Kimberly-Clark has total long-term debt on the 2013 balance sheet with a book value of $5,698 million and a fair value of $6,271 million. The fair value exceeds the book value in part because interest rates in the economy may have declined and/or Kimberly-Clark's credit quality may have improved after issuing the debt. Both factors would cause the fair value of the debt to increase relative to book value.
2. Scheduled maturities of long-term debt for the next 5 years are $312 million in 2014, $353 million in 2015, $302 million in 2016, $962 million in 2017, and $902 million in 2018.

3. During May 2013, the company issued $250 million in floating rate notes due in 2016, $350 million in 2.4% notes due in 2023, and $250 million in 3.7% notes due in 2043. Proceeds were used to repay $500 million of 5.0% notes due in August 2013, to fund investments, and for general corporate purposes.
4. Assuming that the weighted average interest rate at the end of 2013 remains the same in 2014 and the long-term debt remains outstanding for the entire year, interest expense relating to the long-term debt is estimated to be $281.5 million [($5,163 million × 5.2%) + ($200 million × 4.2%) + ($261 million × 0.2%) + ($74 million × 5.6 %)].

Real Report 4.2 Answers Apple Inc.—Contingency

1. With respect to the loss contingency, Apple management believes a material loss is not a reasonable possibility. However, Apple explains that the outcome of litigation is inherently uncertain. Therefore, it warns that although it considers the likelihood of such a loss to be remote, if this legal matter was resolved against Apple for an amount in excess of management's expectations, Apple's financial statements could be materially adversely affected.
2. For the contingent gain, Apple does not recognize the gain in income as of the end of fiscal 2013 because the award is subject to entry of final judgment, partial retrial, and appeal. Under U.S. GAAP, Apple is not permitted to recognize this gain until it is realized (i.e., Apple receives the award payment from Samsung).

Real Report 4.3 Answers Starbucks—Contingent Loss and Subsequent Event

1. The dispute between Starbucks and Kraft involved a contract in which Kraft distributed, marketed, advertised, and promoted Starbucks's packaged coffee products to grocery stores and warehouse clubs in the United States, Canada, Europe, and the United Kingdom. Starbucks discontinued the distribution arrangement with Kraft, alleging material breach of contract.
2. Starbucks did not recognize a loss prior to the arbitrator's ruling because "we could not reasonably estimate the possible loss."
3. On November 12, 2013, the arbitrator ordered Starbucks to pay Kraft $2,227.5 million in damages, plus an estimated $556.6 million in interest and attorneys' fees. The total litigation charge is estimated to be $2,784.1 million.
4. By treating the litigation charge as a subsequent event, Starbucks's 2013 financial statements are considerably more representationally faithful than they would have been had Starbucks only disclosed the loss in the notes. The conditions giving rise to the loss existed on the balance sheet date. The arbitrator's ruling is a very material event, having an enormous impact on Starbucks's reported income for 2013 as well as Starbucks's reported liabilities.

MULTIPLE-CHOICE (AICPA ADAPTED)

Select the best answer for each of the following.

M4-1 **LO 4.1** A donated fixed asset (from a governmental unit) for which the fair value has been determined should be recorded as a debit to Fixed Assets and a credit to:

    a. Contributed Capital
    b. Retained Earnings
    c. Deferred Income
    d. Other Income

M4-2 **LO 4.2** A company receives an advance payment for special-order goods to be manufactured and delivered within 6 months. The advance payment should be reported on the company's balance sheet as a:

    a. deferred charge
    b. contra-asset account
    c. current liability
    d. noncurrent liability

M4-3
LO 4.2

Which of the following may be used to determine fair value based on Level 3 inputs?

	Estimated Market Value	Present Value
a.	No	No
b.	No	Yes
c.	Yes	No
d.	Yes	Yes

M4-4
LO 4.3

On October 2, 2017, a company borrowed cash and signed a 3-year, interest-bearing note on which both the principal and interest are payable on October 2, 2020. At December 31, 2019, the principal and accrued interest should:

a. be reported on the balance sheet as current liabilities
b. be reported on the balance sheet as non-current liabilities
c. be reported on the balance sheet as long-term notes payable
d. not be reported on the balance sheet as liabilities

M4-5
LO 4.3

Land reported in the property, plant, and equipment section of a manufacturing company's balance sheet is reported at:

a. historical cost
b. historical cost, less accumulated depreciation
c. fair value
d. lower of cost or market value

M4-6
LO 4.3

Rent revenue collected 1 month in advance should be accounted for as:

a. revenue in the month collected
b. a current liability for deferred revenue
c. a separate item in shareholders' equity
d. an accrued liability

M4-7
LO 4.5

GAAP related to the disclosure of accounting policies:

a. requires a description of every accounting policy followed by a reporting entity
b. provides a specific listing of all types of accounting policies that must be disclosed
c. requires disclosure of the format for the statement of cash flows
d. requires a description of all significant accounting policies to be included as an integral part of the financial statements

M4-8
LO 4.5

Which of the following contingencies should generally be accrued on the balance sheet when the occurrence of the contingent event is probable and its amount can be reasonably estimated?

	Gain Contingency	Loss Contingency
a.	Yes	Yes
b.	Yes	No
c.	No	Yes
d.	No	No

M4-9
LO 4.5

Which of the following should be disclosed in the Summary of Significant Accounting Policies?

a. rent expense amount
b. maturity dates of long-term debt
c. methods of amortizing intangibles
d. composition of plant assets

M4-10
LO 4.6

The balance sheet provides information about each of the following items, except:

a. operating capability of entity
b. results of entity's operations
c. entity's liquidity
d. financial flexibility of entity

REVIEW EXERCISES

RE4-1
LO 4.1

Match the following terms with the appropriate component of the accounting equation:

(1) Assets
(2) Liabilities
(3) Shareholders' Equity

A. The probable sacrifices of economic benefits arising from the present obligations of a company to transfer assets or provide services in the future as a result of past transactions or events
B. The residual interest in the assets of a company that remains after deducting its liabilities
C. The probable future economic benefits obtained or controlled by a company as a result of past transactions or events

RE4-2 Dorothy Corporation had the following accounts in its year-end adjusted trial balance: Inventories, $23,600; Accounts Receivable, $7,600; Accounts Payable, $7,200; Prepaid Rent, $2,400; Marketable Securities, $3,000; Allowance for Doubtful Accounts, $1,100; and Cash, $1,500. Prepare the current assets section of Dorothy's year-end balance sheet.

LO 4.3

RE4-3 Dorothy Corporation had the following accounts in its year-end adjusted trial balance: Accounts Payable, $7,200; Salaries Payable, $5,800; Income Taxes Payable, $4,000; Short-Term Notes Payable, $2,500; Dividends Payable, $750; Investment in Held-to-Maturity Bonds, $2,750; and Allowance for Doubtful Accounts, $1,100. Prepare the current liabilities section of Dorothy's balance sheet.

LO 4.3

RE4-4 Based on the information in **RE4-2** and **RE4-3**, calculate Dorothy Corporation's working capital and current ratio.

LO 4.6

RE4-5 Toto Company reports the following on its year-end adjusted trial balance: Investment in Held-to-Maturity Bonds, $6,500; Fund to Retire Long-Term Bonds Payable, $7,750; Trademarks, $5,500; and Long-Term Advances to Unconsolidated Affiliated Companies, $3,500. Prepare the long-term investments section of Toto's year-end balance sheet.

LO 4.3

RE4-6 Oz Corporation has the following assets at year-end: Patents (net), $26,000; Land, $50,000; Buildings, $175,000; Accumulated Depreciation: Buildings, $57,500; Investment in Held-to-Maturity Bonds, $12,000; Equipment, $95,000; and Accumulated Depreciation: Equipment, $25,000. Prepare the property, plant, and equipment section of Oz's year-end balance sheet.

LO 4.3

RE4-7 Glenda Corporation has the following assets at year-end: Prepaid Rent, $6,000; Land, $58,000; Trademarks, $37,000; Computer Software Costs, $8,500; Patents, $13,000; Inventories, $17,000; and Goodwill, $11,000. Prepare the intangible assets section of Glenda's year-end balance sheet.

LO 4.3

RE4-8 Wizard Company reports the following on its year-end adjusted trial balance: Long-Term Bonds Payable, $4,500; Unamortized Bond Discount, $600; Accrued Pension Cost, $9,000; Mortgage Payable, $5,000; and Fund to Retire Long-Term Bonds Payable, $8,500. Prepare the long-term liabilities section of Wizard's year-end balance sheet.

LO 4.3

RE4-9 Scarecrow Inc. issues 50,000 shares of $2 par value common stock. The shares are sold for $25 per share. Prepare the journal entry to record the issuance of the stock.

LO 4.3

RE4-10 Tinman Corporation reports the following balances at the end of the current year: Common Stock, $5 par, $50,000; Retained Earnings, $120,000; Additional Paid-in Capital on Common Stock, $200,000; Income Taxes Payable, $9,800; and Accumulated Other Comprehensive Income, $24,500. Prepare the shareholders' equity section of Tinman's year-end balance sheet.

LO 4.3

EXERCISES

E4-1 **Current Assets** Listed here are certain accounts of Jenkins Company at the end of 2016:

LO 4.3

SHOW ME HOW

Account	Debit (Credit)
Land	$12,000
Prepaid Insurance	1,530
Cash on Hand	1,120
Notes Receivable (due 2016)	4,300
Cash in Bank	5,400
Allowance for Doubtful Accounts	(1,100)
Marketable Securities (Short-Term)	3,380
Accumulated Depreciation	(8,700)
Accounts Receivable	15,600
Office Supplies	970
Buildings	27,200
Inventory	19,700

Required:
Prepare the current assets section of Jenkins's balance sheet at the end of 2016.

E4-2 **Plant and Equipment** Your analysis of Moen Corporation's fixed asset accounts at the end of 2016 reveals the following information:

LO 4.3

1. Moen owns two tracts of land. The first, which cost $18,000, is being held as a future building site. It has a current market value of $20,000. The second, which cost $19,000, was purchased 10 years ago. The current office and factory buildings are on this site. The land has a current market value of $56,000.
2. Moen owns two buildings. The office building and the factory building were both built 10 years ago at a cost of $50,000 and $120,000, respectively. At that time, each was expected to have a life of 30 years and a residual value of 10% of original cost. They are being depreciated on a straight-line basis.
3. Moen owns factory machinery with a total cost of $51,000 and accumulated depreciation of $35,300. Included in factory machinery is one machine that cost $7,000 and has accumulated depreciation of $4,200. This machine is being held for resale and is not being used in operations.
4. Moen owns office equipment that cost $14,500 and has a book value of $6,300. It owns office furniture that cost $17,900 and has a book value of $11,400.

Required:
Prepare the property, plant, and equipment section of Moen's 2016 ending balance sheet.

E4-3 **Shareholders' Equity** The following are several of Graf Corporation's accounts at the end of 2016:

LO 4.3

Account	Credit Balance
Common Stock, $10 par	$ 47,100
Bonds Payable (due 2017)	126,000
Additional Paid-in Capital on Preferred Stock	39,600
Retained Earnings	209,000
Premium on Bonds Payable	12,300
Unearned Rent	4,800
Preferred Stock, $100 par	65,400
Additional Paid-in Capital on Common Stock	53,900
Unfunded Accrued Pension Cost	18,400
Treasury Stock (cost)	(7,600) debit
Accumulated Other Comprehensive Income	8,200

Required:
Prepare the shareholders' equity section of Graf's 2016 ending balance sheet.

E4-4 **Classifications on Balance Sheet** A balance sheet may contain the following major sections:

LO 4.3

A. Current assets
B. Long-term investments
C. Property, plant, and equipment
D. Intangible assets
E. Other assets
F. Current liabilities
G. Long-term liabilities
H. Contributed capital
I. Retained earnings
J. Accumulated other comprehensive income

Required:
The following is a list of accounts. Using the letters A through J, indicate in which section of the balance sheet each account would most likely be classified. Also indicate with a check mark (✓) any item that is a contra account. If an account cannot be classified in any of the preceding sections, indicate with an X and explain.

___1. Investments in Marketable Securities
___2. Discount on Bonds Payable (bonds due in 5 years)
___3. Additional Paid-in Capital on Common Stock
___4. Accounts Receivable
___5. Notes Payable (due in 5 years)
___6. Patents (net)
___7. Unrealized Decrease in Fair Value of Available-for-Sale Securities
___8. Preferred Stock
___9. Unearned Rent (to be earned within next 6 months)
___10. Accrued Pension Cost
___11. Trademarks
___12. Deficit
___13. Salaries Payable
___14. Land
___15. Investment in Ace Company Preferred Stock (to be held for 3 years)

E4-5 Classifications on Balance Sheet
LO 4.3

The balance sheet contains the following major sections:

A. Current assets
B. Long-term investments
C. Property, plant, and equipment
D. Intangible assets
E. Other assets
F. Current liabilities
G. Long-term liabilities
H. Contributed capital
I. Retained earnings
J. Accumulated other comprehensive income

Required:
The following is a list of several accounts. Using the letters A through J, indicate in which section of the balance sheet each of the accounts would be classified. Also indicate with a check mark (✓) any item that is a contra account. If an account cannot be classified in any of the preceding sections, indicate with an X and explain.

___ 1. Cash
___ 2. Bonds Payable (due in 8 years)
___ 3. Machinery
___ 4. Deficit
___ 5. Unexpired Insurance
___ 6. Franchise (net)
___ 7. Fund to Retire Preferred Stock
___ 8. Current Portion of Mortgage Payable
___ 9. Accumulated Depreciation
___10. Copyrights
___11. Investment in Held-to-Maturity Bonds
___12. Allowance for Doubtful Accounts
___13. Notes Receivable (due in 3 years)
___14. Property Taxes Payable
___15. Deferred Taxes Payable
___16. Additional Paid-in Capital on Preferred Stock
___17. Premium on Bonds Payable (due in 8 years)
___18. Work in Process
___19. Common Stock, $1 par
___20. Land
___21. Treasury Stock (at cost)
___22. Unrealized Increase in Value of Available-for-Sale Securities

E4-6 Balance Sheet
LO 4.3
LO 4.6

Baggett Company's balance sheet accounts and amounts as of December 31, 2016, are shown in random order as follows:

Account	Debit (Credit)	Account	Debit (Credit)
Income Taxes Payable	$ (3,800)	Additional Paid-in Capital on Preferred Stock	$ (7,900)
Prepaid Items	1,800	Allowance for Doubtful Accounts	(1,600)
Additional Paid-in Capital on Common Stock	(9,300)	Bonds Payable (due 2020)	(23,000)
Land	12,200	Buildings	57,400
Notes Payable (due 2019)	(6,000)	Sinking Fund to Retire Bonds Payable	5,000
Notes Receivable (due 2018)	16,400	Advances from Customers (long-term)	(2,600)
Accounts Receivable	12,600	Cash	4,300
Premium on Bonds Payable	(1,400)	Accumulated Depreciation: Equipment	(9,700)
Accounts Payable	(13,100)	Retained Earnings	(18,300)
Inventory	7,400	Preferred Stock, $100 par	(18,600)
Accumulated Depreciation: Buildings	(21,000)	Wages Payable	(1,400)
Patents (net)	4,600	Common Stock, $10 par	(12,700)
Equipment	28,700		

Required:
1. Prepare a December 31, 2016, balance sheet for Baggett.
2. Compute the debt-to-assets ratio.

E4-7 Balance Sheet Preparation
LO 4.3
LO 4.6
LO 4.7

The December 31, 2016, balance sheet accounts of Hitt Company are shown here in alphabetical order:

Account	Amount	Account	Amount
Accounts Payable	$ 22,400	Equipment	$ 72,400
Accounts Receivable	21,500	Inventory	37,200
Accumulated Depreciation: Buildings	53,000	Land	30,000
Accumulated Depreciation: Equipment	35,100	Marketable Securities (short-term)	6,100
Additional Paid-in Capital on Common Stock	24,000	Patents (net)	9,800
Additional Paid-in Capital on Preferred Stock	11,500	Preferred Stock, $100 par	21,000
Allowance for Doubtful Accounts	800	Retained Earnings	46,200
Bonds Payable (due 2024)	77,000	Revenues	107,000

Buildings	144,000	Salaries Expense	39,000
Cash	2,900	Salaries Payable	2,000
Common Stock, $10 par	30,000	Trademarks	3,700
Current Taxes Payable	10,400	Unrealized Increase in Value of	
Discount on Bonds Payable	6,900	Marketable Securities	1,100

Required:
1. Prepare Hitt's December 31, 2016, balance sheet.
2. Compute the working capital and the current ratio.
3. **Next Level** Discuss how the format of Hitt's balance sheet would be different from Requirement 1 if the company used IFRS.

E4-8
LO 4.3

Balance Sheet Calculations Dawson Company's balance sheet information at the end of 2016 and 2017 is as follows:

	2016	2017
Current assets	$ (a)	$25,000
Long-term liabilities	(b)	34,900
Total contributed capital	(c)	(g)
Long-term investments	19,200	(h)
Retained earnings	50,000	60,000
Total liabilities	(d)	(i)
Intangible assets	10,400	9,200
Current liabilities	14,500	12,300
Common stock, $5 par	(e)	20,000
Total assets	142,200	(j)
Additional paid-in capital	15,000	(k)
Property, plant, and equipment (net)	85,700	92,800
Accumulated other comprehensive income	6,900	7,000
Total shareholders' equity	(f)	(l)

Additional information: The company did not issue any common stock during 2017.

Required:
Next Level Fill in the blanks labeled (a) through (l). All the necessary information is provided. (*Hint:* It is not necessary to calculate your answers in alphabetical order.)

E4-9
LO 4.3

Balance Sheet Calculations Fermer Company's balance sheet information at the end of 2016 and 2017 is as follows:

	2016	2017
Total shareholders' equity	$ (a)	$100,700
Accumulated other comprehensive income	4,800	5,000
Current liabilities	(b)	9,800
Intangible assets	12,600	12,000
Property, plant, and equipment (net)	(c)	87,500
Current assets	19,100	(h)
Total contributed capital	51,000	(i)
Long-term liabilities	(d)	30,200
Retained earnings	40,900	(j)
Total assets	(e)	(k)
Common stock, $10 par	(f)	(l)
Working capital	9,900	10,200
Additional paid-in capital	(g)	36,000
Long-term investments	23,700	(m)
Total liabilities	38,100	(n)

(continued)

Additional information: At the end of 2016, additional paid-in capital is twice the amount of common stock. In 2017, the company issued (sold) 100 shares of common stock.

Required:
Next Level Fill in the blanks labeled (a) through (n). All the necessary information is provided. (*Hint:* It is not necessary to calculate your answers in alphabetical order.)

E4-10 **Correction of Balance Sheet** On December 31, 2016, Stevens Company's bookkeeper prepared the following
LO 4.3 balance sheet with items erroneously classified.

Stevens Company Balance Sheet
For Year Ended December 31, 2016

Current Assets:		Current Liabilities:	
Inventory	$ 6,000	Accounts payable	$ 9,900
Accounts receivable	5,900	Allowance for doubtful accounts	800
Cash	2,300	Salaries payable	1,500
Treasury stock (at cost)	3,300	Taxes payable	2,500
Long-Term Investments:		Long-Term Liabilities:	
Temporary investments in marketable securities	3,200	Bonds payable (due 2020)	11,000
Investment in held-to-maturity bonds	10,000	Unearned rent (for 3 months)	900
Property, Plant, and Equipment:		Shareholders' Equity:	
Land	8,100	Retained earnings	24,200
Office supplies	800	Accumulated depreciation on buildings and	
Buildings and equipment	35,600	equipment	9,200
Intangibles:		Additional paid-in capital on common stock	10,400
Patents (net)	5,000	Common stock, $10 par	12,000
Prepaid insurance (for 6 months)	1,200		
Discount on bonds payable	1,000		
Total Assets	$82,400	Total Credits	$82,400

Required:
Next Level You determine that the account balances listed on the balance sheet are correct but, in certain cases, incorrectly classified. Prepare a properly classified balance sheet for Stevens as of December 31, 2016.

E4-11 **Statement of Shareholders' Equity** On January 1, 2016, Powder Company provided the following shareholders'
LO 4.4 equity section of its balance sheet:

Contributed Capital:	
Preferred stock, $100 par	$ 92,800
Common stock, $5 par	37,400
Additional paid-in capital on preferred stock	21,500
Additional paid-in capital on common stock	58,700
Total contributed capital	$210,400
Retained earnings	185,700
Total Shareholders' Equity	$396,100

During 2016, the following transactions and events occurred and were properly recorded:
1. Powder issued 1,800 shares of common stock at $13 per share.
2. Powder issued 340 shares of preferred stock at $130 per share.
3. Powder earned net income of $38,950.
4. Powder paid a $7 per share dividend on the preferred stock and a $1 per share dividend on the common stock outstanding at the end of 2016.

Required:
Prepare Powder's statement of shareholders' equity (include retained earnings) for 2016.

E4-12 **Statement of Shareholders' Equity** On January 1, 2016, Osgood Film Studios reported the following alphabetical list of shareholders' equity items:

LO 4.4

SHOW ME HOW

Additional paid-in capital on common stock	$170,000
Additional paid-in capital on preferred stock	12,000
Common stock, $2 par	80,000
Preferred stock, $100 par	60,000
Retained earnings	209,000

During 2016, the company sold 3,000 shares of common stock for $10 per share and 500 shares of preferred stock for $125 per share. It also earned income of $99,000 and paid dividends of $8 per share on the preferred stock and $1.50 per share on the common stock outstanding at the end of 2016.

Required:
Prepare Osgood's statement of shareholders' equity (include retained earnings) for 2016.

PROBLEMS

P4-1 **Classifications on Balance Sheet** The current balance sheet of J. J. Arvesen Company contains the following major sections:

LO 4.3

A. Current assets
B. Long-term investments
C. Property, plant, and equipment
D. Intangible assets
E. Other assets

F. Current liabilities
G. Long-term liabilities
H. Contributed capital
I. Retained earnings
J. Accumulated other comprehensive income

Required:
The following is a list of accounts in random order. Using the letters A through J, indicate in which section each account would most likely be classified. Also indicate with a check mark (✓) any item that is a contra account. If an account cannot be classified in any of the preceding sections, indicate with an X and explain.

___ 1. Patents (net)
___ 2. Income Taxes Payable
___ 3. Notes Receivable (due in 5 months)
___ 4. Unearned Rent
___ 5. Discount on Bonds Payable (long-term bonds)
___ 6. Computer Equipment in the Data Processing Center
___ 7. Furniture
___ 8. Land Held for Future Expansion
___ 9. Timberland (net)
___10. Treasury Stock (at cost)
___11. Advances to Sales Personnel
___12. Idle Machinery
___13. Deferred Taxes Payable
___14. Raw Materials
___15. Investment in Held-to-Maturity Bonds
___16. Pollution Control Facilities
___17. Cash from Security Deposits of Customers on Returnable Containers
___18. Donated Capital for Industrial Park Building Site from Toma City
___19. Trademarks
___20. Finished Goods
___21. Cash Dividends Payable
___22. Bond Sinking Fund
___23. Short-Term Investments
___24. Retained Earnings
___25. Advances to Affiliated Company (long-term)
___26. Cash Surrender Value of Life Insurance
___27. Equipment under Capital Lease
___28. Additional Paid-in Capital on Preferred Stock
___29. Interest Receivable (due in 5 months)
___30. Office Supplies
___31. Accrued Pension Cost
___32. Capital Lease Obligation
___33. Investment in 8-Year Certificates of Deposit
___34. Unearned Ticket Sales
___35. Estimated Warranty (6-month) Obligations
___36. Unrealized Decrease in Value of Available-for-Sale Securities
___37. Cash

P4-2
LO 4.3

Balance Sheet without Amounts The following is an alphabetical list of all of White Limnology Company's adjusted trial balance accounts as of December 31, 2016:

Accounts Payable
Accounts Receivable
Accrued Pension Cost
Accumulated Depreciation: Buildings
Accumulated Depreciation: Equipment
Accumulated Depreciation: Machinery
Additional Paid-in Capital on Common Stock
Additional Paid-in Capital on Preferred Stock
Administrative Expenses
Allowance for Doubtful Accounts
Bond Sinking Fund
Bonds Payable (due 2022)
Buildings
Cash in Bank
Cash on Hand
Cash Surrender Value of Life Insurance
Common Stock
Cost of Goods Sold
Deferred Taxes Payable
Dividends Payable
Equipment
Estimated Warranty (1-year) Obligations
Finished Goods
General Expenses
Income Tax Expense
Income Taxes Payable
Interest Expense
Interest Payable

Interest Receivable
Interest Revenue
Investment in Available-for-Sale Securities
Land
Land for Future Plant Site
Loss on Sale of Equipment
Machinery
Mortgage Payable (20 equal annual payments)
Notes Payable (short-term)
Notes Receivable (short-term)
Office Supplies
Patents (net)
Preferred Stock
Premium on Bonds Payable
Prepaid Insurance
Raw Materials
Retained Earnings
Salaries Payable
Sales
Selling Expenses
Temporary Investments in Marketable Securities
Trademarks
Treasury Stock (at cost)
Unearned Rent
Unrealized Increase in Value of Available-for-Sale Securities
Work in Process

Required:
Prepare White Limnology's balance sheet (without amounts) in proper format.

P4-3
LO 4.3

Corrections to Balance Sheet Minett Boatbuilders Company prepared the following balance sheet:

Minett Boatbuilders Company
Balance Sheet for Year Ended December 31, 2016

Working capital	$ 22,800	Noncurrent liabilities	$ 62,000
Other assets	152,000	Shareholders' equity	112,800
Total	$174,800	Total	$174,800

Your analysis of these accounts reveals the following information:

1. Working capital consists of:

Land	$ 12,000
Accounts due from customers	18,000
Accounts due to suppliers	(22,700)
Inventories, including office supplies of $3,500	35,500
Income taxes owed	(16,400)
Wages owed	(3,600)
Note owed to bank (due December 31, 2018)	(17,000)
Securities held as a short-term investment	17,000
	$ 22,800

2. Other assets include:

Cash	$ 12,300
Prepaid insurance	2,400
Buildings and equipment	100,000
Discount on bonds payable	3,000
Investment in available-for-sale securities	29,000
Treasury stock (at cost)	5,300
	$152,000

3. Noncurrent liabilities consist of:

Bonds payable (due 2023)	$ 33,000
Allowance for doubtful accounts	1,400
Additional paid-in capital on preferred stock	2,600
Common stock, $5 par	25,000
	$ 62,000

4. Shareholders' equity includes:

Accumulated depreciation: Buildings and equipment	$ 40,000
Preferred stock, $100 par	12,000
Additional paid-in capital on common stock	15,600
Retained earnings	40,000
Accrued pension cost	6,500
Unrealized decrease in value of available-for-sale securities	(1,300)
	$112,800

Required:

Based on your analysis, prepare a properly classified December 31, 2016, balance sheet for Minett Boatbuilders.

P4-4
LO 4.3

Corrections to Balance Sheet Brandt Company presents the following December 31, 2016, balance sheet:

Brandt Company
Sheet of Balances for Year Ended December 31, 2016

Current assets	$ 44,300	Current liabilities	$ 66,600
Long-term investments	13,600	Long-term liabilities	24,100
Property, plant, and equipment	123,500	Contributed capital	17,000
Intangible assets	7,700	Unrealized capital	22,500
Other assets	13,600	Retained earnings	72,500
Total assets	$202,700	Total equities	$202,700

The following information is also available:

1. Current assets include cash, $3,800; accounts receivable, $18,500; notes receivable (maturity date July 1, 2021), $10,000; and land, $12,000.
2. Long-term investments include a $4,600 investment in available-for-sale securities that are expected to be sold in 2017 and a $9,000 investment in Dray Company bonds that are expected to be held until their December 31, 2019, maturity date.
3. Property, plant, and equipment include buildings costing $63,400, inventory costing $30,500, and equipment costing $29,600.
4. Intangible assets include patents that cost $8,200 (and on which $2,300 amortization has accumulated) and treasury stock that cost $1,800.
5. Other assets include prepaid insurance (which expires on November 30, 2017), $2,900; sinking fund for bond retirement, $7,000; and trademarks that cost $3,700 and are not impaired.
6. Current liabilities include accounts payable, $19,400; bonds payable (maturity date December 31, 2021), $40,000; and accrued income taxes payable, $7,200.
7. Long-term liabilities include accrued wages, $4,100; and mortgage payable (which is due in five equal annual payments starting December 31, 2017), $20,000.
8. Contributed capital includes common stock ($5 par), $11,000; and preferred stock ($100 par), $6,000.

(continued)

9. Unrealized capital includes premium on bonds payable, $4,300; additional paid-in capital on preferred stock, $2,400; additional paid-in capital on common stock, $14,700; and unrealized increase in value of securities available for sale, $1,100.
10. Retained earnings includes unrestricted retained earnings, $37,800; allowance for doubtful accounts, $700; and accumulated depreciation on buildings and equipment of $21,000 and $13,000, respectively.

Required:
Based on the preceding information, prepare a properly classified December 31, 2016, balance sheet for Brandt.

P4-5
LO 4.3
Balance Sheet Calculations Cornerstone Development Company's balance sheet information at the end of 2016 and 2017 is provided in random order, as follows:

	2016	2017
Long-term liabilities	$ (a)	$ 33,100
Accumulated other comprehensive income	8,000	8,900
Working capital	17,900	19,800
Intangible assets	19,100	18,600
Common stock, $10 par	(b)	(i)
Total shareholders' equity	(c)	179,000
Accumulated depreciation	(37,500)	(48,600)
Total liabilities	51,900	(j)
Current assets	(d)	39,800
Retained earnings	83,300	(k)
Total contributed capital	66,700	(l)
Total assets	(e)	(m)
Additional paid-in capital	(f)	(n)
Long-term investments	40,100	(o)
Current liabilities	(g)	(p)
Property, plant, and equipment	(h)	180,000

Additional information: At the end of 2016, (a) the amount of long-term liabilities is twice the amount of current liabilities and (b) there are 2,900 shares of common stock outstanding. During 2017, the company (a) issued 100 shares of common stock for $25 per share, (b) earned net income of $20,600, and (c) paid dividends of $1 per share on the common stock outstanding at year-end.

Required:
Next Level Fill in the blanks lettered (a) through (p). All of the necessary information is provided. (*Hint:* It is not necessary to calculate your answers in alphabetical order.)

P4-6
LO 4.3
Erroneous Balance Sheet Cutler Corporation prepared the following balance sheet:

Cutler Corporation
Balance Report For Year Ended December 31, 2016

Current Assets:			Current Liabilities:		
Cash		$ 6,300	Accounts payable		$ 13,000
Accounts receivable		15,900	Accumulated depreciation:		
Inventory, at higher of cost or market (cost $27,200)		28,000	buildings		17,100
			Wages payable		3,000
Long-Term Investments:			Additional paid-in capital on		
Treasury stock (at cost)		1,400	common stock		23,200
Investment in D Company bonds (at book value)		7,300	Long-Term Liabilities:		
			Bonds payable	$46,000	
Marketable securities, short-term at fair value		10,000	Less: Sinking fund to retire bonds	(6,000)	40,000
Property, Plant, and Equipment:			Preferred stock, $50 par		15,000
Land		11,300	Additional paid-in capital on preferred stock		5,100

Patents	$ 8,000		Accumulated depreciation:	
Less: Accumulated amortization	(2,800)	5,200	Equipment	7,000
Buildings		40,800	Current taxes payable	9,600
Equipment		19,000	Owners' Equity:	
Intangibles:			Common stock, $2 par	8,000
Trademarks		5,700	Unrealized gain on write-up of	
Other Assets:			marketable securities to	
Cash surrender value of life			fair value	1,300
insurance		5,000	Unrealized gain on write-up of	
Discount on bonds payable		3,900	inventory to market value	800
			Retained earnings	16,000
			Allowance for doubtful accounts	700
Total Assets		$159,800	Total Equities	$159,800

Required:
1. **Next Level** Identify the errors made in the Cutler balance sheet.
2. Prepare a corrected, properly classified balance sheet.

P4-7
LO 4.3
AICPA Adapted

Complex Balance Sheet Presented below is the unaudited balance sheet as of December 31, 2016, prepared by Zeus Manufacturing Corporation's bookkeeper.

Zeus Manufacturing Corporation
Balance Sheet for the Year Ended December 31, 2016

Assets		Liabilities and Shareholders' Equity	
Cash	$ 225,000	Accounts payable	$ 133,800
Accounts receivable (net)	345,700	Mortgage payable	900,000
Inventories	560,000	Notes payable	500,000
Prepaid income taxes	40,000	Lawsuit liability	80,000
Investments	57,700	Income taxes payable	61,200
Land	450,000	Deferred tax liability	28,000
Building	1,750,000	Accumulated depreciation	420,000
Machinery and equipment	1,964,000	Total Liabilities	$2,123,000
Goodwill	37,000	Common stock, $50 par; 40,000 shares issued	$2,231,000
Total Assets	$5,429,400	Retained earnings	1,075,400
		Total Shareholders' Equity	$3,306,400
		Total Liabilities and Shareholders' Equity	$5,429,400

Your company has been engaged to perform an audit, during which you discover the following information:
1. Checks totaling $14,000 in payment of accounts payable were mailed on December 31, 2016, but were not recorded until 2017. Late in December 2016, the bank returned a customer's $2,000 check marked "NSF," but no entry was made. Cash includes $100,000 restricted for building purposes.
2. Included in accounts receivable is a $30,000 note due on December 31, 2019, from Zeus's president.
3. During 2016, Zeus purchased 500 shares of common stock of a major corporation that supplies Zeus with raw materials. Total cost of this stock was $51,300, and fair value on December 31, 2016, was $47,000. The decline in fair value is considered temporary. Zeus plans to hold these shares indefinitely.
4. Treasury stock was recorded at cost when Zeus purchased 200 of its own shares for $32 per share in May 2016. This amount is included in investments.
5. On December 31, 2016, Zeus borrowed $500,000 from a bank in exchange for a 10% note payable, maturing December 31, 2021. Equal principal payments are due December 31 of each year beginning in 2017. This note is collateralized by a $250,000 tract of land acquired as a potential future building site, which is included in land.
6. The mortgage payable requires $50,000 principal payments, plus interest, at the end of each month. Payments were made on January 31 and February 28, 2017. The balance of this mortgage was due June 30, 2017. On March 1, 2017, prior to issuance of the audited financial statements, Zeus consummated a noncancelable agreement with the lender to refinance this mortgage. The new terms require $100,000 annual principal

(continued)

payments, plus interest, on February 28 of each year, beginning in 2018. The final payment is due February 28, 2025.
7. The lawsuit liability will be paid in 2017.
8. Of the total deferred tax liability, $5,000 is considered a current liability.
9. The current income tax expense reported in Zeus's 2016 income statement was $61,200.
10. The company was authorized to issue 100,000 shares of $50 par value common stock.

Required:
Prepare a corrected classified balance sheet as of December 31, 2016. This financial statement should include a proper heading, format, and necessary descriptions.

P4-8
LO 4.3
Analyzing Starbucks's Balance Sheet Disclosures Review the financial statements and related notes of **Starbucks** in Appendix A.

Required:
Answer the following questions pertaining to Starbucks's balance sheet as of September 27, 2015, and related information. (*Note*: You do not need to make any calculations. All answers may be found in the financial report.)
1. What was the amount of the current assets and current liabilities?
2. What was the single largest current asset and current liability?
3. What was the amount in the allowance for doubtful accounts?
4. What is the par value of the company's common stock? How many shares were issued and outstanding?
5. What was the total amount of inventory? What were the principal categories of inventory?
6. What costing method was used for inventories?
7. What was the total property, plant, and equipment before and after accumulated depreciation?
8. What was the accumulated depreciation? What method does the company use to depreciate its property, plant, and equipment?
9. What was the long-term debt? When is the debt due?
10. What was the retained earnings balance? What caused retained earnings to change in 2015?
11. What was the accumulated other comprehensive income/(loss) balance?
12. What was the noncontrolling interest balance?

P4-9
LO 4.4
Statement of Shareholders' Equity On January 1, 2016, Knox Company showed the following alphabetical list of shareholders' equity items:

Additional paid-in capital on common stock	$130,000
Additional paid-in capital on preferred stock	6,000
Common stock, $10 par	100,000
Preferred stock, $100 par	50,000
Retained earnings	224,000

During 2016, the following events occurred and were properly recorded by the company:
1. Knox purchased an investment in available-for-sale securities. At year-end, the fair value of the securities had increased by $9,000.
2. Knox issued 2,000 shares of common stock for $25 per share.
3. Knox issued 110 shares of preferred stock for $116 per share.
4. Knox reacquired 400 shares of its common stock as treasury stock at a cost of $26 per share. (*Hint:* Record the reacquisition cost in a Treasury Stock account.)
5. Knox earned net income of $57,000.
6. Knox paid a $7 per share dividend on the preferred stock and a $1.25 per share dividend on the common stock outstanding at the end of 2016 (treasury stock is not entitled to dividends).

Required:
Prepare a statement of shareholders' equity for 2016, including retained earnings.

P4-10
LO 4.3
LO 4.7

Balance Sheet The following is a list (in random order) of KIP International Products Company's December 31, 2016, balance sheet accounts:

Additional Paid-in Capital on Preferred Stock	$ 1,600	Accounts Payable	$16,500
Accounts Receivable	13,800	Prepaid Insurance	900
Dividends Payable	1,800	Discount on Bonds Payable	2,000
Buildings	50,000	Common Stock, $10 par	15,000
Bonds Payable (due 2019)	29,000	Equipment	29,000
Retained Earnings	25,800	Allowance for Doubtful Accounts	700
Office Supplies	1,900	Preferred Stock, $50 par	10,000
Current Income Taxes Payable	4,200	Accumulated Depreciation: Buildings	12,400
Accumulated Depreciation: Equipment	8,300	Current Interest Payable	2,900
Patents (net)	2,400	Investment in Held-to-Maturity Bonds	9,000
Notes Payable (due January 1, 2019)	17,000	Cash	8,200
Inventory	24,400	Treasury Stock (at cost)	1,500
Additional Paid-in Capital on Common Stock	7,700	Accrued Wages	3,700
Sinking Fund for Bond Retirement	4,000	Land	9,500

Required:

1. Prepare a properly classified balance sheet according to U.S. GAAP for KIP as of December 31, 2016.
2. Assume instead that KIP uses IFRS. Prepare its balance sheet as of December 31, 2016.

P4-11
LO 4.3
LO 4.6

Balance Sheet The following is an alphabetical list of Lloyd's Hudson Dealership Inc.'s December 31, 2016, balance sheet accounts and amounts:

Accounts Payable	$20,900	Investment in Available-for-Sale Securities	$16,400
Accounts Receivable	15,300	Land	17,000
Accrued Pension Cost	13,300	Machinery and Equipment	57,800
Accumulated Depreciation: Buildings	32,400	Marketable Securities (short-term)	8,400
Accumulated Depreciation: Machinery and Equipment	30,000	Notes Payable (short-term)	5,000
Allowance for Doubtful Accounts	1,000	Patents (net)	8,600
Bond Sinking Fund	7,700	Preferred Stock, $100 par	30,000
Bonds Payable (due 2024)	29,000	Additional Paid-In Capital on Common Stock	16,300
Buildings	92,500	Additional Paid-In Capital on Preferred Stock	7,000
Cash	7,200	Prepaid Insurance	2,600
Common Stock, $10 par	44,100	Raw Materials	10,100
Deferred Taxes Payable	2,800	Retained Earnings	28,100
Discount on Bonds Payable	2,500	Unearned Rent	5,000
Dividends Payable	5,600	Unrealized Increase in Value of	
Finished Goods	23,800	Available-for-Sale Stock	2,000
Income Taxes Payable	8,900	Wages Payable	2,700
Interest Payable	500	Work in Process	14,700

Required:
1. Prepare a properly classified balance sheet for Lloyd's Hudson Dealership as of December 31, 2016. List the additional parenthetical or note disclosures (if any) that should be made for each item.
2. **Next Level** Compute the current ratio. What does it indicate about Lloyd's Hudson Dealership?

P4-12
LO 4.3
LO 4.6

Balance Sheet from Adjusted Trial Balance The following is the alphabetical adjusted trial balance of Meadows Company on December 31, 2016:

	Debits	Credits
Accounts Payable		$ 9,800
Accounts Receivable	$ 18,000	
Accrued Payables		6,500
Accumulated Depreciation		44,000
Additional Paid-in Capital		50,600
Cash	7,900	
Common Stock, $5 par		29,600
Cost of Goods Sold	175,500	

(continued)

	Debits	Credits
Current Portion of Long-Term Debt		6,200
Deferred Taxes Payable		12,500
Dividends Distributed	7,000	
General Expenses	27,560	
Income Tax Expense	12,340	
Income Taxes Payable		7,500
Interest Expense	4,300	
Inventories	32,000	
Investment in Held-to-Maturity Bonds	36,000	
Long-Term Debt		56,300
Long-Term Receivables	38,600	
Marketable Securities (short-term)	10,100	
Patents (net)	13,000	
Prepaid Insurance	5,000	
Property, Plant, and Equipment	148,000	
Retained Earnings, 1/1/16		64,800
Sales		270,000
Selling Expenses	21,500	
Unrealized Decrease in Value of Available-for-Sale Securities	1,000	
	$557,800	$557,800

Required:
1. Prepare Meadows's December 31, 2016, balance sheet.
2. **Next Level** Compute the debt-to-assets ratio. What does it indicate about Meadows at the end of 2016?

P4-13 **Balance Sheet and Notes** Listed here in random order are Wicks Construction Limited's balance sheet accounts
LO 4.3 and related ending balances as of December 31, 2016:
LO 4.5
LO 4.6

SHOW
ME HOW

Income Taxes Payable	$ 24,700	Short-Term Investments	$19,100
Cash Surrender Value of Life Insurance	8,900	Bonds Payable	80,000
Preferred Stock	40,000	Additional Paid-in Capital on Common Stock	30,300
Premium on Bonds Payable	4,800	Inventories	98,500
Cash	11,600	Accounts Receivable	32,300
Property, Plant, and Equipment (net)	229,300	Patents (net)	18,200
Accounts Payable	58,000	Investment in Bonds	25,000
Common Stock	62,800	Additional Paid-in Capital on Preferred Stock	23,400
Retained Earnings	123,400	Miscellaneous Current Payables	6,200
Land Held for Building Site	19,500	Estimated Liability for Product Warranties	7,300
Allowance for Doubtful Accounts	1,500		

Additional information:
1. The company reports on the balance sheet the total amount for inventories and the net book value of property, plant, and equipment, with the related details for each account disclosed in notes.
2. The straight-line method is used to depreciate buildings, machinery, and equipment, based upon their cost and estimated residual values and lives. A breakdown of property, plant, and equipment shows the following: land at a cost of $32,000, buildings at a cost of $182,400 and a net book value of $120,200, machinery at a cost of $63,900, and related accumulated depreciation of $18,600, and equipment (40% depreciated) at a cost of $53,000.
3. Patents are amortized on a straight-line basis directly to the Patent account.
4. Inventories are listed at the lower of cost or market value using an average cost. The inventories include raw materials, $22,200; work in process, $34,700; and finished goods, $41,600.
5. Common stock has a $10 par value per share, 12,000 shares are authorized, and 6,280 shares have been issued.
6. Preferred stock has a $100 par value per share, 1,000 shares are authorized, and 400 shares have been issued.
7. The investment in bonds is carried at the original cost, which is the face value, and is being held to maturity.
8. Short-term investments in marketable securities were purchased at year-end.
9. The bonds payable mature on December 31, 2021.
10. The company attaches a 1-year warranty on all the products it sells.

Required:
1. Prepare Wicks Construction's December 31, 2016, balance sheet (including appropriate parenthetical notations).
2. Prepare notes to accompany the balance sheet that itemize company accounting policies; inventories; and property, plant, and equipment.
3. **Next Level** Compute the current ratio and the quick ratio. How do these two ratios provide different information about the company's liquidity? Why are these ratios useful?

P4-14 **Comprehensive: Balance Sheet, Schedules, and Notes** The following is an alphabetical listing of Stone Boat Company's balance sheet accounts and account balances on December 31, 2016:

LO 4.3
LO 4.4
LO 4.5
LO 4.6

Accounts Payable	$ 44,200	Income Taxes Payable	$ 19,700
Accounts Receivable	37,100	Inventory	85,300
Accumulated Depreciation	109,300	Investment in Affiliate	30,000
Additional Paid-in Capital on Common Stock	20,000	Long-Term Liabilities (book value)	91,000
Additional Paid-in Capital on Preferred Stock	3,200	Miscellaneous Current Payables	6,800
Allowance for Doubtful Accounts	1,600	Notes Receivable	17,000
Bond Sinking Fund	12,500	Preferred Stock	32,000
Cash	13,800	Property, Plant, and Equipment	296,700
Common Stock	80,000	Retained Earnings	84,600

Additional information:
1. The company reports on the balance sheet the net book value of property and equipment and long-term liabilities (known as control accounts). The related details are disclosed in the notes.
2. The straight-line method is used to depreciate property and equipment based upon cost, estimated residual value, and estimated life. The costs of the assets in this account are: land, $29,500; buildings, $164,600; store fixtures, $72,600; and office equipment, $30,000.
3. The accumulated depreciation breakdown is as follows: buildings, $54,600; store fixtures, $37,400; and office equipment, $17,300.
4. The long-term debt includes 12%, $36,000 face value bonds that mature on December 31, 2021, and have an unamortized bond discount of $1,000; 11%, $48,000 face value bonds that mature on December 31, 2022, have a premium on bonds payable of $1,800, and whose retirement is being funded by a bond sinking fund; and a 13% note payable that has a face value of $6,200 and matures on January 1, 2019.
5. The non-interest-bearing note receivable matures on June 1, 2020.
6. Inventory is listed at lower of cost or market; cost is determined on the basis of average cost.
7. The investment in affiliate is carried at cost. The company has guaranteed the interest on 12%, $50,000, 15-year bonds issued by this affiliate, Jay Company.
8. Common stock has a $10 par value per share, 10,000 shares are authorized, and 1,000 shares were issued during 2016 at a price of $13 per share, resulting in 8,000 shares issued at year-end.
9. Preferred stock has a $50 par value per share, 2,000 shares are authorized, and 140 shares were issued during 2016 at a price of $55 per share, resulting in 640 shares issued at year-end.
10. On January 15, 2017, before the December 31, 2016, balance sheet was issued, a building with a cost of $20,000 and a book value of $7,000 was totally destroyed. Insurance proceeds will amount to only $5,000.
11. Net income and dividends declared and paid during the year were $50,500 and $21,000, respectively.

Required:
1. Prepare Stone Boat's December 31, 2016, balance sheet (including appropriate parenthetical notations).
2. Prepare a statement of shareholders' equity for 2016. (*Hint:* Work back from the *ending* account balances.)
3. Prepare notes that itemize the balance sheet control accounts and those necessary to disclose any company accounting policies, contingent liabilities, and subsequent events.
4. **Next Level** Compute the debt-to-assets ratio at the end of 2016. What is your evaluation of this ratio if it was 39% at the end of 2015?

(continued)

Use the following information for P4-15 and P4-16:

McCormick & Company, Inc. is one of the world's leading producers of spices, herbs, seasonings, condiments, and other flavorings for foods. Its products are sold to consumers, with some of the leading brands of spices and seasonings, as well as to industrial producers of foods. McCormick's consolidated balance sheets for 2012 and 2013 follow.

McCormick: Consolidated Balance Sheets

	Dollar Amounts in Millions	
	2012	2013
Assets		
Current Assets		
Cash and Equivalents	$ 79.0	$ 63.0
Receivables	465.9	495.5
Inventories	615.0	676.9
Prepaid Expenses and Other Assets	125.5	134.8
Total Current Assets	**$1,285.4**	**$1,370.2**
Property and Equipment, Net	547.3	576.6
Goodwill	1,695.3	1,798.5
Intangible Assets, net	323.5	333.4
Investments and Other Assets	313.9	371.0
Total Assets	**$4,165.4**	**$4,449.7**
Liabilities and Shareholders' Equity		
Current Liabilities		
Short-Term Borrowings	$ 140.3	$ 211.6
Current Portion of Long-Term Debt	252.3	2.5
Trade Accounts Payable	375.8	387.3
Other Accrued Liabilities	419.2	461.7
Total Current Liabilities	**$1,187.6**	**$1,063.1**
Long-Term Debt	779.2	1,019.0
Other Long-Term Liabilities	498.4	419.9
Total Liabilities	**$2,465.2**	**$2,502.0**
Shareholders' Equity		
Common Stock	908.2	962.4
Retained Earnings	934.6	970.4
Accumulated Other Comprehensive Loss	(159.9)	(0.3)
Noncontrolling interests	17.3	15.2
Total Shareholders' Equity	**$1,700.2**	**$1,947.7**
Total Liabilities and Shareholders' Equity	**$4,165.4**	**$4,449.7**

P4-15 **Common-Size and Rate of Change Analyses: McCormick** Refer to the information for **McCormick** above.
LO 4.6

SHOW ME HOW

Required:

Compute the common-size balance sheet for 2013 and the rate of change balance sheet for 2013. Which two asset accounts and which two liability and shareholders' equity accounts are the largest relative to total assets in 2013? Which two asset accounts and which two liability and shareholders' equity accounts grew at the fastest rates in 2013? (*Note:* You may find it helpful to enter the data into an Excel spreadsheet for these computations.)

P4-16 **Ratios Analyses: McCormick** Refer to the information for **McCormick** above. Additional information for 2013
LO 4.6 is as follows (amounts in millions):

Total credit sales (all on credit)	$4,123.4
Costs of goods sold	2,457.6
Net income	389.0

Required:

Next Level Compute the following ratios for 2013. Provide a brief description of what each ratio reveals about McCormick.
1. return on common equity
2. debt-to-assets
3. debt-to-equity
4. current

5. quick (McCormick uses cash and equivalents, short-term securities, and receivables in their quick ratio calculation.)
6. inventory turnover days
7. accounts receivable turnover days
8. accounts payable turnover days
9. operating cycle (in days)
10. total asset turnover

Use the following information for P4-17 and P4-18:

The Hershey Company is one of the world's leading producers of chocolates, candies, and confections. It sells chocolates and candies, mints and gums, baking ingredients, toppings, and beverages. Hershey's consolidated balance sheets for 2012 and 2013 follow.

Hershey: Consolidated Balance Sheets

	Dollar Amounts in Millions	
	2012	2013
Assets		
Current Assets		
Cash and Equivalents	$ 728.3	$ 1,118.5
Receivables	461.4	477.9
Inventories	633.3	659.5
Deferred Income Taxes	122.2	52.5
Prepaid Expenses and Other Assets	168.3	178.9
Total Current Assets	$ 2,113.5	$ 2,487.3
Property, Plant and Equipment, Net	1,674.1	1,805.3
Goodwill	588.0	576.6
Other Intangible Assets, net	214.7	195.2
Other Assets	164.5	293.0
Total Assets	$ 4,754.8	$ 5,357.5
Liabilities and Shareholders' Equity		
Current Liabilities		
Accounts Payable	$ 442.0	$ 461.5
Accrued Liabilities	650.9	699.7
Accrued Income Taxes	2.3	79.9
Short-Term Debt	118.2	166.0
Current Portion of Long-Term Debt	257.7	0.9
Total Current Liabilities	$ 1,471.1	$ 1,408.0
Long-Term Debt	1,531.0	1,795.1
Other Long-Term Liabilities	668.7	434.1
Deferred Income Taxes	35.7	104.2
Total Liabilities	$ 3,706.5	$ 3,741.4
Shareholders' Equity		
Common Stock	359.9	359.9
Additional Paid-In Capital	593.0	664.9
Retained Earnings	5,027.6	5,454.3
Treasury Stock (at cost)	(4,558.7)	(4,707.7)
Accumulated Other Comprehensive Loss	(385.1)	(166.6)
Noncontrolling interests	11.6	11.2
Total Shareholders' Equity	$ 1,048.4	$ 1,616.1
Total Liabilities and Shareholders' Equity	$ 4,754.8	$ 5,357.5

P4-17 **Common-Size and Rate of Change Analyses: Hershey** Refer to the information for **Hershey** above.
LO 4.6

Required:

Compute the common-size balance sheet for 2013 and the rate of change balance sheet for 2013. Which two asset accounts and which two liability and shareholders' equity accounts are the largest relative to total assets in 2013? Which two asset accounts and which two liability and shareholders' equity accounts grew at the fastest rates in 2013? (*Note:* You may find it helpful to enter the data into an Excel spreadsheet for these computations.)

P4-18
LO 4.6

Ratios Analysis: Hershey Refer to the information for **Hershey** on the preceding page. Additional information for 2013 is as follows (amounts in millions):

Total credit sales (all on credit)	$7,146.1
Costs of goods sold	3,865.2
Net income	820.5

Required:

Next Level Compute the following ratios for 2013. Provide a brief description of what each ratio reveals about Hershey.
1. return on common equity
2. debt-to-assets
3. debt-to-equity
4. current
5. quick (Hershey uses cash and equivalents, short-term securities, and receivables in their quick ratio calculation.)
6. inventory turnover days
7. accounts receivable turnover days
8. accounts payable turnover days
9. operating cycle (in days)
10. total asset turnover

CASES

COMMUNICATION

C4-1
LO 4.2

Alternative Valuation Methods

A friend who had a bookkeeping course in high school and who is currently a business major says, "I thought that assets were always reported at their historical cost on a company's balance sheet. Recently, however, I heard several accounting majors discussing why a company is required (or elects) to report the fair value of an asset. I know that historical cost is the exchange price paid for an asset, so I can't understand why a company would report any other 'value' for the asset, or how that value could be measured."

Required:
Write a short memo that briefly explains why sometimes a company is required (or elects) to report the fair value of an asset. Then define fair value and explain how it is measured.

C4-2
LO 4.2

Asset Measurement

It is the end of 2016 and you are an accountant for Stone Company. During 2016, sales of the company's products slumped and the company's earnings are expected to be much less than those of 2015. The president comes to you with an idea. He says, "Our company's property, plant, and equipment cost $300,000, and that is the amount we usually report on our balance sheet. However, I just had these assets appraised by an independent appraiser, and she says they are worth $400,000. I think that the company should report the property, plant, and equipment at this amount on its December 31, 2016, balance sheet and should report the $100,000 increase in value as a gain on the 2016 income statement. If we use this approach, it will show how much our company is really worth and increase our earnings. This will make our shareholders happy. What do you think?"

Required:
Prepare a written response to the president.

C4-3
LO 4.5

Contingencies and Subsequent Events

The bookkeeper of a company you are auditing states, "Our balance sheet is dated December 31, the end of our accounting period. I don't understand loss contingencies and subsequent events. Also, I see no reason for disclosing these items on the company's balance sheet because they deal with events that might occur or have occurred *after* the balance sheet date."

Required:
Write a short report to the bookkeeper that explains loss contingencies and subsequent events, as well as the importance of their disclosure on the company's balance sheet.

CREATIVE AND CRITICAL THINKING

C4-4
LO 4.2
Valuation of Assets and Stock

A friend has come to you for advice. He states that he owns several shares of stock in a corporation. He has examined the most recent balance sheet of the corporation and has found that the common stock issued and outstanding totals 40,000 shares, and the market price per share is $25 on the balance sheet date. He is sure that the balance sheet must be in error because, in his words, "the total assets are $1,100,000 and this current value should be the same as the $1,000,000 total value of the outstanding common stock."

Required:
Explain to your friend how the "values" of the various assets of the corporation typically are measured and reported on its balance sheet, and how the "value" of the $1,100,000 total assets is determined. Continue the discussion by explaining to your friend why the "values" of the assets and the stock are not the same.

C4-5 **Ethics and Accounts Receivable Adjustment**

It is February 16, 2017, and you are auditing Davenport Corporation's financial statements for 2016 (which will be issued in March 2017). You read in the newspaper that Travis Corporation, a major customer of Davenport, is in financial difficulty. Included in Davenport's accounts receivable is $50,000 (a material amount) owed to it by Travis. You approach Jim Davenport, president, with this information and suggest that a reduction of accounts receivable and recognition of a loss for 2016 might be appropriate. Jim replies, "Why should we make an adjustment? Ted Travis, the president of Travis Corporation, is a friend of mine; he will find a way to pay us, one way or another. Furthermore, this occurred in 2017, so let's wait and see what happens; we can always make an adjustment later this year. Our 2016 income and year-end working capital are not that high; our creditors and shareholders wouldn't stand for lower amounts than they already are."

Required:
From financial reporting and ethical perspectives, prepare a response to Jim Davenport regarding this issue.

C4-6 **Ethics and Note Due from President**

You are the accountant for Speedy Company and are preparing the financial statements for 2016. Near the end of 2016, Speedy loaned its president $100,000 (a material amount) because she was having financial difficulties. The note was properly recorded as a note receivable by Speedy. You are unsure of how to classify this note on the 2016 ending balance sheet and ask the president when the note is due. She replies, "We never really set a due date; I might repay it in 2017 or maybe in a couple of years when I get more financially secure. It would be best to classify this note as a current asset in the usual manner because that will increase our working capital and current ratio, which will make our creditors and shareholders happy."

Required:
From financial reporting and ethical perspectives, what do you think of the president's suggestion?

C4-7 **Analyzing Starbucks's Accounting Policies**

A company must include a summary of its accounting policies in the notes to its financial statements. **Starbucks** includes this summary as the first note to the consolidated financial statements shown in Appendix A.

Required:
1. Explain what is required to be disclosed about the accounting policies of a company.
2. Review the Starbucks note on its accounting policies and answer the following questions:
    a. What items are classified as cash equivalents?
    b. How are inventories valued, and what inventory costing method(s) is used?
    c. How are property, plant, and equipment stated, and what depreciation method is used?
    d. How much is the allowance for doubtful accounts at the end of 2015? What was the amount of gross receivables?
    e. When does the company test goodwill for impairment?
    f. What items do not appear on the balance sheet as assets or liabilities because the company uses them under operating leases?
    g. How does the company account for treasury stock repurchases?

C4-8 **Analyzing LVMH Group's Balance Sheet**

Review the comparative consolidated balance sheets of **LVMH Group** as of the end of 2013, 2012, and 2011 as shown in the chapter on page 4-46. LVMH prepared these balance sheets using IFRS, and all amounts are expressed in millions of euros.

(continued)

Required:

Answer the following questions pertaining to LVMH Group's balance sheets.

1. What was the amount of the current assets and current liabilities at the end of 2013 and 2012?
2. What was the current ratio at the end of 2013 and 2012? Did LVMH's liquidity increase or decrease in 2013?
3. What was the single largest current asset and current liability?
4. How much has LVMH borrowed in short- and long term debt as of the end of 2013? Did these borrowings increase or decrease in 2013?
5. What is the total amount of liabilities as of the end of 2013 and 2012?
6. What was the total amount of equity as of the end of 2013 and 2012?
7. What was the debt-to-equity ratio as of the end of 2013 and 2012? How did LVMH's leverage change in 2013?
8. What was the inventory turnover rate in 2013? What was the average number of days for inventory turnover in 2013? Does the number of days for inventory turnover for LVMH seem long or short? If so, what aspect of LVMH's business strategy might explain the length of time it takes to turn over inventory? (*Note:* LVMH recognized €10,055 million in cost of sales in 2013.)
9. Are LVMH's noncurrent assets at the end of 2013 primarily tangible, intangible, or financial in nature?
10. What was the amount in investments in associates at the end of 2013?
11. What was the amount of minority interest in equity at the end of 2013?
12. Given your answers to questions 9 and 10, when LVMH has less than 100% ownership in another company, is it more likely that LVMH owns a minority of the equity (less than 50% of the outstanding shares) or a majority?

USING CODIFICATION

C4-9   Researching GAAP

Situation

You are the assistant accountant for Tyler Corporation. It is mid-January 2017 and you are helping to prepare Tyler's balance sheet for December 31, 2016. Tyler will publish this balance sheet on March 1, 2017, after the auditors have completed their work. Tyler has a $100,000 note payable that was issued in 2015 and that is due March 6, 2017. On January 5, 2017, Tyler sold 2,000 shares of its $10 par common stock for $80,000. Its intent is to use these proceeds (plus $20,000 cash it already has on hand) to repay the note payable on March 6. The head accountant says "I'm not sure how to classify the $100,000 note payable on the December 31, 2016, balance sheet. Check this out for me."

Directions

Research the related generally accepted accounting principles and prepare a short memo to the head accountant that explains how Tyler should report the $100,000 note payable on its December 31, 2016, balance sheet.

CHAPTER 5

THE INCOME STATEMENT AND THE STATEMENT OF CASH FLOWS

The Importance of Earnings

While the balance sheet represents a company's financial position, the income statement represents its financial performance. The income statement is an essential statement in the financial reporting system because it reports how well the company performed in generating revenues, incurring expenses, and creating profits for investors, lenders, creditors, and other stakeholders.

Because the bottom-line net income amount on the income statement provides so much useful information for so many stakeholders, it receives more attention from capital markets participants than any other measure of firm performance. When the earnings results are known at the end of each quarter or fiscal year, many publicly listed companies hold press conferences to announce them. Quarterly and annual earnings releases are typically covered by the financial media through broadcast networks like **CNN** and **CNBC**, online media such as **Yahoo! Finance**, as well as print media like *The Wall Street Journal* and *The Financial Times*. Stock prices typically react quickly—rising or falling—depending on whether the earnings news was better or worse than expected. Recall from Chapter 1 the evidence that shows firms that report an increase (a decrease) in earnings compared to the prior year's earnings experience annual stock returns that are on average 19.2% above (16.4% below) market average returns. These results suggest that merely the sign of the change in annual earnings is associated with an average annual 35.6% difference in stock return performance.

LEARNING OBJECTIVES

After reading this chapter you will be able to

LO 5.1 Explain the purposes of an income statement.

LO 5.2 Understand the capital maintenance concept of income.

LO 5.3 Define the elements of an income statement.

LO 5.4 Describe the major components of an income statement.

LO 5.5 Report results from discontinued operations.

LO 5.6 Understand basic earnings per share.

LO 5.7 Report comprehensive income.

LO 5.8 Understand the similarities and differences in how income statements are presented under IFRS versus U.S. GAAP.

LO 5.9 Explain the statement of cash flows and classify cash flows as operating, investing, or financing.

LO 5.10 Apply financial statement analysis techniques to analyze the income statement and cash flow statement information.

LO 5.11 *(Appendix 5.1)* Understand segment reporting and interim reporting.

Stock analysts usually devote tremendous amounts of time developing forecasts for quarterly and annual earnings numbers. For example, at the time of this writing, 27 financial analysts, from firms such as **Goldman Sachs** and **Morgan Stanley**, follow **Starbucks** and frequently issue earnings forecasts. Earnings numbers receive so much attention because they convey useful, value-relevant information to investors and other stakeholders. Income statement information helps investors and other stakeholders evaluate the financial performance of the company and assess whether executives and managers are effectively implementing the company's strategy, generating revenues and growth, controlling costs and expenses, and creating profits.

Because of the important economic consequences associated with earnings numbers, managers face intense pressure to generate earnings numbers that will please investors and stakeholders. Company executives and managers are commonly given compensation packages that include a bonus contingent on whether the company meets or exceeds certain earnings targets established by the board of directors. While the vast majority of company managers strive to generate impressive earnings through legitimate business activities, some companies "manage earnings," manipulating reported earnings numbers to make performance look better than it is. Therefore, investors, lenders, analysts, auditors, and securities regulators such as the SEC must carefully analyze reported earnings numbers.

From the opening vignette, it is clear that the income statement is one of the most important statements in financial reporting. The income statement summarizes the results of a company's financial performance for a period.[1] A company's financial performance is determined primarily by its operating activities (producing and selling goods and services to customers), as well as results from investing activities (such as interest and dividend income) and financing activities (such as interest expense). Although income is largely determined by normal, recurring operating, investing, and financing activities, it can also be impacted by other activities that are infrequent or unusual. A company may generate gains or losses by selling assets or settling liabilities, divesting itself of a major component of its operations, and experiencing unusual or infrequent events. In this chapter, we discuss how a company reports each of these items on the income statement. We also discuss the alternative ways a company may report comprehensive income in its financial statements. In addition, we describe the statement of cash flows because of the important relationships between the income statement, balance sheet, and cash flows from operating, investing, and financing activities.

LEARNING OBJECTIVE 5.1

Explain the purposes of an income statement.

WHAT ARE THE PURPOSES OF THE INCOME STATEMENT?

As noted in Chapter 2, an objective of financial reporting is to provide information that is useful to investors, lenders, creditors, and other external users for evaluating financial performance and assessing the amounts, timing, and uncertainty of future cash flows. A specific objective is to provide information about a company's comprehensive income and its components. Financial statement users are interested in the resources generated and consumed by a company's operations and activities during the period, in order to measure and report the amount of net profit (or loss) generated for the shareholders.

---

[1] This statement is sometimes referred to as a statement of earnings, statement of financial performance, or the profit and loss statement ("the P&L").

The purposes of the income statement are therefore to inform investors, lenders, creditors, and other stakeholders about a company's financial performance so they can:

- *Evaluate the profitability and assess the return on investment in the company.* Shareholders (investors) invest capital to earn a return *on* capital. The income statement informs existing and potential investors about the profitability of the company. Together with the balance sheet, the income statement enables them to determine the rate of return the company is generating relative to the amount of capital invested.
- *Assess the company's operating capability and financial performance for the current period and over time.* The income statement provides information that helps current and potential investors evaluate the company's ability to conduct profitable operating activities. In addition, it provides additional information about other factors that impact income, including income from investments, expenses related to the financing of the company, and tax effects.
- *Evaluate management's performance.* The income statement provides information that helps current and potential investors evaluate how well a company's management has performed in executing company strategy, generating revenues, controlling costs, and creating profits.
- *Predict the company's future income and cash flows.* The income statement is useful for predicting the amounts, timing, and uncertainty of the company's future income and cash flows. If a company's operating activities generate earnings amounts that are persistent and growing, investors and lenders can predict that the company is likely to continue to do so in the future, which typically means higher share values and more favorable borrowing terms.
- *Understand the components of income.* Financial statement users often find that the components of net income are as important as the total amount. A company should report a component of net income separately if it is important for assessing some aspect of financial performance and predicting future income and cash flows. These components include income from ongoing operations, investing and financing activities, taxes, discontinued operations, peripheral activities, unusual activities, and other events and circumstances affecting the company. If a company has separate operating segments, it is also important to disclose income statement information about these segments (see Appendix 5.1).
- *Assess the company's risk.* As described in Chapter 2, *risk* is the uncertainty and variability of the future profitability and cash flows of a company. The greater the uncertainty of future results, the greater the risk associated with an investment in or a loan to the company. Generally, the greater the risk, the higher the expected rate of return. The income statement is useful for determining the risk associated with investing in or extending credit to the company. Evaluating whether the company's income is persistent and growing (versus volatile, unpredictable, declining) helps investors and lenders evaluate this risk.
- *Compare performance against other companies.* Investors are interested in the profitability and risk of investing in a company as compared to other companies in the same industry or other industries. They are also interested in comparing a company's return on investment and operating capability to those of other companies.
- *Assess the impact of economic factors on the company.* Revenues, expenses, gains, and losses that are affected in different ways by changes in economic conditions should be distinguished from one another. For instance, changes in revenues are the joint result of changes in sales volume and selling prices. Information about both types of changes is helpful in evaluating performance and projecting future operating results. In addition, it is helpful to report separately (a) expenses that vary with volume of activity or with various components of income, (b) expenses that are discretionary, and (c) expenses that depend upon other economic factors, such as the level of interest rates or tax rates.

GOT IT?

5-1 In general, how does the income statement help satisfy the objectives of financial reporting?

5-2 What are the purposes of the income statement?

LEARNING OBJECTIVE 5.2

Understand the capital maintenance concept of income.

WHAT IS INCOME?

The purposes of the income statement are important, broad, and multi-dimensional. These purposes should guide companies, accountants, and auditors as they measure and report the elements and components of an income statement.

Accountants and economists have long debated what "income" is and how it should be measured. In accounting and economics, the *capital maintenance concept* is important in understanding income measurement. The accounting equation (Assets = Liabilities + Shareholders' Equity) and accrual accounting provide a useful way to *measure* assets, liabilities, and net income within the capital maintenance concept.

Capital Maintenance Concept

Under the **capital maintenance concept**, a corporation's net income for a period of time is the amount that it could distribute to shareholders without depleting the capital the shareholders have invested.[2] It is the amount of money that can be distributed to shareholders as a return *on* capital, without being a return *of* capital. This concept asserts that shareholders' capital must be maintained and therefore income is measured as the *increase* in capital. To use this concept, the company's income is measured by comparing the beginning and ending common equity capital (net assets) after adjusting for any additional investments by owners (e.g., proceeds from additional issues of shares) or distributions to owners (e.g., dividends) during the period. Applying this concept, lifetime income would be computed as the total amount of cash distributed to shareholders (all of the dividends paid over the life of the company plus the final proceeds received from the liquidation of the net assets) minus the total amount of capital invested by shareholders. Applying this concept to a given period of time, company income would be computed as the difference between the beginning and ending net assets, after any adjustments for additional investments by or distributions to shareholders.[3]

Example: Capital Maintenance Concept

Layla Company had net assets of $45,000 at the beginning and $80,000 at the end of the year, shareholders made additional capital investments of $10,000 during the year, and Layla distributed cash dividends of $2,500 to shareholders during the year. Comparing the ending and the beginning net assets and adjusting for additional investments and dividends, the capital maintenance approach would measure Layla's total income as follows:

Ending net assets	$ 80,000
Less: Beginning net assets	(45,000)
Net change in assets	$ 35,000
Less: Additional investment of capital	(10,000)
Plus: Capital distributed in dividends	2,500
Total income for the year	$ 27,500

---

[2] S. S. Alexander, "Income Measurement in a Dynamic Economy," *Five Monographs on Business Income* (New York: AICPA Study Group on Business Income, 1950), p. 15.

[3] See for instance, E. O. Edwards and P. W. Bell, *The Theory and Measurement of Business Income* (Berkeley: University of California Press, 1970).

Comprehensive Income and Net Income

Following U.S. GAAP and IFRS, companies commonly measure and report two levels of income: net income and comprehensive income.

What Is Comprehensive Income? Consistent with the capital maintenance concept, the FASB developed the concept of **comprehensive income** as follows:

> Comprehensive income is the change in equity of a company during a period from transactions, other events, and circumstances relating to nonowner sources. It includes all changes in equity during a period except those resulting from investments by owners and distributions to owners.[4]

The FASB intends comprehensive income to be a broad concept of income that includes changes in the value of shareholders' equity resulting from (1) transactions, events, and circumstances that are traditionally measured and reported in net income and (2) changes in the values of certain types of assets and liabilities that are reported in other comprehensive income. We discuss the reporting of a company's comprehensive income later in the chapter. First, we focus on its primary component, net income.

What Is Net Income? In **accrual accounting**, a company records the economic effects of transactions, events, and circumstances in the periods when they occur rather than in the periods when it receives or pays cash. The accrual accounting approach to income measures the accomplishments (resources created) and the efforts (resources used up) so that the reported net income measures the results of the company's income-generating activities.[5] In the accrual approach, a corporation's **net income** for a period is measured as follows:

$$\text{Net Income} = \text{Revenues} - \text{Expenses} + \text{Gains} - \text{Losses}$$

This approach measures income based on the net assets created during the period (accomplishments like revenues and gains from asset sales) minus the net assets used up during the period (expenses and losses).

To provide relevant and faithfully represented information about financial performance and income to investors, lenders, and other creditors, the company must determine what, how, and where to report the elements of the income statement:

- *What:* Identify the elements that must be recognized in income.
- *When:* Determine the timing of the recognition of income elements.
- *Where:* Measure and report (classify) the elements on the income statement.

U.S. GAAP and IFRS establish the definitions of the various elements (revenues, expenses, gains, and losses) of net income and the principles that companies must use to measure and report income. We discuss these definitions and principles in this chapter and throughout the book as they relate to specific situations. We describe what elements to recognize in net income, when they should be recognized, and how they should be measured and reported.

GOT IT?

5-3 Define *income* under the *capital maintenance concept*.

5-4 Define *comprehensive income*. What was the intent of the FASB in developing this conceptual definition?

5-5 What is *net income*?

5-6 What three things must a company determine to prepare and report an income statement?

---

[4] "Elements of Financial Statements," *FASB Statement of Financial Accounting Concepts No. 6* (Stamford, CT: FASB, 1985), par. 70.
[5] "Objectives of Financial Reporting by Business Enterprises," *FASB Statement of Financial Accounting Concepts No. 1* (Stamford, CT: FASB, 1978), par. 45.

LEARNING OBJECTIVE 5.3
Define the elements of an income statement.

WHAT ARE THE ELEMENTS OF THE INCOME STATEMENT?

The four elements of the income statement are revenues, expenses, gains, and losses. Each of these elements is defined in *FASB Statement of Financial Accounting Concepts No. 6*.

Revenues

Revenues are increases in assets or settlements of liabilities from delivering or producing goods, rendering services, or other activities that are the company's ongoing major or central operations. Revenues represent increases in future economic benefits from increases in cash, accounts receivable or other types of assets, or reductions in liabilities by satisfying performance obligations to customers who have paid in advance for goods or services. Revenues measure the *accomplishments* of the operating activities in producing and delivering goods and services to customers. The transactions that result in revenues are of various types, depending on the company's operations and when it can recognize revenues.

Revenue Recognition **Revenue recognition** is the process of formally measuring and reporting revenue in a company's financial statements. In May of 2014, the FASB issued new revenue recognition guidance with Accounting Standards Update 2014-09 "Revenue from Contracts with Customers" (becomes effective for annual reporting periods beginning after December 15, 2016). The Update is the result of a joint project with the IASB, and it is an important step forward in revenue recognition guidance.[6] The core principle of the new guidance is that **a company should recognize revenue to depict the transfer of promised goods or services to customers in an amount that reflects the consideration to which the company expects to be entitled in exchange for those goods or services.**

To achieve that core principle, a company should apply the following five steps:

- *Step 1.* Identify the contract(s) with a customer.
- *Step 2.* Identify the performance obligations in the contract.
- *Step 3.* Determine the transaction price.
- *Step 4.* Allocate the transaction price to the performance obligations in the contract.
- *Step 5.* Recognize revenue when (or as) the entity satisfies a performance obligation.

In this section, we briefly describe these steps. Chapter 17 explains and demonstrates these five steps of the revenue recognition model in greater detail.

Step 1: Identify the Contract with a Customer A **contract** is an agreement between two or more parties that creates enforceable rights and obligations. Under the new guidance, a company should apply the revenue recognition requirements to each contract, but only if it is probable that it will collect the consideration to which it will be entitled in exchange for the goods or services that it will transfer to the customer.

Step 2: Identify the Performance Obligations in the Contract A **performance obligation** is a promise in the contract to transfer a good or service to the customer. If a company promises in a contract to transfer more than one good or service to the customer, the company should account for each promised good or service as a separate performance obligation only if it is (1) distinct or (2) a series of distinct goods or services that are substantially the same and have the same pattern of transfer. A good or service that is not distinct should be combined with other promised goods or services until the company identifies a bundle of goods or services that is distinct.

Step 3: Determine the Transaction Price The **transaction price** is the amount of consideration (payment) a company expects to collect in exchange for transferring promised

---
[6] FASB ASC 606: Revenue from Contracts with Customers and IASB IFRS 15: Revenue from Contracts with Customers. This discussion depends heavily on information in FASB ASC 606.

goods or services to a customer, excluding amounts collected on behalf of third parties (i.e., sales taxes). If the payment is variable (e.g., dependent on other factors), the company should determine the best estimate of the transaction price by estimating either the expected value (i.e., probability-weighted amount) or the most likely amount. If the transaction price includes a significant financing component (say, monthly payments over 36 months), then the company should separate the revenue component from the interest component of the transaction price.

Step 4: Allocate the Transaction Price to the Performance Obligations in a Contract If the contract contains a single performance obligation, the transaction price would only relate to that performance obligation. However, if the contract contains more than one performance obligation, the seller would allocate the transaction price to each performance obligation based on the relative stand-alone selling price of the goods and services. The stand-alone selling price is the price for which the company would sell a promised good or service separately to a customer. If the company does not sell the good or service separately, then it will estimate the stand-alone price using all available information.

Step 5: Recognize Revenue When (or as) the Entity Satisfies a Performance Obligation A company should recognize revenue when (or as) it satisfies a performance obligation by transferring control of a promised good or service to a customer. A company should determine whether it satisfies each performance obligation at a specific point in time or over time and recognize revenue accordingly.

Real Report 5.1 shows an excerpt from **The Coca-Cola Company**'s 2013 financial statements explaining Coca-Cola's revenue recognition policy.

REAL REPORT — **REVENUE RECOGNITION 5.1**

The Coca-Cola Company

Notes to Consolidated Financial Statements

Note 1: Business and Summary of Significant Accounting Policies (Partial)

Revenue Recognition
Our Company recognizes revenue when persuasive evidence of an arrangement exists, delivery of products has occurred, the sales price charged is fixed or determinable, and collectability is reasonably assured. For our Company, this generally means that we recognize revenue when title to our products is transferred to our bottling partners, resellers or other customers. In particular, title usually transfers upon shipment to or receipt at our customers' locations, as determined by the specific sales terms of the transactions. Our sales terms do not allow for a right of return except for matters related to any manufacturing defects on our part.

Questions:
1. What criteria did Coca-Cola use to determine revenue recognition in 2013?
2. When the new revenue recognition guidance becomes effective, will the timing of Coca-Cola's revenue recognition likely change dramatically?

Suggested answers to these questions are found at the end of the chapter.

The Timing of Revenues versus Cash Flows Under accrual accounting, a company can recognize revenue when it satisfies performance obligations to customers. Accrual accounting seeks to measure and report when the company generates assets or settles obligations through the revenue-generating process, even though the cash inflows may occur in a different period. Revenue recognition can occur *simultaneously with, prior to,* or *after* the receipt of cash flows from customers. Exhibit 5.1 shows the timing of revenue recognition as it relates to the timing of cash flows from customers.

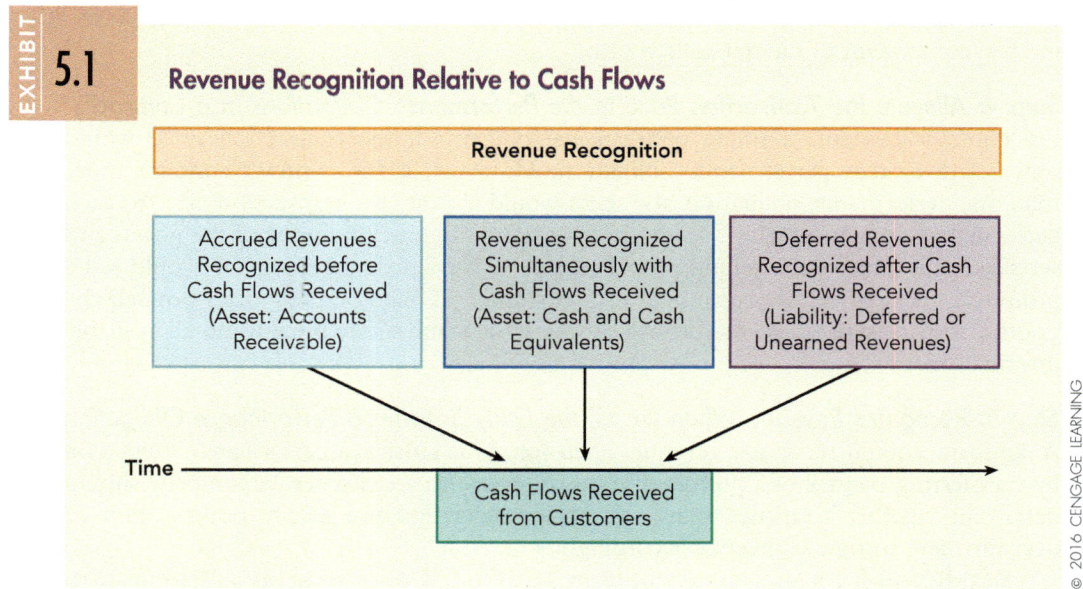

EXHIBIT 5.1 Revenue Recognition Relative to Cash Flows

In most retail operations, revenue recognition occurs simultaneously with cash flows from customers. Stores, restaurants, and other similar operations typically deliver goods or services to their customers and receive payment at the point of sale, thereby simultaneously satisfying performance obligations and collecting payment. **Starbucks**, for example, recognizes revenue and receives payments from customers through retail sales of coffee beverages and similar products in its coffee shops.

In other circumstances, companies may accrue revenues and recognize them on the income statement and as accounts or notes receivable on the balance sheet. The cash flows from these customers will occur in a subsequent period. In these cases, the performance obligations to customers have been satisfied by transferring products or performing services in the current period, and it is probable the company will collect the consideration to which it is entitled under the contract with the customer in a future period. For **Starbucks**, this type of revenue recognition arises when it sells coffee beans and other products to licensees, foodservice distributors, and grocery store chains on commercial terms, with those customers agreeing to pay 30 or 60 days after receipt of the products.

It is also common for some companies to receive cash from customers in advance of satisfying their performance obligations, in which case the companies recognize liabilities (deferred revenues) for performance obligations to their customers. For example, sales of airline tickets, season tickets for sports or entertainment events, subscriptions to magazines or newspapers, insurance premiums, and other arrangements like these involve customers prepaying for goods and services. Under these arrangements, the prepayment from customers triggers a liability (a performance obligation to deliver goods or services). Revenue cannot be recognized until the company satisfies the performance obligation by delivering the goods or services. For **Starbucks**, a large current liability on its 2015 balance sheet is the Stored Value Card Liability ($983.8 million), which primarily represents unearned revenues associated with customers' purchases of gift cards ("Stored Value" cards). **Starbucks** has received the cash payments for these cards, but has not yet satisfied the performance obligations by providing goods or services. It will do so when customers redeem the cards and it delivers coffee beverages or other products to them.

Real Report 5.2 shows brief excerpts from Starbuck's 2015 financial statements, explaining the revenue recognition policies.

REAL REPORT 5.2 — REVENUE RECOGNITION

Starbucks

Notes to Consolidated Financial Statements (partial)

Note 1: Summary of Significant Accounting Policies

Revenue Recognition

Consolidated revenues are presented net of intercompany eliminations for wholly owned subsidiaries and investees controlled by us and for product sales to and royalty and other fees from licensees accounted for under the equity method. Additionally, consolidated revenues are recognized net of any discounts, returns, allowances and sales incentives, including coupon redemptions and rebates.

Company-operated Stores Revenues

Company-operated stores revenues are recognized when payment is tendered at the point of sale. Company-operated store revenues are reported net of sales, use or other transaction taxes that are collected from customers and remitted to taxing authorities.

Licensed Stores Revenues

Licensed stores revenues consist of product sales to licensees, as well as royalties and other fees paid by licensees to use the Starbucks brand. Sales of coffee, tea, food and related products are generally recognized upon shipment to licensees, depending on contract terms. Initial nonrefundable development fees for licensed stores are recognized upon substantial performance of services for new market business development activities, such as initial business, real estate and store development planning, as well as providing operational materials and functional training courses for opening new licensed retail markets. Additional store licensing fees are recognized when new licensed stores are opened. Royalty revenues based upon a percentage of reported sales and other continuing fees, such as marketing and service fees, are recognized on a monthly basis when earned.

CPG, Foodservice and Other Revenues

CPG, foodservice and other revenues primarily consist of sales of packaged coffee and tea as well as a variety of ready-to-drink beverages and single-serve coffee and tea products to grocery, warehouse club and specialty retail stores, sales to our national foodservice accounts, and revenues from sales of products to and license fee revenues from manufacturers that produce and market Starbucks-, Seattle's Best Coffee- and Tazo-branded products through licensing agreements. Sales of coffee, tea, ready-to-drink beverages and related products to grocery and warehouse club stores are generally recognized when received by the customer or distributor, depending on contract terms. Revenues are recorded net of sales discounts given to customers for trade promotions and other incentives and for sales return allowances, which are determined based on historical patterns. Revenues from sales of products to manufacturers that produce and market Starbucks' products through licensing agreements are generally recognized when the product is received by the manufacturer or distributor. License fee revenues from manufacturers are based on a percentage of sales and are recognized on a monthly basis when earned. National foodservice account revenues are recognized when the product is received by the customer or distributor.

Stored Value Cards

Stored value cards, primarily Starbucks Cards, can be loaded at our company-operated and most licensed store locations, online at StarbucksStore.com or via mobile devices held by our customers, and at certain other third party locations, such as grocery stores. When an amount is loaded onto a stored value card at any of these locations, we recognize a corresponding liability for the full amount loaded onto the card, which is recorded within the stored value card liability on our consolidated balance sheets. Stored value cards can be redeemed at company-operated and most licensed stores, as well as online. When a stored value card is redeemed at

(continued)

> a company-operated store or online, we recognize revenue by reducing the stored value card liability. When a stored value card is redeemed at a licensed store location, we reduce the corresponding stored value card liability and cash, which is reimbursed to the licensee.

Suggested answer to this question is found at the end of the chapter.

Question:

1. How does Starbucks describe the differences in revenue recognition policies across the retail, licensed stores, CPG, foodservice and other, and stored value card categories?

Expenses

According to *FASB Statement of Financial Accounting Concepts No. 6*, **expenses** arise from outflows or using up assets or incurring liabilities (or a combination of both) from delivering or producing goods, rendering services, or carrying out other activities that are the company's ongoing major or central operations. Expenses measure and report the *efforts* or *sacrifices* made to conduct business activities. There are many types of transactions and events that cause expenses, depending on a company's various operations and the way it recognizes expenses.

Expense Recognition Within accrual accounting, expenses are measured and recognized in the period in which the resources are used up, the outflows of assets occur, or the liabilities are incurred, even though the cash outflows may occur in a different period. Similar to the recognition of revenues, expenses may be recognized in a period *simultaneously with* cash outflows, *prior to* cash outflows, or *after* cash outflows.

Some expenses for day-to-day operating activities, such as paying wages to employees, are recognized at essentially the same time (or nearly the same time) as when the company pays cash for the resources. Other types of expenses are accrued and recognized in periods in advance of when the company actually pays cash, sometimes many periods in advance. For example, accrued expenses for pension and retirement benefits are often recognized many years prior to when the company pays cash to the employees for these benefits. Still other types of expenses are recognized after cash flows were paid for those resources, which give rise to deferred or prepaid expenses, such as prepaid expenses for insurance or rent. Similarly, cash payments for a long-lived asset like property, plant, and equipment may occur when the asset is purchased, but expense recognition occurs over many years during the asset's service life.

To determine the income related to a company's primary operations during the accounting period, the expenses (efforts) are recognized and matched, when possible, against the revenues (benefits) they help generate. Some types of expenses vary directly with revenues and can be matched to them. However, many expenses cannot be matched directly to revenues, but must be matched to the periods in which the resources are used up or the liabilities are incurred. The FASB has identified the following three expense recognition principles to properly recognize expenses either by matching to revenues or matching to periods:

- **Association of Cause and Effect**. Some expenses are recognized on the basis of a direct association with specific revenues. Some transactions result simultaneously in both a revenue and an expense. Examples include costs of products sold, transportation costs for delivery of goods to customers, and sales commissions.
- **Systematic and Rational Allocation**. Some expenses are recognized in a particular accounting period based on a systematic and rational allocation among the periods in which benefits are provided. Many assets provide benefits for several periods. A portion of the cost of each of these assets is rationally recognized as an expense each period. The allocation system should be based on the expected service life and the consumption of the resource. Examples include depreciation of fixed assets, amortization of intangible assets, and the allocation of prepaid costs.

- **Immediate Recognition.** Some expenses are recognized in the current accounting period because the costs incurred during the period provide no probable future benefits (i.e., they do not result in assets). Examples include management salaries, research and development expenses, and advertising expenses.

Sometimes it is difficult to determine whether an expenditure should be recorded as an expense or as an asset, and, if it is recorded as an asset, when the expense recognition should occur. Exhibit 5.2 is helpful in understanding the relationships among the terms expenditure, asset, and expense.

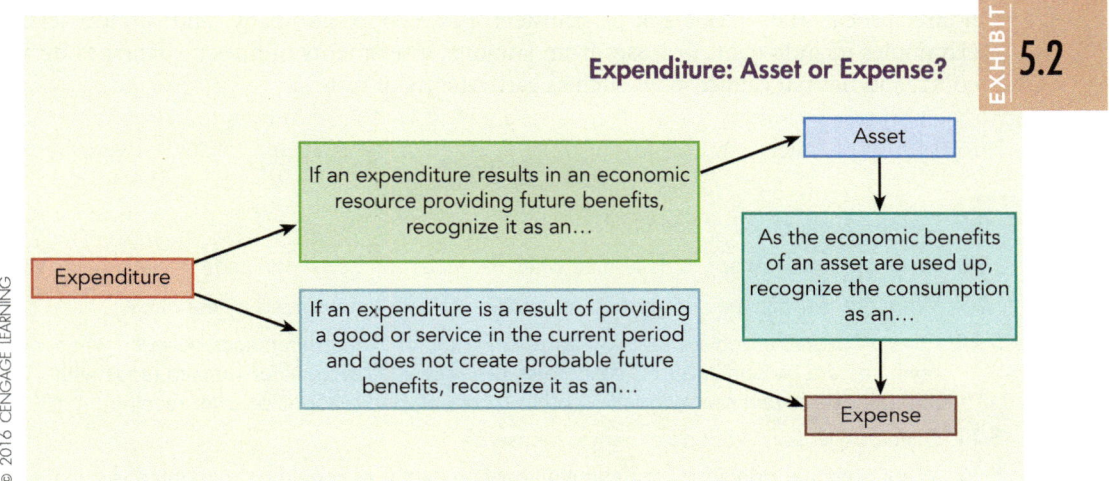

EXHIBIT 5.2 Expenditure: Asset or Expense?

Gains and Losses

Gains and losses, like revenues and expenses, are components of net income.

- **Gains** are increases in the equity (net assets) of a company from peripheral or incidental transactions and other events and circumstances during a period, except those that result from revenues or investments by owners.
- **Losses** are decreases in the equity (net assets) of a company from peripheral or incidental transactions and other events and circumstances during a period, except those that result from expenses or distributions to owners.

However, several differences between revenues and expenses and gains and losses are important in communicating information about a company's performance.

- Revenues and expenses relate to a company's major operating activities. Gains and losses relate to peripheral activities or to the effects of other events and circumstances, some of which may be beyond its control (e.g., loss from flood or a fire).
- Revenues and expenses are reported as gross amounts because they reflect the effects of ongoing business activities that determine earnings. Gains and losses are reported "net" because they typically involve a single transaction that triggers a net increase or decrease in an asset or a liability (e.g., gain on sale of land).
- Revenues are recognized as the company satisfies performance obligations by transferring goods or services to customers, and expenses are recognized as assets are used up or liabilities are incurred. Most gains and losses are recognized in the periods in which the event occurs to trigger the gain or loss, even if the associated cash flows occur in a different period. This could arise, for example, when a company holds a piece of land that appreciates in value over several years. The company will recognize the gain in the period when it sells the land. If it accepts a note receivable from the purchaser of the land, the company will collect the cash flows from the sale over the life of the note.

The definitions of revenues, expenses, gains, and losses do not distinguish precisely between revenues and gains or between expenses and losses. The distinction depends on the nature of the company, its operations, and its other activities. Items that are revenues (expenses) for one company may be gains (losses) for another. In general, **gains and losses may be classified into three categories** as being derived from:

- exchange transactions in which an asset is sold or a liability settled for an amount that differs from the carrying value on the balance sheet. (Examples include a gain or loss on the sale of a piece of used equipment or an investment security.)
- the holding of resources or obligations while their values change. (Examples include losses resulting from writing down inventory from cost to market; gains or losses from changes in the fair value of certain investment securities; and impairment losses on property, plant, and equipment or intangibles.)
- nonreciprocal (i.e., "one-way") transfers between a company and nonowners. (Examples include gains or losses from lawsuits, assessments of fines or damages by a court, and natural catastrophes such as earthquakes or fires.)

> ### GOT IT?
>
> **5-7** Define *revenues*. What operating activities generate revenues?
>
> **5-8** What are the five steps to determine when revenues can be recognized?
>
> **5-9** What are the four specific revenue recognition criteria emphasized by the SEC?
>
> **5-10** Give an example and explanation for each of the following differences between when revenues are recognized and cash flows are received: recognition simultaneous with receipt; accrue revenue recognition prior to receipt; and recognition after receipt.
>
> **5-11** Define *expenses*. What do expenses measure?
>
> **5-12** What are three principles for determining when expenses should be recognized? Give at least one example of an expense that would be recognized under each principle.
>
> **5-13** Define *gains* and *losses*. Give examples of three different types of gains and losses.

LEARNING OBJECTIVE 5.4
Describe the major components of an income statement.

WHAT ARE THE MAJOR COMPONENTS OF THE INCOME STATEMENT?

Although the *form* of the income statement may differ from company to company, its *content* is relatively standard. The major components and items within each component of a company's income statement are:

- Revenues
  - Cost of goods sold
  - Operating expenses
  - Other operating income items (gains and losses)
- Operating income
  - Interest expense
  - Interest and dividend income
  - Unusual and nonrecurring gains and losses
  - Income taxes associated with continuing operations
- Income from continuing operations
- Results from discontinued operations
  - Income (loss) from operations of discontinued components (net of income taxes)
  - Gain (loss) from disposals of discontinued components (net of income taxes)
- Net income
- Earnings per share

Not every company experiences these items every period, nor will they necessarily be listed within each major component in the sequence shown. In addition to these components, U.S. GAAP and IFRS also require companies to report comprehensive income for the period. We describe each section of the income statement, as well as measuring and reporting comprehensive income, in later sections of this chapter.

For full disclosure, a company's financial statements should disclose all material income information that can influence the judgment of informed external users. However, disclosures may be made in several ways. On the income statement, all material income items of the company should be reported on the face of the statement. However, *too much* detail detracts from the readability of the statement. Most companies present a condensed income statement. They aggregate and report all income items within the major components directly on the income statement. Then, supporting schedules and note disclosures supplement this information with additional detail.

In this section, we first describe the two general approaches to income statement presentation—single-step versus multiple-step. After that, we describe each of the major income statement components.

Single-Step and Multiple-Step Formats

The format for reporting *income from continuing operations* may vary from company to company. Many variations of two basic formats, *single-step* and *multiple-step*, are used in actual practice. Under the **single-step income statement** format, a company classifies its items into two groups, revenues and expenses. The company computes its income from continuing operations in a single step as the difference between the totals of the two groups. A variation in this format involves reporting a subtotal for pretax income from continuing operations and then subtracting income tax expense for continuing operations as a separate line item. **Example 5.1** shows a single-step income statement for Banner Corporation.

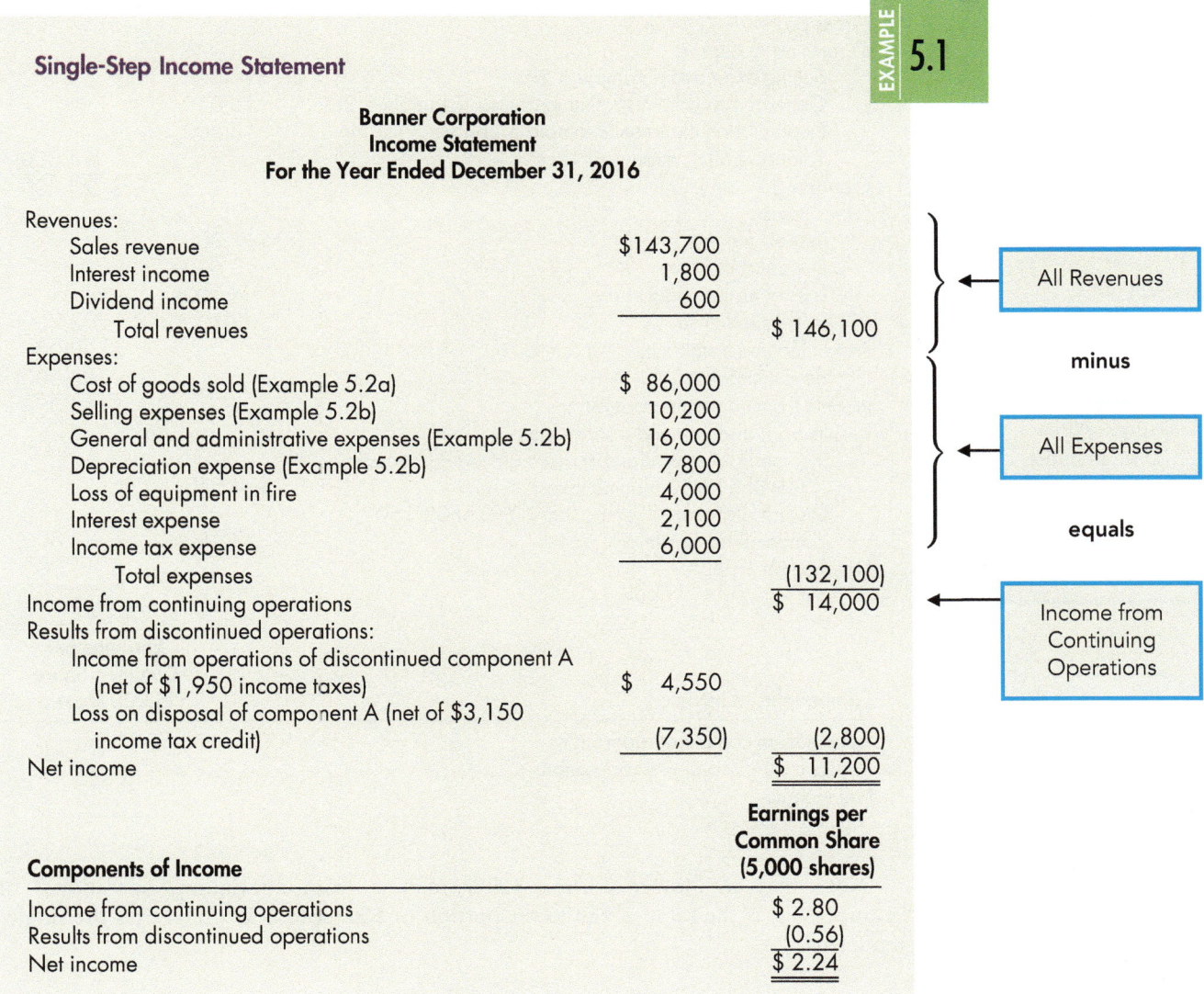

EXAMPLE 5.1

Single-Step Income Statement

Banner Corporation
Income Statement
For the Year Ended December 31, 2016

Revenues:		
Sales revenue	$143,700	
Interest income	1,800	
Dividend income	600	
Total revenues		$ 146,100
Expenses:		
Cost of goods sold (Example 5.2a)	$ 86,000	
Selling expenses (Example 5.2b)	10,200	
General and administrative expenses (Example 5.2b)	16,000	
Depreciation expense (Example 5.2b)	7,800	
Loss of equipment in fire	4,000	
Interest expense	2,100	
Income tax expense	6,000	
Total expenses		(132,100)
Income from continuing operations		$ 14,000
Results from discontinued operations:		
Income from operations of discontinued component A (net of $1,950 income taxes)	$ 4,550	
Loss on disposal of component A (net of $3,150 income tax credit)	(7,350)	(2,800)
Net income		$ 11,200

Components of Income	Earnings per Common Share (5,000 shares)
Income from continuing operations	$ 2.80
Results from discontinued operations	(0.56)
Net income	$ 2.24

All Revenues
minus
All Expenses
equals
Income from Continuing Operations

The single-step format is simple and flexible. However, the number of companies using it is decreasing. Currently, only a small minority of companies use some variation of the single-step format.

Some accountants argue that the simplicity of the single-step format detracts from its usefulness. Specifically, the FASB suggests that the individual items, subtotals, or other parts of a financial statement provide useful information for external decision making. This supports the growing popularity and use of the **multiple-step income statement**, which presents income from continuing operations using various categories and subtotals, such as gross profit, operating income, and income from continuing operations.

Example 5.2 shows Banner Corporation's income statement prepared under a multiple-step approach. **Starbucks**'s 2015 income statement is also prepared under this approach (see Appendix A at the end of the book).

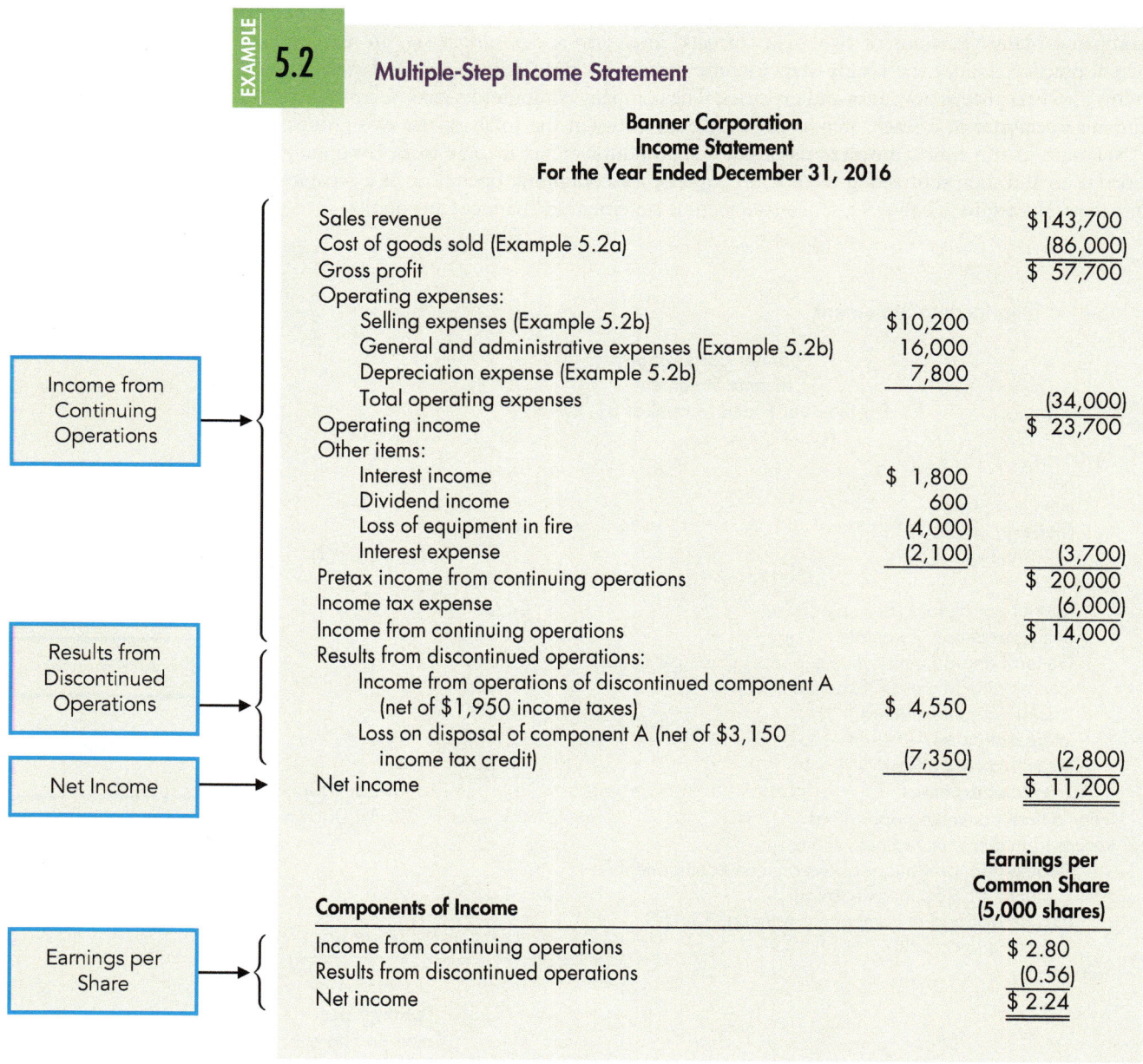

EXAMPLE 5.2 Multiple-Step Income Statement

Banner Corporation
Income Statement
For the Year Ended December 31, 2016

Sales revenue		$143,700
Cost of goods sold (Example 5.2a)		(86,000)
Gross profit		$ 57,700
Operating expenses:		
Selling expenses (Example 5.2b)	$10,200	
General and administrative expenses (Example 5.2b)	16,000	
Depreciation expense (Example 5.2b)	7,800	
Total operating expenses		(34,000)
Operating income		$ 23,700
Other items:		
Interest income	$ 1,800	
Dividend income	600	
Loss of equipment in fire	(4,000)	
Interest expense	(2,100)	(3,700)
Pretax income from continuing operations		$ 20,000
Income tax expense		(6,000)
Income from continuing operations		$ 14,000
Results from discontinued operations:		
Income from operations of discontinued component A		
(net of $1,950 income taxes)	$ 4,550	
Loss on disposal of component A (net of $3,150		
income tax credit)	(7,350)	(2,800)
Net income		$ 11,200

Components of Income	Earnings per Common Share (5,000 shares)
Income from continuing operations	$ 2.80
Results from discontinued operations	(0.56)
Net income	$ 2.24

- Income from Continuing Operations
- Results from Discontinued Operations
- Net Income
- Earnings per Share

Note that the lower portion (after income from continuing operations) of **Example 5.2** is the same as the lower portion of **Example 5.1**, which uses the single-step format.

The primary criticism of the multiple-step format is that variation exists, particularly across different industries, as to which items of revenue and expense should be classified as operating or nonoperating, which can reduce comparability. Nonetheless, the multiple-step format is becoming more popular and is currently being used by the vast majority of firms.

Sales Revenue

Gross sales revenues (or **gross revenues**) are increases in assets or settlements of liabilities from satisfying performance obligations to customers by delivering or producing goods, rendering services, or other activities that are the company's ongoing major or central operations. Gross sales revenue includes the total amounts that the company has generated by delivering goods and services to customers during the period. **Net sales revenues** (or **net revenues**) are the gross sales revenues minus any sales discounts taken by credit customers (or reasonably estimated). Net sales amounts typically exclude any sales taxes or value added taxes the company may have collected from customers because the company will have to remit them to the taxing authority. To increase the predictive value of the sales revenue information, the FASB advocates disclosing sales volume and sales price information. However, many companies discuss this information in the management's discussion and analysis (MD&A) section of their annual report, rather than in the income statement.

Total net revenues reported in **Starbucks**'s 2015 income statement, shown in Appendix A, amounted to $19,162.7 million and include three categories of revenues: company-operated stores ($15,197.3 million), licensed stores ($1,861.9 million), and CPG, foodservice and other ($2,103.5 million). In Note 1, Starbucks discloses that "consolidated revenues are recognized net of any discounts, returns, allowances, and sales incentives, including coupon redemptions and rebates."

Cost of Goods Sold

The **cost of goods sold** is the cost of the inventory items sold to customers during the period.

- If a company uses a *perpetual* inventory system, it records this amount in the cost of goods sold account at the time of each sale and reports the total for the period on its income statement.
- If a company uses a *periodic* inventory system, it does not reduce its inventory at the time of the sale and must calculate its cost of goods sold amount based on a physical inventory taken at the end of each period.

Usually, the computation of the cost of goods sold is shown in a supporting schedule. This schedule starts with the beginning inventory, to which net purchases are added to determine the **cost of goods available for sale**. Net purchases include gross purchases of inventory, plus freight costs and any other costs to acquire and prepare the inventory for sale, and minus any purchases returns, allowances, and discounts. Costs such as shipping, receiving, storing, packaging, and insurance during transport also should be included in net purchases. The ending inventory is subtracted from Cost of Goods Available for Sale to determine Cost of Goods Sold.[7] **Example 5.2a** shows the components of Banner Corporation's cost of goods sold. The cost of goods sold is subtracted from net sales to determine gross profit.

This cost of goods sold schedule assumes Banner Corporation is a merchandising company. In a manufacturing company, the cost of goods manufactured would replace net purchases in the schedule.

In **Starbucks**'s 2015 income statement, the cost of sales is reported together with occupancy costs and amounts to $7,787.5 million. Starbucks includes occupancy costs (rent on company-operated retail coffee shop locations) with the cost of sales (cost of the coffee beans and related ingredients) because both types of costs are essential to Starbucks's core business activities, operating coffee shops to generate retail sales.

---

[7] Note that even if a company uses a perpetual inventory system, it could still prepare a similar schedule of cost of goods sold based on its accounting records.

> **EXAMPLE 5.2a** Cost of Goods Sold
>
> **Banner Corporation**
> **Schedule 1: Cost of Goods Sold**
> **For Year Ended December 31, 2016**
>
> | | | |
> |---|---:|---:|
> | Inventory, January 1, 2016 | | $ 41,000 |
> | Purchases | $80,300 | |
> | Freight-in | 5,500 | |
> | Cost of purchases | $85,800 | |
> | Less: Purchase returns | (2,800) | |
> | Net purchases | | 83,000 |
> | Cost of goods available for sale | | $124,000 |
> | Less: Inventory, December 31, 2016 | | (38,000) |
> | Cost of goods sold | | $ 86,000 |

Operating Expenses

Operating expenses are those primary recurring costs (other than the cost of goods sold) incurred to generate sales revenues and conduct business operations. These expenses typically are classified according to *functional categories.* One way is to show *selling expenses* separately from *general and administrative expenses.* Because of their significance, depreciation expense and amortization expense (excluding amounts included in the cost of goods manufactured) may be shown as a separate category. Research and development expense[8] may also be shown as a separate category. Frequently, aggregate amounts are listed on the income statement for the major categories of operating expenses, with supporting schedules that identify the amounts of the individual expenses in each major category in the notes. **Example 5.2b** shows this supporting schedule for Banner Corporation. The total of the operating expenses is subtracted from the gross profit to determine the operating income, as shown earlier in **Example 5.2**.

Starbucks's 2015 income statement includes four categories of operating expenses: store operating expenses ($5,411.1 million), other operating expenses ($522.4 million), depreciation and amortization expenses ($893.9 million), and general and administrative expenses ($1,196.7 million).

Other Operating Income Items

Gains and losses from asset sales, inventory write-downs, impairment charges, restructuring charges, litigation charges, or other types of gains and losses that are a consequence of normal operating activities will be reported in this section. Note that **Starbucks** reported the litigation charge as part of operating income in 2013. These charges are a consequence of Starbucks's decision to terminate its distribution agreement with **Kraft**, as discussed in Chapter 4. Product distribution is clearly an important aspect of Starbucks's operations. In 2014, Starbucks included in operating income a $20.2 million credit from the litigation charge because the amount Starbucks ultimately had to pay was slightly less than originally estimated in 2013.

In addition, note that Starbucks also includes income from equity investees in operating income. This income represents Starbucks's share of income from joint ventures, which are closely related to Starbucks's central operations and so are included in operating income.[9]

---

[8] Research and development (R&D) expense is the cost incurred in the planned search for new knowledge and the translation of that knowledge into a plan or design for a new product or process or for a significant improvement to an existing product or process. We discuss R&D in Chapter 12.

[9] Accounting for equity investees will be described in Chapter 13.

EXAMPLE 5.2b

Operating Expenses

Banner Corporation
Schedule 2: Operating Expenses
For Year Ended December 31, 2016

Selling Expenses	
Delivery expense	$ 1,800
Advertising expense	3,300
Sales salaries expense	4,100
Sales supplies expense	700
Miscellaneous selling expenses	300
Total selling expenses	$10,200
General and Administrative Expenses	
Administrative salaries	$ 6,900
Office salaries	3,700
Taxes and insurance expenses	2,200
Bad debts expense	1,500
Office supplies expense	700
Miscellaneous expenses	1,000
Total general and administrative expenses	$16,000
Depreciation Expense	
Office equipment	$ 3,300
Store equipment	4,500
Total depreciation expense	$ 7,800

Operating Income (Loss)

Operating income (loss) includes sales revenue, minus the various expenses related to these sales and business activities, and other income items related to operating activities. Financial statement users typically analyze carefully a company's operating income because it represents the company's ability to execute its business strategy and generate profitability from its core, central operations.

Items Resulting from Financing and Investing Activities

Immediately following the operating income section, companies usually report significant recurring items of income and expense, as well as gains and losses, which are not directly related to the primary operations but result from the financing and investing activities of the company. Financing expenses commonly include interest expense on the company's short-term and long-term debt. Investing income includes dividend income, interest income, and realized gains or losses from sales of investment securities. **Starbucks**'s 2015 income statement includes interest income and other, net ($43.0 million) and interest expense ($70.5 million).

Unusual and Nonrecurring Gains and Losses

Gains and losses that are unusual and nonrecurring and not a consequence of normal operating activities will be reported in this section. These could include, for example, the loss from a flood or a fire, or the gain or loss from the extinguishment of debt. As shown in **Example 5.2**, a loss of equipment in a fire is included in this section of Banner Corporation's income statement because the fire is considered to be an unusual event that is not part of the normal operations. **Starbucks**'s 2015 income statement includes two unusual and nonrecurring items: a $390.6 million gain resulting from an acquisition of a joint venture and a $61.1 million loss on the extinguishment of debt.[10]

Pretax Income from Continuing Operations

Before reporting the income tax expense for the period, a company will typically report **pretax income from continuing operations**. Pretax income from continuing operations is operating income plus or minus interest expense, interest and dividend income, other gains and losses, and any unusual or nonrecurring gains and losses. If the company does not have any discontinued operations, this amount is usually simply labeled either pretax income or income before tax.

Income Tax Expense Related to Continuing Operations

Income tax expense related to continuing operations represents an accrued expense for the total amount of income tax (federal, state, and foreign) that a corporation will ultimately have to pay on the income generated during the period. Income tax is typically a significant expense on a corporation's income statement. However, the amount of income taxes actually paid in cash each period is determined according to the rules of the Internal Revenue Code, as well as state and foreign tax regulations. The tax regulations used for determining the *taxable income* that a corporation reports on its income tax return frequently differ from the accounting principles used to determine *pretax financial income* that the corporation reports on its income statement. Additionally, pretax financial income consists of several major components. Because of these differences, two types of tax allocation are necessary.

Interperiod Tax Allocation **Interperiod tax allocation** involves assigning a corporation's tax obligation as an expense across various accounting periods because of temporary (timing) differences between its taxable income and pretax financial income. Generally, interperiod tax allocation requires that:

- annual income tax *expense* for financial reporting be based on pretax *financial* income (and items of other comprehensive income, if any)
- *current* income tax obligation (*liability*) be based on *taxable* income as reported to the tax authorities on the company's tax return
- any *temporary* differences between them give rise to a *deferred tax liability* (or *deferred tax asset*)[11]

Once the total income tax expense for the period is determined, intraperiod (or within period) tax allocation is necessary.[12]

Intraperiod Tax Allocation **Intraperiod tax allocation** involves apportioning a corporation's total income tax expense for a period to the various components of its net income and other comprehensive income items (if any). That is, a portion of the income tax expense is *allocated to*:

- income from continuing operations
- income (loss) from the operations of a discontinued component
- gain (loss) from the disposal of a discontinued component
- any items of other comprehensive income[13]

---

[10] In January, 2015, the FASB adopted Accounting Standards Update 2015-01, "Simplifying Income Statement Presentation by Eliminating the Concept of Extraordinary Items," which is effective for fiscal years beginning after December 15, 2015. The Accounting Standards Update simplifies reporting income statements because it eliminates the concept of "extraordinary gains and losses," which were deemed to be both highly unusual in nature and very infrequent in occurrence given the company's operating environment. Going forward, these types of gains and losses will simply be reported as unusual and nonrecurring. This Accounting Standard Update aligns U.S. GAAP with IFRS.

[11] FASB ASC 740-10-30: Income Taxes, Overall, Initial Measurement.

[12] Accounting for income taxes is the subject of Chapter 18.

[13] In some instances, companies are required to make retrospective adjustments or prior period adjustments to retained earnings, which may also require tax allocation. These adjustments are discussed in Chapter 22.

The rationale behind intraperiod tax allocation is to faithfully represent the after-tax impact of each of the major components of income.

The portion of the total income tax expense for each component of Banner's income statement is calculated in **Example 5.2c**. (For simplicity we assume a constant 30% tax rate on all taxable items in this chapter, and Banner Corporation does not have any items of other comprehensive income.) As shown in **Example 5.2**, the portion of the income tax expense for continuing operations is listed as a separate line item. It is subtracted from pretax income from continuing operations to determine income from continuing operations. However, the results from discontinued operations are shown *net* of the income tax effect. That is, for these items income tax expense (or tax savings in the case of a loss) is deducted directly from each item and only the *after-tax* amount is shown. However, the tax impact on these items should be disclosed, either parenthetically or in a note to the financial statements.

Note that in the 2015 income statement (Appendix A), **Starbucks** reported earnings before income taxes of $3,903.0 million. Starbucks also reported that income tax expense amounted to $1,143.7 million in 2015.

Intraperiod Tax Allocation — EXAMPLE 5.2c

Banner Corporation
Schedule of Intraperiod Allocation of Income Tax Expense
For Year Ended December 31, 2016

Component (Pretax)	Pretax Amount	×	Income Tax Rate	=	Income Tax Expense (Credit)
Income from continuing operations	$ 20,000	×	0.30	=	$ 6,000
Income from operations of discontinued component A	6,500	×	0.30	=	1,950
Loss on disposal of component A	(10,500)	×	0.30	=	(3,150)
Total income tax expense					$ 4,800

Income from Continuing Operations

Income from continuing operations reports the company's income from ongoing, recurring business activities. This section of the income statement includes operating income plus (or minus) income items associated with financing and investing activities (such as interest expense and interest income); gains and losses that are not part of normal, ongoing operating activities; and income taxes. Income from continuing operations excludes the income effects of items that are not continuing, because they are components of the business that are being sold or shut down. Financial statement users find income from continuing operations to be useful information because it summarizes the elements of income that are likely to be recurring and persistent in future periods. Note that if a firm does not have any discontinued operations, then it is not necessary to distinguish income from continuing operations, and instead this amount is simply the bottom-line net income.

Net Income Attributable to Noncontrolling Interests

As described in Chapter 4, some companies recognize a third component of shareholders' equity, known as **noncontrolling interests**. This component of equity only arises when a *parent company* owns a majority of the common shares of a *subsidiary company* but does not own 100% of the shares. In a situation like this, the parent company will consolidate 100% of the subsidiary company's income statement with its own income statement, including all of the revenues, expenses, and net income of the subsidiary. However, the noncontrolling shareholders are entitled to a minority portion of the subsidiary's earnings. For this reason, the parent corporation subtracts the portion of "Net Income Attributable to Noncontrolling Interests" from the total net income of the company, in order to faithfully represent the amount of net income attributable to the common shareholders.

Example ParentCo is a large corporation that owns 77% of the shares of SubCo. Other investors own the other 23% of SubCo's shares. ParentCo's consolidated income statement will report all of its revenues, expenses, and net income combined with all of those from SubCo. After computing total net income, ParentCo will subtract from it an amount equal to 23% of SubCo's net income for the period, which is the portion of SubCo's net income attributable to noncontrolling interests. ■

On its 2015 income statement, **Starbucks** reports total net earnings amounting to $2,759.3 million, and then subtracts $1.9 million in "Net earnings attributable to noncontrolling interests." Starbucks also reports "Net earnings attributable to Starbucks" amounting to $2,757.4 million.[14]

How Does Net Income Affect Retained Earnings?

Retained earnings is the link between a corporation's income statement and its balance sheet. As described in Chapter 4, *retained earnings* is the total amount of corporate earnings that has not been returned to shareholders through dividends, and is a major component of shareholders' equity. The net income (loss) from the income statement is added to (subtracted from) beginning retained earnings. All dividends declared during the accounting period, including cash dividends on preferred stock and common stock as well as any stock dividends (dividends involving the distribution of the company's stock), are subtracted to determine the ending retained earnings balance. Typically, the cash dividends per share are disclosed parenthetically on the statement. If a corporation has any retrospective adjustments or prior period adjustments (which will be described in Chapter 22), these are also included in retained earnings.

Although *not* a required financial statement, whenever a corporation issues an income statement and a balance sheet, it may include a schedule that reconciles the beginning retained earnings balance with the ending retained earnings balance. Some smaller companies report this schedule as a separate financial statement, called the **statement of retained earnings**. More often, companies report this reconciliation within the statement of shareholders' equity, as described in Chapter 4. **Example 5.3** shows Banner Corporation's reconciliation of retained earnings.

EXAMPLE 5.3 Reconciliation of Retained Earnings

Banner Corporation
Reconciliation of Retained Earnings
For Year Ended December 31, 2016

Retained earnings, January 1, 2016	$68,150
Add: Prior period adjustment, correction of understatement of 2015 ending inventory (net of $1,500 income taxes)	3,500
Adjusted retained earnings, January 1, 2016	$71,650
Add: Net income	11,200
Less: Cash dividends declared, $0.50 per share	(2,500)
Retained earnings, December 31, 2016	$80,350

---

[14] Accounting for intercompany investments and noncontrolling interests will be described in more depth in Chapter 13.

> **GOT IT?**
>
> **5-14** What items are included in a company's operating income?
>
> **5-15** What items are included in a company's income from continuing operations? How are these categorized if the company uses (a) a single-step format or (b) a multiple-step format?
>
> **5-16** How are unusual or infrequent gains or losses reported on a company's income statement?
>
> **5-17** What is *interperiod tax allocation*?
>
> **5-18** What is *intraperiod tax allocation*, and why is it necessary? How is the income tax expense related to each major component of income disclosed on the income statement?

HOW DO INCOME STATEMENTS REPORT RESULTS FROM DISCONTINUED OPERATIONS?

LEARNING OBJECTIVE 5.5
Report results from discontinued operations.

A **discontinued operation** arises when a company discontinues or plans to discontinue a business, a component of the business, or a group of components of the business. A **component** of a company involves operations and cash flows that can be clearly distinguished, operationally and for financial reporting purposes, from the rest of the company. A component of a company may be, for instance, a subsidiary, an operating segment (e.g., division), a separate cash-generating unit (e.g., a restaurant or a store), or an asset group. A component may consist of assets (e.g., inventory and property, plant, and equipment) as well as liabilities (e.g., accounts payable and bonds payable).

Reporting Results of Discontinued Operations

To enhance the usefulness of a company's income statement, it is important for the company to report separately the results of its continuing and discontinuing operations and also to highlight the material aspects involving the sale of a discontinued component. When the results from continuing and discontinued operations are reported separately, financial statement users have more useful information to evaluate the company's current period performance and to develop expectations of the company's operations that will be continuing in the future. A company reports *results from discontinued operations* when the disposal of the business or component represents a strategic shift that will have a major effect on a company's operations and financial results. Examples of a strategic shift include the disposal of a major geographic area or a major line of business.

The **results from discontinued operations** section is included on the income statement directly after income from continuing operations. It includes (1) the income (loss) from the operations of the discontinued component until the date of sale and (2) the gain (loss) from its sale, both of which are reported net of income tax.[15]

Example 5.2 illustrates Banner Corporation's results from discontinued operations (the tax amounts are taken from **Example 5.2c**). Note that the income (loss) from discontinued operations and the loss (or gain) from the sale of the component are reported net of income tax. That is, the reported amounts are adjusted directly for the related income tax effects and only the after-tax amounts are included in the computation of net income. Listing these items net of income taxes requires intraperiod tax allocation, as we discussed earlier. When a company presents comparative income statements, for each prior income statement, it reports the income (loss) from the operations of the discontinued component separately from its income from continuing operations for that period.

Real Report 5.3 shows excerpts from the financial statements of **Google, Inc.**, a world leader in web search and online advertising. Google generates revenues primarily by delivering online advertising. However, Google's Motorola Mobile segment also generates revenues by selling mobile wireless devices and related products and services.

---

[15] A company may elect to combine the two amounts on its income statement and then disclose the gain (loss) from the sale in the notes to its financial statements. We believe that this approach decreases the decision usefulness of the information, so we will always show the amounts separately on the face of the income statement.

In April 2013, Google completed the disposition of the Motorola Home segment for roughly $2.6 billion in cash and shares.

5.3 DISCONTINUED OPERATIONS — REAL REPORT

Google, Inc.

Google, Inc.
Consolidated Statements of Income
(in millions, except per share amounts)

	2011	2012	2013
Income from operations	$11,742	$12,760	$13,966
Interest and other income, net	584	626	530
Income from continuing operations before income taxes	12,326	13,386	14,496
Provision for income taxes	2,589	2,598	2,282
Net income from continuing operations	$ 9,737	$10,788	$12,214
Net income (loss) from discontinued operations	0	(51)	706
Net income	$ 9,737	$10,737	$12,920
Net income (loss) per share of Class A and Class B common stock-basic:			
Continuing operations	$ 30.17	$ 32.97	$ 36.70
Discontinued operations	0.00	(0.16)	2.12
Net income (loss) per share of Class A and Class B common stock-basic	$ 30.17	$ 32.81	$ 38.82

Note 8. Discontinued Operations

On April 17, 2013, we completed the disposition of the Motorola Home segment to Arris and certain other persons for consideration of approximately $2,412 million in cash, including cash of $2,238 million received at the date of close and certain post-close adjustments of $174 million received in the third quarter of 2013, and approximately $175 million in Arris' common stock (10.6 million shares). Subsequent to the transaction, we own approximately 7.8% of the outstanding shares of Arris. Additionally, in connection with the disposition, we agreed to indemnify Arris for potential liability from certain intellectual property infringement litigation, for which we recorded an indemnification liability of $175 million, the majority of which was settled subsequent to the disposition.

The disposition resulted in a net gain of $757 million, which was presented as part of net income from discontinued operations in the Consolidated Statements of Income for the year ended December 31, 2013.

The Motorola Home segment results have been presented as a discontinued operation for the years ended December 31, 2012 and 2013. The following table provides the financial results included in net income (loss) from discontinued operations during the periods presented (in millions):

	Year Ended December 31, 2012	Year Ended December 31, 2013
Revenues	$2,028	$804
Loss from discontinued operations before income taxes	(22)	(67)
(Provision for)Benefits from income taxes	(29)	16
Gain on disposal	0	757
Net (loss) income from discontinued operations	$ (51)	$706

Suggested answers to these questions are found at the end of the chapter.

Questions:

1. What components of its operations did Google dispose of in 2013?
2. What was the income or loss from operations of the discontinued businesses in 2012 and 2013? Why does it appear that Google sold this segment?
3. What amount of gain on disposal did Google recognize in income in 2013?

Determining a Discontinued Operation

In April 2014, the FASB adopted an Accounting Standard Update (ASU) to improve the reporting of the results of discontinued operations.[16] The FASB responded to input from stakeholders that too many disposals of small groups of assets that are recurring in nature qualified for discontinued operations presentation under the previous guidance, resulting in financial statements that were less decision-useful for users. Other stakeholders noted that some of the previous guidance on reporting discontinued operations triggered higher costs for financial statement preparers because it was complex and difficult to apply. The ASU addresses those issues by changing the criteria for reporting discontinued operations. The ASU also enhances the convergence of the FASB's and the IASB's reporting requirements for discontinued operations.

A disposal of a component of an entity or a group of components of an entity is required to be reported in discontinued operations if the disposal represents a strategic shift that has (or will have) a major effect on an entity's operations and financial results. Examples of a strategic shift that has (or will have) a major effect on an entity's operations and financial results could include a disposal of a major geographical area, a major line of business, a major equity method investment, or other major parts of an entity.

Example Suppose a merchandise retail chain operates 200 retail stores in malls and 600 supercenter stores throughout the United States. Because of the poor performance of the stores in malls, the company decides to shift its strategy and sell all 200 of the stores in malls. Because the stores in malls are a major part of the company's operations and financial results, disposing of the mall stores represents a strategic shift that should be reported in discontinued operations.

By contrast, suppose the same company decided to dispose of a single store in a specific mall, but would continue to operate the other 199 mall stores. That would not constitute a shift in the company's operations, because it will continue to operate a large number of mall stores, and so it would not be reported in discontinued operations.

Operating Income (or Loss) of a Discontinued Operation

The first element in the results from discontinued operations section is the *operating income (loss)* of the discontinued operation. A company may operate it during part of a year and then sell it before the end of the year, so that it has an operating income or operating loss for part of the year. Therefore, a company reports the operating income (or operating loss) of the discontinued operation from the beginning of the year to the *date of sale* separately from the income from continuing operations of the rest of the company, as shown in Exhibit 5.3.

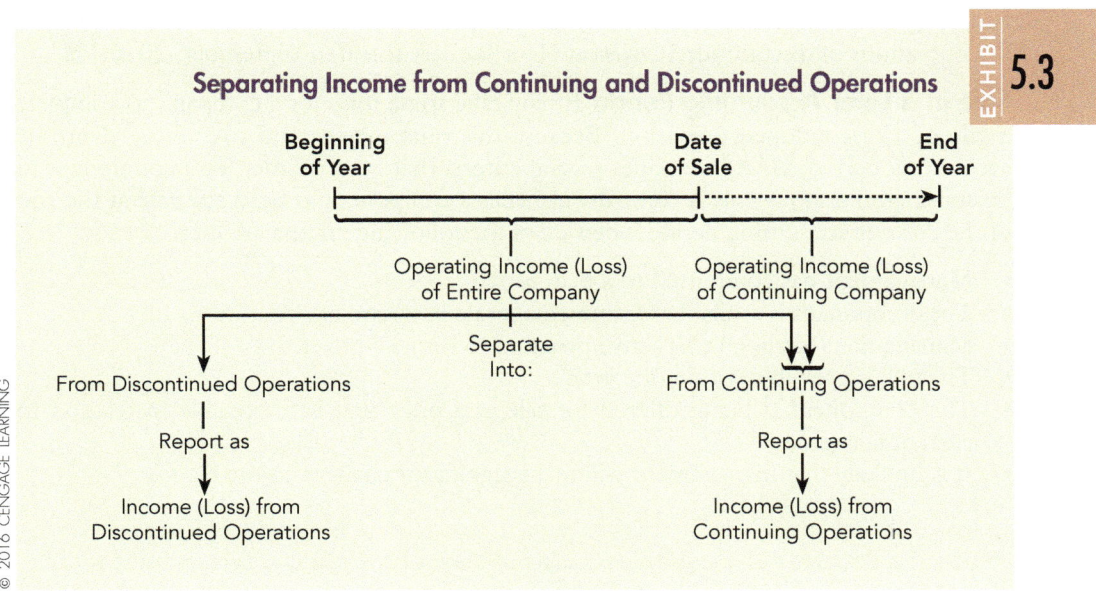

EXHIBIT 5.3 Separating Income from Continuing and Discontinued Operations

[16] FASB ASC 205-20: Presentation of Financial Statements—Discontinued Operations.

The pretax operating income (or loss) of the discontinued operation from the beginning of the year to the date of sale is computed by subtracting the expenses of the discontinued operation from the revenues of the discontinued operation for that period. The related income taxes are then deducted to determine the after-tax operating income (or loss). Note also that if a company reports comparative income statements from prior years with the current year income statement, the prior year income statements are recast so that the operating income (or loss) of the discontinued operation for the prior years are reported separately from the income from continuing operations of the rest of the company.

Gain or Loss on Sale

The second element of the results from discontinued operations section is the gain (loss) on the sale of the discontinued operation. When the sale occurs in the same accounting period that management decided to sell, the calculation of the gain (loss) is straightforward. The company determines the pretax gain (loss) by subtracting the book value of the net assets (assets minus liabilities) of the discontinued operation from the net proceeds received (selling price minus any selling costs, such as broker commissions, legal fees, closing costs). This is similar to accounting for the sale of a single asset. The company then deducts related income taxes from the pretax gain or loss to determine the after-tax gain or loss, which is reported in the results from discontinued operations section.

Example: Sale in Same Accounting Period

In 2016, Stricker Company's management decides to sell Division C, which represents a strategic shift in its operations. On September 30, 2016, Stricker sells Division C for $102,000 and incurs $2,000 of legal fees and closing costs. At the time of the sale, the book values of Division C's assets and liabilities are $150,000 and $80,000, respectively. Stricker is subject to a 30% income tax rate. Based on this information, Stricker calculates a $21,000 after-tax gain on the sale of the division as follows:

Net cash received ($102,000 − $2,000)		$100,000
Book value of net assets of Division C:		
Assets	$150,000	
Liabilities	(80,000)	
Net book value		(70,000)
Pretax gain		$ 30,000
Income taxes (30%)		(9,000)
After-tax gain		$ 21,000

Stricker reports the $21,000 gain on the sale of Division C in the results from discontinued operations section of its 2016 income statement, as well as the income (loss) from the operations of discontinued Division C for January through September, 2016.

Sale in a Later Accounting Period It may take some time for a company to complete a sale of a discontinued operation. Because this time may extend over more than one accounting period, GAAP identifies several criteria that must be met for a component to be considered *held for sale*. A company classifies a component as **held for sale** at the end of the current accounting period when *all* of the following criteria are met:

- Management has committed to a plan to sell.
- The component is available for immediate sale in its present condition.
- Management has begun an active program to locate a buyer.
- The sale is probable within one year.
- The component is being offered for sale at a price that is reasonable in relation to current fair value.
- It is unlikely that management will make significant changes to the plan.[17]

---

[17] FASB ASC 205-20-45-1E: Presentation of Financial Statements: Discontinued Operations: Other Presentation Matters.

When a company classifies a component as held for sale, it reports it on its balance sheet at the lower of (1) its book value (book value of assets minus book value of liabilities) or (2) its fair value minus any costs to sell. If the fair value (minus any costs to sell) is less than the book value, the company records a loss and adjusts the book values of the *assets* of the component. The company reports the loss (after taxes) in the results from discontinued operations section of its income statement. It reports the assets and the liabilities of the component separately in the asset and liability section of its balance sheet. The company must label these assets and liabilities as "held for sale" so that financial statement users understand that these assets and liabilities are associated with the component that is being discontinued.

Example: Sale in a Later Accounting Period

Elmo Company classifies Division M, a component of its operations, as "held for sale" at the end of 2016. Elmo expects to sell Division M in 2017 and estimates that the fair value of Division M is $200,000. For simplicity, assume that any selling costs are immaterial. At the end of 2016, the book value of Division M is $240,000 (consisting of assets with a book value of $330,000 and liabilities with a book value of $90,000). Elmo is subject to a 30% income tax rate. Based on this information, Elmo calculates a pretax loss of $40,000 on the held-for-sale component, as follows:

Fair value of Division M		$ 200,000
Book value of net assets of Division M:		
Assets	$330,000	
Liabilities	(90,000)	
Net book value		(240,000)
Pretax loss		$ (40,000)

To record the loss and decrease the assets, Elmo records the following journal entry at the end of 2016:

Loss on Write-Down of Held-for-Sale Division M (pretax)	40,000	
Assets of Division M		40,000

Elmo reports a $28,000 after-tax loss [$40,000 pretax loss − $12,000 income tax credit ($40,000 × 30%)] in the results from discontinued operations section of its 2016 income statement, along with the income (loss) from the operations of held-for-sale Division M for *all* of 2016. Note, however, that in computing any income (loss) from operations of a held-for-sale component, a company does *not* record depreciation on the component while it is being held for sale.[18] Elmo Company reports $290,000 of assets ($330,000 − $40,000) and $90,000 of liabilities for Division M on its December 31, 2016, balance sheet and identifies these as being held for sale. ■

After a company writes down a held-for-sale component to its fair value, there may be subsequent changes (increases or decreases) in this fair value. The company reports these changes as gains or losses on the income statement and as further adjustments (increases or decreases) to the book value of the component, with one exception. The company cannot increase the book value of the component to an amount higher than the component's book value before it was classified as held for sale. These adjustments are made primarily when the company prepares interim (quarterly) financial statements. The company combines these quarterly gains (losses) and reports only one net gain (loss) in its annual financial statements.

When the company actually completes the sale of a held-for-sale component, it computes any additional gain (loss) on the sale by subtracting the adjusted net book value of the component from the net proceeds received. (If the company was accurate in its estimates, there will be little or no additional gain or loss.) The company reports any after-tax gain (loss) in the results from discontinued operations section of its income statement.

---

[18] FASB ASC 360-10-35: Property, Plant, and Equipment, Overall, Subsequent Measurement.

Disclosures

A company is also required to disclose certain information about the sale (or classification as held for sale) of a discontinued operation in the notes to its financial statements. This information includes:

- a description of the facts and circumstances leading up to the disposal and, if held for sale, the expected manner and timing of the disposal
- the major classes of line items constituting pretax income (loss) of the discontinued operation
- if not separately reported on its income statement, the gain (loss) on the sale and the caption on the income statement that includes the gain (loss)
- either the total operating and investing cash flows of the discontinued operation or the depreciation, amortization, capital expenditures, and significant operating and investing noncash items of the discontinued operation.[19]

GOT IT?

5-19 What items are included in a company's results from discontinued operations? For this purpose, how is a *component* defined?

5-20 Why are results from discontinued operations separated from results from continuing operations on an income statement?

LEARNING OBJECTIVE 5.6
Understand basic earnings per share.

HOW DO WE COMPUTE AND REPORT EARNINGS PER SHARE?

Net income frequently is referred to as the "bottom line" on a company's income statement because it is the sum of income from continuing operations, and results from discontinued operations. To make net income amounts more useful for common equity shareholders, U.S. GAAP and IFRS require a company to report net income on a per-share basis, known as *earnings per share*. **Earnings per share** (**EPS**) is an important ratio in financial statement analysis because investors and analysts often analyze it relative to the market price at which a stock currently is selling to determine the relative attractiveness of that stock. For example, if a company's price-earnings ratio (market price per share divided by earnings per share) is very high (very low) relative to industry average, the company's shares may be viewed as overpriced (underpriced). Earnings per share is the only ratio that GAAP requires companies to disclose. It must be reported on a company's income statement, usually directly below net income.

Basic Earnings per Share

Basic earnings per share is computed as follows:

$$\text{Basic EPS} = \frac{\text{Net Income Available to Common Shareholders}}{\text{Weighted Average Number of Common Shares Outstanding}}$$

To compute the numerator, a company begins with net income attributable to common shareholders (that is, net income after subtracting earnings attributable to noncontrolling interests, if any) and subtracts any preferred stock dividends for the period (if any). Some companies have preferred stock outstanding, which has first priority to dividends, and therefore this amount of income is not available to common shareholders. To compute the denominator, a company computes the weighted average

[19] FASB ASC 205-20-50: Presentation of Financial Statements, Discontinued Operations, Disclosure.

number of shares outstanding during the year, taking into account shares of common stock that may have been outstanding for only part of the year (e.g., shares issued or repurchased during the year).

Example Kellman Company reported net income of $1,000 and was required to pay preferred stock dividends of $50. Net income available to common shareholders would be $950. The company had 1,900 common shares outstanding during the entire year. Basic EPS would be $0.50 ($950 ÷ 1,900 shares). ■

Diluted Earnings per Share

Some companies have complex capital structures that include securities such as convertible preferred stock, convertible bonds, and stock options or warrants that may be converted into shares of common stock. If the conversion of these securities to common stock would dilute the value of the outstanding common shares, they are referred to as **dilutive securities**. Companies with dilutive securities are required to disclose **diluted earnings per share** information, taking into account the effect of these securities on the denominator (and in certain cases the numerator) of the EPS ratio.[20]

Disclosures

All companies are required to report basic and diluted (if applicable) EPS amounts relating to income from continuing operations and net income on their income statements. They are also required to report EPS amounts for the results from discontinued operations on the income statement (or in a note to the financial statements).[21] Some companies disclose an EPS schedule that shows the per-share amounts (after tax) for each of the major components of net income. The schedule often also discloses the number of common shares used in the calculations.

An example of this schedule is shown on Banner Corporation's income statement in **Example 5.2**. The earnings per share disclosure of **Google** is shown in Real Report 5.3 (p. 5-23) and the disclosure of **Starbucks** is shown in Real Report 5.4.

REAL REPORT — **EARNINGS PER SHARE 5.4**

Starbucks

Consolidated Statements of Earnings (in part)

Fiscal Year Ended (amounts in millions, except per share amounts)	Sept. 27, 2015	Sept. 28, 2014	Sept. 29, 2013
Net earnings attributable to Starbucks	$2,757.4	$2,068.1	$ 8.3
Earnings per share—basic	$ 1.84	$ 1.37	$ 0.01
Earnings per share—diluted	$ 1.82	$ 1.35	$ 0.01
Weighted average shares outstanding:			
Basic	1,495.9	1,506.3	1,498.5
Diluted	1,513.4	1,526.3	1,524.5

---

[20] Chapter 16 discusses and demonstrates these earnings per share computations.
[21] FASB ASC 260-10-45: Earnings per Share, Overall, Other Presentation Matters.

> **Note 1: Summary of Significant Accounting Policies (partial)**
>
> *Earnings per Share*
>
> Basic earnings per share is computed on the basis of the weighted average number of shares of common stock outstanding during the period. Diluted earnings per share is computed based on the weighted average number of shares of common stock and the effect of dilutive potential common shares outstanding during the period, calculated using the treasury stock method. Dilutive potential common shares include outstanding stock options and restricted share units (RSUs). Performance-based RSUs are considered dilutive when the related performance criterion has been met.

Suggested answers to these questions are found at the end of the chapter.

Questions:

1. By how much did basic and diluted earnings per share differ for the year ended September 27, 2015? What is the primary cause of this difference?
2. What caused the difference in the weighted average number of shares in the calculation of basic versus diluted earnings per share?

GOT IT?

5-21 What is earnings per share? Where is earnings per share disclosed in a company's financial statements?

5-22 How is basic earnings per share computed?

LEARNING OBJECTIVE 5.7
Report comprehensive income.

HOW DO COMPANIES REPORT COMPREHENSIVE INCOME?

The FASB's definition of comprehensive income is as follows:

> **Comprehensive income** is the change in equity of a company during a period from transactions, other events, and circumstances relating to nonowner sources. It includes all changes in equity during a period except those resulting from investments by owners and distributions to owners.

A company's comprehensive income consists of two parts: net income and other comprehensive income. Currently, under U.S. GAAP there are four items of other comprehensive income:

- unrealized increases (gains) or decreases (losses) in the fair value of available-for-sale investment securities
- certain types of gains, losses, and prior service cost adjustments to net pension plan assets and liabilities
- fair value gains and losses on derivative financial instruments that hedge future cash flows
- translation adjustments from converting the financial statements of foreign subsidiaries into U.S. dollars

We discuss the first three items later in the book; the last item is discussed in an advanced accounting book. If a company has no items of other comprehensive income, then it does not have to report comprehensive income.

Under U.S. GAAP and IFRS, a company can report its comprehensive income (or loss) under two alternatives:

- present net income and comprehensive income in a single continuous performance statement
- present net income on the income statement and present comprehensive income on a separate, but consecutive, statement of comprehensive income

In reporting its comprehensive income, a company must add its other comprehensive income items to its net income. The other comprehensive income items may be reported at their gross amounts or net of tax. If each item is reported at its gross amount, then the tax effects of each item must be reported parenthetically. If the items are reported net of tax, the amount of tax applicable to each item must be reported in the notes to the financial statements. A company is not required to report earnings per share based on comprehensive income.[22]

Example: Comprehensive Income Reporting Alternatives

During the year, Sara Company had revenues of $60,000 and expenses of $40,000, and the income tax rate was 30%. Early in the year, Sara invested $21,000 in available-for-sale securities. At the end of the year, the securities have a fair value of $26,000 which Sara reports on its ending balance sheet. So Sara records a $5,000 unrealized increase in the fair value of these securities.[23] Sara reports its other comprehensive income net of tax.

Alternative 1 If Sara reports its net income and comprehensive income in a single, continuous performance statement, its condensed statement of net income and comprehensive income for the year would appear as follows:

Statement of Net Income and Comprehensive Income	
Revenues	$ 60,000
Expenses	(40,000)
Income before income taxes	$ 20,000
Income tax expense	(6,000)
Net income	$ 14,000
Other comprehensive income: Unrealized increase in fair value of available-for-sale securities (net of $1,500 income taxes)	3,500
Comprehensive income	$ 17,500

Alternative 2 If Sara reports its comprehensive income on a separate but consecutive statement of comprehensive income, its income statement would show net income of $14,000. Its statement of comprehensive income would appear immediately after the income statement, as follows:

Statement of Comprehensive Income	
Net income	$14,000
Other comprehensive income: Unrealized increase in fair value of available-for-sale securities (net of $1,500 income taxes)	3,500
Comprehensive income	$17,500

Exhibit 5.4 shows the relationship of a company's comprehensive income (or loss) components and its "flow" into the company's shareholders' equity accounts, specifically retained earnings and accumulated other comprehensive income (AOCI).

---

[22] FASB ASC 200-10. Accounting Standards Update 2011-05 was issued in June 2011, to become effective for fiscal years beginning after December 15, 2011. By restricting reporting comprehensive income to these two alternatives, this Accounting Standards Update eliminated a prior alternative, which was to report comprehensive income only on the statement of shareholders' equity.

[23] If the company sold some of the securities during the year and recorded a realized gain or loss on these securities, then it would record and report a "reclassification adjustment" as part of its other comprehensive income. We discuss this adjustment in Chapter 13.

EXHIBIT 5.4 The Relationships between Shareholders' Equity, Net Income and Comprehensive Income

```
    Beginning Retained Earnings              Beginning AOCI
+(−) Net Income (Loss)                  +(−) Other Comprehensive Income (Loss)   =   Comprehensive Income (Loss)
 −   Dividends                               _____
    _____
    Ending Retained Earnings                 Ending AOCI
```

In its 2015 financial statements, **Starbucks** reported comprehensive income in a separate statement, immediately following the income statement (see Appendix A). During 2015, Starbucks experienced a $0.9 million after-tax unrealized fair value gain on available-for-sale investment securities as well as unrealized holding gains on various hedging instruments of $33.5 million, net of tax. In addition, Starbucks also experienced losses from foreign currency translation adjustments of $216.7 million, after tax. In 2015, Starbucks reclassified $42.4 million (after tax) of prior unrealized holding gains and translation adjustments in net earnings. In the 2015 comprehensive income statement, Starbucks recognizes other comprehensive income items amounting to a loss of $−224.7 million (after tax). For 2015, Starbucks reported $2,759.3 million in net income (including noncontrolling interests) on its income statement and $2,534.6 million of comprehensive income (including noncontrolling interests) on the statement of comprehensive income.

GOT IT?

5-23 What is included in comprehensive income? Currently, under U.S. GAAP, what are the four items of other comprehensive income?

5-24 What two alternatives does a company have for reporting its comprehensive income under U.S. GAAP and IFRS?

LEARNING OBJECTIVE 5.8
Understand the similarities and differences in how income statements are presented under IFRS versus U.S. GAAP.

U.S. GAAP VERSUS IFRS: SIMILARITIES AND DIFFERENCES IN REPORTING INCOME

INTERNATIONAL DIMENSION

IFRS and U.S. GAAP follow similar but not identical approaches to measuring and reporting net income. Under IFRS, much of a company's income statement content is similar in that IFRS require disclosure of revenues, operating expenses, financing costs, tax expense, net income (loss), results of discontinued operations, and earnings per share. A company is also required to disclose comprehensive income in either a single continuous statement of comprehensive income or in two separate consecutive statements (an income statement and a statement that begins with net income and displays the components of other comprehensive income).

(continued)

Currently several differences exist between IFRS and U.S. GAAP with regard to the presentation of income statement information. Some of the more significant differences include:

- While U.S. GAAP requires either a single-step or multiple-step format for the income statement, there is no prescribed income statement format under IFRS.
- Terminology may differ among companies. For example, some IFRS companies use the term "turnover" to refer to sales or revenues.
- IFRS, unlike U.S. GAAP, require expenses to be classified by their nature or function.
- Under IFRS, if a company has revalued its equipment upward (as discussed in Chapter 4), then it must adjust its related depreciation expense accordingly.
- IFRS allow alternative performance measures, such as earnings before interest, taxes, depreciation and amortization (EBITDA), to be presented on the income statement. Such presentation of non-GAAP performance measures in the financial statements is prohibited by the SEC.
- Under both U.S. GAAP and IFRS, the presentation of discontinued operations is similar. U.S. GAAP and IFRS are also similar in what qualifies as a component that has been disposed of or held for sale. Under both sets of standards, a discontinued operation represents a strategic shift in a company's operations and financial results, such as a disposal of a major geographical area or line of business.
- As a result of recent convergence efforts, the measurement and presentation of earnings per share are similar. However, a few differences exist. The FASB is currently working on revising its earnings per share standard to eliminate any major remaining differences with regard to earnings per share.

IFRS Application The comparative income statements (with amounts in millions of euros) for the years 2013, 2012, and 2011 for **LVMH Group (Moet Hennessy – Louis Vuitton)** are presented below. LVMH manages a portfolio of over 60 of the world's leading brands in luxury goods, with branded products in five different sectors: (1) Wine and Spirits, (2) Fashion and Leather Goods, (3) Perfumes and Cosmetics, (4) Watches and Jewelry, and (5) Selective Retailing. Headquartered in France, LVMH Group prepared these income statements using IFRS.

LVMH Group
Consolidated Income Statements

(EUR millions, except for earnings per share)	Notes	2013	2012	2011
Revenue	23-24	29,149	28,103	23,659
Cost of sales		(10,055)	(9,917)	(8,092)
Gross margin		19,094	18,186	15,567
Marketing and selling expenses		(10,849)	(10,101)	(8,360)
General and administrative expenses		(2,224)	(2,164)	(1,944)
Profit from recurring operations	23-24	6,021	5,921	5,263
Other operating income and expenses	25	(127)	(182)	(109)
Operating profit		5,894	5,739	5,154
Cost of net financial debt		(103)	(140)	(151)
Other financial income and expenses		(96)	126	(91)
Net financial income (expense)	26	(199)	(14)	(242)
Income taxes	27	(1,755)	(1,820)	(1,453)
Income (loss) from investments in associates	7	7	4	6
Net profit before minority interests		3,947	3,909	3,465
Minority interests	17	(511)	(485)	(400)
Net profit, Group share		3,436	3,424	3,065
Basic Group share of net earnings per share *(EUR)*	28	6.87	6.86	6.27
Number of shares on which the calculation is based		500,283,414	499,133,643	488,769,286
Diluted Group share of net earnings per share *(EUR)*	28	6.83	6.82	6.23
Number of shares on which the calculation is based		503,217,497	502,229,952	492,207,492

Note that the income statements of LVMH prepared under IFRS are very similar to those that would be prepared under U.S. GAAP. Revenue amounted to €29,149 million in 2013. A minor difference is that LVMH refers to the portion of its income attributable to noncontrolling interests as "Minority interests" (which was the terminology used previously in U.S. GAAP) and the portion of income attributable to LVMH's common shareholders as "Net profit, Group share."

IFRS Application The comparative comprehensive income statements (with amounts in millions of euros) for the years 2013, 2012, and 2011 for **LVMH Group** are presented below. As described earlier, LVMH Group prepared its comprehensive income statements using IFRS, and they are very similar to those that would be prepared under U.S. GAAP. LVMH reported comprehensive income using Alternative 2, with a separate but consecutive "Consolidated Statement of Comprehensive Gains and Losses."

LVMH Group
Consolidated Statements of Comprehensive Gains and Losses

(EUR millions)	2013	2012[a]	2011[a]
Net profit before minority interests	3,947	3,909	3,465
Translation adjustments	(346)	(99)	190
Tax impact	(48)	(18)	47
	(394)	(117)	237
Change in value of available for sale financial assets	963	(27)	1,634
Amounts transferred to income statement	(16)	(14)	(38)
Tax impact	(35)	(6)	(116)
	912	(47)	1,480
Change in value of hedges of future foreign currency cash flows	304	182	95
Amounts transferred to income statement	(265)	13	(168)
Tax impact	(17)	(50)	21
	22	145	(52)
Gains and losses recognized in equity, transferable to income statement	540	(19)	1,665
Change in value of vineyard land	369	85	25
Tax impact	(127)	(28)	(11)
	242	57	14
Employee benefit commitments: change in value resulting from actuarial gains and losses	80	(101)	(45)
Tax impact	(22)	29	13
	58	(72)	(32)
Gains and losses recognized in equity, not transferable to income statement	300	(15)	(18)
Comprehensive income	4,787	3,875	5,112
Minority interests	(532)	(470)	(429)
Comprehensive income, Group share	4,255	3,405	4,683

[a]The consolidated statements of comprehensive gains and losses as of December 31, 2012 and 2011 have been restated to reflect the retrospective application as of January 1, 2011 of IAS 19 Employee Benefits as amended. See Note 1.2.

Note that for the year 2013, LVMH recognized Net profit before minority interests of €3,947 million. In this statement, LVMH reported that for the year 2013 comprehensive income amounted to €4,787 million. LVMH reported an additional €840 million of gains and losses directly in equity, primarily from translation adjustments (€−394 million), changes in the fair value of available for sale securities (€912 million), changes in the fair value of hedges of future foreign currency cash flows (€22 million), changes in the value of vineyard land (€242 million), and changes in value of employee benefit commitments (pensions) (€58 million). One interesting difference is that the IFRS-based statement separates gains and losses into those that are transferable to the income statement (when realized) and those that are not transferable. Another interesting difference is that IFRS allows companies to use the fair value option for a wider set of assets and liabilities than U.S. GAAP allows, and LVMH uses the fair value option to value its vineyard lands!

IFRS Application The comparative income statements [with amounts in millions of Swiss Francs (CHF)] for the years 2009 and 2010 for **Nestlé Group** are presented below. Nestlé is one of the world's leading companies in nutrition, health, and wellness products. Headquartered in Switzerland, Nestlé prepared these income statements using IFRS.

Nestlé Group
Consolidated Income Statement
For Year Ended 31 December 2010

In millions of CHF	Notes	2010 Continuing operations	2010 Discontinued operations[a]	2010 Total	2009 Continuing operations	2009 Discontinued operations[a]	2009 Total
Sales	3	104 613	5 109	109 722	100 579	7 039	107 618
Cost of goods sold		(44 775)	(1 074)	(45 849)	(43 467)	(1 741)	(45 208)
Distribution expenses		(8 385)	(125)	(8 510)	(8 237)	(183)	(8 420)
Marketing and administration expenses		(36 012)	(1 276)	(37 288)	(34 296)	(1 974)	(36 270)
Research and development costs		(1 403)	(478)	(1 881)	(1 357)	(664)	(2 021)
EBIT Earnings Before Interest, Taxes, restructuring and impairments	3	14 038	2 156	16 194	13 222	2 477	15 699
Other income	4	206	24 535	24 741	466	43	509
Other expenses	4	(2 101)	(14)	(2 115)	(1 196)	(42)	(1 238)
Profit before interest and taxes		12 143	26 677	38 820	12 492	2 478	14 970
Financial income	13	72	22	94	123	56	179
Financial expense	13	(834)	(13)	(847)	(777)	(17)	(794)
Profit before taxes and associates		11 381	26 686	38 067	11 838	2 517	14 355
Taxes	14	(3 343)	(350)	(3 693)	(3 087)	(275)	(3 362)
Share of results of associates	15	1 010	–	1 010	800	–	800
Profit for the year		9 048	26 336	35 384	9 551	2 242	11 793
of which attributable to non-controlling interests		271	880	1 151	291	1 074	1 365
of which attributable to shareholders of the parent (Net profit)		8 777	25 456	34 233	9 260	1 168	10 428
As percentages of sales							
EBIT Earnings Before Interest, Taxes, restructuring and impairments		13.4%	42.2%	14.8%	13.1%	35.2%	14.6%
Profit for the year attributable to shareholders of the parent (Net profit)				31.2%			9.7%
Earnings per share (in CHF)							
Basic earnings per share	16	2.60	7.56	10.16	2.59	0.33	2.92
Fully diluted earnings per share	16	2.60	7.52	10.12	2.58	0.33	2.91

[a] Detailed information related to Alcon discontinued operations is disclosed in Note 2.

Note that the income statements of Nestlé are *very different* from those of LVMH, which were also prepared under IFRS, and are also *very different* from income statements that would be prepared under U.S. GAAP. In particular, take note of the following three differences:

- Nestlé reports the effects of a discontinued operation by showing separate income statement columns for continuing and discontinued operations, which sum to the total income statement column. In 2010, Nestlé disposed of its ownership interests in **Alcon, USA** (a pharmaceutical company) by selling its shares to **Novartis**, a French pharmaceutical company.
- Nestlé does not report operating income but instead reports "EBIT (Earnings Before Interest, Taxes, restructuring and impairments)."
- Nestlé does not report net income but instead reports "Profit for the year."

Source: IAS 1, IAS 33, IFRS 5 (See Appendix C at the end of this book.)

> **GOT IT?**
>
> 5-25 Identify several differences between IFRS and U.S. GAAP in regard to the presentation and content of a company's income statement.

LEARNING OBJECTIVE 5.9
Explain the statement of cash flows and classify cash flows as operating, investing, or financing.

HOW DO COMPANIES REPORT THE STATEMENT OF CASH FLOWS?

Under U.S. GAAP and IFRS, a company prepares a balance sheet to report financial position at the end of the period and an income statement to show financial performance during the period. External users are also very interested in how a company generates and uses cash. How much cash flow is the company generating from its operations? From what sources? How much cash did the company invest to grow? How was the growth financed? Did the company raise cash by issuing debt or use cash to retire debt? How did the company use the proceeds from the issuance of capital stock? These questions cannot be answered directly from the income statement or the balance sheet.

As a result, U.S. GAAP and IFRS require that **a company present a statement of cash flows for the accounting period along with its income statement and balance sheet**. The primary purpose of a **statement of cash flows** is to provide relevant information about a company's cash receipts and cash payments during the period. Because this statement is related to the other financial statements and is an integral part of a company's annual report, we briefly discuss it next and then discuss it more fully in Chapter 21.

Overview and Uses of the Statement of Cash Flows

In Chapter 2, we noted that one of the specific objectives of financial reporting is to provide information to help financial statement users predict the amounts, timing, and uncertainty of a company's future cash flows. Together with the balance sheet and income statement, the statement of cash flows is useful in meeting this objective. Financial statement users analyze the information from the statement of cash flows to assess a company's *risk* (the uncertainty and variability in the company's future performance), *liquidity* (its ability to generate cash flows from operations and convert assets into cash), *financial flexibility* (its ability to adapt to unexpected needs and opportunities), and *operating capability* (its ability to maintain a given level of efficient operations). When used with a company's other financial statements, the statement of cash flows helps external users assess the company's:

- ability to generate positive future cash flows from operations
- ability to meet its obligations
- use of cash for capital expenditures and investments
- capital raised from external financing sources and repayments of external financing
- differences between the company's net income and associated cash receipts and payments
- sources of cash from issuing shares and uses of cash to pay dividends and repurchase shares from common shareholders[24]

Reporting the Statement of Cash Flows

U.S. GAAP and IFRS require that a company must provide **a statement of cash flows to report on a company's cash inflows, cash outflows, and net change in cash from its operating, investing, and financing activities during the accounting period, in a manner that reconciles the beginning and ending cash balances**. This reconciliation causes the statement of cash flows to *articulate* with the balance sheet.

A company's **operating activities** include all the transactions and other events related to its primary business activities, such as those involved in purchasing, producing, selling, and delivering goods for sale, as well as providing services. **Investing activities** include transactions involving buying and selling property, plant, and equipment and intangible assets; buying and selling long-term investments; and lending money and

[24] FASB ASC 230-10-10: Statement of Cash Flows, Overall, Objectives.

collecting on the loans. **Financing activities** include transactions involved in obtaining resources from owners and paying dividends and repurchasing shares, as well as obtaining resources from lenders and repaying the amounts borrowed.

These activities generate cash inflows and outflows that can be categorized according to each activity on the statement of cash flows, as shown in Exhibit 5.5.

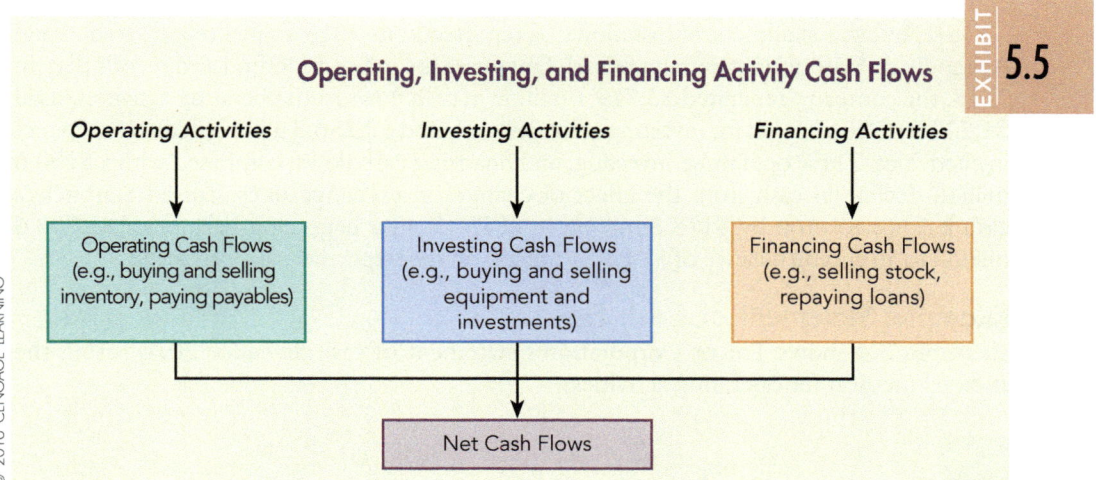

EXHIBIT 5.5 Operating, Investing, and Financing Activity Cash Flows

The statement of cash flows of a company therefore includes three major sections: (1) operating activities, (2) investing activities, and (3) financing activities.[25]

Operating Activities: Indirect Method The *operating activities* section reports the cash receipts and payments from the operating activities of the company. The most common way to prepare this section is called the **indirect method**.[26] Under this method, net income is listed first and then adjustments (additions or subtractions) are made to net income:

- to eliminate certain amounts, such as depreciation expense and amortization expense, that were included in net income but that did not involve a cash inflow or cash outflow for operating activities
- to include the cash flow effects triggered by any changes in the assets (other than cash) and liabilities involved in the company's operating activities (such as changes in accounts receivable, inventory, and payables)

These adjustments are made to convert the net income to the net cash provided by (or used in) operating activities.

Investing Activities The *investing activities* section includes all the cash inflows and outflows involved in the investing activities of the company. The most common cash inflows (receipts) from and cash outflows (payments) for investing activities are:

- receipts from selling and payments for purchasing property, plant, and equipment
- receipts from selling and payments for purchasing investments in stocks and debt securities (e.g., bonds)

Financing Activities The *financing activities* section includes all the cash inflows and cash outflows involved in the financing activities of the company. The most common cash inflows (receipts) from and cash outflows (payments) for financing activities are:

- receipts from the issuance of debt securities (e.g., bonds, mortgages, notes)
- cash flows to repay debt obligations
- receipts from the issuance of shares
- payments to repurchase shares (i.e., treasury stock)
- payments of dividends

---

[25] Transactions involving investing and financing activities that *do not* affect cash receipts or cash payments also are included in a separate schedule accompanying the statement of cash flows. We discuss this schedule in Chapter 21.

[26] According to *Accounting Trends and Techniques* (New York, AICPA, 2010, p. 533), 99% of companies surveyed use the indirect method.

Completing the Statement of Cash Flows To complete the statement of cash flows, the cash inflows and outflows within each section are subtotaled; the subtotals are added to determine the net increase (or decrease) in cash of the company during the accounting period. The net change in cash is then added to or subtracted from the beginning cash balance to reconcile to the ending cash balance reported on the company's year-end balance sheet.[27]

Starbucks's statement of cash flows, as reported in its 2015 annual report, is shown in Appendix A. Starbucks' statement of cash flows uses the indirect method and reveals that, in 2015, the company generated $3,749.1 million in cash flows from operating activities, used $1,520.3 million in cash for investing activities, and used $2,256.5 million in cash for financing activities. These operating, investing, and financing cash flows, combined with a $150.6 million decline in cash from the effect of changes in exchange rates, caused Starbucks's cash balance to drop by $178.3 million in 2015 (from a beginning balance of $1,708.4 million to an ending balance of $1,530.1 million on the respective balance sheets).

Example: Statement of Cash Flows

Example 5.4 shows Trevor Corporation's statement of cash flows for 2016 (using the *indirect* method for operating activities).

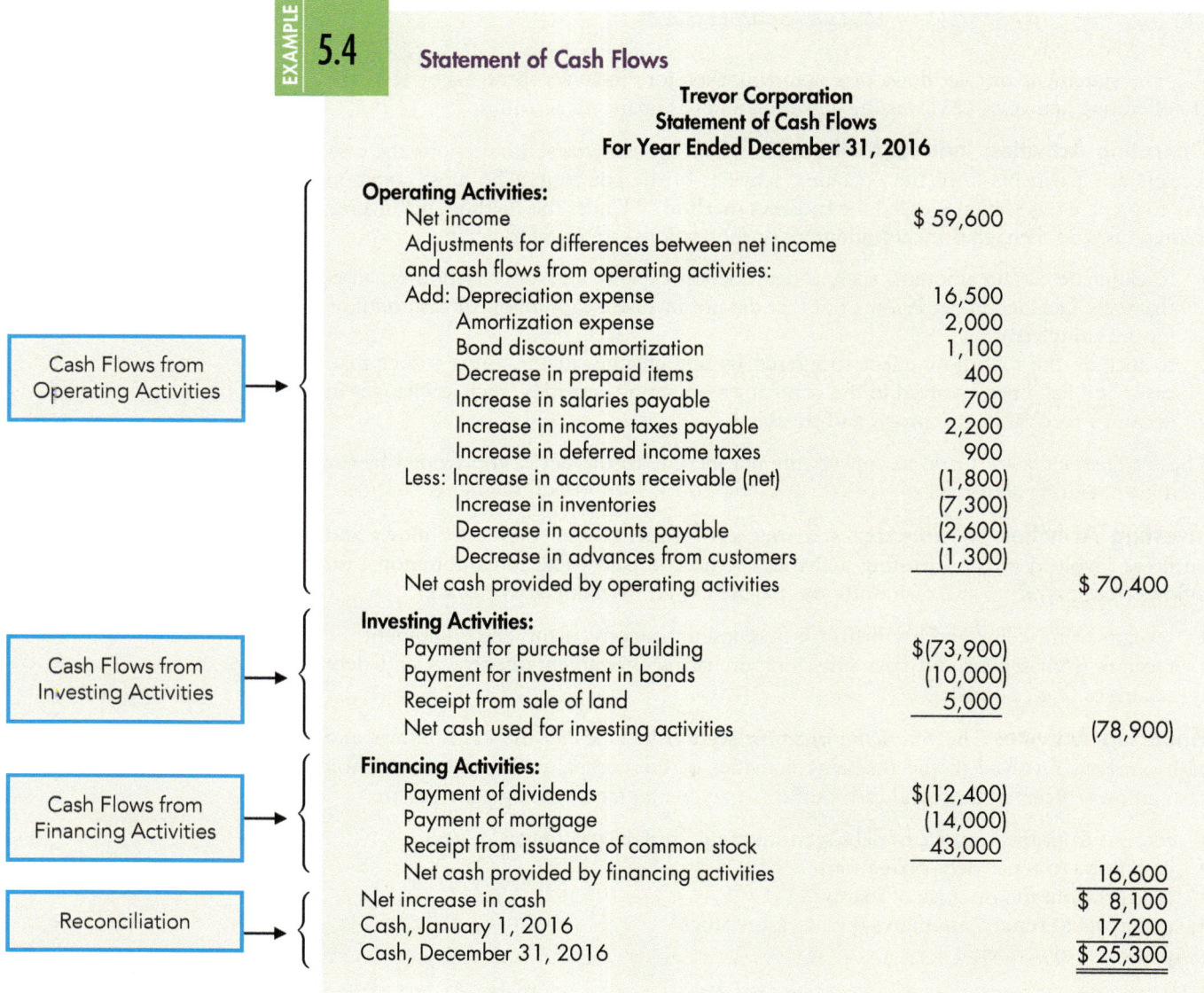

EXAMPLE 5.4

Statement of Cash Flows

Trevor Corporation
Statement of Cash Flows
For Year Ended December 31, 2016

Operating Activities:		
Net income		$ 59,600
Adjustments for differences between net income and cash flows from operating activities:		
Add: Depreciation expense	16,500	
Amortization expense	2,000	
Bond discount amortization	1,100	
Decrease in prepaid items	400	
Increase in salaries payable	700	
Increase in income taxes payable	2,200	
Increase in deferred income taxes	900	
Less: Increase in accounts receivable (net)	(1,800)	
Increase in inventories	(7,300)	
Decrease in accounts payable	(2,600)	
Decrease in advances from customers	(1,300)	
Net cash provided by operating activities		$ 70,400
Investing Activities:		
Payment for purchase of building	$(73,900)	
Payment for investment in bonds	(10,000)	
Receipt from sale of land	5,000	
Net cash used for investing activities		(78,900)
Financing Activities:		
Payment of dividends	$(12,400)	
Payment of mortgage	(14,000)	
Receipt from issuance of common stock	43,000	
Net cash provided by financing activities		16,600
Net increase in cash		$ 8,100
Cash, January 1, 2016		17,200
Cash, December 31, 2016		$ 25,300

Cash Flows from Operating Activities
Cash Flows from Investing Activities
Cash Flows from Financing Activities
Reconciliation

---

[27] As we noted in Chapter 4, a company may report cash and cash equivalents on its balance sheet. It this case, the reconciliation on the statement of cash flows is to the ending cash and cash equivalents.

Note that Trevor had a net cash inflow of $70,400 from its *operating activities* in 2016. This amount was determined by adjusting the $59,600 net income for several differences between its income flows and cash flows. For instance, depreciation expense of $16,500 was added back to net income because it had been deducted as an expense on the income statement but there was no cash outflow. On the other hand, the $1,800 increase in accounts receivable was subtracted because this increase resulted from credit sales, which increased sales revenue (and net income) on the income statement, but provided no cash inflow at the time of the sale. The other adjustments to net income were made for similar reasons, as we discuss more fully in Chapter 21.

The net cash used for *investing activities* was $78,900. The cash outflows were for the purchase of a building and for an investment in bonds. The cash inflow was from the sale of land. The net cash provided by *financing activities* was $16,600. The cash outflows were for the payment of dividends and a mortgage. The cash inflow was from the issuance of common stock. The $8,100 net increase in cash was the result of $70,400 net cash provided by operating activities, minus the $78,900 net cash used for investing activities, plus the $16,600 net cash provided by financing activities. The $8,100 net increase in cash was added to the $17,200 cash balance on January 1, 2016, to reconcile to the $25,300 cash balance on December 31, 2016.

Operating Activities: Direct Method

The other way to report cash flows from operating activities is the **direct method**. The FASB encourages use of the direct method, but relatively few companies use this method. This method separates operating cash inflows from operating cash outflows, which may be useful in estimating future cash flows. Under the direct method, a company's operating cash inflows are listed first, and then the operating cash outflows are deducted to determine the net cash provided by (or used in) operating activities. The most common cash inflows and outflows for operating activities are:

- operating cash inflows
  - collections from customers
  - interest and dividends collected
- operating cash outflows
  - payments to suppliers and employees
  - payments of interest
  - payments of income taxes

Example If Trevor Corporation used the direct method *instead* of the indirect method, the operating cash flows section of **Example 5.4** would be as follows:

Operating Activities:
Cash Inflows:
Collections from customers	$ 248,100	
Interest and dividends collected	3,800	
Cash inflows from operating activities		$ 251,900
Cash Outflows:		
Payments to suppliers and employees	$(143,600)	
Payments of interest	(17,200)	
Payments of income taxes	(20,700)	
Cash outflows for operating activities		(181,500)
Net cash provided by operating activities		$ 70,400

Note that the $70,400 reported as the net cash provided by operating activities is the same under the direct and indirect methods, only the approach to determining the amount is different. The remainder of the statement of cash flows is the same under either method.

> **GOT IT?**
>
> **5-26** What is a *statement of cash flows*? What is its primary purpose?
>
> **5-27** What are the three major sections of the statement of cash flows?
>
> **5-28** When used with a company's other financial statements, what does the statement of cash flows help external users assess?
>
> **5-29** What are the three types of activities that a statement of cash flows reports for a company? Provide examples of transactions for each type of activity.
>
> **5-30** Under the indirect method, how is the net cash provided by operating activities determined in a company's statement of cash flows?

LEARNING OBJECTIVE 5.10

Apply financial statement analysis techniques to analyze the income statement and cash flow statement information.

HOW DO WE ANALYZE THE INFORMATION IN INCOME STATEMENTS AND CASH FLOW STATEMENTS?

As an accounting professional, you need to have a good understanding of how users analyze and interpret financial statement information. This section describes various tools of financial analysis using income statement and cash flow statement information. As in Chapter 4, this section describes several analysis techniques for intracompany comparisons (evaluating a company over time) and intercompany comparisons (comparing two or more companies, either at a point in time or over time). These techniques include common-size and profit margin analysis, rate of change analysis, and ratio analysis.

Common-Size and Profit Margin Analysis

We introduced **common-size analysis** in Chapter 4. Common-size analysis of income statement information typically expresses all of the amounts in terms of percentages of total revenues. Common-size income statements enable users to identify what proportion of each dollar of revenues is absorbed by various expenses, like cost of goods sold as a percent of sales and operating expenses as a percent of sales.

Common-size analysis is also a very useful technique to compute the most commonly used financial statement ratios: profit margins. Financial statement users evaluate profit margins at various levels, reflecting different aspects of the company's financial performance:

- **Gross profit margin** (gross profit divided by total revenues) indicates a company's ability to generate revenues and control the costs of producing and delivering its products and services.
- **Operating margin** (operating income divided by total revenues) indicates a company's ability to generate a profit from its operating activities after covering all of its operating costs.
- **Net profit margin** (net income as a percent of total revenues) is the bottom line proportion of profit per dollar of total revenues.

Common-size analysis of financial statements from several periods enables analysts to identify trends or changes in profit margins over time. Exhibit 5.6 presents **Starbucks**'s income statement information for the fiscal years 2013, 2014, and 2015 in two ways: amounts in millions of dollars and in common-size percentages.

EXHIBIT 5.6

Common-Size and Profit Margin Analysis of Starbucks Corporation's Income Statements

	Dollar Amounts in Millions			Common-Sized		
	2013	2014	2015	2013	2014	2015
Company-operated stores	$11,793.2	$12,977.9	$15,197.3	79.3%	78.9%	79.3%
Licensed stores	1,360.5	1,588.6	1,861.9	9.2%	9.7%	9.7%
CPG, foodservice and other	1,713.1	1,881.3	2,103.5	11.5%	11.4%	11.0%
Total net revenues	**14,866.8**	**16,447.8**	**19,162.7**	**100.0%**	**100.0%**	**100.0%**
Cost of sales including occupancy costs	(6,382.3)	(6,858.8)	(7,787.5)	−42.9%	−41.7%	−40.6%
Gross profit	**8,484.5**	**9,589.0**	**11,375.2**	**57.1%**	**58.3%**	**59.4%**
Store operating expenses	(4,286.1)	(4,638.2)	(5,411.1)	−28.8%	−28.2%	−28.2%
Other operating expenses	(431.8)	(457.3)	(522.4)	−2.9%	−2.8%	−2.7%
Depreciation and amortization	(621.4)	(709.6)	(893.9)	−4.2%	−4.3%	−4.7%
General and administrative expenses	(937.9)	(991.3)	(1,196.7)	−6.3%	−6.0%	−6.2%
Litigation (charge) credit	(2,784.1)	20.2	—	−18.7%	0.1%	0.0%
Income from equity investees	251.4	268.3	249.9	1.7%	1.6%	1.3%
Operating income	**(325.4)**	**3,081.1**	**3,601.0**	**−2.2%**	**18.7%**	**18.8%**
Gain on acquisition of joint venture	—	—	390.6	0.0%	0.0%	2.0%
Loss on extinguishment of debt	—	—	(61.1)	0.0%	0.0%	−0.3%
Interest and other income	123.6	142.7	43.0	0.8%	0.9%	0.2%
Interest expense	(28.1)	(64.1)	(70.5)	−0.2%	−0.4%	−0.4%
Income before income taxes	**(229.9)**	**3,159.7**	**3,903.0**	**−1.5%**	**19.2%**	**20.4%**
Provision for income taxes	(238.7)	1,092.0	1,143.7	−1.6%	6.6%	6.0%
Net income including noncontrolling interests	**8.8**	**2,067.7**	**2,759.3**	**0.1%**	**12.6%**	**14.4%**
Net (income)/loss attributable to noncontrolling interests	(0.5)	0.4	(1.9)	0.0%	0.0%	0.0%
Net income attributable to Starbucks	**$ 8.3**	**$ 2,068.1**	**$ 2,757.4**	**0.1%**	**12.6%**	**14.4%**
Net Income Per Share						
Basic	$ 0.01	$ 1.37	$ 1.84			
Diluted	$ 0.01	$ 1.35	$ 1.82			

These common-size data for Starbucks reveal, for example, that in 2015 company operated-retail revenues amounted to 79.3% of total revenues. The data also show that Starbucks's gross profit margin increased from 57.1% of total net revenues in 2013 to 58.3% in 2014, only to increase again to 59.4% in 2015. Similarly, the common-size percentages show that Starbucks's operating margin was −2.2% of total net revenues in 2013 (because of the litigation charges in 2013, which amounted to 18.7% of revenues). However, Starbucks's operating margin bounced back up to 18.7%, in 2014, and increased slightly further to 18.8% in 2015. Starbucks's net profit margin was only 0.1% of total net revenues in 2013 (again, because of the litigation charges), but then it jumped to 12.6% in 2014 and increased further to 14.4% in 2015. These data reveal that in fiscal 2014 and 2015, Starbucks operated very profitably.

Rate of Change Analysis

In Chapter 4, we also introduced **rate of change analysis**, which is frequently used to compute growth rates. Recall (and, if necessary, review) that in Chapter 4 we also described how to compute compound rates of change to determine the average rate of change compounded over several periods. Rate of change analysis enables users to identify which items on the balance sheet and income statement are growing quickly or slowly over time.

Exhibit 5.7 presents **Starbucks**'s income statement information for the fiscal years 2013, 2014, and 2015 in millions of dollars and in rates of change for 2014 and 2015, as well as the compound rate of change over 2013 to 2015.

EXHIBIT 5.7 Rate of Change Analysis of Starbucks Corporation's Income Statements

	Dollar Amounts in Millions			Rates of Change		
	2013	2014	2015	2014	2015	Compound
Company-operated stores	$11,793.2	$12,977.9	$15,197.3	10.0%	17.1%	13.5%
Licensed stores	1,360.5	1,588.6	1,861.9	16.8%	17.2%	17.0%
CPG, foodservice and other	1,713.1	1,881.3	2,103.5	9.8%	11.8%	10.8%
Total net revenues	**14,866.8**	**16,447.8**	**19,162.7**	**10.6%**	**16.5%**	**13.5%**
Cost of sales including occupancy costs	(6,382.3)	(6,858.8)	(7,787.5)	7.5%	13.5%	10.5%
Gross profit	**8,484.5**	**9,589.0**	**11,375.2**	**13.0%**	**18.6%**	**15.8%**
Store operating expenses	(4,286.1)	(4,638.2)	(5,411.1)	8.2%	16.7%	12.4%
Other operating expenses	(431.8)	(457.3)	(522.4)	5.9%	14.2%	10.0%
Depreciation and amortization	(621.4)	(709.6)	(893.9)	14.2%	26.0%	19.9%
General and administrative expenses	(937.9)	(991.3)	(1,196.7)	5.7%	20.7%	13.0%
Litigation (charge) credit	(2,784.1)	20.2	—	−100.7%	−100.0%	−100.0%
Income from equity investees	251.4	268.3	249.9	6.7%	−6.9%	−0.3%
Operating income	**(325.4)**	**3,081.1**	**3,601.0**	**−1,046.9%**	**16.9%**	**na**
Gain on acquisition of joint venture	—	—	390.6	na	na	na
Loss on extinguishment of debt	—	—	(61.1)	na	na	na
Interest and other income	123.6	142.7	43.0	15.5%	−69.9%	−41.0%
Interest expense	(28.1)	(64.1)	(70.5)	128.1%	10.0%	58.4%
Income before income taxes	**(229.9)**	**3,159.7**	**3,903.0**	**−1,474.4%**	**23.5%**	**na**
Provision for income taxes	(238.7)	1,092.0	1,143.7	−557.5%	4.7%	na
Net income including noncontrolling interests	**8.8**	**2,067.7**	**2,759.3**	**23,396.6%**	**33.4%**	**1,670.8%**
Net (income)/loss attributable to noncontrolling interests	(0.5)	0.4	(1.9)	−180.0%	−575.0%	94.9%
Net income attributable to Starbucks	**$ 8.3**	**$ 2,068.1**	**$ 2,757.4**	**24,816.9%**	**33.3%**	**1,722.7%**
	$ 0.01	$ 1.37	$ 1.84			
	$ 0.01	$ 1.35	$ 1.82			

These growth rates for Starbucks reveal that company-operated store revenues grew by 10.0% from 2013 to 2014 and by 17.1% from 2014 to 2015, resulting in a 13.5% compound growth rate over these 2 years. The growth rate in net income attributable to Starbucks was enormous in 2014 (a whopping 24,816.9% because net income was very low in 2013 due to the litigation charges). In 2015, Starbucks's net income grew by 33.3%. Together, the common-size analysis and the rate of change analysis provide additional information to financial statement users about Starbucks's financial performance in 2015 relative to 2014 and 2013. Starbucks operated very profitably and generated strong growth in revenues and net income during 2014 and 2015.

Ratio Analysis

In Chapter 4, we also described computing and interpreting financial statement analysis ratios. Ratios capture relationships between and among items on financial statements. They are useful indicators of financial position and performance, serving as metrics to evaluate a company's results over time and against its competitors. These ratios reveal useful insights about a company's return on investment, risk, financial flexibility, liquidity, and operating capability. You may want to refer back to Examples 4.4 and 4.7 (pages 4-38 and 4-46), which presented a variety of financial ratios and formulas for Starbucks for 2014 and 2015, to review how these ratios utilize the income statement amounts described in this chapter (net revenues, costs of goods sold, and net income) together with balance sheet data to reveal useful insights about Starbucks.

The most commonly analyzed ratios from the income statement are the various profit margins discussed earlier, including the gross profit margin, operating profit margin, and net profit margin. In this section, we introduce several additional ratios that rely on income statement and cash flow information to assess risk and financial flexibility, and we decompose the rate of return on common equity to show its utilization of both income statement and balance sheet information.

Coverage Ratios Coverage ratios provide insights about a company's risk and financial flexibility because they measure the ability to cover the interest charges associated with debt. These ratios reveal insights about risk and financial flexibility because companies with lower coverage ratios (i.e., less ability to cover or pay for the interest expenses from debt) typically have greater risk and less financial flexibility. The most commonly computed coverage ratio is the **interest coverage ratio**, which can be computed using operating income or cash flows from operations, as follows:

$$\text{Earnings-Based Interest Coverage} = \text{Operating Income} \div \text{Interest Expense}$$

$$\text{Cash Flows-Based Interest Coverage} = \text{Cash Flows from Operations} \div \text{Interest Expense}$$

Computed either way, the coverage ratio is a multiple—the number of times the company earned (either through operating income or cash flows from operations) the amount needed to cover interest expense for the period.

Example For **Starbucks** in 2015, the earnings-based interest coverage ratio is 51.1 and the cash flows-based interest coverage ratio is 53.2. These interest coverage ratios are computed as:

$$\text{Earnings-Based Interest Coverage} = \text{Operating Income} \div \text{Interest Expense}$$
$$= \$3,601.0 \text{ million} \div \$70.5 \text{ million} = 51.1 \text{ times}$$

$$\text{Cash Flows-Based Interest Coverage} = \text{Cash Flows from Operations} \div \text{Interest Expense}$$
$$= \$3,749.1 \text{ million} \div \$70.5 \text{ million} = 53.2 \text{ times}$$

With these computations, it is clear that in 2015, Starbucks generated a substantial amount of operating income and cash flows from operations, many times the amount needed to pay interest charges. ■

Decomposition of Return on Common Equity In Chapter 4, we described the **return on common equity**, which measures the profitability of the company relative to the amount of equity capital invested by the common shareholders. It is computed as:

$$\text{Return on Common Equity} = \text{Net Income} \div \text{Average Common Equity}$$

The return on common equity is informative because it integrates the bottom line of the income statement (net income) with the bottom line of the balance sheet (the amount of equity capital invested by the common shareholders).

The rate of return on common equity is particularly helpful as an analytical tool because it can be broken down into three moving parts—net profit margin times total asset turnover times leverage—using a bit of algebra:

$$\text{Return on Common Equity} = \frac{\text{Net Income}}{\text{Average Common Equity}}$$
$$= \frac{\text{Net Income}}{\text{Total Sales}} \times \frac{\text{Total Sales}}{\text{Average Total Assets}} \times \frac{\text{Average Total Assets}}{\text{Average Common Equity}}$$
$$= \text{Net Profit Margin} \times \text{Total Asset Turnover} \times \text{Leverage}$$

This decomposition is the result of inserting Total Sales as a common numerator and denominator and Average Total Assets as a common numerator and denominator. When all three terms are multiplied, the common numerators and denominators cancel, and the result is the original ratio (Net Income ÷ Average Common Equity). However, the decomposition provides financial statement users very important insights. A company's return on common equity is the joint product of the company's **profitability** (generating profits from revenues: net profit margin) times its **operating capability** (efficiency in utilizing assets to generate revenues) times its **leverage** (the amount of assets relative to the amount of common equity capital). The greater a company's profitability, operating capability, and leverage, the greater should be its total return to common shareholders.

Example To illustrate, in 2015, **Starbucks** generated an impressive 49.7% rate of return for common equity shareholders. That rate of return is the joint product of Starbucks's profitability, operating capability, and leverage, as follows:

$$\text{Return on Common Equity} = \frac{\text{Net Income}}{\text{Total Sales}} \times \frac{\text{Total Sales}}{\text{Average Total Assets}} \times \frac{\text{Average Total Assets}}{\text{Average Common Equity}}$$

$$= \frac{\$2{,}757.4 \text{ million}}{\$19{,}162.7 \text{ million}} \times \frac{\$19{,}162.7 \text{ million}}{(\$12{,}446.1 \text{ million} + \$10{,}752.9 \text{ million})/2}$$

$$\times \frac{(\$12{,}446.1 \text{ million} + \$10{,}752.9 \text{ million})/2}{(\$5{,}818.0 \text{ million} + \$5{,}272.0 \text{ million})/2}$$

$$= 0.144 \times 1.65 \times 2.09 = 0.497$$

Thus, Starbucks's impressive rate of return is due to its 14.4% profit margin per dollar of revenues, times total asset turnover of 1.65 times (it generated $1.65 in total revenue per dollar in average total assets), times leverage of 2.09 (it utilized $2.09 in average total assets per dollar in common shareholders' equity). Together, this means that in 2015, Starbucks generated substantial profits from sales, used assets efficiently to generate sales, and used leverage effectively to finance its assets.

In comparison, during 2014, Starbucks generated a return on common equity of 42.4%, because net profit margin was 12.6%, total asset turnover was 1.48, and leverage was 2.28. Relative to 2014, in 2015 Starbucks was more profitable and more efficient in using its assets to generate revenues, but it was slightly less levered. In combination, these changes lead to a 7.3% increase in the rate of return for common equity shareholders (from 42.4% in 2014 up to 49.7% in 2015). ∎

Earnings Quality and Earnings Management

Analysts, investors, lenders, and securities market regulators (like the SEC) scrutinize reported earnings numbers to assess *earnings quality* and to detect potential *earnings management*. Earnings quality is a concept that is not defined in U.S. GAAP or IFRS nor is it uniformly defined by users of financial statements. In general, **earnings quality** usually refers to the extent to which a company's earnings are relevant and faithful representations of financial performance for the current period and enable financial statement users to develop reasonable expectations of future earnings. High-quality earnings information usually provides relevant and faithful information about the revenues, expenses, gains, and losses of current-period performance. In addition, high-quality earnings information enables users to separate the elements of income that are the result of core operating, investing, and financing activities, which are likely to recur and persist in the future, from those elements that are not likely to recur. When users refer to "earnings quality," they often mean the extent to which earnings numbers of the current period are the results from core, recurring, persistent business activities providing a sound basis to understand the company's performance and forecast future earnings.

When financial statement users or others refer to potential **earnings management**, they are usually referring to the potential for companies to manipulate reported earnings within U.S. GAAP in order to report higher or lower earnings numbers.[28] As the chapter opener points out, earnings numbers trigger important consequences for companies' stock prices and managers' bonuses. Therefore, companies and managers are under great pressure to report earnings results that will satisfy investors, lenders, and other stakeholders. The temptation to manipulate reported earnings can be strong. Even within U.S. GAAP, companies can "manage" to increase (or decrease) earnings in a period by altering such income-related estimates and assumptions as bad debts expense, expected warranty costs, expected pension and retirement benefit costs, and many others. In addition, managers can engage in "real" earnings management transactions by electing to sell available-for-sale securities with accumulated gains; postpone some advertising or research and development expenditures; sale and leaseback transactions involving property, plant, and equipment; or similar tactics. Because of the importance of earnings, and because of the potential for companies to manipulate the reported earnings, financial statement users scrutinize reported earnings very carefully to assess a company's earnings quality and to detect potential earnings management.

GOT IT?

5-31 What are the three most common profit margins financial statement users assess using common-size analysis of an income statement? What do these profit margins indicate?

5-32 What does a financial statement user compute when conducting a rate of change analysis of an income statement?

5-33 What is the rate of return on common equity? What are the three determinants of a company's rate of return on common equity? How do these three determinants affect the rate of return on common equity?

APPENDIX 5.1: SEGMENT AND INTERIM REPORTING

LEARNING OBJECTIVE 5.11
Understand segment reporting and interim reporting.

To provide financial statement users with more timely and relevant financial performance information, companies disclose financial performance separately for major business segments and report financial statements for interim periods (quarterly) within a fiscal year.

Segment Reporting

A company that has subsidiaries prepares its financial statements on a "consolidated" basis. That is, the accounting results of its various legal entities are *aggregated* into a set of financial statements for the entire economic entity (briefly discussed in Chapter 13). Although investors and creditors know the importance of consolidated statements in evaluating overall company performance, the *disaggregation* of total financial data also can be important in their financial analysis because the level of risk, return on investment, and expected future earnings and cash flows may differ significantly across a company's different operating segments.

---

[28] Earnings management has been defined in many ways. One definition is: "When managers use judgment in financial reporting and in structuring transactions to alter financial reports to either mislead some stakeholders about the underlying economic performance of the company or influence contractual outcomes that depend on reported accounting numbers," Paul Healy and James Wahlen, "A Review of the Earnings Management Literature and Its Implications for Standards Setting," *Accounting Horizons* (December 1999), pp. 365–383. In the extreme, explicitly misreporting earnings numbers outside of what is allowed by U.S. GAAP is fraud.

These factors may differ for a number of reasons, including:

- the way that a company is organized and how its segments are operated
- the nature of the product and service markets in which different segments compete
- the conditions in the various geographic areas where different segments operate
- the characteristics of the products, major customers, production processes, and revenue-generating processes of the segments

A company can provide very useful information for investors, lenders, and stakeholders by presenting disaggregated financial information about its operating segments. The FASB, therefore, requires that a company's financial statements include certain disaggregated information about its operating segments.[29]

A company's financial statements might be disaggregated in a number of ways, such as by products and services, geography, legal entity, or type of customer. The way a company identifies its operating segments for financial reporting is through the use of the *management approach*. The management approach is based on the way a company's management organizes the company's segments for making operating decisions and for assessing performance. Thus, a component of a company is an **operating segment** if it:

- engages in business activities to earn revenues and incur expenses
- generates operating results regularly reviewed by the company's chief operating decision maker to make decisions about allocating resources to the segment and assessing its performance
- has discrete financial information available

Not all departments in a company are operating segments. For instance, a corporate headquarters normally does not earn revenues directly and is not an operating segment. Generally, an operating segment has a *segment manager* who is directly accountable for the segment's operating activities and who maintains regular contact with the chief operating decision maker.

Reportable Segments A company does not have to provide financial information about all its operating segments, however. Materiality determines whether or not a segment is a **reportable segment**—one whose operations are significant enough that its financial activities must be reported separately. **An operating segment is significant and is a reportable segment if it passes *any* of the three following tests:**

1. **Revenue Test**. Reported revenues (including sales to external customers and intersegment sales) are 10% or more of the combined revenues of all the company's operating segments.
2. **Profit Test**. The absolute amount of its profit (loss) is 10% or more of the combined reported profits of all operating segments that did not report a loss.[30]
3. **Asset Test**. Segment assets are 10% or more of the combined assets of all operating segments.

There is also an **overall materiality test**, which requires that the reportable segments must be disclosed if their combined revenues are at least 75% of the entire company revenues. The remaining, less significant operating segments are combined and disclosed in an "all other" segment category. If a company has only one operating segment, it does not have disaggregated segment information to report, but it still must disclose the general information and company-wide information discussed next.

---

[29] FASB ASC 280-10-50: Segment Reporting: Overall: Disclosure.
[30] Generally, a company's profit (or loss) is *pretax*. Also, if the combined losses of all operating segments that reported a loss exceed the combined profits as calculated earlier, the combined loss amount is used for this 10% test.

Information Reported The disclosure requirements for segment reporting are summarized as follows:

- *General.* A company must (a) identify how it is organized (e.g., by product lines or geographic areas) and what factors were used to identify its operating segments and (b) describe the types of products and services from which each reportable segment earns its revenues.
- *Profit or Loss.* A company must report its profit or loss for each reportable segment. It must also disclose certain amounts used to compute each segment's profit or loss: (a) revenues (separated into sales to external customers and intersegment sales); (b) interest revenue and interest expense; and (c) depreciation, depletion, and amortization expense.[31]
- *Information about Assets.* A company must report the total assets of each reportable segment. For these assets, a company also must disclose the total capital expenditures for long-lived assets of each reportable segment.
- *Reconciliations.* A company must reconcile the reportable segments' total revenues, total profit or loss, and total assets to the corresponding company totals. The revenues, profit or loss, and assets of the "all other" segment category must be included in these reconciliations.
- *Company-Wide Disclosures.* A company must disclose (a) its revenue from external customers for each product and service and (b) information about geographic areas including (1) revenues from external customers in the United States and in individual foreign countries and (2) total long-lived assets located in the United States and in all foreign countries. If a company's revenues from a single external customer are 10% or more of the company's total revenues, then the company must disclose this fact and identify the segment(s) reporting the revenues.[32]

A company is not required to follow a specific format in making the preceding disclosures. The FASB encourages a company to provide the information in the most useful format for its specific circumstances. Typically, a company will include its segment report and the related narrative discussion in the notes to the financial statements in its annual report. Corporate-level income, expenses, and assets, such as those related to the company's headquarters, are not assigned to any segment and are reported separately.

Thus, a company frequently prepares a worksheet (based on information from internal reports) that assigns its total sales revenues, cost of goods sold, operating expenses, and assets to each operating segment. Based on these assignments, the company performs the revenue, profit, and asset tests to determine the *reportable segments*. The required financial information of the reportable segments (and the "all other" segments) is reported separately in the company's segment report. Because companies vary in their management approaches, it is not practical to illustrate all possible types of segment reports. We do, however, show the way one hypothetical company (Teal Company) discloses its disaggregated financial information in its annual report. **Starbucks** has more extensive disclosures, as shown in Appendix A. In Starbucks's MD&A and in Note 16, Segment Reporting, it discloses information for four reportable segments: Americas; China/Asia Pacific (CAP); Europe, Middle East, and Africa (EMEA); and Channel Development. Note that three reportable segments are organized geographically and one is organized by product/customer type.

Example: Disaggregated Financial Information for Reportable Segments

On its 2016 income statement, Teal Company reports sales of $3,800, cost of goods sold of $2,470, and operating expenses of $620, so that its pretax operating profit is $710 ($3,800 − $2,470 − $620). From this pretax operating profit, the company

---
[31] These are the amounts for the most common items included in a company's pretax income from continuing operations. If an operating segment is evaluated using a more complex "income" measure (or on an after-tax basis), then the company must also disclose any unusual items, equity method income, and other significant noncash items for each reportable segment.

[32] FASB ASC 280-10-50: Segment Reporting: Overall: Disclosure.

deducts interest expense of $80 to report pretax income of $630. Teal also reports total assets of $19,000 on its December 31, 2016, balance sheet. Teal's chief operating officer uses a segment's pretax operating profit to evaluate the segment manager; the company makes no intersegment sales; and interest expense is considered to be incurred at the corporate level. After preparing a worksheet to assign its segment revenues (sales), operating profits (sales minus cost of goods sold and operating expenses), and assets for segment reporting, Teal determines that it has three reportable segments (A, B, and C) and several insignificant operating segments. Teal also identifies $100 of general corporate expenses and $3,000 of general corporate assets.

Example 5.5 shows the schedule and narrative discussion that Teal includes in its annual report. Note that the revenues and pretax profits of the segments are reconciled to the appropriate totals on the income statement. Teal reconciles segment pretax profits to the corporate total pretax income by deducting the general corporate expenses and corporate interest expense. Similarly, the segment assets are reconciled to the total corporate assets.

EXAMPLE 5.5 Segment Reporting

TEAL COMPANY
Operating Segment Financial Results
For Year Ended December 31, 2016

	Reportable Operating Segments			All Other Segments	Totals
	A	B	C		
Segment revenues (sales)	$ 300	$2,530	$ 370	$ 600	$ 3,800
Segment profit (pretax)	$ 70	$ 495	$ 105	$ 140	$ 810
General corporate expenses					(100)
Corporate interest expense					(80)
Pretax income					$ 630
Segment assets	$1,800	$9,400	$2,000	$2,800	$16,000
General corporate assets					3,000
Total assets					$19,000

Notes: The company is organized into three major segments, A, B, and C, which are organized and managed by product line. Operations in Segment A involve production and sales of cynical refrigerator magnets. Operations in Segment B involve production and sales of exotic pet foods. Operations in Segment C involve production and sales of musical candles for birthday cakes. Total revenue by segment includes sales to external customers. The company makes no intersegment sales.

Segment profit is total revenue minus operating expenses. In computing segment profit, none of the following items have been deducted: general corporate expenses, corporate interest expense, or income taxes.

Depreciation for Segments A, B, and C was $20, $300, and $40, respectively. Capital expenditures for the three segments were $100, $400, and $200, respectively. Segment assets are those assets that are used in the company's operations in each segment. General corporate assets are principally cash, investments, and corporate headquarters.

The company only makes sales in the United States. Contracts with the Central Intelligence Agency of the U.S. government account for $600 of the sales to external customers of Segment B.

Conceptual Evaluation The FASB states that the disaggregated reporting requirements are intended to provide information about the different types of operations and the different economic environments in which a company operates to help users (1) better understand the company's current and past performance, (2) better assess its prospects for future net cash flows, and (3) make more informed judgments about the company as a whole. It also required the disclosure of certain segment information in a company's interim reports (discussed in the next section). The FASB expects that this disaggregation will provide more *relevant* information that will improve the *feedback value*, *predictive value*, and *timeliness* of a company's financial reports.

The FASB adopted the management approach to disaggregated reporting to provide a viewpoint of the way a company manages its operations. Furthermore, it felt that because segment managers have a vested interest in the quality of the information used to evaluate them, the information is more likely to be accurate. The FASB expects the current disclosures to have greater *representational faithfulness* and a higher degree of *verifiability*.

There are at least three *comparability* issues, however. First, not all companies are organized in the same way. Therefore, one company's operating segment information may not be comparable to another's. Second, companies vary as to what price a segment is charged when it "purchases" goods from another segment (called "transfer pricing"). So one company's intersegment sales revenue may be based on market prices, while other companies may use full cost or variable cost transfer pricing methods. Finally, if a company allocates expenses in determining each segment's profit, this must be done on a reasonable basis but will vary from one company to another. While these issues may result in reduced comparability across companies, on balance the FASB feels that the current requirements for disaggregated disclosures improve the financial reporting for external users by enhancing the *decision usefulness* of the information.

Interim Financial Reports

Interim financial statements are reports for periods of less than a year. The SEC requires registrants to file interim reports on a quarterly basis (using Form 10-Q). One issue involving interim reports is the difficulty in determining meaningful operating results for intervals of less than a year. Revenues of some businesses are seasonal and fluctuate widely across interim periods. Some companies incur heavy fixed costs in one interim period that benefit the operating activities in other periods. Other companies must estimate costs that will not be paid until later interim periods but that benefit the current one. Estimates also must be made of items such as inventories and income taxes if the interim reports are to be relevant and representationally faithful.

In response to these concerns, U.S. GAAP specifies the disclosures needed to present meaningful information for an interim period of less than a year. The FASB adopts the view that **each interim period is an integral part of an annual period.** Thus, a company must continue to use the GAAP that it used in the preparation of its latest annual report. However, certain principles can be modified for interim reporting purposes so that the results are more informative and articulate better with the annual report results. The FASB has issued additional GAAP to expand and clarify various aspects of interim reporting. The current GAAP focuses primarily on the following income statement items:

- Revenues
- Operating expenses
- Income taxes
- Discontinued operations
- Earnings per share

Revenues A company must recognize revenues from products or services during an interim period in the same manner as during the annual accounting period. In cases where revenues are subject to seasonal variations, like **Toys R' Us**, which experiences a high volume of sales during the holiday season, the company must disclose the seasonal nature of its activities and consider presenting supplemental information regarding revenues for previous periods.

Operating Expenses A company must match the expenses that are directly related to product sales or services against interim revenues in the period the revenues are recognized. These include items such as inventory costs, selling commissions, and warranties. For inventory and cost of goods sold, a company generally must use the same inventory methods (e.g., LIFO, FIFO, weighted average) and make write-downs to market for interim reporting in the same way as it does for annual reporting, with the following exceptions:

- A company that uses a periodic inventory system can estimate gross profit rates (or other estimation methods) to determine its cost of goods sold during interim periods. It must disclose the method used and any significant adjustments from reconciliation with the annual physical inventory.
- If a company using the LIFO method has a temporary partial liquidation of its base-period inventory, but expects to replace that inventory by year-end, its cost of goods sold must include the expected cost to replace the liquidated inventory. Also, the inventory at the interim reporting date must *not* include the effect of the liquidation. Assuming rising prices, this requirement avoids the possibility of showing abnormally high interim period income due to LIFO "liquidation profits," which will be discussed in Chapters 7 and 8.
- A company must recognize a permanent loss due to an inventory market decline by using the lower of cost or market procedures in the interim period during which the decline occurred. It must recognize any recovery of such a loss in a later interim period within the same year as a gain (not to exceed the previously recognized loss). It does not have to recognize a temporary market decline in an interim period.[33]
- If a company uses a standard cost accounting system, it must follow routine annual procedures for all variances. The company must disclose any significant unplanned or unanticipated purchase price or volume variances in the interim period.

Expenses that are not directly associated with product sales (or services) are matched to interim periods using a variety of methods. Expenses that affect the operating activities of more than one interim period are allocated among the interim periods based on an estimate of (1) time expired, (2) benefit received, or (3) activity associated with the periods. These allocations must be consistent with those used for annual reporting purposes. For example, property taxes, advertising costs, depreciation charges, and bad debts expense are allocated among the interim periods. Expenses that relate only to the current interim period are allocated to that period. Arbitrary allocations are not allowed. For example, office utilities, rent expense, and interest costs are expensed as incurred in the interim period. Gains and losses that occur in an interim period are recognized in that interim period. For example, a gain on the sale of land or a loss on the disposal of equipment is recognized in the interim period.[34]

Income Taxes To present fairly the results of operations, at the end of *each* interim period a company must make its best estimate of the effective income tax rate expected to apply for the *entire* year. The effective rate includes the appropriate tax rate on *annual* income from continuing operations. In determining the rate, the company does not consider the income tax related to any items (such as discontinued operations) that are reported separately net of income taxes. Consequently, each quarter the company estimates its annual income from continuing operations and, based on this annual income,

---

[33] FASB ASC 270-10-45: Interim Reporting: Overall: Other Presentation Matters.
[34] FASB ASC 740-270-35: Income Taxes: Interim Reporting: Subsequent Measurement.

estimates its annual income taxes to derive an effective annual income tax rate. It then uses the effective rate to compute the income taxes related to income from continuing operations on a year-to-date basis. The amount of income taxes for the current interim period is the difference between the income tax computed on year-to-date income from continuing operations and the related income taxes reported on previous interim reports of the accounting period.[35] This procedure must be completed for each of the four interim periods; it follows the general principle of intraperiod tax allocation.

Example Trull Corporation reported pretax income of $20,000 at the end of the first quarter and estimated its income tax on this income to be $5,220. (This estimate was made at the end of the first quarter using the technique discussed previously.) Trull now is preparing an interim income statement at the end of the second quarter for that quarter and the first 6 months. It determines that its pretax income from continuing operations for the second quarter is $26,000 and estimates it will earn $25,000 and $29,000 in each of the next two quarters, respectively. The corporate income tax rates are 15% on the first $20,000 of earnings and 30% on earnings in excess of $20,000. As shown in **Example 5.6**, based on an estimated effective income tax rate of 27%, Trull recognizes income tax expense of $12,420 for the first 6 months and $7,200 for the second quarter of operations.

EXAMPLE 5.6

Computation of Interim Income Taxes

1. Estimated Annual Income:

First quarter	$ 20,000	actual income
Second quarter	26,000	actual income
Third quarter	25,000	estimated income
Fourth quarter	29,000	estimated income
	$100,000	estimated annual income

2. Estimated Effective Income Tax Rate:

$$15\% \times \$20{,}000 = \$ 3{,}000$$
$$30\% \times (\$100{,}000 - \$20{,}000) = 24{,}000$$
$$\text{Estimated total tax} = \$27{,}000$$

$$27\% \text{ Effective income tax rate} = \frac{\$27{,}000 \text{ Estimated income tax}}{\$100{,}000 \text{ Estimated income}}$$

3. Estimated Income Tax for First 6 Months:
$46,000 × 27% = $12,420 estimated income tax on first 6 months of income

4. Estimated Income Tax for Second Quarter:

$12,420	estimated income tax on first 6 months of income
(5,220)	estimated income tax on first-quarter income
$ 7,200	estimated income tax on second-quarter income

Discontinued Operations Results of discontinued operations are reported (net of income taxes) in the usual manner in the interim period during which the events occurred. These results are not prorated over the entire annual accounting period. Materiality, however, is determined on the basis of a relationship of the item to the estimated income for the entire *year* and not to the interim period results.

---

[35] FASB ASC 740-270-35: Income Taxes: Interim Reporting: Subsequent Measurement.

Earnings per Share (EPS) Earnings per share computed for each interim period is reported on the face of the interim income statement. A breakdown of EPS related to income from continuing operations and results of discontinued operations is also disclosed.

Preparation and Disclosure of Summarized Interim Financial Data

The accounting procedures a company uses to prepare its interim reports are similar to those for annual reports. Typically, a trial balance of the year-to-date account balances is prepared. The trial balance is entered on a worksheet, spreadsheet, or other working paper. Year-to-date adjusting entries are recorded on the working paper, after which the year-to-date financial statements are prepared. However, the interim accounting procedures differ in several respects from those completed at year-end. In general, companies prepare interim financial statements using the following steps:

- *Step 1.* For a company using a periodic inventory system, the ending inventory for the interim reports is usually based on an estimation technique rather than on a physical inventory. Thus, an estimation technique such as the gross profit method is used to estimate the ending interim inventory.
- *Step 2.* The adjusting entries required at the end of the interim period to bring the accounts up to date usually are recorded only on the working paper and are not entered into the accounts. Adjusting entries are recorded and posted to the accounts only at the end of the year.
- *Step 3.* The accounts are not closed at the end of each interim period. Consequently, in an interim period subsequent to the first period, a company must be careful not to include amounts applicable to previous interim periods in the revenue and expense accounts. To avoid this problem, as we mentioned previously, a company typically prepares the interim income statement on a year-to-date basis and then eliminates the income statement results from any previous interim periods.
- *Step 4.* Interim reports typically are not audited because of the time and cost involved. However, publicly listed companies usually engage the auditors to review the interim financial statement information.

When publicly listed companies report interim summaries of financial information, the following data must be reported at a minimum:

- sales or gross revenues, income taxes, and net income
- earnings per share for each period presented
- seasonal revenues, costs, and expenses
- significant changes in estimates of income taxes
- results of discontinued operations and material unusual or infrequent items
- contingent items
- changes in accounting principles or estimates
- significant changes in financial position (i.e., cash flows)

When a company presents the preceding information on a quarterly basis, it also provides current year-to-date information along with comparable data from the previous year. Companies are encouraged to provide condensed balance sheet and cash flow data for the interim periods to assist external users in their analyses of *financial flexibility* and *liquidity*. A company also must disclose selected information about each of its reportable operating segments. This information includes items such as segment revenues from external customers, intersegment revenues, segment profit or loss, and segment assets.[36] Although interim financial statements are too lengthy to illustrate here, **Starbucks** includes quarterly data in Note 17, Selected Quarterly Financial Information, to its financial statements, as shown in Appendix A.

[36] FASB ASC 280-10-50: Segment Reporting: Overall: Disclosure.

> **GOT IT?**
>
> **5-34** *(Appendix 5.1)* What criteria should a company use under the management approach to determine if a component of the company is an operating segment? Then, what tests determine whether an operating segment is a reportable segment?
>
> **5-35** *(Appendix 5.1)* Why are financial statement users interested in segment and interim financial reports?

REVIEW CENTER

In the chapter opener, we emphasized the importance of the income statement and net income to investors, lenders, analysts, capital markets participants, and company managers. We also identified several objectives you would accomplish after reading the chapter. The objectives are listed below and followed by a brief summary of the key takeaways.

KEY TAKEAWAYS

- The purposes of an income statement include informing stakeholders so they can:
  - evaluate profitability and assess the return on investment in the company
  - assess the company's operating capability and financial performance for the current period and over time
  - evaluate management's performance over time
  - predict the company's future income and cash flows
  - understand the components of income
  - assess the company's risk
  - compare performance against other companies
  - assess the impact of economic factors on the company

LEARNING OBJECTIVE 5.1
Explain the purposes of an income statement.

KEY TAKEAWAYS

- The accrual-based approach to income measurement is consistent with the capital maintenance concept of income. Under the capital maintenance concept, a corporation's net income for a period of time is the amount that it could distribute to shareholders without depleting the amount of capital the shareholders have invested. It is the amount of money that can be distributed to shareholders as a return *on* capital, without being a return *of* capital. A company's income is measured by comparing the beginning and ending net assets of the company after adjusting for any additional investments by owners (such as proceeds from additional issues of shares) or distributions to owners (such as dividends) during the period.
- Comprehensive income is the change in equity of a company during a period from transactions, other events, and circumstances relating to nonowner sources. It includes all changes in equity during a period except those resulting from investments by owners and distributions to owners.
- The income statement is comprised of four elements: revenues, expenses, gains, and losses. A company's net income for an accounting period currently is measured as:

$$\text{Net Income} = \text{Revenues} - \text{Expenses} + \text{Gains} - \text{Losses}$$

LEARNING OBJECTIVE 5.2
Understand the capital maintenance concept of income.

KEY TERMS

accrual accounting, p. 5-5
capital maintenance concept, p. 5-4
comprehensive income, p. 5-5
net income, p. 5-5

LEARNING OBJECTIVE 5.3
Define the elements of an income statement.

KEY TAKEAWAYS
- Revenues are the amounts of consideration to which the company expects to be entitled in exchange for the transfer of goods or services to customers. Revenues arise when companies satisfy performance obligations to customers by transferring goods or performing services. Revenues create increases in assets or settlements of liabilities during a period from delivering goods or providing services to customers in the company's ongoing major or central operations. The FASB has recently passed new revenue recognition guidance. To recognize revenue, a company should apply the following five steps:
    - *Step 1.* Identify the contract(s) with a customer.
    - *Step 2.* Identify the performance obligations in the contract.
    - *Step 3.* Determine the transaction price.
    - *Step 4.* Allocate the transaction price to the performance obligations in the contract.
    - *Step 5.* Recognize revenue when (or as) the entity satisfies a performance obligation.
- Expenses arise from outflows or using up assets or incurring liabilities (or a combination of both) from delivering or producing goods, rendering services, or carrying out other activities that are the company's ongoing major or central operations. Accrual accounting measures and recognizes expenses in the period in which the resources are used up, outflows of assets occur, or liabilities are incurred, even though the cash outflows may occur in different periods. Similar to recognition of revenues, expenses may be recognized in a period simultaneously with cash outflows, prior to cash outflows, or after cash outflows.
- Gains are increases in the equity (net assets) of a company from peripheral transactions and other events and circumstances during a period, except those that result from revenues or investments by owners.
- Losses are decreases in the equity (net assets) of a company from peripheral transactions and other events and circumstances during a period, except those that result from expenses or distributions to owners.
- Gains and losses are similar to revenues and expenses, but they result from peripheral activities that do not directly relate to the operations of the company and are reported net.

KEY TERMS
association of cause and effect, p. 5-10
contract, p. 5-6
expenses, p. 5-10
gains, p. 5-11
immediate recognition, p. 5-11
losses, p. 5-11
performance obligation, p. 5-6
revenue recognition, p. 5-6
revenues, p. 5-6
systematic and rational allocation, p. 5-10
transaction price, p. 5-6

LEARNING OBJECTIVE 5.4
Describe the major components of an income statement.

KEY TAKEAWAYS
- The major components of an income statement are: (1) operating income, (2) income from continuing operations, (3) results from discontinued operations, (4) net income, and (5) earnings per share.
- Income statements may be presented in a single-step format that classifies all items as either revenues or expenses, or it may be reported in a more useful multiple-step format that contains additional classifications of the income statement elements.
- Operating income is determined as net sales minus the cost of goods sold and operating expenses (consisting of selling expenses and general and administrative expenses). Financial statement users typically analyze carefully a company's operating income because it represents the company's ability to execute its business strategy and generate profitability from its central operations.
- Other income items, such as income from investing activities or expenses related to financing activities, are then added to (or deducted from) operating income to determine pretax income from continuing operations, from which income tax expense is deducted to determine income from continuing operations.

- Material gains or losses that are unusual in nature or infrequent in occurrence are reported in the appropriate section of the income statement.
- Income from continuing operations reports the company's income from ongoing business activities. This section of the income statement includes operating income plus (or minus) income items associated with financing and investing activities (such as interest expense and interest income), gains and losses that are not part of normal operating activities, and income taxes. Income from continuing operations is useful information because it summarizes the elements of income that are likely to be recurring in future periods.
- Reporting the impact of income taxes on net income requires intraperiod tax allocation as well as interperiod tax allocation.
- A parent corporation subtracts the portion of "Net Income Attributable to Noncontrolling Interests" from the total net income of the company, in order to faithfully represent the amount of net income attributable to the common shareholders.
- Retained earnings is the link between a corporation's income statement and its balance sheet. Retained earnings is the total amount of corporate earnings that has not been returned to shareholders as dividends and is a major component of shareholders' equity. The net income (loss) amount from the income statement is added to (subtracted from) beginning retained earnings.

KEY TERMS

cost of goods available for sale, p. 5-15
cost of goods sold, p. 5-15
gross revenues, p. 5-15
gross sales revenues, p. 5-15
income from continuing operations, p. 5-19
interperiod tax allocation, p. 5-18
intraperiod tax allocation, p. 5-18
multiple-step income statement, p. 5-14

net revenues, p. 5-15
net sales revenues, p. 5-15
noncontrolling interests, p. 5-19
operating expenses, p. 5-16
operating income (loss), p. 5-17
pretax income from continuing operations, p. 5-18
single-step income statement, p. 5-13
statement of retained earnings, p. 5-20

KEY TAKEAWAYS

LEARNING OBJECTIVE 5.5
Report results from discontinued operations.

- The results of discontinued operations (a component of a company's operations that has been, or will be, eliminated from ongoing operations) consist of two items: (1) the income (or loss) from operations of the discontinued component and (2) the gain (or loss) from the disposal of the component. These items are reported net of taxes.
- A discontinued operation involves the disposal of the business or component that represents a strategic shift that will have a major effect on a company's operations and financial results. Examples of a strategic shift include the disposal of a major geographic area or a major line of business.

KEY TERMS

component, p. 5-21
discontinued operation, p. 5-21
held for sale, p. 5-24

results from discontinued operations, p. 5-21

KEY TAKEAWAYS

LEARNING OBJECTIVE 5.6
Understand basic earnings per share.

- Companies are required to report earnings per share amounts relating to income from continuing operations and net income on their income statements. Basic earnings per share is computed by dividing the net income available to common shareholders by the weighted average number of common shares outstanding throughout the entire year.

KEY EQUATION

Basic EPS = Net Income Available to Common Shareholders ÷ Weighted Average Number of Common Shares Outstanding

KEY TERMS

basic earnings per share, p. 5-26
diluted earnings per share, p. 5-27

dilutive securities, p. 5-27
earnings per share (EPS), p. 5-26

LEARNING OBJECTIVE 5.7
Report comprehensive income.

KEY TAKEAWAYS

- Consistent with the capital maintenance concept, comprehensive income is the change in equity of a company from transactions, other events, and circumstances relating to nonowner sources. It includes all changes in equity during a period except those resulting from investments by owners and distributions to owners. Comprehensive income includes both net income and other comprehensive income.
- Currently, under U.S. GAAP, there are four items of other comprehensive income that are recognized directly in accumulated other comprehensive income in shareholders' equity when they arise, and not included in net income until they are realized in cash flows.
- Under U.S. GAAP, a company can report its comprehensive income (or loss) under two alternatives:
  - following net income in a single, continuous performance statement
  - following the income statement in a separate consecutive statement of comprehensive income

KEY TERM

comprehensive income, p. 5-28

LEARNING OBJECTIVE 5.8
Understand the similarities and differences in how income statements are presented under IFRS versus U.S. GAAP.

KEY TAKEAWAYS

- IFRS and U.S. GAAP follow similar but not identical approaches to measuring and reporting net income. Under IFRS, much of a company's income statement content is similar in that IFRS require disclosure of revenues, operating expenses, financing costs, tax expense, net income (loss), results of discontinued operations, and earnings per share. A company is also required to disclose comprehensive income in either a single continuous statement of comprehensive income or in two separate consecutive statements (an income statement and a statement that begins with net income and displays the components of other comprehensive income).

LEARNING OBJECTIVE 5.9
Explain the statement of cash flows and classify cash flows as operating, investing, or financing.

KEY TAKEAWAYS

- A company's statement of cash flows reports its cash flows from its operating, investing, and financing activities during the accounting period in a manner that reconciles the beginning and ending cash balances. Its purpose is to help users assess a company's liquidity, financial flexibility, and operating capability.
- A company's operating cash flows result from all the transactions and other events related to its primary business activities (e.g., producing and selling goods and services to customers). Its investing cash flows are the cash inflows and outflows resulting from its investing activities (e.g., purchasing equipment). Its financing cash flows are the cash inflows and outflows resulting from its financing activities (e.g., issuing bonds).

KEY TERMS

direct method, p. 5-37
financing activities, p. 5-35
indirect method, p. 5-35

investing activities, p. 5-34
operating activities, p. 5-34
statement of cash flows, p. 5-34

KEY TAKEAWAYS

- Financial statement users analyze income statement and cash flow statement information by applying various analysis techniques for intracompany comparisons (evaluating a company over time) and intercompany comparisons (comparing two or more companies, either at a point in time or over time).
- Users can evaluate return on investment, risk, liquidity, financial flexibility, and operating capability using common-size financial statements including profit margins, rate of change analyses, and various financial ratios.

LEARNING OBJECTIVE 5.10
Apply financial statement analysis techniques to analyze the income statement and cash flow statement information.

KEY TERMS

common size analysis, p. 5-38
coverage ratios, p. 5-41
earnings management, p. 5-42
earnings quality, p. 5-42
gross profit margin, p. 5-38
interest coverage ratios, p. 5-41
leverage, p. 5-42

net profit margin, p. 5-38
operating capability, p. 5-42
operating margin, p. 5-38
profitability, p. 5-42
rate of change analysis, p. 5-39
return on common equity, p. 5-41

KEY CALCULATIONS

Earnings-Based Interest Coverage = Operating Income ÷ Interest Expense

Cash Flows-Based Interest Coverage = Cash Flows from Operations ÷ Interest Expense

$$\text{Return on Common Equity} = \frac{\text{Net Income}}{\text{Average Common Equity}}$$

$$= \frac{\text{Net Income}}{\text{Total Sales}} \times \frac{\text{Total Sales}}{\text{Average Total Assets}} \times \frac{\text{Average Total Assets}}{\text{Average Common Equity}}$$

$$= \text{Net Profit Margin} \times \text{Total Asset Turnover} \times \text{Leverage}$$

KEY TAKEAWAYS

- Financial statement users typically find it useful to evaluate companies on a disaggregated basis. U.S. GAAP therefore requires companies to provide summary financial statement information for each significant reportable operating segment to help external users better understand the way in which they manage their operations.
- While no specific format is specified, extensive disclosures are required that include information on how a company is organized, the types of products and services of each reportable segment, the income and assets of each reportable segment, and how segment data reconcile to company-wide data.
- To provide more timely information, a company prepares interim financial reports that are viewed as an integral part of its annual reporting period.

LEARNING OBJECTIVE 5.11
(Appendix 5.1) Understand segment reporting and interim reporting.

KEY TERMS

asset test, p. 5-44
interim financial statements, p. 5-47
operating segment, p. 5-44
overall materiality test, p. 5-44

profit test, p. 5-44
reportable segment, p. 5-44
revenue test, p. 5-44

EXHIBIT 5.8 Components of Net Income, Comprehensive Income, and Cash Flows

Item	Characteristics	Disclosure
Revenues	Revenues are the amounts of consideration to which the firm is entitled, usually in the form of increases in assets or settlements of liabilities, from satisfying performance obligations to customers.	Top line of the income statement
Expenses	Expenses arise from using up assets or incurring liabilities (or a combination of both) from delivering or producing goods, rendering services, or carrying out other activities that are the company's ongoing major or central operations.	Within various sections of the income statement
Gains	Increases in the equity (net assets) of a company from peripheral transactions and other events and circumstances, except those that result from revenues or investments by owners.	Within various sections of the income statement
Losses	Decreases in the equity (net assets) of a company from peripheral transactions, and other events and circumstances during a period, except those that result from expenses or distributions to owners.	Within various sections of the income statement
Operating Income	Revenues and expenses from primary operating activities, producing and selling goods and services to customers.	Top portion of the income statement
Income from Continuing Operations	Revenues, expenses, gains, and losses from primary operating, investing, and financing activities.	Main body of the income statement
Net Income	Bottom line financial performance of a company for a period: Net Income = Revenues − Expenses + Gains − Losses.	Bottom line of the income statement
Other Comprehensive Income Items	According to U.S. GAAP, four particular types of income items that are recognized directly in accumulated other comprehensive income in equity; when realized, they are recognized in net income.	Two alternatives: (1) with net income in a single continuous income statement; (2) following the income statement in a separate consecutive statement of comprehensive income
Comprehensive Income	Comprehensive income is the change in equity of a company during a period from transactions, other events, and circumstances relating to nonowner sources. It includes all changes in equity during a period except those resulting from investments by owners and distributions to owners.	Two alternatives: (1) with net income in a single continuous income statement; (2) following the income statement in a separate consecutive statement of comprehensive income
Results from Discontinued Operations	The results from discontinued operations include (1) the operating income (loss) of the discontinued component and (2) the gain (loss) from its sale.	Below income from continuing operations on the income statement
Unusual Gains or Losses	Gains or losses that arise from an event or a transaction that is unusual in nature or infrequent in occurrence.	Within various sections of the income statement
Earnings per Share	Net income on a per-share basis.	Below net income on the income statement
Cash Flows from Operating Activities	All of the cash inflows and outflows from the operating activities of the company.	First section of the statement of cash flows
Cash Flows from Investing Activities	All the cash inflows and outflows involved in the investing activities of the company.	Second section of the statement of cash flows
Cash Flows from Financing Activities	All the cash inflows and outflows involved in the financing activities of the company.	Third section of the statement of cash flows

ANSWERS TO REAL REPORT QUESTIONS

Real Report 5.1 Answers The Coca-Cola Company—Revenue Recognition

1. Coca-Cola's revenue recognition criteria are almost identical to the SEC's guidelines. Coca-Cola implements those guidelines by recognizing revenue when title (ownership) to products transfers to bottling partners, resellers, or other customers, either upon shipment or receipt, depending on the specific terms of the sales transactions.
2. Coca-Cola's revenue recognition criteria focus on recognizing revenue when products are transferred to customers. This is consistent with the focus of the new guidance on satisfying performance obligations to customers. Thus, it seems likely that Coca-Cola's revenue recognition timing will not change dramatically under the new standard.

Real Report 5.2 Answers Starbucks Corporation—Revenue Recognition

1. Starbucks recognizes revenue using very different policies across the retail, licensed stores, CPG, foodservice and other, and stored value cards categories. Starbucks recognizes retail revenues at point of sale when customers tender payment. Starbucks recognizes revenues from product sales to licensed stores upon shipment, and revenues from license fees and royalties at various points in time, depending on when they are earned. Starbucks recognizes revenues from product sales (coffee, tea, and related products) to CPG, foodservice, and other customers upon shipment. Starbucks recognizes revenues from stored value cards when redeemed for products. Until then, the outstanding balances are included in the Stored Value Card Liability on the balance sheet.

Real Report 5.3 Answers Google Inc.—Discontinued Operations

1. In 2013, Google discontinued the Motorola Home segment.
2. The loss from operations in fiscal 2012 from discontinued operations was $-51 million. In 2013, the loss from operations was again $-51 million. A company may dispose of components of its business for several reasons, including inadequate or uncertain future prospects, poor earnings or cash flows, and lack of fit with regard to a company's strategic plan. Google likely disposed of these operations because they were not profitable.
3. In 2013, Google recognized a $757 million gain (after tax) on the disposal of the Motorola Home segment.

Real Report 5.4 Answers Starbucks Corporation—Earnings per Share

1. Starbucks's basic and diluted earnings per share amounts for the year ended September 27, 2015, were $1.84 and $1.82, respectively. The difference is $0.02, which is primarily attributable to the difference in the number of shares used to compute basic (1,495.9 million shares) versus diluted (1,513.4 million shares) earnings per share.
2. The difference in Starbucks's weighted average number of shares in the calculation of basis versus diluted earnings per share is attributable to the dilutive effect of common stock equivalents consisting of certain shares subject to stock options and RSUs (restricted stock units).

MULTIPLE-CHOICE (AICPA ADAPTED)

Select the best answer for each of the following.

M5-1
LO 5.3
Which of the following is expensed under the principle of systematic and rational allocation?

a. salespeople's monthly salaries
b. insurance premiums
c. transportation to customers
d. electricity to light office building

M5-2
LO 5.4
The following information is available for Cooke Company for the current year:

Net sales	$1,800,000
Freight-in	45,000
Purchase discounts	25,000
Ending inventory	120,000

The gross margin is 40% of net sales. What is the cost of goods available for sale?

a. $840,000
b. $960,000
c. $1,200,000
d. $1,220,000

M5-3
LO 5.4
The following information is available for Wagner Corporation for the current year:

Sales	$500,000
Beginning inventory	180,000
Ending inventory	95,000
Advertising	45,000
Purchases	215,000

How much is the cost of goods sold?

a. $200,000
b. $300,000
c. $345,000
d. $440,000

M5-4
LO 5.4
Dobbin Corporation, a manufacturer of household paints, is preparing annual financial statements at year end. Because of a recently proven health hazard in one of its paints, the government required Dobbin to recall all cans of this paint sold in the last 6 months. The management of Dobbin estimates that this recall cost $1,000,000. What accounting recognition, if any, should be accorded this situation?

a. no recognition
b. footnote disclosure
c. operating expense of $1,000,000
d. liability of $1,000,000

M5-5
LO 5.4
A loss from the sale of a component of a business enterprise is reported separately as a component of income:

a. after income from continuing operations
b. in income from continuing operations
c. after income tax expense
d. before income from continuing operations

M5-6
LO 5.9
In a statement of cash flows, receipts from sales of property, plant, and equipment generally are classified as:

a. investing activities
b. selling activities
c. operating activities
d. financing activities

REVIEW EXERCISES

RE5-1
LO 5.4
Brandt Corporation had sales revenue of $500,000 for the current year. For the year, its cost of goods sold was $240,000, its operating expenses were $50,000, its interest revenue was $2,000, and its interest expense was $12,000. Brandt's income tax rate is 30%. Prepare Brandt's multiple-step income statement for the current year.

RE5-2
LO 5.4
Refer to **RE5-1**. Prepare a single-step income statement for Brandt Corporation for the current year.

RE5-3
LO 5.4
Shaquille Corporation began the current year with inventory of $50,000. During the year, its purchases totaled $110,000. Shaquille paid freight charges of $8,500 for these purchases. At the end of the year, Shaquille had inventory of $47,800. Prepare a schedule to determine Shaquille's cost of goods sold for the current year.

RE5-4
LO 5.4
Dorno Corporation incurred expenses during the current year as follows: $2,300 delivery expense, $5,500 advertising expense, $13,750 sales salaries expense, $1,250 sales supplies expense, $12,750 office salaries expense, $3,000 insurance expense, and $900 office supplies expense. Prepare schedules to show what amounts Dorno would report on its income statement for total selling expenses and for total general and administrative expenses.

RE5-5 **LO 5.5** Niler Corporation reported the following *after-tax* information for its current fiscal year: $35,000 income from continuing operations, $8,400 income from operations of discontinued Line C, and $12,500 loss on disposal of Line C. Starting with income from continuing operations, prepare a partial income statement for Niler for the current year. Ignore earnings per share.

RE5-6 **LO 5.4** Jordan Corporation reported retained earnings of $225,000 at the beginning of the current year. During the year, Jordan earned net income of $45,000 and paid cash dividends of $3,750. Prepare Jordan's reconciliation of retained earnings for the current year.

RE5-7 **LO 5.5** **LO 5.6** Pallest Corporation reported the following *pretax* information for its current fiscal year: $40,000 income from continuing operations and an $8,000 loss arising from discontinuing a segment (it was simply closed, no gain or loss on sale). Pallest is subject to a 30% income tax rate and had 8,000 shares of common stock outstanding for the year. Starting with pretax income from continuing operations, prepare a partial income statement for Pallest for the current year. Be sure to include earnings per share information.

RE5-8 **LO 5.5** **LO 5.6** Mangold Corporation reported income from continuing operations of $78,400 and loss from discontinuing a segment (net of taxes) of $6,400 for the current year. Mangold had 80,000 common shares outstanding for the entire year. Show how Mangold would report its earnings per share for the current year.

RE5-9 **LO 5.9** Amelia's Bookstore reported net income of $62,000 for the current year. The following information is also available for the year: $5,000 depreciation expense, $5,500 increase in inventory, $2,000 decrease in accounts receivable, and $1,250 decrease in accounts payable. Using the indirect method, prepare the operating activities section of the statement of cash flows for Amelia's for the current year.

RE5-10 **LO 5.9** During the current year, Ross Corporation purchased a warehouse for $45,000, paid $1,000 dividends, sold land for $7,900, and issued $25,000 of common stock. All of these were cash transactions. Show how Ross would report the cash provided by (or used for) its investing and financing activities sections of its statement of cash flows for the current year.

EXERCISES

E5-1 **LO 5.4** **Simple Income Statement** The following are selected items derived from Dibb Company's adjusted trial balance on December 31, 2016:

Loss on sale of land	$ 5,000	Sales (net)	$198,000
Cost of goods sold	130,000	Operating expenses	45,000

Twelve thousand shares of common stock were outstanding the entire year.

Required:
Assuming a 30% income tax rate on all items of income, prepare Dibb's 2016 income statement using (1) a multiple-step format and (2) a single-step format.

E5-2 **LO 5.4** **Simple Income Statement** The following are selected items for Albertson Company as of December 31, 2016:

Purchases (net)	$63,000	Sales (net)	$100,000
Merchandise inventory, January 1, 2016	20,000	Operating expenses	22,000
Gain on sale of equipment	5,000		

The merchandise inventory on December 31, 2016, is $31,000. Ten thousand shares of common stock have been outstanding the entire year. Albertson uses a periodic inventory system.

Required:
Assuming a 30% income tax rate on all items of income, prepare Albertson's 2016 income statement using (1) a multiple-step format and (2) a single-step format.

E5-3
LO 5.4

Income Statement Calculations Revolve Company's income statement information for 2016 and 2017 (a sole proprietorship) is as follows:

	2016	2017
Cost of goods sold	$ (a)	$59,300
Interest expense	600	0
Selling expenses	(b)	10,800
Operating income	21,800	(d)
Sales (net)	96,000	(e)
General expenses	7,900	(f)
Net income	(c)	21,600
Interest revenue	0	600
Gross profit	39,000	40,200

Required:
Next Level Provide the missing amounts for the blanks labeled (a) through (f). All the necessary information is listed. (*Hint*: It is not necessary to calculate your answers in alphabetical order.)

E5-4
LO 5.4

Cost of Goods Sold and Income Statement Schuch Company presents you with the following account balances taken from its December 31, 2016, adjusted trial balance:

Inventory, January 1, 2016	$ 43,000	Purchases returns	$3,500
Selling expenses	35,000	Interest expense	4,000
Purchases	100,000	Sales discounts taken	2,000
Sales	250,000	Gain on sale of property (pretax)	7,000
General and administrative expenses	22,000	Freight-in	5,000

Additional data:
1. A physical count reveals an ending inventory of $22,500 on December 31, 2016.
2. Twenty-five thousand shares of common stock have been outstanding the entire year.
3. The income tax rate is 30% on all items of income.

Required:
1. As a supporting document for Requirements 2 and 3, prepare a separate schedule for Schuch's cost of goods sold.
2. Prepare a 2016 multiple-step income statement.
3. Prepare a 2016 single-step income statement.

E5-5
LO 5.4

Income Statement Calculation O'Connor Company's income statement information for 2016 and 2017 (a sole proprietorship) is as follows:

	2016	2017
Beginning inventory	$ (a)	$ (d)
Sales	206,000	(e)
Purchases	130,000	140,000
Purchases returns and allowances	7,000	6,000
Ending inventory	62,000	(f)
Gross profit	(b)	100,000
Cost of goods sold	114,000	120,000
Selling expenses	35,000	36,000
Transportation-in	2,000	5,000
General and administrative expenses	20,000	(g)
Net income	(c)	43,000

Required:
Next Level Provide the missing amounts for the blanks labeled (a) through (g). All the necessary information is listed. (*Hint*: It is not necessary to calculate your answers in alphabetical order.)

E5-6 **Results of Discontinued Operations** During December 2016, Smythe Company decides to sell Division F (a strategic component of the company). On December 31, 2016, the company classifies Division F as held for sale. On that date, the book values of Division F's assets and liabilities are $950,000 and $600,000, respectively. Smythe expects to sell Division F in 2017 and estimates that the fair value of Division F is $250,000. During 2016, Division F earned revenues of $1,000,000 and incurred expenses of $1,300,000. Smythe is subject to a 30% income tax rate.

LO 5.5

Required:
Prepare the results from discontinued operations section of Smythe's income statement for 2016. Show supporting calculations.

E5-7 **Results of Discontinued Operations** On November 30, 2016, Fleiner Company announced its plans to discontinue the operations of Division P (a major component of the company) by selling the division. On December 31, 2016, Division P had not yet been sold and was classified as held for sale. On this date, Division P had assets with a book value of $920,000 and liabilities with a book value of $610,000. Fleiner estimates that the fair value of Division P on this date is $190,000. During 2016, Division P earned revenues of $920,000 and incurred expenses of $980,000. Fleiner is subject to a 30% income tax rate.

LO 5.5

Required:
Prepare the results from discontinued operations section of Fleiner's income statement for 2016. Show supporting calculations.

E5-8 **Multiple-Step and Single-Step Income Statements** The following items were derived from Gold Company's December 31, 2016, adjusted trial balance:

LO 5.4
LO 5.6
LO 5.8

Cost of goods sold	$101,000	Loss from strike (pretax)	$ 9,000
Sales	195,000	Selling expenses	28,000
General and administrative expenses	20,000	Interest revenue	4,000

Additional data:
1. Seven thousand shares of common stock have been outstanding the entire year.
2. The income tax rate is 30% on all items of income.

Required:
1. Prepare a 2016 multiple-step income statement.
2. Prepare a 2016 single-step income statement.
3. **Next Level** Discuss how Gold Company's income statement in Requirement 1 might be different if it used IFRS.

E5-9 **Income Statement Deficiencies** David Company's income statements for the year ended December 31, 2017 and December 31, 2016, are presented here:

LO 5.5
LO 5.6

AICPA Adapted

SHOW ME HOW

	Year Ended December 31,	
	2017	2016
Net sales	$900,000	$750,000
Costs and expenses:		
Cost of goods sold	$720,000	$600,000
Selling, general, and administrative expenses	112,000	90,000
Other, net	11,000	9,000
Total costs and expenses	$843,000	$699,000
Income from continuing operations before income taxes	$ 57,000	$ 51,000
Income taxes	23,000	21,000
Income from continuing operations	$ 34,000	$ 30,000
Loss on sale of Drexler Division, less applicable income taxes of $8,000	8,000	—
Net income	$ 26,000	$ 30,000
Earnings per share of common stock:		
Net income	$ 2.60	$ 3.00

Additional facts are as follows:

a. The loss from operations of the discontinued Drexler Division (a strategic component of the company) from January 1, 2017 to September 30, 2017 (the portion of the year prior to the date of sale), and from

(continued)

January 1, 2016 to December 31, 2016, is included in David's income statements for the year ended December 31, 2017 and December 31, 2016, respectively, in "other, net."

b. David has a simple capital structure with only common stock outstanding, and the net income per share of common stock was based on the weighted average number of common shares outstanding during each year.

c. David's common stock is listed on the New York Stock Exchange and closed at $13 per share on December 31, 2017, and $15 per share on December 31, 2016.

Required:

Next Level Determine from the additional facts listed whether the presentation of those facts in David's income statements is appropriate. If the presentation is appropriate, discuss the rationale for the presentation. If the presentation is not appropriate, specify the appropriate presentation and discuss its rationale. Do *not* discuss disclosure requirements for the notes to the financial statements.

E5-10 **Multiple-Step and Single-Step Income Statements, and Statement of Comprehensive Income** On December 31, 2016, Opgenorth Company listed the following items in its adjusted trial balance:

LO 5.4
LO 5.6
LO 5.7

Loss from fire (pretax)	$ 8,000	General and administrative expenses	$ 17,000
Interest revenue	2,500	Sales	160,000
Selling expenses	14,000	Unrealized decrease in fair value of	
Cost of goods sold	95,000	available-for-sale securities	1,800
Loss on sale of equipment (pretax)	2,000		

SHOW ME HOW

Additional data:
1. Seven thousand shares of common stock have been outstanding the entire year.
2. The income tax rate is 30% on all items of income.

Required:
1. Prepare a 2016 multiple-step income statement.
2. Prepare a 2016 single-step income statement.
3. Prepare a 2016 statement of comprehensive income.

E5-11 **Net Income and Comprehensive Income** On December 31, 2016, TNT Company derives the following items from its adjusted accounts:

LO 5.4
LO 5.7

Sales (net)	$85,000
Unrealized increase in fair value of	
available-for-sale securities	4,000
Operating expenses	18,000
Cost of goods sold	47,000

Required:
1. Prepare a 2016 multiple-step income statement that includes comprehensive income (disregard earnings per share). Assume TNT faces a 30% income tax rate.
2. Prepare (a) a 2016 multiple-step income statement (disregard earnings per share) and (b) a separate 2016 statement of comprehensive income. Assume TNT faces a 30% income tax rate.

E5-12 **Cost of Goods Sold, Income Statement, and Statement of Comprehensive Income** Gaskin Company derives the following items from its adjusted trial balance as of December 31, 2016:

LO 5.4
LO 5.7

Sales	$139,000	Interest revenue	$ 3,300
Purchases returns	5,200	Purchases discounts taken	2,700
Gain on sale of equipment (pretax)	3,800	Inventory, January 1, 2016	12,100
Freight-in	3,400	Purchases	89,700
Selling expenses	15,600	Administrative expenses	24,200
Unrealized increase in fair value of		Loss from truck accident (pretax)	6,500
available-for-sale securities	2,400		

The following additional information is also available. The December 31, 2016, ending inventory is $14,700. During 2016, 4,200 shares of common stock were outstanding the entire year. The income tax rate is 30% on all items of income.

Required:
1. As a supporting document for Requirements 2 and 3, prepare a separate schedule for Gaskin's cost of goods sold.
2. Prepare a 2016 single-step income statement.
3. Prepare a 2016 multiple-step income statement.
4. Prepare a 2016 statement of comprehensive income.

E5-13
LO 5.9
Net Cash Flow from Operating Activities The following are accounting items taken from Tyrone Shoelaces Company's records for 2016:

a. Net income, $22,900
b. Payment for purchase of land, $4,000
c. Payment for retirement of bonds, $6,000
d. Depreciation expense, $7,800
e. Receipt from issuance of common stock, $7,000
f. Patent amortization expense, $2,700
g. Increase in accounts receivable, $3,400
h. Payment of dividends, $5,000
i. Decrease in accounts payable, $2,600

Required:
Prepare the net cash flow from operating activities section of Tyrone's 2016 statement of cash flows using the indirect method.

E5-14
LO 5.9
Operating Cash Flows: Direct Method The following are various cash flows and other information for Smyczek Company for 2016:

a. Payments of interest, $8,200
b. Receipt from sale of land, $7,900
c. Interest collected, $10,000
d. Payment of dividends, $12,100
e. Depreciation expense, $24,700
f. Collections from customers, $101,600
g. Payments of income taxes, $15,400
h. Receipt from issuance of stock, $18,900
i. Payments to suppliers and employees, $67,500
j. Increase in inventories, $4,600

Required:
Using the direct method, prepare the cash flows from operating activities section of Smyczek's 2016 statement of cash flows.

E5-15
LO 5.9
Statement of Cash Flows The following items involve the cash flow activities of Rocky Horror Picture Co. for 2016:

SHOW ME HOW

a. Net income, $41,000
b. Payment of dividends, $16,000
c. Ten-year, $28,000 bonds payable were issued at face value
d. Depreciation expense, $11,000
e. Building acquired at a cost of $40,000
f. Accounts receivable decreased by $2,000
g. Accounts payable decreased by $4,000
h. Equipment acquired at a cost of $8,000
i. Inventories increased by $7,000
j. Beginning cash balance, $13,000

Required:
Prepare Rocky Horror Picture's statement of cash flows for 2016 using the indirect method.

E5-16
LO 5.9
Statement of Cash Flows The following are several items involving Tejera Company's cash flow activities for 2016:

a. Net income, $60,400
b. Receipt from issuance of common stock, $32,000
c. Payment for purchase of equipment, $41,500
d. Payment for purchase of land, $19,600
e. Depreciation expense, $20,500
f. Patent amortization expense, $1,200
g. Payment of dividends, $21,000
h. Decrease in salaries payable, $2,600
i. Increase in accounts receivable, $10,300
j. Beginning cash balance, $30,700

Required:
Prepare Tejera's statement of cash flows for 2016 using the indirect method.

E5-17 **Classifications** Where would each of the following items most likely be reported in a company's financial statements? Assume the monetary amount of each item is material and the company uses a periodic inventory system.

LO 5.4
LO 5.7
LO 5.9

1. Loss on sale of equipment
2. Office supplies used
3. Unrealized decrease in fair value of available-for-sale securities
4. Freight-in
5. Delivery expense
6. Dividend income
7. Gain from retirement of debt
8. Amortization of license used for sales and marketing
9. Summary of accounting policies
10. Purchases returns and allowances
11. Income tax expense on continuing income
12. Cash dividends declared and paid
13. Loss resulting from tornado damage
14. Merchandise inventory (ending)

E5-18 **Classifications** Where would each of the following items most likely be reported in a company's financial statements? Assume the monetary amount of each item is material.

LO 5.4
LO 5.5
LO 5.7
LO 5.9

1. Bad debts expense
2. Sales discounts taken
3. Depreciation expense on sales equipment
4. Loss from operations of discontinued Division B
5. Earnings per share
6. Gain on sale of land
7. Administrative salaries
8. Cash dividends declared and paid on common stock
9. Gain from sale of discontinued Division B
10. Loss on sale of equipment
11. Advertising expense
12. Merchandise inventory (ending)
13. Loss from write-off of obsolete inventory
14. Cash paid to acquire equipment
15. Unrealized increase in fair value of available-for-sale securities

E5-19 **Rate of Change Analyses** Teicher Company presents the following condensed comparative income statements for 2015, 2016, and 2017:

LO 5.10

	For Years Ended December 31,		
	2017	2016	2015
Sales (net)	$120,000	$100,000	$ 85,000
Cost of goods sold	(72,000)	(55,000)	(45,000)
Gross profit	$ 48,000	$ 45,000	$ 40,000
Operating expenses	(22,000)	(20,000)	(18,000)
Operating income	$ 26,000	$ 25,000	$ 22,000
Other items:			
Dividend revenue	400	500	200
Interest expense	(1,200)	(1,000)	(500)
Income before income taxes	$ 25,200	$ 24,500	$ 21,700
Income tax expense	(8,200)	(8,000)	(6,000)
Net income	$ 17,000	$ 16,500	$ 15,700
Number of common shares	6,000	6,000	5,000
Earnings per share	$ 2.83	$ 2.75	$ 3.14

Required:

Next Level Prepare rate of change analyses for Teicher for 2016 and 2017 using year-to-year growth rates. What favorable or unfavorable trends do your analyses reveal about Teicher Company's financial performance?

E5-20 **Common-Size Analyses** Meagley Company presents the following condensed income statement and balance sheet information for 2016 and 2017:

LO 5.10

Income Statements

	For Years Ended December 31	
	2017	2016
Sales (net)	$100,000	$ 90,000
Cost of goods sold	(60,000)	(51,000)
Gross profit	$ 40,000	$ 39,000
Operating expenses	(21,300)	(21,900)
Interest revenue	1,500	1,400
Interest expense	(3,700)	(2,500)
Income before income taxes	$ 16,500	$ 16,000
Income tax expense	(5,000)	(4,700)
Net income	$ 11,500	$ 11,300
Earnings per share	$ 1.92	$ 1.95

Balance Sheets

	December 31,	
	2017	2016
Cash	$ 3,000	$ 2,000
Receivables (net)	7,000	8,000
Inventories	11,000	12,000
Long-term investments (bonds)	20,000	15,000
Property and equipment (net)	79,000	63,000
Total Assets	$120,000	$100,000
Current liabilities	$ 10,000	$ 11,400
Bonds payable, 10%	37,000	25,000
Common stock, $2 par	12,000	11,600
Additional paid-in capital	21,000	19,500
Retained earnings	40,000	32,500
Total Liabilities and Shareholders' Equity	$120,000	$100,000

Required:

Next Level Prepare Meagley's common-size income statements and balance sheets for 2017 and 2016. What trends do your analyses reveal in Meagley's operations and financial position?

E5-21 **Ratios** Miller Company's condensed income statement for 2016 and December 31, 2016, balance sheet follow:

LO 5.10

Income Statement

Sales (net)	$ 304,400
Cost of goods sold	(183,600)
Gross profit	$ 120,800
Operating expenses	(82,000)
Operating income	$ 38,800
Interest expense	(7,000)
Income before income taxes	$ 31,800
Income taxes	(10,000)
Net income	$ 21,800

(continued)

Balance Sheet

Cash	$ 8,200	Accounts payable	$ 18,000
Receivables (net)	14,700	Other current liabilities	6,800
Inventory	19,300	Bonds payable, 10%	70,000
Property, plant, and equipment (net)	195,800	Common stock, $10 par	80,500
		Additional paid-in capital on common stock	24,000
		Retained earnings	38,700
Total Assets	$238,000	Total Liabilities and Shareholders' Equity	$238,000

Additional information: The common stock was outstanding the entire year and is selling for $16 per share at year-end. On January 1, 2016, the inventory was $21,500, the total assets were $224,000, the accounts payable were $18,800, and the total shareholders' equity was $130,800. The company operates on a 365-day business year.

Required:
Compute the following ratios for Miller (round all computations to two decimal places): (1) gross profit margin, (2) operating profit margin, (3) net profit margin, (4) total asset turnover, (5) return on total assets, (6) return on common equity, (7) current, (8) inventory turnover (in days), and (9) payables turnover (in days).

E5-22 **Ratio Analysis** Byers Company presents the following condensed income statement for 2016 and condensed December 31, 2016, balance sheet:

Income Statement

Sales (net)		$ 267,000
Less:		
Cost of goods sold	$160,000	
Operating expenses	62,000	
Interest expense	11,000	
Income taxes	10,000	
Total expenses		(243,000)
Net income		$ 24,000

Balance Sheet

Cash	$ 10,000	Current liabilities	$ 40,000
Receivables (net)	22,000	Bonds payable, 10%	110,000
Inventory	56,000	Common stock, $10 par	100,000
Long-term investments	30,000	Additional paid-in capital	95,000
Property and equipment (net)	282,000	Retained earnings	55,000
Total Assets	$400,000	Total Liabilities and Shareholders' Equity	$400,000

Additional information:
1. The company's common stock was outstanding the entire year.
2. Dividends of $1.50 per share on the common stock were declared in 2016.
3. On December 31, 2016, common stock is selling for $20 per share.
4. On January 1, 2016, the accounts receivable (net) balance was $24,000, total assets amounted to $380,000, and total shareholders' equity was $241,000.
5. Of the company's net sales, 78% are on credit.
6. The company operates on a 365-day business year.

Required:
Compute the following ratios for Byers (round all computations to two decimals): (1) earnings per share, (2) gross profit margin, (3) operating profit margin, (4) net profit margin, (5) total asset turnover, (6) return on assets, (7) return on common equity, (8) receivables turnover (in days), and (9) interest coverage.

E5-23 **Income Statement and Retained Earnings** Huff Company presents the following items derived from its December 31, 2016, adjusted trial balance:

LO 5.4
LO 5.10

Sales (net)	$124,000	Operating expenses	$30,400
Interest expense	3,700	Common stock, $5 par	22,000
Cost of goods sold	66,200	Retained earnings, 1/1/2016	45,800

SHOW ME HOW

The following information is also available for 2016 and is not reflected in the preceding accounts:
1. The common stock has been outstanding all year. A cash dividend of $1.28 per share was declared and paid.
2. Land was sold at a pretax gain of $6,300.
3. Division X (a major component of the company) was sold at a pretax gain of $4,700. It had incurred a $9,500 pretax operating loss during 2016.
4. A tornado, which is an unusual event in the area, caused a $5,400 pretax loss.
5. The income tax rate on all items of income is 30%.
6. The average shareholders' equity is $90,000.

Required:
1. Prepare a 2016 multiple-step income statement for Huff.
2. Prepare a 2016 retained earnings statement.
3. Compute the 2016 return on common equity (Net Income ÷ Average Shareholders' Equity).

E5-24 **Income Statement and Retained Earnings** Taylor Company uses a periodic inventory system and presents the following items derived from its December 31, 2016, adjusted trial balance:

LO 5.4
LO 5.5
LO 5.10

Operating expenses	$ 35,800	Common stock, $15 par	$45,000
Dividend revenue	1,000	Merchandise inventory, January 1, 2016	24,000
Retained earnings, January 1, 2016	68,700	Purchases (net)	79,200
Sales (net)	139,600		

The following information is also available for 2016 and is not reflected in the preceding accounts:
1. The common stock has been outstanding for the entire year. A cash dividend of $0.84 per share was declared and paid.
2. The income tax rate on all items of income is 30%.
3. The ending merchandise inventory is $27,300.
4. A pretax $4,000 loss was recognized on the sale of Division X (a component of the company). This division had earned a pretax operating income of $1,900 during 2016.
5. Damaged inventory was written off at a pretax loss of $6,600.
6. An earthquake, which is unusual in the area, caused a $3,700 pretax loss.

Required:
1. Prepare a cost of goods sold schedule for Taylor.
2. Prepare a 2016 single-step income statement.
3. Prepare a 2016 retained earnings statement.
4. Compute the 2016 net profit margin (Net Income ÷ Net Sales).

E5-25 **Segment Reporting (Appendix 5.1)** Parks Conglomerate Company does business in several different industries. The following is a 2016 condensed income statement for the entire company:

LO 5.11

Sales		$ 300,000
Less:		
Cost of goods sold	$140,000	
Depreciation expense	30,000	
Other operating expenses	60,000	
Total expenses		(230,000)
Pretax income		$ 70,000
Income tax expense		(21,000)
Net income		$ 49,000
Earnings per share (20,000 shares)		$ 2.45

(continued)

Parks has two major operating segments, A and B. No other operating segment contributes 10% or more of the company's activities. Segments A and B make no sales to each other or to the other segments of the company. An analysis reveals that $2,000 of the total depreciation expense and $6,000 of the total other operating expenses are related to general corporate activities. The *remaining* expenses and total revenues are directly allocable to segment activities according to the following percentages:

	Percent Identified with		
	Segment A	Segment B	Other Segments
Sales	40%	46%	14%
Cost of goods sold	35	50	15
Depreciation expense	40	45	15
Other operating expenses	42	40	18

Required:
Prepare a schedule that reports on the revenues and profit of Segments A and B and the other operating segments of Parks for 2016. Be sure to reconcile these amounts with the related totals on the preceding income statement. Include notes summarizing the depreciation related to each operating segment and the computation of segment profits.

E5-26 **Interim Reporting *(Appendix 5.1)*** Hill Company prepares quarterly and year-to-date interim reports. The following is its interim income statement for the quarter ended March 31, 2016:

LO 5.5
LO 5.11

SHOW ME HOW

Sales (net)		$150,000
Cost of goods sold		(90,000)
Gross profit		$ 60,000
Operating expenses:		
Selling expenses	$18,000	
General expenses	10,600	
Depreciation expense	8,000	(36,600)
Pretax operating income		$ 23,400
Other items:		
Dividend revenue	$ 600	
Interest expense	(1,000)	(400)
Income before income taxes		$ 23,000
Income tax expense		(7,000)
Net income		$ 16,000
Earnings per share (20,000 shares)		$ 0.80

On June 30, 2016, Hill's accountant completed a worksheet in preparation for developing the year-to-date interim income statement. The following are the accounts and amounts listed on the income statement debit and credit columns of this worksheet:

	Debit	Credit
Sales (net)		$340,000
Interest revenue		500
Dividend revenue		1,000
Cost of goods sold	$190,000	
Selling expenses	50,000	
General expenses	20,000	
Depreciation expense	16,000	
Interest expense	2,100	
Income tax expense	19,200	

Required:
Assuming 20,000 shares of common stock have been outstanding for the entire 6 months, prepare:
1. Hill's year-to-date interim income statement for the first 6 months of 2016.
2. Hill's interim income statement for the second quarter of 2016.

PROBLEMS

P5-1
LO 5.5

Results of Discontinued Operations On November 1, 2016, Woods Company announced its plans to sell its subsidiary, Williams Division (a major strategic component of the company). By December 31, 2016, Woods had not sold Williams Division and so it classifies the division as held for sale.

During 2016, Woods recorded the following revenues and expenses for Williams Division and the remainder of the company:

	Williams Division	Remainder of Company
Sales revenues	$170,000	$950,000
Cost of goods sold	119,000	560,000
Operating expenses	42,000	190,000

Woods is subject to a 30% income tax rate.

On December 31, 2016, the net book value of Williams Division is $500,000, consisting of assets of $910,000 and liabilities of $410,000. On this date, Woods estimates that the fair value of Williams Division is $420,000. The company had 50,000 shares of common stock outstanding during all of 2016.

Required:
1. Prepare the journal entry on December 31, 2016, to record the pretax loss on held-for-sale Williams Division. Show supporting calculations.
2. Prepare a 2016 multiple-step income statement for Woods.
3. Show how Williams Division would be reported on Woods's December 31, 2016, balance sheet.

P5-2
LO 5.4
LO 5.5
LO 5.6

Income Statement, Lower Portion At the beginning of 2016, Cameron Company's retained earnings was $212,000. For 2016, Cameron has calculated its pretax income from continuing operations to be $120,000. During 2016, the following events also occurred:
1. During July, Cameron sold Division M (a component of the company). It has determined that the pretax income from the operations of Division M during 2016 totals $39,000 and that a pretax loss of $40,500 was incurred on the sale of Division M.
2. Cameron had 21,000 shares of common stock outstanding during all of 2016. It declared and paid a $1 per share cash dividend on this stock.

Required:
Assuming that all the pretax items are subject to a 30% income tax rate:
1. Complete the lower portion of Cameron's 2016 income statement, beginning with "Pretax Income from Continuing Operations."
2. Prepare an accompanying retained earnings statement.

P5-3
LO 5.4
LO 5.5
LO 5.6

Income Statement, Lower Portion Cunningham Company reports a retained earnings balance of $365,200 at the beginning of 2016. For the year ended December 31, 2016, the company reports pretax income from continuing operations of $150,500. The following information is also available pertaining to 2016:
1. The company declared and paid a $0.72 cash dividend per share on the 30,000 shares of common stock that were outstanding the entire year.
2. The company incurred a pretax $21,000 loss as a result of an earthquake, which is not unusual for the area. This is included in the $150,500 income from continuing operations.
3. The company sold Division P (a component of the company) in May. From January through May, Division P had incurred a pretax loss from operations of $33,000. A pretax gain of $15,000 was recognized on the sale of Division P.

(continued)

Required:

Assuming that all the "pretax" items are subject to a 30% income tax rate:
1. Complete the lower portion of Cunningham's 2016 income statement beginning with "Pretax Income from Continuing Operations." Include any related note to the financial statements.
2. Prepare an accompanying retained earnings statement.

P5-4
LO 5.4
LO 5.5
LO 5.6
LO 5.7

Account Classifications Given the following code letters and components of financial statements, indicate with the appropriate code letter(s) where each item would most likely be reported in the financial statements. Assume the monetary amount of each item is material.

Code Letter	Component
A	Sales revenues (net)
B	Cost of goods sold
C	Selling expenses
D	General and administrative expenses
E	Other items
F	Results from discontinued operations
G	Additions to retained earnings
H	Deductions from retained earnings
I	Notes to financial statements
J	Ending balance sheet

_____ 1. Purchases
_____ 2. Loss on sale of equipment
_____ 3. Utilities expense
_____ 4. Cash dividends declared on common stock
_____ 5. Bad debts expense
_____ 6. Sales salaries
_____ 7. Sales discounts taken
_____ 8. Transportation-in
_____ 9. Net income
_____ 10. Gain on retirement of long-term debt
_____ 11. Purchases returns and allowances
_____ 12. Premium on bonds payable
_____ 13. Gain on sale of land
_____ 14. Interest expense
_____ 15. Delivery expense
_____ 16. Expenses incurred as a result of a strike
_____ 17. Summary of accounting policies
_____ 18. Gain on disposal of Division J
_____ 19. Interest revenue
_____ 20. Additional paid-in capital on common stock
_____ 21. Loss from write-down of obsolete inventory
_____ 22. Administrative salaries
_____ 23. Stock dividends declared on common stock
_____ 24. Operating loss related to discontinued Division J
_____ 25. Additional depreciation on office equipment resulting from decrease in estimated useful life
_____ 26. Gain on sale of factory
_____ 27. Loss from frost damage in southern Wisconsin
_____ 28. Depreciation expense for office equipment
_____ 29. Sales commissions
_____ 30. Promotion expense
_____ 31. Merchandise inventory (beginning)

P5-5 **Financial Statement Violations of U.S. GAAP** The following are the financial statements issued by Allen Corporation for its fiscal year ended October 31, 2016:

LO 5.4
LO 5.6
AICPA Adapted

SHOW ME HOW

Balance Sheet
October 31, 2016

Assets
Cash		$ 15,000
Accounts receivable, net		150,000
Inventory		120,000
Total current assets		$285,000
Patent (Note 3)		250,000
Land		125,000
Total assets		$660,000

Liabilities
Accounts payable		$ 80,000
Accrued expenses		20,000
Total current liabilities		$100,000
Deferred income tax payable (Note 4)		80,000
Total liabilities		$180,000

Shareholders' Equity
Common stock, par $1 (Note 5)	$100,000	
Additional paid-in capital	180,000	
Retained earnings	200,000	480,000
Total liabilities and shareholders' equity		$660,000

Income Statement
For the Fiscal Year Ended October 31, 2016

Sales		$1,000,000
Cost of goods sold		(750,000)
Gross margin		$ 250,000
Expenses:		
Bad debt expense	$ 7,000	
Insurance	13,000	
Lease expenses (Note 1)	40,000	
Repairs and maintenance	30,000	
Pensions (Note 2)	12,000	
Salaries	60,000	(162,000)
Earnings before provision for income tax		$ 88,000
Provision for income tax		(28,740)
Net earnings		$ 59,260
Earnings per common share outstanding		$ 0.5926

Statement of Retained Earnings
For the Fiscal Year Ended October 31, 2016

Retained earnings, November 1, 2015	$150,000
Gain on sale of equipment, net of income tax	25,000
Net earnings for the fiscal year ended October 31, 2016	59,260
	$234,260
Dividends ($0.3426 per share)	(34,260)
Retained earnings, October 31, 2016	$200,000

Notes to Financial Statements:

1. *Long-Term Lease.* Under the terms of a 5-year, noncancelable lease for a building, Allen is obligated to make annual rental payments of $40,000 in each of the next 4 fiscal years.
2. *Pension Plan.* Substantially all employees are covered by Allen's defined benefit pension plan. Pension expense is equal to the total of pension benefits accrued and paid to retired employees during the year. Because it is a defined benefit plan that is paid every year, no pension liability exists.
3. *Patent.* The patent had an estimated remaining life of 10 years at the time of purchase. Allen's patent was purchased from Apex Corporation on January 1, 2016, for $250,000.

(continued)

4. *Deferred Income Tax Payable.* The entire balance in the Deferred Income Tax Payable account arose from tax-exempt municipal bonds that were held during the previous fiscal year, giving rise to a difference between taxable income and reported net earnings for the fiscal year ended October 31, 2016. The deferred liability amount was calculated on the basis of past tax rates.
5. *Warrants.* On January 1, 2015, one common stock warrant was issued to shareholders of record for each common share owned. An additional share of common stock is to be issued upon exercise of 10 stock warrants and receipt of an amount equal to par value. For the 6 months ended October 31, 2016, the average market value for Allen's common stock was $5 per share and no warrants had yet been exercised.
6. *Contingent Liability.* On October 31, 2016, Allen was contingently liable for product warranties in an amount estimated to aggregate $75,000.

Required:

Next Level Review the preceding financial statements and related notes. Identify any inclusions or exclusions from them that would be in violation of GAAP, and indicate corrective action to be taken. Do *not* comment as to format or style. Respond in the following order:
1. Balance sheet
2. Notes
3. Income statement
4. Statement of retained earnings
5. General

P5-6 **Misclassifications** Rox Corporation's multiple-step income statement and retained earnings statement for the year ended December 31, 2016, as developed by its bookkeeper, are shown here:

LO 5.4
LO 5.5

Revenue Statement
December 31, 2016

Sales (net)		$ 179,000
Plus: Income from operations of discontinued Division P (net of $960 income taxes)		2,240
Less: Dividends declared ($1.50 per common share)		(7,500)
Net revenues		$ 173,740
Less: Selling expenses		(19,000)
Gross profit		$ 154,740
Less: Operating expenses:		
Interest expense	$ 4,100	
Loss on sale of Division P (net of $1,200 income tax credit)	2,800	
Cost of goods sold	110,700	
Income tax expense on income from continuing operations	5,370	
Total operating expenses		(122,970)
Operating income		$ 31,770
Miscellaneous items:		
Dividend revenue	$ 1,800	
General and administrative expenses	(24,300)	(22,500)
Income before unusual items		$ 9,270
Unusual items:		
Loss on sale of land	$ (4,800)	
Correction of error in last year's income (net of $1,500 income taxes)	3,500	(1,300)
Net income		$ 7,970

Retained Earnings Statement
December 31, 2016

Beginning retained earnings	$62,850
Add: Net income	7,970
Adjusted retained earnings	$70,820
Less: Loss from theft (net of $2,760 income tax credit)	(6,440)
Ending retained earnings	$64,380

You determine that the account *balances* listed on the statements are correct but are incorrectly classified in certain cases. The company faces a 30% tax rate. No shares of common stock were issued or retired during 2016.

Required:
1. Review both statements and indicate where each incorrectly classified item should be classified.
2. Prepare a correct multiple-step income statement for 2016.
3. Determine the correct beginning balance in retained earnings, and then prepare a correct 2016 retained earnings statement.

P5-7
LO 5.4
LO 5.5

Misclassifications Olson Company's bookkeeper prepared the following income statement and retained earnings statement for the year ended December 31, 2016:

December 31, 2016
Expense and Profits Statement

Sales (net)		$196,000
Less: Selling expenses		(19,600)
Net sales		$176,400
Add: Interest revenue		2,300
Add: Gain on sale of equipment		3,200
Gross sales revenues		$181,900
Less: Costs of operations:		
Cost of goods sold	$120,100	
Correction of overstatement in last year's income because of error (net of $1,650 income tax credit)	3,850	
Dividend costs ($0.50 per share for 8,000 common shares)	4,000	
Unusual loss because of earthquake (net of $1,800 income tax credit)	4,200	(132,150)
Taxable revenues		$49,750
Less: Income tax on income from continuing operations		(12,480)
Net income		$37,270
Miscellaneous deductions		
Loss from operations of discontinued Division L (net of $900 income tax credit)	$2,100	
Administrative expenses	16,800	(18,900)
Net revenues		$18,370

Retained Revenues Statement
For Year Ended December 31, 2016

Beginning retained earnings	$59,300
Add: Gain on sale of Division L (net of $1,350 income taxes)	3,150
Recalculated retained earnings	$62,450
Add: Net revenues	18,370
	$80,820
Less: Interest expense	(3,400)
Ending retained earnings	$77,420

The preceding account *balances* are correct but have been incorrectly classified in certain instances. Assume the income tax amounts are correct and linked to the appropriate items.

Required:
Prepare a corrected 2016 multiple-step income statement and a 2016 retained earnings statement. Before preparing the 2016 retained earnings statement, determine the correct balance as of the beginning of the year.

P5-8
LO 5.4
LO 5.5
AICPA Adapted

Complex Income Statement The following items were derived from Woodbine Circle Corporation's adjusted trial balance on December 31, 2016:

	Debit	Credit
Cash	$ 500,000	
Accounts receivable, net	1,500,000	
Inventory	2,500,000	
Property, plant, and equipment	15,100,000	
Accumulated depreciation		$ 4,900,000
Accounts payable		2,200,000
Income taxes payable		200,000
Notes payable		1,000,000
Common stock ($1 par value)		1,000,000
Additional paid-in capital		5,800,000
Retained earnings, January 1, 2016		3,000,000
Sales—regular		10,100,000
Sales—AL Division		2,000,000
Cost of sales—regular	6,200,000	
Cost of sales—AL Division	900,000	
Administrative expenses—regular	2,000,000	
Administrative expenses—AL Division	300,000	
Interest expense—regular	210,000	
Interest expense—AL Division	140,000	
Loss on sale of AL Division	250,000	
Gain on sale of land		300,000
Income tax expense	900,000	
	$30,500,000	$30,500,000

Other financial data for the year ended December 31, 2016:

Federal Income Taxes

Paid with federal income tax return	$700,000
Accrued	200,000
Total income tax expense (estimated)	$900,000
Tax rate on all types of taxable income	40%

Discontinued Operations

On September 30, 2016, Woodbine sold its Auto Leasing (AL) Division for $4,000,000. The book value of this division was $4,250,000 at that date. For financial statement purposes, this sale was considered as a discontinued operation of a component of the company.

Capital Structure

Common stock, par value $1 per share. Number of shares outstanding during all of 2016	1,000,000

Required:
Using the multiple-step format, prepare a formal income statement for Woodbine for the year ended December 31, 2016, together with the appropriate supporting schedules. All income taxes should be appropriately shown.

P5-9
LO 5.4
LO 5.5

Comprehensive: Comparative Income Statements Tiger Company's accountant for the prepared comparative income statements for 2016 and 2017 as follows:

Comparative Income Statements
For Years Ended December 31

	2017	2016
Sales	$ 3,500,000	$ 4,600,000
Cost of goods sold	(1,600,000)	(2,600,000)
Gross profit	$ 1,900,000	$ 2,000,000
Operating expenses	(1,300,000)	(1,500,000)
Operating income	$ 600,000	$ 500,000
Other items	(200,000)	100,000
Income before income taxes	$ 400,000	$ 600,000
Income tax expense (30%)	(120,000)	(180,000)
Net income	$ 280,000	$ 420,000

Tiger Company's auditor reviewed the accounting records and income statements and discovered the facts described in Items 1 and 2 below. All amounts incurred during 2016 and 2017 are included in the preceding statements.

1. Included in the category "Other Items" (along with other smaller miscellaneous items) were the following:
   a. A loss of $60,000 in 2016 that was considered to be unusual
   b. A $150,000 loss in 2017 from an unusually large write-down of inventory because of obsolescence
   c. A $250,000 gain in 2016 that was considered to be unusual
2. On July 1, 2017, Tiger has announced its intention to sell its backscratcher division. This division is considered a major component of the company. Operating results for this division are included in the company's overall operating results for 2016 and 2017, as shown previously, and are as follows:

	2017 (7/1–12/31)	2017 (1/1–6/30)	2016
Sales	$200,000	$400,000	$700,000
Cost of goods sold	300,000	320,000	290,000
Operating expenses	100,000	180,000	110,000

The division had not been sold by the end of 2017, so the company classified it as held for sale. The division consisted of the following items with book values and fair values on December 31, 2017:

Item	Book Value	Fair Value
Assets	$720,000	$620,000
Liabilities	450,000	510,000

Required:
Prepare corrected comparative income statements for 2017 and 2016 for Tiger. Ignore earnings per share.

P5-10
LO 5.4
LO 5.5
LO 5.7

Comprehensive Income Framework The following is an alphabetical list of accounts for Mack Company:

Accounts Payable
Accounts Receivable
Accumulated Depreciation: Buildings and Office Equipment
Accumulated Depreciation: Store and Delivery Equipment
Administrative Salaries
Advertising Expense
Allowance for Doubtful Accounts
Bad Debts Expense
Bonds Payable
Buildings
Cash
Cash Dividends Declared

Common Stock, $10 par
Delivery Expense
Depreciation Expense: Buildings and Office Equipment
Depreciation Expense: Store and Delivery Equipment
Dividend Income
Dividends Payable
Freight on Purchases
Fund to Retire Long-Term Bonds
Gain on Sale of Division T
Gain on Sale of Equipment
Income Tax Expense
Insurance Expense

(continued)

Interest Expense	Purchases
Interest Income	Purchases Discounts Taken
Interest Payable	Purchases Returns and Allowances
Investment in Securities (Long-Term)	Rent Revenue
Loss from Operations of Discontinued Division T	Retained Earnings, January 1, 2016
Loss on Sale of Office Equipment	Salaries Payable
Merchandise Inventory, January 1, 2016	Sales
Merchandise Inventory, December 31, 2016	Sales Commissions
Miscellaneous Office Expenses	Sales Discounts Taken
Miscellaneous Sales Expenses	Sales Salaries
Mortgage Payable	Stock Dividends Declared
Office Salaries	Unearned Rent
Office Supplies Used	Unexpired Insurance
Paid-in Capital on Common Stock	Unrealized Increase in Fair Value of Available-for-Sale Securities
Prepaid Office Supplies	
Property Tax Expense	Utilities Expense

Required:
Ignoring amounts, select Mack's appropriate accounts and prepare for 2016:
1. A multiple-step income statement with proper subheadings
2. A statement of comprehensive income
3. A retained earnings statement

P5-11 Financial Statement Deficiencies The following is the complete set of financial statements prepared by Oberlin Corporation:

LO 5.4

AICPA Adapted

Statement of Income and Retained Earnings
For the Fiscal Year Ended August 31, 2016

Sales		$ 3,500,000
Less discounts		(35,000)
Net sales		$ 3,465,000
Less cost of goods sold		(1,039,000)
Gross margin		$ 2,426,000
Less:		
Selling expenses	$1,000,000	
General and administrative expenses	1,079,000	(2,079,000)
Operating earnings		$ 347,000
Add other revenues:		
Purchase discounts	$ 10,000	
Gain on increased fair value of real estate	100,000	
Gain on sale of treasury stock	200,000	
Correction of error in last year's statement	90,000	400,000
Ordinary earnings		$ 747,000
Add gain on sale of fixed asset		53,000
Earnings before income tax		$ 800,000
Less income tax expense		(320,000)
Net earnings		$ 480,000
Add beginning retained earnings		2,690,000
		$ 3,170,000
Less:		
Dividends (12% dividend declared but not yet issued)		(120,000)
Contingent liability (Note 2)		(300,000)
Ending retained earnings		$ 2,750,000

Balance Sheet
August 31, 2016

Assets		
Current Assets:		
Cash	$ 80,000	
Accounts receivable, net	110,000	
Inventory	130,000	
Total current assets		$ 320,000
Other Assets:		
Land and building, net	$4,000,000	
Investments in real estate (current value)	1,668,000	
Goodwill (Note 1)	250,000	
Discount on bonds payable	42,000	
Total other assets		5,960,000
Total Assets		**$6,280,000**
Liabilities and Shareholders' Equity		
Current Liabilities:		
Accounts payable	$ 160,000	
Income taxes paycble	300,000	
Dividend payable	120,000	
Total current liabilities		$ 580,000
Other Liabilities:		
Due to Grant Inc. (Note 2)	$ 300,000	
Accrued pension cost	450,000	
Bonds payable (including portion due within 1 year)	1,000,000	
Deferred taxes	58,000	
Total other liabilities		1,808,000
Total liabilities		**$2,388,000**
Shareholders' Equity:		
Common stock	$1,000,000	
Paid-in capital in excess of par	142,000	
Retained earnings	2,750,000	
Total shareholders' equity		3,892,000
Total Liabilities and Shareholders' Equity		**$6,280,000**

Notes to Financial Statements:
1. Goodwill is not being reviewed for impairment. The goodwill was acquired in 2016.
2. The amount, Due to Grant Inc. is contingent upon the outcome of a lawsuit which is currently pending. The amount of loss, if any, is not expected to exceed $300,000.

Required:

Next Level Identify and explain the deficiencies in the presentation of Oberlin's financial statements. There are no arithmetic errors in the statements. Organize your answer as follows:
1. Deficiencies in the statement of income and retained earnings
2. Deficiencies in the balance sheet
3. General comments

If an item appears on both statements, identify the deficiencies for each statement separately.

P5-12
LO 5.9

Comprehensive: Balance Sheet from Statement of Cash Flows Mills Company prepared the following balance sheet at the *beginning* of 2016:

Balance Sheet
January 1, 2016

Assets		Liabilities and Shareholders' Equity	
Cash	$ 1,000	Accounts payable	$ 4,000
Accounts receivable (net)	3,900	Salaries payable	1,100
Inventory	4,700	Total Liabilities	$ 5,100
Land	9,800	Common stock, $10 par	13,500
Buildings and equipment	68,900	Additional paid-in capital	11,200
Less: Accumulated depreciation	(14,100)	Retained earnings	44,400
Total Assets	$74,200	Total Liabilities and Shareholders' Equity	$74,200

At the end of 2016, Mills prepared the following statement of cash flows:

Statement of Cash Flows
For Year Ended December 31, 2016

Operating Activities:		
Net income		$ 5,400
Adjustments for differences between income flows and cash flows from operating activities:		
Add: Depreciation expense		1,900
Decrease in inventory		500
Increase in salaries payable		400
Less: Increase in accounts receivable (net)		(1,100)
Decrease in accounts payable		(1,000)
Net cash provided by operating activities		$ 6,100
Investing Activities:		
Payment for purchase of building	$(13,900)	
Receipt from sale of land	3,000	
Net cash used for investing activities		(10,900)
Financing Activities		
Payment of dividends	$ (3,100)	
Receipt from issuance of bonds	5,700	
Receipt from issuance of common stock	4,500	
Net cash provided by financing activities		7,100
Net increase in cash		$ 2,300
Cash, January 1, 2016		1,000
Cash, December 31, 2016		$ 3,300

Additional information related to the statement of cash flows:
1. The long-term bonds have a face value of $6,000 and were issued on December 31, 2016.
2. The building was purchased on December 30, 2016.
3. The land was sold at its original cost.
4. The common stock which was sold totaled 300 shares and had a par value of $10 per share.

Required:
Next Level Prepare a classified balance sheet for Mills as of December 31, 2016. (*Hint:* Review the information on the statement of cash flows and the balances in the beginning balance sheet accounts to determine the impact on the ending balance sheet accounts.)

P5-13
LO 5.7

Net Income and Comprehensive Income At the beginning of 2016, JR Company's shareholders' equity was as follows:

Common stock, $5 par	$35,000
Additional paid-in capital	49,000
Retained earnings	63,000

During 2016, the following events and transactions occurred:
1. JR recognized sales revenues of $108,000. It incurred cost of goods sold of $62,000 and operating expenses of $12,000.
2. JR issued 1,000 shares of its $5 par common stock for $14 per share.
3. JR invested $30,000 in available-for-sale securities. At the end of the year, the securities had a fair value of $35,000.
4. JR paid dividends of $6,000.

The income tax rate on all items of income is 30%.

Required:
1. Prepare a 2016 income statement for JR which includes net income and comprehensive income (ignore earnings per share).
2. Prepare (a) a 2016 income statement (ignore earnings per share) and (b) a separate 2016 statement of comprehensive income.

P5-14
LO 5.9
Statement of Cash Flows A list of selected items involving Fischer Company's cash flow activities for 2016 is presented here:

a. Patent amortization expense, $3,500
b. Machinery was purchased for $39,500
c. At year-end, bonds payable with a face value of $20,000 were issued for $17,000
d. Net income, $47,200
e. Dividends paid, $16,000
f. Depreciation expense, $12,900

g. Preferred stock was issued for $13,600
h. Investments were acquired for $21,000
i. Accounts receivable increased by $4,300
j. Land was sold at cost, $11,000
k. Inventories increased by $15,400
l. Accounts payable increased by $2,700
m. Beginning cash balance, $19,400

Required:
Prepare Fischer's statement of cash flows for 2016.

P5-15
LO 5.9
Statement of Cash Flows The following are several items involving Mueller Company's cash flow activities for 2016:

a. Net income, $68,000
b. Increase in accounts receivable, $4,400
c. Receipt from sale of common stock, $12,300
d. Depreciation expense, $11,300
e. Dividends paid, $24,500
f. Payment for purchase of building, $65,000
g. Bond discount amortization, $2,700
h. Receipt from sale of long-term investments at cost, $10,600

i. Payment for purchase of equipment, $8,000
j. Receipt from sale of preferred stock, $20,000
k. Increase in income taxes payable, $3,500
l. Payment for purchase of land, $9,700
m. Decrease in accounts payable, $2,900
n. Increase in inventories, $10,300
o. Beginning cash balance, $18,000

Required:
Prepare Mueller Company's statement of cash flows for 2016.

P5-16
LO 5.9
Statement of Cash Flows: Direct Method The following are various cash flows and other information for Leer Company for 2016:

a. Payments of interest, $5,000
b. Depreciation expense, $22,700
c. Receipt from sale of land, $3,100
d. Payments of income taxes, $6,200
e. Beginning cash balance, $16,500
f. Decrease in receivables, $7,400
g. Interest and dividends collected, $6,300
h. Payments of dividends, $5,200

i. Decrease in accounts payable, $8,600
j. Payments to suppliers and employees, $50,300
k. Receipt from issuance of common stock, $11,000
l. Collections from customers, $61,700
m. Payment for purchase of investments, $17,800
n. Net income, $73,400

Required:
Using the direct method for operating cash flows, prepare Leer's 2016 statement of cash flows.

P5-17 **Rate of Change Analyses and Ratios Analyses** The following are Cohen Company's comparative financial statements for 2017, 2016, and 2015:

LO 5.6
LO 5.10

SHOW ME HOW

Comparative Income Statements	For Years Ended December 31,		
	2017	2016	2015
Sales (net)	$102,200	$91,500	$81,700
Cost of goods sold	(61,100)	(52,800)	(47,150)
Gross profit	41,100	38,700	34,550
Selling expenses	(11,400)	(10,000)	(8,900)
Administrative expenses	(8,700)	(7,843)	(6,950)
Interest expense	(3,000)	(4,000)	(4,000)
Total expenses	(23,100)	(21,843)	(19,850)
Income before income taxes	18,000	16,857	14,700
Income tax expense	(5,400)	(5,057)	(4,410)
Net income	$12,600	$11,800	$10,290
Earnings per share	?	?	?

Comparative Retained Earnings Statements	For Years Ended December 31,		
	2017	2016	2015
Beginning retained earnings	$28,800	$20,800	$14,310
Add: Net income	12,600	11,800	10,290
	$41,400	$32,600	$24,600
Less: Dividends distributed	(4,410)	(3,800)	(3,800)
Ending retained earnings	$36,990	$28,800	$20,800

Comparative Balance Sheets	December 31,		
	2017	2016	2015
Cash	$ 4,200	$ 4,000	$ 4,100
Receivables (net)	7,600	7,000	6,200
Inventories	9,800	9,000	8,600
Noncurrent assets	119,390	112,000	107,100
Total Assets	$140,990	$132,000	$126,000
Current liabilities	$ 12,000	$ 10,000	$ 12,000
Bonds payable, 10%	30,000	40,000	40,000
Common stock, $2 par	8,400	7,600	7,600
Additional paid in capital	53,600	45,600	45,600
Retained earnings	36,990	28,800	20,800
Total Liabilities and Shareholders' Equity	$140,990	$132,000	$126,000

Additional information: Credit sales were 65% of net sales in 2016 and 60% in 2017. At the beginning of 2017, 400 shares of common stock were issued, the first sale of stock in several years.

Cohen is concerned. Although it increased the dividends paid per share by 5% in 2017 and its 2017 net income is higher than 2016 net income, the market price of its common stock dropped from $22 per share at the beginning of 2017 to $21 per share at year-end.

Required:
1. For 2015, 2016, and 2017, prepare rate of change analyses for the income statements and balance sheets of Cohen using a year-to-year approach.
2. For 2016 and 2017, compute the following ratios: (a) current, (b) inventory turnover, (c) receivables turnover, (d) net profit margin, (e) earnings per share, (f) return on total assets, (g) return on shareholders' equity, and (h) debt-to-assets.
3. **Next Level** Based on your results, discuss the possible reasons for the decrease in the market price per share in 2017.

P5-18 **Comprehensive: Income Statement and Retained Earnings** The following selected accounts are taken from Crandle Corporation's December 31, 2016, adjusted trial balance:

LO 5.4
LO 5.5
LO 5.6
LO 5.10

Retained Earnings, January 1, 2016	$428,900
Interest Expense	4,900
Depreciation Expense: Sales Equipment	8,500
Advertising Expense	14,100
Common Stock, $10 par	110,000
Administrative and Office Salaries Expense	29,500
Dividend Revenue	900
Sales	366,700
Property Tax Expense	7,700
Gain on Sale of Sales Equipment (pretax)	5,000
Office Supplies Expense	1,800
Transportation-out (deliveries)	6,000
Cost of Goods Sold	191,200
Sales Discounts Taken	5,200
Bad Debt Expense	1,900
Sales Supplies Expense	4,600
Sales Salaries Expense	16,500
Depreciation Expense: Buildings and Office Equipment	10,000
Income Tax Expense	19,560

In addition to the preceding account balances, you have available the following information:
1. In the middle of December 2016, the company incurred a material $5,500 pretax loss as a result of a flood of a river that floods once every 10 years.
2. While making its December 31, 2016, adjusting entries, the company conducted an analysis of its recent favorable experience with uncollectible accounts receivable, and decided to reduce the percentage used in computing bad debt expense. The use of the new percentage resulted in the $1,900 bad debt expense being $500 less than the amount that would have been calculated using the old percentage.
3. On April 1, 2016, the company sold Division M (a component of the company), which had been unprofitable for several years. For the first 3 months of 2016, Division M had incurred a pretax operating loss of $8,800. Division M was sold at a pretax loss of $7,500.
4. The company paid cash dividends of $0.90 per share on its common stock. All the stock was outstanding for the entire year.
5. The company is subject to a 30% income tax rate. The $19,560 Income Tax Expense account balance consists of $21,210 tax on income from continuing operations, less a $1,650 tax credit on the loss because of the flood. It does not include tax credits of $2,640 on the operating loss of Division M, or $2,250 on the loss from sale of Division M.

Required:
1. As supporting documents for Requirement 2, prepare separate schedules for selling expenses and for general and administrative expenses (include each depreciation expense where applicable in these schedules).
2. Prepare a 2016 single-step income statement for Crandle. Include any related note to the financial statements.
3. Prepare a 2016 retained earnings statement.
4. **Next Level** What was Crandle's profit margin for 2016? What is your evaluation of Crandle's 2016 profit margin if last year it was 8%?

P5-19 **Comprehensive: Income Statement and Retained Earnings** Milwaukee Manufacturing Company presents the following partial list of account balances, after adjustments, as of December 31, 2016:

LO 5.4
LO 5.5
LO 5.6
LO 5.8
LO 5.10

SHOW ME HOW

Sales Salaries Expense	$ 27,400	Sales Personnel Travel Expenses	$ 8,300
Miscellaneous Administrative Expenses	3,000	Property Taxes and Insurance Expense	9,000
Sales	463,200	Retained Earnings, January 1, 2016	200,800
Interest Revenue	3,200	Depreciation Expense: Sales Equipment	9,000
Office and Administrative Salaries	30,000	Advertising Expense	15,700
Delivery Expenses	11,700	Miscellaneous Rent Revenue	5,900
Loss on Sale of Factory Equipment (pretax)	4,100	Common Stock, $10 par	200,000
Cost of Goods Sold	232,200	Depreciation Expense: Buildings and Office Equipment	14,400

(continued)

The following information is also available but is not reflected in the preceding accounts:

a. The company sold Division E (a major component of the company) on August 2, 2016. During 2016, Division E had incurred a pretax loss from operations of $16,000. However, because the acquiring company could vertically integrate Division E into its facilities, Milwaukee Manufacturing was able to recognize a $42,000 pretax gain on the sale.

b. On January 2, 2016, without warning, a foreign country expropriated a factory of Milwaukee Manufacturing which had been operating in that country. As a result of that expropriation, the company has incurred a pretax loss of $30,000.

c. The common stock was outstanding for the entire year. A cash dividend of $1.20 per share was declared and paid in 2016.

d. The 2016 income tax expense totals $31,050 and consists of the following:

Tax expense on income from continuing operations	$32,250
Tax credit on Division E operating loss	(4,800)
Tax expense on gain from sale of Division E	12,600
Tax credit on loss from expropriation	(9,000)
	$31,050

Required:
1. As supporting documents for Requirement 2, prepare separate supporting schedules for selling expenses and for general and administrative expenses (include depreciation expense where applicable in these schedules).
2. Prepare a 2016 multiple-step income statement for Milwaukee Manufacturing.
3. Prepare a 2016 retained earnings statement.
4. **Next Level** What was Milwaukee Manufacturing's return on common equity for 2016 if its average shareholders' equity during 2016 was $500,000? What is your evaluation of this return on common equity if its "target" for 2016 was 15%?
5. **Next Level** Discuss how Milwaukee Manufacturing's income statement in Requirement 2 might be different if it used IFRS.

P5-20 **Comprehensive: Income Statement and Supporting Schedules** The following is a partial list of the account balances, after adjustments, of Silvoso Company on December 31, 2016:

LO 5.4
LO 5.5
LO 5.6
LO 5.10

Depreciation Expense: Buildings and Office Equipment	$ 14,500
Sales Commissions and Salaries	18,200
Inventory, January 1, 2016	37,800
Sales Supplies Used	5,600
Retained Earnings, January 1, 2016	83,700
Purchases Returns and Allowances	6,200
Bad Debts Expense	2,700
Transportation-in	13,500
Sales Discounts Taken	4,900
Purchases	173,000
Delivery Expense	7,700
Office Supplies Expense	1,400
Common Stock, $10 par	80,000
Loss on Sale of Office Equipment (pretax)	5,000
Insurance and Property Tax Expense	8,500
Sales	328,600
Rent Revenue	6,900
Office and Administrative Salaries Expense	32,000
Promotion and Advertising Expense	17,000
Purchases Discounts Taken	4,100
Depreciation Expense: Sales Equipment	9,600
Interest Expense	3,700

The following information is also available:
1. The company declared and paid a $0.60 per share cash dividend on its common stock. The stock was outstanding the entire year.
2. A physical count determined that the December 31, 2016, ending inventory is $34,100.
3. A tornado destroyed a warehouse, resulting in a pretax loss of $12,000. The last tornado in this area had occurred 10 years earlier.
4. On May 1, 2016, the company sold an unprofitable division (R). From January through April, Division R (a major component of the company) had incurred a pretax operating loss of $8,700. Division R was sold at a pretax gain of $10,000.
5. The company is subject to a 30% income tax rate. Its income tax expense for 2016 totals $4,230. The breakdown is as follows:

Income Tax Expense (Credit) Related to	Amount
Continuing income	$ 7,440
Operating loss of Division R	(2,610)
Gain on sale of Division R	3,000
Loss from tornado	(3,600)
	$ 4,230

6. The company had average shareholders' equity of $150,000 during 2016.

Required:
1. As supporting documents for Requirement 2, prepare separate supporting schedules for cost of goods sold, selling expenses, general and administrative expenses, and depreciation expense.
2. Prepare a 2016 multiple-step income statement for Silvoso. Include any related note to the financial statements.
3. Prepare a 2016 retained earnings statement.
4. **Next Level** What was Silvoso's return on common equity for 2016? What is your evaluation of Silvoso's return on common equity if last year it was 10%?

P5-21
LO 5.11
Interim Reporting Schultz Company prepares interim financial statements at the end of each quarter. The income statement presented at the end of the first quarter of 2016 is as follows:

Sales (net)		$ 40,000
Cost of goods sold		(23,000)
Gross profit		$ 17,000
Operating expenses:		
Selling expenses	$8,800	
Administrative expenses	4,210	
Total operating expenses		(13,010)
Pretax operating income		$ 3,990
Other items:		
Interest revenue	$ 40	
Rent revenue	300	
Interest expense	(330)	10
Income before income taxes		$ 4,000
Income tax expense		(700)
Net income		$ 3,300
Earnings per share (8,000 shares)		$ 0.41

(continued)

Shown next is the Schultz Company trial balance as of June 30, 2016:

	Debit	Credit
Cash	$ 7,200	
Accounts Receivable (net)	10,300	
Note Receivable (due 9/1/16)	4,000	
Inventory	24,400	
Prepaid Insurance	960	
Property and Equipment	80,000	
Accumulated Depreciation		$ 20,000
Accounts Payable		8,000
Dividends Payable		3,200
Unearned Rent		1,800
Bonds Payable, 10% (due 1/1/2021)		12,000
Discount on Bonds Payable	600	
Common Stock, $1 par		8,000
Additional Paid-in Capital on Common Stock		34,580
Retained Earnings		26,400
Sales (net)		90,000
Cost of Goods Sold	48,600	
Selling Expenses	19,750	
Administrative Expenses	8,170	
	$203,980	$203,980

Additional information:
1. The company uses a perpetual inventory system.
2. The company uses control accounts for selling and administrative expenses.
3. The company records and posts its adjusting entries to its accounts *only at year-end*.
4. Uncollectible accounts average 0.5% of net sales.
5. The $4,000 note receivable was received on March 1, 2016. The 6-month note carries an annual interest rate of 12%, the interest to be collected at the maturity date.
6. The balance in the Prepaid Insurance account represents payment made on January 1, 2016, for a 1-year comprehensive insurance policy.
7. The Property and Equipment account consists of land, $5,000; buildings, $55,000; and equipment, $20,000. The buildings are being depreciated over a 25-year life; the equipment over an 8-year life. Straight-line depreciation is used; residual value is disregarded. No acquisitions have been made in 2016. The depreciation on the buildings is treated as an administrative expense; depreciation on the equipment as a selling expense.
8. On February 1, 2016, the company rented some floor space to another company, receiving 1 year's rent of $1,800 in advance.
9. The bonds pay interest semiannually on January 1 and July 1. Straight-line amortization of the discount is recorded at the end of each year.
10. The company estimates that its pretax income for the second half of 2016 will total $11,550. All items in income are subject to the same income tax rate schedule. The income tax rate schedule is 15% on the first $20,000 of taxable income and 30% on the excess. There is no difference between the company's pretax financial income and taxable income, and no tax credits are available. The company rounds its estimated effective income tax rate to the nearest tenth of a percent. Income taxes will be paid during the first quarter of 2017.
11. On June 29, 2016, the company had declared and recorded (directly in Retained Earnings) a semiannual dividend of $0.40 per share, payable on August 3, 2016.
12. The 8,000 shares of common stock have been outstanding the entire 6 months of 2016.

Required:
1. Prepare a 10-column worksheet to develop the Schultz financial statements for the first 6 months of 2016. (Refer to Chapter 3 for a worksheet illustration, if necessary.)
2. Prepare the income statement for (a) the first 6 months of 2016 and (b) the second quarter of 2016.
3. Prepare a retained earnings statement for the first 6 months of 2016.
4. Prepare the June 30, 2016, balance sheet.

P5-22 **Comparative Income Statements** Century Company, a diversified manufacturing company, had four separate operating divisions engaged in the manufacture of products in each of the following areas: food products, health aids, textiles, and office equipment. Financial data for the 2 years ended December 31, 2017, and 2016 are presented here:

LO 5.4
LO 5.10
LO 5.11
AICPA Adapted

	Net Sales	
	2017	2016
Food products	$3,500,000	$3,000,000
Health aids	2,000,000	1,270,000
Textiles	1,580,000	1,400,000
Office equipment	920,000	1,330,000
	$8,000,000	$7,000,000

	Cost of Sales	
	2017	2016
Food products	$2,400,000	$1,800,000
Health aids	1,100,000	700,000
Textiles	500,000	900,000
Office equipment	800,000	1,000,000
	$4,800,000	$4,400,000

	Operating Expenses	
	2017	2016
Food products	$ 600,000	$ 300,000
Health aids	250,000	150,000
Textiles	200,000	100,000
Office equipment	650,000	750,000
	$1,700,000	$1,300,000

On January 1, 2017, Century adopted a plan to sell the assets and product line of the office equipment division and considered it a component of the company. On September 1, 2017, the division's assets and product line were sold for $2,100,000 cash, resulting in a gain of $640,000.

The company's textiles division had six manufacturing plants that produced a variety of textile products. In April 2017, the company sold one of these plants and realized a gain of $130,000. After the sale, the operations at the plant that was sold were transferred to the remaining five textile plants which the company continued to operate.

In August 2017, the main warehouse of the food products division, located on the banks of the Bayer River, was flooded when the river overflowed. The resulting damage of $420,000 is not included in the financial data given previously. Historical records indicate that the Bayer River normally overflows every 4 to 5 years, causing flood damage to adjacent property.

For the 2 years ended December 31, 2017 and 2016, the company's investments generated interest income of $70,000 and $40,000, respectively.

The provision for income tax expense for each of the 2 years should be computed at a rate of 40%.

Required:
Prepare in proper form a multiple-step comparative income statement for Century for the 2 years ended December 31, 2017, and December 31, 2016. Earnings per share information and footnotes are not required.

P5-23 **Income Statement and Segment Reporting** The following items are based on Reed Company's December 31, 2016, adjusted trial balance:

LO 5.4
LO 5.10
LO 5.11

Cost of goods sold	$121,120	Loss due to flood (pretax)	$ 8,000
Interest expense	4,880	Sales (net)	200,000
Depreciation expense	7,000	Administrative expenses	16,000
Selling expenses	26,000	Interest revenue	1,000

(continued)

Additional information:
1. Reed had 5,000 shares of common stock outstanding the entire year.
2. The income tax rate is 30% on all items.
3. Reed operates several divisions, two of which, Divisions 1 and 2, are reportable operating segments.
4. No intersegment sales are made by any division. Of the total sales (net), Division 1 made 49%; Division 2, 30%; and the remaining segments, 21%.
5. Cost of goods sold as a *percentage of net sales* in each division was: Division 1, 62%; Division 2, 60%; other segments, 58%.
6. Selling expenses consist of sales salaries, sales commissions, delivery costs, advertising, and miscellaneous expenses. These are traceable to the divisions as follows:
   a. Sales salaries ($6,000): $3,000 to Division 1, $2,000 to Division 2, and $1,000 to the remaining segments.
   b. Sales commissions ($4,000): 2% of net sales in all segments.
   c. Delivery costs ($5,000): 60% to Division 1, 30% to Division 2, and 10% to the remaining segments.
   d. Advertising ($10,500): Of the total, $1,200 was spent on general advertising. Of the remainder, $4,600 was spent in Division 1, $3,200 in Division 2, and $1,500 in the other segments.
   e. The miscellaneous selling expenses of $500 are considered common costs and are not allocated to any segments.
7. Administrative expenses consist of bad debts, administrative salaries, property taxes, and miscellaneous expenses. These are allocable to the segments as follows:
   a. Bad debts ($2,000): 1% of net sales in all segments.
   b. Administrative salaries ($10,000): Of the total, $2,100 are considered general corporate salaries. Of the remainder, $3,800 is allocated to Division 1, $2,500 to Division 2, and $1,600 to the other segments.
   c. Property taxes ($3,000): Of the total, $1,600 are general corporate expenses. Of the remainder, 40% is allocable to Division 1, 35% to Division 2, and 25% to the remaining segments.
   d. The miscellaneous administrative expenses of $1,000 are considered common costs and are not allocated to any segments.
8. Depreciation expense is listed as a separate item on the income statement. Of the total, $1,400 is a general corporate expense. Of the remainder, 40% is allocable to Division 1, 30% to Division 2, and 30% to the remaining segments.
9. Interest revenue is from corporate investments in marketable securities. Interest expense is related to corporate bonds used to finance general operating activities.
10. A flood causing the material pretax loss occurred in Division 1.
11. Of the $300,000 total assets on December 31, 2016, 45% are assets of Division 1, 29% are assets of Division 2, 18% are assets of the remaining segments, and 8% are assets related to corporate headquarters.
12. Capital expenditures amounted to $25,000 in Division 1 and $6,000 in Division 2 during 2016 and are included in the total assets on December 31, 2016.

Required:
1. Prepare a 2016 multiple-step income statement for Reed.
2. Prepare a separate schedule that discloses the revenues, profit, and assets of Divisions 1 and 2, and the remaining operating segments.
3. Prepare appropriate segment notes related to depreciation, profit, and capital expenditures.
4. **Next Level** Compute the profit margin *before* income taxes and *pretax* return on identifiable assets for Divisions 1 and 2, and for the other divisions. What do these ratios reveal?

CASES

COMMUNICATION

C5-1 **Revenue Recognition**
LO 5.3 A friend of yours who is not an accounting major states, "I always thought that a company recognizes revenues at the time of sale. Recently, however, I heard that there are five specific steps for revenue recognition and that included in the steps is something about performance obligations to customers (whatever that means). Does that mean companies only recognize revenue when they get paid? But then I also heard that revenue may be recognized before or after the sale. I am confused. Please explain revenue recognition to me."

Required:
Prepare a written response for your friend and explain the revenue recognition criteria. Also include a discussion of the reasons for, and alternative methods of, recognizing revenue in a period other than the period of sale.

C5-2 **Expense Recognition**
LO 5.3 The FASB states that expenses are recognized according to three principles to properly recognize expenses.

Required:
Write a concise report that identifies the three principles, briefly explains each, and provides examples of expenses that would be recognized under each principle.

C5-3 **Cost, Expense, and Loss**
LO 5.3
LO 5.4
AICPA Adapted
You were requested to personally deliver your auditor's report to the board of directors of Sebal Manufacturing Corporation and answer questions posed about the financial statements. While reading the statements, one director asked, "What are the precise meanings of the terms *cost*, *expense*, and *loss*? These terms seem sometimes to identify similar items and other times dissimilar items."

Required:
1. Explain the meanings of the terms (a) *cost*, (b) *expense*, and (c) *loss* as used for financial reporting in conformity with GAAP. In your explanation, discuss the distinguishing characteristics of the terms and their similarities and interrelationships.
2. Classify each of the following items as a cost, expense, loss, or other category, and explain how the classification of each item may change:
   a. Cost of goods sold
   b. Bad debts expense
   c. Depreciation expense for plant machinery
   d. Spoiled goods

C5-4 **Results of Discontinued Operations**
LO 5.5 GAAP deal with, among other issues, defining a "component" and reporting the results of discontinued operations on a company's income statement.

Required:
Identify the elements of a company's results of discontinued operations section of its income statement. Define a *component* and explain how the elements of the section are computed if the company sells a component in the same accounting period that its management decided to sell the component.

C5-5 **Nonrecurring Items**
LO 5.4
LO 5.5
AICPA Adapted
Lynn Company sells a component of its business in the middle of the year. On the date of sale, the net proceeds received were less than the aggregate book value of the component's net assets. The component was operating at a loss from the beginning of the year.

In addition, Lynn had one of its manufacturing plants destroyed by an earthquake during the year. Earthquakes are not uncommon in Lynn's operating environment.

Required:
1. Explain how Lynn should report discontinued operations of a component of its business on its income statement for this year. Do not discuss earnings per share requirements.
2. Explain how Lynn should report the loss from the earthquake on its income statement for this year. Do not discuss earnings per share requirements.

C5-6 **Statement of Cash Flows**
LO 5.9 The president of a company which is being audited for the first time is concerned about all the unnecessary financial information the company is being required to disclose and says, "We have always prepared only a balance sheet and an income statement. Surely these are enough. The only information anyone is interested in is how much we earned and what we have left. Now I am told we must prepare a statement of cash flows. What is this statement, what information does it provide, what are the major sections of the statement, and what is included in each section (under the indirect method)?"

Required:
Prepare a written response that answers the president's questions.

CREATIVE AND CRITICAL THINKING

C5-7 **Accrual Accounting**
LO 5.2
LO 5.3
AICPA Adapted
GAAP requires the use of accruals and deferrals in the determination of income.

Required:
1. Explain how accrual accounting affects the determination of a company's income. Include in your discussion what constitutes accrued and deferred revenues and expenses, and give appropriate examples of each.
2. Contrast accrual accounting with cash accounting.

C5-8 **Capital Maintenance**
LO 5.2
LO 5.10
At the beginning of 1998, the Hill family organized Hill Corporation and issued 8,000 shares of stock to family members for $20 per share. During 2004, it issued an additional 1,600 shares of stock for $25 per share to family members. The 9,600 shares were held by the family until the corporation was liquidated at the end of 2016. At that time, the corporate assets were sold for $600,000, and the $50,000 of corporate liabilities were paid off. The remainder was returned to shareholders. During the 13 years of operation, the corporation had a volatile operating life. It started out slowly but then increased its activities in later years. It had operated in several industry segments, being quite successful in some, not so successful in others. It had survived a major earthquake, but not without incurring significant losses. The corporation paid out dividends of $100,000 during its lifetime.

You are a member of the Hill family who has just inherited a sizable fortune from one of your relatives. Although you were quite young during the operating life of Hill Corporation, you are considering establishing and investing in a new corporation that operates in some of the same lines of business, provided that the corporation would be profitable. You have just received your undergraduate accounting degree and upon investigation find that, with the exception of the preceding information, all the corporate accounting records were destroyed in a recent fire. You have been told that these records were sketchy at best but that a capital maintenance approach to income measurement might yield some useful information.

Required:
Compute the lifetime income of Hill Corporation and comment on what additional information you would desire before making your investment decision.

C5-9 **Ethics and Sale of Operating Component**

It is the end of 2016, and, as an accountant for Newell Company, you are preparing its 2016 financial statements. On December 29, 2016, Newell's management decided to sell one of its major divisions, subject to some legal work that is expected to be completed during the first week in April 2017 (after the 2016 financial statements have been issued). During 2016, the division earned a small operating income that is just enough for the company to report "record earnings" for the year. However, the estimated fair value of the division at the end of 2016 is less than its net book value, so that management anticipates the component will be sold at a loss.

Newell's president stops by your office and says, "You have been doing a fine job. Keep up the good work because you are heading for a promotion in early 2018. Once we report the record earnings for 2016, our shareholders and creditors will be happy. Then I think our earnings for 2017 will be high enough so that the loss we expect to report in 2017 on the sale of the division will not look so bad." After the president leaves your office, you continue preparing the 2016 financial statements.

Required:
From financial reporting and ethical perspectives, what information, if any, will you include about the upcoming sale of the division in the 2016 financial statements?

C5-10 **Analyzing Starbucks's Income Statement and Cash Flow Statement Disclosures**
Review **Starbucks**'s financial statements and notes in Appendix A.

Required:
(*Note:* You do not need to make any calculations.)
1. Does the company use a multiple-step or a single-step format on its income statement? Explain.
2. What was the net earnings attributable to Starbucks for 2015? What was the basic earnings per common share for 2015?
3. What was operating income for 2015? For 2014?
4. How much interest expense was incurred in 2015? In 2014?
5. What was the amount of the income taxes related to income before income taxes for 2015?
6. What was the amount of general and administrative expenses in 2015?
7. What amount of depreciation and amortization expense is reported separately on the income statement for 2015? How much depreciation and amortization expense is added back to net income on the 2015 statement of cash flows? What item on the income statement includes the majority of the difference?
8. What amount of dividends on common stock was paid and declared in 2015? If these amounts differ, where is the difference on the balance sheet?
9. Are Starbucks's revenues seasonal? If so, in which two quarters did Starbucks generate the most revenues in 2014 and 2015?

10. Was the direct or indirect method used to determine the net cash provided by operating activities in 2015? What was the amount?
11. What was the net cash used in investing activities in 2015?
12. What cash was used to pay long-term debt in 2015?

C5-11 **Analyzing LVMH Group's Income Statement and Comprehensive Income Disclosures**

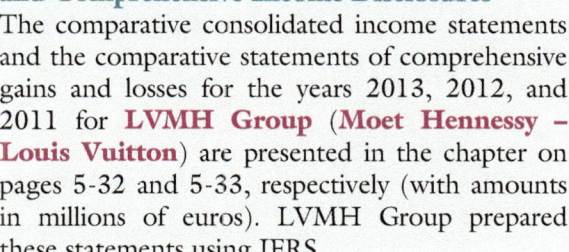

The comparative consolidated income statements and the comparative statements of comprehensive gains and losses for the years 2013, 2012, and 2011 for **LVMH Group** (**Moet Hennessy – Louis Vuitton**) are presented in the chapter on pages 5-32 and 5-33, respectively (with amounts in millions of euros). LVMH Group prepared these statements using IFRS.

Required:
Use the information in these statements to address the following questions:
1. Does LVMH use a multiple-step or a single-step format on its income statement? Explain.
2. What was the gross margin as a percentage of revenue for 2013? For 2012?
3. What was the operating profit margin as a percentage of revenue for 2013? For 2012?
4. What was the net profit margin (net profit, group share) as a percentage of revenue for 2013? For 2012?
5. What were the basic earnings per share and diluted earnings per share for 2013?
6. What do the profit margins computed in Requirements 2, 3, and 4 and the earnings per share figures in Requirement 5 reveal about LVMH's profit performance in 2013 versus 2012?
7. Which amount has a greater impact on the net profit, group share for 2013: income (loss) from investments in associates or minority interests?
8. Does LVMH report comprehensive income using a single continuous statement or consecutive statements?
9. What was the net amount of LVMH's change in value of available-for-sale financial assets that impacted comprehensive gains and losses for 2013? Of this amount, how much was recognized on the income statement in 2013?
10. In 2013, LVMH recognized in comprehensive income a change in the value of vineyard land amounting to €369 million before tax, and €127 million after tax. What amount of this gain, if any, did LVMH recognize on the income statement?

USING CODIFICATION

C5-12 **Researching GAAP**

Situation
Kelly Company, a small corporation, is preparing its 2016 financial statements. At the end of 2016, the company purchased a building for $100,000, paid $20,000 as a down payment, and signed an $80,000 mortgage. Kelly's president is concerned about how to report this transaction on the company's statement of cash flows and has asked you to "look into this issue for me."

Directions
1. Research the related U.S. GAAP using the FASB's Accounting Standards Codification and prepare a short memo to the president that summarizes how to report this transaction on the 2016 statement of cash flows. Cite your reference and applicable paragraph numbers.

TIME VALUE OF MONEY MODULE

LEARNING OBJECTIVES

After reading this chapter you will be able to:

LO M.1 Understand simple interest and compound interest.

LO M.2 Compute and use the future value of a single sum.

LO M.3 Compute and use the present value of a single sum.

LO M.4 Understand annuities, including ordinary annuities and annuities due.

LO M.5 Compute and use the future value of an ordinary annuity.

LO M.6 Compute and use the future value of an annuity due.

LO M.7 Compute and use the present value of an ordinary annuity.

LO M.8 Compute and use the present value of an annuity due.

LO M.9 Compute and use the present value of a deferred ordinary annuity.

LO M.10 Explain the conceptual issues regarding the use of present value in financial reporting.

Interested in Interest?

Suppose a friend approached you with a business proposal and asked you to loan her $1,000 today, with the promise to repay you exactly 1 year later. As a potential lender, you should expect the borrower to repay you more than $1,000 a year from now. The difference in value between an amount today and the same amount in the future is known as the time value of money. Time value of money is usually expressed and measured in terms of interest. Interest is the amount a borrower is required to pay in order to use a lender's money for a period of time, and it is the compensation to the lender for lending money for a period of time. Interest is an expense to the borrower and income to the lender. You might be quite willing to lend the $1,000 to your friend, as long as she is willing to pay you a fair amount of interest for the time value of your money.

Interest and the time value of money impacts the decision making related to the operating, investing, and financing activities of a company. Company executives and managers need to understand the concept of interest when making decisions in which cash paid or received *now* must be compared with amounts that will be received or paid in *the future*. Similarly, investors, lenders, other creditors, and stakeholders apply the principles of the time value of money when making investment, lending, or other resource allocation decisions about a company. Therefore, accountants must be very knowledgeable about applying time value of money techniques, because they are used to determine many measurements and values that a company reports on its financial statements.

For example, on **Starbucks**'s 2015 balance sheet (see Appendix A), time value of money concepts affect the measurement and reporting of many asset accounts, including Starbucks's cash and cash equivalents, short-term investments, long-term investments, as well as liability accounts such as long-term debt. Therefore, time value of money is among the most important concepts and practical techniques in business, particularly accounting, finance, and economics.

We discuss time value of money concepts and practical techniques in this Module and apply them in various chapters when we discuss how a company records and reports cash and receivables (Chapter 6); impairment of noncurrent tangible and intangible assets (Chapters 11 and 12); investment securities and long-term receivables (Chapter 13); financing liabilities such as long-term notes payable, bonds, and the amortization of bond premiums and discounts (Chapter 14); various aspects of employees' postretirement benefits (Chapter 19); and long-term leases (Chapter 20).

Various discounting and compounding techniques can be used to measure either the present values or the future values of different assets and liabilities and various types of transactions. Most discounting and compounding applications can be calculated with arithmetic. In this Module, we illustrate the basic principles of compound interest in a way that leads to your understanding of the formulas that determine present values and future values, as well as how to use the present value and future value factor tables. Note that present and future value computations can also be determined quickly and easily in computer spreadsheet programs such as Excel, as well as with any number of financial calculators. Note that in our examples and computations throughout this Module, many of the calculations are rounded.

WHAT IS THE TIME VALUE OF MONEY?

LEARNING OBJECTIVE M.1
Understand simple interest and compound interest.

Amounts of cash flows that occur on different dates cannot be added or subtracted to produce a meaningful value. For example, if you were to loan your friend $1,000 today and receive $1,000 exactly 1 year from today, you cannot add those two amounts and get a meaningful result because they have different time values. The $1,000 loaned today is worth more to you than the $1,000 to be received in 1 year. This is because of the **time value of money** which provides you, the lender, compensation for delayed consumption, expected inflation, and risk:

$$\text{Time Value of Money} = \text{Compensation for Delayed Consumption} + \text{Compensation for Expected Inflation} + \text{Compensation for Risk}$$

- *Compensation for delayed consumption.* By loaning the $1,000, you are delaying your ability to spend that money on something you might need or want, and so you deserve some compensation as a reward for delayed consumption (a "rent" for the use of your money).
- *Compensation for expected inflation.* By loaning the $1,000, you will lose purchasing power if prices in the economy experience inflation during the next year. The $1,000 you receive in 1 year will not be able to purchase as much as $1,000 can purchase today because of the effects of inflation. So the time value of money includes some compensation for expected inflation to keep your purchasing power whole.
- *Compensation for risk.* By loaning the $1,000, you take some degree of risk that the borrower may not be able to repay some or all of the amount borrowed. So the time value of money usually includes some payment to the lender for bearing risk.

The amount of compensation for each component depends, of course, on the situation in which the money is being lent. For example, you might be quite willing to lend your friend the $1,000 requested in the Module-opening business proposal, as long as the friend would agree to repay $1,080 in 1 year. The $80 is the time value of money, providing you some compensation for delayed consumption, expected inflation, and risk. Time value of money is usually expressed and measured in terms of interest rates or dollar amounts of interest. **Interest** represents the cost to the borrower for the use of money for a period of time, and it is the return to the lender for lending money for a period of time.

In order to add or subtract cash flows that occur at different dates, they must be converted to a common point in time, so that they have the same time values. Cash flows that occur in the future must be restated to present value in order to be combined with current-period cash flows. Alternately, a cash flow occurring in the present must be converted into future value if it is to be combined with cash flows occurring in a future period. The conversion of these future cash flow amounts to the present value is known as **discounting** and involves removing the effects of the time value of money (interest) from those future cash flows. The conversion of current-period cash flows to future value is known as **compounding** and involves adding the time value of money (interest) to determine what a current-period cash flow will be worth in the future.

A company uses the present value or the future value in many situations, such as:

- measuring and reporting certain types of assets and liabilities that represent future cash flows, because many accounting standards under U.S. GAAP and IFRS require the use of present value for measurement and reporting
- estimating the fair values of financial assets and liabilities, because fair value is often determined using present value computations
- decision making involving investing and financing activities (e.g., acquiring property, plant, and equipment using loans or mortgages)

Simple Interest versus Compound Interest

If you are receiving interest payments on savings or an investment, would you rather receive simple interest or compound interest payments? If you are paying interest on a loan, would you rather pay simple interest or compound interest?

- **Simple interest** is interest on the original principal (amount originally received or paid) regardless of the number of time periods that have passed or the amount of interest that has been paid or accrued in the past.
- **Compound interest** is the interest that accrues on both the principal and the past unpaid accrued interest.

An interest rate is usually stated as an *annual* rate. Simple interest is typically computed using the annual rate of interest over the length of time during which interest accumulates. Thus, simple interest is calculated by the following equation:

$$\text{Simple Interest} = \text{Principal} \times \text{Rate} \times \text{Time}$$

where time is either a fraction of a year or a multiple of years. If the term of a note is stated in days, for example, 90 days, the denominator of the time fraction in the preceding equation is usually stated in terms of a full 365-day year.[1] By contrast, compound interest accumulates and *compounds* over each period. Compound interest for a given period is calculated as follows:

$$\text{Compound Interest} = (\text{Principal} + \text{Accumulated Interest}) \times \text{Rate} \times \text{Time}$$

Example: Simple versus Compound Interest

The simple interest on a $10,000, 90-day, 12% note is $295.89 ($10,000 × 0.12 × 90/365). However, if the term of this note is 15 months, the simple interest is $1,500 ($10,000 × 0.12 × 15/12). Observe that simple interest for more than 1 year is still calculated on only the principal amount.[2]

If, on the other hand, the 12% interest is *compounded quarterly* for 15 months (5 quarters), the total compound interest is $1,592.74, as shown in **Example M.1**.

EXAMPLE M.1

Computation of Quarterly Compound Interest

Period	Principal + Accumulated Interest at Beginning of Each Quarter*	×	Rate	×	Time	=	Compound Interest	Principal + Accumulated Interest at End of Each Quarter
1st quarter	$10,000.00	×	0.12	×	1/4		$ 300.00	$10,300.00
2nd quarter	10,300.00	×	0.12	×	1/4		309.00	10,609.00
3rd quarter	10,609.00	×	0.12	×	1/4		318.27	10,927.27
4th quarter	10,927.27	×	0.12	×	1/4		327.82	11,255.09
5th quarter	11,255.09	×	0.12	×	1/4		337.65	11,592.74
Compound interest on $10,000 at 12% compounded for 5 quarters							$1,592.74	

*This value is the amount on which interest is calculated.

Comparing the compound interest to the simple interest, observe that the note with compound interest generated $92.74 of additional interest income because it accrued interest on the prior, accumulated interest. In the compound interest computation, the future amount of principal plus accumulated interest at the end of each quarter becomes the sum used to compute the interest for the following period.

---

[1] Be aware that some commercial settings use a 360-day year. In this practice, the year is assumed to be a period of 12 months of 30 days each.

[2] Although we typically use dollars as the currency units in the examples, the concepts and practical techniques throughout this Module are universal and can be applied with any currency.

Thus, if you are receiving interest payments on this $10,000 note for 15 months, you would rather receive compound interest because you will receive more ($1,592.74) because of the interest on the accumulated interest. If you are paying interest on this $10,000 note, you would rather pay simple interest ($1,500.00), to avoid paying higher interest charges.

To help address the many business issues that involve interest and the time value of money, accountants need to know the various types of compound interest computations. Although there are many variations, there are only four basic types:

- future value of a single sum
- present value of a single sum
- future value of an annuity
- present value of an annuity

GOT IT?

M-1 Explain interest.
M-2 Explain the time value of money and how it can be viewed as compensation.
M-3 Define discounting and compounding.
M-4 Contrast simple interest and compound interest.

HOW DO WE COMPUTE THE FUTURE VALUE OF A SINGLE SUM?

LEARNING OBJECTIVE M.2
Compute and use the future value of a single sum.

In this Module, for each of the time value of money techniques, we will:

1. Explain the ideas and concepts behind the techniques.
2. Describe and explain the formula to use.
3. Explain and demonstrate the time value of money factors and tables to use.
4. Apply the techniques in various examples.

We begin with the future value of a single sum.

The Idea

The **future value of a single sum** is the original sum plus the compound interest, measured as of a specific future date. **Compounding converts a current-period cash flow to a future value by incorporating the time value of money.**

Example: Future Value of a Single Sum

Suppose you invest a single amount of $1,000 in a savings account on January 1, 2016. What will be the future value of the savings account on December 31, 2019, if interest at 6% is compounded annually each year? **Example M.2** illustrates this issue.

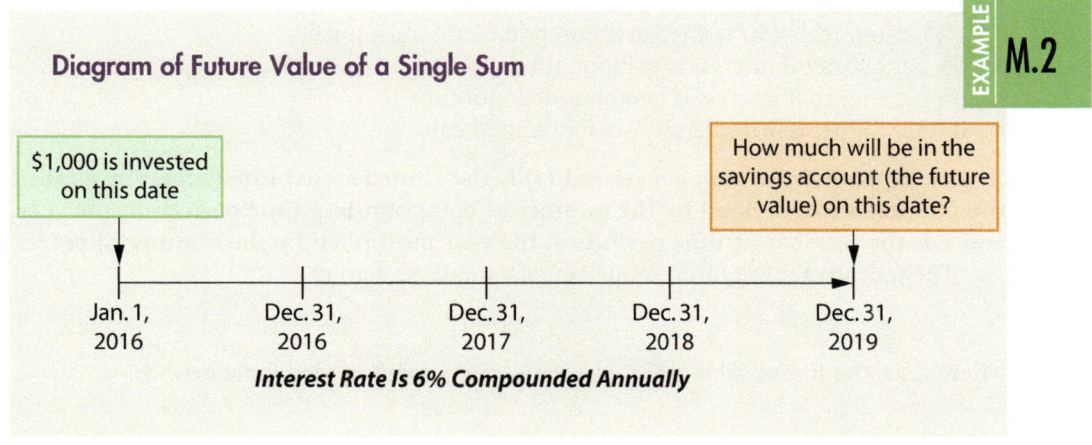

EXAMPLE M.2

Diagram of Future Value of a Single Sum

The future value of $1,000 for 4 years at 6% a year can be calculated as shown in **Example M.2a**. The single sum of $1,000 invested on January 1, 2016, will grow to $1,262.48 by December 31, 2019. This is the future value. The total interest of $262.48 for the 4 years is the compound interest. ■

EXAMPLE M.2a — Calculation of Future Value of Single Sum

(1) Year	(2) Value at Beginning of Year	(3) Annual Compound Interest (Col. 2 × 0.06)	(4) Future Value at End of Year (Col. 2 + Col. 3)
2016	$1,000.00	$60.00	$1,060.00
2017	1,060.00	63.60	1,123.60
2018	1,123.60	67.42	1,191.02
2019	1,191.02	71.46	1,262.48

Formula Approach

The formula to compute the future value of a single sum is:

$$FV = PV \times (1 + i)^n$$

where

FV = future value of a single sum at compound rate of interest i for n periods
PV = present value amount
i = interest rate for each of the stated time periods
n = number of time periods

Example Each amount in Column 4 of **Example M.2a** is 1.06 times the corresponding amount in Column 2. The final future value is therefore $1,000 \times 1.06 \times 1.06 \times 1.06 \times 1.06 = \$1,262.48$. This means that 1.06 has been used as a multiplier four times; that is, 1.06 has been raised to the fourth power. The future value is therefore $1,000 multiplied by 1.06 to the fourth power:

$$FV = PV \times (1 + i)^n = \$1,000 \times (1.06)^4 = \$1,262.48$$ ■

It is important to understand that the interest rate i is the rate of interest applicable for the particular time period during which interest is compounded. The periods used for compounding and the periods used for the interest rate must be consistent. If interest is compounded annually, then an annual rate and the number of annual periods should be used. If interest is compounded monthly, then a monthly rate and the number of months should be used. For example, a stated annual rate of interest of 12% is:

- 12% per year if interest is compounded annually
- 6% per one-half year if interest is compounded semiannually
- 3% per quarter if interest is compounded quarterly
- 1% per month if interest is compounded monthly
- 0.03288% per day if interest is compounded daily

In general, **an interest rate per period (i) is the annual stated rate (sometimes called the nominal rate) divided by the number of compounding time periods in the year, and n is the number of time periods in the year multiplied by the number of years.**

The formula for the future value factor for a single sum is:

$$f_{n,i} = (1 + i)^n$$

where $f_{n,i}$ is the future value of $1 at interest rate i compounded for n periods.

Using the preceding formula for the future value of 1, a short formula for the future compound value of any single amount at compound interest is:

$$FV = PV \times f_{n,i} = PV \times (1 + i)^n$$

Example The future value of $1,000 invested at 6% with interest compounded annually can now be calculated in two steps:

- Step 1. $f_{n=4, i=6\%} = (1.06)^4 = 1.2624796$
- Step 2. $FV = \$1,000 \times (1.06)^4 = \$1,000 \times 1.2624796 = \$1,262.48$

Table Approach

To simplify computations, tables include calculations of the future value factors of a single sum of $1 at different interest rates and for different time periods. They have been constructed using the preceding formula with the appropriate interest rates and time periods.

Example: Future Value of a Single Sum Using Table Approach

Suppose that you need to use tables of the future value of $1 at 2% and 14% for Time Periods 1 through 4 and for 40 periods. These future value factors have been computed and entered in tables as follows:

$f_{n=1, i=2\%} = (1.02)^1 = 1.020000$ $f_{n=1, i=14\%} = (1.14)^1 = 1.140000$
$f_{n=2, i=2\%} = (1.02)^2 = 1.040400$ $f_{n=2, i=14\%} = (1.14)^2 = 1.299600$
$f_{n=3, i=2\%} = (1.02)^3 = 1.061208$ $f_{n=3, i=14\%} = (1.14)^3 = 1.481544$
$f_{n=4, i=2\%} = (1.02)^4 = 1.082432$ $f_{n=4, i=14\%} = (1.14)^4 = 1.688960$
$f_{n=40, i=2\%} = (1.02)^{40} = 2.208040$ $f_{n=40, i=14\%} = (1.14)^{40} = 188.883514$

These factors can be obtained from the tables shown in **Example M.3**. In these tables, each future value factor is for a single sum of $1 for a certain rate and number of periods. We provide more complete tables at the end of this Module.

EXAMPLE M.3

Table of Future Value Factors of $1(1 + i)^n$

Periods	2%	14%
1	1.020000	1.140000
2	1.040400	1.299600
3	1.061208	1.481544
4	1.082432	1.688960
...	...	...
40	2.208040	188.883514

Because the future value factors in **Example M.3** and in Table 1 at the end of this Module are based on the formula $(1 + i)^n$, the table approach can be expressed as:

$$FV = PV \times \text{Factor for } f_{n,i}$$

To calculate the future value that $1,000 today will grow to in 4 years at 6% compounded annually, it is necessary to look up the factor for $f_{n=4, i=6\%}$, namely, 1.262477; then, the calculation is: $FV = \$1,000 \times 1.262477 = \$1,262.48$.

Application

In addition to the straightforward situation of calculating the future value of a single sum at compound interest, you can solve other kinds of problems with *the future value of 1* table.

Example: Finding an Unstated Interest Rate

If $1,000 is invested on January 1, 2016, to earn compound interest, and if the future value on December 31, 2022, is $2,998.70, what is the quarterly interest rate on the investment?

We diagram the facts in **Example M.4**. Using the table approach

$$FV = PV \times \text{Factor for } f_{n,i}$$

and substituting in the formula the amounts shown in **Example M.4**, the factor is determined as follows:

$$\$2{,}998.70 = \$1{,}000 \times \text{Factor for } f_{n=28, i=?}$$

$$\text{Factor for } f_{n=28, i=?} = \frac{\$2{,}998.70}{\$1{,}000.00} = 2.99870$$

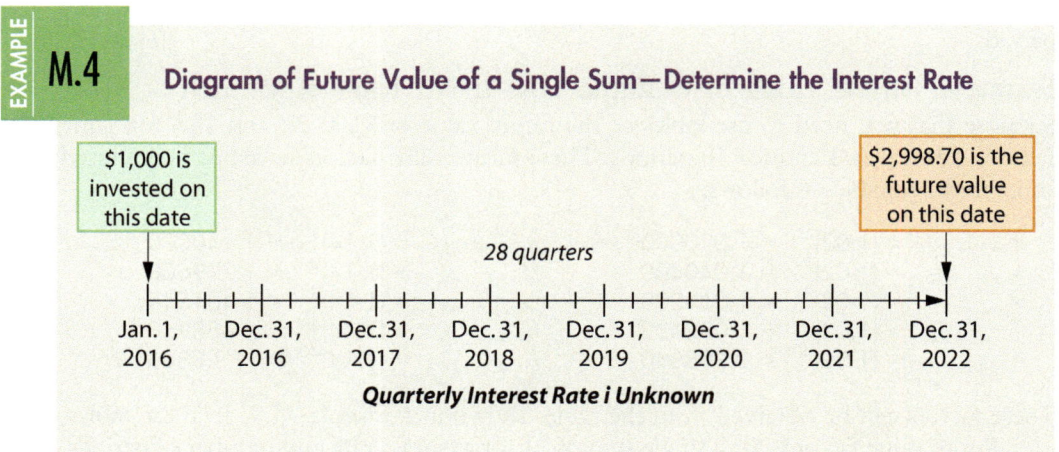

EXAMPLE M.4 Diagram of Future Value of a Single Sum—Determine the Interest Rate

The factor of 2.99870 is the future value of 1 for 28 time periods at an unknown interest rate. Using the future value of 1 table (Table 1) at the end of this Module, you look down the periods (n) column until you get to 28. Then you move horizontally across the columns on the $n = 28$ row to the factor closest to 2.99870. If the value appears in the table, you can determine the interest rate (shown at the top of the column) that produces this value. In this case, 2.99870 is equal to 2.998703 (rounded) located in the 4% column; thus, the quarterly interest rate is 4%. This is often referred to as a stated annual rate of 16%; you should understand, however, that a quarterly rate of 4% compounded four times yields an effective rate of more than 16%. If the factor of 2.99870 does not appear in the table, an interpolation procedure is required to approximate the quarterly interest rate.[3] Calculators, computer software, and Excel that compute the interest rate are widely available. ∎

You can solve other problems by using the future value factor tables. Keep in mind, however, that most tables do not include future value factors for unusual interest rates or time periods. When you are required to compute future values using unusual interest rates or periods, it may be necessary for you to compute the future value factors you need or to use a calculator or computer software.

---

[3] You can use the following six steps to determine an interest rate by linear interpolation: (1) Calculate the compound interest factor as shown in the preceding example. (2) Look up in compound interest tables the two interest rates that yield the next largest and the next smallest factors from the calculated factor determined in Step 1. (3) Determine (a) the difference between the two factors in Step 2 and (b) the difference between the calculated factor from Step 1 and the factor of the smaller interest rate from Step 2. (4) Find the difference between the two interest rates found in Step 2. (5) Apportion the difference in the interest rates in Step 4 by multiplying it by a fraction: The numerator is the difference determined in Step 3b and the denominator is the difference determined in Step 3a. (6) The interest rate is then the lower rate found in Step 2 plus the apportioned difference from Step 5.

> **GOT IT?**
>
> **M-5** Conceptually, what is the difference between a future value and a present value?
> **M-6** How do you compute the future value of a single sum?
> **M-7** Explain the factors in the future value of a single sum table.

HOW DO WE COMPUTE THE PRESENT VALUE OF A SINGLE SUM?

LEARNING OBJECTIVE M.3
Compute and use the present value of a single sum.

For present value of a single sum, we first explain the idea, then show the formula and present value factors using the table approach, and finally demonstrate an application.

The Idea

Present value of a single sum is the value in today's dollars of a cash flow to occur at a future date. *Discounting* **is the process of converting a future cash flow to a present value.**

Example: Present Value of a Single Sum

If $1,000 is worth $1,262.48 when it earns 6% compound interest per year for 4 years, then it follows that $1,262.48 to be received 4 years from now is worth $1,000 today if it is discounted at 6% interest per year. That is, $1,000 is the present value of $1,262.48 discounted at 6% for 4 years, as shown in **Example M.5**.

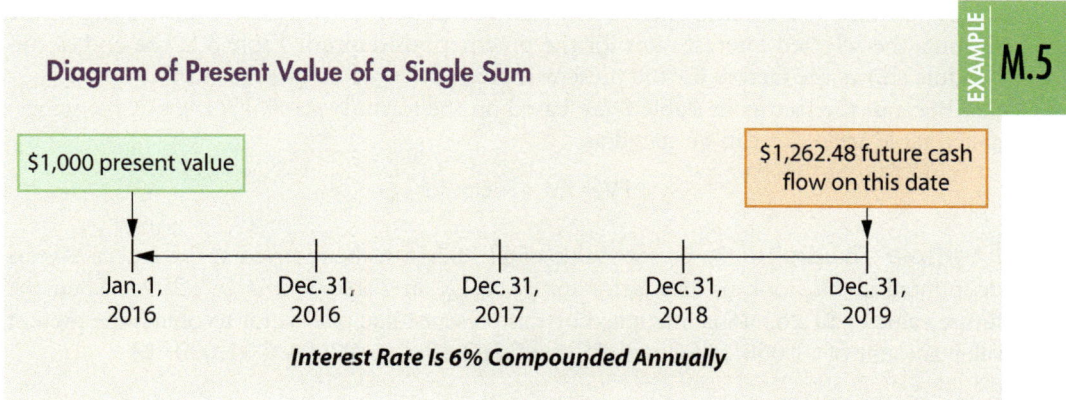

EXAMPLE M.5

Diagram of Present Value of a Single Sum

Interest Rate Is 6% Compounded Annually

Formula and Table Approaches

Because it is straightforward to calculate the present value of $1,262.48 to be received at the end of 4 years discounted at 6% by reversing the process described in the calculation of the future value, we do not show this approach here. Instead, we focus on determining the present value of a single sum by first presenting the formula, and then explaining how to compute and use present value factors.

Formula Approach The present value of a single future amount is the future amount discounted at the applicable interest rate per period over the appropriate number of periods. The formula is expressed as:

$$PV = FV \times \frac{1}{(1+i)^n}$$

where

PV = present value
FV = future value
i = interest rate for each of the stated time periods
n = number of time periods

Note that the present value is the reciprocal value of the future value of a single sum, and this formula is the reciprocal of the future value formula.

Example The present value of $1,262.48 received at the end of 4 years discounted at 6% is $1,000, calculated as follows:

$$PV = \$1{,}262.48 \times \frac{1}{(1.06)^4} = \$1{,}000$$

The formula for the present value factor of 1 is:

$$p_{n,i} = \frac{1}{(1+i)^n}$$

where $p_{n,i}$ is the present value of $1 at interest rate i for n periods. It is now possible to express the formula for the present value of any given future amount as:

$$PV = FV \times p_{n,i}$$

The example of the present value of $1,262.48 to be received 4 years from now with interest of 6% compounded annually can be calculated in two steps:

- *Step 1.* $\quad p_{n=4, i=6\%} = \dfrac{1}{(1.06)^4} = 0.792094$
- *Step 2.* $\quad PV = \$1{,}262.48 \times 0.792094 = \$1{,}000$ ■

Table Approach Tables of present value factors can be constructed using the formula for $p_{n,i}$ for any interest rate and for any number of periods by simply substituting in the formula the selected interest rates for the time periods desired. Table 3 at the end of this Module shows the factors for the present value of 1 ($p_{n,i}$).

Because the factors in Table 3 are based on the formula $p_{n,i} = 1/(1+i)^n$, the generalized table approach can be stated as:

$$PV = FV \times \text{Factor for } p_{n,i}$$

Example To calculate the present value of $1,262.48 to be received at the end of 4 years discounted at 6%, look up the factor for $p_{n=4, i=6\%}$ in Table 3; it is 0.792094. Then the future value of $1,262.48 is multiplied by this present value of 1 factor to obtain the present value amount of $1,000, as follows: $PV = \$1{,}262.48 \times 0.792094 = \$1{,}000$. ■

Application

In addition to calculating the present value of a single sum using compound interest, you can solve other kinds of problems with the present value of 1 table.

Example: Finding an Unstated Interest Rate

If the present value of $10,000 to be paid at the end of 10 years is $3,855.43, what interest rate compounded annually is used in the calculation of the present value?

Example M.6 diagrams the known facts. Because both the present value and the future amount are known, this problem can be solved in two different ways: (1) by using the method we described in the future value section or (2) by using the present value approach we describe here. Because we discussed the future value approach earlier in this Module, we use only the present value approach here to solve the problem. Using the table approach

$$PV = FV \times \text{Factor for } p_{n,i}$$

and substituting in the formula the known amounts shown in **Example M.6**, the factor is determined as follows:

$$\$3{,}855.43 = \$10{,}000.00 \times \text{Factor for } p_{n=10, i=?}$$

$$\text{Factor for } p_{n=10, i=?} = \frac{\$3{,}855.43}{\$10{,}000.00} = 0.385543$$

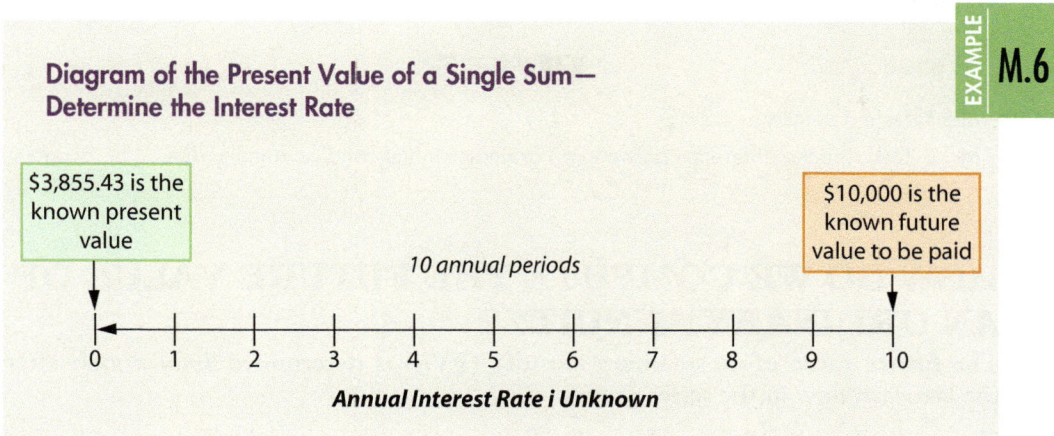

The factor of 0.385543 is the present value of 1 for 10 periods at an unknown interest rate. Using the present value of 1 table (Table 3), you look down the periods (n) column until you get to 10. Then you move horizontally across the columns on the $n = 10$ row to the factor closest to 0.385543. If the amount appears in the table, you can determine the interest rate (shown at the top of the column) that produces this amount. In this case, 0.385543 is in the 10% column. Thus, the annual rate is 10%. If the factor of 0.385543 does not appear in the table, an interpolation procedure is required to approximate the annual interest rate (see Footnote 3).

GOT IT?

M-8 What is the difference between present value and future value?

M-9 How do you compute the present value of a single sum?

M-10 Explain the factors in the present value of a single sum table.

WHAT ARE ANNUITIES?

LEARNING OBJECTIVE M.4
Understand annuities, including ordinary annuities and annuities due.

An **annuity** is a series of equal cash flows (deposits, receipts, payments, withdrawals) occurring at regular intervals with interest compounded at a specified rate. The regular intervals between the cash flows may be any time period—for example, 1 year, 6 months, 1 month, or even 1 day. In solving measurement problems involving the use of annuities, these four conditions must exist:

- periodic cash flows are equal in amount
- time periods between the cash flows are the same length
- interest rate is constant for each time period
- interest is compounded at the end of each time period

Annuities are used in many business contexts and transactions, including leases, bonds, mortgages, pensions, postemployment benefits, and others. An annuity is referred to as an **ordinary annuity** if the cash flows occur on the last day of each period. By contrast, an annuity is referred to as an **annuity due** if the cash flows occur on the first day of each period. For example, if you accept a job offer that will pay you a fixed monthly salary amount on the last day of each month, that would be an ordinary annuity. If you sign a lease for an apartment requiring a fixed amount of monthly rent with rent payments required on the first day of each month, the stream of rent payments would be an annuity due.

GOT IT?

M-11 Define annuity.

M-12 Describe the difference between an ordinary annuity and an annuity due.

LEARNING OBJECTIVE M.5
Compute and use the future value of an ordinary annuity.

HOW DO WE COMPUTE THE FUTURE VALUE OF AN ORDINARY ANNUITY?

The **future value of an ordinary annuity (FV_O)** is determined *immediately* after the last cash flow in the series occurs.

Example: Future Value of an Ordinary Annuity

Assume that you want to calculate the future value of four cash flows of $1,000, each with interest compounded annually at 6%. The first $1,000 cash flow occurs on December 31, 2016, and begins accruing interest at that time. The second, third, and fourth cash flows occur and begin accruing interest on December 31, 2017, 2018, and 2019, respectively, as shown in **Example M.7**.

EXAMPLE M.7

Diagram of Future Value of Ordinary Annuity

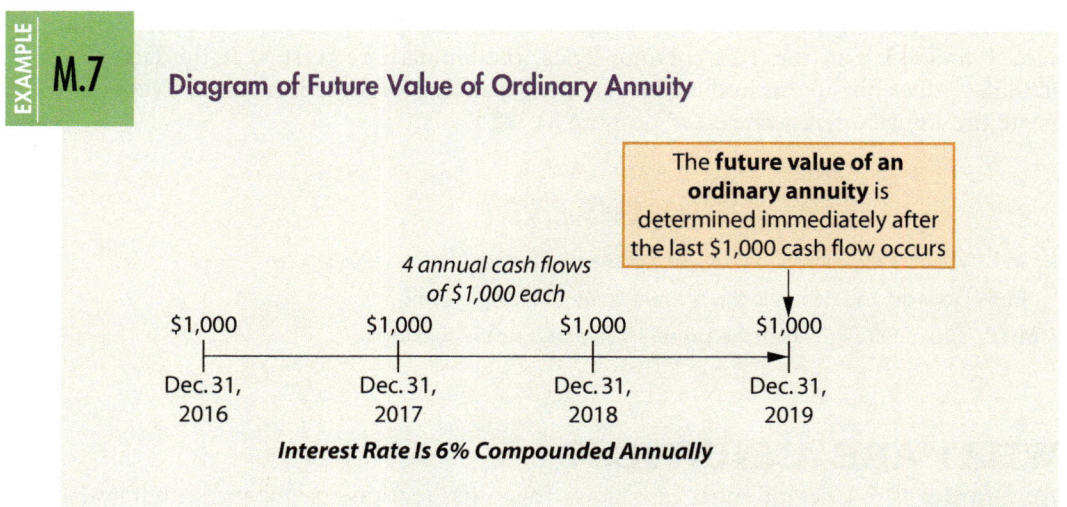

Formula Approach

The formula for the future value of an ordinary annuity of any amount is:

$$FV_O = C \times \left[\frac{(1+i)^n - 1}{i}\right]$$

where

FV_O = future value of an ordinary annuity
C = amount of each cash flow in the annuity
n = number of cash flows (not the number of time periods)
i = interest rate for all of the stated time periods

Example The future value of an ordinary annuity of four cash flows of $1,000 each at 6% compounded annually is as follows:

$$FV_O = \$1{,}000 \times \left[\frac{(1.06)^4 - 1}{0.06}\right] = \$4{,}374.62$$

The formula for the future value factor of an ordinary annuity with cash flows of $1 each period is as follows:

$$f_{O,n,i} = \left[\frac{(1+i)^n - 1}{i}\right]$$

where $f_{O,n,i}$ is the future value of an *ordinary* annuity (denoted O) of n cash flows of $1 each period at interest rate i.

With the preceding formula for $f_{O,n,i}$, it is possible to express another formula for the future value of an ordinary annuity of cash flows C in this manner:

$$FV_O = C \times f_{O,n,i}$$

In a two-step approach, the future value of an ordinary annuity of four cash flows of $1,000 each at 6% compounded annually is calculated as follows:

- Step 1. $f_{O,n=4,i=6\%} = \dfrac{(1.06)^4 - 1}{0.06} = 4.37462$
- Step 2. $\quad FV_O = \$1{,}000 \times 4.37462 = \$4{,}374.62$

This two-step approach is used to solve the problem when factors are not available.

Table Approach

The formula for $f_{O,n,i}$ can be used to construct a table of the future value of any annuity with cash flows of $1 each period for any interest rate. Here, the number of cash flows of $1 and the interest rates are substituted into the formula:

$$\frac{(1+i)^n - 1}{i}$$

Table 2 at the end of this Module shows the factors for $f_{O,n,i}$. Turning to Table 2, observe the following:

- The numbers in the first column (n) represent the number of cash flows.
- The future values are always equal to or larger than the number of cash flows. For example, the future value of four cash flows of 1 each at 6% is 4.374616. This figure comprises two elements: (a) the number of cash flows of 1 each *without* any interest and (b) the compound interest on the cash flows. Note that the last cash flow in the case of an ordinary annuity *does not* earn any interest because it occurs on the last day of the annuity period.

Because Table 2 shows the calculation of $f_{O,n,i}$ or

$$\frac{(1+i)^n - 1}{i}$$

values, the generalized table approach is as follows:

$$FV_O = C \times \text{Factor for } f_{O,n,i}$$

Example To calculate the future value of an ordinary annuity of four cash flows of $1,000 each at 6%, you must look up the $f_{O,n=4,i=6\%}$ factor in the future value of an ordinary annuity of 1 table (Table 2). This factor is 4.374616. Then the amount of each cash flow is multiplied by the Table 2 factor to obtain the future value of $4,374.62:

$$FV_O = \$1{,}000 \times 4.374616 = \$4{,}374.62$$

Applications

The formula for the future value of an annuity (above) has four parameters (FV_O, C, n, and i). As long as you know three of them, you can solve for the fourth. This means you can solve several kinds of problems using a future value of an ordinary annuity of 1 table, such as:

- calculating the future value when the cash flows and interest rate are known (the preceding problem)
- calculating the value of each cash flow when the number of cash flows, interest rate, and future value are known
- calculating the number of cash flows when the amount of each cash flow, interest rate, and future value are known
- calculating an unknown interest rate when the cash flows and the future value are known

Example: Determining the Amount of Annual Cash Flows Needed to Accumulate a Fund to Retire Debt

At the beginning of 2016, Rexson Company issued 10-year bonds with a face value of $1,000,000 due on December 31, 2025. Rexson will accumulate a fund to retire these bonds at maturity. It will make annual deposits to the fund beginning on December 31, 2016. How much must Rexson deposit each year, assuming that the fund will earn 12% interest compounded annually?

Example M.8 diagrams the facts of the problem. The future value and the compound interest rate are known. The amount of each of the 10 deposits (cash flows) is the unknown factor. Starting with the formula:

$$FV_O = C \times \text{Factor for } f_O$$

and then shifting the elements and substituting the known amount and applicable factor (from Table 2), the amount of each annual deposit is $56,984.16, calculated as follows:

$$C = \frac{FV_O}{\text{Factor for } f_{O,n,i}}$$

$$= \frac{FV_O}{\text{Factor for } f_{O, n=10, i=12\%}}$$

$$= \frac{\$1,000,000}{17.548735}$$

$$= \$56,984.16$$

The 10 annual deposits of $56,984.16, plus the compound interest, will accumulate to $1,000,000 by December 31, 2025.

EXAMPLE M.8 — Future Value of an Ordinary Annuity—Determine the Amount of the Cash Flows

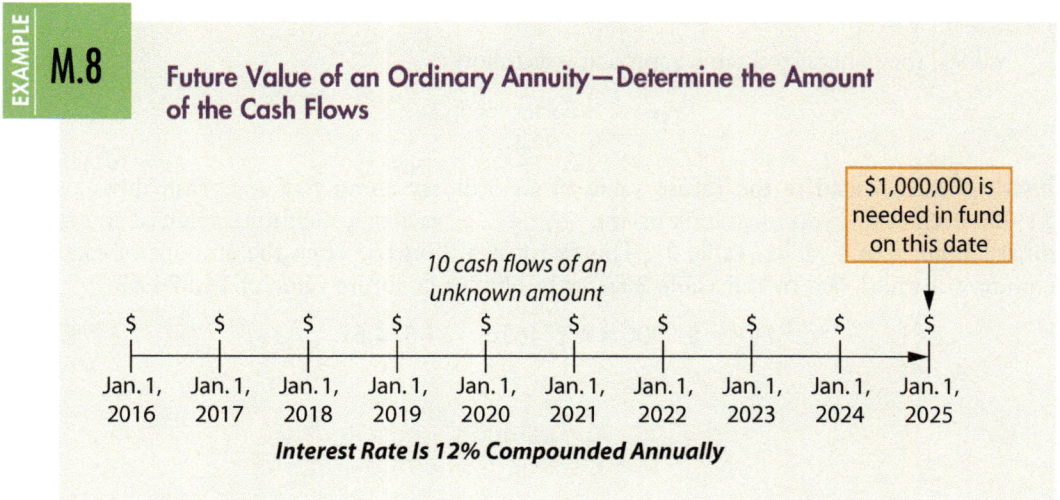

Interest Rate Is 12% Compounded Annually

GOT IT?

M-13 Distinguish between the future value of $1 and the future value of an ordinary annuity of $1.

M-14 How do you compute the future value of an ordinary annuity?

HOW DO WE COMPUTE THE FUTURE VALUE OF AN ANNUITY DUE?

LEARNING OBJECTIVE M.6

Compute and use the future value of an annuity due.

The **future value of an annuity due (FV_D)** is determined 1 period after the last cash flow in the series.

Example: Future Value of an Annuity Due

Assume that you deposit in a fund four payments of $1,000 each beginning January 1, 2016, with the last deposit being made on January 1, 2019. How much will be in the fund on December 31, 2019, one year after the final payment, if the fund earns interest at 6% compounded annually? **Example M.9** diagrams the facts of this problem.

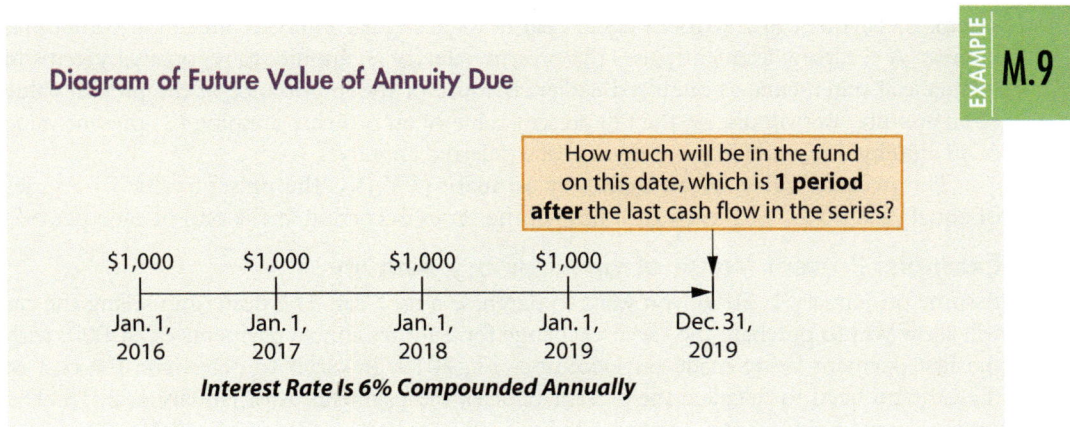

Diagram of Future Value of Annuity Due

EXAMPLE M.9

How much will be in the fund on this date, which is **1 period after** the last cash flow in the series?

$1,000 — Jan. 1, 2016
$1,000 — Jan. 1, 2017
$1,000 — Jan. 1, 2018
$1,000 — Jan. 1, 2019
Dec. 31, 2019

Interest Rate Is 6% Compounded Annually

Table Approach

By observing the information contained in **Examples M.9** and **M.7**, you can determine a quick way to compute the future value of an annuity due.[4] When only the future value of an *ordinary* annuity table is available, **the general rule is to use the future value of an ordinary annuity factor for $n + 1$ cash flows and subtract 1 from the factor.** You can use the factors by completing the following steps.

Example

- **Step 1.** In the *ordinary* annuity table (Table 2), look up the value of $n + 1$ cash flows at 6% (in this example, the value of 5 cash flows at 6%).   5.637093
- **Step 2.** Subtract 1 from the value obtained in Step 1.   (1.000000)
  This is the converted future value factor for an annuity due, $f_{D, n=4, i=6\%}$.   4.637093
- **Step 3.** Multiply the amount of each cash flow, here $1,000, by the converted factor for $f_{D, n=4, i=6\%}$ determined in Step 2:
  $FV_D = \$1,000 \times 4.637093 = \$4,637.09$

---

[4] An alternative approach is to multiply the future value of an ordinary annuity factor by 1 plus the interest rate. Thus, the future value in this example would be computed as $\$1,000 \times (4.374616 \times 1.06) = \$4,637.09$.

Tables of the future value of an annuity due of cash flows of 1 each period are available in some finance books, but not in this book. Therefore, these values must be calculated using the tables for the future value of an *ordinary* annuity. (Note that we do include in this Module a present value of an annuity due table, as we discuss later.)

GOT IT?

M-15 Distinguish between the future value of $1 and the future value of an annuity due of $1.

M-16 How do you compute the future value of an annuity due?

M-17 Distinguish between the future value of an ordinary annuity and the future value of an annuity due. Draw a time line of each.

LEARNING OBJECTIVE M.7
Compute and use the present value of an ordinary annuity.

HOW DO WE COMPUTE THE PRESENT VALUE OF AN ORDINARY ANNUITY?

The present value of an annuity is the present value of a series of equal cash flows that occur in the future. It represents the current period amount of cash that will provide for a receipt or payment of a series of equal cash flows at regular intervals, including compound interest. A company frequently uses the present value of an annuity to report many items in its financial statements, as discussed earlier. Because of the importance of the present value of an annuity, we will discuss the (1) present value of an ordinary annuity, (2) present value of an annuity due, and (3) present value of a deferred annuity.

The **present value of an ordinary annuity (PV_O)** is the present value of a series of equal cash flows, with each cash flow in the series occurring at the end of each period.

Example: Present Value of an Ordinary Annuity

Assume on January 1, 2016, you want to purchase a used car. The dealership selling the car will allow you to purchase the car in exchange for 4 future annual payments of $1,000, with the first payment being made on December 31, 2016. In order to determine the cost of the car, you need to calculate the present value of the payments as of January 1, 2016. The applicable interest rate is 6% compounded annually, as shown in **Example M.10**.

EXAMPLE M.10 Diagram of Present Value of an Ordinary Annuity

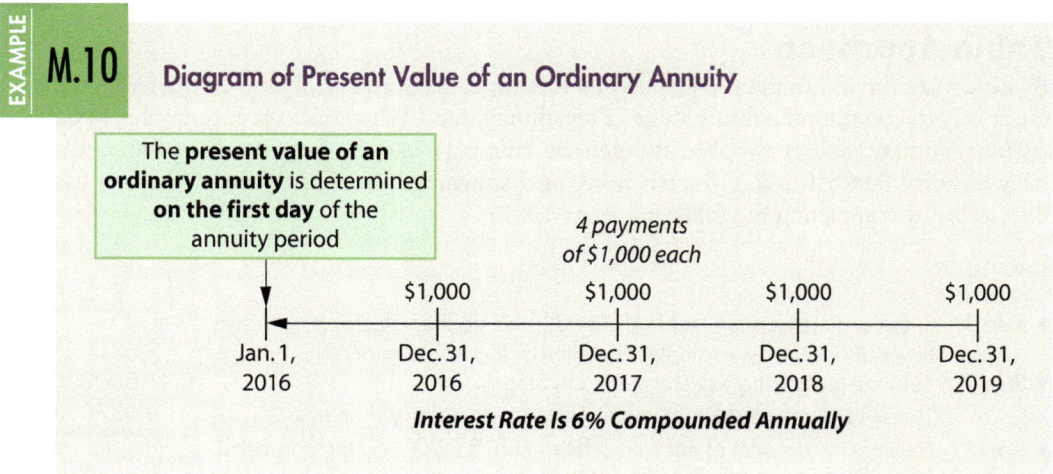

Example: Solving by Determining the Present Value of a Series of Single Sums

The solution to this problem can be determined by using the present value of a series of single sums. For instance, the answer can be calculated in the following two steps: (1) determine the present value of four individual cash flows of $1 each for 1, 2, 3, and 4 years, as shown in **Example M.10a** and (2) sum them and multiply the result by $1,000.

- *Step 1.* The present value of four cash flows of $1 for 1, 2, 3, and 4 years discounted at 6% is determined in Example M.10a.
- *Step 2.* Now it is possible to determine the present value of the four cash flows of $1,000 each by multiplying the $1,000 by 3.465105:
$1,000 × 3.465105 = $3,465.11

The present value on January 1, 2016, is $3,465.11, given an interest rate of 6%.

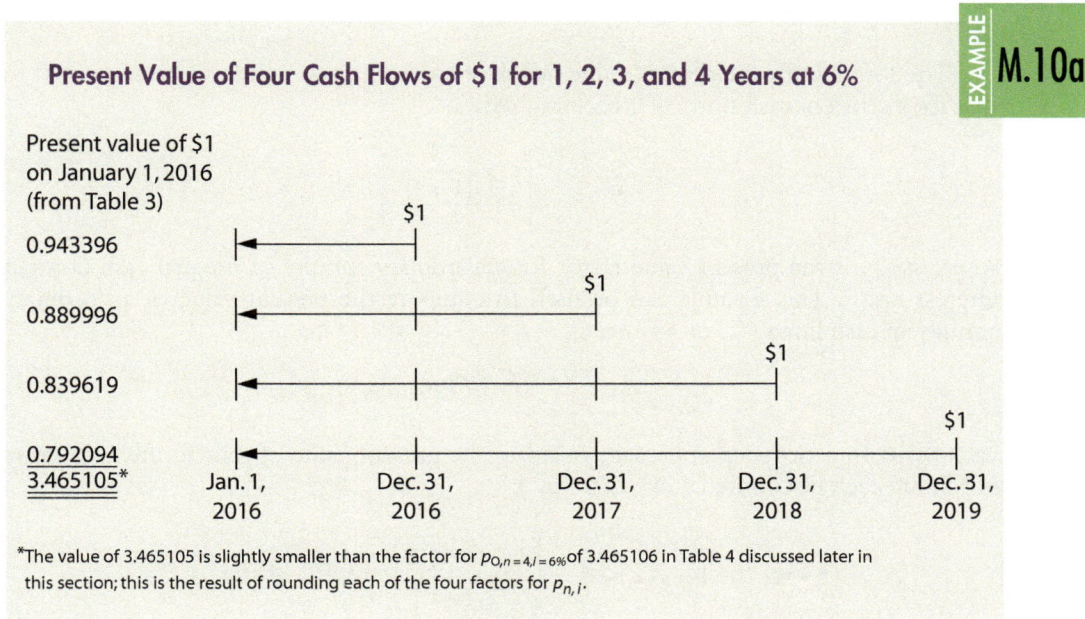

EXAMPLE M.10a

Present Value of Four Cash Flows of $1 for 1, 2, 3, and 4 Years at 6%

Present value of $1 on January 1, 2016 (from Table 3)
0.943396
0.889996
0.839619
0.792094
3.465105*

Jan. 1, 2016 — Dec. 31, 2016 — Dec. 31, 2017 — Dec. 31, 2018 — Dec. 31, 2019

*The value of 3.465105 is slightly smaller than the factor for $p_{O,n=4, i=6\%}$ of 3.465106 in Table 4 discussed later in this section; this is the result of rounding each of the four factors for $p_{n,i}$.

Formula Approach Even though the preceding approach can be used, it is time-consuming for calculations involving a large number of cash flows. The general formula for the present value of an ordinary annuity of any amount is:

$$PV_O = C \times \left[\frac{1 - \frac{1}{(1+i)^n}}{i} \right]$$

where

PV_O = present value of an ordinary annuity
C = amount of each cash flow
n = number of cash flows (not the number of time periods)
i = interest rate for each of the stated time periods

Example The present value of an ordinary annuity of four cash flows of $1,000 each at 6% compounded annually can be calculated as follows:

$$PV_O = \$1,000 \times \left[\frac{1 - \frac{1}{(1.06)^4}}{0.06} \right] = \$3,465.11$$

Based on these calculations and formula, observe that:

- The results are the same as those produced in the first approach, $3,465.11.

- The formula is developed from the formulas for the factors for both the future value of $1(f)$ and the present value of $1(p)$:

$$(1 + i)^n = f$$

$$\frac{1}{(1 + i)^n} = p$$

- The formula can be restated as follows:

$$PV_O = C \times \left(\frac{1 - p}{i}\right)$$

The formula for the present value factor of an ordinary annuity can be converted to that for a series of cash flows of 1 each as follows:

$$p_{O,n,i} = \left[\frac{1 - \frac{1}{(1 + i)^n}}{i}\right]$$

where $p_{O,n,i}$ is the present value factor for an ordinary annuity of n equal cash flows at interest rate i. This formula can be used to compute the present value of an ordinary annuity of cash flows (C) of *any size* as:

$$PV_O = C \times p_{O,n,i}$$

Example In a two-step approach, calculate the present value of four future cash flows of $1,000 each discounted at 6% as follows:

- Step 1. $\quad p_{O, n = 4, i = 6\%} = \left[\dfrac{1 - \dfrac{1}{(1.06)^4}}{0.06}\right] = 3.46511$

- Step 2. $\quad PV_O = \$1{,}000 \times 3.46511 = \$3{,}465.11$

This calculation is exactly the same as that of the first formula except that the process is divided into two steps. ∎

Table Approach The formula for $p_{O,n,i}$ can be used to construct a table of the present value factors for any series of cash flows of $1 each period for any interest rate. All that is necessary is to enter in the formula the desired number of cash flows and the required interest rates. Table 4 at the end of the Module shows the present value factors for $p_{O,n,i}$. Turning to Table 4, observe the following:

- The numbers in the first column (n) represent the number of cash flows of $1 each. In this calculation, the number of cash flows and time periods are equal.
- The present value amounts are always smaller than the number of cash flows of $1. For example, the present value of three cash flows of $1 at 2% is $2.883883.

Because Table 4 shows the present value factors $p_{O,n,i}$ or

$$\frac{1 - \frac{1}{(1 + i)^n}}{i}$$

the generalized table approach is as follows:

$$PV_O = C \times \text{Factor for } P_{O,n,i}$$

Example To calculate the present value on January 1, 2016, of four future payments of $1,000 discounted at 6%, with the first cash flow being paid on December 31, 2016, find the $P_{O, n=4, i=6\%}$ value in the present value of an ordinary annuity of 1 table (Table 4); it is 3.465106. Then multiply this factor by $1,000 to determine the present value figure of $3,465.11:

$$PV_O = \$1,000 \times 3.465106 = \$3,465.11$$

Over the four periods, the annuity yields interest each period as follows:

Period	Beginning Balance	Interest at 6%	Cash Flow	Ending Balance
2016	$3,465.11	$207.91	$(1,000)	$2,673.02
2017	2,673.02	160.38	(1,000)	1,833.40
2018	1,833.40	110.00	(1,000)	943.40
2019	943.40	56.60	(1,000)	0

Applications The formula for the present value of an ordinary annuity (above) has four parameters (PV_O, C, n, and i). As long as you know three of them, you can solve for the fourth. This means you can solve several kinds of problems by using the present value of an ordinary annuity of 1 table. We present one additional example: a problem involving the calculation of the periodic cash flows when the present value and interest rate are known.

Example: Determining the Periodic Cash Flows When the Present Value Is Known

On January 1, 2016, Rex Company borrows $100,000 to finance a plant expansion project. It hopes to be able to pay this amount back with interest at 12% in equal annual payments over a 10-year period, with the payments due on December 31. What is the amount of each payment Rex Company will have to make? **Example M.11** diagrams the facts of the problem.

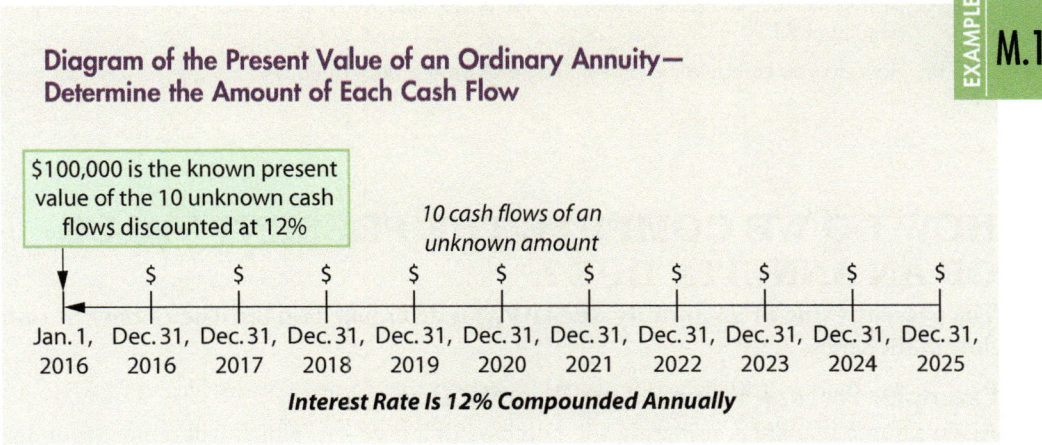

EXAMPLE M.11

Diagram of the Present Value of an Ordinary Annuity—Determine the Amount of Each Cash Flow

$100,000 is the known present value of the 10 unknown cash flows discounted at 12%

10 cash flows of an unknown amount

Jan. 1, 2016, Dec. 31, 2016, Dec. 31, 2017, Dec. 31, 2018, Dec. 31, 2019, Dec. 31, 2020, Dec. 31, 2021, Dec. 31, 2022, Dec. 31, 2023, Dec. 31, 2024, Dec. 31, 2025

Interest Rate Is 12% Compounded Annually

The present value, the compound interest rate, and the number of cash flows are known. The amount of each of the 10 cash flows is the unknown item. We can calculate that the annual cash flow C is $17,698.42, as follows:

$$C = \frac{PV_O}{\text{Factor for } p_{O,n,i}}$$

$$= \frac{PV_O}{\text{Factor for } p_{O, n=10, i=12\%}}$$

$$= \frac{\$100,000}{5.650223}$$

$$= \$17,698.42$$

Remember that each of these payments of $17,698.42 includes (1) a payment of annual interest and (2) a retirement of debt principal. The loan payments, amounts of principal and interest in each payment, and the outstanding balance each period are shown in the following table (known as a loan amortization table). For example, the interest for 2016 is $12,000 (12% × $100,000). Thus, the amount of the payment of principal is $5,698.42 ($17,698.42 − $12,000). For 2017, the interest is $11,316.19 [12% × ($100,000 − $5,698.42)], and the retirement of principal is $6,382.23 ($17,698.42 − $11,316.19). The *last* payment of $17,698.42 on December 31, 2025, will be sufficient to retire the remaining principal and to pay the interest for the tenth year.

Period End Date (Dec. 31)	Beginning Balance	Payment	Interest @ 12%	Principal	Ending Balance
2016	$100,000.00	$17,698.42	$12,000.00	$ 5,698.42	$94,301.58
2017	94,301.58	17,698.42	11,316.19	6,382.23	87,919.35
2018	87,919.35	17,698.42	10,550.32	7,148.10	80,771.25
2019	80,771.25	17,698.42	9,692.55	8,005.87	72,765.38
2020	72,765.38	17,698.42	8,731.85	8,966.57	63,798.81
2021	63,798.81	17,698.42	7,655.86	10,042.56	53,756.24
2022	53,756.24	17,698.42	6,450.75	11,247.67	42,508.57
2023	42,508.57	17,698.42	5,101.03	12,597.39	29,911.18
2024	29,911.18	17,698.42	3,589.34	14,109.08	15,802.10
2025	15,802.10	17,698.42	1896.32*	15,802.10	0.00

*Adjusted $0.07 for rounding

GOT IT?

M-18 Distinguish between the present value of $1 and the present value of an ordinary annuity of $1.

M-19 How do you compute the present value of an ordinary annuity?

LEARNING OBJECTIVE M.8

Compute and use the present value of an annuity due.

HOW DO WE COMPUTE THE PRESENT VALUE OF AN ANNUITY DUE?

The **present value of an annuity due** (PV_D) is determined on the date of the first cash flow in the series.

Example: Present Value of an Annuity Due

Again assume you are considering the purchase of a used car, which will require four annual payments of $1,000 each, but now assume the first payment will be due today and each remaining payment occurs on the first day of the year. To compute the cost of the car, you need to calculate the present value of this annuity on January 1, 2016, the day of the first payment. The interest rate is 6% compounded annually. **Example M.12** shows the facts of this problem.

Formula Approach

As in **Example M.10a** (p. M-17) which computes the present value of an ordinary annuity by summing the present values of each cash flow in the series, the present value of an annuity due can also be determined by summing the present value of each cash flow (note that the first cash flow is already in present value). That approach can be

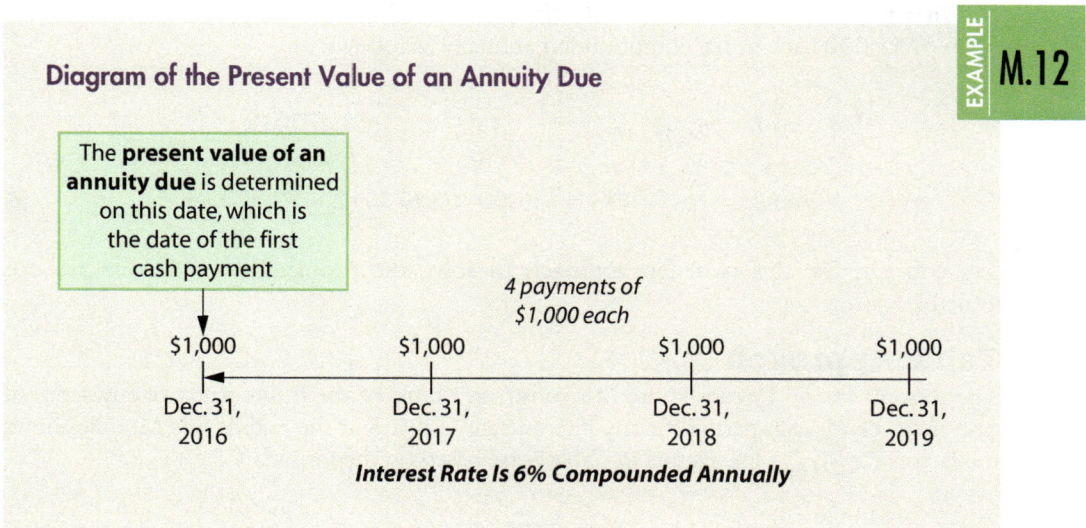

EXAMPLE M.12

cumbersome and time-consuming for a long series of cash flows, in which case the formula approach can be used. The formula for the present value of an annuity due of any cash flow amount is:

$$PV_D = C \times \left[\frac{1 - \frac{1}{(1+i)^{n-1}}}{i} + 1 \right]$$

where

PV_D = present value of an ordinary annuity of a series of cash flows of any amount
C = amount of each cash flow
n = number of cash flows (not the number of time periods)
i = interest rate for each of the stated time periods

Example The present value of an annuity due of four cash flows of $1,000 each at 6% compounded annually is calculated as follows:

$$PV_D = \$1,000 \times \left[\frac{1 - \frac{1}{1.06^3}}{0.06} + 1 \right] = \$3,673.01$$

The formula for the present value factor for an annuity due with cash flows of 1 each is:

$$p_{D,n,i} = \left[\frac{1 - \frac{1}{(1+i)^{n-1}}}{i} + 1 \right]$$

where $p_{D,n,i}$ is the present value of an annuity *due* of n cash flows of $1 each period at interest rate i. Note that the present value of the payments of the annuity due ($3,673.01) is greater than that of the ordinary annuity from the prior example ($3,465.11) because the present value of payments at the start of the period is greater than the present value of payments made at the end of the period.

With the preceding formula for $p_{D,n,i}$, it is possible to express another formula for the present value of an annuity due of cash flows of any size as:

$$PV_D = C \times p_{D,n,i}$$

In a two-step approach, calculate the present value of an annuity due of four cash flows of $1,000 each at 6% compounded annually as follows:

- Step 1. $p_{D, n=4, i=6\%} = \left[\dfrac{1 - \dfrac{1}{1.06^3}}{0.06} + 1 \right] = 3.673012$

- Step 2. $PV_D = \$1{,}000 \times 3.673012 = \$3{,}673.01$ ■

You can use this two-step approach to solve the problem when factors are not available.

Table Approach

The formula for $p_{D,n,i}$ can be used to construct a table of the future value of any series of cash flows of $1 each period for any interest rate. Table 5 at the end of this Module shows the factors for $p_{D,n,i}$. The factors in Table 5 are based on the formula for $p_{D,n,i}$ or

$$\dfrac{1 - \dfrac{1}{(1+i)^{n-1}}}{i} + 1$$

Therefore, computing the present value of an annuity due using the table approach is as follows:

$$PV_D = C \times \text{Factor for } p_{D,n,i}$$

Example To calculate the present value of an annuity due of four cash flows of $1,000 each at 6%, find the $p_{D, n=4, i=6\%}$ factor in the present value of an annuity due table (Table 5). This value is 3.673012. Then multiply the amount of each cash flow by the Table 5 factor to obtain the present value of $3,673.01:

$$PV_D = \$1{,}000 \times 3.673012 = \$3{,}673.01$$ ■

Alternative Table Approach By observing the information contained in **Examples M.12** and **M.10**, you can determine another way to compute the present value of an annuity due.[5] When only the present value of an *ordinary* annuity table is available, **the general rule is to use the present value of an ordinary annuity factor for $n - 1$ cash flows and add 1 to the factor.** You can use the factors to determine the present value of an annuity due with the following steps:

Example

- Step 1. In the ordinary annuity table (Table 4), look up the present value of $n - 1$ cash flows at 6%, in this case, the value of three cash flows at 6%.   2.673012
- Step 2. Add 1 to the value obtained in Step 1.   1.000000
  This is the converted present value factor for $p_{D, n=4, i=6\%}$.   3.673012
- Step 3. Multiply the amount of each cash flow, here $1,000, by the converted factor for $p_{D, n=4, i=6\%}$ determined in Step 2:

$$PV_D = \$1{,}000 \times 3.673012 = \$3{,}673.01$$ ■

---

[5] An alternative approach is to multiply the present value of an ordinary annuity factor by 1 plus the interest rate, which is consistent with the formula:

$$\dfrac{1 - \dfrac{1}{(1+i)^{n-1}}}{i} \times (1 + i)$$

Thus, the present value in this example would be computed as $1,000 × (3.465106 × 1.06) = $3,673.01.

Application

The formula for the present value of an annuity due (above) has four parameters (PV_D, C, n, and i). As long as you know three of them, you can solve for the fourth. This means you can solve many types of problems by using the preceding approaches.

Example: Amount of Each Cash Flow to Be Determined

On January 1, 2016, you purchase an item that costs $10,000. You agree to pay for this item in 10 equal annual installments, with the first installment on January 1, 2016, as a down payment. The equal installments include interest at 8% on the unpaid balance at the beginning of each year. After the interest is deducted, the balance of each payment reduces the principal of the debt. This problem involves the present value of an annuity due and requires the determination of the amount of each of 10 cash flows that have a present value of $10,000 when discounted at an annual rate of 8%. **Example M.13** shows these facts graphically.

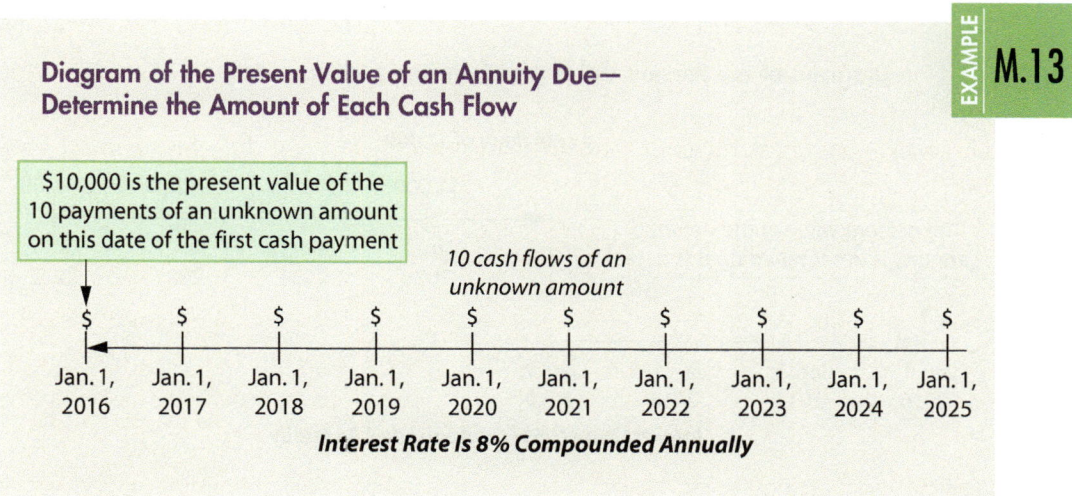

EXAMPLE M.13

Diagram of the Present Value of an Annuity Due— Determine the Amount of Each Cash Flow

The solution to this problem requires the rearrangement of the present value of an annuity due formula:

$$C = \frac{PV_D}{\text{Factor for } p_{D,n,i}}$$

$$= \frac{\$10,000}{7.246888} = \$1,379.90$$

The down payment of $1,379.90 plus nine more payments of this same amount will retire the principal in 9 years, plus pay interest at 8% on the balance of the principal outstanding at the beginning of each year. ■

GOT IT?

M-20 Distinguish between the present value of $1 and the present value of an annuity due of $1.

M-21 How do you compute the present value of an annuity due?

M-22 Distinguish between the future value of an ordinary annuity and the future value of an annuity due. Draw a time line of each.

LEARNING OBJECTIVE M.9
Compute and use the present value of a deferred ordinary annuity.

HOW DO WE COMPUTE THE PRESENT VALUE OF A DEFERRED ANNUITY?

A **deferred ordinary annuity** is an ordinary annuity in which the first payment in the annuity begins on a future date. **The present value of a deferred ordinary annuity ($PV_{deferred}$) is therefore determined on today's date, even though the annuity payments begin two or more periods after today's date.**

Example: Present Value of a Deferred Ordinary Annuity

Suppose that you purchase a used car on January 1, 2016. The car dealership requires four annual receipts of $1,000 each, with the first payment due on January 1, 2020. The interest rate is 6% compounded annually. What is the cost of the used car? That is, what is the present value on January 1, 2016, of the four cash flows of $1,000 each to be paid on January 1, 2020, 2021, 2022, and 2023, discounted at 6%? Example M.14 diagrams the facts of this problem. ■

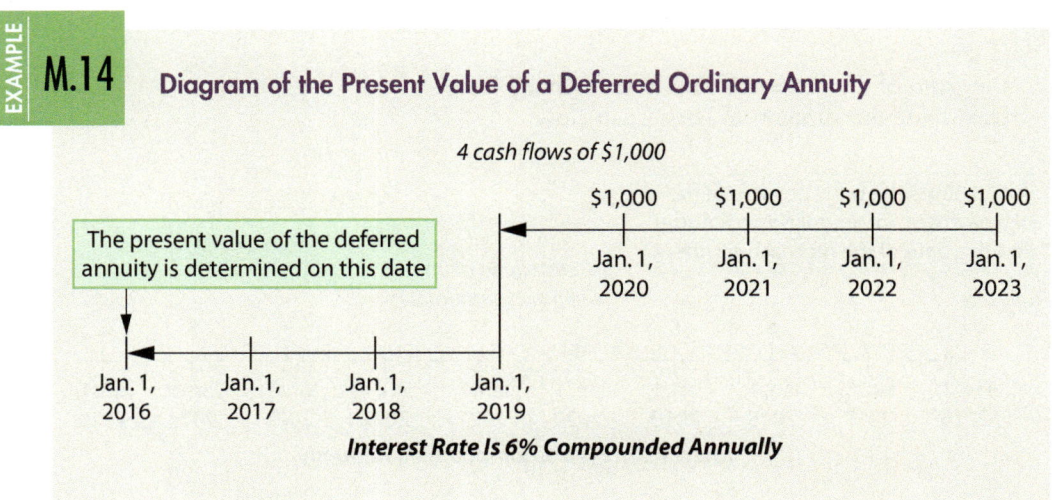

EXAMPLE M.14 Diagram of the Present Value of a Deferred Ordinary Annuity

There are two ways to compute the present value of a deferred annuity. The first method involves a combination of the present value of an ordinary annuity (PV_O) and the present value of a single sum due in the future (PV).

Example To conceptualize this approach, view the deferred annuity as a 4-year ordinary annuity that is deferred for 3 years. For the stated problem, it is necessary to determine first the present value of an *ordinary* annuity of four cash flows of $1,000 each to find a single present value figure discounted to the beginning of the ordinary annuity period, which is January 1, 2019. Note that because the present value of an ordinary annuity table is used, the present value of the four cash flows is computed as of January 1, 2019. That single sum is then discounted for three more periods at 6% to arrive at the present value on January 1, 2016 (today). Using the factors of $1 each, the present value is stated as follows:

$$PV_{deferred} = C \times p_{O,n,i} \times p_{k,i}$$

where

$p_{O,n,i}$ = present value of the ordinary annuity of the n cash flows of 1 at the given interest rate i
$p_{k,i}$ = present value of the single sum of 1 for k periods of deferral

Substituting appropriate factors from Tables 4 and 3, respectively, in this formula, the following solution is obtained:

$$P_{deferred} = C \times p_{O,n,i} \times p_{k,i}$$
$$= \$1,000 \times 3.465106 \times 0.839619$$
$$= \$2,909.37$$

■

An alternative approach involves a combination of two ordinary annuities. For example, it is possible to calculate the present value of an ordinary annuity of $n + k$ cash flows of 1. From this amount is subtracted the present value of the k (the number of periods of deferral, which is 3 years in this example) cash flows of 1. This procedure removes the cash flows that did not occur; yet the discount factor for the three periods of deferral on the four cash flows that are to be received remains in the calculated factor. This difference is multiplied by the value of each cash flow to determine the final present value of the deferred annuity. **Example M.15** illustrates this approach.

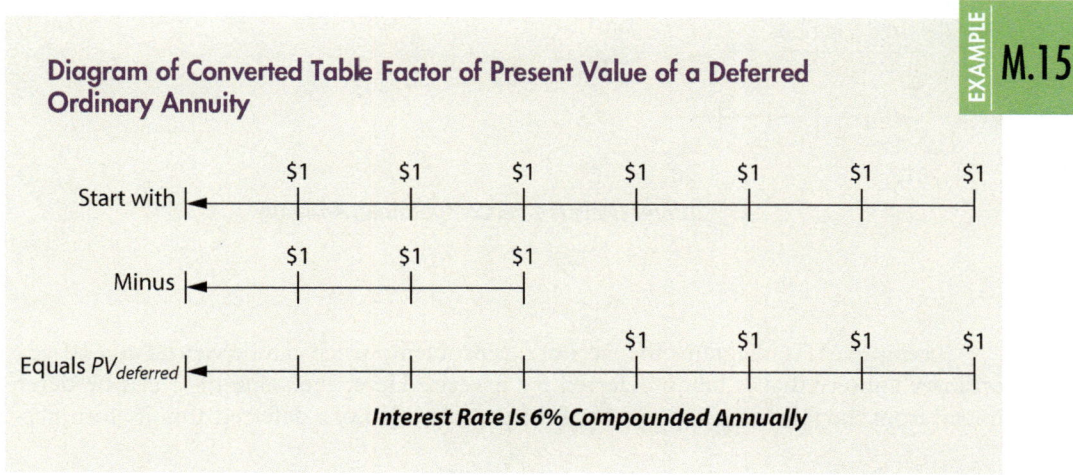

EXAMPLE M.15

Diagram of Converted Table Factor of Present Value of a Deferred Ordinary Annuity

Interest Rate Is 6% Compounded Annually

In effect, the present value of an ordinary annuity of $n + k$ cash flows, minus the present value of an ordinary annuity of the k cash flows, becomes a converted factor for the present value of a deferred annuity, as follows:

$$PV_{deferred} = C \times \text{(Converted Factor for Present Value of Deferred Annuity of 1)}$$

Example Using the factors from Table 4, the converted factor for the deferred ordinary annuity stated in the preceding problem is determined as follows:

$$P_{O, n+k=7, i=6\%} - P_{O, k=3, i=6\%}$$
$$= 5.582381 - 2.673012 = 2.909369$$

The present value of the four cash flows of $1,000 each, deferred three periods, is $2,909.37, calculated as follows:

$$PV_{deferred} = \$1,000 \times 2.909369 = \$2,909.37$$

Note that the two methods produce the same present value. Also, note that the period of deferral is *only* three periods and *not* four because the present value of an ordinary annuity table is used (see **Example M.15** in the second approach). This assumption is required if the problem is to be solved by the use of *ordinary* annuity factors rather than annuity due factors.

Application

In addition to determining the present value of a deferred annuity, other types of problems can be solved by using the previous approaches.

Example: Amount of Each Cash Flow to Be Determined

David Jones wants to invest $50,000 on January 1, 2016, so that he may withdraw 10 annual cash flows of equal amounts beginning January 1, 2022. If the fund earns 12% annual interest over its life, what will be the amount of each of the 10 withdrawals?

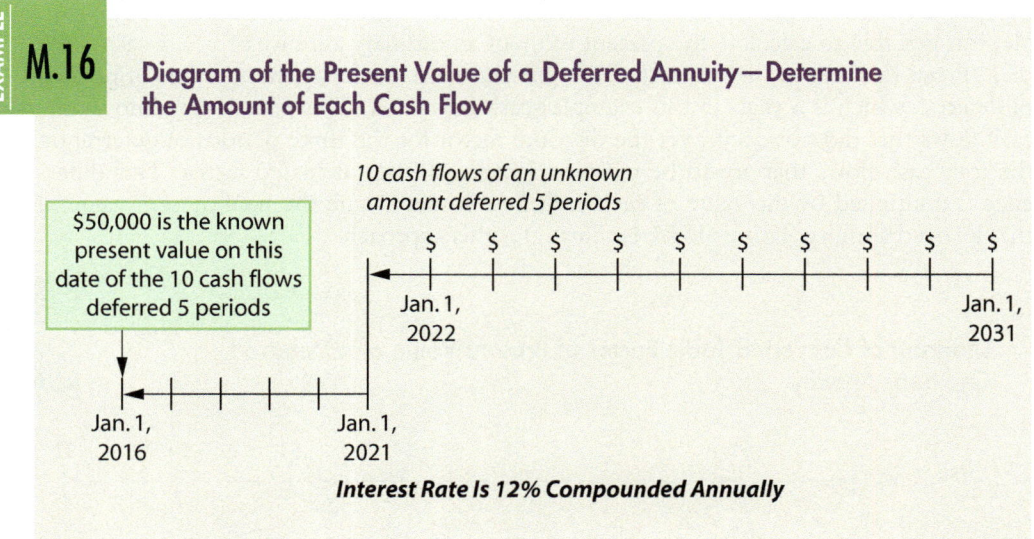

EXAMPLE M.16 Diagram of the Present Value of a Deferred Annuity—Determine the Amount of Each Cash Flow

Example M.16 diagrams the facts of this problem, which can be viewed as a 10-year ordinary annuity that is being deferred for 5 years. Here, the value of C can be determined from the following expression of the present value of a deferred annuity formula:

$$C = \frac{PV_{deferred}}{\text{Converted Factor for Present Value of Deferred Annuity of 1}}$$

Using Table 4, the converted factor for 10 cash flows of $1 each year (Years 6 through 15) deferred 5 years at 12% is as follows:

$$\text{Converted Factor} = p_{O, n+k=15, i=12\%} - p_{O, k=5, i=12\%}$$

$$= 6.810864 - 3.604776 = 3.206088$$

Then the amount of each cash flow is:

$$C = \frac{\$50{,}000}{3.206088} = \$15{,}595.33$$

The accuracy of the answer produced by the second approach can be tested using the amount of each cash flow and the solution from the first approach. The present value of 10 cash flows of $15,595.33 deferred five periods and discounted at 12% must be $50,000 if the first solution is correct. The proof can be calculated as follows:

$$PV_{deferred} = \$15{,}595.33 \times 5.650223 \times 0.567427$$
$$= \$50{,}000$$

A slight rounding-error difference may occur with this method because the solution involves multiplying two factors, $p_{O,n,i}$ and $p_{k,i}$, which are rounded. ■

SUMMARY OF PRESENT AND FUTURE VALUE CALCULATIONS

The present and future value calculations discussed in this Module are summarized by Exhibit M.1.

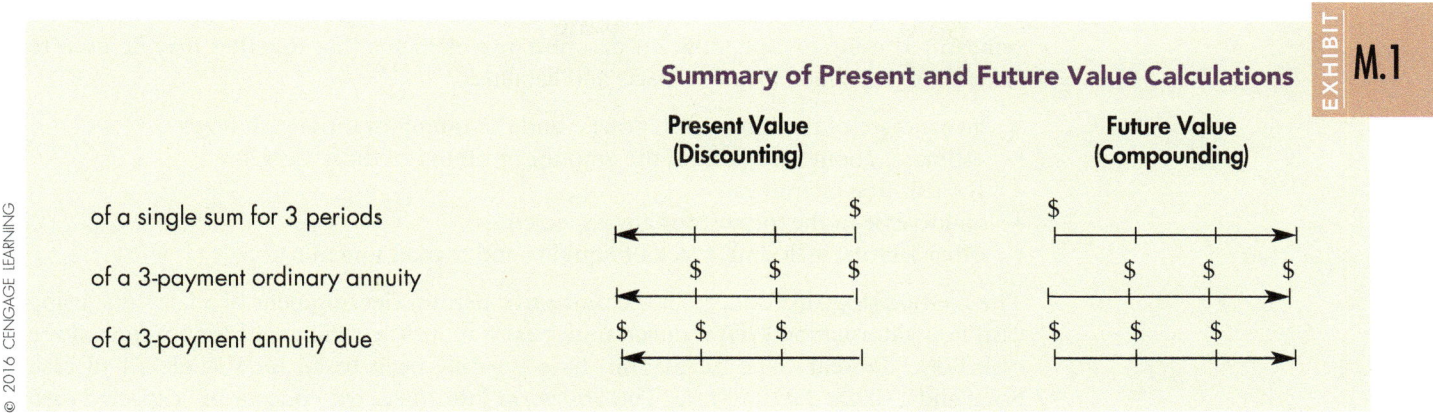

GOT IT?

M-23 What is a deferred ordinary annuity? How does it differ from one that is not deferred? Draw a time line of each.

M-24 How do you compute the present value of a deferred ordinary annuity?

M-25 Explain how to determine the converted factor for any deferred annuity by using the present value of an ordinary annuity table.

HOW DO WE USE PRESENT VALUE TECHNIQUES IN FINANCIAL REPORTING?

LEARNING OBJECTIVE M.10
Explain the conceptual issues regarding the use of present value in financial reporting.

Present values are used in GAAP for a variety of monetary assets and liabilities. A monetary item is cash or a claim to cash flows that is not affected by changes in the prices of specific goods or services. For example, a note receivable is a monetary item, whereas property, plant, and equipment is a nonmonetary item. Monetary items for which present values are used in GAAP include bonds payable and bond investments, long-term notes payable and receivable, leases, and postretirement benefits (e.g., pensions). Accounting principles have not been extended to use present value for nonmonetary items, except for the impairment of noncurrent assets. Therefore, present values are not used for deferred income taxes, warranty obligations, unearned revenue, compensated absences, or nonmonetary assets. We discuss each of these topics in later chapters of this book.

Most accountants would argue that the use of present value creates a *relevant* accounting measurement. For example, in the situations we discussed earlier, present value amounts are more relevant than, for example, the total of the undiscounted cash flows because they represent the equivalent current cash amount. However, present value measurements involve estimation of:

- future cash flows, including the timing, amount, and risk of those cash flows
- interest rates, including the historical rate, current rate, average expected rate, weighted average cost of capital, or incremental borrowing rate

In 2000, the FASB issued *FASB Statement of Financial Accounting Concepts No. 7*, "Using Cash Flow Information and Present Value in Accounting Measurements."[6] The *Statement* provides a framework for using future cash flows as the basis for an accounting measurement of both assets and liabilities. It provides general principles governing the use of present value, as well as the objectives of present value accounting measurements. The *Statement* does not address recognition issues, and therefore does not address when

---

[6] "Using Cash Flow Information and Present Value in Accounting Measurements," *FASB Statement of Financial Accounting Concepts No. 7* (Norwalk, CT: FASB, 2000).

fair value should be based on present value, or when assets or liabilities should be remeasured using present value. It describes five elements that together may be used to determine the value of various assets and liabilities:

- an estimate of the future cash flow(s) and the timing of those cash flows
- estimates about variations in the amount or timing of those cash flows
- the risk-free interest rate
- an increase in the interest for any expected risk
- other factors, including a lack of liquidity and market imperfections

The methodology introduced in the *Statement* permits development of a fair value using cash flow information even if uncertainties exist about the timing and/or amount of the cash flows. Present value calculations have typically been based on a single set of cash flows and a single discount rate. The *Statement* introduces the concept of "expected cash flows" when using present value techniques for accounting measurements. Expected cash flows are a probability-weighted average of the range of possible estimated cash flow amounts and/or estimated timing of cash flows.

Example In regard to differing expected amounts, a company may estimate that there is a 20% probability that the cash flow in a given year will be $1,000, a 50% probability that it will be $1,200, and a 30% probability that it will be $1,400. The company would use the probability-weighted expected cash flow of $1,220 [($1,000 × 0.20) + ($1,200 × 0.50) + ($1,400 × 0.30)] in its present value calculations. Or in regard to the timing of its cash flows, a company might determine that it has a 30% probability of receiving $1,000 in 1 year but a 70% probability of receiving $1,000 in 2 years. The present value would be calculated as [(30% × the present value of $1,000 in 1 year) + (70% × the present value of $1,000 in 2 years)]. ■

The *Statement* also discusses the use of present value to estimate the fair value for a transaction between willing parties or to develop entity-specific measurements. In 2009, the FASB defined fair value as an exit value. Present value techniques may be used to measure fair value, especially when a company is using "Level 3 Inputs," as discussed in Chapter 4.[7]

GOT IT?

M-26 Give two examples of assets and three examples of liabilities that are measured and reported using present values under U.S. GAAP.

REVIEW CENTER

At the beginning of the Module, we described the importance of interest and the time value of money to personal financial decision-making as well as to companies' operating, investing, and financing activities. We also identified several objectives you would accomplish after reading the Module. The objectives are listed below and followed by a brief summary of the key takeaways.

---

[7] FASB ASC 820-10: Fair Value Measurement: Overall.

KEY TAKEAWAYS

- Simple interest is interest on the original principal regardless of the number of time periods that have passed or the amount of interest that has been paid or accrued in the past. Compound interest is the interest that accrues on both the principal and the past unpaid accrued interest.
- The time value of money provides the lender compensation for delayed consumptions, expected inflation, and risk.
- The conversion of these future cash flow amounts to the present value is known as discounting and involves removing the effects of the time value of money (interest) from those future cash flows.
- The conversion of current-period cash flows to future value is known as compounding and involves adding the time value of money (interest) to determine what a current-period cash flow will be worth in the future.

LEARNING OBJECTIVE M.1
Understand simple interest and compound interest.

KEY TERMS

compound interest, p. M-4
compounding, p. M-3
discounting, p. M-3
interest, p. M-3
simple interest, p. M-4
time value of money, p. M-3

KEY CALCULATIONS

Time Value of Money = Compensation for Delayed Consumption + Compensation for Expected Inflation + Compensation for Risk

Simple Interest = Principal × Rate × Time

Compound Interest = (Principal + Accumulated Interest) × Rate × Time

KEY TAKEAWAY

- The future value of a single sum is the original sum plus interest, stated as of a specific future date. The future value may be computed using a formula approach or a table approach (Table 1 at the end of this Module).

LEARNING OBJECTIVE M.2
Compute and use the future value of a single sum.

KEY TERM

future value of a single sum, p. M-5

KEY CALCULATIONS

$$FV = PV \times (1 + i)^n$$

$$f_{n,i} = (1 + i)^n$$

KEY TAKEAWAY

- The present value is today's value of a future cash flow. Discounting is the process of converting the future cash flow to the present value. The present value may be computed using a formula approach or a table approach (Table 3).

LEARNING OBJECTIVE M.3
Compute and use the present value of a single sum.

KEY TERM

present value of a single sum, p. M-9

KEY CALCULATIONS

$$PV = FV \times 1/(1 + i)^n$$

$$p_{n,i} = 1/(1 + i)^n$$

LEARNING OBJECTIVE M.4

Understand annuities, including ordinary annuities and annuities due.

KEY TAKEAWAYS

- An annuity is a series of equal cash flows made at regular intervals with interest compounded at a certain rate.
- An ordinary annuity involves periodic equal cash flows at the end of each period.
- An annuity due involves periodic equal cash flows at the beginning of each period.

KEY TERMS

annuity, p. M-11
annuity due, p. M-11
ordinary annuity, p. M-11

LEARNING OBJECTIVE M.5

Compute and use the future value of an ordinary annuity.

KEY TAKEAWAYS

- The future value of an ordinary annuity is determined immediately after the last cash flow in the series is made. The future value may be computed using a formula approach or a table approach (Table 2).

KEY TERM

future value of an ordinary annuity (FV_O), p. M-12

KEY CALCULATIONS

$$FV_O = C \times \left[\frac{(1+i)^n - 1}{i}\right]$$

$$f_{O,n,i} = \left[\frac{(1+i)^n - 1}{i}\right]$$

LEARNING OBJECTIVE M.6

Compute and use the future value of an annuity due.

KEY TAKEAWAYS

- The future value of an annuity due is determined one period after the last cash flow in the series. An annuity due involves periodic cash flows at the beginning of each period.
- The general rule for determining the future value of an annuity due factor is to take the future value of an ordinary annuity factor (Table 2) for $n + 1$ cash flows and subtract 1 from the factor.

KEY TERM

future value of an annuity due (FV_D), p. M-15

LEARNING OBJECTIVE M.7

Compute and use the present value of an ordinary annuity.

KEY TAKEAWAY

- The present value of an ordinary annuity is determined as of the beginning of the annuity period. The present value may be computed using a formula approach or a table approach (Table 4).

KEY TERM

present value of an ordinary annuity (PV_O), p. M-16

KEY CALCULATIONS

$$PV_O = C \times \left[\frac{1 - \frac{1}{(1+i)^n}}{i}\right]$$

$$p_{O,n,i} = \left[\frac{1 - \frac{1}{(1+i)^n}}{i}\right]$$

KEY TAKEAWAYS

- The present value of an annuity due is determined on the date of the first cash flow in the series. The present value may be computed using a formula approach or a table approach (Table 5).
- The general rule for determining the present value of an annuity due factor is to take the present value of an ordinary annuity factor (Table 4) for $n-1$ cash flows and add 1 to the factor.

KEY TERM

present value of an annuity due (PV_D), p. M-20

KEY CALCULATIONS

$$PV_D = C \times \left[\frac{1 - \frac{1}{(1+i)^{n-1}}}{i} + 1 \right]$$

$$p_{D,n,i} = \left[\frac{1 - \frac{1}{(1+i)^{n-1}}}{i} + 1 \right]$$

LEARNING OBJECTIVE M.8
Compute and use the present value of an annuity due.

KEY TAKEAWAYS

- The present value of a deferred ordinary annuity is determined on today's date, even though the annuity cash flows do not begin for two or more periods in the future.
- The general rule for determining the present value of a deferred ordinary annuity factor is to take the factor for the present value of an ordinary annuity of n Þ k cash flows and subtract the factor for the present value of an ordinary annuity of the k cash flows (with k equal to the number of periods of the deferral).

LEARNING OBJECTIVE M.9
Compute and use the present value of a deferred ordinary annuity.

KEY TERM

deferred ordinary annuity, p. M-24

KEY CALCULATIONS

$$PV_{deferred} = C \times p_{O,n,i} \times p_{k,n,i}$$

KEY TAKEAWAYS

- Present values are used to measure a variety of financial and monetary assets and liabilities. In 2000, the FASB issued *FASB Statement of Financial Accounting Concepts No. 7*, "Using Cash Flow Information and Present Value in Accounting Measurements." This *Statement* provides a framework for using future cash flows as the basis for an accounting measurement of both assets and liabilities. It provides general principles governing the use of present value, as well as the objectives of present value accounting measurements. U.S. GAAP allows the use of present value to measure fair value.

LEARNING OBJECTIVE M.10
Explain the conceptual issues regarding the use of present value in financial reporting.

MULTIPLE-CHOICE (AICPA ADAPTED)

Select the best answer for each of the following.

Use the following information for MM-1 through MM-4:

The following are the present value factors of $1 discounted at 8% for one to five periods. Each item is based on 8% interest discounted annually from day of withdrawal (future) to day of deposit (present).

Periods	Present Value of $1 Discounted at 8% per Period
1	0.926
2	0.857
3	0.794
4	0.735
5	0.681

MM-1
LO M.2
Refer to the present value table information on the previous page. What amount should be deposited in a bank today to grow to $1,000 3 years from today?

a. $\dfrac{\$1,000}{0.794}$
b. $\$1,000 \times 0.926 \times 3$
c. $(\$1,000 \times 0.926) + (\$1,000 \times 0.857) + (\$1,000 \times 0.794)$
d. $\$1,000 \times 0.794$

MM-2
LO M.2
Refer to the present value table information on the previous page. If Kathleen put $3,000 in a savings account today, what amount of cash will be available 2 years from today?

a. $\$3,000 \times 0.857$
b. $\$3,000 \times 0.857 \times 2$
c. $\dfrac{\$3,000}{0.857}$
d. $\dfrac{\$3,000}{0.926} \times 2$

MM-3
LO M.3
Refer to the present value table information on the previous page. What is the present value today of $4,000 to be received 6 years from today?

a. $\$4,000 \times 0.926 \times 6$
b. $\$4,000 \times 0.794 \times 2$
c. $\$4,000 \times 0.681 \times 0.926$
d. cannot be determined from the information given

MM-4
LO M.8
Refer to the present value table information on the previous page. What amount should Brett have in his bank account today, before withdrawal, if he needs $2,000 each year for 4 years, with the first withdrawal to be made today and each subsequent withdrawal at 1-year intervals? (Brett is to have exactly a zero balance in his bank account after the fourth withdrawal.)

a. $\$2,000 + (\$2,000 \times 0.926) + (\$2,000 \times 0.857) + (\$2,000 \times 0.794)$
b. $\dfrac{\$2,000}{0.735} \times 4$
c. $(\$2,000 \times 0.926) + (\$2,000 \times 0.857) + (\$2,000 \times 0.794) + (\$2,000 \times 0.735)$
d. $\dfrac{\$2,000}{0.926} \times 4$

MM-5
LO M.3
On May 1, 2016, a company purchased a new machine that it does not have to pay for until May 1, 2018. The total payment on May 1, 2018, will include both principal and interest. Assuming interest at a 10% rate, the cost of the machine would be the total payment multiplied by what time value of money concept?

a. future value of annuity of 1
b. future value of 1
c. present value of annuity of 1
d. present value of 1

MM-6
LO M.8
An office equipment representative has a machine for sale or lease. If you buy the machine, the cost is $7,596. If you lease the machine, you will have to sign a noncancelable lease and make 5 payments of $2,000 each. The first payment will be paid on the first day of the lease. At the time of the last payment, you will receive title to the machine. The present value of an ordinary annuity of $1 is as follows:

	Present Value of $1 Discounted at		
Number of Periods	10%	12%	16%
1	0.909	0.893	0.862
2	1.736	1.690	1.605
3	2.487	2.402	2.246
4	3.170	3.037	2.798
5	3.791	3.605	3.274

The interest rate implicit in this lease is approximately:

a. 10%
b. 12%
c. between 10% and 12%
d. 16%

MM-7
LO M.8
An accountant wishes to find the present value of an annuity of $1 payable at the beginning of each period at 10% for 8 periods. He has only one present value table, which shows the present value of an annuity of $1 payable at the end of each period. To compute the present value factor he needs, the accountant would use the present value factor in the 10% column for:

a. 7 periods
b. 7 periods and add 1
c. 8 periods
d. 9 periods and subtract 1

MM-8
LO M.8
For which of the following transactions would the use of the present value of an annuity due concept be appropriate in calculating the present value of the asset obtained or liability owed at the date of incurrence?

a. A capital lease is entered into with the initial lease payment due 1 month subsequent to the signing of the lease agreement.
b. A capital lease is entered into with the initial lease payment due upon the signing of the lease agreement.
c. A 10-year, 8% bond is issued on January 2, with interest payable semiannually on July 1 and January 1, yielding 7%.

d. A 10-year, 8% bond is issued on January 2, with interest payable semiannually on July 1 and January 1, yielding 9%.

MM-9
LO M.7
LO M.10
On July 1, 2016, James Rago signed an agreement to operate as a franchisee of Fast Foods Inc. for an initial franchise fee of $60,000. Of this amount, $20,000 was paid when the agreement was signed, and the balance is payable in 4 equal annual payments of $10,000 beginning July 1, 2017. The agreement provides that the down payment is not refundable and no future services are required of the franchisor. Rago's credit rating indicates that he can borrow money at 14% for a loan of this type. Information on present and future value factors is as follows:

Present value of $1 at 14% for 4 periods	0.59
Future value of $1 at 14% for 4 periods	1.69
Present value of an ordinary annuity of $1 at 14% for 4 periods	2.91

Rago should record the acquisition cost of the franchise on July 1, 2016, at:

a. $43,600   c. $60,000
b. $49,100   d. $67,600

MM-10
LO M.8
LO M.10
On January 1, 2016, Ken Company sold a machine to Burns Company. Burns signed a non-interest-bearing note requiring payment of $30,000 annually for 7 years. The first payment was made on January 1, 2016. The prevailing rate of interest for this type of note at the date of issuance was 10%. Information on present value factors is as follows:

Periods	Present Value of $1 at 10%	Present Value of an Ordinary Annuity of $1 at 10%
6	0.56	4.36
7	0.51	4.87

Ken should record the sale in January 2016 at:

a. $107,100   c. $146,100
b. $130,800   d. $160,800

REVIEW EXERCISES

REM-1
LO M.2
What is the future value on January 1, 2022, of $20,000 deposited on January 1, 2016, which accumulates interest at 10% compounded annually?

REM-2
LO M.2
Based on the following annual interest rates, what is the interest rate per period and the frequency of compounding per year in each of the following?
  a. 18% compounded semiannually
  b. 16% compounded quarterly
  c. 15% compounded monthly

REM-3
LO M.3
What is the present value on January 1, 2016, of $40,000 to be received on January 1, 2019, and discounted 8% compounded annually?

REM-4
LO M.3
What is the present value on January 1, 2016, of $10,000 to be received on January 1, 2020, and discounted at 6% compounded quarterly?

REM-5
LO M.3
Next Level Potter wishes to deposit a sum that at 12% interest, compounded semiannually, will permit 2 withdrawals: $40,000 at the end of 4 years and $50,000 at the end of 10 years. Analyze the problem to determine the required deposit, stating the procedure to follow and the tables to use in developing the solution.

REM-6
LO M.5
What is the future value on December 31, 2022, of 6 annual cash flows of $50,000 with the first cash flow being made on December 31, 2016, and interest at 9% compounded annually?

REM-7
LO M.6
What will be the future value on December 31, 2020, of 5 annual $60,000 deposits starting on December 31, 2016, if the amounts earn 8% compounded annually?

REM-8
LO M.7
What is the present value on January 1, 2016, of 7 equal future annual receipts of $30,000 if the first receipt is received on January 1, 2017, and the interest rate is 10% compounded annually?

REM-9
LO M.7
If $80,000 is invested in a fund on December 31, 2016, what is the amount of each of 6 annual withdrawals starting on December 31, 2017, that would deplete the fund if the interest rate earned in the fund is 10% compounded annually?

REM-10 LO M.7 If $90,000 is invested in a fund on December 31, 2016, and 5 equal annual withdrawals of $23,138.32 are made starting on December 31, 2017, that will deplete the fund, what is the interest rate being earned if interest is compounded annually?

REM-11 LO M.7 Samuel Ames owes $20,000 to a friend. He wants to know how much he would have to pay if he paid the debt in 3 annual installments at the end of each year, which would include interest at 14%. Draw a time line for the problem. Indicate what table to use. Look up the table value and place it in a brief formula. Solve.

REM-12 LO M.8 What is the future value on December 31, 2021, of 6 annual cash flows of $50,000 with the first cash flow being made on December 31, 2016, and interest at 9% compounded annually?

REM-13 LO M.8 What is the present value on January 1, 2016, of 7 equal future annual receipts of $30,000 if the first receipt is received on January 1, 2016, and the interest rate is 10% compounded annually?

REM-14 Next Level LO M.2, LO M.3, LO M.5, LO M.7, LO M.8 The following factors are taken from the compound interest tables for the same number of time periods and the same interest rate:

a. 8.137249
b. 50.980352
c. 6.265060
d. 7.142168
e. 0.122892

Identify each of the five compound interest table factors without reference to the tables. Discuss briefly.

EXERCISES

EM-1 LO M.2 **Future Value and Compound Interest** Using the future value tables, solve the following.

Required:
1. What is the value on January 1, 2023, of $40,000 deposited on January 1, 2016, which accumulates interest at 12% compounded annually?
2. What is the value on January 1, 2022, of $10,000 deposited on July 1, 2016, which accumulates interest at 16% compounded quarterly?
3. What is the compound interest on an investment of $6,000 left on deposit for 5 years at 10% compounded annually?

EM-2 LO M.2 **Future Value** Hugh Colson deposited $20,000 in a special savings account that provides for interest at the annual rate of 12% compounded semiannually if the deposit is maintained for 4 years.

Required:
Calculate the balance of the savings account at the end of the 4-year period.

EM-3 LO M.3 **Present Value** Using the present value tables, solve the following problems.

Required:
1. What is the present value on January 1, 2016, of $30,000 due on January 1, 2021, and discounted at 12% compounded annually?
2. What is the present value on July 1, 2016, of $8,000 due January 1, 2021, and discounted at 16% compounded quarterly?
3. What is the amount of the present value discount (the difference between future value and present value) on $8,000 due at the end of 5 years at 10% compounded annually?

EM-4 LO M.5 **Future Value of Annuity** Using appropriate tables, solve the following future value of annuity problems.

Required:
1. What is the future value on December 31, 2022, of 7 annual cash flows of $10,000 with the first cash payment being made on December 31, 2016, and interest at 12% being compounded annually?
2. What is the future value on December 31, 2023, of 7 annual cash flows of $10,000 with the first cash payment made on December 31, 2016, and interest at 12% being compounded annually?

EM-5 **Cash Flow Amounts** Six equal annual contributions are made to a fund, with the first deposit on December 31, 2016.
LO M.5

Required:
Using the future value tables, determine the equal contributions that, if invested at 10% compounded annually, will accumulate to a fund of $30,000 on December 31, 2021.

EM-6 **Cash Flow Amounts** Beginning on January 1, 2017, 5 equal deposits are to be made in a fund.
LO M.5

Required:
Using the appropriate tables, determine the equal deposits if interest at 10% is compounded annually and if $200,000 must be in the fund on
1. January 1, 2021
2. January 1, 2022

EM-7 **Present Value of an Annuity** Samuel David wants to make 5 equal annual withdrawals of $8,000 from a fund that will earn interest at 10% compounded annually.
LO M.7

Required:
How much would Samuel have to invest on:
1. January 1, 2016, if the first withdrawal is made on January 1, 2017?
2. January 1, 2016, if the first withdrawal is made on January 1, 2016?

EM-8 **Cash Flow Amounts** R. Lee Rouse borrows $10,000 that is to be repaid in 24 equal monthly installments payable at the end of each subsequent month with interest at the rate of 1½% per month.
LO M.7

Required:
Using the appropriate table, calculate the equal installments.

EM-9 **Cash Flow Amounts** On January 1, 2016, Charles Jamison borrows $40,000 from his father to open a business. Charles is the beneficiary of a trust created by his aunt from which he will receive $25,000 on January 1, 2026. He signs an agreement to make this amount payable to his father and, further, to pay his father equal annual amounts from January 1, 2017, to January 1, 2025, inclusive, in retirement of the debt. Interest is 12% per year.
LO M.3
LO M.7

Required:
What are the annual payments?

EM-10 **Amount of an Annuity** John Goodheart wishes to provide for 6 annual withdrawals of $3,000 each beginning January 1, 2026. He wishes to make 10 annual deposits beginning January 1, 2016, with the last deposit to be made on January 1, 2025.
LO M.5
LO M.7

Required:
If the fund earns interest compounded annually at 10%, how much is each of the 10 deposits?

EM-11 **Series of Compound Interest Techniques** The following are several situations involving compound interest.
LO M.2
LO M.3
LO M.5
LO M.7

Required:
Using the appropriate table, solve each of the following:
1. Hope Dearborn invests $40,000 on January 1, 2016, in a savings account that earns interest of 8% compounded semiannually. What will be the amount in the fund on December 31, 2021?
2. Ben Johnson receives a bonus of $5,000 each year on December 31. Beginning on December 31, 2016, he deposits his bonus every year in a savings account that earns interest of 12% compounded annually. What will be the amount in the fund on December 31, 2020, after he deposits his bonus received on that date?
3. Ron Sewert owes $30,000 on a non-interest-bearing note due January 1, 2026. He offers to pay the amount on January 1, 2016, provided that it is discounted at 10% on a compound annual discount basis. What would he have to pay on January 1, 2016, under this assumption?
4. June Stickney purchased an annuity on January 1, 2016, which, at a 12% annual rate, would yield $6,000 each June 30 and December 31 for the next 6 years. What was the cost of the annuity to Stickney?

(continued)

5. Five equal annual contributions are to be made to a fund, with the first deposit on December 31, 2016. Determine the equal contributions that, if invested at 10% compounded annually, will produce a fund of $30,000 on December 31, 2021.
6. Beginning on December 31, 2017, 6 equal annual withdrawals are to be made. Determine the equal annual withdrawals if $11,000 is invested at 10% interest compounded annually on December 31, 2016.

EM-12 **Number of Cash Flows** On July 1, 2016, Boston Company purchased a machine at a cost of $80,000. It paid $56,046.06 in cash and signed a 10% note for the difference. This note is to be paid off in annual installments of $5,000 each, payable each July 1, beginning immediately. The $5,000 includes a payment of interest on the balance of the principal at the beginning of each period and a payment on the principal.
LO M.8

Required:
Calculate the number of annual payments to be made by Boston.

EM-13 **Present Value of Leased Asset** On January 1, 2016, Ashly Farms leased a hay baler from Agrico Company. The lease requires Ashly to make $3,000 payments on January 1 of each year for 5 years beginning in 2016. The interest rate is 12%.
LO M.9

Required:
Calculate the present value of Ashly's lease payments as of January 1, 2016.

EM-14 **Amount of an Annuity** Beginning December 31, 2020, 5 equal annual withdrawals are to be made.
LO M.7
LO M.8 **Required:**
LO M.9 Using the appropriate tables, determine the equal annual withdrawals if $25,000 is invested at an interest of 12% compounded annually on:
1. January 1, 2020
2. December 31, 2020
3. January 1, 2017

PROBLEMS

PM-1 **Future Value of an Investment** Using the future value tables, solve the following.
LO M.2
Required:
1. What is the future value on December 31, 2020, of a deposit of $35,000 made on January 1, 2017, assuming interest of 10% compounded annually?
2. What is the future value on December 31, 2020, of a deposit of $10,000 made on January 1, 2017, assuming interest of 16% compounded quarterly?
3. What is the future value on December 31, 2020, of a deposit of $25,000 made on January 1, 2017, assuming interest of 12% compounded semiannually?

PM-2 **Present Value Computations** Using the present value tables, solve the following.
LO M.3
Required:
1. What is the present value on January 1, 2016, of $30,000 due on January 1, 2020, and discounted at 10% compounded annually?
2. What is the present value on January 1, 2016, of $40,000 due on January 1, 2020, and discounted at 11% compounded semiannually?
3. What is the present value on January 1, 2016, of $50,000 due on January 1, 2020, and discounted at 16% compounded quarterly?

PM-3 **Future Value Computations** Using the future values tables, solve the following.
LO M.5
Required:
1. What is the future value on December 31, 2025, of 10 cash flows of $20,000 with the first cash payment made on December 31, 2016, and interest at 10% being compounded annually?

2. What is the future value on June 30, 2026, of 20 cash flows of $15,000 with the first cash payment made on December 31, 2016, and the annual interest rate of 10% being compounded semiannually?
3. What is the future value on December 31, 2026, of 20 cash flows of $15,000 with the first cash payment made on December 31, 2016, and the annual interest rate of 10% being compounded semiannually?

PM-4 **Determining Loan Repayments** Jerry Rockness needs $40,000 to pay off a loan due on December 31, 2025. His
LO M.5 plans included the making of 10 annual deposits beginning on December 31, 2016, in accumulating a fund to pay off the loan. Without making a precise calculation, Jerry made 3 annual deposits of $4,000 each on December 31, 2016, 2017, and 2018, which have been earning interest at 10% compounded annually.

Required:
What is the equal amount of each of the next 7 deposits for the period December 31, 2019, to December 31, 2025, to reach the fund objective, assuming that the fund will continue to earn interest at 10% compounded annually?

PM-5 **Fund to Retire Bonds** At the beginning of 2016, Shanklin Company issued 10-year bonds with a face value of
LO M.5 $1,000,000 due on December 31, 2025. Shanklin wants to accumulate a fund to retire these bonds at maturity by making annual deposits beginning on December 31, 2016.

Required:
How much must Shanklin deposit each year, assuming that the fund will earn 12% interest a year compounded annually?

PM-6 **Cash Flow Amounts** On December 31, 2023, Michael McDowell wants to have $60,000. He plans to make
LO M.7 6 deposits in a fund to provide this amount. Interest is compounded annually at 12%.

Required:
Compute the equal annual amounts that Michael must deposit assuming that he makes the first deposit on:
1. December 31, 2018
2. December 31, 2017

PM-7 **Value of an Annuity** Using the appropriate tables, solve each of the following.
LO M.7
Required:
1. Beginning December 31, 2017, 5 equal withdrawals are to be made. Determine the equal annual withdrawals if $30,000 is invested at 10% interest compounded annually on December 31, 2016.
2. Ten payments of $3,000 are due at annual intervals beginning June 30, 2017. What amount will be accepted in cancellation of this series of payments on June 30, 2016, assuming a discount rate of 14% compounded annually?
3. Ten payments of $2,000 are due at annual intervals beginning December 31, 2016. What amount will be accepted in cancellation of this series of payments on January 1, 2016, assuming a discount rate of 12% compounded annually?

PM-8 **Serial Installments; Amounts Applicable to Interest and Principal** Ronald McDuffie purchases a new car at a
LO M.7 cost of $14,400. He pays $3,000 down and issues an installment note payable by which he promises to pay the balance in 18 equal monthly installments, which include interest at an annual rate of 18% on the remaining unpaid balance at the beginning of each month starting with the first month after the purchase.

Required:
1. Compute the equal installment payments.
2. Compute the interest that will be paid for each of the first two periods. Indicate the amount of each payment that will be a reduction of principal.

PM-9 **Number of Cash Flows** The following are two independent situations.
LO M.2
LO M.5 1. Ted Houser wishes to accumulate a fund of $40,000 for the purchase of a house and lot. He plans to deposit
LO M.7 $4,000 semiannually at the end of each 6 months. Assuming interest at 14% a year compounded semiannually, how many deposits of $4,000 each will be required, and what is the amount of the last deposit?
2. On January 1, 2016, Joan Campbell borrows $20,000 from Susan Rone and agrees to repay this amount in payments of $4,000 a year until the debt is paid in full. Payments are to be of an equal amount and are to include interest at 12% on the unpaid balance of principal at the beginning of each period. Assuming that the

(continued)

first payment is to be made on January 1, 2017, determine the number of payments of $4,000 each to be made and the amount of the final payment.

Required:
Using the appropriate tables, solve each of the preceding situations.

PM-10 **Comprehensive** *Part a.* Reproduced in the following table are the first three lines from the 2% columns of each of several tables of mathematical values. For each of the following items, select from among these fragmentary tables the one from which the amount required can be obtained *most directly* (assuming that the complete table was available in each instance):

LO M.2
LO M.3
LO M.5
LO M.7
AICPA Adapted

Periods	Table A	Table B	Table C	Table D	Table E
0	1.0000		1.0000		
1	0.9804	1.0200	1.0200	1.0000	0.9804
2	0.9612	2.0604	1.0404	0.4950	1.9416
3		3.1216		0.3268	2.8839

1. The amount to which a single sum would accumulate at compound interest by the end of a specified period (interest compounded annually)
2. The amount that must be deposited at the beginning of each of a specific number of years to provide for the accumulation, at annually compounded interest, of $1.02
3. The amount that must be deposited in a fund that will earn interest at a specified rate, compounded annually, in order to make possible the withdrawal of certain equal sums annually over a specified period starting 1 year from date of deposit
4. The amount of interest that will accumulate on a single deposit by the end of a specified period (interest compounded semiannually)
5. The amount that if paid now would settle a debt of larger amount due at a specified future date

Part b. The following tables of values at 10% interest may be used as needed to answer the questions in this part of the problem.

Periods	Future Value of 1 at Compound Interest	Present Value of 1 at Compound Interest	Future Value of Annuity of 1 at End of Each Period	Present Value of Annuity of 1 at End of Each Period
1	1.100	0.9091	1.0000	0.9091
...	...	...	...	...
6	1.7716	0.5645	7.7156	4.3553
7	1.9487	0.5132	9.4872	4.8684
8	2.1436	0.4665	11.4359	5.3349
9	2.3579	0.4241	13.5795	5.7590
10	2.5937	0.3855	15.9374	6.1446
11	2.8531	0.3505	18.5312	6.4951
12	3.1384	0.3186	21.3843	6.8137
13	3.4523	0.2897	24.5227	7.1034
14	3.7975	0.2633	27.9750	7.3667
15	4.1772	0.2394	31.7725	7.6061
16	4.5950	0.2176	35.9497	7.8237

1. Your client will make annual payments of $2,500 into a fund at the close of each year. She has asked you how many $2,500 annual payments will be required to bring the fund to $22,500 assuming that the fund earns interest at 10% compounded annually. Compute the total number of full payments of $2,500 required and the amount of the final payment if it does not require the entire $2,500. Carefully label all computations supporting your answer.
2. Your client wishes to provide for the payment of an obligation of $200,000 due on July 1, 2023. He plans to deposit $20,000 in a special fund each July 1 for 7 years starting July 1, 2017. He wishes to make an initial deposit on July 1, 2016, of an amount that, with its accumulated interest, will bring the fund up to $200,000 at the maturity of the obligation. He expects that the fund will earn interest at the rate of 10% compounded annually. Compute the amount to be deposited July 1, 2016. Carefully label all computations supporting your answer.

PM-11 **Purchase of Asset** William Thomas intends to purchase a tractor on credit. Two local implement dealers have
LO M.7   offered him the following payment plans for identical tractors:
LO M.8
1. Redd Truck & Tractor's plan calls for 5 annual payments of $10,350 with the first payment now and the remaining payments at the beginning of each of the next 4 years.
2. Greene Farm Implements requires semiannual payments of $5,750 at the end of each of the next 10 semi-annual periods, with the first payment to be in 6 months.

Required:
Determine which of the preceding plans offers William the lower present value. The applicable annual interest rate is 10% for both alternatives.

PM-12 **Present Value of an Annuity** John Joshua wants to make 5 equal annual withdrawals of $20,000 from a fund that
LO M.7   will earn interest at 12% compounded annually.
LO M.8
LO M.9 **Required:**
How much would John have to invest on January 1, 2016, if he makes the first withdrawal on:
1. January 1, 2017
2. January 1, 2016
3. January 1, 2020

PM-13 **Present Value of an Annuity** Ralph Benke wants to make 8 equal semiannual withdrawals of $8,000 from a fund
LO M.7   that will earn interest at 11% compounded semiannually.
LO M.8
LO M.9 **Required:**
How much would Ralph have to invest on:
1. January 1, 2016, if the first withdrawal is made on July 1, 2016
2. July 1, 2016, if the first withdrawal is made on July 1, 2016
3. January 1, 2016, if the first withdrawal is made on January 1, 2019

PM-14 **Compound Interest Issues** You are given the following situations:
LO M.7
1. Thomas Petry owes a debt of $7,000 from the purchase of a boat. The debt bears 12% interest payable annually. Thomas will pay the debt and interest in 5 annual installments beginning in 1 year. Calculate the equal annual installments that will pay off the debt and interest at 12% on the unpaid balance.
LO M.8
LO M.9
2. On January 1, 2016, John Cothran offers to buy Ruth House's used tractor and equipment for $4,000 payable in 12 equal semiannual installments which are to include payment of 10% interest on the unpaid balance and payment of a portion of the principal with the first installment to be made on January 1, 2016. Calculate the amount of each of these installments.
3. Nadine Love invests in a $60,000 annuity at 12% compounded annually on March 1, 2016. The first of 15 receipts from the annuity is payable to Love on March 1, 2026, 10 years after the annuity is purchased and on the date Love expects to retire. Calculate the amount of each of the 15 equal annual receipts.

Required:
Using the appropriate tables, solve each of the preceding situations.

PM-15 **Cash Flow Amounts** On January 1, 2016, Philip Holding invests $40,000 in an annuity to provide 8 equal semi-
LO M.7   annual payments. Interest is 10%, compounded semiannually.
LO M.8
LO M.9 **Required:**
Compute the equal semiannual amounts that Philip will receive assuming that the first withdrawal is to be received on:
1. July 1, 2016
2. January 1, 2016
3. July 1, 2019
4. January 1, 2021

PM-16 **Present Value Issues** Nello Construction Company has just purchased several major pieces of road-building
LO M.7   equipment. Because the purchase price is so large, the equipment company is giving Nello an option of choosing
LO M.9   one of four different payment plans:
1. $600,000 immediately in cash.
2. $200,000 down payment now; $65,000 per year for 12 years, beginning at the end of the current year.

(continued)

3. $200,000 down payment now; $25,000 per year for 3 years beginning at the end of the current year; $75,000 per year for 11 years beginning at the end of the fourth year after the purchase.
4. $80,000 now and at the beginning of each of the next 13 years.

Required:
Nello has asked you to decide which payment plan will provide the smallest present value. The expected effective interest rate during the future periods stated above is 12%.

PM-17 **Comprehensive** The following are three independent situations:
LO M.3
LO M.5
LO M.7
LO M.9

1. K. Herrmann has decided to set up a scholarship fund for students. She is willing to deposit $5,000 in a trust fund at the end of each year for 10 years. She wants the trust fund to then pay annual scholarships at the end of each year for 30 years.
2. Charles Jordy is planning to save for his retirement. He has decided that he can save $3,000 at the end of each year for the next 10 years, $5,000 at the end of each year for Years 11 through 20, and $10,000 at the end of each year for Years 21 through 30.
3. Patricia Karpas has $200,000 in savings on the day she retires. She intends to spend $2,000 per month traveling around the world for the next 2 years, during which time her savings will earn 18%, compounded monthly. For the next 5 years, she intends to spend $6,000 every 6 months, during which time her savings will earn 12%, compounded semiannually. For the rest of her life expectancy of 15 years, she wants an annuity to cover her living costs. During this period, her savings will earn 10% compounded annually. Assume that all payments occur at the end of each period.

Required:
1. In Situation 1, how much will the annual scholarships be if the fund can earn 6%? How much at 10%?
2. In Situation 2,
   (a) How much will Charles have at the end of 30 years if his savings can earn 10%? How much at 6%?
   (b) If Charles expects to live for 20 years in retirement, how much can he withdraw from his savings at the end of each year if his savings earn 10%? How much at 6%?
   (c) How much would Charles need to invest today to have the same amount available at the time he retires as calculated in Situation 2(a) at 10%? How much at 6%?
3. In Situation 3, how much will Patricia's annuity be?

PM-18 **Acquisition of Asset** SuMar Company purchased a new piece of machinery by paying $2,000 down and agreeing to pay $1,000 at the end of each year for 5 years. The appropriate interest rate is 8%.
LO M.7
LO M.10

Required:
1. What is the cost of the machinery? What is the present value of the liability at the time of the purchase?
2. Prepare the journal entry to record the purchase of the machinery and the associated liability on SuMar's balance sheet.
3. Prepare a table that shows the interest and ending balance of the liability each year. *(Contributed by Norma C. Powell)*

PM-19 **Asset Purchase Price** BWP Inc. is considering the purchase of an asset. BWP's required rate of return on new assets is 12%. The expected net cash inflows generated by the new asset are as follows:
LO M.3
LO M.7
LO M.9
LO M.10

Years	Amount	Nature of the Cash Inflows
1–4	$3,000	Net operating revenues
5–9	2,500	Net operating revenues
10	2,000	Net operating revenues
10	1,000	Sale of asset

Required:
Given that the net cash inflows can be realized, what is the maximum amount BWP should be willing to pay for the new asset? If BWP pays that amount, at what amount should BWP recognize the asset on the balance sheet? Assume that each cash inflow occurs at the end of the year. *(Contributed by Norma C. Powell)*

CASES

CM-1 **Effective Interest in Various Situations**
LO M.1 On March 1, 2016, White Company purchased $400,000 worth of inventory on credit with terms that require payment in 60 days but allow White to take a 1% discount if it pays in 10 days (often quoted as 1/10, net/60 payment terms). In the past, White has always followed the policy of making payment 30 days after the goods are purchased.

A new member of White's staff has indicated that the company he previously worked for never passed up its cash discounts, and he wonders if this is not a sound policy. It was pointed out, however, that if White were to pay the invoice 10 days earlier, it would have to borrow the necessary funds for the 10 extra days. White's borrowing terms with a local bank are 14% (annual rate) with a 15% compensating balance (a requirement by the bank that White maintain an amount in its account equal to 15% of the loan) for the term of the loan. Most members of White's staff felt that it made little sense to take out a 14% loan with a compensating balance of 15% in order to save 1% on $400,000 by paying the account 10 days earlier than planned.

Required:
1. In terms of simple effective annual interest cost, explain whether it would be to White's advantage to borrow the amount necessary to take the 1% discount by paying the bill 10 days early.
2. It has also been pointed out to White that if it does not take advantage of the cash discount, it should wait the entire 60-day period to pay the full bill rather than pay within 30 days. Explain how your answer to Requirement 1 would change if White undertook this policy.
3. Your answer to Requirement 2 indicates that, in relation to Requirement 1, it has become either more desirable or less desirable to borrow in order to take advantage of the 1% cash discount.
    a. If you said *more desirable,* explain why.
    b. If you said *less desirable,* explain why.

CM-2 **Future Value of Single Investment and Annuity**
LO M.2
LO M.3 Jane Dough was a teller in a large northeastern bank. She was single and approaching age 30, and she considered herself an honest and upright citizen. After considering what she might do to build a retirement plan for the future, she decided to embezzle $1,500,000. Subsequently, she gave herself up to the authorities but did not return the $1,500,000. She was tried, convicted, and sentenced to 20 years in prison. After completing her 20-year term, she returned the $1,500,000 that she had stolen. She then decided to take a world cruise. On the ship, someone asked her how she had accumulated enough money to afford the trip. She replied, "Do you know how much *interest* $1,500,000 will earn in 20 years if invested at an annual rate of 16% compounded quarterly?"

Required:
1. Determine the answer to Jane's question. The table factor for $f_{n=40, i=4\%}$ is 4.801021.
2. Evaluate Jane's retirement decision, assuming that she could have earned $140,000 each year for each of the 20 years she was in prison. Assume that $40,000 is required each year to cover living expenses and that she could have invested the remaining $100,000 at the end of each year to earn interest at 16% compounded annually.

CM-3 **Cost of Insurance Plans**
LO M.7 Johnson Company is considering three different time periods for an insurance policy on its main office building. The premiums on a fire insurance policy covering the building for the amount of $2,000,000 on a 1-year, 3-year, and 5-year basis are as follows:

1 year	$ 4,480
3 years	11,200
5 years	17,920

In each case, the entire premium for the full term of the policy is payable at the beginning of the year in which the policy is purchased.

Required:
Evaluate the present value of the annual cost of each insurance plan assuming a 12% compounded annual discount rate. Which plan do you recommend? State the savings for the company.

CM-4 **Acquisition of Equipment**
LO M.3
LO M.7 Taylor Company's manager has consulted you, the controller, as to which of the following plans you would recommend in acquiring the use of a piece of heavy equipment:
1. Purchase the equipment and pay immediately a cash price of $36,800. The service life of the heavy equipment is estimated to be 5 years,

(continued)

with a resale value at the end of that time of $5,500.
2. Lease the equipment at the rate of $9,100 per year for 5 years, payable at the beginning of each year.

Required:
Assuming that the time value of money is 12%, evaluate the two alternatives and indicate which plan you would recommend to the manager, stating the value of savings to the company.

CM-5 Value of a Note
LO M.3
LO M.10

You have just been promoted to manager at a national CPA firm. A new accountant approaches you with the following situation: He has discovered that the president of your client's company has a brother who is both the major shareholder and the president of a local bank. Your client has a $300,000, 5-year note payable to the bank at 4% interest compounded annually. Because the going interest rate is 16%, the accountant suggests that the note be recorded at its present value using this going rate. The president says that the effective liability is $300,000 and should be reported on the balance sheet at this figure. The note was issued on January 1, 2016, and is due on January 1, 2021.

Required:
1. Explain who is correct.
2. At what amount should the company have valued the note on January 1, 2016, assuming that the accountant's assessment is correct?

COMPOUND INTEREST TABLES

Table 1 Future Value of 1: $f_{n,i} = (1+i)^n$

Table 2 Future Value of an Ordinary Annuity of 1: $f_{O,n,i} = \dfrac{(1+i)^n - 1}{i}$

Table 3 Present Value of 1: $p_{n,i} = \dfrac{1}{(1+i)^n}$

Table 4 Present Value of an Ordinary Annuity of 1: $p_{O,n,i} = \dfrac{1 - \dfrac{1}{(1+i)^n}}{i}$

Table 5 Present Value of Annuity Due: $p_{D,n,i} = \dfrac{1 - \dfrac{1}{(1+i)^{n-1}}}{i} + 1$

TABLE 1

Future Value of 1: $f_{n,i} = (1+i)^n$

n	1.5%	4.0%	4.5%	5.0%	5.5%	6.0%	7.0%
1	1.015000	1.040000	1.045000	1.050000	1.055000	1.060000	1.070000
2	1.030225	1.081600	1.092025	1.102500	1.113025	1.123600	1.144900
3	1.045678	1.124864	1.141166	1.157625	1.174241	1.191016	1.225043
4	1.061364	1.169859	1.192519	1.215506	1.238825	1.262477	1.310796
5	1.077284	1.216653	1.246182	1.276282	1.306960	1.338226	1.402552
6	1.093443	1.265319	1.302260	1.340096	1.378843	1.418519	1.500730
7	1.109845	1.315932	1.360862	1.407100	1.454679	1.503630	1.605781
8	1.126493	1.368569	1.422101	1.477455	1.534687	1.593848	1.718186
9	1.143390	1.423312	1.486095	1.551328	1.619094	1.689479	1.838459
10	1.160541	1.480244	1.552969	1.628895	1.708144	1.790848	1.967151
11	1.177949	1.539454	1.622853	1.710339	1.802092	1.898299	2.104852
12	1.195618	1.601032	1.695881	1.795856	1.901207	2.012196	2.252192
13	1.213552	1.665074	1.772196	1.885649	2.005774	2.132928	2.409845
14	1.231756	1.731676	1.851945	1.979932	2.116091	2.260904	2.578534
15	1.250232	1.800944	1.935282	2.078928	2.232476	2.396558	2.759032
16	1.268986	1.872981	2.022370	2.182875	2.355263	2.540352	2.952164
17	1.288020	1.947900	2.113377	2.292021	2.484802	2.692773	3.158815
18	1.307341	2.025817	2.208479	2.406619	2.621466	2.854339	3.379932
19	1.326951	2.106849	2.307860	2.526950	2.765647	3.025600	3.616528
20	1.346855	2.191123	2.411714	2.653298	2.917757	3.207135	3.869684
21	1.367058	2.278768	2.520241	2.785963	3.078234	3.399564	4.140562
22	1.387564	2.369919	2.633652	2.925261	3.247537	3.603537	4.430402
23	1.408377	2.464716	2.752166	3.071524	3.426152	3.819750	4.740530
24	1.429503	2.563304	2.876014	3.225100	3.614590	4.048935	5.072367
25	1.450945	2.665836	3.005434	3.386355	3.813392	4.291871	5.427433
26	1.472710	2.772470	3.140679	3.555673	4.023129	4.549383	5.807353
27	1.494800	2.883369	3.282013	3.733456	4.244401	4.822346	6.213868
28	1.517222	2.998703	3.429700	3.920159	4.477843	5.111687	6.648838
29	1.539981	3.118651	3.584036	4.116136	4.724124	5.418388	7.114257
30	1.563080	3.243398	3.745318	4.321942	4.983951	5.743491	7.612255

(continued)

Table 1 (concluded)

n	8.0%	9.0%	10.0%	12.0%	14.0%	16.0%	18.0%
1	1.080000	1.090000	1.100000	1.120000	1.140000	1.160000	1.180000
2	1.166400	1.188100	1.210000	1.254400	1.299600	1.345600	1.392400
3	1.259712	1.295029	1.331000	1.404928	1.481544	1.560896	1.643032
4	1.360489	1.411582	1.464100	1.573519	1.688960	1.810639	1.938778
5	1.469328	1.538624	1.610510	1.762342	1.925415	2.100342	2.287758
6	1.586874	1.677100	1.771561	1.973823	2.194973	2.436396	2.699554
7	1.713824	1.828039	1.948717	2.210681	2.502269	2.826220	3.185474
8	1.850930	1.992563	2.143589	2.475963	2.852586	3.278415	3.758859
9	1.999005	2.171893	2.357948	2.773079	3.251949	3.802961	4.435454
10	2.158925	2.367364	2.593742	3.105848	3.707221	4.411435	5.233836
11	2.331639	2.580426	2.853117	3.478550	4.226232	5.117265	6.175926
12	2.518170	2.812665	3.138428	3.895976	4.817905	5.936027	7.287593
13	2.719624	3.065805	3.452271	4.363493	5.492411	6.885791	8.599359
14	2.937194	3.341727	3.797498	4.887112	6.261349	7.987518	10.147244
15	3.172169	3.642482	4.177248	5.473566	7.137938	9.265521	11.973748
16	3.425943	3.970306	4.594973	6.130394	8.137249	10.748004	14.129023
17	3.700018	4.327633	5.054470	6.866041	9.276464	12.467685	16.672247
18	3.996019	4.717120	5.559917	7.689966	10.575169	14.462514	19.673251
19	4.315701	5.141661	6.115909	8.612762	12.055693	16.776517	23.214436
20	4.660957	5.604411	6.727500	9.646293	13.743490	19.460759	27.393035
21	5.033834	6.108808	7.400250	10.803848	15.667578	22.574481	32.323781
22	5.436540	6.658600	8.140275	12.100310	17.861039	26.186398	38.142061
23	5.871464	7.257874	8.954302	13.552347	20.361585	30.376222	45.007632
24	6.341181	7.911083	9.849733	15.178629	23.212207	35.236417	53.109006
25	6.848475	8.623081	10.834706	17.000064	26.461916	40.874244	62.668627
26	7.396353	9.399158	11.918177	19.040072	30.166584	47.414123	73.948980
27	7.988061	10.245082	13.109994	21.324881	34.389906	55.000382	87.259797
28	8.627106	11.167140	14.420994	23.883866	39.204493	63.800444	102.966560
29	9.317275	12.172182	15.863093	26.749930	44.693122	74.008515	121.500541
30	10.062657	13.267678	17.449402	29.959922	50.950159	85.849877	143.370638

TABLE 2

Future Value of an Ordinary Annuity of 1: $F_{O,n,i} = \dfrac{(1+i)^n - 1}{i}$

n	1.5%	4.0%	4.5%	5.0%	5.5%	6.0%	7.0%
1	1.000000	1.000000	1.000000	1.000000	1.000000	1.000000	1.000000
2	2.015000	2.040000	2.045000	2.050000	2.055000	2.060000	2.070000
3	3.045225	3.121600	3.137025	3.152500	3.168025	3.183600	3.214900
4	4.090903	4.246464	4.278191	4.310125	4.342266	4.374616	4.439943
5	5.152267	5.416323	5.470710	5.525631	5.581091	5.637093	5.750739
6	6.229551	6.632975	6.716892	6.801913	6.888051	6.975319	7.153291
7	7.322994	7.898294	8.019152	8.142011	8.266894	8.393838	8.654021
8	8.432839	9.214226	9.380014	9.549109	9.721573	9.897468	10.259803
9	9.559332	10.582795	10.802114	11.026564	11.256260	11.491316	11.977989
10	10.702722	12.006107	12.288209	12.577893	12.875354	13.180795	13.816448
11	11.863262	13.486351	13.841179	14.206787	14.583498	14.971643	15.783599
12	13.041211	15.025805	15.464032	15.917127	16.385591	16.869941	17.888451
13	14.236830	16.626838	17.159913	17.712983	18.286798	18.882138	20.140643
14	15.450382	18.291911	18.932109	19.598632	20.292572	21.015066	22.550488
15	16.682138	20.023588	20.784054	21.578564	22.408663	23.275970	25.129022
16	17.932370	21.824531	22.719337	23.657492	24.641140	25.672528	27.888054
17	19.201655	23.697512	24.741707	25.840366	26.996403	28.212880	30.840217
18	20.489376	25.645413	26.855084	28.132385	29.481205	30.905653	33.999033
19	21.796716	27.671229	29.063562	30.539004	32.102671	33.759992	37.378965
20	23.123667	29.778079	31.371423	33.065954	34.868318	36.785591	40.995492
21	24.470522	31.969202	33.783137	35.719252	37.786076	39.992727	44.865177
22	25.837580	34.247970	36.303378	38.505214	40.864310	43.392290	49.005739
23	27.225144	36.617889	38.937030	41.430475	44.111847	46.995828	53.436141
24	28.633521	39.082604	41.689196	44.501999	47.537998	50.815577	58.176671
25	30.063024	41.645908	44.565210	47.727099	51.152588	54.864512	63.249038
26	31.513969	44.311745	47.570645	51.113454	54.965981	59.156383	68.676470
27	32.986678	47.084214	50.711324	54.669126	58.989109	63.705766	74.483823
28	34.481479	49.967583	53.993333	58.402583	63.233510	68.528112	80.697691
29	35.998701	52.966286	57.423033	62.322712	67.711354	73.639798	87.346529
30	37.538681	56.084938	61.007070	66.438848	72.435478	79.058186	94.460786

(continued)

Table 2 (concluded)

n	8.0%	9.0%	10.0%	12.0%	14.0%	16.0%	18.0%
1	1.000000	1.000000	1.000000	1.000000	1.000000	1.000000	1.000000
2	2.080000	2.090000	2.100000	2.120000	2.140000	2.160000	2.180000
3	3.246400	3.278100	3.310000	3.374400	3.439600	3.505600	3.572400
4	4.506112	4.573129	4.641000	4.779328	4.921144	5.066496	5.215432
5	5.866601	5.984711	6.105100	6.352847	6.610104	6.877135	7.154210
6	7.335929	7.523335	7.715610	8.115189	8.535519	8.977477	9.441968
7	8.922803	9.200435	9.487171	10.089012	10.730491	11.413873	12.141522
8	10.636628	11.028474	11.435888	12.299693	13.232760	14.240093	15.326996
9	12.487558	13.021036	13.579477	14.775656	16.085347	17.518508	19.085855
10	14.486562	15.192930	15.937425	17.548735	19.337295	21.321469	23.521309
11	16.645487	17.560293	18.531167	20.654583	23.044516	25.732904	28.755144
12	18.977126	20.140720	21.384284	24.133133	27.270749	30.850169	34.931070
13	21.495297	22.953385	24.522712	28.029109	32.088654	36.786196	42.218663
14	24.214920	26.019189	27.974983	32.392602	37.581065	43.671987	50.818022
15	27.152114	29.360916	31.772482	37.279715	43.842414	51.659505	60.965266
16	30.324283	33.003399	35.949730	42.753280	50.980352	60.925026	72.939014
17	33.750226	36.973705	40.544703	48.883674	59.117601	71.673030	87.068036
18	37.450244	41.301338	45.599173	55.749715	68.394066	84.140715	103.740283
19	41.446263	46.018458	51.159090	63.439681	78.969235	98.603230	123.413534
20	45.761964	51.160120	57.274999	72.052442	91.024928	115.379747	146.627970
21	50.422921	56.764530	64.002499	81.698736	104.768418	134.840506	174.021005
22	55.456755	62.873338	71.402749	92.502584	120.435996	157.414987	206.344785
23	60.893296	69.531939	79.543024	104.602894	138.297035	183.601385	244.486847
24	66.764759	76.789813	88.497327	118.155241	158.658620	213.977607	289.494479
25	73.105940	84.700896	98.347059	133.333870	181.870827	249.214024	342.603486
26	79.954415	93.323977	109.181765	150.333934	208.332743	290.088267	405.272113
27	87.350768	102.723135	121.099942	169.374007	238.499327	337.502390	479.221093
28	95.338830	112.968217	134.209936	190.698887	272.889233	392.502773	566.480890
29	103.965936	124.135356	148.630930	214.582754	312.093725	456.303216	669.447450
30	113.283211	136.307539	164.494023	241.332684	356.786847	530.311731	790.947991

TABLE 3

Present Value of 1: $p_{n,i} = \dfrac{1}{(1+i)^n}$

n	1.5%	4.0%	4.5%	5.0%	5.5%	6.0%	7.0%
1	0.985222	0.961538	0.956938	0.952381	0.947867	0.943396	0.934579
2	0.970662	0.924556	0.915730	0.907029	0.898452	0.889996	0.873439
3	0.956317	0.888996	0.876297	0.863838	0.851614	0.839619	0.816298
4	0.942184	0.854804	0.838561	0.822702	0.807217	0.792094	0.762895
5	0.928260	0.821927	0.802451	0.783526	0.765134	0.747258	0.712986
6	0.914542	0.790315	0.767896	0.746215	0.725246	0.704961	0.666342
7	0.901027	0.759918	0.734828	0.710681	0.687437	0.665057	0.622750
8	0.887711	0.730690	0.703185	0.676839	0.651599	0.627412	0.582012
9	0.874592	0.702587	0.672904	0.644609	0.617629	0.591898	0.543934
10	0.861667	0.675564	0.643928	0.613913	0.585431	0.558395	0.508349
11	0.848933	0.649581	0.616199	0.584679	0.554911	0.526788	0.475093
12	0.836387	0.624597	0.589664	0.556837	0.525982	0.496969	0.444012
13	0.824027	0.600574	0.564272	0.530321	0.498561	0.468839	0.414964
14	0.811849	0.577475	0.539973	0.505068	0.472569	0.442301	0.387817
15	0.799852	0.555265	0.516720	0.481017	0.447933	0.417265	0.362446
16	0.788031	0.533908	0.494469	0.458112	0.424581	0.393646	0.338735
17	0.776385	0.513373	0.473176	0.436297	0.402447	0.371364	0.316574
18	0.764912	0.493628	0.452800	0.415521	0.381466	0.350344	0.295864
19	0.753607	0.474642	0.433302	0.395734	0.361579	0.330513	0.276508
20	0.742470	0.456387	0.414643	0.376889	0.342729	0.311805	0.258419
21	0.731498	0.438834	0.396787	0.358942	0.324862	0.294155	0.241513
22	0.720688	0.421955	0.379701	0.341850	0.307926	0.277505	0.225713
23	0.710037	0.405726	0.363350	0.325571	0.291873	0.261797	0.210947
24	0.699544	0.390121	0.347703	0.310068	0.276657	0.246979	0.197147
25	0.689206	0.375117	0.332731	0.295303	0.262234	0.232999	0.184249
26	0.679021	0.360689	0.318402	0.281241	0.248563	0.219810	0.172195
27	0.668986	0.346817	0.304691	0.267848	0.235605	0.207368	0.160930
28	0.659099	0.333477	0.291571	0.255094	0.223322	0.195630	0.150402
29	0.649359	0.320651	0.279015	0.242946	0.211679	0.184557	0.140563
30	0.639762	0.308319	0.267000	0.231377	0.200944	0.174110	0.131367

(continued)

Table 3 (concluded)

n	8.0%	9.0%	10.0%	12.0%	14.0%	16.0%	18.0%
1	0.925926	0.917431	0.909091	0.892857	0.877193	0.862069	0.847458
2	0.857339	0.841680	0.826446	0.797194	0.769468	0.743163	0.718184
3	0.793832	0.772183	0.751315	0.711780	0.674972	0.640658	0.608631
4	0.735030	0.708425	0.683013	0.635518	0.592080	0.552291	0.515789
5	0.680583	0.649931	0.620921	0.567427	0.519369	0.476113	0.437109
6	0.630170	0.596267	0.564474	0.506631	0.455587	0.410442	0.370432
7	0.583490	0.547034	0.513158	0.452349	0.399637	0.353830	0.313925
8	0.540269	0.501866	0.466507	0.403883	0.350559	0.305025	0.266038
9	0.500249	0.460428	0.424098	0.360610	0.307508	0.262953	0.225456
10	0.463193	0.422411	0.385543	0.321973	0.269744	0.226684	0.191064
11	0.428883	0.387533	0.350494	0.287476	0.236617	0.195417	0.161919
12	0.397114	0.355535	0.318631	0.256675	0.207559	0.168463	0.137220
13	0.367698	0.326179	0.289664	0.229174	0.182069	0.145227	0.116288
14	0.340461	0.299246	0.263331	0.204620	0.159710	0.125195	0.098549
15	0.315242	0.274538	0.239392	0.182696	0.140096	0.107927	0.083516
16	0.291890	0.251870	0.217629	0.163122	0.122892	0.093041	0.070776
17	0.270269	0.231073	0.197845	0.145644	0.107800	0.080207	0.059980
18	0.250249	0.211994	0.179859	0.130040	0.094561	0.069144	0.050830
19	0.231712	0.194490	0.163508	0.116107	0.082948	0.059607	0.043077
20	0.214548	0.178431	0.148644	0.103667	0.072762	0.051385	0.036506
21	0.198656	0.163698	0.135131	0.092560	0.063826	0.044298	0.030937
22	0.183941	0.150182	0.122846	0.082643	0.055988	0.038188	0.026218
23	0.170315	0.137781	0.111678	0.073788	0.049112	0.032920	0.022218
24	0.157699	0.126405	0.101526	0.065882	0.043081	0.028380	0.018829
25	0.146018	0.115968	0.092296	0.058823	0.037790	0.024465	0.015957
26	0.135202	0.106393	0.083905	0.052521	0.033149	0.021091	0.013523
27	0.125187	0.097608	0.076278	0.046894	0.029078	0.018182	0.011460
28	0.115914	0.089548	0.069343	0.041869	0.025507	0.015674	0.009712
29	0.107328	0.082155	0.063039	0.037383	0.022375	0.013512	0.008230
30	0.099377	0.075371	0.057309	0.033378	0.019627	0.011648	0.006975

TABLE 4

Present Value of an Ordinary Annuity of 1: $p_{O,n,i} = \dfrac{1 - \dfrac{1}{(1+i)^n}}{i}$

n	1.5%	4.0%	4.5%	5.0%	5.5%	6.0%	7.0%
1	0.985222	0.961538	0.956938	0.952381	0.947867	0.943396	0.934579
2	1.955883	1.886095	1.872668	1.859410	1.846320	1.833393	1.808018
3	2.912200	2.775091	2.748964	2.723248	2.697933	2.673012	2.624316
4	3.854385	3.629895	3.587526	3.545951	3.505150	3.465106	3.387211
5	4.782645	4.451822	4.389977	4.329477	4.270284	4.212364	4.100197
6	5.697187	5.242137	5.157872	5.075692	4.995530	4.917324	4.766540
7	6.598214	6.002055	5.892701	5.786373	5.682967	5.582381	5.389289
8	7.485925	6.732745	6.595886	6.463213	6.334566	6.209794	5.971299
9	8.360517	7.435332	7.268790	7.107822	6.952195	6.801692	6.515232
10	9.222185	8.110896	7.912718	7.721735	7.537626	7.360087	7.023582
11	10.071118	8.760477	8.528917	8.306414	8.092536	7.886875	7.498674
12	10.907505	9.385074	9.118581	8.863252	8.618518	8.383844	7.942686
13	11.731532	9.985648	9.682852	9.393573	9.117079	8.852683	8.357651
14	12.543382	10.563123	10.222825	9.898641	9.589648	9.294984	8.745468
15	13.343233	11.118387	10.739546	10.379658	10.037581	9.712249	9.107914
16	14.131264	11.652296	11.234015	10.837770	10.462162	10.105895	9.446649
17	14.907649	12.165669	11.707191	11.274066	10.864609	10.477260	9.763223
18	15.672561	12.659297	12.159992	11.689587	11.246074	10.827603	10.059087
19	16.426168	13.133939	12.593294	12.085321	11.607654	11.158116	10.335595
20	17.168639	13.590326	13.007936	12.462210	11.950382	11.469921	10.594014
21	17.900137	14.029160	13.404724	12.821153	12.275244	11.764077	10.835527
22	18.620824	14.451115	13.784425	13.163003	12.583170	12.041582	11.061240
23	19.330861	14.856842	14.147775	13.488574	12.875042	12.303379	11.272187
24	20.030405	15.246963	14.495478	13.798642	13.151699	12.550358	11.469334
25	20.719611	15.622080	14.828209	14.093945	13.413933	12.783356	11.653583
26	21.398632	15.982769	15.146611	14.375185	13.662495	13.003166	11.825779
27	22.067617	16.329586	15.451303	14.643034	13.898100	13.210534	11.986709
28	22.726717	16.663063	15.742874	14.898127	14.121422	13.406164	12.137111
29	23.376076	16.983715	16.021889	15.141074	14.333101	13.590721	12.277674
30	24.015838	17.292033	16.288889	15.372451	14.533745	13.764831	12.409041

(continued)

Table 4 (concluded)

n	8.0%	9.0%	10.0%	12.0%	14.0%	16.0%	18.0%
1	0.925926	0.917431	0.909091	0.892857	0.877193	0.862069	0.847458
2	1.783265	1.759111	1.735537	1.690051	1.646661	1.605232	1.565642
3	2.577097	2.531295	2.486852	2.401831	2.321632	2.245890	2.174273
4	3.312127	3.239720	3.169865	3.037349	2.913712	2.798181	2.690062
5	3.992710	3.889651	3.790787	3.604776	3.433081	3.274294	3.127171
6	4.622880	4.485919	4.355261	4.111407	3.888668	3.684736	3.497603
7	5.206370	5.032953	4.868419	4.563757	4.288305	4.038565	3.811528
8	5.746639	5.534819	5.334926	4.967640	4.638864	4.343591	4.077566
9	6.246888	5.995247	5.759024	5.328250	4.946372	4.606544	4.303022
10	6.710081	6.417658	6.144567	5.650223	5.216116	4.833227	4.494086
11	7.138964	6.805191	6.495061	5.937699	5.452733	5.028644	4.656005
12	7.536078	7.160725	6.813692	6.194374	5.660292	5.197107	4.793225
13	7.903776	7.486904	7.103356	6.423548	5.842362	5.342334	4.909513
14	8.244237	7.786150	7.366687	6.628168	6.002072	5.467529	5.008062
15	8.559479	8.060688	7.606080	6.810864	6.142168	5.575456	5.091578
16	8.851369	8.312558	7.823709	6.973986	6.265060	5.668497	5.162354
17	9.121638	8.543631	8.021553	7.119630	6.372859	5.748704	5.222334
18	9.371887	8.755625	8.201712	7.249670	6.467420	5.817848	5.273164
19	9.603599	8.950115	8.364920	7.365777	6.550369	5.877455	5.316241
20	9.818147	9.128546	8.513564	7.469444	6.623131	5.928841	5.352746
21	10.016803	9.292244	8.648694	7.562006	6.686957	5.973139	5.383683
22	10.201044	9.442425	8.771540	7.644646	6.742944	6.011326	5.409901
23	10.371059	9.580207	8.883218	7.718434	6.792056	6.044247	5.432120
24	10.528758	9.706612	8.984744	7.784316	6.835137	6.072627	5.450949
25	10.674776	9.822580	9.077040	7.843139	6.872927	6.097092	5.466906
26	10.809978	9.928972	9.160945	7.895660	6.906077	6.118183	5.480429
27	10.935165	10.026580	9.237223	7.942554	6.935155	6.136364	5.491889
28	11.051078	10.116128	9.306567	7.984423	6.960662	6.152038	5.501601
29	11.158406	10.198283	9.369606	8.021806	6.983037	6.165550	5.509831
30	11.257783	10.273654	9.426914	8.055184	7.002664	6.177198	5.516806

TABLE 5

Present Value of Annuity Due: $p_{D,n,i} = \dfrac{1 - \dfrac{1}{(1+i)^{n-1}}}{i} + 1$

n	1.5%	4.0%	4.5%	5.0%	5.5%	6.0%	7.0%
1	1.000000	1.000000	1.000000	1.000000	1.000000	1.000000	1.000000
2	1.985222	1.961538	1.956938	1.952381	1.947867	1.943396	1.934579
3	2.955883	2.886095	2.872668	2.859410	2.846320	2.833393	2.808018
4	3.912200	3.775091	3.748964	3.723248	3.697933	3.673012	3.624316
5	4.854385	4.629895	4.587526	4.545951	4.505150	4.465106	4.387211
6	5.782645	5.451822	5.389977	5.329477	5.270284	5.212364	5.100197
7	6.697187	6.242137	6.157872	6.075692	5.995530	5.917324	5.766540
8	7.598214	7.002055	6.892701	6.786373	6.682967	6.582381	6.389289
9	8.485925	7.732745	7.595886	7.463213	7.334566	7.209794	6.971299
10	9.360517	8.435332	8.268790	8.107822	7.952195	7.801692	7.515232
11	10.222185	9.110896	8.912718	8.721735	8.537626	8.360087	8.023582
12	11.071118	9.760477	9.528917	9.306414	9.092536	8.886875	8.498674
13	11.907505	10.385074	10.118581	9.863252	9.618518	9.383844	8.942686
14	12.731532	10.985648	10.682852	10.393573	10.117079	9.852683	9.357651
15	13.543382	11.563123	11.222825	10.898641	10.589648	10.294984	9.745468
16	14.343233	12.118387	11.739546	11.379658	11.037581	10.712249	10.107914
17	15.131264	12.652296	12.234015	11.837770	11.462162	11.105895	10.446649
18	15.907649	13.165669	12.707191	12.274066	11.864609	11.477260	10.763223
19	16.672561	13.659297	13.159992	12.689587	12.246074	11.827603	11.059087
20	17.426168	14.133939	13.593294	13.085321	12.607654	12.158116	11.335595
21	18.168639	14.590326	14.007936	13.462210	12.950382	12.469921	11.594014
22	18.900137	15.029160	14.404724	13.821153	13.275244	12.764077	11.835527
23	19.620824	15.451115	14.784425	14.163003	13.583170	13.041582	12.061240
24	20.330861	15.856842	15.147775	14.488574	13.875042	13.303379	12.272187
25	21.030405	16.246963	15.495478	14.798642	14.151699	13.550358	12.469334
26	21.719611	16.622080	15.828209	15.093945	14.413933	13.783356	12.653583
27	22.398632	16.982769	16.146611	15.375185	14.662495	14.003166	12.825779
28	23.067617	17.329586	16.451303	15.643034	14.898100	14.210534	12.986709
29	23.726717	17.663063	16.742874	15.898127	15.121422	14.406164	13.137111
30	24.376076	17.983715	17.021889	16.141074	15.333101	14.590721	13.277674

(continued)

Table 5 (concluded)

n	8.0%	9.0%	10.0%	12.0%	14.0%	16.0%	18.0%
1	1.000000	1.000000	1.000000	1.000000	1.000000	1.000000	1.000000
2	1.925926	1.917431	1.909091	1.892857	1.877193	1.862069	1.847458
3	2.783265	2.759111	2.735537	2.690051	2.646661	2.605232	2.565642
4	3.577097	3.531295	3.486852	3.401831	3.321632	3.245890	3.174273
5	4.312127	4.239720	4.169865	4.037349	3.913712	3.798181	3.690062
6	4.992710	4.889651	4.790787	4.604776	4.433081	4.274294	4.127171
7	5.622880	5.485919	5.355261	5.111407	4.888668	4.684736	4.497603
8	6.206370	6.032953	5.868419	5.563757	5.288305	5.038565	4.811528
9	6.746639	6.534819	6.334926	5.967640	5.638864	5.343591	5.077566
10	7.246888	6.995247	6.759024	6.328250	5.946372	5.606544	5.303022
11	7.710081	7.417658	7.144567	6.650223	6.216116	5.833227	5.494086
12	8.138964	7.805191	7.495061	6.937699	6.452733	6.028644	5.656005
13	8.536078	8.160725	7.813692	7.194374	6.660292	6.197107	5.793225
14	8.903776	8.486904	8.103356	7.423548	6.842362	6.342334	5.909513
15	9.244237	8.786150	8.366687	7.628168	7.002072	6.467529	6.008062
16	9.559479	9.060688	8.606080	7.810864	7.142168	6.575456	6.091578
17	9.851369	9.312558	8.823709	7.973986	7.265060	6.668497	6.162354
18	10.121638	9.543631	9.021553	8.119630	7.372859	6.748704	6.222334
19	10.371887	9.755625	9.201712	8.249670	7.467420	6.817848	6.273164
20	10.603599	9.950115	9.364920	8.365777	7.550369	6.877455	6.316241
21	10.818147	10.128546	9.513564	8.469444	7.623131	6.928841	6.352746
22	11.016803	10.292244	9.648694	8.562006	7.686957	6.973139	6.383683
23	11.201044	10.442425	9.771540	8.644646	7.742944	7.011326	6.409901
24	11.371059	10.580207	9.883218	8.718434	7.792056	7.044247	6.432120
25	11.528758	10.706612	9.984744	8.784316	7.835137	7.072627	6.450949
26	11.674776	10.822580	10.077040	8.843139	7.872927	7.097092	6.466906
27	11.809978	10.928972	10.160945	8.895660	7.906077	7.118183	6.480429
28	11.935165	11.026580	10.237223	8.942554	7.935155	7.136364	6.491889
29	12.051078	11.116128	10.306567	8.984423	7.960662	7.152038	6.501601
30	12.158406	11.198283	10.369606	9.021806	7.983037	7.165550	6.509831

PART 2

BUSINESS OPERATING ACTIVITIES

CHAPTER 6
Cash and Receivables

CHAPTER 7
Inventories: Cost Measurement and Flow Assumptions

CHAPTER 8
Inventories: Special Valuation Issues

CHAPTER 9
Current Liabilities and Contingent Obligations

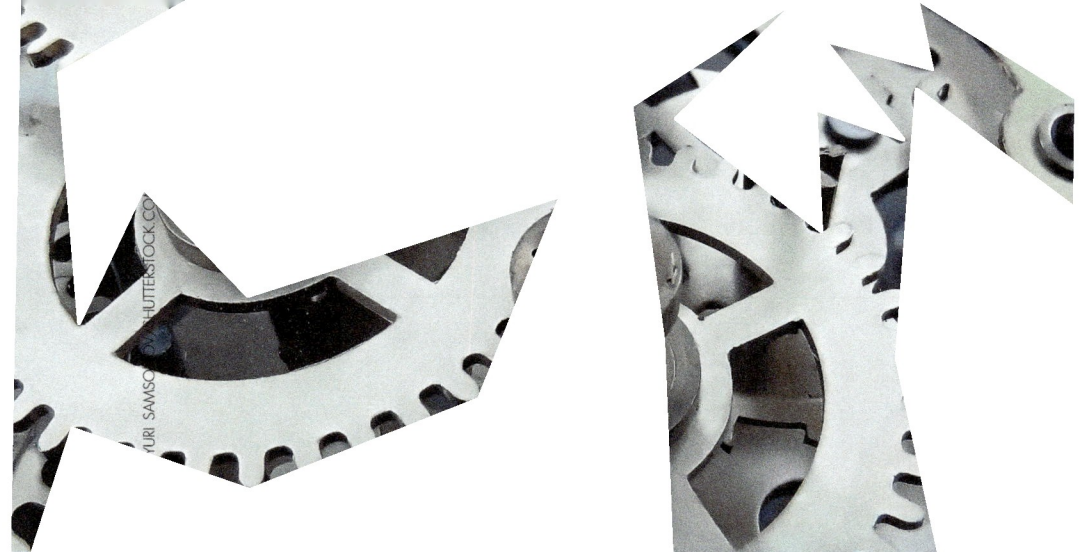

CASH AND RECEIVABLES

Show Me the Money!

From cruising the crystal blue waters of the Caribbean to the rugged beauty of Alaska's Inside Passage, **Royal Caribbean**, like all companies, relies on a steady flow of cash. However, holding large amounts of cash does not maximize a company's profitability because cash earns a low rate of return. A company can improve its performance by investing its excess cash in investment securities or other productive assets which generate higher rates of return. Therefore, management's goal is to hold the minimum amount of cash needed to operate its business, meet debt obligations, and pursue new business opportunities.

One ingredient of successful cash management involves estimating the timing of a company's cash inflows and outflows. This can be particularly difficult for a company whose business is seasonal, like Royal Caribbean. As shown by the fiscal 2013 quarterly financial information on the next page, Royal Caribbean's revenues are relatively stable each quarter but its operating cash flow is significantly higher in the second and third quarters of its fiscal year (April–September) when demand for cruising is greater. Royal Caribbean must properly forecast its cash receipts and expenditures throughout the fiscal year to ensure that it has enough money to operate smoothly.

LEARNING OBJECTIVES

After reading this chapter you will be able to

LO 6.1 Identify items of cash and cash equivalents.

LO 6.2 Understand the importance of cash controls.

LO 6.3 Define and identify different types of receivables.

LO 6.4 Explain the accounting issues associated with accounts receivable.

LO 6.5 Explain the estimation of uncollectible accounts receivable and its effect on the valuation of receivables.

LO 6.6 Explain how to account for secured borrowings and sales of accounts receivable.

LO 6.7 Account for short-term notes receivable.

LO 6.8 *(Appendix 6.1)* Understand how petty cash funds and bank reconciliations are used to control cash.

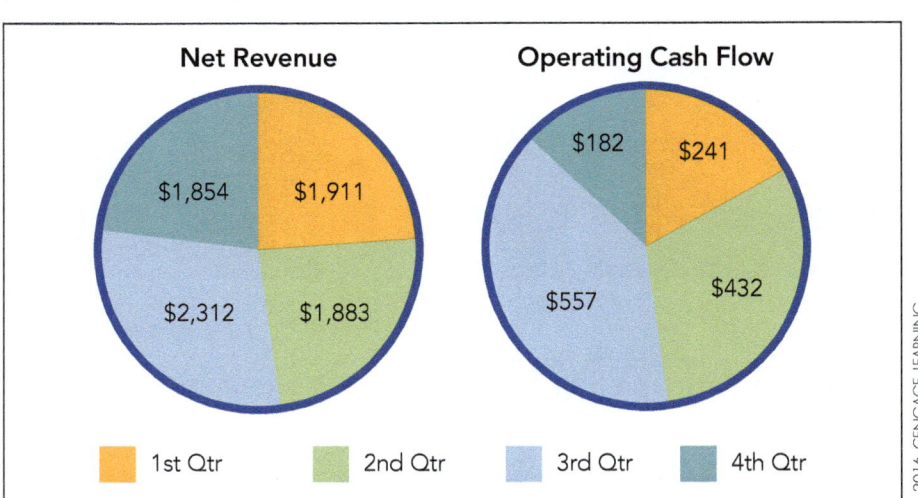

Royal Caribbean: 2013 Quarterly Revenues and Cash Flow Information (Amounts in millions)

A company's cash balance is also influenced by its management of accounts receivable. For example, most companies allow customers to purchase items on credit. If a company extends credit to only the lowest risk customers, it gives up sales, and ultimately cash flow and profit. However, credit policies that are too liberal can lead to excessive bad debt with no future cash collection. Therefore, management must carefully monitor accounts receivable to maximize profits and cash inflows.

In addition, investors and creditors can gain important insights into a company's expected future cash flows by examining its receivables and growth prospects. For example, if accounts receivable increase at a higher rate than sales, it could mean that the company has liberal sales terms or has difficulty collecting amounts owed from its customers. Similarly, an unusual change in the allowance for doubtful accounts relative to the change in accounts receivable may signal future earnings and cash flow difficulties.[1]

Royal Caribbean's effective management of cash and receivables has enabled it to maintain a solid financial foundation that has allowed the company to invest in its core business as well as pursue other profitable opportunities.

Financial statement users focus on a variety of information in making credit and investment decisions. Investors and creditors are interested in a company's **financial flexibility**, which refers to a company's ability to use its financial resources to meet obligations and respond to new business opportunities. These stakeholders are particularly concerned with liquidity. **Liquidity** refers to the availability of a company's liquid assets to settle its obligations. The most common liquid assets (assets that may be quickly converted into cash) are cash, short-term investments, accounts receivable, and notes receivable. In this chapter, we discuss the measurement and valuation procedures for cash, accounts receivable, and notes receivable. We discuss short and long-term investments in Chapter 13.

---

[1] Baruch Lev and S. Ramu Thiagarajan, "Fundamental Information Analysis" *Journal of Accounting Research* Vol. 31, No. 2 (Autumn 1993), pp. 190–215.

WHAT IS CASH?

LEARNING OBJECTIVE 6.1
Identify items of cash and cash equivalents.

Cash, the most liquid of all assets, is the resource used to engage in day-to-day business transactions, pay employees, meet a company's debt obligations, and take advantage of business opportunities when they arise. Cash includes the following:

- coins and currency
- unrestricted funds on deposit with a bank (such as checking accounts and savings accounts[2])
- negotiable instruments (such as checks)
- bank drafts
- undeposited credit card sales receipts

Cash also includes foreign currencies on deposit in foreign banks. For example, a U.S. company may make sales to a European customer, collect the amount owed in Euros, and deposit these funds in a foreign bank until they are needed. These foreign currency amounts are included in cash and are converted to the reporting currency (e.g., U.S. dollar) at each balance sheet date.[3]

To be reported as cash in the current assets section of the balance sheet, the amount must be available to pay current obligations. If there are contractual restrictions that prevent the company from using this money to pay its current debts, it cannot be reported as cash. Consider the following examples:

- **Sinking funds** are accounts into which a company deposits cash over an extended period for a specific purpose. At the end of the period, the cash (plus accumulated interest) is used for the specific purpose (e.g., to retire long-term bonds). Sinking funds are normally reported as long-term investments.
- **Certificates of deposit (CDs)** are financial instruments issued by banks that allow a company to invest cash for specific periods of time. CDs normally are classified as short-term investments.
- **Bank overdrafts** are overdrawn checking accounts. They are reported as current liabilities and should *not* be offset against positive checking or savings account balances in other bank accounts.
- **Postdated checks** from customers are checks dated in the future so they become payable on a date later than the issue date. Postdated checks are included as receivables until the date they become redeemable for cash.
- **Travel advances** are funds or checks given to employees to cover out-of-pocket expenses while traveling on company business. Because travel advances are satisfied when the employee submits receipts for business expenses, they are classified as prepaid items.

In addition, banks may require a portion of any amount loaned to a company to remain on deposit in the bank (usually earning a low interest rate) for the loan period. These required deposits are called **compensating balances** because they "compensate" the bank for granting the loan. For example, a bank loaning a company $100,000 at an interest rate of 12% may require that the company maintain a $10,000 deposit with the bank until the company repays the loan. Such arrangements both reduce the amount of cash available to the borrower and increase the effective interest rate the borrower pays for the use of the funds. In this example, although the stated interest rate is 12%, the effective rate for the actual funds used for a year is 13.33% ($12,000 ÷ $90,000), assuming the $10,000 compensating balance does not earn any interest. To avoid misleading users about the amount of cash available to meet current obligations, the SEC requires

---

[2] Although some banks place restrictions on the withdrawal of funds from savings accounts, they generally are included as a component of cash.

[3] Because the exchange rate between the foreign currency and the reporting currency (e.g., U.S. dollar) may change over time, an exchange gain or loss will be recognized upon conversion to the reporting currency. The accounting for these foreign currency transactions is beyond the scope of this text and covered in advanced accounting courses.

that companies report amounts held as compensating balances against its short-term borrowings in current assets separate from cash. Compensating balances for long-term borrowings are separately reported as noncurrent assets (as either long-term investments or other assets). Compensating balance agreements that do not legally restrict the amount of funds shown on the balance sheet are disclosed in the notes to the financial statements.

Exhibit 6.1 summarizes what is, and what is not, included in cash.

EXHIBIT 6.1 Classification of Cash and Noncash Items

Item	Classification
Coins and currency	Cash
Demand deposits (checking and savings accounts)	Cash
Negotiable instruments (bank drafts, money orders)	Cash
Foreign currencies on deposit in foreign banks	Cash
Sinking funds	Long-term investment
Certificates of deposit	Short-term investment
Bank overdrafts	Current liability
Postdated checks	Receivable
Travel advances	Prepaid expense
Compensating balances	Current or noncurrent asset

Cash and Cash Equivalents

While a few companies use the caption *Cash* on their balance sheets, the majority of companies use a caption such as *Cash and Cash Equivalents*. **Cash equivalents** are short-term, highly liquid investments that are readily convertible into known amounts of cash and so near their maturity that there is little risk of changes in value because of changes in interest rates. Generally, only low risk, highly liquid investments with maturity dates of three months or less from the date acquired by the holder are cash equivalents.[4] Securities such as commercial paper, treasury bills, and money market funds are examples of cash equivalents. Companies combine cash equivalents with cash because of their liquidity and low risk. For instance, as shown in Real Report 6.1, **Royal Caribbean** reported cash and cash equivalents as a current asset and described its cash equivalents in the notes to its financial statements.

LOOKING AHEAD

Many people tend to think of cash equivalents as cash. However, cash equivalents have different characteristics and risks from cash. In their research efforts, both the FASB and the IASB have recognized that combining these different assets may be misleading. Therefore, it is possible that the cash equivalent classification will be removed and cash equivalents will be presented and classified in a manner similar to other short-term investments.

---

[4] FASB ASC 230-10-20: Statement of Cash Flows: Glossary.

> **REAL REPORT**   CASH AND CASH EQUIVALENTS | **6.1**
>
> **Royal Caribbean Cruises, LTD**
> **CONSOLIDATED BALANCE SHEET (in part)**
>
> | (in millions) | December 31, 2013 | December 31, 2012 |
> |---|---|---|
> | ASSETS | | |
> | Current assets: | | |
> | Cash and cash equivalents | $204,687 | $194,855 |
>
> **NOTES TO FINANCIAL STATEMENTS**
> **Note 2: Summary of Significant Accounting Policies (in part)**
>
> *Cash and Cash Equivalents (in part)*
> Cash and cash equivalents include cash and marketable securities with original maturities of less than 90 days.

Royal Caribbean

Question:

1. Why does Royal Caribbean combine cash and cash equivalents into one amount on the balance sheet?

Suggested answer to this question is found at the end of the chapter.

GOT IT?

6-1 What are the components of cash? What items may be confused with cash, but normally are categorized under other balance sheet captions?

6-2 What are *cash equivalents*?

WHY DO BUSINESSES NEED CASH CONTROLS?

LEARNING OBJECTIVE 6.2
Understand the importance of cash controls.

As noted earlier, it is important for a company to effectively manage its cash to ensure that it can fulfill its obligations while earning an adequate return on any excess cash. Because cash is a company's most liquid asset, it's important to protect it from theft, loss, and waste. **Internal control systems** are the policies and procedures a company uses to ensure its financial reports are reliable, its operations (including safeguarding its assets) are effective and efficient, and it complies with applicable laws and regulations. These controls are so important that the Sarbanes-Oxley Act of 2002 requires all publicly traded companies to maintain adequate internal control systems (including internal controls for cash) and independent auditors to issue an opinion on the adequacy of the company's internal controls, noting any weaknesses or deficiencies.

Cash Control Procedures

Internal control over cash is enhanced by routine reviews of the accuracy of recorded cash transactions and the separation of employee duties. Cash control systems can be subdivided into two main functions: control over receipts and control over payments.

Control Over Receipts The control procedures a company adopts for its cash receipts should be designed to safeguard all cash inflows from the time they arrive at the company until they are deposited in its bank account. The key elements in a cash receipts internal control system are as follows:

- immediate counting of receipts by the person opening the mail or the salesperson using the cash register, and subsequent verification by an independent person

- daily recording of all cash receipts in the accounting records
- daily deposit of all receipts in the company's bank account

Control Over Payments The control procedures for payments should ensure that only authorized payments are made for actual company expenditures. The key elements in a cash payments internal control system include the following:

- requiring approval of all expenditures prior to their payment
- making all payments by check (or electronic funds transfer) so there is a record for every company expenditure
- periodically reconciling the cash balance in the bank statement with the company's accounting records

Two important elements of the internal control over cash are a petty cash system and a bank reconciliation, each of which is discussed in more detail in Appendix 6.1 at the end of this chapter.

Electronic Payments

Many companies prepare and process hundreds or even thousands of checks each day to pay their suppliers and employees. Furthermore, they receive and process an equally large number of checks from their customers. Whether for payments or receipts, processing the paperwork for checks is expensive. Therefore, many banks offer **electronic funds transfer (EFT)** to their customers. EFT transfers cash between companies electronically without the need for a check. In addition, banks also use **accounts receivable conversion (ARC)** for faster processing of checks. In ARC, when paper checks arrive at a lockbox, they are converted into electronic payments, and the check itself is destroyed. Finally, the **Check Clearing for the 21st Century Act** (termed **Check 21**) is a law that allows merchants to scan checks and transmit the digital images to the bank instead of sending the actual check. There's even an iPhone app that allows customers to deposit checks by taking a photo of both sides of the check and sending it directly to the bank!

As shown in Exhibit 6.2, between 2009 and 2012, noncash payments grew by 4.4% and had a total value of $79 trillion. Of these noncash payments, more than

EXHIBIT 6.2 **Distribution of the Number and Value of Noncash Payments**

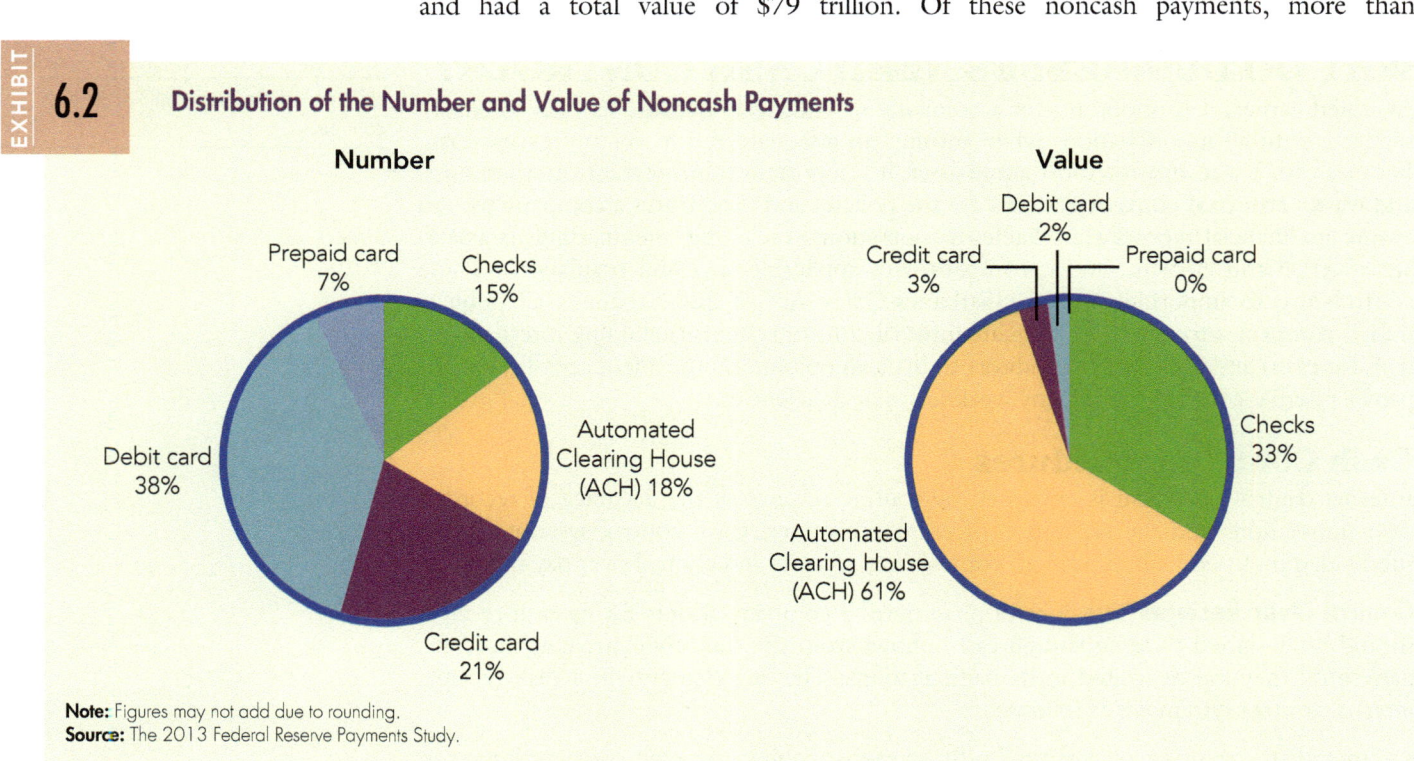

Note: Figures may not add due to rounding.
Source: The 2013 Federal Reserve Payments Study.

three-fourths were made electronically, with debit cards being the most frequently used electronic payment type.

As more companies and banks use EFT, ARC, and Check 21 systems, fewer physical documents (e.g., checks) are processed. Therefore, greater emphasis is being placed on internal control systems as they apply to computer technology because fewer physical source documents are available to verify cash inflows and outflows.

> **GOT IT?**
>
> **6-3** What are *internal control systems?*

WHAT ARE THE DIFFERENT TYPES OF RECEIVABLES?

LEARNING OBJECTIVE 6.3
Define and identify different types of receivables.

Receivables are amounts owed to the company by customers and other parties arising from the company's operations. Most receivables are settled when the customer or borrower pays cash, although others may be settled through the receipt of other assets or services. Additionally, some receivables go unpaid and must be written off as uncollectible. **Companies report receivables that are expected to be collected within one year or the current operating cycle, whichever is longer, on the balance sheet as current assets; the remainder are classified as noncurrent.** Also, a company may group receivables within its classified balance sheet as trade receivables and nontrade receivables.

Trade Receivables Trade receivables arise from the credit sale of the company's products or services to customers. For instance, manufacturers may sell on credit to retailers (or to distributors or other manufacturers), and retailers may sell on credit to consumers. Companies choose to sell on credit in order to increase sales. However, credit sales result in additional costs in managing the collection process, as well as additional risk from bad debts due to nonpayment by customers. Therefore, when companies consider whether to sell on credit, they must evaluate the trade-off between the additional gross profit received from the expected credit sales and the additional expenses incurred due to these credit sales. Most companies have established credit policies that reflect the degree of risk that they are willing to accept to increase sales. However, some companies believe that they can lower costs and increase profits by selling exclusively (or almost exclusively) to customers for cash. Note that credit card sales involving bank credit cards are treated as cash sales, as we discuss later in the chapter.

Trade receivables generally are the majority of a company's total receivables balance. Trade receivables may be subclassified into the following:

- **Accounts receivable**: obligations of customers to pay for goods or services
- **Notes receivable**: unconditional written obligations of customers or suppliers to pay a certain sum of money on a specific date for goods or services

We discuss these subclassifications later in the chapter.

Nontrade Receivables Nontrade receivables arise from transactions that are not directly related to the sale of the company's goods and services. Examples include deposits with utilities, advances to executives and employees, loans made by nonfinancial companies, deposits made to guarantee performance, and declared dividends and accrued interest on investments. Nontrade receivables are reported on the balance sheet as current or noncurrent assets, depending upon the length of their collection period. We discuss nontrade receivables in Chapter 13.

Overview of Accounting for Trade Receivables

Accounting for trade receivables involves a number of issues, as outlined in Exhibit 6.3.

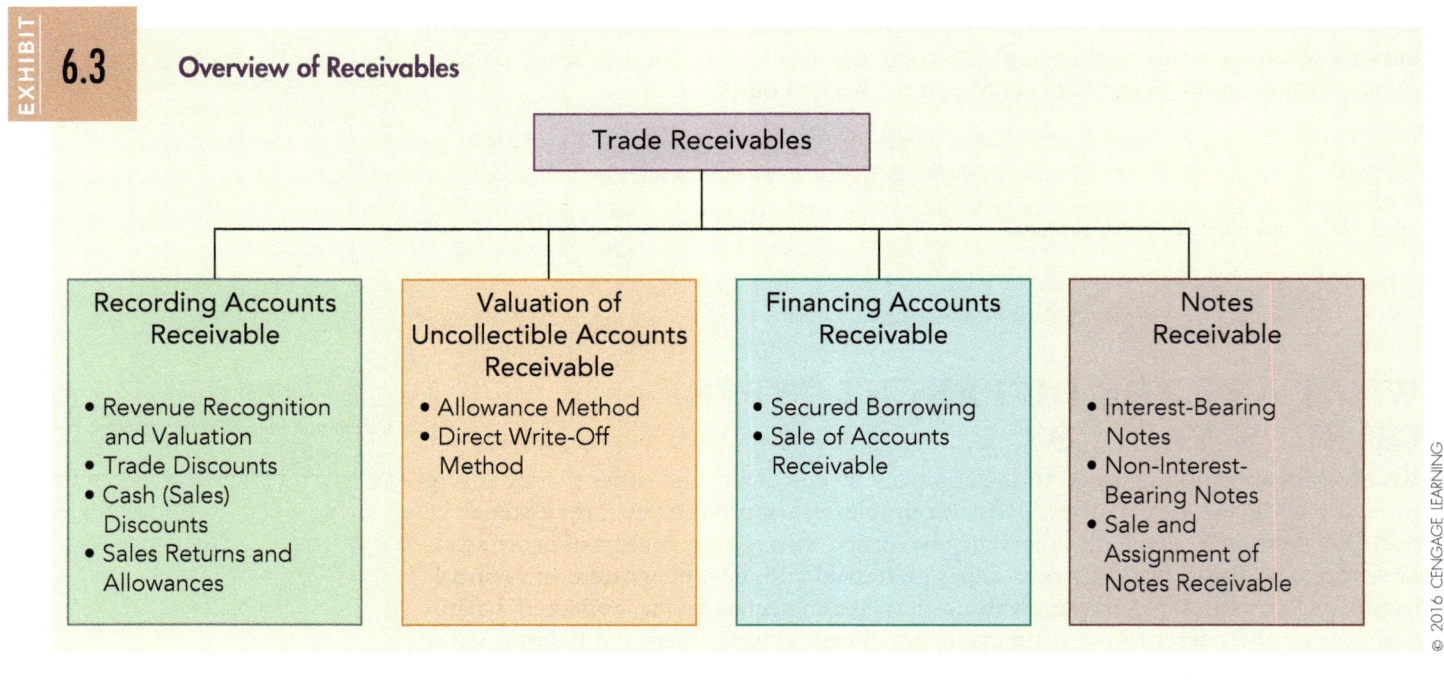

EXHIBIT 6.3 Overview of Receivables

GOT IT?

6-4 How are trade receivables different from nontrade receivables?

LEARNING OBJECTIVE 6.4
Explain the accounting issues associated with accounts receivable.

HOW ARE ACCOUNTS RECEIVABLE RECORDED?

The initial recognition of accounts receivable involves the proper application of the revenue recognition principle, as well as consideration of any trade (or quantity) discounts, cash (or sales) discounts, and sales returns and allowances.

Revenue Recognition and Valuation

A company will often make sales of goods and services to customers by extending short-term credit. As discussed in Chapter 5, a company records revenue from these credit sales by applying the **revenue recognition** principle. **Revenue is recognized when a company satisfies its performance obligation to a customer.** Because revenue is normally recognized when a product or service is delivered, credit sales trigger recognition of both an asset (an account or note receivable) and revenue.

There are two issues related to the valuation of receivables:

- initial recording of the receivables (present value versus maturity value)
- estimation of the probability of collection

GAAP requires receivables to be recorded and reported at their present values. However, GAAP excludes accounts receivable from this rule because the short collection period for most trade receivables (generally 60 days or less) usually makes the difference between a receivable's present value and maturity value immaterial. Consequently, **most short-term trade receivables are recorded initially at their maturity values.**[5]

[5] FASB ASC 835-30-15: Interest: Imputation of Interest.

Whenever a company extends credit, there is a risk that it may not collect all of its receivables. GAAP requires companies to consider the uncertainty of collection in valuing its receivables on its balance sheet. Therefore, **trade receivables are normally valued and reported at net realizable value, which is the amount that the company expects to collect in cash.** We discuss the accounting procedures that deal with the uncertainty of collecting receivables later in this chapter.

Trade Discounts

Companies frequently offer **trade discounts** (or **quantity discounts**) to purchasers as a means to provide incentives to important customers, grant price reductions for large purchases, or to hide real prices from competitors. Trade discounts are usually given as a percentage reduction of the list price of a product, and the transaction price should be recorded at the amount that the company is entitled to receive. For example, assume that a company offers a 10% trade discount to a customer who purchases 100 units of an item with a list price of $80 per unit. The customer is billed $7,200 [$8,000 − (0.10 × $8,000)] as the invoice price. The trade discount of $800 is recorded indirectly by recording the sale and the related receivable at the net of discount price ($7,200).

Cash (Sales) Discounts

Companies may also offer a **cash discount** (or **sales discount**) to induce prompt payment. This discount frequently is expressed using terms such as 2/10, n/30. The first component refers to the discount rate and period, and the second component refers to the invoice due date. Therefore, these terms are read as: The purchaser may subtract a 2% discount from the invoice price if payment is made *within 10 days*; otherwise, the *total invoice price* is due *within 30 days*.

Example Hemingway Company sells $5,000 of merchandise to Fitzgerald Company with terms of 2/10, n/30. If Fitzgerald pays for the merchandise within 10 days, it only has to pay $4,900 [$5,000 − ($5,000 × 0.02)]. By paying within the discount period, Fitzgerald is giving up the use of funds for 20 days (that is, it is accelerating payment by 20 days) to earn a discount of 2%. There is a strong incentive for Fitzgerald to pay within the discount period because the discount equates to a relatively high annual effective interest rate of approximately 36.5% (2% × 365 days per year ÷ 20 days).

Cash discounts are important in the financial management of companies, and the potential effects should be carefully analyzed by both sellers and purchasers. A purchasing company should take advantage of any cash discounts that have a higher effective annual interest rate than the rate it must pay to borrow money. For a selling company, a cash discount has two main positive effects:

- It stimulates faster collection of cash for use in current operations.
- It tends to reduce the losses resulting from uncollectible accounts.

However, the seller should also consider the negative effect of the reduction in total cash inflow due to the high effective interest rate incurred in order to collect receivables sooner. Sellers should attempt to set the cash discount rate at a level so that its positive effects exceed any negative effects.

Recording a Cash (Sales) Discount If a selling company extends cash discounts to its customers, the amount of consideration in the sales contract will vary depending upon whether the customer pays within the discount period or not. GAAP allows companies to use either the net price or the gross price method to account for the variable consideration.

- *Net Price Method:* When the selling company uses the net price method, it assumes the customer will take the discount and records the net invoice price (after deducting the expected cash discount) in both the accounts receivable and the sales revenue accounts at the time of sale. The company estimates this amount using the expected value derived from either a probability-weighted estimate or the most likely amount. When the customer pays and takes the allowable cash discount, the selling company records the cash receipt and reduces the receivable. However, if the customer does *not* take the cash discount, it pays an amount that is greater than the amount in the selling company's accounts receivable account. The company recognizes the difference between the cash received and the original amount of the accounts receivable as revenue.[6]

- *Gross Price Method:* When the selling company expects the customer will not pay within the discount period, it should use the gross price method, which records the total invoice price in both the accounts receivable and the sales revenue accounts at the time of sale. If the customer pays early and takes the allowable cash discount, the company records the difference between the cash received and the original amount of accounts receivable as a reduction in revenue. If the customer does not take the discount, the selling company receives an amount that is equal to the original balance in the accounts receivable account, and no further adjustment is needed.

Conceptually, a company should use the net price method to record sales and receivables associated with customers that it expects will take the discount, whereas it should use the gross price method for customers that are not expected to take the discount. However, the gross price method has two practical advantages over the net price method. First, by reporting receivable accounts at gross amounts, it simplifies communications with customers because discussions are based on the gross amount. Second, the gross price method generally requires less record keeping and is more cost effective. Regardless of which method is used, the reported amount for sales revenue will be the amount that the company expects to be entitled to receive from the customer. Both of these methods are illustrated below.

Example To illustrate the net price and gross price methods, assume the following:

- Howe Corporation sold $8,000 of merchandise to various customers on December 1, 2016, with terms of 2/10, n/30.
- On December 10, Howe received payment on goods originally billed at $5,500.
- On December 30, Howe received payment on goods originally billed at $1,500.
- The remaining $1,000 was not collected by the end of the year.

Assuming that Howe expects all of its customers to pay within the discount period and take the discount, it uses the net price method and computes the transaction price as $7,840 [$8,000 − (0.02 − $8,000)], the most likely amount that it expects to receive from customers. The journal entries to record these transactions under the net price method are shown in **Example 6.1a**.

If customers pay within the discount period, no adjustment is needed because the amount of cash received is equal to the recorded amount of the receivable. However, if customers do *not* take the cash discount and pay an amount greater than originally recorded, the change in the transaction price will be recognized as a credit to Sales Revenue. Finally, at the end of the accounting period, an adjusting entry may be necessary for any cash discounts no longer available on outstanding accounts receivable balances.

Alternatively, Howe may choose to use the gross price method and record the initial transaction at the gross amount of the sale. The journal entries to record this situation are shown in **Example 6.1b**.

Two items are of note if the gross price method is used. First, while no end of period adjustment is required in this example, a company may need to reduce revenues and

---

[6] If a company applies the net price method to a portfolio of sales contracts instead of to a single contract, it is possible that the amount of cash received will be less than the amount estimated at the time of sale. If this occurs, the difference between the cash received and the original amount of the accounts receivable will be recorded as a reduction in revenue.

> **EXAMPLE 6.1a**
>
> **Net Price Method of Accounting for Sales Discounts**
>
> | | | | |
> |---|---|---|---|
> | To record sale on Dec. 1, 2016 | Accounts Receivable [$8,000 − (0.02 × $8,000)]
　　Sales Revenue | 7,840 | 7,840 |
> | To record payment received on Dec. 10, 2016 | Cash
　　Accounts Receivable | 5,390 | 5,390 |
> | To record payment received on Dec. 30, 2016 | Cash
　　Accounts Receivable
　　[$1,500 − ($1,500 × 0.02)]
　　Sales Revenue | 1,500 | 1,470
30 |
> | To adjust the accounts at the end of the period | Accounts Receivable
　　Sales Revenue | 20 | 20 |

> **EXAMPLE 6.1b**
>
> **Gross Price Method of Accounting for Sales Discounts**
>
> | | | | |
> |---|---|---|---|
> | To record sale on Dec. 1, 2016 | Accounts Receivable
　　Sales Revenue | 8,000 | 8,000 |
> | To record payment received on Dec. 10, 2016 | Cash
　　[$5,500 − ($5,500 × 0.02)]
　　Sales Revenue
　　Accounts Receivable | 5,390 | 110
5,500 |
> | To record payment received on Dec. 30, 2016 | Cash
　　Accounts Receivable | 1,500 | 1,500 |
> | To adjust the accounts at the end of the period | No entry required | | |

receivables for any amount due from customers that is expects to receive prior to the end of the discount period. Second, if a customer pays within the discount period, some companies may choose to use a separate account titled "Sales Discounts Taken" that is deducted from Sales Revenue on the income statement to determine net sales.

Sales Returns and Allowances

When a company sells merchandise, the sales contract usually permits customers to return any defective items. Sometimes, contractual agreements also may allow customers to return products that are *not* defective. When the customer returns goods to the seller, the exchange is called a **sales return**. In some cases, when goods are sold that turn out to be defective, the customer may retain the goods and be allowed a reduction in the purchase price, called a **sales allowance**. Companies should **record the estimated amount of future returns and allowances in the period of sale to correctly report net sales revenue and the net realizable value of accounts receivable.**

Example Barclay Corporation sells $500,000 of goods, and the company estimates that returns and allowances will be 2% of sales. To record the sale and its estimate of returns and allowances, Barclay records the following entry in the period of sale (assuming it uses a periodic inventory system):

Accounts Receivable	500,000	
Sales Revenue ($500,000 × 0.98)		490,000
Return Liability ($500,000 × 0.02)		10,000

Barclay records revenue equal to the amount that it expects to be entitled to receive. The difference between the receivable and the revenue is a return liability which represents the company's obligation to return the customer's consideration.[7]

Consequently, when sales returns and allowances of $8,000 actually occur for goods sold on credit, Barclay records this transaction as follows:

Return Liability	8,000	
Accounts Receivable		8,000

*Large retailers with seasonal business, like **Macy's**, typically end their fiscal year around January 31. Because of the one-month delay after the height of their sales (during the holiday season), most returns will have been made, which makes the estimation of returns and allowances easier.*

Many large retailers with seasonal business often set their fiscal year-end a month or two after the heavy selling season so that most of the sales are final and revenues can be reliably measured with less uncertainty and estimation. For these companies (and in cases where returns and allowances are not material), returns and allowances are recorded when they actually occur by debiting Sales Revenue and crediting Accounts Receivable. Then, at the end of the period, any outstanding returns and allowances are estimated and the company decreases Sales Revenue and recognizes a corresponding return liability.

> ### GOT IT?
> **6-5** When is revenue usually recognized?
> **6-6** Explain the differences between trade discounts and cash (sales) discounts.
> **6-7** Briefly explain how to record accounts receivable when cash discounts are involved.
> **6-8** What is a *sales return*? A *sales allowance*? Describe the proper accounting for sales returns and allowances.

LEARNING OBJECTIVE 6.5
Explain the estimation of uncollectible accounts receivable and its effect on the valuation of receivables.

HOW ARE UNCOLLECTIBLE ACCOUNTS RECEIVABLE ESTIMATED?

The preceding discussion focused on recording trade accounts receivable. However, not all accounts receivable will be collected. Some will become bad debts. This uncertainty about the collectibility of accounts receivable represents a loss contingency. GAAP requires companies to estimate loss contingencies and deduct the amounts from income and assets when both of the following conditions are met:

- Information available prior to the issuance of the financial statements indicates that it is probable that an asset has been impaired at the date of the financial statements.
- The amount of the loss can be reasonably estimated.[8]

---
[7] If a company uses a perpetual inventory system, it would also record cost of goods sold (net of the cost of expected returns) and remove the inventory. The difference between Cost of Goods Sold and Inventory would be recorded as a return asset which represents the company's right to recover the goods returned by the customer.
[8] FASB ASC 450-20-25: Contingencies: Loss Contingencies.

Because uncollectible accounts receivable normally meet both conditions, most companies estimate bad debts.[9]

A company can record uncollectible accounts (bad debts) by either of two procedures:

- **Allowance Method**: Companies record uncollectible accounts in the year of sale, based upon an estimate of the amount of uncollectible accounts.
- **Direct Write-Off Method**: Companies record uncollectible accounts when they determine that a specific customer account is uncollectible.

Allowance Method

Under the allowance method, a company forecasts the expected future bad debts in accounts receivable (i.e., a forecast of credit risk). Therefore, it studies the historical data about the actual bad debts it has incurred, its credit risk strategy and policy, industry-wide experiences, and historical trends and economic conditions. It compares this information to its current sales or accounts receivable to determine relationships to use to estimate its current uncollectible accounts. These relationships provide the information the company needs to prepare the adjusting entry to adjust the accounts receivable to the appropriate net realizable value and recognize the estimated bad debt expense for the period.

When the company records the estimate of bad debts, the journal entry is a debit to Bad Debt Expense and a credit to Allowance for Doubtful Accounts (alternatively, Allowance for Bad Debts or Allowance for Uncollectible Accounts). Bad debt expense is normally reported on the income statement as an operating expense. Allowance for Doubtful Accounts is a valuation (contra) account that is offset against Accounts Receivable in the current assets section of the company's balance sheet. Although credit sales create a likelihood of losses from bad debts, the company does not know at the time of sale which actual customer accounts will not be collected. (If they were known, the company would not have extended credit to these customers.) Offsetting Allowance for Doubtful Accounts against Accounts Receivable informs financial statement users of the net realizable value (the amount of cash expected to be collected) of the company's receivables.[10]

It is possible to base the estimate of bad debt expense on relationships between the actual bad debts incurred and (1) credit sales or (2) accounts receivable. These relationships are shown in Exhibit 6.4.

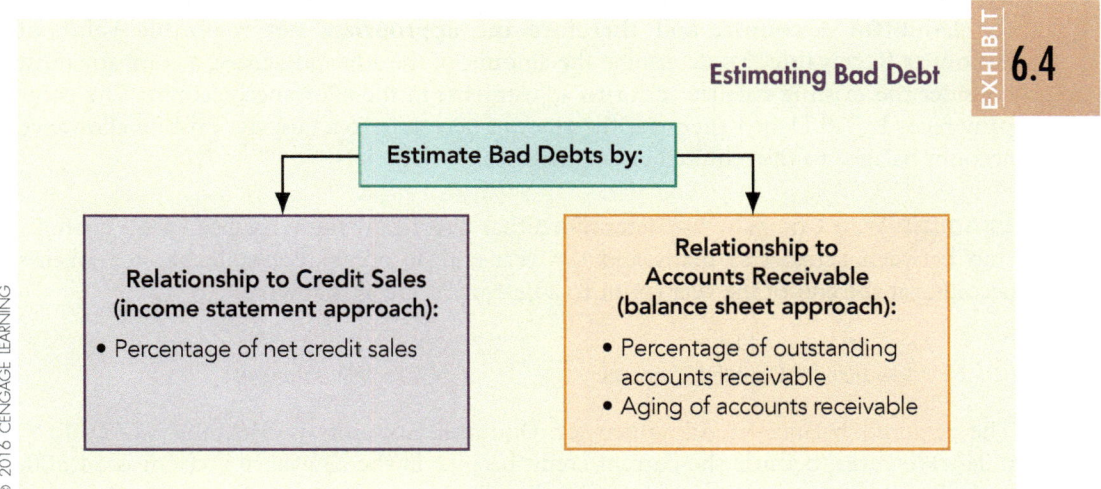

EXHIBIT 6.4 Estimating Bad Debt

[9] Because estimates involve future uncertainties, companies may find it necessary to change their estimates as new information becomes available. These changes in estimate are discussed in Chapter 22.

[10] If a company has other accounts, such as Allowance for Sales Discounts, it also deducts these accounts from Accounts Receivable to determine the net realizable value.

Percentage of Credit Sales Estimating bad debts based on the relationship to credit sales matches current bad debt expenses against current credit sales. This *income statement oriented* method results in recording bad debt expense in the period during which credit sales occur.[11] While companies will often use historical experience to develop the relationship between bad debts and credit sales, historical experience is not always a good predictor of future bad debts. In this situation, the accountant should consider other factors such as changes in the company's credit policies, customer base, and industry and economic conditions.

Example Lema Company's net credit sales during the year were $525,000. Bad debts have historically amounted to 2% of net credit sales, and current conditions indicate that a 2% bad debt loss is likely for the current year. Lema makes the following year-end adjusting entry:

Bad Debt Expense ($525,000 × 0.02)	10,500	
Allowance for Doubtful Accounts		10,500

Because this method focuses on estimating the bad debt expense account, the credit adjustment is simply added to any existing balance in Allowance for Doubtful Accounts.

Although basing bad debt expense on credit sales is a relatively straightforward income statement-based approach, it may not provide the best estimate of the net realizable value of accounts receivable. This is because the existing balance in the allowance account is ignored when making the adjusting entry. Also, if the company materially over- (or under-) estimates the amount of bad debt expense, a change in the accounting estimate may be necessary. Because of these disadvantages, a company may prefer to use a balance sheet approach.

Percentage of Outstanding Accounts Receivable Bad debts may be estimated based on the relationship between the actual amounts not collected and accounts receivable. This approach is *balance sheet oriented* because the resulting accounts receivable is reported on the balance sheet at its estimated net realizable value. A relatively simple balance sheet approach is to base the estimated expense on the historical relationship between the actual bad debts and the outstanding accounts receivable balance at the end of the year.

In using this method, the goal is to determine the ending balance in Allowance for Doubtful Accounts, and therefore the appropriate net realizable value of Accounts Receivable. To determine the amount of the adjusting entry, a company must consider the existing balance (prior to adjustment) in the allowance account. The company records Bad Debt Expense at the amount necessary to adjust the existing allowance account balance to the required ending balance.

Example Weir Company has determined that historically there has been a 4% relationship between actual bad debts and the year-end accounts receivable balance. Weir's accounts at the end of the year (prior to adjustment) are as follows:

Accounts Receivable	475,000
Allowance for Doubtful Accounts	4,500 (credit balance)

The required balance in Allowance for Doubtful Accounts is $19,000 ($475,000 × 0.04). However, because the current credit balance in the allowance account is $4,500, only the amount necessary to increase the allowance account to its required ending

---

[11] Most accountants estimate bad debts based on the historical relationship between bad debts and net credit sales because cash sales do not result in bad debts.

balance is recorded as Bad Debt Expense. In this example, the amount is $14,500 ($19,000 − $4,500), as shown in the following T-account:

Allowance for Doubtful Accounts	
	4,500 (current balance)
	14,500 (required adjustment)
	19,000 (required ending balance)

Based on the preceding information, Weir records the following year-end adjusting entry:

Bad Debt Expense	14,500	
Allowance for Doubtful Accounts		14,500

ETHICAL DILEMMA

As the accountant for SaveMart, the nation's largest retail company, you have performed an extensive analysis and you are convinced that bad debts will be 3% of credit sales this year. While this estimate is higher than last year's estimate of 2%, you feel the increase is warranted because the company, in an effort to stimulate sales, significantly relaxed its credit policy in the current fiscal year. However, if the 3% estimate is used, SaveMart's earnings will fall slightly below analysts' earnings estimates, which some investors consider when valuing SaveMart shares. If the bad debt estimate is lowered to 2.5%, SaveMart will meet analysts' earnings expectations, and you will receive a large bonus in the current period. Because bad debt estimates have historically been between 2% and 3%, you are quite certain that the auditors will accept any estimate in this range. What are your responsibilities?

A potential weakness of basing bad debts on a percentage of total outstanding accounts receivable is that it does not consider the due date of the many individual accounts comprising the total balance. This weakness is overcome by "aging" the accounts receivable.

Aging of Accounts Receivable The length of time an account is outstanding is important in estimating the probability of its future collection because credit risk tends to increase with the age of the account receivable. For example, a company is more likely to collect an account that is 20 days old than one that is 360 days overdue. For this reason, a more sophisticated method of estimating bad debts utilizes information about the ages of accounts receivable in estimating the percentages of bad debts. **A company that "ages" its accounts receivable first classifies the individual accounts receivable based on the length of time they have been outstanding, and then estimates the allowance for bad debts by applying appropriate bad debts percentages to each age category.**

Example The information in **Example 6.2** is taken from the accounts receivable subsidiary ledger of Rhorke Corporation and illustrates estimating bad debts using an aging schedule (or aging analysis).[12] In developing the aging schedule, Rhorke reviewed the unpaid invoices in each customer's account at year-end, classified each of the invoice amounts according to the length of time the invoice has been outstanding, and totaled the amounts in each age group. It then multiplied the total amount in each age group by the applicable estimated uncollectible percentage to determine the estimated amount uncollectible for that age group. It determined the total estimated uncollectible amount by adding the estimated uncollectible amounts related to each age group.

---

[12] A company with few accounts receivable would probably not find an aging analysis to be a useful procedure because each customer could be evaluated individually (specific identification method). Aging is appropriate when there are large numbers of customers who cannot reasonably be evaluated individually at the end of the period. In this example, for simplicity, only a few customers are used.

EXAMPLE 6.2 Aging Analysis

Rhorke Corporation
December 31, 2016

(a) Aging Schedule of Accounts Receivable

Customer	Balance 12/31/16	Under 60 Days	60–120 Days	121–240 Days	241–360 Days	Over 1 Year
Goodwin Co.	$ 33,100	$21,000	$12,100			
Hobson Inc.	14,500					$14,500
Lomas Manufacturing	20,600	15,000	5,600			
McClendon Co.	15,700				$15,700	
Schauer Corporation	37,900	17,500	16,800	$3,600		
	$121,800	$53,500	$34,500	$3,600	$15,700	$14,500

(b) Estimated Uncollectibles

Age	Amount	×	Estimated Percentage Uncollectible	=	Estimated Amounts Uncollectible
Under 60 days	$ 53,500		2%		$ 1,070
60–120 days	34,500		8		2,760
121–240 days	3,600		15		540
241–360 days	15,700		30		4,710
Over 1 year	14,500		50		7,250
	$121,800				$16,330

This analysis indicates that the ending balance of Allowance for Doubtful Accounts should be $16,330 on December 31, 2016. Because the objective in an aging analysis is to determine the ending allowance account balance, a company also considers the previous balance of the allowance account in recording the amount of bad debt expense at the end of the period. If Rhorke has a current $1,350 *credit* balance in its allowance account, the amount of expense necessary to bring the allowance account up to its required balance is $14,980 ($16,330 − $1,350), as shown in the following T-account:

```
          Allowance for Doubtful Accounts
                    | 1,350 (current balance)
                    | 14,980 (required adjustment)
                    | 16,330 (required ending balance)
```

The balance in the allowance account, before adjustment, could be a debit or a credit, for reasons discussed in the subsequent sections. The purpose of the adjustment is to bring the balance in the allowance account up to the required amount. Note that, in this case, the existing *credit* balance in its allowance account is *subtracted* to determine the amount of the adjustment. An existing *debit* balance would be *added* to determine the necessary adjustment amount. Based upon the preceding calculations, Rhorke makes the following year-end adjusting entry:

Bad Debt Expense	14,980	
Allowance for Doubtful Accounts		14,980

Use of the aging method, particularly when the company prepares interim (monthly) financial reports, is very helpful to its credit department. As it prepares each new aging schedule, this method focuses attention on any accounts that have not been collected and that have shifted to an older age category. Frequently, a company will compute its "receivables turnover" (Net Credit Sales ÷ Average Net Accounts Receivable) along with its aging schedule to determine how efficient it is in collecting its accounts receivable.

Writing Off Uncollectible Accounts When a company determines that an individual account is uncollectible, it writes off that account, removing it from Accounts Receivable. The journal entry is a debit to Allowance for Doubtful Accounts and a credit to Accounts Receivable. This write-off simply removes the receivable and the associated amount of allowance for bad debts.

Example Consider the following information for Shy Company:

Accounts Receivable	$175,000
Allowance for Doubtful Accounts	8,750 (credit balance)
Customer account determined to be uncollectible	1,000

At the time of the write-off, Shy makes the following journal entry:

Allowance for Doubtful Accounts	1,000	
Accounts Receivable		1,000

This write-off has *no effect* on the net realizable value of the accounts receivable because the allowance account and the accounts receivable balance are reduced by the same amount. As shown in the following schedule, before the write-off, the net realizable accounts receivable was $166,250 ($175,000 − $8,750). After the write-off, the net carrying value of the accounts receivable is still $166,250, but it now consists of a $174,000 accounts receivable balance and a $7,750 allowance account balance. Similarly, there is no effect on the income statement as a result of this write-off because it did not involve a revenue or an expense account.

	Before Write-Off	Write-Off	After Write-Off
Accounts receivable	$175,000	$(1,000)	$174,000
Less: Allowance for doubtful accounts	(8,750)	1,000	(7,750)
Net realizable value	$166,250		$166,250

It is important to understand that the allowance for uncollectible accounts is an estimate and always involves future uncertainties. The actual losses incurred from bad debts may be greater or less than the amount of estimated expense. Therefore, the balance in the allowance account could be a debit or credit. As new information becomes available, a company may need to change its estimated percentage of bad debts. Such a change is considered to be a change in estimate and is recorded prospectively—treated as an adjustment of bad debt expense in current and future periods. We discuss changes in accounting estimates in Chapter 22.

Collection of an Account Previously Written Off Occasionally a company will receive payment from a customer whose account was already written off. Most accountants favor reestablishing the customer's account receivable and then recording the payment. This procedure has the advantage of providing a complete credit history for each customer account and also eliminates the previous write-off entry.

Example If Uphoff Company receives a $300 payment from a customer whose account had been previously written off, the company makes the following journal entries:

Accounts Receivable	300	
Allowance for Doubtful Accounts		300
Cash	300	
Accounts Receivable		300

Note that the first entry "reverses" the initial write-off and the second entry records the cash collection in the usual manner.

Direct Write-Off Method

In addition to the allowance method discussed previously, a second method of recording uncollectible accounts is the direct write-off method. **When a company uses the direct write-off method, it records bad debt expense when it determines that a specific customer account is uncollectible.** At that time, it writes off the account by debiting Bad Debt Expense and crediting Accounts Receivable.

This method is simple to apply and reports actual bad debt expense rather than an estimate. However, the determination of bad debt expense may not occur until after the period of sale. Therefore, this method does not correctly measure income because it matches the bad debt expenses associated with previous sales against revenues of the current period. It also overstates accounts receivable associated with previous sales. Furthermore, it allows *earnings management* because the company selects the period of write-off (and expense). For these reasons, the direct write-off method is generally not allowed under GAAP, except for situations in which the results of using the direct write-off method do not differ materially from those obtained under the allowance methods. In addition, for most companies, the direct write-off method is required for income tax purposes.

WHY IT MATTERS

Sales and cash flows are essential elements to any company's success, and accounting for accounts receivable involves both of these elements. Therefore, managers, investors, creditors, and others carefully monitor accounts receivable to gain insight into a company's profitability and future cash flow. The *receivables turnover ratio* and the *average collection period* are two measures often used as indicators of the efficiency with which a company collects its receivables and converts them to cash. The **receivables turnover ratio** is calculated as:

$$\text{Receivables Turnover Ratio} = \frac{\text{Net Credit Sales}}{\text{Average Net Receivables}}$$

As a general rule, the higher the receivables turnover ratio the better. An increasing receivables turnover ratio may indicate that a company has less cash tied up in receivables, is collecting receivables at a faster pace, and has fewer uncollectible accounts. A decreasing receivables turnover ratio might indicate that a company has extended more lenient payment terms to customers or is having difficulty in collecting its receivables.

Analysts will often divide the receivables turnover ratio into the number of days in a year to show the average time it takes for a company to collect its receivables. This ratio is calculated as:

$$\text{Average Collection Period} = \frac{365 \text{ days}}{\text{Receivables Turnover Ratio}}$$

(continued)

A comparison of a company's average collection period to the days in its typical credit terms gives an indication of how aggressively the company's credit department collects its receivables.

The receivables turnover ratio and average collection period computation for **Starbucks** is shown below.

(amounts in millions)	2015	2014	2013
Receivables (net)	$ 719.0	$ 631.0	$561.4
Revenue:			
Company-operated stores	15,197.3	12,977.9	
Licensed stores	1,861.9	1,588.6	
Foodservice and Other	2,103.5	1,881.3	
Net Revenues	19,162.7	16,447.8	

If Starbucks uses a traditional calculation of receivables turnover with net revenues in the numerator, it would report a receivables turnover of 28.39 times per year and 27.59 times per year for 2015 and 2014, respectively. However, it is always important to understand the company's business in computing any ratio. For example, these traditional ratios may be misleading for Starbucks because its retail sales are primarily cash sales and its receivables arise mostly from licensing and foodservice activities. Therefore, to gain a clearer picture of Starbucks's collection of receivables, analysts with an understanding of Starbucks's operating environment will often adjust the traditional receivables turnover calculation by including only licensing and foodservice revenues in the numerator, as shown below.

$$2015: \text{Receivables Turnover} = \frac{\$3,965.4}{\left(\frac{\$719.0 + \$631.0}{2}\right)} = 5.87$$

$$2014: \text{Receivables Turnover} = \frac{\$3,469.9}{\left(\frac{\$631.0 + \$561.4}{2}\right)} = 5.82$$

Using the adjusted calculation, Starbucks turned its receivables over 5.87 and 5.82 times per year and took 62.18 days and 62.71 days to collect its receivables for fiscal years 2015 and 2014, respectively.

Over the two-year period examined, the speed of Starbucks's receivable collection was relatively stable, increasing slightly. This suggests that Starbucks was able to increase its cash flow by decreasing the amount of cash tied up in receivables.

GOT IT?

6-9 Discuss the differences between the allowance methods of recording bad debts and the direct write-off method.

6-10 Explain how a company estimates bad debts using (1) the credit sales or income statement approach and (2) the accounts receivable or balance sheet approach.

6-11 Define the *net realizable value* of a company's accounts receivable. How is the net realizable value of accounts receivable reported on the company's balance sheet?

6-12 What method of bad debt estimation categorizes individual accounts receivable based on the length of time outstanding? Why is this length of time an important factor?

6-13 Why does the write-off of uncollectible accounts have no effect on the net realizable accounts receivable on the balance sheet if bad debts are estimated? What is the effect of this write-off on the income statement?

LEARNING OBJECTIVE 6.6
Explain how to account for secured borrowings and sales of accounts receivable.

HOW DO COMPANIES ACCOUNT FOR THE FINANCING OF ACCOUNTS RECEIVABLE

The net realizable value of the accounts receivable reported on a company's balance sheet should be the amount of cash the company expects to collect in its normal operations. However, a company may find that it needs immediate cash and cannot wait until the completion of the normal operating cycle. In order to accelerate the cash inflows from its accounts receivable, a company may choose to "finance" its receivables. In fact, of 500 surveyed companies, 25% reported engaging in some type of financing arrangement related to their accounts receivable.[13]

In today's business environment, many companies specialize in financing other companies' accounts receivable. These finance companies include **Ford Motor Credit Company** (**Ford Credit**), **General Electric Capital Services** (**GECS**), and **Navistar Financial Corporation**, as well as credit card companies such as **VISA**, **MasterCard**, and **American Express**. There are many variations in financing arrangements, including which receivables are involved, which company collects the receivables, who has title, and who bears the credit risk and is responsible for the bad debts. Reporting on these types of arrangements provides important information about a company's liquidity (the availability of a company's liquid assets to settle its obligations) and its financial flexibility (its ability to use its financial resources, such as receivables, to meet its obligations and respond to new business opportunities).

The two basic forms of financing arrangements that companies use to obtain cash from accounts receivable are:

- secured borrowing (pledging or assigning)
- sale of receivables (factoring, securitizations)

In financing arrangements like these, one company (the transferor) transfers the accounts receivable to another company (the transferee).

The accounting issue revolves around whether the risks and rewards associated with the receivables have been transferred. In other words, which company controls the benefits and risks associated with the transferred receivables. In general, the company that "owns" the receivables is the company that has control over the future benefits from them (e.g., the right to collect any amounts owed). With regard to the risks of ownership (e.g., loss from nonpayment of amounts owed), it is important to consider whether the transfer was made *with recourse* or *without recourse*.

- In a transfer with recourse, the transferor retains the risk of ownership and bears any loss from a nonpayment of receivables.
- In a transfer without recourse, the transferee has assumed all the risks of ownership and bears any loss from a nonpayment of receivables.

This assessment of who controls the receivables is critical to determining the proper accounting for their transfer.

GAAP requires that the transferor should record the transfer of financial assets (e.g., accounts receivable) in which it surrenders control to the transferee as a sale when *all* the following conditions are met:

- The transferred assets have been isolated from the transferor (i.e., put beyond the control of the transferor).
- The transferee obtains the right to sell, pledge, or exchange the transferred assets.
- The transferor does not maintain effective control over the transferred assets through an agreement in which it can repurchase the transferred assets before their maturity.

If the transfer meets the conditions for a sale, the transferor records the proceeds, derecognizes (eliminates) the financial assets sold, and records a gain or loss. If the conditions for a sale are *not* met, the transferor records the proceeds from the transfer of financial

[13] *Accounting Trends and Techniques* (New York: AICPA, 2010), p. 164.

assets as a secured borrowing (a liability) with the transferred financial assets serving as collateral. In both situations, the transferor continues to report on its balance sheet any retained interest in the transferred assets.[14] Exhibit 6.5 outlines the accounting for a transfer of accounts receivable.

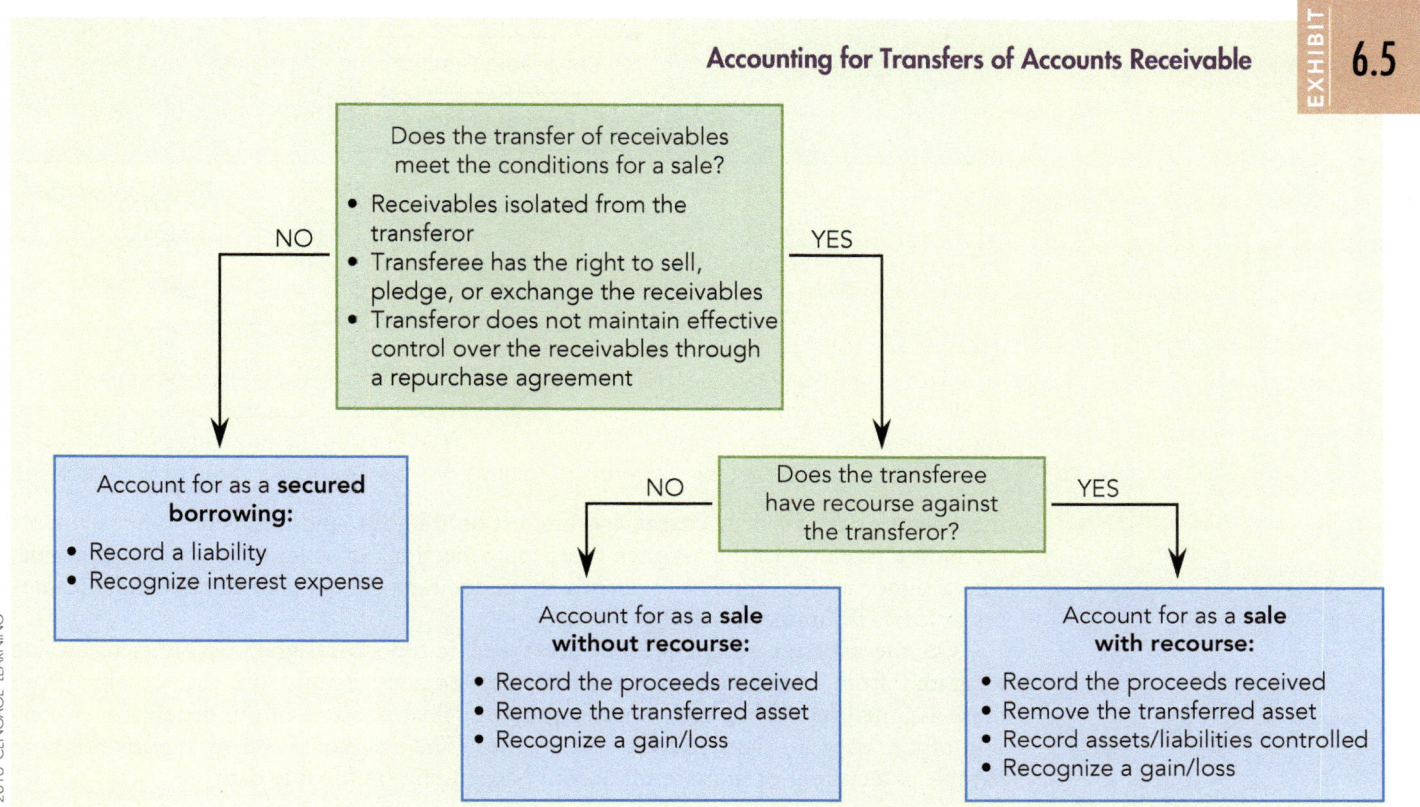

Exhibit 6.5 Accounting for Transfers of Accounts Receivable

Secured Borrowing

In a **secured borrowing**, a company may **assign** or **pledge** its accounts receivable as collateral for a loan. If the company is unable to make payments on the loan, the creditor can require the amounts collected from the accounts receivable be used to repay the amount owed.[15]

Under a basic assignment agreement, the borrowing company (assignor) usually retains ownership of the assigned accounts, incurs any bad debts, collects the amounts due from customers, and uses these funds to repay the loan. Exhibit 6.6 illustrates a typical assignment agreement.

Because the assignor usually retains the risks of ownership, accounts are assigned *with recourse*. This means that if the cash collected from the accounts is not enough to repay the amount owed by the assignor, the assignee (lending company) can demand payment from (has recourse against) the assignor. Normally, the assignor company's relationship with the purchasers of its goods and services is not disrupted because the purchaser continues to make payments directly to the company (*non-notification*) and is unaware of the financing arrangement. Occasionally, the lending company (assignee) will require the assigned accounts to make their payments directly to it (*notification*).

The amount of receivables assigned is usually greater than the amount borrowed to protect the assignee from sales returns and allowances. Under assignment arrangements,

---

[14] FASB ASC 860-10 and FASB ASC 860-20: Broad Transactions: Transfers and Servicing.

[15] If the accounts receivable are transferred to a third party for custodial purposes, the arrangement is commonly referred to as a pledge. Pledged receivables require no special accounting and are generally only disclosed in the notes to the financial statements to indicate that a portion of the accounts receivable balance may not be available to general creditors.

EXHIBIT 6.6 Typical Assignment Agreement

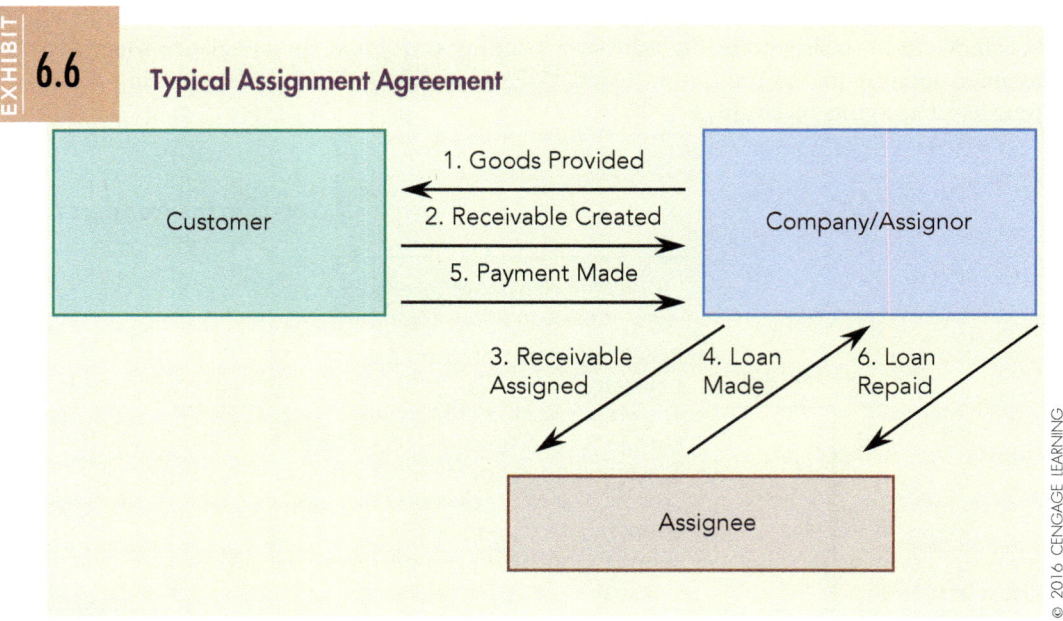

the assignor pays a service charge and interest on the loan, and makes periodic payments (including interest) to the assignee based on collections of assigned accounts receivable. The assignor is also required to absorb any reductions due to sales returns and allowances or losses from uncollectible accounts.

On the assignor company's balance sheet, it reports assigned accounts receivable separately from unassigned accounts receivable because it must use cash receipts from these assigned receivables for a specific purpose. That is, some of the benefits of ownership of the asset are transferred to the assignee. The assignor company reports the note payable as a current or noncurrent liability, depending on the due date.

Example: Assignment

On December 1, 2016, Trussel Company assigns $60,000 of its accounts receivable to a finance company. The finance company advances 80% of the accounts receivable assigned minus a service charge of $500. It also charges an annual interest rate of 12% on any outstanding loan balance. Trussel records this assignment as follows:

Cash [($60,000 × 0.80) − $500]	47,500	
Assignment Service Charge Expense	500	
Notes Payable ($60,000 × 0.80)		48,000
Accounts Receivable Assigned	60,000	
Accounts Receivable		60,000

The first journal entry records the receipt of cash. The Assignment Service Charge Expense account is a cost of borrowed funds, and most companies usually record it as an expense at the time of the advance. The second journal entry reclassifies the receivables as assigned accounts receivable.

On December 31, 2016, Trussel collects $10,000 on assigned accounts. It pays this amount along with the 12% interest for 1 month to the finance company. Trussel records these transactions as follows:

Cash	10,000	
Accounts Receivable Assigned		10,000
Notes Payable	10,000	
Interest Expense ($48,000 × 0.12 × 1/12)	480	
Cash		10,480

The interest expense on any future payments is based upon the balance *remaining* in the Notes Payable account (for example, the interest expense for the next payment in our example is based on the $38,000 note payable balance). During the period in which the note is outstanding, Trussel credits any bad debt losses and sales returns and allowances related to the assigned accounts receivable against the Accounts Receivable Assigned account. After Trussel fully repays the note, it reclassifies any remaining balance in Accounts Receivable Assigned as Accounts Receivable.

On Trussel's December 31, 2016, balance sheet, it reports the assigned accounts and the remaining liability (assuming it is short-term) as follows:

Current Assets		Current Liabilities	
Accounts receivable assigned	$50,000	Notes payable	$38,000

Trussel includes a description of the financing agreement in the notes to its financial statements.

Sale of Accounts Receivable

Two common ways for a company to sell its accounts receivable are **factoring** and **securitization**.

Factoring When a company factors its accounts receivable, it sells individual accounts to a financial institution (called a *factor*). At the time of sale, the factor charges the selling company a commission. The commission usually is based on the amount of receivables transferred and is relatively high, although it varies depending on who bears the risk of noncollection. For example, if the sale is with recourse, the commission will be lower than if the sale is without recourse because the factor bears less risk. The selling company records the commission as an *expense* if it normally factors its accounts receivable, or as a *loss* if it usually does not sell its accounts receivable. In addition to charging a commission, the factor usually will pay only 80% to 90% of the value of the accounts receivable transferred, as a protection against sales returns and allowances. The selling company records the amount withheld (i.e., the 20% to 10%) in a separate Receivable from Factor account to indicate the amount that may be returned by the factor. Because title is transferred, the selling company reduces (credits) Accounts Receivable for the amount of the receivables sold and increases cash. Exhibit 6.7 illustrates a typical factoring transaction.

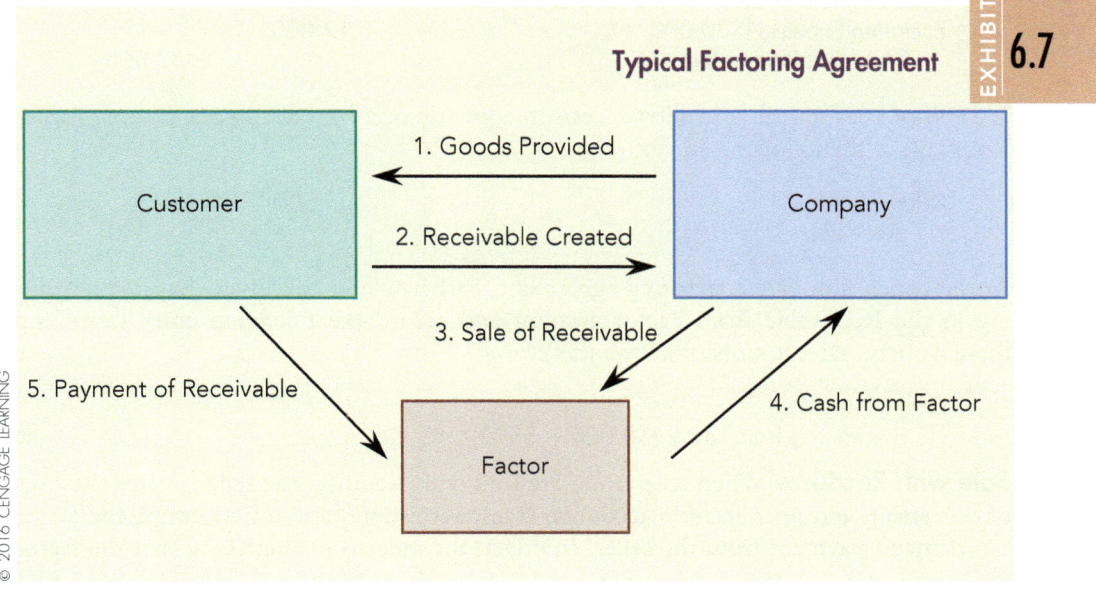

EXHIBIT 6.7 Typical Factoring Agreement

Securitization In a securitization, accounts receivable will be transferred to another entity, usually a trust or subsidiary. This entity then sells financial securities (usually debt instruments) that are collateralized by the accounts receivable, which allow investors to receive cash as the accounts receivable are paid. Because a larger number of investors are involved in a securitization relative to factoring, companies can often securitize much larger amounts.

Recording the Sale of Accounts Receivable

When accounts receivable are sold, the proper accounting depends on whether the sale was without recourse or with recourse.

Sale without Recourse In a sale without recourse, the buyer (or factor) assumes all the risks of ownership. If any receivables are not collected, the factor cannot demand payment from the seller. Because the risks of ownership have been transferred from the seller to the factor and the factor has control of the asset (the accounts receivable), the transaction is accounted for as a sale of accounts receivable. Nonrecourse transactions sometimes (but not always) involve (1) notification of the credit customers to remit the amounts owed directly to the factor and (2) assumption by the factor of all collection activities, setting of credit policies, and losses from uncollectible accounts.

Factoring agreements are common in the furniture and textile industries. Another common example is the sale of home mortgages from one financial institution to another. However, many companies are reluctant to use factoring agreements because their customers may dislike being required to make payments to a company other than the original seller. As such, some companies continue to process payments and maintain customer relationships, even though they remit the payments to the factor. In addition, some companies are reluctant to sell receivables without recourse because they generate a much lower selling price because the factor assumes all the risk of uncollectible receivables.

Example: Sale without Recourse

Farber Corporation sells $80,000 of accounts receivable to a factor without recourse, receives 90% of the value of the factored accounts, and is charged a 15% commission based on the gross amount of factored accounts receivable. Farber records the following journal entry (assuming that it normally factors its accounts receivable):

Cash [($80,000 × 0.90) − ($80,000 × 0.15)]	60,000	
Receivable from Factor ($80,000 × 0.10)	8,000	
Factoring Expense ($80,000 × 0.15)	12,000	
Accounts Receivable		80,000

If $500 of sales returns and allowances subsequently occur on factored accounts, Farber would make the following entry:

Return Liability	500	
Receivable from Factor		500

At the conclusion of the factoring agreement, Farber would collect any balance remaining in the Receivable from Factor account and record the following entry (assuming there were no sales returns or allowances):

Cash	7,500	
Receivable from Factor ($8,000 − $500)		7,500

Sale with Recourse When receivables are sold with recourse, the seller retains the risks of ownership and uncollectible accounts. If any receivables are not collected, the factor can demand payment from the seller. In effect, the seller is guaranteeing that the factor will be paid. Even if the receivables are sold with recourse, as long as the three conditions of a sale are met, the transfer is accounted for as a sale. However, because the seller has a continuing involvement with the receivable, a **financial components approach** must be used. Under this approach, fair values are assigned to components such as the recourse obligation (the estimated amount the seller will have to pay the factor) and any servicing rights. This results in both the factor and the seller recognizing the financial and servicing assets it controls.

Example: Sale with Recourse

Farber Corporation sells $80,000 of accounts receivable with recourse, receives 90% of the value of the transferred accounts receivable, and is charged an 8% commission (lower than the 15% commission without recourse, because the factor is taking less risk) based on the gross amount of the transferred accounts receivable. In addition, the recourse obligation has an estimated fair value of $2,000. Farber records the following journal entry (assuming that it does not normally sell its accounts receivable):

Cash [($80,000 × 0.90) − ($80,000 × 0.08)]	65,600	
Receivable from Factor ($80,000 × 0.10)	8,000	
Loss on Sale of Receivables [($80,000 × 0.08) + $2,000]	8,400	
Recourse Liability		2,000
Accounts Receivable		80,000

Notice that the estimated recourse liability increases the loss on the sale of the receivables.

At the conclusion of the agreement, Farber would collect any balance remaining in the Receivable from Factor account. In addition, if the buyer collects all of the accounts receivable, Farber would eliminate the recourse liability and eliminate the loss. ■

Credit Card Sales Many retail companies make agreements with national credit card companies, which operate either independently or in affiliation with banks. Among the most popular are **VISA**, **MasterCard**, **American Express** and **Capital One**. Under these arrangements, card holders establish a **line of credit** (with the credit card company) which may be used for retail purchases of goods and services. After customers make credit purchases, the retailer deposits the credit card receipts in its bank account (or receives an electronic transfer of cash from the credit card company). The customers then repay the bank or credit card company. These types of agreements are *factoring* agreements.

The retailer accepting these credit cards charges its customers the selling price for goods and services, but is assessed a service charge on credit card sales by the bank or credit card company. This charge is usually a percentage of each sale, and the fee is for the use of a credit and collection department. Thus, the retailer usually records the fee as an operating expense. The individual retailer assumes little or no risk in accepting national credit cards because most risk is borne by the bank or credit card company (except where there is fraud or negligence by the retailer) because the bank or credit card company originally granted the line of credit. The service charge assessed on credit card sales usually varies between 1% and 5% and is partially determined by the annual amount of sales or by exclusive arrangements. In an exclusive arrangement, a retailer will accept only one (or selected) national credit card, and in return, the credit card company charges the retailer a lower service charge. For example, **Sam's Club** accepts only **Discover** and **MasterCard** credit cards (in addition to its own credit card) in its stores.

Example Kerns Shoes sold $1,500 of merchandise on credit which was billed to a national credit card company. If the collection fee charged by the credit card company is

5%, Kerns makes the following journal entry when it deposits the credit card sales receipts (assuming it is using the gross price method of recording sales):

Cash	1,425	
Credit Card Expense ($1,500 × 0.05)	75	
Sales Revenue		1,500

Some large retailers (e.g., **Saks**, **Macy's**, **JCPenney**) have their own credit cards. When a customer makes a credit purchase using a retail company's credit card, the company records accounts receivable in the usual manner.

Disclosure of Financing Agreements of Accounts Receivable

A company should disclose the existence of the transfer of accounts receivable parenthetically or in the notes to its financial statements. In general, management should provide disclosures that allow financial statement users to understand:

- the transferor's continuing involvement, if any, with the transferred assets
- the nature of any restrictions on transferred assets that are reported on the balance sheet
- how servicing assets and liabilities are reported
- how the transfer of financial assets affect a company's balance sheet, income statement, and statement of cash flows

An example of a disclosure related to a transfer of accounts receivable for **Office Depot** is shown in Real Report 6.2.

6.2 DISCLOSURE OF THE TRANSFER OF ACCOUNTS RECEIVABLE — REAL REPORT

Office Depot

Office Depot, Inc.
NOTES TO CONSOLIDATED FINANCIAL STATEMENTS (in part)
Note A: Summary of Significant Accounting Policies (in part)
RECEIVABLES: The Company sells selected accounts receivables on a non-recourse basis to an unrelated financial institution under a factoring agreement in France. The Company accounts for this transaction as a sale of receivables, removes receivables sold from its financial statements, and records cash proceeds when received by the Company as cash provided by operating activities in the Statements of Cash Flows. The financial institution makes available 80% of the face value of the receivables to the Company and retains the remaining 20% as a guarantee until the receipt of the proceeds associated with the factored invoices. The Company activated the arrangement in the fourth quarter of 2012.
    In 2013 and 2012, the Company withdrew $443 million and $53 million, respectively, under the facility. Receivables sold for which the Company did not obtain cash directly from the financial institution are included in Receivables and amount to $10 million and $51 million as of December 28, 2013 and December 29, 2012, respectively. A retention guarantee of $13 million is included in Prepaid expenses and other current assets as of December 28, 2013 and December 29, 2012.

Suggested answers to these questions are found at the end of the chapter.

Questions:

1. Does Office Depot transfer its accounts receivable with or without recourse? What does this mean?
2. Why doesn't Office Depot receive 100% of the value of the accounts receivable that are sold?

> **GOT IT?**
>
> **6-14** Discuss the difference between a secured borrowing (pledging or assigning) and a sale of receivables (factoring).
>
> **6-15** When does a company record the transfer of accounts receivable as a sale? As a secured borrowing (a liability)?

HOW DO COMPANIES ACCOUNT FOR NOTES RECEIVABLE?

LEARNING OBJECTIVE 6.7

Account for short-term notes receivable.

A **note receivable** is a written agreement that gives the holder the right to collect a certain sum of money on a specific date. Notes receivable generally have two attributes that accounts receivable do not have:

- They are negotiable instruments, which means that they are legally transferable among parties and may be used to satisfy debts by the holders of these instruments.
- They usually involve interest, requiring the separation of the receivable into its principal and interest components.

Companies sometimes accept notes receivable when the customers wish to extend the repayment period on an account receivable. Sometimes a company may require notes receivable when it extends credit to new customers, and in some cases, it may require them for all credit sales. However, the majority of notes receivable result from lending transactions. We discuss short-term notes receivable in the following sections. Long-term notes receivable are discussed in Chapter 13.

A company may receive two types of short-term notes receivable: (1) interest-bearing notes and (2) non-interest-bearing notes.

Short-Term Interest-Bearing Notes Receivable

When an interest-bearing note is issued, the amount borrowed (the principal) is listed as the face value, and the interest charged is stated as a specific rate applied to this face value. When a company receives a note, it debits Notes Receivable for the face value. After issuance, it records interest income on the note in the usual fashion, including any year-end adjustments to accrue interest receivable and interest income.

Example On October 1, 2016, Trent Company made a $5,000 credit sale to Jaynik Company and required the company to sign a $5,000, 60-day, 12% note. Trent makes the following entry to record the receipt of the interest-bearing note:

| Oct. 1 | Notes Receivable | 5,000 | |
| | Sales Revenue | | 5,000 |

The collection of the principal and interest (assuming, for simplicity, a 360-day business year) would be recorded as follows:

Dec. 1	Cash	5,100	
	Notes Receivable		5,000
	Interest Income ($5,000 × 0.12 × 60/360)		100

If the note had extended past the end of the year, Trent would have made a year-end adjusting entry to record the interest receivable and recognize the interest income. ■

Bad debt losses may occur on transactions involving short-term notes receivable, particularly when it is common practice to require customers to sign notes for all credit sales. In these cases, the company should assess the likelihood of these losses and establish an Allowance for Doubtful Notes. This procedure is the same as discussed earlier for accounts receivable and results in an increase in its expenses and a decrease in the net realizable value of its notes receivable.

Short-Term Non-Interest-Bearing Notes Receivable

In the case of a non-interest-bearing note, the maturity value (the amount to be collected, which includes both principal and interest) is listed as the face value. Actually, the term "non-interest-bearing" is a misnomer because all notes include interest. For non-interest-bearing notes, the interest is implicitly included in the face value rather than being explicitly stated as a separate rate. A better term would be a note with *no stated interest rate*. GAAP does not *require* current trade receivables to be recorded at their present values because the difference between the present value and the maturity value is not likely to be significant. Consequently, many companies record short-term non-interest-bearing trade notes receivable at their maturity values. This approach, however, overstates sales revenue and understates interest income. A conceptually better approach is to record the note receivable at its present value and to recognize interest income as it is earned.

Example On October 1, 2016, Trent Company signs a $5,100 note with no stated interest rate, due on December 1, 2016, with a present value of $5,000. Trent makes the following entry to record the receipt of the non-interest-bearing note:

Oct. 1	Notes Receivable		5,100	
	Discount on Notes Receivable			100
	Sales Revenue			5,000

The difference between the maturity value and the present value of the note is recorded in a Discount on Notes Receivable account, which represents future interest income that will be recognized as it is earned using the effective interest method. This discount account is a contra account and is deducted from Notes Receivable to report the net realizable value on the balance sheet.

On December 1, 2016, Trent makes the following entries:

Dec. 1	Cash		5,100	
	Notes Receivable			5,100
1	Discount on Notes Receivable		100	
	Interest Income			100

The first entry records the receipt of the face value of the note receivable. The second entry records the amortization of Discount on Notes Receivable and the recognition of Interest Income. ■

Sales or Assignments of Notes Receivable

Occasionally, a company may find that it needs additional cash on a short-term basis, but the company does not wish to borrow money or sell or assign its accounts receivable. In these cases, the company may sell or assign a customer's note receivable to a bank in return for cash. When a company sells or assigns a customer's note receivable at the bank, it transfers the note to the bank in exchange for cash. This financing arrangement is subject to the conditions summarized in Exhibit 6.5 (page 6-21). If all the conditions are met, the company records the transfer as a sale. If the conditions are not met, the company records the transfer as a secured borrowing.

When a customer's note receivable is sold or assigned, the company receives cash (proceeds) equal to the maturity value of the note (face value of the note plus total interest) minus a discount. The discount is determined by multiplying a **discount rate**, which is the interest rate charged by the financial institution, times the maturity value of the note for the discount period. The discount rate has no relationship to the interest rate charged the customer on the note receivable. The **discount period** is the length of time from the date of discount to the maturity date. Any gain or loss from the discounting is computed by comparing the current book value of the note receivable (including accrued interest income) plus any recourse liability to the proceeds received. The company selling or assigning the note makes journal entries on the date of the discount to record any accrued interest income, the proceeds received, and any gain or loss on the discounting of the note. It derecognizes (eliminates) the note on the maturity date.

Example: Selling a Note Receivable

On August 31, 2016, Kasper Corporation sells (with recourse) a customer's note at its bank at a 14% discount rate. Kasper received the note from the customer on August 1. The note is for 90 days, has a face value of $5,000, and carries an interest rate of 12%. The estimated value of the recourse liability is $500. The customer pays the note on the October 30, 2016, maturity date. The calculations on August 31 for the discounted note are as follows (assuming a 360-day business year for simplicity):

Face value of note		$ 5,000.00
Interest to maturity ($5,000 × 0.12 × 90/360)		150.00
Maturity value of note		$ 5,150.00
Discount ($5,150 × 0.14 × 60/360)		(120.17)
Proceeds received		$ 5,029.83
Less:		
Book value of note:		
Face value:	$5,000.00	
Accrued interest income ($5,000 × 0.12 × 30/360)	50.00	(5,050.00)
Recourse liability		(500.00)
Loss from sale of receivable		$ (520.17)

Note that the recourse liability increases the amount of the loss. Kasper makes the following journal entry to record the discounted note on August 31:

Cash	5,029.83	
Loss from Sale of Receivable	520.17	
Notes Receivable		5,000.00
Interest Income		50.00
Recourse Liability		500.00

If the bank collects the entire balance of the note receivable, Kasper would eliminate the recourse liability and increase income (reduce the loss). However, if the bank cannot collect the note receivable from the customer, the bank would require Kasper to pay the maturity value of the note plus a service charge on the dishonored note. Kasper's only recourse is to attempt to collect these amounts from the customer. Consequently, upon default, Kasper would eliminate its recourse liability as it pays the bank the amount owed. In addition, it would establish a Notes Receivable Dishonored account as it attempts to collect the amount from the customer.

For example, assume instead that on November 2, 2016, the bank notified Kasper that the note had not been paid and also charged Kasper a $10 fee. At that time, Kasper would record the following journal entry:

Recourse Liability	500.00	
Notes Receivable Dishonored	4,660.00	
Cash [$5,000 + ($5,000 × 0.12 × 90/360) + $10]		5,160.00

If Kasper does not collect the dishonored note in the future, it recognizes a loss on the default. ■

Notes Receivable Reported at Fair Value

GAAP allows a company to elect to report many types of its financial assets (and financial liabilities) at their fair value. A financial asset involves a contract that gives a company the right to receive cash from another company. As described in Chapter 2, fair value information is considered to be more relevant than historical cost information because it reflects the current cash equivalent price received to sell the financial asset (or paid to transfer the financial liability).

A company may elect to use the fair value option for a single financial asset or for all of the same type of financial assets. Whichever option the company chooses, it must separately report the financial asset(s) valued at fair value from those reported at cost or amortized cost on its balance sheet. It must also report any unrealized gains or losses resulting from changes in the fair value on its income statement. An unrealized gain or loss is computed as the difference between the fair value and the book value of a financial asset.

Example Wilson Company has notes receivable with a book value of $120,000 and a fair value of $150,000. If Wilson elects to use the fair value option for this note receivable, it would make the following adjusting entry to recognize the unrealized holding gain of $30,000 ($150,000 − $120,000) and increase the value of the note receivable:

Notes Receivable	30,000	
Unrealized Holding Gain		30,000

Once Wilson elects to use the fair value option, it must continue to value the note receivable at fair value in all subsequent periods in which it holds the note receivable. The note receivable would be reported at fair value on Wilson's balance sheet and the unrealized holding gain would be reported on Wilson's income statement.

While companies may choose the fair value option for receivables, this chapter focuses on short-term receivables. As a practical matter, a company is unlikely to elect fair value for short-term receivables, and fair values and book values are unlikely to differ much. The measurement and reporting of long-term receivables at fair value is discussed in Chapter 13.

HOW ARE RECEIVABLES DISCLOSED?

In order to improve the reporting of a company's risk, liquidity, and financial flexibility, companies are required to disclose:

- any accounting policies related to their receivables that might be helpful to external users
- major categories of receivables, either in the balance sheet or in the notes to the financial statements
- any valuation accounts (e.g., allowance for doubtful accounts) as well as the methodology used to estimate these amounts
- any receivables designated as collateral
- the fair value of all its financial instruments, either on the balance sheet or in the notes
- all significant concentrations of credit risk

A company typically makes these disclosures in the notes to its financial statements. Real Report 6.3 shows an excerpt from **VF Corporation**'s 2013 annual report illustrating the presentation of receivables.

REAL REPORT — DISCLOSURE OF ACCOUNTS RECEIVABLE | 6.3

VF Corporation

VF Corporation
CONSOLIDATED BALANCE SHEETS

As of December 31,	2013	2012
(in thousands)		
Current Assets: (in part)		
Accounts receivable, less allowance for doubtful account of $45,350 in 2013 and $48,998 in 2012	$1,360,443	$1,222,345

NOTES TO CONSOLIDATED FINANCIAL STATEMENTS (in part)

Note A: Summary of Significant Accounting Policies (in part)

Accounts Receivable (in part)
Trade accounts receivable are recorded at invoiced amounts, less estimated allowances. VF maintains an allowance for doubtful accounts for estimated losses that will result from the inability of customers and licensees to make required payments. All accounts are subject to ongoing review of ultimate collectibility. The allowance is determined based on review of specific customer accounts where collection is doubtful, as well as assessment of the collectability of total receivables considering the aging of balances, anticipated trends and economic conditions. Receivables are written off against the allowance when it is probable the amounts will not be recovered.

Questions:

1. What amount of its accounts receivable does VF believe is uncollectible at the end of 2013?
2. What method does VF use to estimate its allowance for doubtful accounts? Is this method allowable by GAAP?

Suggested answers to these questions are found at the end of the chapter.

With regard to the statement of cash flow presentation of accounts and notes receivable, companies should do the following:

- Include the cash received from collections of its accounts receivable and notes receivable from sales in the operating activities section of its statement of cash flows.
- Include any cash collected from the principal amount of a note receivable in the investing activities section. Any interest received is always included in the operating activities section.
- Report the cash received from the sale of accounts receivable in the operating activities section, if the company normally sells its accounts receivable.
- Report the cash received from selling or assigning a note receivable (that qualifies as a sale) as a cash inflow from an investing activity.
- Report the cash received from secured borrowings in the financing activities section.

INTERNATIONAL DIMENSION

CASH AND RECEIVABLES

IFRS contain the same basic guidance for accounting and reporting for cash and receivables as U.S. GAAP. For example, under IFRS, the reporting of cash and cash equivalents, the accounting for cash (sales) discounts, and the application of

(continued)

the allowance method of accounting for uncollectible accounts are essentially the same. However, some differences do exist.

Classification IFRS classify most receivables in a category termed "loans and receivables," which is not defined under U.S. GAAP. In some instances, IFRS will allow receivables to be classified as "available-for-sale" securities. U.S. GAAP does not allow an "available-for-sale" classification of receivables because they do not meet the definition of a security. Exhibit 6.8 illustrates receivable disclosures for **Nestlé**.

Fair Value Option Both U.S GAAP and IFRS have a fair value option which allows a receivable to be reported at fair value with any changes flowing through income. While the application of the fair value option under IFRS is similar to that of U.S. GAAP, IFRS are more restrictive regarding when the fair value option can be applied. For example, under U.S. GAAP, a company can designate a receivable, upon initial recognition, to be recognized at fair value without meeting any criteria. Under IFRS, this fair value option must satisfy certain qualifying criteria that include showing that (1) the use of the fair value option reduces measurement or recognition inconsistencies (e.g., the "accounting mismatch" that arises from recognizing assets, liabilities, gains, or losses using different measurement attributes) or (2) the receivables are grouped with other financial assets that are managed as part of a risk management or investment strategy that is evaluated on a fair value basis.

Transfers of Financial Assets When financial assets are transferred, U.S. GAAP focuses on whether control has been surrendered in determining whether the transfer is accounted for as a secured borrowing or a sale. Under IFRS, the derecognition of a financial asset is based on whether the seller has transferred substantially all of the risks and rewards of ownership, with control as a secondary test.[16] If the risks and rewards have been transferred, the financial assets are derecognized and accounted for as a sale. If the risk and rewards have not been transferred, the transaction is accounted for as a secured borrowing.

EXHIBIT 6.8

Nestlé's Receivable Disclosures
Notes (in part)

1. Accounting policies (in part)

Loans and Receivables (in part)
Loans and receivables are non-derivative financial assets with fixed or determinable payments that are not quoted in an active market. This category includes the following classes of financial assets: loans; trade and other receivables and cash at bank and in hand.

Subsequent to initial measurement, loans and receivables are carried at amortized cost using the effective interest rate method less appropriate allowances for doubtful receivables.

Allowances for doubtful receivables represent the Group's estimates of losses that could arise from the failure or inability of customers to make payments when due. These estimates are based on the ageing of customers' balances, specific credit circumstances and the Group's historical bad receivables experience.

(continued)

---

[16] With regard to control, IFRS require three criteria to be met for derecognition: (1) transferor has no obligation to repay more than it collects from the customer, (2) transferor may not sell the financial assets to anyone else, and (3) transferor must remit any amounts collected without material delay.

6. Trade and other receivables
6.1 By type

In millions of CHF	2012	2011
Trade receivables	9,915	9,541
Other receivables	3,489	3,799
	13,404	13,340

The five major customers represent 10% (2011: 9%) of trade and other receivables, none of them individually exceeding 5% (2011: 5%).

6.2 Past due and impaired receivables

In millions of CHF	2012	2011
Not past due	10,925	11,326
Past due 1–30 days	1,356	1,119
Past due 31–60 days	445	353
Past due 61–90 days	168	100
Past due 91–120 days	95	90
Past due more than 120 days	798	724
Allowance for doubtful receivables	(383)	(372)
	13,404	13,340

6.3 Allowance for doubtful receivables

In millions of CHF	2012	2011
At 1 January	372	409
Currency retranslations	(5)	(15)
Allowance made during the year	91	59
Amounts used and reversal of unused amounts	(75)	(81)
Reclassified as held for sale	—	
At 31 December	383	372

Based on the historic trend and expected performance of the customers, the Group believes that the above allowance for doubtful receivables sufficiently covers the risk of default.

IFRS Application Assume that Wilson Company transfers $20,000 of accounts receivable, without recourse, to Koboi Inc. for $16,000 cash minus a service charge of $250. Wilson will continue to collect the receivables with the collected amounts remitted to Koboi at the end of each month. Wilson is not allowed to pledge or assign the receivables, and there is no agreement to repurchase the receivables.

Under U.S. GAAP, Wilson has not surrendered control of the receivables because it has not met the criteria for a sale (see Exhibit 6.5, page 6-21) and must account for the transaction as a secured borrowing. That is, the receivables remain on Wilson's balance sheet and a liability is created.

Under IFRS, the nonrecourse nature of the transaction has transferred the risks and rewards of ownership to Koboi. In addition, as a secondary test, Koboi appears to possess control. Therefore, Wilson would be allowed to derecognize the financial asset under IFRS.

(continued)

The journal entries that would be made under U.S. GAAP and IFRS are as follows.

U.S. GAAP			IFRS		
Cash	15,750		Cash	15,750	
Assignment Service			Receivable from		
Charge Expense	250		Factor	4,000	
Notes Payable		16,000	Factoring Expense	250	
			Accounts		
			Receivable		20,000

Sources: IAS 32, IAS 39, IFRS 7, IFRS 9 (See Appendix C at the end of this book.)

GOT IT?

6-16 What is a *note receivable*? How do notes receivable differ from accounts receivable?

6-17 What is a non-interest-bearing note? How does accounting for a short-term non-interest-bearing note differ from a short-term interest-bearing note?

6-18 Why would a company sell or assign its notes receivable? How are transferred notes disclosed on the financial statements during the period between the discount date and maturity date?

6-19 How are the cash proceeds determined when a note receivable is transferred?

6-20 Under IFRS, what criteria must be satisfied in order to recognize receivables at fair value?

6-21 How does IFRS differ from U.S. GAAP with regard to the derecognition of financial assets?

LEARNING OBJECTIVE 6.8
Understand how petty cash funds and bank reconciliations are used to control cash.

APPENDIX 6.1: INTERNAL CONTROLS FOR CASH

Two important elements of cash management include a petty cash fund and a bank reconciliation.

Petty Cash

A petty cash system involves a cash fund under the control of an employee that enables a company to pay for small amounts that might be impractical or impossible to pay by check. For example, a company that requires employees to work overtime may have a policy of sending late-working employees home by taxi. Because taxi drivers may not accept checks, the company may give these employees cash to pay the taxi fare. Small amounts of cash may also be needed to pay for postage, deliveries, small amounts of office supplies, and other items. A company may use a petty cash system for these purposes.

The design and operation of a petty cash system includes the following steps:

- *Step 1.* An employee is appointed petty cash custodian, and the petty cash fund is established at an amount estimated to be enough to cover expenditures over a short period of time.
- *Step 2.* Petty cash vouchers are printed, prenumbered, and given to the custodian of the fund. The vouchers are used as evidence of expenditures. The custodian completes a petty cash voucher each time a payment from the fund is made, but journal entries are *not* recorded at this time. Therefore, at all times the total of the cash in the fund plus the amounts of the vouchers should be equal to the original amount of the fund.

- *Step 3.* When the amount of cash in the petty cash fund becomes low and/or at the end of an accounting period, the vouchers are sorted into expense categories and the remaining cash is counted. The expenses are then recorded, and the fund is replenished. At this time, a Cash Short and Over account is used to record any "shortage" or "overage" between the original petty cash fund balance and the remaining cash in the fund plus the amounts of the petty cash vouchers. The Cash Short and Over account helps to highlight errors and improve internal control.

Example At the beginning of the month, Plath Company established a petty cash fund of $500. The journal entry to record the establishment of the fund is:

Petty Cash	500	
Cash		500

A count at the end of the month shows $67.54 remaining in the petty cash fund, and the sorting of vouchers indicates the following costs were incurred during the month:

Office supplies	$ 34.16
Postage	178.00
Transportation	132.14
Miscellaneous	83.76
Total expenses	$428.06

Because these expenses total $428.06 and the amount needed to replenish the fund is $432.46 ($500 − $67.54), the fund is "short" by $4.40. Plath records (debits) the actual expenses (along with Cash Short and Over), rather than petty cash, as follows when it replenishes the fund:

Office Supplies Expense	34.16	
Postage Expense	178.00	
Transportation Expense	132.14	
Miscellaneous Expense	83.76	
Cash Short and Over	4.40	
Cash		432.46

The $432.46 is given to the fund custodian, and the actual amount of cash in the petty cash fund is now equal to the original fund balance of $500. Plath reports the expenses on its income statement. It reports a debit balance in the Cash Short and Over account at the end of the accounting period as a miscellaneous expense; it reports a credit balance as a miscellaneous revenue. Plath includes the balance of the petty cash fund as part of the Cash amount reported on its balance sheet when it issues financial statements.

Bank Reconciliation

Banks send a monthly statement to each depositor summarizing the activities that have taken place in the depositor's account. These activities include deposits, checks cleared, fees, miscellaneous items, and the ending balance in the checking account. Because the bank is an external, independent party, a good internal control procedure is to use the bank statement to verify the company's Cash balance. A **bank reconciliation** is an analysis of the difference between the company's cash balance in its accounting records and the cash balance reported on its bank statement to determine the correct cash balance.

The bank statement and the company's accounting records usually will not be in complete agreement. Differences can arise from errors and timing. Timing differences occur when the company and the bank record transactions and include the following items:

- *Outstanding Checks.* An **outstanding check** is a check written by the company and deducted from its cash balance that the bank has not yet deducted from the balance reported on the bank statement. On the date a company issues a check, it reduces its Cash account. A period of time is necessary for the check to be received by the payee (recipient of the check), deposited in the payee's bank, and subtracted from the company's bank balance. Therefore, a company has a certain number of outstanding checks at the end of each month that causes its Cash account balance to be less than the balance on the bank statement.

- *Deposits in Transit.* A **deposit in transit** is a cash receipt added to the company's cash balance but not yet added to the balance reported on the bank statement. When a company receives a check, it increases its Cash account. A period of time may pass before the check is deposited by the company and recorded by the bank. At the end of each month, the company may have deposits in transit (either cash or checks) that cause its Cash account balance to be greater than the balance on the bank statement.
- *Charges Made Directly by the Bank.* These represent fees such as service charges, the cost of printing checks, and the cost of stopping payment on checks that a bank deducts directly from the depositor's account and reports on the bank statement. In addition, when the company's bank is unable to collect the amount of the customer's check that was previously deposited, the customer's check is returned to the company, and the bank deducts this amount from the company's bank account. The company now has the responsibility for collecting this "bounced" check from the customer. **NSF (not-sufficient-funds)** is the term used for a customer's check that a company has deposited in its bank account but has not been paid by the customer's bank because there is not enough cash in the customer's account. At the end of the month, the bank lists all of these charges as deductions from the company's cash balance on the bank statement even though the company may not have deducted them from its cash balance in its accounting records. This causes the bank statement balance to be less than the balance in the company's Cash account.
- *Deposits Made Directly by the Bank.* A bank often acts as a collection agency for its customers on items such as notes receivable. In addition, most checking accounts earn interest. Consequently, the bank statement may include cash received by the bank that the company has not yet recorded in its accounting records. In these situations, the bank statement balance is greater than the balance in the company's Cash account.
- *Errors.* Despite the internal control procedures established by the bank and the company, the company may discover errors in either the bank's records or its own records when it prepares the bank reconciliation. For example, a bank may include a deposit or a check from another customer's account or make an error in recording an amount. A company may similarly make an error in recording an amount. For example, a common error is to transpose two numbers, so that the correct amount of $426 is recorded as $462.

Procedures for Preparing a Bank Reconciliation Given the items that might cause a difference between the ending balance in a company's Cash account and the ending cash balance from the bank statement, the company should perform the following in preparing its bank reconciliation:

- *Step 1:* **Compare the deposits listed in the company's records with the deposits shown on the bank statement.** Determine that the deposits in transit included in *last* month's bank reconciliation are listed in this month's bank statement. These deposits do not need any adjustment in the bank reconciliation. If they are *not* shown on the bank statement, investigate to determine if an error or theft has occurred. Identify any deposits for the current month that are not listed on the bank statement. Add the amounts of all the deposits in transit to the ending cash balance of the bank statement in the reconciliation.
- *Step 2:* **Compare the checks listed in the company's records with the checks shown on the bank statement.** Determine that the outstanding checks included in

last month's bank reconciliation are listed in this month's bank statement. These checks do not need any adjustment in the bank reconciliation. If they are *not* shown on the bank statement, investigate to determine if the checks were received by the creditors so that the company's "credit rating" is not affected. Identify any checks for the current month not deducted in the bank statement. Subtract the amounts of all the outstanding checks from the ending cash balance of the bank statement in the reconciliation.

- *Step 3:* **Identify any deposits or charges made directly by the bank that are not included in the company's records.** These include items such as collections of notes receivable, interest earned on the checking account, service charges, and NSF checks which are listed on the bank statement. Add the collections to or subtract the charges from the company's ending cash balance in the bank reconciliation.
- *Step 4:* **Determine the effect of any errors.** If an error is found, the nature of the error determines whether to add the error to or subtract the error from the company's ending cash balance or from the ending cash balance of the bank statement.
- *Step 5:* **Complete the bank reconciliation.** A company is required to report on its balance sheet the amount of cash over which it has control at the end of an accounting period. The bank reconciliation form (shown in Example 6.3) focuses on the form of reconciliation that arrives at an *adjusted*, or *corrected*, cash balance, indicating the amount of cash that a company reports on its balance sheet.
- *Step 6:* **After completing the bank reconciliation, the company makes journal entries to bring its accounts up to date.** The company only makes journal entries for the adjustments it made to *its* records on the bank reconciliation. It does *not* make journal entries for the adjustments it made to the bank statement balance on the reconciliation; the bank will record these adjustments in its accounts at the appropriate time.

Example: Bank Reconciliation

The following example shows the preparation of a bank reconciliation and the required adjusting entries for Craig Corporation for the month ended June 30, 2016. The unadjusted cash balances are as follows:

Cash balance from bank statement, June 30	$12,461.15
Cash balance from company records, June 30	12,437.94

The bank statement disclosed the following information:

- A customer note for $1,200 plus $12 interest was collected on June 29.
- A customer check for $138.14 was returned because of insufficient funds (NSF check).
- The monthly service charge was $15.

A review of the company records disclosed the following:

- A deposit for $1,142.87 at the end of the day on June 30 did not appear on the bank statement.
- Customer checks totaling $327.40 were on hand at the end of June awaiting deposit.
- The following company checks were outstanding at the end of June:

#862	$ 96.19
#864	147.18
#865	263.25

- Check #843, written for $91.20 in payment of an account payable and included with the canceled checks in the bank statement, was erroneously recorded as $19.20 in the company's records.

EXAMPLE 6.3

Bank Reconciliation and Adjusting Entries

Craig Corporation
Bank Reconciliation
June 30, 2016

Cash balance from bank statement			$12,461.15
Add:	Deposit in transit	$1,142.87	
	Checks on hand	327.40	1,470.27
			$13,931.42
Deduct:	Outstanding checks:		
	#862	$ 96.19	
	#864	147.18	
	#865	263.25	(506.62)
Adjusted cash balance			**$13,424.80**
Cash balance from company records			$12,437.94
Add:	Note collected by bank	$1,200.00	
	Interest on note	12.00	1,212.00
			$13,649.94
Deduct:	Bank service charge	$ 15.00	
	NSF check returned	138.14	
	Error in recording check #843	72.00	(225.14)
Adjusted cash balance			**$13,424.80**

Adjusting Entries

June 30	Cash		1,212.00	
		Notes Receivable		1,200.00
		Interest Revenue		12.00
30	Miscellaneous Expense		15.00	
	Accounts Receivable		138.14	
	Accounts Payable		72.00	
		Cash		225.14

The upper part of **Example 6.3** shows the preparation of a bank reconciliation based on this information. After completing the reconciliation, Craig prepares adjusting entries to record those items not previously included in its accounts. These entries are shown in the bottom part of Example 6.3 (with arrows to indicate which items are adjusted). These adjusting entries adjust the Cash account to $13,424.80, the amount that Craig reports as its cash balance (along with any petty cash) on its June 30, 2016, balance sheet. ■

GOT IT?

6-22 *(Appendix 6.1)* What is the purpose of a petty cash system?

6-23 *(Appendix 6.1)* Why are actual expenses, rather than the petty cash account, debited when the fund is replenished?

6-24 *(Appendix 6.1)* What is a *bank reconciliation?* List the causes of the difference between the cash balance listed on a company's bank statement and the balance shown in the company's cash account.

6-25 *(Appendix 6.1)* Why are adjusting entries made after the bank reconciliation is completed? Give an example of an item on a bank reconciliation that requires an adjusting entry.

REVIEW CENTER

At the beginning of the chapter, we discussed how the effective management of cash and receivables is critical to a company's success and identified several key objectives that would highlight accounting's role in this process. These objectives are listed below and followed by a brief summary of the key points.

KEY TAKEAWAYS

LEARNING OBJECTIVE 6.1
Identify items of cash and cash equivalents.

- To be reported as cash, the asset must be readily available to pay current obligations and may not be bound by any contractual or legal restrictions. Cash includes coins and currency, unrestricted funds on deposit with a bank (checking and savings accounts), negotiable instruments (e.g., checks), bank drafts, and undeposited credit card sales receipts.
- Cash does *not* include items such as sinking funds, certificates of deposit, bank overdrafts, postdated checks, travel advances, and compensating balances.
- Cash equivalents are short-term, highly liquid investments with a maturity date of three months or less from the date of purchase. They are often combined with cash for financial reporting purposes.

KEY TERMS

bank overdrafts, p. 6-3
cash, p. 6-3
cash equivalents, p. 6-4
certificates of deposit (CDs), p. 6-3
compensating balances, p. 6-3

financial flexibility, p. 6-2
liquidity, p. 6-2
postdated checks, p. 6-3
sinking funds, p. 6-3
travel advances, p. 6-3

KEY TAKEAWAYS

LEARNING OBJECTIVE 6.2
Understand the importance of cash controls.

- Internal control systems are the policies and procedures a company uses to ensure its financial reports are reliable, its operations are effective and efficient, and it complies with applicable laws and regulations. These internal controls for cash are subdivided into two main functions—control over receipts and control over payments—and include routine reviews of the accuracy of recorded cash transactions and the separation of duties.
- The growth in electronic payments has reduced the number of physical checks being processed. Electronic payments require a strong internal control system to protect a company's assets.

KEY TERMS

accounts receivable conversion (ARC), p. 6-6
Check Clearing for the 21st Century Act (Check 21), p. 6-6

electronic funds transfer (EFT), p. 6-6
internal control systems, p. 6-5

KEY TAKEAWAYS

LEARNING OBJECTIVE 6.3
Define and identify different types of receivables.

- Receivables are amounts owed to the company by customers and other parties arising from the company's operations. A company may group receivables within its balance sheet as either trade receivables or nontrade receivables.
- Trade receivables arise from the sale of the company's products or services to customers and are generally the majority of a company's total receivables balance. Typical trade receivables are accounts receivable and notes receivable.
- Nontrade receivables arise from transactions that are not directly related to the sale of the company's goods and services.

KEY TERMS

accounts receivable, p. 6-7
nontrade receivables, p. 6-7
notes receivable, p. 6-7

receivables, p. 6-7
trade receivables, p. 6-7

LEARNING OBJECTIVE 6.4
Explain the accounting issues associated with accounts receivable.

KEY TAKEAWAYS

- Accounts receivable are normally reported at net realizable value, which is the amount the company expects to receive in cash at the time of collection.
- Trade discounts are recorded indirectly by reducing the sale and the related receivable by the amount of the discount.
- Cash (sales) discounts may be offered to induce prompt payment. Sales Revenue should be recorded at the amount that the company expects to be entitled to receive from the customer. GAAP allows the use of either the gross method or the net method.
- Sales returns and allowances should be recorded as a reduction in sales revenue. In addition, a return liability, which represents the company's obligation to return the customer's consideration, should also be recorded.

KEY TERMS

cash discount, p. 6-9
net realizable value, p. 6-9
quantity discounts, p. 6-9
revenue recognition, p. 6-8

sales allowance, p. 6-11
sales discount, p. 6-9
sales return, p. 6-11
trade discounts, p. 6-9

LEARNING OBJECTIVE 6.5
Explain the estimation of uncollectible accounts receivable and its effect on the valuation of receivables.

KEY TAKEAWAYS

- Because bad debt expense is a cost of granting credit to customers, this expense should be estimated and recorded in the period of the credit sale.
- Companies may record uncollectible accounts (bad debts) by either the allowance method or the direct write-off method. The allowance method is preferred because it enables companies to properly value their receivables and match expenses against revenues in the current period.
- Under the allowance method, bad debt expense may be estimated by using a(n):
  - Percentage of credit sales (an income statement approach): Bad debt expense is recorded at an amount based on an estimate of the percentage of the current sales that will not be collected.
  - Percentage of outstanding receivables (a balance sheet approach): The ending balance in the allowance account is estimated based on the balance in accounts receivable. The bad debt expense account is debited at the amount necessary to adjust the existing allowance account balance to the required ending balance.
  - Aging analysis (a balance sheet approach): Accounts receivable is classified into categories based on their age. The amount in each category is then multiplied by the percentage estimated to be uncollectible and summed to compute the expected uncollectible amounts. Finally, this sum is deducted from the balance in the allowance account to determine the amount to record as a debit to Bad Debts Expense.
- The write-off of an uncollectible account under the allowance method does not affect the carrying value of net accounts receivable.
- Under the direct write-off method, bad debt expense is recorded when it determines that a specific customer account is uncollectible.

KEY TERMS

allowance method, p. 6-13
direct write-off method, p. 6-13

receivables turnover ratio, p. 6-18

KEY TAKEAWAYS

- A company may transfer its receivables to a financing company in order to obtain immediate cash. This transfer is accounted for as either a secured borrowing (pledge or assignment) or a sale of receivables (factoring, securitization), depending upon whether control of the receivables has been surrendered.
  - In a secured borrowing, the transferor does not surrender control over its receivables and records the proceeds from the transfer of receivables as a liability, with the receivables serving as collateral.
  - For a sale of receivables, the transferor surrenders control over its receivables and records the proceeds, derecognizes the receivables sold, and records a gain or loss.
- A sale of receivables can be made with or without recourse.
- In a sale with recourse, the seller retains the risk of ownership and bears any loss from nonpayment of receivables.
- In a sale without recourse, the buyer has assumed all the risks of ownership and bears any loss from a nonpayment of receivables.

LEARNING OBJECTIVE 6.6
Explain how to account for secured borrowings and sales of accounts receivable.

KEY TERMS

assign, p. 6-21
factoring, p. 6-23
financial components approach, p. 6-25
line of credit, p. 6-25

pledge, p. 6-21
secured borrowing, p. 6-21
securitization, p. 6-23

KEY TAKEAWAYS

- Short-term, interest-bearing notes are recorded at the face value of the note receivable, and interest is recognized by applying a specific interest rate to this face value.
- Short-term non-interest-bearing notes receivable are recorded at their maturity value (which includes both principal and implicit interest), and interest income is recognized over the term of the note.
- Similar to accounts receivable, a note receivable may be sold or transferred to a bank in exchange for cash.
- Companies may elect to report financial assets and liabilities at fair value, with any unrealized holding gains or losses reported on the income statement.

LEARNING OBJECTIVE 6.7
Account for short-term notes receivable.

KEY TERMS

discount period, p. 6-29
discount rate, p. 6-28

note receivable, p. 6-27

KEY TAKEAWAYS

- A petty cash system involves assigning a cash fund to an employee who has control over the fund and who pays for small amounts (e.g., postage) that might be impractical or impossible to pay by check. At all times, the amount of the cash in the fund plus the amount of expenditure vouchers should be equal to the original amount in the fund.
- Bank reconciliations provide an external, independent control to verify a company's cash balance. To prepare a bank reconciliation, add the amounts of any deposits in transit to and subtract the amounts of any outstanding checks from the ending bank statement balance. Next, add any collections or subtract any charges made directly by the bank to or from the company's ending cash balance. Then, adjust the ending bank statement balance or company's ending cash balance for any errors and complete the bank reconciliation. Finally, make any journal entries necessary to bring the accounts up to date.

LEARNING OBJECTIVE 6.8
(Appendix 6.1) Understand how petty cash funds and bank reconciliations are used to control cash.

KEY TERMS

bank reconciliation, p. 6-35
deposit in transit, p. 6-36

NSF (not-sufficient-funds), p. 6-36
outstanding check, p. 6-35

ANSWERS TO REAL REPORT QUESTIONS

Real Report 6.1 Answers Royal Caribbean—Cash and Cash Equivalents

1. Cash and cash equivalents are reported as one combined amount because the investment is readily convertible into cash (three months or less at the date of *purcha*se), and the risk that that the short-term investment's value will change significantly due to a change in interest rates is minimal.

Real Report 6.2 Answers Office Depot—Disclosure of the Transfer of Accounts Receivable

1. Office Depot sells its accounts receivable without recourse. A transfer of receivables without recourse implies that the buyer (factor) assumes all the risks of ownership. Therefore, if any receivables are not collected, the factor cannot demand payment from the seller.
2. The financial institution (factor) retains a portion of the receivables as protection against sales returns and allowances and nonpayment by the customer.

Real Report 6.3 Answers VF Corporation—Disclosure of Accounts Receivable

1. VF believes that $45.35 million of its receivables at December 31, 2013, are uncollectible.
2. VF uses both an aging of accounts receivable as well as the specific identification method to estimate its allowance for doubtful accounts. The specific method requires an account-by-account analysis to determine which past due accounts are uncollectible. Both aging and specific identification are generally accepted accounting methods to calculate the allowance for doubtful accounts.

MULTIPLE-CHOICE (AICPA ADAPTED)

Select the best answer for each of the following.

M6-1 **LO 6.1** Which of the following items should be classified under the heading of cash on the balance sheet?

	Postdated Checks	Certificates of Deposit
a.	Yes	Yes
b.	Yes	No
c.	No	No
d.	No	Yes

M6-2 **LO 6.1** Greenfield Company had the following cash balances at December 31, 2016:

Cash in banks	$1,300,000
Petty cash funds (all funds were reimbursed on December 31, 2016)	20,000
Cash legally restricted for additions to plant (expected to be disbursed in 2018)	2,000,000

Cash in banks includes $300,000 of compensating balances against short-term borrowing arrangements at December 31, 2016. The compensating balances are not legally restricted as to withdrawal by Greenfield. In the current assets section of Greenfield's December 31, 2016, balance sheet, what total amount should be reported as cash?

a. $1,020,000
b. $1,320,000
c. $3,020,000
d. $3,320,000

M6-3 **LO 6.5** A company is in its first year of operations and has never written off any accounts receivable as uncollectible. When the allowance method of recognizing bad debt expense is used, the entry to recognize that expense:

a. increases net income
b. decreases current assets
c. has no effect on current assets
d. has no effect on net income

M6-4
LO 6.5
Marmol Corporation uses the allowance method for bad debts. During 2016, Marmol charged $50,000 to bad debt expense and wrote off $45,200 of uncollectible accounts receivable. These transactions resulted in a decrease in working capital of:

a. $0
b. $4,800
c. $45,200
d. $50,000

M6-5
LO 6.5
On January 1, 2016, King Company's Allowance for Doubtful Accounts had a credit balance of $15,000. During 2016, King (1) charged $32,000 to bad debt expense, (2) wrote off $23,000 of uncollectible accounts receivable, and (3) unexpectedly recovered $6,000 of bad debts written off in the prior year. The Allowance for Doubtful Accounts balance at December 31, 2016, should be:

a. $47,000
b. $32,000
c. $30,000
d. $24,000

M6-6
LO 6.5
Prior to adjustments, Barrett Company's account balances at December 31, 2016, for Accounts Receivable and the related Allowance for Doubtful Accounts were $1,200,000 and $60,000, respectively. An aging of accounts receivable indicated that $106,000 of the December 31, 2016, receivables may be uncollectible. The net realizable value of accounts receivable at December 31, 2016, was:

a. $1,034,000
b. $1,094,000
c. $1,140,000
d. $1,154,000

M6-7
LO 6.5
A method of estimating bad debts that focuses on the income statement rather than the balance sheet is the allowance method based on:

a. direct write-off
b. aging the trade receivable accounts
c. credit sales
d. the balance in the trade receivable accounts

M6-8
LO 6.6
When the accounts receivable of a company are sold outright to a company that normally buys accounts receivable of other companies without recourse, the accounts receivable have been:

a. factored
b. assigned
c. pledged
d. collateralized

M6-9
LO 6.7
Tallent Company received a $30,000, 6-month, 10% interest-bearing note from a customer. After holding the note for 2 months, Tallent was in need of cash and sold the note at the United National Bank at a 12% discount rate. The amount of cash received by Tallent from the bank was:

a. $31,260
b. $30,870
c. $30,300
d. $30,240

M6-10
LO 6.7

Under IFRS, which of the following criteria is not necessary for a transfer of financial assets to be treated as a sale?

a. Substantially all of the risks and benefits of ownership have been transferred.
b. There is isolation of the transferred assets from the transferor.
c. The transferor has no obligation to repay more than it collects from the customer.
d. The transferor may not sell the assets to anyone else.
e. All amounts are remitted to the transferee without material delay.

M6-11
LO 6.8
(*Appendix 6.1*) Kingston Company's bank reconciliation for the month of November 2016 follows:

Balance per bank statement, 11/30/16		$18,040
Add: Deposit in transit		4,150
		$22,190
Less: Outstanding checks	$6,300	
Bank credit recorded in error	20	(6,320)
Balance per books, 11/30/16		$15,870

Data for the month of December 2016 follow:

Per bank:	
December deposits	$26,100
December disbursements	22,420
Balance, 12/31/16	21,720

All items that were outstanding as of November 30 cleared through the bank in December, including the bank credit. In addition, $2,500 in checks were outstanding as of December 31, 2016. What is the balance of cash per books at December 31, 2016?

a. $19,220
b. $19,240
c. $21,720
d. $24,220

REVIEW EXERCISES

RE6-1
LO 6.1
On December 31, Harrison Company reports the following assets:

Cash on hand	Savings account	Compensating balance
Checking account	Certificates of deposit	Travel advance
Sinking fund	Negotiable checks	Deposits in a foreign bank

Which of these are included in, and excluded from, cash on the company's balance sheet?

RE6-2
LO 6.2
Lindley Enterprises sells hand-woven rugs. Paige Corporation is a regular customer of Lindley. On June 30, Paige purchased 500 rugs from Lindley for $400,000 on credit. On August 15, Paige paid Lindley in full on its $400,000 balance. Prepare the related journal entries for Lindley.

RE6-3
LO 6.4
Long Corporation is a fabric manufacturing company. On January 20, Long made sales to Lyndsay's Lace in the amount of $15,000 with terms of 2/10, n/30. Lyndsay's paid Long on January 28. Long records accounts receivable and sales at the gross price. Prepare the related journal entries for Long.

RE6-4
LO 6.4
Longmire & Sons made sales on credit to Alderman Sports totaling $500,000 on April 18. Longmire & Sons estimates 3% of its sales to Alderman may be returned. On May 22, $9,000 worth of goods are returned by Alderman. Prepare the related journal entries for Longmire & Sons.

RE6-5
LO 6.5
McKinney & Co. estimates its uncollectible accounts as a percentage of credit sales. McKinney made credit sales of $1,500,000 in 2016. McKinney estimates 2.5% of its sales will be uncollectible. Prepare the journal entry to record bad debt expense for McKinney at the end of 2016.

RE6-6
LO 6.5
Refer to **RE6-5**. At the end of the first quarter of 2017, McKinney & Co. reevaluates its receivables. McKinney's management decides that $8,500 due from Mangold Corporation will not be collectible. This amount was previously included in the allowance account. Prepare the journal entry to record the write-off for McKinney.

RE6-7
LO 6.5
Refer to **RE6-6**. On April 23, 2017, McKinney & Co. receives a check from Mangold Corporation for $8,500. Prepare the journal entry for McKinney to record the collection of the account previously written off.

RE6-8
LO 6.6
On December 1 of the current year, Jordan Inc. assigns $125,000 of its accounts receivable to McLaughlin Company for cash. McLaughlin Company charges a $750 service fee, advances 85% of Jordan's accounts receivable, and charges an annual interest rate of 9% on any outstanding loan balance. Prepare the related journal entries for Jordan.

RE6-9
LO 6.6
Refer to **RE6-8**. On December 31, Jordan Inc. received $50,000 on assigned accounts. Prepare Jordan's journal entries to record the cash receipt and the payment to McLaughlin.

RE6-10
LO 6.6
On December 1, Newton Enterprises sells $100,000 of accounts receivable to a factor without recourse, receives 85% of the value of the factored accounts, and is charged a 10% commission on the gross amount of the factored accounts receivable. Newton normally factors its accounts receivable. Prepare Newton's journal entry.

RE6-11
LO 6.6
Kasey's Cake Shop made $20,000 in sales of wedding cakes in July. All of these sales were on bank credit cards. The credit card company charges a 3.5% collection fee. Prepare Kasey's journal entry to record the credit card sales.

RE6-12
LO 6.7
On June 1, Phillips Corporation sold, with recourse, a note receivable from a customer to a bank. The note has a face value of $15,000 and a maturity value (principal plus interest) of $15,400. The discount is calculated to be $385, and the accrued interest income is $100. The recourse liability is estimated to be $1,000. Prepare the journal entry of Phillips to record the sale of the note receivable.

RE6-13
LO 6.8
(Appendix 6.1) At the end of April, Meyer Company had a $7,890 balance in its cash account, while its bank statement for April showed an ending cash balance of $7,200. The April bank statement showed $10 of interest earned by Meyer on its checking account and a $200 NSF check written by one of Meyer's customers. Meyer's records show a $600 deposit in transit and $100 of outstanding checks at the end of April. Prepare the bank reconciliation of Meyer for April.

EXERCISES

E6-1
LO 6.1

Computing the Cash Balance Listed below are ten items that may be found on a balance sheet.

Required:

Indicate with *yes* or *no* whether each of the items should be included in the cash balance presented on the balance sheet. Also indicate the normal balance sheet treatment for those items not included as cash.

Item	Include in Cash Balance	Classification of Items Excluded
NSF checks	___	___
Savings account	___	___
Compensating balance	___	___
Postdated checks	___	___
IOUs	___	___
Cash on hand	___	___
Cash in sinking fund	___	___
Travel advance	___	___
Bank draft	___	___
Prepaid debit card	___	___

E6-2
LO 6.1

SHOW ME HOW

Reporting Cash on the Balance Sheet Your audit of Watt Corporation discovers the following information:

Reconciled balance in First National Bank checking account	$ 3,525.80
Reconciled balance in City National Bank checking account	(40.20)
Balance in First Federal savings account	34,291.00
Certificate of deposit	30,000.00
Employee's IOU	125.00
Employees' travel advances	1,640.00
Cash on hand (undeposited sales receipts)	1,232.10
Prepaid debit card	600.00
Customer's postdated check	290.40

Required:
1. What amount should be reported as cash on Watt's balance sheet?
2. Describe the balance sheet treatment of the items not included in the cash balance.

E6-3
LO 6.3

SHOW ME HOW

Journal Entry to Separate Receivables An examination of Hutton Corporation's accounting records indicates that all receivables are being recorded in a single account entitled Receivables. An analysis of the account reveals the following:

Accounts receivable (trade)	$15,500
Accounts receivable (officers)	3,600
Interest receivable, due in 3 months	675
Advances to employees	1,800
Notes receivable (trade), due in 3 years	9,000
Deposit to guarantee contract performance	5,000
Utility deposit	500
Total	$36,075

Required:
1. Prepare a journal entry to separate the preceding items into their proper accounts.
2. How would each of the preceding items normally be reflected (current or noncurrent; trade or nontrade receivable) on Hutton's balance sheet?

E6-4
LO 6.4

Accounting for Cash (Sales) Discounts On December 1, 2016, Lynch Incorporated sold $18,000 of merchandise with terms 2/10, n/EOM. On December 11, 2016, collections were made on sales originally billed for $12,000, and on December 31, 2016, additional collections on sales originally billed for $5,000 were received.

Required:
1. Prepare the journal entries to record the sale, collections, and any required year-end adjustments assuming that Lynch records accounts receivable and sales at (a) the gross price and (b) the net price.
2. **Next Level** Assume that Lynch's customer does not have the available cash to pay Lynch within the discount period. How much interest should the customer be willing to pay for a loan to permit them to take advantage of the discount period (assume no additional costs to the loan)?
3. **Next Level** Explain why Lynch's granting of cash (sales) discounts may improve cash flow.

E6-5
LO 6.4

Comparison of Discount Methods Eastman Corporation sells merchandise with a list price of $13,000 on February 1, 2016, with terms of 1/10, n/30. On February 10, 2016, payment was received on merchandise originally billed for $7,500, and the balance due was received on March 1, 2016.

Required:
1. Prepare the journal entries to record the preceding information assuming that Eastman records accounts receivable and sales at (a) the gross price and (b) the net price.
2. **Next Level** What implied annual interest rate is Eastman's customer incurring by failing to take the cash (sales) discount? (Assume a 365-day year.)
3. **Next Level** Which method—recording accounts receivable at the gross price or net price—is theoretically superior? Why?

E6-6
LO 6.4

Returns and Allowances Towbin Products sells merchandise on credit for $7,000 on December 1, 2016. Towbin estimates that returns and allowances will amount to 4% of sales. On December 22, 2016, a customer returns for credit merchandise originally sold on December 1 for $200.

Required:
1. Prepare the journal entries to record the preceding sale and the return of merchandise.
2. How would the preceding information be reflected on Towbin's December 31, 2016, financial statements?
3. **Next Level** What is the conceptual advantage of recording sales returns and allowances as a reduction of revenue?

E6-7
LO 6.4

Accounts Receivable Calculations The following amounts were reported for Cotton, Newton, and Miller Companies:

	Cotton	Newton	Miller
Accounts Receivable, 1/1/2016	$ 502,300	$ 282,100	$ 128,500
Accounts Receivable, 12/31/2016	(a)	311,000	152,700
Cash collections during the year	4,770,900	2,715,200	(c)
Credit sales	4,935,500	(b)	1,571,100

Required:
Next Level Compute the missing amounts.

E6-8
LO 6.5

Estimation versus Direct Write-Off of Bad Debts Blunt Company makes credit sales of $21,000 during the month of February 2016. During 2016, collections are received on February sales of $20,400, accounts representing $600 of these sales are written off as uncollectible, and a $100 account previously written off is collected.

Required:
1. Prepare the journal entries necessary to record the preceding information if (a) bad debts are estimated as 3% of credit sales at the time of sale and (b) the bad debts are recorded as they actually occur.
2. **Next Level** Which method—recording bad debts at the time of sale or when they actually occur—is preferred? Why?

E6-9
LO 6.5

Estimating Bad Debts from Receivables Balances The following information is extracted from Shelton Corporation's accounting records at the beginning of 2016:

Accounts Receivable	$63,000
Allowance for Doubtful Accounts	1,400 (credit)

During 2016, sales on credit amounted to $575,000, $557,400 was collected on outstanding receivables and $2,600 of receivables were written off as uncollectible. On December 31, 2016, Shelton estimates its bad debts to be 4% of the outstanding gross accounts receivable balance.

Required:
1. Prepare the journal entry necessary to record Shelton's estimate of bad debt expense for 2016.
2. Prepare the Accounts Receivable section of Shelton's December 31, 2016, balance sheet.
3. Compute Shelton's receivables turnover. (Round to one decimal place.)
4. If Sheldon uses IFRS, what might be the heading for the accounts receivable section in Requirement 2?

E6-10
LO 6.5

Aging Analysis of Accounts Receivable Cowen's, a large department store located in a metropolitan area, has been experiencing difficulty in estimating its bad debts. The company has decided to prepare an aging schedule for its outstanding accounts receivable and estimate bad debts by the due dates of its receivables. This analysis discloses the following information:

Balance	Age of Receivable	Estimated Percentage Uncollectible
$193,000	Under 30 days	0.8%
114,000	30–60 days	2.0%
73,000	61–120 days	5.0%
41,000	121–240 days	20.0%
25,000	241–360 days	35.0%
19,000	Over 360 days	60.0%
$465,000		

Required:
1. Use the preceding analysis to compute the estimated amount of uncollectible receivables.
2. Prepare the journal entry to record Cowen's estimated uncollectibles, assuming the balance in Allowance for Doubtful Accounts prior to adjustment is:
   a. 0
   b. $3,000 (debit)
   c. $2,800 (credit)

E6-11
LO 6.5

Comparison of Bad Debt Estimation Methods Bradford Company's accounting records on December 31, 2016, provide the following information (prior to adjustment):

Cash sales	$ 93,100	
Net credit sales	262,900	
Total sales (net)		$356,000
Accounts receivable		126,300
Allowance for doubtful accounts		2,150 (credit)

Required:
1. Prepare the journal entries to record the estimate of Bradford's bad debt expense for 2016 assuming:
   a. Bad debts are estimated to be 2% of net credit sales.
   b. Bad debts are estimated to be 5% of gross accounts receivable.
2. **Next Level** Discuss the advantages and disadvantages of the balance sheet and income statement approaches to estimating bad debt.

E6-12
LO 6.5

Inferring Accounts Receivable Amounts At the end of 2016, Karras Inc. had a debit balance of $141,120 in its accounts receivable. Additionally, Karras had a credit balance in its allowance for doubtful accounts of $4,350 and $9,420 at the beginning and end of the year, respectively. During the year, Karras made credit sales of $1,530,000, collected receivables in the amount of $1,445,700, and recorded bad debt expense of $83,750.

Required:
Next Level Compute the amount of accounts receivable that Karras wrote off during the year and the amount of accounts receivable at the beginning of the year.

E6-13
LO 6.5
AICPA Adapted

Receivables—Bad Debts At January 1, 2016, the credit balance in Master Company's Allowance for Doubtful Accounts was $400,000. For 2016, the provision for doubtful accounts is based on a percentage of credit sales. Credit sales for 2016 were $50,000,000 (assume that all of Master's sales are credit sales). Based on the latest available facts, the 2016 provision for doubtful accounts is estimated to be 0.7% of credit sales. During 2016, uncollectible receivables amounting to $410,000 were written off against the allowance for doubtful accounts.

Required:
Prepare a schedule computing the balance in Master's Allowance for Doubtful Accounts at December 31, 2016. Show supporting computations in good form.

E6-14
LO 6.6

Transferring Accounts Receivable White Corporation has entered into an agreement to transfer accounts receivable to Murphy Company. Under the terms of this agreement, White receives 80% of the value of all the transferred accounts receivable (to reflect credit risk) and is charged a 1% service charge, which is based upon the dollar amount of transferred receivables. Interest is charged at an annual interest rate of 12% of any outstanding loan balance. The transferred receivables will continue to be collected by White with any cash flows being remitted to Murphy at the end of each month. White is not allowed to transfer the receivables to anyone else. White normally transfers its accounts receivable. The following selected 2016 transactions relate to this agreement:

Dec. 1 Accounts receivable of $160,000 are transferred.
    11 A sales return of $1,000 on a transferred account is made.
    31 Collections are made on $86,000 of the transferred accounts receivable
        plus interest for the month of December. This amount is remitted to Murphy.

Required:
1. Assume that White uses U.S. GAAP.
   a. Prepare journal entries on White's books to record the preceding transactions.
   b. How would this agreement be reported on White's December 31, 2016, balance sheet (assume the note payable is short-term)?
2. Assume that White uses IFRS:
   a. Prepare journal entries on White's books to record the preceding transactions.
   b. How would this agreement be reported on White's December 31, 2016, balance sheet (assume the note payable is short-term)?

E6-15
LO 6.6

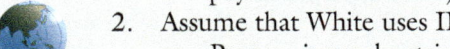

Transfer of Accounts Receivable Inder Corporation is experiencing a temporary cash shortage and decides to transfer a group of its accounts receivable to Newton Company. Inder does not normally transfer its receivables. Newton accepts $80,000 of Inder's accounts receivable, remits 90% of the accounts receivable transferred, and charges a 16% commission on the gross amount of the transferred receivables. Title to the receivables is transferred to Newton, and Newton has the right to assign, pledge, or sell the receivables. During the period, sales returns and allowances on transferred accounts amounted to $1,500.

Required:
1. Prepare all the journal entries necessary by Inder to record the preceding information assuming the transfer was without recourse.
2. Prepare all the journal entries necessary by Inder to record the preceding information assuming the transfer was with recourse and the recourse obligation had an estimated fair value of $4,500.
3. Assume that Inder uses IFRS. How would your answers to Requirements 1 and 2 change?

E6-16
LO 6.6
AICPA Adapted

Generating Cash from Receivables Guide Company requires additional cash for its business. Guide has decided to use its accounts receivable to raise the additional cash as follows:
1. On June 30, 2016, Guide assigned $200,000 of accounts receivable to Cell Finance Company. Guide received an advance from Cell of 85% of the assigned accounts receivable, minus a commission on the advance of 3%. Prior to December 31, 2016, Guide collected $150,000 on the assigned accounts receivable and remitted $160,000 to Cell, $10,000 of which represented interest on the advance from Cell.
2. On December 1, 2016, Guide sold $300,000 of accounts receivable to Factoring Company and received 80% of the value of the factored receivables. Factoring Company charged a 15% commission based on the gross amount of the factored receivables. The receivables were sold without recourse.

Required:
Prepare a schedule showing the expenses reported on the income statement for the year ended December 31, 2016, as a result of the preceding facts. Show all supporting computations.

E6-17 **Interest-Bearing and Non-Interest-Bearing Notes** On December 11, 2016, Hooper Inc. made a credit sale to
LO 6.7 Marshall Company and required Marshall to sign a $12,000, 60-day note.

Required:
Prepare the journal entries necessary to record the receipt of the note by Hooper, the accrual of interest on December 31, 2016, and the customer's repayment on February 9, 2017, assuming:
1. Interest of 12% was assessed in addition to the face value of the note.
2. The note was issued as a $12,000 non-interest-bearing note with a present value of $11,765. The implicit interest rate on the note receivable was 12%. Assume a 360-day year. (Round to the nearest dollar.)

E6-18 **Computing the Proceeds from the Sale of Notes Receivable** Below are several customer notes receivable that
LO 6.7 were sold without recourse.
1. An $8,000, 60-day, non-interest-bearing note sold after 15 days at 12%
2. A $9,000, 12%, 60-day note sold after 30 days at 14%
3. A $6,000, 10%, 90-day note sold after 30 days at 12%
4. A $10,000, 12%, 120-day note sold after 45 days at 15%

Required:
Determine the proceeds from each of the preceding sales of customer notes receivable. (Assume a 360-day year.)

E6-19 **Recording the Sale of Notes Receivable** Singer Corporation was involved in the following events in the current
LO 6.7 year:

June 30	Barney Manufacturing gives Singer a $5,000, 11%, 90-day note for merchandise purchased.
July 15	Dillon Construction Co. gives Singer a $6,000, 10%, 60-day note for merchandise originally purchased, on account, on April 20 of the current year.
30	The Barney and Dillon notes are sold with recourse by Singer at its bank at 12%. The estimated fair value of the recourse liability is $1,500.
Sept. 15	The bank notifies Singer that the Dillon note was paid.
30	The bank notifies Singer that Barney defaulted on the note and charges the amount of principal, interest, and a fee of $10 against Singer's bank account.

Required:
Prepare the journal entries to record the preceding information on Singer's accounting records. Assume that the company does not normally sell its notes. (Assume a 360-day year and round all answers to the nearest penny.)

E6-20 **Petty Cash Transactions** *(Appendix 6.1)* Crown Company established a petty cash fund of $600 for incidental
LO 6.8 expenditures on January 2, 2016. At the end of the month, the count of cash on hand indicated that $57.35 remained in the fund. A sorting of petty cash vouchers disclosed that the following expenses had been incurred during the month, and the fund was replenished.

Postage expense	$250.40
Office supplies expense	165.90
Miscellaneous expense	119.05

Required:
Prepare the journal entries necessary to record Crown's petty cash transactions during January.

E6-21 **Adjusting an Unknown Cash Balance** *(Appendix 6.1)* The information that follows is available from the general
LO 6.8 ledger and the bank statement of Gentry Corporation for the month of August, 2016:

Bank statement balance, August 31	$1,342.50
Note collected by the bank not previously recorded by Gentry	600.00
Interest on the preceding note (not previously recorded)	25.00
NSF check returned with the bank statement (not previously recorded)	212.60
Outstanding checks at the end of August	684.70
Bank service charge for August	12.85
Deposit in transit, August 31	329.42

(continued)

Required:
1. **Next Level** Starting with the bank statement balance, prepare a schedule to determine Gentry's cash balance on August 31, prior to any required adjustments.
2. Prepare a bank reconciliation to determine Gentry's adjusted cash balance on August 31, 2016.
3. Prepare the journal entries necessary to bring Gentry's cash account balance up to date.

E6-22
LO 6.8

Bank Reconciliation *(Appendix 6.1)* The following information is extracted from the bank statement and the accounting records of Sun Corporation for the month of July, 2016:

Cash balance from books, July 31	$1,967.35
Cash balance from bank, July 31	1,980.20
NSF check returned by bank with bank statement	81.00
Note collected by bank on July 31	190.00
Interest on preceding note	5.50
Bank service charge for July	4.40
Outstanding checks at end of July	150.00
Deposit in transit at end of July	247.25

Required:
1. Prepare a bank reconciliation for Sun on July 31, 2016.
2. Prepare the journal entries necessary to adjust Sun's books on July 31, 2016.

E6-23
LO 6.8

Bank Reconciliation and Adjusting Entries *(Appendix 6.1)* Odum Corporation's cash account showed a balance of $17,198 on March 31, 2016. The bank statement balance for the same date indicated a balance of $17,924.55. The following additional information is available concerning Odum's cash balance on March 31:

- Undeposited cash on hand on March 31 amounted to $724.50.
- A customer's NSF check for $173.80 was returned with the bank statement.
- A note for $2,000 plus interest of $25 was collected for Odum by the bank during March. The bank notified Odum of this collection on the bank statement.
- The bank service charge for March was $15.
- A deposit of $951.75 mailed to the bank on March 31 did not appear on the bank statement.

The following checks mailed to creditors had not been processed by the bank on March 31:

#429	$ 57.40
#432	147.50
#433	214.80
#434	191.90

A customer check for $149.50 in payment of his account and listed correctly for that amount on the bank statement had been incorrectly recorded on the accounting records as $194.50.

Required:
1. Prepare a bank reconciliation for Odum on March 31, 2016.
2. Prepare any adjusting journal entries necessary to record the information from Requirement 1.

E6-24
LO 6.8

Computing the Bank Statement Balance *(Appendix 6.1)* Your cashier has notified you that he has misplaced all the bank statements for the past year. You review selected accounting records during the year and discover that the following journal entry was made to reconcile the June 30, 2016, bank statement and the accounting records:

Accounts Receivable	1,520.24	
Miscellaneous Expense	12.50	
Notes Receivable		200.00
Interest Revenue		10.00
Cash		1,322.74

Required:
1. **Next Level** What events might have caused each of the preceding reconciling items to occur?

2. **Next Level** Compute the amount that would have appeared as the balance per bank statement on a bank reconciliation if the preadjustment cash balance in the accounting records was $7,683.70, outstanding checks were $207.50, and no other adjustments were required.
3. **Next Level** Assume that you contact the bank and are informed that a balance of $5,542.90 had been reported on the June 30 bank statement. What does this discrepancy indicate, and how would you begin investigating it?

PROBLEMS

P6-1
LO 6.1
Cash and Other Items The following information has been extracted from Atwood Corporation's accounting records:

Cash on hand (undeposited sales receipts)	$ 1,535
Certificates of deposit	25,000
Customer's note receivable	1,000
Reconciled balance in University National Bank checking account	(350)
Reconciled balance in Second National Bank checking account	9,260
Balance in City Federal savings account	7,410
Customer's postdated check	980
Employee travel advances	1,200
Cash in bond sinking fund	8,300
Bond sinking fund investments	14,600

Required:
1. Determine the balance in Atwood's Cash account.
2. Discuss the balance sheet treatment of any items not included as cash.

P6-2
LO 6.4
Cash Discounts Lambert Corporation sells merchandise at a list price of $70,000 with accompanying terms of 2/10, n/30 on December 8, 2016. By December 18, 2016, Lambert had collected from customers for merchandise originally billed at $46,000. By December 31, 2016, additional collections had been received on sales originally billed for $18,000, and sales returns and allowances of $1,500 had been granted by Lambert. By January 15, 2017, all the remaining balances due had been collected.

Required:
1. Prepare the journal entries to record each of the following items assuming that Lambert records accounts receivable and sales at the gross price:
   a. the sale of the merchandise
   b. collections received by December 18, 2016
   c. collections received by December 31, 2016
   d. sales returns and allowances (*not* estimated in the period of sale)
   e. any required year-end adjustments
   f. any January 1, 2017, reversing entries
   g. the collections received by January 15, 2017

2. Prepare the journal entries to record each of the following items assuming that Lambert records accounts receivable and sales at the net price:
   a. the sale of the merchandise
   b. collections received by December 18, 2016
   c. collections received by December 31, 2016
   d. sales returns and allowances (*not* estimated in the period of sale)
   e. any required year-end adjustments
   f. any January 1, 2017, reversing entries
   g. the collections received by January 15, 2017

3. Calculate the accounts receivable balance that would be reported on Lambert's December 31, 2016, balance sheet if accounts receivable and sales were recorded at (a) the gross price and (b) the net price.

P6-3 **Estimating Bad Debts** Keegan Corporation's accounting records disclosed the following information for 2016:
LO 6.5

Cash sales	$850,000
Net credit sales	720,000
Accounts receivable (12/31/16)	160,000
Allowance for doubtful accounts (12/31/16, prior to adjustment)	1,500 (debit)

Keegan wishes to examine the effect of various alternative bad debt estimation policies.

Required:
1. Prepare the adjusting entry that would be required under each of the following methods:
   a. Bad debts are estimated at 3% of net credit sales.
   b. Bad debts are estimated at 7.5% of gross accounts receivable.
   c. An aging of accounts receivable indicates that half of the outstanding accounts will incur a 3% loss, a quarter will incur a 6% loss, the remaining quarter will incur a 20% loss.
2. **Next Level** Discuss the difference between the income statement and balance sheet approaches to estimating bad debts.

P6-4 **Allowance for Bad Accounts** Installment Jewelry Company has been in business for 5 years but has never had its financial statements audited. Engaged to audit them for 2016, you find that the company's balance sheet carries no allowance for bad accounts. Bad accounts have been expensed as written-off and recoveries credited to income as collected. The company's policy is to write off at December 31 of each year those accounts on which no collections have been received for three months. The installment contracts generally are for 2 years.
LO 6.5
AICPA Adapted

On your recommendation, the company agrees to revise its accounts for 2016 to give effect to bad account treatment on the allowance basis. The allowance is to be based on a percentage of credit sales that is derived from the experience of prior years. Statistics for the past 5 years are shown in the following table:

Year of Sale	Credit Sales	Accounts Written Off					Recoveries
		2012	2013	2014	2015	2016	
2012	$100,000	$550	$1,500	$ 500			
2013	250,000		1,000	4,000	$1,200		$100
2014	300,000			1,300	4,500	$2,700	400
2015	325,000				1,500	5,000	500
2016	275,000					1,400	600

Accounts receivable at December 31, 2016, were as follows:

2015 credit sales	$ 15,000
2016 credit sales	135,000
	$150,000

Required:
Prepare the adjusting journal entry or entries with appropriate explanations to set up the Allowance for Bad Accounts. (Support each item with organized computations; income tax implications should be ignored.)

P6-5 **Allowance for Doubtful Accounts** From inception of operations to December 31, 2015, Harris Corporation provided for uncollectible accounts receivable under the allowance method. Provisions were made monthly at 2% of credit sales; bad debts written off were charged to the allowance account; recoveries of bad debts previously written off were credited to the allowance account; and no year-end adjustments to the allowance account were made. Harris's usual credit terms are net 30 days.
LO 6.5
AICPA Adapted

The balance in the Allowance for Doubtful Accounts was $130,000 at January 1, 2016. During 2016, credit sales totaled $9,000,000, interim provisions for doubtful accounts were made at 2% of credit sales, $90,000 of bad debts were written off, and recoveries of accounts previously written off amounted to $15,000. Harris upgraded its computer facility in November 2016, and an aging of accounts receivable was prepared for the first time as of December 31, 2016. A summary of the aging is as follows:

Classification by Month of Sale	Balance in Each Category	Estimated % Uncollectible
Nov.–Dec. 2016	$1,140,000	2%
July–Oct.	600,000	10
Jan.–June	400,000	25
Prior to 1/1/2016	130,000	75
	$2,270,000	

Based on the review of collectibility of the account balances in the "prior to 1/1/2016" aging category, additional receivables totaling $60,000 were written off as of December 31, 2016. Effective with the year ended December 31, 2016, Harris adopted a new accounting method for estimating the allowance for doubtful accounts at the amount indicated by the year-end aging analysis of accounts receivable.

Required:
1. Prepare a schedule analyzing the changes in the allowance for doubtful accounts for the year ended December 31, 2016. Show supporting computations in good form.
2. Prepare the journal entry for the year-end adjustment to the Allowance for Doubtful Accounts balance as of December 31, 2016.

P6-6
LO 6.3
LO 6.5
AICPA Adapted

Examination of Accounts Receivable You are engaged in the annual examination of Faulane Company, a wholesale office supply business, for the year ended June 30, 2016. You have been assigned to examine the accounts receivable. The following information is available at June 30, 2016.
1. Your review of accounts receivable and discussions with the client disclose that the following items are included in the accounts receivable (of both the control and the subsidiary ledgers):
   a. Accounts with credit balances, representing customer advances, total $1,900
   b. Receivables from officers total $5,300
   c. Advances to employees total $1,250
   d. Accounts that are definitely uncollectible total $1,120
2. Uncollectible accounts are estimated to be 0.50% of the year's net credit sales of $18,125,000.

Required:
Prepare any journal entry (entries) required to:
1. reclassify items that are not trade accounts receivable
2. write off uncollectible accounts
3. adjust the allowance for doubtful accounts

P6-7
LO 6.4
LO 6.5

Aging Accounts Receivable On September 30, 2016 (the end of its fiscal year), Lufkin Corporation reported accounts receivable of $331,750 and an allowance for doubtful accounts of $16,700. During fiscal 2017, the following transactions occurred:

Credit sales (terms, n/EOM)	$2,017,800
Collections on accounts receivable	1,956,000
Accounts receivable written off	16,200

On September 30, 2017, an aging of the accounts receivable balance indicated the following:

Age	Amount	Estimated Percentage Uncollectible
Under 30 days	$169,250	0.8%
30–90 days	100,000	1.6
91–180 days	55,900	5.0
181–360 days	38,200	15.0
Over 360 days	14,000	40.0
	$377,350	

Required:
1. Prepare the journal entries necessary to record the credit sales, collections on account, write-off of accounts receivable, and bad debts expense for Lufkin for fiscal 2017.

(continued)

2. What are Lufkin's September 30, 2017, balances in Accounts Receivable and in its Allowance for Doubtful Accounts, and how will they be disclosed on the September 30, 2017, balance sheet?
3. Compute Lufkin's receivables turnover in days, assuming a 365-day business year. What is your evaluation of its collection policies?

P6-8
LO 6.4
LO 6.5

Reconstructing Accounts Receivable and Expense Journal Entries The 2017 audit of Lane Company's accounting records discloses the following information:

	2016	2017
Accounts receivable (ending)	$186,000	$183,400
Allowance for doubtful accounts (ending)	7,400	7,000
Accounts receivable written off during the year	6,800	7,900
Estimated bad debts for the year	7,200	7,500
Actual gross sales returns and allowances for the year	4,700	6,000
Sales discounts not taken at end of year	0	400
Credit sales during the year (terms, 2/10, n/60)	375,000	380,000
Cash collected on accounts receivable during the year (net of discounts taken)	352,000	367,500

Required:
1. **Next Level** Reconstruct the journal entries that were made by Lane during 2017 to record changes in the following accounts, assuming sales returns and allowances are estimated in the period of sale and the net price method is used to account for sales discounts.
   a. Allowance for Doubtful Accounts
   b. Accounts Receivable
2. What is the 2017 ending balance in each of the accounts in Requirement 1, and how will it be reported on Lane's 2017 financial statements?

P6-9
LO 6.6

Secured Borrowing: Assigning Accounts Receivable Furman Corporation entered into an assignment agreement with a finance company whereby Furman would be advanced 80% of all accounts assigned, minus a $2,000 service charge. The assignment does not meet the conditions for a sale and should be accounted for as a secured borrowing. During the year, $300,000 of accounts receivable were assigned, $220,000 collections were made on outstanding assigned accounts, and $210,000 was remitted to the finance company. This remittance included interest charges of $2,100. Sales returns and allowances on assigned accounts amounted to $5,000.

Required:
1. Prepare the journal entries necessary to record the preceding information.
2. Show how the preceding information would be reported on Furman's year-end balance sheet (assume the note payable is short-term).

P6-10
LO 6.6

Factoring Accounts Receivable Faeber Textile Company frequently factors its accounts receivable. During 2016, Faeber made credit sales of $100,000 to customers, under terms of 2/10, n/30. Faeber records its credit sales using gross price. In 2016, Faeber sold $70,000 of these receivables to a factor. The factor remitted 90% of the accounts receivable factored and charged a 12% commission on the gross amount of the factored receivables. The factoring agreement also requires Faeber to be responsible for any cash discounts taken by customers upon payment of the factored receivables. Faeber is charged for these cash discounts upon reimbursement by the factor. During 2016, the factor collected the remaining amount of the factored receivables, minus the 2% discount on 94% of the collected receivables, and returned the balance owed to Faeber. Faeber collected the remaining amount of the unfactored accounts receivable, minus the 2% discount on 96% of the collected receivables.

Required:
Prepare all the journal entries necessary for Faeber to record the preceding information.

P6-11 **Factoring and Assignment of Accounts Receivable** Lazard Corporation has experienced cash flow problems
LO 6.6 and decides to improve its current cash position by factoring 30% of its receivables, without recourse, and assigning the remainder with the same finance company. The factored receivables meet the conditions for a sale while the assigned receivables do not. The agreement with the finance company stipulates that a 10% commission will be assessed on factored accounts, no service charge is assessed on the assigned accounts, and 15% annual interest will be charged on the outstanding note payable balance related to the assigned accounts. Additionally, the finance company will advance only 80% of the factored and assigned accounts, and Lazard must continue the collection responsibilities on the assigned accounts. At the beginning of the last month of the company's fiscal year, the accounts receivable transferred to the finance company amounted to $187,000. During the month, collections on factored accounts were $46,000, and collections on assigned accounts amounted to $84,000. All collections on assigned accounts plus accrued interest were remitted to the finance company at the end of the month. The remaining amounts owed will be remitted within these months.

Required:
1. Prepare all journal entries to record the preceding information on Lazard's books.
2. How would the accounts related to Lazard's factoring and assignment agreements be reported on Lazard's year-end financial statements?

P6-12 **Recording Note Transactions** The following information is extracted from Tara Corporation's accounting
LO 6.7 records:

May 1 Received a $6,000, 12%, 90-day note from V. Leigh, a customer.
    6 Received a $9,000, 10%, 120-day note from C. Gable, a customer.
    11 Sold the Leigh and Gable notes with recourse at the bank at 13%. In addition, borrowed $10,000 from the bank for 90 days at 12%. The bank remits the face value less the interest. The estimated recourse liability for Leigh and Gable is $84 and $110, respectively.
July 31 The July bank statement indicated that the Leigh note had been paid.
Aug. 10 Repaid the $10,000 borrowed on May 11.
Sept. 4 Received notice that Gable had defaulted on the May 6 note. The bank charged a fee of $10. Paid the amount due on the Gable note to the bank. Informed Gable to pay Tara the entire amount due plus 11% interest on the total of the face amount of the note, the accrued interest, and the fee from the maturity date until Gable remits the amount owed.
    23 Received the amount due from Gable.

Required:
Prepare journal entries to record the preceding information, assuming that Tara usually does not sell its notes. (Assume a 360-day year for the purposes of computing interest and round all calculations to the nearest penny.)

P6-13 **Notes Receivable Transactions** The following notes receivable transactions occurred for Harris Company during
LO 6.7 the last three months of the current year. (Assume all notes are dated the day the transaction occurred.)

Oct. 9 Received a $5,000, 12%, 60-day note from K. Weedon, a customer.
    12 Received a $6,000, 10%, 90-day note from M. Black, a customer.
    15 Sold the Weedon note with recourse at the bank at 14%. The fair value of the recourse liability is estimated to be $1,230.
Nov. 11 Sold the Black note with recourse at the bank at 15%. The fair value of the recourse liability is estimated to be $850.
    16 Received an $8,000, 12%, 60-day note from B. Butcher, a customer.
    20 Received a $6,000, 11%, 120-day note from D. Goldman, a customer.
Dec. 1 Received a $9,000, 13%, 60-day note from S. Lambert, a customer.
    8 Received notice that the Weedon note was paid at maturity.
    10 Sold the Goldman note without recourse at the bank at 13%.

Required:
1. Prepare the journal entries to record the preceding note transactions and the necessary adjusting entries on December 31. (Assume that Harris does not normally sell its notes and uses a 360-day year for the purpose of computing interest. Round all calculations to the nearest penny.)
2. Show how Harris' notes receivable would be disclosed on the December 31 balance sheet. (Assume these are the only note transactions encountered by Harris during the year.)

P6-14 Analyzing Accounts Receivable

LO 6.4, LO 6.5, LO 6.7

Upham Company's June 30, 2016, balance sheet included the following information:

Accounts receivable	$224,000	
Less: Allowance for doubtful accounts	(14,100)	$209,900
Notes receivable*		21,800
Total receivables		$231,700

*The company has a recourse liability of $2,250 for notes receivable sold with recourse.

During the company's fiscal year ending June 30, 2017, the following transactions occurred:

1. Sales on credit — $874,600
2. Collections of accounts receivable — 841,000
3. Accounts receivable written off as uncollectible — 13,800
4. Customer notes received in payment of accounts receivable — 72,000
5. Notes receivable collected — 29,000
6. Notes receivable, previously sold with recourse, were paid at maturity. The associated recourse liability for this note is $800. — 36,000
7. Notes receivable were defaulted. — 2,025
8. Collections on accounts previously written off — 500
9. Bad debts were estimated to be 1.5% of credit sales.

Required:
1. Prepare the journal entries necessary for Upham to record the preceding transactions.
2. Prepare an analysis and schedule that shows the amounts of the accounts receivable, allowance for doubtful accounts, notes receivable, and notes receivable dishonored accounts that will be disclosed on Upham's June 30, 2017, balance sheet.

P6-15 Comprehensive Receivables Problem

LO 6.4, LO 6.5, LO 6.6, LO 6.7

Blackmon Corporation's December 31, 2015, balance sheet disclosed the following information relating to its receivables:

Accounts receivable	$245,000	
Less: Allowance for doubtful accounts	(15,000)	
		$230,000
Notes receivable*		50,000
Total receivables		$280,000

*The company has a recourse liability of $700 related to a note receivable sold to a bank.

During 2016, credit sales (terms, n/EOM) totaled $2,200,000, and collections on accounts receivable (unassigned) amounted to $1,900,000. Uncollectible accounts totaling $18,000 from several customers were written off, and a $1,350 accounts receivable previously written off was collected. Additionally, the following transactions relating to Blackmon's receivables occurred during the year:

Mar. 6 Received payment of $12,460 on a note from Renko Company. The payment included interest income of $460.
31 The March bank statement indicated that the transferred note had been paid at maturity.
May 1 Accepted a 120-day, 13% note from Licata Company in exchange for its account receivable of $4,800.
18 Received a $6,900, 90-day, 12% note from Eagle Manufacturing Corporation for a credit sale.
June 2 Sold both the Licata and Eagle notes with recourse at the bank at 14%. (Assume that Blackmon normally does not sell its notes.) The estimated value of the recourse liability for the Licata and Eagle notes was $650 and $900, respectively.
July 1 Assigned $140,000 of accounts receivable to a finance company. Under the terms of the agreement, Blackmon receives 85% of the value of the accounts assigned, minus a service charge of $5,000, and is charged 1.5% per month on the outstanding loan balance.
6 A sales allowance of $2,500 on an assigned account is allowed by Blackmon.
13 A sales return of $800 on an assigned account is granted by Blackmon.
31 Collections of $50,000 are made on assigned accounts. This amount and one month's interest are remitted to the finance company.
Aug. 31 Assigned accounts of $60,000 are collected, and the remainder of the loan is repaid, including interest.
31 The August bank statement indicated the Eagle note had been paid.
Sept. 1 The bank notified Blackmon that Licata defaulted on its note and charges a fee of $25.
4 Collected the amount due from Licata.
Dec. 31 Collected interest of $5,000 on the outstanding notes receivable.

On December 31, 2016, an aging of the accounts receivable balance indicated the following:

Age	Amount	Estimated Percentage Uncollectible
Under 30 days	$240,487	0.5%
31–60 days	113,421	1.5
61–90 days	30,933	8.0
91–240 days	17,185	35.0
Over 240 days	6,874	70.0
	$408,900	

Required:
1. Prepare the journal entries to record the preceding receivable transactions during 2016 and the necessary adjusting entry on December 31, 2016. Assume a 360-day year for interest calculations and round calculations to the nearest dollar.
2. Prepare the receivables portion of Blackmon's December 31, 2016, balance sheet.
3. Compute Blackmon's accounts receivable turnover in days, assuming a 360-day business year. What is your evaluation of its collection policies?
4. If Blackmon uses IFRS, what might be the heading of the section for the receivables reported in Requirement 2?

P6-16 **Reconciliation of Bank and Company Cash Amounts** *(Appendix 6.1)* Miller Corporation's December 31, **LO 6.8** 2016, bank statement showed a $2,049.25 balance. On this date, Miller's Cash account reflected a $325.60 overdraft. In reconciling these amounts, the following information is discovered:
1. Cash on hand for undeposited sales receipts, December 31, $130.25.
2. Customer NSF check returned with bank statement, $420.40.
3. Cash sales of $640.25 for the week ended December 18 were recorded on the books. The cashier reports this amount missing, and it was not deposited in the bank.
4. Note receivable of $2,500 and interest of $25 collected by the bank and not recorded on the books.
5. Deposit in transit December 31, $350.00.
6. A customer check for $290.40 in payment of its account was recorded on the books at $940.20.
7. Outstanding checks, $2,040.55. Includes a duplicate check of $70.85 to C. Brown, who notified Miller that the original was lost. Miller stopped payment on the original check and has already adjusted the cash account in the accounting records for this amount.

Required:
1. Prepare a December 31 bank reconciliation for Miller.
2. Prepare any journal entries necessary by Miller to record the information from Requirement 1.

P6-17 **Unknown Book Balance** *(Appendix 6.1)* The following information pertains to the Cash account of Nakamoto **LO 6.8** Corporation for the month of July 2016:

Bank statement
Balance July 31	$22,639.54
Service charge for July	15.00
NSF check returned with July bank statement	184.50
Note receivable collected by bank (not previously recorded on the books)	2,000.00
Interest on note collected by bank (not previously recorded on the books)	60.00

Books
Balance July 31		?
Cash on hand awaiting deposit		1,824.42
Outstanding checks:		
#257	$ 42.17	
#271	120.19	
#272	80.82	
Deposit in transit		2,420.98

Required:
1. Prepare a bank reconciliation to determine Nakamoto's adjusted cash balance on July 31.
2. **Next Level** Determine Nakamoto's unadjusted cash balance (per books) on July 31.
3. Prepare the adjusting entries necessary to bring Nakamoto's cash account balance up to date on July 31.

P6-18 **Bank Reconciliation** *(Appendix 6.1)* Daisy Company received a bank statement for February, as follows:
LO 6.8
From: Central Bank, Denver, CO 80222
To: Daisy Company, 1313 Williams St., Denver, CO 80218

Date	Checks	Deposits	Balance
Feb. 1			$4,524.80
7	$2,700.33	$8,642.61	
9	3,484.81		
14	6.00 SC	460.00 CM	
16	274.09		
21	4,133.60	3,385.49	
23	69.69 NSF		
28			$6,344.38

SC = Service Charge   NSF = Check Returned
CM = Credit Memo   DM = Debit Memo

The receipt of $460 on February 14 was for a $445 note collected by the bank, plus $20 current interest, minus a $5 service charge. The company's accounting records contained the following information:

Cash balance on February 28 from the books: $2,610.42

Cash Disbursements		Cash Receipts	
Check No. 155	$2,700.33	Feb. 7	$8,624.61
156	3,484.81	21	3,385.49
157	274.09	All receipts are verified and correct.	
158	589.02		
159	4,133.60		
160	2,742.63		

Required:
1. Prepare a bank reconciliation on February 28, 2016, for Daisy.
2. Prepare the journal entries that Daisy should record as a result of the reconciliation.

P6-19 **Comprehensive Reconciliation** *(Appendix 6.1)* In auditing Train Company, you obtain directly from the bank Train's
LO 6.8 bank statement, canceled checks, and other memoranda which relate to the company's bank account for December 2016.
AICPA In reconciling the bank balance on December 31, 2016, with that shown on Trains's books, you observe the following facts:
Adapted

1. Balance per bank statement $91,174.63
2. Balance per books   59,088.46
3. Outstanding checks, 12/31/16   33,378.82
4. Receipts of 12/31/16 deposited on 1/1/17   5,317.20
5. Service charge for December   22.50
6. Proceeds of bank loan, 12/15/16 omitted from company records (discounted for 3 months at 12% per year)   11,640.00
7. Deposit of 12/20/16 omitted from the bank statement   2,892.41
8. Check of Rome Products Co. charged back on 12/22/16 for lack of countersignature. Redeposited 1/5/17. No entry was made for the chargeback or the redeposit.   873.74
9. Error on bank statement in entering deposit of 12/18/16:
   Correct amount $3,182.40
   Entered in statement   3,181.40   1.00
10. Check No. 3917 of Trait Manufacturing Co. charged in error to company's account   2,690.00
11. Proceeds of note of J. Somers & Co. collected by bank 12/11/16 not entered on books:
    Principal $2,000.00
    Interest   40.00
       $2,040.00
    Less: collection charge   5.00   2,035.00
12. Erroneous debit memo of 12/22/16 to charge company's account with settlement of bank loan, which was paid by check No. 8714 on same date   5,000.00
13. Error on bank statement in entering deposit of 12/4/16
    Entered as $4,817.10
    Correct amount   4,807.10   10.00
14. Deposit of Trait Manufacturing Co. of 12/8/16 credited in error to the company   1,819.20

Required:
1. Prepare a reconciliation of Train's bank account.
2. Prepare journal entries to adjust Train's books to reflect the correct bank balance on December 31, 2016.

CASES

COMMUNICATION

C6-1 Cash Management
LO 6.2

The president of Poor Corporation, who likes to have large balances of cash on hand, has recently been reading articles in highly respected financial magazines about very successful businesses. The president noticed that each company stressed the importance of cash management and cash controls in making it a success. The president comes to you, the accountant, and asks you to explain the concept of cash management and controls.

Required:
Explain the concept of cash management and cash controls.

C6-2 Cash Discounts
LO 6.4

In order to induce prompt payment, Swope Company offers a cash discount of 2% to customers who make payment on their account within 10 days of the invoice date. Swope's bookkeeper is not sure how these discounts should be recorded.

Required:
1. Explain the methods of recording accounts receivable with cash discounts.
2. Discuss the theoretical soundness of each method.

C6-3 Bad Debt Expense
LO 6.5
AICPA Adapted

When a company has a policy of making sales for which credit is extended, it is reasonable to expect a portion of those sales to be uncollectible. As a result, a company must recognize bad debt expense. The two methods of recognizing bad debt expense are the (1) direct write-off method and (2) allowance method.

Required:
1. Describe fully both the direct write-off method and the allowance method of recognizing bad debt expense.
2. Explain the reasons why one of these methods is preferable to the other and the reasons why the other method is not usually in accordance with generally accepted accounting principles.

C6-4 Accounts Receivable
LO 6.6

Moore Company is undergoing a period of financial stress due to the depressed economy. The company is in desperate need of cash. The only liquid asset that the company holds is $500,000 of accounts receivable.

Required:
1. Explain the various types of arrangements that may be used to obtain cash from outstanding accounts receivable.
2. If Moore decides to transfer its accounts receivable, what determines if the transfer is accounted for as a secured borrowing or a sale?

C6-5 Receivables Issues
LO 6.5
LO 6.6
LO 6.7
AICPA Adapted

Magrath Company has an operating cycle of less than one year and provides credit terms for all of its customers. On April 3, 2016, the company factored, without recourse, some of its accounts receivable. Magrath does not normally factor its receivables.

On August 1, 2016, Magrath sold special order merchandise and received an interest-bearing note due April 30, 2017.

Magrath uses the allowance method to account for uncollectible accounts. During 2016, some accounts were written off as uncollectible, and other accounts previously written off as uncollectible were collected.

Required:
1. Explain how Magrath should account for and report the accounts receivable factored on April 3, 2016. Why is this accounting treatment appropriate?
2. Explain how Magrath should report the effects of the interest-bearing note on its income statement for the year ended December 31, 2016, and its December 31, 2016, balance sheet.
3. Explain how Magrath should account for the collection of the accounts previously written off as uncollectible.
4. What are the two basic approaches to estimating uncollectible accounts under the allowance method? What is the rationale for each approach?

CREATIVE AND CRITICAL THINKING

C6-6 **Components of Cash**
LO 6.1 Cash is an important asset of a company.
AICPA
Adapted **Required:**
1. What are the normal components of cash?
2. Under what circumstances, if any, do valuation problems arise in connection with cash?

C6-7 **Receivables Issues**
LO 6.4 Hogan Company uses the net method of accounting for sales discounts. Hogan also offers trade discounts to various groups of buyers. On August 1, 2016, Hogan factored some accounts receivable on a without-recourse basis. Hogan incurred a finance charge.
LO 6.6
LO 6.7
AICPA
Adapted

Hogan also has some notes receivable bearing an appropriate rate of interest. The principal and total interest are due at maturity. The notes were received on October 2, 2016, and mature on October 1, 2017. Hogan's operating cycle is less than one year.

Required:
1. Using the net method, how should Hogan account for the sales discounts at the date of sale? What is the rationale for the amount recorded as sales under the net method?
2. a. Using the net method, what is the effect on Hogan's sales revenues and net income when customers do not take the sales discounts?
   b. What is the effect of trade discounts on sales revenues and accounts receivable? Why?
   c. How should Hogan account for the accounts receivable factored on August 1, 2016? Why?
   d. How should Hogan report the effects of the interest-bearing notes receivable on its December 31, 2016, balance sheet and on its income statement for the year ended December 31, 2016? Why?

C6-8 **Transfer of Accounts and Notes Receivable**
LO 6.6 Tidal Company has significant amounts of trade accounts receivable. In March of this year, Tidal assigned specific trade accounts receivable to Herb Finance Company on a with-recourse, non-notification basis as collateral for a loan. Tidal signed a note and received 70% of the amount assigned. Tidal was charged a 5% finance fee and agreed to pay interest at 12% on the unpaid balance. Some specific accounts of the assigned receivables were written off as uncollectible. The remainder of the trade accounts receivable assigned were collected by Tidal in March and April of this year. Tidal paid Herb Finance in full at the end of April of this year.
LO 6.7
AICPA
Adapted

Tidal also sold some special order merchandise and received a 90-day, 10%, interest-bearing note receivable on July 1 of this year. After 30 days, the note receivable was sold with recourse at 14% at a bank.

Required:
1. Explain how Tidal should account for the transactions described here for the assignment of trade accounts receivable.
2. Explain how Tidal should determine the amount of the discount for the 90-day note receivable sold at the bank.
3. Explain how the sale of the 90-day note receivable should be accounted for.

C6-9 **Ethics and Sales Returns**
LO 6.4 At the end of 2016, the accounting firm for which you work is auditing the books of Debitus Publishing Inc. for the first time. Debitus, a calendar year company, publishes textbooks that are used in colleges and universities across the country. These textbooks are purchased by students through their campus bookstores. Debitus normally makes its biggest sales at the beginning of the fall semester. In the past, Debitus has always recorded sales returns in the spring semester when the campus bookstores return any unsold textbooks. This has been satisfactory because the returns have been immaterial in amount.

In 2015, as a promotional strategy to stimulate sales, Debitus began offering bookstores a reduced price if they ordered more textbooks. There is no penalty for returns of these textbooks if the bookstores cannot sell them to customers. This strategy worked; sales increased by 10% during 2015. In early 2016, however, a substantial amount of unsold textbooks were returned by bookstores to Debitus. Continuing the promotional strategy, sales increased by 15% during 2016.

While reviewing the sales returns account for 2016, you notice that the only entry was for the textbooks returned earlier in the year. You note that these returns amounted to about 5% of the sales for the fall semester of 2015. Because this pattern of returns seems to you to be a trend that will continue, you raise the issue with the company controller as to whether all of the "sales" for the fall semester of 2016 are actually revenue. The controller responds, "Of course they are revenue;

we sold the textbooks. Just because there will be some returns doesn't mean we haven't made sales. Besides, we don't know what percentage the returns will be. They might be as much as 5%, but definitely not more. Furthermore, we have already recorded all those returns at the beginning of 2016 that really applied to 2015. So we already have recorded our fair share of returns for 2016. As long as we record returns consistently, it will all work out. We don't want a drop in earnings for 2016 because of a change in customer returns, our shareholders wouldn't like that. Let's just leave this issue alone."

Required:
From financial reporting and ethical perspectives, what do you think about Debitus's policy in regard to sales returns?

C6-10
LO 6.1
LO 6.3
LO 6.5
Analyzing Starbucks's Cash and Receivables Disclosures
Obtain Starbucks's 2015 annual report either using the "Investor Relations" portion of its web site (do a Web search for Starbucks investor relations) or go to http://www.sec.gov and click "Search for company filings" under "Filings and Forms (EDGAR)."

Required:
1. (a) What were the cash and cash equivalents at the end of 2015? What does the company classify as cash equivalents? (b) Why are cash and cash equivalents combined into one amount on the balance sheet?
2. What were the trade accounts receivable (net) at the end of 2015? At the end of 2014? Given Starbucks's large volume of sales, why isn't the receivables larger?
3. What amount of its accounts receivable does Starbucks believe is uncollectible?
4. What method does Starbucks use to estimate its allowance for doubtful accounts? Is this method allowable by GAAP?

C6-11
LO 6.1
LO 6.5
Analyzing Nestlé's Cash and Receivables Disclosures
Obtain Nestlé's 2012 annual report using the "Investor Relations" portion of its web site (do a Web search for Nestle investor relations).

Required:
1. With regard to Nestlé's cash and cash equivalents:
   a. What amount did Nestlé report as cash and cash equivalents at the end of 2012?
   b. What types of items did Nestlé report as cash equivalents?
   c. Does the classification of cash equivalents differ between IFRS and U.S. GAAP?
2. What amount of its accounts receivable does Nestlé believe is uncollectible?
3. What method does Nestlé use to estimate its allowance for doubtful accounts? Is this method allowable by U.S. GAAP?

USING CODIFICATION

C6-12   Researching GAAP

Situation
Hamilton Company operates in an industry with numerous competitors. It is experiencing a shortage of cash and decides to obtain money from a large bank by using some of its receivables as collateral. Hamilton pledges $100,000 of its receivables, is charged a 12% fee on this amount, and notifies these credit customers to make their payments directly to the bank. Hamilton transfers the receivables to the bank, and the bank assumes the servicing activities, but Hamilton is responsible for all bad debts which it reasonably estimates to be 2% of the receivables amount. When the balance of the receivables pledged is reduced to $3,000, Hamilton is required to "repurchase" the receivables, notify the remaining credit customers to make payments to it, and reassume the servicing activities. The bank has the right to sell the receivables, except to Hamilton's major competitor. Hamilton's president has asked you how to account for (and record) this transaction.

Directions
Research the related generally accepted accounting principles and prepare a short memo to the president that answers his question. Cite your reference and applicable paragraph numbers.

CHAPTER 7

INVENTORIES: COST MEASUREMENT AND FLOW ASSUMPTIONS

Keep Your Eye on the Ball

For companies whose core business model involves selling products to customers, managing inventory represents the most important business activity through which it creates value and serves its customers. Effective production, management, and control of inventory is critical to the profitability and overall performance of all product-focused companies. Management of inventory involves tasks such as managing production and supply chain, making sure that a company has sufficient quantities of the right items, controlling costs, limiting shrinkage (the reduction of inventory because of theft or loss), and controlling the impact of interest costs related to the debt financing of inventory. A well-functioning inventory system allows managers to take advantage of quantity discounts in the purchase of inventory, increase productivity, and lower manufacturing costs by scheduling more efficient production runs. Given the demand and supply uncertainties that exist in business, inventory also serves as a buffer to ensure that adequate goods exist that allow the company to meet customers' needs, including unexpected surges in demand for products. In short, proper inventory management can allow managers to serve their customers, achieve significant operational efficiencies, and enjoy the benefits of economies of scale.

Starbucks reported $1,306.4 million of inventory in 2015, with roasted and unroasted coffee beans representing the majority of this amount.

LEARNING OBJECTIVES

After reading this chapter you will be able to

LO 7.1 Describe the different classifications of inventory and the flow of costs.

LO 7.2 Explain the uses of the perpetual and periodic inventory systems.

LO 7.3 Identify the items to be included in inventory.

LO 7.4 Determine the expenditures included in the cost of inventory.

LO 7.5 Compute ending inventory and cost of goods sold under specific identification, FIFO, average cost, and LIFO.

LO 7.6 Explain the consequences that result from the use of alternative inventory cost flow assumptions.

LO 7.7 Understand and apply dollar-value LIFO.

LO 7.8 Understand inventory disclosures.

Composition of Starbucks's Inventory

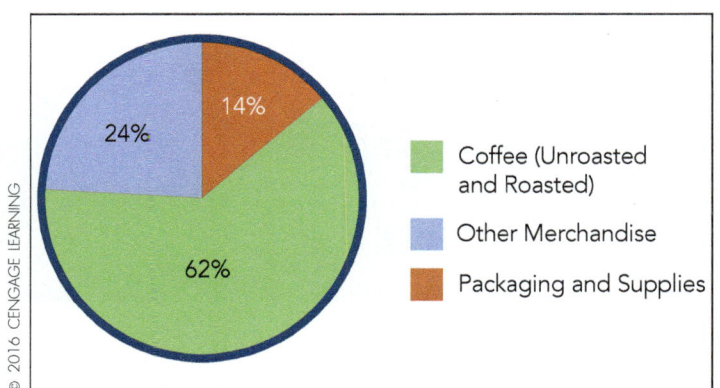

Given the importance of coffee to its business model, Starbucks has vertically integrated its supply chain, working directly with green coffee bean growers around the world. For example, Starbucks operates Farmer Support Centers, staffed with agronomists and sustainability experts, in coffee farming communities to promote best practices in coffee production that improve both coffee quality and yields. Once the coffee beans are harvested by the growers, Starbucks utilizes its supply chain functions to take delivery of the newly harvested beans, ship them, roast them, and package them. For Starbucks, this reduces costs and ensures that the highest quality coffee beans from around the world arrive at its retail locations as efficiently as possible.

What ultimately happens to Starbucks's inventory? The vast majority is used in its retail stores to make cups of coffee for its customers. In addition, some is sold as bags of whole coffee beans, along with food and other merchandise. Starbucks also sells coffee, tea, and other products to various licensees as well as to grocery and warehouse stores such as **Target**, **Wal-Mart**, and **Kroger**. These agreements create "partnerships" that inevitably have conflicts of interest. For example, Starbucks would like to deliver its products as soon as they are produced; however, Target would prefer to receive the items when it is ready to put them on store shelves. Resolving these intercompany conflicts is also a part of effective inventory management. Whether a company is a manufacturer or a merchandiser, inventory should be closely monitored and controlled to increase the company's chance of success.

Inventories are assets of a company that are:
- held for sale to customers in the ordinary course of business
- in the process of production for sale
- used in the production of goods or services that will be made available for sale

The inclusion of an asset in inventory depends on the company's customers and business model. For example, **Ford** includes cars and trucks in inventory because that is what it sells to customers. However, the cars and trucks owned by **Starbucks** will not be part of inventory but, instead, will be included in property, plant, and equipment. Similarly, coffee is inventory for Starbucks, but coffee held by Ford for its employees to enjoy would not be part of Ford's inventory. In addition, some service firms, such as airlines, may also carry inventory, such as jet fuel and in-flight drinks.

As the opening vignette emphasized, inventory is an essential element of operations for all product-focused companies. Naturally, accounting for inventories is important because the purchase, manufacture, and sale of products are critical to the operating success (or failure) of many companies. The valuation of inventory usually has a material effect on a company's balance sheet, typically comprising the largest current asset. In addition, because cost of goods sold represents the cost of inventory sold during a period, the valuation of inventory will have an effect on a company's net income. In fact, cost of goods sold is commonly the single, largest expense on most product-focused companies' income statements. Inventory accounting practices, such as alternative cost flow assumptions and valuation methods, have a significant effect on inventory valuation and income determination. In this chapter, we discuss the classifications of inventory, perpetual and periodic inventory systems, determination of inventory quantities and costs, and alternative inventory cost flow assumptions.

HOW DO COMPANIES CLASSIFY INVENTORY?

LEARNING OBJECTIVE 7.1
Describe the different classifications of inventory and the flow of costs.

A company may use several different accounts to classify inventory, depending on its business. A merchandising company, whether wholesale or retail, purchases goods for resale and does not alter their physical form. Consequently, it needs only one type of inventory account, usually called **merchandise inventory**. For example, **Wal-Mart** does not produce goods. Instead, it is a merchandiser that generates approximately 99% of its revenues from sales of purchased inventory to customers.

Manufacturing companies, like **Sony**, **Toyota**, and **Caterpillar**, change the physical form of the goods and typically use three inventory accounts, usually called raw materials inventory, work-in-process inventory, and finished goods inventory.

Raw Materials Inventory

Raw materials inventory includes the tangible goods acquired for direct use in the production process. The cost of these goods will eventually become part of the cost of the finished product. Raw materials include products purchased from other companies, such as iron ore used by a steel mill or the subassemblies used in the manufacture of appliances.[1] For **Starbucks**, its green coffee beans and supplies are considered raw materials inventory.

Work-in-Process Inventory

Work-in-process inventory (or **goods-in-process inventory**) includes the products that have been started in the manufacturing process but are not yet complete. When the production process is lengthy, such as when **Boeing** produces airplanes over several months, this category of inventory can be quite significant. This partially completed inventory includes three cost components:

- raw materials
- direct labor—the cost of the labor used directly in the manufacture of the product
- manufacturing (or factory) overhead—costs other than raw materials and direct labor that are part of the manufacturing process (e.g., supplies, indirect labor, insurance, utilities, and depreciation on the assets used in the production activities)

Finished Goods Inventory

Finished goods inventory includes the completed manufactured products awaiting sale. The finished goods inventory includes the same three cost components as the work-in-process inventory. The costs are typically combined into a single cost per unit for all the completed units. For example, **Starbucks'** finished goods inventory consists of roasted coffee beans and merchandise such as coffee mugs and presses.

Flow of Inventory Costs

The flow of inventory costs for merchandising and manufacturing companies is shown in Exhibit 7.1.

---

[1] Sometimes a manufacturing company might include in raw materials inventory those materials that are a part of its manufacturing process but are not part of the finished products (e.g., lubricating oil, cleaning supplies for the manufacturing equipment). Typically, these costs are included in an inventory account called factory or manufacturing supplies.

EXHIBIT 7.1 Flow of Inventory Costs

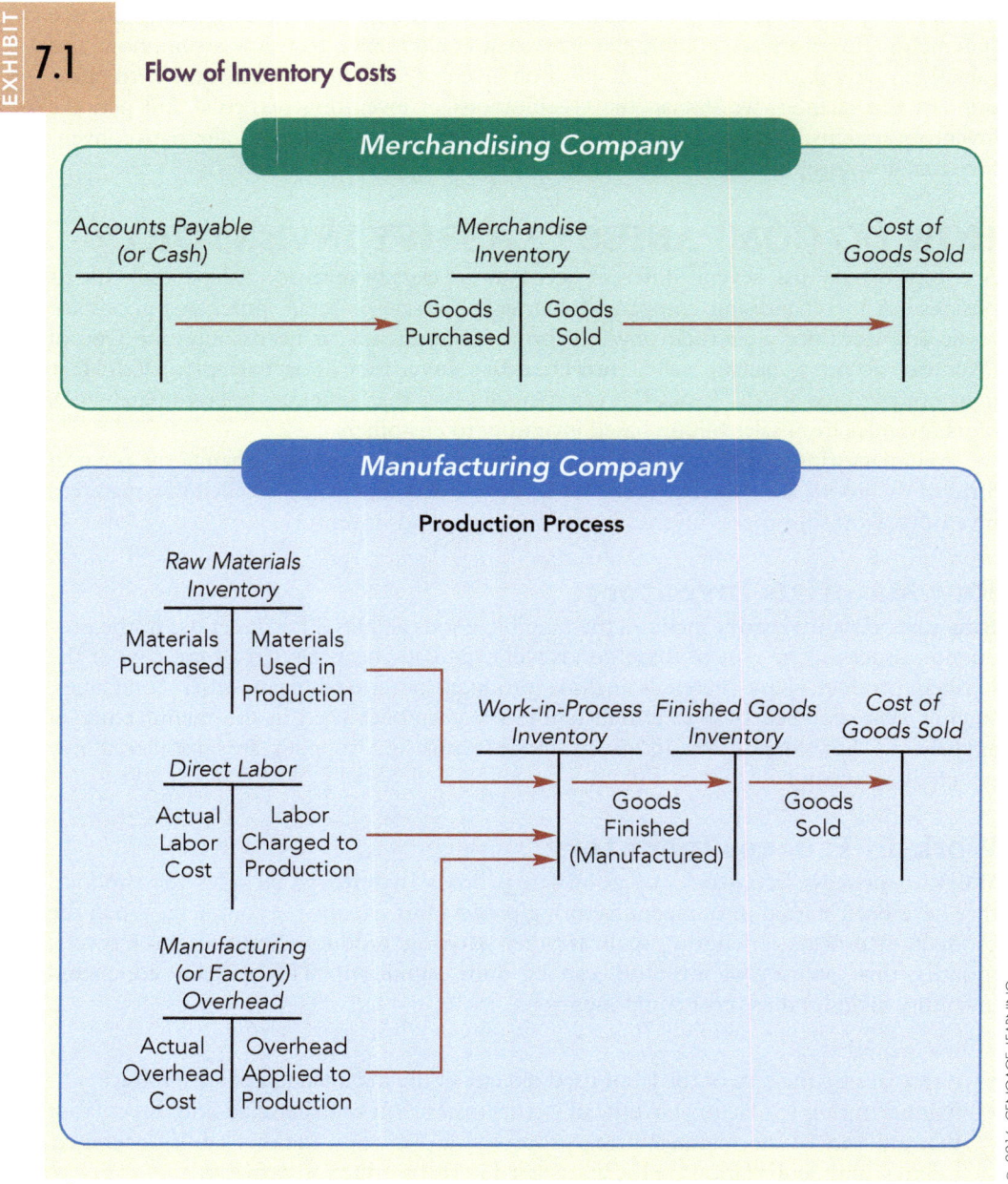

The relationship between cost of goods sold and inventory is given by the cost of goods sold model:

Merchandiser:

$$\text{Beginning Inventory} + \text{Purchases (net)} = \text{Cost of Goods Available for Sale} - \text{Ending Inventory} = \text{Cost of Goods Sold}$$

Manufacturer:

$$\text{Beginning Finished Goods Inventory} + \text{Cost of Goods Manufactured} = \text{Cost of Goods Available for Sale} - \text{Ending Finished Goods Inventory} = \text{Cost of Goods Sold}$$

For both types of companies, the sum of beginning inventory and net purchases (or cost of goods manufactured) represents the **cost of goods available for sale**. The cost of goods available for sale is then allocated between ending inventory and cost of goods sold. The portion of the cost of goods available for sale that remains unsold at the end of the period is the company's ending inventory. The portion of the cost of goods available for sale that is sold becomes cost of goods sold. These relationships are illustrated in Exhibit 7.2.

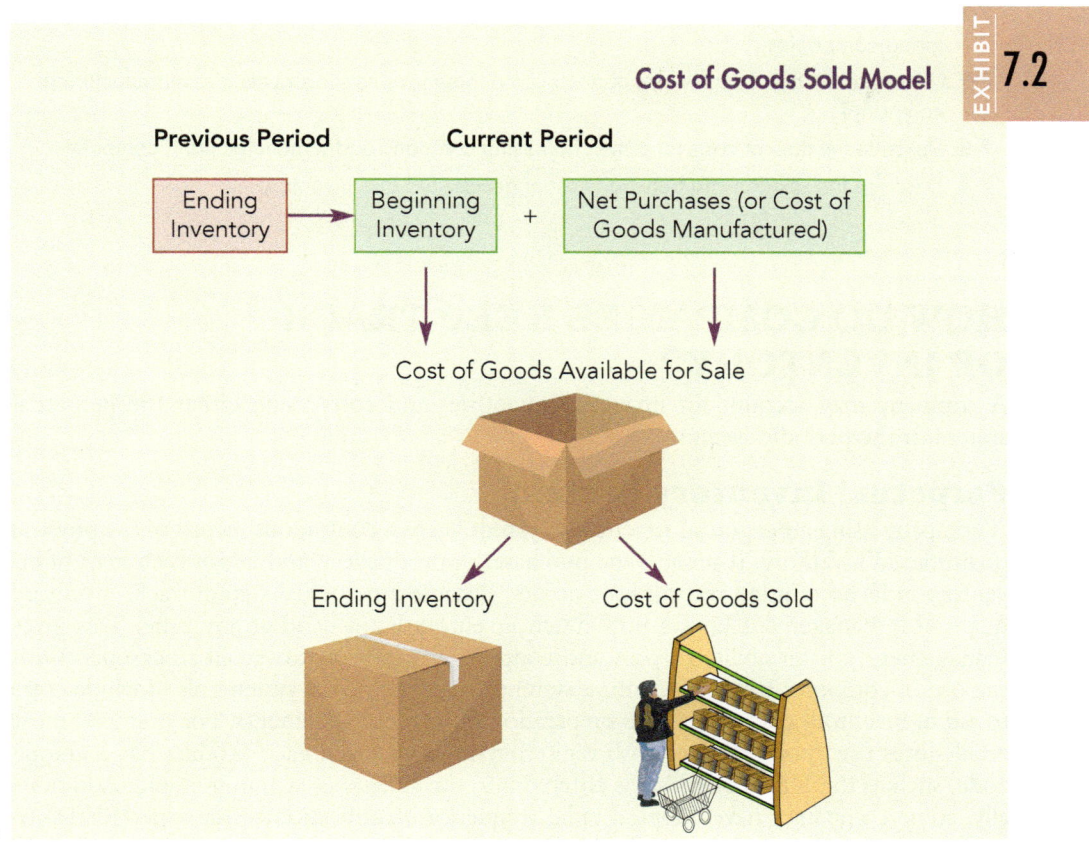

Cost of Goods Sold Model — EXHIBIT 7.2

The importance of this cost allocation process requires a considerable amount of careful measurement and judgment. If a company misstates the amount of ending inventory, it will not only affect the balance sheet but also the income statement because cost of goods sold will also be misstated. This process is discussed later in the chapter.

How Do Companies Report Inventory in Their Financial Statements?

Manufacturing companies will generally disclose, either directly on the balance sheet or in the notes to the financial statements, the dollar amount of each inventory category. The inventory cost that a company reports on its balance sheet and the amount of cost of goods sold that a company reports on its income statement are the final amounts that result from a series of steps. The company must:

- *Step 1.* Decide what items to include in the inventory and count the physical inventory quantities.[2]
- *Step 2.* Determine the costs of the units it purchased or produced during the accounting period, taking into consideration the costs for freight-in and the reductions for purchase discounts, returns, and allowances.
- *Step 3.* Use a cost flow assumption to allocate the cost of goods available for sale between the ending inventory and the cost of goods sold.

Each of these steps is discussed in the following sections.

In addition, a company reports the cash it paid to purchase or produce its inventory, as well as the cash generated by selling inventory, during the period in the operating activities section of its statement of cash flows.

---

[2] As discussed later in the chapter, a physical count of inventory is required only at fiscal year-end.

> **GOT IT?**
>
> **7-1** Distinguish among the types of inventory accounts used for merchandising and manufacturing companies.
>
> **7-2** What are the cost components of each of the three inventory accounts of a manufacturing company?
>
> **7-3** Describe the flow of costs for a merchandising company and a manufacturing company.
>
> **7-4** Describe the relationship between cost of goods sold and inventory.

LEARNING OBJECTIVE 7.2

Explain the uses of the perpetual and periodic inventory systems.

HOW DO COMPANIES KEEP TRACK OF INVENTORY?

A company may account for inventory quantities and costs using either the perpetual system or the periodic system.

Perpetual Inventory System

A company using a **perpetual inventory system** keeps a continuous record of the physical quantities in inventory. It records the purchase, or production, and use of each item of inventory in its accounting records as it occurs. Because a perpetual system tracks inventory quantities, management knows how much inventory is on hand at any time. This gives management greater ability to plan and control inventory and to avoid stock-outs. With the use of computer-based accounting systems, many perpetual systems also include costs to aid in inventory control and the preparation of financial statements. For example, most retail stores use "point of sale" cash register systems in which each product has a unique code, such as the UPC code, that is entered into the system as each unit is sold. Additionally, some companies have adopted radio frequency identification technology (RFID) to track inventory. Both UPC codes and RFID tags enable the retailer to immediately update its inventory and cost of goods sold accounts as each sale is made. Therefore, management knows the dollar amount of inventory and cost of goods sold at all times.

When a company uses a perpetual system, it should take a physical count at least once a year to confirm the balance in the inventory account. Any difference between the physical count and the inventory account balance results from errors in recording, shrinkage, waste, breakage, theft, and other causes. The company adjusts its inventory account and also increases cost of goods sold (or recognizes a loss) for the cost of the difference in the two quantities so that the perpetual records are in agreement with the physical count. The size of the difference provides useful information for inventory control purposes and is another advantage of the perpetual system. For example, **Wal-Mart**'s aggressive response to an estimated $3 billion of inventory shrinkage has been cited as one factor in its improved profitability in subsequent years.

Periodic Inventory System

A company using a **periodic inventory system** does *not* maintain a continuous record of the physical quantities (or costs) of inventory on hand. Instead, it takes physical counts of ending inventory periodically, which should be at least once a year. This is the only time when it knows the physical quantities on hand, and, therefore, the quantities used or sold during the period. A periodic inventory system is adequate for relatively low-cost inventory items, particularly when the costs of maintaining detailed inventory records (e.g., a perpetual inventory system) are likely to be greater than its benefits.

In a periodic system, the company usually records purchases of inventory in a temporary account, Purchases, while the beginning inventory cost remains in the inventory account. Similarly, any purchase discounts, purchase returns and allowances, and freight-in do not affect the inventory account but are recorded in separate accounts (e.g., Purchase

Discounts, Purchase Returns and Allowances, Freight-In). Therefore, net purchases is computed as follows:

$$\text{Net Purchases} = \text{Purchases} + \text{Freight-In} - \text{Purchase Discounts Taken} - \text{Purchase Returns and Allowances}$$

A company then adds the net purchases to the beginning inventory to arrive at cost of goods available for sale. After a physical count of inventory, it determines the balances of ending inventory and cost of goods sold. Specifically, the company determines the cost of the ending inventory by assigning costs to the physical quantities on hand based on the cost flow assumption it is using. Then, it calculates the cost of goods sold by subtracting the ending inventory from the cost of goods available for sale.

WHY IT MATTERS

Effective inventory management and control is a critical ingredient to a company's success. While management wants to keep an adequate supply of inventory on hand to meet customer demands, there is a cost associated with carrying high levels of inventory (e.g., storage costs, risk of obsolescence, damage, theft, insurance, and taxes). Unfortunately, reducing costs by reducing inventory levels can also have adverse consequences such as lost sales, stockouts, and dissatisfied customers. Companies use a variety of tools, such as computerized inventory tracking systems, to manage and control their inventories. The effectiveness of an inventory management program can be evaluated using financial ratios such as inventory turnover and average days in inventory.

Using data obtained from annual reports, the computation of inventory turnover ratios for **Starbucks** and **Panera Bread** are shown below.

(amounts in millions)	Starbucks 2014	Starbucks 2013	Panera Bread 2014	Panera Bread 2013
Cost of goods sold	$6,858.8		$669.860	
Inventories	$1,090.9	$1,111.2	22.811	$21.916

$$\text{Starbucks: Inventory Turnover} = \frac{\$6,858.8}{\left(\frac{\$1,090.9 + \$1,111.2}{2}\right)} = \underline{\underline{6.23}}$$

$$\text{Panera Bread: Inventory Turnover} = \frac{\$669.860}{\left(\frac{\$22.811 + \$21.916}{2}\right)} = \underline{\underline{29.95}}$$

Dividing the inventory turnover into 365 days reveals that Starbucks and Panera Bread hold inventory an average of 58.59 and 12.19 days, respectively. While it may be tempting to conclude that Panera is more effectively managing its inventory, differences in supply chain strategy, size, and business strategy need to be considered. For example, with its emphasis on fresh foods, Panera must turn over its inventory more rapidly than Starbucks. By contrast, Starbucks has a much deeper supply chain than Panera and most of its inventory has a longer shelf life, allowing Starbucks to turn over its inventory more slowly. Similarly, grocery stores, which have relatively low markups on their inventories, must have quicker inventory turns than a high-end, high-markup retailer such as **Tiffany's**. Therefore, users need a good understanding of a company's business strategy and industry in order to use financial information effectively.

Given management's opposing objectives to reduce inventory levels and costs but to keep an adequate supply of inventory on hand to meet customers' demands, additional insights may be gained by examining the change in inventory turnover relative to the ratio of cost of goods sold to sales. For example, between 2013 and 2014, Starbucks's inventory turnover increased from 5.43 to 6.23, while its cost of goods sold to sales ratio decreased from 54.1% to 52.8%. This is consistent with increased demand for Starbucks's products (e.g., comparable store sales were up 6% during the year) coupled with supply chain improvements that led to lower inventory costs.

Comparison of Perpetual and Periodic Inventory Systems

The main difference between a perpetual and a periodic inventory system is that a periodic system only updates the inventory and cost of goods sold accounts at the end of the accounting period. In contrast, a perpetual inventory system updates the inventory and cost of goods sold accounts continually as goods are purchased or sold. **Example 7.1** illustrates the journal entries for the purchase and sale of inventory under each of these inventory systems.

Example Cornett Manufacturing Inc. reported the following information for the current year:

- Beginning inventory................. $50,000 (1,000 units at $50 per unit)
- Purchases on account............... 800,000 (16,000 units at $50 per unit)
- Credit sales............................. 960,000 (12,000 units at $80 per unit)
- Ending inventory..................... 250,000 (5,000 units at $50 per unit)

EXAMPLE 7.1 Journal Entries for Alternative Inventory Systems

	Perpetual Inventory System			Periodic Inventory System		

To record purchase of inventory	Inventory
	    Accounts Payable
		800,000	800,000	Purchases
				    Accounts Payable
					800,000	800,000

To record credit sale of goods	Accounts Receivable
	    Sales Revenue
		960,000	960,000	Accounts Receivable
				    Sales Revenue
					960,000	960,000

	Cost of Goods Sold Inventory (12,000 × $50)	600,000	600,000	No entry		

Adjusting entry at end of period	No Entry			Inventory (ending)
				Cost of Goods Sold
				    Purchases
				    Inventory (beginning)
					250,000
					600,000
						
						800,000
						50,000

Note that both inventory systems report the same amounts for ending inventory ($250,000) and cost of goods sold ($600,000). ■

Differences in the financial statement valuation of ending inventory and cost of goods sold are generally insignificant between the perpetual and periodic inventory systems. However, each inventory system does offer distinct benefits, and any choice between the two inventory systems must weigh the system's advantages against its operating costs. The principle advantage of a periodic system is that it is relatively inexpensive to operate. Because perpetual systems require entering and maintaining more data than periodic systems, the additional costs can be quite substantial for a company with thousands of different items of inventory. However, with technological advances, the costs associated with maintaining perpetual inventory records are rapidly diminishing. The perpetual inventory system has the obvious advantage of making the balances of inventory and cost of goods sold continuously available. This provides management with more timely and relevant information and therefore greater control over inventory than they would have under a periodic inventory system. This can be a significant and extremely valuable advantage in a competitive business environment.

> **GOT IT?**
>
> **7-5** Explain the differences between the perpetual and periodic inventory systems in terms of inventory quantity and cost. Does the use of a perpetual system eliminate the need for taking a physical inventory count?

HOW DO COMPANIES DETERMINE INVENTORY QUANTITIES?

LEARNING OBJECTIVE 7.3
Identify the items to be included in inventory.

The basic criterion for including items in inventory is *economic control* rather than physical possession or legal ownership. In simple situations, all three transfer at the same time. Therefore, in many situations, physical transfer will determine when the seller records the sale and the buyer records the purchase of inventory in their accounting systems. However, because there may be differences in more complex situations, the *economic substance* of the transaction should always take precedence over its *legal form* to determine whether the buyer or the seller has economic control. The following sections discuss several complex situations.

Goods in Transit

When goods are in transit at the end of the accounting period, the shipping terms determine whether the seller or the buyer includes them in its inventory. If the goods are shipped **FOB (free-on-board) shipping point**, control of (and legal title to) the goods is transferred at the shipping point when the seller delivers them to the buyer, or to a transportation company that is acting as an agent for the buyer. Because the buyer has economic control at the shipping point, it will record a purchase of inventory and include those goods in its inventory. At the same time, the seller will record a sale and remove the goods from its inventory.

If goods are shipped **FOB destination**, control of (and legal title to) the goods is not transferred until the goods are delivered to the buyer's destination. Because the seller has economic control until the goods are delivered, it does not record a sale and includes those goods in its inventory until the goods reach the buyer's destination. Similarly, the buyer will not record a purchase, nor an increase in inventory, until the goods are delivered to the buyer's destination.

Exhibit 7.3 illustrates these situations (p. 7-10).

Consigned Goods

Sometimes, a manufacturer or wholesaler may transfer goods to a retailer under a **consignment** arrangement. In this arrangement, the company delivering the goods (the **consignor**) retains economic control and ownership, while the company receiving the goods (the **consignee**) acts as a sales agent of the consignor and attempts to sell the goods to a third party. Such an arrangement gives the consignor access to a broader market of potential customers by encouraging the consignee to stock goods it might not normally carry (because the consignee doesn't have to incur the cost of actually buying the goods or take the risk that the goods might not sell). Because the consignor has economic control (and legal title) of the goods, the consignor retains the goods in its inventory (and does not recognize revenue) until they are sold by the consignee. Similarly, the consignee does *not* record the acquisition of inventory.

Product Financing Arrangements

Some companies will engage in **product financing arrangements** as a way of financing the cost of inventory. In a product financing arrangement, one company "sells" the inventory to a financing company. Then, in a related transaction, the seller agrees to

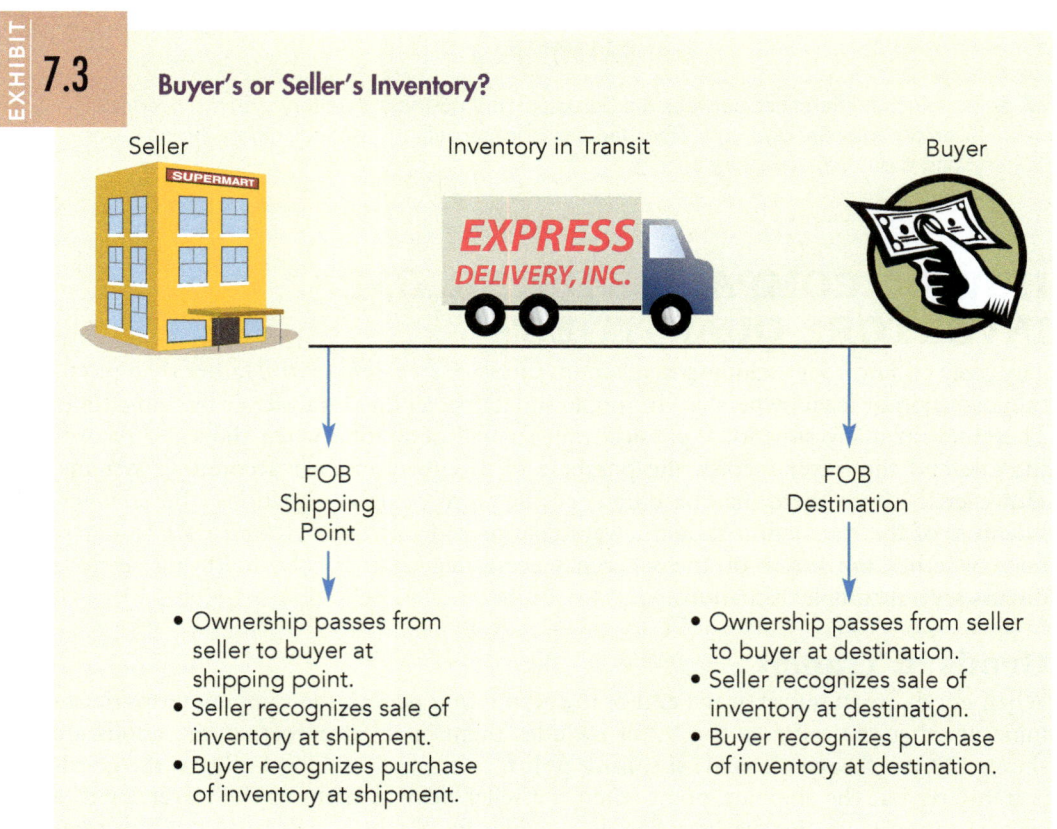

EXHIBIT 7.3 Buyer's or Seller's Inventory?

FOB Shipping Point
- Ownership passes from seller to buyer at shipping point.
- Seller recognizes sale of inventory at shipment.
- Buyer recognizes purchase of inventory at shipment.

FOB Destination
- Ownership passes from seller to buyer at destination.
- Seller recognizes sale of inventory at destination.
- Buyer recognizes purchase of inventory at destination.

purchase the inventory (or a substantially identical item) back from the "financier" at specified prices over specified periods. Typically, the inventory is not delivered to the financier and is repurchased at a higher price, with the difference being an interest charge. Therefore, the substance of a product financing arrangement is that the selling company

Many second-hand stores are operated through consignment arrangements in which the consignees offer used goods like clothing, antiqued, books, records, and toys that it acquired from a consignor.

is borrowing cash from the financier using inventory as collateral (this is often referred to as a "parking" transaction). While legal title to the inventory is transferred to the financier, the seller retains the risk of ownership. Therefore, the inventory remains on the seller's balance sheet at cost. In addition, because the economic benefits remain under the control of the seller, the seller does *not* record sales revenue but instead records the proceeds received as a liability.[3] This procedure captures the economic substance of the transaction, and avoids the overstatement of revenues and income and the understatement of assets and liabilities.

Bill and Hold Sales

In some situations, a company may purchase inventory yet not be ready to take delivery for various reasons such as lack of available space to store the goods or an unanticipated delay in the production schedule. In these cases, the buyer may request that the seller hold the goods to be delivered at a later date. This is known as a **bill and hold sale**. In general, the goods should remain in the inventory of the seller (and no revenue should be recognized) until the seller's performance obligation is satisfied by the buyer obtaining control of the product. In some situations, control is transferred when delivery has occurred. However, in other situations, a buyer may obtain control of a product even though that product remains in a seller's physical possession (e.g., the buyer has the ability to direct the use of, and obtain substantially all of the remaining benefits from, the product even though it has decided not to exercise its right to take physical possession of that product). For a buyer to have obtained control of a product in a bill-and-hold arrangement, it should consider indicators of transfer of control as well as meet all of the following criteria:

- the reason for the bill-and-hold arrangement must be substantive (e.g., the buyer has requested the arrangement).
- the product must be identified separately as belonging to the buyer
- the product currently must be ready for physical transfer to the buyer
- the seller cannot have the ability to use the product or to direct it to another customer.[4]

Under these conditions, the seller should exclude the goods from inventory (and recognize revenue), and the buyer should include the goods in its inventory. Bill and hold arrangements have been abused in the past to improperly inflate revenues. Therefore, any bill and hold agreement should be carefully examined to determine if control has transferred from the seller to the buyer.

Purchase Obligations

To ensure a sufficient supply of inventory, many companies will enter into agreements to purchase inventory well in advance of when the actual purchase will occur. Accounting principles generally do not require a company to record either an asset (inventory) or a **purchase obligation** when entering into a purchase commitment because neither an asset nor a liability is created by placing an order. Therefore, these purchase obligations are not recognized in inventory until delivery. Instead, **if a company has incurred an unconditional purchase obligation at a fixed price or a price to be determined, the company discloses this commitment in a note to its financial statements.**[5] This disclosure provides information that is helpful in the prediction of a company's future cash outflows. For example, in the inventory footnote in its 2015 financial statements, **Starbucks** disclosed $1.085 billion in purchase commitments to acquire coffee.

If a company has an unconditional (noncancelable) purchase obligation to acquire inventory, and the current market price (i.e., replacement cost) is less than the fixed purchase price, the company must recognize the loss in the period in which the decline occurs. This procedure is conservative and provides users of the financial statements with information about the decision-making ability of the management.

---

[3] FASB ASC 470-40-25: Debt: Product Financing Arrangements.
[4] FASB ASC 606-10-55-83: Revenue from Contracts with Customers: Overall: Implementation Guidance and Illustrations
[5] FASB ASC 440-10-50: Commitments: Overall: Disclosure.

Example Morgan Company entered into a noncancelable commitment to purchase inventory at a fixed price of $500,000. The market price (replacement cost) for the same inventory at the end of the year has declined to $450,000. Morgan would make the following year-end adjusting entry:

Loss on Purchase Commitments	50,000	
Accrued Loss on Purchase Commitments		50,000

Morgan reports the accrued loss as a contingent liability on its year-end balance sheet. It writes off the accrued loss when it purchases the goods as follows:

Inventory (or Purchases)	450,000	
Accrued Loss on Purchase Commitments	50,000	
Accounts Payable		500,000

If the market price rises by the time Morgan makes the purchase, it reduces the accrued loss and recognizes a loss recovery. It then records the purchases at the market price (cost) on the date of acquisition. ■

GOT IT?

7-6 What is the general rule used to determine if a company includes an item in inventory? Apply the concept to the accounting for goods in transit and goods on consignment.

7-7 Who records the inventory in a product financing agreement? Why?

7-8 How, and under what conditions, does a company recognize a purchase obligation?

LEARNING OBJECTIVE 7.4
Determine the expenditures included in the cost of inventory.

HOW DO COMPANIES DETERMINE INVENTORY COSTS?

There are two issues in determining inventory costs. The costs attached to each unit *available for sale* are discussed in this section. The costs attached to the *ending inventory* and *cost of goods sold* (the inventory cost flow assumption) will be discussed later in this chapter.

The cost of inventory is the price paid or consideration given to acquire or produce it.[6] Thus, **inventory cost includes costs directly or indirectly incurred in bringing an item to its existing condition and location for sale**. For each item of inventory, a company must make a decision as to whether or not each cost meets this definition. If it does, the company includes it in the cost of the inventory. If it does not, the company immediately recognizes it as an expense. The cost of purchased inventory should include the purchase price (net of purchase discounts and including any sales taxes, import duties, and other taxes applicable to the purchase) plus payments directly related to the inventory, such as freight-in, receiving, unpacking, inspecting, storage, insurance, and personal property taxes. When a company manufactures inventory, it adds the **product costs** that are directly and indirectly incurred in the production activity to the cost of inventory. These costs include acquisition and production costs (including manufacturing overhead).

Another cost that *may* be included in the cost of inventory is the interest cost for amounts a company borrowed to finance the purchase of the inventory. It can be argued that this interest cost is incurred indirectly in order to bring an item to its existing condition and location and, therefore, should be added to the inventory cost. Alternatively, it can be argued that interest costs are period costs associated with borrowing funds for a period of time and not related specifically to the acquisition of a particular inventory item. Under GAAP, interest costs are *not* included in the cost of inventory that is routinely manufactured. However, interest cost is included in the cost of inventory that is manufactured over an extended period of time.

---

[6] FASB ASC 330-10-30: Inventory: Overall: Initial Measurement.

Period costs, such as general and administrative costs and selling costs, are normally expensed because they are not related directly or indirectly to bringing inventory to its existing condition and location for sale. For example, selling costs are not an inventory cost because they relate to the units sold during the period and not to the units held in inventory. Additionally, some costs that could be attached to inventory normally are excluded because of the cost constraint. For example, the costs of operating a shipping and receiving department are necessary to purchasing and delivering inventory in general but are not incurred directly to bring the item to its existing condition and location. Because the practical difficulties involved in allocating these costs to the specific items in inventory often exceed the benefits that result from making the allocation, these costs are normally expensed as incurred. Finally, GAAP requires that abnormal amounts for freight, handling costs, and wasted materials (spoilage) should be expensed in the period and should not be included in the cost of inventory.[7]

Purchase Discounts

Many sellers offer discounts to buyers to encourage prompt payment. These discounts, called **purchase discounts**, may be accounted for by either the gross price method or the net price method. Under the **gross price method**, a company records the purchase at the gross price and records the amount of the discount in the accounting system only if the discount is *taken*. If a periodic inventory system is used, this discount is deducted from the purchases account when computing net purchases (part of the cost of goods sold calculation discussed earlier in the chapter). Under a perpetual inventory system, the purchase discount is deducted from the inventory account. Under the **net price method**, a company records the purchase at its net price and records the amount of the discount in the accounting system only if the discount is *not taken*. This discount lost should be treated as a period expense (e.g., interest expense).

Example Lahiri Company purchases $1,000 of goods under terms of 1/10, n/30 (a 1% discount is allowed if payment is made within 10 days; otherwise, full payment is due within 30 days). The recording of this transaction under the gross price and net price methods is shown in **Example 7.2**.

EXAMPLE 7.2

Alternative Methods of Accounting for Purchase Discounts

	Gross Price Method			Net Price Method		
To record the purchase	Purchases* Accounts Payable	1,000	1,000	Purchases* Accounts Payable	990	990
To record payment within the discount period	Accounts Payable Purchase Discounts* Cash	1,000	10 990	Accounts Payable Cash	990	990
To record payment outside the discount period	Accounts Payable Cash	1,000	1,000	Accounts Payable Purchase Discounts Lost Cash	990 10	1,000
Adjusting entry at end of period if discount has expired and invoice is unpaid	No entry required			Purchase Discounts Lost Accounts Payable	10	10

*The account "Inventory" is used in a perpetual system.

[7] FASB ASC 330-10-30: Inventory: Overall: Initial Measurement.

Conceptual Evaluation of the Two Methods The conceptually correct inventory cost is the invoice price less all available discounts. Therefore, a company should treat the purchase discounts lost under the net price method as a financing (interest) expense for the period and should not include it in inventory cost, **because losing the discount does not increase the economic benefit to be derived from the inventory**. Consistent with the net price method, the gross price method treats any purchase discounts taken as a reduction in inventory cost. However, under the gross price method, any discounts that were lost are included in inventory cost, even though they do not increase the economic benefits of the inventory. Therefore, the conceptually correct inventory cost is always recorded under the net price method, but the gross price method only produces the conceptually correct inventory cost if all discounts are taken.

Another advantage of the net price method is that it isolates the purchase discounts lost, thereby highlighting inefficiencies, which assists the management control process. For example, if a company purchases goods on terms of 2/10, n/30 and does not take the discount, it is paying 2% to delay payment by 20 days (the 30-day maximum minus the 10 days allowed to take the discount), which is an implied annual interest rate of 36.5% (2% × 365/20).

Under the net price method, Accounts Payable reflects the amount of the obligation if the company generally takes the discounts. If the company does not take the discount, the adjusting entry, illustrated in **Example 7.2**, which adds expired discounts to the Accounts Payable balance will ensure that the correct liability (the gross price) appears on the company's balance sheet. Despite the advantages of the net price method, the gross price method is more common because it is simpler to use and the results produced usually are not materially different from the net price method.

GOT IT?

7-9 Discuss the advantages and disadvantages of the two methods of accounting for purchases discounts taken in regard to management's needs, inventory cost, and the valuation of accounts payable.

LEARNING OBJECTIVE 7.5

Compute ending inventory and cost of goods sold under specific identification, FIFO, average cost, and LIFO.

WHAT ARE THE DIFFERENT COST FLOW ASSUMPTIONS?

A company typically starts an accounting period with some units in the beginning inventory and then purchases or produces additional units during the period. Together, these are the goods available for sale. Because the cost of the purchases and production change during the period, the goods available for sale are made up of items with different costs. As discussed earlier, the cost of goods available for sale is then allocated between the cost of goods sold and ending inventory. Which costs should a company use to make this allocation? Unless the company specifically identifies and traces each item of inventory through its operations, it must attach costs to the units of inventory using a **cost flow assumption**. The major cost flow assumptions are specific identification; first-in, first-out (FIFO); average cost; and last-in, first-out (LIFO). Note that there is no requirement that the cost flow assumption be related to the physical flow (except for the specific identification method).

The following sections discuss and apply each cost flow assumption under both the perpetual and the periodic inventory systems using the information for Dalton Company shown in **Example 7.3**. To make the example less complicated, we use a merchandising company, although a manufacturing company follows the same principles.

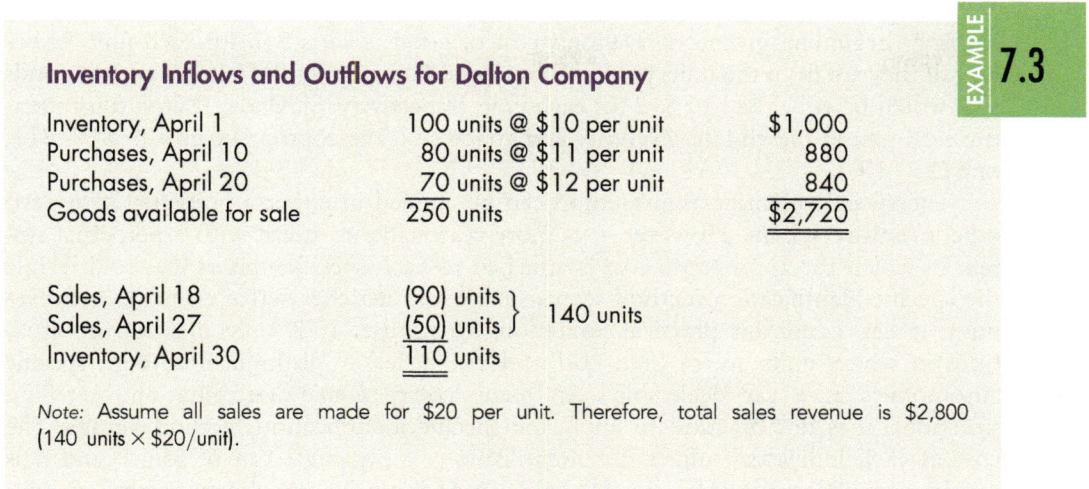

EXAMPLE 7.3

Inventory Inflows and Outflows for Dalton Company

Inventory, April 1	100 units @ $10 per unit	$1,000
Purchases, April 10	80 units @ $11 per unit	880
Purchases, April 20	70 units @ $12 per unit	840
Goods available for sale	250 units	$2,720

Sales, April 18	(90) units ⎱ 140 units	
Sales, April 27	(50) units ⎰	
Inventory, April 30	110 units	

Note: Assume all sales are made for $20 per unit. Therefore, total sales revenue is $2,800 (140 units × $20/unit).

Exhibit 7.4 shows both the unit relationship and the cost flow relationship for Dalton Company.

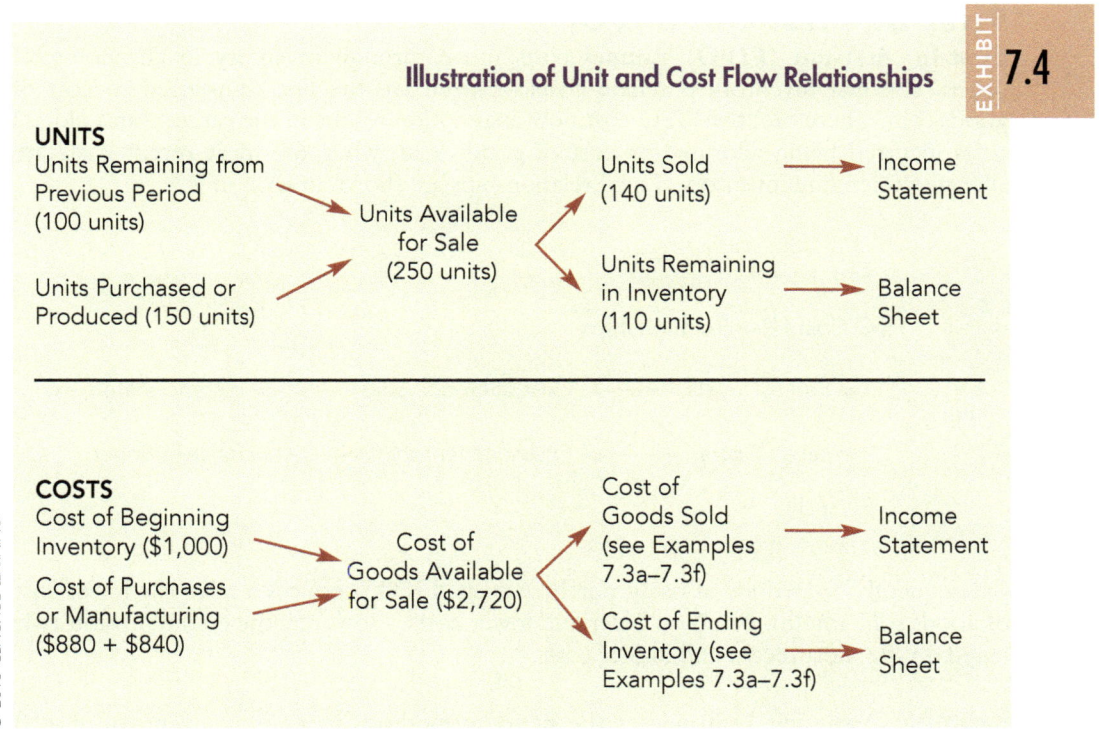

EXHIBIT 7.4 Illustration of Unit and Cost Flow Relationships

UNITS
- Units Remaining from Previous Period (100 units)
- Units Purchased or Produced (150 units)
- → Units Available for Sale (250 units)
- → Units Sold (140 units) → Income Statement
- → Units Remaining in Inventory (110 units) → Balance Sheet

COSTS
- Cost of Beginning Inventory ($1,000)
- Cost of Purchases or Manufacturing ($880 + $840)
- → Cost of Goods Available for Sale ($2,720)
- → Cost of Goods Sold (see Examples 7.3a–7.3f) → Income Statement
- → Cost of Ending Inventory (see Examples 7.3a–7.3f) → Balance Sheet

Note that while the *units* sold and remaining in inventory will be the same under any cost flow assumption, the *cost* allocated to cost of goods sold and ending inventory will depend on the cost flow assumption adopted.

Specific Identification

Under the **specific identification** inventory cost flow assumption, a company identifies each unit sold and each unit remaining in the ending inventory and includes the *actual costs* of those particular units in cost of goods sold and ending inventory, respectively.

For example, Dalton must specifically identify each unit sold on April 27. If all the units are from beginning inventory, Dalton's cost of goods sold is $10 for each unit. However, if they are from the units purchased on April 10 or April 20, Dalton's cost of goods sold would be either $11 or $12 for each unit, respectively. Similarly, Dalton must identify each unit in the ending inventory and attach to it the appropriate cost of $10, $11, or $12.

The specific identification method can be applied in either a perpetual or a periodic inventory system. However, it is more reasonable to use it with a perpetual system in which the appropriate cost is attached to each specific unit as it is sold. While the specific identification method seems simple and matches actual costs against revenues, it has significant practical limitations to its use. It is only practical in situations in which units are of high cost and can be easily distinguished (e.g., specific automobiles at a car dealership). In many complex manufacturing and retailing situations, it is not practical to apply the specific identification method because the cost of each individual unit is not identifiable (e.g., a single can of soup), and it is not known which specific units are sold. In addition, as volume increases, so does the cost of record keeping and the method may become too expensive to use. Therefore, for many companies, it is impractical (if not impossible) to use specific identification.

First-In, First-Out (FIFO)

First-in, first-out (FIFO) assumes costs move through inventory in chronological order. The first inventory purchase costs incurred are the first transferred to cost of goods sold. Therefore, the FIFO cost flow assumption results in the earliest (and oldest) costs incurred being allocated to cost of goods sold, while the most recent costs are allocated to ending inventory. These relationships are shown in Exhibit 7.5.

EXHIBIT 7.5 FIFO Cost Flow Relationships

Consequently, in periods of rising purchase costs, FIFO produces a relatively lower cost of goods sold amount based on older and lower costs. However, the ending inventory is based on the most recent and higher costs.

Example Assuming Dalton uses the periodic method, its ending inventory of 110 units is based on the most recent costs incurred. As shown in **Example 7.3a**, Dalton would start with the most recent purchase (April 20) and accumulate the cost of the purchases until it has accounted for all the units in ending inventory. The resulting amount ($1,280) is Dalton's ending inventory. Dalton would then calculate the cost of goods sold ($1,440) by subtracting the ending inventory from the cost of goods available for sale. Note that cost of goods sold is based on the earliest costs incurred and includes the beginning inventory of 100 units at $10 each and 40 units from the April 10 purchase at $11 each.

EXAMPLE 7.3a

FIFO Cost Flow Assumption (Periodic Inventory System)

Ending Inventory (110 units):
April 10: 40 units @ $11		$ 440
April 20: 70 units @ $12		840
Ending inventory cost		$1,280

Cost of Goods Sold (140 units):

Beginning Inventory	+ Purchases	− Ending Inventory	= Cost of Goods Sold
$1,000	+ $1,720	− $1,280	= $1,440*

*Alternatively,

Beginning inventory:	100 units @ $10	$1,000
April 10:	40 units @ $11	440
Cost of goods sold		$1,440

Example Assuming Dalton uses the perpetual inventory system, it calculates the cost of goods sold of $1,440 and the ending inventory of $1,280 as shown in **Example 7.3b**. Every time inventory is sold, the cost of the earliest purchases that make up cost of goods available for sale is allocated to cost of goods sold, and the cost of the most recent purchases is allocated to ending inventory. Alternatively, ending inventory could be determined by deducting the $1,440 cost of goods sold from the $2,720 cost of goods available for sale.

EXAMPLE 7.3b

FIFO Cost Flow Assumption (Perpetual Inventory System)

Date	Description	Cost of Goods Sold		Inventory Balance	
April 1	Beginning inventory			100 units @ $10/unit =	$1,000
10	Purchase			100 units @ $10/unit =	$1,000
				80 units @ $11/unit =	880
					$1,880
18	Sale (90 units)	90 units @ $10/unit =	$ 900	10 units @ $10/unit =	$ 100
				80 units @ $11/unit =	880
					$ 980
20	Purchase			10 units @ $10/unit =	$ 100
				80 units @ $11/unit =	880
				70 units @ $12/unit =	840
					$1,820
27	Sale (50 units)	10 units @ $10/unit = $100		40 units @ $11/unit =	$ 440
		40 units @ $11/unit = 440	540	70 units @ $12/unit =	840
					$1,280*
		Total cost of goods sold =	$1,440		

*Alternatively,

Beginning Inventory	+ Purchases	− Cost of Goods Sold	= Ending Inventory
$1,000	+ $1,720	− $1,440	= $1,280

Note that the ending inventory and the cost of goods sold under both the perpetual and the periodic systems are identical. This always is true for the FIFO cost flow assumption because the most recent costs incurred always are included in the ending inventory.

Average Cost

Under the **average cost** flow assumption, the cost of ending inventory and cost of goods sold is based on the average of the cost of goods available at a particular point in time. When a company uses the periodic inventory system, the average cost method is known as the **weighted average method**. Under this method, the weighted average cost per unit for the period is computed as follows:

$$\text{Weighted Average Cost per Unit} = \frac{\text{Cost of Goods Available for Sale}}{\text{Units Available for Sale}}$$

The company uses this weighted average cost to determine the cost for the units in both its ending inventory and the cost of goods sold.

Example The weighted average unit cost for Dalton in April is $10.88, as shown in **Example 7.3c**. Dalton uses this weighted average cost per unit to compute the cost of the ending inventory ($1,197) and cost of goods sold ($1,523). Alternatively, Dalton could compute cost of goods sold by deducting the ending inventory from the cost of goods available for sale.

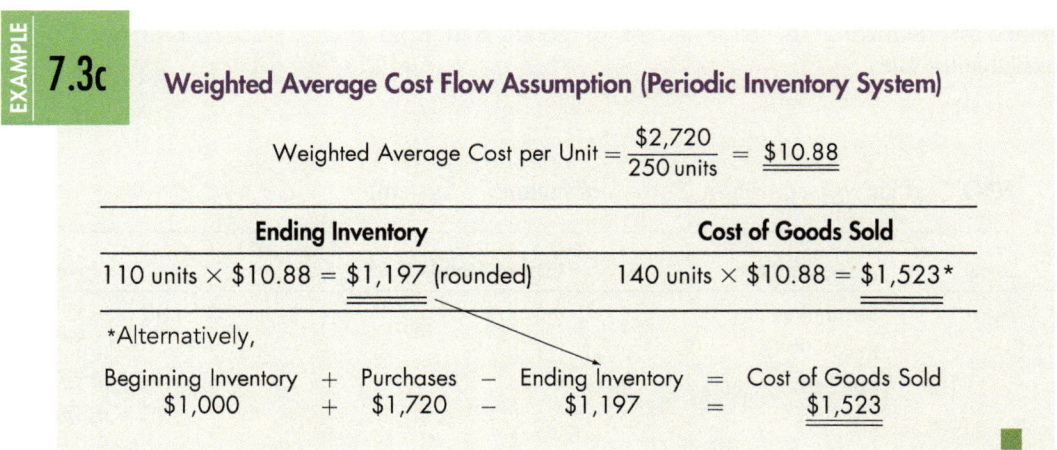

EXAMPLE 7.3c Weighted Average Cost Flow Assumption (Periodic Inventory System)

$$\text{Weighted Average Cost per Unit} = \frac{\$2{,}720}{250 \text{ units}} = \$10.88$$

Ending Inventory	Cost of Goods Sold
110 units × $10.88 = $1,197 (rounded)	140 units × $10.88 = $1,523*

*Alternatively,

Beginning Inventory + Purchases − Ending Inventory = Cost of Goods Sold
$1,000 + $1,720 − $1,197 = $1,523

When a company uses a perpetual inventory system, it applies the same principles. However, it is known as a **moving average method** because a new weighted average cost must be calculated after each purchase, as shown in **Example 7.3d**. The new weighted average is computed in the same way as in the weighted average method. This weighted average cost is used to determine the cost of each sale made until the next purchase, when a new average cost is calculated.

Example As shown in **Example 7.3d**, for Dalton, the weighted average cost after the April 10 purchase is $10.44 (cost of goods available for sale of $1,880 ÷ the number of units available for sale of 180). Therefore, the units sold on April 18 have a cost of $10.44 per unit, resulting in a total cost of goods sold of $940. The purchase on April 20 increases the average cost to $11.125 per unit. Therefore, the 50 units sold on April 27 have a total cost of $556. The total cost of goods sold for April is $1,496 ($940 + $556). Dalton records the ending inventory ($1,224) at the final average cost for the period.

EXAMPLE 7.3d

Moving Average Cost Flow Assumption (Perpetual Inventory System)

Date	Description	Cost of Goods Sold	Inventory Balance	
April 1	Beginning inventory		100 units × $10	= $1,000
10	Purchase 1 (80 units @ $11)		100 units × $10 80 units × $11 180 units	$1,880 ($10.444/unit)[a]
18	Sale (90 units)	90 units × $10.444 = $ 940	90 units × $10.444	= $ 940
20	Purchase (70 units @ $12)		90 units × $10.444 70 units × $12 160 units	$1,780 ($11.125/unit)[b]
27	Sale (50 units)	50 units × $11.125 = 556 Total cost of goods sold = $1,496*	110 units × $11.125	= $1,224

[a] $1,880 ÷ 180 units = $10.444/unit
[b] $1,780 ÷ 160 units = $11.125/unit

*Alternatively,

Beginning Inventory + Purchases − Ending Inventory = Cost of Goods Sold
$1,000 + $1,720 − $1,224 = $1,496

Last-In, First-Out (LIFO)

The **last-in, first-out** (**LIFO**) cost flow assumption allocates the cost of goods available for sale between ending inventory and cost of goods sold based on the assumption that the most recent purchases (the last in) are the first ones sold (the first out). Therefore, the LIFO cost flow assumption results in the most recent costs incurred being allocated to cost of goods sold, while the earliest (and oldest) costs are allocated to ending inventory. These relationships are shown in Exhibit 7.6.

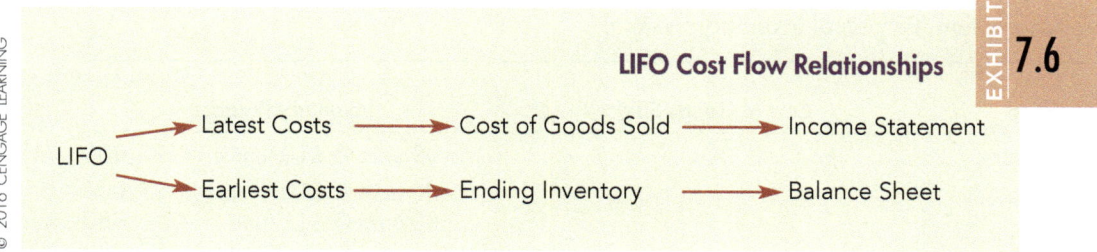

EXHIBIT 7.6 LIFO Cost Flow Relationships

Consequently, in periods of rising costs, LIFO produces a higher cost of goods sold amount based on the most recent costs. However, the ending inventory is based on the oldest and lowest costs.

Under both a periodic and a perpetual inventory system, when the number of units in inventory increases, the company adds a layer of costs to its LIFO inventory. When the number of units in inventory decreases, the company removes costs from its inventory in the reverse order in which it added them—that is, it removes the most recent layers first and includes them in cost of goods sold.

Example Assuming Dalton uses the periodic inventory system, it calculates the ending inventory of $1,110 and the cost of goods sold of $1,610 as shown in **Example 7.3e**. Note that Dalton does not consider the timing of the individual sales. The ending inventory includes the earliest costs, which are the cost of the beginning inventory and the cost of the 10 units from the first purchase on April 10. Dalton computes the cost of goods sold by subtracting the ending inventory from the cost of goods available for sale. This implicitly includes the cost of the 70 units purchased on April 20 ($840) and the cost of 70 units purchased on April 10 ($770).

EXAMPLE 7.3e LIFO Cost Flow Assumption (Periodic Inventory System)

Ending Inventory (110 units):

April 1: 100 units @ $10	$1,000
April 10: 10 units @ $11	110
	$1,110

Cost of Goods Sold (140 units):

Beginning Inventory + Purchases − Ending Inventory = Cost of Goods Sold
$1,000   + $1,720   − $1,110   = $1,610*

*Alternatively,

April 10: 70 units @ $11	$ 770
April 20: 70 units @ $12	840
Cost of goods sold	$1,610

Example Assuming Dalton uses the perpetual inventory system, it calculates the cost of goods sold of $1,580 and the ending inventory of $1,140 as shown in **Example 7.3f**. For each sale, the cost of the most recent purchases that make up cost of goods available for sale is allocated to cost of goods sold, and the cost of the earliest purchases is allocated to ending inventory. Alternatively, ending inventory could be computed by deducting the $1,580 cost of goods sold from the $2,720 cost of goods available for sale.

EXAMPLE 7.3f LIFO Cost Flow Assumption (Perpetual Inventory System)

Date		Description	Cost of Goods Sold		Inventory Balance	
April	1	Beginning inventory			100 units @ $10/unit =	$1,000
	10	Purchase			100 units @ $10/unit =	$1,000
					80 units @ $11/unit =	880
						$1,880
	18	Sale (90 units)	80 units × $11/unit 10 units × $10/unit	$ 980	90 units @ $10/unit =	$ 900
	20	Purchase			90 units @ $10/unit =	$ 900
					70 units @ $12/unit =	840
						$1,740
	27	Sale (50 units)	50 units @ $12/unit =	600	90 units @ $10/unit =	$ 900
					20 units @ $12/unit =	240
						$1,140*
			Total cost of goods sold =	$1,580		

*Alternatively,

Beginning Inventory + Purchases − Cost of Goods Sold = Ending Inventory
$1,000   + $1,720   − $1,580   = $1,140

Note that, in contrast to FIFO, the cost of goods sold and the ending inventory are not the same for the LIFO perpetual method and the LIFO periodic method. This is due to different assumptions about the timing of the sales. Under the periodic method, the entire accounting period (a month in this example) is treated as a single time period, and all the sales are assumed to take place after all the units have been purchased during the period. Therefore, the cost of goods sold includes the costs of the most recent purchases of the period. Under the perpetual method, each event is recorded as it occurs. Therefore, the cost of goods sold is calculated when each sale is made and includes the costs of the most recent purchases at that time.

Comparison of Inventory Cost Flow Assumptions

The cost of goods sold and the inventory amounts for Dalton Company calculated in the preceding examples are summarized in **Example 7.3g**. However, the specific identification method is excluded because, as discussed previously, the results are dependent on the particular units selected for sale. Gross profit is computed as sales ($2,800 for all situations) minus cost of goods sold.

EXAMPLE 7.3g

Effects of Inventory Cost Flow Assumptions

Cost Flow Assumption and Method	Cost of Goods Available for Sale	Cost of Goods Sold	Ending Inventory	Gross Profit
FIFO, periodic	$2,720	$1,440	$1,280	$1,360
FIFO, perpetual	2,720	1,440	1,280	1,360
Weighted average, periodic	2,720	1,523	1,197	1,277
Moving average, perpetual	2,720	1,496	1,224	1,304
LIFO, periodic	2,720	1,610	1,110	1,190
LIFO, perpetual	2,720	1,580	1,140	1,220

In this example, sales, units purchased, and cost of goods available for sale were the same for each method. However, the unit purchase price of inventory rose throughout the period. As a result, observe that in a period of *rising purchase prices*:

- The FIFO method produces the lowest cost of goods sold because it includes the oldest and lowest costs. Therefore, the gross profit (and income) is highest.
- The FIFO method produces the highest cost of ending inventory because it includes the most recent and highest costs.
- The LIFO method produces the highest cost of goods sold and the lowest gross profit (and income) because it includes the most recent and highest costs.
- The LIFO ending inventory is lowest because it includes the earliest and lowest costs.
- The average cost amounts are between the FIFO and LIFO extremes because the ending inventory and the cost of goods sold include an average of both the lower and higher costs of the period.

In this example, Dalton was experiencing rising costs. What would happen if purchase prices were falling during the period? In that situation, the opposite relationships would occur. During a period of *falling purchase prices*, the use of LIFO would produce a higher ending inventory, a lower cost of goods sold, and a higher gross profit (and income) than FIFO. When costs fluctuate (both rise and fall) during a period, no general relationships can be described. The differences between the amounts under the periodic and the perpetual inventory systems for each cost flow assumption result from the different calculations and not from any differences in the logic underlying the cost flow assumptions.

> ### GOT IT?
>
> **7-10** Why does the application of the FIFO, average cost, and LIFO cost flow assumptions produce different amounts for the cost of ending inventory and the cost of goods sold?
>
> **7-11** The costs of which units of cost of goods available for sale (oldest or most recent) are allocated to ending inventory and cost of goods sold under the FIFO, average cost, and LIFO cost flow assumptions?
>
> **7-12** Discuss the LIFO cost flow assumption. Under what conditions would a company's ending inventory differ under a perpetual and a periodic LIFO system?
>
> **7-13** During a period of rising costs, indicate whether the LIFO cost flow assumption results in a larger or a smaller net income as compared to the FIFO cost flow assumption and explain why. Explain how a company's net income would compare during a period of falling costs.

LEARNING OBJECTIVE 7.6

Explain the consequences that result from the use of alternative inventory cost flow assumptions.

WHAT ARE THE CONSEQUENCES OF USING ALTERNATIVE INVENTORY COST FLOW ASSUMPTIONS?

As external users evaluate the profitability, risk, and growth of a company, the impact of the cost flow assumption used can affect a company in many ways—ranging from how much income tax a company pays to the value of its stock. Many arguments can be made in favor of each of the alternative cost flow assumptions. Because FIFO and LIFO represent the two extremes in terms of the costing of inventory, the arguments presented in this section focus on these two cost flow assumptions.

Income Measurement

For financial reporting, the basic objective of accounting for inventory is to report a relevant and representationally faithful balance sheet value for inventory and to achieve a "proper determination of income through the process of matching appropriate costs against revenues."[8] But what are "appropriate" costs? Unfortunately, there is no simple answer as to whether income is better measured under LIFO or FIFO. Both methods match historical costs with revenues, but the major argument in favor of LIFO is that it matches the most *recent* costs with revenue. The most recent costs are closer to replacement costs—the costs the company will have to incur to replace the inventory that was sold. Therefore, LIFO excludes from a company's income some (but not all) of the holding gains that arise when inventory purchase prices are changing.[9] In contrast, FIFO matches the earliest costs with revenue and includes all the holding gains in income. By matching the more recent costs against current revenue, LIFO is said to produce a better measure of current income.

Example Consider the information presented in **Example 7.4** taken from the Dalton Company example. If Dalton sells a unit on April 27 for $20, FIFO produces a gross profit of $10 per unit, which includes a holding gain of $2 per unit ($12 cost to replace the inventory minus $10 cost of goods sold). However, under LIFO, the gross profit of $8 per unit excludes this holding gain because the cost to replace the inventory and the cost of goods sold are the same amount.

---

[8] FASB ASC 330-10-10: Inventory: Overall: Objective.
[9] A holding gain (or inventory profit) is the difference between the purchase price of the inventory and the replacement cost of the units sold.

> **EXAMPLE 7.4**
>
> **Alternative Cost Flow Assumptions and Holding Gains (per Unit)**
>
> | | FIFO | LIFO |
> | --- | --- | --- |
> | Revenue | $ 20 | $ 20 |
> | Cost of goods sold (obtained from **Example 7.3**) | (10) | (12) |
> | Gross profit | $ 10 | $ 8 |
> | Holding gains (excluded from income) | | 2 |
> | | | $ 10 |

To continue this example, suppose that Dalton distributed its income as a dividend. Under FIFO, Dalton would distribute $10 and is left with $10 cash, which is not enough to purchase a unit of inventory at its replacement cost of $12. Thus, the holding gain of $2, which is included in income, does not represent a real increase in wealth because Dalton cannot distribute it to the owners without leaving it worse off in terms of its ability to maintain the same level of inventory. However, under LIFO, Dalton would distribute $8 and it is left with $12 cash, which is enough to purchase a unit of inventory at its replacement cost. Therefore, LIFO is viewed as producing a better measure of income. ■

Income Tax Effects

As we have seen, LIFO produces the highest cost of goods sold and the lowest income under conditions of rising costs. All else being equal, companies would prefer to report higher income rather than lower (recall from Chapter 1 that increases in reported net income are associated with increases in share prices). However, companies also prefer to report lower taxable income and pay lower income taxes. Therefore, although the use of LIFO for inventory may cause a company to report lower net income, the use of LIFO for computing taxable income may result in lower payments for income taxes. For example, by using LIFO for many years, **ExxonMobil** has reduced its income before taxes by $21.3 billion.

The use of LIFO for the computation of federal income taxes presents a special situation. When purchase prices are rising, a company might prefer to use FIFO to report a higher income for financial reporting purposes but use LIFO to prepare its tax return. However, the Internal Revenue Code permits a company to use LIFO for income tax purposes *only if* it also uses LIFO in its financial statements. This requirement is known as the **LIFO conformity rule**. The LIFO conformity rule prevents a company from having "the best of both worlds" by using FIFO for financial reporting and LIFO for income taxes. This is in contrast to many situations in which a company is permitted to use different methods for financial reporting and income tax reporting (e.g., when it uses straight-line depreciation for financial reporting and accelerated depreciation for income tax reporting). A company must decide whether it is willing to report a lower accounting income in order to achieve the advantages of lower cash payments for income taxes.

LOOKING AHEAD

In recent years, there has been considerable discussion on abolishing LIFO. For example, in his fiscal 2016 budget proposal, President Barack Obama has proposed to eliminate LIFO for tax purposes. Assuming rising inventory costs, the Office of Management and Budget estimates that the repeal of LIFO would raise $76 billion over 10 years, as companies report higher inventory values and lower amounts for cost of goods sold—resulting in higher taxable income.

Liquidation of LIFO Layers

A company using the LIFO method may experience a decline in inventory during a period when the unit sales of inventory are more than the units acquired. Therefore, some of the beginning inventory costs are included in cost of goods sold. Because these older units of inventory have lower costs attached to them (assuming rising prices), cost of goods sold is lower and gross profit (and income) is higher than if the liquidation did not occur. This increased amount of income is often referred to as a **LIFO liquidation profit**. LIFO liquidations bring units with a cost from previous years into cost of goods sold and produce an unrealistically high income.

Example Vowell Company was formed in 2012 and uses the LIFO cost flow assumption. Its 2016 beginning inventory of $644,000 is made up of four layers as follows:

2012	10,000 units @ $20/unit =	$200,000
2013	6,000 units @ $22/unit =	132,000
2014	8,000 units @ $24/unit =	192,000
2015	4,000 units @ $30/unit =	120,000
Inventory, January 1, 2016		$644,000

In 2016, Vowell purchases (or manufactures) 50,000 units at $35 per unit but sells 60,000 units. Vowell has an inventory liquidation of 10,000 units. Vowell's cost of goods sold for 2016 includes costs from 2016, 2015, and 2014, as follows:

50,000 units @ $35/unit =	$1,750,000	(2016 costs)
4,000 units @ $30/unit =	120,000	(2015 costs)
6,000 units @ $24/unit =	144,000	(2014 costs)
60,000	$2,014,000	

If, instead, Vowell had purchased (or produced) 60,000 units at $35 each (thus avoiding the LIFO liquidation), Vowell would have had a cost of goods sold in 2016 of $2,100,000 (60,000 units × $35 per unit) consisting entirely of 2016 costs. The difference of $86,000 ($2,100,000 − $2,014,000) is the LIFO liquidation profit (before income taxes). If we assume an income tax rate of 30%, the effect of the LIFO liquidation is to increase gross profit by $86,000, income tax expense by $25,800 ($86,000 × 30%), and net income by $60,200 ($86,000 × 70%). Note that the company's income and income taxes are higher (because cost of goods sold includes older and lower costs) even though there is no economic substance to the higher income. ∎

Public companies are required to disclose the amount of their LIFO liquidation profit so that users of the financial statements may obtain a better understanding of the profit earned by the company. For example, **U.S. Steel** reported LIFO liquidation profits of $27 million and $3 million in 2012 and 2011, respectively.

Earnings Management

As we have seen, a company's liquidation of inventory under LIFO, whether intentional or not, results in higher income (assuming rising costs). Such a liquidation may be caused by economic factors beyond the control of the company, such as a strike or a scarcity of raw materials. Alternatively, the liquidation may result from a strategic management decision such as the adoption of a "just-in-time" inventory system which results in a permanent reduction in the size of the inventory. However, a LIFO liquidation may be deliberately caused by management to increase income. For example, if a company is facing a period of lower income, management can intentionally increase income by delaying purchases until after the end of the fiscal year. An intentional LIFO liquidation to artificially increase income can be viewed as a form of earnings management and is a significant concern. Similarly, a company may manage its income downward by increasing its purchases.

Example Refer back to the Dalton Company periodic LIFO example (**Example 7.3e**) and assume that Dalton purchased an additional 40 units on April 29 at $12 per unit. Because of this additional purchase, ending inventory and cost of goods sold would be computed as shown in **Example 7.5**.

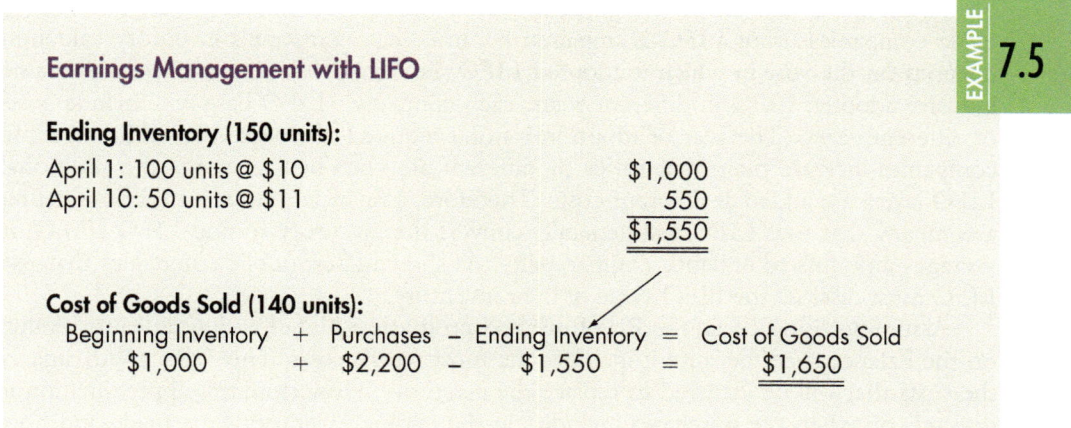

EXAMPLE 7.5

Earnings Management with LIFO

Ending Inventory (150 units):
April 1: 100 units @ $10 $1,000
April 10: 50 units @ $11   550
                              $1,550

Cost of Goods Sold (140 units):
Beginning Inventory + Purchases − Ending Inventory = Cost of Goods Sold
     $1,000   + $2,200   − $1,550   = $1,650

Note that purchasing additional units has increased cost of goods sold by $40 ($1,650 − $1,610) even though unit sales remain unchanged.

Manipulating reported income through the strategic timing of inventory purchases under LIFO does not produce an income measure that is a faithful representation of the performance of the company. However, this earnings management strategy is possible under the LIFO method. The FIFO and average cost methods do not produce unusual results when inventory liquidation occurs, nor are they as susceptible to earnings management.

Management should make decisions about purchasing or manufacturing inventory on the basis of economic and operating factors. The use of LIFO, however, allows management to influence the company's income through the acceleration of, or delay in, acquiring inventory.

ETHICAL DILEMMA

As the CFO of a large manufacturing company, you realize that, although the company performed well over the past fiscal year, reported earnings will fall short of analysts' expectations. Knowing that failure to meet these expectations will likely result in a fall in the company's stock price and possibly the loss of your job, you assemble your most trusted financial experts to provide advice as to how to increase earnings. A plan is developed that would:

- Delay all inventory purchases until the next fiscal year (because you are using LIFO, this delay would result in the liquidation of inventory and a corresponding increase in income)
- Implement a sales program that would allow customers who accepted delivery of merchandise in the current year to defer payment for six months (normal practice requires payment within 30 days)

The financial experts all agree that these two actions are acceptable under GAAP and would allow the company to meet its earnings target. Discuss the ethical implications of these actions.

Inventory Valuation

Assuming rising costs, the LIFO method produces a lower inventory value on a company's balance sheet because the oldest costs remain in this inventory. For companies that either turn over inventory slowly or have used LIFO for many years, the recorded amount of this inventory might have little or no relationship to the costs of the current period or to the costs that will be incurred to replace the inventory and, therefore, will not be a faithful representation of the value of inventory. This low valuation can affect the computation and evaluation of current assets, working capital, total assets, and any financial ratios that include inventory, thereby reducing comparability between companies using LIFO and those using FIFO. Furthermore, comparability between two or more companies using LIFO is impaired because each company's inventory valuation depends on the year in which it adopted LIFO. For example, if companies in the same industry adopted LIFO in different years, each company's LIFO base will include costs of different years. (The year of adoption is not a required disclosure.) In addition, if the companies increase their inventories by different amounts in later years, the additional LIFO layers are added at different costs. Therefore, a financial statement user evaluating a company that uses LIFO will generally convert the inventory to non-LIFO (FIFO or average) amounts to enhance comparability. As shown later, public companies that use LIFO must disclose the FIFO value of their inventory.

Assuming rising costs, the FIFO method produces a higher ending inventory value on the balance sheet because it includes the most recent costs. This value approximates the costs that will be incurred to replace the inventory. How close this approximation is depends on when the purchases included in the ending inventory were made and how fast costs are rising. However, in general, the use of FIFO results in inventory values that are more representationally faithful than those produced by LIFO.

What Does Management Need to Consider in Selecting an Inventory Cost Flow Assumption?

As discussed, there are many financial accounting and tax issues involved in selecting an inventory cost flow assumption. Companies, however, are free to choose whichever cost flow assumption they prefer, regardless of whether the method matches the physical flow of goods. Exhibit 7.7 illustrates the frequency of use of the various inventory cost flow assumptions.

EXHIBIT 7.7 Use of Inventory Cost Flow Assumptions

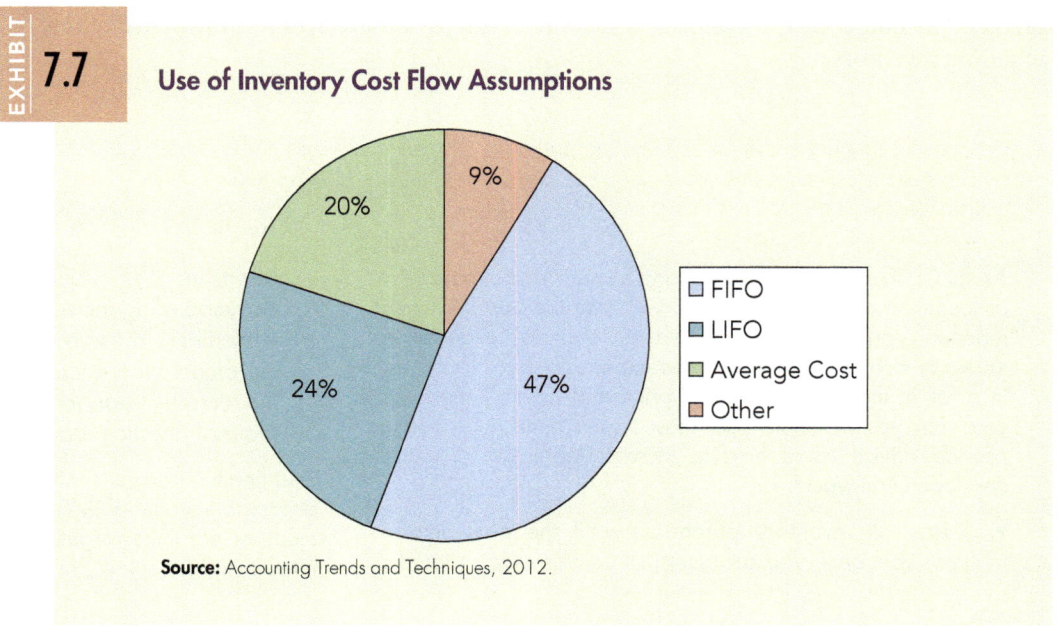

Source: Accounting Trends and Techniques, 2012.

In addition, a company does not have to use the same cost flow assumption for all of its inventory. For example, **Publix Super Markets** values approximately 84% of its inventory using dollar-value LIFO (a form of LIFO discussed in the next section). Publix values the remaining inventory, consisting of seasonal and perishable items, using FIFO. However, once a company adopts a cost flow assumption, it should use that assumption consistently over time in order to enhance the comparability and usefulness of the accounting information.

Real Report 7.1 shows **Panera Bread**'s inventory disclosures.

REAL REPORT 7.1 — DISCLOSURE OF INVENTORY VALUES AND METHODS

Panera Bread

Balance Sheet (in thousands)

Assets (in part)	December 31, 2013	December 25, 2012
Inventories	$21,916	$19,714

Notes to Consolidated Financial Statements (in part)

Note 2: Summary of Significant Accounting Policies (in part)
Inventories—Inventories, which consist of food products, paper goods, and supplies, are valued at the lower of cost or market, with cost determined under the first-in, first-out method.

Note 6: Inventories
Inventories consisted of the following (in thousands):

	December 31, 2013	December 25, 2012
Food:		
Fresh Dough Facilities:		
Raw materials	$ 3,377	$ 3,418
Finished goods	545	420
Bakery Cafes:		
Raw materials	14,329	12,727
Paper goods	3,665	3,149
Total	$21,916	$19,714

Questions:

1. What is the primary cost flow assumption that Panera Bread uses? Discuss how the amounts reported under this assumption compare to amounts reported under alternative cost flow assumptions.
2. In which part of Panera Bread's operations is the majority of its inventory?

Suggested answers to these questions are found at the end of the chapter.

How do companies choose between LIFO and FIFO? Several factors that influence management's selection are discussed below.[10]

---

[10] The discussion in this section is derived from numerous academic studies on the LIFO/FIFO choice. See, for example, B. Cushing and M. LeClere, "Evidence on the Determinants of Inventory Accounting Policy Choice," *The Accounting Review* (April 1992), pp. 355–366; N. Dopuch and M. Pincus, "Evidence on the Choice of Inventory Accounting Methods: LIFO versus FIFO," *Journal of Accounting Research* (Spring 1988), pp. 28–59; D. Morse and G. Richardson, "The LIFO/FIFO Decision," *Journal of Accounting Research* (Spring 1983), pp. 106–127; and J. Hand, "Resolving LIFO Uncertainty—A Theoretical and Empirical Reexamination of 1974–1975 LIFO Adoptions and NonAdoptions," *Journal of Accounting Research* (Spring 1993), pp. 21–49.

Tax Considerations Recall that in a period of *rising* prices, the use of LIFO will result in tax savings for a company. Because of the LIFO conformity rule, a company that wishes to lower its taxes by using LIFO must also use LIFO for financial reporting purposes. Evidence suggests that the anticipated tax benefits from LIFO are the primary reason for its use. However, LIFO does not always produce the lowest taxes. If costs are expected to *fall*, the use of FIFO would result in lower taxes and may be preferred. For example, many high-tech companies with decreasing prices (e.g., **Apple**, **Dell**) use FIFO. Therefore, managers will often forecast the future cash flows produced under each alternative cost flow assumption and select the method that will result in the lowest taxes.

Bookkeeping and Other Related Costs The LIFO method is more costly to use than the FIFO method because of the additional costs of record keeping and financial statement preparation (e.g., keeping track of the LIFO layers for each type of inventory and the requirements imposed by the Internal Revenue Service). For a small company, these additional costs may be greater than the income tax savings that would result from the adoption of LIFO. For larger companies, however, the income tax savings are likely to exceed the additional costs (assuming rising prices).

Conceptual Issues As noted earlier, LIFO provides a better measure of income because it matches the most recent costs against revenues. Conversely, FIFO provides a more accurate inventory valuation on the balance sheet. The selection of LIFO or FIFO is often based on these conceptual grounds.

Stock Price Effects Arguments are made that a company should not adopt LIFO even when its costs are expected to rise. This is because of the lower income that will result and a possible perception that the company is less successful and that its stock price will be lower. Research has shown that capital markets do reduce stock prices when companies switch to LIFO, however, this penalty is not due to lower earnings. Instead, the adoption of LIFO is viewed by the market as a signal that the companies expect rising input prices and inflation in the future, and therefore, lower profitability.

Physical Flow of Goods In most situations, the FIFO and average cost flow assumptions approximate the physical flow of the items in inventory, whereas LIFO does not. For example, a retail clothing store might try to induce a FIFO physical flow on its customers by offering end of season discounts and markdowns on the oldest clothing items first. But the customers may seek more of a LIFO flow if they select the newest, most fashionable items from the shelves. However, accounting principles do not require that the selected cost flow assumption approximate the physical flow of goods. Still, the desire to approximate the physical flow of goods is a major reason given by managers who selected the FIFO cost flow assumption.

Contracting Considerations Management also may be reluctant to adopt LIFO due to contracting considerations. For example, if a company has bond covenants that require it to maintain a current ratio above some minimum level or a debt-to-equity ratio below a maximum level, the use of LIFO (in a period of rising purchase prices) would result in lower assets, income, and shareholders' equity. Therefore, the company's financial flexibility may be limited as it attempts to maintain these ratios. In addition, if management is paid a bonus based on accounting income, the use of LIFO (in periods of rising purchase prices) would lead to lower reported income and lower bonuses.

INTERNATIONAL DIMENSION

INVENTORY ACCOUNTING AND REPORTING

Inventory accounting and reporting requirements under IFRS are generally similar to those under U.S. GAAP. For example, IFRS define inventory similarly to U.S. GAAP and allow the use of the perpetual and periodic inventory systems. Additionally, IFRS, like U.S. GAAP, require a company to initially value its inventory at cost, which includes purchase costs (e.g., purchase price minus cash discounts plus shipping costs), conversion costs (e.g., direct material, labor, overhead), and other costs (e.g., packing costs) necessary to get the inventory to its present location and condition for sale. However, some very important differences do exist.

- IFRS do not allow the use of the LIFO cost flow assumption. The major reason is that LIFO is inconsistent with any presumed physical flow of inventory, an issue that has not been relevant for U.S. GAAP. Also, because LIFO is not permitted to be used for income tax purposes in most countries, there is no international LIFO conformity rule. This results in less incentive to allow the use of LIFO for financial reporting.
- While both U.S. GAAP and IFRS allow the use of multiple acceptable cost flow assumptions, IFRS require that the same assumption be used for all inventories that have a similar nature and use. No such requirement exists under U.S. GAAP.
- Because LIFO is not allowed under IFRS, and U.S. GAAP allows multiple acceptable cost flow assumptions, it is quite common to see U.S. companies with international operations value U.S. inventories using LIFO but value inventories held in subsidiaries that are located in IFRS-based countries with a non-LIFO assumption.

Presented below is the inventory disclosure of **Nestlé**, whose financial statements are prepared under IFRS.

Note 1: Accounting Policies (in part)

INVENTORIES

Raw materials and purchased finished goods are valued at purchase cost. Work in progress and manufactured finished goods are valued at production cost. Production cost includes direct production costs and an appropriate proportion of production overheads and factory depreciation.

Raw material inventories and purchased finished goods are accounted for using the FIFO (first in, first out) method. The weighted average cost method is used of other inventories.

An allowance is established when the net realisable value of an inventory item is lower than the value calculated above.

Note 6: Inventories

in millions of CHF	2013	2012
Raw materials, work in progress and sundry supplies	3,499	3,815
Finished goods	5,138	5,302
Allowance for write-down at net realisable value	(255)	(178)
	8,382	8,939

Source: IAS 2: Inventories (See Appendix C at the end of this book).

> ### GOT IT?
>
> **7-14** Which cost flow assumption, LIFO or FIFO, produces the better measure of current income? Which method produces the better inventory valuation?
>
> **7-15** Discuss the LIFO and FIFO cost flow assumptions relative to the issue of holding gains (inventory profits and inventory liquidation).
>
> **7-16** Explain the issue of inventory liquidation when a company uses the LIFO cost flow assumption. Why is this an issue exclusive to LIFO?
>
> **7-17** What factors might influence management's selection of an inventory cost flow assumption?
>
> **7-18** List the acceptable cost flow assumptions under IFRS. Be sure to explain the reasoning as to why IFRS find certain cost flow assumptions unacceptable.

LEARNING OBJECTIVE 7.7
Understand and apply dollar-value LIFO.

WHAT IS THE DOLLAR-VALUE LIFO METHOD?

The dollar-value LIFO method follows the same cost flow assumption as the LIFO method, but it overcomes three difficulties involved in applying the simple LIFO approach.

- *Record Keeping:* The LIFO method requires a company to keep numerous detailed records of the physical quantities of each item in its inventory and apply unit costs in the LIFO order.
- *LIFO Liquidations:* Fluctuations in the physical quantities of similar inventory items may occur during a period, causing a partial liquidation of its LIFO layers that would remove many of the advantages of LIFO.
- *Technological Change:* As technological changes take place, inventory made with one material is replaced by inventory made with substitute materials, or an outdated design is replaced by a newer design. Strict application of the LIFO method would require a company to start a new LIFO base for the new inventory item, and as the old item is phased out, to reduce its inventory to zero. This would eliminate the advantages of LIFO built up in previous periods.

Dollar-value LIFO overcomes part of the first problem by the use of current costs and cost indexes, and the second and third problems by the use of inventory pools.

Cost Indexes

A **cost index** refers to an internally generated index that relates the current-year cost of inventory to a base-year cost of inventory. A cost index will measure any price level changes that have occurred since the base year and allow a company to isolate the change in cost from the change in physical quantities of inventory. Typically, a company prepares the cost index using a sample of its total inventory. Two methods to compute the cost index are used in practice: *the double-extension method* and the *link-chain method*.

Under the **double-extension method**, a sample of the ending inventory is priced at current-year costs and at base-year costs, and the cost index is computed as follows:

$$\text{Cost Index} = \frac{\text{Ending Inventory at Current-Year Costs}}{\text{Ending Inventory at Base-Year Costs}} \times 100$$

This is known as the double-extension method because the ending inventory is priced and "extended" twice—once at current costs and once at base-year costs. The double-extension method is appropriate for companies that have little change in the characteristics of their inventory items. When changes are frequent, determination of base-year costs for new items is difficult. For example, if a company adopted LIFO in 1993 and develops a new product in 2016, the double-extension method would require the computation of the cost in 1993 of the new product. Because the product did not exist in 1993, the difficulties of such a calculation are obvious. In such situations, the link-chain method should be used.

Under the **link-chain method**, a company prices a sample of the ending inventory at current-year costs and previous-year costs and, therefore, avoids the problems of the double-extension method. The ratio of the current-year current cost to the previous-year current cost is used to compute a cost index for the year. This index is multiplied by the cost index carried forward from the previous year to determine the current-year cumulative index as follows:

$$\text{Cost Index} = \frac{\text{Ending Inventory at Current-Year Costs}}{\text{Ending Inventory at Previous-Year Costs}} \times \text{Previous-Year Cost Index}$$

Inventory Pools

Companies apply dollar-value LIFO to inventory pools by grouping inventory items that are similar as to types of material or use. Some companies may consider their entire inventory as one pool, but usually several pools are used. For example, if Starbucks were to form inventory pools, it may group all of its coffee into a single inventory pool, while its merchandise may be grouped into another pool, and the cups, dairy products, food, supplies, and other products may be grouped into additional pools. The purpose of inventory pools is to maintain the benefits from using LIFO when fluctuations in the physical quantities of similar inventory items occur and when technological change takes place. When the quantity of one item of the inventory pool is reduced, the reduction may be offset with an increase in the quantity of another item in the inventory pool. Therefore, the liquidation of LIFO layers and the loss of the tax benefits of LIFO are normally avoided.

Application of Dollar-Value LIFO

The general principle of the dollar-value LIFO method is that a company is trying to separate the change in the physical quantity of inventory from the change in costs of the inventory. It does this by initially valuing its pool of ending inventory at current cost and using the cost index to "roll back" this cost to the cost at the beginning of the base year (the year in which it adopted LIFO). A comparison of the year's beginning and ending inventory pools at base-year costs indicates whether there has been a real increase (or decrease) in the physical quantity of the inventory. The company then "rolls forward" the increase (or decrease) in the physical quantity to the appropriate current cost level and adds this layer of current cost (or subtracts it from) the beginning inventory to determine its ending inventory. The application of the dollar-value LIFO method requires the following four steps:

- *Step 1.* Value the total ending inventory at current-year costs.
- *Step 2.* Convert (roll back) the ending inventory cost to base-year costs by applying the appropriate cost index as shown below.

$$\frac{\text{Ending Inventory at}}{\text{Base-Year Costs}} = \frac{\text{Ending Inventory at}}{\text{Current-Year Costs}} \times \frac{\text{Base-Year Cost Index}}{\text{Current-Year Cost Index}}$$

- *Step 3.* Compute the base-year change in inventory level by comparing the ending inventory at base-year costs with the beginning inventory at base-year costs.
- *Step 4.* a. If there is an increase in the inventory level at base-year costs, there has been a real increase in the physical quantity of the inventory for the year. Convert (roll forward) this increase to current-year costs by applying the appropriate cost index as shown below.

$$\frac{\text{Layer Increase at}}{\text{Current-Year Costs}} = \frac{\text{Increase at}}{\text{Base-Year Costs}} \times \frac{\text{Current-Year Cost Index}}{\text{Base-Year Cost Index}}$$

Add this layer increase to the dollar-value LIFO inventory cost at the beginning of the year to get the dollar-value LIFO cost of ending inventory.

b. If there is a decrease in the inventory level at base-year costs, there has been a real decrease in the physical quantity of the inventory for the year. This decrease reduces the inventory on a LIFO layer basis. Note that this decrease (shown below) may eliminate more than one layer of LIFO inventory.

$$\frac{\text{Cost Decrease of Most}}{\text{Recently Added Layer(s)}} = \frac{\text{Decrease at}}{\text{Base-Year Costs}} \times \frac{\text{Cost Index of Most Recently Added Layer(s)}}{\text{Base-Year Cost Index}}$$

The dollar-value LIFO cost of ending inventory is the dollar-value LIFO cost at the beginning of the year minus the cost decrease of the most recently added layer(s).

Example: Dollar-Value LIFO

Wagner Company adopted LIFO at the beginning of 2015 and has taken an ending inventory at the current costs for each year as indicated in **Example 7.6**. In addition, Wagner has experienced yearly changes in the level of its costs as indicated by its cost index for each year.

EXAMPLE 7.6 — Data for Wagner Company

Date	Ending Inventory at Current Costs	Cost Index
January 1, 2015	$10,000	100
December 31, 2015	12,100	110
December 31, 2016	13,125	125
December 31, 2017	16,800	140
December 31, 2018	12,360	120

The calculation of the dollar-value LIFO ending inventory is shown in **Example 7.6a**.

EXAMPLE 7.6a — Dollar-Value LIFO Inventory Calculations

	Step 1	Step 2	Step 3	Step 4		
Date	Ending Inventory at Current Costs × Base-Year Cost Index / Current Cost Index = Inventory at Base-Year Costs		Increase (Decrease) at Base-Year Costs × Relevant Cost Index / Base-Year Cost Index = Increase (Decrease) at Relevant Current Costs		Ending Inventory at LIFO	Layers in LIFO Ending Inventory
1/1/15		$10,000	—	—	$10,000	$10,000
12/31/15	$12,100 × 100/110 = 11,000		$1,000 × 110/100 = $1,100		11,100	10,000 ($10,000 @ 100); 1,100 ($1,000 @ 110)
12/31/16	13,125 × 100/125 = 10,500		(500) × 110/100 = (550)		10,550	10,000 ($10,000 @ 100); 550 ($500 @ 110)
12/31/17	16,800 × 100/140 = 12,000		1,500 × 140/100 = 2,100		12,650	10,000 ($10,000 @ 100); 550 ($500 @ 110); 2,100 ($1,500 @ 140)
12/31/18	12,360 × 100/120 = 10,300		(1,500) × 140/100 = (2,100); (200) × 110/100 = (220)		10,330	10,000 ($10,000 @ 100); 330 ($300 @ 110)

The following items are of note:

- The base year is 2015, so the beginning inventory in 2015 needs no adjustment. In 2015, there is a real (quantity) *increase* in inventory of $1,000 (at base-year costs), which is $1,100 in 2015 costs. The ending dollar-value LIFO inventory cost for 2015 is $11,100 which is made up of two layers, the base layer of $10,000 plus the layer added in 2015 of $1,100.
- In 2016, there is a real (quantity) *decrease* in inventory of $500. This decrease is subtracted from the most recently added layer, which is the layer added during 2015. Therefore, Wagner converts the $500 base-year cost decrease using 2015 costs, not 2016 costs, resulting in a decrease of $550 and an ending inventory of $10,550.
- In 2017, Wagner has an increase in inventory at base-year costs, and therefore adds another layer, so that its ending LIFO inventory of $12,650 consists of three layers.
- In 2018, Wagner has a decrease in its cost index. It calculates the ending inventory at base-year costs in the same manner as we discussed previously. In this case, the $1,700 decrease eliminates the $1,500 layer (at base-year costs) added in 2017. Because no layer was added in 2016, Wagner must go back into the 2015 layer to account for the remaining decrease of $200 at base-year costs. The ending LIFO inventory of $10,330 consists of the base inventory plus the remainder of the layer added in 2015.

GOT IT?

7-19 Explain the dollar-value LIFO method of inventory valuation. What are the advantages of dollar-value LIFO as compared to simple LIFO?

7-20 Describe the double-extension and link-chain methods used in dollar-value LIFO and when each should be used.

HOW DO COMPANIES DISCLOSE INVENTORY VALUES AND METHODS?

LEARNING OBJECTIVE 7.8
Understand inventory disclosures.

Exhibit 7.8 shows the relative use of alternative inventory methods and the proportion of the inventory cost determined by LIFO.[11] The trend to shift to LIFO between 1973

EXHIBIT 7.8

Relative Use of Alternative Inventory Methods across Companies and Time

	Number of Companies									
	2011	2009	2006	2000	1997	1991	1988	1982	1979	1976	1973
Methods:										
First-in, first-out (FIFO)	312	325	385	386	415	421	396	373	390	389	394
Last-in, first-out (LIFO)	163	176	228	283	326	361	379	407	374	331	150
Average cost	133	147	159	180	188	200	213	238	241	232	235
Other	72	18	30	38	32	50	50	53	56	50	57
	680	666	802	887	961	1,032	1,038	1,071	1,061	1,002	836
Use of LIFO:										
All inventories	4	4	11	23	17	23	20	28	20	9	8
50% or more inventories	66	82	109	148	170	186	207	206	194	167	49
Less than 50% of inventories	71	78	88	82	99	95	90	88	94	84	78
Not determinable	22	12	20	30	40	57	62	85	66	71	25

Source: *Accounting Trends and Techniques* (New York: AICPA, 1974, 1977, 1980, 1983, 1986, 1989, 1992, 1995, 1998, 2001, 2004, 2007, 2010, and 2012).

---

[11] Data were obtained from a survey of selected industrial, merchandising, technology, and service companies. For years prior to 2009, 600 companies were surveyed. Subsequent to 2009, 500 companies were surveyed.

and 1982 is clearly indicated, although the trend has reversed considerably with the lower inflation in the economy since then. Note that the number of responses exceeded the number of companies surveyed because many companies used more than one inventory method, as indicated by the categories listed in the second section.

LIFO Valuation Allowance (LIFO Reserve)

As noted earlier, a company that uses LIFO for external financial and reporting purposes could report a value for inventory that is not a faithful representation of the current cost of replacing the inventory. Because the use of LIFO reduces the comparability between companies using LIFO and those using FIFO (which is an approximation of current cost), the SEC requires a company that uses LIFO to disclose the amount that the LIFO valuation of inventory differs from the valuation of inventory under FIFO. This difference has a variety of names including valuation allowance or **LIFO reserve**. Because the change in the LIFO reserve during a period represents the difference between LIFO cost of goods sold and cost of goods sold on a FIFO basis, this disclosure can be used to increase comparability by adjusting inventory, cost of goods sold, and income to a FIFO basis. These adjustments are illustrated in the following analysis. The disclosure of the LIFO reserve for **General Mills** is provided in Real Report 7.2 later in the chapter.

WHY IT MATTERS

Analysts often use financial ratios such as inventory turnover and average days in inventory to evaluate the effectiveness of a company's inventory management and control activities. It is important to realize that the accounting choice between FIFO and LIFO can have a significant impact on this evaluation because each method will produce different income statement and balance sheet amounts. Therefore, it is more useful to compare companies that make different accounting choices after first adjusting for these differences. Fortunately, the disclosure of the LIFO reserve allows the following adjustments to be made:

FIFO Inventory = LIFO Inventory + LIFO Reserve
FIFO Cost of Goods Sold = LIFO Cost of Goods Sold
− Increase (or + Decrease) in LIFO Reserve

In addition to the above adjustments, multiplying the total LIFO reserve by the income tax rate gives the cumulative savings in income tax expense since LIFO was adopted. Multiplying the LIFO reserve by the after-tax rate gives the cumulative effect on income.

Using amounts obtained from **Caterpillar**'s annual report, we show this conversion below.

(amounts in millions)	2013	2012
Inventory (as reported, LIFO)	$12,625	$15,547
Add: LIFO Reserve	+ 2,504	+2,750
Inventory (FIFO)	$15,129	$18,297
Cost of Sales (as reported)	$40,727	
Add: Decrease in LIFO Reserve	+ 246	
Cost of Sales (FIFO)	$40,973	

(continued)

Because the LIFO reserve decreased in 2013, Caterpillar reported $246 million more cost of goods sold than would have been reported under FIFO. The inventory turnover computed under LIFO and FIFO is shown below.

$$\text{LIFO Assumption:} \quad \text{Inventory Turnover} = \frac{\$40{,}727}{\frac{\$12{,}625 + \$15{,}547}{2}} = 2.89$$

$$\text{FIFO Assumption:} \quad \text{Inventory Turnover} = \frac{\$40{,}973}{\frac{\$15{,}129 + \$18{,}297}{2}} = 2.45$$

As you can see from these comparative ratios, the use of LIFO or FIFO can produce significant variations. Therefore, any differences should be adjusted so that valid comparisons can be made.

Interim Statements Using LIFO

If a company uses LIFO for annual reporting purposes, it must also use LIFO for interim (i.e., quarterly) reporting purposes. If a company using LIFO experiences a LIFO liquidation at an interim date and forecasts indicate that the liquidation will still exist at the end of the year, the company should include the effect of the LIFO liquidation in its interim financial statements. However, if a company forecasts that the inventory quantity will be replaced so that there is no LIFO liquidation by the end of the annual period, GAAP states that the company should not include the LIFO liquidation in its inventory valuation, and its cost of sales should include the expected cost of replacement of the liquidated LIFO inventory.[12]

Inventory Disclosure

Real Report 7.2 shows an example of **General Mills**'s inventory disclosure. Companies are required to disclose the inventory method, or methods, used. General Mills uses LIFO, shows a breakdown of the components of inventory in the notes to the financial statements, and discloses a LIFO reserve. In addition, LIFO is used for inventories in the United States and FIFO elsewhere.

REAL REPORT 7.2 — EXAMPLE OF DISCLOSURE OF INVENTORY VALUES AND METHODS

General Mills, Inc.
Notes to Consolidated Financial Statements (in part)

Note 2: Summary of Significant Accounting Policies (in part)

INVENTORIES All inventories in the United States other than grain are valued at the lower of cost, using the last-in, first-out (LIFO) method, or market. Grain inventories and all related cash contracts and derivatives are valued at market with all net changes in value recorded in earnings currently. Inventories outside of the United States are valued at the lower of cost, using the first-in, first-out (FIFO) method, or market.

(continued)

---

[12] FASB ASC 270-10-45: Interim Reporting: Overall: Other Presentation Matters.

Note 17: Supplemental Information (in part)		
In Millions	May 26, 2013	May 27, 2012
Inventories:		
Raw materials and packaging	$ 403.0	$ 334.4
Finished goods	1,228.7	1,211.8
Grain	135.6	155.3
Excess of FIFO or weighted-average cost over LIFO cost	(221.8)	(222.7)
Total	$1,545.5	$1,478.8

Inventories of $897.8 million as of May 26, 2013, and $930.2 million as of May 27, 2012, were valued at LIFO. During fiscal 2013 and fiscal 2012, LIFO inventory layers were reduced. Results of operations were not materially affected by these liquidations of LIFO inventory.

Suggested answers to these questions are found at the end of the chapter.

Questions:

1. Why does General Mills use LIFO in the United States and FIFO elsewhere?
2. If the inventory costs of General Mills are rising throughout the world, what is the effect on the financial statements of its use of LIFO?
3. While the results were not material, what is the effect of the LIFO liquidation on General Mills's cost of goods sold and income, assuming rising inventory costs?

GOT IT?

7-21 What is a *LIFO reserve*?

7-22 What is the impact of LIFO inventory liquidation on a company's interim financial statements?

REVIEW CENTER

At the beginning of the chapter, we discussed how the effective management and control of inventory is critical to the profitability and performance of many companies. We also identified several objectives that would highlight accounting's role in this process. These objectives are listed below and followed by a brief summary of the key points.

LEARNING OBJECTIVE 7.1
Describe the different classifications of inventory and the flow of costs.

KEY TAKEAWAYS

- Common inventory classifications used by companies range from a single inventory account (merchandise inventory) for merchandisers and three inventory accounts (raw materials inventory, work-in-process inventory, and finished goods inventory) for manufacturers.
- The relationship between cost of goods sold and inventory is given by the cost of goods sold model:
  - For Merchandisers: Beginning Inventory + Purchases (net) − Ending Inventory = Cost of Goods Sold.
  - For Manufacturers: Beginning Finished Goods Inventory + Cost of Goods Manufactured − Ending Finished Goods Inventory = Cost of Goods Sold.

KEY TERMS

cost of goods available for sale, p. 7-4
finished goods inventory, p. 7-3
goods-in-process inventory, p. 7-3
inventories, p. 7-2

merchandise inventory, p. 7-3
raw materials inventory, p. 7-3
work-in-process inventory, p. 7-3

KEY CALCULATIONS

Merchandiser:

$$\text{Beginning Inventory} + \text{Purchases (net)} = \text{Cost of Goods Available for Sale} - \text{Ending Inventory} = \text{Cost of Goods Sold}$$

Manufacturer:

$$\text{Beginning Finished Goods Inventory} + \text{Cost of Goods Manufactured} = \text{Cost of Goods Available for Sale} - \text{Ending Finished Goods Inventory} = \text{Cost of Goods Sold}$$

KEY TAKEAWAYS

LEARNING OBJECTIVE 7.2
Explain the uses of the perpetual and periodic inventory systems.

- Companies account for inventory quantities and costs using either the perpetual or the periodic inventory system.
- A perpetual inventory system maintains a continuous record of inventory quantities and cost of goods sold, which makes inventory management and control easier.
- A periodic inventory system relies on physical counts of inventory to determine inventory quantities and cost of goods sold, making it relatively inexpensive to operate.

KEY TERMS

periodic inventory system, p. 7-6

perpetual inventory system, p. 7-6

KEY TAKEAWAYS

LEARNING OBJECTIVE 7.3
Identify the items to be included in inventory.

- Economic control is the key factor that a company should consider in determining whether an item is a part of inventory (substance over form).
- When goods are in transit at the end of a period, the shipping terms (FOB shipping point and FOB destination) determine whether the seller or the buyer includes them in inventory.
- In a consignment arrangement, the consignor retains economic control over the goods and includes them in its inventory until they are sold by the consignee.
- The substance of a product financing arrangement is that one company (the seller) is borrowing cash from a financing company using inventory as collateral. Therefore, the inventory remains on the seller's balance sheet at cost.
- In a bill and hold sale, the goods remain in the inventory of the seller until delivery has occurred.
- A company does not record an increase in inventory or a purchase obligation when entering into a purchase commitment.

KEY TERMS

bill and hold sale, p. 7-11
consignee, p. 7-9
consignment, p. 7-9
consignor, p. 7-9

FOB destination, p. 7-9
FOB (free-on-board) shipping point, p. 7-9
product financing arrangements, p. 7-9
purchase obligation, p. 7-11

LEARNING OBJECTIVE 7.4

Determine the expenditures included in the cost of inventory.

KEY TAKEAWAYS

- Inventory costs should include all costs (e.g., purchase price, freight-in, insurance, taxes) that are directly or indirectly incurred in bringing an item to its existing condition and location for sale.
- Purchase discounts may be recorded under the gross price or the net price method.
    - Under the gross price method, a company records the purchase at the gross price and records the amount of the discount only if the discount is taken.
    - Under the net price method, a company records the purchase at its net price and records the amount of the discount only if the discount is not taken.

KEY TERMS

gross price method, p. 7-13	purchase discounts, p. 7-13
net price method, p. 7-13	product costs, p. 7-12
period costs, p. 7-13	

LEARNING OBJECTIVE 7.5

Compute ending inventory and cost of goods sold under specific identification, FIFO, average cost, and LIFO.

KEY TAKEAWAYS

- Because a company carries inventory and the cost of the inventory changes during a period, it uses a cost flow assumption to assign costs to the physical units in ending inventory and cost of goods sold.
- Under the specific identification cost flow assumption, a company identifies the actual cost of each unit in ending inventory and cost of goods sold. This method is appropriate for perpetual inventory systems in which each item can be separately tracked and measured.
- Under the FIFO cost flow assumption, a company includes the earliest costs incurred in the cost of goods sold and includes the most recent costs in the ending inventory.
- Under the LIFO cost flow assumption, a company includes the most recent costs incurred in the cost of goods sold and includes the earliest costs (including costs incurred in previous periods) in the ending inventory.
- Under the average cost flow assumption, a company considers all the costs and units to be combined so that no individual units or costs can be identified. If the company computes an average cost for the period, this method is referred to as the weighted average method. If the company computes an average cost after each acquisition of inventory, the method is referred to as the moving average method.

KEY TERMS

average cost, p. 7-18	moving average method, p. 7-18
cost flow assumption, p. 7-14	specific identification, p. 7-15
first-in, first-out (FIFO), p. 7-16	weighted average method, p. 7-18
last-in, first-out (LIFO), p. 7-19	

LEARNING OBJECTIVE 7.6

Explain the consequences that result from the use of alternative inventory cost flow assumptions.

KEY TAKEAWAYS

- The FIFO cost flow assumption is generally viewed as providing a more relevant inventory valuation and a better approximation of the physical flow of inventory compared to LIFO.
- The LIFO cost flow assumption is generally viewed as providing both a more relevant measure of income when costs are rising, as well as tax benefits. However, it is more susceptible to income distortions because of inventory liquidations or management of inventory quantities.
- The average cost flow assumption produces income measures and inventory valuations that fall between the FIFO and LIFO values.

KEY TERMS

LIFO conformity rule, p. 7-23	LIFO liquidation profit, p. 7-24

KEY TAKEAWAYS

- The dollar-value LIFO method overcomes practical difficulties with applying LIFO through the use of inventory pools and cost indexes.
- Inventory is often included in one or more inventory pools to keep the advantages of LIFO when there are fluctuations in the physical quantities of similar products and/or technological change.
- The general principle of dollar-value LIFO is that a company uses a cost index to convert the current cost of its inventory to a base-year cost, thereby eliminating any cost changes of the inventory and isolating quantity increases (decreases) from cost increases (decreases). The increases (decreases) are then converted to current-year costs to determine the value of ending inventory reported in the financial statements.

LEARNING OBJECTIVE 7.7
Understand and apply dollar-value LIFO.

KEY TERMS

cost index, p. 7-30
double-extension method, p. 7-30
link-chain method, p. 7-31

KEY TAKEAWAYS

- Companies must disclose the inventory method or methods used.
- A company that uses LIFO is required to report a LIFO valuation adjustment (or LIFO reserve), which is the difference in the LIFO inventory valuation and the inventory valuation reported using FIFO.
- If a company uses LIFO for annual reporting purposes, it must also use LIFO for interim reporting.
- A company that has a LIFO liquidation in an interim reporting period but expects to replace the inventory by year-end should remove the impact of the liquidation from its interim financial statements.

LEARNING OBJECTIVE 7.8
Understand inventory disclosures.

KEY TERM

LIFO reserve, p. 7-34

ANSWERS TO REAL REPORT QUESTIONS

Real Report 7.1 Answers Panera Bread—Disclosure of Inventory Values and Methods

1. Panera Bread primarily uses a first-in, first-out (FIFO) cost flow assumption. Because this method assumes that the first costs incurred are the first costs transferred to costs of goods sold, this cost flow assumption (assuming a period of rising prices) produces the highest cost of ending inventory and the lowest cost of goods sold relative to the other cost flow assumptions.
2. As would be expected with a company whose menu promises fresh ingredients, the majority of Panera Bread's inventory is located at it's bakery-cafe operations.

Real Report 7.2 Answers General Mills—Example of Disclosure of Inventory Values and Methods

1. LIFO is generally not allowed by IFRS or for tax purposes in foreign countries. With this tax advantage eliminated and the fact that LIFO is typically more complex and costly to implement, the benefits of FIFO (higher income and balance sheet amounts in periods of rising prices) most likely outweigh any remaining benefits of using LIFO.
2. Given rising inventory costs, General Mills's decision to use LIFO will result in lower inventory values, earnings, and taxes (assuming the use of LIFO for income tax purposes) relative to FIFO.

MULTIPLE-CHOICE (AICPA ADAPTED)

Select the best answer for each of the following.

M7-1
LO 7.3
Goods on consignment should be included in the inventory of:

a. the consignor but not the consignee
b. both the consignor and the consignee
c. the consignee but not the consignor
d. neither the consignor nor the consignee

M7-2
LO 7.3
The following items were included in Venicio Corporation's inventory account on December 31, 2016:

Merchandise out on consignment, at
  sales price, including 40% markup on
  selling price $14,000
Goods purchased, in transit, shipped
  FOB shipping point   12,000
Goods held on consignment by Venicio   9,000

What amount should Venicio report as inventory at December 31, 2016?

a. $21,000   c. $26,000
b. $20,400   d. $35,000

M7-3
LO 7.3
During 2016, R Corp., a manufacturer of chocolate candies, contracted to purchase 100,000 pounds of cocoa beans at $1.00 per pound, delivery to be made in the spring of 2017. Because a record harvest is predicted for 2017, the price per pound for cocoa beans had fallen to $0.80 by December 31, 2016.

Of the following journal entries, the one that would properly reflect in 2016 the effect of the commitment of R Corp. to purchase the 100,000 pounds of cocoa is:

	Debit	Credit
a. Inventory	100,000	
Accounts Payable		100,000
b. Inventory	80,000	
Loss on Purchase Commitments	20,000	
Accounts Payable		100,000
c. Loss on Purchase Commitments	20,000	
Accrued Loss on		
Purchase Commitments		20,000
d. No entry would be necessary in 2016.		

M7-4
LO 7.4
Dixon Menswear Shop purchased shirts from Colt Company on May 28, 2016, and received an invoice with a list price amount of $5,000 and payment terms of 2/10, n/30. Dixon uses the net method to record purchases. Dixon should record purchases of:

a. $4,000   c. $5,000
b. $4,900   d. $5,100

M7-5
LO 7.5
The moving average inventory cost flow assumption is applicable to which of the following inventory systems?

	Periodic	Perpetual
a.	Yes	Yes
b.	Yes	No
c.	No	No
d.	No	Yes

Questions **M7-6** and **M7-7** are based on the following data: City Stationers Inc. had 200 calculators on hand on January 1, 2016, costing $18 each. Purchases and sales of calculators during the month of January were as follows:

Date	Purchases	Sales
Jan. 12		150 @ $28
15	100 @ $20	
27	100 @ $22	
30		100 @ $32

City uses a periodic inventory system. According to a physical count, 150 calculators were on hand at January 31, 2016.

M7-6
LO 7.5
The cost of the inventory on January 31, 2016, under the FIFO method is:

a. $400   c. $3,100
b. $2,700   d. $3,200

M7-7
LO 7.5
The cost of the inventory on January 31, 2016, under the LIFO method is:

a. $400   c. $3,100
b. $2,700   d. $3,200

M7-8
LO 7.5
Assuming no beginning inventory, what can be said about the trend of inventory prices if cost of goods sold computed when inventory is valued using the FIFO method exceeds cost of goods sold when inventory is valued using the LIFO method?

a. Prices decreased.
b. Prices remained unchanged.
c. Prices increased.
d. Price trend cannot be determined from information given.

M7-9
LO 7.7
On December 31, 2015, Kern Company adopted the dollar-value LIFO inventory method. All of Kern's inventories constitute a single pool. The inventory on December 31, 2015, using the dollar-value LIFO inventory method was $600,000. Inventory data for 2016 are as follows:

Dec. 31, 2016 inventory at year-end prices	$780,000
Relevant cost index at year-end (base year 2015)	120

Under the dollar-value LIFO inventory method, Kern's inventory method, Kern's inventory on December 31, 2016, would be:

a. $650,000 c. $660,000
b. $655,000 d. $720,000

M7-10
LO 7.7
When the double-extension approach to the dollar-value LIFO inventory cost flow method is used, the inventory layer added in the current year is multiplied by an index number. How would the following be used in the calculation of this index number?

	Ending Inventory at Current-Year Cost	Ending Inventory at Base-Year Cost
a.	Numerator	Denominator
b.	Numerator	Not Used
c.	Denominator	Numerator
d.	Not Used	Denominator

REVIEW EXERCISES

RE7-1
LO 7.1
On December 31, Pitts Manufacturing Company reports the following assets:

Cash	$ 50,000	Raw materials	$ 74,000
Work in process	176,000	Marketable securities	25,000
Equipment	950,000	Finished goods	150,000
Building	1,200,000	Goodwill	50,000

What is the total amount of Pitts' inventory at year-end?

RE7-2
LO 7.1
On January 1, Pope Enterprises' inventory was $625,000. Pope made $950,000 of net purchases during the year. On its year-end income statement, Pope reported cost of goods sold of $1,025,000. Calculate Pope's December 31 ending inventory.

RE7-3
LO 7.1
Reid & Company uses the periodic inventory system. On January 1, it had an inventory balance of $250,000. During the year, it made $613,000 of net purchases. At the end of the year, a physical inventory showed it had ending inventory of $140,000. Calculate Reid & Company's cost of goods sold for the year.

RE7-4
LO 7.2
Billings Company uses a periodic inventory system. During the year, it made purchases of $402,000. Freight-In related to these purchases was $21,000. Billings was allowed $8,000 in purchase discounts and returned $14,000 of goods to its supplier. Calculate Billings' net purchases.

RE7-5
LO 7.3
Dani Corporation signed a binding commitment on December 2 to purchase inventory at a cost of $300,000 on January 2. By December 31, the market price (replacement cost) of the inventory had declined to $280,000. Prepare Dani's journal entries at year-end and at the date of purchase.

RE7-6
LO 7.4
Stevens Company uses a perpetual inventory system. On July 10, Stevens purchases $50,000 of inventory on credit with payment terms of 2/10, net 30. Using the gross price method, prepare journal entries to record Stevens's purchases on July 10 and the subsequent payment on July 18.

RE7-7
LO 7.4
Using the information in **RE7-6**, prepare journal entries to record Stevens Company's purchases on July 10 and the subsequent payment on August 8.

RE7-8
LO 7.4
Johnson Company uses a perpetual inventory system. On October 23, Johnson purchased $100,000 of inventory on credit with payment terms of 1/15, net 45. Using the net price method, prepare journal entries to record Johnson's purchases on October 23 and the subsequent payment on October 31.

RE7-9 Using the information from **RE7-8**, prepare journal entries to record Johnson's purchase on October 23 and the subsequent payment on November 30.
LO 7.4

RE7-10 Jessie Stores uses the periodic system of calculating inventory. The following information is available for December of the current year when Jessie sold 500 units of inventory.
LO 7.5

	Units	Cost/Unit	Total Cost
Inventory, Dec. 1	300	250	$ 75,000
Purchases, Dec. 8	600	275	165,000
	900		$240,000

Using the FIFO method, calculate Jessie's inventory on December 31 and its cost of goods sold for December.

RE7-11 Using the information from **RE7-10**, calculate Jessie Stores's inventory on December 31 and its cost of goods sold for December using the LIFO method.
LO 7.5

RE7-12 Carla Company uses the perpetual inventory system. The following information is available for January of the current year when Carla sold 1,600 units of inventory on January 14.
LO 7.5

	Units	Cost/Unit	Total Cost
Inventory, Jan. 1	1,500	$0.25	$375
Purchases, Jan. 13	1,100	0.27	297
	2,600		$672

Using the FIFO method, calculate Carla's cost of goods sold for January and its January 31 inventory.

RE7-13 Using the information from **RE7-12**, calculate Carla Company's cost of goods sold for January and its January 31 inventory using the LIFO method.
LO 7.5

RE7-14 On January 1 of Year 1, Dorso Company adopted the dollar-value LIFO method of inventory costing. Dorso's December 31 ending inventory records are as follows:
LO 7.7

Year 1: Current cost, $20,000; Index, 100
Year 2: Current cost, $33,600; Index, 120

Using the dollar-value LIFO method, compute Dorso's December 31 ending inventory for Year 2.

RE7-15 An evaluation of Bryce's Bookstore's inventory was performed in Year 2. It produced the following results:
LO 7.7

Sample of ending inventory at current-year costs = $75,000
Sample of ending inventory at previous-year costs = $69,000

The cost index in Year 1 was 105. Using the link-chain method, compute Bryce's cost index for Year 2.

EXERCISES

E7-1 **Inventory Accounts for a Manufacturing Company** Fujita Company produces a single product. Costs accumulated at the end of the period are as follows:
LO 7.1

SHOW ME HOW

Raw material purchases	$54,000	Production supervisor's salary	$ 20,000
Depreciation on manufacturing equipment	3,000	Shipping costs on units sold	43,500
Sales commissions	20,000	Materials used in production	83,500
Factory labor	36,000	Goods completed	115,000
Property tax on manufacturing equipment	3,500	Cost of units sold	150,000

Assume the beginning raw materials inventory was $62,800, the beginning finished goods inventory was $118,400, and there was no beginning work-in-process inventory.

Required:
Compute the closing account balances of each of the three inventory accounts: Raw Materials, Work in Process, and Finished Goods.

E7-2
LO 7.1

Applying the Cost of Goods Sold Model The following amounts were obtained from the accounting records of Enderle Company:

	2016	2017	2018
Beginning inventory	$38,900	(b)	(d)
Net purchases	(a)	$71,200	$91,820
Ending inventory	42,100	(c)	42,350
Cost of goods sold	83,500	90,800	(e)

Required:
Next Level Compute the missing amounts.

E7-3
LO 7.3

Perpetual versus Periodic Inventory Systems Graham Company is trying to select an inventory system. Below are several statements that pertain to inventory systems.
1. Cost of goods sold is only determined at the end of the period after a physical count of inventory.
2. A physical count of inventory is performed.
3. Purchases of inventory are recorded in a purchases account.
4. Cost of goods sold is determined continually during the period as sales are made.
5. Greater control over inventory is possible.
6. This inventory system is relatively inexpensive to operate.

Required:
Select the inventory system, perpetual or periodic, that is best represented by each statement. If the statement applies to both systems, select "both."

E7-4
LO 7.3

Determining Net Purchases The following amounts were obtained from the accounting records of Newton Company, Washington Inc., and Adams Company:

SHOW ME HOW

	Newton	Washington	Adams
Purchases	$67,200	$102,000	(c)
Freight-In	2,300	(b)	$ 3,475
Purchase discounts	(4,110)	(9,700)	(5,000)
Purchase returns and allowances	(3,180)	(8,250)	(1,210)
Net purchases	(a)	92,600	45,500

Required:
Next Level Compute the missing amounts.

E7-5
LO 7.3

Goods in Transit Gravais Company made two purchases on December 29, 2016. One purchase for $3,000 was shipped FOB destination, and the second for $4,000 was shipped FOB shipping point. Neither purchase had been received nor paid for on December 31, 2016.

Required:
Which of these purchases, if either, does Gravais include in inventory on December 31, 2016? What is the cost?

E7-6
LO 7.3

Items Included in Inventory The following are several items that Golosow Company's controller has questioned regarding their inclusion in inventory:
1. An invoice has been received for goods ordered. The goods were shipped FOB destination but have not been received.
2. Purchases have been ordered and received (shipping terms were FOB destination), but no invoice has arrived.
3. Product was shipped to a customer today, FOB destination, and the invoice mailed.
4. Purchases are in the receiving department, but they are damaged and will be returned.
5. Product is in the shipping department, and the invoice has not been mailed to the customer. Shipping terms are FOB shipping point.
6. Golosow has inventory in its possession from Tate Company. The inventory is to be sold by Golosow under a consignment arrangement with Tate.

Required:
For each of the preceding items, indicate whether Golosow should include them in inventory. Justify your answer.

E7-7
LO 7.3

Loss on Purchase Commitment During 2016, Boge Corporation signed a noncancelable contract to purchase 10,000 bushels of soybeans at $5 per bushel with delivery to be made in 2017. On December 31, 2016, the price of soybeans had fallen to $4.50 per bushel. On May 1, 2017, Boge takes delivery of the soybeans when the price is $4.75 per bushel.

Required:
Prepare the journal entries required on December 31, 2016, and May 1, 2017.

E7-8
LO 7.4

Discounts Hirsch Company buys inventory for $20,000 on terms of 2/10, n/30. It pays within the discount period.

Required:
1. Prepare the journal entries to record the purchase and the payment under both the (a) gross price and (b) net price methods. Assume that Hirsch uses a periodic inventory system.
2. Prepare the journal entries to record the purchase and payment under both the (a) gross price and the (b) net price methods. Assume that Hirsch uses a perpetual inventory system.

E7-9
LO 7.4

Discounts Nelson Company bought inventory for $50,000 on terms of 2/15, n/60. It pays for the first $37,500 of inventory purchased within the discount period and pays for the remaining $12,500 two months later.

Required:
1. Prepare the journal entries to record the purchase and the payment under both the (a) gross price and (b) net price methods. Assume that Nelson uses the periodic inventory system.
2. **Next Level** Which of the two methods yields a conceptually preferable valuation of inventory?

E7-10
LO 7.5

Alternative Inventory Methods Nevens Company uses a periodic inventory system. During November, the following transactions occurred:

Date		Transaction	Units	Cost/Unit
November	1	Balance	500	$3.50
	8	Sale	350	
	13	Purchase	300	4.00
	21	Purchase	200	5.00
	28	Sale	150	

Required:
1. Compute the cost of goods sold for November and the inventory at the end of November for each of the following cost flow assumptions:
   a. FIFO
   b. LIFO
   c. Average cost
2. **Next Level** What can you conclude about the effects of the inventory cost flow assumptions on the financial statements?

E7-11
LO 7.5

Alternative Inventory Methods Park Company's perpetual inventory records indicate the following transactions in the month of June:

	Units	Cost/Unit
Inventory, June 1	200	$3.20
Purchases:		
June 3	200	3.50
June 17	250	3.60
June 24	300	3.65
Sales:		
June 6	300	
June 21	200	
June 27	150	

Required:
1. Compute the cost of goods sold for June and the inventory at the end of June using each of the following cost flow assumptions:
   a. FIFO
   b. LIFO
   c. Average cost (Round unit costs to 3 decimal places and other amounts to the nearest dollar.)
2. **Next Level** Why are the cost of goods sold and ending inventory amounts different for each of the three methods? What do these amounts tell us about the purchase price of inventory during the year?
3. **Next Level** Which method produces the most realistic amount for net income? For inventory? Explain your answer.
4. **Next Level** If Park uses IFRS, which of the previous alternatives would be acceptable and why?

E7-12 **Alternative Inventory Methods** Frate Company was formed on December 1, 2015, and uses the periodic inventory system. The following information is available from Frate's inventory records for Product Ply:

LO 7.5

AICPA Adapted

	Units	Unit Cost
January 1, 2016 (beginning inventory)	800	$ 9.00
Purchases:		
January 6, 2016	1,500	10.00
January 25, 2016	1,200	10.50
February 17, 2016	600	11.00
March 27, 2016	900	11.50

A physical inventory on March 31, 2016, shows 1,600 units on hand.

Required:
Prepare schedules to compute the ending inventory at March 31, 2016, under each of the following inventory methods:
1. FIFO
2. LIFO
3. Weighted average

Show supporting computations in good form.

E7-13 **LIFO, Perpetual and Periodic** Riedel Company's inventory records showed the following transactions for the fiscal period ended June 30:

LO 7.5
LO 7.6

SHOW ME HOW

	Units	Cost/Unit
June 1 Inventory	700	$6.20
June 3 Purchase	400	6.40
June 15 Sales @ $12.00	300	
June 22 Sales @ $12.50	600	
June 30 Purchase	600	6.70

Required:
1. Compute the ending inventory and the cost of goods sold under the LIFO cost flow assumption assuming both a perpetual and a periodic inventory system.
2. **Next Level** Explain the difference in the final inventory valuations.

E7-14 **Dollar-Value LIFO** A company adopted the LIFO method when its inventory was $1,800. One year later its ending inventory was $2,100, and costs had increased 5% during the year.

LO 7.7

Required:
What is the ending inventory using dollar-value LIFO? Round to the nearest dollar.

E7-15 **Dollar-Value LIFO** On January 1, 2015, Sato Company adopted the dollar-value LIFO method of inventory costing. Sato's ending inventory records appear as follows:

LO 7.7

(continued)

Year	Current Cost	Index
2015	$40,000	100
2016	56,100	120
2017	58,500	130
2018	70,000	140

Required:
Compute the ending inventory for the years 2015, 2016, 2017, and 2018, using the dollar-value LIFO method. Round to the nearest dollar.

E7-16 **Dollar-Value LIFO** Belstock Company manufactures one product. On December 31, 2015, Belstock adopted the dollar-value LIFO inventory method. The inventory on that date using the dollar-value LIFO inventory method was $200,000. Inventory data for succeeding years are as follows:

LO 7.7
AICPA Adapted

Year	Inventory at Respective Year-End Prices	Price Index (Base Year 2015)
2016	$231,000	1.05
2017	299,000	1.15
2018	300,000	1.20

Required:
Compute the ending inventory using the dollar-value LIFO method for 2016, 2017, and 2018.

E7-17 **Dollar-Value LIFO** Acute Company manufactures a single product. On December 31, 2015, Acute adopted the dollar-value LIFO inventory method. It computes the inventory on that date using the dollar-value LIFO inventory method as $300,000. Inventory data for succeeding years are as follows:

LO 7.7
AICPA Adapted

Year Ended December 31,	Inventory at Respective Year-End Prices	Relevant Price Index (Base Year 2015)
2016	$363,000	1.10
2017	420,000	1.20
2018	430,000	1.25

Required:
Compute the inventory amounts at December 31, 2016, 2017, and 2018 using the dollar-value LIFO inventory method for each year.

E7-18 **Inventory Pools** Stone Shoe Company adopted dollar-value LIFO on January 1, 2016. The company produces four products and uses a single inventory pool. The company's beginning inventory consists of the following:

LO 7.7

Type	Quantity	Cost per Unit	Total Cost
Running	80,000	$16	$1,280,000
Tennis	30,000	15	450,000
Basketball	60,000	14	840,000
Soccer	40,000	17	680,000
	210,000		$3,250,000

During 2016, the company has the following purchases and sales:

Type	Quantity Purchased	Cost per Unit	Quantity Sold	Selling Price per Unit
Running	150,000	$19	140,000	$40
Tennis	130,000	16	100,000	38
Basketball	100,000	14	90,000	37
Soccer	120,000	18	140,000	42
	500,000		470,000	

Required:
1. Compute the dollar-value LIFO cost of the ending inventory. Round the cost index to 4 decimal places and all other amounts to the nearest dollar.
2. **Next Level** By how much would the company's gross profit differ if it had used four pools instead of a single pool?

E7-19 **FIFO Used Internally, LIFO Used Externally** Grimstad Company uses FIFO for internal reporting purposes
LO 7.8 and LIFO for financial reporting and income tax purposes. At the end of 2016, the following information was obtained from the inventory records:

	2015	2016
Ending inventory, FIFO	$100,000	$140,000
Ending inventory, LIFO	80,000	115,000

Required:
1. Prepare the necessary adjusting journal entry assuming that Grimstad converts the accounts to LIFO at the end of 2016.
2. Indicate how Grimstad would disclose the inventory value on its comparative balance sheets prepared at the end of 2016.
3. **Next Level** By how much would Grimstad's cost of goods sold differ in 2016 if it used FIFO for external reporting?

E7-20 **LIFO and Interim Financial Reports** Assume prices were stable during the period. The following values were
LO 7.8 obtained from the inventory records of Harris Company which has a fiscal year ending on December 31:

Inventory, January 1, 2016, LIFO	$80,000
Inventory, March 31, 2016, LIFO	70,000

SHOW ME HOW

Required:
1. Under what conditions is Harris's inventory liquidation not reflected in its first-quarter interim financial statements?
2. Assuming that the liquidation is not to be reflected, what adjusting entry would Harris make and how would you determine the amount?

PROBLEMS

P7-1 **Applying the Cost of Goods Sold Model** The following amounts were obtained from Stanwick Company's
LO 7.1 accounting records.

		2016		2017
Net sales		$381,220		$423,150
Cost of goods sold:				
Beginning inventory	$36,800		(d)	
Purchases	(a)		296,700	
Goods available for sale	(b)		(e)	
Ending inventory	41,870		(f)	
Cost of goods sold		(c)		295,200
Gross margin		$112,450		(g)

Required:
Next Level Compute the missing amounts.

P7-2
LO 7.3
Items to Be Included in Inventory As the auditor of Hayes Company for the year ended December 31, 2016, you found the following transactions occurred near its closing date:
1. Merchandise received on January 8, 2017, and costing $800 was recorded as inventory on January 8, 2017. An invoice on hand showed the shipment was made FOB shipping point on December 31, 2016. Because the merchandise was not on hand at December 31, 2016, it was not included in the 2016 inventory balance.
2. A product costing $600 was in Hayes's shipping room when the physical inventory was taken. It was not included in the inventory because it was marked "Hold for customer's shipping instructions." Investigation revealed that the customer's order was dated December 18, 2016 but that the case was shipped and the customer billed on January 10, 2017.
3. A machine, made to order for a customer, was finished on December 31, 2016, The customer had inspected it and was satisfied with it. The customer was billed in full for $2,000 on that date. The machine was excluded from inventory, although it was shipped on January 2, 2017.
4. Merchandise costing $800 was received on December 27, 2016, but a purchase was not recorded. The goods were "on consignment from Milliken Company."
5. Merchandise costing $4,000 was received on January 2, 2017, and the related purchase invoice was recorded on January 5, 2017. The invoice showed that the shipment was made on December 29, 2016, FOB destination.

Required:
For each situation, state whether Hayes should include the merchandise in its inventory. Give your reason for the decision on each item.

P7-3
LO 7.3
Valuation of Inventory The inventory on hand at the end of 2016 for Reddall Company is valued at a cost of $94,550. The following items were not included in this inventory:
1. Purchased goods in transit, under terms FOB shipping point, invoice price $4,100, freight costs $220.
2. Goods out on consignment to Marlman Company, sales price $4,200, shipping costs of $250.
3. Goods sold to Grina Co. under terms FOB destination, invoiced for $1,900 which included $178 freight charges to deliver the goods. Goods are in transit.
4. Goods held on consignment by Reddall at a sales price of $2,700 which included sales commission of 20% of sales price.
5. Purchased goods in transit, shipped FOB destination, invoice price $2,100 which included freight charges of $190.

Required:
Determine the cost of the ending inventory that Reddall should report on its December 31, 2016, balance sheet, assuming that its selling price is 140% of the cost of the inventory.

P7-4
LO 7.4
Discounts On April 11, Edwards Construction Company purchased inventory for $30,000 on terms of 2/10, n/30. It pays the account balance on April 21. Edwards uses a periodic inventory system.

Required:
1. Prepare the journal entries to record the purchase and payment using (a) gross price and (b) net price.
2. If the company sold half the inventory during April for $20,000, how much income would it recognize under each method?
3. Assume that the invoice was misfiled and, as a result, the company did not pay until April 30. Prepare the journal entries to record the purchase and payment under each of the methods.
4. If the company sold half the inventory during April for $20,000, how much income would it recognize under each method?
5. **Next Level** Why was there a difference in income for the two methods as reported in Requirement 4?

P7-5
LO 7.5
Cost of Sales As an accountant for Lee Company, your supervisor gave you the following calculations of the gross profit for the first quarter:

Alternative	Sales ($50 per unit)	Cost of Goods Sold	Gross Profit
A	$500,000	$200,000	$300,000
B	500,000	228,000	272,000
C	500,000	213,333	286,667

The three alternative cost flow assumptions are FIFO, average, and LIFO (the alternatives are not necessarily presented in this sequence). Lee uses the periodic inventory system. The computation of the cost of goods sold under each alternative is based on the following data:

	Units	Cost/Unit
Inventory, January 1	12,000	$20
Purchase, January 10	4,000	21
Purchase, February 15	6,000	22
Purchase, March 10	8,000	23

Required:
Prepare schedules computing the ending inventory (in units and dollars) and proving the cost of goods sold shown here under each of the three alternatives.

P7-6 **Alternative Inventory Methods** Garrett Company has the following transactions during the months of April and May:
LO 7.5

Date	Transaction	Units	Cost/Unit
April 1	Balance	400	
17	Purchase	200	$5.50
25	Sale	150	
28	Purchase	100	5.75
May 5	Purchase	250	5.50
18	Sale	300	
22	Sale	50	

The cost of the inventory on April 1 is $5, $4, and $2 per unit, respectively, under the FIFO, average, and LIFO cost flow assumptions.

Required:
1. Compute the inventories at the end of each month and the cost of goods sold for each month for the following alternatives:
   a. FIFO periodic
   b. FIFO perpetual
   c. LIFO periodic
   d. LIFO perpetual
   e. Weighted average (Round unit costs to 4 decimal places.)
   f. Moving average (Round unit costs to 4 decimal places.)

2. **Next Level** Reconcile and explain the difference between the LIFO periodic and the LIFO perpetual results.
3. **Next Level** If Garrett uses IFRS, which of the previous alternatives would be acceptable, and why?

P7-7 **Alternative Inventory Methods** Totman Company has the following transactions during the months of January and February:
LO 7.5

Date	Transaction	Units	Cost/Unit
January 1	Balance	200	
10	Purchase	50	$25
22	Sale	40	
28	Purchase	60	27
February 4	Purchase	40	28
14	Sale	50	
23	Sale	20	

The cost of the inventory at January 1 is $24, $23, and $15 per unit, respectively, under the FIFO, average, and LIFO cost flow assumptions.

Required:
1. Compute inventories at the end of each month and the cost of goods sold for each month for the following alternatives:
   a. FIFO periodic
   b. FIFO perpetual

(continued)

c. LIFO periodic
d. LIFO perpetual
e. Weighted average (Round unit costs to 4 decimal places.)
f. Moving average (Round unit costs to 4 decimal places.)

2. **Next Level** Reconcile and explain the difference between the LIFO periodic and the LIFO perpetual results.
3. **Next Level** If the company had purchased an additional 25 units for $30 each on February 27, compute the cost of goods sold for February under FIFO periodic and LIFO periodic.
4. **Next Level** For February, compute the company's inventory turnover under the FIFO and LIFO periodic methods. Use ending inventory instead of average inventory for convenience. Which measure would you use in your evaluation of the company? How would you convert a monthly inventory turnover into an annual measure to use for comparison with other companies? What assumptions are involved?

P7-8 **Alternative Inventory Methods** Habicht Company was formed in 2015 to produce a single product. The produc-
LO 7.5 tion and sales for the next 4 years were as follows:

	Production		Sales		
	Units	Total Costs	Units	Sales Revenue	Units in Ending Inventory
2015	100,000	$200,000	80,000	$400,000	20,000
2016	120,000	234,000	110,000	550,000	30,000
2017	130,000	247,000	150,000	750,000	10,000
2018	130,000	240,500	120,000	600,000	20,000

Required:
1. Determine the gross profit for each year under each of the following periodic inventory methods:
   a. FIFO
   b. LIFO
   c. Average cost (Round unit costs to 3 decimal places.)
2. **Next Level** Explain whether the company's return on assets (net income divided by average total assets) would be higher under FIFO or LIFO.

P7-9 **Comprehensive** The following information for 2016 is available for Marino Company:
LO 7.3 1. The beginning inventory is $100,000.
LO 7.4 2. Purchases returns of $4,000 were made.
LO 7.5 3. Purchases of $300,000 were made on terms of 2/10, n/30. Eighty percent of the discounts were taken.
4. At December 31, purchases of $20,000 were in transit, FOB destination, on terms of 2/10, n/30.
5. The company made sales of $640,000. The gross selling price per unit is twice the net cost of each unit sold.
6. Sales allowances of $6,000 were made.
7. The company uses the LIFO periodic method and the gross method for purchase discounts.

Required:
1. Compute the cost of the ending inventory before the physical inventory is taken.
2. Compute the amount of the cost of goods sold that came from the purchases of the period and the amount that came from the beginning inventory.

P7-10 **LIFO Liquidation Profit** Hammond Company adopted LIFO when it was formed on January 1, 2014. Since
LO 7.5 then, the company has had the following purchases and sales of its single inventory item:
LO 7.6

Year	Units Purchased	Cost per Unit	Units Sold	Price per Unit
2014	10,000	$5	8,000	$12
2015	12,000	6	9,000	13
2016	15,000	8	14,000	16

In December 2017, the controller realized that because of an unexpected increase in demand, the company had sold 22,000 units but had purchased only 19,000 units during the year. In 2017, each unit had been sold for $19, and each unit purchased had cost $10. The income tax rate is 30%.

Required:
1. **Next Level** If Hammond makes no additional purchases in 2017, how much LIFO liquidation profit will it report?
2. Prepare the appropriate annual report disclosures for 2017.
3. **Next Level** If Hammond purchases an additional 7,000 units in December 2017, how much income tax will the company save?
4. **Next Level** If Hammond purchases the additional 7,000 units, how much income tax has the company saved over the 4-year period by using LIFO instead of the FIFO cost flow assumption?

P7-11
LO 7.7
AICPA Adapted

LIFO and Inventory Pools On January 1, 2013, Grover Company changed its inventory cost flow method to the LIFO cost method from the FIFO cost method for its raw materials inventory. It made the change for both financial statement and income tax reporting purposes. Grover uses the multiple-pools approach under which it groups substantially identical raw materials into LIFO inventory pools. It uses weighted average costs in valuing annual incremental layers. The composition of the December 31, 2015, inventory for the Class F inventory pool is as follows:

	Units	Weighted Average Unit Cost	Total Cost
Base-year inventory—2013	9,000	$10.00	$ 90,000
Incremental layer—2014	3,000	11.00	33,000
Incremental layer—2015	2,000	12.50	25,000
Inventory, December 31, 2015	14,000		$148,000

Inventory transactions for the Class F inventory pool during 2016 were as follows:

- On March 2, 2016, 4,800 units were purchased at a unit cost of $13.50 for $64,800.
- On September 1, 2016, 7,200 units were purchased at a unit cost of $14.00 for $100,800.
- A total of 15,000 units were used for production during 2016.

The following transactions for the Class F inventory pool took place during 2017:

- On January 11, 2017, 7,500 units were purchased at a unit cost of $14.50 for $108,750.
- On May 14, 2017, 5,500 units were purchased at a unit cost of $15.50 for $85,250.
- On December 29, 2017, 7,000 units were purchased at a unit cost of $16.00 for $112,000.
- A total of 16,000 units were used for production during 2017.

Required:
1. Prepare a schedule to compute the inventory (units and dollar amounts) of the Class F inventory pool at December 31, 2016. Show supporting computations in good form.
2. Prepare a schedule to compute the cost of Class F raw materials used in production for the year ended December 31, 2016.
3. Prepare a schedule to compute the inventory (units and dollar amounts) of the Class F inventory pool at December 31, 2017. Show supporting computations in good form.

P7-12
LO 7.7

Dollar-Value LIFO Olson Company adopted the dollar-value LIFO method for inventory valuation at the beginning of 2015. The following information about the inventory at the end of each year is available from Olson's records:

Year	Current Costs	Index
2014	$50,000	100
2015	60,000	108
2016	70,000	115
2017	73,000	125
2018	78,000	135

Required:
1. Calculate the dollar-value LIFO inventory at the end of each year.
2. Prepare the appropriate disclosures for the 2018 annual report if Olson uses current cost internally and LIFO for financial reporting.

P7-13 **Dollar-Value LIFO** Kwestel Company adopted the dollar-value LIFO method for inventory valuation at the beginning of 2015. The following information about the inventory at the end of each year is available from Kwestel's records:

LO 7.7

Year	Current Cost	Index
2014	$ 8,000	100
2015	10,800	120
2016	11,500	130
2017	14,000	145
2018	10,500	125

Required:
Calculate the dollar-value LIFO inventory at the end of each year. Round to the nearest dollar.

P7-14 **Dollar-Value LIFO and Inventory Pools** Webster Company adopted dollar-value LIFO on January 1, 2016. Webster produces three products: X, Y, and Z. Webster's beginning inventory consisted of the following:

LO 7.7

Type	Quantity	Cost per Unit	Total Cost
X	30,000	$4.25	$127,500
Y	10,000	3.50	35,000
Z	25,000	2.00	50,000
	65,000		$212,500

During 2016, Webster had the following purchases and sales:

Type	Quantity Purchased	Cost Per Unit	Quantity Sold	Selling Price per Unit
X	110,000	$4.75	90,000	$10.00
Y	100,000	3.75	85,000	7.50
Z	75,000	2.10	70,000	5.00
	285,000		245,000	

Required:
1. Compute the LIFO cost of the ending inventory assuming Webster uses a single inventory pool. Round cost index to 4 decimal places.
2. Compute the LIFO cost of the ending inventory assuming Webster uses three inventory pools. Round cost indexes to 4 decimal places.

P7-15 **Dollar-Value LIFO—Comprehensive** Kelly Company adopted dollar-value LIFO on January 1, 2015, using two inventory pools each of which includes two types of inventory items. Kelly uses the double-extension method to compute the appropriate cost index. The following information about the inventory at the end of each year is available:

LO 7.7

	Pool 1			Pool 2		
Year	Number of Units	Type	Average Cost per Unit	Number of Units	Type	Average Cost per Unit
2015	20,000	A	$10	40,000	C	$5
	10,000	B	20	20,000	D	8
2016	30,000	A	11	50,000	C	7
	12,000	B	24	22,000	D	9
2017	40,000	A	12	46,000	C	6
	14,000	B	22	20,000	D	8
2018	45,000	A	12	60,000	C	7
	13,000	B	25	25,000	D	8

Required:
1. Compute the cost index for each year for each pool using a base of 100 for each index. Round each cost index to 4 decimal places.
2. Compute the dollar-value LIFO inventory at the end of each year. Round inventory to the nearest dollar.

P7-16 Double-Extension: Dollar-Value LIFO
LO 7.7
AICPA Adapted

On January 1, 2016, Lucas Distributors Inc. adopted the dollar-value LIFO inventory method for income tax and external financial reporting. However, Lucas continued to use the FIFO inventory method for internal accounting and management purposes. In applying the LIFO method, Lucas uses internal conversion cost indexes computed under the double-extension method and a multiple-pools approach under which substantially identical inventory items are grouped into LIFO inventory pools. The following data were available for Inventory Pool No. 1, which is comprised of Products A and B, for the 2 years following the adoption of LIFO:

	FIFO Basis per Records		
	Unit	Unit Cost	Total Cost
Inventory, 1/1/16			
Product A	12,000	$30	$360,000
Product B	8,000	25	200,000
			$560,000
Inventory, 12/31/16			
Product A	17,000	$35	$595,000
Product B	9,000	28	252,000
			$847,000
Inventory, 12/31/17			
Product A	13,000	$40	$520,000
Product B	10,000	32	320,000
			$840,000

Required:
1. Prepare a schedule to compute the internal conversion cost indexes for 2016 and 2017. Round indexes to 2 decimal places.
2. Prepare a schedule to compute the inventory amounts at December 31, 2016, and 2017, using the dollar-value LIFO inventory method.

P7-17 Inventory Valuation
LO 7.1
LO 7.2
LO 7.8
AICPA Adapted

You are engaged in an audit of Roche Mfg. Company for the year ended December 31, 2016. To reduce the workload at year-end, Roche took its annual physical inventory under your observation on November 30, 2016. Roche's inventory account, which includes raw materials and work in process, is on a perpetual basis, and it uses the first-in, first-out method of pricing. It has no finished goods inventory. The company's physical inventory revealed that the book inventory of $60,570 was understated by $3,000. To avoid distorting the interim financial statements, Roche decided not to adjust the book inventory until year-end except for obsolete inventory items. Your audit revealed this information about the November 30 inventory:

- Pricing tests showed that the physical inventory was overpriced by $2,200.
- Footing and extension errors resulted in a $150 understatement of the physical inventory.
- Direct labor included in the physical inventory amounted to $10,000. Overhead was included at the rate of 200% of direct labor. You determined that the amount of direct labor was correct and the overhead rate was proper.
- The physical inventory included obsolete materials recorded at $250. During December, these materials were removed from the inventory account by a charge to cost of sales.

Your audit also disclosed the following information about the December 31, 2016, inventory.

- Total debits to certain accounts during December are:

	December
Purchases	$24,700
Direct labor	12,100
Manufacturing overhead expense	25,200
Cost of sales	68,600

- The cost of sales of $68,600 included direct labor of $13,800.
- Normal scrap loss on established product lines is negligible. However, a special order started and completed during December had excessive scrap loss of $800 which was charged to Manufacturing Overhead Expense.

Required:
1. Compute the correct amount of the physical inventory at November 30, 2016.
2. Without prejudice to your solution to Requirement 1, assume that the correct amount of the inventory at November 30, 2016, was $57,700. Compute the amount of the inventory at December 31, 2016.

P7-18
LO 7.2
LO 7.3
LO 7.4
AICPA Adapted

Comprehensive Allen Company is a wholesale distributor of automotive replacement parts. Initial amounts taken from Allen's accounting records are as follows:

Inventory at December 31, 2016 (based on physical count of goods in Allen's warehouse on December 31, 2016)	$1,250,000
Sales in 2016	9,000,000

Accounts payable at December 31, 2016:

Vendor	Terms	Amount
Baker Company	2% 10 days, net 30	$ 265,000
Charlie Company	Net 30	210,000
Dolly Company	Net 30	300,000
Eager Company	Net 30	225,000
Full Company	Net 30	—
Greg Company	Net 30	—
		$1,000,000

Additional information is as follows:
1. Parts held on consignment from Charlie to Allen, the consignee, amounting to $155,000 were included in the physical count of goods in Allen's warehouse on December 31, 2016, and in accounts payable at December 31, 2016.
2. $22,000 of parts, which were purchased from Full and paid for in December 2016, were sold in the last week of 2016 and appropriately recorded as sales of $28,000. The parts were included in the physical count of goods in Allen's warehouse on December 31, 2016, because the parts were on the loading dock waiting to be picked up by customers.
3. Parts in transit to customers on December 31, 2016, shipped FOB shipping point on December 28, 2016, amounted to $34,000. The customers received the parts on January 7, 2017. Sales of $40,000 to the customers for the parts were recorded by Allen on January 3, 2017.
4. Retailers were holding $210,000 at cost ($250,000 at retail) of goods on consignment from Allen, the consignor, at their stores on December 31, 2016.
5. Goods were in transit from Greg to Allen on December 31, 2016. The cost of the goods was $25,000, and they were shipped FOB shipping point on December 29, 2016.
6. A quarterly freight bill in the amount of $2,000 specifically relating to merchandise purchases in December 2016, all of which was still in the inventory at December 31, 2016, was received on January 4, 2017. The freight bill was not included in either the inventory or in accounts payable at December 31, 2016.
7. All of the purchases from Baker occurred during the last 7 days of the year. These items have been recorded in accounts payable and accounted for in the physical inventory at cost before discount. Allen's policy is to pay invoices in time to take advantage of all cash discounts, adjust inventory accordingly, and record accounts payable, net of cash discounts.

Required:
Prepare a schedule of adjustments to the initial amounts of inventory, accounts payable, and sales. Show the effect, if any, of each of the transactions separately and indicate if the transactions would have no effect on the amount.

CASES

COMMUNICATION

C7-1
LO 7.5
LO 7.6
AICPA Adapted

FIFO and LIFO
A company may compute inventory under one of various cost flow assumptions. Among these assumptions are first-in, first-out (FIFO) and last-in, first-out (LIFO). In the past, some companies have changed from FIFO to LIFO for computing portions or all of their inventory.

Required:
1. Ignoring income tax, explain what effects a change from FIFO to LIFO has on a company's net earnings and working capital.
2. Explain the difference between the FIFO assumption of earnings and operating cycle and the LIFO assumption of earnings and operating cycle.

C7-2
LO 7.4
LO 7.5
LO 7.6
AICPA Adapted

Purchase Discounts, FIFO, and LIFO

Taylor Company, a household appliances dealer, purchases its inventories from various suppliers. Taylor has consistently stated its inventories at the lower of cost (FIFO) or market and uses the gross price method to record purchase discounts.

Required:
1. Taylor is considering alternate methods of accounting for the purchase discounts it takes when paying its suppliers promptly. From a theoretical standpoint, discuss the acceptability of each of the following methods:
    a. income when payments are made
    b. reduction of cost of goods sold for period when payments are made
    c. direct reduction of purchase cost
2. Identify the effects on both the balance sheet and the income statement of a company using the LIFO inventory method instead of the FIFO method over a substantial time period when purchase prices of household appliances are rising. State why these effects take place.

C7-3
LO 7.7
AICPA Adapted

Dollar-Value LIFO

In January, Broome Inc. requested and secured permission from the Commissioner of Internal Revenue to compute inventories under the last-in, first-out (LIFO) method and elected to determine inventory cost under the dollar-value method. Broome Inc. satisfied the Commissioner that cost could be accurately determined by use of an index number computed from a representative sample selected from the company's single inventory pool.

Required:
1. Why should a company include inventories in (a) its statement of financial position and (b) the computation of its net income?
2. The Internal Revenue Code allows some accountable events to be considered differently for income tax reporting purposes and financial accounting purposes, while other accountable events must be reported the same for both purposes. Discuss why it might be desirable to report some accountable events differently for financial accounting purposes than for income tax reporting purposes.
3. Discuss the ways and conditions under which the FIFO and LIFO inventory costing methods produce different inventory valuations. Do not discuss procedures for computing inventory cost.
4. Discuss the specific advantages and disadvantages of using the dollar-value LIFO application as compared to traditional LIFO methods. Ignore income tax considerations.

CREATIVE AND CRITICAL THINKING

C7-4
LO 7.4

Purchase Discounts

Auge Company annually purchases 1,000 tons of raw material at a cost of $100,000 with terms of 2/10, n/30. Auge uses the net price method to account for purchase discounts. Freight costs amount to $10,000 and storage and handling costs to $7,500.

Required:
1. What is the inventory cost?
2. Explain whether your answer to Requirement 1 would change if the discount were not taken.
3. Explain the arguments for and against the use of the net price method.

C7-5
LO 7.5
LO 7.6

LIFO

The 1970s were a period of historically high inflation. The 1976 financial statements of **Ford Motor Company** included the following note:

Note 1 (in part): Inventory valuation. Inventories are stated at the lower of cost or market. In 1976 the company changed its method of accounting from first-in, first-out (FIFO) to last-in, first-out (LIFO) for most of its U.S. inventories.

The change to LIFO reduced net income in 1976 by $81 million or $0.86 a share. There is no effect on prior years' earnings resulting from the change to LIFO in 1976 and, accordingly, prior years' earnings have not been restated. If the FIFO method of inventory accounting had been used by the company, inventories on December 31, 1976, would have been $166 million higher than reported.

Required:
1. Explain the arguments that must have been used in favor of LIFO for the management of Ford to accept a reduction in net income of $81 million.
2. Explain the disadvantages that are likely to result from the adoption of LIFO.
3. Explain why the effect on earnings is $81 million when the effect on the inventory valuation is $166 million.
4. Explain whether your answers to Requirements 1 and 2 would change if you were discussing a change to LIFO for a Ford dealer.

C7-6 Interpretation of GAAP and Ethical Issues
LO 7.6

Robin Smith is considering buying shares in Mah Company. The company has reported an increase in net income this year. On careful reading of the notes to the financial statements, Robin learns that the company had a LIFO liquidation this year. Robin understands what caused the liquidation but has asked you for advice about how to interpret it.

Required:
1. Prepare a short memo to Robin to answer the question.
2. Could a LIFO liquidation profit create ethical issues?

C7-7 Selection of an Inventory Method and Ethical Issues
LO 7.6
LO 7.8

Kelly Company uses FIFO. It has experienced rising costs for the last 5 years and expects that trend to continue. King Company increased the number of LIFO pools it uses to account for its inventory.

Required:
1. Explain why you think each company follows its policy.
2. Does either practice create ethical issues?

C7-8 Analyzing Starbucks's Inventory Disclosures

Obtain **Starbucks's 2015** annual report either using the "Investor Relations" portion of its web site (do a Web search for Starbucks investor relations) or go to http://www.sec.gov and click "Search for company filings" under "Filings and Forms (EDGAR)."

Required:
1. What is the primary cost flow assumption that Starbucks uses? Discuss how the amounts reported under this assumption compare to amounts reported under alternative cost flow assumptions. Explain why you think Starbucks selected this method.
2. What type of inventory system—perpetual or periodic—do you think Starbucks uses?
3. Does Starbucks have any purchase commitments? If so, are they included in inventory?
4. Assume ending inventory for 2013 was $1,111.2 million. Compute the inventory turnover ratio for 2015 and 2014. What is your evaluation of the difference? (Round your answer to two decimal places).
5. Recreate summary journal entries to record the transactions that affected inventory during 2015. (Assume all inventory purchases were on account.)

C7-9 Analyzing Nestlé's Cash and Receivables Disclosures

Obtain **Nestlé**'s 2013 annual report using the "Investor Relations" portion of its web site (do a Web search for Nestlé investor relations).

Required:
1. Which inventory method does Nestlé use? Why doesn't Nestlé use LIFO?
2. Describe the composition of Nestlé's inventory.
3. Assume Nestlé's 2011 ending inventory was CHF 9,255 million. Compute the inventory turnover for 2013 and 2012. What is your evaluation of the difference? (Round your answer to two decimal places).

USING CODIFICATION

C7-10 Researching GAAP

Situation

To pump up sales of all brands, Chapman Inc. is moving aggressively to ship extra cases of inventory into distributors' warehouses and record them as sales, a practice generally known as "trade loading." (Adapted from *Fortune*, April 6, 1992.) Chapman's president has asked you whether these shipments may be recognized as revenue.

Directions

Research the related generally accepted accounting principles and prepare a short memo to the president. Cite your references and applicable paragraph numbers.

C7-11 Researching GAAP

Situation

Fenimore Manufacturing Company uses the average cost method. It has followed a policy of expensing all its manufacturing cost variances. It is considering a change in its policy that will involve allocating them between cost of goods sold and inventory. Fenimore's president has asked you which of these alternative policies is consistent with GAAP.

Directions

Research the related generally accepted accounting principles and prepare a short memo to the president. Cite your references and applicable paragraph numbers.

INVENTORIES: SPECIAL VALUATION ISSUES

Relationships That Matter

LEARNING OBJECTIVES

After reading this chapter you will be able to

LO 8.1 Understand and apply the lower of cost or market rule.

LO 8.2 Explain the valuation of inventory above cost.

LO 8.3 Estimate ending inventory using the gross profit method.

LO 8.4 Apply the retail inventory method to determine ending inventory.

LO 8.5 Understand and apply the dollar-value LIFO retail method.

LO 8.6 Analyze the effects of inventory errors on the financial statements.

LO 8.7 (Appendix 8.1) Apply the lower of cost or market rule in a periodic inventory system.

Inventory management involves decisions that have a major impact on both the balance sheet and the income statement. Accordingly, financial statement users pay close attention to inventory changes as they assess the financial health of companies. In general, when inventory increases faster than sales, analysts normally consider this a negative signal that suggests a company is having difficulties in generating sales. These difficulties may lead to future markdowns and lower income as the company tries to reduce inventory levels. In addition, this inventory buildup may also suggest that the company has obsolete inventory that will lower future income as it is written off.[1] However, not all increases in inventory signal bad news. Increases in raw materials and work-in-process inventories may signal increases in production to meet higher anticipated future demand.[2] Therefore, it's critical that financial statement users properly understand the impact of inventory on the financial statements.

For example, in 1997, **Apple, Inc.**, was an unprofitable company with an inventory turnover of 10.40, or 35 days. Recognizing that this was unacceptably high, Apple reorganized its supply chain and implemented an aggressive inventory management program designed to reduce inventory levels and the associated costs, as well as lessening the company's financial exposure to inventory obsolescence and excess inventory levels. As a result of these actions, by 1999, Apple

---

[1] Baruch Lev and S. Ramu Thiagarajan, "Fundamental Information Analysis," *Journal of Accounting Research* (Autumn 1993), pp. 190–215.

[2] Victor Bernard and James Noel, "Do Inventory Disclosures Predict Sales and Earnings?" *Journal of Accounting, Auditing, and Finance* (Spring 1991), pp. 145–181.

was able to reduce its inventory turnover from over a month to four days while experiencing dramatic increases in profitability. Over the last decade, Apple has been able to sustain this competitive advantage, and, in 2014, its supply chain was ranked as the world's best in Gartner's *Supply Chain Top 25* for the seventh consecutive year.

Perceptive financial statement users also need to understand some special valuation issues related to inventory so that they can more clearly understand inventory's impact on the company's financial performance and position. For example, companies employ a lower of cost or market rule that results in the reporting of inventory losses as soon as they occur instead of when inventory is sold.

Other companies that have large amounts of inventory—such as **Wal-Mart** and **Target** in the United States, **Marks & Spencer** in the United Kingdom, and **Carrefour** in France—may find it either impractical to conduct physical inventory counts to prepare interim reports or inefficient to maintain records of individual inventory purchases. Recognizing the relationship between the costs of inventory purchases and selling prices, these companies use estimation techniques, such as the retail inventory method, to report inventory values and cost of goods sold. Understanding key relationships between inventory and other financial measures is essential for an effective analysis of a company's inventory.

In Chapter 7, we described the various methods used to measure the cost of inventory. However, in certain situations, GAAP allows a company to depart from the historical cost principle in the valuation of inventory. This chapter discusses these alternative valuations—lower of cost or market and valuation above cost. In addition, we examine two methods, the gross profit and the retail inventory methods, by which companies can estimate the value of their inventory. Finally, we discuss the effects of inventory errors on a company's financial statements.

LEARNING OBJECTIVE 8.1
Understand and apply the lower of cost or market rule.

WHAT IS THE LOWER OF COST OR MARKET RULE?

Companies purchase or produce inventory with the expectation of selling it at a profit; however, there are circumstances when this will not occur. For example, an electronics retailer may have an inventory of iPads. When **Apple** releases a newer version with improved features, the selling price of the existing iPad inventory will decline, possibly below the retailer's historical cost. Such declines can also occur for reasons such as competition, damage, obsolescence, or physical deterioration. In situations where the market value of the asset has declined below its cost, valuation of inventory at historical cost will overstate the value of inventory and potentially mislead investors and creditors as to the company's expected future cash inflows. Therefore, GAAP requires the application of the lower of cost or market rule. The **lower of cost or market (LCM) rule** requires that a company write down its inventory to its market value when the inventory's market value has declined to an amount less than its cost. By valuing inventory at the lower of its cost or market value, a company reports a more relevant and representationally faithful value for inventory on its balance sheet. In addition, it reports a loss (or expense) in its income statement in the period in which the asset's value declines rather than in the period the goods are sold.[3] Therefore, the application of the lower of cost or market rule is a conservative approach to the valuation of inventory.

[3] FASB ASC 330-10-35: Inventory: Overall: Subsequent Measurement.

Determining Market Value

To apply the lower of cost or market rule, the company must estimate the market value of inventory and compare it to its cost to determine which amount is lower. The computation of **market value** depends upon the inventory method used to measure inventory cost.

Companies using FIFO, Average Cost, Or Specific Identification If a company uses a cost flow assumption such as first-in, first-out (FIFO), average cost, or specific identification, market value is defined as net realizable value. **Net realizable value (NRV)** is the estimated selling price of the inventory in the ordinary course of business, less reasonably predictable costs of completion, disposal, and transportation.

Companies using LIFO or the Retail Inventory Method If a company uses LIFO or the retail inventory method, market value is defined as the current **replacement cost**—the cost the company would pay to replace the item.[4] When replacement cost is used to measure market value, GAAP imposes an upper (*ceiling*) and a lower (*floor*) constraint as follows:

- *Net Realizable Value (ceiling)*: The market value should not be more than the net realizable value. The ceiling imposes an upper bound on market value that prevents inventory from being valued at an amount that exceeds the net amount the company could realize by selling it.
- *Net Realizable Value minus a Normal Profit Margin (floor)*: The market value should not be less than the net realizable value reduced by an estimate of a normal profit margin or markup. The purpose of the floor is to prevent companies from understating inventory and, thereby, recognizing excessive losses in the current period and excessive profits in future periods when that inventory is sold.

These two constraints determine which "market value" (current replacement cost, net realizable value, or net realizable value minus a normal profit margin) should be compared to cost.

Example Sahara Company uses the LIFO inventory method and has inventory with the following characteristics:

- Selling price $165
- Packaging cost   10
- Transportation cost   15
- Normal profit margin   40

Sahara computes the ceiling and floor as shown in **Example 8.1**.

EXAMPLE 8.1

Computation of Constraints on Market Value

Selling price	$165
Less: Costs of completion (e.g., packaging)	(10)
Costs of disposal (e.g., transportation)	(15)
Ceiling (net realizable value)	$140
Less: Normal profit margin	(40)
Floor (net realizable value less normal profit)	$100

If the current replacement cost is between $100 and $140, it would be used as the market value. If the current replacement cost is above $140, the ceiling would be used; if the current replacement cost is below $100, the floor would be used. The conceptual reasons for imposing these constraints on market value are discussed in the next section. ■

---

[4] By using an entry value (replacement cost) to determine market value of inventory for firms using LIFO or the retail inventory method instead of an exit value (e.g., selling price), there is an inconsistency between market value under the lower cost or market rule and the FASB's definition of fair value, which is an exit value, as discussed in Chapter 4.

Application of the Lower of Cost or Market Rule

To apply the lower of cost or market rule, a company completes four steps:

- *Step 1. Choose an approach to implementing the lower of cost or market rule.* Apply the lower of cost or market rule to each individual inventory item, to each major inventory category, or to the total of inventory.
- *Step 2. Determine the market value.* If a FIFO, average cost, or specific identification cost flow assumption is used, calculate NRV. If LIFO or the retail inventory method is used, calculate the current replacement cost, ceiling, and floor, and select the middle value of the three.
- *Step 3. Compare the market value to cost.* Assign the lower of the selected market value or the historical cost to the value of inventory.
- *Step 4. Report the results in the financial statements.* Report the lower value on the balance sheet. If the company recognizes a loss, report the amount on the income statement as either a separate line item for loss from an inventory write-down or by including it in cost of goods sold (as discussed later).

These steps are shown in Exhibit 8.1.

EXHIBIT 8.1 Applying the Lower of Cost or Market Value

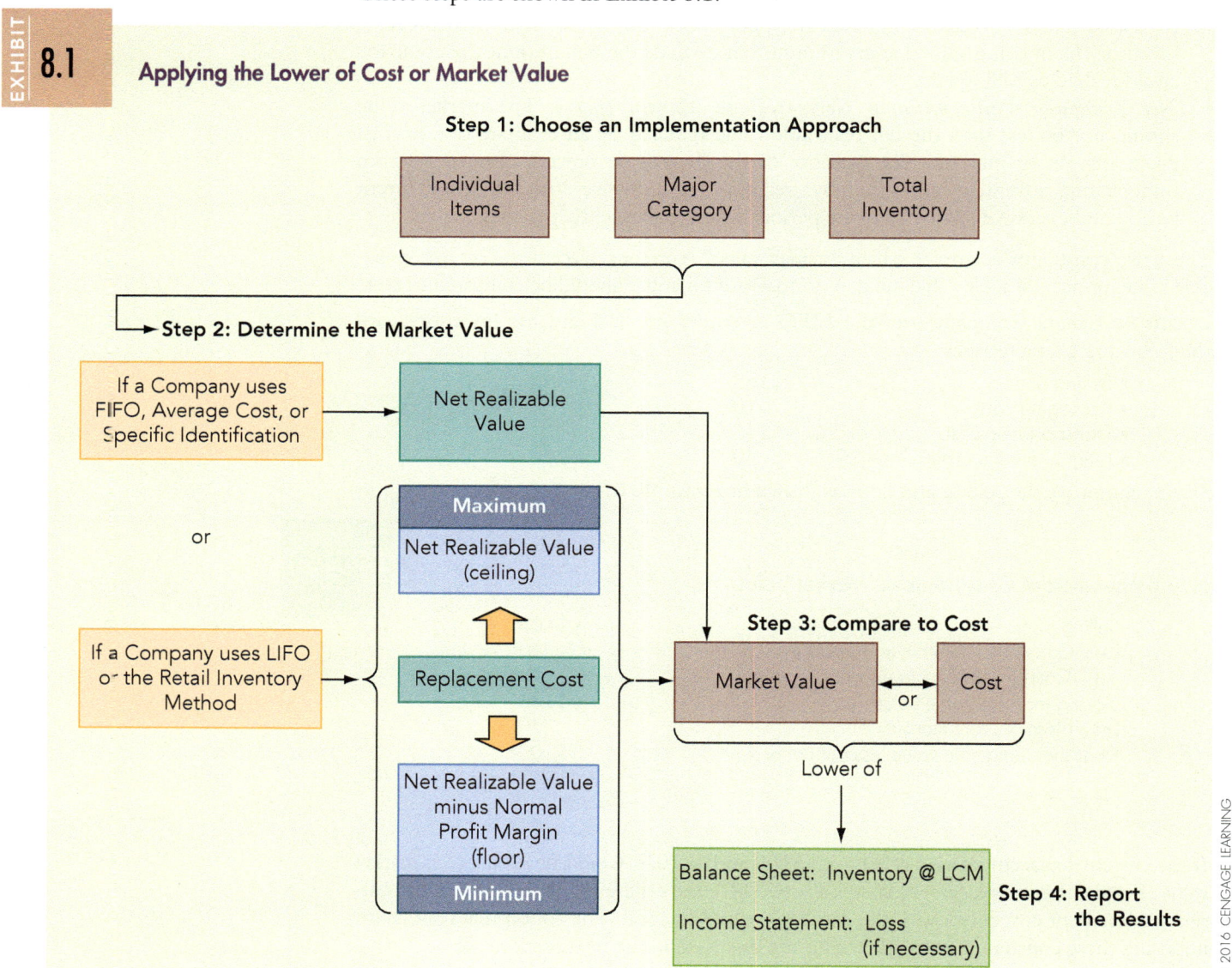

Example Gasparilla Golf Company has five inventory items as of December 31, 2017, with the characteristics shown in **Example 8.2**.

> **EXAMPLE 8.2**
>
> **Information for Lower of Cost or Market Calculations**
>
> | Product | Cost | Replacement Cost | Estimated Selling Price | Cost of Completion, Disposal and Transportation | Normal Profit Margin |
> |---|---|---|---|---|---|
> | Shirts | $28,500 | $30,000 | $33,100 | $1,100 | $4,000 |
> | Pants | 44,500 | 43,000 | 46,000 | 2,000 | 3,000 |
> | Shoes | 10,000 | 15,000 | 12,000 | 500 | 3,500 |
> | Golf Clubs | 33,000 | 34,000 | 34,800 | 3,800 | 2,000 |
> | Golf Balls | 20,000 | 14,000 | 21,300 | 2,300 | 2,500 |

The application of the lower of cost or market rule is shown in **Example 8.2a**. In this example, assume Gasparilla chooses to apply the lower of cost or market rule to each item of inventory. As you review this example, be sure you understand why each market value amount is selected and why the lower of cost or market rule would recognize losses from write-downs of inventory values on Gasparilla's inventory.

> **EXAMPLE 8.2a**
>
> **Applying the Lower of Cost or Market Rule**
>
> **A: If Using FIFO, Average Cost or Specific Identification**
>
> | | Step 1: Choose An Implementation Approach | Step 2: Determine the Market Value | | Step 3: Compare to Cost | | Step 4: Report the Results | |
> |---|---|---|---|---|---|---|---|
> | Product | | NRV* | Market Value | Cost | | Inventory Value | Loss |
> | Shirts | | $32,000 | $32,000 | $28,500 | | $28,500 | $ 0 |
> | Pants | | 44,000 | 44,000 | 44,500 | | 44,000 | 500 |
> | Shoes | | 11,500 | 11,500 | 10,000 | | 10,000 | 0 |
> | Golf Clubs | | 31,000 | 31,000 | 33,000 | | 31,000 | 2,000 |
> | Golf Balls | | 19,000 | 19,000 | 20,000 | | 19,000 | 1,000 |
>
> **B: If Using LIFO or Retail Inventory Method**
>
> | | Step 1: Choose An Implementation Approach | Step 2: Determine the Market Value | | | Step 3: Compare to Cost | | Step 4: Report the Results | |
> |---|---|---|---|---|---|---|---|---|
> | Product | | NRV* | Replacement Cost | NRV minus Normal Profit | Market Value | Cost | Inventory Value | Loss |
> | Shirts | | $32,000 | $30,000 | $28,000 | $30,000 | $28,500 | $28,500 | $ 0 |
> | Pants | | 44,000 | 43,000 | 41,000 | 43,000 | 44,500 | 43,000 | 1,500 |
> | Shoes | | 11,500 | 15,000 | 8,000 | 11,500 | 10,000 | 10,000 | 0 |
> | Golf Clubs | | 31,000 | 34,000 | 29,000 | 31,000 | 33,000 | 31,000 | 2,000 |
> | Golf Balls | | 19,000 | 14,000 | 16,500 | 16,500 | 20,000 | 16,500 | 3,500 |
>
> *NRV = Estimated Selling Price − Costs of Completion, Disposal and Transportation

Note that the reduction of the inventory from cost to market value represents the company's loss; the journal entry to recognize this loss is discussed later. In addition, once the inventory is reduced to market, it is not written back up to cost even if the market value subsequently rises above cost. Effectively, the written-down value becomes the new "cost" for subsequent valuation purposes. ■

Conceptual Evaluation of Ceiling and Floor To better understand the logic for the use of a ceiling and a floor, examine the last two items in Example 8.2a Panel B: golf clubs and golf balls.

For the golf clubs, the replacement cost is greater than the net realizable value (ceiling). Therefore, the net realizable value is used as the market value. Imposing this upper constraint of net realizable value ensures that the reported value for inventory is not overstated and that the full decline in the asset's value is recognized in the period in which it occurs. It would not be representationally faithful to report inventory at a value of $34,000 (replacement cost) when Gasparilla will only realize $31,000 from selling the golf clubs. By recognizing the $2,000 loss ($33,000 cost − $31,000 market value) in the current period, the expected profit from the subsequent sale of the golf clubs is $0. If the ceiling constraint were ignored and the current replacement cost ($34,000) was used as the market value, there would be no write down in the current period, the inventory value would be overstated because the $33,000 cost is greater than the net realizable value, and a loss of $2,000 ($33,000 cost − $31,000 net realizable value) would not be recognized until the golf clubs were sold. Therefore, the upper constraint on market value prevents overstatement of the value of inventory and recognizes any losses in the period that the inventory value falls below its cost.

In contrast, the replacement cost of the golf balls is less than the net realizable value minus a normal profit margin (floor). Therefore, the net realizable value minus a normal profit margin is used as the market value. Imposing this lower constraint of net realizable value minus a normal profit margin prevents an understatement of inventory, an overstatement of losses in the current period due to the write-down, and an excessive profit in the future when the understated inventory is sold. For example, if the company ignored the floor constraint and used the current replacement cost ($14,000) as the market value, it would recognize a loss of $6,000 ($20,000 cost − $14,000 market value) in the current period. In a later period when the golf balls are sold for their net realizable value ($19,000), the company would recognize a $5,000 profit, which is higher than the normal profit margin of $2,500. Thus, the company would report excessive losses followed by excessive profits. Therefore, the lower constraint prevents the profit distortion that would occur by an understatement of inventory and overstatement of losses in the current period.

Approaches to Implementing the Lower of Cost or Market Rule

A company may apply the lower of cost or market rule to each individual item in inventory, to each major inventory category, or to the total of the inventory. When the lower of cost or market rule is applied to each major category or to the total of the inventory, price declines of some of the units in inventory are offset by price increases in other units of inventory in the same category. Therefore, applying the lower of cost or market rule to groups of inventory will usually result in higher inventory valuations and lower losses relative to applying the rule to each individual item of inventory. While all three methods are acceptable, the company should use the method that most clearly reflects periodic income.[5]

Example The three alternative approaches for implementing the lower of cost or market rule for Gasparilla Golf Company are illustrated in **Example 8.2b** (note that the implementation at the individual item level is consistent with **Example 8.2a** Panel A).

When Gasparilla applies the lower of cost or market rule to individual items, the most conservative valuation of inventory, and the greatest loss, is obtained. Conversely, if Gasparilla applies the lower of cost or market rule to total inventory, the highest inventory valuation, and the lowest loss, is obtained. Applying the lower of cost or market rule to major categories of inventory results in an inventory valuation and loss that is between the other methods. ■

While the use of three alternative approaches to account for the same economic event provides companies with flexibility in reporting, it also reduces comparability among companies. Most commonly, companies apply the lower of cost or market rule to each individual item because that approach is required for income tax purposes and it gives the most conservative inventory valuation. Whichever approach a company uses, it should apply the approach consistently over time.

[5] FASB ASC 330-10-35: Inventory: Overall: Subsequent Measurement.

> **EXAMPLE 8.2b**
>
> **Approaches to Implementing Lower of Cost or Market**
>
> | | | | LCM applied to: | | |
> | --- | --- | --- | --- | --- | --- |
> | Inventory | Cost | Market | Individual Items | Inventory Categories | Total Inventory |
> | **Clothing:** | | | | | |
> | Shirts | $ 28,500 | $ 32,000 | $ 28,500 | | |
> | Pants | 44,500 | 44,000 | 44,000 | | |
> | Shoes | 10,000 | 11,500 | 10,000 | | |
> | Total Clothing | $ 83,000 | $ 87,500 | | $ 83,000 | |
> | **Equipment:** | | | | | |
> | Golf Clubs | $ 33,000 | $ 31,000 | 31,000 | | |
> | Golf Balls | 20,000 | 19,000 | 19,000 | | |
> | Total Equipment | $ 53,000 | $ 50,000 | | 50,000 | |
> | **Total** | $136,000 | $137,500 | | | $136,000 |
> | **Inventory Valuation** | | | $132,500 | $133,000 | $136,000 |
> | **Loss Recognition** (Cost less Inventory Valuation) | | | $ 3,500 | $ 3,000 | $ 0 |

Recording the Reduction of Inventory to Market

A company can record the write-down of inventory from cost to market value using either of two methods:

- **Direct Method**—The loss is recorded directly by reducing the company's inventory account and increasing its cost of goods sold account.
- **Allowance Method**—The loss is recorded in a separate inventory valuation account and loss account.

While the two methods result in the same net inventory valuation, the main difference is how the loss is reported. The direct method overstates cost of goods sold by including costs that relate to inventory that has not yet been sold, whereas the allowance method states the loss separately. Therefore, the allowance method is conceptually preferred because it does not comingle the loss with cost of goods sold, and the effects of the write-down can be more clearly identified.

Example Gasparilla Golf Company uses the perpetual FIFO inventory method and applies the lower of cost or market rule to individual items as shown in **Example 8.2b**.[6] The journal entries to record the write-down of inventory from cost to market under the direct and allowance methods at December 31, 2017, would be as follows:

Direct Method

Dec. 31, 2017	Cost of Goods Sold	3,500	
	Inventory (pants)		500
	Inventory (golf clubs)		2,000
	Inventory (golf balls)		1,000
	To record inventory at market.		

Allowance Method

Dec. 31, 2017	Loss Due to Market Valuation	3,500	
	Allowance to Reduce Inventory to Market		3,500
	To record inventory at market.		

[6] The application of the direct and allowance methods for a periodic inventory system is illustrated in Appendix 8.1.

Under either method, the loss ($3,500) and the net value of inventory reported on the balance sheet are the same. However, under the allowance method, the loss can be more easily identified by financial statement users because it is reported separately from cost of goods sold. In addition, the amount reported for cost of goods sold is more representationally faithful because it only includes the cost of goods that were actually sold. ■

Under the direct method, the sale of the inventory in subsequent periods is accounted for as previously discussed—the company would reduce inventory and recognize the related amount as cost of goods sold. If the ending inventory in the future period requires an additional write-down to market, the company would record this write-down by making a journal entry similar to the one above. Under the allowance method, a company would close the allowance account when the goods are sold.

Example Gasparilla sold its inventory that existed on December 31, 2017. Assuming it uses the allowance method, it would record the sales revenue and then make the following entry related to its inventory account:

Cost of Goods Sold	132,500	
Allowance to Reduce Inventory to Market	3,500	
Inventory (at cost)		136,000

If any future write-down of inventory is necessary, the company establishes a "new" allowance account in a manner similar to that previously shown. ■

Reporting Lower of Cost or Market

Under the direct method, the write-down of inventory is recorded directly in inventory and cost of goods sold. Under the allowance method, the write-down is recorded in an allowance account and a loss account. The allowance account is reported as a contra-inventory account in a company's balance sheet. The loss account is reported as a separate line item in a company's income statement. Generally, published financial statements do not disclose the size of the loss and the valuation allowance (unless one, or both, is material) but merely disclose that the company is using the lower of cost or market rule. The inventory disclosure for **Abercrombie & Fitch** is presented in Real Report 8.1.

8.1 ABERCROMBIE & FITCH'S INVENTORY DISCLOSURE — REAL REPORT

Abercrombie & Fitch

Notes to the Financial Statements (in part)

Note 3: Summary of Significant Accounting Policies (in part)

Inventories
Inventories are principally valued at the lower of cost or market on a weighted average basis. The Company writes down inventory through a lower of cost or market adjustment, the impact of which is reflected in cost of goods sold in the Consolidated Statements of Operations and Comprehensive Income. This adjustment is based on management's judgment regarding future demand and market conditions and analysis of historical experience. The lower of cost or market adjustment to inventory as of February 2, 2013, January 28, 2012, and January 29, 2011 was $9.9 million, $13.0 million, and $10.2 million, respectively.

Suggested answers to these questions are found at the end of the chapter.

Questions:

1. What method does Abercrombie & Fitch use to value its inventory?
2. What is the amount of inventory write-downs for the fiscal year ending on February 2, 2013?
3. Does Abercrombie & Fitch record inventory write-downs using the direct or allowance method?

GAAP specifies that if a company experiences a temporary market decline in an interim period, the company should ignore the decline in its interim financial statements. If the company does not expect the inventory price to recover, it should recognize the loss in the interim period in which the decline occurs. If the company recognizes a loss and then reverses it in a later interim period that year, it should recognize a loss recovery and increase the inventory value by the amount of the recovery, but only up to the original cost.[7] Note that under U.S. GAAP, a loss due to the write-down of inventory can only be reversed within the same fiscal year it was originally recognized. Losses recognized in the annual financial statements cannot be recovered.

Conceptual Evaluation of Lower of Cost or Market

The reduction of the value of the inventory to market and the recognition of a loss provide relevant and representationally faithful valuations for a company's balance sheet and income statement. As discussed in Chapter 2, assets are defined as "probable future economic benefits." When the cost of the inventory exceeds the expected benefits, the lower market value is a better measure of the expected benefits because an unrecoverable cost is not an asset. In addition, because a decline in inventory value is an economic event of the period in which the decline occurs, a company should recognize this decline as a reduction in the income of that period.

A major criticism of the lower of cost or market rule is that it is applied only in one direction—inventory value declines are recognized, but value increases are not. While this is obviously inconsistent, it is often justified as being a conservative approach to the valuation of inventory. Conservatism requires a company to recognize losses, both realized and expected, in the period in which they occur. However, it does not allow a company to recognize anticipated gains until they are realized, which is what the lower of cost or market rule achieves. Some users argue that the valuation of inventory at market value is *relevant* because it better reflects the cash flow potential of the inventory and enhances the *predictive value* of the information. In addition, they argue that if the market value of inventory provides a faithful representation of the value of the inventory when it's below historical cost, it also provides a faithful representation when it is above historical cost. However, GAAP does not generally allow the valuation of inventory above its historical cost because that would allow companies to recognize holding gains on inventory in income before those gains are realized by selling the inventory.

Because the lower of cost or market rule requires that a company recognize a loss in the period in which the loss in inventory value occurs, the loss is transferred from the future period of the sale to the current period of the market value decline. Therefore, the company's income will be higher when the inventory is subsequently sold than it otherwise would have been. As such, the accounting more faithfully represents the company's income in both periods. Note, however, that total income over the two periods will be the same whether or not the lower of cost or market rule is used.

INTERNATIONAL DIMENSION

LOWER OF COST OR MARKET

IFRS, like U.S. GAAP, require the use of the lower of cost or market rule to value inventory. However, the following important differences do exist.

- For all companies regardless of inventory cost flow assumption, IFRS define market value as net realizable value (the estimated selling price minus estimated costs of completion and disposal) and do not consider replacement cost

(continued)

---

[7] FASB ASC 270-10-45: Interim Reporting Overall: Other Presentation Matters.

or net realizable value minus a normal profit margin. Therefore, IFRS eliminate the need to use a ceiling and a floor in the determination of market value.
- While U.S. GAAP prohibits the reversal of a write-down of inventory recorded in a previous annual period, IFRS allow the reversal of a previous write-down (but not above its original cost) which is recognized in income.

The excerpt below illustrates the inventory disclosure of **Carrefour**, a large French retailer that uses IFRS. Note that even though inventory is reduced for "depreciation," Carrefour does not depreciate its inventory. Instead, this term is synonymous with the Allowance to Reduce Inventory to Market account. Therefore, users of international financial statements must always be aware of terminology differences that exist between countries.

Notes to the Consolidated Financial Statements (in part)

Note 2: Summary of Significant Accounting Policies

2.10 Inventories (in part)

In accordance with IAS 2-Inventories, goods inventories are measured at the lower of cost and net realizable value. Cost corresponds to the latest purchase price plus all related expenses. Net realizable value corresponds to the estimated selling price in the ordinary course of business, less the estimated costs necessary to make the sale.

Note 22: Inventories

(in millions of euros)	Dec. 31, 2013	Dec. 31, 2012
Inventories at cost	5,978	5,933
Depreciation	(240)	(275)
Inventories, net	5,738	5,658

IFRS Application Godwin Company uses the retail method and reports the following inventory values:

Inventory Item	Net Realizable Value	NRV minus a Normal Profit	Replacement Cost	GAAP Market Value	IFRS Market Value
A	$100	$80	$110	$100	$100
B	100	80	90	90	100
C	100	80	70	80	100

For Item A, IFRS and U.S. GAAP will both define market value as $100. However, for Items B and C, IFRS will result in a greater market valuation ($100 in both cases) relative to U.S. GAAP which would define market as $90 and $80, respectively. Therefore, IFRS will result in market values that are greater than or equal to those reported under U.S. GAAP for companies that use either LIFO or the retail inventory method.

Source: IAS 2. (See Appendix C at the end of this book.)

GOT IT?

8-1 Define the terms *cost* and *market* as used in the lower of cost or market inventory valuation rule.

8-2 For companies that use either LIFO or the retail inventory method, define the upper and lower constraints used in the lower of cost or market rule. What is the purpose of each constraint?

8-3 How may a company apply the lower of cost or market rule to its inventory?

(continued)

8-4 What is the major criticism of the lower of cost or market rule?

8-5 🌐 In applying the lower of cost or market rule to inventory, how do IFRS define market value?

8-6 🌐 With regard to write-downs of inventory under the lower of cost or market rule, how do IFRS differ from U.S. GAAP?

CAN INVENTORY BE VALUED ABOVE COST?

LEARNING OBJECTIVE 8.2

Explain the valuation of inventory above cost.

Normally, a company will not value its inventory above cost. However, under certain circumstances, GAAP does allow a company to report its inventory above cost. This exception must be justified by:

- an inability to determine appropriate costs
- immediate marketability of the inventory at a quoted market price
- the interchangeability of the units of inventory[8]

These conditions generally only apply to commodities, like precious metals, agricultural commodities, oil and gas, and mining commodities. For example, precious metals having a determinable market value with no major cost of marketing may be reported above cost. When goods are reported above cost, this fact should be fully disclosed.

Real Report 8.2 shows an example of valuation at market prices for **ConAgra Foods**. ConAgra justifies this valuation because it is highly certain that the inventory can be sold at the market price. In such a situation, income is earned by production (or through inventory holding gains) rather than by sale.

REAL REPORT — **INVENTORY VALUATION ABOVE COST** — **8.2**

Conagra Foods
Notes to Consolidated Financial Statements

ConAgra Foods

Note 1: Summary of Significant Accounting Policies (in part)
Inventories—We principally use the lower of cost (determined using the first-in, first-out method) or market for valuing inventories other than merchandisable agricultural commodities. Grain and flour inventories are principally stated at market value.

Note 19: Derivative Financial Instruments (in part)
Our operations are exposed to market risks from adverse changes in commodity prices affecting the cost of raw materials and energy.... In the normal course of business, these risks are managed through a variety of strategies, including the use of derivatives. Commodity and commodity index futures and options contracts are used from time to time to economically hedge commodity input prices on items such as natural gas, vegetable oils, proteins, packaging materials, dairy, grains, and electricity.

Questions:

1. What allows ConAgra to value its inventory at market price instead of cost?
2. Why does ConAgra use derivative financial statements?

Suggested answers to these questions are found at the end of the chapter.

GOT IT?

8-7 What are the exceptions to historical cost valuation of inventory allowed under generally accepted accounting principles? Under what conditions is each allowed?

---

[8] FASB ASC 330-10-35: Inventory: Overall: Subsequent Measurement.

LEARNING OBJECTIVE 8.3
Estimate ending inventory using the gross profit method

HOW IS INVENTORY ESTIMATED USING THE GROSS PROFIT METHOD?

Sometimes there are circumstances when it is either impossible or impractical for a company to take a physical count of its inventory in order to determine its value. For example, a natural disaster or fire may destroy the company's inventory. Alternatively, if a company needs to prepare monthly financial statements and has a large quantity of inventory, it may be too expensive and time-consuming to perform a physical count every month. In these situations, a company may estimate its ending inventory by using either the gross profit method or the retail inventory method (discussed in the next section).

The **gross profit method** may be used in the following situations:

- to determine the cost of the inventory for interim financial statements. This method is acceptable provided that the company discloses the method used at the interim date and any significant adjustments that result from reconciliations with the annual physical inventory.[9]
- to check the reasonableness of the reported cost of inventory by an auditor.
- to estimate the cost of inventory that is destroyed by a casualty, such as a fire.
- to estimate the cost of the inventory from incomplete records. For example, if a company's inventory records are destroyed, the inventory can be estimated if the cost of goods available for sale and the sales are known or can be reconstructed.
- to develop budgeted amounts for cost of goods sold and ending inventory from a sales budget.

However, the gross profit method is not acceptable for annual financial statements. Instead, a physical count of inventory is required to verify the inventory quantity.

The gross profit method assumes that a company's gross profit rate in the current period is similar to that of the previous periods. It estimates the cost of ending inventory by using the relationship between cost of goods available for sale, cost of goods sold, and ending inventory in the cost of goods sold model (discussed in Chapter 7). The gross profit method includes the following steps:

- *Step 1.* Calculate the historical gross profit rate:

$$\text{Historical Gross Profit Rate} = \frac{\text{Gross Profit from Prior Periods}}{\text{Net Sales from Prior Periods}}$$

- *Step 2.* Calculate the cost of goods available for sale in the current period:

$$\text{Cost of Goods Available for Sale} = \text{Beginning Inventory} + \text{Net Purchases}$$

- *Step 3.* Estimate the gross profit for the current period:

$$\text{Estimated Gross Profit} = \text{Historical Gross Profit Rate} \times \text{Net Sales Revenue (current period)}$$

- *Step 4.* Estimate the cost of goods sold for the period:

$$\text{Estimated Cost of Goods Sold} = \text{Net Sales Revenue (current period)} - \text{Estimated Gross Profit}$$

- *Step 5.* Determine the estimated cost of the ending inventory:

$$\text{Estimated Ending Inventory} = \text{Cost of Goods Available for Sale} - \text{Estimated Cost of Goods Sold}$$

---

[9] FASB ASC 270-10-45-6: Interim Reporting: Overall: Other Presentation Matters.

Example: Gross Profit Method

Hardin Company has the following information related to its inventory:

Net sales for the period	$130,000
Beginning inventory, cost	10,000
Net purchases for the period	90,000
Estimated historical gross profit rate on net sales	40%[10]

Hardin applies the gross profit method as shown in **Example 8.3**.

EXAMPLE 8.3

Applying the Gross Profit Method

Estimated gross profit rate (given)	40%	Step 1
Beginning inventory, at cost	$ 10,000	
Net purchases	90,000	Step 2
Cost of goods available for sale	$100,000	
Less: Estimated cost of goods sold		
Net sales	$130,000	
Gross profit rate	× 0.40	Step 3
Estimated gross profit	$ 52,000	
Sales	$130,000	
Estimated gross profit	(52,000)	Step 4
Cost of goods sold ($130,000 − $52,000)	(78,000)	
Estimated cost of ending inventory	$ 22,000	Step 5

Evaluation of the Gross Profit Method

The gross profit method can provide a useful estimate of inventory, but its usefulness depends on the accuracy of the gross profit percentage. Four modifications may enhance its accuracy.

First, a company should adjust the historical gross profit rate for known changes in the relationship between its gross profit and net sales. For example, if the company's costs of purchases have increased, but it has not passed on the increases to customers through increased sales prices, it should reduce the historical gross profit percentage accordingly. The company may also need to adjust the historical gross profit rate if its productivity, sales returns and allowances, or purchase returns and allowances have changed.

Second, a company may use a separate gross profit rate for each department or type of inventory that has a different markup percentage. It would then apply separate rates to each department's net sales and add the resulting amounts to compute the total inventory. Use of a single, overall gross profit rate assumes that all types of inventory are sold or held in inventory in equal proportions at all times. Because this is unlikely, use of separate gross profit rates enhances the accuracy of the cost of the ending inventory and the cost of goods sold.

Third, a company may use an average gross profit rate based on several past periods to smooth period-to-period fluctuations. However, use of an average rate assumes that no significant changes occurred over the periods selected for calculating the average rate and that the company made no adjustments to account for such changes. The use of an

---

[10] Sometimes a company will express gross profit as a percent of cost of goods sold instead of as a percent of net sales (for example, as a markup percentage above cost). In this case, it must convert the gross profit percent to a percent of net sales before it can apply the gross profit method, as follows:

$$\text{Gross Profit to Net Sales Ratio} = \frac{\text{Gross Profit to Cost of Goods Sold Ratio}}{1 + \text{Gross Profit to Cost of Goods Sold Ratio}}$$

average rate is particularly appropriate when there are relatively stable costs, selling prices, operating methods, and product mix.

Finally, the ending inventory estimated by the gross profit method is consistent with the cost flow assumption (FIFO, LIFO, average cost) used by the company. This occurs because the gross profit rate is based on past amounts developed from using the particular cost flow assumption. However, if there has been a special situation in the past, such as a write-down of inventory to its market value, or a liquidation of LIFO inventory, the gross profit rate must be adjusted.

> ### GOT IT?
>
> **8-8** Describe five situations in which the gross profit method of estimating inventory would be useful.
>
> **8-9** What is the basic assumption underlying the gross profit method? How may the gross profit percentage for the prior year be modified to provide a better estimate of the inventory value?

LEARNING OBJECTIVE 8.4

Apply the retail inventory method to determine ending inventory.

HOW IS INVENTORY ESTIMATED USING THE RETAIL INVENTORY METHOD?

As an alternative to the gross profit method, the **retail inventory method** can be used to estimate the cost of inventory when there is a consistent pattern between the cost of a company's purchases and its selling prices. This method is widely used by retail stores such as **Wal-Mart**, **Target**, **Saks**, and **Home Depot** where accounting systems are based on retail prices rather than costs, and prices are often set based on a consistent markup above cost.

The retail inventory method has two main advantages compared to the gross profit method:

- The retail method produces a more accurate estimate of current-period ending inventory because it uses a current-period estimate of gross profit. This makes the retail inventory method more sensitive to price changes which results in a more relevant inventory valuation.
- The retail inventory method is allowed for both interim financial reporting and income tax purposes.

Even though the retail inventory method can provide a relatively accurate estimate of ending inventory, a company should still take a physical count of inventory at least once a year for internal control purposes (e.g., to help identify material amounts of inventory theft or misappropriation as well as record-keeping errors).

The retail inventory method requires a company to maintain accounting records that contain the following information:

- beginning inventory at cost and retail value
- goods purchased at cost and retail value
- changes in selling price resulting from additional markups and markdowns
- sales

Note that information related to both beginning inventory and purchases must be provided at both cost and retail values, where retail values are the current selling prices of the goods. With this information, a company using the retail method then performs the following steps:[11]

---

[11] The retail inventory method can be applied for the entire company or for identifiable departments within the company. For simplicity, we will apply the retail method for the entire company.

- *Step 1.* Compute the total goods available for sale at both cost and retail value.
- *Step 2.* Compute the appropriate cost-to-retail ratio, as shown in Exhibit 8.2 (p. 8-16).
- *Step 3.* Compute the ending inventory at retail:

    Ending Inventory at Retail = Retail Value of Goods Available for Sale − Net Sales Revenue

- *Step 4.* Compute the ending inventory at cost:

    Ending Inventory at Cost = Ending Inventory at Retail × Cost-to-Retail Ratio

Example Frazier Company uses the retail inventory method with the average cost flow assumption and has the following information:

	Cost	Retail
Beginning inventory	$10,000	$17,000
Purchases	50,000	83,000
Sales		80,000

The ending inventory at cost is computed as:

	Cost	Retail	
Beginning inventory	$10,000	$17,000	} Step 1
Purchases	50,000	83,000	
Goods available for sale	$60,000	$100,000	

Cost-to-retail ratio: $\dfrac{\$60,000}{\$100,000} = 0.60$ } Step 2

Less: Sales		(80,000)	} Step 3
Ending inventory at retail		$20,000	
Ending inventory at cost (0.60 × $20,000)	$12,000		} Step 4

Retail Inventory Method Terminology

In the preceding example, we assumed that the company made no subsequent changes in retail prices. However, retail stores typically make changes in selling prices after setting the original price. The following seven terms describe these changes:

- **Markup**: the original markup from cost to the original selling price
- **Additional Markup**: an increase above the original selling price
- **Markup Cancellation**: a reduction in the additional markup (the markup cancellation cannot be greater than the additional markup)
- **Net Additional Markup**: the total additional markups minus the total markup cancellations
- **Markdown**: a decrease below the original selling price
- **Markdown Cancellation**: an elimination of all or part of a markdown (the markdown cancellation cannot be greater than the markdown)
- **Net Markdown**: the total markdowns minus the total markdown cancellations

To illustrate the meaning of these terms, suppose that a company purchased an item for $6 and initially priced the item to sell for $10. The markup is $4. If the company subsequently increases the selling price to $12, there is an additional markup of $2. If it then lowers the selling price to $7, there is a markup cancellation of $2 and a markdown of $3. If the company then raises the selling price to $8, there is a markdown cancellation of $1. The original markup is $4, the net additional markup is zero ($2 − $2), and the net markdown is $2 ($3 − $1).

Application of the Retail Inventory Method

To obtain a proper inventory valuation, retailers must include the information contained in net additional markups and net markdowns as inputs of the cost-to-retail ratio. By changing these inputs, companies can use the retail inventory method to develop inventory valuations under different cost flow assumptions. Four alternative valuations can be obtained using different cost-to-retail ratios as described below:

- *FIFO.* Exclude the cost and the retail value of the beginning inventory from the computation of the cost-to-retail ratio for the period. The ratio includes both net additional markups and net markdowns.
- *Average Cost.* Include the cost and the retail value of the beginning inventory and net additional markups and net markdowns in the cost-to-retail ratio.
- *LIFO.* Compute separate ratios for each layer in the beginning inventory and for the purchases of the current period. Include both net additional markups and net markdowns in the cost-to-retail ratio for the current period.
- *Lower of Average Cost or Market.* Include the cost and retail value of the beginning inventory and net additional markups in the cost-to-retail ratio. Net markdowns are excluded from the cost-to-retail ratio. This method is also known as the *conventional retail method.*

The calculation of the cost-to-retail ratio for each of these alternatives is shown in Exhibit 8.2.

EXHIBIT 8.2 **Alternative Cost-to-Retail Ratio Calculations**

	FIFO	Average Cost	LIFO	Lower of Average Cost or Market
Beginning inventory	Exclude	Include	Exclude*	Include
Purchases	Include	Include	Include	Include
Net additional markups	Include	Include	Include	Include
Net markdowns	Include	Include	Include	Exclude

*A separate cost-to-retail ratio is computed for each layer in beginning inventory.

Although these cost-to-retail computations differ, under each approach the net additional markups and net markdowns are added and subtracted in order to compute the retail value of the ending inventory. Also note that additional markups and markdowns are recorded only relative to retail prices.

Each of these methods is demonstrated in the following sections, using the data for Thompson Company given in **Example 8.4**.

EXAMPLE 8.4

Inventory Cost and Retail Value: Thompson Company

	Cost	Retail
Beginning inventory*	$20	$ 40
Purchases	40	80
Net additional markups	—	5
Net markdowns	—	(10)
Goods available for sale	$60	$115
Sales		(66)
Ending inventory at retail		$ 49

*For simplicity, it is assumed that the beginning inventory is valued at a cost of $20 for all flow assumptions.

Example: Retail FIFO

Under the FIFO cost flow assumption, the beginning inventory is excluded from the computation of the cost-to-retail ratio for the period. Thompson would compute the cost of its ending inventory as $26.13, as shown in **Example 8.4a**.

EXAMPLE 8.4a

Retail Inventory Method—FIFO

	Cost	Retail
Purchases	$40	$ 80
Net additional markups		5
Net markdowns		(10)
	$40	$ 75
Cost-to-retail ratio: $\frac{\$40}{\$75} = 0.5333$ (for purchases)		
Beginning inventory	20	40
Goods available for sale	$60	$115
Less: Sales		(66)
Ending inventory at retail		$ 49
Ending inventory at FIFO cost (0.5333 × $49)	$26.13	
Cost of goods sold ($60 − $26.13)	$33.87	

Excluding the beginning inventory from the computation of the cost-to-retail ratio produces the layering effect of FIFO for cost of goods sold. ■

Example: Retail Average Cost

Under the average cost flow assumption, the beginning inventory, net additional markups, and net markdowns are included in the cost-to-retail ratio. Therefore, the cost-to-retail ratio is based on a weighted average of the goods available for sale. **Example 8.4b** shows Thompson's estimation of the cost of its ending inventory.

EXAMPLE 8.4b Retail Inventory Method—Average Cost

	Cost	Retail
Beginning inventory	$20	$ 40
Purchases	40	80
Net additional markups		5
Net markdowns		(10)
Goods available for sale	$60	$115

Cost-to-retail ratio: $\dfrac{\$60}{\$115} = 0.5217$

Less: Sales		(66)
Ending inventory at retail		$ 49
Ending inventory at average cost (0.5217 × $49)	$25.56	
Cost of goods sold ($60 − $25.56)	$34.44	

Because the cost-to-retail ratio is based on the weighted average of costs and retail amounts for all goods available for sale, the resulting estimation of ending inventory and cost of goods sold approximates the amounts that would be obtained under the average cost method. ■

Example: Retail LIFO

When there is an increase in inventory using the LIFO assumption, ending inventory will consist of the beginning inventory plus additional layers added during the current year. To approximate this assumption under the retail method, separate cost-to-retail ratios must be calculated for beginning inventory and purchases. For beginning inventory, the cost-to-retail ratio is the ratio of beginning inventory at retail values divided by beginning inventory at cost. For purchases, the cost-to-retail ratio includes both net additional markups and net markdowns to capture current-period activity. **Example 8.4c** shows the computation of ending inventory and cost of goods sold using the LIFO retail inventory method for Thompson.

EXAMPLE 8.4c Retail Inventory Method—LIFO

	Cost	Retail
Beginning inventory	$20	$ 40

Cost-to-retail ratio: $\dfrac{\$20}{\$35} = 0.57$
(for beginning inventory)

	Cost	Retail
Purchases	40	$ 80
Net additional markups		5
Net markdowns		(10)
		$ 75

Cost-to-retail ratio: $\dfrac{\$40}{\$75} = 0.5333$
(for purchases)

	Cost	Retail
Goods available for sale	$60	$115
Less: Sales		(66)
Ending inventory at retail		$ 49
Ending inventory at LIFO cost:		
$40 × 0.50 (beginning inventory layer)	$20.00	
$9 × 0.5333 (added layer)	4.80	
	$24.80	
Cost of goods sold ($60 − $24.80)	$35.20	

Thompson had sales of $66 which left inventory at a retail value of $49. This inventory consists of two layers—a beginning inventory layer and a layer added in the current year—with each layer converted to cost using its own cost-to-retail ratio. Another way of looking at this example is to see that Thompson sold 88% ($66 ÷ $75) of the goods purchased during the period. Therefore, at cost, the company sold $35.20 (88% × $40) of the purchases, leaving $4.80 ($40 − $35.20) as an added layer in inventory. ■

When there is a decrease in inventory during the period, LIFO assumes that all purchases during the current period are sold, and ending inventory would include only a portion of the beginning inventory. Therefore, there would be no need to compute a cost-to-retail ratio for the purchases of the current period. In more complex situations, the beginning inventory would include LIFO layers, each with its own cost-to-retail ratio, and the inventory would be reduced beginning with the most recently added layers first.

Example: Retail Lower of Average Cost or Market

The retail inventory method can also be used to approximate the valuation of inventory at the lower of cost or market by excluding net markdowns from the computation of the cost-to-retail ratio. The rationale for excluding net markdowns is that companies will normally mark down inventory to indicate a decrease in utility (e.g., obsolescence, lower demand for the goods). Excluding net markdowns will result in a lower cost-to-retail ratio which, consistent with the lower of cost or market rule, leads to a lower approximation of ending inventory. This method is commonly referred to as the **conventional retail method**. Thompson would compute the value of its ending inventory as $23.52, as shown in **Example 8.4d**.

EXAMPLE 8.4d

Retail Inventory Method—Lower of Average Cost or Market

	Cost	Retail
Beginning inventory	$20	$ 40
Purchases	40	80
Net markups		5
	$60	$125

Cost-to-retail ratio: $\frac{\$60}{\$125} = 0.48$

	Cost	Retail
Net markdowns		(10)
Goods available for sale	$60	$115
Less: Sales		(66)
Ending inventory at retail		$ 49
Ending inventory at lower of cost or market (0.48 × $49)	$23.52	
Cost of goods sold ($60 − $23.52)	$36.48	

■

Additional Adjustments under the Retail Method

In addition to the adjustments discussed previously, the application of the retail method is complicated when a company considers other typical costs and activities such as freight charges, purchase discounts, purchase returns and allowances, inventory shrinkage, and employee discounts. The treatment of these items is as follows:

- *Freight charges.* Freight charges are added to the *cost* of purchases because purchases should include all costs incurred to bring the inventory to its existing location and condition.
- *Purchase discounts.* Purchase discounts taken under the gross price method are subtracted from the *cost* of purchases.

- *Purchase returns and allowances.* Any purchase returns and allowances are subtracted from *both the cost and the retail value* of the purchases so as not to distort the computation of the cost-to-retail ratio.
- *Normal inventory shrinkage.* Normal inventory shrinkage due to breakage and theft is a common problem in retail stores, and companies typically estimate and reflect these costs in the retail price of inventory. Therefore, when the retail inventory method is used for interim financial statements, this estimate of normal shrinkage is *subtracted* from cost of goods available at retail (in the same way that sales is subtracted) to determine the ending inventory at retail.
- *Abnormal inventory spoilage.* Abnormal inventory spoilage is not expected and not reflected in the selling price of the inventory. Therefore, any abnormal spoilage would be *subtracted at both cost and retail* to determine the goods available for sale so as not to distort the cost-to-retail ratio.
- *Employee discounts.* Employee discounts—discounts from the normal sales price that are made available to employees—are reflected in the selling price of the inventory and, therefore, are *subtracted* from cost of goods available at retail (in the same way that sales is subtracted) to determine ending inventory at retail.

Conceptual Evaluation of the Retail Inventory Method

Two general assumptions underlie the retail inventory method.

- Items in a company's inventory are sufficiently homogeneous so that all have the same markup, or, if different markups exist, the items in ending inventory are in proportion to those goods available for sale.
- The cost-to-retail ratio remains constant over the accounting period.

If these assumptions are not true, the retail inventory method will not produce accurate estimates of ending inventory. A company can increase the validity of the first assumption by using a separate cost-to-retail ratio for each category of inventory or for each department. The accuracy of the second assumption can be increased by weighting the different cost-to-retail ratios by the volume of activity for inventory items under each ratio.

Because the lower of average cost or market rule is a commonly used version of the retail inventory method, it is important to consider one additional factor relating to this method. The lower of average cost or market rule is accurate only if either markups and markdowns do not exist at the same time or if all the marked-down items have been sold. Therefore, it is critical to assess the underlying assumptions of the retail inventory method to ensure that an accurate estimate of ending inventory is obtained.

Wal-Mart's disclosure of its use of the retail method is shown in Real Report 8.3.

8.3 RETAIL INVENTORY METHOD DISCLOSURE — REAL REPORT

Wal-Mart

Wal-mart Stores
Balance Sheets (in millions)

	January 31, 2013	January 31, 2012
Assets (in part)		
Current Assets:		
Cash and cash equivalents	$ 7,781	$ 6,550
Receivables, net	6,768	5,937
Inventories	43,803	40,714
Prepaid expenses and other	1,588	1,774
Total Current Assets	$59,940	$54,975

> **Notes to Financial Statements (in part)**
>
> **Note 1. Summary of Significant Accounting Policies (in part)**
> **Inventories**
> The Company values inventories at the lower of cost or market as determined primarily by the retail method of accounting, using the last-in, first-out ("LIFO") method for substantially all of the Wal-Mart U.S. segment's inventories. The retail method of accounting results in inventory being valued at the lower of cost or market since permanent markdowns are currently taken as a reduction of the retail value of inventory. The Wal-Mart International segment's inventories are primarily valued by the retail method of accounting, using the first-in, first-out ("FIFO") method. The Sam's Club segment's inventories are valued based on weighted average cost using the LIFO method. At January 31, 2013 and 2012, the Company's inventories valued at LIFO approximate those inventories as if they were valued at FIFO.

Questions:

1. What method does Wal-Mart use to value its inventory? Describe how this method is applied.
2. Why do you think Wal-Mart uses the inventory method you identified in the previous question to value its inventory?
3. Why does Wal-Mart use the retail LIFO inventory method for domestic operations but the retail FIFO inventory method for international operations?

Suggested answers to these questions are found at the end of the chapter.

GOT IT?

8-10 What is the necessary condition for the retail inventory method to provide valid results?

8-11 Explain the meaning of the following terms: markup, additional markup, markup cancellation, net additional markup, markdown, markdown cancellation, and net markdown.

8-12 Describe how a company computes the cost-to-retail ratio for the following cost flow assumptions: FIFO, average cost, LIFO, and lower of average cost or market. Why do the different methods approximate each cost flow assumption?

8-13 What assumptions are necessary for the lower of cost or market retail inventory method to actually produce an inventory value equal to the lower of average cost or market?

8-14 The retail inventory method indicated an inventory value of $80,000. A physical inventory indicated a value of $70,000. Suggest possible causes of this discrepancy.

WHAT IS THE DOLLAR-VALUE RETAIL METHOD?

LEARNING OBJECTIVE 8.5
Understand and apply the dollar-value LIFO retail method.

The previous discussion of the retail LIFO method assumed that there were no changes in the retail price of inventory during the period. However, when prices change during a period, a company can combine the principles of the retail LIFO method with the dollar-value LIFO method (discussed in Chapter 7) to eliminate the effects of this price change. This combination is called the **dollar-value LIFO retail method**. Although no new principles are involved, we provide an illustration of the dollar-value retail LIFO inventory method due to its complexity.

Example Weston Company adopted LIFO on January 1, 2016, and reports the information in **Example 8.5**.

EXAMPLE 8.5 Weston Company Cost and Retail Values and Price Indexes

	2016		2017		2018	
	Cost	Retail	Cost	Retail	Cost	Retail
Jan. 1, inventory	$ 8,000	$ 12,000				
Purchases	20,400	32,000	$25,600	$ 41,000	$26,040	$ 45,000
Net additional markups		3,000		2,000		1,000
Net markdowns		(1,000)		(3,000)		(4,000)
Sales		(29,800)		(32,240)		(42,990)
Price Index:						
Jan. 1, 2016		100				
Dec. 31, 2016		108				
Dec. 31, 2017		115				
Dec. 31, 2018		120				

The cost-to-retail ratio is computed in the same manner described earlier for the LIFO retail method (**Example 8.4c**). That is, the ratio includes both net additional markups and net markdowns but excludes the beginning inventory. The dollar-value LIFO concepts are applied to the retail values using the following steps:

- *Step 1.* The ending inventory at retail is computed by adding the beginning inventory, purchases, and the net additional markups, and subtracting the net markdowns and sales. Alternatively, ending inventory could be computed at year-end by taking a physical inventory and multiplying the units in ending inventory by the current-year retail prices.
- *Step 2.* The ending inventory at retail is converted to base-year retail prices by applying the base-year conversion index:[12]

$$\text{Ending Inventory at Base-Year Retail Prices} = \text{Ending Inventory at Retail} \times \frac{\text{Base-Year Retail Price Index}}{\text{Current-Year Price Index}}$$

- *Step 3.* The change in the inventory at retail in base-year prices is computed by comparing the ending inventory with the beginning inventory when both are measured at retail in base-year prices.
- *Step 4.* The change in the inventory at retail in base-year prices is converted to current-year retail prices by multiplying it by the appropriate conversion index. If there is an increase in inventory, the current year conversion index is:

$$\text{Layer Increase at Current-Year Retail Prices} = \text{Increase at Base-Year Retail Prices} \times \frac{\text{Current-Year Price Index}}{\text{Base-Year Price Index}}$$

If there is a decrease in inventory, the conversion index for the appropriate LIFO layer is:

$$\frac{\text{Decrease at Retail Prices of}}{\text{Most Recently Added Layer}} = \frac{\text{Decrease at Base-}}{\text{Year Retail Prices}} \times \frac{\text{Price Index of Most Recently Added Layer}}{\text{Base-Year Price Index}}$$

Note that for large decreases that affect more than one layer of inventory, the price index applicable to each layer must be used in the conversion index.
- *Step 5.* The change in inventory at current-year retail prices is converted to cost by multiplying it by the cost-to-retail ratio for the appropriate year.

---

[12] Note that the conversion index used here is based on a price index, while the conversion index used in Chapter 7 was based on a cost index. A price index is computed in the same way as a cost index, except that retail prices are used.

- *Step 6.* The ending inventory at cost is computed by adding (subtracting) the increase (decrease) in inventory at cost to the beginning inventory at cost.

Example These steps are illustrated for Weston Company in **Example 8.5a**.

EXAMPLE 8.5a

Dollar-Value LIFO Retail Inventory Method

	2016		2017		2018		
	Cost	Retail	Cost	Retail	Cost	Retail	
Beginning inventory*	$ 8,000	$ 12,000	$ 9,944	$ 16,200	$14,238	$ 23,960	⎫
Purchases	20,400	$32,000	25,600	$41,000	26,040	$45,000	⎪
Net additional markups		3,000		2,000		1,000	⎬ Step 1
Net markdowns		(1,000)		(3,000)		(4,000)	⎪
		34,000		40,000		42,000	⎪
Goods available for sale	$28,400	$ 46,000	$35,544	$ 56,200	$40,278	$ 65,960	⎪
Sales		(29,800)		(32,240)		(42,990)	⎪
Ending inventory at retail		$ 16,200		$ 23,960		$ 22,970	⎭
Ending inventory at retail at base-year prices:							⎫
$16,200 × (100 ÷ 108)		$ 15,000					⎪
$23,960 × (100 ÷ 115)				$ 20,835			⎬ Step 2
$22,970 × (100 ÷ 120)						$ 19,142	⎭
Inventory change at retail base-year prices:							⎫
$15,000 − $12,000		$ 3,000					⎪
$20,835 − $15,000				$ 5,835			⎬ Step 3
$19,142 − $20,835						$ (1,693)	⎭
Change at retail at relevant current prices:							⎫
$3,000 × (108 ÷ 100)		$ 3,240					⎪
$5,835 × (115 ÷ 100)				$ 6,710			⎬ Step 4
($1,693) × (115 ÷ 100)						$ (1,947)	⎭
Change at relevant current costs:*							⎫
$3,240 × 0.60	$ 1,944						⎪
$6,710 × 0.64			$ 4,294				⎬ Step 5
($1,947) × 0.64					$ (1,246)		⎭
Year-end LIFO inventory:							⎫
Base-year layer	$ 8,000		$ 8,000		$ 8,000		⎪
Layer added in 2016	1,944		1,944		1,944		⎪
Layer added in 2017			4,294		4,294		⎬ Step 6
Layer subtracted in 2018 at 2017 costs					(1,246)		⎪
Ending inventory	$ 9,944		$14,238		$12,992		⎭

*2016 cost-to-retail ratio for purchases: $20,400 ÷ $34,000 = 0.60; 2017 cost-to-retail ratio for purchases: $25,600 ÷ $40,000 = 0.64

GOT IT?

8-15 Under what conditions would the dollar-value LIFO retail inventory method be useful?

LEARNING OBJECTIVE 8.6

Analyze the effects of inventory errors on the financial statements.

WHAT ARE THE EFFECTS OF INVENTORY ERRORS?

Errors in the valuation of inventory or the recording of purchases can result in inaccurate values on the company's balance sheet and income statement. The discovery of inventory errors requires careful analysis and adjusting entries to correct the company's accounts. If a company discovers an error in the same accounting period that the error was made, it reverses the erroneous entry and records a correct entry. However, if a company discovers a material error after it has closed the books, it treats the correction as a prior period adjustment (the accounting entries necessary to correct errors are covered in depth in Chapter 22).

Exhibit 8.3 summarizes the effects that three common inventory errors will have if they are not corrected (assuming a periodic inventory system and ignoring income taxes):

EXHIBIT 8.3 Effects of Inventory Errors

I. A purchase on credit is omitted from both the purchases account and ending inventory and is not recorded in the succeeding year.
   A. **Current year**
      1. *Income Statement.* Income is correct because the errors in the purchases and ending inventory offset each other.
      2. *Balance Sheet.* Ending inventory and accounts payable are understated.
   B. **Succeeding year**
      1. *Income Statement.* Income is overstated because beginning inventory is understated, and therefore, cost of goods sold is understated.
      2. *Balance Sheet.* Accounts payable is understated and retained earnings is overstated. Note that if the purchase omitted from the current year was included in the succeeding year, the income would be correct in the second year because the errors would again offset each other. Accounts payable and retained earnings would also be correct.

II. A purchase on credit is omitted from the purchases account but ending inventory is correct.
   A. **Current year**
      1. *Income Statement.* Income is overstated because purchases are understated and therefore cost of goods sold is understated.
      2. *Balance Sheet.* Accounts payable is understated because a purchase has been omitted. Retained earnings is overstated because income is overstated.
   B. **Succeeding year**
      1. *Income Statement.* No effect because the beginning inventory, purchases, and ending inventory are correct.
      2. *Balance Sheet.* Accounts payable is understated and retained earnings is overstated, due to the error in the previous period.

III. Ending inventory is over(under)stated due to quantity and/or costing errors, but purchases are correct.
   A. **Current year**
      1. *Income Statement.* Income is over(under)stated because cost of goods sold is under(over)stated.
      2. *Balance Sheet.* Ending inventory and retained earnings are over(under)stated.
   B. **Succeeding year**
      1. *Income Statement.* Income is under(over)stated because beginning inventory is over(under)stated, and therefore, cost of goods sold is over(under)stated.
      2. *Balance Sheet.* Correct because the errors in inventory and retained earnings in the previous year were counterbalanced in this year.

When analyzing inventory errors, it is helpful to refer to the cost of goods sold model discussed in Chapter 7.

Example Picasso Company's periodic inventory at December 31, 2016, is overstated by $5,000, but purchases are correct. In addition, Picasso correctly values its 2017 ending inventory. This error is illustrated by the following equations:

	Beginning Inventory	+	Purchases	−	Ending Inventory	=	Cost of Goods Sold
2016	Correct		Correct		+$5,000		−$5,000
2017	+$5,000		Correct		Correct		+$5,000

The effect on the financial statements of this error for each year is:

2016: *Income Statement.* Cost of goods sold is understated by $5,000 and income is overstated by $5,000.
Balance Sheet. Ending inventory and retained earnings are overstated by $5,000.

2017: *Income Statement.* Cost of goods sold is overstated by $5,000 and income is understated by $5,000.
Balance Sheet. Ending inventory and retained earnings are correct because the errors have counterbalanced each other.

Note that the total combined income for the two years is correct, as is the ending inventory for the second year. This is referred to as a counterbalancing or self-correcting error. Even though the errors counterbalance, it may still be necessary to restate the financial statements as discussed in Chapter 22. ■

GOT IT?

8-16 Indicate the effect of each of the following errors on the following balance sheet and income statement items for the current and succeeding years: beginning inventory, ending inventory, accounts payable, retained earnings, purchases, cost of goods sold, net income, and earnings per share.

a. The ending inventory is overstated.

b. Merchandise purchased on account and received was not recorded in the purchases account until the succeeding year although the item was included in inventory of the current year.

c. Merchandise purchased on account and shipped FOB shipping point was not recorded in either the purchases account or the ending inventory.

d. The ending inventory was understated as a result of the exclusion of goods sent out on consignment.

APPENDIX 8.1: APPLICATION OF LOWER OF COST OR MARKET IN A PERIODIC INVENTORY SYSTEM

LEARNING OBJECTIVE 8.7
Apply the lower of cost or market rule in a periodic inventory system.

The lower of cost or market rule can be applied in a periodic inventory system by using either the direct or allowance method. While the conceptual ideas are the same as with a perpetual inventory system, the journal entries required to apply each method differ. These differences are illustrated below.

Example Tampa Company has inventory values as shown below.

	Cost	Market	Gain/(Loss)
December 31, 2015	$20,000	$20,000	—
December 31, 2016	25,000	22,000	($3,000)
December 31, 2017	30,000	28,000	($2,000)

Assume that the entire inventory that exists at the end of a year is sold in the subsequent year. If Tampa uses a periodic inventory system, the journal entries for both the direct and allowance methods are shown in **Example 8.6**.

EXAMPLE 8.6

Periodic System: Recording the Reduction of Inventory to Market

	Periodic Inventory System			
	Direct Method		Allowance Method	
December 31, 2016				
1. To close beginning inventory:				
Income Summary	20,000		20,000	
Inventory		20,000		20,000
2. To record ending inventory:				
Inventory	22,000		25,000	
Income Summary		22,000		25,000
3. To record inventory at market:				
Loss Due to Market Valuation	Not required		3,000	
Allowance to Reduce Inventory to Market				3,000
December 31, 2017				
1. To close beginning inventory:				
Income Summary	22,000		22,000	
Allowance to Reduce Inventory to Market			3,000	
Inventory		22,000		25,000
2. To record ending inventory:				
Inventory	28,000		30,000	
Income Summary		28,000		30,000
3. To record inventory at market:				
Loss Due to Market Valuation	Not required		2,000	
Allowance to Reduce Inventory to Market				2,000

Remember from Chapter 3 that, under a periodic inventory system, Tampa must make year-end closing entries to remove beginning inventory and record ending inventory. The first two entries under each method show the necessary closing entries. The third entry under each method shows the adjustment (if necessary) to reduce the inventory from cost to market value.

When the direct method is used, Tampa includes the $3,000 decline in the value of the inventory at the end of 2016 in the year-end closing entry by recording the ending inventory at its lower market value of $22,000. The lower inventory value of $22,000 is the beginning inventory for 2017. At the end of 2017, the market value of $28,000 is included in the closing entry. Therefore, the direct method does not require a third journal entry to reduce inventory to market value.

The allowance method produces the same results; however, it reveals more information about the effect of the lower of cost or market rule on a company's cost of goods sold. In the allowance method, a company records the amount by which the market value of the inventory is below cost in an allowance account, and shows the effect on income in a separate loss account. In the first two entries, the beginning and ending inventory is recorded at cost. For 2016, Tampa records the decline in value of the inventory separately in an allowance account and a loss account. At the end of 2017, Tampa closes both the allowance and inventory accounts to reflect that the ending inventory existing on December 31, 2016, has been sold. Tampa then records the inventory decline for 2017 as the difference between the market value of the inventory and the cost of the inventory. ■

REVIEW CENTER

At the beginning of the chapter, we discussed how understanding key relationships between inventory and other financial measures can assist you in the analysis of a company's inventory as well as its ability to generate a gross profit from sales of inventory. These objectives are listed below and followed by a brief summary of the key points.

KEY TAKEAWAYS

LEARNING OBJECTIVE 8.1
Understand and apply the lower of cost or market rule.

- The lower of cost or market rule requires a company to write down its inventory to market value when the market value of the inventory has declined below its historical cost.
- In applying the lower of cost or market rule, the computation of market value depends upon the inventory cost flow assumption used to measure inventory:
  - If the company uses FIFO, average cost, or specific identification, market value is defined as net realizable value.
  - If a company uses the LIFO or the retail inventory method, market value is defined as the current replacement cost, which is constrained by the net realizable value (ceiling) and the net realizable value minus a normal profit margin (floor).
- The lower of cost or market rule may be applied to individual inventory items (the most conservative approach), to major categories of inventory items, or to the entire inventory.
- The write-down of inventory cost under the lower of cost or market rule can be accomplished by recording the write-down using either the:
  - direct method—recorded directly in the inventory and cost of goods sold accounts
  - allowance method—recorded in an inventory valuation/allowance account and a loss account.
- While the application of the lower of cost or market rule provides conceptually appropriate valuations for a company's balance sheet and income statement, it can be criticized for only recognizing declines in value and not increases in value. Additionally, some critics argue that by recognizing losses in the period of market decline, future income will be higher than it otherwise would have been.

KEY TERMS

allowance method, p. 8-7
direct method, p. 8-7
lower of cost or market (LCM) rule, p. 8-2

market value, p. 8-3
net realizable value, p. 8-3
replacement cost, p. 8-3

LEARNING OBJECTIVE 8.2

Explain the valuation of inventory above cost.

KEY TAKEAWAYS

- Inventory may be valued above cost only in rare circumstances when market values for inventory can be reliably measured, such as for precious metals and certain agricultural and mineral products.

LEARNING OBJECTIVE 8.3

Estimate ending inventory using the gross profit method

KEY TAKEAWAYS

- The gross profit method may be used to estimate ending inventory when it is impractical, infeasible, or impossible to perform a physical count of inventory.
- The gross profit method estimates the cost of inventory with these steps:
  - *Step 1.* Calculate the historical gross rate.
  - *Step 2.* Calculate the cost of goods available for sale in the current period.
  - *Step 3.* Estimate the cost of goods sold for the period.
  - *Step 4.* Estimate the cost of goods sold for the period.
  - *Step 5.* Determine the estimated cost of ending inventory.

KEY TERM

gross profit method, p. 8-12

KEY CALCULATIONS

$$\text{Historical Gross Profit Rate} = \frac{\text{Gross Profit from Prior Periods}}{\text{Net Sales from Prior Periods}}$$

Estimated Gross Profit = Historical Gross Profit Rate × Net Sales Revenue (current period)

LEARNING OBJECTIVE 8.4

Apply the retail inventory method to determine ending inventory.

KEY TAKEAWAYS

- The retail method is a commonly used inventory estimation technique that can produce inventory valuations under FIFO, average cost, LIFO, or lower of average cost or market cost flow assumptions by modifying the calculation of the cost-to-retail ratio.
- Ending inventory is estimated with these steps:
  - *Step 1.* Calculate total goods available for sale at both cost and retail.
  - *Step 2.* Compute the appropriate cost-to-retail ratio.
  - *Step 3.* Compute the ending inventory at retail.
  - *Step 4.* Compute the ending inventory at cost.

KEY TERMS

additional markup, p. 8-15
conventional retail method, p. 8-19
markdown, p. 8-15
markdown cancellation, p. 8-15
markup, p. 8-15

markup cancellation, p. 8-15
net additional markup, p. 8-15
net markdown, p. 8-15
retail inventory method, p. 8-14

KEY CALCULATIONS

Ending Inventory at Retail = Retail Value of Goods Available for Sale − Net Sales Revenue

Ending Inventory at Cost = Ending Inventory at Retail × Cost-to-Retail Ratio

LEARNING OBJECTIVE 8.5

Understand and apply dollar-value LIFO retail method.

KEY TAKEAWAYS

- The dollar-value LIFO retail method combines the principles of the retail LIFO method with the dollar-value LIFO method to approximate ending inventory.
- Under the dollar-value LIFO retail method, a company:
  - Determines its ending inventory at retail.
  - Converts this amount to the ending inventory at base-year retail prices by applying a base-year conversion index.

- Determines the change in inventory at base-year retail prices.
- Converts this amount to current-year retail prices using the appropriate conversion index.
- Converts the change in inventory to cost using the cost-to-retail ratio for the current year.
- Adds (subtracts) the increase (decrease) in inventory to the beginning inventory at cost.

KEY TERM
dollar-value LIFO retail method, p. 8-21

KEY CALCULATIONS

$$\text{Ending Inventory at Base-Year Retail Prices} = \text{Ending Inventory at Retail} \times \frac{\text{Base-Year Retail Price Index}}{\text{Current-Year Price Index}}$$

$$\text{Layer Increase at Current-Year Retail Prices} = \text{Increase at Base-Year Retail Prices} \times \frac{\text{Current-Year Price Index}}{\text{Base-Year Price Index}}$$

$$\text{Decrease at Retail Prices of Most Recently Added Layer} = \text{Decrease at Base-Year Retail Prices} \times \frac{\text{Price Index of Most Recently Added Layer}}{\text{Base-Year Price Index}}$$

KEY TAKEAWAYS

LEARNING OBJECTIVE 8.6
Analyze the effects of inventory errors on the financial statements.

- Errors in the valuation of inventory can result in inaccurate balance sheet and income measurements that affect multiple years.
- Careful analysis is required to determine the effects of such errors and the appropriate correction.

KEY TAKEAWAYS

LEARNING OBJECTIVE 8.7
(Appendix 8.1) Apply the lower of cost or market rule in a periodic inventory system.

- The concepts of the lower of cost or market rule can be applied to a periodic system as well as a perpetual system.
- Under the direct method, any decline in value of the inventory is recorded directly in the ending inventory account and, therefore, directly affects the computation of cost of goods sold.
- While the allowance method produces the same result as the direct method, it reveals more information by recording a decline in inventory value in an allowance account and a loss account.

ANSWERS TO REAL REPORT QUESTIONS

Real Report 8.1 Answers Abercrombie & Fitch—Inventory Disclosure

1. Abercrombie & Fitch values its inventory at lower of cost or market. Cost is determined primarily by the application of the weighted average method.
2. Abercrombie & Fitch reports inventory reserves of $9.9 million as of February 2, 2013.
3. Abercrombie & Fitch uses the direct method based on its statment that the impact of the lower of cost or market adjustment is reflected in cost of goods sold.

Real Report 8.2 Answers ConAgra Foods—Inventory Valuation Above Cost

1. While inventory is normally valued using the lower of cost or market rule, ConAgra is able to value its inventory of grain and flour at market value because of the readily available quoted prices. This represents an exception to the general rule of inventory valuation and should only be used in rare cases.
2. ConAgra uses derivative financial instruments such as commodity and commodity index futures and options contracts as a hedge against price fluctuations of its raw materials. A variety of conditions could occur that would cause the price of its raw materials (e.g., grain, flour) to increase, thereby increasing its cost of goods sold and lowering net income. By using derivatives, the company can protect itself against such price volatility and effectively "lock in" a price for its raw materials.

Real Report 8.3 Answers Wal-Mart—Retail Inventory Method Disclosure

1. Wal-Mart values its inventory at the lower of cost or market using the retail method. The retail inventory method requires records of beginning inventory and goods purchased to be kept at cost (Wal-Mart uses a LIFO assumption) and retail. The retail inventory method then estimates the cost of inventory by applying a cost-to-retail ratio to the ending inventory valued at retail. To achieve a lower of cost or market valuation of the ending inventory, the cost and retail value of the beginning inventory and net markups are included in the computation of the cost-to-retail ratio (net markdowns are excluded). This method is known as the conventional retail method.
2. With inventory over $43 billion, a physical count of inventory is a major undertaking. Wal-Mart most likely uses the retail method because this permits it to compute cost of goods sold and income without having to take a physical count of inventory.
3. Given rising inventory costs, Wal-Mart's use of the LIFO cost flow assumption will result in lower inventory values, earnings, and taxes (assuming the use of LIFO for tax purposes). However, LIFO is not generally allowed for tax purposes in foreign countries. With these benefits removed, the advantages of a FIFO cost flow assumption (higher income and balance sheet amounts) likely outweigh any remaining benefits of using LIFO.

MULTIPLE-CHOICE (AICPA ADAPTED)

Select the best answer for each of the following.

M8-1 LO 8.1 Sienna Company uses the FIFO cost flow assumption. Sierra has inventory with a selling price of $100, packaging costs of $5, and transportation costs of $10. Sienna's normal profit margin is $20. However, due to limited supply of the product from the manufacturer, it would cost Sienna $80 to replace the inventory. What amount should be used as the market value?

a. $65
b. $85
c. $80
d. $100

M8-2 LO 8.1 Moore Company uses the LIFO cost flow assumption and carries Product A in inventory on December 31, 2017, at its unit cost of $9.50. Because of a sharp decline in demand for the product, the selling price was reduced to $10.00 per unit. Moore's normal profit margin on Product A is $2.00, disposal costs are $1.00 per unit, and the replacement cost is $6.50. Under the lower of cost or market rule, Moore's December 31, 2017, inventory of Product A should be valued at a unit cost of:

a. $6.50
b. $7.00
c. $9.00
d. $9.50

M8-3 LO 8.1 A company uses the LIFO cost flow assumption. The replacement cost of an inventory item is below the net realizable value and above the net realizable value minus the normal profit margin. The original cost of the inventory item is above the replacement cost and below the net realizable value. As a result, under the lower of cost or market rule, the inventory item should be valued at the:

a. net realizable value
b. original cost
c. replacement cost
d. net realizable value minus the normal profit margin

M8-4
LO 8.3

The following information is available for Silver Company for the three months ended March 31, 2016:

Merchandise inventory, January 1, 2016	$ 900,000
Purchases	3,400,000
Freight-in	200,000
Sales	4,800,000

The gross margin recorded was 25% of sales. What should be the merchandise inventory at March 31, 2016?

a. $700,000
b. $900,000
c. $1,125,000
d. $1,200,000

M8-5
LO 8.3

Hestor Company's records indicate the following information:

Merchandise inventory, January 1, 2016	$ 550,000
Purchases, January 1 through December 31, 2016	2,250,000
Sales, January 1 through December 31, 2016	3,000,000

On December 31, 2016, a physical inventory determined that ending inventory of $600,000 was in the warehouse. Hestor's gross profit on sales has remained constant at 30%. Hestor suspects some of the inventory may have been taken by some new employees. At December 31, 2016, what is the estimated cost of missing inventory?

a. $100,000
b. $300,000
c. $200,000
d. $700,000

M8-6
LO 8.4

Under the retail inventory method, freight-in would be included in the calculation of the goods available for sale for which of the following?

	Cost	Retail
a.	No	No
b.	No	Yes
c.	Yes	No
d.	Yes	Yes

M8-7
LO 8.4

The retail inventory method would include which of the following in the calculation of the goods available for sale at both cost and retail?

a. freight-in
b. purchases returns
c. markups
d. markdowns

M8-8
LO 8.4

At December 31, 2016, the following information was available from Crisford Company's books:

	Cost	Retail
Inventory, 1/1/16	$14,700	$ 20,300
Purchases	83,300	115,500
Net Additional markups	–	4,200
Available for sale	$98,000	$140,000

Sales for the year totaled $110,600; markdowns amounted to $1,400. Under the approximate lower of average cost or market retail method, Crisford's inventory at December 31, 2016, was:

a. $30,800
b. $28,000
c. $21,560
d. $19,600

M8-9
LO 8.5

Estimates of price-level changes for specific inventories are required for which of the following inventory methods?

a. conventional retail
b. weighted average cost
c. FIFO
d. dollar-value retail LIFO

M8-10
LO 8.6

A company forgets to record a purchase on credit in the purchases account, but ending inventory is correct. The effect of this mistake in the current year is:

	Income	Cost of Goods Sold	Accounts Payable	Retained Earnings
a.	Overstated	Understated	Understated	Overstated
b.	Understated	Overstated	Overstated	Understated
c.	Overstated	Understated	Overstated	Understated
d.	Understated	Overstated	Understated	Overstated

REVIEW EXERCISES

RE8-1
LO 8.1

Brown Company uses the LIFO cost flow assumption and has the following information available regarding each unit of its inventory:

Selling price	$5,200
Costs of completion	250
Current replacement cost	5,000
Normal profit margin	2,400

Based on this information, determine the amount that should be used as the market value to apply the lower of cost or market rule to determine Brown's ending inventory.

RE8-2
LO 8.1
Black Corporation uses the LIFO cost flow assumption. Each unit of its inventory has a net realizable value of $300, a normal profit margin of $35, and a current replacement cost of $250. Determine the amount per unit that should be used as the market value to apply the lower of cost or market rule to determine Black's ending inventory.

RE8-3
LO 8.1
Blue Corporation uses the FIFO cost flow assumption. Each unit of its inventory has a net realizable value of $2,850, a normal profit margin of $1,000, and a current replacement cost of $1,900. Determine the amount per unit that should be used as the market value to apply the lower of cost or market rule to determine Blue's ending inventory.

RE8-4
LO 8.1
Paul Corporation reports the following inventory information:

	Cost	Market
December 31, 2016	$312,000	$298,000

Assuming Paul uses a perpetual inventory system and the direct method, prepare the journal entry to record the reductions to market.

RE8-5
LO 8.1
Using the information provided in **RE8-4**, prepare the journal entry to record the reductions to market for Paul Corporation assuming that it uses the allowance method instead of the direct method.

RE8-6
LO 8.3
Kay's Beauty Supply uses the gross profit method to estimate the cost of ending inventory for in-house interim financial statements. Based on the following information for March, calculate Kay's' ending inventory at March 31.

Cost of goods available for sale	$125,000
Net sales for March	$80,000
Estimated historical gross profit rate on net sales	35%

RE8-7
LO 8.4
Uncle Butch's Hunting Supply Shop reports the following information related to inventory:

	Cost	Retail
Beginning inventory	$ 35,000	$ 92,000
Purchases	75,000	200,000
Net additional markups	—	15,000
Net markdowns	—	(22,000)
Goods available for sale	$110,000	$ 285,000
Sales		(178,000)
Ending inventory at retail		$ 107,000

Calculate Uncle Butch's' ending inventory using the retail inventory method under the FIFO cost flow assumption. Round the cost-to-retail ratio to 3 decimal places.

RE8-8
LO 8.4
Use the information in **RE8-7**. Calculate Uncle Butch's Hunting Supply Shop's ending inventory using the retail inventory method under the average cost assumption. Round the cost-to-retail ratio to 3 decimal places.

RE8-9
LO 8.4
Use the information in **RE8-7**. Calculate Uncle Butch's Hunting Supply Shop's ending inventory using the retail inventory method under the LIFO cost flow assumption. Round the cost-to-retail ratio to 3 decimal places.

RE8-10
LO 8.4
Use the information in **RE8-7**. Calculate Uncle Butch's Hunting Supply Shop's ending inventory using the retail inventory method under the lower of average cost or market assumption. Round the cost-to-retail ratio to 3 decimal places.

RE8-11
LO 8.5
Johnson Corporation had beginning inventory of $20,000 at cost and $35,000 at retail. During the year, it made net purchases of $180,000 at cost and $322,000 at retail. Johnson made sales of $300,000. Assuming a price index of 100 at the beginning of the year and 110 at the end of the year, compute Johnson's ending inventory at cost using the dollar-value LIFO retail method.

RE8-12
LO 8.6
Borys Company's periodic inventory at December 31, 2016 is understated by $10,000, but purchases are correct. Johnson correctly values its 2017 ending inventory. What is the effect of this error on Borys's 2016 and 2017 financial statements?

RE8-13
LO 8.7
Refer to the information provided in **RE8-4**. If Paul Corporation's inventory at January 1, 2016 had a cost and market value of $300,000, prepare the journal entry to record the reductions to market assuming that Paul uses a periodic inventory system and the direct method.

RE8-14
LO 8.7
Refer to the information provided in **RE8-4**. If Paul Corporation's inventory at January 1, 2016 had a cost and market value of $300,000, prepare the journal entry to record the reductions to market for Paul Corporation assuming that Paul uses a periodic inventory system and the allowance method.

EXERCISES

E8-1
LO 8.1

Lower of Cost or Market Stiles Corporation uses the lower of cost or market rule for each of two products in its ending inventory. A profit margin of 30% on the selling price is considered normal for each product. Specific data for each product are as follows:

	Product A	Product B
Historical cost	$ 80	$ 96
Replacement cost	70	98
Estimated cost of disposal	32	30
Estimated selling price	150	120

Required:
1. Assume that Stiles uses the FIFO cost flow assumption. What is the correct inventory value for each product?
2. Assume that Stiles uses the LIFO cost flow assumption. What is the correct inventory value for each product?
3. **Next Level** With regard to requirement 2, what effect does the imposition of the constraints on market value have on the inventory valuations?

E8-2
LO 8.1

Lower of Cost or Market The following information for Tuell Company is available:

	Case 1	Case 2	Case 3	Case 4	Case 5
Cost	$5.00	$5.00	$5.00	$5.00	$5.00
Net realizable value	5.10	5.50	4.80	4.20	4.70
Net realizable value less normal profit	4.80	5.30	4.70	4.00	4.60
Replacement cost	5.30	5.20	4.60	4.10	4.80

Required:
1. Assume Tuell uses the LIFO cost flow assumption. What is the correct inventory value in each of the preceding situations under U.S. GAAP?
2. Assume Tuell uses the average cost inventory cost flow assumption. What is the correct inventory value in each of the preceding situations under U.S. GAAP?
3. What is the correct inventory value in each of the preceding situations if Tuell uses IFRS?
4. Explain any differences between U.S. GAAP and IFRS inventory valuations.

E8-3
LO 8.1

Lower of Cost or Market The following information is taken from Aden Company's records:

Product	Group	Units	Cost/Unit	Market/Unit
A	1	600	$ 1.00	$ 0.80
B	1	250	1.50	1.55
C	2	150	5.00	5.25
D	2	100	6.50	6.40
E	3	80	25.00	24.60

Required:
1. What is the correct inventory value if the company applies the lower of cost or market to each of the following?
   a. individual items
   b. groups of items
   c. the inventory as a whole
2. **Next Level** Are there any conditions under which a company may ignore the decline in the value of inventory below its cost?

E8-4
LO 8.1

Lower of Cost or Market The inventories of Berry Company for the years 2016 and 2017 are as follows:

	Cost	Market
January 1, 2016	$10,000	$10,000
December 31, 2016	13,000	11,500
December 31, 2017	15,000	14,000

Berry uses a perpetual inventory system.

(continued)

Required:
1. Assume the inventory that existed at the end of 2016 was sold in 2017. Prepare the necessary journal entries at the end of each year to record the correct inventory valuation if Berry uses the:
   a. direct method
   b. allowance method
2. **Next Level** Explain any differences in inventory valuation and income between the two methods.

E8-5
LO 8.3

Gross Profit Method: Estimation of Fire Loss On September 28, 2016, a fire destroyed the entire merchandise inventory of Carroll Corporation. The following information is available:

Sales, January 1–September 28, 2016	$560,000
Inventory, January 1, 2016	$170,000
Merchandise purchases, January 1–September 28, 2016 (including $60,000 of goods in transit on September 28, 2016, shipped FOB shipping point)	$472,000
Markup percentage on cost	25%

Required:
What is the estimated inventory on September 28, 2016, immediately prior to the fire?

E8-6
LO 8.3
AICPA Adapted

Gross Profit Method: Estimation of Flood Loss On November 21, 2016, a flood at Hodge Company's warehouse caused severe damage to its entire inventory of Product Tex. Hodge estimates that all usable damaged goods can be sold for $10,000. The following information was available from Hodge's accounting records for Product Tex:

Inventory at November 1, 2016	$100,000
Purchases from November 1, 2016, to date of flood	140,000
Net sales from November 1, 2016, to date of flood	220,000

Based on recent history, Hodge had a gross margin (profit) on Product Tex of 30% of net sales.

Required:
1. Prepare a schedule to calculate the estimated loss on the inventory in the flood, using the gross profit method. Show supporting computations in good form.
2. **Next Level** Describe situations in which the gross profit method may not provide an accurate estimate of ending inventory.

E8-7
LO 8.3

Gross Profit Percentage An accountant sometimes must convert gross profit as a percent of cost of goods sold to gross profit as a percent of sales before the gross profit method can be applied.

Required:
Convert the following gross profit percentages based on the cost of goods sold to gross profit as a percentage of net sales:
1. 20%
2. 25%
3. 40%

E8-8
LO 8.3

Gross Profit Method: Estimation of Theft Loss You are requested by a client on September 28 to prepare an insurance claim for a theft loss that occurred on that day. You immediately take an inventory and obtain the following data:

Inventory, September 1	$38,000	Sales, September 1–September 28	$51,000
Purchases, September 1–September 28	19,000		

The inventory on September 28 indicates that an inventory of $15,000 remains after the theft. During the past year, net sales were made at 50% above the cost of goods sold.

Required:
1. Compute the inventory lost during the theft. Round the gross profit percentage to 3 decimal places.
2. **Next Level** What concerns might you have about the inventory estimation under the gross profit method?

E8-9 **Retail Inventory Method** Harmes Company is a clothing store that uses the retail inventory method. The following information relates to its operations during the year:

LO 8.4

	Cost	Retail
Inventory, January 1	$28,400	$ 40,200
Purchases	65,200	100,000
Markups (net)	—	1,900
Markdowns (net)	—	400
Sales	—	80,000

Required:
Compute the ending inventory by the retail inventory method for the following cost flow assumptions (round the cost-to-retail ratio to 3 decimal places):
1. FIFO
2. average cost
3. LIFO
4. lower of cost or market (based on average cost)

E8-10 **Retail Inventory Method** The following data were available from Hegge Department Store's records for the year ended December 31, 2016:

LO 8.4

AICPA Adapted

	At Cost	At Retail
Merchandise inventory, January 1, 2016	$ 90,000	$130,000
Purchases	330,000	460,000
Markups	—	10,000
Markdowns	—	40,000
Sales	—	480,000

Required:
Using the retail method, what is the estimate of the merchandise inventory at December 31, 2016, valued at the lower of cost or market? Round the cost-to-retail ratio to 3 decimal places.

E8-11 **Retail Inventory Method** The following information relates to the retail inventory method used by Jeffress Company:

LO 8.4

	Cost	Retail
Beginning inventory	$11,160	$18,000
Purchases	54,600	92,400
Freight-in	840	—
Net additional markups	—	600
Net markdowns	—	1,144
Sales	—	94,056

Required:
1. Compute the ending inventory by the retail inventory method using the following cost flow assumptions (round the cost-to-retail ratio to 3 decimal places):
   a. FIFO
   b. average cost
   c. LIFO
   d. lower of cost or market (based on average cost)
2. **Next Level** What assumptions are necessary for the retail inventory method to produce accurate estimates of ending inventory?

E8-12 **Dollar-Value LIFO Retail** Johns Company adopts the dollar-value LIFO retail inventory method on January 1, 2016. The following information for 2016 is obtained from Johns' records:

LO 8.5

	Cost	Retail
Inventory, January 1, 2016	$20,000	$29,000
Purchases	60,000	92,000
Net additional markups	—	1,000
Net markdowns	—	3,000
Sales	—	75,000

The price index on January 1, 2016, was 100, and on December 31, 2016, it was 110.

(continued)

Required:
Compute the cost of the inventory on December 31, 2016. Round the cost-to-retail ratio to 3 decimal places.

E8-13 **Dollar-Value LIFO Retail** Wyatt Company adopts the dollar-value LIFO retail inventory method on January 1, 2016. The company's records reveal that the inventory on January 1, 2016, had a cost of $75,000 and a retail value of $120,000. During 2016, the cost of purchases made was $110,000, and the retail value was $165,000. In addition, net markdowns were $6,000, net additional markups were $8,000, and sales were $147,000. The price index on January 1, 2016, was 100, and the index for 2016 was 110.

LO 8.5

Required:
Compute the cost of inventory on December 31, 2016. Round the cost-to-retail ratio to 3 decimal places.

E8-14 **Dollar-Value LIFO Retail** On December 31, 2015, Davison Company adopted the dollar-value LIFO retail inventory method. Inventory data for 2016 are as follows:

LO 8.5

AICPA Adapted

	LIFO Cost	Retail
Inventory, 12/31/15	$360,000	$500,000
Inventory, 12/31/16	?	$660,000
Increase in price level for 2016		10%
Cost-to-retail ratio for 2016		70%

Required:
Compute the cost of Davison's inventory at December 31, 2016.

E8-15 **Errors** A company that uses the periodic inventory system makes the following errors:

LO 8.6

1. It omits a purchase on credit from the purchases account and the ending inventory.
2. It omits a purchase on credit from the purchases account, but the ending inventory is correct.
3. It overstates the ending inventory, but purchases are correct.

Required:
Indicate the effect of the preceding errors on the income statement and the balance sheet of the current and succeeding years.

E8-16 **Errors** During the course of your examination of the financial statements of Burnett Co., a new client, for the year ended December 31, 2016, you discover the following:

LO 8.6

AICPA Adapted

- Inventory at January 1, 2016, was understated by $6,000.
- Inventory at December 31, 2016, was overstated by $5,000.

During 2016, the company received a $1,000 cash advance from a customer for merchandise to be manufactured and shipped during 2017. It had credited the $1,000 to sales revenue. The company's gross profit on sales is 50%. Net income reported on the 2016 income statement (before reflecting any adjustments for the above items) is $20,000.

Required:
Next Level What is the correct net income for 2016?

E8-17 *(Appendix 8.1)* **Lower of Cost or Market** The inventories of Berry Company for the years 2016 and 2017 are as follows:

LO 8.7

	Cost	Market
January 1, 2016	$10,000	$10,000
December 31, 2016	13,000	11,500
December 31, 2017	15,000	14,000

Berry uses the periodic inventory method.

Required:
1. Assume the inventory that existed at the end of 2016 was sold in 2017. Prepare the necessary journal entries at the end of each year to record the correct inventory valuation if Berry uses the:
   a. direct method
   b. allowance method
2. **Next Level** Refer to your answer for **E8-4**. How does the use of a periodic or perpetual inventory system affect the valuation of inventory?

PROBLEMS

P8-1
LO 8.1

Lower of Cost or Market Palmquist Company has five different inventory items that it values by the lower of cost or market rule applied on an individual item basis. The normal markup on all items is 20% of cost. The following information is obtained from the company's records:

Item	Units	Cost	Replacement Cost	Net Realizable Value
1	500	$10.00	$ 9.10	$ 9.20
2	400	8.00	8.10	7.80
3	300	15.00	13.50	14.00
4	200	18.00	12.00	17.00
5	100	25.00	25.50	25.30

Required:
1. Assume that Palmquist uses the FIFO cost flow assumption. Compute the correct inventory value under the lower of cost or market rule.
2. Assume that Palmquist uses the LIFO cost flow assumption. Compute the correct inventory value under the lower of cost or market rule.
3. Assume that Palmquist uses IFRS. Compute the correct inventory value under the lower of cost or market rule.
4. **Next Level** Explain the differences between the inventory valuations reported under IFRS and U.S. GAAP.

P8-2
LO 8.1

Lower of Cost or Market The following are the inventories for the years 2016, 2017, and 2018 for Parry Company:

	Cost	Market
January 1, 2016	$50,000	$50,000
December 31, 2016	64,000	60,000
December 31, 2017	71,000	70,000
December 31, 2018	75,000	78,000

Required:
1. Assume the inventory that existed at the end of each year was sold in the subsequent year. Prepare journal entries to record the lower of cost or market for each of the following alternatives:
   a. allowance method, perpetual inventory system
   b. direct method, perpetual inventory system
2. **Next Level** Explain any differences in inventory valuation and income between the two methods.

P8-3
LO 8.1

Lower of Cost or Market The inventory records of Frost Company for the years 2016 and 2017 reveal the cost and market of the January 1, 2016, inventory to be $125,000. On December 31, 2016, the cost of inventory was $130,000, while the market value was only $128,000. The December 31, 2017, market value of inventory was $140,000, and the cost was only $135,000. Frost uses a perpetual inventory system.

Required:
1. Assume the inventory that existed at the end of 2016 was sold in 2017. Prepare the journal entries at the end of 2016 and 2017 to record the lower of cost or market under the:
   a. allowance method
   b. direct method
2. Show the presentation of cost of goods sold and inventory on Frost's income statement and balance sheet for 2016 and 2017 under the:
   a. allowance method (assume the cost of goods sold prior to applying the lower of cost or market was $595,000 and $605,000 for 2016 and 2017, respectively)
   b. direct method

P8-4
LO 8.3

Gross Profit Method: Estimation of Fire Loss On January 20, 2017, Stewart Company's records revealed the following information:

Inventory, July 1, 2016	$ 55,300
Purchases, July 1, 2016–January 20, 2017	382,100
Sales, July 1, 2016–January 20, 2017	592,000
Purchases returns	10,400
Purchases discounts taken	6,800
Freight-in	3,500
Sales returns	6,600

(continued)

A fire destroyed the entire inventory on January 20, 2017, except for purchases in transit, FOB shipping point of $6,000, and goods having a selling price of $4,700 that were salvaged from the fire. The salvaged goods had an estimated salvage value of $2,900. The average gross profit on net sales in previous periods was 40%.

Required:
1. Compute the cost of the inventory lost in the fire.
2. **Next Level** If a company discloses that it uses a periodic inventory system, what concerns might you have about its interim financial statements?

P8-5
LO 8.3
AICPA Adapted

Gross Profit Method: Estimation of Flood Loss On June 30, 2016, a flash flood damaged the warehouse and factory of Padway Corporation, completely destroying the work-in-process inventory. There was no damage to either the raw materials or finished goods inventories. A physical inventory taken after the flood revealed the following valuations:

Raw materials	$ 62,000
Work in process	0
Finished goods	119,000

The inventory on January 1, 2016 consisted of the following:

Raw materials	$ 30,000
Work in process	100,000
Finished goods	140,000
	$270,000

A review of the books and records disclosed that the gross profit margin historically approximated 25% of sales. The sales for the first six months of 2016 were $340,000. Raw material purchases were $115,000. Direct labor costs for this period were $80,000, and manufacturing overhead was historically applied at 50% of direct labor.

Required:
Compute the value of the work-in-process inventory lost at June 30, 2016. Show supporting computations in good form.

P8-6
LO 8.4

Retail Inventory Method Turner Corporation uses the retail inventory method. The following information relates to 2016:

	Cost	Retail		Cost	Retail
Inventory, January 1	$ 29,000	$ 45,000	Additional markups	—	$ 50,000
Purchases (gross price)	140,000	190,000	Markup cancellations	—	10,000
Purchases discounts taken	3,000	—	Markdowns	—	15,000
Purchases returns	5,000	8,000	Markdown cancellations	—	3,000
Freight-in	20,000	—	Net Sales	—	190,000
Employee discounts	—	3,000			

Required:
Compute the cost of the ending inventory under each of the following cost flow assumptions (round the cost-to-retail ratio to 3 decimal places):
1. FIFO
2. average cost
3. LIFO
4. lower of cost or market (based on average cost)

P8-7
LO 8.4

Retail Inventory Method EKC Company uses the retail inventory method. The following information for 2016 is available:

	Cost	Retail		Cost	Retail
Inventory, January 1	$100,000	$180,000	Markup cancellations	—	$ 12,000
Purchases (gross price)	320,000	600,000	Markdowns	—	15,000
Purchases discounts taken	6,000	—	Markdown cancellations	—	4,000
Freight-in	16,000	—	Net Sales	—	580,000
Additional markups	—	60,000			

Required:

Compute the cost of the ending inventory under each of the following cost flow assumptions (round the cost-to-retail ratio to 3 decimal places):
1. FIFO
2. average cost
3. LIFO
4. lower of cost or market (based on average cost)

P8-8
LO 8.4
AICPA Adapted

Retail Inventory Method Red Department Store uses the retail inventory method. Information relating to the computation of the inventory at December 31, 2016, is as follows:

	Cost	Retail		Cost	Retail
Inventory at January 1, 2016	$32,000	$80,000	Markups	—	$60,000
Sales	—	600,000	Markup cancellations	—	10,000
Purchases	270,000	590,000	Markdowns	—	25,000
Freight-in	7,600	—	Markdown cancellations	—	5,000

Estimated normal shrinkage is 2% of sales.

Required:
Prepare a schedule to calculate the estimated ending inventory at the lower of average cost or market at December 31, 2016, using the retail inventory method. Show supporting computations in good form. Round the cost-to-retail ratio to 3 decimal places.

P8-9
LO 8.4
LO 8.5

Retail Inventory Method Weber Corporation uses the retail inventory method to estimate its inventory balances. The following information is available on June 30:

	Cost	Retail		Cost	Retail
Inventory, January 1	$25,000	$60,000	Markdowns	—	$7,000
Purchases	75,000	180,000	Additional markups	—	3,000
Sales	—	205,000	Markdown cancellations	—	2,000
Purchases returns	2,000	5,000	Markup cancellations	—	1,000

Required:
1. Compute the inventory on June 30 using the conventional retail inventory method (lower of average cost or market). Round the cost-to-retail ratio to 3 decimal places.
2. Independent of Requirement 1, assume that the June 30 inventory was $80,000 at retail and that the cost-to-retail ratio is 50%. If the price level of the inventory has risen by 5% during the period, compute the cost of the June 30 inventory under the dollar-value retail LIFO method, assuming that the company adopted the method at the beginning of the year.

P8-10
LO 8.5

Dollar-Value LIFO Retail The following information is obtained from Burger Company's records. Burger uses the dollar-value LIFO retail method.

	2016		2017		2018	
	Cost	Retail	Cost	Retail	Cost	Retail
Purchases	$200,000	$420,000	$250,000	$550,000	$240,000	$500,000
Net additional markups	—	20,000	—	30,000	—	10,000
Net markdowns	—	10,000	—	40,000	—	20,000
Sales	—	400,000	—	600,000	—	450,000

The company adopted LIFO on January 1, 2016, when the cost and retail values of the inventory were $50,000 and $100,000, respectively. Burger experienced the following price indexes:

January 1, 2016	100	December 31, 2017	115
December 31, 2016	108	December 31, 2018	120

(continued)

Required:
Compute the cost of the ending inventory for 2016, 2017, and 2018. Round the cost-to-retail ratio to 3 decimal places.

P8-11 **Dollar-Value LIFO Retail** Intella Inc. adopted the dollar-value retail LIFO method on January 1, 2015. The fol-
LO 8.5 lowing data apply to the 4 subsequent years:

		Cost	Retail			Cost	Retail
2015	Inventory, January 1	$40,000	$ 80,000	2017	Purchases	$117,600	$280,000
	Purchases	85,500	190,000		Sales	–	260,000
	Sales	–	200,000	2018	Purchases	147,200	320,000
2016	Purchases	92,000	230,000		Sales	–	300,000
	Sales	–	210,000				

In addition, the following price indexes are available:

January 1, 2015	100	December 31, 2017	120
December 31, 2015	105	December 31, 2018	125
December 31, 2016	110		

Required:
Compute the inventory at the end of each of the 4 years. Round the cost-to-retail ratio to 3 decimal places.

P8-12 **Dollar-Value LIFO Retail and Fire Loss** Golden Company adopted the dollar-value retail LIFO method on
LO 8.5 January 1, 2016. The following information relates to the following 2 years:

	2016		2017 (through September 7)		
	Cost	Retail		Cost	Retail
Inventory, January 1	$ 40,000	$ 90,000	Purchases	$160,000	$350,000
Purchases	100,000	210,000	Sales	–	280,000
Sales	–	200,000	Net additional markups	–	40,000
Net additional markups	–	20,000	Net markdowns	–	70,000
Net markdowns	–	40,000			

In addition, the following price indexes are available:

January 2016	100
December 2016	106
September 2017	110

On September 8, 2017, a fire destroyed the inventory except for goods in transit (properly recorded), FOB shipping point, at a cost of $8,000, and undamaged goods salvaged from the fire which had a retail value of $10,000.

Required:
Compute the cost of the inventory destroyed in the fire. Round the cost-to-retail ratio to 3 decimal places.

P8-13 **Errors** As controller of Lerner Company, which uses a periodic inventory system, you discover the following errors
LO 8.6 in the current year:
1. Merchandise with a cost of $17,500 was properly included in the final inventory, but the purchase was not recorded until the following year.
2. Merchandise purchases are in transit under terms of FOB shipping point. They have been excluded from the inventory, but the purchase was recorded in the current year on the receipt of the invoice of $4,300.
3. Goods out on consignment have been excluded from inventory.
4. Merchandise purchases under terms FOB shipping point have been omitted from the purchases account and the ending inventory. The purchases were recorded in the following year.
5. Goods held on consignment from Talbert Supply Co. were included in the inventory.

Required:
For each error, indicate the effect on the ending inventory and the net income for the current year and on the net income for the following year.

P8-14 **Comprehensive: Inventory Adjustments** Layne Corporation, a manufacturer of small tools, provided the following information from its accounting records for the year ended December 31, 2016:

LO 8.6

AICPA Adapted

Inventory at December 31, 2016 (based on physical count of goods in Layne's plant at cost on December 31, 2016)	$1,750,000
Accounts payable at December 31, 2016	1,200,000
Net sales (sales less sales returns)	8,500,000

Additional information is as follows:
1. Included in the physical count were tools billed to a customer FOB shipping point on December 31, 2016. These tools had a cost of $28,000 and had been billed and included in sales at $35,000. The shipment was on Layne's loading dock waiting to be picked up by the common carrier.
2. Goods were in transit from a vendor to Layne on December 31, 2016. The invoice cost was $50,000, and the goods were shipped FOB shipping point on December 29, 2016.
3. Work-in-process inventory costing $20,000 was sent to an outside processor for plating on December 30, 2016.
4. Tools returned by customers and held pending inspection in the returned goods area on December 31, 2016, were not included in the physical count. On January 8, 2017, the tools costing $26,000 were inspected and returned to inventory. Credit memos totaling $40,000 were issued to the customers on the same date.
5. Tools shipped to a customer FOB destination on December 24, 2016, were in transit at December 31, 2016, and had a cost of $25,000. Upon notification of receipt by the customer on January 2, 2017, Layne issued a sales invoice for $42,000.
6. Goods, with an invoice cost of $30,000, received from a vendor at 5:00 P.M. on December 31, 2016, were recorded on a receiving report dated January 2, 2017. The goods were not included in the physical count, but the invoice was included in accounts payable at December 31, 2016.
7. Goods received from a vendor on December 24, 2016, were included in the physical count. However, the related $60,000 vendor invoice was not included in accounts payable at December 31, 2016, because the accounts payable copy of the receiving report was lost.
8. On January 4, 2017, a monthly freight bill in the amount of $4,000 was received. The bill specifically related to merchandise purchased in December 2016, one-half of which was still in the inventory at December 31, 2016. The freight charges were not included in either the inventory or in accounts payable at December 31, 2016.

Required:
Prepare a schedule of adjustments as of December 31, 2016, to the initial amounts in inventory, accounts payable, and sales. Show separately the effect, if any, of each of the eight transactions on the December 31, 2016, amounts. Indicate if the transactions would have no effect on the initial amount shown.

P8-15 *(Appendix 8.1)* **Lower of Cost or Market** The following are the inventories for the years 2016, 2017, and 2018 for Parry Company:

LO 8.7

	Cost	Market
January 1, 2016	$50,000	$50,000
December 31, 2016	64,000	60,000
December 31, 2017	71,000	70,000
December 31, 2018	75,000	78,000

Required:
1. Assume the inventory that existed at the end of each year was sold in the subsequent year. Prepare journal entries to record the lower of cost or market for each of the following alternatives:
    a. allowance method, periodic inventory system
    b. direct method, periodic inventory system
2. **Next Level** Refer to your answer for **P8-2**. How does the use of the periodic inventory system affect the write-down of inventory to the lower of cost or market?

P8-16 **(Appendix 8.1) Lower of Cost or Market** Frost Company's inventory records for the years 2016 and 2017 reveal
LO 8.7 the cost and market of the January 1, 2016, inventory to be $125,000. On December 31, 2016, the cost of inventory was $130,000, while the market value was only $128,000. The December 31, 2017, market value of inventory was $140,000, and the cost was only $135,000. Frost uses a periodic inventory system. Purchases for 2016 were $100,000 and for 2017 were $110,000.

Required:
1. Assume the inventory that existed at the end of 2016 was sold in 2017. Prepare the journal entries at the end of 2016 and 2017 to record the lower of cost or market under the (a) allowance method and (b) direct method.
2. Prepare the cost of goods sold section of the income statement and show how the company would record the inventory on its balance sheet for 2016 and 2017 under the (a) allowance method and (b) direct method.
3. **Next Level** Refer to your answer for **P8-3**. How does the use of a periodic inventory system versus a perpetual inventory system affect the valuation of inventory and the amount reported as income?

CASES

COMMUNICATION

C8-1 **LCM, Dollar-Value LIFO, and Consignments**
LO 8.1 Caddell Company, a wholesaler, purchases its inventories from various suppliers FOB destination. It incurs substantial warehousing costs. Caddell uses the dollar-value LIFO inventory cost flow method. Caddell also consigns some of its inventories to Reed Company.
AICPA Adapted

Reed also has items for sale that it purchases from other wholesalers. Reed uses the lower of FIFO cost or market inventory method.

Required:
1. When are the purchases from various suppliers generally included in Caddell's inventory? Why?
2. Theoretically, how should Caddell account for the warehousing costs? Why?
3. a. Explain the advantages of using the dollar-value LIFO inventory cost flow method as opposed to the conventional quantity of goods LIFO method.
   b. How does the calculation of dollar-value LIFO differ from the conventional quantity of goods method?
4. Explain how Caddell should account for the inventories consigned to Reed Company.
5. When Reed applies the lower of cost or market rule, what are the ceiling and floor limits?

C8-2 **Retail Inventory Method**
LO 8.4 Sandberg Paint Company, your client, manufactures paint. The company's president, Ms. Sandberg, has decided to open a retail store to sell Sandberg paint as well as wallpaper and other supplies that it would purchase from other suppliers. She has asked you for information about the retail method of pricing inventories at the retail store.
AICPA Adapted

Required:
Prepare a report to the president explaining the retail method of pricing inventories. Your report should include these four points:
1. Description and accounting features of the method
2. Conditions that may distort the results under the method
3. Comparison of the advantages of using the retail method with those of using cost methods of inventory pricing
4. Accounting theory underlying the treatment of net markdowns and net additional markups under the method

CREATIVE AND CRITICAL THINKING

C8-3 **Lower of Cost or Market Rule**
LO 8.1 Blaedon Co. makes ongoing design refinements to lawnmowers that are produced for it by contractors. Blaedon stores the lawnmowers in its own warehouse and sells them at list price, directly to retailers. Blaedon uses the FIFO inventory method. Approximately two-thirds of new lawnmower sales involve trade-ins. For each used lawnmower traded in and returned to Blaedon, retailers receive a $40 allowance regardless of whether the trade-in was associated with a sale of a 2017 or 2018 model. Blaedon's net realizable value on a used lawnmower averages $25.
AICPA Adapted

At December 31, 2017, Blaedon's inventory of new lawnmowers includes both 2017 and 2018 models. When the 2018 model was introduced in September 2017, the list price of the remaining 2017 model lawnmowers was reduced below cost. Blaedon is experiencing rising costs.

Required:
1. At December 31, 2017, how should Blaedon determine the carrying amounts assigned to its lawnmower inventory of:
   a. 2018 models
   b. 2017 models
2. Considering only the 2018 model lawnmower, explain the impact of the FIFO cost flow assumptions on Blaedon's 2017:
   a. income statement amounts
   b. balance sheet amounts

C8-4 **Inventory Valuation Issues**
LO 8.1
AICPA Adapted

Hanlon Company purchased a significant amount of raw materials inventory for a new product that it is manufacturing. Hanlon purchased insurance on these raw materials while they were in transit from the supplier.

Hanlon uses the lower of cost or market rule for these raw materials. The replacement cost of the raw materials is above the net realizable value and both are below the original cost.

Hanlon uses the average cost inventory method for these raw materials. In the last two years, each purchase has been at a lower price than the previous purchase, and the ending inventory quantity for each period has been higher than the beginning inventory quantity for that period.

Required:
1. Explain the theoretically appropriate method that Hanlon should use to account for the insurance costs on the raw materials while they were in transit from the supplier.
2. a. Explain the amount at which Hanlon should report the raw materials inventory on its balance sheet.
   b. In general, explain why the lower of cost or market rule is used to report inventory.
3. Explain what would have been the effect on ending inventory and cost of goods sold had Hanlon used the LIFO inventory method instead of the average cost inventory method for the raw materials. Assume LIFO cost of ending inventory is below both the replacement cost and net realizable value.

C8-5 **Gross Profit**
LO 8.3
AICPA Adapted

Shelly Corporation is an importer and wholesaler. Its merchandise is purchased from several suppliers and is warehoused by Shelly until sold to consumers. In conducting her audit for the year ended June 30, 2016, the corporation's CPA determined that the system of internal control was good. Accordingly, she observed the physical inventory at an interim date, May 31, 2016, instead of at year-end.

The CPA obtained the following information from the general ledger:

Inventory, July 1, 2015	$ 87,500
Physical inventory, May 31, 2016	95,000
Sales for 11 months ended May 31, 2016	840,000
Sales for year ended June 30, 2016	960,000
Purchases for 11 months ended May 31, 2016 (before audit adjustments)	675,000
Purchases for year ended June 30, 2016 (before audit adjustments)	800,000

The CPA's audit disclosed the following information:

Shipments received in May and included in the physical inventory but recorded as June purchases	$7,500
Shipments received in unsalable condition and excluded from physical inventory; credit memos had not been received nor had chargebacks to vendors been recorded:	
Total at May 31, 2016	1,000
Total at June 30, 2016 (including the May unrecorded chargebacks)	1,500
Deposit made with vendor and charged to purchases in April 2016. Product was shipped in July 2016.	2,000
Deposit made with vendor and charged to purchases in May 2016. Product was shipped, FOB shipping point, on May 28, 2016, and was included in May 31, 2016, physical inventory as goods in transit.	5,500
Through the carelessness of the receiving department, a June shipment was damaged by rain. This shipment was later sold in June at its cost of $10,000.	

Required:
In audit engagements in which interim physical inventories are observed, a frequently used auditing procedure is to test the reasonableness of the year-end inventory by the application of gross profit ratios. Prepare in good form the following schedules:
1. Computation of the gross profit ratio for 11 months ended May 31, 2016
2. Computation by the gross profit ratio method of cost of goods sold during June 2016
3. Computation by the gross profit ratio method of June 30, 2016 inventory

C8-6 **Retail Inventory Method**
LO 8.4
AICPA Adapted

Retail Inc. sells normal brand-name household products both from its own store and on consignment through Mall Space Company.

Required:
1. Explain whether Retail should include in its inventory the normal brand-name goods purchased from its suppliers but not yet received if the terms of purchase are FOB shipping point (manufacturer's plant).
2. Explain whether Retail should include freight-in expenditures as an inventoriable cost.
3. Retail purchased cooking utensils for sale in the ordinary course of business three times during the current year, each time at a higher price than the previous purchase. Explain the effect on ending inventory and cost of goods sold if Retail used the weighted average cost method instead of the FIFO method.
4. Explain how and why Retail will treat net markdowns when it calculates the estimated cost of ending inventory using the conventional (lower of cost or market) retail inventory method.
5. Explain what products on consignment are and how they are presented on the balance sheets of Retail and Mall Space Company.

C8-7 **Various Inventory Issues**
LO 8.1
LO 8.4
AICPA Adapted

Diane Company, a retailer and wholesaler of national brand-name household lighting fixtures, purchases its inventories from various suppliers. Diane uses the LIFO inventory method.

Required:
1. a. What criteria are used to determine which of Diane's costs are inventoriable?
   b. Are Diane's administrative costs inventoriable? Defend your answer.
2. a. Diane uses the lower of cost or market rule for its wholesale inventories. Explain the theoretical arguments for that rule.
   b. The replacement cost of the inventories is below the net realizable value less a normal profit margin, which, in turn, is below the original cost. Explain the amount that is used to value the inventories.
3. Diane calculates the estimated cost of its ending inventories held for sale at retail using the conventional (lower of average cost or market) retail inventory method. Explain how Diane would treat the beginning inventories and net markdowns in calculating the cost ratio used to determine its ending inventories.

C8-8 **Various Inventory Issues**
LO 8.1
LO 8.4
AICPA Adapted

Hudson Company, which is both a wholesaler and a retailer, purchases its inventories from various suppliers. Additional facts for Hudson's wholesale operations are as follows:

- Hudson incurs substantial warehousing costs.
- Hudson uses the lower of cost or market rule.
- The replacement cost of the inventories is below the net realizable value and above the net realizable value minus the normal profit margin. The original cost of the inventories is above the replacement cost and below the net realizable value.

Additional facts for Hudson's retail operations are as follows:

- Hudson determines the estimated cost of its ending inventories held for sale at retail using the conventional retail inventory method, which approximates lower of average cost or market.
- Hudson incurs substantial freight-in costs.
- Hudson has net additional markups and net markdowns.

Required:
1. Theoretically, how should Hudson account for the warehousing costs related to its wholesale inventories? Why?
2. a. In general, explain why the lower of cost or market rule is used to report inventory.
   b. At which amount should Hudson report the wholesale inventories on its balance sheet? Explain the application of the lower of cost or market rule in this situation.
3. In the calculation of the cost-to-retail percentage used to determine the estimated cost of its ending retail inventories, how should Hudson treat:
   a. freight-in costs
   b. net additional markups
   c. net markdowns
4. Explain why Hudson's retail inventory method approximates lower of average cost or market.

C8-9 **Ethics and Retail Inventory**
LO 8.4

You are the accountant for the South-Western Division of HiValue Grocery Stores. Late in December, Kelly Cholak, the CEO of the division, stops by your office and says, "I have a couple of questions. I recently received a report from the head office on the first 11 months of the year. We are not doing as well as we budgeted, and they are not happy with the gross profit we have earned. But the good news is that I just got off the phone with a big supplier who has excess inventory and could sell us enough of their products to last us three months. They have offered us a great price—lower than we have paid in a couple of years. Then I remembered that you use that funny LIFO retail inventory method where you play with such confusing numbers. Will the purchase reduce our retail ratio, or whatever you call it, so that our inventory is lower and cost of goods sold higher, because that would only make us look worse? Alternatively, I thought that we could delay this purchase until after January 1, and we might be able to have one of those LIFO liquid profits and make ourselves look good for the year's results. Give these issues some thought and let's have a drink after work today to discuss them."

Required:
From financial reporting and ethical perspectives, how would you reply to Kelly?

C8-10 **Analyzing Starbucks' Inventory Disclosures**
Obtain **Starbucks**' 2015 annual report either using the "Investor Relations" portion of its website (do a web search for Starbucks investor relations) or go to http://www.sec.gov and click "Search for company filings" under "Filings and Forms (EDGAR)."

Required:
1. What classifications are used by Starbucks to value its inventory?
2. How does Starbucks value its inventory?
3. What is the amount of inventory write-downs for 2015? Can you tell if Starbucks records inventory write-downs using the direct or allowance method?

C8-11 **Analyzing Moet Hennessy Louis Vuitton's (LVMH) Inventory Disclosures**

Obtain **Moet Hennessy Louis Vuitton**'s 2013 annual report using the "Investor Relations" portion of its website (do a web search for Moet Hennessy – Louis Vuitton investor relations).

Required:
1. Describe the inventory of LVMH.
2. How does LVMH value its inventory other than wines? Why doesn't LVMH use LIFO?
3. How does LVMH value its wine inventory? What is the justification for this valuation?
4. Did LVMH record any inventory write-downs during the year? If so, what was the dollar amount and can any conclusions be drawn from the pattern or write-downs.

USING CODIFICATION

C8-12 Researching GAAP

Situation
Diversified Inc. is a retailer that sells a variety of goods under three major business units. Its Food Products Division delivers wholesale food products to national grocery store chains. Its Home Appliances Division manufactures and sells home kitchen appliances such as refrigerators, microwave ovens, and dishwashers. Finally, its High Fashion Division is a recognized leader in high-end women's clothing. During his annual review of the company's financial condition, Diversified's president noted that the company's inventory included a material reduction described as an "allowance to reduce inventory to market." While the Home Appliances Division had received a considerable amount of negative publicity relating to fires caused by defective switches in its products, the president felt that any reduction in the market value of these products that was taken in the third quarter was more than offset by the high margins in the High Fashion Division. Therefore, the president felt that no write-down should have been taken. Further, the president noted that the company had replaced the faulty switches in the third fiscal quarter and subsequent sales had shown that the market value of its appliances had partially recovered. All estimates are that the value of the appliance inventory should be completely recovered by the fourth quarter of the next fiscal year.

Directions
Research the related generally accepted accounting principles and prepare a short memo that addresses the president's concerns. Cite your references and applicable paragraph numbers.

CURRENT LIABILITIES AND CONTINGENT OBLIGATIONS

A Risky Proposition

In order to determine if they should provide resources to a company, investors and creditors analyze the risk involved. Financial statement information relating to current liabilities and contingent obligations is particularly useful in the analysis of a company's liquidity, financial flexibility, and credit risk. To assess a company's liquidity, which represents the company's ability to meet its short-term obligations, financial statement users will examine the relationship between a company's current assets and its current liabilities. **Starbucks**'s current liabilities, which represent obligations to employees, suppliers, and other short-term creditors, make up approximately 55% of the company's total liabilities as of the end of fiscal year 2015, as shown below.

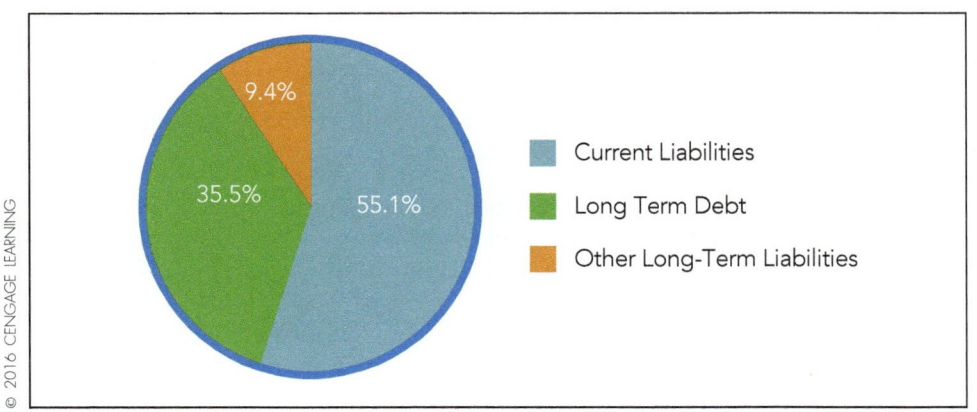

LEARNING OBJECTIVES

After reading this chapter you will be able to

LO 9.1 Explain the characteristics of a liability.

LO 9.2 Describe the nature, classification, and valuation of current liabilities.

LO 9.3 Identify, measure, and record current liabilities based on a contractual amount.

LO 9.4 Understand and record current liabilities whose amounts are determined by operating activities.

LO 9.5 Identify and account for contingent obligations, including warranties and premiums.

LO 9.6 Describe the presentation and disclosure of current liabilities and contingencies.

In 2014, Starbucks paid $2,763.9 million to settle a legal dispute with **Kraft** over distribution rights for Starbucks coffee in grocery stores. Such a large cash payment may raise concerns about Starbucks's liquidity. However, Starbucks's current assets ($4,352.7 million) exceed its current liabilities ($3,653.5 million) by approximately $699 million, and it reports a current ratio (current assets ÷ current liabilities) of 1.19. In addition to examining the current ratio, financial statement users also assess a company's ability to obtain additional short-term financing in the event of temporary cash shortfalls. For example, Starbucks has a $1 billion commercial paper program and a revolving credit facility agreement which allows it to borrow up to $750 million to meet working capital and other needs. With a cash balance of $1,530.1 million and significant borrowing capacity, Starbucks appears to be well-positioned to meet its short-term obligations.

A company's liquidity also affects its financial flexibility—its ability to use its financial resources to adapt to change, take advantage of strategic opportunities, and increase returns to common shareholders. If a company can generate a high return on its net operating assets relative to the cost of borrowing, it can likely increase the level of borrowing and is considered to have greater financial flexibility. In addition, companies that can easily meet their short-term obligations are considered to have greater financial flexibility than companies that are constrained to meet their current obligations. For Starbucks, its ability to generate strong operating cash flows (over $3.7 billion in 2015) coupled with its liquid financial position provides the company with the financial flexibility to invest in its core business and generate favorable returns for its shareholders.

Finally, financial statement users assess a company's credit risk, which refers to a company's ability to pay interest and principal payments on its debt. In addition to the short-term liquidity measures previously discussed, users also consider other factors, such as a company's commitments and contingent obligations. Because the commitments will be paid and the uncertainty associated with contingencies will be resolved on a future date, they can significantly impact a company's credit risk and must be monitored and evaluated by financial statement users for their potential future adverse effects on a company's future cash flows. For example, Starbucks had previously disclosed the legal dispute with Kraft, as well as the fact that an unfavorable outcome might result in a settlement payment of as much as $2.9 billion plus attorney's fees. This amount was not reflected as a liability on the balance sheet until 2013, as an unfavorable outcome was not considered probable. However, with a final settlement of over $2.7 billion, it is crucial for financial statement users to monitor these disclosures.

In this chapter, we focus on current liabilities, including contingent obligations. Your understanding of the topics covered depends on your understanding of the term *liabilities*. Therefore, the initial discussion expands on the concept and definition of a liability presented in the discussion of the balance sheet in Chapter 4. Next, we discuss the nature, definition, and valuation of current liabilities and explain the items that make up three major groups of current liabilities—liabilities arising from contractual arrangements, liabilities arising from operating activities, and contingent liabilities. Finally, we examine the specific methods of reporting current liabilities and contingent obligations on the balance sheet and in the notes to the financial statements.

WHAT ARE LIABILITIES?

LEARNING OBJECTIVE 9.1
Explain the characteristics of a liability.

In its *Conceptual Framework*, the FASB defines *liabilities* as follows:

> Liabilities are the probable future sacrifices of economic benefits arising from present obligations of a company to transfer assets or provide services in the future as a result of past transactions or events.[1]

Given this definition, there are three characteristics of a liability:

- It must involve a present *obligation* that will be settled by a *probable* future sacrifice involving the transfer of assets, provision of services, or other use of assets at a specified or determinable date.
- The company has little or no discretion to avoid the future sacrifice of economic benefits.
- The transaction, event, or arrangement obligating the company has already happened.

Note that this definition does not require a company to know the identity of the recipient before the time of settlement nor is a legally enforceable claim necessary for an obligation to qualify as a liability.[2]

The FASB further explains two of these terms as follows:

- *Probable* refers to what can be expected or believed based on available evidence or logic.
- *Obligations* refers to duties imposed legally or socially which one is bound to do by contract, promise, or moral responsibility. In other words, liabilities include legal as well as equitable and constructive obligations.

Legal liabilities are incurred in transactions that are contractual—determined by written or oral agreements to pay cash or to provide goods or services to other entities in the future. Legal liabilities include such items as accounts payable, notes payable, taxes payable, and wages payable. **Equitable and constructive liabilities** include those obligations where there is *no legal requirement* for assets to be transferred, but a transfer of assets typically occurs as a part of the normal operations of a business.[3] Equitable and constructive obligations include items such as the liability to employees for vacation pay or year-end bonuses when such benefits are part of the company's normal employment practices and are not specified by an employment contract. These are obligations that a company accepts by paying them in the normal course of business even though it is not contractually required and has not announced a policy to do so. We discuss the accounting for both types of liabilities later in this chapter.

LOOKING AHEAD

As part of the joint FASB/IASB Conceptual Framework project, the Boards have recognized that the current definition of a *liability* has several potential shortcomings. For example, the current definition creates ambiguity about whether obligations settled with equity (stock options) are liabilities. To address these shortcomings, the Boards have developed a working definition of *a liability* as "a present economic obligation for which the entity is the obligor." The Boards intend to further develop and refine the working definition of *a liability* after considering the implications of comment letters and redeliberations in other projects.

---

[1] "Elements of Financial Reporting of Business Enterprises," *FASB Statement of Financial Accounting Concepts No. 6* (Stamford, CT: FASB, December 1985), par. 28.
[2] *Ibid.*, par. 36.
[3] *Ibid.*, fn.21 and 22 and par. 38.

The financial accounting issues related to liabilities are important in both balance sheet valuation and income statement measurement. The primary issues discussed in the remainder of this chapter are:

- *Identification* of liabilities—the detection of a company's obligations
- *Valuation and measurement* of the liabilities and the related revenue or expense—the determination of an amount to record for each obligation and to record as a revenue or expense
- *Reporting* on the financial statements—the specific disclosures in both the company's financial statements and the related notes

While liabilities may be classified as either current or long-term, this chapter discusses the preceding issues as they relate to current liabilities. Long-term liabilities are discussed in Chapter 14.

GOT IT?

9-1 Define *liabilities*. Explain the meanings of *probable* and *obligations* in the context of a liability.

9-2 Distinguish between a legal and an equitable or constructive liability. Give an example of each.

9-3 List the three characteristics of a liability. Discuss briefly.

9-4 Before a liability can be reported, a company must know the identity of the recipient. True or false? Justify your answer.

9-5 What are the primary issues in accounting for current liabilities?

LEARNING OBJECTIVE 9.2
Describe the nature, classification, and valuation of current liabilities.

WHAT IS A CURRENT LIABILITY?

The specific meaning, nature, classification, and valuation of current liabilities are important to users of financial statements.

Classification and the Operating Cycle or Year

Current liabilities are obligations that a company must meet within one year or the normal operating cycle, whichever is longer. For most companies, the operating cycle—from cash to inventory to receivables and back to cash—is less than one year, and, therefore, the usual classification criterion is one year. However, in rare instances, for certain companies in which the operating cycle is longer than a year, the length of the operating cycle determines the classification of the liability. For example, for classification of certain assets and liabilities, **Boeing** uses the duration of the related contract or program, which is generally greater than one year, as the operating cycle.

LOOKING AHEAD

As part of the joint FASB/IASB Financial Statement Presentation project, the Boards have proposed that companies base the current and noncurrent classification of assets and liabilities on a fixed period of one year, effectively eliminating the consideration of a company's operating cycle.

Liquidity, Financial Flexibility, and Current Liabilities

Liquidity refers to how quickly a company can convert its assets to cash in order to cover operating costs and pay its liabilities when they become due. The FASB is concerned about reporting information about liquidity because investors and creditors evaluate future cash flows in their decision-making processes. In part, financial statement users predict future cash inflows from liquid assets relative to future cash outflows needed to meet liabilities coming due. For example, the FASB has cited several liquidity ratios, such as the current ratio, as providing useful information to financial statement users.[4] In addition, the SEC requires a company to discuss liquidity in the "Financial Condition, Liquidity, and Capital Resources" section of its Form 10-K.[5] Finally, the AICPA Special Committee on Financial Reporting supports disclosure in the MD&A portion of a company's annual report of the internal and external sources of liquidity, as well as significant unused sources of liquid assets. It also believes that a company should disclose the impact of "illiquidity" on financial flexibility.[6]

Financial flexibility refers to a company's ability to use its financial resources to adapt to change and to take advantage of opportunities. This ability primarily involves the management of cash and other resources to achieve certain financial advantages from both an offensive and defensive point of view. In part, it also involves the potential to create new current and long-term liabilities, to restructure existing debt, and to manage debt in other ways. A more liquid company generally has greater financial flexibility. We discuss these features relating to financial flexibility later in this chapter and in other chapters.

WHY IT MATTERS

Companies experience liquidity problems when their cash inflows are not sufficient to meet their cash outflows. As noted earlier, investors and creditors examine liquidity in assessing a company's financial flexibility and credit risk. In addition, because companies that violate debt covenants[7] could be forced into bankruptcy, managers also closely monitor liquidity. Two useful ratios for assessing a company's liquidity are the **current ratio** and the **quick ratio**, which are computed as follows:

$$\text{Current Ratio} = \frac{\text{Current Assets}}{\text{Current Liabilities}} \qquad \text{Quick Ratio} = \frac{\text{Quick Assets}}{\text{Current Liabilities}}$$

Shown below is selected financial information from the 2013 annual reports for **Nike** and **Under Armour**.

Selected Financial Information (in millions)	Nike 2013	Nike 2012	Under Armour 2013	Under Armour 2012
Current assets	$13,626	$11,845	$1,128.811	$903.598
Quick assets (cash, marketable securities, accounts receivable)	9,082	6,889	557.441	517.365
Current liabilities	3,926	3,882	426.630	252.228

The current and quick ratios are shown below.

	Nike 2013	Nike 2012	Under Armour 2013	Under Armour 2012
Current ratio	3.47	3.05	2.65	3.58
Quick ratio	2.31	1.77	1.31	2.05

(continued)

---

[4] "Reporting Income, Cash Flows, and Financial Flexibility of Business Enterprises," *FASB Proposed Statement of Financial Accounting Concepts* (Stamford, CT: FASB, November 16, 1981), par. 28.
[5] For specific requirements, see Item 303 of SEC Regulation S-K.
[6] "Improving Business Reporting—A Customer Focus," *Report of the AICPA Committee on Financial Reporting* (New York: AICPA, 1994), Appendix II, p. 145.

> In general, financial statement users evaluate the current ratio based on the length of the operating cycle, cash flows from operations, types of current obligations, and types of noncurrent assets available to meet obligations. Financial statement users become concerned when a company's current ratio seems to be too high or too low. A low current ratio may signal that the company does not have sufficient cash and other current assets to meet current obligations. Conversely, a very high current ratio may signal that a company is having difficulties in selling its inventory or that the company is holding too many liquid assets that earn a relatively low rate of return. The quick ratio, a variation of the current ratio, provides a more restrictive measure of liquidity by including only highly liquid assets and excluding inventories and other current assets from the analysis.
>
> An examination of the current and quick ratios above suggests that both Nike and Under Armour appear to have the resources to be able to pay their obligations as they become due. Further, Nike's liquidity has improved between 2012 and 2013, despite the poorly performing economic environment. While Under Armour's liquidity decreased in 2013, both companies still exhibit a low level of short-term liquidity risk.

Classification of Current Liabilities

Most U.S. companies report current liabilities in the first section of liabilities on the balance sheet. Many current liabilities are easily identifiable and have a contractual amount. Some current liabilities, though identifiable, have amounts that are determined by the company's operating activities. Others involve uncertainty about whether the company is obligated (and if so, the amount of the obligation), and this uncertainty will only be resolved when a future event does or does not occur. Exhibit 9.1 classifies the primary types of current liabilities in three groups.[8]

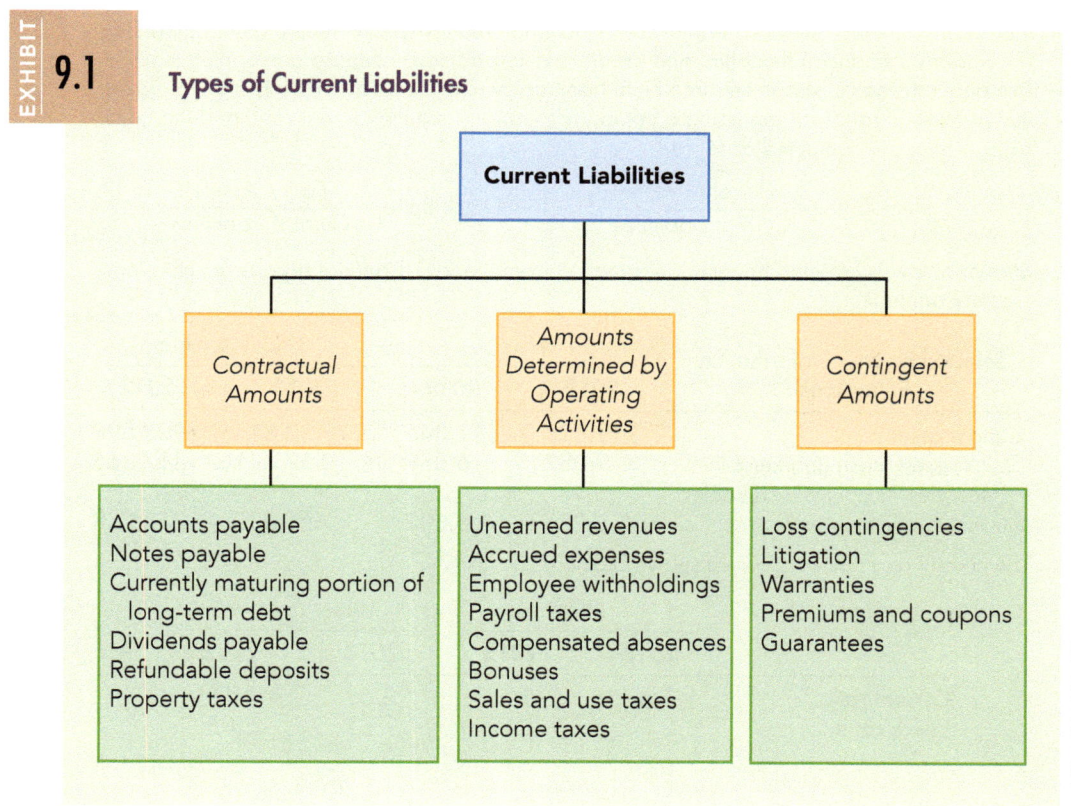

EXHIBIT 9.1 Types of Current Liabilities

[8] Some types of liabilities may fit into more than one category. In addition, there is no requirement that current liabilities be classified into these three categories. Instead, we use these categories simply to organize the text discussion.

How Are Current Liabilities Valued?

Conceptually, a company should record and report its current liabilities at the present value of the required future payments. In practice, however, most current liabilities are measured, recorded, and reported at their maturity or face amount. The difference between the maturity amount and the present value of the maturity amount is usually not material because of the short time period involved—usually one year or less. Although a slight overstatement of liabilities results from reporting current liabilities at their maturity amount, this overstatement is justified on the basis of materiality and the cost constraint.

Real Report 9.1 shows **Nike**'s disclosure of its current liabilities.

REAL REPORT — NIKE'S CURRENT LIABILITIES | 9.1

Nike, Inc.
Consolidated Balance Sheets (in part)

(in millions)	May 31, 2013	May 31, 2012
Current Liabilities:		
Current portion of long-term debt	$ 57	$ 49
Notes payable	121	108
Accounts payable	1,646	1,549
Accrued liabilities	1,986	1,941
Income taxes payable	98	65
Liabilities of discontinued operations	18	170
Total current liabilities	$3,926	$3,882

Notes to the Financial Statements (in part)

Note 5: Accrued liabilities (in part)
Accrued liabilities included the following:

	As of May 31,	
(in millions)	2013	2012
Compensation and benefits, excluding taxes	$ 713	$ 691
Endorsement compensation	264	288
Taxes, other than income taxes	192	169
Dividends payable	188	165
Import and logistics costs	111	133
Advertising and marketing	77	94
Fair value of derivatives	34	55
Other	407	346
Total accrued liabilities	$1,986	$1,941

Questions:

1. Describe Nike's largest current liabilities. What do they represent?
2. Classify each of Nike's current liability accounts using the classification given in Exhibit 9.1.

Suggested answers to these questions are found at the end of the chapter.

GOT IT?

9-6 Define a company's *operating cycle*.

9-7 Why is the liquidity of liabilities important in the accounting for liabilities?

9-8 How does financial flexibility relate to the accounting for liabilities?

9-9 How does materiality affect the accounting for current liabilities?

LEARNING OBJECTIVE 9.3
Identify, measure, and record current liabilities based on a contractual amount.

HOW DO YOU ACCOUNT FOR CURRENT LIABILITIES BASED ON A CONTRACTUAL AMOUNT?

When current liabilities are based on a contractual amount, the liability and its maturity amount are known with reasonable certainty. The accounting issues we discuss in this section for each current liability are (1) identifying the item, (2) measuring it, and (3) recording it in the accounts.

Trade Accounts Payable

Accounts payable (or **trade accounts payable**) are obligations to suppliers arising from purchasing inventory, supplies, or services on credit. Because the credit period is relatively short (e.g., 30 to 90 days), these liabilities are normally recorded at face value and no interest is subsequently charged. For example, **Starbucks** reported $684.2 million of accounts payable at the end of its 2015 fiscal year.

A key concern is ensuring that all accounts payable are recorded in the proper accounting period. Issues often arise when a company purchases inventory near the end of its accounting period and the goods are in transit at year-end. As discussed in Chapter 7, the purchaser should record both the asset and the liability in the accounting period in which the economic control of the goods passes. For goods shipped *FOB shipping point*, economic control of (and legal title to) the goods passes to the purchaser at the shipping point. For goods shipped *FOB destination*, economic control of (and legal title to) the goods is transferred to the purchaser when it receives the merchandise.

The amount of the trade accounts payable usually is determined by reviewing the invoice, which specifies the exact amount owed and the date payment is due. When cash discounts (e.g., 2/10, n/30) are offered, a company has the option to record the purchase (inventory) and the associated liability (accounts payable) using the gross price method or the net price method. The balance reported for accounts payable depends on the method selected. For an illustration of the two methods, refer to Chapter 7.

Notes Payable

A **note payable** is a promissory note that requires the borrower to repay a sum of money on a specific date. Notes payable may be either short term (discussed here) or long term (discussed in Chapter 14). Notes payable normally result from purchasing goods or services on credit or borrowing money. The ability to obtain short-term financing with notes payable is often a key component of a company's working capital strategy.

While the promissory note is the source document a company uses to determine and record the initial amount of the liability, interest also plays a key valuation role. Notes payable are classified as:

- *Interest-bearing*—The principal amount equals the face value of the note, and the interest rate is stated explicitly on the note.
- *Non-interest-bearing*—The note is stated at its maturity value that includes both the principal and interest to maturity. The borrower receives less than the face value, and, therefore, the interest is implied as the difference between the face value of the note and the cash received.

Interest-Bearing Note For an interest-bearing note, the face value of the note is its present value. Therefore, the liability is recorded at an amount equal to the face value of the note. Interest expense then is accrued over the life of the note by applying the stated interest rate to the face value.

Example Titan Corporation uses a perpetual inventory system and purchases merchandise for $7,000 on December 1, 2016, by issuing a $7,000, 12%, 30-day note to the supplier. Titan records the issuance of the note, the accrual of interest, and the payment of the principal and interest (assuming for simplicity, a 360-day business year), respectively, as follows:

December 1, 2016

Inventory	7,000	
Notes Payable		7,000

December 31, 2016

Interest Expense ($7,000 × 0.12 × 30/360)	70	
Interest Payable		70

January 1, 2017

Interest Payable	70	
Notes Payable	7,000	
Cash		7,070

Notes Payable is reported as a current liability on the December 31, 2016, balance sheet along with a current liability, Interest Payable, for the accrued interest.

Non-Interest-Bearing Note Even though the name implies that there is no interest, non-interest-bearing notes do charge interest. However, instead of being explicitly stated, interest is implicit in the face value of the note. This implicit interest, called a *discount on notes payable*, is deducted from the face amount to determine the cash received by the borrower. Interest expense is then recorded over the life of the note as an adjustment of this discounted amount.

Example On April 1, 2016, Trollingwood Corporation borrows money at First National Bank by issuing a $10,000, 3 month, non-interest-bearing note. The note is discounted on a 12% basis. Therefore, Trollingwood receives $9,700 [$10,000 − ($10,000 × 0.12 × 3/12)]. It makes the following journal entry to record the issuance of the note payable:

April 1, 2016

Cash	9,700	
Discount on Notes Payable	300	
Notes Payable		10,000

Observe that $10,000 is the maturity value of the note, but the company records the net liability at its present value—the face amount of the note minus the discount. The discount represents the interest expense applicable to the entire term of the note and is shown on Trollingwood's balance sheet as a contra account to Notes Payable.

At maturity, Trollingwood would make the following entry to recognize interest expense:

June 30, 2016

Interest Expense	300	
Discount on Notes Payable		300

Observe that the reduction in the Discount on Notes Payable account increases the current liability amount shown on the company's balance sheet. After this entry, Discount on Notes Payable has a zero balance, and the carrying value of the note equals its maturity value. In addition, the company repays the maturity value, which includes the $9,700 borrowed plus the $300 total interest recognized (i.e., the amount of the discount).

June 30, 2016

Notes Payable	10,000	
Cash		10,000

In borrowing money, a manager must be aware of the effective interest rate, referred to as the annual percentage rate (or APR), for each source of credit. In the preceding example, the effective interest rate for 3 months can be determined as follows:

$$\text{Effective Interest Rate} = \frac{\text{Total Interest Paid}}{\text{Amount of Cash Borrowed}} = \frac{\$300}{\$9{,}700} = 3.09\%$$

Because the note is for 3 months, the approximate *annual* effective interest rate is 12.36% (3.09% × 12/3 months). Observe that the effective interest rate on the cash actually borrowed is higher than the discount rate of 12%. Federal laws require lenders to disclose the APR to borrowers.

Other Short-Term Financing Techniques: Credit Lines and Commercial Paper In addition to borrowing money by signing a formal note payable, corporations also borrow money on a short-term basis by establishing a line of credit with a bank or by issuing commercial paper. A **line of credit** is an agreement that allows a corporation to borrow up to a prearranged limit. If the line of credit is *noncommitted*, the corporation does not have to follow any formal loan procedures nor complete the normal paperwork. A *committed* line of credit is a more formal process that normally requires a corporation to pay a commitment fee to have access to the funds. The advantage of a line of credit over a regular note payable is that a corporation can only borrow the amount currently needed, and interest is not charged on the portion of the loan that is not used. **Starbucks** reported $150 million in available lines of credit at the end of its 2015 fiscal year.

A second type of short-term borrowing is commercial paper. **Commercial paper** is an unsecured note payable that is commonly used to finance accounts receivable and inventories, as well as to meet other short-term obligations. Commercial paper generally has a maturity ranging from 30 to 270 days. A major benefit of commercial paper is that it does not have to be registered with the SEC as long as it matures before 270 days, making it a very cost-effective way to obtain short-term financing. For example, **Starbucks** maintains a commercial paper program that allows it to issue unsecured notes up to $1 billion to be used primarily for working capital purposes or capital expenditures.

Currently Maturing Portion of Long-Term Debt

Generally, a company classifies the currently maturing portion of long-term debt as a current liability to show the effect on its liquidity. This classification usually arises due to two different situations. First, any long-term debt will become a current liability immediately before the year of retirement.

Example If Browne Company has issued 20-year bonds that mature on July 1, 2017, Browne reports the bonds as a long-term liability in its December 31, 2015 (and prior), balance sheets. However, because the amount is due within one year of December 31, 2016, the bonds would be reported as a current liability on its December 31, 2016, balance sheet. ■

The second situation involves the issuance of installment debt instruments—such as bonds that retire in periodic installments or mortgages requiring monthly or annual installment payments.[9]

Example Assume that on July 1, 2015, Rexlow Corporation issues 9% serial bonds with a face value of $1 million. These bonds are to be retired in installments of $100,000, beginning on July 1, 2017, and for each year thereafter until all bonds are

---

[9] Serial bonds are discussed more fully in an appendix to Chapter 14.

retired. Rexlow's December 31, 2016, balance sheet would show the currently maturing installment of $100,000 as a current liability and the $900,000 (the installments due after December 31, 2017) as a long-term liability. Consequently, on December 31, 2017, Rexlow will report the next $100,000 installment as a current liability and the $800,000 remaining as a long-term liability. The current portion of other long-term debt, such as the current amount of mortgage and lease obligations, is treated in the same manner.

Short-Term Debt Expected to Be Refinanced While short-term debt is generally classified as a current liability, short-term debt that is expected to be refinanced on a long-term basis may be *excluded* from the current liability classification if the company has both:

- intent to refinance the obligation on a long-term basis
- ability to refinance the obligation on a long-term basis

The *intent to refinance* on a long-term basis means that the company intends to refinance the short-term obligations so that the obligation will not require the use of working capital during the next year (or operating cycle, if longer). The *ability to refinance* on a long-term basis means that the company has done one of the following:

- refinanced the obligations by issuing long-term obligations or equity securities after the date of its balance sheet but before the balance sheet is issued
- entered into a long-term financing agreement before it issues its balance sheet that clearly permits the company to refinance the short-term obligations on a long-term basis

If a company has actually refinanced the short-term debt, it excludes from current liabilities *only* that portion of the short-term obligation equal to the proceeds from the new long-term obligations or equity securities that will be used to retire the short-term debt.

Example Rayvon Corporation has $2,000,000 of debt maturing on June 29, 2017. The company borrows $1,500,000 from First National Bank by issuing a 10-year, 12% note on January 10, 2017. Rayvon intends to use the $1,500,000 proceeds to retire a portion of the obligation when it matures. On the December 31, 2016, balance sheet (issued on February 25, 2017), the company reports the debt of $1,500,000 that is expected to be refinanced as a noncurrent liability. It reports the remaining $500,000 that will not be refinanced as a current liability.

When a company relies on a financing agreement to show its ability to refinance, the amount of the short-term debt that it excludes from current liabilities is reduced to an amount that is the *lesser* of:

- the amount available for refinancing under the agreement
- the amount obtainable under the agreement after considering the restrictions included in other agreements
- a reasonable estimate of the minimum amount expected to be available for future refinancing if the amount that could be obtained fluctuates[10]

If the company cannot make a reasonable estimate, it must include the entire outstanding short-term obligation as a current liability.

When a company excludes a short-term obligation to be refinanced from its current liabilities, the notes to its financial statements must include a description of the financing agreement and the terms of any new debt or equity securities issued or expected to be issued as a result of the refinancing. These obligations also may be shown in captions distinct from both the current liabilities and long-term debt, such as "Interim Debt" or "Short-Term Debt Expected to Be Refinanced."

---

[10] FASB ASC 470-10-45: Debt: Overall: Other Presentation Matters.

Three Monthly Entries: October 31–December 31, 2016

Property Tax Expense ($7,200 ÷ 12)	600	
Property Taxes Payable		600

January 15, 2017: Payment of Property Taxes

Property Taxes Payable	1,800	
Prepaid Property Taxes	5,490	
Cash		7,290

Nine Monthly Entries: January 31–September 30, 2017

Property Tax Expense	610	
Prepaid Property Taxes		610

Assuming that Ezell has a calendar fiscal year-end, it reports property tax of $600 per month on its 2016 income statement and an $1,800 ($600 × 3) current liability for property taxes on its December 31, 2016, balance sheet.

Note that the $610 amount in the last journal entry is the result of allocating the $90 difference ($7,290 − $7,200) between the actual and estimated property taxes to the remaining 9-month period ending September 30, 2017. This difference is computed by subtracting the previously estimated property tax expense ($1,800) from the total actual property tax ($7,290) and dividing this difference by the remaining months (9 months) in the year:

$$(\$7{,}290 - \$1{,}800) \div 9 \text{ months} = \$610$$

This difference is considered a change in estimate that is accounted for prospectively.

GOT IT?

9-10 Distinguish between an interest-bearing note and a non-interest-bearing note. How are the proceeds computed for a non-interest-bearing note?

9-11 If a company has $300,000 of 20-year bonds payable that mature in the current year, how are these liabilities classified on the company's balance sheet?

9-12 How should long-term debt that is callable by a creditor be reported in a debtor company's financial statements? Are there any exceptions to this treatment?

9-13 What two criteria must be met before a company can classify short-term debt that is expected to be refinanced as a noncurrent liability?

9-14 How does a company demonstrate the ability to refinance currently maturing short-term debt?

9-15 Distinguish between the balance sheet classification of declared but unpaid cash dividends and stock dividends.

9-16 Donald Company operates a business in Orange County. While Donald uses a calendar fiscal year, Orange County's fiscal year begins in October. How should Donald account for its property taxes assessed by Orange County?

LEARNING OBJECTIVE 9.4

Understand and record current liabilities whose amounts are determined by operating activities.

HOW DO WE ACCOUNT FOR CURRENT LIABILITIES WITH AMOUNTS DETERMINED BY OPERATING ACTIVITIES?

Many current liabilities, such as unearned revenue, wages payable and payroll taxes, bonuses, compensated absences, sales and use taxes, income taxes, and others, are determined by the company's operating activities.

Unearned (Deferred) Revenues

A company's **unearned revenues** (**deferred revenues**) include amounts that it has collected from customers but for which the company has not yet satisfied its performance obligations. Therefore, these amounts cannot be recorded as revenues until the performance obligations are satisfied (e.g., the company provides the product or service to the customer). Unearned revenues are reported as either current liabilities or long-term liabilities, depending upon the length of time it will take the company to satisfy its performance obligations.

Common examples of unearned revenues are amounts collected from customers in advance, such as rent, magazine subscriptions, tickets, gift certificates, airfares, memberships, insurance premiums, and service contracts. **Starbucks** reports $983.8 million of deferred revenue at the end of fiscal 2015 relating to outstanding customer balances on Starbucks cards. Even though Starbucks cards do not expire, Starbucks management believes that its gift cards will be exercised within one year and, therefore, classify the amounts of the cards as current liabilities. The likelihood of a customer redeeming a card that is greater than one year old is considered remote. In these circumstances, Starbucks reduces its liability and recognizes "breakage revenue" for the value of these unredeemed cards. For 2015, Starbucks recognized $39.3 million of breakage revenue.

Example On July 1, 2016, Cook Publishing Company sells $80,000 of two-year magazine subscriptions in advance. Cook makes the following entry when it receives the cash:

July 1, 2016

Cash	80,000	
Unearned Revenue: Subscriptions		80,000

At the end of the year, Cook makes an adjusting entry to record revenue earned from July 1 to December 31.

December 31, 2016

Unearned Revenue: Subscriptions	20,000	
Subscription Revenue [$80,000 ×		
(6 months ÷ 24 months)]		20,000

This entry correctly states the amount of revenue earned during the year as well as the ending balance of its liability—a performance obligation to subscribers. As of December 31, 2016, Cook will report the $40,000 that will be earned in 2017 as a current liability and the remaining $20,000 that will be earned in 2018 as a long-term liability. ■

Accrued Liabilities

Accrued liabilities are expenses that have been incurred but not yet paid. As discussed in Chapter 3, a company usually records these liabilities and the related expenses in an adjusting entry at the end of the accounting period. Most accrued liabilities are current liabilities. Some are definite in amount, while the amounts of others are determined by operating activities. Interest payable—one example of an accrued liability—was discussed earlier in this chapter. Many other common types of accrued liabilities, such as wages payable, utilities payable, income taxes payable, and others, have been discussed in other chapters. Next, we describe several compensation-related accrued liabilities.

Liabilities Related to Compensation

All companies incur liabilities related to compensating their employees. These liabilities include amounts owed to employees for salaries, required withholdings from employees' pay, voluntary deductions from employees' pay, and payroll taxes, as shown in Exhibit 9.2. Because these amounts must be paid within, at most, a few months, they are current

EXHIBIT 9.2 Payroll Taxes and Voluntary Deductions

Employee Withholdings and Payroll Taxes	2014 Rate on Employee	2014 Rate on Employer	2014 Annual Salary per Employee Subject to Tax
Federal income tax	Graduated rates	—	100%
State income tax	Graduated rates	—	100%
F.I.C.A. taxes:			
O.A.S.D.I.	6.20%	6.20%	$117,000
Medicare	1.45%	1.45%	100%*
Federal unemployment tax	—	0.6%	$7,000
State unemployment tax	—	5.4%	$7,000

Voluntary Payroll Deductions

Union dues
Government bonds
Group insurance   } Amount withheld is stated in contract
Retirement savings
Others

*Employers must withhold an additional Medicare tax of 0.9% of wages in excess of $200,000. There is no employer matching contribution.

liabilities. In addition, other compensation-related liabilities, such as compensated absences and bonuses, are also reported as current liabilities.

Employee Withholdings and Payroll Taxes The federal income tax law, most state income tax laws, and some local government laws require employers to withhold from the pay of each employee a legal amount for the anticipated *income taxes payable* by the employee to the respective governmental units. Employers determine the amount to be withheld from each employee's pay by using applicable legal rates or by referring to withholding tax tables. That amount depends on the number of exemptions claimed and the amount of income earned by the employee. The employer must pay withheld amounts to the respective governmental unit at specified times and through specified channels. For example, the withheld federal income taxes must be paid to the Internal Revenue Service either electronically or through local depositories (e.g., banks).

Social security legislation requires that employers withhold **Federal Insurance Contribution Act (F.I.C.A.) taxes** from the wages of each employee under certain conditions. Also, employers must pay their own share of F.I.C.A. taxes for the employee (in addition to the amounts withheld from employees' wages) and remit the sum of both taxes to the Internal Revenue Service along with the income taxes withheld. F.I.C.A. taxes serve to pay:

- Old-Age, Survivor, and Disability Insurance (O.A.S.D.I.) benefits
- Medicare or federal hospital insurance benefits

Together, these taxes are referred to as **social security taxes**. As shown in Exhibit 9.2, the total 2014 F.I.C.A. taxes are 15.30% (6.20% + 1.45% + 6.20% + 1.45%) on the first $117,000 earned by each employee. On income earned by the employee above $117,000, F.I.C.A. taxes of 1.45% are paid by both the employee and employer. The actual tax rates and wage base for future years will be determined by Congress. Because Congress changes these items frequently, for simplicity in the following examples and homework, we use an assumed rate of 16%—8% on the employee and 8% on the employer—and a taxable wage base of $117,000 on *both* F.I.C.A taxes.

The final payroll taxes shown in Exhibit 9.2 are unemployment insurance taxes, another type of social security tax. These taxes are used by governmental units to make payments for a limited time to individuals who become unemployed. The **Federal Unemployment Tax Act (F.U.T.A.)** requires a tax with a maximum rate of 6.0% to be levied on employers of one or more persons, but the rate applies to only the first $7,000 paid to each employee. The law provides, however, that 5.4% of the 6.0% is payable to the state, assuming that the state levies an approved unemployment insurance tax. Thus, in these cases, the net effective federal unemployment tax rate is 0.6%.[14]

Voluntary Payroll Deductions Contractual arrangements between individual employees and employers often result in voluntary payroll deductions for things like group health insurance, accident insurance, life insurance, union dues, and tax-sheltered retirement savings. These payroll deductions are made for the convenience of the employees of a company.

Example: Accounting for Withholdings, Payroll Taxes, and Deductions

Wager Corporation has a weekly payroll of $28,000, all of which is subject to F.I.C.A. tax (8% on employee, 8% on employer), federal unemployment tax (0.6%), and state unemployment tax (5.4%). In addition, federal and state income tax withholdings were $1,980 and 1,000, respectively. Finally, a voluntary payroll deduction of $360 was made for union dues. Wager makes the following two entries to record the payment of the payroll and payroll taxes:

To record salaries and employee withholding items:

Salaries Expense	28,000	
F.I.C.A. Taxes Payable (8% × $28,000)		2,240
Federal Income Taxes Withholding Payable		1,980
State Income Taxes Withholding Payable		1,000
Union Dues Payable		360
Cash		22,420

To record employer payroll taxes:

Payroll Taxes Expense	3,920	
F.I.C.A. Taxes Payable (8% × $28,000)		2,240
Federal Unemployment Taxes Payable (0.6% × $28,000)		168
State Unemployment Taxes Payable (5.4% × $28,000)		1,512

The company reports the various payable accounts as current liabilities. When Wager pays the amounts, it eliminates the related current liability accounts.

ETHICAL DILEMMA

You are on the management team of Crystal Clear Electronics (CCE) Inc., a company that specializes in high-quality home theater systems. In addition to selling these systems, CCE provides custom installation on all purchases and is known for the professionalism of its installation staff. This reputation is due to the rigorous policies its home installation staff must follow. All employees are required to attend bimonthly training sessions, wear CCE uniforms, observe the installation dates and times agreed on by CCE and the customer, and follow any instructions given by CCE as to how to perform the installation.

Faced with shrinking margins and cash flow problems, CCE is looking to cut costs and increase cash flows. You realize that by reclassifying the installation staff as independent contractors, CCE will be able to accomplish both objectives. Because the installation staff would be independent contractors, the company would not have to pay payroll taxes, social security, and Medicare expenses. The reduction in these costs and the corresponding increase in cash flow would certainly help the company's liquidity. Furthermore, such a change would not affect the quality of the service provided and would be virtually invisible to customers. Discuss the ethical implications of this reclassification.

---

[14] Most state laws allow for a reduction of the 5.4% tax through merit-rating plans for those employers who maintain steady employment because that reduces the amount paid from the fund.

Compensated Absences **Compensated absences** include vacation, holiday, illness, or other personal activities for which a company pays its employees. They do not include items such as severance pay, stock options, or long-term fringe benefits. A company recognizes an expense and accrues a liability for employees' compensation for future absences if *all* the following conditions are met:

- The company's obligation is based on the employee's services already rendered.
- The obligation relates to rights that *vest* (the employee will be paid even if employment is terminated) or *accumulate* (unused benefits can be carried forward to a period subsequent to when they were earned).
- Payment of the compensation is probable.
- The amount can be reasonably estimated.[15]

If the company meets the first three conditions but does not accrue a liability because the last condition is not met, it discloses the known facts about these compensated absences in the notes to its financial statements.

A common type of compensated absence is *vacation time* that is allowed to accumulate and for which payment is probable. **Vacation pay is earned as a result of past employment**—the services rendered by the employee. Therefore, the company has incurred an obligation and must recognize an expense and accrue a current liability for the amount of vacation benefits that it expects employees to exercise.

Another frequent compensated absence is *sick pay*, which is treated differently from vacation pay. If sick pay benefits *vest* and are not used by the end of the period, then the employer must recognize an expense and accrue a current liability. If sick pay benefits *accumulate* but do *not* vest, recognition and accrual are optional. The reason for this difference in treatment relates to a fundamental characteristic of a liability—the existence of an obligating event. Some companies permit employees to accumulate unused sick pay and take compensated time off from work even though they are not ill. In other words, the sick pay benefits are vested. In these situations, the company incurs an obligation as the employee earns the benefits because they will be paid in the future, regardless of whether or not the employees are ill. Other companies require that employees receive accumulated sick pay only if they are absent from work because of illness. That is, the benefits do not vest. In this case, the company does not have an obligation until the sickness occurs. Therefore, accounting standards allow companies to choose whether to accrue a liability or not, as shown in Exhibit 9.3.

Just as employees earn paid vacation days and holidays through working for a company, employers recognize expenses and incur liabilities for those paid days off.

When an accrual is made for vacation or sick pay benefits, the company records an expense and related current liability in the period in which the benefits are earned by the employees. In measuring the amount of the accrual, most companies use the rate of pay for the current period instead of the projected rate of pay for the future time of absence. This practice avoids estimates and

[15] FASB ASC 710-10-25: Compensation-General: Overall: Recognition.

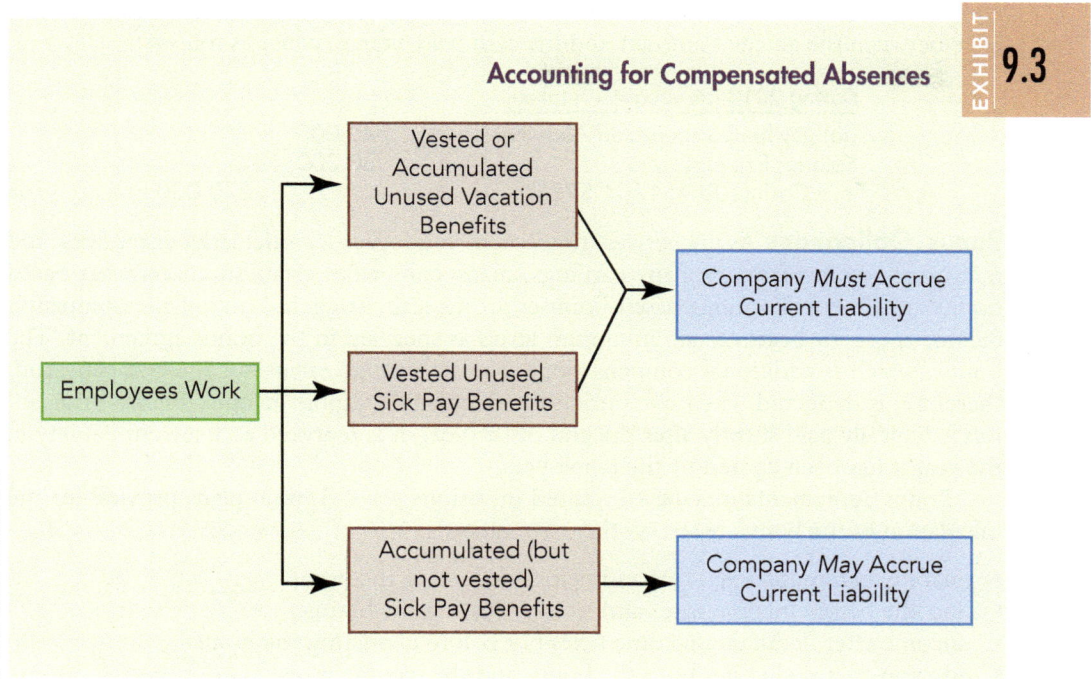

EXHIBIT 9.3 Accounting for Compensated Absences

tends to produce a lower expense and a lower liability. If the amount paid in the future for the compensated absence is larger than the amount of the previous accrual (because of a pay raise or promotion), the company records the difference as an adjustment to the expense in the period of the payment. In other words, the difference is treated as a change in estimate, as we discuss in Chapter 22.

Example: Compensated Absence—Vacation Benefits

Milton Company has 100 employees who are each paid an average of $200 per day. The company has a policy (which meets the conditions set by GAAP) of allowing each employee 12 days of paid vacation per year. The total annual cost of the paid vacations is $240,000 (100 employees × 12 days × $200 per day). Assuming no vacation days were taken in 2017, Milton makes the following entry:

During 2017 (as vacation is earned)

Salaries Expense	240,000	
Liability for Compensated Absences		240,000

This journal entry **recognizes salaries expense in the period during which the employees work and earn the vacation time and *not* during the vacation period**. Milton reports the Liability for Compensated Absences as a current liability on its balance sheet.

The liability for compensated absences will be satisfied when the employees take their vacations. Assuming all of vacation benefits were taken in 2018, Milton would record the payment of vacation pay as follows:

During 2018 (as vacation is taken)

Liability for Compensated Absences	240,000	
Cash		240,000

If the employees received a raise in 2018 so that their average pay rate was $225 per day, the company would treat this increase in pay rate as a change in estimate. That is, the company would reduce the liability by the accrued amount and would record the difference between the accrued amount and the cash paid as an expense as follows:

During 2018 (as vacation is taken)

Liability for Compensated Absences	240,000	
Salaries Expense	30,000	
Cash (100 × 12 × $225)		270,000

Bonus Obligations As incentives to certain employees—particularly executives and managers—to increase company earnings, many companies establish an earnings-based bonus agreement. Earnings-based bonuses are typically triggered only if the company's income meets or beats certain minimum levels as specified in the bonus agreement. The bonus, which is additional compensation, is an operating expense of the company and, therefore, is deducted when computing the company's taxable income. Because the bonus is typically paid shortly after the end of the year, it is reported as a current liability in the year it has been earned by the employees.

Bonus agreements may be structured in various ways. Typical plans provide for the calculation of the bonus based on the corporation's:

- income before income taxes and before deducting the bonus
- income before income taxes and after deducting the bonus
- income after deducting income taxes but before deducting the bonus
- income after deducting both the bonus and the income taxes[16]

Example: Bonus Computation

Bonex Corporation reported income for the current year of $260,000 before deducting income taxes and before a bonus to the chief executive officer. Bonex's effective tax rate is 30% and the bonus rate is 10%. The bonus applies to any income, before deducting income taxes and the bonus, above $100,000. The bonus is calculated as:

$$\text{Bonus} = \text{Income Subject to Bonus Rate} \times \text{Bonus Rate}$$
$$= (\$260{,}000 - \$100{,}000) \times 10\%$$
$$= \$16{,}000$$

Because the bonus is a tax deductible expense, income taxes are computed as follows:

$$\text{Income Taxes} = \text{Income After Deducting Bonus} \times \text{Income Tax Rate}$$
$$= (\$260{,}000 - \$16{,}000) \times 30\%$$
$$= \$73{,}200$$

Bonex records the bonus and income taxes as follows:

To record the bonus:

Salaries Expense	16,000	
Bonus Payable		16,000

To record the income tax expense:

Income Tax Expense	73,200	
Income Taxes Payable		73,200

Bonex reports both the Bonus Payable and Income Taxes Payable as current liabilities on its balance sheet.

Bonuses *may* have an undesirable effect on management's decisions regarding various accounting choices. That is, management might choose an accounting principle,

---

[16] For the latter two approaches, the corporation cannot determine its income tax until it calculates the bonus. Thus, the computation requires solving two simultaneous equations. Due to its complexity, this procedure is not presented here.

method, or procedure only because it increases the company's income, thereby increasing management's bonuses. For example, empirical research suggests that management may use their discretion to manipulate earnings and increase their short-term bonuses.[17]

Sales and Use Taxes

A **sales tax** is a tax levied by a governmental authority (such as a state or local government) on the transfer of certain goods and services. A seller must collect sales tax from the customer and pay the amount—usually on a monthly basis—to the proper governmental authority. For example, when **Starbucks** makes a sale to a customer, it records a liability for sales tax that it collected but has not yet remitted to the tax authority. A **use tax** is a tax levied by a state or local governmental unit on goods bought from a non-sales-tax area or sector. It is levied on the buyer of merchandise purchased for the buyer's own use or consumption. For example, suppose that a company purchases trucks in a state in which it does not operate. When the company registers the trucks in its own state, it has to file a use tax return and pay the tax. A sales tax and a use tax are essentially the same, so in the following examples we only discuss sales tax.

Example: Sales Tax Separate from Sales

Selleroy Company sells merchandise for cash with a retail sales price of $50,000 on which a sales tax of 6% is levied. The company collects $53,000 from its customers and records the collection as follows:

Cash	53,000	
Sales Revenue		50,000
Sales Taxes Payable ($50,000 × 0.06)		3,000

Selleroy owes the $3,000 sales taxes it collected to the state or local government levying the tax. Therefore, the amount is *not* part of revenues but is recorded as a current liability. Later, when Selleroy files the sales tax return and pays the tax to the governmental agency, it eliminates the current liability. ■

Example: Sales Tax Included in Sales

Smally Company collects sales taxes but includes the amount of the sales taxes in the price it charges for the merchandise. Therefore, it records the combined amount of both the sales and the sales taxes in the Sales Revenue account. At the end of January, Sales Revenue shows a credit balance of $169,600. Assuming a 6% sales tax on all goods, Smally computes the amount of sales for the month by dividing Sales Revenue amount by 1 plus the sales tax rate. Thus, Sales Revenue is $160,000 ($169,600 ÷ 1.06), and sales taxes are $9,600 ($169,600 − $160,000 or $160,000 × 0.06). At the end of January, Smally records the following entry to reduce Sales Revenue to the proper amount and create the current liability for sales taxes:

Sales Revenue	9,600	
Sales Taxes Payable		9,600

Income Taxes

The income of corporations is subject to a federal income tax separate from that of individuals. In addition, corporations may be subject to state, local, and foreign income taxes, depending on where the company generates income. The federal corporate income tax imposes a rate schedule for 2013 that is a multistep progressive structure, which ranges from a low of 15% on taxable income of less than $50,000 to 35% on

---

[17] See, for example, P. Healy, "The Effect of Bonus Schemes on Accounting Decisions," *Journal of Accounting and Economics* 7 (1985), pp. 85–107; R. Holthausen, D. Larcker, and R. Sloan, "Annual Bonus Schemes and the Manipulation of Earnings," *Journal of Accounting and Economics* 19 (1995), pp. 29–74; F. Guidry, A. Leone, and S. Rock, "Earnings-based Bonus Plans and Earnings Management by Business-Unit Managers," *Journal of Accounting and Economics* 26 (1999), pp. 113–142.

taxable income over $18,333,333. For simplicity, we assume an effective income tax rate (e.g., 30%) in our discussions and homework. For 2015, **Starbucks** reported $1,143.7 million of income tax expense on $3,903.0 million of earnings before income taxes. This equates to an effective tax rate of approximately 29%.

When a corporation accrues its estimated income taxes for financial statement purposes, it increases both Income Tax Expense and a current liability, Income Taxes Payable. Later, when the corporation pays its actual income taxes, it eliminates the current liability. If the estimated tax amount differs from the actual amount paid, the corporation makes an adjustment to the income tax expense account. This adjustment is considered a change in accounting estimate. In addition, income tax expense normally differs from income taxes payable because GAAP often recognizes revenues and expenses differently than the tax rules and regulations. The accounting for these differences is discussed in Chapter 18.

GOT IT?

9-17 How does unearned revenue arise, and how is it reported on a company's balance sheet?

9-18 Explain the types of liabilities that an employer incurs relating to payroll?

9-19 What are compensated absences? How does a company account for them?

LEARNING OBJECTIVE 9.5
Identify and account for contingent obligations, including warranties and premiums.

HOW DO WE ACCOUNT FOR CONTINGENT OBLIGATIONS?

In the previous sections, we've discussed current liabilities that are based on contractual amounts or arising from a company's operating activities. For these liabilities, the existence of the obligation is known with certainty and the amount is either known or determinable. However, in the normal operations of a company, transactions, events, and commercial arrangements sometimes give rise to uncertainty regarding whether the company will experience a future gain or loss, become obligated to make payments, or become entitled to receive payments. In addition, uncertainties like these often involve uncertain amounts. These uncertainties will ultimately be resolved at some future date. These situations are commonly referred to as "contingencies." Specifically, GAAP defines a **contingency** for a company as:

> an existing condition, situation, or set of circumstances involving uncertainty as to a possible gain (a "*gain contingency*") or loss (a "*loss contingency*") that will be resolved when a future event occurs or fails to occur.[18]

Because the degree of uncertainty can vary greatly and the resolution of this uncertainty can significantly impact a company's cash flows, it is important that financial statement users carefully analyze a company's contingent obligations. We discuss contingent obligations in the following section because they often arise from operating activities and may become formal liabilities. We also discuss the related income statement effects related to the recognition of contingent obligations.

Loss Contingencies

A **loss contingency** is an existing situation in which there is a potential decrease in assets or a potential increase in liabilities, depending on the occurrence of some future event. Examples of loss contingencies include lawsuits, warranties, premiums, and coupon obligations.

---

[18] FASB ASC 450-10-05: Contingencies: Overall: Overview and Background.

The uncertainty associated with loss contingencies can vary widely, and the level of uncertainty influences the accounting for and reporting of the uncertainty. As the degree of uncertainty with regard to the obligating event and the amount of the liability decreases, it increases the need to recognize the loss contingencies in the financial statements. GAAP requires a company to categorize the likelihood of occurrence of a future event that will confirm the loss as:

- **Probable**—The future event is *likely* to occur.
- **Reasonably possible**—The chance of the future event occurring is *more* than remote but *less* than likely.
- **Remote**—The chance of the future event occurring is *slight*.[19]

In addition, the company must assess whether or not it can provide a reasonable estimate of the dollar amount of the contingent loss.

A company accrues an estimated loss from a loss contingency, together with a corresponding liability (or asset impairment), if *both* of the following conditions are met:

- The company has information prior to issuing its financial statements that indicates it is *probable* that a liability has been incurred (or an asset impaired) at the date of the financial statements.
- The company can *reasonably estimate* the amount of the loss. In certain situations, a company's reasonable estimate of the loss may be a range of amounts. When some amount within the range is a better estimate than any other amount in the range, the company should accrue the better estimate. When all amounts within the range are equally likely, the company should accrue the minimum amount in the range because it is not likely that the loss will be less than this minimum.[20]

Note that it is not necessary to know the payee or the date that the liability is to be paid. Generally, a loss contingency is recognized by the following journal entry:

Loss (or expense)	x,xxx	
Liability (or contra-asset)		x,xxx

In some instances, a loss contingency will give rise to an obligation, recognized as a liability. For example, a company should accrue a liability for estimated amounts that will be paid due to the probable result of losing a lawsuit. In addition, insurers (such as life, health, and property-casualty insurers) must estimate and recognize liabilities for amounts that are probable to be paid for claim losses. In other instances, such as exposure to credit risk through making risky loans or accounts receivable, the loss contingency is recognized by reducing an asset (e.g., allowance for doubtful accounts). For example, banks must estimate and recognize allowances for uncollectible amounts in their loan portfolios.[21]

As the uncertainty with respect to the obligating event or amount of the liability increases, the accounting for the contingent obligation shifts from recognition in the financial statements to disclosure in the notes to the financial statements. Specifically, if either of the preceding two conditions are *not* met but there is at least a reasonable possibility that a loss may have been incurred, the company discloses the loss contingency in the notes to its financial statements. The disclosure should indicate the nature of the contingency and give an estimate of the possible loss or range of loss, or state that such an estimate cannot be made. Exhibit 9.4 summarizes the reporting of a loss contingency.

In addition, some remote loss contingencies are also disclosed in the notes. Examples include direct and indirect guarantees[22] of indebtedness of others, obligations of

---

[19] FASB ASC Glossary.
[20] FASB ASC 450-20-30: Contingencies: Loss Contingencies: Initial Measurement.
[21] We discuss loss contingencies that result in the incurrence of a liability in this chapter. Loss contingencies that result in reducing an asset are discussed in other chapters of the book, as appropriate.
[22] An indirect guarantee involves an agreement requiring one company to transfer funds to another company if specified events occur whereby (1) the funds are legally available to creditors of the other company and (2) those creditors may enforce that company's claims against the company under the agreement (FASB ASC Glossary).

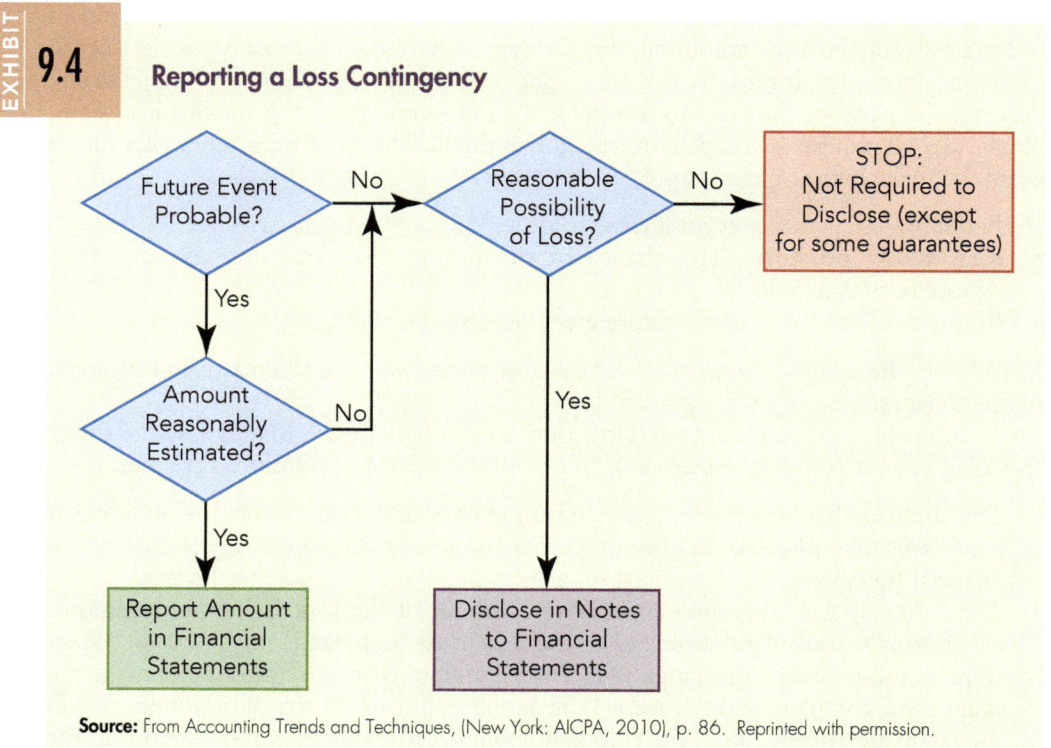

EXHIBIT 9.4 Reporting a Loss Contingency

Source: From Accounting Trends and Techniques, (New York: AICPA, 2010), p. 86. Reprinted with permission.

commercial banks under "standby letters of credit," and guarantees to repurchase receivables that have been sold or otherwise assigned. A common characteristic of these remote contingencies is that the company disclosing the loss contingency has written a guarantee, normally giving an outside party the right to require the guarantor to satisfy the guarantee.[23] The disclosure of this group of guarantees must include the nature and amount of the guarantee and, if estimable, the value of any potential recovery.

Finally, in order to record a liability, the cause of the uncertainty must exist at the balance sheet date. Therefore, no liability will exist for obligations that do not currently exist but instead represent potential future liabilities from exposure to general business risk. For example, companies usually do not record loss contingencies related to the uninsured risk of damage to property by fire, explosion, or other hazards; general or unspecified business risks; or the risk of loss from catastrophes (e.g., hurricanes, earthquakes). For these items, the company's exposure to risk does not mean that a loss or a liability has been incurred.

INTERNATIONAL DIMENSION

CONTINGENT OBLIGATIONS

IFRS and U.S. GAAP are similar in regard to contingencies, but there are some critical differences in terminology, recognition, and measurement.

- *Terminology Differences* Under IFRS, loss contingencies are possible obligations or present obligations that are *not* recognized in the financial statements.

(continued)

---

[23] FASB ASC Glossary.

A *provision* is a liability that is uncertain as to timing or amount and is recognized in the financial statements if it is probable and can be reliably estimated. Therefore, the term provision under IFRS is equivalent to the term contingency under U.S. GAAP.

- *Recognition Differences*
  - In applying the recognition criteria, IFRS define *probable* as "more likely than not" to occur (which implies a greater than 50% likelihood threshold). While this is similar to U.S. GAAP, the lower recognition threshold under IFRS should result in more events qualifying for recognition as a provision under IFRS relative to U.S. GAAP.
  - In a situation where a company cannot determine whether the obligating event has occurred, IFRS require recognition of a liability if it is probable that the event has occurred. U.S. GAAP has no such requirement.
  - IFRS require the disclosure of gain contingencies in the notes to the financial statements if an inflow of economic benefits is probable.
- *Measurement Differences*
  - IFRS require a company to measure a provision at its settlement price on the balance sheet date using present value techniques whenever the effect on the measurement of the liability is material. Contingencies are not measured at present value under U.S. GAAP.
  - If a range of estimates exists and no amount in the range is more likely than any other amount in the range, IFRS require that the mid-point of the range be used to measure the liability, whereas U.S. GAAP uses the minimum amount of the range.

IFRS Application Global Kitchen Products produces a wide variety of kitchen appliances. During the current year, a customer was injured while using one of Global's products and has sued the company. Legal counsel believes that the lawsuit will likely be settled for an amount between $25,000 and $50,000 with no amount being more likely than any other amount.

a. Assuming the loss is considered probable, what is the proper accounting under IFRS and U.S. GAAP? Under IFRS and U.S. GAAP, this litigation qualifies for recognition in the financial statements. Therefore, Global would make the following entries under IFRS and U.S. GAAP:

	IFRS		U.S. GAAP	
Loss from Litigation	37,500		25,000	
Estimated Liability from Lawsuit		37,500		25,000

While both sets of standards require accrual, note that the amount of the accrual differs.

b. Assuming the loss is considered more likely than not, what is the proper accounting under IFRS and U.S. GAAP? The litigation now meets the recognition criteria under IFRS but not under U.S. GAAP. Therefore, Global would make the following entries.

	IFRS		U.S. GAAP
Loss from Litigation	37,500		No entry required
Estimated Liability from Pending Lawsuit		37,500	

Note that IFRS have a lower recognition threshold than under U.S. GAAP.

Source: IAS 37. (See Appendix C at the end of this book.)

Litigation Lawsuits are, by far, the most common type of loss contingency reported by companies. In determining whether to accrue a loss contingency and a liability (or asset impairment), a defendant company should consider the opinion of its legal counsel, the nature of the litigation, its previous experience in similar cases, and management reaction to the lawsuit. For pending litigation, the company will accrue the loss and the related liability (or asset impairment) if:

- the cause of the litigation has occurred *before* the date of its financial statements
- it is *probable* that the outcome of the lawsuit will result in a loss for the company
- the amount of the loss can be *reasonably estimated*

Otherwise, management may decide only to disclose the pending lawsuit in the notes to the financial statements.

In regard to *unfiled* lawsuits and other *unasserted claims*, a company must determine the likelihood that a lawsuit may be filed or the claim or assessment asserted, as well as the probability of an unfavorable outcome. For example, if Patterson Corporation is being investigated for a possible patent infringement lawsuit, it must determine the probability that the lawsuit will be filed and, if so, the likelihood that the lawsuit will be lost. If these future events are probable, if the loss is reasonably estimable, and if the cause for action has occurred before the date of the issuance of the financial statements, it must accrue the loss and related liability.

In practice, companies usually do *not* accrue losses and liabilities for the costs of actual or pending litigation. Given the existing legal environment, it is unlikely that the company will have sufficient evidence to conclude that the likelihood of loss is probable. Further, even if a loss is probable, it is unlikely that a company will conclude that it can reasonably estimate the amount of the loss. Such a disclosure could be used against the company by the plaintiff's legal counsel. Therefore, most losses related to litigation are not recorded until a settlement has been reached.

Apple Inc.'s disclosure of its contingent liabilities is shown in Real Report 9.2.

REAL REPORT 9.2 | LOSS CONTINGENCY DISCLOSURES

Apple Inc.

Apple Inc.
Notes to the Consolidated Financial Statements (in part)

Note 10: Commitments and Contingencies (in part)

Contingencies
The Company is subject to various legal proceedings and claims that have arisen in the ordinary course of business and that have not been fully adjudicated. In the opinion of management, there was not at least a reasonable possibility the Company may have incurred a material loss, or a material loss in excess of a recorded accrual, with respect to loss contingencies. However, the outcome of litigation is inherently uncertain. Therefore, although management considers the likelihood of such an outcome to be remote, if one or more of these legal matters were resolved against the Company in a reporting period for amounts in excess of management's expectations, the Company's consolidated financial statements for that reporting period could be materially adversely affected.

Apple Inc. v. Samsung Electronics Co., Ltd, et al.
On August 24, 2012, a jury returned a verdict awarding the Company $1.05 billion in its lawsuit against Samsung Electronics Co., Ltd and affiliated parties in the United States District Court, Northern District of California, San Jose Division. On March 1, 2013, the District Court upheld $599 million of the jury's award and ordered a new trial as to the remainder. Because the award is subject to entry of final judgment, partial re-trial and appeal, the Company has not recognized the award in its results of operations.

(continued)

VirnetX, Inc. v. Apple Inc. et al.
On August 11, 2010, VirnetX, Inc. filed an action against the Company alleging that certain of its products infringed on four patents relating to network communications technology. On November 6, 2012, a jury returned a verdict against the Company, and awarded damages of $368 million. The Company is challenging the verdict, believes it has valid defenses and has not recorded a loss accrual at this time.

Questions:

1. Is Apple involved in litigation that could result in a loss? If so, what is Apple's justification for not accruing a loss and a related liability?
2. Why doesn't Apple record the gain resulting from the jury award of $1.05 billion in its lawsuit against Samsung Electronics?

Suggested answers to these questions are found at the end of the chapter.

Warranty Obligations

To help promote sales, manufacturers and retailers commonly provide customers a warranty in connection with the sale of a good or service. These warranties can be classified as either:

- **Assurance-type warranties**—a warranty in which the seller promises the customer that the good or service will function as specified in the contract. If it does not function as specified, an assurance-type warranty generally requires the seller, over a specified time after the sale, to correct any defect in the quality of the merchandise sold, to replace the item, or to refund the selling price.
- **Service-type warranties**—a warranty in which the seller provides a service to a customer in addition to the assurance that the delivered good or service will function as specified in the contract. A service-type warranty represents a distinct service and is a separate performance obligation relative to the related good or service.

It may require significant judgment to determine if a warranty is an assurance-type or a service-type warranty. To help make this assessment, companies should consider factors such as legal requirements, the length of the warranty coverage period, and the nature of the tasks the company promises to perform. For example, a 5-year, 100,000-mile warranty on an automobile may represent protection from manufacturing defects (an assurance-type warranty). However, if an automobile manufacturer also offers free oil changes during the first 3 years of the car's life, this would represent a separate performance obligation and be treated as a service-type warranty. Similarly, a smartphone manufacturer might provide a 1-year warranty on defective parts (an assurance-type warranty) as well as a promise to deliver any system upgrades to the customer free of charge for 2 years (a service-type warranty).[24]

Assurance-Type Warranties An assurance-type warranty does not represent a separate performance obligation but rather effectively provides a guarantee of quality. **GAAP requires a company to recognize any warranty costs associated with an assurance-type warranty as an expense in the period during which it makes the sale**. If the warranty period spans two or more accounting periods, the actual use of resources to satisfy the warranty could occur in the period of sale or in a later period. Therefore, in the period of sale, the company must recognize an accrual for the estimated warranty expense over the life of the warranty and a liability for future performance. The company classifies the estimated amount of the warranty liability as either a current liability and/or a

---

[24] Certain arrangements may contain both assurance-type and service-type warranties. If the warranties can be accounted for separately, a company should accrue the costs associated with the assurance-type warranty and defer the revenue allocated to the service-type warranty. If the company cannot account for them separately, the company should treat the warranties as a single performance obligation and allocate revenue to the combined warranty and recognize the revenue over the period in which it provides the warranty services.

long-term liability, depending on when it expects to incur the warranty costs. When the company uses its resources to fulfill the warranty agreement, it decreases both the liability and the asset used to satisfy the warranty.

Example Anglee Machinery Corporation begins production on a new machine in April 2016 and sells 200 of these machines at $6,000 each by December 31, 2016. Each machine carries a one-year warranty. Experience from the sale of similar machinery in the past has shown that the warranty costs will average $150 per unit. Anglee spent $5,000 in 2016 and $25,150 in 2017 to fulfill the warranty agreements for the machines sold in 2016. The company records this information under the expense warranty accrual method for the year 2016 as follows:

<u>Sale of 200 Machines during April–December 2016</u>

Cash or Accounts Receivable ($6,000 × 200)	1,200,000	
Sales Revenue		1,200,000

<u>Recognition of Warranty Expense, April–December 2016</u>

Warranty Expense ($150 × 200)	30,000	
Estimated Warranty Liability		30,000

<u>Payment or Incurrence of Warranty Costs, April–December 2016</u>

Estimated Warranty Liability	5,000	
Cash (or other assets)		5,000

Anglee reports the Warranty Expense as an operating expense on its 2016 income statement. It reports the remaining $25,000 ($30,000 accrued − $5,000 paid) as a current liability, Estimated Warranty Liability, on its December 31, 2016, balance sheet because the warranty period is a year in length.

Anglee records the transactions in 2017 relating to the 200 machines sold in 2016 as follows:

<u>Payment or Incurrence of Warranty Costs during 2017</u>

Estimated Warranty Liability	25,000	
Warranty Expense	150	
Cash (or other assets)		25,150

Note that the actual warranty costs are $150 more than were estimated. Anglee treats this as a change in accounting estimate and debits this amount to Warranty Expense for 2017. ■

Modified Cash Basis Method Under the **modified cash basis method**, a company records assurance-type warranty costs as an expense during the period in which it makes the repairs to merchandise under warranty. This method is conceptually unsound because it recognizes the expense in the period of the *repair*, which may be later than the period of the sale. In addition, it does not appropriately recognize a liability for future warranty costs. However, because the company expects to use resources in the future, a liability *does* in fact exist from the date of sale to the end of the warranty period. The modified cash basis is justified for financial reporting under one of three conditions:

- when the warranty period is relatively short, making the cost of estimating the warranty liability greater than the benefits obtained
- when it is not possible for the company to make a reliable estimate of the warranty obligation amount at the time of sale
- when its results are not materially different from the accrual method described in the previous section

In addition, the modified cash basis is the only method accepted for federal income tax purposes.

Service-Type Warranties Warranties are often priced and sold separately from the product itself. For example, if you purchase electronics from **Best Buy**, you will likely be offered the option to purchase an extended warranty or service contract. When a customer has the option to purchase the warranty and the product separately, the sale of warranty represents a distinct performance obligation. Therefore, it should be treated as a separate sales transaction. Under this method, a company defers revenue from the sale of the service-warranty contract and recognizes it as the performance obligation is satisfied (generally on a straight-line basis over the life of the contract). Any costs necessary to satisfy the warranty are generally expensed as incurred.

Example Waggoner Electronics offers its customers a three-year extended warranty that protects the customer from defects beyond the manufacturer's one-year warranty. On January 2, 2016, Waggoner sells a high-definition television to Matt O'Malley for $3,000. Matt also purchases an extended warranty for $240. Because this is a service-type warranty, Waggoner makes the following entry in 2016 to record the sale of the product and the extended warranty:

Jan. 2	Cash	3,240	
	Sales Revenue		3,000
	Unearned Warranty Revenue		240

Because the extended warranty begins in 2017 after the regular warranty expires, the company reports the $240 balance in Unearned Warranty Revenue as a long-term liability on its December 31, 2016, balance sheet.

If Matt returns the television for warranty service that costs $200 on June 30, 2017, Waggoner would make the following entry:

June 30	Warranty Expense	200	
	Cash (or other assets)		200

Waggoner then makes the following entry in 2017, 2018, and 2019 to recognize warranty revenue:

Dec. 31	Unearned Warranty Revenue	80	
	Warranty Revenue ($240 ÷ 3)		80

At the end of 2017, Waggoner would report the $160 balance in Unearned Warranty Revenue as an $80 current liability and an $80 long-term liability.

Premium, Coupon, and Cash Rebate Obligations

Many companies offer **premiums** such as toys, CDs, and small appliances in exchange for labels, box tops, or wrappers from their products. Other companies offer **coupons** printed in newspapers and magazines that can be used to reduce the purchase price of their products. Still others offer a **cash rebate** when customers return a cash register receipt for the purchase of their products. Many of these offers expire after a specified time, but some do not have an expiration date. While all of these offers are intended to increase a company's sales, the accounting for premiums differs from that for coupons and cash rebates. Generally, premiums result in the recognition of an expense, while coupons and cash rebates result in a reduction of revenue.

Premiums Similar to assurance-type warranties, **GAAP requires that any costs associated with premiums should be recognized as expenses in the period of sale.** Because the period in which the premium is offered may differ from the period in which it is redeemed by the customer, the company must recognize an accrual for the estimated premium expense and the related contingent liability. At the end of the period, the company reports any outstanding premium offer that it expects to be redeemed within the next year as a current liability.

Example On October 1, 2016, American Spaghetti Corporation began offering customers a spaghetti serving fork in return for 30 spaghetti can labels. This offer expires on April 1, 2017. The cost of each spaghetti fork is $2. Based on past experience, the company estimates that only 60% of the labels will be redeemed. During 2016, the company purchased 6,000 spaghetti forks. In 2016, it sold 300,000 cans of spaghetti at $1.80 per can. From these sales, 105,000 labels were returned for redemption in 2016. The company records the following series of journal entries in 2016 to recognize expenses and to record current liabilities:

Purchase of 6,000 Spaghetti Forks

Inventory of Premiums (6,000 × $2)	12,000	
Cash (or Accounts Payable)		12,000

Sale of 300,000 Cans of Spaghetti

Cash (or Accounts Receivable)	540,000	
Sales Revenue (300,000 × $1.80)		540,000

Estimate of the Total Premium Liability

Premium Expense*	12,000	
Estimated Premium Liability		12,000

Redemption of 105,000 Labels

Estimated Premium Liability	7,000	
Inventory of Premiums (105,000 ÷ 30 × $2)		7,000

*Total coupons outstanding	300,000
Estimated percent redeemed	× 60%
Total coupons estimated for redemption	180,000
Premium Expense (180,000 ÷ 30 × $2)	$12,000

The company reports the Premium Expense as a selling expense on its 2016 income statement. The company reports the Inventory of Premiums as a current asset and the Estimated Premium Liability as a current liability on its December 31, 2016, balance sheet because the offer expires in less than a year.

The future redemptions of these labels in 2017 will require a decrease to both the Estimated Premium Liability and Inventory of Premiums accounts. ■

Coupons and Cash Rebates Coupons and cash rebates allow a customer to receive a refund of a portion of the purchase price of a good or service. Generally, the refund payment does not provide a distinct good or service to the seller, and, therefore, the company should treat the expected refund amount as a reduction in revenue at the time of the original sale transaction.[25]

Example On January 1, 2017, Eat Well Cereal Company began offering a cash rebate of $2 to customers who return five coupons contained within cereal boxes. The offer expires on December 31, 2017. Based on historical experience, the company estimates that 30% of the coupons will be redeemed. During 2017, the company sold 1,000,000 boxes of cereal at $4 per box. From these sales, 250,000 coupons were redeemed in 2017 and 50,000 coupons were unredeemed at the end of the year.

---

[25] If the amount payable to the customer is determined to be a payment for a distinct good or service, the company will *not* reduce revenue at the time of the original sales transaction but instead account for the payment in the same way that it accounts for other purchases of goods or services.

Because the rebate does not represent a payment to the customer for a distinct good or service, Eat Well must adjust the transaction price to the amount it expects to receive from the customer. Using the most likely amount, the company computes the expected amount of the rebate ($120,000) and the transaction price ($3,880,000) as follows:

Gross amount of sale (1,000,000 boxes × $4/box)		$4,000,000
Less:		
Total coupons outstanding	1,000,000	
Estimated percent redeemed	× 30%	
Total coupons estimated for redemption	300,000	
Number of coupons required for rebate	÷ 5	
Total number of estimated rebates	60,000	
Value of rebate	× $2	
Expected value of total rebate		120,000
Total transaction price		$3,880,000

The company records the following series of journal entries in 2017 to account for the cash rebate:

Sale of 1,000,000 Boxes of Cereal
Cash (or Accounts Receivable)	4,000,000	
Sales Revenue		3,880,000
Estimated Rebate Liability		120,000

Redemption of 250,000 Coupons
Estimated Rebate Liability	100,000	
Cash (250,000 ÷ 5 × $2)		100,000

Expiration of 50,000 Unredeemed Coupons
Estimated Rebate Liability	20,000	
Sales Revenue (50,000 ÷ 5 × $2)		20,000

Gain Contingencies

If a company has a **gain contingency**, there is a potential increase in its assets or a potential decrease in its liabilities, dependent upon the occurrence of some future event. Examples of gain contingencies include:

- lawsuits in which the company is the plaintiff seeking damages
- favorable resolutions of tax disputes (e.g., audits)
- insurance claims in which the amount to be received from the insurance company for damaged property is expected to exceed the book value of the property

Gain contingencies are usually *not* accrued because to do so might cause income to be recognized prior to its realization. Thus, GAAP takes a conservative approach with regard to gain contingencies. However, gain contingencies may be disclosed in the notes to the financial statements, but care should be taken to avoid misleading users as to the likelihood of realization of the possible gain.[26] In summary, gain contingencies are generally recognized when realized.

GOT IT?

9-20 Define *contingency*. What exactly is the company uncertain about—whether a future event will take place and result in a liability or whether a future event will take place that will confirm that a liability exists from an event that has already taken place?

9-21 How do the matching principle and conservatism enter into the accounting for contingencies?

---

[26] FASB ASC 450-30-25: Contingencies: Gain Contingencies: Recognition.

> **9-22** What two criteria must be met before a loss contingency is reported in a company's financial statements?
>
> **9-23** With regard to a loss contingency, by what date must the event that results in a probable loss have occurred before accrual is required? By what date must information be available for a company to assess the probability that a loss has been incurred?
>
> **9-24** What conditions would have to be met for a company to accrue the loss from a pending lawsuit?
>
> **9-25** 🌐 If a company determines that a provision has a 51% chance of occurring, would it be required to accrue the provision under IFRS? Under U.S. GAAP? Explain your answer.
>
> **9-26** 🌐 If a company that uses IFRS determines that a provision must be accrued and estimates a range of possible outcomes between $60,000 and $100,000 with no one amount being more likely than another, what amount should be accrued as a provision?
>
> **9-27** Identify how to account for warranty costs if the warranty is determined to be an assurance-type warranty? A service-type warranty?
>
> **9-28** Define *gain contingency*. Describe the accounting requirements for a gain contingency.

LEARNING OBJECTIVE 9.6
Describe the presentation and disclosure of current liabilities and contingencies.

HOW ARE CURRENT LIABILITIES AND CONTINGENCIES PRESENTED IN THE FINANCIAL STATEMENTS?

Conceptually, a company should report its three main balance sheet elements—assets, liabilities, and equity—in homogeneous classes. This disclosure is helpful to users in assessing the nature, amount, timing, and liquidity of its resources and obligations. A company can report assets and liabilities as items in its balance sheet in various ways. The FASB has suggested broad guidelines as follows:

- Assets and liabilities with different implications for the *financial flexibility* of the company should be reported as separate items.
- Assets and liabilities with different general *liquidity* characteristics should be reported as separate items.
- Assets and liabilities that differ regarding the measurement attribute should be reported in separate categories.[27]

These guidelines suggest that a company should arrange its current liabilities in a way that will **highlight their liquidity characteristics and their effect on financial flexibility.**

Most companies report current liabilities as the first classification in the Liabilities and Shareholders' Equity section of the balance sheet. Items within the current liability section typically may be listed (1) in the order of their average length of maturity, (2) according to amount (largest to smallest), or (3) in the order of liquidation preference—that is, in the order of their legal claims against assets. A popular way of presenting these items is as follows:

- accounts payable
- notes payable
- accrued liability items
- unearned (deferred) revenue items
- other current liabilities

---

[27] "Reporting Income, Cash Flows, and Financial Flexibility of Business Enterprises," *FASB Proposed Statement of Financial Accounting Concepts, op. cit.*, par. 50 and 51.

These current liabilities are usually recorded and reported at their maturity values. The difference between the maturity amount and the present value of the maturity amount is usually not material because of the short time period involved.

A company discloses any major issues affecting its current liabilities in a note to its financial statements. The notes and other supplemental information about current liabilities should meet the requirement of full disclosure. For example, secured liabilities are clearly identified, along with the related assets pledged as collateral. If the due date of any liability can be extended, that fact and any related details are disclosed. Current liabilities are *not* offset against the assets that the company plans to use for their liquidation, and currently maturing long-term debt is classified as a current liability (unless refinanced). In addition, companies are required to provide product warranty disclosures, including the accounting policy and method used to estimate its warranty liability and a tabular reconciliation of the changes in the warranty liability.

Real Report 9.3 is an excerpt of **General Mills**'s balance sheets showing how it reports its current liabilities along with the related note to the financial statements. This disclosure is representative of the reporting techniques used by most large companies.

REAL REPORT   **DISCLOSURE OF CURRENT LIABILITIES**   **9.3**

General Mills, Inc.
Balance Sheet (in part)

(millions of dollars)	May 26, 2013	May 27, 2012
Liabilities (in part)		
Current Liabilities:		
Accounts payable	$1,423.2	$1,148.9
Current portion of long-term debt	1,443.3	741.2
Notes payable	599.7	526.5
Other current liabilities	1,827.7	1,426.6
Total current liabilities	$5,293.9	$3,843.2

Notes to Consolidated Financial Statements (in part)

Note 8: Debt (in part)
Notes Payable—The components of notes payable and their respective weighted-average interest rates at the end of the period were as follows:

	May 26, 2013		May 27, 2012	
	Notes Payable	Weighted Average Interest Rate	Notes Payable	Weighted Average Interest Rate
U.S. commercial paper	$515.5	0.2%	$412.0	0.2%
Financial institutions	84.2	13.0%	114.5	10.0%
	$599.7	2.0%	$526.5	2.4%

To ensure availability of funds, we maintain bank credit lines sufficient to cover our outstanding short-term borrowings. Commercial paper is a continuing source of short-term financing. We have commercial paper programs available to us in the United States and Europe. In April 2012, we entered into fee-paid committed credit lines, consisting of a $1.0 billion facility scheduled to expire in April 2015 and a $1.7 billion facility scheduled to expire in April 2017. We also have $332.8 million in uncommitted credit lines that support our foreign operations. As of May 26, 2013, there were no amounts outstanding on the fee-paid committed credit lines, and $84.2 million was drawn on the uncommitted lines.

(continued)

Note 17: Supplemental Information (in part)

In Millions	May 26, 2013	May 27, 2012
Other current liabilities:		
Accrued trade and consumer promotions	$ 635.3	$ 560.7
Accrued payroll	417.3	367.4
Dividends payable	279.6	24.5
Accrued taxes	88.0	39.2
Accrued interest, including interest rate swaps	91.2	100.2
Grain contracts	30.0	20.6
Restructuring and other exit costs reserve	19.5	85.9
Derivative payable	4.1	26.1
Miscellaneous	262.7	202.0
Total	$1,827.7	$1,426.6

Suggested answers to these questions are found at the end of the chapter.

Questions:

1. What is the composition of General Mills's short-term notes payable? Are these notes payable properly classified as current liabilities?
2. General Mills reported current assets of $4,298.9 million on May 26, 2013. Compute its current ratio and provide any relevant comments.
3. General Mills reported cost of goods sold of $11,350.2 million for 2013. Compute its payables turnover.

REVIEW CENTER

At the beginning of the chapter, we discussed how the analysis of a company's current liabilities and contingencies helps financial statement users assess the liquidity, financial flexibility, and credit risk of a company. We also identified several objectives you would accomplish after reading the chapter. The objectives are listed below and followed by a brief summary of the key points.

LEARNING OBJECTIVE 9.1
Explain the characteristics of a liability.

KEY TAKEAWAYS

- The characteristics of a liability are that:
  - It must involve a present obligation, which may or may not be legally enforceable, that will be settled by a probable future sacrifice involving the transfer of assets, provision of services, or other use of assets at a specified or determinable date.
  - The company has little or no discretion to avoid the future sacrifice of economic benefits.
  - The transaction, event, or arrangement obligating the company has already happened.

KEY TERMS

equitable and constructive liabilities, p. 9-3   legal liabilities, p. 9-3

LEARNING OBJECTIVE 9.2
Describe the nature, classification, and valuation of current liabilities.

KEY TAKEAWAYS

- Current liabilities are obligations that are due within one year from the balance sheet date. Reporting current liabilities on the balance sheet provides insights into a company's liquidity and financial flexibility and is useful in assessing a company's future cash flows.

- Most current liabilities are measured, recorded, and reported at their maturity amount and can be classified as having contractual amounts, amounts determined by operating activities, or amounts requiring future resolution of uncertainty.

KEY TERMS

current liabilities, p. 9-4
current ratio, p. 9-5
financial flexibility, p. 9-5
liquidity, p. 9-5
quick ratio, p. 9-5

KEY TAKEAWAYS

LEARNING OBJECTIVE 9.3
Identify, measure, and record current liabilities based on a contractual amount.

- Current liabilities in this group result from terms of contracts.
- These liabilities include accounts payable, notes payable (interest-bearing and non-interest-bearing), short-term financing techniques such as lines of credit and commercial paper, current maturities of long-term debt, dividends payable, refundable deposits, and property taxes.
- Accounts payable are normally recorded at face value, after considering cash discounts, and no interest is subsequently charged. A review of the shipping terms is often necessary to ensure that the accounts payable is recorded in the proper time period.
- Interest-bearing notes are recorded at an amount equal to the face value of the note, and interest expense is then accrued over the life of the note by applying the stated interest rate to the face value. For non-interest-bearing notes payable, the implicit interest is deducted from the face amount of the note to determine the cash received by the borrower, and interest expense is recorded over the life of the note as an adjustment to the discount on notes payable.
- The currently maturing portion of long-term debt is classified as a current liability to show the effect on a company's liquidity. In contrast, short-term debt that is expected to be refinanced on a long-term basis may be excluded from the current liability classification if a company has both the intent and ability to refinance the debt on a long-term basis.
- The declaration of cash or property dividends by a company's board of directors creates a current liability if the company expects to distribute the dividend within the following year.
- The classification of a refundable deposit as current or noncurrent depends on the length of time until the deposit will be returned.
- Property taxes should be estimated and accrued in equal monthly amounts during the fiscal year of the taxing authority.

KEY TERMS

accounts payable, p. 9-8
commercial paper, p. 9-10
lien, p. 9-13
line of credit, p. 9-10
note payable, p. 9-8
trade accounts payable, p. 9-8

KEY TAKEAWAYS

LEARNING OBJECTIVE 9.4
Understand and record current liabilities whose amounts are determined by operating activities.

- This classification of liabilities has amounts that are a consequence of conducting operating activities.
- These liabilities include unearned revenues, accrued liabilities, employee withholdings, payroll taxes (F.I.C.A. or social security taxes, F.U.T.A. or unemployment taxes), voluntary payroll deductions, compensated absences, bonus obligations, sales and use taxes, and income taxes.
- Unearned (deferred) revenues are amounts that a company has collected in advance but for which the company has not satisfied its performance obligations. They are

recorded as current or long-term liabilities, depending on when the company expects to satisfy its performance obligation.
- Accrued liabilities are expenses that have been incurred but not yet paid. These are normally recorded as current liabilities as part of the end-of-period adjusting process.
- Mandatory withholdings for income taxes of the employee, as well as voluntary payroll deductions for items such as health insurance and union dues, represent a current liability of the employer.
- In addition to the amounts withheld from employees' pay, a company also has a current liability for payroll taxes—social security, Medicare, unemployment—until these amounts are sent to the appropriate governmental agencies.
- A company's obligation for compensated absences that vest or accumulate must be accrued in the current period if the payment of the obligation is probable and can be reasonably estimated.
- Because bonuses are frequently paid shortly after the end of the year, any amounts owed should be accrued and reported as a current liability in the year it was earned by the employees.
- Sales taxes collected by the seller of goods and certain services are considered a current liability of the seller until remitted to the appropriate tax authority.
- Corporations must pay federal income tax (and sometimes state or foreign income tax) on their income. This amount should be estimated and reported as a current liability until the taxes are paid.

KEY TERMS

accrued liabilities, p. 9-15
compensated absences, p. 9-18
deferred revenues, p. 9-15
Federal Insurance Contribution Act (F.I.C.A.) taxes, p. 9-16

Federal Unemployment Tax Act (F.U.T.A.), p. 9-17
sales tax, p. 9-21
social security taxes, p. 9-16
unearned revenues, p. 9-15
use tax, p. 9-21

LEARNING OBJECTIVE 9.5
Identify and account for contingent obligations, including warranties and premiums.

KEY TAKEAWAYS

- A contingency is an existing uncertainty as to possible gains or losses, where the uncertainty can only be resolved when a future event occurs or fails to occur.
- A loss contingency represents a potential increase in liabilities (or decrease in assets) and is accrued when it is probable that the future confirming event will occur and the amount of the loss can be reasonably estimated. Examples of loss contingencies include litigation, warranty obligations, and premiums.
- If the future confirming event is not probable or cannot be reasonably estimated and there is a reasonable possibility of a loss, the loss contingency is disclosed in the notes to the financial statements.
- Warranties can be classified as either:
  - Assurance-type warranties—a warranty that promises the customer that the good or service provided functions as specified in the contract. Obligations related to assurance-type warranties are estimated and recognized in the period of the sale even though the actual use of resources to satisfy the warranty agreement may not occur until a future period.
  - Service-type warranties—a warranty that provides a service to a customer in addition to the assurance that the delivered good or service functions as specified in the contract. A service-type warranty represents a distinct service and is a separate performance obligation relative to the related good or service provided. Therefore, revenue equal to the warranty costs must be deferred (creating a current liability) and recognized as the performance obligation is satisfied. Any costs necessary to service the warranty are generally expensed as incurred.

- The accounting for obligations relating to premiums is similar to that of assurance-type warranties—any obligation is estimated and recorded in the period of the sale.
- The expected value to be paid to the customer relating to coupons or cash rebates is generally recorded as a reduction in revenue at the time of the original sales transaction.
- Gain contingencies are usually not accrued but are disclosed in the notes to the financial statements. Gain contingencies are generally recognized when realized.

KEY TERMS

assurance-type warranties, p. 9-27
cash rebate, p. 9-29
contingency, p. 9-22
coupons, p. 9-29
gain contingency, p. 9-31
loss contingency, p. 9-22

modified cash basis method, p. 9-28
premiums, p. 9-29
probable, p. 9-23
reasonably possible, p. 9-23
remote, p. 9-23
service-type warranties, p. 9-27

KEY TAKEAWAYS

- Most companies report their current liabilities, in order of liquidity, as the first classification in the liabilities and shareholders' equity section of the balance sheet. Any major issues affecting current liabilities are disclosed in the notes to the financial statements.

LEARNING OBJECTIVE 9.6
Describe the presentation and disclosure of current liabilities and contingencies.

ANSWERS TO REAL REPORT QUESTIONS

Real Report 9.1 Answers Nike, Inc.—Current Liabilities

1. Nike's largest current liabilities are accounts payable and accrued liabilities. Accounts payable represent obligations to suppliers arising from purchasing inventory, supplies, and services on credit. The accrued liabilities represent obligations that have been incurred but not yet paid. The largest of the accrued liabilities include costs relating to compensation such as salaries and wages, as well as endorsement compensation.
2. Nike's liabilities fit into two of the three classifications given in Exhibit 9.1. For example, accounts payable and dividends payable are based on contractual amounts. Accrued compensation and benefits and accrued taxes payable are amounts determined by operating activities. Nike reports no amounts for contingent obligations.

Real Report 9.2 Answers Apple Inc.—Loss Contingency Disclosures

1. Apple is involved in various legal proceedings that could result in loss. However, Apple feels that the likelihood of an outcome that would result in a material loss is remote and, therefore, no accrual of a liability is necessary. In one lawsuit (*VirnetX, Inc. v. Apple Inc. et al.*), the jury has ruled against Apple and awarded damages of $368 million. However, Apple is challenging this verdict, believes it has valid defenses, and does not feel that an adverse outcome is probable. Therefore, no loss accrual is made for this lawsuit.
2. Even though Apple has received a $1.05 billion judgment against Samsung Electronics, no gain has been recorded because the award has not been realized. The gain contingency will only be recognized if, after entry of final judgment and any potential re-trial and appeal, Apple is still awarded an amount by the court.

Real Report 9.3 Answers General Mills—Disclosure of Current Liabilities

1. General Mills's notes payable are primarily composed of commercial paper and other short-term borrowings from financial institutions. Commercial paper is a form of

short-term note payable that typically has a maturity ranging from 30 days to 270 days. Therefore, General Mills properly classified these notes payable as a current liability.
2. The current ratio for General Mills at May 26, 2013, is 0.81 ($4,298.9 million ÷ $5,293.9 million). A ratio less than one could signal liquidity problems because current liabilities exceed current assets. For this reason, General Mills maintains lines of credit sufficient to cover its short-term borrowings. This should alleviate any short-term liquidity concerns.
3. The 2013 payables turnover ratio for General Mills is 8.83 [$11,350.2 million ÷ [($1,148.9 million + $1,423.2 million) ÷ 2]]. Dividing this ratio into 365 days, it appears that General Mills is paying its suppliers, on average, every 41 days.

MULTIPLE-CHOICE (AICPA ADAPTED)

Select the best answer for each of the following.

M9-1 **LO 9.3** The balance in Ashwood Company's accounts payable account at December 31, 2016, was $1,200,000 before any necessary year-end adjustment relating to the following:

- Goods were in transit from a vendor to Ashwood on December 31, 2016. The invoice cost was $85,000, and the goods were shipped FOB shipping point on December 29, 2016. The goods were received on January 2, 2017.
- Goods shipped FOB shipping point on December 20, 2016, from a vendor to Ashwood were lost in transit. The invoice cost was $40,000. On January 5, 2017, Ashwood filed a $40,000 claim against the common carrier.
- Goods shipped FOB destination on December 22, 2016, from a vendor to Ashwood were received on January 6, 2017. The invoice cost was $20,000.

What amount should Ashwood report as accounts payable on its December 31, 2016, balance sheet?

a. $1,260,000 c. $1,325,000
b. $1,285,000 d. $1,345,000

M9-2 **LO 9.3** On September 1, 2016, a company borrowed cash and signed a 1-year, interest-bearing note on which both the principal and interest are payable on September 1, 2017. How will the note payable and the related interest be classified in the December 31, 2016, balance sheet?

	Note Payable	Accrued Interest
a.	Current liability	Noncurrent liability
b.	Noncurrent liability	Current liability
c.	Current liability	Current liability
d.	Noncurrent liability	No entry

M9-3 **LO 9.3** When a company receives a deposit from a customer to protect itself against nonpayment for future services, the deposit should be classified by the company as:

a. revenue
b. a liability
c. part of the allowance for doubtful accounts
d. a deferred credit deducted from accounts receivable

M9-4 **LO 9.4** Bronson Apparel Inc. operates a retail store and must determine the proper December 31, 2016, year-end accrual for the following expenses:

- The store lease calls for fixed rent of $1,000 per month, payable at the beginning of the month, and additional rent equal to 6% of net sales over $200,000 per calendar year, payable on January 31 of the following year. Net sales for 2016 are $800,000.
- Bronson has personal property subject to a city property tax. The city's fiscal year runs from July 1 to June 30, and the tax is payable on June 30. Bronson estimates that its personal property tax will amount to $6,000 for the city's fiscal year ending June 30, 2017.

In its December 31, 2016, balance sheet, Bronson should report accrued expenses of:

a. $39,000 c. $51,000
b. $42,000 d. $54,000

M9-5 **LO 9.4** Morgan Company determined that (1) it has a material obligation relating to employees' rights to receive compensation for future absences attributable to employees' services already rendered, (2) the obligation relates to rights that vest, and (3) payment of the compensation is probable. The amount of Morgan's obligation as of December

31, 2016, is reasonably estimated for the following employee benefits:

Vacation pay $100,000
Holiday pay 25,000

What total amount should Morgan report as its liability for compensated absences on its December 31, 2016, balance sheet?

a. $0
b. $25,000
c. $100,000
d. $125,000

M9-6
LO 9.4

All of Rolf Co.'s employees are entitled to two weeks of paid vacation for each full year in Rolf's employ. Unused vacation time can be accumulated and carried forward to succeeding years and will be compensated at the salary in effect when the vacation is taken. Mary Beal started her employment with Rolf on January 1, 2016. As of December 31, 2016, when Beal's salary was $500 per week, Beal had used none of her vacation time. As of December 2016, Rolf expects to give its employees 10% raises in July 2017. How much should Rolf report as a liability at December 31, 2016, for Beal's accumulated vacation time?

a. $0
b. $500
c. $1,000
d. $1,100

M9-7
LO 9.4

Which of the following is classified as an accrued payroll liability?

	Federal Income Tax Withheld	Employee's Share of F.I.C.A. Taxes
a.	No	Yes
b.	No	No
c.	Yes	No
d.	Yes	Yes

M9-8
LO 9.5

Gain contingencies are usually recognized in the income statement when:

a. realized
b. occurrence is reasonably possible and the amount can be reasonably estimated
c. occurrence is probable and the amount can be reasonably estimated
d. the amount can be reasonably estimated

M9-9
LO 9.5

How should a loss contingency that is reasonably possible and for which the amount can be reasonably estimated be reported?

	Accrued	Disclosed
a.	Yes	No
b.	No	Yes
c.	Yes	Yes
d.	No	No

M9-10
LO 9.5

During 2016, Lawton Company introduced a new line of machines that carry a 3-year assurance-type warranty against manufacturer's defects. Based on industry experience, warranty costs are estimated at 2% of sales in the year of sale, 4% in the year after sale, and 6% in the second year after sale. Sales and actual warranty expenditures for the first 3-year period were as follows:

	Sales	Actual Warranty Expenditures
2016	$ 200,000	$ 3,000
2017	500,000	15,000
2018	700,000	45,000
	$1,400,000	$63,000

What amount should Lawton report as a liability at December 31, 2018?

a. $0
b. $21,000
c. $84,000
d. $105,000

REVIEW EXERCISES

RE9-1
LO 9.3
Rescue Sequences LLC purchased inventory by issuing a $30,000, 10%, 60-day note on October 1. Prepare the journal entries for Rescue Sequences to record the purchase and payment assuming it uses a perpetual inventory system and a 360-day calendar fiscal year. Rescue Sequences LLC uses a perpetual inventory system.

RE9-2
LO 9.3
Use the same information in **RE9-1** except that the note is not interest bearing. Assume that the note is discounted at a 15% rate.

RE9-3
LO 9.3
Cee & Co.'s fiscal year begins April 1. At the beginning of its fiscal year, Cee & Co. estimates that it will owe $17,400 in property taxes for the year. On June 1, its property taxes are assessed at $17,000, which it pays immediately. Prepare the related journal entries for April 1, May 1, and June 1. Then compute the monthly property tax expense that Cee & Co. would record during June through March.

RE9-4
LO 9.4
McFriend Inc. records its liabilities for employees' vacations at the end of each month. For the month of January, McFriend had 50 employees who are paid an average of $176 per day. The company allows 15 paid vacation days per year. Prepare the journal entry to record the vacation accrual for January.

RE9-5
LO 9.4
Assume that for the August 31 payroll, McFriend (see **RE9-4**) pays its employees $120,000 for time worked and $10,000 for vacation taken. Prepare the journal entry to record McFriend's August 20 payroll.

RE9-6
LO 9.4
Smith Company is required to charge customers an 8% sales tax on all goods it sells. At the time of sale, Smith includes the combined amount of both sales and sales tax in the sales account. At the end of May, Smith's sales account for May has a credit balance of $540,000. Prepare the sales tax adjusting journal entry for the end of May.

RE9-7
LO 9.4
Wallace Corporation summarizes the following information from its weekly payroll records during April.

Type of Salary	Gross Pay	F.I.C.A. Tax	Federal Income Tax	State Income Tax	Net Pay
Office Staff	$70,000	$5,600	$5,110	$2,000	$57,290

Prepare the two journal entries to record the payment of the payroll and the accrual of its payroll taxes for April. Assume an 8% F.I.C.A. rate for both employees and the employer. Also assume a 5.4% state unemployment tax rate, a 0.6% federal unemployment tax rate, and that all wages are subject to all payroll taxes. Round to the nearest dollar.

RE9-8
LO 9.4
Borat Company gives annual bonuses after the end of the year. Borat computes the bonuses based on the company's net income after deducting the bonuses but before deducting income taxes. Borat's income before bonuses and income taxes is $565,000 for the current year. The effective income tax rate is 35%, and the bonus rate is 12%. Calculate Borat's bonuses and income taxes for the current year. Round your final answer to two decimal places.

RE9-9
LO 9.5
Dynamo Corporation manufactures toasters. Each toaster comes with a 5-year assurance-type warranty. The toasters sell for $50 each. During Year 1, Dynamo sells 500 toasters. Past experience shows that the average warranty costs are $5 each or $2,500 for these toasters. In Year 1, Dynamo spends $600 for warranty costs on the toasters sold that year. Prepare Dynamo's journal entries related to the sales and warranty in Year 1.

RE9-10
LO 9.5
Landcaster Inc. sells its products with a 2-year service-type warranty. In Year 1, Landcaster sells 60 machines for $2,500 each. Landcaster determines that the machines normally sell for $2,275 each and the service-type warranty could be purchased for $225 per machine. In Year 1, Landcaster pays $5,000 for warranty costs. Prepare Landcaster's journal entries related to the sales and warranty in Year 1.

RE9-11
LO 9.5
After years of experience, Dilcort Company reasonably estimated that a loss from a pending lawsuit was probable at September 30 of the current year. Dilcort Company estimated that the loss would amount to $57,500. Prepare the journal entry, if any, to record the lawsuit at its September 30 year-end.

EXERCISES

E9-1
LO 9.3
Accounts Payable and Cash Discounts On January 4, 2016, Dunbar Company purchased, on credit, 2,500 television sets at $800 each. Terms of the purchase were 2/10, n/30. Dunbar paid for 20% of these sets on January 13 and the remaining 80% on February 1.

Required:
1. Prepare the journal entries on Dunbar Company's books, assuming that it uses the net price method to record its merchandise. (Dunbar uses a perpetual inventory system.)
2. **Next Level** Discuss the conceptual advantage of the net price method compared to the gross price method.

E9-2
LO 9.3
Notes Payable On December 1, 2016, Insto Photo Company purchased merchandise, invoice price $25,000, and issued a 12%, 120-day note to Ringo Chemicals Company. Insto uses the calendar year as its fiscal year and uses the perpetual inventory system.

Required:
Prepare journal entries on Insto's books to record the preceding information, including the adjusting entry at the end of the year and payment of the note at maturity.

E9-3
LO 9.3

Non-Interest-Bearing Notes Payable On November 16, 2016, Clear Glass Company borrowed $20,000 from First American Bank by issuing a 90-day, non-interest-bearing note. The bank discounted this note at 12% and remitted the difference to Clear Glass.

Required:
1. Prepare the journal entries of Clear Glass to record the preceding information, the related calendar year-end adjusting entry, and payment of the note at maturity.
2. Show how the preceding items would be reported on the December 31, 2016, balance sheet.
3. **Next Level** What is Clear Glass Company's effective interest rate?

E9-4
LO 9.3

Discounting of Notes Payable On October 30, 2016, Sanchez Company acquired a piece of machinery and signed a 12-month note for $24,000. The face value of the note includes the price of the machinery and interest. The note is to be paid in four $6,000 quarterly installments. The value of the machinery is the present value of the four quarterly payments discounted at an annual interest rate of 16%.

Required:
1. Prepare all the journal entries required to record the preceding information including the year-end adjusting entry and any payments. Present value techniques should be used.
2. Show how the preceding items would be reported on the December 31, 2016, balance sheet.

E9-5
LO 9.3

Disclosure of Debt On May 1, 2016, Ramden Company issues 13% bonds with a face value of $2 million. The bond contract calls for retirement of the bonds in periodic installments of $200,000, starting on May 1, 2017, and continuing on each May 1 thereafter until all bonds are retired.

Required:
How would the preceding information appear in Ramden's balance sheets on December 31, 2016 and 2017?

E9-6
LO 9.3

Short-Term Debt Expected to Be Refinanced On December 31, 2016, Excello Electric Company had $1 million of short-term notes payable due February 7, 2017. Excello expected to refinance these notes on a long-term basis. On January 15, 2017, the company issued bonds with a face value of $900,000 for $882,000. On January 22, 2017, the proceeds from the bond issue plus additional cash held by Excello on December 31, 2016, were used to liquidate the $1 million of short-term notes. The December 31, 2016, balance sheet is issued on February 12, 2017.

Required:
Prepare a partial balance sheet as of December 31, 2016, showing how the $1 million of short-term notes payable should be disclosed. Include an appropriate footnote for proper disclosure.

E9-7
LO 9.3

Short-Term Debt Expected to Be Refinanced On December 31, 2016, Carrboro Textile Company had short-term debt in the form of notes payable totaling $600,000. These notes were due on June 1, 2017. Carrboro expected to refinance these notes on a long-term basis. On February 1, 2017, Carrboro entered into an agreement with Worldwide Life Insurance Company whereby Worldwide will lend Carrboro $450,000, payable in 5 years at 12%. The money will be available to Carrboro on May 20, 2017. Carrboro issues its December 31, 2016, year-end financial statements on March 2, 2017.

Required:
1. Show how the $600,000 notes payable will be classified on Carrboro Textile's balance sheet on December 31, 2016.
2. **Next Level** What is necessary in order for a company to exclude short-term debt that is expected to be refinanced on a long-term basis from the current liability classification?

E9-8
LO 9.3

Refundable Deposits Party Warehouse Inc. rents a wide variety of products (e.g., tables, chairs, tents) for special events. Upon rental, Party Warehouse requires a deposit which is forfeited if the equipment is not returned at the end of the rental period. Deposits charged are twice the cost of the equipment, and Party Warehouse keeps the equipment in its accounting records until deposits are forfeited. On April 5, a customer rented various products for an event to be held on April 8, and Party Warehouse collected a $10,000 deposit. The products were returned on April 10.

(continued)

Required:
1. Prepare the entries to record the receipt of the deposit and refund of the deposit at the end of the rental period.
2. Assume that the customer only returns 90% of the equipment on April 10. Prepare the entries to record the forfeiture of the deposit.

E9-9
LO 9.3

Unearned Revenue: Gift Certificates On December 5, 2016, Super Circuit Store sold gift certificates totaling $12,000. By December 31, 2016, all but $2,125 worth of these certificates had been redeemed for merchandise. Outstanding certificates were then redeemed by January 15, 2017.

Required:
1. Prepare journal entries on Super Circuit's books to reflect the preceding transactions.
2. How would the gift certificates be reported on Super Circuit's balance sheet on December 31, 2016?

E9-10
LO 9.3

Property Taxes Family Practice Associates has an estimated property tax liability of $7,200 assessed as of January 1, 2016, for the year May 1, 2016, to April 30, 2017. The property tax is paid on September 1, 2016. The property tax becomes a lien against the property on May 1.

Required:
1. Prepare the necessary monthly journal entries to record the preceding information for the period from May 1 to September 30, 2016 (assuming actual taxes are the same as estimated).
2. What would be the amount of the liability on December 31, 2016?

E9-11
LO 9.3

Property Taxes Ames Company is located in a city and county that issue property tax statements in May of each year. The fiscal year for the two local governmental units is May 1 to April 30. Property taxes of $48,000 are assessed against Ames property held on January 1, 2016. The taxes become a lien against Ames property on May 1, 2016. The actual amount of the property taxes of $48,000 is determinable on May 1, 2016; therefore, no estimate of taxes is required. The tax bills are payable in two equal installments on July 10 and September 10.

Required:
Assuming that monthly accruals are recorded, prepare all property tax journal entries for the period May 1 to September 30, 2016.

E9-12
LO 9.4

Compensated Absences Bettinghaus Corporation began business on January 2, 2016, with five employees. Its sick leave and vacation policy follows: Each employee is allowed 8 days of paid sick leave each year and one day of paid vacation leave for each month worked. The accrued vacation leave cannot be taken until the employee has been with the company 1 year. The sick leave, if not used, accumulates to an 18-day maximum. The vacation leave accumulates for 5 years, but at any time the employee may request additional compensation in lieu of taking paid vacation leave. The company records its liability for both compensated absences on a quarterly basis. The daily gross wages for each employee are $160.

Required:
1. Prepare journal entries to record the liability for compensated absences for the first quarter of 2016. Assume no sick leave had been taken by the employees.
2. Prepare a partial interim balance sheet showing how the liability created in Requirement 1 would be reported on March 31, 2016.
3. **Next Level** Discuss the underlying conceptual basis of accounting for compensated absences.

E9-13
LO 9.4

Sales Taxes During August, Hill Sales Company had these summary transactions:
1. cash sales of $210,000, subject to sales taxes of 6%
2. sales on account of $260,000, subject to sales taxes of 6%
3. paid the sales taxes to the state

Required:
Prepare journal entries to record the preceding transactions.

E9-14
LO 9.4

Payroll and Payroll Taxes Rand Company's payroll on December 31 of the current year is as follows:
- total payroll, $500,000
- payroll in excess of $117,000 to each employee, $350,000
- payroll in excess of $7,000 to each employee, $400,000

- income taxes withheld, $85,000
- union dues withheld, $10,000
- tax rates: State unemployment tax, 5.4%; F.I.C.A. tax, 8% for employees and 8% for employers for any amounts over $117,000; federal unemployment tax, 0.6%

Required:
Prepare the journal entries for Rand's payroll and payroll taxes.

E9-15 **Bonus Obligation** Raymond Moss, vice president of Moss Auto Parts, gets an annual bonus of 15% of any income, before deducting bonus and income taxes, above $100,000. Income before bonus and income taxes is $250,000. The effective income tax rate is 30%.

LO 9.4

Required:
1. Compute the amount of Raymond Moss's bonus.
2. Compute the income tax expense.

E9-16 **Loss Contingency** On December 4, 2016, Dan Johnson, delivery truck driver for Farmers Products Inc., ran a stop sign and collided with another vehicle. On January 8, 2017, the driver of the other vehicle filed suit against Farmers Products for damages to the vehicle. Estimated damages to this vehicle were between $6,000 and $10,000 with no amount within the range more likely than any other amount. Farmers Products issued its 2016 financial statements on March 3, 2017.

LO 9.5

Required:
1. Prepare the disclosures and/or journal entries Farmers Products should make in preparing its December 31, 2016, financial statements.
2. If Farmers Products used IFRS, how would the disclosures and/or journal entries differ from those under U.S. GAAP?

E9-17 **Assurance-Type Warranties** On September 1, 2016, Carolina Electronics Company has 1,000 Blu-ray players ready for sale. On October 1, 2016, 900 are sold at $125 each with a 1-year assurance-type warranty. Carolina estimates that the warranty cost on each Blu-ray player sold will probably average $10 per unit. During the final 3 months of 2016, Carolina incurred warranty costs of $4,000, and in 2017 warranty costs were $5,000.

LO 9.5

Required:
1. Prepare the journal entries for the preceding transactions.
2. Show how the preceding items would be reported on the December 31, 2016, balance sheet.
3. Prepare the journal entries for the preceding transactions using the modified cash basis method.
4. **Next Level** Which method produces the better measure of income? Why?

E9-18 **Service-Type Warranties** On August 1, 2016, Pereira Corporation has sold 1,600 Wiglows to Mendez Company at $450 each. Mendez also purchased a 1-year service-type warranty on all the Wiglows for $12 per unit. In 2016, Pereira incurred warranty costs of $9,200. Costs for 2017 were $7,000.

LO 9.5

Required:
1. Prepare the journal entries for the preceding transactions.
2. Show how Pereira would report the items on the December 31, 2016, balance sheet.

E9-19 **Premium Obligation** Sweet Dates Company offers a premium to its customers—a glass bowl (cost to Sweet Dates is $0.90) upon return of 40 coupons. Two coupons are placed in each box of dates sold. The company estimates, on the basis of past experience, that only 70% of the coupons will ever be redeemed. During 2016, 10 million boxes of dates are sold at $0.30 each. Eight million coupons are redeemed during 2016. Sweet Dates purchased 360,000 glass bowls for the plan in 2016.

LO 9.5

Required:
1. Prepare the journal entries related to the sale of dates and the premium plan in 2016.
2. Show how the preceding items would be reported on the December 31, 2016, balance sheet.

E9-20 **Premium Obligation** On the back of its cereal boxes, Tiger Cereal Company offers a premium to its customers. The premium, a toy truck, may be claimed by sending in $1 plus 10 coupons; one coupon is included in each box of cereal sold. Tiger estimates, based on past experience, that 60% of the coupons will be redeemed. During 2016,

LO 9.5

(continued)

Tiger purchased 240,000 toy trucks at $1.25 each for the premium promotion and sold 5,000,000 boxes of cereal at $1.80 per box. In 2016, 2,200,000 coupons were redeemed.

Required:
1. Prepare the journal entries related to the previous promotion (including sales) for 2016.
2. Show how the items related to the premium plan would be reported on the December 31, 2016, balance sheet.
3. **Next Level** What would be the effect on the financial statements if Tiger recorded premium expense as the coupons were redeemed?

E9-21
LO 9.5
Cash Rebates On January 1, 2017, Fro-Yo Inc. began offering customers a cash rebate of $5.00 if the customer mails in 10 proof-of-purchase labels from its frozen yogurt containers. Based on historical experience, the company estimates that 20% of the labels will be redeemed. During 2017, the company sold 5,000,000 frozen yogurt containers at $1 per container. From these sales, 800,000 labels were redeemed in 2017, 150,000 labels were redeemed in 2018, and the remaining labels were never redeemed.

Required:
1. Prepare the journal entries related to the sale of frozen yogurt and the cash rebate offer for 2017 and 2018.
2. **Next Level** Assume that 300,000 labels were redeemed in 2018. Prepare the journal entries related to the cash rebate offer for 2018.

E9-22
LO 9.5
Gain Contingency On December 31, 2016, Braino Tech Inc. learned that its competitor had introduced a product using an accessory to which Braino has exclusive patent rights. Braino planned to file suit and its attorneys estimated that Braino should recover at least $500,000. Braino's December 31, 2016, year-end financial statements were issued March 2, 2017. At that date, Braino still planned to file suit, even though it had not yet done so.

Required:
Next Level Discuss the accounting treatment in regard to the 2016 financial statements of Braino Tech called for by GAAP concerning the described circumstances. Be sure to conceptually justify this treatment.

PROBLEMS

P9-1
LO 9.3
Accounts Payable and Cash Discounts Byrd Company had the following transactions during 2016 and 2017:
1. On December 24, 2016, a computer was purchased on account from Computers International for $60,000. Terms of the sale were 2/10, n/30.
2. Byrd calculated that to forgo the discount for the computer would be the equivalent of paying 36% interest annually for the extra 20 days. Therefore, Byrd went to First Local Bank and signed a $60,000, 30-day note at 12% in order to take advantage of the discount terms. This transaction took place on December 29, 2016. (The account payable was paid on January 2, 2017, and the note was paid at maturity. Assume a 360-day year.)
3. On December 30, 2016, Byrd declared a $2.00 cash dividend to the common shareholders. Ten thousand shares were outstanding on this date. The dividend is to be paid on January 5, 2017.

Required:
1. Prepare the journal entries for Byrd for both 2016 and 2017. Assume that the net price method is used to account for the credit terms.
2. Show how the preceding items would be reported in the current liabilities section of Byrd's December 31, 2016, balance sheet.
3. **Next Level** Assuming Byrd's current assets were $1,200,000 and its current ratio was 2.4 at the end of 2015, compute the current ratio at the end of 2016 (based solely on the effects of the preceding transactions).

P9-2
LO 9.3
Notes Payable and Effective Interest On November 1, 2016, Edwin Inc. borrowed cash and signed a $60,000, 1-year note payable.

Required:
1. Compute the following items assuming (a) an interest-bearing note at 12%, (b) a non-interest-bearing note discounted at 12%:
    a. cash received
    b. effective interest rate
    c. interest expense for 2016

2. Prepare the journal entries for Edwin under each case for 2016 and 2017.
3. **Next Level** Why is the effective rate higher for the non-interest-bearing note?

P9-3
LO 9.3

Trade Note Transactions Adjusto Corporation (which is on a December 31 fiscal year-end) engaged in the following transactions during 2016 and 2017:

2016
Nov. 1   Issued a 120-day, 12% note, face value of $20,000, to Johnson Company to settle an open account of that amount.
Dec. 1   Issued a 90-day, 12% note, face value of $32,000, to Winslow Corporation for the purchase of merchandise (the perpetual inventory method is used).

2017
Mar. 1   Paid the principal and interest on both the Johnson and the Winslow notes.

Required:
Prepare journal entries to record the preceding transactions on Adjusto's books, including the adjusting entries at the end of 2016. Assume a 360-day year.

P9-4
LO 9.3

Short-Term Debt Expected to Be Refinanced Several times during 2016, Palmer Company issued short-term commercial paper totaling $7 million. On December 31, 2016, the company's year-end, Palmer intends to refinance the commercial paper by issuing long-term debt. However, because Palmer had excess cash, $3 million of the liability is liquidated in February 2017 as the commercial paper matures. On March 1, 2017, Palmer issues $9 million of long-term bonds, with $3 million of the proceeds going to replenish the working capital used to liquidate the $3 million of commercial paper, $4 million to pay the remaining balance of the commercial paper due after April, and the remaining $2 million to finance an equipment modernization program at Palmer's plant. Palmer's December 31, 2016, year-end financial statements are issued on March 13, 2017.

Required:
1. **Next Level** How will the $3 million of commercial paper liquidated prior to the refinancing be classified on Palmer's December 31, 2016, balance sheet? Explain your reasoning.
2. **Next Level** How will the remaining $4 million of commercial paper be classified on Palmer's December 31, 2016, balance sheet? Explain your reasoning.

P9-5
LO 9.3

Short-Term Debt Expected to Be Refinanced On December 31, 2016, Atwood Table Company has $8 million of short-term notes payable owed to City National Bank. On February 1, 2017, Atwood negotiates a revolving credit agreement providing for unrestricted borrowings up to $6 million. Borrowings will bear interest at 1% over the prevailing prime rate, will have stated maturities of 120 days, and will be continuously renewable for 120-day periods for 4 years. Atwood plans to refinance as much as possible of the notes outstanding with the proceeds available from this agreement. Assume that Atwood's December 31, 2016, year-end financial statements are issued on March 30, 2017.

Required:
1. Prepare a partial December 31, 2016, balance sheet for Atwood showing how the $8 million short-term debt should be reported.
2. **Next Level** What is the justification for allowing short-term debt that is expected to be refinanced to be classified as a long-term liability.

P9-6
LO 9.3

Non-Interest-Bearing Note Payable: Present Value On January 1, 2016, Northern Manufacturing Company bought a piece of equipment by signing a non-interest-bearing $80,000, 1-year note. The face value of the note includes the price of the equipment and the interest. The effective interest rate is an annual rate of 16%, and the note is to be paid in four $20,000 quarterly installments on March 31, June 30, September 30, and December 31. The price of the equipment is the present value of the four payments discounted at the effective interest rate.

Required:
1. Prepare all journal entries to record the preceding information. Present value techniques should be used.
2. If Northern's financial statements were issued on June 30, 2016, what amount would the company report as notes payable?

P9-7
LO 9.3

Property Taxes Rosen Corporation was formed on December 12, 2015. It plans to close its books annually each December 31. Rosen is located in Lanmark City and Apple County. The fiscal period of these two governmental units runs from July 1 to June 30. The property tax that they assess on property held on January 1 of each year

(continued)

becomes a lien against the property on July 1. The estimated property taxes for Rosen for the period July 1, 2016, to June 30, 2017, are $15,300. The tax bill is mailed in October with a requirement that the tax be paid before December 31. The tax bill received on October 30, 2016, for Rosen revealed an actual tax of $15,705, and the corporation paid this amount on November 30, 2016. Rosen elects to record monthly property tax adjustments for interim statements required by management.

Required:
1. Prepare all property-tax-related entries for Rosen for the period July 1, 2016, to June 30, 2017.
2. Show how the preceding information would be reported on Rosen's December 31, 2016, balance sheet.

P9-8
LO 9.4

Compensated Absences Rexallo Company begins business on January 2, 2016, with 15 employees. Its company policy is to permit each employee to take 6 days of paid sick leave each year and 1½ days of paid vacation leave for each month worked. The sick leave, if not used, accumulates to a 24-day maximum. The vacation leave accumulates for 2 years, but at any time after a 1-year period, the employee may request additional compensation in lieu of taking paid vacation leave. Rexallo prefers to record the liability for compensated absences on a quarterly basis. Assume that the gross salaries for each employee are $100 per day.

The following selected events take place during the first two quarters of 2016:

- On March 31, 2016, the quarterly liability for compensated absences is to be recorded.
- On April 30, 2016, the following $45,000 monthly payroll, including paid vacation and sick leave, is summarized from Rexallo's records:

	Payroll for		
	Time Worked	Vacation Taken	Sick Leave Taken
Salaries	$42,000	$1,800	$1,200

- On June 30, 2016, the quarterly liability for compensated absences is to be recorded.

Required:
1. Prepare journal entries to record the preceding events, ignoring payroll taxes and assuming that both sick leave and vacation time meet the requirements of GAAP for accrual.
2. Prepare a partial interim balance sheet as of June 30, 2016, to disclose the liability created in Requirement 1.
3. **Next Level** Discuss the underlying conceptual basis of accounting for compensated absences.

P9-9
LO 9.4

Payroll and Payroll Taxes Bailey Dry Cleaners has six employees who were paid the following wages during 2016:

Frank Johnson	$ 27,000
Bill Long	18,000
Duff Morse	125,000
Laura Stewart	28,000
Cindy Sharpe	26,000
Melissa Ledbetter	20,000
Total	$244,000

The state allows the company a 1% unemployment compensation merit-rating reduction from the normal rate of 5.4%. The federal unemployment rate is 0.6%. The maximum unemployment wages per employee are $7,000 for both the state and the federal government. Income tax withholdings of 20% are applied to all employees. A F.I.C.A. tax rate of 8% on the employee and 8% on the employer is applied to the first $117,000 of each employee's wages.

Required:
1. Calculate the amount of payroll taxes to be paid by Bailey.
2. Prepare the journal entries to record the payment of payroll and the payroll tax expense.

P9-10
LO 9.4

Bonus Obligation and Income Tax Expense James Kimberley, president of National Motors, receives a bonus of 10% of National's profits above $1,500,000, before the bonus and the corporation's income taxes are deducted. National's effective income tax rate is 30%. Profits before income taxes and his bonus are $5,000,000 for 2016.

Required:
1. Compute the amount of Kimberley's bonus for 2016.
2. Compute National Motors' income tax expense for 2016.
3. Prepare journal entries at the end of 2016 to record the bonus and income taxes.
4. Show how the bonus and income taxes would be reported on National Motors' December 31, 2016, balance sheet.

P9-11
LO 9.4

Sales Taxes Mauldin Company makes sales on which a 5% sales tax is assessed. The following summary transactions were made during 2016:
1. sales for cash of $1,665,400, excluding sales taxes
2. sales on credit of $2,820,500, excluding sales taxes
3. sales taxes of $168,220 were paid to the state government during 2016

Required:
1. Prepare journal entries to record the preceding transactions.
2. Show how the unpaid sales taxes would be reported on Mauldin's December 31, 2016, balance sheet.

P9-12
LO 9.5

Contingencies Fallon Company, a toy manufacturer that also operates several retail outlets, is preparing its December 31, 2016, financial statements. It has identified the following legal situations that may qualify as contingencies:
1. A customer is suing the company for $800,000 in damages because her child was injured in November 2016 while riding an escalator that stopped suddenly in one of its stores. The child was hurt when he tripped and fell while walking "down" an escalator that was going "up." Legal counsel feels that the child is partially at fault, but that it is probable that the lawsuit will be settled for between $50,000 and $100,000, with $80,000 being the most likely amount.
2. Fallon has discovered that a skateboard it began manufacturing and selling in 2016 has defective bearings, sometimes causing a wheel to fall off. Fallon has issued a "recall" notice in newspapers and magazines in which it offers to replace the bearings. It estimates a cost of $200,000 for these repairs. No lawsuits have been filed for injury claims, although the company feels that there is a reasonable possibility that claims may total as high as $2 million.
3. Fallon has an incinerator behind one of its retail outlets which is used to burn cardboard boxes received in shipments of inventory from suppliers. The state environmental protection agency filed suit against the company in August 2016 for air pollution. Fallon expects to stop using the incinerator and begin recycling. However, its lawyers believe that it is probable that a fine of between $40,000 and $60,000 will be levied against the company, although they cannot predict the exact amount.
4. In early 2016, Fallon signed a contract with a computer vendor to install "state of the art" cash registers in all of its retail outlets. Because of the vendor's inability to acquire sufficient cash registers, the vendor canceled the contract. Fallon has filed a breach of contract suit against the vendor, claiming $300,000 in damages. The company's lawyers expect that it will settle the suit "out of court" for $150,000.

Required:
1. **Next Level** For each situation, prepare the journal entry (if any) on December 31, 2016, to record the information for Fallon, and explain your reasoning. If no journal entry is recorded, explain how the information would be disclosed in Fallon's 2016 annual report.
2. How would your answers change if Fallon used IFRS?

P9-13
LO 9.5

AICPA Adapted

Contingencies Greenlaw Inc., a publishing company, is preparing its December 31, 2016, financial statements and must determine the proper accounting treatment for each of the following situations:
1. Greenlaw sells subscriptions to several magazines for a 1, 2, or 3-year period. Cash receipts from subscribers are credited to Unearned Revenue: Magazine Subscriptions, and this account had a balance of $2,500,000 at December 31, 2016. Outstanding subscriptions at December 31, 2016, expire as follows:

    During 2017—$600,000
    During 2018—$900,000
    During 2019—$400,000

2. On January 4, 2016, Greenlaw discontinued collision, fire, and theft coverage on its delivery vehicles and became self-insured for these risks. Actual losses of $45,000 during 2016 were charged to delivery expense. The 2015 premium for the discontinued coverage amounted to $100,000, and the controller wants to set up a

(continued)

reserve for self-insurance by a debit to Delivery Expense of $55,000 and a credit to Reserve for Self-Insurance of $55,000.
3. A suit for breach of contract seeking damages of $1,000,000 was filed by an author against Greenlaw on July 3, 2016. The company's legal counsel believes that an unfavorable outcome is probable. A reasonable estimate of the court's award to the plaintiff is in the range between $100,000 and $500,000. No amount within this range is a better estimate of potential damages than any other amount.
4. During December 2016 a competitor company filed suit against Greenlaw for industrial espionage claiming $2,000,000 in damages. In the opinion of management and company counsel, it is reasonably possible that damages will be awarded to the plaintiff, and the amount of potential damages awarded to the plaintiff is estimated to be $1,500,000.

Required:
1. For each of the preceding situations, prepare the journal entry that should be recorded as of December 31, 2016, or explain why an entry should not be recorded. Show supporting computations in good form.
2. How might your answers to the breach of contract litigation and the industrial espionage litigation change if Greenlaw used IFRS?

P9-14 **Assurance-Type Warranty** Clean-All Inc. sells washing machines with a 3-year assurance-type warranty. In the
LO 9.5 past, Clean-All has found that in the year after sale, warranty costs have been 3% of sales; in the second year after sale, 5% of sales; and in the third year after sale, 7% of sales. The following data are also available:

Year	Sales	Warranty Expenditures
2016	$500,000	$62,000
2017	650,000	82,000
2018	700,000	85,000

Required:
1. Prepare the journal entries for the preceding transactions for 2016–2018. Closing entries are not required.
2. What amount would Clean-All report as a liability on its December 31, 2018, balance sheet, assuming the liability had a balance of $88,200 on December 31, 2015?
3. **Next Level** How would the failure to recognize a contingent liability affect the financial statements?

P9-15 **Service-Type Warranty** Wright Machinery Corporation manufactures automobile engines for major automobile
LO 9.5 producers. The engines sell for $920 per engine. In addition, customers have the option to purchase a service-type warranty for $73 per engine that protects against any defects for a period of 5 years. During 2016, Wright sold 8,000 engines to National Motors. National Motors purchased warranties on all of the engines purchased. During 2016, Wright repaired defective motors at a cost of $94,400.

Required:
Prepare the journal entries for the preceding transactions.

P9-16 **Premium Obligation** Yummy Cereal Company is offering one toy shovel set for 15 box tops of its cereal. Year-to-
LO 9.5 date sales have been off, and it is hoped that this offer will stimulate demand. Each shovel set costs the company $3. The following data are available for the last 3 months of 2016:

Month	Boxes of Cereal Sold	Shovel Sets Purchased by the Company	Box Tops Redeemed by Customers
October	21,000	880	12,000
November	24,000	1,083	16,005
December	33,000	1,697	20,745

It is estimated that only 70% of the box tops will be redeemed. The cereal sells for $2.80 per box.

Required:
1. Prepare journal entries for each month to record sales, shovel set purchases, and redemptions.
2. Assuming Yummy prepares monthly financial statements, indicate how the inventory of premiums and the estimated liability would be disclosed on Yummy's ending balance sheets for October, November, and December.

P9-17 **Comprehensive** Selected transactions of Lizard Lick Corporation during 2016 are as follows:

LO 9.3
LO 9.4

Jan. 5 Purchased merchandise from Boston Company for $30,000; terms, 2/10, n/30. Purchases and accounts payable are recorded by Lizard Lick using the net price method.
26 Paid the January 5 invoice.
Mar. 31 Purchased a van for $19,950 from Hill Sales Company, paying $9,950 in cash and issuing a 12%, 1-year note for the balance of the purchase price.
May 1 Borrowed money from Mebane National Bank by discounting its own 1-year, non-interest-bearing note made out for the maturity value of $50,000 at an interest rate of 12%.
Nov. 2 Received $500 from Carr Mill Playhouse as a deposit to be refunded after certain rental furniture to be used in a play is returned on January 7, 2017.
5 Made sales on credit to Jones Company for $15,000. Sales taxes of $6\frac{1}{2}\%$ were added to the $15,000 price (ignore cost of goods sold).
6 Purchased another van at a cost of $18,000 from a company located in a state that does not levy a sales tax. The entire purchase price was paid in cash. Lizard Lick is located in a state that assesses a use tax of $6\frac{1}{2}\%$ on nonsalable equipment bought outside its sales tax authority. The van and the liability for the use tax are to be recorded.
Dec. 1 Estimated property taxes for the year December 1, 2016, to November 30, 2017, are $36,000 (ignore previous property taxes). The corporation follows the practice of recording its property tax by a monthly accrual starting one month following the lien date. The tax becomes a lien on December 1 and is payable in two installments on May 1 and October 1.
31 Estimated quarterly income taxes for the last quarter of the year are $150,000.

Required:
Prepare journal entries to record the preceding transactions for 2016. Include year-end interest accruals.

P9-18 **Comprehensive** Selected transactions of Shadrach Computer Corporation during November and December of 2016 are as follows:

LO 9.3
LO 9.4
LO 9.5

Nov. 1 Borrowed money from the bank by issuing a non-interest-bearing, $40,000, 90-day note. The note is discounted on a 12% basis.
9 Sold 100 computers with a 1-year assurance-type warranty for $5,000 each on credit (ignore cost of goods sold). Past experience indicates that warranty costs average $125 per computer.
12 Sold 100 software packages at $300 each on credit (ignore cost of goods sold). With each software package, Shadrach offered a premium in the form of a USB drive for the return of one proof of purchase. The offer expires June 30, 2017. The cost of each USB drive is $5, and Shadrach estimates that 80% of the premiums will be redeemed; therefore, 80 USB drives were purchased on credit.
20 Paid $2,900 in fulfillment of the warranty agreement on several of the computers sold on November 9.
30 Accrued monthly vacation pay. Shadrach has 90 employees who are each paid an average of $160 per day. Shadrach has a policy of allowing each employee 12 days' paid vacation per year; the related liability is recorded on a monthly basis. Employees are paid monthly.
30 Paid monthly payroll. Gross salaries were $432,000. No vacations were taken during November. Income tax withholdings of 20% are applicable to the salaries of all employees. A F.I.C.A. tax of 8% for both employees and employers is also applicable. These rates apply to all salaries because no employee's salary has exceeded the maximum wage limit. The state allows the corporation a 1% unemployment compensation merit-rating reduction from the normal rate of 5.4%. The federal unemployment rate is 0.6%. Prior to October, each individual employee had accumulated a gross salary in excess of $7,000 for 2016.
Dec. 14 Twenty proofs of purchase were returned from the November 12 sale.
29 An individual filed suit against Shadrach for damages caused in a November 5 accident that resulted when a member of the sales force hit the individual's car while on personal business. The amount of the suit filed was $1,500. Because the employee was on personal business, the company's insurance company will not pay the claim. In Shadrach's attorney's opinion, the amount of the suit is reasonable; furthermore, the company believes it is likely to lose the suit.
31 Accrued monthly vacation pay.
31 Paid monthly payroll. Gross salaries were $435,000. The salaries included $6,800 of vacation pay in the sales force and $3,200 of vacation pay in the office staff. The F.I.C.A. tax rate still applies to all wages because no employee's salary exceeded the maximum wage limit.
31 Recorded president's bonus. The president receives a 10% bonus on any income over $200,000, before deducting income taxes and the bonus. Shadrach's effective income tax rate is 30%, and income before income taxes and bonus for 2016 was $560,000. The bonus will be paid in January 2017.

(continued)

Required:
Prepare journal entries to record the preceding transactions of Shadrach Computer Corporation for 2016. Include year-end accruals. Round all calculations to the nearest dollar.

CASES

COMMUNICATION

C9-1
LO 9.3

Short-Term Debt Expected to Be Refinanced

While examining the 2016 financial statements of Warder Corporation, you found evidence that the following were not included in its current liabilities on the December 31, 2016, balance sheet:
1. A note payable due and paid by Warder on February 19, 2016. Warder obtained long-term financing equal to this amount paid on February 26, 2016.
2. Note payable due 2 months after the balance sheet date, with refinancing agreement entered into 4 weeks after the balance sheet date.
3. Notes payable of Warder's completely owned subsidiary due its shareholders and payable upon demand.
4. Deposits from customers on equipment ordered by them from Warder.

Required:
Discuss the assumptions needed for Warder to correctly exclude the previously mentioned items from the December 31, 2016, current liabilities. The balance sheet was issued on March 3, 2017.

C9-2
LO 9.5
AICPA Adapted

Loss Contingencies

Part a. The two basic requirements for the accrual of a loss contingency are supported by several basic concepts of accounting. Three of these concepts are the period of time assumption, the recognition principle, and the qualitative characteristic of verifiability.

Required:
Discuss how the two basic requirements for the accrual of a loss contingency relate to the three concepts mentioned above.

Part b. The following three **independent** sets of facts relate to (1) the possible accrual or (2) the possible disclosure by other means of a loss contingency.

Situation I
A company offers a 1-year assurance-type warranty for the product that it manufactures. A history of warranty claims has been compiled and the probable amount of claims related to sales for a given period can be determined.

Situation II
Subsequent to the date of a set of financial statements, but prior to the issuance of the financial statements, a company enters into a contract that will probably result in a significant loss to the company. The amount of the loss can be reasonably estimated.

Situation III
A company has adopted a policy of recording self-insurance for any possible losses resulting from injury to others by the company's vehicles. The premium for an insurance policy for the same risk from an independent insurance company would have an annual cost of $2,000. During the period covered by the financial statements, there were no accidents involving the company's vehicles that resulted in injury to others.

Required:
Explain the accrual and/or type of disclosure necessary (if any) and the reason(s) why such disclosure is appropriate for each of the three independent situations described. Complete your response to each situation before proceeding to the next situation.

C9-3
LO 9.5
AICPA Adapted

Contingency Conditions and Disclosure

Loss contingencies may exist for companies. Write a short memo that answers the following questions.

Required:
1. What conditions should be met for an estimated loss from a loss contingency to be accrued by a charge to income?
2. When is disclosure required, and what disclosure should be made for an estimated loss from a loss contingency that need not be accrued by a charge to income?

CREATIVE AND CRITICAL THINKING

C9-4 **Pending Damage Suit Disclosure**
LO 9.5
On December 15, 2016, a truck driver for Cork Transfer Company negligently rounded a curve that was also a bridge covering several local merchant shops. The truck jumped the guardrail and fell 30 feet onto one of the shops, causing highly flammable chemicals in the truck to explode. Although by February 22, 2017 (the date on which Cork's financial statements for 2016 are issued), no claims had been filed against Cork, the company's legal counsel believes it is probable that some will be filed in the future. However, counsel does not believe it can reasonably estimate the amount of these potential claims.

Required:
Explain the accounting treatment, if any, Cork should give the contingent loss occurring from the wreck in the December 31, 2016, financial statements.

C9-5 **Various Contingency Issues**
LO 9.5
AICPA Adapted
Skinner Company has the following contingencies:
1. Potential costs due to the discovery of a possible defect related to one of its products. These costs are probable and can be reasonably estimated.
2. A potential claim for damages to be received from a lawsuit filed this year against another company. It is probable that proceeds from the claim will be received by Skinner next year.
3. Potential costs due to a promotional campaign in which a cash refund is sent to customers when coupons are redeemed. Skinner estimated, based on past experience, that 70% of the coupons would be redeemed. Forty percent of the coupons were actually redeemed and the cash refunds sent this year. The remaining 30% of the coupons are expected to be redeemed next year.

Required:
1. How should Skinner report the potential costs due to the discovery of a possible product defect? Explain why.
2. How should Skinner report this year the potential claim for damages that may be received next year? Explain why.
3. This year, how should Skinner account for the potential costs and obligations due to the promotional campaign?

C9-6 **Various Contingency Issues**
LO 9.5
AICPA Adapted
At December 31, 2016, Niki Company reviewed the following situations to consider their impact on its 2016 financial statements:
1. In December 2016, Niki became aware of a safety hazard related to one of its products and announced a product recall. Estimates of the probable costs resulting from the hazard include highest, most likely, and lowest amounts.
2. During 2016, Niki received a note for goods sold to a customer. The note was sold, with recourse, to a bank. The customer filed for bankruptcy in December 2016, before the note's 2017 due date.
3. In 2012, Niki moved and assigned the remaining 10 years of its old lease to Pro Company, an unrelated third party. Pro agreed to make all payments due on the assigned lease, but Niki has prime responsibility for the lease to the lessor. At December 31, 2016, it is reasonably possible that Pro will be unable to make all payments due on the assigned lease.

Required:
For each of the preceding situations, state how Niki should report the impact, if any, on its 2016 financial statements, and explain why the reporting is appropriate.

C9-7 **Product and Lawsuit Contingencies**
LO 9.5
AICPA Adapted
Reese Company sells two types of merchandise, Type A and Type B. Each carries a 1-year assurance-type warranty.

- Type A merchandise: Product warranty costs, based on past experience, will normally be 1% of sales.
- Type B merchandise: Product warranty costs cannot be reasonably estimated because this is a new product line. However, the chief engineer believes that product warranty costs are likely to be incurred.

Reese is also being sued for $2,000,000 for an injury caused to a child as a result of alleged negligence while the child was visiting the Reese Company plant in March 2016. The suit was filed in July 2016. Reese's lawyer states that it is probable that Reese will lose the suit and be found liable for a judgment costing anywhere from $200,000 to

(continued)

$900,000. However, the lawyer states that the most probable judgment is $400,000.

Required:
1. How should Reese report the estimated product warranty costs for each of the two types of merchandise mentioned earlier? Explain the rationale for your answer. Do not discuss deferred income tax implications or disclosures that should be made in Reese's 2016 financial statements or notes.
2. How should Reese report the suit in its 2016 financial statements? Explain the rationale for your answer. Include in your answer disclosures, if any, that should be made in Reese's financial statements or notes.

C9-8 **Ethics and Environmental Damage**

Hart Corporation is a chemical company that produces cleaning fluids of different types. It is the main employer in a small town. Stan Hart has been the company president for 15 years and is paid a salary plus a 10% bonus based on pretax income; he is also the major shareholder. After treatment to remove pollutants, Hart has been draining the waste water from its production process into a nearby river for many years. Over the past year (2016), there have been several "fish kills" in the river. At the end of 2016, the Environmental Protection Agency (EPA) filed a $1 million lawsuit against Hart for violation of pollution control laws.

You are an accountant for the firm that is auditing Hart's 2016 financial statements. Preliminary calculations show that Hart earned a pretax income of $600,000 for 2016, before considering the effects of the lawsuit. In a discussion with Stan Hart and Bob Brandt, the company's attorney, you raise the issue of whether or not to report the lawsuit in the company's 2016 financial statements. Stan says, "I've been president of this company for long enough to know that we didn't cause the fish kills. It must be something else. Furthermore, I don't want anything included in the income statement that would jeopardize the company's well-being. The town depends on us. If we shut-down, the town will die." Bob replies, "I generally agree with you, but you need to be realistic. I don't expect the outcome of the lawsuit to be determined for a couple of years. However, there is a pretty good chance the company will lose. If that happens, then there is a 60% chance the loss will be $400,000 and a 40% chance the loss will be $1 million." Stan replies, "Okay, then let's put it in a note to the financial statements."

Required:
From a financial reporting and ethical standpoint, prepare a written report that recommends how to account for the lawsuit.

C9-9 **Analyzing Starbucks's Current Liabilities and Contingencies Disclosures**

Obtain **Starbucks**'s 2015 annual report either using the "Investor Relations" portion of its web site (do a Web search for Starbucks investor relations) or go to http://www.sec.gov and click "Search for company filings" under "Filings and Forms (EDGAR)."

Required:
1. With regard to Starbucks's current liabilities:
   (a) How does Starbucks value its current liabilities and is this valuation justified?
   (b) What were Starbucks's total current liabilities at the end of its 2015 fiscal year. (c) What was the largest current liability? Describe other significant current liabilities as well.
2. What did accrued liabilties consist of at the end of the fiscal year?
3. Is Starbucks involved in litigation? If so, what can be concluded from its disclosures regarding this litigation?
4. Compute Starbucks's current ratio and payables turnover for its 2015 fiscal year and provide any relevant comments.

C9-10 **Analyzing Moet Hennessy Louis Vuitton's (LVMH) Current Liabilities and Contingencies**

Obtain **Moet Hennessy Louis Vuitton**'s 2013 annual report using the "Investor Relations" portion of its web site (do a Web search for Moet Hennessy Louis Vuitton investor relations).

Required:
1. What were the total current liabilities at the end of 2013? What was the largest current liability?
2. Describe LVMH's short-term borrowings at the end of 2013.
3. Did LVMH report any provisions? If so, describe the nature of these provisions?
4. Describe the components of "other current liabilities" as reported by LVMH.

USING CODIFICATION

C9-11 Researching GAAP

Situation

Bogan Company is in need of cash to finance its operations. The company creates a new company, Hall Company, which is wholly owned by Bogan. On November 1, 2016, Bogan sells inventory on credit to Hall for $50,000, which in turn immediately uses the inventory for a $40,000, 12% loan (guaranteed by Bogan) from 8th National Bank. Hall then uses the proceeds from the loan to repay $40,000 of the $50,000 owed to Bogan. Bogan agrees to continue to extend credit for 9 months to Hall for the remaining $10,000. The inventory is Hall's only asset and is stored in a public warehouse. Bogan agrees to pay Hall the $200 monthly storage fee and $400 per month for a financing fee at the end of each month. Bogan also agrees to repurchase the inventory from Hall for $50,000 at the end of July 2017. Bogan uses a perpetual inventory system; the cost of the inventory sold to Hall is $42,000. The president of Bogan has asked you how to account for this series of transactions in 2016.

Directions

1. Research the related generally accepted accounting principles and prepare a short memo to the president that explains how Bogan should record the sale of the inventory on November 1, 2016, and the payment of the fees at the end of November and December. Also explain how Bogan should report the recorded items in its 2016 financial statements. Cite your reference and applicable paragraph numbers.

C9-12 Researching GAAP

Situation

MacKenzie Refrigeration is a manufacturer of residential refrigerators and freezers. MacKenzie manufactures refrigerators for various retailers and sells its products under the retailers own brand name. Each refrigerator it sells comes with a 2-year warranty. Recently, MacKenzie discovered a defective damper control assembly—an automatic valve that periodically opens to let cold air into the refrigerator compartment from the freezer compartment—that is used on its most popular refrigerators. Because of this defect, the valve has a tendency to remain in the open position and allow too much cold air into the refrigerator compartment. Therefore, any food in the refrigerator that contains liquid (e.g., milk, orange juice, meats, fruits) will freeze. MacKenzie's Chief Operations Officer (COO) wishes to issue a product recall to repair the defective assembly which will cost the company approximately $1,000,000 to $1,200,000, or about 5% of its net income. However, the Chief Financial Officer (CFO) believes that such an expense is not necessary. Based on an internal investigation, MacKenzie estimated that approximately one-fourth of all its refrigerators will experience a damper control failure prior to the expiration of the 2-year warranty. The CFO has determined that it will be more cost effective to repair, under the existing warranty program, only those units that fail within the first 2 years. In fact, he argues that the company's refrigeration repair division might actually make money as it charges the customer for repairing the defective assemblies outside of the warranty period. As most of MacKenzie's products are sold under other company's brand names, the CFO argues that there will be minimal impact on the company's image. The Chief Executive Officer (CEO) must present this issue to MacKenzie's board of directors and wants to know the proper accounting treatment of these product recall costs.

Directions

1. Research the related generally accepted accounting principles and prepare a short memo to the Chief Executive Officer that explains how MacKenzie should report the product recall costs. Cite your reference and applicable paragraph numbers.

PART 3

INVESTING ACTIVITIES

CHAPTER 10
Property, Plant, and Equipment: Acquisition and Subsequent Investments

CHAPTER 11
Depreciation, Depletion, Impairment, and Disposal

CHAPTER 12
Intangibles

CHAPTER 13
Investments and Long-Term Receivables

CHAPTER 10

PROPERTY, PLANT, AND EQUIPMENT: ACQUISITION AND SUBSEQUENT INVESTMENTS

To Capitalize or Not to Capitalize, That Is the Question

Acquiring long-lived assets such as property, plant, and equipment usually represents a major use of a company's cash and an important element in its productive strategy. For example, **Verizon Communications**'s property, plant, and equipment is by far the largest asset on its balance sheet and is critically important to its strategy of being one of the world's leading providers of telecommunications services. To sustain its current scale of operations, Verizon replaces items of property, plant, and equipment, such as network equipment and fiber optic cable, as they wear out. In addition, to meet user demands of higher transmission speeds and enhanced data-carrying and multimedia capabilities, Verizon makes additional investments in its technology infrastructure. The chart below shows Verizon's recent capital expenditures for its two major operating segments.

LEARNING OBJECTIVES

After reading this chapter you will be able to

LO 10.1 Describe the characteristics of property, plant, and equipment.

LO 10.2 Identify the costs to be included in the acquisition of property, plant, and equipment.

LO 10.3 Determine the cost of property, plant, and equipment obtained by a nonmonetary exchange of assets.

LO 10.4 Compute the cost of a self-constructed asset, including capitalized interest.

LO 10.5 Describe the accounting for expenditures incurred subsequent to acquisition.

LO 10.6 *(Appendix 10.1)* Explain the accounting for oil and gas properties.

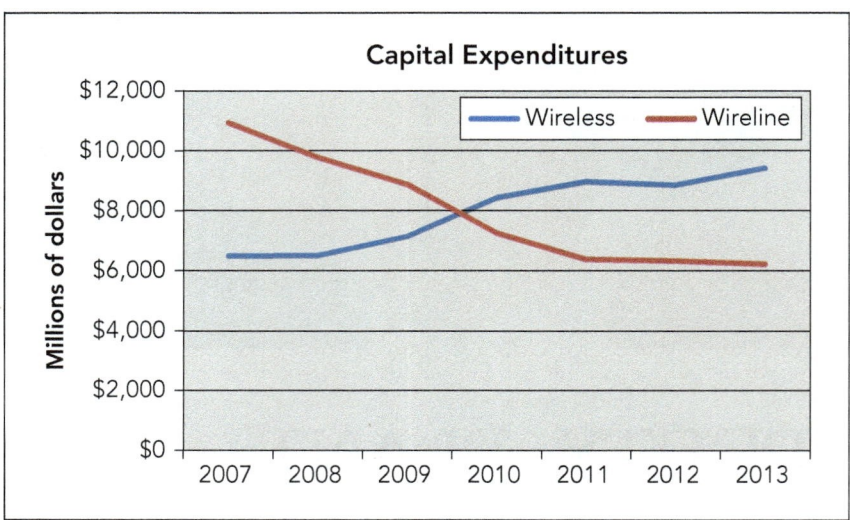

While Verizon's capital expenditures, which totaled over $117 billion between 2007 and 2013, have been relatively flat, it has invested significantly more in its wireless business in recent years. The decline in capital expenditures for the wireline business is primarily due to the completion of the initial deployment of its fiber optic (FiOS) network in 2010. During the same time frame, Verizon's wireless business continued to expand the capacity of its 3G network and build out its 4G LTE network.

As Verizon's experiences indicate, investments in property, plant, and equipment are risky and significantly impact the company's ability to generate growth and profitability. As such, these investments are closely followed by financial statement users. A major accounting issue is whether the expenditures for property, plant, and equipment should be capitalized (recorded as an asset) or expensed in the current period. If the expenditure provides a probable future economic benefit, an asset is created that is subsequently allocated to expense over its useful life. On the other hand, if the expenditure provides no future benefit, it is expensed—no balance sheet asset is created and current period net income is decreased for the full amount of the expenditure. Thus, key issues in the capitalization decision are the recognition of assets and the timing of expenses.

In many cases, the determination of whether an expenditure should be capitalized as an asset or expensed immediately is clear. In other situations, the conclusion is less obvious. In either event, financial statement users should be aware of the financial statement impacts of this decision. First, companies that choose to capitalize rather than expense costs will report higher asset and equity balances. All else equal, this will make them appear more solvent (lower debt-to-assets and debt-to-equity ratios). Second, capitalizing costs in the current period will cause future income to be lower by the amount of the depreciation expense. While the income effect on any single year depends on the actual size of the expenditures, the pattern of reported income will tend to be smoother for companies that capitalize costs because of the systematic allocation of costs through depreciation expense. Therefore, it is crucial for financial statement users to understand the financial statement impacts of the capitalization decision in order to properly assess and forecast a company's growth, profitability, and solvency.

Property, plant, and equipment are important components of a company's assets. They include long-lived assets that a company needs to conduct its business, such as land, office buildings, factories, machinery, equipment, computers, warehouses, retail stores, and delivery vehicles. For many companies, property, plant, and equipment comprise a major portion of total assets. For example, Verizon's property, plant, and equipment represents over 32% of its total assets. This chapter discusses the costs of acquisition and expenditures subsequent to acquisition. In Chapter 11, we discuss the process whereby the cost of property, plant, and equipment is allocated over the periods expected to benefit from the assets' use, and disposal of property, plant, and equipment.

WHAT ARE THE CHARACTERISTICS OF PROPERTY, PLANT, AND EQUIPMENT?

LEARNING OBJECTIVE 10.1

Describe the characteristics of property, plant, and equipment.

Property, plant, and equipment (alternatively called **plant assets** or **fixed assets**) are the tangible long-lived assets that a company uses in the normal operations of its business. To be included in this category, an asset must have three characteristics:

- *The asset must be held for use in operations and not for investment.* Only assets held for use in the normal course of business should be classified as property, plant, and equipment. This characteristic does not imply that the asset must be continuously used. For example, a company includes machinery it owns for standby purposes in case of breakdowns in property, plant, and equipment. Finally, a particular type of asset may be classified as property, plant, and equipment by one company and as inventory by another. For example, the furniture and fixtures in a coffee shop are included in its property, plant, and equipment. However, the companies that sold these items to the coffee shop would categorize them as inventory.
- *The asset must have an expected life of more than one year.* The asset represents future economic benefits, or service potential, that the company will receive over the life of the asset as it is used in the normal course of business. To be included in property, plant, and equipment, the benefits must extend for more than one year. Except for land, the cost of the asset is allocated to expense over the periods in which the asset is used and the benefits are received.
- *The asset must be tangible in nature.* There must be a physical substance that can be seen and touched. In contrast, intangible assets (such as goodwill or patents) and financial assets (such as investment securities or notes receivable) do not have a physical substance.

A company initially records property, plant, and equipment assets at acquisition, or historical, cost. Because the asset is expected to provide economic benefits to the company over a period of more than one year, the company allocates the cost of the asset as an expense to each period in which the asset is used and the company receives benefits. The use of historical cost as the basis for reporting property, plant, and equipment is often justified on the basis that:

- The historical cost is equal to the fair value at the date of acquisition.
- The cost provides a *verifiable* valuation of the asset.
- Gains from holding the asset are recognized only when realized through a sale transaction.

However, the use of historical cost for reporting property, plant, and equipment on a company's financial statements has been criticized as lacking *relevance* if the historical costs become outdated and no longer reflect fair value. For example, many financial statement users question the continued use of historical cost for reporting an asset such as land which may have been purchased many years ago and whose current market value is much greater than its historical cost. Similarly, because depreciation is a process of cost allocation rather than of valuation, the net book value of an asset (cost minus accumulated depreciation) does not necessarily reflect the economic value of the asset.

Unlike stocks and bonds which often have a readily observable price in the capital markets, property, plant, and equipment are not widely traded and generally do not have market prices that are directly observable and verifiable. Therefore, **generally accepted** accounting principles require that a company report its property, plant, and equipment at its depreciated cost (cost minus accumulated depreciation). However, as discussed in Chapter 11, under U.S. GAAP and IFRS, when the asset becomes impaired such that its fair value is less than its book value, the asset must be written down to fair value. Note that, under U.S. GAAP, companies are not allowed to write up an asset if its fair value is above its historical cost. However, IFRS do allow such upward revaluations of property, plant, and equipment.

Because of the significant effects that property, plant, and equipment can have on a company's financial position and income, companies must disclose the following in their financial statements or notes:

- balances of the major classes of depreciable assets, by nature or function
- accumulated depreciation, either by major classes of depreciable assets or in total
- depreciation expense for the period
- a general description of the method or methods used in computing depreciation[1]

Real Report 10.1 shows an example of these disclosures for **Verizon**.

10.1 VERIZON'S PROPERTY, PLANT, AND EQUIPMENT DISCLOSURE — REAL REPORT

Verizon

Note 1: Description of Business and Summary of Significant Accounting Policies (in part)
Plant and Depreciation (in part).

We record plant, property, and equipment at cost. Plant, property, and equipment of wireline and wireless operations are generally depreciated on a straight-line basis. Leasehold improvements are amortized over the shorter of the estimated life of the improvement or the remaining term of the related lease, calculated from the time the asset was placed in service. When the depreciable assets of our wireline and wireless operations are retired or otherwise disposed of, the related cost and accumulated depreciation are deducted from the plant accounts, and any gains or losses on disposition are recognized in income.

We also capitalize interest associated with the acquisition or construction of network-related assets. Capitalized interest is reported as a reduction in interest expense and depreciated as part of the cost of the network-related assets.

Note 4: Plant, Property, and Equipment (in millions)

At December 31,	Lives (years)	2013	2012
Land	–	$ 819	$ 859
Buildings and equipment	15–45	23,857	22,909
Central office and other network equipment	3–15	121,594	113,262
Cable, poles and conduit	11–50	55,240	53,761
Leasehold improvements	5–20	5,877	5,404
Work in progress	–	4,176	4,126
Furniture, vehicles and other	3–20	9,302	9,254
		220,865	209,575
Less accumulated depreciation		131,909	120,933
Total		$ 88,956	$ 88,642

Suggested answers to these questions are found at the end of the chapter.

Questions:

1. What characteristics do these assets possess that allow Verizon to classify them as property, plant, and equipment?
2. At what value does Verizon's report its property, plant, and equipment?
3. Why does Verizon report both the cost of property, plant, and equipment and accumulated depreciation instead of only the net amount?
4. What does work in progress represent?

---

[1] FASB ASC 360-10-50: Property, Plant, and Equipment: Overall: Disclosure.

> **GOT IT?**
>
> **10-1** What characteristics are necessary for a company to include an asset in the category of property, plant, and equipment?
>
> **10-2** What is the *book value* of an asset?
>
> **10-3** What is the relationship between the book value and the fair value of an asset during the life of the asset?

HOW DO WE ACCOUNT FOR THE ACQUISITION OF PROPERTY, PLANT, AND EQUIPMENT?

LEARNING OBJECTIVE 10.2
Identify the costs to be included in the acquisition of property, plant, and equipment.

The major types of assets that a company includes in the category of property, plant, and equipment are land, buildings, equipment, and leasehold improvements. Natural resources, such as timberlands, oil deposits, and mineral deposits, are also included as property, plant, and equipment. While the acquisition of property, plant, and equipment is often straightforward, the situation can be complicated when assets are acquired by a lump-sum purchase, with deferred payments, through the issuance of securities, by donation, in exchange for other assets, or by self-construction. We address each of these complications in the following sections.

Determination of Cost

The **acquisition cost** of property, plant, and equipment includes all costs necessary to obtain the benefits to be derived from the asset. Specifically, any expenditure necessary to obtain the asset and put it in operating condition is capitalized or recorded as part of the cost of the asset. Capitalizable costs include the contract price, minus discounts taken; plus freight, assembly, installation, and testing costs.[2] In addition, the cost associated with an asset retirement obligation—a legal obligation to retire an asset at the end of its useful life—is capitalized as property, plant, and equipment (discussed in more detail later).

Land The recorded cost of land includes the following:

- contract price
- costs of closing the transaction and obtaining title, including commissions, options, legal fees, surveys, title search, insurance, and past due taxes
- costs of preparing the land for its particular use, such as clearing, grading, and removing old buildings (net of any proceeds from salvage) when such improvements have an indefinite life
- government assessments for streets, sidewalks, sewers, and water lines for which the government is responsible for the upkeep and that are permanent in nature

Therefore, when a retailer like **Target** purchases land to build a store or a manufacturer like **Ford** or **Intel** purchases land to construct a production plant, it will capitalize all costs incurred up to the excavation for the building as part of the cost of land. Because land has an indefinite economic life and its residual value is unlikely to be less than its acquisition cost, land is not depreciated.

In some instances, land is reported as an asset but not as property, plant, and equipment. For example, if land is not currently used in operations but purchased for future use, it is more representationally faithful to classify it as an investment. Similarly, if a real estate company purchases land for resale, it should be classified as inventory.

---

[2] GAAP allows a company to either (1) include discounts not taken as part of the cost of the asset or (2) subtract discounts not taken from the cost of the asset and report them as an expense. The rationale for the first alternative is that discounts not taken are viewed as part of the cost of acquiring the asset. The rationale for the second alternative is that, similar to inventory, the benefits to be received from the asset are not affected by whether or not the discount is taken.

Example Marshall Company purchases a parcel of land as a site for a new warehouse for $150,000. Marshall demolished an existing building on the property and began construction of the warehouse. In addition to the purchase price, Marshall incurred the following costs:

Demolition of the old building	$6,000
Title insurance	3,500
Land survey	1,800
Delinquent property taxes	1,100
Current property taxes	800

Marshall was able to sell salvaged materials from the demolished building for $1,000. Marshall would record the land at $161,400 [$150,000 + ($6,000 − $1,000) + $3,500 + $1,800 + $1,100] by making the following journal entry:

Land	161,400	
Property Tax Expense	800	
Cash		162,200

Note that because the payment of delinquent property taxes was necessary to acquire the land, Marshall would include this amount in the cost of the land. However, the current property taxes are recorded as an expense because it was not a necessary cost to acquire the land but is instead a normal operating expense associated with owning and using the land.

Land Improvements A company will often make expenditures that improve the usefulness of the property, such as landscaping, paving, and fencing. Because these improvements have a limited economic life, a company should record the costs of these improvements in a Land Improvements account and depreciate them over their economic lives. Alternatively, if the local government authority is responsible for the continued upkeep of the improvements, the improvements effectively have an indefinite economic life to the company and should not be depreciated. In this case, the company should add the costs of the improvements to the cost of the land.

Buildings The recorded cost of buildings includes the following:

- contract price
- costs of remodeling and reconditioning
- costs of excavation for the specific building
- architectural costs and the costs of building permits
- capitalized interest costs (discussed later in the chapter)

In general, all expenditures related to the acquisition or construction of a building are included as part of the cost of a building.

Equipment Equipment is a broad term that includes machinery, furniture and fixtures, office equipment, vehicles, and similar assets. **Starbucks**, for example, reports equipment that consists of store equipment, roasting equipment, and furniture and fixtures. Any costs necessary to obtain equipment and prepare it for use should be capitalized as property, plant, and equipment. The recorded cost of equipment typically includes the following:

- purchase price, minus any discounts taken, plus sales tax
- transportation costs, plus any insurance costs on the equipment while in transit
- installation or assembly costs
- initial testing costs

Example Devon Company purchases a machine with a contract price of $100,000 on terms of 2/10, n/30. Devon pays within the discount period and incurs transportation costs of $2,500, as well as installation and testing costs of $3,000. Sales tax is $7,000.

During the installation of the machine, uninsured damages of $500 are incurred and paid by the company.

The cost of the machine is $110,500 ($100,000 − $2,000 + $2,500 + $3,000 + $7,000). Devon makes the following journal entry to record these costs:

Machine	110,500	
Repair and Maintenance Expense	500	
Cash		111,000

Note that Devon does not include the $500 of damages in the cost of the asset because it was not a "necessary" cost.

Leasehold Improvements Improvements made by the lessee to leased property that, unless specifically exempted in the lease agreement, revert to the lessor at the end of the lease. Therefore, a lessee capitalizes the cost of a leasehold improvement, such as the interior design of a retail store, and depreciates the cost over its economic life or the life of the lease, whichever is shorter. For example, **Starbucks** reports $5,409.6 million of leasehold improvements related to its coffee shops and depreciates these leasehold improvements over the shorter of their estimated lives or the life of the lease, generally 10 years.

Summary The preceding discussion indicates the general principles to be followed but does not provide solutions for all possible situations. A company's decision to expense a cost immediately, to capitalize it as a depreciable asset (e.g., building, equipment), or to capitalize it as a nondepreciable asset (e.g., land) has an impact on both the company's income statement and balance sheet. **The general procedure is to determine whether incurring the cost will provide economic benefits for the company beyond the current period and, if so, which asset is associated with the expected future benefits.** For example, when a company purchases land, the cost of demolishing an old building on the land is properly capitalized as part of the cost of the land, because it is necessary to demolish the old building to derive the benefits from the land. Also, if the seller had demolished the old building, the selling price for the land presumably would have been higher. In contrast, when a company demolishes an old building on land already owned so that a new building can be erected, the cost is associated with the benefits previously realized from the old building. Therefore, the cost is included in the calculation of the gain or loss on disposal of the old building.

WHY IT MATTERS

Because property, plant, and equipment are often a company's primary productive assets, the analysis of property, plant, and equipment is often concerned with a company's ability to use its investment in fixed assets to generate sales. One measure of the efficiency of which a company uses its property, plant, and equipment is the fixed asset turnover ratio, which computes the number of dollars of sales generated during a period relative to the average dollar invested in fixed assets. Consider the following information from the 2013 10-K of **Verizon** and **AT&T**:

(in millions)	Verizon	AT&T
Net sales (operating revenue)	$120,550	$128,752
Total fixed assets, beginning of year	88,642	109,767
Total fixed assets, end of year	88,956	110,968

(continued)

> Verizon's and AT&T's fixed asset turnover ratio in 2013 is 1.36 and 1.17, respectively, as shown below.
>
> $$\text{Verizon: Fixed Asset Turnover} = \frac{\text{Net Sales}}{\text{Average Fixed Assets}} = \frac{\$120{,}550}{(\$88{,}642 + \$88{,}956) \div 2} = 1.36$$
>
> $$\text{AT\&T: Fixed Asset Turnover} = \frac{\text{Net Sales}}{\text{Average Fixed Assets}} = \frac{\$128{,}752}{(\$109{,}767 + \$110{,}968) \div 2} = 1.17$$
>
> This ratio indicates that for each dollar of fixed assets, Verizon generated $1.36 of sales while AT&T generated $1.17.
>
> Generally, a higher fixed asset turnover ratio indicates greater efficiency in the use of fixed assets to generate revenue. In Verizon's case, the 2013 fixed asset turnover ratio of 1.36 is higher than its 2012 fixed asset turnover ratio of 1.31. This was due to the fact that Verizon generated significant increases in revenues while making only modest new investments in fixed assets, resulting in improved efficiency. However, changes in the fixed asset ratio must be interpreted with caution. For example, a company that is investing heavily in property, plant, and equipment may exhibit a lower fixed asset ratio as it prepares for future growth. On the other hand, a company that decreases its expenditures for property, plant, and equipment could experience an increase in its fixed asset ratio. Therefore, as with all ratios, the fixed asset turnover ratio should be interpreted carefully in light of the company's strategy.

Asset Retirement Obligations

The acquisition of some operational assets creates an **asset retirement obligation**—a legal obligation related to the retirement of the asset. In some instances, asset retirement obligations arise from environmental responsibilities and laws, such as the requirement to decommission nuclear power plants at the end of their useful lives or to reclaim the land after mining or drilling operations have concluded. In other settings, asset retirement obligations can arise from legal arrangements related to the use of an asset. For example, **Starbucks** reports asset retirement obligations of $60.1 million at the end of 2015 related primarily to the future cost of removing leasehold improvements at the termination of its leases for coffee shop locations. GAAP requires recognition of the fair value of an asset retirement obligation as a liability, with an offsetting increase in the carrying value of the related asset.[3] Because most asset retirement obligations do not have a readily observable market value, the fair value of the asset retirement obligation is generally determined by calculating the present value of the estimated future cash outflows required to satisfy the obligation at the end of the asset's useful life.

Example Reed Company spent $100,000 in the interior redesign of a retail store that it acquired through a 10-year lease. The lease requires Reed to restore the leased store to its original condition upon termination of the lease. Reed estimates that in 10 years the restoration costs will be $31,125. Based on Reed's 10% interest rate, the present value of these future restoration costs at the time of the redesign is $12,000. Reed will make the following journal entry to record the leasehold improvement and the associated asset retirement obligation:

Leasehold Improvements	112,000	
Cash		100,000
Asset Retirement Obligation		12,000

Note that the present value of the asset retirement obligation is added to the carrying value of the leasehold improvement.

---

[3] FASB ASC 410-20-25: Asset Retirement and Environmental Obligations: Asset Retirement Obligations: Recognition.

In subsequent periods, the asset is depreciated over its useful life. In addition, the company recognizes **accretion expense**, which is classified as an operating expense and represents the increase of the asset retirement obligation each year that the asset is used.[4] Therefore, on the date the company retires the asset and must pay the retirement obligation, the amount of the liability will equal the estimated retirement costs. Any difference between the actual costs and the amount of the liability is recognized as a gain or loss. Accounting for depreciation and accretion of the asset retirement obligation will be discussed further in Chapter 11.

Lump-Sum Purchase

A company may acquire several fixed assets for a single lump-sum purchase price. To account for the assets on an individual basis, the total purchase price must be allocated among the individual assets. This allocation is necessary because the purchased assets may have different characteristics (e.g., some of the assets may be depreciable and some not, assets may have different economic lives and salvage values) or be depreciated by different methods. **A company allocates the lump-sum acquisition price based on the relative fair values of the individual assets.** If part of the purchase price can be identified with a specific asset, the specifically identified cost should be assigned to that asset with the remainder allocated among the remaining assets based on their relative fair values. Evidence of fair value can be obtained from independent sources such as appraisals, assessed values for property taxes, or other reliable approximations of the assets' market values.

Example Sample Company pays $120,000 for land and a building. An appraisal of the land and building indicates values of $50,000 and $75,000, respectively. Sample allocates the lump-sum purchase price as follows:

	Appraisal Value	Relative Fair Value	×	Total Cost	=	Allocated Cost
Land	$ 50,000	$50,000 ÷ $125,000	×	$120,000	=	$ 48,000
Building	75,000	$75,000 ÷ $125,000	×	$120,000	=	72,000
Total	$125,000					$120,000

Sample records the land at a cost of $48,000 and the building at a cost of $72,000. If the cost of obtaining an appraisal is material, the company should add it to the purchase price so it is allocated to the respective assets.

Deferred (Future) Payments

When a company acquires property, plant, and equipment in exchange for making future payments, such as by issuing notes or bonds or assuming a mortgage, **it records the asset at its fair value or the fair value of the liability on the date of the transaction, whichever is more clearly evident.** Note that GAAP's fair value hierarchy, discussed in Chapter 4, allows a company to measure fair value as the present value of the future payments when observable market values are not available.[5]

Example: Note with Stated Interest Rate

Antush Company purchases equipment by issuing a $7,500, 5-year note with a stated interest rate of 12%, which is equivalent to the market rate of interest. Antush would record the acquisition as follows:

Equipment	7,500	
Notes Payable		7,500

---

[4] Accretion expense (which is similar to interest expense) is computed by multiplying the book value of the liability by the discount rate used to compute the original present value of the asset retirement obligation.
[5] FASB ASC 310-10-30: Receivables: Overall: Initial Measurement.

Example: Non-Interest-Bearing Note

Antush Company purchases equipment by issuing a $10,000 non-interest-bearing 5-year note, when the market rate for obligations of this type is 12%. The note will be paid off at the rate of $2,000 at the end of each year. Because neither the fair value of the equipment nor the note is observable, Antush values the equipment at the present value of the payments, which is $7,210 ($2,000 × 3.604776, the factor from Table 4 of the Time Value of Money Module for 5 years and a 12% rate). Antush records the acquisition of the equipment as follows:

Equipment	7,210	
Discount on Notes Payable	2,790	
Notes Payable		10,000

Issuance of Securities

When a company acquires property, plant, and equipment by issuing securities such as common stock or preferred stock, the company **records the exchange at the fair value of the asset acquired or of the stock issued, whichever is more clearly evident and representationally faithful.** Normally, the two fair value measures would be very similar, but if they are materially different, it is necessary to select one. In some situations, one of the values may be considered more representationally faithful because it is quoted in an active market. For example, if the stock is actively traded on a stock exchange and the asset being acquired is very specialized, the fair value of the stock would be the preferred choice. Alternatively, if the stock is not actively traded but the asset is one that is commonly traded, the asset's fair value would be the better choice. If neither of the two fair values is readily observable, the company must assign the value that it believes to be the most faithful representation of the transaction (a level 3 input in the FASB's fair value hierarchy).

Example Barrett Company issued 10,000 shares of $1 par common stock in exchange for land. Barrett's common stock, as evidenced by recent activity on a stock exchange, has a fair value of $15 per share. Barrett records this transaction as follows:

Land (10,000 shares × $15/share)	150,000	
Common Stock (10,000 shares × $1 par)		10,000
Additional Paid-In Capital on Common Stock		140,000

Assets Acquired by Donation

In certain circumstances, when a company acquires property, plant, and equipment through donation (usually by a governmental unit or an individual), it is a nonreciprocal transfer of nonmonetary assets. A **nonreciprocal transfer** of assets is a receipt of assets without directly paying value in exchange. A strict interpretation of the historical cost concept would require that the asset be valued at zero. However, this approach would not be representationally faithful as it would ignore the economic benefits that the asset provides. Therefore, a company receiving an asset in such an exchange must record the asset at its fair value.

While the donated asset is recorded at fair value, there is some disagreement as to the offsetting credit in this transaction. One view is that the donation represents a contribution of capital. However, the opposing view is that only owners of a company contribute capital, and any donation by a nonowner is more faithfully represented as revenue from performing a service for the donor or as a gain. In general, GAAP requires that a donated asset should be recorded at its fair value with a corresponding increase in either revenue or gain, depending on whether the transaction was part of the company's on-going operations or was a peripheral or incidental transaction.[6]

Example Hrouda Company accepts a donation of a building worth $50,000. Hrouda records the donation as follows:

Building	50,000	
Gain on Receipt of Donated Property		50,000

Hrouda reports the gain in the other items section of its income statement.

INTERNATIONAL DIMENSION

VALUATION OF PROPERTY, PLANT, AND EQUIPMENT

Both U.S. GAAP and IFRS use the same general principles to record the initial value of property, plant, and equipment—the cost necessary to obtain the asset and put it in operating condition. However, the subsequent reporting of property, plant, and equipment can differ. IFRS allow companies to value property, plant, and equipment using either a cost model (cost minus accumulated depreciation, similar to U.S. GAAP) or a revaluation model. Under the revaluation model, a company is allowed to write the value of its property, plant, and equipment up to fair value if fair value can be reliably measured. When a company chooses to revalue its assets to fair value:

- An increase in the fair value of the asset is recognized in other comprehensive income and accumulated in shareholders' equity as a revaluation surplus.
- A decrease in the fair value of the asset first reduces any previously recognized revaluation surplus. Any remaining decrease is recognized as an expense.

If a company chooses to revalue an item of property, plant, and equipment, the entire class of property, plant, and equipment to which the asset belongs must be revalued on a regular basis. Therefore, if a company wishes to revalue a single piece of land, all land that the company owns must be revalued. It should be noted that approximately 7% of surveyed companies using IFRS actually use the revaluation for at least one asset class.[7]

In addition, a company should disclose the effective date of the revaluation, the methods and assumptions used in estimating fair value, the net cost basis of revaluated assets, and the changes to the revaluation surplus account. **LVMH** revalues one item of property, plant, and equipment—vineyard land. For 2013,

(continued)

---

[6] FASB ASC 958-605-25: Not-for-Profit Entities: Revenue Recognition: Recognition. Note that the referenced guidance applies to not-for-profit entities. GAAP does not provide guidance on contributions from governmental entities. Therefore, donations from governmental entities may be accounted for by increasing a contributed capital account called Donated Capital. In this text, we will record all contributions, whether from a nongovernmental or governmental entity, by increasing either a revenue or gain account.

[7] *Accounting Trends & Techniques, IFRS Financial Statements: Best Practices in Presentation and Disclosure* (New York: AICPA) 2012.

this revaluation increased the value of vineyard land by €369 million. The note disclosure related to this revaluation is given below.

Notes to the Consolidated Financial Statements (in part)

1.12 Property, plant, and equipment (in part)
Vineyard land is recognized at the market value at the balance sheet date. This valuation is based on official published data for recent transactions in the same region, (Level 2 of the fair value hierarchy established by IFRS 13). Any difference compared to historical cost is recognized within equity in "Revaluation reserves." If market value falls below acquisition cost, the resulting impairment is charged to the income statement.

6. Property, Plant, and Equipment (in part)
Movements in property, plant, and equipment during 2013 break down as follows:

Gross value (EUR millions)	Vineyard land and producing vineyards	Land and buildings
As of December 31, 2012	2,051	3,865
Acquisitions	5	97
Change in the market value of vineyard land	369	—
Disposals and retirements	—	(133)
Changes in the scope of consolidation	—	71
Translation adjustment	(13)	(131)
Other movements, including transfers	7	(269)
As of December 31, 2013	2,419	3,500

IFRS Application: Revaluation of Property, Plant, and Equipment Harper Company purchased equipment on January 1, 2016, for $100,000. At December 31, 2016, the equipment has a book value of $80,000 (after accumulated depreciation of $20,000), while the fair value, based on an independent appraisal, is determined to be $92,000. If Harper decides to revalue its equipment to fair value, it would make the following journal entry:[8]

Accumulated Depreciation	20,000	
Equipment		20,000

This entry eliminates the previously recorded depreciation against the asset's cost, resulting in a new asset cost of $80,000. Next, Harper would record the unrealized gain as follows:

Equipment	12,000	
Revaluation Surplus (Equipment)		12,000

As a result of these two entries, the equipment is now stated at it fair value of $92,000, which becomes the new basis for purposes of computing depreciation. The revaluation surplus, which represents an unrealized gain from writing the equipment up to its market value, is reported as a component of other comprehensive income. The accumulated balance of the revaluation surplus will be reported as accumulated other comprehensive income in the shareholders' equity section of Harper's balance sheet. ■

Source: IAS 16. (See Appendix C at the end of this book.)

---

[8] An alternative procedure for recording this revaluation is to proportionately restate accumulated depreciation with the change in the gross carrying amount of the asset so that the carrying value of the asset after revaluation equals its revalued amount. This method is rarely used in practice and is not discussed here.

> ## GOT IT?
>
> **10-4** What is the criterion a company uses to decide whether to include an expenditure in the cost of property, plant, and equipment rather than expensing it? Give an example of the types of expenditures that are included in the cost of property, plant, and equipment as a result of the application of this criterion.
>
> **10-5** How does a company categorize land held for investment on its balance sheet?
>
> **10-6** What are *leasehold improvements*? How should a company account for them?
>
> **10-7** What are *asset retirement obligations*? How should a company account for them?
>
> **10-8** When a company purchases several assets for a single lump sum, what principle does it use to allocate the cost among the various assets acquired? Why is it necessary to allocate the cost?
>
> **10-9** How does a company determine the acquisition cost of an asset when it acquires the asset in exchange for securities?
>
> **10-10** 🌐 Explain the primary difference between U.S. GAAP and IFRS with regard to the accounting and reporting of property, plant, and equipment.

HOW DO WE ACCOUNT FOR NONMONETARY ASSET EXCHANGES?

LEARNING OBJECTIVE 10.3
Determine the cost of property, plant, and equipment obtained by a nonmonetary exchange of assets.

In some transactions, a company may acquire property, plant, and equipment in exchange for another nonmonetary asset.[9] A **nonmonetary exchange** is a reciprocal transfer between a company and another entity in which the company acquires nonmonetary assets or services by surrendering other nonmonetary assets or services (e.g., trade-in, swap). **In general, the cost of a nonmonetary asset acquired in exchange for another nonmonetary asset is the fair value of the asset surrendered.** If the fair value of the asset received is more clearly evident than the fair value of the asset surrendered, it can be used to measure the cost of the asset acquired. A gain or loss on the exchange is recognized as the difference between the fair value of the asset surrendered and its book value. When a small amount of cash, often referred to as *boot*, is also given or received, the cost of the asset acquired and the gain or loss on the nonmonetary asset surrendered is determined by these equations.[10]

$$\text{Cost of Asset Acquired} = \text{Fair Value of Asset Surrendered} \begin{cases} + \text{ Cash Paid} \\ \quad \text{or} \\ - \text{ Cash Received} \end{cases}$$

and

$$\text{Gain (Loss)} = \text{Fair Value of Asset Surrendered} - \text{Book Value of Asset Surrendered}$$

Example: Exchanges of Nonmonetary Assets

Example 10.1 shows an exchange of nonmonetary assets between Arnold Company and Carbon Company, both with and without cash included in the exchange. In this example, Arnold entered into an agreement with Carbon to exchange one of its small buildings for a specialized piece of equipment owned by Carbon.

---

[9] A nonmonetary asset is an asset whose amount is *not* fixed by contract or otherwise in terms of a specific number of dollars. Examples include inventories and property, plant, and equipment.

[10] If the cash given or received is less than 25% of the fair value of the transaction, GAAP considers the transaction a nonmonetary exchange (FASB ASC 845-10-25: Nonmonetary Transactions: Overall: Recognition).

EXAMPLE 10.1 Exchange of Nonmonetary Assets

(a) No Cash Included in Exchange

	Arnold Company (Building)	Carbon Company (Equipment)
Cost of asset surrendered	$100,000	$60,000
Accumulated depreciation	54,000	32,000
Book value	$ 46,000	$28,000
Fair value of asset surrendered	$ 40,000	$40,000

Arnold Company			Carbon Company		
Equipment	40,000		Building	40,000	
Accumulated Depreciation	54,000		Accumulated Depreciation	32,000	
Loss on Exchange ($40,000 – $46,000)	6,000		Equipment		60,000
Building		100,000	Gain on Exchange ($40,000 – $28,000)		12,000

(b) Cash Included in Exchange

	Arnold Company (Building)	Carbon Company (Equipment)
Cost of asset surrendered	$100,000	$60,000
Accumulated depreciation	54,000	32,000
Book value	$ 46,000	$28,000
Fair value of asset surrendered	$ 40,000	$35,000
Cash received (paid)	$ 5,000	$ (5,000)

Arnold Company			Carbon Company		
Equipment ($40,000 – $5,000)	35,000		Building ($35,000 + $5,000)	40,000	
Accumulated Depreciation	54,000		Accumulated Depreciation	32,000	
Cash	5,000		Equipment		60,000
Loss on Exchange ($40,000 – $46,000)	6,000		Cash		5,000
Building		100,000	Gain on Exchange ($35,000 – $28,000)		7,000

In Example (a), each company gives up and receives an asset with a fair value of $40,000, which is the fair value of the transaction. Therefore, no cash is exchanged. Arnold records the cost of the acquired equipment at the fair value of $40,000. Because Arnold gives up a building with a fair value of $40,000 and a book value of $46,000, it recognizes a loss of $6,000 ($40,000 – $46,000). Carbon records the cost of the building acquired at the fair value of $40,000 and recognizes a gain of $12,000 ($40,000 – $28,000). Note that the gain or loss is computed based on the difference between the fair value and the book value of the asset surrendered.

In Example (b), the fair value of the assets exchanged differs by $5,000. Therefore, Arnold receives cash of $5,000 so that the fair value surrendered and received by each party is equal. Arnold records the acquired equipment at a cost of $35,000 ($40,000 fair value of the building surrendered minus the $5,000 cash received). Because it gives up a building with a fair value of $40,000 and a book value of $46,000, Arnold recognizes a loss of $6,000. Carbon records the acquired building at a cost of $40,000 ($35,000 fair value of the equipment surrendered plus the $5,000 cash paid) and recognizes a gain of $7,000 ($35,000 – $28,000).

Exception to the General Rule to Use Fair Value for Nonmonetary Exchanges

The conceptual basis of valuing the acquired asset at fair value and allowing for immediate gain or loss recognition is that, in most exchanges, the economic position of the two companies has changed as a result of the exchange. When the company's future cash flows are expected to significantly change as a result of the exchange, the transaction has commercial substance. While most exchanges have commercial substance, it is possible for a company to exchange similar assets and be in the same economic position as before the exchange. If an exchange does *not* have commercial substance and results in a loss, the general rule discussed earlier is followed. If the exchange does *not* have commercial substance and results in a gain, GAAP requires the gain to be deferred by reducing the cost of the asset.[11] GAAP imposes this requirement to prevent companies from recognizing gains from transactions that lack commercial substance (e.g., structuring transactions to exchange economically equivalent assets simply in order to book a gain in income).

Example Messenger Company owns a truck with a book value of $30,000 (cost of $50,000 and accumulated depreciation of $20,000) and a fair value of $33,000. Messenger exchanges the truck and $2,000 for a used truck from Leninger Company that has a fair value of $35,000. Because the trucks are so similar, Messenger's cash flows are not expected to change significantly as a result of this exchange. Messenger would record the truck it received at $32,000, which is the fair value of the asset surrendered plus cash paid ($33,000 + $2,000) minus the $3,000 gain ($33,000 fair value of the truck surrendered − $30,000 book value of the truck surrendered). Messenger would record the exchange as follows:

Truck	32,000	
Accumulated Depreciation	20,000	
Truck		50,000
Cash		2,000

ETHICAL DILEMMA

As the accountant for Magna Corporation, you have been carefully analyzing a nonmonetary exchange of assets that occurred in the current fiscal year. Toward the end of the third quarter, Magna obtained 10 used Ford delivery trucks by exchanging 10 of its own General Motors delivery trucks. Because the fair value of Magna's trucks exceeded their book value, Magna was able to recognize a gain on the transaction. The Ford trucks obtained in the exchange had the same cargo capacity as the General Motors trucks and approximately the same amount of miles on the odometer. In fact, as far as you can tell, other than the manufacturers' names, the trucks were virtually identical! In discussions with management, you determine that, prior to the exchange, third-quarter earnings were slightly lower than analyst expectations, and the exchange appears to be prompted by a desire to record a gain that would increase earnings to meet or beat the analysts' earnings forecasts. As support for the decision to enter into the exchange, management offers a brief memo stating that the new trucks are expected to generate significantly more cash flow than the trucks given up. Therefore, the exchange has commercial substance and GAAP requires the exchange to be recorded at fair value. What is your response?

---

[11] If a nonmonetary exchange which lacks commercial substance results in a gain and cash is received, GAAP allows a portion of the gain to be recognized. The recognized gain is determined based on a proportion of the cash received to the total consideration received:

$$\text{Recognized Gain} = \frac{\text{(Cash Received)}}{\text{(Cash Received + Fair Value of Other Assets Received)}}$$

Because exchanges that lack commercial substance should not be common, we do not illustrate this situation.

> **GOT IT?**
>
> **10-11** At what amount does a company record the cost of a nonmonetary asset acquired in exchange for another nonmonetary asset?
>
> **10-12** At what value does a company recognize a gain or loss that results from an exchange of nonmonetary assets?

LEARNING OBJECTIVE 10.4
Compute the cost of a self-constructed asset, including capitalized interest.

WHAT IS THE COST OF SELF-CONSTRUCTED ASSETS?

Sometimes a company constructs an item of property, plant, and equipment that it intends to use in its operations. For example, **Starbucks** chooses to build some of its assets, such as leasehold improvements in its retail stores, roasting plants, and warehouses. At the end of 2015, Starbucks reported $242.5 million of work in progress related to new store and other asset construction projects. Similar to purchased assets, the cost of a self-constructed asset includes all expenditures necessary to build the asset and put it in operating condition. However, the identification of which expenditures to include deserves a closer look. While there is widespread agreement that the costs directly related to construction—direct material and direct labor—should be added to the cost of the asset, the treatment of two other costs—overhead and interest—have generated considerable debate.

Overhead Costs

Overhead is reported in various accounts on the financial statements. As discussed in Chapter 7, overhead associated with the manufacture of goods held for sale is a product cost that is allocated to inventory, while other overhead is expensed immediately as a period cost. However, when a company constructs a fixed asset, some overhead may relate to the construction of the asset. There are two alternatives for a company to include overhead costs (such as utilities, insurance, and property taxes) in the cost of a self-constructed asset.

- *Allocate a portion of overhead to the self-constructed asset.* Under this full-costing approach, the company allocates fixed and variable overhead to the self-constructed asset in the same manner it allocates overhead to units of inventory produced. Those in favor of this alternative argue that:
    - Construction related overhead is a relevant component of the asset's cost and should be accounted for in the same way as regular products, even though this means that the regular products will be allocated less of the overhead.
    - The cost of the constructed asset will be a more faithful representation of the cost to acquire and prepare the asset for use.
    - Allocating overhead to self-constructed assets enhances comparability with the cost of an equivalent purchased asset because the seller normally would include fixed overhead in its selling price.
- *Include only the incremental overhead in the cost of the self-constructed asset.* Under this alternative, the company includes only the overhead that increases as a result of the construction in the cost of the self-constructed asset. Those in favor of this alternative argue that:
    - To be representationally faithful, the cost of the asset should only include the additional costs incurred to produce it.

- To be comparable, the allocation of overhead to normal operations should not change because the overhead would have been incurred whether or not the construction takes place. To allocate any amount other than the incremental overhead would result in less overhead being allocated to inventory, resulting in lower expenses and higher income. This effect on income is considered undesirable by many people, as income should reflect the success of selling goods and services and not depend on the amount of construction undertaken.

While both arguments have merit, common practice is to allocate both variable overhead and a proportion of fixed overhead to self-constructed assets.[12] Note that if the allocation of overhead causes the cost of the self-constructed asset to be greater than the fair value of the asset, the asset should be recorded at its fair value with the excess recognized as a loss in the current period.

Interest during Construction

It is common for companies to borrow funds to finance long-term construction projects. A question that has caused a great deal of controversy is whether the incremental interest costs associated with construction financing should be capitalized as part of the cost of preparing a self-constructed asset for use or expensed as interest. In addition, if the company uses internally generated funds to finance the construction, should it add imputed interest to the cost of the asset? The FASB considered three alternatives to account for interest during the construction of property, plant, and equipment.

- *Do not capitalize any interest during construction.* Under this alternative, a company would treat interest as a financing cost and would record the interest as an expense during the period incurred. This approach would be consistent with all other interest costs, such as interest on cash borrowed to purchase inventory or to purchase property, plant, and equipment. The principal argument in favor of this alternative is that interest is the price paid for borrowing funds for a period of time, and the benefit received is the availability of the funds. Therefore, interest cost should be expensed during the periods in which the funds are borrowed.
- *Capitalize an amount of interest (actual or imputed) for all funds used for construction.* Under this alternative, a company would assign an interest cost to all funds used in construction, whether borrowed or not. Therefore, the company would have to impute and capitalize an interest cost for the equity funds (common stock, retained earnings) used in construction in addition to the cost of borrowed funds. While it often is argued that this alternative provides the most faithful representation of the economic cost of the asset, the imputed interest cost of the equity funds is subjective and may lack verifiability.
- *Capitalize the actual interest on incremental funds borrowed for the construction.* Under this alternative, a company would treat the cost of borrowed funds as part of the cost of constructing an asset, similar to the treatment of materials and labor. Because the interest cost of the borrowed funds is necessary to obtain the benefits from the asset, the interest cost should not be expensed during construction but capitalized as part of the cost of the asset. The disadvantage of this approach is that it can reduce comparability because the cost of the asset will differ depending on whether debt or equity financing was used for construction.

GAAP views interest cost as an integral part of the cost of construction and uses an approach that is an application of the third alternative above. Specifically, this approach requires the capitalization of a *portion* of the interest incurred for the construction of property, plant, and equipment.

---

[12] This full-costing alternative is supported by the Cost Accounting Standards Board in "Capitalization of Tangible Assets," *CASB Standard 404* (Washington, D.C.: CASB, 1973).

GAAP for Interest Capitalization To implement the approach required by GAAP, a company must address three issues:

- *Does the asset qualify for interest capitalization?* A company is required to capitalize interest on assets that are either constructed for its own use or constructed as discrete projects for sale or lease to others (e.g., long-term construction projects such as ships or real estate developments, as we discuss in Chapter 17). In addition, if a company purchases land and incurs expenditures to develop it for a particular use (e.g., a building or plant site), any interest costs that are associated with these expenditures qualify for interest capitalization and are included as part of the cost of the resulting asset, not the land. Interest *cannot* be capitalized for inventories that are routinely manufactured, assets that are in use or ready for their intended use, or assets that are idle and are not undergoing the activities necessary to get them ready for use.[13]
- *Over what period can interest be capitalized?* The capitalization period begins when (1) expenditures for the asset have begun, (2) activities that are necessary to get the asset ready for its intended use are in progress, and (3) interest cost is being incurred. Interest capitalization continues as long as the three conditions are present.[14] The capitalization period ends when the asset is substantially complete and ready for its intended use.[15]
- *What amount of interest can be capitalized?* The amount of interest capitalized for a qualifying asset is the portion of the interest cost that could have been avoided if the construction had not occurred. This amount is known as **avoidable interest**. A company determines avoidable interest by applying an interest rate to the weighted average accumulated expenditures for the qualifying asset during the capitalization period. The specific steps necessary to determine the amount of avoidable interest that can be capitalized are described next.

---

[13] FASB ASC 835-20-15: Interest: Capitalization of Interest: Scope and Scope Exceptions.
[14] If a company suspends substantially *all* the activities related to the construction of the asset, it suspends interest capitalization until the activities are resumed.
[15] FASB ASC 835-20-25: Interest: Capitalization of Interest: Recognition.

Interest Capitalization Procedures To determine the amount of interest that should be capitalized, a company should follow these four steps:

- *Step 1: Determine the weighted average accumulated expenditures for the period.* **Weighted average accumulated expenditures** are defined as the sum of the construction expenditures weighted by the amount of time that interest cost has been incurred on those expenditures during the construction period. The computation is illustrated in **Example 10.2a** and **10.2b**.
- *Step 2: Determine the appropriate interest rate.* The interest rate depends on the relationship between the weighted average accumulated expenditures and the amounts borrowed specifically for construction.
    - If the weighted average accumulated expenditures are less than or equal to the funds borrowed specifically to finance the construction of a qualifying asset, the company uses the interest rate on that specific borrowing. This computation is illustrated in **Example 10.2a**.
    - If the weighted average expenditures on the asset are greater than the specific borrowing or if no specific borrowing is made, the company uses both the interest rate on the specific borrowing and a weighted average interest rate on all other borrowings. This computation is illustrated in **Example 10.2b**.
- *Step 3: Compute avoidable interest by applying the appropriate interest rate(s) to the weighted average accumulated expenditures.*
- *Step 4: Capitalize the lesser of avoidable interest or actual interest.* The total amount of interest cost that a company capitalizes each period may not exceed the actual interest cost incurred.

These steps are illustrated using the information in **Example 10.2**.

EXAMPLE 10.2

Self-Constructed Asset—Cia Company

On January 1, 2016, Cia Company started the construction of a building to use as its corporate headquarters. The project was completed and ready for occupancy on December 31, 2016. Cia incurred the following expenditures related to construction during 2016:

January 1	$ 200,000
April 1	350,000
October 1	500,000
December 31	150,000
Total	$1,200,000

Cia had a $2,000,000, 12% note payable and a $4,000,000, 13% note payable, both of which are unrelated to the construction project, outstanding during the entire year.

Example: Weighted Average Expenditures Less Than Amount Specifically Borrowed

In order to finance construction, on January 1, 2016, Cia obtained a $1,000,000 construction loan with a 10% interest rate. **Example 10.2a** shows the computation of capitalized interest related to Cia's construction project when weighted average accumulated expenditures are less than the amount specifically borrowed for construction.

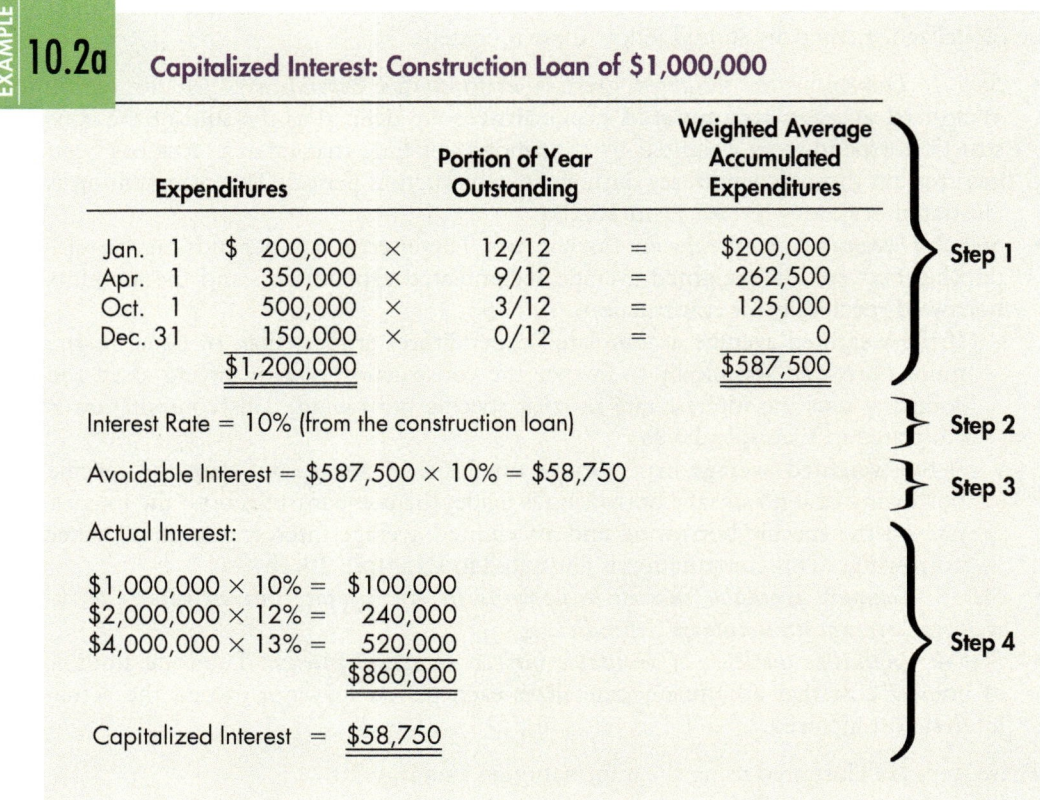

Several items are worth noting. First, the weighted average accumulated expenditures are computed by weighting each expenditure by the amount of time between the date of the actual expenditure and the end of the year or end of the capitalization period, whichever comes first.[16] Because the December 31 expenditure occurred on the last day of the construction period, it received a weighting of 0/12. Second, because Cia borrowed $1,000,000 specifically for this construction project and this amount is greater than the weighted average accumulated expenditures, it uses the 10% rate to determine avoidable interest. Finally, capitalized interest cannot exceed actual interest costs incurred. Therefore, Cia capitalizes the lesser of avoidable interest and actual interest.

Cia would make the following journal entry to record total interest cost incurred, assuming that all interest was paid in cash:

Interest Expense	801,250	
Building (or Construction in Progress)	58,750	
Cash		860,000

In future periods, Cia will depreciate the capitalized interest cost over the useful life of the building. ∎

Example: Weighted Average Expenditures Greater Than Amount Specifically Borrowed

In order to finance construction, on January 1, 2016, Cia obtained a $400,000 construction loan with a 10% interest rate. Cia will finance the remainder of the construction with internally generated funds. **Example 10.2b** shows the computation of capitalized interest related to Cia's construction project when weighted average accumulated expenditures are greater than the amount specifically borrowed for construction.

---

[16] For simplicity, it can be assumed that expenditures are incurred evenly throughout the period. In this case, the average accumulated expenditures are computed as follows: (Beginning Cumulative Costs + Ending Cumulative Costs) ÷ 2.

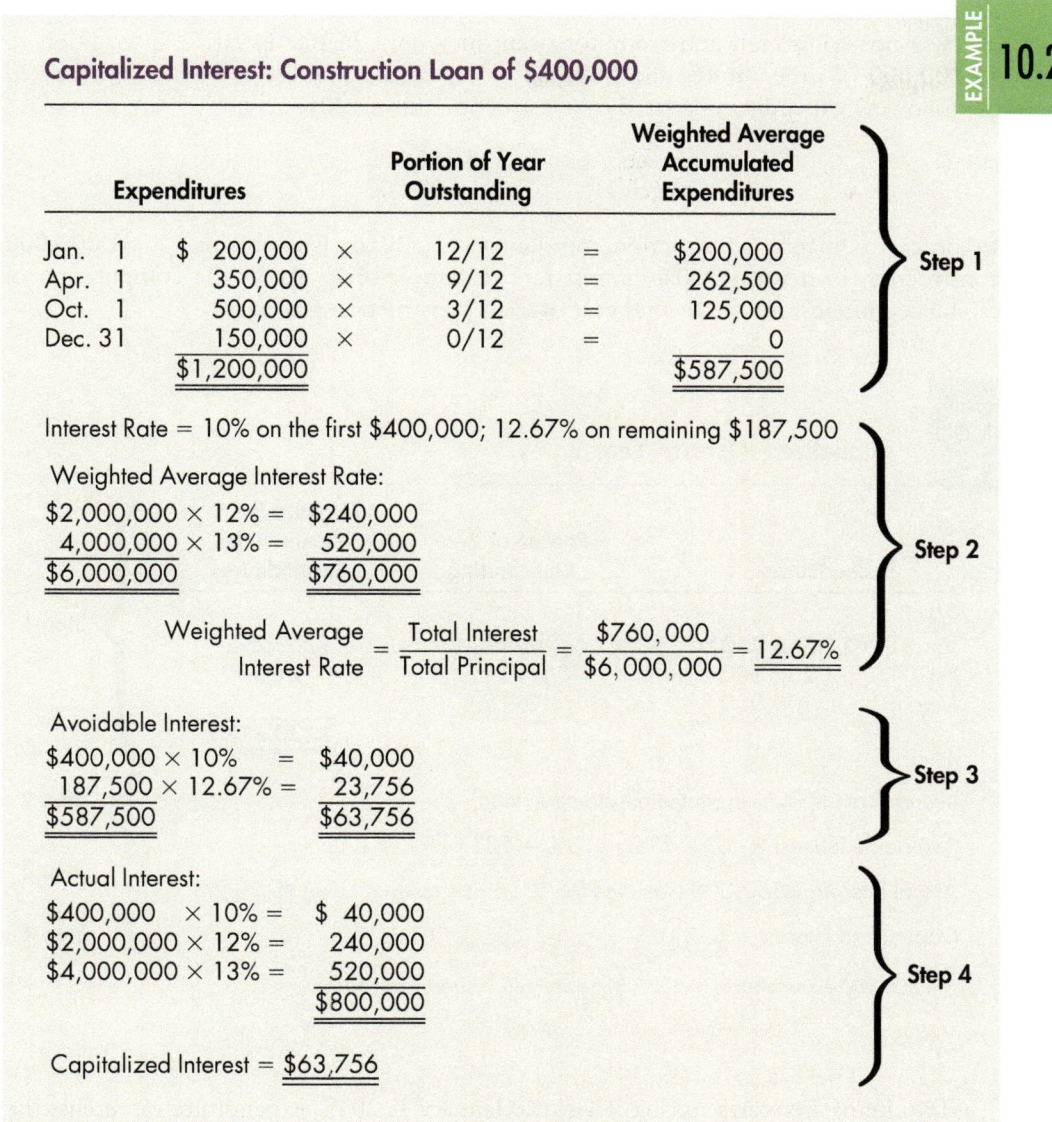

EXAMPLE 10.2b

Capitalized Interest: Construction Loan of $400,000

Expenditures		Portion of Year Outstanding		Weighted Average Accumulated Expenditures
Jan. 1	$ 200,000 ×	12/12	=	$200,000
Apr. 1	350,000 ×	9/12	=	262,500
Oct. 1	500,000 ×	3/12	=	125,000
Dec. 31	150,000 ×	0/12	=	0
	$1,200,000			$587,500

Step 1

Interest Rate = 10% on the first $400,000; 12.67% on remaining $187,500

Weighted Average Interest Rate:
$2,000,000 × 12% = $240,000
4,000,000 × 13% = 520,000
$6,000,000 $760,000

Step 2

$$\frac{\text{Weighted Average}}{\text{Interest Rate}} = \frac{\text{Total Interest}}{\text{Total Principal}} = \frac{\$760,000}{\$6,000,000} = 12.67\%$$

Avoidable Interest:
$400,000 × 10%   = $40,000
187,500 × 12.67% = 23,756
$587,500 $63,756

Step 3

Actual Interest:
$400,000   × 10% = $ 40,000
$2,000,000 × 12% = 240,000
$4,000,000 × 13% = 520,000
                             $800,000

Step 4

Capitalized Interest = $63,756

Because weighted average accumulated expenditures exceed the amount borrowed specifically for construction, the interest rate on the specific borrowing is used to compute avoidable interest for an amount up to the construction-related borrowing. For the excess of weighted average accumulated expenditures over the amount of the construction loan, a weighted average interest rate on other borrowings is used. The presumption is that a company finances construction by first using specific construction-related borrowings and then diverting funds from other borrowings to finance the remainder of the construction costs.

Similar to the previous example, Cia would make the following journal entry to record total interest cost incurred, assuming that all interest was paid in cash:

Interest Expense	736,244	
Building (or Construction in Progress)	63,756	
Cash		800,000

Capitalized Interest—Multiple Accounting Periods It is common for the construction project to extend beyond the end of a company's fiscal year. In this situation, the procedure shown previously is repeated for the subsequent year with one adjustment—the total expenditures plus capitalized interest from the previous year is considered to be an outstanding expenditure as of the first day of the subsequent year.

Example Using the information in **Example 10.2**, assume that Cia's construction project was not completed and ready for occupancy until March 1, 2017. In addition to $1,200,000 of expenditures and $58,750 of capitalized interest in 2016, Cia incurred the following expenditures related to construction during 2017:

February 1 $250,000
March 1 100,000

In order to finance construction, on January 1, 2016, Cia obtained a $1,000,000 construction loan with a 10% interest rate. **Example 10.2c** shows the computation of capitalized interest for the second year of Cia's construction project.

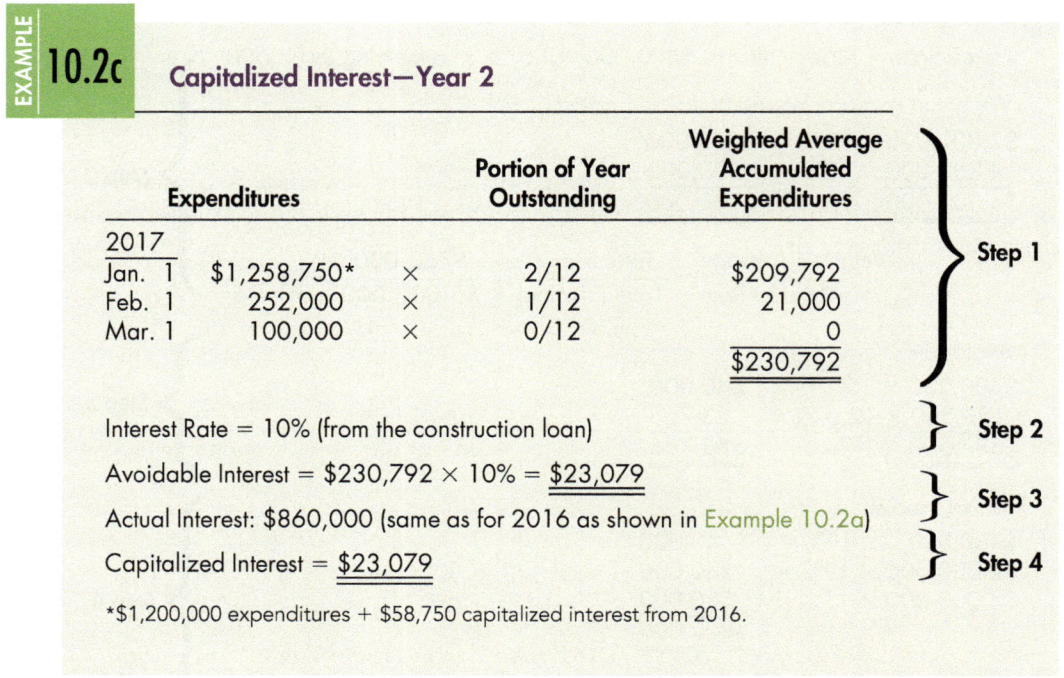

EXAMPLE 10.2c Capitalized Interest—Year 2

	Expenditures		Portion of Year Outstanding	Weighted Average Accumulated Expenditures	
2017					Step 1
Jan. 1	$1,258,750*	×	2/12	$209,792	
Feb. 1	252,000	×	1/12	21,000	
Mar. 1	100,000	×	0/12	0	
				$230,792	

Interest Rate = 10% (from the construction loan)   } Step 2

Avoidable Interest = $230,792 × 10% = $23,079   } Step 3

Actual Interest: $860,000 (same as for 2016 as shown in Example 10.2a)

Capitalized Interest = $23,079   } Step 4

*$1,200,000 expenditures + $58,750 capitalized interest from 2016.

Two items are worth noting. First, the January 1, 2017, expenditure represents the total expenditures plus capitalized interest from 2016. Second, because the capitalization period ends when construction is complete (March 1, 2017), all expenditures receive a weighting from the beginning of the year to the end of the construction period. Cia would make the following journal entries to record total interest cost incurred, assuming that all interest was paid in cash:

Interest Expense	836,921	
Building (or Construction in Progress)	23,079	
Cash		860,000

Impact of Interest Capitalization When a company capitalizes interest costs instead of expensing them, it triggers three effects on the financial statements:

- The company will report higher amounts for property, plant, and equipment due to the capitalized interest being added to the acquisition cost of the equipment.
- The company does not report the capitalized amount of interest as interest expense during the construction period. Therefore, the company will report higher income than it otherwise would if it had expensed the full amount of interest.
- All things being equal, the capitalized interest will result in higher depreciation expense in future periods.

Therefore, the capitalization of interest is essentially a question of asset valuation and timing of the expense recognition, and it is important that financial statement users understand how capitalized interest can affect the analysis of a company's performance over time. To assist in this analysis, GAAP requires that companies disclose both the capitalized interest amount and the total interest cost incurred in the notes to its financial statements. For example, **Starbucks** reported total interest costs of $74.1 million in 2015. Of this amount, $3.6 million was capitalized while $70.5 million was recognized as expense.

In addition, companies may borrow a larger amount than is required for its immediate construction needs and invest the excess funds. GAAP does not allow the interest revenue earned on these funds to be offset against interest cost when determining the amount of interest to be capitalized. Therefore, the interest earned is recognized and reported as interest revenue.

Finally, if a company constructs an asset for less than it would cost to purchase the asset from another company, the construction is reported at the actual construction cost. While an argument can be made that the difference between the construction cost and the purchase price represents income or profit on construction, GAAP does not allow the recognition of income in this situation. Instead, the difference is considered a "savings" from self-construction that will be recognized through reduced depreciation charges in future periods.

INTERNATIONAL DIMENSION

SELF-CONSTRUCTED ASSETS

Both U.S. GAAP and IFRS permit the capitalization of interest on self-constructed assets. However, the determination of the amount of capitalized interest differs.

- While U.S. GAAP permits the capitalization of avoidable interest, IFRS allow for the capitalization of the total amount of borrowing costs of loans obtained specifically for the purpose of constructing a qualifying asset. For any borrowing costs related to funds obtained for general purposes, the interest costs eligible for capitalization are determined similar to U.S. GAAP.
- Under IFRS, any interest revenue from the temporary investment of amounts borrowed specifically for construction is offset against interest costs eligible for capitalization. U.S. GAAP does not allow interest revenue to be offset against interest cost.

IFRS Application In order to finance construction, on January 1, 2016, Cia obtained a $1,000,000 construction loan with a 10% interest rate. The project was completed and ready for occupancy on December 31, 2016. Cia incurred the following expenditures related to construction during 2016:

January 1	$ 200,000
April 1	350,000
October 1	500,000
December 31	150,000
Total	$1,200,000

(continued)

In addition, Cia temporarily invested the excess funds and earned $30,000 in interest revenue.

Under IFRS, Cia would capitalize the entire amount of interest incurred on construction-related borrowings less any interest revenue earned on the temporary investment of the borrowed funds. Therefore, Cia would capitalize $70,000 [total construction-related interest of $100,000 ($1,000,000 × 10%) minus interest revenue of $30,000]. Note that the calculation of weighted average expenditures is not necessary under IFRS. Under U.S. GAAP, Cia would capitalize $58,750 of interest costs (see calculations in **Example 10.2a**).

Source: IAS 23. (See Appendix C at the end of this book.)

GOT IT?

10-13 What are the two common alternative treatments of overhead costs during self-construction of an asset? What are the arguments in favor of each?

10-14 Under what conditions does a company capitalize the interest incurred during self-construction of an asset? Contrast your answer with accounting for interest on a note payable that is not associated with the construction of an asset.

10-15 Explain how a company determines the amount of interest to capitalize when it constructs an asset.

10-16 A company borrows some money, which it uses to acquire a parcel of land on which it plans to construct a building. Before construction of the building begins, a period of time passes while the company obtains the necessary planning permission. May the company capitalize interest during this period? If so, should it capitalize the interest to the land or the building account?

10-17 What are the primary differences between U.S. GAAP and IFRS with regard to the capitalization of interest on self-constructed assets?

LEARNING OBJECTIVE 10.5
Describe the accounting for expenditures incurred subsequent to acquisition.

HOW DO WE ACCOUNT FOR EXPENDITURES SUBSEQUENT TO ACQUISITION?

After initial acquisition, companies make various expenditures relating to property, plant, and equipment for purposes ranging from routine repairs to major overhauls and improvements. The related accounting decision is whether to report these expenditures as investments that enhance property, plant, and equipment or to expense them. Conceptually, if the expenditure is expected to increase the future economic benefits of the asset, it should be capitalized (recorded as an asset). Otherwise, it should be recorded as an expense. An expenditure to acquire property, plant, and equipment or to increase the expected future economic benefits of the asset above those that originally were expected is called a **capital expenditure**. The future economic benefits can be increased by:

- extending the life of the asset
- improving productivity of the asset by enabling the asset to produce more goods at the same cost or by producing the same quantity of goods at a lower cost
- increasing the quality of the product

An expenditure that does not increase the economic benefits but is incurred to maintain the existing benefits is called an **operating expenditure** and is expensed in the period incurred.

From a practical standpoint, many companies establish a lower limit, or *materiality threshold*, on the amount of expenditure that will be capitalized. Any amount that is below this lower limit will be expensed, regardless of whether it provides future benefits or not. Therefore, when making the decision to capitalize or expense a cost, it is important to consistently apply a company's capitalization policy.

In general, subsequent expenditures can be classified as additions, improvements and replacements, rearrangements, and repairs and maintenance.

Additions

An **addition** involves enlarging an existing asset by adding a new component. For example, adding a new wing to a building or installing a pollution-control device on a machine are examples of additions. Expenditures relating to an addition represent an increase in expected future economic benefits and, therefore, are capitalized as an asset.

When an addition involves changing an existing asset, an issue arises as to how to account for the cost of such changes. For example, when a company adds a new wing to a building, it frequently makes alterations to the old building. If these alterations are necessary to acquire and prepare the addition for use, or if the alterations increase the economic benefits originally anticipated for the old building, the cost of alteration is capitalized as an asset. If the alterations do not increase the original benefits of the old building, the cost is expensed. In addition, the cost of any part of the asset that is demolished (e.g., a connecting wall) should be removed from the accounts (unless, of course, the cost of the asset that is removed is immaterial or impractical to measure).

Improvements and Replacements

Improvements and replacements involve the substitution of new parts for old ones and increase the economic benefits to be obtained from the asset. An **improvement** (**betterment**) is the substitution of a better asset for the one currently used, such as the installation of a new solar heating system in a building. A **replacement** (**renewal**) is the substitution of an equivalent asset, such as a new engine in a truck. Expenditures related to improvements and replacements are capitalized as assets. There are three alternative methods for a company to account for such capitalized expenditures, as described below.

Substitution Under this method, the book value of the old asset is removed and a new asset is recorded.

Example Pippa Company decides to replace its old oil furnace with a new gas furnace. The oil furnace has a historical cost of $50,000 with accumulated depreciation of $30,000. The scrap value of the old furnace is $5,000, and the new furnace costs $70,000. Pippa records this transaction as follows:

Furnace	70,000	
Accumulated Depreciation: Furnace	30,000	
Loss on Disposal of Property, Plant, and Equipment ($20,000 – $5,000)	15,000	
Furnace		50,000
Cash ($70,000 – $5,000)		65,000

While this method is conceptually superior, it can only be used when the book value of the old asset is known. The book value of the old asset might not be known if it was acquired as part of a larger asset acquisition. For example, Pippa might not know the cost of the furnace if it was purchased as part of the entire building. In that case, one of the other two alternative methods should be used.

Reduction of Accumulated Depreciation This method reduces accumulated depreciation, thereby increasing the asset's book value, for the cost of the improvement or replacement. This method is appropriate when the expenditure extends the service life of the asset which, in effect, restores some of the service potential of the asset that had previously been depreciated.

Example Bradbury Company incurs a capital expenditure of $60,000 to replace a roof on its factory. Bradbury had not planned to replace the roof, but the replacement has extended the life of the factory. Bradbury records the cost as follows:

Accumulated Depreciation	60,000	
Cash		60,000

Capitalization as a New Asset Under this method, the expenditure is capitalized as a new asset without removing the carrying amount of the old asset. This method is most appropriate for additions. This method is also appropriate for improvements and replacements, particularly if the book value of the old asset has been sufficiently depreciated to an immaterial amount.

Example Heller Company records a capital expenditure of $80,000 to enlarge a factory that increases its usefulness as follows:

Building	80,000	
Cash		80,000

Rearrangement and Moving

The costs of rearranging the facilities within a building or moving them to a new location are capitalized as assets and depreciated over the period expected to benefit. For example, a manufacturing company may rearrange its equipment to achieve a better flow of inventory during the manufacturing process and increase operational efficiency. However, if these costs are immaterial or if it's uncertain that the costs will provide future benefits, the company should expense such costs in the period incurred. Under IFRS, the cost of relocating or reorganizing property, plant, and equipment must be expensed.

Repairs and Maintenance

Routine expenditures for repair and maintenance do not increase the future economic benefits of the asset but, instead, maintain the existing benefits provided by the asset. Therefore, **routine repair and maintenance costs should be expensed in the period incurred**. For example, repairs and maintenance include expenditures such as painting, lubricating a machine, and making periodic adjustments to equipment. Sometimes, repairs cannot be foreseen and do not occur in the ordinary course of business (e.g., emergency repairs to a machine that breaks down during production). Usually, a company expenses the cost of these major repairs. However, if these repairs increase the future benefits of the asset similar to an improvement or a replacement, the cost should be capitalized.

GOT IT?

10-18 What is the distinction between a *capital* and an *operating expenditure*? Give two examples of each.

10-19 Distinguish between *additions* and *improvements/replacements*. How should a company account for each?

10-20 Distinguish between *ordinary repairs and maintenance* and *major repairs*. How should a company account for each?

APPENDIX 10.1: OIL AND GAS PROPERTIES

LEARNING OBJECTIVE 10.6
Explain the accounting for oil and gas properties.

A company faces special issues when accounting for oil and gas properties that are included in its property, plant, and equipment. Conceptually, any exploration costs that provide future benefits should be capitalized. While this poses no problem for exploration activities that discover oil and gas, differences of opinion exist as to the proper accounting for unsuccessful exploration activities. The issue centers on whether unsuccessful exploration efforts ("dry wells") should be expensed as incurred because they will not produce future economic benefits, or whether they are an unavoidable part of the process of discovering the productive wells, and should therefore be considered part of the total capitalized cost associated with the successful wells. Reflecting these two opposing views, two alternative methods of accounting for oil and gas exploration costs exist.

- **Successful-efforts method**—Only those exploration costs that result in the discovery of oil and gas are capitalized as part of the oil and gas reserve and amortized as the oil and gas is produced. The costs of a dry well—exploration that does not result in the discovery of oil or gas—are expensed in the current period.
- **Full-cost method**—All costs incurred in the exploration and discovery of oil and gas—even the costs associated with dry wells—are capitalized as part of the cost of the oil and gas reserves that are discovered, and amortized as the oil and gas is produced.

The principal difference between the two methods concerns the treatment of the cost of dry wells.

Proponents of the *successful-efforts method* argue that a direct relationship between costs incurred and specific reserves discovered (future economic benefits) is required before costs are recorded as assets. Costs of acquisition and development activities that are known not to have resulted in the discovery of reserves do not meet the definition of an asset and should therefore be expensed. In contrast, the *full-cost method* regards the costs of unsuccessful acquisition and exploration activities as necessary for the discovery of reserves. Therefore, all costs incurred in oil and gas drilling are regarded as integral to the development of whatever reserves ultimately result from the efforts as a whole and are thus associated with the company's reserves. Establishing a direct cause-and-effect relationship between drilling costs incurred and specific reserves discovered is not relevant to the full-cost method.

The basic difference between the two methods focuses on the nature of an asset. If the asset is viewed as an individual well, it is appropriate for a company to expense the cost of a dry well because it will produce no future economic benefits. Alternatively, if the asset is viewed as the oil or gas that lies underground, it is appropriate for a company to capitalize the costs of a dry well because the activity was necessary in searching to discover other oil or gas. It is the oil or gas that is discovered that will produce future economic benefits rather than the costs incurred to drill any particular well.

In 1977, GAAP required the use of the successful-efforts method. The FASB cited two primary reasons to justify the adoption of the successful-efforts method. First, an asset is an economic resource that is expected to provide future benefits, so costs that are known not to have resulted in identifiable future benefits should be expensed. Second, financial statements should reflect risk and unsuccessful results. The successful-efforts method highlights the cost of failures and the risks involved in the search for oil and gas reserves.

In a politically motivated decision, the SEC decided not to support the FASB's position. Many of the owners and managers of oil and gas companies that were using the full-cost method objected to its elimination and lobbied Congress. They argued that the use of successful efforts would cause reported income and assets to be lower, and would impair the ability of their companies to raise capital and search for oil and gas. This argument is inconsistent with efficient market research, which indicates that users of financial statements would not be "fooled" by the different reporting of the same underlying economic facts. However, Congress accepted the argument and directed that the SEC must accept the use of the full-cost method in reports filed with it, thereby allowing both methods to continue to be used. Consequently, the FASB suspended the requirement to use the successful-efforts method and companies may choose which method to use.[17]

Because both methods are widely used, difficulties arise for users of financial statements when making comparisons between companies that are each using different methods. Large oil and gas companies generally use the successful-efforts method, whereas small independent producers prefer the full-cost method because it enables them to defer more costs, thereby reducing current expenses and increasing current income. It can be argued that neither method satisfies the needs of users of financial statements because they do not reflect the economic substance of oil and gas exploration. However, GAAP requires extensive disclosures on oil and gas reserves, including:

- estimates of quantities of proven oil and gas reserves—oil and gas reserves which are expected to be recoverable with reasonable certainty
- capitalizable costs related to oil and gas activities
- results of operations of oil- and gas-producing activities
- a standardized measure of discounted future cash flows
- change in standardized future cash flows[18]

GOT IT?

10-21 *(Appendix 10.1)* Distinguish between the *successful-efforts* and *full-cost* methods of accounting for oil and gas properties.

---

[17] Once a company selects one of the two methods to use, it must follow specific rules. See "Codification of Staff Accounting Bulletins, Topic 12" (SEC, 2008) for additional details.
[18] FASB ASC 932-235-50: Extractive Activities—Oil and Gas: Notes to Financial Statements: Disclosure.

REVIEW CENTER

At the beginning of the chapter, we discussed how the investment in property, plant, and equipment impacts a company's reported base of productive assets and its ability to generate income. Specifically, we discussed how the decision to capitalize or expense an expenditure related to property, plant, and equipment affects a company's financial position and profitability. We also identified several objectives you would accomplish after reading the chapter. The objectives are listed below and followed by a brief summary of the key points.

LEARNING OBJECTIVE 10.1
Describe the characteristics of property, plant, and equipment.

KEY TAKEAWAYS

- Property, plant, and equipment are the tangible, long-lived assets that a company uses in the normal course of business to generate revenue.
- To be classified as property, plant, and equipment, an asset must be held for use in operations and not for investment, have an expected life of more than one year, and be tangible in nature.
- Property, plant, and equipment is initially recorded at its acquisition cost, which is subsequently allocated as an expense to each period in which the asset is used, and provides a benefit to the company.
- GAAP requires property, plant, and equipment to be reported at its depreciated cost (cost minus accumulated depreciation).

KEY TERMS

fixed assets, p. 10-3
plant assets, p. 10-3

property, plant, and equipment, p. 10-3

KEY TAKEAWAYS

LEARNING OBJECTIVE 10.2
Identify the costs to be included in the acquisition of property, plant, and equipment.

- The initial cost of the various types of property, plant, and equipment includes all the costs necessary to obtain the asset and put it in operating condition; that is, the acquisition cost includes costs that are necessary to obtain the benefits to be derived from the asset.
- An asset retirement obligation—a legal obligation related to the retirement of property, plant, and equipment—is required to be capitalized at fair value on the date the obligation is incurred, with a corresponding increase in a liability. In subsequent periods, a company depreciates the asset using a systematic and rational method and increases the liability over time by recognizing interest expense (accretion expense).
- The initial valuation of property, plant, and equipment is often complicated by the manner in which the asset is acquired. In these situations, the acquisition cost is generally based on fair value, as noted below.
  - When more than one asset is acquired for a single lump-sum purchase price, the purchase price is allocated to the individual assets based on their relative fair values.
  - Assets acquired on a deferred-payment basis are recorded at the fair value of the asset or the fair value of the liability, whichever can be more clearly determined.
  - Assets acquired through the exchange of stock are recorded at the fair value of the asset or the fair value of the stock, whichever is clearly evident and representationally faithful.
  - Donated assets are recorded at fair value with a corresponding recognition of either a revenue or gain.

KEY TERMS

accretion expense, p. 10-9
acquisition cost, p. 10-5

asset retirement obligation, p. 10-8
nonreciprocal transfer, p. 10-10

KEY TAKEAWAYS

LEARNING OBJECTIVE 10.3
Determine the cost of property, plant, and equipment obtained by a nonmonetary exchange of assets.

- The cost of a nonmonetary asset acquired in exchange for another nonmonetary asset is the fair value of the asset surrendered. If the fair value of the asset received is more clearly evident than the fair value of the asset surrendered, it can be used to measure the cost of the asset acquired.
- Any difference between the fair value of the asset surrendered and its book value is recognized as a gain or loss on the exchange.

KEY TERM

nonmonetary exchange, p. 10-13

KEY TAKEAWAYS

LEARNING OBJECTIVE 10.4
Compute the cost of a self-constructed asset, including capitalized interest.

- The initial cost of self-constructed assets includes direct material, direct labor, variable overhead, and a pro rata share of fixed overhead.
- Interest incurred on borrowed funds to finance construction is viewed as an integral part of construction. If a self-constructed asset qualifies for interest capitalization, avoidable interest (computed by applying an appropriate interest rate to the weighted average accumulated expenditures) is capitalized as long as it does not exceed the actual interest cost incurred during the period.

KEY TERMS

avoidable interest, p. 10-18

weighted average accumulated expenditures, p. 10-19

KEY CALCULATION

Avoidable Interest = Weighted Average Accumulated Expenditures × Appropriate Interest Rate

LEARNING OBJECTIVE 10.5
Describe the accounting for expenditures incurred subsequent to acquisition.

KEY TAKEAWAYS

- In general, subsequent expenditures can be classified as additions, improvements and replacements, rearrangements, and repairs and maintenance.
- Expenditures that increase the future economic benefits of an asset (e.g., extend the useful life of the asset, improve productivity, or increase the quality of the product) are capital expenditures and are added to the cost of the asset.
- Expenditures that simply maintain the existing level of benefits are operating (or revenue) expenditures and are expensed in the current period.

KEY TERMS

addition, p. 10-25
betterment, p. 10-25
capital expenditure, p. 10-24
improvement, p. 10-25

operating expenditure, p. 10-24
renewal, p. 10-25
replacement, p. 10-25

LEARNING OBJECTIVE 10.6
(Appendix 10.1) Explain the accounting for oil and gas properties.

KEY TAKEAWAYS

- A company may account for exploration costs related to oil and gas properties using either the full-cost method, in which the cost of dry holes is capitalized, or the successful-efforts method, in which the cost of dry holes is expensed.

KEY TERMS

full-cost method, p. 10-27

successful-efforts method, p. 10-27

ANSWERS TO REAL REPORT QUESTIONS

Real Report 10.1 Answers Verizon—Property, Plant, and Equipment Disclosure

1. Verizon's plant, property, and equipment have three characteristics. First, all of its fixed assets are used in the course of normal operations. For example, the buildings represent offices and retail stores while the network equipment is used to provide telecommunications service to customers. Second, all of the fixed assets have an expected life greater than 1 year. As noted in the notes to the financial statements, the expected lives range from 3 to 50 years. Finally, all of the fixed assets are tangible in nature.
2. Verizon reports $88,956 million of plant, property, and equipment. Its fixed assets are reported at cost ($220,865 million) minus accumulated depreciation ($131,909 million).
3. Initially, Verizon records its plant, property, and equipment at historical costs. As an asset provides benefit to the company, its cost is allocated as depreciation expense to the periods that the asset provides benefit. GAAP requires that companies report both the historical cost valuation of plant, property, and equipment and the related accumulated depreciation so that financial statement users can see the original cost of the assets as well as the cumulative amount of depreciation expense related to these assets.
4. Work in progress represents the cost of self-constructed plant, property, and equipment that has not yet been completed. When the construction of these assets is completed, the cost will be transferred to the appropriate fixed asset account.

MULTIPLE-CHOICE (AICPA ADAPTED)

Select the best answer for each of the following.

M10-1 **LO 10.2** Hickory Company made a lump-sum purchase of three pieces of machinery for $130,000 from an unaffiliated company. At the time of acquisition, Hickory paid $5,000 to determine the appraised value of the machinery. The appraisal disclosed the following values:

Machine A	$70,000
Machine B	$42,000
Machine C	$28,000

What cost should be assigned to Machines A, B, and C, respectively?

	A	B	C
a.	$45,000	$45,000	$45,000
b.	$65,000	$39,000	$26,000
c.	$67,500	$40,500	$27,000
d.	$70,000	$42,000	$28,000

M10-2 **LO 10.2** A donated plant asset should be recorded at an amount equal to its:

a. historical cost
b. fair value
c. book value on books of donor
d. historical cost or fair value, whichever is more clearly determinable

M10-3 **LO 10.2** Electro Corporation bought a new machine and agreed to pay for it in equal annual installments of $5,000 at the end of each of the next 5 years. Assume a prevailing interest rate of 15%. The present value of an ordinary annuity of $1 at 15% for 5 periods is 3.35. The future amount of an ordinary annuity of $1 at 15% for 5 periods is 6.74. The present value of $1 at 15% for 5 periods is 0.5. How much should Electro record as the cost of the machine?

a. $12,500   c. $25,000
b. $16,750   d. $33,700

M10-4 **LO 10.2** When a company purchases land with a building on it and immediately tears down the building so that the land can be used for the construction of a plant, the costs incurred to tear down the building should be:

a. expensed as incurred
b. added to the cost of the plant
c. added to the cost of the land
d. amortized over the estimated time period between the tearing down of the building and the completion of the plant

M10-5 **LO 10.2** Lyle Inc. purchased certain plant assets under a deferred payment contract. The agreement was to pay $20,000 at the time of purchase and $20,000 at the end of each of the next 5 years. The plant assets should be valued at:

a. present value of a $20,000 ordinary annuity for 5 years
b. $120,000
c. $120,000 minus imputed interest
d. $120,000 plus imputed interest

M10-6 **LO 10.3** Ashton Company exchanged a nonmonetary asset with a cost of $30,000 and accumulated depreciation of $16,000 for another nonmonetary asset worth $12,000. Ashton also received $1,400 cash. In the entry to record this exchange, Ashton should record a:

a. $2,000 gain   c. $600 gain
b. $2,000 loss   d. $600 loss

M10-7 **LO 10.4** Belardo Corporation constructed and manufactured certain assets and incurred the following avoidable interest costs in connection with those activities:

	Avoidable Interest Costs Incurred
Warehouse constructed for Belardo's own use	$20,000
Special-order machine for sale to unrelated customer, produced according to customer's specifications	9,000
Inventories routinely manufactured, produced on a repetitive basis	7,000

All of these assets required an extended period of time for completion. Assuming that the effect of interest capitalization is material, what is the total amount of interest costs to be capitalized?

a. $0   c. $29,000
b. $20,000   d. $36,000

M10-8 **LO 10.5** The following expenditures were among those incurred by Jensen Corporation during the year ended December 31, 2016:

Replacement of tiles on portion of roof that had been leaking	$4,000
Overhaul of machinery that is expected to extend its useful life for another 2 years	6,000

(continued)

How much should be charged to repairs and maintenance in 2016?

a. $0
b. $4,000
c. $6,000
d. $10,000

M10-9
LO 10.5
When a company replaces an old asphalt roof on its plant with a new fiberglass insulated roof, which of the following types of expenditure occurs?

a. ordinary repair
b. addition
c. rearrangement
d. improvement

M10-10
LO 10.5
On January 2, 2016, Yuki Yogurt Company decided to replace its obsolete refrigeration system with a more efficient one. The old system had a book value of $9,000 and a fair value of $1,000. Yuki's new refrigeration system has a fair value of $190,000, for which Yuki paid $189,000 after permitting the contractor to keep the old refrigeration equipment. How much should Yuki capitalize as the cost of the new refrigeration system?

a. $189,000
b. $190,000
c. $197,000
d. $198,000

REVIEW EXERCISES

RE10-1
LO 10.2
On January 1, Duane Company purchases land at a cost of $125,000. Duane incurs costs of $2,000 for the closing fees and surveys. Duane also spent $7,500 on clearing costs to prepare the land for use. What is the cost of land to be recorded by Duane?

RE10-2
LO 10.2
Arlette's Pet Shop purchases a building. The purchase price per the contract is $250,000. The cost of building permits is $3,500. Conversion costs to kennel and pet care facilities total $125,000. What amount should be recorded by Arlette's as the cost of the building?

RE10-3
LO 10.2
Utica Corporation paid $360,000 to purchase land and a building. An appraisal showed that the land is worth $100,000 and the building is worth $300,000. What cost should Utica assign to the land and to the building, respectively?

RE10-4
LO 10.2
Hemingway Company purchases equipment by issuing a 7-year, $350,000 non-interest-bearing note, when the market rate for this type of note is 10%. Hemingway will pay off the note with equal payments to be made at the end of each year. Prepare the journal entry to record Hemingway's acquisition of the equipment.

RE10-5
LO 10.2
Cornett Company, a tennis racket manufacturing company, was given $600,000 worth of property from an independent developer as an incentive to build a factory there. Prepare the journal entry for Cornett to record the receipt of the land.

RE10-6
LO 10.2
On January 1, 2016, Marshall Inc. purchased equipment for $1,000,000 that was to be used in various toxic chemical processes. The asset has a useful life of 20 years. Additionally, Marshall estimates that it will cost $100,000 to remove the asset and restore the site to a suitable use. Based on Marshall's 10% discount rate, the present value of these future restoration costs at the time the equipment is purchased is $14,864. Prepare the entry to record the acquisition of the asset.

RE10-7
LO 10.3
Nabokov Company exchanges assets with Faulkner Company. Nabokov exchanges equipment with a book value of $25,000 and fair market value of $40,000 for Faulkner's land with a cost of $7,500 and fair market value of $38,000. Faulkner also paid Nabokov $2,000 in cash. Compute Nabokov's cost of the land acquired and any gain or loss on the exchange.

RE10-8
LO 10.4
Dexter Construction Corporation is building a student condominium complex; it started construction on January 1, Year 1. Dexter borrowed $2.5 million on January 1 specifically for the project by issuing a 10%, 5-year, $2.5 million note, which is payable on December 31 of Year 3. Dexter also had a 12%, 5-year, $3 million note payable and a 10%, 10-year, $1.8 million note payable outstanding all year. Calculate the weighted average interest rate on the non-construction-specific debt for Year 1.

RE10-9
LO 10.4
Refer to **RE10-8**. In Year 1, Dexter incurred costs as follows:

January 1	$ 300,000
March 1	600,000
June 30	1,000,000
November 1	480,000

Calculate Dexter's weighted average accumulated expenditures.

RE10-10
LO 10.4
Using the information in **RE10-8** and **RE10-9**, calculate Dexter's capitalized interest on the student condominium complex for Year 1.

RE10-11
LO 10.4
Refer to the information in **RE10-8** and **RE10-9**. Assume that Dexter borrowed $1 million specifically for the project by issuing a 10%, 5-year, $1 million note (instead of borrowing $2.5 million as stated in RE10-8). Calculate Dexter's capitalized interest on the student condominium complex in Year 1.

RE10-12
LO 10.5
Rick's Towing Company in Birmingham, Alabama, owns three tow trucks. During the current year, Rick performed maintenance on the trucks and realized he had to make improvements to the engines on two of his trucks. The improvements totaled $55,000. Prepare the journal entries Rick may make under two alternative methods for the improvements made to his trucks.

EXERCISES

E10-1
LO 10.1
LO 10.2
Inclusion in Property, Plant, and Equipment Guthrie Inc. must determine whether the following items are included in property, plant, and equipment:
a. idle equipment awaiting sale
b. machinery kept on hand and used only when other machinery breaks
c. land held for investment
d. the right to publish a literary work
e. progress payments on building being constructed by a contractor
f. fully depreciated assets still being used
g. expenditures to improve leased property
h. equipment leased to others
i. purchase of an asset with an expected life of 9 months
j. obligation to remove leasehold improvement at the termination of a lease

Required:
1. Indicate which items are included in the cost of property, plant, and equipment and which items are excluded from the cost of property, plant, and equipment.
2. **Next Level** For each item excluded from property, plant, and equipment, explain why it was excluded.

E10-2
LO 10.2
LO 10.4
LO 10.5
Determination of Cost Carr Company must determine whether the following items are included in property, plant, and equipment:
a. contract price
b. list price
c. freight costs
d. discounts taken
e. discounts not taken
f. installation costs
g. testing costs
h. cost of major overhaul of equipment
i. costs of grading land prior to construction
j. tax assessment for street improvements
k. delinquent property taxes on acquired property
l. cost of tearing down an old building (already owned) in preparation for new construction
m. cost of insurance during construction
n. avoidable interest costs during construction
o. landscaping costs
p. severance pay for employees dismissed because of the acquisition of a new machine
q. cost of tearing down a building on newly acquired land
r. replacement of an electric motor in a machine

(continued)

s. expansion of the heating/cooling system to accommodate an expansion of a building and certain expected future needs
t. purchase price of a service contract for 2 years on the acquired asset
u. cost of training new employees

Required:
1. Indicate which items are included in the cost of property, plant, and equipment and which items are excluded from the cost of property, plant, and equipment.
2. **Next Level** What is the general rule that should be followed in determining which costs are included in property, plant, and equipment?

E10-3 **Acquisition Costs** Voiture Company manufactures compact, energy-efficient cars. On April 1, it purchased a machine for its assembly line at a contract price of $400,000 with terms of 2/10, n/30. Voiture paid the contract price on April 8 and also incurred installation and transportation costs of $5,000, sales tax of $32,000, and testing costs of $2,000. During testing, the machine was accidentally damaged, so the company had to pay $1,000 to repair it.

LO 10.2
LO 10.5

Required:
Prepare the journal entry to record the acquisition of the machine.

E10-4 **Determination of Acquisition Cost** In January 2016, Cordova Company entered into a contract to acquire a new machine for its factory. The machine, which has a cash price of $215,000, was paid for as follows:

LO 10.2

Down payment	$ 55,000
Note payable in 4 equal annual payments starting in January 2017	$120,000
600 shares of Cordova preferred stock with a mutually agreed value of $100 per share (par value $100)	$ 60,000
Fair rate of interest on the non-interest-bearing note	10%

Required:
1. **Next Level** What principle guides the determination of the cost of the machine?
2. Prepare the journal entry to record the acquisition of the machine.
3. **Next Level** How would your answer change, if at all, if the $215,000 cash price were not available?

E10-5 **Asset Retirement Obligation** Big Cat Exploration erected an oil platform in a remote area of Texas at a cost of $10 million. Bit Cat is legally required to dismantle and remove the platform at the end of its useful life, which is expected to be 10 years. Big Cat estimates that the cost of dismantling and removing the oil rig will be $700,000. Assume that the appropriate discount rate is 8%.

LO 10.2

Required:
Prepare the journal entry to record the acquisition of the oil platform. Round your answer to the nearest dollar.

E10-6 **Acquisition of Land and Building** On February 1, 2016, Edwards Corporation purchased a parcel of land as a factory site for $100,000. It demolished an old building on the property and began construction on a new building that was completed on October 2, 2016. Costs incurred during this period are:

LO 10.2

AICPA
Adapted

Demolition of old building	$ 8,000
Architect's fees	25,000
Legal fees for title investigation and purchase contract	4,000
Construction costs	650,000

Edwards sold salvaged materials resulting from the demolition for $2,000.

Required:
1. At what amount should Edwards record the cost of the land and the new building, respectively?
2. **Next Level** If management misclassified a portion of the building's cost as part of the cost of the land, what would be the effect on the financial statements?

E10-7
LO 10.2

Lump-Sum Purchase Garrett Corporation paid $200,000 to acquire land, buildings, and equipment. At the time of acquisition, Garrett paid $20,000 for an appraisal, which revealed the following values: land, $100,000; buildings, $125,000; and equipment, $25,000.

Required:
1. What cost should the company assign to the land, buildings, and equipment, respectively?
2. Assume that Garrett uses IFRS and chooses to use the revaluation model to value its property, plant, and equipment. At the end of the year, the book value of the land, buildings, and equipment are $88,000, $104,000, and $18,000, respectively. The company determines that the fair value of the land, buildings, and equipment at the end of year is $110,000, $106,000, and $15,000, respectively. Prepare the journal entries that Garrett should make to value its property, plant, and equipment.

E10-8
LO 10.2

Asset Acquired by Donation A developer of a large shopping center donated a building and land to Hetting Co. without charge. The agreement provided that the company employ 350 people for 10 years. The land was appraised at $65,000 and the building at $44,000.

Required:
1. Prepare the journal entry to record the acquisition of the land and building.
2. **Next Level** How should the 10-year agreement be reported in the financial statements?
3. **Next Level** If the title were not to pass until after 10 years, would your answers to Requirements 1 and 2 change?

E10-9
LO 10.3

Exchange of Assets Two independent companies, Denver and Bristol, each own a warehouse, and they agree to an exchange in which no cash changes hands. The following information for the two warehouses is available:

	Denver	Bristol
Cost	$90,000	$45,000
Accumulated depreciation	55,000	25,000
Fair value	30,000	30,000

Required:
1. Assuming the exchange has commercial substance, prepare journal entries for Denver and Bristol to record the exchange.
2. Assuming the exchange does not have commercial substance, prepare journal entries for Denver and Bristol to record the exchange.
3. **Next Level** What is the justification of accounting for the exchange differently when the exchange has commercial substance versus when it does not?

E10-10
LO 10.3

Exchange of Assets Use the same information as in **E10-9**, except that the warehouse owned by Denver has a fair value of $28,000, and therefore, Denver agrees to pay Bristol $2,000 to complete the exchange.

Required:
Assuming the exchange has commercial substance, prepare journal entries for Denver and Bristol to record the exchange.

E10-11
LO 10.3

Exchange of Assets Use the same information as in **E10-9**, except that the warehouse owned by Denver has a fair value of $33,000, and therefore, Bristol agrees to pay Denver $3,000 to complete the exchange.

Required:
Assuming the transaction has commercial substance, prepare journal entries for Denver and Bristol to record the exchange.

E10-12
LO 10.3

Exchange of Assets Goodman Company acquired a truck from Harmes Company in exchange for a machine. The exchange is determined to have commercial substance. The machine cost $30,000, has a book value of $6,000, and has a market value of $9,000. The truck has a cost of $12,000 and a book value of $8,000 on Harmes', books.

Required:
Prepare journal entries for Goodman and Harmes to record the exchange.

E10-13 Exchange of Assets Use the same information as in **E-12**, except that the machine has a market value of $8,500, and, therefore, Goodman agrees to pay $500 to complete the exchange.

LO 10.3

Required:
Prepare journal entries for Goodman and Harmes to record the exchange.

E10-14 Exchange of Assets Minor Baseball Company had a player contract with Doe that was recorded in its accounting records at $145,000. Better Baseball Company had a player contract with Smith that was recorded in its accounting records at $140,000. Minor traded Doe to Better for Smith by exchanging each player's contract. The fair value of each contract was $150,000.

LO 10.3
AICPA Adapted

Required:
What amounts should each company show in its accounting records for the exchange of player contracts?

E10-15 Self-Construction Harshman Company constructed a building for its own use. The company incurred costs of $40,000 for materials and supplies, $68,000 for direct labor, and $7,000 for a supervisor's overtime that was caused by the construction. Harshman uses a factory overhead rate of 50% of direct labor cost. Before construction, the company had received a bid of $162,000 from an outside contractor.

LO 10.4

Required:
1. Assuming common practice is followed, at what value should Harshman capitalize the building?
2. **Next Level** What is the justification for determining the value described in Requirement 1?
3. **Next Level** Would your answer change if the bid from the outside contractor had been $135,000?

E10-16 Interest During Construction Matrix Inc. borrowed $1,000,000 at 8% to finance the construction of a new building for its own use. Construction began on January 1, 2016, and was completed on October 31, 2016. Expenditures related to this building were:

LO 10.4

January 1	$252,000 (includes cost of purchasing land of $150,000)
May 1	310,000
July 1	420,000
October 31	276,000

In addition, Matrix had additional debt (unrelated to the construction) of $500,000 at 9% and $800,000 at 10%. All debt was outstanding for the entire year.

Required:
1. Compute the amount of interest capitalized related to the construction of the building.
2. If the expenditures are assumed to have been incurred evenly throughout the year, compute weighted average accumulated expenditures and the amount of interest capitalized on the building.

E10-17 Interest During Construction Snowbird Company is constructing a building that qualifies for interest capitalization. It is built between January 1 and December 31, 2016. Snowbird made the following expenditures related to this building:

LO 10.4

April 1	$396,000
July 1	400,000
September 1	510,000
December 1	120,000

The company borrowed $500,000 at 12% to help finance the project. In addition, Snowbird had outstanding borrowings of $2 million at 8% and $1 million at 9%.

Required:
1. Compute the amount of interest capitalized related to the construction of the building.
2. **Next Level** What effect does the interest capitalization have on the company's financial statements after it completes the building?

E10-18 Calculating Capitalized Interest Kit Company borrows $5 million at 12% on January 1, 2016, specifically for the purpose of financing the construction of a building that is expected to take 18 months to complete. Kit invests the

LO 10.4

total amount at 11% until it makes payments for the construction project. During the first year of construction, Kit incurs the following expenditures related to this construction project:

January 1	$1,000,000
April 1	1,600,000
October 1	1,200,000
December 31	500,000

Required:
1. Compute the amount of interest expense Kit would capitalize related to the construction of the building.
2. Compute the amount of interest revenue Kit would recognize.
3. Assume that Kit uses IFRS. What amount of interest would be capitalized related to the construction of the building?

E10-19 **Capital and Operating Expenditures** Huxley Company incurs the following expenditures, which may be capital
LO 10.5   expenditures or operating expenditures:

a. cost of installing machinery
b. cost of moving machinery
c. repairs as a result of an accident
d. cost of major overhaul
e. installation of safety device required as a result of OSHA inspection
f. property taxes on land and buildings
g. replacement of the roof on a factory building that extended the life of the building
h. cost of rearranging offices expected to increase operational efficiency
i. cost of annual repainting of offices
j. ordinary repairs

Required:
1. How would Huxley record each of the expenditures under U.S. GAAP?
2. How would your answers change if Huxley uses IFRS?

E10-20 **Expenditures After Acquisition** McClain Company incurred the following expenditures during 2016:
LO 10.5

SHOW
ME HOW

Apr. 9 The air conditioning system in the old manufacturing facility was replaced for $83,000. The old air conditioning system had a cost of $74,000 and a book value of $2,000. The old air conditioning system had no scrap value.
June 29 Annual maintenance of $38,000 was performed.
Sept. 12 The roof of the old manufacturing facility is replaced at a cost of $65,000. This expenditure substantially extended the life of the facility.
Dec. 28 A new wing was added to the manufacturing facility at a cost of $275,000. This expenditure substantially increased the productive capacity of the plant.

Required:
1. Prepare journal entries to record McClain's expenditures for 2016.
2. **Next Level** What is the effect on the financial statements if management had improperly accounted for the:
   a. addition of the new wing to the manufacturing facility
   b. annual maintenance expenditures

E10-21 *(Appendix 10.1)* **Oil and Gas Accounting** In 2016, Lawrence Company spends $4 million drilling oil wells. Sixty
LO 10.6   percent of the drilling is successful and results in commercial quantities of oil being found.

SHOW
ME HOW

Required:
1. How much drilling expense should the company recognize under:
   a. successful-efforts method
   b. full-cost method
2. At what value should the company report the asset, Oil and Gas Properties, on its balance sheet under:
   a. successful-efforts method
   b. full-cost method

PROBLEMS

P10-1
LO 10.2
LO 10.4

Acquisition Costs Mawn Company bought land and built a warehouse during 2016. It improperly debited the following related costs to an account titled Land and Buildings:

Land purchase	$22,000
Demolition of old building	3,000
Legal fees for land acquisition	1,500
Avoidable interest on loan for construction	2,900
Building construction	53,000
Assessment by city for sewer connection—city is responsible for maintenance	1,200
Landscaping (expected to be permanent in nature)	3,500
Equipment purchased for excavation	18,800
Pro rata portion of fixed overhead incurred during construction of building	15,000
Insurance on building during construction	1,000
Profit on construction	12,000
Compensation for injury to construction worker (not covered by the insurance policy purchased by Mawn)	3,000
Modifications to building ordered by building inspectors (due to poor planning by Mawn)	7,500
Deliquent property taxes on land paid in 2016 (land was purchased during the year)	2,500

Required:
Prepare the correcting entries on December 31, 2016, to properly reclassify the preceding items.

P10-2
LO 10.2
LO 10.5

Classification of Costs Associated with Assets The following account balances were included in Bromley Company's balance sheet on December 31, 2015:

Land	$100,000
Land improvements	20,000
Buildings	300,000
Machinery and equipment	500,000

During 2016, the following transactions occurred:
1. Land was acquired for $70,000 for a future building site. Commissions of $4,000 were paid to a real estate agent.
2. A factory and land were acquired from Kent Development Company by issuing 20,000 shares of $3 par common stock. At that time, the stock was selling for $10 per share on the New York Stock Exchange. The independently appraised values of the land and the factory were $60,000 and $180,000, respectively.
3. Equipment was acquired at a cost of $120,000. In addition, sales tax, freight costs, and installation costs were $7,000, $10,000, and $16,000, respectively. During installation, the equipment was damaged, and $2,000 was spent for repairs.
4. A new parking lot was installed at a cost of $30,000.
5. Half the land purchased in Item 1 was prepared as a building site. Costs of $26,000 were incurred to clear the land, and the timber recovered was sold for $3,000. A new building was built for $60,000. Architect's fees relating to construction were $18,000, and imputed interest on equity funds used during construction was $15,000. No debt is outstanding.
6. Costs of $20,000 were incurred to improve some leased office space. The lease will terminate in 2018 and is not expected to be renewed.
7. A group of new machines was purchased under a royalty agreement that provides for payment of annual royalties based on units produced. The invoice price of the machines was $30,000, freight costs were $2,000, and royalty payments for 2016 were $12,000.

Required:
Prepare journal entries to record all the preceding events. Unless otherwise indicated, assume the company makes all payments in cash.

P10-3 **Acquisition Cost** The following transactions of Weber Company occurred during 2016:

LO 10.2
LO 10.5

1. The company acquired a tract of land in exchange for 1,000 shares of $10 par value common stock. The stock was traded on the New York Stock Exchange at $24 on the date of exchange. The land had a book value on the selling company's records of $5,000, and it was believed to be worth "anything up to $30,000."
2. An engine on a truck was replaced. The truck originally cost $10,000 3 years ago and was being depreciated at $2,000 per year. The engine cost $1,000 to replace.
3. The company acquired a tract of land that was believed to have mineral deposits by issuing 500 shares of preferred stock of $50 par value. The preferred stock was rarely traded. The last transaction was 2 months earlier, when 50 shares were sold at $75 per share. The owner of the land was willing to accept cash of $55,000, and an appraisal had shown a value of $60,000.
4. The company purchased a machine with a list price of $8,500 by issuing a 2-year, $10,000 non-interest-bearing note when the market rate of interest was 10%.

Required:
Prepare journal entries to record the preceding events.

P10-4 **Comprehensive** At December 31, 2015, certain accounts included in the property, plant, and equipment section of Townsand Company's balance sheet had the following balances:

LO 10.2
LO 10.5

AICPA
Adapted

Land	$100,000
Buildings	800,000
Leasehold improvements	500,000
Machinery and equipment	700,000

During 2016, the following transactions occurred:

1. Land site number 621 was acquired for $1,000,000. Additionally, to acquire the land, Townsand paid a $60,000 commission to a real estate agent. Costs of $15,000 were incurred to clear the land. During the course of clearing the land, timber and gravel were recovered and sold for $5,000.
2. A second tract of land (site number 622) with a building was acquired for $300,000. The closing statement indicated that the land value was $200,000 and the building value was $100,000. Shortly after acquisition, the building was demolished at a cost of $30,000. A new building was constructed for $150,000 plus the following costs:

Excavation fees	$11,000
Architectural design fees	8,000
Building permit fee	1,000

The building was completed and occupied on September 29, 2016.
3. A third tract of land (site number 623) was acquired for $600,000 and was put on the market for resale.
4. Extensive work was done to a building occupied by Townsand under a lease agreement that expires on December 31, 2025. The total cost of the work was $125,000, which consisted of the following:

Painting of ceilings	$ 10,000 (estimated useful life is 1 year)
Electrical work	35,000 (estimated useful life is 10 years)
Construction of extension to current working area	80,000 (estimated useful life is 30 years)
	$125,000

The lessor, Steinbeck Company, paid one-half of the costs incurred in connection with the extension to the current working area.
5. During December 2016, costs of $65,000 were incurred to improve leased office space. The related lease will terminate on December 31, 2018, and is not expected to be renewed.
6. A group of new machines was purchased under a royalty agreement that provides for payment of royalties based on units of production for the machines. The invoice price of the machines was $75,000, freight costs were $2,000, unloading charges were $1,500, and royalty payments for 2016 were $13,000.

(continued)

Required:
1. Prepare a detailed analysis of the changes in the balance sheet accounts—Land, Buildings, Leasehold Improvements, and Machinery and Equipment—for 2016. Disregard the related accumulated depreciation accounts.
2. List the items in the fact situation that were not used to determine the answer to Requirement 1, and indicate where, or if, these items should be included in Townsand's financial statements.

P10-5 **Assets Acquired by Exchange** Bremer Company made the following exchanges of assets during 2016:
LO 10.3
1. Acquired a more advanced machine worth $10,000 by paying $2,000 cash and giving up a machine that had originally cost $40,000 and has a book value of $12,000.
2. Acquired a building worth $55,000 by paying $5,000 cash and giving up a piece of land that had originally cost $35,000.
3. Acquired a more advanced machine worth $20,000 by paying $5,000 cash and giving up a machine that had originally cost $13,000 and has a book value of $11,000.
4. Acquired a car by giving up a truck that had originally cost $20,000, has a book value of $15,000, and has a "blue book" value of $16,800. In addition, the company received $1,000 cash.

Required:
Prepare Bremer's journal entry for each exchange. Assume all exchanges were determined to have commercial substance.

P10-6 **Assets Acquired by Exchange** Bussell Company exchanged the following assets during 2016:
LO 10.3
a. Acquired a newer machine by paying $4,000 cash and giving up a machine that originally cost $40,000, has a book value of $25,000, and is worth $30,000.
b. Same facts as in Item a, except that the asset being surrendered has a book value of $33,000.
c. Acquired a newer machine by giving up a machine that originally cost $45,000, has a book value of $20,000, and is worth $32,000. In addition, $5,000 cash was received.
d. Same facts as in Item c, except that the asset being surrendered has a book value of $36,000.
e. Acquired a newer machine worth $90,000 by giving up a machine of equal value. The machine surrendered had originally cost $150,000 and has a book value of $80,000.
f. Same facts as in Item e, except that the asset being surrendered has a book value of $94,000.
g. Acquired a building in exchange for land that had originally cost $130,000 and is now worth $200,000.
h. Same facts as in Item g, except that $30,000 was paid.
i. Same facts as in Item g, except that $20,000 was received.

Required:
1. Prepare Bussell's journal entry to record each acquisition. Assume all exchanges were determined to have commercial substance.
2. Consider Item e. Assuming the exchange does not have commercial substance, prepare journal entries to record the exchange.
3. **Next Level** What is the justification of accounting for the exchange differently when the exchange has commercial substance versus when it does not?

P10-7 **Self-Construction** Olson Machine Company manufactures small and large milling machines. Selling prices of
LO 10.4 these machines range from $35,000 to $200,000. During the 5-month period from August 1, 2016, through
CMA December 31, 2016, Olson manufactured a milling machine for its own use. This machine was built as part of the
Adapted regular production activities. The project required a large amount of time from planning and supervisory personnel, as well as that of some of the company's officers, because it was a more sophisticated type of machine than the regular production models.

Throughout the 5-month period, Olson charged all costs directly associated with the construction of the machine to a special account entitled "Asset Construction Account." An analysis of the charges to this account as of December 31, 2016, follows:

ASSET CONSTRUCTION ACCOUNT

Item Description		Cost	
Raw Materials			
Iron castings:			
Main housing, 3 sections		$37,480	
Movable heads, 2 heads @ $3,900		7,800	
Machine bed		4,760	
Table, 2 sections @ $5,500		11,000	$ 61,040
Other raw materials:			
Electrical components and wiring		$28,000	
Worm screws and housing		8,600	
Cutter housings		2,700	
Conveyor system		8,400	
Other parts		2,500	50,200
Direct Labor Costs			
Layout 90 hrs. @ $5.00		$ 450	
Electricians 380 hrs. @ $9.00		3,420	
Machining 1,100 hrs. @ $8.00		8,800	
Heat treatment 100 hrs. @ $7.50		750	
Assembly 450 hrs. @ $7.00		3,150	
Testing 180 hrs. @ $8.00		1,440	18,010
Other Direct Charges			
Repairs and maintenance during testing period		$ 1,340	
Avoidable interest expense from 8/1/16 to 12/31/16		4,260	
Additional labor to assist during machine testing period, 180 hrs. @ $5.00		900	6,500
Balance, December 31, 2016			$135,750

Olson allocates factory overhead to normal production as a percent of direct labor dollars as follows:

	Factory Overhead Rates (applied as a percent of direct labor dollars)		
Departments	Variable	Fixed	Total
Layout and electricians	50%	20%	70%
Machining,* heat treatment, and assembly	50%	50%	100%

*All testing is conducted by employees in the machining department.

Olson uses a flat rate of 40% of direct labor dollars to allocate general and administrative overhead.

During the machine testing period, a cutter head malfunctioned and did extensive damage to the machine table and one cutter housing. This damage was not anticipated and was the result of an error in the assembly operation. Although no additional raw materials were needed to make the machine operational after the accident, the following labor for rework was required:

	Direct Labor Hours
Electric	80
Machining	200
Assembly	100
Testing (conducted by machining department)	20

Olson has included all these labor charges in the asset construction account. In addition, it included in the account the repairs and maintenance charges of $1,340 that it incurred as a result of the malfunction.

Required:
1. Compute, consistent with GAAP and common practice, the amount that Olson should capitalize for the milling machine as of December 31, 2016, when it declares the machine operational.
2. **Next Level** Identify the costs you included in Requirement 1 for which there are acceptable alternative procedures. Describe the alternative procedure(s) in each case.

P10-8 **Interest During Construction** Alta Company is constructing a production complex that qualifies for interest
LO 10.4 capitalization. The following information is available:

- Capitalization period: January 1, 2016, to June 30, 2017
- Expenditures on project:

    2016:
January 1	$ 540,000
May 1	465,000
October 1	600,000

    2017:
March 1	1,500,000
June 30	600,000

- Amounts borrowed and outstanding:
  $1.5 million borrowed at 12%, specifically for the project
  $6 million borrowed on July 1, 2015, at 14%
  $14 million borrowed on January 1, 2011, at 8%

Required:
1. Compute the amount of interest costs capitalized each year.
2. If it is assumed that the production complex has an estimated life of 20 years and a residual value of $0, compute the straight-line depreciation in 2017.
3. **Next Level** Explain the effects of the interest capitalization on the financial statements for both years. Ignore income taxes.

P10-9 **Interest During Construction** Foothills Power Company begins a 2-year construction project on a power plant
LO 10.4 on January 1, 2016. The following information is available:

- The company borrows $10 million on January 1, 2016, at 12%, specifically for use on the project.
- The company's other borrowings are:
  $20 million at 10%
  $60 million at 8%
- The expenditures for the project, incurred evenly each year (excluding capitalized interest from previous years), are as follows:
  $6,000,000 in 2016
  $11,460,000 in 2017
  $1,800,000 in 2018
- The project is completed on March 31, 2018. It took longer than originally planned because the company suspended construction for the last 3 months of 2016 because of a concern about the salability of the electricity produced by the plant.
- Because of reduced demand for electricity, the plant does not begin operations until October 1, 2018.
- The company invests at 11% the unused amounts of the $10 million borrowed specifically for the project.
- Assume all transactions are in cash unless otherwise indicated.

Required:

1. Prepare all the necessary journal entries for each of the 3 years. Record all construction costs in a Construction in Progress inventory account.
2. How would your answer change if Foothills used IFRS?

P10-10 **Events Subsequent to Acquisition** The following selected events occurred for Orwell Company during the first
LO 10.5 quarter of 2016:

Jan. 11		A motor breaks on a machine and is replaced for $2,400. This replacement was expected when the machine was purchased.
Feb. 15		A machine breaks down unexpectedly and requires repairs of $700.
Mar. 10		An accident damages some equipment. Repairs cost $2,000.
	19	A motor breaks on a machine and is replaced for $900. The new motor is of an improved design that increases the capacity of the machine.
	27	Office layout is rearranged at a cost of $700. At the same time, the walls are repainted for $500.

Required:
1. Prepare journal entries for the preceding transactions.
2. Would any of your answers change if the company used IFRS? If so, how?

P10-11 *(Appendix 10.1)* **Oil and Gas Accounting Methods** Iwata Oil Company incurred costs of $6 million during 2016 by drilling for oil. Half the costs resulted in oil being found, and half resulted in dry wells. Iwata expects the oil wells to produce 10% of their capacity each year from 2017 to 2026.
LO 10.6

Required:
1. What amounts appear in the financial statements for 2017 under:
   a. successful-efforts method
   b. full-cost method
2. **Next Level** What financial statement effects might lead some oil companies, particularly small oil companies, to prefer the full-cost method?

CASES

COMMUNICATION

C10-1 Acquisition
LO 10.2
LO 10.3
LO 10.5

AICPA Adapted

Among the principal topics related to the accounting for property, plant, and equipment of a company are acquisition and retirement.

Required:
1. Explain the expenditures that a company capitalizes when it acquires equipment for cash.
2. Assume that a company cannot determine the market value of equipment acquired by reference to a similar purchase for cash. Explain how the company determines the cost of equipment purchased by exchanging it for each of the following 3 items:
   a. Bonds having an established market price.
   b. Bonds that do not have an established market price.
   c. Common stock not having an established market price.
   d. Similar equipment having a determinable market value.
3. Explain the factors that a company uses to determine whether it capitalizes expenditures relating to property, plant, and equipment already in use.

C10-2 Capitalization Issues
LO 10.2
LO 10.5

AICPA Adapted

Bellow Company purchased land for use as its corporate headquarters. A small factory that was on the land when it was purchased was torn down before construction of the office building began. Furthermore, a substantial amount of rock blasting and removal had to be done to the site before construction of the building foundation began. Because the office building was set back on the land, far from the public road, Bellow had the contractor construct a paved road that led from the public road to the parking lot of the office building.

Three years after it occupied the office building, Bellow added four stories to the office building. The four stories had an estimated useful life of 5 years more than the remaining estimated useful life of the original office building.

Required:
Which of the preceding expenditures does the company capitalize? How does it depreciate or amortize each? Explain the rationale for your answers.

C10-3 Cost Issues
LO 10.2
LO 10.5

AICPA Adapted

Deskin Company purchased a new machine to be used in its operations. The new machine was delivered by the supplier, installed by Deskin, and placed into operation. It was purchased under a long-term payment plan for which the interest charges approximated the prevailing market rates. The estimated useful life of the new machine is 10 years, and its estimated residual (salvage) value is significant. Normal maintenance was performed to keep the new machine in usable condition.

Deskin also added a wing to the manufacturing building that it owns. The addition is an integral part of the building. Furthermore, Deskin made significant leasehold improvements to office space used as corporate headquarters.

(continued)

Required:
1. What costs should Deskin capitalize for the new machine?
2. Explain how Deskin should account for the normal maintenance performed on the new machine.
3. Explain how Deskin should account for the wing added to the manufacturing building. Where should the added wing be reported on Deskin's financial statements?
4. Explain how Deskin should account for the leasehold improvements made to its office space. Where should the leasehold improvements be reported on Deskin's financial statements?

CREATIVE AND CRITICAL THINKING

C10-4 Interest Capitalization
LO 10.4 Gold Creek Company has borrowed large amounts of money to purchase 5,000 acres of land, which it will develop as a new ski area over the next 10 years. Development is currently under way on the first 2,000 acres, with trails being cut and ski lifts being built. When the company completes this initial development after 4 years, it will develop the remaining acreage at the rate of approximately 500 acres per year. The company also used some of the money it borrowed to purchase adjacent land, which it will use to expand the ski area if it is successful.

Because this is the first year of the company's existence, it has not developed a policy about interest capitalization. Specifically, it is uncertain about whether it is entitled to capitalize interest on the amounts borrowed to acquire the first 2,000 acres, the total 5,000 acres, the 5,000 acres plus the adjacent land, or the land and the development.

Required:
1. Explain the interest capitalization that is appropriate under these circumstances.
2. How might the decision be influenced if the company were interested in earnings management?

C10-5 Capitalization of Purchase Options
LO 10.2 Morgan Company was planning to expand its production facilities. Therefore, it acquired 1-year options to purchase two alternative sites. Each option cost $5,000 and could not be applied against the contract. One of the sites was bought for $100,000. Morgan was unsure whether to capitalize the land at $100,000, $105,000, or $110,000.

Required:
Write a short report that presents arguments in favor of each alternative.

C10-6 Exchange of Assets
LO 10.2
LO 10.3
AICPA Adapted
You have been hired to examine Brahe Corporation's financial statements for the year ending December 31, 2016. Brahe was organized in January 2016 by Moses and Price, the original owners of options to acquire oil leases on 5,000 acres of land for $350,000. They expected that first the oil leases would be acquired by the corporation and subsequently 180,000 shares of the corporation's common stock would be sold to the public at $6 per share. In February 2016, they exchanged their options, $150,000 cash, and $50,000 of other assets for 75,000 shares of common stock of the corporation. Brahe's board of directors appraised the leases at $600,000, basing the appraisal on the price of other acreage recently leased in the same area. The options were therefore recorded at $250,000 ($600,000 − $350,000 option price).

The options were exercised by the corporation in March 2016, prior to the sale of common stock to the public in April 2016. Leases on approximately 500 acres of land were abandoned as worthless during the year.

Required:
1. Explain why the valuation of assets acquired by a corporation in exchange for its own common stock is sometimes difficult.
2. Explain the reasoning Brahe might use to support valuing the leases at $600,000, the amount of the appraisal by the board of directors.
3. Assuming the board's appraisal was sincere, what steps might Brahe have taken to strengthen its position to use the $600,000 value and to provide additional information if questions were raised about possible overvaluation of the leases?
4. Discuss the propriety of charging 1/10 of the recorded value of the leases against income at December 31, 2016, because leases on 500 acres of land were abandoned during the year.

C10-7 Ethics and Construction Costs

You are the accountant for a division of a company that is constructing a building for its own use. It is January 2017, and you are working on closing the books for 2016. The CEO of the division stops by your office and says, "I have some questions about our building. Although we started construction at the beginning of June this year, we started planning it at the beginning of the previous year. I believe that we can capitalize interest since then. Check to see if we did capitalize some in 2015. If not, we can take it out of this year's expense and get a double dose. Also, I want you to add lots of overhead to the cost of the building so we can increase our profit for this year. For example, you spent quite a bit of time on the project. So perhaps we could add 1/12 of your salary to the cost of the building. You get the idea?" When the CEO leaves, you check the files and find a letter to an architect dated January 2, 2015. There are numerous subsequent letters to and from the architect.

Required:

From financial reporting and ethical perspectives, how would you reply to the CEO?

C10-8 Analyzing Starbucks Corporation's Property, Plant, and Equipment

Obtain **Starbucks**'s 2015 annual report either using the "Investor Relations" portion of its web site (do a Web search for Starbucks investor relations) or go to http://www.sec.gov and click "Search for company filings" under "Filings and Forms (EDGAR)."

Required:
1. What is the value of Starbucks's property, plant, and equipment?
2. What categories of property, plant, and equipment does Starbucks report in its financial statements?
3. What type of asset is work in progress?
4. What is the effect of the capitalization of interest on Starbucks's financial statements?
5. How much cash was used to purchase property, plant, and equipment in 2015?
6. How does Starbucks treat repair and maintenance costs?
7. Compute Starbucks's fixed asset turnover. What does this ratio tell you?

C10-9 Analyzing Moet Hennessy Louis Vuitton's Property, Plant, and Equipment

Obtain **LVMH** (**Moet Hennessy Louis Vuitton**)'s 2013 annual report using the "Investor Relations" portion of its web site (do a Web search for Moet Hennessy Louis Vuitton investor relations).

Required:
1. What is the value of LVMH's property, plant, and equipment?
2. What categories of property, plant, and equipment does LVMH report in its financial statements?
3. How does LVMH value its property, plant, and equipment?

USING CODIFICATION

C10-10 Researching GAAP

Situation

The Tenth National Bank had taken possession of a shopping mall in foreclosure of a mortgage. When the mall was inspected prior to being sold by the bank to a real estate company, it was discovered that it had extensive asbestos problems. An estimate indicated that it would cost $1 million to remove the asbestos. The bank has also purchased an office building for its headquarters. The building was inspected before the purchase and a similar asbestos problem was discovered. An estimate indicated that it would cost $2 million to remove the asbestos, and the bank completed the purchase. The bank's president has asked you how to account for these transactions.

Directions

1. Research the related generally accepted accounting principles and prepare a short memo to the president that answers her question. Cite your references and applicable paragraph numbers.
2. Does this situation create ethical issues?

C10-11 Researching GAAP

Situation

Perry Park Company (a privately held company) was searching for a way to expand its operating capacity even though it was short of cash. Peter, the president of the company, was playing golf and mentioned his concern to his playing partner who owned some land and a building and was interested in disposing of them. After some negotiation, the two agreed to swap the land and building for shares in the company. Peter has asked you how to account for this transaction, including whether the transaction qualifies as an exception to the general rule to use fair value and the value to place on the transaction and its components.

Directions

1. Research the related generally accepted accounting principles and prepare a short memo to the president. Cite your references and applicable paragraph numbers.
2. Does this situation create ethical issues?

CHAPTER 11

DEPRECIATION, DEPLETION, IMPAIRMENT, AND DISPOSAL

Choose Wisely!

As discussed in the previous chapter, companies invest in property, plant, and equipment that is subsequently used in the normal course of operations to generate income. As the future economic benefits, or service potential, of the assets decline, the cost of the asset is allocated to expense. In performing this allocation, managers make choices, estimates, and forecasts that involve a significant amount of judgment and may convey important information about the usefulness of its long-lived assets. By comparing, management's choice of useful life and residual value across firms, financial statement users can identify differences that may warrant further investigation. For example, if Firm A and Firm B compete in the same industry, but Firm A uses a shorter useful life than Firm B, it could imply that Firm A either:

- uses a more conservative useful life forecast
- uses different types of depreciable assets (shorter-lived) for its operations, and/or
- utilizes its assets more heavily in operations (such as running the assets in second or third shifts)

If financial statement users observe that a firm has changed the useful lives of its long-lived assets, it may reveal a change in the composition of a company's assets or a strategic decision to use the assets differently. In addition, the choice of depreciation method can have a significant impact on the timing of expense recognition.

Companies also exercise judgment concerning asset impairments. Accounting standards require companies to evaluate their property, plant, and equipment

LEARNING OBJECTIVES

After reading this chapter you will be able to

LO 11.1 Identify the factors involved in depreciation.

LO 11.2 Calculate depreciation expense using various time-based and activity-based methods.

LO 11.3 Explain the conceptual issues regarding depreciation methods.

LO 11.4 Understand group and composite depreciation methods.

LO 11.5 Understand the disclosure of depreciable assets.

LO 11.6 Understand additional depreciation issues, including partial period depreciation, changes and corrections of depreciation, and depreciation and accretion of asset retirement obligations.

LO 11.7 Test for and account for the impairment of property, plant, and equipment.

LO 11.8 Explain how to account for the disposal of property, plant, and equipment.

LO 11.9 Understand and record depletion of natural resources.

LO 11.10 *(Appendix 11.1)* Understand depreciation for income tax purposes and how it differs from depreciation for financial reporting purposes.

when events or circumstances indicate the carrying value may not be recoverable. This assessment involves estimates of the asset's future cash flows and fair value. For example, in the fourth quarter of 2013, **Radio Shack** recognized impairment losses of $11.2 million related to underperforming retail stores. This impairment is an important part of Radio Shack's turnaround strategy and cash management plan as it attempts to return to profitability.

Management choices that accurately and consistently reflect the use of depreciable assets provide high-quality accounting information to financial statement users. However, this exercise of judgment also creates the potential for bias in the financial reporting process. For example, by overestimating an asset's useful life or salvage value, management can lower current-period depreciation expense and increase reported net income. Similarly, while large impairment charges to write down the book value of depreciable assets will reduce current earnings, the reduced cost basis of the asset produces lower future depreciation charges and higher future income. Therefore, it is critical for managers to make representationally faithful forecasts, assumptions, and estimates about depreciable assets so that financial statements provide important and useful information to enable users to accurately assess the impact of a company's long-lived assets on its profitability.

Property, plant, and equipment are the tangible long-lived assets used by a company to conduct normal operations and generate revenue. In Chapter 10, we discussed how to determine the acquisition cost of these assets as well as whether expenditures subsequent to acquisition should be capitalized or expensed. In this chapter, we discuss the use and eventual disposition of these assets.

Because property, plant, and equipment has long-lived service potential, the expense recognition principle requires that the company allocate the cost of the assets as an expense to each period in which the asset is used and economic resources are consumed. Over the life of the asset, the total cumulative expense is the difference between the purchase price of the asset and its residual value—the estimated amount that company will receive when it disposes of the asset. Terms used to describe this allocation process depend on the type of asset:

- **Depreciation** is the allocation of the cost of *tangible assets*, such as property, plant, and equipment.
- **Depletion** is the allocation of the cost of *natural resources*, such as oil, gas, minerals, and timber.
- **Amortization** is the allocation of the cost of *intangible assets*, such as patents and copyrights. It is also used as a general term to describe the periodic allocation of costs.

These three terms all describe the same principle of allocating the costs of long-lived productive assets to the periods in which those assets are used to conduct business operations. We discuss depreciation and depletion in this chapter and the amortization of intangible assets in Chapter 12.

LEARNING OBJECTIVE 11.1
Identify the factors involved in depreciation.

WHAT ARE THE FACTORS INVOLVED IN DEPRECIATION?

A company considers four factors in computing depreciation expense for a period:

- asset cost
- service life (or useful life)
- residual value (or salvage value)
- methods of cost allocation[1]

---

[1] The service life, residual value, and method of cost allocation are different for income tax purposes under the Modified Accelerated Cost Recovery System (MACRS), which we discuss later in the chapter.

Asset Cost

As described and demonstrated in Chapter 10, the acquisition cost of an asset includes all costs necessary to acquire the asset and prepare it for use in order to obtain the benefits from the asset. These costs include any expenditures necessary to obtain the asset and put it in operating condition, such as the contract price plus freight, assembly, installation, and testing costs.

Service Life

The **service life** (or **useful life**) of an asset is the amount of service or use that a company expects from the asset before its disposal. Service life may be measured in *units of time*, such as years and months, or *units of activity or output*, such as hours of operation of a machine, tons produced for a steel mill, or miles driven for a truck. For example, **Starbucks** measures service life in years, with the service life of equipment ranging from 2 to 15 years, the service life of leasehold improvements being 10 years (the length of a typical Starbucks store lease), and buildings expected to be used for 30 to 40 years.

The factors that limit the service life of an asset can be divided into two general categories:

- *Physical causes:* These factors include wear and tear because of operational use, deterioration and decay that is a function of time (e.g., rust), and damage and destruction.
- *Functional causes:* These factors limit the service life of the asset through obsolescence and inadequacy, *even though the physical life is not exhausted*. Obsolescence is common among technological assets which may lose usefulness because of the development of a new technology. Inadequacy refers to the situation in which an asset is no longer suitable for the size of the company's operations. For example, a warehouse may be physically sound and useful, but may become too small for a growing company's operations.

The service life of an asset is often affected by a combination of these factors. For example, the service life of a truck is likely to be affected by the passage of time (deterioration, decay, and possibly obsolescence) as well as by the amount of use. In addition, the company may be able to increase or decrease the service life by the amount it spends on repairs and maintenance as well as on improvements and replacements. Companies will often rely on the advice of professionals, such as engineers, in the estimation of service life. In other cases, the company will base its estimation on its past experience with the same or similar assets. Ultimately, however, the estimation of service life is a matter of professional judgment.

Residual Value

The **residual value** (or **salvage value**) is the net amount that a company expects to obtain from disposing of an asset at the end of its service life. It is the expected value of the asset at the end of its service life minus disposal costs, such as dismantling, removing, and selling the asset. If a company plans to hold an asset until it is physically exhausted or functionally obsolete, the expected residual value is probably very low and perhaps zero. However, a company may plan to dispose of the asset when it still has considerable economic usefulness to others (e.g., a building). In this case, the expected residual value is the estimated net market value of the asset (the selling price minus disposal costs) at the time of the disposal, which may be relatively high. For example, many airlines sell their planes long before the end of their physical lives and replace them with more technologically advanced planes.

In practice, the residual value may be difficult to estimate due to uncertainty about the future. Therefore, many companies assume a residual value of zero. Alternatively, some companies have a policy in which a standard rate, such as 10% of original cost, is used. These practices are acceptable if they do not have a material effect on the measurement of income and the book value of the asset.

Methods of Cost Allocation

Accounting principles require that a company use a method of cost allocation that is "systematic and rational."[2] In this context, *systematic* means that the calculation should follow a formula and not be determined in an arbitrary manner. *Rational* means that the amount of the depreciation expense each period should relate to the decline in the asset's service potential each period. Although these criteria are very broad and allow numerous methods, three general approaches are used frequently in practice:

- Time-based methods
  - Straight-line
  - Accelerated
    - Sum-of-the-years'-digits
    - Declining-balance
- Activity (or use) methods
- Group or composite methods

Each of these methods is acceptable under GAAP, and companies may apply different methods to different property, plant, and equipment assets. However, once a depreciation method is chosen, it should be consistently applied over time to enhance the comparability of financial information.

GOT IT?

11-1 Briefly explain the meaning of the four factors that are involved in the computation of a company's periodic charge for depreciation.

11-2 What are the primary factors that limit the service life of an asset? For each factor, indicate which depreciation method may be most appropriate.

11-3 Would it be desirable to require all companies to use the same depreciation method?

LEARNING OBJECTIVE 11.2
Calculate depreciation expense using various time-based and activity-based methods.

WHAT ARE THE METHODS OF COST ALLOCATION?

To illustrate the most common depreciation methods, consider the data for Troup Company shown in **Example 11.1**.

Troup Company's Asset Information

Asset cost	$120,000
Date of purchase	January 1, 2015
Estimated residual value	$20,000
Estimated service life	5 years or 10,000 hours
Actual usage	2015 ... 2,100 hours
	2016 ... 2,500
	2017 ... 2,300
	2018 ... 1,800
	2019 ... 1,000

The **depreciation base** (or **depreciable cost**) is computed as follows:

$$\text{Asset Cost} - \text{Estimated Residual Value} = \text{Depreciation Base}$$

---

[2] FASB ASC 360-10-35: Property, Plant, and Equipment: Overall: Subsequent Measurement.

For Troup, this amount is $100,000 ($120,000 − $20,000). The different depreciation methods all allocate the total of $100,000 over the expected service life of the asset. However, the methods differ in the pattern in which the cost is allocated to each year or each unit produced.

Time-Based Methods

A company should use a *time-based method* when the service life of the asset is affected primarily by the passage of time, or if the asset is expected to be used uniformly and continuously over its service life. Two general categories of time-based methods are the straight-line method and the accelerated methods.

The straight-line method is appropriate when a company estimates that the service potential of the asset will decline by an approximately constant amount each period of its useful life. Because the decline in the asset's service potential is constant, the company recognizes an equal amount of depreciation expense each period.

The accelerated methods are appropriate when a company estimates that the service potential of the asset will decline more quickly in the early periods of the asset's useful life than in the later periods. These methods are based on the assumption that an asset is more productive in the earlier years of its service life and a greater proportion of the service potential of the asset is used during those early years. Thus, the accelerated methods recognize depreciation expense that declines each period.

Straight-Line As the name implies, the **straight-line method** allocates an equal amount of an asset's depreciable cost to depreciation expense for each period of the asset's service life. Straight-line depreciation expense is calculated as follows:[3]

$$\text{Straight-Line Depreciation Expense} = \frac{\text{Cost} - \text{Estimated Residual Value}}{\text{Estimated Service Life}}$$

The calculation of straight-line depreciation expense for Troup Company is shown in **Example 11.1a**.

EXAMPLE 11.1a

Straight-Line Depreciation

Year	Book Value of Asset at Beginning of Year	Depreciation Expense	Accumulated Depreciation at Year-End	Book Value at Year-End[b]
2015	$120,000	$20,000[a]	$ 20,000	$100,000
2016	100,000	20,000	40,000	80,000
2017	80,000	20,000	60,000	60,000
2018	60,000	20,000	80,000	40,000
2019	40,000	20,000	100,000	20,000

[a] Depreciation Expense = $\frac{\text{Cost} - \text{Residual Value}}{\text{Service Life}}$

$= \frac{\$120,000 - \$20,000}{5 \text{ years}}$

$= \underline{\$20,000}$ per year

[b] Cost ($120,000) minus accumulated depreciation at year-end

---

[3] Some companies will calculate an annual rate at which the asset should be depreciated. This rate (1 ÷ Estimated Service Life) is called the straight-line rate. Depreciation expense is then computed by multiplying the straight-line rate by the asset's depreciable cost.

Example 11.1a illustrates two important points:

- The straight-line method recognizes the same amount of depreciation expense ($20,000) each year.
- The book value of the asset decreases linearly each year until it equals the estimated residual value at the end of the asset's service life.

Because of its simplicity, the straight-line method is the most widely used depreciation method with approximately 98% of public U.S. companies and 97% of international companies using it for some portion of property, plant, and equipment.[4]

Sum-of-the-Years'-Digits The **sum-of-the-years'-digits method** is an accelerated depreciation method that recognizes a declining depreciation expense each period by applying a decreasing fraction each year to the depreciable base of the asset. The denominator of the fraction is the sum of the years of the asset's service life. Therefore, for an asset with a 5-year life, the sum is $5 + 4 + 3 + 2 + 1 = 15$.[5] The numerator of the fraction is the number of years remaining in the asset's life as of the *beginning* of the year. The fractions for the 5 years of the asset's life are 5/15, 4/15, 3/15, 2/15, and 1/15. The calculation of depreciation expense for Troup Company is shown in **Example 11.1b**.

EXAMPLE 11.1b Sum-of-the-Years'-Digits Depreciation

Year	Depreciation Base	×	Fraction	=	Depreciation Expense	Accumulated Depreciation at Year-End	Book Value at Year-End*
2015	$100,000	×	5/15	=	$ 33,333	$ 33,333	$86,667
2016	100,000	×	4/15	=	26,667	60,000	60,000
2017	100,000	×	3/15	=	20,000	80,000	40,000
2018	100,000	×	2/15	=	13,333	93,333	26,667
2019	100,000	×	1/15	=	6,667	100,000	20,000
					$100,000		

*Cost ($120,000) minus accumulated depreciation at year-end

Note that in this method, the depreciation base remains constant, while the fraction decreases each year. This produces a declining amount for depreciation expense each year, and at the end of the fifth year, the book value of the asset is equal to the estimated residual value ($20,000).

Declining-Balance The **declining-balance methods** are accelerated depreciation methods that recognize a declining depreciation expense amount each period by applying a *constant* rate to the book value of the asset at the beginning of each period. The declining-balance depreciation rate is a multiple of the straight-line rate:

Declining-Balance Depreciation Rate = multiple × Straight-Line Rate

The multiple is often 2, in which case the declining-balance method is called the **double-declining-balance method**.[6] For example, an asset that has a 5-year life would be depreciated at a straight-line rate of 20% per year. The double-declining rate is 40%.

---

[4] *Accounting Trends & Techniques* (New York: AICPA), 2012; and *IFRS Accounting Trends & Techniques* (New York: AICPA), 2012/2013.

[5] The general formula to compute the sum of the years' digits is $n(n+1)/2$. Therefore, for an asset with a 50-year life, the sum is $50(50 + 1)/2 = 1,275$.

[6] The highest rate that can be used is double the straight-line rate. This rate was established as the highest rate by the income tax regulations and was also adopted as the highest rate for financial reporting.

However, an alternative rate could be chosen, such as a 150% declining rate, which is 1½ times the straight-line rate or, in this example, 30% per year.

Depreciation expense for each period of an asset's useful life is computed as follows:

Depreciation Expense = Declining-Balance Rate × Net Book Value at Beginning of Period

Two important points should be noted:

- The periodic depreciation expense declines because the book value decreases each year as the asset depreciates.
- Because the residual value is ignored in the calculation of depreciation expense, the application of the declining-balance method can cause an asset's book value to be different from its residual value at the end of the asset's service life. Therefore, depreciation expense is adjusted toward the end of the asset's service life so that the book value will equal the residual value.

Example 11.1c shows the calculation of depreciation expense for Troup Company using both a 200% and a 150% depreciation rate.

EXAMPLE 11.1c

Declining-Balance Depreciation Methods

(a) Double-Declining-Balance

Year	Book Value of Asset at Beginning of Year	×	Rate	=	Depreciation Expense	Accumulated Depreciation at Year-End	Book Value at Year-End[a]
2015	$120,000	×	40%	=	$ 48,000	$ 48,000	$72,000
2016	72,000	×	40%	=	28,800	76,800	43,200
2017	43,200	×	40%	=	17,280	94,080	25,920
2018	25,920				5,920[b]	100,000	20,000
2019	20,000				—	0	20,000
					$100,000		

(b) 150%-Declining-Balance

Year	Book Value of Asset at Beginning of Year	×	Rate	=	Depreciation Expense	Accumulated Depreciation at Year-End	Book Value at Year-End[a]
2015	$120,000	×	30%	=	$ 36,000	$ 36,000	$84,000
2016	84,000	×	30%	=	25,200	61,200	58,800
2017	58,800	×	30%	=	17,640	78,840	41,160
2018	41,160	×	30%	=	12,348	91,188	28,812
2019	28,812				8,812[b]	100,000	20,000
					$100,000		

[a] Cost ($120,000) minus accumulated depreciation at year-end
[b] Amount necessary to reduce book value to residual value

Note how depreciation expense is adjusted in the last years of the asset's life. Under the double-declining-balance method, the book value at the beginning of 2018 is $25,920. Applying the 40% rate would result in depreciation expense of $10,368 ($25,920 × 40%). However, this would reduce the book value below the estimated residual value. Therefore, the 2018 depreciation expense is only $5,920, which reduces the $25,920 book value to the $20,000 residual value. No depreciation expense is recorded in 2019. A similar issue arises under the 150%-declining-balance method. Applying the 30% rate in 2019 would result in depreciation expense of $8,643.60 ($28,812 × 30%), which would not reduce the book value to the residual value. Consequently, the depreciation expense in 2019 is $8,812, which reduces the book value to the $20,000 residual value.

Many companies that use a declining-balance method avoid these problems by switching from the declining-balance method to the straight-line method during the life of the asset. The change in the depreciation method might be made at the midpoint of the life of the asset, or when the depreciation expense under the straight-line method exceeds the declining-balance depreciation expense. Either method is systematic and rational if the company decides on the policy at the time of purchase and applies it to all assets. In addition, this practice avoids the possible distortion in depreciation expense in the last years of the asset's life.

Activity Methods

When the service life of the asset is affected primarily by the amount the asset is used and not by the passage of time, depreciation expense should be recognized using an **activity method** (also called the **units-of-production method**). Activity, or usage, is usually measured in terms of an input measure such as the number of hours worked or an output measure such as miles driven or units produced. For example, the life of Troup Company's asset, as shown in **Example 11.1**, is estimated to be 10,000 hours of activity.

To compute depreciation expense under the activity method, the depreciation rate is determined as follows:

$$\text{Depreciation Rate} = \frac{\text{Cost} - \text{Residual Value}}{\text{Estimated Usage of the Asset}}$$

Next, depreciation expense is computed as follows:

$$\text{Depreciation Expense} = \text{Depreciation Rate} \times \text{Actual Usage of the Asset}$$

Example 11.1d shows the calculation of the depreciation expense for Troup Company based on an expected 10,000 hours of usage.

EXAMPLE 11.1d Depreciation Based on Activity

Year	Activity Level (hours)	×	Depreciation Rate per hour[a]	=	Depreciation Expense	Accumulated Depreciation at Year-End	Book Value at Year-End[c]
2015	2,100	×	$10	=	$ 21,000	$ 21,000	$99,000
2016	2,500	×	$10	=	25,000	46,000	74,000
2017	2,300	×	$10	=	23,000	69,000	51,000
2018	1,800	×	$10	=	18,000	87,000	33,000
2019	1,000		—		13,000[b]	100,000	20,000
					$100,000		

[a] ($120,000 − $20,000) ÷ 10,000 hours = $10 per hour
[b] Amount necessary to reduce book value to residual value
[c] Cost ($120,000) minus accumulated depreciation at year-end

Note that, similar to the declining-balance method, an adjustment to depreciation expense is necessary toward the end of the asset's service life so that the book value of the asset will equal its estimated residual value.

Although an activity method is appropriate for many assets because their lives are limited by physical causes, it often is not used because of the difficulty of estimating the lifetime units of activity. Also, it would be a costly method to implement because of the need to measure and record the activity level of each asset each period. However, it is the method used for depletion, as we discuss later in the chapter.

Recording Depreciation

Regardless of the depreciation method used, the amount of depreciation expense is generally recorded each period of the asset's service life by making the following journal entry:[7]

```
Depreciation Expense                    xxx
    Accumulated Depreciation                    xxx
```

The credit entry is to a contra-asset account usually called Accumulated Depreciation, or Allowance for Depreciation. A company maintains a separate contra-asset account for each class of asset and should deduct this amount on its balance sheet directly from the cost of that asset class. Alternatively, the company may report the net book value on the balance sheet and disclose the cost and accumulated depreciation in the notes to its financial statements. However, many companies combine all the accumulated depreciation amounts and report only the total, a minimal disclosure that is allowed by GAAP.

While depreciation is normally reported as a current-period expense, a manufacturing company may not expense all its depreciation cost in the period but instead include it as part of manufacturing overhead. **A manufacturing company includes depreciation on manufacturing assets as a cost of inventory by allocating depreciation to each unit of production during the year by increasing the Work-in-Process Inventory account.** The portion of the total depreciation allocated to the units sold appears in the company's income statement as part of the cost of goods sold (and not separately as depreciation expense). Consequently, any depreciation included in the cost of the units produced but not sold remains in the inventory accounts (Work-in-Process or Finished Goods) on the company's balance sheet. Therefore, when a company sells in the current period units produced in previous periods, its cost of goods sold includes some depreciation from previous periods. For example, **Starbucks** reports total depreciation and amortization expense of $933.8 million on its statement of cash flows but only reports $893.9 million of depreciation and amortization expense on its income statement. The difference of $39.9 million is related to roasting and production equipment that is included in cost of sales.

GOT IT?

11-4 What is the *depreciation base*?

11-5 Under what circumstances are straight-line and accelerated methods of depreciation most appropriate?

11-6 A company should use an accelerated depreciation method because of the large decline in the fair value of an asset early in its life. Evaluate this statement.

11-7 Explain how recording depreciation expense affects a company's (a) income statement, (b) balance sheet, and (c) statement of cash flows.

11-8 Under what circumstances is an asset's total depreciation amount not included in a company's current income statement?

---

[7] After the estimated service life of the asset has expired, a company may continue to use the asset. However, because the asset is fully depreciated, no further depreciation expense is recognized.

LEARNING OBJECTIVE 11.3

Explain the conceptual issues regarding depreciation methods.

CONCEPTUAL EVALUATION OF DEPRECIATION METHODS

Depreciation (as well as depletion and amortization) is a process of cost allocation, not asset valuation. The purpose of depreciation is to allocate the cost of an asset to expense in a systematic and rational manner. Although depreciating an asset reduces its book value to reflect the usage of the asset and the decline in the asset's service potential, it is not an attempt to measure and report the fair value of the asset. The asset's book value should represent fair value both at the time the asset is acquired (acquisition cost should reflect fair value) and at the end of the asset's life, when residual value represents the disposal value. During the asset's life, book value will not necessarily equal fair value; however, if fair value is materially lower than net book value, the asset's value must be written down to fair value with an impairment charge (discussed later in the chapter). In addition, depreciation is *not* an attempt to provide funds for the replacement of the asset. Over the life of the asset, accumulated depreciation is merely the sum of the asset's cost that has been expensed.[8]

A company may use any of the previously discussed depreciation methods. While the majority of companies use the straight-line depreciation method because of its simplicity, several other items should be considered in selecting a depreciation method.

Financial Statement Effects

The choice of a particular depreciation method can have a significant impact on a company's income and assets, as you can see by comparing the various depreciation expense amounts and the book value of the asset computed for Troup Company. **Example 11.1e** illustrates these differences.

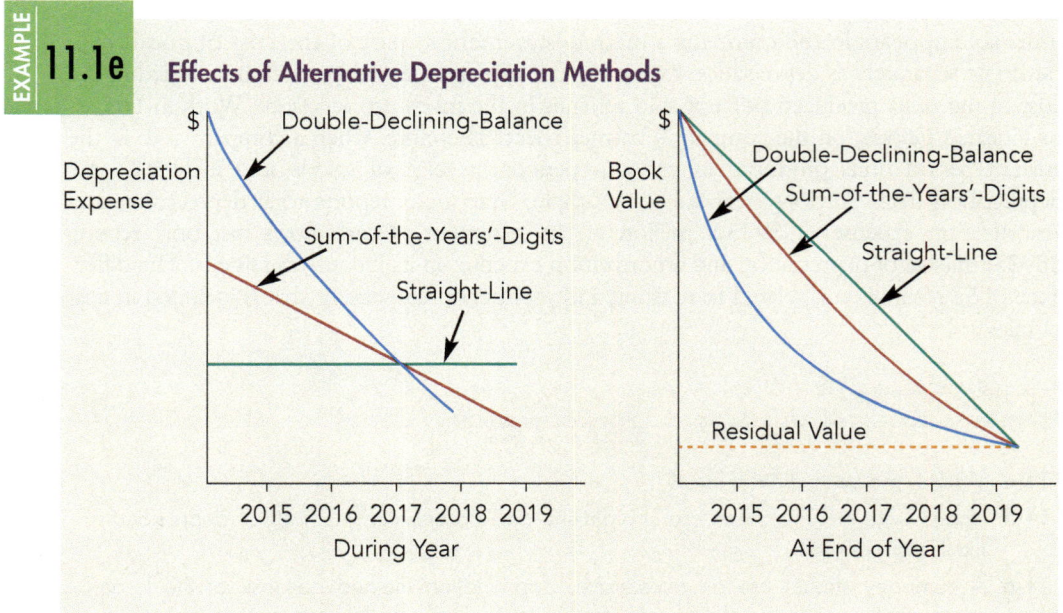

EXAMPLE 11.1e Effects of Alternative Depreciation Methods

While the total amount of depreciation expense over the life of the asset is the same under each method, the yearly amounts of depreciation expense are different. For example, in the early years of an asset's life, the use of the straight-line method results in a smaller amount of reported depreciation expense and a higher reported income relative to the accelerated methods. This situation is reversed in later years. Similarly, in the early

---

[8] Depreciation expense is a tax-deductible expense that produces an income tax savings over the life of an asset. However, the tax savings over the life of the asset will not be sufficient to replace the asset. Depreciation for income taxes is discussed in Appendix 11.1.

years of an asset's life, the use of the straight-line method results in a higher book value of assets relative to the accelerated methods. Financial statement users should understand these relationships to properly compare financial information of companies that use different depreciation methods.

In addition, the depreciation of property, plant, and equipment may make comparisons of the rate of return on assets more difficult. For example, recording depreciation causes the rate of return on total assets (income before financing charges divided by average assets) to increase over time. Refer back to the Troup Company example using the straight-line depreciation method in **Example 11.1a**. Suppose, in addition, that Troup has no interest expense, that net income after depreciation and income taxes is $12,000 per year, and that the company owns only this one asset. The rate of return earned by the company increases each year as shown in **Example 11.2**.

EXAMPLE 11.2

Effect of Depreciation on Rate of Return

Year	Net Income	÷	Average Book Value of Assets	=	Rate of Return
2015	$12,000	÷	$110,000	=	10.9%
2016	12,000	÷	90,000	=	13.3
2017	12,000	÷	70,000	=	17.1
2018	12,000	÷	50,000	=	24.0
2019	12,000	÷	30,000	=	40.0

The increase in the rate of return over the life of the asset would be even more dramatic if an accelerated depreciation method were used. As a result of this relationship, a user should always be careful when analyzing the rate of return. Comparisons between companies with different aged assets can be complicated due to the effect that depreciation has on the rate of return on assets. This is also true when comparing the same company over time – e.g., its rate of return on assets will increase as its asset base gets older.

Other Factors

Two additional factors that are often considered when a company selects a depreciation method are:

- repair and maintenance costs
- the risk associated with the cash flows from the asset

A company often considers the selection of the depreciation method together with the expected repair and maintenance costs associated with the asset. For example, if a company expects consistent repair and maintenance costs over an asset's life, straight-line depreciation may be appropriate as this may imply that the decline in service potential of the asset will remain consistent each period. The use of the straight-line depreciation method and constant repairs and maintenance will result in a consistent total cost (depreciation expense plus repair and maintenance cost) each period. Alternatively, if a company expects increasing repair and maintenance costs over time, the asset might be a good candidate for an accelerated depreciation method as more of the asset's value is consumed early in its life and more repair and maintenance is consumed late in its life. The use of an accelerated depreciation method coupled with increasing repair and maintenance costs may produce a consistent total cost each period. However, repair and maintenance costs would have to increase significantly to offset the decreasing depreciation expense amounts. These two situations are illustrated in Exhibit 11.1 (p. 11-12).

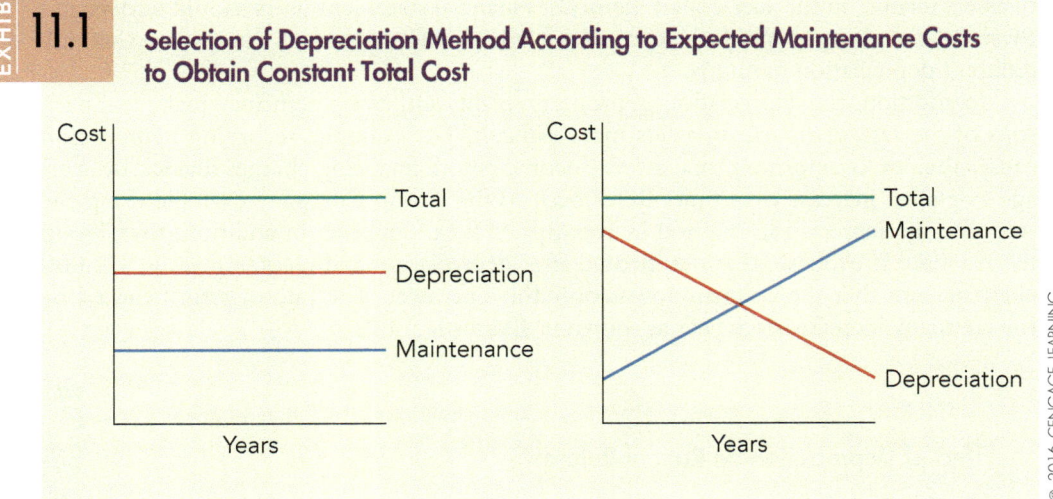

EXHIBIT 11.1 Selection of Depreciation Method According to Expected Maintenance Costs to Obtain Constant Total Cost

Alternatively, a company may expect the service potential of the asset to decline each year for the life of the asset and the repair and maintenance costs to be constant each period or to not rise as fast as the depreciation expense declines. In this case, a declining total cost will be achieved by using an accelerated depreciation method.

In periods of rapid technological change, an asset may become obsolete before the end of its originally estimated useful life. Therefore, there is a greater risk associated with the estimated cash flows produced by the asset near the end of its life than for those at the beginning. Use of an accelerated depreciation method may be appropriate in such situations because the lower depreciation expense recorded late in the asset's life would be consistent with the greater risk that the estimated cash flows will not be realized.

WHY IT MATTERS

While most U.S. companies use the straight-line depreciation method for at least a portion of their assets, they use varying estimates of service lives and residual values, which makes intercompany comparisons much more difficult. However, the required disclosures can be used by analysts to gain insights into a company's property, plant, and equipment. Two useful measures that can be computed are the average age and average useful life of a company's fixed assets.

Consider the following data from **Starbucks**'s and **Panera Bread**'s 2014 annual report.

	Starbucks		Panera Bread	
(in millions)	2014	2013	2014	2013
Gross Property, Plant, and Equipment (excluding Land and Construction in Progress)*	$8,118.8	$7,392.7	$1,369.2	$1,176.3
Accumulated Depreciation	5,062.1	4,581.6	683.3	590.9
Depreciation Expense	700.9	613.7	115.4	97.2
Depreciation Method	Straight-Line		Straight-Line	

*These amounts are excluded because land is not depreciated and no depreciation is taken on self-constructed assets until they are placed in service.

(continued)

Based on the information above, the average useful life of Starbucks's and Panera Bread's property, plant, and equipment can be computed as:[9]

Starbucks:

$$\frac{\text{Average}}{\text{Useful Life}} = \frac{\text{Average Depreciable Assets}}{\text{Depreciation Expense}} = \frac{(\$8{,}118.8 + \$7{,}392.7) \div 2}{\$700.9} = 11.07 \text{ years}$$

Panera Bread:

$$\frac{\text{Average}}{\text{Useful Life}} = \frac{\text{Average Depreciable Assets}}{\text{Depreciation Expense}} = \frac{(\$1{,}369.2 + \$1{,}176.3) \div 2}{\$115.4} = 11.03 \text{ years}$$

For Starbucks, this average useful life is consistent with the fact that the majority of its property, plant, and equipment relates to leasehold improvements that are depreciated over the term of the lease, which is generally 10 years. Similarly, for Panera Bread, the useful life is consistent with the fact that the majority of its assets are depreciated over a term of either 15–20 years (leasehold improvements) or 3–15 years (equipment).

In addition, the average age of Starbucks's property, plant, and equipment can be computed as follows:

$$\text{Average Age}_{2014} = \frac{\text{Accumulated Depreciation}}{\text{Depreciation Expense}} = \frac{\$5{,}062.1}{\$700.9} = 7.2 \text{ years}$$

$$\text{Average Age}_{2013} = \frac{\text{Accumulated Depreciation}}{\text{Depreciation Expense}} = \frac{\$4{,}581.6}{\$613.7} = 7.5 \text{ years}$$

Based on the above analysis, it appears that the average age of Starbucks's fixed assets has decreased during 2014. Similarly, Panera Bread's average age of its fixed assets decreased from 6.1 years to 5.9 years. Analysts may monitor this trend for three reasons. First, the age of a company's assets affects its competitive position because old assets tend to be less efficient than newer assets. Second, the age of assets provides an indication of a company's capital replacement policy and assists analysts in estimating future capital expenditures. Third, all things being equal, a company's return on assets will increase as the company's assets get older, which may affect the company's perceived profitability.

GOT IT?

11-9 What is the objective of accounting for depreciation?

11-10 Does recording depreciation generate funds for the replacement of the asset? Explain.

11-11 Under U.S. GAAP, in a year in which the fair value of an asset rises, should a company record depreciation expense for that asset? Why?

11-12 The manager of a utility stated that since its transmission lines are kept in good condition by regular repairs and maintenance and their efficiency remains constant, the lines do not depreciate. Do you agree with this statement?

---

[9] This formula assumes the use of the straight-line depreciation method and a salvage value of zero.

LEARNING OBJECTIVE 11.4
Understand group and composite depreciation methods.

WHAT ADDITIONAL DEPRECIATION METHODS EXIST?

In the previous section, depreciation expense was calculated for individual items of property, plant, and equipment, which could create a costly and time-consuming record-keeping process for a company with a large number of depreciable assets. To simplify a company's record keeping, some companies use group or composite depreciation methods, which apply conceptually similar methods of depreciation to portfolios of assets. The choice of method depends on the nature of the assets being depreciated. **Group depreciation** is applied to *homogeneous* assets that are expected to have similar service lives and residual values (e.g., laptop computers). **Composite depreciation** is applied to *heterogeneous* assets that are related but have differing service lives and residual values (all the different items of equipment in a company's office).

The group and composite methods recognize that depreciation expense is based on estimates of service lives and residual values and that gains or losses on disposals of single assets are often immaterial. However, the major disadvantages of the two methods are that faulty estimates might be concealed for long periods and gains and losses may be deferred beyond the period in which they actually occurred.

Group Depreciation

A company uses group depreciation when it owns a group of homogeneous assets with similar ages, useful lives, and residual values. For example, a vehicle rental company may depreciate its fleet of rental cars using group depreciation. Under this method, the company:

- capitalizes the total cost of the assets into one account which is treated as one "asset" for purposes of depreciation
- bases the group depreciation rate on the average life of the assets in the group
- calculates the depreciation expense each period by multiplying this rate by the balance in the asset account
- accumulates the depreciation expense in a single contra-asset account

When an item in the group is retired, the company does not recognize a gain or loss on that item because the entire "asset" is not retired. Instead, it records the retirement of an item in the group by a credit to the asset account for the original cost and a debit to the Accumulated Depreciation account for the difference between the cost and the proceeds received. When the final unit in the group is retired, a net gain or loss on the group as a whole is recognized.

Example: Group Depreciation

Minneola Company purchases 10 cars for $20,000 each, and the average expected service life is 3 years with a residual value of $5,000 each. Of those cars, three are sold after 2 years for $8,000 each, five after 3 years for $6,000 each, and two after 4 years for $4,800 each. Minneola computes the group depreciation rate and depreciation expense as follows:

$$\text{Group Depreciation Rate} = \left(\frac{\text{Group Cost} - \text{Group Residual Value}}{\text{Average Life of Group Assets}}\right) \div \text{Group Cost}$$

$$= \left(\frac{\$200{,}000 - \$50{,}000}{3}\right) \div \$200{,}000$$

$$= \$50{,}000 \div \$200{,}000 = \underline{25\%}$$

Group Depreciation Expense = Group Cost × Group Depreciation Rate

Example 11.3 shows the journal entries used to record these events.

> **EXAMPLE 11.3**
>
> **Journal Entries for Group Depreciation**
>
> 1. To record the purchase:
>
> | | | |
> |---|---|---|
> | Cars | 200,000 | |
> | Cash | | 200,000 |
>
> 2. To record the first year's depreciation expense:
>
> | | | |
> |---|---|---|
> | Depreciation Expense (25% × $200,000) | 50,000 | |
> | Accumulated Depreciation | | 50,000 |
>
> 3. To record the second year's depreciation expense:
>
> | | | |
> |---|---|---|
> | Depreciation Expense (25% × $200,000) | 50,000 | |
> | Accumulated Depreciation | | 50,000 |
>
> 4. To record the disposal of three cars at the end of the second year for $8,000 each:
>
> | | | |
> |---|---|---|
> | Cash ($8,000 × 3) | 24,000 | |
> | Accumulated Depreciation | 36,000[a] | |
> | Cars ($20,000 × 3) | | 60,000 |
>
> 5. To record the third year's depreciation expense:
>
> | | | |
> |---|---|---|
> | Depreciation Expense [25% × ($200,000 − $60,000)] | 35,000 | |
> | Accumulated Depreciation | | 35,000 |
>
> 6. To record the disposal of five cars at the end of the third year for $6,000 each:
>
> | | | |
> |---|---|---|
> | Cash | 30,000 | |
> | Accumulated Depreciation | 70,000 | |
> | Cars | | 100,000 |
>
> 7. To record the depreciation expense for the fourth year, the disposal of two cars at the end of the fourth year for $4,800 each, and the *net* gain or loss of the *entire* group:
>
> | | | |
> |---|---|---|
> | Depreciation Expense | 1,000[b] | |
> | Accumulated Depreciation | | 1,000 |
> | Cash | 9,600 | |
> | Accumulated Depreciation | 30,000 | |
> | Loss on Disposal of Property, Plant, and Equipment | 400[c] | |
> | Cars | | 40,000 |
>
> [a] This adjustment to accumulated depreciation is the difference between the cost of the cars and the cash received from disposal. No gain or loss is recognized at this point.
> [b] Because assets are not depreciated below their residual value, the depreciation expense in the last year is the amount needed to reduce the $11,000 book value ($40,000 remaining cost minus $29,000 remaining accumulated depreciation) of the group to the estimated residual value (2 × $5,000).
> [c] The loss is equal to the proceeds of (2 × $4,800) minus the remaining book value of $10,000 ($40,000 − $30,000).

If Minneola purchases a new asset (i.e., more cars) before the group is retired, it computes a new depreciation rate by dividing the new depreciation base (book value at the beginning of the period plus the additional cost minus the estimated residual value of the group) by the new weighted average of the remaining lives of the assets in the group. Alternatively, Minneola could treat each year of car purchases as a separate group.

Composite Depreciation

A company may apply composite depreciation to heterogeneous (dissimilar) assets that are related but have different service lives or residual values. For example, consider a building that consists of the physical structure, a heating/ventilation/air conditioning (HVAC) system, and a roof that each have different useful lives. Composite depreciation may be used to depreciate this integrated asset instead of depreciating each asset separately. Similar to group depreciation, composite depreciation:

- Combines the assets in one asset account and depreciates them accordingly.
- Uses one accumulated depreciation account.
- Does not recognize a gain or loss on each item retired.
- Recognizes a net gain or loss when it retires the final asset.

Example: Composite Depreciation

Granville Company purchases three assets with the following characteristics:

Asset	Cost	Residual Value	Life	Annual Depreciation
A	$25,000	$5,000	10 years	$2,000
B	13,000	1,000	6 years	2,000
C	12,000	—	4 years	3,000
	$50,000	$6,000		$7,000

Assuming that Granville uses straight-line depreciation, it computes the composite depreciation rate as follows:

$$\text{Composite Depreciation Rate} = \text{Annual Depreciation Expense} \div \text{Cost} = \frac{\$7,000}{\$50,000} = 14\%$$

Depreciation expense is then computed as:

$$\text{Composite Depreciation Expense} = \text{Cost of Assets Remaining in Service} \times \text{Composite Depreciation Rate}$$

For Granville, depreciation expense is $7,000 ($50,000 × 0.14). It would continue this process until the book value equals the estimated residual value of $6,000. If the Granville purchases another asset, it may include the asset in the group by adding the cost to the asset account. It then calculates a new composite depreciation rate. ■

INTERNATIONAL DIMENSION

DEPRECIATION

The basic accounting for depreciation is essentially the same under IFRS and U.S. GAAP with both sets of standards allowing the use of the same depreciation methods (straight-line; sum-of-the-years'-digits; declining-balance). However, some differences do exist:

- IFRS require that the estimated useful lives and residual values of the assets, and the depreciation method, be reviewed at least once a year. U.S. GAAP only requires this review when events or circumstances indicate that the estimate has changed.

(continued)

- When an operating asset is made up of individual components that are significant with respect to the total cost of the item (e.g., an airplane and its engines), IFRS require that the initial cost of the operating asset be allocated to the significant components and each component be depreciated separately. For example, an airplane and its engines would be separately capitalized and the airplane is depreciated separately from the engines. This is called **component depreciation**. Under U.S. GAAP, companies are permitted to use component depreciation; however, it is rarely used in practice.
- When a company writes the value of its property, plant, and equipment up to fair value under the revaluation model discussed in Chapter 10, the revalued amount is used to compute subsequent depreciation expense. This issue does not exist under U.S. GAAP as it does not allow upward revaluations of property, plant, and equipment.
- IFRS require that companies disclose the accumulated depreciation for each class of property, plant, and equipment, not just the total amount as allowed by U.S. GAAP.

IFRS Application Across-the-Pond (ATP), Inc., a commuter plane service, purchased an airplane for $80,000,000 on January 1, 2016. The plane is expected to have a service life of 25 years. ATP identified the following components and their service lives:

Component	Amount	Service Life
Frame	$40,000,000	25 years
Engine	30,000,000	10 years
Seats and Other	10,000,000	5 years

If the residual value of the components is zero and ATP uses straight-line depreciation, the amount of depreciation expense recorded in 2016 under IFRS and U.S. GAAP would be:

Component	Cost	Service Life	IFRS Depreciation Expense	U.S. GAAP Depreciation Expense
Frame	$40,000,000	25 years	$1,600,000	
Engine	30,000,000	10 years	3,000,000	
Seats and Other	10,000,000	5 years	2,000,000	
Total	$80,000,000	25 years	$6,600,000	$3,200,000

Under IFRS, ATP would recognize $6,600,000 of depreciation in the first year compared to $3,200,000 under U.S. GAAP. Therefore, all things being equal, ATP would report higher expenses, lower income, and a lower book value of property, plant, and equipment under IFRS. The use of component depreciation, while computationally similar to the computation of depreciation expense under U.S. GAAP, has the potential to result in significant differences relative to U.S. GAAP on a company's financial statements.

Source: IAS 16 (See Appendix C at the end of the book.)

GOT IT?

11-13 How would the upward revaluation of a company's property, plant, and equipment, allowed under IFRS, affect the amount of depreciation expense recorded?

11-14 Compare the group and composite methods of depreciation.

LEARNING OBJECTIVE 11.5
Understand the disclosure of depreciable assets.

HOW ARE DEPRECIABLE ASSETS DISCLOSED?

GAAP requires the following disclosures for depreciation:

- depreciation expense for the period
- balances of major classes of depreciable assets, by nature or function, at the balance sheet date
- accumulated depreciation, either by major classes of depreciable assets or in total, at the balance sheet date
- a general description of the method or methods used in computing depreciation with respect to major classes of depreciable assets[10]

Real Report 11.1 shows the disclosure of these items for **Panera Bread**. Panera Bread reports $106.523 million of depreciation and amortization expense for 2013 in its statement of cash flows, of which $97.2 million was depreciation expense.

11.1 DISCLOSURE OF DEPRECIABLE ASSETS — REAL REPORT

Panera Bread

Notes to Consolidated Financial Statements (in part)

Note 2. Summary of Significant Accounting Policies (in part):

Property, Plant, and Equipment (in part)
Property, equipment, leasehold improvements, and land are stated at cost less accumulated depreciation. Depreciation is provided using the straight-line method over the estimated useful lives of the assets. Leasehold improvements are depreciated using the straight-line method over the shorter of their estimated useful lives or the related reasonably assured lease term. Costs incurred in connection with the development of internal-use software are capitalized in accordance with the accounting standard for internal use software, and are amortized over the expected useful life of the software. The estimated useful lives used for financial statement purposes are:

Leasehold improvements	15–20 years
Machinery and equipment	3–15 years
Furniture and fixtures	2–7 years
Computer hardware and software	3–5 years

Note 7: Property, and Equipment, net (in thousands)

	Dec. 31, 2013	Dec. 25, 2012
Leasehold improvements	$ 607,472	$ 542,081
Machinery and equipment	305,060	265,350
Furniture and fixtures	149,445	130,044
Computer hardware and software	87,316	63,701
Construction in progress	80,108	53,189
Smallwares	27,031	25,152
Land	2,856	2,201
	$1,259,288	$1,081,718
Less: Accumulated depreciation	(589,879)	(509,964)
Property, plant, and equipment, net	$ 669,409	$ 571,754

The Company recorded depreciation expense related to these assets of $97.2 million, $82.7 million, and $74.2 million for the fiscal years ended December 31, 2013, December 25, 2012, and December 27, 2011, respectively.

Suggested answers to these questions are found at the end of the chapter.

Questions:

1. Why do you think Panera Bread selected the straight-line depreciation method?
2. Why does Panera Bread disclose information about the estimates (e.g., useful lives) used in its depreciation calculations?

---

[10] FASB ASC 360-10-50: Property, Plant, and Equipment: Overall: Disclosure.

> **GOT IT?**
>
> **11-15** What disclosures of depreciation are required in a company's financial statements and the accompanying notes?

WHAT ARE SOME ADDITIONAL ISSUES RELATED TO DEPRECIATION?

LEARNING OBJECTIVE 11.6
Understand additional depreciation issues, including partial period depreciation, changes and corrections of depreciation, and depreciation and accretion of asset retirement obligations.

In addition to the previous discussion, there are several special issues related to depreciation that you need to understand:

- depreciation for partial periods
- changes and corrections of depreciation
- depreciation and accretion of asset retirement obligations

Depreciation for Partial Periods

While our previous discussion assumed that assets were purchased on the first day of the fiscal year and disposed of on the last day, this seldom occurs in practice. When acquisition and disposal of assets occur throughout the year, a company should record depreciation expense only for the portion of the year that the asset was used in the operation of the business. While depreciation expense could be computed to the nearest day, such precision is unnecessary given the use of estimates in its calculation. Therefore, three common alternative policies, or conventions, are used to compute depreciation expense for partial periods.

Nearest Whole Month Convention Under the **nearest whole month convention**, assets placed in service on or before the 15th of the month are depreciated for the whole month; assets placed in service after the 15th are *not* depreciated until the next month. Similarly, assets sold on or before the 15th are *not* depreciated for the month; assets sold after the 15th are depreciated for the whole month. Depreciation expense is then based on the fraction of the year (in whole months) the asset is used.

Example: Depreciation to the Nearest Whole Month

Vann Company purchases and places in service a $6,000 asset with a 3-year life and no residual value on August 18. If Vann uses the nearest whole month convention, it should record 4 months (September through December) of depreciation expense in the first year, 12 months of depreciation expense in the second and third years, and 8 months (January through August) of depreciation expense in the fourth year. If Vann uses the straight-line method, it computes depreciation expense as shown in **Example 11.4a**.

EXAMPLE 11.4a

Partial Period Depreciation: Straight-Line

Yearly Depreciation = $6,000 ÷ 3 years = $2,000.

Fiscal Year	Annual Depreciation	Months	Computation	Depreciation Expense
1	$2,000	4	4/12 × $2,000	$ 667
2	2,000	12	12/12 × $2,000	2,000
3	2,000	12	12/12 × $2,000	2,000
4	—	8	8/12 × $2,000	1,333
	$6,000			$6,000

The straight-line calculation is relatively straightforward. Accelerated depreciation methods use similar computations, but they are slightly more complicated, because they allocate the annual amount of depreciation expense into adjacent fiscal years based on the number of months. If Vann uses the *sum-of-the-years'-digits depreciation* method, depreciation expense in each fiscal year is computed as shown in **Example 11.4b**.

EXAMPLE 11.4b Partial Period Depreciation: Sum-of-the-Years'-Digits

Fiscal Year	Annual Depreciation[a]	Months	Computation	Fiscal Year Depreciation Expense
1	$3,000	4	4/12 × $3,000	$1,000
2	2,000	12	(8/12 × $3,000) + (4/12 × $2,000)	2,667
3	1,000	12	(8/12 × $2,000) + (4/12 × $1,000)	1,667
4	—	8	8/12 × $1,000	666[b]
	$6,000			$6,000

[a] Annual depreciation is computed as $6,000 × n/6, where n is the number of years remaining in the asset's life as of the beginning of the year.
[b] Adjusted for $1 rounding error

If Vann Company uses the *double-declining-balance method*, it will calculate annual depreciation and allocate this amount to each fiscal year on the basis of the number of months. This procedure is shown in **Example 11.4c**.

EXAMPLE 11.4c Partial Period Depreciation: Double-Declining-Balance

Fiscal Year	Annual Depreciation[a]	Months	Computation	Fiscal Year Depreciation Expense
1	$4,000	4	4/12 × $4,000	$1,333
2	1,333	12	(8/12 × $4,000) + (4/12 × $1,333)	3,111
3	667	12	(8/12 × $1,333) + (4/12 × $667)	1,111
4	—	8	8/12 × $667	445
	$6,000			$6,000

[a] Annual depreciation is computed as the book value of the equipment at the beginning of the period × the declining-balance rate of 66.67% (1/3 × 2).

Nearest Whole Year Convention Under the **nearest whole year convention**, any assets placed in service during the first 6 months of the year are depreciated for the entire year, and assets placed in service during the second 6 months are not depreciated for that year. Similarly assets disposed of during the first 6 months of a year are not depreciated for that year, while assets disposed of during the last 6 months of a year are depreciated for an entire year. Using the same example, with the straight-line deprecation method there is no depreciation expense recorded in the first fiscal year because the asset was placed in service in the second half of the year. However, the company records a full year of depreciation expense in each of the next 3 years. Under the sum-of-the-years'-digits method, depreciation expense in the 4 fiscal years is $0, $3,000, $2,000, and $1,000, respectively. For the double-declining-balance method, depreciation expense in the 4 fiscal years is $0, $4,000, $1,333, and $667, respectively.

One-Half Year Convention Under the **one-half year convention**, all assets placed in service or sold during the fiscal year are considered to have been placed in service or sold at the midpoint of the year. Therefore, a company would record one-half year's depreciation expense in the year of acquisition and one-half year's depreciation expense in the year of disposal. Using the same information above, Vann Company would compute depreciation expense for each fiscal year for each depreciation method as shown in **Example 11.5**.

EXAMPLE 11.5

Partial Period Depreciation: One-Half Year Convention

Straight-Line

Fiscal Year	Annual Depreciation	Computation	Depreciation Expense
1	$2,000	1/2 × $2,000	$1,000
2	2,000	$2,000	2,000
3	2,000	$2,000	2,000
4	—	1/2 × $2,000	1,000
	$6,000		$6,000

Sum-of-the-Years'-Digits

Fiscal Year	Annual Depreciation	Computation	Depreciation Expense
1	$3,000	1/2 × $3,000	$1,500
2	2,000	(1/2 × $3,000) + (1/2 × $2,000)	2,500
3	1,000	(1/2 × $2,000) + (1/2 × $1,000)	1,500
4	—	1/2 × $1,000	500
	$6,000		$6,000

Double-Declining-Balance

Fiscal Year	Annual Depreciation	Computation	Depreciation Expense
1	$4,000	1/2 × $4,000	$2,000
2	1,333	(1/2 × $4,000) + (1/2 × $1,333)	2,667
3	667	(1/2 × $1,333) + (1/2 × $667)	1,000
4	—	1/2 × $667	333
	$6,000		$6,000

Changes and Corrections of Depreciation

As a result of changes in how the asset is used or the occurrence of economic events, companies may change their depreciation estimates and/or depreciation methods. In addition, companies may make errors in calculating depreciation expense which must be corrected. We give a brief discussion here and discuss these situations more fully in Chapter 22.

Change in Estimate Depreciation expense is based on estimates of service life and residual value. As new or additional information becomes available, a company may find it necessary to revise its estimates of service life, residual value, or both. The change of these estimates will result in a recalculation of depreciation expense, which is accounted for prospectively. A company allocates the remaining book value of the asset at the beginning of the year of the change over the new remaining life, considering the new residual value.

Example In 2011, Kellman Company bought a machine for $200,000. At that time, Kellman estimated the machine would have a useful life of 10 years and a residual value of $20,000. Kellman uses the straight-line method of depreciation and depreciates the machine at a rate of $18,000 per year. On January 1, 2016, when the machine had a book value of $110,000, Kellman determined that the machine would have a remaining useful life of 4 years and a residual value of $10,000. For 2016 through 2019, Kellman would record depreciation expense of:

$$\text{Depreciation Expense} = \frac{\$110{,}000 - \$10{,}000}{4 \text{ years}} = \underline{\$25{,}000}$$ ■

Change in Depreciation Method A change in the depreciation method is also accounted for prospectively. However, this change requires a justification as to why the new method is preferable. For example, a company may change its depreciation method because of a change in the estimated future benefits expected from the asset. When a company changes its depreciation method, the company allocates the book value of the asset at the beginning of the year of the change over the remaining life (considering the residual value) using the new depreciation method. **This change is called a change in accounting estimate that is effected by a change in accounting principle.**[11]

Correction of an Error A correction of an error in depreciation is accounted for as a prior period adjustment. The effect on the current period's financial statements involves a correction to the amount in the accumulated depreciation account and an adjustment to retained earnings (net of income taxes) for the amount of the error in previously reported net income. The company's previous financial statements are also corrected (restated).

Depreciation and Accretion Related to Asset Retirement Obligations

As discussed in Chapter 10, the acquisition and use of operating assets may create an asset retirement obligation (ARO), which is a legal obligation related to the retirement of an asset. The fair value of this obligation is initially recognized as a liability with an offsetting increase in the carrying value of the related asset. In subsequent periods, the asset is depreciated over its service life. In addition, the company recognizes accretion expense and increases the asset retirement obligation each year it uses the asset. Accretion expense is classified as an operating expense and results from the increase in the carrying value of the liability associated with the ARO. It is computed by multiplying the book value of the liability by the discount rate used to compute the original present value of the ARO. For example, as noted in Chapter 10, **Starbucks** has AROs related primarily to the future cost of removing leasehold improvements at the termination of its leases of retail store locations. Starbucks depreciates the cost associated with its ARO over the same term as its leasehold improvements, generally 10 years. While the ARO liability, reported as a long-term liability, has accreted to $60.1 million at the end of 2015, the ARO asset has depreciated to a net value of $5.8 million.

Example Continuing the example from Chapter 10, on January 1, Reed Company spent $100,000 in the interior redesign of a retail store which it had acquired through a 10-year lease. Reed recognized a $12,000 ARO related to this leasehold improvement. Reed depreciates this asset over 10 years using the straight-line method with no residual value. Reed would make the following entry at the end of the year to record depreciation expense:

Depreciation Expense ($112,000 ÷ 10)	11,200	
Accumulated Depreciation		11,200

---

[11] If a company has a policy of switching depreciation methods at a specific point in the service life of an asset, this is *not* considered to be a change in accounting estimate effected by a change in accounting principle.

In addition to this entry, Reed must recognize the increase in the present value of the ARO due to the passage of time. This increase is called **accretion expense**. Assuming a discount rate of 10%, Reed would make the following entry to recognize the accretion of the liability:

Accretion Expense ($12,000 × 10%)	1,200	
Asset Retirement Obligation		1,200

GOT IT?

11-16 Describe the accounting for changes and corrections of depreciation.

11-17 Why is it necessary to record depreciation expense for partial periods? Describe some common conventions that are used to compute partial period depreciation.

11-18 Explain the expenses that are recorded with respect to an asset retirement obligation.

HOW DO WE ACCOUNT FOR THE IMPAIRMENT OF PROPERTY, PLANT, AND EQUIPMENT?

LEARNING OBJECTIVE 11.7
Test for and account for the impairment of property, plant, and equipment.

Property, plant, and equipment is generally reported on the balance sheet at its historical cost minus accumulated depreciation. Because depreciation is a cost allocation process and does not attempt to measure fair value, situations may occur in which the future economic benefit or service potential of an asset decreases below its book value, which is called an **impairment** of an asset.

Measuring property, plant, and equipment properly has important implications for the financial statements. If the fair value of property, plant, and equipment is less than its book value, it could signal that a company's past earnings were overstated because it did not record sufficient depreciation expense in prior years. Therefore, to faithfully represent these assets' values would suggest that a company should write down these assets and recognize a loss. However, if a company writes down the asset by too much, future profits will be overstated because it would record too little depreciation expense in future years. In addition, the write-down itself may signal important information to market participants about the asset's future economic benefits.

GAAP requires that a company review its property, plant, and equipment for impairment whenever events or changes in circumstances indicate that the book value of the property, plant, and equipment may not be recoverable.[12] Examples of such events or changes in circumstances include the following:

- significant decrease in the fair value of the asset
- significant change in the way the asset is used
- significant change in the business or regulatory environment
- costs of constructing the asset that exceed the planned amount
- current-period operating loss
- negative cash flow from operating activities
- expectation that the asset will more likely than not (i.e., more than 50% chance) be sold or otherwise disposed of before the end of its useful life

The accounting for impairments depends on whether the asset is to be held and used or held for sale.

Impairment of Assets to Be Held and Used

After the company identifies events or circumstances that indicate that an asset to be held and used may be impaired, a company will apply the following 2-step procedure to measure and recognize the impairment loss:

- *Step 1. Recoverability Test.* To test for impairment, a company first groups the assets at the lowest level at which identifiable cash flows are largely independent of the cash flows of other groups of assets. (We will use the singular term "asset" to describe the group of assets identified by a company.) Next, a company estimates the future net cash flows expected to result from the use of the asset and its eventual sale. If the total undiscounted expected cash flows are less than the book value of the asset, the book value is not fully recoverable and the company must recognize an impairment loss. If the total undiscounted expected cash flows are greater than or equal to the book value of the asset, the company recognizes no impairment loss.
- *Step 2. Measurement of the Loss.* If the recoverability test indicates an impairment has occurred, **the company measures the impairment loss for an asset that it intends to hold and use as the difference between the asset's book value and its fair value.** The **fair value** is the amount at which the asset could be sold in an orderly transaction between market participants. If quoted market prices are not available, fair value may be measured as the present value of the expected future cash flows (present value techniques are discussed in the Time Value of Money Module). If a company uses present value to estimate fair value, the discount rate should be the rate of return that the company would require for a similar investment with similar risks. For example, this could be the discount rate used to evaluate capital budgeting projects.

Recording and Reporting the Loss When a company recognizes an impairment loss, it writes down the asset to reduce its book value to fair value (as shown in the example that follows). The company reports the impairment loss on the income statement as part of income from continuing operations and reports the reduced book value of the asset on the ending balance sheet. This reduced book value becomes the new "cost" used to compute the depreciation expense over the remaining life of the asset. **Once an asset has been written down, the asset may *not* be written back up if the fair value later increases.**

---

[12] FASB ASC 360-10-35: Property, Plant, and Equipment: Overall: Subsequent Measurement.

Example: Impairment Loss

On January 1, 2013, Hall Company purchased machinery for $3 million. The machinery is held for use and not for sale. Hall is depreciating the machinery over 10 years by the straight-line method to a zero residual value. Late in 2016, because of technological changes in the industry and reduced selling prices for its products, Hall believes that the machinery may be impaired and will have a remaining useful life of 5 years. To test for impairment, Hall estimates that the machinery will produce net cash flows of $300,000 each year for the next 5 years. In addition, Hall uses a discount rate of 16% to evaluate capital budgeting projects of similar risk. Hall tests for impairment and measures the loss as shown in **Example 11.6**.

EXAMPLE 11.6

Impairment Test

Step 1: Recoverability Test
December 31, 2016
Book value:
   Machinery cost $3,000,000
   Less: Accumulated depreciation
      (4 years × $300,000)   (1,200,000) $1,800,000

Undiscounted expected net cash flows (5 × $300,000)   1,500,000
Recoverability: Because $1,500,000 is less than $1,800,000, the company must recognize an impairment loss.

Step 2: Measurement of the Loss
Present Value of the Expected = $300,000 × 3.274294 ($n = 5$, $i = 0.16$ from Table 4
Net Cash Flows (fair value)   in the Time Value of Money Module)
                                = $982,288 (rounded)

Impairment Loss = $982,288 Fair Value − $1,800,000 Book Value
               = $(817,712)

Although GAAP does not specify how to record the write-down, it does indicate that the reduced book value of the asset becomes the new depreciable base. Therefore, we will record the impairment loss as an increase to accumulated depreciation. Hall records the loss as follows:

Loss on Impairment	817,712	
Accumulated Depreciation		817,712

Hall reports the $817,712 loss in income from continuing operations on its 2016 income statement, and the property, plant, and equipment at its fair value of $982,288 ($3,000,000 cost minus $2,017,712 accumulated depreciation) on its 2016 ending balance sheet. Hall will depreciate the remaining depreciable cost of the machinery ($982,288) over its remaining useful life of 5 years for an annual depreciation expense of $196,457.60 ($982,288 ÷ 5 years). ∎

Disclosures A company must disclose the following information in the year of the write-down and the next 2 years:

- description of the impaired asset and the circumstances leading to the impairment
- how the asset's fair value was determined
- amount of the loss
- income statement caption which includes the loss
- operating segment affected (if applicable)

ETHICAL DILEMMA

The fortunes of NetWorth, Inc., are in serious jeopardy. Several years ago, NetWorth was the high-technology darling of Wall Street with the business press constantly heaping praises on NetWorth's innovative business model and solid management team. However, the recession during the last 2 years and increasing competition has certainly dampened its future prospects. During the last 18 months, NetWorth has reported only one profitable quarter, and the Board of Directors is calling for a quick return to profitability. With current quarterly results looking disappointing, the CFO has called on you to perform an extensive analysis of all property, plant, and equipment items in an effort to identify the nonproductive assets and improve operational efficiency. After informing the CFO that preliminary results indicated an impairment loss of almost $700 million must be recognized, you are instructed to increase the impairment amount by $300 million and record a $1 billion impairment loss. When you question the increase in the impairment amount, you are told that upper management thought your estimates of the usefulness of the assets were overly optimistic and that they changed several of your estimates, including the discount rate used in measuring the impairment loss. Because the changes resulted in more conservative financial statements, the CFO was sure you would not object. What is your reaction?

Impairment of Assets Held for Sale

Property, plant, and equipment that a company *intends to sell* is reported at the lower of its book value or net realizable value (fair value minus the costs to sell). The use of net realizable value provides a more faithful representation of the cash flows that the company expects to receive from the sale of the assets. The company recognizes the impairment loss for the amount of the write-down from book value to the net realizable value. Notice that the computation of the impairment loss for held for sale assets, except for the inclusion of costs to sell, is similar to the calculation of the impairment loss for held and used assets. A company does not depreciate assets classified as held for sale, and they should be reported separately in the balance sheet from assets used in operations. Finally, property, plant, and equipment classified as held for sale that are not sold by the end of the period are valued at the lower of book value or net realizable value. Therefore, restoration of the impairment loss is permitted if the net realizable value increases. In this case, a company would recognize a gain to the extent of any previously recognized losses. Under no circumstances may the asset be revalued above the original carrying value. In summary, the impairment test can be summarized as shown in Exhibit 11.2.

Conceptual Evaluation of Asset Impairment

The recognition of an impairment loss is intended to enhance the usefulness of a company's financial statements by recording the loss in the period it is incurred and reporting productive assets at their fair value. Thus, the information is more relevant and helps users assess the return on investment, operating capability, and risk of the company.

However, GAAP allows for significant management flexibility. For example, GAAP does not require annual impairment testing. This gives management flexibility in deciding which assets to include in, and exclude from, each asset grouping. In addition, estimating future cash flows is subjective. For example, the company could use current or expected cost and volume information. Furthermore, the discount rate used to value the cash flows is a management choice. This flexibility could result in earnings management. For example, if the company has already incurred current-year losses, management might prefer to recognize as large an impairment loss as possible, thereby reducing the book value to the lowest possible amount. This would result in lower depreciation expense and higher net income in the future.

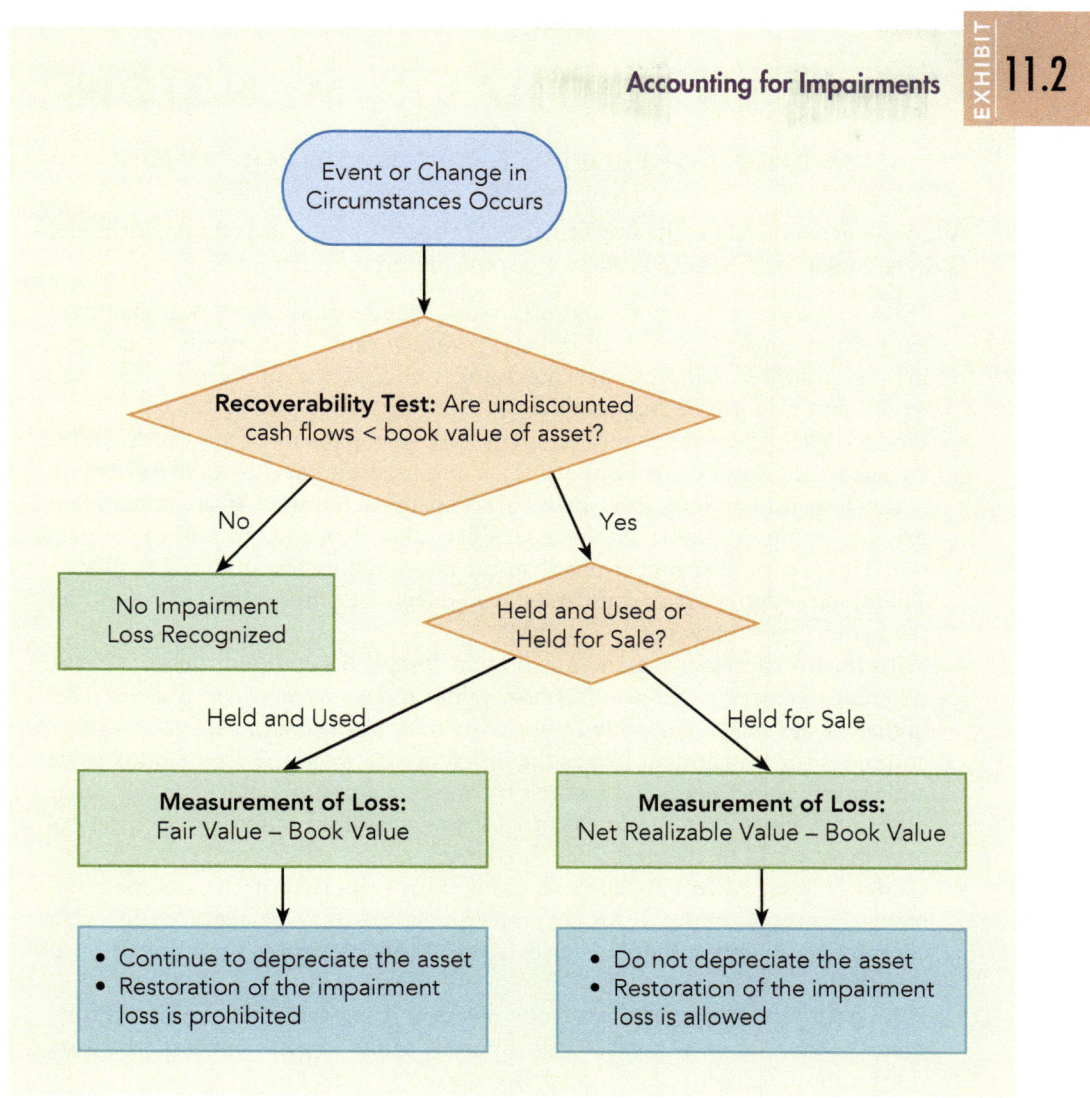

EXHIBIT 11.2 Accounting for Impairments

Four major concerns arise regarding the accounting for impairments:

- Some question whether the fair value of property, plant, and equipment is relevant for assets that will be held and used in normal operations because the asset is not going to be sold in the near term.
- Assuming fair value is relevant (and most believe it is), the cash flows expected by a company from using a specific asset are not necessarily the same as those used to determine the market value of the asset because the company may use the asset differently from other companies. Therefore, the specific cash flows may not result in a faithful representation of fair value.
- The use of undiscounted cash flows for the recoverability test ignores the time value of money.
- The impairment test may differ for identical assets simply because of the depreciation method or service life selected by a company. For example, an asset depreciated by an accelerated method will have a lower book value than one depreciated by the straight-line method. Because of this lower book value, the asset might not fail the recoverability test and, therefore, no impairment loss would be recognized. However, if a straight-line method were used, an impairment loss may have to be recognized.

INTERNATIONAL DIMENSION

IMPAIRMENT OF PROPERTY, PLANT, AND EQUIPMENT

Although accounting for the impairment of property, plant, and equipment under IFRS is similar to U.S. GAAP, there are some important differences.

- IFRS require a company to annually assess whether indicators of impairment exist. In contrast, U.S. GAAP requires a review only when events or changes in circumstances indicate that the book value of the property, plant, and equipment may not be recoverable.
- Under IFRS, there is no recoverability test (comparison of an asset's undiscounted cash flows to its book value) as required under U.S. GAAP. Instead, if the impairment indicators exist, a company determines if an impairment exists by using the higher of the asset's fair value (less costs to sell) or value in use. This is a more stringent test than the recoverabilty test under U.S. GAAP. Therefore, international companies will recognize impairment losses earlier than companies following U.S. GAAP.
- With regard to measuring the impairment loss, IFRS compute the loss as the difference between the asset's book value and its *recoverable amount* (the higher of the asset's fair value minus costs to sell or value in use). U.S. GAAP computes the impairment loss as the difference between the asset's book value and its *fair value*. Because an asset's recoverable amount and its fair value may differ, it is likely that the impairment losses measured under the two sets of principles would be different.
- Under U.S. GAAP, an impairment loss is always reported on the income statement. However, under IFRS, an impairment loss may be reported in other comprehensive income if it reverses a previously recognized upward revaluation of the asset.
- IFRS allow an impairment loss to be reversed if the value is recovered. However, the reversal cannot exceed the amount of the impairment loss (the asset value cannot exceed the original book value). U.S. GAAP does not allow reversal of impairment losses for held and used assets.

IFRS Application On January 1, 2014, Gundrum Company purchased machinery for $1,000,000 and uses the straight-line method of depreciation with a useful life of 5 years and no salvage value. Late in 2016, because of technological changes in the industry and reduced selling prices for its product, Gundrum believes the machinery may be impaired. The current book value of the equipment is $400,000. The asset is expected to generate future net cash flows of $420,000. The asset's fair value is determined to be $304,868 with costs to sell estimated to be $5,000. The impairment loss under IFRS would be $100,132.

Fair value	$304,868	
Less: Costs to sell	5,000	$299,868
Book value		400,000
Impairment loss		$100,132

(continued)

Under U.S. GAAP, there is no impairment loss recognized because the undiscounted cash flows ($420,000) are greater than the book value of the asset ($400,000). Therefore, while the impairment process is similar, measurement differences may still result.

Further, assume that at the beginning of 2018, when the book value of the equipment is $149,934, Gundrum determines that the recoverable amount of the machinery is $185,000. Under IFRS, Gundrum can reverse $35,066 ($185,000 − $149,934) of the previously recognized impairment loss.[13] Gundrum would make the following journal entry to record this reversal.

Machine	35,066	
Loss from Impairment		35,066

U.S. GAAP does not allow reversal of a previously recognized impairment loss.

Source: IAS 36 (See Appendix C at the end of the book.)

GOT IT?

11-19 Explain the meaning of an impaired asset and describe the proper accounting for impaired assets.

11-20 How do IFRS differ from U.S. GAAP in regard to determining if an asset is impaired? What are the implications of this difference?

HOW DO WE ACCOUNT FOR THE DISPOSAL OF PROPERTY, PLANT, AND EQUIPMENT?

LEARNING OBJECTIVE 11.8
Explain how to account for the disposal of property, plant, and equipment.

A company may dispose of property, plant, and equipment by sale, involuntary conversion, abandonment, or exchange. When a disposal occurs, a company recognizes a gain or a loss on the disposal for the difference between the book value of the asset (cost minus accumulated depreciation) and the consideration received. A gain or loss arises because depreciation is a cost allocation process, and its application does not result in the asset being reported at its market value. Therefore, the gain or loss may be considered a correction of the income that has been recorded in the years the asset has been owned. The gain or loss on disposal is normally reported in income from continuing operations in the "Other Income and Expense" category. However, it could be reported as a disposal of a component of a business if it meets the appropriate criteria, as discussed in Chapter 5.

To account for the disposal of property, plant, and equipment, the company first records the depreciation up to the date of the disposal. It then removes the cost of the asset and the related amount of accumulated depreciation from the respective accounts.

Example: Disposal of Machine

Bean Company has a machine that originally cost $10,000, has accumulated depreciation of $7,000 at the beginning of the current year, and is being depreciated at

---

[13] The reversal of the impairment loss cannot increase the book value of the asset above what it would have been had no impairment been previously recognized. In this situation, the reversal of the impairment loss could not increase the machine above $200,000 ($400,000 book value at December 31, 2016, minus $200,000 depreciation in 2017).

$1,000 per year. If the company sells the machine for $1,200 on September 30, it must first depreciate the machine up to the disposal date as follows:

Depreciation Expense	750	
Accumulated Depreciation		750

Once the book value is up to date, the company compares the new book value ($2,250) to the proceeds ($1,200) to determine the gain or loss. Bean records the $1,050 loss ($1,200 − $2,250) as follows:

Cash	1,200	
Accumulated Depreciation	7,750	
Loss on Disposal of Property, Plant, and Equipment	1,050	
Machine		10,000

A company would account for an involuntary disposal, such as when an asset is destroyed by fire, flood, or earthquake or when an asset (such as land) is expropriated by a governmental unit, in the same way.[14] An abandonment is also handled in a similar way, except that there is no receipt of cash, so the loss is equal to the remaining book value. Finally, it is common for a company to develop a plan to dispose of an asset before the actual sale occurs. If the asset meets certain criteria,[15] the asset is considered "held for sale" and no further depreciation is taken. Real Report 11.2 shows the impairment and disposal disclosures of **McDonald's Corporation**.

11.2 IMPAIRMENT AND DISPOSAL DISCLOSURES — REAL REPORT

McDonald's Corporation

Notes to Consolidated Financial Statements (in part)

Note 2. Summary of Significant Accounting Policies (in part):

Long-lived Assets (in part)
Long-lived assets are reviewed for impairment annually in the fourth quarter and whenever events or changes in circumstances indicate that the carrying amount of an asset may not be recoverable. If an indicator of impairment (e.g., negative operating cash flows for the most recent trailing 24-month period) exists for any grouping of assets, an estimate of undiscounted future cash flows produced by each individual restaurant within the asset grouping is compared to its carrying value. If an individual restaurant is determined to be impaired, the loss is measured by the excess of the carrying amount of the restaurant over its fair value as determined by an estimate of discounted future cash flows.

Suggested answers to these questions are found at the end of the chapter.

Questions:

1. How often does McDonald's review its long-lived assets for impairment?
2. With regard to impairments, how does McDonald's measure fair value, and how would this measurement be classified in the fair value hierarchy (Level 1, 2 or 3)?

---

[14] GAAP requires that a gain or loss be recognized when a nonmonetary asset is converted to a monetary asset, even though the company reinvests or is obligated to reinvest the monetary asset in replacement of the nonmonetary asset (FASB ASC 605-40-25: Revenue Recognition: Gains and Losses: Recognition).

[15] These criteria include: (1) management commits to a plan to sell the asset, (2) the asset is available for immediate sale in its present condition, (3) an active effort to locate a buyer is underway, (4) the sale is expected to be completed within 1 year, (5) the selling price of the asset is reasonable, and (6) it is unlikely that the plan of sale will be significantly modified or withdrawn (FASB ASC 360-10-45: Property, Plant, and Equipment: Overall: Other Presentation Matters).

INTERNATIONAL DIMENSION

DISPOSALS OF PROPERTY, PLANT, AND EQUIPMENT

While both IFRS and U.S. GAAP generally measure the gain or loss on disposal as the difference between the asset's book value and the amount received from its sale, this calculation may be slightly different if a company chooses to use the revaluation method and the asset has been written up to fair value, which is only possible under IFRS. Specifically,

- The revaluation surplus should be transferred out of Accumulated Other Comprehensive Income and into Retained Earnings. Under no circumstances can this revaluation surplus be transferred to income.

IFRS Application On January 1, 2015, Danielson Company sold a machine with a book value of $60,000 to Marinelli Company for $70,000. In addition, Danielson had previously revalued the machine to a basis of $180,000, resulting in a $30,000 revaluation surplus. Danielson would record the sale by making the following journal entries:

To record the sale:		
Cash	70,000	
Accumulated Depreciation ($180,000 − $60,000)	120,000	
Machine		180,000
Gain on Disposal of Property, Plant, and		
Equipment ($70,000 − $60,000)		10,000
To remove the revaluation surplus:		
Revaluation Surplus	30,000	
Retained Earnings		30,000

GOT IT?

11-21 How does a company account for the disposal of an asset? How does it report gains and losses on its financial statements?

HOW IS DEPLETION RECORDED?

LEARNING OBJECTIVE 11.9
Understand and record depletion of natural resources.

Natural resources, such as timber, coal deposits, oil and gas reserves, and mineral deposits make up an important part of the productive assets for many companies. For example, at the end of 2013, **BP** had oil and gas properties of over $90 billion, representing approximately 30% of its total assets. Similar to other productive assets, the cost of natural resources is allocated as an expense to each period in which the natural resource provides economic benefits to the company. The allocation of the cost of a natural resource to the periods in which benefits are received is called **depletion**. Although the terminology is different, depletion of natural resources is the same concept as depreciation of property, plant, and equipment. Unlike other productive assets, however, the natural resource is physically consumed as it is used by the company and can only be replaced or restored by an act of nature.

A company determines the cost of natural resources by the same principles used for property, plant, and equipment. Specifically, any expenditure to obtain the rights to the natural resource and bring it to a condition in which it can be used is capitalized as part of the cost of a natural resource. These costs include:

- **Acquisition costs**—amounts paid to acquire the rights to a search for an undiscovered natural resource or to use a discovered resource.
- **Exploration costs**—expenditures, such as drilling a well or excavating a mine, incurred to search for a natural resource.
- **Intangible development costs**—expenditures incurred after the resource is discovered but before production begins that are necessary for production of the resource. These costs include costs for drilling, tunnels, shafts, and wells.
- **Restoration costs** (or **reclamation costs**)—costs incurred to restore a natural resource to its natural state. These costs represent an asset retirement obligation and are added to the cost of the natural resource. The accounting for asset retirement obligations was discussed earlier.

Note that companies often incur costs for equipment or other tangible assets that are necessary for the production of the resource. These tangible development costs are *not* usually included as part of the cost of the natural resource. Instead, these costs are recorded in separate accounts and depreciated over their service life. If the tangible asset cannot be moved and has no alternative future use, it is depreciated over its service life or the life of the natural resource, whichever is shorter.

Because the usefulness of the natural resource is related to the amount of the resource extracted, a company usually records depletion using an activity method. The activity measure is the number of units of the resource that the company expects to extract over the life of the asset. A unit depletion rate is calculated as follows:

$$\text{Unit Depletion Rate} = \frac{\text{Cost} - \text{Residual Value}}{\text{Estimated Recoverable Units}}$$

Next, depletion for a period is calculated as follows:

$$\text{Depletion} = \text{Unit Depletion Rate} \times \text{Units Recovered}$$

As the company recovers the natural resource, it reduces the natural resource and adds the amount of depletion to an inventory account.[16] As the natural resource is sold, the company recognizes an expense, Cost of Goods Sold, related to the asset and reduces the Inventory account. Thus, Cost of Goods Sold only includes the units of the natural resource that are sold, while ending inventory consists of the units on hand at the end of the period.

Example Reggio Company purchases land for $3,000,000 from which it expects to extract 1,000,000 tons of coal, the estimated residual value is $200,000, and it mines 80,000 tons of coal in the first year. It calculates the depletion for that year as follows:

$$\text{Unit Depletion Rate} = (\$3,000,000 - \$200,000) \div 1,000,000 \text{ tons} = \underline{\$2.80 \text{ per ton}}$$

$$\text{Depletion for Year} = \$2.80 \times 80,000 \text{ tons} = \underline{\$224,000}$$

Reggio makes the following journal entry to record the depletion:

Inventory (Coal)	224,000	
Coal Mine		224,000

Assuming that Reggio sells 70,000 tons of coal in the current year, it would make the following entry related to depletion:

Cost of Goods Sold (70,000 tons × $2.80 per ton)	196,000	
Inventory (Coal)		196,000

---

[16] The use of a contra-account, Accumulated Depletion, is also acceptable although it is common.

The nature of natural resources is such that additional capital expenditures may be made in future periods. In addition, the estimation of the remaining number of units is often uncertain and therefore subject to revision based on new geological or scientific information. When a company incurs additional capital expenditures or revises estimated production, it must calculate a new depletion rate. The new depletion rate is based on the current book value of the asset (including the additional capital expenditures), the new estimate of the residual value, and the new estimate of the remaining units as of the beginning of the year.

Example Continuing the preceding example, suppose that at the beginning of the second year of operation of the coal mine, a new estimate indicates that the mine has a capacity to produce another 1,600,000 tons (for a lifetime production of 1,680,000 tons). Reggio computes a new unit depletion rate as follows:

$$\text{Unit Depletion Rate} = \frac{\text{Book Value} - \text{Residual Value}}{\text{Remaining Recoverable Units}}$$

$$= \frac{(\$3,000,000 - \$224,000) - \$200,000}{1,600,000 \text{ tons}}$$

$$= \underline{\underline{\$1.61 \text{ per ton}}}$$

Reggio uses the new unit depletion rate to compute depletion for the second year. ■

GOT IT?

11-22 How does a company determine the cost of a natural resource that is to be depleted?

APPENDIX 11.1: HOW IS DEPRECIATION CALCULATED FOR INCOME TAX PURPOSES?

LEARNING OBJECTIVE 11.10
Understand depreciation for income tax purposes and how it differs from depreciation for financial reporting purposes.

Companies follow different depreciation methods for computing taxable income than for computing income for financial reporting purposes. The use of different methods is appropriate because the purpose of the depreciation methods required by the income tax laws is to stimulate capital investment through the rapid recovery of capital costs. However, the purpose of accounting income is to present fairly the activities of the company over a particular period.

For assets acquired before 1981, depreciation for income tax purposes is based on use of the straight-line, sum-of-the-years'-digits, and declining-balance methods discussed earlier. The asset may not be depreciated below the estimated residual value, and the Internal Revenue Service (IRS) publishes tables that give a range of the estimated lives to use. For assets purchased in 1981 through 1986, the Accelerated Cost Recovery System (ACRS) is used. For assets purchased in 1987 and later, ACRS was modified and is known as the **Modified Accelerated Cost Recovery System (MACRS)**. The following discussion is based on these latest rules.[17]

---

[17] Following the terrorist attacks of September 11, 2001, Congress enacted a temporary change in the MACRS rules. For assets (other than buildings) placed in service between September 10, 2001, and September 11, 2004, a company receives a tax deduction of 30% of the cost of the asset and then applies MACRS procedures to the remaining 70%. To assist in the economic recovery, Congress enacted a temporary change in the MACRS rules. For new assets (other than buildings) placed in service between May 6, 2003, and December 31, 2004, a company receives a tax deduction of 50% of the cost of the asset and then applies MACRS procedures to the remaining 50%. We do not include the effects of these temporary rules in the examples and homework throughout the book.

MACRS Principles

For an asset purchased in 1987 or later, a company's computations of depreciation expense for federal income tax purposes and financial reporting purposes differ in three major respects:

- mandated tax life, which is usually shorter than the economic life
- acceleration of the cost recovery (except for a building)
- elimination of the residual value

Each of these differences tends to cause depreciation expense in the early life of an asset to be higher for income tax purposes than for financial statement reporting. This results in lower income taxes payable in those years. Over the life of an asset, the sum of the total depreciation expense and the gain or loss on disposal for both income tax reporting and financial reporting usually will be the same for both methods. Therefore, a company's taxable income over the asset's life usually will be equal to its income before income taxes reported in its financial statements. You should also note that for income tax reporting, a company may elect to use the straight-line method over the mandated tax life instead of MACRS. Refer to the Internal Revenue Code, or an income tax textbook, for a more detailed and technical discussion.

Shorter Life MACRS establishes lives (recovery periods) of 3, 5, 7, 10, 15, 20, $27\frac{1}{2}$ (residential rental buildings), and 39 (commercial buildings) years. Each asset is classified in one of the categories, and a company uses that life no matter what economic life it uses for financial reporting purposes.

Cost Recovery Methods The depreciation is computed based on the *cost* of the asset, ignoring salvage value. The method used depends on the life of the asset mandated by MACRS, as follows:

Method	MACRS Life (in years)
Double-declining-balance	3, 5, 7, 10
150%-declining-balance	15, 20
Straight-line	$27\frac{1}{2}$, 39

All the depreciation calculations for income tax purposes are based on the half-year convention. That is, a company records depreciation expense for half a year in the year of acquisition and in the last year of the MACRS life. Therefore, the depreciation for tax purposes is spread over one more tax year than the number of calendar years listed previously. Also, when one of the accelerated methods is used, a change is made to the straight-line method in the period in which the straight-line depreciation exceeds the amount calculated under the accelerated method. The IRS has published tables of depreciation rates to simplify the application of these methods, as shown in Exhibit 11.3.

Residual Value The residual value is *not* considered under the MACRS system, and so the asset is depreciated to a zero value at the end of its MACRS life. However, the entire proceeds from the disposal of the asset will be taxable because the entire value received will be a gain.

Example: MACRS

To show the use of the MACRS system and the differences from the calculation of depreciation expense for financial reporting, consider the following facts for an asset purchased by Melville Company on January 1, 2015:

Cost	$200,000
Estimated economic life	8 years
Estimated residual value	$20,000
Depreciation method for financial statements	Straight-line
MACRS life	5 years
MACRS method	200%-declining-balance
Disposal proceeds	$15,000 on January 3, 2023

EXHIBIT 11.3 MACRS Depreciation as a Percentage of the Cost of the Asset

	Tax Life of Asset in Years					
Year of Life	3	5	7	10	15	20
1	33.33%	20.00%	14.29%	10.00%	5.00%	3.750%
2	44.45	32.00	24.49	18.00	9.50	7.219
3	14.81	19.20	17.49	14.40	8.55	6.677
4	7.41	11.52	12.49	11.52	7.70	6.177
5		11.52	8.93	9.22	6.93	5.713
6		5.76	8.92	7.37	6.23	5.285
7			8.93	6.55	5.90	4.888
8			4.46	6.55	5.90	4.522
9				6.56	5.91	4.462
10				6.55	5.90	4.461
11				3.28	5.91	4.462
12					5.90	4.461
13					5.91	4.462
14					5.90	4.461
15					5.91	4.462
16					2.95	4.461
17						4.462
18						4.461
19						4.462
20						4.461
21						2.231

Melville computes the MACRS depreciation expense using the rates from Exhibit 11.3 as follows:

2015:	$200,000 × 20%	=	$ 40,000
2016:	$200,000 × 32%	=	64,000
2017:	$200,000 × 19.20%	=	38,400
2018:	$200,000 × 11.52%	=	23,040
2019:	$200,000 × 11.52%	=	23,040
2020:	$200,000 × 5.76%	=	11,520
			$200,000

Note that the total depreciation expense deductions on the company's income tax returns for 2015 through 2020 are $200,000. Thus, MACRS depreciates the total cost of the asset on an accelerated basis and ignores any residual value. Also note that the MACRS depreciation is spread over 6 tax years, even though the tax life is 5 years. This is because of the half-year MACRS convention. Therefore, the MACRS depreciation expense is zero in 2021 and 2022. The taxable gain in 2023 when the asset is sold is $15,000 because the company has depreciated the asset to a zero residual value. Therefore, the total effect on its taxable income for the years 2015 through 2022 is $185,000 ($200,000 − $15,000).

The depreciation expense for financial reporting purposes is $22,500 [($200,000 − $20,000) ÷ 8] for each of the 8 years of the asset's economic life from 2015 through 2022. The loss on disposal in 2023 is $5,000 ($20,000 book value − $15,000 proceeds). The total effect on the company's income before income taxes for the years 2015 through 2022 on its income statements is $185,000 ($180,000 + $5,000), which is the same as the total effect on taxable income. The different amounts of depreciation expense for income tax reporting and financial reporting in each year result in temporary differences, which require interperiod tax allocation, as we discuss in Chapter 18.

Chapter 11 — Depreciation, Depletion, Impairment, and Disposal

> **GOT IT?**
>
> **11-23** *(Appendix 11.1)* Why might depreciation on a company's financial statements be different from depreciation the company computed for income tax purposes?

REVIEW CENTER

At the beginning of the chapter, we discussed how the exercise of management judgment can convey important information about the usefulness of a company's long-lived assets and affect the quality of accounting information in financial statements. We also identified several objectives you would accomplish after reading the chapter. The objectives are listed below and followed by a brief summary of the key points.

LEARNING OBJECTIVE 11.1
Identify the factors involved in depreciation.

KEY TAKEAWAYS

- Depreciation, depletion, and amortization are allocation processes that allocate the cost of an asset as an expense to each period in which the asset is used.
- The four factors that must be considered in computing depreciation expense are:
  - asset cost—acquisition cost
  - service life—the amount of service or use that a company expects from the asset prior to disposal, measured in units of time or in units of activity
  - residual value—the net amount that a company expects to receive from disposing of an asset at the end of its service life
  - method of cost allocation—a systematic and rational method to allocate the cost of an asset to depreciation expense

KEY TERMS
amortization, p. 11-2
depletion, p. 11-2
depreciation, p. 11-2
residual value, p. 11-3

salvage value, p. 11-3
service life, p. 11-3
useful life, p. 11-3

LEARNING OBJECTIVE 11.2
Calculate depreciation expense using various time-based and activity-based methods.

KEY TAKEAWAYS

- Accounting principles require that the method of cost allocation be systematic and rational.
- Time-based depreciation methods result in a depreciation expense amount that is related to the passage of time.
  - The straight-line method allocates an equal amount of the asset's depreciable cost to each year of the service life.
  - Accelerated methods (sum-of-the-years'-digits and declining-balance) result in periodic depreciation amounts that decline over the asset's service life.
- Activity-based depreciation methods result in a depreciation rate that is based on estimated usage (e.g., number of hours worked or output produced).
- Regardless of the method used, the amount of depreciation expense each period reduces the carrying value of the asset and increases expenses.
- Depreciation on assets used for selling, general, and administrative functions is recorded as a current-period expense on the income statement; however, depreciation on manufacturing assets is recorded as part of the cost of inventory.

KEY TERMS

activity method, p. 11-8
double-declining-balance method, p. 11-6
depreciable cost, p. 11-4
depreciation base, p. 11-4

declining-balance method, p. 11-6
units-of-production method, p. 11-8
straight-line method, p. 11-5
sum-of-the-years'-digits method, p. 11-6

KEY CALCULATIONS

Depreciation Base (Depreciable Cost)

$$\text{Asset Cost} - \text{Estimated Residual Value} = \text{Depreciation Base}$$

Straight-Line Depreciation
Sum-of-the-Years'-Digits

$$\text{Depreciation Expense} = \frac{\text{Cost} - \text{Estimated Residual Value}}{\text{Estimated Service Life}}$$

Declining-Balance

$$\text{Declining-Balance Depreciation Rate} = \text{multiple} \times \text{Straight-Line Rate}$$

$$\text{Depreciation Expense} = \text{Declining-Balance Rate} \times \text{Net Book Value at Beginning of Period}$$

Activity Method (Units-of-Production Method)

$$\text{Depreciation Rate} = \frac{\text{Cost} - \text{Residual Value}}{\text{Estimated Usage of the Asset}}$$

$$\text{Depreciation Expense} = \text{Depreciation Rate} \times \text{Actual Usage of the Asset}$$

KEY TAKEAWAYS

- Depreciation is a process of cost allocation, not asset valuation.
- While a company selects from acceptable depreciation methods that are systematic and rational, this choice can have a significant impact on a company's income measurement, asset valuation, and rate of return on assets.
- The depreciation method should be chosen so that it allocates the cost of the asset over the periods in which the asset is used in operations. Additional factors that should be considered are repair and maintenance costs and the risk associated with the cash flows from the asset.

LEARNING OBJECTIVE 11.3
Explain the conceptual issues regarding depreciation methods.

KEY TAKEAWAYS

- A company may choose to combine multiple assets into one asset account and use group depreciation (for homogeneous assets) or composite depreciation (for heterogeneous assets) to simplify record keeping.
- For both group and composite depreciation methods, the individual assets are capitalized into one asset account, which is treated as a single asset for depreciation purposes. A gain or loss on disposal is only recognized when the final individual asset in the group is sold or disposed.

LEARNING OBJECTIVE 11.4
Understand group and composite depreciation methods.

KEY TERMS

component depreciation, p. 11-17
composite depreciation, p. 11-14

group depreciation, p. 11-14

KEY CALCULATIONS

Group Depreciation

$$\text{Group Depreciation Rate} = \left(\frac{\text{Group Cost} - \text{Group Residual Value}}{\text{Average Life of Group Assets}} \right) \div \text{Group Cost}$$

$$\text{Group Depreciation Expense} = \text{Group Cost} \times \text{Group Depreciation Rate}$$

Composite Depreciation

$$\text{Composite Depreciation Rate} = \text{Annual Depreciation Expense} \div \text{Cost}$$

$$\text{Composite Depreciation Expense} = \text{Cost of Assets Remaining in Service} \times \text{Composite Depreciation Rate}$$

LEARNING OBJECTIVE 11.5
Understand the disclosure of depreciable assets.

KEY TAKEAWAYS

- A company is required to disclose depreciation expense for the period, balances of major classes of depreciable assets by nature or function, accumulated depreciation either by major classes or in total, and a general description of the method or methods used in computing depreciation.

LEARNING OBJECTIVE 11.6
Understand additional depreciation issues, including partial period depreciation, changes and corrections of depreciation, and depreciation and accretion of asset retirement obligations.

KEY TAKEAWAYS

- When assets are not purchased on the first day or disposed of on the last day of a period, a partial year of depreciation expense is computed. Depreciation expense may be allocated to the partial period by one of the following methods:
  - computing depreciation to the nearest whole month
  - computing depreciation to the nearest whole year
  - computing one-half year's depreciation on all assets purchased or sold during the year
- A change in depreciation method (e.g., straight-line to accelerated method) or any change in the estimates used to compute depreciation (e.g., residual value or service life) is accounted for prospectively. A correction of an error in depreciation is accounted for as a prior period restatement.
- The cost related to an asset retirement obligation is depreciated over the life of the related asset. In addition, a company recognizes accretion expense and increases the asset retirement obligation each year it uses the asset.

KEY TERMS

accretion expense, p. 11-23
one-half year convention, p. 11-21
nearest whole month convention, p. 11-19
nearest whole year convention, p. 11-20

KEY CALCULATIONS

Accretion Expense

$$\text{Accretion Expense} = \text{Book Value of the Asset Retirement Obligation} \times \text{Discount Rate}$$

LEARNING OBJECTIVE 11.7
Test for and account for the impairment of property, plant, and equipment.

KEY TAKEAWAYS

- A company must review its property, plant, and equipment for impairment whenever events or changes in circumstances indicate the book value of the asset may not be recoverable.
- When the book value of property, plant, and equipment may not be recoverable, a company should:
  - *Step 1.* Determine if an impairment exists by comparing the undiscounted cash flows to the book value of the asset.
  - *Step 2.* If an impairment exists, measure and recognize the impairment loss as the difference between the book value of the asset and the fair value of the asset.

KEY TERMS

fair value, p. 11-24
impairment, p. 11-23

KEY CALCULATIONS

Recoverability Test

If Book Value > Undiscounted Expected Cash Flows, then

Impairment Loss

Impairment Loss: Fair Value of Asset − Book Value of the Asset

KEY TAKEAWAYS

- A company may dispose of property, plant, and equipment by sale, involuntary conversion, abandonment, or exchange.
- When a company disposes of property, plant, and equipment, it records:
  - Depreciation expense up to the date of the disposal and
  - A gain or loss for the difference between the book value of the asset and the proceeds received.

LEARNING OBJECTIVE 11.8
Explain how to account for the disposal of property, plant, and equipment.

KEY TAKEAWAYS

- Depletion is the allocation of the cost of a natural resource to the periods in which the benefits are received and is normally recorded using an activity method.
- As the natural resource is recovered, the natural resource is reduced and the amount of depletion is added to an inventory account. The natural resource is then expensed as cost of goods sold as the inventory is sold.

LEARNING OBJECTIVE 11.9
Understand and record depletion of natural resources.

KEY TERMS

acquisition costs, p. 11-32
depletion, p. 11-31
exploration costs, p. 11-32
intangible development costs, p. 11-32
reclamation costs, p. 11-32
restoration costs, p. 11-32

KEY CALCULATIONS

$$\text{Unit Depletion Rate} = \frac{\text{Cost} - \text{Residual Value}}{\text{Estimated Recoverable Units}}$$

$$\text{Depletion} = \text{Unit Depletion Rate} \times \text{Units Recovered}$$

KEY TAKEAWAYS

- Depreciation for income tax purposes uses the Modified Accelerated Cost Recovery System (MACRS).
- MACRS, relative to depreciation for financial reporting, usually involves a shorter life, is an accelerated method (except for buildings), and does not recognize a residual value.

LEARNING OBJECTIVE 11.10
(Appendix 11.1) Understand depreciation for income tax purposes and how it differs from depreciation for financial reporting purposes.

KEY TERM

Modified Accelerated Cost Recovery System (MACRS), p. 11-33

ANSWERS TO REAL REPORT QUESTIONS

Real Report 11.1 Answers Panera Bread—Disclosure of Depreciable Assets

1. Straight-line depreciation is the most widely used and easily understood of all the depreciation methods. The straight-line method tends to produce higher income and shareholders' equity amounts compared with the accelerated methods. Furthermore, many of Panera Bread's fixed assets (leasehold improvements, machinery and equipment, furniture and fixtures, computer hardware and software, and smallwares) may provide benefits evenly over time, which is consistent with the results of the straight-line method. Additionally, any benefit derived from using an alternative depreciation method may not exceed the increased costs associated with that method.
2. The depreciation calculation uses varying estimates of service lives and residual values. The disclosure of these items allows users to gain insights into a company's fixed assets. For example, a financial statement user can compute the average fixed life of a company's assets or the average age of its fixed assets. Such analysis may yield insights into the company's competitive position, its capital replacement policy, and its profitability.

Real Report 11.2 Answers McDonald's Corporation—Impairment and Disposal Disclosures

1. McDonald's reviews its long-lived assets for impairment annually in the fourth quarter or when circumstances indicate that an impairment may have occurred. An indicator of impairment that it uses is negative operating cash flow for the most recent trailing 24-month period.
2. McDonald's measures fair value using a discounted cash flow model. In the fair value hierarchy, this would be classified as a Level 3 input. From Chapter 4, Level 3 inputs are unobservable inputs that reflect the company's assumptions about how market participants would price the asset (or liability).

MULTIPLE-CHOICE (AICPA ADAPTED)

Select the best answer for each of the following.

M11-1 **LO 11.2** A method that excludes residual value from the depreciation base for the calculation of depreciation is:

    a. straight-line
    b. sum-of-the-years'-digits
    c. double-declining-balance
    d. activity

M11-2 through M11-4 are based on the following information:
Vorst Corporation's schedule of depreciable assets at December 31, 2016, was as follows:

Asset	Cost	Accumulated Depreciation	Acquisition Date	Residual Value
A	$100,000	$ 64,000	2015	$20,000
B	55,000	36,000	2014	10,000
C	70,000	33,600	2014	14,000
	$225,000	$133,600		$44,000

Vorst takes a full year's depreciation expense in the year of an asset's acquisition and no depreciation expense in the year of an asset's disposition. The estimated useful life of each depreciable asset is 5 years.

M11-2 **LO 11.2** Vorst depreciates Asset A on the double-declining-balance method. How much depreciation expense should Vorst record in 2017 for Asset A?

    a. $32,000   c. $14,400
    b. $25,600   d. $6,400

M11-3 **LO 11.2** Using the sum-of-the-years'-digits method, how much depreciation expense should Vorst record in 2017 for Asset B?

    a. $6,000   c. $11,000
    b. $9,000   d. $12,000

M11-4 **LO 11.2** Vorst depreciates Asset C by the straight-line method. On June 30, 2017, Vorst sold Asset C for $28,000 cash. How much gain (loss) should Vorst record in 2017 on the disposal of Asset C?

    a. $2,800   c. ($5,600)
    b. ($2,800)   d. ($8,400)

M11-5 **LO 11.2** A machine with a 4-year estimated useful life and an estimated 15% residual value was acquired on January 1. Would depreciation expense using the sum-of-the-years'-digits method be higher or lower than depreciation expense using the double-declining-balance method in the first and second years?

	First Year	Second Year
a.	Higher	Higher
b.	Higher	Lower
c.	Lower	Higher
d.	Lower	Lower

M11-6 **LO 11.2** At the end of the expected useful life of a depreciable asset with an estimated 15% residual value, the accumulated depreciation would equal the original cost of the asset under which of the following depreciation methods?

	Straight-Line	Sum-of-the-Years'-Digits
a.	Yes	Yes
b.	No	No
c.	Yes	No
d.	No	Yes

M11-7 **LO 11.4** The composite depreciation method:

    a. is applied to a group of homogeneous assets
    b. is an accelerated method of depreciation
    c. does not recognize gain or loss on the retirement of single assets in the group
    d. excludes residual value from the base of the depreciation calculation

M11-8 **LO 11.6** On July 1, 2015, Mundo Corporation purchased factory equipment for $50,000. Residual value was estimated at $2,000. The equipment will be depreciated over 10 years using the double-declining-balance method. Counting the year of acquisition as one-half year, Mundo should record 2016 depreciation expense of:

a. $7,680
b. $9,000
c. $9,600
d. $10,000

M11-9
LO 11.8
A fixed asset with a 5-year estimated useful life is sold during the second year. How would the use of the straight-line method of depreciation instead of the double-declining-balance method of depreciation affect the amount of gain or loss on the sale of the fixed asset?

	Gain	Loss
a.	No effect	No effect
b.	No effect	Increase
c.	Decrease	Increase
d.	Increase	Decrease

M11-10
LO 11.9
Crowder Company acquired a tract of land containing an extractable natural resource. Crowder is required by the purchase contract to restore the land to a condition suitable for recreational use after it has extracted the natural resource. Geological surveys estimate that the recoverable reserves will be 5,000,000 tons and that the land will have a value of $1,000,000 after restoration. Relevant cost information follows:

Land	$9,000,000
Estimated restoration costs	1,500,000

If Crowder maintains no inventories of extracted material, what should be the depletion per ton of extracted material?

a. $2.10
b. $1.90
c. $1.80
d. $1.60

REVIEW EXERCISES

RE11-1
LO 11.2
Susquehanna Company purchased an asset at the beginning of the current year for $250,000. The estimated residual value is $25,000. Susquehanna estimates that the asset will be used for 10 years and uses straight-line depreciation. Calculate the depreciation expense per year.

RE11-2
LO 11.2
Akron Incorporated purchased an asset at the beginning of Year 1 for $375,000. The estimated residual value is $15,000. Akron estimates that the asset has a service life of 5 years. Calculate the depreciation expense using the sum-of-the-years'-digits method for Years 1 and 2 of the asset's life.

RE11-3
LO 11.2
Albany Corporation purchased equipment at the beginning of Year 1 for $75,000. The asset does not have a residual value and is estimated to be in service for 8 years. Calculate the depreciation expense for Years 1 and 2 using the double-declining-balance method. Round to the nearest dollar.

RE11-4
LO 11.2
Utica Machinery Company purchases an asset for $1,200,000. After the machine has been used for 25,000 hours, the company expects to sell the asset for $150,000. What is the depreciation rate per hour based on activity?

RE11-5
LO 11.2
In Year 1, Utica Machinery Company uses the asset from **RE11-4** for 7,500 hours. Prepare the journal entry to record the depreciation.

RE11-6
LO 11.4
At the beginning of Year 1, Herkimer & Co. purchases a group of seven laptops for its new hires. The laptops are purchased for $2,300 each with a residual value of $500 each. Herkimer expects the laptops to be used for 3 years. Compute the depreciation rate per year for the group.

RE11-7
LO 11.4
At the end of Year 1, Herkimer & Co. sells two laptops for $1,800 each. Based on the information in **RE11-6** in Year 1, prepare the journal entries to record the purchase of the laptops, the depreciation on the laptops, and the sale of the laptops.

RE11-8
LO 11.4
Buffalo, Inc., uses composite depreciation for its assets. Buffalo owns a car with a cost of $25,000, a residual value of $1,500, and a useful life of 5 years; as well as equipment with a cost of $7,500, a residual value of $750, and a useful life of 10 years. Based on this information, calculate Buffalo's composite depreciation rate.

RE11-9
LO 11.6
Assume the same information as in **RE11-2**, except that Akron Incorporated purchased the asset on September 1, Year 1, instead of January 1, Year 1. Calculate the depreciation for Year 1 and Year 2 using the sum-of-the-years'-digits method.

RE11-10 Assume the same information as in **RE11-3**, except that Albany Corporation purchased the asset on April 1, Year 1. Calculate the depreciation for Year 1 and Year 2 using the double-declining-balance method. Round to the nearest dollar.
LO 11.6

RE11-11 Oneonta & Co. owns equipment with a cost of $300,000 and accumulated depreciation of $120,000. The present value of the expected net cash flows from using this equipment is $115,000 (fair value). Calculate the impairment loss.
LO 11.7

RE11-12 At the beginning of the current year, Andy Company has equipment that originally cost $50,000, has $35,000 accumulated depreciation, and is being depreciated at $5,000 per year. Andy sells this equipment for $12,000 at the end of the current year. Prepare journal entries to record both the current year's depreciation and the disposal of the equipment.
LO 11.8

RE11-13 At the beginning of Year 1, Ithaca Incorporated purchased land for $1,500,000 from which it expects to extract 800,000 tons of minerals. The estimated residual value is $250,000. What is Ithaca's unit depletion rate? Assume Ithaca extracted 25,000 tons in Year 1. What is Ithaca's depletion for Year 1 (round to the nearest dollar)?
LO 11.9

RE11-14 *(Appendix 11.1)* Auburn Company purchased an asset on January 1, Year 1, for $150,000. The asset has a MACRS life of 7 years. The residual value of the asset is $35,000. Calculate the depreciation expense for Year 1 and Year 2 using MACRS.
LO 11.10

EXERCISES

E11-1 **Depreciation Methods** Gruman Company purchased a machine for $220,000 on January 2, 2016. It made the following estimates:
LO 11.2

SHOW ME HOW

Service life	5 years or 10,000 hours
Production	200,000 units
Residual value	$20,000

In 2016, Gruman uses the machine for 1,800 hours and produces 44,000 units. In 2017, Gruman uses the machine for 1,500 hours and produces 35,000 units.

Required:
1. Compute the depreciation expense for 2016 and 2017 under each of the following methods:
    a. straight-line
    b. sum-of-the-years'-digits (round to the nearest dollar)
    c. double-declining-balance
    d. activity method based on hours worked
    e. activity method based on units of output
2. For each method, what is the book value of the machine at the end of 2016? At the end of 2017?
3. **Next Level** If Gruman used a service life of 8 years or 15,000 hours and a residual value of $10,000, what would be the effect on (a) depreciation expense and (b) book value under the straight-line, sum-of-the-years'-digits, and double-declining-balance depreciation methods?

E11-2 **Depreciation Methods** Sorter Company purchased equipment for $200,000 on January 2, 2016. The equipment has an estimated service life of 8 years and an estimated residual value of $20,000.
LO 11.2

Required:
Compute the depreciation expense for 2016 under each of the following methods:
1. straight-line
2. sum-of-the-years'-digits
3. double-declining-balance
4. **Next Level** What effect does the depreciation of the equipment have on the analysis of rate of return?

E11-3 **Depreciation Methods** Nickle Company purchased three identical assets for $17,000 on January 2, 2016. Each asset has an expected residual value of $1,000. The depreciation expense for 2016 and 2017 is shown below for three assets:
LO 11.2

Year	Asset A	Asset B	Asset C
2016	$4,000	$6,400	$6,375
2017	4,000	4,800	3,984

Required:
1. **Next Level** Which depreciation method is the company using for each asset?
2. Compute the depreciation expense for 2018 and 2019 for each asset.

E11-4
LO 11.2

Determination of Acquisition Cost On January 1, 2015, Emming Corporation purchased some machinery. The machinery has an estimated life of 10 years and an estimated residual value of $5,000. The depreciation expense on this machinery was $20,000 in 2017.

Required:
Next Level Compute the acquisition cost of the equipment under the following depreciation methods:
1. straight-line
2. sum-of-the-years'-digits
3. double-declining-balance

E11-5
LO 11.2
AICPA Adapted

Comprehensive: Acquisition, Subsequent Expenditures and Depreciation On January 2, 2016, Lapar Corporation purchased a machine for $50,000. Lapar paid shipping expenses of $500, as well as installation costs of $1,200. The company estimated that the machine would have a useful life of 10 years and a residual value of $3,000. On January 1, 2017, Lapar made additions costing $3,600 to the machine in order to comply with pollution-control ordinances. These additions neither prolonged the life of the machine nor increased the residual value.

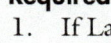

Required:
1. If Lapar records depreciation expense under the straight-line method, how much is the depreciation expense for 2017?
2. Assume Lapar determines the machine has three significant components as shown below.

Component	Amount	Service Life	Salvage Value
A	$25,000	10 years	$3,000
B	15,000	5 years	0
C	11,700	3 years	0

If Lapar uses IFRS, what is the amount of depreciation expense that would be recorded?

E11-6
LO 11.2
LO 11.3

Depreciation and Rate of Return Burrell Company purchased a machine for $20,000 on January 2, 2016. The machine has an estimated service life of 5 years and a zero estimated residual value. The asset earns income before depreciation and income taxes of $10,000 each year. The tax rate is 30%.

Required:
Compute the rate of return earned (on the average net asset value) by the company each year of the asset's life under the straight-line and the double-declining-balance depreciation methods. Assume that the machine is the company's only asset.

SHOW ME HOW

E11-7
LO 11.4

Group Depreciation Loban Company purchased four cars for $9,000 each and expects that they will be sold in 3 years for $1,500 each. The company uses group depreciation on a straight-line basis.

Required:
1. Prepare journal entries to record the acquisition and the first year's depreciation expense.
2. If one of the cars is sold at the beginning of the second year for $7,000, what journal entry is required?

E11-8
LO 11.4

Composite Depreciation Wilcox Company acquires four machines that have the following characteristics:

SHOW ME HOW

Machine	Cost	Estimated Residual Value	Estimated Service Life
A	$26,000	$2,000	6 years
B	19,000	1,000	9 years
C	30,000	5,000	5 years
D	28,000	—	7 years

(continued)

Required:
1. Prepare journal entries to record the acquisition and the first year's depreciation expense, assuming that the composite method is used on a straight-line basis. Round the depreciation rate to 3 decimal places.
2. If the company sells Machine B after 4 years for $10,000, prepare the journal entry. Round all amounts to the nearest dollar.
3. **Next Level** What arguments may be used to support the composite depreciation method?

E11-9 **Depreciation for Partial Periods** Lightning Delivery Company purchased a new delivery truck for $45,000 on April 1, 2016. The truck is expected to have a service life of 10 years or 120,000 miles and a residual value of $3,000. The truck was driven 10,000 miles in 2016 and 13,000 miles in 2017. Lightning computes depreciation expense to the nearest whole month.

LO 11.6

SHOW ME HOW

Required:
1. Compute depreciation expense for 2016 and 2017 (round answers to the nearest dollar) using the:
   a. straight-line method
   b. sum-of-the-years'-digits method
   c. double-declining-balance method
   d. activity method
2. For each method, what is the book value of the machine at the end of 2016? At the end of 2017?
3. **Next Level** Describe the pattern of depreciation expense and book value observed in the above calculations. Under what situations would each method be appropriate?

E11-10 **Depreciation for Partial Periods** Hathaway Company purchased a copying machine for $8,700 on October 1, 2016. The machine's residual value was $500 and its expected service life was 5 years. Hathaway computes depreciation expense to the nearest whole month.

LO 11.6

Required:
1. Compute depreciation expense (rounded to the nearest dollar) for 2016 and 2017 using the:
   a. straight-line method
   b. sum-of-the-years'-digits method
   c. double-declining-balance method
2. **Next Level** Which method produces the highest book value at the end of 2017?
3. **Next Level** Which method produces the highest charge to income in 2017?
4. **Next Level** Over the life of the asset, which method produces the greatest amount of depreciation expense?

E11-11 **Partial Period Depreciation** On May 10, 2016, Horan Company purchased equipment for $25,000. The equipment has an estimated service life of 5 years and zero residual value. Assume that the straight-line depreciation method is used.

LO 11.6

Required:
Compute the depreciation expense for 2016 for each of the following four alternatives:
1. Horan computes depreciation expense to the nearest day. (Use 12 months of 30 days each and round the daily depreciation rate to 2 decimal places.)
2. Horan computes depreciation expense to the nearest month. Assets purchased in the first half of the month are considered owned for the whole month.
3. Horan computes depreciation expense to the nearest whole year. Assets purchased in the first half of the year are considered owned for the whole year.
4. Horan records one-half year's depreciation expense on all assets purchased during the year.

E11-12 **Acquisition Cost and Depreciation** Reveille, Inc., purchased Machine #204 on April 1, 2016, and placed the machine into production on April 3, 2016. The following information is relevant to Machine #204:

LO 11.6

Price	$60,000
Freight-in costs	$2,500
Preparation and installation costs	$3,900
Labor costs during regular production operation	$10,200
Credit terms	2/10, n/30
Total productive output	138,500 units

The company expects that the machine could be used for 10 years, after which the salvage value would be zero. However, Reveille intends to use the machine only 8 years, after which it expects to be able to sell it for $9,800. The invoice for Machine #204 was paid April 10, 2016. The number of units produced in 2016 and 2017 was 23,200 and 29,000, respectively. Reveille computes depreciation expense to the nearest whole month.

Required:

Compute the depreciation expense for 2016 and 2017, using the following methods (round to the nearest dollar):
1. straight-line method
2. sum-of-the-years'-digits method
3. double-declining-balance method
4. activity method based on units of production

(*Originally contributed by Norma C. Powell*)

E11-13 Changes and Corrections of Depreciation Bailand Company purchased a building for $210,000 that had an estimated residual value of $10,000 and an estimated service life of 10 years. Bailand purchased the building 4 years ago and has used straight-line depreciation. At the beginning of the fifth year (before it records depreciation expense for the year), the following *independent* situations occur:
LO 11.6
1. Bailand estimates that the asset has 8 years' life remaining (for a total of 12 years).
2. Bailand changes to the sum-of-the-years'-digits method.
3. Bailand discovers that the estimated residual value has been ignored in the computation of depreciation expense.

Required:

For each of the independent situations, prepare all the journal entries relating to the building for the fifth year. Ignore income taxes.

E11-14 Asset Retirement Obligation On January 1, 2016, Barbosa Company purchased a coal mining site for $1,000,000. Under the terms of the purchase agreement, Barbosa must restore the site to specified conditions at an estimated cost of $125,000. Barbosa estimates that it will be able to operate the site for 20 years. Barbosa uses a 6% discount rate.
LO 11.6

Required:
1. Prepare the journal entry necessary to record the purchase of the coal mining site.
2. Prepare any journal entries needed at December 31 with regard to this mining site.
3. **Next Level** What is the conceptual justification that underlies the accounting for an asset retirement obligation?

E11-15 Asset Impairment On January 1, 2012, Vallahara Company purchased machinery for $650,000, which it installed in a rented factory. It is depreciating the machinery over 12 years by the straight-line method to a residual value of $50,000. Late in 2016, because of increasing competition in the industry, the company believes that its asset may be impaired and will have a remaining useful life of 5 years, over which it estimates the asset will produce total cash inflows of $1,000,000 and will incur total cash outflows of $825,000. The cash flows are independent of the company's other activities and will occur evenly each year. Vallahara is not able to determine the fair value based on a current selling price of the machinery. Vallahara's discount rate is 10%.
LO 11.7

Required:
1. Prepare schedules to determine whether, at the end of 2016, the machinery is impaired and, if so, the impairment loss to be recognized.
2. If the machinery is impaired, prepare the journal entry to record the impairment.
3. If Vallahara uses IFRS and determines that the fair value of the machinery is $200,000 and that it would cost $10,000 to sell the machine, how much would the company recognize as the impairment loss?
4. Assuming that the recoverable amount of the machinery is determined to be $220,000 at the end of 2017, what entry will Vallahara make to record this increase in value under U.S. GAAP? Under IFRS?

E11-16 Disposal of Property, Plant, and Equipment Swann Company sold a delivery truck on April 1, 2016. Swann had acquired the truck on January 1, 2012, for $42,000. At acquisition, Swann had estimated that the truck would have an estimated life of 5 years and a residual value of $5,000. At December 31, 2015, the truck had a book value of $12,400.
LO 11.8

(*continued*)

Required:
1. Prepare any necessary journal entries to record the sale of the truck, assuming it sold for:
   a. $12,000
   b. $9,000
2. How should the gain or loss on disposal be reported on the income statement?
3. Assume that Swann uses IFRS and sold the truck for $12,000. In addition, Swann had previously recorded a revaluation surplus related to this machine of $4,000. What journal entries are required to record the sale?

E11-17 **Disposal of Property, Plant, and Equipment** On July 1, 2016, Osceola Company retired a metal stamping machine that it had originally purchased for $1,500,000. At December 31, 2015, the machine had a book value of $125,000 and was being depreciated on a straight-line basis at $75,000 per year. Osceola sold the machine for $200,000.
LO 11.8

Required:
1. Prepare any journal entries necessary to record the disposal of the machine.
2. **Next Level** How does the disposal of the machine affect the 2016 financial statements?

E11-18 **Depletion** Feller Company purchased a site for a limestone quarry for $100,000 on January 2, 2016. It estimates that the quarry will yield 400,000 tons of limestone. It estimates that its retirement obligation has a fair value of $20,000, after which the land could be sold for $10,000. In 2016, 80,000 tons were quarried and 60,000 tons sold. Costs of production (excluding depletion) are $4 per ton.
LO 11.9

Required:
1. Compute the depletion cost per ton.
2. Compute the total cost of the inventory at December 31, 2016.
3. Compute the total cost of goods sold for 2016.

E11-19 **Depletion** Lorton Company acquired land containing coal. Lorton will restore the land to a condition suitable for recreational use after it has extracted the coal. Geological surveys estimate that the recoverable reserves will be 4,000,000 tons and that the land will have a value of $1 million after restoration. Relevant cost information follows:
LO 11.9
AICPA Adapted

Land	$12,000,000
Estimated fair value of retirement obligation	1,200,000

Required:
If Lorton maintains no inventories of coal, what is the depletion rate per ton of coal?

E11-20 **(Appendix 11.1) Depreciation for Financial Statements and Income Tax Purposes** Dinkle Company purchased equipment for $50,000. The equipment has an estimated residual value of $5,000 and an expected useful life of 10 years. Dinkle uses straight-line depreciation for its financial statements.
LO 11.10

Required:
What is the difference between the company's income before taxes reported on its financial statements and the taxable income reported on its tax return in each of the first 2 years of the asset's life if the asset was purchased on January 2, 2016, and its MACRS life is 5 years?

PROBLEMS

P11-1 **Depreciation Methods** Winsey Company purchased equipment on January 2, 2016, for $700,000. The equipment has the following characteristics:
LO 11.2

Estimated service life	20 years, 100,000 hours, 950,000 units of output
Estimated residual value	$50,000

During 2016 and 2017, the company used the machine for 4,500 and 5,500 hours, respectively, and produced 40,000 and 60,000 units, respectively.

Required:

Compute depreciation expense for 2016 and 2017 under each of the following methods:
1. straight-line method
2. activity method based on hours worked (round the depreciation rate per hour to 2 decimal places)
3. activity method based on units of output (round the depreciation rate per unit to 2 decimal places)
4. sum-of-the-years'-digits method
5. double-declining-balance method
6. 150%-declining-balance method
7. **Next Level** If Winsey used a service life of 16 years, 80,000 hours, or 750,000 units of output, what would be the effect on depreciation expense under the straight-line, sum-of-the-years'-digits, and declining-balance depreciation methods? Round your answers to the nearest dollar.

P11-2
LO 11.2

Depreciation Methods Lord Company purchased a machine on January 2, 2016, for $70,000. The machine had an expected residual value of $10,000, an expected life of 8 years or 24,000 hours, and a capacity to produce 100,000 units. During 2016, Lord produced 12,000 units in 2,500 hours. In 2017, Lord produced 15,000 units in 3,000 hours.

Required:
1. Prepare a schedule showing depreciation expense for 2016 and 2017 and the book value of the asset at the end of 2016 and 2017 for each of the following methods (round your answers to the nearest dollar):
    a. straight-line method
    b. activity method base on hours worked
    c. activity method based on units of output
    d. sum-of-the-years'-digits method
    e. double-declining-balance method
2. **Next Level** Under what conditions would it be appropriate to use each of the depreciation methods discussed above?

P11-3
LO 11.2

Depreciation Methods Sayers Company purchased a building for $250,000 on January 2, 2016. The building has an expected residual value of $20,000 at the end of its expected life of 20 years.

Required:
1. Prepare a schedule showing depreciation expense for 2016 and 2017 and the book value on December 31, 2016, and December 31, 2017, for each of the following methods:
    a. straight-line
    b. sum-of-the-years'-digits
    c. double-declining-balance
    d. 150%-declining-balance
2. **Next Level** Holding all other things equal, what is the effect of depreciation on the rate of return?

P11-4
LO 11.2

Cost of Asset and Depreciation Method Heist Company purchased a machine on January 2, 2016, and uses the 150%-declining-balance depreciation method. The machine has an expected life of 10 years and an expected residual value of $5,000. The following costs relate to the acquisition and use of the machine during the first year of its operations:

Invoice price	$50,000	Testing	$ 1,100
Discounts available and taken	1,000	Normal spoilage of materials during the year	750
Freight	700	Abnormal spoilage of materials during the year	250
Installation	900	Wages of machine operator	15,000

Required:
1. Compute the depreciation expense for 2016 and 2017.
2. **Next Level** What is the effect on the financial statements if the company used the straight-line method instead of the 150%-declining-balance method?

P11-5 **Group and Composite Depreciation** Cheadle Company purchased a fleet of 20 delivery trucks for $8,000 each on January 2, 2016. It decided to use composite depreciation on a straight-line basis and calculated the depreciation from the following schedule:

LO 11.4

Year	Number of Trucks to Be Retired at Year-End	Estimated Residual Value per Truck
2017	2	$4,000
2018	6	4,000
2019	8	2,000
2020	4	—

Cheadle actually retired the trucks according to the following schedule (assume each truck was retired at the beginning of the year):

Year	Number of Trucks Retired	Total Proceeds from Retirements
2017	1	$ 4,000
2018	3	11,000
2019	6	19,000
2020	5	6,000
2021	3	4,000
2022	2	1,000

Required:
1. Prepare the journal entries necessary to record the preceding events.
2. Assume that the company expected all the trucks to last 4 years and be retired for $1,600 each. Using group depreciation, prepare journal entries for all 6 years, assuming the company retired the trucks as shown by the latter schedule.

P11-6 **Composite Depreciation** Borrell Company purchased four delivery trucks on January 2, 2016, for $22,000 each. Borrell expected two of the trucks to last 5 years and have a residual value of $3,500 each. The other two trucks had an expected life of 8 years and no residual value. Borrell uses straight-line depreciation on a composite basis.

LO 11.4

Required:
Prepare journal entries to record the following events:
1. January 1, 2018. One of the two trucks expected to last 5 years is destroyed in an accident. The truck was not insured and the scrap value is $400.
2. January 5, 2018. A new truck is acquired for $26,000. It has an expected life of 4 years and a residual value of $3,920.
3. Depreciation expense for 2018.

P11-7 **Depreciation and Partial Periods** Dinnell Company owns the following assets:

LO 11.6

	Asset		
	A	B	C
Year purchased	2014	2015	2016
Cost	$20,000	$40,000	$100,000
Expected life	5 years	8 years	10 years
Residual value	$2,000	—	$10,000
Depreciation method	Straight-line	Sum-of-the-years'-digits	Double-declining-balance

In the year of acquisition and retirement of an asset, Dinnell records depreciation expense for one-half year. During 2017, Asset A was sold for $7,000.

Required:
Prepare the journal entries to record depreciation on each asset for 2014 through 2017 and the sale of Asset A. Round all answers to the nearest dollar.

P11-8 **Changing Depreciation** Kam Company purchased a machine on January 2, 2016, for $20,000. The machine had an expected life of 8 years and a residual value of $300. The double-declining-balance method of depreciation is used.

LO 11.6

Required:
1. Compute the depreciation expense for each year of the asset's life and book value at the end of each year.
2. Assuming that the company has a policy of always changing to the straight-line method at the midpoint of the asset's life, compute the depreciation expense for each year of the asset's life.
3. Assuming that the company always changes to the straight-line method at the beginning of the year when the annual straight-line amount exceeds the double-declining-balance amount, compute the depreciation expense for each year of the asset's life.

P11-9 **Changes and Corrections of Depreciation** During 2016, Ryel Company's controller asked you to prepare correcting journal entries for the following three situations:

LO 11.6

1. Machine A was purchased for $50,000 on January 1, 2011. Straight-line depreciation has been recorded for 5 years, and the Accumulated Depreciation account has a balance of $25,000. The estimated residual value remains at $5,000, but the service life is now estimated to be 1 year longer than estimated originally.
2. Machine B was purchased for $40,000 on January 1, 2014. It had an estimated residual value of $5,000 and an estimated service life of 10 years. It has been depreciated under the double-declining-balance method for 2 years. Now, at the beginning of the third year, Ryel has decided to change to the straight-line method.
3. Machine C was purchased for $20,000 on January 1, 2015. Double-declining-balance depreciation has been recorded for 1 year. The estimated residual value of the machine is $2,000 and the estimated service life is 5 years. The computation of the depreciation erroneously included the estimated residual value.

Required:
Prepare any necessary correcting journal entries for each situation. Also prepare the journal entry necessary for each situation to record depreciation expense for 2016.

P11-10 **Asset Retirement Obligation** Pete's Petroleum, Inc., an SEC registrant with a calendar year-end, is in the business of constructing and operating offshore oil platforms. Pete's Petroleum is required legally to dismantle and remove the platforms at the end of their useful lives, which is estimated to be 10 years. On January 1, 2016, Pete constructed and began operating an offshore oil platform off the coast of Brazil. The total capitalized cost to construct the platform was $3,700,000. In addition, while the future cost of dismantling the oil platform is difficult to estimate, Pete believes there is a 40% chance that the future cost will be $1,425,000, a 40% chance it will be $1,650,000, and a 20% chance that it will cost $2,125,000. The appropriate discount rate is 12%, and Pete uses the straight-line method of depreciation.

LO 11.6

Required:
1. Prepare the journal entries that Pete should record in 2016 related to the oil platform.
2. Prepare an amortization schedule for the asset retirement obligation.
3. **Next Level** Prepare a table showing the effect of accounting for the asset retirement obligation on assets, liabilities, shareholders' equity, and net income relative to accounting for the associated costs at the end of the asset's service life when the expenditure is made.

P11-11 **Asset Impairment** On January 1, 2011, Borstad Company purchased equipment for $1,180,000. It is depreciating the equipment over 25 years using the straight-line method and a zero residual value. Late in 2016, because of technological changes in the industry and reduced selling prices for its products, Borstad believes that its equipment may be impaired and will have a remaining useful life of 8 years. Borstad estimates that the equipment will produce cash inflows of $400,000 and will incur cash outflows of $295,000 each year for the next 8 years. It is not able to determine the fair value of the equipment based on a current selling price. Borstad's discount rate is 12%.

LO 11.7

Required:
1. Prepare schedules to determine whether, at the end of 2016, the equipment is impaired and, if so, the impairment loss to be recognized.
2. Prepare the journal entry to record the impairment.
3. **Next Level** How would your answer to Requirement 1 change if the discount rate was 16% and the cash flows were expected to continue for 6 years?

(continued)

4. **Next Level** How would your answer change if management planned to implement efficiencies that would save $10,000 each year?

5. Refer to Requirement 1 and assume that the company uses IFRS. It determines that the fair value of the equipment is $570,000 and estimates that it would cost $17,000 to sell the equipment. How much would the company recognize as the impairment loss?

P11-12 **Depletion** On January 2, 2016, Whistler Company purchased land for $450,000, from which it is estimated that
LO 11.9 400,000 tons of ore could be extracted. It estimates that the present value of the cost necessary to restore the land is $80,000, after which it could be sold for $30,000.

During 2016, Whistler mined 80,000 tons and sold 50,000 tons. During 2017, Whistler mined 100,000 tons and sold 120,000 tons. At the beginning of 2018, Whistler spent an additional $100,000, which increased the reserves by 60,000 tons. In 2018, Whistler mined 140,000 tons and sold 130,000 tons. Whistler uses a FIFO cost flow assumption.

Required:
1. Calculate the depletion included in the income statement and ending inventory for 2016, 2017, and 2018. Round the depletion rate to 2 decimal places.
2. Prepare the natural resources section of the balance sheet on December 31, 2016, 2017, and 2018, assuming that an accumulated depletion account is used.
3. Assume Whistler's discount rate was 8%. What is the balance in the asset retirement obligation at 2016, 2017, and 2018?

P11-13 **Depletion** On July 1, 2016, Amplex Company purchased a coal mine for $2 million. The estimated capacity of the
LO 11.9 mine was 800,000 tons. During 2016, Amplex mines 10,000 tons of coal per month and sells 9,000 tons per month. The selling price is $30 per ton and production costs (excluding depletion and depreciation) are $8 per ton. At the end of the mine's life, Amplex estimates that the present value of the cost to restore the land is $300,000, after which it can be sold for $100,000. Amplex also purchased some temporary housing for the miners at a cost of $170,000. The housing has an expected life of 10 years but is expected to be sold for $10,000 at the end of the mine's life. The housing is depreciated using the activity method. Amplex uses the FIFO cost flow assumption and its discount rate is 10%.

Required:
1. Compute the company's expenses included on the 2016 income statement.
2. Compute the cost of the company's inventory at December 31, 2016.
3. In January 2017, a new estimate indicated that the capacity of the mine was only 500,000 tons at that time. Compute the company's expenses included on the 2017 income statement if the company mines and sells 10,000 tons per month. Round the depletion rate to 3 decimal places.

P11-14 **(Appendix 11.1) Depreciation for Financial Statements and Income Tax Purposes** Hunter Company pur-
LO 11.10 chased a light truck on January 2, 2016 for $18,000. The truck, which will be used for deliveries, has the following characteristics:

Estimated life: 5 years
Estimated residual value: $3,000
Depreciation method for financial statements: straight-line method
Depreciation for income tax purposes: MACRS (3-year life)
From 2016 through 2020, each year, Hunter had sales of $100,000, cost of goods sold of $60,000, and operating expenses (excluding depreciation) of $15,000. The truck was disposed of on December 31, 2020, for $2,000.

Required:
1. Prepare an income statement for financial reporting through pretax accounting income for each of the 5 years, 2016 through 2020.
2. Prepare, instead, an income statement for income tax purposes through taxable income for each of the 5 years, 2016 through 2020.
3. Compare the total income for all 5 years under Requirements 1 and 2.

P11-15 **Comprehensive** Logan Corporation, a manufacturer of steel products, began operations on October 1, 2015.
LO 11.2 Logan's accounting department has started the fixed asset and depreciation schedule shown as follows:

AICPA Adapted

Assets	Acquisition Date	Cost	Salvage Value	Depreciation Method	Estimated Life in Years	Depreciation Expense Year Ended September 30 2016	2017
Land A	October 1, 2015	(1)___	N/A	N/A	N/A	N/A	N/A
Building A	October 1, 2015	(2)___	$47,500	Straight-line	(3)___	$14,000	(4)___
Land B	October 3, 2015	(5)___	N/A	N/A	N/A	N/A	N/A
Building B	Under construction	$210,000 to date	—	Straight-line	30	—	(6)___
Donated equipment	October 3, 2015	(7)___	2,000	150%-declining-balance	10	(8)___	(9)___
Machinery A	October 3, 2015	(10)___	5,500	Sum-of-the-years'-digits	10	(11)___	(12)___
Machinery B	October 1, 2016	(13)___	—	Straight-line	15	—	(14)___

You have been asked to complete this schedule. In addition to determining that the data already on the schedule are correct, you have obtained the following information from Logan's records and personnel:
1. Depreciation expense is computed from the first of the month of acquisition to the first of the month of disposition.
2. Land A and Building A were acquired together for a lump-sum price of $812,500. At the time of acquisition, the land had an appraised value of $72,000, and the building had an appraised value of $828,000.
3. Land B was acquired on October 3, 2015, in exchange for 3,000 newly issued shares of Logan's common stock. At the date of acquisition, the stock had a par value of $5 per share and a fair value of $25 per share. During October 2015, Logan paid $10,400 to demolish an existing building on this land so that it could construct a new building.
4. Construction of Building B on the newly acquired land began on October 2, 2016. By September 30, 2017, Logan had paid $210,000 of the estimated total construction costs of $300,000. Estimated completion and occupancy are July 2018.
5. Certain equipment was donated to the corporation by a local university. An independent appraisal of the equipment when donated placed the fair value at $16,000 and the salvage at $2,000.
6. Machinery A's total cost of $110,000 includes installation expense of $550 and normal repairs and maintenance of $11,000. Salvage value is estimated at $5,500. Machinery A was sold on February 1, 2017.
7. On October 1, 2016, Machinery B was acquired with a down payment of $4,000 and the remaining payments to be made in 10 annual installments of $4,000 each beginning October 1, 2017. The prevailing interest rate was 10%. The data that follow were abstracted from present value tables:

Present Value of $1.00 at 10%		Present Value of Annuity of $1.00 in Arrears at 10%	
10 years	0.386	10 years	6.145
11 years	0.350	11 years	6.495
15 years	0.239	15 years	7.606

Required:
For each numbered blank in the schedule, supply the correct amount. Round each answer to the nearest dollar. Show supporting computations in good form.

P11-16 **Comprehensive** On January 2, 2016, Brock Corporation purchased a tract of land (site number 101) with a build-
LO 11.2 ing for $600,000. Additionally, Brock paid a real estate broker's commission of $36,000, legal fees of $6,000, and
LO 11.6 title guarantee insurance of $18,000. The closing statement indicated that the land's value was $500,000 and the
AICPA building's value was $100,000. Shortly after acquisition, the building was razed at a cost of $75,000.
Adapted

Brock entered into a $3,000,000 fixed-price contract with Barnett Builders, Inc., on March 2, 2016, for the construction of an office building on land site number 101. The building was completed and occupied on September 30, 2017. Additional construction costs were incurred as follows:

Plans, specifications, and blueprints	$12,000
Architects' fees for design and supervision	95,000

(continued)

The company estimates that the building will have a 40-year life from the date of completion and decides to use the 150%-declining-balance depreciation method.

To finance the construction cost, Brock borrowed $3,000,000 on March 2, 2016. The loan is payable in 10 annual installments of $300,000 plus interest at the rate of 14%. Brock's weighted average accumulated expenditures related to the construction of the building were as follows:

For the period March 2 to December 31, 2016	$ 900,000
For the period January 1 to September 30, 2017	2,300,000

Required:
1. Prepare a schedule that discloses the individual costs making up the balance in the Land account with respect to land site number 101 as of September 30, 2017.
2. Prepare a schedule that discloses the individual costs that the company should capitalize in the Office Building account as of September 30, 2017. Show supporting computations in good form.
3. Prepare a schedule showing the depreciation expense computation of the office building for the year ended December 31, 2017.

P11-17 Comprehensive On December 31, 2016, Vail Company owned the following assets:

LO 11.2
LO 11.6
LO 11.8

Asset	Date of Purchase	Cost	Accumulated Depreciation	Life in Years	Residual Value
Building	1/1/2014	$50,000	$ 3,750[a]	40	$ 0
Office machinery	1/1/2014	20,000	9,760[b]	10	2,000
Office fixtures	1/1/2014	30,000	20,000[c]	5	5,000

[a] Straight-line depreciation
[b] Double-declining-balance depreciation
[c] Sum-of-the-years'-digits depreciation

Vail computes depreciation and amortization expense to the nearest whole year. During 2017, Vail engaged in the following transactions:

Jan. 3 Extended the building at a cost of $30,000. The extension provided an addition to the service potential of the building.

Mar. 7 Sold a piece of office machinery that had originally cost $4,000 and that had accumulated depreciation of $1,952 on December 31, 2016. The machine was sold for $3,000.

May 17 Purchased office fixtures and office machinery for $9,200. The supplier reduced the price because of the joint purchase. If purchased separately, the office fixtures would have cost $6,000 and the office machinery $4,000. Delivery costs paid by Vail were $200. The machinery was accidentally damaged during installation and cost $230 to repair. The office fixtures have an estimated life of 5 years and a residual value of $250. The office machinery has an estimated life of 10 years and a residual value of $500.

Aug. 10 Exchanged the president's desk (classified as office fixtures) for a larger desk belonging to a friend of the president. The desk had cost $600 and had accumulated depreciation on December 31, 2016, of $400 and an estimated residual value of $100. The new desk had a value of $900 and $700 cash was paid.

Oct. 20 Serviced and adjusted the office machinery at a cost of $125.

Required:
1. Check the accuracy of the accumulated depreciation balances at December 31, 2016. Round to the nearest whole dollar in all requirements.
2. Prepare journal entries to record the preceding events in 2017, as well as the year-end recording of depreciation expense.
3. Prepare an Accumulated Depreciation account for each category of assets, enter the beginning balance, post the journal entries from Requirement 2, and compute the ending balance.

P11-18 Comprehensive: Errors Soon after December 31, 2016, the auditor requested a depreciation schedule for trucks of Jarrett Trucking Company, showing the additions, retirements, depreciation, and other data affecting the income of the company in the 4-year period 2013 to 2016, inclusive. The following data were in the Trucks account as of January 1, 2013:

LO 11.2
LO 11.6
LO 11.8

Truck no. 1	Purchased January 1, 2010	$12,000
Truck no. 2	Purchased July 1, 2010	10,400
Truck no. 3	Purchased January 1, 2012	12,800
Truck no. 4	Purchased July 1, 2012	15,000
	Balance January 1, 2013	$50,200

The Accumulated Depreciation—Trucks account, previously adjusted to January 1, 2013, and duly entered in the ledger, had a balance on that date of $16,460. This amount represented the straight-line depreciation on the four trucks from the respective dates of purchase, based on a 5-year life and no residual value. No debits had been made to this account prior to January 1, 2013.

Transactions between January 1, 2013, and December 31, 2016, and their record in the ledger were as follows:

1. July 1, 2013: Truck no. 1 was sold for $1,000 cash. The entry was a debit to Cash and a credit to Trucks, $1,000.
2. January 1, 2014: Truck no. 3 was traded for a larger one (no. 5) with a 5-year life. The agreed purchase price was $12,000. Jarrett paid the other company $1,780 cash on the transaction. The entry was a debit to Trucks, $1,780, and a credit to Cash, $1,780.
3. July 1, 2015: Truck no. 4 was damaged in a wreck to such an extent that it was sold as junk for $50 cash. Jarrett received $950 from the insurance company. The entry made by the bookkeeper was a debit to Cash, $1,000, and credits to Miscellaneous Revenue, $50, and Trucks, $950.
4. July 1, 2015: A new truck (no. 6) was acquired for $20,000 cash and debited at that amount to the Trucks account. The truck has a 5-year life.

Entries for depreciation had been made at the close of each year as follows: 2013, $8,840; 2014, $5,436; 2015, $4,896; 2016, $4,356.

Required:

1. **Next Level** For each of the 4 years, calculate separately the increase or decrease in earnings arising from the company's errors in determining or entering depreciation or in recording transactions affecting trucks.
2. Prove your work by one compound journal entry as of December 31, 2016; the adjustment of the Trucks account is to reflect the correct balances, assuming that the books have not been closed for 2016.

P11-19 **Comprehensive** Information for Blake Corporation's property, plant, and equipment for 2016 is:

LO 11.2
LO 11.6
LO 11.8
AICPA
Adapted

Account Balances at January 1, 2016

	Debit	Credit
Land	$ 150,000	
Building	1,200,000	
Accumulated Depreciation		$263,100
Machinery and Equipment	900,000	
Accumulated Depreciation		250,000
Automotive Equipment	115,000	
Accumulated Depreciation		84,600

Depreciation Method and Useful Life

Building: 150%-declining-balance; 25 years.
Machinery and equipment: Straight-line; 10 years.
Automotive equipment: Sum-of-the-years'-digits; 4 years.
Leasehold improvements: Straight-line.
The residual value of the depreciable assets is immaterial.
Depreciation is computed to the nearest month.

Transactions during 2016 and other information were as follows:

a. On January 2, 2016, Blake purchased a new car for $10,000 cash and a trade-in of a 2-year-old car with a cost of $9,000 and a book value of $2,700. The new car has a cash price of $12,000; the market value of the trade-in is not known.
b. On April 1, 2016, a machine purchased for $23,000 on April 1, 2011, was destroyed by fire. Blake recovered $15,500 from its insurance company.

(continued)

c. On May 1, 2016, costs of $168,000 were incurred to improve leased office premises. The leasehold improvements have a useful life of 8 years. The related lease, which terminates on December 31, 2022, is renewable for an additional 6-year term. The decision to renew will be made in 2022 based on office space needs at that time.

d. On July 1, 2016, machinery and equipment were purchased at a total invoice cost of $280,000; additional costs of $5,000 for freight and $25,000 for installation were incurred.

e. Blake determined that the automotive equipment comprising the $115,000 balance at January 1, 2016, would have been depreciated at a total amount of $18,000 for the year ended December 31, 2016.

Required:
1. For each asset classification, prepare schedules showing depreciation and amortization expense, and accumulated depreciation and amortization that would appear on Blake's income statement for the year ended December 31, 2016, and on the balance sheet at December 31, 2016, respectively.
2. Prepare a schedule showing the gain or loss from disposal of assets that would appear in Blake's income statement for the year ended December 31, 2016.
3. Prepare the property, plant, and equipment section of Blake's December 31, 2016, balance sheet.

P11-20 **Comprehensive** Pell Corporation's Property, Plant, and Equipment and Accumulated Depreciation accounts had the following balances at December 31, 2015:

LO 11.2
LO 11.6
LO 11.8
AICPA
Adapted

	Property, Plant, and Equipment	Accumulated Depreciation
Land	$ 350,000	$ —
Land Improvements	180,000	45,000
Building	1,500,000	350,000
Machinery and Equipment	1,158,000	405,000
Automobiles	150,000	112,000

Depreciation method and useful lives:

- Land improvements: Straight-line; 15 years.
- Building: 150%-declining-balance; 20 years.
- Machinery and equipment: Straight-line; 10 years.
- Automobiles: 150%-declining-balance; 3 years.
- Depreciation is computed to the nearest month. No salvage values are recognized.

Transactions during 2016:
1. On January 2, 2016, machinery and equipment were purchased at a total invoice cost of $260,000, which included a $5,500 charge for freight. Installation costs of $27,000 were incurred.
2. On March 31, 2016, a machine purchased for $58,000 on January 3, 2012, was sold for $36,500.
3. On May 1, 2016, expenditures of $50,000 were made to repave parking lots at Pell's plant location. The work was necessitated by damage caused by severe winter weather.
4. On November 2, 2016, Pell acquired a tract of land with an existing building in exchange for 10,000 shares of Pell's $20 par common stock, which had a market price of $38 a share on this date. Pell paid legal fees and title insurance totaling $23,000. The last property tax bill indicated assessed values of $240,000 for land and $60,000 for building. Shortly after acquisition, the building was razed at a cost of $35,000 in anticipation of new building construction in 2017.
5. On December 31, 2016, Pell purchased a new automobile for $15,250 cash and trade-in of an automobile purchased for $18,000 on January 1, 2015. The new automobile has a cash value of $19,000.

Required:
1. Prepare a schedule analyzing the changes in each of the plant assets during 2016, with detailed supporting computations. Disregard the related Accumulated Depreciation accounts.
2. For each asset classification, prepare a schedule showing depreciation expense for the year ended December 31, 2016.
3. Prepare a schedule showing the gain or loss from each asset disposal that Pell would recognize in its income statement for the year ended December 31, 2016.

P11-21 **Comprehensive** Lurch Company's December 31, 2015, balance sheet follows:

LO 11.2
LO 11.8

Assets		
Cash		$ 540,000
Inventory		450,000
Prepaid rent		60,000
Machine	$ 500,000	
Less: Accumulated depreciation	(135,000)	365,000
		$1,415,000

Liabilities and Equities	
Accounts payable	$ 400,000
Common stock, $10 par	300,000
Additional paid-in capital	515,000
Retained earnings	200,000
	$1,415,000

During 2016, the following transactions occurred:
1. To avoid paying monthly rent of $5,000 on existing plant facilities, the company decided to buy a tract of land and construct a building of its own on it. On January 2, 2016, Lurch exchanged 6,000 shares of its common stock to acquire the land; the stock was selling for $25 per share. Construction of the building also began on January 2, 2016. At the time, Lurch borrowed funds by issuing a 1-year, $500,000 note at 12% to help finance the project. The principal and interest on the note are due January 3, 2017. Construction costs (paid in cash) that occurred evenly throughout the year totaled $700,000. The building was completed on December 30, 2016, and the move-in to the new building was to occur during the next week.
2. On January 2, 2016, Lurch exchanged its one existing machine plus $50,000 for a newer machine with a fair value of $430,000. The new machine is to be depreciated using straight-line depreciation based on an economic life of 5 years and a residual value of $55,000.
3. Lurch uses a FIFO perpetual inventory system. Lurch sold $350,000 of its inventory for $700,000 cash, paid for its beginning accounts payable, and purchased $480,000 of inventory on account during the year.
4. On July 31, 2016, Lurch declared and paid a $2.50 per share cash dividend to its shareholders.
5. Lurch is subject to a 30% income tax rate, and income taxes are accrued at year-end.

Required:
Prepare Lurch's income statement and statement of retained earnings for the fiscal year ended December 31, 2016, and a balance sheet as of December 31, 2016. Show all supporting journal entries and computations made during 2016. (*Contributed by Scott I. Jerris*)

CASES

COMMUNICATION

C11-1 **Operating and Capital Expenditures**
LO 11.1
AICPA Adapted

Property, plant, and equipment generally represents a material portion of the total assets of most companies. Accounting for the acquisition and usage of such assets is, therefore, an important part of the financial reporting process.

Required:
1. Distinguish between operating and capital expenditures and explain why this distinction is important.
2. Briefly define depreciation as used in accounting.
3. Identify the factors that are relevant in determining annual depreciation expense and explain whether these factors are determined objectively or whether they are based on judgment.
4. Explain why depreciation expense is usually shown in the net cash flow from operating activities section of the statement of cash flows.

C11-2 **Capitalization and Depreciation**
LO 11.1
LO 11.2
LO 11.3
AICPA Adapted

Gehl Company purchased significant amounts of new equipment this year to be used in its operations. The equipment was delivered by the suppliers, installed by Gehl, and placed into operation. Gehl purchased some for cash with discounts available for

(*continued*)

prompt payments. It purchased some under long-term payment plans, for which the interest charges approximate prevailing rates. In addition, Gehl disposed of some equipment that it had purchased in a prior year. As a result, Gehl is studying its capitalization and depreciation policies.

Required:
1. What costs should Gehl capitalize for the new equipment purchased this year?
2. What factors cause the equipment to lose its future economic benefit?
3. Briefly explain the following:
    a. the objective of depreciation accounting (do not discuss specific methods)
    b. the factors that should be considered in computing the equipment's depreciation expense
4. What theoretical justifications are there for the use of accelerated depreciation methods?
5. How should Gehl account for and report the disposal of the automobile?

C11-3 **Straight-Line and Composite Depreciation**
LO 11.2
LO 11.4
AICPA Adapted

Portland Co. uses the straight-line depreciation method for depreciable assets. All assets are depreciated individually, except manufacturing machinery, which is depreciated by the composite method.

During the year, Portland exchanged a delivery truck with Maine Co. for a larger delivery truck. It paid cash equal to 10% of the larger truck's value.

Required:
1. Explain the factors that should influence Portland's selection of the straight-line depreciation method.
2. Explain how Portland should account for and report the truck exchange transaction.
3. What benefits should Portland derive from using the composite method rather than the individual basis for manufacturing machinery?
4. How should Portland calculate the manufacturing machinery's annual depreciation expense in its first year of operation?

CREATIVE AND CRITICAL THINKING

C11-4 **Depreciation Concepts**
LO 11.1
LO 11.2
LO 11.3
AICPA Adapted

Depreciation continues to be one of the most controversial, difficult, and important problem areas in accounting.

Required:
1. Explain the conventional accounting concept of depreciation accounting, and discuss its conceptual merit with respect to (a) the value of the asset, (b) the amount(s) expensed, and (c) the discretion of management in selecting the method.
2. Answer the following:
    a. Explain the factors that should be considered when applying the conventional concept of depreciation to the determination of how the value of a newly acquired computer system should be assigned to expense for financial reporting purposes. (Ignore income tax considerations for this case.)
    b. What depreciation methods might be used for the computer system?

C11-5 **Depreciation Concepts**
LO 11.1
LO 11.10

The following two statements concern depreciation:
1. "Because our plant was shut down for part of the year, we will not depreciate it. Depreciating it for the full year would increase our costs and overstate the inventory."
2. "I think we should have increasing depreciation expense each period because it will increase the funds recovered near the end of the asset's life when maintenance costs are high and we will need to replace the asset. Also, I think tax rates will be higher toward the end of the asset's life, so we will be better off to have a larger amount of depreciation expense then."

Required:
Prepare a short report that evaluates each of the following statements separately.

C11-6 **Ethics and Depreciation Issues**

You are auditing the financial records of a company and are reviewing the depreciation computations. Included in the assets are two buildings and numerous machines in each building. One of the buildings is used to manufacture components of toys and the other for assembly and packing, using the manufactured components as well as others purchased from suppliers. You see that the company uses straight-line depreciation over 40 years for the buildings and 20 years for the machinery. You decide to ask the CFO about these calculations, and he replies, "We use 40 years for the buildings because it is close to the 39 we use for tax. And our best guess is that we will replace the machines twice while we use the building. And the method is easy to use and most companies use it, don't they? Or have things changed that much since I was in college?" You feel as if you have annoyed the CFO with your questions, so you decide to leave. As you walk back to your office, you recall from earlier in the audit that the company uses FIFO and LIFO for different segments of its inventory and that all top-level managers receive bonuses based on reported income.

Required:

From financial reporting and ethical perspectives, what depreciation methods and lives would you recommend?

C11-7 **Analyzing Starbucks's Property, Plant, and Equipment Disclosures**

Obtain **Starbucks**'s 2015 annual report either using the "Investor Relations" portion of its web site (do a Web search for Starbucks investor relations) or go to http://www.sec.gov and click "Search for company filings" under "Filings and Forms (EDGAR)."

Required:

1. Which depreciation method does Starbucks use? Why do you think Starbucks selected this method?
2. What are the useful lives of the various classes of Starbucks's property, plant, and equipment?
3. a. Does Starbucks report all of its depreciation expense in a single line item on its income statement?
   b. What amount did Starbucks report as depreciation and amortization for 2015, 2014 and 2013? Do these amounts result in an increase to cash?
4. a. What amount does Starbucks report for impairment and disposition losses for 2015, 2014, and 2013? Where are impairment and disposition losses reported?
   b. What is the conceptual justification for Starbucks's combination of impairment and disposition losses?
   c. With regard to impairments, how does Starbucks measure fair value, and how would this measurement be classified in the fair value hierarchy (Level 1, 2, or 3)?

C11-8 **Analyzing Nestlé's Property, Plant, and Equipment**

Obtain **Nestlé**'s 2013 annual report using the "Investor Relations" portion of its web site (do a Web search for Nestlé investor relations).

Required:

1. What is the value of Nestlé's property, plant, and equipment?
2. What categories of property, plant, and equipment does Nestlé report on its financial statements?
3. Which depreciation method does Nestlé use?
4. What are the useful lives of the various classes of Nestlé's property, plant, and equipment?
5. For 2013, how much did Nestlé report for:
   a. depreciation expense
   b. capital expenditures
   c. disposals
   d. impairments
6. Compute the average useful life and the estimated average age of the property, plant, and equipment.

USING CODIFICATION

C11-9 Researching GAAP

Situation

Magic Movie Company has been formed to produce films for showing in movie theaters. The president knows that there are some unusual accounting issues regarding asset valuation and income recognition and has asked for your advice.

Directions
1. Research the related generally accepted accounting principles and prepare a short memo to the president. Cite your references and applicable paragraph numbers.
2. Does this situation allow opportunities for earnings management?

C11-10 Researching GAAP

Situation

Scientific Software sells software to the oil industry. Its policy is to recognize revenue when it signs a licensing agreement for the software. It uses a 13-year amortization period for the software products it capitalizes. The president has asked you to evaluate these revenue recognition and amortization policies.

Directions
1. Research the related generally accepted accounting principles and prepare a short memo to the president. Cite your references and applicable paragraph numbers.
2. Why do you think the company might have selected a 13-year amortization period?

CHAPTER 12

INTANGIBLES

Where's the Value?

LEARNING OBJECTIVES

After reading this chapter you will be able to

LO 12.1 Explain the accounting for intangible assets, including initial valuation, amortization, and impairment.

LO 12.2 Identify and explain the accounting issues related to research and development costs.

LO 12.3 Understand the disclosures related to intangibles.

LO 12.4 Explain the accounting treatment for specific identifiable intangible assets, including trademarks and trade names, copyrights, franchises, patents, and computer software costs.

LO 12.5 Account for unidentifiable intangibles, including internally developed and purchased goodwill.

Even though intangible assets do not have a physical or financial nature and, therefore, cannot be touched or spent, they can create an enormous value for companies. In fact, with the move to a more knowledge-based economy over the last several decades, intangible assets are replacing tangible assets as key value drivers for the economy. For example, the **World Bank** estimates that intangible assets are not only the single most important component of wealth but the fastest growing one as well—averaging approximately 77% of worldwide assets.[1] At the national level, investment in tangible capital by U.S. companies has been relatively flat—averaging about 11.4% of gross domestic product (GDP). However, the average rate of intangible capital investment has more than doubled—from 5.9% to 12.8%—since 1948.[2] Finally, a study by **Accenture** estimates that, on average, 60% of a company's market value is tied to intangible assets. In addition, 49% of the executives surveyed indicated that their company primarily relies on intangible assets to create shareholder wealth.

Given the importance of intangible assets, the key question is: How should they be measured and reported? For situations in which intangible assets are acquired in an external transaction, this issue is relatively straightforward—measure and report them at their acquisition cost. For example, in 2013, **Google** was involved in numerous acquisitions which increased intangible assets by $1,540 million. At the end of 2013, Google reported the following intangible assets:

---

[1] World Bank. "The Changing Wealth of Nations: Measuring Sustainable Development in the New Millennium" (December 2010).
[2] Corrado and Hulten (2010) "How Do You Measure a Technological Revolution." *The American Economic Review* (May): 99–104.

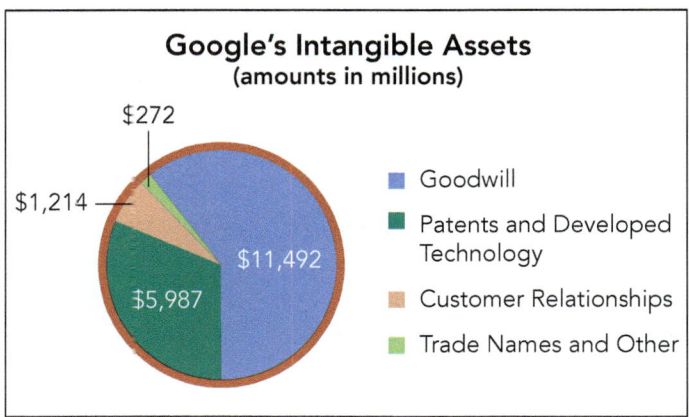

Google's Intangible Assets (amounts in millions)
- Goodwill: $11,492
- Patents and Developed Technology: $5,987
- Customer Relationships: $1,214
- Trade Names and Other: $272

In the absence of an external transaction, how are intangible assets measured and reported? While accountants could rely on estimates from valuation experts, the nature of intangible assets will most likely result in widespread differences in opinion about any estimated value. Because of their subjective nature, intangible asset value estimates are relevant but not necessarily representationally faithful information, and accountants generally take the conservative approach of expensing the development of any internally developed intangibles. Therefore, for many companies, major resources that have been internally developed will not be recognized and reported as assets on the balance sheet. For example, the value of **Starbucks**'s brand name and the "Starbucks Experience™" (its unique customer experience which is a function of service, beverage quality, and store atmosphere) do not appear on its balance sheet. On the other hand, the goodwill from Starbucks Corporation's acquisition of **Teavana** lead to recognition of $467.5 million in goodwill and $120.8 million of other intangible assets. While intangible assets, such as trademarks, patents, customer lists, and goodwill, can give a company a competitive advantage in the marketplace, the measurement issues that exist with regard to these assets pose a significant challenge for financial reporting and company valuation.

As we discussed in Chapter 10, tangible noncurrent assets have a physical substance that can be seen and touched. Chapter 13 will discuss noncurrent assets that are financial in nature, such as long-term investments and notes receivable. In contrast to tangible and financial assets, **intangible assets** do not have a physical or financial nature but do have value based on the rights and privileges they convey to the company that owns and uses them. These rights and privileges often arise from legal or contractual rights. For example, the **Starbucks** logo is a registered trademark that is protected under federal law and excludes others from using the same logo or one that is "confusingly similar." In addition, Starbucks has contract-based patents ranging from coffee-brewing technology to the cardboard sleeve that insulates its coffee cups.

Intangible and tangible noncurrent assets do have characteristics in common, as both:

- are held for use in the ordinary course of business and not for investment—although they are "used" in very different ways
- have a useful life of more than one year
- derive their value from their ability to generate economic benefits
- are expensed by a company in the periods in which the assets are used in operations (if the assets have finite lives)

However, intangible assets generally have a higher degree of uncertainty regarding their future economic benefits. In large part, this is due to the fact that their intangible nature makes them harder to separate and sell relative to tangible assets.

HOW DO WE ACCOUNT FOR INTANGIBLE ASSETS?

LEARNING OBJECTIVE 12.1
Explain the accounting for intangible assets, including initial valuation, amortization, and impairment.

Intangible assets can be either *externally acquired* or *internally developed*. Intangible assets that are externally acquired are purchased from others, either in a separate transaction (such as acquiring a license) or as part of a business acquisition (such as a merger or takeover). By contrast, a company internally develops intangibles when it engages in business activities, such as advertising or research and development, that enhance the company's capabilities but do not involve the purchase of an identifiable asset. For example, in 2013, Merck spent $7,503 million on the internal development of intangibles by engaging in research and development activities to create new products. This contrasts with 2009, when Merck purchased $40,952 million of intangible assets by acquiring Schering-Plough. The accounting for such expenditures differs greatly based on whether these intangibles were internally developed or externally acquired.

Initial Valuation of Intangible Assets

The external acquisition of an intangible asset provides a faithful representation of its future economic benefits. Therefore, **purchased intangible assets are capitalized at their acquisition cost**—the cost to obtain the asset and prepare it for use. On the other hand, **internally developed intangible assets are generally expensed** because the future economic benefits associated with them are difficult to measure, and the costs incurred to develop them are often difficult to measure separately from the normal, ongoing operating costs of the business. However, any direct costs, such as legal and filing costs associated with establishing the rights associated with an intangible asset, may be capitalized.

In addition, intangible assets may be classified according to whether they are *identifiable or unidentifiable*. **Identifiable intangible assets** are intangible assets that can be separated from the company and sold, transferred, licensed, rented, or exchanged. For example, Starbucks's identifiable intangible assets consist of trademarks, patents, and copyrights. Other common identifiable intangible assets are franchise rights, customer lists and relationships, noncompete agreements, and licenses. **Unidentifiable intangible assets** *cannot* be separated from the entity and sold, transferred, licensed, rented, or exchanged. The primary unidentifiable intangible asset is goodwill. Starbucks reported $1,575.4 million of goodwill at the end of 2015. This represented approximately 75.2% of its total intangible assets.

Based on these classifications, a company accounts for the cost of its intangible assets as summarized in Exhibit 12.1 (p. 12-4).

Four main points with regard to the initial valuation of intangible assets are illustrated in Exhibit 12.1:

- *Purchased Identifiable Intangible Assets.* Companies account for purchased identifiable intangible assets, such as a patent or trademark, in a similar manner to that of tangible assets, as discussed in Chapter 10.
- *Purchased Unidentifiable Intangible Assets.* A company capitalizes the cost of a purchased unidentifiable intangible asset, which is called goodwill. Goodwill can be acquired only through the purchase of another company. We discuss the nature of and accounting for goodwill in more detail later in this chapter.
- *Internally Developed Identifiable Intangible Assets.* When a company internally develops an intangible asset, such as a patent, it can capitalize only *certain* costs. For example, the capitalized costs of an internally developed patent include the legal and related costs of establishing and successfully defending the rights associated with the patent but *not* the costs leading to the development of the product or process being patented. A company includes those latter costs in research and development expenses as incurred. We discuss the accounting for research and development costs later in this chapter.

- *Internally Developed Unidentifiable Intangible Assets.* A company expenses the costs of internally developed unidentifiable intangible assets as incurred, even though they may be expected to have benefits extending beyond the current period. Examples of these costs include advertising, employee training, and customer relationships. This procedure is justified because either the costs incurred and/or the expected life of the benefits cannot be faithfully represented.

EXHIBIT 12.1 **Classification and Accounting for Intangible Assets**

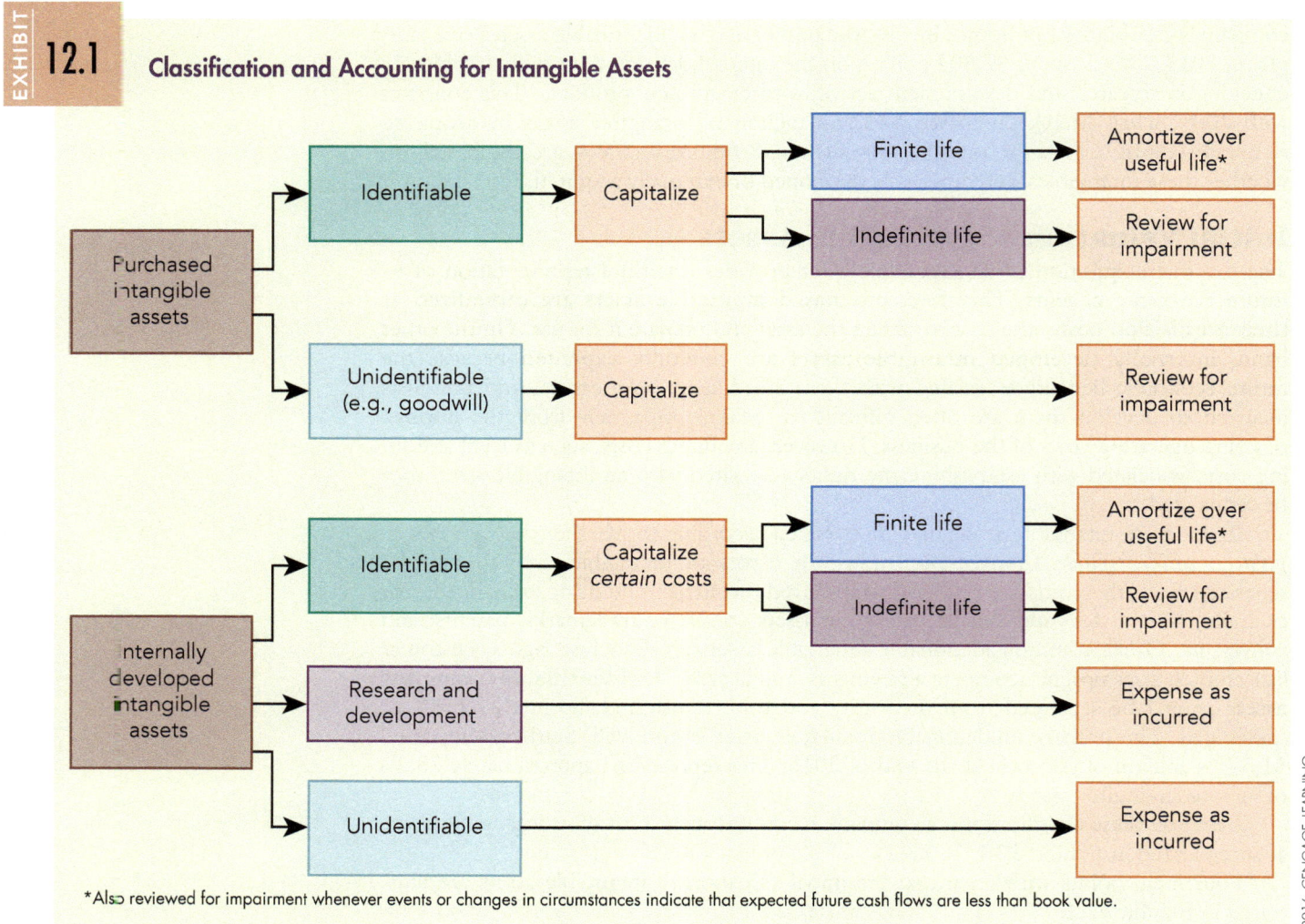

*Also reviewed for impairment whenever events or changes in circumstances indicate that expected future cash flows are less than book value.

Amortization and Impairment of Intangible Assets

Subsequent to acquisition, two main accounting issues relating to capitalized intangible assets are amortization and impairment. The allocation of the cost of intangible assets in a systematic and rational manner over the asset's useful life is called **amortization**. An **impairment** of an intangible asset occurs when the fair value of the asset is less than its carrying value. Intangible assets are separated into two categories to determine whether they are amortized and how they are reviewed for impairment. The two categories are:

- intangible assets with a finite, or limited, life
- intangible assets with an indefinite life

Intangible Assets with a Finite Life An identifiable intangible asset that has a finite life is amortized over its useful life. The useful life is the period over which the intangible asset is expected to be used in operations and to contribute directly or indirectly to the future cash flows of the company. Factors that a company should consider in estimating the useful life of an intangible asset include the:

- expected legal, technological, or contractual life
- expected use of the intangible asset
- expected useful life of a related a related asset (e.g., mineral rights that relate to a depleting asset)
- legal, regulatory, or contractual provisions that enable renewal or extension of the intangible asset's legal or contractual life without substantial economic cost, if any
- effects of obsolescence, demand, competition, and other economic factors
- level of maintenance costs required to obtain the expected future cash flows from the asset[3]

The amortization of intangible assets follows the same principles as the depreciation of tangible assets. The amount of an intangible asset to be amortized is the cost minus the residual value. In general, the residual value of the intangible asset is assumed to be zero unless, at the end of its useful life, the intangible asset has value to another company. The amortization method selected should be systematic and rational, reflecting the pattern in which the economic benefits of the intangible asset are used or consumed in the operations of the business. If the company cannot reliably determine this pattern, it should use the straight-line method. As with tangible assets, amortization expense is normally reported as a current-period operating expense. In certain circumstances (e.g., the amortization expense related to a patent on a manufacturing process), amortization expense may be considered a production cost and included in the cost of inventory. Amortization expense may be credited to either the intangible asset itself or a contra-asset account, usually called Accumulated Amortization.

Example Schultz Company purchases a patent for $85,000 and amortizes it using the straight-line method over 10 years (the time period it expects to use the patent) with no expected residual value. The journal entries to record the acquisition and the amortization for the first year are as follows:

Patent	85,000	
Cash		85,000
Amortization Expense ($85,000 ÷ 10 years)	8,500	
Patent (or Accumulated Amortization: Patent)		8,500

Schultz reports the $76,500 ($85,000 − $8,500) book value of the patent in the intangible assets section of its balance sheet. If, in future periods, Schultz revises its estimate of the useful life of the intangible asset, this change in estimate is accounted for by computing a new periodic amortization expense amount based on the remaining book value of the asset and the revised useful life. ■

GAAP requires that a company review its intangible assets that are subject to amortization for impairment whenever events or circumstances indicate that its book value may not be recoverable.[4] Testing for impairment of intangible assets with a finite life consists of two steps:

- *Step 1: Recoverability Test.* If the total undiscounted cash flows expected to result from the use of the intangible asset are less than the asset's book value, the company must recognize an impairment loss because the book value of the asset is not recoverable.
- *Step 2: Measurement of the Loss.* The impairment loss is measured as the difference between the asset's fair value and its book value.

---

[3] FASB ASC 350-30-35: Intangibles—Goodwill and Other: General Intangibles Other than Goodwill: Subsequent Measurement.
[4] FASB ASC 350-30-35: Intangibles—Goodwill and Other: General Intangibles Other than Goodwill: Subsequent Measurement.

When a company recognizes an impairment loss, it writes down the asset to reduce its book value to fair value. A company reports an impairment loss as part of income from continuing operations on its income statement and reports the reduced book value of the asset on its ending balance sheet. This impairment test follows the same procedures discussed in Chapter 11 for tangible property, plant, and equipment.

Example Because of technological developments in its industry, Schultz Company decides to review its patent, which has a book value of $68,000, for impairment. Schultz estimates that the future net cash flows from this patent are $40,000. Because the expected cash flows are less than the book value, Schultz must recognize an impairment loss. The fair value of the patent, measured as the present value of the expected future cash flows, is $25,000. Schultz records the impairment of the patent as follows:

Loss on Impairment ($25,000 − $68,000)	43,000	
Patent		43,000

After recording the impairment loss, the reduced book value of the intangible asset is amortized over the asset's remaining useful life. If the patent subsequently experiences a substantial recovery of its value, restoration of the previously recognized impairment loss is prohibited under U.S. GAAP. However, as we discuss later, IFRS do allow the impairment loss to be reversed.

Intangible Assets with an Indefinite Life Some identifiable intangible assets, such as trademarks and trade names, have a potentially indefinite life. The asset's useful life is considered indefinite when there is no foreseeable limit on the period of time over which the intangible asset is expected to be used in operations and to contribute to a company's cash flows. **An intangible asset with an indefinite life is not amortized but is reviewed for impairment.**[5] A company must review these intangible assets for impairment annually, *or* more frequently when events or circumstances indicate the intangible asset may be impaired. If events change, an indefinite-lived intangible asset may be reclassified as an intangible asset with a finite life and amortized over its remaining life.

The impairment test for an intangible asset with an indefinite life differs from the impairment test for an intangible asset with a finite life because there is no recoverability test. An intangible asset with an indefinite life is impaired when its fair value is less than its book value.[6] The impairment loss is the amount by which the fair value of the intangible asset is less than its carrying value. The loss is recorded by increasing an impairment loss account and decreasing the intangible asset account.

Example Norton Company purchased a trademark 2 years ago for $60,000. Norton considered the trademark to have an indefinite life, and, at the beginning of the year, it has a carrying value of $60,000. At the end of the current year, Norton determines that the fair value of the trademark is $20,000. Norton records the $40,000 impairment loss ($20,000 fair value − $60,000 cost) as follows:

Loss on Impairment	40,000	
Trademark		40,000

Norton reports the impairment loss as a component of income from continuing operations on its income statement and reports the $20,000 fair value of the trademark in the intangible asset section of its balance sheet. Subsequently, the company must compare the fair value with the $20,000 carrying value to determine if the trademark is again impaired. In addition, restoration of any previously recognized impairment loss is prohibited under U.S. GAAP (but not under IFRS). ■

---

[5] FASB ASC 350-30-35: Intangibles—Goodwill and Other: General Intangibles Other than Goodwill: Subsequent Measurement.
[6] The fair value of an intangible asset is the amount at which the asset could be sold in an orderly transaction between market participants. The quoted market price in an active market is the best measure of fair value. However, because a quoted market price is often unavailable for an intangible asset, a company may estimate the value by using the value of similar assets, or by using present value techniques.

Goodwill is an unidentifiable intangible asset with an indefinite useful life that is only recognized when one company purchases another company. **Goodwill** is defined and measured as the excess of the purchase price over the fair value of the acquired company's identifiable net assets. We discuss the recognition and impairment of goodwill in a later section of this chapter.

> **GOT IT?**
>
> **12-1** How are intangible assets distinguished from tangible assets? What do they have in common?
>
> **12-2** How are identifiable intangible assets distinguished from unidentifiable intangible assets?
>
> **12-3** Explain how a company accounts for the cost of its intangible assets.
>
> **12-4** Are all intangible assets amortized? If not, which ones are not? Why?
>
> **12-5** Which amortization method is required for intangible assets? Are there any exceptions?
>
> **12-6** What factors should a company consider in estimating the useful life of an intangible asset?

HOW DO WE ACCOUNT FOR RESEARCH AND DEVELOPMENT COSTS?

LEARNING OBJECTIVE 12.2

Identify and explain the accounting issues related to research and development costs.

Research and development (R&D) activities are defined as follows:

- **Research** is the planned search or critical investigation aimed at discovering new knowledge with the hope that such knowledge will be useful in developing a new product or process or in significantly improving an existing product or process.
- **Development** is the translation of research findings into a plan or design for a new product or process or for significantly improving an existing product or process. It includes the conceptual formulation, design, and testing of product alternatives, construction of prototypes, and operation of pilot plants. It does not include routine or periodic alterations to existing products, production lines, manufacturing processes, and other ongoing operations. It does not include market research or market testing activities.[7]

Exhibit 12.2 shows examples of activities that are included as R&D and those that are excluded from R&D.

EXHIBIT 12.2 Examples of Activities Included in and Excluded from R&D

Included in R&D
- (a) laboratory research aimed at discovery of new knowledge
- (b) searching for applications of new research findings or of other knowledge
- (c) conceptual formulation and design of possible product or process alternatives
- (d) testing in search for or evaluation of product or process alternatives
- (e) modification of the formulation or design of a product or process
- (f) design, construction, and testing of preproduction prototypes and models
- (g) design of tools, jigs, molds, and dies involving new technology

(continued)

---

[7] FASB ASC 730-10-20: Research and Development: Overall: Glossary.

> **EXHIBIT 12.2** (Continued)
>
> (h) design, construction, and operation of a pilot plant that is not of a scale economically feasible to the company for commercial production
> (i) engineering activity required to advance the design of a product to the point that it meets specific functional and economic requirements and is ready for manufacture
>
> **Excluded from R&D**
>
> (a) engineering follow-through in an early phase of commercial production
> (b) quality control during commercial production, including routine testing of products
> (c) troubleshooting in connection with breakdowns during commercial production
> (d) routine, ongoing efforts to refine, enrich, or otherwise improve upon the qualities of an existing product
> (e) adaptation of an existing capability to a particular requirement or customer's need as part of a continuing commercial activity
> (f) seasonal or other periodic design changes to existing products
> (g) routine design of tools, jigs, molds, and dies
> (h) activity, including design and construction engineering, related to the construction, relocation, rearrangement, or start-up of facilities or equipment other than (1) pilot plants and (2) facilities or equipment whose sole use is for a particular research and development project
> (i) legal work in connection with patent applications or litigation, and the sale or licensing of patents
>
> **Source:** FASB ASC 730-10-55: Research and Development: Overall: Implementation Guidance and Illustrations.

Many companies spend large sums each year on research and development activities. In its 2013 10-K, **Google** made the following disclosure regarding R&D:

> **Research**
>
> We continue to develop new products and services and to enhance our existing ones through research and product development and the licensing and acquisition of third-party businesses and technology. Our product development philosophy is to launch innovative products early and often, and then iterate rapidly to make those products even better. We often post early-stage products at test locations online or directly on Google.com. We then use data and user feedback to decide if and how to invest further in those products. Our research and development expenses were $5.2 billion, $6.8 billion, and $8.0 billion in 2011, 2012, and 2013, respectively.

In addition, at the end of 2013, approximately 39% of Google's employees were classified as related to R&D. Clearly, R&D activities represent a substantial investment. Other industries, such as pharmaceuticals, also invest heavily in R&D. For example, **Johnson and Johnson** and **GlaxoSmithKline** spent $8.183 billion and £3.923 billion, respectively, on R&D in 2013. If these activities are successful, they create valuable intangible resources such as a patented product or process. However, in many cases, R&D activities are unsuccessful and do not produce any direct future benefits for the company.

GAAP requires that **a company expense all its research and development costs as incurred**.[8] Even though R&D projects may produce future benefits, at the time the costs are incurred, there is a high degree of uncertainty about which R&D projects will produce future benefits and which will not. Furthermore, even if the benefits provided by R&D activities could be estimated, it would be difficult to provide a faithful representation of the estimated useful life or how the resources will be used in operations, which is necessary to determine the proper amount of periodic amortization. For companies with significant R&D costs, immediate expensing of R&D may lead to assets being understated, resulting in financial statements being less relevant and faithfully representative. After considering the advantages and disadvantages of capitalizing versus immediate expensing of R&D costs, the FASB decided to require that R&D be expensed in the belief that this approach would be easier to implement and would likely lead to greater comparability between companies.[9] However, if a company performs R&D for other companies under a contractual arrangement, the cost of the R&D activity is capitalized as inventory and expensed when the company recognizes the revenue from the contract.

The costs for the following elements of R&D activities are *included* in R&D costs, and thus are expensed as incurred:

- materials, equipment, and facilities
- personnel
- intangible assets purchased from others
- contract services—the costs of services performed by others in connection with the R&D activities of an enterprise
- indirect costs—R&D includes a reasonable allocation of indirect costs; however, general and administrative costs that are not clearly related to R&D activities are not included as R&D costs[10]

If the materials, equipment, facilities, and intangible assets purchased from others have *alternative future uses* (in other R&D or non-R&D activities), a company follows normal accrual procedures. For example, a company includes the salaries, wages, and other costs of R&D personnel in R&D expense as payments are made or costs are accrued. It also records the costs of materials in inventory and includes them as R&D expense as the materials are used. Finally, a company capitalizes the cost of a machine that has alternative future uses (even if only in other R&D projects) and depreciates this cost over the asset's estimated useful life with the depreciation included in R&D expense.

However, if the materials, equipment, facilities, and intangibles purchased from others have *no alternative future uses* and are used in a single R&D project, their cost is immediately expensed as R&D. For example, if a company can use inventory or a machine only for one R&D project, the company includes the total acquisition costs in R&D expense in the period it incurs the cost.

---

[8] FASB ASC 730-10-25: Research and Development: Overall: Recognition.

[9] In addition, income tax regulations allow a company to immediately expense its R&D costs. Therefore, immediately expensing R&D for financial reporting eliminates a potential significant difference between financial income and taxable income.

[10] FASB ASC 730-10-25: Research and Development: Overall: Recognition.

Example Kent Company incurred and paid the following costs for R&D activities:

Material used from inventory	$ 50,000
Wages and salaries	90,000
Allocation of general and administrative costs	20,000
Depreciation on building housing multiple R&D activities	25,000
Machine purchased for R&D project that has no alternative future uses	30,000
Total	$215,000

Kent includes all these costs in R&D expense, including the entire cost of the machine with no alternative future uses, and records them as follows:

Research and Development Expense	215,000	
Cash		140,000
Inventory		50,000
Accumulated Depreciation: Building		25,000

If the machine had alternative future uses and was being depreciated on a straight-line basis over 5 years, Kent would include only the $6,000 depreciation expense related to the machine in R&D expense. Therefore, total R&D expense would be $191,000 ($50,000 + $90,000 + $20,000 + $25,000 + $6,000), and the journal entry would be as follows:

Research and Development Expense	191,000	
Cash		110,000
Inventory		50,000
Accumulated Depreciation: Building		25,000
Accumulated Depreciation: Machine		6,000

In-Process R&D

When a company that is performing R&D activities is acquired by another company, the acquiring company must allocate a portion of the purchase price to the R&D activities that are purchased. This intangible asset is called **in-process R&D (IPR&D)**. IPR&D is initially capitalized at fair value and treated as an intangible asset with an indefinite life until the R&D activities are completed or abandoned. Once the project is completed, the IPR&D is accounted for as either a finite-life or an indefinite-life intangible asset, depending on its nature. If the project is abandoned, the IPR&D is immediately expensed.[11]

Start-Up Costs

Start-up costs are broadly defined as the costs incurred for one-time activities related to:

- opening a new facility or commencing a new operation
- introducing a new product or service
- conducting business in a new territory or with an entirely new class of customer
- initiating a new process in an existing facility

Start-up costs include organization costs such as legal fees, stock certificate costs, underwriting fees, and accounting fees associated with forming a new company. Because these costs are incurred with the expectation of obtaining future benefits, it can be argued that start-up costs are an intangible asset with an indefinite life. **However, GAAP requires that the costs of start-up activities be expensed as incurred.**[12] Similar to R&D costs, this conservative accounting treatment is justified due to the high level of uncertainty with regard to the amount and timing of any future benefits relating to these costs.

---

[11] FASB ASC 350-30-35: Intangibles—Goodwill and Other: General Intangibles Other than Goodwill: Subsequent Measurement.
[12] FASB ASC 720-15-25: Other Expense: Start-Up Costs: Recognition.

> **GOT IT?**
>
> **12-7** What is meant by the terms *research* and *development*?
>
> **12-8** What activities are included in R&D? Which are excluded?
>
> **12-9** What elements of R&D activities does a company include in R&D costs?

HOW ARE INTANGIBLE ASSETS DISCLOSED?

LEARNING OBJECTIVE 12.3
Understand the disclosures related to intangibles.

At the end of each period when a company presents a balance sheet, it should disclose the following:

- for intangible assets that are amortized—the total cost, accumulated amortization, amortization expense, and estimated amortization expense for the next 5 years. Amortization expense should be included with the related line items of expenses (cost of goods sold, selling, general, administrative, R&D), as appropriate, in income from continuing operations
- for intangible assets that are not amortized—the cost of each major class of intangible asset
- the total of all identifiable intangible assets as a separate line item (asset) on the balance sheet
- for any intangible asset impairment other than goodwill—the facts leading to the impairment, the amount of the impairment loss, and the method of determining the fair value of the intangible asset; any impairment losses should be included in income from continuing operations
- for goodwill—the amount of goodwill acquired and the amount of any impairment losses recognized; any impairment loss should be reported as a separate line item in income from continuing operations, unless the impairment is related to a discontinued operation

In addition, if intangible assets are acquired during the period, GAAP requires a company to disclose:

- cost of any intangible assets acquired
- residual value and the weighted average amortization period for intangible assets that are amortized
- cost of any research and development acquired and written off, and where it is included on the income statement

Real Report 12.1 shows **Merck**'s disclosures of intangible assets.

REAL REPORT | **DISCLOSURE OF INTANGIBLE ASSETS** | **12.1**

Merck & Co.
Consolidated Balance Sheet (in part)
(in millions)

Assets (in part)	Dec. 31, 2013	Dec. 31, 2012
Goodwill	$12,301	$12,134
Other intangibles, net	23,801	29,083

(continued)

Notes to the Financial Statements (in part)

Note 2: Summary of Accounting Policies (in part)

Goodwill

Goodwill represents the excess of the consideration transferred over the fair value of net assets of businesses purchased. Goodwill is assigned to reporting units and evaluated for impairment on at least an annual basis, or more frequently if impairment indicators exist, by first assessing qualitative factors to determine whether it is more likely than not that the fair value of a reporting unit is less than its carrying amount. If the Company concludes it is more likely than not that the fair value of a reporting unit is less than its carrying amount, a quantitative fair value test is performed. Based upon the Company's most recent annual impairment test completed as of October 1, 2013, the Company concluded goodwill was not impaired.

Acquired Intangibles

Acquired intangibles include products and product rights, tradenames and patents, which are recorded at fair value, assigned an estimated useful life, and are amortized primarily on a straight-line basis over their estimated useful lives ranging from 3 to 40 years (see Note 7). The Company periodically evaluates whether current facts or circumstances indicate that the carrying values of its acquired intangibles may not be recoverable. If such circumstances are determined to exist, an estimate of the undiscounted future cash flows of these assets, or appropriate asset groupings, is compared to the carrying value to determine whether an impairment exists. If the asset is determined to be impaired, the loss is measured based on the difference between the carrying value of the intangible asset and its fair value, which is determined based on the net present value of estimated future cash flows.

Note 7: Goodwill and Other Intangibles (in part)

The following table summarizes goodwill activity by segment:

(in millions)	Pharmaceutical	All Other	Total
Goodwill balance December 31, 2012	$10,086	$2,048	$12,134
Acquisitions	103	188	291
Divestitures	(45)	—	(45)
Other	(79)	—	(79)
Goodwill balance December 31, 2013	$10,065	$2,236	$12,301

Other intangibles at December 31 consisted of:

	2013			2012		
	Gross Carrying Amount	Accumulated Amortization	Net	Gross Carrying Amount	Accumulated Amortization	Net
Products and product rights	$41,691	$21,216	$20,475	$41,932	$16,678	$25,254
In-process R&D	1,856	—	1,856	2,393	—	2,393
Tradenames	1,632	310	1,322	1,521	236	1,285
Other	958	810	148	896	745	151
Total	$46,137	$22,336	$23,801	$46,742	$17,659	$29,083

Acquired intangibles include products and product rights, tradenames and patents, which are recorded at fair value, assigned an estimated useful life, and are amortized primarily on a straight-line basis over their estimated useful lives.

During 2013 and 2012, the Company recorded impairment charges related to marketed products of $486 million and $118 million, respectively, within *Material and*

(continued)

production costs. Of the amount recorded in 2013, $330 million resulted from lower cash flow projections for *Saphris/Sycrest*, due to reduced expectations in international markets and in the United States. These revisions to cash flows indicated that the *Saphris/Sycrest* intangible asset value was not recoverable on an undiscounted cash flows basis. The Company utilized market participant assumptions and considered several different scenarios to determine its best estimate of the fair value of the intangible asset related to *Saphris/Sycrest* that, when compared with its related carrying value, resulted in the impairment charge noted above. The remaining $156 million of impairment charges in 2013 resulted from lower cash flow projections for *Rebetol* due to reduced expectations in Japan and Europe. These revisions to cash flows indicated that the *Rebetol* intangible asset value was not recoverable on an undiscounted cash flows basis. The Company utilized market participant assumptions to determine its best estimate of the fair value of the intangible asset related to *Rebetol* that, when compared with its related carrying value, resulted in the impairment charge noted above.

IPR&D represents the fair value assigned to incomplete research projects that the Company acquires through business combinations which, at the time of acquisition, have not reached technological feasibility. Amounts capitalized as IPR&D are accounted for as indefinite-lived intangible assets, subject to impairment testing until completion or abandonment of the projects. Upon successful completion of each project, the Company will make a separate determination as to the[RM2][JPJ3] useful life of the assets and begin amortization. During 2013, 2012 and 2011, $346 million, $78 million and $666 million, respectively, of IPR&D was reclassified to products and product rights upon receipt of marketing approval in a major market.

Aggregate amortization expense primarily recorded within *Materials and production costs* was $4.8 billion in 2013, $5.0 billion in 2012 and $5.1 billion in 2011. The estimated aggregate amortization expense for each of the next five years is as follows: 2014, $4.3 billion; 2015, $4.1 billion; 2016, $3.4 billion; 2017, $3.1 billion; 2018, $1.6 billion.

Questions:

1. What types and amounts of intangible assets does Merck have at the end of 2013?
2. What were the total impairment charges related to intangible assets during 2013? How did Merck determine fair value for the impairment test?
3. What is in-process research and development? What happens to in-process research and development once the project is completed?
4. How much amortization expense does Merck expect over the next 5 years?

Suggested answers to these questions are found at the end of the chapter.

IDENTIFIABLE INTANGIBLE ASSETS

While the prior section discussed general accounting procedures for identifiable intangible assets, this section examines the accounting treatment for some of the more common intangible assets. Specifically, these assets can be classified into five basic categories related to:

- marketing
- customers
- artistic works
- contracts
- technology[13]

LEARNING OBJECTIVE 12.4

Explain the accounting treatment for specific identifiable intangible assets, including trademarks and trade names, copyrights, franchises, patents, and computer software costs.

---

[13] FASB ASC 805-20-55: Business Combinations: Identifiable Assets and Liabilities, and Any Noncontrolling Interest: Implementation Guidance and Illustrations.

For example, in 2013, **Microsoft** reported the following amounts and useful lives related to these categories of intangible assets:

(in millions)	Net Carrying Amount	Weighted Average Life
Marketing-related (trade-names)	$1,249	15 years
Technology-based	275	5 years
Customer-related	114	5 years
Contract-based	10	4 years

Marketing-Related Intangible Assets

Marketing-related intangible assets are resources used to market or promote a company's products or services. For example, as part of its marketing strategy to improve the customer experience, **Starbucks** offers the Starbucks Mobile App for iPhone, Android, and Blackberry. The amount paid to **mFoundry** for developing this app is recorded as a marketing-related intangible asset. Also included in this category are trademarks and trade names, trade dress (unique color, shape, or package design), Internet domain names, and noncompete agreements.

A **trademark** (or **trade name**) is a word, name, phrase, or symbol that identifies the source of a product and distinguishes it from the products of other companies. For example, Starbucks Coffee® and Starbucks's logo are examples of trademarks. If a company internally develops a trademark, it capitalizes costs, such as attorney fees and registration costs, that are necessary to obtain the intangible asset, but excludes any R&D costs. If the trademark is purchased from another company, the acquiring company capitalizes the purchase price. Registration of a trademark or trade name with the U.S. Patent and Trademark Office establishes a right to exclusive use of that trademark or trade name for 10 years. This right is renewable indefinitely as long as the trademark or trade name is used continuously. Therefore, trademarks are typically considered to have an indefinite life and are not amortized (unless the company later decides its useful life is no longer indefinite). The company must review the trademark for impairment at least annually.

Similarly, an **Internet domain name** is used to identify a particular Internet address. The cost of registering the Internet domain name (if internally developed) or the purchase price of the Internet domain name (if purchased from a third party) is capitalized as an intangible asset. The market value of Internet domain names can be quite large. For example, **Facebook** purchased the Internet domain name "FB.com" for $8.5 million. Because Internet domain names are renewable indefinitely, they are considered intangible assets with an indefinite life.

Customer-Related Intangible Assets

Customer-related intangible assets arise from the relationship between a company and its customers. Included in this category are customer lists, order or production backlogs, and customer relationships. If these assets are developed internally, the cost of developing them is expensed. However, if customer-related intangibles purchased from another company are included as part of a business combination, the amount of the purchase price relating to the intangible asset is capitalized. For example, **Google** reported assets for purchased customer relationships with a net value of $703 million at the end of its 2013 fiscal year. Customer-related intangible assets are generally considered to have a finite life and are amortized on a straight-line basis.

Acquired customer-related intangible assets can be considerable among financial institutions. Banks will recognize "core deposit intangible assets" for the value of the depositor base of acquired banks. For example, **Bank of America** reported core deposit intangibles with a gross value of over $3.5 billion at the end of its 2013 fiscal year. Similarly, insurers will recognize intangible assets for "policyholder acquisition costs." For example, **AFLAC** recognized over $8.7 billion of policy acquisition costs on its 2013 balance sheet.

Artistic-Related Intangible Assets

Artistic-related intangible assets represent the right to reproduce, copy, or perform artistic works such as plays, operas, ballets, books or other literary works, music compositions and lyrics, photographs, motion pictures, television programs, and even accounting textbooks. When these rights are protected by copyrights, a company records an intangible asset. A **copyright** is a grant by the federal government that gives the owner the exclusive right to publish, sell, or otherwise control literary or artistic products for the life of the author plus 70 years. A company capitalizes the cost of acquiring and successfully defending a copyright. Any research and development costs incurred relating to the artistic work are expensed as incurred. The capitalized cost of the copyright is amortized over its useful life.

It is possible that a fully amortized copyright may subsequently develop a significant value, such as in the case of some old films or music. Under U.S. GAAP, increases in the market value of intangible assets are not recognized in the financial statements.

Contract-Based Intangible Assets

Contract-based intangible assets represent the value of rights arising from contractual arrangements. Included in this category are franchise agreements, licensing and royalty agreements, construction permits, broadcast rights, and use rights (e.g., drilling, mining, timber-cutting rights). For example, in 2011, **NBC** obtained the U.S. broadcast rights for the 2014, 2016, 2018, and 2020 Olympic games for approximately $4.4 billion. NBC will capitalize this amount and amortize it over its useful life, which ends with the broadcast of the 2020 Olympic games.

One of the more common contract-based intangible assets is a franchise agreement. **Franchises** are contractual agreements in which, for a royalty percentage of sales, the franchisor gives the franchisee the right to perform certain functions or sell certain products or services. In addition, the franchisor may agree to provide certain services to the franchisee. Many franchises exist between governments and companies, such as a franchise to provide a monopoly service (e.g., utilities) or to use public property to provide a service (e.g., a ferry). A common example of a franchise between two companies is in the restaurant business, where many individual restaurants of national chains such as **McDonald's** are locally owned and operated under the terms of a franchise agreement. Similar to a franchise, some companies operate under license agreements that allow them to operate under another company's brand. For example, **Starbucks**, which does not franchise, licenses the rights to run coffee shops. In fact, at the end of fiscal 2015, Starbucks had 10,808 licensed stores worldwide, which represented 47% of its total stores.

A franchisee or licensee capitalizes the initial cost it pays to acquire the franchise or license, but it expenses any continuing fees that it pays in subsequent years. If the franchise or license has a finite legal life, the franchisee or licensee amortizes the initial cost over its useful life. If, the franchise or license is granted in perpetuity, it is considered to have an indefinite life and should not be amortized. However, it would be tested for impairment at least annually.

Technology-Based Intangible Assets

Technology-based intangible assets are assets that represent technological advancement and provide economic benefits to companies through either legal or contractual protection. Examples include patents, computer software, databases, and trade secrets (e.g., secret recipes or formulas).

Patent A **patent** is an exclusive right granted by the federal government that gives the owner control of the manufacture, sale, or other use of an invention for 20 years from the date of filing. A patent has value if it gives the company a competitive advantage over its competitors by enabling the company to obtain higher income by selling products at a higher price, producing products at a lower cost, or producing a product for which there is less competition. If the patent is purchased from a third party, the purchase price is capitalized as an intangible asset. If the patent is developed internally, only the costs directly associated with obtaining the legal rights (e.g., legal and filing fees paid to secure the patent) and successfully defending those rights are capitalized. Any R&D costs to develop the patent are expensed as incurred.

Companies that develop a patented technology often license the technology patent to other companies to use for their products. For example, **Qualcomm** developed and patented much of the technology behind mobile phones. Today, the company licenses this technology to other mobile phone manufacturers who pay Qualcomm a fee to use the technology. Licenses often are granted to others to use the invention covered by a patent. To properly account for amounts received under such agreements, a company must first determine whether the license represents a distinct performance obligation. If so, the company next considers the nature of the promise. If the license is determined to represent a "right to access" the intellectual property throughout the license period, revenue will be recognized over the license period. However if the license grants a "right to use" the intellectual property as it exists at a point in time, revenue is recognized at the beginning of the license period.[14] A company should disclose any material license agreements in the notes to its financial statements.

In addition, a company may find it necessary to defend the patent against infringement by others. A company capitalizes the unrecovered costs of successfully defending the legal validity of a patent because the benefits of the patent are maintained for its remaining economic life. If the company loses the lawsuit, it immediately expenses all legal costs and writes off the remaining book value of the patent because there is no remaining economic value.

Patents cannot be renewed and are considered an intangible asset with a finite life. However, the value of a patent might expire before the end of its legal life by the actions of other companies that produce a competing product without violating the patent, or through technological change or a change in demand for the product. Therefore, a company should amortize the cost of a patent over its expected *useful* life if it is shorter than 20 years.

In other situations, the effective life of the patent may be extended beyond 20 years by obtaining new patents on modifications and improvements to the original invention. If the new patent provides similar protection as the original patent, any unamortized cost of the original patent is added to the capitalized cost of the new patent, and the total amount is amortized over the shorter of the new patent's expected useful life or 20 years.

Software Development Costs **Software development costs** are the costs of designing, coding, and testing software to be sold, licensed, or leased to third parties, as well as preparing related documentation and training materials. GAAP requires that these costs be treated as R&D expense until the technological feasibility of the product is

---

[14] FASB ASC 606-10-55-54 through 55-64: Revenue from Contracts with Customers: Overall: Implementation Guidance and Illustrations.

established.[15] **Technological feasibility** is established either on the date the company completes a detailed program design or, in its absence, when it completes a working model of the product. After this date, a company capitalizes all software development costs until the product is available for general release to customers. For example, in 2009, **Apple** capitalized $71 million in software development costs related to the development of the Mac OS X operating system. After the product is ready for general release, any software development costs are expensed as incurred.[16]

Exhibit 12.3 summarizes the accounting for software development costs.

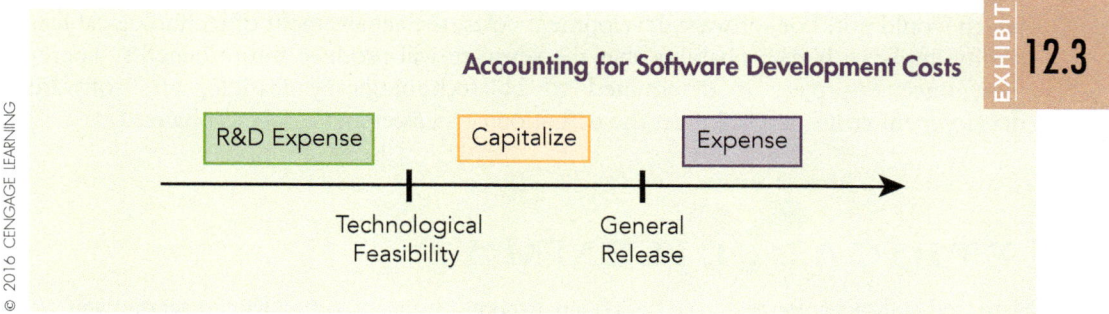

EXHIBIT 12.3 Accounting for Software Development Costs

The company amortizes the capitalized software development costs incurred during the period between technological feasibility and general release over the expected life of the product, which typically will be a relatively short period, such as 3 to 5 years. Amortization expense is calculated as the greater amount resulting from the following two methods:

- percent-of-revenue method—calculated as the ratio of current revenues from the software to the total amount of current and anticipated future revenues from the software multiplied by the cost of the asset
- straight-line method

Example Verlon Corp. develops computer video games for sale. A new development project reached technological feasibility at the end of June 2016, and the project was available for general release to customers on January 1, 2017. Development costs incurred prior to June 30 were $1,600,000, and costs incurred from July 1 to December 31 were $1,200,000. Revenues in 2017 from the sale of the new product were $4,000,000, and the company anticipates another $12,000,000 in revenues. The economic life of the software is 3 years.

Verlon will include the $1,600,000 incurred prior to the determination of technological feasibility as R&D expense. The $1,200,000 incurred after technological feasibility was determined but before general release to customers would be capitalized in 2016 as follows:

Software Development Costs	1,200,000	
Cash		1,200,000

In 2017, Verlon would calculate amortization expense related to the software development costs as the greater of:

$$\text{Percent-of-Revenue Method} \quad \frac{\$4,000,000}{\$4,000,000 + \$12,000,000} \times \$1,200,000 = \$300,000$$

$$\text{Straight-Line Method} \quad \frac{\$1,200,000}{3 \text{ years}} = \$400,000$$

---

[15] FASB ASC 985-20-25: Software: Costs of Software to Be Sold, Leased or Marketed: Recognition.
[16] Products are often released soon after technological feasibility is established. Therefore, the majority of software development costs will be included in R&D.

Because the straight-line method produces the greater amortization, Verlon would record amortization for 2017 as follows:

Amortization Expense	400,000	
Software Development Costs		400,000

The capitalization of a portion of software development costs is inconsistent with the accounting treatment of R&D. What is the justification for this inconsistency? Remember that FASB chose to require the expensing of all R&D costs due to the high degree of uncertainty about which R&D projects would produce future benefits and which would not. For software development costs, the achievement of technological feasibility implies a high probability that the software will produce future benefits. Therefore, once a project is determined to be technologically feasible, any software development costs incurred meet the definition of an asset and can be capitalized.

ETHICAL DILEMMA

Quality Technology Systems (QTS) is a high-technology company that focuses on developing software that controls and manages industrial machinery used in automated manufacturing processes. As an accountant for QTS, one of your responsibilities is to determine which expenditures can be capitalized as software development costs. Because you are not an expert in software design, you rely extensively on status reports provided by the company's engineering department and have, over the years, developed a friendship with one of the engineers. Based on the latest status report, you have decided that a new wireless operating system had reached technological feasibility, which resulted in the capitalization of approximately $1,000,000 during the current quarter.

During lunch today, you mention to the engineer that you were impressed at the progress they had made on the wireless operating system. After making you promise that you would not repeat anything he says, the engineer responded that the project has really been time consuming, and he wasn't sure if it would ever result in a functioning technology. In fact, recent setbacks had resulted in much of the previous work being scrapped and the project effectively having to start over from scratch. He further confided in you that he overheard a conversation between the CEO and the chief engineer in which the CEO instructed the engineer to do whatever it takes to achieve technological feasibility by the end of the quarter. What are your responsibilities upon learning of these events?

Software Development for Internal Use The costs that are incurred in the preliminary stage of developing internal-use computer software (e.g., conceptual formulation and evaluation of alternatives) are expensed as incurred.[17] Once the preliminary stage is completed and management agrees to fund the development of the software, the company capitalizes the software costs. These capitalized costs are amortized using the straight-line method over the estimated useful life of the software. Training costs for using the software are expensed as incurred. Costs incurred for upgrades and enhancements of the software are capitalized if they meet the capitalization criteria. However, costs incurred for maintaining the software are expensed as incurred. Impairment is measured and recognized similar to other intangible assets with a finite life.

GOT IT?

12-10 How does a company record a patent worth $100,000 if: (a) it has just purchased it for $90,000? (b) the company has internally developed it at a cost of $50,000 and paid $1,000 in legal and filing fees?

12-11 Which costs associated with a franchise are capitalized as an intangible asset?

12-12 What justifies the different treatment given to software development costs compared to R&D costs?

12-13 Over how many years are patents amortized? Trademarks?

---

[17] FASB ASC 350-40-25: Intangibles—Goodwill and Other: Internal-Use Software: Recognition.

HOW DO WE ACCOUNT FOR UNIDENTIFIABLE INTANGIBLES?

LEARNING OBJECTIVE 12.5
Account for unidentifiable intangibles, including internally developed and purchased goodwill.

The identifiable intangible assets discussed in the previous section can be separated from the company and sold, transferred, licensed, rented, or exchanged. However, other types of intangible assets generate economic benefits for a company but cannot be separated and specifically associated with an identifiable right. These unidentifiable intangibles are often called *goodwill*. Accounting for goodwill depends on whether it is internally developed or purchased through a transaction.

Internally Developed Goodwill

All companies strive to internally develop goodwill through product quality, effective marketing, customer relations, employee training and relations, community service, and other activities. For example, one of **Starbucks**'s key strategies is to increase the value of the Starbucks brand by delivering a consistently positive consumer experience. This "Starbucks Experience" is a function of service, beverage quality, and store atmosphere. While these efforts certainly generate goodwill for Starbucks, this customer experience is not recorded as an asset on its balance sheet. Similarly, a company that is close to its raw materials or its major customers may have an advantageous geographical location that is not recorded in its balance sheet. Internally developed goodwill, such as product quality, reputation, customer relations, human resources, or geographical location, is distinguished from other identifiable intangible assets by two characteristics:

- It is not separable from the other assets of a company. For example, the outstanding reputation of a company's employees cannot be sold to another company, and the geographical location cannot be sold without selling the other assets of the company.
- Measuring the value of internally developed goodwill would be very difficult and less representationally faithful than measuring the value of identifiable intangible assets.

Capitalizing internally developed goodwill would raise issues similar to those for R&D, such as which costs should be capitalized and which should be expensed. For example, do some or all of the company's marketing costs provide benefits for just the current period, or do they also provide benefits for future periods? Because of these characteristics, **the costs associated with *internally developed goodwill* are expensed as incurred**.

Purchased Goodwill

When one company acquires another company, the price paid is often much greater than the book value of the net assets acquired. Four factors can account for the difference between the value of the company as a whole and the book value of the net assets (assets minus liabilities):

- Many assets are listed on the balance sheet at amounts different from their fair market value. For example, land is reported at historical cost, and buildings and equipment are reported at depreciated cost, which may differ from fair value.
- Identifiable intangible assets may be unrecorded or undervalued. As we discussed earlier in the chapter, many costs to internally develop intangible assets, such as R&D, are expensed as incurred. This results in internally developed intangibles either not being recorded or recorded at costs associated with obtaining the intangible asset—not their fair market values.
- Unidentifiable intangible assets, such as internally developed goodwill of the target company, may exist but not be recognized on the target company's balance sheet.
- The acquirer may have simply paid too much. (We discuss goodwill impairment in a later section.)

When a company is purchased by another company, previously developed but unrecognized goodwill can be separately identified and recognized by the acquirer. The **purchased goodwill** is the difference between the purchase price of the acquired company and the fair value of its identifiable net assets.[18] Goodwill is recorded as an asset by the acquiring company because a transaction has occurred and the exchange price allows for a faithful representation of the value of the goodwill. Therefore, goodwill is a residual value determined only after an acquisition and only after the acquired company's other assets and liabilities are identified and measured at fair value.

Example: Recording the Purchase of Goodwill

Sara Company acquires Trevor Company and purchases its net assets for $790,000 cash. An independent valuation of Trevor's net assets results in the following reported fair market values in comparison to book values:

Trevor Company

	Book Value	Fair Value
Cash	$ 75,000	$ 75,000
Accounts receivable	180,000	180,000
Inventory	150,000	210,000
Property, plant, and equipment	270,000	325,000
Trademark	—	130,000
Notes payable	(530,000)	(530,000)
Identifiable net assets	$ 145,000	$ 390,000

The differences between book values and fair values can result from numerous factors. For example, for inventory, this difference could be due to the use of LIFO, which, in periods of rising prices, results in a lower book value of ending inventory relative to its current market value. For property, plant, and equipment, the depreciation process can lead to a divergence of book value from fair value.

Note that Trevor had a trademark with a book value of zero but an estimated value of $130,000. In recording the purchase, Sara assigns a value to any identifiable assets and liabilities, whether tangible or intangible. The difference between the fair value of the identifiable net assets ($390,000) and the purchase price ($790,000) is recorded as goodwill.

Sara would record the identifiable net assets of Trevor at their fair value and record the following journal entry:

Cash	75,000	
Accounts Receivable	180,000	
Inventory	210,000	
Property, Plant, and Equipment	325,000	
Trademark	130,000	
Goodwill	400,000	
Notes Payable		530,000
Cash		790,000

Impairment of Goodwill

Goodwill is considered to have an indefinite life, and, therefore, it is not amortized. However, a company must review its goodwill for impairment at least annually or

---

[18] FASB ASC 805-30-30: Business Combinations: Goodwill or Gain from Bargain Purchase, Including Consideration Transferred: Initial Measurement.

whenever events or changes in circumstances occur that would indicate an impairment may exist. Examples include:

- macroeconomic conditions such as a deterioration in general economic conditions, limitations on accessing capital, or other developments in the equity and credit markets
- industry and market considerations such as a deterioration in the business environment or increased competition
- cost factors such as increases in raw materials, labor, or other costs
- a decline in financial performance of the company
- changes in management, key personnel, strategy, or customers
- events affecting a reporting unit (e.g., an expectation that a reporting unit may be sold, adverse changes in a reporting unit's key business drivers)

Because goodwill is an unidentifiable intangible asset that cannot be separated from the company itself, the goodwill must be assigned to a reporting unit within the company. A **reporting unit** is an operating segment or component of a company for which discrete financial information is available that is regularly reviewed by management. Because goodwill only produces cash flows in connection with other assets, it is tested for impairment within the context of its reporting unit.

A company may first assess qualitative factors (such as those discussed above) that indicate whether further impairment testing is necessary.[19] If, after performing this qualitative assessment, a company determines that it is more likely than not that the fair value of the reporting unit is *greater than* its carrying value, it does not have to perform any other impairment testing. If this qualitative assessment indicates that it is more likely than not that the fair value of the reporting unit is *less than* its carrying value, a company must perform a two-step quantitative impairment test.

- *Step 1.* Determine if an impairment has occurred by comparing the fair value of the reporting unit with its book value, including goodwill.[20] If the fair value of the reporting unit is greater than the book value, goodwill is not considered to be impaired, and the second step is not necessary. If the fair value of the reporting unit is *less than* its book value, the second step of the impairment test must be performed to measure the *amount* of the impairment loss, if any.
- *Step 2.* Measure and recognize an impairment loss for the amount by which the implied fair value of the goodwill is less than its carrying value.
  - The implied fair value of a reporting unit's goodwill is the excess of the fair value of the reporting unit over the fair value of the identifiable net assets of the reporting unit.
  - The impairment loss is the difference between the carrying value of the goodwill and the implied fair value of the goodwill. The recognition of an impairment loss reduces the carrying value of the goodwill to the implied fair value.

Any impairment loss is reported as a separate line item on the company's income statement as part of income from continuing operations.

Example: Goodwill Impairment

Kent Company purchased Devon Company as a subsidiary several years ago. Devon is considered a reporting unit of Kent. At the end of 2016, Devon has a net book value (assets minus liabilities) of $3.6 million, which includes goodwill of $400,000. On that date, Kent estimates that the fair value of Devon is $3 million. In addition, Kent determines that the fair value of Devon's identifiable net assets, excluding goodwill, is $2.7 million. To test for the impairment of its goodwill, Kent performs the following two-step test:

- *Step 1.* Kent compares Devon's $3 million fair value to its $3.6 million book value. Because the fair value is less than book value, an impairment loss is indicated and Kent must perform the second step.

---

[19] FASB ASC 350-20-35-3A: Intangibles—Goodwill and Other, Goodwill, Subsequent Measurement.
[20] Impairment tests must be performed on other assets of the reporting unit prior to testing goodwill for impairment.

- *Step 2.* Kent then determines whether it needs to recognize an impairment loss. Kent calculates an impairment loss of $100,000 as follows:

    Implied Goodwill = Fair Value of Devon − Fair Value of Devon's Net Identifiable Assets
    = $3 million − $2.7 million = $300,000

    Impairment Loss = Carrying Value of Goodwill − Implied Value of Goodwill
    = $400,000 − $300,000 = $100,000

    Kent records the $100,000 impairment loss as follows:

Impairment Loss on Goodwill	100,000	
Goodwill		100,000

    Kent reports the $100,000 impairment loss as part of income from continuing operations and the new (reduced) $300,000 carrying value of goodwill on its ending balance sheet.

    Note also that the book value of Devon's identifiable net assets is $3,200,000 ($3,600,000 − $400,000 goodwill). Because the fair value of the identifiable net assets is $2,700,000, Kent also has an impairment of its assets other than goodwill (e.g., property, plant, and equipment) and should recognize additional impairment losses of $500,000 ($2,700,000 − $3,200,000) on the relevant assets (assuming the recorded amounts are not considered to be recoverable). The impairment of these other assets is discussed in other chapters.

Bargain Purchase

The discussion and examples in this chapter have assumed that the price paid for the company is greater than the fair value of the identifiable net assets acquired. However, it is possible that the cash paid is less than the fair value of the identifiable net assets acquired. While such a situation is not common, it may occur if there is a forced liquidation or distressed sale. In this case, there is a *bargain purchase*. If such a purchase transaction does occur, negative goodwill is *not* recorded. Instead, the acquiring company recognizes a gain on the bargain purchase equal to the difference between the purchase price and the fair value of the identifiable net assets acquired. Bargain purchase gains occurred a number of times in the aftermath of the credit crisis, as healthy banks bought distressed banks (with FDIC assistance and subsidies).

INTERNATIONAL DIMENSION

INTANGIBLE ASSETS

While IFRS and U.S. GAAP define intangible assets similarly, significant differences exist in the accounting for intangible assets. Specifically:

- IFRS allow a company to capitalize more of the cost of internally generated intangible assets than allowed under U.S. GAAP. Under IFRS, a company must classify activities leading to the generation of an intangible asset into a research phase and a development phase. Costs incurred during the research phase are expensed as incurred. However, costs incurred in the development phase may be capitalized if the company can demonstrate technical and economic feasibility.
- IFRS allow intangible assets to be revalued to fair value. Under this revaluation model, any upward revaluation of the intangible asset is reflected in an account

(continued)

called "Revaluation Surplus" which is included in shareholders' equity as a component of accumulated other comprehensive income. Any downward revaluation first reduces the revaluation surplus, with any remainder recognized as a loss on the income statement. Because fair value must be determined by reference to an active market and active markets for intangible assets are not common, the revaluation model is not commonly used in practice.

- For all intangible assets, with either finite or indefinite lives, IFRS use a one-step approach to determine if an impairment loss exists. This single-step approach uses the same calculation (described below) to both determine if an impairment loss exists and measure the amount of the impairment loss.
- For intangible assets other than goodwill, an impairment loss is calculated under IFRS as the difference between the carrying value of the intangible asset and its recoverable amount. The recoverable amount is the higher of the fair value minus costs to sell or value-in-use. Value-in-use is the present value of the cash flows expected from the future use of the asset. Because U.S. GAAP does not apply the value-in-use concept, the definition of fair value and the resulting amount of the impairment loss may be different between the two sets of standards.
- For goodwill, IFRS calculate the impairment loss as the difference between the carrying amount of the cash-generating unit, including any goodwill, and the recoverable amount of the cash-generating unit. A **cash-generating unit** is the smallest identifiable group of assets that generates cash inflows that are largely independent of the cash inflows from other assets or groups of assets.
- For all intangible assets other than goodwill, IFRS allow an impairment loss to be reversed if the value is recovered. Reversal of impairment losses is prohibited under U.S. GAAP.

IFRS Application Placebo Inc. has been actively working on a project, named Excalibur, with the goal of producing a drug that will both lower a person's LDL (bad cholesterol) and raise a person's HDL (good cholesterol). At the end of April 2015, Placebo determined that the drug was both technically and economically feasible. From January to April of 2015, Placebo incurred $500,000 of costs related to this drug. Placebo incurred $2,800,000 in costs from May to December of 2015. What amount would Placebo capitalize, and what amount would be expensed under IFRS and U.S. GAAP?

	IFRS	U.S. GAAP
Capitalize	$2,800,000	$ 0
Expense	500,000	3,300,000

Under IFRS, any expenditures prior to determining technical and economic feasibility are considered to have occurred during the research phase and are expensed. Any expenditures after that time are considered part of the development phase and are capitalized. U.S. GAAP expenses all R&D costs as incurred.

At the beginning of 2016, Placebo obtains a patent for the drug for $10,000. Because a competitor is developing a competing drug with additional benefits that is expected to enter the market in 10 years, Placebo estimates that its cholesterol drug will only provide future economic benefits over the next 10 years. Assuming that Placebo uses IFRS, it records amortization expense of $281,000 [($2,800,000 + $10,000) ÷ 10 years] during 2016. At the end of 2016, the intangible asset has a book value of $2,529,000 ($2,810,000 − $281,000).

At the beginning of 2017, Placebo learns that early trials of the competitors' drug were extremely discouraging. Therefore, it expects the economic benefits

(continued)

from its cholesterol drug to extend beyond the original 10-year period. Placebo estimates that the fair value of its drug is $2,700,000. As discussed in Chapter 10, IFRS allow a company to revalue its productive assets to fair value. Therefore, applying this revaluation model, Placebo would make the following journal entry:

Intangible Asset: Excalibur	171,000	
Revaluation Surplus ($2,700,000 − $2,529,000)		171,000

As a result of this entry, the intangible asset is now stated at it fair value of $2,700,000, which becomes the new basis for purposes of computing amortization. The revaluation surplus, which represents an unrealized gain from writing the intangible asset up to its fair value, is reported as a component of other comprehensive income.

Source: IFRS 3, IAS 36, IAS 38. (See Appendix C at the end of this book.)

GOT IT?

12-14 List four factors that cause the market value of the company as a whole to be greater than the book value of the company.

12-15 Under what conditions is goodwill capitalized at acquisition? Expensed at acquisition? Explain the arguments used to justify this accounting.

12-16 Under what conditions is purchased goodwill amortized? Explain how a company determines if goodwill is impaired.

12-17 It has been proposed that purchased goodwill should be written off immediately to shareholders' equity. Evaluate the arguments in favor of and against this proposal.

12-18 What is meant by the term *bargain purchase*? How is it recorded?

12-19 How does the measurement and reporting of impaired intangible assets differ between IFRS and U.S. GAAP?

12-20 Explain how research and development expenditures are treated under IFRS.

REVIEW CENTER

At the beginning of the chapter, we discussed the importance of intangible assets for the economy as well as the significant measurement challenges that exist with regard to these assets. We also identified several objectives you would accomplish after reading the chapter. The objectives are listed below and followed by a brief summary of the key points.

LEARNING OBJECTIVE 12.1

Explain the acccunting for intangible assets, including initial valuation, amortization, and impairment.

KEY TAKEAWAYS

- A purchased identifiable intangible asset is capitalized as an asset at its acquisition cost while the cost associated with an internally developed intangible asset is generally expensed (although certain costs may be capitalized).
- The cost of a purchased identifiable intangible asset with a finite life is amortized over its useful life. An intangible asset subject to amortization is also tested for impairment whenever events or circumstances indicate that its book value may not be

recoverable. The impairment test for intangible assets with a finite life follows the same two-step procedure used to determine and measure the impairment of tangible property, plant, and equipment.
- The cost of a purchased identifiable intangible with an indefinite life not amortized. Instead, it is reviewed for impairment annually, or more frequently if events or circumstances indicate that the intangible asset may be impaired. The impairment test for purchased identifiable intangible assets with an indefinite life is a one-step procedure in which the impairment loss is computed as the amount by which the asset's fair value is less than its carrying value.

KEY TERMS

amortization, p. 12-4
goodwill, p. 12-7
identifiable intangible assets, p. 12-3

impairment, p. 12-4
intangible assets, p. 12-2
unidentifiable intangible assets, p. 12-3

KEY TAKEAWAYS

LEARNING OBJECTIVE 12.2
Identify and explain the accounting issues related to research and development costs.

- Research and development costs, which include expenditures for materials, equipment, facilities, personnel, purchased intangible assets, contract services, and other indirect costs, are required to be expensed as incurred.
- In-process R&D is initially capitalized at fair value and treated as an intangible asset with an indefinite life until the R&D activities are completed or abandoned.
- Costs associated with the start-up of a process or business are expensed in the period incurred.

KEY TERMS

development, p. 12-7
in-process R&D (IPR&D), p. 12-10

research, p. 12-7
start-up costs, p. 12-10

KEY TAKEAWAYS

LEARNING OBJECTIVE 12.3
Understand the disclosures related to intangibles.

- A company must disclose its total research and development expense.
- Intangible assets and goodwill are distinguished from tangible assets in the financial statements.
- A company must also disclose amortization expense, impairment losses, method and period of amortization, as well as other disclosures.

KEY TAKEAWAYS

LEARNING OBJECTIVE 12.4
Explain the accounting treatment for specific identifiable intangible assets, including trademarks and trade names, copyrights, franchises, patents, and computer software costs.

- Identifiable intangible assets can be separated from the company and sold, transferred, licensed, rented, or exchanged. These intangible assets may be classified as related to:
    - marketing (e.g., trademark, Internet domain name)
    - customers (e.g., customer lists, customer relationships)
    - artistic works (e.g., copyright)
    - contracts (e.g., franchise agreement, broadcast rights)
    - technology (e.g., patent, software development costs)
- While the accounting procedures for each of these intangible assets follow the same general procedures discussed earlier, accounting issues unique to each type of asset exist.

KEY TERMS

copyright, p. 12-15
franchises, p. 12-15
Internet domain names, p. 12-14
patent, p. 12-16

software development costs, p. 12-16
technological feasibility, p. 12-17
trademark, p. 12-14
trade name, p. 12-14

LEARNING OBJECTIVE 12.5
Account for unidentifiable intangibles, including internally developed and purchased goodwill.

KEY TAKEAWAYS
- Goodwill is an intangible asset that provides economic benefits but cannot be separated and specifically associated with an identifiable right.
  - The costs associated with internally developed goodwill are expensed as incurred.
  - Purchased goodwill, measured as the difference between the purchase price of the acquired company and the fair value of the reported identifiable net assets, is capitalized and reviewed for impairment annually at the reporting unit level.
- A two-step approach is used to test for an impairment of goodwill:
  - *Step 1.* Determine if an impairment has occurred by comparing the fair value of the reporting unit with its book value, including goodwill.
  - *Step 2.* Measure and recognize an impairment loss for the amount by which the implied fair value of goodwill is less than its carrying value.

KEY TERMS
cash-generating unit, p. 12-23
purchased goodwill, p. 12-20
reporting unit, p. 12-21

ANSWERS TO REAL REPORT QUESTIONS

Real Report 12.1 Answers Merck—Disclosure of Intangible Assets
1. Merck has net identifiable intangible assets of $23,801 million. These identifiable intangible assets consist of products and product rights, tradenames, patents, and in-process research and development. In addition, Merck reports goodwill of $12,301 million.
2. During 2013, Merck recorded impairment charges related to products of $486 million. Merck used market participant assumptions to determine its estimate of fair value—a level three fair value measurement.
3. IPR&D represents the fair value assigned to incomplete research projects acquired through business combinations that have not yet reached technological feasibility. Upon successful completion of each project, Merck reclassifies the IPR&D and begins amortization. During 2013, $346 million of IPR&D was reclassified to the product and product rights intangible asset.
4. Merck estimates $16.5 billion of amortization expense over the next 5 years. This amount is computed as $4.3 billion + $4.1 billion + $3.4 billion + $3.1 billion + $1.6 billion.

MULTIPLE-CHOICE (AICPA ADAPTED)

Select the best answer for each of the following.

M12-1
LO 12.1 What is the proper time or time period over which to amortize an intangible asset if there is no forseeable limit on the period of time over which the intangible assets is expected to be used in operations?

    a. 40 years   c. immediately
    b. 50 years   d. not amortized

M12-2
LO 12.2 Plaza Company originated late in 2015 and began operations on January 2, 2016. Plaza is engaged in conducting market research studies on behalf of manufacturers. Prior to the start of operations, the following costs were incurred:

Attorney's fees in connection with organization of Plaza	$ 4,000
Improvements to leased offices prior to occupancy	7,000
Meetings of incorporators, state filing fees, and other company expenses	5,000
	$16,000

What is the amount of expense recognized for 2016?

    a. $16,000   c. $7,000
    b. $9,000   d. $4,000

M12-3 Frye Company incurred R&D costs in 2016 as follows:
LO 12.2

Equipment acquired for use in multiple R&D projects	$1,000,000
Depreciation on the equipment	150,000
Materials used	200,000
Wages and salaries of R&D personnel	500,000
Outside consulting fees	100,000
Appropriately allocated indirect costs	250,000

The total R&D expenses reported in Frye's 2016 income statement should be:

a. $650,000
b. $900,000
c. $1,200,000
d. $1,800,000

M12-4 Which of the following assets typically are amortized?
LO 12.4

	Patents	Trademarks
a.	No	No
b.	Yes	Yes
c.	No	Yes
d.	Yes	No

M12-5 Which of the following amounts incurred in connection with a trademark should be capitalized?
LO 12.1
LO 12.4

	Cost of a Successful Defense	Registration Fees
a.	Yes	No
b.	Yes	Yes
c.	No	Yes
d.	No	No

M12-6 A purchased patent has a remaining legal life of 15 years. It should:
LO 12.1
LO 12.4

a. be expensed in the year of acquisition
b. be amortized over 15 years regardless of its useful life
c. be amortized over its useful life if less than 15 years
d. not be amortized

M12-7 During 2012, Traco Machine Company spent $176,000 on R&D costs for an invention. This invention was patented on January 2, 2013, at a nominal cost that was expensed in 2013. The patent had a legal life of 20 years and an estimated useful life of 8 years. In January 2017, Traco paid $16,000 for legal fees in a successful defense of the patent. Amortization for 2017 should be:
LO 12.1
LO 12.4

a. $0
b. $1,000
c. $4,000
d. $26,000

M12-8 Sherwood Corporation incurred $68,000 of R&D costs in its laboratory to develop a patent that was granted on January 2, 2016. Legal fees and other costs associated with registration of the patent totaled $13,600. Sherwood estimates that the economic life of the patent will be 8 years. What amount should Sherwood charge to patent amortization expense for the year ended December 31, 2016?
LO 12.1
LO 12.2
LO 12.4

a. $0
b. $800
c. $1,700
d. $10,200

M12-9 Goodwill represents the excess of the purchase price of an acquired company over the:
LO 12.5

a. sum of the fair values assigned to tangible assets acquired minus liabilities assumed
b. sum of the fair values assigned to identifiable assets acquired minus liabilities assumed
c. sum of the fair values assigned to intangible assets acquired minus liabilities assumed
d. book value of an acquired company

M12-10 Flint Corporation's general ledger as of December 31, 2016, includes the following accounts:
LO 12.2
LO 12.4
LO 12.5

Corporation (start-up) costs	$ 5,000
Deposits with advertising agency (will be used to promote goodwill)	8,000
Discounts on bonds payable	15,000
Excess of purchase price over fair value of the identifiable net assets of acquired company	70,000
Trademarks	12,000

In the preparation of Flint's balance sheet as of December 31, 2016, what should be reported as total intangible assets?

a. $82,000
b. $87,000
c. $95,000
d. $110,000

REVIEW EXERCISES

RE12-1 Steel Magnolia Incorporated purchased a trademark 7 years ago for $275,000. Steel Magnolia believed the trademark would have an indefinite life. At the end of 2017, the corporation believes the fair value of the trademark is $189,000. Record the impairment loss for Steel Magnolia.
LO 12.1

RE12-2 Match the following items with the correct accounting treatment (A through C):
LO 12.1
LO 12.2
1. research and development costs
2. intangibles with an indefinite life
3. intangibles with a finite life

A. review for impairment
B. amortize over useful life
C. expense when incurred

RE12-3 Notting Hill Company incurred the following costs for R&D activities:
LO 12.2

Material used from inventory	$15,000
Equipment purchased (with cash) for R&D with no other use	85,000
Depreciation on building housing multiple R&D activities	10,000
Wages and salaries paid to R&D employees	38,500

Prepare Notting Hill's journal entry(ies) to record its R&D.

RE12-4 Hook Corp. incurred the following start-up costs, all paid in cash:
LO 12.2

Legal fees	$75,000
Accounting fees	35,000
Promotional fees	15,000
Staff training fees	13,000

Prepare Hook's journal entry to record the start-up costs, all paid in cash.

RE12-5 Mystic Pizza Company purchased a patent from Prime Pizza Plus on January 1, 2016, for $72,000. The patent
LO 12.1 has a remaining legal life of 9 years. Prepare the journal entries to record the acquisition and the amortization for
LO 12.4 2016, assuming Mystic Pizza amortizes its patents using the straight-line method over the life of the asset.

RE12-6 Mystic Pizza Company purchases a franchise from NY Pizzeria Inc. for $96,000 on June 1, 2016. The franchise
LO 12.1 will last 8 years. Record Mystic Pizza's purchase of the franchise on June 1 and adjusting entry at the end of
LO 12.4 2016.

RE12-7 Closer & Co. incurred and paid the following costs for internal-use software:
LO 12.4
- $12,000 in the preliminary stage of development
- $17,000 in external direct material and service costs used in developing the internal-use software
- $23,000 in payroll costs for employees working on the project
- $3,500 in interest costs while developing the software

RE12-8 Prepare Closer's initial journal entry(s) to record its internal-use software.
LO 12.4 Identify which of the following are (1) expensed as incurred, (2) amortized and reviewed for impairment whenever
LO 12.5 events or circumstances indicate that the book value may not be recoverable, or (3) reviewed for impairment only.

a. patent
b. licenses, granted in perpetuity
c. goodwill
d. copyright
e. trademark
f. computer software costs (after technological feasibility has been established)
g. research and development (R&D)

RE12-9 Grand Champion Inc. purchased America's Sweethearts Corporation on January 1, 2016. At the time, America's
LO 12.5 Sweethearts had the following assets and liabilities (stated at fair value):

Cash	$ 62,000
Accounts receivable	138,000
Inventory	185,000
Property, plant, and equipment	300,000
Patent	65,000
Accounts payable	200,000
Notes payable	325,000

Grand Champion paid $900,000 for America's Sweethearts. Record the purchase by Grand Champion.

RE12-10 Using the information from **RE12-9**, assume that America's Sweethearts is a reporting unit of Grand Champion.
LO 12.5 At the end of 2017, America's Sweethearts has a fair value of $720,000 and a book value of $850,000, which includes any goodwill recorded in **RE12-9**. Of this fair value, $350,000 is attributable to identifiable assets net of (or identifiable net assets) liabilities. Calculate the impairment loss of goodwill (if any) and record the appropriate journal entry.

EXERCISES

E12-1
LO 12.1
LO 12.2
LO 12.4

Cost of a Patent Befort Company filed for a patent on a new type of machine. The application costs totaled $12,000. R&D costs incurred to create the machine were $75,000. In the year in which the company filed for and received the patent, it spent $20,000 in the successful defense of a patent infringement suit.

Required:
1. At what amount should the company capitalize the patent?
2. **Next Level** How would you determine the economic life of the patent?

E12-2
LO 12.1
LO 12.4

Cost of a Patent On January 4, 2016, Franc Company purchased for $27,000 a patent that had been filed 8 years earlier. The patent covers a manufacturing process that the company plans to use for 15 years. On January 3, 2017, the company paid its lawyers $10,000 for successfully defending the patent in a lawsuit.

Required:
Prepare all the journal entries associated with the patent in 2016 and 2017.(Round all calculations to the nearest dollar.)

E12-3
LO 12.1
LO 12.4

Cost of a Trade Name On January 11, 2016, Hughes Company applied for a trade name. Legal costs associated with the application were $20,000. In January 2017, the company incurred $8,000 of legal fees in a successful defense of its trade name. The trade name was not impaired in 2016 and 2017.

Required:
1. Compute the ending carrying value of the trade name for 2016 and 2017.
2. **Next Level** Should the company amortize the trade name? Under what circumstances would the trade name be amortized?

E12-4
LO 12.1
LO 12.4

Cost of a Copyright Gansac Publishing Company signed a contract with an author to publish her book. The signing took place on January 1, 2016, and a payment of $20,000 was made to obtain a copyright. Gansac expects to sell 200,000 books evenly between 2016 and 2020 at a price of $10 per book.

SHOW ME HOW

Required:
1. Prepare journal entries to record the events related to the copyright and sales of the book during 2016 and 2017, assuming that sales were as projected.
2. **Next Level** How would your answer change if Gansac expected sales of the book to be 100,000 copies in 2016, 80,000 copies in 2017, and 20,000 copies over the remainder of the copyright's useful life?

E12-5
LO 12.2

Research and Development Activities Bouden Company performed the following activities during 2016:
a. built an oil shale plant to test the feasibility of large-scale exploitation
b. tested a new type of machine to evaluate its potential usefulness in production
c. modified a machine to make it suitable for filling a customer's order
d. designed a new plant to produce the same products more efficiently
e. tested alternative production methods in an attempt to increase efficiency

Required:
Which of the activities are considered R&D? Justify your reasons for each answer.

E12-6
LO 12.2

Research and Development Costs Danielson Inc. incurred the following costs during 2016:
a. current-period depreciation expense on the building housing the R&D activities
b. cost of a market research study
c. current-period depreciation expense on a machine used in multiple R&D activities
d. salary of the director of R&D
e. salary of the vice president who spends one-third of her time overseeing the R&D activities
f. pension costs for the salaries in Items d and e

Required:
1. Which of the following are included in R&D costs of the current period? Justify each answer.
2. **Next Level** What is the justification of expensing all costs that are classified as R&D?

E12-7
LO 12.2

Research and Development Costs KLK Clothing Company manufactures professional clothing for women. In order to keep costs low while still producing quality clothes, KLK conducts many R&D projects. On a current project, KLK researchers used $35,000 of cotton and $27,000 of wool from its inventory. KLK paid its researchers $30,000 cash in wages and purchased a special weaving machine for $60,000 cash. The machine was not suitable for use in production activities and was not expected to be used in other research projects. In addition, depreciation expense related to the project's research lab amounted to $20,000.

Required:
Prepare the journal entry to record KLK's R&D costs.

E12-8
LO 12.2

Research and Development Costs Cressman Company incurred R&D costs for various projects in 2016 as follows:

Materials used for research	$ 240,000
Materials used for development	160,000
Equipment acquired that will have alternative uses in future research projects for 4 years	2,000,000
Personnel costs of employees involved in research	600,000
Personnel costs of employees involved in development	400,000
Consulting fees paid to outsiders for research	20,000
Consulting fees paid to outsiders for development	80,000
Indirect costs reasonably allocable for research	130,000
Indirect costs reasonably allocable for development	70,000

Required:
1. What is the amount of Cressman's R&D expenses for 2016 if it uses U.S. GAAP?
2. How would your answer change if Cressman uses IFRS? Assume that the company can demonstrate that the projects are expected to generate future economic benefits.

E12-9
LO 12.2
AICPA Adapted

Research and Development Costs In 2016, Lalli Corporation incurred R&D costs as follows:

Materials used from inventory	$100,000
Personnel in R&D lab	100,000
Allocation of the cost of utilities and maintenance costs of the R&D facility	50,000
	$250,000

These costs relate to a product that will be marketed in 2017. The company estimates that these costs will be recouped by December 31, 2017.

Required:
1. What is the amount of R&D costs expensed in 2016?
2. **Next Level** Would your answer change if the materials were purchased and not used or if the utilities and maintenance costs were related to the corporate offices?

E12-10
LO 12.2

Start-Up Costs Kling Company was organized in late 2016 and began operations on January 2, 2017. Prior to the start of operations, it incurred the following costs:

Costs of hiring new employees	$ 3,000
Attorney's fees in connection with the organization of the company	12,000
Improvements to leased offices prior to occupancy (10-year lease)	6,000
Costs of pre-opening advertising	5,000

Required:
1. What amount should the company expense in 2016? In 2017?
2. **Next Level** What is the justification of the accounting treatment of these costs?

E12-11
LO 12.1
LO 12.4
LO 12.5

Various Intangible Assets Barnum Company acquired several small companies at the end of 2015, and based on the acquisitions, reported the following intangible assets on its December 31, 2015, balance sheet:

Patent	$20,000
Trade name	35,000
Internet domain name	10,000
Goodwill	90,000

The company's accountant determines the patent has an expected life of 10 years and no expected residual value, and it will generate approximately equal benefits each year. The company expects to use the trade name for the foreseeable future. The company plans to continue to use the Internet domain name of the smaller companies until it can integrate the companies into its existing operations. This procedure is expected to take 4 years.

Required:

How much amortization expense should the company recognize on each intangible asset in 2016?

E12-12 Cost of Intangibles Brush Company engaged in the following transactions at the beginning of 2016:

LO 12.1
LO 12.4

a. Purchased a patent (Patent A) for $70,000 that had originally been filed in January 2010. The purchase was made to protect another patent (Patent B) that the company had filed for in January 2012 and subsequently received.
b. Purchased the rights to a novel by a best-selling novelist in exchange for 10,000 shares of $10 par value common stock selling for $60 per share. The book is expected to sell 1,500,000 copies over the next 3 years with no significant sales of the novel expected beyond 3 years.
c. Purchased the franchise to operate a ferry service from the state government for $10,000. A bridge has been planned to replace the ferry, and the bridge is expected to be completed in 5 years. Brush hopes that the ferry will continue as a tourist attraction, but profits are expected to be only 20% of those earned before the bridge is opened.
d. Paid $28,000 of legal costs to successfully defend the patent acquired in Transaction a.
e. Paid a race car driver $50,000 to have the Brush Company name prominently displayed on the race car for 2 years.

Required:

1. Prepare the journal entries to record the preceding transactions.
2. Prepare the journal entries to record the amortization of intangible assets for 2016, if appropriate. Amortize over the legal life unless a better alternative is indicated.

E12-13 Cost of Patents Davis Research Company engaged in the following 5 transactions during 2016:

LO 12.1
LO 12.2
LO 12.4

1. Purchased a patent for $35,000. Legal costs of $5,000 were also incurred.
2. Costs paid to improve patent:

Engineering costs	$20,000
Assembling and testing prototypes	10,000
Other R&D costs	25,000

3. Licensed a manufacturing process to another company and received $80,000 as an advance payment.
4. Successfully defended a patent infringement suit at a cost of $12,000.
5. Earned $5,000 of the advance payment on the licensed manufacturing process in Item 4.

Required:

Prepare journal entries to record the preceding transactions.

E12-14 Intangibles: Balance Sheet Presentation and Income Statement Effects Barb Company has provided information on intangible assets as follows:

LO 12.1
LO 12.2
LO 12.3
LO 12.4

AICPA Adapted

1. A patent was purchased from Lou Company for $1,500,000 on January 1, 2015. Barb estimated the remaining useful life of the patent to be 10 years. The patent was carried in Lou's accounting records at a net book value of $1,250,000 when Lou sold it to Barb.
2. During 2016, a franchise was purchased from Rink Company for $500,000. In addition, 5% of revenue from the franchise must be paid to Rink. Revenue from the franchise for 2016 was $2,000,000. Barb estimates the useful life of the franchise to be 10 years and takes a full year's amortization in the year of purchase.
3. Barb incurred R&D costs in 2016 as follows:

Materials and equipment	$120,000
Personnel	140,000
Indirect costs	60,000
	$320,000

Barb estimates that these costs will be recouped by December 31, 2017.

(continued)

4. On January 1, 2016, Barb estimates, based on new events, that the remaining life of the patent purchased on January 1, 2015, is only 5 years from January 1, 2016.

Required:
1. Prepare the intangibles assets section of Barb's balance sheet at December 31, 2016. Show supporting computations.
2. Prepare a schedule showing the income statement effects for the year ended December 31, 2016, as a result of the previously mentioned facts. Show supporting computations.

E12-15 Impairment of Trademark Probst Company acquired a trademark several years ago at a cost of $60,000. Probst has never considered the trademark to be impaired. However, at the end of 2016, Probst has determined that the trademark is impaired because of a change in market conditions. It estimates that the trademark has a fair value of $40,000 at the end of 2016.

LO 12.1
LO 12.4

Required:
1. Prepare Probst's journal entry (if any) to record the impairment of its trademark at the end of 2016.
2. **Next Level** Assume Probst uses IFRS. If Probst estimates that the cost of selling the trademark is zero but the value-in-use is $45,000, prepare Probst's journal entry to record the impairment of its trademark at the end of 2016. Explain any differences between the impairment loss calculated under IFRS and the impairment loss calculated under U.S. GAAP.
3. Assume, instead, that Probst estimated that the trademark had a fair value of $70,000 at the end of 2016. How would Probst account for this if it were using (a) U.S. GAAP or (b) IFRS?

E12-16 Software Development Costs In 2016, eGames spent $8,000,000 developing new software. Of this amount, $5,300,000 was spent before July 2016—when technological feasibility was established. The product was marketed to consumers beginning in September 2016. eGames estimates total revenue of $20,000,000 to be earned during the software's 3-year life (calculated from the September 1 product release date). During 2016, revenue of $10,000,000 was recognized.

LO 12.1
LO 12.4

Required:
1. Prepare the 2016 journal entries to record the development costs.
2. Compute the amount of amortization to be recognized in 2016 and prepare the appropriate journal entry, if any.
3. **Next Level** What is the justification for treating software development costs differently from R&D costs?

E12-17 Goodwill Elm Company is considering purchasing EKC Company. EKC's balance sheet at December 31, 2016, is as follows:

LO 12.5

Cash	$ 50,000	Current liabilities	$ 60,000
Accounts receivable	70,000	Bonds payable	200,000
Inventory	120,000	Common stock	300,000
Property, plant, and equipment (net)	600,000	Retained earnings	280,000
	$840,000		$840,000

At December 31, 2016, Elm discovered the following about EKC:
a. No allowance for uncollectible accounts has been established. An allowance of $5,000 is considered appropriate.
b. The LIFO inventory method has been used. The FIFO inventory method would be used if EKC were purchased by Elm. The FIFO inventory valuation of the December 31, 2016, ending inventory would be $180,000.
c. The fair value of the property, plant, and equipment (net) is $730,000.
d. The company has an unrecorded patent that is worth $120,000.
e. The book values of the current liabilities and bonds payable are the same as their market values.

Required:
1. Compute the value of the goodwill if Elm pays $1,350,000 for EKC.
2. **Next Level** Why would the book value of a company's identifiable net assets differ from its market value?

E12-18 Goodwill Marino Company had the following balance sheet on January 1, 2016:

LO 12.5

Cash	$ 10,000	Accounts payable	$ 30,000
Inventory	40,000	Notes payable	100,000
Property, plant, and equipment	200,000		
Patent	20,000	Shareholders' equity	140,000
	$270,000		$270,000

On January 2, 2016, Paul Company purchased Marino by acquiring all its outstanding shares for $300,000 cash. On that date, the fair value of the inventory was $30,000, and the fair value of the equipment was $240,000. In addition, the fair value of a previously unrecorded customer list was $25,000. For all other amounts, the book value of January 1, 2016, equaled fair value.

Required:
1. Compute the goodwill associated with the purchase of Marino.
2. Prepare the journal entry necessary at January 1, 2016, to record the acquisition of Marino.

E12-19 Impairment of Goodwill Several years ago, Blaha Company purchased Husker Company as a subsidiary. At that time, Blaha recorded goodwill of $100,000 related to the purchase. Since that time, the company has not considered the goodwill to be impaired. However, at the end of 2016, Blaha decides to evaluate the goodwill for impairment because of technological changes in the industry. Husker (which is considered a reporting unit of Blaha) has a book value (including the goodwill) of $800,000. Blaha estimates that the fair value of Husker is $720,000, of which it allocates $660,000 to Husker's identifiable assets and liabilities.

LO 12.5

SHOW ME HOW

Required:
1. Prepare the journal entry (if any) for Blaha to record the impairment of its goodwill at the end of 2016.
2. Assume that Blaha uses IFRS and has estimated the recoverable amount of Husker (which qualifies as a cash-generating-unit) to be $740,000. Prepare the journal entry for Blaha to record the impairment of its goodwill at the end of 2016.

E12-20 Intangibles Jolis Company has provided information on the following items:

LO 12.1
LO 12.2
LO 12.4
LO 12.5

1. A patent was purchased from Totley Company for $500,000 on January 1, 2015. At that time, Jolis estimated the remaining useful life to be 10 years. The patent was carried on Totley's books at $20,000 when it sold the patent.
2. On March 2, 2016, a franchise was purchased from Unal Company for $240,000. In addition, 8% of the revenue from the franchise must be paid to Unal. Revenue earned during 2016 was $620,000. Jolis believes that the life of the franchise is indefinite and that the franchise is not impaired at the end of 2016.
3. R&D costs were incurred as follows: (a) materials and equipment, $50,000; (b) personnel, $80,000; and (c) indirect costs, $40,000. The costs were incurred to develop a product that will go on sale in 2017 and will have an expected life of 5 years.
4. A trade name had been purchased for a sugar substitute at the beginning of 2012 for $80,000. In January 2016, it was suspected that the product caused cancer. Its fair value was estimated to be zero and the trade name was abandoned.
5. The company purchased the net assets of Lansing Company on September 1, 2016, for $950,000, and Lansing was liquidated. Lansing had the following book (fair) values: cash, $50,000 ($50,000); inventory, $150,000 ($160,000); property, plant, and equipment, $750,000 ($900,000); accounts payable, $75,000 ($75,000); and notes payable, $175,000 ($175,000). Any goodwill is not impaired at the end of 2016.

Required:
Prepare journal entries for Jolis for 2016. The company uses the straight-line method of amortization computed to the nearest month over the maximum allowable life. Assume that the company pays all costs in cash, unless otherwise indicated.

PROBLEMS

P12-1 Cost of Intangibles Byrd Corporation engaged in the following transactions at the beginning of 2016:

LO 12.1
LO 12.2
LO 12.4

a. Purchased a Hogburger franchise for a 5-year, $60,000, 10% interest-bearing note. The franchise has an indefinite life providing the terms of the franchise are not violated.

(continued)

b. Sold a trade name for $50,000. The trade name had a carrying value of $5,000.
c. Paid an advertising agency $60,000 for advertisements to promote a new trade name. The advertisements will begin in 2017.
d. Incurred legal fees of $5,000 to register a new trade name.
e. Purchased the copyright to a new movie for $500,000. The movie is made during 2016 at a cost of $15 million. It will begin showing in 2017 and is expected to gross $10 million during 2017, $20 million during 2018, and $10 million during 2019.

Required:
1. Prepare journal entries to record the preceding transactions, including any appropriate adjusting entries for 2016.
2. **Next Level** With regard to the copyright in Transaction e, what factors should Byrd consider in selecting an amortization method.

P12-2
LO 12.1
LO 12.2
LO 12.4

Correct Classification of Intangibles During the current year, Cartwright Corporation's accountant recorded numerous transactions in an account entitled Intangible Assets, as follows:

Date	Description	Amount
Jan. 2	Paid incorporation fees.	$17,500
11	Paid legal fees for the organization of the company.	7,500
25	Paid for large-scale advertising campaign for the year.	15,000
Apr. 1	Acquired land for $15,000 and a building for $20,000 to house the R&D activities. The building has a 20-year life.	35,000
May 15	Purchased materials exclusively for use in R&D activities. Of these materials, 20% are left at the end of the year and will be used in the same project next year. (They have no alternative use.)	15,000
June 30	Paid expenses related to obtaining a patent.	10,000
Dec. 11	Purchased an experimental machine from an inventor. The machine is expected to be used for a particular R&D activity for 2 years, after which it will have no residual value.	12,000
31	Paid salaries of employees involved in R&D.	30,000

Required:
Prepare adjusting journal entries to eliminate the Intangible Assets account and correctly record all the items, including appropriate amortization adjustments. Cartwright amortizes patents over 10 years.

P12-3
LO 12.1
LO 12.4

Correcting Entries for Patents During the year-end audit of Cressman Corporation's financial statements for 2016, you discover the following items:
1. Cressman capitalized $57,000 to the Patent account at the beginning of 2015 for the cost of a patent. This amount included $50,000 of R&D costs. The patent was amortized over a 20-year life in 2015 and 2016.
2. At the beginning of 2015, Cressman paid its lawyers $8,000 to successfully defend a patent infringement suit regarding the patent in Item 1. Cressman debited this cost to Legal Fees Expense.
3. At the beginning of 2016, Cressman purchased a patent for $30,000 from Baylor Company to prevent potential competition. It recorded the cost in the Patent account and amortized this cost over the remaining legal life of the patent obtained in Item 1 (19 years). However, Cressman agreed to a suggestion by the auditors that the life of the original patent obtained in Item 1 was protected for only 7 more years as of the beginning of 2016.

Required:
Prepare adjusting and correcting journal entries on December 31 for 2016.

P12-4
LO 12.2

R&D Costs Halpern Company's controller prepared the following income statement and balance sheet at the end of the first year of the company's existence:

Income Statement	
Sales revenue	$ 40,000
Cost of sales	(20,000)
Operating expenses	(8,000)
Net income	$ 12,000

Balance Sheet

Cash	$ 33,000	Accounts payable	$ 5,000
Inventory	24,000	Notes payable	40,000
R&D costs	30,000	Common stock	50,000
Property, plant, and equipment (net)	20,000	Retained earnings	12,000
	$107,000		$107,000

Investigation shows that R&D costs include, among others, $8,000 of operating costs because "the company is not yet operating at capacity." In addition, R&D costs include $5,000 of materials that were wasted during early production because "our employees made some unnecessary mistakes."

Required:
Prepare the financial statements according to GAAP.

P12-5 **Intangibles** Bailey Company was formed in January 2014 and is preparing its financial statements under GAAP for the first time at the end of 2016. Its general ledger at December 31, 2016, includes the following assets:

LO 12.1
LO 12.4
LO 12.5

Patent	$120,000
Copyright	140,000
Trade name	150,000
Computer software	90,000
Start-up costs	30,000
Intellectual capital	150,000
Goodwill	90,000

As the recently hired accountant for Bailey, you have been asked to make sure that the company's accounting for intangible assets follows GAAP. Based on your investigation, you determine the following:

- The patent acquired in January 2016 has an expected life of 15 years and no residual value, and it will generate approximately equal benefits each year.
- Bailey will use the copyright and trade name for the foreseeable future.
- The computer software was purchased in January 2016 and is used in the Bailey's 20 offices around the country. It is expected to be replaced with new software at the beginning of 2018.
- Bailey previously capitalized the expected value of its "human resources" as intellectual capital, with a corresponding increase in additional paid-in capital.
- The trade name and goodwill arose from an acquisition of a subsidiary company at the end of 2015. Because of a significant adverse change in the market, you decide that both assets are impaired. You estimate that the fair value of the trade name is $50,000. The subsidiary company, which qualifies as a reporting unit, has a book value of $500,000, including the goodwill of $90,000. You estimate that the subsidiary's fair value is $300,000, of which $250,000 is allocated to its identifiable assets and liabilities.

Required:
Assume no adjusting entries have been made. Prepare journal entries to provide the correct information under GAAP at the end of 2016.

P12-6 **Impairment** Wember Company acquired a subsidiary company on December 31, 2012, and recorded the cost of the intangible assets it acquired as follows:

LO 12.1
LO 12.4
LO 12.5

Patent	$100,000
Trade name	80,000
Goodwill	150,000

The patent is being amortized by the straight-line method over an expected life of 10 years with no residual value. Amortization has been recorded for the current year. The trade name was considered to have an indefinite life.

Because of the success of the subsidiary in the past, Wember has not previously considered any of the intangible assets to be impaired. However, in 2016, because of a current recession and technological changes in the subsidiary's industry, Wember decides to review all of its intangible assets for impairment and record any adjustments at December 31, 2016.

(continued)

Wember estimates that the fair value of the patent is $42,000. The company estimates the fair value of the trade name to be $90,000 but decides that it now has a limited life of 5 years. The subsidiary company, which qualifies as a reporting unit, has a book value of $700,000, including the goodwill of $150,000. Wember estimates that the fair value of the subsidiary company is $400,000, of which it allocates 80% to the identifiable assets and liabilities.

Required:
1. Prepare journal entries for Wember to record the impairment of its intangible assets at December 31, 2016.
2. Prepare journal entries for Wember to record the amortization expense for its intangibles at December 31, 2017.

P12-7 **Goodwill** Hamilton Company's balance sheet on January 1, 2016, was as follows:

LO 12.5

Cash	$ 30,000	Accounts payable	$ 20,000
Accounts receivable	80,000	Bonds payable	120,000
Marketable securities (short-term)	40,000	Pension liability	50,000
Inventory	100,000	Common stock	200,000
Property, plant, and equipment (net)	200,000	Retained earnings	60,000
	$450,000		$450,000

Korbel Company is considering purchasing Hamilton (a privately held company) and discovers the following about Hamilton:

a. No allowance for doubtful accounts has been established. A $10,000 allowance is considered appropriate.
b. Marketable securities are valued at cost. The current market value is $60,000.
c. The LIFO inventory method is used. The FIFO inventory of $140,000 would be used if the company is acquired.
d. Land, included in property, plant, and equipment, which is recorded at its cost of $50,000, is worth $120,000. The remaining property, plant, and equipment is worth 10% more than its depreciated cost.
e. The company has an unrecorded trademark that is worth $70,000.
f. The company's bonds are currently trading for $130,000.
g. The pension liability is understated by $40,000.

Required:
1. Compute the amount of goodwill if Korbel agrees to pay $500,000 cash for Hamilton.
2. **Next Level** What are the reasons that the book value of Hamilton's net identifiable assets differ from their market value?
3. Prepare the journal entry to record the acquisition on the books of Korbel assuming Hamilton is liquidated.
4. If Korbel agrees to pay only $400,000 cash, how much goodwill exists?
5. If Korbel pays only $400,000 cash, prepare the journal entry to record the acquisition on its books, assuming Hamilton is liquidated.

P12-8 **Intangibles: Expense and Disclosure** Munn Inc. had the following intangible account balance at December 31, 2015:

LO 12.1
LO 12.3   Patent $168,000

LO 12.4 Information relating to Munn's patent and transactions involving other intangible assets during 2016 includes the
AICPA   following:
Adapted

a. The patent was purchased from Grey Company for $192,000 on January 1, 2014, at which time the remaining legal life was 16 years. On January 1, 2016, Munn determined that the useful life of the patent was only 8 years from the date of acquisition.
b. On January 2, 2016, in connection with the purchase of a trademark from Cody Corporation, the parties entered into a noncompete agreement and a consulting contract. Munn paid Cody $800,000, of which three-quarters was for the trademark and one-quarter was for Cody's agreement not to compete for a 5-year period in the line of business covered by the trademark. Munn considers the life of the trademark to be indefinite. Under the consulting contract, Munn agreed to pay Cody $50,000 annually on January 2 for 5 years. The first payment was made on January 2, 2016. The trademark is not impaired at the end of 2016.

Required:
1. Prepare a schedule of the expenses for 2016 relating to Munn's intangible asset balances at December 31, 2015, and transactions during 2016.
2. Prepare the intangible assets section of Munn's balance sheet at December 31, 2016.

P12-9
LO 12.1
LO 12.2
LO 12.4
LO 12.5
AICPA Adapted

Comprehensive Lee Manufacturing Corporation was incorporated on January 3, 2015. The corporation's financial statements for its first year's operations were not examined by a CPA. You have been engaged to examine the financial statements for the year ended December 31, 2016, and your examination is substantially completed. Lee's trial balance at December 31, 2016, appears as follows:

	Debit	Credit
Cash	$ 61,000	
Accounts receivable	92,500	
Allowance for doubtful accounts		$ 500
Inventories	38,500	
Machinery	75,000	
Equipment	29,000	
Accumulated depreciation		10,000
Patent	85,000	
Leasehold improvements	26,000	
Prepaid expenses	10,500	
Organization costs	29,000	
Goodwill	24,000	
Licensing Agreement No. 1	50,000	
Licensing Agreement No. 2	49,000	
Accounts payable		147,500
Unearned revenue		12,500
Common stock		300,000
Retained earnings, January 1, 2016	27,000	
Sales		768,500
Cost of goods sold	466,000	
Selling and general expenses	173,000	
Interest expense	3,500	
Total	$1,239,000	$1,239,000

The following information relates to accounts that may yet require adjustment:

1. Patents for Lee's manufacturing process were acquired January 2, 2016, at a cost of $68,000. An additional $17,000 was spent in December 2016 to improve machinery covered by the patents and charged to the Patent account. Depreciation on fixed assets has been properly recorded for 2016 in accordance with Lee's practice which provides a full year's depreciation for property on hand June 30 and no depreciation otherwise. Lee uses the straight-line method for all depreciation and amortization and amortizes its patents over their legal life.

2. On January 3, 2015, Lee purchased Licensing Agreement No. 1, which was believed to have an indefinite useful life. The balance in the Licensing Agreement No. 1 account includes its purchase price of $48,000 and costs of $2,000 related to the acquisition. On January 1, 2016, Lee purchased Licensing Agreement No. 2, which has a life expectancy of 10 years. The balance in the Licensing Agreement No. 2 account includes its $48,000 purchase price and $2,000 in acquisition costs, but it has been reduced by a credit of $1,000 for the advance collection of 2017 revenue from the agreement. In late December 2015, an explosion caused a permanent 60% reduction in the expected revenue-producing value of Licensing Agreement No. 1, and in January 2017 a flood caused additional damage that rendered the agreement worthless.

3. The balance in the Goodwill account includes (a) $8,000 paid December 30, 2015, for newspaper advertising for the next 4 years following the payment, and (b) legal costs of $16,000 incurred for Lee's incorporation on January 3, 2015.

4. The Leasehold Improvements account includes (a) the $15,000 cost of improvements with a total estimated useful life of 12 years, which Lee, as tenant, made to leased premises in January 2015; (b) movable assembly line equipment costing $8,500 that was installed in the leased premises in December 2016; and (c) real estate taxes of $2,500 paid by Lee in 2016, which under the terms of the lease should have been paid by the landlord. Lee paid its rent in full during 2016. A 10-year nonrenewable lease was signed January 3, 2015, for the leased building that Lee used in manufacturing operations.

5. The balance in the Organization Costs account includes costs incurred during the organizational period.

Required:
Prepare a worksheet (spreadsheet) to adjust accounts that require adjustment and prepare financial statements. Formal adjusting journal entries and financial statements are not required. No intangible assets are impaired at the end of 2016. Ignore income taxes.

P12-10 Comprehensive Information concerning Tully Corporation's intangible assets is as follows:

LO 12.1
LO 12.2
LO 12.3
LO 12.4
AICPA Adapted

a. On January 1, 2016, Tully signed an agreement to operate as a franchisee of Rapid Copy Service Inc. for an initial franchise fee of $85,000. Of this amount, $25,000 was paid when the agreement was signed, and the balance is payable in 4 annual payments of $15,000 each beginning January 1, 2017. The agreement provides that the down payment is not refundable and no future services are required of the franchisor. The present value at January 2, 2016, of the 4 annual payments discounted at 14% (the implicit rate for a loan of this type) is $43,700. The agreement also provides that 5% of the revenue from the franchise must be paid to the franchisor annually. Tully's revenue from the franchise for 2016 was $900,000. Tully estimates the useful life of the franchise to be 10 years.

b. Tully incurred $78,000 of experimental and development costs in its laboratory to develop a patent, which was granted on January 2, 2016. Legal fees and other costs associated with registration of the patent totaled $16,400. Tully estimates that the useful life of the patent will be 8 years.

c. A trademark was purchased from Walton Company for $40,000 on July 1, 2013. Expenditures for successful litigation in defense of the trademark totaling $10,000 were paid on July 1, 2016. Tully estimates that the useful life of the trademark will be 20 years from the date of acquisition.

Required:
1. Prepare the intangible assets section of Tully's balance sheet at December 31, 2016. Prepare supporting schedules showing related computations.
2. Prepare a schedule showing all expenses resulting from the transactions that would appear on Tully's income statement for the year ended December 31, 2016. Show supporting computations or reference supporting schedules prepared for part 1.

P12-11 Comprehensive Bryant Corporation was incorporated on December 1, 2015, and began operations one week later. Before closing the books for the fiscal year ended November 30, 2016, Bryant's controller prepared the following financial statements:

LO 12.1
LO 12.2
LO 12.3
LO 12.4
AICPA Adapted

Balance Sheet
November 30, 2016

Assets			Liabilities and Shareholders' Equity		
Current Assets:			Current Liabilities:		
Cash		$ 180,000	Accounts payable and accrued expenses		$ 592,000
Accounts receivable	480,000		Income taxes payable		168,000
Less: Allowance for doubtful accounts	(59,000)	430,000	Total current liabilities		$ 760,000
Inventories		430,000	Shareholders' Equity:		
Prepaid insurance		15,000	Common stock, $10 par value		$ 400,000
Total current assets		$1,046,000	Retained earnings		392,000
Property, plant, and equipment	426,000		Total shareholders' equity		$ 792,000
Less: Accumulated depreciation	(40,000)				
R&D costs		120,000			
Total Assets		$1,552,000	Total Liabilities and Shareholders' Equity		$1,552,000

Income Statement
For Year Ended November 30, 2016

Net sales		$2,950,000
Operating expenses:		
Cost of goods sold	$1,670,000	
Selling and administrative	650,000	
Depreciation	40,000	
Research and development Expense	30,000	
Total expenses		$2,390,000
Income before income taxes		$ 560,000
Income tax expense		168,000
Net income		$ 392,000

Bryant is in the process of negotiating a loan for expansion purposes, and the bank has requested audited financial statements. During the course of the audit, the following additional information was obtained:

a. Included in selling and administrative expenses were $5,000 of software development expense related to costs incurred on software being developed for sale to others. The technological feasibility of the software has been established.
b. Based on an aging of the accounts receivable as of November 30, 2016, it was estimated that $36,000 of the receivables will be uncollectible.
c. Inventories at November 30, 2016, did not include work-in-process inventory costing $12,000 sent to an outside processor on November 26, 2016.
d. A $3,000 insurance premium paid on November 30, 2016, on a policy expiring one year later was charged to insurance expense.
e. On June 1, 2016, a production machine purchased for $24,000 was charged to repairs and maintenance expense. For financial and tax purposes, Bryant depreciates machines of this type using the straight-line method over a 5-year life with no salvage value.
f. R&D costs of $150,000 were incurred in the development of a patent that Bryant expects to be granted during the fiscal year ending November 30, 2017. Bryant initiated a 5-year amortization of the $150,000 total cost during the fiscal year ended November 30, 2016.
g. During December 2016, a competitor company filed suit against Bryant for patent infringement, claiming $200,000 in damages. Bryant's legal counsel believes that an unfavorable outcome is probable. This lawsuit is deemed to be a subsequent event that should be recognized in the current fiscal year and a reasonable accrual based on an estimate of the court's award to the plaintiff is $50,000.
h. The 30% effective tax rate was determined to be appropriate for calculating the provision for income taxes for the fiscal year ended November 30, 2016. Ignore computation of the deferred portion of income taxes.

Required:
1. Prepare the necessary correcting entries.
2. Prepare a corrected balance sheet for Bryant as of November 30, 2016, and a corrected income statement for the year ended November 30, 2016.

CASES

COMMUNICATION

C12-1 Patents
LO 12.1
LO 12.4
AICPA Adapted

In examining Samson Manufacturing Company's books, you find on the December 31, 2016, balance sheet the item, "Costs of patents, $308,440." Referring to the ledger accounts, you note the following items regarding one patent acquired in 2013:

2013	Legal costs incurred in defending the validity of the patent	$3,500
2015	Legal costs in prosecuting an infringement suit	7,900
2015	Legal costs (additional expenses) in the infringement suit	1,500
2015	Cost of improvements (unpatented) on the patented device	4,800

There are no credits in the account, and the company has not recorded any amortization for any of the patents. There are three other patents issued in 2010, 2012, and 2013; all were developed by the staff of Samson. The patented articles are presently very marketable, but are estimated to be in demand only for the next few years.

Required:
Discuss the accounting issues related to the items included in the Patent account.

C12-2 Patent and R&D
LO 12.1
LO 12.2
LO 12.4
AICPA Adapted

Clonal Inc., a biotechnology company, developed and patented a diagnostic product called Trouver. Clonal purchased some research equipment to be used exclusively for Trouver and other research equipment to be used on Trouver and subsequent research projects. Clonal defeated a legal challenge to its Trouver patent and began production and marketing operations for the product.

Clonal allocated its corporate headquarters' costs to its research division as a percentage of the division's salaries.

Required:
1. What is the definition of *research* and of *development* as defined by GAAP?
2. Briefly indicate the justification for the existing GAAP relating to R&D costs.

(continued)

3. Explain how Clonal should report the equipment purchased for Trouver on its income statements and balance sheets.
4. Explain how Clonal should report the legal costs incurred in defending Trouver's patent on its statement of cash flows.
5. Explain how Clonal should classify its corporate headquarters' costs allocated to the research division on its income statement.

C12-3 Goodwill
LO 12.5
AICPA Adapted

Elson Corporation, a retail fuel oil distributor, has increased its annual sales volume to a level three times greater than the annual sales of a dealer it purchased in 2012 in order to begin operations.

The board of directors recently received an offer to negotiate the sale of Elson to a large competitor. As a result, the majority of the board wants to increase the stated value of goodwill on the balance sheet to reflect the larger sales volume developed through intensive promotion and the current market price of fuel oil. A few of the board members, however, would prefer to eliminate goodwill altogether from the balance sheet in order to prevent "possible misinterpretations." Goodwill was recorded properly in 2012.

Required:
1. Explain the meaning of the term *goodwill*.
2. Explain why the book and fair values of the goodwill of Elson may differ.
3. Discuss the propriety of (a) increasing the stated value of goodwill prior to the negotiations and (b) eliminating goodwill completely from the balance sheet prior to negotiations.

CREATIVE AND CRITICAL THINKING

C12-4 Intangibles
LO 12.1
LO 12.4

Some intangible assets that companies may report on their balance sheets include patents, copyrights, trade names, software development costs, and goodwill.

Required:
1. Discuss which of these intangible assets would typically be amortized and which would not typically be amortized.
2. Which of these intangibles must be reviewed for impairment annually?

C12-5 Patents
LO 12.1
LO 12.4
AICPA Adapted

On June 30, 2016, your client, Sprauge Corporation, was granted two patents covering plastic cartons that it has been producing and marketing profitably for the past 3 years. One patent covers the manufacturing process, and the other covers the related products.

Sprauge executives tell you that these patents represent the most significant breakthroughs in the industry in the past 30 years. The products have been marketed under the registered trademarks Safetainer, Duratainer, and Sealrite. Your client has already granted licenses under the patents to other manufacturers in the United States and abroad, and they are producing substantial royalties.

On July 1, Sprauge commenced patent infringement actions against several companies whose names you recognize as those of substantial and prominent competitors. Sprauge management is optimistic that these suits will result in a permanent injunction against the manufacture and sale of the infringing products and collection of damages for loss of profits caused by the alleged infringement. The financial vice president has suggested that the patents be recorded at the discounted value of expected net royalty receipts.

Required:
1. Explain the meaning of *discounted value of expected net receipts*.
2. How would such a value be calculated for net royalty receipts?
3. Explain the basis of valuation of Sprauge's patents that would be generally accepted in accounting.
4. Assuming no practical problems of implementation and ignoring generally accepted accounting principles, explain the ideal basis of valuation for patents.
5. Explain what would be the preferable theoretical basis of amortization.
6. Explain what recognition, if any, the company should make of the infringement litigation in the financial statements for the year ending September 30, 2016.

C12-6 Television Rights and Player Contracts
LO 12.1
LO 12.4

In 1975, a trial was held to settle a tax dispute between the owners of the Atlanta Falcons, a National Football League franchise, and the Internal Revenue Service. In 1966, the owners had paid $8.5 million to purchase the franchise. They considered $50,000 to be the cost of the franchise (which is not depreciable for income tax reporting), $727,000 was deferred interest, and the remaining $7.7 million was claimed to be the cost of the players' contracts and options. The dispute centered on several variables:

- How much of the purchase price was assignable to television rights?
- Can the value assignable to television rights be amortized? If so, what is the expected life?
- How much of the purchase price was assignable to player contracts and options?
- Over what life should the value assigned to the players be amortized?
- What is the value of the franchise?

Required:
1. As an independent accountant, explain the approach you would take and the information you would need to provide advice to the court for the resolution of the points in dispute.
2. Do these valuation issues also create ethical issues?

C12-7 **Broadcast Rights**
LO 12.1
LO 12.4
NBC paid $401 million for the rights to televise the 1992 Summer Olympic Games, and it was widely reported that it had a loss of more than $60 million. CBS purchased the rights to the 1992 and 1994 Winter Olympic Games for a combined $543 million. CBS reported a $322 million pretax loss on its baseball and football contracts in 1991.

Required:
1. Under what conditions, if any, should NBC and CBS have written down the value of their assets?
2. Does this situation allow opportunities for earnings management?

C12-8 **Ethics and Intangibles**

You are auditing the financial records of a company, and you are aware that it has grown quickly in the last few years by acquiring other companies. You look up the disclosure in last year's annual report which states, "The company amortizes its intangibles over periods ranging from 3 to 15 years." As you review the company's records, you find that the company made an acquisition of a "high-tech" company 3 years ago and has not recognized any impairment on the related goodwill. In the last 6 years, the company has made five other acquisitions and has not recognized any impairment related to them. Included in the acquisitions are several patents that are amortized over 9 years and some intangibles with indefinite lives.

Required:
From financial reporting and ethical perspectives, discuss the issues raised by this situation.

C12-9 **Analyzing Coca-Cola's Intangibles Disclosures**
Obtain Starbucks's 2015 annual report either using the "Investor Relations" portion of its website (do a web search for Starbucks investor relations) or go to http://www.sec.gov and click "Search for company filings" under "Filings and Forms (EDGAR)."

Required:
1. What was the total amount of intangible assets that Starbucks reported at the end of its 2015 fiscal year, and what was the amount of each component?
2. Do you think that Starbucks has additional intangible assets that are not recorded on the balance sheet? Why? How would this issue affect your understanding of the company's financial performance?
3. Is any information provided on the intangible assets that were purchased during the year?
4. What is the average remaining useful life of the intangible assets with a finite life?
5. Why does Starbucks amortize some of its intangible assets but not others? How much amortization expense does Starbucks expect to recognize over the next 5 years?

C12-10 **Analyzing Nestlé's Intangibles Disclosures**
Obtain Nestlé's 2013 annual report using the "Investor Relations" portion of its website (do a web search for Nestlé investor relations).

Required:
1. What was the total amount of intangible assets that Nestlé reported at the end of 2013, and what was the amount of each component?
2. What is the value of Nestlé's intangible assets (other than goodwill) with an indefinite life?
3. Does Nestlé capitalize its R&D costs related to new products? Why or why not?
4. Compute the estimated average useful life of the intangible assets with a finite life.
5. Did Nestlé report any impairments of intangible assets? If so, provide a brief discussion of what the impairment related to and its amount.

USING CODIFICATION

C12-11 Researching GAAP

Situation

After securing lease commitments from several major stores, Bay Lake Shops Inc. was organized and built a shopping center in a growing suburb. The shopping center would have opened on schedule on January 2, 2017, if it had not been struck by a severe tornado in December. Instead, it opened for business on October 2, 2017. All the additional construction costs incurred as a result of the tornado were covered by insurance.

In July 2016, in anticipation of the scheduled January opening, a permanent staff was hired to promote the shopping center, obtain tenants for the uncommitted space, and manage the property. A summary of some of the costs incurred in 2016 and the first 9 months of 2017 follows:

	2016	Jan. 1 to Sept. 30, 2017
Interest on mortgage bonds	$60,000	$90,000
Cost of obtaining tenants	28,000	58,000
Promotional advertising	34,000	34,000

The promotional advertising campaign was designed to familiarize shoppers with the center. Had the company known in time that the center would not open until October 2017, it would not have made the 2016 expenditure for promotional advertising. The company had to repeat the advertising in 2017.

All the tenants who had leased space in the shopping center at the time of the tornado accepted the October occupancy date on condition that the monthly rental charges for the first 9 months of 2017 be canceled.

Directions

Research the related generally accepted accounting principles and prepare a short memo to the president that explains how the company should treat each of the costs for 2016 and the first 9 months of 2017. Cite your references and applicable paragraph numbers.

C12-12 Researching GAAP

Situation

Gilmatt Company developed a new product that it planned to sell directly to customers and to promote heavily because of "stiff" competition in the marketplace. Its marketing department did extensive market surveys and developed a marketing plan for this product. The plan called for a series of television commercials and magazine advertisements. The television commercials aired for 2 months (September and October) in 2016 to (a) advertise the product and (b) indicate to viewers that "$5-off" coupons would be appearing in forthcoming magazine advertisements. The magazine advertisements appeared evenly over a 3-month period from November 2016 through January 2017 and further promoted the product, as well as included the coded $5-off coupons (which expired at the end of February 2017). Gilmatt expected 20,000 coupons to be redeemed. During November and December 2016, Gilmatt sold 2,000 units of the new product at the $50 regular price and 8,000 units at the $45 coded-coupon price. In January 2017, the company sold another 3,000 units at $50 each and 7,000 units at $45 each. It expects customers to redeem another 5,000 coupons before the coupons expire. It is now late January 2017, and Gilmatt is preparing its 2016 annual report.

The marketing department has prepared the following schedule of its 2016 costs related to the advertising and promotion of the new product: supervisor's salary, $10,000; payroll of employees working on magazine advertising copy, $40,000; depreciation, $7,500; cost of television commercials (independently produced), $180,000; cost of magazine space for advertisements, $100,000; and cost of television airtime, $300,000.

Directions

Research the related generally accepted accounting principles and indicate how Gilmatt should report the costs of marketing the new product and the related sales revenues on its 2016 financial statements. Cite your reference and applicable paragraph numbers.

CHAPTER 13

INVESTMENTS AND LONG-TERM RECEIVABLES

Investing for the Future

Companies often invest in the debt and equity securities of other companies for a variety of reasons, including obtaining additional income. For example, **Apple Inc.** generates approximately 42% of its operating cash flows for the year in its first fiscal quarter, but it needs cash throughout the year. Because its operating cash inflows do not coincide with its operating cash outflows, Apple must manage its cash to meet its short-term obligations, while investing excess cash to earn a return. It does this by investing its excess cash in marketable debt and equity securities and selling these marketable securities when it needs cash. At the end of its 2015 fiscal year, Apple had over $184 billion of such investments that allowed it to earn additional income in the form of interest or dividends, as well as profits from the potential price appreciation of the securities. By contrast, at the end of fiscal 2015, Starbucks held $81.3 million in short-term and $312.5 million in long-term investment securities.

In addition to obtaining additional income, a company may invest in another company to improve its competitive position. By purchasing shares of a supplier, customer, or other valuable business, the investing company is able to exert significant influence over that company's activities. The return from such an investment comes in the form of increased profits and growth. For example, **Starbucks** has investments that give it significant influence over several international companies that are licensed to operate Starbucks's retail stores. In addition, Starbucks recently acquired **Teavana** to capitalize on the fast-growing, and profitable, tea market. Finally, Starbucks has also strategically invested in a joint venture with **PepsiCo** called the North America Coffee Partnership, which produces and distributes Frappuccino®

LEARNING OBJECTIVES

After reading this chapter you will be able to

LO 13.1 Explain the classification and valuation of investments.

LO 13.2 Account for investments in debt securities classified as held-to-maturity, including amortization of bond premiums and discounts.

LO 13.3 Account for investments in debt and equity securities classified as trading.

LO 13.4 Account for investments in debt securities classified as available-for-sale.

LO 13.5 Understand transfers between categories and impairment of debt and equity securities.

LO 13.6 Account for intercompany investments using the equity method.

LO 13.7 Understand disclosures of investments.

LO 13.8 Account for additional types of investments, including long-term receivables.

LO 13.9 (Appendix 13.1) Account for derivative financial instruments.

beverages and other espresso drinks to grocery stores and other outlets. At the end of its 2015 fiscal year, Starbucks had $306.4 million of such strategic investments.

A major challenge of accounting for investments relates to the use of fair value measurements. In order to provide relevant information, a company that does not have control or significant influence over the investee generally reports the investment at fair value because it provides the most relevant information about the value of the investments to financial statement users. Because the value of investment securities can change dramatically in a short period of time, accounting information that reflects fair value allows financial statement users to better evaluate a company's investment strategies, as well as its financial flexibility and liquidity. However, the changes in fair value introduce uncertainty which could produce less predictable earnings. In addition, the representational faithfulness of fair value estimates may diminish when securities markets become illiquid. Addressing these issues is critical if accounting wishes to convey the most useful information to investors, creditors, and other lenders.

Companies invest excess cash in financial instruments for numerous reasons that range from earning interest, dividends, or capital gains to developing a strategic relationship.[1] In this chapter, we focus on investments in debt and equity securities. A **debt security** represents a creditor relationship with another company. Thus, investments in debt securities include:

- U.S. treasury securities
- municipal and corporate bonds
- convertible debt
- commercial paper
- preferred stock that has certain debt-like features

An **equity security** represents an ownership interest in another company. Thus, investments in equity securities include:

- common stock
- preferred stock
- stock options, rights, and warrants
- put and call options

When a company invests in debt securities and equity securities that have a readily determinable fair value, they are classified as investments on the balance sheet. If the investment is in a relatively small proportion of another company's equity securities, it is measured at fair value. If the investment is in a debt security, it is measured at either fair value or amortized cost, depending on the company's intent to hold or sell the securities. The entire group of securities is often referred to as a portfolio of **marketable securities** (or **investment securities**).[2] However, if a company owns a relatively large proportion of the outstanding equity shares of another company, different methods of accounting apply. If the investment allows the company to significantly influence the investee's

---

[1] The FASB defines a financial instrument as cash, evidence of an ownership interest in an entity, or a contract that both (1) imposes on one entity a contractual obligation either to deliver cash or another financial instrument to a second entity or to exchange other financial instruments on potentially unfavorable terms with the second entity and (2) conveys to that second entity a contractual right either to receive cash or another financial instrument from the first entity or to exchange other financial instruments on potentially favorable terms with the first entity. (FASB ASC Master Glossary)

[2] Marketable securities are securities that have readily determinable fair values. A fair value is considered readily determinable if a sales price is currently available on a securities exchange (e.g., the New York Stock Exchange) or in an over-the-counter market for which prices are publicly reported. Nonmarketable securities are those that are not publicly traded. GAAP does not require that nonmarketable securities be reported at fair value. Consequently, most companies report them at historical cost, often referred to as the cost method.

decisions, the company will use the equity method. If the investment is sufficient for the investor to control the investee, consolidation accounting applies. This chapter focuses on the accounting for a wide variety of investments in the marketable debt and equity securities of other companies.[3]

In addition, companies commonly include other items in the investments category on the balance sheet, such as long-term receivables, the cash surrender value of life insurance policies, and sinking funds. The recording and reporting for these types of investments are also discussed in this chapter.

HOW ARE INVESTMENTS CLASSIFIED AND REPORTED?

LEARNING OBJECTIVE 13.1
Explain the classification and valuation of investments.

When a company's investment is not sufficiently large enough to allow it to control or exert significant influence over the other company, the investment is considered a **minority passive investment**. Generally, an investment is considered passive when a company owns less than 20% of the voting common stock of the investee. At acquisition, a company classifies each passive investment in debt and equity securities into one of three categories:

1. *Held-to-Maturity Securities.* Investments in **held-to-maturity securities** are debt securities for which the company has the *positive intent and ability* to hold until maturity, which is not the same as the absence of an intent to sell.[4] Any sales of these securities prior to their maturity should be rare and should be due to a change in circumstances, such as the tax status of the investment, the credit quality of the issuer, or other isolated, nonrecurring, and unusual events for the company. A company does not classify a security as being held-to-maturity if it intends to hold the security for an indefinite period. Therefore, the classification is *not* appropriate if the security might be sold for reasons such as a change in market interest rates or a need for liquid funds.[5]

2. *Trading Securities.* All equity securities and investments in debt securities that are purchased and held principally to sell in the near term are classified as **trading securities**.[6] Trading generally involves active and frequent buying and selling, and the securities are held with the intent to profit on short-term changes in price. Financial institutions such as banks, insurers, and security brokers and dealers generally hold sizable portfolios of trading securities. For example, **Citibank** reported almost $286 billion of trading assets at December 31, 2013. It is much less common for companies that are not financial institutions to hold trading portfolios; nevertheless, for 2015, **Starbucks** reported $65.8 million of investments classified as trading securities, primarily equity mutual funds and equity exchange-traded funds.

3. *Available-for-Sale Securities.* Investments classified as **available-for-sale securities** are debt securities that are not classified as held-to-maturity or trading. Available-for-sale securities are investments the company intends to hold for an indefinite period. Such securities could be held for a long period of time or could be sold if the price of the security becomes attractive or the company needs the funds from the sale. For example, at the end of 2015, **Starbucks** reported $15.5 million of short-term available-for-sale investments and $312.5 million of long-term available for sale investments.

---

[3] In January 2016, the FASB issued Accounting Standards Update 2016-01: Recognition and Measurement of Financial Assets and Liabilities (FASB ASC 825-10: Financial Instruments — Overall) which is effective for fiscal years beginning after December 15, 2017. This chapter presents GAAP with regard to financial instruments as amended by this Update.

[4] FASB ASC 320-10-25: Investments—Debt and Equity Securities: Overall: Recognition.

[5] Sales of held-to-maturity debt securities are considered to be at maturity if (1) the security is sold near enough to its maturity that interest rate risk is substantially eliminated or (2) the sale occurs after the company has collected a substantial portion (e.g., 85%) of the principal.

[6] If an investment in an equity security does not have a readily determinable fair value, it may be measured at cost less impairment, plus or minus any observable price changes of an identical or similar investment of the same issuer. Any change in the basis of these equity investments will be reported in current earnings.

All equity securities with readily determinable fair values must be categorized as trading securities and reported at fair value. The accounting for debt securities differs based on management intent. While these three classifications provide information about managers' intent regarding their debt investments, they may be criticized as creating the potential for inconsistency in the application of GAAP. For example, companies holding identical debt securities could account for those securities using three different methods. Therefore, allowing classification of investments in debt securities based on management intent may create a lack of comparability among these debt investments both for an individual company as well as among companies.

A company reports its held-to-maturity securities at amortized cost. Because holders of these securities have the intent and ability to hold the securities until maturity, any changes in fair value prior to the maturity date are not a primary concern in predicting the level and riskiness of cash flows. Therefore, U.S. GAAP allows the use of amortized cost measurement for held-to-maturity securities because it is a faithful representation of the amount invested.

A company reports its investments in trading securities at fair value on the balance sheet with any changes in fair value reported on the income statement as part of net income. Investments classified as available-for-sale are also reported at fair value on the balance sheet; however, any changes in fair value are reported as other comprehensive income and shown in accumulated other comprehensive income in the shareholders' equity section of the balance sheet. As Chapter 4 describes, fair value is the amount that would be received if a security is sold in an orderly transaction between market participants.[7] For marketable investment securities, fair value is generally determined as the number of units of the security times the quoted selling price. Fair value provides a relevant measure of these investments because it provides users with more timely measures of the future cash flows that could be realized from the securities (as compared to the acquisition or historical cost of those securities). This information helps users evaluate the performance of a company's investment strategies. It also provides an indication of the *financial flexibility*, or *solvency*, of companies, particularly for financial institutions that have a large portion of their assets in such securities. Using fair values to measure trading and available-for-sale securities results in "unrealized holding gains and losses," which are the changes in fair value from one period to another. (discussed later in the chapter).

In addition to passive investments, a company may invest in the debt or equity securities of other corporations to establish long-term relationships with suppliers or to obtain significant influence over the companies' activities. Significant influence generally occurs when the investor owns between 20% and 50% of the voting common stock of the investee. These types of investments are considered **minority active investments** (or **equity method investments**). When the investor has significant influence over the investee, the *equity method* is used to account for the investment, as we discuss later in the chapter.

Consolidation occurs when the investor *controls* the investee through an investment in equity securities. Legal control occurs when the investor owns more than 50% of the voting common stock of the investee. However, control can also be defined as the power to direct the use of the assets of the investee in essentially the same way as the company can use its own assets. Therefore, a company may possess effective control at a lower ownership level than legal control.[8] When the investor controls the investee, the investment is considered a **majority active investment**. GAAP requires the majority investor to issue consolidated financial statements, which are the combined financial statements of both companies.[9]

Exhibit 13.1 provides an overview of the various categories and methods for recording and reporting investments in securities.

---
[7] FASB ASC Glossary.

[8] The 20% and 50% levels of ownership are guidelines in determining whether significant influence or control exists. A company may own less than 20% of the voting common stock of the investee and still be considered to have significant influence. Similarly, a company owning less than 50% of the voting common stock may have effective control. The determination of whether significant influence or control exists depends on the full set of circumstances and requires the exercise of professional judgment.

[9] Although the underlying concepts of consolidation accounting are briefly discussed in a later section, the preparation of consolidated financial statements is covered in advanced accounting texts.

EXHIBIT 13.1 Accounting for Investments

Accounting Methods for Investments

	Balance Sheet	Income Statement	Unrealized Holding Gains and Losses
Equity Securities			
1. No significant influence: Trading	Fair value	Dividends, realized gains/losses	Net income
2. Significant influence	Equity method	Proportion of investee's income	Not recognized; disclosed in footnotes
3. Control	Consolidation	Proportion of investee's income	Not recognized
Debt Securities			
1. Trading	Fair value	Interest, realized gains/losses	Net income
2. Available-for-sale	Fair value	Interest, realized gains/losses	Other comprehensive income
3. Held-to-maturity	Amortized cost	Interest, realized gains/losses	Not recognized; disclosed in footnotes

Fair Value Option

As noted in earlier chapters, GAAP allows companies to report most financial instruments at fair value, with unrealized gains and losses recognized in income in the period in which they occur. This fair value option is generally a choice made when a company first purchases a financial asset or incurs a financial liability and must be applied on an instrument-by-instrument basis. The choice as to whether or not to use the fair value option is an irrevocable decision. With regard to financial assets, the effect of the application of the fair value option is to measure the financial assets at fair value on the balance sheet with unrealized gains and losses recognized in net income, consistent with the treatment of trading securities.

In addition, the fair value option allows companies to report certain financial liabilities at fair value, which may provide a more relevant view of the company's exposure to interest rate risk.[10] For example, financial institutions manage their interest rate risk by coordinating their holdings of financial assets and liabilities, effectively creating a hedge against such risk. Therefore, the fair value option allows companies to avoid the earnings volatility that may exist if only one side of their portfolio of financial instruments were reported at fair value.

GOT IT?

13-1 Why do companies purchase securities of other corporations?

13-2 Provide brief definitions for the following terms: (a) *debt security*, (b) *equity security*, and (c) *fair value*.

13-3 What are the three categories of minority passive investments in debt and equity securities? Describe the criteria used to classify the investments into these three categories.

13-4 How are each of the three categories of minority passive investments reported on the balance sheet?

13-5 Identify the accounting methods a company uses for investments of 20% or more in the voting common stock of the investee.

---

[10] The FASB does not require liabilities to be reported at fair value because of the difficulty of determining which liabilities should be reported at fair value and obtaining a reliable value for those liabilities that do not trade in an established market. In addition, not all companies manage risk in the same way. Therefore, the benefits of using fair value for liabilities of these companies may not be worth the additional cost.

LEARNING OBJECTIVE 13.2

Account for investments in debt securities classified as held-to-maturity, including amortization of bond premiums and discounts.

HOW ARE INVESTMENTS IN HELD-TO-MATURITY SECURITIES MEASURED AND REPORTED?

When a company has the positive ability and intent to hold a debt security to maturity, it can be reported as a held-to-maturity security. The accounting for investments in held-to-maturity debt securities is as follows:

- The investment is initially recorded at cost.
- The investment is subsequently reported at amortized cost on the ending balance sheet(s).[11]
- Unrealized holding gains and losses are *not* recognized on the balance sheet or the income statement but are disclosed in the notes to the financial statements.
- Interest income is recognized in net income as it is earned, along with any realized gains and losses on sales (but these should be rare given the held-to-maturity classification).

Recording Initial Cost

Investments in debt securities are initially recorded at cost. Cost is determined as the price paid to acquire the debt securities, which can be measured as the principal amount, or face value, of the debt plus any premium or minus any discount at acquisition.[12] As discussed more completely in Chapter 14, debt securities, such as bonds, that carry a stated interest rate above the prevailing market interest rate for securities with a similar amount of risk sell at an amount above their face value. This is termed selling at a *premium*. This premium results in reported interest income being less than the cash received for interest. Debt securities carrying a stated interest rate below the prevailing market rate for securities with a similar amount of risk sell at an amount below their face value. This is termed selling at a *discount*. The discount results in reported interest income being greater than the cash received for interest.

Example Drinkwitz Company invests in bonds that it intends to hold to maturity. The bonds have a face value of $100,000 and mature on December 31, 2020. Drinkwitz pays $99,000 on January 1, 2018. Interest is payable semiannually on June 30 and December 31. Drinkwitz records this purchase on January 1, 2018, as follows:

Investment in Held-to-Maturity Debt Securities	99,000	
Cash		99,000

Note that Drinkwitz includes the $1,000 discount ($100,000 face value − $99,000 cost) directly in the investment account.[13]

Recognition of Interest Income and Amortization of Bond Premiums and Discounts

Investments in held-to-maturity debt securities that are purchased at a premium (discount) result in a market, or effective, interest rate that is below (above) the stated rate. When a company receives the interest on these investments, the cash receipt is based on the stated rate of interest. However, **the amount of interest income recognized each**

---

[11] Amortized cost is the remaining amount (e.g., carrying value) of the investment after any premium or discount has been amortized each period and interest revenue is recognized.

[12] Other costs, such as brokerage fees, necessary for the acquisition are also included in the cost of the securities. However, these amounts would then be allocated among each security purchased to determine its cost. For simplicity, we do not discuss this procedure.

[13] Companies may record any premiums or discounts in a separate valuation account. However, this is not common practice in accounting for investments. Therefore, these journal entries are not shown.

accounting period is based on the effective (or market) interest rate determined at the time of acquisition. Interest income is computed as follows:

Interest Income = Effective Interest Rate × Book Value of the Investment at Beginning of Period × Time

Consequently, a portion of any premium or discount is amortized over the remaining life of the bonds. **This amortization is equal to the difference between the amount of interest income and the cash receipt.** This process is known as the **effective interest method** (or **interest method**) of amortization.

An alternative procedure to record interest income and account for premiums and discounts is the *straight-line method*, in which the discount or premium is amortized to interest income in equal amounts each period during the life of the debt security. GAAP requires use of the effective interest method, unless the use of the straight-line method does not result in a material difference in the amount of interest income recognized in any year. These methods are discussed in greater detail in Chapter 14.

Example: Accounting for Premiums

Colburn Company invests in bonds that will be held to maturity. The bonds have a face value of $100,000, and Colburn pays $102,458.71 on January 1, 2018, resulting in a premium of $2,458.71 ($102,458.71 − $100,000). The bonds carry a stated interest rate of 13% payable semiannually on June 30 and December 31. The bonds mature on December 31, 2020, and have an effective interest rate of 12%. Colburn records the acquisition on January 1, 2018, as follows:

Investment in Held-to-Maturity Debt Securities	102,458.71	
Cash		102,458.71

Example 13.1 shows the schedule for computing interest income, the premium amortization, and the carrying value under the effective interest method for these investments.

EXAMPLE 13.1

Investment Interest Income and Premium Amortization Schedule: *Effective Interest Method*

Date	Cash (Debit)[a]	Interest Income (Credit)[b]	Investment in Debt Securities (Credit)[c]	Carrying Value of Investment in Debt Securities[d]
1/1/18				$102,458.71
6/30/18	$6,500.00	$6,147.52	$352.48	102,106.23
12/31/18	6,500.00	6,126.37	373.63	101,732.60
6/30/19	6,500.00	6,103.96	396.04	101,336.56
12/31/19	6,500.00	6,080.19	419.81	100,916.75
6/30/20	6,500.00	6,055.01	444.99	100,471.76
12/31/20	6,500.00	6,028.24[e]	471.76	100,000.00

[a] $100,000 (face value) × 0.13 (stated rate of interest) × 6/12 months.
[b] Previous Investment Carrying Value × 0.12 (effective interest rate) × 6/12 months.
[c] Amount from a − Amount from b.
[d] Previous Investment Carrying Value − Amount from c.
[e] Difference of $0.07 due to rounding.

Using the effective interest method, Colburn records the first interest receipt on June 30, 2018, for the investment purchased at a premium, as follows:

Cash	6,500.00	
Investment in Held-to-Maturity Debt Securities		352.48
Interest Income		6,147.52

Note that Colburn credits the premium amortization directly to the investment account. Over the remaining life, Colburn records a similar entry every 6 months, using the amounts in the amortization schedule from Example 13.1.

By contrast, if Colburn uses the straight-line method, it would amortize the $2,458.71 premium over the 6 remaining semiannual periods ($2,458.71 ÷ 6 = $409.79) and make the following entry every 6 months:

Cash	6,500.00	
Investment in Held-to-Maturity Debt Securities		409.79
Interest Income		6,090.21

Example: Accounting for Discounts

Colburn Company invests in bonds that will be held to maturity. The bonds have a face value of $100,000, and Colburn pays $97,616.71 on January 1, 2018, resulting in a discount of $2,383.29 ($100,000 − $97,616.71). The bonds carry a stated interest rate of 13% payable semiannually on June 30 and December 31. The bonds mature on December 31, 2020, and have an effective interest rate of 14%. Colburn records the acquisition on January 1, 2018, as follows:

Investment in Held-to-Maturity Debt Securities	97,616.71	
Cash		97,616.71

Example 13.2 illustrates the schedule for computing interest income, the discount amortization, and the carrying value under the effective method for these bonds.

EXAMPLE 13.2

Investment Interest Income and Discount Amortization Schedule: *Effective Interest Method*

Date	Cash (Debit)[a]	Interest Income (Credit)[b]	Investment in Debt Securities (Debit)[c]	Carrying Value of Investment in Debt Securities[d]
1/1/18				$ 97,616.71
6/30/18	$6,500.00	$6,833.17	$333.17	97,949.88
12/31/18	6,500.00	6,856.49	356.49	98,306.37
6/30/19	6,500.00	6,881.45	381.45	98,687.82
12/31/19	6,500.00	6,908.15	408.15	99,095.97
6/30/20	6,500.00	6,936.72	436.72	99,532.69
12/31/20	6,500.00	6,967.31[e]	467.31	100,000.00

[a] $100,000 (face value) × 0.13 (stated rate of interest) × 6/12 months.
[b] Previous Investment Carrying Value × 0.14 (effective interest rate) × 6/12 months.
[c] Amount from b − Amount from a.
[d] Previous Investment Carrying Value + Amount from c.
[e] Difference of $0.02 due to rounding.

Colburn records the first interest receipt on June 30, 2018, using the effective interest method for the investment purchased at a discount, as follows:

Cash	6,500.00	
Investment in Held-to-Maturity Debt Securities	333.17	
Interest Income		6,833.17

Note that Colburn debits the discount amortization directly to the investment account.

If Colburn uses the straight-line method, it would amortize the $2,383.29 discount over the 6 remaining semiannual periods ($2,383.29 ÷ 6 = $397.22) and make the following entry every 6 months:

Cash	6,500.00	
Investment in Held-to-Maturity Debt Securities	397.22	
Interest Income		6,897.22

Amortization for Bonds Acquired between Interest Dates

Investments in held-to-maturity debt securities may be acquired between interest dates. When a company purchases debt securities between interest payment dates, it normally pays both the purchase price and the interest accrued on the debt securities from the most recent interest payment date to the date of purchase. The interest amount received is typically debited to Interest Income. On the next interest payment date, the company receives interest for the entire period and records interest income as usual.[14]

Example Tallen Company purchased 9% bonds with a face value of $200,000 at par plus accrued interest on March 1, 2018. Interest on these bonds is payable June 30 and December 31, and the bonds mature December 31, 2020 (34 months after the date of purchase). Tallen records the acquisition on March 1, 2018, as follows:

Investment in Held-to-Maturity Debt Securities	200,000	
Interest Income ($200,000 × 0.09 × 2/12)	3,000	
Cash		203,000

If the investment was purchased at a premium or discount, it would be amortized over the remaining life of the debt securities as shown in the previous section.

Tallen records the first interest receipt on June 30, 2018, as follows:

Cash ($200,000 × 0.09 × 6/12)	9,000	
Interest Income		9,000

Note that the actual amount of interest income recognized in Tallen's income statement for the 6 months ending June 30, 2015, is $6,000 ($9,000 − $3,000), which represents interest earned for the 4 months it owned the investment.

Sale of a Held-to-Maturity Investment Prior to Maturity

Selling an investment in held-to-maturity securities before the maturity date should be rare because the sale may violate the reason for their classification. However, circumstances may arise (e.g., a significant deterioration of the issuer's creditworthiness, a tax law change that eliminates the tax exempt status of the debt security, or other isolated, nonrecurring or unusual events) which would cause a company to sell a held-to-maturity debt security prior to its maturity. When such a sale occurs, a company first accrues any interest income and amortizes any premium or discount on the investment from the last interest date to the sale date. This procedure is necessary to record the correct amount of interest income and to determine the carrying value of the investment on the date of the sale. The carrying value of the investment is then subtracted from the sales price (*excluding* any accrued interest) to determine the gain or loss that is recorded. In addition, any interest earned since the last interest date is collected from the purchaser.

Example On March 31, 2019, Colburn Company sells $100,000, 13% bonds classified as held-to-maturity for $102,000 plus accrued interest. The bonds were purchased on January 1, 2018, for $97,616.71 and have a maturity date of December 31, 2020.

---

[14] This procedure reduces the record keeping for the first interest receipt and is discussed more completely in Chapter 14.

The effective interest rate at the time the bonds were purchased was 14%. Colburn amortizes the bond discount by the effective interest method (see **Example 13.2**) and reports the investment's carrying value at January 1, 2019, as $98,306.37. Colburn records the following entries on March 31, 2019:

Investment in Held-to-Maturity Debt Securities	190.72	
[($98,306.37 × 0.14 × 3/12) − ($100,000 × 0.13 × 3/12)]		
Interest Income		190.72
Cash ($102,000 + $3,250)	105,250.00	
Interest Income ($100,000 × 0.13 × 3/12)		3,250.00
Investment in Held-to-Maturity Debt Securities		
($98,306.37 from Example 13.2 + $190.72)		98,497.09
Gain on Sale of Debt Securities		3,502.91

The first journal entry amortizes the discount up to the date of sale, which increases the investment's carrying value to $98,497.09 ($98,306.37 + $190.72). In the second journal entry, Colburn collects the sales price plus the $3,250 interest earned in the 3 months since the last interest payment date and eliminates the current carrying value of the investment account. Colburn computes the gain on the sale by comparing the carrying value of the investment account on the sale date ($98,497.09) with the $102,000 selling price of the investment. Colburn reports this gain as part of income from continuing operations. ■

If held-to-maturity debt securities are sold in response to other circumstances (e.g., change in market interest rates, the need for liquidity), the company's intent to hold the other debt securities to maturity may be called into question or "tainted." If this occurs, the company may be forced to reclassify other held-to-maturity securities to either the trading or available-for-sale categories. The transfer of securities between investment categories is discussed in a later section.

GOT IT?

13-6 Briefly summarize the accounting for an investment in debt securities held to maturity.

13-7 When are investments in debt securities held to maturity purchased at a premium? How does the amortization of a premium under the effective interest method affect interest income?

13-8 When are investments in debt securities held to maturity purchased at a discount? How does the amortization of a discount under the effective interest method affect interest income?

13-9 Briefly describe the two methods available to determine interest income and account for premiums and discounts on investments in bonds held to maturity.

LEARNING OBJECTIVE 13.3

Account for investments in debt and equity securities classified as trading.

HOW ARE INVESTMENTS IN TRADING SECURITIES MEASURED AND REPORTED?

All investments in equity securities and investments in debt securities that are actively bought and sold with the intention to profit on short-term changes in price are classified as trading securities. The accounting for trading securities applies the most complete fair value measurement approach, as follows:

- The investment is initially recorded at cost (which equals fair value on the date of purchase).
- The investment is subsequently reported at fair value on the balance sheet.

- Unrealized holding gains and losses resulting from changes in the fair value of the securities are included in net income each period.
- Interest and dividend income, as well as realized gains and losses on sales, are included in net income each period.

The accounting for trading securities is illustrated in the following sections using the information for Kent Company shown in **Example 13.3**.

EXAMPLE 13.3

Investment in Trading Securities

- On May 1, 2018, Kent Company purchases the following securities:

Able Company common stock	100 shares at $50 per share
Baker Company common stock	300 shares at $80 per share
Charlie Company preferred stock	200 shares at $120 per share
Delta Company 10% bonds	Face value of $15,000, acquired at par. Interest is paid on April 30 and October 31 each year.

- Kent intends to actively buy and sell the debt investments to profit on short-term price changes. Therefore, Kent appropriately classifies the debt securities as an investment in trading securities.
- Kent received $3,000 of dividends during 2018 related to the common stock investments.

Recording the Initial Cost of Trading Securities

A company records the purchase of investments in trading securities at the acquisition price of the securities.

Example The total cost of the trading securities purchased by Kent is $68,000 [(100 shares × $50) + (300 shares × $80) + (200 shares × $120) + $15,000]. Kent records the purchase as follows:

Investment in Trading Securities	68,000	
Cash		68,000

Recording Interest and Dividend Income

Interest income related to investments in debt securities is recorded as it is earned during the period. Because companies only receive cash related to interest periodically (e.g., semiannually), interest income should be accrued as time passes (using either the effective or straight-line method). In contrast, companies are not obligated to pay dividends on equity securities. Therefore, dividend income is recorded when dividends are declared by the company's board of directors.

Example On May 31, 2018, and every month Kent holds the investment in Delta Company bonds, Kent will accrue one month of interest as follows:

Interest Receivable	125	
Interest Income ($15,000 × 0.10 × 1/12)		125

If Kent had purchased the Delta Company bonds at a premium or discount, it would compute the interest income using the effective interest (or straight-line) method and amortize a portion of the premium or discount, as discussed earlier.

On October 31, 2018, Kent receives the semiannual interest payment and records it as follows:

Cash	750	
Interest Receivable		750

Kent records the $3,000 of dividends it received related to its investments in the stock of Able, Baker, and Charlie as follows:

Cash	3,000	
Dividend Income		3,000

If Able, Baker, or Charlie had declared dividends at year-end but Kent had not yet received them, it would debit Dividends Receivable instead of Cash. ■

Recognition of Unrealized Holding Gains and Losses

On its balance sheet, a company reports any investments in trading securities at fair value. An increase in the fair value of investment securities is an **unrealized holding gain**, while a decrease in the fair value of investment securities is an **unrealized holding loss**. The gain or loss is unrealized because the securities have not been sold. For investments in trading securities, a company reports its unrealized gains and losses as part of net income. Notice that for investments in trading securities, a company reports *both* its realized and unrealized gains and losses in its net income.

For investments in trading securities, the Unrealized Holding Gain/Loss account is a temporary account that is closed to Retained Earnings during the closing process. A debit balance in the account represents a net unrealized loss. A credit balance in the account represents a net unrealized gain.

Example On December 31, 2018, the fair value of Kent's investment in trading securities is $71,000 as follows:

Security	Cost	12/31/18 Fair Value	Cumulative Change in Fair Value
100 shares of Able Company common stock	$ 5,000	$ 6,000	$1,000
300 shares of Baker Company common stock	24,000	23,500	(500)
200 shares of Charlie Company preferred stock	24,000	26,000	2,000
$15,000 face value of Delta Company bonds	15,000	15,500	500
Totals	$68,000	$71,000	$3,000

Kent records the $3,000 net increase in the value of the securities, an unrealized holding gain, as follows:

Investment in Trading Securities	3,000	
Unrealized Holding Gain/Loss—Trading Securities		3,000

On its December 31, 2018, balance sheet, Kent reports the investment as an asset at the $71,000 fair value of the securities.[15] Because trading securities are frequently bought and sold, the investment will be reported as a current asset, and the Unrealized Holding Gain/Loss is included in net income of the current period.[16] The disclosure of investments in trading securities is shown later in the chapter.

To illustrate subsequent increases or decreases in fair value, suppose that on December 31, 2019, the fair value of the investment in trading securities held by Kent is $66,000 as follows:

Security	12/31/18 Fair Value	12/31/19 Fair Value	Change in Fair Value
100 shares of Able Company common stock	$ 6,000	$ 6,100	$ 100
300 shares of Baker Company common stock	23,500	22,700	(800)
200 shares of Charlie Company preferred stock	26,000	23,200	(2,800)
$15,000 face value of Delta Company bonds	15,500	14,000	(1,500)
Totals	$71,000	$66,000	$(5,000)

---

[15] Alternatively, a company may choose to record any changes in fair value in a valuation account, Allowance for Change in Value of Investment. We illustrate the use of a valuation account in the discussion of investments in available-for-sale securities.

[16] The fair value method is not allowed for federal tax purposes. Therefore, the inclusion of unrealized gains/losses in net income and its exclusion from taxable income creates a temporary difference which leads to the recognition of deferred income taxes, as discussed in Chapter 18.

Kent determines the amount of the year-end adjustment by comparing the fair value of the investments at the end of the period with the fair value of the investments at the beginning of the period. Therefore, Kent records a $5,000 unrealized holding loss as follows:

Unrealized Holding Gain/Loss—Trading Securities	5,000	
Investment in Trading Securities		5,000

On its December 31, 2019, balance sheet, Kent reports the investment in trading securities as an asset at the $66,000 fair value of the securities.[17] It reports the $5,000 unrealized holding loss in its 2019 income statement. ■

Realized Gains and Losses on Sales of Trading Securities

A company reports realized gains and losses on sales of investments in trading securities in net income. The realized gain or loss is measured as the difference between the selling price and the fair value of the security on the previous balance sheet.

Example On March 1, 2020, Kent sold the 100 shares of Able Company common stock for $6,000. The fair value at the previous balance sheet was $6,100. Kent recognizes a loss of $100 ($6,000 selling price − $6,100 fair value at the previous balance sheet) as follows:

Cash	6,000	
Loss on Sale of Trading Securities	100	
Investment in Trading Securities		6,100

At the end of 2020, Kent reports the fair values of the securities it still owns. On December 31, 2020, the total fair value of the remaining securities is $62,300 as follows:

Security	12/31/19 Fair Value	12/31/20 Fair Value	Cumulative Change in Fair Value
300 shares of Baker Company common stock	$22,700	$23,500	$ 800
200 shares of Charlie Company preferred stock	23,200	24,100	900
$15,000 face value of Delta Company bonds	14,000	14,700	700
Totals	$59,900	$62,300	$2,400

Kent records the increase in value (unrealized holding gain) as follows:

Investment in Trading Securities	2,400	
Unrealized Holding Gain/Loss—Trading Securities		2,400

Kent reports the $100 realized loss on the sale of its investment in the Able Company common stock and the $2,400 unrealized holding gain (on the Baker, Charlie, and Delta securities) in its 2020 net income. ■

GOT IT?

13-10 Briefly summarize the accounting for an investment in trading securities.

13-11 Briefly describe how to determine and record any subsequent increases or decreases in the fair value of an investment in trading securities.

13-12 Briefly describe how to determine and record the gain or loss on the sale of an investment in trading securities.

---

[17] A company preparing interim (quarterly) financial statements would use the same accounting procedures each quarter.

LEARNING OBJECTIVE 13.4

Account for investments in debt securities classified as available-for-sale.

HOW ARE INVESTMENTS IN AVAILABLE-FOR-SALE SECURITIES MEASURED AND REPORTED?

Investments in debt securities that are not classified as held-to-maturity or trading are classified as available-for-sale. The accounting for investments in available-for-sale securities is as follows:

- The investment is initially recorded at cost (which equals fair value on the acquisition date).
- The investment is subsequently reported at fair value on the balance sheet.
- Unrealized holding gains and losses resulting from changes in the fair value of the securities are reported as a component of other comprehensive income each period. The cumulative unrealized holding gains and losses are reported in the accumulated other comprehensive income section of shareholders' equity.
- Interest income is included in net income each period.
- When a security is sold, realized gains and losses are included in net income, and any unrealized holding gains or losses must be reclassified from accumulated other comprehensive income into net income.

The accounting for available-for-sale securities is illustrated in the following sections using the information for Morgan Company shown in **Example 13.4**.

EXAMPLE 13.4 **Investment in Available-for-Sale Securities**

- On January 1, 2018, Morgan Company purchases bonds for $195,000.
- The bonds have a face value of $200,000
- The bonds pay interest semiannually on June 30 and December 31 at a stated interest rate of 10%
- The bonds mature on December 31, 2027 (10 years)
- Morgan does not intend to hold the debt securities to maturity nor does it intend to actively buy and sell them. Therefore, Morgan appropriately classifies the securities as available-for-sale investments.
- Morgan uses the straight-line method of amortization.

Recording the Initial Cost of Available-for-Sale Securities

A company records the purchase of investments in available-for-sale securities at the acquisition price of the securities, which can be measured as the principal amount of the debt plus any premium or minus any discount at acquisition. The concept, computation, and recognition of the initial cost of investments in available-for-sale securities is identical to that required for investments in held-to-maturity securities.

Example Using the information in Example 13.4, Morgan records the purchase as follows:

Investment in Available-for-Sale Securities	195,000	
Cash		195,000

Note that similar to the accounting for investments in held-to-maturity securities, the $5,000 discount is included directly in the investment account.

Recording Interest and Dividend Income

Interest income related to investments in debt securities accrues continuously over time. Similar to the accounting for investments in held-to-maturity securities, any interest income is computed using the effective interest (or straight-line) method.

Example On June 30, 2018, Morgan records the first semiannual interest receipt (using the straight-line method) for the investment as follows:

Cash ($200,000 × 0.10 × 6/12)	10,000	
Investment in Available for Sale Securities ($5,000 ÷ 20)	250	
Interest Income		10,250

Note that Morgan records the discount amortization directly to the investment account. A similar entry would be made periodically over the remaining time that Morgan holds the investment.

Recognition of Unrealized Holding Gains and Losses

On its balance sheet, a company reports any investments in available-for-sale securities at fair value through the use of a valuation account named Allowance for Change in Fair Value of Investments. This allowance account is an adjunct/contra account to the investment account. A debit balance in the allowance account represents an increase in fair value above the amortized cost of the investment (an unrealized holding gain). A credit balance in the allowance account represents a decrease in fair value below the amortized cost of the investment (an unrealized holding loss). The use of an allowance account allows the company to report the investment at fair value while maintaining a record of the amortized cost of the investment.

    The company reports any unrealized holding gains and losses in other comprehensive income for the period. For available-for-sale securities, a credit *change* in the Unrealized Holding Gain/Loss account represents the net unrealized holding gains on the securities for the period, while a debit *change* in this account represents the net unrealized holding losses on the securities for the period. A *credit balance* in the account represents the *cumulative* net unrealized holding gains and is reported as a positive element in the accumulated other comprehensive income section of shareholders' equity. A *debit balance* in the account represents the *cumulative* net unrealized holding *losses* and is reported as a negative element in the accumulated other comprehensive income section of shareholders' equity. In summary, for available-for-sale securities, a company reports the *realized* gains and losses in net income but reports *unrealized* gains and losses in other comprehensive income.

Example On December 31, 2018, the amortized cost of Morgan's investment in available-for-sale securities was $195,500 ($195,000 acquisition cost + $500 amortization of discount). The fair value of the investment at that date was determined to be $199,000. Morgan records the $3,500 difference between the amortized cost and the fair value of the investment, an unrealized holding gain, as follows:

Allowance for Change in Fair Value of Investments	3,500	
Unrealized Holding Gain/Loss—Available-for-Sale Securities		3,500

On its December 31, 2018, balance sheet, Morgan reports the investment as an asset at the $199,000 fair value of the securities. If Morgan holds multiple available-for-sale investments and some are determined to be current and some noncurrent, the asset account is separated between the current and noncurrent components, as shown later in the chapter. The use of an allowance account to record the changes in the fair values of the securities allows a company to retain information about the amortized cost of each security that will be used to compute the realized gain or loss on the sale of a security.[18]

---

[18] Alternatively, a company may choose to record any changes in the fair value directly in the investment account, similar to what was shown for trading securities. However, this method makes it more difficult to determine information needed for transactions in subsequent periods; therefore, we do not use this method for investments in available-for-sale securities.

Morgan reports the $3,500 increase in fair value as an unrealized holding gain in its other comprehensive income for 2018. Because this is the first year that Morgan owns marketable securities, the balance in the Unrealized Holding Gain/Loss account equals the unrealized holding gain/loss for the year. Therefore, it also reports the $3,500 credit balance in the Unrealized Holding Gain/Loss account as an addition to Accumulated Other Comprehensive Income in the shareholders' equity section of its balance sheet.[19] This disclosure is shown later in the chapter.

To illustrate subsequent increases or decreases in fair value, suppose that on December 31, 2019, the fair value of Morgan's investment in available-for-sale securities is $198,000. The amortized cost of this investment on 12/31/19 is $196,000 ($195,500 book value at 12/31/18 + $500 amortization for 2019). Note that Morgan continues to amortize the discount based on the investment's *original* acquisition cost.

Once a company has established an allowance account, it determines the amount of the period-end adjustment by first computing the required amount in the allowance account as the difference between the fair value and the amortized cost of the investment. At December 31, 2019, the required amount of Morgan's allowance account is a $2,000 debit balance ($198,000 fair value − $196,000 amortized cost). Next, the amount of the period-end adjustment is computed by comparing the required amount in the allowance account with the previous balance in the account. For Morgan, the previous balance at December 31, 2018, was a $3,500 debit balance. Therefore, Morgan credits the allowance account for $1,500 at the end of 2019 to record the decline in fair value, an unrealized holding loss, as follows:

Unrealized Holding Gain/Loss—Available-for-Sale Securities	1,500	
Allowance for Change in Fair Value of Investments		1,500

On its December 31, 2019, balance sheet, Morgan reports the investment as an asset at the $198,000 fair value of the securities ($196,000 amortized cost + $2,000 allowance). It reports the $1,500 decrease in fair value as an unrealized holding loss in its other comprehensive income for 2019. It also reports the $2,000 *credit balance* in the Unrealized Holding Gain/Loss account as an addition to accumulated other comprehensive income in the shareholders' equity section of its balance sheet.

Realized Gains and Losses on Sales of Available-for-Sale Securities

A company reports realized gains and losses on sales of investments in available-for-sale securities in net income. The realized gain or loss is measured as the selling price minus the *amortized cost* of a debt security. Because the security is no longer in the portfolio of available-for-sale securities, the related balances in the Allowance for Change in Fair Value of Investment and Unrealized Holding Gain/Loss accounts reported at the previous balance sheet date for the security sold must be "reversed" by making a reclassification adjustment. This reclassification adjustment serves two purposes. First, it eliminates the allowance account that is associated with the investment that was sold. Second, it adjusts other comprehensive income for the previous amount of unrealized gain or loss which is now being realized.

Example On March 31, 2020, Morgan sold its investment in available-for-sale securities for $197,000. The amortized cost of the securities at March 31, 2020, was $196,125 ($196,000 amortized cost at 12/31/19 + $125 amortization during 2020). Morgan records the sale and the reclassification adjustment on March 31, 2020, in two journal entries as follows:

---

[19] The amounts included in other comprehensive income for the year and accumulated other comprehensive income are reported net of tax. For simplicity, we do not include the tax effects in this discussion.

Cash	197,000		
Investment in Available-for-Sale Securities		196,125	
Gain on Sale of Available-for-Sale Securities		875	
Unrealized Holding Gain/Loss—Available-for-Sale Securities	2,000		
Allowance for Change in Fair Value of Investment		2,000	

The first journal entry records the sale and the realized gain of $875 ($197,000 selling price − $196,125 amortized cost) in 2020. The second journal entry reverses (eliminates) the $2,000 unrealized gain that had accumulated from January 1, 2018 (the date the company purchased the securities), until December 31, 2019 (the most recent balance sheet date). This unrealized gain had previously been reported in other comprehensive income, and this reclassification adjustment avoids a double-counting of this gain in Morgan's comprehensive income.[20] The net effect on comprehensive income for the period in which the gain is realized is a $1,125 loss (an $875 realized gain in net income minus a $2,000 elimination of the previous amount of the unrealized gain in other comprehensive income).

ETHICAL DILEMMA

As you complete the audit of Blanket Insurance Company, an interesting item comes to your attention. One of the staff accountants on the job noted that at the end of each quarter, the company sold a portion of its investments classified as available-for-sale. With each sale, Blanket was able to recognize a gain and increase income so that it would be able to just meet analyst forecasts. As the audit manager, you began to look into this finding and an interesting pattern emerged. For the last 5 years, if the company's income appeared to fall short of the analysts' expectations, Blanket would sell available-for-sale investments that had increased in value and recognize a gain that would allow Blanket to meet the analysts' forecasts. Because the company has a significant investment portfolio, you overlooked the strategic timing of these sales of appreciated securities in previous years. In discussions with Blanket's management, the CEO noted that this practice was part of the company's financial reporting strategy. Also, the CEO argued that the recognition of these gains and losses was entirely within GAAP. What is your reaction to the CEO's comments?

Summary and Conceptual Discussion

Exhibit 13.2 summarizes the accounting issues we have discussed for the three categories of investments in securities.

EXHIBIT 13.2 Summary of Accounting for Marketable Investments

Classification	Initially Record at:	Report on Balance Sheet at:	Recognize Unrealized Holding Gains/Losses in:	Recognize Interest and/or Dividend Income in:	Recognize Realized Gains/Losses in:
Held-to-maturity	Cost	Amortized cost	No recognition	Net income	Net income*
Trading	Cost	Fair value	Net income	Net income	Net income
Available-for-sale	Cost	Fair value	Other comprehensive income	Net income	Net income

*Sales of held-to-maturity securities should be rare.

---

[20] A sale of an investment in securities at a loss would be recorded in the same way. The company would record the sale and realized loss in the first journal entry and would eliminate any cumulative unrealized gain or loss and allowance on that security.

Three items are of particular interest. First, a company measures and reports investments in trading and available-for-sale securities for which the investor has no significant influence at fair value. The FASB believes that the use of fair value for financial instruments that are part of a trading or available-for-sale portfolio provides relevant information that reflects the underlying economics of a company's investments. In addition, for these types of investments, fair value provides more useful information for financial statement users in evaluating the performance of a company's investment strategies as well as understanding and analyzing a company's risk. However, for some investments, the FASB believes the use of fair value may not be as relevant because a company's business strategy is to realize the value of its investment through collection of contractual cash flows (principal and interest).[21] Therefore, U.S. GAAP permits the use of amortized cost for investments expected to be held to maturity. The FASB made this exception to the use of fair value restrictive. A company that wishes to use amortized cost must establish, for each investment in a debt security, the positive intent and ability to hold the security until maturity to be able to classify the investment as held-to-maturity. Thus, the accounting for marketable securities at both fair value and historical cost is an example of a mixed-attribute measurement model.

Second, FASB requires all investments in equity securities to be classified as trading securities. Equity securities cannot be classified as held-to-maturity because they do not have specified maturity dates. Further, the FASB believes that reporting equity investments at fair value with changes in the fair value presented in net income is the most relevant measurement attribute for equity investments. This conclusion is based largely on the fact that the primary way companies ultimately realize the value of equity investments is by selling the investment.

Finally, one of the major differences between the accounting for investments in trading and available-for-sale securities is the treatment of unrealized holding gains and losses. Because trading securities are actively managed, the FASB concluded that income measurement for those securities is more relevant if it includes the results of changes in fair value—the unrealized holding gains and losses. Therefore, a company's net income includes the results of economic events that occur in the period and provides a better measure of the company's *return on investment*. However, partly in response to the political pressure from banks and other financial institutions, the FASB concluded that including unrealized holding gains and losses in income for available-for-sale securities could create volatility in a company's reported net income. Such volatility may not represent the way that the company manages its business and the impact of economic events of the period. Therefore, unrealized holding gains and losses on available-for-sale securities are not included in net income but instead are reported as a component of other comprehensive income.

By allowing unrealized holding gains and losses on investments in available-for-sale investments to temporarily bypass the income statement until they are realized, current accounting standards provide a company with the ability to manage its earnings through a practice known as *gains trading*. This practice involves selectively selling investments that have risen in value so that a company can include the gains in income, while not selling investments that have declined in value and thereby avoid recognizing the losses. Thus, companies are able to "manage" the amount of net income they report by selecting which securities to sell. Note, however, that this practice does not permit companies to manage comprehensive income because the reclassification adjustment corrects comprehensive income for the amount of gain or loss that

---

[21] For additional discussion, see the Basis of Conclusions in FASB Accounting Standards Update (ASU) 2016-01.

had been unrealized in prior periods. Astute analysts and financial statement users should compare realized gains and losses in net income against reclassification adjustments in comprehensive income to try to detect whether a company is engaging in gains trading.

> ### GOT IT?
>
> **13-13** Briefly summarize the accounting for an investment in available-for-sale securities.
>
> **13-14** Briefly describe how to determine and record any subsequent increases or decreases in the fair value of an investment in available-for-sale securities.
>
> **13-15** Briefly describe how to determine and record the gain or loss on the sale of an investment in available-for-sale securities.

HOW DO WE ACCOUNT FOR TRANSFERS AND IMPAIRMENTS?

LEARNING OBJECTIVE 13.5
Understand transfers between categories and impairment of debt and equity securities.

Two additional issues arise in accounting for investments—one involves transfers between investment categories and the second involves impairments of investments.[22]

Transfers of Investments between Categories

At each reporting date, a company should assess the appropriateness of the classification of its investments in debt securities. If the classification previously used is no longer appropriate, the investment should be reclassified and transferred into the appropriate category. **The transfer of a security between investment categories is accounted for at fair value at the time of the transfer.** In the journal entry to record the transfer, the fair value is used as the "new" carrying value of the investment, and the "old" carrying value is eliminated. However, the accounting for any related unrealized gain or loss depends on the type of transfer.

- A transfer *from the trading* category into any other category—No accounting for the unrealized holding gain or loss is needed because it has already been recognized in net income.
- A transfer *into the trading* category from any other category—The previous unrealized holding gain or loss is recognized immediately in net income and eliminated from accumulated other comprehensive income.
- A transfer *into the available-for-sale* category *from the held-to-maturity* category—The difference between the held-to-maturity security's amortized cost and the fair value at the time of transfer gives rise to an unrealized holding gain or loss, which is included in other comprehensive income.
- A transfer of a debt security *into the held-to-maturity* category *from the available-for-sale* category—The unrealized holding gain or loss on the date of transfer will continue to be reported as a separate component of accumulated other comprehensive income and also represents a premium or discount that is

---

[22] When a company adopts Accounting Standards Update 2016-01: Recognition and Measurement of Financial Assets and Liabilities, it should apply the guidance by making a cumulative-effect adjustment to the balance sheet as of the beginning of the fiscal year of adoption.

amortized over the remaining life of the security consistent with the effective interest method.

Note that transfers into or out of the trading category should be rare, as should transfers *from* the held-to-maturity category.

Example: Transfer *into* Trading *from* Available-for-Sale

In early 2019, Haigh Company purchased bonds it classified as available-for-sale investments. The bonds have a face value of $5,000 and were purchased at par. On December 31, 2019, the bonds had a fair value of $6,100, resulting in an unrealized gain presented in other comprehensive income of $1,100. In 2020, when the bonds had a fair value of $6,300, Haigh transfers the bonds into the trading category. Haigh records the transfer as follows:

Investment in Trading Securities	6,300	
Investment in Available-for-Sale Securities		5,000
Gain on Transfer of Securities		1,300
Unrealized Holding Gain/Loss—Available-for-Sale Securities	1,100	
Allowance for Change in Fair Value of Investments		1,100

In the first journal entry, the investment is transferred to the trading securities account at its fair value ($6,300) and the amortized cost of the securities ($5,000) is removed from the available-for-sale securities account. The difference results in a realized gain of $1,300, which is included in net income for 2020. In the second journal entry, Haigh eliminates the unrealized holding gain of $1,100 that was reported in accumulated other comprehensive income at December 31, 2019, as well as the related allowance account. This reclassification amount is included in other comprehensive income for the period. Note that the net effect of this transfer increases comprehensive income in 2020 by $200 ($1,300 gain on transfer − $1,100 elimination of the unrealized holding gain in other comprehensive income). The net amount of gain in comprehensive income reflects the change in the fair value of these securities during the period ($6,300 at the end of the period − $6,100 at the beginning of the period), adjusted by amortization of the premium or discount ($0 because the bonds were purchased at par).

Example: Transfer *into* Available-for-Sale *from* Held-to-Maturity

Devon Company has bonds it classified as an investment in held-to-maturity securities. The bonds have a face value of $10,000, and the company purchased them at par. When the fair value of the bonds is $9,500, Devon transfers the bonds into the available-for-sale category. Because an investment in available-for-sale securities is recorded at cost with an allowance account to adjust the carrying value to fair value (with a corresponding adjustment to the Unrealized Holding Gain/Loss account), Devon records the transfer as follows:

Investment in Available-for-Sale Securities	10,000	
Investment in Held-to-Maturity Securities		10,000
Unrealized Holding Gain/Loss—Available-for-Sale Securities	500	
Allowance for Change in Fair Value of Investments		500

If Devon purchased bonds being held to maturity at a premium or discount, it would record the investment in available-for-sale securities at the amortized cost, and it would compute the adjustment to the allowance and unrealized holding gain/loss accounts by comparing the fair value to the amortized cost. Note that, because the transfer casts doubt on whether Devon can faithfully represent other securities as held-to-maturity, Devon may be required to reclassify all of its held-to-maturity securities to available-for-sale.

Example: Transfer *into* Held-to-Maturity *from* Available-for-Sale

Assume the same facts for Devon Company, except that it currently classifies the bonds as available-for-sale and transfers them into the held-to-maturity category. The bonds had a fair value of $9,700 on the previous balance sheet date. In this case, Devon records the investment in held-to-maturity securities at the current fair value of $9,500 and eliminates the previous $300 ($9,700 − $10,000) holding loss reported in the allowance account and in accumulated other comprehensive income. It creates a new shareholders' equity account, Unrealized Holding Gain/Loss—Held-to-Maturity Securities for the $500 unrealized holding loss on the date of transfer. Devon records the transfer as follows:

Investment in Held-to-Maturity Securities	9,500	
Unrealized Holding Gain/Loss—Held-to-Maturity Securities	500	
Investment in Available-for-Sale Securities		10,000
Allowance for Change in Fair Value of Investments	300	
Unrealized Holding Gain/Loss—Available-for-Sale Securities		300

In later periods, Devon amortizes the $500 discount in the Investment in Held-to-Maturity Securities account using the effective interest method over the remaining life of the bonds. The $500 unrealized holding loss is also amortized as an adjustment to interest income, using the effective interest method over the remaining life of the bonds, and this amount offsets the amortization of the discount.

Impairments

At each reporting date, a company should evaluate its investment in held-to-maturity and available-for-sale debt securities to determine if an **impairment** exists. This evaluation involves three steps:[23]

- *Step 1. Determine whether the investment is impaired.* An investment is considered impaired when its fair value is less than its cost. The company assesses impairment for each individual security.
- *Step 2. Evaluate whether the impairment is other than temporary.* The company must evaluate whether it will be able to recover the cost of the investment. A debt security's impairment is **other-than-temporary** if the company: (a) has decided to sell the security, or (b) considers it more likely than not that it will be required to sell the security before the recovery of its amortized cost basis. In making its other-than-temporary impairment assessment, a company should consider all information relevant to the collectibility of the security such as the remaining payment terms of the security, prepayment speeds, the financial condition of the issuer, expected defaults, and the value of any underlying collateral.[24]
- *Step 3. If the impairment is other than temporary, recognize a loss equal to the difference between the cost of the investment and its fair value.* The company includes the amount of the write-down in net income and the fair value becomes the new carrying value of the investment. Under U.S. GAAP, this loss cannot be restored for any subsequent increases in fair value.

---

[23] FASB ASC 320-10-35: Investments—Debt Securities: Overall: Subsequent Measurement.

[24] The SEC has also been involved in the issue of how the "other than temporary" criterion is to be applied by publicly traded companies. It suggests that a company should consider the length of time a security has been impaired and the amount by which the fair value is less than cost; the financial condition and near-term prospects of the investee; and the intent and ability of the company to retain its investment for long enough to allow for any anticipated recovery in fair value.

Example Tracey Company has a bond investment categorized as held-to-maturity, which has a carrying value of $21,500 and a fair value of $6,500. If it considers the decline in value to be other than temporary, Tracey records the decline of $15,000 ($21,500 − $6,500) as follows:

Impairment Loss	15,000	
Investment in Held-to-Maturity Securities		15,000

The $6,500 fair value becomes the new carrying value of the security, and Tracey computes interest income using the effective interest method based on the new effective interest rate computed.

A similar procedure is followed for an investment in a debt security classified as available-for-sale which has a decline in value that is considered to be other than temporary. Because a company is already reporting the security at fair value by using an allowance account, it establishes the fair value as the new cost basis. It eliminates the allowance and unrealized holding gain/loss accounts and records the loss from the write-down as an impairment loss. Any subsequent changes in fair value (that are considered to be temporary) are recognized as unrealized holding gains and losses in other comprehensive income.

LOOKING AHEAD

The FASB is considering an impairment model based on current expected credit losses (CECL). Under this approach, a company should recognize current expected credit losses for any investments measured at amortized cost. Under the CECL model, a company would evaluate financial assets with similar characteristics on a collective (pool) basis. An estimate of expected credit losses is then developed after considering all available information relevant to assessing the collectability of contractual cash flows. This information would include qualitative and quantitative factors relating to the environment in which the company operates and factors specific to the borrow. The estimate of expected credit losses should consider all contractual cash flows over the life of the financial asset, including expected prepayments and should always reflect the risk of loss, even if that risk is remote.

In addition, for any investment in debt securities classified as available-for-sale, an allowance approach would be used for recognizing credit losses. Such an approach would allow a company to recognize reversals of credit losses. The measurement of the expected credit losses for these securities will be limited to the difference between fair value and amortized cost.

GOT IT?

13-16 Briefly describe how to record the transfer of an investment in a debt security from (a) the held-to-maturity category to the available-for-sale category and (b) the available-for-sale category to the held-to-maturity category.

HOW DO YOU ACCOUNT FOR MINORITY ACTIVE INVESTMENTS?

LEARNING OBJECTIVE 13.6
Account for intercompany investments using the equity method.

When an investor company owns a sufficiently large percentage of common stock of another company, it is able to exert significant influence over the financial and operating policies of the investee company. For example, the investor could influence the investee's dividend policy in response to its own cash needs, the desire to raise its income, or tax considerations. In addition, the investor may use its influence to create favorable operating relationships with the investee. Significant influence is determined by factors such as:

- representation on the board of directors
- participation in policy-making processes
- material intercompany transactions
- interchange of managerial personnel
- technological dependency

In the absence of evidence to the contrary, **an investment of *20% or more* in the outstanding common stock of the investee leads to the *presumption* of significant influence and the use of the equity method.**[25]

The equity method recognizes that a material economic relationship exists between the investor and the investee. Because of this relationship, accounting for an investment as a trading security, which recognizes income when dividends are declared, is not appropriate because the investor could influence the amount and timing of the investee's dividend payments and therefore the amount of income it recognizes. The result would be that the earnings of the investee that were generated under the investor's influence may not be faithfully represented in the investor's financial statements. Therefore, the **equity method** of accounting is used to account for investments in which significant influence exists. The equity method requires the investor to recognize as income (or loss) each period its proportionate share of the net income (or loss) of the investee. For example, **Starbucks** reported income related to its equity method investees of $191 million for 2015.[26] The objective of the equity method is to reflect the economic substance of the investor's underlying claim on the net income and net assets of the investee rather than the legal form of two separate entities. The use of the equity method more closely fits the requirements of accrual accounting because the investor's share in investee income is reported by the investor during the period in which it is earned rather than when cash is received. The equity method, therefore, supplies more relevant information for decision makers.

When determining how to account for an investment, it's important to understand how much the investment allows the company to control or influence decisions. In the absence of evidence to the contrary, an investment of 20% or more in the outstanding common stock of the investee leads to the presumption of significant influence and the use of the equity method.

---

[25] If an investor has significant influence but holds *less* than a 20% investment, the investor should use the equity method. On the other hand, there are situations in which an investor holds 20% or more of the outstanding common stock of the investee and does *not* have the ability to exercise significant influence over the investee. In these cases, the investor would *not* use the equity method. (FASB ASC 320-10-15: Investments—Equity Method and Joint Ventures: Overall: Scope and Scope Exceptions.)

[26] Starbucks reports $249.9 million of income from equity method investees on the income statement. However, as disclosed in Note 6, Equity and Cost Investments (Appendix A), this amount includes $58.9 million of gross profit from transactions with the investees. Therefore, the net amount of income from equity method investees is $191 million.

Accounting Procedures

To apply the equity method, an investor:

- Initially records the investment at its acquisition cost.
- Subsequently records income and an increase in the carrying value of the investment account when income is reported by the investee. The amount of income recorded is based on the investor's percentage of ownership in the investee.
- Records dividends received (or receivable) as reductions in the carrying value of the investment account when they are paid (or declared) by the investee.

In addition, the investor must make certain adjustments to its investment income. The most frequent are to:

- Record the proportionate share of the investee's equity adjustments for other comprehensive income as increases or decreases to the investment account with corresponding adjustments in equity.
- Depreciate the proportionate share of any difference between the fair values and book values of the investee's depreciable assets that is implied by the acquisition price being greater than the book value of the investee. In the event the investor cannot determine the fair value of the specific investee assets, the entire excess of the acquisition price of the investment over the proportionate book value is treated as goodwill and is *not* amortized.[27]

In summary, the investor accounts for the investment and income under the equity method as follows:

Investment = Acquisition Cost + Investor's Share of Investee Income − Dividends Received

where

Investor's Share of Investee Income = (Investee's Net Income × Ownership %) − Adjustments

and

Dividends Received = Total Dividends Paid by Investee × Ownership %

Example: Equity Method

Panther Company purchases 4,200 shares of Salsa Company's outstanding common stock on January 1, 2016. On that date, Salsa had 16,800 shares outstanding; therefore, Panther's investment is 25% and significant influence is presumed to exist. Panther paid $125,000 for the shares and, on the date of acquisition, obtains the following information concerning Salsa:

	Balance Sheet Book Value	Fair Value
Depreciable assets (remaining life, 10 years)	$400,000	$450,000
Other non-depreciable assets (e.g., land)	190,000	246,000
Total	$590,000	$696,000
Liabilities	$200,000	$220,000
Common stock	250,000	
Retained earnings	140,000	
Total	$590,000	

There were no intercompany transactions during the year. Salsa paid a $20,000 dividend on August 27, 2016, and reported net income for 2016 of $81,000. Panther records these events as follows:

To record the original investment on January 1, 2016:

Investment in Stock: Salsa Company	125,000	
Cash		125,000

---

[27] In addition, the investor recognizes deferred income taxes for any difference between income reported under the equity method for financial reporting purposes and dividend income reported for income tax purposes. Deferred taxes are discussed in Chapter 18.

To record the receipt of dividends on August 27, 2016:

Cash	5,000	
Investment in Stock: Salsa Company (0.25 × $20,000)		5,000

The effect of this transaction is simply to exchange one asset (Investment in Stock: Salsa Company) for another (Cash).

To record Panther's 25% share in the year's net income on December 31, 2016:

Investment in Stock: Salsa Company	20,250	
Investment Income (0.25 × $81,000)		20,250

Note that Panther increases the investment account by its share of the total net income.

To depreciate the increase in the recorded value of depreciable assets:

Investment Income	1,250	
Investment in Stock: Salsa Company ($12,500 ÷ 10)		1,250

The depreciable assets have a fair value that exceeds book value by $50,000 ($450,000 − $400,000) and the remaining useful life of the assets is 10 years. Because it owns 25% of Salsa's shares, it therefore owns 25% of this increase in asset value, so Panther depreciates $12,500 (0.25 × $50,000) of the additional depreciable asset value over the remaining useful life of the assets. This results in additional depreciation of $1,250 ($12,500 ÷ 10 years), which Panther records directly as a deduction from the investment income and the investment on December 31, 2016.

The investment must also be reviewed for impairment as we discuss later in the chapter.[28]

Panther computes the carrying value of its Investment in Stock: Salsa Company account by adding the reported income for the year and deducting the dividends and depreciation expense. The carrying value of the investment is computed as follows:

Investment in Salsa Company

Acquisition price January 1, 2016		$125,000
Add: Share of 2016 reported income		20,250
		$145,250
Less: Dividends received August 27, 2016	$5,000	
Depreciation of excess fair value of assets ($12,500 ÷ 10)	1,250	(6,250)
Carrying value		$139,000

This investment is reported in the long-term investment's section of Panther's December 31, 2016, balance sheet.

The total amount of investee income that Panther reports on its income statement for 2016 is $19,000. This amount is computed as follows:

Income from Investment

Share of 2016 income	$20,250
Less: Depreciation of excess fair value of acquired assets	(1,250)
Net Investment income	$19,000

---

[28] According to FASB ASC 323-10-35: (Investments—Equity Method and Joint Ventures: Overall: Subsequent Measurement), any implied goodwill at the purchase of equity investments is *not* reviewed for impairment.

INTERNATIONAL DIMENSION

ACCOUNTING FOR INVESTMENTS

Several key differences in the accounting for investments exist between U.S. GAAP and IFRS as follows:

- *Classification and Measurement*: IFRS has three classification categories for debt and equity investments: amortized cost, fair value through other comprehensive income (FVOCI), and fair value through profit and loss (FVPL). Unlike U.S. GAAP where all equity securities are classified as trading and the classification of an investment in debt securities is based on management intent, IFRS classify investments in marketable debt securities based on the company's business model for managing financial assets and the characteristics of the contractual cash flows of the financial asset. If the objective of the business model is (a) to hold the asset and collect the contractual cash flows and (b) the cash flows represent solely payments of principal and interest (SPPI), the debt investment is initally recognized at fair value and subsequently measured at amortized cost. If the objective of the business model is achieved by collecting contractual cash flows (consisting of SPPI) *and* selling financial assets, the debt investment is measured at fair value through other comprehensive income. If the debt security does not meet the business model or cash flow characteristics conditions, it is classified as fair value through profit and loss. All equity investments are classified as FVPL and are initially measured at fair value with any change recorded through profit or loss. A company may make an irrevocable election at initial recognition to classify equity investments that it does not hold for trading as FVOCI.
- *Fair Value Option*: In both U.S. GAAP and IFRS, at initial recognition companies are given a fair value option to choose whether to record the changes in value of any financial asset or liability on the balance sheet and in net income. However, IFRS only allow this fair value option if reporting changes in fair value though profit and loss would eliminate a measurement or recognition inconsistency (sometimes called an "accounting mismatch") that would arise from measured assets and liabilities on different measurement bases.
- *Impairments*: For investments classified as amortized cost or FVOCI, IFRS require an expected loss impairment model in which expected credit losses are measured through a loss allowance at an amount equal to either (a) the 12-month expected credit losses or (b) full lifetime expected credit losses. In addition, IFRS allow for the reversal of these impairment losses with the amount of the reversal recognized in income. No such reversals are allowed under U.S. GAAP.

The application of the equity method is generally the same under IFRS and U.S. GAAP. However, several items should be noted:

- One major terminology difference is that IFRS use the term *associate* to refer to what would be referred to as an *equity method investee* under U.S. GAAP.
- IFRS do not address whether an investor's interest that is represented by something other than an equity instrument but that is similar in substance to an equity instrument (e.g., in-substance common stock) gives rise to significant influence over the investee. U.S. GAAP contains more detailed guidance on such non-equity interests.
- IFRS define joint venture arrangements and account for joint ventures by either the equity method or proportionate consolidation. Under proportionate consolidation, companies would report consolidated financial statements including their proportionate share of the joint venture. Under U.S. GAAP, proportionate consolidation is generally not permitted.

Source: IAS 28, 31, IFRS 9 (See Appendix C at the end of this book.)

Special Issues

When a company applies the equity method, it may encounter issues such as impairments of the equity investment or changes in the level of ownership of the investee.

Impairment: Other Than Temporary The investor must recognize "other than temporary" declines in the value of investments accounted for under the equity method. Evidence of these declines may be provided by the bankruptcy of the investee, by lengthy declines in the fair value of the stock, or by a number of years of operating losses. These events bring into question the ability of the investee to sustain income sufficient to justify the carrying value of the investment. When a decline is considered to be other than temporary, the investor debits a loss account and credits the investment account for the difference between the carrying value of the investment and the fair value. If the fair value of the investment later increases, the investor does *not* recognize the recovery in value.

Change to Equity Method When an investor currently accounting for an equity investment as a trading security acquires enough additional common shares during a year to obtain significant influence over the investee, the investor is required to adopt the equity method of accounting. When the equity method is adopted, the investor restates its investment in the investee by debiting the investment account and crediting Retained Earnings for its *previous* percentage of investee income (minus dividends) for the period from the original date of acquisition to the date that significant influence was obtained. This is a retrospective adjustment.[29] Thereafter, the equity method is applied in the usual manner based on the *current* percentage ownership.

Example On January 2, 2018, Short Company purchased as its only investment 15% of the outstanding common stock of Jones Corporation for $150,000, which it classified as a trading security. At that time, Jones's book value of net assets was $1,000,000. At the end of 2018, Jones reported net income of $300,000 and paid dividends of $60,000. Because the market value of Jones's shares at the end of 2018 was $186,000, Short wrote up the carrying value of the investment to fair value. On January 2, 2019, to exert significant influence on Jones, Short purchased an additional 25% of its outstanding common stock for $310,000.

The journal entries that Short recorded in 2018 and 2019 related to this information are shown in the upper portion of **Example 13.5**.

While most of these entries have been previously discussed, the last three entries for 2019 in which Short accounts for its *previous* 15% ownership under the equity method deserve an explanation. First, Short applies the equity method retrospectively by recognizing $45,000 ($300,000 × 0.15) of the 2018 net income of Jones as an increase in its Investment account and in Retained Earnings. Second, it also reduces its Investment account and Retained Earnings by $9,000 for its share of the 2018 dividends of Jones. (Note that Retained Earnings was adjusted directly for the share of net income and dividends because these are from the *prior* year.) Finally, Short reverses its December 31, 2018, adjustment to increase the carrying value of the investment. (Note that Short must debit Retained Earnings because the unrealized holding gain was recognized in income in the *prior* year) Because the purchase price of the shares was equal to their underlying book value, no additional depreciation was recorded.

The lower portion of Example 13.5 explains the rationale behind the adjustments. Note that the book value of the net assets of Jones was $1,240,000 on January 2, 2019. By increasing the $150,000 initial investment for the $45,000 share of 2018 net income and decreasing it for the $9,000 share of the 2018 dividends, the book value of the Investment account is $186,000, or 15% of the $1,240,000 net assets of Jones on

---

[29] Retrospective adjustments are discussed in more detail in Chapter 22.

EXAMPLE 13.5 Journal Entries to Illustrate a Change to the Equity Method

Trading Security

Date	Account	Debit	Credit
1/2/18	Investment in Trading Securities	150,000	
	Cash		150,000
12/31/18	Cash	9,000[a]	
	Dividend Income		9,000
12/31/18	Investment in Trading Securities	36,000	
	Unrealized Holding Gain/Loss: Trading Securities		36,000

Change to Equity Method

Date	Account	Debit	Credit
1/2/19	Investment in Stock: Jones Corporation	310,000	
	Cash		310,000
1/2/19	Investment in Stock: Jones Corporation	186,000	
	Investment in Trading Securities		186,000
1/2/19	Investment in Stock: Jones Corporation	45,000[b]	
	Retained Earnings		45,000
1/2/19	Retained Earnings	9,000	
	Investment in Stock: Jones Corporation		9,000
1/2/19	Retained Earnings	36,000	
	Investment in Trading Securities		36,000

Comparison of Book Values

	Jones Corporation Net Assets	Investment in Jones
Book value, 1/2/18	$1,000,000	$150,000
+ Net income for 2018	300,000	45,000
− Dividends for 2018	(60,000)	(9,000)
Book value, 1/2/19	$1,240,000	$186,000 (15%)[c]
Additional investment (25%)		310,000 (25%)
Book value, 1/2/19 (40%)		$496,000 (40%)

[a] $60,000 × 0.15
[b] $300,000 × 0.15
[c] $186,000 ÷ $1,240,000

January 2, 2019. Increasing the $186,000 for the $310,000 (25%) additional investment results in an Investment account balance of $496,000, or 40% of the net assets. From this point on, Short will apply the equity method using the 40% ownership interest.

Change from Equity Method Sometimes an investor using the equity method sells a portion of the investment so that its portion of ownership falls below 20%, or the investor may lose significant influence over the investee. Under these conditions, the use of the equity method is no longer appropriate, and the investor no longer accrues its share of investee income. However, previously recorded income remains as a part of the book value of the investment account. The investor then accounts for the investment as a trading security.[30]

Consolidated Financial Statements When an investor using the equity method acquires *control* over the investee's operations, the entity concept is enhanced by

---

[30] The investment may also be accounted for under the cost method as described in FASB ASC 325-20: Investments—Other: Cost Method Investments.

preparing financial statements for the combined set of companies. However, the two (or more) companies continue to maintain separate accounting records. During the year, the investor accounts for its investment in the investee by the equity method, as previously discussed. At the end of the year, the two sets of financial statements of the investor and investee are combined (and the investment account is eliminated) and reported in one consolidated set of financial statements.

The logic of consolidation accounting is to present financial statements for a single economic entity, even though there are separate legal entities. The two guiding principles for the preparation of consolidated financial statements are:

- The entity cannot make a profit by selling to itself. That is, intercompany sales and profits must be eliminated from the consolidated financial statements.
- The entity cannot own or owe itself. That is, intercompany receivables and payables must be eliminated from the consolidated financial statements.

Discussion of the preparation of consolidated financial statements is included in advanced accounting textbooks.

GOT IT?

13-17 Discuss the rationale behind the use of the equity method for an investment in common stock.

13-18 Briefly describe the accounting for an investment in common stock under the equity method.

13-19 Discuss the appropriate accounting treatment to use when (a) an investor acquires enough additional common stock during a year to change from accounting for the investment as a trading security to using the equity method and (b) an investor using the equity method sells enough common stock so that its portion of ownership falls below 20%.

13-20 How does IFRS categorize minority passive investments? Describe how this classification is determined.

13-21 Describe the accounting treatment under IFRS of investments accounted for at fair value.

13-22 How would the reversal of an impairment loss on an available-for-sale equity security be treated under IFRS? How does this compare with the treatment under U.S. GAAP?

13-23 Morgan Inc. and Parker Company are considering entering into a joint venture arrangement. Under IFRS, what accounting alternatives are available to Morgan and Parker with respect to this joint venture? How does this compare with the options under U.S. GAAP?

HOW ARE INVESTMENTS DISCLOSED IN THE FINANCIAL STATEMENTS?

LEARNING OBJECTIVE 13.7
Understand disclosures of investments.

For minority passive investments, a company is required to make the following major disclosures for each major type of security:

- *Trading Securities.* A company should disclose:
  - aggregate fair value
  - change in the net unrealized holding gain or loss that is included in each income statement
- *Available-for-Sale Securities.* For each balance sheet date, a public company should disclose:
  - aggregate fair value
  - gross unrealized holding gains and losses
  - amortized cost

For each income statement period, a company should disclose:
- proceeds from sales and the gross realized gains and losses on those sales
- basis on which cost was determined (e.g., the average cost method)
- gross gains and gross losses included in net income from transfers of securities from this category into the trading category
- change in the net unrealized holding gain or loss included as a separate component of other comprehensive income

- *Held-to-Maturity Securities.* For each balance sheet date, a public company should disclose
  - aggregate fair value
  - gross unrecognized holding gains and losses
  - amortized cost
  - the related realized or unrealized gain or loss and the circumstances leading to the decision to sell or transfer the security

As noted in Chapter 4, the FASB has established a three-tiered hierarchy that distinguishes among different inputs used to determine fair value. Although the relevance of fair values is obvious, the FASB did recognize that the representational faithfulness of Level 2 and Level 3 inputs may be questioned. To allow financial statement users to assess the valuation techniques and inputs used to develop fair value measurements as well as the effect on net income or other comprehensive income, several additional disclosures related to fair value are required. In addition to the fair value measurement of the investment, companies must also disclose:

- level within the fair value hierarchy of the fair value measurement
- for fair value measurements using significant unobservable inputs (Level 3), a reconciliation of the beginning and ending balances
- description of the valuation technique used for Level 2 or Level 3 fair value measurements

Investments in trading securities are always classified as current assets on a company's classified balance sheet. Investments in available-for-sale securities are classified as current or noncurrent assets depending on whether or not they will mature or be sold within one year or the operating cycle, whichever is longer. Investments in held-to-maturity securities are classified as noncurrent assets unless they mature within the next year.[31]

Cash flows from purchases, sales, and maturities of available-for-sale securities and held-to-maturity securities are classified as cash flows from investing activities. The gross amounts of inflows and outflows are reported for each category. Even though interest received on debt securities is related to an investing activity, U.S. GAAP requires any cash received for interest to be included in the operating section of the statement of cash flows. Cash flows from purchases, sales, and maturities of trading securities are generally classified as cash flows from operating activities if trading in these securities is a normal part of operations. However, for companies that do not routinely invest in trading securities, the related cash flows can be classified as cash flows from investing activities.

For minority active (or equity method) investments, a company should make the following major disclosures:

- name of each investee and the percentage of ownership of its common stock
- investor's accounting policies with respect to equity method investments
- aggregate value of each investment based on the quoted market price (if available)

Real Report 13.1 shows the disclosures of **Apple** in its 2015 annual report.

---

[31] FASB ASC 320-10-45: Investments—Debt and Equity Securities: Overall: Other Presentation Matters.

REAL REPORT 13.1: DISCLOSURE OF INVESTMENTS

Notes to Consolidated Financial Statements (in part): Apple Inc.

Note 1: Summary of Significant Accounting Policies (in part)

Financial Instruments (in part)

Cash Equivalents and Marketable Securities

The Company's marketable debt and equity securities have been classified and accounted for as available-for-sale. Management determines the appropriate classification of its investments at the time of purchase and reevaluates the designations at each balance sheet date. The Company classifies its marketable debt securities as either short-term or long-term based on each instrument's underlying contractual maturity date. Marketable debt securities with maturities of 12 months or less are classified as short-term and marketable debt securities with maturities greater than 12 months are classified as long-term. Marketable equity securities, including mutual funds, are classified as either short-term or long-term based on the nature of each security and its availability for use in current operations. The Company's marketable debt and equity securities are carried at fair value, with unrealized gains and losses, net of taxes, reported as a component of Accumulated Other Comporehensive Income ("AOCI") in shareholders' equity, with the exception of unrealized losses believed to be other-than-temporary which are reported in earnings in the current period. The cost of securities sold is based upon the specific identification method.

Note 2: Financial Instruments (in part)

Cash, Cash Equivalents and Marketable Securities (in part)

The following tables show the Company's cash and available-for-sale securities' adjusted cost, gross unrealized gains, gross unrealized losses and fair value by significant investment category recorded as cash and cash equivalents or short- or long-term marketable securities as of September 26, 2015 and September 27, 2014 (in millions):

	2015						
	Adjusted Cost	Unrealized Gains	Unrealized Losses	Fair Value	Cash and Cash Equivalents	Short-Term Marketable Securities	Long-Term Marketable Securities
Cash	$ 11,389	$ 0	$ 0	$ 11,389	$11,389	$ 0	$ 0
Level 1:							
Money market funds	1,798	0	0	1,798	1,798	0	0
Mutual funds	1,772	0	(144)	1,628	0	1,628	0
Subtotal	3,570	0	(144)	3,426	1,798	1,628	0
Level 2:							
U.S. Treasury securities	34,902	181	(1)	35,082	0	3,498	31,584
U.S. agency securities	5,864	14	0	5,878	841	767	4,270
Non-U.S. government securities	6,356	45	(167)	6,234	43	135	6,066
Certificates of deposit and time deposits	4,347	0	0	4,347	2,065	1,405	877
Commercial paper	6,016	0	0	6,016	4,981	1,035	0
Corporate securities	116,908	242	(985)	116,165	3	11,948	104,214
Municipal securities	947	5	0	952	0	48	904
Mortgage- and asset-backed securities	16,121	87	(31)	16,177	0	17	16,160
Subtotal	191,461	574	(1,184)	190,851	7,933	18,853	164,065
Total	$206,420	$574	$(1,328)	$205,666	$21,120	$20,841	$164,065

	2014						
	Adjusted Cost	Unrealized Gains	Unrealized Losses	Fair Value	Cash and Cash Equivalents	Short-Term Marketable Securities	Long-Term Marketable Securities
Cash	$ 10,232	$ 0	$ 0	$ 10,232	$10,232	$ 0	$ 0
Level 1:							
Money market funds	1,546	0	0	1,546	1,546	0	0
Mutual funds	2,531	1	(132)	2,400	0	2,400	0
Subtotal	4,077	1	(132)	3,946	1,546	2,400	0
Level 2:							
U.S. Treasury securities	23,140	15	(9)	23,146	12	607	22,527
U.S. agency securities	7,373	3	(11)	7,365	652	157	6,556
Non-U.S. government securities	6,925	69	(69)	6,925	0	204	6,721
Certificates of deposit and time deposits	3,832	0	0	3,832	1,230	1,233	1,369
Commercial paper	475	0	0	475	166	309	0
Corporate securities	85,431	296	(241)	85,486	6	6,298	79,182
Municipal securities	940	8	0	948	0	0	948
Mortgage- and asset-backed securities	12,907	26	(49)	12,844	0	25	12,859
Subtotal	141,023	417	(379)	141,061	2,066	8,833	130,162
Total	$155,332	$418	$(511)	$155,239	$13,844	$11,233	$130,162

The Company may sell certain of its marketable securities prior to their stated maturities for strategic reasons including, but not limited to, anticipation of credit deterioration and duration management. The maturities of the Company's long-term marketable securities generally range from one to five years.

As of September 26, 2015, the Company considers the declines in market value of its marketable securities investment portfolio to be temporary in nature and did not consider any of its investments other-than-temporarily impaired. The Company typically invests in highly-rated securities, and its investment policy generally limits the amount of credit exposure to any one issuer. The policy generally requires investments to be investment grade, with the primary objective of minimizing the potential risk of principal loss. Fair values were determined for each individual security in the investment portfolio. When evaluating an investment for other-than-temporary impairment, the Company reviews factors such as the length of time and extent to which fair value has been below its cost basis, the financial condition of the issuer and any changes thereto, changes in market interest rates, and the Company's intent to sell, or whether it is more likely than not it will be required to sell, the investment before recovery of the investment's cost basis.

Suggested answers to these questions are found at the end of the chapter.

Questions:

1. What was the pretax amount of the gross unrealized holding gain and gross unrealized holding loss on available-for-sale securities that Apple included in other comprehensive income for 2015?
2. How much did Apple include in accumulated other comprehensive income (pretax) at the end of its 2015 fiscal year for available-for-sale securities?
3. How much gain or loss related to marketable securities did Starbucks include on its income statement for 2015? Were any impairment losses recognized?

> **GOT IT?**
>
> **13-24** Show the balance sheet disclosures of an investment in available-for-sale securities that a company classifies as current and has a fair value in excess of cost.

WHAT IS THE ACCOUNTING FOR OTHER TYPES OF INVESTMENTS?

LEARNING OBJECTIVE 13.8
Account for additional types of investments, including long-term receivables.

In addition to investments in debt and equity securities of other companies, other items are often classified on a company's balance sheet under the investments category. These include long-term receivables, the cash surrender value of life insurance, and investments in funds.

Long-Term Notes Receivable

Companies may acquire long-term notes receivable as a result of lending cash to another entity. However, except for financial institutions, long-term notes receivable are acquired primarily as a result of an exchange for property, goods, or services.

When a company receives a note in exchange for property, goods, or services, it should presume that the stipulated interest rate on the note is fair unless:

- no interest rate is stated
- the stated interest rate is clearly unreasonable
- the face value of the note is materially different from the cash sales price of the property, goods, or services, or from the fair value of the note on the transaction date

In any of these situations, **the note receivable is recorded at the fair value of the property, goods, or services or the fair value of the note, whichever is more clearly determinable. If neither of these values can be determined, the note is recorded at its present value by using the *borrower's* incremental interest rate.** The effective interest method is used to record the periodic interest income. Recording the note at its fair value (present value) and using the effective interest method results in the correct asset valuation and in the proper timing of income recognition.

Example: Exchange of Equipment for Note Receivable

Joyce Company accepts a $10,000, non-interest-bearing, 5-year note on January 1, 2016, in exchange for used equipment it sold to Marsden Company. Because Joyce cannot determine the fair value of the equipment or the note, it uses Marsden's incremental borrowing rate, which is 12%, to determine a present value of $5,674.27 ($10,000 × 0.567427 from Present Value of 1 Table in the TVM Module) for the note. The equipment had originally cost Joyce $8,000 and had a book value of $5,000 on the date of sale. Joyce records the following journal entries for the exchange and the first two interest receipts:

January 1, 2016		
Notes Receivable	10,000.00	
Accumulated Depreciation	3,000.00	
Discount on Notes Receivable ($10,000 − $5,674.27)		4,325.73
Equipment		8,000.00
Gain on Sale of Equipment		674.27
December 31, 2016		
Discount on Notes Receivable	680.91	
Interest income [($10,000 − $4,325.73) × 0.12]		680.91
December 31, 2017		
Discount on Notes Receivable	762.62	
Interest income {[$10,000 − ($4,325.73 − $680.91)] × 0.12}		762.62

At the date of exchange, Joyce records the difference between the present value and face value of the note in a Discount on Notes Receivable account. This account is a contra-account and is subtracted from the Notes Receivable account to report the carrying (book) value of the note in the investments section on Joyce's balance sheet. Joyce computes the $674.27 gain by comparing the book value ($5,000) of the equipment with the present value ($5,674.27) of the note.[32] At the end of each year, Joyce records interest income using the effective interest method. By the maturity date, it will have amortized the entire discount to Interest Income, and the carrying value will equal the face value of the note. ■

Loan Fees and Loan Origination Costs Lending activities precede the payment of funds and generally include efforts to identify and attract potential borrowers and to originate a loan or loan commitment. The nonrefundable fees charged to borrowers for these activities are called **loan origination fees** (or **commitment fees**). Generally, any loan origination or commitment fees are deferred and recognized over the life of the loan as an increase in the interest income related to the note receivable.[33] Likewise, any direct loan origination costs are deferred and recognized over the life of the loan as a decrease in the interest income. In either case, a new, effective interest rate is computed for the loan.

Impairment of a Loan A loan (note receivable) is impaired if it is *probable* that the creditor will be unable to collect all amounts due according to the contractual terms of the loan agreement.[34] Impairment occurs when there is a delay or reduction in the payment of the principal or interest. The creditor, often a financial institution, applies its normal loan review procedures in making this determination. A loan is *not* impaired even if there is a delay in making interest or principal payments provided the creditor expects to collect all amounts due, including interest accrued during the period of delay. When a loan is deemed to be impaired, the creditor computes the present value of the expected future cash flows of the impaired loan using the effective interest rate on the loan. The effective interest rate is the original (contractual) interest rate on the loan (adjusted for any loan fees, discount, or premium). The creditor recognizes the amount by which the present value is less than the recorded investment in the loan by increasing Bad Debt Expense and Allowance for Doubtful Notes. Alternatively, the creditor may measure the impairment based on the loan's market price, or the fair value of the collateral, net of the costs of selling the loan or the collateral, if it expects repayment of the loan to be provided solely by the underlying collateral.

Once the creditor has written down the loan, it computes the interest income each period by multiplying the carrying value of the loan by the effective interest rate. It recognizes the interest income as a reduction of the allowance account.[35] If there are additional changes in the amount or timing of an impaired loan's expected cash flows, or if actual cash flows are different than expected cash flows, the creditor recalculates the amount of the impairment. It recognizes the difference, whether an increase or decrease, as an adjustment to Bad Debt Expense and the Allowance account.

---

[32] If the exchange takes place in the middle of the year, Joyce must make a depreciation adjusting entry to bring the book value of the equipment up to date. If Joyce receives cash in addition to the note, it computes the gain by comparing the book value of the equipment with the sum of the cash received plus the present value of the note.

[33] FASB ASC 310-20-25: and 35 Receivables, Nonrefundable Fees and Other Costs: Recognition and Subsequent Measurement.

[34] FASB ASC 310-10-35: Receivables: Overall: Subsequent Measurement.

[35] This method is the conceptually preferred method for recognizing income. Alternatively, the entire change in the present value (the bad debt expense *and* the interest revenue) can be recognized as a single amount and reported as an increase or decrease in bad debt expense. However, because the two alternatives were inconsistent with the accounting for impaired loans required by bank and thrift regulators, FASB ASC 310-10-35 allows the use of any method of income recognition, such as cash basis or cost recovery, even though the current value of the impaired loan may be less than the present value of the expected cash flows discounted at the loan's effective interest rate. Thus, the FASB allows a reduction of *comparability* in order to reduce implementation *costs* for companies. Because illustrations of all the methods are beyond the scope of the book, we use the conceptually preferred effective interest method.

Example: Impairment of Loan

Snook Company has a $100,000 note receivable from Ullman Company that it is carrying at face value. The original loan agreement specifies that interest of 8% is payable each December 31 and the principal is to be paid on December 31, 2021. Ullman paid the interest due on December 31, 2016, but informed Snook at that time that it probably would miss the next 2 years' interest payments because of its financial difficulties. After that, it expects to resume the $8,000 annual interest payments, but the principal payment would be made one year late with interest paid for that additional year. The different cash flows are shown in **Example 13.6**.

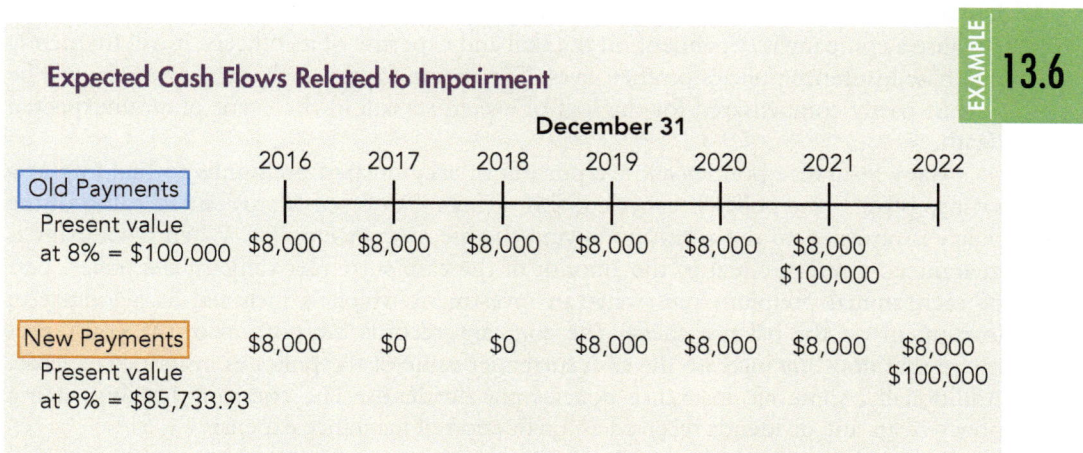

EXAMPLE 13.6

Expected Cash Flows Related to Impairment

On December 31, 2016, Snook computes the present value of the impaired loan as shown below. Note that Snook discounts the principal for 6 years, the period from December 31, 2016, to December 31, 2022, but discounts the interest for only 4 years, deferred 2 years, because Ullman will not pay interest for 2 years.

Present Value of Principal = $100,000 × present value of a single sum for 6 years at 8%
(from Time Value of Money Module)
= $100,000 × 0.630170
= $63,017.00

Present Value of Interest = $8,000 × present value of an annuity for 4 years at 8%
deferred 2 years (from Time Value of Money Module)
= $8,000 × 3.312127 × 0.857339
= $22,716.93

Value of the Impaired Loan = $63,017.00 + $22,716.93
= $85,733.93

At December 31, 2016, Snook recognizes the impairment of $14,266.07 ($100,000 carrying value − $85,733.93 present value) as follows:

Bad Debt Expense	14,266.07	
Allowance for Doubtful Notes		14,266.07

The carrying value of the debt after recording the impairment is $85,733.93 ($100,000 − $14,266.07). At December 31, 2017, Snook recognizes interest income of $6,858.71 (8% × $85,733.93) as follows:

Allowance for Doubtful Notes	6,858.71	
Interest Income		6,858.71

The carrying value of the debt is now $92,592.64 ($85,733.93 + $6,858.71). At December 31, 2018, Snook recognizes interest income of $7,407.41 (8% × $92,592.64). This eliminates the balance in the Allowance for Doubtful Notes account, and the carrying value of the receivable is now $100,000. Snook will recognize interest income of $8,000 each year for 2019 through 2022 as the cash payment is received. Snook will eliminate the $100,000 carrying value on December 31, 2022, when it receives the principal payment. If Snook's expectations of future cash flows decrease (increase) before December 31, 2018, it would debit (credit) Bad Debt Expense and credit (debit) the Allowance account for the decrease (increase) in the present value. In either situation, the company would recognize interest income each year. ■

Cash Surrender Value of Life Insurance

Because a company is dependent on the skill and expertise of its officers, it will frequently purchase insurance policies on their lives. The reason for this is that the company will be at least partly compensated for the loss of executive skill in the event of an unexpected death.

Many insurance policies allow a portion of accumulated premiums to build up as a savings plan. If the policy is canceled, this savings plan or **cash surrender value** of the policy is returned to the company buying the life insurance policy. When a company is guaranteed a return equal to the amount of the cash surrender value of the policy, part of each annual premium represents an investment which is included as a long-term investment on the balance sheet. The company records the portion of the yearly premium that does *not* increase the cash surrender value of the policy as insurance expense. Additionally, some life insurance policies pay dividends. The company holding such a policy treats any dividends received as a reduction of insurance expense.

Example At the beginning of the year, Mele Corporation pays an annual insurance premium of $5,500 to cover the lives of its officers. It records the payment as follows:

Prepaid Insurance	5,500	
Cash		5,500

According to the terms of the insurance contract, the cash surrender value of the policies increases from $7,200 to $8,300 during that year. The adjusting entry at the end of the year to increase the cash surrender value is as follows:

Insurance Expense	4,400	
Cash Surrender Value of Life Insurance ($8,300 − $7,200)	1,100	
Prepaid Insurance		5,500

Upon the death of any of the insured officers, Mele would collect the face amount of the insurance policy and credit the Cash Surrender Value account to close out the balance in the account related to this policy. The difference between the proceeds and the cash surrender value is normally reported as an ordinary gain, because collecting insurance proceeds is a usual operating procedure. For income tax purposes, the premiums are not tax deductible and the gain is not taxable. ■

Investments in Funds

Companies may place assets in special funds for specific purposes, and some of these assets then are restricted from use in normal operations because of indenture or other contractual arrangements. Special funds may be current, if they are expected to be used within one year, or they may be long term. The most common long-term funds are as follows:

- funds used to accumulate cash to retire long-term liabilities (**sinking funds**)
- funds used to retire preferred stock (**stock redemption funds**)
- funds used to purchase long-term assets (**plant expansion funds**)

A company reports its long-term funds as investments on its balance sheet. It is important to understand the distinction between a fund and an appropriation, or restriction, of retained earnings. A fund actually sets aside cash and other assets to accomplish specific objectives. In contrast, an appropriation of retained earnings discloses legal or contractual restrictions limiting the use of cash for payment of dividends or share repurchases (as we discuss in Chapter 16). An appropriation does not set aside any cash.

Accounting for long-term funds requires separate accounts, and the funds may be placed in trust with a separate legal entity. In essence, the fund is accounted for as an individual set of books. This company makes journal entries to these accounts to record its:

- initial and/or periodic cash contributions to the sinking fund
- investments in various securities to earn dividends and interest
- expenses to administer the fund
- unrealized increases and decreases in value
- sale of the securities to acquire cash to retire the bonds.

The company reports any revenues, expenses, gains, and losses in the usual manner on its income statement.

APPENDIX 13.1: DERIVATIVE FINANCIAL INSTRUMENTS

LEARNING OBJECTIVE 13.9

Account for derivative financial instruments.

Companies have always held or issued financial instruments. However, derivatives of those financial instruments create interesting accounting issues. Companies often use derivatives to reduce the risk of adverse changes in interest rates, commodity prices, and foreign currency exchange rates. Some companies also use derivatives to take risk or speculate on future movements of economic factors, such as interest rates, commodity prices, or foreign currencies. It is important for financial statements to show the effects of that risk management and risk-taking. Here, we discuss recording and reporting issues as they relate to selected derivative transactions.

A **financial instrument** is cash, evidence of an ownership interest in an entity, or a contract that both:

- imposes on one entity a contractual obligation to deliver cash or another financial instrument to a second entity or to exchange other financial instruments on potentially unfavorable terms with the second entity
- conveys to that second entity a contractual right to receive cash or another financial instrument from the first entity or to exchange other financial instruments on potentially favorable terms with the first entity[36]

Thus, financial instruments include cash, accounts and notes receivable, accounts and notes payable, and investments in debt and equity securities, as well as bonds payable and common stock.

A **derivative financial instrument** (or simply **derivative**) derives its value from an underlying asset, market price, interest rate, foreign exchange rate, or index. Derivatives include futures, forwards, swaps, and option contracts. Derivative contracts can be very complex, and they involve the following concepts:[37]

- A derivative's cash flows or fair value must fluctuate and vary based on the changes in the fair value of one or more underlying variables.
- The contract must be based on one or more notional (defined later) amounts or payment provisions or both. The underlying and notional amounts determine the amount of the settlement.
- Many contracts require no initial net investment.
- The contract may be readily settled by a net cash payment.

[36] FASB ASC Glossary.
[37] FASB ASC 815-10: Derivatives and Hedging: Overall.

A recent study indicated that more than $639 trillion of derivative contracts (notional amount) are outstanding worldwide. Derivative contracts have been in the news in recent years and include situations in which **Procter & Gamble** sustained significant losses, **Bankers Trust** has been sued by numerous clients, **Barings Bank** in London was bankrupted, **Orange County**, **California**, lost millions of dollars, and **Fannie Mae** restated its results by $9 billion.

A **hedge** is a means of protecting against a financial loss by mitigating exposure to changes in values of underlying assets, liabilities, or future cash flows. A derivative may help mitigate exposure to a risk if, for example, the value of the derivative increases when the value of the hedged item decreases. Alternately, a derivative can help mitigate a risk exposure if cash flows received from the derivative contract offset cash flows paid out of the hedged item. For a derivative to be considered a hedge, it must be "highly effective" in offsetting a substantial amount of risk exposure associated with changes in fair values or cash flows of the hedged item. The three types of hedges are:

- fair value hedges
- cash flow hedges
- hedges of foreign currency exposures of net investments in foreign operations

GAAP requires a different accounting treatment for each type of hedge. Accounting for derivatives can be very complex. To explain the basic issues, we show the accounting for a fair value hedge using an interest-rate swap and discuss the accounting issues for a cash flow hedge.[38] In our examples, we use simplifying assumptions (such as a flat yield curve) so that you can understand the basic accounting issues and avoid many real-world complexities regarding valuation.

An **interest-rate swap** is an agreement in which two companies agree to exchange the interest payments on debt over a specified period. The interest payments are based on a principal amount that often is referred to as a **notional** amount because the swap does not involve an actual exchange of principal at either inception or maturity. A company might use an interest-rate swap if, for example, it held a variable rate note receivable (where the interest rate on the note changed periodically with an index) but wanted to lock in the interest income it would earn on that note. In that situation, the company could engage in an interest-rate swap arrangement in which the company *receives* a fixed rate of interest and *pays* a variable rate. In such a hedge, the counterparty to the interest-rate swap is a company (often a financial institution) that *receives* a variable rate of interest and *pays* a fixed rate.

Although we discuss investments in this chapter, we focus on accounting for a derivative of a financial instrument that is a liability because they are more common for nonfinancial companies. However, a derivative can result in either an asset or a liability being recognized by either party, as market conditions change. The other company involved in the original transaction, a bank in our example, has a financial instrument that is an asset.

Fair Value Hedge

A fair value hedge protects against the risk from changes in value caused by *fixed* terms, rates, or prices. For example, a company with an outstanding financial debt obligation that has a fixed interest rate faces interest rate risk because if interest rates fall, the fair value of the debt will increase (making it more costly for the company if it decides to retire the debt before maturity). To mitigate this fair value risk, the company enters into an interest-rate swap to receive a fixed rate of interest and pay a variable rate. If interest rates fall, the value of the debt obligation increases, but the fair value of the interest-rate swap (asset) increases, offsetting (hedging) the fair value of the debt obligation. If interest rates rise, it will pay a higher rate on the swap than the fixed rate, so the fair value of the swap will decline (become a liability), hedging the decline in the fair value of the debt obligation (liability). Another example would be a company that purchases a commodity, such as oil. If the

---

[38] Hedges of foreign currency exposures are beyond the scope of this book.

company wishes to hedge the fair value of the oil, it can agree to a fixed price futures contract to sell the oil at a specified future date. If, for example, the market price of oil decreases, the fair value of the oil the company owns will fall, but the value of the future contract fixing the future selling price will rise, hedging the fair value of the oil. If the market price for oil rises, the fair value of the company's oil increases, but the fair value of the futures contract falls. Again the fair value of the oil has been hedged. In each case, the company has converted a fixed-rate contract (for interest or oil) into a variable-rate contract.

For a fair value hedge, GAAP requires a company to recognize in its current *net income*:

- any gain or loss from a change in the fair value of the derivative (fair value hedge)
- any gain or loss from the change in the fair value of the financial instrument or other item being hedged, along with any interest income or expense

As a result, the company reports both the derivative and the financial instrument on its balance sheet at their respective fair values. Note that GAAP requires the use of the *fair value method* in the valuation of derivatives *and* the related hedged financial instruments.

Example: Interest-Rate Swap That Is a Fair Value Hedge

Laki Company has had a $1 million, 6% fixed-rate bank loan (the financial instrument) from MidAmerica Bank outstanding for several years. On January 1, 2016, when the $1 million loan (debt) has 5 years remaining, Laki contracts with Jordan Investment Bank (a swaps dealer) for a 5-year interest-rate swap (the derivative) with a $1 million notional amount. Laki agrees to *receive* from Jordan a fixed interest rate of 6% and to *pay* Jordan an interest rate each year that is variable. The variable rate is the LIBOR (London Interbank Offer Rate) interest rate at the beginning of each year. In other words, Laki has converted ("swapped") its fixed interest rate debt into the variable LIBOR interest rate debt. If the LIBOR interest rate debt is 5.3% at January 1, 2016, the company has converted 6% debt into 5.3% debt for that year. This type is called a "matched" swap because the notional amount is the same as the actual loan amount and the fixed interest rate on the derivative is equal to the fixed interest rate paid on the loan. Therefore, the derivative is an effective hedge of the risk of interest rate changes. **Example 13.7** summarizes the facts for the loan and swap involving Laki, MidAmerica Bank, and Jordan Investment Bank.

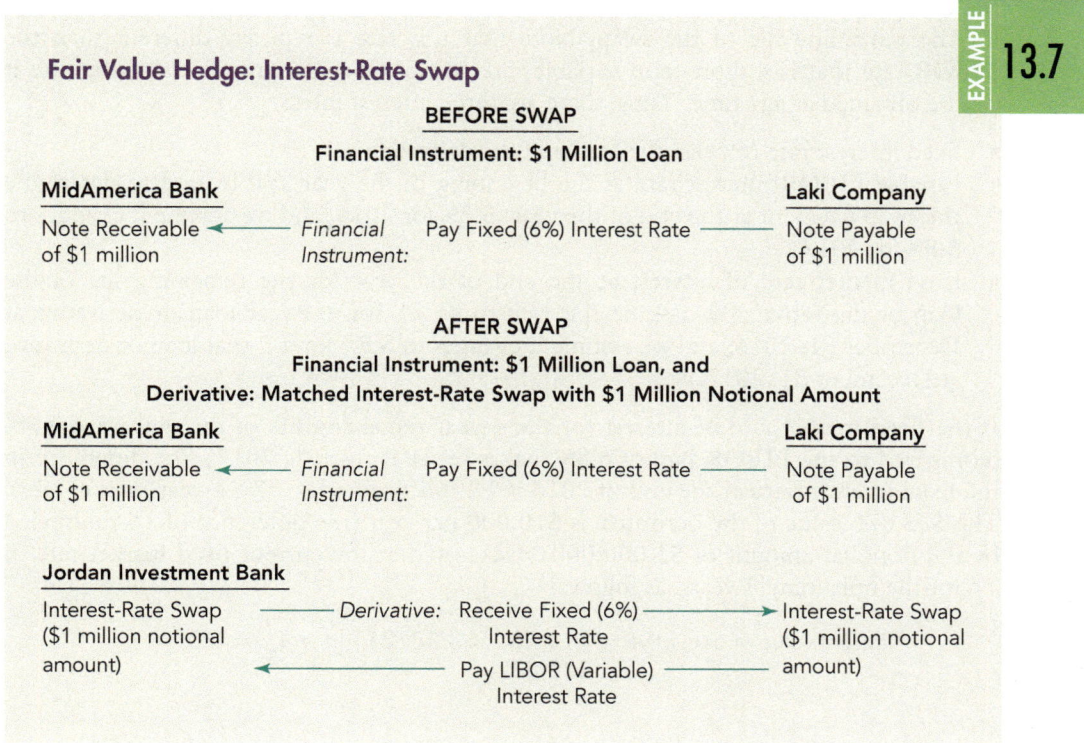

EXAMPLE 13.7

Laki recorded the following journal entry for the financial instrument (the original loan):

Cash	1,000,000	
Notes Payable		1,000,000

Laki accounts for the derivative (the fair value hedge) in 2016 and 2017, as follows:

Interest Payment on Loan: December 31, 2016
Laki pays MidAmerica the fixed rate of 6% on the $1 million loan and records this as interest expense, as follows:

Interest Expense	60,000	
Cash		60,000

Interest-Rate Swap Payment: December 31, 2016
Because the LIBOR rate that was set at January 1, 2016, is 5.3%, there is a net payment (settlement) between Laki and Jordan. Because Laki owes to Jordan the 5.3% LIBOR rate and receives from Jordan the fixed 6% rate, it receives from Jordan the *net* 0.7% on the notional amount of $1 million, or $7,000. Laki records the cash received as a *decrease* to interest expense, as follows:

Cash	7,000	
Interest Expense		7,000

Thus, Laki records a total interest expense of $53,000 ($60,000 − $7,000) in 2016, which is the equivalent of the variable rate of 5.3% on the $1 million loan.

Fair Values and Gains and Losses: December 31, 2016
The fair value method uses market values to recognize the value of derivatives if they are available, such as for futures contracts traded on exchanges. However, many derivatives are forward contracts that are custom-designed for the two entities, and market values are not readily available for such distinctive contracts, as in this example. In these cases, discounted cash flows are used to value the derivative.

Laki determines the gain or loss for 2016 on the derivative (fair value hedge) by computing the net present value of the future cash flows over the remaining life of the derivative. It is based on the difference between the fixed interest rate contracted in the derivative and the current market fixed interest rate applied to the notional amount for the remaining life of the swap. Note that this rate is typically different than the LIBOR rate that is a short-term variable rate and has no inherent fair value because it can be obtained at any time. Thus, there are three interest rates:

- fixed interest rate (6%) on the loan and the derivative
- variable LIBOR interest rate at the beginning of the year that is used to determine the swap payment at the end of the year (5.3% for 2016, and we assume it changes to 6.8% for 2017)
- fixed market rate of interest at the end of the year for the remaining life of the loan or derivative (We assume this rate to be 7% for a 4-year loan or derivative at December 31, 2016, and we assume it changes to 5.5% for a 3-year loan or derivative at December 31, 2017.)

If the fixed market rate of interest for the 4-year remaining life of the derivative is 7% (compared to the LIBOR rate of 6.8% that is set at January 1, 2017), the difference in the fixed interest rates at the end of 2016 is 1% (6% fixed rate − 7% 4-year market rate). The $33,872 value of the derivative is $10,000 per year (the difference of 1% multiplied by the notional amount of $1,000,000) discounted at the current fixed market rate of 7% for the remaining 4 years, as follows:

$$\text{Present value of derivative} = \$10,000 \times 3.387211 \ (n = 4, i = 0.07)$$
$$= \$33,872$$

A swap derivative *liability* and *loss* exist because the 7% current market rate is higher than the 6% fixed interest rate that Laki receives on the derivative. Laki records the liability and loss as follows:

Loss in Value of Derivative	33,872	
Liability from Interest-Rate Swap		33,872

Because interest rates have changed, the value of Laki's debt (financial instrument) has also changed. The increase in interest rates decreases the value of the debt. The current value of the debt is computed based on the 7% market rate as follows:

Present value of principal = $\$1,000,000 \times 0.762895$ ($n = 4, i = 0.07$)
= $\$762,895$

Present value of interest = $\$60,000 \times 3.387211$ ($n = 4, i = 0.07$)
= $\$203,233$

Total present value of debt = $\$762,895 + \$203,233$
= $\$966,128$

Laki recognizes the $33,872 ($1,000,000 − $966,128) decrease in the value of the debt and the related *gain* as follows:

Notes Payable	33,872	
Gain in Value of Debt		33,872

Laki reports both the $33,872 gain in the value of the debt and the $33,872 loss in value of the derivative in the other items section of its 2016 income statement. There is no net effect because it is an effective hedge. Laki reports the $33,872 derivative liability and the $966,128 ($1,000,000 − $33,872) value of the note payable on its December 31, 2016, balance sheet. Therefore, its total liability in regard to this debt is $1,000,000.

Interest Payment on Loan: December 31, 2017
Laki pays MidAmerica the fixed rate of 6% on the $1 million loan and records this as interest expense, as follows:

Interest Expense	60,000	
Cash		60,000

Interest-Rate Swap Payment: December 31, 2017
Assume that at the beginning of 2017 the LIBOR interest rate is 6.8%. Because Laki pays Jordan the LIBOR 6.8% rate and receives from Jordan the fixed 6% rate, it pays to Jordan the *net* 0.8% on the notional amount of $1 million, or $8,000. Laki records the payment as an *increase* in interest expense, as follows:

Interest Expense	8,000	
Cash		8,000

Thus, Laki records a total interest expense of $68,000 ($60,000 + $8,000) in 2017, which is the equivalent of the variable rate of 6.8% on the $1 million loan.

Fair Values and Gains and Losses: December 31, 2017
Laki again determines the gain or loss for 2017 on the derivative (fair value hedge) by computing the net present value of the future cash flows over the remaining life of the derivative. It is again based on the difference between the fixed interest rate contracted in the derivative and the current market fixed interest rate, applied to the notional amount for the remaining life of the swap. Assume that at December 31, 2017, the 3-year fixed interest rate is 5.5%. Thus, the difference in fixed interest rates at the end of 2017 is 0.5% (6% fixed rate − 5.5% 3-year market rate). The $13,490 value of the derivative is $5,000 per year (the difference of 0.5% multiplied by the notional amount of

$1,000,000) discounted at the current market rate of 5.5% for the remaining 3 years, computed as follows:

$$\text{Present value of derivative} = \$5,000 \times 2.697933 \ (n = 3, i = 0.055)$$
$$= \$13,490$$

A swap derivative *asset* and *gain* exist because the current 5.5% market rate is lower than the 6% fixed interest rate that Laki receives on the derivative. So Laki has moved from a $33,872 liability at the end of 2016 to a $13,490 asset position at the end of 2017, and has a $47,362 ($33,872 + $13,490) gain which it records as follows:

Liability from Interest-Rate Swap	33,872	
Asset from Interest-Rate Swap	13,490	
Gain in Value of Derivative		47,362

Again, because interest rates have changed, the value of Laki's debt (financial instrument) has also changed. The decrease in interest rates increases the value of the debt. The current value of the debt is computed based on the 5.5% current market rate as follows:

$$\text{Present value of principal} = \$1,000,000 \times 0.851614 \ (n = 3, i = 0.055)$$
$$= \$851,614$$

$$\text{Present value of interest} = \$60,000 \times 2.697933 \ (n = 3, i = 0.055)$$
$$= \$161,876$$

$$\text{Total present value of debt} = \$851,614 + \$161,876$$
$$= \$1,013,490$$

Laki recognizes the $47,362 ($1,013,490 current value − $966,128 previous value) increase and the related loss as follows:

Loss in Value of Debt	47,362	
Notes Payable		47,362

Laki reports the $47,362 gain in value of the derivative and the $47,362 loss in value of the debt in the other items section of its 2017 income statement. There is no net effect for this effective hedge. It reports the $13,490 derivative asset as a long-term investment and the $1,013,490 ($966,128 + $47,362) value of the note payable on its December 31, 2017, balance sheet. Note that Laki's *net* liability in regard to the debt is still $1,000,000. Laki would account for the loan and the derivative (fair value hedge) in a similar manner for the years 2018 through 2021.

In summary, Laki has converted a fixed interest rate bank loan into a variable interest rate loan with this interest-rate swap. Laki pays a variable net interest rate on this loan and reports the amount each year as interest expense on its income statement. Laki reports the derivative asset or liability and the related financial instrument (note payable) on its balance sheet at their respective fair values. There is no effect from the change in the fair value of this derivative on the income statement because the change in the fair value of the derivative is offset by the change in the fair value of the financial instrument (i.e., an effective hedge of the fixed rate debt). Note that when a hedge is not perfect or is ineffective (e.g., the notional amount is not equal to the actual principal amount), then a net amount is reported on the income statement. The financial reporting reflects Laki's interest rate risk management strategy. Laki discloses the characteristics of its financial instrument and derivative in the notes to its financial statements.

Cash Flow Hedge

A cash flow hedge protects against the risk caused by *variable* prices, costs, rates, or terms that cause future cash flows to be uncertain. A cash flow hedge is a hedge of an expected transaction that will probably occur in the future, but the amount of the transaction has not been fixed. This contrasts with a fair value hedge that protects against the risk from changes in value caused by *fixed* terms, rates, or prices related to existing assets or liabilities.

For example, a company with a variable rate debt that enters into an interest-rate swap to receive a variable rate of interest and pay a fixed rate protects itself against paying a higher rate of interest if interest rates increase. Of course, it will pay a higher rate than the variable rate if interest rates fall. The company has hedged the future cash flows for interest payments because it converted a variable-rate contract into a fixed-rate contract.

For a cash flow hedge, GAAP requires a company to recognize in its current *other comprehensive income* any gain or loss from a change in the fair value of the derivative (cash flow hedge). The company reports the derivative at its fair value and the related accumulated other comprehensive income in its shareholders' equity on its ending balance sheet. The company does *not* recognize in its financial statements any change in value of the financial instrument being hedged because the derivative is intended to hedge the future cash flows associated with that financial instrument rather than the fair value of the instrument itself. When the hedged expected transaction occurs, the company transfers the accumulated other comprehensive income to its current net income.

Example: Interest-Rate Swap That Is a Cash Flow Hedge

Assume the same facts as for the fair value hedge, except that Laki has a 5.3% (for 2016) variable rate $1 million loan (debt) with MidAmerica Bank that is based on the LIBOR rate. It enters into an interest-rate swap with Jordan Investment Bank in which it will receive a variable (5.3% for 2016) interest rate and pay a 6% fixed rate. Because this hedge protects against the risk caused by variable interest rates, it is a cash flow hedge. **Example 13.8** summarizes the facts for the loan and swap involving Laki, MidAmerica Bank, and Jordan.

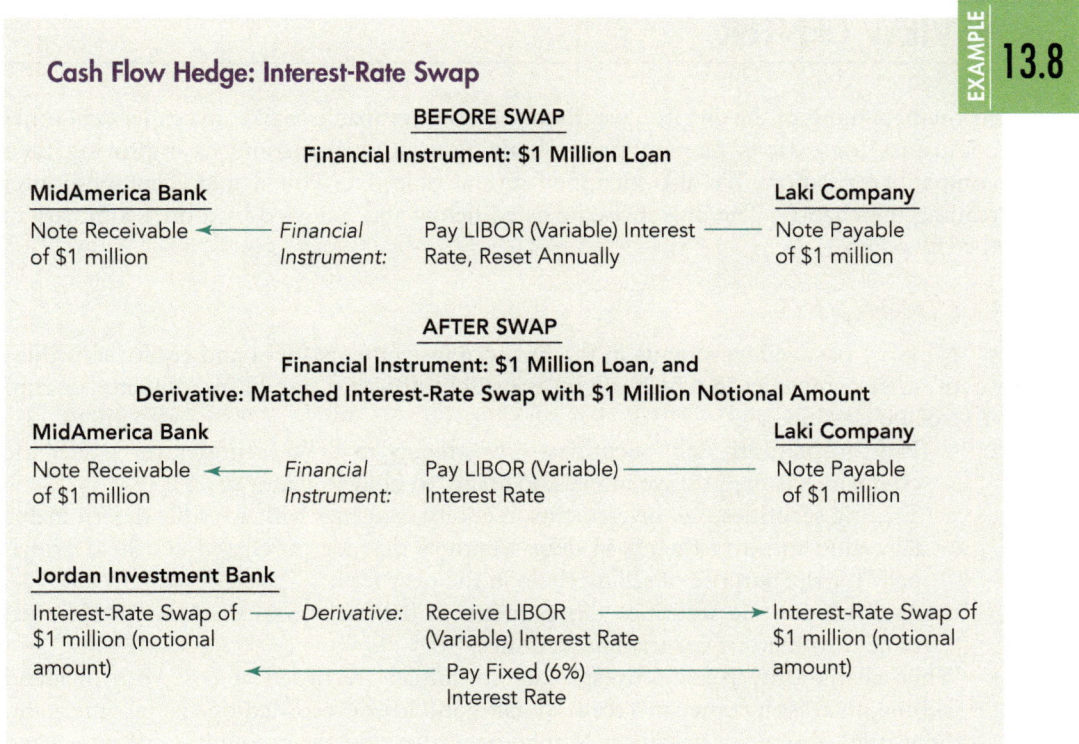

EXAMPLE 13.8

Laki reports this swap at its fair (present) value on the balance sheet and reports any change in the fair value for the period in other comprehensive income. It reports the total change in fair value as accumulated other comprehensive income in the shareholders' equity section of its balance sheet. This type of interest-rate swap does not hedge the liability. Instead, it hedges the future interest payments. Thus, as Laki makes each interest payment, a hedged expected transaction occurs and Laki must transfer an amount from the accumulated other comprehensive income to its net income, based on the change in the present value. In this case, Laki must compute the present value of each interest payment separately. Because each payment occurs at a different point on the yield curve, Laki would use a different interest rate to determine its present value. These procedures are beyond the scope of this book. ■

GOT IT?

13-25 Describe the steps necessary for a company to determine the value at which to record a non-interest-bearing note receivable exchanged for property, goods, or services.

13-26 If a company receives a note in exchange for property, goods, or services, when and for what calculations is the borrower's incremental rate used?

13-27 Why is the cash surrender value of a life insurance policy on which the company is the beneficiary carried as an investment? How does the company determine the increase in this amount and the amount of insurance expense determined each year?

13-28 What is a *fund*? Distinguish between a fund and an appropriation of retained earnings.

13-29 What is a hedge? Describe the differences between a fair value and a cash flow hedge.

13-30 Explain the accounting differences between a fair value hedge and a cash flow hedge.

REVIEW CENTER

At the beginning of the chapter, we discussed how companies make investments in other companies for reasons ranging from obtaining additional income to improving their competitive position. We also identified several objectives you would accomplish after reading the chapter. The objectives are listed below and followed by a brief summary of the key points.

LEARNING OBJECTIVE 13.1
Explain the classification and valuation of investments.

KEY TAKEAWAYS

- Minority passive investments in the financial instruments (debt and equity securities) of other companies in which the investor does not have significant influence or control are classified as:
  - Held-to-maturity debt securities—investments in debt securities for which the company has the positive intent and ability to hold to maturity
  - Trading securities—all investments in equity securities with a readily determinable fair value and investments in debt securities that are purchased and held principally for the purpose of selling them in the near term
  - Available-for-sale securities—investments in debt securities that are not classified as held-to-maturity or trading securities
- While all minority passive investments are initially recorded at cost with dividend income, interest income, and realized gains and losses recorded on the income statement, the subsequent valuation of these securities and the recognition of unrealized gains and losses depend on their classification.
- Minority active investments, ownership of between 20% and 50% of a company's voting stock, give the investor significant influence over the investee and are accounted for under the equity method.

- When an investor controls the investee, the investment is considered a majority active investment and consolidation is appropriate.
- GAAP also gives companies the option to report financial instruments at fair value, with unrealized gains and losses recognized in income.

KEY TERMS

available-for-sale securities, p. 13-3
consolidation, p. 13-4
debt security, p. 13-2
equity security, p. 13-2
held-to-maturity securities, p. 13-3
majority active investment, p. 13-4

marketable securities (investment securities), p. 13-2
minority active investments (equity method investments), p. 13-4
minority passive investment, p. 13-3
trading securities, p. 13-3

KEY TAKEAWAYS

LEARNING OBJECTIVE 13.2
Account for investments in debt securities classified as held-to-maturity, including amortization of bond premiums and discounts.

- Investments in held-to-maturity debt securities are initially recorded at cost and subsequently reported at amortized cost, with any premium or discount amortized over the remaining life of the security.
- Unrealized holding gains and losses are not recognized.
- Interest income, as well as realized gains and losses on sales (if any), are included in net income of the current period.

KEY TERM

effective interest method (interest method) p. 13-7

KEY CALCULATION

Interest Income = Effective Interest Rate × Book Value of the Investment at Beginning of Period × Time

KEY TAKEAWAYS

LEARNING OBJECTIVE 13.3
Account for investments in debt and equity securities classified as trading.

- Investments in debt and equity trading securities are initially recorded at cost and subsequently reported at fair value.
- Unrealized holding gains and losses, which result from increases or decreases in the fair value of the securities, are included in net income of the period.
- Interest and dividend income, as well as realized gains and losses on sales, are included in net income of the current period.

KEY TERMS

unrealized holding loss, p. 13-12   unrealized holding gain, p. 13-12

KEY TAKEAWAYS

LEARNING OBJECTIVE 13.4
Account for investments in debt securities classified as available-for-sale.

- Investments in available-for-sale debt securities are initially recorded at cost and subsequently reported at fair value.
- Unrealized holding gains and losses are reported as a component of other comprehensive income of the period. The cumulative net unrealized holding gains or losses are reported in the accumulated other comprehensive income section of shareholders' equity on the balance sheet.
- Realized gains and losses are included in net income for the current period and, when the security is sold, any unrealized holding gains or losses must be reclassified from accumulated other comprehensive income into net income.
- Interest income is included in net income of the current period.

KEY CALCULATION

Realized Gain or Loss on Debt Security = Selling Price − Amortized Cost

LEARNING OBJECTIVE 13.5

Understand transfers between categories and impairment of debt and equity securities.

KEY TAKEAWAYS

- The transfer of a security between categories is accounted for at the fair value at the time of the transfer.
- Depending on the classification of the security transferred, the unrealized gain or loss is either eliminated or established.
- An impairment occurs when there is an other than temporary decline below the amortized cost of a debt security classified as available-for-sale or held-to-maturity. The company writes down the amortized cost of the security to the fair value and includes the amount of the write-down in net income as a realized loss.

KEY TERMS

impairment, p. 13-21   other than temporary, p. 13-21

LEARNING OBJECTIVE 13.6

Account for intercompany investments using the equity method.

KEY TAKEAWAYS

- An investor company uses the equity method when it is able to exercise significant influence over the operating and financial policies of an investee. Significant influence is presumed if the investor owns between 20% and 50% of the investee's outstanding common stock.
- Under the equity method:
  - The initial investment is recorded at cost, is increased by the investor's proportionate share of the investee's reported income, and is reduced by the investor's proportionate share of any dividends declared.
  - The investor depreciates its proportionate share of any difference between the fair value and the book value of the investee's depreciable assets by reducing the investment account.
  - If a company changes its accounting for investments to the equity method, a retrospective restatement (adjustment) is made to adjust the accounts to the balance they would have shown if the equity method had always been used.
  - If the equity method is no longer appropriate (e.g., the investor's ownership percentage falls below 20%), the company will normally account for the investment as a trading security.

KEY TERM

equity method, p. 13-23

KEY CALCULATIONS

Investment = Acquisition Cost + Investor's Share of Investee Income − Dividends Received

where

Investor's Share of Investee Income = (Investee's Net Income × Ownership %) − Adjustments

and

Dividends Received = Total Dividends Paid by Investee × Ownership %

LEARNING OBJECTIVE 13.7

Understand disclosures of investments.

KEY TAKEAWAYS

- For trading securities, a company must disclose the aggregate fair value of the securities and the change in the net unrealized holding gain or loss that is included in each income statement.
- For available-for-sale securities, a company must disclose, for each balance sheet date, the aggregate fair value, gross unrealized holding gains and gross unrealized holding losses, and amortized cost by major security types. For each income statement period, the company must disclose (1) the proceeds from the sales and the gross realized gains and losses on those sales as well as the basis on which cost was determined, (2) the gross gains and gross losses included in net income from transfers of securities from this

category into the trading category, and (3) the change in the net unrealized holding gain or loss included as a separate component of other comprehensive income.
- For held-to-maturity securities, a company must disclose for each balance sheet date the aggregate fair value, gross unrealized holding gains, gross unrealized holding losses, and amortized cost by major security types. For any sales or transfers from this category, the disclosures must include the amortized cost, the related realized or unrealized gain or loss, and the circumstances leading to the decision to sell or transfer security.

KEY TAKEAWAYS

- Long-term receivables are classified as investments and recorded at the fair value of the property, goods, or services, or the fair value of the note, whichever is more clearly determinable.
- A loan is impaired if it is probable that the creditor will be unable to collect all amounts due according to the contractual terms of the loan agreement.
- Other items classified as investments include the cash surrender value of life insurance and investments in funds.

LEARNING OBJECTIVE 13.8
Account for additional types of investments, including long-term receivables.

KEY TERMS

cash surrender value, p. 13-36
loan origination fees (commitment fees), p. 13-34
plant expansion funds, p. 13-36
sinking funds, p. 13-36
stock redemption funds, p. 13-36

KEY TAKEAWAYS

- A derivative derives its value from an underlying financial instrument.
- A hedge is a means of protecting against a financial loss.
  - A *fair value hedge* protects against the risk from changes in value caused by fixed terms, rates, or prices. A company recognizes in its current net income any gain or loss from a change in the fair value of the derivative (fair value hedge) and any gain or loss from the change in the fair value of the financial instrument being hedged, along with any interest income or expense. As a result, the company reports both the derivative and the financial instrument on its balance sheet at their respective fair values.
  - A *cash flow hedge* protects against the risk caused by variable prices, costs, rates, or terms that cause future cash flows to be uncertain. A cash flow hedge is a hedge of an expected transaction that will probably occur in the future, but the amount of the transaction has not been fixed. A company recognizes in its current other comprehensive income any gain or loss from a change in the fair value of the derivative (cash flow hedge). The company reports the derivative at its fair value and the related accumulated other comprehensive income in its shareholders' equity on its ending balance sheet.

LEARNING OBJECTIVE 13.9
(Appendix 13.1) Account for derivative financial instruments.

KEY TERMS

derivative, p. 13-37
derivative financial instrument, p. 13-37
financial instrument, p. 13-37
hedge, p. 13-38
interest-rate swap, p. 13-38
notional, p. 13-38

ANSWERS TO REAL REPORT QUESTIONS

Real Report 13.1 Answers Apple Inc.—Disclosure of Investments

1. Other comprehensive income for 2015 included any change in the unrealized gains and losses from securities that are classified as available-for-sale. The total pretax unrealized gains and losses for Apple for 2015 and 2014 are shown below.

(in millions)	2015	2014	Net Change
Gross Unrealized Gain	$ 574	$ 418	$ 156
Gross Unrealized Loss	(1,328)	(511)	(817)
Net Unrealized Loss			$(661)

Apple's other comprehensive income for 2015 would report a pretax unrealized gain of $156 million and a pretax unrealized loss of $817 million. Therefore, the net unrealized loss would be $661 million.

2. Accumulated other comprehensive income would include the cumulative unrealized gains and losses for the available-for-sale securities. At the end of 2015, Apple has a cumulative pretax gross unrealized loss of $754 million ($574 million gross unrealized gain minus $1,328 million gross unrealized loss).

3. On its income statement for 2015, Apple did not appear to report any gains/losses from the sale of marketable securities classified as available-for-sale as none were disclosed in the annual report. In addition, Apple reported no impairment loss on these securities after considering factors such as the length of time and extent to which fair value has been below its cost basis, the financial condition of the issuer, and Apple's intent to sell, or whether it is more likely than not that it will be required to sell, the investment before the recovery of its cost basis.

MULTIPLE-CHOICE (AICPA ADAPTED)

Select the best answer for each of the following.

M13-1 **LO 13.2** On January 1, 2016, Weaver Company purchased as held-to-maturity debt securities $500,000 face value of Park Corporation's 8% bonds for $456,200. The bonds were purchased to yield 10% interest and pay interest annually. The bonds mature on January 1, 2021. Weaver uses the effective interest method of amortization. What amount should Weaver report on its December 31, 2016, balance sheet as an investment in held-to-maturity debt securities?

a. $450,580
b. $456,200
c. $461,820
d. $466,200

M13-2 **LO 13.3** On its December 31, 2015, balance sheet, Fay Company reported investments, classified as trading securities, at a market value of $183,000. There was no change during 2016 in the composition of Fay's portfolio of marketable equity securities. Pertinent data are as follows:

Security	Cost	Market Value at 12/31/15	Market Value at 12/31/16
A	$ 60,000	$ 62,000	$ 63,000
B	45,000	42,000	40,000
C	80,000	79,000	78,500
Totals	$185,000	$183,000	$181,500

What amount of loss on these securities should be included in Fay's income statement for the year ended December 31, 2016?

a. $0
b. $1,500
c. $2,000
d. $3,500

M13-3 **LO 13.3** During 2018, Anthony Company purchased securities as a long-term investment and classified them as trading. Pertinent data are as follows:

Security	Cost	Market Value at 12/31/18
A	$ 20,000	$ 18,000
B	40,000	30,000
C	90,000	93,000
Totals	$150,000	$141,000

The net holding gain or loss included in Anthony's income statement for the year should be:

a. $0
b. $3,000 gain
c. $9,000 loss
d. $12,000 loss

M13-4 **LO 13.4** On July 1, 2016, Aldrich Company purchased as an available-for-sale security $200,000 face value, 9% U.S. Treasury notes for $194,000. The notes mature July 1, 2017, and pay interest semiannually on January 1 and July 1. The notes were sold on December 1, 2016, for $199,000. Aldrich normally uses straight-line amortization on all of its notes. In its income statement for the year ended December 31, 2016, what amount should Aldrich report as a gain on the sale of the available-for-sale security?

   a. $2,500   c. $5,000
   b. $3,500   d. $6,000

M13-5
LO 13.4 In 2018, Cromwell Corporation purchased bonds of Oliver Company at par for $300,000 and classified the investment as available-for-sale. In 2019, the market value declined to $200,000. In 2020, the market value of the Fleming stock rose to $230,000, and the stock was sold. How much should Cromwell record as a realized gain or loss in its determination of net income for 2020?

   a. $0   c. $70,000 loss
   b. $30,000 gain   d. $100,000 loss

M13-6
LO 13.4 When the market value of a company's portfolio of available-for-sale securities is lower than its cost, the difference should be:

   a. accounted for as a valuation allowance deducted from the asset to which it relates
   b. accounted for as an addition in the shareholders' equity section of the balance sheet
   c. accounted for as a liability
   d. disclosed and described in a note to the financial statements but not accounted for

M13-7
LO 13.5 A security in a portfolio of available-for-sale securities is transferred to the trading category. The security should be transferred between the corresponding portfolios at:

   a. book value at date of transfer if higher than the fair value at date of transfer
   b. fair value at date of transfer, regardless of its cost
   c. cost, regardless of the fair value at date of transfer
   d. lower of its cost or fair value at date of transfer

M13-8
LO 13.6 On January 2, 2016, Portela Inc. bought 30% of the outstanding common stock of Bracero Corporation for $258,000 cash. Portela accounts for this investment by the equity method. At the date of acquisition of the stock, Bracero's property, plant, and equipment had a fair value in excess of its book value of $150,000. Bracero's property, plant, and equipment has a remaining life of 10 years. Bracero's net income for the year ended December 31, 2016, was $180,000. During 2016, Bracero declared and paid cash dividends of $20,000. On December 31, 2016, Portela should have carried its investment in Bracero in the amount of:

   a. $258,000   c. $306,000
   b. $301,500   d. $312,000

M13-9
LO 13.3
LO 13.4
LO 13.6 Cash dividends declared out of current earnings were distributed to an investor. How will the investor's investment account be affected by those dividends under each of the following accounting methods?

	Trading Security	Equity Method
a.	Decrease	No effect
b.	No effect	Decrease
c.	Decrease	Decrease
d.	No effect	No effect

M13-10
LO 13.8 On January 1, 2016, Parke Company accepted a $36,000, non-interest-bearing, 3-year note from a major customer in exchange for used equipment. The equipment had originally cost Parke $200,000 and had a book value of $20,000 on the date of the sale. At the 12% imputed interest rate for this type of loan, the present value of the note is $25,500 at January 1, 2016. Parke uses the effective interest rate. What is the carrying value of the note receivable on Parke's December 31, 2016, balance sheet?

   a. $28,560   c. $32,500
   b. $29,000   d. $36,000

REVIEW EXERCISES

RE13-1
LO 13.2 On January 1, 2018, Gatrong Corporation purchased 12%, 5-year Fleming Corporation bonds with a face value of $200,000. It expects to hold these bonds until maturity. The bonds pay interest semiannually on June 30 and December 31. Gatrong paid $215,443, a price that yields a 10% effective annual interest rate. Prepare the journal entry of Gatrong to record the purchase of the bonds.

RE13-2
LO 13.2 Refer to the information in **RE13-1**. Prepare the journal entry on June 30 for Gatrong to record the first interest receipt, using the effective interest method. Round to the nearest dollar.

RE13-3
LO 13.3
On July 1, 2018, Wolfpack Corporation purchased securities which it intends to buy and sell frequently. These securities consisted of (a) Todd Corporation 10%, 5-year bonds with a face value of $20,000 which were purchased for $18,500 and (b) 300 shares of Cornett Company common stock which were purchased at $40 per share. Prepare the July 1 journal entry to record the purchase of these trading securities.

RE13-4
LO 13.3
Refer to the information in **RE13-3**. Assume that on December 31, 2018, Wolfpack received interest on the Todd Corporation bonds as well as a $3 dividend per share interest on the Cornett Company stock. Wolpack uses the straight-line method to amortize premiums and discounts. Prepare the December 31 journal entries to record the receipt of the interest and the receipt of the dividends.

RE13-5
LO 13.3
Refer to the information in **RE13-3**. Assume that on December 31, 2018, the investment in Todd Corporation bonds has a market value of $22,300, and the investment in Cornett Company stock has a market value of $10,500. Prepare the year-end journal entry to record the unrealized gain or loss.

RE13-6
LO 13.3
Refer to the information in **RE13-3**. Assume that on February 1, 2019, Wolfpack sold its investment in Cornett stock for $10,000. Prepare the journal entries of Wolfpack to record the sale.

RE13-7
LO 13.4
On April 30, 2018, Aggie Corporation purchased Smith Corporation 10%, 5-year bonds with a face value of $12,000 at par plus four months of accrued interest. Prepare the April 30 journal entry to record the purchase of these available-for-sale securities.

RE13-8
LO 13.4
Refer to the information in **RE13-7**. Assume that on June 30, Aggie received interest on the Smith Corporation bonds. Prepare the June 30 journal entries to record the receipt of the interest.

RE13-9
LO 13.4
Refer to the information in **RE13-7**. Assume that on December 31, 2018, the investment in Smith Corporation bonds has a market value of $12,300. Prepare the year-end journal entry to record the unrealized gain or loss.

RE13-10
LO 13.4
Refer to the information in **RE13-7**. Assume that on February 1, 2019, Aggie sold its investment in Smith Corporation for $12,500. Prepare the journal entries of Aggie Corporation to record the sale and adjustment of the unrealized gain or loss.

RE13-11
LO 13.5
On February 1, 2019, Razorback Corporation decides to transfer its available-for-sale securities to the trading category. These securities had been purchased for $9,400 early in 2018 and had a fair value of $11,700 on December 31, 2018. On February 1, 2019, the securities have a fair value of $12,500. Prepare the journal entries to record the transfer.

RE13-12
LO 13.5
On September 30, Franz Corporation notices a decline in value of its investment in held-to-maturity bonds that it believes to be other than temporary. On that date, the carrying value of the bonds is $38,500 and the fair value is $22,980. Prepare the journal entry to record the impairment.

RE13-13
LO 13.6
On January 1, 2016, Tiger Company purchased 6,720 shares of Eagle Corporation's common stock when Eagle had 22,400 shares outstanding. On that date, the following information pertained to Eagle:

Balance Sheet

	Book Value	Fair Value
Depreciable assets (remaining life, 8 years)	$600,000	$620,000
Other non-depreciable assets	290,000	300,000
Total	$890,000	$920,000
Liabilities	$300,000	$330,000
Shareholders' equity	590,000	
Total	$890,000	

During 2016, Eagle earned net income of $120,000 and paid total dividends of $48,000. Prepare the journal entries of Tiger related to its share of Eagle's net income and dividends in 2016.

RE13-14
LO 13.8
On January 1, Kilgore Inc. accepts a $20,000 non-interest-bearing, 5-year note from Dieland Company for equipment. Neither the fair value of the note nor the equipment is determinable. Kilgore had originally purchased the equipment for $18,000, and the equipment has a book value of $14,000 on January 1. Kilgore knows Dieland's incremental borrowing rate of 9%. Prepare the journal entry for Kilgore to record the sale of the equipment on January 1.

RE13-15
LO 13.8
Moontake Corporation holds a $250,000 note receivable from Golden Company. Based on present value computations, it now appears that the Golden note is impaired and that Golden will only be able to pay back 87% of the principal at maturity. Prepare the journal entry for Moontake to record the impairment.

RE13-16
LO 13.8
At the beginning of the year, Commodore Company paid its $12,000 annual insurance premium for life insurance on its officers. The cash surrender value of the life insurance policies increased during the year from $8,500 to $10,000. Prepare the journal entries of Commodore to record the annual payment at the beginning of the year and the adjustment needed at the end of the year to recognize the change in surrender value.

EXERCISES

E13-1
LO 13.1
Classification of Investments The following investments occurred in 2018 for Mole Company.

a. Mole purchased 5% of the common stock on Brandon Company, a business which has a history of paying large quarterly dividends. Mole wishes to hold the securities for the forseeable future in order to receive these dividends.
b. Mole purchased a bond that will mature in 10 years. Mole purchased this bond because it expects that over the next 6 months, interest rates will fall, causing the bond price to increase. At that time, Mole plans to sell the bonds to earn a profit.
c. Mole purchased $100,000 of Wilson Company's convertible bonds. Mole has no intention of converting the bonds or selling the debt in the near future.
d. Mole purchased 30% of the common stock in a supplier in an effort to have more input into the quality of the raw materials it receives.
e. Mole purchased bonds for Collier Company with a face value of $100,000 for $95,000. The bonds pay interest of 8% semiannually. Mole has the ability and intent to hold the bonds to maturity and collect the principal and interest.

Required:
1. Classify each investment as either held-to-maturity, trading, available-for-sale, or an equity method investment.
2. **Next Level** Discuss the basis upon which the classification of each investment is based.
3. **Next Level** How would each of these investments be classified under IFRS?

E13-2
LO 13.2
Held-to-Maturity Securities and Amortization of a Discount On January 1, 2018, Kelly Corporation acquired bonds with a face value of $500,000 for $483,841.79, a price that yields a 10% effective annual interest rate. The bonds carry a 9% stated rate of interest, pay interest semiannually on June 30 and December 31, are due December 31, 2021, and are being held to maturity.

Required:
Prepare journal entries to record the purchase of the bonds and the first two interest receipts using the:
1. straight-line method of amortization
2. effective interest method of amortization

E13-3
LO 13.2
Purchase of Bonds between Interest Dates On March 31, 2018, Brodie Corporation acquired bonds with a par value of $400,000 for $425,800. The bonds are due December 31, 2023, carry a 12% annual interest rate, pay interest on June 30 and December 31, and are being held to maturity. The accrued interest is included in the acquisition price of the bonds. Brodie uses straight-line amortization.

Required:
1. Prepare journal entries for Brodie to record the purchase of the bonds and the first two interest receipts.
2. **Next Level** If Brodie failed to separately record the interest at acquisition, explain the errors that would occur in the company's financial statements (no calculations are required).

E13-4
LO 13.2
Purchase, Discount Amortization, and Sale of Bond Investment On November 1, 2017, Reid Corporation acquired bonds with a face value of $700,000 for $673,618.61. The bonds carry a stated rate of interest of 10%, were purchased to yield 11%, pay interest semiannually on April 30 and October 31, were purchased to be held to maturity, and are due October 31, 2021. On November 1, 2018, in contemplation of a major acquisition, the bonds were sold for $700,000. Reid is on a fiscal year accounting period ending October 31 and uses the effective interest method.

(continued)

Required:

Prepare journal entries to record the purchase of the bonds, the interest receipts on April 30, 2018, and October 31, 2018, and the sale of the bonds.

E13-5
LO 13.2

Investment Discount Amortization Schedule On January 1, 2018, Rodgers Company purchased $200,000 face value, 10%, 3-year bonds for $190,165.35, a price that yields a 12% effective annual interest rate. The bonds pay interest semiannually on June 30 and December 31.

Required:
1. Record the purchase of the bonds.
2. Prepare an investment interest income and discount amortization schedule using the effective interest method.
3. Record the receipts of interest on June 30, 2018, and June 30, 2020.

E13-6
LO 13.2

Investment Premium Amortization Schedule On January 1, 2018, Lynch Company acquired 13% bonds with a face value of $50,000. The bonds pay interest on June 30 and December 31 and mature on December 31, 2020. Lynch paid $51,229.35, a price that yields a 12% effective annual interest rate.

Required:
1. Record the purchase of the bonds.
2. Prepare an investment interest income and premium amortization schedule using the effective interest method.
3. Record the receipts of interest on June 30, 2018, and December 31, 2020.

E13-7
LO 13.2

Purchase, Premium Amortization, and Sale of Bond Investment Glover Corporation purchased bonds with a face value of $300,000 for $307,493.34 on January 1, 2018. The bonds carry a face rate of interest of 12%, pay interest semiannually on June 30 and December 31, were purchased to be held to maturity, are due December 31, 2020, and were purchased to yield 11%. On January 1, 2019, in contemplation of a major acquisition, the bonds were sold for $300,000. Glover uses the effective interest method.

Required:
1. Prepare journal entries to record the purchase of the bonds, the first two interest receipts, and the sale of the bonds.
2. **Next Level** Discuss the considerations involved when held-to-maturity debt securities are sold prior to their maturity date.

E13-8
LO 13.3

Trading Securities Midwest Bank invests in trading securities. At the beginning of December 2018, the bank held no trading securities. During December of 2018, it entered into the following trading securities transactions:

Dec. 10   Purchased 500 shares of Carroll Company common stock for $76 per share.
     21   Purchased 800 shares of Dynamo Company common stock for $34 per share.

At the end of December, the Carroll Company common stock had a quoted market price of $79 per share, and the Dynamo Company common stock had a quoted market price of $33 per share.

Required:

1. Prepare journal entries to record the preceding information.
2. What is the unrealized holding gain or loss, and where is it reported in the 2018 financial statements?
3. Show how the bank reports the trading securities on its December 31, 2018, balance sheet.
4. **Next Level** If Midwest uses IFRS, how would the accounting be different from U.S. GAAP?

E13-9
LO 13.3

Trading Securities Southeast Bank invests in trading securities and prepares quarterly financial statements. At the beginning of the fourth quarter of 2018, the bank held as trading securities 200 shares of Eglan Company common stock that originally cost $5,500. At that time, these securities had a fair value of $5,200. During the fourth quarter, the bank engaged in the following trading securities transactions:

Oct. 26   Purchased 300 shares of Farrell Company common stock for $35 per share.
Nov. 26   Sold 200 shares of Eglan common stock for $25 per share.
Dec. 10   Purchased 400 shares of Gray Company common stock for $41 per share.

On December 31, 2018, the quoted market prices of the shares were as follows: Eglan Company, $52 per share; Farrell Company, $38 per share; and Gray Company, $40 per share.

Required:
1. Prepare journal entries to record the preceding information for the fourth quarter.
2. Show what the bank reports on its fourth quarter 2018 income statement for these trading securities.
3. Show how the bank reports these trading securities on its balance sheet at the end of the fourth quarter of 2018.
4. **Next Level** What justification does the FASB give for its treatment of unrealized holding gains and losses for trading securities?

E13-10
LO 13.4

SHOW ME HOW

Available-for-Sale Securities On December 31, 2018, Marsh Company held Xenon Company bonds in its portfolio of available-for-sale securities. The bonds have a par value of $15,000, carry a 10% annual interest rate, mature in 2025, and had originally been purchased at par. The market value of the bonds at December 31, 2018 was $13,000. The December 31, 2018, balance sheet showed the following:

Assets	
Investment in available-for-sale securities	$15,000
Less: Allowance for change in value of investment	(2,000)
	$13,000
Shareholders' Equity	
Unrealized holding gain/loss	$ (2,000)

On January 1, 2019, Marsh acquired bonds of Yellow Company with a par value of $16,000 for $16,200. The Yellow Company bonds carry an annual interest rate of 12% and mature on December 31, 2023. Additionally, Marsh acquired Zebra Company bonds with a face value of 18,000 for $17,600. The Zebra Company bonds carry an 8% annual interest rate and mature on December 31, 2028. At the end of 2019, the respective market values of the bonds were: Xenon, $14,000; Yellow, $17,000; and Zebra, $20,000. Marsh classifies all of the debt securities as available-for-sale as it does not intend to hold them to maturity nor does it intend to actively buy and sell them. Assume that Marsh uses the straight-line method to amortize any discounts or premiums.

Required:
1. Prepare the journal entries necessary to record the purchase of the investments on January 1, 2019, the annual interest payments on December 31, 2019, and the adjusting entry needed on December 31, 2019.
2. What would Marsh disclose on its December 31, 2019, balance sheet related to these investments?

E13-11
LO 13.4

Available-for-Sale Securities At the beginning of 2018, Ace Company had the following portfolio of investments in available-for-sale debt securities (all of which were acquired at par value):

Security	Cost	1/1/2018 Fair Value
A	$20,000	$25,000
B	30,000	29,000
Totals	$50,000	$54,000

During 2018, the following transactions occurred:

May 3	Purchased C debt securities at their par value for $50,000.
July 1	Sold all of the A securities for $25,000 plus interest of $1,000.
Dec. 31	Received interest of $7,600 on the B and C securities. Additionally the following information was available:

Security	12/31/18 Fair Value
B	$29,000
C	52,500

Required:
1. Prepare journal entries to record the preceding information.
2. What is the balance in the Unrealized Holding Gain/Loss account on December 31, 2018?
3. **Next Level** What justification does the FASB give for its treatment of unrealized holding gains and losses for available-for-sale securities?

E13-12 **Available-for-Sale Securities** At the end of 2018, Terry Company prepared the following schedule of investments
LO 13.4 in available-for-sale debt securities (all of which were acquired at par value):

(continued)

Company	Amortized Cost	12/31/18 Fair Value	Cumulative Change in Fair Value
Morgan Company	$35,000	$34,200	$ (800)
Nance Company	50,000	53,100	3,100
Totals	$85,000	$87,300	$2,300

During 2019, the following transactions occurred:

July 1   Purchased Oscar Company debt securities with a par value of 100,000 for $98,000. The securities carry an annual interest rate of 10%, mature on December 31, 2021, and pay interest seminannually on July 1 and December 31. Terry uses the straight-line method to amortize any discounts or premiums.

Oct. 11   Sold all of the Morgan Company securities for $33,000 plus interest of $1,300.

Dec. 31   Received interest of $6,000 on the Nance Company and Oscar Company debt securities, and the following year-end total market values were available: Nance Company debt securities, $55,000; Oscar Company debt securities, $96,000.

Required:
1. Prepare journal entries to record the preceding information.
2. Show how the preceding items are reported on Terry's December 31, 2019, balance sheet. Assume all investments are noncurrent.
3. **Next Level** If Terry uses IFRS, how would the accounting for investments be different from U.S. GAAP?

E13-13 **Transfer Between Categories** On December 31, 2015, Leslie Company held an investment in bonds of Kaufmann Company which it categorized as being held to maturity. At that time, the 8%, $100,000 face value bonds had a carrying value of $107,023.56 and were being amortized using the effective interest method based on a market rate of 7%. Interest on these bonds is paid annually each December 31.

LO 13.5

On December 31, 2016, after recording the interest earned, Leslie decided to reclassify the Kaufmann bonds to its available-for-sale category in anticipation of a major restructuring. At that time, the ending quoted market price for the bonds was $105,000.

SHOW ME HOW

Required:
Prepare the journal entries on December 31, 2016, to record the interest earned and the reclassification.

E13-14 **Impairment** On June 1, 2016, Hansen Company purchased ten $1,000 Francisco Company bonds at par and classified them as held-to-maturity. In 2017, Francisco experienced financial difficulties and Hansen reduced the carrying value of each bond by 40%. In 2018, Francisco improved its financial condition, and Hansen believed that each bond was now worth $900 based on current market yields.

LO 13.5

Required:
1. Prepare the journal entries for Hansen to record the above events under U.S. GAAP.
2. How would your answers change if the company uses IFRS?

E13-15 **Equity Method** Miller Corporation acquired 30% of the outstanding common stock of Crowell Corporation for $160,000 on January 1, 2018, and obtained significant influence. The purchase price of the shares was equal to their book value. During 2018, the following information is available for Crowell:

LO 13.6

Mar. 31   Declared and paid a cash dividend of $50,000.
June 30   Reported semiannual earnings of $120,000 for the first half of 2018.
Sept. 30   Declared and paid a cash dividend of $50,000.
Dec. 31   Reported semiannual earnings of $140,000 for the second half of 2018.

SHOW ME HOW

Required:
1. Prepare journal entries for Miller to reflect the preceding information.
2. What is the balance in Miller's investment account on December 31, 2018? Show your computations.

E13-16 **Equity Method** On January 1, 2018, Field Company acquired 40% of North Company by purchasing 8,000 shares for $144,000 and obtained significant influence. On the date of acquisition, Field calculated that its share of the excess of the fair value over the book value of North's depreciable assets was $15,000 and that the purchased goodwill was $12,000. At the end of 2018, North reported net income of $45,000 and paid dividends of $0.70 per share. Field depreciates its depreciable assets over a 12-year remaining life.

LO 13.6

Required:
1. Prepare all the journal entries of Field to record the preceding information for 2018.
2. **Next Level** What is the conceptual justification for the use of the equity method?

E13-17 **Equity Method** On January 1, 2018, Jones Company acquires a 30% interest in Fink Company by purchasing
LO 13.6 3,000 of its 10,000 common shares for $16 per share and obtains significant influence. On the date of acquisition, the net assets of Fink were as shown here:

	Book Value	Fair Value
Non-depreciable assets (for example, land)	$ 15,000	$ 25,000
Depreciable assets (10-year remaining life)	90,000	115,000
	$105,000	$140,000
Liabilities	$ 10,000	$ 15,000

During 2018, Fink earned income of $22,000 and paid dividends of $6,000.

Required:
Prepare all journal entries on Jones's books to record the acquisition, dividends, and income from the investment in Fink. Show supporting calculations.

E13-18 **Notes Receivable** On January 1, 2016, Crouser Company sold land to Chad Company, accepting a 2-year,
LO 13.8 $150,000, non-interest-bearing note due January 1, 2018. The fair value of the land was $123,966.90 on the date of sale. The company purchased the land for $120,000 on January 1, 2010.

Required:
Prepare all the journal entries on Crouser's books for January 1, 2016, through January 1, 2018, in regard to the Chad note.

E13-19 **Notes Receivable** On January 1, 2016, Worthylake Company sold used machinery to Brown Company, accepting
LO 13.8 a $25,000, non-interest-bearing note maturing on January 1, 2018. Worthylake carried the machinery on its books at a cost of $22,000 and a current book value of $15,000. Neither the fair value of the machinery nor the note was determinable at the time of sale; however, Brown's incremental borrowing rate was 12%.

Required:
Prepare the journal entries on Worthylake's books to record:
1. sale of the machinery
2. related adjusting entries on December 31, 2016, and 2017
3. payment of the note by Brown on January 1, 2018

E13-20 **Note Receivable in Installments** On January 1, 2016, Tabor Company sold land with a book value of $50,000
LO 13.8 to Wilson Company, accepting a $60,000 note, payable in three $20,000 annual installments beginning December 31, 2016. The note carried no stated interest rate and the fair values of the land and the note were not determinable. An appropriate interest rate for this note is 12%.

Required:
Prepare the journal entries on Tabor's books to record (1) the sale and (2) the annual interest income and receipt of each $20,000 installment.

E13-21 **Notes Receivable and Income** On January 1, 2016, Pitt Company sold a patent to Chatham Inc. which had a car-
LO 13.8 rying value on Pitt's books of $10,000. Chatham gave Pitt a $60,000, non-interest-bearing note payable in five
AICPA equal annual installments of $12,000 with the first payment due and paid on January 1, 2017. There was no estab-
Adapted lished price for the patent, and the note has no ready market value. The prevailing rate of interest for a note of this type at January 1, 2016, is 12%.

Required:
1. Prepare a schedule showing the income or loss before income taxes that Pitt should record for the years ended December 31, 2016 and 2017. Show supporting computations in good form.
2. **Next Level** If Pitt inadvertently failed to discount the note and instead recorded it at its gross value, what would be the effect on income or loss before income taxes for the year ended December 31, 2016?

E13-22 **Loan Impairment** Perry National Bank has a note receivable of $200,000 from Mogren Company that it is carry-
LO 13.8 ing at face value and is due on December 31, 2020. Interest on the note is payable at 9% each December 31.

(continued)

Mogren paid the interest due on December 31, 2016, but informed the bank that it would probably miss the next 2 years' interest payments because of its financial difficulties. After that, it expected to resume its annual interest payments, but it would make the principal payment one year late, with interest paid for that additional year at the time of the principal payment.

Required:
1. Compute the value of the impaired loan on December 31, 2016.
2. Prepare the journal entries from 2016 to 2021 for the bank to record the above events.

E13-23 **Loan Impairment** Oaks National Bank has a note receivable of $500,000 from Haldane Company that it is carrying at face value, and it is due on December 31, 2022. Interest on the note is payable at 6% each December 31. Haldane paid the interest due on December 31, 2016, but informed the bank that it would probably miss the next 3 years' interest payments because of its financial difficulties. After that, it expected to resume its annual interest payments, but it would make the principal payment 2 years late, with interest paid for the additional years. On January 1, 2019, the bank received new information and now expected Haldane to pay the interest for 2019 through 2024 on December 31 of each year.

LO 13.8

Required:
1. Compute the value of the impaired loan on December 31, 2016.
2. Prepare the journal entries from 2016 to 2024 for the bank to record the above loan impairment events.

E13-24 **Cash Surrender Value of Life Insurance** Westford Corporation purchases life insurance policies on its officers, and these policies all carry a cash surrender value clause. At the beginning of 2016, Westford paid $13,300 in life insurance premiums for one year. During 2016, the cash surrender value of the policies increased from $98,450 to $103,900. At the beginning of 2017, Westford's vice president died in an automobile accident. The policy carried on this officer paid $50,000, and the cash surrender value of the policy was $6,480.

LO 13.8

Required:
Prepare journal entries to record the preceding information on Westford's books.

E13-25 **Sinking Funds Entries** The following information is available concerning Nunan Corporation's sinking fund:

LO 13.8

2016
- Jan. 1   Established a sinking fund to retire an outstanding bond issue by contributing $425,000.
- Feb. 3   Purchased securities for $400,000.
- July 30   Sold securities originally costing $48,000 for $45,000.
- Dec. 31   Collected dividends and interest on the remaining securities in the amount of $49,000; the securities had a market value of $355,000 at this time.

2017
- Dec. 31   Collected dividends and interest on the remaining securities in the amount of $40,000.
- 31   Paid sinking fund expenses of $4,500.
- 31   Sold the remaining securities in the fund for $360,000.
- 31   Retired an outstanding bond issue of $500,000 with the cash from the fund and transferred the remaining fund balance back to the Cash account.

Required:
Prepare journal entries to record the preceding transactions for Nunan.

E13-26 *(Appendix 13.1)* **Derivatives** Anglar Company has a $3 million, 7% bank loan from Castle Rock Bank. On January 1, 2016, when the $3 million loan has 3 years remaining, Anglar contracts with Susan Investment Bank to enter into a 3-year interest-rate swap with a $3 million notional amount. Anglar agrees to receive from Susan a fixed interest rate of 7% and to pay Susan an interest amount each year that is variable based on the LIBOR interest rate at the beginning of the year. The interest payments are made at year-end. The applicable interest rate on the swap is reset each year after the annual interest payment is made. The LIBOR interest rate is 6.6% at the beginning of 2016. The 3-year fixed interest rate is 8% at December 31, 2016.

LO 13.9

Required:
1. Prepare the journal entries of Anglar for the bank loan and derivative for 2016. Round answers to the nearest dollar.
2. Prepare the appropriate disclosures in Anglar's financial statements for 2016.

PROBLEMS

P13-1
LO 13.2
Premium Amortization on Bond Investment and Partial Sale of the Investment Using the Effective Interest Method On January 1, 2018, Hyde Corporation purchased bonds with a face value of $300,000 for $308,373.53. The bonds are due June 30, 2021, carry a 13% stated interest rate, and were purchased to yield 12%. Interest is payable semiannually on June 30 and December 31. On March 31, 2019, in contemplation of a major acquisition, the company sold one-half the bonds for $159,500 including accrued interest; the remainder were held until maturity.

Required:
Prepare the journal entries to record the purchase of the bonds, each interest payment, the partial sale of the investment on March 31, 2019, and the retirement of the bond issue on June 30, 2021.

P13-2
LO 13.2
Bond Investment Discount Amortization Schedule Tudor Company acquired $500,000 of Carr Corporation bonds for $487,706.69 on January 1, 2018. The bonds carry an 11% stated interest rate, pay interest semiannually on January 1 and July 1, were issued to yield 12%, and are due January 1, 2021.

Required:
1. Prepare an investment interest income and discount amortization schedule using the:
   a. straight-line method
   b. effective interest method
2. Prepare the July 1, 2020, journal entries to record the interest income under both methods.

P13-3
LO 13.2
Discount Amortization on Bonds Purchased Between Interest Dates On October 1, 2018, Jenkins Corporation bought bonds with a face value of $200,000 for $199,175, which included accrued interest. The bonds are due December 31, 2020, and carry a face rate of interest of 10.5%. Interest on the bonds is payable semiannually on June 30 and December 31. Jenkins uses the straight-line method to amortize the discount.

Required:
1. Prepare journal entries to record the purchase of the bonds, each interest receipt, and the retirement of the issue on December 31, 2020.
2. **Next Level** If Jenkins failed to separately record the interest at acquisition, explain the errors that would occur in the company's financial statements (no calculations are required).

P13-4
LO 13.2
Bond Investment Premium Amortization Schedule Mercer Corporation acquired $400,000 of Park Company's bonds on June 30, 2018, for $409,991.12. The bonds carry a 12% stated interest rate and pay interest semiannually on June 30 and December 31. The appropriate market interest rate is 11%, and the bonds are due June 30, 2021.

Required:
1. Prepare an investment interest income and premium amortization schedule, using the:
   a. straight-line method
   b. effective interest method
2. Prepare journal entries to record the December 31, 2018, and December 31, 2020, interest receipts using both methods.

P13-5
LO 13.2
Discount Amortization on Bond Investment and Partial Sale of Investment Using Effective Interest Method On January 1, 2018, Mark Corporation purchased bonds with a face value of $500,000 for $475,413.60. The bonds are due December 31, 2020, carry a 10% stated rate, and were purchased to yield 12%. Interest is payable semiannually on June 30 and December 31. On January 1, 2020, in contemplation of a major acquisition, one-fourth of the bonds were sold for $127,000. The remainder were held until maturity.

Required:
Prepare journal entries to record the purchase of the bonds, each interest payment, the partial sale of the investment on January 1, 2020, and the retirement of the bond issue on December 31, 2020.

P13-6
LO 13.3

Trading Securities The investment manager of 4th National Bank invests some of the bank's financial resources in trading securities. During the last quarter of 2018, the following transactions occurred in regard to these trading securities:

Nov. 5   Purchased 200 shares of Morgan Company common stock at $86 per share.
19   Purchased 300 shares of Parker Company preferred stock at $63 per share.
29   Sold 100 shares of Morgan Company common stock at $89 per share.
Dec. 15   Purchased 400 shares of Tathem Company common stock at $37 per share.
17   Sold 100 shares of Parker Company preferred stock at $62 per share.

On December 31, 2018, the market values of the shares were as follows: Morgan, $87 per share; Parker, $61 per share; and Tathem, $37.25 per share. The bank held no trading securities at the beginning of the last quarter of 2018.

Required:
1. Prepare journal entries to record the preceding information.
2. Show what the bank reports on its fourth quarter 2018 income statement for these trading securities.
3. Show how the bank reports these trading securities on its December 31, 2018, balance sheet.

P13-7
LO 13.3

Trading Securities 8th State Bank prepares interim financial statements and follows an investment strategy of investing in trading securities. At the beginning of the third quarter of 2018, the bank held the following portfolio of trading securities:

Security	Cost	June 30, 2018 Fair Value
100 shares of Gordan Company common stock	$ 2,900	$ 2,800
600 shares of Olivia Company common stock	12,000	12,600
Totals	$14,900	$15,400

During the third quarter of 2018, the bank entered into the following trading securities transactions:

July 2   Received dividends of $1.50 per share on the Gordan Company common stock.
14   Sold 600 shares of Olivia Company common stock for $20 per share.
Aug. 9   Purchased 300 shares of Porter Company common stock for $36 per share.
24   Sold 100 shares of Gordan Company common stock for $30 per share.
Sept. 17   Purchased 500 shares of Union Company common stock for $22 per share.

On September 30, 2018, the Porter Company common stock had a quoted market price of $36.50 per share and the Union Company common stock had a quoted market price of $21 per share.

Required:
1. Prepare journal entries to record the preceding information.
2. Show what the bank reports on its third quarter 2018 income statement for these trading securities.
3. Show how the bank reports these trading securities on its September 30, 2018, balance sheet.

P13-8
LO 13.3

Investments in Equity Securities Noonan Corporation prepares quarterly financial statements and invests its excess funds in marketable securities. At the end of 2018, Noonan's portfolio of trading investments consisted of the following equity securities:

Security	Number of Shares	Cost per Share	Fair Value per Share
Keene Company	500	$60	$60
Sachs Inc.	800	43	44
Bacon Company	400	70	72

During the first half of 2019, Noonan engaged in the following investment transactions:

Jan. 6   Sold one-half of the Sachs shares for $45 per share.
Feb. 3   Purchased 700 shares of Jackson Corporation common stock for $45 per share.
Mar. 31   Dividends of $2,500 were received on the investments, and the following information is available on market prices:

Security	Fair Value per Share
Keene Company	$59
Sachs Inc.	45
Bacon Company	70
Jackson Corporation	43

Apr. 14   Purchased 300 shares of Quinn Company preferred stock for $52 per share.
May 11   Sold the remainder of the Sachs shares for $42 per share.
June 30   Dividends of $2,800 were received on investments, and the following information is available:

Security	Fair Value per Share
Keene Company	$62
Bacon Company	69
Jackson Corporation	46
Quinn Company	50

Required:
1. Record Noonan's investment transactions for January 6 through June 30, 2019.
2. Show the items of income or loss from investment transactions that Noonan reports for each of the first and second quarters of 2019.
3. Show how the preceding items are reported on the first and second quarter 2019 ending balance sheets, assuming that management expects to dispose of the Keene and Sachs securities within the next year.

P13-9   **Investments in Trading Securities** Manson Incorporated reported investments in trading securities of $60,495
LO 13.3   as a current asset on its December 31, 2018, balance sheet. An analysis of Manson's investments on December 31, 2018, reveals the following:

Equity Security	Cost	Fair Value
400 shares of Turben Company, common	$14,275	$13,590
500 shares of Cook Corp. common stock	12,650	13,175
700 shares of Hill Corp. common stock	17,450	18,180
200 shares of Web Engines, preferred stock	19,100	15,550
Totals	$63,475	$60,495

During 2019, the following transactions related to Manson's investments occurred:

Jan. 6   Received a $265 dividend on the Turben Company common stock.
Mar. 31   Received the semiannual dividend of $500 on the Web Engines preferred stock. The following information is available concerning Manson's investments:

Equity Security	Fair Value
Turben Company	$13,470
Cook Corp.	13,765
Hill Corp.	18,940
Web Engines	15,500

June 30   Received a $375 dividend on the Cook Corp. common stock and a $700 dividend on the Hill Corp. common stock. The information is available concerning Manson's investments:

Equity Security	Fair Value
Turben Company	$13,300
Cook Corp.	14,125
Hill Corp.	19,300
Web Engines	15,400

July 6   Sold the Turben Company common stock for $13,750.
Sept. 29   Received the semiannual dividend of $500 on the Web Engines preferred stock. The following information is available concerning Manson's investments:

(continued)

Equity Security	Fair Value
Cook Corp.	$14,230
Hill Corp.	19,500
Web Engines	15,900

Nov. 2   Sold the Hill Corp. common stock for $19,780.
Dec. 30   Received a $375 dividend on the Cook Corp. common stock. The following information is available:

Equity Security	Fair Value
Cook Corp.	$14,280
Web Engines	16,400

Required:
1. Assuming Manson prepares quarterly financial statements, prepare journal entries to record the preceding information.
2. Show the items of income or loss from investment transactions that Manson reports for each quarter of 2019.
3. Show how Manson's investments are reported on the balance sheet on March 31, 2019; June 30, 2019; September 30, 2019; and December 31, 2019.

P13-10   **Available-for-Sale Securities** Holly Company invests its excess cash in marketable securities. At the beginning of
LO 13.4   2019, it had the following portfolio of investments in available-for-sale debt securities:

Security	Par Value	Amortized Cost	12/31/18 Fair Value
Igor Company 5% bonds, maturing on Dec. 31, 2028	$10,000	$ 8,400	$ 9,400
Ozone Company 6% bonds, maturing on Dec. 31, 2023	$20,000	23,100	21,700
Totals		$31,500	$31,100

During 2019, the following transactions occurred:

Mar. 31   Purchased Union Company 8% bonds with a face value of $10,000 for $10,000 plus accrued interest; interest is payable on the bonds each June 30 and December 31.
Mar. 31   Sold the Ozone Company investment for $22,000 plus accrued interest.
June 30   Received the semiannual interest on the Union Company bonds.
Dec. 31   Received the annual interest on the Igor Company bonds and the semiannual interest on the Union Company bonds.

The December 31 closing market prices were as follows: Igor Company bonds, $9,000; and Union Company 8% bonds, $10,100. Holly uses the straight-line method to amortize any discounts or premiums.

Required:
1. Prepare journal entries to record the preceding information.
2. Show what is reported on Holly's 2019 income statement.
3. Assuming the investment in Igor Company bonds is considered to be a current asset and the investment in Union Company bonds is considered to be a noncurrent asset, show how all the items are reported on Holly's December 31, 2019, balance sheet.
4. What is Holly's unrealized holding gain or loss on available-for-sale securities in 2019?

P13-11   **Investment in Available-for-Sale Bonds** The following information relates to Starr Company's investment in
LO 13.4   available-for-sale bonds for 2018:

Jan. 1   Purchased $30,000 face value of Bradford Company 8% bonds for $29,100. The market rate of interest is 10%, and interest on the bonds is payable each June 30 and December 31.
     1   Purchased $40,000 face value of Morris Company 10% bonds for $40,400. The market rate of interest is 9.8%, and interest on the bonds is payable each June 30 and December 31.

June 30   Collected the interest and the following information is available:

Security	Fair Value
Bradford Company 8%	$29,160
Morris Company 10%	40,800

July 1   Purchased $25,000 face value of Whipple Corporation 11% bonds for $23,000. The market rate of interest is 12%, and interest on the bonds is payable each June 30 and December 31.

Nov. 30   Sold the Whipple bonds for $22,750 plus accrued interest.

Dec. 31   Starr collected the interest, sold the Morris bonds for $40,800, and the following information is also available:

Security	Fair Value
Bradford Company 8% bonds	$28,800

Required:
1. Prepare journal entries to record the previous information for 2018. Use the effective interest method and round all amounts to the nearest *dollar*. Assume that Starr prepares semiannual financial statements.
2. Show the items of income or loss from investment transactions that Starr reports for each 2018 semiannual income statement.
3. Show how the investment items are reported on each of the 2018 semiannual balance sheets, assuming that management expects to dispose of all investments within one year of purchase.

P13-12   **Investments in Available-for-Sale Bonds** During 2018, Dana Company decided to begin investing its idle cash in marketable securities. The information contained below relates to Dana's 2018 marketable security transactions:

LO 13.4

Apr. 1   Purchased $20,000 face value of Solomon Inc. 12% bonds at par plus accrued interest; interest on the bonds is payable each June 30 and December 31.

June 30   Received the semiannual interest on the Solomon bonds and a $0.25 per share dividend on the Blair common stock.

Nov. 1   Purchased $30,000 face value of Edwards Company 11% bonds at par plus accrued interest; interest on the bonds is payable each June 1 and December 1.

Dec. 1   Received the interest on the Edwards bonds and sold the bonds for $30,300.

31   Received the interest on the Solomon bonds. At year-end, the market price of the Solomon bonds was $20,200.

Required:
1. Record Dana's investment transactions for 2018.
2. Show the items of income or loss on temporary investments Dana reports on its 2018 income statement.
3. Show the carrying value of Dana's investment account on its December 31, 2018, balance sheet.

P13-13   **Investments, Petty Cash, Bank Reconciliation** During the first quarter of 2018, Payne Corporation entered into the following transactions:

LO 13.3
LO 13.4

Jan. 1   Acquired 150 shares of Block Corporation common stock for $20 per share, 200 shares of Bridle Corporation common stock for $30 per share, and 100 shares of Alpha Corporation common stock for $25 per share. These are the only shares the company owns and all are classified as trading securities.

Feb. 1   Purchased 12% Atom Company bonds with a face value of $20,000 at par, plus accrued interest. Interest on the bonds is payable February 28 and August 31 each year, and the bonds are due August 31, 2019. Also purchased 10% Bradford Company bonds with a face value of $12,000 at par, plus accrued interest. Interest on the bonds is payable March 31 and September 30, and the bonds are due September 30, 2022. These are the only bonds the company owns and all are classified as available-for-sale securities.

(continued)

Feb. 1   Established a petty cash fund for incidental expenditures at $500.
28   Received the semiannual interest on the Atom Company bonds.
28   A count of cash on hand indicated that $125.50 remained in the petty cash fund. A sorting of petty cash vouchers disclosed that $110.00 was spent for postage, $170.65 was spent for office supplies, $45.00 was spent for transportation, and $43.50 was spent for miscellaneous items. The fund was replenished.
Mar. 31   Received first quarter dividends of $1,500 and the semiannual interest on the Bradford Company bonds.
31   The fair value of Payne's trading securities is $10,200 and the fair value of its available-for-sale securities is $32,400.
31   A count of cash on hand indicated that $230.50 remained in the petty cash fund. A sorting of petty cash vouchers disclosed that $140.00 was spent for postage, $75.30 was spent for office supplies, and $54.20 was spent for miscellaneous items. The fund was replenished.

The bank statement and the accounting records of Payne for the month of March 2018 indicated that the cash collected from the dividends and the Bradford Company bond interest was deposited on March 31 but did not appear on the March bank statement. There were no other deposits in transit. The bank statement showed a balance on March 31 of $13,459.75, which included collection of a $1,500 note and $100 of interest by the bank for Payne. Also listed was a $20 bank service charge and a $75.60 NSF check returned by the bank. The cash balance per the accounting records on March 31 was $11,689.95, which included checks totaling $2,365.40 that had not yet cleared the bank.

Required:
1. Prepare journal entries to record the preceding transactions of Payne for the first quarter of 2018.
2. Prepare a bank reconciliation for Payne for March 31, 2018.
3. Prepare any journal entries necessary to adjust Payne's books on March 31, 2018.

P13-14   **Comparison of Fair Value and Equity Methods** On January 1, 2018, Snow Corporation purchased 20% of the 200,000 outstanding shares of common stock of Garvey Company for $4.00 per share as a long-term investment. The purchase price of the shares was equal to their book value. The following information is available about Garvey for 2018 and 2019:

LO 13.3
LO 13.6

End of 2018	Reported net income	$80,000
	Cash dividends declared and paid	$30,000
	Market value of shares	$3.80 per share
End of 2019	Reported net income	$90,000
	Cash dividends declared and paid	$35,000
	Market value of shares	$4.25 per share

Required:
1. Prepare journal entries to record this information, assuming:
   a. Snow accounts for the investment as a trading security.
   b. Snow uses the equity method.
2. Assume 10,000 of the Garvey shares are sold on January 4, 2020, by Snow for $4.30 per share. Prepare the journal entry for this sale, assuming:
   a. Snow accounts for the investment as a trading security.
   b. Snow uses the equity method.

P13-15   **Application of Equity Method** On January 1, 2016, Doe Company purchased 3,000 of the 10,000 common shares outstanding of Ray Company for $15 per share and obtained significant influence. Doe amortizes its patents over 10 years. Ray's December 31, 2015, condensed balance sheet is shown here:

LO 13.6

Current assets	$ 10,000	Liabilities	$ 50,000
Fixed assets (net)	100,000	Common stock, no par	30,000
Patents (net)	40,000	Retained earnings	70,000
	$150,000		$150,000

Doe was unable to determine the fair value of Ray's identifiable net assets shown on the preceding balance sheet. It did, however, determine that Ray uses the straight-line method (no residual value) to depreciate its fixed assets and to amortize its patents over 20 years and 10 years, respectively. At the end of 2016, Ray disclosed the following condensed income statement and retained earnings statement for 2016:

Revenues	$100,000	Beginning retained earnings	$ 70,000
Expenses	(68,000)	Add: Net income	32,000
Net income	$ 32,000		$102,000
		Less: Cash dividends	(20,000)
		Ending retained earnings	$ 82,000

Required:
Prepare all the 2016 journal entries that Doe should make related to this investment. Show and label all supporting calculations.

P13-16 **Recording Investments Under the Equity Method** Harper Corporation acquired 80,000 of the 200,000 outstanding shares of Moore Corporation on April 1, 2016, for $400,000 and obtained significant influence. The following information concerning Moore is available on the date of acquisition:

LO 13.6

	Book Value	Fair Value
Depreciable assets (remaining life, 15 years)	$ 600,000	$ 700,000
Other assets	500,000	450,000
Total	$1,100,000	$1,150,000
Liabilities	$ 300,000	$ 320,000
Common stock	250,000	
Retained earnings	550,000	
Total	$1,100,000	

Subsequently, Moore paid a cash dividend of $40,000 on August 31, 2016, and reported net income of $155,000 on December 31, 2016.

Required:
1. Prepare journal entries for Harper to record the preceding information.
2. What is the balance in Harper's investment account on December 31, 2016? Show all computations.
3. Prepare Harper's net cash flow from operating activities section of its 2016 statement of cash flows under the indirect method, assuming Harper reported $200,000 of net income. Ignore income taxes.

P13-17 **Equity Method and Subsequent Sale** On January 1, 2016, Easton Corporation acquired 30% of the outstanding common shares of Feeley Corporation for $140,000, purchased 25% of the outstanding common shares of Holmes Company for $82,500, and obtained significant influence in both situations. On this date, the financial statements of Feeley and Holmes disclosed the following information:

LO 13.6

	Feeley	Holmes
Current assets	$190,000	$140,000
Long-term assets	370,000	180,000
	$560,000	$320,000
Liabilities	$120,000	$ 90,000
Common stock (no par)	200,000	150,000
Retained earnings	240,000	80,000
	$560,000	$320,000

During 2016, Feeley reported a loss of $70,000 and paid dividends of $40,000; Holmes reported income of $45,000 and paid dividends of $28,000. On January 1, 2017, Easton sold all the Holmes shares for $90,000. Assume Easton records both investments under the equity method and considers that any difference between each purchase price and the respective book value of the net assets acquired is goodwill.

Required:
Prepare journal entries to record (1) the purchase of the Feeley and Holmes shares, (2) the recognition of investment income, (3) the receipt of investee dividends, and (4) the sale of the Holmes shares.

P13-18 Change to Equity Method On January 1, 2018, Lion Company paid $600,000 for 10,000 shares of Wolf Company's voting common stock, which was a 10% interest in Wolf. Lion does not have the ability to exercise significant influence over the operating and financial policies of Wolf. Lion received dividends of $1.00 per share from Wolf on October 2, 2018. Wolf reported net income of $400,000 for the year ended December 31, 2018, and the ending market price of its shares was $63.

LO 13.6

On July 2, 2019, Lion paid $1,950,000 for 30,000 additional shares of Wolf's voting common stock, which represents a 30% investment in Wolf. The fair values of all of Wolf's assets, net of liabilities, were equal to their book values of $6,500,000. As a result of this transaction, Lion has the ability to exercise significant influence over the operating and financial policies of Wolf. Lion received dividends of $1.00 per share from Wolf on April 2, 2019, and $1.35 per share on October 1, 2019. Wolf reported net income of $500,000 for the year ended December 31, 2019, and $200,000 for the 6 months ended December 31, 2019.

Required:
1. For Lion, show the dividend income for 2018, as well as the December 31, 2018, unrealized holding gain or loss for the trading securities and carrying value of the investment account.
2. Assuming that Lion issues comparative financial statements for 2018 and 2019, show the investment income for 2018 and 2019, as well as the December 31, 2018 and 2019 carrying value of the investment account.

P13-19 Notes Receivable On January 1, 2016, Somerville Corporation sold a used truck to Cornelius Company and accepted a $28,000 non-interest-bearing note due January 1, 2019. Somerville carried the truck on its books at a cost of $30,000 and a current book value of $23,000. Neither the fair value of the truck nor the note was available at the time of the sale; however, Cornelius's incremental borrowing rate was 12%.

LO 13.8

Required:
1. Prepare the journal entries on Somerville's books to record:
   a. sale of the truck
   b. related adjusting entries on December 31, 2016, 2017, and 2018
   c. collection of the note on January 1, 2019
2. Prepare the notes receivable portion of Somerville's December 31, 2016, 2017, and 2018 balance sheets.

P13-20 Notes Receivable On January 1, 2016, Lisa Company sold machinery with a book value of $118,000 to Mark Company. Mark signed a $180,000 non-interest-bearing note, payable in three $60,000 annual installments on December 31, 2016, 2017, and 2018. The fair value of the machinery was $149,211.12 on the date of sale. The machinery had been purchased by Lisa at a cost of $160,000.

LO 13.8

Required:
1. Prepare all the journal entries on Lisa's books for January 1, 2016, through December 31, 2018.
2. Prepare the notes receivable portion of Lisa's balance sheet on December 31, 2016 and 2017.

P13-21 Comprehensive Notes Receivable On January 1, 2016, Seaver Company sold land with a book value of $23,000 to Bench Company. Bench paid $15,000 down and signed a $15,000 non-interest-bearing note, payable in two $7,500 annual installments on December 31, 2016, and 2017. Neither the fair value of the land nor of the note is determinable. Bench's incremental borrowing rate is 12%. Later in the year, on July 1, 2016, Seaver sold a building to Hane Company, accepting a 2-year, $100,000 non-interest-bearing note due July 1, 2018. The fair value of the building was $82,644.60 on the date of the sale. The building had been purchased at a cost of $90,000 on January 1, 2011, and had a book value of $67,500 on December 31, 2015. It was being depreciated on a straight-line basis (no residual value) over a 20-year life.

LO 13.8

Required:
1. Prepare all the journal entries on Seaver's books for January 1, 2016, through December 31, 2017, in regard to the Bench note.
2. Prepare all the journal entries on Seaver's books for July 1, 2016, through July 1, 2018, in regard to the Hane note.
3. Prepare the notes receivable portion of Seaver's balance sheet on December 31, 2016 and 2017.

P13-22 **Cash Surrender Value of Life Insurance** On January 1, 2015, Kehoe Corporation insured the lives of its president, vice president, controller, and treasurer for $100,000 each. The annual premium on each policy is $4,200, payable on January 1 of each year, and the cash surrender values for the policies increase by 4% of the annual premiums paid. Premium payments were made on the scheduled date by Kehoe through 2017, and the following dividends were received at the end of the year on each policy: 2015, $450; 2016, $575; 2017, $550. On February 1, 2018, the treasurer died and Kehoe collected the face value of his policy plus 11 months' premium.

LO 13.8

Required:

Prepare journal entries to record the preceding information for the years 2015 through 2018. Round calculations to the nearest dollar.

P13-23 *(Appendix 13.1)* **Derivatives** Danburg Company has a $5 million, 9% bank loan outstanding with its local bank. On January 1, 2016, when the loan has 4 years remaining, Danburg contracts with Bradford Investment Bank to enter into a 4-year interest-rate swap with a $5 million notional amount. Danburg agrees to receive from Bradford a fixed interest rate of 9% and to pay Bradford an interest amount each year that is variable based on the LIBOR interest rate at the beginning of the year. The interest payments are made at year-end. The applicable interest rate on the swap is reset each year after the annual interest payment is made. The LIBOR interest rate is 8.6% and 9.5% at the beginning of 2016 and 2017, respectively. The 3-year fixed interest rate is 10% at December 31, 2016, and the 2-year rate is 8% at December 31, 2017.

LO 13.9

Required:
1. Prepare the journal entries of Danburg for the bank loan and derivative for 2016 and 2017. Round calculations to the nearest dollar.
2. Prepare the appropriate disclosures in Danburg's financial statements for 2016 and 2017.

CASES

COMMUNICATION

C13-1 **Realized and Unrealized Losses: Minority Passive Investments**

LO 13.1

An important part of the accounting for minority passive investments is the distinction between investments categorized as trading, available-for-sale, or held-to-maturity.

Required:
1. When a company has excess cash, what types of securities may it invest in?
2. Explain why a company invests in debt and equity securities.
3. Explain how the distinction between the three categories is made.
4. Discuss the distinction between realized and holding gains and losses on investments in debt and equity securities.
5. Explain how a company discloses realized and holding gains and losses on investments in equity securities on its financial statements.

C13-2 **Investments in Securities**

LO 13.3
LO 13.4
LO 13.5

Cane Company has two portfolios of investments in marketable debt securities. It classifies one as trading securities and the other as available-for-sale securities. Cane does not have the ability to exercise significant influence over any of the companies in either portfolio. It sold some securities from each portfolio during the year. Cane reclassified one of the securities in the available-for-sale category to the trading category when its fair value was less than its amortized cost. At the beginning and end of the year, the aggregate cost of each portfolio exceeded its aggregate market value by different amounts.

Required:
1. Explain how Cane measures and reports the income statement effects of the securities sold during the year from each portfolio.
2. Explain how Cane accounts for the reclassified security.
3. Explain how Cane reports the effects of changes in the fair value of investments in each portfolio on its balance sheet as of the end of the year and on its income statement for the year. Do not discuss the securities sold.
4. Explain gains trading. Can Cane use gains trading on either portfolio? Does gains trading raise ethical issues?

C13-3
LO 13.6
AICPA Adapted

Equity Method

The most common method of accounting for unconsolidated subsidiaries is the equity method.

Required:
Answer the following questions with respect to the equity method.
1. Under what circumstances does a company apply the equity method?
2. At what amount does a company record the initial investment and what events subsequent to the initial investment (if any) change this amount?
3. How does a company recognize investment earnings under the equity method, and how does it determine the amount?

CREATIVE AND CRITICAL THINKING

C13-4
LO 13.2
LO 13.3
LO 13.4
AICPA Adapted

Investments in Stocks and Bonds

Victoria Company has investments in marketable securities classified as trading and available-for-sale. At the beginning of the year, the aggregate market value of each portfolio exceeded its amortized cost. During the year, Victoria sold some securities from each portfolio. At the end of the year, the aggregate amortized cost of each portfolio exceeded its market value.

Victoria also has investments in bonds classified as held-to-maturity, all of which were purchased for face value. During the year, some of these bonds held by Victoria were called prior to their maturity by the bond issuer. Three months before the end of the year, additional similar bonds were purchased for face value plus 2 months' accrued interest.

Required:
1. Explain how Victoria accounts for:
   a. sale of securities from each portfolio
   b. each equity securities portfolio at year-end
2. Explain how Victoria accounts for the disposition prior to their maturity of the long-term bonds called by their issuer.
3. Explain how Victoria reports the purchase of the additional similar bonds at the date of the acquisition.

C13-5
LO 13.4
LO 13.5
AICPA Adapted

Available-for-Sale Securities

The following are four *unrelated* situations involving investments in available-for-sale securities:

Situation I
A portfolio of available-for-sale debt securities with an aggregate fair value in excess of amortized cost includes one particular security whose fair value has declined to less than one-half of its amortized cost. The decline in value is considered to be other than temporary.

Situation II
The portfolio of available-for-sale debt securities includes securities that have an amortized cost in excess of fair value of $500. The remainder of the portfolio has a net fair value in excess of amortized cost of $1,000.

Situation III
An available-for-sale debt security, whose fair value is currently less than its amortized cost, is reclassified as a trading security.

Situation IV
A company's portfolio of available-for-sale securities consists of the bonds of one company. At the end of the prior year, the fair value of the security was 95% of amortized cost, and the effect was properly reflected in an allowance account. However, at the end of the current year, the fair value of the debt security had appreciated to 102% of the amortized cost.

Required:
Explain the effect on classification, carrying value, and earnings for each of the preceding situations.

C13-6
LO 13.6
AICPA Adapted

Change in Percent Ownership

For the past 5 years, Herbert has maintained an investment (properly accounted for and reported upon) in Broome amounting to a 10% interest in the voting common stock of Broome. The purchase price was $700,000 and the underlying net equity in Broome at the date of purchase was $620,000. On January 2 of the current year, Herbert purchased an additional 15% of the voting common stock of Broome for $1,200,000; the underlying net equity of additional investment at January 2 was $1,000,000. Broome has been profitable and has paid dividends annually since Herbert's initial acquisition.

Required:
Discuss how this increase in ownership affects the accounting for and reporting upon the investment in Broome. Include in your discussion adjustments, if any, to the amount shown prior to the increase in investment to bring the amount into conformity with GAAP. Also include how the company would report in current and subsequent periods.

C13-7 Ethics and Investments
LO 13.4
LO 13.6

You are an accountant for Davanzo Company. The president of the company calls you into her office and says, "I want to ask you about two issues. First, we need to sell one of our investments to raise $1 million because I think I have found a better investment. We could sell the bonds of Company X, which are currently worth $1 million even though they have an amortized cost basis of $950,000. But I don't want to sell them because I like the steady stream of cash flow we get related to interest. Or we could sell the bonds in that dog, Company Z. These bonds are also worth $1 million, but they cost us $1.2 million. I hate to admit we made such a big mistake, and if they can somehow avoid bankruptcy, we may actually recover our investment. And then there's that loss. I don't want to report that. Second, I am going to use the $1 million to buy about 20% of the shares of Company M, but I seem to remember that there is some accounting rule that might affect how much we buy. I was also wondering about buying some of Company M's convertible preferred stock so we can convert that into a large ownership position in the future. Let me know what you think." You are aware that Company M is a new company that is not yet listed on the stock market, has been making losses, and is expected to continue making losses for a few more years.

Required:
From financial reporting and ethical perspectives, discuss the issues raised by this situation.

C13-8 Analyzing Starbucks's Investments Disclosures

Obtain **Starbucks**'s 2015 annual report either using the "Investor Relations" portion of its website (do a web search for Starbucks investor relations) or go to http://www.sec.gov and click "Search for company filings" under "Filings and Forms (EDGAR)."

Required:
1. What amount did Starbucks report as the fair value of available-for-sale securities? Trading securities? What level inputs were used to determine these fair values?
2. How much did Starbucks report as an unrealized holding gain/loss for 2015 for each class of marketable security? Where were these amounts reported?
3. Explain why Starbucks has cost method investments.
4. What amount did Starbucks report as equity method investments for its 2015 fiscal year? Are any assets and liabilities of equity method investees reflected on Starbucks's financial statements?

C13-9 Analyzing Nestlé's Disclosure of Investments

Obtain **Nestlé**'s 2013 annual report using the "Investor Relations" portion of its website (do a web search for Nestlé investor relations).

Required:
1. What is the value of Nestlé's financial assets at December 31, 2013?
2. What was the carrying value of Nestlé's financial assets classified as fair value through net income (FVNI)? Describe the accounting for these assets.
3. What was the carrying value of Nestlé's financial assets classified as available-for-sale? Describe the accounting for these assets.
4. What are associates? How much has Nestlé invested in these associates, and how does it account for this investment group?

USING CODIFICATION

C13-10 Researching GAAP

Situation

Middleton Company has operated a successful retail business for many years that has generated significant amounts of excess cash. Middleton invests this excess cash in equity and debt securities and has appropriately classified all of its investments as either available-for-sale or held-to-maturity. As Middleton prepares its financial statements for the current fiscal year, its auditors have questioned whether any of the investments are other than temporarily impaired. Middleton had never considered this issue before and needs guidance as to how to test these securities for impairment.

Directions

1. Research the related generally accepted accounting principles and prepare a short memo to Middleton that provides guidance as to how available-for-sale and held-to-maturity investment securities should be evaluated for impairment.

PART 4

FINANCING ACTIVITIES

CHAPTER 14
Financing Liabilities: Bonds and Long-Term Notes Payable

CHAPTER 15
Contributed Capital

CHAPTER 16
Retained Earnings and Earnings per Share

CHAPTER 14

FINANCING LIABILITIES: BONDS AND LONG-TERM NOTES PAYABLE

Leverage: A Double-Edged Sword

A company's **capital structure** refers to the mix of debt and equity it uses to finance its operations. Most companies consider debt financing because they can use debt to increase earnings, a concept known as **financial leverage**. If a company invests borrowed money in assets that generate profits that are greater than the after-tax cost of the debt, the excess profits will increase the return on equity for the company's shareholders.

For example, assume three companies each have income before interest expense and taxes of $150 and an effective tax rate of 40%, but differ in terms of financial leverage, as shown in the table below. Because Raleigh Company is not leveraged, its return on equity will be 9%. However, Auburn and Bloomington companies are using financial leverage to generate greater returns on equity for their shareholders even though each company has lesser net income.

	Raleigh Company	Auburn Company	Bloomington Company
Average Assets	$1,000	$1,000	$1,000
Debt (10% interest rate)	0	500	800
Average Equity	1,000	500	200
Earnings before Interest Expense and Taxes	150	150	150
Interest Expense (Debt × 10%)	0	50	80
Earnings before Taxes	150	100	70
Tax Expense (Earnings before Taxes × 40%)	60	40	28
Net Income	90	60	42
Return on Equity (Net Income ÷ Average Equity)	9%	12%	21%

LEARNING OBJECTIVES

After reading this chapter you will be able to

- **LO 14.1** Explain the reasons for issuing long-term financing liabilities, such as bonds and notes payable.
- **LO 14.2** Understand the characteristics of bonds payable.
- **LO 14.3** Compute the issue price of bonds payable.
- **LO 14.4** Record the issuance of bonds payable.
- **LO 14.5** Amortize bond discounts and bond premiums.
- **LO 14.6** Explain extinguishment of liabilities.
- **LO 14.7** Understand bonds with equity characteristics.
- **LO 14.8** Account for long-term notes payable.
- **LO 14.9** Understand the disclosure of long-term liabilities.
- **LO 14.10** (Appendix 14.1) Understand troubled debt restructurings.

Results may not always be so positive. Because debt requires interest and principal payments at specified times, companies consider debt financing to be a more risky source of financial capital than equity financing (which does not require specified payments of principal or interest). If the economy becomes troubled, the company's return on assets is less than the after-tax cost of debt, shareholders' earnings are reduced, and return on equity will deteriorate rapidly. In extreme cases, the company may be unable to pay the required amounts and be forced to declare bankruptcy.

Companies such as **Verizon** and **AT&T** are considered highly leveraged, while **Starbucks Corporation** has a relatively small amount of debt, and **Chipotle Mexican Grill** has no financial debt. Because financial leverage magnifies the financial effects of both good and bad years, an understanding of the benefits and risks of financial leverage is critical to analyzing a company's return and risk.

A company classifies an item as a *long-term liability* if the obligation is not expected to be repaid within 1 year of the balance sheet date or the current operating cycle whichever is longer. The most common examples of long-term liabilities are bonds payable, long-term notes payable, lease obligations, pension obligations, deferred income taxes, and other long-term deferrals. In this chapter, we examine the recording and reporting requirements for financial liabilities, such as bonds payable and long-term notes payable. **Financial liabilities** are contractual obligations that require one entity to deliver cash or another financial asset to another party and normally result from the firm raising cash for operating and investing activities.[1] Long-term liabilities may also result from operating activities, such as offering employees pensions or incurring deferred taxes, which we discuss elsewhere in this book.

LEARNING OBJECTIVE 14.1
Explain the reasons for issuing long-term financing liabilities, such as bonds and notes payable.

WHY DO COMPANIES ISSUE LONG-TERM FINANCING LIABILITIES?

Companies seeking to obtain financial resources can consider issuing long-term debt instruments, which result in a long-term liability. A company might issue long-term debt rather than offer other types of securities for the following reasons:

- *Debt financing may be the only available source of funds.* Many small- and medium-sized companies have difficulty attracting equity capital (i.e., common stock) because investors think they are too risky. Debt securities are seen as a less risky investment because interest and principal are required to be paid on specific dates. Also, some types of debt (such as a mortgage) are secured by a lien against specific company assets which allows the creditor to recover collateral if the debt is not paid.
- *Debt financing typically has a lower cost of capital than equity.* Historically, because debt has a lesser investment risk than stock, investors in debt securities typically expect a lower rate of return than investors in equity securities.
- *Debt financing offers an income tax advantage.* Interest payments to debt holders are deductible as interest expense by a corporation for income tax purposes, whereas dividend payments on equity securities are not.
- *Debt does not carry voting rights.* Corporate shareholders may not want to share ownership and can maintain control by issuing debt rather than equity.

---

[1] The ASC Master Glossary defines a financial liability as a contractual obligation (1) to deliver cash or another financial instrument to another entity, or (2) to exchange other financial instruments on potentially unfavorable conditions with another entity.

- *Debt financing offers the opportunity for financial leverage.* By investing borrowed funds, a company expects **to earn a return greater than the interest it will pay for the use of the funds, thereby benefiting the shareholders**. Earnings in excess of after-tax interest charges increase earnings per share. However, if the return falls below the effective interest rate, earnings per share will decline. Expectations of current and future earnings, inflation, and the debt/equity relationship influence the rate of interest needed to issue debt.

> ### GOT IT?
> **14-1** Why does debt financing typically have a lower cost of capital than equity financing?
>
> **14-2** Why does issuing debt result in an income tax advantage when compared to issuing equity?

WHAT ARE THE CHARACTERISTICS OF BONDS PAYABLE?

LEARNING OBJECTIVE 14.2
Understand the characteristics of bonds payable.

Some companies looking to raise financial capital choose to issue bonds. To understand bonds, knowledge of the following terms is essential:

- **Bond:** A debt instrument in which a company agrees to pay the holder the face value at the maturity date and usually to pay periodic interest on the face value at a specified rate. Thus, the company that issues the bonds (the issuer) is borrowing money from the holder of the bonds (the lender).
- **Face Value** (or **Par Value**): The amount of money that the issuer agrees to pay at maturity. It is the same concept as the principal of a note.
- **Maturity Date:** The date on which the issuer of the bond agrees to pay the bondholder the face value (plus any final amount of interest owed).
- **Contract Rate** (or **Stated**, **Face**, or **Nominal Rate**): The interest rate the issuer of the bond agrees to pay each period until maturity.
- **Bond Certificate:** A legal document that provides evidence of ownership and specifies the face value, the annual interest rate, the maturity date, and other characteristics of the bond issue.
- **Bond Indenture:** A document (contract) that defines the rights of the bondholders and the obligations of the issuer.

Bonds usually are issued by corporations, such as **Disney**, **GE**, and **Coca-Cola**, and government entities to borrow large amounts of money. Corporations usually issue bonds so that each bond has a face value of $1,000. The entire bond issue may be sold to one purchaser or to numerous individual purchasers. Thus, a $1 million bond issue includes 1,000 bonds, each with a $1,000 face value. In addition, bonds commonly pay interest twice each year (semiannually) on dates stated on the bond certificate. Therefore, the semiannual interest rate is usually one-half of the annual rate.

Characteristics of Bonds

Different companies issue bonds that may have different characteristics, as shown in Exhibit 14.1. While some of these characteristics are mutually exclusive, several can be combined for a bond issue. The characteristics of a particular bond issue are listed on the bond certificates for that issue and spelled out in detail in the bond indenture. A company may also include in the bond indenture certain restrictive covenants to protect the bondholders and improve the marketability of a bond issue. These restrictions may include limitations on dividends, adherence to certain minimum working capital amounts, maintenance of a debt/equity ratio below some maximum level, or prohibition of issuing additional bonds with superior status in the event of bankruptcy. In this chapter, we focus primarily on the accounting for debenture bonds which are the most common types of bonds.

EXHIBIT 14.1 Characteristics of Bonds

Debenture Bonds	Debenture bonds are not secured by specific property. Their marketability is based on the general credit rating of the company. Generally, a company must have a long history of profitability and positive cash flows, as well as expectations of future positive earnings and cash flows, to sell debenture bonds. Debenture bondholders are considered to be general creditors, with the same rights as other creditors if the issuer fails to pay the interest or principal and declares bankruptcy.
Mortgage Bonds	Mortgage bonds are secured by a lien against specific property of the company. If the company becomes bankrupt and is liquidated, the holders of these bonds have first claim against the proceeds of the sale of the assets that secure their debt. If the proceeds from the sale of pledged assets are not sufficient to repay the debt, mortgage bondholders become general creditors for the balance of the unpaid debt.
Zero-Coupon Bonds (Deep-Discount Bonds)	Zero-coupon bonds are bonds on which the interest is not paid until the maturity date. That is, the bonds are sold at a price considerably below their face value, interest accrues until maturity, and then the bondholders are paid the interest along with the principal at maturity.
Callable Bonds	Callable bonds are bonds that the company has the option to repay (call) at a predetermined price (usually at a premium above face value) for a specified period. That is, the company has the right to require the bondholders to return the bonds before the maturity date with the company paying the predetermined price and interest to date.
Convertible Bonds	Convertible bonds give bondholders the option to convert the bonds into a predetermined number of common equity shares of the issuing company. Thus, upon conversion, the bondholder becomes a shareholder of the company.
Serial Bonds	Serial bonds are issued at one time, but portions of the total face value mature in a series of periodic installments at different future dates. For example, a serial bond issued in 2016 may have a face value of $50,000, and bonds with a face value of $10,000 mature each year for 5 years from 2022 through 2026.

The Bond Issue Process

When a company issues bonds, it may offer them to the public or privately to an institution, such as a financial institution like **Wells Fargo**, or a pension fund. When the bonds are offered to the public, the company usually deals with an underwriter (a stockbrokerage firm or an investment banker). The underwriter agrees on a price for the bonds, pays the company for them, and then sells the bonds to its clients. Because the issuing company avoids having to find the purchasers and being involved in cash transactions with each purchaser, it pays the underwriter a fee for this service.

At the time of the sale, the underwriter negotiates with the company to determine an appropriate selling price. The selling price is based on the terms of the bond issue (such as the stated rate of interest and the length of time to maturity) and factors such as the general bond market conditions, the relative risk of the bonds, and the expected state of the economy. The underwriter determines the effective rate (yield) that it believes best reflects the current market conditions for the particular bond issue. The **effective rate (yield)** is the market rate at which the bonds are actually sold.[2] The yield on the bonds may be different from the contract (stated) rate set by the company and printed

---

[2] After a company has issued bonds, their yield will fluctuate in the bond market as changes occur in the risk premium and expected inflation rate. It is the yield at the time of issuance, however, that is relevant to the company in accounting for the bonds.

on the bond certificates. This difference may result from a difference of opinion between the underwriter and the company about the correct yield. It may also result from a change of economic conditions between the date the company set the terms of the bond issue and the date it was issued.

> ### GOT IT?
>
> **14-3** What is a *bond*? Define *face value, maturity date, contract rate, bond certificate,* and *bond indenture.*
>
> **14-4** What is the difference between a mortgage bond and a debenture bond?
>
> **14-5** What are callable bonds? Convertible bonds?
>
> **14-6** Why do the stated (contract) rate and the effective rate (yield) of interest on bonds frequently differ?

HOW IS THE ISSUE PRICE OF BONDS PAYABLE COMPUTED?

LEARNING OBJECTIVE 14.3

Compute the issue price of bonds payable.

The selling price of the bonds payable is determined by summing the present value of the principal and interest payments discounted at the effective interest (yield) rate. Three alternatives are possible for a company selling bonds:

- **At Par:** Purchasers of the bonds pay the face value of the bonds. The effective interest (yield) rate is equal to the contract interest rate.
- **At a Discount:** Purchasers of the bonds pay an amount less than the face value of the bonds. The effective interest rate is greater than the contract interest rate.
- **At a Premium:** Purchasers of the bonds pay an amount greater than the face value of the bonds. The effective interest rate is less than the contract interest rate.

Example: Bonds Issued at Par

Jet Company decides to sell $100,000 of 5-year bonds that pay semiannual interest with a contract rate of 12% when the effective interest rate is also 12%. Because the contract rate is equal to the effective rate, the bonds will sell at par value. **To determine this selling price, the effective rate is applied to both the future principal and periodic interest payments**, as shown in the following computations. In present value analyses (see the Time Value of Money Module) when interest is paid semiannually, the effective rate is divided by the interest periods per year to determine the effective rate per semiannual period, computed for Jet as follows:

$$12\% \div 2 \text{ periods} = 6\% \text{ semiannual rate}$$

Similarly, the time to maturity is expressed in semiannual periods:

$$5\text{-year bonds} \times 2 \text{ periods} = 10 \text{ semiannual periods}$$

The selling price is computed as follows:

Present value of principal: $100,000 × 0.558395[a]	$ 55,839.50
Present value of interest payments: $6,000[b] × 7.360087[c]	44,160.50[d]
Selling price	$100,000.00

[a] From Present Value of 1 Table ($n = 10$, $i = 0.06$)
[b] $100,000 × 0.12 × 1/2
[c] From Present Value of an Ordinary Annuity of 1 Table ($n = 10$, $i = 0.06$)
[d] Difference of $0.02 due to rounding

Example: Bonds Issued at a Discount

Jet Company decides to sell the $100,000 of 5-year bonds when the effective interest rate is 14%. Recall that the bonds have a contract rate of 12% and because the contract rate is less than the effective rate, the bonds will sell at a discount to par value. The discount of $7,023.61 is computed using the semiannual 7% effective rate as follows:

Present value of principal: $100,000 × 0.508349[a]	$ 50,834.90
Present value of interest payments: $6,000[b] × 7.023582[c]	42,141.49
Selling price	$ 92,976.39
Face value	$100,000.00
Selling price	(92,976.39)
Discount	$ 7,023.61

[a]From Present Value of 1 Table (n = 10, i = 0.07)
[b]$100,000 × 0.12 × 1/2
[c]From Present Value of an Ordinary Annuity of 1 Table (n = 10, i = 0.07)

Example: Bonds Issued at a Premium

If Jet Company sells the bonds when the effective rate is 10%, the bonds will sell at a premium to par value. The premium of $7,721.71 is computed as follows (to compute the present value, the effective rate is expressed on a semiannual basis, 5%, and the time to maturity is expressed in semiannual periods, 10):

Present value of principal: $100,000 × 0.613913[a]	$ 61,391.30
Present value of interest payments: $6,000 × 7.721735[b]	46,330.41
Selling price	$ 107,721.71
Selling price	$ 107,721.71
Face value	(100,000.00)
Premium	$ 7,721.71

[a]From Present Value of 1 Table (n = 10, i = 0.05)
[b]From Present Value of an Ordinary Annuity of 1 Table (n = 10, i = 0.05)

Face Value and Price

On financial web sites, like **Yahoo! Finance** and **InvestinginBonds.com**, a bond's price is often quoted as a percentage of the face value. For example, bonds with a face value of $100,000 that are quoted at 103 (meaning 103% of the face value) are selling for $103,000—that is, at a premium of $3,000. Alternatively, bonds with a $200,000 face value quoted at 98 are selling for $196,000 ($200,000 × 0.98), a $4,000 discount.

It is important to understand why bonds sell at a price different from the face value, and, therefore, the yield is different from the contract rate. The difference between the price paid and the face value essentially adjusts the yield to the issuer and the purchaser.

- When bonds are sold at a discount, the yield is higher than the contract rate. The discount between the lower purchase price and the face value at maturity, along with the contract interest received by the purchaser each period, result in a yield that is greater than the contract rate.
- When bonds are sold at a premium, the yield is lower than the contract rate. The premium between the higher selling price and the face value, along with the contract interest received by the purchaser each period, results in a yield lower than the contract rate.

These relationships are summarized in Exhibit 14.2.

EXHIBIT 14.2 Bond Yields versus Contract Rates

Bonds Sold at	Yield Compared to Contract Rate	Interest Over the Life of the Bonds
Premium ↑	Yield < Contract Rate	Interest Expense < Interest Paid
Par	Yield = Contract Rate	Interest Expense = Interest Paid
Discount ↓	Yield > Contract Rate	Interest Expense > Interest Paid

When the bonds yield a rate either lower (for bonds sold at a premium) or higher (for bonds sold at a discount) than the contract rate, the interest expense recorded by the issuing company each period is different from the interest paid.

- When bonds are sold at a premium, the interest expense is less than the interest paid.
- When bonds are sold at a discount, the interest expense is more than the interest paid.

The difference between the interest expense and the interest payment is the amount of the premium or discount amortized by the issuing company in the period (which we discuss later).

GOT IT?

14-7 Why do bond discounts and bond premiums arise at the time of sale?

14-8 How is the amount of proceeds from a bond issue determined once the market (yield) rate of interest is specified?

HOW IS THE ISSUANCE OF BONDS PAYABLE RECORDED?

LEARNING OBJECTIVE 14.4
Record the issuance of bonds payable.

At the time of issue, the issuing company records the face value of bonds in a Bonds Payable account and the proceeds received as a debit to the Cash account.

- If the bonds are issued at a premium, the issuer will record the premium in a separate account titled Premium on Bonds Payable.
- When bonds are issued at a discount, the issuer will record the discount in a separate account titled Discount on Bonds Payable.

Example: Recording the Issuance of Bonds Payable

Return to the Jet Company examples discussed earlier.

Bonds Issued at Par When Jet issued bonds payable at par, it would record the sale as follows:

Cash	100,000	
Bonds Payable		100,000

Bonds Issued at a Discount When Jet issued bonds payable at a discount, it would record the sale as follows:

Cash	92,976.39	
Discount on Bonds Payable	7,023.61	
Bonds Payable		100,000

The Discount on Bonds Payable account is a *contra* account and is subtracted from the Bonds Payable account on the balance sheet. The book value (carrying value) of the bond issue at any time is the face value minus any unamortized discount:

$$\text{Book Value} = \text{Face Value} - \text{Unamortized Discount}$$

Bonds Issued at a Premium When Jet issued bonds payable at a premium, it would record the sale as follows:

Cash	107,721.71	
Bonds Payable		100,000.00
Premium on Bonds Payable		7,721.71

The Premium on Bonds Payable account is an *adjunct* account and is added to the Bonds Payable account in the long-term liability section of the balance sheet. The book value (carrying value) of the bond issue at any time is the face value plus any unamortized premium:

$$\text{Book Value} = \text{Face Value} + \text{Unamortized Premium}$$

Bonds Issued between Interest Payment Dates

Recall that the interest on bonds usually is paid semiannually on specific dates indicated on the bond certificates. Bonds often are sold after their authorization date and between interest payment dates. In such cases, the issuing company must pay interest only for the period of time the bonds are outstanding—that is, from the sale date to the next interest payment date. When a company sells bonds between interest dates, the company normally will collect from the investors both the selling price and the interest accrued on the bonds from the interest payment date prior to the date of sale. This procedure reduces the record keeping for the first interest payment. This interest amount collected typically is *credited* to Interest Expense and is **computed by multiplying the face value by the stated interest rate for the fraction of the year from the interest payment date prior to the sale date**. On the next interest payment date, the company pays each bondholder 6 months of interest and records Interest Expense as usual. Exhibit 14.3 illustrates this situation.

Example On March 1, 2016, Grimes Corporation issues $800,000 of 10-year bonds dated January 1, 2016, at par. The bonds have a contract (stated) interest rate of 12% and pay interest semiannually on January 1 and July 1. On March 1, because 2 months have elapsed since the interest payment date prior to the sale, Grimes collects $16,000 ($800,000 × 0.12 × 2/12) accrued interest in addition to the face value. Grimes records the issue of the bonds on March 1, 2016, as follows:

Cash	816,000	
Interest Expense		16,000
Bonds Payable		800,000

On July 1, 2016, Grimes records the first semiannual interest payment as follows:

Interest Expense ($800,000 × 0.12 × 6/12)	48,000	
Cash		48,000

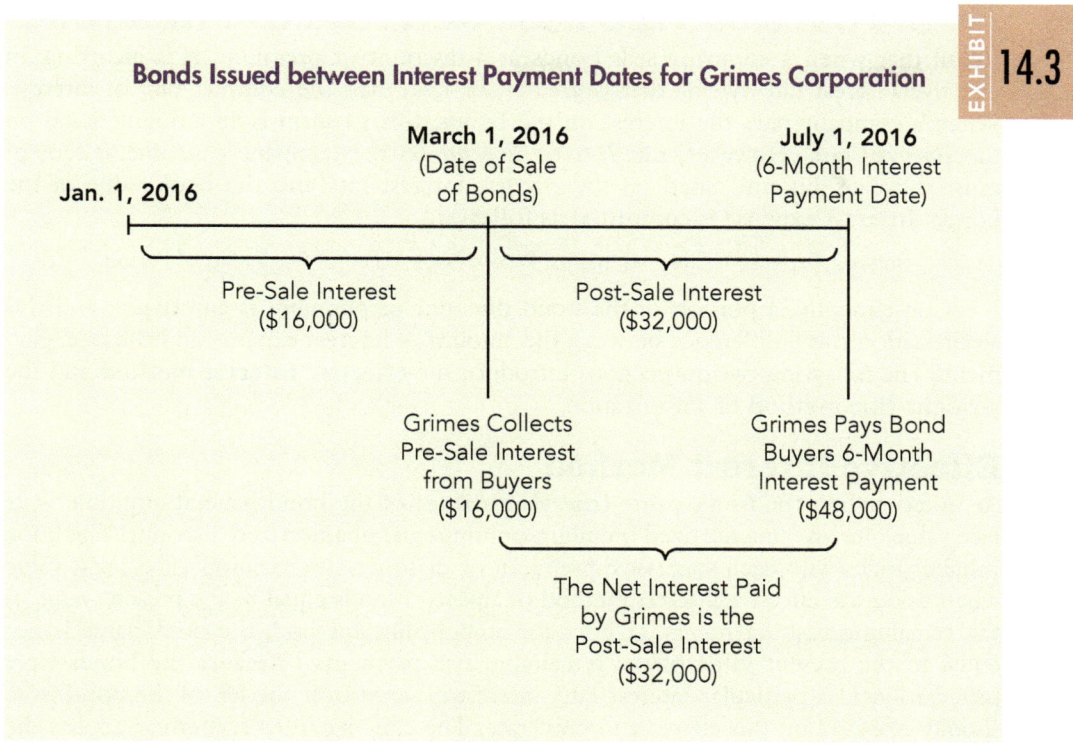

EXHIBIT 14.3 Bonds Issued between Interest Payment Dates for Grimes Corporation

As a result of the preceding journal entries, on July 1, 2016, the Interest Expense account has a debit balance of $32,000 ($48,000 − $16,000) representing the interest ($800,000 × 0.12 × 4/12) since the bonds were issued.

Alternatively, it is possible to record the previous transaction by using a liability account because part of the proceeds (i.e., the accrued interest) will be repaid in the future. Using this approach, Grimes would record the original transaction as follows:

Cash	816,000	
Interest Payable		16,000
Bonds Payable		800,000

On July 1, 2016, Grimes would record the first interest payment as follows:

Interest Expense ($800,000 × 0.12 × 4/12)	32,000	
Interest Payable	16,000	
Cash		48,000

Companies generally use the first method because it has less potential for errors in later transactions. Also, this method enables a company to develop a single routine in its computerized accounting system for recording and distributing all interest payments. ■

GOT IT?

14-9 Distinguish between bond premiums and discounts.

14-10 Why does the recorded amount of interest expense for the first interest payment differ from the expense recorded for other interest payments when bonds are issued between interest payment dates?

LEARNING OBJECTIVE 14.5
Amortize bond discounts and bond premiums.

HOW TO AMORTIZE DISCOUNTS AND PREMIUMS

Recall that when a company sells bonds at a discount or premium, it is incurring an effective interest rate (yield) that is greater, or less, than the contract rate of interest. When a company pays the interest on the bonds, this *payment* is an amount based on the *contract* rate. However, the *Interest Expense* on the company's income statement must show an amount based on the *effective* interest rate and the book value of the bonds. **Interest expense is computed as follows:**

$$\text{Interest Expense} = \text{Effective Interest Rate} \times \text{Book Value at Beginning of Period}$$

Consequently, a portion of the bond discount or premium is amortized, and this amortization is the difference between the amount of interest expense and the cash payment. The following two subsections introduce the **effective interest method** and the **straight-line method** of amortization.

Effective Interest Method

As noted earlier, the **book value** (**carrying value**) of the bond issue at any time is its face value plus any unamortized premium or minus any unamortized discount. The book value changes with each successive premium or discount amortization. The book value when using the effective interest method of amortization is equal to the present value of the remaining cash payments. (Under the straight-line method, the book value is not equal to the present value of the remaining cash payments.) Because the bonds were issued to yield a particular interest rate, interest expense over the life of the bond issue should be based on this effective interest rate. The effective interest method applies the semiannual yield to the book value of the bonds at the beginning of each successive semiannual period to determine the interest expense for that period. In this procedure, **the discount or premium amortization is the difference between the interest expense computed under the effective interest method and the cash payment.** This method is based on the compound interest techniques discussed in the Time Value of Money Module. The relationships among the interest paid, interest expense, and the amortization are shown in Exhibit 14.4.

EXHIBIT 14.4 Interest and Amortization

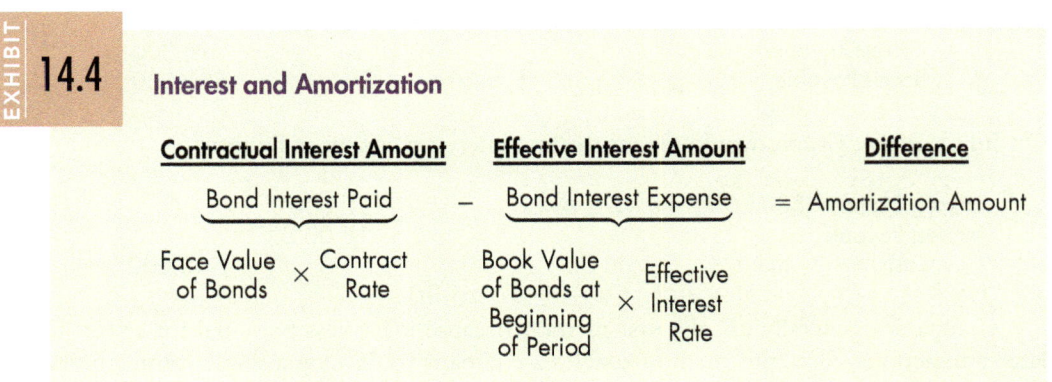

Example: Bond Discount (Effective Interest Method)

After Jet Company sold bonds for $92,976.39 (yielding an effective annual interest rate of 14%), it records the first interest payment under the effective interest method as follows:

June 30, 2016		
Interest Expense ($92,976.39 × 0.14 × 1/2)	6,508.35	
Discount on Bonds Payable ($6,508.35 − $6,000.00)		508.35
Cash ($100,000 × 0.12 × 1/2)		6,000.00

After the first interest entry, the book value of the bonds payable would increase by $508.35 (the amount of discount amortized) from $92,976.39 to $93,484.74. This new book value is used to determine interest expense for the second interest payment:

December 31, 2016
Interest Expense ($93,484.74 × 0.14 × 1/2)   6,543.93
   Discount on Bonds Payable ($6,543.93 − $6,000.00)   543.93
   Cash   6,000.00

Example: Bond Premium (Effective Interest Method)

Alternatively, if Jet Company sold the bonds for $107,721.71 (equivalent to an annual yield rate of 10%), it records the first interest payment under the effective interest method as follows:

June 30, 2016
Interest Expense ($107,721.71 × 0.10 × 1/2)   5,386.09
Premium on Bonds Payable ($6,000.00 − $5,386.09)   613.91
   Cash ($100,000 × 0.12 × 1/2)   6,000.00

After this interest date, Jet would decrease the book value of its bonds payable by $613.91 from $107,721.71 to $107,107.80. This new book value will be used to determine interest expense for the next interest period:

December 31, 2016
Interest Expense ($107,107.80 × 0.10 × 1/2)   5,355.39
Premium on Bonds Payable ($6,000.00 − $5,355.39)   644.61
   Cash   6,000.00

After this second interest period, the bonds payable will have a book value of $106,463.19, which is equal to the beginning of the period book value less the premium amortized during the period ($107,107.80 − $644.61). In addition, it is important to understand that the book value will be equal to the discounted value of the remaining cash flows. After the first two interest dates, the book value of $106,463.19 is equal to the discounted cash flows over the remaining eight interest periods:

Present value of principal: $100,000 × 0.676839[a] $ 67,683.90
Present value of interest: $6,000 × 6.463213[b]   38,779.29[c]
Selling price $106,463.19

[a] From Present Value of 1 Table (n = 8, i = 0.05)
[b] From Present Value of an Ordinary Annuity of 1 Table (n = 8, i = 0.05)
[c] Difference of $0.01 due to rounding

WHY IT MATTERS

Investors, creditors, and others are interested in a company's long-run solvency and stability. As companies acquire more debt, risk typically increases for debt holders and common equity shareholders. This risk arises from two sources. First, debt usually requires periodic interest payments, and failure to make these payments can lead to default and possibly bankruptcy. Second, in the event of bankruptcy, the creditors' claims are satisfied first. Two

(continued)

ratios that provide evidence of this risk that can affect a company's long-run solvency and stability are:

- The **debt-to-assets ratio**, which measures the proportion of assets financed with debt capital rather than equity capital.
- The **times-interest-earned ratio**, which indicates the number of times the firm's operating income could cover the interest charges.

Both ratios are indicators of credit risk, although in different directions. Higher debt-to-assets ratios, as compared to competitors or industry averages, indicate more financial leverage and greater credit risk, whereas higher times-interest-earned ratios indicate less risk. Below are excerpts from **AT&T**'s and **Verizon**'s 2012 annual reports.

	Verizon		AT&T	
(in millions)	2012	2011	2012	2011
Total Assets	$225,222	$230,461	$272,315	$270,442
Total Liabilities	192,065	194,491	179,953	164,908
Interest Expense	2,571	2,827	3,444	3,535
Income before Income Taxes	9,897	10,483	10,439	6,716

The debt-to-assets ratios are computed as follows:

Verizon

2012: Total Liabilities ÷ Total Assets = $192,065 ÷ $225,222 = 0.85
2011: Total Liabilities ÷ Total Assets = $194,491 ÷ $230,461 = 0.84

AT&T

2012: Total Liabilities ÷ Total Assets = $179,953 ÷ $272,315 = 0.66
2011: Total Liabilities ÷ Total Assets = $164,908 ÷ $270,442 = 0.61

Subtracting this ratio from 100%, stockholders contributed 15% and 16% of the total assets for Verizon in 2012 and 2011, respectively. AT&T's shareholders contributed 34% and 39% in 2012 and 2011, respectively. The interest coverage ratio is computed as follows:

Verizon

2012: Pretax Operating Income ÷ Interest Expense = ($9,897 + $2,571) ÷ $2,571 = 4.85
2011: Pretax Operating Income ÷ Interest Expense = ($10,483 + $2,827) ÷ $2,827 = 4.71

AT&T

2012: Pretax Operating Income ÷ Interest Expense = ($10,439 + $3,444) ÷ $3,444 = 4.03
2011: Pretax Operating Income ÷ Interest Expense = ($6,716 + $3,535) ÷ $3,535 = 2.90

These results show that Verizon has a higher degree of financial leverage at the end of 2012. However, both Verizon and AT&T have increased their leverage slightly from 2011 to 2012, which is usually viewed as becoming more risky. In both cases, the interest coverage ratio indicates that more than enough operating income is available to pay interest, which reduces the riskiness of the two companies.

Bond Interest Schedules—Effective Interest Method

Schedules may be developed to show the interest expense, amortization of discounts and premiums, and book values using the effective interest method. **Example 14.1** illustrates a schedule for Jet Company's bonds issued at a discount. **Example 14.2** illustrates a schedule for these bonds issued at a premium. Note that **the amount of interest expense using the effective interest method is based on a constant rate applied to the remaining book value of the bonds**. (In contrast, under the straight-line method, the amount of interest expense remains constant.)

EXAMPLE 14.1

Bond Interest Expense and Discount Amortization Schedule: Effective Interest Method

12% Bonds Sold to Yield 14%

Date	Cash (Credit)[a]	Effective Interest Expense (Debit)[b]	Amortization of Bond Discount (Credit)[c]	Book Value of Bonds[d]
01/01/16				$ 92,976.39
06/30/16	$6,000.00	$6,508.35	$508.35	93,484.74
12/31/16	6,000.00	6,543.93	543.93	94,028.67
06/30/17	6,000.00	6,582.01	582.01	94,610.68
12/31/17	6,000.00	6,622.75	622.75	95,233.43
06/30/18	6,000.00	6,666.34	666.34	95,899.77
12/31/18	6,000.00	6,712.98	712.98	96,612.75
06/30/19	6,000.00	6,762.89	762.89	97,375.64
12/31/19	6,000.00	6,816.29	816.29	98,191.93
06/30/20	6,000.00	6,873.44	873.44	99,065.37
12/31/20	6,000.00	6,934.63[e]	934.63	100,000.00

[a] Credit to cash amounts are equal to $100,000 (face value) × 0.12 (stated annual interest rate) × 1/2 (year).
[b] Effective interest expense amounts are determined as the previous book value × 0.14 (effective interest rate) × 1/2 (year)
[c] Amortization amounts are determined as cash interest payments minus the effective interest expense amounts.
[d] Previous book value + Amortization amount
[e] Difference of $0.05 due to rounding

EXAMPLE 14.2

Bond Interest Expense and Premium Amortization Schedule: Effective Interest Method

12% Bonds Sold to Yield 10%

Date	Cash (Credit)[a]	Effective Interest Expense (Debit)[b]	Amortization of Bond Premium (Debit)[c]	Book Value of Bonds[d]
01/01/16				$107,721.71
06/30/16	$6,000.00	$5,386.09	$613.91	107,107.80
12/31/16	6,000.00	5,355.39	644.61	106,463.19
06/30/17	6,000.00	5,323.16	676.84	105,786.35
12/31/17	6,000.00	5,289.32	710.68	105,075.67
06/30/18	6,000.00	5,253.78	746.22	104,329.45
12/31/18	6,000.00	5,216.47	783.53	103,545.92
06/30/19	6,000.00	5,177.30	822.70	102,723.22
12/31/19	6,000.00	5,136.16	863.84	101,859.38
06/30/20	6,000.00	5,092.97	907.03	100,952.35
12/31/20	6,000.00	5,047.65[e]	952.35	100,000.00

[a] Credit to cash amounts are equal to $100,000 (face value) × 0.12 (stated annual interest rate) × 1/2 (year).
[b] Effective interest expense amounts are determined as the previous book value × 0.10 (effective interest rate) × 1/2 (year).
[c] Amortization amounts are determined as cash interest payments minus the effective interest expense amounts.
[d] Previous book value − Amortization amount
[e] Difference due to $0.03 rounding

Straight-Line Method

With the straight-line method of amortization, the discount or premium to interest expense is amortized in equal amounts each period during the life of the bonds.

Example: Bond Discount (Straight Line)

Recall that Jet Company sells bonds for $92,976.39 on January 1, 2016. The bonds have a face value of $100,000 and a 12% stated annual interest rate. Interest is paid semiannually on June 30 and December 31, and the bonds mature on December 31, 2020. Thus, the bonds have a 5-year life, with 10 semiannual interest periods. Jet records the sale on January 1, 2016, as follows:

Cash	92,976.39	
Discount on Bonds Payable	7,023.61	
Bonds Payable		100,000.00

On the first interest payment date, Jet records both the cash payment and discount amortization. It computes the discount amortization per period as:[3]

$$\text{Discount Amortization per Period} = \text{Total Discount} \div \text{Number of Interest Periods}$$
$$\$702.36 = \$7,023.61 \div 10$$

The interest expense is calculated as the sum of the cash payment and the discount amortization:

$$\text{Straight-Line Interest Expense} = \text{Coupon Interest Payment} + \text{Discount Amortization}$$
$$\$6,702.36 = \$6,000.00 + \$702.36$$

Jet records the first interest payment on June 30, 2016, as follows:

Interest Expense ($6,000.00 + $702.36)	6,702.36	
Discount on Bonds Payable ($7,023.61 ÷ 10)		702.36
Cash ($100,000 × 0.12 × 1/2)		6,000.00

In this case, the interest expense is higher than the cash paid, indicating that the effective rate is higher than the stated rate. Jet makes a similar journal entry to record the second interest payment on December 31, 2016, and every 6 months after that. After this second entry, the long-term liabilities section of Jet's December 31, 2016, balance sheet includes the following:

Bonds Payable	$100,000.00
Less: Discount on Bonds Payable	(5,618.89)
	$ 94,381.11

Note that the unamortized discount of $5,618.89 ($7,023.61 − $702.36 − $702.36) is subtracted from the $100,000 face value of the bonds to determine the $94,381.11 book value.

Example: Bond Premium (Straight Line)

The straight-line amortization of a bond premium follows the same methods. In our second example, when the effective rate was 10%, Jet Company sold bonds on January 1, 2016, for $107,721.71. In this case, the premium amortization per semiannual period is:

$$\text{Premium Amortization per Period} = \text{Total Premium} \div \text{Number of Interest Periods}$$
$$\$7,721.71 \div 10 = \$772.17$$

---

[3] Note that the maturity date of bonds is established on the date they are authorized. When bonds are issued later than the authorization date, any discount or premium is amortized over the *remaining life* until the maturity date.

Interest expense is the cash payment minus the premium amortization:

Straight-Line Interest Expense = Coupon Interest Payment − Premium Amortization
$6,000.00 − $772.17 = $5,227.83

Jet records the sale and first interest payment as follows:

January 1, 2016
Cash	107,721.71	
Bonds Payable		100,000.00
Premium on Bonds Payable		7,721.71

June 30, 2016
Interest Expense ($6,000.00 − $772.17)	5,227.83	
Premium on Bonds Payable ($7,721.71 ÷ 10)	772.17	
Cash ($100,000 × 0.12 × 1/2)		6,000.00

Here the interest expense is lower than the cash paid, indicating an effective rate lower than the stated rate. After a similar journal entry to record the second interest payment, Jet's December 31, 2016, balance sheet includes the following:

Bonds Payable	$100,000.00
Add: Premium on Bonds Payable	6,177.37
	$106,177.37

Note that the $6,177.37 ($7,721.71 − $772.17 − $772.17) unamortized premium is added to the $100,000 face value of the bonds to determine the $106,177.37 book value. ■

In both situations, the total discount or premium will be amortized by the maturity date, and the book value will equal the maturity value.

Accruing Bond Interest

In the previous examples, the semiannual interest payments coincided with the company's fiscal year. However, frequently companies issue bonds with interest payment dates that differ from the fiscal year. In such cases, the company must accrue interest expense and interest payable and recognize partial period amortization of the bond premium or discount at the end of the fiscal year.

Example Olivia Company issues $200,000 of 10%, 5-year bonds on October 1, 2016, for $185,279.87. Interest on these bonds is payable each October 1 and April 1. On October 1, 2016, Olivia records this issuance of the bonds as follows:

Cash	185,279.87	
Discount on Bonds Payable	14,720.13	
Bonds Payable		200,000.00

At the end of the fiscal year, December 31, 2016, Olivia must accrue interest and amortize the discount for the months of October, November, and December. Thus, it must compute and record the amount of interest expense in 2016 for these 3 months. Olivia records this adjusting entry (assuming straight-line amortization) as follows:

Interest Expense	5,736.01	
Discount on Bonds Payable [($14,720.13 ÷ 5) × 3/12]		736.01
Interest Payable ($200,000 × 0.10 × 3/12)		5,000.00

Typically, the company will record a reversing entry on January 1, 2017, so that it can make the April 1, 2017, entry to record interest expense as usual. If the company does not make a reversing entry, when it records interest expense it eliminates the Interest Payable account and records the 3 months of interest expense incurred in 2017. ■

If a company uses the effective interest method to amortize a premium or discount, it determines the amount of interest expense it accrues on December 31, 2016, by computing the semiannual effective interest cost for the next interest and amortization period, and allocating this amount over the number of months of interest being accrued.

Example Return to the Olivia example discussed earlier, but assume that the effective annual interest rate is 12% and Olivia uses the effective interest method. In order to accrue interest expense at December 31, 2016, Olivia first calculates the amount of semiannual interest for the 6-month period from October 1, 2016, to April 1, 2017, as follows:

$$\$185,279.87 \times 0.12 \times 1/2 = \$11,116.79$$

There are 6 months in the interest period and the elapsed time since the date of issue (October 1) to the fiscal period end is 3 months; therefore, the company expenses $5,558.40, or 3/6 of the $11,116.79 semiannual interest charge. It computes the amount of discount amortization as the difference between the effective interest expense, $5,558.40, and the $5,000.00 ($200,000 × 0.10 × 3/12) amount of interest owed, or $558.40. Using the effective interest method of discount amortization, Olivia records the accrued interest on December 31, 2016, as follows:

Interest Expense	5,558.40	
Discount on Bonds Payable		558.40
Interest Payable		5,000.00

Zero-Coupon Bonds

As defined in Exhibit 14.1, zero-coupon bonds are bonds sold at a "deep" discount. As the name implies, zero-coupon bonds pay no interest each period. The only cash outflow for the bonds is the payment of the face value on the maturity date. The calculation of the selling price follows the principles we discussed earlier; that is, it is the present value (based on the yield) of the face value. A company records the issuance of zero-coupon bonds in the usual way; it debits the discount account for the difference between the selling price and the face value.

Even though the bonds pay no interest each period, the company must still recognize the amount of interest expense incurred each period on the amount borrowed. It computes the interest expense, as we discussed earlier, by multiplying the yield times the book value of the bonds at the beginning of the period. (Alternatively, the company may use the straight-line method.) Because the company makes no cash payment for interest each period, it recognizes the interest expense each period as a decrease (credit) in the discount account (and therefore increases the book value of the bonds). The accounting for a non-interest-bearing note is illustrated on page 14-29. Accounting for a zero-coupon bond follows the same procedures.

Debt Issuance Costs

Debt issuance costs represent the costs associated with issuing debt and include legal, finance and accounting fees, printing costs and registration fees. These costs are paid for by the company issuing debt and result in a reduction of the amount received. In addition, they are presented as a direct deduction from the carrying value of the debt. Conceptually, a company could expense the issue costs or defer them and compute a new yield. However, GAAP requires debt issuance costs to be amortized to interest expense over the life of the bond issue by either the straight-line or effective interest methods.[4]

---

[4] FASB ASU 2015-03 Simplifying the Presentation of Debt Issuance Costs.

Example On January 1, 2016, Graham Company issues 10-year bonds with a face value of $500,000 at 104, or $520,000 ($500,000 × 1.04). Costs connected with the issue totaled $8,000. Graham records this issue as follows:

Cash	520,000	
Premium on Bonds Payable (0.04 × $500,000)		20,000
Bonds Payable		500,000
Deferred Debt Issuance Costs	8,000	
Cash		8,000

Graham amortizes the deferred debt issuance costs of $8,000 to interest expense (i.e., debit Interest Expense and credit Deferred Debt Issuance Costs) each year over the 10-year life of the bonds. In the balance sheet the unamortized deferred debt issuance costs are reported as a direct deduction from the carrying value of the debt. ∎

Fair Value Option

As discussed in Chapter 4, both GAAP and IFRS allow a company to value any financial instrument at fair value. Under GAAP, fair value is defined as an exit value. The fair value option allows a company to value any of its bonds payable (or any other financial liability) at fair value. This decision must be made at the time the bonds payable or other financial liability is issued and then must be continually applied throughout the life of the liability. To measure fair value, a company must use the valuation method consistent with the fair value hierarchy. For example, a company might decide that it is most appropriate to value its bonds payable by discounting the future cash flows using an estimate of the current market yield. When a company chooses this fair value option for a debt instrument, it reports:

- the debt instrument on its balance sheet separately from any debt instruments that are not reported at fair value
- any change in the fair value that is not related to changes in instrument-specific credit risk in its income statement for that period
- any change in the fair value resulting from a change in the instrument-specific credit risk as a separate component of other comprehensive income

Real Report 14.1 shows the liabilities section of **Bank of America**'s 2012 balance sheet, which discloses a number of its financial instrument liabilities measured at fair value and disclosed parenthetically.

REAL REPORT 14.1   FINANCIAL LIABILITIES AT FAIR VALUE

Bank of America Corporation and Subsidiaries
CONSOLIDATED BALANCE SHEET (continued)

Bank of America Corporation

	December 31	
(Dollars in millions)	2012	2011
Liabilities		
Deposits in U.S. offices:		
Noninterest-bearing	$ 372,546	$ 332,228
Interest-bearing (includes $2,262 and $3,297 measured at fair value)	654,332	624,814
Deposits in non-U.S. offices:		
Noninterest-bearing	7,573	6,839
Interest-bearing	70,810	69,160
Total deposits	1,105,261	1,033,041

(continued)

	December 31	
(Dollars in millions)	2012	2011
Federal funds purchased and securities loaned or sold under agreements to repurchase (includes **$42,639** and $34,235 measured at fair value)	$ 293,259	$ 214,864
Trading account liabilities	73,587	60,508
Derivative liabilities	46,016	59,520
Commercial paper and other short-term borrowings (includes **$4,074** and $6,558 measured at fair value)	30,731	35,698
Accrued expenses and other liabilities (includes **$16,594** and $15,743 measured at fair value and **$513** and $714 of reserve for unfunded lending commitments)	148,579	123,049
Long-term debt (includes **$49,161** and $46,239 measured at fair value)	275,585	372,265
Total liabilities	**1,973,018**	**1,898,945**

Suggested answers to these questions are found at the end of the chapter.

Questions:

1. What is the total amount of Bank of America's liabilities valued at fair value as of December 31, 2012?
2. Why would financial statement users be concerned with the amount of liabilities recorded at fair value?
3. Why do you think that Bank of America only values a portion of its long-term debt at fair value?

GOT IT?

14-11 What two methods may a company use to amortize a premium or discount over the life of a bond issue? Briefly describe each method.

14-12 How is the amount of interest expense a company records each period affected by the amortization of a bond discount using the straight-line method?

14-13 How is the amount of interest expense a company records each period affected by the amortization of a bond premium using the straight-line method?

LEARNING OBJECTIVE 14.6

Explain extinguishment of liabilities.

HOW DO WE ACCOUNT FOR THE EXTINGUISHMENT OF LIABILITIES?

The agreement between the bondholders and the issuing company always includes a specified maturity date. On this date, the company agrees to repay the face value of the bonds to the bondholders. At this time, any premium or discount will be completely amortized so that the book value of the bonds is equal to the face value. Under certain circumstances, bonds may be retired (extinguished) prior to their scheduled maturity date.

Over the past three decades, both of the accounting standard setting boards have considered the various circumstances under which liabilities should be considered to be extinguished and what, if any, gain or loss should be recognized on that extinguishment. Under GAAP, a liability is derecognized for financial reporting purposes if one of the following occurs:[5]

- debtor pays the creditor and is relieved of its obligation for the liability
- debtor is released legally from being the primary obligor under the liability

[5] FASB ASC 405-20-40: Liabilities, Extinguishment of Liabilities.

Bonds Retired at Maturity

On the balance sheet issued within 1 year prior to the maturity date, a company reclassifies the face value (and any related premium or discount) of the bonds to be retired from a noncurrent (long-term) to a current liability. On the maturity date after the last interest payment is recorded, any premium or discount on bonds payable is fully amortized. Therefore, the book value of the bonds is equal to the maturity value. The company records the retirement of bonds on the maturity date by a debit to Bonds Payable (to eliminate the liability) and a credit to Cash.

Bonds Retired Prior to Maturity

Many companies will issue long-term financing instruments, such as bonds or notes, including a **call provision**. A call provision gives the issuing company the option to recall and repay the debt issue prior to maturity, usually at a prestated percentage above the face value of the debt. Companies might call a bond for the following reasons:

- to repay the debt to reduce their level of debt
- to eliminate any restrictions on operations included in the bond contract
- to take advantage of favorable changes in market conditions

Because the call price is generally set above the issue price, a loss occurs when the company recalls the debt.

An alternative method of retiring bonds prior to their maturity is for the company to purchase them on the open market, if they are traded. Then a gain or loss arises depending on the relationship between the book value and the market value of the bonds.

Any gain or loss is reported in the period of extinguishment and is included as a component of income from continuing operations.[6]

Example: Retirement Prior to Maturity

Rodgers Corporation originally issued $100,000 of 12% bonds at 97 on January 1, 2016. The bonds have a 10-year life, pay interest on January 1 and July 1, and are callable at 105 plus accrued interest. Assume, for simplicity, that Rodgers amortizes the discount by the straight-line method. On June 30, 2021, the company calls the bonds. First, Rodgers records the current interest expense and liability, including the amortization of the discount that expired since the last interest payment, as follows:

Interest Expense	6,150	
Discount on Bonds Payable [($3,000 ÷ 10) × 1/2]		150
Interest Payable ($100,000 × 0.12 × 1/2)		6,000

Rodgers then records the reacquisition of the bonds as follows:

Bonds Payable	100,000	
Interest Payable	6,000	
Loss on Bond Redemption	6,350[a]	
Discount on Bonds Payable		1,350[b]
Cash [($100,000 × 1.05) + $6,000]		111,000

[a] Call price (excluding interest) $ 105,000
  Face value $ 100,000
  Unamortized discount   (1,350)
    Less: Carrying value   (98,650)
    Loss on bond redemption $ 6,350

[b] Original discount $ 3,000
  Amortization on straight-line basis for 5 1/2 years = 5.5 × $300   (1,650)
  Unamortized discount 6/30/21 $ 1,350

Rodgers reports the loss of $6,350 in income from continuing operations on its 2021 income statement.

---

[6] FASB ASC 470-50-45: Debt, Modifications and Extinguishments.

In addition to retirement at maturity or prior to maturity, a liability can be extinguished through loan **defeasance**, in which the debtor is legally released from being the primary obligor of the liability. This situation arises when:

- an affiliated company agrees to become the primary obligor for the bonds
- the issuing company transfers a sufficient amount of assets (such as investment securities) into a legally separate entity (such as a trust) to be used for bond retirement at maturity

The parent company derecognizes the liability (e.g., bonds payable) from its balance sheet, recognizes a reduction in an investment account (either an investment in affiliate account or an investment securities account), and reports a gain or loss on the transaction, if appropriate. The bond issuer may still be required to disclose a contingent liability if the issuer has been released from being the primary obligor because a third party has assumed the debt, but the creditor requires the issuer to be a guarantor of the third party's debt.

GOT IT?

14-14 What is a call provision? Why do companies often include call provisions on bond issues?

14-15 Distinguish between bond retirements and bond refundings.

14-16 When do companies recognize gains and losses from the extinguishment of debt? Where are the gains and losses disclosed on the income statement?

LEARNING OBJECTIVE 14.7
Understand bonds with equity characteristics.

HOW DO WE ACCOUNT FOR BONDS WITH EQUITY CHARACTERISTICS?

A company may issue bonds that allow creditors to ultimately become shareholders either by attaching stock warrants to the bonds or including a conversion feature in the bond indenture. **Stock warrants** give holders the option to purchase a specified number of common shares at a predetermined price for a period of time, whereas **conversion** allows bondholders to exchange bonds for common equity shares at a predetermined exchange ratio. In either case, the bondholder has acquired a dual set of rights:

- the right to receive interest and principal repayments on the bonds
- the right to acquire common stock, either by exercising the warrants and purchasing shares or by exchanging bonds for shares, and thereafter to participate in future dividends and the potential appreciation of the market value of the company's common stock

Conceptually, it can be argued that the economic substance of issuing bonds with either detachable warrants or a conversion feature is similar (but not identical) because both give bondholders the rights to acquire common shares. For consistency, therefore, a portion of the proceeds of a bond issue carrying either of these features could be assigned to shareholders' equity. However, GAAP differs in its treatment of these securities.

Bonds Issued with Detachable Stock Warrants

When a company issues bonds with detachable stock warrants, these warrants represent rights that enable the security holder to acquire a specified number of common shares at a given price within a certain time period. Stock warrants are attached to bonds to increase their marketability. They generally result in either a lower interest rate or greater proceeds when compared with other bond issues with similar risk but without such rights. (The terms *stock warrants* and *stock rights* often are used interchangeably.) Because these warrants are detachable, they sometimes trade separately from the bonds on the open market.

GAAP requires that a portion of the proceeds of bonds issued with detachable warrants be allocated to the stock warrants and accounted for as additional paid-in capital. This allocation is based on the relative fair values of the bonds and warrants as soon as both elements trade separately on the open market. The allocation is made as follows:

$$\text{Amount Assigned to Bonds} = \frac{\text{Market Value of Bonds without Warrants}}{\text{Market Value of Bonds without Warrants} + \text{Market Value of Warrants}} \times \text{Issuance Price}$$

$$\text{Amount Assigned to Warrants} = \frac{\text{Market Value of Warrants}}{\text{Market Value of Bonds without Warrants} + \text{Market Value of Warrants}} \times \text{Issuance Price}$$

Amount Assigned to Bonds + Amount Assigned to Warrants = Issuance Price

Example: Bonds Issued with Detachable Warrants

Grant Company sold $800,000 of 12% bonds at 101, or $808,000. Each $1,000 bond carried 10 warrants, and each warrant allows the holder to acquire one share of $5 par common stock for $25 per share. After issuance, the bonds are quoted at 99 *ex rights* (without the rights attached), and the warrants (rights) are quoted at $3 each. Grant calculates the values assigned to each security as follows:

$$\text{Value Assigned to Bonds} = \frac{\$990 \times 800}{(\$990 \times 800) + (\$3 \times 800 \times 10)} \times \$808,000$$

$$= \frac{\$792,000}{\$792,000 + \$24,000} \times \$808,000 = \$784,235.29$$

$$\text{Value Assigned to Warrants} = \frac{\$3 \times 800 \times 10}{(\$990 \times 800) + (\$3 \times 800 \times 10)} \times \$808,000$$

$$= \frac{\$24,000}{\$792,000 + \$24,000} \times \$808,000 = \$23,764.71$$

In the denominator of each equation, note that the $792,000 fair value of the bonds without warrants is computed by multiplying the $990 (99 ex rights) quoted price times the 800 bonds. The fair value of the warrants is determined by multiplying the $3 quoted price times the 8,000 warrants (800 × 10). Grant records the transaction as follows:

Cash	808,000.00	
Discount on Bonds Payable ($800,000.00 − $784,235.29)	15,764.71	
Bonds Payable		800,000.00
Common Stock Warrants		23,764.71

This journal entry recognizes the fact that the bonds with detachable warrants are hybrid financing instruments comprised of two components: bonds (liabilities) and warrants (options) on common shares (common equity). Each warrant is assigned a value of $2.971 ($23,764.71 ÷ 8,000). If 500 of the warrants were later exercised at the $25 per share exercise price, Grant would record the following journal entry:

Cash ($25 × 500)	12,500.00	
Common Stock Warrants ($2.971 × 500)	1,485.50	
Common Stock ($5 × 500)		2,500.00
Additional Paid-In Capital on Common Stock		11,485.50

If the remaining 7,500 warrants expire, Grant would record the following journal entry:

Common Stock Warrants ($23,764.71 − $1,485.50)	22,279.21	
Additional Paid-In Capital from Expired Warrants		22,279.21

This journal entry transfers the value assigned to the warrants to the existing shareholders.

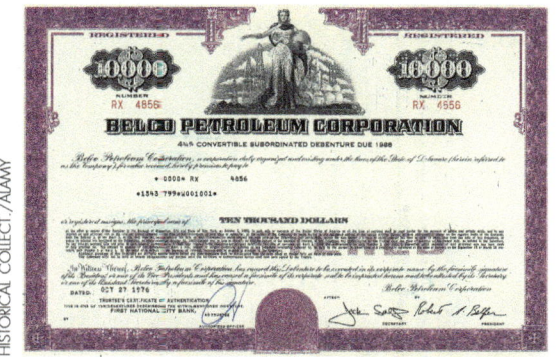

Convertible Bonds

A company may also issue **convertible bonds** that are convertible into common stock. At conversion, the bondholder (creditor) exchanges the bonds for a specified number of common shares and becomes a shareholder. Debt securities that are convertible into common stock are hybrid financing instruments that often play a role in corporate financing, and this role appears to be growing.

Most financial analysts agree that a company sells convertible bonds for one of three primary reasons:

- The company wants to increase its equity capital at a later date and decides that the issuance of convertible bonds is the best way to do so.
- The company wants to increase its debt and finds the conversion feature necessary to make the bonds sufficiently marketable at a reasonable interest rate.
- The company may wish to issue lower risk convertible debt now, while giving bondholders an option on the upside of the company's common stock.

Several other factors motivate companies to issue convertible bonds rather than common stock. For example, a company may wish to:

- avoid potential downward price pressures on its stock which could result from a large new issue of common stock
- avoid the direct sale of common stock when it believes its stock currently is undervalued in the market
- penetrate that segment of the capital market that is unwilling or unable to participate in a direct common stock issue
- minimize the costs associated with selling securities

For similar reasons, companies may issue convertible preferred stock (discussed in Chapter 15). In this chapter, we focus only on accounting for convertible bonds.

Recording the Issuance Conceptually, there are two methods for recording the issuance of convertible debt. The company could attribute part of the proceeds from the sale of the security to the conversion privilege and allocate this amount to shareholders' equity, or the company could treat the issue solely as debt.

Advocates of the first position argue that because both the conversion feature and the right to receive interest are valuable to an investor, the conversion feature often carries a lower interest rate or a higher selling price (or both) than might otherwise have been available. Because the conversion feature is valuable, an amount equal to the difference between the price at which the bonds might have been sold without the conversion privilege and the actual issue price should be allocated to additional paid-in capital. While this position was originally included in GAAP, it was removed due to opposition from corporate interests.

In most cases, GAAP requires companies to treat the proceeds from the issuance of convertible debt solely as debt.[7] The argument is that the debt and the conversion option are not separable for trading purposes and that separate values are not reliable. Thus, a company records the issuance of convertible debt in the same manner as the issuance of nonconvertible debt, without separately recording a value for the conversion feature. However, the FASB is considering revisiting this issue and requiring that the equity component be separately valued, as we discuss later in the chapter.

Recording the Conversion When bondholders convert bonds into common stock, a company must determine the amount to record as shareholders' equity. If the conversion takes place between interest dates, the company first must record interest expense,

[7] FASB ASC 470-20: Debt, Debt with Conversion and Other Options.

interest payable, and any discount or premium amortization to bring the book value of the bonds up to date. There are two GAAP methods for a company to record the conversion of the bonds:

- **Book Value Method:** The common method used in practice is to record the common stock and additional paid-in capital at the book value of the convertible bonds on the date of conversion. Under the book value method, no gain or loss is recorded upon conversion.
- **Market Value Method:** In specific situations, such as when the issuer calls the bonds, the market value method is used.[8] Under this method, common stock and additional paid-in capital are recorded at the market value of the shares issued on the date of conversion, and a loss is recorded. The loss is computed by comparing the market value of the shares with the book value of the bonds at the time of conversion. This loss is reported in income from continuing operations on the company's income statement.

Example: Conversion of Bonds

Shannon Corporation has outstanding convertible bonds with a face value of $10,000. It has just paid interest on these bonds, and the bonds have a book value of $10,500. Each $1,000 bond is convertible into 40 shares of common stock (par value $20 per share). If all the bonds are converted into common stock when the market value of Shannon's common stock is $26.50 per share, the accounting for the conversion under the two methods would be as follows:

Book Value Method

Bonds Payable	10,000	
Premium on Bonds Payable	500	
Common Stock (40 × 10 × $20)		8,000
Additional Paid-In Capital from Bond		
Conversion ($10,500 − $8,000)		2,500

Market Value Method

Bonds Payable	10,000	
Premium on Bonds Payable	500	
Loss on Conversion ($10,600 − $10,500)	100	
Common Stock (40 × 10 × $20)		8,000
Additional Paid-In Capital from Bond		
Conversion (40 × 10 × $6.50)		2,600

Induced Conversions A company that has issued convertible bonds may want to induce conversion of these bonds to common stock to reduce interest costs, improve its debt/equity ratio, or for other reasons. To induce conversion, the company may add a "sweetener" to the convertible bond issue so that the conversion privileges are changed or additional consideration is paid to the bondholder.

Induced conversions typically involve situations in which the issuer changes conversion privileges for outstanding convertible bonds, usually offering additional consideration for a limited period of time. The changed terms often reduce the original conversion price resulting in one of the following:

- issuance of additional shares of common stock
- issuance of warrants or other securities not included in the original conversion terms
- payment of cash to bondholders who convert during the specified time period

When convertible bonds are converted to common stock in such a situation, the debtor company recognizes an expense equal to the excess of the fair value of the common stock (and any other consideration) transferred in the transaction over

---

[8] FASB ASC 470-20-40-5: Debt, Debt with Conversion and Other Options, Derecognition, Conversion Upon Issuer's Exercise of Call Option.

the fair value of the common stock issuable under the original conversion terms. The fair values are measured on the date the inducement offer is accepted by the convertible bondholders.[9]

Example Matthews Company issued convertible bonds with a face value of $10,000 at par. At the time of issuance, the conversion terms allowed each $1,000 bond to be converted into 40 shares of no-par common stock. To induce conversion, Matthews later changed the conversion terms so that each bond is convertible into 50 shares of no-par common stock if conversion is made in 60 days. All the bonds are converted within the time limit when the market price of the common stock is $30 per share. Bond conversion expense is calculated as:

Fair value of no-par common stock issued to induce conversion	10 bonds × 50 common shares per bond × $30 per common share =	$15,000
Less: Fair value of no-par common stock under original contract	10 bonds × 40 common shares per bond × $30 per common share =	12,000
Bond conversion expense		$ 3,000

Under the book value method, Matthews records the bond conversion expense at $3,000, eliminates the $10,000 par value of the bonds payable, and records the no-par common stock at $13,000 as follows:

Bonds Payable	10,000	
Bond Conversion Expense	3,000	
Common Stock, no par		13,000

If Matthews had decided instead to use the market value method, it would have recorded the common stock at its fair value of $15,000 and the bond conversion expense at $5,000 and removed the $10,000 par value of bonds payable. Matthews reports the bond conversion expense in its income from continuing operations. ∎

Convertible Bonds That Require Recognition of an Equity Component There are three cases in which an equity component must be recognized when issuing convertible bonds. The first case is when a company issues a convertible bond that initially has a beneficial conversion feature. A beneficial conversion feature is one in which the conversion price is below the fair value of the stock into which it is convertible. The second case occurs when the convertible debt is issued at a significant premium. The final case occurs when the company may settle the convertible debt by paying cash to the owner of the bond. These cash settled convertible bonds normally settle in one of three ways:

- Net Share Settlement: The bond issuer pays the face value of the bonds in cash and delivers shares for the in-the-money amount of the conversion option.
- Cash or Stock in Any Combination: The bond issuer pays some combination of cash and common stock in a total amount equal to conversion value.
- Cash Settlement: The bond issuer pays cash equal to conversion value.

Example Jordy Company issues a $1,000 bond that pays annual interest of 1% and is convertible into 50 shares of its $5 par value common stock at the end of 3 years. Jordy may also settle the bond through a cash payment equal to the principal amount. It sells the bond for its face value of $1,000. At the date of issuance, the company's common stock is selling for $18 per share, so the stock price only has to increase by at least $2 per share before the conversion becomes "in the money" (50 shares × $20 = $1,000).

---

[9] FASB ASC 470-20-40-26: Debt, Debt with Conversion and Other Options.

When a convertible bond can be settled by paying cash, the company must separately report the debt and the conversion feature.[10] The company estimates the debt component as equal to the fair value of a similar bond without a conversion feature. The difference between this amount and the selling price of the bond is allocated to Additional Paid-In Capital: Conversion Feature. For example, suppose Jordy Company estimates that the current market rate on a 3-year bond is 12%. Then, it would value the bond as follows:

Present value of principal: $1,000 × 0.711780[a]	$711.78
Present value of interest: $10[b] × 2.401831[c]	24.02
Implicit value of the convertible debt	$735.80

[a] From Present Value of 1 Table ($n = 3$, $i = 0.12$)
[b] $1,000 × 0.01
[c] From Present Value of an Ordinary Annuity of 1 Table ($n = 3$, $i = 0.12$)

Jordy would allocate the difference between the selling price of the convertible debt ($1,000) and its implicit value ($735.80) to the conversion feature and record the issuance of the bond as follows:

Cash	1,000.00	
Discount on Bonds Payable	264.20	
Bonds Payable		1,000.00
Additional Paid-In Capital: Conversion Feature		264.20

At the end of the first year, Jordy records the interest as follows:

Interest Expense ($735.80 × 0.12)	88.30	
Discount on Bonds Payable		78.30
Cash		10.00

Note that Jordy's interest expense is $88.30, compared to the $10 it would have been if the conversion feature had not been separately valued. Over the life of the bond, Jordy recognizes the interest expense using the effective interest method to accrete (or increase) the bond's carrying value to its $1,000 face value at the end of 3 years.

If the owner of the bond chooses the cash settlement at the end of 3 years (which would occur if the stock price is still below $20 per share), Jordy would record the following:

Bonds Payable	1,000.00	
Cash		1,000.00

Alternatively, if the owner of the bond chooses the conversion feature at the end of 3 years (which would occur if the stock price is above $20 per share), Jordy would record the following:

Bonds Payable	1,000.00	
Additional Paid-In Capital: Conversion Feature	264.20	
Common Stock		250.00
Additional Paid-In Capital from Bond Conversion		1,014.20

Real Report 14.2 shows the debt note from **Encore Capital Group**'s 2012 annual report describing Encore's 3% convertible senior notes which may be settled with a cash payment.

---

[10] FASB ASC 470-20-30: Debt, Debt with Conversion and Other Options, Initial Measurement. If the debt is convertible before the maturity date, the company uses the expected life to compute the present value and to amortize the discount.

14.2 CASH SETTLED CONVERTIBLE BONDS — REAL REPORT

Encore Capital Group

Note 11: Debt

The Company is obligated under borrowings, as follows (in thousands):

	December 31, 2012	December 31, 2011
Revolving credit facility	$258,000	$305,000
Term loan facility	148,125	—
Propel facility	117,601	—
Senior secured notes	72,500	75,000
Convertible notes	115,000	—
Less: Debt discount	(14,442)	—
Capital lease obligations	9,252	8,950
	$706,036	$388,950

Convertible Senior Notes

On November 27, 2012, Encore sold $100.0 million in aggregate principal amount of 3.0% convertible senior notes due November 27, 2017 in a private placement transaction. On December 6, 2012, the initial purchasers exercised, in full, their option to purchase an additional $15.0 million of the convertible senior notes, which resulted in aggregate principal amount of $115.0 million of the convertible senior notes outstanding (collectively, the "Convertible Notes"). Interest on the Convertible Notes is payable semi-annually, in arrears, on May 27 and November 27 of each year, beginning on May 27, 2013. The Convertible Notes are the Company's general unsecured obligations. The Convertible Notes will be convertible into cash up to the aggregate principal amount of the Convertible Notes to be converted and the Company will pay or deliver, as the case may be, cash, shares of the Company's common stock or a combination of cash and shares of the Company's common stock, at the Company's election, in respect of the remainder, if any, of the Company's conversion obligation in excess of the agreegate principal amount of the Convertible Notes being converted. The Convertible Notes will be convertible at an initial conversion rate of 31.6832 shares of the Company's common stock per $1,000 principal amount of Convertible Notes, subject to adjustment upon certain events, which is equivalent to an initial conversion price of approximately $31.56 per share of the Company's common stock.

Authoritative guidance related to debt with conversion and other options requires that issuers of convertible debt instruments that, upon conversion, may be settled fully or partially in cash, must separately account for the liability and equity components in a manner that will reflect the entity's nonconvertible debt borrowing rate when interest cost is recognized in subsequent periods. Additionally, debt issuance costs are required to be allocated in proportion to the allocation of the liability and equity components and accounted for as debt issuance costs and equity issuance costs, respectively.

Interest expense related to the Convertible Notes was as follows (in thousands):

	Year Ended December 31, 2012
Interest expense—stated coupon rate	$307
Interest expense—amortization of debt discount	260
Total interest expense—convertible notes	$567

Suggested answers to these questions are found at the end of the chapter.

Questions:

1. What is the maturity amount of the Convertible Senior Notes sold by Encore on November 27, 2012, and when do the notes become due and pay interest?
2. For the Convertible Senior Notes, what amount of interest would be paid each annual fiscal period?
3. For the 3% Convertible Senior Notes, what amount of interest was expensed for the year ended December 31, 2012? Was this amount greater than or less than the cash interest paid for the year ended December 31, 2012?

INTERNATIONAL DIMENSION

FINANCING LIABILITIES

IFRS for long-term financing liabilities are generally similar to U.S. GAAP; however, there are some differences:

- Both GAAP and IFRS require the use of the effective interest method; however, GAAP allows the use of the straight-line method if the results are not materially different from those obtained by using the effective interest method.[11] In addition, under IFRS premiums and discounts are not recorded and disclosed separately as they are under GAAP. Bonds payable are simply disclosed at their net amount.
- IFRS contain a general principle that an instrument would be classified as a financial liability when it contains an obligation to transfer resources (e.g., cash or other assets) regardless of the legal form of the instrument. U.S. GAAP has a similar definition of liabilities, but instead addresses the classification of specific instruments. Therefore, instruments that are classified as equity under U.S. GAAP may be classified as liabilities under IFRS.
- IFRS require a company that issues a compound financial instrument containing both liability and equity components to report each component separately on its balance sheet. While this is similar to U.S. GAAP with respect to bonds with detachable stock warrants, IFRS require companies that issue convertible debt to report the debt instrument and the conversion option (an equity instrument) separately, regardless of whether the conversion feature can be settled in stock or cash.

IFRS Application On January 1, 2016, Chivay Corporation, a Norwegian company, originally issued €500,000 of 10-year bonds that pay annual interest with a contract rate of 8%. Transaction costs connected with the issuance totaled €7,200. Chivay received proceeds after deducting the transaction costs of €476,263.15, which is equivalent to an effective rate for the bonds of 8.731%.[12] Chivay would record the issuance of the bonds as follows:

Cash	476,263.15	
Bonds Payable		476,263.15

Chivay records its first interest payment on December 31, 2016, as follows:

Interest Expense (476,263.15 × 8.731%)	41,582.54	
Bonds Payable		1,582.54
Cash (500,000 × 8%)		40,000.00

Chivay would report a bonds payable liability of €477,845.69 (476,263.15 + 1,582.54) in its December 31, 2016, balance sheet. Note that IFRS net the bond discounts and premiums and any debt issuance costs against the principal.

Source: IAS 32 (See Appendix C at the end of this book.)

---

[11] FASB ASC 835-30-55-2: Interest, Imputation of Interest.

[12] An accurate interest rate can be obtained by solving for the implicit interest rate that equates the net proceeds of €476,263.15 with the present value of the principal plus the present value of the interest payments. See the Time Value of Money Module for a demonstration.

> **GOT IT?**
>
> **14-17** Why does a company issue a bond with detachable warrants (rights)? At what value is each of these securities recorded at the time of the bond issuance?
>
> **14-18** What are convertible bonds? Why would a company issue convertible debt?
>
> **14-19** What two alternative methods are available to account for the issuance of convertible debt? What method did GAAP finally require? Why?
>
> **14-20** If a company that uses IFRS had a significant amount of convertible debt, how would its debt-to-equity ratio be affected relative to if the company had used U.S. GAAP?

LEARNING OBJECTIVE 14.8
Account for long-term notes payable.

HOW DO WE ACCOUNT FOR LONG-TERM NOTES PAYABLE?

A long-term note is economically similar to a debenture bond because it represents a future obligation of the borrower to repay debt in more than a year. Also, in many cases, no collateral backs the note. Like bonds, long-term notes generally require payments of interest on the borrowed funds, and the rate of interest charged will depend on such factors as the credit risk of the borrower, the length of time until maturity, and other issues. Although GAAP addresses the accounting for most notes payable, it specifically exempts normal trade transactions not exceeding 1 year, as we discussed in Chapter 6.[13]

In some commercial arrangements, corporate lenders will lend financial capital to companies or employees, and the long-term notes will *not* require explicit interest payments. These lending arrangements are sometimes used to maintain favorable customer, supplier, or employee relations or to ensure future services. GAAP provides guidelines for cases in which a long-term note does not stipulate a rate of interest or the stated interest rate is clearly below market. The basic principle is that, regardless of how a note is structured legally, **GAAP recognizes the underlying economics of the arrangement, requiring the borrower to record the note payable at its present value and use the effective interest method to record the interest expense.**[14] This means that the accounting for a note is based on its economic substance and not its legal form, thereby providing more relevant and representationally faithful information about the borrowing arrangement to financial statement users. When the present value of the note is known, the borrower calculates the interest rate implicit in the transaction and uses this rate to apply the effective interest method. When present value is not known, the borrower uses its incremental interest rate to determine the present value and to apply the effective interest method. **The incremental interest rate is the rate that the borrower would be required to pay to obtain similar financing in the credit market at the time the note is issued.** The three major categories of notes are as follows:

- notes exchanged for cash
- notes exchanged for cash and rights or privileges
- notes exchanged for property, goods, or services

Notes Payable Issued for Cash

When a company borrows cash and issues a long-term note payable bearing a stated (and fair) interest rate, it records the note initially at its face value (because it is equal to

---

[13] FASB ASC 835-30-15 and 35: Interest, Imputation of Interest, Scope and Scope Exceptions and Subsequent Measurement.
[14] The straight-line method may be used if the results obtained are not materially different from the effective interest method.

the present value). Subsequently, it records interest payments and accruals as debits to Interest Expense and credits to Cash or Interest Payable. Upon payment at maturity, it eliminates the Notes Payable account.

When the interest rate agreed to in a note is not fair, (e.g., a long-term non-interest-bearing note), the borrower must use an **imputed interest rate**, which is an estimated interest rate based on the rate that an independent borrower and an independent lender would negotiate for a similar transaction under comparable terms and conditions. Accounting standards require interest to be imputed in the following situations:

- when a note is non-interest-bearing or no interest rate is stated
- when an interest rate is stated but the interest rate is unrealistically low[15]

In both cases, an accountant is required to view the substance of a lending transaction and cannot rely on the stated interest rate.

When a long-term, non-interest-bearing note is exchanged solely for cash, the note is assumed to have a present value equal to the cash proceeds. The difference between the cash proceeds and the face value of the note is recorded as a discount and amortized over the life of the note by the effective interest method. To apply the effective interest method, a company must determine the implicit (effective) interest rate of the note. Because the cash received is the present value of the note and the face value is the future value of the note at maturity, the effective (implicit) interest rate is the rate that equates the future value on the maturity date to the present value.

Example: Note Payable Issued for Cash

On January 1 of the current year, Backes Company issues a 3-year, non-interest-bearing note with a face value of $8,000 and receives $5,694.24 in exchange. Backes records the issuance of the note as follows:

Cash	5,694.24	
Discount on Notes Payable	2,305.76	
Notes Payable		8,000.00

The discount account is a contra account and is subtracted from the Notes Payable account on Backes's balance sheet to report the carrying (book) value of the note.[16]

In order to determine the implicit interest rate, Backes must solve for the interest rate that equates the present value of $5,694.24 with the future value of $8,000 at the end of 3 years. As demonstrated in the Time Value of Money Module, solve the following formula for the present value of 1 factor:

$$\text{Present Value} = \text{Future Value} \times \text{PV of 1 (3 periods, } i = ?)$$
$$\$5{,}694.24 = \$8{,}000 \times \text{PV of 1 (3 periods, } i = ?)$$
$$\$5{,}694.24 \div \$8{,}000 = \text{PV of 1 (3 periods, } i = ?)$$
$$0.711780 = \text{PV of a single sum (3 periods, } i = ?)$$

The value of 0.711780 is the present value of 1 factor from the Present Value of 1 Table in the Time Value of Money Module. The interest rate can be solved by reading across the 3 period row until the value 0.711780 is found. The present value factor represents an interest rate of 12%.

---

[15] FASB ASC 835-30-05-2: Interest, Imputation of Interest, Overview and Background.

[16] An alternative method is to record the Notes Payable account at its present value without the use of a Discount on Notes Payable account. In this case, the adjusting entries for interest involve a debit to Interest Expense and a credit directly to the Notes Payable account. When a company uses this method, it discloses the difference between the maturity value and the carrying value parenthetically on its balance sheet as the amount of the discount.

Backes computes the interest expense each year by multiplying the 12% effective interest rate by the carrying value at the beginning of the year. This amount also increases the carrying value of the note by reducing the discount. Backes computes the interest each year as follows:

	Year 1	Year 2	Year 3
Note payable	$ 8,000.00	$ 8,000.00	$ 8,000.00
Less: Unamortized discount	(2,305.76)	(1,622.45)[a]	(857.14)[b]
Carrying value at beginning of year	$ 5,694.24	$ 6,377.55	$ 7,142.86
Effective interest rate	× 0.12	× 0.12	× 0.12
Interest expense and discount amortization	$ 683.31	$ 765.31	$ 857.14

[a] $2,305.76 − $683.31
[b] $1,622.45 − $765.31

Backes records the $683.31 interest expense for the first year as follows:

| Interest Expense ($5,694.24 × 0.12) | 683.31 | |
| Discount on Notes Payable | | 683.31 |

Backes records interest expense for the next 2 years in the same way so that the Discount on Notes Payable account has a zero balance at the end of the third year. Therefore, the carrying value at the end of the third year is $8,000 (the face value of the note), and the repayment involves a debit to Notes Payable and credit to Cash for the $8,000 face value of the note. ■

Notes Payable Exchanged for Cash and Rights or Privileges

Long-term notes exchanged for cash may include special rights or privileges. A company must consider these rights or privileges when accounting for such long-term notes. For instance, a company might sign a contract with a customer in which the company borrows cash from the customer on a non-interest-bearing basis with the understanding that the customer has the right to purchase certain goods from the company at less than prevailing prices over the period of the contract. A portion of the consideration received from the customer for the note is, in essence, a prepayment for future purchases. For the company issuing the note:

- the note is recorded at its present value at the time of issuance by discounting the maturity value using the incremental interest rate of the borrower
- interest expense is recorded each period over the life of the note using the effective interest method
- the difference between the cash proceeds and the present value of the note is recorded as unearned revenue, and revenue is recognized over the life of the contract using appropriate revenue recognition criteria

For instance, revenue might be recognized on a per-unit basis as goods are sold, or evenly throughout the contract on a straight-line basis.

Example: Exchange for Cash and Rights or Privileges

Rose Company borrows $100,000 by issuing a 3-year, non-interest-bearing note to a customer. In addition, Rose agrees to sell fixed amounts of inventory to the customer at reduced prices over a 5-year period. Rose's incremental borrowing rate is 12%, so the present value of $100,000 to be repaid at the end of 3 years is $71,178 ($100,000 × 0.711780, from the Present Value of 1 Table). The customer agrees to purchase the fixed amounts of inventory each year over the 5-year period so that a straight-line method of revenue recognition is appropriate (any additional inventory purchases over the fixed amounts will be at the normal, undiscounted price). Rose records the following journal entries during the first 2 years:

Issuing the Note

Cash	100,000.00	
Discount on Notes Payable ($100,000 − $71,178)	28,822.00	
Notes Payable		100,000.00
Unearned Revenue		28,822.00

End of First Year

Interest Expense ($71,178 × 0.12)	8,541.36	
Discount on Notes Payable		8,541.36
Unearned Revenue ($28,822 ÷ 5 years)	5,764.40	
Sales Revenue		5,764.40

End of Second Year

Interest Expense [($71,178 + $8,541.36) × 0.12]	9,566.32	
Discount on Notes Payable		9,566.32
Unearned Revenue	5,764.40	
Sales Revenue		5,764.40

Recording the transactions according to these procedures results in the proper recognition of both the revenue and expense components, so the financial statements can provide relevant and representationally faithful information about this agreement. The company's income statement recognizes revenue as it earns it over the 5-year purchase agreement and recognizes the expense over the 3-year life of the loan. The company's balance sheet recognizes a liability for the present value of the note payable and a liability for the obligation associated with unearned revenue in the inventory purchase agreement.

Notes Payable Exchanged for Property, Goods, or Services

When a note is exchanged solely for property, goods, or services in an external transaction, GAAP says that the stated rate of interest should be presumed fair. This presumption can be overcome only if:

- no interest is stated, or
- stated rate of interest is clearly unreasonable, or
- face value of the note is materially different from the cash sales price of the property, goods, or services, or the fair value of the note, at the date of the transaction.[17]

In any of these cases, the note is recorded at the fair value of the property, goods, or services, or the fair value of the note, whichever can be measured with greater reliability. The interest rate implicit in the transaction is used to calculate the interest expense and the carrying value of the note each period using the effective interest method. If neither of these fair values is determinable, the note is recorded at its present value by discounting the future cash flow(s) using the incremental interest rate of the borrower. The incremental interest rate then is used to apply the effective interest method to determine the interest expense and the carrying value of the note.

If the liability and asset had been erroneously recorded at the face value of the note, both would be overstated in the current period. Additionally, this would result in an overstatement of depreciation expense (or cost of goods sold) and an understatement of interest expense over the life of the asset and note, respectively. Recording the asset and the note at fair (present) value results in correct asset and liability valuations and in the proper timing of expense recognition.

[17] FASB ASC 835-30-25: Interest, Imputation of Interest.

Example: Exchange for Property

On January 1, 2016, Madsen Company purchases used equipment from Jordan Company, issuing a non-interest-bearing, $10,000, 5-year note in exchange. Neither the fair value of the equipment nor that of the note is determinable, so Madsen uses its incremental interest rate to compute the present value. If Madsen's incremental borrowing rate is 12%, the present value of $10,000 to be repaid at the end of 5 years at 12% is $5,674.27 ($10,000 × 0.567427, from Present Value of 1 Table). Assume the remaining asset life is 10 years (no residual value). Madsen records the issuance of the note, the first two interest payments, and annual straight-line depreciation as follows:

January 1, 2016		
Equipment	5,674.27	
Discount on Notes Payable	4,325.73	
Notes Payable		10,000.00
December 31, 2016		
Interest Expense [($10,000 − $4,325.73) × 0.12]	680.91	
Discount on Notes Payable		680.91
Depreciation Expense	567.43	
Accumulated Depreciation ($5,674.27 ÷ 10)		567.43
December 31, 2017		
Interest Expense {[$10,000 − ($4,325.73 − $680.91)] × 0.12}	762.62	
Discount on Notes Payable		762.62
Depreciation Expense	567.43	
Accumulated Depreciation		567.43

This example assumes that a 12% interest rate is appropriate for the transaction, but a borrower should attempt to determine the fair values of the property and of the note before applying its incremental interest rate. If either the fair value of the property or of the note is used, the note payable is recorded at the fair value, and the company must find the implicit interest rate that equates the recorded (fair) value to the face value over the term of the loan.

For example, assume in the previous example that Madsen determines that the fair value of the equipment is $6,209.21. From the Present Value of 1 Table, the rate that equates $6,209.21 to $10,000 at the end of 5 years is 10%.[18] Madsen would record the note payable initially at $6,209.21, and then would record the interest expense of 10% on the carrying value of the note each year over the life of the note.

This example also assumes the issuance of a non-interest-bearing note. As discussed earlier, the same principles apply in the case where a note carries a stated interest rate that is unreasonable. For example, assume that on January 1, 2016, Fox Company issues a $30,000, 3-year note bearing interest of 2% for equipment when its incremental borrowing rate is 10%. If the fair value of the equipment or the note is not determinable, Fox records the transaction using the present value of the future cash flows with the 10% rate for the 3-year life. In this case, it records the equipment and note at $24,031.56 [($30,000 face value × 0.751315) + ($600 annual interest × 2.486852)]. It then applies the effective interest method using the 10% rate at the end of each year to determine the interest expense. For instance, at the end of 2016, it debits Interest Expense for $2,403.16 ($24,031.56 × 0.10), credits Cash for $600 ($30,000 × 0.02), and increases the book value of the note by $1,803.16. ∎

Guarantees

Sometimes a company may **guarantee** another company's debt. For example, suppose Fischer Company sells a product to Metcalf Company for $10 million. Since Metcalf does not have sufficient cash, it decides to obtain a bank loan to finance the purchase. However, its financial status is such that the bank will not provide an unsecured loan. So

---

[18] $6,209.21/$10,000 = 0.620921. In the n = 5 row, we find 0.620921 in the 10% column.

ETHICAL DILEMMA

TLM, Inc., a struggling software development company, has been experiencing cash flow problems. To address working capital deficiencies, TLM entered into an agreement with one of its customers, Sunrise, Inc., and issued a 2-year, non-interest-bearing note with a face value of $5,000,000 and received $4,853,310 in exchange. This equates to an effective (implicit) interest rate of 1.5%. TLM's normal borrowing rate is 10%. As the accountant for TLM, you question how the company obtained such a low interest rate and learn that the CEO made an oral side-agreement with Sunrise to provide free software support (e.g., installation, troubleshooting) over the next 5 years. You therefore conclude that the note and future interest charges should be recorded at the market interest of 10%, resulting in larger yearly interest charges. Furthermore, the value of the software support should be recorded as unearned revenue and recognized over the next 5 years. Upper management disagrees with your conclusion and tells you that the interest expense required under your assessment would turn the company's small positive net income into a net loss, as well as cause TLM to be in violation of existing debt covenants. Furthermore, the CEO states that the verbal agreement is nonbinding and to record revenue in such a situation would be earnings management. The CEO instructs you to record the transaction as if the side-agreement did not exist. What are your responsibilities?

Fischer agrees to guarantee Metcalf's loan from the bank so that it can make the sale. GAAP requires Fischer to determine the fair value of the guarantee and recognize it as a liability.[19] The company has a liability because it has an obligation to "stand ready" to perform over the life of the guarantee if the specific triggering events or conditions occur. For Fischer, it would have to repay the bank loan if Metcalf defaulted. In addition to recognizing a liability, Fischer would reduce the profit it recognizes on the sale.

GAAP does not explicitly state how the guarantee is to be accounted for in future periods. However, it is presumed that the company would determine the fair value each period and recognize the change in value in its income for the period. In most situations, the fair value would decrease each period and a gain would be recognized.

GAAP also requires the company to make certain disclosures including the nature of the guarantee, its approximate term, how it arose, and the events or circumstances that would require the company to perform under the guarantee. Other disclosures include the maximum potential future undiscounted payments that the company could be required to make and the current carrying value of the liability. This GAAP does not apply to some guarantees, such as insurance and warranty contracts.

GOT IT?

14-21 When a company exchanges a long-term, non-interest-bearing note for cash and no interest rate is stated, how does it determine the effective interest?

14-22 Describe the steps necessary for a company to determine the value at which to record a non-interest-bearing note payable exchanged for property, goods, or services.

14-23 What is the incremental interest rate of a borrower? When and for what calculations is this rate used if a company exchanges a note for property, goods, or services?

WHAT SHOULD BE DISCLOSED FOR LONG-TERM LIABILITIES?

LEARNING OBJECTIVE 14.9
Understand the disclosure of long-term liabilities.

We discussed how balance sheets report long-term financing from bonds and notes payable earlier in the chapter. However, companies' balance sheets often disclose the book value of the liability net of any premiums or discounts and do not separately disclose the premiums or discounts. We also discussed how company income statements report any gains or losses on the retirement of long-term liabilities.

---
[19] FASB ASC 460-10: Guarantees.

Companies generally report cash flows associated with long-term liability transactions in the financing section of the statement of cash flows:

- Cash received from the issuance of notes payable or bonds payable—whether issued at face value, at a premium, or at a discount—is reported as a cash inflow from financing activities.
- Cash paid to retire bonds payable or notes payable is reported as a cash outflow for financing activities.

Cash paid for interest, however, is included in the operating activities section. Even though the interest paid is related to a financing activity, GAAP requires it to be included in operating activities because the related interest expense is included in the company's income statement. Under IFRS, firms have the option of disclosing interest payments in either the operating or financing activities section of the cash flow statement. However, once a decision is made it must be applied consistently.

If a company has amortized a discount (premium) on bonds payable, under the indirect method for the statement of cash flows, the company adds (subtracts) the amortization of the discount (premium) to net income in the operating activities section. It also includes any gains or losses on the retirement of its long-term liabilities as adjustments to net income in the operating activities section of its statement of cash flows when prepared using the indirect method. If a company converts bonds into common stock, it discloses this transaction as a noncash financing activity.

A company also must disclose the various characteristics of its long-term debt. It normally does so in the notes to its financial statements. Real Report 14.3 shows **Nike**'s disclosure of its long-term debt. Also included are disclosures about scheduled repayments of long-term debt, interest payments, capitalized interest, and lines of credit.

14.3 DISCLOSURE OF DEBT — REAL REPORT

Nike

Note 8 — Long-Term Debt

Long-term debt, net of unamortized premiums and discounts and swap fair value adjustments, comprises the following:

Scheduled Maturity (Dollars in millions)	Original Principal	Interest Rate	Interest Payments	Book Value Outstanding As of May 31, 2013	2012
Corporate Bond Payables:[4]					
July 23, 2012[1]	$ 25	5.66%	Semi-Annually	$ —	$ 25
August 7, 2012[1]	$ 15	5.40%	Semi-Annually	—	15
October 1, 2013	$ 50	4.70%	Semi-Annually	50	50
October 15, 2015[1]	$ 100	5.15%	Semi-Annually	111	115
May 1, 2023[5]	$ 500	2.25%	Semi-Annually	499	—
May 1, 2043[5]	$ 500	3.63%	Semi-Annually	499	—
Promissory Notes:[2]					
April 1, 2017	$ 40	6.20%	Monthly	40	—
January 1, 2018	$ 19	6.79%	Monthly	19	—
Japanese Yen Notes:					
August 20, 2001 through November 20, 2020[3]	¥9,000	2.60%	Quarterly	34	50
August 20, 2001 through November 20, 2020[3]	¥4,000	2.00%	Quarterly	15	22
Total				1,267	277
Less current maturities				57	49
TOTAL LONG-TERM DEBT				**$ 1,210**	**$ 228**

(1) *The Company has entered into interest rate swap agreements whereby the Company receives fixed interest payments at the same rate as the note and pays variable interest payments based on the six-month LIBOR plus a spread. The swaps have the same notional amount and maturity date as the corresponding note. At May 31, 2013, the interest rates payable on these swap agreements ranged from approximately 0.3% to 0.4%.*

(2) *The Company assumed a total of $59 million in bonds payable on May 30, 2013 as part of its agreement to purchase certain Corporate properties, which was treated as a non-cash financing transaction. The property serves as collateral for the debt. The purchase of these properties was accounted for as a business combination where the total consideration of $85 million was allocated to the land and buildings acquired; no other tangible or intangible assets or liabilities resulted from the purchase. The bonds mature in 2017 and 2018 and the Company does not have the ability to re-negotiate the terms of the debt agreements and would incur significant financial penalties if the notes are paid off prior to maturity.*

(3) *NIKE Logistics YK assumed a total of ¥13.0 billion in loans as part of its agreement to purchase a distribution center in Japan, which serves as collateral for the loans. These loans mature in equal quarterly installments during the period August 20, 2001 through November 20, 2020.*

(4) *Senior unsecured obligations rank equally with our other unsecured and unsubordinated indebtedness.*

(5) *The bonds carry a make whole call provision and are redeemable at any time prior to maturity. The bonds also feature a par call provision payable 3 months and 6 months prior to the scheduled maturity date for the bonds maturing on May 1, 2023 and May 1, 2043, respectively.*

The scheduled maturity of long-term debt in each of the years ending May 31, 2014 through 2018 are $57 million, $7 million, $108 million, $45 million and $25 million, respectively, at face value.

The fair value of the Company's long-term debt, including the current portion, was approximately $1,219 million at May 31, 2013 and $283 million at May 31, 2012.

The fair value of long-term debt is estimated based upon quoted prices of similar instruments (level 2).

Questions:

Suggested answers to these questions are found at the end of the chapter.

1. As of May 31, 2013, approximately what percentage of Nike's long-term debt will be coming due over its next 5 fiscal years?
2. Was Nike's long-term corporate bonds payable due in 2023 and 2024 issued at a premium or discount?
3. What amount of interest does Nike pay each month on its promissory notes?

GOT IT?

14-24 When a company retires long-term financing liabilities, what information should be reported on the statement of cash flows?

14-25 How do GAAP and IFRS differ in the reporting of interest expense on the statement of cash flows?

APPENDIX 14.1: TROUBLED DEBT RESTRUCTURINGS

LEARNING OBJECTIVE 14.10
Understand troubled debt restructurings.

Some companies experiencing difficulty in repaying long-term debt obligations enter into financial arrangements with their creditors in order to avoid bankruptcy. GAAP states that a **troubled debt restructuring** occurs when a creditor for economic or legal reasons related to a debtor's financial difficulties grants a concession to the debtor that it would not otherwise consider. A troubled debt restructuring may include, but is not limited to, one or any combination of the following:

- **modification of terms** of a debt, such as:
  - reduction of the stated interest rate for the remaining original life of the debt
  - extension of the maturity date at a stated interest rate lower than the current market rate for new debt with similar risk
  - reduction of the face amount or maturity amount of the debt
  - reduction of accrued interest
- issuance or other granting of an equity interest to the creditor by the debtor to satisfy a debt unless the equity interest is granted under existing terms for converting the debt into an equity interest
- transfer of receivables, real estate, or other assets from the debtor to the creditor to satisfy a debt[20]

How Does a Debtor Account for Troubled Debt Restructuring?

We first discuss the debtor's accounting for a troubled debt restructuring. Later we discuss the creditor's accounting.

Modification of Terms When a restructuring agreement involves only a modification of terms, the carrying value of the liability (face value of the debt plus any unpaid accrued interest) is compared to the undiscounted future cash payments (principal plus interest) specified by the new terms:

- If the undiscounted total future cash payments are equal to or greater than the carrying value of the liability, the debtor does not recognize a gain, the carrying value of the liability is not reduced, and interest expense is recognized in future periods using an imputed interest rate.
- If the future cash payments are less than the carrying value of the liability, the debtor recognizes a gain, the carrying value of the liability is reduced, and interest expense is not recognized in future periods.

When there is a modification of terms and the total cash to be repaid over the remaining life of the loan is equal to or greater than the carrying value of the liability, the debtor completes the following steps:

- Debtor makes no adjustment to the carrying value.
- Debtor recognizes annual interest expense using the effective interest method. The imputed interest rate used is the rate that equates the total amount of cash to be paid with the current carrying value of the debt.
- Debtor records a portion of each cash payment as interest expense and records the remainder as a reduction in the carrying value of the liability.

Example: No Gain Recognized by the Debtor

On December 31, 2016, Chapin Company restructures a $1,178,073 debt with its bank (a note payable of $1,100,000 plus accrued interest of $78,073). The bank makes the following modifications:

- forgives the $78,073 of accrued interest and $100,000 of principal
- extends the maturity date from December 31, 2016, to December 31, 2021
- reduces the interest rate from 10% to 8%

The total future cash payments under the new terms are $1,400,000 (principal of $1,000,000 at the end of 5 years and interest of $80,000 at the end of each year for 5 years). Because the *undiscounted* amount of the principal and interest to be paid ($1,400,000) exceeds the carrying value of the liability ($1,178,073), Chapin does not record a gain and, therefore, does not reduce the carrying value of the liability. It records

---

[20] For debtors this topic is covered in FASB ASC 470-60: Debt, Troubled Restructurings by Debtors. For creditors this topic is covered in FASB ASC 310-40: Receivables, Troubled Debt Restructurings by Creditors.

the difference of $221,927 as interest expense over the next 5 years by using the effective interest method. It determines the interest expense each period by multiplying the effective interest rate times the carrying value at the beginning of the period.

The effective interest rate is that rate which discounts the principal of $1,000,000 and the interest payments of $80,000 to the $1,178,073 carrying value of the note. This discounting procedure involves two present value calculations, as summarized in Exhibit 14.5.

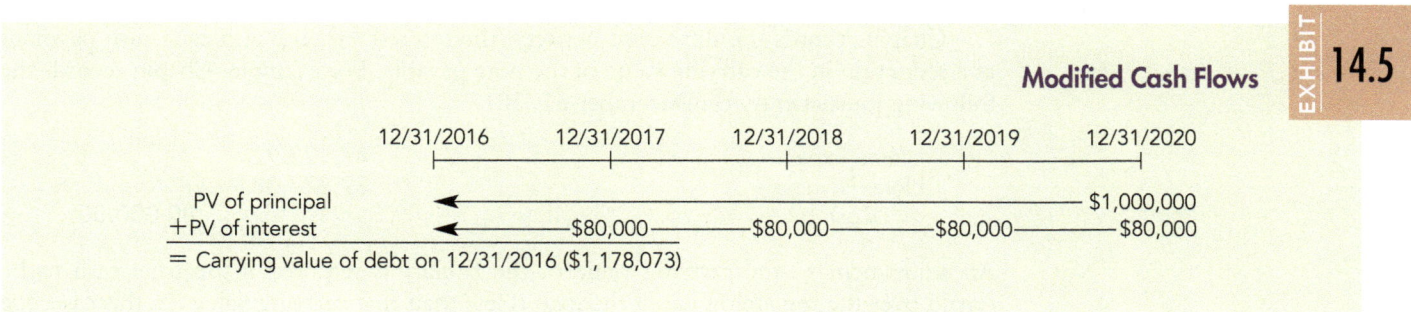

Modified Cash Flows — EXHIBIT 14.5

This rate is 4%, as demonstrated below.

Present Value of Interest Payments:
(Present Value of an Ordinary Annuity Table in
 Time Value of Money Module, n = 5, i = 0.04) $80,000 × 4.451822 = $ 356,146
Present Value of Principal:
(Present Value of 1 Table in Time Value of Money
 Module, n = 5, i = 0.04) $1,000,000 × 0.821927 =   821,927
Carrying Value of the Debt on 12/31/2016 $1,178,073

On December 31, 2016, Chapin transfers the accrued Interest Payable balance to the Notes Payable account as follows:

Interest Payable	78,073	
Notes Payable		78,073

The Notes Payable account now contains the entire $1,178,073 carrying value of the note. Chapin computes the interest expense to be recorded in each period by applying the effective interest rate of 4% to the carrying value of the note each year. **Example 14.3** illustrates the computation of the interest expense and principal reduction for each year of Chapin's restructuring agreement.

EXAMPLE 14.3

Debt Restructuring Agreement: Schedule to Compute Interest Expense

Date	Cash Credit[a]	Interest Expense Debit[b]	Notes Payable Debit[c]	Carrying Value of Note[d]
12/31/16				$1,178,073.00
12/31/17	$ 80,000	$47,122.92	$ 32,877.08	1,145,195.92
12/31/18	80,000	45,807.84	34,192.16	1,111,003.76
12/31/19	80,000	44,440.15	35,559.85	1,075,443.91
12/31/20	80,000	43,017.76	36,982.24	1,038,461.67
12/31/21	1,080,000	41,538.33[e]	1,038,461.67	0

[a] Cash payments are specified in the terms of restructuring agreement.
[b] Previous carrying value times the effective interest rate of 4%.
[c] Cash payment amount minus the amount attributable to interest expense.
[d] Previous carrying value of the note minus the amount of the cash payment attributable to reducing the note payable balance.
[e] Difference of $0.14 due to rounding.

In reviewing **Example 14.3**, note that each cash payment is separated into its interest and principal components as follows:

$$\text{Carrying Value} \times \text{Imputed Interest Rate} = \text{Interest Expense}$$
$$\$1{,}178{,}073.00 \times 4\% = \$47{,}122.92$$

$$\text{Modified Cash Interest Payment} - \text{Interest Expense} = \text{Principal Reduction}$$
$$\$80{,}000.00 - \$47{,}122.92 = \$32{,}877.08$$

Chapin records the difference between the interest expense and each cash payment as a reduction in the carrying value of the note payable. For example, Chapin records the following journal entry on December 31, 2017:

Interest Expense	47,122.92	
Notes Payable	32,877.08	
Cash		80,000.00

An adjustment to the carrying value of the liability is required if the total cash to be repaid over the remaining life of the loan is less than that carrying value. In this case, the debtor recognizes a gain equal to the excess of the carrying value (face value plus accrued interest) over the sum of the future payments. ∎

Example: Gain Recognized by the Debtor

Assume that Chapin was allowed the terms stated previously (reduction of principal by $100,000, forgiveness of $78,073 of accrued interest, and extension of repayment period by 5 years) except that the stated interest rate was reduced to 3%. The aggregate future cash payments in this case total $1,150,000 ($1,000,000 principal and $30,000 interest per year for 5 years). This amount is $28,073 less than the carrying value of $1,178,073 ($1,100,000 face value + $78,073 accrued interest). Chapin reports this amount as a gain in its income from continuing operations for 2016, eliminates the accrued interest, and credits the difference between the gain and the accrued interest to the Notes Payable account so that the balance is now $1,150,000. Chapin records the restructuring on December 31, 2016, as follows:

Interest Payable	78,073	
Notes Payable		50,000
Gain on Debt Restructure		28,073

Each future cash payment reduces the carrying value of the payable, and Chapin does not recognize interest expense since the effective interest rate is 0%. That is, since the amount to be repaid is less than the original carrying value of the liability, the creditor is, in effect, accepting repayment without an accompanying interest charge. Chapin records the first cash payment on December 31, 2017, as follows:

Notes Payable	30,000	
Cash		30,000

The reduction of the Notes Payable account by $30,000 each year for 5 years will reduce this account to $1,000,000. This amount will then be eliminated at the time of the lump-sum principal payment at the end of the fifth year. ∎

Equity or Asset Exchange When a debtor satisfies a liability by exchanging an equity interest or an asset of lesser value, it records the transfer on the basis of the fair value of the equity interest or asset transferred and recognizes a gain on the debt restructuring. Also, when an asset is exchanged, if the fair value is greater or less than its carrying value, the debtor also records a gain or loss on the disposal of the asset.

Example: Equity Exchange

On December 31, 2016, Chapin repays the note payable and the accrued interest totaling $1,178,073 by issuing 35,000 shares of its own common stock to the bank. The shares have a par value of $10 per share and are selling currently for $25 per share on the open market. Chapin records the stock at the fair value of $875,000 (35,000 shares × $25), reduces the liability by $1,178,073, and recognizes a gain of $303,073 ($1,178,073 − $875,000). Chapin records the debt restructuring as follows:

Notes Payable	1,100,000	
Interest Payable	78,073	
Common Stock (35,000 × $10)		350,000
Additional Paid-In Capital on Common Stock		525,000
Gain on Debt Restructure		303,073

Example: Asset Exchange

Assume the same information as the equity exchange except that Chapin repays the liability by transferring land it owns to the bank. The land has a fair value of $800,000 and cost Chapin $600,000 5 years ago. Chapin recognizes a gain of $378,073 ($1,178,073 − $800,000) on the restructuring and a gain of $200,000 ($800,000 − $600,000) on the disposal of the land. Chapin records the debt restructuring as follows:

Notes Payable	1,100,000	
Interest Payable	78,073	
Gain on Debt Restructure		378,073
Gain on Disposal of Land		200,000
Land		600,000

Equity or Asset Exchange Combined with a Modification of Terms A troubled debt restructuring can include an equity or asset exchange as well as a modification of terms. In this case, the following steps are necessary:

- Debtor records the equity or asset transfer first at the fair value as we discussed previously.
- Debtor compares the remaining carrying value of the liability, after deducting the fair value of the equity or assets transferred, to the total undiscounted future cash payments specified under the new terms.
    - If the remaining carrying value is less than the total payments, the debtor does not recognize a gain, does not reduce the carrying value of the liability, and recognizes interest expense in future periods using an imputed interest rate.
    - If the remaining carrying value is greater than the total payments, the debtor recognizes a gain and reduces the carrying value of the liability, but does not record interest expense in future periods.

The accounting procedures to be followed in these two situations are the same as those discussed earlier.

Disclosure of Restructuring Agreements The following disclosures are required for debtors who have entered into restructuring agreements:

- description of the principal changes in terms and/or the major features of settlement for each restructuring agreement
- aggregate gain on debt restructures and the related income tax effect
- per share amount of the aggregate gain on restructuring, net of the related income tax effect
- aggregate gain or loss recognized during the period on transfers of assets
- information on any contingent payments[21]

---

[21] For debtors this topic is covered in FASB ASC 470-60-50: Debt, Troubled Restructurings by Debtors, Disclosure. For creditors this topic is covered in FASB ASC 310-40-50: Receivables, Troubled Debt Restructurings by Creditors, Disclosure.

The following is an example of the disclosure required for Chapin's exchange of equity securities discussed previously (ignoring income taxes):

> During the year, Chapin Company gave common stock with a fair value of $875,000 to the bank in exchange for full settlement of a 10% note in the amount of $1,100,000 and accrued interest of $78,073. As a result of this exchange, the company recognized a gain of $303,073 and increased earnings per share by $0.11.

How Does a Creditor Account for Troubled Debt Restructuring?

Under GAAP, some of the elements of accounting for the creditor in a troubled debt restructuring are the mirror image of that for the debtor, while other elements are quite different.

Modification of Terms The accounting for a modification of terms differs for debtors and creditors because the creditor must recognize a new value for the loan. In this case, the creditor completes the following steps:

- Creditor values the investment in the restructured loan by discounting the total future cash flows specified by the new contractual terms to their present value.
- Creditor records a loss as the difference between the present value of the future cash flows and the carrying value of the receivable.
- Creditor uses the original (contractual) interest rate on the loan (i.e., the same interest rate used for a loan impairment) as the effective interest rate in the present value calculation, and not the rate specified in the restructuring agreement.[22]

A loan whose terms are modified in a troubled debt restructuring usually will have been identified as impaired in a previous period. We discussed the GAAP for an impaired loan in Chapter 13.

Example: Modification of Terms

To illustrate the accounting for a modification of terms in a troubled debt restructuring, consider the first Chapin example. Assume that the loan was from Tenth National Bank and that the bank has not recognized a previous impairment. The bank's note receivable is $1,100,000 and the accrued interest is $78,073. On December 31, 2016, the bank restructures the note so that the new principal is $1,000,000, payable in 5 years, with an interest rate of 8% (i.e., the annual interest payment is $80,000). Since 10% is the original interest rate on the loan to Chapin, the loan is valued as follows:

Present Value of Principal = $1,000,000 × Present Value of a Single Sum for 5 Years at 10% (from the Present Value of 1 Table)
= $1,000,000 × 0.620921
= $620,921.00

Present Value of Interest = $80,000 × Present Value of an Annuity for 5 Years at 10% (from the Present Value of an Ordinary Annuity of 1 Table)
= $80,000 × 3.790787
= $303,262.96

Value of the Restructured Loan = $620,921.00 + $303,262.96
= $924,183.96

---

[22] FASB ASC 310-40-35: Receivables, Troubled Debt Restructurings by Creditors, Subsequent Remeasurement.

On December 31, 2016, the bank records a loss of $253,889.04 ($1,178,073 − $924,183.96) on the restructuring as follows:

Loss on Restructured Loan	253,889.04	
Interest Receivable		78,073.00
Notes Receivable		175,816.04

The carrying value of Notes Receivable is now $924,183.96 ($1,100,000 − $175,816.04).

In later periods, the bank earns interest at the original rate of 10% applied to the current carrying value. The bank recognizes interest revenue for 2017 of $92,418.40 (10% × $924,183.96) on December 31, 2017, as follows:

Cash	80,000.00	
Notes Receivable	12,418.40	
Interest Revenue		92,418.40

After 5 years of recording interest under the effective interest method, Notes Receivable will grow to the principal amount of $1,000,000. ■

It is important to note the following difference between the accounting by the debtor and creditor for a modification of terms:

- Debtor does *not* record the liability at a present value and, therefore, either recognizes no interest expense at all or recognizes an interest expense that is based on a below-market rate that was never part of the contractual agreement.
- Creditor records the receivable at a present value and, therefore, recognizes interest revenue at the original contractual rate.

Equity or Asset Exchange The accounting by the creditor (e.g., the bank) for a troubled debt restructuring that involves an equity or asset exchange is a mirror image of the accounting by the debtor. Thus, when a creditor receives an equity interest or asset to satisfy the receivable, the creditor records the equity or asset investment at fair value, eliminates the carrying value of the receivable, and recognizes a loss.

Example 14.4 shows the journal entries used by Tenth National Bank to record the equity and asset exchanges for the troubled debt restructuring of Chapin Company. It is helpful to observe the mirror image by contrasting the bank's journal entries with those of Chapin shown earlier.

EXAMPLE 14.4

Creditor Journal Entries for Troubled Debt Restructuring

Equity Exchange			
12/31/16	Investment in Chapin	875,000	
	Loss on Restructured Loan	303,073	
	Notes Receivable		1,100,000
	Interest Receivable		78,073
Asset Exchange			
12/31/16	Land	800,000	
	Loss on Restructured Loan	378,073	
	Notes Receivable		1,100,000
	Interest Receivable		78,073

Equity or Asset Exchange Combined with Modification of Terms When an equity interest or asset is received and a modification of terms is made, the creditor completes the following steps:

- *Step 1.* Creditor records the equity or asset first at its fair value.
- *Step 2.* Creditor then discounts the future cash receipts to their present value at the effective (contractual) rate of interest.

- *Step 3.* Creditor records a loss as the difference between the carrying value of the receivable and the sum of the fair value of the equity interest or asset plus the present value of the future cash flows.

Exhibit 14.6 provides a summary of the GAAP we have discussed.

EXHIBIT 14.6 Creditor Accounting for Troubled Debt Restructuring

	Modification of Terms		Equity or Asset Exchange	
	Debtor	**Creditor**	**Debtor**	**Creditor**
(a)	If undiscounted cash flows ≥ carrying value, no gain and impute new interest rate	Compute present value using the original (contractual) interest rate	Record at fair value, recognize gain	Record at fair value, recognize loss
(b)	If undiscounted cash flows ≤ carrying value, recognize gain (no interest recognized)			

Conceptual Evaluation of Accounting for Troubled Debt Restructurings

When the original GAAP was issued, many accountants and financial statement users criticized the accounting principles for troubled debt restructurings. With the issuance of revised GAAP, these criticisms apply only to the accounting by the debtor because there is no longer a mirror image between the debtor and creditor, as discussed earlier. The critics argue that the GAAP for the debtor (i.e., a limited or no gain) leads to inconsistencies in recording events that have similar economic substance (i.e., a modification of terms and an asset or equity exchange). They view a modification of terms as an economic event that should be recorded at a present value. In other words, they argue that the debtor should follow the GAAP that is now required for the creditor.

At the time that the original GAAP was issued, it was widely believed that the rules to be followed by the creditor in a modification of terms were the result of lobbying by financial institutions. These institutions argued that the recognition of large losses under the fair value approach would undermine the public's confidence in the banking system and have an adverse effect on the economy. A counterargument was that the nonrecognition of losses enabled banks to continue in business longer than they should have, resulting in larger payments by taxpayers to "bail out" failing banks.

Since the GAAP for the creditor has now been superceded, it seems logical that the GAAP for the debtor should also be modified. However, some supporters of the original GAAP point out that the FASB was just being conservative in its approach so as to minimize the gain recognized by a financially distressed debtor in a restructuring. Therefore, the choice of the GAAP for debtors is based on whether a person believes that conservatism or the recognition of fair value is more important to external decision makers.

GOT IT?

14-26 When does a troubled debt restructuring occur? What three conditions may be involved in a troubled debt restructuring?

14-27 Under what conditions would a debtor company recognize a gain after modifying the terms of its borrowing agreement?

REVIEW CENTER

At the beginning of the chapter, we discussed how the use of debt can benefit shareholders by increasing the company's return on equity. However, the use of debt makes the company more risky. We also identified several objectives you would accomplish after reading the chapter. The objectives are listed below and followed by a brief summary of the key points.

KEY TAKEAWAYS

- Companies issue long-term debt for a variety of reasonsy:
  - Debt may be the only source of financing for the company.
  - Debt may have a lower cost of capital than equity.
  - Debt may provide income tax benefits.
  - Debt does not carry voting rights.
  - Debt increases financial leverage.

LEARNING OBJECTIVE 14.1
Explain the reasons for issuing long-term financing liabilities, such as bonds and notes payable.

KEY TERMS

capital structure, p. 14-1
financial leverage, p. 14-1
financial liabilities, p. 14-2

KEY TAKEAWAYS

- A bond is a type of debt instrument in which a company agrees to pay the holder the face value at the maturity date and usually to pay interest periodically at a specified rate on the face value.
- The face value (or par value) is the amount of money that the issuer agrees to pay at maturity.
- The maturity date is the date on which the issuer of the bond agrees to pay the face value to the holder.
- The contract rate is the rate at which the issuer of the bonds agrees to pay interest each period until maturity.
- When bonds are issued, companies usually enlist an underwriter to negotiate the bond terms and sell the bonds.
- The effective rate (yield) is the market rate at which the bonds are actually sold.

LEARNING OBJECTIVE 14.2
Understand the characteristics of bonds payable.

KEY TERMS

bond, p. 14-3
bond certificate, p. 14-3
bond indenture, p. 14-3
contract rate, p. 14-3
effective rate, p. 14-4
face rate, p. 14-3

face value, p. 14-3
maturity date, p. 14-3
nominal rate, p. 14-3
par value, p. 14-3
stated rate, p. 14-3
yield, p. 14-4

KEY TAKEAWAYS

- The selling price of a bond is based on the relationship between the yield (effective rate) and the contract rate of interest.
- If the yield is equal to the contract rate, the bonds sell at par and the periodic interest expense is equal to the interest paid.
- If the yield is lower than the contract rate, the bonds sell at a premium and the periodic interest expense is less than the interest paid.

LEARNING OBJECTIVE 14.3
Compute the issue price of bonds payable.

- If the yield is greater than the contract rate, the bonds sell at a discount and the periodic interest expense is greater than the interest paid.
- For both premiums and discounts, the straight-line method results in a constant amount of interest expense each semiannual period even though the book value of the liability changes each period.
- The straight-line method results in the same interest entry being made on each interest date.
- At the bond's maturity date, the company will pay the principal amount of the bonds payable to the creditor and debit Bonds Payable and credit Cash.

KEY TERMS

at a discount, p. 14-5
at a premium, p. 14-5
at par, p. 14-5

LEARNING OBJECTIVE 14.4
Record the issuance of bonds payable.

KEY TAKEAWAYS

- The book value of a bond is the face value plus any unamortized premium or minus any unamortized discount.
- At the time of sale, the company records the face value of the bonds in a Bonds Payable account, and it records any premium or discount in a separate account entitled Premium on Bonds Payable or Discount on Bonds Payable.
- A premium account is an adjunct account, and a discount account is a contra account.
- When a bond is sold between interest payment dates, the issuing company will normally collect the selling price plus any accrued interest since the last interest payment date.

KEY CALCULATIONS

Book Value for Bonds Issued at a Premium = Bond Face Value + Unamortized Premium

Book Value for Bonds Issued at a Discount = Bond Face Value − Unamortized Discount

LEARNING OBJECTIVE 14.5
Amortize bond discounts and bond premiums.

KEY TAKEAWAYS

- Under the effective interest method, interest expense is calculated by multiplying the effective interest rate by the beginning of period book value.
- The discount or premium amortization is the difference between the interest expense and the cash payment.
- For both premiums and discounts, the straight-line method results in a constant amount of interest expense each interest period even though the book value of the liability changes each period.
- The straight-line method results in the same interest entry being made on each interest date.
- Debt issuance costs are presented as a direct deduction from the carrying value of the debt and amortized to Interest Expense over the life of the bond issue by either the straight-line or effective interest methods of amortization.
- GAAP and IFRS allow a company to value any financial instrument, including its financial liabilities, at fair value.

KEY CALCULATIONS

Effective Interest Expense for Interest Period = Book Value of Bonds at Beginning of Period × Effective Interest Rate for Interest Period

Effective Interest Premium Amortization per Period = Contractual Interest − Effective Interest

Effective Interest Discount Amortization per Period = Contractual Interest + Effective Interest

Straight-Line Premium Amortization per Period = Total Premium/Number of Interest Periods

Straight-Line Discount Amortization per Period = Total Discount/Number of Interest Periods

KEY TERMS

book value, p. 14-10
carrying value, p. 14-10
debt-to-assets ratio, p. 14-12

effective interest method, p. 14-10
straight-line method, p. 14-10
times-interest-earned ratio, p. 14-12

KEY TAKEAWAYS

LEARNING OBJECTIVE 14.6
Explain extinguishment of liabilities.

- A liability is extinguished for financial reporting purposes when either (1) the debtor pays the creditor and is relieved of its obligation for the liability, or (2) the debtor is released legally from being the primary obligor under the liability.
- If bonds are extinguished prior to their maturity date, any difference between the book value of the bonds and the amount paid to retire the bonds is recognized as either a gain or loss in income from continuing operations.

KEY CALCULATIONS

Loss on Bond Redemption = Call Price − Carrying Value of Bonds Payable on Redemption Date
(if carrying value of bonds payable on redemption date is greater than call price record a gain)

KEY TERMS

call provision, p. 14-19

defeasance, p. 14-20

KEY TAKEAWAYS

LEARNING OBJECTIVE 14.7
Understand bonds with equity characteristics.

- A company may issue bonds that allow creditors to ultimately become shareholders by attaching stock warrants to the bonds or including a conversion feature. In either case, the investor has acquired the right to receive principal payments and interest on the bonds and the right to either acquire common stock by exercising the warrants or by converting the bonds into common equity shares.
- If bonds are issued with detachable stock warrants that give the bondholder the option to acquire shares of stock, the issue price is allocated between the bonds and the warrants based on their relative fair values.
- In most cases, GAAP requires that the issuance of such bonds is accounted for solely as debt due to the inseparability of the debt and conversion options and the lack of sufficiently reliable market valuations.
- Companies may record the conversion of bonds into stock using either the book value method (the equity is recorded at the book value of the debt) or the market value method (the equity is recorded at market value, which generally results in a loss).
- When convertible bonds are issued with a beneficial conversion, or issued at a significant premium or may be settled with a cash payment, an equity component should be recognized at issuance.
- The company estimates the debt component as equal to the fair value of a similar bond without a conversion feature. The difference between this amount and the selling price of the bond is allocated to Additional Paid-In Capital: Conversion Feature.

KEY CALCULATIONS

For bonds issued with detachable warrants:

$$\text{Amount Assigned to Bonds} = \frac{\text{Market Value of Bonds without Warrants}}{\text{Market Value of Bonds without Warrants} + \text{Market Value of Warrants}} \times \text{Issuance Price}$$

$$\text{Amount Assigned to Warrants} = \frac{\text{Market Value of Warrants}}{\text{Market Value of Bonds without Warrants} + \text{Market Value of Warrants}} \times \text{Issuance Price}$$

Amount Assigned to Bonds + Amount Assigned to Warrants = Issuance Price

KEY TERMS

conversion, p. 14-20
convertible bonds, p. 14-22
stock warrants, p. 14-20

LEARNING OBJECTIVE 14.8
Account for long-term notes payable.

KEY TAKEAWAYS

- A note payable is recorded at its present value, and the effective interest method is used to record the subsequent interest.
- When a note is exchanged for cash and special rights or privileges, these rights and privileges represent unearned revenue (measured as the difference between the cash proceeds and the present value of the note), which is recognized over the life of the contract.
- A note exchanged for property, goods, or services is recorded at the fair value of the property, goods, or services, or the fair value of the note, whichever can be measured with greater reliability. If neither of these fair values is determinable, the note is recorded at its present value by discounting the future cash flow(s) using the incremental interest rate of the borrower.

KEY TERMS

guarantee, p. 14-32
imputed interest rate, p. 14-29

LEARNING OBJECTIVE 14.9
Understand the disclosure of long-term liabilities.

KEY TAKEAWAYS

- A company must disclose many characteristics of its long-term debt, including the book value, interest rates, maturity dates, scheduled repayments for each of the next 5 years, interest expense, interest paid, and capitalized interest.
- It normally makes these disclosures in the notes to its financial statements.

LEARNING OBJECTIVE 14.10
(Appendix 14.1) Understand troubled debt restructurings.

KEY TAKEAWAYS

- A troubled debt restructuring occurs when a creditor, for economic or legal reasons related to a debtor's financial difficulties, grants a concession to the debtor that it would not otherwise consider.
- A troubled debt restructuring may include a modification of terms, the issuance or other granting of an equity interest, and the transfer of an asset.
- If the future cash payments are less than the carrying value of the liability, the debtor recognizes a gain, the carrying value of the liability is reduced, and interest expense is not recognized in future periods.
- If the undiscounted total future cash payments are equal to or greater than the carrying value of the liability, the debtor does not recognize a gain, the carrying value of the liability is not reduced, and interest expense is recognized in future periods using an imputed interest rate.
- The accounting for a modification of terms by the creditor results in the recognition of a new value for the loan.
- The accounting by the creditor for a troubled debt restructuring that involves an equity or asset exchange is a mirror image of the accounting by the debtor.

KEY TERMS

modification of terms, p. 14-36
troubled debt restructuring, p. 14-35

ANSWERS TO REAL REPORT QUESTIONS

Real Report 14.1 Answers Bank of America—Financial Liabilities at Fair Value

1. Bank of America reports $114,730 million of liabilities at fair value at the end of 2012:

Deposits in U.S. offices	$ 2,262
Federal funds purchased and securities loaned or sold under agreements to repurchase	42,639
Commercial paper and other short-term borrowings	4,074
Accrued expenses and other liabilities	16,594
Long-term debt	49,161

   This represents approximately 6.0% of the company's total liabilities.
2. As interest rates change, the market value of liabilities will also change. This allows users of the financial statements to assess the firm's ability to repay its debts at an amount that is greater or less than the liabilities book value.
3. There are a number of reasons but most commonly debt that is being hedged with derivative securities is reported at fair value to make the accounting simpler.

Real Report 14.2 Answers Encore Capital Group—Cash Settled Convertible Bonds

1. The maturity of the Convertible Senior Notes is $115 million, and the notes mature on November 27, 2017. Interest is paid semiannually on May 27 and November 27 of each year.
2. The notes have a face value of $115 million and a stated interest rate of 3% so annual interest would be $3,450,000.
3. Encore recognized interest expense of $567,000 for the year ended December 31, 2012, and paid $307,000. The difference was due to amortization of the debt discount relating to the conversion feature.

Real Report 14.3 Answers Nike—Disclosure of Debt

1. $242 million of Nike's debt comes due over the next 5 fiscal years; this is approximately 19.1% of the company's total long-term debt ($242 million/$1,267 million).
2. These corporate bonds were issued at a discount, given that the book values provided are less than the original principal (face values) of the bonds.
3. The 2023 and 2024 promissory notes would pay $206,667 and $107,583 per month, respectively.

MULTIPLE-CHOICE (AICPA ADAPTED)

Select the best answer for each of the following.

M14-1
LO 14.3 On January 1, 2015, Bay Company issues bonds with a face value of $850,000 that pay 9% interest semiannually and mature in 15 years. The market interest rate at the date of issuance is 8%. What is the issue price of the bond?

   a. $850,000.00
   b. $923,491.41
   c. $815,386.52
   d. $567,656.32

M14-2
LO 14.4 Should legal fees and underwriting costs associated with issuing bonds be expensed as incurred?

	Legal Fees	Underwriting Costs
a.	No	No
b.	No	Yes
c.	Yes	No
d.	Yes	Yes

M14-3
LO 14.4 On April 1, 2016, Granville Corporation issued, at 98 plus accrued interest, 400 of its 10%, $1,000 bonds. The bonds are dated January 1, 2016 and mature on

January 1, 2023. Interest is payable semiannually on January 1 and July 1. From the bond issuance, Granville would realize net cash receipts of:

a. $382,000
b. $392,000
c. $397,000
d. $402,000

M14-4
LO 14.4
When the interest payment dates of a bond are May 1 and November 1, and a bond issue is sold on June 1, the amount of cash received by the issuer will be:

a. increased by accrued interest from June 1 to November 1
b. increased by accrued interest from May 1 to June 1
c. decreased by accrued interest from June 1 to November 1
d. decreased by accrued interest from May 1 to June 1

M14-5
LO 14.5
For the issuer of a 10-year term bond, the amount of amortization using the effective interest method would increase each year if the bond was sold at a:

	Discount	Premium
a.	No	No
b.	Yes	Yes
c.	No	Yes
d.	Yes	No

M14-6
LO 14.5
On January 1, 2016, when the market rate for bond interest was 14%, Lenoir Corporation issued bonds in the face amount of $500,000 with interest at 12% payable semiannually. The bonds mature on December 31, 2023, and were issued at a discount of $53,180. How much of the discount should be amortized by the effective interest method at July 1, 2016?

a. $1,277
b. $2,659
c. $3,191
d. $3,723

M14-7
LO 14.6
When the issuer of bonds exercises the call provision to retire the bonds, the excess of the cash paid over the carrying amount of the bonds should be recognized separately as a(n):

a. expense
b. prior period adjustment
c. loss from continuing operations
d. loss from discontinued operations

M14-8
LO 14.7
When the cash proceeds from a bond issued with detachable stock purchase warrants exceed the sum of the par value of the bonds and the fair value of the warrants, the excess should be credited to:

a. Additional Paid-In Capital
b. Retained Earnings
c. Premium on Bonds Payable
d. Detachable Stock Warrants Outstanding

M14-9
LO 14.7
On December 31, 2015, Dare Corporation had outstanding 8%, $2,000,000 face value convertible bonds maturing on December 31, 2019. Interest is payable annually on December 31. Each $1,000 bond is convertible into 60 shares of Dare's $10 par value common stock. On January 2, 2017, when the Premium on Bonds Payable account balance was $45,000, an individual holding 200 of the bonds exercised the conversion privilege when the market value of Dare's common stock was $18 per share. Using the book value method, Dare's entry to record the conversion should include a credit to Additional Paid-In Capital of:

a. $80,000
b. $84,500
c. $96,000
d. $125,000

M14-10
LO 14.7
On July 1, 2014, Rix Corporation had $10,000,000 of 9% bonds outstanding. The maturity date is June 30, 2019. Interest is paid semiannually every June 30 and December 31. All the bonds were redeemed on July 1, 2014, at 98. At the time of the bond redemption, there was unamortized bond premium of $60,000 and unamortized debt issuance costs of $100,000. What is the amount of the gain on the bond redemption?

a. $80,000 gain
b. $160,000 gain
c. $240,000 gain
d. $0

M14-11
LO 14.8
On January 1, 2016, Onslow Company borrowed $360,000 from a major customer evidenced by a non-interest-bearing note due in 3 years. Onslow agreed to supply the customer's inventory needs for the loan period at lower than market price. At the 12% imputed interest rate for this type of loan, the present value of the note is $255,000 at January 1, 2016. What amount of interest expense should be included in Onslow's 2016 income statement?

a. $43,200
b. $35,000
c. $30,600
d. $0

M14-12
LO 14.10
(Appendix 14.1) Pamlico Company has a $500,000, 15%, 3-year note dated January 1, 2016, payable to Forest National Bank. On December 31, 2017, the bank agreed to settle the note and unpaid interest of $75,000 for $50,000 cash and marketable securities having a current market value of $375,000. Pamlico's acquisition cost of the securities is $385,000. Ignoring income taxes, what amount should Pamlico report as a gain from the debt restructuring on its 2016 income statement?

a. $65,000
b. $75,000
c. $140,000
d. $150,000

REVIEW EXERCISES

RE14-1
LO 14.3
On January 1, Canglon, Inc., issues 10%, 5-year bonds with a face value of $150,000 when the effective rate is 12%. Interest is to be paid semiannually. Prepare calculations to prove that the selling price of the bonds is $138,959.90.

RE14-2
LO 14.5
Refer to the information in **RE14-1**. Assume Canglon uses the effective interest method to amortize the discount. Prepare the journal entry to record the first interest payment.

RE14-3
LO 14.3
On January 1, Lightfoot Corporation issues 10%, 5-year bonds with a face value of $275,000 when the effective interest rate is 9%. Interest is to be paid semiannually. Prepare calculations to prove that the selling price of the bonds is $285,880.07.

RE14-4
LO 14.5
Refer to the information in **RE14-3**. Lightfoot uses the effective interest method to amortize the premium. Prepare the journal entry to record the first interest payment.

RE14-5
LO 14.4
On January 1, 2016, North Company issued $2,000,000 of bonds with a stated rate of 10% that are due to mature December 31, 2025, and pay interest semiannually. The market rate of interest was 9% at the date of issuance. Prepare the journal entry for the sale of the bonds on January 1, 2016.

RE14-6
LO 14.4
On January 1 (the authorization date) of the current year, Temple Company issues $500,000 of 9% bonds at 103. These bonds pay interest on June 30 and December 31. Prepare the journal entry to record the issuance of the bonds.

RE14-7
LO 14.4
Use the information in **RE14-6**, except assume that Temple issues its bonds on March 1 at par, plus accrued interest. Prepare the journal entries to record the issuance of the bonds (adjust interest expense for the accrued interest) and the first semiannual interest payment.

RE14-8
LO 14.4
LO 14.5
Bangles Corporation issued 5-year, 11% bonds with a face value of $300,000 on April 1 for $288,000. Interest is paid semiannually at October 1 and April 1. Prepare the journal entries to record the issuance on April 1 and the first interest payment on October 1. Use the straight-line method to amortize the discount.

RE14-9
LO 14.4
LO 14.5
Use the information in **RE14-8**, except assume that the bonds are sold for $318,000. Prepare the journal entries to record the issuance on April 1 and the first interest payment on October 1. Use the straight-line method to amortize the premium.

RE14-10
LO 14.6
On June 1, Fignon Company recalls bonds with a face value of $200,000 and a current book value of $190,000. Fignon pays $192,000 to retire the bonds. Prepare the journal entry to record the retirement of the bonds.

RE14-11
LO 14.7
Langdon & Co. issues bonds with a face value of $50,000 for $51,000. Each $1,000 bond carries 10 warrants, and each warrant allows the holder to acquire one share of $1 par common stock for $40 per share. Immediately after the issuance, the bonds are quoted at 99 ex rights and the warrants are quoted at $5 each. Calculate the value to be assigned to the bonds and to the warrants.

RE14-12
LO 14.7
Nolan Corporation has outstanding convertible bonds with a face value of $15,000 and a current book value of $17,500. Each $1,000 bond is convertible into 25 shares of common stock (par value $5 per share). All the bonds are converted into common stock when the market value of Nolan's common stock is $50 per share. Using the book value method, prepare the journal entry for Nolan to record the conversion.

RE14-13
LO 14.7
Branson Corporation issued $500,000 of convertible bonds at par value. The bonds were issued with a stated interest rate of 3%. Each $1,000 bond is convertible into 20 shares of the corporation's $1 par value common stock. Branson may also elect to settle bonds with a cash payment in lieu of issuing stock. Similar bonds without the conversion feature would have sold for $455,000. Prepare the journal entry for Branson to record the issuance of the convertible bonds.

RE14-14
LO 14.8
On January 1, Boater Company issues a $20,000 non-interest-bearing, 5-year note for equipment. Neither the fair value of the note nor the equipment is determinable. Boater's incremental borrowing rate is 9%. The asset has a useful life of 7 years. Prepare the journal entry for Boater to record the issuance of the note on January 1.

RE14-15
LO 14.8
On January 2, 2016, Jennings Company purchases machinery and equipment and borrows $200,000 on a 5-year non-interest-bearing note. The principal of $200,000 will be paid at the maturity date of December 31, 2020. To place a fair value on the transaction, the accountant will impute an interest rate and use that rate to compute the present value of the note. Assuming that an 8% interest rate is applicable, record the journal entry for interest expense for the year ended December 31, 2016.

EXERCISES

E14-1
LO 14.3
Determining the Proceeds from Bond Issues Madison Corporation is authorized to issue $500,000 of 5-year bonds dated June 30, 2016, with a stated rate of interest of 11%. Interest on the bonds is payable semiannually, and the bonds are sold on June 30, 2016.

Required:
Determine the proceeds that the company will receive if it sells (1) the bonds to yield 12% and (2) the bonds to yield 10%.

E14-2
LO 14.4
Recording Bond Issue and Interest Payments Synergy Corporation is authorized to issue $1,200,000 of 8% bonds. Interest on the bonds is payable semiannually; the bonds are dated January 1, 2016, and are due December 31, 2021.

Required:
Prepare the journal entries to record the following:

a. January 1, 2016   Sold the bonds at par
b. June 30, 2016   First interest payment
c. December 31, 2016   Second interest payment

E14-3
LO 14.4
Recording Bond Issue and Interest Payments Burris Corporation is authorized to issue $800,000 of 9% bonds. Interest on the bonds is payable semiannually; the bonds are dated January 1, 2016, and are due December 31, 2020.

Required:
Prepare the journal entries to record the following:

a. April 1, 2016   Sold the bonds at par plus accrued interest
b. June 30, 2016   First interest payment
c. December 31, 2016   Second interest payment

E14-4
LO 14.4
Recording Bond Issuance On January 1, 2016, Knorr Corporation issued $1,000,000 of 9%, 5-year bonds dated January 1, 2016. The bonds pay interest annually on December 31. The bonds were issued to yield 10%. Debt issuance costs associated with the bonds totaled $18,000.

Required:
Prepare the journal entries to record the following:

January 1, 2016   Sold the bonds at an effective rate of 10%
December 31, 2016   First interest payment using the effective interest method
December 31, 2016   Amortization of bond issue costs using the straight-line method
December 31, 2017   Second interest payment using the effective interest method
December 31, 2017   Amortization of bond issue costs using the straight-line method

E14-5
LO 14.5
Straight-Line Premium Amortization On January 1, 2016, Hackman Corporation issued $1 million face value 12% bonds dated January 1, 2016, for $1,023,000. The bonds pay interest semiannually on June 30 and December 31 and are due December 31, 2020. Hackman uses the straight-line amortization method.

Required:
Record the issuance of the bonds and the first two interest payments.

E14-6 **Straight-Line Discount Amortization** Bryan Company issued $500,000 of 10% face value bonds on January 1, 2016, for $486,000. The bonds are due December 31, 2018, and pay interest semiannually on June 30 and December 31. Bryan uses the straight-line amortization method.
LO 14.5

Required:
Prepare the journal entries to record the issuance of the bonds and the first two interest payments.

E14-7 **Effective Interest Discount Amortization** Chowan Corporation issued $100,000 of 10% bonds dated January 1, 2016, for $96,832.72 on January 1, 2016. The bonds are due December 31, 2019, were issued to yield 11%, and pay interest semiannually on June 30 and December 31. Chowan uses the effective interest method of amortization.
LO 14.5

Required:
Prepare the journal entries to record the issue of the bonds on January 1, 2016, and the interest payments on June 30, 2016, December 31, 2016, and June 30, 2017. In addition, prepare a bond interest expense and discount amortization schedule for the bonds through June 30, 2017.

E14-8 **Effective Interest Premium Amortization** Polk Incorporated issued $200,000 of 13% bonds on July 1, 2016, for $206,801.60. The bonds were dated January 1, 2016, pay interest on each June 30 and December 31, are due December 31, 2020, and were issued to yield 12%. Polk uses the effective interest method of amortization.
LO 14.5

Required:
Prepare the journal entries to record the issue of the bonds on July 1, 2016, and the interest payments on December 31, 2016, and June 30, 2017. In addition, prepare a bond interest expense and premium amortization schedule for the bonds through June 30, 2017.

E14-9 **Effective Interest Amortization of Premium or Discount** Taylor Company issued $100,000 of 13% bonds on January 1, 2016. The bonds pay interest semiannually on June 30 and December 31 and are due December 31, 2018.
LO 14.5

Required:
1. Assume the company sells the bonds for $102,458.71 to yield 12%. Prepare the journal entries to record:
   a. the sale of the bonds
   b. each 2016 semiannual interest payment and premium amortization, using the effective interest method
2. Assume the company sells the bonds for $97,616.71 to yield 14%. Prepare the journal entries to record:
   a. the sale of the bonds
   b. each 2016 semiannual interest payment and discount amortization, using the effective interest method

E14-10 **Bond Amortization Tables** On January 1, 2016, Calvert Company issues 12%, $100,000 face value bonds for $103,545.91, a price to yield 10%. The bonds mature on December 31, 2017. Interest is paid semiannually on June 30 and December 31.
LO 14.5

Required:
1. Prepare a bond interest expense and premium amortization schedule using the straight-line method.
2. Prepare a bond interest expense and premium amortization schedule using the effective interest method.
3. Prepare the journal entries to record the interest payments on June 30, 2016, and December 31, 2016, using both methods.

E14-11 **Effective Interest versus Straight-Line Discount Amortization** Burr Motor Company, a manufacturer of small- to medium-sized electric motors, needs additional funds to market a revolutionary new motor. Burr has arranged for private placement of a $50,000, 5-year, 11% bond issue. Interest on these bonds is paid annually each year on August 31. The issue was dated and sold on September 1, 2015, for proceeds of $48,197.61 to yield 12%. Burr Motor Company has December 31 fiscal year-end.
LO 14.5

Required:
1. Prepare a bond interest expense and discount amortization schedule showing interest expense for each interest period using the effective interest method. (Round to the nearest whole dollar.)
2. Prepare journal entries to record the issuance of the bonds and the interest entries for 2016 and 2017 using (a) the effective interest method and (b) the straight-line method.

E14-12 Effective Interest versus Straight-Line Premium Amortization On October 1, 2016, Ball Company issued 9% bonds dated October 1, 2016, with a face amount of $200,000. The bonds mature in 10 years. Interest is paid semiannually on March 31 and September 30. The proceeds from the bond issuance were $205,294.53 to yield 8.5%. Ball Company has a December 31 fiscal year-end and does not use reversing entries.

LO 14.6

Required:
1. Prepare journal entries to record the issuance of the bonds and the interest payments for 2016 and 2017 using the effective interest method.
2. Prepare journal entries to record the issuance of the bonds and the interest payments for 2016 and 2017 using the straight-line method.

E14-13 Redemption of Bonds Prior to Maturity Hill Corporation issued $1,500,000 of 11% bonds at 98 on January 2, 2014. Interest is paid semiannually on June 30 and December 31. The bonds had a 10-year life from the date of issue, and the company uses the straight-line method of amortization. On March 31, 2017, Hill recalls the bonds at the call price of 107 plus accrued interest.

LO 14.6

Required:
Prepare the journal entries to record the reacquisition (recall) of Hill's bonds.

E14-14 Extinguishment of Bonds Prior to Maturity On January 1, 2008, Davis Corporation issued $3,000,000 of 8% bonds at 103. Interest is paid annually on December 31 of each year. The bonds mature on December 31, 2027, and the company uses the straight-line method of amortization. On January 2, 2016, Davis reacquired the bonds and recognized a loss of $96,000.

LO 14.6

Required:
Next Level Calculate the reacquisition price of the bonds on January 2, 2016, and prepare the journal entry to record the reacquisition of Davis's bonds.

E14-15 Extinguishment of Bonds Prior to Maturity On December 1, 2014, Cone Company issued its 10%, $2 million face value bonds for $2.3 million, plus accrued interest. Interest is payable on November 1 and May 1. On December 31, 2016, the book value of the bonds, inclusive of the unamortized premium, was $2.1 million. On July 1, 2017, Cone reacquired the bonds at 98 plus accrued interest. Cone appropriately uses the straight-line method for the amortization because the results do not materially differ from those of the effective interest method.

LO 14.6

AICPA Adapted

Required:
Prepare a schedule to compute the gain or loss on this redemption of debt. Show supporting computations in good form.

E14-16 Premium Amortization and Partial Retirement Rockwood Company issued $100,000 of 10% bonds on November 1, 2016, at 103. Interest on the bonds is payable on November 1 and May 1 of each year, and the maturity date is November 1, 2026. Rockwood retired bonds with a face value of $20,000 on February 1, 2018, at 98 plus accrued interest. Rockwood uses straight-line amortization and reverses any calendar year-end adjusting entries.

LO 14.5
LO 14.6

Required:
1. Prepare the journal entry to record the issuance of the bonds on November 1, 2016.
2. Prepare all the journal entries to record the interest expense during 2017.
3. Prepare the journal entries to record the retirement of $20,000 of the bonds on February 1, 2018.

E14-17 Convertible Bonds On January 1, 2015, when its $30 par value common stock was selling for $80 per share, a corporation issued $10 million of 10% convertible debentures due in 10 years. The conversion option allowed the holder of each $1,000 bond to convert it into six shares of the corporation's $30 par value common stock. The debentures were issued for $11 million. At the time of issuance, the present value of the bond payments was $8.5 million, and the corporation believes the difference between the present value and the amount paid is attributable to the conversion feature. On January 1, 2016, the corporation's $30 par value common stock was split 3 for 1. On January 1, 2017, when the corporation's $10 par value common stock was selling for $90 per share, holders of 40% of the convertible debentures exercised their conversion options. The corporation uses the straight-line method for amortizing any bond discounts or premiums.

LO 14.7

AICPA Adapted

Required:
1. Prepare the journal entry to record the original issuance of the convertible debentures.
2. Prepare the journal entry to record the exercise of the conversion option, using the book value method. Show supporting computations in good form.

E14-18 **Induced Conversion** On July 1, 2017, Tuttle Company had bonds payable outstanding with a face value of $200,000 and a book value of $194,000. The interest on these bonds was paid on June 30. When these bonds were issued, each $1,000 bond was convertible into 20 shares of $10 par common stock. To induce conversion, on June 15, 2017, the terms were changed so that each bond was convertible into 22 shares of common stock if the conversion was made within 30 days. All the bonds were converted on July 1, 2017, when the market price of the common stock was $50 per share.

LO 14.7

Required:
Next Level Using the book value method, record the conversion of the bonds on July 1, 2017.

E14-19 **Detachable Stock Warrants** Conroe Corporation sold $500,000 of 13% bonds at 107. Each $1,000 bond carried 20 warrants, and each warrant allowed the holder to acquire one share of $10 par value common stock for $20 per share. Subsequent to the issuance of the securities, the bonds were quoted at 102 ex rights, and the warrants were quoted at $4 each.

LO 14.7

SHOW ME HOW

Required:
1. Determine the value to be assigned to the bonds and the warrants and prepare the journal entry to record the issuance of the convertible bonds.
2. Assume that 4,000 warrants are subsequently exercised. Prepare the journal entry for the issuance of the common stock.

E14-20 **Bonds with Detachable Warrants** On July 1, 2016, Salem Corporation issued $3 million of 12% bonds payable in 10 years. The bonds pay interest semiannually. The bonds include detachable warrants giving the bondholder the right to purchase for $30, one share of $1 par value common stock at any time during the next 10 years. Salem sold the bonds for $3 million. The value of the warrants at the time of issuance was $200,000.

LO 14.7

AICPA Adapted

Required:
Prepare in general journal format the entry to record the issuance of the bonds.

E14-21 **Convertible Bond Entries** On July 2, 2015, McGraw Corporation issued $500,000 of convertible bonds. Each $1,000 bond could be converted into 20 shares of the company's $5 par value stock. On July 3, 2017, when the bonds had an unamortized discount of $7,400 and the market value of the McGraw shares was $52 per share, all the bonds were converted into common stock.

LO 14.4
LO 14.7

SHOW ME HOW

Required:
1. Prepare the journal entry to record the conversion of the bonds under (a) the book value method and (b) the market value method.
2. Compute the company's debt-to-equity ratio (total liabilities divided by total shareholders' equity, as described in Chapter 6) under each alternative. Assume the company's other liabilities are $2 million and shareholders' equity before the conversion is $3 million.
3. Assume the company uses IFRS and issued the bonds for $487,500 on July 2, 2015. On this date, it determined that the fair value of each bond was $930 and the fair value of the conversion option was $45 per bond. Prepare the journal entry to record the issuance of the bonds.

E14-22 **Convertible Bond Entries** On January 2, 2016, Lindsay Corporation issued $800,000 of 8% convertible bonds at par. The bonds mature in 10 years and pay interest semiannually on June 30 and December 31. Each $1,000 bond could be converted into 26 shares of the company's $2.50 par value common stock. Alternatively, Lindsay has the right to settle the bonds in cash instead of issuing common stock. Similar bonds without the conversion feature would carry a 10% stated interest rate.

LO 14.7

Required:
Prepare the journal entry to record the issuance of the bonds.

E14-23 Long-Term Notes Payable On January 1, 2016, Johnson Corporation issued a 2-year note due December 31, 2017, with a face value of $10,000, receiving $7,694.68 in exchange.

LO 14.8

Required:
Prepare the journal entries to account for the note:
1. on the date the note is issued
2. at the end of 2016
3. at the end of 2017

E14-24 Note Payable Exchanged for Cash and Rights Spath Company borrows $75,000 by issuing a 4-year, non-interest-bearing note to a customer on January 1, 2016. In addition, Spath agrees to sell inventory to the customer at reduced prices over a 5-year period. Spath's incremental borrowing rate is 12%. The customer agrees to purchase an equal amount of inventory each year over the 5-year period so that a straight-line method of revenue recognition is appropriate.

LO 14.8

Required:
Prepare the journal entries on Spath's books for 2016 and 2017. (Round answers to 2 decimal places.)

E14-25 Exchange of a Note Payable for an Asset Webb Corporation purchased an asset from Shaw Corporation on January 1, 2016. Shaw accepted a 3-year, non-interest-bearing note of $18,000 due December 31, 2018, in exchange for the asset. Neither the fair value of the asset nor that of the note is available. Webb's incremental borrowing rate is 12%.

LO 14.8

Required:
Prepare the journal entries to record the issuance of the note, retirement, and any interest expense on the books of Webb on each of the following dates:
1. January 1, 2016
2. December 31, 2016
3. December 31, 2017
4. December 31, 2018

E14-26 Note Payable Issued in Exchange for an Asset On January 1, 2016, Sanders Corporation purchased equipment having a fair value of $68,301.30 by issuing a non-interest-bearing, $100,000, 4-year note due December 31, 2019.

LO 14.8

Required:
Prepare the journal entries to record (1) the purchase of the equipment, (2) the annual interest charges over the life of the note, and (3) the repayment of the note.

E14-27 Note Payable in Installments On January 1, 2016, Billips Corporation purchased equipment having a fair value of $72,054.94 by issuing a $90,000 note, payable in three $30,000 annual installments beginning December 31, 2016.

LO 14.8

Required:
Prepare (1) the journal entry to record the purchase of the equipment, (2) a schedule to compute the annual interest expense, and (3) the journal entries to record yearly interest expense and note repayments over the life of the note.

E14-28 (Appendix 14.1) Troubled Debt Restructuring (Debtor)—Modification of Terms On January 1, 2016, Northfield Corporation becomes delinquent on a $100,000, 14% note to First National Bank, on which $16,651 of interest has accrued. On January 2, 2016, the bank agrees to restructure the note. It forgives the accrued interest, extends the repayment date to December 31, 2018, and reduces the interest rate to 10%.

LO 14.10

Required:
Prepare a schedule for Northfield to compute the annual interest expense in regard to the preceding note for each year of the restructuring agreement.

E14-29 (Appendix 14.1) Troubled Debt Restructuring (Debtor)—Equity and Asset Exchange On January 1, 2016, Boonville Corporation is delinquent on a $300,000 note to Great National Bank on which $66,000 of interest has accrued. On January 2, 2016, Boonville enters into a debt restructuring agreement with the bank.

LO 14.10

Required:

Prepare the journal entries for Boonville to record the restructuring agreement assuming:
1. the bank accepts 10,000 shares of Boonville's $10 par common stock that is currently selling for $35 per share in full settlement of the debt
2. the bank accepts land with a fair value of $342,000 in full settlement of the debt. The land is being carried on Boonville's books at a cost of $324,000.

E14-30 *(Appendix 14.1)* **Troubled Debt Restructuring (Creditor)—Modification of Terms** On December 31, 2016, Central Bank agrees to a restructuring of a 12% note with a $200,000 face value and $60,000 of accrued interest owed to the bank by Carter Company. The bank agrees to forgive the accrued interest, extend the maturity date to December 31, 2019, and reduce the annual interest rate to 6%. Carter paid the interest due on December 31, 2017.

LO 14.10

Required:
1. Prepare the journal entry for Central Bank to record the restructuring of the note on December 31, 2016.
2. Prepare the journal entry for Central Bank to record the receipt of the interest on December 31, 2017.

E14-31 *(Appendix 14.1)* **Troubled Debt Restructuring (Creditor)—Equity and Asset Exchange** Refer to the debt restructuring information in **E14-29**.

Required:

Prepare the journal entries for Great National Bank to record the restructuring agreement assuming:
1. the bank accepts the 10,000 shares of Boonville's stock
2. the bank accepts the land

PROBLEMS

P14-1 **Computation of Selling Price and Debt Issuance Costs** Barnett Industries, Inc., issued $600,000 of 8% bonds on January 1, 2016. The bonds pay interest semiannually on July 1 and January 1. The maturity date on these bonds is December 31, 2025. The firm uses the effective interest method of amortizing discounts and premiums. The bonds were sold to yield an effective interest rate of 9%. Barnett incurred legal and investment banking fees of $22,000 in issuing the bonds and amortizes these costs annually on a straight-line basis.

LO 14.3
LO 14.4

Required:
1. Calculate the selling price of the bonds.
2. Prepare journal entries for the issuance of the bonds and debt issuance costs.

P14-2 **Computation of Effective Interest Rate** On June 30, 2016, Gaston Corporation sold $800,000 of 11% face value bonds for $761,150.96. On December 31, 2016, Gaston sold $700,000 of this same bond issue for $734,645.28. The bonds were dated January 1, 2016, pay interest semiannually on each December 31 and June 30, and are due December 31, 2023.

LO 14.3

Required:
Compute the effective yield rate on each issuance of Gaston's 11% bonds.

P14-3 **Amortizing Debt Issuance Costs and Bond Premiums** On January 1, 2016, Gates Corporation issued $100,000 of 5-year bonds due December 31, 2020, for $103,604.79 minus debt issuance costs of $3,000. The bonds carry a stated rate of interest of 13% payable annually on December 31 and were issued to yield 12%. The company uses the effective interest method of amortization to amortize any discounts or premiums and the straight-line method to amortize the debt issuance costs.

LO 14.5
LO 14.6

Required:
Prepare the journal entries to record the issuance of the bonds, all the interest payments, premium amortizations, debt issuance cost amortizations, and the repayment of the bonds. In addition, prepare a bond interest expense and premium amortization schedule for the bonds.

P14-4
LO 14.5
LO 14.6

Premium Amortization Schedule with Retirement Before Maturity Hillis Corporation issued $600,000 of 13% bonds on January 1, 2015, for $614,752.24. The bonds are due December 31, 2017, were issued to yield 12%, and pay interest semiannually on June 30 and December 31. Hillis uses the effective interest method.

Required:
1. Prepare a bond interest expense and premium amortization schedule.
2. Assume the company retired the bonds on September 30, 2017, for $630,000, which includes accrued interest. Prepare the journal entry to record the bond retirement.

P14-5
LO 14.5
LO 14.6

Comprehensive Bats Corporation issued $800,000 of 12% face value bonds for $851,705.70. The bonds were dated and issued on April 1, 2016, are due March 31, 2020, and pay interest semiannually on September 30 and March 31. Bats sold the bonds to yield 10%.

Required:
1. Prepare a bond interest expense and premium amortization schedule using the straight-line method.
2. Prepare a bond interest expense and premium amortization schedule using the effective interest method.
3. Prepare any adjusting entries for the end of the fiscal year, December 31, 2016, using the:
   a. straight-line method of amortization
   b. effective interest method of amortization
4. Assume the company retires the bonds on June 30, 2017, at 103 plus accrued interest. Prepare the journal entries to record the bond retirement using the:
   a. straight-line method of amortization
   b. effective interest method of amortization

P14-6
LO 14.5
LO 14.6

Discount Amortization Schedule and Retirement Before maturity, Foster Incorporated sold $500,000 of 12% bonds on January 1, 2016, for $470,143.47, a price that yields a 14% interest rate. The bonds pay interest semiannually on June 30 and December 31 and are due December 31, 2019. Foster uses the effective interest method.

Required:
1. Prepare an interest expense and discount amortization schedule.
2. Assume the company reacquired the bonds on July 1, 2018, at 104. Prepare journal entries to record the bond retirement.

P14-7
LO 14.5
LO 14.6
LO 14.9

Comprehensive Wilbury Corporation issued $1 million of 13.5% bonds for $985,071.68. The bonds are dated and issued October 1, 2016, are due September 30, 2020, and pay interest semiannually on March 31 and September 30. Assume an effective yield rate of 14%.

Required:
1. Prepare a bond interest expense and discount amortization schedule using the straight-line method.
2. Prepare a bond interest expense and discount amortization schedule using the effective interest method.
3. Prepare adjusting entries for the end of the fiscal year December 31, 2016, using the:
   a. straight-line method of amortization
   b. effective interest method of amortization
4. If income before interest and income taxes of 30% in 2017 is $500,000, compute net income under each alternative.
5. Assume the company retired the bonds on June 30, 2017, at 98 plus accrued interest. Prepare the journal entries to record the bond retirement using the:
   a. straight-line method of amortization
   b. effective interest method of amortization
6. Compute the company's times interest earned (pretax operating income divided by interest expense) for 2017 under each alternative.

P14-8
LO 14.6

Bond Refunding Baxter Corporation issued $400,000 of 11% bonds for $385,279.91 on January 1, 2016. The bonds pay interest semiannually on June 30 and December 31, were issued to yield 12%, and are due on December 31, 2020. Interest is amortized using the effective interest method, and the bonds are callable at 105. In 2018, Baxter wishes to take advantage of more favorable market interest rate conditions and issues $450,000 of 11%, 10-year bonds at 102 on June 1. Interest on these bonds is payable each May 31 and November 30. Sufficient proceeds from this issue are used to recall the original issue on July 1, 2018.

Required:
1. Prepare the journal entries to record (a) the original issue, (b) the new issue, and (c) the recall of the old issue.
2. **Next Level** If the company were required to reflect the current yield each year, explain how it would account for the bonds. For simplicity, assume that the yield changes from 12% to 11% on January 1, 2018. No calculations are required.

P14-9
LO 14.7
Convertible Bonds Wedge Corporation issued $1,500,000 of 10% convertible bonds for $1,620,000 on March 1, 2016. The bonds are dated March 1, 2016, pay interest semiannually on August 31 and February 28, and the premium is amortized using the straight-line method. The bonds are due on February 28, 2026, and each $1,000 bond is convertible into 25 shares of Wedge's $10 par common stock. On March 1, 2018, when the shares were selling for $28 per share, $300,000 of bonds were converted. On September 1, 2020, when the shares were selling for $30 per share, the remainder of the bonds were converted.

Required:
1. Prepare the journal entries to record each bond conversion using (a) the book value method and (b) the market value method.
2. **Next Level** If the company were required under GAAP to assign a value to the conversion feature, explain how the valuation would be determined (no calculations are required).
3. Compute the company's debt-to-equity ratio (total liabilities divided by total shareholders' equity, as mentioned in Chapter 6) under each alternative. Assume the company's other liabilities are $3 million, and that shareholders' equity before conversion is $3.5 million. Compute the ratio right before and right after the March 1, 2018, transaction under each alternative.
4. Assume the company uses IFRS and issued the bonds for $1,620,000 on March 1, 2016. On this date, it determined that the fair value of each bond was $1,040 and the fair value of the conversion option was $40 per bond. Prepare the journal entry to record the issuance of the bonds.

P14-10
LO 14.7
Bonds with Detachable Warrants On January 1, 2016, Berlin Corporation issued $500,000 of 11.5% bonds due January 1, 2023, at 102. The bonds pay interest semiannually on June 30 and December 31. Each $1,000 bond carried 20 warrants, and the exchange of two warrants allowed the holder to acquire one share of $10 par common stock for $50. Shortly after the time of issue, the bonds were quoted at 98 ex rights and each individual warrant was quoted at $5. Subsequently, on March 31, 2016, 8,000 rights were exercised.

Required:
1. Prepare the journal entry to record the bond issue.
2. Prepare the journal entries on March 31, 2016, to record the exchange of the warrants for common shares.

P14-11
LO 14.8
Notes Payable Lubbock Corporation acquires machinery from South Company in exchange for a $20,000 non-interest-bearing, 5-year note on June 30, 2016. The note is due on June 30, 2021. The machinery has a fair value of $11,348.54, is subject to straight-line depreciation, and has an estimated life of 10 years (no residual value). Lubbock's fiscal year ends June 30.

Required:
Prepare the journal entries on each of the following dates to record the preceding information for Lubbock:
1. June 30, 2016
2. June 30, 2017
3. June 30, 2018
4. June 30, 2019
5. June 30, 2020
6. June 30, 2021

P14-12
LO 14.8
Notes Payable in Installments Hamlet Corporation purchases computer equipment at a price of $100,000 on January 1, 2016, paying $40,000 down and agreeing to pay the balance in three $20,000 annual installments beginning December 31, 2016. It is not possible to value either the equipment or the $60,000 note directly; however, Hamlet's incremental borrowing rate is 12%.

Required:
1. Prepare a schedule to compute the interest expense and discount amortization on the note.
2. Prepare all the journal entries for Hamlet to record the issuance of the note, each annual interest expense, and the three annual installment payments.

P14-13 Comprehensive An examination of the accounting records of Durham Corporation on January 1, 2016 (after reversing entries had been made for all accrued interest at the end of 2015) disclosed the following information regarding the company's long-term debt:

LO 14.5
LO 14.6
LO 14.7
LO 14.8

12.5% bonds, dated January 1, 2012, paying interest semiannually on June 30 and December 31, and due December 31, 2018		$1,300,000
11% convertible bonds, dated April 1, 2014, paying interest semiannually on March 31 and September 30, and due March 31, 2019		$ 500,000
Discount on convertible bonds payable		(17,500)
		$ 482,500
9% bonds, dated March 1, 2015, paying interest annually on February 28, and due February 28, 2020		$ 100,000
Discount on bonds payable		(3,960)
		$ 96,040
4-year, non-interest-bearing note issued January 1, 2015 (Durham's incremental borrowing rate on the date the note was issued was 10%.)		$ 80,000
Discount on note payable		(19,895)
		$ 60,105

Additional information disclosed in the notes to Durham's 2015 financial statements:
1. The conversion option allows the holder of each $1,000 bond to exchange it for 30 shares of $10 par common stock. Durham uses the book value method to record conversions of bonds to common stock.
2. Each $1,000 bond of the 9% bonds dated March 1, 2015, carries 15 detachable warrants. The company had recorded the 1,500 warrants on the bonds at $4,800 in a Common Stock Warrants account. The exchange of three warrants allows the holder to acquire one share of $10 par common stock for $27.
3. The discount on the convertible bonds and the discount on the 9% bonds with detachable warrants are being amortized using the straight-line method.
4. The discount on the note payable is being amortized annually using the effective interest method.

During 2016, Durham engaged in the following long-term debt transactions:

Jan. 1   Issued 11%, $800,000 face value bonds for $820,302, a price to yield 10%. Interest on these bonds is payable semiannually on June 30 and December 31, and they are due December 31, 2018. The effective interest method is to be used to amortize the premium. The bonds are callable at 107.
May 1   600 warrants from the 9% bonds were exercised when the common stock was selling for $42 per share.
Sept. 30   Convertible bonds of $100,000 were exchanged when the common stock was selling for $45 per share.
Nov. 1   Retired $200,000 of the bonds issued on January 1, 2016, at the call price plus accrued interest.

Required:
1. Prepare the journal entries for Durham to record all the transactions that occurred during 2016 relating to the preceding information.
2. Prepare the long-term debt section of Durham's balance sheet on December 31, 2016.

P14-14 (Appendix 14.1) Troubled Debt Restructuring (Debtor) Oakwood Corporation is delinquent on a $2,400,000, 10% note to Second National Bank that was due January 1, 2016. At that time, Oakwood owed the principal amount plus $34,031.82 of accrued interest. Oakwood enters into a debt restructuring agreement with the bank on January 2, 2016.

LO 14.10

Required:
Prepare the journal entries for Oakwood to record the debt restructuring agreement and all subsequent interest payments assuming the following independent alternatives:
1. The bank extends the repayment date to December 31, 2019, forgives the accrued interest owed, reduces the principal by $200,000, and reduces the interest rate to 8%.
2. The bank extends the repayment date to December 31, 2019, forgives the accrued interest owed, reduces the principal by $200,000, and reduces the interest rate to 1%.
3. The bank accepts 160,000 shares of Oakwood's $5 par value common stock, which is currently selling for $14.50 per share, in full settlement of the debt.
4. The bank accepts land with a fair value of $2,300,000 in full settlement of the debt. The land is being carried on Oakwood's books at a cost of $2,200,000.

P14-15 *(Appendix 14.1)* **Troubled Debt Restructuring (Creditor)** Refer to the debt restructuring information listed in **P14-14**.
LO 14.10

Required:
For each of the independent alternatives listed in the "additional information disclosed" sections 1 through 4 of **P14-14**, prepare the journal entries for Second National Bank to record the debt restructuring agreement and all subsequent interest receipts.

P14-16 *(Appendix 14.1)* **Comprehensive—Loan Impairment and Troubled Debt Restructuring** Tenth National
LO 14.10 Bank has a $200,000, 12% note receivable from Priday Company that is due on December 31, 2019. On December 31, 2016, Priday misses the interest payment due on that date. The bank expects that the company will also miss the next payment, but will pay the principal on the maturity date. On December 31, 2017, Priday misses the interest payment due on that date. On December 31, 2018, Priday pays half the interest payment due on that date and is not expected to pay the other half.

In early January 2019, the bank and the company agree to a loan restructuring because of the financial condition of the company. The bank forgives the unpaid interest, extends the loan to December 31, 2021, and reduces the interest rate to 6%. The market rate for the loan is estimated to be 10% at this time.

Required:
1. Compute the value of the impaired loan on December 31, 2016.
2. Prepare the journal entries from 2016 to 2021 for the bank to record the above events. Assume that Priday makes all required payments under the modified agreement.

CASES

COMMUNICATION

C14-1 Capital Expansion and Financing
LO 14.1
LO 14.7
Your company is rapidly growing and needs additional capital to expand the online retailing portion of its business model. One group of the board of directors proposes that the company issue $800,000 of additional common stock, while a separate group of the board is in favor of issuing the same amount of long-term bonds. As a possible compromise, the company's investment banker suggests that the company issue convertible bonds. The board asks you to write a memo examining the advantages and disadvantages of convertible bonds. The company currently has 200,000 common shares outstanding, and the stock is currently trading at a price of $30 per share. The company's effective interest rate is 10%; however, the investment banker believes that the convertible debt could be issued at a 6% interest rate.

Required:
Write a memo to the board of directors detailing how convertible bonds work and the advantages and disadvantages of the security. In addition, provide details on how the issuance of the security would affect the financial statements compared to if the company simply issued debt or common stock.

C14-2 Various Bond Characteristics
LO 14.2
LO 14.4
LO 14.5
LO 14.6
LO 14.7
One way for a corporation to accomplish long-term financing is through the issuance of long-term debt instruments in the form of bonds.

AICPA Adapted

Required:
1. Explain how to account for the proceeds from bonds issued with detachable stock purchase warrants.
2. Contrast a serial bond with a term (straight) bond.
3. For a 5-year term bond issued at a premium, why is the amortization in the first year of the life of the bond different using the interest method of amortization as opposed to the straight-line method? Include in your discussion whether the amount of amortization in the first year of the life of the bond is higher or lower using the interest method as opposed to the straight-line method.
4. When a company sells a bond issue between interest dates at a discount, what journal entry does it make, and how is the subsequent amortization of bond discount affected? Include in your discussion an explanation of how the amounts of each debit and credit are determined.

(continued)

5. Explain how to account for and classify the gain or loss from the reacquisition of a long-term bond prior to its maturity.

C14-3
LO 14.4
LO 14.7
AICPA Adapted

Convertible and Nonconvertible Bonds

On February 1, 2010, Aubrey Company sold its 5-year, $1,000 par value, 9% bonds, which were convertible at the option of the investor into Aubrey Company common stock at a ratio of 10 shares of common stock for each bond. Aubrey sold the convertible bonds at a discount. Interest is payable annually each February 1. On February 1, 2016, Mel Company, an investor in the Aubrey Company convertible bonds, tendered 1,000 bonds for conversion into 10,000 shares of Aubrey Company common stock, which had a market value of $110 per share at the date of the conversion.

On May 1, 2016, Aubrey sold its 10-year, $1,000 par value, 10% nonconvertible term bonds dated April 1, 2016. Interest is payable semiannually, and the first interest payment date is October 1, 2016. Due to market conditions, the company sold the bonds at an effective interest rate (yield) of 12%.

Required:
1. Explain how Aubrey accounts for the conversion of the convertible bonds into common stock under both the book value and market value methods. Discuss the rationale for each method.
2. Were the nonconvertible term bonds sold at par, at a discount, or at a premium? Discuss the rationale for your answer.
3. Identify and discuss the effects on Aubrey's 2016 income statement associated with the nonconvertible term bonds.

CREATIVE AND CRITICAL THINKING

C14-4
LO 14.7
AICPA Adapted

Recording Convertible Debt

Zakin Co. recently issued $1,000,000 face value, 10%, 30-year subordinated debentures at 97. The debentures are redeemable at 103 upon demand by the issuer at any date upon 30 days notice 10 years after the issue. Each $1,000 debenture is convertible into 80 shares of $10 par common stock of the company at the conversion price of $12.50 per share.

Required:
1. Explain how the conversion feature of convertible debt has a value to the:
   a. issuer
   b. purchaser
2. Management of Zakin has suggested that in recording the issuance of the debentures, it should assign a portion of the proceeds to the conversion feature.
   a. What are the arguments for according separate accounting recognition to the conversion feature of the debentures?
   b. What are the arguments supporting accounting for the convertible debentures as a single element?
3. Assume that the company assigns no value to the conversion feature upon issue of the debentures. Assume further that 5 years after issue, debentures with a face value of $100,000 and book value of $97,500 are tendered for conversion on an interest payment date when the market price of the debentures is 104 and the common stock is selling at $14 per share and that the company records the conversion as follows:

Bonds Payable	100,000	
Bond Discount		2,500
Common Stock		80,000
Premium on Common Stock		17,500

Discuss the propriety of the preceding accounting treatment.

C14-5
LO 14.7
LO 14.8
AICPA Adapted

Debt with Detachable Stock Warrants

Incurring long-term debt with an arrangement whereby lenders receive an option to buy common stock during all or a portion of the time the debt is outstanding is a frequently used corporate financing practice. In some situations, the result is achieved through the issuance of convertible bonds; in others, the debt instruments and the warrants to buy stock are separate.

Required:
1. Assess the above transactions and answer the following questions:
   a. Explain the differences that exist in current accounting for original proceeds of the issuance of convertible bonds and of debt instruments with separate warrants to purchase common stock.

b. Explain the underlying rationale for the differences described in Requirement 1a.
c. Summarize the arguments that have been presented for the alternative accounting treatment.

2. At the start of the year, AB Company issued $6 million of 7% notes along with warrants to buy 400,000 shares of its $10 par value common stock at $18 per share. The notes mature over the next 10 years, starting 1 year from date of issuance, with annual maturities of $600,000. At the time, AB had 3,200,000 shares of common stock outstanding, and the market price was $23 per share. The company received $6,680,000 for the notes and the warrants. For AB, 7% was a relatively low borrowing rate. If offered alone, at this time, the notes would have been issued at a 20% to 24% discount. Prepare journal entries for the issuance of the notes and warrants for the cash consideration received.

C14-6 Long-Term Notes Payable
LO 14.8
AICPA Adapted

Business transactions often involve the exchange of property, goods, or services for notes or similar instruments that may stipulate no interest rate or an interest rate that varies from prevailing rates.

Required:
1. When a company exchanges a note for property, goods, or services, what value does it place on the note:
   a. if it bears interest at a reasonable rate and is issued in a bargained transaction entered into at arm's length? Explain.
   b. if it bears no interest and/or is not issued in a bargained transaction entered into at arm's length? Explain.
2. If the recorded value of a note differs from the face value, explain:
   a. how the company should account for the difference.
   b. how the company should present this difference in the financial statements.

C14-7 Bonds: Sale, Interest, and Recall
LO 14.3
LO 14.4
LO 14.5
LO 14.6
AICPA Adapted

On March 2, 2016, Wesley Company sold its 5-year, $1,000 face value, 8% bonds dated March 2, 2016, at an effective annual interest rate (yield) of 10%. Interest is payable semiannually, and the first interest payment date is September 2, 2016. Wesley uses the interest method of amortization and incurred debt issuance costs in preparing and selling the bond issue. Wesley can call the bonds at 101 at any time on or after March 2, 2017.

Required:
1. Based on the above information, answer the following questions:
   a. How does the company determine the selling price of the bonds?
   b. Specify, how the company presents all items related to the bonds in a balance sheet prepared immediately after the bond issue is sold.
2. What items related to the bond issue does Wesley include in its 2016 income statement, and how does it determine each?
3. Will the amount of bond discount amortization using the interest method of amortization be lower in the second or third year of the life of the bond issue? Why?
4. Assuming that the bonds are called in and retired on March 2, 2017, how does Wesley report the retirement of the bonds on the 2017 income statement?

C14-8 Bonds: Issuance, Expense, and Conversion
LO 14.4
LO 14.5
LO 14.6
LO 14.7
AICPA Adapted

On January 1, 2016, Brewster Company issued 2,000 of its 5-year, $1,000 face value, 11% bonds dated January 1 at an effective annual interest rate (yield) of 9%. Brewster uses the effective interest method of amortization. On December 31, 2017, Brewster extinguished the 2,000 bonds early through acquisition in the open market for $1,980,000.

On July 1, 2016, Brewster issued 5,000 of its 6-year, $1,000 face value, 10% convertible bonds dated July 1 at an effective annual interest rate (yield) of 12%. The bonds are convertible at the option of the investor into Brewster's common stock at a ratio of 10 shares of common stock for each bond. Brewster uses the effective interest method of amortization. On July 1, 2017, an investor in Brewster's convertible bonds tendered 1,500 bonds for conversion into 15,000 shares of Brewster's common stock, which had a market value of $105 per share at the date of the conversion.

Required:
1. Using the information about Brewster, answer the following questions:
   a. Were the 11% bonds issued at par, at a discount, or at a premium? Why?
   b. Is the amount of interest expense for the 11% bonds using the effective interest method of amortization higher in the first or second year of the life of the bond issue? Why?

(continued)

2. Using the information about Brewster, explain the following:
   a. How is a gain or loss on early extinguishment of debt determined? Does the early extinguishment of the 11% bonds result in a gain or loss? Why?
   b. How does Brewster report the early extinguishment of the 11% bonds on the 2017 income statement?
3. Based on the information provided about Brewster, answer the following questions:
   a. Does recording the conversion of the 10% convertible bonds into common stock under the book value method affect net income? What is the rationale for the book value method?
   b. Does recording the conversion of the 10% convertible bonds into common stock under the market value method affect net income? What is the rationale for the market value method?

C14-9 **Analyzing AB InBev's Debt Disclosures**
LO 14.8

Obtain **AB InBev**'s 2012 annual report using the "Investor Relations" portion of its web site (do a Web search for AB InBev investor relations).

Required:
1. Examine note 23. What was the total amount of Interest-Bearing Loans and Borrowings outstanding at the end of fiscal year 2012? What amount was due within 1 year?
2. Examine the cash flow statement. What amount of interest was paid by AB InBev in 2012?
3. What amount of interest expense did AB InBev record in 2012? How does the company refer to interest expense?

C14-10 **Ethics and Long-Term Liabilities**
LO 14.1
LO 14.7

You are an accountant for Taos Company, which has two items of long-term convertible debt on its balance sheet. Taos's president calls you into his office and says, "We are too leveraged. So, you remember that convertible debt we issued at the beginning of the year? Let's figure out the value of the conversion feature and assign that to equity so that we can reduce the amount we report as debt. And I have also been thinking about that convertible debt we issued at par 5 years ago. If you remember, each $1,000 bond is convertible into 25 shares. Now that our shares are trading at $70, obviously that is no longer debt. So let's classify that debt as equity now."

Required:
From financial reporting and ethical perspectives, discuss the issues raised by this situation.

C14-11 **Analyzing Coca-Cola's Long-Term Debt Disclosures**

Obtain **The Coca-Cola Company**'s 2012 annual report either using the "Investor Relations" portion of its web site (do a Web search for Coca-Cola investor relations) or go to http://www.sec.gov and click "Search for company filings" under "Filings and Forms (EDGAR)."

Required:
1. What was the difference between the interest expense and interest paid in 2012?
2. How much long-term debt will mature each year from 2013 through 2017?
3. What was the weighted average interest rate on the company's long-term debt for the year ended December 31, 2012?
4. Was the current yield at December 31, 2012, on the company's long-term debt the same as, greater than, or less than the average yield at issuance? At December 31, 2011?

USING CODIFICATION

C14-12 Researching GAAP

Situation

You are beginning the 2016 audit of Alta Tierra Company's long-term debt, and you determine that the company's long-term note payable requires that it comply with certain financial covenants. The note payable is dated January 1, 2013, has a face value of $1,000,000, is due December 31, 2022, and is held by First Bank of Apex. The note payable requires that Alta Tierra maintain a minimum current ratio of 1.25, and any violation of the covenant allows the lender to call the debt. You find that Alta Tierra's year-end current ratio is 1.1. Alta Tierra's Chief Financial Officer, Tony Plush, informs you that the company is in violation of the debt covenant but has been granted a waiver by First Bank of Apex, so there are no consequences to the violation. The waiver allows Alta Tierra 90 days from year-end to increase its current ratio to above 1.25. Your audit partner believes that the violation is an issue and is concerned that the long-term debt must be reclassified as current.

Directions

Research the related generally accepted accounting principles and prepare a short memo to your audit partner that answers whether the long-term debt should be reclassified. How would your answer change if First Bank of Apex granted a 15-month waiver as opposed to the 90-day waiver? How would your answer change if Alta Tierra met the 2016 year-end covenant, but it was probable that the first quarter 2017 current ratio covenant would be violated? Cite your references and applicable paragraph numbers.

C14-13 Researching GAAP

Situation

Clare Company is constructing a new warehouse facility. On May 15, 2016, the company issued $2,500,000 of short-term notes payable due March 15, 2017, to finance construction of the warehouse. On December 31, 2016, Clare intends to refinance the short-term notes payable by issuing long-term debt. However, because Clare has excess cash on January 12, 2017, it retires $800,000 of the short-term notes payable.

On January 20, 2017, Clare completes a $5,000,000 long-term debt offering. Clare uses the proceeds from the long-term debt to:

- retire the remaining $1,700,000 of short-term notes payable on March 15, 2017
- pay $3,300,000 of warehouse construction costs during 2017

As the financial statements for 2016 are being prepared, Steve Share, president of Clare Company, wants to make sure that all $2,500,000 of short-term notes payable are reclassified as long-term because the company borrowed enough to repay the total amount. As the accountant for Clare Company, you know that you can classify short-term debt that is going to be refinanced as a long-term liability but are not certain how much.

Directions

Research the related generally accepted accounting principles and prepare a short memo to the president of Clare Company that describes how the short-term notes payable should be classified in the 2016 balance sheet. Cite your references and applicable paragraph numbers.

CHAPTER 15

CONTRIBUTED CAPITAL

Stock Buybacks Gain Momentum

During 2013 the stock market experienced some of the largest 1-year gains in history, with the S&P 500 index increasing by more than 30%. Going hand in hand with these large stock market increases has been the repurchase by U.S. companies of their own common and preferred shares. In total, U.S. corporations included in the S&P 500 index repurchased $477 billion of stock during 2013. **ExxonMobil Corporation**, for example, repurchased $15 billion of its own stock during its 2013 fiscal year, while **Pfizer** purchased over $12 billion of its own stock. As you can see the growth in stock buybacks has been significant since 2009:

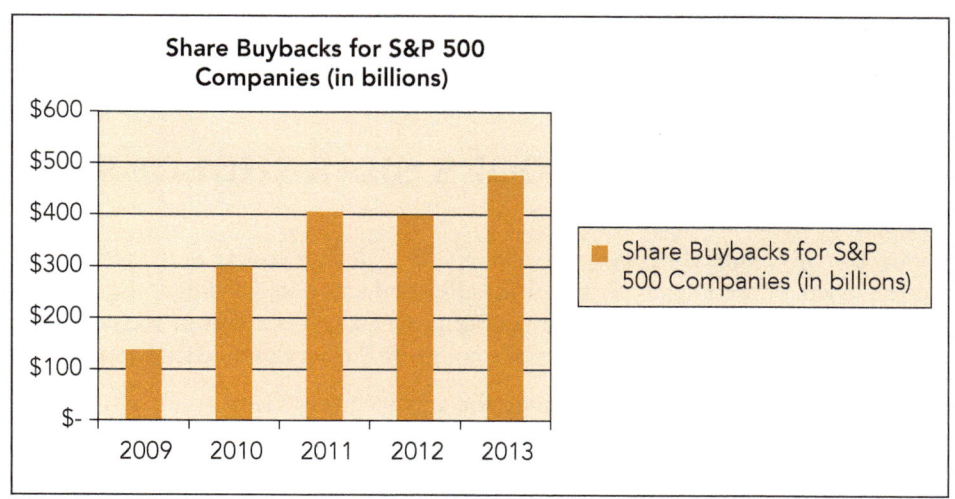

LEARNING OBJECTIVES

After reading this chapter you will be able to

LO 15.1 Define equity and explain the corporate form of organization, including its advantages and disadvantages.

LO 15.2 Know the rights and terms that apply to capital stock.

LO 15.3 Account for the issuance of capital stock.

LO 15.4 Describe noncompensatory share purchase plans.

LO 15.5 Describe and account for share-based compensation plans.

LO 15.6 Describe the characteristics of preferred stock.

LO 15.7 Understand the accounting for treasury stock.

LO 15.8 Know the components of contributed capital and how they are reported in financial statements.

Apple made one of the largest stock buybacks in 2013 when it announced in April that it would increase its share repurchase program from $10 billion to $60 billion. As a very profitable company, Apple had started its 2013 fiscal year with over $100 billion of cash and investments on its balance sheet. While Apple's operations (e.g., designing, producing, and selling iPods, iPads, iPhones, and Mac computers) generated double-digit returns, its cash and investments were only earning 1% to 2% per year. For this reason, Tim Cook, Apple's CEO, felt that returning capital to shareholders was a good use of its cash: "We believe so strongly that repurchasing our shares represents an attractive use of our capital that we have dedicated the vast majority of the increase in our capital return program to share repurchases."

Research shows that the capital markets usually react favorably when firms announce stock repurchase plans, as investors often interpret this action as a signal that the firm believes its shares are undervalued. Repurchase plans also provide companies with a flexible means of returning capital to shareholders who wish to sell their shares and help them avoid making a commitment to pay dividends to all shareholders. In addition, many firms repurchase shares to obtain the shares they need to satisfy employees' stock options exercises. However, some investors believe that shareholders would be better served if companies reinvested more of their money in research and development or for expanding operations.

The previous chapters focused primarily on changes in assets and liabilities and their impact on net income (and equity). The main focus of Chapters 15 and 16 is on investments by owners, distributions to owners, and stock-based compensation plans, as they apply to corporations.

In Chapter 15, we primarily discuss topics related to contributed capital. These issues include the formation of a corporation, terminology relating to capital stock, issuance of capital stock, compensatory share (stock) option plans, the Contributed Capital section of shareholders' equity, and reacquisition of capital (treasury) stock. In Chapter 16, we primarily discuss issues related to earned capital, including retained earnings, dividends, and earnings per share.

LEARNING OBJECTIVE 15.1
Define equity and explain the corporate form of organization, including its advantages and disadvantages.

WHAT INFORMATION DOES SHAREHOLDERS' EQUITY PROVIDE?

FASB Statement of Financial Accounting Concepts No. 6 defines **equity** as the residual interest in the assets of a company that remains after deducting its liabilities.[1] Equity in a company is the ownership interest that arises from owners' investments in the company. Owners' investments can finance the assets of a company through two general approaches:

- contributing capital directly in exchange for an ownership claim (such as investing cash to purchase shares of stock issued by the company)
- choosing to reinvest the income generated by the company

Therefore, the balance sheet accounting for financing activities by common equity shareholders typically involves *contributed capital accounts* (such as common equity at par and

[1] "Elements of Financial Statements of Business Enterprises," *FASB Statement of Financial Accounting Concepts No. 6* (Stamford, CT: FASB, 1985), par. 49.

additional paid-in capital) and *earned capital accounts* (such as retained earnings and accumulated other comprehensive income).

A corporation records the results of all its stock transactions in capital stock accounts and additional paid-in capital accounts. It then lists and adds together these accounts in the **Contributed Capital** section of its shareholders' equity. Any net income that has been reinvested in the corporation and not paid out to shareholders as dividends is reported in the **Retained Earnings** section of shareholders' equity. Also, shareholders' equity may increase or decrease as a result of other comprehensive income. A corporation reports this element of its capital structure in an **Accumulated Other Comprehensive Income** section of shareholders' equity. Retained earnings and accumulated other comprehensive income are discussed in Chapter 16.

The basic framework of a corporation's shareholders' equity is as follows:

Shareholders' Equity

Contributed Capital:	
Capital stock	$ xx
Additional paid-in capital	xx
Retained earnings	xx
Accumulated other comprehensive income	xx
Total Shareholders' Equity	$x,xxx

A company's equity changes as it earns net income and declares dividends. In addition, equity changes because of transactions between the company and its owners and other comprehensive income transactions and events, as summarized in Exhibit 15.1.[2]

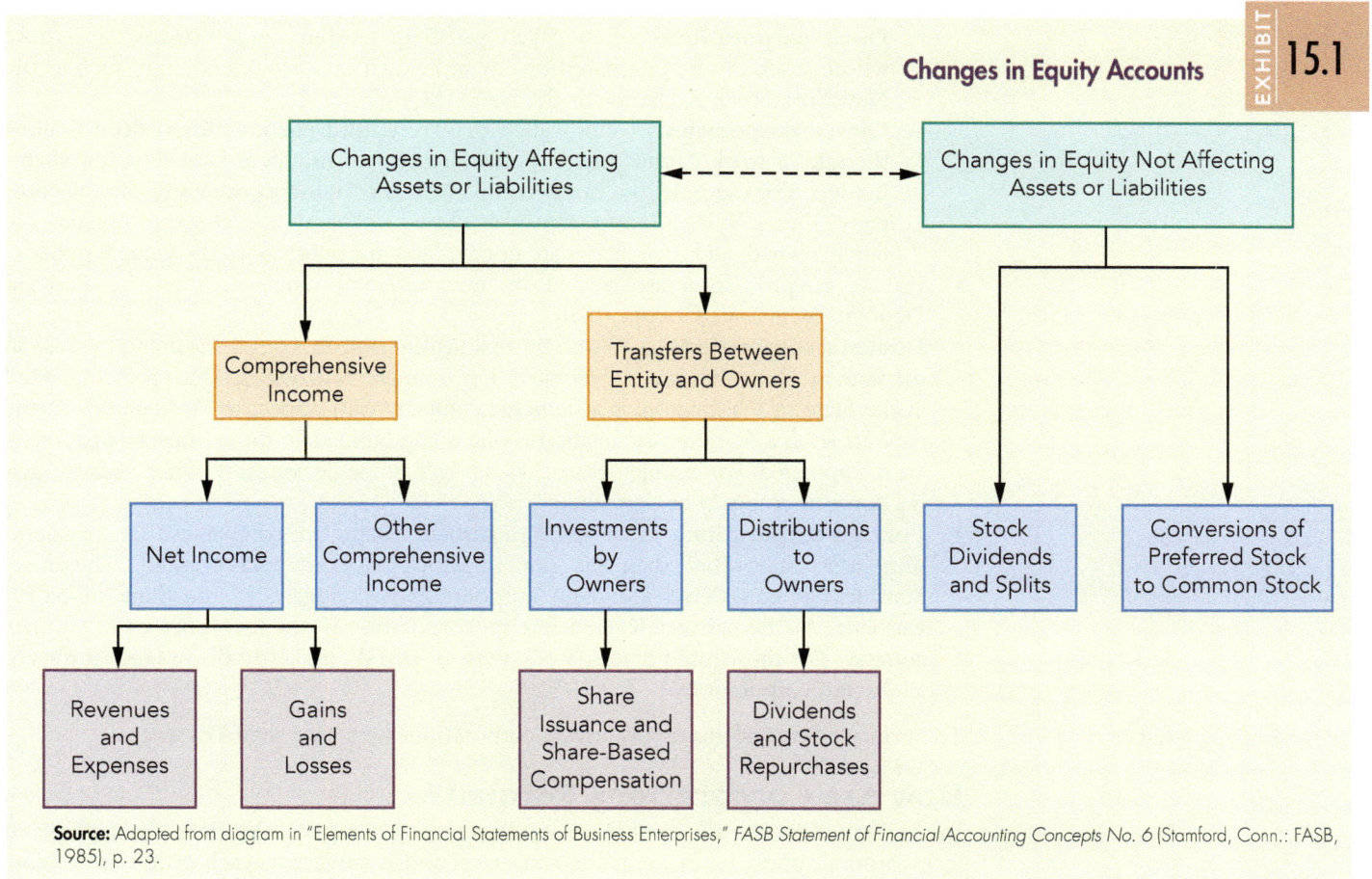

Changes in Equity Accounts — EXHIBIT 15.1

Source: Adapted from diagram in "Elements of Financial Statements of Business Enterprises," *FASB Statement of Financial Accounting Concepts No. 6* (Stamford, Conn.: FASB, 1985), p. 23.

[2] *Ibid*, par. 60–63.

HOW ARE CORPORATIONS ORGANIZED?

Starbucks Corporation, like most large companies, is organized as a corporation. This means that it is a separate legal entity from its owners, who are referred to as **shareholders** (or **stockholders**). While there is a greater number of sole proprietorships and partnerships, corporations are typically much larger organizations and produce and sell many more goods and services.

A corporation offers several advantages over other organization forms. One primary advantage of the corporate form is the ability to raise large amounts of capital by issuing shares of stock. Although a corporation actually is a collection of individual owners, it is a legal entity that is separate from and independent of these individuals. Thus, ownership is readily transferable between investors. Another primary advantage is that shareholders (owners) ordinarily have **limited legal liability**, meaning they bear no personal liability for the corporation's debts and risk, only their capital investment. However, corporations generally pay more taxes than other organizational forms because the corporate income tax rate is generally higher than the individual income tax rate. In addition, a corporation's income is taxed twice—once at the corporate level as income is earned and again at the investor level when dividends are distributed to shareholders.

How Are Corporations Classified?

Corporations may be classified as follows:

- **Corporations** include *stock* companies, such as **Microsoft** and **Samsung Electronics**, that issue shares of stock to shareholders and operate for profit, and also nonstock companies that do not operate for profit, such as some universities and hospitals. Stock companies include open and closed corporations.
    - **Open corporations** (often called **publicly traded corporations**) are those whose stock can be purchased by any individual on a stock exchange such as the New York Stock Exchange or the NASDAQ.
    - **Closed corporations** (often called **privately held corporations**) do not allow the sale of stock to the general public. This stock usually is held by a few shareholders. For example, the candy company **Mars, Incorporated** and the toy company **The LEGO Group** are both closed corporations. Both companies are family owned, and their shares are not available for purchase to the general public.
- **Public corporations** are owned by governmental units, such as the **Federal Deposit Insurance Corporation**.
- **Domestic corporations**, as viewed by a particular state, are companies doing business in the state in which they are incorporated. For example, **Starbucks**, which is incorporated in the State of Washington, is a domestic company with respect to Washington. At the national level, a domestic corporation is one doing business in the country in which they are incorporated. For example, Starbucks is a U.S. domestic company, while **Volkswagen** is a domestic company of Germany.
- **Foreign corporations**, as viewed by a particular state, are companies that are operating in a state other than the one in which they are incorporated. Therefore, Starbucks is considered a foreign corporation with regard to the State of North Carolina. At the national level, a foreign corporation is one incorporated in another country. For the United States, **Volkswagen**, **BMW**, and **Vodafone Group plc** are all foreign corporations.

The primary focus of this text is private corporations that issue shares of stock.

How Are Corporations Formed?

In the United States, a **corporation** is a legal entity of a particular state. An application to incorporate must be made at the state level and is subject to each state's laws. Normally, incorporation requires that one or more individuals apply for approval to form a corporation. The application includes the following:

- names of the individual incorporators
- corporate name, address, and nature of business
- types, par value (if any), and number of shares of capital stock to be issued
- any other information required by the state's law

The application may also include the names and addresses of the initial subscribers to the capital stock, number of subscribed shares, subscription price, and down payment (if any).

If approved, the application is referred to as the **articles of incorporation** (or **corporate charter**). A shareholders' meeting will then be held. At this meeting, capital stock is initially issued to the incorporators, a board of directors is elected, rules (bylaws) regulating the corporate operations are established, and executive officers ("top management") of the corporation are appointed by the board of directors.

For a corporation to perform its functions, the state gives it various rights and powers. These include the right to enter into contracts; to hold, buy, and sell property; to sue and be sued; and to continue indefinitely.

A corporation also has a number of responsibilities. A corporation may engage only in the activities for which it was established, it must adhere to state and federal laws concerning the conduct of business and distribution of income, and it must pay state and federal taxes. Because a corporation's management has the responsibility to abide by state and federal laws and to safeguard and ensure the proper use of capital contributed by a diverse set of owners, accounting for corporate capital is important.

GOT IT?

15-1 What information is contained in a corporation's articles of incorporation?

15-2 What is the difference between (a) a public and privately held corporation, (b) an open and closed corporation, and (c) a domestic and foreign corporation (as viewed by a particular state)?

15-3 What are the three components and the basic framework of shareholders' equity?

HOW IS THE CAPITAL STRUCTURE OF A CORPORATION DEFINED?

LEARNING OBJECTIVE 15.2
Know the rights and terms that apply to capital stock.

Ownership in a corporation is represented by a **stock certificate**, a serially numbered document that indicates the number of shares owned and the par value (if any). Exhibit 15.2 (p. 15-6) shows a number of companies' stock certificates, including **Pixar** and **Coca-Cola**. Because stock certificates are easily transferred from one investor to another, state laws require that each corporation keep appropriate records of its shareholders. Investors can be individuals, other corporations, mutual funds, trust or pension funds, banks, insurers, and many other types of entities. Many corporations employ an independent **transfer agent** (such as a bank) to handle the issuance of stock certificates, as well as a **registrar** to maintain the shareholder records.

Capital Stock and Shareholders' Rights

Capital stock refers to the shares of stock issued by the corporation and owned by its shareholders. Each shareholder has various rights. Generally, these rights include the following:

- right to a dividend when it is declared
- right to elect directors and to establish corporate policies (**voting right**)
- right (called a **preemptive right**) to maintain a proportionate interest in the ownership of the corporation by purchasing a proportionate (pro rata) share of additional capital stock if issued
- right to share in the distribution of the assets of the corporation if it is liquidated

EXHIBIT 15.2 Illustration of a Stock Certificate

These rights may be modified or waived for some types of capital stock or in specific circumstances. For instance, shareholders who own a certain class of stock may be entitled to vote only on particular issues. Another instance involves waiving the preemptive right to allow a corporation to raise significant capital or acquire another company by issuing a large number of additional shares of stock.

A corporation may issue capital stock in exchange for cash, for nonmonetary assets, to retire debt, and as part of a compensatory share plan. It may issue two basic types of stock, generally designated as common stock and preferred stock.

Common stock is capital stock that carries all of the rights of ownership. Some corporations issue more than one class of common stock such as Class A and Class B common stock. In this situation, usually one type of common stock has greater voting rights than the other to maintain control over the corporate activities. For example, at the end of 2012, **Nike** had approximately 90 million Class A common shares and 368 million Class B common shares. Class A holders have the right to elect 75% of the company's board of directors, while Class B holders get to elect only 25% of the board.

In exchange for certain other privileges, **preferred stock** usually is not granted all of the common stock's rights. We discuss the various stock transactions, as well as the characteristics and privileges of preferred stock, later in this chapter.

Basic Terminology

It is important to understand the following terms regarding capital stock and related transactions:

- **Authorized capital stock** is the number of shares of capital stock (both preferred and common) that a corporation may issue as stated in its corporate charter.

- **Issued capital stock** is the number of shares of capital stock that a corporation has issued to its shareholders as of a specific date.
- **Outstanding capital stock** is the number of shares of capital stock that a corporation has issued to shareholders and that are still being held by shareholders as of a specific date.
- **Treasury stock** is the number of shares of capital stock that a corporation has issued to and reacquired from shareholders but not retired. The number of treasury shares is the difference between the number of issued shares and the number of outstanding shares.
- **Subscribed capital stock** is the number of shares of capital stock that a corporation will issue upon the completion of an installment purchase contract with an investor.

Legal Capital

To protect the corporation's creditors, state laws have established the concept of **legal capital** as the amount of shareholders' equity that is restricted for purposes of dividends and other distributions. A corporation may not pay dividends or reacquire capital stock if such a transaction would impair its legal capital. The definition of legal capital varies among states. An investor must refer to the corporate laws of each state to determine the corporate legal capital in that state. However, in most states, the par value or stated value of the issued capital stock represents some or all of the legal capital.

Par Value Stock Historically, the primary way a corporation establishes its legal capital is by issuing par value stock. The **par value** of a corporation's capital stock (either common or preferred) is a designated dollar amount per share that is established in the articles of incorporation and is printed on each stock certificate. When a corporation issues par value stock, most states designate that the par value of all its issued stock is the legal capital, which is computed as follows:

Legal Capital = Par Value per Share × Number of Shares Issued

The par value of a share often is set very low—perhaps $5, $1, or even less per share.

It is important to note that the par value of a stock has no relation to its market value. Capital stock normally sells at a price much higher than the par value, which results in the legal capital being a small portion of the total proceeds received. For example, **Starbucks** has sold stock to investors for $42.6 million and only $1,500,000 of that amount is par value.

Stock rarely sells initially for less than its par value, because it is illegal to do so in most states. If such a sale occurs, the stock is said to have been sold at a *discount*, in which case the shareholder is contingently responsible to contribute sufficient additional capital to meet the corporation's legal capital requirements.

No-Par Stock To avoid the contingent liability that would arise if stock were issued at less than par value, many states allow corporations to issue **no-par capital stock**. As the term implies, this stock does not carry a par value. When a corporation issues no-par stock, some states require that the corporation designate the entire proceeds received as legal capital. Many states, however, allow the corporate board of directors to establish a **stated value** per share of no-par stock. This stated value, when multiplied by the number of shares issued, generally determines the amount of the corporation's legal capital. The accounting for stated value stock is consistent with accounting for par value stock.

The concept of legal capital has had a significant effect on corporate reporting practices, particularly as they apply to the accounting for shareholders' equity. A corporation creates capital stock accounts (for either common stock or preferred stock) to accumulate at least part of the legal capital. It uses Additional Paid-in Capital accounts for the remainder of the capital contributed by shareholders.

Additional Paid-in Capital

As indicated earlier, a corporation may issue capital stock in a variety of transactions. In each of these transactions, the exchange price is likely to be significantly higher than the par or stated value of the stock. State law requires the corporation to record the par or stated value. Sound accounting practice also requires the corporation to identify, measure, and record the excess value received (the difference between the exchange price and the par value) in each type of stock transaction. The corporation records this excess in a specific **Additional Paid-in Capital** account. While most companies use the term Additional Paid-in Capital, you may also see the terms:

- *Capital in Excess of Par (or Stated) Value*
- *Paid-in Capital in Excess of Par (or Stated) Value*
- *Additional Capital*

Because this additional paid-in capital is likely to arise from a variety of transactions, a corporation may create a single Additional Paid-in Capital *control* account and then have a subsidiary ledger containing separate additional paid-in capital accounts for each different source. When this occurs, it reports only the control account balance on its balance sheet. In this chapter, we assume a control account is *not* used and, instead, each source has its own Additional Paid-in Capital account.

WHY IT MATTERS

One key ratio used to evaluate a company's profitability is the **return on shareholders' equity** (**ROE**). This ratio shows how many dollars of net income were earned for every dollar invested by the owners and is computed as:

$$\text{ROE} = \text{Net Income} \div \text{Average Shareholders' Equity}$$

While the overall ROE can be useful, many financial statement users prefer a more detailed examination of the components of this ratio. The DuPont model enables the analyst to "decompose" the ROE ratio into three major components as shown below.

$$\text{ROE} = \text{Profitability} \times \text{Efficiency} \times \text{Financial Leverage}$$

$$= \frac{\text{Net Income}}{\text{Net Sales}} \times \frac{\text{Net Sales}}{\text{Average Assets}} \times \frac{\text{Average Assets}}{\text{Average Shareholders' Equity}}$$

The formula above provides the financial statement analyst insights into whether a change in ROE is caused by a change in profitability (Income/Sales), a change in efficiency (Sales/Average Assets), or a change in financial leverage (Average Assets/Average Equity).

Below is information obtained from Nike's and Under Armour's 2012 financial statements (in millions):

(in millions)	Nike 2012	Nike 2011	Under Armour 2012	Under Armour 2011
Average assets	$15,232	$14,709	$1,038	$ 797
Average shareholders' equity	10,112	9,799	727	567
Net sales	24,128	20,862	1,835	1,473
Net income	2,223	2,133	129	97

(continued)

Nike's ROE for 2012 and 2011 can be computed as:

2012: ROE = $2,223/$24,128 × $24,128/$15,232 × $15,232/$10,112
= 0.092 × 1.584 × 1.506
= 21.9%

2011: ROE = $2,133/$20,862 × $20,862/$14,709 × $14,709/$9,799
= 0.102 × 1.418 × 1.501
= 21.7%

In the same way, Under Armour's ROE can be computed as:

2012: ROE = $129/$1,835 × $1,835/$1,038 × $1,038/$727
= 0.070 × 1.768 × 1.428
= 17.7%

2011: ROE = $97/$1,473 × $1,473/$797 × $797/$567
= 0.066 × 1.848 × 1.406
= 17.1%

This analysis indicates that Nike has stronger profitability, but Under Armour is more efficient with more sales per dollar of average assets. It also shows that Nike uses more leverage in its capital structure with approximately $1.50 in average assets for each $1.00 of shareholders' equity, compared to Under Armour with roughly $1.43 in average assets for each $1.00 in equity. Both companies had strong and consistent ROEs over the period.

ETHICAL DILEMMA

Muddy Water Inc. catches and supplies fresh seafood to a variety of restaurants across the country. While the company remains profitable, increased competition from South American seafood suppliers has lowered the company's return on equity (Net Income ÷ Average Shareholders' Equity) to a level that the board of directors finds unacceptable. In response to these competitive pressures, the company decides to modernize its processing plants in hopes that the resulting increase in efficiency will lead to lower costs and higher profit margins. You are in charge of assembling a team to develop financing options. After carefully analyzing the various options, your team recommends that the modernization be financed by issuing stock.

The CEO, however, discusses the matter with another business professional who informs her that issuing stock would only increase shareholders' equity, which would lower the company's return on equity, while debt financing might actually help the company reach its return on equity targets. The CEO now advocates financing the modernization with debt instead of equity.

While you confirm that this may be true, you inform the CEO that the debt option is much riskier, and the required interest payments would lower the company's net income and put the company in a shaky cash position. The CEO states that she understands the risk, but that she really needs to reach the return on equity target to achieve bonuses for her executive team, and any cash flow concerns will not surface until after she retires in two years. Do you have any ethical responsibilities to report the CEO's decision to the board of directors?

GOT IT?

15-4 List the various rights of a shareholder. Which do you consider to be the most important?

15-5 What is the meaning of the following terms: (a) authorized capital stock, (b) issued capital stock, (c) outstanding capital stock, and (d) treasury stock? What is the difference between the number of issued and outstanding capital shares?

15-6 What is a corporation's legal capital, and why is it important?

15-7 How is a corporation's legal capital determined, assuming its capital stock has a par value, a stated value, or no par value?

15-8 How does preferred stock differ from common stock?

LEARNING OBJECTIVE 15.3
Account for the issuance of capital stock.

HOW DO WE ACCOUNT FOR THE ISSUANCE OF CAPITAL STOCK?

When a corporation issues only one class of capital stock, it is referred to as common stock. Common shareholders have a residual interest in the net assets of a corporation. Unless waived or modified, common shareholders generally have all the rights discussed earlier in the chapter. Corporations may issue capital stock under a number of scenarios, and we describe the proper accounting for each of these transactions next. Because most capital stock is common stock, our examples are in terms of common stock. However, the journal entries we show apply equally to preferred stock.

Authorization

The corporate charter contains the authorization to issue capital stock. A corporation usually records this authorization in a memorandum journal entry. The entry identifies the number of authorized shares, the par or stated value per share, and, in the case of preferred stock, any preference provisions. Generally, the corporation creates a separate account for each class of capital stock and makes a similar memorandum entry in each account.

Issuance for Cash

In the case of par value stock issued for cash, the corporation records the difference between the proceeds and the total par value in an Additional Paid-in Capital account.

Example Apex Corporation issues 500 shares of its $5 par common stock for $16 per share. The corporation records the transaction as follows:

Cash ($16 × 500)	8,000	
Common Stock, $5 par value ($5 × 500)		2,500
Additional Paid-in Capital on Common Stock		5,500

If, instead, the stock were no-par stock with a stated value of $5 per share, it would record the preceding transaction as follows:

Cash ($16 × 500)	8,000	
Common Stock, $5 stated value ($5 × 500)		2,500
Additional Paid-in Capital on Common Stock		5,500

Note that, with the exception of the terminology change, accounting for the issuance of no-par stock with a stated value is identical to that of par value stock. For both of these situations, the number of shares issued can be determined as follows:

$$\text{Number of Common Shares Issued} = \frac{\text{Total Amount in the Common Stock Account}}{\text{Par or Stated Value of the Shares}}$$

Alternatively, Apex may be authorized to issue no-par stock without a stated value. In this case, the entire amount of the proceeds is the legal capital and is recorded in the capital stock account as follows:

Cash ($16 × 500)	8,000	
Common Stock, no-par (500 shares)		8,000

Note that, in this journal entry, it is necessary to include the number of *shares* issued because it cannot be determined by dividing the total increase in the Common Stock account by the par value per share. In the remaining examples of stock issuances, we assume a par value for the stock.

Stock Issuance Costs

A corporation may incur various costs that arise from issuing its capital stock. They include items such as legal fees, accounting fees, stock certificate costs, underwriter's fees, promotional costs, and postage. When these costs are incurred at the initial issuance of stock at the time of incorporation, they are considered an organization expense. After the initial incorporation, any costs incurred to issue capital stock are considered to be normal financing costs and are recorded as a reduction of the proceeds received from the issuance. Specifically, additional paid-in capital is reduced for the amount of these costs.

Stock Subscriptions

Investors sometimes agree to purchase capital stock from a corporation and pay at a later date. This creates a legally binding subscription contract between the corporation and the future shareholder. This contract requires the investor to buy a certain number of shares at an agreed-upon price, with payment spread over a specified time period. The contract often requires a down payment and may require the investor to issue the company a promissory note. The contract will also set forth what will happen if the investor is not able to pay and defaults. Normally, the corporation does not treat the shares of capital stock as issued until the investor has completed full payment of the subscription price.

Example: Subscription Contract

Varina Corporation enters into a subscription contract with an investor. The contract requires the investor to purchase 1,000 shares of $6 par common stock at a price of $15 per share. The contract further requires a down payment of $3 per share, with the remaining $12 per share collectible at the end of one month. Varina will issue stock to each subscriber after it receives payment in full. Varina records the subscription as follows:

Cash ($3 × 1,000)	3,000	
Subscriptions Receivable: Common Stock ($12 × 1,000)	12,000	
Common Stock Subscribed ($6 × 1,000)		6,000
Additional Paid-in Capital on Common Stock		9,000

Note that the balance to be received is recorded in a Subscriptions Receivable account. There is disagreement as to how a corporation should report the subscriptions receivable on its balance sheet. Some argue that because the subscription contract is legally binding, the receivable should be reported as an asset on the corporation's balance sheet. Others contend that Subscriptions Receivable should be listed as a contra-shareholders' equity account so that the amount of capital contributed will not be overstated. The SEC supports this view by requiring a corporation to report its subscriptions receivable as a contra-shareholders' equity account on financial statements filed with it.

In addition, a Common Stock Subscribed account is credited for the par value of the shares subscribed because the shares have not yet been issued. Given that the corporation expects the contract to be completed, the Common Stock Subscribed account is reported in the Contributed Capital section of its shareholders' equity. Additional Paid-in Capital is credited for the entire difference between the subscription price (the proceeds) and the par value of the subscribed stock under the assumption that the contract will be completed and the stock fully paid for.

When the corporation receives payment, it debits Cash and credits the Subscriptions Receivable account. Once the corporation has received full payment for the subscription, it makes a journal entry to transfer the balance in the Common Stock Subscribed account to the Common Stock account, and issues stock certificates for the number of subscribed shares fully paid for by the investor. Assuming that Varina received the $12 per share final payment from its investors at the end of the month, it makes the following journal entries:

Cash (1,000 × $12)	12,000	
Subscriptions Receivable: Common Stock		12,000
Common Stock Subscribed (1,000 × $6)	6,000	
Common Stock, $6 par		6,000

Combined Sales of Stock

Sometimes companies will bundle two or more securities and issue them together. These combined transactions may include combinations of common stock, preferred stock, or long-term bonds or notes. For example, **Black and Decker, Inc.,** sold $632.5 million of convertible preferred equity units. Each equity unit sold by Black and Decker contained shares of preferred stock and a note payable.

When a corporation issues different types of securities in a combined sale, it allocates the proceeds between the securities based on the relative fair value of each security. If the fair value of only one of the securities is known, the fair value amount is assigned to that security. The remaining proceeds are assigned to the security with the unknown fair value.

Example Fairway Corporation issues 100 "equity units" of securities for $82.80 per unit, or a total of $8,280. Each equity unit includes two shares of $10 par common stock and one share of $50 par preferred stock. If the separate fair values are $16 per share for the common stock and $60 per share for the preferred stock, Fairway makes the following journal entry and supporting computations:

Cash	8,280	
Common Stock, $10 par (200 shares)		2,000
Additional Paid-in Capital on Common Stock		880
Preferred Stock, $50 par (100 shares)		5,000
Additional Paid-in Capital on Preferred Stock		400

Supporting Computations:

Aggregate Fair Value
Common Stock: $16 × 2 shares × 100 equity units = $3,200
Preferred Stock: $60 × 1 share × 100 equity units = 6,000
$9,200

Allocation

Common Stock: $\dfrac{\$3{,}200}{\$9{,}200} \times \$8{,}280 = \$2{,}880$

Preferred Stock: $\dfrac{\$6{,}000}{\$9{,}200} \times \$8{,}280 = \dfrac{\$5{,}400}{\$8{,}280}$

Note that Fairway's journal entry separates the fair value assigned to each class of stock into the par value and additional paid-in capital.

If only the separate fair value of $16 per share for the common stock is known, Fairway assigns $3,200 ($16 × 2 shares × 100 equity units) of the proceeds to the common stock and allocates the remainder of $5,080 to the preferred stock, as follows:

Cash	8,280	
Common Stock, $10 par		2,000
Additional Paid-in Capital on Common Stock		1,200
Preferred Stock, $50 par		5,000
Additional Paid-in Capital on Preferred Stock		80

In the rare case when none of the securities has a market value, a corporation must estimate the fair values and make a reasonable allocation to the various elements of equity.

Nonmonetary Issuance of Stock

In some cases, a corporation may issue capital stock for assets other than cash or for services performed. This type of transaction is called a **nonmonetary exchange**. The corporation must assign an appropriate value to the transaction so it can record the exchange properly. This valuation is a particularly troublesome issue when it involves intangible assets such as patents, copyrights, or organization costs. The general rule is to **record the exchange at the fair value of the stock issued or the asset received, whichever can be measured with greater representational faithfulness.** For instance, at the time of the exchange, the stock may be selling on the stock market at a specified price, but a verifiable value of the asset may be difficult to determine. In this case, the stock market price is used as the fair value at which to record the exchange transaction.

Example: Fair Value of Stock Known

Dunn Corporation issues 200 shares of $5 par common stock for a patent. The stock currently is selling for $22 per share on the open market, and no significant impact on the market price by the issuance of the additional shares is expected.[3] Dunn assigns a value of $4,400 to the exchange and records the transaction as follows:

Patent ($22 × 200)	4,400	
Common Stock, $5 par		1,000
Additional Paid-in Capital on Common Stock		3,400

Alternatively, the stock may be closely held and not actively traded. Therefore, using the fair value of the assets received may provide a more representationally faithful value of the transaction. This value may be based on recent transactions involving similar assets or on an appraisal by an independent appraiser.

Example: Fair Value of Asset Known

Omaha Corporation issues 500 shares of $8 par common stock that is not widely traded for an acre of land. An independent appraiser indicates the land has a value of $30,000. Omaha uses the appraisal value of the land as the fair value and records the transaction as follows:

Land	30,000	
Common Stock, $8 par		4,000
Additional Paid-in Capital on Common Stock		26,000

Stock Splits

The market price of a corporation's common stock may increase to the point where it discourages investments by some investors. For example, **Starbucks** has executed six 2-for-1 stock splits since its initial public offering. Therefore, an investor who purchased 100 shares of Starbucks's common stock at its initial public offering in 1992 would now own 6,400 shares. If Starbucks had never split its stock, the individual share price would have increased to more than $3,840 at the end of 2015, making the purchase of even one share prohibitive for many small investors.

Many corporations believe that wide distribution of ownership increases the liquidity of their shares in the capital market, improves their public image, increases the demand for their stock, and may increase product sales to these shareholders. To reduce the market price so that it falls within desired "trading range" of most investors, a corporation may authorize a stock split. A **stock split** proportionally decreases market price and the par value per share of stock and increases the number of shares issued. Generally, a stock split also results in a proportional increase in the number of shares authorized. **A *reverse* stock split increases the par value per share and proportionally decreases the number of shares issued.**

---

[3] If a large number of additional shares is issued, this may significantly reduce the market price of the shares. In this case, the corporation does not record the transaction until the reduced market price is known.

In the investor relations section of its web site, **The Coca-Cola Company** provides this information about its stock splits:

> Stock splits must be recommended by management to the Board of Directors and then approved by the Company's shareowners. Also, there must be enough shares authorized to affect a split. Stock of The Coca-Cola Company has split 11 times since 1919 in an effort to lower the absolute price per share to a more attractive and convenient purchase level; however, there is not a predetermined price ceiling or set time frame for a stock split to occur.

Example Angier Corporation has 250,000 authorized shares and 60,000 shares issued and outstanding of $10 par common stock. Angier declares a 2-for-1 stock split and a reduction in par value to $5 per share. After the split, 500,000 shares are authorized, and a total of 120,000 shares of $5 common stock are issued and outstanding. Generally, a stock split will cause a corresponding decrease in the market price per share because more shares have a claim on the same amount of a company's net assets.

When a corporation has a stock split, it generally does not recall the existing shares. Instead, each shareholder is informed of the new par value per share and is issued an additional number of shares to compensate for the split. From an accounting standpoint, a stock split has no dollar effect on any element of the corporation's shareholders' equity. Consequently, a stock split has no effect on total shareholders' equity. In the previous example, the total par value of the issued common stock is $600,000 prior to and after the stock split.

A corporation ordinarily records a stock split by a memorandum entry that indicates the new par value, the total number of shares issued, and the impact (if any) on the number of authorized shares. For instance, Angier's memorandum entry might read as follows:

> The board of directors split the common stock two for one, increasing the issued stock from 60,000 to 120,000 shares. The par value of the stock has been reduced from $10 per share to $5 per share, and the authorized shares have been increased to 500,000 shares.

Stock Warrants

Stock warrants represent the right to purchase additional shares of common stock at an established price, usually referred to as the *exercise price*. The **exercise price** (or **strike price**) is the price at which the holder of a warrant has the right to buy or sell the common stock. Stock warrants may be issued in several ways. In some cases, warrants may be given to existing shareholders as evidence of their preemptive right. For example, if a corporation's board of directors authorizes the issuance of additional shares, it may fulfill this preemptive right by issuing stock warrants to each present shareholder who may then exercise them to acquire additional shares of stock. A corporation may also issue warrants to shareholders to encourage the rapid sale of new issuances of stock.

At the time a corporation issues warrants, it makes a memorandum entry listing the number of additional shares that it may be required to issue through the exercise of the stock rights. This entry also provides information for disclosing the outstanding warrants in the notes to its financial statements. If the holders exercise the warrants, the corporation makes the usual journal entry to record the issuance of the stock. If the rights expire, it makes another memorandum entry noting the expiration.

Warrants may be issued separately or in conjunction with other securities, such as a bond or preferred stock. These warrants are referred to as **detachable warrants** because they can be separated from the other security and traded independently. Accounting for detachable warrants gives rise to two questions:

- Should the warrants be treated separately from the accompanying security?
- How is the value of the warrant determined?

When a company issues warrants with either a bond or preferred stock, it is important to recognize that the company is issuing a bundle containing two distinct securities, a warrant that allows the holder to purchase common stock and either a debt instrument or preferred share. The proceeds from the sale of the combined securities should be allocated to the two securities according to the proportionate fair market values as of the issue date (as discussed earlier in this chapter). In Chapter 14, we discussed the accounting for bonds issued with warrants; below we show the accounting for warrants issued with preferred stock.

Example Rehage Company issues 1,000 shares of $50 par value preferred stock with detachable warrants for $106,000 on January 1, 2016. Each share of preferred stock is issued with 5 detachable stock warrants. Each warrant entitles the holder to purchase one share of common stock for $50. The warrants expire in 2 years. The fair market value of the preferred stock is $72,000 on January 1, 2016, and the warrants sell for $8 per warrant. Rehage records the issuance of the preferred shares and warrants by making the following journal entry and supporting computations:

Cash	106,000.00	
Preferred Stock		50,000.00
Additional Paid-in Capital on Preferred Stock		18,142.86
Paid-in Capital—Common Stock Warrants		37,857.14

Supporting Computations:

Aggregate Fair Value

Preferred Stock =	$ 72,000
Common Stock Warrants: 5,000 warrants × $8 =	40,000
	$112,000

Allocation
Preferred Stock: ($72,000/$112,000) × $106,000 = $68,142.86
Common Stock Warrants: ($40,000/$112,000) × $106,000 = $37,857.14

Assume that on July 1, 2019, the warrants are exercised to purchase common stock (with a par value of $10 per share). The exercise price is $50 per share. Rehage should make the following entry:

Cash (5,000 warrants × $50)	250,000.00	
Paid-in Capital—Common Stock Warrants	37,857.14	
Common Stock (5,000 common shares × $10 par value)		50,000.00
Additional Paid-in Capital on Common Stock		237,857.14

When the warrants are exercised, the Paid-in Capital—Common Stock Warrants account is eliminated. The buyer of the stock has given consideration of $50 per share in cash but has also given warrants that had been assigned a value of $37,857.14.

INTERNATIONAL DIMENSION

SHAREHOLDERS' EQUITY

Under IFRS, the accounting for shareholders' equity is similar to that of U.S. GAAP. However, some differences do exist:

- Terminology:
  - Shareholders' equity is normally referred to as *capital and reserves*.
  - The capital stock account is generally called either *issued capital* or *share capital*.
  - Additional paid-in capital is often referred to as *share premium*.
  - Retained earnings is normally referred to as a *reserve account*.
- IFRS allow companies to revalue (upward and downward) their property, plant, and equipment and intangible assets. When a company increases its asset values because of a revaluation to fair value, it also credits a revaluation surplus, or reserve, account. (A decrease because of revaluation would reduce this revaluation account, or if no balance exists in the revaluation account, the downward adjustment would be recognized as a loss on the income statement.)

IFRS Application These differences are illustrated in Exhibit 15.3 which provides the equity section from the balance sheet of **LVMH**'s most recent financial report.

EXHIBIT 15.3 LVMH's Liabilities and Equity

LIABILITIES AND EQUITY (EUR millions)	Notes	2013	2012	2011
Share capital	15.1	152	152	152
Share premium account	15.1	3,849	3,848	3,801
Treasury shares and LVMH-share settled derivatives	15.2	(451)	(414)	(485)
Cumulative translation adjustment	15.4	(8)	342	431
Revaluation reserves		3,900	2,731	2,637
Other reserves		15,817	14,341	12,770
Net profit, Group share		3,436	3,424	3,065
Equity, Group share		26,695	24,424	22,371
Minority interests	17	1,028	1,084	1,055
Total equity		**27,723**	**25,508**	**23,426**
Long-term borrowings	18	4,159	3,836	4,132
Non-current provisions	19	1,755	1,756	1,530
Deferred tax		3,934	3,960	3,925
Other non-current liabilities	20	6,403	5,456	4,506
Non-current liabilities		**16,251**	**15,008**	**14,093**
Short-term borrowings	18	4,688	2,976	3,134
Trade accounts payable		3,308	3,134	2,952
Income taxes		382	442	443
Current provisions	19	322	335	349
Other current liabilities	21	3,000	2,595	2,716
Current liabilities		**11,700**	**9,482**	**9,594**
Total liabilities and equity		**55,674**	**49,998**	**47,113**

Source: IAS 1 and IAS 32. (See Appendix C at the end of this book.)

> ### GOT IT?
>
> **15-9** What amount of the proceeds from the issuance of no-par, no-stated-value stock is recorded in the Capital Stock account?
>
> **15-10** What is a stock subscription? How does a corporation report the accounts Subscriptions Receivable and Preferred Stock Subscribed on its balance sheet? Why?
>
> **15-11** How would you record the proceeds received from the combined issuance by a corporation of shares of common stock with shares of preferred stock?
>
> **15-12** If a corporation issues capital stock for an asset other than cash, what amount would you use to record the transaction?
>
> **15-13** What is a stock split? How do stock splits affect each element of a corporation's shareholders' equity?
>
> **15-14** If a French company using IFRS revalued its property, plant, and equipment upwards due to an increase in its fair value, where would the revaluation appear on its financial statements? How would the company account for a subsequent downward revaluation?

HOW DO COMPANIES ACCOUNT FOR NONCOMPENSATORY SHARE PURCHASE PLANS?

LEARNING OBJECTIVE 15.4
Describe noncompensatory share purchase plans.

Corporations may have a **noncompensatory share purchase plan** that enables employees to buy shares of stock, usually at a discount from market price. This plan may be established to raise capital or to obtain more widespread employee ownership of the corporate stock. A share purchase plan is noncompensatory if the plan conveys no compensation to employees. Three criteria must be met for a share purchase plan to be noncompensatory:

- All employees who meet specific employment qualifications may participate in the plan on an equal basis.
- The discount from the market price does not exceed the per-share amount of stock issuance costs avoided by not issuing the stock to the public. A purchase discount of up to 5% automatically complies with this criterion.
- The plan has no option features other than the following: (a) employees are allowed a short time (no longer than 31 days) from the date the purchase price is set to decide whether to enroll in the plan, and (b) the purchase price is based solely on the market price of the stock on the purchase date, and employees are permitted to cancel their participation before the purchase date and obtain a refund of any amounts previously paid.[4]

Any plan that does not meet all three of these criteria is considered a compensatory plan. If the plan is noncompensatory, the corporation makes a memorandum entry indicating the number of additional shares that may be acquired. If employees exercise the stock purchase rights, the corporation makes the usual journal entry to record the stock issuance. If not exercised, it makes a memorandum entry noting the expiration. **Starbucks'** describes its employee stock purchase plan (ESPP) in its annual report as follows:

> *ESPP*
>
> Our ESPP allows eligible employees to contribute up to 10% of their base earnings toward the quarterly purchase of our common stock, subject to an annual maximum dollar amount. The purchase price is 95% of the fair market value of the stock on the last business day of the quarterly offering period. The number of shares issued under our ESPP was 0.5 million in fiscal 2015.

---

[4] FASB ASC 718-50-25: Compensation-Stock Compensation, Employee Share Purchase Plans, Recognition.

> **GOT IT?**
>
> **15-15** What are restricted shares and share appreciation rights? Why are they advantageous to an employee?
>
> **15-16** What are the criteria for a noncompensatory share option plan, and what is the purpose behind a noncompensatory plan?

LEARNING OBJECTIVE 15.5
Describe and account for share-based compensation plans.

WHAT ARE SHARE-BASED COMPENSATION PLANS?

In addition to cash salaries, many corporations use share-based compensation plans to provide employees additional benefits. A **share-based compensation plan** is a compensation arrangement in which employees receive share options, shares of stock, or cash payments based on the change in stock price instead of cash bonus. The accounting objective of share-based compensation plans is to recognize compensation expense over the periods in which the employees perform a service and earn the share-based award.

A **compensatory share option plan** is intended to provide additional compensation to selected employees within the corporation by awarding them options to purchase the company's stock. **Restricted share awards** and **share appreciation rights** are also intended to provide additional compensation by awarding employees shares in the company or cash bonuses tied to changes in the company's stock price. For example, **Starbucks**' share-based compensation programs include both share option plans and restricted share awards. These compensation plans are both time-vested programs, in which the employee must remain an employee of Starbucks for a certain length of time to receive the compensation, and performance-based awards, in which the compensation is awarded to the employees if certain financial goals are met.

Overview of Compensatory Share Option Plans

In developing a compensatory share option plan, a company's objective is to better align the company's goals with those of management and its owners. Awarding options on shares in the company should motivate executives and employees to manage the company in a way that increases stock price. If this happens, both the managers and shareholders benefit. In addition, by awarding share options that become exercisable after a certain length of time (often 3 years after the grant date), it provides incentives for managers and employees to remain with the company for that period, reducing employee turnover.

Share options became extremely prevalent in the 1990s as boards of directors developed new employment contracts that involved options to enhance compensation packages without having to expend cash. Under a common type of plan, a corporation grants selected employees the rights to purchase shares of stock at an exercise price sometime in the future in exchange for their services. The date on which the company provides the share options to the employees is called the **grant date**. For instance, a corporation may grant an employee the right to purchase 1,000 shares of common stock at the end of three years at an exercise (strike) price of $20 per share. If the market price increases to $35 per share at the end of 3 years, the employee can exercise the option and acquire shares with a value of $35,000 ($35 × 1,000) by paying only $20,000 ($20 × 1,000).

Intrinsic Value Initially, GAAP required the use of the *intrinsic value method*. Under the **intrinsic value method**, a corporation measured the total options-based compensation cost for each employee as follows:

$$\text{Total Options-Based Compensation Cost} = \text{Number of Share Options} \times \left(\text{Market Price of the Stock on Date of Grant} - \text{Exercise Price of the Share Option} \right)$$

The company recognized this compensation cost as an expense on a straight-line basis over the years from the date of grant to the date the shares could first be purchased. Normally companies set the exercise price equal to or slightly above the market price on the grant date. Therefore, under the intrinsic value method, companies generally deemed the compensation cost to be zero and recognized no compensation expense.

Fair Value In response to the need for high-quality transparent financial reporting that faithfully represented the underlying substance of the arrangement, the FASB, along with the IASB, updated the accounting for share-based compensation plans. The change by the FASB and IASB required the use of the fair value method, which measures options-based compensation expense using the fair values of the options granted, and provides a more relevant and representationally faithful measure of an employee's total compensation.

Political Controversy In the early 1990s, the FASB issued an *Exposure Draft* which would have required companies to use the fair value method to account for compensatory share option plans. The Exposure Draft was extremely controversial, resulting in various groups, such as technology companies and venture capital firms, vigorously opposing and lobbying against the fair value method. These efforts threatened the very existence of the FASB. As a result of political pressure, the FASB revised the Exposure Draft and issued a standard for stock-option-based compensation that allowed a company the choice of using the fair value method or the intrinsic method to account for its compensatory share option plans. Almost all companies continued to use the intrinsic value method and recognized little, if any, compensation expense related to these plans.

The serious financial reporting failures that occurred in the early 2000s led many groups to revisit the share-based compensation issue. These groups felt that because compensation expense was not recognized under the intrinsic value method, many companies' income statements were misleading and contributed to many of the financial reporting problems. In response to the need for high-quality "transparent" financial reporting that faithfully represented the underlying substance of the arrangement, the FASB, along with the IASB, updated the accounting for share-based compensation plans to require the use of the fair value method.[5]

Because the fair value method affects both a corporation's income statement and balance sheet, GAAP addresses several related issues. These issues include:

- how to measure the fair value of share-based compensation issued for employees' services
- how to recognize and report the related compensation expense
- what additional disclosures should be made for the plan

Exhibit 15.4 (p. 15-20) details the recommended method of accounting for share-based compensation plans and will help you see the "big picture" before we discuss the detailed accounting issues.

How Do We Account for Compensatory Share Option Plans?

The fair value of a share option in a compensatory plan should be measured based on the market price of an option with the same or similar terms and conditions. Because similar options normally don't exist, fair value must be estimated using an option pricing model, such as the Black-Scholes-Merton option pricing model, at the grant date. On this date, the corporation becomes contingently obligated to issue common stock to the employee who fulfills the service requirements of the plan (e.g., working for the corporation for a certain number of years or reaching certain performance goals). Once the fair

---

[5] FASB ASC 718-10-30-21 states that it should be possible to reasonably estimate the fair value of most equity share options and other equity instruments at the date they are granted. However, in the rare case that it is not possible to reasonably estimate an equity instruments fair value, the intrinsic value may be used.

EXHIBIT 15.4 Accounting for Share-Based Compensation Plans

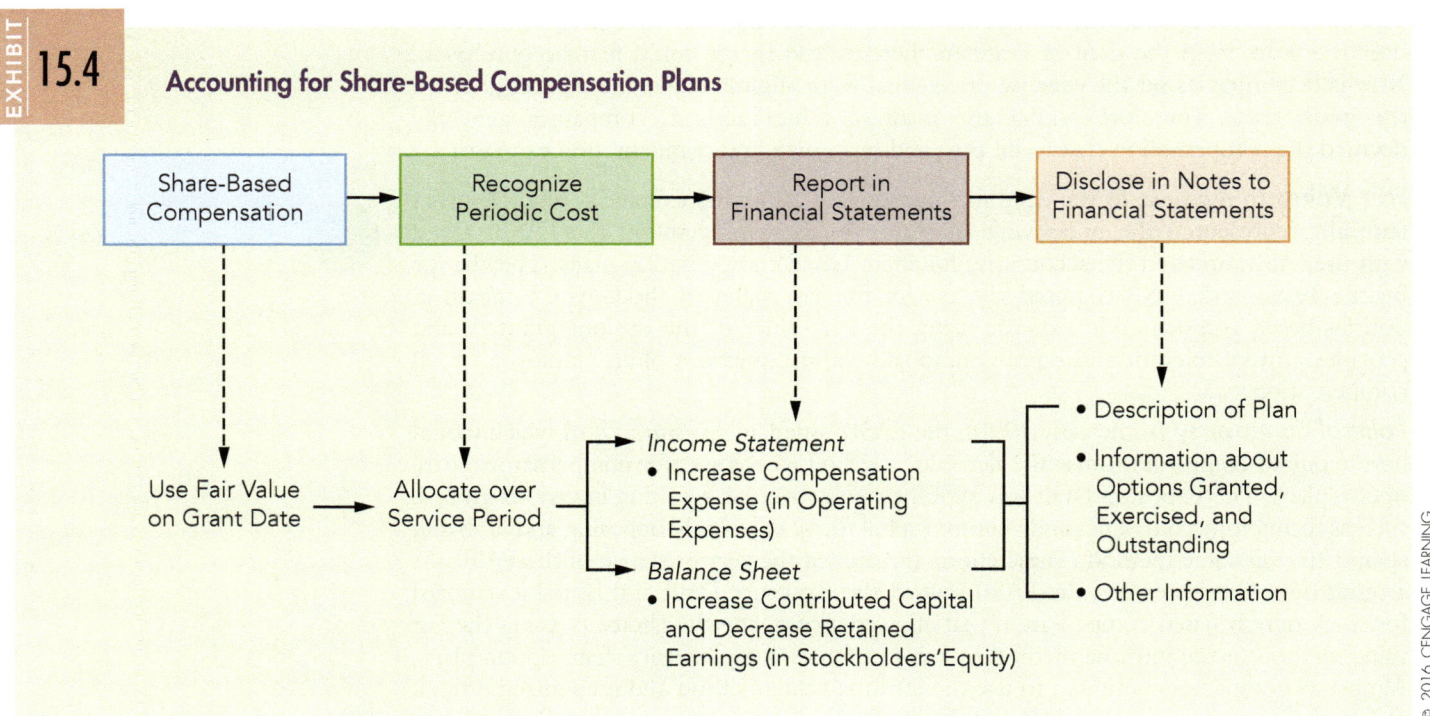

value is measured on the grant date, it is not remeasured for later changes in the underlying variables of the option pricing model.[6]

Option Pricing Model The option pricing model that a corporation uses must take into account the following variables as of the grant date:

- exercise price
- expected life of the option
- current market price of the underlying common stock
- expected volatility of the stock price
- expected dividends on the stock
- risk-free interest rate for the expected term of the option

While we do not illustrate complex option pricing models, it is helpful to understand how the option pricing variables affect the fair value of the option. Using the basic option model (for an option on a share for which market price will exceed the exercise price), we can observe that an option's value is determined as follows:

$$\text{Option Value (Fair Value)} = \text{Current Stock Price} - \text{Present Value of Exercise Price}$$

Examining this basic equation, we can observe that the following factors will increase the value of the option:

- a higher current market price of the stock.
- a lower exercise price.
- a higher interest rate used to calculate the present value of the exercise price.
- a longer time period until the option expires.
- a more volatile stock price.

---

[6] When a company has a stock split or a stock dividend (discussed in Chapter 16), the number of share options, the fair value, and the exercise price are adjusted proportionately. For example, if the company issues a 100% stock dividend, the number of options would be doubled, and the fair value and the exercise price are halved.

For instance, a higher market price of the stock means that there is a greater difference between this price and the exercise price; hence, the option is more valuable. The more complex option pricing models expand on this equation by including expected dividends and volatility variables in the equation.[7] For simplicity, in the examples that follow and the end-of-chapter exercises and problems, we always assume a fair value (option value) for each option on the grant date.

The cost recognized by a company for its share-based compensation plan is the total fair value of the share options that actually become vested. Share options become **vested** on the date the employee fulfills the service requirement and takes ownership of the share options. A corporation recognizes the total compensation cost as compensation expense over the required service period using the straight-line method. The service period is the time period that the employee must work for the company in exchange for the share options. Generally, the service period is the same as the vesting period.

If the corporation expects that a significant number of employees will forfeit their nonvested share options (because they will not fulfill the service requirements for vesting), then it records the compensation expense each year based on an estimate of the number of options expected to vest. The estimated total compensation cost is determined at the grant date as follows:

$$\text{Estimated Total Compensation Cost} = \text{Fair Value per Option} \times \text{Estimate of the Number of Share Options Expected to Vest}$$

If additional information becomes available after the grant date and estimated forfeitures change, the change is included in compensation expense in the year of the change (as illustrated in a later example).

The corporation records the compensation expense[8] each year as follows:

```
Compensation Expense                       xxx
    Paid-in Capital from Share Options            xxx
```

The corporation includes the compensation expense as an operating expense on its income statement. It includes the Paid-in Capital from Share Options account balance in the Contributed Capital section of shareholders' equity on its ending balance sheet.

GAAP deals with many different types of share-based compensation plans. For example, share option plans can either be *fixed* (where all the terms are fixed on the date of grant) or *performance-based* (where the number of options to be earned or the exercise price varies). In addition, some share-based plans provide compensation based on share appreciation while others offer restricted shares.

Example: Fixed Share Option Plan

On January 1, 2016, Fox Corporation adopts a compensatory share option plan and grants 9,000 share options (to acquire 9,000 shares of common stock) with a maximum life of 10 years to 30 selected employees. The $50 exercise price is equal to the market price of the stock on this grant date. All the options vest at the end of 3 years if the employee is still employed by the company. This plan is called a **fixed share option plan** because all the terms (e.g., exercise price, number of shares) are set ("fixed") on the grant date.

Due to normal employee turnover rates, Fox expects 10% of the options to be forfeited by employees before they vest. Therefore, at the beginning of 2016, it uses a 10% forfeiture rate in its compensation cost (and expense) calculations. At the end of 2018, a total of 7,500 share options for 25 employees actually vest and the other 1,500 are forfeited.

---

[7] For an explanation of option pricing, see J. Marlow, *Option Pricing: Black-Scholes Made Easy: A Visual Way to Understand Stock Options, Option Prices, and Stock-Market Volatility* (New York: Wiley, 2001).

[8] In many cases, the amount of compensation expense a corporation recognizes for financial reporting purposes in a given year will be different than the amount of compensation expense it reports on its income tax return. This issue is discussed in Chapter 18.

Using an option pricing model in accordance with GAAP, Fox determines that the fair value of each option is $18 on the grant date. The total options-based estimated compensation cost on the grant date is determined as follows:

$$\begin{aligned}\text{Total Options-Based Estimated Compensation Cost} &= \text{Fair Value per Option} \times \text{Number of Options Expected to Vest} \\ &= \$18 \times (9{,}000 \times 0.9) \\ &= \$145{,}800\end{aligned}$$

On January 1, 2016 (the grant date), Fox makes a memorandum entry to summarize the terms of the compensatory share option plan as follows:

Memorandum entry: On January 1, 2016, the company granted compensatory share options to 30 employees. The plan allows each employee to exercise 300 options to acquire the same number of shares of the company's common stock at an exercise price of $50 per share. The options vest at the end of 3 years and expire at the end of 10 years. The estimated fair value of the options expected to be exercised is $145,800.

Example 15.1 shows the compensation computations for Fox's fixed compensatory share option plan over the 3-year service period. The 2016 compensation expense is computed as follows:

$$\$145{,}800 \div 3 \text{ years} = \$48{,}600$$

On December 31, 2016, Fox records the compensation expense as follows:

Compensation Expense	48,600	
Paid-in Capital from Share Options		48,600

EXAMPLE 15.1 Fixed Compensatory Share Option Plan

	2016	2017	2018
Estimated (actual) total compensation cost	$145,800[a]	$145,800	$135,000[b]
Fraction of service period expired	× 1/3	× 2/3	× 3/3
Estimated compensation expense to date	$ 48,600	$ 97,200	$135,000
Previously recognized compensation expense	(0)	(48,600)	(97,200)
Current compensation expense	$ 48,600	$ 48,600	$ 37,800

[a] $18 Fair value per option × (9,000 options × 0.90 retention rate)
[b] $18 Fair value per option × 7,500 options actually vested

The computation of the 2017 compensation expense is consistent with the previous calculation. Because two-thirds of the service period has expired, $97,200 ($145,800 × 2/3) of the cost is the compensation expense to date. Because Fox recorded $48,600 compensation expense in 2016, it recognizes $48,600 ($97,200 − $48,600) as compensation expense in 2017. On December 31, 2017, Fox records the compensation expense as follows:

Compensation Expense	48,600	
Paid-in Capital from Share Options		48,600

The last year of the service period is 2018. Because actual forfeitures were different from the estimated forfeitures, Fox must adjust the computation of the compensation expense for this difference. Total compensation expense is $135,000 (7,500 Share Options × $18 Fair Value). Therefore, the 2018 compensation expense is $37,800, which represents the total actual compensation cost minus the previously recognized compensation cost. The December 31, 2018, journal entry is as follows:

Compensation Expense	37,800	
Paid-in Capital from Share Options		37,800

After this journal entry, Fox has recorded the entire compensation cost as an expense over the 3-year service period. Also, the Paid-in Capital from Share Options account has a balance of $135,000 because each of the 7,500 vested share options was recorded at its fair value of $18.[9] ■

When an employee exercises share options, the employee delivers the option certificates and pays the exercise price per share to the corporation in exchange for the stock. The corporation records the issuance of the common stock at **a price that is the sum of the cash received plus the previously recorded value of the share options received.**

Example On January 5, 2019, one employee exercises options to purchase 300 shares of Fox Corporation's $10 par common stock. On this date, the stock is selling for $70 per share on the stock market. Fox records this transaction as follows:

Cash (300 × $50)	15,000	
Paid-in Capital from Share Options (300 × $18)	5,400	
Common Stock, $10 par		3,000
Additional Paid-in Capital on Common Stock		17,400

The common stock is recorded at a price of $68 ($50 Exercise Price + $18 Option Price). The current market price of $70 is *not* used because these shares were awarded to the employee based on the terms (and values) set in the compensation agreement on the grant date. If an employee does not exercise share options before they expire, the amount recorded in the Paid-in Capital from Share Options account for these options is transferred to Additional Paid-in Capital. ■

Performance-Based Share Option Plans Many companies tie share option awards to employees meeting certain performance goals, such as increasing sales or meeting profitability targets. As earnings or profitability increases, the terms of the plan may involve a decrease in the exercise price or an increase in the number of options awarded to the employees.

In these **performance-based share option plans** (or **variable-term share option plans**) one or more terms are *not* fixed at the grant date. These plans are set up so that the terms will vary depending on how well the selected employees perform during the service period.

Example: Performance-Based Share Option Plan

Assume that the terms of Fox Corporation's performance-based plan adopted on January 1, 2016, are the same as in the previous example (3-year vesting and service period, $50 exercise price, $18 fair value per option) except that Fox grants each of the 30 selected employees a *maximum* of 300 share options. The options vest in differing numbers depending on the increase in market share of Fox's products over the 3-year service period. The terms are as follows:

---

[9] In *graded vesting*, a certain percentage of the share options vest each year (rather than in *cliff vesting* where all the options vest at the end of the service period). In the case of graded vesting, in addition to adjusting each year's computations for the estimated retention rate, the computations must also be adjusted for the percentage of options that vest in that year. See FASB ASC 718-20-55.

Performance-based plans motivate and incentivize employees by rewarding them with share options for achieving or exceeding goals set by management.

By December 31, 2018:

- If the market share has increased by at least 5%, at least 100 share options will vest for each employee on that date.
- If the market share has increased by at least 10%, another 100 share options will vest for each employee, for a total of 200.
- If the market share has increased by more than 20%, all 300 share options will vest for each employee.

In a performance-based plan, the estimated total fair value depends on the number of options that are expected to be earned during the vesting period. For Fox's plan, on the grant date it bases the estimated total options-based compensation cost on the estimate of market growth over the 3-year vesting period. This cost then is adjusted in later years for any changes in the expected or actual market share growth. On the grant date, Fox estimates that its market share will increase between 10% and 20%, so it assumes 200 share options will vest for each employee. Furthermore, on the grant date, Fox estimates the forfeiture rate on the share options to be 8%, but changes it to 12% at the end of 2017. At the end of 2018, Fox determines that its market share has increased over the 3-year period by more than 20% (so that 300 share options actually vest for each employee). In addition, at the end of 2018, 25 employees vest in 7,500 share options.

Example 15.2 shows the computations for Fox's performance-based compensatory share option plan over the 3-year service period. In 2016, the $99,360 estimated total compensation cost is based on the 200 share options expected to vest and an expected forfeiture rate of 8%. At the end of 2017, the $95,040 estimated total compensation cost is based on the same expected share options, but on an expected 12% forfeiture rate. At the end of 2018, the $135,000 actual total compensation cost is based on the 7,500 actual share options that vest in the plan. Fox allocates the compensation cost to Compensation Expense each year using the same procedure as we showed in the previous example.

EXAMPLE 15.2

Performance-Based Compensatory Share Option Plan

	2016	2017	2018
Estimated (actual) total compensation cost	$99,360[a]	$95,040[b]	$135,000[c]
Fraction of service period expired	× 1/3	× 2/3	× 3/3
Estimated compensation expense to date	$33,120	$63,360	$135,000
Previously recognized compensation expense	(0)	(33,120)	(63,360)
Current compensation expense	$33,120	$30,240	$71,640

[a] (200 Options × 30 Employees) × 0.92 Retention Rate × $18 Fair Value per Option
[b] (200 Options × 30 Employees) × 0.88 Retention Rate × $18 Fair Value per Option
[c] 7,500 Options Vested × $18 Fair Value per Option; Actual Total Compensation Cost

Fox would report the following journal entries:

December 31, 2016
Compensation Expense   33,120
    Paid-in Capital from Share Options   33,120

December 31, 2017
Compensation Expense   30,240
    Paid-in Capital from Share Options   30,240

December 31, 2018
Compensation Expense   71,640
    Paid-in Capital from Share Options   71,640

INTERNATIONAL DIMENSION

SHARE-BASED PAYMENT PLANS

As a result of convergence efforts by the FASB and the IASB, the treatment for share-based payments under U.S. GAAP and IFRS is similar. Both generally require share-based payments to employees to be measured at the fair value on the date of grant, where fair value is measured based on the market value of the equity or a valuation technique. However, minor differences still exist as detailed below.

- Under U.S. GAAP, plans that are open to all employees and do not provide significant benefits are considered noncompensatory and no compensation expense is recorded for the small purchase discount provided to employees. Under IFRS, these types of plans would be considered compensatory and compensation expense equal to the purchase discount is recorded.
- If share options vest ratably or in installments, IFRS require each installment to be treated as an individual arrangement. Under U.S. GAAP, a company may elect to treat each installment individually or recognize compensation over the longest vesting period.
- If the share-based compensation plan is modified under U.S. GAAP, a new fair value is calculated and used to determine compensation expense for the remainder of the service period. Under IFRS, if the fair value of the modified plan is less than the fair value of the original plan, no reduction in compensation cost is recognized.

> **IFRS Application** On January 1, 2016, Heat Corporation grants 5,000 share options to its employees which will vest on December 31, 2017, if sales grow by 50% by that date. Based on past results, this appears to be a reasonable growth target for the company. Heat expenses the share options on a straight-line basis and determines that the fair value of an option on the date of grant is $16.
>
> On January 3, 2017, due to a reduction in business, the share option plan is modified so that only a more achievable 35% growth rate is needed in order for the options to vest. On January 3, 2017, the share options are recalculated and fair value is determined to be $12 per option.
>
> Given this information, Heat would recognize the following amounts of compensation expense over the service period under U.S. GAAP and IFRS.
>
> **U.S. GAAP**
>
> **December 31, 2016**
> Compensation Expense*   40,000
>   Paid-in Capital from Share Options   40,000
>
> *(5,000 Share Options × $16 Fair Value per Option) = $80,000
> Total Compensation Cost ÷ 2 Years
>
> **December 31, 2017**
> Compensation Expense*   20,000
>   Paid-in Capital from Share Options   20,000
>
> *(5,000 Share Options × $12 Fair Value per Option) = $60,000
> Total Compensation Cost less $40,000 previously recognized
>
> **IFRS**
>
> **December 31, 2016**
> Compensation Expense*   40,000
>   Paid-in Capital from Share Options   40,000
>
> *(5,000 Share Options × $16 Fair Value per Option) = $80,000
> Total Compensation Cost ÷ 2 Years
>
> **December 31, 2017**
> Compensation Expense*   40,000
>   Paid-in Capital from Share Options   40,000
>
> *No reduction in compensation expense is recognized under IFRS.
>
> **Source:** IFRS 2. (See Appendix C at the end of this book.)

Restricted Share Unit Plans and Share Appreciation Rights

Although options-based compensation plans provide selected employees with the opportunity to buy shares of stock with a market value in excess of the exercise price, these plans have some disadvantages. At the time of exercise, the employee must have enough cash to pay the exercise price and any income taxes. For some employees, this creates a significant cash flow problem. For this and other reasons, corporations have developed share-based plans involving restricted shares and share appreciation rights.

Restricted Share Unit Plans Under a **restricted share unit plan**, employees are awarded restricted share units that allow the employee to receive shares once certain goals are met. These goals may be time-based, such as continuing as an employee for a certain number of years, or performance-based, such as reaching certain financial goals. If the employee does not reach the stated goals, the restricted share units are forfeited.[10]

---
[10] There are also restricted share plans in which employees are granted actual shares of stock on the date of grant. While the employee becomes an actual shareholder on the date of grant, the company maintains physical possession of the shares, restricting the employee's ability to sell the shares, until the employee reaches certain goals. In a restricted share plan, a company would record Deferred Compensation (a contra-equity account) on date of grant while crediting Common Stock and Additional Paid-in Capital. As the shares vest, Compensation Expense is recognized, and the Deferred Compensation account is eliminated.

Starbucks describes its restricted share plan of restricted share units (RSUs) as follows:

> *RSUs*
>
> We have both time-vested and performance-based RSUs. Time-vested RSUs are awarded to eligible employees and entitle the grantee to receive shares of common stock at the end of a vesting period, subject solely to the employee's continuing employment. Our performance-based RSUs are awarded to eligible employees and entitle the grantee to receive shares of common stock if we achieve specified performance goals for the full fiscal year in the year of award and the grantee remains employed during the subsequent vesting period. The fair value of RSUs is based on the closing price of Starbucks common stock on the award date. Expense for performance-based RSUs is recognized when it is probable the performance goal will be achieved.

Compensation cost for restricted share unit plans is determined using the fair value method and is calculated as follows:

$$\text{Estimated Total Compensation Cost} = \text{Market Price of the Share on Date of Grant} \times \text{Estimated Number of Restricted Share Units to Vest}$$

In a *time-based plan*, estimated total compensation cost is allocated to Compensation Expense on a straight-line basis over the time period in which the employee must provide service. In a *performance-based plan*, estimated total compensation cost is allocated to Compensation Expense in the period in which it is probable that the performance goal will be achieved.[11]

Consistent with the treatment of share options, if additional information becomes available after the grant date and estimated forfeitures change, the change is included in compensation expense in the year of the change.

Example: Time-Based Restricted Share Plan

On January 3, 2016, Ginger Corporation hires a new Director of Internal Audit. In addition to salary and other benefits, the employment package grants 10,000 restricted share units of Ginger common stock that vest in 3 years if the director is still an employee. On January 3, 2016, the $5 par value common stock is trading at $63 per share. Ginger Corporation estimates that the director will meet the vesting requirements and all shares will be awarded. The grant date fair value of the restricted share award would be calculated as follows:

$$\$630{,}000 = \$63 \text{ Market Price} \times 10{,}000 \text{ Restricted Share Units}$$

Ginger would recognize $210,000 ($630,000 ÷ 3 years) of compensation expense for each year of the 3 required service years as follows:

December 31, 2016
Compensation Expense	210,000	
Paid-in Capital from Restricted Share Units		210,000

This journal entry would also be made at December 31, 2017 and 2018. If the Director of Internal Audit is still an employee at the end of 3 years, the shares would vest with the employee and no longer be restricted. Ginger would then issue 10,000 common shares to the employee as shown by the following journal entry:

December 31, 2018
Paid-in Capital from Restricted Share Units	630,000	
Common Stock (10,000 × $5 Par Value)		50,000
Additional Paid-in Capital on Common Stock		580,000

---

[11] FASB ASC 718-10-30: Compensation-Stock Compensation, Overall, Initial Measurement.

If the Director of Internal Audit left Ginger in March 2018 (prior to the completion of the 3-year service period), Ginger would make the following journal entry to reverse the 2 years of compensation expense previously recorded:

Paid-in Capital from Restricted Share Units	420,000	
Compensation Expense		420,000

Share Appreciation Rights Share appreciation rights (SARs) are rights granted to selected employees that enable them to receive cash, shares, or a combination of both equal to the *excess* of the market value over a stated price of the corporation's stock on the date of *exercise*. One advantage of a SARs plan is that the employee can receive the market appreciation of the corporation's stock in cash on the date of exercise, without paying cash to actually acquire the shares.

A company accounts for a SARs plan using the fair value method; however, for SARs, the fair value can only be determined on the date the rights are exercised because the cash payment is a function of the stock price on that date.[12] Therefore, for a SARs plan, a company:

- estimates the total compensation cost at the end of *each* year based on the fair value of the SARs *at that time*
- records compensation expense over the service period based on these estimates (and any corrections of previous estimation errors)
- makes additional adjustments to compensation expense at the end of each year *after* the service period has expired and up to the date of exercise

This process is shown in Exhibit 15.5.

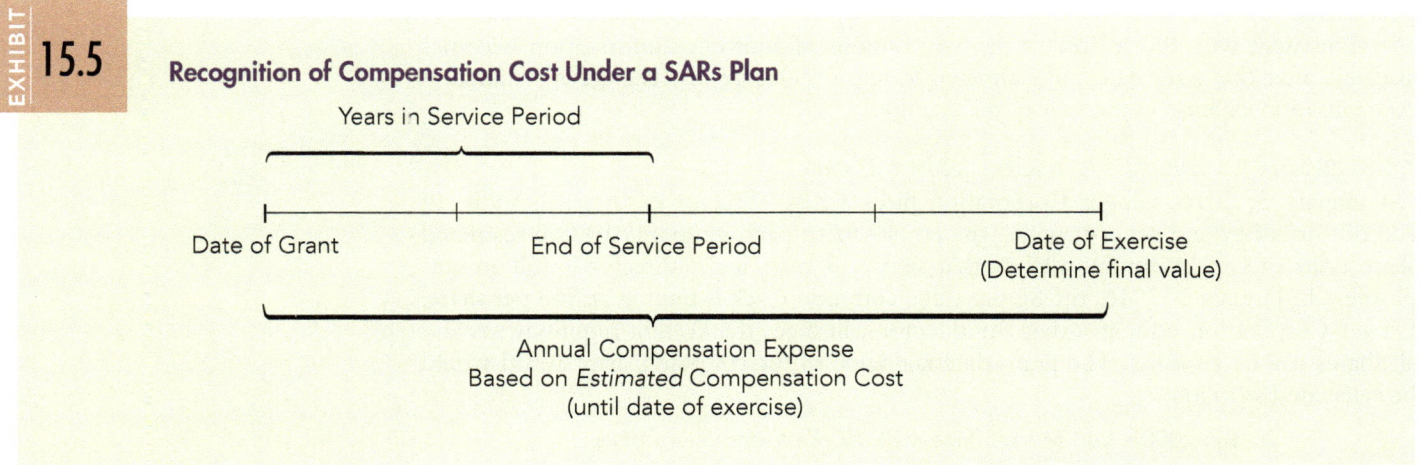

EXHIBIT 15.5 Recognition of Compensation Cost Under a SARs Plan

Accounting for a SARs plan also differs from the accounting for a compensatory share option plan in two ways:

- The adjustments that are made at the end of each year to compensation expense after the service period has expired (until the date of exercise) are based on the difference between 100% of the estimated total compensation cost and the accrued compensation expense recognized to date.
- The credit entry recognizes an accrued compensation liability account if the company can be required to pay cash to the employee on the date of exercise.[13]

---

[12] FASB ASC 718-30-5: Compensation–Stock Compensation, Awards Classified as Liabilities, Overview and Background.
[13] FASB ASC 718-10-25: Compensation-Stock Compensation, Overall, Recognition.

Example: Accounting for a SARs Plan

On January 1, 2016, when the market price is $60 per share, Wolf Corporation grants share appreciation rights to a selected employee. (For simplicity, in this example we show the calculations for Olivia Essman, one executive who is expected to remain employed by the company. If more employees were involved, estimates of turnover would be included in the calculations, as we showed in earlier examples.) Under the SARs plan, Olivia will receive cash for the difference between the quoted market price and $60 for 1,000 shares of Wolf's common stock on the date of exercise. The service period is 4 years and the rights must be exercised within 10 years from the grant date.

On the grant date, using an option pricing model, Wolf estimates that the fair value of each SAR is $17. Therefore, the corporation makes a *memorandum entry* on January 1, 2016, indicating that the estimated fair value of this SAR award is $17,000 ($17 × 1,000 shares).

At the end of each year until the date of exercise, Wolf estimates the fair value of each SAR on that date. We show the year-end fair value per SAR in **Example 15.3**. Olivia exercises the rights on December 31, 2020, when the quoted market price of Wolf's common stock was $94 per share. The calculations of the annual compensation expense are shown in **Example 15.3**. At the end of each year, Wolf records the SAR compensation by debiting Compensation Expense and crediting SAR Compensation Payable for the amount calculated in the last column of **Example 15.3**. For instance, on December 31, 2016, Wolf makes the following journal entry:

Compensation Expense	5,000	
SAR Compensation Payable		5,000

EXAMPLE 15.3

SAR Annual Compensation Expense

Date	Fair Value per SAR	Estimated Total Compensation Cost[a]	Percent Accrued[b]	Total Compensation Expense to Date[c]	Accrued Compensation Expense to Date[d]	Yearly Compensation Expense[e]
12/31/16	$20	$20,000	25%	$ 5,000	—	$ 5,000
12/31/17	30	30,000	50	15,000	$ 5,000	10,000
12/31/18	18	18,000	75	13,500	15,000	(1,500)
12/31/19[f]	26	26,000	100	26,000	13,500	12,500
12/31/20[g]	34	34,000	100	34,000	26,000	8,000
						$34,000

[a] Fair value per SAR × 1,000 shares; at end of 2016, $20 × 1,000 shares
[b] Service years to date ÷ Total service period; at end of 2016, 1 ÷ 4 = 25%
[c] Amount from footnote a × Percent from footnote b; at end of 2016, $20,000 × 0.25
[d] Amount for previous year from footnote c
[e] Amount from footnote c − Amount from footnote d
[f] End of service period
[g] Date of exercise

An exception to this procedure occurs in 2018. Because the fair value at the end of 2018 decreased below that of initial fair value determined at the end of 2016, Wolf makes an adjusting entry *debiting* SAR Compensation Payable and *crediting* Compensation Expense for $1,500 to reduce the total accrued liability.[14] On December 31, 2020,

---
[14] The SAR Compensation Payable account can never have a debit *balance* because the cumulative compensation expense can never be negative.

Wolf makes the following journal entry to recognize the SAR compensation expense for 2020 and to record the exercise of the rights:

Compensation Expense	8,000	
SAR Compensation Payable	26,000	
Cash [($94 Market Price − $60 Option Price) × 1,000]		34,000

Note that by the end of 2020, Wolf has recognized total compensation expense of $34,000 for this SAR plan, the amount paid to Olivia on the date of exercise. ∎

Additional Disclosures

A corporation must disclose several items of information about its share-based compensation plans. This information includes the following:

- A description of the plans, including the general terms, and the potential effect of the plans on shareholders. This information should include service period, number of shares authorized for grants of options, and maximum term of options granted. Information should also be included about the number and weighted average exercise prices for share-based compensation granted, vested, expired, and forfeited during the year.
- The effect of the compensation cost arising from share-based payments on the income statement, as well as the tax-related benefit and any portion of compensation cost that is capitalized as part of the cost of an asset.
- A description of the method and assumptions (e.g., risk-free interest rate, expected life, and volatility) used during the year to estimate the fair values for share-based compensation plans.
- The cash flow effects resulting from share-based payments.
- The total intrinsic value of options exercised or share units converted, share liabilities paid, and the total fair value of shares vested during the year.[15]

Illustration of Disclosure Real Report 15.1 shows Note 12 of **Starbucks**'s 2015 10-K.

15.1 DISCLOSURE OF SHARE-BASED COMPENSATION PLANS   REAL REPORT

Starbucks

Note 12: Employee Stock and Benefit Plans

We maintain several equity incentive plans under which we may grant non-qualified stock options, incentive stock options, restricted stock, restricted stock units ("RSUs"), or stock appreciation rights to employees, non-employee directors and consultants. We issue new shares of common stock upon exercise of stock options and the vesting of RSUs. We also have an employee stock purchase plan ("ESPP").

As discussed in Note 1, Summary of Significant Accounting Policies, on April 9, 2015, we effected a two-for-one stock split of our $0.001 par value common stock for shareholders of record as of March 30, 2015. All share and per-share data presented in this note has been retroactively adjusted to reflect this stock split.

As of September 27, 2015, there were 96.3 million shares of common stock available for issuance pursuant to future equity-based compensation awards and 14.3 million shares available for issuance under our ESPP.

Stock-based compensation expense recognized in the consolidated financial statements (in millions):

Fiscal Year Ended	Sep 27, 2015	Sep 28, 2014	Sep 29, 2013
Options	$ 37.8	$ 41.8	$ 37.1
RSUs	172.0	141.4	105.2
Total stock-based compensation expense recognized in the consolidated statements of earnings	$209.8	$183.2	$142.3

---

[15] FASB ASC 718-10-50: Compensation-Stock Compensation, Overall, Disclosure.

Fiscal Year Ended	Sep 27, 2015	Sep 28, 2014	Sep 29, 2013
Total related tax benefit	$ 72.3	$ 63.4	$ 49.8
Total capitalized stock-based compensation included in net property, plant and equipment and inventories on the consolidated balance sheets	$ 1.9	$ 1.9	$ 1.8

Stock Option Plans

Stock options to purchase our common stock are granted at the fair value of the stock on the grant date. The majority of options become exercisable in four equal installments beginning a year from the grant date and generally expire 10 years from the grant date. Options granted to non-employee directors generally vest over one to three years. Nearly all outstanding stock options are non-qualified stock options.

The fair value of stock option awards was estimated at the grant date with the following weighted average assumptions for fiscal years 2015, 2014, and 2013:

	Employee Stock Options Granted During the Period		
Fiscal Year Ended	2015	2014	2013
Expected term (in years)	4.2	4.5	4.8
Expected stock price volatility	22.3%	26.8%	34.0%
Risk-free interest rate	1.1%	1.1%	0.7%
Expected dividend yield	1.6%	1.3%	1.6%
Weighted average grant price	$39.89	$40.12	$25.62
Estimated fair value per option granted	$ 6.58	$ 8.36	$ 6.44

The expected term of the options represents the estimated period of time until exercise, and is based on historical experience of similar awards, giving consideration to the contractual terms, vesting schedules and expectations of future employee behavior. Expected stock price volatility is based on a combination of historical volatility of our stock and the one-year implied volatility of Starbucks traded options, for the related vesting periods. The risk-free interest rate is based on the implied yield available on U.S. Treasury zero-coupon issues with an equivalent remaining term. The dividend yield assumption is based on our anticipated cash dividend payouts. The amounts shown above for the estimated fair value per option granted are before the estimated effect of forfeitures, which reduce the amount of expense recorded in the consolidated statements of earnings.

Stock option transactions for the year ended September 27, 2015 *(in millions, except per share and contractual life amounts)*:

	Shares Subject to Options	Weighted Average Exercise Price per Share	Weighted Average Remaining Contractual Life (Years)	Aggregate Intrinsic Value
Outstanding, September 28, 2014	39.6	$18.93	5.8	$ 754
Granted	6.4	39.89		
Exercised	(11.3)	14.99		
Expired/forfeited	(1.1)	32.38		
Outstanding, September 27, 2015	33.6	23.81	6.0	1,150
Exercisable, September 27, 2015	21.1	16.75	4.7	872
Vested and expected to vest, September 27, 2015	32.4	23.29	5.9	1,125

(continued)

The aggregate intrinsic value in the table above, which is the amount by which the market value of the underlying stock exceeded the exercise price of outstanding options, is before applicable income taxes and represents the amount optionees would have realized if all in-the-money options had been exercised on the last business day of the period indicated.

As of September 27, 2015, total unrecognized stock-based compensation expense, net of estimated forfeitures, related to nonvested options was approximately $32 million, before income taxes, and is expected to be recognized over a weighted average period of approximately 2.6 years. The total intrinsic value of options exercised was $358 million, $258 million, and $539 million during fiscal years 2015, 2014, and 2013, respectively. The total fair value of options vested was $36 million, $44 million, and $56 million during fiscal years 2015, 2014, and 2013, respectively.

RSUs

We have both time-vested and performance-based RSUs. Time-vested RSUs are awarded to eligible employees and non-employee directors and entitle the grantee to receive shares of common stock at the end of a vesting period, subject solely to the employee's continuing employment or the non-employee director's continuing service. The majority of RSUs vest in two equal annual installments beginning a year from the grant date. Our performance-based RSUs are awarded to eligible employees and entitle the grantee to receive shares of common stock if we achieve specified performance goals during the performance period and the grantee remains employed during the subsequent vesting period.

RSU transactions for the year ended September 27, 2015 *(in millions, except per share and contractual life amounts)*:

	Number of Shares	Weighted Average Grant Date Fair Value per Share	Weighted Average Remaining Contractual Life (Years)	Aggregate Intrinsic Value
Nonvested, September 28, 2014	10.8	$31.17	1.0	$407
Granted	6.7	38.56		
Vested	(5.1)	26.73		
Forfeited/canceled	(1.7)	36.10		
Nonvested, September 27, 2015	10.7	36.35	1.0	620

For fiscal 2014 and 2013, the weighted average fair value per RSU granted was $40.07 and $25.12, respectively. As of September 27, 2015, total unrecognized stock-based compensation expense related to nonvested RSUs, net of estimated forfeitures, was approximately $126 million, before income taxes, and is expected to be recognized over a weighted average period of approximately 2.3 years. The total fair value of RSUs vested was $137 million, $103 million and $104 million during fiscal years 2015, 2014, and 2013, respectively.

Suggested answers to these questions are found at the end of the chapter.

Questions:

1. The market price of Starbucks's shares at the end of fiscal 2015 was $57.99 per share. Assuming that all of the share (stock) options exercised during fiscal 2015 were exercised at year-end, what was the "profit" or "loss" made by employees who exercised their options in fiscal 2015?
2. How many options are currently exercisable at the end of fiscal 2015? How many shares does Starbucks have reserved for future grants under its share option plan?
3. How much compensation expense did Starbucks recognize during fiscal 2013 related to share-based awards?
4. What assumptions does Starbucks use to determine the compensation expense related to share options?
5. How many restricted share units vested during fiscal 2015? What was the fair value of the restricted share units that vested?

Conceptual Evaluation

From a conceptual standpoint, by requiring corporations to use a fair value method of accounting for their compensatory share option plans, current GAAP increases the *relevance* of the accounting information because it shows the fair value of the share options. Although some argue that the *reliability* of the accounting information is decreased because of the use of complex estimates, this is similar to using estimates for items such as depreciation, bad debts, and postemployment benefits (discussed in Chapter 19). Others argue that the reliability is increased because the result is more *representationally faithful* in that the accounting information better depicts the economic obligation. Use of the fair value method provides a more relevant measure of a corporation's *return on equity (ROE)* and *earnings per share (EPS)* because compensation expense (based on fair value) is included in the corporation's net income. Similarly, a better assessment of *risk* is possible because external users can evaluate the likelihood of the exercise of the share options. Finally, *comparability* is improved because external users can better contrast the terms of different plans with the information provided in the notes to the financial statements.

On the other hand, there are several criticisms of the way the fair value method is applied in current GAAP. The fair value of the share options is measured only on the grant date using an option pricing model. This fair value is not further adjusted for changes in the variables of the model, even though some of these variables (e.g., volatility and risk-free interest rate) change with changes in the underlying economy. Not allowing adjustment of the fair value may distort reporting of the real value of the share options. However, not adjusting is consistent with generally accepted accounting principles that are based on acquisition costs for assets and original obligating amounts for liabilities.

GOT IT?

15-17 Under the fair value method, how does a corporation determine the total compensation cost for a share-based compensation plan? How does it recognize this amount as compensation expense?

15-18 What is the difference between a fixed compensation plan and a performance-based compensation plan?

WHAT CHARACTERISTICS DESCRIBE PREFERRED STOCK?

LEARNING OBJECTIVE 15.6
Describe the characteristics of preferred stock.

Some investors consider certain shareholder rights to be more important than others. Therefore, they are willing to give up some rights in exchange for preferences for other rights. To attract these investors, a corporation may issue a class of capital stock called *preferred stock*. The preferred stock contract identifies the shareholders' rights as well as the rights of the corporation. Various preferred stock characteristics may be specified in the contract, including:

- preference as to dividends
- accumulation of dividends
- participation in excess dividends
- convertibility into common stock
- attachment of stock warrants
- callability by the corporation
- mandatory redemption at a future maturity date
- preference as to assets upon liquidation of the corporation
- lack of voting rights

Preference as to Dividends

Holders of preferred stock have a preference as to dividends because a corporation must pay any applicable dividends to preferred shareholders before a dividend may be paid to common shareholders. Given that most preferred stock is issued with a par value, the preferred dividend may be expressed as a percentage of this par value. If no-par stock is issued, the preferred dividend is expressed as a dollar amount per share.

Example Tusker Corporation has outstanding 5,000 shares of 6%, $100 par preferred stock. In this case:

- Each preferred shareholder is entitled to a $6 ($100 × 0.06) annual dividend per share.
- The corporation must pay $30,000 of dividends (6% × $100 × 5,000 shares) to preferred shareholders before it may pay any dividends to common shareholders.

A preference as to dividends does not guarantee, however, that a corporation will pay a preferred dividend in any given year. This is because dividend payments are at the discretion of the board of directors. To protect preferred shareholders further, a corporation may issue *cumulative preferred stock*.

Cumulative Preferred Stock

A corporation's shareholders are not legally entitled to share in dividends unless these dividends have been declared by its board of directors. If dividends are not declared in a particular year, a holder of **noncumulative preferred stock** will never be paid a dividend for that year. For this reason, corporations seldom issue noncumulative preferred stock because investors think this feature is a distinct disadvantage.

Most preferred stock is **cumulative preferred stock**. If a corporation fails to declare a dividend on cumulative preferred stock at the stated rate on the usual dividend date, the amount becomes **dividends in arrears**. Dividends in arrears accumulate from period to period. A corporation cannot pay common shareholders any dividends until it has paid the preferred dividends in arrears. The dividends in arrears are *not* a liability to the corporation, because no liability exists until the dividend declaration. Nonetheless, this information is very important to investors and other interested parties in predicting future cash flows, and so a corporation discloses dividends in arrears in a note to its financial statements.

Example Kali Corporation has outstanding 1,000 shares of 10%, $100 par cumulative preferred stock. Each share of stock is entitled to a $10 annual dividend (10% × $100 Par Value). If Kali does not pay dividends in 2016 and 2017, preferred shareholders would be entitled to dividends in arrears of:

- $10,000 at the end of 2016
- $20,000 at the end of 2017

At the end of 2018, Kali would have to pay $30,000 (for 3 years) to preferred shareholders before it could pay any dividends to common shareholders.

Participating Preferred Stock

When preferred stock is **participating preferred stock**, preferred shareholders share with the common shareholders in any additional dividends. Additional dividends are paid only after preferred shareholders have been paid their stated dividend amount and common shareholders have been paid at a rate equal to that paid on the preferred stock.

For example, if Pierce Corporation has 9%, $100 par participating preferred stock and $10 par common stock outstanding, it must pay preferred shareholders $9 per share (9% of the $100 par) and common shareholders 90 cents per share (9% of the $10 par). Then, if the total dividends paid are greater than the amount needed to meet these dividend requirements, an extra dividend arises.

Participating preferred stock may be either fully or partially participating. **Fully participating preferred shareholders** share equally with the common shareholders in any extra dividends. When a corporation pays extra dividends, they are distributed to the fully participating preferred shareholders and common shareholders proportionately based on the respective total par values of each class of stock. **Partially participating preferred shareholders** share in extra dividends, but this participation is limited to a fixed rate or amount per share.

Convertible Preferred Stock

Convertible preferred stock allows shareholders, at their option and under specified conditions, to convert the shares of preferred stock into common stock of the corporation. Usually the conversion provisions stipulate the conditions and a specific exchange ratio. This exchange ratio is modified, however, if there is a stock split. Because most preferred stock is not participating, the conversion feature allows the holder to exchange the dividend preferences attached to preferred stock for the rights to net assets held by common shareholders. This feature is attractive to investors because the exchange ratio tends to tie the market price of the preferred stock to the market price of the common stock when that price is rising. This increases the value of the preferred stock. Conversely, the preferred stock dividend rate tends to stabilize the market price of the preferred stock when common stock prices are falling.

Theoretically, both the preferred features and the option to convert into common stock equity are valuable to (and paid for by) an investor in convertible preferred stock. Conceptually, then, a corporation could separate the proceeds received when it issues the stock into preferred and common shareholders' equity. However, because of the inseparability of the stock and conversion option, no value is assigned to the conversion provision when preferred stock is issued. Therefore, a corporation accounts for the issuance of convertible preferred stock in the same way as for the issuance of nonconvertible stock. This method of accounting places more importance on the legal form of the security than the economic substance of the transaction.

Accounting for the *conversion* of preferred to common stock is very straightforward because the *book value method* is used. (We discussed the book value method in relation to convertible debt in Chapter 14.) Under the book value method, the corporation eliminates the contributed capital (that is, the par value and additional paid-in capital) associated with the preferred stock and replaces it with the par (or stated) value of the common stock. If the total contributed capital eliminated for the preferred stock is more than the common stock par value, the corporation records the excess as an increase in additional paid-in capital related to the conversion. If the total is less, the corporation reduces retained earnings because it is considered to be a dividend distribution to the preferred shareholders. The book value method is used because it does not result in a corporation recording a gain or loss on a transaction involving its own capital stock, which would violate the concept of income.

Example: Conversion of Preferred Stock

Pender Corporation originally issued 500 shares of $100 par convertible preferred stock at $120 per share. If each preferred share may be converted into four shares of $20 par common stock and all the shares are converted, Pender makes the following journal entry at conversion:

Preferred Stock, $100 par	50,000	
Additional Paid-in Capital on Preferred Stock	10,000	
Common Stock, $20 par (4 × 500 × $20)		40,000
Additional Paid-in Capital from Preferred Stock Conversion		
($60,000 − $40,000)		20,000

The conversion of preferred to common stock changes the components of shareholders' equity, but does not affect the corporation's total shareholders' equity.

Preferred Stock with Stock Warrants

A corporation may also attach *warrants* to preferred stock to enhance their attractiveness. As we discussed earlier in the chapter and in Chapter 14 for bonds payable, these **warrants** represent rights that allow the holder to purchase additional shares of common stock at a specified price over some future period. This period frequently involves a number of years, and in some cases no time limit is set. The longer the time period, the greater the attractiveness of such warrants, because stock prices over the long run tend to increase. Because these warrants are separable (*detachable*) from the preferred stock, they usually begin trading on the stock market at some market price. This happens whether the specified purchase price of the common stock is greater than, less than, or the same as the current market price.

Theoretically, an investor in preferred stock with attached (detachable) warrants is investing in dual rights, each of which has a value. These rights include:

- right to dividends that will be paid on the preferred stock
- right to the market value appreciation of the common stock that may be purchased as a result of the warrants

To faithfully represent the issuance of these securities, the economic substance of the event should take precedence over the legal form of the security. GAAP states that **the proceeds from the issuance of preferred stock with attached warrants is allocated to preferred shareholders' equity and to common shareholders' equity, based on the relative independent fair values of the two securities at the time of issuance.**[16]

Example: Issuance of Preferred Stock and Exercise of Warrants

Belmont Corporation issues 1,000 shares of $100 par value preferred stock at a price of $120 per share. It attaches a warrant to each share of stock that allows the holder to purchase one share of $10 par common stock at $40 per share. Immediately after the issuance, the preferred stock begins selling ex rights (without rights attached) on the market for $119 per share. The warrants begin selling for $6 each. Based on the $119,000 ($119 × 1,000 shares) and $6,000 ($6 × 1,000 shares) relative market values of the preferred stock (ex rights) and the warrants, respectively, Belmont makes the following journal entry to allocate the $120,000 ($120 × 1,000 shares) issuance price and supporting computations:

Cash ($120 × 1,000 shares)	120,000	
Preferred Stock, $100 par		100,000
Additional Paid-in Capital on Preferred Stock		14,240
Common Stock Warrants		5,760

Supporting Computations:

Preferred Stock: $\dfrac{\$119{,}000}{\$119{,}000 + \$6{,}000} \times \$120{,}000 = \$114{,}240$

Common Stock Warrants: $\dfrac{\$6{,}000}{\$119{,}000 + \$6{,}000} \times \$120{,}000 = \dfrac{5{,}760}{\$120{,}000}$

If the warrants did not begin trading, the corporation must make the allocation based on an estimate of the value paid for the warrants.

Belmont lists the Common Stock Warrants account as an element of contributed capital in its shareholders' equity. Assuming all warrants are exercised, Belmont makes the following journal entry to record the issuance of the 1,000 shares of common stock in exchange for the warrants and $40 per share:

Cash ($40 × 1,000 shares)	40,000	
Common Stock Warrants	5,760	
Common Stock, $10 par		10,000
Additional Paid-in Capital on Common Stock		35,760

[16] FASB ASC 470-20-25: Debt, Debt with Conversion and Other Options, Recognition.

If any warrants are not exercised, the corporation makes a journal entry debiting Common Stock Warrants and crediting Additional Paid-in Capital from Expired Warrants to transfer the value assigned to the warrants to the existing common shareholders.

Callable Preferred Stock

Preferred stock frequently has a *call* provision. **Callable preferred stock** may be retired (called) under specified conditions by a corporation at its discretion. The corporation includes the specified conditions and call price in the stock contract. The call price is greater than the issuance price and usually establishes a ceiling on the market value of the preferred stock. Typically, the stock contract requires the payment of dividends in arrears before the call is made. Occasionally, callable preferred stock also will be convertible. In this case, the call price may be lower than the issuance price but usually will be higher than the par value. When a corporation recalls convertible preferred stock, the corporation will ordinarily allow the shareholder the choice of conversion or call.

When a corporation *issues* callable preferred stock, no special accounting is required. The corporation credits the difference between the issuance price and par value to Additional Paid-in Capital. Upon *call*, the corporation eliminates the par value in the preferred stock account and the additional paid-in capital associated with the called preferred stock. If the call price exceeds the total of these amounts, the corporation debits the difference to Retained Earnings because it is treated as a dividend distribution.

Example: Calling Preferred Stock

Li Corporation has outstanding 1,000 shares of $100 par callable preferred stock that were issued at $110 per share and that has no dividends are in arrears. If the call price is $112 per share, Li makes the following journal entry to record the call of these shares:

Preferred Stock, $100 par	100,000	
Additional Paid-in Capital on Preferred Stock	10,000	
Retained Earnings ($112,000 − $110,000)	2,000	
Cash ($112 × 1,000 shares)		112,000

The call and retirement of preferred stock causes a permanent reduction in the corporation's shareholders' equity.

Redeemable Preferred Stock

In contrast to convertible preferred stock and callable preferred stock, some preferred stock is redeemable. **Redeemable preferred stock** may either be subject to mandatory redemption at a specified future maturity date for a specified price or redeemable at the option of the holder (instead of being callable at the option of the issuer). Redeemable preferred stock has a key characteristic of a liability because of the obligation of a cash outflow in the future that the company has no ability to prevent. Therefore, a corporation with mandatorily redeemable preferred stock is required to report the preferred stock as a *liability*. If both the maturity date and redemption price are fixed, at the end of each year the corporation reports the liability at the present value of the amount to be paid at settlement. To determine the present value, the corporation uses the implicit interest rate when it issued the redeemable preferred stock. It records interest expense for the change in the present value during the year. If either the maturity date or the redemption price is not known, at the end of each year, the corporation reports the liability at its current market value. It records interest expense for the change in market value during the year.[17] The corporation is also required to disclose the redemption

---

[17] FASB ASC 480-10-35: Distinguishing Liabilities from Equity, Overall, Subsequent Measurement.

features, shares issued and redeemed, and other related issues in the notes to its financial statements. Preferred stock that is redeemable at the option of the holder is *not* reported as a liability. It is reported in shareholders' equity.

Preference in Liquidation

If a corporation is liquidated, the preferred stock contract usually allows the preferred shareholders **liquidation preference** over the common shareholders (but secondary to the creditors) with respect to the corporate assets. The preference is typically expressed as a percentage of (or equal to) the par value. It also frequently requires the payment of dividends in arrears. This liquidation preference is important to external users. A corporation discloses this information either parenthetically in its shareholders' equity section or in the notes accompanying its financial statements.[18]

Voting Rights

In exchange for the previously discussed provisions, the preferred stock contract often states that the holder has no voting rights. Otherwise, the preferred shareholder has full voting rights.

GOT IT?

15-19 Define the following terms regarding preferred stock: (a) dividend preference, (b) cumulative, (c) participating, (d) convertible, (e) warrants, (f) callable, and (g) redeemable.

15-20 How is a preferred stock similar to a long-term bond? How is it similar to common stock?

LEARNING OBJECTIVE 15.7
Understand the accounting for treasury stock.

WHAT IS TREASURY STOCK AND HOW IS IT ACCOUNTED FOR?

In most states, a corporation may reacquire its own previously issued capital stock. **Treasury stock** is a corporation's own capital stock that (1) has been fully paid for by shareholders, (2) has been legally issued, (3) is reacquired by the corporation, and (4) is being held by the corporation for possible future reissuance. A corporation typically pays cash to reacquire its capital stock, but it may exchange other assets.

A corporation may acquire treasury stock to:

- use for share option, bonus, and employee purchase plans
- use in the conversion of convertible preferred stock or bonds
- distribute excess cash to shareholders (instead of paying or increasing dividends)
- use in acquiring other companies
- signal to the capital market that the company managers believe the shares are underpriced and that they are willing to use corporate funds to repurchase them
- reduce the number of shares held by hostile shareholders and thereby reduce the likelihood of being acquired by another company
- use for the issuance of a stock dividend

Treasury stock is *not* an asset of a corporation because the corporation cannot own itself. Instead, a corporation treats treasury stock as a reduction of its shareholders' equity, as we will discuss later. In addition, a corporation cannot recognize a gain or loss when reacquiring its own stock. This restricts a corporation from influencing its net income by buying and selling its own stock.

---

[18] FASB ASC 505-10-50: Equity, Overall, Disclosure.

To ensure that treasury stock is handled in the best interests of the shareholders, states have passed laws regulating corporate activities as follows:

- A corporation must acquire treasury stock for some legitimate corporate purpose.
- Treasury stock does not vote, has no preemptive rights, ordinarily cannot participate in any type of dividends, and has no rights at liquidation.
- Treasury stock does participate in stock splits, because the par value must be revised.
- The acquisition of treasury stock does not formally reduce a corporation's legal capital.
- Treasury stock transactions may reduce retained earnings but may never increase retained earnings.

The original issuance of capital stock causes an increase in a corporation's shareholders' equity and the number of shares outstanding. Its reacquisition has an opposite effect—a reduction in shareholders' equity and the number of shares outstanding. If the reacquired capital stock is formally retired (discussed more fully in a later subsection), the shares revert to authorized but unissued shares, and the corporation's legal capital is appropriately reduced. If the shares are *not* retired, the corporation may reissue the treasury stock at a price above or below the acquisition price or the par value. Ordinarily, the board of directors does not need to consider the par value when treasury stock is reissued because it met the legal capital requirements when it originally issued the stock. Upon reissuance, the corporation again increases its shareholders' equity and the number of shares outstanding.

A corporation may account for treasury stock transactions by either the **cost method** or the **par value method (or stated value method)**. Both are GAAP, although they affect the various components of shareholders' equity differently. Because the cost method is used by the vast majority of companies that hold treasury stock, we discuss and illustrate this method in the following section. We briefly discuss the par value method in a later section.

Cost Method

Under the cost method, when the corporation reacquires its capital stock, it assumes it will reissue rather than retire the stock. Therefore, it debits an account entitled Treasury Stock (and credits Cash or another appropriate asset account) for the *cost* paid to reacquire the shares. During the period between reacquisition and reissuance, the corporation treats the Treasury Stock account as a contra-shareholders' equity account.

When the corporation reissues the treasury shares, it reduces (credits) the Treasury Stock account for the *cost* of the shares reissued and records the difference between the cash received and the cost of the reissued shares as an adjustment of shareholders' equity. If the cash received exceeds the cost of the reissued treasury stock, it records the excess as an increase in additional paid-in capital from treasury stock. If the cash is less than the cost, it records the "deficit" as a reduction of additional paid-in capital from treasury stock. If the additional paid-in capital from treasury stock is insufficient to absorb the deficit, the corporation records the remainder as a reduction in retained earnings. Because a corporation may reacquire treasury stock at different dates and at different costs, it will need to specifically identify which shares are reissued or make a cost flow assumption, such as first-in, first-out or average cost to record the reduction in the Treasury Stock account.

Example: Treasury Stock: Cost Method

Ball Corporation is authorized to issue 20,000 shares of $10 par common stock and enters into several treasury stock transactions. These transactions (1 through 5) are listed in **Example 15.4** (p. 15-40), followed by the journal entries to record the transactions.

> **EXAMPLE 15.4 Journal Entries for Treasury Stock: Cost Method**
>
> 1. Issuance of 6,000 shares of $10 par common stock for $12 per share:
>
> | | | |
> |---|---:|---:|
> | Cash | 72,000 | |
> | Common Stock, $10 par | | 60,000 |
> | Additional Paid-in Capital on Common Stock | | 12,000 |
>
> 2. Reacquisition of 1,000 shares of common stock at $13 per share:
>
> | | | |
> |---|---:|---:|
> | Treasury Stock | 13,000 | |
> | Cash | | 13,000 |
>
> 3. Reissuance of 600 shares of treasury stock at $15 per share:
>
> | | | |
> |---|---:|---:|
> | Cash | 9,000 | |
> | Treasury Stock (600 shares at $13 per share) | | 7,800 |
> | Additional Paid-in Capital from Treasury Stock | | 1,200 |
>
> 4. Reissuance of another 200 shares of treasury stock at $8 per share:
>
> | | | |
> |---|---:|---:|
> | Cash | 1,600 | |
> | Additional Paid-in Capital from Treasury Stock | 1,000 | |
> | Treasury Stock (200 shares at $13 per share) | | 2,600 |
>
> 5. Reissuance of another 100 shares of treasury stock at $10 per share:
>
> | | | |
> |---|---:|---:|
> | Cash | 1,000 | |
> | Additional Paid-in Capital from Treasury Stock | 200 | |
> | Retained Earnings | 100 | |
> | Treasury Stock (100 shares at $13 per share) | | 1,300 |

In Journal Entry 4, note that the treasury stock was reissued at less than par. However, this is not relevant because the legal capital requirements were met in Journal Entry 1. Only the *cost* of the treasury stock is used to determine the impact on additional paid-in capital.[19]

After Journal Entry 4, the additional paid-in capital related to common treasury stock transactions is $200 ($1,200 − $1,000). In Transaction 5, Ball reissues 100 shares of treasury stock at $10 per share. When Ball records this transaction, it reduces the Additional Paid-in Capital from Treasury Stock account to zero and records the remaining deficit as a reduction of Retained Earnings. The accounting for no-par treasury stock follows the same procedures. ∎

Balance Sheet Presentation If a corporation holds treasury stock on the balance sheet date, it deducts the Treasury Stock account from the total of contributed capital, retained earnings, and accumulated other comprehensive income (if any). For example, assume that retained earnings is $40,000 *prior to* recording any treasury stock transactions and that Ball Corporation prepares its shareholders' equity section immediately after recording Transactions 1–5 of the preceding example. We show Ball's shareholders' equity section of its balance sheet in **Example 15.5**.

---

[19] Some corporations prepare a slightly different journal entry from that shown in Transaction 4 when they reissue treasury stock at substantially less than cost. This involves reducing the additional paid-in capital from all the *original* issuances of the same class of stock by an average pro rata amount per share. Any deficit below the average original issuance price is then debited to Retained Earnings. For example, recall from Transaction 1 that the original issuance price of $12 per share resulted in a $2 per share increase in additional paid-in capital (because this is the only issuance, the $2 excess per share is also the *average* excess per share). The reissuance price of $8 per share in Transaction 4 is $5 below the per share cost of the treasury stock, this would result in the corporation recording Transaction 4 as follows:

Cash	1,600	
Additional Paid-in Capital on Common Stock ($2 per share)	400	
Retained Earnings ($3 per share)	600	
Treasury Stock (200 shares at $13)		2,600

> **EXAMPLE 15.5**
>
> **Treasury Stock and Shareholders' Equity**
>
> **Shareholders' Equity**
> Contributed Capital:
>   Common stock, $10 par (20,000 shares authorized, 6,000 shares
>   issued, of which 100 are being held as treasury stock) $ 60,000
>   Additional paid-in capital on common stock   12,000
>   Total contributed capital $ 72,000
> Retained earnings   39,900
> Accumulated other comprehensive income   10,000
>   Total contributed capital, retained earnings, and accumulated
>   other comprehensive income $121,900
>   Less: Treasury stock (100 shares at cost)   (1,300)
> Total Shareholders' Equity $120,600

Retirement of Treasury Stock Accounted for Using the Cost Method Occasionally, a corporation's board of directors may decide to retire treasury stock. As a result, the corporation's legal capital is reduced. In the journal entry a corporation makes to record the retirement, it offsets the cost of the retired shares in the Treasury Stock account against both the par value in the Capital Stock account and a pro rata share from the Additional Paid-in Capital (on common or preferred) account. Any difference between these amounts and the cost of the treasury stock either is debited to Retained Earnings or credited to an Additional Paid-in Capital from Treasury Stock account. For example, assume Ball Corporation retires the remaining 100 shares of treasury stock from the previous example. The journal entry to record the retirement is:

Common Stock, $10 par	1,000	
Additional Paid-in Capital on Common Stock*	200	
Retained Earnings	100	
Treasury Stock (100 shares at $13 per share)		1,300

*$\dfrac{\$12,000}{6,000} \times 100 \text{ shares} = \$200$

Note that the pro rata reduction per share in additional paid-in capital on common stock was computed based on the current balance in Additional Paid-in Capital on Common Stock ($12,000) divided by the number of shares *issued* (6,000). After retirement, it accounts for the shares as authorized but unissued stock.

Par Value Method If a corporation uses the par value method to account for treasury stock, it treats the *reacquisition* of capital stock as an event entirely separate from the stock's *reissuance*. When the corporation reacquires its capital stock, it debits the Treasury Stock (either common or preferred) account for the *par* value of the stock and debits the original Additional Paid-in Capital (on common or preferred) account for an amount based on the average price received from all the *original* issuances of the stock.

- If the reacquisition price is less than the original average issuance price, it credits the excess to a new Additional Paid-in Capital from Treasury Stock account.
- If the reacquisition price is more than the original average issuance price, it first records the deficit as a reduction of Additional Paid-in Capital from Treasury Stock

(if any) and then as a reduction of Retained Earnings (as a kind of dividend paid upon reacquisition).

During the period between reacquisition and reissuance, the corporation treats the Treasury Stock account as a contra-capital stock account. Because fewer shares are outstanding, it deducts the Treasury Stock account from the Capital Stock (common or preferred) account to reduce the total par value.

When the corporation reissues the treasury stock, it increases its contributed capital (and the number of outstanding shares) by crediting the Treasury Stock account at *par* and crediting the existing Additional Paid-in Capital (on common or preferred) account for the excess of the proceeds over the par value.

- If the cash received is less than par, it reduces the Additional Paid-in Capital account.
- If no additional paid-in capital exists related to this class of stock, it debits Retained Earnings.
- If the corporation retires treasury stock, it debits the Capital Stock account and credits the Treasury Stock account for the par value of the retired stock.

Example: Treasury Stock: Par Value Method

Brown Corporation is authorized to issue 20,000 shares of $5 par common stock and enters into several treasury stock transactions. These transactions (1–5) are listed in **Example 15.6**, followed by the journal entries Brown makes to record the transactions.

EXAMPLE 15.6

Journal Entries for Treasury Stock: Par Value Method

1. Issuance of 6,000 shares of $5 par common stock for $12 per share:

Cash	72,000	
Common Stock, $5 par		30,000
Additional Paid-in Capital on Common Stock		42,000

2. Reacquisition of 1,000 shares of common stock at $13 per share:

Treasury Stock	5,000	
Additional Paid-in Capital on Common Stock	7,000	
Retained Earnings	1,000	
Cash		13,000

3. Reissuance of 600 shares of treasury stock at $15 per share:

Cash	9,000	
Treasury Stock (600 shares at $5 per share)		3,000
Additional Paid-in Capital on Common Stock		6,000

4. Reissuance of another 200 shares of treasury stock at $8 per share:

Cash	1,600	
Treasury Stock (200 shares at $5 per share)		1,000
Additional Paid-in Capital on Common Stock		600

5. Retires 100 shares of treasury stock:

Common Stock	500	
Treasury Stock (100 shares at $5 per share)		500

> ### GOT IT?
>
> **15-21** What is treasury stock, and why might a corporation acquire treasury stock?
>
> **15-22** If a corporation uses the cost method to account for treasury stock, the treasury stock "event" is treated as though it consists of two elements. If it uses the par value method, the reacquisition and reissuance transactions are viewed as separate events. Explain the accounting differences resulting from these concepts.
>
> **15-23** How does a corporation report the Treasury Stock account under the cost method of accounting for treasury stock? Under the par value method?
>
> **15-24** What accounting procedures are involved under the cost method when a corporation retires treasury stock?

HOW IS THE CONTRIBUTED CAPITAL SECTION STRUCTURED?

LEARNING OBJECTIVE 15.8
Know the components of contributed capital and how they are reported in financial statements.

A corporation includes the results of the various transactions involving its issuance of capital stock in the Contributed Capital (or Paid-in Capital) section of shareholders' equity on its balance sheet. Contributed capital is usually separated into the par (or stated) value of the outstanding capital stock (or, in the case of no-par stock, the total proceeds received from the stock issue) and the additional paid-in capital arising from the different transactions. A corporation's Contributed Capital section may include:

- Capital stock
    - par value of preferred stock
    - par value of common stock
    - common (or preferred) stock subscribed
    - stock warrants
    - stock dividends to be distributed (discussed in Chapter 16)
- Additional paid-in capital
    - on preferred stock
    - on common stock
    - from other sources (e.g., stock splits, preferred stock conversions, treasury stock)

In addition to reporting the specific amounts for the Capital Stock and Additional Paid-in Capital accounts, a corporation is required to disclose certain other information. For each class of stock, this disclosure includes the par value and the number of shares authorized, issued, and outstanding. The FASB also requires the following disclosures about preferred and common shares:[20]

- preferred stock dividend rate
- preferred stock characteristics
- any dividends in arrears
- any relevant details relating to the common stock

A corporation may present this information parenthetically adjacent to each capital stock account or in a note to its financial statements. As discussed in the next chapter, a schedule summarizing the changes in these various components of contributed capital is also an integral part of a corporation's financial statements. To illustrate the preceding contributed capital framework, **Example 15.7** presents the Contributed Capital section of a hypothetical company, Newsom Corporation.

---

[20] FASB ASC 505-10-50: Equity, Overall, Disclosure.

EXAMPLE 15.7 Newsom Corporation, Contributed Capital, December 31, 2016

Shareholders' Equity
Contributed Capital:

Preferred stock, $100 par (9%, cumulative, convertible, 10,000 shares authorized, 4,300 shares issued and outstanding)	$ 430,000
Common stock, $5 par (80,000 shares authorized, 32,800 shares issued and outstanding)	164,000
Common stock subscribed, $5 par (3,600 shares at a subscription price of $34 per share)	18,000
Paid-in capital from share options	23,000
Additional paid-in capital on preferred stock	107,500
Additional paid-in capital on common stock	590,400
Additional paid-in capital from conversion of preferred stock into common stock	10,100
Total contributed capital	$1,343,000

Real Report 15.2 shows the contributed capital of **Starbucks**'s shareholders' equity section of its comparative balance sheets dated September 27, 2015, and September 28, 2014, and the accompanying Note 11 (in part), which describes the capital stock.

REAL REPORT 15.2 CONTRIBUTED CAPITAL

Starbucks

	Sep 27, 2015	Sep 28, 2014
Shareholders' equity:		
Common stock ($0.001 par value) — authorized, 2,400.0 shares; issued and outstanding, 1,485.1 and 1,499.1 shares, respectively	1.5	0.7
Additional paid-in capital	41.1	39.4

Note 11: Equity

As discussed in Note 1, Summary of Significant Accounting Policies, on April 9, 2015, we effected a two-for-one stock split of our $0.001 par value common stock for shareholders of record as of March 30, 2015. All share data presented in this note has been retroactively adjusted to reflect this stock split.

In addition to 2.4 billion shares of authorized common stock with $0.001 par value per share, we have authorized 7.5 million shares of preferred stock, none of which was outstanding at September 27, 2015.

Included in additional paid-in capital in our consolidated statements of equity as of September 27, 2015 and September 28, 2014 is $39.4 million related to the increase in value of our share of the net assets of Starbucks Japan at the time of its initial public stock offering in fiscal 2002. Also included in additional paid-in capital as of September 27, 2015 is $1.7 million, which represents the difference between the carrying value of the remaining outstanding noncontrolling interests in Starbucks Japan prior to obtaining full ownership and the cash paid to acquire the noncontrolling interests. Refer to Note 2, Acquisitions and Divestitures, for further discussion.

We repurchased 29.0 million shares of common stock at a total cost of $1.4 billion, and 21.0 million shares at a total cost of $769.8 million for the years ended September 27, 2015 and September 28, 2014, respectively. On July 23, 2015, we announced that our Board of Directors approved an increase of 50 million shares to our ongoing share repurchase program. As of September 27, 2015, 52.7 million shares remained available for repurchase under current authorizations.

Questions:

1. What is the par value of Starbucks's common stock? How many more shares can Starbucks issue as of September 27, 2015?
2. How many shares of common stock did Starbucks repurchase and retire during the fiscal year ended September 27, 2015? What was the effect of these transactions on shareholders' equity? What was the average price paid per share acquired during fiscal 2015?
3. How many classes of capital stock have been authorized by Starbucks?

Suggested answers to these questions are found at the end of the chapter.

GOT IT?

15-25 What are the two components of a corporation's contributed capital, and what might be included in each component?

15-26 What additional disclosures about preferred and common shares does the FASB require?

REVIEW CENTER

At the beginning of the chapter, we discussed how stock repurchase programs grew significantly during 2013. Specifically, we focused on **Apple**'s large buyback program and the reasons investors may view treasury stock transactions positively or negatively. We also identified several objectives you would accomplish after reading the chapter. The objectives are listed below and followed by a brief summary of the key points.

KEY TAKEAWAYS

- Equity is the residual interest in the assets of the company that remains after deducting its liabilities.
- A corporation is a legal entity of a particular state, and its articles of incorporation state the types, par value, and number of shares of capital stock to be issued.
- A corporation's owners (shareholders) have limited liability.
- A corporation may enter into contracts, hold property, sue and be sued, and continue in perpetuity.

LEARNING OBJECTIVE 15.1
Define equity and explain the corporate form of organization, including its advantages and disadvantages.

KEY TERMS

Accumulated Other Comprehensive Income, p. 15-3
articles of incorporation, p. 15-5
closed corporations, p. 15-4
Contributed Capital, p. 15-3
corporate charter, p. 15-5
corporation, p. 15-4
domestic corporations, p. 15-4
equity, p. 15-2

foreign corporations, p. 15-4
limited legal liability, p. 15-4
open corporations, p. 15-4
privately held corporations, p. 15-4
public corporations, p. 15-4
publicly traded corporations, p. 15-4
Retained Earnings, p. 15-3
shareholders, p. 15-4
stockholders, p. 15-4

KEY TAKEAWAYS

- Capital stock represents the basic ownership interest in a corporation and possesses various rights including:
  ○ the right to share in the corporation's profits by receiving a dividend when it is declared
  ○ the right to elect directors and establish corporate policies (voting right)

LEARNING OBJECTIVE 15.2
Know the rights and terms that apply to capital stock.

- the right to maintain a proportionate share in the ownership of the corporation when new stock is issued (preemptive right)
- the right to share in the distribution of the assets if the corporation is liquidated
- The terms that apply to capital stock include authorized, issued, and outstanding capital stock, par (or stated) value, and additional paid-in capital.
- Legal capital, the amount of shareholders' equity that cannot be distributed to shareholders, is based on the par value or stated value of the capital stock.
- While par and stated values have no direct relationship to market value, these values are needed in many states to properly separate a corporation's legal capital from its other capital accounts.
- Additional Paid-in Capital represents any capital contributed by shareholders in excess of the par or stated value.
- Shareholders' equity is generally separated into three primary components: Contributed Capital, Retained Earnings, and Accumulated Other Comprehensive Income.

KEY CALCULATION

Legal Capital = Par Value per Share × Number of Shares Issued

KEY TERMS

Additional Paid-in Capital, p. 15-8
authorized capital stock, p. 15-6
capital stock, p. 15-5
common stock, p. 15-6
issued capital stock, p. 15-7
legal capital, p. 15-7
no-par capital stock, p. 15-7
outstanding capital stock, p. 15-7
par value, p. 15-7
preemptive right, p. 15-5

preferred stock, p. 15-6
registrar, p. 15-5
return on shareholders' equity (ROE), p. 15-8
stated value, p. 15-7
stock certificate, p. 15-5
subscribed capital stock, p. 15-7
transfer agent, p. 15-5
treasury stock, p. 15-38
voting right, p. 15-5

LEARNING OBJECTIVE 15.3
Account for the issuance of capital stock.

KEY TAKEAWAYS

- When common stock is issued for cash, the total par value (Number of Shares × Par Value per Share) is recorded in the Common Stock account, with any excess recorded as Additional Paid-in Capital.
- Common stock issued with a stated value is treated in the same manner.
- For stock with no par value, the total amount received from the sale is recorded as Common Stock.
- Stock issuance costs that arise from the initial issuance of stock to the public are recorded as an expense. When the costs relate to subsequent issuances of stock, they are treated as a reduction of additional paid-in capital.
- When stock is issued on a subscription basis, the initial entry results in a debit to Cash for the subscription price received, a debit to Subscriptions Receivable (a contra-equity account) for any cash not yet received, a credit to Common Stock Subscribed (a contributed capital account) for the par value of the subscribed shares that have not yet been issued, and a credit to Additional Paid-in Capital for any excess of the subscription price.
- If more than one class of security (common stock, preferred stock, bonds) is issued for a single price, the proceeds are allocated to the different securities based on their relative fair values.
- Capital stock issued for services or assets other than cash should be recorded at the fair value of the stock issued or noncash consideration received, whichever is more representationally faithful.
- A stock split increases the number of shares issued and proportionately decreases the par value per share, resulting in no dollar impact to any element of shareholders' equity. A reverse split works in the opposite manner.

- Stock warrants represent the right to purchase additional shares of common stock at an established price, usually referred to as the exercise price. Warrants that are issued with other securities and are detachable should be accounted for independently.

KEY CALCULATION

$$\text{Number of Common Shares Issued} = \frac{\text{Total Amount in the Common Stock Account}}{\text{Par or Stated Value of the Shares}}$$

KEY TERMS

detachable warrants, p. 15-15
exercise price, p. 15-14
nonmonetary exchange, p. 15-13
stock split, p. 15-13
stock warrants, p. 15-14
strike price, p. 15-14

KEY TAKEAWAYS

LEARNING OBJECTIVE 15.4
Describe noncompensatory share purchase plans.

- A share purchase plan, which is available to all employees to buy shares directly from their company and only provides a small discount on the purchase price, is referred to as a noncompensatory share purchase plan.
- For noncompensatory plans, the sale of shares to employees is simply recorded at the discounted amount.

KEY TERM

noncompensatory share purchase plan, p. 15-17

KEY TAKEAWAYS

LEARNING OBJECTIVE 15.5
Describe and account for share-based compensation plans.

- A share-based compensation plan is intended to provide additional compensation to selected employees within the corporation. The employees receive share options, shares of stock, cash tied to changes in stock price, or other equity instruments in exchange for their services.
- The accounting objective of share-based compensation plans is to recognize compensation expense over the periods in which the employees perform a service and earn the share-based award.
- Share-based compensation plans are accounted for using the fair value method. Under this method, the total compensation cost associated with a share-based compensation plan is the total fair value of the share-based compensation that actually becomes vested by the employee.
- In a fixed share option plan, all terms (e.g., exercise price, number of shares) are set at the grant date, which allows a company to measure total compensation cost at the grant date. Any subsequent adjustments to compensation cost involve only changes in estimated forfeitures.
- In a performance-based share option plan, one or more of the terms (e.g., exercise price, number of shares) vary with performance, which requires compensation cost to be adjusted during the vesting period in response to changes in the terms of the share option plan.
- Restricted share plans are accounted for using the fair value method, with compensation cost allocated over the required service period. The nonvested shares do not have full rights until the service period or performance benchmarks are met.
- Stock appreciation rights (SARs) allow employees to receive cash, stock, or a combination of both equal to the increase of the stock price over a stated value on the date of exercise.
    - SARs are accounted for using the fair value method, with compensation expense recorded over the service period.
    - The value of the SAR plan is estimated based on the fair value of the SARs on the date of grant and is later adjusted each year until the SARs are exercised.
    - Any adjustments to compensation expense that occur after the service period has expired are accounted for in the period the estimate is revised.

KEY CALCULATIONS

Total Options-Based Compensation Cost:

$$\text{Total Options-Based Compensation Cost} = \text{Number of Share Options} \times \left(\text{Market Price of the Stock on Date of Grant} - \text{Exercise Price of the Share Option} \right)$$

Option Fair Value:

$$\text{Option Value (Fair Value)} = \text{Current Stock Price} - \text{Present Value of Exercise Price}$$

Estimated Total Compensation Cost:

$$\text{Estimated Total Compensation Cost} = \text{Fair Value per Option} \times \text{Estimate of the Number of Share Options Expected to Vest}$$

Compensation Cost for Restricted Share Plan:

$$\text{Compensation Cost for Restricted Share Plan} = \text{Market Price of the Share on Date of Grant} \times \text{Number of Restricted Shares Awarded}$$

KEY TERMS

compensatory share option plan, p. 15-18
fixed share option plan, p. 15-21
grant date, p. 15-18
intrinsic value method, p. 15-18
performance-based share option plans, p. 15-23

restricted share awards, p. 15-18
restricted share unit plan, p. 15-26
share appreciation rights (SARs), p. 15-18
share-based compensation plan, p. 15-18
variable-term share option plans, p. 15-23
vested, p. 15-21

LEARNING OBJECTIVE 15.6
Describe the characteristics of preferred stock.

KEY TAKEAWAYS

- Preferred stock may have (1) a preference as to dividends, (2) accumulation of dividends, (3) participation in excess dividends, (4) convertibility into common stock, (5) attachment of stock warrants (rights), (6) callability by the corporation, (7) redemption at a future maturity date, (8) preference as to assets if the corporation is liquidated, and (9) lack of voting rights.

KEY TERMS

callable preferred stock, p. 15-37
convertible preferred stock, p. 15-35
cumulative preferred stock, p. 15-34
dividends in arrears, p. 15-34
fully participating preferred shareholders, p. 15-35
liquidation preference, p. 15-38

noncumulative preferred stock, p. 15-34
partially participating preferred shareholders, p. 15-35
participating preferred stock, p. 15-34
redeemable preferred stock, p. 15-37
warrants, p. 15-36

LEARNING OBJECTIVE 15.7
Understand the accounting for treasury stock.

KEY TAKEAWAYS

- Treasury stock is a corporation's own capital stock that it has reacquired. Treasury stock is not an asset; a corporation cannot recognize a gain or loss when reacquiring (or reissuing) its own stock.
- When treasury stock is accounted for using the cost method, it debits the Treasury Stock account for the amount paid. When it reissues treasury stock, it debits Cash for the proceeds received, credits the Treasury Stock account for the cost, and credits (or debits) Additional Paid-in Capital from Treasury Stock for the difference.
- When treasury stock is accounted for using the par value method, the Treasury Stock account (reported as a contra-capital account) is recorded at par value with any reissuance of treasury stock accounted for in a manner similar to that of an original issuance of stock.
- The retirement of treasury stock involves a reduction in the legal capital of the company.

KEY TERMS

treasury stock, p. 15-38
cost method, p. 15-39

par value method (or stated value method), p. 15-39

KEY TAKEAWAYS

- Contributed capital usually includes capital stock (par value of preferred and common stock) and additional paid-in capital (on preferred and common stock).
- The FASB also requires that companies disclose the following information about its preferred and common shares:
  - preferred stock dividend rate
  - preferred stock characteristics
  - any dividends in arrears
  - any relevant details relating to common stock

LEARNING OBJECTIVE 15.8
Know the components of contributed capital and how they are reported in financial statements.

ANSWERS TO REAL REPORT QUESTIONS

Real Report 15.1 Answers Starbucks Corporation—Disclosure of Share-Based Compensation Plans

1. During fiscal 2015, 11,300,000 options were exercised at a weighted average exercise price of $14.99 per share. If these options were exercised when the share price was $56.99, these employees made a "profit" of $42.00 per share ($56.99 − $14.99) or $474,600,000 (11,300,000 shares × $42.00 profit per share).
2. At the end of fiscal 2015, 21,100,000 options were currently exercisable at a weighted average price of $16.75, and Starbucks has 96.3 million shares of common stock available for issuance pursuant to future equity-based compensation awards. Given that Starbucks granted 6.4 million awards in 2015, the amount reserved for future awards appears to be adequate.
3. Starbucks recognized total stock-based compensation expense of $209,800,000 in fiscal 2015. $37,100,000 of this total was related to share options and $1,725,000,000 was related to restricted share units.
4. Starbucks determined the fair value of the compensation expense using the following assumptions:
   - expected term
   - expected stock price volatility
   - risk-free interest rate
   - expected dividend yield
   - weighted-average grant price
   - estimated fair value per option granted
5. 5,100,000 restricted share units vested during fiscal year 2015. Given a weighted average grant date fair value per share of $38.56, the fair value of the vested restricted share units was $196,656,000.

Real Report 15.2 Answers Starbucks Corporation—Contributed Capital

1. The par value of Starbucks common stock is $0.001 per share. Starbucks has authorized 2,400 million shares of common stock and has issued and outstanding shares at September 27, 2015 of 1,485.1 million, so the company may issue 914.9 million additional shares.
2. Starbuck's repurchased and retired 29,000,000 shares of common stock during fiscal 2015. This reduced Additional Paid-in Capital by $1.4 billion. The average price paid for a share of common stock was $48.28.
3. Starbucks has authorized both preferred and common, however, the company has not issued any preferred shares.

MULTIPLE-CHOICE (AICPA ADAPTED)

Select the best answer for each of the following.

M15-1
LO 15.3
On July 14, Peterman Corporation exchanged 1,000 shares of its $8 par value common stock for a plot of land. Peterman's common stock is listed on the NYSE and traded at an average price of $21 per share on July 14. The land was appraised by independent real estate appraisers on July 14 at $23,000. As a result of this exchange, Peterman's additional paid-in capital will increase by:

a. $0
b. $8,000
c. $13,000
d. $15,000

M15-2
LO 15.3
Cary Corporation has 50,000 shares of $10 par common stock authorized. The following transactions took place during 2016, the first year of the corporation's existence:

- Sold 5,000 shares of common stock for $18 per share.
- Issued 5,000 shares of common stock in exchange for a patent valued at $100,000.

At the end of Cary's first year, total contributed capital amounted to:

a. $40,000
b. $90,000
c. $100,000
d. $190,000

M15-3
LO 15.3
What is the most likely effect of a stock split on the par value per share and the number of shares outstanding?

	Par Value per Share	Number of Shares Outstanding
a.	Decrease	Increase
b.	Decrease	No effect
c.	Increase	Increase
d.	No effect	No effect

M15-4
LO 15.3
Polk Corporation was organized on January 2, 2016, with authorized capital of 100,000 shares of $10 par value common stock. During 2016, Polk had the following transactions:

Jan. 12 Issued 20,000 shares at $12 per share
Apr. 23 Issued 1,000 shares for legal services when the market price was $14 per share

What should be the amount of additional paid-in capital at December 31, 2016?

a. $4,000
b. $14,000
c. $40,000
d. $44,000

M15-5
LO 15.3
During 2016, Bradley Corporation issued for $110 per share, 5,000 shares of $100 par value convertible preferred stock. One share of preferred stock can be converted into 3 shares of Bradley's $25 par value common stock at the option of the preferred shareholder. On December 31, 2017, all of the preferred stock was converted into common stock. The market value of the common stock at the conversion date was $40 per share. What amount should be credited to the Common Stock account on December 31, 2017?

a. $375,000
b. $500,000
c. $550,000
d. $600,000

M15-6
LO 15.3
LO 15.6
Amlin Corporation was incorporated on January 1, 2016, with the following authorized capitalization:

- 20,000 shares of common stock, no par value, stated value $40 per share
- 5,000 shares of 5% cumulative preferred stock, par value $10 per share

During 2016, Amlin issued 12,000 shares of common stock for a total of $600,000 and 3,000 shares of preferred stock at $16 per share. In addition, on December 21, 2016, subscriptions for 1,000 shares of preferred stock were taken at a purchase price of $17. These subscribed shares were paid for on March 4, 2017. What should Amlin report as total contributed capital on its December 31, 2016, balance sheet issued on February 1, 2017?

a. $520,000
b. $648,000
c. $665,000
d. $850,000

M15-7
LO 15.5
On January 1, 2016, Stoner Corporation granted compensatory share options to key employees for the purchase of shares of the company's common stock at $25 per share. The options are intended to compensate employees for the next 2 years. The options are exercisable within a 4-year period beginning January 1, 2018, by grantees still in the employ of the company. The fair value of each option was $7 on the date of grant. Stoner expects to distribute 10,000 shares of treasury stock when options are exercised. The treasury stock was acquired by Stoner during 2015 at a cost of $28 per share and was recorded under the cost method. How much should Stoner charge to

compensation expense for the year ended December 31, 2016?

a. $70,000 c. $30,000
b. $35,000 d. $15,000

M15-8 When treasury stock is purchased for cash at more than its par value, what is the effect on total shareholders' equity under each of the following methods?
LO 15.7

	Cost Method	Par Value Method
a.	Increase	Increase
b.	Decrease	Decrease
c.	No effect	Decrease
d.	No effect	No effect

M15-9 Preferred stock that may be retired by the corporation at its option is known as:
LO 15.7

a. convertible c. cumulative
b. redeemable d. callable

M15-10 When treasury stock accounted for by the cost method is subsequently sold for more than its purchase price, the excess of the cash proceeds over the carrying value of the treasury stock should be recognized as:
LO 15.8

a. an ordinary gain
b. an increase in additional paid-in capital
c. income from continuing operations
d. an increase in retained earnings

REVIEW EXERCISES

RE15-1 Brown Corporation issues 800 shares of its $5 par common stock for $20 per share. Prepare the journal entry to record this transaction.
LO 15.3

RE15-2 Heart Corporation entered into a subscription contract with several subscribers. The contract requires the subscribers to purchase 2,000 shares of $4 par common stock at a price of $20 per share. The contract requires a down payment of $5 per share, with the remaining $15 per share collectible at the end of one month. The stock will be issued to each subscriber upon full payment. Prepare the journal entry to record this transaction.
LO 15.3

RE15-3 Blue Corporation issues 200 "packages" of securities for $80 per package, or a total of $16,000. Each package includes 4 shares of $5 par common stock and one share of $30 par preferred stock. If the separate market values are $20 per share for the common stock and $70 per share for the preferred stock, what journal entry will Blue make to record this transaction?
LO 15.3

RE15-4 Sun Corporation issues 500 shares of $8 par common stock for a patent. The stock is currently selling for $37 per share on the open market, and no significant impact on the market price is expected by the issuance of the additional shares. Prepare the journal entry to record this transaction.
LO 15.3

RE15-5 **Next Level** Morgan Corporation issues 500 "packages" of securities for $180 per package. Each package includes 10 shares of $1 par value common stock and 2 shares of $50 par value preferred stock. The separate market value of the common stock was $8 at the time of the sale and Morgan credits the Common Stock account for $5,000 and the Additional Paid-in Capital on Common Stock account for $29,615.38. What was the separate market value of the preferred stock on the date of the sale, and what journal entry would Morgan make to record this transaction?
LO 15.5

RE15-6 Given the following information from Fire Corporation's fixed share option compensation plan, prepare the journal entry to record its current compensation expense for Year 2.
LO 15.5

Estimated compensation expense to date	Year 1	Year 2
	$54,357	$89,990

RE15-7 On January 1, Year 1, Phoenix Corporation adopts a performance-based share option plan for 25 executives, with the number of shares based on the yearly increase in sales. At the end of Year 1, based on a 10% increase in sales, it expects that each executive will be granted 150 options and that the fair value of an option expected to vest is $15.75. Phoenix expects a turnover rate of 15% over the 3-year service period. Determine the compensation expense for Year 1 for this plan.
LO 15.5

RE15-8
LO 15.5
On January 2, 2016, Brust Corporation grants its new CFO 2,000 restricted share units. Each of the time-vested restricted share units entitles the CFO to receive one share of Brust common stock if she remains an employee of the company for 4 years. On January 2, 2016, shares of Brust's $1 par value common are trading at $29.50 per share. The company estimates that the CFO will complete all 4 years of required service with the company. Prepare the journal that Brust should make each year to account for the restricted share units.

RE15-9
LO 15.5
On January 1, Year 1, Salt Lake Corporation grants share appreciation rights to its CEO. Under the plan, the CEO will receive cash for the difference between the quoted market price over a $50 option price for 1,000 shares of the company's common stock on the exercise date. The service period is 3 years. The fair value per SAR is $15 at the end of Year 1 and $27 at the end of Year 2. Determine the compensation expense for Year 2.

RE15-10
LO 15.6
Assume Cole Corporation originally issued 300 shares of $50 par convertible preferred stock at $110 per share. If each preferred share may be converted into 6 shares of $8 par common stock and all the shares are converted, what journal entry will Cole make to record the conversion?

RE15-11
LO 15.6
Violet Corporation issues 1,200 shares of $150 par value preferred stock at a price of $200 per share. It attaches a warrant to each share of stock that allows the holder to purchase one share of $20 par common stock at $50 per share. Given that the portion of the proceeds attributable to the preferred stock totals $230,303 and the portion attributable to the common stock warrants totals $9,697, what journal entry would Violet make to allocate the $240,000 ($200 × 1,200) issuance price?

RE15-12
LO 15.6
Assume that Lily Corporation has outstanding 1,500 shares of $150 par callable preferred stock that were issued at $175 per share, and that no dividends are in arrears. If the call price is $185 per share, what journal entry will Lily make to record the recall of these shares?

RE15-13
LO 15.7
Tulip Corporation uses the cost method to account for treasury stock transactions. What journal entry would Tulip make to record the reacquisition of 2,000 shares of its common stock at $12 per share? After the treasury stock transaction, Tulip made the following journal entry when it reissued the treasury shares:

Cash	34,000	
Treasury Stock		24,000
Paid-in Capital—Treasury Stock		10,000

Next Level At what price per share were the treasury shares reissued?

EXERCISES

E15-1
LO 15.3
Par Value and No-Par Stock Issuance Caswell Corporation is authorized to issue 10,000 shares of common stock. It sells 6,000 shares at $19 per share.

SHOW ME HOW

Required:
Record the sale of the common stock, given the following independent assumptions:
1. The stock has a par value of $10 per share.
2. The stock is no-par stock, but the board of directors has assigned a stated value of $8 per share.
3. The stock has no par and no stated value.

E15-2
LO 15.3
Combined Sale of Stock Maxville Company issues 300 shares of $50 par preferred stock and 1,000 shares of $10 par common stock in a "package" sale. Total proceeds received amount to $39,000.

Required:
Record the transaction for each independent assumption shown:
1. The common stock has a current market value of $19 per share; the current market value of preferred stock is not known.
2. The common stock and the preferred stock have a current market value per share of $22 and $60, respectively.

E15-3
LO 15.3
Sale of Stock with Bonds Pilsen Company issues 12% bonds with a face value of $10,000 and 600 shares of $10 par common stock in a combined sale, receiving total proceeds of $23,000.

Required:
Record the transaction for each independent assumption shown:
1. The common stock has a current market value of $21 per share; the market value of the bonds is not known.
2. The common stock has a current market value of $24.50 per share; the bonds are selling at 98.

E15-4
LO 15.3
Issuance of Stock for Land Putt Company issues 500 shares of $100 preferred stock to Drive Corporation in exchange for land. This land was carried on Drive's books for $40,000.

Required:
1. Prepare the journal entry to record the acquisition of the land for each of the following independent situations:
   a. The preferred stock is currently selling for $120 per share. No appraisal is available on the land.
   b. The land is appraised at $65,000. There have been no recent sales of the preferred stock.
   c. The preferred stock is currently selling for $125 per share. The land is appraised at $64,000.
2. **Next Level** For Requirement 1(c), discuss why you chose the value used in the journal entry.

E15-5
LO 15.3
Stock Subscription On February 3, Teel Corporation enters into a subscription contract with several subscribers for 5,000 shares of $10 par common stock at a price of $16 per share. The contract requires a down payment of 25%, with the remaining balance to be paid on May 3. The stock will be issued to each subscriber upon full payment.

Required:
Prepare journal entries to record the following:
1. The February 3 receipt of the down payment and signing of the contract.
2. The May 3 receipt of the full remaining balance from subscribers. The market price is currently $17 per share.

E15-6
LO 15.5
Fixed Compensatory Share Option Plan Nadal Company has 20 executives to whom it grants compensatory share options on January 1, 2016. At that time, it grants each executive the right to purchase 100 shares of its $5 par common stock at $40 per share after a 3-year service period. The value of each option is estimated to be $10.25 on the grant date. Based on its average employee turnover rate each year, Nadal expects that 2 executives will not vest in the plan. At the end of 2018, Nadal confirms that the actual turnover was the same as expected. On January 5, 2019, 3 executives exercise their options.

Required:
Prepare Nadal's memorandum entry on the grant date and journal entries for 2016 through 2019 in regard to its compensatory share option plan (round all calculations to the nearest whole number).

E15-7
LO 15.5
Fixed Share Option Compensation Plan On January 1, 2016, Pepin Company adopts a compensatory share option plan for its 50 executives. The plan allows each executive to purchase 200 shares of its $2 par common stock for $30 per share after completing a 3-year service period. Pepin estimates the value of each option to be $14 on the grant date, and the company expects that 15% of the options will be forfeited and uses this rate in its compensation cost calculations in 2016. At the end of 2018, Pepin determined that the actual turnover was 7 executives for the entire service period. On January 6, 2019, 8 executives exercise their options.

Required:
1. Prepare a schedule of Pepin's compensation computations for its compensatory share option plan for 2016 through 2018 (round all computations to the nearest dollar).
2. Prepare Pepin's memorandum entry on the grant date and journal entries for 2016 through 2019 in regard to this plan.

E15-8
LO 15.5
Performance-Based Share Option Plan On January 1, 2016, Rhine Company adopts a performance-based share option plan for its 80 key executives. Each executive is granted a maximum of 70 share options, but the number of options that vest depends on the percentage increase in Rhine's sales over a 3-year service period. If by December 31, 2018, sales have increased by at least 10%, 50 options will vest for each executive; if sales have increased by at least 15%, all 70 options will vest. On the grant date, Rhine estimates that its sales will increase by 12% over the service period, and that its employee turnover rate over the 3-year service period will be 6%. It also determines that

(continued)

the fair value of an option expected to vest is $13.40. At the end of 2018, actual sales had increased by 16% for the service period, and the actual turnover was 6 key executives for the service period.

Required:
1. Prepare a schedule of Rhine's computations for its compensatory share option plan for 2016 through 2018 (round all computations to the nearest dollar).
2. Prepare the compensation expense journal entry for 2016.

E15-9 **Restricted Share Units** On January 2, 2016, Dekker Company grants each of its 15 new employees 200 restricted
LO 15.5 share units. Each of the time-vested restricted share units entitles the employee to receive one share of Dekker common stock if they remain an employee of the company for 2 years. On January 2, 2016, shares of Dekker's $2 par value common are trading at $52 per share. Dekker estimates that 12 of the 15 employees will complete 2 years of service with the company. At the end of 2017, Dekker reported that four employees left the company before completing the service period.

Required:
1. Prepare a schedule of Dekker's computations for its restricted share unit plan for 2016 and 2017 (round all computations to the nearest dollar).
2. Prepare all journal entries for the restricted share unit plan for 2016 and 2017.

E15-10 **Share Appreciation Rights** On January 1, 2016, as a form of executive compensation, Wadlin Corporation grants
LO 15.5 share appreciation rights to Robert Brandt. These rights entitle Brandt to receive cash equal to the excess of the quoted market price over a $20 option price for 4,000 shares of the company's common stock on the exercise date. The service period is 3 years (which Brandt is expected to complete), and the rights must be exercised within 5 years. Brandt exercises his rights on December 31, 2019. The fair value per SAR was as follows: 12/31/16, $3.00; 12/31/17, $4.20; 12/31/18, $4.00; and 12/31/19, $5.00. The quoted market price per share of common stock was $25 on December 31, 2019.

Required:
1. Prepare a schedule to compute the compensation expense related to this SAR plan for 2016 through 2019.
2. Prepare the December 31, 2019, journal entry related to this SAR plan.

E15-11 **Convertible Preferred Stock** On January 2, 2016, Bray Corporation issues 900 shares of $100 par convertible
LO 15.6 preferred stock for $117 per share. On January 7, 2017, all the preferred shareholders convert their shares to common stock.

Required:
1. Prepare the January 2, 2016, journal entry to record the issuance of the preferred stock.
2. Prepare the January 7, 2017, journal entry to record the conversion, assuming the preferred stock contract states that:
   a. each share of preferred stock is convertible into 7 shares of $10 par common stock
   b. each share of preferred stock is convertible into 12 shares of $10 par common stock

E15-12 **Callable Preferred Stock** On March 4, 2016, Hein Corporation issues 1,000 shares of $100 par preferred stock
LO 15.6 for $125 per share. The stock is not callable by the corporation until 3 years have expired. On April 7, 2019, all the stock is called by Hein.

Required:
1. Prepare the journal entry to record the issuance of the stock.
2. Prepare the journal entry to record the recall:
   a. at a price of $140 per share
   b. at a price of $108 per share

E15-13 **Stock Rights with Preferred Stock** Nelson Corporation issues 6,000 shares of $100 par preferred stock at a price
LO 15.6 of $112 per share. A stock warrant is attached to each share of preferred stock that enables the holder to purchase one share of $10 par common stock for $25. Immediately after issuance, the preferred stock begins selling ex rights for $110 per share. The warrants (which expire in 30 days) also begin trading for $4 per warrant.

Required:
1. Prepare the journal entry to record the sale of the preferred stock.
2. Prepare the journal entry to record the issuance of 5,000 shares of common stock in exchange for 5,000 warrants and $25 per share.
3. Prepare the journal entry to record the expiration of 1,000 warrants.

E15-14 **Various Journal Entries** Lodi Company is authorized to issue 100,000 shares of no-par, $6 stated-value common stock and 10,000 shares of 9%, $100 par preferred stock. It enters into the following transactions:

LO 15.3
LO 15.6

1. Accepts a subscription contract to 7,000 shares of common stock at $42 per share and receives a 30% down payment.
2. Collects the remaining balance of the subscription contract and issues the common stock.
3. Acquires a building by paying $3,000 cash and issuing 3,000 shares of common stock and 900 shares of preferred stock. Common stock is currently selling at $46 per share; preferred stock has no current market value. The building is appraised at $225,000.
4. Sells 1,000 shares of common stock at $47 per share.
5. Sells 900 shares of preferred stock at $112 per share.
6. Declares a three-for-one stock split on the common stock, reducing the stated value to $2.00 per share.

Required:
Prepare memorandum and journal entries to record the preceding transactions.

E15-15 **Treasury Stock, Cost Method** On January 1, Lorain Corporation had 2,000 shares of $5 par common stock authorized and outstanding. These shares were originally issued at a price of $26 per share. In addition, 500 shares of $50 par preferred stock were outstanding. These were issued at a price of $75 per share. During the year, the following stock transactions occurred:

LO 15.7

SHOW ME HOW

1. March 3: Lorain reacquired 100 shares of its own common stock at a cost of $24 per share.
2. April 27: It sold 25 shares of the common stock acquired on March 3 for $33 per share.
3. July 10: It sold 25 shares of the common stock acquired on March 3 for $22 per share.
4. October 12: It retired the remaining shares acquired on March 3.

Required:
Prepare journal entries to record the treasury stock transactions of Lorain, assuming it uses the cost method.

E15-16 **Contributed Capital** Adams Company's records provide the following information on December 31, 2016:

LO 15.8

SHOW ME HOW

Account Title	Amount
Additional Paid-in Capital on Preferred Stock	$ 17,000
Common Stock	75,000
Premium on Bonds Payable	4,000
Preferred Stock	80,000
Bonds Payable	100,000
Preferred Stock Subscribed	20,000
Retained Earnings	121,000
Additional Paid-in Capital on Common Stock	84,000

Additional information:
1. Common stock has a $5 par value, 50,000 shares are authorized, 15,000 shares have been issued and are outstanding.
2. Preferred stock has a $100 par value, 3,000 shares are authorized, 800 shares have been issued and are outstanding. Two hundred shares have been subscribed at $120 per share. The stock pays an 8% dividend, is cumulative, and is callable at $130 per share.
3. Bonds payable mature on January 1, 2020. They carry a 12% annual interest rate, payable semiannually.

Required:
Prepare the Contributed Capital section of the December 31, 2016, balance sheet for Adams. Include appropriate parenthetical notes.

E15-17 Treasury Stock, Cost Method (and IFRS Revaluation) Holland Incorporated's records provide the following information on January 1, 2016:

LO 15.3
LO 15.7
LO 15.8

Preferred stock, $50 par (5,000 shares authorized, issued, and outstanding)	$250,000
Common stock, $10 par (20,000 shares authorized, 10,000 shares issued and outstanding)	100,000
Additional paid-in capital on preferred stock	50,000
Additional paid-in capital on common stock	80,000
Retained earnings	95,000

During 2016, the following transactions were recorded by Holland:
1. Reacquired 250 shares of preferred stock for $53 per share.
2. Reacquired 500 shares of common stock for $20 per share.
3. Sold 200 shares of the common stock acquired in Transaction 2 for $27 per share.
4. Sold 250 shares of preferred stock acquired in Transaction 1 for $59 per share.
5. Sold 100 shares of the common stock acquired in Transaction 2 for $18 per share.

Required:
1. Prepare journal entries to record the stock transactions of Holland assuming it uses the cost method of accounting for treasury stock.
2. Prepare the shareholders' equity section of the Holland balance sheet at December 31, 2016, assuming 2016 net income was $30,000 and dividends distributed were $10,000.
3. **Next Level** Assume that Holland is using IFRS. At the end of 2016, Holland revalued its property, plant, and equipment upward by $40,000. Discuss how Holland's shareholders' equity items would be different under IFRS, and then, based on your answer, repeat Requirement 2.

E15-18 Treasury Stock, Cost and Par Value Methods On January 1, West Company had outstanding 10,000 shares of $10 par common stock, which had been originally issued at an average price of $35 per share. During the year, West engaged in the following treasury stock transactions:

LO 15.8

1. Reacquired 1,000 shares of its common stock for $33 per share.
2. Reissued 600 shares of the treasury stock for $35 per share.
3. Reissued 300 shares of the treasury stock for $32 per share.
4. Retired the remaining 100 shares of treasury stock.

Required:
Prepare journal entries to record the preceding treasury stock transactions for West assuming it uses (1) the cost method and (2) the par value method.

E15-19 Treasury Stock, No Par Propst-Steele Production Corporation's accounting records provide the following information:

LO 15.8

1. Issued 5,000 shares of no-par common stock at $15 per share.
2. Issued an additional 5,000 shares of no-par common stock at $17 per share.
3. Reacquired 500 shares of its no-par common stock at a cost of $12.50 per share.
4. Reissued 200 of its treasury shares at $14 per share.
5. Reissued the remaining treasury shares at $11 per share.

Required:
Prepare journal entries to account for the preceding stock transactions of Propst-Steele Production, assuming it uses the cost method for treasury stock.

PROBLEMS

P15-1 Subscriptions On August 3, 2016, the date of incorporation, Quinn Company accepts separate subscriptions for 1,000 shares of $100 par preferred stock at $104 per share and 9,000 shares of no-par, no-stated-value common stock for $22 per share. The subscription contracts require a 10% down payment, with the balance due by November 1, 2016. Shares are issued to each subscriber upon full payment. On November 1, Quinn received the remaining balances for the shares of preferred stock and common stock.

LO 15.3

Required:
Prepare journal entries to record all the transactions related to:
1. the preferred stock
2. the common stock

P15-2
LO 15.3

Stock Rights to Shareholders Nichols Electronics Corporation has been experiencing a steadily growing demand for its products. In order to meet this demand, a major expansion of production facilities is necessary. Nichols plans to raise the money for this proposed expansion by issuing 10,000 shares of $50 par preferred stock and 50,000 shares of $10 par common stock. These shares were previously authorized but have not yet been issued.

There are presently 200,000 shares of $10 par common stock issued and outstanding. To maintain the preemptive right of the current shareholders, the board of directors authorizes the issuance of stock rights to the current common shareholders on March 2, 2016. The current market price of the common stock at this date is $24 per share. Each common shareholder is to receive one stock warrant for each share of common stock owned. One additional share of common stock may be purchased at any time prior to April 7, 2016, for $23 and 4 of the stock warrants.

There are presently 20,000 shares of the $50 par preferred stock issued and outstanding. They were selling for $78 per share on March 4, 2016. No preemptive right applies to the preferred stock. In order to assure the sale of the additional 10,000 shares of the preferred stock, the board of directors also authorizes one stock warrant to be attached to each share of preferred stock in the new issue. One of these stock warrants allows the preferred shareholder to purchase one share of $10 par common stock for $18 per share at any time prior to April 7, 2016. The preferred shares with warrants attached are issued on March 5, 2016, at a price of $83 per share. The warrants begin trading in the market at $6 each.

Required:
1. Prepare the entry to record the issuance of the common stock warrants on March 2, 2016.
2. Prepare journal entries to record the following transactions:
    a. The sale of the 10,000 shares of $50 par preferred stock with detachable warrants on March 5, 2016.
    b. The exercise on March 19, 2016, of 6,000 of the stock warrants that had been attached to the preferred stock (the common stock price is currently $24 per share and the preferred stock is selling ex rights for $79 per share).
    c. The exercise on April 2, 2016, of 120,000 stock warrants issued in conjunction with the preemptive right (the common stock is currently selling at $23.50 per share).
    d. The 4,000 stock warrants related to the preferred stock and the 80,000 stock warrants related to the preemptive right expire on April 6, 2016.

P15-3
LO 15.5

Fixed Share Option Compensation Plan On January 1, 2016, Roswall Corporation's common stock is selling for $55 per share. On this date, Roswall creates a compensatory share option plan for its 60 key employees. The plan document states that each employee may purchase 500 shares of its $10 par common stock for $55 per share after working for the company for 3 years. On this date, based on an option pricing model, Roswall estimates that each option has a value of $18. Roswall expects that employee turnover rate will be 15% over the service period. Because of lower turnover, at the end of 2017, Roswall changes its estimated turnover rate to 12% for the entire service period. At the end of 2018, the options vest for 54 employees. On January 13, 2019, 10 executives exercise their options when the stock is selling for $75 per share.

Required:
1. Prepare a schedule of Roswall's compensation computations for its compensatory share option plan for 2016 through 2018 (round all computations to the nearest dollar).
2. Prepare Roswall's memorandum entry for the grant date and journal entries for 2016 through 2019 in regard to this plan.
3. Show how the account(s) related to the plan is (are) reported in the shareholders' equity section of Roswall's balance sheet on December 31, 2017.

P15-4
LO 15.5

Performance-Based Share Option Compensation Plan Connors Company has 70 executives to whom it grants compensatory share options on January 1, 2016. The plan grants each executive options to acquire a maximum of 100 shares of the company's $5 par common stock at $50 per share after completing 3 years of continuous service. However, the number of options that vest depends on the increase in the company's market share over the 3-year

(continued)

period. The following schedule shows the number of options granted to each executive based on the increase in market share by the end of the service period:

Increase in Market Share	Number of Share Options Granted
0 to 4%	40
5 to 8%	60
More than 8%	100

Based on past trends, on the grant date, Connors predicts that its market share will increase about 3% by the end of 2018. At the end of 2017, due to its improved market position over the previous 2 years, Connors revises this estimate to 7%. At the end of 2018, Connors determines that its market share has increased 9% over the 3-year period.

On the grant date, Connors estimates that (1) the fair value of each option is $16.25, and (2) its employee turnover rate will be 9% over the service period. At the end of 2017, because of increased resignations, Connors changes its estimated turnover rate to 12% for the service period. At the end of 2018, 59 executives vest in the plan. On January 17, 2019, 30 executives exercise their options when the stock is selling for $68 per share.

Required:
1. Prepare a schedule of Connors's compensation computations for its compensatory share option plan for 2016 through 2018 (round all computations to the nearest dollar).
2. Prepare Connors's memorandum entry on the date of grant and journal entries for 2016 through 2019 in regard to this plan.
3. Show how the account(s) related to the plan is (are) reported in the shareholders' equity section of Connors's balance sheet on December 31, 2017.
4. **Next Level** Do you see a problem with your answer to Requirement 3 and the eventual value of the vested share options? How might this problem be avoided?

P15-5 **Performance-Based Share Option Compensation Plan** On January 1, 2016, Pierce Company establishes a
LO 15.5 performance-based share option plan for its 80 top executives. The terms of the plan are that each executive is granted a maximum of 200 options after completing a 3-year service period. The exact number of options granted, however, depends on the percentage increase in sales over the 3-year period. The terms are: (1) if sales increase between 0% and 3%, each executive is granted 90 options; (2) if sales increase between 4% and 6%, each executive is granted 140 options; and (3) if sales increase at least 7%, each executive is granted the maximum number of options. Each option entitles the executive to acquire one share of the company's $10 par common stock at a price of $45. The options expire at the end of 4 years.

On the grant date, Pierce uses an option pricing model to estimate that the fair value of each share option is $15.50. Pierce's employee turnover rate is expected to be 16% over the service period. At the end of 2017, because of lower turnover, Pierce revises its estimated turnover rate to 14% for the service period. At the end of 2018, options vest for 68 executives. On February 3, 2019, 50 executives exercise their options when the market price of the company's common stock is $62 per share. During the remainder of the year, the market price declines so that at the end of 2019 the other 18 executives allow their options to expire.

Based on a projection of past trends, on the grant date Pierce estimates that its sales will increase about 5% by the end of 2018. This estimate appears accurate through 2017. However, in the last half of 2018, sales increase so much that at the end of 2018 Pierce determines that its total sales have increased by 7% over the 3-year service period. All inventory is shipped by Pierce to its customers under FOB destination terms.

Required:
1. Prepare a schedule of Pierce's compensation computations for its compensatory share option plan for 2016 through 2018 (round all computations to the nearest dollar).
2. Prepare Pierce's memorandum and journal entries for 2016 through 2019 in regard to this plan.
3. Show how the account(s) related to the plan is (are) reported in the shareholders' equity section of Pierce's December 31, 2017, balance sheet.
4. **Next Level** Do you see any problems with the way the terms of Pierce's compensatory share option plan are structured? Explain.

P15-6 **Share Appreciation Rights** Holden Company has a share appreciation rights plan for its key executives. This SAR plan gives each qualifying executive the right to receive cash, stock, or a combination of both equal to the excess of the quoted market price over the option price of the company's $10 par common stock on the date of exercise. The key characteristics and requirements of this SAR plan are as follows:

LO 15.5

- Option price: Market price on date of grant
- Service period: 4 years
- Exercise limit: Within 6 years after the service period has expired

On January 1, 2015, Sarah Mendelson was granted SARs to 10,000 shares of the company's common stock under the requirements of the SAR plan. She is expected to complete the service period and receive cash on the date of exercise. On December 31, 2019, Mendelson exercised her rights to receive $27,000 cash and the remainder in common stock. The fair value per SAR was as follows: 12/31/15, $4.00; 12/31/16, $4.10; 12/31/17, $3.80; 12/31/18, $5.50; and 12/31/19, $6.00. The quoted market price per share of common stock was $16 on January 1, 2015, and $22 on December 31, 2019.

Required:
1. Prepare a schedule to compute the compensation expense related to this SAR plan for 2015 through 2019.
2. Prepare the journal entries related to the SAR plan on December 31, 2015, through December 31, 2019.

P15-7 **Issuances of Stock** Cada Corporation is authorized to issue 10,000 shares of $100 par, convertible, callable preferred stock and 80,000 shares of no-par, no-stated-value common stock. There are currently 7,000 shares of preferred and 30,000 shares of common stock outstanding. The following are several *alternative* transactions:

LO 15.3
LO 15.6

1. Purchased land by issuing 640 shares of preferred stock and 1,000 shares of common stock. Preferred and common are currently selling at $113 and $36 per share, respectively. No reliable appraisal of the land is available.
2. Same as Transaction 1, except that land is appraised at $104,000, and the preferred stock has no current market value.
3. Issued, for $99,000 cash, a combination of 400 shares of preferred stock and bonds payable with a face value of $50,000. Currently, the preferred stock is selling for $120 per share and the bonds at 104.
4. Same as Transaction 3, except that the bonds do not have a current market value.
5. Same as Transaction 3, except that the preferred stock does not have a current market value.
6. Preferred shareholders (who had originally paid the corporation $110 per share for their stock) convert 6,500 preferred shares into 19,500 shares of common stock. The current market prices of the preferred stock and the common stock are $120 and $41 per share, respectively.
7. The corporation calls the 7,000 shares of preferred stock (originally issued at $110 per share) at $123 per share. Common stock is currently selling for $42 per share. Shareholders elect *not* to convert into common stock.
8. Same as Transaction 7, except that shareholders owning 2,000 shares of preferred stock elect to convert each share into 3 shares of common stock. The remaining 5,000 preferred shares are retired.

Required:
Next Level Prepare the journal entry necessary to record each transaction. Below each entry, explain your reason for the values used.

P15-8 **Issuances of Stock** Epple Corporation is authorized to issue 20,000 shares of $100 par, convertible, callable preferred stock and 100,000 shares of $10 stated value common stock. Currently, Epple has outstanding 6,000 shares of preferred stock and 40,000 shares of common stock. The following are several *alternative* transactions:

LO 15.3
LO 15.6

1. Acquired a patent by issuing 2,500 shares of common stock and bonds with the face value of $100,000. The stock is currently selling for $27 per share and the bonds are selling at 98.
2. Sold, for $96,000 cash, a "package" consisting of 500 shares of preferred stock and 2,000 shares of common stock. Currently, the preferred and common stock are independently selling for $112 and $22 per share, respectively.
3. Purchased land by issuing 300 shares of preferred stock and 1,000 shares of common stock. The common stock is selling for $25 per share, but the preferred stock is not being actively traded. The value of the land is appraised at $57,000.
4. The corporation calls the 6,000 shares of preferred stock (originally issued at $108 per share) at a call price of $112 per share. Common stock is currently selling for $23 per share. The shareholders elect *not* to convert into common stock.

(continued)

5. Same as Transaction 4, except that shareholders owning 4,000 shares of preferred stock elect to convert each share into 5 shares of common stock. The remaining 2,000 shares of preferred stock are retired.
6. Upon approval by the state, the board of directors decides to split the common stock two for one, reducing the stated value to $5 per share and increasing the authorization to 200,000 shares. (Remember, only 40,000 shares are issued and outstanding.)

Required:

Next Level Prepare the journal entry necessary to record each transaction. Below each entry, explain your reason for the values used.

P15-9 **Comprehensive** Young Corporation has been operating successfully for several years. It is authorized to issue
LO 15.3 24,000 shares of no-par common stock and 6,000 shares of 8%, $100 par preferred stock. The Contributed Capital
LO 15.6 section of its January 1, 2016, balance sheet is as follows:
LO 15.7

8% preferred stock, $100 par	$190,000
Common stock, no par	184,000
Additional paid-in capital on preferred stock	15,200
	$389,200

Part a. A shareholder has raised the following questions:
1. What is the legal capital of the corporation?
2. At what average price per share has the preferred stock been issued?
3. How many shares of common stock have been issued (the common stock has been issued at an average price of $23 per share)?

Part b. The company engaged in the following transactions in 2016:

Mar. 2 Issued 350 shares of the 8% preferred stock at a price of $122 per share.
Apr. 5 Sold 900 shares of common stock for $34 per share.
  13 Issued 400 shares of common stock in exchange for land. The stock is currently selling at $33 per share.
June 1 Reacquired 500 shares of common stock at $36 per share. The company uses the cost method to account for treasury stock.
Oct. 19 Issued for $27,000 a combination of 500 shares of common stock and 100 shares of preferred stock. The common and preferred stock are currently selling for $35 and $125 per share, respectively.
Nov. 16 Reissued the 500 shares of treasury stock at $38 per share.
Dec. 31 Distributed an $8-per-share dividend on all preferred stock outstanding and a $2-per-share dividend on all common stock outstanding on this date (debit Retained Earnings and credit Cash for each dividend).

Required:
1. Answer the questions in Part *a*.
2. Prepare journal entries to record the transactions in Part *b*.
3. Prepare the Contributed Capital section of Young's December 31, 2016, balance sheet.

P15-10 **Comprehensive** The shareholders' equity section of Superior Corporation's balance sheet as of December 31,
LO 15.3 2015, is as follows:
LO 15.6
LO 15.8 **Shareholders' Equity**

Preferred stock, $100 par value; authorized, 300,000 shares; issued, 30,000 shares	$3,000,000
Common stock, $5 par value; authorized, 2,000,000 shares; issued, 400,000 shares	2,000,000
Paid-in capital in excess of par—preferred	90,000
Paid-in capital in excess of par—common	850,000
Retained earnings	3,000,000
	$8,940,000

The following events occurred during 2016:

Jan. 5 10,000 shares of authorized and unissued common stock were sold for $8 per share.
  16 10,000 shares of authorized and unissued preferred stock were sold for $109 per share.
Apr. 1 80,000 shares of common stock were repurchased for the treasury at a price of $19 per share. Superior uses the cost method to account for treasury stock.
Sept. 1 3,000 shares of preferred stock are issued in exchange for a piece of land. The land has an appraised value of $336,000. The preferred stock currently trades on the New York Stock Exchange at a price of $109 per share.
Dec. 1 25,000 shares of treasury stock are reissued at a price of $24 per share.

Required:
1. Prepare journal entries for each of the above transactions.
2. Calculate the number of authorized, issued, and outstanding common shares as of December 31, 2016.
3. Calculate Superior's legal capital at December 31, 2016.

P15-11 **Treasury Stock Analysis** Ray Holt Corporation has retained you as a consultant on accounting policies and proce-
LO 15.7 dures. During 2016, the company engaged in a number of treasury stock transactions, having foreseen an opportunity to report its treasury stock as an asset and to recognize a profit in trading its own stock. The transactions were as follows:
1. Reacquired 100 shares of its $10 par common stock at $20 per share. The shares had originally been issued at $23 per share.
2. Reacquired 150 shares of its $10 par common stock at $24 per share. The shares had originally been issued at $23 per share.
3. Reacquired 50 shares of its $100 par preferred stock at $140 per share. The shares had originally been issued at $170 per share.
4. Sold all common treasury shares held at $25 per share.
5. Reacquired 150 shares of its $100 par preferred stock at $130 per share. The shares had originally been issued at $170 per share.
6. Retired all preferred shares held in the treasury.

Required:
1. **Next Level** Is the corporation correct in assuming that its treasury stock is an asset and that it can recognize a profit or gain from its treasury stock transactions? Explain.
2. **Next Level** Prepare an analysis of treasury stock accounting for Mr. Robert Richter, the controller. This analysis should contain proper journal entries for each of the treasury stock transactions occurring during 2016, prepared using the cost method discussed in the chapter.
3. **Next Level** Conclude the analysis by discussing how "gains" on treasury stock are reported and how treasury stock is reported on a corporation's balance sheet.

P15-12 **Comprehensive** Byrd Company's Contributed Capital section of its January 1, 2016, balance sheet is as follows:
LO 15.3
LO 15.5
LO 15.6
LO 15.7
LO 15.8

Preferred stock (6%, $50 par, 8,000 shares authorized, 3,400 shares issued and outstanding)	$170,000
Common stock ($10 stated value, 30,000 shares authorized, 12,000 shares issued and outstanding)	120,000
Additional paid-in capital on preferred stock	12,800
Additional paid-in capital on common stock	72,000
Total contributed capital	$374,800

During 2016, Byrd entered into the following transactions:

Jan. 4 Established a compensatory share option plan for its key executives. The options vest after a 3-year service period. The estimated fair value of the options expected to be exercised is $81,000.
Apr. 23 Sold 300 shares of preferred stock at $55 per share.
June 7 Sold 600 shares of common stock at $17 per share.
Sept. 21 Purchased building by paying $9,000 cash and issuing 800 shares of common stock and 450 shares of preferred stock. Common and preferred stock are currently selling for $19 and $57 per share, respectively.
Oct. 12 Reacquired 900 shares of common stock at $19.50 per share. The company uses the cost method to account for treasury stock.
Nov. 15 Issued for $32,000 a combination of 700 shares of common stock and 12% bonds with a face value of $20,000. The common stock is currently selling for $18 per share. No market value exists for the bonds.
Dec. 14 Reissued the 900 shares of treasury stock at $20.50 per share.
28 Distributed a $3.00-per-share dividend on all outstanding preferred stock and a $1.50-per-share dividend on all common stock outstanding on this date (debit Retained Earnings and credit Cash for each dividend).

Required:
1. Prepare memorandum and journal entries to record the preceding transactions.
2. Prepare the Contributed Capital section of Byrd's December 31, 2016, balance sheet.

P15-13 Contributed Capital A partial list of the accounts and ending account balances taken from the post-closing trial balance of Jordan Corporation on December 31, 2016, is as follows:

LO 15.8

Account Title	Amount
Retained Earnings	$410,000
Bonds Payable	220,000
Common Stock Subscribed	60,000
Long-Term Investments in Stock	210,000
Additional Paid-in Capital on Common Stock	460,000
Premium on Bonds Payable	30,000
Common Stock	500,000
Preferred Stock Subscribed	35,000
Additional Paid-in Capital on Preferred Stock	112,000
Preferred Stock	300,000
Additional Paid-in Capital from Treasury Stock	4,000
Unrealized Increase in Value of Securities Available for Sale	3,000
Common Stock Option Warrants	20,000

Additional information:
1. Common stock is no-par, with a stated value of $10 per share. 90,000 shares are authorized, 50,000 shares are issued and outstanding, and 6,000 shares have been subscribed at a price of $28 per share.
2. Preferred stock has a $50 par value, 8,000 shares are authorized, 6,000 shares are issued and outstanding, and 700 shares have been subscribed at a price of $70 per share. Each share is cumulative, is convertible into 5 shares of common stock, and pays a 7% annual dividend. Dividends are not in arrears.
3. Bonds payable mature on July 1, 2025. They carry a 12% annual interest rate, payable semiannually. The premium is being amortized using the straight-line method.

Required:
Prepare the Contributed Capital section of the December 31, 2016, balance sheet for Jordan. Include appropriate parenthetical notes for the common and preferred stock.

P15-14 Contributed Capital The following is a partial list of the accounts and ending account balances taken from the post-closing trial balance of Clett Corporation on December 31, 2016:

LO 15.8

Common Stock Subscribed	$ 10,000
Premium on Bonds Payable	50,000
Preferred Stock	400,000
Trading Investments in Common Stock	110,000
Bonds Payable	500,000
Common Stock	150,000
Additional Paid-in Capital on Preferred Stock	76,000
Available-for-Sale Investments in Bonds	90,000
Preferred Stock Subscribed	100,000
Retained Earnings	610,000
Additional Paid-in Capital on Common Stock	542,000
Unrealized Decrease in Value of Securities Available for Sale	6,000

Additional information:
1. The bonds payable mature on December 31, 2026. They carry a 12% interest rate, payable semiannually. The premium is being amortized using the straight-line method.
2. The 7.5% preferred stock is cumulative and convertible into 3 shares of common stock. It has a par value of $100 per share, 20,000 shares are authorized, 4,000 shares are issued and outstanding, and 1,000 shares have been subscribed at $125 per share.
3. The common stock has a par value of $5 per share, 100,000 shares are authorized, 30,000 shares are issued and outstanding, and 2,000 shares have been subscribed at $41 per share.

Required:
Prepare the Contributed Capital section of the December 31, 2016, balance sheet for Clett. Include appropriate parenthetical notes for the common and preferred stock.

P15-15 Reconstruct Journal Entries At the end of its first year of operations, Leo Company lists the following accounts and ending account balances related to stock transactions and dividends:

LO 15.3
LO 15.8

Account	Balance Debit	Balance Credit
Cash (from stock and for dividends paid)	$250,000	
Subscriptions Receivable: Common Stock	14,000	
Subscriptions Receivable: Preferred Stock	33,600	
Equipment	69,000	
Preferred Stock Subscribed (for 300 shares)		$ 30,000
8% Preferred Stock, $100 par (2,300 shares)		230,000
Additional Paid-in Capital on Preferred Stock		33,000
Common Stock Subscribed (2,000 shares)		10,000
Common Stock, $5 stated value (9,000 shares)		45,000
Additional Paid-in Capital on Common Stock		46,000
Retained Earnings		2,600

During the first year, the following events occurred:
1. Subscription contracts were entered into for common stock at $9 per share and preferred stock at $112 per share. Common stock subscriptions required a $2-per-share down payment. Preferred stock subscriptions required no down payment. Shares (either common or preferred) were issued to subscribers upon full payment.
2. One thousand shares of common stock were sold for $11 per share, and the stock was issued to shareholders.
3. Equipment with an appraised value of $69,000 was acquired by issuing 600 shares of preferred stock. The appraised value of the equipment was used to record the transaction.
4. Net income of $30,000 was closed to Retained Earnings from Income Summary at the end of the year.
5. Dividends of $8 per share on all the preferred stock outstanding and $1 per share on all the common stock outstanding were distributed at the end of the year (the company debited Retained Earnings and credited Cash for each dividend).

Required:
Next Level On the basis of the preceding information, reconstruct all the journal entries that the company made to record the stock transactions, net income, and dividends. It may be helpful to begin by using T-accounts and entering the ending balances.

P15-16 Treasury Stock, Cost Method Bush-Caine Company reported the following data on its December 31, 2015, balance sheet:

LO 15.7
LO 15.8

Preferred stock, $50 par	$ 50,000
Additional paid-in capital on preferred stock	4,000
Common stock, $10 par	100,000
Additional paid-in capital on common stock	80,000
Retained earnings	95,000

The following transactions were reported by the company during 2016:
1. Reacquired 200 shares of its preferred stock at $57 per share.
2. Reacquired 500 shares of its common stock at $16 per share.
3. Sold 100 shares of preferred treasury stock at $58 per share.
4. Sold 200 shares of common treasury stock at $17 per share.
5. Sold 100 shares of common treasury stock at $9 per share.
6. Retired the shares of common stock remaining in the treasury.

The company maintains separate treasury stock accounts and related additional paid-in capital accounts for each class of stock.

Required:
1. Prepare the journal entries required to record the treasury stock transactions using the cost method.
2. Assuming the company earned a net income in 2016 of $30,000 and declared and paid dividends of $10,000, prepare the shareholders' equity section of its balance sheet at December 31, 2016.

15-64   Chapter 15   Contributed Capital

P15-17 **Comprehensive** Udall Corporation's post-closing trial balance at December 31, 2016, was as follows:

LO 15.8

AICPA Adapted

	Debit	Credit
Accounts Payable		$ 290,000
Accounts Receivable	$ 550,000	
Accumulated Depreciation—Building and Equipment		200,000
Additional Paid-in Capital—on Common Stock		1,560,000
Additional Paid-in Capital from Treasury Stock		250,000
Allowance for Doubtful Accounts		30,000
Bonds Payable		400,000
Building and Equipment	1,100,000	
Cash	220,000	
Common Stock ($1 par value)		150,000
Dividends Payable on Preferred Stock		4,000
Inventories	620,000	
Land	380,000	
Available-for-Sale Investments	285,000	
Trading Investments	215,000	
Preferred Stock ($50 par value)		500,000
Prepaid Expenses	40,000	
Retained Earnings		231,000
Treasury Stock—Common (at cost)	180,000	
Accumulated Other Comprehensive Income	25,000	
Totals	$3,615,000	$3,615,000

At December 31, 2016, Udall had the following number of common and preferred shares:

	Common	Preferred
Authorized	500,000	50,000
Issued	150,000	10,000
Outstanding	140,000	10,000

The dividends on preferred stock are $4 cumulative. In addition, the preferred stock has a preference in liquidation of $50 per share.

Required:
1. Prepare the shareholders' equity section of Udall's balance sheet at December 31, 2016.
2. **Next Level** Assume that Udall is using IFRS. At the end of 2016, Udall revalued its property, plant, and equipment upward by $70,000. Discuss how Udall's shareholders' equity items would be different under IFRS, and then, based on your answer, repeat Requirement 1.

CASES

COMMUNICATION

C15-1 **Corporate Form of Organization**

LO 15.1 Most large companies are organized as corporations. Furthermore, corporations are often classified as privately held or public corporations, with privately held corporations further distinguished as open or closed corporations.

Required:
1. List and briefly explain the advantages and disadvantages of the corporate form of organization.
2. Briefly explain the differences between publicly traded and private corporations. What distinguishes an open corporation from a closed corporation?

C15-2 **Issuance of Security Packages**

LO 15.3 Occasionally, a corporation will combine securities into a "package" (for example, common stocks, preferred stocks, bonds) and issue these securities as a single unit.

Required:
Assuming that two securities (common stock and preferred stock) are issued as a unit, explain the alternative ways of valuing the separate stocks of the unit in an exchange for (1) cash or (2) an asset(s) other than cash.

C15-3 Share Options
LO 15.4
AICPA Adapted

A corporation has a noncompensatory share purchase plan for all its employees and a compensatory share option plan for some of its corporate officers.

Required:
1. Compare and contrast the accounting at the date the stock is issued for the noncompensatory share purchase plan with that for the compensatory share option plan.
2. What entry should be made for the compensatory share option plan at the date of the grant?

C15-4 Capital Stock
LO 15.2
LO 15.7
AICPA Adapted

Capital stock is an important area of a corporation's equity section. Generally the term *capital stock* embraces common and preferred stock issued by a corporation.

Required:
1. What are the basic rights inherent in ownership of common stock, and how are they exercised?
2. What is preferred stock? Discuss the various preferences afforded preferred stock.

C15-5 Treasury Stock
LO 15.7

A corporation sometimes engages in treasury stock transactions.

Required:
1. Define *treasury stock*.
2. Why would a corporation acquire treasury stock?
3. Briefly explain the cost method of accounting for the reacquisition and reissuance of treasury stock. Assume the treasury stock is common stock and has a par value.
4. Briefly explain the balance sheet presentation of treasury stock under this method.

CREATIVE AND CRITICAL THINKING

C15-6 Share Option Compensation Plans
LO 15.4
LO 15.5
AICPA Adapted

On November 6, 2015, Gunpowder Corp.'s board of directors approved a share option plan for key executives. On January 2, 2016, a specific number of share options were granted. These options were exercisable between January 2, 2018, and December 31, 2020, at 90% of the quoted market price on January 2, 2016. The service period is for 2016 and 2017. Some options were forfeited when an executive resigned in 2017. All other options were exercised during 2018.

Required:
1. How should Gunpowder determine the compensation expense, if any, for the share option plan in 2016?
2. What is the effect of forfeiture of the share options on Gunpowder's financial statements for 2017?
3. What is the effect of the share option plan on the balance sheet at December 31, 2018? Be specific as to the changes in balance sheet accounts between November 6, 2015, and December 31, 2018.

C15-7 Share Appreciation Rights
LO 15.4
LO 15.5

Instead of a fixed compensatory share option plan, Wright Company is considering providing its key executives with a plan that involves share appreciation rights (SAR).

Required:
1. Explain what is meant by a SAR plan.
2. Identify the key differences between accounting for a SAR plan and a fixed compensatory share option plan.
3. Briefly summarize the steps in accounting for a SAR plan (assume that the executive is expected to receive cash on the date of exercise).

C15-8 Compensatory Share Option Plan
LO 15.4
LO 15.5

Tom Twitlet, president of Twitlet Corporation, is considering establishing a compensatory share option plan for the company's 20 top executives. Tom wants to set the terms of the plan so that the number of options the executives can exercise increases based on a specified increase in the company's future earnings. Tom wants to make sure that the plan cannot be manipulated but, in addition, it should properly motivate the executives to stay with the company and make it successful. Given this concern, he wants to know how the increase in earnings should be specified: Should it be a dollar amount or a percentage change, and should the change in earnings be compared to the company's past results or against industry results? He also is interested in understanding how to

(continued)

determine the service period of the plan. Finally, Tom wants to understand the accounting for the plan and how it will affect the company's financial statements.

Required:
Prepare a memo to Tom that briefly explains the issues involved in specifying the terms used in the plan and accounting for the terms of this type of compensatory share option plan.

C15-9 Convertible Preferred Stock and Warrants
LO 15.3
LO 15.6
The shareholders' equity of a corporation may include both preferred stock and common stock. Preferred stock may (1) be convertible into common stock or (2) be issued with warrants attached enabling the acquisition of common stock.

Required:
Discuss the following three items:
1. The similarities and differences between these types of preferred stock.
2. Theoretically, the appropriate accounting treatment for the proceeds from the issuance of both types of preferred stock.
3. Which accounting treatment is generally acceptable for each type and why? In your answer, you may want to make an analogy to the accounting for convertible bonds and bonds issued with attached common stock warrants that was discussed in Chapter 14.

C15-10 Treasury Stock
LO 15.8
AICPA Adapted
For numerous reasons, a corporation may reacquire shares of its own capital stock. When a corporation purchases treasury stock, it has two options as to how to account for the shares: (1) the cost method and (2) the par value method.

Required:
Write a short report that compares and contrasts the cost method with the par value method for each of the following:
1. Purchase of shares at a price less than par value.
2. Purchase of shares at a price greater than par value.
3. Subsequent resale of treasury shares at a price less than purchase price, but more than par value.
4. Subsequent resale of treasury shares at a price greater than both purchase price and par value.
5. Effect on net income.

C15-11 Analyzing Coca-Cola's Contributed Capital
Obtain **The Coca-Cola Company**'s 2012 annual report either using the "Investor Relations" portion of its web site (do a Web search for Coca-Cola investor relations) or go to http://www.sec.gov and click "Search for company filings" under "Filings and Forms (EDGAR)."

Required:
1. How many shares of preferred stock were authorized and issued at the end of 2012?
2. How many shares of common stock were authorized and issued at the end of 2012? What is the par value per share?
3. What does the company call its additional paid-in capital? What was the amount at the end of 2012?
4. How many shares of treasury stock did the company hold at the end of 2012? What was the average cost per share?
5. How many shares of treasury stock did the company reacquire during 2012? What was the average cost per share?
6. Briefly describe the company's 2008 Stock Option Plan. What was the weighted average fair value of the share options the company granted in 2012? How much was the company's total stock-based compensation expense for 2012, and where was it reported? How many share options were granted and exercised during 2012, and how many were outstanding at the end of 2012? At what weighted average price per share were the options exercised in 2012?

C15-12 Ethics and Share Options
LO 15.4
Smaller Corporation has been in operation for several years. Each year, around the holidays, Smaller gives a cash bonus to each of its employees and records the bonuses as compensation expense. Smaller has reached the point at which it is now making a reasonable return on its shareholders' equity. At the end of the current year, the company president is considering establishing a compensatory share option plan for Smaller's key executives, instead of paying cash bonuses to any of its employees. At this time, the market price and the planned option (exercise) price of the company's common stock are the same. The plan would allocate a specified number of options to each executive based on the executive's level within the company and meeting Smaller's targeted income goals. The service period would be 3 years and the options would have to be exercised within 10 years.

You are the controller for Smaller and one of the key executives who would participate in the plan. You also already own a substantial number of shares of Smaller common stock. The company president comes to you for advice about this plan and says, "If Smaller establishes this plan, it will work out for all of us. It looks like the plan is pretty valuable, since an option pricing model shows a high fair value for each option. The corporation will be saving cash because it won't have to pay bonuses to either the executives or the other employees. But executives will manage better because their share options will depend on meeting the company's targeted income. Because the market price and the option price are the same, there won't be any compensation cost or expense related to this plan. Furthermore, since no bonuses would be paid to any employees, the corporation will decrease its compensation expense. This will increase its net income and earnings per share compared to last year, as well as its return on shareholders' equity. So the stock value will go up. This seems like a win-win situation for everyone. Am I right on this?" Do you think Smaller should adopt this compensatory share option plan?

Required:
From financial reporting and ethical perspectives, how would you reply to the president?

USING CODIFICATION

C15-13 Researching GAAP
LO 15.8

Situation

Russell International, a publicly traded company, reacquired 500,000 shares of its common stock during July 2017 at a cost of $25 per share. The current market price of the stock was $20 per share when the 500,000 shares were reacquired.

The shares that were reacquired had been owned by a group of minority shareholders who had been dissatisfied with Russell's earnings trend, stock price, and dividends paid. In fact, these minority shareholders had been so disgruntled that they had filed a suit against Russell's directors during 2016. The minority shareholders' suit claimed damages of $3 million because of the board's failure to fulfill its fiduciary responsibility to maximize shareholders' value.

In August 2017, the minority shareholders' suit was dropped, with neither Russell nor its directors having to offer or pay a settlement. Russell accounts for its treasury stock transactions using the cost method.

Directions
1. Research the related generally accepted accounting principles and explain how Russell should account for the treasury stock transaction. Cite your reference and applicable paragraph numbers. (*Contributed by Daryl G. Krause*)

C15-14 Researching GAAP
LO 15.3
LO 15.6

Situation

Bowsher Company had 10% bonds payable outstanding with a total face value of $185,000. Each bond had an individual face value of $1,000 and paid interest semiannually on June 30 and December 31. On July 1 of the current year, the 10% bonds had a total book value of $210,000. At that time, because of a financial restructuring, the company executed an "exchange agreement" in which all of these 10% bonds were extinguished. In exchange for each bond, the bondholders were given cash of $125, six shares of 7%, $100 preferred stock, and 50 warrants that allow the holder to acquire 50 shares of $5 par common stock for $25 per share. On July 1, the 7% preferred stock was selling at $106 per share and the warrants were selling at $5 each on the open market. You are the assistant accountant for Bowsher and have been asked by the head accountant to recommend how to record this transaction.

CHAPTER 16

RETAINED EARNINGS AND EARNINGS PER SHARE

Apple Decides to Once Again Pay a Dividend

In July 2012, **Apple** declared that it would once again pay a cash dividend on its common shares. The company, whose stock was trading at a price of $615 per share, announced that it would begin paying a quarterly dividend of $2.65 cents per share. With approximately 900 million shares outstanding, Apple paid out about $10.6 billion in dividends during its 2013 fiscal year. It was the first dividend that the company had paid since December 1995.

While $10.6 billion is a lot of money to return to shareholders, it is important to note that at the time of the announcement Apple had almost $100 billion in cash and short-term investments and had generated over $50 billion in cash flows from operating activities during the previous fiscal year 2012.

The declaration of a dividend was a major change for Apple, which previously had plowed all of its earnings back into the business so that it could grow quickly by developing new products and services. However, as Apple matured and its growth leveled, the company's cash balance began to grow. In fact, cash and investments on Apple's balance sheet grew from $33.7 billion at the end of its 2009 fiscal year to over a $110 billion at the time of the dividend announcement.

In addition to this buildup of cash, Apple had no short- or long-term debt and, with a current ratio of 1.50, had no liquidity issues. This allowed Apple to return the excess cash to shareholders by both offering dividends and agreeing to repurchase over $60 billion of its outstanding common shares.

LEARNING OBJECTIVES

After reading this chapter you will be able to

LO 16.1 Explain the accounting and reporting for different types of dividends.

LO 16.2 Discuss the accounting for prior period adjustments and restrictions of retained earnings.

LO 16.3 Explain the various components of shareholders' equity and related disclosures.

LO 16.4 Compute basic earnings per share (EPS) including the computation of weighted average common shares.

LO 16.5 Compute diluted earnings per share including the identification of potential common shares.

Apple's decision to begin paying a cash dividend and to repurchase shares is part of a growing trend that started in 2003. Prior to 2003, both the number of companies paying dividends and the average dividend yield, which represents the annual dividend divided by the company's stock price, had steadily declined. However, with the reduction in the individual tax rate on dividend income from a maximum rate of 35% to 15%, more companies started paying out dividends.

Tax rates, however, are not the only reason companies pay dividends. Dividends serve as a signal from management that the company is healthy, its earnings are stable, and future cash flows are expected to be available to sustain dividend payments. While the financial crisis caused many companies to reduce their dividend payout ratios, most analysts expect dividend payout ratios and dividend yields to continue to grow in the future as the world economy recovers and grows.

Shareholders' equity refers to the shareholders' claims to the business. In Chapter 15, we examined contributed capital, the first element of shareholders' equity. Contributed capital represents the shareholders' direct investments in a corporation. In this chapter, we continue discussing shareholders' equity by focusing on retained earnings, dividends, the preparation of the statement of shareholders' equity, and earnings per share.

WHAT COMPRISES RETAINED EARNINGS?

Retained earnings is the primary link between a corporation's income statement and balance sheet. As described in Chapter 1, shareholders' equity arises from contributed capital and earned capital. Contributed capital typically arises when the corporation issues shares to shareholders, who invest capital directly in the company. Earned capital arises as the corporation generates earnings for the shareholders and reinvests the earnings in the company, minus any dividends the company has paid to common shareholders. A corporation uses its **Retained Earnings** account to summarize the earned capital component of its shareholders' equity, which primarily comprises the cumulative amount of net income over the life of the corporation minus the cumulative amount of dividends paid out to shareholders. Other factors that occur infrequently but can affect retained earnings include retrospective and prior period adjustments and appropriations, which are described in the following sections.

Most corporations use the account title Retained Earnings, with other corporations using titles with very similar meanings (such as *Reinvested Income* or other variations). A number of corporations have *negative* retained earnings and use the term *Retained Earnings (Deficit)* or *Accumulated Deficit*. A **deficit**, or a negative retained earnings balance, is the result of a corporation's accumulated prior net losses or dividends in excess of its earnings.

LEARNING OBJECTIVE 16.1
Explain the accounting and reporting for different types of dividends.

HOW DO WE ACCOUNT FOR DIVIDENDS?

When a corporation generates net income, it increases the retained earnings component of shareholders' equity. When a corporation issues a cash or property dividend, it has the opposite effect on retained earnings. The payment of a cash dividend or distribution of a property dividend decreases assets and reduces retained earnings. A stock dividend, on the other hand, occurs when a company distributes additional shares to existing shareholders, instead of distributing cash or property. Stock dividends increase contributed capital and decrease retained earnings.

Requirements to Distribute Dividends

To pay cash or property dividends, a corporation must meet legal requirements and have assets available for distribution.

Legal Requirements The board of directors is responsible for establishing a dividend policy and determining the amount, timing, and type of dividends to be declared. It must consider the articles of incorporation, applicable state regulations for dividends, the impact on legal capital (established to protect corporate creditors), and compliance with debt covenants and other contractual agreements as well as the financial well-being of the corporation.

Legal requirements for dividends vary from state to state, but most states require a corporation to have a positive (credit) retained earnings balance before it may declare dividends. Also, the amount of dividends generally cannot exceed this retained earnings balance. Usually, a corporation must restrict the amount of retained earnings available for dividends by the cost of treasury shares repurchased. Also, contractual agreements (such as long-term bond covenants) may restrict a corporation from declaring dividends. Corporate legal counsel is responsible for reviewing applicable state laws and corporate contracts to determine the legality of dividends. Nonetheless, accountants also should be aware of state regulations and contractual obligations, particularly as they affect restrictions of dividends.

Financial Status Besides meeting legal requirements, the board of directors must evaluate the financial desirability of a particular dividend. In this case, the board may consult with the corporate accountants and financial executives. Consideration should be given to the corporation's *financial flexibility* and *operating capability*. Factors that management may take into account when considering a dividend would be:

- impact of a dividend on its cash and working capital
- ability to finance capital expansion projects
- ability to meet short-term debt obligations
- effect on the stock market price per share
- ability to maintain a liquidity "cushion" against possible future deteriorating economic conditions should be evaluated

For the declaration of a dividend to be a positive strategic decision, it must be in both the short- and long-term financial interests of shareholders.

WHAT ARE THE DIFFERENT TYPES OF DIVIDENDS?

A corporation's board of directors may consider several types of dividends, including cash, property, scrip, stock, and liquidating dividends. The impact of each type of dividend upon a corporation's capital structure is as follows:

Type of Dividend	Impact on Contributed Capital	Impact on Retained Earnings	Impact on Shareholders' Equity
Cash, property and scrip dividends	No change	Decrease	Decrease
Stock dividends	Increase	Decrease	No change
Liquidating dividends	Decrease	No change	Decrease

Cash Dividends

The most common type of dividend is the cash dividend—the distribution of cash by the corporation to its common and/or preferred shareholders. Unless described otherwise, the simple term *dividends* refers to cash dividends.

Four dates are important for a cash dividend (or any type of dividend):

- declaration date
- ex-dividend date
- date of record
- date of payment

For instance, on April 24, 2014, **Starbucks** declared a $0.26-per-share quarterly dividend, payable on May 23, 2014, to shareholders of record on May 8, 2014. The ex-dividend date for this dividend was May 6, 2014.

On the declaration date, the board of directors formally declares that a dividend will be paid to *shareholders of record* on a specific future date, typically four to six weeks later. On this declaration date, the corporation becomes legally liable to pay the dividend. Before this date, shareholders ordinarily cannot require that a dividend be paid; dividend policy has been legally entrusted to the board of directors. Because the corporation incurs a liability on the declaration date, it records the following journal entry:

Retained Earnings (or Dividends Declared)	xxx	
Dividends Payable		xxx

Two items are of note:

- Most corporations reduce (debit) Retained Earnings directly. However, some corporations use a contra-retained earnings account titled Dividends Declared for the dividends related to each class of stock.
- The corporation either increases (credits) a current liability, Dividends Payable, or increases separate liability accounts for the amounts owed to each class of shareholder.

After the declaration date, the outstanding stock of the corporation trading in the open market normally sells "with dividends attached" (that is, at a higher market price that includes the amount of the future dividend payment). The ex-dividend date occurs several days before the date of record to enable the corporation to update its *shareholders' ledger* by the date of record. The ex-dividend date is important to investors because **on the ex-dividend date the stock stops selling with dividends attached**. Any purchaser of the stock on or after this date will not receive the current dividend. No accounting entry is required on the ex-dividend date.

The date of record is used by the corporation to set a date on which to record its registered shareholders. Only registered shareholders are entitled to receive a dividend payment. The **date of record** usually occurs several weeks after the declaration date, a day or two after the ex-dividend date, and several weeks before the payment date, as specified in the dividend provisions. On the date of record, the corporation makes a memorandum entry indicating that the date of record has been reached and showing the future dividend payment date.

On the **date of payment, the corporation distributes the dividend payments and makes a journal entry to eliminate the liability and reduce cash.** After the date of payment, the corporation has completed the dividend process. It reports the payment of dividends as a cash outflow in the financing section of its statement of cash flows.

Exhibit 16.1 summarizes the accounting procedures for a cash dividend.

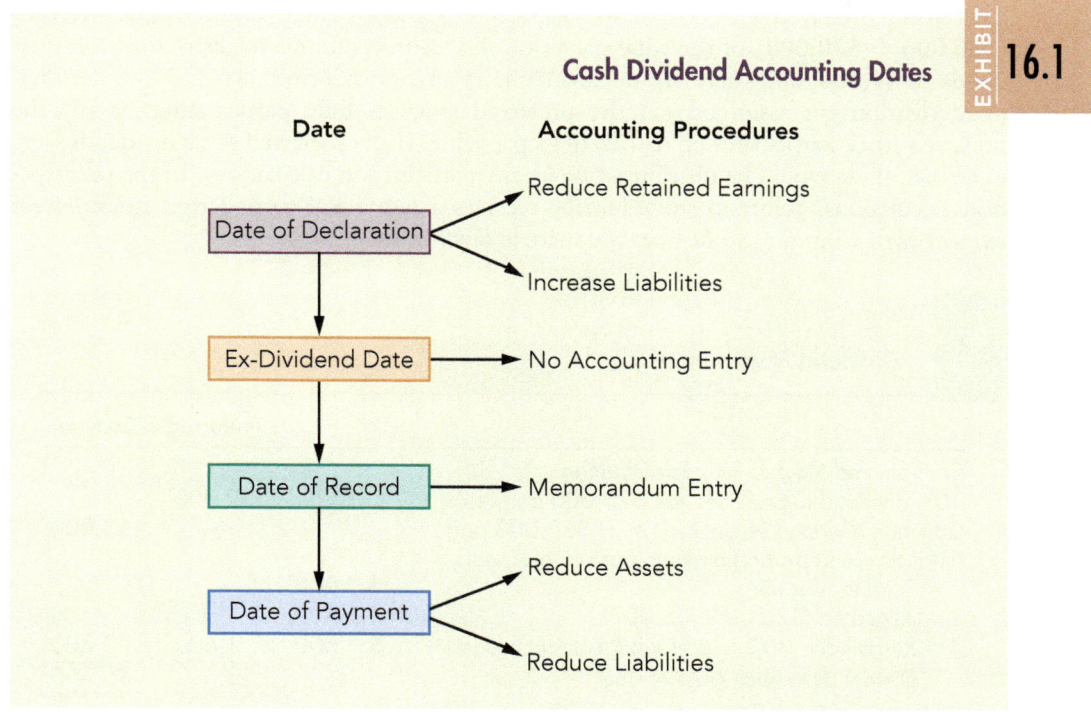

EXHIBIT 16.1 Cash Dividend Accounting Dates

Example: Declaration and Payment of Dividends

On November 2, 2016, Bengal Corporation's board of directors declares preferred dividends totaling $25,000 and common dividends totaling $40,000. These dividends are payable on December 14, 2016, to shareholders of record on November 23, 2016. Bengal makes the following journal entries to record the dividend:

November 2, 2016
Retained Earnings	65,000	
Dividends Payable: Preferred Stock		25,000
Dividends Payable: Common Stock		40,000

November 23, 2016
Memorandum entry: The company will pay dividends on December 14, 2016, to preferred and common shareholders of record as of today, the date of record.

December 14, 2016
Dividends Payable: Preferred Stock	25,000	
Dividends Payable: Common Stock	40,000	
Cash		65,000

If its accounting period ends before the dividend payment, Bengal reports the Dividends Payable account(s) as a current liability on its balance sheet. If it uses the contra account, Dividends Declared, it closes this account directly to Retained Earnings as part of the year-end closing process. ∎

Participating Preferred Stock Usually, the amounts of dividends payable to each class of stock can be easily determined. In certain cases, however, preferred stock may be either fully or partially participating. In these cases, a corporation must compute the dividends payable to preferred and common shareholders. Recall from Chapter 15 that *fully participating* preferred stock shares equally with the common stock in any extra dividends. These extra dividends are distributed proportionally, based on the respective *total* par values of each class of stock. *Partially participating* preferred stock is limited in its participation to a fixed rate (based on the respective par value) or amount per share.

Example: Participating Preferred Stock Dividends

Edgecombe Corporation has issued 10%, participating, cumulative preferred stock with a total par value of $20,000 and common stock with a total par value of $30,000. Therefore, preferred stock is 40% ($20,000 ÷ $50,000) and common stock is 60% ($30,000 ÷ $50,000) of the total par value. Edgecomb intends to distribute cash dividends of $9,000, and there are no dividends in arrears. **Example 16.1** shows the dividend distribution assuming (a) the preferred stock is fully participating or (b) the preferred stock participates up to 12% of its par value. If any preferred stock dividends were in arrears, these would be distributed *before* any participation calculations. In the participation calculations, common stock initially receives a rate equal to preferred stock *for the current year*. Common stock does *not* share in any dividends in arrears.

EXAMPLE 16.1 Dividend Distribution

		Preferred	Common
(a) Preferred Stock Is Fully Participating			
10% dividend to preferred (on $20,000 par)		$2,000	
Common dividend (equal to 10% of $30,000 par)			$3,000
Extra dividend proportionate to par values:			
Total to allocate	$ 9,000		
Allocated ($2,000 + $3,000)	(5,000)		
Remainder (40% to preferred, 60% to common)	$ 4,000	1,600	2,400
Dividends to each class of stock		$3,600	$5,400
(b) Preferred Stock Participates up to 12%			
10% dividend to preferred		$2,000	
Common dividend (equal to 10% of par)			$3,000
2% dividend on par of preferred (2% × $20,000)		400	
2% dividend on par of common (2% × $30,000)			600
Remainder to common ($9,000 − $6,000 allocated)			3,000
Dividends to each class of stock		$2,400	$6,600

ETHICAL DILEMMA

Mark Kellman, CEO of AM Technologies (AMT), has just learned that, for the third time in four months, a key executive has left the company to pursue a better-paying opportunity with a competitor. Mark is concerned that, without a proper incentive compensation plan, AMT will lose other key executives and the company's future could be in jeopardy. Mark determined that the executives expected AMT's stock to generate only modest returns in the stock market over the next several years, meaning that AMT's stock option plan would not produce the large gains that were historically observed. Mark has therefore proposed eliminating the stock option plan and replacing it with a restricted stock plan. Under Mark's plan, company executives would be given shares of restricted stock that could not be sold unless the executive remained with AMT for 10 years. If an employee were to leave prior to that period, the shares would be forfeited. Mark believes that such a plan would increase retention.

The restricted stock plan has three other features that make it attractive. First, because restricted stock consists of actual shares rather than the option to buy future shares, AMT will grant fewer shares than it would under the stock option plan, resulting in lower compensation expense and higher income. Second, executives would also receive dividend payments on the restricted stock, even if the stock has not vested. Therefore, by increasing the dividend, AMT could actually pay the executives a "cash bonus" without having to recognize compensation expense. Finally, employees will have something of value, even if the stock price doesn't increase. As the accountant for AMT, what is your reaction to Mark's proposal?

Property Dividends

Occasionally, a corporation will declare a **property dividend** that is payable in assets other than cash. These dividends are sometimes referred to as dividends in kind. For example, a corporation paying a property dividend might distribute marketable securities of other companies that it owns for the property dividend because they can be distributed easily to the shareholders, and as liquid assets the shareholders can easily sell the securities for cash if they wish. However, companies sometimes pay property dividends with any assets (such as inventory or land) designated by its board of directors.

A property dividend is classified as a *nonreciprocal, nonmonetary transfer to owners*. That is, the corporation enters into an exchange in which it gives up something of value (the asset) but for which it receives no asset or service in return. Also, because no cash is involved, the exchange is a nonmonetary transfer. GAAP requires a corporation to record a property dividend at the fair value of the asset transferred.[1] Therefore, the corporation would remove the asset distributed by crediting the asset account for the book value of the asset, it would debit Retained Earnings by the amount of the fair value of the asset distributed, and it would recognize a gain (or loss) in income if the asset fair value is greater than (less than) book value. The net effect on retained earnings, after deducting the fair value of the property dividend and recognizing a gain (or loss), is that retained earnings is reduced by the book value of the asset distributed.

The logic behind using fair value for a property dividend is that the corporation could have sold the asset distributed in the dividend for cash and used the proceeds (fair value) to pay a cash dividend. The fair value is determined *on the declaration date* (because this is the date the dividend becomes a legal liability) by referring to existing stock or bond market prices, recent cash exchanges of similar assets, or objective independent appraisals.

Example: Investment Securities (Bonds) Distributed as Property Dividend

Freestone Corporation's board of directors declares a property dividend, payable in investment securities, which are bonds issued by Bandera Company. The bonds are recorded as an investment asset by Freestone and classified as "available for sale" (in accordance with GAAP). The bonds are carried on Freestone's books at a fair value of $40,000, which was also the purchase price of the bonds. However, due to a decrease in interest rates since the last balance sheet date, their current fair value is $43,000. On the declaration date, Freestone revalues the investment account to its current fair value and records the dividend obligation at this value so that the amounts of both the gain and the dividend liability are properly reported. Freestone makes the following journal entries to record this property dividend:

Declaration Date

Investment in Bandera Company Bonds		
($43,000 – $40,000)	3,000	
Gain on Disposal of Investments		3,000
Retained Earnings	43,000	
Property Dividends Payable		43,000

Date of Payment

Property Dividends Payable	43,000	
Investment in Bandera Company Bonds		43,000

On the date of payment, Freestone does not adjust the gain or loss, even though the fair value may have changed since the declaration date. It reports the gain or loss in the other items section of its income statement. If Freestone will not pay the dividend until next year, it reports the dividend liability as a current liability on its balance sheet.

---

[1] FASB ASC 845-10-30: Nonmonetary Transactions, Overall, Initial Measurement.

In the case where a corporation distributes an "available-for-sale" debt security as a property dividend and there is a previously recorded unrealized increase or decrease in fair value, the computation of the gain or loss is more complex. The corporation is carrying its investment in available-for-sale securities (whether current or noncurrent) at the fair value (by use of an Allowance account) of the securities *on the last balance sheet date*. It is also reporting an "unrealized gain (or loss)" amount (whose balance is the difference between the cost and the fair value) in the Accumulated Other Comprehensive Income section of its shareholders' equity, as discussed in Chapter 13. However, the realized gain or loss on this type of property dividend is computed as the difference between the fair value of the securities *on the declaration date* and the original *cost* of the securities. The corporation must record a journal entry on the declaration date to revalue the investment (by adjusting the Allowance account), to record the realized gain or loss, and to eliminate the unrealized gain (loss) in value for these securities.

Example: Available-for-Sale Security Distributed as Property Dividend

Clay Corporation declares a property dividend on March 15, 2017, payable in Donley Company bonds. Clay purchased the Donley bonds early in 2016 for $24,000, and they were reported as an available-for-sale investment at a fair value of $29,000 (i.e., at a cost of $24,000 plus an allowance for a change in value of $5,000, along with an unrealized increase in value of $5,000 reported in its accumulated other comprehensive income) on the December 31, 2016, balance sheet. If the market value is $31,000 on March 15, 2017, the gain is $7,000, computed by comparing the current fair value ($31,000) to the original cost ($24,000). Clay makes the following journal entries on the declaration date to record this property dividend:

Allowance for Change in Fair Value of Investments	2,000	
Unrealized Holding Gain/Loss: Available-for-Sale Securities	5,000	
Gain on Sale of Investments		7,000
Retained Earnings	31,000	
Property Dividends Payable		31,000

Clay makes the following journal entry on the date of payment to record the distribution of the securities to shareholders:

Property Dividends Payable	31,000	
Investment in Available-for-Sale Securities		24,000
Allowance for Change in Fair Value of Investments		7,000

Scrip Dividends

As discussed earlier, in establishing dividend policy, the board of directors must consider both the legal requirements and the corporation's financial status. A corporation may have adequate retained earnings to meet the legal dividend requirements but insufficient cash to justify a current cash dividend. In this case, it may declare a **scrip dividend** and issue promissory notes (called "scrip") requiring it to pay dividends at some future date. It makes the usual journal entries on the declaration date (although some companies may credit Notes Payable instead of Dividends Payable) and date of payment. When the notes carry an interest rate, the corporation should make any necessary entries (e.g., adjusting entries) to record interest expense. Additionally, the dividend liability will be classified as short- or long-term depending on the maturity date of the scrip. Scrip dividends are rare, because corporations with liquidity problems typically do not commit to future cash outflows.

Internationally, scrip dividends have a different meaning. Many corporations such as **HSBC** and **Royal Dutch Shell** have scrip dividend programs in which investors can elect to receive additional common shares instead of cash. These are not stock dividends but an election by shareholders to purchase shares with the cash they would have received in dividends.

Stock Dividends

A corporation may also declare and distribute a stock dividend. A **stock dividend** is a proportional (pro rata) distribution of additional shares of a corporation's own stock to its shareholders.

A stock dividend usually consists of the same class of shares; that is, a common stock dividend is declared on common stock outstanding. This type of distribution is called an *ordinary* stock dividend. The distribution of a different class of stock (common on preferred or preferred on common) sometimes is called a *special* stock dividend. A corporation usually issues a stock dividend out of authorized but unissued shares, although it may use shares of treasury stock. Unlike other dividends, a corporation may legally rescind the declaration of a stock dividend before distribution. A stock dividend also differs from other dividends in that *no corporate assets are distributed*. Each shareholder maintains the same percentage ownership in the corporation before and after the distribution.

Shareholders often view stock dividends favorably even though (1) they receive no corporate assets, (2) their percentage ownership does not change, (3) the total market value of their investment remains the same (the increased number of shares outstanding will cause the market price per share to decrease proportionately; for example, a 10% stock dividend will cause the market share price to fall 10%), and (4) future cash dividends may be limited (retained earnings is decreased by the amount of the stock dividend and most states set legal dividend restrictions based on positive retained earnings). However, the following factors may enhance the perceived attractiveness of a stock dividend:

- The shareholders may view the stock dividend as a signal of corporate growth or sound financial strategy.
- Other investors may view the stock dividend in a favorable light, and increased trading in the stock may cause the market price *not* to decrease proportionally to the increased number of shares.
- The corporation may state that it will pay the same fixed cash dividend per share, in which case individual shareholders will receive higher total future cash dividends.
- If the market price is relatively high, a stock dividend might cause the price to decrease to a lower trading range, making the stock more liquid and therefore more attractive to additional investors so that the market price may eventually rise.

Conceptual Issues for Stock Dividends The economic substance of a stock dividend is that it is not really a "dividend" but instead is similar to a stock split. In both cases, even though the number of shares increases, a corporation does not distribute any assets to the shareholders, and each shareholder's percentage ownership stays the same. So, the corporation's total assets and shareholders' equity remain unchanged. Because they have similar economic substance, in theory, a corporation *should* record a stock dividend like a stock split.

From an accounting standpoint, however, a corporation does *not* account for a stock dividend like a stock split, but instead retained earnings is decreased and contributed capital is increased by the amount of the "dividend." When a company records a stock dividend, it does not change total shareholders' equity. This treatment is based on an "opportunity cost" argument. That is, the corporation should record the "dividend" at the fair value of the stock because this is the value it forgoes to issue the stock dividend.

Under this method, the fair value may be determined by assuming the stock is sold for cash at the current market price and the proceeds used to pay a cash dividend. The appropriate fair value at which to record the stock dividend is the market price *after* the declaration of the dividend. If a very small number of shares were issued in a stock dividend, this would cause only a small decrease in the market price. Larger stock dividends would cause greater decreases in the market price. To use this fair value approach, a method for estimating the decrease in fair value would need to be developed. However, no such method has been implemented. Instead, a distinction is made between "small" and "large" stock dividends, and different accounting principles apply to each.

GAAP for Stock Dividends A small stock dividend is viewed as a simultaneous sale of stock and payment of a dividend. **Therefore, a corporation accounts for a *small* stock dividend by transferring from retained earnings to contributed capital an amount equal to the fair value of the additional shares issued.** In distinguishing between a small and a large stock dividend, GAAP states that **fair value is ordinarily the appropriate value to use whenever the stock dividend is less than 20% to 25% of the previously outstanding shares.**[2]

State legal requirements govern the *minimum* amount that a corporation must capitalize (transfer from retained earnings to contributed capital as part of legal capital) for a stock dividend. Generally, this amount is the par or stated value of the additional shares distributed. The accounting for a large stock dividend relates to this legal capital. **Therefore, a corporation accounts for a *large* stock dividend by transferring from retained earnings to contributed capital an amount equal to the par value of the additional shares issued.** In this case, GAAP suggests that the use of the term *dividend* be avoided or, when this is not possible because of legal restrictions, the transaction should be described in terminology such as *a stock split effected in the form of a dividend.*[3]

Given the argument that a stock dividend should be based on fair value, use of par value to record a large stock dividend seems inappropriate. Par value has no direct relationship to fair value. Also, use of par value for large stock dividends and fair value for small stock dividends can lead to inconsistent accounting results. For example, assume a corporation with 2,000 shares of $10 par common stock outstanding issued a 15% (300 shares) small stock dividend when the market price per share is $40. In this case, it would reduce retained earnings and increase contributed capital by $12,000. If it issued a 50% (1,000 shares) large stock dividend, the corporation would reduce retained earnings and increase contributed capital by only $10,000. In this example, a small stock dividend has a greater effect on the components of the corporation's shareholders' equity than a large stock dividend! Nonetheless, use of fair value to record a small stock dividend and use of par value to record a large dividend are generally accepted accounting principles. Exhibit 16.2 shows the effects on the various elements of shareholders' equity of a small and large stock dividend, respectively.

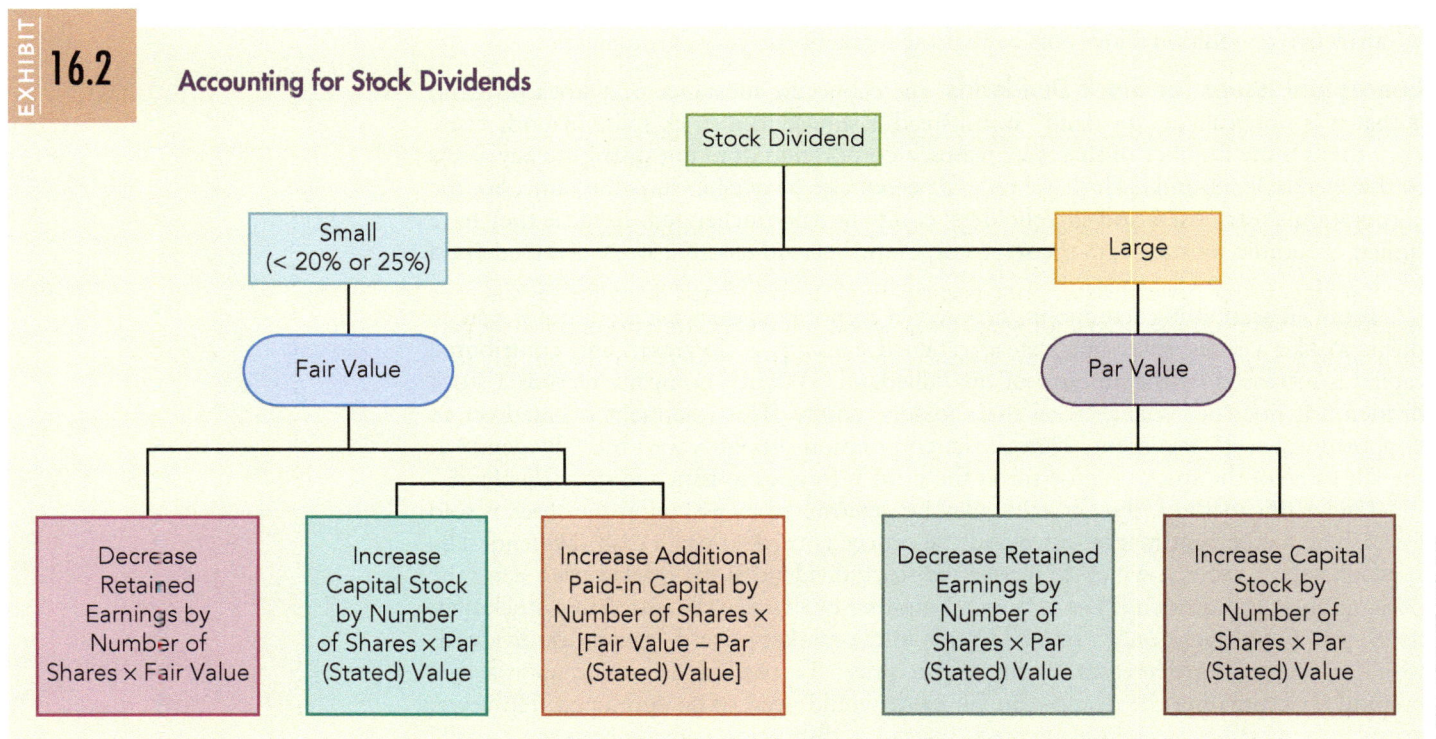

EXHIBIT 16.2 Accounting for Stock Dividends

[2] GAAP (FASB ASC 505-20-25-3: Equity, Glossary, Recognition) still uses the range of 20%–25%; however, the SEC has refined the cutoff to 25% of outstanding shares.
[3] FASB ASC 505-20-30: Equity, Stock Dividends and Stock Splits, Initial Measurement.

Example: Stock Dividends

To show the accounting for the two sizes of stock dividend, assume Querry Corporation has the following shareholders' equity prior to the stock dividend:

Common stock, $10 par (20,000 shares issued and outstanding)	$200,000
Additional paid-in capital	180,000
Retained earnings	320,000
Total shareholders' equity	$700,000

Example: Small Stock Dividend

Assume that Querry Corporation declares and issues a 10% stock dividend. On the declaration date, the stock is selling for $23 per share. Querry records the 2,000-share stock dividend at the fair value of $46,000, as shown in the following journal entries:

Declaration Date

Retained Earnings	46,000	
Common Stock to Be Distributed		20,000
Additional Paid-in Capital from Stock Dividend		26,000

Date of Issuance

Common Stock to Be Distributed	20,000	
Common Stock, $10 par		20,000

Querry's resulting shareholders' equity is as follows:

Common stock, $10 par (22,000 shares issued and outstanding)	$220,000
Additional paid-in capital	206,000
Retained earnings	274,000
Total shareholders' equity	$700,000

Note that the amounts of the components of Querry's shareholders' equity have changed, but its total shareholders' equity ($700,000) remains the same as before the small stock dividend.

If a corporation prepares a balance sheet after the declaration, but before the issuance of the stock dividend, it reports the Common Stock to Be Distributed account as a component of contributed capital. **The account is *not* a liability like the dividend payable accounts related to other types of dividends because it will not be satisfied by the distribution of assets.** Instead, it is a temporary shareholders' equity item representing the legal capital related to the stock to be issued. As shown, it is eliminated when the stock is issued.

Treasury stock normally does not participate in a small stock dividend because the dividend is based on the outstanding shares of stock. However, treasury stock may participate in a large stock dividend because the dividend is considered to be similar to a stock split.

Example: Large Stock Dividend

Assume, *instead*, that Querry declares and issues a 40% stock dividend when the stock is selling for $23 per share. In this case, Querry uses the par value of $80,000 for the 8,000 shares to record the stock dividend as follows:

Declaration Date

Retained Earnings	80,000	
Common Stock to Be Distributed		80,000

Date of Issuance

Common Stock to Be Distributed	80,000	
Common Stock, $10 par		80,000

The resulting shareholders' equity is as follows:

Common stock, $10 par (28,000 shares issued and outstanding)	$280,000
Additional paid-in capital	180,000
Retained earnings	240,000
Total shareholders' equity	$700,000

Note again that Querry's total shareholders' equity ($700,000) remains the same as before the large stock dividend. ∎

Fractional Shares In the case of a stock dividend, the number of shares that many shareholders own will not entitle them to receive additional whole shares from the dividend. For example, if a corporation declared a 10% stock dividend, a shareholder owning 43 shares would be entitled to 4.3 additional shares. Some corporations have a policy of not issuing fractional shares. These corporations usually offer shareholders the following two alternatives:

- Shareholders receive cash equal to the market price of the fractional share, in which case the corporation accounts for the cash it pays as a cash dividend and issues fewer shares.
- Shareholders pay in sufficient cash to receive a full share, in which case the corporation records the stock dividend in the usual manner and adjusts contributed capital for the cash it receives.

Stock Splits

As discussed in Chapter 15, a stock split results in a corporation issuing additional shares, or in the case of a reverse stock split, reducing the number of shares outstanding. However, a stock split does not affect retained earnings. Rather it results in a change in the par value amount and a proportional increase (or decrease) in the number of shares issued and outstanding. Firms do not record a journal entry for a stock split; however, they do make a memorandum entry to document the stock split, reflecting the impact of the split on the numbers of shares authorized, issued, and outstanding.

Liquidating Dividends

Liquidating dividends represent a return of contributed capital rather than a distribution of retained earnings. A corporation usually declares a liquidating dividend when it is ceasing or reducing operations. However, there are cases when a healthy company will declare a liquidating dividend. For example, **Cypress Semiconductor Corporation** stated that its March 2014 dividend will be paid from sources other than the company's retained earnings and for this reason will be treated as a return of capital. A liquidating dividend also may arise when a corporation with natural resources pays a dividend based on earnings before depletion. That portion of the dividend equal to the amount of depletion is considered the liquidating dividend.

When a corporation pays a dividend that is in part (or in total) a liquidating dividend, it must adhere to state legal requirements in recording the dividend. It records the *normal* portion of the dividend as a reduction of retained earnings and the *liquidating* portion as a reduction of contributed capital. The latter may be recorded as a debit either to an additional paid-in capital account or to a special contra-contributed capital account entitled, for instance, Contributed Capital Distributed as a Liquidating Dividend. The corporation should disclose the liquidating dividend in a note to its financial statements to notify shareholders that a portion of contributed capital is being returned.

> **GOT IT?**
>
> **16-1** What are the four important dates in regard to a cash dividend? What journal entry does the corporation make on each date?
>
> **16-2** How does the ex-dividend date differ from the date of record?
>
> **16-3** What is fully participating preferred stock? Partially participating preferred stock?
>
> **16-4** Discuss how a corporation records the declaration of a property dividend.
>
> **16-5** Distinguish between an ordinary and a special stock dividend.
>
> **16-6** Distinguish between small and large stock dividends. What amounts does a corporation use to record the declaration of each dividend?
>
> **16-7** How does the accounting for a liquidating dividend differ from that for a normal cash dividend?

HOW DO WE ACCOUNT FOR PRIOR PERIOD ADJUSTMENTS (RESTATEMENTS)?

LEARNING OBJECTIVE 16.2
Discuss the accounting for prior period adjustments and restrictions of retained earnings.

Corporations are required to report a few events as either retrospective adjustments or **prior period adjustments** (**restatements**) of retained earnings. These can arise from changes in accounting principles, change in accounting entity, and corrections of errors of prior periods.[4] The specific accounting treatment of these items will be discussed in Chapter 22. The following discussion illustrates prior period adjustments by focusing on corrections of errors and their impact on retained earnings.

A corporation may make an error in the financial statements of one accounting period that it does not discover until a later period. These errors may be due to oversights, incorrect use of existing facts, mathematical mistakes, or errors in applying accounting principles. Usually these errors affect an asset or liability and a revenue or expense of a prior year. A corporation is required to treat corrections of all material errors as prior period adjustments (restatements) of retained earnings. That is, when the error is corrected, the asset or liability account balance is corrected (debited or credited), and the offsetting credit or debit (which involved a revenue or expense previously closed to retained earnings) is made directly to the Retained Earnings account. Any related impact on income taxes is similarly recorded.

Example: Prior Period Adjustment

In 2017, Rycker Corporation discovers that it inadvertently did not accrue $10,000 of interest expense for 2016. This material error overstated 2016 income before income taxes by a similar amount. Assuming a related income tax effect of $3,000, Rycker makes the following correcting entries in 2017:

Retained Earnings	10,000	
Interest Payable		10,000
Income Tax Refund Receivable (or Payable)	3,000	
Retained Earnings		3,000

When a corporation makes a prior period adjustment, it reports the item (net of the applicable income taxes) as an adjustment of the beginning balance of retained earnings on its statement of retained earnings. If Rycker's January 1, 2017, retained earnings balance was $102,400, it reports the correction on its December 31, 2017, statement of retained earnings as a prior period adjustment as follows:

Retained earnings, as previously reported January 1, 2017	$102,400
Less: Correction of overstatement in 2016 net income due to interest expense understatement (net of $3,000 income taxes)	(7,000)
Adjusted retained earnings, January 1, 2017	$ 95,400

---
[4] FASB ASC 250-10-45: Accounting Changes and Error Corrections, Overall, Other Presentation Matters.

Rycker then completes the remaining portion of the statement as shown in Exhibit 16.3 (p. 16-16). It discloses the effect of the error on the prior year's net income and earnings per share in the period in which the correction is made. With these disclosures, users can see the impact of the error on the company's financial statements. If Rycker presents comparative financial statements, it makes corresponding adjustments to its net income, retained earnings, asset, or liability account balances for all the periods reported.[5]

Restrictions (Appropriations) of Retained Earnings

Sometimes, because of debt covenants or other financial or legal constraints, a corporation must use the *assets* represented by retained earnings for specific activities, including financing ongoing operations and long-term expansion projects, or paying the principal and interest on debt securities.

To indicate that a certain portion of assets and therefore a certain portion of retained earnings is not available for dividends, a corporation may restrict (appropriate) retained earnings. A **restriction** (**appropriation**) of retained earnings means that the board of directors makes a commitment that a portion of retained earnings is unavailable for dividends. It is important to understand that such a policy does *not* directly restrict the use of any assets. It merely requires that the corporation not distribute any assets that would reduce restricted retained earnings. A board of directors may restrict retained earnings (1) to meet legal requirements or (2) to meet contractual restrictions.

Certain states require restrictions of retained earnings when a corporation reacquires its own stock as treasury stock. Usually, retained earnings are reduced by an amount equal to the cost of the treasury shares. The argument for this is that acquiring treasury stock is similar in substance to a dividend because it returns cash to shareholders, and therefore reduces the amount of retained earnings that can be paid in dividends.

A corporation also may restrict retained earnings because of a contractual agreement. This type of agreement may be made when a corporation issues long-term bonds. To provide some assurance that sufficient assets will be kept in the corporation to satisfy bondholders' claims (and not paid out to shareholders in dividends), the bond provisions (sometimes called "debt covenants") may require the restriction of a certain amount of retained earnings.

Corporations disclose restrictions of retained earnings in a note (or sometimes by parenthetical notations) to the financial statements. In the note, a clear description of the legal or contractual provisions and the amount of the restriction is required.

Example Johnstone Corporation has a $300,000 retained earnings balance when it acquires treasury stock at a cost of $20,000. Johnstone would report the $300,000 retained earnings balance and disclose the restriction of retained earnings as follows:

Retained earnings (see *Note A*)	$300,000

Notes to the Financial Statements
Note A: Retained earnings are restricted in the amount of $20,000, the cost of the treasury stock.

When a corporation cancels a restriction (for instance, because it no longer has treasury stock), it removes the note in its financial statements.

GOT IT?

16-8 How does a corporation record and report a correction of a material error made in a previous year in its current year's financial statements?

16-9 For what reasons would a corporation restrict its retained earnings? How does it report a restriction?

[5] Ibid.

HOW DO COMPANIES REPORT CHANGES IN SHAREHOLDERS' EQUITY?

LEARNING OBJECTIVE 16.3
Explain the various components of shareholders' equity and related disclosures.

A corporation may engage in various transactions that affect some component of its shareholders' equity. *FASB Statement of Financial Accounting Concepts No. 5* suggests that a full set of financial statements should show investments by and distributions to owners during the period. To inform users of a corporation's financial statements about its capital activities, GAAP states:

> ... disclosure of changes in the separate accounts comprising stockholders' equity (in addition to retained earnings) and of the changes in the number of shares of equity securities during at least the most recent annual fiscal period ... is required to make the financial statements sufficiently informative.[6]

Thus, a corporation must disclose the changes in the different classes of common stock, additional paid-in capital, retained earnings, accumulated other comprehensive income, and treasury stock in its annual report. The purpose is to report the changes in the corporation's financial structure to help users assess changes in its financial flexibility, profitability, and risk. Most corporations prepare a statement of shareholders' equity that includes an analysis of the changes in these items. The statement of shareholders' equity is usually reported in matrix form, with the columns representing the various claims of equity shareholders (common stock at par, additional paid-in capital, retained earnings, etc.) and the rows reporting changes in each of those elements during the period. The ending amounts in this statement then tie to the shareholders' equity section of the year-end balance sheet.

Examples 16.2 and **16.3** show a statement of shareholders' equity and an excerpt from the balance sheet showing the ending shareholders' equity for the hypothetical Bardwell Corporation.[7]

EXAMPLE 16.2

Bardwell Corporation, Statement of Shareholders' Equity for 2016

Explanation	Common Stock — Shares Issued	Common Stock — Par Value	Additional Paid-in Capital — Common Stock	Additional Paid-in Capital — Treasury Stock	Common Stock Option Warrants	Retained Earnings	Accumulated Other Comprehensive Income	Treasury Stock (Cost)	Total Shareholders' Equity
Balances, 1/1/2016	10,000	$50,000	$170,000	$2,300	$11,200	$322,000	$15,200	$(7,500)	$563,200
Issued for cash	1,100	5,500	22,000						27,500
Reissued treasury stock				2,700				4,500	7,200
Issued for exercise of share options	300	1,500	5,400		(900)				6,000
Compensation expense for share options					3,300				3,300
Unrealized increase in value of available-for-sale securities							4,800		4,800
Net income						97,000			97,000
Cash dividends						(32,800)			(32,800)
Balances, 12/31/2016	11,400	$57,000	$197,400	$5,000	$13,600	$386,200	$20,000	$(3,000)	$676,200

---

[6] FASB ASC 505-10-50-2: Equity, Overall, Disclosure.
[7] Bardwell Corporation reports its comprehensive income in a separate financial statement.

EXAMPLE 16.3 — Bardwell Corporation, Shareholders' Equity Section of the Balance Sheet on December 31, 2016

Contributed Capital:	
Common stock, $5 par (30,000 shares authorized, 11,400 shares issued, of which 100 shares are being held as treasury stock)	$ 57,000
Additional paid-in capital on common stock	197,400
Additional paid-in capital from treasury stock	5,000
Common stock option warrants	13,600
Total contributed capital	$273,000
Retained earnings (see Note A)	386,200
Accumulated other comprehensive income:	
Unrealized increase in value of available-for-sale securities	20,000
Total contributed capital, retained earnings, and accumulated other comprehensive income	$679,200
Less: Treasury stock (at cost)	(3,000)
Total Shareholders' Equity	$676,200

Notes to the Financial Statements

Note A: Retained earnings are restricted regarding dividends in the amount of $3,000, the cost of the treasury stock.

Accumulated Other Comprehensive Income

As discussed in Chapters 4 and 5, a corporation is required to report its total comprehensive income for the accounting period. Comprehensive income includes both net income and "other comprehensive income." Other comprehensive income (loss) might include the following four items:

- unrealized increases (gains) or decreases (losses) in the fair value of investments in available-for-sale securities
- translation adjustments from converting the financial statements of a company's foreign operations into U.S. dollars
- gains and losses on certain types of derivative financial instruments that are designated as cash flow hedges
- certain types of pension plan gains, losses, and prior service cost adjustments

A corporation may report its comprehensive income (net of income taxes) on the face of its income statement or in a separate statement of comprehensive income that immediately follows the income statement.

Statement of Retained Earnings

Although not a required separate financial statement, many small corporations include a statement of retained earnings in their financial statements. To disclose the earnings, dividends, prior period and retroactive adjustments, and other reductions, we suggest the format shown in Exhibit 16.3.

EXHIBIT 16.3 — Statement of Retained Earnings for 2016

Retained earnings, as previously reported, January 1, 2016
  Plus (minus): Prior period and retrospective adjustments (net of income tax effect)
Adjusted retained earnings, January 1, 2016
  Plus (minus): Net income (loss)
  Minus: Dividends (specifically identified, including per share amounts)
      Reductions because of retirement or reacquisition of capital stock
      Reductions because of conversion of bonds or preferred stock
Retained earnings, December 31, 2016

A corporation may include the retained earnings statement as a separate statement within the financial statements, as a supporting schedule directly beneath the income statement, or, as is common, in the statement of shareholders' equity. Although the format in Exhibit 16.3 includes all items affecting retained earnings, the following three items are relatively rare:

- reductions due to prior period and retroactive adjustments
- reductions because of conversions
- reductions because of the retirement of capital stock

A retained earnings statement usually includes only adjustments to retained earnings for net income and dividends. Any restrictions of retained earnings are disclosed in a note to the financial statements.

Miscellaneous Changes in Shareholders' Equity

In rare instances, a corporation may increase shareholders' equity for events not related to the issuance of stock or to retained earnings. For example, as discussed in Chapter 10, it is possible for a corporation to receive donated assets (e.g., a plant site) from a governmental unit to induce it to locate in a particular community. As this is a nonreciprocal, nonmonetary transfer, the corporation records the asset at its fair value. It records the resulting credit in a Donated Capital account. A corporation lists these items separately in its shareholders' equity.

Noncontrolling Interest

Many companies, including **Starbucks**, report the line item "noncontrolling interest" in shareholders' equity. In addition, the income statement has net earnings including noncontrolling interest and net earnings attributable to noncontrolling interests. Noncontrolling interests is not an account but instead represents a portion of a subsidiary that is not owned by a parent corporation. For example, if Starbucks owns 95% of the outstanding equity of another company, the 5% that is owned by other investors and not by Starbucks is the noncontrolling interest.

Under GAAP, the noncontrolling interest reported on the balance sheet represents that amount of net assets in the subsidiary that are owned by shareholders other than the parent corporation. The noncontrolling interest is reported in this manner because the parent corporation consolidates all 100% of the assets and liabilities of its controlled subsidiaries, even though it may not own all 100% of the assets and liabilities. The portion of net assets that is not owned by the parent is then reported as a separate portion of equity called the noncontrolling interest.

The same procedure is used on the income statement for the noncontrolling interest. The parent company includes 100% of the revenues, expenses, and net income of its controlled subsidiaries even if it does not own all 100% of the subsidiary. The portion of net income attributable to the noncontrolling interest is subtracted from total net income to obtain net income for the parent company. Continuing with the prior example, 5% of the earnings of Starbucks's subsidiary would be subtracted as "net income attributable to noncontrolling interests."

The specific details of accounting for consolidated financial statements and noncontrolling interests are saved for an advanced course.

To illustrate, review the shareholders' equity portion of **Starbucks**'s consolidated balance sheet and consolidated statements of equity shown in Real Report 16.1.

16.1 SHAREHOLDERS' EQUITY AND RELATED CHANGES — REAL REPORT

Starbucks Corporation

STARBUCKS CORPORATION
CONSOLIDATED BALANCE SHEETS
(In millions, except per share data)

	Sep 27, 2015	Sep 28, 2014
Shareholders' equity:		
Common stock ($0.001 par value) — authorized, 2,400.0 shares; issued and outstanding, 1,485.1 and 1,499.1 shares, respectively	1.5	0.7
Additional paid-in capital	41.1	39.4
Retained earnings	5,974.8	5,206.6
Accumulated other comprehensive income/(loss)	(199.4)	25.3
Total shareholders' equity	5,818.0	5,272.0
Noncontrolling interest	1.8	1.7
Total equity	5,819.8	5,273.7
TOTAL LIABILITIES AND EQUITY	$12,446.1	$10,752.9

STARBUCKS CORPORATION
CONSOLIDATED STATEMENTS OF EQUITY
(in millions, except per share data)

	Common Stock Shares	Common Stock Amount	Additional Paid-in Capital	Retained Earnings	Accumulated Other Comprehensive Income/(Loss)	Shareholders' Equity	Noncontrolling Interest	Total
Balance, September 30, 2012	749.3	$0.7	$39.4	$5,046.2	$22.7	$5,109.0	$5.5	$5,114.5
Net earnings	—	—	—	8.3	—	8.3	0.5	8.8
Other comprehensive income/(loss)	—	—	—	—	44.3	44.3	—	44.3
Stock-based compensation expense	—	—	144.1	—	—	144.1	—	144.1
Exercise of stock options/vesting of RSUs, including tax benefit of $259.9	14.4	0.1	366.7	—	—	366.8	—	366.8
Sale of common stock, including tax benefit of $0.2	0.3	—	20.4	—	—	20.4	—	20.4
Repurchase of common stock	(10.8)	—	(288.5)	(255.6)	—	(544.1)	—	(544.1)
Cash dividends declared, $0.445 per share	—	—	—	(668.6)	—	(668.6)	—	(668.6)
Noncontrolling interest resulting from divestiture	—	—	—	—	—	—	(3.9)	(3.9)
Balance, September 29, 2013	753.2	$0.8	$282.1	$4,130.3	$67.0	$4,480.2	$2.1	$4,482.3
Net earnings	—	—	—	2,068.1	—	2,068.1	(0.4)	2,067.7
Other comprehensive income/(loss)	—	—	—	—	(41.7)	(41.7)	—	(41.7)
Stock-based compensation expense	—	—	185.1	—	—	185.1	—	185.1
Exercise of stock options/vesting of RSUs, including tax benefit of $114.8	6.5	—	154.8	—	—	154.8	—	154.8
Sale of common stock, including tax benefit of $0.2	0.3	—	22.3	—	—	22.3	—	22.3
Repurchase of common stock	(10.5)	(0.1)	(604.9)	(164.8)	—	(769.8)	—	(769.8)
Cash dividends declared, $0.550 per share	—	—	—	(827.0)	—	(827.0)	—	(827.0)
Balance, September 28, 2014	749.5	$0.7	$39.4	$5,206.6	$25.3	$5,272.0	$1.7	$5,273.7
Net earnings	—	—	—	2,757.4	—	2,757.4	1.9	2,759.3
Other comprehensive income/(loss)	—	—	—	—	(193.6)	(193.6)	(31.1)	(224.7)
Stock-based compensation expense	—	—	211.7	—	—	211.7	—	211.7
Exercise of stock options/vesting of RSUs, including tax benefit of $131.3	14.6	—	224.4	—	—	224.4	—	224.4

	Common Stock		Additional Paid-in Capital	Retained Earnings	Accumulated Other Comprehensive Income/(Loss)	Shareholders' Equity	Noncontrolling Interest	Total
	Shares	Amount						
Sale of common stock, including tax benefit of $0.2	0.6	—	23.5	—	—	23.5	—	23.5
Repurchase of common stock	(29.0)	—	(459.6)	(972.2)	—	(1,431.8)	—	(1,431.8)
Cash dividends declared, $0.680 per share	—	—	—	(1,016.2)	—	(1,016.2)	—	(1,016.2)
Two-for-one stock split	749.4	0.8	—	(0.8)	—	—	—	—
Noncontrolling interest resulting from acquisition	—	—	—	—	—	—	411.1	411.1
Purchase of noncontrolling interest	—	—	1.7	—	(31.1)	(29.4)	(381.7)	(411.1)
Balance, September 27, 2015	1,485.1	$1.5	$41.1	$5,974.8	$(199.4)	$5,818.0	$1.8	$5,819.8

Questions:

1. How many shares of treasury stock were acquired in fiscal year 2015? At what average price were these shares acquired?
2. What was Starbucks's other comprehensive income for fiscal year 2015, and what was Starbucks's ending 2015 balance in Accumulated Other Comprehensive Income? Examine Starbucks's consolidated statements of equity to determine what transactions affected comprehensive income during fiscal year 2015.
3. What were the total dividends declared during fiscal year 2015? How much did dividends change from 2014 to 2015?
4. How many shares of common stock were issued for stock option compensation in 2015? At what average price were the common shares issued?

Suggested answers to these questions are found at the end of the chapter.

INTERNATIONAL DIMENSION

SHAREHOLDERS' EQUITY

Under IFRS, a corporation's shareholders' equity (sometimes called shareholders' interests) consists of two sections: (1) share capital and (2) other equity. Within the equity section, one major difference with regard to the components of shareholders' equity is that IFRS permit the reporting of a Revaluation Reserve. The Revaluation Reserve is the result of IFRS allowing, but not requiring, the revaluation to fair value of some intangible assets; property, plant, and equipment; and some inventories. In addition, GAAP and IFRS differ in how changes in shareholders' equity are reported. IFRS require that the statement of shareholders' equity be presented as a primary financial statement. GAAP, however, permits the statement of shareholders' equity to be presented as a primary financial statement or within the financial footnotes. However, the SEC requires that publicly registered companies must present a statement of shareholders' equity.

Many of the disclosures required for shareholders' capital are similar to those required under U.S. GAAP. Companies are required to disclose information about:

- number of shares authorized, issued, and outstanding; par value; reacquired shares and rights; preferences; and restrictions regarding dividends
- changes in the above items from the previous period
- any externally imposed capital requirements that result in restrictions

Source: IAS 1. (See Appendix C at the end of this book.)

EARNINGS PER SHARE

In addition to reporting net income, corporations are also required by GAAP to report earnings per share information on their income statements. Earnings per share is one of the pieces of financial information most closely examined by financial analysts, investors, and the financial press. On the most basic level, **earnings per share** represent the amount of net income associated with each share of common stock. When a financial website or newspaper reports on a company's earnings, it normally reports the earnings per share as a summary of the company's performance during the period. Earnings per share information is relevant to these users in evaluating *return on investment* and *risk* of a corporation. Recall the Nichols and Wahlen study discussed in Chapter 1 regarding the relation between companies' changes in net income and changes in stock prices in the capital markets. According to the study, companies that reported an increase in earnings over the prior fiscal year experienced stock returns that beat market average returns by roughly 19.2%. Those companies that had earnings that decreased from the prior fiscal year had stock returns 16.4% lower than the market average.[8] The amount of earnings per share, the change in earnings per share from the previous period, and the trend in earnings per share are all important indicators of a corporation's profitability for investors.

One ratio used to evaluate return and risk is the **price/earnings ratio**, which investors often use in intercompany comparisons of share price relative to profitability. The price/earnings ratio is computed as follows:

$$\text{Price/Earnings Ratio} = \frac{\text{Market Price per Share of Common Stock}}{\text{Earnings per Share}}$$

As this book goes to press, **Under Armour** and **Nike** had price/earnings ratios of 63 and 25, respectively. Under Armour's price/earnings ratio indicates that the stock is selling for a price of 63 times the most recent year's earnings per share. The difference in the ratios indicates that, compared to Nike, investors are more optimistic about the future of Under Armour and expect that it will have a higher growth in earnings per share.

GOT IT?

16-10 What changes does a corporation include in its statement of shareholders' equity?

16-11 What items might a corporation include in the Accumulated Other Comprehensive Income section of its shareholders' equity?

16-12 What is the suggested format for the statement of retained earnings? What are the two most common elements in this statement?

LEARNING OBJECTIVE 16.4
Compute basic earnings per share (EPS) including the computation of weighted average common shares.

HOW ARE BASIC EARNINGS PER SHARE (EPS) COMPUTED?

Due to the importance of EPS as a summary measure of company performance, the accounting rules for its calculation are detailed and specific. When computing earnings per share, the company's capital structure will determine what type of information will need to be reported. There are two types of corporate capital structures—simple and

---

[8] D. Craig Nichols and James Wahlen, "How Do Earnings Numbers Relate to Stock Returns? A Review of Classic Accounting Research with Updated Evidence," *Accounting Horizons* (December 2004), pp. 263–286.

complex. The difference depends on whether the firm has issued securities that could convert into common stock:

- A **simple capital structure** is one that simply consists of common stock outstanding, with no convertible claims on common stock.
- A **complex capital structure** is one that has both common stock outstanding and securities that could convert into common equity and be potentially dilutive, such as stock options, convertible debt, or convertible preferred shares.

A corporation with a simple capital structure is required to report basic earnings per share.[9] **Basic earnings per share** (sometimes called **earnings per common share**) is computed as follows:

$$\text{Basic Earnings per Share} = \frac{\text{Net Income} - \text{Preferred Dividends}}{\text{Weighted Average Number of Common Shares Outstanding}}$$

Example: Basic Earnings per Share

During 2016, Branson Corporation reports net income of $48,000, and declares and pays dividends of $8,000 on its nonconvertible preferred stock. It also declares and pays dividends of $12,000 on its 16,000 shares of common stock that have been outstanding for the entire year. Branson computes its basic earnings per share for 2016 as follows:

$$\frac{\$48,000 - \$8,000}{16,000} = \$2.50$$

Note that Branson deducts the dividends on its preferred dividends but not the dividends on its common stock in computing its basic earnings per share. This is because the numerator of the basic earnings per share calculation is the earnings available to common shareholders, and preferred dividends must be paid before common dividends may be distributed.

Branson reports its basic earnings per share on its 2016 income statement, directly below net income. If it had a net loss, it would have reported the basic loss per share. It also reports basic earnings per share (or basic loss per share) for each comparative income statement presented.

Several complexities affect the numerator and denominator of the earnings per share equation. Although we discuss these issues for basic earnings per share, they also apply to corporations that report diluted earnings per share (discussed in a later section).

Numerator Calculations

Only the amount of *earnings available to common shareholders* is used in the numerator of the earnings per share computation. If a corporation has outstanding *noncumulative* preferred stock, it deducts the dividends declared during the current period from the net income to determine the earnings available to common shareholders (as in the previous example). If the corporation has *cumulative* preferred stock outstanding, it deducts the dividends for the *current* period, *whether declared or not*. It discloses the amount of the dividends deduction in the notes to its financial statements, as shown in **Example 16.8** (p. 16-33).

Denominator Calculations

In determining the weighted average number of shares a company should use in the denominator of its earnings per share calculation, it must consider when the shares were issued and if the shares were issued in a stock split or dividend.

[9] FASB ASC 260-10-45: Earnings Per Share, Overall, Other Presentation Matters.

Weighted Average Shares Because a corporation generates net income over the entire year, the earnings relate to the common shares outstanding during the year. If a corporation has not issued or reacquired any shares and the number of shares outstanding has remained constant during the year, it uses the number of common shares outstanding at the end of the accounting period as the denominator. If a corporation has issued or reacquired common shares during the period, the denominator is the weighted average number of common shares outstanding during the period.

As the company issues more shares or repurchases shares, the revised number of common shares outstanding is multiplied by the fraction for the year they are outstanding. This process continues for the entire period and the amounts are totaled to determine the weighted average number of common shares.

Example: Weighted Average Shares

Alamance Corporation had 15,000 shares of common stock outstanding at the beginning of the year. On March 1, it issued 2,700 shares; on July 1, it issued another 3,300 shares; and on December 1, it reacquired 600 shares as treasury stock. The weighted average number of common shares the corporation uses in computing its earnings per share is 18,850 shares, as shown in **Example 16.4**. Alamance discloses this number in the notes to its financial statements.

EXAMPLE 16.4 Weighted Average Shares

Months Shares Are Outstanding	Shares Outstanding	×	Fraction of Year Outstanding	=	Equivalent Whole Units
January–February	15,000	×	2/12	=	2,500
March–June	17,700	×	4/12	=	5,900
July–November	21,000	×	5/12	=	8,750
December	20,400	×	1/12	=	1,700
			Total weighted average common shares		18,850

Note that for simplicity, the nearest whole month is used to determine the fraction of the year each layer of shares was outstanding. In practice, corporations will base their weighted average calculations on the actual number of days outstanding.

Stock Dividends or Splits In the Alamance example, each issuance and repurchase of common stock was a result of a cash transaction. However, a company's shares outstanding can change as a result of a stock dividend or stock split, which are noncash events. These events do not affect shareholders' total investment in the corporation, instead only changing the number of shares outstanding. Because these events do not affect the company's net assets, the company gives *retroactive* recognition to these events for all comparative income statements that it presents.[10] This retroactive adjustment results in comparable earnings per share amounts for all periods presented in the financial statements, based on the most recent capital structure.

---

[10] A corporation must also give retroactive recognition if the stock dividend or split occurs after the end of the accounting period but before it issues its financial statements.

The simplest way of giving retroactive recognition is to first assume (for earnings per share computations) that the stock dividend or split occurred at the *beginning* of the earliest comparative period. Then assume that all stock transactions between this beginning date and the *actual* date of the stock dividend or split included the additional shares resulting from the assumed dividend or split. To illustrate the importance of maintaining comparability, suppose the company had the same level of earnings in two consecutive years and engaged in a 2-for-1 stock split in the second year. Without the retroactive adjustment to the number of shares outstanding, earnings per share would be half that of the prior year, which would be misleading because net income remained the same.

Example: Stock Dividend and Split

Vance Corporation begins operations in January 2016 and issues 5,000 shares of common stock that are outstanding during all of 2016. On December 10, 2016, it issues a 2-for-1 stock split, so that shareholders now have 200% more shares than prior to the split. At the end of 2016, the weighted average number of shares that it uses in the earnings per share computation for 2016 is 10,000 (5,000 × 200% × 12/12) because the 2-for-1 stock split is *assumed* to have occurred on January 1, 2016.

During 2017, Vance enters into the following transactions:

- On June 1, 2017, the corporation issues 5,000 shares of common stock.
- On August 9, 2017, it issues a 20% stock dividend.
- On October 1, 2017, it issues 2,000 shares of stock.

At the end of 2017, when Vance reports comparative earnings per share for 2016 and 2017, the weighted average numbers of shares it uses in the computation are 12,000 shares for 2016 and 16,000 shares for 2017, as shown in **Example 16.5**.

EXAMPLE 16.5

Comparative Weighted Average Shares

Retroactive Recognition of Stock Split and Stock Dividend: At End of 2017, for 2016 and 2017

Months Shares Are Outstanding	Actual Shares Outstanding	Assumed Shares Outstanding	×	Fraction of Year Outstanding	=	Equivalent Whole Units
2016						
January–December	5,000	5,000 × 200% × 120% = 12,000	×	12/12	=	12,000
				Total weighted average common shares		12,000
2017						
January–May	10,000	10,000 × 120% = 12,000	×	5/12	=	5,000
June–July	15,000	15,000 × 120% = 18,000	×	2/12	=	3,000
August–September	18,000	15,000 × 120% = 18,000	×	2/12	=	3,000
October–December	20,000	(15,000 × 120%) + 2,000 = 20,000	×	3/12	=	5,000
				Total weighted average common shares		16,000

In **Example 16.5**, for comparative purposes at the end of 2017, the 2-for-1 stock split actually issued on December 10, 2016, *and* the 20% stock dividend actually issued on August 9, 2017, are both *assumed* to have occurred on January 1, 2016. Under this assumption, 12,000 shares of stock would have been outstanding during all of 2016. Similarly, during 2017, 12,000 shares initially would have been outstanding. The 5,000 shares issued on June 1, 2017, would have increased by 20% to 6,000 shares, resulting in 18,000 shares outstanding until October 1, 2017. The 2,000 shares actually issued on

October 1, 2017, would not have increased because this issuance occurred after the actual stock dividend. The resulting weighted average number of shares is 16,000 at the end of 2017. Although these assumptions do not reflect the actual timing of the transactions, they are necessary to compute comparable earnings per share amounts for each year. ■

> # WHY IT MATTERS
>
> Investors, creditors, and others use various measures to assess how effective a company has been at meeting its profit objective. While one such measure (earnings per share) has been discussed earlier in the chapter, two other measures are often used—price/earnings ratio and dividend yield.
>
> The price/earnings ratio measures the market's assessment of the future earnings potential of the company. Using information obtained from its 2013 annual report, General Mills's price/earnings ratio at May 1, 2014, can be computed as:
>
> $$\text{Price/Earnings Ratio} = \frac{\text{Market Price per Common Share}}{\text{Earnings per Share}} = \frac{\$52.68}{\$2.86} = 18.42$$
>
> While price/earnings ratios should be evaluated in the context of the industry in which the company operates, higher price/earnings ratios relative to other similar companies are generally interpreted as a positive signal regarding a company's future prospects.
>
> Another useful measure of shareholder profitability is dividend yield. This ratio provides investors with information pertaining to the rate of return that was received in cash dividends. For General Mills, the dividend yield as of May 1, 2014, was:
>
> $$\text{Dividend Yield} = \frac{\text{Dividends per Common Share}}{\text{Market Price per Common Share}} = \frac{\$1.64}{\$52.68} = 3.1\%$$
>
> The dividend yield, together with the percentage change in the market price of the stock held during the period, is the total return on the shareholders' investment.

Components of Earnings per Share

Net income is the bottom line earnings amount on a corporation's income statement. If the net income includes any results from discontinued operations, the corporation must report separate earnings per share amounts for *both* income from continuing operations and net income on its income statement. It is also required to disclose the earnings per share related to the results from discontinued operations. The corporation may report these component amounts on its income statement or in the notes to its financial statements.[11] When a corporation has deducted preferred dividends in the computation of total earnings per share, it also deducts these dividends from the income related to continuing operations to reconcile the earnings per share amounts.

Each of these earnings per share component amounts is based on the same weighted average number of shares. When reported on the income statement, the components are summed to report the total earnings per share. The intent is to show the contribution of each income statement component to the total earnings per share.

Example: Basic Earnings per Share

Example 16.6 provides a comprehensive illustration of the computation of basic earnings per share for Caswell Corporation. ■

---

[11] FASB ASC 260-10-45: Earnings Per Share, Overall, Other Presentation Matters. These disclosures are also required for diluted earnings per share, as we discuss later.

EXAMPLE 16.6

Computation and Reporting of Basic Earnings per Share

1. Income statement information for Caswell Corporation:
   a. Net income for 2016 is $14,000.
   b. Income from discontinued operations (net of income taxes) of $3,600 is included in net income.
2. Shareholders' equity information (end of 2016):
   a. Preferred stock, 8%, $100 par, $30,000
   b. Common stock, $10 par, $60,000
3. Additional information:
   a. No preferred stock was issued or reacquired during 2016.
   b. Preferred dividends were declared during 2016 at the stated rate.
   c. A review of the Common Stock account shows that on January 1, 2016, 2,000 shares of common stock were outstanding. On April 1, 500 shares of common stock were issued for cash. On June 1, a 2-for-1 stock split occurred, resulting in 5,000 total common shares. On November 1, 1,000 shares of common stock were issued for cash.
4. Basic earnings per share computations for 2016:
   a. Net income available to common shareholders:

Net Income	$14,000
Less: Preferred dividends	(2,400)
Net income—common shareholders	$11,600

   b. Preferred dividends: $30,000 × 0.08 = $2,400
   c. Weighted average shares:

Initial shares, including stock split effects:	
(2,000 × 200% stock split) × 3/12 =	1,000
Initial shares plus shares issued in April:	
(2,500 × 200%) × 7/12 =	2,917
Include shares outstanding from November share issue:	
[(2,500 × 200%) + 1,000] × 2/12 =	1,000
Weighted average common shares	4,917

   d. Basic earnings per share: $11,600 ÷ 4,917 = $2.36

5. Condensed income statement presentation of Caswell for 2016:

Income before discontinued operations	$10,400
Discontinued operations (net of income taxes)	3,600
Net income	$14,000
Basic earnings per share (see Note A):	
Income before discontinued operations	$ 1.63
Income from Discontinued operations	0.73
Net income	$ 2.36

6. Note A to financial statements: Preferred dividends of $2,400 are deducted from income before discontinued operations and net income to determine earnings available to common stock. The resulting amounts of $8,000 and $11,600 divided by the 4,917 weighted average number of common shares yield $1.63 and $2.36 basic earnings per share, respectively. A total of 6,000 common shares were outstanding at the end of 2016.

> **GOT IT?**
>
> **16-13** What is a simple capital structure?
>
> **16-14** How is basic earnings per share computed for a corporation with a simple capital structure?
>
> **16-15** What is the weighted average number of shares for computing earnings per share, and how is it calculated?
>
> **16-16** On what date are stock dividends and splits considered to be issued for computing earnings per share?

LEARNING OBJECTIVE 16.5

Compute diluted earnings per share including the identification of potential common shares.

WHEN DO COMPANIES REPORT DILUTED EARNINGS PER SHARE?

Many corporations have complex capital structures. Their capital structures include securities such as share options and warrants, convertible preferred stock, convertible bonds, participating securities, differing classes of common stock, and contingent shares. These securities are referred to as **potential common shares** if they can be used by the holder to acquire common stock. Because conversion of these securities would change the number of common shares outstanding, they are considered in computing a corporation's earnings per share.

A corporation with a complex capital structure is required to report both basic and diluted earnings per share amounts on the face of its income statement. Basic earnings per share is computed, as discussed earlier, under the assumptions of a simple capital structure. **Diluted earnings per share** (**DEPS**) **shows the earnings per share after including *all* potential common shares that would decrease earnings per share.** It considers these potential common shares in addition to the weighted average common shares calculation discussed previously. In this section, we discuss only the more common types of potential common shares—stock options and warrants, and convertible preferred stock and bonds.

Potential common shares are included in the calculation of diluted earnings per share only if they have a potentially *dilutive* effect on (that is, decrease) earnings per share. Depending on stock prices and other factors, some potential common shares may be dilutive and others may not be, and given how stock prices change over time, some potential common shares may be dilutive in one period but not another. For example, if a firm's share price is $30, vested stock options with an exercise price of only $25 would be dilutive, whereas those with an exercise price of $31 would not be. Next year, if the stock price rises to $35, both sets of stock options would be dilutive. Thus, a corporation may include a potential common share in the diluted earnings per share computation in one accounting period and not in another. Consequently, you must be familiar with the types of potential common shares, the tests to determine the dilution of each security, and the diluted earnings per share computations.

Computing Diluted Earnings per Share

To evaluate the dilutive effect of each security, a corporation must include potential common shares in the diluted earnings per share (DEPS) calculations in a certain order. Therefore, the steps for computing DEPS are as follows:

- *Step 1*. Compute basic earnings per share for the company.
- *Step 2*. Include all dilutive share options and warrants and compute a *tentative* DEPS.
- *Step 3*. Develop a ranking of the impact of each convertible preferred stock and convertible bond on *tentative* DEPS, from the *most dilutive* effect on EPS to the least dilutive effect on EPS.

- *Step 4.* Beginning with the most dilutive convertible bond or convertible preferred stock first, add each dilutive convertible security into DEPS from most dilutive to least dilutive. Compute a new *tentative* DEPS after each security is added.
- *Step 5.* Determine the lowest calculated tentative DEPS and report as the diluted earnings per share.

Exhibit 16.4 shows a flowchart summarizing these steps. The following discussion explains Steps 2 through 5 for computing diluted earnings per share.

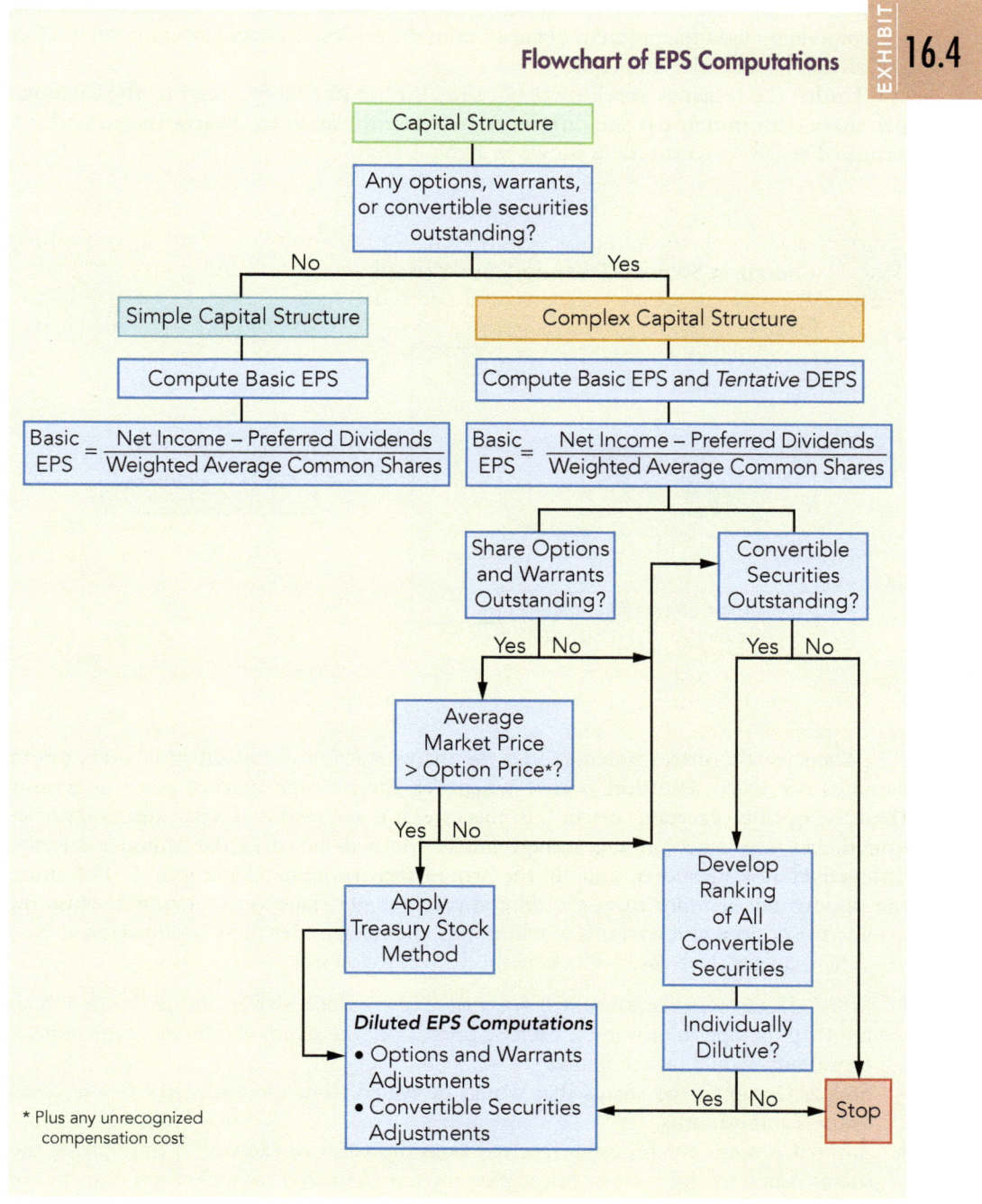

EXHIBIT 16.4 Flowchart of EPS Computations

*Plus any unrecognized compensation cost

Share Options and Warrants

A corporation always first considers share options and share warrants in its diluted earnings per share calculations. However, they are *only* included in diluted earnings per share if they are *dilutive*. Share options and warrants will not be dilutive if they are out of the money (that is, the exercise price of the option or warrant is higher than the market price). Because the exercise of share options or warrants does not affect the corporation's net income, the focus is on the earnings per share denominator. **The treasury stock method is used to determine the change in the number of shares.** This method assumes the company uses the proceeds received from the exercise of options or warrants (exercise price × number of shares issued) to acquire as many treasury shares as possible (hence, the name "treasury share method"), and then only issues the minimum number of additional shares. In this method, we first compute the impact on common shares under the assumption (for earnings per share computations) that the dilutive options and warrants were exercised at the beginning of the period (or at the time they were issued, if issued during the accounting period). Then, we assume that the corporation used the proceeds obtained from the exercise to reacquire common stock at the *average* market price during the period.

Under the **treasury stock method**, the number of shares added to the earnings per share denominator is the difference between the assumed shares issued and the assumed shares reacquired, as shown in Exhibit 16.5.

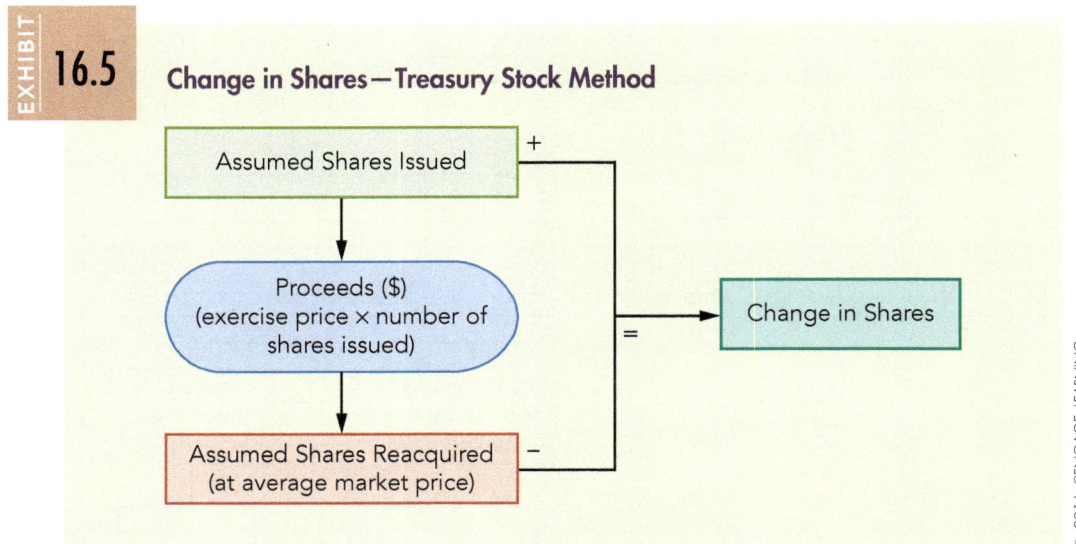

EXHIBIT 16.5 Change in Shares—Treasury Stock Method

Whenever the shares issued exceed the shares reacquired, the effect is a dilution of earnings per share. **Dilution occurs whenever the average market price is greater than the option (exercise) price.**[12] In this case, it is assumed that fewer shares are reacquired than are issued. If the average market price is less than the option price, the assumed exercise would be antidilutive (would *increase* earnings per share). Therefore, the options are *excluded* from the diluted earnings per share computation because we assume the options and warrants would not be exercised under these circumstances.

The steps for the treasury stock method are as follows:

- *Step 1.* Determine the *average market price* of common shares during the period (if less than the option or warrant exercise price, stop; the assumed exercise of the options or warrants would be antidilutive).[13]
- *Step 2.* Compute the shares that would be issued from the assumed exercise of all options and warrants.
- *Step 3.* Compute the proceeds received from the assumed exercise by multiplying the shares issued by the exercise price [plus any unrecognized compensation cost (net of tax) per share—explained below].
- *Step 4.* Compute the assumed shares that would be reacquired by dividing the proceeds (Step 3) by the average market price (Step 1).

[12] The option price is adjusted for any unrecognized compensation cost, as we discuss later.
[13] Computing the average market price of common shares for quarterly and year-to-date periods can involve complex calculations. For simplicity, we always provide the average market price.

- *Step 5.* Compute the incremental common shares that would need to be issued (shares assumed issued minus shares assumed reacquired; the results of Step 2 minus Step 4). Add this number of shares to the weighted average in order to compute diluted earnings per share.

Step 3 needs further explanation. Recall from Chapter 15 that a corporation uses the fair value method to account for its compensatory share option plan. It determines its total compensation cost on the grant date (based on the estimated fair value of the stock) and recognizes a portion of this cost as an expense over the service period. For its earnings per share, the portion of the compensation cost (net of tax) that the corporation has *not* yet recognized as compensation expense is included in the proceeds received from the assumed exercise of compensatory share options.[14] This approach estimates the fair value per share that the corporation would receive from the share options for the common stock assumed issued before the service period has expired. That is, if an employee exercised a share option before the service period had expired, the corporation would require the employee to pay both the option price and a "premium" for the early exercise. The unrecognized compensation cost per share is an estimate of this premium. By adding this amount to the exercise price, the computation includes an estimate of the amount of cash the corporation would receive at the point of early exercise. The computation of the unrecognized compensation cost is complex; for simplicity, in the text and homework we always state the amount per share of any unrecognized compensation cost (net of tax) that should be included in the computation of the proceeds.

Example: Share Options

Plummer Corporation has compensatory share options for employees to purchase 1,000 common shares at an exercise price of $18 per share throughout the year, and the average market price for the common stock during the year was $25 per share. The unrecognized compensation cost (net of tax) related to the share options is $2 per share. The net increase in the denominator is 200 shares, which has a dilutive effect on earnings per share. The share calculation is as follows:

Shares issued from assumed exercise	1,000
Shares assumed reacquired: $\dfrac{\text{Proceeds}}{\text{Average Market Price per Share}} = \dfrac{1{,}000 \times (\$18 + \$2)}{\$25} = \dfrac{\$20{,}000}{\$25} =$	(800)
Assumed increment in common shares for computing diluted earnings per share	200

After Plummer has computed the number of incremental shares resulting from the assumed exercise of the options or warrants, it adds the increase to the weighted average number of common shares used in the denominator of the basic earnings per share. Then it divides the net income minus preferred dividends by the new denominator to determine the tentative diluted earnings per share. If no convertible securities are outstanding, this tentative figure is the final diluted earnings per share. We show this procedure later in Part 4 of **Example 16.8** (p. 16-33). ■

Convertible Securities

Convertible bonds and convertible preferred stock are considered for inclusion in diluted earnings per share after share options and warrants. A corporation includes convertible securities in its diluted earnings per share only if they are *dilutive*. It must be careful to include the individual convertible securities, one at a time, in the proper sequence. If it does not, it may make a mistake by including an antidilutive security in diluted earnings per share. That is, **a convertible security that may appear to be individually dilutive may, in fact, be antidilutive in combination with other convertible securities.**

To determine the sequence in which to include convertible securities in diluted earnings per share, the securities are ranked by their potential impact on diluted earnings per share. To compute this impact, the **if-converted method** is used. Under this

---
[14] FASB ASC 260-10-45: Earnings Per Share, Overall, Other Presentation Matters.

method, **each convertible stock or bond is *assumed* (for computing diluted earnings per share) to have been converted into common stock at the beginning of the earliest period reported** (or on the date of issuance of the security, if later).

This assumed conversion causes two changes in the earnings per share calculation—an increase in the denominator and an increase in the numerator:

- The denominator increases by the number of common shares issued in the assumed conversion.
- If bonds are assumed to be converted into common stock, net income in the numerator increases because the corporation would not have to pay interest expense (net of income taxes) for the converted bonds.[15] If preferred stock is assumed to be converted into common stock, the numerator increases because the corporation would not have to pay preferred dividends on the converted preferred shares.

The impact of each convertible security on the corporation's diluted earnings per share is computed as follows:

$$\text{Impact on DEPS} = \frac{\text{Increase in Earnings per Share Numerator}}{\text{Increase in Earnings per Share Denominator}}$$

After the corporation has computed the impact on DEPS for each convertible security, it ranks the securities starting with the *most dilutive* and ending with the *least dilutive* security at the *bottom* of the ranking. Beginning with the most dilutive security, the corporation sequentially enters the dilutive securities into its diluted earnings per share computations. The **security, which *causes the greatest decrease* in diluted earnings per share, is the most dilutive convertible security and is the first (after options and warrants) to be included in diluted earnings per share.** The ranking enables the corporation to sequentially include dilutive convertible securities in its diluted earnings per share in the descending order of their individual dilutive effect on earnings per share.

Example 16.7 shows the calculation of the impact of each convertible security on diluted earnings per share and the ranking for a corporation that has four convertible securities outstanding the entire year. As you can see, Security C has the most dilutive impact on diluted earnings per share because the numerator would only increase by $8,000 while the denominator would increase by 5,000 shares. It is the first convertible security (after options and warrants) to be included in diluted earnings per share (assuming it is dilutive).

EXAMPLE 16.7 **Computation of Impact of Convertible Securities on Diluted Earnings per Share**

A. Summary of Convertible Securities

Security	Description
A	9% convertible preferred stock. Dividends of $5,400 were declared during the year. The preferred shares are convertible into 3,000 shares of common stock.
B	10% convertible bonds. Interest expense (net of income taxes) of $4,800 was recorded during the year. The bonds are convertible into 1,920 shares of common stock.
C	8% convertible preferred stock. Dividends of $8,000 were declared during the year. The preferred shares are convertible into 5,000 shares of common stock.
D	7% convertible bonds. Interest expense (net of income taxes) of $6,300 was recorded during the year. The bonds are convertible into 3,150 shares of common stock.

(continued)

---

[15] The pretax savings in interest expense includes the interest paid or accrued plus any bond discount amortization or minus any bond premium amortization. The net-of-tax interest-expense savings is computed by multiplying the pretax interest-expense savings times one minus the effective income tax rate.

B. Computations and Rankings

Security	Impact on *Tentative* DEPS	Order in Ranking
A	$\dfrac{\$5{,}400}{3{,}000} = \$1.80$	2
B	$\dfrac{\$4{,}800}{1{,}920} = \$2.50$	4 - Least Dilutive Effect on EPS
C	$\dfrac{\$8{,}000}{5{,}000} = \$1.60$	1 - Most Dilutive Effect on EPS
D	$\dfrac{\$6{,}300}{3{,}150} = \$2.00$	3

Computation of Tentative and Final Diluted Earnings per Share

A corporation computes its diluted earnings per share in the following sequence:

- *Step 1.* Calculate basic earnings per share.
- *Step 2.* Compute the incremental shares from the assumed exercise of share options and warrants. Add the incremental shares to the denominator from basic earnings per share, and calculate an initial tentative diluted earnings per share.
- *Step 3.* Include the dilutive convertible securities in diluted earnings per share in sequential order according to their dilutive effect on tentative diluted earnings per share. Starting with the most dilutive convertible security (based on the ranking discussed earlier), include it in diluted earnings per share if its impact is *less* than the initial tentative diluted earnings per share. This involves computing a new numerator and denominator by adding the increase in the numerator and the increase in the denominator resulting from the assumed conversion to the amounts used to compute the initial tentative diluted earnings per share.[16] This procedure is shown in Exhibit 16.6. This results in a second (and lower) tentative diluted earnings per share.

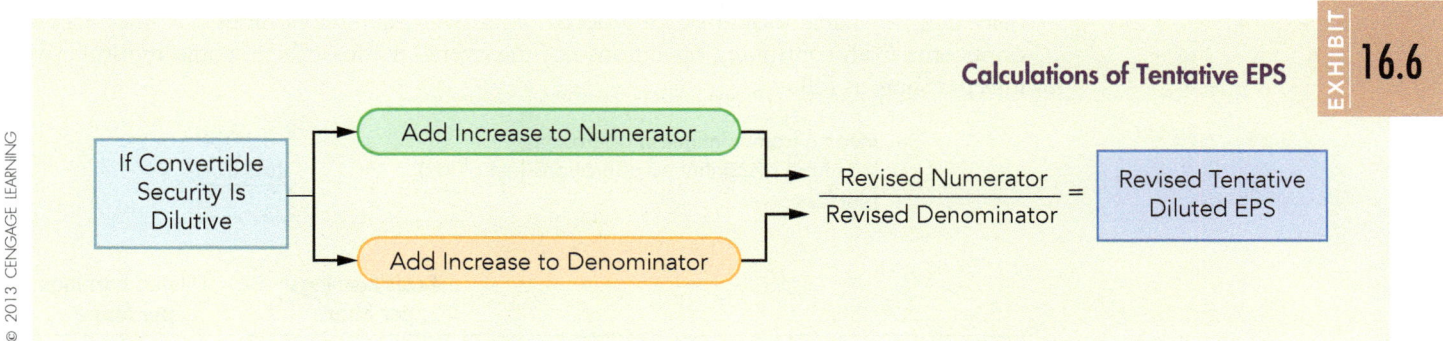

EXHIBIT 16.6 Calculations of Tentative EPS

- *Step 4.* Repeat with each dilutive security in the ranking until the impact of the next convertible security is *antidilutive* (or until all dilutive securities are used). Any remaining securities in the ranking are antidilutive and are excluded from diluted earnings per share.
- *Step 5.* Final diluted earnings per share is the last tentative figure. It contains all the dilutive convertible securities included in the tentative diluted earnings per share computations.

---

[16] If no share options or warrants are outstanding, the corporation adds the increases in the numerator and denominator resulting from the assumed conversion of the top-ranked convertible security to the numerator and denominator it used to compute its basic earnings per share.

Special Issues Related to Diluted Earnings per Share

If a corporation reports a *loss from continuing operations*, then it does not include potential common shares in calculating diluted earnings per share. This is true even if it reports a positive overall net income due to having income from discontinued operations.[17]

Example Davis Corporation reports a loss from continuing operations of $75,000 and income from discontinued operations (net of tax) of $97,000 for total net income of $22,000. Davis has 50,000 weighted average common shares outstanding. In addition, Davis has a convertible bond that is convertible into 12,000 common shares. When calculating earnings per share, the potentially dilutive shares would be ignored because they are antidilutive to the loss from continuing operations. Davis would report earnings per share as follows:

Loss from continuing operations		$(75,000)
Income from discontinued operations (net of tax)		97,000
Net income		22,000

	Basic Earnings per Share	Diluted Earnings per Share
Loss from continuing operations	$(1.50)	$(1.50)
Income from discontinued operations (net of tax)	1.94	1.94
Net income	$ 0.44	$ 0.44

In this situation, diluted earnings per share would be computed in the same manner as basic earnings per share.[18]

If the corporation reports *income from continuing operations* and results of discontinued operations in its net income, it tests for dilution based on income from continuing operations not overall net income. The corporation compares the impact from dilutive securities to the initial tentative diluted earnings per share related to *income from continuing operations* not the initial total diluted earnings per share related to net income.

Example Ryan Corporation reports income from continuing operations of $30,000 and a loss from discontinued operations of $63,000 (net of tax) for an overall net loss of $33,000. Ryan has 40,000 weighted average common shares outstanding and has a convertible bond that is convertible into 15,000 common shares. To determine if the potentially dilutive shares should be considered, Ryan will examine earnings per share based on income from continuing operations not the overall net loss. Ryan would report earnings per share as follows:

Income from continuing operations		$ 30,000
Loss from discontinued operations (net of tax)		(63,000)
Net loss		$(33,000)

	Basic Earnings per Share	Diluted Earnings per Share
Loss from continuing operations	$ 0.75	$ 0.55
Income from discontinued operations (net of tax)	(1.58)	(1.15)
Net income	$(0.83)	$(0.60)

In this case, the dilutive shares are used to calculate dilutive earnings per share because they dilute earnings per share from continuing operations.[19]

---

[17] FASB ASC 260-10-45: Earnings Per Share, Overall, Other Presentation Matters.
[18] FASB ASC 260-10-45-20: Earnings Per Share, Overall, Other Presentation Matters.
[19] FASB ASC 260-10-45-18: Earnings Per Share, Overall, Other Presentation Matters.

Example 16.8 shows the computation of diluted earnings per share for Randolph Corporation, assuming the following:

- Share options are outstanding.
- Both convertible bonds and convertible preferred stock are outstanding.
- The convertible bonds are dilutive, but the convertible preferred stock is antidilutive.

The computations result in diluted earnings per share of $1.94. Note that Randolph reports *both* basic and diluted earnings per share on its income statement. Note, also, that if no ranking had been prepared and if both the convertible preferred stock and bonds had been included in diluted earnings per share, the corporation would have reported an erroneous $1.96 [($2,000 + $800 + $224) ÷ (985 + 400 + 160)] diluted earnings per share.

EXAMPLE 16.8

Computation and Reporting of Diluted Earnings per Share

1. Income statement information for Randolph Corporation:
   a. Net income for 2016 is $2,800.
   b. The income tax rate is 30%.
2. Balance sheet information:
   a. 900 shares of common stock were outstanding the entire year.
   b. Options were outstanding the entire year. The assumed exercise of these options would result in an increment of 85 shares of common stock.
   c. 100 shares of 8%, $100 par (and issuance price) convertible preferred stock were outstanding the entire year. $800 dividends were declared on this stock in 2016. Each share of preferred stock is convertible into 4 shares of common stock.
   d. Convertible bonds, $5,000 face value were outstanding the entire year. These bonds have a stated rate of 6% interest, but were issued at a discount. Bond interest expense of $320 was recorded in 2016; the total discount is being amortized at the rate of $20 per year. Each $1,000 bond is convertible into 32 shares of common stock.
3. Impact on diluted earnings per share and resulting ranking:

Security	Impact	Ranking
Preferred	$\dfrac{\$800}{100 \times 4} = \dfrac{\$800}{400} = \$2.00$	2
Bonds	$\dfrac{[(\$5,000 \times 0.06) + \$20] \times (1 - 0.3)}{5 \times 32} = \dfrac{\$224}{160} = \$1.40$	1

4. Diluted earnings per share computations for 2016:

Explanation	Earnings (Adjustments)	÷	Shares (Adjustments)	=	Earnings Per Share
Basic earnings per share	$2,000[a]	÷	900	=	$2.22 Basic
Increment in shares (options)			85		
DEPS$_1$ earnings and shares	$2,000	÷	985	=	$2.03 DEPS$_1$[b]
Savings in interest expense (bonds)	224[c]				
Increment in shares (bonds)			160[d]		
Diluted earnings and shares	$2,224	÷	1,145	=	$1.94 Diluted[e]

[a] $2,000 = $2,800 Net income − $800 Preferred dividends
[b] $1.40 is less than $2.03; therefore, the convertible bonds are individually dilutive and are included in diluted earnings per share.
[c] $224 = [($5,000 × 0.06) + $20] × (1 − 0.3)
[d] 160 Shares = 5 Bonds × 32 Common shares
[e] The $2.00 impact on diluted earnings per share of the convertible preferred stock is more than $1.94; therefore, inclusion of the preferred stock in diluted earnings per share would be antidilutive.

(continued)

> **EXAMPLE 16.8 (Continued)**
>
> 5. Condensed income statement presentation of Randolph Corporation for 2016:
>
> | | |
> |---|---:|
> | Net income | $2,800 |
> | Earnings per share (see Note A): | |
> | Basic earnings per share | $ 2.22 |
> | Diluted earnings per share | $ 1.94 |
>
> 6. Note A to financial statements: Basic earnings per share is based on 900 average common shares outstanding. Preferred dividends of $800 are deducted from net income to determine earnings available to common shareholders. Diluted earnings per share is based on 900 average common shares outstanding plus 245 incremental shares from giving effect to the assumed exercise of share options and the conversion of 6% convertible bonds. Earnings available to common shareholders are adjusted for the $224 savings in interest expense (net of taxes). The 8% convertible preferred stock is antidilutive and is not included in diluted earnings per share. A total of 900 common shares were outstanding at the end of 2016.

Additional Considerations

The previous sections focused on the main issues related to computing earnings per share. Several other issues are relevant to basic and diluted earnings per share.

Conversion Ratios After issuing convertible securities or share options, a corporation may declare a stock dividend or stock split. Typically, the "conversion ratio" for convertible securities and stock options is proportionally adjusted for the stock dividend or split. For instance, assume a share of preferred stock is convertible into four shares of common stock before a 2-for-1 stock split on the common stock. *After* the stock split, the preferred stock is convertible into eight shares of common stock. The corporation uses the *current* conversion ratio for convertible securities and share options in its diluted earnings per share computations.

Contingent Issuances A corporation may be obligated to issue common shares in the future if certain conditions are met. This stock is referred to as contingently issuable common stock. Issuance may depend on satisfying certain conditions, such as attaining or maintaining a certain level of earnings. If the conditions have been met before issuance, the corporation considers these shares to be outstanding for both basic and diluted earnings per share purposes. If the conditions have not been met, if dilutive, the corporation includes the shares in diluted earnings per share. They are included based on the number of shares that would be issuable if the end of the accounting period were the end of the contingency period of the shares.

Additional Disclosures When a corporation reports its basic and diluted earnings per share on its income statement, it also is required to make additional disclosures in the notes to its financial statements. These include a schedule or note identifying and reconciling the numerators and denominators on which it calculated both basic and diluted earnings per share. For example, Randolph could disclose the information included in the schedule in Part 4 of **Example 16.8**. The schedule or note also includes information that:

- Identifies the amount of preferred dividends deducted to determine the income available to common shareholders.
- Describes the potential common shares that were *not* included in the diluted earnings per share computation because they were antidilutive.
- Describes any material impact on the common shares outstanding of transactions after the close of the accounting period but before the issuance of the financial report.[20]

[20] FASB ASC 260-10-50: Earnings Per Share, Overall, Disclosure.

For example, Randolph would disclose the information in Part 6 of **Example 16.8**.

EPS Disclosure Illustration

Starbucks's 2015 annual report includes earnings per share disclosures, as shown in Real Report 16.2. Starbucks's dilutive securities include not only stock options but also restricted stock units (RSUs). Restricted stock units differ from stock options in that the employee is receiving an award of actual common stock that vest based on performance or time. In the case of Starbucks, the company offers both time- and performance-based RSU awards.

REAL REPORT — **EARNINGS PER SHARE DISCLOSURES** — **16.2**

Starbucks Corporation

STARBUCKS CORPORATION
CONSOLIDATED STATEMENTS OF EARNINGS
(in millions, except per share data)

	Sep 27, 2015	Sep 28, 2014	Sep 29, 2013
Net earnings attributable to Starbucks	$2,757.4	$2,068.1	$ 8.3
Earnings per share — basic	$ 1.84	$ 1.37	$ 0.01
Earnings per share — diluted	$ 1.82	$ 1.35	$ 0.01
Weighted average shares outstanding:			
Basic	1,495.9	1,506.3	1,498.5
Diluted	1,513.4	1,526.3	1,524.5

Note 14: Earnings per Share

Calculation of net earnings per common share ("EPS") — basic and diluted *(in millions, except EPS)*:

Fiscal Year Ended	Sep 27, 2015	Sep 28, 2014	Sep 29, 2013
Net earnings attributable to Starbucks	$2,757.4	$2,068.1	$ 8.3
Weighted average common shares outstanding (for basic calculation)	1,495.9	1,506.3	1,498.5
Dilutive effect of outstanding common stock options and RSUs	17.5	20.0	26.0
Weighted average common and common equivalent shares outstanding (for diluted calculation)	1,513.4	1,526.3	1,524.5
EPS — basic	$ 1.84	$ 1.37	$ 0.01
EPS — diluted	$ 1.82	$ 1.35	$ 0.01

Potential dilutive shares consist of the incremental common shares issuable upon the exercise of outstanding stock options (both vested and non-vested) and unvested RSUs, calculated using the treasury stock method. The calculation of dilutive shares outstanding excludes out-of-the-money stock options (i.e., such options' exercise prices were greater than the average market price of our common shares for the period) because their inclusion would have been antidilutive. We had no out-of-the-money stock options as of September 27, 2015 and September 29, 2013, respectively. There were 5.3 million out-of-the-money stock options as of September 28, 2014.

Questions:

Suggested answers to these questions are found at the end of the chapter.

1. Why was the average number of common shares used in the diluted earnings per share computation more than the weighted average number of common shares used in the basic earnings per share computation?
2. To answer this question, you will also need to examine the information in Starbucks's Note 12, which provides information about the company's employee stock and benefit plans. At September 27, 2015, how many stock options were exercisable, and how many were vested and expected to vest? How does this amount compare to the number of dilutive shares used by Starbucks to compute diluted earnings per share?

INTERNATIONAL DIMENSION

COMPUTING EARNINGS PER SHARE

Due to convergence efforts, IFRS and U.S. GAAP are similar in regard to computing and reporting basic and diluted earnings per share. In addition, the FASB and the IASB have both issued Exposure Drafts that, if adopted, would even more closely align the calculations of earnings per share for U.S. GAAP and IFRS. The main differences that need to be resolved are as follows:

- When applying the treasury stock method for potentially dilutive share options, IFRS do not require a company to include any unrecognized compensation cost in the assumed proceeds from issuing the stock. The exclusion of unrecognized compensation cost would result in lower earnings per share amounts under IFRS as compared to U.S. GAAP.
- U.S. GAAP requires that any contingently convertible debt securities that convert when a company's stock price reaches a certain level are always included in dilutive earnings per share, even if the target stock price has not been reached. Under IFRS, the additional shares would only be included in diluted earnings per share if the target stock price had been reached at the financial statement date. The inclusion of these contingent shares by GAAP would result in lower basic earnings per share amounts.
- For contracts that may be settled in issuance of shares or payment of cash, IFRS require the if-converted method to be used which assumes that the contract will be settled in shares. However, under U.S. GAAP if a cash settlement is presumed, companies are allowed to ignore the dilutive effects of the contract and treat the settlement as an adjustment to earnings.
- Finally, U.S. GAAP does not allow the presentation of non-GAAP EPS amounts, whereas IFRS do allow such presentation in the notes to the financial statements.

Except for some additional complex issues that are beyond the scope of this book, the remaining computations for earnings per share would be the same. If these differences can be resolved, U.S. GAAP and IFRS for earnings per share will be very similar.

IFRS Application In January 2016, Eurotron Corporation awarded its employees 15,000 compensatory share options. The share options have an exercise price of $20 per share option. In addition, the unrecognized compensation cost (net of tax) relating to the share options is $3.50 per share option. Eurotron has 60,000 shares of common stock outstanding during all of 2016 and the stock sold at an average price of $48. For the year 2016, Eurotron reported net income of $45,000. Under U.S. GAAP, the unrecognized compensation cost would be added to the exercise price when calculating the number of shares assumed reacquired under the treasury stock method, while under IFRS the amount is currently excluded.

(continued)

	Change in Shares—U.S. GAAP	Change in Shares—IFRS
Shares issued from assumed exercise	15,000	15,000
Shares assumed reacquired	7,344 [15,000 × ($20.00 + $3.50) ÷ $48]	6,250 (15,000 × $20.00 ÷ $48)
Assume increment in common shares for computing diluted earnings per share	7,656	8,750

Eurotron would present the same basic earnings per share amount of $0.75 ($45,000 Net income ÷ 60,000 Shares) under U.S. GAAP and IFRS. However, when calculating diluted earnings per share Eurotron would report $0.67 ($45,000 Net income ÷ 67,656 Shares) under U.S. GAAP and $0.65 ($45,000 Net income ÷ 68,750 Shares) under IFRS.

Source: IAS 33. (See Appendix C at the end of this book.)

GOT IT?

16-17 Identify several securities that might be found in the complex capital structure of a corporation.

16-18 What two earnings per share figures generally are reported by a corporation with a complex capital structure? Besides common shares outstanding, what additional securities are included in the second earnings per share calculation?

16-19 What is the treasury stock method? How is the increase in the diluted earnings per share denominator determined under the treasury stock method?

16-20 Discuss how to develop a ranking for determining in which order to include convertible securities in a corporation's diluted earnings per share calculations.

16-21 What additional disclosures does a corporation make concerning the basic and diluted earnings per share it reports on its income statement?

16-22 A company with potentially dilutive share options is preparing its financial statements under IFRS. Compared to the U.S. GAAP financial statements, would its EPS be higher or lower under IFRS?

16-23 Hoke Company suffers a large loss of one of its major manufacturing facilities due to a fire. Management believes that this loss is both unusual and infrequent and estimates the per share effect of the loss to be $0.25 per share. Under IFRS, how would this loss be shown in the presentation of EPS?

REVIEW CENTER

At the beginning of the chapter, we discussed **Apple**'s decision to once again start paying dividends. When making investment decisions, investors research a company's dividend yield and earnings per share ratio to assess the company's performance and determine how it compares to its competitors. We also identified several objectives you would accomplish after reading the chapter. The objectives are listed below and followed by a brief summary of the key points.

Chapter 16 Retained Earnings and Earnings per Share

LEARNING OBJECTIVE 16.1
Explain the accounting and reporting for different types of dividends.

KEY TAKEAWAYS

- Four important dates for any type of dividend are the:
  - Declaration date—the date the board of directors formally declares that a dividend will be paid and the dividend becomes a liability of the company
  - Ex-dividend date—the date the stock stops selling with the right to receive dividends (usually several days before the date of record)
  - Date of record—only registered owners of stock on this date will receive a dividend
  - Date of payment—the date the dividend is distributed and the liability is eliminated
- A corporation records the declaration of a cash dividend by debiting Retained Earnings and crediting Dividends Payable. It records the payment by debiting Dividends Payable and crediting Cash.
- A property dividend (a dividend payable in assets other than cash) is recorded at fair value, which involves revaluing the property to be distributed to fair value and recognizing a gain or loss for the difference between the fair value and the carrying value.
- A company without enough cash to justify paying a cash dividend may declare a scrip dividend, which obligates the company to pay the dividend plus interest at a future date.
- A stock dividend, the distribution of additional shares of stock to a company's shareholders, does not change total shareholders' equity and is accounted for based on the size of the dividend:
  - A small stock dividend (less than 20% or 25% of the outstanding shares) transfers the fair value of the shares issued from retained earnings to contributed capital.
  - A large stock dividend (more than 20% or 25% of the outstanding shares) transfers the par value of the shares issued from retained earnings to contributed capital.
- Liquidating dividends are a return of contributed capital rather than a distribution of retained earnings.

KEY TERMS

date of payment, p. 16-5
date of record, p. 16-4
declaration date, p. 16-4
deficit, p. 16-2
ex-dividend date, p. 16-4

liquidating dividends, p. 16-12
property dividend, p. 16-7
Retained Earnings, p. 16-2
scrip dividend, p. 16-8
stock dividend, p. 16-9

LEARNING OBJECTIVE 16.2
Discuss the accounting for prior period adjustments and restrictions of retained earnings.

KEY TAKEAWAYS

- Retroactive adjustments and prior period adjustments (restatements) are reported as adjustments of the beginning balance of retained earnings, net of taxes, on the statement of retained earnings. When the adjustment is made, the asset or liability account balance is adjusted, and the offsetting credit or debit (which involved a revenue or expense previously closed to Retained Earnings) is made directly to the Retained Earnings account. Any related impact on income taxes is similarly recorded.
- A restriction of retained earnings, to meet legal requirements or contractual restrictions, indicates that a portion of retained earnings is unavailable for dividends.

KEY TERMS

appropriation, p. 16-14
prior period adjustments
 (restatements), p. 16-13

restriction, p. 16-14

LEARNING OBJECTIVE 16.3
Explain the various components of shareholders' equity and related disclosures.

KEY TAKEAWAYS

- A statement of shareholders' equity is used to disclose the changes in different classes of common stock, additional paid-in capital, retained earnings, accumulated other comprehensive income, and treasury stock.

- A statement of retained earnings is often used to disclose the items affecting retained earnings—net income (loss), dividends, prior period (and retrospective) adjustments, and other reductions.
- Under GAAP, the noncontrolling interest reported in the balance sheet represents that amount of net assets in the subsidiary that is controlled by shareholders other than the parent corporation.
- Accumulated other comprehensive income may be reported on the face of the income statement, in a separate statement of comprehensive income, or in the statement of shareholders' equity.

KEY CALCULATIONS

$$\text{Price/Earnings Ratio} = \frac{\text{Market Price per Share of Common Stock}}{\text{Earnings per Share}}$$

$$\text{Dividend Yield} = \frac{\text{Dividends per Common Share}}{\text{Market Price per Common Share}}$$

KEY TERMS

earnings per share, p. 16-20 price/earnings ratio, p. 16-20

KEY TAKEAWAYS

LEARNING OBJECTIVE 16.4
Compute basic earnings per share (EPS) including the computation of weighted average common shares.

- Basic earnings per share is computed by dividing a company's earnings available to common shareholders by the weighted average number of common shares outstanding.
- A company that has a simple capital structure (only common stock is outstanding) is required to report separate basic earnings per share amounts for income from continuing operations and net income on its income statement, with any per share amounts related to discontinued operations disclosed either on the income statement or in the notes to the financial statements.
- Preferred dividends reduce earnings available to common shareholders unless the preferred stock is noncumulative and no dividends were declared during the year.
- In the event of a stock dividend or stock split, the number of common shares outstanding at the date of the split is retroactively adjusted as if the stock dividend or split occurred at the beginning of the earliest period presented.

KEY CALCULATION

$$\text{Basic Earnings per Share} = \frac{\text{Net Income} - \text{Preferred Dividends}}{\text{Weighted Average Number of Common Shares Outstanding}}$$

KEY TERMS

basic earnings per share, p. 16-21 earnings per common share, p. 16-21
complex capital structure, p. 16-21 simple capital structure, p. 16-21

KEY TAKEAWAYS

LEARNING OBJECTIVE 16.5
Compute diluted earnings per share including the identification of potential common shares.

- When securities that have the potential to dilute earnings per share exist (e.g., share options and warrants, convertible preferred stock, and convertible bonds), the company has a complex capital structure and is required to report basic and diluted earnings per share. These securities are included in diluted EPS only if they decrease EPS.
- The treasury stock method, used to calculate the dilutive effect of share options and warrants, assumes that the options or warrants were exercised at the beginning of the earliest period presented and that any proceeds obtained from this exercise were used

to reacquire common stock at the average market price. The difference between the shares assumed to be issued and the shares assumed to be repurchased is the dilutive effect of the share options or warrants.
- The if-converted method is used to determine the dilutive effect for all other potentially dilutive securities (e.g., convertible preferred stock or convertible bonds). Under this method:
  - The individual impact of each potentially dilutive security is computed (both numerator and denominator effects) as if the security were converted into common stock at the beginning of the earliest period presented.
  - The securities are ranked in order of their dilutive impact on earnings per share, with the most dilutive security being considered first for inclusion in diluted earnings per share.

KEY CALCULATION

$$\text{Impact of each convertible security on diluted earnings per share} = \frac{\text{Increase in Earnings per Share Numerator}}{\text{Increase in Earnings per Share Denominator}}$$

KEY TERMS

diluted earnings per share (DEPS), p. 16-26
if-converted method, p. 16-29
potential common shares, p. 16-26
treasury stock method, p. 16-28

ANSWERS TO REAL REPORT QUESTIONS

Real Report 16.1 Answers Starbucks Corporation—Shareholders' Equity and Related Changes

1. During fiscal year 2015, Starbucks acquired 29.0 million shares of treasury stock at an average price of $49.37 per share ($1,431.8 million/29.0 million shares).
2. Starbucks reported an other comprehensive loss of $199.4 million for fiscal year 2015; this consists of a net of tax unrealized holding gain related to hedging instruments of $33.5 million, currency translation adjustment loss of $216.7 (net of a tax credit) million, and an unrealized holding gain net of tax on available-for-sale securities of $0.9 million. In addition, Starbucks recorded a loss due to a reclassification adjustment of $42.4, net of tax. The balance in accumulated other comprehensive income at September 27, 2015, is ($199.4) million. This amount can be found in the shareholders' equity section of the partial balance sheet as well as the consolidated statements of equity.
3. Total dividends declared were $1,016.2 million. This was an increase of $189.2 million dollars from fiscal year 2014 when dividends of $872.0 million were declared.
4. During fiscal 2015, Starbucks issued 14.6 million shares of common stock for stock options at an average price per share of $15.37 [increase in shareholders' equity due to stock option transactions of $224.4 million ($224.4 million/14.6 million shares)].

Real Report 16.2 Answers Starbucks Corporation—Earnings per Share Disclosures

1. Starbucks issues stock options and RSUs to its employees because the average market price was greater than the exercise price these securities were dilutive.
2. Note 12 discloses that at September 27, 2015, Starbucks had 33.6 million stock options/RSUs outstanding. Of this amount, 21.1 million options were exercisable. Employees had 32.4 million shares that were vested and expected to vest. Using the weighted average shares outstanding information in the income statement, the stock options and RSUs result in 17.5 million incremental common shares for computing diluted earnings per share.

MULTIPLE-CHOICE (AICPA ADAPTED)

Select the best answer for each of the following.

M16-1 Cash dividends on the $10 par value common stock of Garrett Company were as follows:
LO 16.1
LO 16.3

1st quarter of 2016	$ 800,000
2nd quarter of 2016	900,000
3rd quarter of 2016	1,000,000
4th quarter of 2016	1,100,000

The 4th-quarter cash dividend was declared on December 21, 2016, to shareholders of record on December 31, 2016. Payment of the 4th-quarter cash dividend was made on January 18, 2017.

In addition, Garrett declared a 5% stock dividend on its $10 par value common stock on December 3, 2016, when there were 300,000 shares issued and outstanding and the market value of the common stock was $20 per share. The shares were issued on December 24, 2016.

What was the effect on Garrett's shareholders' equity accounts as a result of the preceding transactions?

	Common Stock	Additional Paid-in Capital	Retained Earnings
a.	$0	$0	$3,800,000 dr
b.	$150,000 cr	$0	$3,950,000 dr
c.	$150,000 cr	$150,000 cr	$4,100,000 dr
d.	$300,000 cr	$300,000 dr	$3,800,000 dr

M16-2 A prior period adjustment should be reflected, net of applicable income taxes, in the financial statements of a business entity in the:
LO 16.2

a. retained earnings statement after net income but before dividends
b. retained earnings statement as an adjustment of the opening balance
c. income statement after income from continuing operations
d. income statement as part of income from continuing operations

M16-3 Prince Corporation's accounts provided the following information at December 31, 2016:
LO 16.3

Total income since incorporation	$840,000
Total cash dividends paid	260,000
Total value of stock dividends distributed	60,000
Additional paid-in capital from treasury stock	140,000

What should be the current balance of retained earnings?

a. $520,000   c. $610,000
b. $580,000   d. $670,000

M16-4 Effective May 1, the shareholders of Baltimore Corporation approved a 2-for-1 split of the company's common stock and an increase in authorized common shares from 100,000 shares (par value $20 per share) to 200,000 shares (par value $10 per share). Baltimore's shareholders' equity items immediately before issuance of the stock split shares were as follows:
LO 16.3

Common stock, $20 par (100,000 shares authorized, 50,000 shares outstanding)	$1,000,000
Additional paid-in capital (premium of $3 per share on issuance of common stock)	150,000
Retained earnings	1,350,000

What should be the balances in Baltimore's Additional Paid-in Capital and Retained Earnings accounts immediately after the stock split is effected?

	Additional Paid-in Capital	Retained Earnings
a.	$0	$500,000
b.	$150,000	$350,000
c.	$150,000	$1,350,000
d.	$1,150,000	$350,000

M16-5 Kent Corporation was organized on January 1, 2014. On that date, it issued 200,000 shares of $10 par value common stock at $15 per share (400,000 shares were authorized). During the period January 1, 2014, through December 31, 2016, Kent reported net income of $750,000 and paid cash dividends of $380,000. On January 5, 2016, Kent purchased 12,000 shares of its common stock at $12 per share. On December 28, 2016, 8,000 treasury shares were sold at $8 per share. Kent used the cost method of accounting for treasury shares. What is Kent's total shareholders' equity as of December 31, 2016?
LO 16.3

a. $3,290,000   c. $3,338,000
b. $3,306,000   d. $3,370,000

M16-6
LO 16.4
For purposes of computing the weighted average number of shares outstanding during the year, a midyear event that must be treated as occurring at the beginning of the year is the:

a. issuance of stock warrants
b. purchase of treasury stock
c. sale of additional common stock
d. declaration and issuance of a stock dividend

M16-7
LO 16.4
In determining basic earnings per share, dividends on nonconvertible cumulative preferred stock should be:

a. deducted from net income only if declared
b. deducted from net income whether declared or not
c. added back to net income whether declared or not
d. disregarded

M16-8
LO 16.4
Hyde Corporation's capital structure at December 31, 2015, was as follows:

	Shares Issued and Outstanding
Common stock	100,000
Nonconvertible preferred stock	20,000

On July 2, 2016, Hyde issued a 10% stock dividend on its common stock and paid a cash dividend of $2.00 per share on its preferred stock. Net income for the year ended December 31, 2016, was $780,000. What should be Hyde's 2016 basic earnings per share?

a. $7.80
b. $7.09
c. $7.68
d. $6.73

M16-9
LO 16.5
Iredell Company has 2,500,000 shares of common stock outstanding on December 31, 2015. An additional 500,000 shares of common stock were issued on April 2, 2016, and 250,000 more on July 2, 2016. On October 1, 2016, Iredell issued 5,000, $1,000 face value, 7% convertible bonds. Each bond is dilutive and convertible into 40 shares of common stock. No bonds were converted into common stock in 2016. What is the number of shares to be used in computing basic earnings per share and diluted earnings per share, respectively, for the year ended December 31, 2016?

a. 2,875,000 and 2,925,000
b. 2,875,000 and 3,075,000
c. 3,000,000 and 3,050,000
d. 3,000,000 and 3,200,000

M16-10
LO 16.5
At December 31, 2016, Talbot Corporation had 90,000 shares of common stock and 20,000 shares of convertible preferred stock outstanding, in addition to 9% convertible bonds payable in the face amount of $2,000,000. During 2016, Talbot paid dividends of $2.50 per share on the preferred stock. The preferred stock is convertible into 20,000 shares of common stock. The 9% convertible bonds are convertible into 30,000 shares of common stock. Net income for 2016 was $970,000. Assume an income tax rate of 30%. How much is the diluted earnings per share for the year ended December 31, 2016?

a. $7.83
b. $8.82
c. $9.35
d. $10.22

REVIEW EXERCISES

RE16-1
LO 16.1
Edgefield Corporation has issued 10%, participating, cumulative preferred stock with a total par value of $22,000 and common stock with a total par value of $66,000. Therefore, the preferred stock par value is 1/4 and the common stock par value is 3/4 of the total par value. Edgefield intends to distribute cash dividends of $14,000, and there are no dividends in arrears. What is the dividend distribution to each class of stock if the preferred stock is fully participating?

RE16-2
LO 16.1
York Corporation declares a property dividend, payable in bonds of Laurens Company, which are classified as "available for sale." The bonds are recorded at a fair value of $58,000 (there is a $0 balance in Allowance for Change in the Value of Investment in Available-for-Sale Securities), but at the time of the property dividend have a current value of $67,000. Prepare the journal entries to record the declaration of this property dividend.

RE16-3
LO 16.1
Pickens Corporation declares and issues a 10% stock dividend. On the date of declaration, the stock is selling for $30 per share. Assuming that there were 50,000 shares previously outstanding, with a $10 par value, prepare the journal entry on the date of declaration to record Pickens's stock dividend.

RE16-4
LO 16.1
Use the same facts as in **RE16-3**, but instead assume that Pickens declares and issues a 50% stock dividend when the stock is selling for $30 per share. Prepare the journal entry on the date of declaration to record Pickens's stock dividend.

RE16-5
LO 16.3
Given the following current year information, calculate Adair Corporation's retained earnings balance on December 31.
- Net income, $95,400
- Common stock dividends declared, $32,000
- Retained earnings, January 1, $122,250

RE16-6
LO 16.2
In Year 2, Adams Corporation discovered that it forgot to accrue interest expense of $40,000 in Year 1. This overstatement of pretax income was material. The related income tax effect of this error was $12,000 for Year 1. Record the correcting entries in Year 2.

RE16-7
LO 16.4
Howard Corporation had 10,000 shares of common stock outstanding at the beginning of the year. On July 1, it issued 5,000 shares, and on September 1, it reacquired 600 shares as treasury stock. What is the weighted average number of common shares Howard will use in computing its earnings per share?

RE16-8
LO 16.4
Given the following year-end information for Somerset Corporation, compute its basic earnings per share.
- Net income, $13,000
- Preferred dividends declared, $4,000
- Weighted average common shares for the year, 4,500

RE16-9
LO 16.5
Aiken Corporation has compensatory share options for employees to purchase 4,000 common shares at $12 per share outstanding the entire year. The average market price for the common stock during the year was $20 per share. The unrecognized compensation cost (net of tax) related to the share options is $1 per share. What is the assumed increment in the denominator for computing Aiken's diluted earnings per share?

RE16-10
LO 16.5
Marlboro Corporation has 9% convertible preferred stock outstanding. It declared preferred dividends of $5,625 during the year. The preferred shares are convertible into 4,500 shares of common stock. Compute the impact of these convertible preferred shares on Marlboro's diluted earnings per share.

RE16-11
LO 16.5
Sarasota Corporation has 9% convertible bonds outstanding. It recorded interest expense (net of income taxes) of $6,300 on these bonds during the year. The bonds are convertible into 2,500 shares of common stock. Compute the impact of these convertible bonds on Sarasota's diluted earnings per share.

RE16-12
LO 16.5
Given the following year-end information, compute Greenwood Corporation's basic and diluted earnings per share.
- Net income, $15,000
- The income tax rate, 30%
- 4,000 shares of common stock were outstanding the entire year.
- 500 shares of 10%, $50 par (and issuance price) convertible preferred stock were outstanding the entire year. Dividends of $2,500 were declared on this stock during the year. Each share of preferred stock is convertible into 5 shares of common stock.

EXERCISES

E16-1
LO 16.1

Various Dividends Carlyon Company listed the following items in its December 31, 2015, financial statements:

Investment in Man Company bonds	$ 25,000
Dividends payable: preferred	4,000
Dividends payable: common	40,000
Preferred stock, 8%, $100 par	100,000
Common stock, $10 par	400,000
Additional paid-in capital on preferred stock	20,000
Additional paid-in capital on common stock	210,000
Retained earnings	270,000

(continued)

During 2016, the following transactions occurred:

Feb. 2 Paid the semiannual dividends declared on December 15, 2015.
Mar. 5 Declared a property dividend, payable to common shareholders on April 5 in Man Company bonds being held to maturity. The bonds (which have a book value of $25,000) have a current market value of $31,000.
Apr. 5 Paid the property dividend.
July 6 Declared a $4 per share semiannual cash dividend on preferred stock and a $1.10 per share semiannual dividend on common stock, to be paid on August 17.
Aug. 17 Paid the cash dividends.
Oct. 15 Declared a 2% stock dividend on common stock to be issued on December 3. The current market price is $22 per share.
Dec. 3 Issued the stock dividend.
28 Declared a $4 and $1.20 per share semiannual cash dividend on preferred and common stock, respectively, to be paid on February 15, 2017.

Required:
Next Level Prepare journal entries to record the preceding transactions.

E16-2 **Dividends** Andrews Company has $80,000 available to pay dividends. It has 2,000 shares of 10%, $100 par, preferred stock and 30,000 shares of $10 par common stock outstanding. The preferred stock is selling for $125 per share, and the common stock is selling for $20 per share.
LO 16.1

Required:
1. **Next Level** Determine the amount of dividends to be paid to each class of shareholder for each of the following independent assumptions:
   a. Preferred stock is nonparticipating and noncumulative.
   b. Preferred stock is nonparticipating and cumulative. Preferred dividends are 2 years in arrears at the beginning of the year.
   c. Preferred stock is fully participating and cumulative. Preferred dividends are 1 year in arrears at the beginning of the year.
2. For 1(a), compute the dividend yield on the preferred stock and the common stock.

E16-3 **Various Dividends** Stamboul Company lists the following condensed balance sheet as of the beginning of 2016:
LO 16.1

Current assets	$ 60,000
Investment in Ostend bonds	9,000
Fixed assets (net)	200,000
	$269,000
Current liabilities	$ 30,000
Common stock, no par	150,000
Retained earnings	89,000
	$269,000

Stamboul is considering the impact of various types of dividends on this balance sheet. Each dividend would be declared and paid in 2016. These include:
1. Cash dividend of $1.00 per share on the 15,000 shares outstanding.
2. Stock dividend of 5% on the 15,000 shares outstanding when the market price is $17 per share.
3. Property dividend consisting of the $9,000 (book value) investment in Ostend bonds being held to maturity. This investment has a current market value of $13,000. (For Requirement 2, assume any gain or loss is to be reflected in retained earnings. Disregard income taxes.)
4. Scrip dividend of $0.80 per share on the 15,000 shares outstanding. The scrip earns interest at a 12% annual rate and is to be declared on January 30 and paid on December 30, 2016. (For Requirement 2, assume any interest expense is to be reflected in retained earnings. Disregard income taxes.)
5. Cash dividend consisting of a $0.70 per share normal dividend and a $0.30 per share liquidating dividend.

Required:
For each preceding *independent* dividend:
1. Prepare the appropriate journal entries for the declaration and payment or distribution of the dividend.
2. Prepare a condensed balance sheet after each dividend has been *paid* or distributed.

E16-4 **Stock Dividend** The shareholders' equity of Raven Company is as shown:

LO 16.1

Common stock, $10 par	$250,000
Additional paid-in capital on common stock	150,000
Retained earnings	200,000
	$600,000

Raven is considering the declaration and issuance of a stock dividend at a time when the market price is $30 per share.

Required:
1. Assuming the board of directors recommends a 6% stock dividend, prepare:
   a. the journal entry at the date of declaration
   b. the journal entry at the date of issuance
   c. shareholders' equity after the issuance
2. Assuming, instead, that a 40% stock dividend is recommended, answer a, b, and c of Requirement 1.

E16-5 **Stock Dividend Comparison** Although Oriole Company has enough retained earnings legally to declare a dividend, its working capital is low. The board of directors is considering a stock dividend instead of a cash dividend. The common stock is currently selling at $34 per share. The following is Oriole's current shareholders' equity:

LO 16.1

Common stock, $10 par	$ 400,000
Additional paid-in capital on common stock	800,000
Total contributed capital	$1,200,000
Retained earnings	1,300,000
Total shareholders' equity	$2,500,000

Required:
1. Assuming a 15% stock dividend is declared and issued, prepare the shareholders' equity section immediately after the date of issuance.
2. Assuming, instead, that a 30% stock dividend is declared and issued, prepare the shareholders' equity section immediately after the date of issuance.
3. **Next Level** What unusual result do you notice when you compare your answers from Requirement 1 with Requirement 2? From a theoretical standpoint, how might this have been avoided?

E16-6 **Prior Period Adjustments** Scobie Company began 2016 with a retained earnings balance of $142,400. During an examination of its accounting records on December 31, 2016, Scobie found it had made the following material errors, for both financial reporting and income tax reporting, during 2015.

LO 16.2

SHOW ME HOW

1. Depreciation expense of $15,000 inadvertently had been recorded twice for the same machine.
2. No accrual had been made at year-end for interest; therefore, interest expense had been understated by $4,000.

Scobie's net income after taxes during 2016 was $60,000. The company has been subject to a 30% income tax rate for the past several years. It declared and paid dividends of $13,000 during 2016.

Required:
1. Prepare whatever journal entries in 2016 are necessary to correct Scobie's books for its previous errors. Make your corrections directly to the Retained Earnings account.
2. Prepare the statement of retained earnings for 2016.

E16-7 **Restrictions** Pemberton Company has a retained earnings balance of $400,000 at the end of 2016. During 2016, it had issued $100,000 of 5-year, 12%, long-term bonds. The bond provisions require that each year over the 5-year period an additional $20,000 of retained earnings be unavailable for dividends. This restriction is in addition to any other retained earnings restrictions that the company might make. At the end of 2016, Pemberton held treasury stock costing $15,000.

LO 16.3

Required:
Show how Pemberton would report its retained earnings in its 2016 financial statements. Include a note to the financial statements fully describing the restrictions.

E16-8 Retained Earnings Statement Rolt Company began 2016 with a $120,000 balance in retained earnings. During the year, the following events occurred:
LO 16.3
1. The company earned net income of $80,000.
2. A material error in net income from a previous period was corrected. This error correction increased retained earnings by $9,800 after related income taxes of $4,200.
3. Cash dividends totaling $13,000 and stock dividends totaling $17,000 were declared.
4. One thousand shares of callable preferred stock that originally had been issued at $110 per share were recalled and retired at the beginning of 2016 for the call price of $120 per share.
5. Treasury stock (common) was acquired at a cost of $20,000. State law requires a restriction of retained earnings in an equal amount. The company reports its retained earnings restrictions in a note to the financial statements.

Required:
1. Prepare a statement of retained earnings for the year ended December 31, 2016.
2. Prepare the note to disclose the restriction of retained earnings.

E16-9 Retained Earnings Statement On January 1, 2016, Castillo Company had a retained earnings balance of $206,000. During 2016, the following events occurred:
LO 16.3
1. Treasury stock (common) was acquired at a cost of $14,000. State law requires a restriction of retained earnings in an equal amount. The company reports its retained earnings restrictions in a note to the financial statements.
2. Cash dividends totaling $9,000 and stock dividends totaling $6,000 were declared and distributed.
3. Net income was $58,000.
4. Two thousand shares of callable preferred stock were recalled and retired at a price of $150 per share. This stock had originally been issued at $130 per share.
5. A material error in net income for a previous period was corrected. This error correction decreased retained earnings by $12,600 after a related income tax credit of $5,400.

Required:
1. Prepare a statement of retained earnings for the year ended December 31, 2016.
2. Prepare a note to disclose the restriction of retained earnings.

E16-10 Shareholders' Equity Herrera Manufacturing Corporation completed the following transactions during its first year of operation, 2016:
LO 16.3
1. The state authorized the issuance of 30,000 shares of $5 par common stock; 15,000 shares were issued at $22 per share.
2. The state authorized the issuance of 6,000 shares of $50 par preferred stock. All 6,000 shares were issued at $70 per share.
3. Herrera reacquired 1,000 shares of its outstanding common stock at $18 per share. The cost method is used to account for treasury stock.
4. Herrera invested $50,000 of excess cash, not needed to finance operations, in long-term available-for-sale debt securities. At year-end, the market value of these securities was $47,500.
5. Herrera sold 500 shares of treasury stock for $23 per share.
6. Net income for the first year of operations was $16,000. No dividends were declared.

Required:
Prepare the shareholders' equity section (and any related notes to the financial statements) of Herrera's balance sheet as of December 31, 2016.

E16-11 Changes in Shareholders' Equity The shareholders' equity section of Flores Design Company's December 31, 2015, balance sheet appeared as follows:
LO 16.3

Contributed Capital:	
Preferred stock, $100 par (10,000 shares authorized, 1,250 shares issued)	$125,000
Additional paid-in capital on preferred stock	55,000
Common stock, $10 par (60,000 shares authorized, 15,000 shares issued)	150,000
Additional paid-in capital on common stock	105,000
Total contributed capital	$435,000
Retained earnings	78,000
Contributed capital and retained earnings	$513,000
Less: Treasury stock (300 shares of common at $14 per share)	(4,200)
Total Shareholders' Equity	$508,800

During 2016, the company entered into the following transactions affecting shareholders' equity:
1. Issued 250 shares of preferred stock at $164 per share.
2. Issued 3,000 shares of common stock at $17 per share.
3. Reacquired 200 of its own common shares as treasury stock for $15 per share.
4. Reissued 250 shares of treasury stock at $17 per share (FIFO basis).
5. Net income for 2016 was $46,500. Dividends of $25,000 were distributed.

Required:
1. Prepare a statement of shareholders' equity for the year ended December 31, 2016, for Flores.
2. Compute the return on shareholders' equity for 2016.

E16-12 **Weighted Average Shares** At the beginning of 2014, Hardin Company had 220,000 shares of $10 par common
LO 16.4 stock outstanding. During the year, it engaged in the following transactions related to its common stock:

Mar. 1	Issued 45,000 shares of stock at $22 per share.
June 1	Issued a 15% stock dividend.
July 1	Issued 10,000 shares of stock at $27 per share.
Aug. 31	Issued a 2-for-1 stock split on outstanding shares, reducing the par value to $5 per share.
Oct. 31	Reacquired 95,000 shares as treasury stock at a cost of $30 per share.
Nov. 30	Reissued 45,000 treasury shares at a price of $33 per share.

Required:
Determine the following:
1. weighted average number of shares outstanding for computing the current earnings per share
2. number of common shares outstanding at December 31, 2014

E16-13 **Weighted Average Shares** At the beginning of the current year, Hardin Company had 20,000 shares of $10 par
LO 16.4 common stock outstanding. During the year, it engaged in the following transactions related to its common stock, so that at year-end it had 63,800 shares outstanding:

Apr. 1	Issued 5,000 shares of stock.
June 1	Issued 4,000 shares of stock.
July 1	Issued a 10% stock dividend.
Sept. 30	Issued a 2-for-1 stock split, reducing the par value to $5 per share.
Oct. 1	Reacquired 1,000 shares as treasury stock.
Nov. 30	Reissued the 1,000 shares of treasury stock.

Required:
Determine the weighted average number of shares outstanding for computing the current earnings per share.

E16-14 **Earnings per Share** The 2015 balance sheet for Guthrie Corporation revealed the following information:
LO 16.4
- Common stock, $10 par, 50,000 shares issued and outstanding
- Preferred stock, $100 par, 6%, cumulative stock, 1,000 shares issued and outstanding

During 2016, Guthrie reported net income of $225,000 and engaged in the following stock transactions:

Mar. 1	Issued 10,000 shares of common stock for cash.
Apr. 1	Reacquired 2,000 shares of common stock as treasury stock.
Aug. 1	Resold 1,000 shares of treasury stock for cash.
Sept. 1	Declared and issued a 50% stock dividend on common stock.

Required:
1. Determine if Guthrie has a simple or complex capital structure.
2. Calculate the weighted average number of shares of stock that should be used to calculate EPS for the 2016 income statement.
3. Compute the basic EPS that would be disclosed by Guthrie.

E16-15 Earnings per Share Rodgers Corporation reported basic earnings per share of $1.25 for the year ended December 31, 2016. Rodgers had 8,000 shares of cumulative, nonconvertible $100 par, 12% preferred stock outstanding during all of 2016. The company began 2016 with 200,000 shares of common stock outstanding and ended the year with 400,000 share of common stock outstanding, due to issuing 200,000 shares on July 1, 2016.

LO 16.4

SHOW ME HOW

Required:

Next Level Determine Rodgers's net income for 2016.

E16-16 Weighted Average Shares Jumbo Corporation reported the following information about its stock on its December 31, 2015, balance sheet:

LO 16.4

Preferred stock, $100 par value, 6% cumulative, 30,000 shares authorized 1,000 shares issued and outstanding	$100,000
Common stock, $10 par value, 150,000 shares authorized 50,000 shares issued and outstanding	500,000

Jumbo Corporation engaged in the following stock transactions during 2016:

Mar. 1   Issued 10,000 shares of common stock for cash.
Apr. 1   Purchased 2,000 shares of common stock as treasury stock.
Aug. 1   Resold 1,000 shares of treasury stock.
Sept. 1 Declared and distributed a 50% stock dividend on common stock.

Required:
1. Does Jumbo Corporation have a simple or complex capital structure?
2. Calculate the number of shares that Jumbo would use to calculate basic EPS for its 2016 income statement.

E16-17 Comparative Earnings per Share Lucas Company reports net income of $5,125 for the year ended December 31, 2016, its first year of operations. On January 4, 2016, Lucas issued 9,000 shares of common stock. On August 2, 2016, it issued an additional 3,000 shares of stock, resulting in 12,000 shares outstanding at year-end.

LO 16.4

During 2017, Lucas earned net income of $16,400. It issued 2,000 additional shares of stock on March 3, 2017, and declared and issued a 2-for-1 stock split on November 3, 2017, resulting in 28,000 shares outstanding at year-end.

During 2018, Lucas earned net income of $23,520. The only common stock transaction during 2018 was a 20% stock dividend issued on July 2, 2018.

Required:
1. Compute the basic earnings per share that would be disclosed in the 2016 annual report.
2. Compute the 2016 and 2017 comparative basic earnings per share that would be disclosed in the 2017 annual report.
3. Compute the 2016, 2017, and 2018 comparative basic earnings per share that would be disclosed in the 2018 annual report.

E16-18 Basic Earnings per Share Monona Company reported net income of $29,975 for 2016. During all of 2016, Monona had 1,000 shares of 10%, $100 par, nonconvertible preferred stock outstanding, on which the year's dividends had been paid. At the beginning of 2016, the company had 7,000 shares of common stock outstanding. On April 2, 2016, the company issued another 2,000 shares of common stock so that 9,000 common shares were outstanding at the end of 2016. Common dividends of $17,000 had been paid during 2016. At the end of 2016, the market price per share of common stock was $17.50.

LO 16.4

Required:
1. Compute Monona's basic earnings per share for 2016.
2. Compute the price/earnings ratio for 2016.

E16-19 Basic Earnings per Share Lyon Company shows the following condensed income statement information for the year ended December 31, 2016:

LO 16.4

Income before discontinued operations	$29,936
Less: Loss from discontinued operations loss (net of income tax)	(2,176)
Net income	$27,760

Lyon declared dividends of $6,000 on preferred stock and $17,280 on common stock. At the beginning of 2016, 10,000 shares of common stock were outstanding. On May 1, 2016, the company issued 2,000 additional common shares, and on October 31, 2016, it issued a 20% stock dividend on its common stock. The preferred stock is not convertible.

Required:
1. Compute the 2016 basic earnings per share.
2. Show the 2016 income statement disclosure of basic earnings per share.
3. Draft a related note to accompany the 2016 financial statements.

E16-20 **Earnings per Share Disclosure** Extreme Company reported the following information about its stock on its
LO 16.4 December 31, 2016, balance sheet:

Preferred stock, $2 par value, 5% cumulative, 300,000 shares authorized, 120,000 shares issued and outstanding	$240,000
Common stock, $1 par value, 500,000 shares authorized, 240,000 shares issued and outstanding	240,000

The following amounts were taken from Extreme's income statement:

Income from continuing operations before income taxes	$ 680,000
Income tax expense	(204,000)
Income from continuing operations	$ 476,000
Loss from discontinued operations, net of $13,000 tax benefit	(36,000)
Net income	$ 440,000

The only stock issued during 2016 was 80,000 shares of common stock issued on June 30, 2016. No dividends were declared during 2016.

Required:
1. Calculate all earnings per share amounts for 2016.
2. Are dividends on preferred stock taken into account when calculating earnings per share even if they are not declared? If so, why?

E16-21 **Impact on EPS and Rankings** Mills Company had five convertible securities outstanding during all of 2016. It
LO 16.5 paid the appropriate interest (and amortized any related premium or discount using the straight-line method) and dividends on each security during 2016. Each convertible security is described in the following table. The corporate income tax rate is 30%.

Security	Description
9.5% preferred stock	$200,000 par value. Issued at 112. Each $100 par preferred stock is convertible into 4.2 shares of common stock.
11.0% bonds	$220,000 face value. Issued at par. Each $1,000 bond is convertible into 44 shares of common stock.
8.0% preferred stock	$150,000 par value. Issued at par. Each $100 par preferred stock is convertible into 3.8 shares of common stock.
10.0% bonds	$100,000 face value. Issued at 94. Discount being amortized over 20-year life. Each $1,000 bond is convertible into 55 shares of common stock.
9.0% bonds	$200,000 face value. Issued at 108. Premium being amortized over 25-year life. Each $1,000 bond is convertible into 48 shares of common stock.

Required:
1. Prepare a schedule that lists the impact of the assumed conversion of each convertible security on diluted earnings per share.
2. Prepare a ranking of the order in which the securities would be included in the diluted earnings per share computations.

E16-22 Convertible Preferred Stock, Convertible Bonds, and EPS Francis Company has 24,000 shares of common stock outstanding at the beginning of 2016. Francis issued 3,000 additional shares on May 1 and 2,000 additional shares on September 30. It also has two convertible securities outstanding at the end of 2016. These are:

LO 16.5

1. Convertible preferred stock: 2,500 shares of 8.5%, $50 par, preferred stock were issued on January 2, 2013, for $60 per share. Each share of preferred stock is convertible into 3 shares of common stock. Current dividends have been declared and paid. To date, no preferred stock has been converted.
2. Convertible bonds: Bonds with a face value of $250,000 and an interest rate of 5.5% were issued at par in 2015. Each $1,000 bond is convertible into 20 shares of common stock. To date, no bonds have been converted.

Francis earned net income of $72,500 during 2016. The income tax rate is 30%.

Required:
1. Compute the number of shares of common stock that Francis should use in calculating basic earnings per share for 2016.
2. Calculate basic earnings per share for 2016.
3. Calculate diluted earnings per share for 2016 and the incremental EPS of the preferred stock and convertible bonds.
4. **Next Level** Assume the same facts as above except that net income included a loss from discontinued operations of $18,000 net of income taxes. Compute *basic* EPS and show how it should be reported to shareholders. You do not have to calculate diluted EPS for this case.

E16-23 Share Options, EPS Marion Company has 30,000 shares of common stock outstanding during all of 2016. This common stock has been selling at an average market price of $45 per share. Marion also has outstanding for the entire year compensatory share options to purchase 4,000 shares of common stock at $32 per share. The unrecognized compensation cost (net of tax) relating to these share options is $3 per share. During 2016, Marion earned income of $36,000 after income taxes of 30%.

LO 16.5

Required:
1. Compute Marion's 2016 diluted earnings per share.
2. **Next Level** Assume Marion uses IFRS. Discuss what Marion would do differently for computing earnings per share, and then compute its earnings per share.

E16-24 Convertible Preferred Stock and EPS Palo Alto Company earned net income of $43,800 during 2016. At the beginning of 2016, it had 10,000 shares of common stock outstanding; an additional 4,000 shares were issued on July 2. During 2016, 600 shares of 8%, $100 par, convertible preferred stock were outstanding the entire year. Dividends on this preferred stock were paid in 2016. Each share is convertible into 5 shares of common stock. The corporate income tax rate is 30%.

LO 16.5

Required:
Compute the 2016 diluted earnings per share.

E16-25 Convertible Bonds and EPS Dream Corporation reported net income of $44,000 for 2016. The company has 10,000 shares of common stock issued and outstanding for all of 2016 and no preferred stock. During 2015, Dream issued $400,000 of 8% convertible bonds at par value. Each $1,000 bond can be converted into 24 shares of common stock. No bonds have been converted as of December 31, 2016. Dream has a 30% tax rate.

LO 16.5

Required:
1. Calculate the earnings per share amounts that Dream should disclose on its 2016 income statement.
2. How will the calculations of earnings per share change if the convertible bonds are antidilutive?

E16-26 Convertible Bonds and EPS Tama Company's capital structure consists of common stock and convertible bonds. At the beginning of 2016, Tama had 15,000 shares of common stock outstanding; an additional 4,500 shares were issued on May 4. The 7% convertible bonds have a face value of $80,000 and were issued in 2013 at par. Each $1,000 bond is convertible into 25 shares of common stock; to date, none of the bonds have been converted. During 2016, the company earned net income of $79,200 and was subject to an income tax rate of 30%.

LO 16.5

Required:
Compute the 2016 diluted earnings per share.

E16-27 **Convertible Securities and Earnings per Share** Percy Company has 15,000 shares of common stock outstanding during all of 2016. It also has 2 convertible securities outstanding at the end of 2016. These are:
LO 16.5

1. Convertible preferred stock: 1,000 shares of 9%, $100 par, preferred stock were issued in 2015 for $140 per share. Each share of preferred stock is convertible into 3.5 shares of common stock. The current dividends have been paid. To date, no preferred stock has been converted.
2. Convertible bonds: Bonds with a face value of $100,000 and an interest rate of 10% were issued at par on July 1, 2016. Each $1,000 bond is convertible into 35 shares of common stock. To date, no bonds have been converted.

Percy earned net income of $54,000 during 2016. Its income tax rate is 30%.

Required:
Compute the 2016 diluted earnings per share. What earnings per share amount(s) would Percy report on its 2016 income statement?

E16-28 **Convertible Securities and Earnings per Share** Francis Company has 20,000 shares of common stock outstanding during all of 2016. It also has two convertible securities outstanding at the end of 2016. These are:
LO 16.5

SHOW ME HOW

1. Convertible preferred stock: 2,000 shares of 9.5%, $50 par, preferred stock were issued on January 2, 2016, for $60 per share. Each share of preferred stock is convertible into 3 shares of common stock. Current dividends have been declared. To date, no preferred stock has been converted.
2. Convertible bonds: Bonds with a face value of $200,000 and an interest rate of 5.7% were issued at par in 2015. Each $1,000 bond is convertible into 22 shares of common stock. To date, no bonds have been converted.

Francis earned net income of $61,500 during 2016. Its income tax rate is 30%.

Required:
Compute the 2016 diluted earnings per share. What earnings per share amount(s) would Francis report on its 2016 income statement?

PROBLEMS

P16-1 **Dividends** Keener Company has had 1,000 shares of 7%, $100 par preferred stock and 40,000 shares of $5 stated-value common stock outstanding for the last 3 years. During that period, dividends paid totaled $6,000, $28,000, and $30,000 for each year, respectively.
LO 16.1

Required:
Compute the amount of dividends that Keener must have paid to preferred shareholders and common shareholders in each of the 3 years, given the following 3 independent assumptions:
1. Preferred stock is nonparticipating and noncumulative.
2. Preferred stock is nonparticipating and cumulative.
3. Preferred stock is fully participating and cumulative.

P16-2 **Dividends** Otter Tail, Inc., began operations in January 2012 and had the following reported net income or loss for each of its 5 years of operations:
LO 16.1

AICPA Adapted

2012	$ 150,000	loss
2013	130,000	loss
2014	120,000	loss
2015	250,000	income
2016	1,000,000	income

At December 31, 2016, Otter Tail's capital stock was comprised of the following:

Common stock, $10 par (100,000 shares authorized; 50,000 shares issued and outstanding)	$ 500,000
Preferred stock, 4% noncumulative and nonparticipating, $100 par (1,000 shares authorized, issued, and outstanding)	100,000
Preferred stock, 8% cumulative and fully participating, $100 par (10,000 shares authorized, issued, and outstanding)	1,000,000

(continued)

Otter Tail has never paid a cash or stock dividend. There has been no change in the capital accounts since Otter Tail began operations. The appropriate state law permits dividends only from retained earnings.

Required:

Prepare a worksheet showing the maximum amount available for cash dividends on December 31, 2016, and how it would be distributable to the holders of the common shares and each of the preferred shares. Show supporting computations in good form.

P16-3 **Corrections, Dividends, Retained Earnings Statement** On January 1, 2016, Kittson Company had a retained earnings balance of $218,600. It is subject to a 30% corporate income tax rate. During 2016, Kittson earned net income of $67,000, and the following events occurred:
LO 16.1
LO 16.2

1. Cash dividends of $3 per share on 4,000 shares of common stock were declared and paid.
2. A small stock dividend was declared and issued. The dividend consisted of 600 shares of $10 par common stock. On the date of declaration, the market price of the company's common stock was $36 per share.
3. The company recalled and retired 500 shares of $100 par preferred stock. The call price was $125 per share; the stock had originally been issued for $110 per share.
4. The company discovered that it had erroneously recorded depreciation expense of $45,000 in 2015 for both financial reporting and income tax reporting. The correct depreciation for 2015 should have been $20,000. This is considered a material error.

Required:

1. Prepare journal entries to record Items 1 through 4.
2. Prepare Kittson's statement of retained earnings for the year ended December 31, 2016.

P16-4 **Corrections** You've been hired to perform an audit of Hubbard Company for the year ended December 31, 2016. You find the following account balances related to shareholders' equity:
LO 16.2

Preferred stock, $100 par	$ 30,000
Common stock, $10 par	65,000
Capital surplus	(16,400)
Retained earnings	150,000

Because of the antiquated terminology and negative balance, you examine the Capital Surplus account first and find in it the following entries:

	Credit (Debit)
Additional paid-in capital on common stock	$ 27,100
Capital from donated land	16,000
Treasury stock (500 common shares at cost)	(7,500)
Additional paid-in capital on preferred stock	3,000
Stock dividend (50%)	(20,000)
Prior period adjustment (net of income taxes)	(12,000)
Loss from fire (uninsured), 2015	(18,000)
Property dividend declared	(6,000)
Cash dividends declared	(24,000)
Balance	$(41,400)

Your examination of the Preferred Stock and Common Stock accounts reveals that the amounts shown correctly state the total par value of the issued capital stock. The Retained Earnings account contains the accumulated earnings of the company, with the exception of any items of retained earnings that were inappropriately debited or credited to the Capital Surplus account.

Required:

1. Prepare whatever journal entries are necessary to eliminate the Capital Surplus account and to correct Hubbard's shareholders' equity accounts.
2. Prepare a corrected shareholders' equity section of Hubbard's December 31, 2016, balance sheet. Include any related notes to its financial statements.

P16-5
LO 16.3

Stock Dividends, Splits Alert Company's shareholders' equity prior to any of the following events is as follows:

Preferred stock, 8%, $100 par	$100,000
Common stock, $10 par	150,000
Additional paid-in capital on preferred stock	16,000
Additional paid-in capital on common stock	220,000
Retained earnings	264,000
	$750,000

The company is considering the following *alternative* items:
1. An 8% stock dividend on the common stock when it is selling for $30 per share.
2. A 30% stock dividend on the common stock when it is selling for $32 per share.
3. A *special* stock dividend to common shareholders consisting of 1 share of preferred stock for every 100 shares of common stock. The preferred stock and common stock are selling for $123 and $31 per share, respectively.
4. A 2-for-1 stock split on the common stock, reducing the par value to $5 per share (assume the same date for declaration and issuance). The market price is $30 per share on the common stock.
5. A property dividend to common shareholders consisting of 100 bonds issued by West Company. These bonds are carried on the Alert Company books as an available-for-sale investment at a fair value of $48,000 (which is also its cost); it has a current value of $54,000.
6. A cash dividend, consisting of a normal dividend and a liquidating dividend, on both the preferred and the common stock. The 10% preferred dividend includes a 2% liquidating dividend, and the $2.30 per share common dividend includes a $0.30 per share liquidating dividend (separate liquidating dividend contra accounts should be used).

Required:
For each of the preceding *alternative* items:
1. Record (a) the journal entry at the date of declaration and (b) the journal entry at the date of issuance.
2. Compute the balances in the shareholders' equity accounts immediately after the issuance (any gains or losses are to be reflected in the retained earnings balance; ignore income taxes).

P16-6
LO 16.1
LO 16.2
LO 16.3

Retained Earnings Statement Olivia Company began 2016 with a Retained Earnings account balance of $180,000. During 2016, the following 8 events occurred and were properly recorded by the company:
1. Bonds payable with a face value of $100,000 were issued on January 1 at 98. The bonds mature in 10 years. The bond provisions require the restriction of retained earnings (by means of a note to the financial statements) equal to one-half the face value of the bonds during the period the bonds are outstanding.
2. On April 13, Olivia reissued 2,400 shares of treasury stock for $25 per share. The company had reacquired these shares in 2014 at a cost of $20 per share. At that time, it had restricted retained earnings (by means of a note to the financial statements) in an amount equal to the cost of the treasury shares.
3. On January 5, Olivia recalled and retired 800 shares of $100 par preferred stock at the call price of $120 per share. The stock had originally been issued for $108 per share.
4. During June, Olivia declared and issued a 2-for-1 stock split on its common stock, reducing the par value from $10 to $5 per share. Immediately prior to the split, 10,000 shares of common stock were outstanding. The stock market price on the date of the split was $25 per share.
5. In August, Olivia declared and issued a 15% stock dividend when the common stock was selling at $13 per share.
6. During December, Olivia declared and paid its annual $1.30 per share cash dividend on the outstanding common stock.
7. Net income amounted to $72,000.
8. During the year-end audit, it was found that in 2015, Olivia had recorded depreciation on a particular machine twice. The error resulted in a $13,000 overstatement of depreciation during 2015. It was also found that, due to an oversight, a $10,000 loss on the sale of land was omitted from the 2015 income statement. Both items are material. The company has been subject to a 30% income tax rate for several years.

Required:
Prepare Olivia's statement of retained earnings and any related notes to its financial statements for the year ended December 31, 2016.

P16-7
LO 16.1
LO 16.2
LO 16.3
AICPA
Adapted

Comprehensive Oakwood Inc. is a public enterprise whose shares are traded in the over-the-counter market. At December 31, 2015, Oakwood had 6,000,000 authorized shares of $10 par value common stock, of which 2,000,000 shares were issued and outstanding. The shareholders' equity accounts at December 31, 2015, had the following balances:

Common stock	$20,000,000
Additional paid-in capital on common stock	7,500,000
Retained earnings	6,470,000

Transactions during 2016 and other information relating to the shareholders' equity accounts were as follows:
1. On January 5, 2016, Oakwood issued at $54 per share, 100,000 shares of $50 par value, 9%, cumulative convertible preferred stock. Each share of preferred stock is convertible, at the option of the holder, into 2 shares of common stock. Oakwood had 600,000 authorized shares of preferred stock.
2. On February 2, 2016, Oakwood reacquired 20,000 shares of its common stock for $16 per share. Oakwood uses the cost method to account for treasury stock.
3. On April 27, 2016, Oakwood sold 500,000 shares (previously unissued) of $10 par value common stock to the public at $17 per share.
4. On June 18, 2016, Oakwood declared a cash dividend of $1 per share of common stock, payable on July 13, 2016, to shareholders of record on July 2, 2016.
5. On November 9, 2016, Oakwood sold 10,000 shares of treasury stock for $21 per share.
6. On December 14, 2016, Oakwood declared the yearly cash dividend on preferred stock, payable on January 14, 2017, to shareholders of record on December 31, 2016.
7. On January 18, 2017, before the books were closed for 2016, Oakwood became aware that the ending inventories at December 31, 2015, were understated by $300,000 (the after-tax effect on 2015 net income was $210,000). The appropriate correcting entry was recorded the same day.
8. After correcting the beginning inventory, net income for 2016 was $4,500,000.

Required:
1. Prepare a statement of retained earnings for Oakwood for the year ended December 31, 2016. Assume that only single-period financial statements for 2016 are presented.
2. Prepare the shareholders' equity section of Oakwood's balance sheet at December 31, 2016.

P16-8
LO 16.1
LO 16.2
LO 16.3
AICPA
Adapted

Comprehensive Dakota Corporation had the following shareholders' equity account balances at December 31, 2015:

Preferred stock	$1,800,000
Additional paid-in capital on preferred stock	90,000
Common stock	5,150,000
Additional paid-in capital on common stock	3,500,000
Retained earnings	4,000,000
Unrealized decrease in value of marketable equity securities	245,000
Treasury common stock	270,000

Transactions during 2016 and other information relating to the shareholders' equity accounts were as follows:
1. Dakota's preferred and common shares are traded on the over-the-counter market. At December 31, 2015, Dakota had 100,000 authorized shares of $100 par, 10%, cumulative preferred stock; and 3,000,000 authorized shares of no-par common stock with a stated value of $5 per share.
2. On January 9, 2016, Dakota formally retired all 30,000 shares of its treasury common stock and had them revert to an unissued basis. The treasury stock had been acquired on January 20, 2015. The shares were originally issued at $10 per share.
3. Dakota owned 10,000 shares of Bush Inc. common stock purchased in 2013 for $750,000. The Bush stock was included in Dakota's short-term marketable securities portfolio at the end of 2015 at a value of $650,000. On February 13, 2016, Dakota declared a dividend in kind of 1 share of Bush for every 100 shares of Dakota common stock held by shareholders of record on February 27, 2016. The market price of Bush common stock was $63 per share on February 13, 2016. The dividend in kind was distributed on March 12, 2016.
4. On April 2, 2016, 250,000 stock rights were issued to the common shareholders permitting the purchase of 1 new share of common stock in exchange for 1 right and $11 cash. On April 23, 2016, 210,000 stock rights were exercised when the market price of Dakota's common stock was $13 per share. Dakota issued new shares to settle the transaction. The remaining 40,000 rights were not exercised and expired.

5. On December 10, 2016, Dakota declared the yearly cash dividend on preferred stock, payable on January 14, 2017, to shareholders of record on December 31, 2016.
6. After the year-end adjustment, the Unrealized Decrease in Value of Marketable Equity Securities account had a debit balance of $135,000 at December 31, 2016.
7. On January 14, 2017, before the accounting records were closed for 2016, Dakota became aware that rent income for the year ended December 31, 2015, was overstated by $500,000. The after-tax effect on 2015 net income was $275,000. The appropriate correcting entry was recorded the same day.
8. After correcting the rent income, net income for 2016 was $2,600,000.

Required:
1. Prepare Dakota's statement of retained earnings for the year ended December 31, 2016. Assume that only single-period financial statements for 2016 are presented.
2. Prepare the shareholders' equity section of Dakota's balance sheet at December 31, 2016.

P16-9
LO 16.1
LO 16.2
LO 16.3

Comprehensive Dana Company reported the following amounts in the shareholders' equity section of its December 31, 2015, balance sheet:

Preferred stock, 9%, $100 par (10,000 shares authorized, 1,000 shares issued)	$100,000
Common stock, $10 par (20,000 shares authorized, 9,000 shares issued)	90,000
Additional paid-in capital on preferred stock	20,000
Additional paid-in capital on common stock	99,000
Retained earnings	330,000

During 2016, Dana's net income was $83,000 and its dividends on preferred and common stock were $9,900 and $17,600, respectively. In addition, the following transactions affected its shareholders' equity:
1. Purchased 750 shares of its outstanding common stock as treasury stock for $22 per share.
2. Sold 500 shares of treasury stock at $27 per share. The company uses the cost method to account for treasury stock.
3. Retired 200 of the common shares held in the treasury.
4. Issued 100 shares of preferred stock for $125 per share.
5. The aggregate market value of the company's long-term investments in available-for-sale debt securities dropped below the carrying value of these securities at year-end. The difference between the carrying value and the year-end market value totals $10,000 (net of taxes).

Required:
1. Prepare Dana's statement of shareholders' equity for 2016. (*Hint:* This statement will include more than 10 numerical columns.) Assume Dana reports its comprehensive income in this statement.
2. Prepare the shareholders' equity section of Dana's balance sheet as of December 31, 2016. Include any related notes to its financial statements.

P16-10
LO 16.1
LO 16.2
LO 16.3

Comprehensive The shareholders' equity section of Gaines Industries's balance sheet appeared as follows at December 31, 2015:

Contributed Capital:	
Preferred stock, 8%, $100 par (5,000 shares authorized, 3,000 shares issued)	$ 300,000
Common stock, $10 par (25,000 shares authorized, 20,000 shares issued of which 500 shares are being held as treasury stock)	200,000
Additional paid-in capital on preferred stock	120,000
Additional paid-in capital on common stock	280,000
Common stock option warrants	32,000
Total contributed capital	$ 932,000
Retained earnings	260,000
Total contributed capital and retained earnings	$1,192,000
Less: Treasury stock (500 common shares at $31)	(15,500)
Total Shareholders' Equity	$1,176,500

(continued)

During 2016, the following chronological transactions were recorded:
1. Gaines issued 1,000 shares of common stock for $40 per share.
2. Gaines has a share option plan for key executives. In accordance with the plan, the shares under option and the option price per share for each executive are known on the grant date. During 2016, no new options were granted, and compensation expense of $3,000 was recorded in regard to the existing options.
3. Share options to 500 common shares were exercised in 2016 at an option price of $30 per share. The share option value originally recorded in the Common Stock Option Warrants account in regard to these shares amounted to $3 per share.
4. Gaines reissued 200 shares of its treasury stock for $41 per share.
5. Gaines accepted land in an industrial park for a factory building site from the Columbus Development Association. The fair value of the land is estimated by an independent appraiser to be $50,000.
6. The law firm of Crook, Rezich, and Romero agreed to accept 100 shares of preferred stock in lieu of legal fees. At the time, the preferred stock was selling for $142 per share.
7. Net income for 2016 of $182,000 was transferred from Income Summary to Retained Earnings. Dividends on preferred and common were $24,800 and $43,000, respectively (debit Retained Earnings and credit Cash).

Required:
1. Prepare journal entries to record the preceding 2016 transactions for Gaines.
2. Prepare the statement of shareholders' equity for 2016. (*Hint:* This statement will require 10 numerical columns.)
3. Prepare the shareholders' equity section of the December 31, 2016, balance sheet. Include appropriate notes to the financial statements.
4. Compute the return on shareholders' equity for 2016.

P16-11 **Shareholders' Equity** Raun Company had the following equity items as of December 31, 2016:
LO 16.3
AICPA Adapted

Preferred stock, 9% cumulative, $100 par, convertible
Paid-in capital in excess of par value on preferred stock
Common stock, $1 stated value
Paid-in capital in excess of stated value on common stock
Retained earnings

The following additional information about Raun was available for the year ended December 31, 2016:
1. There were 2 million shares of preferred stock authorized, of which 1 million were outstanding. All 1 million shares outstanding were issued on January 2, 2013, for $120 a share. The preferred stock is convertible into common stock on a 1-for-1 basis until December 31, 2022; thereafter, the preferred stock ceases to be convertible and is callable at par value by the company. No preferred stock has been converted into common stock, and there were no dividends in arrears at December 31, 2016.
2. The common stock has been issued at amounts above stated value per share since incorporation in 1992. Of the 5 million shares authorized, 3,580,000 were outstanding at January 1, 2016. The market price of the outstanding common stock has increased slowly but consistently for the last 5 years.
3. Raun has an employee share option plan where certain key employees and officers may purchase shares of common stock at 100% of the market price at the date of the option grant. All options are exercisable in installments of one-third each year, commencing 1 year after the date of the grant, and expire if not exercised within 4 years of the grant date. On January 1, 2016, options for 70,000 shares were outstanding at prices ranging from $47 to $83 a share. Options for 20,000 shares were exercised at $47 to $79 a share during 2016. During 2016, no options expired and additional options for 15,000 shares were granted at $86 a share. The 65,000 options outstanding at December 31, 2016, were exercisable at $54 to $86 a share; of these, 30,000 were exercisable at that date at prices ranging from $54 to $79 a share.
4. Raun also has an employee share purchase plan whereby the company pays one-half and the employee pays one-half of the market price of the stock at the date of the subscription. During 2016, employees subscribed to 60,000 shares at an average price of $87 a share. All 60,000 shares were paid for and issued late in September 2016.
5. On December 31, 2016, there was a total of 355,000 shares of common stock set aside for the granting of future share options and for future purchases under the employee share purchase plan. The only changes in the shareholders' equity for 2016 were those described previously, the 2016 net income, and the cash dividends paid.

Required:
Prepare the shareholders' equity section of Raun's balance sheet at December 31, 2016. Substitute, where appropriate, X's for unknown dollar amounts. Use good form and provide full disclosure. Write appropriate notes as they should appear in the published financial statements.

P16-12 **Comprehensive** Isanti Inc. finances its capital needs approximately one-third from long-term debt and two-thirds from equity. At December 31, 2015, Isanti had the following liability and equity items:

LO 16.1
LO 16.2
LO 16.3
AICPA
Adapted

11% debenture bonds payable, face amount	$5,000,000
Premium on bonds payable	352,400
Common stock	8,000,000
Additional paid-in capital	2,295,000
Retained earnings	2,465,000
Treasury stock, at cost	325,000

Transactions during 2016 and other information relating to Isanti's liabilities and equity accounts were as follows:

1. The debenture bonds were issued on December 31, 2013, for $5,378,000 to yield 10%. The bonds mature on December 31, 2025. Interest is payable annually on December 31. Isanti uses the interest method to amortize bond premium.
2. Isanti's common stock shares are traded on the over-the-counter market. At December 31, 2015, Isanti had 2,000,000 authorized shares of $10 par common stock.
3. On January 15, 2016, Isanti reissued 15,000 of its 25,000 shares of treasury stock for $225,000. The treasury stock had been acquired on February 24, 2015.
4. On March 2, 2016, Isanti issued a 5% stock dividend on all issued shares. The market price of Isanti's common stock at the time of issuance was $14 per share.
5. On November 2, 2016, Isanti borrowed $4,000,000 at 9%, evidenced by an unsecured note payable to United Bank. The note is payable in five equal annual principal installments of $800,000. The first principal and interest payment is due on November 2, 2017.
6. On December 31, 2016, Isanti owned 10,000 shares of Ryan Corp.'s common stock, which represented a 1% ownership interest. Isanti treats this marketable equity investment as a long-term investment in available-for-sale securities. The stock was purchased on November 2, 2016, at $20 per share. The market price was $18 per share on December 31, 2016.
7. Isanti's net income for 2016 was $2,860,000.

Required:
1. Prepare the long-term liabilities section of Isanti's December 31, 2016, balance sheet, including all disclosures applicable to each obligation.
2. Prepare the shareholders' equity section of Isanti's December 31, 2016, balance sheet.
3. Prepare a schedule showing interest expense for the year ended December 31, 2016.

P16-13 **Comprehensive** Truman Co. is a publicly held company whose shares are traded in the over-the-counter market. The shareholders' equity at December 31, 2015, is comprised of the following:

LO 16.1
LO 16.2
LO 16.3
AICPA
Adapted

Preferred stock, $100 par value, 6% cumulative (5,000 shares authorized, 2,000 issued and outstanding)	$ 200,000
Common stock, $1 par value (150,000 shares authorized, 100,000 issued and outstanding)	100,000
Additional paid-in capital	800,000
Retained earnings	1,586,000
Total shareholders' equity	$2,686,000

Transactions during 2016 and other information relating to the shareholders' equity accounts were as follows:

- February 2, 2016—Issued 13,000 shares of common stock to Wolf Co. in exchange for land. On the date issued, the stock had a market price of $11 per share. The land had a carrying value on Wolf's books of $135,000 and an assessed value for property taxes of $90,000.
- March 2, 2016—Purchased 5,000 shares of its own common stock to be held as treasury stock for $14 per share. Truman uses the cost method to account for treasury stock. Transactions in treasury stock are legal in Truman's state of incorporation.

(continued)

- May 11, 2016—Declared a property dividend of marketable securities held by Truman to common shareholders. The securities had a carrying value of $600,000; fair values on relevant dates were:

Date of declaration (May 11, 2016)	$720,000
Date of record (May 28, 2016)	758,000
Date of distribution (June 4, 2016)	736,000

- October 1, 2016—Reissued 2,000 shares of treasury stock for $16 per share.
- November 2, 2016—Declared a cash dividend of $1.50 per share to all common shareholders of record November 16, 2016. The dividend was paid on November 26, 2016.
- December 21, 2016—Declared the required annual cash dividend on preferred stock for 2016. The dividend was paid on January 4, 2017.
- January 14, 2017—Before closing the accounting records for 2016, Truman became aware that no amortization had been recorded for 2015 for a patent purchased on July 1, 2015. The patent was properly capitalized at $320,000 and had an estimated useful life of 8 years when purchased. Truman's income tax rate is 30%. The appropriate correcting entry was recorded on the same day.
- Adjusted net income for 2016 was $838,000.

Required:

Determine the amounts of each of the following items. Show supporting calculations.
1. Prior period adjustment
2. Preferred dividends
3. Common dividends—cash
4. Common dividends—property
5. Number of common shares issued at December 31, 2016
6. Total legal capital of common stock issued
7. Additional paid-in capital, including treasury stock transactions
8. Total dollar amount of treasury stock
9. Numerator used in calculation of 2016 earnings per share for the year

P16-14 **Comprehensive** Gray Company lists the following shareholders' equity items on its December 31, 2015, balance sheet:

LO 16.1
LO 16.3

Contributed Capital:	
Preferred stock, 8%, $100 par	$120,000
Common stock, $10 par	180,000
Additional paid-in capital on preferred stock	21,600
Additional paid-in capital on common stock	90,000
Total contributed capital	$411,600
Retained earnings	230,000
Accumulated other comprehensive income:	
Unrealized increase in value of available-for-sale securities	6,000
Total contributed capital, retained earnings, and accumulated other comprehensive income	$647,600
Less: Treasury stock (2,000 shares of common at $21 per share, acquired on March 3, 2015)	(42,000)
Total Shareholders' Equity	$605,600

The following stock transactions occurred during 2016:

Jan.	4	Issued 3,000 shares of common stock at $25 per share.
	30	Paid the annual 2015 per share dividend on preferred stock and the $2 per share dividend on common stock. These dividends had been declared on December 31, 2015.
Mar.	2	Issued 400 shares of preferred stock at $125 per share.
May	7	Reissued 600 shares of treasury stock at $24 per share.
June	15	Split the common stock 2-for-1, reducing the par value to $5 per share.
July	2	Declared a 5% stock dividend on the outstanding common stock, to be issued on August 3. The stock is selling for $14 per share.
Aug.	3	Issued the stock dividend.
Oct.	1	Declared a property dividend payable to common shareholders on November 1. The dividend consists of 200 Lamb Company bonds that are classified as an available-for-sale investment. The bonds had been acquired at a cost of $24,000 and have a carrying value of $30,000. The bonds are currently selling for $32,000.
Nov.	1	Issued the property dividend to common shareholders.
Dec.	31	Declared the annual per share dividend on the outstanding preferred stock and a $1 per share dividend on the outstanding common stock, to be paid on January 30, 2017.

Required:
1. Prepare journal entries to record the preceding transactions.
2. Prepare the December 31, 2016, shareholders' equity section (assume that 2016 net income was $225,000).

P16-15 **Comprehensive** Included in the December 31, 2015, Jacobi Company balance sheet was the following shareholders' equity section:
LO 16.1
LO 16.3

Contributed Capital:
Preferred stock, 6%, $100 par		$200,000	
Additional paid-in capital on preferred stock		12,000	$ 212,000
Common stock, $5 par		$150,000	
Additional paid-in capital on common stock		240,000	390,000
Total contributed capital			$ 602,000
Retained earnings			627,000
Accumulated other comprehensive income (loss):			
Unrealized decrease in value of available-for-sale securities			(41,000)
Total contributed capital, retained earnings, and accumulated other comprehensive income			$1,188,000
Less: Treasury stock (1,000 shares of common stock at cost, acquired on 2/3/2015)			(20,000)
Total Shareholders' Equity			$1,168,000

The company engaged in the following stock transactions during 2016:

Jan.	4	Paid the semiannual dividend on the outstanding preferred stock and a $1.60 per share annual dividend on the outstanding common stock. These dividends had been declared on December 1, 2015.
	5	Issued 500 shares of preferred stock at $110 per share.
	22	Issued 4,000 shares of common stock at $23 per share.
Apr.	2	Reissued 700 shares of treasury stock at $24 per share.
May	14	Declared a 10% stock dividend on the outstanding common stock, payable on June 29. The common stock is currently selling for $25 per share.
June	4	Declared the semiannual cash dividend on the outstanding preferred stock, payable on July 5.
	29	Issued the stock dividend declared on May 14.
July	5	Paid the cash dividend declared on June 4.
	20	Split the common stock 2-for-1 and reduced the par value to $2.50 per share.
Aug.	3	Declared a property dividend, payable to common shareholders on September 14. The dividend consists of an available-for-sale investment in 50 Drot Company bonds. The bonds had been acquired for $45,000, but have a carrying value of $30,000. The bonds are currently selling for $20,000.
Sept.	14	Paid the property dividend declared on August 3.
Dec.	3	Declared the semiannual cash dividend on the outstanding preferred stock and a $0.90 per share annual dividend on the outstanding common stock.

Required:
1. Prepare journal entries to record the preceding transactions.
2. Prepare the December 31, 2016, shareholders' equity section (assume that 2016 net income was $270,000).

P16-16 **Comprehensive** Cory Company's shareholders' equity on January 1, 2016, is as follows:
LO 16.1
LO 16.2
LO 16.3

Preferred stock, 8%, $100 par, callable at $116	$100,000
Preferred stock, 7%, $100 par	150,000
Common stock, $10 par	220,000
Additional paid-in capital on preferred stock	50,000
Additional paid-in capital on common stock	110,000
Retained earnings	182,200
	$812,200

In January 2016, Cory recalled and retired the 8% preferred stock. This stock originally had been issued for $105 per share. In April, it declared and issued a 10% stock dividend on the common stock; the stock was then selling for $16 per share. This was the only issuance of common or preferred stock during the year. During November, Cory reacquired as treasury stock 1,000 shares of its common stock at $18 per share (it uses the cost method for treasury stock). State law requires a restriction of retained earnings equal to the cost of all treasury shares held. Cory discloses this

(continued)

restriction by means of a note to the financial statements. In December, the annual cash dividends on the outstanding preferred stock and a $1 per share cash dividend on the outstanding common stock were declared and paid. At the end of December, net income of $87,000 was closed from Income Summary to Retained Earnings. During the year-end audit, it was found that two errors had been made during 2015 for both financial reporting and income tax reporting. First, depreciation on certain machinery in the amount of $10,000 was inadvertently omitted. Second, a mathematical mistake was made in the calculation of the accumulated depreciation related to the sale of equipment. Consequently, the reduction in accumulated depreciation and the amount of the gain recognized were both understated by $8,000. Both errors are considered material. Cory has been subject to a 30% income tax rate for the past several years.

Required:
1. Prepare journal entries to record the preceding transactions.
2. Prepare Cory's statement of retained earnings and any related notes to its financial statements for the year ended December 31, 2016.

P16-17 **Ratio Analysis** Graham Railways Inc. is evaluating its operations and provides the following information:
LO 16.4

	2016	2015	2014
Net income	$ 62,854	$ 45,852	$ 35,456
Total assets at year-end	$381,500	$246,250	$145,490
Common shares outstanding	56,000	49,000	41,000
Weighted average number of common shares outstanding	52,500	47,500	41,000
Total liabilities at year-end	$206,100	$117,800	$ 52,690
Dividends per common share	$0.40	$0.35	$0.25
Common shareholders' equity at year-end	$175,400	$128,450	$ 92,800
Ending share price	$24.20	$18.75	$14.40

Required:
For each of the years 2014 through 2016, calculate Graham Railways's earnings per share and dividend yield ratio. The company has no preferred stock or other potentially dilutive securities outstanding.

P16-18 **Income Statement and Basic EPS** Mantego Company listed the following selected pretax items as of December
LO 16.4 31, 2016:

	Debit	Credit
Preferred stock, 8%, $100 par, nonconvertible		$ 60,000
Common stock, $5 par		90,000
Sales		206,000
Cost of goods sold	$131,000	
Gain on disposal of discontinued Division B		8,000
Operating expenses	19,250	
Loss from operations of discontinued Division B	20,000	

Additional information:
The preferred shares had been outstanding the entire year; annual dividends were declared and paid in 2016. During 2016, 2,000 common shares were issued on July 2, and 6,000 common shares were issued on November 3. Common dividends of $12,500 were declared and paid in 2016. The company is subject to a 30% income tax rate.

Required:
Prepare Mantego's 2016 income statement (multiple-step) and the related note.

P16-19 **Comparative Income Statements and Basic EPS** Anoka Company reported the following selected items in the
LO 16.4 shareholders' equity section of its balance sheet on December 31, 2016, and 2017:

	December 31,	
	2017	2016
Preferred stock, 7%, 100 par, nonconvertible	$50,000	$50,000
Common stock, $10 par	84,000	70,000

In addition, it listed the following selected pretax items as of December 31, 2016 and 2017:

	December 31, 2017		December 31, 2016	
	Debit	Credit	Debit	Credit
Sales		$140,000		$124,300
Income from discontinued operations		—		6,000
Cost of goods sold	$80,000		$75,000	
Operating expenses	20,000		18,000	
Loss from discontinued operations	9,000		—	

The preferred shares were outstanding during all of 2016 and 2017; annual dividends were declared and paid in each year. During 2016, 2,000 common shares were sold for cash on October 4. During 2017, a 20% stock dividend was declared and issued in early May. At the end of 2016 and 2017, the common stock was selling for $25.75 and $32.20, respectively. The company is subject to a 30% income tax rate.

Required:
1. Prepare the comparative 2016 and 2017 income statements (multiple-step), and the related note that would appear in Anoka's 2017 annual report.
2. **Next Level** Compute the price/earnings ratio for 2017. How does this compare to 2016? Why is it different?

P16-20 **Earnings per Share** Winona Company began 2016 with 10,000 shares of $10 par common stock and 2,000
LO 16.5 shares of 9.4%, $100 par, convertible preferred stock outstanding. On April 2 and June 1, respectively, the company issued 2,000 and 6,000 additional shares of common stock. On November 16, Winona declared a 2-for-1 stock split. The preferred stock was issued in 2015. Each share of preferred stock is currently convertible into 4 shares of common stock. To date, no preferred stock has been converted. Current dividends have been paid on both preferred and common stock. Net income after taxes for 2016 totaled $109,800. The company is subject to a 30% income tax rate. The common stock sold at an average market price of $24 per share during 2016.

Required:
1. Prepare supporting calculations for Winona and compute its:
   a. basic earnings per share
   b. diluted earnings per share
2. Show how Winona would report the earnings per share on its 2016 income statement. Include an accompanying note to the financial statements.

3. **Next Level** Assume Winona uses IFRS. Discuss what Winona would do differently for computing earnings per share, and then repeat Requirement 1 under IFRS.

P16-21 **Impact on EPS, Rankings, and Computations** Waseca Company had 5 convertible securities outstanding dur-
LO 16.4 ing all of 2016. It paid the appropriate interest (and amortized any related premium or discount using the straight-
LO 16.5 line method) and dividends on each security during 2016. Each of the convertible securities is described in the following table:

Security	Description
10.2% bonds	$200,000 face value. Issued at par. Each $1,000 bond is convertible into 28 shares of common stock.
12.0% bonds	$160,000 face value. Issued at 110. Premium being amortized over 20-year life. Each $1,000 bond is convertible into 47 shares of common stock.
9.0% bonds	$200,000 face value. Issued at 95. Discount being amortized over 10-year life. Each $1,000 bond is convertible into 44 shares of common stock.
8.3% preferred stock	$120,000 par value. Issued at 108. Each $100 par preferred stock is convertible into 3.9 shares of common stock.
7.5% preferred stock	$180,000 par value. Issued at par. Each $100 par preferred stock is convertible into 6 shares of common stock.

(continued)

Additional data:

Net income for 2016 totaled $119,460. The weighted average number of common shares outstanding during 2016 was 40,000 shares. No share options or warrants are outstanding. The effective corporate income tax rate is 30%.

Required:
1. Prepare a schedule that lists the impact of the assumed conversion of each convertible security on diluted earnings per share.
2. Prepare a ranking of the order in which each of the convertible securities should be included in diluted earnings per share.
3. Compute basic earnings per share.
4. Compute diluted earnings per share.
5. Indicate the amount(s) of the earnings per share that Waseca would report on its 2016 income statement.

P16-22 **Comprehensive: EPS** Roseau Company is preparing its annual earnings per share amounts to be disclosed on its 2016 income statement. It has collected the following information at the end of 2016:

LO 16.4
LO 16.5

1. Net income: $120,400. Included in the net income is income from continuing operations of $130,400 and a loss from discontinued operations (net of income taxes) of $10,000. Corporate income tax rate: 30%.
2. Common stock outstanding on January 1, 2016: 20,000 shares.
3. Common stock issuances during 2016: July 6, 4,000 shares; August 24, 3,000 shares.
4. Stock dividend: On October 19, 2016, the company declared a 10% stock dividend that resulted in 2,700 additional outstanding shares of common stock.
5. Common stock prices: 2016 average market price, $30 per share; 2016 ending market price, $27 per share.
6. 7% preferred stock outstanding on January 1, 2016: 1,000 shares. Terms: $100 par, nonconvertible. Current dividends have been paid. No preferred stock issued during 2016.
7. 8% convertible preferred stock outstanding on January 1, 2016: 800 shares. The stock was issued in 2015 at $130 per share. Each $100 par preferred stock is currently convertible into 1.7 shares of common stock. Current dividends have been paid. To date, no preferred stock has been converted.
8. Bonds payable outstanding on January 1, 2016: $100,000 face value. These bonds were issued several years ago at 97 and pay annual interest of 9.6%. The discount is being amortized in the amount of $300 per year. Each $1,000 bond is currently convertible into 22 shares of common stock. To date, no bonds have been converted.
9. Compensatory share options outstanding: Key executives may currently acquire 3,000 shares of common stock at $20 per share. The options were granted in 2015. To date, none have been exercised. The unrecognized compensation cost (net of tax) related to the options is $4 per share.

Required:
1. Compute the basic earnings per share. Show supporting calculations.
2. Compute the diluted earnings per share. Show supporting calculations.
3. Show how Roseau would report these earnings per share figures on its 2016 income statement. Include an explanatory note to the financial statements.

P16-23 **Convertible Securities and Earnings per Share** At the beginning of 2016, Microbee Honey Corporation had 90,000 shares of $1.00 par value common stock issued and outstanding. During 2016, the following common stock transactions have taken place:

LO 16.5

Feb. 1,	Issued 40,000 shares at a price of $32 per share.
Apr. 1,	Declared and distributed a 10% stock dividend. The market price on that date was $36.
June 1	Repurchased 16,000 shares for the treasury at a price of $33 per share.
Aug. 1	Reissued 5,000 shares from the treasury at a price of $45 per share.
Nov. 30	Declared a 2-for-1 stock split. The market price on that date was $56.

For 2016, Microbee reported $575,000 of net income. In addition, the company had the following securities outstanding:

1. 22,000 stock options issued on March 1, 2016. The stock options have an exercise price of $15, and none had been exercised as of December 31, 2016.
2. 5,000 shares of $100 par value, 12% cumulative convertible preferred stock. Each share of preferred stock is convertible into 15 shares of common stock. The shares were issued in 2012.
3. $600,000 of 9% convertible bonds issued at par. The bonds were issued in 2014 and as of December 31, 2016, none had been converted into common shares. Each $1,000 bond is convertible into 32 shares of common stock.

All option exercise prices and conversion ratios have been adjusted for stock dividends and stock splits that occurred during the year.

Microbee has an effective tax rate of 36% and had an average stock price during 2016 of $37 adjusted for stock splits and dividends.

Required:
1. Calculate basic earnings per share for Microbee for 2016.
2. Calculate tentative DEPS and incremental DEPS for each dilutive security.
3. What would Microbee report for basic and diluted earnings per share for 2016?

P16-24 **Comprehensive: EPS** Frost Company has accumulated the following information relevant to its 2016 earnings per share.
LO 16.4
LO 16.5
1. Net income for 2016: $150,500.
2. Bonds payable: On January 1, 2016, the company had issued 10%, $200,000 bonds at 110. The premium is being amortized in the amount of $1,000 per year. Each $1,000 bond is currently convertible into 22 shares of common stock. To date, no bonds have been converted.
3. Bonds payable: On December 31, 2014, the company had issued $540,000 of 5.8% bonds at par. Each $1,000 bond is currently convertible into 11.6 shares of common stock. To date, no bonds have been converted.
4. Preferred stock: On July 3, 2015, the company had issued 3,800 shares of 7.5%, $100 par, preferred stock at $108 per share. Each share of preferred stock is currently convertible into 2.45 shares of common stock. To date, no preferred stock has been converted and no additional shares of preferred stock have been issued. The current dividends have been paid.
5. Common stock: At the beginning of 2016, 25,000 shares were outstanding. On August 3, 7,000 additional shares were issued. During September, a 20% stock dividend was declared and issued. On November 30, 2,000 shares were reacquired as treasury stock.
6. Compensatory share options: Options to acquire common stock at a price of $33 per share were outstanding during all of 2016. Currently, 4,000 shares may be acquired. To date, no options have been exercised. The unrecognized compensation cost (net of tax) related to these options is $5 per share.
7. Miscellaneous: Stock market prices on common stock averaged $41 per share during 2016, and the 2016 ending stock market price was $40 per share. The corporate income tax rate is 30%.

Required:
1. Compute the basic earnings per share. Show supporting calculations.
2. Compute the diluted earnings per share. Show supporting calculations.
3. Indicate which earnings per share figure(s) Frost would report on its 2016 income statement.

P16-25 **Earnings per Share** The controller of Red Lake Corporation has requested assistance in determining income, basic earnings per share, and diluted earnings per share for presentation on the company's income statement for the year ended September 30, 2017. As currently calculated, Red Lake's net income is $540,000 for fiscal year 2016–2017.
LO 16.4
LO 16.5

AICPA Adapted

Your working papers disclose the following opening balances and transactions in the company's capital stock accounts during the year:
1. Common stock (at October 1, 2016, stated value $10, authorized 300,000 shares; effective December 1, 2016, stated value $5, authorized 600,000 shares):
   Balance, October 1, 2016—issued and outstanding 60,000 shares
   December 1, 2016—60,000 shares issued in a 2-for-1 stock split
   December 1, 2016—280,000 shares (stated value $5) issued at $39 per share
2. Treasury stock—common:
   March 3, 2017—purchased 40,000 shares at $38 per share
   April 1, 2017—sold 40,000 shares at $40 per share
3. Noncompensatory stock purchase warrants, Series A (initially, each warrant was exchangeable with $60 for 1 common share; effective December 1, 2016, each warrant became exchangeable for 2 common shares at $30 per share):
   October 1, 2016—25,000 warrants issued at $6 each
4. Noncompensatory stock purchase warrants, Series B (each warrant is exchangeable with $40 for 1 common share):
   April 1, 2017—20,000 warrants authorized and issued at $10 each

(continued)

5. First mortgage bonds, 5½%, due 2026 (nonconvertible; priced to yield 5% when issued):
   Balance October 1, 2016—authorized, issued, and outstanding—the face value of $1,400,000
6. Convertible debentures, 7%, due 2033 (initially, each $1,000 bond was convertible at any time until maturity into 20 common shares; effective December 1, 2016, the conversion rate became 40 shares for each bond):
   October 1, 2016—authorized and issued at their face value (no premium or discount) of $2,400,000

The following table shows the average market prices for the company's securities during 2016–2017:

	Average for Year Ended September 30, 2017
Common stock	37.50*
First mortgage bonds	87
Convertible debentures	115
Series A warrants	15
Series B warrants	9½

*$Adjusted for stock split

Required:
Prepare a schedule computing:
1. the basic earnings per share
2. the diluted earnings per share that should be presented on Red Lake's income statement for the year ended September 30, 2017

A supporting schedule computing the numbers of shares to be used in these computations should also be prepared. Assume an income tax rate of 30%.

P16-26 **Earnings per Share** Olmstead Corporation's capital structure is as follows:

LO 16.4
LO 16.5
AICPA
Adapted

	December 31	
	2016	2015
Outstanding shares of:		
Common stock	336,000	300,000
Nonconvertible preferred stock	10,000	10,000
8% convertible bonds	$1,000,000	$1,000,000

The following additional information is available:
1. On September 1, 2016, Olmstead sold 36,000 additional shares of common stock.
2. Net income for the year ended December 31, 2016, was $750,000.
3. During 2016, Olmstead paid dividends of $3 per share on its nonconvertible preferred stock.
4. The 8% convertible bonds are convertible into 40 shares of common stock for each $1,000 bond.
5. Unexercised compensatory share options to purchase 30,000 shares of common stock at $20.50 per share were outstanding at the beginning and end of 2016. The average market price of Olmstead's common stock was $36 per share during 2016. The market price was $33 per share at December 31, 2016. The unrecognized compensation cost (net of tax) related to the options is $2 per share.
6. Warrants to purchase 20,000 shares of common stock at $38 per share were attached to the preferred stock at the time of issuance. The warrants, which expire on December 31, 2021, were outstanding at December 31, 2016.
7. Olmstead's effective income tax rate was 30% for 2015 and 2016.

Required:
(Show supporting computations in good form, and round earnings per share to the nearest penny.)
1. Compute the number of shares that should be used for the computation of basic earnings per share for the year ended December 31, 2016.
2. Compute the basic earnings per share for the year ended December 31, 2016.
3. Compute the number of shares that should be used for the computation of diluted earnings per share for the year ended December 31, 2016.
4. Compute the diluted earnings per share for the year ended December 31, 2016.

CASES

COMMUNICATION

C16-1 **Dividends and Journal Entries**
LO 16.1
AICPA Adapted

Problems may be encountered in accounting for transactions involving the shareholders' equity section of the balance sheet.

Required:
1. Explain the significance of the four dates that are important in accounting for cash dividends to shareholders. State the journal entry, if any, needed at each date.
2. Assume retained earnings can be used for stock dividends distributable in shares. What is the effect of an ordinary 10% common stock dividend on retained earnings and total shareholders' equity?

C16-2 **Stock Dividends and Splits**
LO 16.1
AICPA Adapted

Stock splits and stock dividends may be used by a corporation to change the number of shares of its stock outstanding.

Required:
1. Explain what is meant by a stock split effected in the form of a dividend.
2. From an accounting viewpoint, explain how a stock split effected in the form of a dividend differs from an ordinary stock dividend.
3. How should a stock dividend that has been declared but not yet issued be classified in a statement of financial position? Why?

C16-3 **Earnings per Share**
LO 16.4
LO 16.5
AICPA Adapted

Earnings per share (EPS) is the most featured single financial statistic about modern corporations. Daily published quotations of stock prices also include a "times earnings" figure for many securities that is based on EPS. Often, the focus of analysts' discussions will be on the EPS of the corporations receiving their attention.

Required:
1. Explain how dividends or dividend requirements on any class of preferred stock that may be outstanding affect the computation of basic EPS.
2. One of the technical procedures applicable in diluted EPS computations is the "treasury stock method." Briefly describe the circumstances under which it might be appropriate to apply the treasury stock method.
3. In the case of convertible bonds that are assumed to be converted and are dilutive, explain how they are handled for purposes of diluted EPS computations.

C16-4 **Complex Capital Structure**
LO 16.5
AICPA Adapted

The earnings per share data required of a company depend on the nature of its capital structure. A corporation may have a simple capital structure and compute only "basic earnings per share" or it may have a complex capital structure and have to compute basic earnings per share and "diluted earnings per share."

Required:
Define the term *complex capital structure* and discuss the disclosures (both financial and explanatory) necessary for earnings per share when a corporation has a complex capital structure.

CREATIVE AND CRITICAL THINKING

C16-5 **Dividends and Treasury Stock**
LO 16.1
AICPA Adapted

Brady Company has 30,000 shares of $10 par value common stock authorized and 20,000 shares issued and outstanding. On August 13, 2016, Brady purchased 1,000 shares of treasury stock for $12 per share. Brady uses the cost method to account for treasury stock. On September 14, 2016, Brady sold 500 shares of the treasury stock for $14 per share.

In October 2016, Brady declared and distributed 2,000 shares as a stock dividend from unissued shares when the market value of the common stock was $16 per share.

On December 21, 2016, Brady declared a $1 per share cash dividend, payable on January 11, 2017, to shareholders of record on December 31, 2016.

Required:
1. How should Brady account for the cash dividend, and how would it affect Brady's balance sheet at December 31, 2016? Explain why.

(continued)

2. How should Brady account for the stock dividend, and how would it affect Brady's shareholders' equity at December 31, 2016? Explain why.
3. How should Brady account for the purchase and sale of the treasury stock, and how should the treasury stock be presented in Brady's balance sheet at December 31, 2016?

C16-6 **Convertible Securities**
LO 16.5 Public enterprises are required to present earnings per share data on the face of the income statement.
AICPA Adapted

Required:
In regard to the computation of diluted earnings per share, discuss:
1. the effect of dilutive convertible securities
2. the effect of antidilutive convertible securities

C16-7 **Share Options and EPS**
LO 16.5 Jones Company has adopted a traditional share option plan for its officers and other employees. This plan is properly considered a compensatory plan.
AICPA Adapted

Required:
Explain how this plan will affect diluted earnings per share.

C16-8 **Analyzing Coca-Cola's Retained Earnings and EPS**
Obtain **The Coca-Cola Company**'s 2013 annual report either using the "Investor Relations" portion of its web site (do a Web search for Coca-Cola investor relations) or go to http://www.sec.gov and click "Search for company filings" under "Filings and Forms (EDGAR)."

Required:
1. What does the company call its retained earnings? What was the amount at the end of 2013?
2. What was the balance of accumulated other comprehensive income on December 31, 2013? What caused it to change during 2013 and by what amounts?
3. What was the company's basic net income per share for 2013? How much preferred dividends were subtracted in the computation of this income per share? What was the average number of common shares outstanding used in the computation of this income per share? What was the company's diluted net income per share for 2013? How does this amount compare to 2012? What potential common shares were included?
4. What were the dividends per share and in total for 2013?
5. Compute the return on shareholders' equity for 2013. How does this compare to 2012 (the shareholders' equity was $31,635 million at the end of 2011)?

C16-9 **Ethics and EPS Adjustment**
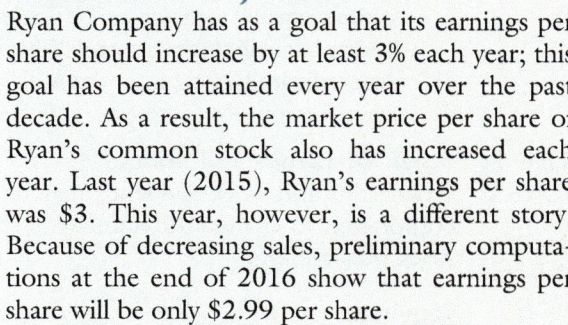
Ryan Company has as a goal that its earnings per share should increase by at least 3% each year; this goal has been attained every year over the past decade. As a result, the market price per share of Ryan's common stock also has increased each year. Last year (2015), Ryan's earnings per share was $3. This year, however, is a different story. Because of decreasing sales, preliminary computations at the end of 2016 show that earnings per share will be only $2.99 per share.

You are the accountant for Ryan. Ryan's controller, Jim Nastic, has come to you with some suggestions. He says, "I've noticed that the decrease in revenues has been primarily related to credit sales. Since we have fewer credit sales, I believe we are justified in reducing our bad debts expense from 4% to 2% of net sales. I also think that because of the decreased sales, we won't use our factory equipment as much, so we can extend its estimated remaining life from 10 to 15 years for computing our straight-line depreciation expense. Based on my calculations, if we make these changes, Ryan's 2016 earnings per share will be $3.06. This will sure make our shareholders happy, not to mention our CEO. You may even get a promotion. What do you think?"

Required:
From financial reporting and ethical perspectives, prepare a response to Jim regarding his suggestions.

USING CODIFICATION

C16-10 Researching GAAP

Situation

In 2016, its first year of operations, Kanbec Corporation appropriately reported basic earnings per share of $1.05 on its income statement. During 2017, the company instituted a share option plan and is required to report both basic and diluted earnings per share of $1.12 and $0.98, respectively, on its 2017 income statement. In its 2017 annual report, Kanbec presents comparative income statements for 2016 and 2017.

Directions

Research the related generally accepted accounting principles and prepare a short memo to Kanbec's president that explains how to report the 2016 and 2017 comparative earnings per share in its 2017 annual report. Cite your reference and applicable paragraph numbers.

PART 5

SPECIAL TOPICS IN FINANCIAL REPORTING

CHAPTER 17
Advanced Issues in Revenue Recognition

CHAPTER 18
Accounting for Income Taxes

CHAPTER 19
Accounting for Postretirement Benefits

CHAPTER 20
Accounting for Leases

CHAPTER 21
The Statement of Cash Flows

CHAPTER 22
Accounting for Changes and Errors

CHAPTER 17

ADVANCED ISSUES IN REVENUE RECOGNITION

Always Be Selling

Starbucks recognizes revenue from multiple sources each day. In exchange for fees and royalties, Starbucks licenses its name, trademarks, logos, products, and methods to licensees who own and operate coffee shops. It also distributes and sells its products to retail outlets such as grocery stores as well as to food service companies that provide Starbucks's coffee and tea to hotels, dormitories, corporate cafeterias, and other organizations. In addition, Starbucks is involved in a partnership that produces and sells ready-to-drink versions of its products. However, as shown below, the majority of its 2015 revenues (79.3%) come from the coffee shops that Starbucks owns and operates, which sell everything from coffee and tea to CDs. In these stores, the bulk of the company's revenue is recognized at the point of sale, which, for most companies, is the normal point of revenue recognition.

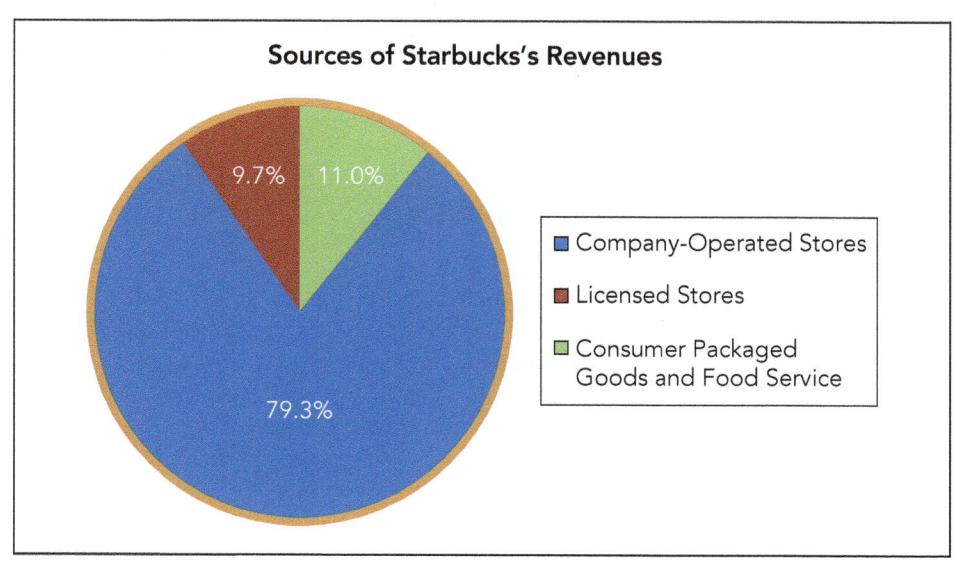

LEARNING OBJECTIVES

After reading this chapter you will be able to

LO 17.1 Understand and explain the core principle of revenue recognition.

LO 17.2 Describe how a company identifies a contract with a customer.

LO 17.3 Examine how a company identifies the performance obligations in a contract.

LO 17.4 Understand how a company determines the transaction price of a contract.

LO 17.5 Describe how to allocate the transaction price to the performance obligations in a contract.

LO 17.6 Account for revenue as the company satisfies the performance obligations in the contract.

LO 17.7 Describe the company's required revenue recognition disclosures.

LO 17.8 Understand the accounting for long-term contracts in which revenue is recognized over time versus at a point in time.

However, the point of sale is not when all of Starbucks's revenues are recognized. Many customers purchase coffee and other products by using a Starbucks's Stored Value Card which they have preloaded with cash. In these cases, the customers have transferred money to Starbucks prior to the sale of coffee. Because Starbucks has not yet satisfied its performance obligation, it cannot yet recognize revenue. Instead, it reports a liability to the customer which will be satisfied when the customer redeems the card for a cup of coffee or other products. Stored value cards have become a popular gift. In 2014, Americans spent over $124 billion on stored value or gift cards.[1] In addition to giving them as gifts, customers also purchase stored value cards for personal convenience. One issue for companies when determining revenue from stored value cards is that the balance of the card may never be fully redeemed if the customer loses or forgets about the card (referred to as *breakage* or *spillage*). The issue of sold but never fully redeemed stored value cards creates an interesting but difficult accounting issue for the companies issuing the cards. When should a company remove the liability and recognize revenue from stored value cards that it expects might never be redeemed in full? Starbucks recognizes breakage revenue when, based on historical experience, it deems the likelihood of redemption to be remote. In 2015, Starbucks recognized $39.3 million of breakage revenue.

Revenue is a key performance metric used by investors and other stakeholders in assessing a company's past performance, future growth potential, and financial health. Therefore, to aid financial statement users in understanding a company's operations, a company's revenue recognition policy must faithfully represent the revenues it is generating.

For many financial statement users, revenue is one of the most important and carefully scrutinized items reported in the financial statements. In this chapter, we discuss the conceptual and practical issues of revenue recognition. We first provide an overview of the 5-step revenue recognition model. While many revenue transactions are straightforward, others can be quite complex. Therefore, we examine each step in detail, with emphasis on applying these concepts to different scenarios (e.g., recognizing revenue when a contract contains a number of performance obligations and when performance obligations are satisfied over time). Finally, we examine the presentation and disclosure requirements designed to help users understand the nature, amount, timing, and uncertainty of revenue and cash flows generated from contracts with customers.

LEARNING OBJECTIVE 17.1
Understand and explain the core principle of revenue recognition.

WHEN CAN COMPANIES RECOGNIZE REVENUE?

After over 10 years of discussion, exposure drafts, and comment letters, in May 2014, the FASB and the IASB completed their revenue recognition project and issued *Revenue from Contracts with Customers*, a comprehensive, principles-based revenue recognition model that specifies how and when companies should recognize revenue.[2] The main goals of the revenue project were relatively straightforward—convergence, consistency,

---

[1] Conference Executive Board, "Gift Cards State of the Union 2014," CEB Tower Group, https://www.cebglobal.com/financial-services/tower-group/gift-cards.html.
[2] FASB ASC 606: Revenue from Contracts with Customers and IFRS 15, Revenue from Contracts with Customers.

and transparency. Both the FASB and the IASB recognized that companies' revenue numbers are of primary importance to users of financial statements in assessing company performance. In addition, the two Boards recognized that, in a global economy, it was important to have a revenue number that was comparable across national borders. The new standard is based on **the core principle that a company should recognize revenue to depict the transfer of promised goods or services to customers in an amount that reflects the consideration to which the entity expects to be entitled in exchange for those goods or services**.

The FASB defines **revenues** as follows:

> Revenues are increases in assets or settlements of liabilities during a period from delivering or producing goods, rendering services, or other activities that are the company's ongoing major or central operations.[3]

This definition implies an asset–liability approach to revenue recognition in which revenues are recognized and measured based on changes in assets and liabilities. In general, when a company enters into a sales contract with a customer, it receives the right to consideration from the customer while also assuming a performance obligation to transfer goods or services to the customer. Revenues are recognized when the company's net position (contract assets minus contract liabilities) in the revenue contract increases as it satisfies a performance obligation. Therefore, revenues represent increases in assets (future economic benefits from increases in cash, accounts receivable, or other types of assets) or settlements of liabilities (such as performance obligations to customers who have paid in advance for goods or services) that occur as a result of the company's ongoing primary operating activities in delivering goods and services to customers. Thus, revenues measure the *accomplishments* of the operating activities during the accounting period.

The 5-Step Revenue Recognition Model

The FASB provides a 5-step model for evaluating when a company should recognize revenue. Exhibit 17.1 (p. 17-4) shows the five steps that companies must undertake to achieve the core principle.

The five steps appear straightforward; however, each step requires a systematic analysis of the terms and conditions of the contract with the customer that involves professional judgment. The FASB believes that the application of the revenue recognition model will bring discipline compared to the "earned and realized" approach to revenue recognition that was previously used, resulting in a more representationally faithful and consistent recognition of revenue.

Companies must begin to apply the new standard in fiscal years starting after December 15, 2016. However, the FASB allows firms to defer adoption for one year, if needed. Companies may choose to apply the new standard to prior years using either a retrospective approach or a cumulative effect approach. Under the retrospective approach, companies would apply the new revenue recognition methods in each fiscal period presented in the financial report, with a prior period adjustment to retained earnings for the cumulative effect of the new standard on all prior years. Under the cumulative effect approach, companies would apply the new standard only to the current period. However, companies would also recognize the cumulative effects of the new standard on prior years presented in the financial report as a prior period adjustment to retained earnings in the current period.

The new revenue recognition standard applies to all contracts with customers. However, it excludes certain types of contracts, transactions, and arrangements that are within

---

[3] FASB ASC 606-10-20: Revenues from Contracts with Customers, Overall, Glossary.

EXHIBIT 17.1 5-step Revenue Recognition Model

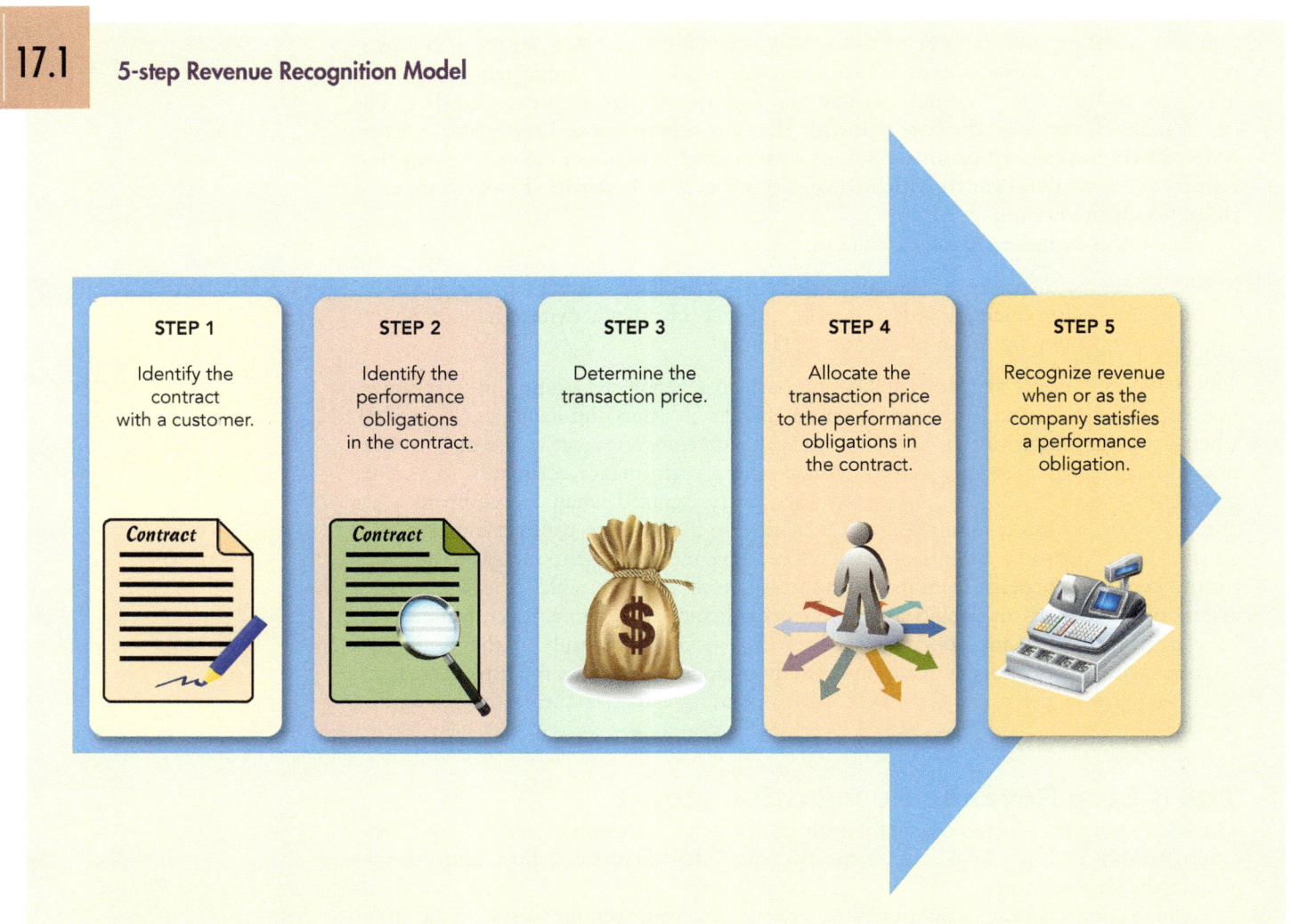

the scope of other standards. Specifically, the following types of contracts are not covered by the new revenue standard:

- leases
- insurance contracts
- financial instruments
- guarantees
- nonmonetary exchanges between two companies in the same line of business in order to facilitate sales to customers

In addition, the revenue recognition standard excludes items such as interest and dividends that are part of a company's ordinary activities.

While the revenue recognition standard applies to every individual contract with each customer, for practical purposes companies may apply this guidance to a portfolio of contracts with similar characteristics. Such an approach is acceptable if the company reasonably expects the revenue recognized under a portfolio approach to not differ materially from the revenue recognized under an individual contract approach. For example, Starbucks sells coffee through its retail coffee shops under the same sales terms and conditions to a large number of individual customers every day. Therefore, it is appropriate for Starbucks to apply the revenue recognition standard to its portfolio of retail customers. Similarly, Starbucks generates revenues from many different licensees around the world, and so it is appropriate for Starbucks to apply the new standard to its portfolio of licensees.

> ### GOT IT?
>
> **17-1** What is the core principle of revenue recognition?
>
> **17-2** How does the FASB define revenues?
>
> **17-3** When a company recognizes revenue during a period, what does it also recognize in its balance sheet?
>
> **17-4** Identify the five steps in the revenue recognition model.

HOW DO YOU IDENTIFY A CONTRACT WITH A CUSTOMER?

LEARNING OBJECTIVE 17.2
Describe how a company identifies a contract with a customer.

The first step in the revenue recognition model requires identifying both the contract and the customer. A **customer** is a party that has entered into a contract with a company to obtain goods or services that are an output of that company's ordinary activities. A **contract** is an agreement between two or more parties that creates enforceable rights and obligations. A contract may be written, oral, or implied by customary business practices. For example, when purchasing a cup of coffee at a Starbucks's location, it is not required that a customer sit down with a barista and sign a formal contract to get a coffee. The exchange of money for coffee implies a contract. Therefore, the existence of a contract depends upon the facts and circumstances of each transaction.

A company should only apply the revenue recognition standard to contracts that meet all of the following criteria:

- All of the parties to the contract approve the contract (in writing, orally, or by implication) and commit to performing their obligations under the contract.
- The company is able to identify each party's rights regarding the goods or services to be transferred.
- The company is able to identify the payment terms for the goods or services to be transferred. This does not imply that the transaction price has to be fixed or explicitly stated. In fact, the transaction price may vary due to discounts or rebates.
- The contract has commercial substance. This means that the contract must change the timing, amount, or probability of the company's future cash flows.
- It is probable that the company will collect the consideration to which it is entitled in exchange for the goods or services that it will transfer to the customer.

What Are the Issues in Identifying a Contract?

While identifying a contract seems quite simple, a number of significant issues arise such as accounting for termination rights, determining when contracts should be combined, accounting for contract modifications, and examining collectability.

Termination Rights A contract does not qualify for revenue recognition and no revenue can be recognized if the contract is wholly unperformed and either party can unilaterally cancel the contract before performance without compensating the other party. A **wholly unperformed contract** is one in which the seller has not transferred the goods or services to the customer nor has it received, or is entitled to receive, consideration in exchange for the promised goods or services. Therefore, no revenue recognition can occur until performance under the contract occurs.

Example On January 1, 2018, Harper Company enters into a contract to deliver goods to Young Corporation for $100,000. The contract terms allow cancellation without penalty by either party at any time prior to delivery of the goods. For this reason, the contract does not qualify for revenue recognition and no journal entry is required on

January 1, 2018, because neither party has performed under the contract (e.g., Harper has not delivered the goods and Young has not paid for the goods) and the contract can be unilaterally cancelled without compensation to the other party. However, once either party performs, the appropriate journal entry must be made. If Harper delivers, then Harper should recognize an account receivable and revenue; if Young pays, then Harper should recognize cash and a deferred revenue liability.

Combining Contracts While many sales transactions involve a single contract, there may be legal or commercial reasons to use multiple contracts with a customer. A company must combine two or more contracts and account for them as a single contract if it enters into the contracts at or near the same time with the same customer[4] and one or more of the following criteria are met:

- The company negotiates the contracts as a package with a single commercial objective.
- The amount of consideration to be paid in one contract is dependent upon the price or performance of the other contract.
- All or some of the goods or services promised in the contracts comprise a single performance obligation.

The key objective is to combine contracts when the economics of the revenues to be recognized from the transaction can only be understood with reference to the arrangement as a whole.

Example Suppose Willard Company enters into a contract to deliver 10,000 pairs of running shoes to Go The Distance, a regional chain of retail stores for runners. At the same time, and because Go The Distance enters into such a large contract, Willard signs a separate contract for $10,000 to deliver, stock shelves, and set up retail displays for the shoes in each of the Go The Distance retail locations. Because the separate delivery contract is negotiated at the same time as the purchase contract and represents a single commercial objective (delivery of a large order of shoes to a customer's retail locations), these two contracts should be combined for revenue recognition purposes.

Contract Modifications Companies often modify their respective rights and performance obligations during a contract. An agreed-upon change in the goods or services that are to be delivered and/or the price of the contract is referred to as a **contract modification** (or **change order** or **contract amendment**). A modification may be written, oral, or implied by customary business practices and may occur even if the seller and buyer have not agreed on how the modification will ultimately affect the scope or price of the goods or services in the contract. A contract modification may result in either a new contract that must be accounted for separately from the original contract or as part of the existing contract. Exhibit 17.2 (p. 17-7) briefly outlines the accounting for contract modifications.

The seller accounts for a contract modification as a *separate contract* if both of the following conditions are met:

- The contract modification adds promised goods or services that are *distinct*—the customer can benefit from the good or service on its own (or with other readily available goods or services) and the promised good or service is separable from other promises in the contract.
- The price of the contract increases by an amount of *consideration that reflects the entity's stand-alone selling prices* of the additional promised goods or services.

---

[4] Only contracts entered into at or near the same time can be considered for combination. Any subsequent contracts or promises made to a customer are generally accounted for as a contract modification or new contract.

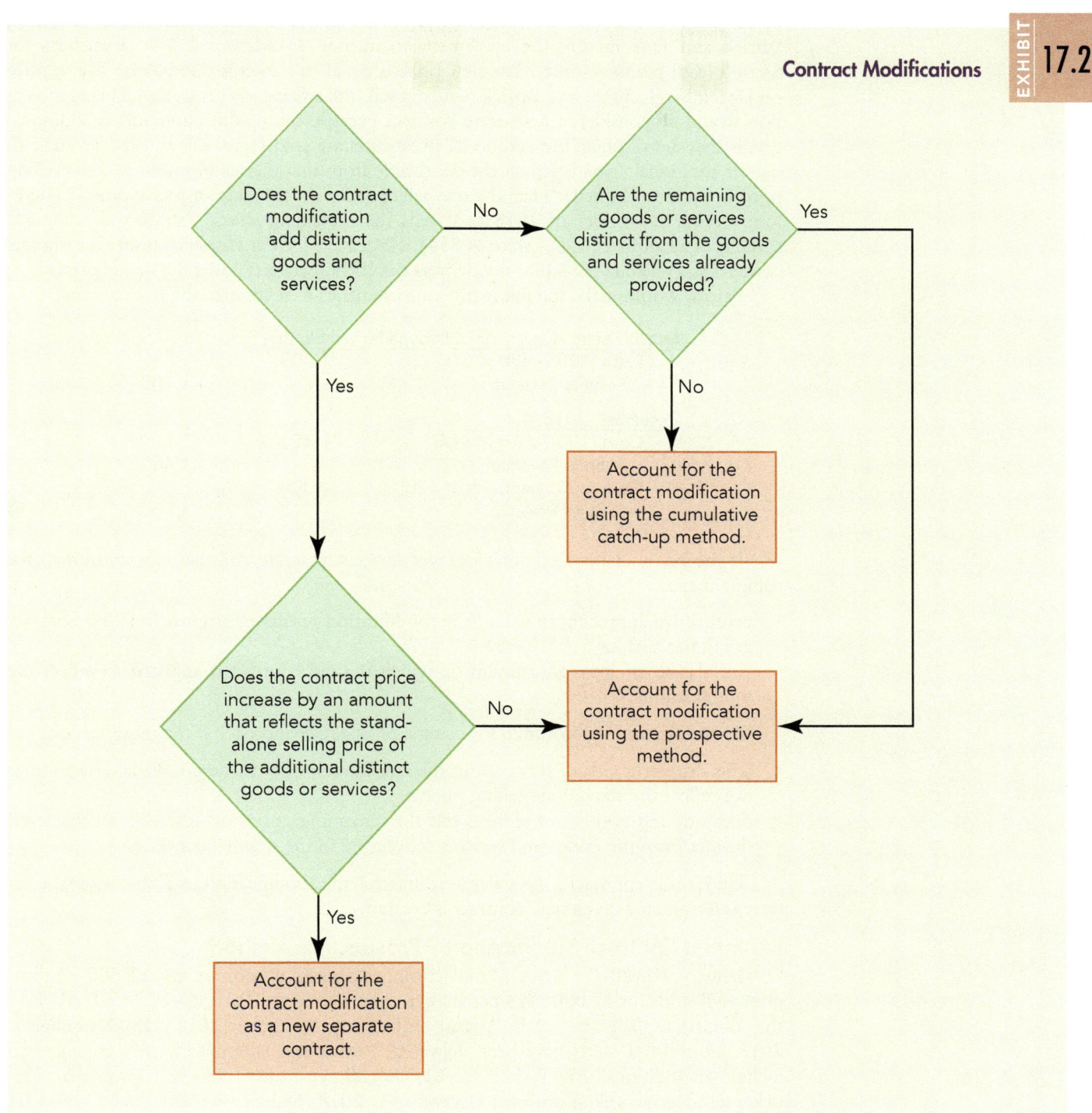

Contract Modifications — EXHIBIT 17.2

If both of these criteria are met, they suggest that the economics of the new contract stand alone from the original contract. The contract modification is therefore a separate contract, so the seller applies the revenue recognition model to the new, separate contract.

Example: Contract Modification Resulting in a Separate Contract

On January 10, 2018 Patrick Manufacturing agrees to a contract to sell 500 custom-printed T-shirts for $7,000 ($14 per shirt) to Jane Company. Patrick is expected to transfer the T-shirts to Jane starting in August and ending in December 2018, at a rate of 100 shirts per month. On December 1, 2018, after 400 T-shirts have been delivered, Patrick and Jane modify the agreement to include an additional 200 sweatshirts for $4,000 ($20 per sweatshirt). The new price is equal to Patrick's stand-alone selling price on December 1, 2018, and Patrick regularly sells the sweatshirts separately. This modification would be considered a separate contract because the modification added additional goods that are distinct (the additional sweatshirts are sold separately and the promise to deliver additional shirts is separately identifiable from the original promise) and the selling price is equal to the seller's stand-alone selling price on the date of modification. Therefore, during December of 2018 as it sells the remaining shirts, Patrick will recognize revenue of $1,400 [100 T − shirts × $14] as it delivers the last 100 shirts under the original contract and revenue of $4,000 as it delivers the 200 sweatshirts under the new contract.

Patrick would make the following journal entries to recognize the transactions:

Monthly entry August, 2018 through November 2018:
Cash (100 T-shirts × $14)   1,400
    Sales Revenue   1,400

December, 2018:
Cash (100 T-shirts × $14)   1,400
    Sales Revenue   1,400
Cash (200 sweatshirts × $20)   4,000
    Sales Revenue   4,000

If the contract modification does *not* create a separate contract it is accounted for using either a:

- prospective approach, in which the modification results in essentially a new contract going forward, or
- cumulative catch-up adjustment, in which the old contract is adjusted to reflect the modifications.

A modification is accounted for using a prospective approach if the modification:

- adds distinct goods or services but the consideration for those goods or services does not reflect the standalone selling price or
- does not add goods and services but the remaining goods or services are considered distinct from the goods and services transferred in the original contract.

Under this approach, the seller accounts for the modification as if the original contract is terminated and a new contract is created.

Example: Contract Modification—Prospective Method

On January 10, 2018 Patrick Manufacturing agrees to a contract to sell 500 custom-printed T-shirts for $7,000 ($14 per shirt) to Jane Company. Patrick is expected to deliver the T-shirts to Jane starting in August and ending December 2018. On December 1, 2018, after 400 T-shirts have been delivered, Patrick and Jane modify the agreement to include an additional 200 T-shirts for $1,000 ($5 per T-shirt), which is lower than Patrick's stand-alone selling price on December 1, 2018. Because the additonal T-shirts are distinct (the additional 200 T-shirts are distinct from the original 500 shirts) and the selling price does *not* reflect the stand-alone selling price of the goods, this modification would *not* be considered a separate contract. Instead, Patrick should use a prospective approach and account for the goods as if the original contract is terminated and a new contract is created. The $1,400 of revenue remaining from the original contract (100 shirts × $14) is combined with the revenue related to the modification ($1,000), and Patrick will recognize revenue of $8 per shirt ($2,400 total revenue ÷ 300 shirts) as it delivers shirts in December of 2018.

When the remaining goods or services that are to be delivered are *not* distinct from the goods and services transferred in the original contract, the modification is viewed as part of the existing contract (e.g., part of a single performance obligation that is partially satisfied at the date of the contract modification). In this situation, a cumulative catch-up approach is used. Under this approach, the revenue account is adjusted at the time of the contract modification for the cumulative amount of revenue that would have been recognized in prior periods if the new contract terms had existed.

Example: Contract Modification—Cumulative Catch-Up Method

Assume Patrick Manufacturing and Jane Company have entered into the same contract as in the prior examples (500 shirts at $14 per shirt for a total of $7,000). On December 1, 2018, after 400 T-shirts have been delivered, Patrick and Jane modify the agreement to reduce the price of the remaining 100 undelivered T-shirts to only $9 per shirt, which is lower than Patrick's stand-alone selling price on December 1, 2018. In this case the promise to deliver the remaining 100 T-shirts is not distinct from the original promise to deliver T-shirts. Therefore, Patrick should use a cumulative catch-up approach and account for the goods as if the original contract specified total revenues of $6,500 (an average of $13 per shirt; 400 shirts × $14 plus 100 shirts × $9]. Patrick should therefore only recognize $5,200 in revenue for the 400 shirts it has already delivered [400 shirts × $13]. Because Patrick had previously recognized $5,600 (400 shirts × $14), it must reduce revenue by $400 ($5,600 − $5,200) at the time of the modification by making the following journal entry:

Sales Revenue	400	
Unearned Revenue		400

In addition, Patrick would recognize the remaining $1,300 in revenue (100 shirts × $13 new average selling price) as it delivers the 100 remaining shirts by making the following journal entry:

Unearned Revenue	400	
Cash	900	
Sales Revenue		1,300

Collectability For a contract to be considered for potential revenue recognition, it must be probable that the seller will collect the expected consideration in exchange for the goods or services that it has promised to transfer to the customer. This requires a company to examine **collectability**. This probability assessment should reflect the customer's ability and intent to pay (the customer's credit risk), as well as any price concessions expected to be provided to the customer. Any amounts that the seller does not expect to collect result in a reduction of the contract price. The seller should use the adjusted (collectable) price as the starting point to apply the remaining steps of the revenue recognition model.

Example

In an attempt to establish a presence in a new region of the country, Wall Company entered into a contract on June 1, 2018 with Pittman Corporation and delivers 5,000 units of its product for $1,000,000.

On June 30, 2018 Wall shipped 5,000 units to Pittman and recorded the following journal entry:

Accounts Receivable	1,000,000	
Sales Revenue		1,000,000

During July 2018 there was a sudden downturn in economic conditions and Wall expects Pittman to have difficulty paying the full amount. In an effort to maintain this business relationship, Wall grants Pittman a $200,000 price concession on July 30, 2018. While a contract exists, the contract price should now be $800,000 ($1,000,000 − $200,000) and Wall would recognize the price concession by recording the following journal entry:

Sales Revenue	200,000	
Accounts Receivable		200,000

GOT IT?

17-5 What is a contract? What form can a contract take?

17-6 What is the proper accounting for a wholly unperformed contract?

17-7 If a seller enters into more than one contract with a specific customer, when should the contracts be combined and treated as a single contract?

17-8 When should a seller account for a contract modification as a separate contract?

LEARNING OBJECTIVE 17.3

Examine how a company identifies the performance obligations in a contract.

HOW DO YOU IDENTIFY PERFORMANCE OBLIGATIONS IN A CONTRACT?

A **performance obligation** is a promise in a contract with a customer to transfer goods or services. The promise may be explicit, such that a source document details the terms of the performance obligation. On the other hand, the promise may be implicit and establish a **constructive obligation** in which the seller creates a compelling expectation that it will provide the promised goods or services based on its customary business practices, published policies, or specific statements. In addition, performance obligations do not have to be legally enforceable. For example, many companies offer customer loyalty programs that may be legally cancelled at any time; however, these companies still have performance obligations with respect to these loyalty programs. Examples of performance obligations are illustrated in Exhibit 17.3.

EXHIBIT 17.3 Examples of Performance Obligations

- Building, designing, manufacturing, or creating an asset for a customer
- Transferring produced goods or reselling purchased goods
- Granting a right to use an intangible asset
- Standing ready to provide goods or services in the future
- Performing contractually agreed-upon tasks
- Arranging for another party to transfer goods or services

The proper identification of performance obligations is a critical step in applying the revenue recognition model and requires significant judgment because the satisfaction of performance obligations ultimately determines the amount and timing of revenue recognition. Many performance obligations are easy to identify, such as the promise to deliver a cup of coffee by **Starbucks**. However, many others can be complicated, such as performance obligations under contracts with upfront payments, licensing agreements, and principal–agent relationships, all of which are discussed in this section.

When examining the terms of a contract, the seller must evaluate the promised goods or services to determine whether each good or service (or bundle of goods or services) is distinct. A promised good or service is considered distinct if both of the following criteria are met:

- The promised good or service is *capable of being distinct* because the customer is able to benefit from the good or service either on its own or together with other resources that are readily available to the customer.[5] For example, if the seller normally sells the goods or services separately, that would be evidence that the customer could benefit from the goods or services on their own.
- The promised good or service is *distinct within the context of the contract* because the seller's promise to transfer the good or service to the customer is separately identifiable from other promises in the contract.

Determining whether a promise is **separately identifiable** within the contract will require significant judgment on the part of the accounting team. In making this decision the seller would conclude that the promise is separately identifiable if:

- the good or service is not significantly integrated with other promised goods or services offered by the seller, or
- the good or service does not significantly modify or customize another good or service promised in the contract, or
- the good or service is not highly dependent on, or highly interrelated with, other promised goods or services.

If the promise to deliver goods or services is distinct, the performance obligation is accounted for separately. If a promised good or service is not distinct, the seller combines it with the other promised goods or services to which it relates until it has identified a bundle of promised goods or services that is "distinct." Once a distinct bundle of goods or services is identified, a separate performance obligation exists.

Example Tung, a software company, enters into a contract with Costello Corp. for its accounting software. The contract includes the sale of the Tung accounting software license, installation and customization of the software for Costello. Tung sells the software license and installation service separately. The installation service is also performed by many other companies and results in customization of the software so that it integrates with Costello's other computing software.

To determine its performance obligations within the contract, Tung must first assess whether the two promised goods and services (software license and installation service) are distinct. While the software and installation services are capable of being distinct (e.g., software is sold separately, installation may be performed by other companies), they are not distinct within the context of this contract. Because the software is significantly modified and customized by the installation service, the software and installation service are essentially being used as inputs to produce an integrated accounting software system. This represents a significant integration of goods and services. For this reason, the software and installation services are not distinct and would be combined into one performance obligation.

Based on this analysis, Tung concludes that there is only one performance obligation in the contract.

If the installation services did not significantly modify the software, the installation service would be considered distinct within the context of the contract. In this situation, Tung would have two separate performance obligations (software license and installation services). ■

Upfront Payments

It is common for companies to receive **upfront payments**—payments from customers before a product or service is delivered. These upfront payments are often nonrefundable and labeled as setup fees, activation fees, initiation fees, or membership fees. In some

---

[5] Readily available resources are goods or services that are sold separately by a company or others in the market, as well as resources that the customer has already obtained.

situations, the cash payment may be for goods or services to be redeemed in the future at the customer's request (e.g., gift cards). In other situations, upfront payments are for goods or services to be delivered in the future, such as fares for flights or cruises, season tickets for entertainment events, insurance premiums, advertising, rent, and others. When a company receives an upfront payment, it must determine the performance obligation to which the upfront fee relates. Revenue should not be recognized until the performance obligation is satisfied.

Example: Upfront Initiation Fees

Mill Health Club enters into contracts with customers for one year of access to its gym, swimming pool, and racquetball courts for $1,200 per year. Mill also charges a $180 nonrefundable initiation fee to compensate for the administrative tasks to register the customer. Registering the customer is not considered a performance obligation because it does not transfer a good or service to a customer. Instead, Mill's performance obligation is to provide the customer the right to access its facilities. Because this performance obligation is satisfied over time, the upfront fee is recognized on a straight-line basis over the 1-year contract period. Similarly, the $1,200 fee is recognized as revenue of $100 each month of the contract period.

In this scenario Mill would make the following journal entries:

At the time of sale:		
Cash	1,380	
Unearned Revenue		1,380
Monthly entry:		
Unearned Revenue	115	
Sales Revenue ($1,380 ÷ 12)		115

Assume, however that Mill allows customers to renew their membership without having to pay another initiation fee upon renewal. Further, Mill determines that its customers, on average, remain members for 5 years. Mill determines the total transaction price of $6,180 [$180 upfront fee + ($1,200 per year × 5 years)] and allocates it evenly over the 5-year expected contract length. Therefore, Mill would recognize revenue of $1,236 per year ($6,180 ÷ 5 years).[6] In this case the $180 initiation fee would be recognized as unearned revenue when received and allocated to revenue over the expected contract period.

Licensing

As we discussed at the beginning of the chapter, **Starbucks** receives 9.7% of its total revenue from **licensing** agreements. Under these agreements, Starbucks licenses its trademarks and sells product to licensed stores, grocery companies, and food service accounts in exchange for payments. It describes the arrangement in the following manner:

> **Licensed Store Revenues**
> Licensed store revenues consist of product and equipment sales to licensees, as well as royalties and other fees paid by licensees to use the Starbucks brand. Sales of coffee, tea, food and related products are generally recognized upon shipment to licensees, depending on contract terms. Shipping charges billed to licensees are also recognized as revenue, and the related shipping costs are included in cost of sales including occupancy costs on our consolidated statements of earnings.

---

[6] Conceptually, the customer has received a material right (the option to renew the contract). In this situation, the seller should include the upfront fee in the transaction price, determine the stand-alone selling price of the renewal option, allocate a portion of the transaction price to the renewal option, and recognize revenue when the renewal option is exercised or forfeited. However, as a practical expedient, GAAP allows revenue related to the upfront fee to be recognized over the expected period the goods or services will be provided.

> Initial nonrefundable development fees for licensed stores are recognized upon substantial performance of services for new market business development activities, such as initial business, real estate and store development planning, as well as providing operational materials and functional training courses for opening new licensed retail markets. Additional store licensing fees are recognized when new licensed stores are opened. Royalty revenues based upon a percentage of reported sales, and other continuing fees, such as marketing and service fees, are recognized on a monthly basis when earned.

Revenue from licensing poses two unique challenges for sellers. The first challenge is that sellers must identify whether the performance obligation associated with a license is distinct from other performance obligations in the arrangement. If the rights under a license are separable from related goods and services, and the benefits from the license to the customer are not dependent on or integrated with a related product or service, then the license is considered distinct. On the other hand, any license that is a part of a tangible good and is essential to the functionality of the good or benefits the customer only in conjunction with a related service is *not* considered distinct.

Example Trident Software Company licenses its accounting software to Eagle Corporation and also enters into a contract to install the software. Trident sells the software license with or without installation. The accounting software is not modified or customized by the customer. In this case, the software license is distinct from the installation service because the software is licensed separately (capable of being distinct) and the license is separable from other promises in the contract (distinct within the context of the contract). Therefore, there are two performance obligations in the contract—granting the license and the installation services. ∎

Example Airwaves, a telecommunications company, licensed intellectual property from RadioTech relating to next generation wireless transmission technology. In addition, RadioTech provides research and development (R&D) services as part of the contract. Given the specialized nature of the intellectual property being licensed, RadioTech is the only company able to provide these R&D services. In this situation, the license is *not* distinct because Airwaves can only benefit from the license in conjunction with the R&D services provided by RadioTech. Therefore, the license and the R&D services are considered a single performance obligation. ∎

The second issue for licensing involves the nature of the license. GAAP identifies two types of licenses: those that provide access to the seller's intellectual property throughout the license period and those that provide use of the intellectual property as it exists at the point in time when the license is granted. A grant of a license that provides access for the length of the contract agreement results in a performance obligation that is satisfied over time. For example, when **Microsoft** licenses its enterprise resource planning software platform for a 2-year period, including software upgrades, it results in a performance obligation satisfied over time. A license that conveys no other expectations from the seller results in a performance obligation that is satisfied at a point in time. For example, when Microsoft licenses its Office software to a customer, with no expectation that it will provide any additional services or upgrades, it recognizes satisfaction of the performance obligation when it transfers the license and software to the customer.

Principal—Agent Contract Consideration

The identification of a company's performance obligation is complicated when a principal–agent relationship exists. The **principal**'s performance obligation is to provide goods or services to customers, while an **agent**'s performance obligation is to arrange for goods or services to be provided by the principal to the customer. For example, many companies sell goods through the **Amazon** website where Amazon never takes possession of the goods nor does it control the shipping to the customer. So, one might wonder which company has primary responsibility for fulfilling the contract: Is Amazon the principal seller with a performance obligation to the customer, or is it merely an agent that is facilitating the transaction for the seller?

GAAP provides indicators for determining if a company may be an agent, such that it does not control the goods or services provided to the customer. Exhibit 17.4 lists these indicators.

EXHIBIT 17.4 Indicators That a Company May Be an Agent

- Another company is primarily responsible for fulfilling the contract.
- The company does not have inventory risk before and after the goods have been ordered by a customer, during shipping, or upon return.
- The company does not have discretion in establishing prices for the goods and services.
- The company's consideration is in the form of a commission.[7]

No single indicator is more important than another and management must use judgment in assessing if it is a principal or an agent. If management, based on the answers to these indicators, concludes that it is an agent and not the principal seller of the goods or services, then it would recognize commission revenue for the net amount of consideration retained after paying the principal for the goods or services provided to the customer. If the answers to these indicators suggest that the company is the principal, it would recognize the gross amount received from the customer as revenue when the performance obligation is satisfied.

Returning to the case of Amazon, in transactions in which it has inventory risk or latitude in setting prices and selecting suppliers, Amazon considers itself the principal and records revenue at the gross amount. In cases where Amazon is not primarily obligated it considers itself the agent and records the net amount of commissions earned.

Example Blues Corp. sells products directly through its website. In addition Blues also lets independent sellers list products on its website and sell those products to customers. Blues charges independent sellers a 15% sales commission for sales made through their websites. On January 5, 2018, Blues sold a television directly from its inventory for a price of $1,399 and an independent seller sold a $900 unlocked smart phone through its website. Blues records the sales as follows:

Cash	1,399	
Sales Revenue		1,399
Cash (15% × $900)	135	
Commission Revenue		135

---

[7] Under IFRS, there is one additional indicator which states that the company is not exposed to any credit risk for the amount receivable from the customer in exchange for the goods or services.

> ### GOT IT?
>
> **17-9** What is a performance obligation? Do performance obligations need to be legally enforceable?
>
> **17-10** How does the seller determine if a performance obligation is distinct?
>
> **17-11** How should the seller treat promised goods and services that are not distinct within a contract?
>
> **17-12** Are upfront payments considered separate performance obligations?

HOW DO YOU DETERMINE THE TRANSACTION PRICE?

LEARNING OBJECTIVE 17.4
Understand how a company determines the transaction price of a contract.

The third step in determining the amount of revenue to be recognized is to determine the **transaction price**—the amount of **consideration** to be recognized the entity expects to be entitled in exchange for providing the promised goods or services to the customer. A seller determines the transaction price by examining the terms of the contract and how it normally conducts business. Often, the transaction price is easy to determine because the seller receives fixed cash payments when it transfers the promised goods or services. However, in other situations, the seller must take into account other factors that affect the transaction price such as:

- the time value of money
- variable consideration
- noncash consideration
- consideration payable to a customer

We discuss each of these considerations in this section.

Time Value of Money

When a customer pays a seller either well before or well after the promised goods or services are transferred, a sales contract contains a significant financing, or interest, component. The seller then determines the transaction price by discounting the promised amount of future consideration to reflect the time value of money.[8] The seller should use the same discount rate it would use if it were to enter into a separate financing transaction with the customer. The objective is for the seller to recognize revenue at the amount that would have been recognized had the customer paid cash for the promised goods or services at the time of transfer. In effect, the contract is separated into a revenue element and a financing element. The revenue element is accounted for consistent with the revenue recognition model discussed in this chapter, while the financing element is accounted for consistent with the long-term financing principles discussed in Chapter 14.

Example On January 1, 2018, Beckham Company sold goods to Adams Company in exchange for a 3-year, non-interest-bearing note with a face value of $20,000. If Beckham entered into a separate financing transaction with Adams, an appropriate interest rate would be 12%. To determine the transaction price, Beckham would discount the contract price of $20,000 at a 12% interest rate for three periods. Therefore, the

---

[8] For revenue contracts without a significant financing component, the seller measures the transaction price as the amount of consideration to which it is entitled and does *not* adjust for customer credit risk because collectability is assessed at the time the contract is identified—Step 1 of the revenue recognition model.

transaction price would be $14,235.60 ($20,000 × 0.711780).[9] When Beckham delivers the goods to Adams on January 1, 2018, it records the following journal entry:

Notes Receivable	20,000.00	
Sales Revenue		14,235.60
Discount on Notes Receivable		5,764.40

Note that the contract has now been separated into a revenue element ($14,235.60), which is recognized as the performance obligation is satisfied, and a financing element ($5,764.40), which is recognized as interest income over the term of the note. At the end of the year, Beckham would record interest income as follows:

Discount on Notes Receivable	1,708.27	
Interest Income ($14,235.60 × 12%)		1,708.27

The financing element should be reported separately from the revenue element on a company's income statement. In practice, companies are not required to adjust the consideration for the time value of money if the time period between the customer's payment and the company's transfer of goods or services is less than one year.

Variable Consideration

In many cases, the amount expected to be received from the customer may be uncertain. The amount of consideration that will ultimately be received can vary due to contract terms that include incentives, discounts, allowances, rebates, penalties, performance bonuses, price concessions, and/or royalties. These items can make determining the consideration expected to be received from the customer difficult. In order to determine the transaction price when there is **variable consideration**, the seller must:

- Step 1: Estimate the total amount to which it expects to be entitled (the variable consideration).
- Step 2: Determine whether there is an **applicable constraint** on the variable consideration. An applicable constraint is a contract term that could cause the amount of consideration received to be less than the amount expected.

When a contract contains an uncertain, variable amount of consideration, GAAP requires that a company only recognize total consideration in an amount the seller expects to receive when the uncertainty is resolved. Stated in the negative, GAAP requires that companies should not recognize 100% of revenue now if there is a chance that the revenue amount could be significantly reduced later when the uncertainty is resolved.

Step 1: Determining Variable Consideration Amounts To estimate the variable consideration, a company uses either the **expected value approach** or the **most likely amount approach**.

- Under the expected value approach, a company identifies the range of possible outcomes and the probabilities associated with each outcome. The expected value is then calculated as the sum of the probability-weighted amounts in this range.
- Under the most likely amount approach, the consideration is the single most likely amount within a range of possible variable consideration amounts.

Note that the approach used is not a "free choice", rather the company should use the approach that provides the best prediction of the amount of consideration to which the company expects to be entitled. The approach should be consistently applied throughout the contract and the estimate updated at the end of each reporting period. This updating may result in the amount of revenue recognized changing as additional information is received.

---

[9] The present value factor of 0.711780 is obtained from the Present Value of 1 Table in the Time Value of Money Module.

Example BonJovi Corporation enters into a contract to build a new football stadium. The promise to transfer the stadium is a performance obligation. The promised consideration is $80 million but could vary depending on the date of completion and final inspection. The contract states that for every day after August 15, 2018, that the stadium is not available to be used as a football stadium, the promised consideration is reduced by $500,000. For every day prior to August 15, 2018, that the stadium is available to be used as a football stadium, the promised consideration is increased by $500,000. The contract also states that if the stadium receives a safety inspection rating from government inspectors that is above 95 points, BonJovi will receive a performance bonus of $10 million.

BonJovi estimates the following completion schedule:

Expected Completion Date	Probability	Bonus/(Penalty)
August 12, 2017	15%	$ 1,500,000
August 13, 2017	17	1,000,000
August 14, 2017	24	500,000
August 15, 2017	14	0
August 16, 2017	15	(500,000)
August 17, 2017	9	(1,000,000)
August 18, 2017	6	(1,500,000)

In addition, BonJovi estimates that there is an 85% chance that the stadium will receive a safety inspection above 95 points.

If BonJovi uses the expected value approach to determine the variable consideration, it would take the sum of the following probability-weighted amounts of consideration:

15% × ($80,000,000 + $1,500,000) =	$12,225,000
17% × ($80,000,000 + $1,000,000) =	$13,770,000
24% × ($80,000,000 + $500,000) =	$19,320,000
14% × ($80,000,000) =	$11,200,000
15% × ($80,000,000 − $500,000) =	$11,925,000
9% × ($80,000,000 − $1,000,000) =	$ 7,110,000
6% × ($80,000,000 − $1,500,000) =	$ 4,710,000
Expected value	$80,260,000
Expected value of safety bonus (85% × $10,000,000)	8,500,000
Total variable consideration	$88,760,000

Assuming instead that BonJovi used the most likely amount approach, the most likely completion date is August 14, 2018. Therefore, it would determine the variable consideration as $90,500,000 ($80,000,000 + $500,000 completion bonus + $10,000,000 safety bonus). ∎

Step 2: Assessing Whether an Applicable Constraint Exists Once the variable consideration has been estimated, a company may only include it in the transaction price to the extent that it is probable that a significant reversal of the revenue previously recognized will not occur.[10] This constraint on variable consideration is aimed at preventing "over-recognition" of revenue in one period that would have to be reversed when the uncertainty associated with the variable consideration is resolved.

Example Tiger Corporation enters into a one-year contract with Walker Inc. to provide setup and cleaning services at events for a fixed fee of $500,000. Tiger is also entitled to performance bonuses based on customer satisfaction surveys and health inspection reports. The performance bonus can be one of four amounts: $0, $25,000, $50,000 or $100,000 under the contract. Based on its prior experience with contracts of this type, Tiger estimates the probabilities for each bonus amount as:

---

[10] FASB ASC 606-10-32-11: Revenue from Contracts with Customers, Overall, Measurement. Note that IFRS use the term "highly probable" instead of "probable;" however, the Board believes that the interpretation of these terms will be similar.

Tiger's Bonus Amount	Probability of Receiving Bonus
$ 0	25%
$ 25,000	45%
$ 50,000	20%
$100,000	10%

Under the expected value approach, Tiger estimates the variable consideration is $31,250 [($0 × 25%) + ($25,000 × 45%) + ($50,000 × 20%) + ($100,000 × 10%)], but Tiger must also consider the applicable constraint on the variable consideration. The bonus agreement limits the amount of variable consideration to one of four amounts. So, in this case Tiger can only recognize variable consideration of $25,000 because any amount greater than $25,000 would be subject to reversal unless the next level of bonus ($50,000) is received. ■

Noncash Consideration

If the customer promises consideration in a form other than cash, the seller includes the fair value of the noncash consideration in the transaction price. If the seller is unable to estimate the fair value of the noncash consideration received, it should estimate fair value indirectly based on the stand-alone selling prices of the promised goods or services.

Example Frank Company enters into a contract to deliver goods to Walters Company. In exchange for the goods, Walters promises to give Frank 1,000 shares of its $1 par value common stock. At the date the goods are delivered, Walters's common stock has a fair value of $20. Frank appropriately classifies the securities it receives as trading securities. Frank makes the following journal entry when it satisfies its performance obligation to Walters:

Investment in Trading Securities (1,000 shares × $20 per share)	20,000	
Sales Revenue		20,000

In addition, customers sometimes contribute goods or services to a company in order to assist in the fulfillment of a company's performance obligation. If a company has control of the customer's contributed goods or services, it should include the customer's contribution in the determination of the transaction price.

Example Build Company contracts with Pear Inc. to build 100,000 mobile phones. Pear agrees to pay Build $5 million and contributes certain parts with a fair value of $1 million to assist in the manufacture of the phones to Pear's specifications. If Build concludes that it has control over the contributed parts, the transaction price would be $6 million ($5 million + $1 million). ■

Consideration Payable to a Customer

Under certain types of sales arrangements, some companies may make payments to their customers. Such payments are often in the form of discounts, refunds, coupons, rebates, or free services but may also be for goods or services that the customer provides. If a seller pays, or expects to pay, consideration to the customer, the seller accounts for that consideration as a reduction in the transaction price. However, if the payment is for a distinct good or service that the customer transfers to the seller, then the payment is accounted for in the same way as other purchases from suppliers.

Example Tractor Company manufactures and sells riding lawnmowers. It is currently running a promotion in which it pays a $200 rebate to any customer that purchases a lawnmower over $1,500. The rebate form must be returned within 180 days of the original sale. Given its historical experience and the ease of obtaining a rebate, Tractor expects all qualifying customers to receive the rebate. Assume that Tractor sells and delivers a $2,000 lawnmower. Tractor would determine the transaction price to be $1,800 ($2,000 − $200) and recognize revenue of $1,800 when the customer takes delivery of the lawnmower. In addition, Tractor would recognize a liability for the expected rebate and make the following journal entries:

Cash	2,000	
Rebate Liability		200
Sales Revenue		1,800

If the customer returns the rebate form within the rebate period, Tractor would record the following journal entry:

Rebate Liability	200	
Cash		200

If at the end of the rebate period the form was not returned, Tractor would update the transaction price of the lawnmower and record the following journal entry:

Rebate Liability	200	
Sales Revenue		200

GOT IT?

17-13 What is the seller's main objective when determining the transaction price?

17-14 How should the seller measure revenue when it expects to receive consideration in a form other than cash?

HOW DO YOU ALLOCATE THE TRANSACTION PRICE TO THE PERFORMANCE OBLIGATIONS IN THE CONTRACT?

LEARNING OBJECTIVE 17.5
Describe how to allocate the transaction price to the performance obligations in a contract.

Once the performance obligations have been identified and the transaction price has been determined, the seller must allocate the transaction price to the performance obligations in the contract. If the contract contains only one performance obligation, then the transaction price only relates to that performance obligation and no allocation is needed.

However, contracts with customers sometimes contain multiple distinct performance obligations. For example, a cellular network operator, like **AT&T** or **Verizon**, generally sells a cell phone along with a service contract that provides voice, text, and data service. Similarly, a real estate company may rent office space that also includes parking spots and cleaning services. Because the distinct performance obligations are considered separate units of accounting, revenue is recognized for the goods and services once each performance obligation is satisfied.

When a contract contains more than one performance obligation, the seller allocates the transaction price to each performance obligation in proportion to the relative stand-alone selling prices of those goods and services. The stand-alone selling price is the price at which the seller would sell a promised good or service separately to a customer. If the stand-alone selling price is not readily observable, the company should use its best estimate of what it would sell the goods or services for separately. To obtain an estimate of the stand-alone selling price, GAAP suggests the three approaches shown in Exhibit 17.5.

Whichever estimation method is used, the seller should apply it in a consistent fashion.

Example CoCo Communications enters into a contract with a customer to sell voice, text, and data services for $60 per month. Each service is appropriately determined to be a separate performance obligation that is satisfied at a different point in time. CoCo regularly sells voice service for $28 and text services for $24.50 under similar circumstances to similar customers. Therefore, the stand-alone selling price of the voice and text services are directly observable. CoCo determines that the selling prices for the data service is highly variable and uncertain. Using an acceptable estimation method, CoCo estimates

> **EXHIBIT 17.5** Methods to Estimate the Stand-Alone Price
>
> **Adjusted Market Assessment Approach**
>
> The **adjusted market assessment approach** requires the seller to consider the market in which the good or service is sold and estimate the price that a customer in that market would be willing to pay. Inputs for this approach would include such things as competitors' prices, adjusted for factors specific to the seller, such as market position or cost structure. A single good or service could have more than one stand-alone selling price if it is sold in multiple markets. Discounts offered by an entity when a good or service is sold separately should be considered when estimating stand-alone selling prices.
>
> **Expected Cost Plus a Margin Approach**
>
> Using the **expected cost plus a margin approach**, the seller forecasts the unobservable stand-alone price by estimating the cost of satisfying a performance obligation and then adding a gross profit margin. Costs included in the estimate should be consistent with those the seller would normally consider in setting stand-alone prices. Both direct and indirect costs should be considered.
>
> Factors to consider when assessing if a margin is reasonable could include:
> - Gross margins achieved on stand-alone sales of similar products
> - Market data related to historical margins within an industry
> - Industry sales price averages
> - Market conditions
> - Profit objectives
>
> **Residual Approach**
>
> The **residual approach** involves the seller deducting from the total transaction price the sum of the estimated stand-alone selling prices of other goods and services in the contract. What is left over, the residual, is the unobserved stand-alone price for the remaining goods or services. The residual approach may only be used if one of the following criteria is met:
> - The entity sells the same good or service to different customers (at or near the same time) for a broad range of amounts (i.e., the selling price is highly variable because a representative stand-alone selling price is not discernible from past transactions or other observable evidence).
> - The entity has not yet established a price for that good or service, and the good or service has not previously been sold on a stand-alone basis (i.e., the selling price is uncertain).

the selling price for the data service to be $17.50. If CoCo sold each service separately, the total transaction price would be $70 ($28 + $24.50 + $17.50). However, this estimation results in a $10 discount in the total transaction price ($60 − $70). If CoCo does not have sufficient evidence to support allocation of the discount to a specific service, it allocates the discount based on the relative stand-alone prices. This results in the following allocation of the $70 transaction price to the separate performance obligations:

Voice service: ($28 ÷ $70) × $60 = $24

Text service: ($24.50 ÷ $70) × $60 = $21

Data service: ($17.50 ÷ $70) × $60 = $15

However, sometimes sellers regularly discount certain goods or services in a contract, but not other goods and services. If the seller (1) regularly sells each distinct promised good or service (or bundle of promised goods or services) on a stand-alone basis and (2) has observable evidence that the discount relates to one or more specific performance obligations, the seller should allocate the discount only to those performance obligations.

Example Assume the same information for CoCo in the previous example except that CoCo determined that the $10 discount arose only due to the data service. Because it has sufficient evidence to allocate the discount to a specific service, it should allocate the discount to that service only. Therefore, CoCo makes the following allocation of the $70 transaction price to the separate performance obligations:

Voice service: $28 stand-alone price = $28.00

Text service: $24.50 stand-alone price = $24.50

Data service: $17.50 − $10 discount = $7.50

Changes in Transaction Price

After the initial allocation of the transaction price, the transaction price may change if the contract includes consideration that is variable or contingent upon some threshold or event being met or achieved. For any changes in the transaction price over the life of the contract,[11] the seller should update the amounts allocated to the performance obligations in the same manner as the original allocation. Any amounts allocated to a performance obligation that has already been satisfied are recognized as revenue (or a reduction in revenue) in the period of the change.

Example: Change in Circumstances

During the first quarter of 2018, Buzz City sells 1,000 embroidered hoodies to Hornets Corporation for $30 per hoodie. Buzz City provides a 15% discount if a customer purchases more than 2,500 hoodies during a calendar year. Because Hornets Corporation is a new customer, Buzz City does not assume that it will achieve the sales volume necessary to get the discount. However, during the second quarter of 2018, Hornets purchase an additional 4,000 hoodies. Buzz City would record the following journal entries for the sales to Hornets:

Quarter 1, 2018:
Cash (1,000 × $30)	30,000	
Sales Revenue		30,000

Quarter 2, 2018:
Cash	97,500	
Sales Revenue		97,500*

*Quarter 2 revenue: 4,000 hoodies sold × $25.50 ($30 less a 15% volume discount)	= $102,000
Less: Volume discount from Quarter 1: 1,000 × $4.50 (15% volume discount)	= (4,500)
Quarter 2 Revenue	$ 97,500

GOT IT?

17-15 How does the seller allocate the transaction price when a contract contains multiple performance obligations?

17-16 What is the best evidence of a good's or service's stand-alone selling price?

17-17 If the stand-alone selling price of a good or service is not readily observable, what approaches might a company use to obtain an estimate of the stand-alone selling price?

WHEN SHOULD YOU RECOGNIZE REVENUE?

LEARNING OBJECTIVE 17.6
Account for revenue as the company satisfies the performance obligations in the contract.

The final step in the revenue recognition model is for the seller to determine when a performance obligation is satisfied in order to recognize revenue. A seller satisfies a performance obligation by transferring control of a promised good or service to a customer. Each good or service is considered an asset, and control of that asset by the customer

---

[11] These changes in the transaction price are due to changes in variable consideration. GAAP does not permit a reallocation of the transaction price due to changes in the stand-alone selling prices of the promised goods or services.

represents their ability to direct its use and obtain substantially all of its remaining benefits.[12] Control also allows the customer to restrict or prevent other companies from directing the use of or obtaining benefits from the good or service.

To determine if the customer has obtained control of a promised good or service, the seller would observe whether:

- The seller is entitled to payment.
- Legal title has been transferred from the seller to the customer.
- Physical possession has been transferred from the seller to the customer.
- The significant risks and rewards of ownership have transferred to the customer.
- The customer has accepted the goods or services.

Observing any one (or more) of these indicators usually establishes that the customer has control of the good or service.

A performance obligation is satisfied at either a point in time or over time. Many times a performance obligation is satisfied at the point in time at which the good or service is transferred, as when **Starbucks** provides a customer with a cup of coffee. However, there are many cases where a performance obligation will be satisfied over time, as in the case of a publisher delivering newspapers to a customer (subscriber) during an annual subscription, or Starbucks's subscription service, which delivers coffee or tea to a subscriber on a set schedule.

For a performance obligation to be satisfied over time, at least one of the following three criteria must be met:

1. **The customer simultaneously receives and consumes the benefits of the seller's performance as the seller performs.** This criterion primarily relates to service contracts. For example, a payroll processing company enters into a 12-month contract to process payroll each week for a customer. In this case, the customer receives and consumes the benefits as each weekly payroll transaction is processed, and, therefore, the payroll processing company satisfies its performance obligation over time. If it had processed 70% of the payroll transactions during the current fiscal period, the payroll processing company would recognize 70% of the transaction price as revenue in its current period income statement.

2. **The seller's performance creates or enhances an asset (e.g., work in progress) that the customer controls as the asset is created or enhanced.** This criterion relates to a situation in which the customer controls the work in process as the seller manufactures the goods or provides services. Many construction contracts and research and development contracts would fall under this criterion. For example, a technology company contracts with a construction company to build a manufacturing plant on land owned by the technology company. The plant is built to the technology company's specifications, progress payments are made during construction, and the project can be cancelled by the technology company at any point. If cancelled, the plant construction to date belongs to the technology company. Because the technology company controls the plant as it is being built, the performance obligation is satisfied over time and revenue is recognized by the construction company as the plant is built.

3. **The seller's performance does not create an asset with an alternative use to the seller. In addition, the seller has a right to payment for performance completed to date.** The last criterion is important to sellers that create goods or services specifically for a customer that the seller would not be able to resell to any other customer. For example, a consulting firm contracts with a large restaurant chain to develop a sustainability plan for its restaurants. The consulting firm's performance obligation is to provide a monthly report to the restaurant company, and if the restaurant company cancels the contract, it must pay for the work performed by the consulting firm up to the date of cancellation. The consulting firm would recognize revenue from the contract over time as it completes the work.

If none of the criteria is met, the performance obligation is satisfied at the point in time that the good or service is transferred.

[12] Under U.S. GAAP, the benefits derived from an asset represent the potential cash flows that can be obtained directly or indirectly from the asset.

Example On January 12, 2018, Brew Company enters into a contract with Roaster Inc. to construct a large-scale coffee roasting machine for its business. The machine has a cost of $180,000 and will be delivered to Brew's location on February 2, 2019, at which time Brew must pay Roaster. If Brew cancels the contract, Roaster can sell the machine to another customer. On February 2, 2019, the machine is delivered and accepted by Brew. Because none of the three criteria for revenue recognition over time are met, Roaster cannot recognize revenue until that point. Specifically, Roaster will recognize revenue on February 2, 2019, the day on which it has satisfied its performance obligation with the delivery and acceptance of the machine by Brew.

Example Mast Company enters into a contract to manufacture a cruise ship for Windward Company. The ship is designed and manufactured to Windward's specifications and represents a single performance obligation for Mast. Physical possession of and title to the cruise ship remain with Mast during construction. Windward can cancel the contract at any time but would be obligated to pay Mast for the costs incurred plus a normal profit margin. Any work in process remains the property of Mast; however, it would require significant costs to rework the ship to make it useful for another customer. Because Mast has a right to payment and the significant rework costs result in the ship not having an alternative use for Mast, the performance obligation is satisfied over time, and Mast should recognize revenue over time.

Methods for Revenue Recognition When Performance Obligations are Satisfied Over Time

When a seller determines that a performance obligation is satisfied over time, it must measure its progress toward complete satisfaction of the performance obligation to determine the timing of revenue recognition. To measure progress over time, companies use various methods that can be classified as either of the following:

- **Output methods**: Measure progress over time based on *results achieved* to date compared to the total expected results of the contract (e.g., units produced, units delivered, contract milestones reached). Output methods use direct measurements of the value of the goods and services transferred to the customer during completion of the contract.
- **Input methods**: Measure progress over time based on the seller's *efforts* to satisfy the performance obligation (e.g., costs incurred, labor hours worked, machine hours worked, time lapsed).

Theoretically, output methods are preferable to input methods because, by measuring actual performance to date, they provide a more faithful representation of progress. However, it is sometimes difficult to directly observe output measures. In those situations, an input method will produce a more reliable measure of progress.

Two popular input methods are as follows:

- **Cost-to-cost method**: Measure progress toward satisfaction of the performance obligation by comparing the costs incurred to date with the expected total costs for the contract.
- **Efforts-expended method**: Measure progress toward satisfaction of the performance obligation by the work performed to date, such as labor hours, labor dollars, machine hours, or material quantities, compared to the expected total work to be performed in the contract.

Once the progress toward satisfaction of the performance obligation is determined, revenue is recognized each period as follows:

$$\text{Current Period Revenue} = \text{Progress Percentage} \times \text{Allocated Transaction Price} - \text{Previously Recognized Revenue}$$

Example: Cost-to-Cost Method

On January 1, 2018, Grande Construction Company enters into a contract with a customer to build an office complex for a fixed price of $25 million. Grande estimates that it will take 20 months to complete the project and appropriately determines that the contract has a single performance obligation that is satisfied over time. To measure progress toward satisfying the performance obligation, Grande decides to use the cost-to-cost input method. The total estimated contract costs are $22 million. Grande reports the actual costs incurred, the estimated costs to complete the contract, and the progress toward completion in 2018 and 2019 as follows:

	2018	2019
Actual cost incurred to date	$ 9,900,000	$21,000,000
Estimated cost to complete	12,100,000	0
Total estimated costs	$22,000,000	$21,000,000
Progress toward completion*	45%	100%

*Actual costs incurred to date ÷ Total estimated costs

Grande would use the progress toward completion percentage to determine the amount of revenue to recognize each period. In this situation, Grande would recognize revenue of $11,250,000 (45% × $25,000,000) in 2018 and revenue of $13,750,000 [(100% × $25,000,000) − $11,250,000] in 2019.

Contract Costs

A company may incur costs in obtaining or fulfilling a contract. For example, a real estate developer that is competing for a contract to build new stores for **Target** may incur bidding costs along with costs to develop a construction budget that must be submitted before any contract is awarded. In addition, a company that sells coffee bean roasting machines to **Starbucks** may award its salesperson a sales commission for closing the sale. GAAP requires capitalization of the incremental costs to obtain a contract.[13] **Incremental costs** are the costs the seller incurred by obtaining the contract that would not have been incurred if the contract had not been obtained. To be an incremental cost, the following criteria must be met:

- The costs must relate directly to a contract or an anticipated contract that the company can specifically identify.
- The costs must generate or enhance resources that will be used in satisfying future performance obligations.
- The costs must be expected to be recovered.

In the examples above, the sales commission would be considered an incremental cost because it would not have been incurred if the vendor had not sold the coffee roasting machines and the cost is expected to be recovered. The bidding and budget development costs are not incremental because these costs are incurred whether the company wins the contract or not.

Incremental costs are capitalized as an asset when incurred and then amortized to expense using a method that is consistent with the recognition of revenue from the related contract. For example, on January 1, 2018, Roasting Company enters into a contract to supply 480 coffee roasting machines to a regional coffee shop. The machines will be delivered at a rate of 20 machines per month over 2 years. The salesperson received a $24,000 sales commission on the date the contract was signed. The company would recognize an asset for the prepaid sales commission and amortize it to sales commission expense on a monthly basis consistent with the delivery of the machines. For contracts

---

[13] FASB ASC 340-40-25-1: Other Assets and Deferred Costs, Contracts with Customers, Recognition.

where the amortization period would be less than one year, companies may directly expense incremental costs.

> **GOT IT?**
>
> **17-18** How does a seller satisfy a performance obligation? When does this occur?
>
> **17-19** What evidence would suggest that a performance obligation is satisfied and that the customer has control of the good or service?
>
> **17-20** If the seller's performance creates an asset (e.g., work in progress) that the customer controls as the asset is created, would the performance obligation be satisfied at a point in time or over time?
>
> **17-21** Describe input and output methods used to measure progress over time for performance obligations that are satisfied over time.

WHAT ARE THE REQUIRED DISCLOSURES FOR REVENUE RECOGNITION?

LEARNING OBJECTIVE 17.7

Describe the company's required revenue recognition disclosures.

The revenue recognition standard provides considerable guidance on the presentation of contract assets, contract liabilities, and revenue. In addition, the standard requires extensive disclosures regarding revenue.

Presentation

As discussed earlier, the FASB's definition of revenue implies an asset–liability approach to revenue recognition. The revenue recognition model is based on the idea that a contract asset or contract liability is generated when either the buyer or seller performs under the contract. Companies are required to present these contract assets and contract liabilities on their balance sheets.

When a seller has satisfied a performance obligation but the customer has not yet paid, the seller records either a receivable or a contract asset. A **receivable** represents the seller's *unconditional* right to receive consideration from a customer. On the other hand, a **contract asset** arises when the seller's right to consideration from a customer is *conditional* upon something other than the passage of time (e.g., the seller must satisfy another performance obligation before it is entitled to bill the customer for the goods or services). Companies should present receivables and contract assets separately on the balance sheet.[14] If a company has a contract asset and its right to consideration becomes unconditional, the company must reclassify the contract asset as a receivable.

A **contract liability** represents the seller's performance obligation and arises when a customer's payment of consideration occurs prior to the seller's performance under the contract. This contract liability is often referred to as Unearned Revenue and should be presented on the seller's balance sheet.

Finally, revenue from contracts with customers should be presented or disclosed separately from the seller's other sources of revenue. For example, if a company has both sales revenue from contracts with customers and revenue from lease arrangements, these two sources of revenue should be presented separately.

Disclosure

In order for financial statement users to understand the nature, amount, timing, and uncertainty of revenue and cash flows, companies should disclose both qualitative and quantitative information about contracts with customers, as well as any significant

---

[14] Companies are not required to use the term "contract asset" (or "contract liability") but should disclose enough information for users to distinguish between unconditional and conditional rights to consideration.

judgments in applying the revenue recognition guidance. Companies' disclosures would include:

- Disaggregation of revenue into categories that allow users to determine how revenue is affected by economic factors such as type of good or service, geography, market or type of customer, and type of contract.
- Reconciliation of the opening and closing balances of contract assets and liabilities. In addition, qualitative and quantitative information about significant changes in contract balances should be disclosed.
- Information about performance obligations, including a description of the obligations. Companies are also required to disclose the transaction price allocated to unsatisfied performance obligations and when the obligations will be satisfied.
- Significant judgments used by the company to recognize revenue for performance obligations satisfied over time and why the method is appropriate. In addition, companies must disclose how they determine transfer of control for performance obligations satisfied at a point in time.

GOT IT?

17-22 What information must a company disclose about its performance obligations?

17-23 What types of disclosures must companies make to allow users to understand how revenue is by affected economic factors?

LEARNING OBJECTIVE 17.8
Understand the accounting for long-term contracts in which revenue is recognized over time versus at a point in time.

WHAT ARE THE METHODS TO ACCOUNT FOR LONG-TERM CONTRACTS?

Long-Term Contracts

Companies like **Boeing**, **General Electric**, and **United Technologies** engage in long-term construction contracts in which they agree to construct an asset for another entity over an extended period. Long-term construction contracts involve projects such as buildings, airplanes, ships, roads, bridges, and dams, which can take several years to complete. Such contracts may involve advance payments by the buyer to help the seller finance the construction and to establish the buyer's ownership interest in the asset under construction. The contract also may include specific responsibilities of the seller, such as the use of certain materials, achievement of certain safety and technical specifications, and the completion of production on a specific timetable. At completion, the buyer typically inspects and approves the finished asset before the final transfer of title takes place.

Because the construction process usually extends over more than one period, the question arises as to whether the construction company should recognize revenue over time or at a point in time. To make this determination, the construction company should analyze whether it satisfies any of the criteria (discussed earlier on page 17-22) for a performance obligation to be satisfied over time. If it meets any of these criteria, revenue will be recognized over time based on the measure of progress

Long-term construction contracts, which involve projects that take several years to complete, like building bridges, typically require the use of the percentage-of-completion method.

toward satisfaction of the performance obligation. If it does not meet any of these criteria, revenue will be recognized at a point in time, typically the date of the final delivery of the asset.

Most long-term contracts are accounted for as single performance obligations because the separate performance obligations within the contract are often not distinct. In addition, this performance obligation is normally satisfied over time because:

- The buyer and seller obtain enforceable rights, including the right of the buyer to enforce specific performance.
- The buyer usually makes progress payments providing evidence of the buyer's ownership interest.
- The buyer has the right to take over the work in progress.

Given these factors, the construction company's performance creates or enhances an asset that the customer controls. The recognition of revenue over time for long-term contracts generally produces a *more relevant* measure of periodic income because income includes the results of the accomplishments during the each period throughout the long-term construction period. In addition, it provides a more representationally faithful measure of performance relative to point-in-time recognition.

In some circumstances, a company may not be able to reasonably measure its progress toward satisfaction of the performance obligation. In that situation, a company should recognize revenue at the point in time that the project is complete and the customer takes delivery. We discuss these situations below.

How Do We Account for Long-Term Contracts over Time?

Once a company determines its long-term contract performance obligation is satisfied over time, it must select an input or output method (as discussed earlier on page 17-23) to measure progress and recognize revenue over time. The company then uses an inventory account, **Construction in Progress**, to record all costs incurred on the project. In addition, it adds the gross profit that it recognizes on the project to the Construction in Progress account, so that at the end of the period, inventory is valued at cost plus gross profit recognized (i.e., net realizable value). As the company completes portions of the contract, it can typically bill the customer for a partial payment of the total contract price. When these partial billings are made, the company debits a receivable account and credits the **Partial Billings** account. The company reports the balance in the Partial Billings account on its balance sheet as a contra account to the Construction in Progress account. This results in the net balance sheet amount being an asset if Construction in Progress exceeds Partial Billings or a liability if Partial Billings exceeds Construction in Progress.

If the project's total estimated cost exceeds the contract price, the company expects a loss on the project. In this situation, the company must recognize the total expected loss in the current year and reduce the carrying value of the inventory.[15]

The following sections provide examples to illustrate how to account for long term contracts when revenue is recognized over time, when revenue is recognized at a point in time, and how to treat long-term contracts that will result in losses.

Example: Long-Term Contract Revenue Recognized over Time

Cameron Company contracted to construct a stadium that takes 3 years to complete. Cameron has agreed to a contract price of $700,000, estimates total contract costs of $500,000, and expects a gross profit of $200,000. **Example 17.1** shows the contract price, costs incurred, estimated costs to complete, partial billings, and collections. Cameron estimates the percentage completed using the cost-to-cost method.

---

[15] We discuss the recognition of losses later in the chapter.

EXAMPLE 17.1 Cameron Company: Stadium Construction Contract Amounts

	2017	2018	2019
Construction costs incurred during the year	$100,000	$186,000	$314,000
Estimated costs to complete the contract	400,000	264,000	—
Partial billings to customer	80,000	350,000	270,000
Collections from customer	50,000	330,000	320,000
Total contract price: $700,000			

The gross profit recognized each year is shown in **Example 17.1a**.

EXAMPLE 17.1a Gross Profit Recognition: Revenue Recognized Over Time

	2017	2018	2019
Construction costs incurred to date	$ 100,000	$ 286,000	$ 600,000
Estimated costs to complete	400,000	264,000	—
Total estimated costs	$ 500,000	$ 550,000	$ 600,000
Percent complete (construction cost incurred to date ÷ total estimated costs)	20%	52%	100%
Revenue to date (% complete × $700,000 contract price)	$ 140,000	$ 364,000	$ 700,000
Revenue recognized for the year (revenue to date − revenue previously recognized)	$ 140,000	$ 224,000	$ 336,000
Construction cost (expense) incurred for the year	(100,000)	(186,000)	(314,000)
Gross profit recognized	$ 40,000	$ 38,000	$ 22,000

2017: In 2017, the contract is 20% complete. Therefore, Cameron recognizes $140,000 of revenue in the current period (20% × $700,000). Cameron also recognizes $100,000 of construction expense for 2017 (20% × $500,000),[16] resulting in gross profit of $40,000. Note that the contract is 20% complete, and Cameron recognizes 20% of the $200,000 projected gross profit.

2018: In 2018, Cameron follows the same procedure. The total costs incurred *to date* are $286,000 (the sum of the costs incurred in 2017 and 2018). At this point, estimated costs to complete the project have been revised and are now estimated to be $264,000. Therefore, the project is 52% complete [$286,000 ÷ ($286,000 + $264,000)]. For 2018, Cameron recognizes $224,000 of revenue [(52% × $700,000) − $140,000], construction expense of $186,000 [(52% × $550,000) − $100,000], and gross profit of $38,000. Note that it is important to differentiate between the amounts recognized in the current period and the cumulative totals. The contract is 52% complete, resulting in a profit *recognized to date* of $78,000 (52% × $150,000). This amount includes the $40,000 and $38,000 gross profit recognized in each of the 2 years.

2019: In 2019, Cameron completes the contract at a total cost of $600,000. The revenue for *2019* is $336,000, which is the total revenue of $700,000 minus the revenue

---

[16] Under the cost-to-cost method, construction expenses recognized for the year are equal to the construction costs incurred during the year (unless a loss is expected on the contract, as we discuss later). Therefore, the construction expense computations are simplified, as we show in Example 17.1a. If this method is not used, construction expenses recognized in a given year may differ from the actual yearly construction costs incurred.

to date of $364,000 ($140,000 + $224,000). Construction costs for *2019* are $314,000, resulting in gross profit of $22,000 for 2019. Note that the total gross profit for the 3 years is $100,000 ($40,000 + $38,000 + $22,000), which reflects the total revenue minus the total actual costs ($700,000 − $600,000). ■

Example: Long-Term Contract Revenue Recognized at a Point in Time

If a company cannot make reasonably dependable estimates of the progress toward satisfaction of the performance obligation, it should recognize revenue at the point in time that the project is complete and the customer takes delivery. In effect, this method is just like the production and sale of any unit of inventory. The recording and reporting of inventory costs and partial billings are handled in the same way as they were in the previous example when revenue was recognized over time. While the revenue and periodic income amounts recognized are *more verifiable* because they are based on final results rather than on estimates, these amounts are *less relevant* because a company's revenue and net income does not reflect its performance for that period.

Assume the same facts for Cameron Company except that Cameron determines that it cannot make reasonably dependable estimates of the progress toward satisfaction of the performance obligation. Therefore, it recognizes the entire amount of revenue, expenses, and gross profit at the end of 2019—the point in time that the contract is complete. The total construction costs incurred over the 3 years (recorded in Construction in Progress) are $600,000 ($100,000 + $186,000 + $314,000). The revenue recognized is the total contract price of $700,000. Therefore, Cameron recognizes zero revenue and gross profit in 2017 and 2018, and then in 2019 recognizes the entire $700,000 of revenue and the entire $100,000 of gross profit ($700,000 − $600,000).

Example 17.1b provides the journal entries to record Cameron's activities when revenue is recognized both over time and at a point in time.

EXAMPLE 17.1b

Journal Entries to Record Stadium Construction

	Revenue Recognized Over Time		Revenue Recognized at a Point in Time	
2017				
1. To record construction costs:				
Construction in Progress	100,000		100,000	
Accounts Payable, Raw Materials Inventory, Cash, etc.		100,000		100,000
2. To record partial billings:				
Accounts Receivable	80,000		80,000	
Partial Billings		80,000		80,000
3. To record collections:				
Cash	50,000		50,000	
Accounts Receivable		50,000		50,000
4. To record gross profit:				
Construction Expense	100,000		No Entry	
Construction in Progress	40,000			
Sales Revenue		140,000		
2018				
1. To record construction costs:				
Construction in Progress	186,000		186,000	
Accounts Payable, Raw Materials Inventory, Cash, etc.		186,000		186,000

(continued)

> **EXAMPLE 17.1b** (Continued)

	Revenue Recognized Over Time		Revenue Recognized at a Point in Time	
2. To record partial billings:				
Accounts Receivable	350,000		350,000	
Partial Billings		350,000		350,000
3. To record collections:				
Cash	330,000		330,000	
Accounts Receivable		330,000		330,000
4. To record gross profit:				
Construction Expense	186,000		No Entry	
Construction in Progress	38,000			
Sales Revenue		224,000		
2019				
1. To record construction costs:				
Construction in Progress	314,000		314,000	
Accounts Payable, Raw				
Materials Inventory, Cash, etc.		314,000		314,000
2. To record partial billings:				
Accounts Receivable	270,000		270,000	
Partial Billings		270,000		270,000
3. To record collections:				
Cash	320,000		320,000	
Accounts Receivable		320,000		320,000
4. To record gross profit and to close out Construction in Progress and Partial Billings:				
Construction Expense	314,000		No Entry	
Construction in Progress	22,000			
Sales Revenue		336,000		
Partial Billings	700,000		No Entry	
Construction in Progress		700,000		
Partial Billings	No Entry		700,000	
Construction Revenue				700,000
Construction Expense	No Entry		600,000	
Construction in Progress				600,000

Several key points can be observed:

- For 2017 through 2019, the accounting for the construction costs, the billings to the customer, and the collection of cash are the same for both methods.
- When revenue is recognized over time, the company recognizes the gross profit (calculated in **Example 17.1a**) each year by journal entries to revenue and expense accounts. The difference between these two amounts, the gross profit, is debited to Construction in Progress. This increases the asset value from cost to net realizable value and eventually to the contract selling price.
- When revenue is recognized at a point in time, the company does not recognize revenue, expense, or gross profit in 2017 or 2018, so no journal entries are required.
- In 2019, when the contract is completed, closing entries for the contract are required. When revenue is recognized over time, the company closes Partial Billings against Construction in Progress. Note that both accounts will reflect the selling

price. When revenue is recognized at a point in time, the company recognizes the total gross profit on the contract at the completion date. It does this by closing Partial Billings against Construction Revenue because both accounts include the selling price. It also closes Construction in Progress against Construction Expense because both accounts include the cost. At the end of the period, it closes the revenue and expense accounts to Income Summary.

Example 17.1c shows how Cameron reports its activities for this contract under each situation. To complete the income statement under each situation, Cameron deducts its operating expenses from the gross profit to determine its net income. On the balance sheet under each situation, it offsets Partial Billings against Construction in Progress. At the end of 2017, Construction in Progress exceeds Partial Billings, so Cameron reports the net amount as inventory in the current assets section of its balance sheet. At the end of 2018, Partial Billings exceeds Construction in Progress, so Cameron reports the net amount as a current liability on its balance sheet. Note that the difference in the book values under the two situations is equal to the gross profit to date on the contract. Thus, at December 31, 2017, the book value when revenue is recognized over time is $60,000 and, when revenue is recognized at a point in time, it is $20,000. The difference of $40,000 is the gross profit for 2017.

EXAMPLE 17.1c

Financial Statement Reporting

1. Revenue Recognized Over Time	2017	2018	2019
Income Statement (partial):			
Sales revenue	$ 140,000	$ 224,000	$ 336,000
Construction expense	(100,000)	(186,000)	(314,000)
Gross profit	$ 40,000	$ 38,000	$ 22,000
Balance Sheet (partial; end of year):			
Current Assets			
Accounts receivable	$ 30,000	$ 50,000	
Inventories			
Construction in progress	$ 140,000		
Less: Partial billings	(80,000)		
Costs and recognized profit not yet billed	$ 60,000		
Current Liabilities			
Partial billings		$ 430,000	
Less: Construction in progress		(364,000)	
Billings in excess of costs and recognized profit		$ 66,000	

Notes to Financial Statements: Summary of Significant Accounting Policies (in part): The company reports profits from its long-term construction contracts over time. Profits are accrued based on the ratio of cost incurred to total estimated costs. Costs include direct material, direct labor, and job-related overhead. General and administrative expenses are charged to operations as incurred and are not allocated to contract costs.

2. Revenue Recognized at a Point in Time	2017	2018	2019
Income Statement (partial):			
Construction revenue	—	—	$ 700,000
Construction expense	—	—	(600,000)
Gross profit			$ 100,000

(continued)

EXAMPLE 17.1c (Continued)

2. Revenue Recognized at a Point in Time	2017	2018	2019
Balance Sheet (partial; end of year):			
Current Assets			
Accounts receivable	$ 30,000	$ 50,000	
Inventories			
Construction in progress	$100,000		
Less: Partial billings	(80,000)		
Excess of costs over related billings	$ 20,000		
Current Liabilities			
Partial billings		$ 430,000	
Less: Construction in progress		(286,000)	
Excess of billings over related costs		$ 144,000	

Notes to Financial Statements: Summary of Significant Accounting Policies (in part): The company reports profits from long-term construction contracts at the completion of the project. Under this method, billings and costs are accumulated during the period of construction, but no profits are recorded before the contract is either completed. Costs include direct labor, direct materials, and job-related overhead. General and administrative expenses are charged to operations as incurred and are not allocated to contract costs.

ETHICAL DILEMMA

Titanic Inc. is a construction company that specializes in the construction of commercial cruise ships. Titanic appropriately recognizes revenue from its construction contracts over time where the progress toward satisfaction of the performance obligation is determined by the cost-to-cost method. That is, Titanic recognizes sales and gross profit as work is performed based on the ratio of actual costs incurred to the estimated total costs of the contract. As the accountant for Titanic, you recently informed the CEO that labor difficulties, which caused the company to halt construction earlier in the year, would cause Titanic to fall short of its revenue projections. The CEO calmly replied that he still had "a few tricks up his sleeve," and the company would meet these projections.

Later in the month, as you were completing your quarterly physical inspection of the various construction projects, you noticed large amounts of material on hand waiting to be used in the various projects. Several of the workers commented that most of this material had been delivered over the last 2 weeks, and if any more were to arrive, they wouldn't have any place to store it. In fact, most of this material was not even going to be needed in the construction process for several more weeks! Returning to the corporate offices, you discovered that the CEO had personally placed the order for this material. The CEO explained to you that he had managed to negotiate a fantastic deal with some of the suppliers if Titanic would take possession of the materials immediately. (A later review of the invoices revealed that the purchase price for this material was equal to the average market price during the month.) Furthermore, the CEO noted that he really wanted the company to complete the projects ahead of schedule to take advantage of the large cash incentives being offered for early completion of the contract, and he didn't want the projects to be delayed because of lack of the necessary materials. Remembering the CEO's earlier comment about meeting earnings projections, you wonder if this purchase of materials was one of the tricks the CEO had up his sleeve. What are the potential effects of this purchase of materials on the company's financial statements, and is this action ethical?

Example: Losses on Long-Term Contracts

There are two types of losses that can arise during long-term construction contracts:

- *Loss in the Current Period.* This type of loss occurs when the estimate of future costs may indicate that there is a loss in the current period but a profit is still expected on the overall contract. We treat this type of loss as a change in accounting estimate (discussed in greater detail in Chapter 22) because it results from changing cost estimates during the construction process.

- *Overall Loss on the Contract.* This type of loss occurs when the contractor expects total costs will be greater than contract revenue. When there is an overall expected loss on the contract, GAAP requires that a company immediately recognize the total estimated loss on the entire contract regardless of whether it is recognizing revenue over time or at a point in time.

The next two examples demonstrate the appropriate accounting in each of these loss scenarios.

Example: Loss in Current Period

To show the computation of a loss for the current period, suppose that Cameron is recognizing long-term contract revenue over time and, in 2018, estimates that the costs to complete are $364,000 instead of $264,000. Assuming that the data for 2017 are the same as in **Example 17.1**, Cameron recognizes an $18,000 loss in 2018, which it calculates as follows:

	2018
Construction costs incurred to date	$ 286,000
Estimated costs to complete	364,000
Total estimated costs	$ 650,000
Progress percentage ($286,000 ÷ $650,000)	44%
Revenue to date (44% × $700,000)	$ 308,000
Revenue recognized for year ($308,000 − $140,000)	$ 168,000
Construction costs incurred for year	(186,000)
Current period loss	$ (18,000)

If the costs in 2019 are $364,000 as expected, Cameron recognizes the remaining 56% of the revenue, or $392,000. Therefore, Cameron reports a gross profit of $28,000 in 2019, with a total profit over the 3 years of the contract of $50,000 ($40,000 − $18,000 + $28,000). This is equal to the total revenue of $700,000 minus the total cost of $650,000. If Cameron were recognizing revenue at a point in time, no adjustment is needed in 2018 because the company expects an overall profit on the contract.

Example: Overall Loss on Contract

More complicated situations arise when the estimated total costs exceed the contract price, so that an overall loss on the contract is anticipated. In the next two examples, we demonstrate the appropriate accounting for contract losses when revenue is recognized over time and at a point in time.

Revenue Recognized over Time Suppose, at the end of 2018, Cameron Company estimates that its costs to complete are $429,000 and expected total costs will be $715,000 ($286,000 + $429,000). Therefore, an overall loss of $15,000 is expected by the end of the contract, and Cameron has to remove the gross profit to date and recognize the loss of $15,000 in 2018. It recognizes the revenue for 2018 in the normal way, as shown in **Example 17.2**. The total expense recognized in 2018 includes two components:

- the amount needed to create a cumulative profit of zero
- the amount of the overall loss recognized in prior periods

EXAMPLE 17.2

Calculation of Revenues and Expenses When a Loss Is Expected on the Contract

	Current Year	Total to Date
2017		
Construction revenue	$ 140,000[a]	$ 140,000
Construction expense	(100,000)[b]	(100,000)
Gross profit	$ 40,000	$ 40,000

(continued)

EXAMPLE 17.2 (Continued)

	Current Year	Total to Date
2018		
Construction revenue	$ 140,000	$ 280,000
Construction expense	(195,000)[d]	(295,000)[c]
Gross profit	$ (55,000)	$ (15,000)
2019		
Construction revenue	$ 420,000	$ 700,000
Construction expense	(420,000)	(715,000)
Gross profit	$ 0	$ (15,000)

[a] (20% × $700,000)
[b] (20% × $500,000)

[c]
Contract price	$700,000
Progress percentage	40%
Cost of earned revenue before loss provision	$280,000
Estimated total loss	15,000
Construction expense to date	$295,000

[d]
Cumulative construction expense	$ 295,000
Less: Construction expense in previous year	(100,000)
Current construction expense	$ 195,000

Because the revenue to date is $280,000 and the expense recognized in 2017 was $100,000, the company recognizes an expense of $180,000 in 2018 to make the cumulative profit equal to zero. In addition, it recognizes a provision for the overall loss of $15,000, resulting in a total expense for 2018 of $195,000. Cameron records the revenue and expense as shown in the following journal entry:

Construction Expense	195,000	
Construction in Progress		40,000
Construction Revenue		140,000
Provision for Loss on Contract		15,000

The credit to the Construction in Progress account removes the increase in value resulting from the gross profit recognized in 2017. Therefore, the account includes only the project costs incurred to date. The Provision for Loss on Contract is reported as a contra account to Construction in Progress (minus Partial Billings), or it may be reported as a liability. Note that the negative gross profit of $55,000 ($140,000 − $195,000) is equal to the gross profit of $40,000 in 2017 that is reversed plus the anticipated loss of $15,000.

If costs in 2019 are $429,000 as projected, the company recognizes a zero gross profit in 2019. The revenue recognized is the remaining amount of $420,000 ($700,000 − $140,000 − $140,000) left to be recognized on the contract. The expense is also $420,000. Thus, Cameron recognizes no additional losses in 2019 because it recognized the total loss on the contract in the year in which it was first estimated (2018).

Cameron debits the costs incurred on the contract in 2019 to the Construction in Progress account in the normal way up to a total of $700,000 ($414,000 in 2019). The balance in the Construction in Progress account should not exceed the contract price because the asset value cannot be greater than the total proceeds to be received on the contract. However, Cameron actually incurred $429,000 of costs to complete the project in 2019. Total costs amount to $715,000 even though the revenue from the contract will only be $700,000. Therefore, the additional $15,000 of costs incurred over $700,000 are debited to the Provision for Loss on Contract account, which eliminates the $15,000 balance established in the account at the end of 2018.

Cameron records the construction costs, revenue, and expense in 2019 as follows:

Construction in Progress	414,000	
Provision for Loss on Contract	15,000	
Cash, Accounts Payable, etc.		429,000
Construction Expense	420,000	
Construction Revenue		420,000

Revenue Recognized at a Point in Time Under this method, Cameron recognizes the loss in 2018 because there is an overall loss on the contract. It records this loss as follows:

Construction Expense	15,000	
Provision for Loss on Contract		15,000

Cameron debits an expense account to recognize the loss because the construction activity is *not* an incidental or peripheral activity. Note that there is no credit to the Construction in Progress account because, when revenue is recognized at a point in time, Cameron did not add the gross profit to the Construction in Progress account in previous years.

Cameron would recognize a gross profit or loss if the actual costs incurred in 2019 were less, or greater, than its estimated amount. This procedure is consistent with accounting for a change in estimate.

GOT IT?

17-24 Under what circumstances does a company recognize revenue over time for long-term contracts?

17-25 How does a company classify the following accounts in its financial statements: Construction in Progress, Partial Billings, Construction Revenue, and Construction Expense?

REVIEW CENTER

At the beginning of the chapter, we examined the various sources of **Starbucks**'s revenues and introduced the core principle of revenue recognition. In addition, we described the 5-step model companies use to determine revenue recognition. We also identified several objectives you would accomplish after reading the chapter. The objectives are listed below and followed by a brief summary of the key points.

KEY TAKEAWAYS

- Revenues are increases in assets or settlements of liabilities during a period from delivering or producing goods, rendering services, or other activities that are the company's ongoing major or central operations.
- The core principle of revenue recognition is that a company should recognize revenue to depict the transfer of promised goods or services to customers in an amount that reflects the consideration to which the entity expects to be entitled in exchange for those goods or services.

LEARNING OBJECTIVE 17.1
Understand and explain the core principle of revenue recognition.

- The 5-step revenue recognition model used to apply this core principle involves the following steps: (1) identify the contract, (2) identify the performance obligation, (3) determine the transaction price, (4) allocate the transaction price, and (5) recognize revenue when or as the company satisfies a performance obligation.

KEY TERM
revenues, p. 17-3

LEARNING OBJECTIVE 17.2
Describe how a company identifies a contract with a customer.

KEY TAKEAWAYS
- The revenue recognition model is applied to contracts that meet the following criteria:
  - All of the parties approve the contract (in writing, orally, or by implication).
  - The company is able to identify each party's rights and obligations under the contract.
  - The company is able to identify the payment terms of the goods or services to be transferred.
  - The contract has commercial substance.
  - It is probable the company will collect the consideration to which it is entitled.
- The main issues in identifying a contract relate to:
  - *Contract Terminations.* A contract does not exist if the contract is wholly unperformed and either of the parties can unilaterally cancel the contract without compensating the other party.
  - *Combination of Contracts.* The key objective is to combine contracts when the economics of the transaction can only be understood with reference to the arrangement as a whole.
  - *Contract Modifications.* A contract modification may result in either a new contract that must be accounted for separately from the original contract or as part of the existing contract.
  - *Collectability.* In order for there to be a contract, the seller must conclude that it is probable that it will collect the consideration in the contract in exchange for the goods or services that it has promised to transfer to the customer.

KEY TERMS
change order, p. 17-6
collectability, p. 17-9
contract, p. 17-5
contract amendment, p. 17-6

contract modification, p. 17-6
customer, p. 17-5
wholly unperformed contract, p. 17-5

LEARNING OBJECTIVE 17.3
Examine how a company identifies the performance obligations in a contract.

KEY TAKEAWAYS
- The identification of performance obligations is critical because the satisfaction of the performance obligations ultimately determines the amount and timing of revenue recognition.
- One of the main complications involves contracts that involve the sale of a bundle of goods or services. Does each good or service create a distinct separate performance obligation or, due to the interrelatedness of the goods or services, should they be combined into a single performance obligation? A promised good or service is considered distinct if both of the following criteria are met:
  - The promised good or service is capable of being distinct because the customer is able to benefit from the good or service either on its own or together with other resources that are readily available to the customer.
  - The promised good or service is *distinct within the context of the contract* because the seller's promise to transfer the good or service to the customer is separately identifiable from other promises in the contract.

- When a company receives an upfront payment, it must determine the performance obligation to which the upfront fee relates. Revenue should not be recognized until the performance obligation is satisfied.
- In a licensing arrangement, the seller must identify whether a performance obligation is distinct from other performance obligations in the contract and the nature of the license.
  - If the nature of the license is to provide access to the intellectual property throughout the license period, revenue is recognized over time.
  - If the nature of the license is to provide use of the intellectual property as it exists at the point in time the license is granted, revenue is recognized at a point in time.
- In a principal–agent relationship, the principal would record the gross amount received from the customer as revenue when the performance obligation is satisfied, and the agent records commission revenue for the net amount of consideration retained after paying the principal for the goods or services provided to the customer.

KEY TERMS

agent, p. 17-14
constructive obligation, p. 17-10
licensing, p. 17-12
performance obligation, p. 17-10

principal, p. 17-14
separately identifiable, p. 17-11
upfront payments, p. 17-11

KEY TAKEAWAYS

LEARNING OBJECTIVE 17.4
Understand how a company determines the transaction price of a contract.

- The determination of the transaction price includes consideration of the following:
  - *Time Value of Money.* When a contract has a significant financing component, the seller determines the transaction price by discounting the promised amount of consideration to reflect the time value of money.
  - *Variable Consideration.* The amount expected to be received from the customer can vary due to contract terms that include such things as incentives, discounts and allowances, rebates, penalties, performance bonuses, price concessions, and royalties. In order to determine the transaction price when there is variable consideration, the seller must estimate the total amount of consideration it expects to receive. This can be achieved by using the sum of the probability-weighted amounts or most likely amount approach.
  - *Noncash Consideration.* If the customer promises consideration in a form other than cash, the seller includes the fair value of the noncash consideration in the transaction price.
  - *Consideration Payable to a Customer.* If a seller pays, or expects to pay, consideration to the customer, the seller accounts for that consideration as a reduction in the transaction price unless the payment to the customer is in exchange for distinct goods or services that the customer transfers to the seller.

KEY TERMS

applicable constraint, p. 17-16
consideration, p. 17-15
expected value approach, p. 17-16

most likely amount approach, p. 17-16
transaction price, p. 17-15
variable consideration, p. 17-16

KEY TAKEAWAYS

LEARNING OBJECTIVE 17.5
Describe how to allocate the transaction price to the performance obligations in a contract.

- If the contract contains a single performance obligation, the transaction price would only relate to that performance obligation.
- If the contract contains more than one performance obligation, the seller would allocate the transaction price to each performance obligation based on the relative stand-alone selling price of the goods and services.

- If the stand-alone selling price of a good or service is not observable, the seller may estimate it using one of the following approaches:
  - *Adjusted Market Assessment Approach.* Analyze the market in which the good or service is sold and estimate the amount that the company believes a customer would be willing to pay.
  - *Expected Cost Plus a Margin Approach.* Forecast the cost of satisfying a performance obligation and add an appropriate gross margin to obtain the stand-alone price.
  - *Residual Approach.* Determine the stand-alone selling prices of the other goods and services in the contract and subtract these amounts from the total transaction price to estimate the unobservable price.

KEY TERMS

adjusted market assessment approach, p. 17-20

expected cost plus a margin approach, p. 17-20

residual approach, p. 17-20

LEARNING OBJECTIVE 17.6

Account for revenue as the company satisfies the performance obligations in the contract.

KEY TAKEAWAYS

- The seller recognizes revenue when a performance obligation is satisfied.
- Performance obligations are satisfied when the seller transfers control of the promised good or service to a customer. Control allows the customer to restrict or prevent other companies from directing the use of or obtaining benefits from the good or service.
- Performance obligations may be settled over time or at a point in time. If any of the following conditions are met, the performance obligation is satisfied over time:
  - The customer simultaneously receives and consumes the benefits of the seller's performance as the seller performs.
  - The seller's performance creates or enhances an asset (e.g., work in progress) that the customer controls as the asset is created or enhanced.
  - The seller's performance does not create an asset with an alternative use to the seller. In addition, the seller has a right to payment for performance completed to date.
- For performance obligations accounted for over time, a company can determine the progress toward satisfaction of the performance obligation by using either:
  - input methods that recognize revenue based on the seller's efforts to satisfy the performance obligation (e.g., costs incurred, labor hours worked, time lapsed), or
  - output measures that use the results achieved to date (e.g., units delivered, units produced, contract milestones reached)
- If the performance obligation is not accounted for over time, it is satisfied at the point in time that the good or service is transferred.
- GAAP requires capitalization of the incremental costs to obtain a contract.

KEY TERMS

cost-to-cost method, p. 17-23
efforts-expended method, p. 17-23
incremental costs, p. 17-24

input methods, p. 17-23
output methods, p. 17-23

KEY CALCULATION

$$\text{Current Period Revenue} = \text{Progress Percentage} \times \text{Allocated Transaction Price} - \text{Previously Recognized Revenue}$$

KEY TAKEAWAYS

- GAAP requires companies to disclose qualitative and quantitative information about contracts with customers and any significant judgments in applying the revenue recognition guidance. Both the FASB and the IASB stated that companies should provide information about contracts with customers so that users are able to assess the amount, timing, and uncertainty of revenues and cash flows.
- Required disclosures include:
  - Disaggregation of revenue into categories that allow users to determine how revenue is affected by economic factors such as type of good or service, geography, market or type of customer, and type of contract.
  - Reconciliation of contract balances from the opening balance to the closing balance of contract assets and liabilities.
  - Information about performance obligations including a description of the obligations. Companies will also be required to disclose the transaction price allocated to unsatisfied performance obligations and when the obligations would be satisfied.

LEARNING OBJECTIVE 17.7
Describe the company's required revenue recognition disclosures.

KEY TERMS

contract asset, p. 17-25
contract liability, p. 17-25
receivable, p. 17-25

KEY TAKEAWAYS

- Most long-term contracts are accounted for as a single performance obligation. The performance obligation in the contract may be accounted for over time or at a point in time.
- For long-term contracts accounted for over time:
  - The total revenue recognized to date is computed by multiplying the progress toward satisfaction of the performance obligation by the estimated total revenue.
  - The total revenue to be recognized in the current period is computed by subtracting the total revenue recognized to date from the total revenue recognized in prior periods.
  - The Construction in Progress account is increased by the amount of gross profit (revenues minus expenses).
  - Any partial billings are recorded in a contra account to Construction in Progress. If the net amount is a debit, it is reported as an asset; if the net amount is a credit, it is reported as a liability.
- For long-term contracts accounted for at a point in time:
  - The company does not recognize revenue, expense, or gross profit until the project is complete and the customer takes delivery.
  - The accounting for project costs, billings to the customer, and the collection of cash is the same as for contracts accounted for over time.
- A loss (negative gross profit) on long-term contracts may be either:
  - a loss in the current period but a profit is still expected on the overall contract. This type of loss is accounted for as a change in estimate.
  - an overall loss on the contract. Immediate recognition of the total estimated loss is required.

LEARNING OBJECTIVE 17.8
Understand the accounting for long-term contracts in which revenue is recognized over time versus at a point in time.

KEY TERMS

Construction in Progress, p. 17-27
Partial Billings, p. 17-27

MULTIPLE-CHOICE

Select the best answer for each of the following.

M17-1 A company should recognize revenue when:
LO 17.1
   a. the revenue is earned
   b. the contract is signed
   c. the seller satisfies the performance obligation
   d. the consideration is received

M17-2 A contract between one or more parties creates:
LO 17.2
   a. the date that cash is paid by the customer
   b. enforceable rights and obligations for the parties
   c. revenue for recognition
   d. the fixed amount of payments for the good or service

M17-3 Morgan Company and its customer agree to modify their existing contract. Under which of the following situations would the modification result in a new contract?
LO 17.2
   a. The modification adds distinct goods or services, and the contract price increases by an amount that reflects the stand-alone selling price of additional goods or services.
   b. The modification only affects the transaction price.
   c. The modification adds distinct goods or services but does not change the contract price.
   d. The modification does not add distinct goods or services but does not affect the transaction price.

M17-4 Chlorine Corp. has a contract to deliver pool products to the community aquatic center. The contract with the aquatic center states that the first 1,000 gallons of chemicals will cost $36 per gallon. However, the cost will drop to $30 per gallon for all purchases over 1,000 gallons. Based on its experience, Chlorine Corp. estimates that the aquatic center will use 1,400 gallons of chemicals.
LO 17.4

What transaction price per gallon should Chlorine use for this contract?

   a. $36.00   c. $34.29
   b. $33.00   d. $30.00

M17-5 Orange Construction Company enters into a long-term contract to build a new stadium. The contract is for $400 million and work is expected to be completed on June 30, 2019. Orange will receive a $20 million bonus if the work is completed by June 30, 2019. Orange has built numerous stadiums and believes that there is a 90% chance that it will complete the project on time. What is the amount of the transaction price?
LO 17.4

   a. $400 million
   b. $418 million
   c. $0 because the transaction price is variable
   d. $420 million

M17-6 On July 15, 2017, Matrix Corp. sells 20,000 snow shovels to a distributor for $15 per shovel. The distributor pays the amount on July 15, 2017, and has the right to return any of the snow shovels for any reason within 180 days for a full refund. Matrix uses the expected value method to estimate that 8% of the snow shovels will be returned and it is probable that no more than 8% of the shovels will be returned. How much sales revenue should Matrix recognize on July 15, 2017, for this sale?
LO 17.6

   a. $0   c. $24,000
   b. $300,000   d. $276,000

M17-7 In accounting for a long-term construction contract in which the performance obligations will be satisfied at a point in time and for which there is a projected profit, the balance in the Construction in Progress account at the end of the first year of work would be:
LO 17.6

   a. zero
   b. the same as if revenue is recognized over time
   c. lower than if revenue is recognized over time
   d. higher than if revenue is recognized over time

M17-8 Warren Construction Company has consistently recognized revenue from its long-term contracts as the performance obligations were met over time. In 2017, Warren started work on a $6,000,000 construction contract, which was completed in 2018. The accounting records disclosed the following data:
LO 17.8

	2017	2018
Progress billings	$2,200,000	$3,800,000
Costs incurred	1,800,000	3,600,000
Collections	1,400,000	4,600,000
Estimated cost to complete	3,600,000	—

How much gross profit should Warren have recognized in 2017?

   a. $200,000   c. $300,000
   b. $220,000   d. $400,000

M17-9
LO 17.8
On April 1, 2015, Pine Construction Company entered into a fixed-price contract to construct an apartment building for $6,000,000. Pine will satisfy the performance obligations in the contract over time and appropriately accounts for this contract. Information relating to the contract is as follows:

	At December 31, 2017	At December 31, 2018
Percentage of completion	20%	60%
Estimated costs at completion	$4,500,000	$4,800,000
Gross profit recognized (cumulative)	$ 300,000	$ 720,000

What is the amount of contract costs incurred during the year ended December 31, 2018?

a. $1,200,000
b. $1,920,000
c. $1,980,000
d. $2,880,000

M17-10
LO 17.6
A customer obtains control over a good or service when:

a. the customer takes physical possession of the good or service
b. the customer has the ability to direct the use of the good or service and obtain substantially all of the remaining benefits from the good or service
c. the customer pays for the good or service
d. the seller receives final payment

REVIEW EXERCISES

RE17-1
LO 17.2
CustomTee Inc. contracts with various customers to sell T-shirts. In the case of sales, CustomTee's normal accounting policy requires a written and signed sales agreement. On July 1, in response to a special last-minute phone call from a regular customer, CustomTee delivered 500 T-shirts for $5,000. Does CustomTee have an enforceable contract?

RE17-2
LO 17.2
Yankee Corp. agrees to provide Albany Company 24 months of coaching services. The contract sets the price at $4,000 per month, which is the normal stand-alone price that Yankee charges. After 16 months, Yankee and Albany agree to modify the contract. Yankee reduces the fee for the 8 remaining months to $3,800 per month, and Albany agrees to a 24-month extension at a cost of $3,600 per month. At the time that the contract is modified, Yankee is charging other customers $3,750 per month for the coaching service. Should Yankee and Albany treat the modification as a separate contract?

RE17-3
LO 17.2
Assume the same facts as in **RE17-2**. If Yankee determines that the additional services are distinct from the goods and services transferred in the original contract, how would it account for the modification?

RE17-4
LO 17.2
East Georgia Community Hospital enters into a contract to provide $15,000 of elective medical care to a patient. After a review of the patient's ability and intent to pay, the hospital does not expect to collect the full contract price of $15,000. However, the hospital occasionally performs "discounted" procedures to members of the community to enhance its standing in the local area. While the hospital invoiced the customer for the full amount of the services, it only expects to collect $10,000. What amount of revenue should the hospital recognize?

RE17-5
LO 17.3
LongDrive sells a specialized golf club that has core plugs to shift weight in the club head and produce different ball flights. LongDrive sells the golf club and replacement core plugs separately, and no other company sells either item. Customers can use the golf club without the replacement core plugs, but the replacement core plugs are not usable without the golf club. LongDrive sells the golf club and four replacement core plugs to a customer. The golf club is shipped on April 1, 2017, and the replacement plugs are shipped on May 1, 2017. How many performance obligations does LongDrive have with respect to this sale?

RE17-6
LO 17.3
Modine Homes Inc. enters into a contract to design and build a cabana and pool for a customer. Modine will design the cabana and pool and is responsible for the overall management of the project. The project includes providing the customer with a design and a plan for implementing and executing the design. The project also includes getting the site ready, excavation for the pool, construction, plumbing, electrical, and all other services needed to complete the project. Modine is in the business of managing full projects but also sells all of these goods and services on an individual basis. How many performance obligations will Modine have with respect to the cabana and pool project?

RE17-7
LO 17.3
VolleyElite runs a volleyball program consisting of camps, tournaments, and specialized coaching. VolleyElite charges customers $500 per year for access to its facilities and programs. In addition, VolleyElite charges each customer a $100 registration fee. The fee is not refundable and must be paid at the initiation of the contract. Should the registration fee be considered a separate performance obligation from the yearly dues?

RE17-8
LO 17.3
Enterprise Solutions Inc. licenses its productivity software to Blackmon Company for $100,000, payable at contract inception. Enterprise agrees to provide semiannual software upgrades over the 5-year length of the contract to enable Blackmon to benefit from any technological advancement. Enterprise concludes that the software license is not distinct from the promised upgrades. What journal entries are necessary for Enterprise to account for this transaction?

RE17-9
LO 17.3
Assume the same facts as in **RE17-8**, except that Enterprise does not agree to provide software updates. What journal entry is necessary for Enterprise to record this transaction?

RE17-10
LO 17.3
Magical Memories sells Florida theme park vacation packages to various customers throughout the United States. Magical Memories receives a 5% commission based on the total price of the vacation package. A customer purchased the Deluxe Package valued at $15,000. Prepare Magical Memories's journal entries to record sale of the vacation package, the receipt of cash from the customer, and the remittance to the theme park.

RE17-11
LO 17.4
On January 1, Morris Company offered a customer a 10% trade discount if the customer purchases 1,000 units of an item within the next 6 months. Each item sells for $100. Based on the customer's previous purchase history, Morris believes there is a 60% chance that the customer will purchase more than 1,000 units. In January, the customer purchases 200 units on credit. How much revenue should Morris recognize related to this customer?

RE17-12
LO 17.4
Robotics Inc. contracts with a customer to build a custom robot to be used in the customer's manufacturing operations for $2,000,000. If the robot is delivered and operational by January 1, the customer will pay Robotics a $200,000 performance bonus. For every week that the robot is not operational, the bonus is reduced by $100,000. Robotics estimates the following possible outcomes and probabilities:

Completed by January 1	40%
One week late	40%
Two weeks late	20%

Determine the transaction price that Robotics should use for this contract when it is signed.

RE17-13
LO 17.4
CoolShoes sells its elite tennis shoes to sports retailers throughout the country. When introducing its new RF17 shoes that sell for $125 per pair, the company includes a $15 rebate form. The rebate form can be used when the customer ultimately purchases the shoes. CoolShoes sells 100 pairs of shoes and estimates that 80% of the rebate forms will be returned by customers for a rebate. Determine the transaction price that CoolShoes should use when recognizing revenue from sale of one pair of the RF17 shoe.

RE17-14
LO 17.4
Using the information in **RE17-13**, what journal entry would CoolShoes make to record the sale of 100 pairs of RF17 shoes on account to a retailer?

RE17-15
LO 17.5
GameDay sells recreational vehicles along with secure parking storage to customers. GameDay sells the FB7 model for $62,000, and this price includes one year of secure parking storage. GameDay also sell secure parking storage separately for $8,000 per year, and customers can purchase the FB7 model without secure parking storage for $60,000. If a customer purchases the FB7 model with secure parking storage, how should GameDay allocate the transaction price?

RE17-16
LO 17.8
Clorad Corporation contracts with a customer to construct a building. It appropriately determines that it has one performance obligation which is satisfied over time. Using the following information for Year 1, compute Clorad's (a) total estimated costs for the contract, (b) revenue to date, and (c) gross profit recognized.

Year 1 (of 4-year project):

Construction costs incurred during the year	$ 174,000
Estimated costs to complete the contract	426,000
Partial billings to customers	100,000
Collections from customers	25,000
Total contract price	1,000,000

RE17-17 Using the information provided in **RE17-16**, prepare the journal entries to record Year 1's (a) construction costs, (b) partial billings, (c) cash collections, and (d) gross profit.
LO 17.8

RE17-18 Wells Corporation appropriately determined that Construction Project A was a single performance obligation that is satisfied over time. For this project, Wells had previously recognized revenue of $250,000 out of a total of $800,000 for the project. During the current year, Wells accumulated the following information about this project:
LO 17.8

- construction costs incurred for the year, $92,000
- construction costs incurred to date (including this year's costs), $200,000
- estimated costs to complete, $300,000

Based on the previous information, prepare a schedule to determine the amount of loss that Wells should recognize for the current year.

RE17-19 Lark Corporation appropriately determined that each of its long-term projects represents a single performance obligation that is satisfied over time. At the end of the current year, Lark estimates that its costs to complete a project exceed the contract price, so that an overall loss on the contract is anticipated. What journal entry will Lark record at the end of the current year, given the following information?
LO 17.8

- Revenue to date is $350,000 ($175,000 of which is to be recognized in the current year).
- The expense recognized previously was $100,000.
- An overall loss of $30,000 is anticipated.

EXERCISES

E17-1 **Revenue Recognition Model** Cass Company enters into a contract with Dearborn Inc. to sell it $50,000 of goods with delivery on May 10, 2017. Cass manufactured the goods at a cost of $33,000. The contract is signed on April 15, 2017, at which time Dearborn pays Cass $25,000. Cass delivers the goods on May 10, 2017, and Cass pays the final $25,000 on that date.
LO 17.1

Required:
1. On what date does a contract exist between Cass and Dearborn?
2. What are Cass's performance obligations in the contract?
3. What is the transaction price?
4. Does this transaction price need to be allocated?
5. Prepare Cass's journal entries related to the contract with Dearborn.

E17-2 **Identifying a Contract** Consider each of the following scenarios:
LO 17.2
a. A seller orally agrees with one of its best customers to deliver goods in exchange for $10,000. While the seller's practice is to obtain a written sales agreement, the seller delivered these goods to the customer without a written agreement due to the customer's urgent need.
b. A seller agrees to provide accounting services to a customer for the next year in exchange for $40,000. While the two parties are negotiating the terms of the agreement and the specific services to be performed, the seller begins to perform some services as a gesture of good faith.
c. A seller has a written agreement to deliver goods to a customer for $50 per unit. The price will drop to $45 per unit if the customer purchases more than 2,000 units per month.
d. A seller had a written agreement and provided custodial services to a customer for $2,000 per month in a previous year. The contract expired on December 31, 2016. During negotiations for a new contract in January 2017, custodial services were provided at the previous monthly rate and paid for by the buyer. The seller and the customer agree to a new contract on February 1, 2017. The seller is concerned whether a contract existed in January 2017 and whether revenue can be recognized.

Required:
1. Determine if a contract exists for each of the scenarios.
2. If it is determined that a contract exists but the seller believes it is probable that it will not collect the expected consideration, how does this affect the seller's ability to recognize revenue?

E17-3 **Contract to Deliver Goods** On August 1, 2017, Aiken Corporation enters into a contract with Benton Corp. to sell it $25,000 of goods. Aiken will deliver the goods on August 30, 2017, and Benton will pay the full amount upon acceptance. The goods were manufactured by Aiken at a cost of $18,000. Both Aiken and Benton consider the acceptance of the goods on August 30 a formality given that Benton has purchased the same goods from Aiken numerous times without incident. On August 30, 2017, Aiken delivers the goods and Benton transfers cash to Aiken.

LO 17.2

Required:
1. Does an enforceable contract exist between Aiken and Benton on August 1, 2017?
2. Prepare the journal entries in August 2017 necessary to account for this transaction. Assume Aiken uses a perpetual inventory system.
3. **Next Level** Assume that the contract is noncancelable. Would this condition allow Aiken to recognize revenue on August 1, 2017?

E17-4 **Contract Modification** On January 1, 2017, Spring Fashions Inc. enters into a contract with a southeast retail company to provide 500 dresses for $62,500 ($125 per dress) over the next 10 months. On October 1, 2017, after 450 of the dresses had been delivered (50 dresses per month), the contract is modified.

LO 17.2
LO 17.6

Required:
1. Fifty dresses were delivered each month for the first 9 months of 2017. Prepare Spring Fashions's monthly journal entry to record revenue.
2. Assume that the contract is modified to sell, once the original 500 dresses are delivered, an additional 100 dresses at $110 per dress, which is the stand-alone selling price on October 1, 2017. Assume the dresses are delivered evenly in November and December 2017. Prepare the journal entries to record the contract modification.

E17-5 **Determine the Transaction Price** On January 1, 2017, Loud Company enters into a 2-year contract with a customer for an unlimited talk and 5 GB data wireless plan for $65 per month. The contract includes a smartphone for which the customer pays $299. Loud also sells the smartphone and monthly service plan separately, charging $649 for the smartphone and $65 for the monthly service for the unlimited talk and 5 GB data wireless plan.

LO 17.5

SHOW ME HOW

Required:
1. Calculate the transaction price for the smartphone and unlimited talk and 5 GB data wireless plan assuming that Loud allocates consideration based on stand-alone prices.
2. Record the initial journal entry for Loud Company's sale of a 2-year contract on January 1, 2017, and the monthly journal entry.

E17-6 **Contract Modification** Assume the same facts as in **E17-5**. On July 1, 2017, the customer realizes that she needs less data in her wireless plan and downgrades to the unlimited talk and 2 GB data plan for the remaining term of the contract (18 months). The unlimited talk and 2 GB data plan is priced at $55 per month. The $55 per month is Loud's current stand-alone price for this plan that is available to all customers.

LO 17.2
LO 17.6

Required:
1. How should Loud account for this contract modification?
2. Provide Loud's new monthly revenue recognition journal entry.

E17-7 **Contract Modification** Assume the same facts as in **E17-5** and ignore **E17-6**. On July 1, 2017, the customer realizes that she needs a text messaging plan and adds an unlimited text messaging plan for the remaining term of the contract (18 months). The unlimited text messaging plan is priced at $15 per month. This is the current pricing for this plan available to all customers.

LO 17.2
LO 17.6

Required:
1. How should Loud account for this contract modification?
2. Provide Loud's new monthly revenue recognition journal entry.

E17-8 **Identifying Performance Obligations** Sanderson Construction Company provides a variety of construction services, ranging from general contracting services to specialized subcontracting services (e.g., electrical, plumbing services). Sanderson entered into a contract to construct a building for a customer. The contract identifies Sanderson as responsible for site preparation and all aspects of construction, including laying the foundation, framing, interior "rough-in" (e.g., plumbing, electrical, drywall), and exterior and interior finishing.

LO 17.3

Required:
Identify Sanderson's performance obligations.

E17-9 **Identifying Performance Obligations** GrillMaster Inc. sells an industry-leading line of outdoor charcoal and gas grills to customers through its online store as well as national home improvement stores. While the majority of the company's grills is mass produced, the company also provides custom grill products as part of its high-end line of products. Three independent scenarios are described below.

LO 17.3

a. GrillMaster Inc. agrees to provide an outdoor gas grill, replacement parts, and installation of the grill to a customer as part of its "Get Ready for Summer" promotion. The replacement parts and installation services are available from other vendors.
b. GrillMaster agrees to provide a custom gas grill and replacement parts to a customer utilizing a proprietary grilling technology. Due to the proprietary nature of the product, no other vendor sells either product. The grill is delivered on April 1, 2017, and the replacement parts are delivered in the following month.
c. Assume the same facts as in b, but because of production delays, GrillMaster delivers the replacement parts prior to delivery of the grill.

Required:
List each performance obligation in the contract.

E17-10 **Upfront Payments** WaterWorld Inc. operates an aquarium and water park in Orlando, Florida. In addition to daily admission tickets, WaterWorld offers two other ticket options. First, it offers an annual pass for $600 that allows unlimited access to the aquarium and theme park for one year from the date of purchase. In addition, it offers a Summer Fun Pass that allows unlimited access to the waterpark for June, July, and August for $450. Both pass options require full payment at the time of purchase. On April 1, 2017, WaterWorld entered into a contract with a customer to purchase an annual pass. On that same date, it entered into another contract with a customer to purchase a Summer Fun Pass.

LO 17.3
LO 17.5

SHOW ME HOW

Required:
1. Prepare WaterWorld's journal entries in 2017 related to the annual pass.
2. Prepare WaterWorld's journal entries related to the Summer Fun Pass.

E17-11 **License** On January 1, 2017, Crockett Pharmaceuticals granted a 5-year license of its patent rights to a drug compound to Tubbs Company for $10 million. As part of the agreement, Crockett also agrees to manufacture and supply the drug to Tubbs. Crockett is the only company capable of manufacturing the drug. However, Crockett plans to continue its R&D activities and seek for ways to enhance the drug's effectiveness. Any new discoveries are not covered by the license agreement.

LO 17.3
LO 17.5

Required:
1. Identify Crockett's performance obligations in this contract.
2. Prepare Crockett's journal entry with regard to the license agreement on January 1, 2017.
3. Assuming Crockett manufactures and delivers the drug to Tubbs evenly over the 5-year period, how much revenue related to the license is recognized in 2017?
4. Assume that other companies could manufacture the drug. Prepare the journal entry on January 1, 2017, under this scenario.

E17-12 **Variable Consideration** Jonas Consulting enters into a contract to provide cost management consulting services over a one-year period for $10,000 per month. At the end of the contract, Jonas will either give the customer a $24,000 refund or be entitled to an additional $24,000, depending on the level of cost savings. The company believes there is an 80% chance that it will be entitled to an additional $24,000 and a 20% chance it will give a refund of $24,000. In addition, Jonas believes it is probable that a significant reversal of any previously recognized revenue will not occur. The contract performance is determined to be satisfied over time.

LO 17.4

Required:
1. Determine the monthly transaction price that Jonas should use for recording the contract and prepare Jonas's journal entry at the end of the first month of the contract using the most likely amount approach.
2. **Next Level** What is the objective of determining the transaction price based on the amount of variable consideration?

E17-13 **Variable Consideration** On March 1, 2017, Elkhart enters into a new contract to build a specialized warehouse for $7 million. The promise to transfer the warehouse is determined to be a performance obligation. The contract states that if the warehouse is usable by November 30, 2017, Elkhart will receive a bonus of $600,000. For every

LO 17.4

(continued)

week after November 30 that the warehouse is not usable, the bonus will decrease by $150,000. Elkhart provides the following completion schedule:

Expected Completion Date	Probability
November 30, 2017	60%
December 7, 2017	20
December 14, 2017	10
December 21, 2017	5
December 28, 2017	5

Required:
1. Assume that Elkhart uses the expected value approach. What amount should Elkhart use for the transaction price?
2. Assume that Elkhart uses the most likely amount approach. What amount should Elkhart use for the transaction price?
3. **Next Level** What is the purpose of assessing whether a constraint on the variable consideration exists?

E17-14 Right of Return On January 5, 2017, ShoeKing Corporation sells for cash 500 pairs of volleyball shoes to FootAction, a shoe retailer, for $70 each. FootAction has the right to return the shoes for any reason up to March 31, 2017, for a full refund. The cost of each pair of shoes is $32. ShoeKing predicts that it is probable that 40 pairs of the shoes will be returned. ShoeKing uses the perpetual method for inventory.

LO 17.4

Required:
1. Prepare ShoeKing's journal entry on January 5, 2017, to account for this transaction.
2. Assume that FootAction returns 35 pairs of shoes on March 31, 2017. Prepare the journal entry to record this return.

E17-15 Volume Discount On January 1, 2017, Piper Company entered into an agreement with Save-Mart to sell its most popular product, the gadget. The contract stipulates that the price per unit will decrease as Save-Mart purchases higher volumes of the gadget, as follows:

LO 17.4

Sales Volume	Price per Unit
0 to 1,000 units	$50
1,001 to 2,000 units	45
2,001 to 3,000 units	40
3,001 units and above	35

The contract states that Save-Mart pays Piper the unit price based on the current sales volume. Once a volume threshold is reached, the price is retroactively reduced to the applicable price per unit. Based on its past experience with similar contracts, Piper believes that the total sales volume for the year will be 1,800 units and uses the most likely amount approach to estimate variable consideration. In addition, Piper concludes it is probable that a significant reversal in the amount of cumulative revenue recognized will not occur once the uncertainty surrounding the variable consideration is resolved.

Required:
1. Determine the transaction price per unit that Piper should use to record revenue.
2. Assume that Save-Mart purchases 800 units in the first quarter of 2017 and 900 units in the second quarter of 2017. Prepare Piper's journal entries to record the sales in the first and second quarters.
3. Given the higher than expected sales volume in the first half of the year, Piper increases its estimate of the sales volume to 2,800 units. Prepare the journal entry to record this change in estimate.

E17-16 Time Value of Money On January 1, 2017, Fulton Inc. enters into a contract with Gibson to deliver goods. Gibson pays $100,000 at the time the contract is signed, at which time the goods are transferred and Fulton's performance obligation is complete. In addition, Gibson agrees to pay Fulton $100,000 on December 31, 2017, and December 31, 2018. If Fulton entered into a financing arrangement with Gibson it would charge an interest rate of 9%.

LO 17.4

Required:
1. Determine the transaction price for the contract with Gibson.
2. Prepare the journal entries to record Fulton's 2017 sales revenue and interest revenue.
3. **Next Level** What is the objective of adjusting the transaction price to reflect the time value of money?

E17-17 Noncash Consideration On February 1, 2017, Silicon Rentals contracts with Zurgg Technology to provide 6 months of office services in exchange for 18,000 shares of Zurgg's common stock. The contract is signed on that date and works starts immediately. Silicon appropriately determines that its performance obligation is satisfied over time and each month it receives 3,000 shares of Zurgg Technology common stock. The fair value of Zurgg's common stock at February 28, 2017, and March 31, 2017, is $40 and $31, respectively.

LO 17.4

Required:
1. Prepare Silicon's journal entries related to recognize service revenue for February and March.
2. Assume that Silicon could not estimate the fair value of Zurrgg's common stock. How would Silicon determine fair value?

E17-18 Consideration Payable to a Customer On December 1, 2017, AwakeAllNight Inc. sells 5,000 super caffeinated candy bars to Campus Grocers. The candy bars sell for $3 per bar. In addition, AwakeAllNight pays Campus Grocers a $900 "placement fee" to ensure that its candy bars are always stocked prominently by the cash register. The $900 is paid at the end of each month based on the results of random inspections of Campus Grocers by AwakeAllNight to ensure that the terms of the contract are being followed.

LO 17.4

Required:
1. Determine the transaction price for AwakeAllNight's revenue contract.
2. Prepare AwakeAllNight's journal entries to recognize sales revenue and pay Campus Grocers the placement fee.

E17-19 Allocation of Transaction Price Rix Company sells home appliances and provides installation and service for its customers. On April 1, 2017, a customer purchased a dishwasher that Rix normally sells for $1,000. In addition, the customer purchased the installation service and a 3-year service contract, with stand-alone selling prices of $200 and $400, respectively. Because the customer purchased all three items as a bundle, Rix charged the customer $1,400.

LO 17.5

Required:
1. How should the transaction price be allocated among the products?
2. Prepare the journal entries to recognize revenue related to each product in 2017.

E17-20 Allocation of Transaction Price Assume the same facts as in **E17-19**, except that Rix cannot directly observe the stand-alone selling prices of the installation and service contracts. However, Rix has determined that the cost of the installation services is $150 and historical margins relative to cost average 20%. Therefore, Rix estimates the stand-alone selling price of the installation services using an expected cost plus a margin approach.

LO 17.5

Rix decides to use an adjusted market assessment approach to estimate the selling price of the service contract. Based on information obtained from competitors, Rix determines the average selling price of a similar service contract to be $350. Rix believes that it has a higher cost structure than its competitors and that it should increase this estimate by 10% to achieve an acceptable margin.

Required:
1. Determine the stand-alone selling price of each good or service.
2. How should the transaction price be allocated among the products? (Round your answer to the nearest dollar.)

E17-21 Allocation of Transaction Price Crazy Computer Store sells a back-to-school bundle that consists of a laptop computer, printer, and tablet to a customer for $2,400. Crazy Computer also sells the products on a stand-alone basis for the following amounts: the laptop for $1,800, the printer for $350, and the tablet for $500. The customer receives a $250 discount for buying the three products as a bundle. Crazy Computer normally sells the laptop and printer as a package for a price of $1,900. The tablet is normally not discounted.

LO 17.5

Required:
1. How should the transaction price be allocated among the products?
2. Prepare the journal entry when Crazy sells a back-to-school bundle for cash.

E17-22 Timing of Revenue Recognition Each of the following is an independent situation that relates to the recognition of revenue:

LO 17.6

a. Collection of a fare by an airline when the passenger makes a reservation
b. Receipt of payment for delivery services prior to the delivery of the goods

(continued)

c. Sale of an annual pass to a theme park
d. Construction of a home in a subdivision prior to a buyer being identified
e. Payment of insurance coverage at the beginning of the coverage period

Required:
For each situation, indicate if the company should recognize revenue over time or at a point in time. Also, indicate the company's performance obligation and be as specific as possible as to the time period it is satisfied.

E17-23 Long-Term Contracts In 2017, Tarlo Company agrees to construct a highway for Brice County over a 3-year period (2017 through 2019). The contract price is $1,200,000, and the construction costs (both actual and estimated) total $705,000 for the 3 years. Tarlo's estimate of progress toward satisfaction of the performance obligation at the end of each year is as follows: 2017, 20%; 2018, 75%; 2019, 100%.

LO 17.6
LO 17.8

Required:
1. Prepare a schedule showing the amount of gross profit that Tarlo recognizes each year assuming the performance obligation is determined to be satisfied over time.
2. Prepare a schedule showing the amount of gross profit that Tarlo recognizes each year assuming the performance obligation is satisfied at a point in time.

E17-24 Long-Term Contracts King Construction Company began work on a contract in 2017. The contract price is $4,000,000, and King determined that its performance obligation was satisfied over time. Other information relating to the contract is as follows:

LO 17.8

	2017
Costs incurred during the year	$ 800,000
Estimated costs to complete, December 31	2,400,000
Billings during the year	600,000
Collections during the year	400,000

Required:
1. How much gross profit or loss does King recognize in 2017?
2. **Next Level** Prepare the appropriate sections of the 2017 income statement and ending balance sheet.

E17-25 Long-Term Contracts Koolman Construction Company began work on a contract in 2017. The contract price is $3,000,000, and the company determined that its performance obligation was satisfied over time. Other information relating to the contract is as follows:

LO 17.8

	2017	2018
Costs incurred during the year	$ 600,000	$ 700,000
Estimated costs to complete, December 31	1,400,000	1,200,000
Billings during the year	500,000	850,000
Collections during the year	400,000	800,000

Required:
1. Compute the gross profit or loss recognized in 2017 and 2018.
2. Prepare the appropriate sections of the income statement and ending balance sheet for each year.

E17-26 Long-Term Contracts Newberg Construction Corporation contracted to construct a building for $400,000. Construction began in 2017 and was completed in 2018. Data relating to the contract are as follows:

LO 17.8

	Year Ended December 31,	
	2017	2018
Costs incurred	$200,000	$110,000
Estimated costs to complete	100,000	—

Newberg determined that its performance obligation was satisfied over time.

Required:
For the years ended December 31, 2017 and 2018, respectively, how much gross profit should Newberg report?

PROBLEMS

P17-1
LO 17.1
LO 17.2
LO 17.3
LO 17.4
LO 17.5
LO 17.6

Revenue Recognition Alternatives Each of the following independent situations relates to the recognition of revenue:

a. On June 2, 2017, a customer books travel on an airline, paying $500 for a round-trip ticket that departs July 15, 2017, and returns July 20, 2017. In addition, once the round-trip ticket is used, the airline credits the passenger's frequent-flier account for 500 miles. The airline determines that each frequent-flier point has a value of $0.01.

b. On May 1, 2017, a retailer enters into a contract with a construction company. The construction company will build a new warehouse for the retailer at a price of $2 million. The retailer will make four equal payments to the construction company over the 1-year construction period, starting on May 1, 2017, and then every 4 months. The retailer can cancel construction at any time and will own any construction to date; however, it must pay the construction company for work done up to the cancellation date. The building is completed on April 30, 2017.

c. Morning Donut agrees to supply donuts and coffee on a daily basis to a local business. The contract starts on January 1, 2017, and runs for 1 year. Morning Donut charges $400 per week for the donuts and coffee.

d. The Raleigh Knights sell four season tickets to a customer. The Knights play 10 regular season games, and the cost of one season ticket is $250.

Required:
For each situation, use the 5-step process to determine when revenue can be recognized. Determine (1) if a contract exists, (2) the performance obligations in the contract, (3) the transaction price in the contract, (4) how the transaction price is allocated to the performance obligations, and (5) when revenue is recognized.

P17-2
LO 17.2
LO 17.6

SHOW ME HOW

Contract Modification JustKitchens Inc. provides services to restaurants and hotels. The company supplies paper products, tableware, cookware, restaurant and kitchen equipment, and cleaning supplies. On January 2, 2017, JustKitchens enters into a contract with a local restaurant chain to provide its services for 3 years at a cost of $10,000 per year. The restaurant chain pays the total contract fee on January 2, 2017. JustKitchens's stand-alone selling price is also $10,000 per year.

After 2 years, the restaurant asks to modify the contract. On January 2, 2019, the companies agree to reduce the fee for the third year to $9,000 in exchange for extending the contract for 2 additional years at a fee of $11,000 per year. This modification is agreed to by both parties, and on that date the restaurant chain pays for the additional 2 years of service. The $11,000 fee for the additional years is the same as JustKitchens's stand-alone price.

Required:
1. How should JustKitchens account for the contract modification?
2. Prepare the journal entry that JustKitchens would make over the life of the contract.

P17-3
LO 17.2
LO 17.6

Contract Modification On January 1, 2017, ForeRunner Inc. enters into a contract with a sporting goods company to provide 100 GPS-enabled watches for $25,000 ($250 per watch) over the next 6 months. On April 1, 2017, when 80 of the watches have been delivered, the contract is modified.

Required:
1. Assume 30, 20, and 30 watches were delivered in January, February, and March, respectively. Prepare ForeRunner's journal entries to record revenue for each of these months.
2. Assume the contract is modified to include an additional 40 watches at $205 per watch, which is the stand-alone selling price on April 1, 2017. Assume that 20 watches are sold to the sporting goods company in April, May and June. Prepare the journal entries to record the watch sales in April, May and June.
3. Assume the contract is modified to include an additional 40 watches at $205 per watch, which does *not* represent the stand-alone selling price on April 1, 2017. Assume that 20 watches are sold to the sporting goods company in April, May and June. Prepare the journal entries to record the watch sales in April, May and June.
4. Assume that the contract is modified to reduce the price of the remaining 20 watches from the original order of 100 watches to $205 per watch, which is significantly lower than the stand-alone selling price on April 1, 2017. Assume 10, 5, and 5 watches are sold in April, May, and June, respectively. Prepare the journal entries to record the watch sales in April, May and June.

P17-4
LO 17.3
LO 17.4
LO 17.8

Variable Consideration and Performance Obligations Satisfied over Time On January 2, 2017, TI enters into a contract with Drewry Corp. to build a new piece of equipment. The contract price is $3 million, and construction is expected to take 18 months. Drewry is billed and pays $1,500,000 of the contract price on January 2, 2017, and will pay the balance at completion.

TI estimates that the cost of construction will be $2.2 million.
Drewry includes two performance bonuses in the contract:

- U.S. Bonus: If the equipment design receives a U.S. patent by March 15, 2018, Drewry will pay a $300,000 bonus.
- International Bonus: If the equipment receives approval for international distribution by January 31, 2018, Drewry will pay a $1,000,000 bonus.

The bonuses are payable when a U.S. patent is approved and when international distribution is approved.

On the date the contract is signed, IT estimates that there is an 80% chance it will receive U.S. patent protection by March 15, 2018, but only a 30% chance that the equipment will be approved for international distribution.

TI received a U.S. patent on the equipment design on November 15, 2017, and immediately billed Drewry and received its bonus payment. On December 31, 2017, TI has incurred $1,760,000 of contract costs and is 80% complete. TI won approval for international distribution on January 15, 2018, and completed the equipment project on April 15, 2018, at a cost of $2,200,000.

Required:
1. Identify the performance obligations in the contract.
2. Provide the journal entries that TI should make to recognize revenue from the contract.

P17-5
LO 17.4
LO 17.6

Time Value of Money, Incremental Contract Costs Palantir Corp. sells specialized equipment to the healthcare industry. Palantir pays its sales agents a salary plus a 5% commission on sales. Sales agents employed by the company sold 10 Osgilith MRI machines during January 2017. The MRI machine sells for $45,600 due at the end of 12 months. Alternatively, customers may elect to pay $40,000 at delivery and installation. All customers purchasing machines during January elected to pay at the end of the 12-month period.

Required:
1. Determine the transaction price of the Osgilith MRI machines, and discuss how Palantir would account for the sales commission.
2. Discuss whether the delayed payment contract contains a significant financing component.
3. Prepare the journal entries for 2017 for the Osgilith MRI machines sold by Palantir to customers who elect the delayed payment option. Assume that Palantir determines that an appropriate annual discount rate for the transaction is 14%.
4. Prepare the 2017 journal entries that Palantir would make for the 10 Osgilith MRI machines that are sold if customers elect to pay at delivery.

P17-6
LO 17.7

Long-Term Contracts In 2017, Dreyer Corporation began construction work under a 3-year contract, which represents a single performance obligation. The contract price is $800,000, and the performance obligation is satisfied over time. The financial statement presentations relating to this contract on December 31, 2017, follow:

Balance Sheet

Accounts receivable		$15,000
Construction in progress	$ 50,000	
Less: Progress billings	(47,000)	
Cost of uncompleted contract in excess of billings		3,000

Income Statement

Gross profit (before tax) on the contract	$10,000

Required:
1. How much cash did Dreyer collect during 2017?
2. What percentage complete is Dreyer as of the end of 2017?
3. What is the estimated gross profit before tax on the contract as of the end of 2017?

P17-7 **Long-Term Construction Contracts** Fender Construction Company receives a contract to construct a building
LO 17.8 over a period of 3 years for a price of $700,000. The contract represents a single performance obligation that will
be satisfied over time. Information relating to the performance of the contract is summarized as follows:

	2017	2018	2019
Construction costs incurred during the year	$150,000	$242,000	$168,000
Estimated costs to complete	350,000	168,000	—
Billings during the year	120,000	250,000	330,000
Collections during the year	100,000	260,000	340,000

Required:
1. Prepare journal entries for all 3 years.
2. Assume that the contract represents a single performance obligation that will be satisfied at a point in time. Prepare journal entries for all 3 years.

P17-8 **Volume Discounts** SoccerHawk Merchandise Inc. enters into a 6-month contract to sell soccer balls to City
LO 17.2 Soccer. The contract contains the following price scale:
LO 17.4
LO 17.6

Sales Volume	Price per Soccer Ball
First 300 soccer balls sold	$22
Next 200 soccer balls sold	19
Next 250 soccer balls sold	17
Additional soccer balls sold	15

On the date the contract is signed, SoccerHawk estimates based on past experience that there is a 20% chance it will sell 450 soccer balls, a 45% chance it will sell 600 soccer balls, and a 25% chance it will sell 800 soccer balls.

The company sells the following soccer balls during the 6-month contract:

	Number of Soccer Balls
Month 1	155
Month 2	60
Month 3	125
Month 4	75
Month 5	85
Month 6	60
Total sales	560 balls

Required:
1. On the date that the contract is signed should SoccerHawk make a journal entry? Why or why not?
2. Determine the transaction price that SoccerHawk should use when recording monthly revenue (round your answer to the nearest penny). Round average cost per unit to the nearest cent.
3. Prepare the journal entries for SoccerHawk assuming that City Soccer pays the amount due at the end of each month based on the sales to date.

P17-9 **Gift Cards** Escargot Inc. is a 5-star restaurant in Cincinnati. The restaurant sells 500 gift cards during January
LO 17.3 2017. Each gift card has a face value of $300. The gift cards never expire, although based on industry experience,
LO 17.4 Escargot expects that 12% of the balances will never be redeemed. During February 2017, $45,000 of gift cards are
LO 17.6 redeemed, and in March 2017 another $80,000 is redeemed.

Required:
1. Prepare journal entries for Escargot's gift card transactions for January through March.
2. Assume that at the end of March, due to the popularity of the restaurant, Escargot reduces its estimate of the amount of gift cards that will go unused to 8%. During April, gift cards worth $10,000 are used. Prepare any necessary journal entries.

P17-10 **Long-Term Construction Contracts** Jorg is building an office building for Wilmington Company for
LO 17.8 $20,000,000. The contract has the following characteristics:

- The office building is built to the customer's specifications and the customer can make changes to these specifications over the contract term.

(continued)

- Progress payments are made by the customer throughout construction.
- The customer can cancel the contract at any time (with a termination penalty); any work in process is the property of the customer.

Jorg provides you with the following details:

	December 31,		
	2017	2018	2019
Costs incurred to date	$8,000,000	$16,000,000	$18,000,000
Estimated costs to complete	6,000,000	3,000,000	—
Billings to date	8,000,000	16,000,000	20,000,000
Collections to date	6,000,000	12,000,000	18,000,000

Required:
1. Calculate the estimated total gross profit on the contract as of December 31, 2017, 2018, and 2019.
2. Calculate the percentage of completion for 2017, 2018, and 2019.
3. Calculate the amount of income (loss) Jorg will recognize for 2017, 2018, and 2019.
4. Prepare all journal entries related to this project for Jorg for all 3 years.
5. How will this project be carried on the balance sheet for 2017, 2018, and 2019?

P17-11 **Revenue Recognition Model** Blackmon Company provides locator services to the city transportation departments. Blackmon's service involves installing a dedicated hardware transmitter in each city bus. This transmitter provides real-time information to a central logistics center that provides a manager with detailed information as to bus location, speed, current weather, and traffic patterns. The manager can then reroute buses to improve efficiency of operations and increase customer satisfaction. Customers generally sign two separate contracts: one contract governs the sale of the hardware devices, while the second governs the provision of the locator services.

LO 17.2
LO 17.3
LO 17.6

On January 1, 2017, a customer purchased Blackmon's service by signing a contract for 100 devices for $480,000, the normal selling price. In addition, the customer signed a separate 12-month service contract for $2,000 per month ($20 per month per unit, which is the standard selling price for the service). This amount is billed on a monthly basis, and the customer pays for January service on January 31, 2017. The hardware device can only be used with Blackmon's services and there are currently no other competitors making devices that work with the Blackmon service. The customer may cancel at any time; however, the amount paid for the device is nonrefundable. The customer is given the right to renew the service contract at the existing rate each December, and the average life of a customer contract is 5 years. The customer takes delivery of the device on January 1, 2017, and begins the locator service on that date.

Required:
1. Identify the contract(s) for accounting purposes.
2. How many performance obligations exist? When will the performance obligation(s) be satisfied?
3. Prepare Blackmon's journal entries for January 2017.
4. Assume that other competitors sell a similar locator service comparable to Blackmon's. Would this fact change your previous answers?

CASES

COMMUNICATION

C17-1 **Revenue Recognition**
LO 17.1 Prior to ASU 2014-09 changing the principles underlying revenue recognition, companies recognized revenue when it was earned and realized. The principles of earned and realized were replaced with a core principle which states that companies should recognize revenue to depict the transfer of promised goods or services to customers in an amount that reflects the consideration to which the entity expects to be entitled in exchange for those goods or services. To accomplish this core principle, the FASB and the IASB stated that companies should follow a 5-step process.

Required:
Discuss the 5-step process that companies should use to accomplish the core principle of revenue recognition.

C17-2 **Identifying a Contract**
LO 17.2
The first step in the revenue recognition process is determining if a contract is in place between the seller and the customer. A contract is an agreement between two or more parties that creates enforceable rights and obligations. The standard states that a contract may be written, oral, or implied by customary business practices. To be a contract, the accounting standard states that it must meet five criteria.

Required:
Discuss the criteria necessary for a contract to be considered under the revenue recognition process. How would a company account for a contract that does not meet the criteria?

C17-3 **Stand-Alone Selling Price**
LO 17.4
Luke's Gameday Company sells a package of goods and services to its customers. The package includes four FCS Championship football tickets, a reserved parking space, a pregame party, and four pregame sideline passes. The package sells for $18,000. Because the stand-alone selling for the pregame party and sideline passes is not observable, Luke's Gameday Company is interested in determining how to allocate the transaction price to each underlying performance obligation.

Required:
Discuss what methods are available for estimating a stand-alone selling price for a good or service when the stand-alone selling price is not directly observable. Which method is preferred?

C17-4 **Variable Consideration**
LO 17.4
One of the more difficult issues that companies face in recognizing revenue is determining the transaction price. In cases where the consideration in a contract includes a variable amount, an entity should estimate the amount of consideration to which it is entitled in exchange for transferring the promised goods or services.

Required:
Discuss the methods a company may use to estimate variable consideration and the situations in which one method may be preferred over another.

C17-5 **Publishing and Revenue Recognition**
LO 17.6
After the presentation of your report on the examination of the financial statements to the board of directors of Savage Publishing Company, one of the new directors says he is surprised the income statement assumes that revenue is recognized over the period consistent with the publication of every issue of the company's magazine. He feels that the "crucial event" in the process of recognizing revenue in the magazine business is the cash sale of the subscription. He does not understand why—other than for the smoothing of income—most of the revenue cannot be "recognized" in the period of the sale.

Required:
Explain the propriety of timing the recognition of revenue in Savage Publishing's accounts with:
1. the cash sale of the magazine subscription
2. the publication of the magazine every month

CREATIVE AND CRITICAL THINKING

C17-6 **Contract Identification**
LO 17.2
On October 1, 2017, Graham's Weed&Feed Inc. signs a contract to maintain the grounds for BigData Corp. The contract ends on March 31, 2018, and has a monthly payment of $3,200. The contract does not include any stipulations for additional periods. On June 1, Graham's Weed&Feed and BigData sign a new 12-month contract that is retroactive to April 1, 2018. The monthly fee for the new contract is $4,000 per month and is also retroactive to April 1, 2018.

During April and May of 2018, while the new contract was being negotiated, Graham's Weed&Feed continued to maintain the grounds, and BigData continued to pay $3,200 per month. BigData was satisfied with Graham's Weed&Feed's performance, and the only issue during negotiations was the monthly fee.

Required:
Determine if a valid contract exists between Graham's Weed&Feed and BigData during April and May 2018.

C17-7 **Contract Modification**
LO 17.2
On January 1, 2017, Mopps Corp. agrees to provide Conklin Company 3 years of cleaning and janitorial services. The contract sets the price at $12,000 per year, which is the normal stand-alone price that Mopps charges. On December 31, 2018, Mopps and Conklin agree to modify the contract. Mopps reduces the fee for the third year to $10,000, and Conklin agrees to a 4-year extension that will extend services through December 31, 2023, at a price of $15,000 per year. At the time that the contract is modified, Mopps is charging other customers $13,500 for the cleaning and janitorial service.

(continued)

Required:

Should Mopps and Conklin treat the modification as a separate contract? If so how should Mopps account for the contract modification on December 31, 2018? Support your opinion by discussing the application to this case of the factors that need to be considered for determining the accounting for contract modifications.

C17-8 **Recognizing Revenue over Time versus Point in Time**
LO 17.6

On November 1, 2017, Olivia's Art Shoppe agreed to a contract with Tobacco Road Company to create 10 murals for the company's corporate headquarters. The contract has a transaction price of $800,000. The contract has the following features:

- All of the murals will be delivered and installed on February 1, 2018.
- Tobacco Road can cancel the contract at any point in time. Any murals created before cancellation will remain the property of Olivia's Art Shoppe.
- Tobacco Road paid $50,000 on November 1, 2017, and will pay the balance on February 1, 2018.

Olivia's Art Shoppe is nationally known and demand for its large murals is very high. On December 31, 2017, the CFO of Olivia's Art Shoppe determines that 7 of the 10 murals have been completed and recognizes $560,000 (7/10 × $800,000) of revenue.

Required:

Is the accounting for the murals by Olivia's CFO consistent with GAAP? Support your opinion by discussing the application to this case of the factors that need to be considered for revenue recognition.

C17-9 **Revenue Recognition Control**
LO 17.6

Revenue for a company is recognized for accounting purposes when the customer obtains control over the good or service. In some situations, revenue is recognized at a point in time; in other cases, accountants would recognize revenue over time. (Ignore income taxes.)

Required:
1. Explain when it would be appropriate to recognize revenue over time as opposed to a point in time.
2. How would a seller determine if a customer has obtained control over a good or service?

C17-10 **Revenue Recognized over Time**
LO 17.6
LO 17.8

Village Company is accounting for a long-term construction contract where revenue is recognized over time. The project is built to the customer's specifications, and the customer can make changes as construction is ongoing. It is a 3-year, fixed-fee contract that is presently in its first year. The latest reasonable estimates of total contract costs indicate that the contract will be completed at a profit. Village will submit progress billings to the customer and has reasonable assurance that collections on these billings will be received in each year of the contract. The contract can be cancelled at any time by the customer who will retain control of any work done to date.

Required:
1. When should revenue from contracts be accounted for over time versus at a point in time?
2. What facts in the preceding situation indicate that Village should account for this long-term construction contract over time?
3. How would the income recognized in each year of this long-term construction contract be determined using the cost-to-cost method of determining progress toward satisfaction of the performance obligation?
4. What is the effect on income, if any, of the progress billings and the collections on these billings?

CHAPTER 18

ACCOUNTING FOR INCOME TAXES

Global Tax Strategy

Tax implications arise from almost every decision a company makes—from how to structure a transaction to where to locate domestic and foreign operations. As business has become more global, companies have put a greater emphasis on creating effective international tax strategies that lower their overall effective tax rate in comparison to the statutory tax rate as set in the Internal Revenue Code. The company's **effective tax rate** is its income tax expense divided by its pretax financial income, while the **statutory tax rate** is the tax rate set in the Internal Revenue Code. For example, during 2013, **Google** operated in over 50 different countries, almost all of which have different tax laws and tax rates. Through various tax strategies, specifically the use of transfer pricing, Google is able to reduce its overall tax burden. In 2013, Google was able to lower its effective tax rate by almost 20% by shifting activities and income to countries with lower tax rates than the United States. Other companies such as **General Electric**, **Microsoft**, and **Intel** have been just as successful and have decreased their effective tax rates by over 10% through international tax management.

Because of these tax strategies, companies sometimes recognize revenues and expenses for financial reporting purposes at a different point than for income tax purposes. These differences are called *temporary differences* and result in future tax savings or future payable amounts which are reported on a company's balance sheet as deferred tax assets (for future deductible amounts) and deferred tax liabilities (for future taxable amounts). By reporting the amount of a company's deferred tax assets and deferred tax liabilities, companies provide information to help financial statement users to understand a company's tax strategies.

LEARNING OBJECTIVES

After reading this chapter you will be able to

LO 18.1 Understand accounting issues related to income taxes.

LO 18.2 Apply interperiod income tax allocation and explain the accounting for temporary differences.

LO 18.3 Record and report deferred tax liabilities and deferred tax assets.

LO 18.4 Understand and explain the accounting for permanent differences.

LO 18.5 Explain and account for operating loss carrybacks and carryforwards.

LO 18.6 Describe and apply intraperiod tax allocation.

LO 18.7 Examine presentation and disclosure issues related to accounting for income taxes.

LO 18.8 Understand and explain the accounting for uncertain tax positions.

This has created one major problem for U.S. companies operating in foreign countries—how to repatriate, or return, foreign-earned profits to the United States without incurring additional taxes. The United States utilizes a worldwide tax system in which every dollar of income earned by a U.S. company anywhere in the world is taxed at U.S. rates when the companies bring the profits back to the United States. Therefore, companies with international profits earned in countries with low tax rates, such as Ireland's 12.5% corporate tax rate, are leaving their cash overseas and not bringing it back to the United States, where it would be taxed an additional 22.5%. For example, at the end of 2013, Google reported $38.9 billion of cumulative foreign earnings that are permanently invested overseas. In total, the U.S. Senate Finance Committee reported that Google's untaxed foreign profits doubled from $1 trillion in 2008 to over $2.1 trillion at the end of 2013. As you can imagine, as business becomes more global, the issue of foreign-earned income and international tax strategies will become even more important.

Corporations report their business results to numerous stakeholders, of which, two of the most important are financial statement users and tax authorities. However, the objectives of financial reporting as established by the FASB and the objectives of tax reporting as established by the U.S. Congress in the Internal Revenue Code are very different. The objective of financial reporting is to provide useful information to decision makers about companies' cash flows, financial performance, resources, and obligations. This information enables external users to make intelligent investment and credit decisions, as discussed in Chapter 1. The overall objective of tax reporting under the Internal Revenue Code, on the other hand, is to obtain funds, in an equitable manner, to operate the federal government. Additionally, tax laws are frequently used to stimulate and regulate the economy and achieve various public policy goals.

As a result of their differing objectives, there are striking differences in accounting methods for financial reporting as governed by U.S. GAAP and income tax reporting in the United States as governed by the Internal Revenue Code.[1] Often these two systems recognize revenues and expenses in different periods and different amounts. For these reasons, **the income statement reported under GAAP is very different from the tax return reported under the Internal Revenue Code.** These different objectives give rise to a difference between income tax expense recognized on the income statement and income taxes paid to the government. If a corporation reports different revenues and/or expenses for financial reporting than it does for income tax reporting, it must determine the:

- deferred income tax liabilities and/or assets to report on its balance sheet
- income tax expense to subtract from its pretax financial income[2] on its income statement

This chapter discusses the procedures used to determine and report these items.

---

[1] Corporations may be subject to federal, state, and foreign income taxes as well as other forms of tax such as sales taxes, payroll taxes, and property taxes. In this chapter, we limit the discussion to financial reporting for federal income taxes.

[2] The terms *financial income, financial accounting income, book income,* and *accounting income* are synonymous and may be used interchangeably. Because the FASB uses the term *financial income* in its discussion of accounting for income taxes, we use that term throughout this chapter.

WHAT ARE THE ACCOUNTING ISSUES RELATED TO INCOME TAXES?

LEARNING OBJECTIVE 18.1
Understand accounting issues related to income taxes.

The accounting for income taxes creates a number of financial reporting issues affecting assets, liabilities, shareholders' equity, the provision for income taxes, and net income. **Pretax financial income** determined under GAAP is normally not equal to the amount of **taxable income** as determined by the Internal Revenue Code (IRC). These differences generally arise either because of measurement differences or timing differences between GAAP and IRC rules, which can be categorized into three groups as illustrated in Exhibit 18.1.

- *Temporary Differences:* A corporation reports some items of revenue and expense in one period for financial accounting purposes, but in an earlier or later period for income tax purposes. These items cause temporary timing differences between the corporation's pretax financial income and taxable income resulting in deferred tax assets and liabilities.
- *Permanent Differences:* Some items of revenue and expense that a corporation reports for financial accounting purposes are never reported for income tax purposes under the Internal Revenue Code. In addition, some items that are allowable deductions for income tax reporting do not qualify as expenses under GAAP. These items cause permanent measurement and timing differences between the corporation's pretax financial income and taxable income.[3]
- *Operating Loss Carrybacks and Carryforwards:* When a corporation reports an operating loss in a given year, the IRC allows the corporation to carry back the loss to offset taxable income reported in previous years, and/or carry forward the loss to offset future taxable income. These will result in tax refunds in the case of operating loss carrybacks and deferred tax assets in the case of operating loss carryforwards.

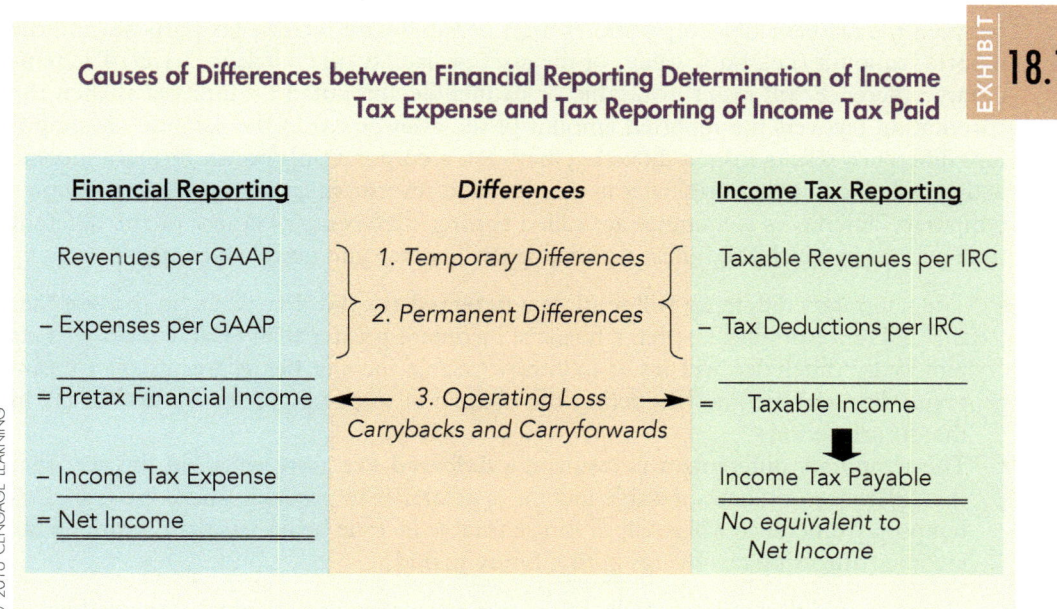

EXHIBIT 18.1 Causes of Differences between Financial Reporting Determination of Income Tax Expense and Tax Reporting of Income Tax Paid

---

[3] In addition, tax credits are a form of permanent difference. The tax code provides specific tax credits that a corporation may deduct from its current income tax payable. Tax credits cause a permanent difference between the corporation's pretax financial income and taxable income.

> ### GOT IT?
>
> **18-1** What source is used to determine income tax expense, and what source is used to determine income tax paid?
>
> **18-2** Identify the three groups of possible differences between pretax financial income and taxable income (or between income tax expense and income taxes payable).
>
> **18-3** How does the objective of tax reporting under the Internal Revenue Code differ from the objective of financial reporting under GAAP?

LEARNING OBJECTIVE 18.2

Apply interperiod income tax allocation and explain the accounting for temporary differences.

WHAT ARE THE BASIC ISSUES FOR INTERPERIOD INCOME TAX ALLOCATION?

Differences between a corporation's pretax financial income and taxable income arise from both temporary and permanent differences. Because temporary differences ultimately reverse companies must allocate income tax obligations across periods to income tax expense. This process is referred to as **interperiod income tax allocation**. For a temporary difference in which the amount of tax payable in the current period is lower than tax expense (because the company has delayed paying tax), the company has a liability to pay the difference in some future period (a deferred tax liability). Conversely, a temporary difference in which the amount of tax payable in the current period is greater than tax expense (because the company has essentially prepaid taxes) gives rise to an asset because the company will have the benefit of the taxes paid in some future period (a deferred tax asset). On the other hand, *permanent differences* between pretax financial income and taxable income never reverse and do *not* trigger interperiod tax allocation.

Temporary Differences

For financial reporting purposes, a **temporary difference** is measured as the difference between the tax basis of a corporation's asset or liability for income tax purposes and the reported amount (i.e., book value) of the asset or liability on its balance sheet. The temporary difference will result in taxable or deductible amounts in future years when the corporation recovers the reported amount of the asset or settles the liability.[4] A temporary difference results from a difference between a corporation's pretax financial income and taxable income that originates in one year and reverses in later years. A corporation's temporary differences sometimes are called **timing differences** because of the different time periods in which they affect pretax financial income and taxable income.

- The temporary difference will result in a **deferred tax liability** when, in the year that the difference originates, pretax financial income is greater than taxable income. This temporary difference will result in *future* taxable income being greater than future pretax financial income (triggering the obligation to pay a greater amount of tax in that future period).
- The temporary difference will result in a **deferred tax asset** when, in the year that the difference originates, taxable income is greater than pretax financial income. This temporary difference will result in future taxable income being less than future pretax income (triggering tax savings in that future period).

Temporary differences generally relate to a corporation's individual assets and liabilities and may be classified into four groups,[5] as shown in Exhibit 18.2 (p. 18-5).

---
[4] Temporary differences also include items that a corporation cannot identify with a particular asset or liability for financial reporting but which (a) result from events that it has recognized in the financial statements and (b) will result in taxable or deductible amounts in future years based on provisions in the tax law.

[5] FASB ASC 740-10-25 identifies four other temporary differences: (1) a reduction in the tax basis of depreciable assets because of an investment tax credit accounted for by the deferred method, (2) a reduction in the tax basis of depreciable assets because of other tax credits, (3) an increase in the tax basis of assets because of indexing whenever the local currency is the functional currency, and (4) business combinations accounted for by the purchase method. Because these temporary differences occur less frequently, we do not discuss them in this chapter.

Temporary Differences — EXHIBIT 18.2

Temporary Differences Creating Deferred Tax Liabilities

Future Taxable Income Will Be Greater Than Future Pretax Financial Income

1. *Revenues or gains are included in pretax financial income before they are included in taxable income.*

   For example:
   a. Gross profit from sales revenue accounted for on an accrual basis for financial reporting purposes but on the installment (cash) basis for tax purposes.
   b. Gross profit on long-term construction contracts may be recognized for financial reporting purposes over the construction period. But, for income tax purposes, it may be recognized by certain corporations once the construction project is complete.
   c. Investment income may be recognized under the equity method for financial reporting purposes. But, for income tax purposes, it is recognized in periods when dividends are received.
   d. Unrealized holding gains on trading securities are recognized when they occur for financial reporting purposes. However, for income tax purposes, gains are not recognized until realized.
   e. Income earned in a foreign country that has a lower tax and is expected to be repatriated back to the United States in a future period.

2. *Expenses or losses are deducted to compute taxable income before they are subtracted to compute pretax financial income.*

   For example:
   a. Depreciable assets may be depreciated on an accelerated basis under the Modified Accelerated Cost Recovery System (MACRS) over the prescribed tax life (discussed in Chapter 11) for income tax purposes, but for financial reporting purposes, they may be depreciated using the straight-line method over a different period.
   b. Interest and taxes on certain self-construction projects may be deducted as incurred in arriving at taxable income. However, these costs may be capitalized in certain instances as a part of the cost of the self-constructed assets for financial reporting.
   c. Prepaid expenses are deducted on the tax return in the period paid. However, for financial reporting purposes, they are not recognized until the period used.

Temporary Differences Creating Deferred Tax Assets

Future Taxable Income Will Be Less Than Future Pretax Financial Income

3. *Revenues or gains are included in taxable income before they are included in pretax financial income.*

   For example:
   a. Items such as rent, interest, and royalties received in advance are taxable when received. However, they are not recognized as revenue for financial reporting purposes until the service actually has been provided.
   b. Gains on "sales and leasebacks" are taxed at the date of sale, but are reported over the life of the lease contract for financial reporting purposes.

4. *Expenses or losses are subtracted to compute pretax financial income before they are deducted to compute taxable income.*

   For example:
   a. Product warranty costs, bad debt expense, and losses on inventories may be estimated and recorded as expenses in the current year for financial reporting purposes. However, they may not be deducted until actually incurred to determine taxable income (for instance, in the period when the warranty costs are paid or the bad debts are written off).

(continued)

> **EXHIBIT 18.2 (Continued)**
>
> b. Compensatory share option plans require the recognition of expense during the periods in which employee service is provided. However, a tax deduction is not allowed until the employees exercise the share options.
> c. Indirect costs of producing inventory may be recorded as expenses in the current year for financial reporting purposes. However, these costs may be capitalized in the cost of inventory and therefore deducted as part of cost of goods sold in a later year to determine taxable income.
> d. A contingent loss may be expensed for financial reporting purposes if a loss is probable and is reasonably estimable, but it may not be deducted in arriving at taxable income until it is actually paid.

Interperiod Income Tax Allocation: Conceptual Issues

The FASB identified two objectives of accounting for income taxes.[6]

- A corporation should recognize the amount of its income tax payable or refund for the current year.
- A corporation should recognize deferred tax liabilities for **future taxable amounts**, and deferred tax assets for **future tax deductible amounts**, so that the balance sheet recognizes the future tax consequences that will arise from all past transactions, events, and arrangements that it has reported in its financial statements or income tax returns.

In order to accomplish these objectives, the FASB concluded that a **comprehensive asset and liability approach** was necessary for financial accounting and reporting for income taxes. The comprehensive asset and liability approach means that a tax asset or liability will result when there are timing differences between the accounting value and tax value of an asset or liability.

The FASB concluded that interperiod tax allocation is appropriate because income taxes are an expense of doing business for a corporation and should be accrued and deferred just like other expenses which results in the recognition of deferred assets and liabilities. In addition, the allocation of income tax expense should be based on *all* temporary differences, regardless of how significant and how often they reoccur. Finally, it concluded that deferred tax assets and liabilities should be measured using the enacted tax rates that will be in existence when the temporary differences reverse because that is when the cash flows will occur.

To implement the comprehensive asset and liability approach, the FASB listed four principles that a corporation is to apply to account for its income taxes. A corporation must:

- recognize a current tax liability (asset) for the estimated income tax payable (refund) on its income tax return for the current year[7]
- recognize a deferred tax liability or asset for the estimated future tax effects of each temporary difference
- measure its deferred tax liabilities and assets based on the provisions of the enacted tax law; the effects of possible (but not yet enacted) future changes in tax laws or rates are not anticipated[8]
- reduce the amount of deferred tax assets, if necessary, by the amount of any tax benefits that, based on available evidence, are not expected to be realized.

---

[6] FASB ASC 740-10-10: Income Taxes, Overall, Objectives.

[7] Because a corporation may make estimated tax payments during the year, the current tax liability or asset that it reports on its ending balance sheet may be different than its total tax payable or refund. If a corporation has an "uncertain tax position," this also may affect the tax liability or asset. In the chapter, we assume this is *not* the case, but we briefly discuss uncertain tax positions at the end of the chapter.

[8] If the enacted laws provide for a future change in tax rates or laws, we use the enacted future rates and rules. If a change in tax rates or rules is expected but not yet enacted, we use what is current as this book goes to print.

Thus, a corporation uses interperiod income tax allocation to determine its deferred tax assets and liabilities for all temporary differences. These deferred items are measured based on the currently enacted income tax rates and laws. The corporation adjusts its deferred tax assets and liabilities when changes in the income tax rates or laws are enacted.

Deferred Tax Liability Chapter 4 discussed the following three characteristics of a liability established in *FASB Statement of Financial Accounting Concepts No. 6*:

- It involves a responsibility that will be settled by a sacrifice requiring the transfer of assets, provision of services, or other use of assets in the future.
- The responsibility obligates the corporation, so that it has little or no discretion to avoid the future sacrifice.
- The transaction or other event obligating the corporation has already occurred.

Temporary differences that will result in higher tax payments for a corporation in future years meet the first characteristic because (a) the deferred tax consequences stem from the tax law and are a responsibility to the government, (b) settlement will involve a future payment of taxes, and (c) settlement will result from events specified by the existing tax law. They meet the second characteristic because income taxes will be payable when the temporary differences result in taxable amounts in future years. The third characteristic is met because the events that resulted in the deferred tax liability have already occurred.

Deferred Tax Asset The three characteristics of an asset are:

- It is expected to provide future economic benefits for the company.
- The company has obtained the rights to the benefits and controls other entities' access to it.
- The transaction, arrangement, or event resulting in the company's right to or control of the benefit has already occurred.[9]

Temporary differences that will result in deductible amounts in future years meet the first characteristic because the deductible amounts will reduce future taxable income and will provide future economic benefits to the company through reduced taxes paid. The second characteristic is met because the corporation will have an exclusive right to the reduced taxes paid. Finally, the third characteristic is met because the events that resulted in the deferred tax asset have already occurred.

Measurement After a corporation has identified a future taxable or deductible amount, it measures the temporary difference to record the amount of the deferred tax liability or deferred tax asset to report in its financial statements. The FASB addressed two issues regarding the measurement of deferred tax liabilities and assets: the applicable income tax rates and whether a valuation allowance should be created for deferred tax assets.

Applicable Income Tax Rate The U.S. federal corporate income tax is assessed based on a progressive rate schedule, in which higher income amounts are taxed at higher rates. However, once a corporation's taxable income exceeds a relatively low threshold amount, its entire taxable income essentially is taxed at a single flat rate (35% in 2014). For deferred taxes, the FASB decided to require companies to use the **marginal tax rate**—the enacted income tax rate expected to apply to its *last* dollar of taxable income—in the periods when it expects the deferred tax liability or asset to be settled or realized. Therefore, most corporations are required to use a single flat rate in their deferred tax calculations.[10]

---

[9] "Elements of Financial Statements of Business Enterprises," *FASB Statement of Financial Accounting Concepts No. 6* (Stamford, CT: FASB, 1985), par. 26 and 36.

[10] Corporations for which graduated rates are a significant factor must use an "average graduated tax rate" approach for measuring their deferred tax liabilities and assets. We do not discuss this approach in this book.

Valuation Allowance The second issue—the possible use of a valuation allowance (a contra account to reduce the reported asset value) for deferred tax assets—was more controversial. A corporation will realize the tax benefits from a deferred tax asset only if it will have enough future taxable income from which to subtract the future deductible amount. If there is sufficient uncertainty about a corporation's future taxable income, the FASB decided that it must establish a valuation allowance to reduce its deferred tax asset(s) to the realizable amount. (This approach is similar to reporting accounts receivable at a gross amount and then reducing the amount by an allowance for doubtful accounts.)

But how much uncertainty is sufficient, and how does a corporation make a judgment about the realizable amount? In regard to sufficiency, the FASB applied a "more likely than not" (a likelihood of more than 50%) criterion to measure uncertainty. In other words, a corporation must recognize a valuation allowance if, based on available evidence, it is *more likely than not* that the deferred asset will *not* be fully realized.

To make a judgment about the realizable amount, a corporation should consider all available evidence, both positive and negative, in determining whether it needs a valuation allowance. Positive evidence that a corporation will realize the tax benefits from a deferred tax asset includes, for instance, a history of profitability or existing contracts and prudent and feasible tax-planning strategies.[11] These may be sufficient for a corporation to conclude that it does not need a valuation allowance.

The Board stated that it would be difficult for a corporation to conclude that a valuation allowance is *not* needed when there is negative evidence, such as cumulative losses in recent years. It also provided other examples of negative evidence, such as:

- a history of unused operating loss carryforwards
- losses expected in the near future years
- unsettled circumstances (such as a lawsuit) that are potentially unfavorable

The Board noted, however, that other positive evidence (e.g., a strong earnings history and expected future profitability) may overcome negative evidence, making a valuation allowance unnecessary. A corporation must use good judgment in weighing the verifiable positive and negative evidence to determine if it needs a valuation allowance for some or all of a deferred tax asset.

If a corporation does establish a valuation allowance, a future change in circumstances may cause a change in judgment about the realizability of the related deferred tax asset. There also may be a change in tax laws or rates that would affect the amount of previously recorded deferred tax assets and liabilities. Therefore, the corporation must evaluate its valuation allowance on each balance sheet date. In each of the preceding situations, the corporation includes the effect of the change as an adjustment to the income tax expense related to its income from continuing operations in the year of the change.[12]

GOT IT?

18-4 What is a temporary difference? Give two examples.

18-5 What four principles did the FASB conclude were necessary to implement the objectives of the comprehensive asset and liability approach?

18-6 What are the two objectives of accounting for income taxes identified by the FASB?

18-7 What are the three characteristics of a liability, and why does a deferred tax liability of a corporation meet these characteristics?

18-8 What are the three characteristics of an asset, and why does a deferred tax asset of a corporation meet these characteristics?

---

[11] A tax planning strategy is an action a corporation ordinarily would not take except to ensure that it can realize a deductible temporary difference (e.g., acceleration of taxable income).

[12] FASB ASC 740-10-30: Income Taxes, Overall, Initial Measurement.

HOW ARE CURRENT AND DEFERRED TAXES RECORDED AND REPORTED UNDER INTERPERIOD INCOME TAX ALLOCATION?

LEARNING OBJECTIVE 18.3
Record and report deferred tax liabilities and deferred tax assets.

To measure and record the amount of its current and deferred income taxes, a corporation completes the following steps, as illustrated in Exhibit 18.3.

- *Step 1.* Determine the company's taxable income and income tax payable for the year by applying the applicable tax rate to the current taxable income.
- *Step 2.* Identify the temporary differences and classify each as either a future taxable amount or a future deductible amount.
- *Step 3.* Measure the year-end deferred tax liability for each future taxable amount using the applicable tax rate.
- *Step 4.* Measure the year-end deferred tax asset for each future deductible amount using the applicable tax rate.
- *Step 5.* Reduce deferred tax assets by a valuation allowance if, based on available evidence, it is *more likely than not* that some or all of the year-end deferred tax assets will not be realized in tax savings in future years.
- *Step 6.* Record the income tax expense (including the deferred tax expense or benefit), income tax payable, change in deferred tax liabilities and/or deferred tax assets, and change in valuation allowance (if any).

EXHIBIT 18.3 Determination of Current and Deferred Income Taxes

Step 1: Determine taxable income.

| Balance Sheet | Journal Entry |

Taxable Income × Applicable Tax Rate → Income Tax Payable → Income Tax Payable

Step 2: Identify the temporary differences and classify as either a future taxable amount or a future deductible amount.

Step 3: Measure the year-end deferred tax liability for each future taxable amount.

Future Taxable Amount × Applicable Tax Rate → Deferred Tax Liability Balance → Change in Deferred Tax Liability

Step 4: Measure the year-end deferred tax asset for each future deductible amount.

Future Deductible Amount × Applicable Tax Rate → Deferred Tax Asset Balance → Change in Deferred Tax Asset

Step 5: Establish a valuation allowance for deferred tax assets, if necessary.

Unrealizable Amount of Year-End Deferred Tax Asset × Applicable Tax Rate → Deferred Tax Asset Valuation Allowance Balance → Change in Valuation Account

Step 6: Record income tax expense.

Income Tax Payable ± Change in Deferred Tax Liability ± Change in Deferred Tax Asset ± Change in Valuation Allowance = Income Tax Expense

Basic Entries

As Exhibit 18.3 shows, the corporation first determines taxable income by applying the Internal Revenue Code. It then determines the amount the company will have to pay the government, as follows:

$$\text{Taxable Income} \times \text{Applicable Tax Rate(s)} = \text{Income Tax Payable}$$

The income tax expense for the period will differ from the income tax payable when changes occur during the period in deferred tax liabilities, deferred tax assets, or the valuation allowance. The amount of this change is combined with the amount of its income tax payable (or refund) to determine the amount of its income tax expense (or benefit) for the year. Note that the change in the deferred tax liabilities or assets during the year represents a corporation's deferred tax expense or benefit.

Example Grazie Company is in its first year of business. The company earns pretax income for the year, and reports a deferred tax liability of $1,600 at the end of the year. Grazie makes the following journal entry (amounts assumed):

Income Tax Expense	11,600	
Income Taxes Payable		10,000
Deferred Tax Liability		1,600

For a similar situation involving a single deferred tax asset of $1,300 (and *no* valuation allowance) instead of a deferred tax liability, Grazie makes the following journal entry (amounts assumed):

Income Tax Expense	12,800	
Deferred Tax Asset	1,300	
Income Taxes Payable		14,100

Grazie determines the amount of the income tax payable by multiplying the taxable income for the year by the current tax rate(s). For simplicity, we assume here (and in the later examples and homework) that the corporation does *not* make estimated income tax payments during the year. Therefore, it records the entire obligation for the year as income taxes payable.

In subsequent years, Grazie calculates the amount of the change to the deferred tax liability (asset) in the journal entry by determining the amount of the year-end deferred tax liability (asset) and comparing this ending amount to the beginning amount of the deferred tax liability (asset). The corporation reports the net amount of the year-end deferred tax liability (asset) on its ending balance sheet, classified as "noncurrent," as we discuss in a later section. ■

Example If, in the last example, Grazie previously had no valuation allowance related to the deferred tax asset but determined that a $400 allowance was necessary at the end of the year, it would make the following additional journal entry (amounts assumed):

Income Tax Expense	400	
Allowance to Reduce Deferred Tax Asset to		
Realizable Value		400

Grazie combines the $400 debit to Income Tax Expense with the $12,800 amount of Income Tax Expense from the journal entry in the last example to determine its $13,200 *total* Income Tax Expense. Achebe subtracts the Allowance account from the Deferred Tax Asset account on its ending balance sheet to report the expected net realizable value of the deferred tax asset. ■

When a corporation has more than one future taxable amount or future deductible amount, permanent differences, and changes in enacted future tax rates, completion of the steps listed earlier becomes more complex.

Example: Deferred Tax Liability—Single Future Taxable Amount

In 2016, Track Company purchased an asset at a cost of $6,000. For financial reporting purposes, the asset has a 4-year life, has no residual value, and is depreciated by the straight-line method. For income tax purposes, the asset is depreciated under MACRS using the 200%-declining-balance method over a 3-year life (no residual value), as discussed in Chapter 11. Prior to 2016, Track had no deferred tax liability or asset. The difference between the company's depreciation expense for financial reporting purposes and income tax purposes is the only temporary difference between its pretax financial income and taxable income.[13] In 2016, Track has taxable income of $7,500 (after deducting the MACRS depreciation). The enacted income tax rate for 2016 and all future years is 30%.

Based on the preceding information:

- The depreciation expense for 2016 is $1,500 [$6,000 ÷ 4 years] for financial reporting purposes and $2,000 [$6,000 × 33.33% (from Exhibit 11.3 in Chapter 11)] for income tax purposes.
- At the end of 2016, the asset has a book value of $4,500 for financial reporting purposes and a book value of $4,000 for income tax purposes, as shown in the top part of **Example 18.1**.

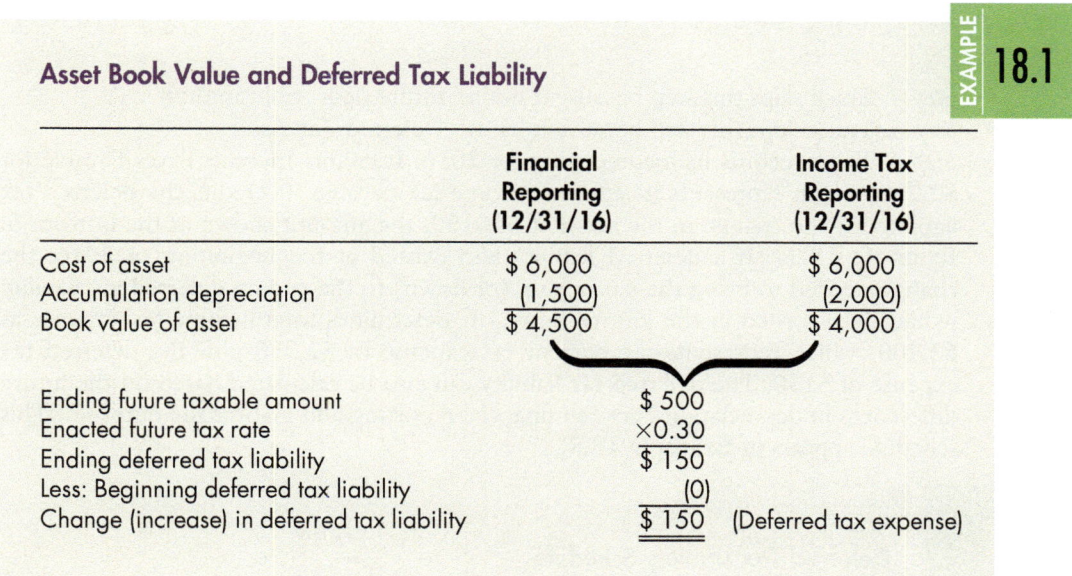

EXAMPLE 18.1

Asset Book Value and Deferred Tax Liability

	Financial Reporting (12/31/16)	Income Tax Reporting (12/31/16)
Cost of asset	$ 6,000	$ 6,000
Accumulation depreciation	(1,500)	(2,000)
Book value of asset	$ 4,500	$ 4,000

Ending future taxable amount	$ 500	
Enacted future tax rate	×0.30	
Ending deferred tax liability	$ 150	
Less: Beginning deferred tax liability	(0)	
Change (increase) in deferred tax liability	$ 150	(Deferred tax expense)

The $500 difference in book values is the result of a temporary difference in depreciation expense that originated in 2016 and caused taxable income to be lower than pretax financial income in that year. This difference will reverse in years 2017 to 2019 because tax depreciation expense will be *lower* than financial depreciation expense by $500 over that period. We show this schedule in **Example 18.2**. Thus, the $500 is the ending *future taxable amount* for 2016 because future taxable income will be *higher* than future pretax financial income.

Track Company applies the steps listed on page 18-9 to determine its current and deferred income taxes:

- *Step 1.* Track measures taxable income of $7,500 and then determines the income tax payable for 2016 as $2,250 ($7,500 taxable income × 0.30 current tax rate).
- *Step 2.* Track identifies the temporary depreciation expense difference as a future taxable amount for 2016, as shown in **Example 18.1**.
- *Step 3.* Track measures the year-end deferred tax liability for the future taxable amount as $150 by multiplying the $500 total future taxable amount times the 30% enacted future tax rate, as shown in the middle of Exhibit 18.1 (p. 18-3).

---

[13] In reality, a corporation would have several depreciable assets of different ages and with varying lives, perhaps resulting in both originating (and deductible) and reversing (and taxable) depreciation differences in a given year. For simplicity, when dealing with depreciable assets in the text and homework, we generally focus on a single depreciable asset, with depreciation causing a reversing (taxable) difference in the future.

EXAMPLE 18.2 Financial and Income Tax Depreciation Schedule

Depreciation Expense

Year	Financial Depreciation	Income Tax Depreciation
2017	$1,500[a]	$2,667[b]
2018	1,500	889[c]
2019	1,500	444[d]
Total	$4,500	$4,000

[a] Straight-line depreciation: $6,000 ÷ 4 years = $1,500 Depreciation expense per year
[b] $6,000 × 44.45% from Exhibit 11.3
[c] $6,000 × 14.81% from Exhibit 11.3
[d] $6,000 × 7.41% from Exhibit 11.3; $1 rounding error

- *Step 4.* Track skips this step because it has no future deductible amount.
- *Step 5.* Track skips this step because it has no Deferred Tax Asset.
- *Step 6.* Track records its income taxes for 2016. It credits Income Taxes Payable for $2,250, which represents its current income tax payable. It credits the deferred tax liability for the change in the account of $150, the amount shown at the bottom of **Example 18.1**. [If a deferred liability had existed at the beginning of 2016, the change needed to bring the balance up (or down) to the ending deferred tax liability would be recorded in the journal entry.] It determines total income tax expense as $2,400, which represents the current tax expense of $2,250 plus the deferred tax expense of $150. The deferred tax liability can also be calculated based on the future differences in depreciation between financial reporting and income tax purposes. This schedule appears in **Example 18.3**.

EXAMPLE 18.3 Deferred Tax Liability Schedule

Deferred Tax Liability

	2017	2018	2019	
Financial depreciation	$ 1,500	$1,500	$1,500	
Income tax depreciation	(2,667)	(889)	(444)	
Taxable amount*	$(1,167)	$ 611	$1,056	= $500
Income tax rate	×0.30	×0.30	×0.30	
Deferred tax liability (rounded)	$ (350) +	$ 183 +	$ 317	= $150

*Higher (lower) income tax depreciation expense results in lower (higher) taxable income.

Track makes the following journal entry at the end of 2016:

Income Tax Expense ($2,250 + $150)	2,400	
Income Taxes Payable		2,250
Deferred Tax Liability		150

Track reports the $2,400 income tax expense on its 2016 income statement. The company reports the $2,250 in income taxes payable as a current liability on its 2016 ending balance sheet. As we discuss in a later section, the company reports the noncurrent deferred tax liability of $150 on its ending balance sheet.

Examining the information in **Example 18.3** in 2017, the deferred tax liability would be credited for $350, resulting in a total deferred tax liability of $500. Starting with 2018, the temporary difference would start reversing and the deferred tax liability would be debited for $183, leaving a deferred tax liability of $317. In the final year of the temporary difference, the deferred tax liability would be debited for $317 and the deferred tax liability would be reduced to zero. ■

Example: Deferred Tax Liability—Single Future Taxable Amount and Multiple Tax Rates

Assume the same information as in the previous example, in which Track Company acquires an asset in 2016 that has a financial book value of $4,500 and a tax basis of $4,000 at the end of 2016, creating a future taxable amount of $500. Now also assume that the income tax rate for 2016 is 40%, but Congress has enacted tax rates of 35% for 2017, 33% for 2018, and 30% for 2019 and beyond. In the previous example, the calculation of the deferred tax liability is straightforward because a 30% tax rate is applicable to all the future years in which the depreciation temporary difference reverses and results in higher taxable income. However, when future tax rates are different than current tax rates, the calculation of deferred tax rates becomes more complicated. The calculation requires a company to:

- prepare a schedule to determine the reversing difference (i.e., taxable amount) for each future year
- multiply each yearly taxable amount by the applicable tax rate to determine the additional income tax payable (deferred taxes) for that year
- sum the yearly deferred taxes to determine the total deferred tax liability

In this example, Track first prepares a schedule to compute the 2017 through 2019 depreciation expense for financial reporting and income tax purposes, as illustrated in the upper portion of **Example 18.4**. Based on the differences in depreciation expense for

---

EXAMPLE 18.4

Depreciation and Deferred Tax Schedules

Depreciation Expense

Year	Financial Depreciation	Income Tax Depreciation
2017	$1,500[a]	$2,667[b]
2018	1,500	889[c]
2019	1,500	444[d]
Total	$4,500	$4,000

Deferred Tax Liability

	2017		2018		2019		
Financial depreciation	$ 1,500		$1,500		$1,500		
Income tax depreciation	(2,667)		(889)		(444)		
Taxable amount[e]	$(1,167)	+	$ 611	+	$1,056	=	$500
Income tax rate	×0.35		×0.33		×0.30		
Deferred tax liability[f]	$ (408)	+	$ 202	+	$ 317	=	$111

[a] Straight-line depreciation: $6,000 ÷ 4 years = $1,500 Depreciation expense per year
[b] $6,000 × 44.45% from Exhibit 11.3
[c] $6,000 × 14.81% from Exhibit 11.3
[d] $6,000 × 7.41% from Exhibit 11.3; $1 rounding error
[e] Higher (lower) income tax depreciation results in lower (higher) taxable income.
[f] Amounts rounded to nearest dollar

financial reporting and income tax purposes, Track prepares a schedule to calculate its deferred tax liability, as illustrated in the lower portion of **Example 18.4**.

For each year, Track deducts the income tax depreciation expense from the financial reporting depreciation expense to determine the taxable amount. Given the enacted tax rates for the respective years, the deferred tax liability would increase in 2014 and then reverse back to zero at the end of 2019. Thus, the total deferred tax liability is $111 at the end of 2016. Because the taxable income for 2016 is $7,500, the income tax payable is $3,000 ($7,500 × 0.40) based on the 40% tax rate for 2016. Track makes the following journal entry at the end of 2016:

Income Tax Expense ($3,000 + $111)	3,111	
Income Taxes Payable		3,000
Deferred Tax Liability		111

Track reports the income tax expense, income taxes payable, and a deferred tax liability in its financial statements.

Examining the information in **Example 18.4**, in 2017 Deferred Tax Liability would be credited for $408, resulting in a total deferred tax liability of $519. Starting with 2018, the temporary difference would start reversing and Deferred Tax Liability would be debited for $202, leaving a deferred tax liability of $317. In the final year of the temporary difference, Deferred Tax Liability would be debited for $317 and the deferred tax liability would be reduced to zero. ■

Example: Deferred Tax Asset—Single Future Deductible Amount

Klemper Company has been operating profitably for several years selling a product on which it provides a 3-year assurance-type warranty. It expects to continue to be profitable in the future. For financial reporting purposes, Klemper estimates its future warranty costs over the full 3-year warranty period for all of the products sold that year, and records a warranty expense and liability at year-end. For income tax purposes, the company is not allowed to deduct its warranty costs until they are paid. This difference in reporting warranty costs is the only temporary difference between the company's pretax financial income and taxable income. It is a *future deductible amount* (resulting in a deferred tax asset) because in future years the warranty costs that Klemper deducts for income tax purposes will exceed the warranty expense it deducts for financial reporting purposes. This will cause its future taxable income to be *lower* than its future pretax financial income. Assume that at the beginning of 2016, Klemper had a deferred tax asset of $330 related to the warranty liability on its balance sheet. At the end of 2016, Klemper estimates that its ending warranty liability is $1,400, as shown in **Example 18.5**.

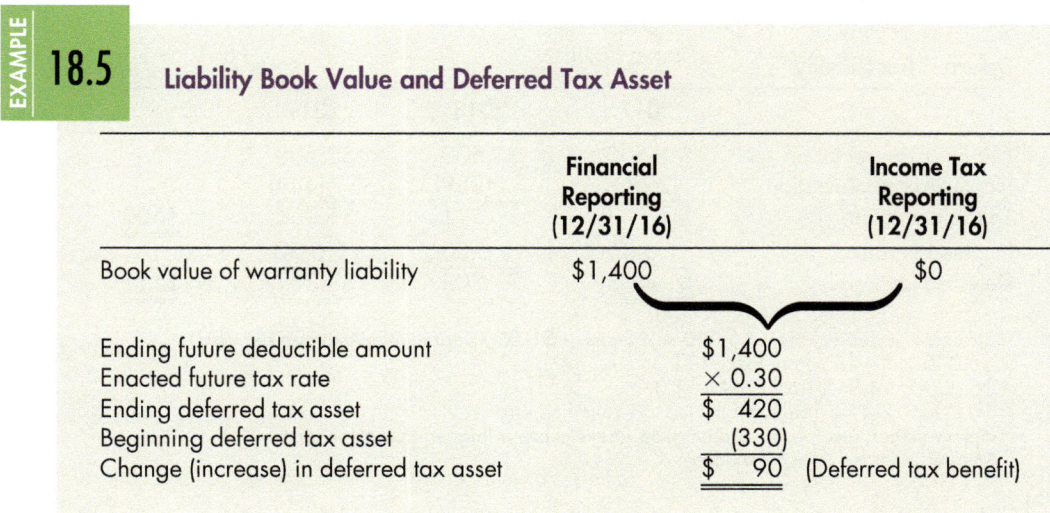

EXAMPLE 18.5 Liability Book Value and Deferred Tax Asset

	Financial Reporting (12/31/16)	Income Tax Reporting (12/31/16)
Book value of warranty liability	$1,400	$0
Ending future deductible amount		$1,400
Enacted future tax rate		× 0.30
Ending deferred tax asset		$ 420
Beginning deferred tax asset		(330)
Change (increase) in deferred tax asset		$ 90 (Deferred tax benefit)

In 2016, Klemper has taxable income of $5,000. The income tax rate for 2016 is 30%, and no change in the tax rate has been enacted for future years.

Klemper applies the steps listed on page 18-9 to determine its current and deferred income taxes:

- *Step 1.* Klemper determines taxable income to be $5,000 and then measures the current year's tax payable for 2016 as $1,500 ($5,000 × 0.30).
- *Step 2.* Klemper identifies the warranty liability as the only temporary difference and classifies it as a future deductible amount for 2016, as shown in **Example 18.5**.
- *Step 3.* Klemper skips this step because it has no future taxable amount.
- *Step 4.* Klemper measures the year-end deferred tax asset as $420 by multiplying the future deductible amount of $1,400 times the 30% enacted future tax rate, as shown in the middle of **Example 18.5**.
- *Step 5.* Klemper skips this step because it does not need a valuation allowance. The company has a successful earnings history and expects to be profitable in the future, which will enable it to realize the benefits of the future deductible amount.
- *Step 6.* Klemper records its income taxes for 2016. It credits Income Taxes Payable for $1,500, which represents its current income tax payable. It debits Deferred Tax Asset for the change in the account of $90, calculated as the $420 ending deferred tax asset minus the beginning amount of $330, as shown in the bottom part of Example 18.5. This $90 change in the deferred tax asset is subtracted from the $1,500 income taxes payable to determine the $1,410 debit to Income Tax Expense for 2016.

Klemper makes the following journal entry at the end of 2016:

Income Tax Expense ($1,500 − $90)	1,410	
Deferred Tax Asset	90	
Income Taxes Payable		1,500

Klemper reports the deferred tax asset on its balance sheet, as we discuss in a later section.

Example: Deferred Tax Asset and Valuation Allowance

Assume the same information as in the previous example, except that during the past few years Klemper Company's sales and profits have been declining. At the end of 2016, because of uncertain future economic conditions, Klemper determines that it is "more likely than not" that $600 of the ending $1,400 future deductible amount will not be realized. Therefore, in addition to the income tax entry made in the previous example, Klemper also records a valuation allowance of $180 ($600 × 0.30) at the end of 2016 as follows:

Income Tax Expense	180	
Allowance to Reduce Deferred		
Tax Asset to Realizable Value		180

Klemper subtracts the $180 ending balance in the allowance account from the $420 deferred tax asset ending balance to report the realizable value of $240 on its ending balance sheet as follows:

Deferred tax asset	$ 420
Less: Allowance to reduce deferred tax asset to realizable value	(180)
Net deferred tax asset	$ 240

In 2017 and future years, the company must review all available evidence to determine whether it needs to adjust (increase or decrease) the valuation allowance.

Change in Income Tax Laws or Rates

In our previous examples, the corporation determined the balances of its deferred tax liabilities (or assets) at the end of a given year by applying the currently enacted income tax rate(s) and laws to its future taxable and future deductible temporary differences. Occasionally, Congress may change the income tax laws or rates so that they differ from the laws or rates a corporation previously used to calculate its deferred tax liabilities and assets. A corporation must recognize the financial statement impact of this congressional action because it is an event that has material economic consequences for the corporation.

When a change in the income tax laws or rates occurs, a corporation adjusts the deferred tax liabilities and assets for the effect of the change. It makes the adjustment to the balance of each deferred tax liability and asset as of the beginning of the year in which the change is made, and includes the resulting tax effect in the income tax expense related to its income from continuing operations.[14] The amounts of the adjustments are the differences between each of the deferred tax liability and deferred tax asset balances at the beginning of the year, based on the newly enacted laws or rates, and their respective balances that were computed under the old laws and rates.

Example Triumph Company has one deferred tax liability at the end of 2016 of $120 as a result of a temporary future taxable amount of $400 and one deferred tax asset of $90 as a result of a future deductible amount of $300. If, in May 2017, Congress increases the income tax rate from 30% to 35%, then Triumph's deferred tax liability will have increased to $140 ($400 × 0.35) and its deferred tax asset will have increased to $105 ($300 × 0.35). Therefore, the company increases the deferred tax liability deferred tax asset by the effect of the change in the income tax rate. In May 2017, Triumph records the increase and recognizes the additional income tax expense as follows:

Income Tax Expense	5	
Deferred Tax Asset	15	
Deferred Tax Liability		20

Triumph increases the income tax expense by $5 on its 2017 income statement and reports the deferred tax liability at $140 and the deferred tax asset at $105. At the end of 2017, the company computes its deferred taxes in the usual manner, except that it uses the newly enacted 35% income tax rate. ■

GOT IT?

18-9 When does a corporation establish a valuation allowance? Give an example of positive evidence that might be used to justify that a valuation allowance is not needed.

18-10 List the steps necessary to measure and record a corporation's current and deferred income taxes.

18-11 How does a corporation determine its deferred taxes under GAAP?

18-12 Briefly describe the adjustment of a deferred tax liability (or asset) and the related income statement disclosure for a change in the income tax rate.

LEARNING OBJECTIVE 18.4
Understand and explain the accounting for permanent differences.

HOW DO WE ACCOUNT FOR PERMANENT DIFFERENCES?

A **permanent difference** is a difference between a corporation's pretax financial income and taxable income in an accounting period that will *never* reverse in a later accounting period. In the United States, these differences arise because the U.S. Congress sets economic policies and establishes provisions of the tax code that impose a tax burden on, or provide a tax subsidy to, a particular segment of the economy. There are three types of permanent differences between a corporation's pretax financial income and taxable income, as illustrated in Exhibit 18.4.

[14] FASB ASC 740-10-45: Income Taxes, Overall, Other Presentation Matters.

EXHIBIT 18.4 Three Types of Permanent Differences

1. **Nontaxable Financial Accounting Revenues:** Revenues that are recognized under GAAP for financial reporting purposes but are never taxable.
   For example:
   a. Interest on municipal bonds. For income tax purposes, the interest received by a corporation on an investment in municipal bonds generally is not taxable. The provision enables municipalities to offer bonds that pay a relatively lower rate of interest than corporate bonds of a similar quality. This reduces the cost of borrowing for these municipalities.
   b. Life insurance proceeds payable to a corporation upon the death of an insured employee. For income tax purposes, the proceeds received are not taxable to the corporation. Instead, they are treated as partial compensation for the loss of the employee.
2. **Nondeductible Financial Accounting Expenses:** Expenses that are recognized under GAAP for financial reporting purposes but are never deductible for income tax purposes.
   For example:
   a. Cap on top management compensation. Limits the tax deductibility of management compensation paid to the CEO and other highly compensated employees at $1 million per executive unless it qualifies as substantially performance based.
   b. Life insurance premiums on officers. For income tax purposes, the periodic premiums for life insurance policies on officers are not deductible as expenses. This procedure is consistent with the treatment of the insurance proceeds discussed in 1(b).
   c. Fines. For income tax purposes, fines or other expenses related to the violation of a law are not deductible.
3. **Allowable Tax Deductions:** Deductions that are allowed for income tax purposes but do not qualify as expenses under GAAP.
   For example:
   a. Percentage depletion in excess of cost depletion. Certain corporations that own wasting assets are allowed to deduct percentage depletion in excess of the cost depletion on a wasting asset from their revenues for income tax purposes. This provision of the tax code was designed to encourage exploration for natural resources.
   b. Special dividend deduction. For income tax purposes, corporations are allowed a special deduction (usually 70% or 80%) for certain dividends from investments in equity securities.

Permanent differences affect *either* a corporation's reported pretax financial income *or* its taxable income, *but not both.* Permanent differences do *not* have deferred tax consequences because they do not create future taxable amounts or future deductible amounts. Permanent differences cause a company's **effective tax rate** (income tax expense ÷ income before income taxes) to be different than the tax code or **statutory tax rate**. A corporation that has nontaxable revenue or additional deductions for income tax purposes will report a lower taxable income (compared to its pretax financial income). A corporation with expenses that are not tax deductible will report a higher taxable income.

Example: Permanent and Temporary Differences

Sand Company has been in operation for several years and has earned income in each of those years. For *financial reporting purposes,* at the end of 2016, Sand reports pretax financial income of $75,500. Included in the calculation of this income are the following items:

- interest revenue of $7,500 on investments in municipal bonds
- accrued revenue of $8,000 under GAAP, not yet collected in cash
- accrued rent revenue of $3,000 for the first year of a 3-year rental contract; all $9,000 in rent was collected in advance

For *income tax purposes*, Sand reports revenue when cash is collected. It also reports rent revenue for tax purposes when cash is collected. Sand had a deferred tax liability of $300 related to an accrued revenue temporary difference of $1,000 at the beginning of 2016. The enacted income tax rate for 2016 and all future years is 30%.

To determine Sand's current and deferred income taxes, the company must first compute its 2016 taxable income. This amount is $66,000, as shown in **Example 18.6**. In preparing the schedule in Example 18.6, there is one permanent difference and two temporary differences. The permanent difference ($7,500 tax-exempt interest revenue) is deducted from pretax financial income to determine taxable income. Although the interest revenue is included in pretax financial income, it is not taxable. Thus, it is ignored for deferred tax calculations because it will *never* reverse and never be taxable.

EXAMPLE 18.6 — **Computation of 2016 Taxable Income**

Pretax financial income	$75,500
Less: Tax-exempt interest revenue on municipal bonds (permanent difference)	(7,500)
Excess of accrued revenue over cash-basis revenue (temporary difference)	(8,000)[a]
Add: Excess of rent collected in advance over rent revenue (temporary difference)	6,000[b]
Taxable Income	$66,000

[a] $8,000 revenue recognized under the accrual method for financial reporting
[b] $6,000 rent collected in advance and reported for income taxes, in addition to the $3,000 rent revenue already recognized for financial reporting

---

The $8,000 *excess* of the accrued revenue included in pretax financial income is subtracted because less cash is collected and taxed in the current year. This difference is a *future taxable amount* because it will be included in future taxable income when the cash is collected. On the other hand, the $6,000 *excess* of rent collected in advance is added to pretax financial income because more cash ($9,000) is collected and taxed than reported as rent revenue ($3,000) in pretax financial income. This difference is a *future deductible amount* because future taxable income will be less than future pretax financial income when the rent is recognized as rent revenue for financial reporting purposes.

Sand applies the steps listed on page 18-9 to determine its current and deferred income taxes:

- *Step 1.* Sand determines taxable income of $66,000 for 2016 (from **Example 18.6**) and measures the income tax payable for 2016 as $19,800 ($66,000 taxable income × 0.30).
- *Step 2.* a. Sand identifies the temporary accrual-based revenue difference of $9,000 ($1,000 beginning + $8,000 increase during 2016) as a *future taxable amount* for 2016. This amount is the difference between the book value of the accounts receivable that it reported under the accrual method for financial reporting purposes and the book value of the receivable that it reported under the cash-basis method for income tax purposes.
  b. Sand identifies the temporary rent difference of $6,000 ($6,000 book value of unearned rent reported for financial reporting purposes less the $0 book value reported for income tax purposes) as a *future deductible amount* for 2016.
- *Step 3.* Sand measures the 2016 year-end deferred tax liability as $2,700 by multiplying the $9,000 total future taxable amount times the 30% enacted future tax rate.

- Because the company had a $300 beginning deferred tax liability, it must increase this liability by $2,400 ($2,700 − $300).
- *Step 4.* Sand measures the 2016 year-end deferred tax asset as $1,800 by multiplying the $6,000 total future deductible amount times the 30% enacted future tax rate.
- *Step 5.* Sand skips this step because its $9,000 total future taxable amount is greater than its $6,000 total future deductible amount so that it does not need a valuation allowance for the deferred tax asset.
- *Step 6.* Sand records its income taxes for 2016. It credits Income Taxes Payable for its $19,800 current income tax payable. It credits (increases) Deferred Tax Liability for $2,400. It debits (increases) Deferred Tax Asset for $1,800. It determines the $20,400 debit to Income Tax Expense by adding $2,400 to and subtracting $1,800 from the $19,800 Income Taxes Payable ($20,400 = $19,800 + $2,400 − $1,800).

Sand makes the following journal entry at the end of 2016:

Income Tax Expense	20,400	
Deferred Tax Asset	1,800	
Income Taxes Payable		19,800
Deferred Tax Liability		2,400

The permanent difference will result in Sand reporting an effective tax rate of 27.02% ($20,400 ÷ $75,500), which is different from the applicable tax rate of 30%. ∎

GOT IT?

18-13 What is a permanent difference? Give two examples.

18-14 Describe an operating loss carryback. List the two conceptual questions concerning accounting for a carryback.

18-15 How is a corporation's effective tax rate calculated?

HOW DO WE ACCOUNT FOR OPERATING LOSS CARRYBACKS AND CARRYFORWARDS?

LEARNING OBJECTIVE 18.5
Explain and account for operating loss carrybacks and carryforwards.

Previous sections and examples dealt with the recognition of a deferred tax liability or asset when a corporation had taxable *income* in the current year. This section deals with the situation where a corporation has a *loss* for income tax purposes in the current year, resulting in an operating loss carryback or carryforward for income tax purposes.

The tax code allows a corporation reporting an operating loss for income tax purposes in the current year to carry this loss back in order to offset previous taxable income and claim a tax refund or carry it forward to offset future taxable income. The corporation may first carry a reported operating loss back 2 years (in sequential order, starting with the *earliest* of the 2 years). This procedure is called an **operating loss carryback**. In this case, the corporation files amended income tax returns showing lower taxable income for those years and receives a refund of income taxes previously paid. Operating loss carrybacks can provide significant refunds for companies. For example, the homebuilding company **Pulte Homes** was able to claim an $800 million tax refund as a result of operating loss carrybacks.

If a corporation's taxable income for the past 2 years is not enough to offset the amount of the currently reported operating loss, it then sequentially carries forward the loss for up to as many as 20 years and offsets the loss against future taxable income, if there is any. This procedure is called an **operating loss carryforward**. The corporation then pays lower income taxes in the future based on lower future taxable income. **Ford Motor Company**, for example, experienced operating losses and recognized operating

loss carryforwards each year during the period 2006 to 2009. As the company rebounded during 2010, it was able to start applying $15 billion of operating loss carryforwards against its taxable income.

Exhibit 18.5 shows a diagram of the operating loss carryback and carryforward sequence. A corporation also may elect to decline the carryback and, instead, only carry forward an operating loss. Unless higher future income tax rates have been enacted, most corporations do not make this election because an operating loss carryback will result in a definite and immediate income tax refund. However, a carryforward will reduce income taxes payable in future years only to the extent that taxable income is earned.

EXHIBIT 18.5 Operating Loss Carrybacks and Carryforwards

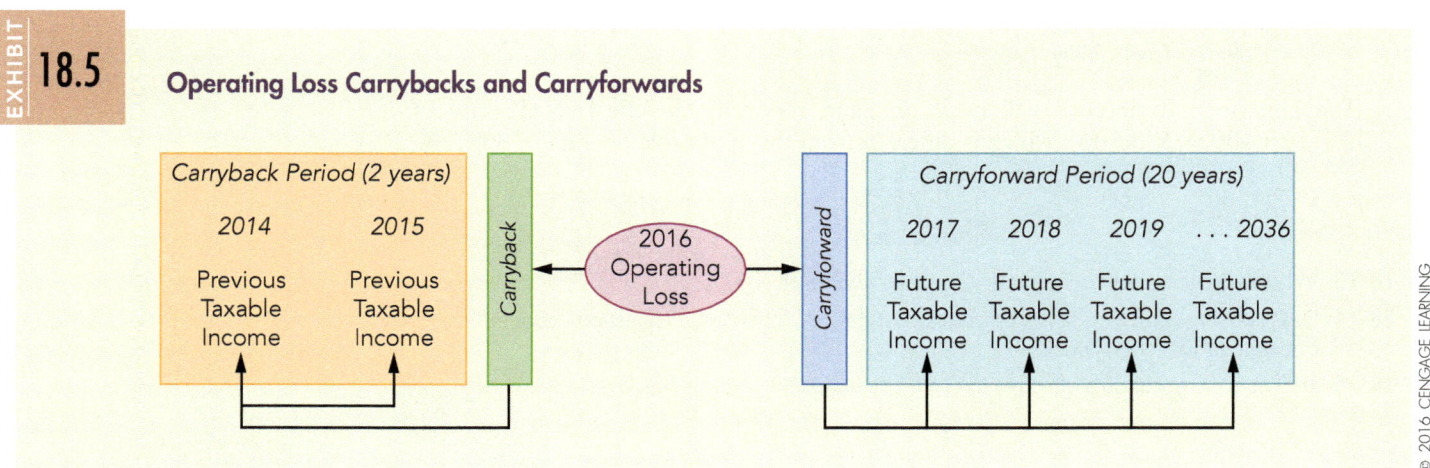

Conceptual Issues

When a corporation reports an operating loss for financial reporting purposes in a given year, there are several important accounting questions about valuing assets, recognizing income tax expense, and reporting net income.

The FASB concluded that the GAAP for the financial reporting of operating loss carrybacks and carryforwards is as follows:

Operating Loss Carrybacks A corporation must recognize the tax benefit of an operating loss carryback in the period of the loss as an asset (current receivable) on its balance sheet and as a reduction of the tax expense which reduces the loss on its income statement. The FASB concluded that, even though the tax benefit is a refund of taxes paid in prior years, the corporation's prior income only enables use of the carryback and is what gives value to the carryback. For this reason, it is the corporation's current operating loss that creates the tax benefit, and so it is recognized as a reduction in current period tax expense. In addition, the FASB determined that the corporation incurring the operating loss should recognize a current receivable for the tax benefit of the carryback. The recognition of a receivable by a corporation for the tax benefit of an operating loss carryback is conceptually sound. The corporation will realize the tax benefit as an income tax refund when the refund is issued by the federal government. Thus, it is an economic benefit (asset).

Operating Loss Carryforwards A corporation must recognize the tax benefit of an operating loss carryforward in the period of the loss as a deferred tax asset. However, it must reduce the deferred tax asset by a valuation allowance if, based on the available evidence, it is more likely than not that the corporation will not realize some or all of the deferred tax asset.[15] Initially, the FASB debated on whether to recognize the loss carryforward in the period of the loss or to defer recognition until the asset is realized. The FASB concluded that the asset should be recognized in the period of the loss for the following reasons:

- The tax effects are an economic resource of the corporation because it has a right to and control over the future tax benefit, if it is able to generate sufficient future taxable income.
- The corporation recognizes the tax benefit in income in the year in which the operating loss generated the benefit.

Therefore, a corporation handles operating loss carryforwards in the same manner as the future deductible amounts discussed earlier in the chapter. That is, at year-end:

- The corporation measures a deferred tax asset for an operating loss carryforward using the enacted future tax rate.
- If necessary, it measures a valuation allowance and deducts the amount from the deferred tax asset to determine its net realizable value.
- In the year-end journal entry to record its current and deferred taxes, the corporation treats any increase (decrease) in the deferred tax asset and valuation allowance as an adjustment of its income tax expense (benefit).

It is more likely that a corporation will need a valuation allowance for a deferred tax asset related to an operating loss carryforward if the operating loss itself provides negative evidence as to the likelihood of having sufficient future taxable income to realize the tax benefits.

Example: Operating Loss Carryback

Lewis Company reports a pretax operating loss of $90,000 in 2016 for both financial reporting and income tax purposes. Assume that reported pretax financial income and taxable income for the previous 2 years had been: 2014—$40,000 (tax rate 25%); and 2015—$70,000 (tax rate 30%). Thus, the $110,000 total pretax income in the previous 2 years is more than enough to offset the $90,000 pretax operating loss. When Lewis carries back its 2016 operating loss, it is entitled to a tax refund of $25,000, calculated as shown in **Example 18.7**.

EXAMPLE 18.7

Refund from Operating Loss Carryback

Year	Pretax Financial Income and Taxable Income Offset by Carryback	×	Income Tax Rate	=	Income Tax Refund
2014	$40,000	×	0.25	=	$10,000
2015	50,000	×	0.30	=	15,000
	$90,000				$25,000

Note in **Example 18.7** that all of the 2014 income of $40,000 is offset by the $90,000 operating loss carryback, but only $50,000 of the $70,000 income in 2015 is offset because the carryback is first applied to the earlier year. Therefore, the

---

[15] FASB ASC 740-10-30: Income Taxes, Overall, Initial Measurement.

remaining $20,000 of the 2015 income remains available to offset any operating losses that might occur in 2017. At the end of 2016, Lewis makes the following journal entry:

Income Tax Refund Receivable	25,000	
Income Tax Benefit from Operating Loss Carryback		25,000

Lewis reports the receivable on its balance sheet as a current asset until it collects the receivable. The company reports the operating loss carryback tax benefit in the lower portion of its 2016 income statement as follows:

Pretax operating loss	$(90,000)
Less: Income tax benefit from operating loss carryback	25,000
Net loss	$(65,000)

Example: Operating Loss Carryforward and Valuation Allowance

Clark Company reports a pretax operating loss of $60,000 in 2016 (its first year of operation) for both financial reporting and income tax purposes. The income tax rate is 30% and no change in the tax rate has been enacted for future years. Because the company had no income prior to 2016, it cannot carry back the operating loss. Because it carries forward the operating loss, Clark reports a deferred tax asset at the end of 2016 for the deferred tax consequences (future tax benefit) of the carryforward. It calculates the deferred tax asset to be $18,000 ($60,000 × 0.30). Clark makes the following journal entry at the end of 2016:

Deferred Tax Asset	18,000	
Income Tax Benefit from Operating Loss Carryforward		18,000

Because Clark has no history of taxable income and has insufficient positive evidence of future taxable income, it must also reduce the deferred tax asset by a valuation allowance. If we assume the company establishes a valuation allowance for the entire amount of the deferred tax asset, it also makes the following journal entry at the end of 2016:

Income Tax Benefit from Operating Loss Carryforward	18,000	
Allowance to Reduce Deferred Tax Asset to Realizable Value		18,000

Clark reports the $60,000 operating loss as a net loss on its 2016 income statement because it did not realize any tax benefit from the operating loss carryforward in 2016. The deferred tax asset, offset by the valuation allowance, normally is reported on a company's balance sheet, but the net amount is zero in this example. However, Clark discloses both the deferred tax asset and the valuation allowance amounts in the notes to its 2016 financial statements. Clark also discloses the operating loss carryforward as follows in a note to its 2016 financial statements:

> The company has a $60,000 operating loss carryforward that can be used within 20 years to offset future taxable income and reduce income taxes.

Now assume that in 2017, Clark operates successfully and earns pretax operating income of $100,000 for both financial reporting and income tax purposes. The company realizes the tax benefit of the operating loss carryforward in 2017 as a reduction of its income tax payable. It offsets the $60,000 carryforward from 2016 against the $100,000 pretax income in 2017, resulting in taxable income of $40,000. Based on the 30% income tax rate, its income taxes payable and income tax expense are $12,000 ($40,000 × 0.30). Because the company has used up the tax benefit of the operating loss carryforward, it eliminates the deferred asset and related valuation allowance. Clark makes the following journal entry at the end of 2017:

Income Tax Expense	12,000	
Allowance to Reduce Deferred Tax Asset to Realizable Value	18,000	
Income Taxes Payable		12,000
Deferred Tax Asset		18,000

The lower portion of Clark's 2017 income statement is as follows:

Pretax operating income	$100,000
Less: Income tax expense	(12,000)
Net income	$ 88,000

The effect of the operating loss carryforward is to reduce the company's income tax expense for 2017 from $30,000 ($100,000 × 0.30)—the amount without the tax benefit of the carryforward—to $12,000, so that its 2017 net income (after tax) is increased by $18,000. ∎

In some cases, a corporation's pretax operating income of a given year is not enough to offset the entire amount of an operating loss carryforward. In this situation, it offsets a portion of the operating loss against the income and continues to carry forward the remainder as a deferred tax asset. This amount would be disclosed in the notes to the financial statements. For instance, if Clark had earned only $50,000 pretax operating (and taxable) income in 2017, then it would offset this taxable income with $50,000 of the $60,000 operating loss carryforward and would pay no income taxes for 2017. The company would report income tax expense of $15,000 ($50,000 × 0.30) and would reduce its deferred tax asset by $15,000. It would eliminate the $3,000 ($18,000 − $15,000) deferred tax asset (30% of the $10,000 remaining operating loss carryforward) in a future year(s) when it realized the tax benefit.

ETHICAL DILEMMA

Classical Notes Inc. manufactures and sells classical sheet music. Over the last several years, interest in classical music has decreased and, as a result, Classical Notes has reported annual losses over this period. However, recent scientific evidence that classical music stimulates brain development has sparked renewed interest in classical music, resulting in the company reporting operating profit of $80,000 in the most recent year. This is the first operating profit reported by the company in 5 years. At the end of the current fiscal year, Classical Notes has recognized $4,000,000 of deferred tax assets, net of a $1,000,000 valuation allowance, which primarily consists of operating loss carryforwards that will expire evenly over the next 10 years.

As the recently hired accountant for Classical Notes, you are in charge of preparing the income tax accrual for the current year. You are particularly concerned with the amount of the valuation allowance (which was decreased from $1.9 million to $1 million in the current year) and have requested a meeting with the CEO concerning this matter. During the meeting, you inform the CEO that you think the valuation allowance is too small and should be increased by at least $500,000. You have based your conclusions on the fact that the company has reported historical operating losses in 4 of the last 5 years. Furthermore, the current operating profit was due largely to a one-time surge in the demand for classical music and all economic analyses expect this demand to level off within the next year. Therefore, you do not think the company will have sufficient future taxable income to use the operating loss carryforwards.

The CEO is extremely upset at your recommendation. She informs you that the company's fortunes have finally turned around and the demand for classical music will continue to grow despite what the experts say. Furthermore, if the valuation allowance is increased, it would cause the company to report a net loss for the year and send the wrong signal to the market. After a heated exchange, the CEO tells you that the amount of the valuation allowance is a judgment call, and as the experienced leader of the company, it is her judgment that the valuation allowance is appropriate. She then instructs you to drop the matter and leave the major decisions to her. What is your response?

Example: Comprehensive Illustration

The examples in the previous sections showed the accounting for temporary differences separately from operating losses. In this comprehensive example, we show a temporary difference, an operating loss carryback, and an operating loss carryforward.

Hilltop Company begins operations in 2013 and is profitable through 2015. In 2016, the company reports a pretax financial loss of $8,000 and a taxable loss of $8,800. In 2017 and 2018, Hilltop is again profitable, although at the end of 2016 the company felt that future profits were not likely. The income tax rate is 30%. **Example 18.8** shows Hilltop's pretax financial income (loss) and taxable income (loss) for the years 2013 through 2018, as well as its income taxes payable (receivable). It is assumed that the only difference between pretax financial income (loss) and taxable income (loss) in any year results from additional (MACRS) depreciation reported for income tax purposes.

EXAMPLE 18.8 Income Taxes Payable or Receivable

Year	Pretax Financial Income (Loss)	Depreciation Difference	Taxable Income (Loss)	Income Taxes Payable (Receivable)
2013	$ 2,000	$ 800	$ 1,200	$ 360[a]
2014	3,000	1,320	1,680	504[a]
2015	2,000	880	1,120	336[a]
2016	(8,000)	800	(8,800)	(840)[b]
2017	2,200	700	1,500	0[c]
2018	7,000	600	6,400	570[d]

[a] Taxable income × 0.30 income tax rate
[b] $2,800 carryback to years 2014 and 2015, resulting in tax refund of $840; remaining carryforward of $6,000 ($8,800 − $2,800).
[c] $1,500 taxable income offset by carryforward, therefore no income taxes owed; remaining carryforward of $4,500 ($6,000 − $1,500).
[d] $6,400 taxable income offset by $4,500 carryforward; $1,900 × 0.30

As shown in **Example 18.8**, Hilltop pays $360 of income taxes in 2013, $504 in 2014 and $336 in 2015. In 2016, $2,800 of the $8,800 operating loss is carried back to offset the 2014 and 2015 taxable income, resulting in a tax refund of $840. Note that the 2016 operating loss is *not* carried back to 2013 because of the 2-year carryback limitation. In 2017 and 2018, the $6,000 remaining operating loss is carried forward and (1) offsets the $1,500 taxable income in 2017 so that no income taxes are paid and (2) offsets $4,500 of the $6,400 taxable income in 2018 so that $570 of income taxes are paid.

For financial reporting purposes, Hilltop must determine its deferred tax liability (or deferred tax asset) and income tax expense (or refund) for each year. Both the depreciation expense taxable temporary difference and the operating loss carryforward for each year affect the company's deferred taxes. **Example 18.9** shows these calculations. Note that the depreciation taxable temporary difference increases each year by the difference in depreciation expense for financial reporting purposes and income tax purposes shown in **Example 18.8**.

EXAMPLE 18.9

Deferred Tax Information

Year	Depreciation Temporary Difference			Operating Loss Carryforward
	Beginning	Addition	Ending[a]	
2013	$ 0	$ 800	$ 800	—
2014	800	1,320	2,120	—
2015	2,120	880	3,000	—
2016	3,000	800	3,800	(6,000)[b]
2017	3,800	700	4,500	(4,500)[c]
2018	4,500	600	5,100	—

[a] Beginning depreciation temporary difference + Additional difference for current year
[b] $8,800 taxable loss − $2,800 operating loss carryback for years 2015 and 2014 (see Example 18.8)
[c] $6,000 operating loss carryforward from 2016 − $1,500 taxable income in 2017 (see Example 18.8)

The operating loss carryforward of $6,000 at the end of 2016 is the $8,800 operating loss in 2016 minus the $2,800 operating loss carryback, as discussed earlier. The operating loss carryforward at the end of 2017 is only $4,500, because $1,500 was used to offset the taxable income in 2017. The following "timeline" diagram further explains the relationships between the taxable incomes and the operating loss carrybacks and carryforwards for the various years:

	2013	2014	2015	2016	2017	2018
Taxable income before adjustments	$1,200	$ 1,680	$ 1,120	$(8,800)	$ 1,500	$ 6,400
Loss carryback (to 2014)		(1,680) ◄———		1,680		
Loss carryback (to 2015)			(1,120) ◄———	1,120		
		2016 Operating Loss Carryforward ———►		(6,000)		
Loss carryforward (to 2017)				1,500 ———►	(1,500)	
Loss carryforward (to 2018)				4,500 ——————————————————►		(4,500)
Taxable income				$ 0	$ 0	$ 1,900

Example 18.10 shows the computations of Hilltop's deferred tax liability and asset (and valuation allowance) for each year, based on the information in Example 18.9. As shown in Example 18.9, Hilltop has $800 additional depreciation expense for tax purposes at the end of 2013, which will result in taxable income of the same amount in future years. As shown in Example 18.10, applying the 30% tax rate to the future taxable amount results in a deferred tax liability of $240 at the end of 2013. Because there was a $0 deferred tax liability at the beginning of 2013, the company makes a $240 adjustment (credit) to the deferred tax liability. Hilltop makes similar computations for 2014 through 2018.

At the end of 2016, the $6,000 operating loss carryforward results in an ending deferred tax asset of $1,800 ($6,000 × 0.30). Because there was a $0 deferred tax asset at the beginning of 2016, Hilltop recognizes an $1,800 deferred tax asset. A valuation allowance is required at the end of 2016 because the company does not expect to be profitable in future years. However, the valuation allowance does not have to be for the full amount of the deferred tax asset resulting from the operating loss carryforward. This is because Hilltop has an existing depreciation temporary difference that will result in additional future taxable income against which to offset the operating loss carryforward. Because the operating loss carryforward is $6,000, but the total ending depreciation taxable temporary difference is $3,800 at the end of 2016 (see Example 18.9), a valuation

EXAMPLE 18.10 Annual Deferred Taxes

	Deferred Tax Liability			Deferred Tax Asset			Valuation Allowance		
Year	Beginning	Ending[a]	Adjustment	Beginning	Ending	Adjustment	Beginning	Ending	Adjustment
2013	$ 0	$ 240	$240	—	—	—	—	—	—
2014	240	636	396	—	—	—	—	—	—
2015	636	900	264	—	—	—	—	—	—
2016	900	1,140	240	—	$1,800[b]	$ 1,800	—	$660[c]	$ 660
2017	1,140	1,350	210	$1,800	1,350[d]	(450)	$660	0[e]	(660)
2018	1,350	1,530	180	1,350	0	(1,350)	—	—	—

[a] Ending depreciation taxable temporary difference (from Example 18.9) × 0.30
[b] $6,000 operating loss carryforward (from Example 18.9) × 0.30
[c] [$6,000 carryforward − $3,800 ending depreciation temporary difference (from Example 18.9)] × 0.30
[d] $4,500 operating loss carryforward × 0.30
[e] ($4,500 carryforward − $4,500 ending depreciation temporary difference) × 0.30

allowance of only $660 [($6,000 − $3,800) × 0.30] is required and the company makes an adjustment (credit) for that amount.

At the end of 2017, Hilltop has a $1,350 deferred tax asset ($ 4,500 operating loss carryforward × .30), which requires a $450 adjustment (credit) to that account. Because the $4,500 total ending depreciation taxable temporary difference is the same as the $4,500 remaining operating loss carryforward, it does not need a valuation allowance. This requires an adjustment (debit) of $660 to the Valuation Allowance account. In 2018, Hilltop uses the $4,500 remaining operating loss carryforward to offset an equal amount of taxable income, so it eliminates (credits) the $1,350 related Deferred Tax Asset.

At the end of each year, the company prepares a journal entry to record its income taxes, based on the information in **Examples 18.8** and **18.10**. For instance, at the end of 2016, Hilltop makes the following journal entry:

Income Tax Refund Receivable	840	
Deferred Tax Asset	1,800	
Deferred Tax Liability		240
Allowance to Reduce Deferred Tax Asset to Realizable Value		660
Income Tax Benefit from Operating Loss Carryback		840
Income Tax Benefit from Operating Loss Carryforward		900

The $840 income tax benefit from the operating loss carryback relates to the income tax refund receivable. The $900 income tax benefit from the operating loss carryforward is the net amount that the company will realize in future years and that is related to the deferred tax asset, valuation allowance, and deferred tax liability.

Hilltop reports operating loss carryback and carryforward tax benefits on its 2016 income statement as follows:

Pretax operating loss			$(8,000)
Less:	Income tax benefit from operating loss carryback	$840	
	Income tax benefit from operating loss carryforward	900	1,740
Net loss			$(6,260)

The company discloses the remaining operating loss carryforwards in 2016 and 2017 in a note accompanying the respective year's financial statements. ■

> **GOT IT?**
>
> **18-16** Describe an operating loss carryforward. List the two conceptual questions concerning accounting for a carryforward.
>
> **18-17** Briefly summarize the GAAP for the financial reporting of operating loss carrybacks and carryforwards.

HOW DOES INTRAPERIOD INCOME TAX ALLOCATION AFFECT THE INCOME STATEMENT?

LEARNING OBJECTIVE 18.6
Describe and apply intraperiod tax allocation.

Intraperiod income tax allocation is the allocation of a corporation's total income tax expense for a period to the various components of income that are reported in the income statement, comprehensive income, and/or the statement of shareholders' equity. GAAP requires intraperiod income tax allocation to income (or loss) related to discontinued operations, retrospective adjustments, and prior period adjustments, as well as gains and losses included in other comprehensive income.[16] When a corporation has these items, it allocates income taxes between them and income from continuing operations. A corporation *matches* its income tax expense against the major components of its pretax income to give a faithful representation of the after-tax impact of each of these items.

For intraperiod income tax allocation purposes, on its income statement a corporation reports the income tax expense applicable to its pretax income from continuing operations separately from income tax related to other components of income. The amount of income tax expense is based on the normal income tax rates applied to this income. The disclosure of the tax effect on its income from continuing operations is important because external users are interested in the after-tax profitability of the corporation's business activities that are expected to continue. However, the corporation reports the income or loss from the operations of a discontinued component, the gain or loss from the disposal of a discontinued segment, retrospective adjustments and prior period adjustments (reported in the column for retained earnings in the statement of shareholders' equity), and any other comprehensive income items *net* of the related income tax effects (reported in the column for accumulated other comprehensive income in the statement of shareholders' equity). That is, for these items the corporation deducts the income tax expense (or tax savings, which is called a tax *credit* in the case of a loss) directly from each item and reports only the *after-tax* amount. It discloses the amount of the income tax expense or tax credit for each of these items either parenthetically or in a note to its financial statements. The corporation determines the amount of the income tax expense or tax credit for each item by applying the marginal (incremental) tax rate to each item.

Example: Intraperiod Income Tax Allocation

Kalloway Company reports the following *pretax* financial (and taxable) income items for 2016:

Income from continuing operations (revenues of $270,000 minus expenses of $190,000)	$80,000
Gain on disposal of discontinued Division X	18,000
Loss from operations of discontinued Division X	(5,000)
Prior period adjustment (error in calculating bad debt expense for 2015)	(8,000)
Amount subject to income taxes	$85,000

---

[16] Currently, there are four items of other comprehensive income, as discussed in Chapter 5. For instance, when a company records a change in the unrealized increase (decrease) shareholders' equity account for investments in available-for-sale securities, this causes a change in the deferred tax liability (or asset). In the journal entry to record the change in the deferred tax liability (or asset), the offsetting entry is a reduction of the unrealized increase (decrease) account.

The company is subject to income tax rates of 20% on the first $50,000 of income and 30% on all income in excess of $50,000. **Example 18.11** shows the schedule to allocate the total income tax expense, and **Example 18.12** shows Kalloway's 2016 income statement[17] and schedule of retained earnings as it would appear within the statement of shareholders' equity as a result of applying intraperiod income tax allocation.

EXAMPLE 18.11 Schedule of Income Tax Expense for 2016

Component (Pretax)	Pretax Amount	×	Income Tax Rate	=	Income Tax Expense (Credit)
Income from continuing operations	$50,000	×	0.20	=	$10,000
	30,000	×	0.30	=	9,000
Gain on disposal of discontinued Division X	18,000	×	0.30	=	5,400
Loss from operations of discontinued Division X	(5,000)	×	0.30	=	(1,500)
Prior period adjustment	(8,000)	×	0.30	=	(2,400)
Total income tax expense					$20,500

As shown in **Example 18.11**, the total income taxes for Kalloway in 2016 are $20,500. Kalloway generated $80,000 in pretax income from continuing operations, for which it computes income tax expense applicable to its pretax income from continuing operations of $19,000 [(0.20 × $50,000) + (0.30 × $30,000)]. This provision for income tax does *not* consider the tax consequences of any items not included in pretax income from continuing operations. To determine the tax consequences of the discontinued operations, and the prior period adjustment, the company computes each of the related income tax effects in **Example 18.11** by multiplying each item by the marginal tax rate (30%) by the pretax gain or loss.[18] Kalloway makes the following journal entry to record its 2016 intraperiod income tax allocation:

Income Tax Expense	19,000	
Gain on Disposal of Division X	5,400	
Loss from Operations of Discontinued Division X		1,500
Retained Earnings (prior period adjustment)		2,400
Income Taxes Payable		20,500

Note that the debit to Income Tax Expense of $19,000 relates *only* to the income taxes applicable to income from continuing operations. Because the company reports its results of discontinued operations, and prior period adjustments on the financial statements *net* of their respective income tax effects, it debits or credits each of these items directly (as shown in the journal entry) to reduce the account balance to its after-tax amount.

In terms of financial statement presentation, Kalloway reports the $19,000 income tax expense applicable to pretax income from continuing operations on its income statement in **Example 18.12** on a separate line directly below pretax income from continuing operations, and it subtracts this amount to determine its income from continuing

---

[17] For simplicity, in Example 18.12 and related homework we do not include earnings per share information.

[18] In our example, only two tax rates were in effect, and the income from continuing operations was large enough that the gain and losses were taxed at a single marginal rate. It is possible for several tax rates to be in effect at the same time, and for the total income to be increased or decreased by other gains and losses, so that more than one marginal tax rate may be applicable. In these cases, a corporation uses a weighted averaging process to determine the appropriate tax effects on the gains and losses. This process is beyond the scope of this book.

operations. Kalloway reports the gain on the disposal of the discontinued Division X, and the loss from the operations of the discontinued Division X *net of income tax* on its income statement in **Example 18.12**, and it discloses each related income tax effect in parentheses. It reports the prior period adjustment net of its income tax effect in the schedule of retained earnings within the statement of shareholders' equity in the lower portion of **Example 18.12**.

EXAMPLE 18.12

Kalloway Company
Income Statement
For Year Ended December 31, 2016

Revenues (listed separately)		$ 270,000
Expenses (listed separately)		(190,000)
Pretax income from continuing operation		$ 80,000
Income tax expense		(19,000)
Income from continuing operations		$ 61,000
Results of discontinued operations:		
Gain on disposal of discontinued Division X		
(net of $5,400 income taxes)	$12,600	
Loss from operations of discontinued Division X		
(net of $1,500 income tax credit)	(3,500)	9,100
Net income		$ 70,100

Schedule of Retained Earnings within Statement of Shareholders' Equity
For Year Ended December 31, 2016

Retained earnings, January 1, 2016	$ 435,000
Less: Prior period adjustment, understatement of 2015 bad debt expense (net of $2,400 income tax credit)	(5,600)
Adjusted retained earnings, January 1, 2016	$ 429,400
Add: Net income	70,100
	$ 499,500
Less: Cash dividends	(23,500)
Retained Earnings, December 31, 2016	$ 476,000

In this example, we assume that taxable income and pretax financial income are the same. If a corporation's taxable income is not the same as its pretax financial income because of temporary differences, the total income tax expense is the sum of the income tax payable and the adjustments to the deferred tax liabilities and assets. In this case, the corporation must determine the impact of the adjustments on each component of pretax financial income before it can properly allocate the income tax expense. For adjustments of (1) a valuation allowance because of changes in circumstances and (2) deferred tax liabilities and assets because of changes in tax rates or laws, the corporation includes the amounts of the adjustments in its income tax expense related to continuing operations.[19] ∎

GOT IT?

18-18 What is intraperiod income tax allocation? How is income tax expense reported on a corporation's income statement and retained earnings statement?

18-19 Why must a corporation match its income tax expense against the major components of its pretax income?

---

[19] FASB ASC 740-20-45: Income Taxes, Intraperiod Tax Allocation, Other Presentation Matters.

LEARNING OBJECTIVE 18.7
Examine presentation and disclosure issues related to accounting for income taxes.

HOW ARE INCOME TAX ITEMS PRESENTED AND DISCLOSED IN THE FINANCIAL STATEMENTS?

GAAP specifies what is required for reporting deferred tax liabilities and assets on a corporation's balance sheet and disclosures in the notes to the corporation's financial statements.

Balance Sheet Presentation

At the end of 2015 the FASB released ASU 2015-17 which simplifies the balance sheet classification of deferred taxes.[20] The new presentation requirements become effective for annual reporting periods beginning after December 15, 2016 and require that all deferred tax assets and liabilities be classified as noncurrent amounts. A corporation would combine the noncurrent deferred tax asset and noncurrent deferred tax liability and report a net noncurrent deferred tax asset or liability.

Previously, GAAP required that deferred taxes for each tax paying jurisdiction (for example state, federal, international) be presented as a net current asset or liability and net noncurrent asset or liability. ASU 2015-17 aligns GAAP presentation of deferred income taxes with IFRS.[21]

Example: Balance Sheet Presentation

Anicar Company has the four deferred tax items shown in Example 18.13. In this situation, Anicar combines the $6,000 credit balance of the deferred tax liability resulting from accrual-based revenue (Item 1) with the $12,000 credit balance of the deferred tax liability related to depreciation (Item 2), resulting in a $18,000 deferred tax liability. In addition, Anicar combines the $3,400 debit balance of deferred tax asset resulting from warranty costs (Item 3) with the $2,500 debit balance of the deferred tax asset resulting from unearned rent, resulting in a deferred tax asset of $5,900. (Item 4) Assuming that each of the temporary differences resulted from federal income tax regulations (i.e. the same tax jurisdiction) Anicar would report a $12,100 ($18,000 − $5,900) *noncurrent* deferred tax liability in its balance sheet.

EXAMPLE 18.13 Schedule of Deferred Assets and Liabilities

Deferred Tax Accounts	Account Balance	Related Balance Sheet Account
Deferred Tax Liabilities		
1. Accrual-based revenues	$ 6,000 credit	Accounts receivable
2. Depreciation	12,000 credit	Property, plant, and equipment
Deferred Tax Assets		
3. Assurance-type warranty costs	3,400 debit	Warranty liability
4. Rent revenue (long-term)	2,500 debit	Unearned rent

---

[20] ASU 2015-17 Balance Sheet Classification of Deferred Taxes.
[21] This "offsetting" applies to each tax jurisdiction for example state income taxes, federal income taxes and international income taxes. Assuming that different jurisdictions result in different net deferred tax asset and liabilities a corporation may have both a noncurrent deferred tax and a noncurrent deferred tax liaiblity.

Financial Statement Disclosures

To help users evaluate a corporation's income taxes, GAAP also requires extensive income tax disclosures in the notes to the financial statements (or directly on the statements themselves). We briefly summarize the major disclosures. For the net deferred tax liability or asset, it discloses:

- causes of the deferred tax assets and liabilities
- total deferred tax liabilities
- total deferred tax assets
- total valuation allowance and the net change in the allowance

For income taxes (or provision for income taxes as some companies, such as **Starbucks**, refer to it) it discloses:

- amount of income tax expense or benefit allocated to continuing operations, discontinued operations, retrospective adjustments, prior period adjustments, and gains and losses included in other comprehensive income
- significant components of income tax expense related to continuing operations for each year. These can include (1) current tax expense or benefit (i.e., income tax payable or refund), (2) deferred tax expense or benefit, (3) tax credits, (4) benefits of operating loss carryforwards, and (5) adjustments of the valuation allowance for changes in circumstances.[22]

For the reconciliation of the statutory U.S. federal tax rate to the effective tax rate, companies also disclose:

- U.S. federal income tax amount and the statutory rate
- amounts of income tax expense attributable to states and foreign countries
- effects of differences in tax rates associated with taxable income generated in various states and countries
- other effects impacting the effective tax rate for the period

The intraperiod allocation of income taxes on the face of a corporation's income statement (and schedule of retained earnings within the statement of changes in shareholders' equity, or comprehensive income) partially satisfies the preceding disclosure requirements. A corporation typically discloses the remaining information in a note to its financial statements. Real Report 18.1 (p. 18-32) provides the 2015 income tax footnote disclosure from Starbucks Corporation's annual report. These disclosures provide inputs for the analysis of interperiod income taxes.

REAL REPORT — ANALYSIS OF INCOME TAXES — **18.1**

Note 13: Income Taxes — Starbucks

Components of earnings/(loss) before income taxes (in millions):

Fiscal Year Ended	Sep 27, 2015	Sep 28, 2014	Sep 29, 2013 Total	Sep 29, 2013 Litigation charge	Sep 29, 2013 All Other
United States	$2,837.2	$2,572.4	$(674.0)	$(2,784.1)	$2,110.1
Foreign	1,065.8	587.3	444.1	—	444.1
Total earnings/(loss) before income taxes	$3,903.0	$3,159.7	$(229.9)	$(2,784.1)	$2,554.2

(continued)

---

[22] FASB ASC 740-10-50: Income Taxes, Overall, Disclosure.

Provision/(benefit) for income taxes (in millions):

Fiscal Year Ended	Sep 27, 2015	Sep 28, 2014	Sep 29, 2013 Total	Sep 29, 2013 Litigation charge	Sep 29, 2013 All Other
Current taxes:					
U.S. federal	$ 801.0	$ 822.7	$ 616.6	$ —	$616.6
U.S. state and local	150.1	132.9	93.8	—	93.8
Foreign	172.2	128.8	95.9	—	95.9
Total current taxes	1,123.3	1,084.4	806.3	—	806.3
Deferred taxes:					
U.S. federal	56.5	12.0	(898.8)	(922.3)	23.5
U.S. state and local	4.0	(4.9)	(144.0)	(148.7)	4.7
Foreign	(40.1)	0.5	(2.2)	—	(2.2)
Total deferred taxes	20.4	7.6	(1,045.0)	(1,071.0)	26.0
Total income tax expense/(benefit)	$1,143.7	$1,092.0	$ (238.7)	$(1,071.0)	$832.3

Reconciliation of the statutory U.S. federal income tax rate with our effective income tax rate:

Fiscal Year Ended	Sep 27, 2015	Sep 28, 2014	Sep 29, 2013 Total	Sep 29, 2013 Litigation charge	Sep 29, 2013 All Other
Statutory rate	35.0 %	35.0 %	35.0%	35.0%	35.0 %
State income taxes, net of federal tax benefit	2.8	2.6	15.8	3.5	2.4
Benefits and taxes related to foreign operations	(2.1)	(1.9)	37.5	—	(3.4)
Domestic production activity deduction	(2.2)	(0.7)	8.1	—	(0.7)
Domestic tax credits	(0.2)	(0.2)	2.8	—	(0.3)
Charitable contributions	(0.3)	(0.4)	3.9	—	(0.3)
Gain resulting from acquisition of joint venture	(3.7)	—	—	—	—
Other, net	—	0.2	0.7	—	(0.1)
Effective tax rate	29.3%	34.6 %	103.8%	38.5%	32.6 %

Our effective tax rate in fiscal 2013 was significantly affected by the litigation charge we recorded as a result of the conclusion of our arbitration with Kraft. In order to provide a more meaningful analysis of tax expense and the effective tax rate, the tables above present separate reconciliations of the effect of the litigation charge. The deferred tax asset related to the litigation charge is estimated to be recovered over a period of 15 years; the deferred tax asset has been classified between current and non-current consistent with the expected recovery period for income tax reporting purposes.

U.S. income and foreign withholding taxes have not been provided on approximately $2.8 billion of cumulative undistributed earnings of foreign subsidiaries and equity investees. We intend to reinvest these earnings for the foreseeable future. If these amounts were distributed to the U.S., in the form of dividends or otherwise, we would be subject to additional U.S. income taxes, which could be material. Determination of the amount of unrecognized deferred income tax liabilities on these earnings is not practicable because of the complexities with its hypothetical calculation, and the amount of liability, if any, is dependent on circumstances existing if and when remittance occurs.

Tax effect of temporary differences and carryforwards that comprise significant portions of deferred tax assets and liabilities *(in millions)*:

	Sep 27, 2015	Sep 28, 2014
Deferred tax assets:		
Property, plant and equipment	$ 121.4	$ 78.5
Accrued occupancy costs	98.4	58.8
Accrued compensation and related costs	81.7	75.3
Other accrued liabilities	49.0	27.6
Asset retirement obligation asset	29.0	18.6
Stored value card liability	99.1	63.4
Asset impairments	26.2	49.5
Tax credits	20.8	20.3
Stock-based compensation	135.5	131.5
Net operating losses	93.4	104.4
Litigation charge	931.0	1,002.0
Other	104.5	77.0
Total	$1,790.0	$1,706.9
Valuation allowance	(143.7)	(166.8)
Total deferred tax asset, net of valuation allowance	$1,646.3	$1,540.1
Deferred tax liabilities:		
Property, plant and equipment	(217.5)	(148.2)
Intangible assets and goodwill	(177.3)	(92.9)
Other	(114.1)	(89.4)
Total	(508.9)	(330.5)
Net deferred tax asset	$1,137.4	$1,209.6
Reported as:		
Current deferred income tax assets	$ 381.7	$ 317.4
Long-term deferred income tax assets	828.9	903.3
Current deferred income tax liabilities (included in Accrued liabilities)	(5.4)	(4.2)
Long-term deferred income tax liabilities (included in Other long-term liabilities)	(67.8)	(6.9)
Net deferred tax asset	$1,137.4	$1,209.6

The valuation allowance as of September 27, 2015 and September 28, 2014 is primarily related to net operating losses and other deferred tax assets of consolidated foreign subsidiaries. The net change in the total valuation allowance was a decrease of $23.1 million and an increase of $6.3 million for fiscal 2015 and 2014, respectively.

As of September 27, 2015, we had state tax credit carryforwards of $32.0 million with an expiration date of fiscal 2024 and foreign net operating loss carryforwards of $309.5 million, the majority of which has no expiration date.

Questions:

Suggested answers to these questions are found at the end of the chapter.

1. Starbucks reports Income Tax Expense on its fiscal 2015 income statement of $1,143.7 million. How much of this tax benefit is current tax expense (benefit), and how much is deferred tax expense (benefit)?
2. What was the amount of valuation allowance established by Starbucks for its deferred tax asset as of September 27, 2015?
3. What is the main contributor of future taxable amounts for Starbucks? What is the main contributor of future deductible amounts for Starbucks?
4. What amount of foreign-earned income has Starbucks decided to permanently reinvest in its foreign subsidiaries?

> **GOT IT?**
>
> **18-20** How are deferred tax liabilities and assets reported on a corporation's balance sheet?
>
> **18-21** What are the four required disclosures a corporation must make regarding its provision for income taxes and effective tax rate?

LEARNING OBJECTIVE 18.8
Understand and explain the accounting for uncertain tax positions.

WHAT ARE ACCOUNTING ISSUES RELATED TO UNCERTAIN TAX POSITIONS?

Earlier in the chapter, we discussed various transactions involving tax deductions. The tax treatment of many transactions is not always clear-cut. Companies and the IRS often disagree on whether certain types of transactions trigger taxable income or tax deductions, the period in which the amount should be taxed or can be deducted, and the amount of the income or deduction, if any. Because GAAP did not provide a confidence threshold that must be met for a company to recognize the benefits from a **tax position** (current or future tax deduction) in its financial statements, considerable diversity developed in practice for these **uncertain tax positions**. Many companies recorded the tax benefits on an "as-filed" basis. That is, they recognized any current or deferred tax assets or liabilities when they took the related tax position. They frequently recorded a valuation allowance to reduce any current or deferred tax benefit if it was *more likely than not* that an adjustment to the tax benefit would be required. Because of the variety of approaches that companies used to recognize the tax benefits associated with their uncertain tax positions, the FASB provided additional guidance on the recognition and measurement of all income tax positions.[23]

The first step for a company in applying this guidance is to determine whether to recognize an uncertain tax position by evaluating whether the tax position is "more likely than not" (greater than 50% probability) of being upheld during a tax audit by the IRS, based on the technical merits of the position. Assuming that a tax position meets the recognition criteria, the second step is for the company to measure the tax benefit as the largest dollar amount that is above the "more likely than not" threshold.[24]

The difference between the tax benefit recognized in the financial statements and the tax benefit reflected in the tax return would result in either an increase in the income tax liability, an increase in a deferred tax liability (if the difference relates to a taxable temporary difference), or a decrease in a deferred tax asset (if the difference is due to a deductible temporary difference). Among the required disclosures are:

- a table that reconciles the beginning and ending balances of the unrecognized tax benefits
- the total amount of the unrecognized tax benefits that, if recognized, would affect the effective tax rate
- a discussion of the tax positions that management believes are reasonably possible to change significantly in the next 12 months.[25]

---

[23] FASB ASC 740-10-25: Income Taxes, Overall, Recognition.
[24] FASB ASC 740-10-30: Income Taxes, Overall, Initial Measurement.
[25] If a company's estimate of the tax benefit changes because of new information, the subsequent recognition and measurement is based on its best estimate as of the reporting date. In the case of a decreased estimate, the company may have to "derecognize" the tax benefit which may result in accrued interest and penalties.

Example: Uncertain Tax Position

Wolf Company claims a research and experimentation tax credit of $1,000,000 on its tax return. Historically, the IRS has challenged whether some of the expenditures meet the definition of "qualified research expenses." Before Wolf can recognize the tax benefit, it must first determine if the tax position is "more likely than not" to be upheld during a tax audit by the IRS. Based on the technical merits of the position, the company believes that all the expenditures are valid and supportable, and the majority will be upheld in a tax audit. Wolf has met the recognition threshold and must now determine the amount of the benefit to recognize.

Wolf estimates the following probability distribution of possible outcomes.

Dollar Amount of Tax Benefit That Management Anticipates Will Be Upheld	Probability That the Tax Position Will Be Upheld	Cumulative Probability That the Tax Position Will Be Upheld
$1,000,000	30%	30%
910,000	30	60
850,000	40	100

Because $910,000 is the largest dollar amount above the cumulative 50% probability threshold, the company will recognize a current tax benefit of $910,000 in its financial statements. The $90,000 difference between the tax credit claimed on the tax return ($1,000,000) and the amount estimated to be ultimately upheld ($910,000) is the "unrecognized tax benefit" and is recorded as a noncurrent liability because the company does not expect settlement within the next year. The ultimate settlement, at an amount greater or less than $90,000, would be accounted for in the period of settlement.

Starbucks's uncertain tax position disclosure is presented in Real Report 18.2.

REAL REPORT 18.2 — STARBUCKS'S UNCERTAIN TAX POSITION DISCLOSURE

Uncertain Tax Positions — Starbucks

As of September 27, 2015, we had $150.4 million of gross unrecognized tax benefits of which $101.7 million, if recognized, would affect our effective tax rate. We recognized expense of $0.7 million, expense of $5.9 million, and a benefit of $0.8 million of interest and penalties in income tax expense, prior to the benefit of the federal tax deduction, for fiscal 2015, 2014 and 2013, respectively. As of September 27, 2015 and September 28, 2014, we had accrued interest and penalties of $11.3 million and $10.6 million, respectively, before the benefit of the federal tax deduction, included within other long-term liabilities on our consolidated balance sheets.

The following table summarizes the activity related to our unrecognized tax benefits (in millions):

	Sep 27, 2015	Sep 28, 2014	Sep 29, 2013
Beginning balance	$112.7	$ 88.8	$75.3
Increase related to prior year tax positions	7.9	1.4	8.9
Decrease related to prior year tax positions	(0.9)	(2.2)	(9.3)
Increase related to current year tax positions	32.0	26.7	19.3
Decrease related to current year tax positions	(0.6)	(1.9)	(0.4)
Decreases related to settlements with taxing authorities	(0.7)	(0.1)	—
Decreases related to lapsing of statute of limitations	—	—	(5.0)
Ending balance	$150.4	$112.7	$88.8

(continued)

> We are currently under examination, or may be subject to examination, by various jurisdictions inside and outside the U.S. as well as U.S. state and municipal taxing jurisdictions for fiscal years 2006 through 2014. We are no longer subject to U.S. federal or state examination for years prior to fiscal year 2010, with the exception of one state and one city. We are no longer subject to examination in any material international markets prior to 2006.
>
> There is a reasonable possibility that $31.2 million of the currently remaining unrecognized tax benefits may be recognized by the end of fiscal 2016 as a result of a lapse of the statute of limitations and expected consent from taxing authorities.

Suggested answers to these questions are found at the end of the chapter.

Questions:

1. What was the change in Starbucks's gross unrecognized tax benefits from September 28, 2014, to September 27, 2015?
2. What amount of unrecognized tax benefit did Starbucks recognize in fiscal 2015 due to settlements with taxing authorities?
3. Did the increase in Starbucks's total amount of unrecognized tax benefits in 2015 change more as a result of current or prior-year tax positions?

INTERNATIONAL DIMENSION

ACCOUNTING FOR DEFERRED TAX ASSETS AND LIABILITIES

IFRS for deferred income taxes differ in certain respects from U.S. GAAP. Both IFRS and U.S. GAAP generally require the comprehensive allocation of temporary differences using a balance sheet (or asset/liability) approach. However, there are a number of significant differences between IFRS and U.S. GAAP with regard to the recognition, measurement, and presentation of deferred tax assets and liabilities.

- IFRS allow a company to recognize a deferred tax asset up to the amount for which it is probable that the company will have sufficient future taxable income against which to utilize the deferred tax asset. Therefore, valuation allowances for deferred tax assets are not recorded. Under U.S. GAAP, deferred tax assets are recognized in full and then reduced by a valuation allowance for the portion that is not expected to be realized. It is important to note that the net amount will be the same under both sets of standards.
- Under U.S. GAAP, the recognition threshold for deferred tax assets is defined as *more likely than not*. Although IFRS define "probable" as "more likely than not" for contingencies, this definition is currently not specifically included in IAS 12 Income Taxes for deferred taxes. Therefore, differences in application might arise.
- IFRS allow an upward revaluation of certain assets to fair value (e.g., property, plant, and equipment). The difference between the carrying amount of the revalued asset and its taxable basis is considered a temporary difference,

(continued)

which results in the recognition of a deferred tax amount that is reported in shareholders' equity. No such upward revaluations are allowed under U.S. GAAP.
- Under IFRS, the measurement of a company's deferred tax assets and liabilities is based on enacted tax rates or substantially enacted tax rates (under IFRS "substantially enacted" means virtually certain). IFRS also bases the measurement of deferred tax assets and liabilities on how the tax laws of the country in which it is located allow it to recover or settle the deferred tax asset or liability. Under U.S. GAAP, only enacted tax rates can be used, and it is assumed that the deferred tax asset or liability will be recovered or settled in a manner consistent with its current use in the business.
- IFRS provide no specific guidance on the recognition of deferred tax liabilities related to uncertain tax positions. However, within its current income tax project, the IASB has proposed guidance similar to that in U.S. GAAP.
- IFRS require that the tax effects of any equity adjustments (e.g., asset revaluations) be reported directly in equity.

IFRS Application Lavalle Company, a French company reporting under IFRS, reports a pretax operating loss of €85,000 in 2016 (its first year of operation) for both financial reporting and income tax purposes. The income tax rate is 25%, and there is no significant probability that a change in the tax rate will be enacted for future years. French law allows for both operating loss carrybacks and loss carryforwards; however, because Lavalle had no income prior to 2016, it cannot carry back the operating loss.

Based on all available evidence, it appears probable that Lavalle will not be able to realize €54,000 of the operating loss carryforward due to its competitive marketplace. Lavalle would make the following journal entry for 2016 to recognize the portion of the operating loss carryforward that it is likely to realize:

Deferred Tax Asset [(€85,000 − €54,000) × 25%]	7,750	
Income Tax Benefit from Loss Carryforward		7,750

If Lavalle was reporting under GAAP, it would have made the following entries:

Deferred Tax Asset [(€85,000) × 25%]	21,250	
Income Tax Benefit from Loss Carryforward		21,250
Income Tax Benefit from Loss Carryforward [(€54,000) × 25%]	13,500	
Allowance to Reduce Deferred Tax Asset to Realizable Value		13,500

In both cases, the income tax benefit from loss carryforward is €7,750. However, under IFRS, only the portion of the deferred tax asset that is considered probable to be realized is recognized, whereas under GAAP, the full amount of the deferred tax asset is recognized and then a valuation allowance is applied for the portion not likely to be realized.

In February 2017, due to an improved business climate and new business strategy, Lavalle now believes that it is probable that it will be able to utilize the

(continued)

full amount of its operating loss carryforward. Lavalle would make the following journal entry in early 2017 to recognize the remaining portion of the operating loss carryforward that previously was unrecorded:

Deferred Tax Asset [(€54,000) × 25%]	13,500	
Income Tax Benefit from Loss Carryforward		13,500

If Lavalle was reporting under U.S. GAAP, the change would have been recorded by reversing the allowance account:

Allowance to Reduce Deferred Tax Asset to Realizable Value [(€54,000) × 25%]	13,500	
Income Tax Benefit from Loss Carryforward		13,500

Because it is now probable that the remaining portion of the operating loss carryforward is expected to be realized, Lavalle will be able to recognize the benefit.

Source: IAS 12 (See Appendix C at the end of this book.)

GOT IT?

18-22 What are the two steps that a company must complete for an uncertain tax position?

18-23 If a company believes that it is more likely than not to have future taxable income against which it can use its deferred tax asset, how might the accounting treatment of this deferred tax asset differ under U.S. GAAP and IFRS?

REVIEW CENTER

At the beginning of the chapter, we discussed the role that taxes have in planning and decision making for global companies and the effect this can have on effective tax rates and operations. We also identified several objectives you would accomplish after reading the chapter. The objectives are listed below and followed by a brief summary of the key points.

LEARNING OBJECTIVE 18.1
Understand accounting issues related to income taxes.

KEY TAKEAWAYS

- The objectives of financial reporting under GAAP and IFRS differ from the objectives of tax reporting under the Internal Revenue Code. This causes a company's pretax financial income and income tax expense (computed under GAAP) to differ from its taxable income and income tax payable.
- Differences between a company's pretax financial income and its taxable income arise from both temporary and permanent differences and operating loss carrybacks and carryforwards.

KEY TERMS

effective tax rate, p. 18-1
pretax financial income, p. 18-3

statutory tax rate, p. 18-1
taxable income, p. 18-3

KEY TAKEAWAYS

LEARNING OBJECTIVE 18.2
Apply interperiod income tax allocation and explain the accounting for temporary differences.

- Temporary (timing) differences arise when a company reports a revenue or an expense in one period for financial accounting purposes but in an earlier or later period for income tax purposes. This causes a difference between a company's tax basis of its assets or liabilities and the book value of the assets or liabilities in the financial statements, which creates either a:
  - future taxable amount, which increases taxable income in the future (deferred tax liability), or
  - future deductible amount, which decreases taxable income in the future (deferred tax asset)
- In accounting for income taxes, a company should:
  - recognize the amount of its income tax payable or refund for the current year
  - recognize deferred tax liabilities or assets for the future tax consequences of events that have been reported in the financial statements or income tax returns
- A deferred tax liability is the increase in future taxes payable due to currently existing temporary differences that will give rise to future taxable amounts. A deferred tax asset is the reduction in future taxes payable due to currently existing temporary differences that will give rise to future deductible amounts.
- Deferred tax liabilities and assets are measured using the enacted tax rate that will be in existence when the temporary differences result in future taxable or deductible amounts.
- A deferred tax asset should be reduced by a valuation allowance if it is more likely than not that the deferred tax asset will not be realized (e.g., the future deductible amount will not be used because of insufficient future taxable income).

KEY TERMS

comprehensive asset and liability approach, p. 18-6
deferred tax asset, p. 18-4
deferred tax liability, p. 18-4
future taxable amounts, p. 18-6
future tax deductible amounts, p. 18-6
interperiod income tax allocation, p. 18-4
marginal tax rate, p. 18-7
temporary difference, p. 18-4
timing differences, p. 18-4

KEY TAKEAWAYS

LEARNING OBJECTIVE 18.3
Record and report deferred tax liabilities and deferred tax assets.

- The following steps are necessary to measure and record a company's current and deferred income taxes:
  - *Step 1.* Calculate the current period taxable income and then measure the current income tax payable by multiplying the current taxable income by the applicable tax rate.
  - *Step 2.* Identify any temporary differences and classify them as future taxable amounts or future deductible amounts.
  - *Step 3.* Calculate the deferred tax liability for each future taxable amount using the applicable tax rate.
  - *Step 4.* Calculate the deferred tax asset for each future deductible amount using the applicable tax rate.
  - *Step 5.* Reduce any deferred tax assets by a valuation allowance if necessary.
  - *Step 6.* Prepare journal entries to record income tax expense, the income tax payable, the change in deferred liabilities and/or deferred tax assets, and the change in the valuation allowance (if any).

- Two basic journal entries are required to account for income taxes:
  - The first journal entry is based on the fact that income tax expense consists of an amount payable in the current period (income taxes payable) and an amount deferred until a later period (deferred expense or benefit). Note that a company's deferred tax expense or benefit is the change in its deferred tax liabilities and deferred tax assets during the year.
  - The second journal entry adjusts the valuation allowance (if necessary) with a matching adjustment to income tax expense. The valuation allowance is reported as a contra-account to the deferred tax asset.
- When there are multiple enacted tax rates, the company prepares a schedule to determine the amounts of temporary differences that will reverse each year and uses the applicable enacted tax rate for each year to compute the deferred tax liability or asset.
- A change in income tax laws or rates requires an adjustment of the deferred tax liabilities and deferred tax assets as of the beginning of the year in which the change is made, with the resulting tax effect included in income tax expense relating to income from continuing operations.

KEY CALCULATION

Income Tax Payable = Taxable Income × Applicable Tax Rate(s)

LEARNING OBJECTIVE 18.4
Understand and explain the accounting for permanent differences.

KEY TAKEAWAYS

- Permanent differences arise from revenues or expenses that are recognized for financial reporting purposes but never affect taxable income, or deductions that reduce taxable income but never qualify as expenses for financial reporting.
- Permanent differences never reverse and do not require interperiod income tax allocation. Permanent differences affect companies' effective tax rates.

KEY TERMS

effective tax rate, p. 18-17
permanent difference, p. 18-16
statutory tax rate, p. 18-17

KEY CALCULATION

Effective Tax Rate = Income Tax Expense ÷ Income before Income Taxes

LEARNING OBJECTIVE 18.5
Explain and account for operating loss carrybacks and carryforwards.

KEY TAKEAWAYS

- If a company has an operating loss for income tax purposes (tax deductible expenses exceed taxable revenue), it can choose to either:
  - carry the operating loss back 2 years (in sequential order starting with the earliest year) to offset previous taxable income and create a refund of income taxes previously paid; any remaining loss can then be carried forward sequentially for 20 years to offset future taxable income
  - forgo the operating loss carryback and choose to carry forward sequentially the operating loss for 20 years to offset future taxable income.
- The income tax benefit of an operating loss carryback is recognized in the year the operating loss occurs as a current receivable on the balance sheet and as a reduction of the operating loss on the income statement.
- The income tax benefit of an operating loss carryforward is recognized in the year the operating loss occurs as a deferred tax asset (reduced by a valuation allowance, if necessary) on the balance sheet and as a reduction of the operating loss on the income statement.

KEY TERMS

operating loss carryback, p. 18-19   operating loss carryforward, p. 18-19

KEY TAKEAWAYS

LEARNING OBJECTIVE 18.6
Describe and apply intraperiod tax allocation.

- Intraperiod income tax allocation is the allocation of a corporation's total income tax expense for a period to the various components of its income statement, the schedule of retained earnings within the statement of shareholders equity, and the comprehensive income within the statement of shareholders' equity.
  - Intraperiod tax allocation is based on the concept of linking components of income tax expense against the major components of pretax income to provide more useful information to external users.
  - Income or loss from a discontinued component, retrospective adjustments, prior period adjustments, and any other comprehensive income item are reported net of the related income tax effects where the income tax effect is based on the company's marginal tax rate.

KEY TERM

intraperiod income tax allocation, p. 18-27

KEY TAKEAWAYS

LEARNING OBJECTIVE 18.7
Examine presentation and disclosure issues related to accounting for income taxes.

- A company reports deferred tax liabilities and assets as a net noncurrent amount for financial reporting.
- For the net deferred tax liability or asset, it discloses:
  - causes of the deferred tax assets and liabilities
  - total deferred tax liabilities
  - total deferred tax assets
  - total valuation allowance and the net change in the allowance
- For income tax expense, it discloses:
  - amount of income tax expense or benefit allocated to continuing operations, discontinued operations, retrospective adjustments, prior period adjustments, and gains and losses included in other comprehensive income
  - significant components of income tax expense related to continuing operations for each year
- For the reconciliation of the statutory U.S. federal tax rate to the effective tax rate, companies also disclose:
  - U.S. federal income tax amount and the statutory rate amounts of income tax expense attributable to states and foreign countries
  - effects of differences in tax rates associated with taxable income generated in various states and countries
  - other effects impacting the effective tax rate for the period

KEY TAKEAWAYS

LEARNING OBJECTIVE 18.8
Understand and explain the accounting for uncertain tax positions.

- Companies often enter into transactions that are expected to result in a tax benefit (current or future tax deduction), which is called a tax position. If the company is not certain that the Internal Revenue Service will agree that the transaction will result in a tax benefit, it is referred to as an uncertain tax position.
- Companies and the IRS often disagree on whether certain types of transactions trigger taxable income or tax deductions, the period in which the amount should be taxed or can be deducted, and the amount of the income or deduction, if any. Because of this, the FASB provides additional guidance on the recognition and measurement of all uncertain income tax positions.

- For an uncertain tax position, a company completes two steps. First, it evaluates whether the tax position is "more likely than not" to be upheld during its audit. If so, the second step is to measure the tax benefit as the largest dollar amount above the more likely than not threshold.

KEY TERMS

income tax position, p. 18-34

uncertain tax position, p. 18-34

ANSWERS TO REAL REPORT QUESTIONS

Real Report 18.1 Answers Starbucks—Analysis of Income Taxes

1. Starbucks's current tax expense is $1,123.3 million [$1,123.3 = $801.0 (Federal) + $150.1(State) + $172.2 (Foreign)]. It reports a deferred tax expense of $20.4 million [$20.4 = $56.5(Federal) + $4.0(State) + ($40.1)(Foreign)].
2. Starbucks reports a valuation allowance of $143.7 million at September 27, 2015.
3. The main contributor of future taxable amounts for Starbucks is Property, Plant and Equipment, which created a deferred tax liability of $217.5 million as of September 27, 2015. The main contributor of future deductible amounts for Starbucks is the litigation charge resulting from the arbitration with Kraft, which created a deferred tax asset of $931.0 million as of September 27, 2015. Stock based compensation, which created a deferred tax asset of $135.5 million as of September 27, 2015, is normally the largest contributor to deferred tax assets.
4. Starbucks has decided to permanently reinvest approximately $2.8 billion in its foreign subsidiaries as of September 27, 2015.

Real Report 18.2 Answers Starbucks—Uncertain Tax Position Disclosure

1. Starbucks's unrecognized tax benefits changed by $37.7 million from September 28, 2014, to September 27, 2015.
2. During fiscal year 2015, Starbucks reduced its unrecognized tax benefits due to settlements with taxing authorities by $0.7 million.
3. The increase in Starbucks's total amount of unrecognized tax benefits in 2015 as a result of current-year tax positions was greater. The change due to prior-year tax positions was $7.0 million ($7.9 million − $0.9 million) versus a change due to current-year tax positions of $31.4 million ($32.0 million − $0.6 million).

MULTIPLE-CHOICE (AICPA ADAPTED)

Select the best answer for each of the following.

M18-1 **LO 18.1** Which of the following is *not* a cause of a difference between pretax financial income and taxable income in a given period?

a. operating loss carrybacks and carryforwards
b. permanent differences
c. applicable tax rates
d. temporary differences

M18-2 **LO 18.2** Which of the following is an argument in favor of the asset/liability method of interperiod income tax allocation?

a. Deferred taxes are the result of historical transactions and should be reported in a similar manner.
b. Taxes are an expense of doing business and should be accrued and deferred like other expenses, which results in the recognition of deferred assets and liabilities.
c. The predictive value of future cash flows is increased when deferred taxes are reported based on enacted tax rates in effect when the temporary difference originates.

d. Historical tax rates are more verifiable, and, therefore, the deferred tax amount is more reliable.

M18-3 The FASB came to which of the following conclusions regarding interperiod income tax allocation?
LO 18.2

a. The partial allocation approach should be applied.
b. The net-of-tax method of income tax allocation should be used.
c. Nonallocation of income tax expense is appropriate.
d. The asset/liability method of income tax allocation should be used.

M18-4 Prior to and during 2016, Shadrach Company reported tax depreciation at an amount higher than the amount of financial depreciation, resulting in a book value of the depreciable assets of $24,500 for financial reporting purposes and of $20,000 for tax purposes at the end of 2016. In addition, Shadrach recognized a $3,500 estimated liability for legal expenses in the financial statements during 2016; it expects to pay this liability (and deduct it for tax purposes) in 2020. The current tax rate is 30%, no change in the tax rate has been enacted, and the company expects to be profitable in future years. What is the amount of the net deferred tax liability at the end of 2016?
LO 18.3

a. $300
b. $450
c. $1,050
d. $1,350

M18-5 At the beginning of 2016, Conley Company purchased an asset at a cost of $10,000. For financial reporting purposes, the asset has a 4-year life with no residual value and is depreciated by the straight-line method beginning in 2016. For tax purposes, the asset is depreciated under MACRS using a 5-year recovery period. Prior to 2016, Conley had no deferred tax liability or asset. The difference between depreciation for financial reporting purposes and income tax purposes is the only temporary difference between pretax financial income and taxable income. The current income tax rate is 30%, and no change in the tax rate has been enacted for future years. In 2016 and 2017, taxable income will be higher or lower than financial income by what amount?
LO 18.3

	2016	2017
a.	higher by $150	lower by $210
b.	higher by $500	lower by $700
c.	lower by $500	higher by $700
d.	lower by $1,500	higher by $100

M18-6 Oliver Company earned taxable income of $7,500 during 2016, its first year of operations. A reconciliation of pretax financial income and taxable income indicated that an additional $2,500 of accelerated depreciation was deducted for tax purposes and that an estimated expense of $5,800 was deducted for financial reporting purposes. The estimated expense is not expected to be deductible for tax purposes until 2019, when the liability is paid. The current tax rate is 30%, and no change in the tax rate has been enacted for future years. The resulting journal entry for 2016 would be:
LO 18.3

a. Income Tax Expense   1,260
   Deferred Tax Asset   1,740
       Deferred Tax Liability   750
       Income Taxes Payable   2,250
b. Income Tax Expense   1,260
   Deferred Tax Asset   990
       Income Taxes Payable   2,250
c. Income Tax Expense   3,240
       Deferred Tax Liability   990
       Income Taxes Payable   2,250
d. Income Tax Expense   3,000
       Deferred Tax Liability   750
       Income Taxes Payable   2,250

M18-7 A permanent difference is a difference between pretax financial income and taxable income in an accounting period that will never reverse in a later period. Which of the following is *not* an example of a permanent difference?
LO 18.4

a. fine for air pollution
b. percentage depletion in excess of cost depletion on a wasting asset
c. interest on municipal bonds
d. rent received in advance

M18-8 In 2016, Swope Company reports a pretax operating loss of $70,000 for both financial reporting and income tax purposes. Pretax financial income and taxable income for the previous 3 years had been: 2013—$15,000 (tax rate 20%), 2014—$24,000 (tax rate 25%), and 2015—$49,000 (tax rate 30%). The current tax rate is 30%, and no change in the tax rate has been enacted for future years. At the end of 2016, the journal entry recorded would contain an income tax benefit from an operating loss carryback of:
LO 18.5

a. $0
b. $18,300
c. $19,800
d. $19,950

M18-9 Brooks Company reported a prior period adjustment of $12,000 in pretax financial "income" and taxable income for 2017. The prior period
LO 18.6

(continued)

adjustment was the result of an error in calculating bad debt expense for 2016. The current tax rate is 30%, and no change in the tax rate has been enacted for future years. When the company applies intraperiod income tax allocation, the prior period adjustment will be shown on the:

a. income statement at $12,000
b. income statement at $8,400 (net of $3,600 income taxes)
c. retained earnings statement at $12,000
d. retained earnings statement at $8,400 (net of $3,600 income taxes)

M18-10 Which component of current income is not disclosed on the income statement net of tax effects?
LO 18.6

a. gain on sale of discontinued component
b. gain on disposal of milling machine
c. gain from sale of discontinued segment
d. loss from operations of discontinued component

REVIEW EXERCISES

RE18-1 Parker Company identifies depreciation as the only difference for future taxable amounts. In Year 1, its depreciation
LO 18.2 for financial reporting purposes is $9,000 and $10,500 for income tax reporting purposes. Parker has an income tax rate of 35%. Explain whether this is a deferred tax asset or deferred tax liability, and calculate the amount.

RE18-2 Refer to **RE18-1**. Assume that Parker's taxable income for Year 1 is $150,000. Prepare the journal entry to record
LO 18.3 Parker's income tax expense.

RE18-3 In the current year, Madison Corporation had $50,000 of taxable income at a tax rate of 25%. During the year,
LO 18.3 Madison began offering warranties on its products and has a warranty liability for financial reporting purposes of $5,000 at the end of the year. Warranty expenses are not deductible until paid for income tax purposes. Prepare the journal entry to record Madison's income taxes at the end of the year.

RE18-4 Refer to **RE18-3**. Prepare the additional journal entry necessary for Madison Corporation assuming that the corpora-
LO 18.3 tion decides that it is "more likely than not" that $500 of the $5,000 future deductible amount will not be realized.

RE18-5 Turnip Company purchased an asset at a cost of $10,000 with a 10-year life during the current year. Turnip uses
LO 18.3 differing depreciation methods for financial reporting and income tax purposes. The depreciation expense during the current year for financial reporting is $1,000 and for income tax purposes is $2,000. Turnip is subject to a 30% enacted future tax rate. Prepare a schedule to compute Turnip's (a) ending future taxable amount, (b) ending deferred tax liability, and (c) change in deferred tax liability (deferred tax expense) for the current year.

RE18-6 Carrot Company has been profitable in the past and expects to remain profitable in the future. Carrot sells a prod-
LO 18.3 uct for which it provides a 5-year warranty. For financial reporting purposes, Carrot estimates its future warranty costs and records a warranty expense and liability at year-end, whereas for income tax purposes the company deducts its warranty costs when paid. At the beginning of the current year, Carrot had a deferred tax asset of $500 related to the warranty liability on its balance sheet. At the end of the current year, the company estimates that its ending warranty liability is $2,000. Carrot had current year taxable income of $10,000 and is subject to an enacted future tax rate of 30%. Prepare a schedule to compute Carrot's (a) ending future deductible amount, (b) ending deferred tax asset, and (c) change in deferred tax asset for the current year (deferred tax benefit).

RE18-7 Compute Radish Company's taxable income given the following information:
LO 18.3
LO 18.4
- Excess of accrual-basis sales over cash-basis sales for taxes $ 6,000
- Tax-exempt interest revenue on municipal bonds 3,000
- Pretax financial income 55,000
- Excess of rent collected in advance over rent revenue 8,000

RE18-8 Sky Company reports a pretax operating loss of $50,000 in Year 3 for both financial reporting and income tax pur-
LO 18.5 poses. Its reported pretax financial income and taxable income for the previous 2 years had been: Year 1: $20,000 (tax rate 30%) and Year 2: $30,000 (tax rate 35%). Calculate Sky's income tax refund for Year 3.

RE18-9 Tally & Co. incurred a pretax operating loss of $100,000 in its first year of operations for both financial reporting
LO 18.5 and income tax purposes. However, it expects to be profitable in the future. Its expected future income tax rate is 25%. Prepare Tally & Co.'s journal entry to record its operating loss carryforward.

RE18-10 Kline Company has the following items of pretax financial (and taxable) "income" for the current year:

LO 18.6

Income from continuing operations	$100,000
Gain on disposal of discontinued Division B	23,000
Loss from operations of discontinued Division B	(11,000)

Kline is subject to income tax rates of 30% on the first $40,000 of income and 35% on all income in excess of $40,000. Prepare a schedule to calculate Kline's intraperiod income tax expense (and credit) amounts.

RE18-11 Barth James Inc. has the following deferred tax assets and liabilities: $12,000 noncurrent deferred tax asset, and $10,500 noncurrent deferred tax liability. Show how Barth James would report these deferred tax assets and liabilities on its balance sheet.

LO 18.7

RE18-12 Cole Company had a deferred tax liability of $1,000 at the end of Year 1 when the tax rate was 20%. In Year 2, Congress increases the income tax rate from 20% to 30%. Record the journal entry Cole would make to adjust for this change.

LO 18.3

EXERCISES

E18-1 **Future Taxable Amount** Arrow Company began operations at the beginning of 2016. At the end of 2016, Arrow reported taxable income of $20,800 and pretax financial income of $22,200 because of a single temporary difference. The income tax rate for the current year is 30%, but Congress has enacted a 40% tax rate for 2017 and beyond.

LO 18.3

Required:
Prepare Arrow's income tax journal entry at the end of 2016.

E18-2 **Change in Tax Rates** At the end of 2016, Sentry Company reported a deferred tax liability of $6,120 based on an income tax rate of 30%. On January 2, 2017, Congress changed the income tax rate to 35%.

LO 18.3

Required:
1. Calculate the amount of the adjustment to Sentry's 2016 year-end deferred tax liability.
2. Prepare the journal entry to correct Sentry's deferred tax liability.

E18-3 **Temporary Difference** At the end of 2016, its first year of operations, Slater Company reported a book value for its depreciable assets of $40,000 for financial reporting purposes and $33,000 for income tax purposes. Slater earned taxable income of $97,000 during 2016. The company is subject to a 30% income tax rate, and no change has been enacted for future years. The depreciation was the only temporary difference between taxable income and pretax financial income.

LO 18.3

Required:
1. Prepare Slater's income tax journal entry at the end of 2016.
2. Show how the deferred taxes would be reported on Slater's December 31, 2016, balance sheet.

E18-4 **Single Temporary Difference: Multiple Rates** At the end of 2016, Fulhage Company reported taxable income of $9,000 and pretax financial income of $10,600. The difference is due to depreciation for tax purposes in excess of depreciation for financial reporting purposes. The income tax rate for the current year is 40%, but Congress has enacted tax rates of 35% for 2017 and 30% for 2018 and beyond.

LO 18.3

Fulhage has calculated the excess of its financial depreciation over its tax depreciation for future years as follows: 2017, $600; 2018, $700; and 2019, $300. Prior to 2016, the company had no deferred tax liability or asset.

Required:
Prepare Fulhage's income tax journal entry at the end of 2016.

E18-5 **Future Deductible Amount** Pito Company has been in operation for several years. During those years, the company has been profitable and it expects to continue to be profitable in the foreseeable future. At the beginning of 2016, Pito has a deferred tax asset of $360 pertaining to one future deductible amount. During 2016, Pito earned

LO 18.3

(continued)

taxable income of $51,000 which was taxed at a rate of 30% (no change in the tax rate has been enacted for future years). At the end of 2016, the book value of the current liability to which the deferred tax asset relates for financial reporting purposes exceeded the book value for income tax purposes by $6,000.

Required:
1. Prepare Pito's income tax journal entry at the end of 2016.
2. Show how the deferred tax asset is reported on Pito's December 31, 2016, balance sheet.

E18-6 **Valuation Account** At the end of 2016, its first year of operations, Beattie Company reported taxable income of $38,000 and pretax financial income of $34,400. The difference is due to the way the company handles its warranty costs. For tax purposes, Beattie deducts the warranty costs as they are paid. For financial reporting purposes, Beattie provides for a year-end estimated warranty liability based on future expected costs. Beattie is subject to a 30% tax rate for 2016, and no change in the tax rate has been enacted for future years. Based on verifiable evidence, the company decides it should establish a valuation allowance of 60% of its ending deferred tax asset.

LO 18.3

Required:
1. Prepare Beattie's income tax journal entry at the end of 2016.
2. Prepare the lower portion of Beattie's 2016 income statement.

E18-7 **Deferred Tax Asset and Valuation Account** Zeta Corporation reported taxable income for 2016 of $200,000. The enacted tax rate for 2016 is 40%. During 2016, Zeta became the defendant in a lawsuit. The lawsuit has not been resolved at the end of the period, but Zeta's lawyers believe that it is probable that the company will be held liable. The legal office estimated that the amount of loss will be $80,000. As a result, the lawsuit has been recognized as a contingent liability. However, the legal obligation is not deductible for tax purposes during 2016. The lawsuit represents the only difference between financial income and taxable income for the year.

LO 18.3

Required:
1. Assume that Zeta Corporation has been quite profitable in past periods and expects to continue that pattern in the future. Record a journal entry to recognize tax expense, tax payable, and deferred tax for 2016.
2. Assume that there is substantial doubt about whether Zeta Corporation will be profitable in future periods. As a result, the company believes that one-half of the future deduction for legal costs will not be realized. Record a journal entry to recognize tax expense, tax payable, and deferred tax for the year.
3. **Next Level** Explain what circumstances require that a valuation allowance account should be utilized when deferred tax is recognized. How should that account be presented on the financial statements?
4. Prepare your answer to Requirement 2 assuming that Zeta prepares financial statements according to IFRS.

E18-8 **Income Taxes** Thun Company has been in operation for several years. It has both a deductible and a taxable temporary difference. At the beginning of 2016, its deferred tax asset was $690, and its deferred tax liability was $750. The company expects its future deductible amount to be "deductible" in 2017 and its future taxable amount to be "taxable" in 2018. In 2015, Congress enacted income tax rates for future years as follows: 2016, 30%; 2017, 34%; and 2018, 35%. At the end of 2016, Thun reported income taxes payable of $25,800, an increase in its deferred tax liability of $300, and an ending balance in its deferred tax asset of $860. Thun has prepared the following schedule of items related to its income taxes for 2016.

LO 18.3

Item	Amount
Taxable income for 2016	_____
Future taxable amount, 12/31/16	_____
Increase in future deductible amount during 2016	_____
Income tax expense for 2016	_____

Required:
Fill in the blanks in the preceding schedule. Show your calculations.

E18-9 **Originating and Reversing Difference** Tanner Corporation begins operations in 2015 and reports the following amounts of pretax financial income and taxable income for the years 2015 through 2019. Tanner has only one temporary difference and only one originating or reversing difference occurs in any single year. Tanner is subject to a tax rate of 30% for all the years.

LO 18.3

Year	Pretax Financial Income	Taxable Income
2015	$70,000	$ 50,000
2016	85,000	75,000
2017	90,000	90,000
2018	82,000	92,000
2019	93,000	113,000

Required:
1. Prepare the income tax journal entry for each year.
2. **Next Level** What do you notice about the balance in the deferred taxes over the 5 years?

E18-10 **Multiple Temporary Differences** Vickers Company reports taxable income of $4,500 for 2016. Vickers has two temporary differences between pretax financial income and taxable income at the end of 2016. The first difference is expected to result in taxable amounts totaling $2,470 in future years. The second difference is expected to result in deductible amounts totaling $1,360 in future years. Vickers has a deferred tax asset of $372 and a deferred tax liability of $690 at the beginning of 2016. The current tax rate is 30%, and no change in the tax rate has been enacted for future years. Vickers has positive, verifiable evidence of future taxable income.

LO 18.3

Required:
Prepare Vickers's income tax journal entry at the end of 2016.

E18-11 **Multiple Tax Rates** For the year ended December 31, 2016, Nelson Co.'s income statement showed income of $435,000 before income, tax expense. To compute taxable income, the following differences were noted:

LO 18.3

Income from tax-exempt municipal bonds	$ 60,000
Depreciation deducted for tax purposes in excess of depreciation recorded on the books	120,000
Proceeds received from life insurance on death of an insured employee	100,000
Corporate tax rate for 2016	30%
Enacted tax rate for future periods	35%

Required:
1. Calculate taxable income and tax payable for tax purposes.
2. Prepare Nelson's income tax journal entry at the end of 2016.

E18-12 **Temporary and Permanent Differences** Lin has just completed its first year of operations and has a number of differences between its pretax financial income and taxable income. The differences at the end of 2016 are as follows:

LO 18.3
LO 18.4

a. Lin recorded $7,000 of interest revenue on municipal bonds during 2016.
b. $15,000 of accrual-basis sales were recognized in income during 2016. They are expected to be received in cash during January 2017.
c. Depreciation on machinery totaled $28,000 using straight-line depreciation for financial statements. Lin's tax accountant recorded $36,000 of depreciation on the company's tax return.
d. Lin was fined $3,000 for violating certain labor laws during 2016. Lin paid the fine during 2016 and agreed to ensure future violations would not occur.
e. Bryant Corporation has agreed to rent space from Lin in 2017. In December 2016, Lin received $7,500 from Bryant in advance for rent.
f. For 2016, Lin reported $9,500 of warranty expense on its income statement. The company's warranty liability at the end of 2016 was $6,250. Lin expects additional warranty costs to be paid during 2017.

Required:
1. For each item, determine if it results in a temporary or permanent difference. If the item results in a temporary difference, determine if it results in a deferred tax asset or deferred tax liability.
2. For each item, determine if it initially results in pretax financial income being greater than or less than taxable income.
3. **Next Level** Discuss why permanent differences do not impact future periods' taxable income and how these differences affect tax rates.

E18-13 **Temporary and Permanent Differences** Assume the following facts for Munoz Company in 2016. Munoz reported pretax financial income of $800,000. In addition, Munoz reported the following differences between its pretax financial income and taxable income:

LO 18.3
LO 18.4

- Interest income of $80,000 was received during 2016 from an investment in municipal bonds. This income is exempt for tax purposes.
- Rent income of $40,000 was collected in 2015 and included for tax purposes during that year. For financial statement purposes, it will be reported as earned equally in 2016 and 2017.
- An asset with a 5-year life was purchased during 2016; straight-line depreciation for book purposes was $40,000. MACRS depreciation expense for 2016 was $100,000.
- Warranty expense of $20,000 was recognized on the 2016 income statement, while $5,000 was recognized for tax purposes. (Assume a 1-year warranty contract.)

The balance of the Deferred Tax Asset account (debit) at January 1, 2016, was $16,000 as a result of the rent income temporary difference. The tax rate for all years was 40%. Munoz has positive verifiable evidence of future taxable income.

Required:
1. Calculate the amount of Munoz's 2016 taxable income.
2. Prepare Munoz's income tax journal entry at the end of 2016.
3. Calculate Munoz's effective income tax rate for 2016.

E18-14 **Operating Loss** At the end of 2016, Keil Company reports a pretax operating loss of $80,000 for both financial reporting and income tax purposes. Prior to 2016, Keil had been successful and had reported and paid taxes on the following pretax financial income and taxable income: 2013, $37,000; 2014, $50,000; and 2015, $54,000. Keil had been subject to tax rates of 20% in 2013, 25% in 2014, and 30% in 2015.

LO 18.5

Required:
1. Prepare Keil's income tax journal entry at the end of 2016.
2. Prepare the lower portion of Keil's 2016 income statement.

E18-15 **Operating Loss** At the end of 2016, its first year of operations, Swelland Company reported a pretax operating loss of $32,000 for both financial reporting and income tax purposes. At that time, Swelland had no positive verifiable evidence that it would earn future taxable income. However, due to successful management, the company reported pretax operating income (and taxable income) of $70,000 in 2017. During both years, the income tax rate was 30%, and no change had been enacted for future years.

LO 18.5

Required:
1. Prepare Swelland's income tax journal entries at the end of 2016.
2. Prepare Swelland's income tax journal entry at the end of 2017.
3. Prepare the lower portion of Swelland's 2017 income statement.

E18-16 **Operating Loss** Baxter Company began operations in 2012 and was profitable through 2015, during which time the tax rate was 30%. At the end of 2016, Baxter reported a pretax operating loss of $135,000 for both financial reporting and income taxes. Because the tax rate was increased to 40% in 2016, Baxter elects to forgo any carryback of the operating loss. In 2017, Baxter reported pretax operating income of $150,000.

LO 18.5

Required:
1. Prepare Baxter's income tax journal entry at the end of 2016.
2. Prepare the lower portion of Baxter's 2016 income statement.
3. **Next Level** Explain why Baxter elected to forgo any carryback in 2016.
4. Prepare Baxter's income tax journal entry at the end of 2017.
5. Prepare the lower portion of Baxter's 2017 income statement.

E18-17 **Intraperiod Tax Allocation** Wright Company reports the following information for the year ended December 31, 2016:

LO 18.6

Pretax income from continuing operations	$160,000ᵃ
Pretax income from operations of discontinued Division M	27,000
Pretax loss on disposal of Division M	(45,000)
Pretax correction of error in understating depreciation in 2015	(8,000)
Retained earnings, January 1, 2016	410,000
Cash dividends during 2016	48,000
Income tax payable	41,000ᵇ

ᵃOf this amount, revenues are $400,000 and expenses are $240,000.
ᵇOf this amount, $6,750 relates to the pretax income from the operations of discontinued Division M; pretax loss on the disposal of Division M resulted in an income tax savings of $11,250; and pretax correction of the depreciation error resulted in an income tax savings of $2,000.

Required:
1. Prepare the year-end journal entry necessary to record the 2016 intraperiod income tax allocation in regard to the preceding information.
2. Prepare Wright's 2016 income statement and statement of retained earnings.

E18-18 **Calculating Intraperiod Income Taxes** EyeBeam Corporation reports the following *pretax* accounting (and taxable) income items during 2016:

LO 18.6

Income from continuing operations	$ 90,000*
Loss from operations of a discontinued division	(10,000)
Gain from the disposal of the discontinued division	25,000

*Of this amount, revenues are $320,000 and expenses are $230,000.

Required:
1. Prepare the journal entry necessary to record the 2016 intraperiod income tax allocation in regard to the preceding information. Assume a tax rate of 15% on the first $40,000 of income and a rate of 30% on income in excess of $40,000.
2. Prepare EyeBeam's 2016 income statement.

E18-19 **Disclosure of Intraperiod Tax Allocation** Lester Corporation reports $119,000 of both *pretax* accounting "income" and taxable income in 2016. In addition to income from continuing operations (of which revenues are $500,000), included in this "income" is a $17,000 loss from operations of discontinued Division W, a $15,000 gain on the disposal of Division W, and a $14,000 correction of an error due to the understatement of bad debt expense in 2015. Lester is subject to a 20% tax rate on the first $50,000 of income and a rate of 25% on income in excess of $50,000.

LO 18.6

SHOW ME HOW

Required:
1. Show how this information is disclosed on Lester's 2016 income statement.
2. Prepare Lester's 2016 statement of retained earnings. (Assume a beginning retained earnings balance of $191,000 and cash dividends during 2016 amounting to $65,000.)

E18-20 **Balance Sheet Presentation** Thiel Company reports the following deferred tax items at the end of 2016:

LO 18.7

SHOW ME HOW

Deferred Tax Item #	Account Balance	Related Asset or Liability creating the deferred tax item
1	$ 6,700 debit	Current asset
2	7,200 credit	Current liability
3	10,600 debit	Noncurrent asset
4	15,500 credit	Noncurrent liability

Required:
Show how the preceding deferred tax items are reported on Thiel's December 31, 2016, balance sheet.

E18-21 **Uncertain Tax Position** At the end of the current year, Boyd Company claims a $200,000 tax credit on its income tax return. Boyd is uncertain whether the IRS will accept this credit. It studies the IRS regulations and determines that it is more likely than not that the IRS will accept all or some of this tax credit. Based on this research, Boyd estimates the following probability distribution of possible outcomes:

LO 18.8

Dollar Amount of Tax Benefit That It Anticipates Will Be Upheld	Probability That the Tax Position Will Be Upheld	Cumulative Probability That the Tax Position Will Be Upheld
$200,000	25%	25%
150,000	45	70
100,000	30	100

Required:
For the current year, determine (1) the amount that Boyd will recognize as a current tax benefit and (2) the amount that it will record as the unrecognized tax benefit.

PROBLEMS

P18-1 **Definitions** The FASB has defined several terms in regard to accounting for income taxes. Below are various code letters (for terms) followed by definitions.

LO 18.2

Code Letter	Term	Code Letter	Term
A	Future deductible amount	H	Deferred tax consequences
B	Income tax payable (or refund)	I	Future taxable amount
C	Operating loss carryback	J	Deferred tax liability
D	Valuation allowance	K	Temporary difference
E	Deferred tax asset	L	Income tax expense (or benefit)
F	Operating loss carryforward	M	Deferred tax expense (or benefit)
G	Taxable income		

_____ 1. The deferred tax consequences of future deductible amounts and operating loss carryforwards
_____ 2. A difference between the tax basis of an asset or liability and its reported amount in the financial statements that will result in taxable or deductible amounts in future years when the reported amount of the asset or liability is recovered or settled, respectively
_____ 3. Temporary difference that results in taxable amounts in future years when the related asset or liability is recovered or settled, respectively
_____ 4. The future effects on income taxes, as measured by the applicable enacted tax rate and provisions of the enacted tax law, resulting from temporary differences and operating loss carryforwards at the end of the current year
_____ 5. The change during the year in a corporation's deferred tax liabilities and assets
_____ 6. The deferred tax consequences of future taxable amounts
_____ 7. The portion of a deferred tax asset for which it is more likely than not that a tax benefit will not be realized
_____ 8. Temporary difference that results in deductible amounts in future years when the related asset or liability is recovered or settled, respectively
_____ 9. The sum of income tax payable and deferred tax expense (or benefit)
_____ 10. The amount of income taxes paid or payable (or refundable) for the current year
_____ 11. An excess of tax deductible expenses over taxable revenues in a year that may be carried forward to reduce taxable income in a future year
_____ 12. The excess of taxable revenues over tax deductible expenses and exemptions for the year
_____ 13. An excess of tax deductible expenses over taxable revenues in a year that may be carried back to reduce taxable income in a prior year

Required:
Indicate which term belongs with each definition by inserting the corresponding code letter on the line preceding the definition.

P18-2
LO 18.3
LO 18.4

Temporary and Permanent Differences In the current year, you are calculating a diversified company's deferred taxes. Based on an analysis of the company's current taxable income and pretax financial income, you have identified the following items that create differences between the two amounts and that may result in differences between the company's future taxable income and its future pretax financial income:

_____ 1. Percentage depletion deducted for taxes in excess of cost depletion for financial reporting
_____ 2. Warranty costs to be deducted for taxes that were deducted as warranty expense for financial reporting
_____ 3. Gross profit to be recognized for taxes under the completed-contract method that was recognized for financial reporting under the percentage-of-completion method
_____ 4. Officers' life insurance premium expense deducted for financial reporting
_____ 5. Rent revenue to be recognized for financial reporting that was reported for taxes when collected in advance
_____ 6. Loss from writedown of inventory that was recognized for financial reporting but that will be deducted for taxes when the inventory is sold
_____ 7. Interest revenue on municipal bonds recognized for financial reporting
_____ 8. Loss due to contingent liability that was deducted for financial reporting that will be deducted for taxes when the liability is actually paid
_____ 9. Gross profit to be recognized under the cash-basis method for tax purposes that was recognized on an accrual basis for financial reporting
_____ 10. Depreciation to be recognized for financial reporting in excess of MACRS depreciation to be deducted for tax purposes
_____ 11. Investment income that has been recognized under the equity method for financial reporting that will be recognized as fully taxable for tax purposes when dividends are collected

Required:
For each difference, indicate whether it is a temporary difference (T) or a permanent difference (P) by placing the appropriate letter on the line provided. If the difference is a temporary difference, also indicate for the current year whether it will result in a future taxable amount (FT) or a future deductible amount (FD).

P18-3
LO 18.3

Multiple Temporary Differences Wilcox Company has prepared the following reconciliation of its pretax financial income with its taxable income for 2016:

Pretax financial income		$3,000
Add:	Estimated expense on 1-year warranties recognized for financial reporting in excess of actual warranty costs deducted for income taxes	100
Less:	MACRS depreciation deducted for income taxes in excess of depreciation recognized for financial reporting	(150)
Taxable income		$2,950

At the beginning of 2016, Wilcox had a deferred tax liability of $495. The current tax rate is 30%, and no change in the tax rate has been enacted for future years. At the end of 2016, Wilcox anticipates that actual warranty costs will exceed estimated warranty expense by $100 next year and that financial depreciation will exceed tax depreciation by $1,800 in future years. Wilcox has earned income in all past years and expects to earn income in the future.

Required:
1. Prepare Wilcox's income tax journal entry at the end of 2016.
2. Prepare the lower portion of Wilcox's 2016 income statement.
3. Show how the income tax items are reported on Wilcox's December 31, 2016, balance sheet.

P18-4
LO 18.3

Interperiod Tax Allocation Klerk Company had four temporary differences between its pretax financial income and its taxable income during 2016 as follows:

Number	Temporary Difference
1	Gross profit on certain sales is recognized under the accrual method for financial reporting and under the cash-basis method for income taxes.
2	MACRS depreciation is used for income taxes; a different depreciation method is used for financial reporting.
3	Rent receipts are included in taxable income when collected in advance; rent revenue is recognized under the accrual method for financial reporting.
4	Warranty expense is estimated for financial reporting; warranty costs are deducted as incurred for income taxes.

(continued)

At the beginning of 2016, Klerk had a deferred tax liability of $84,300 related to Temporary Difference #2 and a deferred tax asset of $21,090 related to Temporary Difference #4. Based on its tax records, Klerk earned taxable income of $270,000 for 2016. Kerk's accountant has prepared the following schedule showing the total future taxable and deductible amounts at the end of 2016 for its four temporary differences:

Future Taxable Amounts		Future Deductible Amounts	
#1	#2	#3	#4
$77,900	$241,000	$20,000	$55,300

The company has a history of earning income and expects to be profitable in the future. The income tax rate for 2016 is 40%, but in 2015 Congress enacted a 30% tax rate for 2017 and future years.

During 2016, for financial accounting purposes, Klerk reported revenues of $750,000 and expenses of $447,100. The deferred taxes related to Temporary Differences #1, #2, and #4 are considered to be noncurrent by the company; the deferred tax related to Temporary Difference #3 is considered to be current.

Required:
1. Prepare Klerk's income tax journal entry for 2016.
2. Prepare a condensed 2016 income statement for Klerk.
3. Show how the income tax items are reported on Klerk's December 31, 2016, balance sheet.

P18-5 **Deferred Taxes: Multiple Rates** Wicks Corporation began operations on January 1, 2016. At the end of 2016,
LO 18.3 Wicks reported pretax financial income of $60,000 and taxable income of $57,700, due to two temporary differences. The income tax rate is 30% for 2016 through 2018, but Congress has enacted a tax rate of 35% for 2019 and beyond. To determine its deferred taxes, Wicks prepared the following schedule of expected future taxable and deductible amounts for the two temporary differences:

	2017	2018	2019	2020
Future taxable amounts	$4,900	$4,200	$ 4,600	$4,100
Future deductible amount			(15,500)	

Required:
1. Prepare Wicks's income tax journal entry at the end of 2016. Assume a valuation allowance is not required.
2. Prepare the lower portion of the 2016 income statement for Wicks.

P18-6 **Interperiod Tax Allocation** Quick Company reports the following revenues and expenses in its pretax financial
LO 18.3 income for the year ended December 31, 2016:

Revenues	$ 229,600
Expenses	(160,100)
Pretax financial income	$ 69,500

The revenues included in pretax financial income are the same amount as the revenues included in the company's taxable income. A reconciliation of the expenses reported for pretax financial income to the expenses reported for taxable income, however, reveals four differences:
1. Depreciation deducted for financial reporting exceeded depreciation deducted for income taxes by $11,000.
2. Percentage depletion deducted for income taxes exceeded cost depletion deducted for financial reporting by $15,600.
3. Warranty costs deducted for income taxes exceeded warranty expenses deducted for financial reporting by $8,900.
4. Legal expense of $9,800 was deducted for financial reporting; it will be deducted for income taxes when paid in a future year.

Quick expects its percentage depletion to exceed its cost depletion in each of the next 5 years by the same amount as in 2016. At the end of 2016, the other three expenses are expected to result in total future taxable or deductible amounts as follows:

	Totals
Future Taxable Amounts	
Depreciation expense difference	$63,000
Future Deductible Amounts	
Warranty expense difference	48,400
Legal expense difference	9,800

At the beginning of 2016, Quick had a deferred tax liability of $22,200 related to the depreciation difference and a deferred tax asset of $17,190 related to the warranty difference. The income tax rate for 2016 is 35%, but in 2015 Congress enacted a 30% rate for 2017 and future years.

Required:
1. Compute Quick's taxable income for 2016.
2. Prepare Quick's income tax journal entry for 2016. Assume no valuation allowance is necessary.
3. Prepare a condensed 2016 income statement for Quick.

P18-7
LO 18.3

Deferred Tax Liability: Depreciation At the beginning of 2016, its first year of operations, Cooke Company purchased an asset for $100,000. This asset has an 8-year economic life with no residual value, and it is being depreciated by the straight-line method for financial reporting purposes. For tax purposes, however, the asset is being depreciated using the MACRS (200%, 5-year life) method.

During 2016, Cooke reported pretax financial income of $51,500 and taxable income of $44,000. The depreciation temporary difference caused the difference between the two income amounts. The tax rate in 2016 was 30%, and no change in the tax rate had been enacted for future years.

Required:
1. Prepare a schedule that shows for each year, 2016 through 2023, (a) MACRS depreciation, (b) straight-line depreciation, (c) the annual depreciation temporary difference, and (d) the accumulated temporary difference at the end of each year.
2. Prepare a schedule that computes for each year, 2016 through 2023, (a) the ending deferred tax liability and (b) the change in the deferred tax liability.
3. Prepare Cooke's income tax journal entry at the end of 2016.
4. **Next Level** Explain what happens to the balance of the deferred tax liability at the end of 2016 through 2023.

P18-8
LO 18.3

Deferred Tax Liability: Depreciation Gire Company began operations at the beginning of 2016, at which time it purchased a depreciable asset for $60,000. For 2016 through 2019, the asset was depreciated on the straight-line basis over a 4-year life (no residual value) for financial reporting. For income tax purposes, the asset was depreciated using MACRS (200%, 3-year life).

For 2016 through 2019, Gire reported pretax financial income and taxable income of the following amounts (the differences are due solely to the depreciation temporary differences):

Year	Pretax Financial Income	Taxable Income
2016	$24,998	$20,000
2017	38,670	27,000
2018	27,886	34,000
2019	29,446	40,000

Over the entire 4-year period, Gire was subject to an income tax of 30%, and no change in the tax rate had been enacted for future years.

Required:
1. Prepare a schedule that shows for each year, 2016 through 2019, the (a) MACRS depreciation, (b) straight-line depreciation, (c) annual depreciation temporary difference, and (d) accumulated temporary difference at the end of each year.
2. Prepare Gire's income tax journal entry at the end of (a) 2016, (b) 2017, (c) 2018, and (d) 2019. (Round to the nearest dollar.)
3. Prepare the lower portion of Gire's income statement for (a) 2016, (b) 2017, (c) 2018 and (d) 2019.

P18-9
LO 18.3
LO 18.4

Interperiod Tax Allocation Peterson Company has computed its pretax financial income to be $66,000 in 2016 *after* including the effects of the appropriate items from the following information:

1. Depreciation taken for tax purposes	$40,000
2. Officers' life insurance premium expense recorded on accounting records	15,000
3. Interest revenue on investment in municipal bonds recorded on accounting records	25,000
4. Percentage depletion taken for tax purposes in excess of cost depletion taken for financial reporting purposes	10,000

5. Depreciation taken for financial reporting purposes	$48,000
6. Actual product warranty costs deducted for tax purposes	20,000
7. Excess of accrual-basis sales over cash-basis sales recognized for tax purposes	11,000
8. Estimated product warranty expense recorded on accounting records	27,000

Peterson's accountant has prepared the following schedule showing the future taxable and deductible amounts at the end of 2016 for its three temporary differences:

	Totals
Future Taxable Amounts	
Depreciation difference	$33,800
Accrual-basis vs. cash-basis excess	26,700
Future Deductible Amounts	
Warranty difference	56,500

At the beginning of 2016, Peterson had a deferred tax liability of $12,540 related to the depreciation difference and $4,710 related to the accrual-basis sales difference. In addition, it had a deferred tax asset of $14,850 related to the warranty difference. The current tax rate is 30%, and no change in the tax rate has been enacted for future years.

Required:
1. Compute Peterson's taxable income for 2016.
2. Prepare Peterson's income tax journal entry for 2016 (assume no valuation allowance is necessary).
3. **Next Level** Identify the permanent differences in Items 1 through 8 and explain why you did or did not account for them as deferred tax items in Requirement 2.

P18-10 **Operating Loss** Ross Company has been in business for several years, during which time it has been profitable.
LO 18.5 For each of those years, Ross reported (and paid taxes on) taxable income in the same amount as pretax financial income based on the following revenues and expenses:

	Revenues	Expenses
2012	$182,000	$150,000
2013	220,000	170,000
2014	253,000	180,000
2015	241,000	196,000

Ross was subject to the following income tax rates during this period: 2012, 20%; 2013, 25%; 2014, 30%; and 2015, 25%. During 2016, Ross experienced a severe decrease in the demand for its products. The company tried to offset this decrease with an expensive marketing campaign, but was unsuccessful. Consequently, at the end of 2016, Ross determined that its revenues were $60,000 and its expenses were $193,000 during 2016 for both income taxes and financial reporting.

Ross decided to carry back its 2016 operating loss because it was not confident it could earn taxable income in the future carryforward period. The income tax rate was 30% in 2016, and no change in the tax rate had been enacted for future years.

In 2017, Ross developed and introduced a new product that proved to be in high demand. On June 1, 2017, Ross received a refund check from the government based on the tax information it filed at the end of 2016. For 2017, Ross reported revenues of $181,000 and expenses of $155,000 for both income taxes and financial reporting. The applicable income tax rate was 30%.

Required:
1. Prepare Ross's income tax journal entries at the end of 2016.
2. Prepare Ross's 2016 income statement. Include a note for any operating loss carryforward.
3. Prepare the journal entry to record the receipt of the refund check on June 1, 2017.
4. Prepare the income tax journal entry at the end of 2017.
5. Prepare Ross's 2017 income statement.

P18-11 **Operating Loss** Refer to the information in **P18-10** and modify it as follows: Ross Company decided to carry back
LO 18.5 its 2016 operating loss. Furthermore, since Ross had already begun to develop the new product at the end of 2016 and had contracts for its sale in 2017, the company was confident at the end of 2016 that it would earn sufficient taxable income in the future carryforward period.

Required:
1. Prepare Ross's income tax journal entries at the end of 2016.
2. Prepare Ross's 2016 income statement. Include a note for any operating loss carryforward recognition.
3. Prepare the journal entry to record the receipt of the refund check on June 1, 2017.
4. Prepare the income tax journal entry at the end of 2017.
5. Prepare Ross's 2017 income statement.

P18-12 **Balance Sheet Reporting and Tax Rate Change** At the end of 2015, Dolf Company prepared the following
LO 18.7 schedule of its deferred tax items (based on the currently enacted tax rate of 30%):

Deferred Tax Item #	Account Balance	Related Asset or Liability causing the deferred tax item
1	$ 8,400 debit	Current asset
2	10,200 debit	Noncurrent asset
3	5,700 credit	Current liability
4	17,700 credit	Noncurrent liability

On April 30, 2016, Congress changed the income tax rate to 40% for 2016 and future years. At the end of 2016, Dolf reported taxable income of $62,500 for 2016. At that time, Dolf determined that its deferred tax items should have balances as follows at the end of 2016 (based on the 40% tax rate): #1, $10,700 debit; #2, $15,000 debit; #3, $7,000 credit; #4, $25,900 credit.

Required:
1. Show how the deferred tax items are reported on Dolf's December 31, 2015, balance sheet.
2. Prepare the April 30, 2016, journal entry to correct Dolf's deferred tax items.
3. Prepare Dolf's income tax journal entry at the end of 2016.
4. Show how the current and deferred tax items are reported on Dolf's December 31, 2016, balance sheet.
5. Calculate the total income tax expense for 2016.

P18-13 **Comprehensive** Colt Company reports *pretax* financial "income" of $143,000 in 2016. In addition to pretax
LO 18.3 income from continuing operations (of which revenues are $295,000), the following items are included in this pre-
LO 18.4 tax "income:"
LO 18.6
LO 18.7

Loss from disposal of Division B	(10,000)
Income from operations of discontinued Division B	16,000
Prior period adjustment	(8,000)

SHOW ME HOW

Colt's taxable income totals $93,000 in 2016. The difference between the pretax financial income and the taxable income is due to the excess of tax depreciation over financial depreciation on assets used in continuing operations.

At the beginning of 2016, Colt had a retained earnings balance of $310,000 and a deferred tax liability of $8,100. During 2016, Colt declared and paid dividends of $48,000. It is subject to tax rates of 15% on the first $50,000 of income and 30% on income in excess of $50,000. Based on proper interperiod tax allocation procedures, Colt has determined that its 2016 ending deferred tax liability is $14,100.

Required:
1. Prepare a schedule for Colt to allocate the total 2016 income tax expense to the various components of pretax income.
2. Prepare Colt's income tax journal entry at the end of 2016.
3. Prepare Colt's 2016 income statement.
4. Prepare Colt's 2016 statement of retained earnings.
5. Show the related income tax disclosures on Colt's December 31, 2016, balance sheet.

P18-14 **Comprehensive** At the beginning of 2016, Norris Company had a deferred tax liability of $6,400, because of the use
LO 18.3 of MACRS depreciation for income tax purposes and units-of-production depreciation for financial reporting. The
LO 18.4 income tax rate is 30% for 2015 and 2016, but in 2015 Congress enacted a 40% tax rate for 2017 and future years.
LO 18.6
LO 18.7 Norris's accounting records show the following *pretax* items of financial income for 2016: income from continuing operations, $120,000 (revenues of $352,000 and expenses of $232,000); gain on disposal of Division F, $23,000; loss from operations of discontinued Division F, $10,000; and prior period adjustment, $15,000, due to

(continued)

an error that understated revenue in 2015. All of these items are taxable; however, financial depreciation for 2016 on assets related to continuing operations exceeds tax depreciation by $5,000. Norris had a retained earnings balance of $161,000 on January 1, 2016, and declared and paid cash dividends of $32,000 during 2016.

Required:
1. Prepare Norris's income tax journal entry at the end of 2016.
2. Prepare Norris's 2016 income statement.
3. Prepare Norris's 2016 statement of retained earnings.
4. Show the related income tax disclosures on Norris's December 31, 2016, balance sheet.

P18-15 **Comprehensive** Jayryan Company sells products in a volatile market. The company began operating in 2014 and reported (and paid taxes on) taxable income in 2014 and 2015. It has one taxable temporary difference (future taxable amount) and reconciled its taxable income to its pretax financial income for 2014 and 2015 as follows:

LO 18.3
LO 18.4
LO 18.6
LO 18.7

	2014	2015
Taxable income	$25,000	$53,000
Temporary difference	2,500	4,800
Pretax financial income	$27,500	$57,800

In 2016, because of a downturn in the market, Jayryan reported a taxable loss of $90,000, and it was uncertain as to future profits. A temporary difference of $2,700 resulted in an $87,300 pretax operating loss for financial reporting. In 2017 and 2018, Jayryan was again profitable and reported the following items:

	2017	2018
Taxable income	$7,000	$19,000
Temporary difference	2,300	2,800
Pretax financial income	$9,300	$21,800

The income tax rate has been 30% since 2012, and no change in the tax rate has been enacted for future years.

Required:
1. Prepare a schedule that shows Jayryan's income taxes payable (or receivable) for each year, 2014 through 2018.
2. Prepare a schedule that shows the deferred tax information (change in temporary difference and operating loss carryforward) for each year, 2014 through 2018.
3. Prepare a schedule that shows the deferred taxes for each year, 2014 through 2018.
4. Based on the schedule prepared in Requirement 3, prepare Jayryan's income tax journal entry at the end of 2016.
5. Prepare a partial income statement for 2016. Include a note for any operating loss carryforward.

CASES

COMMUNICATION

C18-1 **Asset/Liability Method and Temporary Differences**
LO 18.2

Interperiod tax allocation is necessary because there are differences in the timing of revenues and expenses between a corporation's financial statements and its federal income tax returns.

Required:
1. Identify the two goals and four basic principles of accounting for income taxes.
2. Briefly explain interperiod income tax allocation under generally accepted accounting principles.
3. List the four groups of items that result in temporary differences and give examples for each group.

C18-2 **Interperiod Tax Allocation**
LO 18.2 A friend in a business policy class says, "I always thought the income taxes reported on a

corporation's income statement were the same as the income taxes paid during that period.

Now I am not so sure because some other students mentioned interperiod income tax allocation. Also, I have heard about comprehensive and partial allocation. I am confused. Please explain this to me."

Required:
Prepare a written response for your friend. In your discussion, be sure to discuss permanent and temporary differences and to compare comprehensive allocation with partial allocation. Include the reasons for interperiod allocation and comprehensive allocation.

C18-3 **Operating Losses**
LO 18.5 The Internal Revenue Code allows a corporation to carry back or carry forward an "operating loss" for a given year.

Required:
1. Describe an operating loss carryback and a carryforward.
2. For a carryback, identify and briefly explain the two important conceptual questions.
3. For a carryforward, identify and briefly explain the two important conceptual questions.
4. Briefly summarize the generally accepted accounting principles for the financial reporting of (a) an operating loss carryback and (b) an operating loss carryforward.

C18-4 **Interperiod and Intraperiod Tax Allocation**
LO 18.2
LO 18.6 Income tax allocation is an integral part of generally accepted accounting principles. Income tax allocation consists of both intraperiod and interperiod tax allocation.

Required:
1. Explain the difference between interperiod and intraperiod income tax allocation.
2. Explain how a corporation discloses its income tax expense (or credit) for the year under intraperiod allocation.
3. Provide an example of intraperiod tax allocation on a corporation's income statement that includes income from continuing operations, a loss from the sale of a discontinued component, and a gain from the operations of the discontinued. Assume a 30% tax rate.

CREATIVE AND CRITICAL THINKING

C18-5 **Deferred Tax Assets and Liabilities**
LO 18.2 A friend says to you, "I don't understand how taxable temporary differences can be 'liabilities' and how deductible temporary differences can be 'assets.' It seems to me that these temporary differences relate only to the future and that accounting is based on 'historical cost.' In addition, the government frequently changes the tax laws, so no one knows what the future tax laws will be."

Required:
Prepare a written response for your friend that explains why deferred tax assets and deferred tax liabilities are recognized and reported on a corporation's balance sheet. Include a discussion of a valuation allowance.

C18-6 **Interperiod Tax Allocation**
LO 18.2
AICPA Adapted Chris Green, CPA, is auditing Rayne Co.'s 2016 financial statements. For the year ended December 31, 2016, Rayne is applying GAAP for income taxes. Rayne's controller, Dunn, has prepared a schedule of all differences between financial statement and income tax return income. Dunn believes that as a result of pending legislation, the enacted tax rate at December 31, 2016, will be increased for 2017. Dunn is uncertain which differences to include and which rates to apply in computing deferred taxes. Dunn has requested an overview of GAAP from Green.

Required:
Prepare a brief memo to Dunn from Green that identifies the objectives of accounting for income taxes, defines temporary differences, explains how to measure deferred tax assets and liabilities, and explains how to measure deferred income tax expense or benefit.

C18-7 **Permanent and Temporary Differences**
LO 18.3
LO 18.4 To implement interperiod income tax allocation, an accountant must be able to distinguish between permanent and temporary differences. The following is a list of three differences between a corporation's pretax financial income and taxable income:

a. Estimated warranty costs (covering a 3-year warranty) are expensed for financial reporting purposes at the time of sale but are deducted for tax purposes when incurred.
b. MACRS depreciation for income tax purposes exceeds straight-line depreciation for financial reporting purposes.
c. Percentage depletion for tax purposes exceeds cost depletion for financial reporting purposes.

(continued)

Required:
1. Define (a) *permanent difference* and (b) *temporary difference*.
2. Define interperiod income tax allocation and briefly describe its application under generally accepted accounting principles.
3. Indicate and explain whether each of the three differences listed in this case should be treated as a temporary or permanent difference.

C18-8 Analyzing Coca-Cola's Income Tax Disclosures
Obtain **The Coca-Cola Company**'s 2013 annual report either using the "Investor Relations" portion of its website (do a web search for Coca-Cola investor relations) or go to http://www.sec.gov and click "Search for company filings" under "Filings and Forms (EDGAR)."

Required:
1. What was the total income tax expense relating to income before income taxes for 2013? How much of this was current? How much was deferred?
2. What were the total deferred tax assets at the end of 2013? Total deferred tax liabilities? Net deferred tax liability?
3. How much was the noncurrent deferred tax liability at the end of 2013, and where was it reported?
4. How much were the operating loss carryforwards at the end of 2013? Over what time periods must these be utilized?

C18-9 Analyzing Nestlé's Income Tax Disclosures
Obtain **Nestlé**'s 2013 annual report using the "Investor Relations" portion of its website (do a web search for Nestlé investor relations).

Required:
1. What was the total income tax expense relating to profit before taxes and associates for 2013? How much of this was current? How much was deferred? What makes up the balance of taxes from continuing operations?
2. What is the amount of Nestlé's 2013 permanent differences? How does Nestlé refer to permanent differences in its reconciliation of taxes?
3. What is the net amount of Nestlé's deferred tax assets and liabilities at December 31, 2013? What are the three largest causes of temporary differences for Nestlé?

USING CODIFICATION

C18-10 Researching GAAP

Situation
Golf-Travel Inc. is a U.S. company that provides travel packages for individual golfers and corporate golf outings. The company has mainly focused on U.S. customers but has decided to expand its business globally. Ben Watson, the company's CEO, has decided that the best location for the company's European operations is Ireland. While Mark obviously appreciated all of the golf related history in Ireland, he was also attracted by Ireland's low 12.5% corporate tax rate.

In January 2016, Golf-Travel formally opened its European operations, called Europe-Golf, in Portmarnock, Ireland, as a wholly owned subsidiary of Golf-Travel. During 2016, the subsidiary's performance exceeded expectations by hosting almost 400 individual golf trips and 200 corporate outings. At the end of the year, the subsidiary reported pretax income of €324,260 and the subsidiary paid Irish taxes of €40,533, leaving a net income of €283,727.

Directions
Ben Watson has asked you, Golf-Travel's Chief Financial Officer, to research the generally accepted accounting principles and write a memo that summarizes the tax issue of earnings of foreign subsidiaries. He is interested in understanding the different financial statement reporting issues of a strategy that remits the earnings back to the United States versus a strategy of permanently reinvesting the earnings back into the Irish subsidiary.

CHAPTER 19

ACCOUNTING FOR POSTRETIREMENT BENEFITS

Who Cares about Pensions... and Why?

Whether you are just starting your career or have been employed for many years, it is important to plan for the income and financial resources that will allow you to enjoy your retirement years in comfort and leisure. From a business perspective, in order to attract and retain high quality employees, most companies offer some type of compensation package that will provide their workers with payments and other benefits during retirement. With pension assets at the beginning of 2013 for companies in the S&P 500 totaling over $1.7 trillion and pension liabilities totaling over $2.1 trillion, these retirement plans are certainly significant.

Retirement benefits raise an important, challenging, and interesting opportunity in accounting—how do we account *today* for promises and obligations companies have made to pay employees' retirement benefits *many years in the future*? In many respects, accrual accounting faces its toughest challenge, and provides its most useful information, when it bridges a long time span between when economic effects occur (such as creating pension assets and liabilities today) and when the related cash flows occur (paying retirees' pensions benefits many years from now).

Because of their long-term nature, small changes in forecast assumptions and estimates can result in large changes in pension plan obligations. For example, since 1990, average life expectancy in the United States has increased by 6% from 75.2 years to 79.8 years in 2013.[1] In retirement terms, this means that individuals who retire at age 65 will have retirements lasting 45% longer, which substantially

[1] World Health Organization, Life Expectancy, 2013.

LEARNING OBJECTIVES

After reading this chapter you will be able to

LO 19.1 Understand the characteristics of pension plans.

LO 19.2 Explain the GAAP for pension plans, including computing pension expense and recognizing pension liabilities and assets.

LO 19.3 Account for defined benefit pension plans.

LO 19.4 Understand several important additional issues related to accounting for pension plans.

LO 19.5 Explain and account for other postretirement benefit plans (OPRBs).

increases the amounts of benefits that guaranteed benefit pension plans are going to have to pay to their retirees.

Corporate pension plan assets and liabilities are important for investors, lenders, and other creditors because substantial net pension assets can significantly improve the financial health and earnings of a company, while a substantial net pension liability can be a real financial health hazard that may create a headwind for future growth in profits. In addition, the accounting for pension plan assets and liabilities is extremely important for the employees and retirees who depend on the future benefits from retirement plans.

According to the World Health Organization, the average life expectancy of a male and female born in the United States in 2013 has increased to 77.4 and 82.2 years, respectively. Consequently, more people are living long into retirement causing them to depend more on retirement income, such as pensions. In this chapter, we focus on the recording, reporting, and disclosure procedures for company pension plans under GAAP. In addition to pensions, many employers provide other postretirement benefits to their employees. We discuss the accounting for these benefits later in the chapter.

LEARNING OBJECTIVE 19.1
Understand the characteristics of pension plans.

WHAT ARE THE CHARACTERISTICS OF PENSION PLANS?

A **pension plan** is a contract between a company and its employees under which the company agrees to pay benefits into a fund, which will then make payments to the employees after they retire. While the exact nature of each pension agreement varies greatly from company to company (and may also vary between employees within a company), in most pension plans, both the employer and the employee make contributions into a pension fund which provides for retirement payments.

The legal statutes that govern pension plans generally require that the pension fund be managed by an independent asset management company, such as **Fidelity Investments** or **Vanguard**. The managers of the pension fund are entrusted with the assets of the pension fund and are expected to invest them to earn a return (in the form of interest, dividends, and capital appreciation) so that adequate funds are available to pay the company's retirees during retirement. The pension fund is also responsible for making payments to the retirees and maintaining retiree account records.

Accounting for pensions and other retirement benefits involves a considerable amount of terminology, so it is important that you understand the terms very clearly. We will define the terms as we proceed, but for your reference, Exhibit 19.1 includes many of the key terms and definitions.

EXHIBIT 19.1 Key Terms Related to Pension Plans

Accumulated Benefit Obligation. The actuarial present value of all the benefits attributed by the pension benefit formula to employee service rendered before a specified date. The amount is based on current and past compensation levels of employees and, therefore, includes no assumptions about future salary increases.

Actual Return on Plan Assets. The difference between the fair value of the plan assets at the end of the period and the fair value at the beginning of the period, adjusted for contributions and payments of benefits during the period.

(continued)

Actuarial Assumptions. Estimates of the occurrence of future events affecting pension costs, such as mortality, withdrawal, disablement and retirement, changes in compensation, and discount rates.

Actuarial Funding Method. Any technique that actuaries use in determining the amounts and timing of employer contributions to provide for pension benefits.

Discount Rate. The rate at which the pension benefits can be effectively settled (e.g., the rate implicit in current prices of annuity contracts that could be used to settle the pension obligation). The discount rate is used in computing the service cost, the projected benefit obligation, and the interest cost. The discount rate is also referred to as the settlement rate.

Expected Return on Plan Assets. An amount calculated by applying the expected long-term rate of return on plan assets to the fair market value of the plan assets at the beginning of the period.

Gain or Loss. A change in the value of the projected benefit obligation (or the plan assets) resulting from experience different from that assumed or from a change in an actuarial assumption.

Prior Service Cost. The cost of retroactive benefits granted in a plan amendment or at the initial adoption of the plan. The cost is the present value of the additional benefits attributed by the pension benefit formula.

Projected Benefit Obligation. The actuarial present value, at a specified date, of all the benefits attributed by the pension benefit formula to employee service rendered prior to that date. The amount includes future increases in compensation that the company projects it will pay to employees during the remainder of their employment, provided the pension benefit formula is based on those future compensation levels. The projected benefit obligation differs from the accumulated benefit obligation because it includes anticipated future salary increases.

Service Cost. The actuarial present value of benefits attributed by the pension benefit formula to services of employees during the current period. If the pension benefit formula is based on future compensation levels (e.g., average of the final five years' salary), the service cost is based on those future compensation levels.

Vested Benefit Obligation. The actuarial present value of the vested benefits, which are those benefits that the employees have the right to receive even if the employee no longer works for the employer.

What Types of Pensions Plans Are There?

There are two types of pension plans that employers tend to provide to employees—*defined benefit plans* and *defined contribution plans*. In a **defined benefit plan**, the company promises to pay its employees certain amounts of benefits after retirement. The amount of the future benefit is usually determined by a formula that is based on the employee's compensation levels and length of service to the company. These benefits are usually paid out to the employees monthly during retirement. The amount that the company contributes into the pension plan depends on how much is needed to pay current and future retirees. It is the responsibility of the company to contribute sufficient assets to ensure that there are enough resources to allow the payments to retirees that are promised in the pension plan contract.

In a **defined contribution plan**, the company simply promises to contribute a defined amount to the employee's pension account each month, as the employee earns those contributions. Unlike a defined benefit plan, the company makes no promises about how much future benefits the employee will receive upon retirement. The company's contribution into the pension fund is based on a formula. The employees' future benefits are the result of the amount that can be provided by the contributions made during the employee's service to the company and the returns earned on the investment of those contributions.

These two types of plans involve *very* different risks to the company and the employees. With a defined benefit plan, most of the risks lie with the company because the payments to the retired employees are defined by the pension contract and the company has the obligation to ensure that those amounts are paid, perhaps many years in the future. If the company does not contribute enough to the pension fund, or if the pension fund does not earn enough in interest, dividends, and capital appreciation, the company will have to make additional contributions into the plan. In contrast, with a defined contribution plan, most of the risks lie with the employees because the company satisfies its obligations once it makes the required contribution to the pension fund for that period. Because the obligations and risks of these two types of plans are very different, so is the accounting for them.

In addition, companies' pension plans can be either *noncontributory* or *contributory*. In a **noncontributory plan**, the entire pension cost is borne by the employer (company). Under a **contributory plan**, employees share part of the cost of the plan and make contributions from their salaries into the pension fund. For simplicity, we discuss noncontributory plans in this chapter.

Pension plans may be either *qualified* or *nonqualified* with respect to Internal Revenue Code (IRC) rules and regulations. Many companies design their pension plans to be qualified, which means the plan covers the majority of the company's employees and limits contributions to a certain amount. **Qualified pension plans** have the following advantages:

- Employer contributions into the plan qualify as tax deductions.
- Pension fund earnings are exempt from income taxes.
- Employer contributions to the pension fund are not taxable to the employees until they receive their pension benefits. In addition, benefits are not subject to payroll taxes.

While the tax advantages of qualified plans are significant, most companies also provide **nonqualified pension plans** that are not governed by the IRC rules and regulations. These plans are normally initiated so that companies can provide additional benefits to highly compensated employees by not limiting the company's pension plan contribution. However, they do not provide the tax advantages of qualified plans.

There are many estimates and assumptions that are required when preparing the accounting for a defined benefit pension plan. Some estimates that the company must make include:

- how many employees will remain with the company until retirement
- the length of time the employee will draw retirement benefits
- what amount the employees' retirement benefits will be during their retirement
- what pension fund assets will be available to pay retirement benefits

Most companies employ actuaries to determine the appropriate estimates and assumptions and to establish the appropriate funding policies for the pension plan. **Actuaries** are certified professionals who are trained to determine future risk, estimate probabilities of future events, make price decisions, estimate present and future values, and formulate investment strategies. The accountants and actuaries must jointly determine the proper financial presentation of pensions.

It is important that you note that the focus of this chapter is on *accounting for the employer* as opposed to the employees, the pension fund, or asset management company. Because the pension fund is an independent entity, we will not discuss in any detail the accounting presentation that must be made on the financial statements of the pension fund. Accounting for the pension fund as a separate legal entity is somewhat distinct from the accounting for the employer and must be treated separately. Exhibit 19.2

summarizes the relationships among the employees, the company, and the asset management company for a noncontributory defined benefit pension plan.

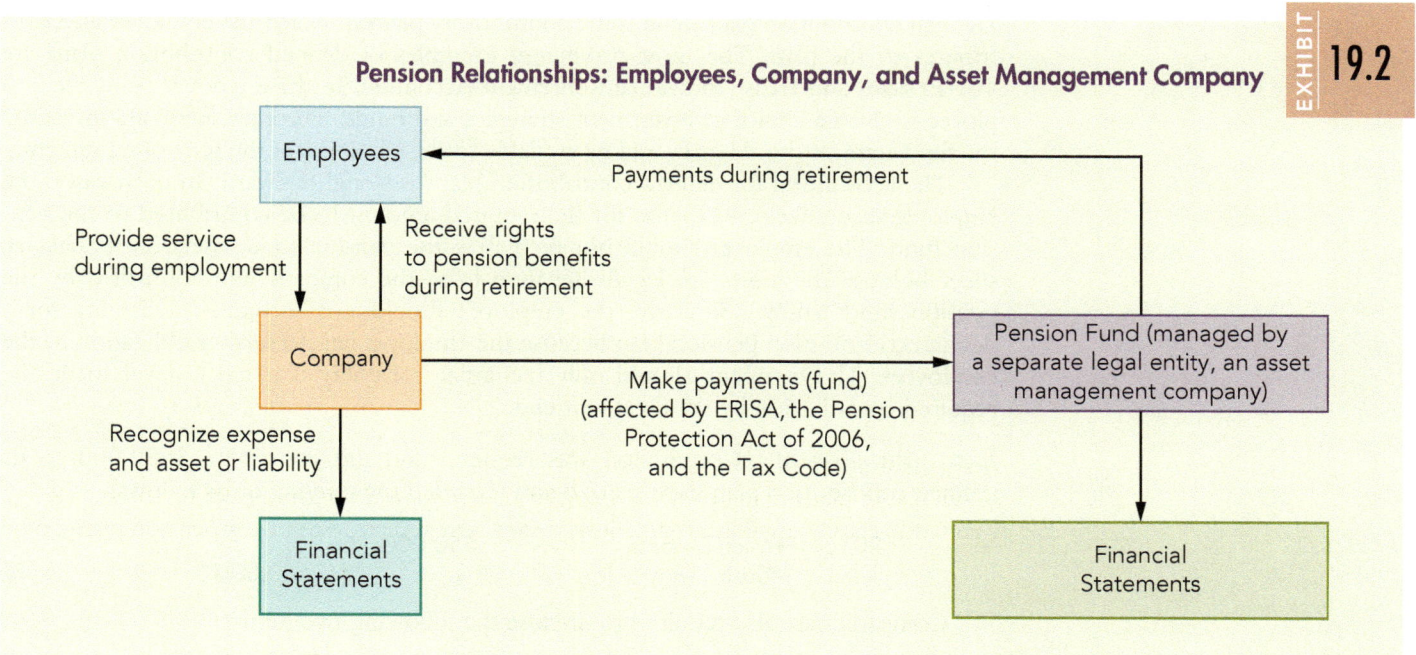

GOT IT?

19-1 What is a pension plan? Explain how yearly income of retired employees is determined under a defined benefit pension plan.

19-2 What is service cost? How does this differ from prior service cost?

19-3 Distinguish between a defined benefit pension plan and a defined contribution pension plan.

19-4 Distinguish between contributory and noncontributory pension plans.

HOW DO COMPANIES ACCOUNT FOR PENSION PLANS?

LEARNING OBJECTIVE 19.2
Explain the GAAP for pension plans, including computing pension expense and recognizing pension liabilities and assets.

Accounting for the costs of pension plans was initially established in 1966 when GAAP was amended to require the use of the accrual method to recognize pension expenses. Prior to that time, companies generally recognized pension expense as retirement benefits were paid (the cash basis). However, it was not until 1980 that GAAP required limited balance sheet recognition of pension plan liabilities. Only when the obligation to pay benefits *greatly* exceeded plan assets was a *portion* of the pension plan liability recorded (and pension plan assets were never recorded). Since that time, additional GAAP has been established for disclosure requirements and balance sheet recognition of the net pension plan asset or liability.

Accounting for Defined Contribution Plans

With a defined contribution plan, the employer and/or employee contribute to the pension fund during the employee's service based on the terms of the pension agreement. The company makes no guarantee that the employee will receive a certain amount of benefits during retirement. Instead, the retirement payments are dependent on the contributions to the fund and on the investment performance of the fund. Normally, an employer is required to contribute a specific amount every year, established by an agreement between the company and its employees or by a resolution of the board of directors. Defined contribution plans tend to be contributory plans in which the employee also contributes to the plan. The most prominent examples of defined contribution plans are 401(k) plans and IRAs (Individual Retirement Accounts). In these types of plans the employee is given a choice of investment strategies and funds. Through successful investing, the fund amount should grow and be available to the employee at the time of retirement.

The accounting for defined contribution plans is straightforward. In most cases, the employer recognizes an expense for the required amount to be contributed to the pension fund. The employer should not recognize the pension fund assets on its balance sheet because the assets are legally separate from the company and controlled by the pension fund trustee. Similarly, the employer should not recognize a liability for a defined contribution pension plan because the employer has no further obligation to the employees. The company should only recognize a liability if it has not yet made the required contribution by the fiscal year end.

Example Hiawatha Corporation was required and did contribute $650,000 to its defined contribution plan during 2016 and recorded the transaction as follows:

2016	Pension Expense	650,000	
	Cash		650,000

Companies are also required to disclose the following two items:

- a description of the plan, including employee groups covered, the basis for determining contributions, and the nature and effect of significant matters affecting the comparability of the information for all periods presented
- the amount of the pension expense recognized during the period[2]

Exhibit 19.3 provides **Starbucks Corporation**'s 2015 disclosure of its employees' defined contribution plans.

EXHIBIT 19.3

Starbucks's Defined Contribution Disclosure

NOTES TO CONSOLIDATED FINANCIAL STATEMENTS

Note 12 Employee Stock and Benefit Plans (partial)

Defined Contribution Plans

We maintain voluntary defined contribution plans, both qualified and non-qualified, covering eligible employees as defined in the plan documents. Participating employees may elect to defer and contribute a portion of their eligible compensation to the plans up to limits stated in the plan documents, not to exceed the dollar amounts set by applicable laws.

Our matching contributions to all US and non-US plans were $70.9 million, $73.0 million and $54.7 million in fiscal years 2015, 2014, and 2013, respectively.

As can be seen from Exhibit 19.3, Starbucks matched its employees' contributions and recognized pension expense of $70.9 million dollars in 2015. This resulted in Starbucks and its employees contributing a total of $141.8 million into employees' defined contribution pension funds.

---

[2] FASB ASC 715-70-50: Compensation – Retirement Benefits, Defined Contribution Plans, Disclosure.

How Do Companies Account for Defined Benefit Plans?

In a defined benefit pension plan, employees are promised future payments based on the formula in a pension plan contract. Normally these contracts specify that the benefit payment will be a function of how long the employee works for the company (called the service life) and their future salary level multiplied by a fraction determined by the contract. For example, a company may have a retirement plan under which an employee who retires at age 65 would receive annual retirement income according to the following formula:

Average of Final 5 Years' Salary × Number of Years of Service × 0.025

An individual who worked 30 years for the company and had an average salary during their last 5 years of employment of $128,000 would receive annual pension benefit payments of $96,000 per year.

The accounting issues for defined benefit plans are much more challenging than those for defined contribution plans. It is important to recognize that accounting for defined benefit pension plans has both unique balance sheet and income statement issues. In order to understand these issues it is important to first understand the main issues of the pension expense and then understand the pension liability and plan assets.

What Are the Components of Pension Expense?

GAAP uses the term **net periodic pension cost** when discussing the cost of a pension plan that is recognized in an employer's financial statements during an accounting period. This term is used as opposed to pension expense because a company may capitalize some of its net periodic pension cost as part of an asset, such as inventory or property, plant, and equipment.[3] For simplicity, we will use the term **pension expense** and assume that none of the pension costs are capitalized. The pension expense that a company recognizes is a function of the changes in the pension obligation and pension plan assets. As shown below, pension expense includes five components: service cost, interest cost, return on plan assets, amortization of prior service cost, and gain or loss. Each of these components is explained in the following sections.

Service Cost	Present Value of Benefits Earned During the Year Using the Discount Rate
+ Interest Cost	Projected Benefit Obligation at Beginning of the Year × Discount Rate
− Expected Return on Plan Assets	Fair Value of Plan Assets at the Beginning of the Year × Expected Long-Term Rate of Return on Plan Assets
+ Amortization of Prior Service Cost	Present Value of Additional Benefits Granted at Adoption or Modification of the Plan Amortized over the Remaining Service Lives of Active Employees
+ or − Gain or Loss	Immediate Recognition or Amortization of the Cumulative Net Gain or Loss from Previous Periods Using the Corridor Method or Other Reasonable Method
= Pension Expense	

Service Cost The **service cost** is the increase in the projected benefit obligation due to employees providing service to the company during the current period. The amount is specifically defined as the present value of the benefits attributed by the pension benefit formula to the service provided by employees during the current period as determined by the actuary. The service cost is computed as a present value of the retirement benefits earned in the current period, using the *discount* rate selected by the company. The discount rate will vary as economic conditions change. If the rate increases (decreases), the present value decreases (increases). Exhibit 19.4 (p. 19-8) illustrates the calculation of the service cost.

Interest Cost The **interest cost** is the increase in the projected benefit obligation due to the passage of time. The **projected benefit obligation** is the present value of the

---

[3] If the related amount of pension cost pertains to employees whose compensation is capitalized as part of the cost of preparing assets for use, then the related pension costs would be expensed through cost of goods sold or depreciation.

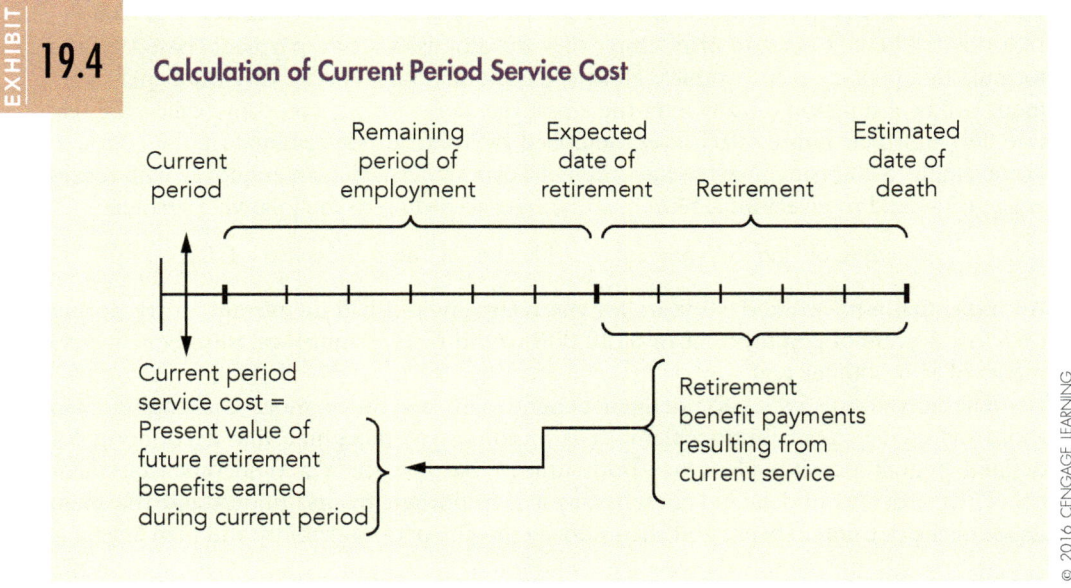

EXHIBIT 19.4 Calculation of Current Period Service Cost

future retirement payments earned by the employees to date (based on their expected future compensation levels). The interest cost is calculated as follows:

$$\text{Interest Cost} = \frac{\text{Projected Benefit Obligation}}{\text{at the Beginning of the Period}} \times \text{Discount Rate}^4$$

Interest on the projected benefit obligation accrues because of the passage of time and the interest cost is added in the computation of pension expense.

Return on Plan Assets There are two returns that affect pension expense: the *actual return on plan assets* and the *expected return on plan assets*.

- The **actual return on plan assets** is the change in the plan assets due to dividends, interest earned, and the unrealized and realized changes in the fair value of the pension plan assets. Plan assets are held by the pension asset manager and consist of investments in securities such as stocks and bonds, as well as other investments. The actual return can be either positive or negative.
- The **expected return on plan assets** is the expected increase in the plan assets due to investing activities. The expected return is calculated by multiplying the fair value of the plan assets at the beginning of the period by the expected long-term rate of return on plan assets.[5] The rate of return reflects the average rate of earnings expected on the assets invested to provide for the benefits included in the projected benefit obligation.

GAAP specifies that the actual return should be used when calculating pension expense. However, GAAP requires that the expected return on plan assets is subtracted in calculating pension expense because the earnings on the pension plan assets offset the interest cost on the projected benefit obligation. The difference between the actual return and expected return is an unexpected gain or loss on plan assets for

---

[4] The discount rate is also referred to as the settlement rate. The company uses a discount rate that reflects the rate at which the pension benefits could be effectively settled when it computes the service cost, the projected benefit obligation, and the accumulated benefit obligation. For example, if the company could settle its obligation by purchasing an annuity from an insurance company for each employee, it would use the rate on that annuity as the appropriate discount rate. Companies are required by the SEC to evaluate the rate each year.

[5] The expected (assumed) long-term rate of return on plan assets used to compute the expected return on assets is based on the average rate of earnings expected on the funds invested (or to be invested). Actual experience is considered along with the rates of return expected to be available in the future.

(continued)

the period. The unexpected gain or loss is included in the gain or loss component of pension expense. Together, these two amounts equal the actual return, as required by GAAP.

Amortization of Prior Service Cost Sometimes a company will amend its pension plan to include provisions that grant additional retroactive benefits to employees based on their employment in prior periods. These amendments result in an increase in the projected benefit obligation. Retroactive benefits may also be granted at the initial adoption of a plan. The cost of these retroactive benefits is the **prior service cost**. The prior service cost is reported as a liability and as a negative element of other comprehensive income at the date of the plan amendment. The prior service cost is then amortized each period and included in the computation of pension expense. The amount amortized is also reported as a component of other comprehensive income. We illustrate the required journal entries later in the chapter.[6]

Gain or Loss The **gain** or **loss** arises because estimates and assumptions are made about many of the items included in the computation of pension costs and benefits. These include future compensation levels, the interest (discount) rate, employee turnover, retirement rates, life expectancy, and expected returns on the pension plan assets. Actual experience will not necessarily turn out to be the same as these expectations. As a result, the *actual* projected benefit obligation and the *actual* fair value of the pension plan assets at year-end will not be equal to the *expected* projected benefit obligation and the *expected* fair value of the pension plan assets. This difference between actual and expected amounts creates a gain or loss. As a result, gains and losses result from:

- changes in the actuarial assumptions used to calculate the projected benefit obligation
- experience that differs from what was expected in measuring the obligation and expected return on the pension plan assets[7]

Gains occur when actual experience is more favorable than expected. For example, if future compensation levels are lower than expected, the projected benefit obligation will be smaller and the defined benefit plan will experience a gain. Losses occur when the actual experience is unfavorable. It is important to distinguish between the impact on the company as compared to the impact on the employees. For example, a longer life span is obviously better for employees. However, it creates a loss to the company because it will have to make more pension payments than expected.

Current accounting guidance provides three methods for companies to recognize gains and losses in pension expense:

- immediate recognition in pension expense
- minimum amortization using the corridor approach
- any systematic and rational approach that results in faster amortization than the corridor approach

Any gain or loss that is not recognized in pension expense in the period it occurs is recognized as a component of other comprehensive income.

Most companies do not immediately recognize the entire gain or loss because it might create significant fluctuations in pension expense. Instead, many companies use the **corridor approach** in which amortization of any net gain or loss is included in the pension expense of a given year if the beginning of the year cumulative net gain or loss (included in accumulated other comprehensive income) exceeds a "corridor." **The corridor is defined as 10% of the greater of the beginning of the year projected**

---

[6] Plan amendments may also decrease future benefits, resulting in a decrease in the projected benefit obligation. In this situation, the amortized amount of prior service cost reduces pension expense each period.

[7] In addition, gains and losses can occur because of the use of the market-related value of the plan assets, as we explain in the next section. These gains and losses are handled in a manner similar to those for changes in the projected benefit obligation, so for simplicity, we do not discuss them further.

benefit obligation or the beginning of the year fair value of the plan assets. If amortization is required, the minimum amortization is computed as follows:

$$\text{Minimum Corridor Amortization} = \frac{\text{Cumulative Net Gain or Loss at the Beginning of the Year} - \text{Corridor at the Beginning of the Year}}{\text{Average Remaining Service Period of the Active Employees Expected to Receive Benefits under the Pension Plan}}$$

The amortization of a net gain is subtracted in the computation of pension expense, while amortization of a net loss is added in the computation of pension expense. Companies may also amortize the net gain or loss in a faster manner, for example, **Honeywell** expenses immediately all amounts outside the corridor, while **AT&T** and **Verizon** expense all gains and losses immediately.

To summarize, the gain or loss component of pension expense generally consists of one of the following two items:

- amortization of any net loss from previous periods (added to compute pension expense)
- amortization of any net gain from previous periods (deducted to compute pension expense)

Note that the amortization of a *reduction* in prior service cost would be deducted in the pension expense calculation.

Pension Obligation

In a defined benefit plan, the amounts to be paid to retirees in the future represent an obligation of the company. Because these are future payments, they must be discounted back to the current period using the company's **discount rate** to obtain the company's *current* obligation. The resulting amount, which is based on expected future salary levels, is called the *projected benefit obligation*. As stated earlier, the projected benefit obligation is the actuarial present value of all the benefits attributed by the pension benefit formula to employee service rendered prior to that date. The change in the projected benefit obligation is determined as follows:

```
  Beginning Projected Benefit Obligation
+ Prior Service Cost
= Adjusted Beginning Projected Benefit Obligation
+ Service Cost for Period
+ Interest Cost on Projected Benefit Obligation
+ Actuarial Losses (or − Actuarial Gains)
− Benefit Payments to Retirees
= Ending Projected Benefit Obligation
```

Companies must also disclose information about their accumulated benefit obligations and vested benefit obligations. The **accumulated benefit obligation** is the present value of benefits attributed to employee service provided before a specified date based on current salary levels. The **vested benefit obligation** is the present value of the benefits the employee is entitled to receive even if the employee is no longer employed by the company. The projected benefit obligation will provide the largest and most conservative measure of the pension obligation while the vested benefit will be the smallest measure.

Pension Assets

To pay for the retirement benefits promised to employees, companies with defined benefit pension plans contribute cash into a pension fund managed by a pension management company. The funds are invested to earn interest and dividends and achieve capital appreciation. Actuaries develop an **actuarial funding method** to determine the amounts and timing of employer contributions that will be needed over time to provide for current and future pension benefit payments.

When discussing the valuation of pension assets, GAAP uses the term *market-related value* to describe the value of plan assets. The **market-related value** is either the fair market value at the end of each accounting period or a calculated value that recognizes changes in fair value in a systematic or rational manner over not more than 5 years. The use of the calculated value was provided by GAAP to reduce the volatility in pension expense. For simplicity, we will always use the fair value of the plan assets as the market-related value. The use of the fair value of plan assets makes the accounting for pension plan assets much simpler than the accounting for the projected benefit obligation, which requires many more estimates and assumptions.

The value of plan assets is calculated by the pension plan asset management company as follows:

$$\begin{array}{l} \text{Beginning Fair Value of Pension Plan Assets} \\ + \text{ Actual Return on Plan Assets} \\ + \text{ Contributions (Amount Funded) by the Company}^8 \\ - \text{ Payments to Retirees} \\ \hline = \text{Ending Fair Value of Pension Plan Assets} \end{array}$$

The Funded Status of the Defined Benefit Plan The difference between the projected benefit obligation and the fair value of the pension plan assets at the end of the period is the **funded status** of the pension plan. The company reports this amount as an accrued pension cost liability (in the case of an underfunded plan) or prepaid pension cost asset (in the case of an overfunded plan) on its year-end balance sheet. Note that if a company has multiple plans (perhaps associated with different groups of employees or with different subsidiaries), it must report the amounts in funded status as assets separately from the amounts underfunded as liabilities. (It cannot net the pension assets and liabilities across separate plans.) Because either a liability or an asset can occur for a given plan (but not both at the same time), we use a single title for the account, **Accrued/Prepaid Pension Cost**. This account will have a credit balance if the plan is underfunded and a debit balance if it is overfunded.

When a company recognizes pension expense, the difference between the pension expense and the amount contributed to the pension plan is recorded in the Accrued/Prepaid Pension Cost account. **If the amount in Accrued/Prepaid Pension Cost does not equal the difference between the projected benefit obligation and the fair value of the plan assets, the company must adjust the balance in Accrued/Prepaid Pension Cost to properly reflect the funded status of the pension plan.** In effect, the company compares the underfunded (or overfunded) amount to the balance in Accrued/Prepaid Pension Cost and makes a journal entry for the difference.

- When a company's pension plan is underfunded, the adjusting journal entry involves a debit to Other Comprehensive Income and a credit to Accrued/Prepaid Pension Cost to increase the liability.
- If the company's pension plan is overfunded, the adjusting journal entry involves a debit to Accrued/Prepaid Pension Cost to increase the asset and a credit to Other Comprehensive Income.

The reason for adjusting other comprehensive income instead of recording additional pension expense is that the adjustment represents a past change in the funded status of the plan that will be recognized in future periods as a component of pension expense.

---

[8] Our discussion focuses on noncontributory defined benefit plans. In a contributory plan, employees also make contributions. In these plans employees' contributions simultaneously increase the pension obligation and assets.

This adjustment to Other Comprehensive Income can be separated into two components:

- retroactive benefits (prior service cost) that have been granted and are amortized into pension expense
- gains or losses (which include the difference between the actual and expected return on plan assets, as well as any actuarial gains or losses)

These adjustments related to the two components are explained below.

Example: Prior Service Cost Adjustment

Poole Company awards retroactive pension benefits to its employees when it adopts its pension plan on January 1, 2016, and incurs $900,000 of prior service costs. Poole records this initial award as:

Other Comprehensive Income: Prior Service Cost	900,000	
Accrued/Prepaid Pension Cost		900,000

This journal entry recognizes a liability (accrued pension cost) due to the increased benefits.

If Poole amortizes the prior service cost to pension expense over a period of 15 years, the company makes the following journal entry:

Accrued/Prepaid Pension Cost	60,000	
Other Comprehensive Income: Prior Service Cost		60,000

This second journal entry is necessary to avoid "double counting" the company's comprehensive income. Recall from Chapter 5 that a company's comprehensive income for a period includes both its net income (loss) and its other comprehensive income (loss). As discussed above, the company initially recorded the total amount of the prior service cost as a negative component (i.e., loss) of its other comprehensive income. Because a portion of this prior service cost is now amortized and reduces net income (by increasing pension expense), this second entry reduces the negative component of its other comprehensive income for the same amount. ■

Example: Gain/Loss Adjustment

Poole Company determined that it had a $40,000 loss (including the difference between the actual and expected return on plan assets as well as any actuarial gains or losses) for the current year. It recorded the loss at the end of the year by making the following entry:

Other Comprehensive Income	40,000	
Accrued/Prepaid Pension Cost		40,000

In addition, the company makes a second journal entry to amortize the gain or loss. Assuming that amortization for the year was $15,000, Poole makes the following entry:

Accrued/Prepaid Pension Cost	15,000	
Other Comprehensive Income		15,000

Because the company initially recorded the total amount of the loss in its other comprehensive income, this second entry avoids "double counting" the company's comprehensive income, following the same logic as previously discussed for the amortization of prior service cost. ■

The company reports its other comprehensive income (net of tax), as discussed in Chapter 5.[9]

- If the accrued/prepaid pension cost has a credit balance (because the projected benefit obligation is greater than the fair value of plan assets), the company reports the accrued pension cost as a liability.
- If the accrued/prepaid pension cost has a debit balance (because the fair value of plan assets is greater than the projected benefit obligation), the company reports the prepaid pension cost as an asset.

Typically, the amount is classified as noncurrent. The company reports the prior service cost and gains or losses not yet recognized in pension expense as accumulated other comprehensive income, an element of shareholders' equity on its year-end balance sheet.

In summary, a company may report the following pension plan asset, liability, and accumulated other comprehensive income items, depending on the circumstances, on its balance sheet:[10]

Assets	Liabilities
Prepaid pension cost (debit balance)	Accrued pension cost (credit balance)

	Shareholders' Equity
	Accumulated other comprehensive income: Prior service cost and/or: • loss not yet amortized to pension expense (negative element) • gain not yet amortized to pension expense (positive element)

Disclosures for Defined Benefit Pension Plans Under U.S. GAAP and IFRS, the disclosure requirements for defined benefit pension plans of employers are very detailed and are intended to provide users with relevant information.[11] We summarize the major required disclosures below.

- narrative description of investment policies and strategies, including target allocations for each major category of plan assets and other factors that are pertinent to an understanding of the investment goals, risk management strategies, and permitted and prohibited investments
- narrative description of the basis used to determine the expected rate of return on plan assets
- other information that would be useful in understanding the risk associated with each asset category and the rate of the return on plan assets
- benefits expected to be paid in each of the next 5 years and the total for the next 5 years
- expected contributions to be made by the company to the plan in the next year
- reconciliation of the beginning and ending balances of the projected benefit obligation, including the amounts of the service cost, interest cost, actuarial gains and losses, benefits paid, and plan amendments

---

[9] A company is required to show its other comprehensive income net of taxes. Therefore, in addition to the journal entries presented later in the chapter, a company would also record deferred taxes. For instance, suppose a company debits Other Comprehensive Income: Net Gain/Loss and credits Accrued/Prepaid Pension Cost to adjust for the underfunding of its pension plan. In this case, the company would record a second journal entry debiting Deferred Tax Asset and crediting Other Comprehensive Income: Net Gain/Loss for the amount of the tax effect. For simplicity, we do not deal with deferred taxes in this chapter. See Chapter 18 for a more complete discussion of deferred taxes.

[10] A company that has more than one postemployment plan must aggregate all overfunded plans and report one net asset amount and aggregate all underfunded plans and report one net liability amount.

[11] FASB ASC 715-20-50: Compensation – Retirement Benefits, Defined Benefit Plans – General, Disclosure. There are additional disclosures beyond those we have listed.

- reconciliation of the beginning and ending balances of the fair value of the plan assets, including the actual return on plan assets, contributions by the company, and benefits paid
- funded status of the plan and the amounts recognized on the balance sheet with the current and noncurrent portions of the liability reported separately if the company prepares a classified balance sheet
- amount of pension expense, including the service cost, interest cost, expected return on plan assets, amortization of any prior service cost, and amortization of any net gains or losses
- amounts of the prior service cost and the net gain or loss that remain in accumulated other comprehensive income
- discount rate, rate of compensation increase, and expected long-term rate of return on the plan assets
- amounts and types of securities included in the plan assets, including a separate disclosure using the guidelines and format used for investment securities (The disclosure should include the fair value of each major category of plan assets and the level of the fair value hierarchy for the significant inputs.)

Real Report 19.1 shows the pension disclosures for **Honeywell**.

19.1 PENSION DISCLOSURES (PARTIAL) — REAL REPORT

Honeywell

Note 23: Pension and Other Postretirement Benefits

We sponsor both funded and unfunded U.S. and non-U.S. defined benefit pension plans covering the majority of our employees and retirees. Pension benefits for substantially all U.S. employees are provided through non-contributory, qualified and non-qualified defined benefit pension plans. U.S. defined benefit pension plans comprise 76 percent of our projected benefit obligation. All non-union hourly and salaried employees joining Honeywell for the first time after December 31, 2012, are not eligible to participate in Honeywell's U.S. defined benefit pension plans. Non-U.S. employees, who are not U.S. citizens, are covered by various retirement benefit arrangements, some of which are considered to be defined benefit pension plans for accounting purposes. Non-U.S. defined benefit pension plans comprise 25 percent of our projected benefit obligation.

	Pension Benefits			
	U.S. Plans		Non-U.S. Plans	
	2013	2012	2013	2012
Change in benefit obligation:				
Benefit obligation at beginning of year	$17,117	$15,600	$5,272	$4,648
Service cost	272	256	58	48
Interest cost	677	738	215	221
Plan amendments	14	—	—	—
Actuarial (gains) losses	(975)	1,493	72	372
Acquisitions	190	—	44	—
Benefits paid	(1,005)	(970)	(198)	(188)
Settlements and curtailments	—	—	—	(16)
Other	—	—	60	187
Benefit obligation at end of year	16,290	17,117	5,523	5,272
Change in plan assets:				
Fair value of plan assets at beginning of year	14,345	12,836	4,527	3,958
Actual return on plan assets	3,191	1,654	428	336

	Pension Benefits			
	U.S. Plans		Non-U.S. Plans	
	2013	2012	2013	2012
Company contributions	28	825	183	271
Acquisitions	168	—	45	—
Benefits paid	(1,005)	(970)	(198)	(188)
Settlements and curtailments	—	—	—	(16)
Other	—	—	52	166
Fair value of plan assets at end of year	16,727	14,345	5,037	4,527
Funded status of plans	$ 437	$ (2,772)	$ (486)	$ (745)
Amounts recognized in Consolidated Balance Sheet consist of:				
Prepaid pension benefit cost[1]	$ 839	$ —	$ 120	$ 87
Accrued pension liability[2]	(402)	(2,772)	(606)	(832)
Net amount recognized	$ 437	$ (2,772)	$ (486)	$ (745)

[1] Included in Other Assets on Consolidated Balance Sheet
[2] Included in Other Liabilities - Non-Current on Consolidated Balance Sheet

The components of net periodic benefit cost and other amounts recognized in other comprehensive (income) loss for our significant plans for the years ended December 31, 2013, 2012, and 2011 include the following components:

	Pension Benefits					
	U.S. Plans			Non-U.S. Plans		
Net Periodic Benefit Cost	2013	2012	2011	2013	2012	2011
Service cost	$ 272	$ 256	$ 232	$ 58	$ 48	$ 59
Interest cost	677	738	761	215	221	239
Expected return on plan assets	(1,076)	(1,020)	(1,014)	(308)	(291)	(284)
Amortization of transition obligation	—	—	—	2	2	2
Amortization of prior service cost (credit)	23	28	33	(2)	(2)	(2)
Recognition of actuarial losses	—	707	1,568	51	250	234
Settlements and curtailments	—	—	24	—	2	1
Net periodic benefit (income) cost	$ (104)	$ 709	$ 1,604	$ 16	$ 230	$ 249

Other Changes in Plan Assets and Benefits Obligations Recognized in Other Comprehensive (Income) Loss	U.S. Plans			Non-U.S. Plans		
	2013	2012	2011	2013	2012	2011
Actuarial (gains)/losses	$(3,090)	$ 859	$ 1,628	$(48)	$ 327	$ 368
Prior service cost (credit)	14	—	5	—	—	—
Transition obligation recognized during year	—	—	—	(2)	(2)	(2)
Prior service (cost) credit recognized during year	(23)	(28)	(33)	2	2	2

(continued)

Other Changes in Plan Assets and Benefits Obligations Recognized in Other Comprehensive (Income) Loss	U.S. Plans			Non-U.S. Plans		
	2013	2012	2011	2013	2012	2011
Actuarial losses recognized during year	—	(707)	(1,568)	(51)	(250)	(234)
Foreign exchange translation adjustments	—	—	—	3	23	(11)
Total recognized in other comprehensive (income) loss	$(3,099)	$ 124	$ 32	$ 96	$ 100	$ 123
Total recognized in net periodic benefit (income) cost and other comprehensive (income) loss	$(3,203)	$ 833	$ 1,636	$(80)	$ 330	$ 372

The estimated prior service cost (credit) for pension benefits that will be amortized from accumulated other comprehensive (income) loss into net periodic benefit cost in 2014 are expected to be $23 million and $(2) million for U.S. and Non-U.S. benefit plans, respectively.

Net Periodic Benefit Cost	Other Postretirement Benefits Years Ended December 31,		
	2013	2012	2011
Service cost	$ —	$ 1	$ 1
Interest cost	44	53	69
Amortization of prior service (credit)	(13)	(14)	(34)
Recognition of actuarial losses	27	34	38
Settlements and curtailments	(42)	(6)	(167)
Net periodic benefit (income) cost	$ 16	$ 68	$ (93)

Other Changes in Plan Assets and Benefits Obligations Recognized in Other Comprehensive (Income) Loss	Years Ended December 31,		
	2013	2012	2011
Actuarial (gains) losses	$(108)	$ 34	$ 6
Prior service (credit)	(175)	(1)	(21)
Prior service credit recognized during year	13	14	34
Actuarial losses recognized during year	(27)	(34)	(38)
Settlements and curtailments	42	6	167
Total recognized in other comprehensive (income) loss	$(255)	$ 19	$148
Total recognized in net periodic benefit (income) cost and other comprehensive (income) loss	$(239)	$ 87	$ 55

The estimated net loss and prior service (credit) for other postretirement benefits that will be amortized from accumulated other comprehensive (income) loss into net periodic benefit cost in 2013 are expected to be $24 and $(20) million, respectively.

Major actuarial assumptions used in determining the benefit obligations and net periodic benefit cost for our significant benefit plans are presented in the following table.

	Pension Benefits					
	U.S. Plans			Non-U.S. Plans		
	2013	2012	2011	2013	2012	2011
Actuarial assumptions used to determine benefit obligations as of December 31:						
Discount rate	4.89%	4.06%	4.89%	4.29%	4.29%	4.84%
Expected annual rate of compensation increase	4.50%	4.50%	4.50%	2.81%	3.55%	3.67%
Actuarial assumptions used to determine net periodic benefit (income) cost for years ended December 31:						
Discount rate	4.06%	4.89%	5.25%	4.29%	4.84%	5.40%
Expected rate of return on plan assets	7.75%	8.00%	8.00%	6.99%	7.03%	7.06%
Expected annual rate of compensation increase	4.50%	4.50%	4.50%	3.55%	3.67%	3.79%

The discount rate for our U.S. pension and other postretirement benefits plans reflects the current rate at which the associated liabilities could be settled at the measurement date of December 31. To determine discount rates for our U.S. pension and other postretirement benefit plans, we use a modeling process that involves matching the expected cash outflows of our benefit plans to a yield curve constructed from a portfolio of high quality, fixed-income debt instruments. We use the average yield of this hypothetical portfolio as a discount rate benchmark. The discount rate used to determine the other postretirement benefit obligation is lower principally due to a shorter expected duration of other postretirement plan obligations as compared to pension plan obligations.

Our expected rate of return on U.S. plan assets of 7.75 percent is a long-term rate based on historical plan asset returns over varying long-term periods combined with current market condition and broad asset mix considerations. We review the expected rate of return on an annual basis and revise it as appropriate.

For non-U.S. benefit plans, none of which was individually material, assumptions reflect economic assumptions applicable to each country.

Pension Benefits

Included in the aggregate data in the tables above are the amounts applicable to our pension plans with accumulated benefit obligations exceeding the fair value of plan assets. Amounts related to such plans were as follows:

	December 31,			
	U.S. Plans		Non-U.S. Plans	
	2013	2012	2013	2012
Projected benefit obligation	$576	$17,117	$911	$4,670
Accumulated benefit obligation	$569	$16,288	$855	$4,426
Fair value of plan assets	$174	$14,345	$307	$3,837

(continued)

Accumulated benefit obligation for our U.S. defined benefit pension plans were $15.7 and $16.3 billion and our Non-U.S. defined benefit plans were $5.3 and $5.0 billion at December 31, 2013 and 2012, respectively.

Our asset investment strategy for our U.S. pension plans focuses on maintaining a diversified portfolio using various asset classes in order to achieve our long-term investment objectives on a risk adjusted basis. Our actual invested positions in various securities change over time based on short and longer- term investment opportunities. To achieve our objectives, we have established long-term target allocations as follows: 60-70 percent equity securities, 10-20 percent fixed income securities and cash, 5-15 percent real estate investments, and 10-20 percent other types of investments. Equity securities include publicly-traded stock of companies located both inside and outside the United States. Fixed income securities include corporate bonds of companies from diversified industries, mortgage-backed securities, and U.S. Treasuries. Real estate investments include direct investments in commercial properties and investments in real estate funds. Other types of investments include investments in private equity and hedge funds that follow several different strategies. We review our assets on a regular basis to ensure that we are within the targeted asset allocation ranges and, if necessary, asset balances are adjusted back within target allocations.

Our non-U.S. pension assets are typically managed by decentralized fiduciary committees with the Honeywell Corporate Investments group providing standard funding and investment guidance. Local regulations, local funding rules, and local financial and tax considerations are part of the funding and investment allocation process in each country. While our non-U.S. investment policies are different for each country, the long-term investment objectives are generally the same as those for the U.S. pension assets.

Suggested answers to these questions are found at the end of the chapter.

Questions:

1. How much was Honeywell's Net periodic benefit (income) cost for its U.S. defined benefit plans for 2013 and 2012? What were the largest and smallest components?
2. Was Honeywell's 2013 actual return on plan assets for its U.S. defined benefit plans greater or less than the expected (projected) return?
3. How much are Honeywell's accumulated and projected benefit obligations for its U.S. defined benefit plans at the end of 2013? Why is the projected benefit obligation different from the accumulated benefit obligation?
4. Is Honeywell in a net asset or a net liability position for its pension plans at the end of 2013 and 2012?
5. If Honeywell had used a lower discount rate for its U.S. defined benefit plans during 2013, what would be the effect on its 2013 pension expense and 2013 projected benefit obligation?

GOT IT?

19-5 Define projected benefit obligation. How does this differ from an accumulated benefit obligation?

19-6 What is a company's accrued/prepaid pension cost? When is a company's accrued/prepaid pension cost a liability, and when is it an asset?

19-7 List the disclosures a company must make for its defined benefit pension plan.

19-8 When is a pension plan qualified? What are the advantages of a qualified pension plan?

19-9 List and briefly define the five components of pension expense.

19-10 In regard to pension plans, define assumptions. What is the relationship between a gain or loss and an assumption?

DEMONSTRATING ACCOUNTING FOR DEFINED BENEFIT PENSION PLANS

LEARNING OBJECTIVE 19.3
Account for defined benefit pension plans.

In order to demonstrate the accounting for defined benefit plans, we illustrate various situations using assumed amounts based on the information in **Example 19.1** for National Company.

> **EXAMPLE 19.1**
>
> **Information Related to National Company's Pension Plan**
>
> a. National adopts a pension plan on January 1, 2016. The plan does not grant retroactive benefits to employees.
> b. The service cost each year is: 2016, $400,000; 2017, $420,000; and 2018, $432,000.
> c. The projected benefit obligation at the beginning of each year is: 2016, $0; 2017, $400,000; and 2018, $840,000.
> d. The discount rate is 10%.
> e. The expected rate of return on plan assets is 10%, which is also equal to the actual rate of return.
> f. National adopts a policy of funding an amount equal to the pension expense and makes the payment to the pension fund management company at the end of each year.[12]
> g. Benefit payments of $20,000 are paid to retired employees at the end of each year (beginning in 2017).

Example 19.1a: Pension Expense Equal to Pension Funding

Based on the information in **Example 19.1**, the calculation of pension expense and the related journal entries for National can be determined for each year as follows:

2016

The service cost of $400,000 is the only component of the pension expense in 2016. This situation occurs because the company has:

- no interest cost (No employees had pension coverage before 2016; National has no projected benefit obligation at the beginning of the year and, therefore, no interest cost.)
- no expected return on plan assets (National had no pension plan assets at the beginning of the year. Its expense recognition and funding were made at the end of the first year.)
- no prior service cost
- no gain or loss

Because National funds an amount equal to the pension expense, it records the following journal entry on December 31, 2016:

Pension Expense	400,000	
Cash		400,000

The projected benefit obligation and the fair value of the plan assets are the same ($400,000) at the end of 2016 which means that the pension plan is fully funded and

---

[12] Companies are required by law to make payments to funding agencies on a quarterly basis. For simplicity, in all examples and homework we assume a single annual payment is made at the end of each year.

the company does not report a pension asset or liability on its December 31, 2016, balance sheet. Also, no adjusting entry is needed because there are no prior service costs and no gains or losses.

2017

The calculation of the pension expense for 2017 is more complex because it now has three components: service cost, interest cost, and expected return on plan assets. National computes its pension expense for 2017 as follows:

Service cost (given in Example 19.1)	$420,000
Interest cost ($400,000 PBO at 1/1/2017 × 10% discount rate)	40,000
Expected return on plan assets ($400,000 plan assets at 1/1/2017 × 10% expected return)	(40,000)
Pension expense	$420,000

National funds an amount equal to the expense and records the following journal entry on December 31, 2017:

Pension Expense	420,000	
Cash		420,000

At the end of 2017, the projected benefit obligation and fair value of plan assets are calculated as:

Projected Benefit Obligation:

1/1/2017 projected benefit obligation balance	=	$400,000
+ Service cost for 2017	=	420,000
+ Interest cost for 2017	=	40,000
− Payment to retired employees for 2017	=	(20,000)
12/31/2017 projected benefit obligation balance	=	$840,000

Fair Value of Pension Plan Assets:

1/1/2017 fair value of plan assets balance	=	$400,000
+ Actual return on plan assets for 2017	=	40,000
+ 2017 Contribution into pension plan	=	420,000
− Payment to retired employees for 2017	=	(20,000)
12/31/2017 fair value of plan assets balance	=	$840,000

Again, the projected benefit obligation is equal to the fair value of plan assets resulting in the pension plan being fully funded. For this reason, National does not report a pension asset or liability on its December 31, 2017, balance sheet. Also, no adjusting entry is needed because there are no prior service costs and no gains or losses. Note also that the $20,000 payment to retired employees that reduces both the projected benefit obligation and the fair value of pension plan assets is made by the pension fund manager, and *not* by the company.

2018

For 2018, the service cost is $432,000. The projected benefit obligation and the plan assets at the beginning of 2018 are both $840,000. Therefore, National computes its pension expense for 2018 as follows:

Service cost (given in Example 19.1)	$432,000
Interest cost ($840,000 PBO at 1/1/2018 × 10% discount rate)	84,000
Expected return on plan assets ($840,000 plan assets at 1/1/2018 × 10% expected return)	(84,000)
Pension expense	$432,000

Because the company funds an amount equal to the expense, it records the following journal entry on December 31, 2018:

Pension Expense	432,000	
Cash		432,000

At the end of 2018, the projected benefit obligation and fair value of the pension plan assets are calculated as:

Projected Benefit Obligation:
1/1/2018 projected benefit obligation balance	=	$ 840,000
+ Service cost for 2018	=	432,000
+ Interest cost for 2018	=	84,000
− Payment to retired employees for 2018	=	(20,000)
12/31/2018 projected benefit obligation balance	=	$1,336,000

Fair Value of Pension Plan Assets:
1/1/2018 fair value of plan assets balance	=	$ 840,000
+ Actual return on plan assets for 2018	=	84,000
+ 2018 contribution into pension plan	=	432,000
− Payment to retired employees for 2018	=	(20,000)
12/31/2018 fair value of plan assets balance	=	$1,336,000

At the end of 2018, the projected benefit obligation is $1,336,000, and the fair value of the pension plan assets is also $1,336,000. Therefore, the pension plan is fully funded and the company does not report a pension asset or liability on its December 31, 2018, balance sheet. Also, no adjusting entry is needed because there are no prior service costs and no gains or losses.

Note that the interest cost and the expected return on the plan assets offset each other in this example. This situation occurs because the discount rate and the expected long-term rate of return on plan assets are both 10% and because the company funds an amount equal to the expense. ■

Example 19.1b: Pension Funding Greater Than Pension Expense

Assume the same facts for National Company as in **Example 19.1a**, except that instead of funding an amount equal to the pension expense, the company funds $405,000 in 2016, $425,000 in 2017, and $435,000 in 2018.[13] Because National provides *more* assets to the pension fund, the expected return on those assets each year is higher, and therefore, the pension expense is less because of the higher expected return.

2016

National's pension expense in 2016 is the $400,000 service cost, so the journal entry on December 31, 2016, is as follows:

Pension Expense	400,000	
Accrued/Prepaid Pension Cost	5,000	
Cash		405,000

Because National funds $405,000 in 2016 when the expense is $400,000, it recognizes an asset, Accrued/Prepaid Pension Cost, of $5,000.

At the end of 2016, the $400,000 projected benefit obligation is $5,000 less than the $405,000 fair value of the pension plan assets so the pension plan is *overfunded* by $5,000. The $5,000 debit balance in Accrued/Prepaid Pension Cost reflects the overfunded status of the pension plan and no adjustment is necessary because there are no prior service costs or gains or losses. National reports this overfunded amount as its pension plan asset, Prepaid Pension Cost, on its December 31, 2016, balance sheet. It is important to note that if the pension plan were underfunded because the projected obligation exceeded the fair value of plan assets, National would recognize a noncurrent liability, Accrued Pension Cost.

2017

In 2017, the only difference from **Example 19.1a** in the computation of the pension expense is the increased expected return on the plan assets caused by the larger amount contributed to the pension plan. National computes its pension expense for 2017 as follows:

---

[13] In this and future examples, the amount funded each year is at least equal to the service cost plus one-seventh of any prior service cost. This amount is in accordance with the rules established in the Pension Protection Act of 2006, as we discuss later.

Service cost	$420,000
Interest cost ($400,000 PBO at 1/1/2017 × 10% discount rate)	40,000
Expected return on plan assets ($405,000 plan assets at 1/1/2017 × 10% expected return)	(40,500)
Pension expense	$419,500

The entry to record pension expense and funding of $425,000 in 2017 is recorded as:

December 31, 2017:

Pension Expense	419,500	
Accrued/Prepaid Pension Cost	5,500	
Cash		425,000

The balance in the Accrued/Prepaid Pension Cost account is now a debit of $10,500 ($5,000 + $5,500), representing an asset.

At the end of 2017, the projected benefit obligation and fair value of the pension plan assets are calculated as follows:

Projected Benefit Obligation:

1/1/2017 projected benefit obligation balance	=	$400,000
+ Service cost for 2017	=	420,000
+ Interest cost for 2017	=	40,000
− Payment to retired employees for 2017	=	(20,000)
12/31/2017 projected benefit obligation balance	=	$840,000

Fair Value of Pension Plan Assets:

1/1/2017 fair value of plan assets balance	=	$405,000
+ Actual return on plan assets for 2017	=	40,500
+ 2017 Contribution into pension plan	=	425,000
− Payment to retired employees for 2017	=	(20,000)
12/31/2017 fair value of plan assets balance	=	$850,500

At the end of 2017, the fair value of the pension plan assets is $850,500 which is $10,500 greater than the projected benefit obligation. This means that the pension plan is *overfunded* by $10,500 ($850,500 − $840,000). However, no adjustment is necessary because there are no prior service costs or gains or losses, and the $10,500 debit balance in Accrued/Prepaid Pension Cost reflects the overfunded status of the pension plan. National reports this overfunded amount as a noncurrent pension plan asset, Prepaid Pension Cost, on its December 31, 2017, balance sheet.

2018

In 2018, the computation of the pension expense is again affected by the increased expected return on the plan assets. Therefore, National computes its pension expense for 2018 as follows:

Service cost	$432,000
Interest cost ($840,000 PBO at 1/1/2018 × 10% discount rate)	84,000
Expected return on plan assets ($850,500 plan assets at 1/1/2018 × 10% expected return)	(85,050)
Pension expense	$430,950

The following journal entry is made on December 31, 2018, to record pension expense, funding and the change in the Accrued/Prepaid Pension Cost account:

December 31, 2018:

Pension Expense	430,950	
Accrued/Prepaid Pension Cost	4,050	
Cash		435,000

The balance in the asset account is now $14,550 ($10,500 + $4,050).

At the end of 2018, the projected benefit obligation and fair value of the pension plan assets are calculated as:

Projected Benefit Obligation:

1/1/2018 projected benefit obligation balance	=	$840,000
+ Service cost for 2018	=	432,000
+ Interest cost for 2018	=	84,000
− Payment to retired employees for 2018	=	(20,000)
12/31/2018 projected benefit obligation balance	=	$1,336,000

Fair Value of Pension Plan Assets:

1/1/2018 fair value of plan assets balance	=	$850,500
+ Actual return on plan assets for 2018	=	85,050
+ 2018 contribution into pension plan	=	435,000
− Payment to retired employees for 2018	=	(20,000)
12/31/2018 fair value of plan assets balance	=	$1,350,550

The pension plan is *overfunded* by $14,550 ($1,350,550 − $1,336,000), and National reports this overfunded amount as its pension plan asset, Prepaid Pension Cost, on its December 31, 2018, balance sheet. Again no adjustment is needed to the account because there is no prior service cost or gains/losses.

ETHICAL DILEMMA

Cloud Nine Airlines provides airline service to most major cities in the continental United States. Due mainly to high fuel costs and the reduced demand for air travel, Cloud Nine has been generating very low earnings over the past 5 years and is just able to generate enough cash flow to pay many of its short-term operating costs. Since its start in 1975, Cloud Nine has provided its pilots, crew members, and ground crew a defined benefit plan. Many of the company's employees are now nearing retirement, and Cloud Nine's projected benefit obligation is becoming very significant. Although the company has been making contributions into the plan, the large stock market declines in 2009 and 2010 have left Cloud Nine's pension plan considerably underfunded. In fact, at the end of 2012, the funded status of Cloud Nine's pension plans was at 68%.

In July 2013, Brad Richter, the Chief Financial Officer, comes into your office to discuss the pension plans with you. Brad is very happy that the stock market has had a stronger performance lately and states that the improving market and economic conditions justify changing the pension plan assumptions. Specifically, he asks that you increase the expected return on plan assets from 6.5% to 8.0% and also increase the discount rate from 4.2% to 5.0%. Brad states he has spoken with the company's actuary and independent accountant and that they have no issues with the changes in estimates.

As the accountant for Cloud Nine, you are in charge of preparing the financial statements and related note disclosures for the current year. You know that recent actual returns on pension assets over the previous 2 years have averaged 4.8% since the major stock market decline and that 10-year U.S. Treasury bond interest rates have been averaging 3.5% over the last 5 years. For these reasons, you tell Brad that there is no cause to change the pension assumptions. Brad is clearly agitated by your response and states that, as the CFO, these types of decisions are his alone and that he is not asking you to make the change but telling you to make the change. If you make the changes Brad wants, how will those assumptions affect Cloud Nine's pension obligation and pension expense? How would you handle this situation?

Example 19.1c: Expected Return Different from Actual Return

Assume the same facts for National Company as in **Example 19.1**, except that:

- Instead of funding an amount equal to the pension expense, National funds $415,000 in 2016, $425,000 in 2017, and $440,000 in 2018.
- The expected return is 11% each year, whereas the *actual return* is 12% each year.

In this example, National provides *more* assets to the pension fund and expects to earn a higher return on those assets. Therefore, the pension expense is less to compensate for the expected higher return. Assume that any gain or loss is not immediately recognized in pension expense but rather deferred and recognized as a component of Other Comprehensive Income by the company.[14]

2016

National's pension expense in 2016 is the $400,000 service cost and the journal entry on December 31, 2016, is as follows:

Pension Expense	400,000	
Accrued/Prepaid Pension Cost	15,000	
Cash		415,000

National recognizes an asset, Accrued/Prepaid Pension Cost, of $15,000 because National funds $415,000 in 2016 when the expense is only $400,000. At the end of

---

[14] In this example, the higher actual return compared to the expected return creates an "unrecognized gain," as discussed earlier in the chapter. However, as discussed later in the chapter, the gain does not exceed the corridor, so no amortization is necessary.

2016, the $415,000 fair value of the pension plan assets is $15,000 more than the $400,000 projected benefit obligation so the pension plan is *overfunded* by $15,000. Because there is neither prior service cost nor gains/losses, the $15,000 balance in the Accrued/Prepaid Pension Cost account already reflects the overfunded status of the pension plan. National reports this overfunded amount as its pension plan asset, Prepaid Pension Cost, on its December 31, 2016, balance sheet.

2017

National contributed $415,000 on December 31, 2016, and expects to earn an 11% rate of return on its plan assets. National computes the pension expense for 2017 as follows:

Service cost	$420,000
Interest cost ($400,000 PBO at 1/1/2017 × 10% discount rate)	40,000
Expected return on plan assets ($415,000 plan assets at 1/1/2017 × 11% expected return)	(45,650)
Pension expense	$414,350

National funds $425,000 in 2017 and records the following journal entry on December 31, 2017:

Pension Expense	414,350	
Accrued/Prepaid Pension Cost	10,650	
Cash		425,000

The balance in the asset account is now $25,650 ($15,000 + $10,650).

At the end of 2017, National computes the projected benefit obligation and fair value of the pension plan assets as follows:

Projected Benefit Obligation:			*Fair Value of Pension Plan Assets:*		
1/1/2017 projected benefit obligation balance	=	$400,000	1/1/2017 fair value of plan assets balance	=	$415,000
+ Service cost for 2017	=	420,000	+ Actual return on plan assets for 2017 ($415,000 × 12%)	=	49,800
+ Interest cost for 2017	=	40,000	+ 2017 contribution into pension plan	=	425,000
− Payment to retired employees for 2017	=	(20,000)	− Payment to retired employees for 2017	=	(20,000)
12/31/2017 projected benefit obligation balance	=	$840,000	12/31/2017 fair value of plan assets balance	=	$869,800

At the end of 2017, National's pension plan is overfunded by $29,800 ($869,800 − $840,000). Given that the Accrued/Prepaid Pension Cost account has a debit balance of $25,650, the account must be increased by $4,150 ($29,800 − $25,650) which requires the following journal entry:

Accrued/Prepaid Pension Cost	4,150	
Other Comprehensive Income: Net Gain/Loss		4,150

This journal entry recognizes the "gain" that results from the actual return ($49,800) being greater than the expected return ($45,650).[15] After this journal entry, the Accrued/Prepaid Pension Cost account has a $29,800 debit balance, which is the amount by which the company's pension plan is overfunded. National reports this overfunded amount as its pension plan asset, Accrued/Prepaid Pension Cost, on its December 31, 2017, balance sheet. The credit of $4,150 is included in other comprehensive income for 2017 and is also reported as a component of accumulated other comprehensive income on its December 31, 2017, balance sheet.

---

[15] In the case where the actual return is less than the expected return, the Other Comprehensive Income: Net Gain/Loss would be debited and the pension asset decreased by crediting Accrued/Prepaid Pension Cost.

2018

As shown in the computations at the end of 2017, National's plan assets at the beginning of 2018 are $869,800. National continues to expect to earn 11% on its plan assets. National computes its pension expense for 2018 as follows:

Service cost	$432,000
Interest cost ($840,000 PBO at 1/1/2018 × 10% discount rate)	84,000
Expected return on plan assets ($869,800 plan assets at 1/1/2018 × 11% expected return)	(95,678)
Pension expense	$420,322

Because the company funds $440,000 in 2018, it records the following journal entry on December 31, 2018:

Pension Expense	420,322	
Accrued/Prepaid Pension Cost	19,678	
Cash		440,000

The balance in the Accrued/Prepaid Pension Cost asset account is now $49,478 ($29,800 + $19,678).

At the end of 2018, the projected benefit obligation and fair value of the pension plan assets is computed as follows:

Projected Benefit Obligation:

1/1/2018 projected benefit obligation balance	=	$ 840,000
+ Service cost for 2018	=	432,000
+ Interest cost for 2018	=	84,000
− Payment to retired employees for 2018	=	(20,000)
12/31/2018 projected benefit obligation balance	=	$1,336,000

Fair Value of Pension Plan Assets:

1/1/2018 fair value of plan assets balance	=	$ 869,800
+ Actual return on plan assets for 2018 ($869,800 × 12%)	=	104,376
+ 2018 contribution into pension plan	=	440,000
− Payment to retired employees for 2018	=	(20,000)
12/31/2018 fair value of plan assets balance	=	$1,394,176

Comparing the projected benefit obligation to the fair value of plan assets shows that the pension plan is *overfunded* by $58,176 ($1,394,176 − $1,336,000). The overfunded amount is compared to the current balance in the Accrued/Prepaid Pension Cost account, which has a debit balance of $49,478, to determine that the account must be increased by $8,698 ($58,176 − $49,478). To record the increase, National records the following journal entry:

Accrued/Prepaid Pension Cost	8,698	
Other Comprehensive Income: Net Gain/Loss		8,698

This adjustment recognizes the "gain" that results from the actual return ($104,376) being greater than the expected return ($95,678).[16] After this journal entry, the Accrued/Prepaid Pension Cost account has a $58,176 debit balance, which is the amount by which the company's pension plan is overfunded. National reports this overfunded amount as its pension plan asset, Accrued/Prepaid Pension Cost, on its December 31, 2018, balance sheet. In addition the credit of $8,698 is included in other comprehensive income for 2018. The balance in accumulated other comprehensive income is $12,848 ($4,150 + $8,698), which represents the cumulative gain not recognized in pension expense. National reports this amount on its December 31, 2018, balance sheet. ■

It is important that you understand the impact of the *expected* and *actual* rates of return on plan assets. A company uses the expected return to compute its pension expense for the year. However, the actual return for the year increases the value of the plan assets at the end of the year. In the next year, the company multiplies those actual plan assets by the expected return to compute the amount that it subtracts to compute its pension expense. In its pension plan disclosures, the company includes the actual

---

[16] The company may also decide to immediately recognize gains and losses in pension expense. In this case, the company would not debit or credit Other Comprehensive Income: Net Gain/Loss for the amount of the gain or loss but rather would debit or credit Pension Expense directly.

return on its plan assets in the reconciliation of the beginning and ending balances of the fair value of its plan assets.

Disclosure

To improve the usefulness of a company's disclosures about its defined benefit pension plan, as discussed earlier, the company must report certain information in the notes to its financial statements, in addition to the amounts contained in its financial statements. GAAP requires disclosure of, among other items, a reconciliation of the beginning and ending amounts of the projected benefit obligation, a reconciliation of the beginning and ending fair value of the plan assets, the components of the pension expense, and the discount rate used and the expected long-term rate of return on plan assets.

Note that in the reconciliation of the beginning and ending fair value of the plan assets, a company discloses the *actual* return on its pension plan assets. In the schedule listing the components of the pension expense, however, the company discloses the *expected* return on the pension plan assets. This aspect of the pension plan disclosures is important because it enables external users to compare the difference between the expected and actual returns to evaluate how well the pension funds are being managed.

Example 19.1d: Disclosure of Defined Benefit Pension Plan Information

The disclosures for National Company for 2018, using the facts from **Example 19.1c**, are presented below.

National Company
Disclosure of Defined Benefit Pension Plan Information (2018)

Reconciliation of the beginning and ending amounts of the projected benefit obligation:

Beginning 1/1/2018 projected benefit obligation	$ 840,000
Service cost	432,000
Interest cost	84,000
Actuarial gains and losses	0
Benefits paid	(20,000)
Plan amendments	0
Ending 12/31/2018 projected benefit obligation	$1,336,000

Reconciliation of the beginning and ending fair value of the plan assets:

Beginning 1/1/2018 fair value of plan assets	$ 869,800
Actual return on plan assets	104,376
Contributions	440,000
Benefits paid	(20,000)
Ending 12/31/2018 fair value of plan assets	$1,394,176

Components of 2018 pension expense:

Service cost	$ 432,000
Interest cost	84,000
Expected return on plan assets	(95,678)
Amortization of prior service cost	0
Amortization of gains and losses	0
Total pension expense	$ 420,322

Items not yet recognized as a component of pension expense:

Other comprehensive income: Net gain/loss	$ 12,848

Assumptions:
Discount rate: 10%
Expected long-term rate of return on plan assets: 11%

Examples **19.1a**, **19.1b**, and **19.1c** showed relatively simple computations of pension expense and the related pension liability or asset. The remaining examples deal with prior service cost and gain/loss amortization.

Example 19.1e: Pension Expense Including Amortization of Prior Service Cost

Assume the same facts for National Company as in **Example 19.1c**, except that the company awarded retroactive benefits to the employees when it adopted the pension plan on January 1, 2016. National's actuary computed the prior service cost to be $2 million. This amount creates the beginning balance of the projected benefit obligation on January 1, 2016. To fund this projected benefit obligation, National decided to increase its total contributions for each year:

- Year 2016: $705,000
- Year 2017: $715,000
- Year 2018: $730,000

For simplicity, also assume that the company amortizes the prior service cost by the straight-line method over the remaining 20-year average service life of its active employees. This results in prior service cost amortization of $100,000 ($2,000,000 ÷ 20) per year.

2016

National records this projected benefit obligation for the prior service cost at the inception of the plan (1/1/2016) as follows:

Other Comprehensive Income: Prior Service Cost	2,000,000	
Accrued/Prepaid Pension Cost		2,000,000

This entry records the prior service cost as a liability because it is an obligation to the company's employees, and also as a negative element of other comprehensive income.

National's pension expense in 2016 now has three components—service cost, interest cost on the projected benefit obligation, and amortization of prior service cost. Therefore, it computes the pension expense for 2016 as follows:

Service cost	$400,000
Interest cost ($2,000,000 × 10%)	200,000
Amortization of prior service cost	100,000
Pension expense	$700,000

Given that National funds $705,000 in 2016, it records the following journal entry at December 31, 2016:

Pension Expense	700,000	
Accrued/Prepaid Pension Cost	5,000	
Cash		705,000

It is important to recognize that the 2016 pension expense includes $100,000 amortization of prior service cost, which results in the need for an adjusting entry at December 31, 2016, as follows:

Accrued/Prepaid Pension Cost	100,000	
Other Comprehensive Income: Prior Service Cost		100,000

This entry reduces the amount of prior service cost included in Accumulated Other Comprehensive Income from $2,000,000 to $1,900,000 to avoid "double counting" the portion of the prior service cost that was amortized and reduced net income. National reports $1,900,000 as a negative element of other comprehensive income for

2016 and as a negative element of accumulated other comprehensive income on its December 31, 2016, balance sheet.

At the end of 2016, the projected benefit obligation and fair value of the pension plan assets is computed as follows:

Projected Benefit Obligation:			Fair Value of Pension Plan Assets:		
Beginning projected benefit obligation	=	$2,000,000	1/1/2016 fair value of plan assets balance	=	$ 0
+ Service cost for 2016	=	400,000	+ Actual return on plan assets for 2017 ($0 × 12%)	=	0
+ Interest cost for 2016	=	200,000	+ 2016 contribution into pension plan	=	705,000
Ending projected benefit obligation	=	$2,600,000	12/31/2016 fair value of plan assets balance	=	$705,000

This results in the pension plan being *underfunded* by $1,895,000 ($2,600,000 − $705,000). No further adjustment is necessary because there are no gains or losses, and the $1,895,000 ($2,000,000 − $5,000 − $100,000) credit balance in Accrued/Prepaid Pension Cost is the amount by which the pension plan is underfunded. National reports this underfunded amount as a noncurrent pension plan liability, Accrued/Prepaid Pension Cost, on its December 31, 2016, balance sheet.

2017

National's beginning projected benefit obligation is $2,600,000, and the company computes the pension expense for 2017 as follows:

Service cost	$420,000
Interest cost ($2,600,000 × 10%)	260,000
Expected return on plan assets ($705,000 × 11%)	(77,550)
Amortization of prior service cost	100,000
Pension expense	$702,450

The pension expense journal entry on December 31, 2017, is:

Pension Expense	702,450	
Accrued/Prepaid Pension Cost	12,550	
Cash		715,000

The 2017 pension expense amount includes $100,000 amortization of prior service cost. As this amount is now included in pension expense, National must record an adjusting entry as follows:

Accrued/Prepaid Pension Cost	100,000	
Other Comprehensive Income: Prior Service Cost		100,000

This entry reduces the amount of prior service cost included in Accumulated Other Comprehensive Income from $1,900,000 to $1,800,000. National reports $100,000 as a positive element of other comprehensive income for 2017.

At the end of 2017, National computes the projected benefit obligation and fair value of the pension plan assets as follows:

Projected Benefit Obligation:			Fair Value of Pension Plan Assets:		
1/1/2017 projected benefit obligation balance	=	$2,600,000	1/1/2017 fair value of plan assets balance	=	$ 705,000
+ Service cost for 2017	=	420,000	+ Actual return on plan assets for 2017 ($705,000 × 12%)	=	84,600
+ Interest cost for 2017	=	260,000	+ 2017 contribution into pension plan	=	715,000
− Payment to retired employees for 2017	=	(20,000)	− Payment to retired employees for 2017	=	(20,000)
12/31/2017 projected benefit obligation balance	=	$3,260,000	12/31/2017 fair value of plan assets balance	=	$1,484,600

This results in the pension plan being *underfunded* by $1,775,400 ($3,260,000 − $1,484,600). However, the Accrued/Prepaid Pension Cost account has a credit balance of $1,782,450 ($1,895,000 beginning balance − $12,550 − $100,000), which means the account must be decreased by $7,050. To accomplish this, National records the following journal entry:

Accrued/Prepaid Pension Cost	7,050	
Other Comprehensive Income: Net Gain/Loss		7,050

Note that this adjustment is necessary to recognize the gain that resulted from the actual return ($84,600) being greater than the expected return ($77,550). After this journal entry, the Accrued/Prepaid Pension Cost account has a $1,775,400 credit balance, which is the amount by which the company's pension plan is underfunded. National reports this underfunded amount as its pension plan liability, Accrued/Prepaid Pension Cost, and $1,792,950 as a negative element of Accumulated Other Comprehensive Income on its December 31, 2017, balance sheet.

2018

On January 1, 2018, National computes the pension expense for 2018 as follows:

Service cost	$ 432,000
Interest cost ($3,260,000 × 10%)	326,000
Expected return on plan assets ($1,484,600 × 11%)	(163,306)
Amortization of prior service cost	100,000
Pension expense	$ 694,694

The company funds $730,000 in 2018 and records the following journal entry on December 31, 2018:

Pension Expense	694,694	
Accrued/Prepaid Pension Cost	35,306	
Cash		730,000

Once again, the 2018 pension expense includes the $100,000 amortization of prior service cost, and National records an adjusting entry as follows:

Accrued/Prepaid Pension Cost	100,000	
Other Comprehensive Income: Prior Service Cost		100,000

This entry reduces the amount of prior service cost included in Accumulated Other Comprehensive Income from $1,800,000 to $1,700,000 to avoid "double counting" the portion of the prior service cost that was amortized and reduced net income. National reports $100,000 as a positive element of other comprehensive income for 2018.

At the end of 2018, the projected benefit obligation and fair value of the pension plan assets is computed as follows:

Projected Benefit Obligation:

1/1/2018 projected benefit obligation balance	=	$3,260,000
+ Service cost for 2018	=	432,000
+ Interest cost for 2018	=	326,000
− Payment to retired employees for 2018	=	(20,000)
12/31/2018 projected benefit obligation balance	=	$3,998,000

Fair Value of Pension Plan Assets:

1/1/2018 fair value of plan assets balance	=	$1,484,600
+ Actual return on plan assets for 2018 ($1,484,600 × 12%)	=	178,152
+ 2018 contribution into pension plan	=	730,000
− Payment to retired employees for 2018	=	(20,000)
12/31/2018 fair value of plan assets balance	=	$2,372,752

Therefore, the pension plan is *underfunded* by $1,625,248 ($3,998,000 − $2,372,752). Because the Accrued/Prepaid Pension Cost account has a credit balance of $1,640,094 ($1,775,400 beginning balance − $35,306 − $100,000), the account must be decreased by $14,846 ($1,625,248 − $1,640,094), so National records the following journal entry:

Accrued/Prepaid Pension Cost	14,846	
Other Comprehensive Income: Net Gain/Loss		14,846

Note that this adjustment is necessary to recognize the gain that resulted from the actual return ($178,152) being greater than the expected return ($163,306). After this journal entry, the Accrued/Prepaid Pension Cost account has a $1,625,248 credit balance, which is the amount by which the company's pension plan is underfunded. National reports this underfunded amount as a noncurrent pension plan liability, Accrued/Prepaid Pension Cost, and $1,678,104 as a negative element of Accumulated Other Comprehensive Income on its December 31, 2018, balance sheet. ■

Example 19.2: Corridor Amortization of Net Gain or Loss (to Extent Recognized)

Earlier, we discussed the situations that cause a gain or loss in previous periods:

- changes in the actuarial assumptions used to calculate the projected benefit obligation
- experience that differs from what was expected in measuring the obligation and expected return on the pension plan assets

The gain or loss can be recognized immediately or it can be deferred and amortized in future periods to pension expense. The minimum amount that must be amortized is determined by using a method called *corridor* amortization. Because most companies use the corridor method and because it determines the minimum amount of amortization, we examine the calculations in this section.

When a net gain or loss exceeds the corridor amount, the excess amount is amortized over the remaining service life of active employees. Corridor amortization involves three steps:

- *Step 1.* The cumulative net gain or loss at the beginning of the year is calculated.
- *Step 2.* **The corridor is calculated as 10% of the greater of the beginning projected benefit obligation or beginning of the period fair value of plan assets.**
- *Step 3.* If the net gain or loss exceeds the corridor, the amount in excess of the corridor is amortized over the remaining service life of active employees. A company *adds* any amortization of a net loss to pension expense. It *subtracts* any amortization of a net gain from pension expense.

Example 19.2 shows the computation of the corridor and net gain or loss included in pension expense for Hall Company for years 2016 through 2019. Hall has had a

EXAMPLE 19.2 **Computation of Corridor and Amortization of Net Gain or Loss**

Year	Beginning Cumulative Net Loss (Gain)	Beginning Projected Benefit Obligation: Actual	Beginning Fair Value of Plan Assets	Corridor[a]	Excess Net Loss (Gain)[b]	Amortized Net Loss (Gain)[c]
2016	$13,000	$110,000	$100,000	$11,000	$2,000	$200
2017	(2,300)	135,000	130,000	13,500	—[d]	—
2018	18,700	168,000	170,000	17,000	1,700	170
2019	27,500	230,000	215,000	23,000	4,500	450

[a] 10% of the greater of the actual projected benefit obligation or the fair value of the plan assets at the beginning of the year
[b] Absolute Value of the Cumulative Net Loss (Gain) − Corridor
[c] Excess Net Loss (Gain) ÷ Average Remaining Service Life (10 years)
[d] Because the absolute value of the cumulative net loss (gain) is less than the corridor, there is no excess net loss (gain).

defined benefit pension plan for its employees for several years. The amounts of the cumulative net loss (gain), the projected benefit obligation (actual), and the fair value of the plan assets are based on information provided by the company's actuary and pension fund asset manager.

Step 1

To compute the amortization, the first step is to determine the cumulative net gain or loss at the beginning of the year. Hall calculates the amounts in the Cumulative Net Loss (Gain) column of **Example 19.2** at the beginning of the year, based on previous periods. Thus, for instance, the $13,000 amount of cumulative net loss at the beginning of 2016 is a result of experience different from that assumed and changes in actuarial assumptions in periods prior to 2016. In this example, we have assumed large amounts of gains and losses to better illustrate the calculations. Also, note that we show a cumulative net *loss* without parentheses because the related amortization is *added* to pension expense, whereas we show a *gain* in parentheses because the amortization is *deducted*.

Step 2

Hall's actuary and asset management company also calculate the amounts in the Projected Benefit Obligation and the Fair Value of Plan Assets columns at the beginning of the year. Hall has a $110,000 projected benefit obligation and a $100,000 fair value of the plan at the beginning of 2016. These amounts are used to determine the **corridor** amount, as illustrated for Hall in **Example 19.2**.

Step 3

Next, Hall determines if the cumulative net gain or loss needs to be amortized. **At a minimum, a company amortizes any cumulative net gain or loss in a given year if, at the beginning of the year, the (absolute value of the) cumulative net gain or loss exceeds the corridor.** This 10% threshold (the corridor) is intended to reduce fluctuations in pension expense. In many cases, the corridor will not be exceeded, so no amortization is recorded. Also, if a company had a large cumulative net gain (loss) at the beginning of a given year, pension expense would only be affected by the amortization of the cumulative net gain (loss) in excess of the corridor amount.

In **Example 19.2**, the amount in the corridor column for a given year is 10% of the higher of the actual projected benefit obligation or the fair value of the plan assets at the beginning of that year. Thus, in 2016, Hall computes the $11,000 corridor as 10% of the $110,000 actual projected benefit obligation because it is the higher of the two amounts. In 2018, however, it computes the $17,000 corridor as 10% of the $170,000 fair value of the plan assets.

The amount in the Excess Net Loss (Gain) column for a given year is the excess of the (absolute value of the) cumulative net loss (gain) over the corridor at the beginning of that year. Thus, in 2016, the $2,000 excess net loss is the difference between the $13,000 cumulative net loss and the $11,000 corridor. In 2017, however, the corridor exceeds the cumulative net gain, so there is no excess.

The amount in the Amortized Net Loss (Gain) column for a given year is the adjustment to pension expense. The company computes each amortization amount by dividing the excess net loss (gain) for that year by the average remaining service life of the active employees expected to receive benefits under the plan. In this example, assume a 10-year average service life for all years. In reality, the company may have to recompute the average service life each year for changes in its employee work force. For instance, in 2016 the $200 amortization that Hall *adds* to pension expense as the amortized net loss is determined by dividing the $2,000 excess net loss by the 10-year average service life. We discussed the journal entry to record pension expense earlier in the chapter. In addition, Hall would record the following:

Accrued/Prepaid Pension Cost	200	
Other Comprehensive Income: Net Gain/Loss		200

This entry decreases the net loss reported in accumulated other comprehensive income by $200 and is similar to the adjustment for the amortization of the prior service cost discussed earlier.

Pension Spreadsheet

Example 19.3 shows a spreadsheet prepared using the amounts in Example 19.1e. There are three important aspects of this spreadsheet:

- The amounts at the bottom of the "Pension Expense" columns provide the information that National uses to determine the debit (dr) to the Pension Expense account, and the credits (cr) to the Cash and the Accrued/Prepaid Pension Cost accounts.
- The ending projected benefit obligation and plan assets amounts for one year are the beginning amounts for the next year.
- The calculations for the projected benefit obligation, amortization of prior service cost, and the plan assets provide much of the information that National would use to adjust its Other Comprehensive Income (and Accrued/Prepaid Pension Cost), as well as to disclose its pension plan information in the notes to its financial statements.

EXAMPLE 19.3 Pension Plan Spreadsheet

Item	2016 Amount	2016 Pension Expense	2017 Amount	2017 Pension Expense	2018 Amount	2018 Pension Expense
Beginning projected benefit obligation	$2,000,000[a]		$2,600,000		$3,260,000	
× Discount rate	× 0.10		× 0.10		× 0.10	
= Interest cost	$ 200,000 →	$200,000	$ 260,000 →	$260,000	$ 326,000 →	$326,000
Beginning projected benefit obligation	2,000,000		2,600,000		3,260,000	
+ Service cost	400,000 →	400,000	420,000 →	420,000	432,000 →	432,000
Benefits paid	(0)		(20,000)		(20,000)	
= Ending projected benefit obligation	$2,600,000		$3,260,000		$3,998,000	
Beginning plan assets	$ 0		$ 705,000		$1,484,600	
× Expected rate of return	× 0.11		× 0.11		× 0.11	
= Expected return	$ 0 →	(0)	$ 77,550 →	(77,550)	$ 163,306 →	(163,306)
Beginning plan assets	$ 0		$ 705,000		$1,484,600	
+ Actual return[b]	0		84,600		178,152	
+ Contributions	705,000		715,000		730,000	
− Benefits paid	(0)		(20,000)		(20,000)	
= Ending plan assets	$ 705,000		$1,484,600		$2,372,752	
Prior service cost	$2,000,000		$2,000,000		$2,000,000	
÷ Average service life (years)[c]	÷ 20		÷ 20		÷ 20	
= Amortization of prior service cost	$ 100,000 →	100,000	$ 100,000 →	100,000	$ 100,000 →	100,000
Net gain or loss[d]	$ 0 →	0	$ 0 →	0	$ 0 →	0
Total pension expense		$700,000 dr		$702,450 dr		$694,694 dr
Contribution (cash)		705,000 cr		715,000 cr		730,000 cr
Adjustment to accrued/prepaid pension cost		$ 5,000 dr		$ 12,550 dr		$ 35,306 dr

[a] Prior service cost at adoption of plan
[b] The actual return is assumed to be 12% each year × Beginning plan assets
[c] Or times amortization fraction
[d] Calculated using the corridor approach (Example 19.2)

INTERNATIONAL DIMENSION

DEFINED BENEFIT PENSION ACCOUNTING

In June 2011, the IASB amended IAS 19, *Employee Benefits*, significantly changing its method of accounting for pensions. Prior to this amendment, the basic principles of accounting for defined benefit plans under IFRS were the same as U.S. GAAP. However, the amendment resulted in IFRS being significantly different from GAAP. Changing the accounting for defined benefit plans has been a long-time project of the FASB, and these changes by the IASB make it more likely that GAAP will change to converge with IFRS.

The major result of the IASB amendments was to remove many of the smoothing devices in pension accounting. Under the new accounting standards, companies will recognize all changes in their projected benefit obligation and plan assets in the current period. These changes will be recorded in pension expense or other comprehensive income, which means these accounts will become more variable.

Specifically, pension expense will have two components: service cost and net interest.

- The service cost represents the increase in the pension obligation as a result of employees providing service during the period.
- The net interest component is determined by multiplying the company's discount rate by the net pension obligation or net pension asset. This calculation combines the interest expense and expected return components used to determine pension expense under GAAP.

In a particular year, if the amount funded exceeds the pension expense, the difference would decrease the accrued pension liability (if underfunded) or increase the prepaid pension asset (if overfunded). Conversely, in a year when the amount funded is less than the pension expense, the difference would increase the pension liability or decrease the pension asset. Any changes in the projected benefit obligation resulting from changes in estimates or assumptions and changes in the plan assets due to the difference in expected and actual returns are considered remeasurements and are immediately recognized as a component of other comprehensive income. In addition, the remeasurement amount increases or decreases the accrued pension liability or prepaid pension asset, as appropriate. The main result of these changes is that anticipated changes in the pension plan (i.e., service cost and interest) will be recognized in the income statement through pension expense. Unanticipated changes resulting from changes in experience and assumptions will be recorded in other comprehensive income (so some smoothing effects remain). Net income should be less volatile because gains and losses on the projected benefit obligation and plan assets will be recorded in other comprehensive income.

One additional difference is that changes in the projected benefit obligation resulting from plan amendments are recognized immediately in pension expense through the service cost component. Companies may elect to report this prior service cost component of net income. Under U.S. GAAP, any plan amendments resulting in prior service cost are deferred through other comprehensive income and then amortized to pension expense over the remaining years of future service.

(continued)

IFRS Application Klammer Corporation is a German company that provides a defined benefit pension program to its employees. At the beginning of 2016, Klammer's pension plan had €920 million of pension obligations and €775 million of plan assets. Therefore, Klammer reported accrued pension cost in its statement of financial position of €145 million.

The company uses a discount rate of 6% and reported service cost of €55 million related to 2016. In addition, Klammer's 2016 contribution to the pension fund was €47 million and the pension fund paid out €44 million in benefits to employees. The pension fund also reported that its actual return on plan assets was €51.5 million.

Klammer's 2016 pension expense is calculated as follows:

Service cost	= € 55 million
+ Net interest expense (€920 beginning PBO − €775 beginning plan assets) × 6% discount rate	= € 8.7 million
Pension expense	= €63.7 million

Remeasurements on the pension plan would be determined by examining the projected benefit obligation and plan assets for gains and losses resulting from changes in assumptions or experience. Klammer's expected return on plan assets was €46.5 million (€775 million × 6%). The difference between the actual and expected return results in a remeasurement gain of €5.0 million (€51.5 million − €46.5 million) which is recorded in other comprehensive income.

In addition, Klammer calculates the projected benefit obligation and fair value of the pension plan assets at the end of 2016 as follows:

Projected Benefit Obligation:		Fair Value of Pension Plan Assets:	
1/1/2016 projected benefit obligation balance	= €920.0 million	1/1/2016 fair value of plan assets balance	= €775.0 million
+ Service cost for 2016	= 55.0 million	+ Actual return on plan assets for 2016	= 51.5 million
+ Interest cost for 2016 (€920 million × 6%)	= 55.2 million	+ 2016 contribution into pension plan	= 47.0 million
− Payment to retired employees for 2016	= (44.0 million)	− Payment to retired employees for 2016	= (44.0 million)
12/31/2016 projected benefit obligation balance	= €986.2 million	12/31/2016 fair value of plan assets balance	= €829.5 million

Given that Klammer contributes €47 million into the pension plan in 2016, it would record pension expense as:

Pension Expense	63.7 million	
Other Comprehensive Income		5.0 million
Accrued/Prepaid Pension Cost		11.7 million
Cash		47.0 million

At the end of the period Klammer will show an accrued pension liability of €156.7 million. This amount is equal to the beginning balance of €145 million plus the increase in accrued pension cost during the period.

Source: IAS 19 (See Appendix C at the end of this book.)

> **GOT IT?**
>
> **19-11** When applying the corridor approach, what are the three steps in determining the amount of amortization of net gain or loss?
>
> **19-12** 🌐 List and define the potential components of pension expense under amended IAS 19. In addition, how are differences between expected and actual returns treated?
>
> **19-13** 🌐 Compare how prior service cost is treated under amended IAS 19 relative to its treatment under U.S. GAAP.

WHAT ARE THE ADDITIONAL ISSUES RELATED TO ACCOUNTING FOR PENSIONS?

LEARNING OBJECTIVE 19.4
Understand several important additional issues related to accounting for pension plans.

Several other issues have an impact on pension accounting. These include conceptual issues, reporting issues, and technical issues.

Conceptual Issues

The accounting for prior service cost and the pension liability has been controversial because of the conceptual issues surrounding the topics.

Prior Service Cost Accounting for prior service cost has been controversial due to its complexity and economic consequences. When examining how to initially account for prior service cost, accounting regulators considered four alternatives:

1. *Account for prior service cost prospectively.* This method would require the prior service cost to be expensed in the current and future periods, and no liability be recorded when the cost arises. It is argued that this method does not provide a faithful representation because all the services performed by the employees were completed in previous periods. Also, the lack of recognition of a pension obligation is a violation of the concept of a liability.
2. *Recognize the total amount as an expense in the period in which it arises (i.e., the current period) and record a liability.* This procedure also does not provide a faithful representation because the services were performed by the employees in previous periods and not in the current period.
3. *Recognize the liability and reduce other comprehensive income, and then amortize the prior service cost as a component of pension expense. In addition, the liability is reduced and other comprehensive income is increased as the prior service amount is amortized.* This procedure does not faithfully represent pension expense because the services were performed by the employees in previous periods and are expensed in the current and future periods.
4. *Decrease retained earnings (as a retrospective adjustment because they reflect prior service) and record a liability.* This procedure would violate the all-inclusive income concept because the total amounts would never be included in the income statement.

Accounting regulators settled on the third alternative of recognizing a liability and reducing other comprehensive income. While this approach has the advantage of recognizing the liability in full, it is not representationally faithful. By recording the prior service cost amount in other comprehensive income, it postpones the impact on net income until the periods in which the prior service costs are amortized. Most accountants felt that the second alternative of recognizing a liability and expense in the current period was the best alternative. However, many constituents argued that it would create negative economic consequences in that it might tend to discourage companies from adopting, or changing, pension plans because of the related effect (i.e., decrease) on net income of the current period.

Presentation of Pension Plan Assets An additional conceptual issue involves the disclosure of assets in the pension plan. *Assets* are probable future economic benefits obtained or controlled by a company as a result of past transactions or events. As indicated earlier, a company that has a pension plan typically makes periodic payments to a separate legal entity, the pension fund asset manager. This entity assumes the responsibility for safeguarding and investing the pension assets (to earn a return on the assets), and for making benefit payments to retired employees. There are two alternative views for accounting by the employer for these pension assets:

- *Funding is a discharge of the pension liability.* This alternative does not view the net assets of the pension plan held by the asset manager as assets of the employer. The principal reasons are that: (1) the funding agency is a separate legal entity (e.g., a trust) with legal title to the plan assets; (2) the assets can be used only for the benefit of the employees and retirees, and ordinarily cannot be returned to the employer; (3) the employer's obligation is to make contributions to the funding agency, and the agency pays the actual pension benefits; and (4) the employer's obligation may be limited by termination of the plan.
- *The pension liability is not discharged until the retiree receives the pension payment.* This alternative views the pension plan assets as assets of the employer as long as the employer remains obligated to provide benefits defined by the plan. In addition, the pension trust is a legal device controlled by the employer for funding the pension obligation. Although the asset manager holds legal title to the assets, the employer is at risk with regard to the assets and ultimately reaps the rewards of economic ownership of them. If the assets grow, the employer's future contributions will be reduced. If the assets do not grow, or if losses are sustained, future contributions will be increased.

The second alternative is the approach required by GAAP, except that the projected benefit obligation is netted against the pension plan assets to determine the underfunding (liability) or overfunding (asset). It is also important to note that, in cases where a company has multiple defined benefit pension plans, the plans cannot be netted against each other and must be reported separately on the balance sheet.

Pension Liabilities Another conceptual issue regarding accounting for pension plans involves identifying and recording pension plan liabilities. *Liabilities* are probable future sacrifices of economic benefits arising from present obligations of a company to transfer assets or provide services in the future as a result of past transactions or events.

Generally, it is agreed that a pension is a form of deferred compensation. An employer's pension obligation may be viewed as an obligation to make contributions to the plan, or as an obligation to employees for pensions promised. A company cannot know the exact amount of the pension obligation for each employee until the employee (or related beneficiary) dies. Therefore, actuaries can only estimate the amount of the obligation using assumptions about employee turnover, life expectancy, and other variables.

In making the decision on what liability should be used in pension accounting, regulators examined five alternatives to determine which best met the recognition-measurement criteria of a liability:

1. *Contributions Based on an Actuarial Funding Method.* Under this alternative, it is argued that the employer has an obligation to make contributions to the plan rather than directly to employees. In this scenario, the employer's liability would be based on the actuarial funding method used for funding the plan, in which case the only recorded pension liability would be for contributions due but not yet paid.
2. *Amount Attributed to Employee Service to Date.* This alternative is based on the concept that the employer's pension obligation arises as the employees work and that the transaction resulting in the obligation is the employees' service. The pension

transaction is an exchange whereby employees render service for pension benefits (deferred compensation) in addition to current compensation. The resulting obligation for deferred compensation (the projected benefit obligation) is recorded in a manner similar to current compensation.
3. *Termination Liability.* This alternative would be based on the argument that the employer's obligation should be limited to the amount that it must pay when the plan is terminated. Those disagreeing believe that a company is a going concern and that an assumption of plan termination would be inappropriate unless there is clear evidence to the contrary.
4. *Amount of Vested Benefits.* Under this alternative, the employer's obligation would be based on the vested benefits earned by the employees. Nonvested benefits are contingent on and result from future services and, therefore, create a liability only as they become vested in future periods. Those disagreeing believe that vesting is a legal transaction and that it is probable that a portion of the nonvested benefits will become vested and, therefore, meet the definition of a liability.
5. *Amount Payable to Retirees.* This alternative is a form of "pay-as-you-go" accounting whereby the employer's liability arises only during the period in which pension benefits will be paid to employees. Under this alternative, the liability would be readily measurable. Those disagreeing believe that this approach is a violation of the accrual concept of accounting.

Accounting regulators settled on the second alternative. The only exception made is that the projected benefit obligation is netted against the pension plan assets to determine the underfunding (liability) or overfunding (asset).

Reporting Issues

We now turn from conceptual issues to reporting issues for statement of cash flows disclosures and vested benefits.

Statement of Cash Flows Disclosures
A company reports the cash it paid to fund its pension plan as a cash outflow in the operating activities section of its statement of cash flows. If a company uses the indirect method to report its operating cash flows, it adds any increase in its accrued pension cost (liability), or any decrease in its prepaid pension cost (asset), to net income in the operating activities section of its statement of cash flows. It subtracts from net income any decrease in its accrued pension cost (liability), or any increase in its prepaid pension cost (asset). Note that this adjustment is only for the amount of the accrual for the difference between the expense and the funding. It does not include the amount of the adjustment for the over- or underfunding because that amount did not affect net income.

Vested Benefits
Vested benefits are pension benefits earned by employees that are not contingent on future service with the company. That is, the employees will receive retirement benefits based on service to date, even if they terminate employment. The Employee Retirement Income Security Act (ERISA) specifies the minimum vesting requirements that companies must follow. A company must disclose the vested portion of the accumulated benefit obligation. Also, the vesting provisions affect calculations made by the company's actuary because it is necessary to estimate the number of employees who will leave before vesting of their pension benefits occurs.

Technical Issues

We now turn to the technical issues involving calculating the amortization of prior service cost, the Employee Retirement Income Security Act of 1974, the Pension Protection Act of 2006, pension settlements and curtailments, and multiemployer plans.

Calculation of Amortization of Prior Service Cost
In **Example 19.1e**, the calculation of pension expense included the amortization of a prior service cost and an "average

life" of 20 years was used to determine the amount of the amortization. While this straight-line amortization method is allowed, another method of calculating the amount of the amortization of prior service cost exists. This preferred method assigns an equal amount to each future service period for each active participating employee who is expected to receive future benefits under the plan. Because the FASB did not give this method a title, we will refer to it as the "years-of-future-service" method.

Example: Amortization of Prior Service Cost

At the beginning of 2018, Watt Company has nine employees who are participating in its pension plan and who are expected to receive benefits. One employee (A) is expected to retire after 3 years, one (B) after 4, two (C and D) after 5, two (E and F) after 6, and three (G, H, and I) after 7 years. **Example 19.4** shows the computation of the amortization fraction.

EXAMPLE 19.4 Computation of Amortization Fraction

Employees	Expected Years of Future Service	Number of Service Years Rendered in Each Year						
		2016	2017	2018	2019	2020	2021	2022
A	3	1	1	1				
B	4	1	1	1	1			
C, D	5	2	2	2	2	2		
E, F	6	2	2	2	2	2	2	
G, H, I	7	3	3	3	3	3	3	3
Total		9	9	9	8	7	5	3
Amortization fraction		9/50	9/50	9/50	8/50	7/50	5/50	3/50

First, Watt computes the number of service years rendered by the nine employees in each calendar year. Thus, in 2016, there are 9 service years rendered, while in 2020 there are only 7 service years rendered because employees A and B have retired. The total number of these service years is 50. Next, Watt computes the amortization fraction for each year by dividing the total service years in each calendar year by the total of 50. In 2016, 9/50 is the amortization fraction, whereas in 2020, 7/50 is the fraction.

If we assume that Watt's actuary computed the total prior service cost at the beginning of 2016 to be $400,000, the company calculates the amount of the amortization each year as shown in **Example 19.4a**.

Watt includes the calculated amount of amortization in the total pension expense on its income statement for each year. The remaining prior service cost is the balance at the end of the previous year minus the amount amortized for the year.

To compute the alternative straight-line amortization, Watt calculates the average remaining service life of the participating employees. Watt computes the total number of service years rendered (50) by adding the expected years of service for all employees and dividing by the number of employees. Using the information from **Example 19.4**, this gives an average service life of 5.56 years:

$$\frac{3(A) + 4(B) + 5(C) + 5(D) + 6(E) + 6(F) + 7(G) + 7(H) + 7(I)}{9 \text{ employees}} = 5.56 \text{ years}$$

Under the straight-line amortization method, Watt amortizes $71,942 ($400,000 ÷ 5.56 years) each year from 2016 through 2020 to increase the pension expense. In 2021, the amortization is only $40,290, the amount needed to reduce the remaining prior service cost to zero. Note that if an amendment caused a decrease in future

EXAMPLE 19.4a

Amortization of Prior Service Cost: Years-of-Future-Service Method

Year	Total Prior Service Cost[a]	Amortization Fraction[b]	Amortization to Increase Pension Expense[c]	Remaining Prior Service Cost[d]
2016	$400,000	9/50	$72,000	$328,000
2017	400,000	9/50	72,000	256,000
2018	400,000	9/50	72,000	184,000
2019	400,000	8/50	64,000	120,000
2020	400,000	7/50	56,000	64,000
2021	400,000	5/50	40,000	24,000
2022	400,000	3/50	24,000	—

[a] Computed by actuary
[b] From Example 19.4
[c] $400,000 × Amortization Fraction
[d] Balance from End of Previous Year (or Initial Balance) − Amortization for the Current Year

benefits, the resulting "negative" prior service cost is amortized in the same manner to decrease pension expense each period. ■

Pension Legislation The primary purpose of the Employee Retirement Income Security Act of 1974 (ERISA) is to create standards for the operation and maintenance of pension funds and prevent abuses in the handling of these funds. ERISA provides guidelines for employee participation in pension plans, vesting provisions, minimum funding requirements, financial statement disclosure, and the administration of the plan. ERISA also created the Pension Benefit Guaranty Corporation (PBGC), an organization that provides benefits to employees covered by plans that have been terminated (usually because of the bankruptcy of the sponsoring company). The PBGC receives an annual fee for every employee covered by a pension plan that is subject to the PBGC.

The *Pension Protection Act of 2006* made many changes to the requirements that company pension plans must follow, including minimum funding requirements. A company must fund its pension plan each year at an amount that at least equals the service cost for the year plus the amount needed to amortize any underfunding over a maximum of 7 years.

Pension Plan Settlements and Curtailments In recent years, many companies have either *settled* (terminated) or *reduced* (curtailed) their defined benefit pension plans. Some have settled their defined benefit pension plans and substituted defined contribution plans. Others have reduced the benefits to be paid to employees, while continuing the defined benefit pension plans. **GAAP requires that a company include the net gain or loss from a settlement or curtailment in its net income of the period.**

Multiemployer Plans In our examples, we assumed that the pension plan is a single-employer plan. That is, the plan is maintained by one company for its employees. In contrast, a **multiemployer plan** involves two or more unrelated companies in which assets contributed by each company are available to pay benefits to the employees of all the involved companies. Generally, these plans result from collective-bargaining agreements with unions. Each company recognizes as pension expense the required contribution for the period. In other words, these plans are treated as defined contribution plans. Cash-basis accounting is allowed because of the difference in the nature of the obligation of the company and the difficulty of obtaining *reliable* information for each separate company.

GOT IT?

19-14 What are the two alternative views for presentation of pension plan assets by the employer? Which is consistent with GAAP?

19-15 Conceptually, what are the four possible alternative methods for accounting for the prior service cost that arises from pension plan modifications? Which one is required by GAAP?

19-16 What are the five possible alternative methods of determining the extent of a company's pension plan liability? Which one is required by GAAP?

19-17 Does GAAP specify the minimum amount that a company must pay into its pension fund each year? If not, how is the amount determined?

19-18 What is a pension plan settlement? Curtailment? How should the net gain or loss from a settlement or curtailment be accounted for by a company?

19-19 Where should a company report the cash it paid to fund its pension plan when preparing its statement of cash flows?

LEARNING OBJECTIVE 19.5

Explain and account for other postretirement benefit plans (OPRBs).

HOW DO YOU ACCOUNT FOR OTHER POSTRETIREMENT BENEFITS?

In addition to providing pensions to their employees, many companies also provide two types of additional benefits: *other postemployment benefits* and *other postretirement benefits*.

Other postemployment benefits (**OPEBs**) are provided to former employees after employment but *before* retirement. Other postemployment benefits include payments such as termination benefits, job training and counseling and supplemental unemployment benefits. Under GAAP, a company must accrue the cost of these benefits during employment and recognize the amount as an expense and a liability if the four criteria for the recognition of compensated absences are met, as we discussed in Chapter 9. If any one of the criteria is not met, the company records the expense and liability when the liability is probable and the amount can be reasonably estimated, in accordance with accounting for contingencies.[17]

In the rest of this section, we discuss **other postretirement benefits (OPRBs)**, which include all forms of benefits provided to former employees *after* their retirement, other than pensions. Healthcare benefits typically are the most significant of these other postretirement benefits, but some companies also provide dental benefits, eye care, tuition assistance, life insurance, legal services, and financial advisory services. Our discussion focuses on accounting for healthcare benefits because they usually are the largest dollar amount, present the greatest measurement difficulties, and are the most controversial.

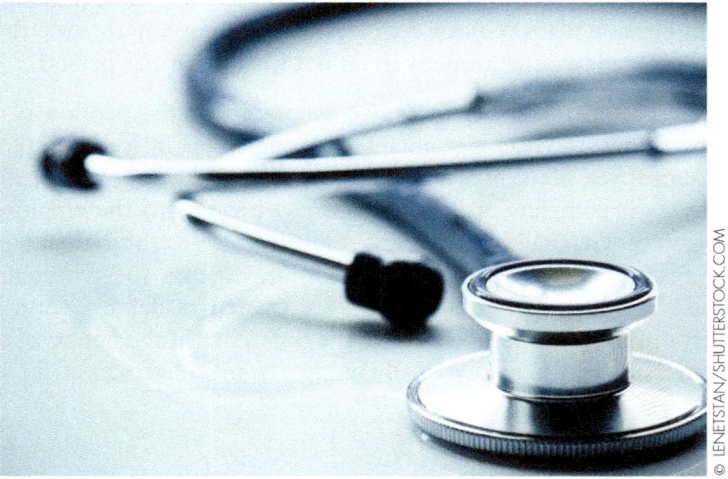

[17] FASB ASC 712-25: Compensation – Nonretirement Postemployment Benefits, Recognition.

GAAP requires that a company accrue the cost of OPRBs during the periods in which its employees earn the benefits.[18] In contrast to the cash-basis accounting for OPRBs that was originally used, this accrual accounting requirement has had a dramatic impact on the financial statements of many companies, by improving the statement's relevance and representational faithfulness.

Conceptual Overview of Other Postretirement Benefits

It is easy to argue that accrual accounting is more *relevant* than cash-basis accounting because costs are recognized as expenses in the periods in which the benefits are earned. For OPRBs, the benefits are earned while the employee is working, not when he or she is retired. Therefore, the *relevance* of a company's income statement is enhanced by inclusion of the OPRB expense. In addition, the recognition of OPRB obligations enhances the relevance of the balance sheet.

However, the measurement problems associated with OPRBs created considerable controversy. Because of the numerous assumptions about future benefits required to measure OPRB costs, it can be argued that OPRB costs cannot be measured with sufficient *representational faithfulness to* warrant the increased relevance. The measurement of the various amounts used in accounting for OPRBs is even more difficult than for pensions. For example, healthcare plans agree to pay for some or all of a service, the amount and timing of which are unknown. However, pension payments are tied to more predictable variables of length of service and pay levels. Also, healthcare plans require an estimate of such items as the medical-cost trend rate and marital and dependency status during retirement. Furthermore, because of the totally new information that is required, companies were concerned that the costs of implementation would be fairly high and might well exceed the benefits obtained.

Those who favored the new principles argued that knowledge of these costs is essential for rational decision making by management and that accounting includes many estimates. Also, they argued that this OPRB cost information is useful for lending and investment decisions and that such decisions are never based on certainty. Therefore, they argued that it is better for a company to record the information based on the best estimates and provide disclosures of the subjectivity of the amounts rather than to report only cash payments.

Similarities to and Differences from Pensions Because pensions and OPRBs are both postretirement benefits, it is helpful to understand their similarities and differences in considering GAAP for OPRBs. The basic argument that accounting for OPRBs should be similar to the principles used for pensions is they both involve the concept of a liability. Recall that a *liability* of a company is a probable future sacrifice of economic benefits arising from present obligations of the company to transfer assets or provide services to other entities in the future as a result of past transactions or events. The term *obligations* includes not only legal duties defined in a contract, but also equitable and constructive obligations based on promises or moral responsibility.

Some argue that a company offering OPRBs is essentially providing deferred compensation to employees because the benefits received during retirement were earned during the period of employment. Therefore, the company incurs an obligation as its employees provide services. GAAP follows this viewpoint.

Others argue that many OPRBs do not have the same explicit legal contract as a pension agreement, and the obligation of the company to continue to provide benefits may not be formally stipulated in a contract. Some argue that there is no liability if the company has the right to withdraw the benefits. Some also argue a company has no obligation for OPRBs until its employees retire because they must retire to obtain the benefit. However, recent court decisions have not allowed companies to withdraw rights

---

[18] FASB ASC 715-10: Compensation-Retirement Benefits, Overall and FASB ASC 715-60: Compensation-Retirement Benefits, Defined Benefit Plans, Other Postretirement.

from retired employees and made it difficult to withdraw rights already earned by current employees. This has created constructive obligations in which the future sacrifices are probable. Therefore, the concept of a liability appears to have been satisfied.

The major differences between healthcare OPRBs and pensions are as follows:

- *Beneficiary.* While the beneficiary of a pension plan is generally the retired employee, a company usually provides OPRBs to the retired employee, spouse, and dependents up to, say, age 21.
- *Benefit.* The pension benefit is defined as a fixed dollar amount that is paid monthly. The OPRB, however, usually is not limited in amount because benefits are paid no matter how long or serious the illness, benefits are paid as used, and the amount of benefits varies geographically. Also, the amount is difficult to predict because of the incidence of new illnesses and the use of new treatments.
- *Funding.* Companies fund pension plans because of ERISA requirements, and the contributions are tax-deductible. On the other hand, companies often do not fund OPRBs because there are no legal requirements and, although the payments for OPRB services are tax-deductible, the contributions into the plan are not tax-deductible.

Accounting Principles

GAAP requires that companies follow accounting principles for OPRBs that closely parallel those for pensions. (Because we assume that you have studied the discussion of accounting for pensions, this section is simplified. However, it may be helpful to review those principles as we discuss the OPRB principles.)

Two additional concepts need to be understood.

- The **expected postretirement benefit obligation** (**EPBO**) is the actuarial present value of the benefits a company expects to pay under the terms of the postretirement benefit plan. The present value amount is measured as of the balance sheet date, and it is based on the benefits that employees will receive after their expected retirement dates.
- The **accumulated postretirement benefit obligation** (**APBO**) is the actuarial present value of the benefits attributed to employee service rendered to a specific date.

Prior to the date in which the employee becomes fully eligible for the benefits, the APBO is the portion of the EPBO attributed to that employee's service rendered to that date. On or after the full eligibility date, the APBO and EPBO for an employee are the same. Thus, **the difference between the EPBO and APBO is the amount of the benefits that has been earned to date versus the total amount of benefits expected to be paid to employees.**

Net Postretirement Benefit Expense

The net postretirement benefit expense[19] that a company reports on its income statement generally includes the following components:

$$\begin{aligned} &\text{Service Cost} \\ &+ \text{Interest Cost} \\ &- \text{Expected Return on Plan Assets} \\ &+ \text{Amortization of Prior Service Cost} \\ &\pm \text{Amortization of Net Gain or Loss} \\ &= \text{OPRB Expense} \end{aligned}$$

Service Cost The *service cost* is the actuarial present value of the expected postemployment benefit obligation attributed to services of the employees during the current period. Typically, a company provides OPRB benefits on an all-or-nothing basis. That is,

---

[19] GAAP uses this term rather than the more commonly used term, OPEB, because other benefits such as layoff benefits may be paid after employment but before retirement.

benefits are generally not defined in terms of years of service. Therefore, an equal amount of the expected benefits is attributed to each year of the attribution period (discussed later). The discount (interest) rate used to calculate the service cost is the rate of return on high quality fixed-income investments currently available.

Interest Cost The *interest cost* is the increase in the accumulated postretirement benefit obligation due to the passage of time. Because the OPRB is a deferred compensation plan in which future payments are discounted to their present values, interest accrues because of the passage of time. Interest cost is calculated as follows:

$$\text{Interest Cost} = \text{Accumulated Postretirement Benefit Obligation at the Beginning of the Period} \times \text{Discount Rate}$$

The interest rate used to calculate the accumulated postretirement benefit obligation is the same rate as that used for the service cost. The interest cost is added to the computation of the postretirement benefit expense.

Expected Return on Plan Assets The *expected return on plan assets* is the expected increase in the plan assets due to investing activities. Plan assets are held by the separate fund management company and include investments in securities such as stocks and bonds, as well as other investments. The expected return is calculated as follows:

$$\text{Expected Return} = \text{Fair Value of Plan Assets at the Beginning of the Period} \times \text{Expected Long} - \text{Term Rate of Return on Plan Assets}$$

The rate of return reflects the average rate of earnings expected on the assets invested to provide for the benefits included in the projected benefit obligation. If the OPRB plan is not funded, the expected return on plan assets is zero. Because OPRBs often are *not* funded, we do not discuss this component further.

Amortization of Prior Service Cost The *prior service cost* is the increase (decrease) in the accumulated postretirement benefit obligation that results from plan amendments (and at the initiation of the plan). It is recorded as a liability and as a negative element of other comprehensive income at the date of the plan amendment. The prior service cost is then amortized each period and included in the computation of the OPRB expense. The required journal entries are discussed later in the chapter. **The prior service cost is amortized by assigning an equal amount to each remaining year of service until full eligibility for benefits is reached for each plan participant active at the date of amendment.** If all or almost all of a plan's participants are fully eligible for benefits, the prior service cost is amortized instead, based on the remaining life expectancy of the plan participants. Straight-line amortization over the average remaining years of service to full eligibility is also allowed for simplicity. The amortization amount is added in the computation of the postretirement benefit expense if the benefits are increased and subtracted if the benefits are decreased.

Amortization of the Net Gain or Loss *Gains* and *losses* are changes in the amount of either the accumulated postretirement benefit obligation or fair value of the plan assets resulting from experience different from that assumed, or from changes in assumptions. The entire gain or loss is *not* recognized in the period in which it occurs. Any gain or loss that is not recognized in OPRB expense in the period it occurs is recognized as a component of other comprehensive income. Amortization of any net gain or loss included in other comprehensive income is included in the postretirement benefit expense of a given year if, at the beginning of the year, the cumulative net gain or loss from previous periods included in accumulated other comprehensive income exceeds a "corridor."[20] If amortization is required, the minimum amortization is the excess divided by the average

---

[20] The corridor is defined as 10% of the greater of the accumulated postemployment benefit obligation or the fair value of the plan assets.

remaining service period of active plan participants (or if most of the plan participants are retired, over their average remaining life expectancy). The total amount of any gain (loss) recognized is deducted (added) in the computation of the postretirement benefit expense.

OPRB Liability

Because a company usually does not fund the plan, it increases a liability, **accrued postretirement benefit cost**, each period by an amount equal to the expense. The company decreases this account by payments made to retired employees. As with pensions, GAAP also requires that the difference between the accumulated postretirement benefit obligation and the plan assets be recognized as a liability on the balance sheet.

Attribution Period

Attribution is the process of assigning the cost of postretirement benefits to periods of employee service. The attribution period begins with the date of hire or the date that credit for service begins, and ends on the date that the employee is eligible for full benefits, as shown in Exhibit 19.5. Thus, the expected postretirement benefit obligation is attributed to the periods of employee service until the full eligibility date. However, the measurement of the accumulated postretirement benefit obligation at the full eligibility date is based on the benefits an employee is expected to receive and the expected retirement date. This results in the **attribution period** (**recognition period**) and the measurement period being different. Specifically, the period over which a company recognizes the service cost is based only on the period to full eligibility. However, measurement of the service cost is based on the period beyond that date to the expected retirement date.

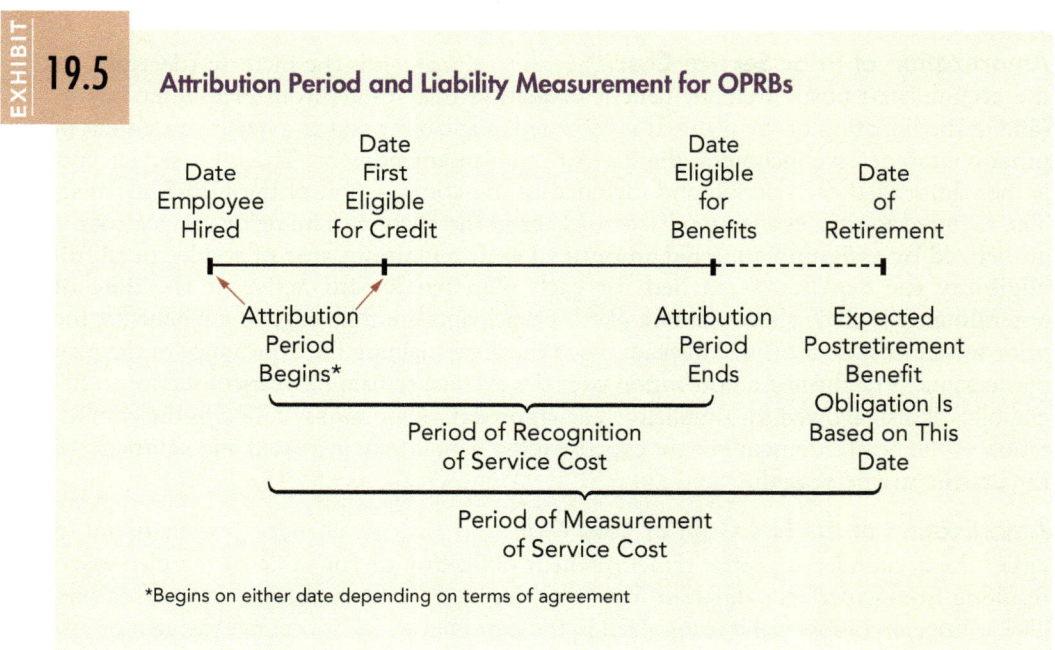

EXHIBIT 19.5 Attribution Period and Liability Measurement for OPRBs

*Begins on either date depending on terms of agreement

Differences from Accounting for Pensions

GAAP requires accounting principles that closely parallel the accounting for pensions. Three major differences are:

- Although the attribution period is defined in the same way, the effect is different because the benefit formulas for most pension plans link benefits to years of service and salary levels. The result is that, for pension plans, the expected retirement date

and date of full eligibility are the *same*. For many OPRBs, however, the attribution process causes the two dates to be *different*.
- The interest component of the net postretirement benefit expense is based on the accumulated postretirement benefit obligation. However, the interest component of the pension expense is based on the projected benefit obligation.
- The OPRB liability (or asset) is the difference between the accumulated postretirement benefit obligation (which is based on the benefits employees will receive for services rendered to date) and the fair value of the OPRB plan assets. However, the pension liability (or asset) is the difference between the projected benefit obligation (which is based on expected future pay increases) and the fair value of the pension plan assets.

OPRB Disclosure

GAAP requires disclosures for OPRBs that are similar to those discussed for pension plans. In addition, it requires the following disclosures (not required for pensions):[21]

- the assumed healthcare cost trend rates
- the effect of a 1% increase and a 1% decrease in the assumed healthcare cost trend rates on the aggregate of the service cost and the interest cost, as well as on the accumulated postretirement benefit obligation for healthcare benefits
- a description of the direction and pattern of change in the assumed healthcare cost trend rates, together with the ultimate trend rate(s) and when that rate is expected to be achieved
- if applicable, the amounts and types of securities included in the plan assets and the approximate amount of future benefits covered by insurance contracts
- if applicable, the cost of providing special or contractual termination benefits provided during the period and a description of the event
- an explanation of any significant change in the benefit obligation or plan assets not otherwise apparent from the other disclosures

Example: Accounting for OPRBs

Livingston Company adopts a healthcare plan for retired employees on January 1, 2016. At that time, Livingston has two employees and one retired employee. **Example 19.5** provides information related to this plan. To determine eligibility for benefits, Livingston retroactively gives credit to the date of hire for each employee.

Livingston recognizes the accumulated postretirement benefit obligation on January 1, 2016, as follows:

Other Comprehensive Income: Prior Service Cost	100,000	
Accrued Postretirement Benefit Cost		100,000

Livingston makes the following three journal entries to record the OPEB items at December 31, 2016. It records the expense for the year and, because the plan is not funded, the accompanying liability as follows:

Postretirement Benefit Expense	31,100	
Accrued Postretirement Benefit Cost		31,100

The second entry records the payment of retirement benefits:

Accrued Postretirement Benefit Cost	1,500	
Cash		1,500

---

[21] FASB ASC 715-20-50 Compensation – Retirement Plans, Defined Benefit Plans General, Disclosure.

> ## EXAMPLE 19.5 Accrual of Postretirement Healthcare Benefits
>
> **BASIC INFORMATION**
>
> - The plan is started on January 1, 2016, and is not funded.
> - The discount rate is 10%.
> - All employees were hired at age 25.
> - All employees become eligible for full benefits at age 55.
> - Employee Claire was paid $1,500 postretirement healthcare benefits in 2016.
> - The company elects to use straight-line amortization for any prior service cost.
>
> *Additional information on January 1, 2016*
>
> | Employee | Status | Age | Expected Retirement Age | Accumulated Postretirement Benefit Obligation[a] |
> |---|---|---|---|---|
> | Angie | Employee | 47 | 65 | $ 15,000 |
> | Brian | Employee | 53 | 65 | 60,000 |
> | Claire | Retired | 70 | — | 25,000 |
> | | | | | $100,000[b] |
>
> [a] Actuarially determined at January 1, 2016.
> [b] This amount is the prior service cost.
>
> **Computation of Postretirement Benefit Expense for 2016**
>
> | | |
> |---|---|
> | Service cost | $ 1,100[a] |
> | Interest cost | 10,000[b] |
> | Expected return on plan assets | 0 |
> | Amortization of prior service cost | 20,000[c] |
> | Gain or loss | 0 |
> | | $31,100 |
>
> [a] Actuarially determined based on expected postretirement benefit obligation. Note that there is no service cost for Claire because she has passed the date for full eligibility.
> [b] Accumulated Postretirement Benefit Obligation at January 1, 2016 × Discount Rate, or $100,000 × 10%.
> [c] $100,000 ÷ 5, or $20,000. Employee Claire has reached eligibility for full benefits. Employees Angie and Brian have 8 and 2 years of service, respectively, to reach the full eligibility date (age 55). Therefore, the average remaining service period is (8 + 2) ÷ 2 = 5 years..

The third entry reduces the prior service cost included in Accumulated Other Comprehensive Income from $100,000 to $80,000 to avoid "double counting" the portion of the prior service cost that was amortized and reduced net income:

Accrued Postretirement Benefit Cost	20,000	
Other Comprehensive Income: Prior Service Cost		20,000

This results in a balance in the accrued postretirement benefit cost of $109,600 ($100,000 + $31,100 − $1,500 − $20,000). In addition, at the end of 2016, the accumulated postretirement benefit obligation is calculated as follows:

1/1/2016 accumulated postretirement benefit obligation balance	= $100,000
+ Service cost for 2016	= 1,100
+ Interest cost for 2016	= 10,000
− Payment of retirement benefits for 2016	= (1,500)
12/31/2016 accumulated postretirement benefit obligation balance	= $109,600

Because the plan is not funded, the credit balance in the Accrued Postretirement Benefit Cost account reflects the underfunded status of the OPRB plan and no adjustment is necessary. Livingston reports this underfunded amount as its OPRB plan liability on its December 31, 2016, balance sheet. ■

GOT IT?

19-20 Why do pension plans tend to be funded while OPRB plans are unfunded?

19-21 What are other postemployment benefits? How are they distinguished from other postretirement benefits?

19-22 List and briefly define the five components of OPRB expense.

19-23 How does accounting for other postretirement benefits differ from accounting for defined benefit pension plans?

REVIEW CENTER

At the beginning of the chapter, we discussed the importance of accounting for pension and postretirement benefits as well as the challenges that they present. We also identified several objectives you would accomplish after reading the chapter. The objectives are listed below and followed by a brief summary of the key points.

KEY TAKEAWAYS

- A pension plan requires a company to provide income to its retired employees in return for services they provided during their employment and can be classified as either a:
  - defined contribution plan if the employer's annual contribution is based on a formula but no commitment is made as to the future benefits to be paid to employees
  - defined benefit plan if it promises fixed retirement benefits determined by a formula that is usually based on the employee's earnings and length of service

LEARNING OBJECTIVE 19.1
Understand the characteristics of pension plans.

KEY TERMS

actuaries, p. 19-4
contributory plan, p. 19-4
defined benefit plan, p. 19-3
defined contribution plan, p. 19-3

noncontributory plan, p. 19-4
nonqualified pension plans, p. 19-4
pension plan, p. 19-2
qualified pension plans, p. 19-4

KEY TAKEAWAYS

- For a defined contribution pension plan, pension expense is equal to the company's required contribution. The company does not recognize a pension obligation (unless it has not satisfied the contribution requirement) nor does it recognize any plan assets.
- For a defined benefit pension plan, pension expense consists of five components:
  - Service cost—the actuarial present value of the benefits earned by employees during the year (the discount rate used is a settlement rate reflecting the rate at which the pension benefits could be effectively settled)

LEARNING OBJECTIVE 19.2
Explain the GAAP for pension plans, including computing pension expense and recognizing pension liabilities and assets.

- Interest cost—the increase in the projected benefit obligation (the present value of the benefits earned by employees based on their expected future compensation levels) due to the passage of time
- Expected return on plan assets—the expected increase in plan assets that are invested
- Amortization of prior service cost—the amortization of the cost of retroactive benefits granted to employees
- Amortization of gain or loss—the amortization of the change in the projected benefit obligation and the fair value of the pension plan assets resulting from actual experience being different from that which is assumed
• Because pension expense (determined by GAAP) usually differs from the amount funded, the difference is recorded as either a(n):
  - Asset—prepaid pension cost—if pension expense is less than the amount funded
  - Liability—accrued pension cost—if pension expense is greater than the amount funded
• The difference between the projected benefit obligation and the fair value of the pension plan assets at the end of the year is the funded status of the pension plan. The company reports it as an accrued pension cost liability (in the case of an underfunded plan) or prepaid pension cost asset (in the case of an overfunded plan) on its year-end balance sheet.

KEY CALCULATIONS

Interest Cost = Projected Benefit Obligation at the Beginning of the Period × Discount Rate

$$\text{Minimum Corridor Amortization} = \frac{\text{Cumulative Net Gain or Loss at the Beginning of the Year} - \text{Corridor at the Beginning of the Year}}{\text{Average Remaining Service Period of the Active Employees Expected to Receive Benefits under the Pension Plan}}$$

Pension Expense = Service Cost + Interest Cost − Expected Return on Plan Assets + Amortization of Prior Service Cost + or − Gain or Loss

Beginning Projected Benefit Obligation
+ Prior Service Cost
= Adjusted Beginning Projected Benefit Obligation
+ Service Cost for Period
+ Interest Cost on Projected Benefit Obligation
+ Actuarial Losses (or − Actuarial Gains)
− Benefit Payments to Retirees
= Ending Projected Benefit Obligation

Beginning Fair Value of Pension Plan Assets
+ Actual Return on Plan Assets
+ Contributions (Amount Funded) by the Company
− Payments to Retirees
= Ending Fair Value of Pension Plan Assets

KEY TERMS

Accrued/Prepaid Pension Cost, p. 19-11
accumulated benefit obligation, p. 19-10
actual return on plan assets, p. 19-8
actuarial funding method, p. 19-10
corridor, p. 19-9

corridor approach, p. 19-9
discount rate, p. 19-10
expected return on plan assets, p. 19-8
funded status, p. 19-11
gain, p. 19-9

interest cost, p. 19-7
loss, p. 19-9
market-related value, p. 19-11
net periodic pension cost, p. 19-7
pension expense, p. 19-7

prior service cost, p. 19-9
projected benefit obligation, p. 19-7
service cost, p. 19-7
vested benefit obligation, p. 19-10

KEY TAKEAWAYS

LEARNING OBJECTIVE 19.3
Account for defined benefit pension plans.

- Service cost and interest cost (computed as the discount rate multiplied by the projected benefit obligation at the beginning of the period) increase pension expense.
- The expected return (computed as the fair value of the plan assets at the beginning of the period multiplied by the expected long-term rate of return) is a reduction in pension expense. The actual return increases the plan assets.
- The difference between pension expense and the amount funded is recorded in a liability/asset account, accrued/prepaid pension cost.
- If a company grants retroactive benefits to its employees, the prior service cost is recorded as an increase in a liability and a decrease in other comprehensive income. It is amortized into pension expense using either the straight-line method over the average remaining service life of the employees or the years-of-future-service method. The amortized amount is also recorded as a reduction in accrued/prepaid pension cost and an increase in other comprehensive income.
- Current accounting guidance provides three methods for companies to recognize gains and losses in pension expense:
  - immediate recognition in pension expense
  - minimum amortization using the corridor approach
  - any systematic and rational approach that results in faster amortization than the corridor approach
- The excess of the net gain or loss over a corridor amount (determined as 10% of the greater of the projected benefit obligation or the fair value of the plan assets at the beginning of the period) is the minimum amount amortized into pension expense on a straight-line basis over the average remaining service life of the employees.

KEY TAKEAWAYS

LEARNING OBJECTIVE 19.4
Understand several important additional issues related to accounting for pension plans.

- Several conceptual issues arise in accounting for pensions:
  - Any prior service cost is recognized as a liability and expensed in the current and future periods (arguably a violation of the matching concept).
  - The under- or overfunded amount of the pension plan is reported on the employer's balance sheet.
- Other issues that impact pension accounting include statement of cash flow disclosures, vested benefits, calculation of the amortization period for prior service cost, pension legislation, pension settlements and curtailments, termination benefits paid to employees, and multiemployer plans.

KEY TERM
multiemployer plan, p. 19-39

KEY TAKEAWAYS

LEARNING OBJECTIVE 19.5
Explain and account for other postretirement benefit plans (OPRBs).

- Other postretirement benefits, or OPRBs, include all forms of benefits paid to former employees after their retirement, other than pensions. The cost of OPRBs is accrued during the periods that the employees earn the benefits by providing service.
- While the accounting for OPRBs is similar to that of pensions, two concepts should be understood:
  - The expected postretirement benefit obligation (EPBO) is the actuarial present value of the benefits a company expects to pay.

- The accumulated postretirement benefit obligation (APBO) is the actuarial present value of the benefits attributed to employee service rendered to a specific date.
- Similar to pensions, the net postretirement benefit expense consists of service cost, interest cost (discount multiplied by the APBO at the beginning of the period), expected return (generally zero because the OPRB is usually not funded), amortization of prior service cost, and amortization of gain or loss.
- An OPRB liability is recorded because the amount of the postretirement benefit expense is greater than the amount funded.
- Similar to pensions, any underfunding is reported as a liability on the balance sheet.
- The cost of OPRBs is recognized over the attribution period (generally beginning with the date of hire and ending on the date the employee is eligible for full benefits). However, the APBO at the full eligibility date is measured from the date of hire to the expected retirement date.

KEY CALCULATION

OPRB Expense = Service Cost + Interest Cost − Expected Return on Plan Assets
+ Amortization of Prior Service Cost + or − Amortization of Net Gain or Loss

KEY TERMS

accrued postretirement benefit cost, p. 19-44
accumulated postretirement benefit obligation (APBO), p. 19-42
attribution period, p. 19-44
attribution, p. 19-44
expected postretirement benefit obligation (EPBO), p. 19-42

other postemployment benefits (OPEBs), p. 19-40
other postretirement benefits (OPRBs), p. 19-40
recognition period, p. 19-44

ANSWERS TO REAL REPORT QUESTIONS

Real Report 19.1 Answers Honeywell—Pension Disclosures

1. Honeywell's Net periodic benefit (income) cost for its Primary defined benefit plan in 2013 was $104 million (income). For 2012, Honeywell recognized Net periodic benefit cost (expense) of $709 million. The expected return on plan assets was the largest component in 2013 and 2012, while amortization of prior service cost was the smallest.
2. The actual return on Honeywell's Primary plan assets of $3,191 million was greater than the expected return of $1,076 million.
3. At the end of 2013, the accumulated benefit obligation for the U.S. plan was $15,700 million, and the U.S. plan projected benefit obligation was $16,290 million. The difference in these amounts is due to the fact that the projected benefit obligation includes projected salary increases while the accumulated benefit obligation is based on current employee salaries.
4. For its U.S. plans, Honeywell is in a net asset position of $437 million at the end of fiscal year 2013. This amount is equal to the fair value of the plan assets of $16,727 million minus the projected benefit obligation of $16,290 million. However, at the end of 2012, Honeywell was in a net liability position of $2,772 million (projected benefit obligation of $17,117 million minus $14,345 fair value of plan assets).
5. The use of a lower discount rate during 2013 would increase the ending balance in the projected benefit obligation, increase the balance in the accrued pension cost, increase service cost, decrease the actuarial loss, and decrease interest cost for 2013. However, interest cost in 2014 would be higher (because of the increase in the projected benefit obligation at the end of 2013) relative to the amount that would have been reported if the discount rate were not changed.

MULTIPLE-CHOICE (AICPA ADAPTED)

Select the best answer for each of the following.

M19-1 The actuarial present value of all the benefits attributed by the pension benefit formula to employee service rendered before a specified date based on expected future compensation levels is the:
LO 19.1

a. projected benefit obligation
b. prior service cost
c. service cost
d. accumulated benefit obligation

M19-2 On January 1, 2016, Soloman Company changes the factor in the benefit formula from 0.02 to 0.022, retroactive to the adoption of the plan. The amendment will result in a(n):
LO 19.2

a. decrease in projected benefit obligation
b. increase in service cost
c. decrease in pension expense
d. increase in plan assets

M19-3 A company with a defined benefit pension plan makes all of the following disclosures except the:
LO 19.2

a. amount of the pension expense, showing each of the components separately
b. estimates of contributions for the next 5 years
c. funded status of the plan
d. discount rate

Refer to the following information for M19-4 through M19-6. Spath Company adopted a noncontributory defined benefit pension plan on January 1, 2016. Spath uses the benefit/years-of-service method, which results in the following information:

	2016	2017
Service cost	$300,000	$450,000
Amount funded	240,000	390,000
Discount rate	10%	10%
Expected rate of return	10%	10%

The actual rate of return is equal to the expected return, and the company has not made any payments to retirees.

M19-4 Refer to the information for Spath Company above. What is the pension expense for the year ended December 31, 2017?
LO 19.2
LO 19.3

a. $390,000 c. $456,000
b. $426,000 d. $480,000

M19-5 Refer to the information for Spath Company above. In the journal entry to record pension expense, what is the amount of the credit entry to accrue pension cost on December 31?
LO 19.2
LO 19.3

	2016	2017
a.	$ 0	$ 60,000
b.	$60,000	$ 60,000
c.	$60,000	$ 66,000
d.	$60,000	$126,000

M19-6 Refer to the information for Spath Company to the left. As of December 31, 2017, what is the balance in the pension plan asset fund?
LO 19.2
LO 19.3

a. $456,000 c. $654,000
b. $630,000 d. $840,000

M19-7 Which of the following is not a component of pension expense?
LO 19.2
LO 19.3

a. amount funded
b. service cost
c. expected return on plan assets
d. interest cost

M19-8 Davison Company has a noncontributory defined benefit pension plan for its employees. During 2016, the pension plan has a discount rate of 8%, service cost of $98,000, plan assets as of 1/1/16 of $432,000, and an expected return on plan assets of $34,560. On December 31, 2016, Davison contributed $90,000 to the pension plan, resulting in a credit to Accrued/Prepaid Pension Cost of $6,300. What is the amount of the projected benefit obligation on January 1, 2016?
LO 19.2
LO 19.3

a. $332,000 c. $410,750
b. $345,600 d. $432,000

M19-9 McCollum Company amended its noncontributory defined benefit pension plan at the beginning of 2013. The prior service cost related to this amendment amounts to $240,000. Information regarding the four participating employees is as follows:
LO 19.4

Employee	Expected to Retire After
A	Year 1
B	Year 2
C	Year 4
D	Year 5

Using the straight-line method, what is the amount of prior service cost to be amortized in 2016?

a. $0 c. $60,000
b. $40,000 d. $80,000

M19-10 A company records a loss and a liability for termination benefits paid to employees when the:
LO 19.4

a. employee accepts the offer
b. amount can be reasonably estimated
c. employee accepts the offer or the amount can be reasonably estimated
d. employee accepts the offer and the amount can be reasonably estimated

REVIEW EXERCISES

RE19-1 Crabtree Company's pension expense for the current year is $200,000, and the company funds $185,000. Prepare the journal entry Crabtree will make on December 31.
LO 19.2
LO 19.3

RE19-2 Oak Company's pension expense for the current year is $300,000, and the company funds $327,000. Prepare the journal entry Oak will make on December 31.
LO 19.2
LO 19.3

RE19-3 Pinecone Company has plan assets of $500,000 at the beginning of the current year and expects to earn 12% on its plan assets during the year. Pinecone's service cost is $230,000, and its interest cost is $55,000. Compute Pinecone's pension expense for the current year.
LO 19.2
LO 19.3

RE19-4 Palm Company's actuary has computed its prior service cost to be $5,000,000. Palm amortizes the prior service cost by the straight-line method over the remaining 25-year service life of its active employees. During the current year, Palm also recognizes $330,000 of service cost and $22,000 of interest cost. Compute Palm's pension expense for the current year.
LO 19.2
LO 19.3

RE19-5 Raspberry Company's actuary has computed its prior service cost to be $8,000,000. Raspberry amortizes the prior service cost by the straight-line method over the remaining 20-year service life of its active employees. During the current year, Raspberry also recognizes service cost of $560,000 and interest cost of $100,000. At the beginning of the year, the plan assets were $1,500,000, and the company expects to earn 10% on its plan assets. Compute Raspberry's pension expense for the current year.
LO 19.2
LO 19.3

RE19-6 **Next Level** At the end of the current year, Maple Company has a projected benefit obligation of $439,000 for its pension plan, and the fair value of its pension plan assets is $450,000. Maple has a debit balance of $5,000 in its Accrued/Prepaid Pension Cost account. Prepare the journal entry to adjust its Accrued/Prepaid Pension Cost account. Assume that the difference between the projected benefit obligation and the fair value of the pension plan assets is due to the actual return on plan assets being different from the expected return on plan assets. Indicate why and where (and the amount) Maple would report its Accrued/Prepaid Pension Cost.
LO 19.2
LO 19.3

RE19-7 **Next Level** At the end of the current year, Chelsey Company has a projected benefit obligation of $600,000 for its pension plan, and the fair value of its pension plan assets is $580,000. Chelsey has a credit balance of $32,000 in its Accrued/Prepaid Pension Cost account. Prepare the journal entry to adjust its Accrued/Prepaid Pension Cost account. Assume that the difference between the projected benefit obligation and the fair value of the pension plan assets is due to the actual return on plan assets being different from the expected return on plan assets. Indicate why and where (and the amount) Chelsey would report its Accrued/Prepaid Pension Cost.
LO 19.2
LO 19.3

RE19-8 At the beginning of the current year, Willow Company adopts a pension plan and awards retroactive benefits to its employees. Willow's actuary computes these prior service costs to be $280,000. Willow amortizes the prior service costs by the straight-line method over the remaining 14-year service life of its active employees. Prepare the journal entries to record the prior service costs and the related year-end adjusting entry for the current year.
LO 19.2
LO 19.3

RE19-9 Given the following information for Tyler Company's pension plan at the beginning of the year, calculate the corridor, excess net loss (gain), and amortized net loss (gain). Assume an average remaining service life of 15 years.
LO 19.2
LO 19.3

Cumulative net loss	$ 25,000
Projected benefit obligation: actual	220,000
Fair value of pension plan assets	200,000

RE19-10 At the beginning of Year 1, Cactus Company has three employees: A, B, and C. Employee A has 3 expected years of future service, Employee B has 4 expected years of future service, and Employee C has 5 expected years of future service. Using the year-of-future-service method, compute the amortization fraction for Years 1 through 5 that Cactus would use to amortize its prior service cost.
LO 19.4

RE19-11 Bluebird Company has an accumulated postretirement benefit obligation (prior service cost) of $500,000 at the beginning of the year, and the average remaining service life of its employees is 20 years. The service cost for the year is $5,000. Bluebird uses a discount rate of 8%. Given this information, calculate Bluebird's postretirement benefit expense for the current year.
LO 19.5

EXERCISES

E19-1 **Pension Expense** Bailey Company has had a defined benefit pension plan for several years. At the end of 2016, Bailey's actuary provided the following information for 2016 regarding the pension plan: (1) service cost, $115,000; (2) expected return on plan assets, $14,000; (3) amortization of net loss, $2,000; (4) interest cost on projected benefit obligation, $16,000; and (5) amortization of prior service cost, $4,000. Bailey decides to fund an amount at the end of 2016 equal to its pension expense.
LO 19.2
LO 19.3

Required:
1. Compute the amount of Bailey's pension expense for 2016 and prepare the related journal entry.
2. **Next Level** If Bailey had decided to fund an amount less than the 2016 pension expense, how would the company's balance sheet be affected?

E19-2 **Pension Expense and Liability** On December 31, 2016, Robey Company accumulated the following information for 2016 in regard to its defined benefit pension plan:
LO 19.2
LO 19.3

Service cost	$105,000
Interest cost on projected benefit obligation	12,000
Expected return on plan assets	11,000
Amortization of prior service cost	2,000

On its December 31, 2015, balance sheet, Robey had reported an accrued/prepaid pension cost liability of $14,000.

Required:
1. Compute the amount of Robey's pension expense for 2016.
2. Prepare all the journal entries related to Robey's pension plan for 2016 if it funds the pension plan in the amount of (a) $108,000, (b) $107,000, and (c) $112,000.
3. **Next Level** Assuming Robey's beginning 2016 Accumulated Other Comprehensive Income: Prior Service Cost balance was $60,000 what would be its ending balance?
4. **Next Level** How much would Robey need to fund its pension plan for 2016 in order to report an accrued/prepaid pension cost asset of $5,000 at the end of 2016?

E19-3 **Interest Cost and Return on Assets** On December 31, 2016, Palmer Company determined that the 2016 service cost on its defined benefit pension plan was $120,000. At the beginning of 2016, Palmer had pension plan assets of $520,000 and a projected benefit obligation of $600,000. Its discount rate (and expected long-term rate of return on plan assets) for 2016 was 10%. There are no other components of Palmer's pension expense; the company had an accrued/prepaid pension cost liability at the end of 2015.
LO 19.2
LO 19.3

Required:
1. Compute the amount of Palmer's pension expense for 2016.
2. Prepare the journal entry to record Palmer's 2016 pension expense if it funds the pension plan in the amount of (a) $128,000 and (b) $120,000.

E19-4 **Pension Expense Different Than Funding: One Year** Verna Company has had a defined benefit pension plan for several years. At the end of 2016, Verna accumulated the following information: (1) service cost for 2016, $127,000; (2) projected benefit obligation, 1/1/2016, $634,000; (3) discount rate, 9%; (4) plan assets, 1/1/2016,
LO 19.2
LO 19.3

(continued)

$389,000; and (5) expected long-term rate of return on plan assets, 9%. There are no other components of Verna's pension expense. Verna had an accrued/prepaid pension cost liability at the end of 2015. Verna contributed $128,000 to the pension plan at the end of 2016.

Required:

Compute the amount of Verna's pension expense for 2016 and prepare the related journal entry.

E19-5
LO 19.2
LO 19.3

Pension Expense Different Than Funding: Multiple Years Baron Company adopted a defined benefit pension plan on January 1, 2015. The following information pertains to the pension plan for 2016 and 2017:

	2016	2017
Service cost	$160,000	$172,000
Projected benefit obligation (1/1)	120,000	289,600
Plan assets (1/1)	120,000	294,600
Company contribution (funded 12/31)	165,000	175,000
Discount rate	8%	8%
Expected long-term (and actual) rate of return on plan assets	8%	8%

There are no other components of Baron's pension expense.

Required:

1. Compute the amount of Baron's pension expense for 2016 and 2017.
2. Prepare the journal entries to record the pension expense for 2016 and 2017.

E19-6
LO 19.2
LO 19.3

Determination of Projected Benefit Obligation Several years ago, Lewad Company established a defined benefit pension plan for its employees. The following information is available for 2016 in regard to its pension plan: (1) discount rate, 10%; (2) service cost, $142,000; (3) plan assets (1/1), $659,000; and (4) expected return on plan assets, $65,900. There is no amortization of prior service cost, and there is no gain or loss. On December 31, 2016, Lewad contributed $143,000 to the pension plan, resulting in a credit to Accrued/Prepaid Pension Cost of $8,200.

Required:

1. Compute the amount of Lewad's projected benefit obligation on January 1, 2016.
2. **Next Level** How would a decrease in the discount rate affect Lewad's pension expense?

E19-7
LO 19.2
LO 19.3

Pension Expense Different Than Funding: Multiple Years Carli Company adopted a defined benefit pension plan on January 1, 2015, and funded the entire amount of its 2015 pension expense. The following information pertains to the pension plan for 2016 and 2017:

SHOW ME HOW

	2016	2017
Service cost	$200,000	$215,000
Projected benefit obligation (1/1)	180,000	396,200
Plan assets (1/1)	180,000	406,400
Company contribution (funded 12/31)	212,000	220,000
Discount rate	9%	9%
Expected long-term (and actual) rate of return on plan assets	8%	8%

There are no other components of Carli's pension expense.

Required:

1. Compute the amount of Carli's pension expense for 2016 and 2017.
2. Prepare the journal entries to record the pension expense for 2016 and 2017.
3. **Next Level** If the actual return on plan assets was greater than the expected return in 2016 how would it effect the calculation of pension expense?

E19-8
LO 19.2
LO 19.3

Pension Expense and Liability Farber Company adopted a defined benefit pension plan on January 1, 2016, at which time it awarded retroactive benefits to its employees. This prior service cost amounted to $200,000, which the company did not fund. Farber planned to amortize this prior service cost in the amount of $10,000 per year. Farber determined its pension expense (which included the prior service cost amortization) to be $75,000 for

2016, of which the company funded $74,000. At the end of 2016, the fair value of the pension plan assets was $74,000 and Farber's projected benefit obligation was $265,000.

Required:

Prepare all the journal entries related to Farber's pension plan for 2016. Include a brief explanation for each journal entry.

E19-9 **Pension Expense and Liability** Pitchford Company adopted a defined benefit pension plan on January 1, 2016, at which time it awarded retroactive benefits to its employees. The following information is available in regard to this plan:

LO 19.2
LO 19.3

Prior service cost on 1/1/16 related to retroactive benefits:	$300,000 (not funded)
Planned amortization of prior service cost	$ 25,000 per year
Pension expense for 2016 ($95,000 funded)	$105,000*
Fair value of plan assets, end of 2016	$ 95,000
Projected benefit obligation, end of 2016	$380,000

*Includes amortization of prior service cost

Required:

Prepare all the journal entries related to Pitchford's pension plan for 2016. Include a brief explanation for each journal entry.

E19-10 **Prior Service Cost** On January 1, 2016, Smith Company adopted a defined benefit pension plan. At that time, Smith awarded retroactive benefits to its employees, resulting in a prior service cost that created a projected benefit obligation of $1,250,000 on that date (which it did not fund). Smith decided to amortize the prior service cost by the straight-line method over the 20-year average remaining service life of its active participating employees. Smith's actuary has also provided the following additional information for 2016 and 2017: (1) service cost: 2016, $147,000; 2017, $153,000; (2) expected (and actual) return on plan assets: 2017, $33,000; and (3) projected benefit obligation: 1/1/2017, $1,522,000. The discount rate was 10% in both 2016 and 2017. Smith contributed $330,000 and $350,000 to the pension fund at the end of 2016 and 2017, respectively. There are no other components of Smith's pension expense.

LO 19.2
LO 19.3

Required:

1. Compute the amount of Smith's pension expense for 2016 and 2017.
2. Prepare all the journal entries related to Smith's pension plan for 2016 and 2017.
3. **Next Level** If the prior service cost was vested, explain how Smith's pension expense for 2016 would be different under amended IAS 19.

E19-11 **Net Gain or Loss** Lee Company has a defined benefit pension plan. During 2015, for the first time, Lee experienced a difference between its expected and actual projected benefit obligation. At the beginning of 2016, Lee's actuary accumulated the following information related to Lee's pension plan:

LO 19.2
LO 19.3

Net loss (1/1/2016)	$ 44,000
Actual projected benefit obligation (1/1/2016)	228,000
Fair value of plan assets (1/1/2016)	260,000

On December 31, 2016, Lee is in the process of computing the net gain or loss to include in its pension expense for 2016. Lee has determined that the average remaining service life of its employees is 9 years. There was no difference between the company's expected and actual return on plan assets in 2016.

Required:

Compute the amount of the net gain or loss to include in the pension expense for 2016, assuming that Lee uses the corridor approach. Indicate whether it is an addition to or a subtraction from pension expense.

E19-12 **Net Gain or Loss** Hudson Company's actuary has provided the following information concerning the company's defined benefit pension plan at the end of 2016:

LO 19.2
LO 19.3

Fair value of plan assets (1/1/2016)	$350,000
Actual projected benefit obligation (1/1/2016)	360,000
Expected projected benefit obligation (1/1/2016)	424,000
Average remaining service life of employees	10 years

The difference between the actual and expected projected benefit obligation first occurred in 2015.

(continued)

Required:
1. Compute the amount of the gain or loss for Hudson's pension plan at the beginning of 2016, assuming that Hudson uses the corridor approach.
2. Compute the amount of the net gain or loss to include in Hudson's pension expense for 2016. Indicate whether it is an addition to or a subtraction from pension expense.
3. **Next Level** If Hudson Company is using IFRS, how would the gain or loss be treated?

E19-13 **Straight-Line Amortization** At the beginning of 2016, Brent Company amended its defined benefit pension plan. The amendment entitled five active participating employees to receive increased future benefits based on their prior service. Brent's actuary determined that the prior service cost for this amendment amounts to $330,000. Employee A is expected to retire after 1 year, employee B after 2, employee C after 3, employee D after 4, and employee E after 5 years.

LO 19.4

Required:
Using the straight-line method, (1) compute the average remaining service life, and (2) prepare a schedule to amortize the prior service cost.

E19-14 **Years-of-Future-Service Amortization** Refer to the information provided in **E19-13**.

LO 19.4

Required:
Using the years-of-future-service method, prepare a set of schedules to determine (1) the amortization fraction for each year and (2) the amortization of the prior service cost.

E19-15 **Methods to Amortize Prior Service Cost** Wolz Company, a small business, has had a defined benefit pension plan for its employees for several years. At the beginning of 2016, Wolz amended the pension plan; this amendment provides for increased benefits based on services rendered by certain employees in prior periods. Wolz's actuary has determined that the related prior service cost amounts to $140,000. Wolz has four participating employees who are expected to receive the increased benefits. The following is a schedule identifying the employees and their expected years of future service:

LO 19.4

SHOW ME HOW

Employee Numbers	Expected Years of Future Service
1	2
2	3
3	4
4	5

Required:
1. **Next Level** Using the straight-line method, (a) compute the average remaining service life and (b) prepare a schedule to amortize the prior service cost.
2. **Next Level** Using the years-of-future-service method instead, prepare a set of schedules to determine (a) the amortization fraction for each year and (b) the amortization of the prior service cost.

E19-16 **Accounting for an OPRB Plan** On January 1, 2016, Flash and Dash Company adopted a healthcare plan for its retired employees. To determine eligibility for benefits, the company retroactively gives credit to the date of hire for each employee. The following information is available about the plan:

LO 19.5

SHOW ME HOW

Service cost	$ 30,000
Accumulated postretirement benefit obligation (1/1/16)	120,000
Expected return on plan assets	0
Amortization of Prior service cost	10,000
Payments to retired employees during 2016	5,000
Interest rate	10%
Average remaining service period of active plan participants (1/1/16)	12 years

Required:
1. Compute the OPRB expense for 2016 if the company uses the average remaining service life to amortize the prior service cost.
2. Prepare all the required journal entries for 2016 if the plan is not funded.

PROBLEMS

P19-1 **Pension Expense Worksheet** When Turner Company adopted its defined benefit pension plan on January 1, 2016, it awarded retroactive benefits to its employees. These retroactive benefits resulted in a prior service cost of $980,000 that created a projected benefit obligation of the same amount on that date (which it did not fund). Turner decided to amortize the prior service cost using the years-of-future-service method. Turner's actuary and funding agency have provided the following additional information for 2016 and 2017: (1) service cost: 2016, $187,000; 2017, $189,000; (2) plan assets: 1/1/2016, $0; 1/1/2017, $342,000; (3) expected long-term (and actual) rate of return on plan assets: 2017, 9%; (4) discount rate for both 2016 and 2017: 8%; and (5) amortization fraction for prior service cost: 2016, 80/980; 2017, 79/980. Turner contributed $342,000 and $336,000 to the pension fund at the end of 2016 and 2017, respectively. No retirement benefits were paid in either year. There are no other components of Turner's pension expense. Ignore any adjustment of accumulated other comprehensive income.

LO 19.3

Required:
Prepare a pension plan worksheet that includes the calculation of Turner's pension expense for 2016 and 2017, the reconciliation of the beginning and ending projected benefit obligation for 2016 and 2017, the reconciliation of the beginning and ending plan assets for 2016 and 2017, and the journal entry to record the pension expense at the end of 2016 and 2017, indicating whether each component is a debit or credit.

P19-2 **Pension Expense Worksheet** Carpenter Company adopted a defined benefit pension plan for its employees on January 1, 2016. At the time of adoption, the pension contract provided for retroactive benefits for the company's active participating employees. These retroactive benefits resulted in a prior service cost of $1,860,000 that created a projected benefit obligation of the same amount on that date. Carpenter decided to amortize the prior service cost by the straight-line method over the 20-year average remaining service life of the employees. The following additional information is also available for 2016 and 2017: (1) discount rate for both 2016 and 2017: 8%; (2) company contribution (funded 12/31): 2016, $550,000; 2017, $530,000; (3) expected long-term rate of return on plan assets: 9%; (4) actual rate of return on plan assets, 10%; (5) service cost: 2016, $257,000; 2017, $264,000; and (6) plan assets: 1/1/2016, $0. Carpenter paid pension benefits of $30,000 each year. Carpenter uses the corridor approach to amortize gains or losses. There are no other components of Carpenter's pension expense. Ignore any adjustment of accumulated other comprehensive income.

LO 19.3

Required:
Prepare a pension plan worksheet that includes the calculation of Carpenter's pension expense for 2016 and 2017, the reconciliation of the beginning and ending projected benefit obligation for 2016 and 2017, the reconciliation of the beginning and ending plan assets for 2016 and 2017, and the journal entry to record the pension expense at the end of 2016 and 2017, indicating whether each component is a debit or credit.

P19-3 **Components of Pension Expense** Nelson Company has a defined benefit pension plan for its employees. At the end of 2016 and 2017, the following information is available in regard to this pension plan:

LO 19.2
LO 19.3

	2016	2017
Expected return on plan assets	$ 27,000	$ 28,000
Amortization of net gain	3,000	—
Amortization of net loss	—	4,000
Amortization of prior service cost	7,000	6,000
Company contribution (funded 12/31)	220,000	248,000
Interest cost on projected benefit obligation	42,000	45,000
Service cost	211,000	217,000
Prior Service Cost (as of 1/1)	96,000	89,000

Required:
1. Compute the amount of Nelson's pension expense in 2016 and 2017.
2. Based on the available information, prepare all the journal entries related to Nelson's pension plan for 2016 and 2017.
3. **Next Level** If the prior service cost was vested, explain how Nelson Company's pension expense for 2016 would be different under IFRS.

P19-4
LO 19.2
LO 19.3

Pension Expense Different Than Funding On January 1, 2016, Parkway Company adopted a defined benefit pension plan. At that time, Parkway awarded retroactive benefits to its employees, resulting in a prior service cost of $2,180,000 on that date (which it did not fund). Parkway decided to amortize this cost by the straight-line method over the 16-year average remaining service life of its active participating employees. Parkway's actuary and funding agency have also provided the following additional information for 2016 and 2017:

	2016	2017
Service cost	$ 340,000	$ 348,000
Projected benefit obligation (1/1)	2,180,000*	2,738,000
Plan assets (1/1)	0	670,000
Discount rate	10%	10%
Expected long-term (and actual) rate of return on plan assets	—	9%

*Due to the prior service cost

Parkway contributed $670,000 and $700,000 to the pension fund at the end of 2016 and 2017, respectively. There are no other components of Parkway's pension expense. At the end of 2017, the projected benefit obligation was $3,359,800 and the fair value of the pension plan assets was $1,430,300.

Required:
1. Compute the amount of Parkway's pension expense for 2016 and 2017.
2. Prepare all the journal entries related to Parkway's pension plan for 2016 and 2017.
3. What is the total accrued/prepaid pension cost at the end of 2017? Is it an asset or a liability?

P19-5
LO 19.2
LO 19.3

Pension Expense Different Than Funding Lane Company was incorporated in 2004. Because it had become successful, Lane established a defined benefit pension plan for its employees on January 1, 2016. Due to the loyalty of its employees, Lane granted retroactive benefits to them. These retroactive benefits resulted in $1,240,000 of prior service cost on that date. Lane decided to amortize this cost using the years-of-future-service method. Lane's actuary and funding agency have provided the following additional information for 2016 and 2017:

	2016	2017
Expected long-term (and actual) rate of return on plan assets	—	9%
Amortization fraction for prior service cost	48/620	46/620
Discount rate	9%	9%
Plan assets (1/1)	$0	$690,000
Projected benefit obligation (1/1)	$1,240,000*	$1,814,600
Service cost	$463,000	$475,000

*Due to the prior service cost

Lane contributed $690,000 and $660,000 to the pension fund at the end of 2016 and 2017, respectively. No retirement benefits were paid in 2016 or 2017. There are no other components of Lane's pension expense. At the end of 2017, the projected benefit obligation was $2,452,914 and the fair value of the pension plan assets was $1,412,100.

Required:
1. Compute the amount of Lane's pension expense for 2016 and 2017.
2. Prepare all the journal entries related to Lane's pension plan for 2016 and 2017.
3. What is the total accrued/prepaid pension cost at the end of 2017? Is it an asset or a liability?
4. Prepare a schedule that reconciles the beginning and ending amounts of the projected benefit obligation for 2017.

P19-6
LO 19.2
LO 19.3

Net Gain or Loss For several years, Kent Company has had a defined benefit contribution plan for its employees. During those years, Kent experienced differences between its expected and actual projected benefit obligation. These differences resulted in a cumulative net gain or loss at the beginning of each subsequent year. The following schedule summarizes the amounts related to the preceding information for the years 2016 through 2018:

Year	Cumulative Net Loss (Gain)*
2016	$25,000
2017	26,000
2018	36,500

*At beginning of year

Kent's actuary and funding agency have also provided the following information about the company's actual projected benefit obligation and fair value of plan assets at the beginning of each year:

Year	Projected Benefit Obligation	Plan Assets
2016	$220,000	$200,000
2017	275,000	270,000
2018	320,000	325,000

Kent uses the corridor approach and amortizes any excess gain or loss by the straight-line method over the average remaining service life of its active participating employees. Because of a consistent pattern of employee hirings and retirements, this average service life has remained at 20 years for 2016 through 2018.

Required:
Prepare a schedule to compute the amount of the net gain or loss to include in Kent's pension expense for 2016 through 2018. Indicate whether the gain or loss is added to or subtracted from the pension expense.

P19-7 **Pension Liability Adjustments** In Fisk Company's negotiations with its employees' union on January 1, 2016,
LO 19.2 the company agreed to an amendment that increased the employee benefits based on services rendered in prior
LO 19.3 periods. This resulted in an $80,000 prior service cost that increased the projected benefit obligation of the company. Due to financial constraints, Fisk decided not to fund the total increase in its pension obligation at that time.

Prior to 2016, it had been Fisk's policy to fund only some of its pension expense each year so that the fair value of the plan assets at the end of the year was less than the year-end projected benefit obligation. As a result, Fisk reported an accrued/prepaid pension cost liability of $40,000 on its December 31, 2015, balance sheet.

Fisk appropriately amortized the prior service cost over a 10-year service life as a component of pension expense in 2016 and 2017. The resulting pension and other information for 2016 and 2017 are as follows:

Year	Pension Expense	Company Contribution[a]	Projected Benefit Obligation[b]	Fair Value of Plan Assets[b]
2016	$137,000	$125,000	$579,000	$455,000
2017	152,900	142,000	769,400	642,500

[a]Funded December 31
[b]At year-end

Required:
1. Prepare all the journal entries related to Fisk's pension plan for 2016.
2. List the amounts of any accounts related to Fisk's pension plan to be reported on the company's December 31, 2016, balance sheet. Indicate in what sections they would be reported.
3. Prepare all the journal entries related to Fisk's pension plan for 2017.
4. List the amounts of any accounts related to Fisk's pension plan to be reported on the company's December 31, 2017, balance sheet. Indicate in what sections they would be reported.

P19-8 **Determination of Pension Plan Amounts** Various pension plan information of Kerem Company for 2016 and
LO 19.2 2017 is as follows:
LO 19.3

	2016	2017
Service cost	$100,000	(j)
Interest cost on projected benefit obligation	54,000	(g)
Discount rate	9%	9%
Amortization of prior service cost	4,000	4,000
Plan assets (fair value), 1/1*	500,000	615,000
Projected benefit obligation, 1/1**	(a)	720,000
Expected long-term rate of return on plan assets	(b)	11%
Amortization of net loss	(d)	700
Accrued pension cost (liability), 12/31	(f)	(k)
Average service life of employees	10 years	10 years
Pension expense	(e)	110,850
Cumulative net loss, 1/1	68,000	(i)
Expected return on plan assets	50,000	(h)
Corridor	(c)	72,000

*1/1/2018: $762,000
**1/1/2018: $857,800

(continued)

Required:
Next Level Fill in the blanks lettered (a) through (k). All the necessary information is listed. It is not necessary to calculate your answers in alphabetical order.

P19-9
LO 19.4

SHOW ME HOW

Amortization of Prior Service Cost On January 1, 2016, Baznik Company adopted a defined benefit pension plan. At that time, Baznik awarded retroactive benefits to certain employees. These retroactive benefits resulted in a prior service cost of $1,200,000 on that date (which it did not fund). Baznik has six participating employees who are expected to receive the retroactive benefits. Following is a schedule that identifies the participating employees and their expected years of future service as of January 1, 2016:

Employee	Expected Years of Future Service
A	1
B	3
C	4
D	5
E	5
F	6

Baznik decided to amortize the prior service cost to pension expense using the years-of-future-service method. The following are the amounts of the components of Baznik's pension expense, in addition to the amortization of the prior service cost for 2016 and 2017:

	2016	2017
Service cost	$469,000	$507,000
Interest cost on projected benefit obligation	108,000	159,930
Expected return on plan assets	—	85,000

Baznik contributed $850,000 and $830,000 to the pension fund at the end of 2016 and 2017, respectively.

Required:
1. **Next Level** Prepare a set of schedules for Baznik to determine (a) the amortization fraction for each year and (b) the amortization of the prior service cost.
2. **Next Level** Prepare all the journal entries related to Baznik's pension plan for 2016 and 2017.

P19-10
LO 19.2
LO 19.3
LO 19.4

Comprehensive Jay Company has had a defined benefit pension plan for several years. At the beginning of 2016, Jay amended the plan; this amendment provided for increased benefits to employees based on services rendered in prior periods. The prior service cost related to this amendment totaled $88,000. As a result, the projected benefit obligation increased. Jay decided not to fund the increased obligation at the time of the amendment, but rather to increase its periodic year-end contributions to the pension plan.

The following information for 2016 has been provided by Jay's actuary and funding agency and obtained from a review of its accounting records:

Projected benefit obligation (12/31)	$808,090
Service cost	183,000
Discount rate	9%
Cumulative net loss (1/1)	64,500
Company contribution to pension plan (12/31)	200,000
Projected benefit obligation (1/1)*	513,000
Plan assets, fair value (12/31)	698,000
Accrued pension cost (liability) (1/1)	33,000*
Expected (and actual) return on plan assets	48,000
Plan assets, fair value (1/1)	480,000
Retirement benefits paid	30,000

*Before the increase of $88,000 due to the prior service cost from the amendment

Jay decided to amortize the prior service cost and any excess cumulative net loss by the straight-line method over the average remaining service life of the participating employees. It has developed the following schedule concerning these 50 employees:

Employee Numbers	Expected Years of Future Service*	Employee Numbers	Expected Years of Future Service*
1–5	2	26–30	12
6–10	4	31–35	14
11–15	6	36–40	16
16–20	8	41–45	18
21–25	10	46–50	20

*Per employee

Required:
1. Compute the average remaining service life and prepare a schedule to determine the amortization of the prior service cost of Jay for 2016.
2. Prepare a schedule to compute the net gain or loss component of pension expense for 2016.
3. Prepare a schedule to compute the pension expense for 2016.
4. Prepare all the journal entries related to Jay's pension plan for 2016.
5. What is Jay's total accrued/prepaid pension cost at the end of 2016? Is it an asset or liability?

P19-11 **Comprehensive** TAN Company has a defined benefit pension plan for its employees. The plan has been in existence for several years. During 2015, for the first time, TAN experienced a difference between its expected and actual projected benefit obligation. This resulted in a cumulative "experience" loss of $29,000 at the end of 2015, which it recorded and which did not change during 2016. TAN amortizes any excess loss by the straight-line method over the average remaining service life of its active participating employees. It has developed the following schedule concerning these 40 employees:

LO 19.2
LO 19.3
LO 19.4

Employee Numbers	Expected Years of Future Service*	Employee Numbers	Expected Years of Future Service*
1–5	3	21–25	15
6–10	6	26–30	18
11–15	9	31–35	21
16–20	12	36–40	24

*Per employee

TAN makes its contribution to the pension plan at the end of each year. However, it has not always funded the entire pension expense in a given year. As a result, it had an accrued pension cost liability of $65,000 on December 31, 2015.

In addition to the preceding information, the following set of facts for 2016 and 2017 has been assembled, based on information provided by TAN's actuary and funding agency, and obtained from its accounting records:

	2016	2017
Plan assets, fair value (12/31)	$620,500	$860,550
Cumulative net loss (1/1)	29,000	29,000
Expected (and actual) return on plan assets	40,500	62,050
Company contribution to pension plan (12/31)	175,000	178,000
Projected benefit obligation (1/1)	470,000*	686,000
Discount rate	10%	10%
Service cost	169,000	175,000
Plan assets, fair value (1/1)	405,000	620,500

*Includes the cumulative net loss at the end of 2015.

Required:
1. Calculate the average remaining service life of TAN's employees. Compute to one decimal place.
2. Prepare a schedule to compute the net gain or loss component of pension expense for 2016 and 2017, assuming that the company uses the corridor approach. For simplicity, assume the average remaining life calculated in Requirement 1 is applicable to both years.
3. Prepare a schedule to compute the pension expense for 2016 and 2017.
4. Prepare all the journal entries related to TAN's pension plan for 2016 and 2017.
5. What is TAN's total accrued/prepaid pension cost at the end of 2016? Is it an asset or liability?

P19-12 Accounting for an OPRB Plan

LO 19.5 On January 1, 2016, Vasby Software Company adopted a healthcare plan for its retired employees. To determine eligibility for benefits, Vasby retroactively gives credit to the date of hire for each employee. The service cost for 2016 is $8,000. The plan is not funded, and the discount rate is 10%. All employees were hired at age 28 and become eligible for full benefits at age 58. Employee C was paid $7,000 for postretirement healthcare benefits in 2016. On December 31, 2016, the accumulated postretirement benefit obligation for Employees B and C were $77,000 and $41,500, respectively. Additional information on January 1, 2016, is as follows:

Employee Status	Age	Expected Retirement Age	Accumulated Postretirement Benefit Obligation
1. Employee	31	65	$ 14,000
2. Employee	55	65	70,000
3. Retired	67	—	45,000
			$129,000

Required:
1. Compute the OPRB expense for 2016 if Vasby uses the average remaining service life to amortize the prior service cost.
2. Prepare all the required journal entries for 2016 if the plan is not funded.

CASES

COMMUNICATION

C19-1 Financial Reporting for a Defined Benefit Pension Plan
LO 19.2

Fink Company is considering establishing a defined benefit pension plan for its employees. Fink's president is slightly familiar with GAAP and understands that accounting for a defined benefit pension plan may result in certain items being included in the financial statements of the sponsoring company. The president has come to you for help in better understanding these items.

Required:
List each item, summarize how it is calculated, and briefly explain its meaning.

C19-2 Pension Cost Components
LO 19.2
AICPA Adapted

Carson Company sponsors a single-employer IRS qualified defined benefit pension plan. The plan provides that pension benefits are determined by age, years of service, and compensation. Among the components that should be included in the net pension cost recognized for a period are service cost, interest cost, and expected return on plan assets.

Required:
1. What is a qualified pension plan? How does it differ from a nonqualified plan?
2. What types of assumptions must a company make when accounting for a defined benefit pension plan? Are assumptions also needed when accounting for a defined contribution? Explain.
3. Explain how Carson should determine the service cost component of the net pension cost.
4. Explain how Carson should determine the interest cost component of the net pension cost.
5. Explain how Carson should determine the expected return on plan assets component of the net pension cost.

C19-3 Pension and Future Vacation Costs
LO 19.1
LO 19.2
AICPA Adapted

Essex Company has a single-employer defined benefit pension plan and a compensation plan for future vacations for its employees.

Required:
1. Define the interest cost component of net pension cost for a period. Explain how Essex should determine the interest cost component of its net pension cost for a period.
2. Define prior service cost. Explain how Essex should account for prior service cost.
3. What conditions must be met for Essex to accrue compensation for future vacations? Explain the theoretical rationale for accruing compensation for future vacations.

C19-4 Conceptual Issues
LO 19.4

In this chapter, the conceptual issues related to pension liabilities and pension plan assets are discussed.

Required:

Explain how GAAP resolves each of these three conceptual issues.

C19-5 Other Postretirement Benefits
LO 19.5

Companies often provide their employees with postretirement benefits other than pensions. These benefits may include health insurance, life insurance, and disability benefits.

Required:

Explain how the accounting for these other postretirement benefits is similar or dissimilar to accounting for pensions.

CREATIVE AND CRITICAL THINKING

C19-6 Income Smoothing
LO 19.2

Income smoothing is the concept of reducing the period-to-period fluctuations in revenues and expenses in order to decrease the variability of reported income. GAAP generally does not support income smoothing; however, a friend of yours, after studying GAAP, claims, "The use of expected returns and the corridor approach in pension accounting results in income smoothing."

Required:

Describe the methods by which GAAP avoids year-to-year fluctuations in the amount of pension expense.

C19-7 Pension Issues
LO 19.2

MacAdams Company had engaged in large amounts of R&D to develop a new product that would put the company ahead of its Japanese competition. As a result, the company's profits were severely reduced, and the president was concerned about the possibility of a takeover by a European competitor. The president was discussing the situation with the controller and said, "Your accounting principles make me so mad. Here we are working hard to develop a product to beat the rest of the world, and you won't let me treat any of those costs as an asset."

The controller replied, "I understand your frustration. And please remember they are not 'my' principles."

"I know," responded the president. "Do you have any suggestions?"

"Well," the controller replied, "we can't adjust R&D expense, but we can reduce our pension expense. One easy way to increase our profits would be for the board of directors to vote to increase the discount rate used for computing the present values and to increase the expected rate of return on plan assets. Both of those would have the effect of reducing the pension expense."

"Great idea. I will have to remember that when it is time for the year-end bonuses."

Required:

Write a short report evaluating the controller's suggestion.

C19-8 OPRB Issues
LO 19.5

"Will it cost your company your company? Ready for one of the most difficult challenges ever to confront corporate America? One that is estimated to cost up to $400 billion. New FASB regulations will force companies to measure and post as a debit their health expense obligation to current and *future* retirees.... We'll help you minimize the financial impact of these regulations and still enable you to remain responsive to the benefit needs of employees." (Excerpts from an advertisement by CIGNA, a large insurance company.)

"Forget about retiring with all-expenses-paid health care from your employer. About 65% of U.S. companies have reduced benefits. Some have asked retirees to pay more of the costs, while others have eliminated the plans altogether. Blame soaring medical expenses and a new accounting rule that requires companies to post long-term retiree medical benefits as liabilities on their balance sheets." (Adapted from *BusinessWeek*, August 24, 1992, p. 39.)

Required:

1. Critically evaluate the content of the advertisement.
2. Explain why companies may have reduced benefits when they adopted new GAAP.

C19-9 Analyzing Coca-Cola's Postretirement Benefit Disclosures
LO 19.2
LO 19.5

Obtain **The Coca-Cola Company**'s 2013 annual report either using the "Investor Relations" portion of its website (do a web search for Coca-Cola investor relations) or go to http://www.sec.gov

(continued)

and click "Search for company filings" under "Filings and Forms (EDGAR)." Answer each of the questions for (a) the company's pension benefits and (b) the company's other benefits.

Required:
1. How much are Coca-Cola's Pension Benefits expense and Other Benefits expense in 2013?
2. How much are Coca-Cola's actual and expected return on plan assets for its Pension Benefits plans for 2013?
3. How much are Coca-Cola's Projected Benefit obligation and accumulated benefit obligation at December 31, 2013, for its Pension Benefits plans?
4. Is each of Coca-Cola's Pension Benefits and Other Benefits plans in a net asset or liability position at December 31, 2013?
5. Conceptually, what were the effects of the increase in the discount rate in 2013 on the amounts disclosed by the company (no calculations are required)?

C19-10 Ethics and Pensions

You are an accountant for Lanthier Company. Lanthier's president calls you into the office and says, "We have to find a way to reduce our pension costs. They are too high, and they are making us uncompetitive against our foreign competitors whose employees have state-funded pensions. I think we might have to abandon our defined benefit plan, but I know the employees would not be happy about that. I was also thinking that perhaps we could raise the discount rate we use up to the high end of the acceptable range. I also think we need a trustee who will pursue a more aggressive investment strategy for the pension funds; that way we can raise our expected rate of return."

Required:
From financial reporting and ethical perspectives, discuss the issues raised by this situation.

USING CODIFICATION

C19-11 Researching GAAP

Situation
Panther Company currently sponsors a defined benefit pension plan for its employees. At the end of 2016, the plan had a projected benefit obligation of $1,456,000 and fair value of plan assets of $1,629,000. Panther recognized a net pension asset in its balance sheet of $173,000 at the end of 2016. Due to the plans overfunded position, Allison Costello, Panther's CFO, is interested in finding out if it is possible to settle or curtail the plan. Specifically, she is interested in purchasing a portfolio of high-quality bonds that have principal and interest payment dates very similar to the estimated dates pension benefits would be paid.

Directions
1. Research the GAAP and prepare a short memo to Allison Costello that provides guidance on the following issues:

1. What is a pension settlement and pension curtailment?
2. Can the company recognize a gain or loss if it settles its pension plan? What is the amount of the gain or loss?
3. Can the company recognize a gain or loss if it curtails its pension plan? What is the amount of the gain or loss?
4. Would Allison Costello's plan of purchasing high quality bonds qualify as a settlement of a pension plan? Why or why not?

CHAPTER 20

ACCOUNTING FOR LEASES

Where Are All the Buildings?

At the end of fiscal year 2015, **Starbucks** operated 12,235 retail store locations and 12 warehouse, roasting, manufacturing, and distribution facilities totaling 3,780,000 square feet. The company also used an additional 1,000,000 square feet of office space in Seattle for corporate headquarters and other administrative purposes. However, according to Starbucks's Property, Plant, and Equipment footnote (Note 7 in Appendix A), only $411.5 million of buildings are recorded in the company's consolidated balance sheet. This is less than one-third of the total of furniture and fixtures and significantly less than the $5.4 billion of leasehold improvements that Starbucks had made as of the end of fiscal 2015. So you might wonder, where are all the buildings?

Starbucks, like many retailers, leases its retail locations instead of purchasing them. The reasons for this strategy range from allowing more flexibility in store locations to receiving extra benefits from landlords for being a shopping mall's anchor store that is expected to enhance consumer traffic and benefit the other retailers.

In addition, certain leases provide beneficial accounting treatment. By not recording the leased property and the related obligation on its balance sheet, Starbucks appears less risky (e.g., lower debt-to-equity ratio) and more profitable (e.g., higher return on assets) than it would otherwise. However, this accounting treatment did require Starbucks to report rent expense (which it includes in occupancy costs) of $1,137.8 million for 2015. Even though Starbucks recognizes rent expense related to the leased retail locations, growing companies with operating leases generally report less depreciation expense than companies that own retail locations, and less interest expense than companies that use debt to finance retail locations. These financial reporting advantages are important to many companies.

LEARNING OBJECTIVES

After reading this chapter you will be able to

LO 20.1 Explain how to classify leases.

LO 20.2 Explain the advantages and disadvantages of leasing.

LO 20.3 Account for a lessee's operating and capital leases.

LO 20.4 Understand statement of cash flow presentation and disclosure by the lessee.

LO 20.5 Account for a lessor's operating, direct financing, and sales-type leases.

LO 20.6 Understand statement of cash flow presentation and disclosure by the lessor.

LO 20.7 (Appendix 20.1) Examine lease issues related to sale-leaseback transactions, real estate leases, and modification and changes of lease provisions.

Leasing is not just important for retail locations. Almost any asset can either be leased or purchased. Among the most popular leased items are cars, photocopiers, computers, airplanes, railroad boxcars, and buildings. Without the ability to lease, companies would find it more difficult to obtain the right to use property and equipment or upgrade the equipment necessary to operate their business, which, in turn, would adversely affect business and economic growth. Clearly, leasing is an important financial transaction for many companies.

The accounting for leases has an important effect on companies' financial statements. This chapter focuses on long-term leases involving depreciable property such as equipment, machinery, and trucks. We examine operating and capital leases and the disclosures associated with them. We also discuss sale-leaseback transactions, leases of real estate and property attached to real estate, and certain other specialized lease issues in Appendix 20.1.

HOW ARE LEASES CLASSIFIED?

LEARNING OBJECTIVE 20.1
Explain how to classify leases.

For accounting purposes, GAAP defines a **lease** as "an agreement conveying the right to use property, plant, or equipment (land or depreciable assets or both) usually for a stated period of time."[1] A lease involves both a lessee and a lessor:

- A **lessee** acquires the right to use the leased asset in exchange for making future lease payments.
- A **lessor** gives up the right to use the leased asset in exchange for the receipt of future lease payments.

U.S. GAAP recognizes two types of leases: *operating* and *capital*. The basic concept of GAAP is that **a lease that transfers substantially all the risks and benefits of ownership from the lessor to the lessee is, in economic substance, a purchase by the lessee and a sale by the lessor.** This type of lease is a **capital lease**. For the lessee, a capital lease is in substance an asset acquisition and the incurrence of a related liability to make future payments. From the lessor's perspective, it is viewed as either the sale of an asset and the creation of a financial instrument (a receivable under a *sales-type lease*) or as only the creation of a financial instrument (a receivable under a *direct financing lease*). A lease that does *not* transfer substantially all the risks and benefits of ownership is classified as an **operating lease**. An operating lease is viewed by both the lessee and the lessor as a rental agreement, conveying the rights to use an asset for a finite period, but not conveying the majority of the benefits or risks of the asset.

GAAP specifies that a lessee should consider a lease as a transfer of the majority of the risks and benefits of ownership and account for the lease as a capital lease if it meets any one of the following four **capitalization criteria** in Exhibit 20.1.

The fourth criterion in Exhibit 20.1 refers to the present value of the minimum lease payments. For the lessee, **minimum lease payments** are the expected payments over the term of the lease, including:

- minimum periodic payments required by the lease
- payment required by a bargain purchase option (if one exists)
- any guaranteed residual value
- any payments resulting from failure to renew or extend the lease

---
[1] FASB ASC Master Glossary.

> **Lease Capitalization Criteria** — EXHIBIT 20.1
>
> 1. The lease transfers ownership of the property to the lessee by the end of the lease term.
> 2. The lease contains a bargain purchase option.
> 3. The lease term is equal to 75% or more of the estimated economic life of the leased property.
> 4. The present value of the minimum lease payments is equal to 90% or more of the fair value of the leased property to the lessor.[2]

If a lease does not meet any of the four capitalization criteria the lease is classified as an *operating lease*, and the lessee does *not* recognize an asset or a liability. Under an operating lease, the lessee simply recognizes rent expense each period and discloses the terms of the lease in a footnote.

To qualify as a capital lease for the lessor, GAAP adds a second step to the decision framework. A lessor classifies a lease as a capital lease if it meets any one of the four capitalization criteria that are listed in Exhibit 20.1 *and* meets both of the recognition criteria in Exhibit 20.2.

> **Additional Lease Capitalization Criteria for Lessors** — EXHIBIT 20.2
>
> 1. The collectibility of the minimum lease payments is reasonably assured (i.e., predictable).
> 2. No important uncertainties surround the amount of unreimbursable costs yet to be incurred by the lessor under the lease.

These additional criteria apply only to the lessor and are necessary for the lessor to record the sale portion of a capital lease transaction. For the lessor, the lease is a capital lease if it meets one of the four capitalization criteria and both of the recognition criteria. If the lease is classified as a capital lease, the lessor will account for it as either a *sales-type capital lease* or a *direct financing capital lease*. If the fair value of the leased property at the inception of the lease is greater than its cost of carrying value, the lease will be classified a **sales-type capital lease** and a manufacturer's or dealer's profit will be recorded by the lessor. Otherwise, the lease will be classified as a **direct-financing capital lease** and no manufacturer's or dealer's profit will recognized at the inception of the lease.

For the lessor, the lease is an *operating lease* only if it does not meet any of the four capitalization criteria *or* fails *one* of the recognition criteria. In this case, the lessor recognizes rent revenue each period, and the leased asset remains on its balance sheet.

> **GOT IT?**
>
> **20-1** List the four criteria used to determine if a lease is classified as a capital lease by the lessee.
> **20-2** What is the difference between the lessee and lessor?
> **20-3** From a lessor's standpoint, a capital lease must meet one or more of the capitalization criteria of a capital lease as well as two additional criteria. Describe these two additional criteria.

---

[2] Criteria 3 and 4 do not apply if the beginning of the lease term falls within the last 25% of the total estimated economic life. This qualification was added by the FASB to prevent the possible manipulation of the kinds of leases that may result from renewal options. For example, without this qualification, for a machine having an estimated useful life of 25 years and placed under five successive 5-year leases, the first four leases would be classified as operating leases and the last lease would be classified as a capital lease.

INTERNATIONAL DIMENSION

ACCOUNTING FOR LEASES

Although the FASB and IASB have issued new lease accounting guidance that greatly changes accounting for leases, it is important to recognize the similarities and differences between current U.S. GAAP and IFRS. IFRS focus more on the *substance* of the lease agreement rather than the *form*. For this reason, IAS 17 Leases is generally less detailed and is considered more principles-based, while U.S. GAAP lease guidance has more specific form-driven requirements and is generally considered rules-based. To illustrate this point, it is important to examine the five capitalization criteria under IAS 17:

1. The lease transfers ownership of the asset to the lessee by the end of the lease term.
2. The lessee has the option to purchase the asset at a price which is expected to be sufficiently lower than fair value at the date the option becomes exercisable that, at the inception of the lease, it is reasonably certain that the option will be exercised.
3. The lease term is for the *major part* of the economic life of the asset, even if title is not transferred.
4. At the inception of the lease, the present value of the minimum lease payments amounts to at least *substantially all* of the fair value of the leased asset.
5. The leased assets are of a specialized nature such that only the lessee can use them without major modifications being made.[4]

As you can see, the criteria are similar to U.S. GAAP except that IFRS do not contain the "bright-lines" contained in U.S. GAAP. For example, in the third criteria, IFRS use the major part of the economic life of the asset instead of 75% that is used in U.S. GAAP. In addition, in the fourth criteria, IFRS use the term *substantially all* of the fair value of the leased asset as opposed to U.S. GAAP which uses 90%. IAS 17 also contains other conditions that require leases to be capitalized that are not specified under U.S. GAAP. These following conditions would require the lease to be capitalized:

1. if the lessee is entitled to cancel the lease, but the contract requires the lessee to assume the lessor's losses associated with the cancellation
2. if any gains or losses from fluctuations in the fair value of the residual value are rebated to the lessee
3. the lessee has the ability to continue to lease for an additional period at a rent that is substantially lower than market rent[5]

In addition, under IAS 17, a lease meeting one of the capitalization criteria is termed a *finance lease*, whereas GAAP uses the term *capital lease*. U.S. GAAP also contains more detailed disclosures related to lease payments over the next 5 years and the period after 5 years; however, IFRS do not require this disclosure.

Source: IAS 17 Leases (See Appendix C at the end of this book.)

LEARNING OBJECTIVE 20.2

Explain the advantages and disadvantages of leasing.

WHAT ARE THE ADVANTAGES OF LEASING?

Almost anyone who has been in the market for a new car has been confronted with a choice to lease or buy. The lease versus buy decision can be answered by examining the benefits and costs of leasing and making lease payments as opposed to purchasing the

---

[4] IAS 17.10.
[5] IAS 17.11.

asset and making loan payments. Because leasing is a popular method of financing, it is important to examine its advantages as well as its disadvantages.

What Are the Advantages and Disadvantages to the Lessee?

From the lessee's point of view, the advantages (and disadvantages) of leasing may result from financing and strategic issues and include risk reduction and tax issues. However the main issue for many lessees revolves around financial reporting.

Financing Issues When making a loan for a purchase of an asset, banks or lenders normally require an initial payment and finance only a portion of the asset in order to protect themselves in case of default. A lease, however, may provide almost 100% financing, so that the lessee acquires the use of the asset by making little or no initial cash payment. However, the lessor usually charges a higher rate of interest for this benefit, making leasing more expensive for the lessee in the long run relative to purchasing the asset.

The leasing arrangement creates a secured claim on only the leased equipment and not on all assets, as is the case if the company issued general debt to support the purchase of the asset. However, in some circumstances, a lease agreement can offer a lower interest rate than a loan agreement. This can occur when the lessee has a lower tax rate than the lessor, making the depreciation deduction on the leased asset more valuable to the lessor. The lease can be structured so that the lessor receives this tax benefit, and the lessee makes smaller lease payments.

Strategic Issues Many companies cannot afford or do not want the cash outflows associated with purchasing an asset. Some companies, like **Starbucks**, prefer to lease a location for only 10 years, so they do not have to use capital to buy the asset. In addition, leases provide an exit option (through termination of the lease) that may be less costly than if the company was required to sell the asset. Also, many assets are not for sale and can only be leased—such as prime locations in office buildings or retail malls.

Risk Reduction Issues The lease may allow the lessee to reduce risk. One of the greatest risks in purchasing an asset, especially a technology asset, is obsolescence risk, or the risk that the asset will no longer be competitive. Many times, leases are structured so that if equipment becomes obsolete, the lessee can return it or substitute newer equipment. By doing this, the lease transfers risk from the lessee to the lessor. However, the lessee, by not taking an ownership position, gives up the right to any appreciation in the value of the asset. In addition, leases usually contain more restrictive provisions on how the asset can be used.

Tax Issues By deducting lease payments, the lessee can write off the full cost of the asset. If land is being leased, this means the tax deductible lease payment includes a cost of using the land (which would not be tax deductible if owned). The tax benefit is critical for some companies.

Financial Reporting Issues For operating leases, the lease does not add a liability or asset to the lessee's balance sheet (although operating lease commitments are required note disclosures). Therefore, it does not affect certain liquidity, financial leverage, and profitability ratios that use balance sheet and income statement data, such as the current ratio, the debt-to-asset ratio, the debt-equity ratio, and the rate of return on assets. As a result, these ratios tend to be "better" because the leased asset and liability are omitted from the balance sheet. In particular, omitting the liability from the balance sheet may add to the perceived borrowing capacity of the lessee. However, financial analysts can use footnote data to adjust reported balance sheet amounts to include lease commitments before computing these ratios, which reduces this advantage. The financial reporting issue is crucial for some companies. If a lessee structures a lease to avoid meeting the capitalization criteria, it can obtain the use of a resource without recognizing an asset or a liability on its balance sheet. This is one mechanism among many that are sometimes referred to as *off-balance-sheet financing*.

Example: Buying versus Leasing

In 2016, BuyCo and LeaseCo have the following identical financial data prior to any new acquisitions:

Current assets	$2,100,000	Current liabilities	$1,000,000
Noncurrent assets	2,900,000	Noncurrent liabilities	1,600,000
	$5,000,000	Shareholders' equity	2,400,000
			$5,000,000

On December 31, 2016, BuyCo purchases equipment with a 10-year life, at a cost of $2,825,112. BuyCo signs a 10-year, 12% note requiring $500,000 to be paid at the end of each year, starting on December 31, 2017. The payments include interest at 12% on the beginning-of-year principal balance. The remainder of each annual payment reduces the principal.

Because this transaction is a purchase by the issuance of debt, BuyCo records the asset purchased and the note payable (part of which is a current liability). Because of the purchase, BuyCo's noncurrent assets increase by the amount of the new equipment, its current liabilities increase by the present value of the first $500,000 payment discounted at 12%, and its noncurrent liabilities increase by the present value of the last 9 payments discounted at 12%.[3] BuyCo's balance sheet is as follows:

Current assets	$2,100,000	Current liabilities	$1,000,000
Noncurrent assets	2,900,000	Lease obligation—current	446,429[a]
Leased equipment	2,825,112	Noncurrent liabilities	1,600,000
	$7,825,112	Lease obligation—noncurrent	2,378,683[b]
		Shareholders' equity	2,400,000
			$7,825,112

[a] Present value of first annual payment discounted at 12%: $500,000 × 0.892857
[b] Present Value of 10 Annual Payments − First Annual Payment Classified as Current: $2,825,112 − $446,429

Considering these changes, note the effect on two of BuyCo's balance sheet ratios:

	Before Acquisition	After Acquisition
Current ratio	2.10	1.45[a]
Debt to shareholders' equity	1.08	2.26[b]

[a] Current Assets of $2,100,000 ÷ Current Liabilities of $1,446,429 ($1,000,000 + $446,429)
[b] Debt of $5,425,112 ($1,446,429 + $3,978,683) ÷ Shareholders' Equity of $2,400,000

By taking on debt, BuyCo's current ratio falls significantly, which negatively affects users' assessments of the company's liquidity. In addition, BuyCo's debt to shareholders' equity ratio more than doubles. This may affect the perceptions of long-term creditors or shareholders as to the solvency risk of the company. These adverse changes, coupled with the impact that the purchase has on the rate of return on assets in 2017, might impair BuyCo's borrowing capacity or its ability to sell stock.

At the end of 2016, LeaseCo leases identical equipment, agreeing to pay $500,000 rent each year for the next 10 years. If the interest rate is 12%, then the present value of 10 payments of $500,000 discounted at 12% is $2,825,112 ($500,000 × 5.650223). If LeaseCo classifies the lease as a capital lease, it records an asset and a liability, and the effects on its balance sheet are the same as the effects of the purchase on BuyCo's balance sheet. However, if the lease is classified as an operating lease, LeaseCo does not record an asset or a liability. The current ratio after the lease remains at 2.10, and the ratio of debt to shareholders' equity remains at 1.08. Also, the rate of return on assets in 2017 (assuming that plant expansion was profitable) is significantly higher than for BuyCo, even though LeaseCo acquires equipment identical to that acquired by BuyCo. ∎

---

[3] The present value calculations in this chapter use factors from the tables in the Time Value of Money Module.

In this example, two virtually identical economic events are reported very differently in the financial statements of the two companies. Although many companies lease certain assets, some prefer to structure the transaction as an operating lease agreement to avoid capitalizing the lease payments as assets and liabilities. This strategy reduces the impact that reporting the asset and liability has on key balance sheet ratios.

What Are the Advantages and Disadvantages to the Lessor?

The preceding discussion is based on the lessee's point of view. The opposite effects occur for the lessor. For an operating lease, the asset remains on the lessor's balance sheet. The lessor also recognizes rent revenue periodically, usually at an amount equal to the amount of the rent receipts. For a capital lease, the lessor derecognizes the leased asset and records the related receivable. These alternatives affect the financial statements and ratios of the lessor.

From the lessor's point of view, the main advantages and disadvantages of leasing an asset relative to selling the asset are as follows:

- Leasing provides a method of indirectly making a sale while still maintaining many of the advantages of ownership, including security in the asset and tax benefits.
- Leasing enables the lessor to earn profit on the transfer of an asset over the term of the lease.
- A disadvantage for the lessor is additional risk of default (in the event the lessee fails to pay) and obsolescence that result from the lease contract.

Understanding Leasing

Accounting for leasing involves a considerable amount of terminology. It is important to understand these terms clearly. Exhibit 20.3 lists many of the key terms and definitions that we use throughout the chapter.

EXHIBIT 20.3 — Key Terms Related to Leasing

Bargain purchase option. A contract provision allowing the lessee to purchase the leased asset at the end of the life of the lease at a price so favorable that the exercise of the option appears, at the inception of the lease, to be reasonably assured.

Bargain renewal option. A contract provision allowing the lessee to renew the lease for a rental that is so favorable that the exercise of the option by the lessee appears, at the inception of the lease, to be reasonably assured.

Estimated economic life of leased asset. Regardless of the lease term, the estimated remaining period during which the asset is expected to be usable for the purpose that was intended at the inception of the lease, with normal repairs and maintenance.

Estimated residual value of leased asset. The estimated fair value of the leased asset at the end of the lease term. (Note that this value is a different concept from the estimated residual value at the end of the *economic* life of the asset.)

Executory costs. Costs, such as insurance, maintenance, and property taxes, that may be paid either by the lessor or the lessee. Normally, it is expected that the cost should be borne by the party to the contract who controls the asset essentially in the manner of an owner.

Fair value of leased asset. The price that would be received to sell the asset in an orderly transaction between market participants that are independent of the lessor. If the lessor is a manufacturer or dealer, the fair value of the asset at the inception of the lease is normally the selling price. If the lessor is not a manufacturer or dealer, the fair value is *usually* the cost of the asset to the lessor.

(continued)

EXHIBIT 20.3 (Continued)

Guaranteed residual value. The portion of the estimated residual value of the leased asset that is guaranteed by the lessee or by a third party unrelated to the lessor.

Inception of the lease. The date of the lease agreement; or, if the leased asset is being constructed, the date that title passes to the lessor.

Initial direct costs. Costs incurred by the lessor to originate a lease. These costs also include costs directly related to specified activities performed by the lessor for that lease, such as evaluating the lessee's financial condition, negotiating lease terms, preparing and processing lease documents, and closing the transaction.

Interest rate implicit in the lease. The interest (discount) rate that, when applied on a present value basis to the sum of the minimum lease payments and any unguaranteed residual value accruing to the lessor, causes the resulting total present value to be equal to the fair value of the leased asset to the lessor.

Lease receivable (gross investment in the lease). The sum of the undiscounted (1) *minimum lease payments* plus (2) any unguaranteed residual value accruing to the benefit of the lessor at the end of the lease.

Lease term. The fixed, noncancelable term of the lease plus (1) any periods covered by bargain renewal options, (2) any periods for which failure to renew the lease imposes a significant penalty on the lessee, (3) any periods covered by ordinary renewal options preceding the exercise date of a bargain purchase option, and (4) any periods during which the lessor has the option to renew or to extend the lease. The lease term, however, in no case extends beyond the date a bargain purchase option becomes exercisable.

Lessee's incremental borrowing rate. The rate that, at the inception of the lease, the lessee would have incurred to borrow, over a similar term, the cash necessary to purchase the leased asset.

Manufacturer's profit (loss) [dealer's profit (loss)]. This profit or loss is the difference between the following two items: (1) the fair value of the asset at the inception of the lease and (2) the cost or carrying amount of the leased asset.

Minimum lease payments. These are the payments that are required to be paid by the lessee to the lessor over the life of the lease. Specifically, for a lease that contains a *bargain purchase option*, the minimum lease payments also include the payment required by the bargain purchase option. Otherwise, the minimum lease payments include (1) the minimum periodic payments plus (2) any guaranteed residual value and (3) any payments on failure to renew or extend the lease. Executory costs are *not* included in minimum lease payments.

Noncancelable lease term. The portion of the lease term that is cancelable only under any of the following conditions: (1) the occurrence of some remote contingency; (2) permission of the lessor; (3) the lessee enters into a new lease with the same lessor; or (4) the lessee incurs a penalty in such amount that continuation of the lease appears, at inception, reasonably assured.

Unguaranteed residual value. The portion of the estimated residual value of the leased asset that is not guaranteed by the lessee or by a third party unrelated to the lessor.

GOT IT?

20-4 List five benefits to the lessee of leasing versus purchasing an asset.

20-5 Assume that a lessee leases equipment and insists on terms that qualify it as an operating lease, barely escaping the qualification as a capital lease. Discuss the impact that such an operating lease has on financial statements and related financial information as compared to the effect that a capital lease would have.

20-6 What components make up the minimum lease payments of a typical capital lease?
20-7 Under IAS 17 what are the two types of lease classifications defined by IFRS?
20-8 Discuss the similarities and differences between the capitalization criteria for finance leases under IAS 17 and the criteria for capitalizing leases under U.S. GAAP.

LOOKING AHEAD

The Future of Lease Accounting
Many users have been critical of lease accounting since 1976 when the FASB approved the lease framework. The main criticism has focused on whether the four capitalization criteria fully capture the transfer of risks and benefits of ownership from the lessor to the lessee. The first two criteria, the transfer of ownership and bargain purchase option, are included in a lease agreement when both parties clearly want ownership to transfer to the lessee. However, there is more controversy about the third and fourth criteria because they are fairly easy to avoid. For example, a company can use an optimistic estimate of the length of the economic life of the leased asset so the lease term is less than 75% of that period. Similarly, companies often want to effectively protect the lessor's risk related to the asset's residual value without meeting the definition of a guaranteed residual value. This would make the present value of the minimum lease payments less than 90% of the asset's fair value. For example, third-party guarantees of the residual value have been widely used to protect the lessor while keeping the present value of the minimum lease payments is less than 90% of the fair value of the leased asset. Many believe the relevance and representational faithfulness of lease accounting would be enhanced by having a simple rule for capitalization of leases as opposed to certain leases that meet one of the four capitalization criteria.

Specifically, the application of current leasing standards causes the balance sheet and the income statement to omit relevant information about a company's rights and obligations under operating leases (although operating lease commitments are disclosed in the notes). In response to these criticisms, in 2006, the IASB and FASB began joint deliberations on a new approach to accounting for leases. These deliberations resulted in the two bodies issuing a joint exposure draft of a proposed Accounting Standards Update in August 2010. After numerous comments from preparers, auditors, and external users, the two boards issued a second exposure draft in May 2013. Finally, during the first quarter of 2016, the FASB and IASB released new standards to account for leases (Leases, which is Topic 842 in U.S. GAAP and is IFRS 16). The new accounting for leases will become effective for companies in 2019 although early adoption will be permitted.

In the new standards, the core principle for lessees is that a company should recognize an asset and liability arising from a lease. For lessors, the core principle is that lease transactions should be classified by whether the lease is effectively a financing or a sale.

The following table provides a summary of significant changes for accounting for lease transactions.

Model:	US GAAP-Topic 842	IFRS 16
Lessee Accounting Model	Two types of leases for lessees: 1. Finance leases – Balance sheet and income statement effects will be consistent with current U.S. GAAP for capital leases. This accounting will apply to most assets other than land and buildings. 2. Operating leases – Income statement effects will be consistent with current U.S. GAAP for operating leases (i.e., one total lease or rent expense amount). Balance sheets will recognize lease liabilities and right-of-use assets equal to the present value of the remaining lease payments. This lease classification would apply to most leases of land and buildings.	One type of lease for lessees: 1. All leases will be recognized on the balance sheet consistent with current accounting for IFRS finance leases. 2. New standard requires balance sheet recognition of a right-of-use asset and a lease liability. 3. New standard requires that the income statement report amortization of the right-of-use asset separately from interest expense on the lease liability.

(continued)

	3. The current lease capitalization criteria rules are replaced with a set of criteria similar to current IRFS requirements based on the substance of the lease terms. Lease classification will require judgment and are discussed below.
Lessor Accounting Model	U.S. GAAP and IFRS accounting for lessors will converge. 1. Lessors will account for leases using accounting that is substantially equivalent to current U.S. GAAP for sales-type leases, direct-financing leases, and operating leases. 2. The classification criteria to determine lease type will be consistent with the previous IFRS accounting for leases, which is IAS 17.

Definition of a Lease
The new standard defines a lease as "a contract that conveys the right to control the use of identified property, plant or equipment (an identified asset) for a period of time in exchange for consideration." Control over the use of the identified asset means that the customer has both:

1. The right to obtain substantially all of the economic benefits from the use of the asset, and
2. The right to direct the use of the asset.

An identified asset is specified explicitly or implicitly in the contract and is physically distinct. So, a specific floor of an office building (such as, the 3rd floor of a 10-floor building) is specific and would qualify, but simply saying 10% of a 10-floor office building would not qualify because it is not physically distinct. The right to use means the lessee has the ability to direct the use and obtain the benefits of the identified asset. This broadens the current definition of leases by applying a right-of-use model to all lease arrangements. Under the new definition, it is likely more types of transactions will fall under lease provisions.

Lease Classification
Under U.S. GAAP, the classification criteria for leases have been changed to become more consistent with international rules. In leases of assets other than land and buildings, a lease will be considered a finance lease (lessee) or a direct-financing/sales-type lease (lessor) unless one of the following two criteria are met:

- The lease term is for an insignificant part of the total economic life of the underlying asset.
- The present value of the lease payments is insignificant relative to the fair value of the underlying asset at the commencement date.

If either of the criteria are met, then the lease will be classified as an operating lease for the lessee and lessor.

For leases where the underlying asset is land or a building, a lease would be considered an operating lease for the lessee and lessor unless one of the following two criteria are met:

- The lease term is the major part of the remaining economic life of the underlying asset.
- The present value of the lease payments accounts for substantially all of the fair value of the underlying asset at the commencement date.

If either of the criteria are met, then the lease will be classified as a finance lease (lessee) or a direct-financing/sales-type lease (lessor).

For lessees under IFRS, no classification is required because all leases are recognized on the balance sheet. For lessors, under IFRS 16 a lease will be classified as a finance lease if it transfers substantially all the risks and rewards incidental to ownership of an underlying asset. When no substantial transfer exists, the lease will be considered an operating lease.

Lessee Accounting
Under U.S. GAAP, *all* leases with a term greater than 12 months would be recognized on the balance sheet. Leases would be classified as finance or operating leases, and both types would result in the recognition of a right-of use asset and a lease liability when the lessee initially signs the lease, obtains the right to use the asset, and incurs an obligation to make lease payments. The lessee will record a right-of-use asset equal to the present value of the lease payments plus any initial direct costs and a lease liability equal to the present value of the lease payments.

(continued)

The main difference between the two types of leases is that finance leases will trigger amortization of the right-of-use asset separately from interest expense on the lease liability (this results in an accelerated expense pattern with more expense in the early years of the lease). Operating leases will result in a single total lease expense (a straight-line expense pattern).

Under IFRS, a single lease accounting model will exist for lessees. At the beginning of the lease, the lessee will recognize a right-of-use asset and a lease liability. Lessees using IFRS will have an accelerated expense pattern with amortization of the right-to-use asset and interest expense on the lease liability being larger in the earlier years of the lease.

Lessor Accounting
Lessor accounting remains relatively unchanged from current accounting. Even though the classification criteria have changed, U.S. GAAP accounting for lessors will continue with capital leases (direct-financing and sales-type) and operating leases. The same is true under IFRS 16.

HOW DOES A LESSEE ACCOUNT FOR AND REPORT ITS LEASES?

LEARNING OBJECTIVE 20.3
Account for a lessee's operating and capital leases.

A lessee must account for a lease either as a capital or operating lease. We demonstrate the accounting and reporting issues for lessees in this section.

Example: Operating Lease Accounting by a Lessee
Starling Company and Cardinal Company sign a lease agreement that contains the terms and provisions listed in **Example 20.1**.

EXAMPLE 20.1

Terms and Provisions of Lease Agreement between Starling Company (Lessor) and Cardinal Company (Lessee) Dated January 1, 2016

1. The lease term is 5 years. The lease is noncancelable and requires equal payments of $50,000 at the beginning of each year.
2. The cost, and also fair value, of the equipment to Starling Company at the inception of the lease is $300,000. The equipment has an estimated economic life of 10 years and has a zero estimated residual value at the end of this time.
3. There is no guarantee of the residual value by Cardinal Company.
4. The equipment reverts to Starling at the end of the 5 years. That is, the lease contains no bargain purchase option and no agreement to transfer ownership at the end of the lease.
5. Cardinal's incremental borrowing rate is 12.5% per year.
6. For Starling, the interest rate implicit in the lease is 12%.
7. The present value of an annuity due of 5 payments of $50,000 each at 12% is $201,867 (4.037349 × $50,000 = $201,867.45).

Cardinal will classify this lease as an operating lease because it does not meet any of the four capitalization criteria, as shown in **Example 20.1a** (p. 20-12).

Cardinal records the following journal entries each year, from 2016 to 2020:

Jan. 1	Prepaid Rent	50,000	
	Cash		50,000
Dec. 31	Rent Expense	50,000	
	Prepaid Rent		50,000

If Cardinal prepares quarterly interim statements, it reports the expired portion of prepaid rent as an expense and the unexpired portion of prepaid rent as an asset.

> **EXAMPLE 20.1a** Application of Lessee Classification Criteria by Cardinal
>
> | | Criteria Met? | Remarks |
> |---|---|---|
> | **Capitalization Criteria** | | |
> | 1. Transfer of ownership at end of lease | No | |
> | 2. Bargain purchase option | No | |
> | 3. Lease term is 75% or more of economic life | No | It is 50% (5 years ÷ 10 years) |
> | 4. Present value of minimum lease payments is 90% or more of fair value | No | The present value is $201,867.45, or 67% of the $300,000 fair value |
>
> **Decision:** A capital lease must meet one or more of the capitalization criteria; otherwise, the lease is an operating lease.
> **Conclusion:** The lease is an operating lease. It does not meet any of the criteria.

Cardinal does not report the rented equipment in its balance sheet; however, it discloses the future minimum rental payments and other information in the notes to its financial statements, as we discuss at the end of this section.

Contingent Rental Payments by the Lessee—Operating Lease

Leases are often structured so that the lessee pays a set rental payment each period plus an additional amount based on usage or determined by a change in an index, like the consumer price index. These additional payments are termed **contingent rental payments** because they are contingent on some future event occurring. If the contingent rental payments are included in an operating lease agreement, the rental payments should be expensed when it is likely the contingency will be met. For example, **Starbucks**'s discussion of its operating leases states:

> **Operating Leases**
>
> We lease retail stores, roasting, distribution and warehouse facilities, and office space for corporate administrative purposes under operating leases.
>
> Certain leases provide for contingent rent, which is determined as a percentage of gross sales in excess of specified levels. We record a contingent rent liability in accrued occupancy costs within accrued liabilities on our consolidated balance sheets and the corresponding rent expense when specified levels have been achieved or when we determine that achieving the specified levels during the fiscal year is probable.

Capital Lease Accounting by a Lessee

When an asset is leased under a capital lease, **the lessee records, at the beginning of the lease term, an asset and a liability equal to the sum of the present value of the minimum lease payments during the lease term.**[6] In accounting for the asset and

---
[6] FASB ASC 840-30-30: Leases, Capital Leases, Initial Measurement.

liability, the lessee must consider executory costs, the discount rate, contingent rental payments, amortization of the leased asset, and reduction of the lease obligation.

Executory Costs Costs related to the ownership of the leased asset such as insurance, maintenance, and property taxes are called executory costs. Executory costs may be paid by either the lessee or the lessor, depending on how the lease contract is written. However, because the risks and benefits of ownership have been transferred in a capital lease, the lessee usually incurs these costs and many capital leases require the lessee to pay the executory costs directly. Executory costs are expensed as incurred by the lessee and not included when determining the present value of the minimum lease payments.

Alternatively, the lessor may pay the executory costs directly and add them to the periodic lease amounts. In this situation, the lessee *excludes* the executory costs from the minimum lease payments. Therefore, **the minimum lease payment is the lease payment minus the executory costs paid by the lessor.** This is because part of the lease payment is a reimbursement by the lessee of

Often the lease contract is written so that the lessee incurs the executory costs involved with leasing an asset—such as maintenance for a leased building.

the executory costs paid by the lessor. If the executory costs are not specifically stated in the lease contract, the lessee estimates the amount of the executory costs included in each lease payment in order to determine the amount to subtract from each lease payment before computing the present value. The lessee expenses the portion of the total lease payment that is for the executory costs.

Discount Rate The lessee computes the present value of the minimum lease payments by using the lower of either the:

- lessee's *incremental borrowing rate*
- lessor's *implicit interest rate* in the lease, if known by the lessee (or if it is practicable for the lessee to learn)[7]

The **incremental borrowing rate** is the interest rate that the lessee normally would pay to borrow money to finance the purchase of the asset (e.g., the interest rate on a secured loan with the asset as collateral for the same term as the life of the lease). The **implicit interest rate** is the interest rate used by the lessor to compute the minimum lease payments necessary to recover the fair value of the leased asset. Because the lessee is acquiring the use of an asset by financing, the incremental borrowing rate it would face to borrow money to acquire an asset is appropriate. However, if the lessee knows the implicit rate used by the lessor and if this rate is lower than the incremental borrowing rate, it should use the implicit rate as this is the actual cost of financing.

In many leases, the lessor usually will disclose its implicit interest rate. If it does not, the lessee can compute the implicit rate if it knows the fair value of the asset and either the guaranteed residual value, the bargain purchase option price, or the lessor's estimate of the unguaranteed residual value.

Contingent Rental Payments by Lessee—Capital Lease If a capital lease contains contingent rental payments, GAAP either includes or excludes them from the minimum lease payment based on the type of contingency:

- If the contingent rental payment is based on usage of the asset, such as percentage of sales, number of copies made, or miles driven, the contingent rental payment is

[7] FASB ASC 840-10-25-31: Leases, Overall, Recognition.

excluded from the minimum lease payments. This is based on the view that if the asset is not used there is no contingent payment.
- If the contingent rental payment is based on a rate or index, such as an inflation index or government interest rate, the contingent rental payment is *included* in the minimum lease payments. In calculating the contingent rental payment to be included in the minimum lease payment, it is assumed that the rate or index will stay the same over the entire lease term. The lessee expenses any difference between the actual lease payment and the estimated payment.

For simplicity, in the examples we do not include contingent rental payments.

Amortization of Leased Asset Because the lessee records a long-lived asset, it must recognize an expense for the use of the asset by systematically allocating the cost of the asset over its service life, which is the shorter of either the economic life of the asset or the lease term. Technically, GAAP uses the term *amortization* rather than *depreciation*, because the leased asset is an intangible asset—the right to use the asset. However, the lessee often includes the leased asset in the property, plant, and equipment section of its balance sheet. If the asset is written off over the estimated economic life of the property, the term that is usually used in practice is *depreciation*. If the asset is written off over a shorter period of time (the term of the lease), practice usually uses the term *amortization*. To simplify the discussion, we use *depreciation* in this chapter.

The lessee depreciates the asset over its estimated *economic* life to its estimated residual value if the capital lease agreement either:

- transfers ownership of the asset to the lessee
- includes a bargain purchase option

The lessee uses the estimated economic life because it expects to acquire ownership of the asset.

If the capital lease does not transfer ownership of the asset to the lessee and does not include a bargain purchase option, the lessee depreciates the leased asset over the lease term because its right to the use of the asset ceases at the end of the lease. In addition, the lessee should only depreciate the leased asset down to its guaranteed residual value.[8] The lessee uses a depreciation method (e.g., straight-line, double-declining-balance) that is consistent with its normal policy for similar, owned assets. Exhibit 20.4 summarizes the depreciation of leased property by the lessee.

EXHIBIT 20.4 Depreciation of Leased Property by the Lessee

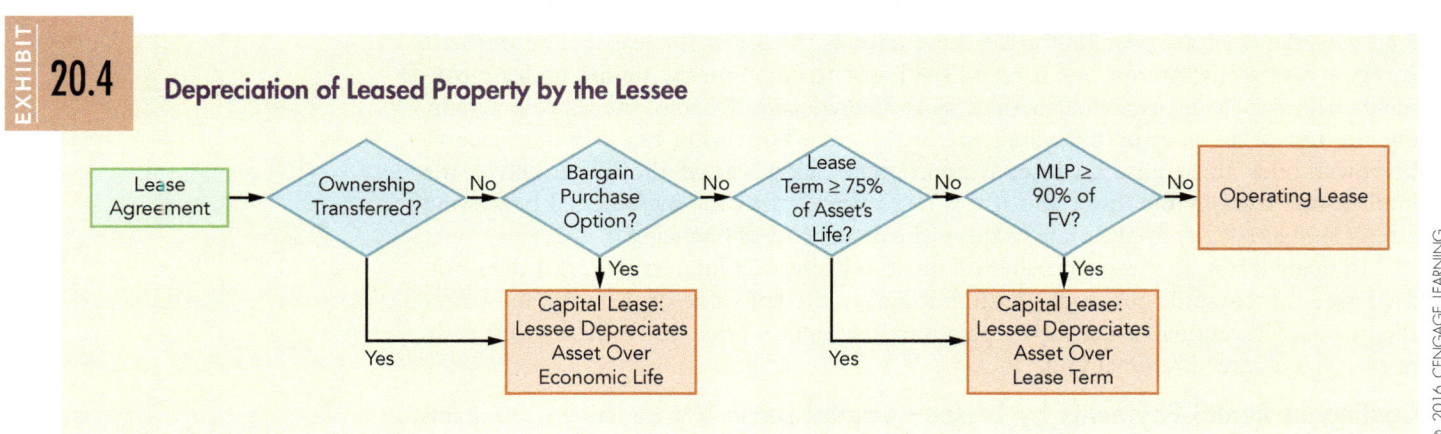

Reduction of the Lease Obligation Because the lessee records a liability, it computes interest expense and the reduction of the principal for each lease payment using the effective interest method demonstrated in Chapter 14. This method computes interest

---
[8] FASB ASC 840-30-35: Leases, Capital Leases, Subsequent Measurement.

expense each period by applying the discount rate (either the incremental borrowing rate or the implicit interest rate, as appropriate) to the outstanding balance of the lease obligation at the beginning of each period.

Example: Equipment Is Leased and Lease Does Not Transfer Ownership or Provide a Bargain Purchase Option

Hawk Company (the lessee) and Dove Leasing Company (the lessor) sign a lease agreement dated January 1, 2016, in which Hawk leases equipment from Dove beginning January 1, 2016. The lease contains the terms and provisions shown in **Example 20.2**.

EXAMPLE 20.2

Terms and Provisions of Lease Agreement between Dove Leasing Company (Lessor) and Hawk Company (Lessee) Dated January 1, 2016

1. The lease term is 4 years. The lease is noncancelable and requires equal payments of $32,923.45 at the end of each year.
2. The cost, and also fair value, of the equipment to Dove at the inception of the lease is $100,000. The equipment has an estimated economic life of 4 years and has a zero estimated residual value at the end of this time.
3. Hawk does not guarantee the residual value.
4. Hawk agrees to pay executory costs for maintenance of $4,000 per year directly on December 31 of each year.
5. The equipment reverts to Dove at the end of the 4 years; that is, the lease contains no transfer of ownership or bargain purchase option.
6. Hawk's incremental borrowing rate is 12.5% per year.
7. Hawk uses the straight-line method to record depreciation on similar equipment.
8. For Dove, the interest rate implicit in the lease is 12%. Hawk knows this rate.
9. The present value of an ordinary annuity of four payments of $32,923.45 each at 12% is $100,000 (3.037349 × $32,923.45).

First, Hawk (the lessee) determines that the lease is a capital lease, as shown in **Example 20.2a**.

EXAMPLE 20.2a

Application of Lease Classification Criteria by Hawk Company (Lessee)

	Criteria Met?	Remarks
Capitalization Criteria		
1. Transfer of ownership at end of lease	No	Title reverts to lessor
2. Bargain purchase option	No	
3. Lease term is 75% or more of economic life	Yes	100% of estimated life
4. Present value of minimum lease payments is 90% or more of fair value	Yes	The present value is $100,000, or 100% of fair value

Decision: A capital lease must meet one or more of the capitalization criteria; otherwise, the lease is an operating lease.
Conclusion: The lease is a capital lease. It meets two of the four criteria.

Because it is a capital lease, Hawk records the leased asset at the present value of the minimum lease payments using the 12% interest rate implicit in the lease. We assume that Hawk knows this rate, and the rate is lower than its incremental borrowing rate of 12.5%. Hawk also ensures that the capitalized amount does not exceed the fair value of the leased asset. Hawk pays the executory costs directly and expenses these costs as incurred.

Hawk records the acquisition of the leased asset, the depreciation, and the annual payments for 2 years as follows:

Initial Recording of Capital Lease on January 1, 2016
Leased Equipment	100,000.00	
Capital Lease Obligation		100,000.00

Hawk records both the asset and the liability at the present value of the minimum lease payments ($100,000) rather than the nominal value of $131,693.80 (4 × $32,923.45).[9]

First Annual Payment on Capital Lease on December 31, 2016
Interest Expense (12% × $100,000)	12,000.00	
Capital Lease Obligation ($32,923.45 − $12,000)	20,923.45	
Cash		32,923.45

The annual payment is comprised of both interest and principle. Note that this lease requires the payment to be made at the end of the year. Thus, the annuity is an ordinary annuity. If the lease requires the payments to be made at the beginning of the year, it is an annuity due (shown later in this chapter).

The lessee depreciates the asset over the lease term because the lease does not include a transfer of ownership or a bargain purchase option. The lessee uses the straight-line method, and the annual depreciation is $25,000 ($100,000 ÷ 4).

The balance sheet of Hawk for December 31, 2016, includes the Leased Equipment minus the Accumulated Depreciation in the property, plant, and equipment section of its assets. It divides the Capital Lease Obligation between current liabilities and long-term liabilities, as we discuss in the next section.

Recognition of Annual Depreciation of Leased Equipment on December 31, 2016
Depreciation Expense: Leased Equipment	25,000.00	
Accumulated Depreciation: Leased Equipment		25,000.00

The payment of executory costs such as insurance, maintenance, and property taxes is recorded in regular operating expense accounts. This entry occurs each December 31 for the four year lease term.

Payment of Executory Costs on December 31, 2016
Maintenance Expense	4,000.00	
Cash		4,000.00

The amount of the second payment is the same as that for 2016, but the payment for interest is the effective rate of 12% multiplied by the balance of the lease obligation at the beginning of 2017.

- The interest is 12% × $79,076.55 ($100,000 − $20,923.45), or $9,489.19.
- The remainder of the annual payment is the reduction of the principal of $23,434.26 ($32,923.45 − $9,489.19).

Second Annual Payment and Recognition of Interest Expense on December 31, 2017
Interest Expense [12% × ($100,000 − $20,923.45)]	9,489.19	
Capital Lease Obligation ($32,923.45 − $9,489.19)	23,434.26	
Cash		32,923.45

[9] It is acceptable for the lessee to record the liability at the gross amount with an accompanying debit to a contra-liability account, Discount on Capital Lease Obligation, for $31,693.80. This alternative procedure may be useful when the lessee prepares the required disclosures that we discuss later.

Example 20.2b shows the interest expense and the reduction of the capital lease obligation over the life of the lease.

EXAMPLE 20.2b

Summary of Lease Payments and Interest Expense of Hawk Company (Lessee)

(1) Date	(2) Annual Lease Payment	(3) Interest at 12% on Unpaid Obligation[a]	(4) Reduction of Capital Lease Obligation[b]	(5) Balance of Capital Lease Obligation[c]
January 1, 2016	—	—	—	$100,000.00
December 31, 2016	$32,923.45	$12,000.00	$20,923.45	79,076.55
December 31, 2017	32,923.45	9,489.19	23,434.26	55,642.29
December 31, 2018	32,923.45	6,677.07	26,246.38	29,395.91
December 31, 2019	32,923.45	3,527.54[d]	29,395.91	—

[a] Column 5 at beginning of year × 12%
[b] Column 2 − Column 3
[c] Column 5 at beginning of year − Column 4
[d] Adjusted for rounding error of $0.03

Under the straight-line method, the depreciation entry for 2017 is the same as that for 2016.

Recognition of Annual Depreciation on December 31, 2017

Depreciation Expense: Leased Equipment	25,000.00	
Accumulated Depreciation: Leased Equipment		25,000.00

The journal entries for 2018 and 2019 follow a pattern similar to those presented for 2016 and 2017.

Classification of Capital Lease Obligation When a lessee classifies its capital lease obligation on its balance sheet, it considers the usual criteria for classifying portions of the lease obligation as current or noncurrent.[10] A lessee may use two approaches to measure the amount of the current liability: the present value of next year's payments or the change in the present value of the total lease obligation.

Present Value of Next Year's Payments Under the present value of next year's payments approach, the amount of the lessee's current liability is the payment(s) the lessee will make in the next year discounted to the balance sheet date. For Hawk, the current liability each year is $29,395.93 (0.892857 × $32,923.45). The remaining portion of the obligation (the present value of all future lease payments beyond next year) is classified as a noncurrent liability. This method is conceptually sound and consistent with the theoretical measurement of liabilities. In this chapter, we use the present value of next year's payments to determine the current liability portion of the lease obligation.

Change in the Present Value The change in present value approach may be used by a lessee to measure the amount of its current liability. In this approach, the current liability is the amount by which the total balance of the lease liability will decrease in the next year. For Hawk, the current portion of the liability on December 31, 2016, is $23,434.26 ($79,076.55 − $55,642.29), and on December 31, 2017, it is $26,246.38 ($55,642.29 − $29,395.91). Note that the current liability on December 31, 2018, (the balance sheet preceding the final year's lease payment) is the same for each approach (with minor differences for rounding).

[10] FASB ASC 840-30-45: Leases, Capital Leases, Other Presentation Matters.

Example: Lease Payments Are Made at the Beginning of the Year

Assume that all the lease provisions described in **Example 20.2** (p. 20-15) are the same *except* that Hawk Company is required to make the lease payments in advance, on January 1 of each year, and that the *cost* (and also fair value) of the equipment is $112,000. The annuity calculation is now the present value of an *annuity due* rather than that of an ordinary annuity:

Present Value of Four Payments of $32,923.45 in Advance at 12% = $32,923.45 × 3.401831
= $112,000 (rounded)

Example 20.3 shows the information for the interest expense and the reduction of the capital lease obligation for each period.

EXAMPLE 20.3 **Summary of Lease Payments in Advance and Interest Expense of Hawk Company (Lessee)**

(1) Date	(2) Annual Lease Payment	(3) Interest at 12% on Unpaid Obligation[a]	(4) Balance of Capital Lease Obligation[b]
January 1, 2016	Before the initial lease payment		$112,000.00
January 1, 2016	$32,923.45		79,076.55
December 31, 2016		$9,489.19	88,565.74[d]
January 1, 2017	32,923.45[c]		55,642.29
December 31, 2017		6,677.07	62,319.36[d]
January 1, 2018	32,923.45		29,395.91
December 31, 2018		3,527.54[e]	32,923.45[d]
January 1, 2019	32,923.45		0

[a] Column 4 at beginning of year × 12%
[b] Column 4 at beginning of year − Column 2 + Column 3
[c] Each lease payment, after the initial payment, includes the accrued interest for the previous year.
[d] $32,923.45 of this amount is a current liability; it will be paid January 1 of the next year. The remaining amount is a noncurrent liability.
[e] Adjusted for $0.03 rounding error

The journal entries through January 1, 2017, are as follows. To begin, Hawk records both the asset and the obligation at the present value of the minimum future lease payments.

Initial Recording of Capital Lease on January 1, 2016
Leased Equipment   112,000.00
    Capital Lease Obligation   112,000.00

The first payment is entirely a reduction of principal because no interest has accrued. (The preceding two journal entries could be made as one compound entry.)

First Annual Payment in Advance on January 1, 2016
Capital Lease Obligation   32,923.45
    Cash   32,923.45

The straight-line depreciation is $112,000 ÷ 4 years, or $28,000.

Recognition of Annual Depreciation of Leased Equipment on December 31, 2016
Depreciation Expense: Leased Equipment   28,000.00
    Accumulated Depreciation: Leased Equipment   28,000.00

Even though Hawk will not make the next payment until January 1, 2017, the accrual concept requires that the lessee recognize interest expense in the year that it is incurred. The lessee separates the Capital Lease Obligation into its current and noncurrent portions in its year-end balance sheet. In the December 31, 2016, balance sheet, it reports $32,923.45 as a current liability and the remaining part, $55,642.29, as a long-term liability.

Recognition of Interest Expense on Capital Lease on December 31, 2016
Interest Expense [($112,000 − $32,923.45) × 12%]   9,489.19
    Accrued Interest on Capital Lease Obligation[11]   9,489.19

The lessee also recognizes expenses of $4,000 for maintenance and other executory costs each year on December 31.

Payment of executory costs on December 31, 2016
Maintenance Expense   4,000.00
    Cash   4,000.00

The interest applicable to 2017 is $9,489.19, as shown in **Example 20.3**. The remaining entries follow the pattern of those for 2017.

Second Annual Payment in Advance on January 1, 2017
Accrued Interest on Capital Lease Obligation   9,489.19
Capital Lease Obligation   23,434.26
    Cash   32,923.45

ETHICAL DILEMMA

The Chocolate Hut Inc. is a national retailer that specializes in selling a variety of high-end chocolate products. As a former auditor of the Chocolate Hut, you were recently approached to become the controller for the company. After accepting the position, you began a review of several areas of operating risk faced by the company. During this review, you noted that the company made extensive use of operating leases for its 300 retail stores as well as the majority of its property, plant, and equipment. During a meeting to discuss this issue, the CFO stated that the company, like many retailers, has chosen to lease many of its assets due to the advantages of leasing. In particular, the CFO stated that the financial reporting benefits are particularly attractive. If Chocolate Hut were forced to record an asset and liability for the assets currently under operating leases, its debt ratio would be so adversely affected that the company would face considerable difficulty in attempting to obtain debt financing, putting the future of the company in considerable doubt. While you understand these benefits, you are particularly concerned that many of Chocolate Hut's operating leases for its more profitable stores will soon expire. Based on your knowledge of the real estate markets in these areas, you question whether the company will be successful in renewing the leases. The CFO stated that the renewals will not be a problem because she has personally executed side agreements for all of the company's operating leases that will require Chocolate Hut to renew the leases indefinitely. If these side agreements were included in the original lease agreements, the company would be forced to classify the leases as capital leases. However, by having the renewal option contained in a separate contract, the company is able to classify the leases as operating leases.

You are shocked by this admission. When you audited Chocolate Hut, you personally reviewed the lease documents and were never made aware of the side agreements. If you had been aware of their existence, you certainly would have insisted that the two contracts were, in substance, one contract and demanded that the company reclassify the leases as capital leases. To insist at this point that the company reclassify the leases would most certainly cost you your current job with Chocolate Hut, and the fact that you never discovered these side agreements may lead others to perceive you as an incompetent auditor which would make finding another job extremely difficult. What course of action do you take?

---

[11] If not material, the lessee may credit this amount to the liability account, Capital Lease Obligation.

Other Lessee Capitalization Issues

A lessee may also sign a lease agreement that includes a bargain purchase option, or a guaranteed residual value. Accounting for these features is described below.

Example: Bargain Purchase Option

Pheasant Company leases equipment for 4 years and agrees to pay $40,000 at the end of each year. The lease also includes an option to pay $2,000 at the end of the fourth year to purchase the asset. Because this amount is significantly lower than the expected fair value at the end of the fourth year, Pheasant is very likely to exercise the option. Therefore, it is a bargain purchase option. Pheasant's incremental borrowing rate is 11%, and the lessor's implicit interest rate is 10%. The cost and fair value of the equipment is $128,160.63. This lease qualifies as a capital lease because there is a bargain purchase option. The lessee records the leased equipment at the present value of the minimum lease payments, including the bargain purchase option, based on the lower 10% rate, calculated as follows:

Present value of the annual payments discounted at 10% ($40,000 × 3.169865)	$126,794.60
Add: Present value of the single sum of $2,000 (the bargain purchase option) discounted at 10% ($2,000 × 0.683013)	1,366.03
Present value of the minimum lease payments	$128,160.63

The lessee records the leased asset as follows:

Leased Equipment	128,160.63	
Capital Lease Obligation		128,160.63

The accounting by the lessee follows the same principles as in the previous capital lease examples. However, because it is highly likely the lessee will exercise the bargain purchase option, the lessee depreciates the Leased Equipment of $128,160.63 over its estimated *economic life* (not over the term of the lease) to its estimated residual value (*not* the bargain purchase option of $2,000). The lessee reduces the liability account, Capital Lease Obligation, by the effective interest method, as previously illustrated. However, at the end of the fourth year, it has a balance of $2,000. When the lessee exercises the bargain purchase option, it debits Capital Lease Obligation and credits Cash for $2,000.

Impact of Guaranteed Residual Value The lessee may agree to guarantee part or all of the residual value. That is, it guarantees that the value of the leased asset at the end of the lease term will be at least the stated amount of the guarantee. If the asset is not worth this guaranteed value, the lessee must pay the lessor any difference between this smaller value and the guaranteed value. A lessor would generally prefer a guaranteed residual value because it transfers the risk associated with the future value of the asset to the lessee. The guaranteed residual value is included in the minimum lease payments. Therefore, the lessee capitalizes the present value of the amount guaranteed.

Example: Guaranteed Residual Value

Partridge Company leases equipment for 4 years that cost the lessor $147,284.99 (its fair value) and agrees to make rental payments of $40,000 at the end of each year. The equipment has an estimated residual value of $30,000 at the end of the fourth year, and Partridge guarantees the entire amount of this residual value. There is no transfer of ownership or bargain purchase option. Assume an appropriate interest rate of 10%. This lease is a capital lease because the present value of the minimum lease payments, including the guaranteed residual amount, is $147,284.99 (calculation below), which is greater than 90% of the fair value of the leased property ($147,284.99).

Present value of the annual lease payments discounted at 10% ($40,000 × 3.169865)	$126,794.60
Add: Present value of the guaranteed residual value discounted at 10% ($30,000 × 0.683013)	20,490.39
Present value of minimum lease payments	$147,284.99

The lessee records the leased equipment at the present value of the minimum lease payments (which includes the guaranteed residual value) as follows:

Leased Equipment	147,284.99	
Capital Lease Obligation		147,284.99

The accounting for the lease follows the same principles as in the previous capital lease examples. The lessee depreciates the asset over the *lease term* down to the guaranteed residual value. It reduces the liability using the effective interest method, so that at the end of the fourth year the liability has a balance of $30,000.

The final journal entry to remove the asset and eliminate the liability depends on the condition of the leased asset and the terms of the lease agreement. Based on the previous information for Partridge Company, at the end of the fourth year after recording the depreciation, interest, and reduction of the liability, Partridge has the following accounts and balances:

Account	Balance
Leased Equipment	$147,284.99 (debit)
Accumulated Depreciation: Leased Equipment	117,284.99 (credit)
Capital Lease Obligation	30,000.00 (credit)

If the fair value of the leased asset is less than $30,000, the lessee may pay part of the liability by returning the asset to the lessor. It then pays the remainder in cash and recognizes a loss on disposal of the asset. If Partridge returns the leased equipment to the lessor, both Partridge and the lessor agree that the equipment is worth only $17,000. Partridge pays the lessor $13,000 in cash and records the disposal as follows:

Accumulated Depreciation: Leased Equipment	117,284.99	
Capital Lease Obligation	30,000.00	
Loss on Disposal of Leased Equipment	13,000.00	
Leased Equipment		147,284.99
Cash		13,000.00

If the fair value is more than $30,000, the lessee may pay the liability in full by returning the asset to the lessor. In this case, the lessee does not recognize a gain. Remember, this is the accounting when the residual value is guaranteed. If the residual value was *unguaranteed*, the lessee would ignore this residual value in accounting for the lease. ■

GOT IT?

20-9 Describe briefly the procedures followed by the lessee to account for a capital lease.

20-10 Owens Company leased equipment for 4 years at $50,000 a month with an option to renew the lease for 6 years at $2,000 per month or to purchase the equipment for $25,000 (a price considerably less than the expected fair value) after the initial lease term of 4 years. How does Owens record this transaction?

20-11 McFarland Corporation leased equipment under a lease calling for the payment of $50,000 a year in rent. At the end of the current year, when the capital lease had a remaining term of 20 years, McFarland subleased the asset for a rental of $75,000 a year for 20 years. The new lease is acceptable to the lessor, who agrees that McFarland has completed its primary obligation. When will McFarland report the gain from this transaction? Explain.

LEARNING OBJECTIVE 20.4
Understand statement of cash flow presentation and disclosure by the lessee.

HOW DOES THE LESSEE PRESENT LEASE CASH FLOWS AND DISCLOSE LEASES?

This section describes how lessees present operating and capital lease cash flows in the statement of cash flows and discusses disclosure requirements for leases.

Lessee Statement of Cash Flows Presentation

If a lessee records a lease as an operating lease, it classifies each lease payment as a use of cash in the operating activities section of its statement of cash flows. If a lessee records a lease as a capital lease, it reports a noncash investing and financing activity at the signing of the lease agreement. For each lease payment, it classifies the portion of each cash outflow that reduces the lease obligation as a use of cash in the financing activities section.

Disclosure Requirements

GAAP requires certain disclosures by the lessee for both operating and capital leases. The basic disclosures are summarized in Exhibit 20.5. The lessee discloses this information in its balance sheet or in the notes to its financial statements.[12]

EXHIBIT 20.5 Disclosure Requirements for Lessee: Operating and Capital Leases

Operating Leases:
- Rental expense for each period
- Operating leases having lease terms in excess of one year:
    - Future minimum rental payments required as of the date of the latest balance sheet presented, for each of the five succeeding fiscal years and in total
    - The total of minimum rentals to be received in the future under noncancelable subleases

Capital Leases:
- Gross amount of assets recorded under capital leases by major classes according to nature or function
- Future minimum lease payments for each of the 5 succeeding fiscal years and in total with separate deductions from the total (1) for the amount of executory costs included in the minimum lease payments and (2) for the amount of the imputed interest required to reduce the net minimum lease payments to present value
- Total of minimum sublease rentals to be received in the future under noncancelable subleases
- Assets, accumulated depreciation, depreciation expense, and liabilities

For all leases, a general description of the lessee's leasing arrangements including the following:
- The existence and term of renewal or purchase options and escalation clauses
- Restrictions imposed by lease agreements, such as those concerning dividends, additional debt, and further leasing

---

[12] FASB ASC 840-30-50: Leases, Capital Leases, Disclosure.

Noodles & Company's lease disclosure from its 2013 annual report is shown in Real Report 20.1.

| REAL REPORT | LEASE OBLIGATIONS | 20.1 |

13. Leases

The Company leases restaurant facilities, office space and certain equipment under operating leases that expire on various dates through December 2029. Lease terms for traditional shopping centers generally include a base term of 10 years, with options to extend these leases for additional periods of 5 to 15 years. Typically, the lease includes rent escalations, which are expensed on a straight-line basis over the lease term. The difference between rent expense and cash paid for rent is recognized as deferred rent. Rent expense for 2013, 2012 and 2011 was approximately $29.5 million, $24.6 million and $20.9 million, respectively.

Future minimum lease payments required under existing leases as of December 31, 2013 are as follows (in thousands):

2014	$ 33,912
2015	34,351
2016	33,279
2017	30,689
2018	26,368
Thereafter	89,330
	$247,929

Noodles & Company

Suggested answers to these questions are found at the end of the chapter.

Questions:

1. Why do you think Noodles & Company has chosen to use long-term operating leases instead of buying the assets?
2. Do you think that Noodles's footnote disclosure contains enough information for users to understand the obligation in the same way as if it was on the balance sheet?
3. Noodles & Company reported total assets of $187,802 thousand and total liabilities of $63,329 thousand at the end of 2013, if Noodles's operating leases were classified as capital leases, what would the effect be on Noodles's debt ratio (total liabilities to total assets)? For simplicity, assume that lease payments are made as a single annual payment at the beginning of each year and the amounts listed thereafter are paid at the beginning of Year 5. Assume an interest rate of 10%.

GOT IT?

20-12 Describe the difference between how a lessee would report the cash flows associated with an operating lease and a capital lease.

20-13 What must a lessee disclose for all leases whether classified as operating or capital?

20-14 What disclosures are lessees required to make for capital leases?

HOW DOES A LESSOR ACCOUNT FOR AND REPORT A LEASE?

LEARNING OBJECTIVE 20.5
Account for a lessor's operating, direct financing, and sales-type leases.

Recall that a lessor, such as **Caterpillar**, **Ford** or **John Deere**, classifies a lease as follows:

- *Operating Lease.* A lease that does not meet any of the four capitalization criteria or does not meet both of the recognition criteria.
- *Sales-Type Capital Lease.* A sales-type lease results in a manufacturer's or dealer's profit (or loss) and meets one or more of the capitalization criteria and both of the recognition criteria.

- *Direct Financing Capital Lease.* A direct financing lease does not result in a manufacturer's or dealer's profit (or loss) and meets one or more of the capitalization criteria and both of the recognition criteria.

We discuss the accounting method for each of the leases in the following sections.

Lessor Accounting for an Operating Lease

Under an operating lease, a lessor retains substantially all the risks and benefits of ownership. The lessor keeps the leased asset on its balance sheet and reports it as a noncurrent asset separate from property, plant, and equipment held for the lessor's own use.[13] It will also report, on the income statement, depreciation on the leased asset. The lessor records the rental receipts as revenue when they are earned. If the lessor pays executory costs, it recognizes those costs as expenses when incurred.

Example: Operating Lease

Starling Company leases a piece of equipment to Cardinal Company for 5 years under the terms described in **Example 20.1** (p. 20-11). Cardinal agrees to pay $50,000 at the beginning of each year. In addition, Starling purchased the equipment at a cost of $300,000. The equipment has an estimated life of 10 years, and Starling uses the straight-line method of depreciation. On January 10, 2016, Starling pays the annual insurance premium of $2,000, and on December 15, 2016, it pays for repairs of $1,500. Assume that there are no initial direct costs involved in this lease. Starling records the preceding information as follows:

Purchase of Equipment to Be Leased on January 1, 2016

Equipment Leased to Others	300,000	
Cash (or Notes Payable)		300,000

We show the purchase of the equipment to reinforce your understanding of its classification separate from property, plant, and equipment held for Starling's own use. If Starling already owned the equipment, it would debit Equipment Leased to Others and credit the Equipment account (and eliminate any related Accumulated Depreciation).

Starling collects the annual rental payments at the beginning of each year and records them as Deferred Rental Revenue (a liability). If the amount is receivable at this date but not yet collected, Rent Receivable is debited.

Collection of Annual Payment on Operating Lease on January 1, 2016

Cash	50,000	
Deferred Rental Revenue		50,000

Under operating leases, the lessor usually pays executory costs such as insurance, property tax, and repairs and maintenance. It records these costs as operating expenses in the periods in which they are incurred. If Starling prepares monthly or quarterly interim statements, it reports the unexpired portion of the expense as an asset, Prepaid Insurance.

Payment of Annual Insurance Premium on January 10, 2016

Insurance Expense	2,000	
Cash		2,000

The repair expense is another example of an executory cost paid by the lessor.

Payment of Repairs on December 15, 2016

Repair Expense	1,500	
Cash		1,500

---

[13] FASB ASC 840-20-50: Leases, Operating Leases, Disclosure.

Starling records depreciation on the leased equipment over its 10-year economic life. It reports the leased equipment and the accompanying accumulated depreciation on its balance sheet in an account separate from property, plant, and equipment held for its own use.

Recognition of Annual Revenue on Operating Lease on December 31, 2016
Deferred Rental Revenue	50,000	
Rental Revenue		50,000

Recognition of Annual Depreciation Expense on December 31, 2016
Depreciation Expense: Equipment Leased to Others	30,000	
Accumulated Depreciation: Equipment Leased to Others		30,000

Initial Direct Costs Involved in an Operating Lease *Initial direct costs* are costs that a lessor incurs directly for negotiating and originating a lease. These costs include such things as legal fees, credit verification fees, and commissions. For an operating lease, the lessor records these costs as an asset and allocates them as an operating expense in proportion to the rental receipts over the term of the operating lease. This procedure results in an appropriate matching of the initial direct costs as an expense against the rental revenue.

Direct Financing Leases (Lessor)

Under a direct financing lease, the lessor is usually a financial institution (or a financial subsidiary of a manufacturing company). The lessor treats the lease as a sale of the asset at a fair value equal to its cost or carrying value and records an accompanying receivable. Because there is no manufacturer's or dealer's profit (or loss) in a direct financing lease, **the net amount at which the lessor records the receivable must be equal to the cost or carrying value of the property**. The *net* receivable is equal to the present value of the future lease payments to be received.

There are, however, two components of the net receivable. The first component is the **gross receivable** (the total undiscounted cash flows) and is composed of both:

- *undiscounted* minimum lease payments, which include any guaranteed residual value, to be received by the lessor
- any unguaranteed residual value accruing to the benefit of the lessor[14]

Note that the gross receivable includes the residual value, whether guaranteed or unguaranteed. The second component is the *unearned interest* (the interest to be earned over the life of the lease). This amount is measured as the difference between the gross receivable (the Lease Receivable[15] account) and the cost or carrying value of the leased property. This unearned interest account is a contra account, and the lessor deducts this account from the Lease Receivable account to determine its net investment in the direct financing lease. The lessor reports this net investment on its balance sheet and divides the amount between the current and noncurrent asset sections. The current asset portion is determined by using the present value of next year's payments approach or by using the change in present value approach, as explained earlier for the lessee's accounting.

We illustrate the lessor's accounting under the gross method which is consistent with the presentation in the FASB Codification. The lessor may also record the asset at the net amount consistent with lessee accounting.

---

[14] FASB ASC 840-30-30: Leases, Capital Leases, Initial Measurement.

[15] The title "Minimum Lease Payments Receivable" is appropriate when there is a *guaranteed* residual value. The title "Gross Investment in the Lease" is most appropriate if there is an *unguaranteed* residual value because then the lessor has not "sold" the residual value. For simplicity, we use the title "Lease Receivable."

The lessor determines its interest revenue each period using the effective interest method to produce a constant periodic rate of return on the net investment in the lease. At the beginning of the lease, the net investment is equal to the original cost of the asset if it is new or the carrying value if it has been owned in previous periods. The interest rate implicit in the lease is the rate that, when applied to the gross receivable, will discount that amount to a present value that is equal to the net receivable.

Example: Direct Financing Lease with No Guaranteed Residual Value and Payments Made at End of Year

Osprey Leasing Company (a financial institution) leases equipment to Tanager Company, as shown in **Example 20.4**.

EXAMPLE 20.4

Terms and Provisions of Lease Agreement between Osprey Leasing Company (Lessor) and Tanager Company (Lessee) Dated January 1, 2016

1. The lease term is 4 years. The lease is noncancelable and requires equal payments of $32,923.45 at the end of each year.[16]
2. The cost, and also fair value, of the equipment to Osprey at the inception of the lease is $100,000. The equipment has an estimated economic life of 4 years and has a zero estimated residual value at the end of this time.
3. Tanager does not guarantee the residual value.
4. Tanager agrees to pay executory costs for maintenance of $4,000 per year directly on December 31 of each year.
5. The equipment reverts to Osprey at the end of the 4 years; that is, the lease contains no transfer of ownership or bargain purchase option.
6. Tanager's incremental borrowing rate is 12.5% per year.
7. Tanager uses the straight-line method to record depreciation on similar equipment.
8. For Osprey, the interest rate implicit in the lease is 12%. Tanager knows this rate.
9. The present value of an ordinary annuity of four payments of $32,923.45 each at 12% is $100,000 (3.037349 × $32,923.45).
10. The collectibility of the lease payments is reasonably assured, and there are no uncertainties involved in the lease.
11. There are no initial direct costs of negotiating and closing the lease transaction.

As shown in **Example 20.4a**, based on the capitalization criteria and revenue recognition criteria, the lease is a direct financing rather than a sales-type lease because the fair (present) value of the property is equal to its cost.

---

[16] Osprey (the lessor) calculates the annual rental payments it charges as follows:

$$\text{Annual Payments} = \frac{\text{Present Value Equal to the Cost of Equipment}}{\text{Present Value of an Annuity for 4 Periods at 12\%}}$$

$$= \frac{\$100,000}{3.037349}$$

$$= \$32,923.45$$

> **EXAMPLE 20.4a**
>
> **Application of Lease Classification Criteria by Osprey Leasing Company (Lessor)**
>
> | | Criteria Met? | Remarks |
> |---|---|---|
> | **Capitalization Criteria** | | |
> | 1. Transfer of ownership | No | |
> | 2. Bargain purchase option | No | |
> | 3. Lease term is 75% or more of economic life | Yes | 100% of economic life |
> | 4. Present value of minimum lease payments is 90% or more of fair value | Yes | The present value is $100,000, or 100% of fair value |
> | **Recognition Criteria** | | |
> | 1. Collectibility reasonably assured | Yes | |
> | 2. No uncertainties | Yes | |
>
> **Decision:** If the lease meets one or more of the capitalization criteria and both of the recognition criteria, and there is no manufacturer's or dealer's profit or loss, it is a direct financing lease.
>
> **Conclusion:** The lease is a direct financing lease because the appropriate criteria are met and there is no manufacturer's or dealer's profit or loss. The present (fair) value of the lease payments equals the cost of the property.

Osprey first acquires the equipment at its fair value of $100,000 and records it as follows:

Acquisition of Equipment to Be Leased

Equipment Leased to Others	100,000	
Cash		100,000

Osprey (the lessor) records the Lease Receivable at the sum of the undiscounted annual payments to be collected from Tanager (the lessee) plus the undiscounted unguaranteed residual value. Because there are no executory costs or unguaranteed residual value, Osprey records this asset at $131,693.80 (4 × $32,923.45). The beginning balance of the account, Unearned Interest: Leases, is the difference between the Lease Receivable account and the cost or carrying value of the leased asset. For Osprey, this difference is $31,693.80 ($131,693.80 − $100,000). Osprey records the following:

Initial Recording of the Lease on January 1, 2016

Lease Receivable	131,693.80	
Equipment Leased to Others		100,000.00
Unearned Interest: Leases		31,693.80

The effect of this transaction is to replace the leased equipment with a monetary asset (the lease receivable) of an equal amount. Again, note that Osprey records the receivable at the amount of the gross (undiscounted) cash flows plus the estimated unguaranteed residual value of the leased asset (zero in this case). The Unearned Interest: Leases account is a contra-account to the Lease Receivable account. Osprey removes the Equipment Leased to Others account because, in substance, this is a disposal of an asset even though legal transfer of ownership has not occurred.

Collection of Annual Payment at End of First Year on December 31, 2016

Cash	32,923.45	
Lease Receivable		32,923.45

Because the lease receivable is reported at its gross amount, it is reduced by the total amount of cash received.

Recognition of Interest Revenue for First Year on December 31, 2016
Unearned Interest: Leases   12,000.00
    Interest Revenue: Leases   12,000.00

Osprey amortizes the Unearned Interest account using the effective interest method by recognizing the interest revenue as 12% of the net investment at the beginning of the period (which is the January 1, 2016, balance of the Lease Receivable minus the balance of the Unearned Interest: Leases):

$$12\% \times (\$131{,}693.80 - \$31{,}693.80) = \$12{,}000.00$$

Osprey separates the receivable into its current and noncurrent portions for reporting the lease on its balance sheet. It calculates the current and noncurrent amounts of the net investment that it reports on its December 31, 2016, balance sheet as follows:

	Current	Noncurrent
Lease receivable	$32,923.45	$ 65,846.90[a]
Unearned interest: leases	(3,527.52)	(16,166.27)[b]
Net investment	$29,395.93	$ 49,680.63

[a] 2 × $32,923.45
[b] [$32,923.45 − ($32,923.45 × 0.797194)] + [$32,923.45 − ($32,923.45 × 0.711780)]

Note that the $29,395.93 current portion plus the $49,680.63 noncurrent portion sum to the $79,076.55 (with a $0.01 rounding error) total Net Investment on December 31, 2016, shown in **Example 20.4b**.

EXAMPLE 20.4b Summary of Lease Payments Received and Interest Revenue Earned by Osprey Leasing Company (Lessor)

(1) Date	(2) Annual Lease Payment Received	(3) Interest Revenue at 12% on Net Investment[a]	(4) Amount of Net Investment Recovered[b]	(5) Lease Receivable[c]	(6) Unearned Interest Leases[d]	(7) Net Investment[e]
January 1, 2016				$131,693.80	$31,693.80	$100,000.00
December 31, 2016	$32,923.45	$12,000.00	$20,923.45	98,770.35	19,693.80	79,076.55
December 31, 2017	32,923.45	9,489.19	23,434.26	65,846.90	10,204.61	55,642.29
December 31, 2018	32,923.45	6,677.07	26,246.38	32,923.45	3,527.54	29,395.91
December 31, 2019	32,923.45	3,527.54[f]	29,395.91	0	0	0

[a] Column 7 at beginning of year × 12%
[b] Column 2 − Column 3
[c] Annual Lease Payment × Number of Years Remaining on Lease, or Previous Balance − Column 2
[d] Previous Balance − Column 3
[e] Column 5 − Column 6
[f] Adjusted for $0.03 rounding error

Collection of Annual Payment for Second Year on December 31, 2017
Cash   32,923.45
    Lease Receivable   32,923.45

Osprey records the receipt of the payment for the second period in the same way as during the first period.

Recognition of Interest Revenue for Second Year on December 31, 2017
Unearned Interest: Leases	9,489.19	
Interest Revenue: Leases		9,489.19

The calculation of the 2017 interest revenue by the effective interest method follows the same procedure as that for 2016. The calculation for 2017 is 12% of the January 1, 2017, balance in the Lease Receivable account minus the balance of the Unearned Interest: Leases. For 2017, the interest revenue is:

$$12\% \times (\$100{,}000 - \$20{,}923.45) = \$9{,}489.19$$

Example 20.4b shows the interest revenue and the reductions in the receivable and the unearned interest over the life of the lease. Osprey would use the information shown in **Example 20.4b** to record the journal entries for the remaining years of the lease. At the end of 2019, its net investment is zero. ■

Example: Direct Financing Lease with an Unguaranteed Residual Value at the End of the Lease and Payments Received in Advance

The following example is similar to the preceding example, except it demonstrates lessor accounting when there is an unguaranteed residual value and payments are received in advance. On January 1, 2016, Condor Bank leases equipment to Kestrel Company, with the terms and provisions of the lease shown in **Example 20.5**. This lease is a capital lease because the provisions of the lease agreement meet one or more of the capitalization criteria and both of the recognition criteria. The lease is a direct financing lease because it does not include any manufacturer's or dealer's profit, and the fair (present) value of the property is equal to its cost.

EXAMPLE 20.5

Terms and Provisions of Lease Agreement between Condor Bank (Lessor) and Kestrel Company (Lessee) Dated January 1, 2016

1. The cost, and fair value, of the equipment is $11,149.06.
2. The initial direct costs incurred by Condor Bank are not material.
3. The term of the lease is 4 years, with annual payments of $3,000 received at the beginning of each year.
4. The estimated economic life of the equipment is 5 years, the lease is for only 4 years, and there is an estimated residual value of $2,000 at the end of the lease. Kestrel Company does not guarantee any of the estimated residual value.
5. The lease payments are determined at an amount such that Condor will earn a 14% annual rate of return on its net investment.
6. Kestrel pays all the executory costs.
7. The equipment reverts to Condor at the end of the fourth year. The lease contains no renewal or bargain purchase options.
8. The present value of the minimum lease payments receivable for the lessor plus the unguaranteed residual value is $11,149.06, calculated as follows:

Present value of 4 amounts of $3,000 in advance at 14% (3.321632 × $3,000)	= $ 9,964.90
Add: Present value of the unguaranteed residual value at 14% for 4 periods (0.592080 × $2,000)	= 1,184.16
Total present value	= $11,149.06

9. The collectibility of the payments is reasonably assured, and there are no uncertainties involved in the lease.

Condor records the acquisition of the equipment and the lease for the year 2016 using the amounts from **Example 20.5** (p. 20-29). Condor records the Lease Receivable at $14,000 (the undiscounted 4 annual rental payments totaling $12,000, plus the $2,000 unguaranteed residual value). Note that the discounted amount of the $2,000 unguaranteed residual value is included in the receivable to determine the net investment. Condor records the Unearned Interest at $2,850.94; thus, the net receivable is the cost of the equipment of $11,149.06. Because the transaction is considered a disposal of an asset, Condor also credits the Equipment account.

Acquisition of the Equipment
Equipment Leased to Others	11,149.06	
Cash		11,149.06

Initial Recording of Lease on January 1, 2016
Lease Receivable	14,000.00	
Equipment Leased to Others		11,149.06
Unearned Interest: Leases		2,850.94

The payments are collected in advance so an additional journal entry on January 1, 2016, reduces the net investment that will earn interest.

Collection of Annual Payment for First Year on January 1, 2016
Cash	3,000.00	
Lease Receivable		3,000.00

As shown in **Example 20.5a**, the interest earned during 2016 is $1,140.87. Condor uses the information shown in **Example 20.5a** to record the entries for the remaining years. At the end of the lease, there will be $2,000 left in the Lease Receivable account. When Condor receives the asset, it records it at the lowest of the cost, carrying value, or fair value. Condor records a loss if the asset value is less than $2,000.

Recognition of Interest Revenue for First Year on December 31, 2016
Unearned Interest: Leases	1,140.87	
Interest Revenue: Leases		1,140.87

EXAMPLE 20.5a Summary of Lease Payments Received in Advance and Interest Revenue Earned by Condor Bank (Lessor)

(1) Date	(2) Annual Lease Payment Received	(3) Interest Revenue at 14% on Net Investment[a]	(4) Lease Receivable[b]	(5) Unearned Interest: Leases[c]	(6) Net Investment[d]
January 1, 2016			$14,000	$2,850.94	$11,149.06
January 1, 2016	$3,000		11,000		8,149.06[e]
December 31, 2016		$1,140.87		1,710.07	9,289.93
January 1, 2017	3,000		8,000		6,289.93
December 31, 2017		880.59		829.48	7,170.52[e]
January 1, 2018	3,000		5,000		4,170.52
December 31, 2018		583.87		245.61	4,754.39[e]
January 1, 2019	3,000		2,000[f]		1,754.39
December 31, 2019		245.61		0	2,000.00[f]

[a] Column 6 at beginning of year × 14%
[b] Annual Lease Payment × Number of Years Remaining on Lease + $2,000 Residual Value, or Previous Balance − Column 2
[c] Previous Balance − Column 3
[d] Lease Receivable balance − Unearned Interest = Leases balance
[e] $3,000 of each of these December 31 balances is a current asset; the remaining amount is a noncurrent asset
[f] Estimated unguaranteed residual value

Initial Direct Costs Involved in a Direct Financing Lease

The accounting for initial direct costs incurred by the lessor is different for direct financing and sales type leases. Recall that for an operating lease, the lessor records these initial direct costs as an asset and allocates them as an operating expense over the term of the operating lease.

GAAP states that the *initial direct costs* of a completed lease transaction include the following two types of costs:

- Costs that result directly from and are essential to the leasing transaction and would not have been incurred by the lessor if the transaction had not occurred.
- Costs of the lessor related to evaluating the lessee's financial condition, negotiating terms, preparing and processing lease documents, and closing the transaction.[17]

Because the lessor does not recognize any revenue at the time it signs a direct financing lease, it defers the initial direct costs. This accounting procedure requires that the lessor determine a *new* (lower) implicit rate that will discount the remaining future minimum lease payments to the net investment at the inception of the lease.[18] It expenses all other lease-related costs, such as the costs of advertising, servicing existing leases, unsuccessful lease originations, supervision, and administration, as incurred.

Example If a lessor incurs initial direct costs of $5,000 on a direct financing lease, it records the costs as follows:

Unearned Interest: Leases	5,000	
Cash		5,000

The initial direct costs are deferred and expensed over the lease term as interest revenue is recognized. The reduction in the Unearned Interest: Leases account increases the net investment, but the future cash flows remain unchanged, resulting in a lower implicit rate. The lower rate results in less interest revenue being recognized each period. This achieves the goal of deferring the initial direct costs and including them as a reduction of income over the life of the lease. ■

The calculation of the new implicit rate requires the use of compound interest techniques discussed in the Time Value of Money Module. Instead of showing this calculation, we assume a new implicit rate and list it in the related homework assignments.

Sales-Type Leases (Lessor)

In a sales-type lease, like a direct financing lease, the lessor "sells" the asset and records a receivable.[19] A sales-type lease differs from a direct financing lease in that the fair value of the asset is greater (or less) than its cost or carrying value resulting in **manufacturer's profit (loss)** [**dealer's profit (loss)**]. The manufacturer's or dealer's profit or loss is the difference between the following two items:

- present value of the minimum lease payments computed at the interest rate implicit in the lease (i.e., the sale proceeds)
- cost or carrying value of the asset plus any initial direct costs minus the present value of the unguaranteed residual value accruing to the benefit of the lessor[20]

Example: Sales-Type Lease

On January 1, 2016, Solitaire Company leases specialty equipment to Meadowlark Company with the terms and provisions of the lease shown in **Example 20.6**. Solitaire is a manufacturer of the specialty equipment being leased and records the manufacturing costs of the equipment

---

[17] FASB ASC 840-20-25-17: Leases, Operating Leases, Recognition.
[18] FASB ASC 840-30-35: Leases, Capital Leases, Subsequent Measurement.
[19] A lessor may not classify a lease involving real estate as a sales-type lease unless the lease agreement provides for the transfer of title to the lessee at or shortly after the end of the lease term.
[20] FASB ASC 840-30-35: Leases, Capital Leases, Subsequent Measurement.

for $120,000 in the normal manner.[21] The company determines that the lease qualifies as a sales-type lease based on the capitalization and revenue recognition criteria in **Example 20.6a**.

EXAMPLE 20.6

Terms and Provisions of Lease Agreement between Solitaire Company (Lessor) and Meadowlark Company (Lessee) Dated January 1, 2016

1. The cost of the equipment is $120,000. The fair value is $190,008.49.
2. No initial direct costs are incurred by Solitaire Company.
3. The term of the lease is 10 years, with annual payments of $30,000 received at the beginning of each year. The estimated economic life of the equipment is also 10 years.
4. Meadowlark Company agrees to pay all executory costs.
5. Meadowlark is given an option to buy the equipment for $500 at the end of the lease term, December 31, 2022. This is a bargain purchase option.
6. The interest rate implicit in the lease is 12%.
7. The present value of 10 payments of $30,000 at 12% on an annuity-due basis, plus the present value of the bargain purchase option, is $190,008.49, calculated as follows:

   Present value of 10 amounts in advance at
      12% (6.328250 × $30,000)   = $189,847.50
   Plus: Present value of $500 discounted at
      12% (0.321973 × $500)   =   160.99
   Total present value   = $190,008.49

8. The collectibility of the payments is reasonably assured, and there are no uncertainties involved in the lease.

EXAMPLE 20.6a

Application of Lease Classification Criteria by Solitaire Company (Lessor)

	Criteria Met?	Remarks
Capitalization Criteria		
1. Transfer of ownership	No	
2. Bargain purchase option	Yes	
3. Lease term is 75% or more of economic life	Yes	100% of life
4. Present value of minimum lease payments is 90% or more of fair value	Yes	The present value is $190,008.49, or 100% of estimated fair value
Recognition Criteria		
1. Collectibility reasonably assured	Yes	
2. No uncertainties	Yes	

Decision: If the lease meets one or more of the capitalization criteria and both recognition criteria and there is a manufacturer's or dealer's profit or loss, it is a sales-type lease.

Conclusion: The lease is a sales-type lease, because appropriate criteria are met and the selling price ($190,008.49) exceeds the cost ($120,000), resulting in manufacturer's or dealer's profit. That is, the present (fair) value of the lease payments is greater than the cost of the property.

---

[21] If the lessor was a dealer in the asset being leased the asset would be recorded at the dealer's acquisition cost.

Solitaire records the information relevant to the lease for 2016 in the following manner:

Initial Recording of the Sales-Type Lease on January 1, 2016

Lease Receivable	300,500.00	
Sales Revenue		190,008.49
Unearned Interest: Leases		110,491.51
Cost of Asset Leased	120,000.00	
Inventory (or Equipment Held for Lease)		120,000.00

The first journal entry records the "sale" of the asset. Because this lease contains a bargain purchase option, Solitaire (the lessor) records the lease receivable at the sum of the undiscounted annual rental payments ($300,000) plus the undiscounted amount of the bargain purchase option ($500). It records the $190,008.49 sales revenue at the present value of the minimum lease payments, which is equal to:

Present Value of the Annual Payments ($189,847.50)
+ Present Value of the Bargain Purchase Option ($160.99)

The accounting for the bargain purchase option is the same as that for a guaranteed residual value because each is included in the minimum lease payments. Thus, the present value of the bargain purchase option (or a guaranteed residual value) is included as a part of the sales price of the equipment.

The Unearned Interest: Leases amount of $110,491.51 is the difference between the receivable of $300,500 (the gross investment) and the sales revenue of $190,008.49. In general, the Unearned Interest: Leases amount is the difference between the gross investment in the lease and the sum of the present value of the two components of the gross investment:

- present value of the minimum lease payments
- present value of any unguaranteed residual value accruing to the lessor

The second journal entry records the cost of the asset leased as an expense at its cost ($120,000) because there is no unguaranteed residual value. Solitaire reports a gross profit of $70,008.49 ($190,008.49 sales revenue − $120,000.00 cost of asset leased) on this sales-type lease at the time of the transfer of the asset.

Collection of Annual Payment for First Year on January 1, 2016

Cash	30,000.00	
Lease Receivable		30,000.00

The lease provisions require that payments are collected in advance at the beginning of each year. Also, remember that this collection reduces the net investment (the amount on which interest revenue is calculated) by $30,000.00.

Recognition of Interest Revenue for First Year on December 31, 2016

Unearned Interest: Leases	19,201.02	
Interest Revenue: Leases		19,201.02

Solitaire amortizes the Unearned Interest: Leases account using the effective interest method. It recognizes interest as 12% of the net investment *after* the collection of the first rent, or $19,201.02, calculated as follows:

12% × [($300,500 − $30,000) − $110,491.51] = $19,201.02

Solitaire's journal entries for the following 9 years will show a similar pattern. After it records the entries for the tenth year, its net investment on December 31, 2022, will be $500, the amount of the bargain purchase option. ■

Initial Direct Costs Involved in a Sales-Type Lease

The accounting for the lessor's initial direct costs is different under a sales-type lease. If a lessor does incur initial direct costs on a sales-type lease, it expenses them in the period in which the lease is initiated.[22] The lessor may report the initial direct costs in one of two ways:

- added to the expense Cost of Asset Leased
- included as a selling expense entitled Initial Direct Sales-Type Lease Expense

Either procedure results in an appropriate recognition of these expenses in the period in which they are incurred.

Unguaranteed and Guaranteed Residual Values

As discussed in the introduction to sales-type leases, the lessor deducts the present value of any *unguaranteed* residual value from the cost or carrying value of the asset when it recognizes the expenses associated with the signing of the lease. **The unguaranteed residual value is *not* included in sales revenue because it represents a portion of the asset that is *not* sold.**

The present value of any *guaranteed* residual value, on the other hand, is *not* subtracted from the expenses (e.g., Cost of Asset Leased) and is included in sales. Because both the expense and the revenue items contain the present value of the guaranteed residual value, the gross profit is the same as if the residual value is unguaranteed.

The major difference is that the sales revenue and expenses for a sales-type lease with an unguaranteed residual value are both reduced by the present value of the unguaranteed residual value. This method of accounting for the unguaranteed residual value in a sales-type lease indicates that there has been a total transfer of the risks and benefits to the lessee that is usually associated with ownership of an asset.

GOT IT?

20-15 What is the basic difference between the accounting procedures used by a lessor for a sales-type lease and those used for a direct financing lease?

20-16 Why are compound interest concepts appropriate and applicable in accounting for a direct financing lease?

20-17 Describe briefly the accounting procedures followed by the lessor for an operating lease.

LEARNING OBJECTIVE 20.6
Understand statement of cash flow presentation and disclosure by the lessor.

HOW DOES THE LESSOR PRESENT LEASE CASH FLOWS AND DISCLOSE LEASES?

In this section, we describe how lessors present operating and capital lease cash flows in the statement of cash flows and discuss disclosure requirements for leases.

Lessor Statement of Cash Flow Presentation

Presentation of leases in the lessor's cash flow statement is dependent on the classification of the lease. If a lessor records a lease as an operating lease, it classifies each lease receipt as a cash inflow in the operating activities section of its statement of cash flows. If a lessor records a lease as a direct financing lease, it classifies any cash paid to purchase the asset as a cash outflow in the investing activities section. Then, for each lease receipt, it classifies the interest portion as a cash inflow in the operating activities section and the reduction of the lease receivable as a cash inflow in the investing activities section. If a

---

[22] FASB ASC 840-30-35: Leases, Capital Leases, Subsequent Measurement.

lessor records a lease as a sales-type lease, it classifies any cash paid to purchase the asset as a cash outflow in the operating activities section. Then, for each lease receipt, it classifies the receipt as a cash inflow in the operating activities section.

Disclosure Requirements

Exhibit 20.6 shows the basic disclosures for operating, direct financing, and sales-type leases for a lessor whose leasing activities are a significant part of its business activities.[23]

EXHIBIT 20.6 Disclosure Requirements for Lessor: Operating, Direct Financing, and Sales-Type Leases

Operating Leases:
- Cost and carrying amount, if different, of property on lease or held for leasing by major classes of property and the amount of the total accumulated depreciation
- Minimum future rentals on noncancelable leases for each of the 5 succeeding fiscal years and in total
- Total contingent rentals included in income for each period

Direct Financing and Sales-Type Leases:
- The components of the net investment in direct financing and sales-type leases including:
  ○ Future minimum lease payments to be received, including any profit thereon
  ○ Unguaranteed residual values accruing to the benefit of the lessor
  ○ For direct financing leases only, initial direct costs
  ○ Unearned income

For all leases, a general description of the lessor's leasing arrangements including the following:
- Future minimum lease payments to be received for each of the 5 succeeding fiscal years and in total
- Total contingent rentals included in revenue for each period

GOT IT?

20-18 Describe the difference between how a lessor would report the cash flows associated with an operating lease and a capital lease.

20-19 What disclosures are lessors required to make for various types of leases?

APPENDIX 20.1: SPECIALIZED LEASE ISSUES AND CHANGES IN LEASE PROVISIONS

LEARNING OBJECTIVE 20.7
Examine lease issues related to sale-leaseback transactions, real estate leases, and modification and changes of lease provisions.

There are a number of leasing issues, such as sale-leasebacks, real estate leases, and modifications to lease agreements that require additional discussion, which we provide in this appendix.

Sale-Leaseback Transactions

Companies like **Southwest Airlines**, **Hyatt Hotels**, and **Tiffany and Company** have all recently realized gains from **sale-leaseback transactions**. If a company has limited cash or decides it does not want to be responsible for owning a property, it may sell an asset (often land and buildings, but not real property exclusively) and then immediately

---
[23] FASB ASC 840-30-50: Leases, Capital Leases, Disclosure.

lease it back from the buyer. This kind of transaction may be advantageous to both the lessee and lessor: The lessee receives cash from the sale that is needed for its activities, and may derive a tax advantage. The lessor acquires an asset. The sale of the asset and the leaseback are considered to be a single transaction that is like a secured loan, with the creditor obtaining legal title to the asset. The sales price of the asset, any profit earned, and the minimum lease payments must be considered together.

Purchaser-Lessor's Accounting for a Sale-Leaseback Transaction The purchaser-lessor follows the principles discussed earlier in the chapter to account for the purchase of the asset and the immediate lease of it back to the seller. From the lessor's point of view, no new issues are involved.

Seller-Lessee's Accounting for a Sale-Leaseback Transaction If the lease meets at least one of the four capitalization criteria, the seller-lessee accounts for the lease as a capital lease and any profit from the sale of the asset is initially deferred and then amortized in proportion to the depreciation of the leased asset. If none of the capitalization criteria are met, the seller-lessee accounts for the lease as an operating lease and any profit on the sale is deferred and amortized in proportion to the payments over the period of time it expects the asset to be used.

However, when the fair value of the property at the time of the transaction is less than its undepreciated cost, the seller-lessee *recognizes a loss immediately* up to the amount of the difference between the undepreciated cost and fair value.[24]

The primary new issue from the seller-lessee's viewpoint is the accounting for the profit or loss on the sale of the property.

Example: Sale-Leaseback (Seller-Lessee Accounting)

On January 1, 2016, Harrier Railroad built 10 boxcars costing $400,000. Because of a cash flow problem, Harrier decided to sell these boxcars immediately to Longspur Financial for $600,000 and then lease them back under the conditions shown in **Example 20.7**.

EXAMPLE 20.7

Terms and Provisions of Lease Agreement between Longspur Financial and Harrier Railroad Dated January 1, 2016

1. Title to the boxcars will be transferred to Harrier (the seller-lessee) at the end of the lease term.
2. The estimated economic life of the equipment is 20 years, with no expected residual value at the end of this time.
3. The cost of the boxcars to Harrier (the seller-lessee) is $400,000. The selling price to Longspur (the purchaser-lessor) is $600,000; thus, this amount becomes the new cost of the equipment to the seller-lessee.
4. The term of the lease is 15 years, with annual payments of $92,771.13 in advance at the beginning of each year.
5. The interest rate implicit on the lease is 16%. Harrier knows this rate, and the rate equals its incremental borrowing rate.
6. The present value of 15 payments of $92,771.13 at 16% on an annuity-due basis is $600,000, calculated as follows:

    Present value of 15 amounts in advance at 16% = 6.467529 × $92,771.13
    = $600,000 (rounded)

7. The lease qualifies as a capital lease to Harrier because it meets the capitalization criteria.
8. Harrier agrees to pay all executory costs.

---

[24] FASB ASC 840-40-25: Leases, Sale-Leaseback Transactions, Recognition.

The accounting entries to record the information related to the sale-leaseback for Harrier (the seller-lessee) for 2016 are as follows:

Build 10 Boxcars

Boxcars	400,000.00	
Cash		400,000.00

Sale of the Boxcars to Longspur Financial on January 1, 2016

Cash	600,000.00	
Boxcars		400,000.00
Unearned Gain on Sale-Leaseback		200,000.00

Harrier includes the Unearned Gain on Sale-Leaseback in the liability section of its balance sheet.

Initial Recording of the Leaseback as a Capital Lease on January 1, 2016

Leased Boxcars	600,000.00	
Capital Lease Obligation		600,000.00

Annual Payment on January 1, 2016

Capital Lease Obligation	92,771.13	
Cash		92,771.13

Payment of Executory Costs on Various Dates in 2016 (amounts assumed)

Insurance Expense	2,600.00	
Repairs and Maintenance Expense	2,300.00	
Property Tax Expense	9,700.00	
Cash		14,600.00

Recording Depreciation of Boxcars on December 31, 2016

Depreciation Expense: Leased Boxcars	30,000.00	
Accumulated Depreciation: Leased Boxcars		30,000.00

Harrier uses the straight-line method and a life of 20 years because ownership is transferred at the end of the lease. Depreciation for 2016 is $30,000 ($600,000 ÷ 20).

Amortization of Unearned Gain on Sale-Leaseback on December 31, 2016

Unearned Gain on Sale-Leaseback	10,000.00	
Gain on Sale-Leaseback (or Depreciation Expense: Leased Boxcars)		10,000.00

The amortization is $10,000 ($200,000 ÷ 20). Note that Harrier amortizes the Unearned Gain on Sale-Leaseback and recognizes the gain over a 20-year period. For a capital lease, GAAP requires that a seller-lessee recognize any gain using the same rate that it used to depreciate the leased asset. For an operating lease, the seller-lessee defers such gain (or loss) and amortizes the amount in proportion to the lease payments over the period it expects to use the leased assets. A loss would be recorded by the seller-lessee if the book value or carrying amount were larger than the fair value of the asset. The seller-lessee recognizes the entire amount of this loss in the year of the sale-leaseback.

Recognition of Interest Expense on December 31, 2016

Interest Expense	81,156.62	
Capital Lease Obligation		81,156.62

This year-end adjusting entry is the same as that made for any capital lease for which the payment is made in advance. Harrier calculates the amount as $81,156.62 [16% × ($600,000 − $92,771.13)]. ■

Real Estate Leases

In this chapter, we discussed operating and capital leases of real property, such as equipment, that is consumed as it is used. Leases involving real estate pose special issues because the asset, land, is not consumed as it is used.[25] Exhibit 20.7 shows the differences in the classification of leases involving real estate.

EXHIBIT 20.7 Classification of Leases Involving Real Property

I. **General Criteria for Classifying Leases**

Column A Capitalization Criteria Applicable to Both Lessees and Lessors	Column B Revenue Recognition Criteria Applicable to Lessors Only
1. Transfer of ownership 2. Contains bargain purchase option 3. Lease term is 75% or more of economic life 4. Present value of minimum lease payments is 90% or more of fair value	1. Collectability reasonably assured 2. No uncertainties surround the amount of unreimbursable costs yet to be incurred by the lessor

II. **Lease of Land Only**

A. Lessee

1. *Capital lease.* Lease must meet either Criterion 1 or 2 in Column A (Part I). (Criteria 3 and 4 are *not* applicable.)
2. *Operating lease.* Lease must not meet either Criterion 1 or 2 in Column A (Part I).

B. Lessor

1. *Sales-type lease.* Lease must:
   a. meet either Criterion 1 or 2 in Column A (Part I), *and*
   b. meet both criteria in Column B (Part I), *and*
   c. result in a dealer's profit or loss.
2. *Direct financing lease.* Lease must meet:
   a. either Criterion 1 or 2 in Column A (Part I), *and*
   b. both criteria in Column B (Part I).
3. *Operating lease.* Lease that does *not* qualify as a sales-type or direct financing lease.

III. **Lease of Both Land and Buildings**

A. Lease of both land and buildings that transfers ownership or contains a bargain purchase option

1. Lessee

   a. *Capital lease.* The lease is a capital lease because one or more of the criteria of Column A (Part I) are met. Land and buildings are separately capitalized.

2. Lessor

   a. *Sales-type lease.* The two assets, land and buildings, are considered as a single unit and the lease must:
      (1) meet either Criterion 1 or 2 in Column A (Part I), *and*
      (2) meet both criteria in Column B (Part I), *and*
      (3) result in a dealer's profit or loss.
   b. *Direct financing lease.* The lease of the two assets combined must meet:
      (1) either Criterion 1 or 2 in Column A (Part I), *and*
      (2) both criteria in Column B (Part I).

(continued)

---

[25] FASB ASC 840-30-25: Leases, Overall, Recognition.

B. If lease meets neither Criterion 1 nor Criterion 2 in Column A (Part I), and if fair value of land is less than 25% of fair value of both land and buildings. (The land portion is ignored and the classification is determined using the characteristics of building.)

1. Lessee
a. *Capital lease.* Lease must meet either Criterion 3 or 4 in Column A (Part I).
b. *Operating lease.* Lease meets none of the criteria in Column A (Part I).

2. Lessor
a. *Sales-type lease.* Lease must:
(1) meet either Criterion 3 or 4 in Column A (Part I), *and*
(2) meet both criteria in Column B (Part I), *and*
(3) result in a dealer's profit or loss.
b. *Direct financing lease.* Lease must meet:
(1) either Criterion 3 or 4 in Column A (Part I), *and*
(2) both criteria in Column B (Part I).
c. *Operating Lease.* Lease that does *not* qualify as a sales-type or direct financing lease.

C. If lease meets neither Criterion 1 nor Criterion 2 in Column A (Part I), and if fair value of land is more than 25% of fair value of both land and buildings. (The lease is separated into land and building portions.)

1. Lessee
a. *Land portion.* Always an operating lease
b. *Building portion.* Classified by remaining criteria of Column A (Part I)

2. Lessor
a. *Land portion.* Always an operating lease
b. *Building portion.* Classified by remaining criteria of Columns A and B (Part I)

Lease of Land Only When a lessee enters into a lease for land, it accounts for the lease as a capital lease only if the lease transfers ownership at the end of the lease, or includes a bargain purchase option. Otherwise, the lessee accounts for the lease as an operating lease. This is because the criteria dealing with the 75% of the estimated economic life and the 90% of the fair value of the leased property do *not* apply to leases of land.

The lessee does not depreciate the asset, Leased Land Under Capital Leases, because title to the land is expected to be transferred, and land is not subject to depreciation.

The lessor accounts for the lease of land as a sales-type lease if all of the following are met:

- lease transfers ownership or contains a bargain purchase option
- lease meets both the collectability and uncertainty criteria
- there is a dealer's profit or loss

If the criteria for a sales-type lease are met but there is no dealer's profit or loss, the lease qualifies as a direct financing one. Otherwise, it is an operating lease.

Lease of Both Land and Buildings That Transfers Title or Contains a Bargain Purchase Option When both land and buildings are leased, a new issue arises as to the classification of the lease because one portion involves a depreciable asset with an estimated economic life and the other involves a nondepreciable asset. This lease is accounted for either as:

- a lease of both land and buildings that meets the transfer of ownership and bargain purchase criteria of Column A (Part I) of Exhibit 20.7
- a lease of both land and buildings that does *not* meet either the transfer of ownership or bargain purchase criteria

Lessee's Accounting For a capital lease of land and buildings that transfers ownership or contains a bargain purchase option, the lessee allocates the present value of the minimum lease payments between the two leased assets in proportion to their fair values at the inception of the lease. It depreciates the amount assigned to Leased Buildings over the estimated economic life of the buildings. It does *not* depreciate the amount assigned to Leased Land.

Lessor's Accounting The lessor accounts for the lease as a single unit, either as a direct financing, a sales-type, or an operating lease. The term **single unit** means that for a sales-type or direct financing lease, the lessor uses one Lease Receivable account to record the appropriate values for the lease of both land and buildings. In the original lease entry, however, the lessor credits both the land and the buildings accounts.

Lease of Land and Buildings That Does Not Transfer Title or Include a Bargain Purchase Option
The accounting for this transaction is dependent on the value of the land in relationship to the total value of the transaction. In cases where the fair value of the land is greater than 25% of the total transaction, the land is considered a material part of the transaction.

Value of Land Is Less Than 25% If a lease of land and buildings does not transfer ownership or include a bargain purchase option, it is a capital lease if it meets one of the other two criteria. If the fair value of the land is less than 25% of the total fair value of the leased property at the inception of the lease, the land is considered to be immaterial. Therefore, *both* the lessee and the lessor treat the land and buildings as a single unit. Note that the estimated economic life of the building is used as the economic life of the unit.

- *Lessee's Accounting.* If the lease transfers ownership or contains a bargain purchase option, the lessee classifies the lease as a capital lease and recognizes the leased land and buildings as a single asset. It depreciates the total amount over the term of the lease, even though it is implicitly depreciating the land portion of the asset. If the lease does not meet any of the criteria, it is an operating lease.
- *Lessor's Accounting.* If the lease meets either Criterion 3 or 4 of Column A (Part I) of Exhibit 20.7 and both of the revenue recognition criteria of Column B (Part I), the lessor accounts for the lease as a single unit, as either a direct financing or a sales-type lease as appropriate. Otherwise, the lease is an operating lease.

Value of Land Is More Than 25% On the other hand, if at the inception of the lease, the land represents 25% or more of the fair value of the leased property, the amount of the land is considered to be a material amount. Then, both the lessee and the lessor must treat the land and the buildings separately for purposes of applying the criteria listed in Exhibit 20.7. In this case, the lessee and lessor separate the minimum lease payments into amounts applicable to land and to buildings. Because the lease of the land results in an operating lease, the best way to make the preceding calculation is to determine the fair value of land, and then use the appropriate interest rate to determine the periodic minimum lease payments applicable to the land portion, as follows:

$$\text{Incremental Borrowing Rate} \times \text{Fair Value of Land} = \text{Periodic Minimum Lease Payment Applicable to Land}$$

The periodic minimum lease payments applicable to both land and buildings minus the amount calculated is the amount attributed to the buildings.

- *Lessee's Accounting.* Once the amount assigned to the buildings is determined, if the building portion of the lease meets either capitalization Criterion 3 or 4 of Column A (Part I) of Exhibit 20.7, the lessee accounts for it as a capital lease. The lessee depreciates the present value amount assigned to the asset, Leased Buildings, over the life of the lease. It accounts for the land portion of the lease separately as an operating lease. Therefore, if the buildings portion of the lease meets neither capitalization Criterion 3 nor 4 of Column A (Part I) of Exhibit 20.7, the lessee accounts for both the buildings and the land as a single operating lease.
- *Lessor's Accounting.* If the buildings portion of the lease meets either capitalization Criterion 3 or 4 of Column A (Part I) and both revenue recognition criteria, the lessor accounts for the lease as a direct financing or sales-type lease, depending on

whether there is a manufacturer's or dealer's profit or loss. It accounts for the land portion of the lease separately as an operating lease. If the buildings portion of the lease does not meet the relevant criteria, the lessor accounts for both the buildings and land as a single operating lease.

Lease Involving Equipment as Well as Real Estate If a lease involves both equipment and real estate, the portion of the minimum lease payments for the equipment portion of the lease is estimated. The equipment then is treated separately when applying the criteria listed in Exhibit 20.7. It is accounted for separately according to its classification by both the lessee and lessor. The accounting for the remaining real estate portion follows the accounting standards described earlier in the chapter.

Changes in Lease Provisions

Lease contracts contain many provisions, including renewal, extension, or purchase options, and penalties. Lessees and lessors may opt to change certain provisions that, in effect, change the classification of the lease. If at any time the lessee and lessor change a lease (other than by renewing or extending its term) so that the lease would have been classified differently *had the changed terms been in effect at the beginning of the lease term*, the revised agreement is considered a new agreement. The new agreement is reclassified as operating, direct financing, or sales-type, according to the capitalization and revenue recognition criteria discussed earlier.

GAAP also addresses the issue of renewals and extensions. A change in an operating lease to a direct financing or sales-type lease presents the fewest issues because the accounting for the new lease would be similar to that described earlier in the chapter. The most complex issue involves a change in either a sales-type or direct financing lease.

Impact of Renewal of Lease on Guarantee of Residual Value Suppose, for example, a lessee records a lease as a capital lease while the lessor records it as a direct financing lease, and the lease contains a guarantee of the residual value of the leased property. If at the end of the lease term the lessee elects to renew the lease, this election would cancel the guarantee of residual value. The renewal, however, is *not* treated as a new agreement, because there is no change in the lease classification. The lessee adjusts the remaining balances of the asset and obligation from the original lease. The amount of the adjustment is equal to the difference between the present value of the future minimum lease payments under the new renewal agreement and the existing present balance of the obligation.

Changes to Sales-Type or Direct Financing Lease Prior to Lease Term Expiration That Change the Lease to an Operating Lease If changes are made in either sales-type or direct financing lease provisions before the expiration of the lease, and if these changes would have caused the original agreement to be classified as an operating lease, the lessor removes the remaining net investment from its accounts. It replaces the Lease Receivable with an asset at its original cost, fair value, or carrying amount, whichever is lowest, and reports any net adjustment as an operating loss in the period of change. It then accounts for the new lease as any other operating lease.

An exception occurs when a guarantee or penalty becomes inoperative. In this case, if the renewal or extension results in an operating lease, the lessor continues to account for the existing lease as either a sales-type or direct financing lease (depending on the original classification) to the end of its original term. It then accounts for the renewal or extension as any other operating lease. The accounting by the lessee follows a similar pattern.

Renewal of Sales-Type or Direct Financing Lease Resulting in a New Lease That Qualifies as a Sales-Type Lease The accounting for a renewal of sales-type and direct financing leases that results in a lease that qualifies again as a sales-type lease is complex. When an existing sales-type or direct financing lease is renewed *during the term* of the lease, the lessor *cannot* classify the renewal lease as a sales-type lease even though it meets the necessary criteria. This renewal lease has to be treated as a direct financing lease.

If the renewal takes place *at the end* of the lease (or during the last few months of the existing lease), the lease change can qualify as a sales-type lease.

Renewal Occurring During Lease Term The FASB concluded that if a lessor treated a renewal of a sales-type or direct financing lease as a sales-type lease at the time of an interim renewal, a "second sale" would result in recognition of revenue before its realization. For this reason, GAAP requires that a lessor classify a renewal of an existing sales-type or direct financing lease that *otherwise qualifies as a sales-type lease* as a direct financing lease if the lease change occurs *during the term* of the lease.

Renewal Occurring at End of Lease Term If the renewal occurs at the end of the lease term, and if the new agreement qualified as a sales-type lease (according to the capitalization and revenue recognition criteria discussed earlier), GAAP requires the lessor to account for the renewal as a sales-type lease at the end of the original term of the existing lease.

Many other changes may be made in lease terms. These often involve complex changes in accounting and, thus, require careful consideration. The preceding discussion indicates the scope of the issues. An accountant faced with new changes should carefully research the FASB Accounting Standards Codification before taking action on a particular change.

GOT IT?

20-20 From the seller-lessee's point of view, what is the primary accounting issue involved in accounting for a sale-leaseback transaction as compared to other lessee transactions? Discuss.

20-21 Under what conditions would a change in lease provisions result in a lease being considered a new agreement?

REVIEW CENTER

At the beginning of the chapter, we discussed how Starbucks leases many of its retail stores and facilities and the effects these leases have on Starbucks's financial statements. We also identified several objectives you would accomplish after reading the chapter. The objectives are listed below and followed by a brief summary of the key points.

LEARNING OBJECTIVE 20.1
Explain how to classify leases.

KEY TAKEAWAYS

- A lessee is the party that acquires the right to use the asset, and the lessor is the party that gives up the right to use the asset.
- A lease that transfers substantially all the risks and benefits of ownership is a capital lease and is accounted for in a similar manner to a purchase by the lessee and as a sale by the lessor.
- A lease that does not transfer substantially all of the risks and benefits of ownership is treated as an operating lease and is accounted for as a rental agreement.
- If a lease meets any one of the four capitalization criteria, the lessee classifies it as a capital lease and records an asset and a related liability; otherwise, the lessee classifies it as an operating lease.
- If the lease meets one of the four capitalization criteria and both recognition criteria, the lessor classifies the lease as either a:
  - Sales-type capital lease if the fair value of the leased property at the inception of the lease differs from its cost or carrying value (profit or loss exists)

- Direct financing capital lease if there is no manufacturer's or dealer's profit or loss at the inception of the lease

Otherwise, the lessor classifies it as an operating lease.

KEY TERMS

capital lease, p. 20-2
capitalization criteria, p. 20-2
direct financing capital lease, p. 20-3
lease, p. 20-2
lessee, p. 20-2
lessor, p. 20-2
minimum lease payments, p. 20-2
operating lease, p. 20-2
sales-type capital lease, p. 20-3

KEY TAKEAWAYS

LEARNING OBJECTIVE 20.2
Explain the advantages and disadvantages of leasing.

- Compared to buying, the advantages of leasing for the lessee are related to less costly financing, reduced risk, lower taxes, and off-balance-sheet financing.
- From the lessor's viewpoint, the benefits of leasing may be the ability to indirectly make a sale and earn additional profit (interest) on the leased asset.

KEY TERMS

bargain purchase option, p. 20-7
bargain renewal option, p. 20-7
dealer's profit (loss), p. 20-7
estimated economic life of leased asset, p. 20-7
estimated residual value of leased asset, p. 20-7
executory costs, p. 20-7
fair value of leased asset, p. 20-7
guaranteed residual value, p. 20-8
inception of the lease, p. 20-8
initial direct costs, p. 20-8
interest rate implicit in the lease, p. 20-8
lease receivable (gross investment in the lease), p. 20-8
lease term, p. 20-8
lessees incremental borrowing rate, p. 20-8
manufacturer's profit (loss), p. 20-8
minimum lease payments, p. 20-8
noncancelable lease term, p. 20-8
unguaranteed residual value, p. 20-8

KEY TAKEAWAYS

LEARNING OBJECTIVE 20.3
Account for a lessee's operating and capital leases.

- A lessee accounts for an operating lease as a rental agreement. The lessee records rent expense each period and does not report the leased equipment or any related obligation for future payments on the balance sheet.
- For a capital lease, the lessee records the leased asset and a liability equal to the present value of the minimum lease payments at the beginning of the lease term.
- Executory costs (such as insurance, maintenance, and property taxes) are not considered part of the minimum lease payment and are excluded from any present value calculations.
- The lessee uses the lower of the lessee's incremental borrowing rate or the lessor's interest rate implicit in the lease (if it is known by the lessee) in any present value calculations.
- The lessee depreciates the leased asset over its estimated economic life if it expects to acquire the asset at the end of the lease term (e.g., the lease agreement transfers ownership to the lessee or contains a bargain purchase option), or the lease term if the lessor is expected to retain ownership of the leased asset at the end of the lease term.
- Each lease payment consists of interest expense and a reduction of the principal of the recorded liability, computed using the effective interest method.
- The lease obligation is classified as current or noncurrent on the balance sheet using either the present value of next year's payments approach or the change in present value approach.
- If a lease contains a bargain purchase option, the bargain purchase option is viewed as an additional lease payment and is included in the computation of the present value of the minimum lease payments.

- If the lessee guarantees the residual value of the leased asset, it views the guaranteed residual value as an additional payment and includes this amount in the calculation of the present value of the minimum lease payments.
- Contingent rental payments depend on some future event occurring such as sales, miles driven, or a change in inflation. If the contingent rental payment is determined by usage, it is excluded from minimum lease payments. If the contingent rental payment is determined by an index or rate, it is included in minimum lease payments.

KEY TERMS

contingent rental payments, p. 20-12
executory costs, p. 20-7
implicit interest rate, p. 20-13
incremental borrowing rate, p. 20-13

LEARNING OBJECTIVE 20.4
Understand statement of cash flow presentation and disclosure by the lessee.

KEY TAKEAWAYS

- When preparing its statement of cash flows, a lessee reports operating lease cash flows in the operating activities section and capital lease cash flows in the financing activities section.
- Beyond a general description of the lessee's leasing arrangement, the lessee must also disclose specific information about lease payments for both operating and capital leases. Of specific importance is information on the future minimum lease payments for each of the succeeding 5 years and the total of all payments after year 5. This disclosure is made separately for operating and capital leases.

LEARNING OBJECTIVE 20.5
Account for a lessor's operating, direct financing, and sales-type leases.

KEY TAKEAWAYS

- A lessor accounts for an operating lease as a rental agreement.
  - The lessor records rental revenue each period and includes the leased equipment on its balance sheet as part of property, plant, and equipment.
  - The lessor depreciates the leased equipment over its estimated economic life.
  - Executory costs paid by the lessor are recorded as operating expenses and matched against rental revenue.
  - Any initial direct costs (costs incurred from directly originating the lease) are recorded as an asset and amortized over the lease term.
- For a direct financing lease, the lessor removes the carrying value of the leased equipment and records a gross receivable equal to the undiscounted minimum lease payments plus any unguaranteed residual value. The difference between the gross receivable and the carrying value of the leased property is recorded as unearned interest revenue (a contra-account to the lease receivable).
  - The gross receivable includes the residual value, whether it is guaranteed or unguaranteed.
  - Executory costs are not included in the gross receivable or the present value calculations.
  - The lessor's net investment in the lease (the lease receivable minus unearned revenue) is reported as current or noncurrent using the present value of next year's payments approach or the change in present value approach.
  - Interest revenue is recorded each period and is computed using the effective interest method based on the interest rate implicit in the lease.
  - Initial direct costs are deferred and recognized over the lease term by reducing unearned interest revenue based on a newly computed implicit interest rate.
- For a sales-type lease, the lessor recognizes a manufacturer's or dealer's profit or loss at the inception of the lease in addition to interest revenue over the lease term (like in a direct financing lease).
  - The manufacturer's or dealer's profit is measured as the difference between the present value of the minimum lease payments (sales revenue) and the cost of the

asset minus the present value of the unguaranteed residual value (cost of asset leased).
- If the residual value is guaranteed by the lessee, the present value of this amount is not subtracted from the cost of the asset and is included in sales revenue.
- Initial direct costs are expensed at the inception of the lease.

KEY TERMS

dealer's profit (loss), p. 20-31
gross receivable, p. 20-25
manufacturer's profit (loss), p. 20-31

KEY TAKEAWAYS

LEARNING OBJECTIVE 20.6
Understand statement of cash flow presentation and disclosure by the lessor.

- When preparing its statement of cash flows, a lessor reports operating lease cash flows in the operating activities section.
- If a lessor records a direct financing lease, the interest cash receipts are reported in the operating activities section and the recovery of the lease receivable cash flows are reported in the investing activities section.
- If a lessor records a sales-type lease, the cash receipts are reported in the operating activities section.
- Beyond a general description of the lessor's leasing arrangement, the lessor must also disclose specific information about lease rentals for operating leases and the components of net investment in direct financing and sales-type capital leases.

KEY TAKEAWAYS

LEARNING OBJECTIVE 20.7
(Appendix 20.1) Examine lease issues related to sale-leaseback transactions, real estate leases, and modification and changes of lease provisions.

- The primary issue in a sale-leaseback is that the seller-lessee recognizes a loss in the period of the transaction, but defers any gain and amortizes it over the remaining life of the lease.
- When lease provisions are changed in such a way that the lease would have been classified differently had the changed terms been in effect at the beginning of the lease term, the revised agreement is considered a new agreement.
- Leases of real estate follow special rules that are summarized in Exhibit 20.7 (p. 20-38).

KEY TERMS

sale-leaseback transactions, p. 20-35   single unit, p. 20-40

ANSWERS TO REAL REPORT QUESTIONS

Real Report 20.1 Answers Noodles & Company—Lease Obligations

1. Operating leases provide many benefits to the lessee. The use of long-term operating leases for stores and equipment may provide Noodles considerable flexibility. (In addition, many of Noodles's locations are not available for purchase and must be leased.) For example, renewal options may allow Noodles to continue to operate profitable locations, and for less profitable locations, Noodles may have lower expenses due to contingent rentals. Additionally, relocating these stores can be accomplished relatively easily by choosing not to exercise renewal options. Such flexibility can lead to a significant reduction in the company's risk. In addition, the use of operating leases provides a financial reporting benefit in that the lease does not add an asset or liability to Noodles's balance sheet, which generally results in "better" liquidity, solvency, and return on asset ratios.

2. The lease footnote does not provide all of the information needed to understand the lease in the same way as if it were capitalized and on the balance sheet. For example, we do not have information about:

   - gross amount of the assets under operating leases and where the assets would be classified on the balance sheet
   - age of the assets being leased and the average length of the leases
   - present value of the minimum lease payments
   - interest rate used in lease calculations

3. The classification of Noodles's operating leases as capital leases would result in a deterioration of Noodles's debt ratio. Noodles's 2013 debt ratio is 33.7% ($63,329 in total liabilities/$187,802 in total assets). Assuming an interest rate of 10% and annual lease payments in advance, assets and liabilities would both be increased by the present value of the lease payments of approximately $189,177 thousand (see calculation below). This would more than triple the total liabilities on Noodles's balance sheet and would result in an increase in Noodles's debt ratio to 67.0% ($252,506 in total liabilities/$376,979 in total assets). (All amounts in thousands.)

Year	Min. Lease Payment	PV Factor	Present Value
2014	$33,912.00	1	$ 33,912
2015	34,351.00	0.909091	31,228
2016	33,279.00	0.826446	27,503
2017	30,689.00	0.751315	23,057
2018	26,368.00	0.683013	18,010
2019	89,330.00	0.620921	55,467
			$189,177

MULTIPLE-CHOICE (AICPA ADAPTED)

Select the best answer for each of the following.

M20-1 The present value of the minimum lease payments should be used by the lessee in the determination of a(n):
LO 20.3

	Capital Lease Liability	Operating Lease Liability
a.	Yes	No
b.	Yes	Yes
c.	No	Yes
d.	No	No

M20-2 East Company leased a new machine from North Company on May 1, 2016, under a lease with the following information:
LO 20.3

Lease term	10 years
Annual rental payable at beginning of each lease year	$40,000
Useful life of machine	12 years
Implicit interest rate	14%
Present value factor for an annuity of 1 in advance for 10 periods at 14%	5.95
Present value factor for 1 for 10 periods at 14%	0.27

East has the option to purchase the machine on May 1, 2023, by paying $50,000, which approximates the expected fair value of the machine on the option exercise date. On May 1, 2016, East should record a capitalized lease asset of:

a. $251,500   c. $224,500
b. $238,000   d. $198,000

M20-3 For a lease that transfers ownership of the property to the lessee by the end of the lease term, the lessee should:
LO 20.3

a. record the minimum lease payment as an expense
b. amortize the capitalizable cost of the property using the interest method
c. depreciate the capitalizable cost of the property in a manner consistent with the lessee's normal depreciation policy for owned assets, except that the period of depreciation should be the lease term
d. depreciate the capitalizable cost of the property in a manner consistent with the lessee's normal depreciation policy for owned assets

Refer to the following information for M20-4 and M20-5.
Fox Company, a dealer in machinery and equipment, leased equipment to Tiger Inc. on July 1, 2016. The lease is

appropriately accounted for as a sale by Fox and as a purchase by Tiger. The lease is for a 10-year period (the useful life of the asset) expiring June 30, 2026. The first of 10 equal annual payments of $500,000 was made on July 1, 2016. Fox had purchased the equipment for $2,675,000 on January 1, 2016, and established a list selling price of $3,375,000 on the equipment. Assume that the present value at July 1, 2016, of the rent payments over the lease term, discounted at 12% (the appropriate interest rate), was $3,165,000.

M20-4 Refer to the information for Fox Company above. What is the amount of profit on the sale and the amount of interest income that Fox should record for the year ended December 31, 2016?
LO 20.5

a. $0 and $159,900
b. $490,000 and $159,900
c. $490,000 and $189,900
d. $700,000 and $189,900

M20-5 Refer to the information for Tiger Inc. above. Assuming that Tiger uses straight-line depreciation, what is the amount of depreciation and interest expense that Tiger should record for the year ended December 31, 2016?
LO 20.3

a. $158,250 and $159,900
b. $158,250 and $189,900
c. $168,750 and $159,900
d. $168,750 and $189,900

M20-6 For a 6-year capital lease, the portion of the minimum lease payment applicable in the third year to the reduction of the obligation should be:
LO 20.3

a. less than in the second year
b. more than in the second year
c. the same as in the fourth year
d. more than in the fourth year

M20-7 On January 2, 2016, Lafayette Machine Shops Inc. signed a 10-year noncancelable lease for a heavy-duty drill press, stipulating annual payments of $15,000 starting at the end of the first year, with title passing to Lafayette at the expiration of the lease. Lafayette treated this transaction as a capital lease. The drill press has an estimated useful life of 15 years with no salvage value. Lafayette uses straight-line depreciation for all of its fixed assets.
LO 20.3

Aggregate lease payments were determined to have a present value of $92,170, based on implicit interest of 10%. For 2016, Lafayette should record:

	Interest Expense	Depreciation Expense
a.	$0	$0
b.	$7,717	$6,145
c.	$9,217	$6,145
d.	$9,217	$9,217

M20-8 At its inception, the lease term of an equipment lease is 65% of the estimated remaining economic life of the leased property. This lease contains a bargain purchase option. The lessee should record the equipment lease as:
LO 20.3

a. neither an asset nor a liability
b. an asset but not a liability
c. an expense
d. an asset and a liability

M20-9 Rent received in advance by the lessor for an operating lease should be recognized as revenue
LO 20.5

a. when received
b. at the lease's inception
c. in the period specified by the lease
d. at the lease's expiration

M20-10 On August 1, 2016, Kern Company leased a machine to Day Company for a 6-year period requiring payments of $10,000 at the beginning of each year. The machine cost $48,000, which is the fair value at the lease date, and has a useful life of 8 years with no residual value. Kern's implicit interest rate is 10%, and present value factors are as follows:
LO 20.5

Present value for an annuity due of
$1 at 10% for 6 periods   4.791
Present value for an annuity due of
$1 at 10% for 8 periods   5.868

Kern appropriately recorded the lease as a direct financing lease. At the inception of the lease, the gross Lease Receivables account balance should be:

a. $60,000   c. $48,000
b. $58,680   d. $47,910

REVIEW EXERCISES

RE20-1 Next Level Keller Corporation (the lessee) entered into an equipment lease with Dallo Company (the lessor) on January 1 of Year 1. Use the following information to decide whether this lease qualifies as an operating or capital lease for Keller, and give an explanation using the four classification criteria.
LO 20.3

1. The equipment reverts back to the lessor at the end of the lease, and there is no bargain purchase option.
2. The lease term is 8 years and requires annual payments of $10,000 at the end of each year.

(continued)

3. The equipment's fair value at lease inception is $100,000. Assume that the present value of minimum lease payments is $50,000.
4. The equipment has an estimated economic life of 20 years and has zero residual value at the end of this time.

RE20-2 **Next Level** Garvey Company (the lessee) entered into an equipment lease with Richie Company (the lessor) on January 1 of Year 1. Use the following information to decide whether this lease qualifies as an operating or capital lease for Garvey, and give an explanation using the four classification criteria.
LO 20.3
1. The equipment reverts back to the lessor at the end of the lease, and there is no bargain purchase option.
2. The lease term is 5 years and requires Garvey to make annual payments of $65,949.37 at the end of each year.
3. The discount rate is 10%, which is implicit in the lease. Garvey knows this, and this rate is lower than its incremental borrowing rate.
4. The equipment's fair value at the lease inception is $250,000. The present value of an ordinary annuity of five payments of $65,949.37 each at 10% is $250,000.
5. The equipment has an estimated economic life of 7 years and has zero residual value at the end of this time. Straight-line depreciation is used for similar assets.

RE20-3 Use the information in **RE20-2**. Prepare the journal entries that Garvey Company would make in the first year of the lease assuming the lease is classified as a capital lease. Assume that Garvey is required to make payments on December 31 each year.
LO 20.3

RE20-4 Use the information in **RE20-2**. Prepare the journal entries that Garvey Company would make in the first year of the lease assuming the lease is classified as a capital lease. However, assume that Garvey is now required to make the $65,949.37 payments on January 1 each year and that the fair value at the lease inception is now $275,000 ($65,949.37 × 4.169865).
LO 20.3

RE20-5 Montevallo Corporation leased equipment from Folio Company. The lease term is 10 years, requires payments of $25,000 at the end of each year, and contains a bargain purchase option. At the end of the lease, Montevallo has an option to pay $4,000 (which is much less than the estimated fair value at that time) to purchase the equipment. The equipment has a fair value at the inception of the lease of $175,000 and an estimated useful life of 20 years. The lease agreement stipulates that Folio receive a rate of return of 8% each year, which is lower than Montevallo's incremental borrowing rate. Calculate the present value of the minimum lease payments.
LO 20.3

RE20-6 Use the information in **RE20-5**. However, assume that there is no bargain purchase option and that Montevallo guarantees the $20,000 estimated residual value at the end of the 10-year lease. Calculate the present value of the minimum lease payments. Round your answer to the nearest dollar.
LO 20.3

RE20-7 Use the information in **RE20-1**. Prepare the journal entry that Keller Corporation would make each year, assuming the lease is classified as an operating lease.
LO 20.5

RE20-8 Use the following information to decide whether this equipment lease qualifies as an operating, sales-type, or direct financing lease to a *lessor*.
LO 20.1
LO 20.5
a. • There is no transfer of ownership at the end of the lease term.
   • There is no bargain purchase option.
   • The lease term is 72% of the economic life of the leased property.
   • The present value of minimum lease payments is 100% of the fair value of the leased property to the lessor.
   • The cost of the leased property is less than the fair value.
   • The collectability of the minimum lease payments is reasonably assured.
   • No important uncertainties surround the amount of unreimbursable costs yet to be incurred by the lessor under the lease.
b. Same as (a), except that the cost of the leased property equals its fair value.
c. • Same as (a), except that the present value of minimum lease payments is only 50% of the fair value of the leased asset.
   • The collectability of the minimum lease payments is not predictable.
   • There are important uncertainties surrounding the amount of unreimbursable costs yet to be incurred by the lessor.

RE20-9 Use the information in **RE20-2**. Prepare the journal entries that Richie Company (the lessor) would make in the first year of the lease assuming the lease is classified as a direct financing lease. Assume that the lessee is required to make payments on December 31 each year. Also assume that Richie had purchased the equipment at a cost of $250,000.
LO 20.5

RE20-10 Use the information in **RE20-2**. Prepare the journal entries that Richie Company (the lessor) would make in the first year of the lease assuming the lease is classified as a sales-type lease. Assume that the lessee is required to make payments on December 31 each year. Also assume that Richie had purchased the equipment at a cost of $200,000.
LO 20.5

EXERCISES

E20-1 **Determining Type of Lease and Subsequent Accounting** On January 1, 2016, Caswell Company signs a 10-year cancelable (at the option of either party) agreement to lease a storage building from Wake Company. The following information pertains to this lease agreement:
LO 20.1
LO 20.3
1. The agreement requires rental payments of $100,000 at the end of each year.
2. The cost and fair value of the building on January 1, 2016, is $2 million.
3. The building has an estimated economic life of 50 years, with no residual value. Caswell depreciates similar buildings according to the straight-line method.
4. The lease does not contain a renewable option clause. At the termination of the lease, the building reverts to the lessor.
5. Caswell's incremental borrowing rate is 14% per year. Wake set the annual rental to ensure a 16% rate of return (the loss in service value anticipated for the term of the lease).
6. Executory costs of $7,000 annually, related to taxes on the property, are paid by Wake.

Required:
1. Examine and evaluate each capitalization criteria and determine what type of lease this is for the lessee.
2. Prepare appropriate journal entries on the lessee's books to reflect the signing of the lease agreement and to record the payments and expenses related to this lease for the years 2016 and 2017.

E20-2 **Lessee Accounting with Payments Made at Beginning of Year** Adden Company signs a lease agreement dated January 1, 2016, that provides for it to lease heavy equipment from Scott Rental Company beginning January 1, 2016. The lease terms, provisions, and related events are as follows:
LO 20.1
LO 20.3

SHOW ME HOW

1. The lease term is 4 years. The lease is noncancelable and requires annual rental payments of $20,000 to be paid in advance at the beginning of each year.
2. The cost, and also fair value, of the heavy equipment to Scott at the inception of the lease is $68,036.62. The equipment has an estimated life of 4 years and has a zero estimated residual value at the end of this time.
3. Adden agrees to pay all executory costs.
4. The lease contains no renewal or bargain purchase option.
5. Scott's interest rate implicit in the lease is 12%. Adden is aware of this rate, which is equal to its borrowing rate.
6. Adden uses the straight-line method to record depreciation on similar equipment.
7. Executory costs paid at the end of the year by Adden are:

2016	2017
Insurance, $1,500	Insurance, $1,300
Property taxes, $6,000	Property taxes, $5,500

Required:
1. **Next Level** Examine and evaluate each capitalization criteria and determine what type of lease this is for Adden.
2. Prepare a table summarizing the lease payments and interest expense for Adden.
3. Prepare journal entries for Adden for the years 2016 and 2017.

E20-3 **Lessee Accounting Issues** Sax Company signs a lease agreement dated January 1, 2016, that provides for it to lease computers from Appleton Company beginning January 1, 2016. The lease terms, provisions, and related events are as follows:
LO 20.1
LO 20.2
LO 20.3
1. The lease term is 5 years. The lease is noncancelable and requires equal rental payments to be made at the end of each year.
2. The computers have an estimated life of 5 years, a fair value of $300,000, and a zero estimated residual value.
3. Sax agrees to pay all executory costs.

SHOW ME HOW

(continued)

4. The lease contains no renewal or bargain purchase option.
5. The annual payment is set by Appleton at $83,222.92 to earn a rate of return of 12% on its net investment. Sax is aware of this rate, which is equal to its borrowing rate.
6. Sax uses the straight-line method to record depreciation on similar equipment.

Required:

1. **Next Level** Examine and evaluate each capitalization criteria and determine what type of lease this is for Sax.
2. Calculate the amount of the asset and liability of Sax at the inception of the lease (round to the nearest dollar).
3. Prepare a table summarizing the lease payments and interest expense.
4. Prepare journal entries for Sax for the years 2016 and 2017.
5. **Next Level** If the lease term is 3 years and the annual payment is $110,000, how would Sax classify the lease under (a) U.S. GAAP and (b) IFRS?

E20-4
LO 20.3

Lessee Accounting for Capital Lease On January 1, 2016, Concord Corp. signs a contract to lease manufacturing equipment from Stone Inc. Concord agrees to make lease payments of $47,500 per year. Additional information pertaining to the lease is as follows:
1. The term of the noncancelable lease is 3 years, with a renewal option at the end of the lease term. Payments are due every January 1, beginning January 1, 2016.
2. The fair value of the manufacturing equipment on January 1, 2016, is $150,000. The equipment has an economic life of 7 years.
3. Concord guarantees that the equipment will have a residual value of $15,000 at the end of the lease term.
4. Concord Corp. depreciates similar assets using the double-declining-balance method.
5. Concord's incremental borrowing rate is 15% per year; Stone's implicit interest rate is 10.5% and known by Concord.
6. Concord pays $2,500 per year for maintenance of the equipment and $1,000 in property taxes.

Required:
1. Next Level Examine and evaluate each capitalization criteria and determine what type of lease this is for Concord.
2. Calculate the amount of the asset and liability to be reported by Concord at the inception of the lease (round to the nearest dollar).
3. Prepare a table summarizing the lease payments and interest expense.
4. Prepare journal entries for Concord for the entire lease period. Assume that the equipment has a fair value of $9,500 at the end of the 3-year lease term.

E20-5
LO 20.2
LO 20.3

Comparisons of Operating and Sales-Type Leases On January 1, 2016, Nelson Company leases certain property to Queens Company at an annual rental of $60,000 payable in advance at the beginning of each year for 8 years. The first payment is received immediately. The leased property, which is new, cost $275,000 and has an estimated economic life of 8 years and no residual value. The interest rate implicit in the lease is 12% and the lease is noncancelable. Nelson had no other costs associated with this lease. It should have accounted for this lease as a sales-type lease but mistakenly treated it as an operating lease.

Required:
Next Level Compute the effect on income before income taxes during the first year of the lease as a result of Nelson's classification of this lease as an operating rather than a sales-type lease. Round your answer to the nearest dollar.

E20-6
LO 20.5

Lessor Accounting Issues Ramallah Company leases heavy equipment to Terrell Inc. on January 2, 2016, on the following terms:

1. Forty-eight lease rentals of $1,600 at the end of each month are to be paid by Terrell, and the lease is noncancelable.
2. The cost of the heavy equipment to Ramallah was $60,758.
3. Ramallah will account for this lease using the direct financing method. The difference between total rental receipts ($1,600 × 48 = $76,800) and the cost of the equipment ($60,758) was computed to yield a return of 1% per month over the lease term.

Required:
Next Level Prepare journal entries for Ramallah (the lessor) to record the lease contract and the receipt of the first lease rental on January 31, 2016. Record the part of the $16,042 Unearned Interest that was earned during the first month and carry calculations to the nearest dollar.

E20-7
LO 20.5

Lessor Accounting with Receipts at End of Year Berne Company (lessor) enters into a lease with Fox Company to lease equipment to Fox beginning January 1, 2016. The lease terms, provisions, and related events are as follows:
1. The lease term is 4 years. The lease is noncancelable and requires annual rental payments of $50,000 to be made at the end of each year.
2. The equipment costs $130,000. The equipment has an estimated life of 4 years and an estimated residual value at the end of the lease term of zero.
3. Fox agrees to pay all executory costs.
4. The interest rate implicit in the lease is 12%.
5. The initial direct costs are insignificant and assumed to be zero.
6. The collectibility of the rentals is reasonably assured, and there are no important uncertainties surrounding the amount of unreimbursable costs yet to be incurred by the lessor.

Required:
1. **Next Level** Determine if the lease is a sales-type or direct financing lease from Berne's point of view (calculate the selling price and assume that this is also the fair value).
2. Prepare a table summarizing the lease receipts and interest revenue earned by the lessor.
3. Prepare journal entries for Berne, the lessor, for the years 2016 and 2017.

E20-8
LO 20.5

Lessor Accounting with Receipts at Beginning of Year Edom Company, the lessor, enters into a lease with Davis Company to lease equipment to Davis beginning January 1, 2016. The lease terms, provisions, and related events are as follows:
1. The lease term is 5 years. The lease is noncancelable and requires annual rental receipts of $100,000 to be made in advance at the beginning of each year.
2. The equipment costs $313,000. The equipment has an estimated life of 6 years and, at the end of the lease term, has an unguaranteed residual value of $20,000 accruing to the benefit of Edom.
3. Davis agrees to pay all executory costs.
4. The interest rate implicit in the lease is 14%.
5. The initial direct costs are insignificant and assumed to be zero.
6. The collectibility of the rentals is reasonably assured, and there are no important uncertainties surrounding the amount of unreimbursable costs yet to be incurred by the lessor.

Required:
1. **Next Level** Determine if the lease is a sales-type or direct financing lease from Edom's point of view (calculate the selling price and assume that this is also the fair value).
2. Prepare a table summarizing the lease receipts and interest revenue earned by the lessor.
3. Prepare journal entries for Edom, the lessor, for the years 2016 and 2017.

E20-9
LO 20.5

Determining Type of Lease and Subsequent Accounting Ravis Rent-A-Car Company leases a car to Ira Reem, an employee, on January 1, 2016. The term of the noncancelable lease is 4 years. The following information about the lease is provided:
1. Title to the car passes to Ira on the termination of the lease with no additional payment required by the lessee.
2. The cost and fair value of the car to Ravis Rent-A-Car is $8,400. The car has an economic life of 5 years.
3. The lease payments are determined at an amount that will yield Ravis Rent-A-Car a rate of return of 10% on its net investment.
4. Collectibility of the lease payments is reasonably assured.
5. There are no important uncertainties surrounding the amount of unreimbursable costs yet to be incurred by the lessor.
6. Equal annual lease payments are due at the end of each year.

Required:
1. **Next Level** Determine if the lease is an operating, sales-type, or direct financing lease from Ravis Rent-A-Car's point of view. Why?
2. Prepare a table summarizing the lease receipts and interest revenue earned by the Ravis Rent-A-Car for the 4-year lease term.
3. Prepare the journal entries for 2016 and 2017 to record the lease agreement, the lease receipts, and the recognition of income on the books of Ravis Rent-A-Car.

E20-10 Guaranteed and Unguaranteed Residual Values Grygiel Company leases a machine with a fair value of $50,000 to Baker Company. The lease has a life of 6 years and requires a $10,000 payment at the end of each year. The lease does not include a transfer of ownership or a bargain purchase option, and the life of the lease is less than 75% of the expected economic life of the machine. The collectibility of the lease payments is reasonably assured, and there are no uncertainties involved in the lease. Round your answers to the nearest dollar.

LO 20.5

Required:
1. **Next Level** If Grygiel requires a return of 10%, compute the machine's expected residual value.
2. **Next Level** If the residual value is guaranteed by Baker, how would each company classify the lease?
3. **Next Level** If the residual value is not guaranteed by Baker, how would each company classify the lease?

E20-11 Lessor Accounting Issues Rexon Company leases equipment to Ten-Care Company beginning January 1, 2016. The lease terms, provisions, and related events are as follows:

LO 20.1
LO 20.5

1. The lease term is 8 years. The lease is noncancelable and requires equal rental payments to be made at the end of each year.
2. The cost, and also fair value, of the equipment is $500,000. The equipment has an estimated life of 8 years and has a zero estimated value at the end of that time.
3. Ten-Care agrees to pay all executory costs.
4. The lease contains no renewal or bargain purchase option.
5. The interest rate implicit in the lease is 14%.
6. The initial direct costs are insignificant and assumed to be zero.
7. The collectibility of the rentals is reasonably assured, and there are no important uncertainties surrounding the amount of unreimbursable costs yet to be incurred by the lessor.

Required:
1. **Next Level** Assuming that the lease is a direct financing lease from Rexon's point of view, calculate the amount of the equal rental receipts.
2. Prepare a table summarizing the lease receipts and interest revenue earned by Rexon.
3. Prepare journal entries for Rexon for the years 2016 and 2017.

E20-12 Lessee and Lessor Accounting Issues Lessor Leasing Company agrees to provide Lessee Company with equipment under a noncancelable lease for 5 years. The equipment has a 5-year life, cost Lessor $30,000, and will have no residual value when the lease term ends. Lessee agrees to pay all executory costs ($500 per year) throughout the lease period. On January 1, 2016, the equipment is delivered. Lessor expects a 14% return. The five equal annual rents are payable in advance starting January 1, 2016.

LO 20.3
LO 20.5

Required:
1. Assuming this is a direct financing lease for the lessor and a capital lease for the lessee, prepare a table summarizing the lease and interest payments suitable for use by either party.
2. **Next Level** On the assumption that both companies adjust and close books each December 31, prepare journal entries relating to the lease for both companies through December 31, 2016, based on data derived in the table. Assume that Lessee depreciates similar equipment by the straight-line method.

E20-13 Lessee and Lessor Accounting Issues The following information is available for a noncancelable lease of equipment that is classified as a sales-type lease by the lessor and as a capital lease by the lessee. Assume that the lease payments are made at the beginning of each month, interest and straight-line depreciation are recognized at the end of each month, and the residual value of the leased asset is zero at the end of a 3-year life.

LO 20.3
LO 20.5

Cost of equipment to lessor (Anson Company)	$50,000
Initial payment by lessee (Bullard Company) at inception of lease	2,000
Present value of remaining 35 payments of $2,000 each discounted at 1% per month	58,817

Required:
1. Record the lease (including the initial receipt of $2,000) and the receipt of the second and third installments of $2,000 in Anson's accounts. Carry computations to the nearest dollar.
2. Record the lease (including the initial payment of $2,000), the payment of the second and third installments of $2,000, and monthly depreciation in Bullard's accounts. The lessee records the lease obligation at net present value. Carry computations to the nearest dollar.

E20-14 Lease Income and Expense Reuben Company retires a machine from active use on January 2, 2016, for the express purpose of leasing it. The machine had a carrying value of $900,000 after 12 years of use and is expected to have 10 more years of economic life. The machine is depreciated on a straight-line basis. On March 2, 2016, Reuben leases the machine to Owens Company for $180,000 a year for a 5-year period ending February 28, 2021. Under the provisions of the lease, Reuben incurs total maintenance and other related costs of $20,000 for the year ended December 31, 2016. Owens pays $180,000 to Reuben on March 2, 2016. The lease was properly classified as an operating lease.

LO 20.3
LO 20.5

Required:
1. Compute the income before income taxes derived by Reuben from this lease for the calendar year ended December 31, 2016.
2. Compute the amount of rent expense incurred by Owens from this lease for the calendar year ended December 31, 2016.

E20-15 Sale-Leaseback (Appendix 20.1) On January 1, 2016, Stimpson Company sells land to Barker Company for $2.5 million and then immediately leases it back. The relevant information is as follows:

LO 20.7

1. The land was carried on Stimpson's books at a value of $2 million.
2. The term of the noncancelable lease is 25 years.
3. The lease agreement requires equal rental payments of $363,746 at the end of each year.
4. The incremental borrowing rate of Stimpson is 15%. Stimpson is aware that Barker set the annual rental to ensure a rate of return of 14%.
5. The land has a fair value of $2.5 million on January 1, 2016.
6. Stimpson has the option of purchasing the land for $150 at the end of 25 years.
7. Stimpson pays all executory costs. These costs consist of insurance and property taxes amounting to $12,000 per year.
8. There are no important uncertainties surrounding the amount of unreimbursable costs yet to be incurred by the lessor, and the collectibility of the rentals is reasonably assured.

Required:
1. Prepare the journal entries for the seller-lessee, Stimpson, for 2016 to reflect the sale and leaseback agreement. In calculating the present value of the lease payments, ignore the $150 bargain purchase option as immaterial.
2. **Next Level** Describe briefly the accounting treatment of the gain by the seller-lessee. Prepare any journal entry that Stimpson should make relating to the gain at year-end 2016.

PROBLEMS

P20-1 Determining Type of Lease and Subsequent Accounting On January 1, 2016, Ballieu Company leases specialty equipment with an economic life of 8 years to Anderson Company. The lease contains the following terms and provisions:

LO 20.3

- The lease is noncancelable and has a term of 8 years.
- The annual rentals are $35,000, payable at the beginning of each year.
- The interest rate implicit in the lease is 14%.
- Anderson agrees to pay all executory costs and is given an option to buy the equipment for $1 at the end of the lease term, December 31, 2024.
- The cost of the equipment to the lessor is $150,000, and the fair retail value is approximately $185,100.
- The lessor incurs no material initial direct costs.
- The collectibility of the rentals is reasonably assured, and there are no important uncertainties surrounding the amount of unreimbursable costs yet to be incurred by the lessor.
- The lessor estimates that the fair value is expected to be significantly greater than $1 at the end of the lease term.

The lessor calculates that the present value on January 1, 2016 of 8 annual payments in advance of $35,000 discounted at 14% is $185,090.68 (the $1 purchase option is ignored as immaterial).

Required:
1. **Next Level** Identify the classification of the lease transaction from Ballieu's point of view. Give the reasons for your classification.

(continued)

2. Prepare all the journal entries for Ballieu for the years 2016 and 2017.
3. Discuss the disclosure requirements for the lease transaction in Ballieu's notes to the financial statements.

P20-2
LO 20.1
LO 20.3

Determining Type of Lease and Subsequent Accounting On January 1, 2016, Alice Company leases equipment for 5 years, agreeing to pay $70,000 annually (including executory costs) at the beginning of each year under the non-cancelable lease. Superior Equipment Company, the lessor, agrees to remit all executory costs, estimated to be $3,450 per year. The cost and also fair value of the equipment is $305,000. Its estimated life is 10 years. The estimated residual value at the end of 5 years is $64,000 and is not guaranteed by Alice; at the end of 10 years, it is $5,000. There is no bargain purchase option in the lease or any agreement to transfer ownership at the end of the lease to the lessee. The implicit interest rate is 12%. During 2016, Superior Equipment pays property taxes of $650, maintenance costs of $1,600, and insurance of $1,200. There are no important uncertainties surrounding the amount of unreimbursable costs yet to be incurred by the lessor. Straight-line depreciation is considered the appropriate method by both companies.

Required:
1. **Next Level** Identify the type of lease involved for Alice and Superior Equipment and give reasons for your classifications.
2. Prepare appropriate journal entries for 2016 for the lessee and lessor.
3. **Next Level** If the residual value at the end of 5 years is guaranteed by Alice, identify the type of lease and briefly explain why. Prepare journal entries for 2016 and 2017 for the lessee and lessor. Also prepare the journal entries for the lessee and the lessor when the lessee pays the guaranteed residual value.

P20-3
LO 20.3
LO 20.5

Accounting for Leases by Lessee and Lessor Scupper Farms, the lessee, and Tyrrell Equipment, the lessor, sign a lease agreement on January 1, 2016, that provides for Scupper to lease a cultivator from Tyrrell. The lease terms, provisions, and other related events are as follows:

- The lease is noncancelable and has a term of 6 years.
- The annual rentals are $56,100 (including executory costs), payable at the beginning of each year.
- Tyrrell agrees to pay all executory costs, which are expected to be $1,100 annually, including property taxes of $500, insurance of $350, and maintenance of $250.
- The cultivator has an estimated economic life of 6 years.
- Scupper guarantees a residual value of $60,000 at the end of 6 years.
- The interest rate implicit in the lease is 14%, which is known by Scupper.
- Scupper's incremental borrowing rate is 15%, and it uses the sum-of-the-years'-digits method to record depreciation on similar equipment.
- The cost and fair value of the cultivator to Tyrrell is $271,154.68.
- The lessor incurs no material initial direct costs.
- The collectibility of the rentals is reasonably assured, and there are no important uncertainties surrounding the amount of unreimbursable costs yet to be incurred by the lessor.

Required:
1. **Next Level** Identify the type of lease involved for both Scupper and Tyrrell and give reasons for your classifications.
2. Prepare the journal entries for both Scupper and Tyrrell for 2016. (*Hint*: Scupper should expense executory costs when annual payments are made to Tyrrell.)

P20-4
LO 20.1
LO 20.2
LO 20.3

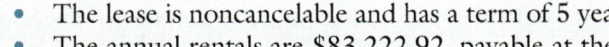

Lessee Accounting Issues Timmer Company signs a lease agreement dated January 1, 2016, that provides for it to lease equipment from Landau Company beginning January 1, 2016. The lease terms, provisions, and related events are as follows:

- The lease is noncancelable and has a term of 5 years.
- The annual rentals are $83,222.92, payable at the end of each year, and provide Landau with a 12% annual rate of return on its net investment.
- Timmer agrees to pay all executory costs at the end of each year. In 2016, these were insurance, $3,760; property taxes, $5,440. In 2017: insurance, $3,100; property taxes, $5,330.
- There is no renewal or bargain purchase option.

Timmer estimates that the equipment has a fair value of $300,000, an economic life of 5 years, and a zero residual value. Timmer's incremental borrowing rate is 16%, it knows the rate implicit in the lease, and it uses the straight-line method to record depreciation on similar equipment.

Required:
1. Calculate the amount of the asset and liability of Timmer at the inception of the lease. (Round to the nearest dollar.)
2. Prepare a table summarizing the lease payments and interest expense.
3. Prepare journal entries on the books of Timmer for 2016 and 2017.
4. **Next Level** Prepare a partial balance sheet in regard to the lease for Timmer for December 31, 2016. Use the change in present value approach to classify the capital lease obligation between current and noncurrent.
5. If the lease term is 3 years with an annual payment of $120,000 and Timmer does not know the rate implicit in the lease, how would Timmer classify the lease under (a) U.S. GAAP and (b) IFRS?

P20-5
LO 20.5

Direct Financing Lease Calder Company, the lessor, enters into a lease with Darwin Company, the lessee, to provide heavy equipment beginning January 1, 2016. The lease terms, provisions, and related events are as follows:

- The lease is noncancelable, has a term of 8 years, and has no renewal or bargain purchase option.
- The annual rentals are $65,000, payable at the end of each year.
- The interest rate implicit in the lease is 15%.
- Darwin agrees to pay all executory costs.
- The cost and fair value of the equipment to the lessor is $308,021.03.
- The lessor incurs no material initial direct costs.
- The collectibility of the rentals is reasonably assured, and there are no important uncertainties surrounding the amount of unreimbursable costs yet to be incurred by the lessor.
- The lessor estimates that the fair value at the end of the lease term will be $50,000 and that the economic life of the equipment is 9 years.

The following present value factors are relevant:

- $PVOA_{n=8, i=15\%} = 4.487322$
- $PV_{n=8, i=15\%} = 0.326902$
- $PV_{n=1, i=15\%} = 0.869565$

Required:
1. Prepare a table summarizing the lease receipts and interest revenue earned by the lessor for this direct financing lease.
2. State why the lease is a direct financing lease.
3. Prepare journal entries for Calder for the years 2016, 2017, and 2018.
4. **Next Level** Prepare partial balance sheets for December 31, 2016, and December 31, 2017, showing how the accounts should be reported. Use the present value of next year's payment approach to classify the capital lease obligation. In addition, calculate how the accounts would be reported under the change in present value approach.

P20-6
LO 20.5

Direct Financing Lease with Unguaranteed Residual Value Lessor Company and Lessee Company enter into a 5-year, noncancelable, direct financing lease on January 1, 2016, for a new computer that cost Lessor $400,000 (useful life is 5 years). The fair value is also $400,000. Lessor expects a 12% return over the 5-year period of the lease. The computer will have an estimated unguaranteed residual value of $20,000 at the end of the fifth year of the lease. The lease provisions require 5 equal annual amounts, payable each January 1, beginning with January 1, 2016. Lessee pays all executory costs. The computer reverts to the lessor at the termination of the lease. Assume there are no initial direct costs, no important uncertainties surrounding the amount of unreimbursable costs yet to be incurred by the lessor, and that the collectibility of rentals is reasonably assured.

Required:
1. Show how Lessor should compute the annual rental amounts.
2. Prepare a table summarizing the lease and interest receipts that would be suitable for Lessor.
3. Prepare the journal entries for Lessor for the years 2016, 2017, and 2018.

P20-7
LO 20.5

Sales-Type Lease with Receipts at End of Year Lamplighter Company, the lessor, agrees to lease equipment to Tilson Company, the lessee, beginning January 1, 2016. The lease terms, provisions, and related events are as follows:

- The lease is noncancelable and has a term of 8 years.
- The annual rentals are $32,000, payable at the end of each year.
- Tilson agrees to pay all executory costs.

(continued)

- The interest rate implicit in the lease is 14%.
- The cost of the equipment to the lessor is $110,000.
- The lessor incurs no material initial direct costs.
- The collectibility of the rentals is reasonably assured, and there are no important uncertainties surrounding the amount of unreimbursable costs yet to be incurred by the lessor.
- The lessor estimates that the fair value at the end of the lease term will be $20,000 and that the economic life of the equipment is 9 years.

Required:
1. Calculate the selling price implied by the lease and prepare a table summarizing the lease receipts and interest revenue earned by the lessor for this sales-type lease.
2. **Next Level** State why this is a sales-type lease.
3. Prepare journal entries for Lamplighter for the years 2016, 2017, and 2019.
4. Prepare partial balance sheets for Lamplighter for December 31, 2016, and December 31, 2017, showing how the accounts should be disclosed.

P20-8
LO 20.5
Initial Direct Costs and Related Issues On January 1, 2016, Amity Company leases a crane to Baltimore Company. The lease contains the following terms and provisions:

- The lease is noncancelable and has a term of 10 years.
- The lease does not contain a renewal or bargain purchase option.
- The annual rentals are $4,000, payable at the beginning of each year.
- Baltimore agrees to pay all executory costs.
- The cost and fair value of the equipment to the lessor is $24,913.94.
- The lessor incurs initial direct costs of $1,364.98.
- The interest rate implicit in the lease is 12.5%.
- After including the initial direct costs, the implicit rate is 12%.
- The collectibility of the rentals is reasonably assured, and there are no important uncertainties surrounding the amount of unreimbursable costs yet to be incurred by the lessor.
- The lessor estimates that the fair value at the end of the lease term will be $3,000 and that the economic life of the crane is 12 years.

Required:
1. **Next Level** What are initial direct costs? Discuss the accounting treatment of these costs. Are they treated in the same manner for (a) an operating lease, (b) a sales-type lease, and (c) a direct financing lease?
2. From the lessor's viewpoint, is the preceding lease a sales-type or direct financing lease? Give reasons to support your conclusion.
3. Prepare the journal entries for Amity for 2016.

P20-9
LO 20.5

Lessor's Income Statement Dahlia Company has two divisions, Astor Division, which started operating in 2014, and Tulip Division, which started operating in 2015. Astor leases medical equipment to hospitals. All of its leases are appropriately recorded as operating leases for accounting purposes except for a major lease entered into on January 1, 2016, which is appropriately recorded as a sale-type lease for accounting purposes.

Under long-term contracts, Tulip constructs wastewater treatment plants for small communities throughout the United States. All of its long-term contracts are appropriately recorded for accounting purposes under the percentage-of-completion method, except for two contracts which are appropriately recorded for accounting purposes under the completed-contract method because of a lack of dependable estimates at the time of entering into these contracts.

For the year ended December 31, 2016, the following information is available:

Astor Division:
Operating Leases. Revenues from operating leases were $800,000. The cost of the related leased equipment is $3,700,000, which is being depreciated on a straight-line basis over a 5-year period. The estimated residual value of the leased equipment at the end of the 5-year period is $200,000. No leased equipment was acquired or constructed in 2016. Maintenance and other related costs and the costs of any other services rendered under the provisions of the leases were $70,000 in 2016.

Lease Recorded as a Sale. The January 1, 2016, lease recorded as a sale is for a 6-year period expiring December 31, 2021. The cost of this leased equipment is $3,500,000. This leased equipment is estimated to have no residual value at the end of the lease. Maintenance and other related costs, and the costs of any other services rendered under the provisions of this lease, all of which were paid by the lessee, were $120,000 in 2016. Equal annual payments under the lease are $750,000 and are due on January 1. The first payment was made on January 1, 2016. The present value for an annuity of $1 in advance at 10% is as follows:

Number of Periods	Present Value
5	4.170
6	4.791
7	5.355

Tulip Division:
Long-Term Contracts: Percentage-of-Completion Method. Long-term contracts recorded under the percentage-of-completion method aggregate $6,000,000. Costs incurred on these contracts were $1,500,000 in 2015 and $3,000,000 in 2016. Estimated additional costs of $1,000,000 are required to complete these contracts. Revenues of $1,740,000 were recognized in 2015. A total of $4,800,000 has been billed, of which $4,600,000 has been collected. No long-term contracts recorded under the percentage-of-completion method were completed in 2016.

Long-Term Contracts: Completed-Contract Method. The two long-term contracts recorded under the completed-contract method were started in 2015. One is a $5,000,000 contract. Costs incurred were $1,400,000 in 2015 and $1,600,000 in 2016. A total of $3,100,000 has been billed and $2,800,000 collected. Although it is difficult to estimate the additional costs required to complete this contract, indications are that this contract will prove to be profitable.

The second contract is for $4,000,000. Costs incurred were $1,200,000 in 2015 and $2,600,000 in 2016. A total of $3,300,000 has been billed, and $2,900,000 has been collected. Although it is difficult to estimate the additional costs required to complete this contract, indications are that there will be a loss of approximately $550,000.

Dahlia Company:
Selling, general, and administrative expenses exclusive of amounts specified earlier were $600,000 in 2016. Other income exclusive of amounts specified earlier was $50,000 in 2016.

Required:
Prepare Dahlia's income statement for the year ended December 31, 2016, stopping at income (loss) before income taxes. Show supporting schedules and computations in good form. *Ignore income tax and deferred tax considerations.* Notes are *not* required.

P20-10 **Various Lease Issues for Lessor and Lessee** Lessee Company leases heavy equipment on January 1, 2016, under
LO 20.3   a capital lease from Lessor Company with the following lease provisions:
LO 20.5

- The lease is noncancelable and has a term of 10 years.
- The lease does not contain a renewal or bargain purchase option.
- The annual rentals are $27,653.77, payable at the beginning of each year.
- Lessee agrees to pay all executory costs.
- The interest rate implicit in the lease is 12%, which is known by Lessee.
- The residual value of the property at the end of 10 years is estimated to be zero.
- The cost and fair value of the equipment to the lessor is $175,000.
- The lessor incurs no material initial direct costs.
- The collectibility of the rentals is reasonably assured, and there are no important uncertainties surrounding the amount of unreimbursable costs yet to be incurred by the lessor.
- Lessee's incremental borrowing rate is 15%, and it uses the straight-line method to record depreciation on similar equipment.
- In 2016, the lessee pays insurance of $1,900, property taxes of $1,300, and maintenance of $600.
- In 2017, the lessee pays insurance of $1,800, property taxes of $1,200, and maintenance of $500.

Required:
1. **Next Level** Identify the type of lease involved for the lessee and the lessor, and give reasons for your classifications.
2. Prepare all the journal entries for both the lessee and the lessor for 2016 and 2017.

P20-11 **Various Lease Issues for Lessor and Lessee** Benjamin Company has rented new equipment to Murrell Builders
LO 20.3   that cost $50,000. This equipment has a life of 4 years and no residual value at the end of that time. The lease is noncan-
LO 20.5   celable and is signed on January 1, 2016. Murrell assumes all normal risks and executory costs of ownership. The title to

(continued)

the property is transferred to Murrell at the end of the 4 years. Benjamin computes the rents on the basis of a 14% return. The lessee's incremental borrowing rate is also 14%. The collectibility of rentals is reasonably assured, and there are no important uncertainties surrounding the amount of unreimbursable costs yet to be incurred by the lessor.

Required:
1. Assuming the annual rentals are payable at the end of each year, complete the following:
   a. lessor computation of periodic rental receipts
   b. lessee computation of the present value of the special property rights under the lease
   c. a table summarizing lease and interest payments that would be suitable for both lessor and lessee
2. Assuming the annual rentals are payable at the start of each year, compute the same three items listed in Requirement 1.
3. Prepare the journal entries for the lessor and lessee for Requirement 2 throughout 2016. Use the straight-line depreciation method.
4. Indicate the asset and liability amounts that the lessor and lessee would report on their balance sheets at December 31, 2016, under Requirement 2.

P20-12 Various Lease Issues Farrington Company leases a computer from Wilson Company. The lease includes the following provisions:
LO 20.3
LO 20.5

- The lease is noncancelable and has a term of 8 years.
- The annual rentals are $60,000, payable at the end of each year.
- Farrington agrees to pay all executory costs and has an option to purchase the computer for $1,000 at the end of the life of the lease.
- The interest rate implicit in the lease is 12%, which is known to Farrington.
- Farrington estimates that the computer has an economic life of 12 years and a value of $70,000 at the end of 8 years.
- Farrington's incremental borrowing rate is 16%, and it uses the straight-line method to record depreciation on similar equipment.
- The computer cost Wilson $200,000 to manufacture.
- The lessor incurs initial direct costs of $10,000.
- The collectibility of the rentals is reasonably assured, and there are no important uncertainties surrounding the amount of unreimbursable costs yet to be incurred by the lessor.

Required:
1. **Next Level** What is the correct classification of the lease for the lessee and lessor? Explain whether the lease meets *each* of the required criteria.
2. Assuming that the lease is signed on January 1, 2016, prepare all journal entries for 2016 for the lessor.
3. **Next Level** After 6 years, because of changes in the technology, the lessee and lessor independently conclude that the computer's expected residual value at the end of the life of the lease is only $10,000. Discuss how the lessor should account for the change.

P20-13 Comprehensive Landlord Company and Tenant Company enter into a noncancelable, direct financing lease on January 1, 2016, for new heavy equipment that cost the Landlord $300,000 (useful life is 6 years with no residual value). The fair value is also $300,000. Landlord expects a 14% return over the 6-year period of the lease. Lease provisions require 6 equal annual amounts payable each January 1, beginning with January 1, 2016. Tenant pays all executory costs. The heavy equipment reverts to the lessor at the termination of the lease. Assume that there are no initial direct costs. The collectibility of the rentals is reasonably assured, and there are no important uncertainties surrounding the amount of unreimbursable costs yet to be incurred by the lessor.
LO 20.1
LO 20.3
LO 20.5

Required:
1. **Next Level** (a) Show how Landlord should compute the annual rental amounts. (b) Discuss how the Tenant Company should compute the present value of the lease rights. What additional information would be required to make this computation?
2. **Next Level** Prepare a table summarizing the lease and interest receipts that would be suitable for Landlord. Under what conditions would this table be suitable for Tenant?
3. Assuming that the table prepared in Requirement 2 is suitable for both the lessee and the lessor, prepare the journal entries for both firms for the years 2016 and 2017. Use the straight-line depreciation method for the leased equipment. The executory costs paid by the lessee are in 2016: insurance, $700 and property taxes, $800; in 2017: insurance, $600 and property taxes, $750.

4. **Next Level** Show the items and amounts that would be reported on the comparative 2016 and 2017 income statements and ending balance sheets for both the lessor and the lessee. Include appropriate notes to the financial statements.

P20-14 **Sale-Leaseback** *(Appendix 20.1)* On January 1, 2016, Orr Company sells heavy equipment to Foible Company
LO 20.7 for $3 million and then immediately leases it back. The relevant information is as follows:

- Orr Company purchased the heavy equipment on January 1, 2016, for $2,100,000.
- The lease is noncancelable and has a term of 8 years.
- The annual rentals are $603,908.50, payable at the end of each year.
- The seller-lessee agrees to pay all executory costs.
- The interest rate implicit in the lease is 12%.
- The purchaser-lessor incurs no material initial direct costs.
- The collectibility of the rentals is reasonably assured, and there are no important uncertainties surrounding the amount of unreimbursable costs yet to be incurred by the lessor.
- Orr's incremental borrowing rate is 12%, and the company estimates that the economic life of the equipment is 8 years.
- The present value on January 1, 2016, of 8 payments of $603,908.50, discounted at 12%, is $3 million ($603,908.50 × 4.967640).
- The executory costs for 2016 are:

Repairs and maintenance	$10,200
Property taxes	20,500
Insurance	18,000

Required:
1. **Next Level** What type of lease is this to the seller-lessee? Discuss.
2. Prepare the journal entries for both the seller-lessee and the purchaser-lessor for 2016 to reflect the purchase of the heavy equipment by Orr and the sale and leaseback agreement. Assume that Orr uses the straight-line depreciation method.

P20-15 **Determining Types of Leases** *(Appendix 20.1)* Rigdon Company leases 50 acres of land to Christmas Tree Inter-
LO 20.7 national on January 1, 2016. The provisions of the lease are as follows:

- The lease is noncancelable and has a term of 25 years.
- The annual rentals are $10,000, payable at the end of each year.
- The lease contains no bargain purchase option and the land reverts to Rigdon at the end of the lease.
- The incremental borrowing rate of Christmas Tree is 12%.
- The cost of the land to Rigdon is $60,000.
- The fair value is $78,431.39.
- The lessor incurs no material initial direct costs.
- The collectibility of the rentals is reasonably assured, and there are no important uncertainties surrounding the amount of unreimbursable costs yet to be incurred by the lessor.

Required:
1. Determine the classification of this lease for both the lessor and the lessee.
2. **Next Level** Why are the final two criteria (lease term 75% of economic life and present value of lease payments 90% of fair value) not applicable when classifying a lease of land?

CASES

COMMUNICATION

C20-1 **Miscellaneous Lease Issues**
LO 20.1 On January 1, 2016, Von Company entered into
LO 20.3 two noncancelable leases for new machines to be
AICPA used in its manufacturing operations. The first lease
Adapted does not contain a bargain purchase option. The lease term is equal to 80% of the estimated economic life of the machine. The second lease contains a bargain purchase option. The lease term is equal to 50% of the estimated economic life of the machine.

(continued)

Required:
1. Explain the theoretical basis for requiring lessees to capitalize certain long-term leases. Do *not* discuss the specific criteria for classifying a lease as a capital lease.
2. Explain how a lessee should account for a capital lease at its inception.
3. Explain how a lessee should record each minimum lease payment for a capital lease.
4. Explain how Von should classify each of the two leases.

C20-2 Initial Direct Costs
LO 20.5

Efland Company leases equipment to Orange Company. Efland pays $3,000 initial direct costs in negotiating the lease.

Required:
1. Explain what initial direct costs are.
2. Indicate precisely how Efland should account for initial direct costs if this lease is (a) an operating lease, (b) a sales-type lease, and (c) a direct financing lease.
3. For a sales-type lease, GAAP requires that: "The cost or carrying amount, if different, of the leased property, plus any initial direct costs ... less the present value of the unguaranteed residual value accruing to the benefit of the lessor, computed at the interest rate implicit in the lease, shall be charged against income in the same period." Does this provision require that initial direct costs for sales-type leases be charged to cost of goods sold? Discuss the reasons for this accounting treatment.

C20-3 Sales-Type Lease Issues
LO 20.5

Jordan Industries manufactures and leases to its customers 5-ton construction dump trucks. The lease arrangements are usually as follows:
1. Payments on the lease are due for 5 years after its inception, but the present value is not greater than 90% of the fair value of the trucks at the time of sale.
2. The trucks revert to Jordan at the end of the lease. Estimated economic life of the trucks is 10 years.
3. No substantial uncertainties exist as to future payments Jordan must make, and potential customers are thoroughly checked for creditworthiness before the trucks are leased to them.
4. Jordan's accountant has informed the company that there are advantages from a reporting standpoint in treating the leases as sales-type instead of operating leases.

Required:
1. Discuss the reasons why Jordan would want to treat the leases as sales-type instead of operating leases.
2. Explain what Jordan should do to treat the leases properly as sales-type leases.

C20-4 Classification of Leases
LO 20.1
LO 20.3
LO 20.5
AICPA Adapted

Part a. Capital leases and operating leases are the two classifications of leases for the lessee.

Required:
1. Explain how a capital lease is accounted for by the lessee, both at the inception of the lease and during the first year of the lease, assuming the lease transfers ownership of the property to the lessee by the end of the lease.
2. Explain how an operating lease is accounted for by the lessee, both at the inception of the lease and during the first year of the lease, assuming equal monthly payments are made by the lessee at the beginning of each month of the lease. Describe the change in accounting, if any, when rental payments are not made on a straight-line basis.

Do not discuss the criteria for distinguishing between capital leases and operating leases.

Part b. Sales-type leases and direct financing leases are two of the classifications of leases for the lessor.

Required:
Write a short report that compares and contrasts a sales-type lease with a direct financing lease as follows:
a. Gross investment in the lease
b. Amortization of unearned interest income
c. Manufacturer's or dealer's profit

Do not discuss the criteria for distinguishing between the leases described above and operating leases.

C20-5 Sale-Leaseback *(Appendix 20.1)*
LO 20.7
AICPA Adapted

On January 1, 2016, Metcalf Company sold equipment for cash and leased it back. As seller-lessee, Metcalf retained the right to substantially all of the remaining use of the equipment.

The term of the lease is 8 years. There is a gain on the sale portion of the transaction. The lease portion of the transaction is classified appropriately as a capital lease.

Required:
1. Explain the theoretical basis for requiring lessees to capitalize certain long-term leases. Do *not* discuss the specific criteria for classifying a lease as a capital lease.

2. Consider the facts in the case and answer the following questions.
   a. Explain how Metcalf should account for the sale portion of the sale-leaseback transaction at January 1, 2016.
   b. Explain how Metcalf should account for the leaseback portion of the sale-leaseback transaction at January 1, 2016.
3. Explain how Metcalf should account for the gain on the sale portion of the sale-leaseback transaction during the first year of the lease.

CREATIVE AND CRITICAL THINKING

C20-6 **Capitalized and Operating Leases**
LO 20.3
AICPA Adapted

On January 1, Borman Company, a lessee, entered into three noncancelable leases for brand new equipment: Lease J, Lease K, and Lease L. None of the three leases transfers ownership of the equipment to Borman at the end of the lease term. For each of the three leases, the present value of the minimum lease payments at the beginning of the lease term, excluding that portion of the payments representing executory costs such as insurance, maintenance, and taxes to be paid by the lessor, including any profit thereon, is 75% of the fair value of the equipment to the lessor at the inception of the lease.

The following information is peculiar to each lease:

a. Lease J does not contain a bargain purchase option. The lease term is equal to 80% of the estimated economic life of the equipment.
b. Lease K contains a bargain purchase option. The lease term is equal to 50% of the estimated economic life of the equipment.
c. Lease L does not contain a bargain purchase option. The lease term is equal to 50% of the estimated economic life of the equipment.

Required:
1. Explain how Borman should classify each of the preceding three leases. Discuss the rationale for your answer.
2. What amount, if any, should Borman record as a liability at the inception of the lease for each of the preceding three leases?
3. Assuming that the minimum lease payments are made on a straight-line basis, how should Borman record the minimum lease payment for each of the preceding three leases?

C20-7 **Capital Lease Issues**
LO 20.1
LO 20.3
AICPA Adapted

On January 1, 2016, Lani Company entered into a noncancelable lease for a machine to be used in its manufacturing operations. The lease transfers ownership of the machine to Lani by the end of the lease term. The term of the lease is 8 years. The minimum lease payment made by Lani on January 1, 2016 was one of eight equal annual payments. At the inception of the lease, the criteria established for classification as a capital lease by the lessee were met.

Required:
1. Explain the theoretical basis for the accounting standard that requires certain long-term leases to be capitalized by the lessee. Do not discuss the specific lease as a capital lease.
2. Explain how Lani should account for this lease at its inception and determine the amount to be recorded.
3. Explain what expenses related to this lease Lani will incur during the first year of the lease and how they will be determined.
4. Explain how Lani should report the lease transaction on its December 31, 2016, balance sheet.

C20-8 **Types of Leases and Related Issues**
LO 20.1
LO 20.3
LO 20.5
AICPA Adapted

Circuit Village Company entered into a lease arrangement with Thomas Leasing Company for a certain machine. Thomas's primary business is leasing, and it is not a manufacturer or dealer. Circuit Village will lease the machine for a period of 4 years, which is 50% of the machine's economic life. Thomas will take possession of the machine at the end of the initial 4-year lease and lease it to another smaller company that does not need the most current version of the machine. Circuit Village does not guarantee any residual value for the machine and will not purchase the machine at the end of the lease term. Circuit Village's incremental borrowing rate is 16%, and the implicit rate on the lease is 14%. Circuit Village has no way of knowing or estimating the implicit rate used by Thomas. Using either rate, the present value of the minimum lease payments is between 90% and 100% of the fair value of the machine at the time of the lease agreement. Circuit Village has agreed to pay all executory costs directly, and no allowance for these costs is included in the lease payments. Thomas is reasonably certain that Circuit Village will pay all lease payments, and because it has agreed to pay all executory costs, there are no important uncertainties regarding costs to be incurred by Thomas.

(continued)

Required:
1. With respect to Circuit Village (the lessee), answer the following:
   a. What type of lease has been entered into? Explain the reason for your answer.
   b. How should Circuit Village compute the appropriate amount to record for the lease or asset acquired?
   c. What accounts will be created or affected by this transaction, and how will the lease or asset or other cost be matched with earnings?
2. With respect to Thomas (the lessor), answer the following:
   a. What type of leasing arrangement has been entered into? Explain the reason for your answer.
   b. How should this lease be recorded by Thomas, and how are the appropriate amounts determined?
   c. How should Thomas determine the appropriate amount of earnings to be recognized from each lease payment?

C20-9 Disclosure of Leases and Related Issues
LO 20.4
LO 20.6
United Manufacturing Company manufactures and leases computers to its customers. During 2016, the following lease transactions take place:
1. On January 1, a computer is leased to Superior Microelectronics Industries and is guaranteed by United against obsolescence. The present value of the lease payments is greater than 90% of the fair value of the computer to both United and Superior.
2. Also on January 1, a computer is leased to Pitt Steel Company. Because of Pitt's unstable financial condition, its incremental borrowing rate is substantially greater than United's rate implicit in the lease (which Pitt did not know and could not estimate).

Required:
1. For the first transaction, explain on whose financial statements the leased computer is shown.
2. Explain under what conditions in the second transaction the computer could fail to be shown on either United's or Pitt Steel's balance sheets at December 31, 2016.

C20-10 Sale-Leaseback *(Appendix 20.1)*
LO 20.7
AICPA Adapted
On December 31, 2015, Port Co. sold 6-month-old equipment at fair value and leased it back. There was a loss on the sale. Port pays all insurance, maintenance, and taxes on the equipment. The lease provides for eight equal annual payments, beginning December 31, 2016, with a present value equal to 85% of the equipment's fair value and sales price. The lease's term is equal to 80% of the equipment's useful life. There is no provision for Port to reacquire ownership of the equipment at the end of the lease term.

Required:
1. Consider the facts in the case and answer the following questions.
   a. Explain why it is important to compare an equipment's fair value to its lease payments' present value and its useful life to the lease term.
   b. Evaluate Port's leaseback of the equipment in terms of each of the four criteria for determination of a capital lease.
2. Explain how Port should account for the sale portion of the sale-leaseback transaction at December 31, 2015.
3. Explain how Port should report the leaseback portion of the sale-leaseback transaction on its December 31, 2016, balance sheet.

C20-11 Analyzing Coca-Cola's Leases
Obtain **The Coca-Cola Company**'s 2013 annual report either using the "Investor Relations" portion of its website (do a web search for Coca-Cola investor relations) or go to http://www.sec.gov and click "Search for company filings" under "Filings and Forms (EDGAR)."

Required:
1. What types of properties does Coca-Cola lease? Does Coca-Cola utilize capital leases or operating leases? How can we know?
2. What is the amount of Coca-Cola's total minimum operating lease payments as of December 31, 2013?

C20-12 Analyzing LVMH's Leases

Obtain **LVMH (Moet Hennessy – Louis Vuitton)**'s 2013 annual report using the "Investor Relations" portion of its website (do a web search for Moet Hennessy – Louis Vuitton investor relations).

Required:
1. What amount of LVMH's 2013 commercial lease expense is considered fixed? Variable?
2. What is the fixed amount of LVMH's operating lease payments coming due within 1 year of December 31, 2013? Between 1 and 5 years?

3. Does LVMH utilize capital leases? What term is used for these leases under IFRS?

C20-13 Ethics and Leasing

You are an accountant for ABC Mining Company, and the CFO gives you a copy of a recent lease agreement to record. As you read the agreement, you discover the company has leased 12 trucks from XYZ Finance Co. The fair value of the trucks is $2.4 million. ABC has agreed to pay $250,000 semiannually, in advance. The lease term is 5 years, and the lessor's implicit rate is 8%. There is no option or requirement to purchase the trucks. This all seems straightforward, especially when you remember that the company recently borrowed from a bank and agreed to a 10% interest rate. Also, you recall that the company owns some similar trucks and depreciates them over 8 years. You are about to leave the office early to meet some friends when you notice that there is a contingent rental of $97,592, payable by ABC and starting with the seventh semiannual payment, if the Consumer Price Index prevailing at the beginning of the lease increases in any one of the first 3 years of the lease.

Required:
From financial reporting and ethical perspectives, discuss the issues raised by this situation.

USING CODIFICATION

C20-14 Capital Lease Issues
LO 20.1
LO 20.3

Situation

Cliborn Retail Company negotiated a lease for a retail store in a new shopping center that included 30 stores. The accountant for Cliborn, Gail Naugle, was given the lease agreement to analyze. She looked into whether the lease was a capital lease. The lease did not include a transfer of ownership or an option to purchase. The lease term was for 20 years, and the present value of the minimum lease payments was $100,000. Unsure of the fair market value of the property or its life, she called the lessor's controller.

"That is easy," he replied. "There is no fair value because we would never sell a single store in a shopping center. And, let's see, 20 years divided by 75% is about 27 years, so the life of the property must be at least that much."

Directions

1. Assuming that you are Gail, research the generally accepted accounting principles and prepare a short memo to the controller of Cliborn that summarizes how to classify the lease. Cite your reference and applicable paragraph numbers.

C20-15 Capital Lease Issues
LO 20.1
LO 20.3

Situation

Stirbis Company was negotiating a lease for a new building that would be used as a warehouse. Stirbis's accountant, Shannon Fenimore, had been invited to join Jim Stirbis (the president) in a meeting where the lease agreement was settled. The president of the company that owned the building said, "I assume you want an operating lease."

"That is correct," replied Jim.

The president responded, "So we will not include a transfer of ownership or an option to purchase. Anyway, I am sure you do not want to get into the real estate business."

"No, of course not."

"And we agree that the lease term is 30 years."

"Yes, but that seems to present some problems. We would have to argue that the life of the building is more than 40 years."

"You should not have any trouble persuading your auditors to agree to that."

"Maybe not. But the present value of the $53,040 annual lease payment is $500,000, which is the fair value of the building."

"That is a problem. But I think I have a solution. We will adjust the annual payment to $45,000, so that the present value is only 85% of the fair value. Then we will add a clause that you also pay 1% of your total sales, up to a maximum of $8,040 each year."

Directions

1. Assuming that you are Shannon, research the generally accepted accounting principles and prepare a short memo to the president of Stirbis that summarizes how to classify the lease. Cite your reference and applicable paragraph numbers.

CHAPTER 21

THE STATEMENT OF CASH FLOWS

Starbucks Turns Coffee Beans into Cash

Examining **Starbucks**'s cash flow statement in Appendix A we see that in fiscal 2015, Starbucks reduced its cash balance by $178.3 million, from $1,708.4 million to $1,530.1 million. For investors, lenders, and other creditors to understand what is driving Starbucks's cash increase, they must be able to understand and assess its statement of cash flows. In fact, the conceptual framework states that one of the objectives of financial accounting is to provide information about the amounts, timing, and uncertainty of future cash flows. The statement of cash flows is important because it allows users to understand how the company is generating cash and how it is using cash with each of the three categories of business activities—operating, investing, or financing. For example, during the 2015 fiscal year Starbucks generated $3,749.1 million in cash flows from operating activities. During that same fiscal year, investing activities used cash of $1,520.3 million as Starbucks built more stores and made acquisitions of other companies. The financing activities section of the cash flow statement also shows that Starbucks returned cash of over $2.2 billion to investors and creditors during the period.

The statement of cash flows also allows users to compare and reconcile the accrual accounting amounts presented in the income statement with related cash flows. For example, users would want to know why, in 2014, Starbucks reported net income of $2,067.7 million but actually had a decrease in cash of $867.3 million; whereas in 2013 net income was only $8.8 million and cash increased by $1,387.1 million. The main cause of these differences relates to the litigation charge that Starbucks accrued during its 2013 fiscal year which reduced net

LEARNING OBJECTIVES

After reading this chapter you will be able to

LO 21.1 Understand and define operating, investing, and financing activities.

LO 21.2 Explain the direct and indirect methods for reporting operating cash flows.

LO 21.3 Prepare a statement of cash flows using the visual inspection method.

LO 21.4 Prepare a statement of cash flows using the spreadsheet method.

LO 21.5 Account for special items affecting the statement of cash flows.

LO 21.6 *(Appendix 21.1)* Understand and prepare the operating activities section under the direct method.

income but did not affect cash flows from operating activities. By contrast, in fiscal 2014, Starbucks actually paid $2,763.9 million to settle the litigation charge liability, which of course reduced operating cash flows that year.

The statement of cash flows also provides information to help users understand the company's cash flows to and from entities with which it does business, such as employees, customers, suppliers, creditors, and investors. For example, in 2015, the company raised $848.5 million in cash by issuing long-term debt, but it also used $610.1 million to repay a long-term debt obligation. In addition, over this 3-year period, Starbucks paid out $2,340.6 million in dividends to its shareholders and paid $2,782.8 million to repurchase shares of its common stock.

As these examples reveal, the statement of cash flows provides information about how a company is generating and using cash flows, providing insights into the company's operating, investing, and financing strategies. The use of cash flow information, along with information contained in the balance sheet and income statement, helps financial statement users better understand a company's past financial performance and its future prospects.

Users of financial statements are interested in the operating, investing, and financing activities of companies. For a particular company, they ask questions such as:

- What is the relationship between net income and cash provided by operations?
- Were the company's operations a source or a use of cash?
- What investments and growth activities took place?
- How were activities financed?
- What were the proceeds received from issuing capital stock or debt, and how were the funds used?

Each of these questions relates to the cash flows of the company. The FASB recognized the importance of providing answers to these questions by stating that financial reporting should provide information about a company's:

- methods for obtaining and spending cash
- data on borrowing and repayment of debt
- capital transactions, including cash dividends and other distributions of resources to owners
- other factors that may affect its liquidity or solvency.[1]

To satisfy these objectives, GAAP requires a company to present a *statement of cash flows* for the accounting period along with its income statement and balance sheet.[2] The statement of cash flows is an integral part of a company's financial statements and the subject of this chapter.

LEARNING OBJECTIVE 21.1
Understand and define operating, investing, and financing activities.

WHAT INFORMATION DOES THE STATEMENT OF CASH FLOWS PROVIDE, AND HOW IS IT REPORTED?

In Chapter 2, we noted that one of the specific objectives of financial reporting is to provide information about the amount, timing, and uncertainty of a company's cash flows. Investors, lenders, and other creditors need useful information about a company's cash

---

[1] "Conceptual Framework for Financial Reporting," *FASB Statement of Financial Accounting Concepts No. 8* (Stamford, CT: FASB, 1978), paragraph OB20.
[2] FASB ASC 230-10-15: Statement of Cash Flows, Overall, Scope and Scope Exceptions.

inflows and outflows, borrowings and repayments, and capital transactions (including dividends). A company's receivables, payables, and inventory are links between its operations and its cash inflows and outflows. Information about these relationships is useful in understanding the operations of the company.

The primary purpose of a company's statement of cash flows is to provide relevant information about its cash receipts and cash payments during an accounting period. The FASB states that the information in a statement of cash flows, if used with information in the other financial statements, helps external users assess:

- a company's ability to generate positive future net cash flows
- a company's ability to meet its obligations and pay dividends
- a company's need for external financing
- the reasons for differences between a company's net income and related cash receipts and payments
- both the cash and noncash aspects of a company's financing and investing transactions during the accounting period[3]

What Classifications Are Used in the Statement of Cash Flows?

To help financial statement users develop expectations for the amounts, timing, and uncertainty of future cash flows, a company classifies and reports cash flows related to similar business activities.[4] According to GAAP, a company's statement of cash flows for the accounting period must clearly show:

- cash provided by or used in its operating activities
- cash provided by or used in its investing activities
- cash provided by or used in its financing activities
- net increase or decrease in its cash, reconciling the change from the beginning cash balance to the ending cash balance reported on the year-end balance sheet

Operating Activities A company's **operating activities** are part of the day-to-day business activities of a company—acquiring (purchasing or manufacturing), selling, and delivering goods and services to customers. Cash inflows from operating activities include *cash receipts from*:

- sale of goods or services to customers
- collection of accounts receivable
- collection of interest on loans
- receipts of dividends on investments in equity securities

Cash outflows for operating activities include *cash payments to*:

- suppliers for inventory and other goods and services used in operations
- employees
- governmental authorities for taxes
- lenders for interest (unless capitalized)
- other suppliers for various expenses

Starbucks's main operating activity providing cash is generating revenues by selling coffee and other products to customers in its retail stores, while paying for inventory and employees is its main cash operating outflow.

Investing Activities A company's investing activities are those transactions that involve acquiring and selling productive assets and investments needed to achieve the operating objectives of the business. **Investing activities** include transactions involving *cash receipts from*:

- sale of property, plant, and equipment
- sale of investments classified as available for sale and held-to-maturity
- repayment of principal from loans made to other companies

---

[3] FASB ASC 230-10-10: Statement of Cash Flows, Overall, Objectives.
[4] "Recognition and Measurement in Financial Statements of Business Enterprises," *FASB Statement of Financial Accounting Concepts No. 5* (Stamford, CT: FASB, 1984), par. 20.

Cash outflows for investing activities include *cash payments to*:

- acquire property, plant, and equipment
- acquire investments classified as available for sale and held-to-maturity
- make loans to other companies

In 2013 through 2015, **Starbucks**'s main investing activity that used cash was purchasing plant, property, and equipment, which was the result of Starbucks rapid expansion in opening new stores. In those same years, Starbucks received large amounts of cash from sales and maturities of investment securities, but also used large amounts to purchase investment securities. In 2013 and 2015, Starbucks also used large amounts of cash to acquire other companies.

Financing Activities A company's **financing activities** include its transactions involving obtaining resources from owners and providing them with a return on their investment as well as borrowing money from creditors and repaying those obligations. Cash inflows from financing activities include *cash receipts from* issuing:

- equity securities (i.e., common stock and preferred stock)
- financing instruments (i.e., bonds, short-term or long-term notes, mortgages, capital leases, and other short- or long-term borrowings)

Cash outflows for financing activities include *cash payments for*:

- dividends
- repurchase of the company's equity securities
- repayments of amounts borrowed through financing instruments

Most borrowings and repayments of borrowings are financing activities. However, the settlement of liabilities, such as accounts payable incurred to acquire inventory and salaries payable, is an operating activity.

In 2015, **Starbucks**'s largest financing cash payments were to investors for dividends and repurchase of common stock. In addition, that year Starbucks raised $848.5 million by issuing long-term debt, used $610.1 million to repay long-term debt, and used $360.8 million to purchase non-controlling interests.

Noncash Investing and Financing Activities Most financing and investing activities of a company affect its cash; however, some transactions (such as buying land by issuing common stock) are "simultaneous" investing and financing activities that do not affect its cash. Examples of these transactions include:

- acquisitions of assets by issuing equity securities (noncash investing and financing activities)
- acquisitions of assets by assuming liabilities such as capital lease obligations (noncash investing and financing activities)
- exchanges of debt securities or preferred stock for equity securities such as the conversion of bonds or preferred stock for common stock (noncash financing activities)
- exchanges of assets for assets (noncash investing activities)
- exchanges of liabilities for liabilities (noncash financing activities)

While these transactions do not affect cash, they are important in providing an overall picture of a company's investing and financing activities as well as its prospective cash flows. The company is required to report these items either in a separate schedule or narrative explanation that accompanies the statement of cash flows.

Cash and Cash Equivalents As we discussed in Chapter 6, as part of its cash management procedures, a company may invest its cash in short-term, highly liquid investments, such as treasury bills, commercial paper, and money market funds. These investments are called *cash equivalents* and, instead of reporting "Cash" as a current asset on its balance sheet, the company reports "Cash and Cash Equivalents." In this case, the company's statement of cash flows explains the change during the accounting period in its *cash and* *cash equivalents*. For example, examining **Starbucks**'s cash flow statement you can see that it explains the net increase (decrease) in cash and cash equivalents. In this chapter, for simplicity, we focus only on changes in *cash*.

Presentation and Content of the Statement of Cash Flows

Example A typical statement of cash flows for Winslow Corporation is shown in Example 21.1.

Typical Statement of Cash Flows

EXAMPLE 21.1

Winslow Corporation
Statement of Cash Flows
For Year Ended December 31, 2016

Operating Activities:		
Net income		$ 42,000
Adjustments for noncash income items:		
Add: Depreciation expense	24,000	
Less: Gain on sale of land	(2,700)	
Adjustments for cash flow effects from working capital items:		
Decrease in accounts receivable	7,800	
Increase in inventory	(6,000)	
Decrease in accounts payable	(21,000)	
Increase in salaries payable	2,400	
Net cash provided by operating activities		$ 46,500
Investing Activities:		
Payment for purchase of building	$(84,000)	
Payment for purchase of equipment	(12,000)	
Proceeds from sale of land	30,000	
Net cash used for investing activities		(66,000)
Financing Activities:		
Proceeds from issuance of common stock	$ 54,000	
Proceeds from issuance of bonds	36,000	
Payment of dividends	(27,000)	
Payment of note payable	(39,000)	
Net cash provided by financing activities		24,000
Net increase in cash (see Schedule 1)		$ 4,500
Cash, January 1, 2016		32,700
Cash, December 31, 2016		$ 37,200
Schedule 1: Investing and Financing Activities Not Affecting Cash		
Investing Activities:		
Acquisition of land by issuance of common stock		$(18,000)
Financing Activities:		
Issuance of common stock for land		18,000

Operating Activities A company reports the net cash provided by or used in its operating activities in the first section of its statement of cash flows. A company will be successful in the long run only if it is able to generate positive cash flows from its operations. This situation occurs when the cash received from selling goods or services exceeds the cash paid to provide the goods or services. Generating positive cash from operations generally is the most important cash flow activity of a company. External users can compare the company's net cash flow from operating activities with the same information from previous years to detect favorable or unfavorable trends, which will impact the company's liquidity, financial flexibility, operating capability, and risk. They can compare this information with the same information from other companies for the same purposes.

Winslow Corporation provided a net cash inflow of $46,500 from its operating activities during 2016.

Investing Activities A company reports the cash inflows and outflows from its investing activities in the second section of the statement of cash flows. It lists each investing cash inflow and outflow separately and subtotals the amounts to determine the net cash used by or provided by investing activities.

During 2016, Winslow paid cash of $84,000 to purchase a building and paid cash of $12,000 to purchase equipment. It received cash of $30,000 from the sale of land, at cost. The net result was that Winslow used $66,000 cash for its investing activities.

Financing Activities A company reports the cash inflows and outflows from its financing activities in the third section of the statement of cash flows. It lists each financing cash inflow and outflow separately and subtotals the amounts to determine the net cash provided by or used for financing activities.

During 2016, Winslow had cash inflows of $54,000 and $36,000 from issuing common stock and bonds, respectively. It had a cash payment of $27,000 for dividends and a $39,000 cash payment for a note payable. The net result was that $24,000 cash was provided by its financing activities.

Net Change in Cash and Reconciliation The net increase or decrease in cash is determined by adding the amounts of the net cash flows from operating activities, investing activities, and financing activities.

The $46,500 net cash provided by operating activities, minus the $66,000 net cash used for investing activities, plus the $24,000 net cash provided by financing activities resulted in a $4,500 net increase in cash for Winslow in 2016. This $4,500 net increase in cash reconciles the $32,700 beginning cash balance to the $37,200 ending cash balance.

Noncash Items A company reports its investing and financing activities not affecting cash in a separate schedule accompanying the statement of cash flows. It lists each investing and/or financing activity and offsets the related amounts against each other.

During 2016, Winslow engaged in a simultaneous investing and financing transaction. It acquired land costing $18,000 by issuing common stock. The investing portion of the transaction was the acquisition of the land, while the financing portion was the issuance of common stock. Schedule 1 shows the investing activity as an $18,000 "outflow" which is offset by the $18,000 "inflow" from the financing activity. Although no cash was exchanged, both items are listed to show all of Winslow's investing and financing activities during 2016.

What Information Does the Statement of Cash Flows Help Financial Statement Users Understand?

By reviewing a company's statement of cash flows, external users can see how a company obtained and used its cash, as well as the types of investing and financing activities that did not affect cash. They can examine the items in each section to see if important changes have occurred.

Example Winslow's investing activities involving the acquisition of the building and equipment in 2016 may indicate an increase in its operating capability. In addition, Winslow's financing activities involving the issuance of both bonds and common stock in 2016 reveal a change in its capital structure and may indicate a change in its financial flexibility and risk.

A comparison with other companies can also show, for instance, whether the company is obtaining or using a greater proportion of its cash from financing or investing activities rather than operations. This may be important in assessing the relative risk of investing in the company. External users can evaluate the likelihood of future cash dividends, as well as the need for additional cash to finance existing operations or the expansion of operations. They also can evaluate the ability of the company to pay current obligations, make periodic interest payments, and pay off long-term debt when the debt reaches its maturity date. Thus, a company's statement of cash flows provides external users with information about its liquidity, financial flexibility, operating capability, and risk. In so doing, the statement enhances both the predictive value and confirmatory value and, therefore, the *decision usefulness* of a company's financial statements to help fulfill the objectives of financial reporting.

WHY IT MATTERS

Information from the statement of cash flows enables financial statement users to assess a company's liquidity and risk. Previously, you learned that the current ratio and quick ratio can be used to assess liquidity. These ratios provide a measure of assets available at a specific point in time to meet current liabilities. The **operating cash flow ratio** provides a measure of resources generated *over a period of time*, which a company may be able to use to meet current liabilities and is computed as:

$$\text{Operating Cash Flow Ratio} = \frac{\text{Cash Flow from Operating Activities}}{\text{Average Current Liabilities}}$$

For example, **Starbucks**'s balance sheets reported $3,653.5 million of current liabilities in at the end of 2015, and $3,038.7 million of current liabilities at the end of 2014. Starbucks also reported $3,749.1 million of cash flows from operating activities for fiscal year 2015. Analysts would calculate its operating cash flow ratio as:

$$\frac{\$3,749.1}{(\$3,653.5 + \$3,038.7)/2} = \$1.12$$

This ratio tells analysts that the company generated approximately $1.12 from operating activities during the year for every dollar of current liabilities. This measurement provides a dynamic measurement of the resources available for meeting current obligations.

Another cash flow ratio examined by analysts to assess risk is the **operating cash flow to total liabilities ratio**, which provides recognition of a company's ability to generate cash flows from operations to pay its debt. This ratio is computed as:

$$\text{Operating Cash Flow to Total Liabilities Ratio} = \frac{\text{Cash Flow from Operating Activities}}{\text{Average Total Liabilities}}$$

For **Starbucks**, the ratio would be calculated as:

$$\frac{\$3,749.1}{(\$6,626.3 + \$5,479.2)/2} = \$0.62$$

When comparing ratios between two companies, a higher ratio indicates that the company is less risky. Similarly, when comparing these ratios for a given company over time, increasing ratios indicate a company is becoming less risky, whereas decreasing ratios indicate a company is facing greater risk in generating cash flows sufficient to cover its liabilities.

Cash Inflows and Outflows

To understand a company's cash flows, the relationships between the *changes* in balance sheet accounts and the company's cash flows must be analyzed.

- A company's *inflows* of cash are caused by *decreases* in its assets (other than cash) and by *increases* in liabilities and shareholders' equity during the accounting period.
- A company's *outflows* of cash are caused by *increases* in its assets (other than cash) and *decreases* in liabilities and in shareholders' equity during the accounting period.

The difference between the inflows and outflows is the change in cash.

Inflows of Cash There are three categories of a company's inflows (increases) of cash:

- *Decreases in Assets.* The sale or other disposal of assets (other than cash) typically causes a direct increase in cash when cash is received or collected in exchange for the assets (such as selling an investment security for cash or collecting a receivable in cash). In some cases, however, a decrease in assets *implies* an increase (savings) in cash because the asset being consumed was purchased for cash in a prior period. For example, a decrease in a prepaid expense asset implies a savings of cash *during the current* period.
- *Increases in Liabilities.* The issuance or incurrence of liabilities typically causes a direct increase in cash when cash is borrowed (such as issuing a note payable for cash). In some cases, the incurrence of a liability *implies* an increase in cash even though the cash flow may not have literally occurred during the period. For example, incurring an increase in wages payable or accounts payable represents additional borrowing by the company, which implies a positive cash flow *during the current* period, even though the employees or suppliers did not literally lend cash to the company.
- *Increases in Shareholders' Equity.* Shareholders' equity increases mainly because of net income and additional investments by owners. Additional investments cause an increase in cash because cash is received in exchange for the common stock issued. Net income is slightly more complicated because the inflows and outflows of cash for operating activities are different from the revenues and expenses included in net income (we discuss this topic later).

Outflows of Cash There are also three categories of a company's outflows (decreases) of cash:

- *Increases in Assets.* The acquisition of assets (other than cash) typically causes a decrease in cash because cash is paid in exchange for the assets. Again, in some cases, however, an increase in assets *implies* a decrease (use) of cash, even though cash may not have literally been used to acquire the asset *during the current* period. For example, an increase in receivables implies a use of cash because the company has, in effect, extended credit to customers, even though the company has not literally loaned customers cash.
- *Decreases in Liabilities.* The payment of liabilities typically causes a decrease in cash when cash is paid to satisfy the liabilities. Again, in some cases, the reduction of a liability *implies* a use of cash even though the cash flow may not have literally occurred during the period. For example, reducing unearned or deferred revenues represents satisfying liabilities to customers who have prepaid for goods or services, which implies a use of cash during the period, even though the company did not literally pay cash to the customers.
- *Decreases in Shareholders' Equity.* Shareholders' equity may decrease as a result of several transactions. Two common transactions are the payment of dividends and the acquisition of treasury stock. In each case, a decrease in shareholders' equity is accompanied by a decrease in cash.

ETHICAL DILEMMA

Kyma Inc. manufactures and sells a variety of high-end electronic devices. Its most popular product, a portable satellite radio receiver, has been a market leader for years and has helped the company amass a large amount of cash. However, Kyma's financial performance has been somewhat disappointing over the last 2 years. Specifically, Kyma's return on assets has decreased by two percentage points, and its stock price has been stagnant. As Kyma's accountant, the CEO has asked you to provide an analysis of the causes of these disappointing results and a recommendation that would increase the company's performance measures. Your examination of the company's financial results reveals that Kyma's large cash balance may be a factor in its disappointing performance. While the large cash balance increases the company's liquidity, the majority of these funds are invested in short-term, risk-free financial instruments that yield approximately 2%. This low return is a significant cause of the company's declining return on assets measure and has many investors calling for an increased dividend, which the CEO is adamantly against. Instead of paying a dividend, you suggest that Kyma use the excess cash to finance its customers' purchases of the company's products. The interest rate charged to provide this financial assistance will be much higher than the rate earned by Kyma's current investment strategy, and this increased return is expected to add at least one percentage point to the company's return on assets.

The CEO is very excited about this proposal, but he is concerned about how the increased receivables created by the loans to customers will affect the company's cash flow from operating activities. You state that while this is not specifically addressed by GAAP, you feel that because customer loans arise from the sale of Kyma's products, the associated cash outflow should be classified as an operating activity. The CEO disagrees and decides that the cash outflow associated with the lending transaction is an investing activity. He reasons that because GAAP does not specifically address this issue, he has an obligation to the shareholders to make the company's financial statements look as good as possible. If Kyma classifies the lending transaction as an operating activity, it would report declining cash flow from operations and send an incorrect signal to the market as to the company's future. Furthermore, the CEO states that because the matter is simply a classification issue that does not change the company's total cash flow, no one would be hurt by classifying the transaction as an investing activity. How do you respond to the CEO's statements?

GOT IT?

21-1 What information does the statement of cash flows help users assess?

21-2 Briefly describe the three types of activities a company reports in its statement of cash flows.

21-3 Thompson Company sold a piece of equipment that had an original cost of $22,000 and a carrying value of $10,000 for $13,000 in cash. How would this information be reported on a statement of cash flows prepared using the indirect method?

21-4 Give two examples of a company's (a) cash inflows from investing activities and (b) cash outflows for investing activities.

21-5 Give two examples of a company's (a) cash inflows from financing activities and (b) cash outflows for financing activities.

21-6 Give two examples of a company's investing and financing activities not affecting cash.

HOW ARE CASH FLOWS FOR OPERATING ACTIVITIES REPORTED?

LEARNING OBJECTIVE 21.2
Explain the direct and indirect methods for reporting operating cash flows.

The calculation of a company's net cash flow from operating activities is usually the most detailed part of its statement of cash flows. To prepare this section, it is helpful to understand the relationship between the accruals that determine revenues and expenses and the cash flows related to revenues and expenses in a company's operating cycle.

Exhibit 21.1 provides a summary of this relationship. Revenue and expenses in the income statement are related to cash inflows and outflows in the operating activities of the cash flow statement. The changes in the accrual accounts allow us to convert the revenues and expense to cash flows.

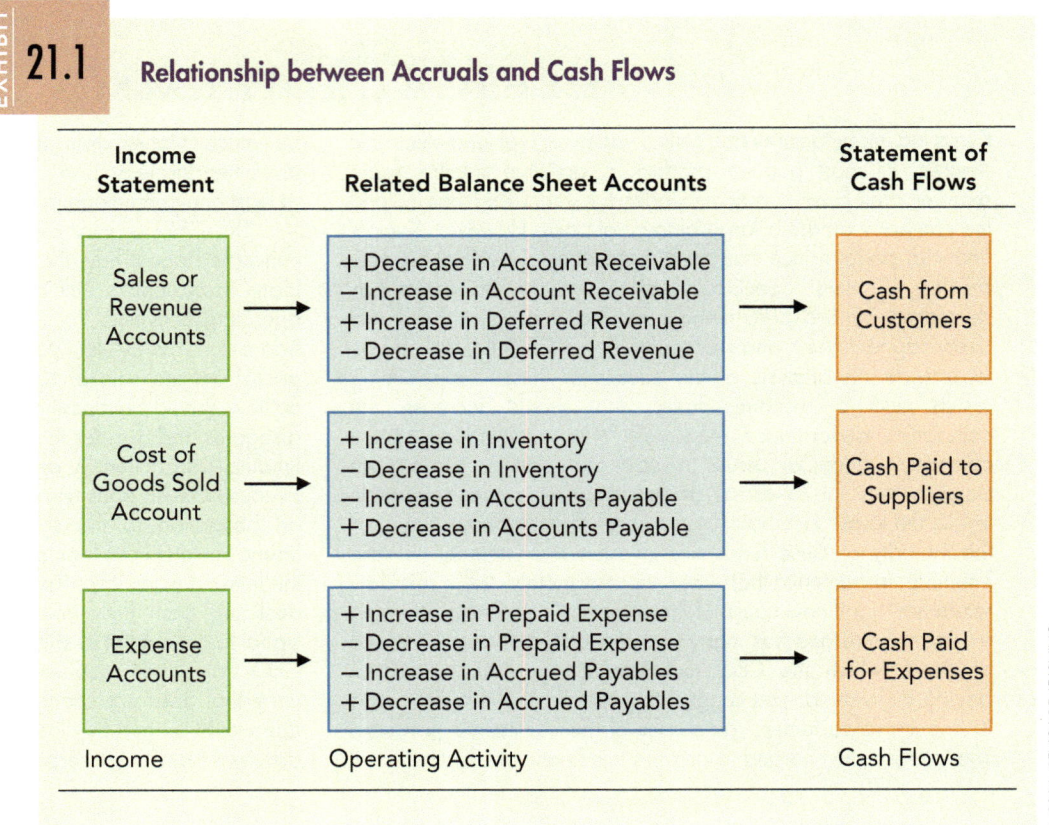

EXHIBIT 21.1 Relationship between Accruals and Cash Flows

As you can see from Exhibit 21.1, the relationship between the accruals that determine revenues and expenses and the cash flows related to revenues and expenses results in the company's net income and its net cash flow from operating activities being different. The difference is a result of when the company records revenues and expenses and when it receives and pays cash. A company "adjusts" for these changes to calculate its net cash flow from operating activities.

There are also "noncash" changes in certain noncurrent asset and liability accounts that affect a company's net income but do not result in a cash inflow or outflow for operating activities. For instance, depreciation expense reduces net income (and noncurrent assets), but there is no cash outflow for operating activities. The recording of amortization expense for intangible assets and the depletion of natural resources also reduce net income (and noncurrent assets) but have no related operating cash outflow. In addition, when a company sells an asset and records a gain or loss, the gain or loss affects net income, but the entire cash flow from the sale is recorded as an investing activity. Therefore, the gain or loss must be adjusted when calculating net cash flow from operating activities. A company must analyze each of the changes in these noncurrent asset accounts to help determine the effect on its net cash flow from operating activities.

Direct Method

GAAP allows a company to choose one of two ways to report its net cash flow from operating activities on its statement of cash flows: the *direct method* or the *indirect method*. Under the **direct method**, a company computes operating cash inflows and deducts its operating cash outflows to determine its net cash flow from operating activities.

Operating Cash Inflows Under the direct method, a company reports its cash inflows from operating activities in three categories: collections from customers, interest and dividends collected, and other operating receipts, if any. Generally, these cash inflows from operating activities are calculated by an analysis of income statement and balance sheet items as follows:

- *Collections from Customers.* Sales revenue, plus decrease in accounts receivable or minus increase in accounts receivable, and plus increase in deferred revenues or minus decrease in deferred revenues
- *Interest and Dividends Collected.* Interest revenue and dividend revenue, plus decrease in interest/dividends receivable or minus increase in interest/dividends receivable, and plus amortization of premium on investment in bonds or minus amortization of discount on investment in bonds
- *Other Operating Receipts.* Other operating revenues, minus gains on disposals of assets and liabilities, and minus investment income recognized under the equity method

Operating Cash Outflows A company reports its cash outflows from operating activities in the following five categories:

- *Payments to Suppliers.*[5] Cost of goods sold, plus increase in inventory or minus decrease in inventory, plus decrease in accounts payable or minus increase in accounts payable
- *Payments to Employees.* Salaries (wages) expense, plus decrease in salaries payable or minus increase in salaries payable
- *Other Operating Payments.* Other operating expenses, plus increase in prepaid items or minus decrease in prepaid items; minus depreciation, depletion, and amortization expense; minus losses on disposals of assets and liabilities; minus investment loss recognized under the equity method
- *Payments of Interest.* Interest expense, plus decrease in interest payable or minus increase in interest payable, plus amortization of premium on bonds payable or minus amortization of discount on bonds payable
- *Payments of Income Taxes.* Income tax expense, plus decrease in income taxes payable or minus increase in income taxes payable, plus decrease in deferred tax liability or minus increase in deferred tax liability[6]

Under the direct method, the company's net cash provided by (or used in) operating activities is the difference between these cash inflows and cash outflows.

Diagram of Operating Cash Flows Under the *direct* method, a company computes the cash inflows from operating activities by adjusting the various revenue accounts for changes in certain asset accounts and deferred revenues, and to eliminate certain "noncash" revenues (gains). The company computes the cash outflows for operating activities by adjusting the various expense accounts for changes in certain liability (and asset) accounts and deferred revenues, and to eliminate certain "noncash" expenses (losses).

Exhibit 21.2 shows these adjustments. The adjustments may have to be modified depending on the way that the company reports and classifies the related items in its financial statements. For instance, an increase in deferred revenue of an airline would be due to selling tickets in advance. In this case, the adjustment would be to sales revenue. On the other hand, an increase in deferred revenue of a retail company may be due to a collection of rent in advance. In this case, the adjustment is to other revenue instead of sales revenues.

---

[5] The Accounting Standards Codification (FASB ASC 230-10-45: Statement of Cash Flows, Overall, Other Presentation Matters) combines payments to suppliers and payments to employees into one category. However, it encourages companies to provide further breakdowns of operating cash receipts and operating cash payments, when useful.

[6] For a company that has a deferred tax asset, it adds an increase in the deferred tax asset to income tax expense or subtracts a decrease. It handles a change in a related valuation allowance (contra account) in the opposite way.

EXHIBIT 21.2 — Major Adjustments to Convert Income Statement Amounts to Operating Cash Flows

Income Statement Amounts	Adjustments	Operating Cash Receipts and Payments	Net Operating Cash Flows
Sales revenue	+ Decrease in accounts receivable *or* − Increase in accounts receivable + Increase in deferred revenues *or* − Decrease in deferred revenues	= Collections from customers	Cash inflows from operating activities
Interest revenue and dividend revenue	+ Decrease in interest receivable *or* − Increase in interest receivable + Amortization of premium on investment in bonds *or* − Amortization of discount on investment in bonds	= Interest and dividends collected	
Other revenues	− Gains on disposals of assets and liabilities[a] − Investment income (equity method)[a]	= Other operating receipts	
Cost of goods sold	+ Increase in inventory *or* − Decrease in inventory + Decrease in accounts payable *or* − Increase in accounts payable	= Payments to suppliers	Cash outflows for operating activities
Salaries expense	+ Decrease in salaries payable *or* − Increase in salaries payable	= Payments to employees	
Other expenses	+ Increase in prepaid items *or* − Decrease in prepaid items − Depreciation, depletion, and amortization expense[a] − Losses on disposals of assets and liabilities[a] − Investment loss (equity method)[a]	= Other operating payments	
Interest expense	+ Decrease in interest payable *or* − Increase in interest payable + Amortization of premium on bonds payable *or* − Amortization of discount on bonds payable	= Payments of interest	
Income tax expense	+ Decrease in income taxes payable *or* − Increase in income taxes payable[b] + Decrease in deferred tax liability[b] *or* − Increase in deferred tax liability	= Payments of income taxes	

[a] Unless listed as separate items on income statement
[b] A change in a deferred tax asset is handled in an opposite manner.

In the following example, we focus on payments to suppliers, payments to employees, and payments for income taxes. We provide a more detailed example in the appendix to this chapter.

Example: Direct Method

Quant Corporation presents the following simplified income statement information for the year ended December 31, 2016:

Sales revenue		$70,000
Less:		
Cost of goods sold	$(29,000)	
Salaries expense	(13,000)	
Depreciation expense	(8,000)	
Loss on sale of equipment	(2,500)	
		(52,500)
Income before income taxes		$17,500
Income tax expense		(4,000)
Net income		$13,500

Further analysis reveals the following changes in its current asset and current liability accounts for 2016:

- Accounts receivable decreased by $2,600.
- Inventory increased by $2,000.
- Accounts payable decreased by $7,000.
- Salaries payable increased by $800.

Under the direct method, Quant computes cash collected from customers as:

$70,000 sales revenue + $2,600 decrease in accounts receivable = $72,600

This adjustment is made because the company's cash collections exceeded its sales during the year, which caused accounts receivable to decrease. Because this is the only cash receipt, cash inflows from operating activities are $72,600.

Cash paid to suppliers is computed as:

$29,000 cost of goods sold + $2,000 increase in inventory + $7,000 decrease in accounts payable = $38,000

These adjustments are made because the company's inventory purchases not only replaced the cost of goods sold but also increased the inventory on hand by $2,000, increasing the cash outflows to suppliers. In addition, cash outflows to suppliers were increased further because the company paid off some of the accounts payable, reducing the outstanding balance by $7,000.

Cash paid to employees is computed as:

$13,000 salaries expense − $800 increase in salaries payable = $12,200

This adjustment is made because the cash paid for salaries was less than its salaries expense, which caused an increase in salaries payable.

Because there was no change in income tax payable or income tax receivable, it indicates that the entire $4,000 of income tax expense was paid in cash. Therefore, cash outflows for operating activities total $54,200 ($38,000 + $12,200 + $4,000). Note that the depreciation expense is *not* included in the net cash flows from operating activities because it did not result in an outflow of cash. In addition, the loss on the sale of equipment is not included because the cash flow related to the sale is included in the investing activities section.

Quant reports the cash flows from operating activities on its statement of cash flows as follows:

Operating Activities:
Cash inflows:
 Cash collected from customers $72,600
  Cash inflows from operating activities $72,600
Cash outflows:
 Cash paid to suppliers $(38,000)
 Cash paid to employees   (12,200)
 Cash paid for income taxes   (4,000)
  Cash outflows for operating activities   (54,200)
Net cash provided by operating activities $18,400

The direct method has the advantage of reporting a company's operating cash inflows separately from its operating cash outflows, which may be useful in estimating future cash flows. However, the direct method is criticized because it does not reconcile the net income reported on a company's income statement to the net cash provided by operating activities reported on its statement of cash flows. Also, the direct method does not show how the changes in the elements (i.e., current assets and current liabilities) of a company's operating cycle affected its operating cash flows.

Indirect Method

The *indirect method* for reporting a company's net cash flow from operating activities resolves the two criticisms of the direct method. Under the **indirect method**, a company's net income is adjusted (reconciled) to its net cash flow from operating activities. To do so, net income is listed first and then *adjustments* (additions or subtractions) are made to net income:

- Add back noncash expenses, such as depreciation and amortization expense, deferred income taxes, and share based compensation expense.
- Add back noncash charges, such as restructuring and impairment charges.
- Subtract noncash revenues, such as equity method income and excess tax benefits from share based compensations awards.
- Add back losses or subtract gains recognized in income from the sale of assets, so that the full amount of the proceeds from the sale can be reported in the investing activities section.
- Subtract increases and add back decreases in current operating assets (other than cash) and add back increases and subtract decreases in current operating liabilities to adjust for accruals and deferrals effects on cash flows.

Under the indirect method, a company's net income is converted from an *accrual* basis to a *cash flow* basis. In this manner, the indirect method provides information about the lead and lag intervals between the company's net income and operating cash flows.

GAAP recommends the direct method but allows the use of either the direct method or the indirect method. However, if a company uses the direct method on its statement of cash flows, it must also include a schedule that reconciles its net income to its net cash flow provided by (or used in) operating activities (i.e., the indirect method). Most companies use the indirect method because of its historical use and the extra schedule required under the direct method. (This includes **Starbucks**, as shown in

Appendix A.) However, companies that use the indirect method must report the interest paid and income taxes paid.

Example: Indirect Method

Refer back to Quant Corporation's income statement and additional information shown earlier. Under the indirect method, Quant reports the net cash flow from operating activities on its statement of cash flows as follows:

Operating Activities:
Net income	$13,500
Adjustments for noncash income items:	
Add back: Depreciation expense	8,000
Add back: Loss on sale of equipment	2,500
Adjustments for cash flows from working capital items:	
Decrease in accounts receivable	2,600
Increase in inventory	(2,000)
Decrease in accounts payable	(7,000)
Increase in salaries payable	800
Net cash provided by operating activities	$18,400

It is important to understand how each adjustment is used to convert the net income to the net cash provided by operating activities.

- The $8,000 depreciation expense is *added back* to the $13,500 net income because it had been deducted to determine net income even though it did not involve an outflow of cash.
- The $2,500 loss is *added back* to net income because it also had been deducted to determine net income. By adjusting out the loss, the entire amount of the sale of the equipment is able to be reported in the investing activities section.
- The $2,600 decrease in accounts receivable is added to net income because it reflects additional cash receipts from operations.
- The $800 increase in salaries payable resulted in an increase in expenses and a decrease in net income. It is added to net income because it did not involve a cash payment for operations during this period.
- The $2,000 increase in inventory and the $7,000 decrease in accounts payable are both deducted from net income because they represent additional operating cash payments to suppliers.

Note that by using either the direct or indirect method, net cash provided by operating activities is the same amount ($18,400). ■

Major Adjustments In the Quant example of the indirect method, we made only a few simple adjustments to convert the net income to the net cash flow from operating activities. Many companies include many adjustments involving noncash expenses and income items, increases and decreases in its current assets and current liabilities, as well as other noncurrent accounts. Exhibit 21.3 (p. 21-17) lists the major adjustments used to convert a company's net income to its net cash flow from operating activities. We explain these adjustments in the examples later in the chapter.

INTERNATIONAL DIMENSION

STATEMENT OF CASH FLOWS

IFRS require a company to include a cash flow statement as one of its basic financial statements. These standards define operating, investing, and financing activities in a manner similar to U.S. GAAP. In addition, a company may present its operating cash flows under either the indirect or direct method. However, some differences do exist:

- Contrary to U.S. GAAP, IFRS do not require a company using the direct method to reconcile its net income to its operating cash flows.
- When using the indirect method, IFRS do not specify the particular income line item that must begin the operating activities section. A company could begin the section under IFRS with operating income.
- Differences in the way a company presents certain items under IFRS as compared to U.S. GAAP also exist. Under IFRS, a company is:
  - required to report as an investing cash outflow the cash paid for any development costs that it capitalized as an intangible asset
  - allowed to report dividends and interest paid as either an operating cash outflow or a financing cash outflow
  - allowed to report dividends and interest received as either an operating cash inflow or an investing cash inflow
  - allowed to report bank overdrafts as a financing cash inflow
  - allowed to report payments of income taxes identified with financing or investing transactions as financing or investing cash outflows
  - allowed to report its cash flow per share
  - allowed more freedom in netting cash receipts and payments

IFRS also encourage a company to disclose any undrawn borrowing facilities that may be available for future operating activities; the cash flows that represent increases in its operating capacity separately from the cash flows that are needed to maintain its operating capacity; and the operating, investing, and financing activities of each of its reported industry and geographic segments.

The application of IFRS also permits recognition of several types of noncash transactions that affect only balance sheet accounts, which U.S. GAAP does not permit. For example, under IFRS, a company is allowed to write the value of its property, plant, and equipment and intangible assets up to fair value with a corresponding increase in shareholders' equity (a revaluation surplus account). Even though no cash is involved in these transactions, the company must "reconstruct" the related journal entries on its spreadsheet for its statement of cash flows to properly account for the changes in these balance sheet accounts. IFRS also permit a company to reverse a previous inventory write-down taken under the lower-of-cost-or-market rule as well as to reverse any impairment losses related to a loan (note receivable). These reversals are recognized in income, but do not involve cash.

Finally, as discussed in Chapter 12, under IFRS a company may capitalize development costs (that are part of its R&D) as an intangible asset. It then must amortize the cost as a noncash expense on its income statement. Similar to other noncash income items (e.g., gains, losses, depreciation expense) under the indirect method, the company would reconstruct the related journal entries on its spreadsheet to subtract from (or add to) its net income any of these amounts to reconcile its net income to the net cash flow from operating activities.

Source: IAS 7 Statement of Cash Flows (See Appendix C at the end of this book.)

EXHIBIT 21.3 Adjustments to Convert Net Income to Net Cash Flow from Operating Activities—Indirect Method

Net Income

Plus

Adjustments for Noncash Income Items
- Depreciation, depletion, and amortization expense
- Loss (net) on disposal (or impairment) of assets or liabilities
- Loss under the equity method
- Amortization of discount on bonds payable
- Amortization of premium on investment in bonds
- Increase in deferred tax liability
- Decrease in deferred tax asset
- Increase in accrued pension cost
- Decrease in prepaid pension cost

Decreases in Current Assets
- Decrease in accounts receivable
- Decrease in interest receivable
- Decrease in inventory
- Decrease in prepaid expenses
- Decreases in other current assets*

Increases in Current Liabilities
- Increase in accounts payable
- Increase in salaries payable
- Increase in interest payable
- Increase in income taxes payable
- Increase in deferred revenues
- Increases in other current liabilities*

Minus

Adjustments for Noncash Income Items
- Gain (net) on disposal of assets or liabilities
- Income under the equity method
- Amortization of premium on bonds payable
- Amortization of discount on investment in bonds
- Decrease in deferred tax liability
- Increase in deferred tax asset
- Decrease in accrued pension cost
- Increase in prepaid pension cost

Increases in Current Assets
- Increase in accounts receivable
- Increase in interest receivable
- Increase in inventory
- Increase in prepaid expenses
- Increases in other current assets*

Decreases in Current Liabilities
- Decrease in accounts payable
- Decrease in salaries payable
- Decrease in interest payable
- Decrease in income taxes payable
- Decrease in deferred revenues
- Decreases in other current liabilities*

Equals

Net Cash Flow from Operating Activities

*Related to operating activities.

GOT IT?

21-7 Two companies each incur interest expense of $16,000 and pay dividends of $30,000. In addition, the companies receive interest and dividends from investments of $8,000 and $12,000, respectively. How would the statements of cash flows differ if one company uses IFRS and the other uses U.S. GAAP?

21-8 How is the reporting of income taxes paid different under IFRS compared to U.S. GAAP?

21-9 What are the two ways to calculate and report a company's net cash flow from operating activities? Briefly describe each method.

21-10 List the three operating cash inflows that a company reports under the direct method.

21-11 List the five operating cash outflows that a company reports under the direct method.

LEARNING OBJECTIVE 21.3

Prepare a statement of cash flows using the visual inspection method.

HOW IS A STATEMENT OF CASH FLOWS PREPARED UNDER THE VISUAL INSPECTION METHOD?

To prepare its statement of cash flows, a company needs the following information:

- beginning and ending balance sheets
- income statement
- shareholders' equity or retained earnings statement

in addition, the preparer will need other information obtained from the accounting records that explains the changes in its balance sheet accounts.

There are two methods that you may use to prepare a company's statement of cash flows: the *visual inspection method* or the *spreadsheet method*. Under the **visual inspection method**, you review the company's financial statements and prepare its statement of cash flows without using a spreadsheet. This method may be used when a company's financial statements are simple and when the relationships between changes in account balances can be easily analyzed. Due to the popularity of the indirect method, we discuss preparing the statement of cash flows using the indirect method in this section and preparation under the direct method is saved for the appendix. There are four steps in the visual inspection method:

- *Step 1.* Prepare the heading for the statement of cash flows and list the three sections: Operating Activities, Investing Activities, and Financing Activities.[7] List the company's net income as the first item in the operating activities section.
- *Step 2.* Calculate the increase or decrease that occurred during the accounting period in each balance sheet account (except cash) and determine whether it caused an inflow or outflow of cash. If so, report it in the appropriate category: Operating Activities, Investing Activities, or Financing Activities.
- *Step 3.* If no cash flow occurred in Step 2, determine whether the increase or decrease was (a) the result of a noncash income statement item or (b) a simultaneous investing and/or financing transaction. If (a), then determine the adjustment (addition or subtraction) to convert net income to the net cash flow from operating activities. If (b), then identify the components of the simultaneous investing and/or financing activity and report them in a separate note or schedule.
- *Step 4.* Complete the various sections of the statement of cash flows (based on the analysis in Steps 2 and 3). Check that the sum of the three subtotals of the sections equals the net change in cash. Also check that the sum of the net change in cash and the beginning cash balance is equal to the ending cash balance reported on the balance sheet.

Steps 2 and 3 do not have to be completed in sequential order. What is important is a complete analysis of the relevant information. While the visual inspection method is simple, its disadvantage is that it does not provide supporting documentation for the statement of cash flows.

Knowledge of the visual inspection method is helpful in understanding the more complex spreadsheet method.

Example: Visual Inspection Method

To understand how to prepare a statement of cash flows using the visual inspection method, we discuss a comprehensive example using Manning Company (a service company). Throughout the example, we refer to Manning's condensed financial information for 2016 in **Example 21.2**.

---

[7] If the company engaged in any investing and financing transactions not affecting cash, you must also prepare the heading for a schedule of Investing and Financing Activities Not Affecting Cash in Step 1 of Exhibit 21.3.

EXAMPLE 21.2

Manning Company: Condensed Financial Information

Income Statement Information for 2016

Service revenues		$ 31,800
Operating expenses:		
Depreciation expense	$ 2,300	
Interest expense	1,400	
Other expenses	18,100	(21,800)
Income before income taxes		$ 10,000
Income tax expense		(3,000)
Net income		$ 7,000

Retained Earnings Information for 2016

Beginning retained earnings	$11,300
Add: Net income	7,000
	$18,300
Less: Dividends	(3,500)
Ending retained earnings	$14,800

Balance Sheet Information

	Balances	
Accounts	**12/31/15**	**12/31/16**
Cash	$ 4,000	$ 6,600
Accounts receivable	6,300	9,000
Land	9,000	6,000
Buildings and equipment	48,000	60,000
Accumulated depreciation	(12,500)	(14,800)
Total Assets	$ 54,800	$ 66,800
Accrued expenses	$ 7,500	$ 9,000
Notes payable, 10%	14,000	21,000
Common stock, $10 par	22,000	22,000
Retained earnings	11,300	14,800
Total Liabilities and Shareholders' Equity	$ 54,800	$ 66,800

Supplemental Information for 2016:

- A building was purchased for cash during the year. No equipment was purchased during the year.
- Land was sold for cash during the year.
- No buildings or equipment were sold during the year.
- A note payable was issued at the end of the year.

Example 21.2a shows the statement of cash flows prepared from the information in **Example 21.2**. After preparing the heading and listing the sections of the statement of cash flows, the $2,600 net increase in cash is determined. This increase is computed by subtracting the $4,000 cash balance on the beginning balance sheet from the $6,600 cash balance on the ending balance sheet. Then, the $7,000 net income is obtained from the income statement and listed as the first item in the net cash flow from operating activities section (Step 1). The following discussion explains the remaining steps in the visual inspection method by reviewing the items in each section of the statement.

> **EXAMPLE 21.2a Simple Statement of Cash Flows**
>
> **Manning Company**
> **Statement of Cash Flows**
> **For Year Ended December 31, 2016**
>
> | | | |
> |---|---:|---:|
> | **Operating Activities:** | | |
> | Net income | | $ 7,000 |
> | Adjustments for noncash income items: | | |
> | Add: Depreciation expense | | 2,300 |
> | Adjustments for cash flow effects from working capital items: | | |
> | Increase in accounts receivable | | (2,700) |
> | Increase in accrued expenses | | 1,500 |
> | Net cash provided by operating activities | | $ 8,100 |
> | **Investing Activities:** | | |
> | Payment for purchase of building | $(12,000) | |
> | Proceeds from sale of land, at cost | 3,000 | |
> | Net cash used for investing activities | | (9,000) |
> | **Financing Activities:** | | |
> | Proceeds from issuance of note | $ 7,000 | |
> | Payment of dividends | (3,500) | |
> | Net cash provided by financing activities | | 3,500 |
> | Net increase in cash | | $ 2,600 |
> | Cash, January 1, 2016 | | 4,000 |
> | Cash, December 31, 2016 | | $ 6,600 |

Operating Activities In this section, there are three adjustments to convert the net income to the net cash flow from operating activities. The first adjustment involves the $2,300 depreciation expense. This amount is obtained from the income statement in **Example 21.2**. It is also the $2,300 increase (from $12,500 to $14,800) in the accumulated depreciation account on the balance sheets during the year.[8] Because depreciation is deducted in computing net income but does not cause a cash outflow, the $2,300 depreciation expense is added to net income.

The second adjustment involves the $1,500 increase (from $7,500 to $9,000 in **Example 21.2**) in accrued expenses. Accrued expenses increased, which implies a positive cash flow—we have incurred more expenses than we paid for during the period. Consequently, the $1,500 increase in accrued expenses is added to net income.

The third adjustment involves the $2,700 increase (from $6,300 to $9,000) in accounts receivable. Accounts receivable increased during the year because revenues on credit exceeded the cash collections on account. Therefore, service revenues and net income are greater than the related cash receipts. Consequently, the $2,700 increase in accounts receivable is deducted from net income.

As a result of the preceding adjustments, the net cash flow from Manning's operating activities is $8,100 in 2016, as shown in **Example 21.2a**. Note that, with the exception of depreciation, the adjustments to net income involve changes in current assets (except cash) and current liabilities.

---

[8] No buildings or equipment were sold during the year. If they had been sold, the accumulated depreciation account would have decreased. The related cash flow analysis would have been more complicated. We discuss this situation later in the spreadsheet method.

Investing Activities There are only two cash flows from investing activities: one cash payment and one cash receipt. During 2016, the Buildings and Equipment account increased by $12,000, from $48,000 to $60,000, as shown on the balance sheets in **Example 21.2**. Because there were no sales of buildings or equipment, this increase is the result of the purchase of a building, an investing activity, which required a cash payment of $12,000. This cash payment is listed as the first item in this section. During 2016, the Land account decreased by $3,000 (from $9,000 to $6,000) as a result of the sale of land, an investing activity. Because the proceeds from selling the land were equal to the cost of the land, there is no gain or loss.[9] The $3,000 cash receipt is listed as the second item in this section. As a result of these two cash flows, Manning uses a net cash of $9,000 for investing activities in 2016, as shown in **Example 21.2a**.

Financing Activities There are also two cash flows from financing activities: one cash receipt and one cash payment. During 2016, the Notes Payable account increased by $7,000 (from $14,000 to $21,000) as shown in **Example 21.2**. This increase is the result of issuing a note, a financing activity, which provided a cash receipt of $7,000 that is listed as the first item in this section. There was no change in the Common Stock account during the year, so there is no cash inflow or outflow related to common stock. During 2016, the company declared and paid dividends of $3,500. The amount of the dividends is obtained from the retained earnings statement in **Example 21.2**. The $3,500 cash payment of dividends, a financing activity, is listed as the second item in this section. As a result of these two cash flows, net cash inflow of $3,500 is provided by Manning's financing activities during 2016, as shown in **Example 21.2a**.

It is important to note that GAAP requires that a company report the cash inflows and cash outflows for related investing activities as well as for related financing activities *separately* and *not* "net" them against each other.[10]

Summary In preparing the three sections of the cash flow statement in **Example 21.2a**, it is important to account for all the changes in the assets, liabilities, and shareholders' equity accounts during 2016, as listed in **Example 21.2**. Note that, with the exception of depreciation, the adjustments to net income in the net cash flow from operating activities section involve changes in current asset and current liability accounts that are *part of the company's operating cycle*. On the other hand, all of the cash receipts and payments listed in the cash flows from investing activities section and the cash flows from financing activities section involve changes in noncurrent asset, noncurrent liability, and shareholders' equity accounts.

In general, current assets and liabilities that are not part of the company's operating cycle are not accounted for in the operating activities section. This would include accounts such as short-term notes receivable, short-term notes payable, changes in available-for-sale securities, and dividends payable. In addition, there are noncurrent assets and liabilities, such as bond discounts and premiums and deferred income taxes, that are part of the operating cycle that would affect operating activities.

The statement of cash flows in **Example 21.2a** is now complete. The $8,100 net cash provided by operating activities, minus the $9,000 net cash used for investing activities, plus the $3,500 net cash provided by financing activities, equals the $2,600 net increase in cash. And, the $2,600 net increase in cash, added to the $4,000 beginning cash balance, is equal to the $6,600 ending cash balanorted on the company's December 31, 2016, balance sheet).

---

[9] We discuss the reporting of the sale of noncurrent assets at a gain or loss in a later example.
[10] FASB ASC 230-10-45: Statement of Cash Flows, Overall, Other Presentation Matters.

Disclosure Real Report 21.1 shows the statement of cash flows for **Chipotle Mexican Grill, Inc**. Chipotle uses the indirect method to report net cash flow from operating activities. Additionally, the effect of foreign exchange rate changes on cash is disclosed separately after net cash flow from financing activities.

21.1 STATEMENT OF CASH FLOWS — REAL REPORT

Chipotle Mexican Grill, Inc.

Chipotle Mexican Grill, Inc.
Consolidated Statement Of Cash Flows *(in thousands)*

	Years ended December 31		
	2013	**2012**	**2011**
Operating activities			
Net income	$ 327,438	$ 278,000	$ 214,945
Adjustments to reconcile net income to net cash provided by operating activities:			
Depreciation and amortization	96,054	84,130	74,938
Deferred income tax provision (benefit)	2,103	(18,057)	11,935
Loss on disposal of assets	6,751	5,027	5,806
Bad debt allowance	19	1,046	239
Stock-based compensation expense	63,657	64,276	41,382
Excess tax benefit on stock-based compensation	(38,379)	(73,210)	(38,786)
Other	507	522	2,501
Changes in operating assets and liabilities:			
Accounts receivable	(7,238)	(9,438)	(2,970)
Inventory	(1,950)	(2,180)	(1,816)
Prepaid expenses and other current assets	(6,806)	(5,954)	(5,399)
Other assets	(1,354)	(20,539)	(7,350)
Accounts payable	2,052	7,849	9,432
Accrued liabilities	12,020	21,307	17,451
Income tax payable/receivable	44,334	59,357	66,555
Deferred rent	25,715	23,765	19,624
Other long-term liabilities	3,857	4,062	2,609
Net cash provided by operating activities	528,780	419,963	411,096
Investing activities			
Purchases of leasehold improvements, property and equipment	(199,926)	(197,037)	(151,147)
Acquisition of interests in equity method investment	—	—	(586)
Purchases of investments	(387,639)	(213,462)	(183,251)
Maturities of investments	159,250	55,000	124,766
Net cash used in investing activities	(428,315)	(355,499)	(210,218)
Financing activities			
Acquisition of treasury stock	(138,903)	(217,092)	(63,508)
Proceeds from employee stock plan transactions	316	481	574
Excess tax benefit on stock-based compensation	38,379	73,210	38,786
Other financing payments	(143)	(133)	(120)
Net cash used in financing activities	(100,351)	(143,534)	(24,268)

(continued)

	Years ended December 31		
	2013	2012	2011
Effect of exchange rate changes on cash and cash equivalents	536	380	(205)
Net change in cash and cash equivalents	650	(78,690)	176,405
Cash and cash equivalents at beginning of period	322,553	401,243	224,838
Cash and cash equivalents at end of period	$ 323,203	$ 322,553	$ 401,243
Supplemental disclosures of cash flow information			
Income taxes paid	$ 160,973	$ 138,385	$ 56,270
Increase (decrease) in purchases of leasehold improvements, property and equipment accrued in accounts payable	$ (1,736)	$ 4,455	$ 3,249

Questions:

Suggested answers to these questions are found at the end of the chapter.

1. Over the 3-year period, what have consistently been the two largest adjustments to reconcile Chipotle's net income to net cash provided by operating activities?
2. What information can be discovered about the use of cash to invest in the growth of Chipotle's retail stores?
3. Did Chipotle increase or decrease inventory during 2013? By how much?
4. Examining the financing activities section, how much cash did Chipotle return to common shareholders between 2011 and 2013?

GOT IT?

21-12 What is the visual inspection method? List the steps in this method.

HOW IS THE STATEMENT OF CASH FLOWS PREPARED USING THE SPREADSHEET METHOD?

LEARNING OBJECTIVE 21.4
Prepare a statement of cash flows using the spreadsheet method.

Companies usually use the **spreadsheet method** to prepare their statements of cash flows. Under this method, a company uses a spreadsheet to:

- record its cash receipts and payments according to the operating, investing, and financing sections of the statement of cash flows
- record the investing and financing activities *not* affecting cash
- account for the *change* in each asset, liability, and shareholders' equity account

The spreadsheet method is designed to determine the changes in each balance sheet account and then reconstruct the implied effects of those changes on cash. The spreadsheet itself provides an effective and efficient tool to reconstruct the cash flow implications of all of the changes impacting the balance sheet. This method is most often used because it enables a company to analyze its complex transactions in a concise format. A common way of preparing an electronic spreadsheet is to use a software program such as Microsoft Excel. Because the spreadsheet method is used in more complex situations, it is helpful to follow a series of steps.

The Spreadsheet Method: A Four-Step Process

After gathering information from the financial statements and supplemental information from the accounting records, a company completes a series of four steps to prepare the spreadsheet and its statement of cash flows:

- *Step 1.* Preparing the spreadsheet
- *Step 2.* Completing the spreadsheet
- *Step 3.* Preparing the final spreadsheet entry
- *Step 4.* Preparing the statement of cash flows

There are three issues related to the spreadsheet method:

- After starting with net income, there is no required order in which the spreadsheet entries are constructed, but most companies proceed line by line through each account on the balance sheet. You should develop a method to account for all the changes in the noncash accounts in an orderly way.
- You may have to make *more than one* spreadsheet entry to reconcile the change in an account. For instance, the change in the Land account may be the result of both a sale and a purchase of land. In these cases, both the cash receipt and cash payment are accounted for and reported separately.
- The spreadsheet entries are *not* posted to any accounts. They are recorded on the spreadsheet only to help prepare the statement of cash flows.

Comprehensive Example (Spreadsheet Method)

To understand how to prepare a spreadsheet and statement of cash flows, we discuss a comprehensive example using Rivers Company. This example is not all-inclusive but is intended to provide a general framework for how to use a spreadsheet to analyze similar operating, investing, and financing transactions. Throughout the example, we refer to Rivers Company's condensed financial information in **Example 21.3**. Here, we include letters of the alphabet in parentheses beside amounts or items of information. These letters correspond to the letters we use to explain the spreadsheet entries in **Example 21.3a** (p. 21-28). Entries (a) through (j) relate to operating activities and generally affect current assets and current liabilities. Entries (k) through (v) generally affect noncurrent assets, noncurrent liabilities, and shareholders' equity items and relate to investing and financing activities. Entry (w) represents the change in cash.

EXAMPLE 21.3

Rivers Company: Condensed Financial Information

Income Statement Information for 2016

Sales		$ 88,020
Less: Cost of goods sold	$(52,200)	
Other operating expenses	(15,800)	
Depreciation expense: equipment	(2,820) (b)	
Depreciation expense: building	(5,100) (c)	
Patent amortization expense	(600) (d)	
Bond interest expense	(1,100)	
Loss on sale of building	(2,100)	
Income tax expense	(3,630)	
Plus: Gain on sale of land	1,700	(81,650)
Net Income		$ 6,370 (a)

(continued)

Balance Sheet Information

Accounts	Balances 12/31/15	Balances 12/31/16
Cash	$ 3,200	$ 5,900 (w)
Accounts receivable	5,600	7,600 (e)
Inventories	7,300	7,000 (f)
Prepaid expenses	1,200	1,400 (g)
Land	10,000	18,200
Equipment	35,000	35,000
Accumulated depreciation: equipment	(12,000)	(14,820)
Buildings	144,000	149,000
Accumulated depreciation: buildings	(39,300)	(39,600)
Leased equipment	0	5,300
Patents (net)	5,000	4,400
Total Assets	$160,000	$179,380
Accounts payable	$ 8,600	$ 7,300 (h)
Income taxes payable	1,500	2,130 (i)
Interest payable	0	500 (j)
Note payable	0	2,600
Obligation under capital lease	0	5,300
Bonds payable, 10%	0	10,000
Discount on bonds payable	0	(900)
Deferred tax liability	1,920	2,100
Preferred stock, $100 par	6,000	0
Additional paid-in capital on preferred stock	1,000	0
Common stock, $10 par	34,000	37,400
Additional paid-in capital on common stock	67,000	73,700
Retained earnings	39,980	39,250
Total Liabilities and Shareholders' Equity	$160,000	$179,380

Retained Earnings Information for 2016

Beginning retained earnings		$ 39,980
Add: Net income		6,370
		$ 46,350
Less: Stock dividends	$ (3,100)	
Cash dividends	(4,000) (v)	(7,100)
Ending Retained Earnings		$ 39,250

Supplemental Information for 2016

(k) On December 31, 2016, the company borrowed $2,600 from a bank by issuing a 12%, 90-day note payable.

(l) During the year, additional land was acquired at a cost of $10,400.

(m) During the year, land that cost $2,200 was sold for $3,900, resulting in a $1,700 gain.

(n) During the year, a new building was acquired at a cost of $15,000.

(o) During the year, the company sold a building that cost $10,000 and had a book value of $5,200. The company received cash proceeds of $3,100 and recorded an ordinary of $2,100.

(p) On December 31, 2016, the company leased equipment under a long-term capital lease, recording the lease at $5,300.

(q) On January 1, 2016, the company issued $10,000 of long-term bonds for $9,000. The bonds pay interest semiannually on July 1 and January 1 at a 10% annual rate and mature in 10 years on January 1, 2023.

(continued)

> **EXAMPLE 21.3 (Continued)**
>
> (r) The company uses straight-line amortization for the bond discount in (q); consequently, bond discount amortization was $100 for the year.
> (s) On January 1, 2016, 60 shares of preferred stock with a total par value of $6,000 and book value of $7,000 were converted into 240 shares of common stock. The required book value method was used to record the conversion.
> (t) Taxable income was less than pretax accounting income for the year, increasing the deferred tax liability by $180.
> (u) During the year, a stock dividend was declared and issued. The stock dividend involved 100 shares of $10 par common stock. The market value of the stock on the declaration date was $31 per share.

Step 1: Preparing the Spreadsheet Step 1 involves setting up the spreadsheet. Prepare the column headings and enter the account titles (column A), their beginning and ending balances (columns B and C), and the changes in the account balances in the appropriate columns (column D). The columns are totaled to check for accuracy. Next list the major headings on the spreadsheet: Cash Flows from Operating Activities, Cash Flows from Investing Activities, Cash Flows from Financing Activities, and Investing and Financing Activities Not Affecting Cash. Enough space is left under each section so that the cash flows may be listed accordingly. **Example 21.3a** shows these accounts and their headings for Rivers Company.

Step 2: Completing the Spreadsheet Account for all the changes in the noncash accounts that occurred during the current period. *Reconstruct* the journal entries that caused the changes in the noncash accounts directly on the spreadsheet, in terms of the implied effects on cash inflows and outflows for operating, investing, and financing activities. In this step, you are reconstructing the entries on the spreadsheet to prepare the statement of cash flows. Use the following *general rules*:

- *Start with net income.* Net income is adjusted on the spreadsheet to reconcile it to the net cash flow from operating activities. The entry on the spreadsheet to list net income and to explain the impact on retained earnings is a debit to Net Income in the Operating Activities section and a credit to Retained Earnings.[11]
- *Account for the changes in the current asset (except cash) and current liability accounts.* When the changes in the current assets and current liabilities relate to the company's *operating activities*, the impacts of these changes on cash are listed as *adjustments (additions or deductions)* to *net income* in the Operating Activities section of the spreadsheet. Review each operating current asset (except cash) and operating current liability account. Make an entry on the spreadsheet to record the change (debit or credit) in that account and the adjustment [credit (deduction) or debit (addition)] to net income. If changes in current assets or current liabilities do not reflect cash flows from operating activities, then make the corresponding entries in the Investing Activities or the Financing Activities section, as appropriate.
- *Account for the changes in the noncurrent accounts.* Review each noncurrent account and determine the entry responsible for its change. Identify whether the transaction involves an operating, investing, or financing activity. If the transaction involved an investing or financing activity, make the entry on the spreadsheet with the following changes:

---

[11] The entry to show a net loss involves a debit to Retained Earnings and a credit to Net Loss.

- If the entry affects cash, list the item as a debit (receipt) or credit (payment) under the proper heading: Investing Activities or Financing Activities.
- If the entry involves an operating activity and affects a noncash income statement item (e.g., depreciation, gain, or loss), show it as an adjustment to net income in the Operating Activities section.
- If the entry does not affect an operating activity or cash, it is a simultaneous financing and/or investing transaction. For this type of transaction, create expanded entries to record both the financing and/or investing activities.

Spreadsheet Entries for Operating Activities Entry (a) records net income as the first item on the spreadsheet in the Operating Activities section, with the corresponding entry as a credit to retained earnings. Adjustments are then made for noncash expenses and for changes in current assets and current liabilities.

Noncash Expenses A review of the expenses on the income statement in **Example 21.3a** shows three "noncash" expenses: depreciation expense on equipment, depreciation expense on buildings, and patent amortization expense. Each of these is added back to net income to help reconcile it to the net cash flow from operating activities, as shown in Entries (b), (c), and (d). Entries (b) and (d) fully explain the changes in Accumulated Depreciation: Equipment and Patents (net) accounts. Entry (o), which we discuss later, is also recorded to explain the change in the Accumulated Depreciation: Buildings account.

Changes in Current Assets A review of the changes in the current assets (except cash) reveals several additional adjustments that are made to help reconcile the net income to the net cash flow from operating activities. Accounts receivable increased by $2,000 during the year because the company collected less cash than the credit sales it made, which implies a cash outflow. Entry (e) adjusts net income for this implied cash outflow.[12]

Inventories decreased by $300 during the year, indicating that the company purchased less inventory than it recorded as cost of goods sold, which implies a cash savings. Entry (f) adjusts net income for this implied operating cash inflow. Prepaid expenses increased by $200 during the year, indicating that the company paid more cash for these items than the amount of expense it included in other operating expenses. Entry (g) adjusts net income for the higher operating cash outflow.

Changes in Current Liabilities Accounts payable decreased by $1,300 during the year. This decrease indicates that the company's cash payments to suppliers were greater than credit purchases for inventory. Entry (h) adjusts net income for the higher cash outflow. Both income taxes payable and interest payable increased during the year, indicating that the company paid less cash than it reported as the respective expenses. Entries (i) and (j) adjust net income for the lower cash outflows.

No adjustment is made to *operating* activities for the $2,600 increase in the current liability, notes payable. This is because the increase was due to a *financing* activity, which we summarized in the supplemental information of **Example 21.3a**. To record the cash receipt from this financing activity, Entry (k) is made. At this point, we have accounted for the cash flow implications from all the changes in the current assets (except cash) and current liabilities.

Spreadsheet Entries for Investing and Financing Activities Turning to the noncurrent assets and liabilities, a review of the supplemental information is needed to identify the various investing and financing activities.

---

[12] For simplicity, we show accounts receivable at its net amount. If accounts receivable are provided with an allowance for doubtful accounts, then both the change in the accounts receivable and the allowance account should be included in the spreadsheet. An increase in the allowance account is the result of bad debt expense, which is a noncash charge and would be added to net income.

EXAMPLE 21.3a Cash Flows Spreadsheet for 2016 (Rivers Company)

Rivers Company
Cash Flows Worksheet
For Year Ended Dec. 31, 2016

Account Titles	Balances 12/31/15	Balances 12/31/16	Change Increase (Decrease)	Worksheet Entries Debit	Worksheet Entries Credit
Debits					
Cash	3,200	5,900	2,700	(w) 2,700	
Noncash Accounts:					
Accounts Receivable (net)	5,600	7,600	2,000	(e) 2,000	
Inventories	7,300	7,000	(300)		(f) 30
Prepaid Expenses	1,200	1,400	200	(g) 200	
Land	10,000	18,200	8,200	(l) 10,400	(m) 2,200
Equipment	35,000	35,000	0		
Buildings	144,000	149,000	5,000	(n) 15,000	(o) 10,000
Leased Equipment	0	5,300	5,300	(p-2) 5,300	
Patents (net)	5,000	4,400	(600)		(d) 600
Discount on Bonds Payable	0	900	900	(q) 1,000	(r) 100
Totals	211,300	234,700	23,400		
Credits					
Accumulated Depreciation:					
Equipment	12,000	14,820	2,820		(b) 2,820
Accumulated Depreciation:					
Buildings	39,300	39,600	300	(o) 4,800	(c) 5,100
Accounts Payable	8,600	7,300	(1,300)	(h) 1,300	
Income Taxes Payable	1,500	2,130	630		(i) 630
Interest Payable	0	500	500		(j) 500
Note Payable	0	2,600	2,600		(k) 2,600
Obligation under Capital Lease	0	5,300	5,300		(p-1) 5,300
Bonds Payable, 10%	0	10,000	10,000		(q) 10,000
Deferred Tax Liability	1,920	2,100	180		(t) 180
Preferred Stock, $100 par	6,000	0	(6,000)	(s-2) 6,000	
Additional Paid-in Capital					
on Preferred Stock	1,000	0	(1,000)	(s-2) 1,000	
Common Stock, $10 par	34,000	37,400	3,400		(s-1) 2,400
					(u) 1,000
Additional Paid-in Capital					
on Common Stock	67,000	73,700	6,700		(s-1) 4,600
					(u) 2,100
Retained Earnings	39,980	39,250	(730)	(u) 3,100	(a) 6,370
				(v) 4,000	
Totals	211,300	234,700	23,400	56,800	56,800

(Lower portion shown on facing page)

Changes in Land During the year, the company both purchased and sold land; both are investing activities. The acquisition of land resulted in a $10,400 cash payment, which is recorded in Entry (l). Land that cost $2,200 was sold for $3,900, which is reported as a cash receipt from an investing activity. The resulting gain of $1,700

EXAMPLE 21.3a

Cash Flows Spreadsheet for 2016 (Rivers Company) (continued)

	A	B	C	D	E		F	
46	Cash Flows from Operating Activities:							
47	Net income				(a)	6,370		
48	Add: Depreciation expense: equipment				(b)	2,820		
49	Depreciation expense: buildings				(c)	5,100		
50	Patent amortization expense				(d)	600		
51	Decrease in inventories				(f)	300		
52	Increase in income taxes payable				(i)	630		
53	Increase in interest payable				(j)	500		
54	Ordinary loss on sale of building				(o)	2,100		
55	Bond discount amortization				(r)	100		
56	Increase in deferred tax liability				(t)	180		
57	Less: Increase in accounts receivable						(e)	2,000
58	Increase in prepaid expenses						(g)	200
59	Decrease in accounts payable						(h)	1,300
60	Gain on sale of land						(m)	1,700
61	Cash Flows from Investing Activities:							
62	Payment for purchase of land						(l)	10,400
63	Proceeds from sale of land				(m)	3,900		
64	Payment for purchase of building						(n)	15,000
65	Proceeds from sale of building				(o)	3,100		
66	Cash Flows from Financing Activities:							
67	Proceeds from issuance of short-term note payable				(k)	2,600		
68	Proceeds from issuance of bonds				(q)	9,000		
69	Payment of dividends						(v)	4,000
70	Investing and Financing Activities Not Affecting Cash:							
71	Incurrence of capital lease obligation for equipment				(p-1)	5,300		
72	Acquisition of equipment under capital lease						(p-2)	5,300
73	Issuance of common stock to convert preferred stock				(s-1)	7,000		
74	Conversion of preferred stock to common stock						(s-2)	7,000
75	Net increase in cash						(w)	2,700
76	Totals					49,600		49,600
77								

($3,900 − $2,200) increased net income but did not involve a cash inflow. Therefore, the gain is *subtracted* from net income. Therefore, Entry (m) is made.[13] Note that Entries (l) and (m) account for the $8,200 increase in the Land account.

Changes in Buildings and Ordinary Loss The acquisition of a new building during the year resulted in a $15,000 cash payment for an investing activity, which is recorded in Entry (n). GAAP requires that a company report its cash flows from discontinued operations as investing or financing activities and exclude them from its net cash flows from operating activities.[14] During the year, Rivers sold a building with a cost of $10,000 and a book value of $5,200. The company received cash proceeds of $3,100 from the purchaser and recognized an ordinary loss of $2,100, which reduced net income. The proceeds from the sale are recorded as a cash receipt from an investing activity. The loss

---

[13] If the land was sold at a loss, the loss would decrease net income even though there was no outflow of cash for operating activities. In this case, the spreadsheet entry would be modified so that Loss on Sale of Land is *debited* under the heading Operating Activities to *add back* the loss to net income in a manner similar to depreciation expense.

[14] FASB ASC 230-10-45: Statement of Cash Flows, Overall, Other Presentation Matters.

did not involve a cash outflow, and requires an adjustment in the Operating Activities section. Therefore, Entry (o) is made to record the cash receipt, eliminate the book value, and *add back* the loss to net income. Because spreadsheet Entry (o) is complex, the journal entry is provided below.

(o)

Investing Activities: Proceeds from sale of Building	3,100	
Accumulated Depreciation: Building	4,800	
Operating Activities: Ordinary Loss	2,100	
Buildings		10,000

Entries (n) and (o) fully account for the $5,000 increase in the Building account, and Entries (c) and (o) account for the $300 increase in the Accumulated Depreciation account. The Ordinary Loss is shown on the spreadsheet as an addition to net income, along with the other added items.

Change in Leased Equipment At the end of the year, the company leased equipment under a capital lease, recording the asset and liability at $5,300. Although not affecting cash, this is a simultaneous investing and financing transaction, and the company reports both activities in a schedule accompanying the statement of cash flows. Entries (p-1) and (p-2) record these events.

Changes in Bonds Payable and Related Discount On January 1, the company issued bonds payable with a face value of $10,000, at a discount, receiving proceeds of $9,000. This is a financing activity, and the cash receipt is recorded in Entry (q). Note that the $1,000 debit to Discount on Bonds Payable does not equal the net change ($900) in the account. This is because the company amortized part of the discount during the year. On the income statement in **Example 21.3**, note that the bond interest expense is $1,100; however, the cash paid or owed on the bonds is 10% of $10,000, or $1,000. The additional $100 of interest expense is due to the discount amortization. This amortization increased interest expense and reduced net income but did not involve a cash outflow. To adjust for the lower operating cash outflow, Entry (r) is made. The $900 increase in Discount on Bonds Payable is now accounted for. The adjustment for the amortization of a premium on bonds payable would be handled in a similar but opposite way. Bond premium amortization reduces interest expense to an amount *less* than the operating cash outflow. Therefore, the spreadsheet entry would involve a debit to Premium on Bonds Payable and a credit to Operating Activities: Bond Premium Amortization for the amount of the premium amortization.

Some users suggest that bond premium amortization involves repayment of the originally incurred obligation rather than interest and should therefore be classified as a financing activity rather than as an operating activity. IFRS allow, but do not require, the categorization of interest as a financing activity. However, U.S. GAAP requires that the premium amortization be treated as an adjustment within the operating activities section.

Change in Preferred Stock During the year, 60 shares of convertible preferred stock with a total par value of $6,000 and a book value of $7,000 were converted to 240 shares of $10 par common stock; the company accounted for the transaction by the required book value method. Although not affecting cash, two simultaneous financing activities involving the exchange of equity securities occurred that the company reports in a schedule accompanying the statement of cash flows. Entries (s-1) and (s-2) record these events. Note that Entry (s-1) did not account for all the changes in the Common Stock and Additional Paid-in Capital on Common Stock accounts. Entry (u) also affects these accounts, as we discuss below.

Change in Deferred Taxes The deferred tax liability increased by $180 because the company's income tax expense was higher than the actual income taxes it paid (because of a temporary difference between pretax financial income and taxable income). To adjust net income for the lower operating cash outflow, Entry (t) is made.

Stock Dividend The company declared and issued a stock dividend during the year. It recorded the transaction at the market price of the stock. Recall that stock dividends affect only shareholders' equity accounts and do not involve the transfer of cash to shareholders or the exchange of equity securities. Consequently, the issuance of a stock dividend is *not* considered to be a financing activity and is *not* reported on a company's statement of cash flows. However, to account for the $3,100 effect on the company's shareholders' equity accounts, Entry (u) is made in the spreadsheet.

Cash Dividends The $730 net decrease in retained earnings is a function of three changes: Entry (a) increased retained earnings for the net income of $6,370, while Entry (u) decreased it for the stock dividend of $3,100. The remaining decrease in retained earnings was due to the declaration and payment of $4,000 in cash dividends. This payment is a financing activity and is recorded in Entry (v).

Step 3: Preparing the Final Spreadsheet Entry In Step 2, a check of the debit and credit entries in the upper portion of the spreadsheet shows that all the changes in the noncash accounts have been accounted for. A final spreadsheet entry is made to record the increase in cash and to bring the debit and credit column totals into balance.[15] This is Entry (w). The debit and credit totals in the upper portion of **Example 21.3a** are $56,800 and in the lower portion are $49,600. The spreadsheet for Rivers Company is now complete.

Step 4: Preparing the Statement of Cash Flows The fourth step of the spreadsheet method involves preparing the statement of cash flows and accompanying schedule. This step uses the information developed in the lower part of the spreadsheet along with the beginning and ending cash balances. To prepare the statement of cash flows:

- Under the major sections of the statement, list the various cash receipts and payments.
- Under the operating activities section, list adjustment for noncash items first and adjustments for cash flow effects from working capital items second.
- Subtotal the items under each major section and add or subtract the subtotals to determine the net change in cash.
- Add the net change in cash to the beginning cash balance to determine the ending cash balance.
- In an accompanying schedule, list the various investing and financing activities not affecting cash.

Example 21.3b shows the statement of cash flows and the accompanying schedule of investing and financing activities not affecting cash for Rivers Company. Note that in the Investing Activities section, the company reports the payment for the purchase of land separately from the receipt from the sale of land. Similarly, it reports the payment for the purchase of the building separately from the receipt from the building destroyed by the earthquake. Note also that the reconciliation of the beginning and ending cash balances at the bottom of the statement of cash flows enables a user to trace the change in cash to related amounts on the company's balance sheets. Finally, note that the schedule of investing and financing activities not affecting cash discloses the $5,300 noncash transaction that had both an investing and financing element, and the $7,000 noncash transaction that involved two financing elements. ■

---

[15] For a net decrease in cash, an opposite entry (a debit to Net Decrease in Cash and a credit to Cash) is made.

EXAMPLE 21.3b Comprehensive Statement of Cash Flows

Rivers Company
Statement of Cash Flows
For Year Ended December 31, 2016

Operating Activities:		
Net income		$ 6,370
Adjustments for noncash income items:		
Depreciation expense: equipment	2,820	
Depreciation expense: buildings	5,100	
Patent amortization expense	600	
Gain on sale of land	(1,700)	
Loss on sale of building	2,100	
Bond discount amortization	100	
Increase in deferred tax liability	180	
Adjustments for cash flow effects from working capital items:		
Increase in accounts receivable	(2,000)	
Decrease in inventories	300	
Increase in prepaid expenses	(200)	
Decrease in accounts payable	(1,300)	
Increase in income taxes payable	630	
Increase in interest payable	500	
Net cash provided by operating activities		$ 13,500
Investing Activities:		
Payment for purchase of land	$(10,400)	
Proceeds from sale of land	3,900	
Payment for purchase of building	(15,000)	
Proceeds from sale of building	3,100	
Net cash used for investing activities		(18,400)
Financing Activities:		
Proceeds from issuance of short-term note payable	$ 2,600	
Proceeds from issuance of bonds	9,000	
Payment of dividends	(4,000)	
Net cash provided by financing activities		7,600
Net increase in cash (see Schedule 1)		$ 2,700
Cash, January 1, 2016		3,200
Cash, December 31, 2016		$ 5,900
Schedule 1: Investing and Financing Activities Not Affecting Cash		
Investing Activities:		
Acquisition of equipment under capital lease		$ (5,300)
Financing Activities:		
Issuance of capital lease obligation for equipment		5,300
Conversion of preferred stock to common stock		(7,000)
Issuance of common stock to convert preferred stock		7,000

GOT IT?

21-13 Briefly describe the spreadsheet method of analyzing the information for a company's statement of cash flows. (Do not list the steps in preparation.)

HOW ARE SPECIAL ITEMS ACCOUNTED FOR IN THE STATEMENT OF CASH FLOWS?

LEARNING OBJECTIVE 21.5
Account for special items affecting the statement of cash flows.

The previous examples and discussion focused on common items involved in preparing the statement of cash flows. In this section, we examine some transactions that require additional attention.

Sale of Depreciable Asset

When a company sells a depreciable asset, it normally results in a gain or loss, computed as the difference between the current book value and selling price. When the company records the transaction, it increases cash, removes the asset's cost and related accumulated depreciation), and recognizes a gain or loss that it reports on its income statement. When preparing the statement of cash flows using the indirect method, the gain (loss) must be subtracted from (added back to) net income, and the total proceeds from the sale must be reported as a cash inflow in the investing section.

Assets like computer equipment can depreciate rapidly as the technological environment advances.

Example: Sale of Depreciable Asset

During the year, Austin Company sold equipment with a cost of $2,200 and accumulated depreciation of $700 for $2,100. Austin recorded the following journal entry for the sale:

Cash	2,100	
Accumulated Depreciation	700	
Equipment		2,200
Gain on Sale of Equipment		600

Because the $2,100 selling price (proceeds) was more than the $1,500 ($2,200 − $700) net book value, the company recorded a Gain on Sale of Equipment for $600.

The proceeds of $2,100 are a cash receipt from an *investing* activity. The gain increased net income, but there was no cash inflow from *operating* activities. In preparing the spreadsheet entry for this transaction, two modifications are made:

- Instead of debiting Cash, Proceeds from Sale of Equipment in the Investing Activities section is debited for the $2,100.
- Gain on Sale of Equipment is *credited* in the Operating Activities section to *subtract* the gain from net income to avoid double counting and to correctly show the cash provided by operating activities.

On the statement of cash flows, the gain of $600 is subtracted from net income, and the total sale proceeds of $2,100 are reported as a cash inflow in the investing section. The sale of equipment (or other depreciable assets) at a loss is handled in a similar manner, except that Loss on Sale of Equipment is *debited* under Net Cash Flow from Operating Activities to *add back* the loss to net income because it did not involve an operating cash outflow. ■

Retirement of Bonds

A company computes the gain or loss on the retirement of bonds by comparing the current book value of the bonds payable to the retirement price. When the company records the transaction, it decreases cash, eliminates the book value (face value and any related premium or discount), and recognizes a gain or loss that it reports on its income statement. At the end of the year, this journal entry must be properly reconstructed on the spreadsheet to account for the changes in the various accounts. On the statement of cash flows, the gain (loss) must be subtracted from (added back to) net income, and the total proceeds to retire the bonds be reported as a cash outflow in the financing section.

Example: Retirement of Bonds

During the year, Cypress Creek Company paid $8,900 to retire bonds with a face value of $10,000 and a book value of $9,700. Cypress Creek recorded the following journal entry at the time of the retirement:

Bonds Payable	10,000	
Discount on Bonds Payable		300
Cash		8,900
Gain on Retirement of Bonds Payable		800

Because the cash paid was less than the book value, the company also recorded an $800 ($9,700 − $8,900) Gain on Retirement of Bonds Payable.

The cash paid of $8,900 is a cash payment for a *financing* activity. The gain increased net income, but there was no cash inflow from *operating* activities. In preparing the spreadsheet entry for this transaction, two modifications are made:

- Instead of crediting Cash, Financing Activities: Payment to Retire Bonds is credited for $8,900.
- Instead of crediting gain, Operating Activities: Gain on Retirement of Bonds is credited for $800 to *subtract* the gain from net income to correctly show the cash provided by operating activities.

On the statement of cash flows, the $800 gain is subtracted from net income, and the total amount of $8,900 paid to retire the bonds is reported as a cash outflow in the financing section. The retirement of bonds payable at a loss is handled in a similar manner, except that Operating Activities: Loss on Retirement of Bonds is debited to *add back* the loss to net income because it did not involve an operating cash outflow. ■

Interest Paid and Income Taxes Paid

GAAP requires a company using the indirect method of reporting its operating cash flows to also disclose its interest *paid* and income taxes *paid*. This disclosure may be made in a separate schedule, narrative description, or the notes to the financial statements. Interest *expense* is affected by the cash paid, accruals, any premium or discount amortizations on bonds (or notes) payable, and any amounts capitalized. Income tax *expense* is affected by the cash paid, accruals, and changes in deferred income taxes. Exhibit 21.4 illustrates the necessary adjustments to convert interest expense to interest paid and to convert income tax expense to income taxes paid.[16]

Example: Interest and Income Taxes

Refer to the Rivers Company information shown in **Examples 21.3** and **21.21a**. To determine its interest paid and income taxes paid for 2016, Rivers prepares the following schedules:

Bond interest expense	$1,100	Income tax expense	$3,630
− Increase in interest payable	(500)	− Increase in income taxes payable	(630)
− Bond discount amortization	(100)	− Increase in deferred tax liability	(180)
Interest paid	$ 500	Income taxes paid	$2,820

Based on these computations, Rivers reports interest paid of $500 and income taxes paid of $2,820 as a separate disclosure with its 2016 statement of cash flows. ■

---

[16] A company may have a valuation allowance related to its deferred tax asset. Because the valuation allowance is a contra account, it handles any changes in the account in the opposite way to that of the deferred tax asset.

EXHIBIT 21.4 Adjustments to Calculate Income Tax and Interest Paid

Interest	Income Taxes
Interest *expense*	**Income tax *expense***
+ Decrease in interest payable	+ Decrease in income taxes payable
or	*or*
− Increase in interest payable	− Increase in income taxes payable
+ Amortization of premium on bonds payable	+ Decrease in deferred tax liability
+ Interest capitalized	
or	*or*
− Amortization of discount on bonds payable	− Increase in deferred tax liability
= **Interest *paid***	+ Increase in deferred tax asset
	or
	− Decrease in deferred tax asset
	= **Income taxes *paid***

Short- and Long-Term Investments

As discussed in Chapter 13, a company recognizes investment securities as either trading, available-for-sale, or held-to-maturity securities.

Available-for-Sale Securities U.S. GAAP requires companies to report investments (whether current or long-term) in available-for-sale debt securities as assets at fair value (by using an allowance account) on its year-end balance sheet. It also includes any resulting unrealized increase or decrease in fair value as a component of accumulated other comprehensive income[17] in shareholders' equity. When the company sells this current or long-term investment, it eliminates the fair value (cost and allowance accounts) of the security as well as any cumulative unrealized increase or decrease in fair value from its accounting records. It also records a realized gain or loss on the sale. It computes the realized gain or loss by comparing the proceeds to the *amortized cost* of the security.

Because the company used an allowance account and an unrealized increase or decrease account to value the investment in available-for-sale securities, it must carefully analyze any changes in these accounts to determine the impact (if any) on its statement of cash flows.

- The company reports an increase in the investment account due to the *purchase* of the securities on its statement of cash flows as a cash payment for an investing activity. The entry on the spreadsheet to prepare the statement is also made in the usual manner.
- The company does *not* report any changes in the allowance and the unrealized increase or decrease accounts resulting from a *revaluation to fair value at year-end* on its statement of cash flows. However, it must account for the changes on the spreadsheet.
- The company reports a decrease in the investment account because of the *sale* of the securities on its statement of cash flows as a cash receipt from an investing activity in the usual manner. However, the spreadsheet entry must reconcile the changes in the investment, allowance, unrealized increase/decrease, and realized gain (or loss) accounts.

---

[17] The company would first include the periodic *change* in the unrealized increase or decrease in value in its other comprehensive income for the period.

Example: Purchase and Sale of an Available-for-Sale Investment

On November 28, 2016, Hays Company purchased 400 of Bear Company's bonds for $40,000 and classified them as available-for-sale securities. On December 31, 2016, the fair value of the bonds has risen to $42,000, so that the company reported the available-for-sale investment securities as a current asset of $42,000 ($40,000 cost + $2,000 allowance). It also reported a $2,000 unrealized increase in value of available-for-sale securities as a component of its accumulated other comprehensive income in its shareholders' equity on the December 31, 2016, balance sheet. For its cash flow analysis, Hays would make the following spreadsheet entries at the end of 2016 to reconcile the $42,000 change in the carrying value of the investment:

Investment in Available-for-Sale Securities	40,000	
Investing Activities: Payment for Purchase of Available-for-Sale Securities		40,000
Allowance for Change in Value of Investment	2,000	
Unrealized Increase in Value of Available-for-Sale Securities		2,000

The debit portion of the first entry is listed in the upper part of the spreadsheet. This helps to reconcile the change in the investment account. The credit portion of the first entry is listed in the lower part of the spreadsheet and accounts for the cash payment for the purchase of the investment. The company reports this $40,000 cash payment in its 2016 statement of cash flows. Both the debit and credit portions of the second entry are listed in the upper portion of the spreadsheet and complete the reconciliation of the changes in the allowance and unrealized increase accounts. The company does *not* include this portion of the increase in the carrying value of the investment on its 2016 statement of cash flows because there was no cash flow.

Now suppose that Hays Company sold its investment in Bear Company bonds for $45,000 on January 16, 2017. Hays would make the following spreadsheet entries at the end of 2017 to reconcile the changes in the various accounts:

Investing Activities: Receipt from Sale of Investment	45,000	
Investment in Available-for-Sale Securities		40,000
Operating Activities: Gain on Sale of Investment		5,000
Unrealized Increase in Value of Available-for-Sale Securities	2,000	
Allowance for Change in Value of Investment		2,000

These two journal entries (1) record the $45,000 investing cash inflow from the sale of the securities, (2) treat the $5,000 gain on the sale as a subtraction from net income to reconcile it to the net cash flow from operating activities, and (3) reconcile the changes in the investment, allowance, and unrealized increase accounts. The company reports the first two items on its 2017 statement of cash flows in the usual manner.

Held-to-Maturity Securities A company may also make a long-term investment in debt securities (e.g., bonds) that it expects to hold to maturity.

- It amortizes any premium or discount each year as an adjustment to interest revenue and reports the investment at its amortized cost on the year-end balance sheet. For cash flow reporting purposes, it reports the purchase as a cash payment for investing activities.
- The company also adds any premium amortization on this type of investment to net income in the operating activities section of the statement of cash flows because the amortization reduced interest revenue to an amount lower than the cash received.
- The company subtracts any discount amortization from net income because the amortization increased interest revenue to an amount higher than the cash received.

Each of these adjustments helps reconcile the net income to the net cash flow from operating activities.

Trading Securities A company may also make short-term investments in trading securities. GAAP requires that a company report the cash flows from purchases, sales, and maturities of trading securities as either operating or investing cash flow activities, based on the nature and purpose for which the securities were acquired. Also, as discussed in Chapter 13, GAAP requires a company to report investments in trading securities at their fair value and report any resulting unrealized holding gain or loss in net income. Consequently, for reporting its operating cash flows under the indirect method, a company adds (deducts) an unrealized holding loss (gain) on trading securities to (from) net income to help adjust net income from an accrual basis to a cash basis.

Equity Method Investments The equity method of accounting for investments also creates a need for a noncash adjustment. As discussed in Chapter 13, the equity method results in recognition of revenue and an increase in the investment account equal to the investor's share of the investee's net income or net loss. In addition, the equity investment account is decreased (and the Cash account is increased) for any share of the investee's dividends received.

Example: Equity Method Investments

Graham Products owns 30% of US Toys and accounts for its investment using the equity method. US Toys reported net income of $10,000 and paid $2,000 in dividends. Graham would record the following entries to recognize its share of income and dividends:

Investment in US Toys (30% × $10,000)	3,000	
Investment Income: Ordinary		3,000
Cash (30% × $2,000)	600	
Investment in US Toys		600

To calculate the amount of the adjustment required in the operating activities section of the statement of cash flows, the company would subtract $2,400, which is the investment income from the equity investment in US Toys minus its share of dividends ($3,000 − $600). ∎

Cash Dividends Declared

In the previous examples, whenever we discussed cash dividends, we assumed that the dividends were declared *and* paid in the current year. The declaration and payment of cash dividends is a financing activity that causes a decrease in both retained earnings and cash.

In some instances, a company will declare a cash dividend in the *current* year and pay the cash dividend in the *next* year. In this case, the cash dividend is handled differently in preparing the spreadsheet for the statement of cash flows. The declaration of the cash dividend is recorded on the spreadsheet as a decrease (debit) in Retained Earnings and an increase (credit) in Dividends Payable. Because no cash outflow occurs in the current year, the company does not report dividends paid on its statement of cash flows. In the next year, the company records the payment of the cash dividends on the spreadsheet as a decrease (debit) in Dividends Payable and a decrease (credit) in Cash. The company then reports the dividends paid as a cash payment in the financing activities section of its statement of cash flows.

When a company follows a policy of declaring a dividend in one year and paying the dividend in the next year, its Dividends Payable account balance will change during each year. A comparison of the change in the account balance to the dividends reported on the retained earnings statement will determine the spreadsheet entry necessary to account for the cash dividends.

Cash Flows for Compensatory Share Option Plans

In Chapter 15, we showed how a corporation records its estimated compensation expense for a compensatory share option plan. In Chapter 18, we explained how recording this compensation expense for financial reporting purposes but not recording any compensation expense for income tax purposes results in a deferred tax asset for the future deductible amount. Although both of these journal entries affect net income, neither involves a cash flow. Therefore, on the corporation's statement of cash flows, under the indirect method, the increase in compensation expense must be *added* back to net income and the increase in the deferred tax asset must be *subtracted* from net income to help determine the net cash flow from operating activities.

When employees exercise the share options, the cash flow treatment is more complicated, and we only provide a brief overview here.

- First, the company records the gross proceeds received from the employees exercising options (the number of options exercised times the exercise price) as a cash inflow in the financing section.
- Second, if the company uses cash to purchase shares in the open market and then sells those shares to the employees exercising options, the cash paid to acquire treasury shares is reported as a use of cash in the financing section.

In Chapter 18, we explained that in the year an employee exercises the share options, the corporation is allowed to take a tax deduction for compensation expense equal to the difference between the market price of the shares on the exercise date and the exercise price. However, for financial reporting purposes, the corporation has already recorded all of the compensation expense during the service period. So, when the share options are exercised, the corporation has higher pretax financial income than taxable income because the previous future deductible difference has "reversed." Therefore, it eliminates the deferred tax asset (that it had previously recorded during the service period) and increases income tax expense. For cash flow purposes, this decrease in the deferred tax asset is *added* back to net income under the indirect method to help determine the net cash flow from operating activities.

If the actual market price for the share used to record the compensation expense for income tax purposes is the same as the estimated fair value of the option (based on the option pricing model) used to record the compensation expense for financial reporting purposes, then there are no additional cash flow issues. However, it is likely that the share price and the option fair value will differ, so a "permanent" difference will likely exist that provides a tax benefit by reducing the corporation's income tax expense and income taxes payable. Therefore, GAAP requires that the corporation compute the excess realized tax benefit as the difference between the compensation expense reported for income tax purposes and the compensation expense recorded for financial reporting purposes. The excess realized tax benefit is reported as a cash inflow from financing activities because it relates to the issuance of stock, which is a financing activity. The corporation is also required to *subtract* the excess realized tax benefit from net income to help determine its net cash flow from operating activities on its statement of cash flows.[18] The amount is subtracted because it reduced income tax expense but did not involve an operating cash savings.

Example: Compensatory Share Option Expense

Rehage Corporation reported net income of $500,000 and had a tax deduction of $800,000 in the current year for compensation expense because employees exercised share options. In previous years, for financial reporting purposes, Rehage had recorded compensation expense of $700,000 for this compensatory share option plan. If Rehage is subject to a 30% tax rate and uses the indirect method to report its cash flows from operating activities, then it would report the $30,000 [($800,000 − $700,000) × 0.30] excess realized tax benefit on its statement of cash flows for the current year as follows:

Operating Activities:	
Net income	$500,000
Less: Excess tax benefits from compensatory stock option plan	(30,000)
Financing Activities:	
Excess tax benefits from compensatory stock option plan	$ 30,000

[18] FASB ASC 230-10-45: Statement of Cash Flows, Overall, Other Presentation Matters.

Changes in Foreign Currency Exchange Rates

When a company has foreign subsidiaries, the foreign operations are normally transacted in the foreign currency. However, when the parent corporation prepares its consolidated financial statements, it needs to translate the subsidiaries' results back to the parent's currency. Because currency rates change throughout the period, the parent company must disclose the "reporting currency equivalent" of the "foreign currency" cash flows using the exchange rates in effect at the time of the cash flows. The parent company may use a weighted average exchange rate for the period if this yields similar results. On the statement of cash flows, the parent company reports the effect of exchange rate changes on cash balances held in foreign currencies as a separate part of the reconciliation of the change in cash during the period.[19]

GOT IT?

21-14 Dunn Company recognized a $5,000 unrealized holding gain on investment in **Starbucks**'s long-term bonds during 2013. The company classified its investment as an available-for-sale security. How would this information be reported on a statement of cash flows prepared using the indirect method?

21-15 Jordan Company recognized a $5,000 unrealized holding gain on investment in **Starbucks**'s common stock during 2013. The company classified its investment as a trading security. How would this information be reported in a statement of cash flows prepared using the indirect method?

21-16 Indicate how a company computes the amount of interest and income taxes that it paid during the year.

21-17 What adjustment is required to the operating activities section prepared using the indirect method for a company's equity method investment income?

APPENDIX 21.1: PREPARE THE OPERATING ACTIVITIES SECTION UNDER THE DIRECT METHOD

LEARNING OBJECTIVE 21.6
Understand and prepare the operating activities section under the direct method.

When a company uses the direct method to prepare the information for its statement of cash flows, it may use either the visual inspection method or the spreadsheet method. This depends on the complexity of its accounting information. The information is obtained, however, in a slightly different manner. Normally, under the direct method, a company obtains the information for its statement of cash flows from the following working papers:

- *Post-closing trial balance (or balance sheet) from previous period.* Recall from Chapter 3 that a post-closing trial balance contains the debit and credit balances of all the *permanent* accounts in a company's general ledger. In other words, a post-closing trial balance of the previous period contains the same information as the *ending balance sheet* of the *previous* period.
- *Adjusted trial balance of current period.* Recall from Chapter 3 that an adjusted trial balance contains the debit and credit balances (after adjustments but before closing) of all the temporary and permanent accounts in a company's general ledger. In other words, an adjusted trial balance of the current period contains the *balance sheet, income statement*, and *retained earnings statement* information for the *current* period.

---

[19] FASB ASC 830-230-45: Foreign Currency Matters, Statement of Cash Flows, Other Presentation Matters.

In addition, the company needs other information to explain the changes in its balance sheet (permanent) accounts (other than cash). This information is obtained from its accounting records. In complex situations, use of the post-closing trial balance of the prior period and the adjusted trial balance of the current period is the most efficient way to prepare the statement of cash flows. In simpler situations, however, the statement may be developed based on the information contained in the beginning and ending balance sheets, the income statement, and the retained earnings statement of the current year.

Visual Inspection—Direct Method

Under the visual inspection approach, the steps to complete the statement of cash flows using the direct method for operating activities are similar to those for the indirect method, except that the information for the cash flows from operating activities section is computed as follows:

- Make adjustments to the applicable revenues for the period (e.g., to sales revenue for change in accounts receivable and deferred revenues) to determine the amounts of collections from customers, interest and dividends collected, and other operating receipts.
- Make adjustments to the applicable expenses for the period (e.g., to cost of goods sold for changes in inventory and accounts payable) to determine the amounts of payments to suppliers, payments to employees, other operating payments, payments of interest, and payments of income taxes.

Exhibit 21.2 is helpful for making these adjustments. Once the operating activities section is completed, the investing activities section and the financing activities section are completed by analyzing the changes in the other balance sheet accounts in the same way as we discussed for the indirect method.

Example: Visual Inspection Method

The following income statement items were taken from Candid Company's adjusted trial balance at the end of 2016:

	Debit	Credit
Sales revenue		$94,000
Interest revenue		5,400
Cost of goods sold	$43,000	
Salaries expense	18,500	
Depreciation expense	11,000	
Other expenses	4,700	
Interest expense	9,200	
Income tax expense	3,900	

A comparison of the post-closing trial balance for 2015 with the adjusted trial balance for 2016 shows the following *changes* in selected balance sheet accounts:

Accounts receivable	$ 8,200 credit (decrease)
Interest receivable	1,200 debit (increase)
Inventory	6,300 debit (increase)
Prepaid expenses	600 debit (increase)
Accumulated depreciation	11,000 credit (increase)
Accounts payable	4,800 credit (increase)
Salaries payable	500 debit (decrease)
Discount on bonds payable	200 credit (decrease)
Income taxes payable	300 credit (increase)
Deferred tax liability	400 credit (increase)

Based on the preceding information, Candid prepares **Example 21.4** to determine each of the operating cash inflows and outflows.

EXAMPLE 21.4

Schedule to Compute Cash Flows

Income Statement Amounts		Adjustments			Operating Cash Flows	
Sales revenue	$94,000	+ Decrease in accounts receivable of	$8,200	=	$102,200	Collections from customers
Interest revenue	5,400	− Increase in interest receivable of	1,200	=	4,200	Interest collected
					$106,400	Operating cash inflows
Cost of goods sold	43,000	{ + Increase in inventory of − Increase in accounts payable of	6,300 4,800 }	=	$ 44,500	Payments to suppliers
Salaries expense	18,500	+ Decrease in salaries payable of	500	=	19,000	Payments to employees
Other expenses	4,700	+ Increase in prepaid expenses of	600	=	5,300	Other operating payments
Interest expense	9,200	− Decrease in discount on bonds payable (amortization) of	200	=	9,000	Payments of interest
Income tax expense	3,900	{ − Increase in income taxes payable of − Increase in deferred tax liability of	300 400 }	=	3,200	Payments of income taxes
					$ 81,000	Operating cash outflow
					$ 25,400	Net cash provided by operating activities

Operating Cash Inflows The $94,000 of sales revenue is increased by the $8,200 decrease in accounts receivable to determine the $102,200 collections from customers. This is because the company's cash collections exceeded its sales during the year. The $5,400 interest revenue is decreased by the $1,200 increase in interest receivable to determine the $4,200 interest collected because the company received less cash than it recorded as interest revenue. The total operating cash inflows were $106,400 in 2016.

Operating Cash Outflows The $43,000 cost of goods sold is adjusted for two items. It is increased for the $6,300 increase in inventory because the company's purchases exceeded its cost of goods sold. It is decreased by the $4,800 increase in accounts payable because the company's cash payments were less than its purchases. Thus, payments to suppliers totaled $44,500 in 2016. The $18,500 of salaries expense is increased by the $500 decrease in salaries payable to determine the $19,000 paid to employees, because salaries paid exceeded salaries expense. The $4,700 of other expenses are increased by the $600 increase in prepaid expenses to determine the $5,300 other operating payments, because the company's cash payments for prepaid items exceeded its expenses. Note that the $11,000 depreciation expense is the same as the $11,000 credit to accumulated depreciation. Because this is a "noncash" income statement item and is listed separately from other operating expenses, no adjustment is made for operating cash flows.

The decrease in the discount on bonds payable resulted from the amortization of the discount. Recall that the amortization of the discount on bonds payable increases interest expense to an amount greater than the cash the company paid for interest. Therefore, the $200 decrease in the discount on bonds payable is subtracted from the $9,200 interest expense to determine the $9,000 interest paid. The $3,900 income tax expense is decreased by the $300 increase in income taxes payable and the $400 increase in the deferred tax liability to determine the $3,200 payments of income taxes, because the company paid less taxes currently than it recorded as an expense. The total operating cash outflows were $81,000 in 2016, so that $25,400 net cash was provided by operating activities during 2016 as shown at the bottom of **Example 21.4**.

Example 21.4a shows the cash flows from operating activities section of Candid Company's statement of cash flows, under the direct method. The company includes cash flows from investing activities and the cash flows from financing activities in the usual manner to complete the statement of cash flows.

EXAMPLE 21.4a Operating Cash Flows (Direct Method)

Candid Company
Statement of Cash Flows (Partial)
For Year Ended December 31, 2016

Operating Activities:		
Cash inflows:		
Collections from customers	$102,200	
Interest collected	4,200	
Cash inflows from operating activities		$106,400
Cash outflows:		
Payments to suppliers	$ (44,500)	
Payments to employees	(19,000)	
Other operating payments	(5,300)	
Payments of interest	(9,000)	
Payments of income taxes	(3,200)	
Cash outflows for operating activities		(81,000)
Net cash provided by operating activities		$ 25,400

Spreadsheet Method

Under the spreadsheet method, the steps completed using the direct method are very similar to those of the indirect method:

- *Step 1.* Preparing the spreadsheet
- *Step 2.* Completing the spreadsheet
- *Step 3.* Preparing the final spreadsheet entry
- *Step 4.* Preparing the statement of cash flows

Comprehensive Example (Spreadsheet Method, Direct Method)

Refer to the information obtained from Finley Company's accounting records in **Example 21.5**. In addition, the following information was included in Finley's accounting records for 2016:

- Land costing $2,000 was sold for $2,800.
- Equipment was purchased at a cost of $24,700.
- Common stock was issued for $10,000.
- Dividends of $3,500 were declared and paid.

Appendix 21.1: Prepare the Operating Activities Section under the Direct Method

EXAMPLE 21.5

Cash Flows Spreadsheet for 2016 (Finley Company)

	A	B	C	D	E	F	G	H		I	
1	Finley Company										
2	Cash Flows Worksheet										
3	For Year Ended Dec. 31, 2016										
4											
5		12/31/2015		12/31/2016							
6		Post-Closing		Adjusted							
7		Trial Balance		Trial Balance		Change		Worksheet Entries			
8	Accounts	Debit	Credit	Debit	Credit	Debit	Credit	Debit		Credit	
9	Cash	5,300		9,800		4,500		(r)	4,500		
10	Accounts Receivable	9,600		10,900		1,300		(i)	1,300		
11	Inventory	12,500		11,000			1,500			(j)	1,500
12	Land	22,000		20,000			2,000			(n)	2,000
13	Buildings and Equipment	82,600		107,300		24,700		(o)	24,700		
14	Accumulated Depreciation		32,800		41,900		9,100			(h)	9,100
15	Accounts Payable		10,300		12,100		1,800			(k)	1,800
16	Salaries Payable		1,100		800	300		(l)	300		
17	Interest Payable		300		500		200			(m)	200
18	Notes Payable		34,000		34,000		0				
19	Common Stock, no par		30,000		40,000		10,000			(p)	10,000
20	Retained Earnings		23,500		20,000	3,500		(q)	3,500		
21	Sales Revenue				98,700		98,700			(a)	98,700
22	Interest Revenue				2,500		2,500			(b)	2,500
23	Gain on Sale of Land				800		800			(n)	800
24	Cost of Goods Sold			51,000		51,000		(c)	51,000		
25	Salaries Expense			23,000		23,000		(d)	23,000		
26	Depreciation Expense			9,100		9,100		(h)	9,100		
27	Other Expenses			1,900		1,900		(e)	1,900		
28	Interest Expense			4,000		4,000		(f)	4,000		
29	Income Tax Expense			3,300		3,300		(g)	3,300		
30	Totals	132,000	132,000	251,300	251,300	126,600	126,600	126,600		126,600	
31	Cash Flows from Operating Activities:										
32	Collections from customers							(a)	98,700	(i)	1,300
33	Interest and dividends collected							(b)	2,500		
34	Other operating receipts										
35	Payments to suppliers							(j)	1,500	(c)	51,000
36								(k)	1,800		
37	Payments to employees									(d)	23,000
38										(l)	300
39	Other operating payments									(e)	1,900
40	Payments of interest							(m)	200	(f)	4,000
41	Payments of income taxes									(g)	3,300
42	Cash Flows from Investing Activities:										
43	Proceeds from sale of land							(n)	2,800		
44	Payment for purchase of equipment									(o)	24,700
45	Cash Flows from Financing Activities:										
46	Proceeds from issuance of common stock							(p)	10,000		
47	Payment of dividends									(q)	3,500
48	Net increase in cash									(r)	4,500
49	Totals								117,500		117,500
50											

Step 1: Preparing the Spreadsheet Complete Step 1 by entering the accounts and amounts of the trial balances (columns A–E); the changes in the accounts are entered in either column F or G, depending on if it is a debit or credit change. Then, based on

the preceding information, Entries (a) through (r) are entered in columns H and I of the spreadsheet to complete it. Next, list on the spreadsheet the major headings, Operating Activities, Investing Activities, Financing Activities, and Investing and Financing Activities Not Affecting Cash. Enough space is left under each heading so that the cash flows may be listed accordingly. **Example 21.5** shows the spreadsheet, the accounts, and their headings for Finley Company.

Step 2: Completing the Spreadsheet Step 2 involves accounting for all the changes in the noncash accounts that occurred during the current period. *Reconstruct* the journal entries that caused the changes in the noncash accounts directly on the spreadsheet, making the necessary modifications to show the cash receipts and payments related to operating, investing, and financing activities.

Start with the usual revenue and expense accounts. The changes in these accounts during the year represent potential operating cash receipts or payments. Therefore, the entry on the spreadsheet is to debit or credit the related operating cash inflow or outflow caption and to credit or debit the revenue or expense account. Observe that these changes represent potential cash flows. They may have to be adjusted later for changes in certain current assets (e.g., accounts receivable) and current liabilities (e.g., accounts payable), as well as other accounts, to show the actual cash flows.

Note that there are two exceptions to the previous procedures:

- The spreadsheet entries for any noncash revenues and expenses (e.g., depreciation expense) are made in the usual manner, without any modifications.
- Spreadsheet entries are *not* prepared at this time to account for gains or losses. The changes in these accounts will be accounted for later when dealing with the investing or financing transactions to which they relate (e.g., retirement of bonds at a gain).

Entries (a) and (b) account for the sales revenue and interest revenue and record the "unadjusted" collections from customers and receipts of interest. (There are no other operating receipts.) Entries (c), (d), (e), (f), and (g) account for the cost of goods sold, salaries expense, other expenses, interest expense, and income tax expense, and record the "unadjusted" payments to suppliers, payments to employees, payments of interest, other operating payments, and payments of income taxes.

Entry (h) accounts for the depreciation expense and increase in accumulated depreciation. Note that it is made in the normal manner in the upper part of the spreadsheet and, therefore, has no effect on the operating cash flows. The entry is necessary, however, to help account for the changes in all the income statement and balance sheet accounts.

After accounting for the usual revenue and expense accounts, the preparer next *accounts for the changes in the current asset (except cash) and current liability accounts.* Because most of the changes in the current assets and current liabilities relate to the *operating activities*, the impacts of these changes on cash are listed as adjustments to the related operating cash inflow or outflow. There are several exceptions to this procedure. These exceptions involve changes in short-term notes receivable and notes payable, changes in temporary investments (i.e., marketable securities), and changes in dividends payable. These changes are the results of investing or financing activities and are handled like the changes in the noncurrent accounts.

Entries (i) through (m) account for the effect of the changes in the current assets and current liabilities on the "unadjusted" operating cash flows recorded earlier. Entry (i) reduces (adjusts) the collections from customers because of the increase in accounts receivable. Entries (j) and (k) reduce (adjust) the payments to suppliers because of the decrease in inventory and the increase in accounts payable. Entry (l) increases (adjusts) the payments to employees because of the decrease in salaries payable. Finally, Entry

(m) reduces (adjusts) the interest payments because of the increase in interest payable. There are no adjustments to the other operating payments or to the payments of income taxes in this example.

The final part of Step 2 is to a*ccount for the changes in the remaining current assets (except cash) and current liabilities, as well as the changes in noncurrent accounts.* Review each account and determine the entry responsible for its change. Identify whether the transaction involves an operating, investing, or financing activity. If the transaction involves an investing or financing activity, make the entry on the spreadsheet with the following changes:

- If the entry affects cash, replace a debit to Cash with either an investing or financing cash inflow section and list the item as a debit (receipt) under the proper heading of the spreadsheet. Replace a credit to Cash with a proper cash outflow section and list the item as a credit (payment) under the proper heading of the spreadsheet. In the case of a transaction involving a gain or loss, record the gain or loss portion of the spreadsheet entry in the usual manner.
- If the entry does not affect an operating activity or cash, it is a "simultaneous" financing and/or investing transaction. For this type of transaction, create "expanded" entries on the spreadsheet to record both the financing and/or investing activities. The first entry shows the financing aspect of the exchange, while the second entry shows the investing aspect. These types of transactions are disclosed on a schedule accompanying the statement of cash flows.

Entries (n) through (q) record the investing and financing cash flows. Entry (n) records the $2,800 investing cash receipt (proceeds) from the sale of land costing $2,000. Note that the $800 gain is recorded in the usual way. Entry (o) records the investing cash payment for the purchase of equipment. Entry (p) records the financing cash receipt (proceeds) from the sale of common stock. Entry (q) records the financing cash payment of dividends.

Step 3: Preparing the Final Spreadsheet Entry

In Step 3, a check of the debit and credit entries in the upper portion of the spreadsheet shows that all the changes in the noncash accounts have been accounted for. A final spreadsheet entry is made to record the increase in cash and to bring the debit and credit column totals into balance. This is Entry (r). The debit and credit totals in the upper portion of **Example 21.5** are $126,600 and in the lower portion are $117,500. The spreadsheet for Finley is now complete.

Step 4: Preparing the Statement of Cash Flows

The fourth and final step of the spreadsheet method involves preparing the statement of cash flows and accompanying schedule. Use the information developed in the lower part of the spreadsheet along with the beginning and ending cash balances. Under the major sections of the statement, list the various cash receipts and payments. Subtotal the items under each major section and add or subtract the subtotals to determine the net change in cash. Add the net change in cash to the beginning cash balance to determine the ending cash balance. In an accompanying schedule, list the various investing and financing activities not affecting cash.

Example 21.5a shows Finley Company's statement of cash flows, prepared from the spreadsheet in **Example 21.5**. Note that the only difference between this statement, prepared under the direct method, and a statement of cash flows prepared under the indirect method is in the presentation of the cash flows from operating activities.

> **EXAMPLE 21.5a** **Statement of Cash Flows (Direct Method)**

Finley Company
Statement of Cash Flows
For Year Ended December 31, 2016

Operating Activities:		
Cash inflows:		
Collections from customers	$ 97,400	
Interest and dividends collected	2,500	
Cash inflows from operating activities		$ 99,900
Cash outflows:		
Payments to suppliers	$(47,700)	
Payments to employees	(23,300)	
Other operating payments	(1,900)	
Payments of interest	(3,800)	
Payments of income taxes	(3,300)	
Cash outflows for operating activities		(80,000)
Net cash provided by operating activities		$ 19,900
Investing Activities:		
Proceeds from sale of land	$ 2,800	
Payment for purchase of equipment	(24,700)	
Net cash used for investing activities		(21,900)
Financing Activities:		
Proceeds from issuance of common stock	$ 10,000	
Payment of dividends	(3,500)	
Net cash provided by financing activities		6,500
Net increase in cash		$ 4,500
Cash, January 1, 2016		5,300
Cash, December 31, 2016		$ 9,800

GOT IT?

21-18 *(Appendix 21.1)* Define the direct method of reporting the cash flows from operating activities of a company.

21-19 *(Appendix 21.1)* Briefly describe how to determine each of the operating cash inflows and operating cash outflows under the direct method.

REVIEW CENTER

At the beginning of the chapter, we examined how Starbucks's cash flow statement explained how the company decreased its cash balance during fiscal 2015. The statement provides users the ability to understand the amount, timing, and uncertainty of future cash flows. We also identified several objectives you would accomplish after reading the chapter. The objectives are listed below and followed by a brief summary of the key points.

KEY TAKEAWAYS

LEARNING OBJECTIVE 21.1
Understand and define operating, investing, and financing activities.

- The statement of cash flows provides relevant information about a company's cash receipts and cash payments that is useful for assessing its liquidity, financial flexibility, operating capability, and risk.
- A company's cash flows are reported as:
  - Operating activities—cash receipts and cash payments relating to the day-to-day operating activities of the company (generally resulting from transactions that affect income)
  - Investing activities—cash receipts and cash payments relating to the acquisition and disposition of assets such as property, plant, and equipment, notes receivable, intangibles, and investments in other companies
  - Financing activities—cash receipts and cash payments relating to the external financing of a company such as the issuance and repurchase of common stock, issuance and repayment of debt financing instruments, and payment of dividends
- A company's statement of cash flows must clearly show the cash flows from operating, investing, and financing activities as well as the net increase or decrease in cash and a reconciliation of the beginning and ending cash balance reported on the balance sheet. Furthermore, significant noncash activities must be reported in either a separate schedule or narrative explanation that accompanies the statement of cash flows.

KEY TERMS

financing activities, p. 21-4
investing activities, p. 21-3
operating activities, p. 21-3
operating cash flow ratio, p. 21-7
operating cash flow to total liabilities ratio, p. 21-7

KEY CALCULATIONS

$$\text{Operating Cash Flow Ratio} = \frac{\text{Cash Flow from Operating Activities}}{\text{Average Current Liabilities}}$$

$$\text{Operating Cash Flow to Total Liabilities Ratio} = \frac{\text{Cash Flow from Operating Activities}}{\text{Average Total Liabilities}}$$

Cash Flows from Operating Activities + Cash Flows from Investing Activities + Cash Flows from Financing Activities = Change in Cash and Cash Equivalents

KEY TAKEAWAYS

LEARNING OBJECTIVE 21.2
Explain the direct and indirect methods for reporting operating cash flows.

- The calculation of a company's net cash flow from operating activities involves an adjustment of net income for differences in when the company records revenues and expenses and when it receives and pays cash, as well as for noncash items (e.g., depreciation and amortization expenses) that affect net income but do not result in a cash receipt or payment. These adjustments are made using either the direct or indirect method.
- The direct method calculates and reports a company's net cash flow from operating activities by computing the company's cash inflows for each operating activity and then deducting its cash outflows for each operating activity.
- The direct method requires that each income statement account be analyzed and adjusted for changes in current assets or liabilities, certain noncurrent assets or liabilities, and any noncash items.
- If the direct method is used, a company must include a reconciliation of net income to net cash flow from operating activities.
- The indirect method calculates a company's net cash flow from operating activities by converting its net income from an accrual basis to a cash flow basis.

- The indirect method adjusts net income for changes in the appropriate current assets or liabilities, certain noncurrent assets or liabilities, and any noncash items.
- The indirect method is the most commonly used method for the preparation of net cash flow from operating activities.
- A company's investing and financing activities are identified through an analysis of the changes in the balance sheet accounts (generally noncurrent assets and liabilities) and a review of any supplemental information provided.

KEY TERMS

direct method, p. 21-10　　　　　　　　　　indirect method, p. 21-14

KEY CALCULATIONS

Sales or Revenue Accounts + Decrease (− Increase) in Accounts Receivable or + Increase (− Decrease) in Deferred Revenue = Cash Received from Customers

Cost of Goods Sold Accounts { + Increase (− Decrease) in Inventory, + Decrease (− Increase) in Accounts Payable } = Cash Paid to Suppliers

Expense Accounts + Increase (− Decrease) in Prepaid Expense or + Decrease (− Increase) in Accrued Payables = Cash Paid for Expenses

LEARNING OBJECTIVE 21.3
Prepare a statement of cash flows using the visual inspection method.

KEY TAKEAWAYS

- The statement of cash flows may be prepared by using either the visual inspection method or the spreadsheet method. Under either method, all of the changes in the assets (except cash), liabilities, and shareholders' equity accounts during the period are explained.
- To complete a simple statement of cash flows, use the visual inspection method.
  - Step 1. First, prepare the heading and major sections and list the net change in cash at the bottom.
  - Step 2. Next, list net income under the operating activities section.
  - Step 3. Then list the increase or decrease in each balance sheet account as a cash receipt or payment (or adjustment) in the appropriate operating, investing, or financing section.
  - Step 4. Subtotal each section, add them together to calculate the net change in cash, and then add the net change in cash to the beginning cash balance to determine the ending cash balance.
  - Step 5. Verify that this amount is the same as the ending cash balance reported on the balance sheet.

KEY TERM

visual inspection method, p. 21-18

LEARNING OBJECTIVE 21.4
Prepare a statement of cash flows using the spreadsheet method.

KEY TAKEAWAYS

- In more complicated situations, companies use the spreadsheet method to prepare the statement of cash flows.
- When preparing the statement of cash flows using the spreadsheet method, the four steps are preparing the spreadsheet, completing the spreadsheet, preparing the final spreadsheet entry, and preparing the statement of cash flows.
- To complete a statement of cash flows, using the spreadsheet method:
  - Step 1. First, set up a spreadsheet that shows the change in the balance of each balance sheet account at the top and the sections of the statement of cash flows (and a section for noncash investing and financing activities) at the bottom.

- Step 2. Second, make spreadsheet entries to account for the changes in all the noncash balance sheet accounts, making modifications to show the cash receipts and payments for operating, investing, and financing activities.
- Step 3. Make a final spreadsheet entry to record the net change in cash.
- Step 4. Total the debit and credit spreadsheet entries in the upper and lower portions to verify that the respective totals are equal.

KEY TERM

spreadsheet method, p. 21-23

KEY TAKEAWAYS

LEARNING OBJECTIVE 21.5
Account for special items affecting the statement of cash flows.

- The sale of a depreciable asset generally involves an increase in cash (classified as an investing activity), the elimination of the book value of the asset, and the recognition of a gain or loss (the difference between the book value and the proceeds from the sale) which requires an adjustment to net income in the operating activities section of the statement of cash flows prepared under the indirect method.
- The retirement of bonds generally involves an outflow of cash (classified as a financing activity), the elimination of the book value of the bonds, and the recognition of a gain or loss (the difference between the book value of the bonds and cash paid to retire the bonds) which requires an adjustment to net income in the operating activities section of the statement of cash flows prepared under the indirect method.
- A company using the indirect method must disclose the interest paid and the income taxes paid in a separate schedule, narrative description, or the notes to the financial statements.
- Cash receipts or payments relating to the sale or purchase of investments in available-for-sale securities are classified as a cash inflow or outflow from investing activities. However, the unrealized change in the market value of these securities is not included on the statement of cash flows.
- The sale or purchase of debt securities classified as held-to-maturity is recorded as a cash inflow or outflow from investing activities. The amortization of any premium or discount related to this long-term investment is a noncash item requiring an adjustment to net income in the operating activities section of the statement of cash flows prepared under the indirect method.
- Investments accounted for under the equity method require a noncash adjustment equal to the difference between the investment income recognized from the investment and any dividends received.
- The recognition of compensation expense (a noncash item) related to compensatory share option plans results in an increase in a deferred tax asset. On a statement of cash flows prepared under the indirect method, a corporation must add the increase in compensation expense and subtract the increase in the deferred tax asset in determining net cash flow from operating activities. When the share options are exercised, cash flows received for the exercise price are reported as cash inflows in the financing section. If cash flows are used to acquire shares to sell to employees exercising options, they are reported as cash outflows in the financing section. The decrease in the deferred tax asset is added back to net income in the operating activities section of the statement of cash flows.

KEY TAKEAWAYS

LEARNING OBJECTIVE 21.6
(Appendix 21.1) Understand and prepare the operating activities section under the direct method.

- To compute the operating cash flows under the direct method, it is important to make adjustments to the applicable revenues and expenses for the period.
- To complete the operating activities section of the statement of cash flows, using the direct method:
  - Step 1. First, determine the operating cash inflows by adjusting the applicable revenues for changes in related balance sheet accounts to determine the collections from customers, interest and dividends collected, and other operating receipts.

- Step 2. Next, determine the operating cash outflows by adjusting to the applicable expenses for changes in related balance sheet accounts to determine the amount of payments to suppliers, payments to employees, payments of interest, payments for other operating items, and payments for income taxes.
- Step 3. Subtract the total operating cash outflows from the total operating cash inflows to determine the net cash flow from operating activities.

ANSWERS TO REAL REPORT QUESTIONS

Real Report 21.1 Answers Chipotle Mexican Grill, Inc.—Statement of Cash Flows

1. The two largest adjustments to reconcile Chipotle's net incomes to net cash provided by operating activities have been depreciation and amortization and stock-based compensation expense.
2. During 2012 and 2013, Chipotle increased its investment in leasehold improvements, property and equipment to almost $200 million per year.
3. Chipotle's inventory during 2013 increased. We know this because the inventory is a use of cash in the operating activities section. Inventory increased by $1,950,000.
4. Over the 3-year period, Chipotle returned $419,503,000 to shareholders through the acquisition of treasury stock.

MULTIPLE-CHOICE (AICPA ADAPTED)

Select the best answer for each of the following.

M21-1 **LO 21.1** Which of the following would be considered a cash outflow for investing activities?

a. cash paid to purchase product for inventory
b. cash paid to reacquire common stock
c. cash paid to repay debt
d. cash paid to purchase equipment

M21-2 **LO 21.2** In a statement of cash flows (indirect method), the amortization of patents of a company with substantial operating profits should be presented as a(n):

a. cash flow from investing activities
b. cash flow from financing activities
c. deduction from net income
d. addition to net income

M21-3 **LO 21.2** The net cash provided by operating activities in Seat's statement of cash flows for 2016 was $8,000,000. For 2016, depreciation on fixed assets was $3,800,000, amortization of patents was $100,000, and dividends on common stock were $2,000,000. Based on the preceding information, Seat's net income for 2016 was:

a. $2,100,000   c. $8,000,000
b. $4,100,000   d. $11,900,000

M21-4 **LO 21.2** The retirement of long-term debt by the issuance of common stock should be presented in a statement of cash flows as a:

	Cash Flow from Financing Activities	Cash Flow from Investing Activities
a.	No	No
b.	No	Yes
c.	Yes	No
d.	Yes	Yes

M21-5 **LO 21.2** Saratoga Company reports sales of $200,000 and interest revenue of $17,000 for the current year. During the year, accounts receivable increased by $21,000 and interest receivable decreased by $3,000. Under the direct method, Saratoga would report cash inflows from operating activities of:

a. $235,000   c. $241,000
b. $193,000   d. $199,000

M21-6 **LO 21.3** Selected information from Brook Corporation's accounting records and financial statements for 2016 follows:

Net cash provided by operating activities	$1,500,000
Mortgage payable issued to acquire land and building	1,800,000
Common stock issued to retire preferred stock	500,000
Proceeds from sale of equipment	400,000
Cost of office equipment purchased	200,000

On the statement of cash flows for the year ended December 31, 2016, Brook should disclose a net increase in cash in the amount of:

a. $1,700,000 c. $3,700,000
b. $2,400,000 d. $4,200,000

M21-7
LO 21.3
The net income for Mountain Corporation was $4,000,000 for the year ended December 31, 2016. Additional information is as follows:

Depreciation on fixed assets	$2,000,000
Proceeds from sale of land	200,000
Increase in accounts payable	300,000
Dividends on preferred stock	400,000

The net cash provided by operating activities in the statement of cash flows for the year ended December 31, 2016, should be:

a. $6,000,000 c. $6,300,000
b. $6,100,000 d. $6,500,000

M21-8
LO 21.3
Smith Company provided the following information on selected transactions for 2016:

Net income	$20,000,000
Proceeds from short-term borrowings	1,200,000
Proceeds from long-term borrowings	4,000,000
Purchases of fixed assets	3,200,000
Decrease in inventories	8,000,000
Proceeds from sale of Smith's common stock	2,000,000
Depreciation expense	500,000

What is the net increase in cash for the year ended December 31, 2016, as a result of the preceding information?

a. $32,500,000 c. $16,500,000
b. $25,700,000 d. $12,500,000

M21-9
LO 21.1
LO 21.3
Which of the following need not be disclosed in a schedule accompanying the statement of cash flows as an investing and financing activity not affecting cash?

a. acquisition of fixed assets in exchange for capital stock
b. dividend distributed in capital stock of the company (stock dividend)
c. retirement of a bond issue through the issuance of another bond issue
d. conversion of convertible debt to capital stock

M21-10
LO 21.1
LO 21.3
The following information was taken from Oregon Corporation's accounting records for 2016:

Proceeds from issuance of preferred stock	$4,000,000
Dividends paid on preferred stock	400,000
Bonds payable converted to common stock	2,000,000
Payment for purchase of machinery	500,000
Proceeds from sale of plant building	1,200,000
2% stock dividend on common stock	300,000
Gain on sale of plant building	200,000

Oregon's statement of cash flows for the year ended December 31, 2016, should show the following amounts for investing and financing activities, based on the preceding information:

	Net Cash Flow from Investing Activities	Net Cash Flow from Financing Activities
a.	$700,000	$3,600,000
b.	$700,000	$3,900,000
c.	$900,000	$3,900,000
d.	$900,000	$5,600,000

REVIEW EXERCISES

RE21-1
LO 21.2
Identify these cash flows as either investing activities (I) or financing activities (F).

a. payment for purchase of a building
b. payment of dividends
c. proceeds from sale of land, at cost
d. proceeds from issuance of note
e. proceeds from issuance of bonds

RE21-2
LO 21.2
Given the following information, convert Lark Company's sales revenue from its income statement into collections from customers for its statement of cash flows.

• Sales revenue	$80,000
• Increase in accounts receivable	20,000
• Increase in deferred revenue	10,000

RE21-3
LO 21.2
Given the following information, convert Cardinal Company's cost of goods sold from its income statement into payments to suppliers for its statement of cash flows.

- Cost of goods sold $50,000
- Increase in inventory 23,000
- Decrease in accounts payable 15,000

RE21-4
LO 21.2
Given the following information, convert Robin Company's salaries expense from its income statement into payments to employees for its statement of cash flows.

- Salaries expense $40,000
- Increase in salaries payable 18,000

RE21-5
LO 21.3
In the current year, Harrisburg Corporation had net income of $35,000, a $9,000 decrease in accounts receivable, a $7,000 increase in inventory, an $8,000 increase in salaries payable, a $13,000 decrease in accounts payable, and $10,000 in depreciation expense. Using the indirect method, prepare the operating activities section of its statement of cash flows based on this information.

RE21-6
LO 21.3
Tifton & Co. had the following cash transactions during the current year:

Proceeds from issuance of common stock	$400,000
Payment of dividends	100,000
Payment for purchase of land	75,000
Proceeds from issuance of bonds payable	300,000
Payment for purchase of treasury stock	80,000
Proceeds from sale of equipment	100,000
Payment for purchase of building	500,000

Prepare the investing activities section of Tifton's statement of cash flows.

RE21-7
LO 21.3
Refer to the information in **RE21-6**. Prepare the financing activities section of Tifton & Co.'s statement of cash flows.

RE21-8
LO 21.1
LO 21.3
Trenton Corporation has the following items. Specify what will be added (A) or subtracted (S) in the operating activities section of the statement of cash flows prepared under the indirect method.

____ Increase in inventory
____ Decrease in accounts receivable
____ Increase in interest receivable
____ Increase in salaries payable
____ Increase in income taxes payable
____ Decrease in deferred tax asset
____ Decrease in deferred tax liability
____ Gain on disposal of assets or liabilities
____ Depreciation expense

RE21-9
LO 21.1
LO 21.3
Lime Corporation participated in a simultaneous investing and financing transaction where it acquired a building costing $50,000 by issuing common stock. Show how Lime would report this transaction in regard to its statement of cash flows.

RE21-10
LO 21.2
LO 21.3
In the current year, Harrisburg Corporation collected $100,000 from its customers and paid out $30,000 to suppliers, $20,000 to employees, and $8,000 for income taxes. Using the direct method, prepare the operating activities section of its statement of cash flows based on this information.

RE21-11
LO 21.4
Providence Company sold equipment for $25,000 cash. The equipment had originally cost $35,000 and had accumulated depreciation of $15,000. Prepare the spreadsheet entry (in journal entry format) to record this transaction for Providence's statement of cash flows.

RE21-12
LO 21.4
Annapolis Corporation paid $270,000 to retire bonds with a face value of $300,000 and a book value of $290,000. Prepare the spreadsheet entry (in journal entry format) to record the retirement of these bonds for Annapolis's statement of cash flows.

RE21-13 Given the following information, compute Lemon Company's interest paid.
LO 21.5

- Decrease in interest payable — $1,000
- Bond premium amortization — 750
- Bond interest expense — 5,000

RE21-14 Given the following information, compute Peach Company's income taxes paid.
LO 21.5

- Decrease in income taxes payable — $ 600
- Income tax expense — 4,400

EXERCISES

E21-1 **Ratio Analysis** Following are totals from selected financial statements of Magdalene Corporation for the years ended December 31, 2016 and 2017:
LO 21.1

SHOW ME HOW

	12/31/16	12/31/17
Cash flows provided by operating activities	$102,000	$ 82,000
Cash flows provided by investing activities	16,000	33,000
Cash flows used by financing activities	(40,000)	(25,000)
Net increase in cash	$ 78,000	$ 90,000
Net income	$ 60,000	$ 24,000
Current assets	126,000	144,000
Total assets	560,000	650,000
Current liabilities	92,000	116,000
Total liabilities	344,000	410,000

Required:

1. **Next Level** Calculate the operating cash flow ratio for the year ended December 31, 2017. What information does this provide about the company?
2. **Next Level** Calculate the operating cash flow to total liabilities ratio for the year ended December 31, 2017. What information does this provide about the company?

E21-2 **Visual Inspection** Gordon Company's accounting records provided the following changes in account balances and other information for 2016:
LO 21.3

SHOW ME HOW

	Net Changes for 2016	
	Debit	Credit
Cash	$ 1,000	
Accounts Receivable		$ 1,100
Inventory	2,000	
Buildings and Equipment	8,800	
Accumulated Depreciation		2,900
Accounts Payable	900	
Common Stock, no par		5,500
Retained Earnings		3,200
	$12,700	$12,700

Additional information: Net income totaled $5,800. Dividends were declared and paid. Equipment was purchased for $8,800. No buildings and equipment were sold during the year. One hundred shares of common stock were sold for $55 per share. The ending cash balance was $4,200.

Required:
Using visual inspection, prepare a 2016 statement of cash flows for Gordon.

E21-3 **Visual Inspection** Noble Company's accounting records provided the following changes in account balances and other information for 2016:

LO 21.3

	Net Changes for 2016	
	Debit	Credit
Cash		$ 2,000
Accounts Receivable	$ 1,900	
Inventory		2,400
Land		1,700
Buildings and Equipment	23,000	
Accumulated Depreciation		4,500
Accounts Payable		1,600
Salaries Payable	600	
Bonds Payable		5,000
Common Stock, no par		3,000
Retained Earnings		5,300
	$25,500	$25,500

Additional information: Net income was $9,900. Dividends were declared and paid. Land was sold for $1,700. No land was purchased. A building was purchased for $23,000. No buildings and equipment were sold. Bonds payable were issued at the end of the year. Two hundred shares of stock were issued for $15 per share. The beginning cash balance was $4,800.

Required:
Using visual inspection, prepare a 2016 statement of cash flows for Noble.

E21-4 **Balance Sheet** The following beginning balance sheet and statement of cash flows for 2016 are available for Fazzi Company:

LO 21.3

Balance Sheet January 1, 2016

Cash	$ 900	Accounts payable	$ 1,600
Accounts receivable		2,300	Notes payable	3,900
Land		4,900	Common stock, $5 par	4,500
Equipment	$20,000		Additional paid-in capital	1,800
Less: Accumulated depreciation	(9,100)	10,900	Retained earnings	7,200
Total Assets		$19,000	Total Liabilities and Shareholders' Equity	$19,000

Statement of Cash Flows For Year Ended December 31, 2016

Operating Activities:		
Net income		$ 3,900
Adjustments for differences between income flows and cash flows from operating activities:		
Add: Depreciation expense		900
Increase in accounts payable		100
Less: Increase in accounts receivable		(700)
Gain on sale of land		(200)
Net cash provided by operating activities		$ 4,000
Investing Activities:		
Payment for purchase of equipment	$(5,000)	
Proceeds from sale of land	1,200	
Net cash used for investing activities		(3,800)
Financing Activities:		
Proceeds from issuance of common stock (200 shares)	$ 2,600	
Payment of long-term note	(900)	
Payment of dividends	(1,300)	
Net cash provided by financing activities		400
Net increase in cash		$ 600
Cash, January 1, 2016		900
Cash, December 31, 2016		$ 1,500

Required:

Next Level On the basis of this information, prepare a balance sheet for Fazzi as of December 31, 2016.

E21-5 **Classification of Cash Flows** The following are several transactions and events that might be disclosed on a company's statement of cash flows:
LO 21.1
LO 21.2
LO 21.3
a. issuance of common stock
b. purchase of building
c. net income
d. increase in accounts receivable
e. depreciation expense
f. sale of land at cost
g. conversion of bonds to common stock
h. increase in accounts payable
i. payment of cash dividends
j. issuance of a stock dividend

Required:
1. Identify in which section (if any) of the statement of cash flows each of the preceding items would appear and indicate whether it would be an inflow (addition) or outflow (subtraction).
2. **Next Level** Under IFRS, how may the payment of cash dividends be classified?

E21-6 **Net Cash Flow from Operating Activities** Hyde Company's records for 2016 provide the following information:
LO 21.1
LO 21.2
LO 21.3

a. amortization of premium on bonds payable, $600
b. purchase of equipment, $6,000
c. depreciation expense, $7,400
d. decrease in accounts receivable, $800
e. decrease in accounts payable, $2,800
f. issuance of long-term note for cash, $4,200
g. increase in inventories, $7,500

h. gain on sale of land, $8,000
i. increase in prepaid assets, $500
j. declaration and payment of cash dividends, $1,800
k. increase in wages payable, $300
l. patent amortization expense, $1,000
m. net income, $10,800

Required:
Prepare the operating activities section of the 2016 statement of cash flows for Hyde Company.

E21-7 **Statement of Cash Flows** The following is a list of items for Witts Company's 2016 statement of cash flows:
LO 21.1
LO 21.2
LO 21.3

a. receipt from sale of equipment, $2,700
b. increase in inventory, $3,900
c. net income, $13,500
d. payment for purchase of building, $29,000
e. depreciation expense, $8,700
f. receipt from issuance of bonds, $8,000
g. increase in prepaid expenses, $800

h. loss on sale of equipment, $2,200
i. payment of dividends, $5,200
j. decrease in accounts receivable, $1,700
k. issuance of common stock for land, $6,900
l. decrease in accounts payable, $1,500
m. beginning cash balance, $10,200

Required:
1. Prepare the statement of cash flows.
2. **Next Level** Under IFRS, what alternative treatment of the payment of dividends is allowed? How would this affect the statement of cash flows?

E21-8 **Erroneous Statement of Cash Flows** Andell Company's 2016 statement of cash flows, as developed by its bookkeeper, is shown here:
LO 21.1
LO 21.3

Cash Flows Statement December 31, 2016

Inflows of Cash	
Operating Activities	
Net income	$10,600
Add: Proceeds from sale of equipment	4,400
Proceeds from issuance of stock	4,300
Less: Payment for investment in bonds	(6,000)
Payment of long-term note	(5,000)
Net cash inflows from operations	$ 8,300

(continued)

Cash Flows Statement December 31, 2016

Other Inflows		
Decrease in accounts receivable	$ 2,100	
Depreciation expense	4,800	
Total other inflows of cash		6,900
Total inflows of cash		$ 15,200
Outflows of Cash		
Payment for purchase of land	$(5,200)	
Decrease in accounts payable	(2,800)	
Payment of dividends	(3,000)	
Gain on sale of equipment	(700)	
Total outflows of cash		(11,700)
Net increase in cash		$ 3,500
Cash, December 31, 2016		11,700
Cash, January 1, 2016		$ 8,200

You determine that the *amounts* of the items listed on the statement are correct, but in certain circumstances, incorrectly classified.

Required:

Next Level Prepare a corrected 2016 statement of cash flows for Andell.

E21-9
LO 21.4

Partially Completed Spreadsheet Hanks Company has prepared the following changes in account balances for the spreadsheet to support its 2016 statement of cash flows:

	A	B	C	D
1				
2		Increase	Worksheet Entries	
3	Account Title	(Decrease)	Debit	Credit
4	Debits			
5	Cash	$ 830		
6	Noncash Accounts			
7	Accounts Receivable	(290)		
8	Inventory	1,280		
9	Investments	1,550		
10	Land	(700)		
11	Equipment	2,300		
12	Patents (net)	(100)		
13	Total	$4,870		
14	Credits			
15	Accumulated Depreciation	$ 350		
16	Accounts Payable	120		
17	Bonds Payable	2,000		
18	Premium on Bonds Payable	300		
19	Common Stock, $2 par	480		
20	Additional Paid-in Capital on			
21	Common Stock	1,120		
22	Retained Earnings	500		
23	Total	$4,870		
24				

Additional information: The net income was $1,300. Depreciation expense was $350, and patent amortization expense was $100. At the end of 2016, long-term investments were purchased at a cost of $1,550. Land that cost $700 was sold for $900. On December 31, 2016, bonds payable with a face value of $2,000 were issued for equipment valued at $2,300. Two hundred shares of common stock were issued at $7 per share. Forty shares of common stock were issued as a "small" stock dividend, the relevant market price being $5 per share. Cash dividends declared and paid totaled $600.

Required:

On the basis of the preceding information, complete the spreadsheet.

E21-10 **Spreadsheet** The following 2016 information is available for Payne Company:

LO 21.4

Comparative Balance Sheets

	January 1, 2016	December 31, 2016
Cash	$ 400	$ 600
Accounts receivable	220	200
Inventory	370	610
Land	250	410
Equipment	2,070	2,200
Less: Accumulated depreciation	(310)	(400)
Total Assets	$3,000	$3,620
Accounts payable	$ 800	$ 500
Notes payable (long-term)	900	720
Common stock, no par	600	1,000
Retained earnings	700	1,400
Total Liabilities and Shareholders' Equity	$3,000	$3,620

Partial additional information: The net income for 2016 totaled $1,600. During 2016, the company sold, for $390, equipment that cost $390 and had a book value of $300. The company sold land for $200, resulting in a loss of $40. The remaining change in the Land account resulted from the purchase of land through the issuance of common stock.

Required:

Making whatever additional assumptions that are necessary, prepare a spreadsheet to support the 2016 statement of cash flows for Payne.

E21-11 **Spreadsheet and Statement** The following 2016 information is available for Stewart Company:

LO 21.4

SHOW ME HOW

Condensed Income Statement for 2016

Sales	$ 9,000
Cost of goods sold	(6,000)
Other expenses	(2,000)
Loss on sale of equipment	(260)
Gain on sale of land	400
Net income	$ 1,140

Comparative Balance Sheets

	December 31, 2015	December 31, 2016
Cash	$ 700	$1,130
Accounts receivable	450	310
Inventory	350	400
Land	300	500
Equipment	1,600	1,800
Less: Accumulated depreciation	(200)	(150)
Total Assets	$3,200	$3,990
Accounts payable	$ 600	$ 750
Bonds payable (due 1/1/2018)	1,000	1,000
Common stock, $10 par	900	1,400
Retained earnings	700	840
Total Liabilities and Shareholders' Equity	$3,200	$3,990

Partial additional information:

- The equipment that was sold for cash had cost $400 and had a book value of $300.
- Land that was sold brought a cash price of $530.
- Fifty shares of stock were issued at par.

(continued)

Required:
Making whatever additional assumptions that are necessary,
1. Prepare a spreadsheet to support a 2016 statement of cash flows for Stewart.
2. Prepare the statement of cash flows.

E21-12 **Fixed Asset Transactions** The following is an Equipment account and its associated Accumulated Depreciation
LO 21.5 account:

Equipment				Accumulated Depreciation			
Beg. balance	49,000	Machine A	8,100	Related to Mach. A	6,300	Beg. balance	29,000
Machine C	25,000	Machine B	5,200	Related to Mach. B	4,600	Depreciation	12,000
End. balance	60,700					End. balance	30,100

Additional information:
- Machine A was sold at a gain of $900.
- Machine B was sold for its scrap value of $200.
- Machine C was acquired during the year.

Required:
Next Level Analyze the two accounts and show, in journal entry form, the entries that would be made in preparation of the statement of cash flows to reflect all of the changes listed in the accounts.

E21-13 **Retirement of Debt** Moore Company is preparing its statement of cash flows for the current year. During the year,
LO 21.5 the company retired two issuances of debt and properly recorded the transactions. These transactions were as follows:
1. Paid cash of $18,000 to retire bonds payable with a face value of $20,000 and a book value of $18,300.
2. Paid cash of $38,000 to retire bonds payable with a face value of $35,000 and a book value of $37,000.

Required:
Record, in journal entry form, the entries that Moore would make for the preceding transactions on its spreadsheet to prepare its statement of cash flows.

E21-14 **Interest and Income Taxes** Staggs Company has prepared its 2016 statement of cash flows. In conjunction with
LO 21.5 this statement, it plans to disclose the interest and income taxes it paid during 2016. The following information is available from its 2016 income statement and beginning and ending balance sheet:

Income Statement	
Interest expense	$12,000
Income tax expense	35,000

Balance Sheet		
	Cr. Bal. 01/01/16	Cr. Bal. 12/31/16
Interest payable	$ 600	$ 2,300
Income taxes payable	5,000	3,000
Bonds payable	80,000	80,000
Premium on bonds payable	9,000	8,100
Deferred taxes payable	3,300	4,400

Required:
1. Compute the amounts of interest paid and income taxes paid by Staggs for 2016.
2. **Next Level** Under IFRS, how would interest paid and income taxes paid be reported?

E21-15 **Investments** On October 4, 2016, Collins Company purchased 100 bonds of Steph Company for $6,400 as a
LO 21.5 short-term investment in securities classified as available for sale. On December 31, 2016, the bonds had a fair value of $6,300, and on February 8, 2017, Collins sold the bonds for $6,700.

Required:
In journal entry form, prepare the spreadsheet entries to record these transactions for Collins Company's 2016 and 2017 statement of cash flows.

E21-16 Statement of Cash Flows The following is a list of the items for Lombardo Company's 2016 statement of cash flows:

LO 21.1
LO 21.3
LO 21.5

SHOW ME HOW

a. depreciation expense, $4,200
b. proceeds from sale of land, $5,600
c. payment of dividends, $5,000
d. net income, $7,900
e. conversion of bonds to common stock, $7,000
f. increase in accounts payable, $3,100
g. proceeds from issuance of note, $6,200
h. gain on sale of land, $1,800
i. payment for purchase of building, $13,000
j. increase in accounts receivable, $2,700
k. ending cash balance, $13,900

Required:
Prepare the statement of cash flows.

E21-17 Investing Activities and Depreciable Assets Verlando Company had the following account balances and information available for 2016:

LO 21.3
LO 21.5

	January 1, 2016	December 31, 2016
Land	$ 45,000	$ 85,000
Buildings and equipment	100,000	210,000
Accumulated depreciation: buildings and equipment	50,000	36,000
Investment in available-for-sale securities	16,000	29,000
Patents, net	10,000	25,200
Unrealized gain on available-for-sale securities	500	2,300
Retained earnings	150,000	200,000

During 2016, Verlando recorded the following transactions affecting these accounts:

a. Land with a carrying value of $35,000 was sold at a loss of $6,000.
b. Land and equipment were purchased with cash during the period.
c. Equipment with an original cost of $20,000 that had a book value of $4,000 was written off as obsolete.
d. A building with an original cost of $60,000 and accumulated depreciation of $25,000 was sold at a $23,000 gain.
e. Depreciation expense and amortization expense were recorded.
f. Net income for the year was $60,000.
g. A patent was acquired during the year in exchange for 1,200 shares of common stock with a par value of $1 per share and a market value of $26 per share.
h. Additional marketable securities were purchased during the year.
i. Verlando Company has no notes payable in the liabilities section of its balance sheet.

Required:
1. **Next Level** Assuming that Verlando uses the indirect method to determine operating cash flows, what is the amount of depreciation expense and amortization expense that would be added back to net income?
2. Prepare the investing activities section of the statement of cash flows for the year ended December 31, 2016.
3. Prepare the disclosure for significant noncash transactions for the statement of cash flows for the year ended December 31, 2016.

E21-18 (Appendix 21.1) Operating Cash Flows Spreadsheet Method Refer to the information for Stewart Company in E21-11.

LO 21.6

Required:
Based only on the information presented and using the direct method, prepare the cash flows from operating activities section of the 2016 statement of cash flows for Stewart using the spreadsheet method.

E21-19 (Appendix 21.1) Operating Cash Flows The following is accounting information taken from Woodrail Company's adjusted trial balance for 2016:

LO 21.6

SHOW ME HOW

	Debit	Credit
Sales		$75,000
Interest Revenue		4,300
Cost of Goods Sold	$43,600	
Salaries Expense	13,600	
Interest Expense	5,400	
Income Tax Expense	3,000	

(continued)

In addition, the following changes occurred in selected accounts during 2016:

Accounts Receivable	$5,700 credit
Inventory	9,800 debit
Accounts Payable	7,000 credit
Salaries Payable	900 debit
Interest Payable	300 credit

Required:
Using the direct method, prepare the cash flows from operating activities section of the 2016 statement of cash flows for Woodrail.

E21-20 *(Appendix 21.1)* **Statement of Cash Flows** The following is a list of items to be included in Estes Company's 2016 statement of cash flows:
LO 21.6

a. payments to suppliers, $31,500
b. other operating receipts, $1,200
c. payments of dividends, $4,000
d. payments of income taxes, $5,000
e. collections from customers, $68,400
f. payment for purchase of equipment, $18,500
g. payments to employees, $19,300

h. interest and dividends collected, $7,100
i. other operating payments, $900
j. proceeds from issuance of bonds, $11,300
k. payments of interest, $8,400
l. proceeds from sale of investments, $6,000
m. beginning cash balance, $28,400

Required:
1. Prepare the statement of cash flows using the direct method for operating cash flows.
2. **Next Level** Under IFRS, which items may be classified differently than under U.S. GAAP?

E21-21 *(Appendix 21.1)* **Visual Inspection** The following changes in account balances were taken from Walson Company's adjusted trial balance at the end of 2016:
LO 21.6

	Net Changes for 2016	
	Debit	Credit
Cash	$ 2,100	
Accounts Receivable	8,700	
Inventory		$ 2,500
Land		1,900
Buildings and Equipment	10,400	
Accumulated Depreciation		6,800
Accounts Payable	4,500	
Salaries Payable		800
Income Taxes Payable		1,000
Common Stock, no par		9,000
Retained Earnings	4,000	
Sales		69,000
Cost of Goods Sold	34,000	
Salaries Expense	17,200	
Depreciation Expense	6,800	
Income Tax Expense	3,300	
Totals	$91,000	$91,000

In addition, the following information was obtained from the company's records:

- Land was sold, at cost, for $1,900.
- Dividends of $4,000 were declared and paid.
- Equipment was purchased for $10,400.
- Common stock was issued for $9,000.
- Beginning cash balance was $17,000.

Required:
Using visual inspection and the direct method, prepare Walson's 2016 statement of cash flows. (A separate schedule reconciling net income to cash provided by operating activities is not necessary.)

E21-22 Direct and Indirect Methods Dauve Company reported the following condensed income statement for 2016:

LO 21.2
LO 21.3
LO 21.6

SHOW ME HOW

Sales		$100,000
Cost of goods sold		(58,000)
Gross profit		$ 42,000
Operating expenses:		
Depreciation expense	$ 8,000	
Salaries expense	12,000	(20,000)
Income before income taxes		$ 22,000
Income tax expense		(6,600)
Net income		$ 15,400

During 2016, the following changes occurred in the company's current assets and current liabilities:

	Increase (Decrease)
Cash	$ 3,700
Accounts receivable	(5,500)
Inventories	8,900
Accounts payable (purchases)	(4,600)
Salaries payable	2,800

Required:
1. By visual inspection, prepare the net cash flow from the operating activities section of Dauve's 2016 statement of cash flows using the indirect method.
2. By visual inspection, prepare the net cash flow from the operating activities section of Dauve's 2016 statement of cash flows using the direct method.

PROBLEMS

P21-1 Classifications of Cash Flows A company's statement of cash flows and the accompanying schedule of investing
LO 21.1 and financing activities not affecting cash may contain the following major sections:

   a. Operating Activities
   b. Investing Activities
   c. Financing Activities
   d. Investing and Financing Activities Not Affecting Cash

The following is a list of items that might appear on a company's statement of cash flows or in the accompanying schedule.

   _____ 1. decrease in accounts payable
   _____ 2. payment of dividends
   _____ 3. increase in income taxes payable
   _____ 4. proceeds from issuance of note
   _____ 5. payment for purchase of available-for-sale temporary investments
   _____ 6. amortization of premium on investment in bonds
   _____ 7. increase in prepaid expenses
   _____ 8. payment of note
   _____ 9. gain on sale of equipment

(continued)

10. proceeds from sale of land
_____ 11. net income
_____ 12. payment for acquisition of building
_____ 13. depreciation expense
_____ 14. issuance of common stock for land
_____ 15. proceeds (principal) from collection of note
_____ 16. amortization of discount on bonds payable
_____ 17. decrease in deferred taxes payable
_____ 18. proceeds from issuance of bonds
_____ 19. issuance of stock dividend
_____ 20. payment for purchase of treasury stock
_____ 21. depletion expense
_____ 22. increase in inventory
_____ 23. conversion of preferred stock to common stock
_____ 24. proceeds from issuance of stock
_____ 25. lease of equipment under capital lease
_____ 26. proceeds from sale of patent

Required:
Using the letters A through D, indicate in which section of the statement of cash flows (or the accompanying schedule) the preceding items would most likely be classified. After each letter, indicate with a plus (+) or a minus (−) whether the items would be reported as an increase (inflow) or decrease (outflow). Indicate with an X an item that would not be reported on the statement (or the accompanying schedule).

P21-2 **Net Cash Flow from Operating Activities** Verna Company's records provided the following information for
LO 21.1 2016:
LO 21.2

a. decrease in accounts payable, $4,600
b. loss on sale of land, $1,900
c. increase in inventory, $7,800
d. increase in income taxes payable, $2,700
e. net income, $68,400
f. patent amortization expense, $1,600
g. ordinary loss, $6,200
h. decrease in deferred taxes payable, $2,500
i. amortization of discount on bonds payable, $1,300
j. payment of cash dividends, $24,000
k. depletion expense, $5,000
l. decrease in salaries payable, $1,400
m. decrease in accounts receivable, $3,500
n. gain on sale of equipment, $6,100
o. proceeds from issuance of stock, $57,000
p. ordinary gain, $3,700
q. depreciation expense, $10,000
r. amortization of discount on investment in bonds, $1,500

Required:
Prepare the operating activities section of Verna's 2016 statement of cash flows.

P21-3 **Statement of Cash Flows** The following is a list of the items to be included in the preparation of Warrick
LO 21.3 Company's 2016 statement of cash flows:

a. net income, $59,200
b. payment for purchase of building, $98,000
c. increase in accounts receivable, $7,400

d. proceeds from issuance of common stock, $37,100
e. increase in accounts payable, $4,500
f. proceeds from sale of land, $7,000
g. depreciation expense, $12,600
h. payment of dividends, $36,000
i. gain on sale of land, $5,300
j. decrease in inventory, $3,700
k. payment for purchase of long-term investments, $9,600
l. amortization of discount on bonds payable, $1,900
m. proceeds from issuance of note, $18,000
n. increase in deferred taxes payable, $5,000
o. equipment acquired by capital lease, $19,500
p. decrease in salaries payable, $2,300
q. beginning cash balance, $20,300

Required:
1. Prepare the statement of cash flows.
2. Assume the company's preferred stock has been selling for $120 per share during 2016. How many shares would the company have had to issue to avoid having a decrease in cash during the year? Where would this issuance have been reported in the statement of cash flows?

P21-4 **Statement of Cash Flows** The following is a list of the items to be included in the preparation of Trone
LO 21.3 Company's 2016 statement of cash flows:

a. ordinary gain, $9,200
b. proceeds from issuance of note, $25,000
c. decrease in accounts receivable, $5,000
d. payment for purchase of patent, $19,800
e. increase in inventory, $6,700
f. payment of dividends, $30,000
g. decrease in accounts payable, $4,000
h. proceeds from sale of investments, $8,500
i. amortization of premium on bonds payable, $2,100
j. net income, $49,200
k. common stock exchanged for land, $14,000
l. payment for purchase of equipment, $39,400
m. loss on sale of investments, $4,800
n. decrease in deferred taxes payable, $3,600
o. proceeds from issuance of preferred stock, $52,800
p. payment to retire bonds, $37,800
q. depreciation expense, $10,700
r. ending cash balance, $22,100

Required:
1. Prepare the statement of cash flows.
2. **Next Level** What would have happened if the company had not issued the note during 2016? How did the issuance of the note affect the company's debt ratio (discussed in Chapter 6) at the end of 2016?

P21-5
LO 21.4

Partially Completed Spreadsheet The following partially completed spreadsheet has been prepared for Perrin Company's 2016 statement of cash flows:

	A	B	C	D	E	F
1						
2		Balances		Change	Worksheet Entries	
3	Account Titles	12/31/15	12/31/16	Increase (Decrease)	Debit	Credit
4	Debits					
5	Cash	800	1,540			
6	Noncash Accounts:					
7	Accounts Receivable	1,500	2,180			
8	Inventory	3,100	6,055			
9	Investments in Stock	—	2,800			
10	Land	6,000	9,200			
11	Buildings	20,000	20,000			
12	Office Equipment	4,000	6,100			
13	Delivery Equipment	3,000	5,900			
14	Treasury Stock	—	2,000			
15	Totals	38,400	55,775	?		
16						
17	Credits					
18	Accumulated Depreciation	7,000	8,500			
19	Accounts Payable	3,300	3,695			
20	Wages Payable	600	500			
21	Bonds Payable	—	5,000			
22	Premium on Bonds Payable	—	240			
23	Common Stock, $10 par	6,000	8,200			
24	Additional Paid-in Capital	9,000	13,640			
25	Retained Earnings	?	?	3,500		
26	Totals	38,400	55,775	?		
27						

Additional relevant information:

a. Beginning retained earnings $12,500
   Plus: Net income 8,000
   $20,500
   Less: Stock dividends $ 840
   Cash dividends 3,660 (4,500)
   Ending retained earnings $16,000

b. Accumulated depreciation is a contra account for all the depreciable assets. Depreciation on these assets totaled $2,200 for the year.

c. On January 1, 2016, the company issued 10% bonds with a face value of $5,000 at 106. Interest was paid semi-annually on June 30 and December 31. The bonds mature on January 1, 2021. Straight-line amortization is used for bond discount or premium. Bond interest expense was $440.

d. Land was purchased for $3,200 during the year.

e. Two hundred shares of common stock were issued for delivery equipment valued at $2,900 and office equipment valued at $3,100.

f. Twenty shares of stock were issued as a stock dividend. The market price per share was $42.

g. Office equipment with a cost of $1,000 and a book value of $300 was sold for $50.

h. Fifty shares of its own common stock were reacquired by the company as treasury stock. The company purchased the shares for $40 per share.

i. One hundred shares of Doe Company stock were purchased for $28 per share at year-end.

Required:
Complete the spreadsheet.

P21-6
LO 21.4

Spreadsheet and Statement of Cash Flows The following information was taken from Lamberson Company's accounting records:

	Account Balances	
	January 1, 2016	December 31, 2016
Debits		
Cash	$ 1,400	$ 2,400
Accounts Receivable (net)	2,800	2,690
Marketable Securities (at cost)	1,700	3,000
Allowance for Change in Value	500	800
Inventories	8,100	7,910
Prepaid Items	1,300	1,710
Investments (long-term)	7,000	5,400
Land	15,000	15,000
Buildings and Equipment	32,000	46,200
Discount on Bonds Payable	—	290
	$69,800	$85,400
Credits		
Accumulated Depreciation	$16,000	$16,400
Accounts Payable	3,800	4,150
Income Taxes Payable	2,400	2,504
Wages Payable	1,100	650
Interest Payable	—	400
Note Payable (long-term)	3,500	—
12% Bonds Payable	—	10,000
Deferred Taxes Payable	800	1,196
Convertible Preferred Stock, $100 par	9,000	—
Common Stock, $10 par	14,000	21,500
Additional Paid-in Capital	8,700	13,700
Unrealized Increase in Value of Marketable Securities	500	800
Retained Earnings	10,000	14,100
	$69,800	$85,400

Additional information for the year:

a.
Sales	$ 39,930
Cost of goods sold	(19,890)
Depreciation expense	(2,100)
Wages expense	(11,000)
Other operating expenses	(1,000)
Bond interest expense	(410)
Dividend revenue	820
Gain on sale of investments	700
Loss on sale of equipment	(200)
Income tax expense	(2,050)
Net income	$ 4,800

b. Dividends declared and paid totaled $700.
c. On January 1, 2016, convertible preferred stock that had originally been issued at par value were converted into 500 shares of common stock. The book value method was used to account for the conversion.
d. Long-term nonmarketable investments that cost $1,600 were sold for $2,300.
e. The long-term note payable was paid by issuing 250 shares of common stock at the beginning of the year.
f. Equipment with a cost of $2,000 and a book value of $300 was sold for $100. The company uses one Accumulated Depreciation account for all depreciable assets.
g. Equipment was purchased at a cost of $16,200.
h. The 12% bonds payable were issued on August 31, 2016, at 97. They mature on August 31, 2026. The company uses the straight-line method to amortize the discount.

(continued)

i. Taxable income was less than pretax accounting income, resulting in a $396 increase in deferred taxes payable.
j. Short-term marketable securities were purchased at a cost of $1,300. The portfolio was increased by $300 to a $3,800 fair value at year-end by adjusting the related allowance account.

Required:
1. Prepare a spreadsheet to support Lamberson Company's 2016 statement of cash flows.
2. Prepare the statement of cash flows.
3. **Next Level** Compute the cash flow from operations to sales ratio and the profit margin ratio for 2016. What is the primary reason for the difference in the results of the ratios?

P21-7 **Spreadsheet and Statement of Cash Flows** The following information is available for Bott Company:
LO 21.4

	Account Balances	
	December 31, 2015	December 31, 2016
Debits		
Cash	$ 1,800	$ 2,000
Accounts Receivable	4,600	4,720
Notes Receivable (short-term)	0	1,000
Inventories	12,000	9,700
Prepaid Items	1,700	1,380
Land	11,000	17,100
Buildings and Equipment	78,000	110,000
Patent	4,400	4,000
Treasury Stock (common, at cost, $25 per share)	2,500	1,000
Totals	$116,000	$150,900
Credits		
Accumulated Depreciation	$ 24,000	$ 31,800
Accounts Payable	6,000	8,210
Salaries Payable	2,600	3,500
Miscellaneous Current Payables	1,400	1,200
Interest Payable	0	140
12% Bonds Payable	0	7,000
Premium on Bonds Payable	0	650
Convertible Preferred Stock, $50 par	9,000	6,500
Additional Paid-in Capital on Preferred Stock	3,000	2,500
Common Stock, $10 par	18,000	23,500
Additional Paid-in Capital on Common Stock	28,800	41,150
Retained Earnings	23,200	24,750
Totals	$116,000	$150,900

Additional information for the year:

a. Beginning retained earnings, unadjusted — $23,200
   Less: Prior period adjustment—correction of understatement of depreciation
   (net of income taxes) — (1,300)
   Adjusted beginning retained earnings — $21,900
   Add: Net income — 11,500
   — $33,400
   Less: Cash dividends — $(4,000)
   Stock dividends (150 shares at $31 per share) — (4,650) (8,650)
   Ending retained earnings — $24,750

b. Last year, depreciation expense was inadvertently understated in the amount of $1,800. The correction was made this year to Accumulated Depreciation and to Retained Earnings as a prior period adjustment. The company also received a related income tax refund of $500.
c. Sixty shares of treasury stock (common) were reissued at $30 per share.

d. Bonds payable with a face amount of $7,000 were issued for $7,750 on April 30, 2016. The bonds mature on April 30, 2021, and pay interest semiannually. The straight-line method is used to amortize the bond premium. Interest expense totaled $460 for 2016.
e. Fifty shares of preferred stock (originally issued at $60 per share) were converted into 100 shares of common stock.
f. Land costing $2,900 was sold for $3,800.
g. Three hundred shares of common stock were sold for $33 per share.
h. Equipment costing $32,000 was purchased during the year.
i. Land was acquired at a cost of $9,000 during the year.
j. Depreciation expense was $6,000.
k. Patent amortization was $400.
l. The company loaned money to one of its executives and received a $1,000 short-term note receivable on December 31, 2016. The note matures 90 days from the date of issuance.

Required:
1. Prepare a spreadsheet to support a statement of cash flows for 2016.
2. Prepare Bott Company's 2016 statement of cash flows. Show the reconciliation of the net income to the net cash provided by operating activities in a separate schedule accompanying the statement.

P21-8
LO 21.4
Spreadsheet from Trial Balance Heinz Company's post-closing trial balance as of December 31, 2015, and the adjusted trial balance as of December 31, 2016, are shown here:

	December 31, 2015 Post-Closing Trial Balance		December 31, 2016 Adjusted Trial Balance	
Cash	$ 2,700		$ 3,520	
Accounts Receivable	5,900		6,215	
Inventories	15,300		15,530	
Prepaid Items	1,400		1,000	
Investments in Bonds (long-term)	8,300		7,300	
Land	16,300		19,000	
Buildings	68,700		60,700	
Accumulated Depreciation: Buildings		$ 35,000		$ 34,500
Equipment	29,600		25,600	
Accumulated Depreciation: Equipment		14,200		14,700
Patents (net)	8,700		9,185	
Accounts Payable		8,900		9,195
Interest Payable		630		300
Wages Payable		2,500		2,600
Bonds Payable		23,000		17,000
Discount on Bonds Payable		0	715	
Common Stock, $10 par		22,000		22,650
Additional Paid-in Capital		15,320		15,970
Retained Earnings		35,350		35,350
	$156,900	$156,900		
Sales (net)				49,550
Cost of Goods Sold			23,800	
Wages Expense			16,510	
Other Operating Expenses			1,100	
Depreciation Expense: Buildings			2,700	
Depreciation Expense: Equipment			3,100	
Patent Amortization			815	
Interest Expense			1,715	
Loss (Ordinary) on Sale of Investments			200	
Interest Revenue				790
Gain (Ordinary) on Exchange of Assets				1,300
Income Tax Expense			500	
Ordinary Loss on sale of building			2,600	
Dividends Declared			2,100	
Totals			$203,905	$203,905

(continued)

A review of the accounting records reveals the following additional information:

a. Bonds payable with a face value, book value, and market value of $14,000 were retired on June 30, 2016.
b. Bonds payable with a face value of $8,000 were issued at 90.25 on August 1, 2016. They mature on August 1, 2021. The company uses the straight-line method to amortize the bond discount.
c. The company sold a building that had an original cost of $8,000 and a book value of $4,800. The company received $2,200 in cash for the building and recorded a loss of $2,600.
d. Equipment with a cost of $4,000 and a book value of $1,400 was exchanged for an acre of land valued at $2,700. No cash was exchanged.
e. Long-term investments in bonds being held to maturity with a cost of $1,000 were sold for $800.
f. Sixty-five shares of common stock were exchanged for a patent. The common stock was selling for $20 per share at the time of the exchange.

Required:
Prepare a spreadsheet to support a statement of cash flows for 2016.

P21-9
LO 21.4
Prepare Ending Balance Sheet On December 31, 2016, a fire destroyed a significant portion of Richey Company's accounting records. Only the January 1, 2016, balance sheet, the statement of cash flows for 2016, and several additional documents were saved as follows:

Balance Sheet
January 1, 2016

Assets			
Current assets:			
Cash			$ 1,900
Accounts receivable			5,100
Inventories			13,900
Prepaid items			1,300
Total current assets			$22,200
Property, plant, and equipment:			
Land			$12,000
Buildings	$60,000		
Equipment	20,000	$ 80,000	
Less: Accumulated depreciation		(29,000)	51,000
Total property, plant, and equipment			$63,000
Patents (net)			$ 7,100
Total Assets			$92,300
Liabilities			
Current liabilities:			
Accounts payable			$ 5,500
Income taxes payable			4,100
Miscellaneous payables			1,200
Total current liabilities			$10,800
Long-term liabilities:			
10% bonds payable (due 12/31/2022)		$ 15,000	
Less: Discount on bonds payable		(1,000)	14,000
Total liabilities			$24,800
Shareholders' Equity			
Preferred stock, $100 par		$ 17,000	
Additional paid-in capital on preferred stock		1,500	$18,500
Common stock, $10 par		$ 14,000	
Additional paid-in capital on common stock		11,200	25,200
Retained earnings			23,800
Total shareholders' equity			$67,500
Total Liabilities and Shareholders' Equity			$92,300

Statement of Cash Flows
For Year Ended December 31, 2016

Operating Activities:		
Net income	$10,000	
Adjustments for differences between income flows and cash flows from operating activities:		
Add: Depreciation expense	5,100	
Patent amortization expense	600	
Loss on sale of land	400	
Decrease in accounts receivable (net)	1,100	
Decrease in inventories	3,010	
Increase in income taxes payable	190	
Increase in miscellaneous payables	200	
Bond discount amortization	100	
Less: Gain on sale of equipment	(180)	
Gain on sale of patent	(1,100)	
Increase in prepaid items	(120)	
Decrease in accounts payable	(400)	
Net cash provided by operating activities		$18,900
Investing Activities:		
Purchase of building by issuance of mortgage and cash	$(43,000)	
Less: Issuance of mortgage	20,000	
Payment for purchase of building	$(23,000)	
Proceeds from sale of land	2,800	
Proceeds from sale of equipment	500	
Proceeds from sale of patent	2,100	
Net cash used for investing activities		(17,600)
Financing Activities:		
Proceeds from issuance of common stock (150 shares)	$3,000	
Payment of dividends	(5,000)	
Net cash used for financing activities		(2,000)
Net decrease in cash (see Schedule 1)		$ (700)
Cash, January 1, 2016		1,900
Cash, December 31, 2016		$ 1,200

Schedule 1: Investing and Financing Activities Not Affecting Cash

Investing Activities:	
Acquisition of land by issuance of preferred stock (40 shares)	$(4,800)
Financing Activities:	
Issuance of preferred stock to acquire land	4,800

The remaining financial documents reveal the following additional data:

- The new building was acquired on December 31, 2016. The related mortgage requires equal annual repayments of the principal over a 5-year period beginning December 31, 2018.
- The company issued a stock dividend of 200 shares of common stock on December 14, 2016. On the date of declaration, the stock was selling for $18 per share.
- The equipment that was sold had an original cost of $1,900.

Required:
Next Level Prepare a December 31, 2016, balance sheet for Richey. Include supporting calculations.

P21-10 **Infrequent Transactions** The following transactions were recorded on the books of Baxter Company during the current year.
LO 21.2
LO 21.5

a. Issued a "small" common stock dividend of 400 shares. The par value is $10 per share, and the relevant market price was $20 per share.

b. Exchanged equipment with a cost of $10,000 and a book value of $3,800 for land valued at $12,000, paying an additional $8,500 in cash.

(continued)

c. Converted preferred stock ($100 par) with a total par value of $20,000 and a book value of $22,800 to 1,500 shares of its $10 par common stock. The book value method was used to account for the conversion.

c. Recorded a loss of $4,200 as a result of retiring bonds payable with a face value of $30,000 and a related premium of $5,000 by paying $39,200.

e. Recorded an ordinary gain of $6,000 as a result of a sale of a building costing $100,000 and having an associated book value of $70,000. Cash received from the sale totaled $76,000.

f. Acquired equipment by entering into a capital lease. The lease required payments of $5,000 in advance; the present value of the lease payments (before the initial payment) was $34,000.

Required:

Next Level For each of the preceding items, discuss *if* and illustrate *how* the transaction would be recorded on the spreadsheet to support the statement of cash flows. Use a journal entry format for your illustrations.

P21-11 **Erroneous Statement of Cash Flows** Ryan Company's bookkeeper prepared the following 2016 statement of cash flows:
LO 21.3
LO 21.5

Flows of Cash Statement
December 31, 2016

Sources (Inflows) of Cash		
Net Source from Operations		
Net income	$ 47,800	
Add: Cash receipt from sale of land	6,500	
Inflow from issuing 10% bonds payable	25,000	
Depreciation expense	13,200	
Reduction in inventory	1,900	
Less: Outflow to buy equipment	(16,400)	
Increase in prepaid expenses	(700)	
Cash (principal) paid on long-term note	(9,500)	
ordinary gain	(2,000)	
Total source from operations		$ 65,800
Other Sources (Inflows) of Cash		
Loss on sale of land	$ 2,300	
Increase in accounts payable	1,000	
Cash from issuing preferred stock	38,700	
Patent amortization expense	2,100	
Total other sources of cash		44,100
Sources (Financing) Not Affecting Cash		
Issuance of common stock for patent		11,000
Total inflows of cash		$120,900
Uses (Outflows) of Cash		
To purchase building	$(62,000)	
Increase in accounts receivable	(7,800)	
For acquiring marketable securities	(7,100)	
Decrease in income taxes payable	(1,400)	
Total uses of cash		(78,300)
Uses (Investing) Not Affecting Cash		
Acquisition of patent by issuing common stock		(11,000)
Net inflow before dividends		$ 31,600
Less: Cash dividends		(24,000)
Net Increase in Cash		$ 7,600
Cash, January 1, 2016		15,300
Cash, December 31, 2016		$ 22,900

After a thorough investigation, you have determined that the *amounts* of the items listed on the statement are correct. However, you notice several items that are incorrectly classified and reported.

Required:

Next Level Prepare a corrected 2016 statement of cash flows for Ryan.

P21-12 **Comprehensive** Angel Company has prepared its financial statements for the year ended December 31, 2016, and
LO 21.3 for the 3 months ended March 31, 2017. You have been asked to prepare a statement of cash flows for the 3
LO 21.4 months ended March 31, 2017. The company's balance sheet data at December 31, 2016, and March 31, 2017,
LO 21.5 and its income statement data for the 3 months ended March 31, 2017, follow. You are satisfied as to the correctness of the amounts presented.

	Balance Sheet Data	
	December 31, 2016	March 31, 2017
Cash	$ 25,300	$ 79,400
Marketable investments (at cost)	17,500	8,300
Allowance for decrease in value	(1,000)	(900)
Accounts receivable	24,320	49,320
Inventory	31,090	48,590
Total current assets	$ 97,210	$184,710
Land	40,000	18,700
Building	250,000	250,000
Equipment	—	81,500
Accumulated depreciation	(15,000)	(16,250)
Equity investment (30% ownership of Titan Company)	61,220	67,100
Other assets	15,100	15,100
Totals	$448,530	$600,860
Accounts payable	$ 21,220	$ 38,417
Income taxes payable	—	13,529
Total current liabilities	$ 21,220	$ 51,946
Bonds payable	50,000	115,000
Discount on bonds payable	(2,300)	(2,150)
Deferred taxes payable	510	846
Preferred stock	30,000	—
Common stock	80,000	110,000
Unrealized decrease in value of marketable investments	(1,000)	(900)
Dividends declared	—	(8,000)
Retained earnings	83,100	147,118
Other liabilities	187,000	187,000
Totals	$448,530	$600,860

	Income Statement Data for the 3 Months Ended March 31, 2017
Sales	$242,807
Gain on sale of marketable investments	2,400
Equity method earnings from Titan investment (30% ownership)	5,880
Ordinary gain on condemnation of land	8,560
Total revenues	$259,647
Cost of sales	$157,354
General and administrative expenses	22,010
Depreciation	1,250
Interest expense	1,150
Income taxes	13,865
Total expenses	$195,629
Net income	$ 64,018

(continued)

Your discussion with the company's controller and a review of the financial records have revealed the following information:

a. On January 7, 2017, the company sold marketable securities for cash. These securities had cost $9,200, and had a fair value of $8,600 at December 31, 2016. The remaining marketable securities were adjusted to their $7,400 fair value on March 31, 2017, by adjustment of the related allowance account. The dividend and interest revenue on these marketable securities is not material.
b. The company's preferred stock was converted into common stock at a rate of one share of preferred for two shares of common. The preferred stock and common stock have par values of $2 and $1, respectively.
c. On January 16, 2017, 3 acres of land were condemned. An award of $29,860 in cash was received on March 24, 2017. Purchase of additional land as a replacement is not contemplated by the company.
d. On March 25, 2017, the company purchased equipment for cash.
e. On March 26, 2017, bonds payable were issued by the company at par for cash.
f. The equity investment representing a 30% ownership interest in Titan Company included an amount of $9,600 attributable to an increase in the recorded value of depreciable assets at December 31, 2016. This increase is being depreciated at a quarterly rate of $480.

Required:
1. Prepare a spreadsheet to support the statement of cash flows for Angel for the 3 months ended March 31, 2017.
2. Prepare the statement of cash flows.

P21-13 **Comprehensive** The following are Farrell Corporation's balance sheets as of December 31, 2016, and 2015, and the statement of income and retained earnings for the year ended December 31, 2016:

LO 21.3
LO 21.4
LO 21.5

Balance Sheets

	December 31 2016	December 31 2015	Increase (Decrease)
Assets			
Cash	$ 225,000	$ 180,000	$ 45,000
Accounts receivable, net	295,000	305,000	(10,000)
Inventories	549,000	431,000	118,000
Investment in Hall Inc. at equity	73,000	60,000	13,000
Land	350,000	200,000	150,000
Plant and equipment	624,000	606,000	18,000
Less: Accumulated depreciation	(139,000)	(107,000)	(32,000)
Patent	16,000	20,000	(4,000)
Total Assets	$1,993,000	$1,695,000	$298,000
Liabilities and Shareholders' Equity			
Accounts payable and accrued expenses	$ 604,000	$ 563,000	$ 41,000
Note payable, long-term	150,000	—	150,000
Bonds payable	160,000	210,000	(50,000)
Deferred taxes payable	41,000	30,000	11,000
Common stock, $10 par	410,000	400,000	10,000
Additional paid-in capital	196,000	175,000	21,000
Retained earnings	432,000	334,000	98,000
Treasury stock, at cost	—	(17,000)	17,000
Total Liabilities and Shareholders' Equity	$1,993,000	$1,695,000	$298,000

Statement of Income and Retained Earnings
For the Year Ended December 31, 2016

Net sales		$1,950,000
Operating expenses:		
Cost of sales	$1,150,000	
Selling and administrative expenses	505,000	
Depreciation	53,000	
		$1,708,000
Operating income		$ 242,000
Other (income) expense:		
Interest expense	$ 15,000	
Equity in net income of Hall Inc.	(13,000)	
Loss on sale of equipment	5,000	
Amortization of patent	4,000	
		$ 11,000
Income before income taxes		$ 231,000
Income taxes:		
Current	$ 79,000	
Deferred	11,000	
Provision for income taxes		$ 90,000
Net income		$ 141,000
Retained earnings, January 1, 2016		334,000
		$ 475,000
Cash dividends, paid August 13, 2016		43,000
Retained earnings, December 31, 2016		$ 432,000

Additional information:

a. On January 2, 2016, Farrell sold equipment costing $45,000, with a book value of $24,000, for $19,000 cash.
b. On April 2, 2016, Farrell issued 1,000 shares of common stock for $23,000 cash.
c. On May 14, 2016, Farrell sold all of its treasury stock for $25,000 cash.
d. On June 1, 2016, Farrell paid $50,000 to retire bonds with a face value (and book value) of $50,000.
e. On July 2, 2016, Farrell purchased equipment for $63,000 cash.
f. On December 31, 2016, land with a fair market value of $150,000 was purchased through the issuance of a long-term note in the amount of $150,000. The note bears interest at the rate of 15% and is due on December 31, 2018.
g. Deferred taxes payable represent temporary differences relating to the use of accelerated depreciation methods for income tax reporting and the straight-line method for financial statement reporting.

Required:
1. Prepare a spreadsheet to support a statement of cash flows for Farrell for the year ended December 31, 2016, based on the preceding information.
2. Prepare the statement of cash flows.

P21-14 **(Appendix 21.1) Operating Cash Flows** Refer to the information for Lamberson Company in **P21-6**.

LO 21.6

Required:
1. Using the direct method, prepare the operating activities section of the 2016 statement of cash flows for Lamberson.
2. *(Optional).* If you completed **P21-6** earlier, prepare the remaining portion of the statement of cash flows. (A separate schedule reconciling net income to cash provided by operating activities is not necessary.)

P21-15 **(Appendix 21.1) Statement of Cash Flows** The following is a list of the items to be included in the preparation of Yellow Company's 2016 statement of cash flows:

LO 21.6

a. proceeds from sale of land, $2,100
b. payments of interest, $5,000
c. equipment acquired by capital lease, $7,200

(continued)

d. proceeds from issuance of preferred stock, $11,000
e. other operating payments, $1,300
f. interest and dividends collected, $4,700
g. payments to employees, $20,300
h. payment for purchase of investments, $12,100
i. collections from customers, $54,500
j. payments of income taxes, $2,900
k. payment of dividends, $5,200
l. other operating receipts, $1,600
m. payments to suppliers, $29,500
n. beginning cash balance, $29,700

Required:
Prepare the statement of cash flows using the direct method for operating cash flows.

P21-16 *(Appendix 21.1)* **Spreadsheet and Statement** Refer to the information for Farrell Corporation in **P21-13**.
LO 21.6

Required:
1. Using the direct method for operating cash flows, prepare a spreadsheet to support a 2016 statement of cash flows. (*Hint:* Combine the income statement and December 31, 2016, balance sheet items for the adjusted trial balance. Use a retained earnings balance of $291,000 in this adjusted trial balance.)
2. Prepare the statement of cash flows. (A separate schedule reconciling net income to cash provided by operating activities is not necessary.)

P21-17 *(Appendix 21.1)* **Comprehensive** The following are Adair Company's December 31, 2015, post-closing trial
LO 21.6 balance and the December 31, 2016, adjusted trial balance:

Accounts	12/31/15 Post-Closing Trial Balance		12/31/16 Adjusted Trial Balance	
	Debit	Credit	Debit	Credit
Cash	2,700		3,300	
Accounts Receivable	7,300		6,200	
Inventory	8,100		9,900	
Investments in Bonds	10,000		18,600	
Property and Equipment	105,300		133,300	
Accumulated Depreciation		42,400		49,200
Accounts Payable		8,100		8,500
Salaries Payable		1,300		700
Interest Payable		0		300
Notes Payable		0		9,000
Common Stock, no par		43,600		58,100
Retained Earnings		38,000		31,500
Sales				89,000
Cost of Goods Sold			48,800	
Depreciation Expense			6,800	
Salaries Expense			12,000	
Other Operating Expenses			1,700	
Interest Revenue				1,200
Interest Expense			900	
Income Tax Expense			6,000	
Totals	133,400	133,400	247,500	247,500

A review of the accounting records reveals the following additional information for 2016:

- Investments in bonds to be held to maturity were purchased at year-end for $8,600.
- A building was purchased for $28,000.

- A note payable was issued for $9,000.
- Common stock was issued for $14,500.
- Dividends of $6,500 were declared and paid.

Required:
1. Using the direct method for operating cash flows, prepare a spreadsheet to support the 2016 statement of cash flows for Adair.
2. Prepare the statement of cash flows. (A separate schedule reconciling net income to cash provided by operating activities is not necessary.)

P21-18 *(Appendix 21.1)* **Complex Spreadsheet** Refer to the information for Heinz Company in **P21-8**.
LO 21.6

Required:
Using the direct method for operating cash flows, prepare a spreadsheet to support a 2016 statement of cash flows.

CASES

COMMUNICATION

C21-1 Financial Statement Interrelationships
LO 21.1 Prepare an outline of the general format of the statement of cash flows (indirect method). Include examples of cash inflows and outflows that would be reported under each major section. Finally, discuss the information that is disclosed on the income statement, balance sheet, and statement of cash flows, respectively, that is not disclosed on the other statements.

C21-2 Statement of Cash Flows
LO 21.1
LO 21.2 A friend of yours is taking an introductory accounting course. He says, "I understand the income statement and balance sheet, but I am confused by the statement of cash flows and accompanying schedule. What is this statement, what is it useful for, what are its major sections, and what items are reported in each section and the accompanying schedule? I need to understand this statement better so I can do well in my class."

Required:
Prepare a written response to your friend's questions.

C21-3 Cash Flow Activities
LO 21.1
LO 21.2 A company's statement of cash flows shows its cash inflows, cash outflows, and net change in cash from the operating, investing, and financing activities during an accounting period.

Required:
Prepare a short memo that defines a company's operating, investing, and financing activities and identifies the cash inflows and cash outflows related to each activity.

C21-4 Operating, Investing, and Financing
LO 21.1 Activities
LO 21.2 The following is information about three different companies.
1. Noon Wakeup Company is a software game development company that creates titles for the Android operating system. The company recently launched its first software title. The company is expanding its operations by hiring additional developers and administrative staff. Noon Wakeup is not yet profitable, but it expects to show a profit within 2 years. Investors view the company as being on the cutting edge with its technology and have continued to invest in the company. Noon Wakeup has not yet borrowed money, but is considering doing so in the future.
2. Steel Grid Company is a textile company located in Waynesboro, NC. The company is experiencing its 20th year of profitability. Management is concerned by the recent economic downturn in the textile business, which has hurt sales in the 3 most recent fiscal years. Next year the company expects to just break even. For this reason, the company is not expanding and is only replacing fully depreciated equipment in its machine intensive manufacturing business. Steel Grid-prides itself in paying dividends and having no debt on its balance sheet.

(continued)

3. Device Driver Company is a technology manufacturing company located in Bloomington, IN. The company has just introduced its 10th new product and is the leader in market share for its industry. The company continues to invest in new equipment and property and to expand by purchasing its competitors. The company has yet to pay dividends, but it is considering doing so in the future. The company's largest current asset is cash, as a result of its high profit margin; because of this, the company has no need for external sources of cash.

Required:
For each company, prepare a report examining whether you think the company's current cash flows from each activity (operating, investing, and financing) will be positive (the activity provides cash) or negative (the activity uses cash). Provide support for your answers.

C21-5 Operating Cash Flows
LO 21.2
There are two methods to calculate and report a company's net cash provided by (or used in) operating activities.

Required:
Prepare a short memo that identifies the two methods and explains the calculations necessary for each method.

C21-6 Spreadsheet Method
LO 21.4
The spreadsheet method is commonly used to analyze the information for preparing a company's statement of cash flows. This method involves the completion of several steps.

Required:
Explain the method and list and briefly discuss the steps in this method.

CREATIVE AND CRITICAL THINKING

C21-7 Financing and Investing Activities Not Involving Cash
LO 21.1
LO 21.2
AICPA Adapted

The statement of cash flows is normally a required basic financial statement for each period for which an earnings statement is presented. The statement should include a separate schedule listing the financing and investing activities not involving cash.

Required:
1. What are financing and investing activities not involving cash?
2. What are two types of financing and investing activities not involving cash?
3. Explain what effect, if any, each of the following seven items would have on the statement of cash flows.
    a. accounts receivable
    b. inventory
    c. depreciation
    d. deferred tax liability
    e. issuance of long-term debt in payment for a building
    f. payoff of current portion of debt
    g. sale of a fixed asset resulting in a loss or gain

C21-8 Inflows and Outflows
LO 21.1
LO 21.5
AICPA Adapted

Alfred Engineering Company is a young and growing producer of electronic measuring instruments and technical equipment. You have been retained by Alfred to advise it in the preparation of a statement of cash flows. For the fiscal year ended October 31, 2016, you have obtained the following information concerning certain events and transactions of Alfred:

1. The amount of reported earnings for the fiscal year was $800,000.
2. Depreciation expense of $240,000 was included in the earnings statement.
3. Uncollectible accounts receivable of $30,000 were written off against the allowance for uncollectible accounts. Also, $37,000 of bad debts expense was included in determining earnings for the fiscal year, and the same amount was added to the allowance for uncollectible accounts.
4. A gain of $4,700 was realized on the sale of a machine; it originally cost $75,000, of which $25,000 was undepreciated on the date of sale.
5. On July 2, 2016, a building and land were purchased for $600,000; Alfred gave in payment $100,000 cash, $200,000 market value of its unissued common stock, and a $300,000 mortgage.
6. Alfred owns 25,000 shares of Field Corporation, which represents 40% of the company. Alfred accounts for the investment using the equity method. Field paid a cash dividend of $1.50 per share on August 3, 2016. For the year ended December 31, 2016, Field reported net income of $225,000.

7. On August 3, 2016, $700,000 of Alfred's convertible preferred stock was converted into $140,000 par value of its common stock. The preferred stock was originally issued at par.
8. The board of directors declared a $320,000 cash dividend on October 19, 2016, payable on November 16, 2016, to shareholders of record on November 5, 2016.

Required:

For each of the eight items, explain whether each is an inflow or outflow of cash and explain how it should be disclosed in Alfred's statement of cash flows (indirect method) for the fiscal year ended October 31, 2016. If any item is neither an inflow nor outflow of cash, explain why it is not and indicate the disclosure, if any, that should be made of the item in Alfred's statement of cash flows for the fiscal year ended October 31, 2016.

C21-9 Analyzing Coca-Cola's Cash Flow Disclosures

Obtain **The Coca-Cola Company**'s 2013 annual report either using the "Investor Relations" portion of its website (do a web search for Coca-Cola investor relations) or go to http://www.sec.gov and click "Search for company filings" under "Filings and Forms (EDGAR)."

Required:
1. What was the net cash provided by operating activities for 2013? What method was used to determine this amount? What was the largest positive and negative adjustment to net income?
2. What was the net cash used in investing activities for 2013? What was the largest investing cash outflow? Investing cash inflow?
3. What was the net cash used in financing activities for 2013? What was the largest financing cash inflow? Financing cash outflow?
4. What was the interest paid in 2013? Income taxes paid?
5. Compute the operating cash flow ratio for 2013. How does this result compare to the operating cash flow ratio for 2012 (current liabilities at the end of fiscal year 2011 were $24,283 million)? Is this a positive or negative signal for investors, why?

C21-10 Ethics and Cash Flows

You are the accountant for Nello Company, which manufactures specialty equipment. Nello has been in financial difficulty, so its suppliers require purchases to be paid in cash. Furthermore, Nello has long-term debt with a debt covenant that requires it to maintain a 1:1 acid-test (quick) ratio. Nello's employees work a 5-day week, Monday through Friday.

On Wednesday morning during the last week of the current year, Sam (the production supervisor) comes to you and says, "I don't understand it. We have this large special order from a customer that must be delivered at the end of the first week in January. Once we get the raw materials, it is going to take 5 solid days of work without overtime to produce the order. If Bob (the president) would let me order the raw materials this morning, we could have them by late today. This would give us 2 days this week and the 4 days after New Year's Day (Monday) of next week to complete the order without incurring overtime costs. But Bob says we must wait until next Tuesday to order the materials. This means we will have to work double time that Wednesday through Friday to finish the order. That overtime cost is going to really increase next year's factory salary expense, so our profit and operating cash flows from that order will be very low. Please talk to him."

When you approach Bob about buying the raw materials this morning, he says, "If we purchase those materials today, we will have to write a check. And that means our cash flow from operating activities for this year will be much lower, which our shareholders won't like. Furthermore, our quick ratio will go down from 1.01:1 to 0.90:1, so our creditors may be upset. I know our profit and operating cash flows for next year will be lower if we delay the purchase, but that seems to be the best decision. Don't you agree?"

Required:

From financial reporting and ethical perspectives, how would you respond to Bob?

USING CODIFICATION

C21-11 Researching GAAP

Situation

You are the new accountant for 12th National Bank and are preparing its 2016 statement of cash flows. The bank reports net income of $75,800 on its 2016 income statement. Included in this net income are the following items: $6,700 gain on sale of trading securities, $1,200 unrealized holding gain on trading securities, and $5,100 loss on sale of securities available for sale. Among its 2016 transactions, the bank sold trading securities with a carrying value of $22,900 for $29,600, and purchased trading securities for $65,200. The bank sold securities available for sale with a cost (and carrying value) of $58,700 for $53,600, and purchased securities available for sale for $39,400. It also made routine 90-day loans of $47,500 to customers and collected $20,000 principal on these customer loans. As a result of the preceding information, the bank's trading securities account increased by $43,500, the securities available for sale account decreased by $19,300, and the loans receivable account increased by $27,500. The bank uses the indirect approach to report operating cash flows on its statement of cash flows.

Directions

1. Research the applicable GAAP and prepare a written memo to the 12th National Bank's auditors that explains how you plan to report the preceding items on the bank's 2016 statement of cash flows. Cite your reference and applicable paragraph numbers.

CHAPTER 22

ACCOUNTING FOR CHANGES AND ERRORS

A Change for the Better

LEARNING OBJECTIVES

After reading this chapter you will be able to

- **LO 22.1** Identify the types of accounting changes and explain the methods of reporting each type of change.
- **LO 22.2** Account for a change in accounting principle.
- **LO 22.3** Account for a change in estimate.
- **LO 22.4** Identify a change in a reporting entity.
- **LO 22.5** Account for a correction of an error.

The primary objective of financial reporting is to provide useful information about a company that assists investors, lenders, and other creditors in making decisions about providing resources to the company. To achieve this objective, both the FASB and the IASB have identified *comparability*, which includes *consistency*, as a qualitative characteristic that enhances the decision-usefulness of financial information. Ideally, the consistent application of accounting methods and procedures from period to period should produce comparable information that helps users identify and explain similarities and differences between two or more sets of economic facts. However, because we live in a dynamic and changing economic environment, it is often necessary for a company to sacrifice consistency to improve the usefulness of its accounting information. In these situations, the rules governing the recognition and disclosure of accounting changes are designed to enhance comparability and inform users on how the changes affect current-period financial statements.

Accounting changes may occur for a variety of reasons. Sometimes, the FASB will require companies to follow a new approach or apply a new method of accounting. For example, the recently issued standard on revenue recognition led to a mandatory change in the accounting for revenue from contracts with customers. In other cases, a company may voluntarily change from one acceptable accounting principle to another acceptable principle, for example, changing from the average cost method of accounting for inventory to the FIFO method. In addition, the application of accounting principles requires a company to make many estimates for items such as uncollectible accounts receivable, the useful life of a depreciable asset, and the return rate for warranties. As the economic environment changes, changing such estimates is a necessary consequence of applying accrual accounting principles.

While not classified as an accounting change, errors also affect the comparability of financial information. When a material error is discovered, GAAP requires that the financial statements be restated to enhance comparability. As shown below, after peaking in 2006, the number of financial restatements has decreased dramatically and remains low relative to the more than 15,000 businesses that file financial statements with the SEC.

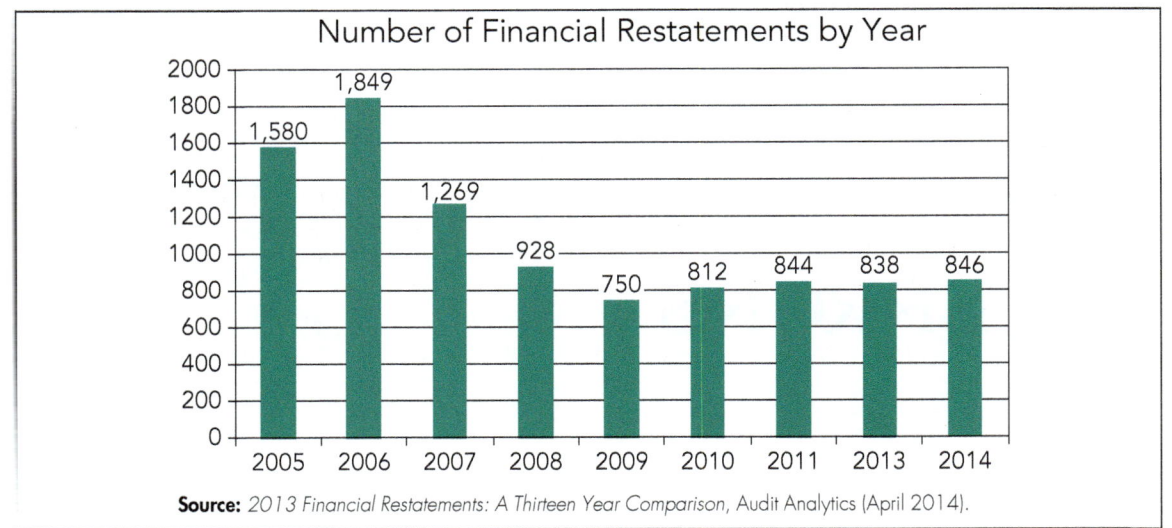

Source: *2013 Financial Restatements: A Thirteen Year Comparison*, Audit Analytics (April 2014).

In addition, the severity of the restatements—measured by factors such as the impact on income and the average number of restatement issues identified—has also remained low. For example, during 2013, restatements had an average negative impact on income of $3.2 million, the lowest in the last seven years. Further, in 2013, the average restatement involved only 1.61 financial accounting issues, significantly lower than the 2.43 restatements per year in 2005.

Although accounting changes occur infrequently, they can dramatically affect the financial statements of a company and distort the comparability of financial information. Therefore, rules to account for changes exist to ensure that the financial information presented provides relevant information that faithfully represents the company's financial position and economic performance.

While accounting changes decrease the comparability and consistency of financial information, such change is inevitable as companies respond to the dynamic business environment. Accountants need to report these accounting changes in a way that provides investors, lenders, and other creditors with information useful in their decision-making processes. The primary topic of this chapter is accounting and reporting the effects of a change in an accounting principle and a change in an estimate. In addition, we discuss a closely related issue—the accounting to correct errors in the financial statements.

WHAT ARE THE TYPES OF ACCOUNTING CHANGES, AND HOW ARE THEY REPORTED?

> **LEARNING OBJECTIVE 22.1**
> Identify the types of accounting changes and explain the methods of reporting each type of change.

GAAP defines three types of accounting changes[1] as follows:

- *Change in an Accounting Principle.* **Changes in accounting principle** represent a change from one generally accepted accounting principle to another generally accepted accounting principle. For example, if **Starbucks** changed its inventory cost flow assumption from average cost to FIFO, this would be a change in accounting principle. A change in the method of applying an accounting principle is also a change in accounting principle. For example, if a company that previously applied the lower of cost or market rule to its individual inventory items now applies the test to its inventory as a whole, this would be a change in the method of applying an accounting principle.
- *Change in an Accounting Estimate.* **Changes in accounting estimate** are a revision of an estimate used in the accounting process. This type of change is inherent in the periodic presentation of financial statements and occurs as the result of new or additional information and experience. For example, if, because of advances in coffee brewing technology, Starbucks changed the estimated life of its coffee brewing equipment from 7 to 4 years, this would be a change in estimate.
- *Change in a Reporting Entity.* **Changes in a reporting entity** represent a change in the type of entity being reported. When a parent company owns subsidiaries, it operates and reports financial results in a consolidated manner. If the parent company acquires or sells off a subsidiary, the reporting entity has changed. For example, Starbucks recently acquired 100% ownership and operating control over **Teavana**. This acquisition changed Starbucks's corporate entity and the company now reports Teavana as part of its consolidated financial statements.

In addition to the preceding accounting changes, GAAP specifies another category that requires adjustment to the financial statements:

- *Errors.* **Errors** are the result of mathematical mistakes, mistakes in the application of GAAP, or the oversight or misuse of facts that existed when the financial statements were prepared. For example, if a company incorrectly counts its inventory, the financial statements will contain an error.

While errors are not accounting changes per se, they are discussed in this chapter because the correction of an error involves corrections to the reported financial statements similar to accounting changes.

Method of Reporting Accounting Changes and Errors

If a company makes an accounting change, GAAP provides two possible methods of reporting the change:

- *Retrospective Adjustment Method.* The **retrospective adjustment method** requires that any previously issued financial statements reported for comparative purposes be revised to reflect the impact of the accounting change.
- *Prospective Method.* The **prospective method** does not require an adjustment to previously issued financial statements. Instead, the accounting change is accounted for in the current and future periods.

Additionally, if an error is discovered, a company will correct the error by making a prior period adjustment. Prior period adjustments are discussed in a later section.

The major advantage of the retrospective adjustment method is that it achieves comparability and consistency between accounting periods. Because all of the financial statements that are presented at a given date are revised and presented based on the same

---

[1] FASB ASC 250-10: Accounting Changes and Error Corrections: Overall.

accounting principles, financial statement users are able to make more meaningful comparisons with the previous years' financial statements. Therefore, the retrospective adjustment method provides a more faithful representation of financial information by presenting the effect of prior economic events and transactions in the period in which they occurred instead of the period in which an accounting change is made.

However, the retrospective adjustment method does have some disadvantages. First, the cost of determining the effect of an accounting change and revising prior period financial statements could be greater than the benefits obtained from the increase in comparability. Second, a retrospective adjustment may reduce the public's confidence in the reported financial information because numbers that users have previously relied upon as correct have now changed. Finally, revising prior period financial statements may impact a company's contractual arrangements (e.g., bonus agreements, bond indentures, royalties, or profit sharing plans), which are tied to financial statement measures. The need to revisit and adjust the contract terms for the accounting change can impose significant costs on the company.

An advantage of the prospective approach is that once financial statements are prepared according to GAAP, the reported information does not change. This method views accounting changes as an inherent part of accounting. If a company prepares financial statements using acceptable principles and estimates made with the best information available at that time, a future change in either the principle or the estimate should not affect the previously reported information. Instead, changing to a new principle or a new estimate that reflects new information should be accounted for prospectively (in current and future periods). A second advantage is that the prospective method is relatively easy to implement and imposes less cost on the company relative to the retrospective adjustment method.

The disadvantage of the prospective method is that the information in the current period is less comparable to the previously reported information. Therefore, financial statement users, with limited access and knowledge to company-specific information, must adjust the financial information in order to make meaningful comparisons.

According to GAAP:

- **A change in an accounting principle is accounted for by the retrospective application of the new accounting principle.**[2]
- **A change in an accounting estimate is accounted for prospectively.**
- **A change in a reporting entity is accounted for by a retrospective adjustment so that all the financial statements presented are for the same entity.**
- **An error is accounted for as a prior period adjustment (prior period restatement).**

GOT IT?

22-1 Describe the three types of accounting changes.

22-2 Describe the two possible methods that a company could use to report the effect of accounting changes. Give one reason in favor of and one reason against each alternative.

LEARNING OBJECTIVE 22.2

Account for a change in accounting principle.

HOW DO WE ACCOUNT FOR A CHANGE IN ACCOUNTING PRINCIPLE?

The application of GAAP requires a company to make many decisions as to the accounting principles that it will use. For example, a company must choose whether to use FIFO, LIFO, or average cost to value inventory. Once a company adopts an accounting

---

[2] If it is not practical to determine the cumulative effect of applying a change in any accounting period, the new principle is applied as if the change was made prospectively at the earliest date practical. This impracticability exception is discussed later in the chapter.

principle, it should be consistently followed. However, a company may choose to change its accounting principles in order to provide more useful information in response to changing economic conditions.

A change in accounting principle includes:

- change from one generally accepted accounting principle to another generally accepted accounting principle[3]
- change in accounting principle because an Accounting Standard Update has been issued and the former principle is no longer generally accepted
- change in the method of applying an accounting principle

Thus, a change in an accounting principle can be either a *voluntary* change or a *mandatory* change. However, a change in an accounting principle does *not* include:

- initial adoption of a generally accepted accounting principle because of events or transactions occurring for the first time or that were previously immaterial. For example, if **Starbucks**, which currently uses average cost to value its inventory, adopts FIFO for all *newly acquired* inventory but continues to use average cost for *previously acquired* inventory, this would not be a change in accounting principle. Instead, Starbucks would describe the nature of the change and its effect on net income of the period of the change, together with the earnings per share amounts, in the notes to the financial statements.
- adoption or modification of an accounting principle for transactions or events that are clearly different in substance from those previously occurring.
- change to a generally accepted accounting principle from a principle that is *not* generally accepted. This would be treated as a correction of an error. For example, assume that a coffee company had a policy of recognizing the entire amount of revenue related to coffee sales when a gift card is sold. If it later changed this policy to recognize revenue as the gift card was redeemed and coffee delivered to a customer, this change would be reported as the correction of an error.

Once a company adopts an accounting principle, it should apply that principle consistently from period to period. Any change in accounting principle must be justified on the grounds that the new principle is preferable to the old.[4] *Preferable* means that the new method represents an improved method of measuring business operations in the particular circumstances. For example, **Nike** justified its change to FIFO by stating that "this change was predicated on the fact that the LIFO method no longer matches the realities of how we do business." The issuance of an *Accounting Standards Update* is sufficient support for a change in accounting principle and does not require special justification.[5] That is, a newly mandated principle is automatically considered to be preferable.

Retrospective Adjustment Method

A company accounts for a change in accounting principle by the retrospective application of the new accounting principle to all prior periods as follows:

- *Step 1.* Compute the cumulative effect of the change to the new accounting principle as of the beginning of the first period presented.
- *Step 2.* Prepare a journal entry to adjust the book values of the assets and liabilities (including income taxes) that are affected by the change so that their balances reflect the amounts that would have existed under the newly adopted accounting principle. An

---

[3] If a company makes an accounting change in conjunction with an initial public offering (the first sale of common stock to the public), this is a change in accounting principle and retrospective adjustment is required.

[4] The SEC requires that when a publicly traded company makes an accounting change, the auditor must submit a letter indicating whether the change is to an alternative principle that, in the auditor's judgment, is preferable under the circumstances. There is no requirement that the auditor make a statement about the preferability of the accounting principles that the company is currently using.

[5] In conjunction with the issuance of a new standard, the FASB often specifies transition rules that indicate how the new standard should be applied (e.g., retrospectively or prospectively). In these instances, the transition rules should be followed.

offsetting adjustment is made to the beginning balance of Retained Earnings for the cumulative effect of the change (net of taxes).
- *Step 3.* Adjust the financial statements of the current period and each prior period to reflect the specific effects of applying the new accounting principle. Therefore, the comparative financial statements would appear as if the newly adopted accounting principle was used in every period presented.
- *Step 4.* Disclose the following information:
  - nature and reason for the change in accounting principle, including an explanation of why the new principle is preferable
  - description of the prior period information that has been retrospectively adjusted
  - effect of the change on income, earnings per share, and any other financial statement line item for the current period and the prior periods retrospectively adjusted
  - cumulative effect of the change on retained earnings (or other appropriate component of equity) at the beginning of the earliest period presented

The FASB requires the use of the retrospective adjustment method for changes in accounting principle because it provides financial statement users with more useful information by enhancing the comparability and consistency of the information.

Example: Retrospective Adjustment

Werner Company decided to change from the LIFO to the FIFO inventory method at the beginning of 2017 because the FIFO method better represented the flow of inventory. This was considered a change to a preferable accounting principle. **Example 22.1** shows selected information for Werner.

EXAMPLE 22.1 Selected Information for Werner Company

1. Werner Company starts operations on January 1, 2015.
2. Werner changes from the LIFO method to the FIFO method on January 1, 2017.
3. Werner reports the previous year's financial statements for comparative purposes. Therefore, the beginning of the first period presented is January 1, 2016.
4. Retained earnings on December 31, 2015, and December 31, 2016, (before the effects of the accounting change) are $231,000 and $525,000, respectively. Werner paid no dividends in 2015, 2016, and 2017.
5. Werner's tax rate is 30%, and there are no temporary or permanent differences.
6. Werner pays its income taxes in a single payment in the following year.
7. Werner must repay the taxes saved by using LIFO according to IRS rules but has *not* yet made any payments.
8. Werner has 100,000 shares outstanding and no potentially dilutive securities.
9. Werner calculated its inventory and cost of goods sold amounts under LIFO and FIFO as follows:

	Inventory		Cost of Goods Sold	
	LIFO Method	FIFO Method	LIFO Method	FIFO Method
12/31/2015	$ 70,000	$120,000	$720,000	$670,000
12/31/2016	90,000	160,000	780,000	760,000
12/31/2017	130,000	210,000	860,000	850,000

(continued)

10. Werner's income statement prepared under the LIFO method is as follows:

Werner Company
Income Statement
For Years Ended 12/31/2017, 12/31/2016, and 12/31/2015

	2017	2016	2015
Sales	$2,000,000	$1,700,000	$1,500,000
Cost of goods sold	(860,000)	(780,000)	(720,000)
Operating expenses	(550,000)	(500,000)	(450,000)
Income before income taxes	$ 590,000	$ 420,000	$ 330,000
Income tax expense	(177,000)	(126,000)	(99,000)
Net income	$ 413,000	$ 294,000	$ 231,000
Earnings per share	$ 4.13	$ 2.94	$ 2.31

Step 1 To retrospectively adjust the financial statements, Werner first computes the cumulative effect of the change to FIFO as of the beginning of the first period presented. Because the 2016 financial statements will be presented for comparative purposes, the cumulative difference between LIFO and FIFO inventory is $70,000 ($160,000 − $90,000). This is also the cumulative difference between the LIFO and FIFO income before taxes.

Step 2 Next, Werner prepares the appropriate current-year journal entry to reflect the financial statement effects of the accounting change. Therefore, at the beginning of 2017, Werner records the retrospective adjustment as follows:

Inventory	70,000	
Retained Earnings		49,000
Deferred Tax Liability		21,000

After this entry, the Inventory account at the beginning of 2017 reflects the FIFO valuation $160,000 ($90,000 LIFO balance + $70,000 cumulative effect adjustment). The $49,000 increase in Retained Earnings represents the cumulative effect of the change from LIFO to FIFO for 2015 and 2016, net of income taxes. Because the company previously used LIFO, it reports lower income before taxes and pays lower taxes than it would have under FIFO. Therefore, the $21,000 increase to the Deferred Tax Liability account represents the amount that Werner is obligated to repay for the income taxes it saved from using LIFO in 2015 and 2016.

Step 3 Next, Werner adjusts the financial statements so that they appear as if the newly adopted accounting principle was used in every period presented. **Example 22.1a** (p. 22-8) shows Werner's revised income statements for 2016 and 2017 prepared using the FIFO method.

Note that the difference in the income statements is due to the fact that cost of goods sold under FIFO is less than cost of goods sold under LIFO. This net of tax difference of $14,000 [($780,000 − $760,000) × (1 − 0.30)] in 2016 and $7,000 [($860,000 − $850,000) × (1 − 0.30)] in 2017 caused net income to be higher in each of the 2 years. Although we don't show the balance sheet, Werner would also have reported inventory of $210,000 and $160,000 on its 2017 and 2016 balance sheets, respectively.

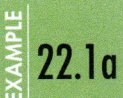

22.1a Revised Comparative Income Statements (FIFO)

Werner Company
Income Statement
For Years Ended 12/31/2016 and 12/31/2017

	2017	2016 As adjusted
Sales	$2,000,000	$1,700,000
Cost of goods sold	(850,000)	(760,000)
Operating expenses	(550,000)	(500,000)
Income before income taxes	$ 600,000	$ 440,000
Income tax expense	(180,000)	(132,000)
Net income	$ 420,000	$ 308,000
Earnings per share	$ 4.20	$ 3.08

Werner also adjusts its beginning retained earnings for the cumulative effect of the change from LIFO to FIFO (net of taxes) for 2016 and 2017. **Example 22.1b** shows Werner's revised retained earnings statements for these years.

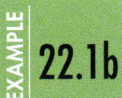

22.1b Comparative Retained Earnings Statements (FIFO)

Werner Company
Retained Earnings Statement
For Years Ended 12/31/2017 and 12/31/2016

	2017	2016
Beginning unadjusted retained earnings	$525,000	$231,000
Plus: Adjustment for the cumulative effect on prior years of retrospectively applying the FIFO inventory method (net of income taxes of $21,000 in 2017 and $15,000 in 2016)	49,000	35,000
Adjusted beginning retained earnings	$574,000	$266,000
Net income	420,000	308,000
Ending retained earnings	$994,000	$574,000

Notice that the $35,000 cumulative effect adjustment in 2016 is the after-tax effect changing from LIFO to FIFO for 2015 [($720,000 − $670,000) × (1 − 0.3)]. Therefore, the $266,000 adjusted beginning retained earnings is the retained earnings balance that Werner would have reported at the beginning of 2016 if it had been using FIFO during 2015. Similarly, the $525,000 unadjusted beginning retained earnings for 2017 is adjusted for the net of tax cumulative effect of the change from LIFO to FIFO for *all previous years* {[($720,000 − $670,000) + ($780,000 − $760,000)] × (1 − 0.3)}.

Step 4 Finally, Werner makes the appropriate disclosures of this accounting change. Section 1 of **Example 22.1c** shows Werner's discussion of the nature and reason for the change from LIFO to FIFO, an explanation of why the new principle is preferable, and a description of the prior period information that has been retrospectively adjusted. In Section 2 of Example 22.1c, Werner discloses the effects of the change from the LIFO method to the FIFO method on the financial statements.[6]

> **EXAMPLE 22.1c**
>
> **Disclosure of the Effects of a Change in Accounting Principle**
>
> **Section 1: Description of Accounting Change**
>
> On January 1, 2017, the company changed its method of valuing its inventory and cost of goods sold to the FIFO method from the LIFO method used in all previous years. The new method of accounting for inventory and cost of goods sold was adopted to better recognize the physical flow of goods in the company's business. The financial statements of prior years have been retrospectively adjusted to apply the new method. The effect on retained earnings at January 1, 2016 was an increase of $35,000.
>
> **Section 2: Effects on Financial Statements**
>
> The following financial statement line items for 2017 and 2016 were affected by the change from the LIFO to the FIFO inventory method.
>
> **Werner Company**
> **Income Statement Effects**
> **For Year Ended 12/31/2016**
>
> | | As Originally Reported under LIFO | As Adjusted to FIFO | Effect of Change |
> |---|---|---|---|
> | Sales | $1,700,000 | $1,700,000 | $ 0 |
> | Cost of goods sold | (780,000) | (760,000) | 20,000 |
> | Operating expenses | (500,000) | (500,000) | 0 |
> | Income before income taxes | $ 420,000 | $ 440,000 | $20,000 |
> | Income tax expense | (126,000) | (132,000) | (6,000) |
> | Net income | $ 294,000 | $ 308,000 | $14,000 |
> | Earnings per share | $ 2.94 | $ 3.08 | $ 0.14 |
>
> **Werner Company**
> **Income Statement Effects**
> **For Year Ended 12/31/2017**
>
> | | As Computed under LIFO | As Reported under FIFO | Effect of Change |
> |---|---|---|---|
> | Sales | $2,000,000 | $2,000,000 | $ 0 |
> | Cost of goods sold | (860,000) | (850,000) | 10,000 |
> | Operating expenses | (550,000) | (550,000) | 0 |
> | Income before income taxes | $ 590,000 | $ 600,000 | $10,000 |
> | Income tax expense | (177,000) | (180,000) | (3,000) |
> | Net income | $ 413,000 | $ 420,000 | $ 7,000 |
> | Earnings per share | $ 4.13 | $ 4.20 | $ 0.07 |
>
> *(continued)*

---

[6] GAAP allows companies to disclose the effect of a retrospective adjustment on the entire financial statement or on just the line items affected.

EXAMPLE 22.1c (Continued)

Werner Company
Balance Sheet Effects
12/31/2016

	As Originally Reported under LIFO	As Adjusted under FIFO	Effect of Change
Inventory	$ 90,000	$160,000	$70,000
Deferred tax liability	0	15,000*	15,000
Retained earnings	525,000	574,000	49,000

*$50,000 × 0.3

Werner Company
Balance Sheet Effects
12/31/2017

	As Computed under LIFO	As Reported under FIFO	Effect of Change
Inventory	$130,000	$210,000	$80,000
Deferred tax liability	0	21,000**	21,000
Retained earnings	938,000	994,000	56,000

**$70,000 × 0.3

Werner Company
Statement of Cash Flows Effects
For Year Ended 12/31/2016

	As Originally Reported under LIFO	As Adjusted under FIFO	Effect of Change
Net income	$294,000	$308,000	$ 14,000
Adjustments to reconcile net income to net cash provided by operating activities:			
Increase in inventory	(20,000)	(40,000)	(20,000)
Increase in income taxes payable	27,000	33,000	6,000
Net cash provided by operating activities	$301,000	$301,000	$ 0

Werner Company
Statement of Cash Flows Effects
For Year Ended 12/31/2017

	As Computed under LIFO	As Reported under FIFO	Effect of Change
Net income	$413,000	$420,000	$ 7,000
Adjustments to reconcile net income to net cash provided by operating activities:			
Increase in inventory	(40,000)	(50,000)	(10,000)
Increase in income taxes payable	51,000	54,000	3,000
Net cash provided by operating activities	$424,000	$424,000	$ 0

Direct and Indirect Effects

In **Example 22.1** (p. 22-6), we assumed that the change in the accounting principle used for inventory was the only item affecting the previous year's income. In more complex situations, a change in accounting principle might have an interactive effect on other items that affect prior years' income. For example, a company might have bonus arrangements with management, profit sharing plans for employees, or royalty payments, all of which are based on the company's income. In these cases, a change in an accounting principle has both a *direct* and an *indirect* effect on the company's income of prior years.

The **direct effect of a change in accounting principle** is the amount by which a company's prior years' income is increased or decreased specifically as a result of the change in accounting principle. An **indirect effect of a change in accounting principle** is the amount by which the company's prior years' income is affected by how the change in principle affects other elements of income. For example, suppose Werner Company also has a bonus arrangement with management based on net income. If the company had used FIFO instead of LIFO in prior years, the direct effect is an increase in income because of a lower cost of goods sold. However, this increase in income would have been partially offset by the recognition of higher bonus expense (an indirect effect).

In situations in which a change in accounting principle has both a direct and indirect effect on prior years' income, **a company recognizes only the *direct effect* (net of applicable income taxes) in determining the amount of the retrospective adjustment**. Therefore, the indirect effects that would have been recognized if the newly adopted principle had been used in prior periods are *not* included in the retrospective adjustment but would be accounted for in the current period.

Example: Indirect Effects

Werner Company's total pretax difference from the change to FIFO was $70,000 ($50,000 + $20,000) at January 1, 2017. Werner pays a bonus of 10% of its income before income taxes and bonus to employees. If the bonus contract requires that Werner pay the incremental amount due based on the FIFO amounts, Werner would recognize a compensation expense of $7,000 ($70,000 × 10%) in 2017, the year it adopted the new accounting principle. Note that taxes would be lower by $2,100 ($7,000 × 30%) because of the additional expense of $7,000. If the bonus contract does not require payment of this incremental amount, the amounts and disclosures illustrated earlier would be unaffected by any indirect effects of prior periods and would only be adjusted for the direct effect of the bonus on reported income in 2017. ■

Impracticability of Retrospective Adjustment

Sometimes, it may not be practicable to determine the effect of applying a change in accounting principle to a prior period. Retrospective adjustment is considered impracticable if any of the following conditions exist:

- The company cannot, after reasonable effort, determine the effect on prior periods.
- Retrospective adjustments depend on management's intent that cannot be independently verified.
- Significant estimates are required that cannot be objectively verified.[7]

If retrospective adjustment is impracticable, the new accounting principle should be applied prospectively as of the earliest date practicable.

For example, a change *to* LIFO would require the company to make subjective assumptions about LIFO cost layers as well as determinations of whether any LIFO liquidations have occurred in the past. Because such records are probably not maintained, it would be impracticable to retrospectively adjust the financial statements. Therefore, the company would apply the new accounting principle in the year of the change without adjusting the financial statements of prior years. It would disclose

---

[7] FASB ASC 250-10-45: Accounting Changes and Error Corrections: Overall: Other Presentation Matters.

information similar to that shown in Section 1 of **Example 22.1c** (p. 22-9). If, however, the company had sufficient information to retrospectively adjust to the new accounting principle for some, but not all, of the prior periods presented, it would apply the retrospective adjustment as of the earliest date practicable. Note also that if a company provides a summary of its financial results for a specific amount of years, it must retrospectively adjust its disclosures for those periods, if practicable.

Accounting Changes in Interim Financial Statements

If a company makes a change in accounting principle in an interim period, it reports the change using the retrospective adjustment method in its interim financial statements. For example, if a company changes from LIFO to FIFO during the third quarter of its fiscal year, it must restate the prior interim periods (the first and second quarters). The company does this by applying the newly adopted accounting principle to those interim periods and reporting the cumulative effect of the change in retained earnings at the beginning of the first interim period. Companies cannot evoke the impracticability exception for interim periods in the year in which the change is made. Therefore, the new principle is applied retrospectively to, at a minimum, the beginning of the year in which the change is made.

> **GOT IT?**
>
> **22-3** Describe two situations in which a company could justify a change in an accounting principle.
>
> **22-4** What steps are necessary to apply the retrospective adjustment method?
>
> **22-5** Does the adoption of a new accounting principle for events or transactions occurring for the first time represent a change in accounting principle?
>
> **22-6** What are direct and indirect effects of a change in accounting principle? How does a company account for any direct and indirect effects?
>
> **22-7** In which situations may it be impracticable for a company to apply the retrospective adjustment method? What is the correct accounting in such situations?
>
> **22-8** How does a company report a change in an accounting principle in its interim financial statements?

LEARNING OBJECTIVE 22.3
Account for a change in estimate.

HOW DO WE ACCOUNT FOR A CHANGE IN AN ACCOUNTING ESTIMATE?

The application of GAAP requires a company to make estimates for items such as uncollectible accounts receivable, inventory obsolescence, service lives and residual values of depreciable assets, recoverable mineral reserves, warranty costs, pension costs, and the periods that it expects to be benefited by a deferred cost. In fact, virtually every number on the balance sheet involves an estimate. Because estimating future events is an inherently uncertain process, changes in estimates are inevitable as new events occur, as more experience is acquired, or as additional information is obtained. For example, **Starbucks** makes the following statement regarding estimates in its annual report:

> *Estimates and Assumptions*
>
> Preparing financial statements in conformity with accounting principles generally accepted in the United States of America ("GAAP") requires management to make estimates and assumptions that affect the reported amounts of assets, liabilities, revenues and expenses. Examples include, but are not limited to, estimates for asset and goodwill impairments, stock-based compensation forfeiture rates, future asset
>
> *(continued)*

> retirement obligations and inventory reserves; assumptions underlying self-insurance reserves and income from unredeemed stored value cards; and the potential outcome of future tax consequences of events that have been recognized in the financial statements. Actual results and outcomes may differ from these estimates and assumptions.

GAAP requires that a **company account for a change in an accounting estimate in the period of the change and future periods if affected**.[8] Therefore, a change in an accounting estimate does *not* result in a retrospective adjustment. Instead, the new estimate is incorporated into the accounting records *prospectively beginning in the period of the change*. In addition to including the revised amounts in the financial statements, a company discloses the effect of the change on its income from continuing operations, net income, and the related earnings per share amounts of the current period in the notes to its financial statements. This disclosure is not required for estimates made each period in the ordinary course of accounting for items such as uncollectible accounts or inventory obsolescence, unless the change is material.

Example: Change in Estimate

Harris Company owns an asset with an original cost of $100,000, an estimated life of 20 years, and an estimated residual value of zero. Harris uses the straight-line method of depreciation. Straight-line depreciation expense of $5,000 has been recorded each year, so the asset's book value at the end of 8 years is $60,000 [$100,000 − (8 × $5,000)]. At the beginning of the ninth year of the asset's life, Harris changes the estimate of the asset's service life to a total of 23 years, so that 15 years now remain. Harris also revises its estimate of the asset's residual value to $7,500. Harris calculates a revised periodic depreciation expense based on the current book value, the estimated residual value, and the new estimated remaining service life as follows:

$$\text{Depreciation Expense} = \frac{(\$60,000 - \$7,500)}{15 \text{ years}} = \underline{\underline{\$3500}}$$

Therefore, Harris records depreciation expense in current and future periods of $3,500 per year.

In addition, if the income tax rate is 30% and the company has 10,000 shares outstanding, the after-tax effect of such a change is an increase in income from continuing operations and net income (because of lower depreciation expense) of $1,050 [($5,000 − $3,500) × 0.70]. The effect on earnings per share is an increase of $0.105 per share ($1,050 ÷ 10,000). Harris discloses these amounts in the notes to its financial statements. ■

A Change in Principle Distinguished from a Change in an Estimate

Sometimes it is difficult for a company to distinguish between a change in an accounting principle and a change in an estimate. For example, a company may change from capitalizing and amortizing a cost to recording it as an expense when incurred because future benefits associated with the cost have become doubtful. The company adopted the new accounting method because of the change in estimated benefits, and therefore, the change in method is *inseparable* from the change in estimate. The company is required to account for such a change as a *change in estimate*. This is often referred to as a **change in accounting estimate effected by a change in accounting principle**.

An additional complexity arises with respect to the depreciation (as well as amortization or depletion) of the cost of an asset over its useful life. Remember that the selection

---

[8] FASB ASC 250-10-45: Accounting Changes and Error Corrections: Overall: Other Presentation Matters.

of a depreciation method should be based on systematic and rational criteria. When a company changes its depreciation method, the change should reflect a change in the estimated amount or timing of the future benefits to be received from the asset. Because the change in depreciation method is made to reflect changes in estimates of future benefits, it is not possible to separate the effects of the change in principle from the effects of the change in estimate. Therefore, **a change in the depreciation method is treated as a change in an estimate under GAAP.**[9]

Example: Change in Estimate Effected by a Change in Principle

At the beginning of 2015, Dowson Company purchased an asset for $20,000, which had an estimated life of 4 years and a zero residual value. Dowson was depreciating the asset using the sum-of-the-years'-digits method and decided to switch to the straight-line method at the beginning of 2017 because of a change in the estimated pattern of benefits the asset produces. Straight-line and sum-of-the-years'-digits methods produce the annual depreciation expense amounts (ignoring taxes) shown in **Example 22.2**.

EXAMPLE 22.2 Effect of Alternative Depreciation Methods

	Method	
Year	Sum-of-the-Years'-Digits	Straight-Line
2015	$ 8,000	$ 5,000
2016	6,000	5,000
2017	4,000	5,000
2018	2,000	5,000
	$20,000	$20,000

Dowson depreciates the book value of the asset at the beginning of 2017 over the remaining life of the asset. In this case, under the sum-of-the-years'-digits method, the asset has a book value at the beginning of 2017 of $6,000 ($20,000 − $8,000 − $6,000) which is depreciated by the straight-line method over the remaining life of 2 years. Therefore, depreciation expense is $3,000 per year ($6,000 ÷ 2 years) for 2017 and 2018. Because Dowson accounts for the change prospectively, the only effect in the year of the change (2017) is that Dowson reports $3,000 of depreciation expense instead of the $4,000 that it would have reported under the sum-of-the-years'-digits method. No change is made in the financial statements for years 2015 and 2016. Dowson is also required to disclose the effect of the change on its income from continuing operations, net income, and the related earnings per share amounts of the current period in the notes to its financial statements.

GOT IT?

22-9 Define a *change in estimate*. What is the proper accounting for a change in estimate?

22-10 What distinguishes a change in an accounting principle from a change in an estimate? What is the proper accounting if the two changes cannot be distinguished from each other?

22-11 How is a change in depreciation method accounted for? Why?

[9] Ibid.

HOW DO WE ACCOUNT FOR A CHANGE IN A REPORTING ENTITY?

The third type of change defined by GAAP is a change in a reporting entity which results in financial statements that, in effect, are those of a different reporting entity. A change in an accounting entity is limited mainly to presenting consolidated or combined financial statements in place of the statements of individual companies, changing specific subsidiaries that make up the group of companies for which consolidated financial statements are presented, or changing the companies included in combined financial statements.[10]

A company accounts for a change in reporting entity as a retrospective adjustment so that all the financial statements it presents are for the same entity.[11] In addition, a company includes in the notes to its financial statements of the period in which it makes the change a description of the change as well as the reason for it, and the effect of the change on net income, other comprehensive income, and related earnings per share amounts for all periods presented. However, financial statements of later periods need not repeat these disclosures. Additional discussion of accounting for a change in reporting entity is included in advanced accounting textbooks.

LEARNING OBJECTIVE 22.4
Identify a change in a reporting entity.

GOT IT?

22-12 Describe a *change in a reporting entity*. How does a company account for such changes?

HOW DO WE ACCOUNT FOR A CORRECTION OF AN ERROR?

Anyone can make an error. Examples include the use of an accounting principle that is not generally accepted or an estimate that does not fully consider the information available; mathematical miscalculations, such as the incorrect computation of inventory; logical errors, such as the omission of the residual value in the calculation of straight-line depreciation; or an oversight, such as the omission of a deferral or accrual (e.g., the failure to accrue warranty costs).

LEARNING OBJECTIVE 22.5
Account for a correction of an error.

What happens when a company makes a material error in the financial statements of a prior period that it does not discover until the current period? If a company makes a material error, it must correct the error as soon as it is discovered. The correction of an error is *not* an accounting change under GAAP. **A company accounts for the correction of a material error of a past period that it discovers in the current period as a prior period adjustment (prior period restatement).**

As noted in the chapter opening vignette, the number of restatements has decreased dramatically since 2006 and remains relatively low. However, the causes of

---

[10] FASB Codification Glossary.
[11] FASB ASC 250-10-45: Accounting Changes and Error Corrections: Overall: Other Presentation Matters.

restatements have remained largely the same. Some of the more common issues involved in restatements in 2013 included:

- revenue recognition
- expense recognition
- deferred, stock-based, or executive compensation
- liabilities, payables, reserves and accrual estimate failures
- debt, quasi-debt, and other equity issues
- accounts/loans receivable, investments, and cash
- cash flow statement classification errors
- tax expense, deferral and other issues
- inventory, vendor and/or cost of sales issues

While large restatements, such as **Fannie Mae**'s $6.3 billion restatement in 2004 and **American International Group**'s (**AIG**) $5.2 billion restatement in 2005, received considerable attention in the financial press, many restatements are much smaller in size and result from the growing complexity of transactions and simple misapplication of accounting principles. For example, in 2013, the average negative impact on net income of restatements was $3.2 million, the lowest in the last 7 years.[12]

A prior period adjustment requires a company to perform the following steps:

- *Step 1.* Compute the cumulative effect of the error on prior period financial statements. This represents the amounts that would have been in the financial statements if an error had not been made.
- *Step 2.* Prepare a journal entry to adjust the book values of those assets and liabilities (including income taxes) affected by the error. An offsetting adjustment is made to the beginning balance of Retained Earnings to report the cumulative effect of the error correction (net of taxes) for each period presented.
- *Step 3.* Adjust the financial statements of each prior period to reflect the specific effects of correcting the error. Each item in each financial statement that is affected by the error must be restated to the appropriate amount.
- *Step 4.* Disclose the following information:
  - a statement that the previously issued financial statements have been restated because of an error, along with a description of the nature of the error
  - the effect of the correction of the error on each financial statement line item and any per share amounts for each prior period presented
  - the cumulative effect of the change on retained earnings (or other appropriate component of equity) at the beginning of the earliest period presented

Therefore, the effect of a prior period restatement is very similar to a retrospective adjustment method required for changes in accounting principle.

Real Report 22.1 provides an illustration of the disclosure of a restatement made by **Barnes & Noble**.

22.1 DISCLOSURE OF RESTATEMENT — REAL REPORT

Barnes & Noble

Notes to Consolidated Financial Statements (in part)

2. Restatement of Prior Period Financial Statements (in part)
The Company has restated its previously reported consolidated financial statements for the years ended April 28, 2012 and April 30, 2011, including the opening stockholders' equity balance, in order to correct certain previously reported amounts.

(continued)

---

[12] *2013 Financial Restatements: A Thirteen Year Comparison*, Audit Analytics (April 2014).

In fiscal 2013, management determined that the Company had incorrectly overstated certain accruals for the periods prior to April 27, 2013, as a result of inadequate controls over its Distribution Center accrual reconciliation process. In accordance with ASC 250-10-S99-2, *Considering the Effects of Prior Year Misstatements when Quantifying Misstatements in Current Year Financial Statements* (ASC 250), the Company recorded an adjustment to decrease cost of sales by $6,700 ($4,027 after tax) and $8,460 ($5,084 after tax) to correctly present the statement of operations for fiscal 2012 and 2011, respectively. The Company also decreased accounts payable by $89,500 and $96,200 at April 30, 2011 and April 28, 2012, respectively; increased income taxes payable included in Accrued Liabilities in the consolidated Balance Sheets by $14,939 and $18,598 at April 30, 2011 and April 28, 2012, respectively; and increased retained earnings by $74,561 and $78,588, net of tax at April 30, 2011 and April 28, 2012, respectively.

In addition, in reviewing the Company's components of deferred income tax assets and liabilities, management determined that deferred income tax liability in the amount of $26,026, net, was related to a transaction in which gain was reported for both accounting and tax purposes prior to 2010. Accordingly, management concluded that this deferred income tax liability should be reversed. In accordance with ASC 250, the Company recorded an adjustment to decrease deferred tax liability and increase retained earnings by $26,026 at May 1, 2010. The cumulative effect of these adjustments increased previously reported retained earnings by $95,503 at May 1, 2010.

In fiscal 2013, management determined that the Company had not accrued a tenant allowance related to one of its properties in fiscal 2012. The Company recorded an adjustment to increase receivable, net and other long-term liabilities by $9,450 in fiscal 2012.

The following tables set forth the correction to each of the individual affected line items in the consolidated balance sheets as of April 30, 2011 and April 28, 2012 and the consolidated statement of operations for fiscal 2011 and 2012. The restated amounts presented below reflect the impact of these corrections, as well as adjustments of $52,072 and $47,026 related to the current portion of deferred rent and tenant allowances on the April 30, 2011 and April 28, 2012 balance sheet, respectively. The Company did not present tables for the adjustments within the consolidated cash flow statement since all of the adjustments were within the operating section of the consolidated cash flow statement. The above corrections and adjustments did not effect total cash flows from operating activities, financing activities or investing activities for any period presented. The Company did not present tables for the adjustments within the consolidated cash flow statement since all of the adjustments were within the operating section of the consolidated cash flow statement. The above corrections and adjustments did not effect total cash flows from operating activities, financing activities or investing activities for any period presented.

The financial information included in the accompanying financial statements and notes thereto reflect the affects of the corrections and other adjustments described in the preceding discussion and tables.

Balance Sheet Data:

(In thousands, except per share data)	As of April 28, 2012			
	As Previously Reported	Corrections	Other Adjustments	Restated
Liabilities and Shareholders' Equity				
Current liabilities:				
Accounts payable	$ 959,423	(96,200)	—	$ 863,223
Accrued liabilities	546,495	18,598	47,026	612,119
Gift card liabilities	321,362	—	—	321,362
Total current liabilities	1,827,280	(77,602)	47,026	1,796,704
Long-term debt	324,200	—	—	324,200
Deferred taxes	268,774	(26,026)	—	242,748
Other long-term liabilities	405,065	8,464	(47,026)	366,503

(continued)

Balance Sheet Data:	As of April 28, 2012			
(In thousands, except per share data)	As Previously Reported	Corrections	Other Adjustments	Restated
Redeemable Preferred Shares; $.001 par value; 5,000 shares authorized; 204 shares issued	192,273	—	—	192,273
Shareholders' equity:				
Common stock; $.001 par value; 300,000 shares authorized; 91,376 shares issued	91	—	—	91
Additional paid-in capital	1,340,909	—	—	1,340,909
Accumulated other comprehensive loss	(16,635)	—	—	(16,635)
Retained earnings	481,574	104,614	—	586,188
Treasury stock, at cost, 33,722 shares	(1,058,282)	—	—	(1,058,282)
Total Shareholders' equity	747,657	104,614	—	852,271
Commitments and contingencies	—	—	—	—
Total liabilities and shareholders' equity	$ 3,765,249	9,450	—	$ 3,774,699

Statement of Operations Data:	Fiscal 2011		
(In thousands, except per share data)	As Previously Reported	Corrections	Restated
Sales	$6,998,565	—	$6,998,565
Cost of sales and occupancy	5,205,712	(8,460)	5,197,252
Gross profit	1,792,853	8,460	1,801,313
Selling and administrative expenses	1,629,465	—	1,629,465
Depreciation and amortization	228,647	—	228,647
Operating income (loss)	(65,259)	8,460	(56,799)
Interest expense, net and amortization of deferred financing fees	(57,350)	—	(57,350)
Income (loss) before income taxes (benefit)	(122,609)	8,460	(114,149)
Income taxes (benefit)	(48,652)	3,376	(45,276)
Net income (loss)	(73,957)	5,084	(68,873)
Net loss attributable to noncontrolling interests	37	—	37
Net income (loss) attributable to Barnes & Noble, Inc.	$ (73,920)	5,084	$ (68,836)
Diluted income (loss) per common share			
Net income (loss) attributable to Barnes & Noble, Inc.	$ (1.31)	0.09	$ (1.22)

(continued)

Statement of Operations Data:		Fiscal 2012	
(In thousands, except per share data)	As Previously Reported	Corrections	Restated
Sales	$7,129,199	—	$7,129,199
Cost of sales and occupancy	5,218,383	(6,700)	5,211,683
Gross profit	1,910,816	6,700	1,917,516
Selling and administrative expenses	1,739,452	—	1,739,452
Depreciation and amortization	232,667	—	232,667
Operating income (loss)	(61,303)	6,700	(54,603)
Interest expense, net and amortization of deferred financing fees	(35,304)	—	(35,304)
Income (loss) before income taxes (benefit)	(96,607)	6,700	(89,907)
Income taxes (benefit)	(27,740)	2,673	(25,067)
Net income (loss)	$ (68,867)	4,027	$ (64,840)
Diluted income (loss) per common share			
Net income (loss)	$ (1.41)	0.07	$ (1.34)

Questions:

1. What were the errors that required Barnes & Noble to restate its financial statements?
2. What effect did these errors have on Barnes & Noble's 2011 and 2012 income statements and 2012 balance sheet?
3. What effect did these errors have on the statement of cash flows?

Suggested answers to these questions are found at the end of the chapter.

Error Analysis

Because errors happen in unpredictable and often illogical ways, it is difficult to generalize the kinds of errors that a company might make and the journal entries that may be required to correct them. Many errors are discovered automatically through proper use of the double-entry accounting system. Others are found by the company's internal or external auditors before being included in the financial statements. Obviously, if the error is found before financial statements are prepared, the company should reverse the erroneous entry and prepare the correct one. Other errors escape detection until after they are included in a company's issued financial statements. These errors, which are the focus of this section, can be categorized according to the effect they have on the financial statements.

Errors Affecting Only the Balance Sheet Some errors affect only the presentation of balance sheet accounts. For example, a company may include a note receivable as an account receivable or it may incorrectly record a journal entry (e.g., a company may have debited Accounts Receivable when it should have debited Cash). When this type of error is discovered, the company reclassifies the item to the proper account and restates any comparative financial statements presented.

Errors Affecting Only the Income Statement Errors that affect only income statement accounts usually result from the misclassification of items. For example, a company may include interest revenue with sales revenue. Errors of this kind require reclassification but do not affect the total amount reported as net income. If the error is discovered prior to the issuance of the financial statements, the company makes an entry to reclassify the item. However, if the error occurred in a prior period, the company does not make a correcting journal entry because the current year income statement accounts are correctly stated. (Remember that the prior year income statement accounts have been closed to Retained Earnings). Instead, it restates any comparative financial statements presented.

Errors Affecting Both the Income Statement and Balance Sheet

An error may affect both an income statement account and a balance sheet account, such as the failure to accrue a liability at the end of the period. These types of errors can be classified as *counterbalancing* or *noncounterbalancing*.

Counterbalancing errors are those that are automatically corrected in the next accounting period, even if they are not discovered.

Example Consider the financial statement impact if Pattinson Company fails to accrue $2,000 of interest. The error understates interest expense on the income statement and omits interest payable from the balance sheet. Therefore, this error, ignoring taxes, results in the following financial statement effects in the year of the error:

Revenues	Expenses	Net Income	Assets	Liabilities	Shareholders' Equity
Correct	Understated ($2,000)	Overstated $2,000	Correct	Understated ($2,000)	Overstated $2,000

In the next period, when the company pays the interest and records the entire payment as an expense, the following financial statement effects are observed:

Revenues	Expenses	Net Income	Assets	Liabilities	Shareholders' Equity
Correct	Overstated $2,000	Understated ($2,000)	Correct	Correct	Correct

The overstatement of interest expense causes net income to be understated in an amount equal to the overstatement in the first period. Therefore, the retained earnings balance is now correct and the interest payable is no longer understated. The errors have counterbalanced resulting in no balance sheet account errors at the end of the second period.

Whether or not a counterbalancing error requires a correcting journal entry depends on *when* the error is discovered. For example, if Pattinson discovers the error before it has counterbalanced, a journal entry to correct the error is required. If Pattinson discovers the error after it has counterbalanced, no correcting entry is necessary. However, **any financial statements presented for comparative purposes should always be restated**—even if a correcting journal entry is not required. This restatement is necessary to enhance the comparability of the financial information presented, which assists users in analyzing trends and other financial ratios.

Noncounterbalancing errors are those that are not offset in the next accounting period. Therefore, noncounterbalancing errors take more than two accounting periods to correct themselves.

Example Consider the financial statement impact if Stewart Company erroneously records the purchase of a long-lived productive asset costing $10,000 as supplies expense. If Stewart should have capitalized the asset in property, plant, and equipment and recorded $1,000 of depreciation expense, the effects of the error (ignoring taxes) on the company's financial statements of the period in which it made the error are as follows:

- Supplies expense is overstated by $10,000.
- Depreciation expense is understated by $1,000 ($10,000 ÷ 10).
- Net income is understated by $9,000.
- Retained earnings is understated by $9,000.
- Property, plant, and equipment is understated by $10,000.
- Accumulated depreciation is understated by $1,000.

The understatement of the asset and the depreciation expense continues until the end of the asset's life. At this point, the balance sheet accounts are correct for the first time since the error was made.

ETHICAL DILEMMA

As Coruscant Industries' controller, you've just finished an exhausting year and finally issued Coruscant's annual report. After being surprised by the disappointing net income a year earlier, the board of directors charged you with improving the company's fortunes. Reviewing the previous year's financial results, you determined that the primary reason for Coruscant's disappointing results was higher than expected cost of goods sold. Seeking to improve the efficiency of operations and lower cost of goods sold, you aggressively implemented several cost-containment measures to address this problem, which resulted in numerous complaints from the manufacturing supervisors. Despite these criticisms, the current annual report, which just met the analysts' projections of net income, should serve as validation that you successfully responded to the board of directors' challenges. As a reward for your efforts, you've decided to take a few days off to work on your golf game.

As you are preparing to leave the office, you receive an e-mail from Yvette, a first-year staff accountant whom you had asked to double-check the accuracy of the current year inventory count. Yvette informs you that, while the current year inventory records appear in order, she discovered an error in the beginning inventory records. It appears that you inadvertently transposed two numbers in the previous year's inventory balance, resulting in a material understatement of the previous year's ending inventory. She says that, since the current year inventory records are accurate, the error "self-corrected" and there is no need to adjust the current year financial statements. Do you agree with Yvette's assessment? What ethical considerations does this situation present?

Error Correction

The approach to correcting an error is difficult to generalize because of the variety of errors that may occur. While each error may be unique and must be examined carefully, the following steps provide a basic framework for the analysis and correction of an error:

- *Step 1.* Analyze the original erroneous journal entry and determine what accounts and/or amounts were recorded in error.
- *Step 2.* Determine the journal entry that should have been recorded.
- *Step 3.* Evaluate whether the error has caused additional errors in other accounts.[13]
- *Step 4.* Prepare the correcting entry (or entries). Any corrections of the revenues and expenses for prior years are recorded as adjustments to Retained Earnings.

Note that the correcting entry includes an adjustment to Retained Earnings because the prior years' revenue and expense accounts have been closed to the Retained Earnings account.

Although it is not possible to give examples of every type of error, the following examples illustrate some of the more common types of errors. In each situation, the facts must be carefully examined, with particular consideration given to the time periods involved, when the error was discovered, and the possibility of additional errors resulting from the initial error. In addition, remember that the cumulative effect of the error correction should be shown net of taxes. However, for simplicity, the correction of the errors in the subsequent examples ignores the potential impact on taxable income, income tax expense, and deferred income taxes. For these examples, assume all errors are material.

---

[13] For example, if a company incorrectly records the purchase of property, plant, and equipment as an expense, the error will directly affect the value recorded as a fixed asset. In addition, it will cause additional errors because no depreciation will be taken if no fixed asset is recorded.

INTERNATIONAL DIMENSION

ACCOUNTING CHANGES

Because of convergence efforts, IFRS are similar to U.S. GAAP. However, several differences still exist:

- While both IFRS and U.S. GAAP require errors to be corrected by restating previously issued financial statements, IFRS allow an impracticability exception to this requirement. If restatement is impracticable for all prior periods, the error can be corrected by restating the financial statements for the earliest period practicable (which may be the current period). This exception could result in the correction of an error in a period other than that in which it initially occurred. U.S. GAAP only allows an impracticability exception for changes in accounting principle.
- IFRS do not address when the indirect effects of a change in accounting principle should be reported nor the disclosures required. Under U.S. GAAP, indirect effects are accounted for in the current period. Therefore, differences in the accounting for indirect effects may exist.
- The disclosure requirements of IFRS for accounting changes and error corrections are considered less extensive than those required under U.S. GAAP.

Source: *IAS 8* (See Appendix C at the end of this book.)

Example: Omission of Unearned Revenue

In December 2016, Huggins Company received $10,000 as a prepayment for renting a building to another company for all of 2017. Huggins recorded this transaction by a debit to Cash and a credit to Rent Revenue. The erroneous entry and the entry that should have been made (*Steps 1* and *2*) are shown below:

Original (Erroneous) Entry			**Entry That Should Have Been Made**		
Cash	10,000		Cash	10,000	
Rent Revenue		10,000	Unearned Revenue		10,000

This error caused no additional errors in other accounts (*Step 3*). Finally, if Huggins discovers the overstatement of income in 2017, it corrects the error by making the following entry (*Step 4*):

Retained Earnings	10,000	
Rent Revenue		10,000

The correcting entry decreases Retained Earnings to correct the 2016 overstatement of income and recognizes Rent Revenue in the proper year. Alternatively, Huggins could have credited Unearned Revenue and made a subsequent adjusting journal entry to reduce unearned revenue and recognize rent revenue.

If Huggins discovers the error in 2018, it does not make a correcting entry because the amount has counterbalanced. However, the 2016 and 2017 financial statements would be restated as discussed earlier.

Example: Failure to Accrue Revenue

On December 31, 2016, Huggins failed to accrue interest revenue of $500 that it had earned but not received on an outstanding note receivable. The erroneous entry and the entry that should have been made (*Steps 1* and *2*) are shown below:

Original (Erroneous) Entry
No entry made

Entry That Should Have Been Made
Interest Receivable   500
    Interest Revenue   500

This error caused no additional errors in other accounts (*Step 3*). If Huggins discovers the understatement of income in 2017, it makes the following entry (*Step 4*):

Interest Revenue   500
    Retained Earnings   500

This correcting entry increases Retained Earnings to correct the understatement of income in 2016. In addition, assuming that Huggins increased interest revenue when it received cash in 2017, the entry reduces interest revenue to correct the overstatement of interest revenue in 2017. If the error was discovered prior to the receipt of cash related to interest, Huggins would debit Interest Receivable.

If Huggins discovers the error in 2018, it does not make a correcting entry because the amount has counterbalanced. However, the 2016 and 2017 financial statements would be restated as discussed earlier. ■

Example: Omission of Prepaid Expense

In December 2016, Huggins paid $1,000 for insurance coverage for the year 2017 and 2018. It recorded the original entry as a debit to Insurance Expense and a credit to Cash and did not record a year-end adjustment. The erroneous entry and the entry that should have been made (*Steps 1* and *2*) are shown below:

Original (Erroneous) Entry
Insurance Expense   1,000
    Cash   1,000

Entry That Should Have Been Made
Prepaid Insurance   1,000
    Cash   1,000

This error caused no additional errors in other accounts (*Step 3*). If Huggins discovers the understatement of income at the end of 2017, it makes the following entry (*Step 4*):

Insurance Expense   500
Prepaid Insurance   500
    Retained Earnings   1,000

This correcting entry increases Retained Earnings to correct the understatement of income in 2016. In addition, it recognizes $500 of Insurance Expense in 2017 and $500 of Prepaid Insurance which will be used in 2018.

If Huggins discovered the error in 2018, the correcting entry is:

Insurance Expense   500
    Retained Earnings   500

In this situation, $500 of the error has counterbalanced, leaving only $500 to be corrected. Once again, Huggins restates the 2016 and 2017 financial statements if it presents them for comparative purposes. ■

Example: Error in Ending Inventory

At December 31, 2016, Huggins, which uses a periodic inventory system, recorded its ending inventory at $50,000 based on a physical count. During 2017, it discovered that the correct inventory value should have been $55,000 because it made an error in the inventory count. Because it understated the ending inventory for 2016 by $5,000, it overstated cost of goods sold for 2016, and understated income. Notice that there is no journal entry to analyze (*Steps 1* and *2*) for this error. This error caused no additional errors in other accounts (*Step 3*). If Huggins discovers the understatement of income in 2017, it makes the following entry (*Step 4*):

Inventory	5,000	
Retained Earnings		5,000

This correcting entry increases Retained Earnings and Inventory to correct the error that occurred in 2016.

If Huggins discovers the error in 2018, it does not make a correcting entry because the amount has counterbalanced. However, the 2016 and 2017 financial statements would be restated because the error in the inventory affects cost of goods sold in both years. ■

Example: Error in Purchases of Inventory

During December 2016, Huggins made a purchase of inventory on credit that it had not paid at year's end. It recorded this transaction incorrectly at $17,000 although the invoice price of the inventory was $27,000. The erroneous entry and the entry that should have been made (*Steps 1* and *2*) are shown below:

Original (Erroneous) Entry			Entry That Should Have Been Made		
Purchases	17,000		Purchases	27,000	
Accounts Payable		17,000	Accounts Payable		27,000

The understatement of Purchases caused an understatement of Cost of Goods Sold in 2016 (assuming that Huggins recorded the ending inventory correctly) and an overstatement of income. This error caused no additional errors in other accounts (*Step 3*). If Huggins discovers the overstatement of income at the end of 2017, it makes the following entry (*Step 4*):

Retained Earnings	10,000	
Accounts Payable		10,000

This correcting entry decreases Retained Earnings to correct the overstatement of income in 2016. In addition, it correctly states Huggins's liability to its creditor.

Because of the creditor's demand for payment, it is difficult to conceive of such an error remaining undetected until 2018. However, if that did happen, Huggins would make the entry shown above. Because the ending inventory was correct, the error was not counterbalanced, and Huggins has overstated its income for 2016 and retained earnings until it makes the correction. ■

Example: Failure to Accrue Estimated Bad Debts

Huggins, which uses the aging method to estimate bad debts, failed to accrue an allowance for doubtful accounts of $7,000 in its 2016 financial statements. The erroneous entry and the entry that should have been made (*Steps 1* and *2*) are shown below:

Original (Erroneous) Entry	Entry That Should Have Been Made		
No entry made	Bad Debt Expense	7,000	
	Allowance for Doubtful Accounts		7,000

The result of this error was the understatement of bad debt expense and an overstatement of income by $7,000. This error caused no additional errors in other accounts (*Step 3*). If Huggins discovers the understatement of income in 2017, it makes the following entry (*Step 4*):

Retained Earnings	7,000	
Allowance for Doubtful Accounts		7,000

This correcting entry decreases Retained Earnings to correct the overstatement of income in 2016. In addition, the increase in the Allowance for Doubtful accounts corrects the overstatement of net accounts receivable. Alternatively, if Huggins discovers the error at the end of 2017 after it makes its estimate of doubtful accounts, it has overstated the bad debt expense for 2017 because part of the charge relates to the 2016 error. Therefore, the correcting entry would be:

Retained Earnings	7,000	
Bad Debt Expense		7,000

Example 22.3 shows a schedule that summarizes the effects of Huggins's multiple errors on its income before income taxes for the years affected. The schedule includes each of the errors. The net effect of the errors is to reduce Huggins's pretax income for 2016 by $20,500, increase pretax income for 2017 by $4,000, reduce assets by $6,500, and increase liabilities by $10,000 on its 2017 balance sheet. If the income tax rate is 30% and the correction of each of these errors affects taxable income, the 2016 errors enable the company to obtain a tax refund of $6,150 (30% × $20,500). Therefore, Huggins would make the following entry:

Income Tax Refund Receivable	6,150	
Retained Earnings		6,150

EXAMPLE 22.3

Summary of Corrections of Errors Discovered in 2017

Error	Effect of Correction on Income 2016	Effect of Correction on Income 2017	Increases on Balance Sheet December 31, 2017
Omission of unearned revenue	$(10,000)	$10,000	
Failure to accrue interest revenue	500	(500)	
Omission of prepaid expense (2-year insurance policy)	1,000	(500)	Prepaid insurance $500
Error in ending inventory	5,000	(5,000)	
Error in purchases	(10,000)		Accounts payable $10,000
Failure to accrue estimated bad debts	(7,000)		Allowance for doubtful accounts $7,000
Total pretax effect	$(20,500)	$ 4,000	
Less: Income tax effect	6,150		
After-tax effect	$(14,350)		

GOT IT?

22-13 How does a company report an error of a prior period that it discovers in the current period?

22-14 Describe two errors that affect only a company's balance sheet.

22-15 Describe two errors that affect only a company's income statement.

22-16 What is a *counterbalancing error?* Describe two errors that are counterbalanced in the following period.

22-17 What is a *noncounterbalancing error?* Describe two errors that are not counterbalanced in the following period.

22-18 Why does a company correct errors even after they have counterbalanced?

22-19 How does the accounting for an indirect effect of a change in accounting principle differ between IFRS and U.S. GAAP?

22-20 If a company that uses IFRS discovers an error but determines that it is impracticable to restate its financial statements for all prior periods, what alternatives does IFRS allow? How does this compare with U.S. GAAP?

REVIEW CENTER

At the beginning of the chapter, we discussed how the dynamic and changing business environment may require accounting changes. In response to these changes, accounting recognition and disclosure rules are designed to enhance comparability and ensure that financial statements provide relevant information that faithfully represents the company's financial position and economic performance. We also identified several objectives you would accomplish after reading the chapter. The objectives are listed below and followed by a brief summary of the key points.

LEARNING OBJECTIVE 22.1
Identify the types of accounting changes and explain the methods of reporting each type of change.

KEY TAKEAWAYS

- GAAP defines three types of accounting changes:
  - Change in an accounting principle—A change from one generally accepted accounting principle to another generally accepted accounting principle, including a change in the method of applying an accounting principle
  - Change in an accounting estimate—A revision of an estimate used in the accounting process due to new or additional information or experience
  - Change in a reporting entity—A change in the type of entity being reported
- In addition, another category that requires adjustment, but is not considered an accounting change, is errors.
- There are two possible methods for a company to report an accounting change:
  - Retrospective adjustment method—The current period's financial statements, along with any other financial statements presented, are revised as if the newly adopted principle had always been used.
  - Prospective method—An accounting change is accounted for in current and future periods.

KEY TERMS

changes in a reporting entity, p. 22-3
changes in accounting estimate, p. 22-3
changes in accounting principle, p. 22-3
errors, p. 22-3
prospective method, p. 22-3
retrospective adjustment method, p. 22-3

LEARNING OBJECTIVE 22.2
Account for a change in accounting principle.

KEY TAKEAWAYS

- A company accounts for a change in accounting principle by the retrospective application of the new accounting principle to all prior periods as follows:
  - *Step 1.* Compute the cumulative effect of the change to the new accounting principle as of the beginning of the first period presented.
  - *Step 2.* Prepare a journal entry to adjust the book values of those assets and liabilities (including income taxes) that are affected by the change so that their balances reflect the amounts that would have existed under the newly adopted accounting principle. An offsetting adjustment is made to the beginning balance of Retained Earnings for the cumulative effect of the change (net of taxes).
  - *Step 3.* Adjust the financial statements of each prior period to reflect the specific effects of applying the new accounting principle.
  - *Step 4.* Disclose relevant information in the notes to the financial statements. A company should only recognize the direct effect (net of applicable income taxes) in determining the amount of the retrospective adjustment. If it is impracticable to apply the retrospective adjustment method, GAAP requires companies to apply the new accounting principle prospectively as of the earliest date practicable.

- When a change in accounting principle has both direct and indirect effects on a company's income, only the direct effect of the change in accounting principle is included in the retrospective adjustment. Any indirect effects incurred are included in the year in which the accounting change is made.
- In situations for which it is impracticable to retrospectively adjust the financial statements for a change in accounting principle, a company may apply the new accounting principle as if the change was made prospectively as of the earliest date practicable.

KEY TERMS

direct effect of a change in accounting principle, p. 22-11

indirect effect of a change in accounting principle, p. 22-11

KEY TAKEAWAYS

LEARNING OBJECTIVE 22.3
Account for a change in estimate.

- A change in an accounting estimate is accounted for prospectively in the period of the change, or the period of the change and future periods if the change affects both.
- If a change in accounting estimate cannot be distinguished from a change in accounting principle (e.g., a change in depreciation, depletion, or amortization method), it is considered a change in estimate effected by a change in accounting principle and is accounted for prospectively.

KEY TERM

change in accounting estimate effected by a change in accounting principle, p. 22-13

KEY TAKEAWAYS

LEARNING OBJECTIVE 22.4
Identify a change in a reporting entity.

- A change in a reporting entity occurs when:
  - a company presents consolidated or combined statements in place of statements of individual companies
  - there is a change in the specific subsidiaries that make up the group of companies for which consolidated financial statements are presented, or
  - the companies included in the combined financial statements change.
- A change in reporting entity is accounted for by retrospectively adjusting the financial statements of all prior periods presented.

KEY TAKEAWAYS

LEARNING OBJECTIVE 22.5
Account for a correction of an error.

- An error results from mathematical mistakes or mistakes in the application of GAAP.
- A company accounts for a material error of a past period that it discovers in the current period as a prior period adjustment (prior period restatement) as follows:
  - *Step 1.* Compute the cumulative effect of the error on prior period financial statements.
  - *Step 2.* Prepare a journal entry to adjust the book values of those assets and liabilities (including income taxes) that are affected by the error and make an offsetting adjustment to the beginning balance of Retained Earnings to report the cumulative effect of the error correction (net of taxes) for each period presented.
  - *Step 3.* Adjust the financial statements of each prior period to reflect the specific effects of correcting the error.
  - *Step 4.* Disclose relevant information in the notes to the financial statements.

- Errors can be classified as:
  - Affecting only the balance sheet—Reclassification of the balance sheet amounts affected and a restatement of comparative financial statements are required.
  - Affecting only the income statement—Reclassification of the income statement amounts affected is required if the error is discovered prior to the issuance of the financial statements. If the error occurred in a prior period, comparative financial statements must be restated.
  - Affecting both the income statement and the balance sheet—A correcting journal entry and restatement of the financial statements may be required.
- If an error is a counterbalancing error (e.g., the error automatically corrects in the next accounting period), a correcting journal entry is needed if the error is discovered during the second year. If the error is discovered after the second year, no correcting journal entry is needed, but the financial statements should be restated so that they are not misleading.
- If an error is a noncounterbalancing error (e.g., the error will not automatically correct in the next accounting period), a correcting journal entry is needed and any applicable financial statements must be restated.
- Every error should be carefully examined to determine how the transaction *was* recorded versus how it *should have been* recorded and then the appropriate journal entry to correct the error can be made.

KEY TERMS

counterbalancing errors, p. 22-20
noncounterbalancing errors, p. 22-20
prior period adjustment, p. 22-15
prior period restatement, p. 22-15

ANSWERS TO REAL REPORT QUESTIONS

Real Report 22.1 Answers Barnes & Noble—Disclosure of Restatement

1. Barnes & Noble made three errors. First, Barnes & Noble overstated accruals (accounts payable) related to its Distribution Center—an error caused by inadequate internal controls. Second, Barnes & Noble recorded a deferred tax liability related to a gain. However, the gain was reported for both accounting and tax purposes, and, therefore, no deferred tax liability should have been reported. Finally, Barnes & Noble failed to accrue a tenant allowance on one of its properties.
2. The errors caused an overstatement of Barnes & Noble's net loss of $5,084,000 for 2011 and $4,027,000 for 2012. In 2011, cost of sales was overstated by $8,460,000 and income tax expense was overstated by $3,376,000. In 2012, cost of sales was overstated by $6,700,000 and income tax expense was overstated by $2,673,000. On its 2012 balance sheet, the correction of these errors caused Barnes & Noble's retained earnings to increase by $104,614,000. In addition, its accounts receivable were understated by $9,450,000, its current liabilities were overstated by $30,576,000, its deferred taxes overstated by $26,026,000, and its other long-term liabilities overstated by $38,562,000.
3. These errors were all adjustments within the operating section of the statement of cash flows. Therefore, the total cash flows from operating activities, investing activities, and financing activities were not affected.

MULTIPLE-CHOICE (AICPA ADAPTED)

Select the best answer for each of the following.

M22-1
LO 22.2
The cumulative effect of an accounting change should generally be reported as an adjustment to the beginning balance of retained earnings in the period in which the change is made for a:

	Change in Accounting Principle	Change in Accounting Estimate
a.	Yes	Yes
b.	No	Yes
c.	Yes	No
d.	No	No

M22-2
LO 22.2
When a change in accounting principle is made during the year, the cumulative effect on retained earnings is determined:

a. during the year using the weighted average method
b. as of the date of the change
c. as of the beginning of the year in which the change is made
d. as of the end of the year in which the change is made

M22-3
LO 22.2
On January 1, 2016, Belmont Company changed its inventory cost flow method to the FIFO method from the LIFO method. Belmont can justify the change which was made for both financial statement and income tax reporting purposes. Belmont's inventories were $4,000,000 on the LIFO basis at December 31, 2015. Supplementary records maintained by Belmont showed that the inventories would have totaled $4,800,000 at December 31, 2015, on the FIFO basis. Ignoring income taxes, the adjustment for the effect of changing to the FIFO method from the LIFO method should be reported by Belmont as an:

a. $800,000 adjustment to cost of goods sold on the 2016 income statement
b. $800,000 increase to the 2016 beginning balance of retained earnings
c. $800,000 gain on the 2016 income statement
d. $800,000 decrease to the 2016 beginning balance of retained earnings

M22-4
LO 22.3
A change in the expected service life of an asset arising because additional information has been obtained is:

a. an accounting change that should be reported by restating the financial statements of all prior periods represented

b. an accounting change that should be reported in the period of change and future periods if the change affects both
c. a correction of an error
d. not an accounting change

M22-5
LO 22.3
During 2016, White Company determined that machinery previously depreciated over a 7-year life had a total estimated useful life of only 5 years. An accounting change was made in 2016 to reflect the change in estimate. If the change had been made in 2015, accumulated depreciation at December 31, 2015, would have been $1,600,000 instead of $1,200,000. As a result of this change, the 2016 depreciation expense was $100,000 greater than it would have been if no change were made. The income tax rate was 30% in both years. What is the proper amount of the adjustment to White's January 1, 2016, balance of retained earnings?

a. $0
b. $100,000
c. $280,000
d. $400,000

M22-6
LO 22.3
Generally, how should a change in accounting estimate that is affected by a change in accounting principle be reported?

	Prospective Method	Retrospective Adjustment Method
a.	No	No
b.	Yes	Yes
c.	No	Yes
d.	Yes	No

M22-7
LO 22.3
On January 2, 2014, Garr Company acquired machinery at a cost of $320,000. This machinery was being depreciated by the double-declining-balance method over an estimated useful life of 8 years, with no residual value. At the beginning of 2016, Garr changed to the straight-line method of depreciation. Ignoring income tax considerations, the required adjustment to the 2016 beginning balance of retained earnings is:

a. $0
b. $60,000
c. $65,000
d. $140,000

M22-8
LO 22.4
A company has included in its consolidated financial statements this year a subsidiary acquired several years ago that was appropriately excluded from consolidation last year. This results in:

a. an accounting change that should be reported prospectively

b. an accounting change that should be reported by retrospectively restating the financial statements of all prior periods presented
c. neither an accounting change nor a correction of an error
d. a correction of an error

Use the following information for M22-9 and M22-10:

Shannon Corporation began operations on January 1, 2016. Financial statements for the years ended December 31, 2016 and 2017, contained the following errors:

	December 31	
	2016	2017
Ending inventory	$16,000 understated	$15,000 overstated
Insurance expense	$10,000 overstated	$10,000 understated
Prepaid insurance	$10,000 understated	—

In addition, on December 31, 2017, fully depreciated machinery was sold for $10,800 cash, but the sale was not recorded until 2018. There were no other errors during 2016 or 2017, and no corrections have been made for any of the errors.

M22-9 Refer to the information for Shannon Corporation above. Ignoring income taxes, what is the total effect of the errors on 2017 net income?
LO 22.5

a. net income understated by $1,800
b. net income overstated by $5,800
c. net income overstated by $11,000
d. net income overstated by $14,200

M22-10 Refer to the information for Shannon Corporation above. Ignoring income taxes, what is the total effect of the errors on the amount of working capital (current assets minus current liabilities) at December 31, 2017?
LO 22.5

a. working capital overstated by $4,200
b. working capital understated by $5,800
c. working capital understated by $6,000
d. working capital understated by $9,800

REVIEW EXERCISES

RE22-1 The two methods of reporting an accounting change are (a) retrospective adjustment and (b) prospectively.
LO 22.1 Indicate which method is used for the following changes:

1. change in reporting entity
2. change in accounting principle
3. change in accounting estimate

RE22-2 Heller Company began operations in 2016 and used the LIFO method to compute its $300,000 cost of goods sold
LO 22.2 for that year. At the beginning of 2017, Heller changed to the FIFO method. Heller determined that its cost of goods sold under FIFO would have been $250,000 in 2016. For 2017, Heller's cost of goods sold under FIFO was $360,000, while it would have been $410,000 under LIFO. Heller is subject to a 30% income tax rate. Compute the cumulative effect of the retrospective adjustment on prior year's income (net of taxes) that Heller would report on its retained earnings statement for 2017.

RE22-3 Refer to **RE22-2**. Assume the pretax cumulative effect adjustment is $50,000. Prepare the journal entry that Heller
LO 22.2 Company would make at the beginning of 2017 to record the cumulative effect of the change from LIFO to FIFO.

RE22-4 Refer to **RE22-2**. Assume Heller Company had sales revenue of $510,000 in 2016 and $650,000 in 2017. Prepare
LO 22.2 Heller's partial income statements (through gross profit) for 2016 and 2017.

RE22-5 Bloom Company had beginning unadjusted retained earnings of $400,000 in the current year. At the beginning of
LO 22.2 the current year, Bloom changed its inventory method from LIFO to FIFO, and the cumulative effect (net of taxes) of this change was $28,000. In addition, Bloom earned net income of $150,000 and paid dividends of $30,000 in the current year. Prepare Bloom's retained earnings statement for the current year.

RE22-6 Suppose that Blake Company's total pretax difference from a change to FIFO was $100,000 and the company pays
LO 22.2 a bonus of 5% of its income before income taxes and bonus to employees. If Blake pays an additional bonus based on the change in income, would it recognize any expense? If so, when and how much?

RE22-7
LO 22.3
Bliss Company owns an asset with an estimated life of 15 years and an estimated residual value of zero. Bliss uses the straight-line method of depreciation. At the beginning of the sixth year, the asset's book value is $200,000 and Bliss changes the estimate of the asset's life to 25 years, so that 20 years now remain in the asset's life. Explain how this change will be accounted for in Bliss's financial statements, and compute the current and future annual depreciation expense.

RE22-8
LO 22.5
At the end of 2016, Framber Company received $8,000 as a prepayment for renting a building to a tenant during 2017. The company erroneously recorded the transaction by debiting Cash and crediting Rent Revenue in 2016 instead of 2017. Upon discovery of this error in 2017, what correcting journal entry will Framber make? Ignore income taxes.

RE22-9
LO 22.5
At the end of 2016, Cortex Company failed to accrue interest revenue of $3,200 that it had earned but not received on an outstanding note receivable. Instead, Cortex increased interest revenue in 2017 when it received the cash. Upon discovery of this error in 2017, what correcting journal entry will Cortex make? Ignore income taxes.

RE22-10
LO 22.5
At the end of 2016, Jayrad Company paid $6,000 for insurance coverage for 2017. It recorded this by debiting Insurance Expense and crediting Cash, but failed to record a year-end adjustment. Upon discovery of this error at the end of 2017, what correcting journal entry will Jayrad Company make? Ignore income taxes.

RE22-11
LO 22.5
At the end of 2016, Manny Company recorded its ending inventory at $350,000 based on a physical count. During 2017, the company discovered the correct inventory value at the end of 2016 should have been $400,000 because it made a counting error. Upon discovery of this error in 2017, what correcting journal entry will Manny make? Ignore income taxes.

RE22-12
LO 22.5
Abrat Company failed to accrue an allowance for doubtful accounts of $13,500 in 2016. Upon discovery of this error in 2017 prior to making its estimate of doubtful accounts, what correcting journal entry should Abrat make? Ignore income taxes.

EXERCISES

E22-1
LO 22.1
Identification and Effects of Changes and Errors The following are independent events:
a. Changed from the LIFO to the FIFO inventory cost flow assumption.
b. Reduced remaining service life of machinery from 10 to 8 years.
c. Changed from an accelerated method to the straight-line method of depreciating assets.
d. Wrote-down inventories because of obsolescence.
e. Received damages won in a court suit instigated 5 years ago.
f. Discovered that costs were recorded as an expense in a previous period but should have been recorded as an item of property, plant, and equipment.
g. Wrote down property, plant, and equipment because of closure of inefficient plants.
h. Changed from the successful-efforts method to the full-cost accounting method for oil exploration costs.

Required:
1. Indicate what type of accounting change or error, if any, is represented by each of the preceding items and the method of accounting (retrospective adjustment, prospective, or prior period adjustment) for the item in the financial statements of the current year.
2. **Next Level** Indicate the effect on the financial statements of the item (e.g., which accounts or line items are affected and is the effect an increase or a decrease).

E22-2
LO 22.1
Identification and Effects of Changes and Errors The following are independent events:
a. Changed from the FIFO to the LIFO inventory cost flow assumption.
b. Wrote off patent due to the introduction of a competing product.
c. Changed accounting policy of not accruing interest on notes payable to accruing interest.
d. Increased allowance for uncollectible accounts from 2% to 4% of credit sales.
e. Changed from straight-line to double-declining-balance method.
f. Increased the rate used to compute warranty costs.
g. Purchased another company that requires the presentation of consolidated financial statements in place of unconsolidated financial statements.

(continued)

Required:
1. Indicate what type of accounting change or error, if any, is represented by each of the preceding items and the method of accounting (retrospective adjustment, prospective, or prior period adjustment) for the item in the financial statements of the current year.
2. **Next Level** Indicate the effect on the financial statements of the item (e.g., which accounts or line items are affected and can increases or decreases generally be expected).

E22-3 **Identification and Accounting for Changes and Errors** The following are independent events:
LO 22.1
LO 22.2
a. A partnership is preparing to become a corporation and sell stock to the public. At this time, it decides to switch from accelerated to straight-line depreciation.
b. A company has been debiting half its advertising costs to an intangible asset account and amortizing these costs over 3 years.
c. A company has been using accelerated depreciation. It now estimates that the pattern of benefits to be received in the future will be equal each period, so it decides to change to the straight-line depreciation method.
d. A company has been using straight-line depreciation for its property, plant, and equipment. It is now buying a new type of machine and elects to use accelerated depreciation on the new machine.
e. A company switches from capitalizing certain expenditures to expensing them due to the issuance of an Accounting Standards Update that makes capitalization of these expenditures no longer generally accepted.

Required:
Identify the correct accounting treatment for the changes (if any) related to the preceding events.

E22-4 **Change in Inventory Cost Flow Assumption** At the beginning of 2017, Brett Company decided to change from the FIFO to the average cost inventory cost flow assumption for financial reporting purposes. The following data are available in regard to its pretax operating income and cost of goods sold:
LO 22.2

SHOW ME HOW

Year	Reported Income Before Income Taxes	Excess of Average Cost of Goods Sold Over FIFO Cost of Goods Sold	Adjusted Income Before Income Taxes
Prior to 2016	$1,600,000	$130,000	$1,470,000
2016	600,000	50,000	550,000
2017	700,000		

The income tax rate is 30%, and the company received permission from the IRS to also make the change for income tax purposes. Brett has a simple capital structure, with 100,000 shares of common stock outstanding. Brett computed its reported income before income taxes in 2017 using the newly adopted inventory cost flow method. Brett's 2016 and 2017 revenues were $1,500,000 and $1,750,000, respectively. Its retained earnings balances at the beginning of 2016 and 2017 (unadjusted) were $1,120,000 and $1,540,000, respectively. Brett paid no dividends in any year.

Required:
1. Prepare the journal entry at the beginning of 2017 to reflect the change.
2. At the end of 2017, prepare comparative income statements for 2017 and 2016. Notes to the financial statements are not necessary.
3. At the end of 2017, prepare comparative retained earnings statements for 2017 and 2016.

E22-5 **Change in Inventory Method** Fava Company began operations in 2015 and used the LIFO inventory method for both financial reporting and income taxes. At the beginning of 2016, the anticipated cost trends in the industry had changed, so that it adopted the FIFO method for both financial reporting and income taxes. Fava reported revenues of $300,000 and $270,000 in 2016 and 2015, respectively. Fava reported expenses (excluding income tax expense) of $125,000 and $120,000 in 2016 and 2015, which included cost of goods sold of $55,000 and $45,000, respectively. An analysis indicates that the FIFO cost of goods sold would have been lower by $8,000 in 2015. The tax rate is 30%. Fava has a simple capital structure with 15,000 shares of common stock outstanding during 2015 and 2016. It paid no dividends in either year.
LO 22.2

Required:
1. Prepare the journal entry to reflect the change.
2. At the end of 2016, prepare the comparative income statements for 2016 and 2015. Notes to the financial statements are not necessary.
3. At the end of 2016, prepare the comparative retained earnings statements for 2016 and 2015.

E22-6 **Change in Inventory Cost Flow Assumption** Berg Company began operations on January 1, 2016, and uses
LO 22.2 the FIFO method in costing its raw materials inventory. During 2017, management is contemplating a change to
AICPA the LIFO method and is interested in determining what effect such a change will have on net income. Accordingly,
Adapted the following information has been developed:

	2016	2017
FIFO—ending inventory	$240,000	$270,000
LIFO—ending inventory	—	210,000
Income before income taxes (computed under the FIFO method)	120,000	170,000

Required:
What is the effect on income before income taxes in 2017 of a change to the LIFO method?

E22-7 **Change in Oil and Gas Accounting** Delta Oil Company uses the successful-efforts method to account for oil
LO 22.2 exploration costs. Delta started business in 2014 and prepared the following income statements:

	2014	2015
Revenue	$1,000,000	$3,000,000
Other expenses	400,000	1,300,000
Exploration expenses	120,000	238,000
Income before income taxes	$ 480,000	$1,462,000
Income tax expense (30%)	144,000	438,600
Net income	$ 336,000	$1,023,400
Earnings per share	$ 3.36	$ 10.23

The company choose to change to the full-cost method at the beginning of 2016. Under the full-cost method, Delta capitalizes all exploration costs of the Oil and Gas Properties asset account on its balance sheet. It determines the exploration and amortization expense amounts under the full-cost method to be as follows:

	2014	2015	2016
Exploration expense	$ 0	$ 0	$ 0
Amortization expense	8,000	18,200	42,000

In addition, Delta reported revenue of $9,000,000 and other expenses of $4,200,000 in 2016. With the 2016 financial statements, the company issues comparative statements for the previous 2 years.

Required:
1. Prepare the journal entry to reflect the change.
2. Prepare the comparative income statements and the comparative statements of retained earnings for 2016, 2015, and 2014. Notes to the financial statements are not necessary.
3. **Next Level** Discuss the advantages and disadvantages of accounting for a change in this manner.

E22-8 **Change in Inventory Method** In 2017, Frost Company, which began operations in 2015, decided to change
LO 22.2 from LIFO to FIFO because management believed that FIFO better represented the flow of their inventory. Management prepared the following analysis showing the effect of this change:

Ending Inventory	LIFO	FIFO	Cumulative Difference
12/31/2015	$240,000	$273,000	$33,000
12/31/2016	245,000	301,000	56,000
12/31/2017	256,000	328,000	72,000

Frost reported net income of $2,500,000, $2,400,000, and $2,100,000 in 2015, 2016, and 2017, respectively. The tax rate is 30%.

Required:
1. Prepare the journal entry necessary to record the change.
2. What amount of net income would Frost report in 2015, 2016, and 2017?
3. If Frost's employees received a bonus of 10% of income before deducting the bonus and income taxes in 2015 and 2016, what would be the effect on net income for 2015, 2016, and 2017?

E22-9 Changes in Depreciation Gundrum Company purchased equipment on January 1, 2012 for $850,000. The equipment was expected to have a useful life of 10 years and a salvage value of $30,000. Gundrum uses the straight-line method of depreciation. At the beginning of 2017, Gundrum determined the total estimated life of the equipment was 13 years and the residual value would be $10,000 at the end of that time.

LO 22.3

Required:
Prepare any entry needed in 2017 to account for this change.

E22-10 Changes in Warranty Costs Newton Company introduced a line of laptop computers in 2016 that carry a 1-year assurance-type warranty. Based on experience with other computers that it sells, Newton estimated warranty costs as 3% of net sales. Net sales of the laptop in 2016 were $5,000,0000, and Newton recorded warranty expense of $150,000. In 2017, based on the previous years' warranty costs, Newton revises its estimate of warranty costs to 1% of net sales. In 2017, Newton reported $8,000,000 in net sales of the laptop.

LO 22.3

Required:
1. Prepare any entry needed in 2017 to account for this change.
2. **Next Level** Discuss the advantages and disadvantages of accounting for a change in this manner.

E22-11 Changes and Corrections of Depreciation On January 1, 2011, Klinefelter Company purchased a building for $520,000. The building had an estimated life of 20 years and an estimated residual value of $20,000. The company has been depreciating the building using straight-line depreciation. At the beginning of 2017, the following *independent* situations occur:

LO 22.3
LO 22.5

a. The company estimates that the building has a remaining life of 10 years (for a total of 16 years).
b. The company changes to the sum-of-the-years'-digits method.
c. The company discovers that it had ignored the estimated residual value in the computation of the annual depreciation each year.

Required:
For each of the independent situations, prepare all journal entries related to the building for 2017. Ignore income taxes.

E22-12 Effects of Errors The following are independent errors made by a company that uses a periodic inventory system:

LO 22.5

a. failure to record a purchase of inventory on credit (however, inventory was properly counted at the end of the period)
b. expensing the purchase of a machine
c. failure to accrue wages
d. failure to record an allowance for uncollectibles
e. including collections in advance as revenue
f. including payments in advance as expenses
g. failure to accrue warranty costs
h. discount on a note payable issued for purchase of a machine is ignored
i. failure to record depreciation expense on assets purchased during the year

Required:
Next Level Indicate the effect of each of the preceding errors on the company's assets, liabilities, shareholders' equity, and net income in the year in which the error occurs. State whether the error causes an overstatement (+), an understatement (−), or no effect (NE).

E22-13 Journal Entries to Correct Errors The following are independent errors made by a company that uses the periodic inventory system:

LO 22.5

a. Goods in transit, purchased on credit and shipped FOB destination, $10,000, were included in purchases but not in the physical count of ending inventory.
b. Purchase of a machine for $2,000 was expensed. The machine has a 4-year life, no residual value, and straight-line depreciation is used.
c. Wages payable of $2,000 were not accrued.
d. Payment of next year's rent, $4,000, was recorded as rent expense.
e. Allowance for doubtful accounts of $5,000 was not recorded. The company normally uses the aging method.
f. Equipment with a book value of $70,000 and a fair value of $100,000 was sold at the beginning of the year. A 2-year, non-interest-bearing note for $129,960 was received and recorded at its face value, and a gain of $59,960 was recognized. No interest revenue was recorded and 14% is a fair rate of interest.

Required:
1. **Next Level** Indicate the effect of each of the preceding errors on the company's assets, liabilities, shareholders' equity, and net income in the year in which the error occurs. State whether the error causes an overstatement (+), an understatement (−), or no effect (NE).
2. Prepare the correcting journal entry or entries required at the beginning of the year for each of the preceding errors, assuming the company discovers the error in the year after it was made. Ignore income taxes.

E22-14 **Journal Entries to Correct Errors** Refer to the information in **E22-13**.
LO 22.5
Required:
Prepare the correcting journal entries if the company discovers each error 2 years after it is made and it has closed the books for the second year. Ignore income taxes.

E22-15 **Correcting Journal Entries for Errors** The following are independent errors:
LO 22.5
a. In January 2016, repair costs of $9,000 were debited to the Machinery account. At the beginning of 2016, the book value of the machinery was $100,000. No residual value is expected, the remaining estimated life is 10 years, and straight-line depreciation is used.
b. All purchases of materials for construction contracts still in progress have been immediately expensed. It is discovered that the use of these materials was $10,000 during 2015 and $12,000 during 2016.
c. Depreciation on manufacturing equipment has been excluded from manufacturing costs and treated as a period expense. During 2016, $40,000 of depreciation was accounted for in that manner. Production was 15,000 units during 2016, of which 3,000 remained in inventory at the end of the year. Assume there was no inventory at the beginning of 2016.

Required:
Prepare journal entries for the preceding errors discovered during 2017. Ignore income taxes.

E22-16 **Omission of Accruals and Prepayments** Dudley Company failed to recognize the following accruals. It also
LO 22.5 recorded the prepaid expenses and unearned revenues as expenses and revenues, respectively, in the following year when paid or collected.

	2015	2016	2017
Prepaid expenses	$500	$ 900	$1,100
Accrued expenses	800	700	950
Revenue received in advance	300	400	1,300
Revenue earned but not received	600	1,000	1,200

The reported pretax income was $20,000 in 2015, $25,000 in 2016, and $23,000 in 2017.

Required:
1. Compute the correct pretax income for 2015, 2016, and 2017.
2. Prepare the journal entries necessary in 2017 if the errors are discovered at the end of that year. Ignore income taxes.
3. Prepare the journal entries necessary in 2018 if the errors are discovered at the end of that year. Ignore income taxes.

PROBLEMS

P22-1 **Identification and Effects of Changes and Errors** On January 2, 2016, Quo Inc. hired Reed as its controller.
LO 22.1 During the year, Reed, working closely with Quo's president and outside accountants, made changes in accounting
AICPA policies, corrected several errors dating from 2015 and before, and instituted new accounting policies. Quo's 2016
Adapted financial statements will be presented in comparative form with its 2015 financial statements. Items a through i represent Quo's transactions.

a. Quo manufactures heavy equipment to customer specifications on a contract basis. Due to the issuance of a new Accounting Standard Update, it switched the accounting method for these long-term contracts because the former method is no longer acceptable.

(continued)

b. As a result of a production breakthrough, Quo determined that manufacturing equipment previously depreciated over 15 years should be depreciated over 20 years.

c. The equipment that Quo manufactures is sold with a 5-year warranty. Because of a production breakthrough, Quo reduced its computation of warranty costs from 3% of sales to 1% of sales.

d. Quo changed from LIFO to FIFO to account for its finished goods inventory.

e. Quo sells extended service contracts on its products. Because related services are performed over several years, in 2016 Quo changed from the cash method to the accrual method of recognizing income from these service contracts.

f. During 2016, Quo determined that an insurance premium paid and entirely expensed in 2015 was for the period January 1, 2015, through January 1, 2017.

g. Quo changed its method of depreciating office equipment from an accelerated method to the straight-line method to more closely reflect the pattern of benefits.

h. Quo instituted a pension plan for all employees in 2016 and adopted GAAP. Quo had not previously had a pension plan.

i. During 2016, Quo increased its investment in Worth Inc. from a 10% interest, purchased in 2015, to 60%. As a result of its increased investment, Quo changed its method of accounting for investment in subsidiary from the fair value method to the consolidation method.

Required:
1. Indicate how Quo should classify each transaction.
2. Indicate the proper accounting treatment (retrospective adjustment, prior period adjustment, prospective) for each transaction.

P22-2 **Changes in Inventory Cost Flow Assumption** At the beginning of 2017, Flynne Company decided to change
LO 22.2 from the LIFO to the FIFO inventory cost flow assumption. The following data are available:

Year	Reported Income Before Income Taxes	Excess of LIFO Cost of Goods Sold Over FIFO Cost of Goods Sold	Adjusted Income Before Income Taxes
Prior to 2016	$240,000	$42,000	$282,000
2016	80,000	18,000	98,000
2017	70,000	16,000	

The tax rate is 30%. Flynne has a simple capital structure and 10,000 shares of common stock outstanding. Assume that the balance in retained earnings is the sum of the company's reported income amounts (net of tax) and that the reported income before income taxes in 2017 uses the newly adopted method. Flynne's revenues for 2016 and 2017 were $225,000 and $230,000, respectively. Flynne's operating expenses (other than cost of goods sold) for 2016 and 2017 were $32,000 and $40,000, respectively.

Required:
1. Prepare the journal entry at the beginning of 2017 to reflect the change.
2. At the end of 2017, prepare comparative income statements for 2017 and 2016.
3. At the end of 2017, prepare comparative retained earnings statements for 2017 and 2016.
4. Prepare a note to the comparative financial statements that discusses the nature and reason for the change from LIFO to FIFO and discloses the effects of the change on the company's income statements for 2016 and 2017. (Ignore the effects on the balance sheet and statement of cash flows because there is insufficient information to calculate these changes.)
5. **Next Level** Explain how your answer to Requirement 2 would change if the employees received a bonus of 10% of income before deducting the bonus and income taxes and the company paid additional bonuses for prior years in 2017.

P22-3 **Change from FIFO to Average Cost** Koopman Company began operations on January 1, 2015, and uses the
LO 22.2 FIFO inventory method for financial reporting and the average cost inventory method for income taxes. At the beginning of 2017, Koopman decided to switch to the average cost inventory method for financial reporting. It had previously reported the following financial statement information for 2016:

Income Statement	2016	Retained Earnings Statement	2016
Revenues	$100,000	Beginning retained earnings	$ 15,000
Cost of goods sold	(60,000)	Add: Net income	10,500
Gross profit	$ 40,000		$ 25,500
Operating expenses	(25,000)	Less: Dividends	(6,000)
Income before income taxes	$ 15,000	Ending retained earnings	$ 19,500
Income tax expense	(4,500)		
Net income	$ 10,500		
Earnings per share	$ 1.05		

Balance Sheet (12/31/16)			
Cash	$ 9,000	Accounts payable	$ 3,000
Inventory	38,000	Income taxes payable	1,800
Other assets	64,100	Deferred tax liability	4,800
		Common stock, no par	82,000
		Retained earnings	19,500
	$111,100		$111,100

An analysis of the accounting records discloses the following cost of goods sold under the FIFO and average cost inventory methods:

	FIFO Cost of Goods Sold	Average Cost of Goods Sold
2015	$50,000	$57,000
2016	60,000	69,000
2017	70,000	80,000

There are no indirect effects of the change in inventory method. Revenues for 2017 total $130,000; operating expenses for 2017 total $30,000. Koopman is subject to a 30% income tax rate in all years; it pays the income taxes payable of a current year in the first quarter of the next year. Koopman had 10,000 shares of common stock outstanding during all years; it paid dividends of $1 per share in 2017. At the end of 2017, Koopman had cash of $10,000, inventory of $24,000, other assets of $70,800, accounts payable of $4,500, and income taxes payable of $6,000. It desires to show financial statements for the current year and previous year in its 2017 annual report.

Required:
1. Prepare the journal entry to reflect the change in methods at the beginning of 2017. Show supporting calculations.
2. Prepare the 2017 financial statements. Notes to the financial statements are not necessary. Show supporting calculations.

P22-4 **Change from LIFO to Average Cost** Schmidt Company began operations on January 1, 2015, and used the
LO 22.2 LIFO inventory method for both financial reporting and income taxes. However, at the beginning of 2017, Schmidt decided to switch to the average cost inventory method for financial and income tax reporting. It had previously reported the following financial statement information for 2016:

Income Statement	2016	Retained Earnings Statement	2016
Revenues	$128,000	Beginning retained earnings	$ 27,000
Cost of goods sold	(78,000)	Add: Net income	17,500
Gross profit	$ 50,000		$ 44,500
Operating expenses	(25,000)	Less: Dividends	(6,000)
Income before income taxes	$ 25,000	Ending retained earnings	$ 38,500
Income tax expense	(7,500)		
Net income	$ 17,500		
Earnings per share	$ 1.75		

Balance Sheet (12/31/16)			
Cash	$ 8,000	Accounts payable	$ 4,000
Inventory	42,000	Income taxes payable	7,500
Other assets	60,000	Common stock, no par	60,000
		Retained earnings	38,500
	$110,000		$110,000

(continued)

An analysis of the accounting records discloses the following cost of goods sold under the LIFO and average cost inventory methods:

	LIFO Cost of Goods Sold	Average Cost of Goods Sold
2015	$62,000	$56,000
2016	78,000	69,000
2017	90,000	80,000

There are no indirect effects of the change in inventory method. Revenues for 2017 total $130,000; operating expenses for 2017 total $30,000. Schmidt is subject to a 30% income tax rate in all years; it pays all income taxes payable in the next quarter. Assume that any deferred tax liability was paid in the subsequent year. Schmidt had 10,000 shares of common stock outstanding during all years; it paid dividends of $1 per share in 2017. At the end of 2017, Schmidt had cash of $12,000, inventory of $34,000, other assets of $76,000, income taxes payable of $6,000, and accounts payable of $3,000. It desires to show financial statements for the current year and previous year in its 2017 annual report.

Required:
1. Prepare the journal entry to reflect the change in method at the beginning of 2017. Show supporting calculations.
2. Prepare the 2017 financial statements. Notes to the financial statements are not necessary. Show supporting calculations.

P22-5
LO 22.2

Change in Accounting for Construction Contracts Since Goode Oil Company was formed in 2015, it has used the full-cost method for financial reporting and recorded all exploration costs in an asset account called Oil and Gas Properties. At the beginning of 2017, it changes to the successful-efforts method. Goode previously had reported pretax income of $2,200,000 and $2,000,000 in 2015 and 2016, respectively.

Analysis of the accounting records discloses that the company incurred the following exploration expenses based on the successful-efforts method:

	2015	2016
Exploration expenses	$550,000	$780,000

In 2017, Goode reported pretax income of $3,100,000 under the successful-efforts method. The tax rate is 30%. Goode has a simple capital structure with 100,000 shares of common stock outstanding. It paid no dividends.

Required:
1. Prepare the journal entry to reflect the change in method at the beginning of 2017.
2. If the company also presents the 2015 and 2016 financial statements for comparative purposes, prepare the income statement disclosures (starting with income before income taxes) and retained earnings disclosures that are required in 2017.
3. What items (if any) would be restated on the financial statements?

P22-6
LO 22.2
AICPA Adapted

Change in Accounting for Inventory Kraft Manufacturing Company manufactures two products: Mult and Tran. At December 31, 2016, Kraft used the FIFO inventory method. Effective January 1, 2017, Kraft changed to the LIFO inventory method. The cumulative effect of this change is not determinable, and, as a result, the ending inventory of 2016, for which the FIFO method was used, is also the beginning inventory for 2017 for the LIFO method. Any layers added during 2017 should be costed by reference to the first acquisitions of 2017, and any layers liquidated during 2017 should be considered a permanent liquidation.

The following information was available from Kraft's inventory records for the 2 most recent years:

	Mult		Tran	
	Units	Unit Cost	Units	Unit Cost
2016 purchases:				
January 7	5,000	$4.00	22,000	$2.00
April 17	12,000	4.50		
November 9	17,000	5.00	18,500	2.50
December 14	10,000	6.00		
2017 purchases:				
February 12	3,000	7.00	23,000	3.00
May 21	8,000	7.50		
October 15	20,000	8.00		
December 24			15,500	3.50
Units on hand:				
December 31, 2016	15,000		14,500	
December 31, 2017	16,000		13,000	

Required:
Compute the effect on income before income taxes for the year ended December 31, 2017, resulting from the change from the FIFO to the LIFO inventory method.

P22-7 **First Issuance of Financial Statements** Jackson Company has decided to issue common stock to the public in
LO 22.2 2017. This will be the first public sale, and therefore, the company will issue its first publicly available financial statements since it was formed in 2014. The financial statements that it has prepared for its own use follow:

Income Statements

	For Years Ended December 31,		
	2014	2015	2016
Sales	$100,000	$130,000	$180,000
Cost of goods sold	(35,000)	(45,000)	(65,000)
Gross profit	$ 65,000	$ 85,000	$115,000
Other expenses	(62,500)	(75,000)	(83,200)
Income before income taxes	$ 2,500	$ 10,000	$ 31,800
Income tax expense	(750)	(3,000)	(9,540)
Net income	$ 1,750	$ 7,000	$ 22,260

Balance Sheets

	December 31		
	2014	2015	2016
Cash	$ 5,500	$ 12,500	$ 9,960
Accounts receivable	30,000	50,000	63,000
Inventory	40,000	60,000	65,000
Equipment	100,000	100,000	140,000
Less: Accumulated depreciation	(20,000)	(52,000)	(79,200)
	$155,500	$170,500	$198,760
Current liabilities	$ 19,250	$ 27,250	$ 33,250
Notes payable	50,000	50,000	50,000
Common stock	84,500	84,500	84,500
Retained earnings	1,750	8,750	31,010
	$155,500	$170,500	$198,760

(continued)

These financial statements are audited for the first time at the beginning of 2017, and the following facts are discovered:

- The company has not made any allowance for noncollection of accounts receivable. An allowance of 1% of total sales is considered appropriate. Uncollectible accounts of $630 should have been written off in 2016.
- The notes payable are to officers of the company and have an interest rate of 12%. They were issued on January 1, 2014. No interest has been accrued or paid. (Assume simple interest and no compounding.)
- The company has been using MACRS over a 5-year life for both financial reporting and income tax purposes. It has been decided that the straight-line method should have been used for financial reporting, based on an economic life of 10 years and a zero residual value, with a full year's depreciation being recorded in the year of acquisition. No disposals of property, plant, and equipment have occurred.
- After adjustments, with the exception of depreciation, expenses deducted for financial accounting purposes are the same as those deducted for income tax purposes.
- The company is subject to a 30% income tax rate and pays its taxes at the end of each year.

Required:
1. Prepare the financial statements for 2014, 2015, and 2016 that the company would issue at the beginning of 2017.
2. **Next Level** Describe what method the company would use to account for each item if the financial statements for all 3 years had been publicly issued previously.

P22-8 **Changes and Corrections of Depreciation** At the beginning of 2017, Holden Company's controller asked you
LO 22.3 to prepare correcting entries for the following three situations:
LO 22.5
1. Machine X was purchased for $100,000 on January 1, 2012. Straight-line depreciation has been recorded for 5 years, and the Accumulated Depreciation account has a balance of $45,000. The estimated residual value remains at $10,000, but the service life is now estimated to be 1 year longer than originally estimated.
2. Machine Y was purchased for $40,000 on January 1, 2015. It had an estimated residual value of $4,000 and an estimated service life of 8 years. It has been depreciated under the sum-of-the-years'-digits method for 2 years. Now, the company has decided to change to the straight-line method.
3. Machine Z was purchased for $80,000 on January 1, 2016. Double-declining-balance depreciation has been recorded for 1 year. The estimated residual value is $8,000 and the estimated service life is 5 years. The computation of the depreciation erroneously included the estimated residual value.

Required:
Prepare any necessary correcting journal entries for each situation. Also prepare the journal entry for each situation to record the depreciation for 2017. Ignore income taxes.

P22-9 **Error Correction** At the end of 2017, while auditing Sandlin Company's books, *before* the books have been
LO 22.5 closed, you find the following items:

a. A building with a 30-year life (no residual value, depreciated using the straight-line method) was purchased on January 1, 2017, by issuing a $90,000 non-interest-bearing, 4-year note. The entry made to record the purchase was a debit to Building and a credit to Notes Payable for $90,000; 12% is a fair rate of interest on the note.
b. The inventory at the end of 2017 was found to be overstated by $15,000. At the same time, it was discovered that the inventory at the end of 2016 had been overstated by $35,000. The company uses the perpetual inventory system.
c. For the last 3 years, the company has failed to accrue salaries and wages. The correct amounts at the end of each year were: 2015, $12,000; 2016, $18,000; and 2017, $10,000.

Required:
1. Prepare journal entries to correct the errors. Ignore income taxes.
2. Assume, instead, that the company discovered the errors *after* it had closed the books. Prepare journal entries to correct the errors. Ignore income taxes.

P22-10 **Error Correction** At the beginning of 2017, Tanham Company discovered the following errors made in the
LO 22.5 preceding 2 years:

	2015	2016
Overstatement of ending inventory	$5,000	$2,000
Omission of wages payable	700	800
Omission of allowance for doubtful accounts	1,300	1,700
Prepayment of insurance recorded as expense	500	200

Reported net income was $27,000 in 2015 and $35,000 in 2016. The allowance for doubtful accounts had a zero balance at the beginning of 2015. No accounts were written off during 2015 or 2016. Ignore income taxes.

Required:
1. What is the correct net income for 2015 and 2016?
2. Prepare the adjusting journal entry in 2017 to correct the errors.

P22-11 **Error Correction** A review of Anderson Corporation's books indicates that the errors and omissions pertaining to the balance sheet accounts shown as follows had not been corrected during the applicable years.

LO 22.5

The net income per the books is: 2014, $10,000; 2015, $12,000; 2016, $15,000; and 2017, $20,000. No dividends were declared during these years and no adjustments were made to retained earnings. The Retained Earnings balance on December 31, 2017, is $50,000.

December 31	Ending Inventory Overvalued	Ending Inventory Undervalued	Omissions			
			Prepaid Expense	Unearned Revenues	Accrued Expense	Accrued Revenues
2014	$ —	$4,000	$600	$ —	$300	$ —
2015	3,000	—	—	500	—	700
2016	2,000	—	400	—	100	—
2017	—	1,000	900	200	350	800

Required:
Determine the correct net income for the years 2014, 2015, 2016, and 2017, and the adjusted balance sheet accounts as of December 31, 2017. Ignore possible income tax effects.

P22-12 **Error Correction** Cask Company's bookkeeper, who has maintained its accounting records since the company's formation in January 2014, has prepared the unaudited financial statements. In your examination of these statements at the end of 2016, you discover the following items:

LO 22.5

1. Sales taxes collected from customers have been included in the Sales account. The Sales Tax Expense account is debited when the sales taxes are remitted to the state in the month following the sale. All sales are subject to a 6% sales tax. Total sales (excluding sales tax) for the 3 years 2014 through 2016 were $200,000, $300,000, and $500,000, respectively. The Sales Tax Expense account balance for the 3 years was $10,000, $15,000, and $26,000, respectively.
2. An account payable of $15,000 for merchandise purchased in December 2014 was recorded in January 2015. The merchandise was not included in inventory at December 31, 2014. Cask uses a periodic inventory system.
3. Merchandise with a cost of $4,000 was included twice in the December 31, 2015, inventory. Cask uses a periodic inventory system.
4. The company has used the direct write-off method of accounting for bad debts. Accounts written off in the 3 years 2014 through 2016 were $2,000, $4,500, and $6,500, respectively. The appropriate balances of Allowance for Doubtful Accounts at the end of 2014 through 2016 are $5,000, $6,000, and $8,200, respectively.
5. On January 1, 2015, 12%, 10-year bonds with a face value of $600,000 were issued at 102. The premium was credited to Additional Paid-in Capital. The bonds pay interest on June 30 and December 31, and use of the straight-line amortization method is appropriate.
6. Travel advances to the sales personnel of $18,000 were included as selling expenses for 2015. The travel occurred in 2016.
7. Salaries payable at the end of each year have not been accrued. Appropriate amounts at the end of 2014 through 2016 are $10,000, $11,000, and $7,000, respectively.
8. Installation, freight, and testing costs of $25,000 on a machine purchased in January 2014 were expensed at that time. The machine has a life of 5 years and a residual value of $10,000.

Required:
Analyze the effects of the errors on income for the 2014, 2015, and 2016 ending balance sheet (ignore income taxes), according to the following format:

Explanation	Income 2014		Income 2015		Income 2016		Balance Sheet December 31, 2016		
	Amount		Amount		Amount		Amount		
	Debit	Credit	Debit	Credit	Debit	Credit	Debit	Credit	Account

P22-13 **Comprehensive** Gray Company's financial statements showed income before income taxes of $4,030,000 for the year ended December 31, 2017, and $3,330,000 for the year ended December 31, 2016. Additional information is as follows:

LO 22.1
LO 22.2
LO 22.3
LO 22.5
AICPA Adapted

- Capital expenditures were $2,800,000 in 2017 and $4,000,000 in 2016. Included in the 2017 capital expenditures is equipment purchased for $1,000,000 on January 1, 2017, with no salvage value. Gray used straight-line depreciation based on a 10-year estimated life in its financial statements. As a result of additional information now available, it is estimated that this equipment should have only an 8-year life.
- Gray made an error in its financial statements that should be regarded as material. A payment of $180,000 was made in January 2017 and charged to expense in 2017 for insurance premiums applicable to policies commencing and expiring in 2016. No liability had been recorded for this item at December 31, 2016.
- The allowance for doubtful accounts reflected in Gray's financial statements was $7,000 at December 31, 2017, and $97,000 at December 31, 2016. During 2017, $90,000 of uncollectible receivables were written off against the allowance for doubtful accounts. In 2016, the provision for doubtful accounts was based on a percentage of net sales. The 2017 provision has not yet been recorded. Net sales were $58,500,000 for the year ended December 31, 2017, and $49,230,000 for the year ended December 31, 2016. Based on the latest available facts, the 2017 provision for doubtful accounts is estimated to be 0.2% of net sales.
- A review of the estimated warranty liability at December 31, 2017, which is included in "other liabilities" in Gray's financial statements, has disclosed that this estimated liability should be increased $170,000.
- Gray has two large blast furnaces that it uses in its manufacturing process. These furnaces must be periodically relined. Furnace A was relined in January 2011 at a cost of $230,000 and in January 2016 at a cost of $280,000. Furnace B was relined for the first time in January 2017 at a cost of $300,000. In Gray's financial statements, these costs were expensed as incurred. Since a relining will last for 5 years, Gray's management feels it would be preferable to capitalize and depreciate the cost of the relining over the productive life of the relining. Gray has decided to make a change in accounting principle from expensing relining costs as incurred to capitalizing them and depreciating them over their productive life on a straight-line basis with a full year's depreciation in the year of relining. This change meets the requirements for a change in accounting principle under GAAP.

Required:
1. For the years ended December 31, 2017 and 2016, prepare a worksheet reconciling income before income taxes as given previously with income before income taxes as adjusted for the preceding additional information. Show supporting computations in good form. Ignore income taxes and deferred tax considerations in your answer. The worksheet should have the following format:

	Year Ended December 31	
	2017	2016
Income before income taxes, before adjustments	$4,030,000	$3,330,000
Adjustments		
Net adjustments		
Income before income taxes, after adjustments	$	$

2. As of January 1, 2017, compute the retrospective adjustment of retained earnings for the change in accounting principle from expensing to capitalizing relining costs. Ignore income taxes and deferred tax considerations in your answer.

P22-14 **Comprehensive** Ingalls Corporation is in the process of negotiating a loan for expansion purposes. The books and records have never been audited, and the bank has requested that an audit be performed. Ingalls has prepared the following comparative financial statements for the years ended December 31, 2017 and 2016:

LO 22.3
LO 22.5
AICPA Adapted

Balance Sheet		
	As of December 31,	
	2017	2016
Assets		
Current Assets:		
Cash	$ 163,000	$ 82,000
Accounts receivable	392,000	296,000
Allowance for doubtful accounts	(37,000)	(18,000)
Investment in available-for-sale securities	78,000	78,000

Balance Sheet

	As of December 31,	
	2017	2016
Inventory	207,000	202,000
Total current assets	$ 803,000	$ 640,000
Property, plant, and equipment:		
Equipment	$ 167,000	$ 169,500
Accumulated depreciation	(121,600)	(106,400)
Total property, plant, and equipment	$ 45,400	$ 63,100
Total Assets	$ 848,400	$ 703,100
Liabilities and Shareholders' Equity		
Liabilities:		
Accounts payable	$ 121,400	$ 196,100
Shareholders' equity:		
Common stock, par value $10, authorized 50,000 shares, issued and outstanding 20,000 shares	$ 260,000	$ 260,000
Retained earnings	467,000	247,000
Total shareholders' equity	$ 727,000	$ 507,000
Total Liabilities and Shareholders' Equity	$ 848,400	$ 703,100

Statement of Income

	For the Years Ended December 31,	
	2017	2016
Sales	$1,000,000	$ 900,000
Cost of sales	(430,000)	(395,000)
Gross profit	$ 570,000	$ 505,000
Operating expenses	$ 210,000	$ 205,000
Administrative expenses	140,000	105,000
	$ (350,000)	$(310,000)
Net income	$ 220,000	$ 195,000

During the course of the audit, the following additional facts were determined:

- An analysis of collections and losses on accounts receivable during the past 2 years indicates a drop in anticipated losses because of bad debts. After consultation with management, it was agreed that the loss experience rate on sales should be reduced from the recorded 2% to 1%, beginning with the year ended December 31, 2017.
- An analysis of the available-for-sale securities revealed that this portfolio consisted entirely of short-term investments in marketable securities that were acquired in 2016. The total market valuation for these investments as of the end of each year was as follows: December 31, 2016, $81,000; December 31, 2017, $62,000.
- The merchandise inventory at December 31, 2016, was overstated by $4,000, and the merchandise inventory at December 31, 2017, was overstated by $6,100.
- On January 2, 2016, equipment costing $12,000 (estimated useful life of 10 years and residual value of $1,000) was incorrectly charged to Operating Expenses. Ingalls records depreciation via the straight-line method. In 2017, fully depreciated equipment (with no residual value) that originally cost $17,500 was sold as scrap for $2,500. Ingalls credited the proceeds of $2,500 to Equipment.
- An analysis of 2016 operating expenses revealed that Ingalls charged to expense a 3-year insurance premium of $2,700 on January 15, 2016.

Required:
1. Prepare the journal entries to correct the books at December 31, 2017. The books for 2017 have not been closed. Ignore income taxes.
2. Prepare a schedule showing the computation of corrected net income for the years ended December 31, 2017 and 2016, assuming that any adjustments are to be reported on comparative statements for the 2 years. The first items on your schedule should be the net income for each year. Ignore income taxes. (Do not prepare financial statements.)

CASES

COMMUNICATION

C22-1 **Accounting Changes**
LO 22.1
LO 22.2　There are three types of accounting changes: changes
LO 22.3　in accounting principles, changes in accounting esti-
LO 22.4　mates, and changes in reporting entities.

Required:
Explain the differences and similarities between each of these types of changes, and explain the correct accounting for each. Include a discussion of the advantages and disadvantages of the required accounting method.

C22-2 **Accounting Changes**
LO 22.1
LO 22.2　The various types of accounting changes may sig-
LO 22.3　nificantly affect the presentation of a company's fi-
LO 22.4　nancial statements and also affect the trends shown
AICPA　on its comparative financial statements and histori-
Adapted　cal summaries.

Required:
1. Explain a change in accounting principle and how a company reports it in the period of the change.
2. Explain a change in accounting estimate and how a company reports it in the period of the change.
3. Explain a change in reporting entity and how a company reports it. Give an appropriate example of a change in reporting entity.

C22-3 **Accounting Changes**
LO 22.1
LO 22.2　Berkeley Company, a manufacturer of many dif-
LO 22.3　ferent products, changed its inventory method
LO 22.4　from FIFO to LIFO. The LIFO method was
AICPA　determined to be preferable.
Adapted
In addition, Berkeley changed the residual values used in computing depreciation for its office equipment. It made this change on January 1, 2016, because it obtained additional information.

On December 31, 2016, Berkeley changed the specific subsidiaries comprising the group of companies for which consolidated financial statements are presented.

Required:
1. What kind of accounting change is each of the preceding three situations? For each situation, indicate whether or not the company should show:
   a. retrospective application of a new accounting principle
   b. effects on the financial statements of the current and future periods
   c. restatement of the financial statements of all prior periods
2. Why does the company have to disclose a change in accounting principle?

CREATIVE AND CRITICAL THINKING

C22-4 **Transition Methods for a Change in**
LO 22.1 **Accounting Principle**
LO 22.2
When the FASB issues a new generally accepted accounting principle, it may require companies to apply the new principle prospectively, or to account for the change by the retrospective adjustment method.

Required:
Why do you think that the FASB requires one of two different transition methods when a company adopts a newly required accounting principle? Do you agree with the use of two alternative methods?

C22-5 **Accounting Changes**
LO 22.1
LO 22.3　It is important in accounting theory to be able to
LO 22.4　distinguish the types of accounting changes.
LO 22.5
Required:
AICPA
Adapted　1. If a public company desires to change from the sum-of-the-years'-digits depreciation method to the straight-line method for its fixed assets, what type of accounting change would this be? Discuss the permissibility of this change.
2. If a public company obtained additional information about the service lives of some of its fixed assets that showed that the service lives previously used should be shortened, what type of accounting change would this be? Include in your discussion how the change is reported in the year of the change and what disclosures are made in the financial statements or notes.
3. If a company discovers halfway through a building's life that it ignored the residual value of the building in computing the straight-line depreciation, what type of accounting change would this be? Include in your discussion how the change is reported in the year of the change, and what disclosures are made in the financial statements or notes.

4. Changing specific subsidiaries comprising the group of companies for which consolidated financial statements are presented is an example of what type of accounting change? What effect does it have on the consolidated income statements?

C22-6 **Ethics, Enron, Arthur Andersen, and Accounting Changes**

In 2001, **Enron Corporation** filed financial statements in which it did not consolidate various special purpose entities, thereby keeping large amounts of debt off its balance sheet. The company has since declared bankruptcy and admitted that it violated GAAP. Enron's auditor, **Arthur Andersen LLP**, issued an unqualified audit opinion stating that Enron had followed GAAP. Instead, Enron should have changed its accounting principles to conform to GAAP, and Andersen should not have issued an unqualified opinion.

The U.S. Department of Justice began an investigation of Enron and Arthur Andersen. Some employees of Arthur Andersen shredded certain documents related to the audit. As a result, the firm was found guilty of obstruction of justice and therefore was no longer able to perform audits. Only a few of the Arthur Andersen partners and employees were involved in the audit and even fewer in the shredding. However, thousands of Arthur Andersen employees lost their jobs.

Required:
From an ethical perspective, discuss whether the actions of the Department of Justice were fair with regard to the employees of Arthur Andersen.

C22-7 **Ethics and Accounting Changes and Errors**

You are auditing the financial records of a company and reviewing the property, plant, and equipment records. Included in the assets are two buildings and numerous machines in each building. One of the buildings is used to manufacture components of toys; the other is used for assembly and packing, using the manufactured components as well as others purchased from suppliers. You see that the company has changed from the straight-line to the double-declining-balance depreciation method at the beginning of the year. You also discover that a $90,000 repair was added to the cost of the building in the previous year. You decide to ask the CFO about these calculations, and she replies, "We decided to change the depreciation method because toys have such short lives and get obsolete so fast. You know how kids always want the latest fad. And that is partly why we are also going to recognize an asset impairment of $150,000 this year. And, as for that $90,000, those repairs should make the building last longer. But, anyway, the amount wasn't material to our depreciation calculations." As you walk back to your office, you recall from earlier in the audit that the company uses LIFO for its inventory and that income before income taxes has been around $1 million for each of the last several years.

Required:
From financial reporting and ethical perspectives, discuss the issues raised by this situation.

C22-8 **Analyzing Kellogg's Accounting Change Disclosures**

Obtain **Kellogg**'s 2012 annual report either using the "Investor Relations" portion of its website (do a web search for Kellogg's investor relations) or go to http://www.sec.gov and click "Search for company filings" under "Filings and Forms (EDGAR)."

Required:
1. Did Kellogg's report any changes in accounting principles between 2010 and 2012? If so, describe the reason for the change in principle and how Kellogg's accounted for the change?
2. What was the financial statement impact of the change on net income, assets, liabilities, and equity?
3. What types of estimates did Kellogg's discuss in its financial statements?

C22-9 **Analyzing LVMH's Accounting Change Disclosures**

Obtain **LVMH (Moet Hennessy – Louis Vuitton)**'s 2013 annual report using the "Investor Relations" portion of its website (do a web search for Moet Hennessy – Louis Vuitton investor relations).

Required:
1. Did LVMH report any changes in accounting principle between 2011 and 2013? If so, describe the reason for the change in principle and the how LVMH accounted for this change.
2. What is LVMH's policy regarding the use of estimates?

USING CODIFICATION

C22-10 Researching GAAP
AICPA Adapted

Sometimes a business entity may change its method of accounting for certain items. It may classify the change as a change in accounting principle, a change in accounting estimate, or a change in reporting entity. The following are three situations faced by Hyde Company relating to accounting changes.

Situation I
Hyde determined that the depreciable lives of its fixed assets are presently too long to fairly match the cost of the fixed assets with the revenue produced. Hyde decided at the beginning of the current year to reduce the depreciable lives of all of its existing fixed assets by 5 years.

Situation II
On December 31, 2015, Hyde owned 51% of Patten Company, at which time Hyde reported its investment using the cost method, owing to political uncertainties in the country in which Patten was located. On January 2, 2016, the management of Hyde was satisfied that the political uncertainties were resolved and the assets of the company were in no danger of nationalization. Accordingly, Hyde will prepare consolidated financial statements for Hyde and Patten for the year ended December 31, 2016.

Situation III
Hyde decides in January 2016 to adopt the straight-line method of depreciation for equipment. The straight-line method will be used for new acquisitions, as well as for previously acquired equipment for which depreciation had been provided on an accelerated basis.

Directions
For each of the preceding situations, research the related generally accepted accounting principles and prepare a short memo to the president that explains the following: type of accounting change; manner of reporting the change under current generally accepted accounting principles, including a discussion, where applicable, of how amounts are computed; effect of the change on the balance sheet and income statement; and note disclosures that would be necessary. Cite your references and applicable paragraph numbers.

STARBUCKS CORPORATION'S ANNUAL REPORT (EXCERPTS)

A-2	Form	Starbucks 10K Cover Page
A-2	Item 1	Business
A-7	Item 6	Selected Financial Data
A-9	Item 7	Management's Discussion and Analysis of Financial Condition and Results of Operations
A-20	Item 8	Financial Statements and Supplementary Data
A-26	Notes	Notes to Consolidated Financial Statements
A-54	Item 9	Controls and Procedures

Appendix A Starbucks Corporation's Annual Report (Excerpts)

UNITED STATES SECURITIES AND EXCHANGE COMMISSION
Washington, DC 20549
Form 10-K

☒ ANNUAL REPORT PURSUANT TO SECTION 13 OR 15(d) OF THE SECURITIES EXCHANGE ACT OF 1934
For the Fiscal Year Ended September 27, 2015
or
☐ TRANSITION REPORT PURSUANT TO SECTION 13 OR 15(d) OF THE SECURITIES EXCHANGE ACT OF 1934
For the transition period from   to   .
Commission File Number: 0-20322

Starbucks Corporation
(Exact Name of Registrant as Specified in its Charter)

Washington	91-1325671
(State of Incorporation)	*(IRS Employer ID)*

2401 Utah Avenue South, Seattle, Washington 98134
(206) 447-1575
(Address of principal executive offices, zip code, telephone number)

Securities Registered Pursuant to Section 12(b) of the Act:

Title of Each Class	Name of Each Exchange on Which Registered
Common Stock, $0.001 par value per share	Nasdaq Global Select Market

Securities Registered Pursuant to Section 12(g) of the Act: None

Indicate by check mark if the registrant is a well-known seasoned issuer, as defined in Rule 405 of the Securities Act.   Yes ☒   No ☐
Indicate by check mark if the registrant is not required to file reports pursuant to Section 13 or Section 15(d) of the Act.   Yes ☐   No ☒
Indicate by check mark whether the registrant: (1) has filed all reports required to be filed by Section 13 or 15(d) of the Securities Exchange Act of 1934 during the preceding 12 months (or for such shorter period that the registrant was required to file such reports), and (2) has been subject to such filing requirements for the past 90 days.   Yes ☒   No ☐
Indicate by check mark whether the registrant has submitted electronically and posted on its corporate Web site, if any, every Interactive Data File required to be submitted and posted pursuant to Rule 405 of Regulation S-T (§ 232.405 of this chapter) during the preceding 12 months (or for such shorter period that the registrant was required to submit and post such files).   Yes ☒   No ☐
Indicate by check mark if disclosure of delinquent filers pursuant to Item 405 of Regulation of S-K (§ 229.405 of this chapter) is not contained herein, and will not be contained, to the best of the registrant's knowledge, in definitive proxy or information statements incorporated by reference in Part III of this Form 10-K or any amendment to this Form 10-K.   ☐
Indicate by check mark whether the registrant is a large accelerated filer, an accelerated filer, a non-accelerated filer, or a smaller reporting company. See the definitions of "large accelerated filer," "accelerated filer" and "smaller reporting company" in Rule 12b-2 of the Exchange Act. (Check one):

Large accelerated filer	☒	Accelerated filer	☐
Non-accelerated filer	☐ (Do not check if a smaller reporting company)	Smaller reporting company	☐

Indicate by check mark whether the registrant is a shell company (as defined in Rule 12b-2 of the Act).   Yes ☐   No ☒

The aggregate market value of the voting stock held by non-affiliates of the registrant as of the last business day of the registrant's most recently completed second fiscal quarter, based upon the closing sale price of the registrant's common stock on March 29, 2015 as reported on the NASDAQ Global Select Market was $69 billion. As of November 6, 2015, there were 1,484.8 million shares of the registrant's Common Stock outstanding.

DOCUMENTS INCORPORATED BY REFERENCE
Portions of the definitive Proxy Statement for the registrant's Annual Meeting of Shareholders to be held on March 23, 2016 have been incorporated by reference into Part III of this Annual Report on Form 10-K.

PART I

Item 1. *Business*

General

Starbucks is the premier roaster, marketer and retailer of specialty coffee in the world, operating in 68 countries. Formed in 1985, Starbucks Corporation's common stock trades on the NASDAQ Global Select Market ("NASDAQ") under the symbol "SBUX." We purchase and roast high-quality coffees that we sell, along with handcrafted coffee, tea and other beverages and a variety of fresh food items, including snack offerings, through company-operated stores. We also sell a variety of coffee and tea products and license our trademarks through other channels such as licensed stores, grocery and foodservice accounts. In addition to our flagship Starbucks Coffee brand, we sell goods and services under the following brands: Teavana, Tazo, Seattle's Best Coffee, Evolution Fresh, La Boulange and Ethos.

Our objective is to maintain Starbucks standing as one of the most recognized and respected brands in the world. To achieve this, we are continuing the disciplined expansion of our global store base, adding stores in both existing, developed markets such as the U.S., and in newer, higher growth markets such as China, as well as optimizing the mix of company-operated and licensed stores in each market. In addition, by leveraging the experience gained through our traditional store model, we continue to offer consumers new coffee and other products in a variety of forms, across new categories, and through diverse channels. We also believe our Starbucks

Global Responsibility strategy, commitments related to ethically sourcing high-quality coffee and contributing positively to the communities we do business in, and being an employer of choice are contributors to our objective.

In this Annual Report on Form 10-K ("10-K" or "Report") for the fiscal year ended September 27, 2015 ("fiscal 2015"), Starbucks Corporation (together with its subsidiaries) is referred to as "Starbucks," the "Company," "we," "us" or "our."

Segment Financial Information

We have four reportable operating segments: 1) Americas, which is inclusive of the U.S., Canada, and Latin America; 2) China/Asia Pacific ("CAP"); 3) Europe, Middle East, and Africa ("EMEA") and 4) Channel Development. We also have several non-reportable operating segments, including Teavana, Seattle's Best Coffee, Evolution Fresh, and our Digital Ventures business, as well as certain developing businesses such as the Starbucks Reserve® Roastery & Tasting Room, which are combined and referred to as All Other Segments. Revenues from our reportable segments and All Other Segments as a percentage of total net revenues for fiscal 2015 were as follows: Americas (69%), CAP (13%), EMEA (6%), Channel Development (9%) and All Other Segments (3%).

Our Americas, CAP, and EMEA segments include both company-operated and licensed stores. Our Americas segment is our most mature business and has achieved significant scale. Certain markets within our CAP and EMEA operations are still in the early stages of development and require a more extensive support organization, relative to their current levels of revenue and operating income, than our Americas operations. In certain markets within CAP and EMEA, occupancy costs and store operating expenses can be higher than in the Americas segment due to higher rents for prime store locations or costs of compliance with country-specific regulatory requirements. The Americas and EMEA segments also include certain foodservice accounts, primarily in Canada and the U.K.

Our Channel Development segment includes roasted whole bean and ground coffees, premium Tazo® teas, Starbucks- and Tazo-branded single-serve products, a variety of ready-to-drink beverages, such as Frappuccino®, Starbucks Doubleshot® and Starbucks Refreshers® beverages, and other branded products sold worldwide through channels such as grocery stores, warehouse clubs, specialty retailers, convenience stores, and U.S. foodservice accounts.

Starbucks segment information is included in Note 16, Segment Reporting, to the consolidated financial statements included in Item 8 of Part II of this 10-K.

Revenue Components

We generate nearly all of our revenues through company-operated stores, licensed stores, consumer packaged goods ("CPG") and foodservice operations.

Company-operated and Licensed Store Summary as of September 27, 2015

	Americas	As a % of Total Americas Stores	CAP	As a % of Total CAP Stores	EMEA	As a % of Total EMEA Stores	All Other Segments	As a % of Total All Other Segments Stores	Total	As a % of Total Stores
Company-operated stores	8,671	59%	2,452	45%	737	31%	375	90%	12,235	53%
Licensed stores	6,132	41%	3,010	55%	1,625	69%	41	10%	10,808	47%
Total	14,803	100%	5,462	100%	2,362	100%	416	100%	23,043	100%

The mix of company-operated versus licensed stores in a given market will vary based on several factors, including our ability to access desirable local retail space, the complexity and expected ultimate size of the market for Starbucks, and our ability to leverage the support infrastructure in an existing geographic region.

Company-operated Stores

Revenue from company-operated stores accounted for 79% of total net revenues during fiscal 2015. Our retail objective is to be the leading retailer and brand of coffee and tea in each of our target markets by selling the finest quality coffee, tea and related products, as well as complementary food and snack offerings, and by providing each customer with a unique *Starbucks Experience*. The *Starbucks Experience* is built upon superior customer service, as well as clean and well-maintained stores that reflect the personalities of the communities in which they operate, thereby building a high degree of customer loyalty.

Our strategy for expanding our global retail business is to increase our market share in a disciplined manner, by selectively opening additional stores in new and existing markets, as well as increasing sales in existing stores, to support our long-term strategic objective to maintain Starbucks standing as one of the most recognized and respected brands in the world. Store growth in specific existing markets will vary due to many factors, including the maturity of the market, economic conditions, consumer behavior and local business practices.

Company-operated store data for the year-ended September 27, 2015:

	Stores Open as of Sep 28, 2014	Opened	Closed	Transfers	Net	Stores Open as of Sep 27, 2015
Americas:						
U.S.	7,303	312	(56)	—	256	7,559
Canada	983	41	(15)	—	26	1,009
Brazil	89	18	(4)	—	14	103
Puerto Rico	20	—	(1)	(19)	(20)	—
Total Americas	8,395	371	(76)	(19)	276	8,671

China/Asia Pacific[1]:						
Japan	—	77	(13)	1,009	1,073	1,073
China	823	212	(9)	—	203	1,026
Thailand	203	36	(2)	—	34	237
Singapore	106	14	(4)	—	10	116
Total China/Asia Pacific	1,132	339	(28)	1,009	1,320	2,452
EMEA:						
U.K.	506	4	(18)	(64)	(78)	428
Germany	152	2	(5)	—	(3)	149
France	78	—	(2)	—	(2)	76
Switzerland	55	1	—	—	1	56
Austria	17	1	—	—	1	18
Netherlands	9	1	—	—	1	10
Total EMEA	817	9	(25)	(64)	(80)	737
All Other Segments:						
Teavana	365	11	(5)	—	6	371
Evolution Fresh	4	—	(1)	—	(1)	3
Starbucks Reserve® Roastery & Tasting Room	—	1	—	—	1	1
Total All Other Segments	369	12	(6)	—	6	375
Total company-operated	10,713	731	(135)	926	1,522	12,235

[1] China/Asia Pacific store data includes the transfer of 1,009 Japan stores from licensed stores to company-operated as a result of the acquisition of Starbucks Japan in the first quarter of fiscal 2015.

Starbucks® company-operated stores are typically located in high-traffic, high-visibility locations. Our ability to vary the size and format of our stores allows us to locate them in or near a variety of settings, including downtown and suburban retail centers, office buildings, university campuses, and in select rural and off-highway locations. We are continuing the expansion of our various store formats, including Drive Thru and express stores, to provide a greater degree of access and convenience for our customers.

Starbucks® stores offer a choice of coffee and tea beverages, as well as other premium coffee, tea and related products, including distinctively packaged roasted whole bean and ground coffees, a variety of premium single-serve and ready-to-drink coffee and tea products, juices and bottled water. Starbucks® stores also offer an assortment of fresh food and snack offerings, including selections focusing on high-quality ingredients, nutritional value and great flavor. A focused selection of beverage-making equipment and accessories are also sold in our stores. Each Starbucks® store varies its product mix depending upon the size of the store and its location. To complement the in-store experience, our company-operated Starbucks® stores in the U.S., Canada, and certain other international markets also provide customers free access to wireless internet.

Retail sales mix by product type for company-operated stores:

Fiscal Year Ended	Sep 27, 2015	Sep 28, 2014	Sep 29, 2013
Beverages	73%	73%	74%
Food	19%	18%	18%
Packaged and single-serve coffees and teas	3%	4%	4%
Other[1]	5%	5%	4%
Total	100%	100%	100%

[1] "Other" primarily consists of sales of ready-to-drink beverages, serveware and coffee-making equipment, among other items.

In fiscal 2014, we moved ready-to-drink beverage revenues from the "Food" category to the "Other" category and combined packaged and single-serve teas, which were previously included in the "Other" category, with packaged and single-serve coffees, which are now categorized as "Packaged and single-serve coffees and teas."

Additionally, we revised our discount allocation methodology in fiscal 2014 to more precisely allocate sales discounts to the various revenue product categories. None of these changes had a material impact on the composition of our retail sales mix by product type.

Stored Value Cards

The Starbucks Card and our other branded stored value card programs are designed to provide customers with a convenient payment method, support gifting, and increase the frequency of store visits by cardholders, in part through the related My Starbucks Rewards® loyalty program where available, as discussed below. Stored value cards are issued to customers when they initially load them with an account balance. They can be obtained in our company-operated and most licensed stores in North America, China, Brazil, and many of our markets in the EMEA segment, as well as on-line, via the Starbucks® mobile app, and through other retailers, including a number of other international locations. Customers may access their card balances by utilizing their stored value card or the Starbucks® mobile app in participating stores, which also include certain Teavana® and Evolution Fresh™ locations. Using the Mobile Order and Pay functionality of the Starbucks® mobile app, customers can also place orders in advance for pick-up at certain participating locations in the U.S. Customers who register their card in the U.S., Canada, and certain other countries are automatically enrolled in the My Starbucks Rewards® program and can receive various benefits depending on factors such as the number of reward points ("Stars") earned in a 12-month period. Refer to Note 1, Summary of Significant Accounting Policies, included in Item 8 of Part II of this 10-K, for further discussion of our stored value cards and loyalty program.

Licensed Stores

Revenues from our licensed stores accounted for 10% of total net revenues in fiscal 2015. Licensed stores generally have a lower gross margin and a higher operating margin than company-operated stores. Under the licensed model, Starbucks receives a reduced share of the total store revenues, but this is more than offset by the reduction in our share of costs as these are primarily incurred by the licensee.

In our licensed store operations, we leverage the expertise of our local partners and share our operating and store development experience. Licensees provide improved, and at times the only, access to desirable retail space. Most licensees are prominent retailers with in-depth market knowledge and access. As part of these arrangements, we sell coffee, tea, food and related products to licensees for resale to customers and receive royalties and license fees from the licensees. We also sell certain equipment, such as coffee brewers and espresso machines, to our licensees for use in their operations. Employees working in licensed retail locations are required to follow our detailed store operating procedures and attend training classes similar to those given to employees in company-operated stores. For Teavana® and Seattle's Best Coffee®, as well as Starbucks® stores within certain markets, we also use traditional franchising and include these stores in the results of operations from our other licensed stores.

Licensed store data for the year-ended September 27, 2015:

	Stores Open as of Sep 28, 2014	Opened	Closed	Transfers	Net	Stores Open as of Sep 27, 2015
Americas[1]:						
U.S.	4,659	357	(54)	—	303	4,962
Mexico	434	73	(1)	—	72	506
Canada	462	23	(136)	—	(113)	349
Other	241	55	—	19	74	315
Total Americas	5,796	508	(191)	19	336	6,132
China/Asia Pacific[2]:						
South Korea	700	149	(18)	—	131	831
China	544	244	(3)	—	241	785
Taiwan	323	41	(8)	—	33	356
Philippines	240	24	—	—	24	264
Japan	1,060	22	(15)	(1,009)	(1,002)	58
Other	625	101	(10)	—	91	716
Total China/Asia Pacific	3,492	581	(54)	(1,009)	(482)	3,010
EMEA:						
U.K.	285	65	(1)	65	129	414
Turkey	220	44	(4)	—	40	260
United Arab Emirates	115	18	(2)	—	16	131
Russia	87	21	(4)	—	17	104
Spain	86	4	(1)	—	3	89
Kuwait	72	5	—	—	5	77

Saudi Arabia	67	8	(4)	—	4	71
Other	391	92	(3)	(1)	88	479
Total EMEA	1,323	257	(19)	64	302	1,625
All Other Segments:						
Teavana	29	8	(2)	—	6	35
Seattle's Best Coffee	13	—	(7)	—	(7)	6
Total All Other Segments	42	8	(9)	—	(1)	41
Total licensed	**10,653**	**1,354**	**(273)**	**(926)**	**155**	**10,808**

(1) Americas store data includes the closure of 132 Target Canada licensed stores in the second quarter of fiscal 2015.

(2) China/Asia Pacific store data includes the transfer of 1,009 Japan stores from licensed stores to company-operated as a result of the acquisition of Starbucks Japan in the first quarter of fiscal 2015.

Consumer Packaged Goods

Revenues from sales of consumer packaged goods comprised 8% of total net revenues in fiscal 2015. Our consumer packaged goods business includes both domestic and international sales of packaged coffee and tea as well as a variety of ready-to-drink beverages and single-serve coffee and tea products to grocery, warehouse clubs and specialty retail stores. It also includes revenues from product sales to and licensing revenues from manufacturers that produce and market Starbucks-, Seattle's Best Coffee- and Tazo-branded products through licensing agreements.

Foodservice

Revenues from foodservice accounts comprised 3% of total net revenues in fiscal 2015. We sell Starbucks® and Seattle's Best Coffee® roasted whole bean and ground coffees, a selection of premium Tazo® teas, Starbucks VIA® Ready Brew, and other coffee and tea-related products to institutional foodservice companies that service business and industry, education, healthcare, office coffee distributors, hotels, restaurants, airlines and other retailers. We also sell our Seattle's Best Coffee® through arrangements with national accounts. The majority of the sales in this channel come through national broadline distribution networks with SYSCO Corporation, U.S. Foodservice™, and other distributors.

Product Supply

Starbucks is committed to selling the finest whole bean coffees and coffee beverages. To ensure compliance with our rigorous coffee standards, we control coffee purchasing, roasting and packaging, and the global distribution of coffee used in our operations. We purchase green coffee beans from multiple coffee-producing regions around the world and custom roast them to our exacting standards for our many blends and single origin coffees.

The price of coffee is subject to significant volatility. Although most coffee trades in the commodity market, high-altitude *arabica* coffee of the quality sought by Starbucks tends to trade on a negotiated basis at a premium above the "C" coffee commodity price. Both the premium and the commodity price depend upon the supply and demand at the time of purchase. Supply and price can be affected by multiple factors in the producing countries, including weather, natural disasters, crop disease, general increase in farm inputs and costs of production, inventory levels and political and economic conditions. Price is also impacted by trading activities in the *arabica* coffee futures market, including hedge funds and commodity index funds. In addition, green coffee prices have been affected in the past, and may be affected in the future, by the actions of certain organizations and associations that have historically attempted to influence prices of green coffee through agreements establishing export quotas or by restricting coffee supplies.

We buy coffee using fixed-price and price-to-be-fixed purchase commitments, depending on market conditions, to secure an adequate supply of quality green coffee. Price-to-be-fixed contracts are purchase commitments whereby the quality, quantity, delivery period, and other negotiated terms are agreed upon, but the date, and therefore the price, at which the base "C" coffee commodity price component will be fixed has not yet been established. For these types of contracts, either Starbucks or the seller has the option to select a date on which to "fix" the base "C" coffee commodity price prior to the delivery date. Until prices are fixed, we estimate the total cost of these purchase commitments. Total green coffee purchase commitments as of September 27, 2015 were $1.1 billion, comprised of $819 million under fixed-price contracts and an estimated $266 million under price-to-be-fixed contracts. As of September 27, 2015, approximately $38 million of our price-to-be-fixed contracts were effectively fixed through the use of futures contracts. All price-to-be-fixed contracts as of September 27, 2015 were at the Company's option to fix the base "C" coffee commodity price component. Total purchase commitments, together with existing inventory, are expected to provide an adequate supply of green coffee through fiscal 2016.

We depend upon our relationships with coffee producers, outside trading companies and exporters for our supply of green coffee. We believe, based on relationships established with our suppliers, the risk of non-delivery on such purchase commitments is remote.

To help ensure the future supply of high-quality green coffee, and to reinforce our leadership role in the coffee industry, Starbucks operates seven farmer support centers. The farmer support centers are staffed with agronomists and sustainability experts who work with coffee farming communities to promote best practices in coffee production designed to improve both coffee quality and yields.

In addition to coffee, we also purchase significant amounts of dairy products, particularly fluid milk, to support the needs of our company-operated stores. We believe, based on relationships established with our dairy suppliers, that the risk of non-delivery of sufficient fluid milk to support our stores is remote.

Products other than whole bean coffees and coffee beverages sold in Starbucks® stores include tea and a number of ready-to-drink beverages that are purchased from several specialty suppliers, usually under long-term supply contracts. Food products, such as La Boulange™ pastries, breakfast sandwiches and lunch items, are purchased from national, regional and local sources. As we continue to develop our food program, we expect the amount of food products purchased to become more significant to our operations. We also purchase a broad range of paper and plastic products, such as cups and cutlery, from several companies to support the needs of our retail stores as well as our manufacturing and distribution operations. We believe, based on relationships established with these suppliers and manufacturers, that the risk of material non-delivery of these items is remote.

Competition

Our primary competitors for coffee beverage sales are specialty coffee shops and quick-service restaurants. In almost all markets in which we do business, there are numerous competitors in the specialty coffee beverage business. We believe that our customers choose among specialty coffee retailers primarily on the basis of product quality, service and convenience, as well as price. We continue to experience direct competition from large competitors in the U.S. quick-service restaurant sector and the U.S. ready-to-drink coffee beverage market, in addition to well-established companies in many international markets. We also compete with restaurants and other specialty retailers for prime retail locations and qualified personnel to operate both new and existing stores.

Our coffee and tea products sold through our Channel Development segment compete directly against specialty coffees and teas sold through grocery stores, warehouse clubs, specialty retailers, convenience stores, and U.S. foodservice accounts and compete indirectly against all other coffees and teas on the market.

Item 6. *Selected Financial Data*

The following selected financial data is derived from the consolidated financial statements. All per-share data has been retroactively adjusted to give effect to the two-for-one stock split discussed in Note 1, Summary of Significant Accounting Policies, included in Item 8 of Part II of this 10-K. The data below should be read in conjunction with "Management's Discussion and Analysis of Financial Condition and Results of Operations," "Risk Factors," and the consolidated financial statements and notes.

Financial Information (in millions, except per share data):

As of and for the Fiscal Year Ended [1]	Sep 27, 2015 (52 Wks)	Sep 28, 2014 (52 Wks)	Sep 29, 2013 (52 Wks)	Sep 30, 2012 (52 Wks)	Oct 2, 2011 (52 Wks)
Results of Operations					
Net revenues:					
Company-operated stores	$ 15,197.3	$ 12,977.9	$ 11,793.2	$ 10,534.5	$ 9,632.4
Licensed stores	1,861.9	1,588.6	1,360.5	1,210.3	1,007.5
CPG, foodservice and other	2,103.5	1,881.3	1,713.1	1,532.0	1,060.5
Total net revenues	$ 19,162.7	$ 16,447.8	$ 14,866.8	$ 13,276.8	$ 11,700.4
Operating income/(loss) [2]	$ 3,601.0	$ 3,081.1	$ (325.4)	$ 1,997.4	$ 1,728.5
Net earnings including noncontrolling interests [2]	2,759.3	2,067.7	8.8	1,384.7	1,248.0
Net earnings attributable to noncontrolling interests	1.9	(0.4)	0.5	0.9	2.3
Net earnings attributable to Starbucks [2]	2,757.4	2,068.1	8.3	1,383.8	1,245.7
EPS — diluted [2]	1.82	1.35	0.01	0.90	0.81
Cash dividends declared per share	0.680	0.550	0.445	0.360	0.280
Net cash provided by operating activities	3,749.1	607.8	2,908.3	1,750.3	1,612.4
Capital expenditures (additions to property, plant and equipment)	1,303.7	1,160.9	1,151.2	856.2	531.9
Balance Sheet					
Total assets	$ 12,446.1	$ 10,752.9	$ 11,516.7	$ 8,219.2	$ 7,360.4
Long-term debt (including current portion)	2,347.5	2,048.3	1,299.4	549.6	549.5
Shareholders' equity	5,818.0	5,272.0	4,480.2	5,109.0	4,384.9

[1] Our fiscal year ends on the Sunday closest to September 30.

[2] Fiscal 2013 results include a pretax charge of $2,784.1 million resulting from the conclusion of our arbitration with Kraft Foods Global, Inc. The impact of this charge to net earnings attributable to Starbucks and diluted EPS, net of the related tax benefit, was $1,713.1 million and $1.12 per share, respectively.

Comparable Store Sales:

Fiscal Year Ended	Sep 27, 2015 (52 Wks)	Sep 28, 2014 (52 Wks)	Sep 29, 2013 (52 Wks)	Sep 30, 2012 (52 Wks)	Oct 2, 2011 (52 Wks)
Percentage change in comparable store sales [3]					
Americas					
Sales growth	7%	6%	7%	8%	8%
Change in transactions	3%	2%	5%	6%	5%
Change in ticket	4%	3%	2%	2%	2%
China/Asia Pacific					
Sales growth	9%	7%	9%	15%	22%
Change in transactions	8%	6%	7%	11%	20%
Change in ticket	1%	—%	2%	3%	2%
EMEA					
Sales growth	4%	5%	—%	—%	3%
Change in transactions	2%	3%	2%	—%	3%
Change in ticket	1%	2%	(2)%	—%	—%
Consolidated					
Sales growth	7%	6%	7%	7%	8%
Change in transactions	3%	3%	5%	6%	6%
Change in ticket	4%	3%	2%	1%	2%

[3] Includes only Starbucks® company-operated stores open 13 months or longer. Comparable store sales exclude the effect of fluctuations in foreign currency exchange rates.

Store Count Data:

As of and for the Fiscal Year Ended	Sep 27, 2015 (52 Wks)	Sep 28, 2014 (52 Wks)	Sep 29, 2013 (52 Wks)	Sep 30, 2012 (52 Wks)	Oct 2, 2011 (52 Wks)
Net stores opened/(closed) and transferred during the year:					
Americas [4,5]					
Company-operated stores	276	317	276	228	32
Licensed stores	336	381	404	280	215
China/Asia Pacific [6,7]					
Company-operated stores	1,320	250	239	152	74
Licensed stores	(482)	492	349	296	192
EMEA [8]					
Company-operated stores	(80)	(9)	(29)	10	25
Licensed stores	302	180	129	101	79
All Other Segments [9]					
Company-operated stores	6	12	343	—	6
Licensed stores [10]	(1)	(24)	(10)	(4)	(478)
Total	1,677	1,599	1,701	1,063	145
Stores open at year end:					
Americas [4,5]					
Company-operated stores	8,671	8,395	8,078	7,802	7,574
Licensed stores	6,132	5,796	5,415	5,011	4,731

China/Asia Pacific[6,7]					
Company-operated stores	2,452	1,132	882	643	491
Licensed stores	3,010	3,492	3,000	2,651	2,355
EMEA[8]					
Company-operated stores	737	817	826	855	845
Licensed stores	1,625	1,323	1,143	1,014	913
All Other Segments[9]					
Company-operated stores	375	369	357	14	14
Licensed stores[10]	41	42	66	76	80
Total	23,043	21,366	19,767	18,066	17,003

[4] Americas store data has been adjusted for the sale of store locations in Chile to a joint venture partner in the fourth quarter of fiscal 2013 by reclassifying historical information from company-operated stores to licensed stores, and to exclude Seattle's Best Coffee and Evolution Fresh, which are reported within All Other Segments.

[5] Americas store data includes the closure of 132 Target Canada licensed stores in the second quarter of fiscal 2015.

[6] China/Asia Pacific store data has been adjusted for the transfer of certain company-operated stores to licensed stores in the fourth quarter of fiscal 2014.

[7] China/Asia Pacific store data includes the transfer of 1,009 Japan stores from licensed stores to company-operated as a result of the acquisition of Starbucks Japan in the first quarter of fiscal 2015.

[8] EMEA store data has been adjusted for the acquisition of store locations in Austria and Switzerland in the fourth quarter of fiscal 2011 by reclassifying historical information from licensed stores to company-operated stores, and the transfer of certain company-operated stores to licensed stores in the fourth quarter of fiscal 2012 and in the second and fourth quarters of fiscal 2014.

[9] Includes 337 Teavana® stores acquired in the second quarter of fiscal 2013.

[10] Includes the closure of 475 licensed Seattle's Best Coffee® locations in Borders Bookstores during fiscal 2011.

Item 7. *Management's Discussion and Analysis of Financial Condition and Results of Operations*

General

Our fiscal year ends on the Sunday closest to September 30. The fiscal years ended on September 27, 2015, September 28, 2014 and September 29, 2013 all included 52 weeks. Starbucks 2016 fiscal year will include 53 weeks, with the 53rd week falling in our fourth fiscal quarter. All references to store counts, including data for new store openings, are reported net of related store closures, unless otherwise noted.

Financial Highlights

- Total net revenues increased 17% to $19.2 billion in fiscal 2015 compared to $16.4 billion in fiscal 2014.

- Global comparable store sales grew 7% driven by a 4% increase in average ticket and a 3% increase in the number of transactions.

- Consolidated operating income increased to $3.6 billion in fiscal 2015 compared to operating income of $3.1 billion in fiscal 2014. Fiscal 2015 operating margin was 18.8% compared to 18.7% in fiscal 2014. The operating margin expansion was primarily driven by sales leverage, partially offset by the impact of our ownership change in Starbucks Japan and increased salaries and benefits due to increased store partner (employee) investments.

- Earnings per share ("EPS") for fiscal 2015 increased to $1.82, compared to EPS of $1.35 in fiscal 2014, primarily due to the gain resulting from the fair value adjustment of our preexisting equity interest in Starbucks Japan upon acquisition, which increased EPS by $0.26 per share in fiscal 2015. The remaining increase was primarily due to improved sales leverage and the incremental tax benefit related to domestic manufacturing deductions claimed for the current year and on U.S. corporate income tax returns for fiscal years 2010 through 2014.

- Cash flows from operations were $3.7 billion in fiscal 2015 compared to $607.8 million in fiscal 2014. The increase was primarily driven by lapping the prior year payment of $2.8 billion for the Kraft arbitration matter. The remaining change of $377 million was primarily due to strong earnings, partially offset by unfavorable changes in working capital accounts, mainly due to timing.

- Capital expenditures were $1.3 billion in fiscal 2015 compared to $1.2 billion in fiscal 2014.

- We returned $2.4 billion to our shareholders in fiscal 2015 through share repurchases and dividends compared to $1.6 billion in fiscal 2014.

Overview

Starbucks results for fiscal 2015 demonstrate the continued strength of our global business model and our ability to successfully make disciplined investments in our business and our partners (employees). Our net revenues grew 17% over fiscal 2014 and all reportable segments drove an increase in consolidated operating income. Consolidated operating margin expanded to 18.8% from 18.7% in fiscal 2014, largely driven by sales leverage, partially offset by the 90 basis point impact of our ownership change in Starbucks Japan as well as increased salaries and benefits due to investments in our store partners (employees) in the Americas segment. The ownership change in Starbucks Japan reflects the change in accounting from a joint venture to a consolidated market and includes the acquisition-related transaction and integration costs.

The Americas segment continued to perform well in fiscal 2015, with revenues growing 11% to $13.3 billion, primarily driven by comparable store sales growth of 7%, comprised of a 4% increase in average ticket and a 3% increase in number of transactions, as well as incremental revenues from 612 net new store openings over the last 12 months. Growth in our core beverages, paired with the success of our food offerings and beverage innovation, drove the increase in comparable store sales. Americas operating margin grew 80 basis points to 24.2% in fiscal 2015, primarily driven by sales leverage, partially offset by increased salaries and benefits due to investments in our store partners (employees) and digital platforms related to in-store initiatives. Looking forward, we expect to continue to drive revenue growth and moderate margin expansion through new stores and leveraging investments in both our store partners (employees) and our digital platforms, such as Mobile Order and Pay.

Our fiscal 2015 China/Asia Pacific segment results reflect the impact of fully consolidating Starbucks Japan since October 31, 2014. Incremental revenues from the change in ownership of Starbucks Japan were the primary driver of the 112% increase in segment revenues, to $2.4 billion. Also contributing were increased sales from the opening of 767 net new stores over the past year, along with a 9% increase in comparable store sales, primarily driven by an 8% increase in transactions. Operating income grew 34%, to $501 million, while operating margin declined 1,210 basis points to 20.9%. The overall operating margin decline was due to the 1,410 basis point impact of the ownership change in Starbucks Japan, which was partially offset by 200 basis points of expansion primarily due to sales leverage. We expect this segment will become a more significant contributor to overall company revenue growth in the future as we look forward to continued net new store openings and the first full year of consolidating Starbucks Japan. In fiscal 2016, we also expect China to continue to move towards being one of our largest international markets, primarily driven by expanding our retail store presence and increasing transaction growth.

Our EMEA segment revenues declined 6% to $1.2 billion, primarily driven by unfavorable foreign currency translation of approximately $116 million. This was partially offset by revenue growth of $38 million that was primarily driven by incremental revenues from 238 net new licensed store openings over the past year. EMEA operating margin expanded 460 basis points to 13.8% in fiscal 2015, primarily due to sales leverage driven by our ongoing portfolio shift to higher-margin licensed stores. We expect our continued disciplined licensed store expansion and focus on the customer experience in this region will result in improved operating performance, with operating margin approaching 15% in fiscal 2016.

The Channel Development segment revenues grew 12% to $1.7 billion in fiscal 2015, primarily due to increased sales of premium single-serve products, driven by sales of Starbucks- and Tazo-branded K-Cup® portion packs, and improved packaged coffee sales. Operating margin increased 180 basis points to 37.8%, primarily driven by leverage on cost of sales and increased income due to strong performance by our North American Coffee Partnership joint venture. We continue to expand customer occasions outside of our retail stores and through our developing international presence. For fiscal 2016, we expect moderate margin expansion primarily driven by growing our premium single-serve category with innovative new beverages, including the ready-to-drink market.

Fiscal 2016 — The View Ahead

For fiscal 2016, we expect revenue growth in excess of 10%, driven by strong comparable store sales slightly above the mid-single digits, the addition of approximately 1,800 net new stores, and a 53rd fiscal week, which is expected to contribute an incremental 2% to our revenue growth rate. Approximately one-half of net new store openings will be in our China/Asia Pacific segment, with approximately 40% coming from the Americas and the remaining 10% from the EMEA segment.

We expect consolidated operating margin and earnings per share to increase slightly in fiscal 2016 when compared to our fiscal 2015 results, primarily due to leverage on revenue growth and a 53rd fiscal week, which we expect to contribute approximately $0.06 to earnings per share, partially offset by continued investments in our store partners (employees) in the Americas segment and the development of these initiatives in our international markets, as well as digital innovation.

The effective tax rate for fiscal 2016 is expected to be between 34% to 35%.

Capital expenditures in fiscal 2016 are expected to be approximately $1.4 billion, primarily for new stores and store renovations, as well as for other investments to support our ongoing growth initiatives.

Acquisitions and Divestitures

See Note 2 Acquisitions and Divestitures, to the consolidated financial statements included in Item 8 of Part II of this 10-K for information regarding acquisitions and divestitures.

RESULTS OF OPERATIONS — FISCAL 2015 COMPARED TO FISCAL 2014

Consolidated results of operations *(in millions)*:

Revenues

Fiscal Year Ended	Sep 27, 2015	Sep 28, 2014	% Change
Net revenues:			
Company-operated stores	$ 15,197.3	$ 12,977.9	17.1 %
Licensed stores	1,861.9	1,588.6	17.2
CPG, foodservice and other	2,103.5	1,881.3	11.8
Total net revenues	**$ 19,162.7**	**$ 16,447.8**	**16.5 %**

Total net revenues increased $2.7 billion, or 17%, over fiscal 2014, primarily due to increased revenues from company-operated stores (contributing $2.2 billion). The growth in company-operated store revenues was primarily driven by incremental revenues from the acquisition of Starbucks Japan (approximately $1.1 billion), an increase in comparable store sales (approximately 7% growth, or $852 million) and incremental revenues from 550 net new Starbucks® company-operated store openings over the past 12 months (approximately $590 million). Partially offsetting these increases was the impact of unfavorable foreign currency translation (approximately $252 million).

Licensed store revenue growth also contributed $273 million to the increase in total net revenues, primarily resulting from the opening of 1,075 net new Starbucks® licensed stores over the past 12 months and improved comparable store sales as well as increased La Boulange food sales to our licensees in the Americas segment. Partially offsetting these increases was a decrease in licensed store revenues resulting from the impact of our ownership change in Starbucks Japan (approximately $45 million).

CPG, foodservice and other revenues increased $222 million, primarily due to increased sales of premium single-serve products (approximately $116 million), U.S. packaged coffee (approximately $55 million) and foodservice sales (approximately $40 million).

Operating Expenses

Fiscal Year Ended	Sep 27, 2015	Sep 28, 2014	Sep 27, 2015	Sep 28, 2014
			% of Total Net Revenues	
Cost of sales including occupancy costs	$ 7,787.5	$ 6,858.8	40.6%	41.7%
Store operating expenses	5,411.1	4,638.2	28.2	28.2
Other operating expenses	522.4	457.3	2.7	2.8
Depreciation and amortization expenses	893.9	709.6	4.7	4.3
General and administrative expenses	1,196.7	991.3	6.2	6.0
Litigation credit	—	(20.2)	—	(0.1)
Total operating expenses	15,811.6	13,635.0	82.5	82.9
Income from equity investees	249.9	268.3	1.3	1.6
Operating income	**$ 3,601.0**	**$ 3,081.1**	**18.8%**	**18.7%**
Store operating expenses as a % of related revenues			35.6%	35.7%

Cost of sales including occupancy costs as a percentage of total net revenues decreased 110 basis points, primarily driven by sales and operating leverage on cost of sales (approximately 60 basis points), driven by strong sales and initiatives in our supply chain, such as improvements in sourcing, as well as sales leverage on occupancy costs (approximately 40 basis points).

Store operating expenses were flat as a percentage of total net revenues. Store operating expenses as a percentage of company-operated store revenues, decreased 10 basis points, primarily driven by sales leverage (approximately 50 basis points) and decreased expenses, largely salaries and benefits, due to the shift to more licensed stores in EMEA (approximately 40 basis points), partially offset by increased investments in store partners (employees) and digital platforms related to in-store initiatives (approximately 100 basis points) in the Americas segment.

Other operating expenses as a percentage of total net revenues decreased 10 basis points. Excluding the impact of company-operated store revenues, other operating expenses were flat, primarily due to sales leverage (approximately 70 basis points), partially offset by increased marketing (approximately 20 basis points), largely due to timing, the impairment of certain assets in the Americas segment (approximately 20 basis points) and the impact of our ownership change in Starbucks Japan (approximately 20 basis points).

Depreciation and amortization expenses as a percentage of total net revenues increased 40 basis points, primarily due to the impact of our ownership change in Starbucks Japan (approximately 30 basis points).

General and administrative expenses as a percentage of total net revenues increased 20 basis points, primarily driven by the impact of our ownership change in Starbucks Japan (approximately 10 basis points).

The $20 million decrease in litigation credit for fiscal 2015 was due to lapping a prior year credit related to a reduction of our estimated prejudgment interest payable associated with the Kraft arbitration, as a result of paying our obligation earlier than anticipated.

Income from equity investees decreased $18 million, primarily due to the impact of our ownership change in Starbucks Japan and the absence of income from our Malaysia joint venture sold in the fourth quarter of fiscal 2014, partially offset by improved performance from our North American Coffee Partnership and China joint ventures. As a percentage of total revenues, income from equity investees decreased 30 basis points, primarily due to the impact of our ownership change in Starbucks Japan (approximately 30 basis points).

The overall increase in operating margin of 10 basis points was driven by the changes discussed above, including the impact of our ownership change in Starbucks Japan and the acquisition-related transaction and integration costs, which contributed unfavorably to operating margin (approximately 90 basis points).

Other Income and Expenses

Fiscal Year Ended	Sep 27, 2015	Sep 28, 2014	Sep 27, 2015	Sep 28, 2014
			% of Total Net Revenues	
Operating income	$ 3,601.0	$ 3,081.1	18.8%	18.7%
Gain resulting from acquisition of joint venture	390.6	—	2.0	—
Loss on extinguishment of debt	(61.1)	—	(0.3)	—
Interest income and other, net	43.0	142.7	0.2	0.9

Interest expense	(70.5)	(64.1)	(0.4)	(0.4)
Earnings before income taxes	3,903.0	3,159.7	20.4	19.2
Income taxes	1,143.7	1,092.0	6.0	6.6
Net earnings including noncontrolling interests	2,759.3	2,067.7	14.4	12.6
Net earnings/(loss) attributable to noncontrolling interests	1.9	(0.4)	—	—
Net earnings attributable to Starbucks	$ 2,757.4	$ 2,068.1	14.4 %	12.6 %
Effective tax rate including noncontrolling interests			29.3 %	34.6 %

During the first quarter of fiscal 2015, we recorded a gain of $391 million as a result of remeasuring our preexisting 39.5% ownership interest in Starbucks Japan to fair value upon acquisition.

During the fourth quarter of fiscal 2015, we recorded a loss of $61 million related to the redemption of our $550 million of 6.250% Senior Notes (the "2017 notes"), which were originally scheduled to mature in August 2017. The loss primarily relates to the optional redemption premium outlined in the 2017 notes indenture, as well as expenses related to the previously capitalized original issuance costs and accelerated amortization of the unamortized discount.

Net interest income and other decreased $100 million, primarily due to lapping the gain on the sale of our equity interest in our Malaysia joint venture (approximately $68 million) in the prior year and net unfavorable fair value adjustments from derivative instruments used to manage our risk of commodity price fluctuations (approximately $25 million) in fiscal 2015.

Interest expense increased $6 million primarily due to incurring a full quarter of interest in the first quarter of fiscal 2015 on the long-term debt we issued in December of fiscal 2014 as well as the reclassification of $2 million from accumulated other comprehensive income to interest expense related to remaining unrecognized losses from interest rate contracts associated with the 2017 notes redeemed in the fourth quarter of fiscal 2015.

Our tax rate is affected by recurring items, such as tax rates in foreign jurisdictions and the relative amounts of income we earn in those jurisdictions, as well as discrete items that may occur in any given year, but are not consistent from year to year. The effective tax rate for fiscal 2015 was 29.3% compared to 34.6% for fiscal 2014. The decrease in the rate for fiscal 2015 was primarily due to the 3.7% impact of the gain associated with the remeasurement of our preexisting 39.5% ownership interest in Starbucks Japan upon acquisition, which was almost entirely non-taxable, as well as the 1.5% incremental tax benefit related to domestic manufacturing deductions claimed in fiscal 2015 on U.S. corporate income tax returns for fiscal years 2010 through 2015.

Segment Information

Results of operations by segment *(in millions)*:

Americas

Fiscal Year Ended	Sep 27, 2015	Sep 28, 2014	Sep 27, 2015	Sep 28, 2014
			As a % of Americas Total Net Revenues	
Net revenues:				
Company-operated stores	$ 11,925.6	$ 10,866.5	89.7%	90.7%
Licensed stores	1,334.4	1,074.9	10.0	9.0
Foodservice and other	33.4	39.1	0.3	0.3
Total net revenues	**13,293.4**	**11,980.5**	**100.0**	**100.0**
Cost of sales including occupancy costs	4,845.0	4,487.0	36.4	37.5
Store operating expenses	4,387.9	3,946.8	33.0	32.9
Other operating expenses	122.8	100.4	0.9	0.8
Depreciation and amortization expenses	522.3	469.5	3.9	3.9
General and administrative expenses	192.1	167.8	1.4	1.4
Total operating expenses	10,070.1	9,171.5	75.8	76.6
Operating income	**$ 3,223.3**	**$ 2,809.0**	**24.2%**	**23.4%**
Store operating expenses as a % of related revenues			36.8%	36.3%

Revenues

Americas total net revenues for fiscal 2015 increased $1.3 billion, or 11%, primarily due to increased revenues from company-operated stores (contributing $1.1 billion) and licensed stores (contributing $260 million).

The increase in company-operated store revenues was driven by a 7% increase in comparable store sales (approximately $745 million), as well as incremental revenues from 318 net new Starbucks® company-operated store openings over the past 12 months (approximately $455 million). Partially offsetting these increases was unfavorable foreign currency translation (approximately $139 million), primarily driven by the strengthening of the U.S. dollar against the Canadian dollar.

The increase in licensed store revenues was primarily due to higher product sales to and royalty revenues from our licensees, resulting from increased La Boulange™ food sales to our licensees beginning in the first quarter of fiscal 2015, as well as the opening of 317 net new licensed stores over the past 12 months and improved comparable store sales.

Operating Expenses

Cost of sales including occupancy costs as a percentage of total net revenues decreased 110 basis points, primarily driven by leverage on cost of sales (approximately 60 basis points), lower commodity costs (approximately 30 basis points), mainly dairy, and sales leverage on occupancy costs (approximately 30 basis points).

Store operating expenses as a percentage of total net revenues increased 10 basis points. As a percentage of company-operated store revenues, store operating expenses increased 50 basis points, primarily driven by increased investments in store partners (employees) and digital platforms related to in-store initiatives (approximately 130 basis points), partially offset by sales leverage (approximately 100 basis points).

Other operating expenses as a percentage of total net revenues increased 10 basis points. Excluding the impact of company-operated store revenues, other operating expenses were flat, primarily driven by sales leverage (approximately 60 basis points), offset by the impairment of certain assets in the region (approximately 60 basis points).

Depreciation and amortization expenses as a percentage of total revenues were flat, primarily driven by sales leverage (approximately 10 basis points), offset by incremental costs from investments in our existing store portfolio (approximately 10 basis points).

The combination of these changes resulted in an overall increase in operating margin of 80 basis points over fiscal 2014.

China/Asia Pacific

Fiscal Year Ended	Sep 27, 2015	Sep 28, 2014	Sep 27, 2015	Sep 28, 2014
			As a % of China/Asia Pacific Total Net Revenues	
Net revenues:				
Company-operated stores	$ 2,127.3	$ 859.4	88.8%	76.1%
Licensed stores	264.4	270.2	11.0	23.9
Foodservice and other	4.2	—	0.2	—
Total net revenues	**2,395.9**	**1,129.6**	**100.0**	**100.0**
Cost of sales including occupancy costs	1,071.5	547.4	44.7	48.5
Store operating expenses	609.8	221.1	25.5	19.6
Other operating expenses	62.2	48.0	2.6	4.2
Depreciation and amortization expenses	150.7	46.1	6.3	4.1
General and administrative expenses	120.8	58.5	5.0	5.2
Total operating expenses	2,015.0	921.1	84.1	81.5
Income from equity investees	119.6	164.0	5.0	14.5
Operating income	**$ 500.5**	**$ 372.5**	**20.9%**	**33.0%**
Store operating expenses as a % of related revenues	119.6	164.0	28.7%	27.7%

Discussion of our China/Asia Pacific segment results below reflects the impact of fully consolidating Starbucks Japan due to the ownership change from an equity method joint venture to a company-operated market since the acquisition date of October 31, 2014. Under the joint venture model, we recognized royalties and product sales within revenue and related product cost of sales as well as our proportionate share of Starbucks Japan's net earnings, which we recognized within income from equity investees. This resulted in a lower gross margin and a very high operating margin. Under the company-operated ownership model, Starbucks Japan's operating results are reflected in most income statement lines of this segment and have an operating margin more in line with that of our other retail businesses.

Revenues

China/Asia Pacific total net revenues for fiscal 2015 increased $1.3 billion, or 112%, largely due to increased revenues from company-operated stores (approximately $1.3 billion). The increase in company-operated store revenues was primarily driven by incremental revenues from the acquisition of Starbucks Japan (approximately $1.1 billion). Also contributing were incremental revenues from the opening of 247 net new company-operated stores over the past 12 months (approximately $160 million) and a 9% increase in comparable store sales (approximately $74 million).

Licensed store revenues decreased $6 million, primarily due to our ownership change in Starbucks Japan to mostly company-operated stores (approximately $45 million). This decrease was partially offset by increased product sales to and royalty revenues from licensees (approximately $27 million), resulting from the opening of 520 net new licensed store openings over the past 12 months, improved comparable store sales, and incremental revenues from the ownership changes in Australia and Malaysia (approximately $17 million) in the fourth quarter of fiscal 2014.

Operating Expenses

Cost of sales including occupancy costs as a percentage of total net revenues decreased 380 basis points, primarily due to the impact of our ownership change in Starbucks Japan (approximately 230 basis points) and the shift in our cost of sales mix resulting from growth of company-operated stores, which have a higher gross margin (approximately 50 basis points). Sales leverage (approximately 40 basis points) also contributed.

Store operating expenses as a percentage of total net revenues increased 590 basis points. As a percentage of company-operated store revenues, store operating expenses increased 300 basis points, primarily driven by the impact of our ownership change in Starbucks Japan (approximately 410 basis points), partially offset by the sale of our Australia retail operations in the fourth quarter of fiscal 2014 (approximately 70 basis points) and sales leverage (approximately 50 basis points).

Other operating expenses as a percentage of total net revenues decreased 160 basis points. Excluding the impact of company-operated store revenues, other operating expenses increased 540 basis points, primarily due to the impact of our ownership change in Starbucks Japan (approximately 350 basis points) as well as increased salaries and benefits largely due to increased headcount to support growth in our China market (approximately 150 basis points).

Depreciation and amortization expenses as a percentage of total revenues increased 220 basis points, primarily due to the impact of our ownership change in Starbucks Japan (approximately 210 basis points).

General and administrative expenses as a percentage of total revenues decreased 20 basis points, primarily due to sales leverage (approximately 40 basis points) and the impact of the sale of our Australia retail operations in the fourth quarter of fiscal 2014 (approximately 20 basis points), which includes lapping professional fees associated with the sale. The impact of our ownership change in Starbucks Japan contributed unfavorably (approximately 60 basis points).

Income from equity investees decreased $44 million, primarily due to the impact of our ownership change in Starbucks Japan and absence of income from our Malaysia joint venture sold in the fourth quarter of fiscal 2014, partially offset by improved performance from our China joint venture. As a percentage of total net revenues, income from equity investees declined 950 basis points, primarily due to the impact of our ownership change in Starbucks Japan (approximately 870 basis points).

The overall decrease in operating margin of 1,210 basis points over fiscal 2014 was primarily driven by the impact of our ownership change in Starbucks Japan (approximately 1,410 basis points), partially offset by 200 basis points of margin expansion driven by the other items discussed above.

EMEA

Fiscal Year Ended		Sep 27, 2015		Sep 28, 2014	Sep 27, 2015	Sep 28, 2014
					As a % of EMEA Total Net Revenues	
Net revenues:						
Company-operated stores	$	911.2	$	1,013.8	74.9%	78.3%
Licensed stores		257.2		238.4	21.1	18.4
Foodservice		48.3		42.6	4.0	3.3
Total net revenues		**1,216.7**		**1,294.8**	**100.0**	**100.0**
Cost of sales including occupancy costs		582.5		646.8	47.9	50.0
Store operating expenses		308.7		365.8	25.4	28.3
Other operating expenses		51.8		48.2	4.3	3.7
Depreciation and amortization expenses		52.0		59.4	4.3	4.6
General and administrative expenses		56.6		59.1	4.7	4.6
Total operating expenses		1,051.6		1,179.3	86.4	91.1
Income from equity investees		3.1		3.7	0.3	0.3
Operating income	**$**	**168.2**	**$**	**119.2**	**13.8%**	**9.2%**
Store operating expenses as a % of related revenues					33.9%	36.1%

Revenues

EMEA total net revenues for fiscal 2015 decreased $78 million, or 6%. The decrease was primarily due to a decline in company-operated store revenues (approximately $103 million), which was largely due to unfavorable foreign currency translation (approximately $94 million). Also contributing to the decrease in company-operated revenues was the shift to more licensed stores in the region, which includes net store closures as well as the absence of revenues from the conversion of certain stores in the U.K. from company-operated to licensed. This decline was partially offset by 4% growth in comparable store sales.

Licensed store revenues increased $19 million, or 8%, primarily due to higher product sales to and royalty revenues from our licensees (approximately $45 million), resulting from the opening of 238 net new licensed stores over the past 12 months and improved comparable store sales, partially offset by unfavorable foreign currency translation (approximately $22 million).

Operating Expenses

Cost of sales including occupancy costs as a percentage of total net revenues decreased 210 basis points, primarily due to favorable foreign currency exchange (approximately 130 basis points). We buy and sell products, primarily roasted coffee, in multiple currencies throughout the region depending on the functional currency of each market. Differences in those rates generated favorable foreign currency exchange for fiscal 2015 resulting in a benefit in cost of sales. Sales leverage(approximately 40 basis points) also contributed to the decrease.

Store operating expenses as a percentage of total net revenues decreased 290 basis points. As a percentage of company-operated store revenues, store operating expenses decreased 220 basis points primarily due to gains on the sales of certain store assets in the region (approximately 150 basis points) as well as decreased expenses, largely salaries and benefits, driven by the shift to more licensed stores (approximately 40 basis points).

Other operating expenses as a percentage of total net revenues increased 60 basis points. Excluding the impact of company-operated store revenues, other operating expenses decreased 20 basis points, primarily driven by the gain on the sale of certain assets in the region (approximately 40 basis points) and improved collection results (approximately 20 basis points). These decreases were partially offset by increased costs to grow our non-retail operations in the region (approximately 50 basis points), largely driven by higher marketing costs.

The combination of these changes resulted in an overall increase in operating margin of 460 basis points over fiscal 2014.

Channel Development

Fiscal Year Ended	Sep 27, 2015	Sep 28, 2014	Sep 27, 2015	Sep 28, 2014
			As a % of Channel Development Total Net Revenues	
Net revenues:				
CPG	$ 1,329.0	$ 1,178.8	76.8%	76.2%
Foodservice	401.9	367.2	23.2	23.8
Total net revenues	**1,730.9**	**1,546.0**	**100.0**	**100.0**
Cost of sales	974.8	882.4	56.3	57.1
Other operating expenses	210.5	187.0	12.2	12.1
Depreciation and amortization expenses	2.7	1.8	0.2	0.1
General and administrative expenses	16.2	18.2	0.9	1.2
Total operating expenses	1,204.2	1,089.4	69.6	70.5
Income from equity investees	127.2	100.6	7.3	6.5
Operating income	**$ 653.9**	**$ 557.2**	**37.8%**	**36.0%**

Revenues

Channel Development total net revenues for fiscal 2015 increased $185 million, or 12%, over the prior year, primarily driven by higher sales of premium single-serve products (approximately $97 million) and U.S. packaged coffee (approximately $42 million), as well as an increase in foodservice sales (approximately $35 million).

Operating Expenses

Cost of sales as a percentage of total net revenues decreased 80 basis points, primarily due to leverage on cost of sales (approximately 100 basis points).

Other operating expenses as a percentage of total net revenues increased 10 basis points, primarily driven by increased marketing (approximately 60 basis points), largely due to new premium single-serve product launches. This increase was partially offset by lower professional fees (approximately 30 basis points) and sales leverage (approximately 20 basis points).

Income from equity investees increased $27 million, driven by higher income from our North American Coffee Partnership joint venture, primarily due to increased sales of bottled Frappuccino® and Starbucks Doubleshot® beverages, largely driven by new product launches and higher sales volumes.

The combination of these changes contributed to an overall increase in operating margin of 180 basis points over fiscal 2014.

All Other Segments

Fiscal Year Ended	Sep 27, 2015	Sep 28, 2014	% Change
Net revenues:			
Company-operated stores	$ 233.2	$ 238.2	(2.1)%
Licensed stores	5.9	5.1	15.7
CPG, foodservice and other	286.7	253.6	13.1
Total net revenues	**525.8**	**496.9**	**5.8**
Cost of sales including occupancy costs	316.5	287.2	10.2
Store operating expenses	104.7	104.5	0.2
Other operating expenses	76.5	74.6	2.5
Depreciation and amortization expenses	16.3	15.2	7.2
General and administrative expenses	36.6	42.2	(13.3)
Total operating expenses	550.6	523.7	5.1
Operating loss	**$ (24.8)**	**$ (26.8)**	**(7.5)%**

All Other Segments primarily includes Teavana, Seattle's Best Coffee, Evolution Fresh, and Digital Ventures, as well as certain developing businesses such as the Starbucks Reserve® Roastery & Tasting Room.

Total net revenues for All Other Segments increased $29 million over the prior year, primarily driven by higher Seattle's Best Coffee® (approximately $23 million) and e-commerce (approximately $8 million) sales.

Total operating expenses increased $27 million, primarily due to an increase in cost of sales.

FINANCIAL CONDITION, LIQUIDITY AND CAPITAL RESOURCES

Cash and Investment Overview

Starbucks cash and investments were $1.9 billion and $2.2 billion as of September 27, 2015 and September 28, 2014, respectively. We actively manage our cash and investments in order to internally fund operating needs, make scheduled interest and principal payments on our borrowings, make acquisitions, and return cash to shareholders through common stock cash dividend payments and share repurchases. Our investment portfolio primarily includes highly liquid available-for-sale securities, including corporate debt securities, government treasury securities (foreign and domestic), mortgage and asset-backed securities, state and local government obligations and agency obligations. As of September 27, 2015, approximately $1.0 billion of cash and investments were held in foreign subsidiaries.

Borrowing capacity

Our $750 million unsecured, revolving credit facility (the "2013 credit facility") with various banks, of which $150 million may be used for issuances of letters of credit, is available for working capital, capital expenditures and other corporate purposes, including acquisitions and share repurchases. During the second quarter of fiscal 2015, we extended the duration of our credit facility, which is now set to mature on January 21, 2020, and amended certain facility fees and borrowing rates. Starbucks has the option, subject to negotiation and agreement with the related banks, to increase the maximum commitment amount by an additional $750 million. Borrowings under the credit facility will bear interest at a variable rate based on LIBOR, and, for U.S. dollar-denominated loans under certain circumstances, a Base Rate (as defined in the credit facility), in each case plus an applicable margin. The applicable margin is based on the better of (i) the Company's long-term credit ratings assigned by Moody's and Standard & Poor's rating agencies and (ii) the Company's fixed charge coverage ratio, pursuant to a pricing grid set forth in the credit facility. The current applicable margin is 0.565% for Eurocurrency Rate Loans and 0.00% for Base Rate Loans. The credit facility contains provisions requiring us to maintain compliance with certain covenants, including a minimum fixed charge coverage ratio, which measures our ability to cover financing expenses. As of September 27, 2015, we were in compliance with all applicable covenants. No amounts were outstanding under our credit facility as of September 27, 2015. During the first quarter of fiscal 2016, we replaced the 2013 credit facility with a new $1.5 billion unsecured, revolving credit facility (the "2016 credit facility") with various banks, which is now set to mature on November 6, 2020. The terms and conditions of the 2016 credit facility are substantially consistent with those of the 2013 credit facility.

Under our commercial paper program, we may issue unsecured commercial paper notes up to a maximum aggregate amount outstanding at any time of $1 billion, with individual maturities that may vary but not exceed 397 days from the date of issue.

Amounts outstanding under the commercial paper program are required to be backstopped by available commitments under our credit facility discussed above. As of September 27, 2015, availability under our commercial paper program was approximately $750 million (which represents the full committed credit facility amount, as the amount of outstanding letters of credit was not material as of September 27, 2015). The proceeds from borrowings under our commercial paper program may be used for working capital needs, capital expenditures and other corporate purposes, including share repurchases, business expansion, payment of cash dividends on our common stock or the financing of possible acquisitions. In the fourth quarter of fiscal 2015, we issued and subsequently repaid commercial paper borrowings of $93 million for general corporate purposes. We had no other borrowings under our commercial paper program during fiscal 2015.

In June 2015, we issued additional long-term debt in an underwritten registered public offering, which consisted of $500 million of 7-year 2.700% Senior Notes (the "2022 notes") due June 2022, and $350 million of 30-year 4.300% Senior Notes (the "2045 notes") due June 2045. Interest on the 2022 notes and the 2045 notes is payable semi-annually on June 15 and December 15 of each year, commencing on December 15, 2015. See Note 9, Debt, to the consolidated financial statements included in Item 8 of Part II of this 10-K for details of the components of our long-term debt.

As discussed in Note 3, Derivative Financial Instruments, to the consolidated financial statements included in Item 8 of Part II of this 10-K, during the first quarter of fiscal 2015, we entered into forward-starting interest rate swap agreements to hedge the variability in cash flows due to changes in the benchmark interest rate related to the 2022 notes. During the third quarter of fiscal 2015, we entered into forward-starting interest rate swap agreements to hedge the variability in cash flows due to changes in the benchmark interest rate related to the 2045 notes. The swap agreements were cash settled in the third quarter of fiscal 2015 at the time the 2022 notes and the 2045 notes were priced. The resulting net losses from these agreements are included in accumulated other comprehensive income and will be amortized as an increase to interest expense on the consolidated statements of net earnings over the lives of the 2022 notes and the 2045 notes.

In July 2015, we redeemed our $550 million of 6.250% Senior Notes (the "2017 notes") that were originally scheduled to mature in August 2017. See Note 9, Debt, to the consolidated financial statements included in Item 8 of Part II of this 10-K for details of the components of our long-term debt.

We continually evaluate liquidity and funding needs and anticipate issuing long-term debt in fiscal 2016 to provide us with financial flexibility. As discussed further in Note 3, Derivative Financial Instruments, to the consolidated financial statements included in Item 8 of Part II of this 10-K, during the fourth quarter of fiscal 2015, we entered into forward-starting interest rate swap agreements to hedge the variability in cash flows due to changes in the benchmark interest rate related to this anticipated debt issuance.

The indentures under which all of our Senior Notes were issued require us to maintain compliance with certain covenants, including limits on future liens and sale and leaseback transactions on certain material properties. As of September 27, 2015, we were in compliance with all applicable covenants. See Note 9, Debt, to the consolidated financial statements included in Item 8 of Part II of this 10-K for details of the components of our long-term debt.

Use of Cash

We expect to use our available cash and investments, including additional potential future borrowings under the credit facility and commercial paper program, to invest in our core businesses, including capital expenditures, new product innovations, related marketing support and partner investments, return cash to shareholders through common stock cash dividend payments and share repurchases, as well as other new business opportunities related to our core businesses. Further, we may use our available cash resources to make proportionate capital contributions to our equity method and cost method investees. We may also seek strategic acquisitions to leverage existing capabilities and further build our business in support of our growth agenda. Acquisitions may include increasing our ownership interests in our equity method and cost method investees. Any decisions to increase such ownership interests will be driven by valuation and fit with our ownership strategy.

We believe that future cash flows generated from operations and existing cash and investments both domestically and internationally will be sufficient to finance capital requirements for our core businesses in those respective markets as well as shareholder distributions for the foreseeable future. Significant new joint ventures, acquisitions and/or other new business opportunities may require additional outside funding. We have borrowed funds domestically and continue to believe we have the ability to do so at reasonable interest rates; however, additional borrowings would result in increased interest expense in the future.

As described in Note 2, Acquisitions and Divestitures, to the consolidated financial statements included in Item 8 of Part II of this 10-K, in September 2014, we entered into a tender offer bid agreement with Starbucks Japan and our former joint venture partner, Sazaby League, Ltd., to acquire the remaining 60.5% ownership interest in Starbucks Japan for approximately $876 million, through a two-step tender offer. In the first quarter of fiscal 2015, we funded the first tender offer step with $509 million in offshore cash. We funded the second tender offer step in the second quarter of fiscal 2015 and the related cash-out procedure during the remainder of fiscal 2015, which required a combined total of $362 million in offshore cash. The remaining $6 million of the purchase price represents cash that was unclaimed by minority shareholders as of September 27, 2015 and is recorded in accrued liabilities on our consolidated balance sheets. There are no legal restrictions on the remaining unclaimed balance.

We consider the majority of undistributed earnings of our foreign subsidiaries and equity investees as of September 27, 2015 to be indefinitely reinvested and, accordingly, no U.S. income and foreign withholding taxes have been provided on such earnings. We have not, nor do we anticipate the need to, repatriate funds to the U.S. to satisfy domestic liquidity needs; however, in the event that we need to repatriate all or a portion of our foreign cash to the U.S., we would be subject to additional U.S. income taxes, which could be material. We do not believe it is practicable to calculate the potential tax impact of repatriation, as there is a significant amount of uncertainty around the calculation, including the availability and amount of foreign tax credits at the time of repatriation, tax rates in effect, and other indirect tax consequences associated with repatriation.

During each of the first three quarters of fiscal 2014, we declared and paid a cash dividend to shareholders of $0.13 per share. In the fourth quarter of fiscal 2014 and each of the first three quarters of fiscal 2015 we declared a cash dividend of $0.16 per share. Cash returned to shareholders through dividends in fiscal 2015 and 2014 totaled $958.7 million and $783.1 million, respectively. In the fourth quarter of fiscal 2015, we declared a cash dividend of $0.20 per share to be paid on November 27, 2015 with an expected payout of approximately $297.0 million.

During fiscal years 2015 and 2014, we repurchased 29.0 million and 21.0 million shares of common stock, respectively, or $1.4 billion and $769.8 million, respectively, under share repurchase authorizations. On July 23, 2015, we announced that our Board of Directors approved an increase of 50 million shares to our ongoing share repurchase program. The number of remaining shares authorized for repurchase at September 27, 2015 totaled 52.7 million.

Other than normal operating expenses, cash requirements for fiscal 2016 are expected to consist primarily of capital expenditures for new company-operated stores; remodeling and refurbishment of, and equipment upgrades for, existing company-operated stores; systems and technology investments in our stores and in the support infrastructure; and additional investments in manufacturing capacity. Total capital expenditures for fiscal 2016 are expected to be approximately $1.4 billion.

Cash Flows

Cash provided by operating activities was $3.7 billion for fiscal 2015, compared to $607.8 million for fiscal 2014. The increase was driven by lapping the prior year payment of $2.8 billion for the Kraft arbitration matter. The remaining change of $377 million was primarily due to increased earnings, partially offset by changes in working capital accounts mainly due to timing.

Cash used by investing activities totaled $1.5 billion for fiscal 2015, compared to $817.7 million for fiscal 2014. The change was primarily due to the use of cash to acquire Sazaby's 39.5% ownership interest in Japan in the first quarter of fiscal 2015, as well as lapping the liquidation of a significant portion of our offshore investment portfolio in the fourth quarter of fiscal 2014 in order to fund the acquisition of Starbucks Japan. Additions to property, plant and equipment also contributed, driven by increased store renovations and additions for new store openings.

Cash used by financing activities for fiscal 2015 totaled $2.3 billion, compared to $623.3 million for fiscal 2014. The change was primarily due to increased cash returned to shareholders through higher share repurchases and dividend payments compared to fiscal 2014 and cash used to redeem our 2017 notes, as discussed above, as well as cash used to fund the second tender offer step and the cash-out procedure of the Starbucks Japan acquisition in fiscal 2015. These changes were partially offset by incremental proceeds from the long-term debt we issued in June of fiscal 2015 over the prior year's issuance.

Contractual Obligations

The following table summarizes our contractual obligations and borrowings as of September 27, 2015, and the timing and effect that such commitments are expected to have on our liquidity and capital requirements in future periods (*in millions*):

Contractual Obligations [1]	Total		Payments Due by Period		
		Less than 1 Year	1 - 3 Years	3 - 5 Years	More than 5 Years
Operating lease obligations [2]	$ 5,669.5	$ 1,032.4	$ 1,632.3	$ 1,172.9	$ 1,831.9
Financing lease obligations [3]	47.1	3.2	6.4	6.4	31.1
Debt obligations					
Principal payments	2,350.0	—	400.0	350.0	1,600.0
Interest payments [4]	821.2	67.9	130.6	118.4	504.3
Purchase obligations [5]	1,257.1	884.0	284.7	76.0	12.4
Other obligations [6]	122.7	19.2	28.3	13.0	62.2
Total	$ 10,267.6	$ 2,006.7	$ 2,482.3	$ 1,736.7	$ 4,041.9

[1] Income tax liabilities for uncertain tax positions were excluded as we are not able to make a reasonably reliable estimate of the amount and period of related future payments. As of September 27, 2015, we had $159.3 million of gross unrecognized tax benefits for uncertain tax positions, which includes accrued interest and penalties.

[2] Amounts include direct lease obligations, excluding any taxes, insurance and other related expenses.

[3] Amounts consist of build-to-suit lease arrangements primarily related to the Starbucks Japan acquisition, which are described further in Note 2, Acquisitions and Divestitures, to the consolidated financial statements included in Item 8 of Part II of this 10-K.

[4] Amounts exclude any gain or loss upon settlement of related interest rate swap agreements, which are described further in Note 3, Derivative Financial Instruments, to the consolidated financial statements included in Item 8 of Part II of this 10-K.

[5] Purchase obligations include agreements to purchase goods or services that are enforceable and legally binding on Starbucks and that specify all significant terms. Green coffee purchase commitments comprise 86% of total purchase obligations.

[6] Other obligations include other long-term liabilities primarily consisting of asset retirement obligations and hedging instruments.

Starbucks currently expects to fund these commitments primarily with operating cash flows generated in the normal course of business.

Off-Balance Sheet Arrangements

Off-balance sheet arrangements relate to operating lease and purchase commitments detailed in the footnotes to the consolidated financial statements included in Item 8 of Part II of this 10-K.

APPLICATION OF CRITICAL ACCOUNTING POLICIES

Critical accounting policies are those that management believes are both most important to the portrayal of our financial condition and results and require the most difficult, subjective or complex judgments, often as a result of the need to make estimates about the effect of matters that are inherently uncertain. Judgments and uncertainties affecting the application of those policies may result in materially different amounts being reported under different conditions or using different assumptions.

Our significant accounting policies are discussed in Note 1, Summary of Significant Accounting Policies, to the consolidated financial statements included in Item 8 of Part II of this 10-K. We believe that of our significant accounting policies, the following policies involve a higher degree of judgment and/or complexity.

We consider financial reporting and disclosure practices and accounting policies quarterly to ensure that they provide accurate and transparent information relative to the current economic and business environment. During the past three fiscal years, we have not made any material changes to the accounting methodologies used to assess the areas discussed below, unless noted otherwise.

Property, Plant and Equipment and Other Finite-Lived Assets

We evaluate property, plant and equipment and other finite-lived assets for impairment when facts and circumstances indicate that the carrying values of such assets may not be recoverable. When evaluating for impairment, we first compare the carrying value of the asset to the asset's estimated future undiscounted cash flows. If the estimated undiscounted future cash flows are less than the carrying value of the asset, we determine if we have an impairment loss by comparing the carrying value of the asset to the asset's estimated fair value and recognize an impairment charge when the asset's carrying value exceeds its estimated fair value. The adjusted carrying amount of the asset becomes its new cost basis and is depreciated over the asset's remaining useful life.

Long-lived assets are grouped with other assets and liabilities at the lowest level for which identifiable cash flows are largely independent of the cash flows of other assets and liabilities. For company-operated store assets, the impairment test is performed at the individual store asset group level. The fair value of a store's assets is estimated using a discounted cash flow model. For other long-lived assets, fair value is determined using an approach that is appropriate based on the relevant facts and circumstances, which may include discounted cash flows, comparable transactions, or comparable company analyses.

Our impairment calculations contain uncertainties because they require management to make assumptions and to apply judgment to estimate future cash flows and asset fair values. Key assumptions used in estimating future cash flows and asset fair values include projected revenue growth and operating expenses, as well as forecasting asset useful lives and selecting an appropriate discount rate. For company-operated stores, estimates of revenue growth and operating expenses are based on internal projections and consider the store's historical performance, the local market economics and the business environment impacting the store's performance. The discount rate is selected based on what we believe a buyer would assume when determining a purchase price for the store. These estimates are subjective and our ability to realize future cash flows and asset fair values is affected by factors such as ongoing maintenance and improvement of the assets, changes in economic conditions, and changes in operating performance.

During fiscal 2015, there were no significant changes in any of our estimates or assumptions that had a material impact on the outcome of our impairment calculations. However, as we periodically reassess estimated future cash flows and asset fair values, changes in our estimates and assumptions may cause us to realize material impairment charges in the future.

Goodwill and Indefinite-Lived Intangible Assets

We evaluate goodwill and indefinite-lived intangible assets (primarily trade names and trademarks) for impairment annually during our third fiscal quarter, or more frequently if an event occurs or circumstances change that would indicate that impairment may exist. When evaluating for impairment, we may first perform a qualitative assessment to determine whether it is more likely than not that a reporting unit or intangible asset group is impaired. If we do not perform a qualitative assessment, or if we determine that it is not more likely than not that the fair value of the reporting unit or intangible asset group exceeds its carrying amount, we calculate the estimated fair value of the reporting unit or intangible asset group. Fair value is the price a market participant would pay for the reporting unit or intangible asset and is typically calculated using an income approach, such as a discounted cash flow or relief-from-royalty method. For certain reporting units, where deemed appropriate, we may also utilize a market approach. Under the market approach, fair value is estimated by reviewing prices in market transactions involving identical or comparable assets or liabilities with a similar risk profile. If the carrying amount of the reporting unit or intangible asset group exceeds the estimated fair value, an impairment charge is recorded to reduce the carrying value to the estimated fair value.

Our decision to perform a qualitative impairment assessment for an individual reporting unit in a given year is influenced by a number of factors, inclusive of the size of the reporting unit's goodwill, the significance of the excess of the reporting unit's estimated fair value over carrying value at the last quantitative assessment date, the amount of time in between quantitative fair value assessments and the date of acquisition. During fiscal 2015, as part of our annual goodwill impairment analysis, we performed the qualitative assessment for approximately $941 million, or 60%, of our total goodwill balance of $1.6 billion, the majority of which resides in our Japan retail, U.S. company-operated and Canada company-operated reporting units. Our Japan retail reporting unit, which was acquired in fiscal 2015, represented approximately $730 million of the goodwill balance that was assessed qualitatively.

As part of our ongoing operations, we may close certain stores within a reporting unit containing goodwill due to underperformance of the store or inability to renew our lease, among other reasons. We may abandon certain assets associated with a closed store, including leasehold improvements and other non-transferable assets. When a portion of a reporting unit that constitutes a business is to be disposed of, the associated goodwill is included in the carrying amount when determining any loss on disposal. Our evaluation of whether the portion of a reporting unit being disposed of constitutes a business occurs on the date of abandonment. Although an operating store meets the accounting definition of a business prior to abandonment, it does not constitute a business on the closure date because the remaining assets on that date do not constitute an integrated set of assets that are capable of being managed for the purpose of providing a return to investors. As a result, when closing individual stores, we do not include goodwill in the calculation of any loss on disposal of the related assets. If store closures are indicative of potential impairment of goodwill at the reporting unit level, we perform an evaluation of our reporting unit goodwill when such closures occur.

Our impairment calculations contain uncertainties because they require management to make assumptions and to apply judgment when performing a qualitative assessment or when estimating future cash flows and asset fair values. Key assumptions used in estimating future cash flows and asset fair values typically include projected revenue growth and operating expenses related to existing businesses, product innovation and new store concepts, as well as selecting an appropriate discount rate. For indefinite-lived intangible assets, management also makes assumptions around the royalty rate that could hypothetically be charged by a licensor of the asset to an unrelated licensee. For a goodwill reporting unit, estimates of revenue growth and operating expenses are based on internal projections considering the reporting unit's past performance and forecasted growth, strategic initiatives, local market economics and the local business environment impacting the reporting unit's performance. The discount rate is selected based on the estimated cost of capital for a market participant to operate the reporting unit in the region. For indefinite-lived intangible assets, estimates of revenue growth are based on internal projections considering the intangible asset group's past performance and forecasted growth, and the royalty rate used is based on observed market royalty rates for similar licensing arrangements, adjusted for our particular facts and circumstances. The discount rate is selected based on the estimated cost of capital that reflects the risk profile of the related business. These estimates are highly subjective judgments and our ability to realize the future cash flows used in our fair value calculations is affected by factors such as the success of strategic initiatives, changes in economic conditions, changes in our operating performance, and changes in our business strategies, including retail initiatives and international expansion.

For fiscal 2015, we determined the fair value of our material reporting units and intangible asset groups were significantly in excess of their carrying values. Accordingly, we did not recognize any material impairment charges during the current fiscal year. During fiscal 2015, there were no significant changes in any of our estimates or assumptions that had a material impact on the outcome of our impairment calculations. However, as we periodically reassess estimated future cash flows and asset fair values, changes in our estimates and assumptions may cause us to realize material impairment charges in the future.

Income Taxes

We recognize deferred tax assets and liabilities based on the differences between the financial statement carrying amounts and the respective tax bases of our assets and liabilities. Deferred tax assets and liabilities are measured using current enacted tax rates expected to apply to taxable income in the years in which we expect the temporary differences to reverse. We routinely evaluate the likelihood of realizing the benefit of our deferred tax assets and may record a valuation allowance if, based on all available evidence, we determine that some portion of the tax benefit will not be realized. Changes in tax laws and rates may affect recorded deferred tax assets and liabilities and our effective tax rate in the future; however, we do not expect changes from recently enacted tax laws to be material to the consolidated financial statements.

In evaluating our ability to recover our deferred tax assets within the jurisdiction from which they arise, we consider all available positive and negative evidence, including scheduled reversals of deferred tax liabilities, projected future taxable income, tax-planning strategies, and results of operations. In projecting future taxable income, we consider historical results and incorporate assumptions about the amount of future state, federal, and foreign pretax operating income adjusted for items that do not have tax consequences. Our assumptions regarding future taxable income are consistent with the plans and estimates we are using to manage the underlying businesses. In evaluating the objective evidence that historical results provide, we consider three years of cumulative operating income/(loss).

In addition, our income tax returns are periodically audited by domestic and foreign tax authorities. These audits include review of our tax filing positions, including the timing and amount of deductions taken and the allocation of income between tax jurisdictions. We evaluate our exposures associated with our various tax filing positions and recognize a tax benefit only if it is more likely than not that the tax position will be sustained upon examination by the relevant taxing authorities, including resolutions of any related appeals or litigation processes, based on the technical merits of our position. For uncertain tax positions that do not meet this threshold, we record a related liability. We adjust our unrecognized tax benefit liability and income tax expense in the period in which the uncertain tax position is effectively settled, the statute of limitations expires for the relevant taxing authority to examine the tax position, or when new information becomes available. As discussed in Note 13, Income Taxes, to the consolidated financial statements included in Item 8 of Part II of this 10-K, there is a reasonable possibility that our unrecognized tax benefit liability will be adjusted within 12 months due to the expiration of a statute of limitations and expected consent from taxing authorities.

We have generated income in certain foreign jurisdictions that has not been subject to U.S. income taxes. We intend to reinvest these earnings for the foreseeable future. While we do not expect to repatriate cash to the U.S. to satisfy domestic liquidity needs, if these amounts were distributed to the U.S., in the form of dividends or otherwise, we would be subject to additional U.S. income taxes, which could be material. Determination of the amount of unrecognized deferred income tax liabilities on these earnings is not practicable because such liability, if any, is dependent on circumstances existing if and when remittance occurs.

Our income tax expense, deferred tax assets and liabilities, and liabilities for unrecognized tax benefits reflect management's best assessment of estimated current and future taxes to be paid. Deferred tax asset valuation allowances and our liabilities for unrecognized tax benefits require significant management judgment regarding applicable statutes and their related interpretation, the status of various income tax audits, and our particular facts and circumstances. Although we believe that the judgments and estimates discussed herein are reasonable, actual results could differ, and we may be exposed to losses or gains that could be material. To the extent we prevail in matters for which a liability has been established, or are required to pay amounts in excess of our established liability, our effective income tax rate in a given financial statement period could be materially affected.

RECENT ACCOUNTING PRONOUNCEMENTS

See Note 1, Summary of Significant Accounting Policies, to the consolidated financial statements included in Item 8 of Part II of this 10-K for a detailed description of recent accounting pronouncements.

Item 8. *Financial Statements and Supplementary Data*

STARBUCKS CORPORATION
CONSOLIDATED STATEMENTS OF EARNINGS
(in millions, except per share data)

Fiscal Year Ended	Sep 27, 2015	Sep 28, 2014	Sep 29, 2013
Net revenues:			
Company-operated stores	$ 15,197.3	$ 12,977.9	$ 11,793.2
Licensed stores	1,861.9	1,588.6	1,360.5
CPG, foodservice and other	2,103.5	1,881.3	1,713.1
Total net revenues	19,162.7	16,447.8	14,866.8
Cost of sales including occupancy costs	7,787.5	6,858.8	6,382.3
Store operating expenses	5,411.1	4,638.2	4,286.1
Other operating expenses	522.4	457.3	431.8
Depreciation and amortization expenses	893.9	709.6	621.4
General and administrative expenses	1,196.7	991.3	937.9
Litigation charge/(credit)	—	(20.2)	2,784.1
Total operating expenses	15,811.6	13,635.0	15,443.6
Income from equity investees	249.9	268.3	251.4
Operating income/(loss)	3,601.0	3,081.1	(325.4)
Gain resulting from acquisition of joint venture	390.6	—	—
Loss on extinguishment of debt	(61.1)	—	—
Interest income and other, net	43.0	142.7	123.6
Interest expense	(70.5)	(64.1)	(28.1)
Earnings/(loss) before income taxes	3,903.0	3,159.7	(229.9)
Income tax expense/(benefit)	1,143.7	1,092.0	(238.7)
Net earnings including noncontrolling interests	2,759.3	2,067.7	8.8
Net earnings/(loss) attributable to noncontrolling interests	1.9	(0.4)	0.5
Net earnings attributable to Starbucks	$ 2,757.4	$ 2,068.1	$ 8.3
Earnings per share — basic	$ 1.84	$ 1.37	$ 0.01
Earnings per share — diluted	$ 1.82	$ 1.35	$ 0.01
Weighted average shares outstanding:			
Basic	1,495.9	1,506.3	1,498.5
Diluted	1,513.4	1,526.3	1,524.5

See Notes to Consolidated Financial Statements.

STARBUCKS CORPORATION
CONSOLIDATED STATEMENTS OF COMPREHENSIVE INCOME
(in millions)

	Sep 27, 2015	Sep 28, 2014	Sep 29, 2013
Net earnings including noncontrolling interests	$ 2,759.3	$ 2,067.7	$ 8.8
Other comprehensive income/(loss), net of tax:			
Unrealized holding gains/(losses) on available-for-sale securities	1.4	1.6	(0.6)
Tax (expense)/benefit	(0.5)	(0.6)	0.2
Unrealized gains/(losses) on cash flow hedging instruments	47.6	24.1	47.1
Tax (expense)/benefit	(16.8)	(7.8)	(24.6)
Unrealized gains/(losses) on net investment hedging instruments	4.3	25.5	32.8
Tax (expense)/benefit	(1.6)	(9.4)	(12.1)
Translation adjustment	(222.7)	(75.8)	(41.6)
Tax (expense)/benefit	6.0	(1.6)	0.3
Reclassification adjustment for net (gains)/losses realized in net earnings for available-for-sale securities, hedging instruments, and translation adjustment	(65.9)	(1.5)	46.3
Tax expense/(benefit)	23.5	3.8	(3.5)
Other comprehensive income/(loss)	(224.7)	(41.7)	44.3
Comprehensive income including noncontrolling interests	2,534.6	2,026.0	53.1
Comprehensive income/(loss) attributable to noncontrolling interests	(29.2)	(0.4)	0.5
Comprehensive income attributable to Starbucks	$ 2,563.8	$ 2,026.4	$ 52.6

See Notes to Consolidated Financial Statements.

STARBUCKS CORPORATION CONSOLIDATED BALANCE SHEETS
(in millions, except per share data)

	Sep 27, 2015	Sep 28, 2014
ASSETS		
Current assets:		
Cash and cash equivalents	$ 1,530.1	$ 1,708.4
Short-term investments	81.3	135.4
Accounts receivable, net	719.0	631.0
Inventories	1,306.4	1,090.9
Prepaid expenses and other current assets	334.2	285.6
Deferred income taxes, net	381.7	317.4
Total current assets	4,352.7	4,168.7
Long-term investments	312.5	318.4
Equity and cost investments	352.0	514.9
Property, plant and equipment, net	4,088.3	3,519.0
Deferred income taxes, net	828.9	903.3
Other long-term assets	415.9	198.9
Other intangible assets	520.4	273.5
Goodwill	1,575.4	856.2
TOTAL ASSETS	$ 12,446.1	$ 10,752.9
LIABILITIES AND EQUITY		
Current liabilities:		
Accounts payable	$ 684.2	$ 533.7
Accrued liabilities	1,760.7	1,514.4
Insurance reserves	224.8	196.1
Stored value card liability	983.8	794.5
Total current liabilities	3,653.5	3,038.7
Long-term debt	2,347.5	2,048.3
Other long-term liabilities	625.3	392.2
Total liabilities	6,626.3	5,479.2
Shareholders' equity:		
Common stock ($0.001 par value) — authorized, 2,400.0 shares; issued and outstanding, 1,485.1 and 1,499.1 shares, respectively	1.5	0.7
Additional paid-in capital	41.1	39.4
Retained earnings	5,974.8	5,206.6
Accumulated other comprehensive income/(loss)	(199.4)	25.3
Total shareholders' equity	5,818.0	5,272.0
Noncontrolling interest	1.8	1.7
Total equity	5,819.8	5,273.7
TOTAL LIABILITIES AND EQUITY	$ 12,446.1	$ 10,752.9

See Notes to Consolidated Financial Statements.

STARBUCKS CORPORATION
CONSOLIDATED STATEMENTS OF CASH FLOWS
(in millions)

Fiscal Year Ended	Sep 27, 2015	Sep 28, 2014	Sep 29, 2013
OPERATING ACTIVITIES:			
Net earnings including noncontrolling interests	$ 2,759.3	$ 2,067.7	$ 8.8
Adjustments to reconcile net earnings to net cash provided by operating activities:			
Depreciation and amortization	933.8	748.4	655.6
Litigation charge	—	—	2,784.1
Deferred income taxes, net	21.2	10.2	(1,045.9)
Income earned from equity method investees	(190.2)	(182.7)	(171.8)
Distributions received from equity method investees	148.2	139.2	115.6
Gain resulting from acquisition/sale of equity in joint ventures and certain retail operations	(394.3)	(70.2)	(80.1)
Loss on extinguishment of debt	61.1	—	—
Stock-based compensation	209.8	183.2	142.3
Excess tax benefit on share-based awards	(132.4)	(114.4)	(258.1)
Other	53.8	36.2	23.0
Cash provided/(used) by changes in operating assets and liabilities:			
Accounts receivable	(82.8)	(79.7)	(68.3)
Inventories	(207.9)	14.3	152.5
Accounts payable	137.7	60.4	88.7
Accrued litigation charge	—	(2,763.9)	—
Income taxes payable, net	87.6	309.8	298.4
Accrued liabilities and insurance reserves	124.4	103.9	47.3
Stored value card liability	170.3	140.8	139.9
Prepaid expenses, other current assets and other long-term assets	49.5	4.6	76.3
Net cash provided by operating activities	3,749.1	607.8	2,908.3
INVESTING ACTIVITIES:			
Purchases of investments	(567.4)	(1,652.5)	(785.9)
Sales of investments	600.6	1,454.8	60.2
Maturities and calls of investments	18.8	456.1	980.0
Acquisitions, net of cash acquired	(284.3)	—	(610.4)
Additions to property, plant and equipment	(1,303.7)	(1,160.9)	(1,151.2)
Proceeds from sale of equity in joint ventures and certain retail operations	8.9	103.9	108.0
Other	6.8	(19.1)	(11.9)
Net cash used by investing activities	(1,520.3)	(817.7)	(1,411.2)

FINANCING ACTIVITIES:			
Proceeds from issuance of long-term debt	848.5	748.5	749.7
Repayments of long-term debt	(610.1)	—	(35.2)
Cash used for purchase of non-controlling interest	(360.8)	—	—
Proceeds from issuance of common stock	191.8	139.7	247.2
Excess tax benefit on share-based awards	132.4	114.4	258.1
Cash dividends paid	(928.6)	(783.1)	(628.9)
Repurchase of common stock	(1,436.1)	(758.6)	(588.1)
Minimum tax withholdings on share-based awards	(75.5)	(77.3)	(121.4)
Other	(18.1)	(6.9)	10.4
Net cash used by financing activities	(2,256.5)	(623.3)	(108.2)
Effect of exchange rate changes on cash and cash equivalents	(150.6)	(34.1)	(1.8)
Net (decrease)/increase in cash and cash equivalents	(178.3)	(867.3)	1,387.1
CASH AND CASH EQUIVALENTS:			
Beginning of period	1,708.4	2,575.7	1,188.6
End of period	$ 1,530.1	$ 1,708.4	$ 2,575.7
SUPPLEMENTAL DISCLOSURE OF CASH FLOW INFORMATION:			
Cash paid during the period for:			
Interest, net of capitalized interest	$ 69.5	$ 56.2	$ 34.4
Income taxes, net of refunds	$ 1,072.2	$ 766.3	$ 539.1

See Notes to Consolidated Financial Statements.

STARBUCKS CORPORATION
CONSOLIDATED STATEMENTS OF EQUITY
(in millions, except per share data)

	Common Stock		Additional Paid-in Capital	Retained Earnings	Accumulated Other Comprehensive Income/(Loss)	Shareholders' Equity	Noncontrolling Interest	Total
	Shares	Amount						
Balance, September 30, 2012	749.3	$ 0.7	$ 39.4	$ 5,046.2	$ 22.7	$ 5,109.0	$ 5.5	$ 5,114.5
Net earnings	—	—	—	8.3	—	8.3	0.5	8.8
Other comprehensive income/(loss)					44.3	44.3	—	44.3
Stock-based compensation expense	—	—	144.1	—	—	144.1	—	144.1
Exercise of stock options/vesting of RSUs, including tax benefit of $259.9	14.4	0.1	366.7	—	—	366.8	—	366.8
Sale of common stock, including tax benefit of $0.2	0.3	—	20.4	—	—	20.4	—	20.4
Repurchase of common stock	(10.8)	—	(288.5)	(255.6)	—	(544.1)	—	(544.1)
Cash dividends declared, $0.445 per share	—	—	—	(668.6)	—	(668.6)	—	(668.6)
Noncontrolling interest resulting from divestiture	—	—	—	—	—	—	(3.9)	(3.9)
Balance, September 29, 2013	753.2	$ 0.8	$ 282.1	$ 4,130.3	$ 67.0	$ 4,480.2	$ 2.1	$ 4,482.3
Net earnings	—	—	—	2,068.1	—	2,068.1	(0.4)	2,067.7
Other comprehensive income/(loss)					(41.7)	(41.7)	—	(41.7)
Stock-based compensation expense	—	—	185.1	—	—	185.1	—	185.1
Exercise of stock options/vesting of RSUs, including tax benefit of $114.8	6.5	—	154.8	—	—	154.8	—	154.8
Sale of common stock, including tax benefit of $0.2	0.3	—	22.3	—	—	22.3	—	22.3
Repurchase of common stock	(10.5)	(0.1)	(604.9)	(164.8)	—	(769.8)	—	(769.8)
Cash dividends declared, $0.550 per share	—	—	—	(827.0)	—	(827.0)	—	(827.0)
Balance, September 28, 2014	749.5	$ 0.7	$ 39.4	$ 5,206.6	$ 25.3	$ 5,272.0	$ 1.7	$ 5,273.7
Net earnings	—	—	—	2,757.4	—	2,757.4	1.9	2,759.3
Other comprehensive income/(loss)					(193.6)	(193.6)	(31.1)	(224.7)

Stock-based compensation expense	—		—		211.7		—		—		211.7		—		211.7
Exercise of stock options/vesting of RSUs, including tax benefit of $131.3	14.6		—		224.4		—		—		224.4		—		224.4
Sale of common stock, including tax benefit of $0.2	0.6		—		23.5		—		—		23.5		—		23.5
Repurchase of common stock	(29.0)		—		(459.6)		(972.2)		—		(1,431.8)		—		(1,431.8)
Cash dividends declared, $0.680 per share	—		—		—		(1,016.2)		—		(1,016.2)		—		(1,016.2)
Two-for-one stock split	749.4		0.8		—		(0.8)		—		—		—		—
Noncontrolling interest resulting from acquisition	—		—		—		—		—		—		411.1		411.1
Purchase of noncontrolling interest	—		—		1.7		—		(31.1)		(29.4)		(381.7)		(411.1)
Balance, September 27, 2015	1,485.1	$	1.5	$	41.1	$	5,974.8	$	(199.4)	$	5,818.0	$	1.8	$	5,819.8

See Notes to Consolidated Financial Statements.

STARBUCKS CORPORATION
NOTES TO CONSOLIDATED FINANCIAL STATEMENTS
Fiscal Years ended September 27, 2015, September 28, 2014 and September 29, 2013

Note 1: Summary of Significant Accounting Policies

Description of Business

We purchase and roast high-quality coffees that we sell, along with handcrafted coffee and tea beverages and a variety of fresh food items, through our company-operated stores. We also sell a variety of coffee and tea products and license our trademarks through other channels such as licensed stores, grocery and national foodservice accounts.

In this 10-K, Starbucks Corporation (together with its subsidiaries) is referred to as "Starbucks," the "Company," "we," "us" or "our."

We have four reportable operating segments: 1) Americas, which is inclusive of the U.S., Canada, and Latin America; 2) China/Asia Pacific ("CAP"); 3) Europe, Middle East, and Africa ("EMEA") and 4) Channel Development. We also have several non-reportable operating segments, including Teavana, Seattle's Best Coffee, Evolution Fresh, and our Digital Ventures business, as well as certain developing businesses such as the Starbucks Reserve® Roastery & Tasting Room, which are combined and referred to as All Other Segments. Unallocated corporate operating expenses, which pertain primarily to corporate administrative functions that support the operating segments but are not specifically attributable to or managed by any segment, are presented as a reconciling item between total segment operating results and consolidated financial results.

Additional details on the nature of our business and our reportable operating segments are included in Note 16, Segment Reporting, of these Consolidated Financial Statements.

Principles of Consolidation

Our consolidated financial statements reflect the financial position and operating results of Starbucks, including wholly-owned subsidiaries and investees that we control. Investments in entities that we do not control, but have the ability to exercise significant influence over operating and financial policies, are accounted for under the equity method. Investments in entities in which we do not have the ability to exercise significant influence are accounted for under the cost method. Intercompany transactions and balances have been eliminated.

Fiscal Year End

Our fiscal year ends on the Sunday closest to September 30. Fiscal years 2015, 2014 and 2013 included 52 weeks.

Estimates and Assumptions

Preparing financial statements in conformity with accounting principles generally accepted in the United States of America ("GAAP") requires management to make estimates and assumptions that affect the reported amounts of assets, liabilities, revenues and expenses. Examples include, but are not limited to, estimates for inventory reserves, asset and goodwill impairments, assumptions underlying self-insurance reserves, income from unredeemed stored value cards, stock-based compensation forfeiture rates, future asset retirement obligations, and the potential outcome of future tax consequences of events that have been recognized in the financial statements. Actual results and outcomes may differ from these estimates and assumptions.

Cash and Cash Equivalents

We consider all highly liquid instruments with maturities of three months or less at the time of purchase, as well as credit card receivables for sales to customers in our company-operated stores that generally settle within two to five days, to be cash equivalents. We maintain cash and cash equivalent balances with financial institutions that exceed federally-insured limits. We have not experienced any losses related to these balances and we believe credit risk to be minimal.

Our cash management system provides for the funding of all major bank disbursement accounts on a daily basis as checks are presented for payment. Under this system, outstanding checks are in excess of the cash balances at certain banks, which creates book overdrafts. Book overdrafts are presented as a current liability in accrued liabilities on our consolidated balance sheets.

Investments

Available-for-sale Securities

Our short-term and long-term investments consist primarily of investment-grade debt securities, all of which are classified as available-for-sale. Available-for-sale securities are recorded at fair value, and unrealized holding gains and losses are recorded, net of tax, as a component of accumulated other comprehensive income. Available-for-sale securities with remaining maturities of less than one year and those identified by management at the time of purchase to be used to fund operations within one year are classified as short-term. All other available-for-sale securities are classified as long-term. We evaluate our available-for-sale securities for other than temporary impairment on a quarterly basis. Unrealized losses are charged against net earnings when a decline in fair value is determined to be other than temporary. We review several factors to determine whether a loss is other than temporary, such as the length and extent of the fair value decline, the financial condition and near-term prospects of the issuer, and whether we have the intent to sell or will more likely than not be required to sell before the securities' anticipated recovery, which may be at maturity. Realized gains and losses are accounted for using the specific identification method. Purchases and sales are recorded on a trade date basis.

Trading Securities

We also have a trading securities portfolio, which is comprised of marketable equity mutual funds and equity exchange-traded funds. Trading securities are recorded at fair value with unrealized holding gains and losses recorded in net interest income and other on our consolidated statements of earnings. Our trading securities portfolio approximates a portion of our liability under our Management Deferred Compensation Plan ("MDCP"), which is included in accrued compensation and related costs, within accrued liabilities on our consolidated balance sheets. Changes in our MDCP liability are recorded in general and administrative expenses on our consolidated statements of earnings.

Equity and Cost Method Investments

We evaluate our equity and cost method investments for impairment annually and when facts and circumstances indicate that the carrying value of such investments may not be recoverable. We review several factors to determine whether the loss is other than temporary, such as the length and extent of the fair value decline, the financial condition and near-term prospects of the investee, and whether we have the intent to sell or will more likely than not be required to sell before the investment's anticipated recovery. If a decline in fair value is determined to be other than temporary, an impairment charge is recorded in net earnings.

Fair Value

Fair value is the price we would receive to sell an asset or pay to transfer a liability (exit price) in an orderly transaction between market participants. For assets and liabilities recorded or disclosed at fair value on a recurring basis, we determine fair value based on the following:

Level 1: The carrying value of cash and cash equivalents approximates fair value because of the short-term nature of these instruments. For trading and U.S. government treasury securities and commodity futures contracts, we use quoted prices in active markets for identical assets to determine fair value.

Level 2: When quoted prices in active markets for identical assets are not available, we determine the fair value of our available-for-sale securities and our over-the-counter forward contracts, collars, and swaps based upon factors such as the quoted market price of similar assets or a discounted cash flow model using readily observable market data, which may include interest rate curves and forward and spot prices for currencies and commodities, depending on the nature of the investment. The fair value of our long-term debt is estimated based on the quoted market prices for the same or similar issues or on the current rates offered to us for debt of the same remaining maturities.

Level 3: We determine the fair value of our auction rate securities using an internally-developed valuation model, using inputs that include interest rate curves, credit and liquidity spreads, and effective maturity.

Assets and liabilities recognized or disclosed at fair value on a nonrecurring basis include items such as property, plant and equipment, goodwill and other intangible assets, equity and cost method investments, and other assets. We determine the fair value of these items using Level 3 inputs, as described in the related sections below.

Derivative Instruments

We manage our exposure to various risks within our consolidated financial statements according to a market price risk management policy. Under this policy, we may engage in transactions involving various derivative instruments to hedge interest rates, commodity prices and foreign currency denominated revenue streams, inventory purchases, assets and liabilities, and investments in certain foreign operations. We record all derivatives on our consolidated balance sheets at fair value. We generally do not offset derivative assets and liabilities in our consolidated balance sheets or enter into derivative instruments with maturities longer than three years. Refer to Note 3, Derivative Financial Instruments, for further discussion of our derivative instruments. We do not enter into derivative instruments for trading purposes.

We use various types of derivative instruments including forward contracts, commodity futures contracts, collars and swaps. Forward contracts and commodity futures contracts are agreements to buy or sell a quantity of a currency or commodity at a predetermined future date, and at a predetermined rate or price. A collar is a strategy that uses a combination of a purchased call option and a sold put option with equal premiums to hedge a portion of anticipated cash flows, or to limit the range of possible gains or losses on an underlying asset or liability to a specific range. A swap agreement is a contract between two parties to exchange cash flows based on specified underlying notional amounts, assets and/or indices.

Cash Flow Hedges

For derivative instruments that are designated and qualify as a cash flow hedge, the effective portion of the derivative's gain or loss is reported as a component of other comprehensive income ("OCI") and recorded in accumulated other comprehensive income ("AOCI") on our consolidated balance sheets. The gain or loss is subsequently reclassified into net earnings when the hedged exposure affects net earnings.

To the extent that the change in the fair value of the contract corresponds to the change in the value of the anticipated transaction using forward rates on a monthly basis, the hedge is considered effective and is recognized as described above. The remaining change in fair value of the contract represents the ineffective portion, which is immediately recorded in net interest income and other on our consolidated statements of earnings.

Cash flow hedges related to anticipated transactions are designated and documented at the inception of each hedge by matching the terms of the contract to the underlying transaction. Cash flows from hedging transactions are classified in the same categories as the cash flows from the respective hedged items, which is discussed further at Note 3, Derivative Financial Instruments. Once established, cash flow hedges generally remain designated as such until the hedge item impacts net earnings, or the anticipated transaction is no longer likely to occur. For dedesignated cash flow hedges or for transactions that are no longer likely to occur, the related accumulated derivative gains or losses are recognized in net interest income and other or interest expense on our consolidated statements of earnings based on the nature of the underlying transaction.

Net Investment Hedges

For derivative instruments that are designated and qualify as a net investment hedge, the effective portion of the derivative's gain or loss is reported as a component of OCI and recorded in AOCI. The gain or loss will be subsequently reclassified into net earnings when the hedged net investment is either sold or substantially liquidated.

To the extent that the change in the fair value of the forward contract corresponds to the change in value of the anticipated transactions using spot rates on a monthly basis, the hedge is considered effective and is recognized as described above. The remaining change in fair value of the forward contract represents the ineffective portion, which is immediately recognized in net interest income and other on our consolidated statements of earnings.

Derivatives Not Designated As Hedging Instruments

We also enter into certain foreign currency forward contracts, commodity futures contracts, collars and swaps that are not designated as hedging instruments for accounting purposes. The change in the fair value of these contracts is immediately recognized in net interest income and other on our consolidated statements of earnings.

Normal Purchase Normal Sale

We enter into fixed-price and price-to-be-fixed green coffee purchase commitments, which are described further at Note 5, Inventories. For both fixed-price and price-to-be-fixed purchase commitments, we expect to take delivery of and to utilize the coffee in a reasonable period of time and in the conduct of normal business. Accordingly, these purchase commitments qualify as normal purchases and are not recorded at fair value on our balance sheets.

Receivables, net of Allowance for Doubtful Accounts

Our receivables are mainly comprised of receivables for product and equipment sales to and royalties from our licensees, as well as receivables from our CPG and foodservice business customers. Our allowance for doubtful accounts is calculated based on historical experience, customer credit risk and application of the specific identification method. As of September 27, 2015 and September 28, 2014, the allowance for doubtful accounts was $10.8 million and $6.7 million, respectively.

Inventories

Inventories are stated at the lower of cost (primarily moving average cost) or market. We record inventory reserves for obsolete and slow-moving inventory and for estimated shrinkage between physical inventory counts. Inventory reserves are based on inventory obsolescence trends, historical experience and application of the specific identification method. As of September 27, 2015 and September 28, 2014, inventory reserves were $33.8 million and $31.2 million, respectively.

Property, Plant and Equipment

Property, plant and equipment, which includes assets under capital leases, are carried at cost less accumulated depreciation. Cost includes all direct costs necessary to acquire and prepare assets for use, including internal labor and overhead in some cases. Depreciation is computed using the straight-line method over estimated useful lives of the assets, generally ranging from 2 to 15 years for equipment and 30 to 40 years for buildings. Leasehold improvements are amortized over the shorter of their estimated useful lives or the related lease life, generally 10 years. For leases with renewal periods at our option, we generally use the original lease term, excluding renewal option periods, to determine estimated useful lives. If failure to exercise a renewal option imposes an economic penalty to us, we may determine at the inception of the lease that renewal is reasonably assured and include the renewal option period in the determination of the appropriate estimated useful lives.

The portion of depreciation expense related to production and distribution facilities is included in cost of sales including occupancy costs on our consolidated statements of earnings. The costs of repairs and maintenance are expensed when incurred, while expenditures for refurbishments and improvements that significantly add to the productive capacity or extend the useful life of an asset are capitalized. When assets are disposed of, whether through retirement or sale, the net gain or loss is recognized in net earnings. Long-lived assets to be disposed of are reported at the lower of their carrying amount or fair value less estimated costs to sell.

We evaluate property, plant and equipment for impairment when facts and circumstances indicate that the carrying values of such assets may not be recoverable. When evaluating for impairment, we first compare the carrying value of the asset to the asset's estimated future undiscounted cash flows. If the estimated undiscounted future cash flows are less than the carrying value of the asset, we determine if we have an impairment loss by comparing the carrying value of the asset to the asset's estimated fair value and recognize an impairment charge when the asset's carrying value exceeds its estimated fair value. The fair value of the asset is estimated using a discounted cash flow model based on forecasted future revenues and operating costs, using internal projections. Property, plant and equipment assets are grouped at the lowest level for which identifiable cash flows are largely independent of the cash flows of other assets and liabilities. For company-operated store assets, the impairment test is performed at the individual store asset group level.

We recognized net disposition charges of $12.5 million, $14.7 million, and $17.4 million and net impairment charges of $25.8 million, $19.0 million, and $12.7 million in fiscal 2015, 2014, and 2013, respectively. The nature of the underlying asset that is impaired or disposed of will determine the operating expense line on which the related impact is recorded on our consolidated statements of earnings. For assets within our retail operations, net impairment and disposition charges are recorded in store operating expenses. For all other assets, these charges are recorded in cost of sales including occupancy costs, other operating expenses, or general and administrative expenses.

Goodwill

We evaluate goodwill for impairment annually during our third fiscal quarter, or more frequently if an event occurs or circumstances change, such as material deterioration in performance or a significant number of store closures, that would indicate that impairment may exist. When evaluating goodwill for impairment, we may first perform a qualitative assessment to determine whether it is more likely than not that a reporting unit is impaired. If we do not perform a qualitative assessment, or if we determine that it is not more likely than not that the fair value of the reporting unit exceeds its carrying amount, we calculate the estimated fair value of the reporting unit. Fair value is the price a willing buyer would pay for the reporting unit and is typically calculated using a discounted cash flow model. For certain reporting units, where deemed appropriate, we may also utilize a market approach for estimating fair value. If the carrying amount of the reporting unit exceeds the estimated fair value, an impairment charge is recorded to reduce the carrying value to the estimated fair value.

As part of our ongoing operations, we may close certain stores within a reporting unit containing goodwill due to underperformance of the store or inability to renew our lease, among other reasons. We may abandon certain assets associated with a closed store, including leasehold improvements and other non-transferable assets. When a portion of a reporting unit that constitutes a business is to be disposed of, goodwill associated with the business is included in the carrying amount of the business in determining any loss on disposal. Our evaluation of whether the portion of a reporting unit being disposed of constitutes a business occurs on the date of abandonment. Although an operating store meets the accounting definition of a business prior to abandonment, it does not constitute a business on the closure date because the remaining assets on that date do not constitute an integrated set of assets that are capable of being managed for the purpose of providing a return to investors. As a result, when closing individual stores, we do not include goodwill in the calculation of any loss on disposal of the related assets. As noted above, if store closures are indicative of potential impairment of goodwill at the reporting unit level, we perform an evaluation of our reporting unit goodwill when such closures occur. There were no material goodwill impairment charges recorded during fiscal 2015, 2014, and 2013.

Other Intangible Assets

Other intangible assets consist primarily of finite-lived intangible assets, which mainly consist of acquired and reacquired rights, trade secrets, licensing agreements, contract-based patents and copyrights, are amortized over their estimated useful lives, and are tested for impairment using a similar methodology to our property, plant and equipment, as described above.

Indefinite-lived intangibles, which consist primarily of trade names and trademarks, are tested for impairment annually during the third fiscal quarter, or more frequently if an event occurs or circumstances change that would indicate that impairment may exist. When evaluating other intangible assets for impairment, we may first perform a qualitative assessment to determine whether it is more likely than not that an intangible asset group is impaired. If we do not perform the qualitative assessment, or if we determine that it is not more likely than not that the fair value of the intangible asset group exceeds its carrying amount, we calculate the estimated fair value of the intangible asset group. Fair value is the price a willing buyer would pay for the reporting unit and is typically calculated using an income approach, such as a relief-from-royalty model. If the carrying amount of the intangible asset group exceeds the estimated fair value, an impairment charge is recorded to reduce the carrying value to the estimated fair value. In addition, we continuously monitor and may revise our intangible asset useful lives if and when facts and circumstances change.

There were no other intangible asset impairment charges recorded during fiscal 2015, 2014, and 2013.

Insurance Reserves

We use a combination of insurance and self-insurance mechanisms, including a wholly-owned captive insurance entity and participation in a reinsurance treaty, to provide for the potential liabilities for certain risks, including workers' compensation, healthcare benefits, general liability, property insurance, and director and officers' liability insurance. Liabilities associated with the risks that are retained by us are not discounted and are estimated, in part, by considering historical claims experience, demographics, exposure and severity factors, and other actuarial assumptions.

Revenue Recognition

Consolidated revenues are presented net of intercompany eliminations for wholly-owned subsidiaries and investees controlled by us and for product sales to and royalty and other fees from licensees accounted for under the equity method. Additionally, consolidated revenues are recognized net of any discounts, returns, allowances and sales incentives, including coupon redemptions and rebates.

Company-operated Store Revenues

Company-operated store revenues are recognized when payment is tendered at the point of sale. Company-operated store revenues are reported net of sales, use or other transaction taxes that are collected from customers and remitted to taxing authorities.

Licensed Store Revenues

Licensed store revenues consist of product and equipment sales to licensees, as well as royalties and other fees paid by licensees to use the Starbucks brand. Sales of coffee, tea, food and related products are generally recognized upon shipment to licensees, depending on contract terms. Shipping charges billed to licensees are also recognized as revenue, and the related shipping costs are included in cost of sales including occupancy costs on our consolidated statements of earnings.

Initial nonrefundable development fees for licensed stores are recognized upon substantial performance of services for new market business development activities, such as initial business, real estate and store development planning, as well as providing operational materials and functional training courses for opening new licensed retail markets. Additional store licensing fees are recognized when new licensed stores are opened. Royalty revenues based upon a percentage of reported sales, and other continuing fees, such as marketing and service fees, are recognized on a monthly basis when earned.

CPG, Foodservice and Other Revenues

CPG, foodservice and other revenues primarily include sales of packaged coffee and tea as well as a variety of ready-to-drink beverages and single-serve coffee and tea products to grocery, warehouse clubs and specialty retail stores, sales to our national foodservice accounts, and revenues from sales of products to and license fee revenues from manufacturers that produce and market Starbucks-, Seattle's Best Coffee- and Tazo-branded products through licensing agreements. Sales of coffee, tea, ready-to-drink beverages and related products to grocery and warehouse club stores are generally recognized when received by the customer or distributor, depending on contract terms. Revenues are recorded net of sales discounts given to customers for trade promotions and other incentives and for sales return allowances, which are determined based on historical patterns.

Revenues from sales of products to manufacturers that produce and market Starbucks-, Seattle's Best Coffee- and Tazo-branded products through licensing agreements are generally recognized when the product is received by the manufacturer or distributor. License fee revenues from manufacturers are based on a percentage of sales and are recognized on a monthly basis when earned. National foodservice account revenues are recognized, when the product is received by the customer or distributor.

Sales to customers through CPG channels and national foodservice accounts, including sales to national distributors, are recognized net of certain fees paid to the customer. We characterize these fees as a reduction of revenue unless we are able to identify a sufficiently separable benefit from the customer's purchase of our products such that we could have entered into an exchange transaction with a party other than the customer in order to receive such benefit, and we can reasonably estimate the fair value of such benefit.

Stored Value Cards

Stored value cards, primarily Starbucks Cards, can be loaded at our company-operated and most licensed store locations, online at StarbucksStore.com or via mobile devices held by our customers, and at certain other third party locations, such as grocery stores. When an amount is loaded onto a stored value card at any of these locations, we recognize a corresponding liability for the full amount loaded onto the card, which is recorded within stored value card liability on our consolidated balance sheets.

Stored value cards can be redeemed at company-operated and most licensed stores, as well as online. When a stored value card is redeemed at a company-operated store or online, we recognize revenue by reducing the stored value card liability. When a stored value card is redeemed at a licensed store location, we reduce the corresponding stored value card liability and cash, which is reimbursed to the licensee.

There are no expiration dates on our stored value cards, and we do not charge service fees that cause a decrement to customer balances. While we will continue to honor all stored value cards presented for payment, management may determine the likelihood of redemption, based on historical experience, is deemed to be remote for certain cards due to long periods of inactivity. In these circumstances, if management also determines there is no requirement for remitting balances to government agencies under unclaimed property laws, unredeemed card balances may then be recognized as breakage income, which is included in net interest income and other on our consolidated statements of earnings. In fiscal 2015, 2014, and 2013, we recognized breakage income of $39.3 million, $38.3 million, and $33.0 million, respectively.

Loyalty Program

Starbucks has a loyalty program called My Starbucks Rewards® ("MSR"). Customers in the U.S., Canada, and certain other countries who register their Starbucks Card are automatically enrolled in that program. They earn loyalty points ("Stars") with each purchase at participating Starbucks®, Teavana®, and Evolution Fresh™ stores, as well as on certain packaged coffee products purchased in select Starbucks® stores, online, and through CPG channels. After accumulating a certain number of Stars, the customer earns a reward that can be redeemed for free product that, regardless of where the related Stars were earned within that country, will be honored at company-operated stores and certain participating licensed store locations in that same country.

We defer revenue associated with the estimated selling price of Stars earned by our program members towards free product as each Star is earned, and a corresponding liability is established within stored value card liability on our consolidated balance sheets. The estimated selling price of each Star earned is based on the estimated value of the product for which the reward is expected to be redeemed, net of Stars we do not expect to be redeemed, based on historical redemption patterns. Fully earned rewards generally expire if unredeemed after approximately 30 days. Stars generally expire if inactive for a period of one year.

When a customer redeems an earned reward, we recognize revenue for the redeemed product and reduce the related loyalty program liability.

Marketing & Advertising

Our annual marketing expenses include many components, one of which is advertising costs. We expense most advertising costs as they are incurred, except for certain production costs that are expensed the first time the advertising takes place.

Marketing expenses totaled $351.5 million, $315.5 million and $306.8 million in fiscal 2015, 2014, and 2013, respectively. Included in these costs were advertising expenses, which totaled $227.9 million, $198.9 million and $205.8 million in fiscal 2015, 2014, and 2013, respectively.

Store Preopening Expenses

Costs incurred in connection with the start-up and promotion of new store openings are expensed as incurred.

Leases

Operating Leases

We lease retail stores, roasting, distribution and warehouse facilities, and office space for corporate administrative purposes under operating leases. Most lease agreements contain tenant improvement allowances, rent holidays, lease premiums, rent escalation clauses and/or contingent rent provisions. We recognize amortization of lease incentives, premiums and minimum rent expenses on a straight-line basis beginning on the date of initial possession, which is generally when we enter the space and begin to make improvements in preparation for intended use.

For tenant improvement allowances and rent holidays, we record a deferred rent liability within accrued liabilities, or other long-term liabilities, on our consolidated balance sheets and amortize the deferred rent over the terms of the leases as reductions to rent expense in cost of sales including occupancy costs on our consolidated statements of earnings.

For premiums paid upfront to enter a lease agreement, we record a prepaid rent asset in prepaid expenses and other current assets on our consolidated balance sheets and amortize the deferred rent over the terms of the leases as additional rent expense in cost of sales including occupancy costs on our consolidated statements of earnings.

For scheduled rent escalation clauses during the lease terms or for rental payments commencing at a date other than the date of initial possession, we record minimum rent expense on a straight-line basis over the terms of the leases in cost of sales including occupancy costs on our consolidated statements of earnings.

Certain leases provide for contingent rent, which is determined as a percentage of gross sales in excess of specified levels. We record a contingent rent liability in accrued occupancy costs within accrued liabilities on our consolidated balance sheets and the corresponding rent expense when specified levels have been achieved or when we determine that achieving the specified levels during the fiscal year is probable.

When ceasing operations of company-operated stores under operating leases, in cases where the lease contract specifies a termination fee due to the landlord, we record such expense at the time written notice is given to the landlord. In cases where terms, including termination fees, are yet to be negotiated with the landlord, we will record the expense upon signing of an agreement with the landlord. In cases where the landlord does not allow us to prematurely exit the lease, but allows for subleasing, we estimate the fair value of any sublease income that can be generated from the location and recognize an expense equal to the present value of the remaining lease payments to the landlord less any projected sublease income at the cease-use date.

Lease Financing Arrangements

We are sometimes involved in the construction of leased buildings, primarily stores. When we qualify as the deemed owner of these buildings due to significant involvement during the construction period under build-to-suit lease accounting requirements and do not qualify for sales recognition under sales-leaseback accounting guidance, we record the cost of the related buildings in property, plant and equipment. The offsetting lease financing obligations are recorded in other long-term liabilities, with the current portion recorded in in accrued occupancy costs within accrued liabilities on our consolidated balance sheets. These assets and obligations are amortized in depreciation and amortization and interest expense, respectively, on our consolidated statements of earnings based on the terms of the related lease agreements.

Asset Retirement Obligations

We recognize a liability for the fair value of required asset retirement obligations ("ARO") when such obligations are incurred. Our AROs are primarily associated with leasehold improvements, which, at the end of a lease, we are contractually obligated to remove in order to comply with the lease agreement. At the inception of a lease with such conditions, we record an ARO liability and a corresponding capital asset in an amount equal to the estimated fair value of the obligation. We estimate the liability using a number of assumptions, including store closing costs, cost inflation rates and discount rates, and accrete to its projected future value over time. The capitalized asset is depreciated using the same depreciation convention as leasehold improvement assets. Upon satisfaction of the ARO conditions, any difference between the recorded ARO liability and the actual retirement costs incurred is recognized as a gain or loss in cost of sales including occupancy costs on our consolidated statements of earnings. As of September 27, 2015 and September 28, 2014, our net ARO assets included in property, plant and equipment were $5.8 million and $4.1 million, respectively, and our net ARO liabilities included in other long-term liabilities were $60.1 million and $28.4 million, respectively. The increases in our net ARO assets and net ARO liabilities in fiscal 2015 were primarily due to the acquisition of Starbucks Japan, which is discussed in Note 2, Acquisitions and Divestitures.

Stock-based Compensation

We maintain several equity incentive plans under which we may grant non-qualified stock options, incentive stock options, restricted stock, restricted stock units ("RSUs") or stock appreciation rights to employees, non-employee directors and consultants. We also have an employee stock purchase plan ("ESPP"). RSUs issued by us are equivalent to nonvested shares under the applicable accounting guidance. We record stock-based compensation expense based on the fair value of stock awards at the grant date and recognize the expense over the related service period following a graded vesting expense schedule. Expense for performance-based RSUs is recognized when it is probable the performance goal will be achieved. Performance goals are determined by the Board of Directors and may include measures such as earnings per share, operating income and return on invested capital. The fair value of each stock option granted is estimated on the grant date using the Black-Scholes-Merton option valuation model. The assumptions used to calculate the fair value of options granted are evaluated and revised, as necessary, to reflect market conditions and our historical experience. The fair value of RSUs is based on the closing price of Starbucks common stock on the award date, less the present value of expected dividends not received during the vesting period. Compensation expense is recognized over the requisite service period for each separately vesting portion of the award, and only for those options expected to vest, with forfeitures estimated at the date of grant based on our historical experience and future expectations.

Foreign Currency Translation

Our international operations generally use their local currency as their functional currency. Assets and liabilities are translated at exchange rates in effect at the balance sheet date. Income and expense accounts are translated at the average monthly exchange rates during the year. Resulting translation adjustments are reported as a component of OCI and recorded in AOCI on our consolidated balance sheets.

Income Taxes

We compute income taxes using the asset and liability method, under which deferred income taxes are recognized based on the differences between the financial statement carrying amounts and the respective tax basis of our assets and liabilities. Deferred tax assets and liabilities are measured using current enacted tax rates expected to apply to taxable income in the years in which we expect the temporary differences to reverse. The effect of a change in tax rates on deferred taxes is recognized in income in the period that includes the enactment date.

We routinely evaluate the likelihood of realizing the benefit of our deferred tax assets and may record a valuation allowance if, based on all available evidence, we determine that some portion of the tax benefit will not be realized. In evaluating our ability to recover our deferred tax assets within the jurisdiction from which they arise, we consider all available positive and negative evidence, including scheduled reversals of deferred tax liabilities, projected future taxable income, tax-planning strategies, and results of recent operations. If we determine that we would be able to realize our deferred tax assets in the future in excess of their net recorded amount, we would make an adjustment to the deferred tax asset valuation allowance, which would reduce the provision for income taxes.

In addition, our income tax returns are periodically audited by domestic and foreign tax authorities. These audits include review of our tax filing positions, including the timing and amount of deductions taken and the allocation of income between tax jurisdictions. We evaluate our exposures associated with our various tax filing positions and recognize a tax benefit from an uncertain tax position only if it is more likely than not that the tax position will be sustained upon examination by the relevant taxing authorities, including resolutions of any related appeals or litigation processes, based on the technical merits of our position. The tax benefits recognized in the financial statements from such a position are measured based on the largest benefit that has a greater than 50% likelihood of being realized upon ultimate settlement. For uncertain tax positions that do not meet this threshold, we record a related liability. We adjust our unrecognized tax benefit liability and income tax expense in the period in which the uncertain tax position is effectively settled, the statute of limitations expires for the relevant taxing authority to examine the tax position, or when new information becomes available.

Starbucks recognizes interest and penalties related to income tax matters in income tax expense on our consolidated statements of earnings. Accrued interest and penalties are included within the related tax liability on our consolidated balance sheets.

Stock Split

On April 9, 2015, we effected a two-for-one stock split of our $0.001 par value common stock for shareholders of record as of March 30, 2015. All share and per-share data in our consolidated financial statements and notes has been retroactively adjusted to reflect this stock split. We adjusted shareholders' equity to reflect the stock split by reclassifying an amount equal to the par value of the additional shares arising from the split from retained earnings to common stock during the second quarter of fiscal 2015, resulting in no net impact to shareholders' equity on our consolidated balance sheets.

Earnings per Share

Basic earnings per share is computed based on the weighted average number of shares of common stock outstanding during the period. Diluted earnings per share is computed based on the weighted average number of shares of common stock and the effect of dilutive potential common shares outstanding during the period, calculated using the treasury stock method. Dilutive potential common shares include outstanding stock options and RSUs. Performance-based RSUs are considered dilutive when the related performance criterion has been met.

Common Stock Share Repurchases

We may repurchase shares of Starbucks common stock under a program authorized by our Board of Directors, including pursuant to a contract, instruction or written plan meeting the requirements of Rule 10b5-1(c)(1) of the Securities Exchange Act of 1934. Under applicable Washington State law, shares repurchased are retired and not displayed separately as treasury stock on the financial statements. Instead, the par value of repurchased shares is deducted from common stock and the excess repurchase price over par value is deducted from additional paid-in capital and from retained earnings, once additional paid-in capital is depleted.

Recent Accounting Pronouncements

In September 2015, the Financial Accounting Standards Board ("FASB") issued guidance on the recognition of adjustments to preliminary amounts recognized in a business combination, which removes the requirement to retrospectively account for these adjustments. The guidance will become effective for us at the beginning of our first quarter of fiscal 2017. We will apply the guidance prospectively and do not expect the adoption will have a material impact on our consolidated financial statements.

In July 2015, the FASB issued guidance on the subsequent measurement of inventory, which changes the measurement from lower of cost or market to lower of cost and net realizable value. The guidance will require prospective application at the beginning of our first quarter of fiscal 2018, but permits adoption in an earlier period. We are currently evaluating the impact this guidance will have on our consolidated financial statements and the timing of adoption.

In April 2015, the FASB issued guidance on the financial statement presentation of debt issuance costs. This guidance requires debt issuance costs to be presented in the balance sheet as a reduction of the related debt liability rather than an asset. The guidance will become effective for us at the beginning of our first quarter of fiscal 2017 and will only result in an immaterial change in presentation of these costs on our consolidated balance sheets.

In February 2015, the FASB issued guidance that changes the evaluation criteria for consolidation and related disclosure requirements. This guidance introduces evaluation criteria specific to limited partnerships and other similar entities, as well as amends the criteria for evaluating variable interest entities with which the reporting entity is involved and certain investment funds. The guidance will become effective for us at the beginning of our first quarter of fiscal 2017. We do not expect the adoption of this guidance will have a material impact on our consolidated financial statements.

In May 2014, the FASB issued guidance outlining a single comprehensive model for entities to use in accounting for revenue arising from contracts with customers that supersedes most current revenue recognition guidance. This guidance requires an entity to recognize revenue when it transfers promised goods or services to customers in an amount that reflects the consideration to which the entity expects to be entitled in exchange for those goods or services. The original effective date of the guidance would have required us to adopt at the beginning of our first quarter of fiscal 2018. In July 2015, the FASB approved an optional one-year deferral of the effective date. The new guidance may be applied retrospectively to each prior period presented or retrospectively with the cumulative effect recognized as of the date of adoption. We are currently evaluating the overall impact this guidance will have on our consolidated financial statements, as well as the expected timing and method of adoption. Based on our preliminary assessment, we determined the adoption will change the timing of recognition and classification of our stored value card breakage income, which is currently recognized using the remote method and recorded in net interest income and other. The new guidance will require application of the proportional method and classification within total net revenues on our consolidated statements of earnings. Additionally, the new guidance requires enhanced disclosures, including revenue recognition policies to identify performance obligations to customers and significant judgments in measurement and recognition. We are continuing our assessment, which may identify other impacts.

In April 2014, the FASB issued guidance that changes the criteria for reporting discontinued operations. To qualify as a discontinued operation under the amended guidance, a component or group of components of an entity that has been disposed of or is classified as held for sale must represent a strategic shift that has or will have a major effect on the entity's operations and financial results. This guidance also expands related disclosure requirements. The guidance will become effective for us at the beginning of our first quarter of fiscal 2016. We do not expect the adoption of this guidance will have a material impact on our financial statements.

In July 2013, the FASB issued guidance on the financial statement presentation of an unrecognized tax benefit when a net operating loss carryforward, a similar tax loss, or a tax credit carryforward exists. This guidance requires the unrecognized tax benefit to be presented in the financial statements as a reduction to a deferred tax asset. When a deferred tax asset is not available, or the asset is not intended to be used for this purpose, the unrecognized tax benefit should be presented in the financial statements as a liability and not netted with a deferred tax asset. The guidance became effective for us at the beginning of our first quarter of fiscal 2015 and did not have a material impact on our consolidated financial statements.

In March 2013, the FASB issued guidance on a parent's accounting for the cumulative translation adjustment upon derecognition of certain subsidiaries or groups of assets within a foreign entity or of an investment in a foreign entity. This guidance requires a parent to release any related cumulative translation adjustment into net income only if the sale or transfer results in the complete or substantially complete liquidation of the foreign entity in which the subsidiary or group of assets had resided. The guidance became effective for us at the beginning of our first quarter of fiscal 2015 and did not have a material impact on our consolidated financial statements.

Note 2: Acquisitions and Divestitures

Fiscal 2015

During the fourth quarter of fiscal 2015, we sold our company-operated retail store assets and operations in Puerto Rico to Baristas Del Caribe, LLC, converting these operations to a fully licensed market, for a total of $8.9 million. This transaction resulted in a pre-tax gain of $3.7 million, which was included in net interest income and other on the consolidated statements of earnings.

On September 23, 2014, we entered into a tender offer bid agreement with Starbucks Coffee Japan, Ltd. ("Starbucks Japan"), at the time a 39.5% owned equity method investment, and our former joint venture partner, Sazaby League, Ltd. ("Sazaby"), to acquire the remaining 60.5% ownership interest in Starbucks Japan. Acquiring Starbucks Japan further leverages our existing infrastructure to continue disciplined retail store growth and expand our presence into other channels in the Japan market, such as consumer packaged goods ("CPG"), licensing and foodservice. This acquisition was structured as a two-step tender offer.

On October 31, 2014, we acquired Sazaby's 39.5% ownership interest in Starbucks Japan through the first tender offer step for ¥55 billion in cash, or $509 million with Japanese yen converted into U.S. dollars at a reference conversion rate of 108.13 JPY to USD, based on a spot rate that approximates the rate as of the acquisition date, bringing our total ownership in Starbucks Japan to a controlling 79% interest.

The following table summarizes the allocation of the total consideration to the fair values of the assets acquired and liabilities assumed as of October 31, 2014 *(in millions)* :

Consideration:		
Cash paid for Sazaby's 39.5% equity interest	$	508.7
Fair value of our preexisting 39.5% equity interest		577.0
Total consideration	$	1,085.7
Fair value of assets acquired and liabilities assumed:		
Cash and cash equivalents	$	224.4
Accounts receivable, net		37.4
Inventories		26.4
Prepaid expenses and other current assets		35.7
Deferred income taxes, net (current)		23.4
Property, plant and equipment		282.9
Other long-term assets		141.4
Other intangible assets		323.0
Goodwill		815.6
Total assets acquired		1,910.2
Accounts payable		(54.5)
Accrued liabilities		(115.9)
Stored value card liability		(36.5)
Deferred income taxes (noncurrent)		(90.7)
Other long-term liabilities		(115.8)
Total liabilities assumed		(413.4)
Noncontrolling interest		(411.1)
Total consideration	$	1,085.7

During fiscal 2015, the acquisition date fair value of goodwill increased due to revisions that decreased the acquisition date fair value of accrued liabilities and deferred income taxes (noncurrent) and increased the acquisition date fair value of other-long-term liabilities. None of the adjustments had a material effect on our current or interim period consolidated financial statements.

The assets acquired and liabilities assumed are reported within our China/Asia Pacific segment. Other current and long-term assets acquired primarily include various deposits, specifically lease and key money deposits. Accrued liabilities and other long-term liabilities assumed primarily include the financing obligations associated with the build-to-suit leases discussed below, as well as asset retirement obligations.

The intangible assets are finite-lived and include reacquired rights, licensing agreements with Starbucks Japan's current licensees and Starbucks Japan's customer loyalty program. The reacquired rights of $305.0 million represent the fair value, calculated over the remaining original contractual period, to exclusively operate licensed Starbucks® retail stores in Japan. These rights will be amortized on a straight-line basis through March 2021, or over a period of approximately 6.4 years. The licensing agreements were valued at $15.0 million and will be amortized on a straight-line basis over a period of approximately 10.9 years, which is based on the remaining terms of the respective licensing agreements. The customer loyalty program was valued at $3.0 million and will be amortized on a straight-line basis over a period of 4.0 years, which represents the period during which we expect to benefit from these customer relationships.

Below is a tabular summary of the acquired intangible assets as of September 27, 2015, for which the gross balances in total are $33.7 million lower than as of the October 31, 2014 acquisition date due to foreign currency translation *(in millions)* :

	Sep 27, 2015		
	Gross Carrying Amount	Accumulated Amortization	Net Carrying Amount
Reacquired rights	$ 273.2	$ (39.0)	$ 234.2
Licensing agreements	13.4	(1.1)	12.3
Customer loyalty program	2.7	(0.6)	2.1
Total acquired finite-lived intangible assets	$ 289.3	$ (40.7)	$ 248.6

Amortization expense for these finite-lived intangible assets for the year ended September 27, 2015 was $41.0 million and is estimated to be approximately $44 million each year for the next five years and approximately $29 million thereafter.

The $815.6 million of goodwill represents the intangible assets that do not qualify for separate recognition and primarily includes the acquired customer base, the acquired workforce including store partners in the region that have strong relationships with these customers, the existing geographic retail and online presence, and the expected geographic presence in new channels. The goodwill was allocated to the China/Asia Pacific segment and is not deductible for income tax purposes. Due to foreign currency translation, the balance of goodwill related to the acquisition declined $85.1 million to $730.5 million as of September 27, 2015.

As a part of this acquisition, we acquired a significant number of operating leases, including $7.5 million of favorable lease assets, which are included in prepaid expenses and other current assets and other long-term assets, and $15.5 million of unfavorable lease liabilities, which are included in accrued liabilities and other long-term liabilities on the consolidated balance sheets. The fair values of these assets and liabilities were determined based on market terms for similar leases as of the date of the acquisition, and will be amortized on a straight-line basis as rent expense, or a reduction of rent expense, respectively, in cost of sales including occupancy costs on the consolidated statements of earnings over the remaining terms of the leases, for which the weighted-average period was 9.4 years as of the October 31, 2014 acquisition date. We recorded a net reduction of rent expense of $0.8 million for the year ended September 27, 2015, in connection with the leases acquired.

Additionally, we acquired a number of build-to-suit lease arrangements that are accounted for as financing leases. Starbucks Japan is the deemed owner of buildings under build-to-suit lease accounting requirements since Starbucks Japan has significant involvement with the respective lessors and does not qualify for sales recognition under sale-leaseback accounting guidance. Accordingly, we have recorded the acquired buildings in property, plant and equipment, and the assumed lease financing obligations, representing the related future minimum lease payments, in other long-term liabilities, with the current portion recorded in accrued occupancy costs within accrued liabilities on the consolidated balance sheets. These financing obligations will be amortized based on the terms of the related lease agreements.

The table below summarizes our estimated minimum future rental payments under the acquired non-cancelable operating leases and lease financing arrangements as of September 27, 2015 *(in millions)*:

	Operating Leases	Lease Financing Arrangements
Year 1	$ 83.7	$ 2.8
Year 2	66.5	2.8
Year 3	49.0	2.8
Year 4	37.5	2.8
Year 5	30.3	2.7
Thereafter	129.4	24.8
Total minimum lease payments	$ 396.4	$ 38.7

The fair value of the noncontrolling interest in Starbucks Japan was estimated by applying the market approach. Specifically, the fair value was determined based on the purchase price we expected to pay for the remaining 21% noncontrolling interest, which was comprised of a set market price and a premium above the market price. The market price premium is a customary business practice for public tender offer transactions in Japan, so we believe this is what a market participant would pay and should be included in the fair value determination.

As a result of this acquisition, we remeasured the carrying value of our preexisting 39.5% equity method investment to fair value, which resulted in a pre-tax gain of $390.6 million that was presented separately as gain resulting from acquisition of joint venture within other income and expenses on the consolidated statements of earnings. The fair value of $577.0 million was calculated using an average of the income and market approach. The income approach fair value measurement was based on significant inputs that are not observable in the market and thus represents a fair value measurement categorized within Level 3 of the fair value hierarchy. Key assumptions used in estimating future cash flows included projected revenue growth and operating expenses, as well as the selection of an appropriate discount rate. Estimates of revenue growth and operating expenses were based on internal projections and considered the historical performance of stores, local market economics and the business environment impacting the stores' performance. The discount rate applied was based on Starbucks Japan's weighted-average cost of capital and included a company-specific risk premium. The market approach fair value measurement was based on the implied fair value of Starbucks Japan using the purchase price of Sazaby's 39.5% ownership interest and the expected purchase price of the 21% remaining noncontrolling interest.

We began consolidating Starbucks Japan's results of operations and cash flows into our consolidated financial statements beginning after October 31, 2014. For the year ended September 27, 2015, Starbucks Japan's net revenues and net earnings included in our consolidated statements of earnings were $1.1 billion and $108.5 million, respectively.

The following table provides the supplemental pro forma revenue and net earnings of the combined entity had the acquisition date of Starbucks Japan been the first day of our first quarter of fiscal 2014 rather than during our first quarter of fiscal 2015 *(in millions)*:

	Pro Forma (unaudited)	
	Year Ended	
	Sep 27, 2015	Sep 28, 2014
Revenue	$ 19,254.5	$ 17,646.4
Net earnings attributable to Starbucks[1]	2,380.9	2,449.9

[1] The pro forma net earnings attributable to Starbucks for fiscal 2014 includes the acquisition-related gain of $390.6 million, and transaction and integration costs of $13.6 million for the year ended September 28, 2014.

The amounts in the supplemental pro forma earnings for the periods presented above fully eliminate intercompany transactions, apply our accounting policies and reflect adjustments for additional occupancy costs, depreciation and amortization that would have been charged assuming the same fair value adjustments to leases, property, plant and equipment and acquired intangibles had been applied on September 30, 2013. These pro forma results are unaudited and are not necessarily indicative of results of operations that would have occurred had the acquisition actually occurred in the prior year period or indicative of the results of operations for any future period.

We initiated the second tender offer step on November 10, 2014 to acquire the remaining 21% ownership interest held by the public shareholders and option holders of Starbucks Japan's common stock, with the objective of acquiring all of the remaining outstanding shares including outstanding stock options. At the close of the second tender offer period on December 22, 2014, we funded the second tender offer step to acquire an additional 14.7% ownership interest for ¥31 billion in cash, or $258 million with Japanese yen converted into U.S. dollars at a reference conversion rate of 120.39 JPY to USD. However, we did not complete the second tender offer nor obtain control of these shares until the settlement date of December 29, 2014, which was the first day of our second quarter of fiscal 2015.

Subsequent to the completion of the second tender offer step, we commenced a cash-out procedure under Japanese law (the "Cash-out") to acquire all remaining shares of Starbucks Japan (an approximate 6.3% interest). On March 26, 2015, we obtained control of these shares resulting in 100% ownership of Starbucks Japan. The purchase price for the Cash-out was ¥13.5 billion, or $109 million. During the third quarter of fiscal 2015, we settled ¥9.6 billion, or $78 million, of the purchase price in cash, with Japanese yen converted into U.S. dollars at a reference conversion rate of 123.87 JPY to USD. During the fourth quarter of fiscal 2015, we settled ¥3.2 billion, or $26 million, of the purchase price in cash, with Japanese yen converted into U.S. dollars at a reference conversion rate of 120.72 JPY to USD. The remaining ¥674 million ($6 million) was recorded in accrued liabilities on our consolidated balance sheets and represents cash that was unclaimed by minority shareholders as of September 27, 2015. There are no legal restrictions on the remaining unclaimed balance.

For the first quarter of fiscal 2015, net earnings attributable to noncontrolling interests in our consolidated statement of earnings related to Starbucks Japan reflects the 21% of minority shareholders' interests that we did not own as of the end of the first quarter of fiscal 2015. For the second quarter of fiscal 2015, net earnings attributable to noncontrolling interests in our consolidated statement of earnings related to Starbucks Japan reflects the approximate 6.3% of minority shareholders' interests that we did not obtain control of until March 26, 2015.

The following table shows the effects of the change in Starbucks ownership interest in Starbucks Japan on Starbucks equity:

	Year Ended	
	Sep 27, 2015	Sep 28, 2014
Net earnings attributable to Starbucks	$ 2,757.4	$ 2,068.1
Transfers (to)/from the noncontrolling interest:		
Increase/(decrease) in additional paid-in capital for purchase of interest in subsidiary	1.7	—
Change from net earnings attributable to Starbucks and transfers (to)/from noncontrolling interest	$ 2,759.1	$ 2,068.1

During the year ended September 27, 2015, we incurred approximately $11.9 million of acquisition-related costs, such as regulatory, legal, and advisory fees, which we have recorded within unallocated corporate general and administrative expenses.

Fiscal 2014

During the fourth quarter of fiscal 2014, we sold our Australian company-operated retail store assets and operations to the Withers Group, converting these operations to a fully licensed market, for a total of $15.9 million. This transaction resulted in a pre-tax gain of $2.4 million, which was included in net interest income and other on our consolidated statements of earnings. On an after-tax basis, this transaction resulted in a loss that was not material to our financial statements.

Fiscal 2013

During the fourth quarter of fiscal 2013, we sold our 82% interest in Starbucks Coffee Chile S.A. to our joint venture partner Alsea, S.A.B. de C.V., converting this market to a 100% licensed market, for a total purchase price of $68.6 million, which includes final working capital adjustments. This transaction resulted in a gain of $45.9 million, which was included in net interest income and other on our consolidated statements of earnings.

In the third quarter of fiscal 2013, we acquired 100% ownership of a coffee farm in Costa Rica for $8.1 million in cash. The fair value of the net assets acquired on the acquisition date primarily comprised property, plant and equipment.

On December 31, 2012, we acquired 100% of the outstanding shares of Teavana Holdings, Inc. ("Teavana"), a specialty retailer of premium loose-leaf teas, authentic artisanal teawares and other tea-related merchandise, to elevate our tea offerings as well as expand our domestic and global tea footprint. We acquired Teavana for $615.8 million in cash. Of the total cash paid, $12.2 million was excluded from the purchase price allocation below as it represented contingent consideration receivable, all of which has been settled. At closing, we also repaid $35.2 million for long-term debt outstanding on Teavana's balance sheet, which was recognized separately from the business combination. The following table summarizes the allocation of the purchase price to the fair values of the assets acquired and liabilities assumed on the closing date *(in millions)*:

	Fair Value at Dec 31, 2012
Cash and cash equivalents	$ 47.0
Inventories	21.3
Property, plant and equipment	59.7
Other intangible assets	120.8
Goodwill	467.5
Other current and noncurrent assets	19.8
Current liabilities	(36.0)
Deferred income taxes (noncurrent)	(54.3)
Long-term debt	(35.2)
Other long-term liabilities	(7.0)
Total consideration	$ 603.6

The assets acquired and liabilities assumed are reported within All Other Segments. Other current and noncurrent assets acquired primarily include prepaid expenses, trade receivables, and deferred tax assets. In addition, we assumed various current liabilities primarily consisting of accounts payable, accrued payroll-related liabilities and other accrued operating expenses. The intangible assets acquired as part of the transaction include the Teavana trade name, tea blends and non-compete agreements. The Teavana trade name was valued at $105.5 million and determined to have an indefinite life, based on our expectation that the brand will be used indefinitely and has no contractual limitations. The intangible asset related to the tea blends was valued at $13.0 million and will be amortized on a straight-line basis over a period of 10 years, and the intangible asset related to the non-compete agreements was valued at $2.3 million and will be amortized on a straight-line basis over a period of 3 years. The $467.5 million of goodwill represents the intangible assets that do not qualify for separate recognition, primarily including Teavana's established global store presence in high traffic mall locations and other high-sales-volume retail venues, Teavana's global customer base, and Teavana's "Heaven of tea" retail experience in which store employees engage and educate customers about the ritual and enjoyment of tea. The goodwill was allocated to All Other Segments and is not deductible for income tax purposes.

Note 3: Derivative Financial Instruments

Interest Rates

Depending on market conditions, we enter into interest rate swap agreements to hedge the variability in cash flows due to changes in the benchmark interest rate related to anticipated debt issuances. These agreements are cash settled at the time of the pricing of the related debt. The effective portion of the derivative's gain or loss is recorded in accumulated other comprehensive income ("AOCI") and is subsequently reclassified to interest expense over the life of the related debt.

During the first quarter of fiscal 2015, we entered into forward-starting interest rate swap agreements with an aggregate notional amount of $250.0 million related to the $500 million of 7-year 2.700% Senior Notes (the "2022 notes") due in June 2022 issued in the third quarter of fiscal 2015. During the third quarter of fiscal 2015, we entered into forward-starting interest rate swap agreements with an aggregate notional amount of $250.0 million related to the $350 million of 30-year 4.300% Senior Notes (the "2045 notes") due in June 2045 issued in the third quarter of fiscal 2015. We cash settled these swap agreements at the time of the pricing of the 2022 and the 2045 notes, effectively locking in the benchmark interest rate in effect at the time the swap agreements were initiated. In July 2015, we redeemed our $550 million of 6.250% Senior Notes (the "2017 notes") originally scheduled to mature in August 2017. In connection with the redemption in the fourth quarter of fiscal 2015, we reclassified $2.0 million from accumulated other comprehensive income to interest expense on our consolidated statements of earnings related to remaining unrecognized losses from interest rate contracts entered into in conjunction with the 2017 notes and designated as cash flow hedges. In the fourth quarter of fiscal 2015, we entered into forward-starting interest rate swap agreements with an aggregate notional amount of $125 million related to an anticipated debt issuance in fiscal 2016. Refer to Note 9, Debt, for details of the components of our long-term debt.

Foreign Currency

To reduce cash flow volatility from foreign currency fluctuations, we enter into forward and swap contracts to hedge portions of cash flows of anticipated revenue streams and inventory purchases in currencies other than the entity's functional currency. The effective portion of the derivative's gain or loss is recorded in AOCI and is subsequently reclassified to revenue or cost of sales including occupancy costs when the hedged exposure affects net earnings.

In connection with the acquisition of Starbucks Japan that is discussed in Note 2, Acquisitions and Divestitures, we entered into cross-currency swap contracts during the first and third quarters of fiscal 2015 to hedge the foreign currency transaction risk of certain yen-denominated intercompany loans with a total notional value of ¥86.5 billion, or approximately $717 million as of September 27, 2015. Gains and losses from these swaps offset the changes in value of interest and principal payments as a result of changes in foreign exchange rates, which are also recorded in net interest income and other on the consolidated statements of earnings. We recognize the difference between the U.S. dollar interest payments received from the swap counterparty and the U.S. dollar equivalent of the Japanese yen interest payments made to the swap counterparty in interest income and other, net or interest expense on our consolidated statements of earnings. This difference varies over time and is driven by a number of market factors, including relevant interest rate differentials and foreign exchange rates. These swaps have been designated as cash flow hedges and mature in September 2016 and November 2024 at the same time as the related loans. There are no credit-risk-related contingent features associated with these swaps, although we may hold or post collateral depending upon the gain or loss position of the swap agreements.

We also enter into forward contracts to hedge the foreign currency exposure of our net investment in certain foreign operations. The effective portion of the derivative's gain or loss is recorded in AOCI and will be subsequently reclassified to net earnings when the hedged net investment is either sold or substantially liquidated.

As a result of our acquisition of Starbucks Japan, we reclassified the pretax cumulative net gains in AOCI of $7.2 million related to our net investment derivative instruments used to hedge our preexisting 39.5% equity method investment in Starbucks Japan into earnings, which was included in the gain resulting from acquisition of joint venture line item on the consolidated statements of earnings. These gains offset the cumulative translation adjustment loss balance associated with our preexisting investment included in the calculation of the remeasurement gain, which is described further in Note 2, Acquisitions and Divestitures.

To mitigate the translation risk of certain balance sheet items, we enter into foreign currency swap contracts that are not designated as hedging instruments. Gains and losses from these derivatives are largely offset by the financial impact of translating foreign currency denominated payables and receivables; both are recorded in net interest income and other on our consolidated statements of earnings.

Commodities

Depending on market conditions, we enter into coffee futures contracts and collars (the combination of a purchased call option and a sold put option) to hedge a portion of anticipated cash flows under our price-to-be-fixed green coffee contracts, which are described further in Note 5, Inventories. The effective portion of the derivative's gain or loss is recorded in AOCI and is subsequently reclassified to cost of sales including occupancy costs when the hedged exposure affects net earnings.

To mitigate the price uncertainty of a portion of our future purchases of dairy products and diesel fuel, we enter into swaps, futures and collars that are not designated as hedging instruments. Gains and losses from these derivatives are recorded in net interest income and other and help offset price fluctuations on our dairy purchases and the financial impact of diesel fuel fluctuations on our shipping costs, which are included in cost of sales including occupancy costs on our consolidated statements of earnings.

Gains and losses on derivative contracts designated as hedging instruments included in AOCI and expected to be reclassified into earnings within 12 months, net of tax (*in millions*):

	Net Gains/(Losses) Included in AOCI		Net Gains/(Losses) Expected to be Reclassified from AOCI into Earnings within 12 Months	Contract Remaining Maturity (Months)
	Sep 27, 2015	Sep 28, 2014		
Cash Flow Hedges:				
Interest rates	$ 30.1	$ 36.4	$ 3.5	4
Cross-currency swaps	(27.8)	—	—	111
Foreign currency - other	29.0	10.6	19.2	35
Coffee	(5.7)	(0.7)	(2.5)	12
Net Investment Hedges:				
Foreign currency	1.3	3.2	—	0

Pretax gains and losses on derivative contracts designated as hedging instruments recognized in other comprehensive income ("OCI") and reclassifications from AOCI to earnings (*in millions*):

	Year Ended			
	Gains/(Losses) Recognized in OCI Before Reclassifications		Gains/(Losses) Reclassified from AOCI to Earnings	
	Sep 27, 2015	Sep 28, 2014	Sep 27, 2015	Sep 28, 2014
Cash Flow Hedges:				
Interest rates	$ (6.8)	$ 0.5	$ 3.2	$ 5.0
Cross-currency swaps	11.4	—	46.2	—
Foreign currency - other	52.0	24.0	26.1	8.0
Coffee	(9.0)	(0.4)	(3.5)	(13.1)
Net Investment Hedges:				
Foreign currency	4.3	25.5	7.2	—

Pretax gains and losses on derivative contracts not designated as hedging instruments recognized in earnings (*in millions*):

	Gains/(Losses) Recognized in Earnings	
	Sep 27, 2015	Sep 28, 2014
Foreign currency	$ 27.1	$ 1.7
Coffee	(0.2)	—
Dairy	(3.8)	12.6
Diesel fuel	(9.0)	(1.0)

Notional amounts of outstanding derivative contracts *(in millions)*:

	Sep 27, 2015	Sep 28, 2014
Interest rates	$ 125	$ —
Cross-currency swaps	717	—
Foreign currency - other	577	542
Coffee	38	45
Dairy	43	24
Diesel fuel	14	17

The fair values of our derivative assets and liabilities are included in Note 4, Fair Value Measurements, and additional disclosures related to cash flow hedge gains and losses included in accumulated other comprehensive income, as well as subsequent reclassifications to earnings, are included in Note 11, Equity.

Note 4: Fair Value Measurements

Assets and Liabilities Measured at Fair Value on a Recurring Basis (in millions):

	Balance at Sep 27, 2015	Quoted Prices in Active Markets for Identical Assets (Level 1)	Significant Other Observable Inputs (Level 2)	Significant Unobservable Inputs (Level 3)
Assets:				
Cash and cash equivalents	$ 1,530.1	$ 1,530.1	$ —	$ —
Short-term investments:				
Available-for-sale securities				
Corporate debt securities	10.2	—	10.2	—
Foreign government obligations	2.0	—	2.0	—
State and local government obligations	3.3	—	3.3	—
Total available-for-sale securities	15.5	—	15.5	—
Trading securities	65.8	65.8	—	—
Total short-term investments	81.3	65.8	15.5	—
Prepaid expenses and other current assets:				
Derivative assets	50.8	—	50.8	—
Long-term investments:				
Available-for-sale securities				
Agency obligations	8.6	—	8.6	—
Corporate debt securities	121.8	—	121.8	—
Auction rate securities	5.9	—	—	5.9
Foreign government obligations	18.5	—	18.5	—
U.S. government treasury securities	104.8	104.8	—	—
State and local government obligations	9.7	—	9.7	—

Mortgage and other asset-backed securities	43.2	—	43.2	—
Total long-term investments	312.5	104.8	201.8	5.9
Other long-term assets:				
Derivative assets	54.7	—	54.7	—
Total assets	$ 2,029.4	$ 1,700.7	$ 322.8	$ 5.9
Liabilities:				
Accrued liabilities:				
Derivative liabilities	$ 19.2	$ 3.6	$ 15.6	$ —
Other long-term liabilities:				
Derivative liabilities	14.5	—	14.5	—
Total liabilities	$ 33.7	$ 3.6	$ 30.1	$ —

	Balance at Sep 28, 2014	Fair Value Measurements at Reporting Date Using		
		Quoted Prices in Active Markets for Identical Assets (Level 1)	Significant Other Observable Inputs (Level 2)	Significant Unobservable Inputs (Level 3)
Assets:				
Cash and cash equivalents	$ 1,708.4	$ 1,708.4	$ —	$ —
Short-term investments:				
Available-for-sale securities				
Corporate debt securities	4.9	—	4.9	—
Foreign government obligations	33.7	—	33.7	—
U.S. government treasury securities	10.9	10.9	—	—
State and local government obligations	12.7	—	12.7	—
Certificates of deposit	1.0	—	1.0	—
Total available-for-sale securities	63.2	10.9	52.3	—
Trading securities	72.2	72.2	—	—
Total short-term investments	135.4	83.1	52.3	—
Prepaid expenses and other current assets:				
Derivative assets	28.7	0.9	27.8	—
Long-term investments:				
Available-for-sale securities				
Agency obligations	8.9	—	8.9	—
Corporate debt securities	130.9	—	130.9	—
Auction rate securities	13.8	—	—	13.8

Foreign government obligations	17.4	—	17.4	—
U.S. government treasury securities	94.8	94.8	—	—
State and local government obligations	6.7	—	6.7	—
Mortgage and other asset-backed securities	45.9	—	45.9	—
Total long-term investments	318.4	94.8	209.8	13.8
Other long-term assets:				
Derivative assets	18.0	—	18.0	—
Total assets	$ 2,208.9	$ 1,887.2	$ 307.9	$ 13.8
Liabilities:				
Accrued liabilities:				
Derivative liabilities	$ 2.4	$ 0.4	$ 2.0	$ —

There were no material transfers between levels and there was no significant activity within Level 3 instruments during the periods presented. The fair values of any financial instruments presented above exclude the impact of netting assets and liabilities when a legally enforceable master netting agreement exists.

Available-for-sale Securities

Long-term investments generally mature within 4 years. Proceeds from sales of available-for-sale securities were $600.6 million, $1.5 billion, and $60.2 million for fiscal years 2015, 2014 and 2013, respectively. The increase in fiscal 2014 was due to the liquidation of a significant portion of our offshore investment portfolio in the fourth quarter of fiscal 2014 in anticipation of funding the acquisition of Starbucks Japan. Realized gains and losses on sales and maturities of available-for-sale securities were not material for fiscal years 2015, 2014, and 2013. Gross unrealized holding gains and losses on available-for-sale securities were not material as of September 27, 2015 and September 28, 2014.

Trading Securities

Trading securities include equity mutual funds and exchange-traded funds. Our trading securities portfolio approximates a portion of our liability under our Management Deferred Compensation Plan ("MDCP"), a defined contribution plan. Our MDCP liability was $98.3 million and $106.4 million as of September 27, 2015 and September 28, 2014, respectively, which is included in accrued compensation and related costs within accrued liabilities on the consolidated balance sheets. The changes in net unrealized holding gains and losses in the trading securities portfolio included in earnings for fiscal years 2015, 2014 and 2013 were a net loss of $4.5 million, and net gains of $1.2 million, and $11.7 million, respectively. Gross unrealized holding gains and losses on trading securities were not material as of September 27, 2015 and September 28, 2014.

Derivative Assets and Liabilities

Derivative assets and liabilities include foreign currency forward contracts, commodity futures contracts, collars and swaps, which are described further in Note 3, Derivative Financial Instruments.

Assets and Liabilities Measured at Fair Value on a Nonrecurring Basis

Assets and liabilities recognized or disclosed at fair value on a nonrecurring basis include items such as property, plant and equipment, goodwill and other intangible assets, equity and cost method investments, and other assets. These assets are measured at fair value if determined to be impaired. Impairment of property, plant, and equipment is included at Note 1, Summary of Significant Accounting Policies. During fiscal 2015 and 2014, there were no other material fair value adjustments.

Fair Value of Other Financial Instruments

The estimated fair value of our long-term debt based on the quoted market price (Level 2) is included at Note 9, Debt.

Note 5: Inventories *(in millions)*

	Sep 27, 2015	Sep 28, 2014
Coffee:		
Unroasted	$ 529.4	$ 432.3
Roasted	279.7	238.9
Other merchandise held for sale	318.3	265.7
Packaging and other supplies	179.0	154.0
Total	$ 1,306.4	$ 1,090.9

Other merchandise held for sale includes, among other items, serveware and tea. Inventory levels vary due to seasonality, commodity market supply and price fluctuations.

As of September 27, 2015, we had committed to purchasing green coffee totaling $819 million under fixed-price contracts and an estimated $266 million under price-to-be-fixed contracts. As of September 27, 2015, approximately $38 million of our price-to-be-fixed contracts were effectively fixed through the use of futures contracts. Price-to-be-fixed contracts are purchase commitments whereby the quality, quantity, delivery period, and other negotiated terms are agreed upon, but the date, and therefore the price, at which the base "C" coffee commodity price component will be fixed has not yet been established. For these types of contracts, either Starbucks or the seller has the option to "fix" the base "C" coffee commodity price prior to the delivery date. Until prices are fixed, we estimate the total cost of these purchase commitments. We believe, based on relationships established with our suppliers in the past, the risk of non-delivery on such purchase commitments is remote.

Note 6: Equity and Cost Investments *(in millions)*

	Sep 27, 2015	Sep 28, 2014
Equity method investments	$ 306.4	$ 469.3
Cost method investments	45.6	45.6
Total	$ 352.0	$ 514.9

Equity Method Investments

As of September 27, 2015, we had a 50% ownership interest in each of the following international equity method investees: President Starbucks Coffee (Shanghai); Starbucks Coffee Korea Co., Ltd.; President Starbucks Coffee Corporation (Taiwan) Company Limited; and Tata Starbucks Limited (India). In addition, we had a 49% ownership interest in Starbucks Coffee España, S.L. ("Starbucks Spain"). These international entities operate licensed Starbucks® retail stores.

We also license the rights to produce and distribute Starbucks-branded products to our 50% owned joint venture, The North American Coffee Partnership with the Pepsi-Cola Company, which develops and distributes bottled Starbucks® beverages, including Frappuccino® coffee drinks, Starbucks Doubleshot® espresso drinks, Starbucks Refreshers® beverages, and Starbucks Discoveries Iced Café Favorites®.

On September 23, 2014, we entered into a two-step tender offer bid agreement to acquire the remaining 60.5% interest in Starbucks Japan, at the time a 39.5% owned equity method investment. Upon the completion of the first tender offer step in the first quarter of fiscal 2015, we obtained a controlling interest in Starbucks Japan and began consolidating its results instead of applying equity method accounting. See further discussion at Note 2, Acquisitions and Divestitures.

In the fourth quarter of fiscal 2014, we sold our 50% equity method ownership interest in our Malaysian joint venture, Berjaya Starbucks Coffee Company Sdn. Bhd., to our joint venture partner, Berjaya Food Berhad, for a total purchase price of $88.0 million. This transaction resulted in a gain of $67.8 million, which was included in net interest income and other on our consolidated statements of earnings.

In the fourth quarter of fiscal 2013, we acquired a 49% equity method ownership interest in Starbucks Spain from our licensee partner Sigla S.A. (Grupo Vips) for approximately $33 million in cash.

Our share of income and losses from our equity method investments is included in income from equity investees on our consolidated statements of earnings. Also included in this line item is our proportionate share of gross profit resulting from coffee and other product sales to, and royalty and license fee revenues generated from, equity investees. Revenues generated from these related parties were $153.4 million, $219.2 million, and $205.1 million in fiscal years 2015, 2014, and 2013, respectively. Related costs of sales were $94.5 million, $121.2 million, and $115.4 million in fiscal years 2015, 2014, and 2013, respectively. As of September 27, 2015 and September 28, 2014, there were $36.7 million and $54.9 million of accounts receivable from equity investees, respectively, on our consolidated balance sheets, primarily related to product sales and royalty revenues.

Summarized combined financial information of our equity method investees, which represent 100% of the investees' financial information (*in millions*):

Financial Position as of	Sep 27, 2015	Sep 28, 2014
Current assets	$ 402.8	$ 701.3
Noncurrent assets	578.8	873.9
Current liabilities	490.0	615.6
Noncurrent liabilities	38.7	79.1

Results of Operations for Fiscal Year Ended	Sep 27, 2015	Sep 28, 2014	Sep 29, 2013
Net revenues	$ 2,688.0	$ 3,461.3	$ 3,018.7
Operating income	426.4	467.7	434.8
Net earnings	392.1	382.6	358.0

Cost Method Investments

As of September 27, 2015, we had $19 million invested in equity interests of entities that develop and operate Starbucks® licensed stores in several global markets. We have the ability to acquire additional interests in some of these cost method investees at certain intervals. Depending on our total percentage ownership interest and our ability to exercise significant influence over financial and operating policies, additional investments may require a retroactive application of the equity method of accounting. We also had a $25 million investment in the preferred stock of Square, Inc.

During the fourth quarter of fiscal 2013, we sold our 18% interest in Starbucks Coffee Argentina S.R.L. to our joint venture partner Alsea, S.A.B. de C.V., for a total purchase price of $4.4 million. This transaction resulted in a loss of $1.0 million, which was included in net interest income and other on our consolidated statements of earnings.

During the second quarter of fiscal 2013, we sold our 18% interest in Cafe Sirena S. de R.L. de CV (a Mexican limited liability company), to our controlling joint venture partner, SC de Mexico, S.A. de CV, owned by Alsea, S.A.B. de C.V., for a total purchase price of $50.3 million, which included final working capital adjustments. This transaction resulted in a gain of $35.2 million, which was included in net interest income and other on our consolidated statements of earnings.

Note 7: Supplemental Balance Sheet Information *(in millions)*

Property, Plant and Equipment, net

	Sep 27, 2015	Sep 28, 2014
Land	$ 46.6	$ 46.7
Buildings	411.5	278.1
Leasehold improvements	5,409.6	4,858.4
Store equipment	1,707.5	1,493.3
Roasting equipment	542.4	410.9
Furniture, fixtures and other	1,281.7	1,078.1
Work in progress	242.5	415.6
Property, plant and equipment, gross	9,641.8	8,581.1
Accumulated depreciation	(5,553.5)	(5,062.1)
Property, plant and equipment, net	$ 4,088.3	$ 3,519.0

Accrued Liabilities

	Sep 27, 2015	Sep 28, 2014
Accrued compensation and related costs	$ 522.3	$ 437.9
Accrued occupancy costs	137.2	119.8
Accrued taxes	259.0	272.0
Accrued dividends payable	297.0	239.8
Other	545.2	444.9
Total accrued liabilities	$ 1,760.7	$ 1,514.4

Note 8: Other Intangible Assets and Goodwill

Indefinite-Lived Intangible Assets

(in millions)	Sep 27, 2015	Sep 28, 2014
Trade names, trademarks and patents	$ 202.8	$ 197.5
Other indefinite-lived intangible assets	15.1	15.1
Total indefinite-lived intangible assets	$ 217.9	$ 212.6

Additional disclosure regarding changes in our intangible assets due to acquisitions is included at Note 2, Acquisitions and Divestitures.

Goodwill

Changes in the carrying amount of goodwill by reportable operating segment *(in millions)*:

	Americas	China/Asia Pacific	EMEA	Channel Development	All Other Segments	Total
Balance at September 29, 2013						
Goodwill prior to impairment	$ 230.2	$ 75.1	$ 62.2	$ 23.8	$ 480.2	$ 871.5
Accumulated impairment charges	(8.6)	—	—	—	—	(8.6)
Goodwill	$ 221.6	$ 75.1	$ 62.2	$ 23.8	$ 480.2	$ 862.9
Impairment	—	—	—	—	(0.8)	(0.8)
Other[1]	(2.6)	(0.2)	(3.1)	—	—	(5.9)
Balance at September 28, 2014						
Goodwill prior to impairment	$ 227.6	$ 74.9	$ 59.1	$ 23.8	$ 480.2	$ 865.6
Accumulated impairment charges	(8.6)	—	—	—	(0.8)	(9.4)
Goodwill	$ 219.0	$ 74.9	$ 59.1	$ 23.8	$ 479.4	$ 856.2
Acquisition/(divestiture)	(2.5)	815.6	—	—	—	813.1
Impairment	—	—	—	—	(0.5)	(0.5)
Other[1]	(5.3)	(86.4)	(1.7)	—	—	(93.4)
Balance at September 27, 2015						
Goodwill prior to impairment	$ 219.8	$ 804.1	$ 57.4	$ 23.8	$ 480.2	$ 1,585.3
Accumulated impairment charges	(8.6)	—	—	—	(1.3)	(9.9)
Goodwill	$ 211.2	$ 804.1	$ 57.4	$ 23.8	$ 478.9	$ 1,575.4

[1] Other is primarily comprised of changes in the goodwill balance as a result of foreign currency translation.

Finite-Lived Intangible Assets

	Sep 27, 2015			Sep 28, 2014		
(in millions)	Gross Carrying Amount	Accumulated Amortization	Net Carrying Amount	Gross Carrying Amount	Accumulated Amortization	Net Carrying Amount
Acquired and reacquired rights	$ 308.6	$ (52.5)	$ 256.1	$ 36.8	$ (10.1)	$ 26.7
Acquired trade secrets and processes	27.6	(8.2)	19.4	27.6	(5.4)	22.2
Licensing agreements	13.4	(1.1)	12.3	—	—	—
Trade names, trademarks and patents	24.5	(13.0)	11.5	21.6	(11.6)	10.0
Other finite-lived intangible assets	6.5	(3.3)	3.2	3.8	(1.8)	2.0
Total finite-lived intangible assets	$ 380.6	$ (78.1)	$ 302.5	$ 89.8	$ (28.9)	$ 60.9

Amortization expense for finite-lived intangible assets was $50.0 million, $8.7 million, and $7.7 million during fiscal 2015, 2014, and 2013, respectively.

Estimated future amortization expense as of September 27, 2015 (*in millions*):

Fiscal Year Ending		
2016	$	53.2
2017		52.9
2018		51.5
2019		51.2
2020		51.1
Thereafter		42.6
Total estimated future amortization expense	$	302.5

Additional disclosure regarding changes in our intangible assets due to acquisitions is included at Note 2, Acquisitions and Divestitures.

Note 9: Debt

Revolving Credit Facility and Commercial Paper Program

Our $750 million unsecured, revolving credit facility with various banks, of which $150 million may be used for issuances of letters of credit, is available for working capital, capital expenditures and other corporate purposes, including acquisitions and share repurchases. During the second quarter of fiscal 2015, we extended the duration of our credit facility, which is now set to mature on January 21, 2020, and amended certain facility fees and borrowing rates. Starbucks has the option, subject to negotiation and agreement with the related banks, to increase the maximum commitment amount by an additional $750 million. Borrowings under the credit facility will bear interest at a variable rate based on LIBOR, and, for U.S. dollar-denominated loans under certain circumstances, a Base Rate (as defined in the credit facility), in each case plus an applicable margin. The applicable margin is based on the better of (i) the Company's long-term credit ratings assigned by Moody's and Standard & Poor's rating agencies and (ii) the Company's fixed charge coverage ratio, pursuant to a pricing grid set forth in the credit facility. The current applicable margin is 0.565% for Eurocurrency Rate Loans and 0.00% for Base Rate Loans. The credit facility contains provisions requiring us to maintain compliance with certain covenants, including a minimum fixed charge coverage ratio, which measures our ability to cover financing expenses. As of September 27, 2015, we were in compliance with all applicable covenants. No amounts were outstanding under our credit facility as of September 27, 2015.

Under our commercial paper program, we may issue unsecured commercial paper notes up to a maximum aggregate amount outstanding at any time of $1 billion, with individual maturities that may vary, but not exceed 397 days from the date of issue. Amounts outstanding under the commercial paper program are required to be backstopped by available commitments under our credit facility discussed above. As of September 27, 2015, availability under our commercial paper program was approximately $750 million (which represents the full committed credit facility amount, as the amount of outstanding letters of credit was not material as of September 27, 2015). The proceeds from borrowings under our commercial paper program may be used for working capital needs, capital expenditures and other corporate purposes, including share repurchases, business expansion, payment of cash dividends on our common stock or the financing of possible acquisitions. In the fourth quarter of fiscal 2015, we issued and subsequently repaid commercial paper borrowings of $93 million for general corporate purposes. We had no other borrowings under our commercial paper program during fiscal 2015 or fiscal 2014, and there were no amounts outstanding as of September 27, 2015 or September 28, 2014.

Long-term Debt

In July 2015, we redeemed our $550 million of 6.250% Senior Notes (the "2017 notes") originally scheduled to mature in August 2017. The redemption resulted in a charge of $61.1 million, which is presented separately as loss on extinguishment of debt within other income and expenses on our consolidated statements of earnings. This loss primarily relates to the optional redemption payment as outlined in the 2017 notes indenture, as well as non-cash expenses related to the previously capitalized original issuance costs and accelerated amortization of the unamortized discount. In connection with the redemption, we also reclassified $2.0 million from accumulated other comprehensive income to interest expense on our consolidated statements of earnings related to remaining unrecognized losses from interest rate contracts entered into in conjunction with the 2017 notes and designated as cash flow hedges.

In June 2015, we issued additional long-term debt in an underwritten registered public offering, which consisted of $500 million of 7-year 2.700% Senior Notes (the "2022 notes") due June 2022, and $350 million of 30-year 4.300% Senior Notes (the "2045 notes") due June 2045. Interest on the 2022 and 2045 notes is payable semi-annually on June 15 and December 15 of each year, commencing on December 15, 2015.

In December 2013, we issued $400 million of 3-year 0.875% Senior Notes (the "2016 notes") due December 2016, and $350 million of 5-year 2.000% Senior Notes (the "2018 notes") due December 2018, in an underwritten registered public offering. Interest on the 2016 and 2018 notes is payable semi-annually on June 5 and December 5 of each year.

In September 2013, we issued $750 million of 10-year 3.85% Senior Notes (the "2023 notes") due October 2023, in an underwritten registered public offering. Interest on the 2023 notes is payable semi-annually on April 1 and October 1 of each year.

Components of long-term debt including the associated interest rates and related fair values (*in millions, except interest rates*):

Issuance	Sep 27, 2015		Sep 28, 2014		Stated Interest Rate	Effective Interest Rate [1]
	Face Value	Estimated Fair Value	Face Value	Estimated Fair Value		
2016 notes	$ 400.0	$ 400	$ 400.0	$ 400	0.875%	0.941%
2017 notes	—	—	550.0	625	6.250%	—%
2018 notes	350.0	354	350.0	353	2.000%	2.012%
2022 notes	500.0	503	—	—	2.700%	2.819%
2023 notes	750.0	790	750.0	786	3.850%	2.860%
2045 notes	350.0	355	—	—	4.300%	4.348%
Total	2,350.0	2,402	2,050.0	2,164		
Aggregate unamortized discount	2.5		1.7			
Total	$ 2,347.5		$ 2,048.3			

[1] Includes the effects of the amortization of any premium or discount and any gain or loss upon settlement of related treasury locks or forward-starting interest rate swaps utilized to hedge the interest rate risk prior to the debt issuance.

The indentures under which the above notes were issued also require us to maintain compliance with certain covenants, including limits on future liens and sale and leaseback transactions on certain material properties. As of September 27, 2015, we were in compliance with each of these covenants.

The following table summarizes our long-term debt maturities as of September 27, 2015 (*in millions*):

Fiscal Year	Total
2016	$ —
2017	400.0
2018	—
2019	350.0
2020	—
Thereafter	1,600.0
Total	$ 2,350.0

Interest Expense

Interest expense, net of interest capitalized, was $70.5 million, $64.1 million, and $28.1 million in fiscal 2015, 2014 and 2013, respectively. In fiscal 2015, 2014, and 2013, $3.6 million, $6.2 million, and $10.4 million, respectively, of interest was capitalized for asset construction projects.

Note 10: Leases

Rent expense under operating lease agreements *(in millions)*:

Fiscal Year Ended	Sep 27, 2015	Sep 28, 2014	Sep 29, 2013
Minimum rent	$ 1,026.3	$ 907.4	$ 838.3
Contingent rent	111.5	66.8	56.4
Total	$ 1,137.8	$ 974.2	$ 894.7

Minimum future rental payments under non-cancelable operating leases and lease financing arrangements as of September 27, 2015 *(in millions)*:

Fiscal Year Ending	Operating Leases	Lease Financing Arrangements
2016	$ 1,032.4	$ 3.2
2017	892.5	3.2
2018	739.8	3.2
2019	624.0	3.2
2020	548.9	3.2
Thereafter	1,831.9	31.1
Total minimum lease payments	$ 5,669.5	$ 47.1

We have subleases related to certain of our operating leases. During fiscal 2015, 2014, and 2013, we recognized sublease income of $11.9 million, $13.3 million, and $9.3 million, respectively. Additionally, as of September 27, 2015, the gross carrying value of assets related to build-to-suit lease arrangements accounted for as financing leases was $66.8 million with associated accumulated depreciation of $2.5 million. We had no built-to-suit lease arrangements as of September 28, 2014.

Note 11: Equity

As discussed in Note 1, Summary of Significant Accounting Policies, on April 9, 2015, we effected a two-for-one stock split of our $0.001 par value common stock for shareholders of record as of March 30, 2015. All share data presented in this note has been retroactively adjusted to reflect this stock split.

In addition to 2.4 billion shares of authorized common stock with $0.001 par value per share, we have authorized 7.5 million shares of preferred stock, none of which was outstanding at September 27, 2015.

Included in additional paid-in capital in our consolidated statements of equity as of September 27, 2015 and September 28, 2014 is $39.4 million related to the increase in value of our share of the net assets of Starbucks Japan at the time of its initial public stock offering in fiscal 2002. Also included in additional paid-in capital as of September 27, 2015 is $1.7 million, which represents the difference between the carrying value of the remaining outstanding noncontrolling interests in Starbucks Japan prior to obtaining full ownership and the cash paid to acquire the noncontrolling interests. Refer to Note 2, Acquisitions and Divestitures, for further discussion.

We repurchased 29.0 million shares of common stock at a total cost of $1.4 billion, and 21.0 million shares at a total cost of $769.8 million for the years ended September 27, 2015 and September 28, 2014, respectively. On July 23, 2015, we announced that our Board of Directors approved an increase of 50 million shares to our ongoing share repurchase program. As of September 27, 2015, 52.7 million shares remained available for repurchase under current authorizations.

During fiscal years 2015 and 2014, our Board of Directors declared the following dividends (*in millions, except per share amounts*):

	Dividend Per Share	Record date	Total Amount	Payment Date
Fiscal Year 2015				
First quarter	$0.16	February 5, 2015	$240.1	February 20, 2015
Second quarter	$0.16	May 7, 2015	$240.1	May 22, 2015
Third quarter	$0.16	August 6, 2015	$239.0	August 21, 2015
Fourth quarter	$0.20	November 12, 2015	$297.0	November 27, 2015
Fiscal Year 2014				
First quarter	$0.13	February 6, 2014	$196.4	February 21, 2014
Second quarter	$0.13	May 8, 2014	$195.5	May 23, 2014
Third quarter	$0.13	August 7, 2014	$195.3	August 22, 2014
Fourth quarter	$0.16	November 13, 2014	$239.8	November 28, 2014

Comprehensive Income

Comprehensive income includes all changes in equity during the period, except those resulting from transactions with our shareholders. Comprehensive income is comprised of net earnings and other comprehensive income. Accumulated other comprehensive income reported on our consolidated balance sheets consists of foreign currency translation adjustments and the unrealized gains and losses, net of applicable taxes, on available-for-sale securities and on derivative instruments designated and qualifying as cash flow and net investment hedges.

Changes in accumulated other comprehensive income ("AOCI") by component, for year ended September 27, 2015, net of tax:

(in millions)	Available-for-Sale Securities	Cash Flow Hedges	Net Investment Hedges	Translation Adjustment	Total
September 27, 2015					
Net gains/(losses) in AOCI, beginning of period	$ (0.4)	$ 46.3	$ 3.2	$ (23.8)	$ 25.3
Net gains/(losses) recognized in OCI before reclassifications	0.9	30.8	2.7	(185.6)	(151.2)

	Available-for-Sale Securities	Cash Flow Hedges	Net Investment Hedges	Translation Adjustment	Total
Net (gains)/losses reclassified from AOCI to earnings	(0.6)	(51.5)	(4.6)	14.3	(42.4)
Other comprehensive income/(loss) attributable to Starbucks	0.3	(20.7)	(1.9)	(171.3)	(193.6)
Purchase of noncontrolling interest	—	—	—	(31.1)	(31.1)
Net gains/(losses) in AOCI, end of period	$ (0.1)	$ 25.6	$ 1.3	$ (226.2)	$ (199.4)

(in millions)	Available-for-Sale Securities	Cash Flow Hedges	Net Investment Hedges	Translation Adjustment	Total
September 28, 2014					
Net gains/(losses) in AOCI, beginning of period	$ (0.5)	$ 26.8	$ (12.9)	$ 53.6	$ 67.0
Net gains/(losses) recognized in OCI before reclassifications	1.0	16.3	16.1	(77.4)	(44.0)
Net (gains)/losses reclassified from AOCI to earnings	(0.9)	3.2	—	—	2.3
Other comprehensive income/(loss) attributable to Starbucks	0.1	19.5	16.1	(77.4)	(41.7)
Net gains/(losses) in AOCI, end of period	$ (0.4)	$ 46.3	$ 3.2	$ (23.8)	$ 25.3

Impact of reclassifications from AOCI on the consolidated statements of earnings *(in millions)*:

	Amounts Reclassified from AOCI Fiscal Year Ended		Affected Line Item in the Statements of Earnings
	Sep 27, 2015	Sep 28, 2014	
Gains/(losses) on cash flow hedges			
Interest rate hedges	$ 3.2	$ 5.0	Interest expense
Cross-currency swaps	46.2	—	Interest income and other, net
Foreign currency hedges	14.0	5.1	Revenue
Foreign currency/coffee hedges	8.6	(10.0)	Cost of sales including occupancy costs
Gains/(losses) on net investment hedges [1]	7.2	—	Gain resulting from acquisition of joint venture
Translation adjustment [2]			
Starbucks Japan	(7.2)	—	Gain resulting from acquisition of joint venture
Other	(7.1)	—	Interest income and other, net
	64.9	0.1	Total before tax
	(23.1)	(3.3)	Tax (expense)/benefit
	$ 41.8	$ (3.2)	Net of tax

[1] Release of pretax cumulative net gains in AOCI related to our net investment derivative instruments used to hedge our preexisting 39.5% equity method investment in Starbucks Japan.

[2] Release of cumulative translation adjustments to earnings upon sale or liquidation of foreign business.

Note 12: Employee Stock and Benefit Plans

We maintain several equity incentive plans under which we may grant non-qualified stock options, incentive stock options, restricted stock, restricted stock units ("RSUs"), or stock appreciation rights to employees, non-employee directors and consultants. We issue new shares of common stock upon exercise of stock options and the vesting of RSUs. We also have an employee stock purchase plan ("ESPP").

As discussed in Note 1, Summary of Significant Accounting Policies, on April 9, 2015, we effected a two-for-one stock split of our $0.001 par value common stock for shareholders of record as of March 30, 2015. All share and per-share data presented in this note has been retroactively adjusted to reflect this stock split.

As of September 27, 2015, there were 96.3 million shares of common stock available for issuance pursuant to future equity-based compensation awards and 14.3 million shares available for issuance under our ESPP.

Stock-based compensation expense recognized in the consolidated financial statements *(in millions)*:

Fiscal Year Ended	Sep 27, 2015	Sep 28, 2014	Sep 29, 2013
Options	$ 37.8	$ 41.8	$ 37.1
RSUs	172.0	141.4	105.2
Total stock-based compensation expense recognized in the consolidated statements of earnings	$ 209.8	$ 183.2	$ 142.3
Total related tax benefit	$ 72.3	$ 63.4	$ 49.8
Total capitalized stock-based compensation included in net property, plant and equipment and inventories on the consolidated balance sheets	$ 1.9	$ 1.9	$ 1.8

Stock Option Plans

Stock options to purchase our common stock are granted at the fair value of the stock on the grant date. The majority of options become exercisable in four equal installments beginning a year from the grant date and generally expire 10 years from the grant date. Options granted to non-employee directors generally vest over one to three years. Nearly all outstanding stock options are non-qualified stock options.

The fair value of stock option awards was estimated at the grant date with the following weighted average assumptions for fiscal years 2015, 2014, and 2013:

Fiscal Year Ended	Employee Stock Options Granted During the Period		
	2015	2014	2013
Expected term (in years)	4.2	4.5	4.8
Expected stock price volatility	22.3%	26.8%	34.0%
Risk-free interest rate	1.1%	1.1%	0.7%
Expected dividend yield	1.6%	1.3%	1.6%
Weighted average grant price	$ 39.89	$ 40.12	$ 25.62
Estimated fair value per option granted	$ 6.58	$ 8.36	$ 6.44

The expected term of the options represents the estimated period of time until exercise, and is based on historical experience of similar awards, giving consideration to the contractual terms, vesting schedules and expectations of future employee behavior. Expected stock price volatility is based on a combination of historical volatility of our stock and the one-year implied volatility of Starbucks traded options, for the related vesting periods. The risk-free interest rate is based on the implied yield available on U.S. Treasury zero-coupon issues with an equivalent remaining term. The dividend yield assumption is based on our anticipated cash dividend payouts. The amounts shown above for the estimated fair value per option granted are before the estimated effect of forfeitures, which reduce the amount of expense recorded in the consolidated statements of earnings.

Stock option transactions for the year ended September 27, 2015 *(in millions, except per share and contractual life amounts)*:

	Shares Subject to Options	Weighted Average Exercise Price per Share	Weighted Average Remaining Contractual Life (Years)	Aggregate Intrinsic Value
Outstanding, September 28, 2014	39.6	$ 18.93	5.8	$ 754
Granted	6.4	39.89		
Exercised	(11.3)	14.99		

Expired/forfeited	(1.1)	32.38		
Outstanding, September 27, 2015	33.6	23.81	6.0	1,150
Exercisable, September 27, 2015	21.1	16.75	4.7	872
Vested and expected to vest, September 27, 2015	32.4	23.29	5.9	1,125

The aggregate intrinsic value in the table above, which is the amount by which the market value of the underlying stock exceeded the exercise price of outstanding options, is before applicable income taxes and represents the amount optionees would have realized if all in-the-money options had been exercised on the last business day of the period indicated.

As of September 27, 2015, total unrecognized stock-based compensation expense, net of estimated forfeitures, related to nonvested options was approximately $32 million, before income taxes, and is expected to be recognized over a weighted average period of approximately 2.6 years. The total intrinsic value of options exercised was $358 million, $258 million, and $539 million during fiscal years 2015, 2014, and 2013, respectively. The total fair value of options vested was $36 million, $44 million, and $56 million during fiscal years 2015, 2014, and 2013, respectively.

RSUs

We have both time-vested and performance-based RSUs. Time-vested RSUs are awarded to eligible employees and non-employee directors and entitle the grantee to receive shares of common stock at the end of a vesting period, subject solely to the employee's continuing employment or the non-employee director's continuing service. The majority of RSUs vest in two equal annual installments beginning a year from the grant date. Our performance-based RSUs are awarded to eligible employees and entitle the grantee to receive shares of common stock if we achieve specified performance goals during the performance period and the grantee remains employed during the subsequent vesting period.

RSU transactions for the year ended September 27, 2015 *(in millions, except per share and contractual life amounts)*:

	Number of Shares	Weighted Average Grant Date Fair Value per Share	Weighted Average Remaining Contractual Life (Years)	Aggregate Intrinsic Value
Nonvested, September 28, 2014	10.8	$ 31.17	1.0	$ 407
Granted	6.7	38.56		
Vested	(5.1)	26.73		
Forfeited/canceled	(1.7)	36.10		
Nonvested, September 27, 2015	10.7	36.35	1.0	620

For fiscal 2014 and 2013, the weighted average fair value per RSU granted was $40.07 and $25.12, respectively. As of September 27, 2015, total unrecognized stock-based compensation expense related to nonvested RSUs, net of estimated forfeitures, was approximately $126 million, before income taxes, and is expected to be recognized over a weighted average period of approximately 2.3 years. The total fair value of RSUs vested was $137 million, $103 million and $104 million during fiscal years 2015, 2014, and 2013, respectively.

ESPP

Our ESPP allows eligible employees to contribute up to 10% of their base earnings toward the quarterly purchase of our common stock, subject to an annual maximum dollar amount. The purchase price is 95% of the fair market value of the stock on the last business day of the quarterly offering period. The number of shares issued under our ESPP was 0.5 million in fiscal 2015.

Deferred Compensation Plan

We have a Deferred Compensation Plan for Non-Employee Directors under which non-employee directors may, for any fiscal year, irrevocably elect to defer receipt of shares of common stock the director would have received upon vesting of restricted stock units. The number of deferred shares outstanding related to deferrals made under this plan is not material.

Defined Contribution Plans

We maintain voluntary defined contribution plans, both qualified and non-qualified, covering eligible employees as defined in the plan documents. Participating employees may elect to defer and contribute a portion of their eligible compensation to the plans up to limits stated in the plan documents, not to exceed the dollar amounts set by applicable laws.

Our matching contributions to all U.S. and non-U.S. plans were $70.9 million, $73.0 million, and $54.7 million in fiscal years 2015, 2014, and 2013, respectively.

Note 13: Income Taxes

Components of earnings/(loss) before income taxes *(in millions)*:

Fiscal Year Ended	Sep 27, 2015	Sep 28, 2014	Sep 29, 2013		
			Total	Litigation charge	All Other
United States	$ 2,837.2	$ 2,572.4	$ (674.0)	$ (2,784.1)	$ 2,110.1
Foreign	1,065.8	587.3	444.1	—	444.1
Total earnings/(loss) before income taxes	$ 3,903.0	$ 3,159.7	$ (229.9)	$ (2,784.1)	$ 2,554.2

Provision/(benefit) for income taxes *(in millions)*:

Fiscal Year Ended	Sep 27, 2015	Sep 28, 2014	Sep 29, 2013		
			Total	Litigation charge	All Other
Current taxes:					
U.S. federal	$ 801.0	$ 822.7	$ 616.6	$ —	$ 616.6
U.S. state and local	150.1	132.9	93.8	—	93.8
Foreign	172.2	128.8	95.9	—	95.9
Total current taxes	1,123.3	1,084.4	806.3	—	806.3
Deferred taxes:					
U.S. federal	56.5	12.0	(898.8)	(922.3)	23.5
U.S. state and local	4.0	(4.9)	(144.0)	(148.7)	4.7
Foreign	(40.1)	0.5	(2.2)	—	(2.2)
Total deferred taxes	20.4	7.6	(1,045.0)	(1,071.0)	26.0
Total income tax expense/(benefit)	$ 1,143.7	$ 1,092.0	$ (238.7)	$ (1,071.0)	$ 832.3

Reconciliation of the statutory U.S. federal income tax rate with our effective income tax rate:

Fiscal Year Ended	Sep 27, 2015	Sep 28, 2014	Sep 29, 2013		
			Total	Litigation charge	All Other
Statutory rate	35.0 %	35.0 %	35.0%	35.0%	35.0 %
State income taxes, net of federal tax benefit	2.8	2.6	15.8	3.5	2.4
Benefits and taxes related to foreign operations	(2.1)	(1.9)	37.5	—	(3.4)
Domestic production activity deduction	(2.2)	(0.7)	8.1	—	(0.7)
Domestic tax credits	(0.2)	(0.2)	2.8	—	(0.3)
Charitable contributions	(0.3)	(0.4)	3.9	—	(0.3)
Gain resulting from acquisition of joint venture	(3.7)	—	—	—	—
Other, net	—	0.2	0.7	—	(0.1)
Effective tax rate	29.3 %	34.6 %	103.8%	38.5%	32.6 %

Our effective tax rate in fiscal 2013 was significantly affected by the litigation charge we recorded as a result of the conclusion of our arbitration with Kraft. In order to provide a more meaningful analysis of tax expense and the effective tax rate, the tables above present separate reconciliations of the effect of the litigation charge. The deferred tax asset related to the litigation charge is estimated to be recovered over a period of 15 years; the deferred tax asset has been classified between current and non-current consistent with the expected recovery period for income tax reporting purposes.

U.S. income and foreign withholding taxes have not been provided on approximately $2.8 billion of cumulative undistributed earnings of foreign subsidiaries and equity investees. We intend to reinvest these earnings for the foreseeable future. If these amounts were distributed to the U.S., in the form of dividends or otherwise, we would be subject to additional U.S. income taxes, which could be material. Determination of the amount of unrecognized deferred income tax liabilities on these earnings is not practicable because of the complexities with its hypothetical calculation, and the amount of liability, if any, is dependent on circumstances existing if and when remittance occurs.

Tax effect of temporary differences and carryforwards that comprise significant portions of deferred tax assets and liabilities *(in millions)*:

	Sep 27, 2015	Sep 28, 2014
Deferred tax assets:		
Property, plant and equipment	$ 121.4	$ 78.5
Accrued occupancy costs	98.4	58.8
Accrued compensation and related costs	81.7	75.3
Other accrued liabilities	49.0	27.6
Asset retirement obligation asset	29.0	18.6
Stored value card liability	99.1	63.4
Asset impairments	26.2	49.5
Tax credits	20.8	20.3
Stock-based compensation	135.5	131.5
Net operating losses	93.4	104.4
Litigation charge	931.0	1,002.0
Other	104.5	77.0
Total	$ 1,790.0	$ 1,706.9
Valuation allowance	(143.7)	(166.8)
Total deferred tax asset, net of valuation allowance	$ 1,646.3	$ 1,540.1
Deferred tax liabilities:		
Property, plant and equipment	(217.5)	(148.2)
Intangible assets and goodwill	(177.3)	(92.9)
Other	(114.1)	(89.4)
Total	(508.9)	(330.5)
Net deferred tax asset	$ 1,137.4	$ 1,209.6
Reported as:		
Current deferred income tax assets	$ 381.7	$ 317.4
Long-term deferred income tax assets	828.9	903.3
Current deferred income tax liabilities (included in Accrued liabilities)	(5.4)	(4.2)
Long-term deferred income tax liabilities (included in Other long-term liabilities)	(67.8)	(6.9)
Net deferred tax asset	$ 1,137.4	$ 1,209.6

The valuation allowance as of September 27, 2015 and September 28, 2014 is primarily related to net operating losses and other deferred tax assets of consolidated foreign subsidiaries. The net change in the total valuation allowance was a decrease of $23.1 million and an increase of $6.3 million for fiscal 2015 and 2014, respectively.

As of September 27, 2015, we had state tax credit carryforwards of $32.0 million with an expiration date of fiscal 2024 and foreign net operating loss carryforwards of $309.5 million, the majority of which has no expiration date.

Uncertain Tax Positions

As of September 27, 2015, we had $150.4 million of gross unrecognized tax benefits of which $101.7 million, if recognized, would affect our effective tax rate. We recognized expense of $0.7 million, expense of $5.9 million, and a benefit of $0.8 million of interest and penalties in income tax expense, prior to the benefit of the federal tax deduction, for fiscal 2015, 2014 and 2013, respectively. As of September 27, 2015 and September 28, 2014, we had accrued interest and penalties of $11.3 million and $10.6 million, respectively, before the benefit of the federal tax deduction, included within other long-term liabilities on our consolidated balance sheets.

The following table summarizes the activity related to our unrecognized tax benefits *(in millions)*:

	Sep 27, 2015	Sep 28, 2014	Sep 29, 2013
Beginning balance	$ 112.7	$ 88.8	$ 75.3
Increase related to prior year tax positions	7.9	1.4	8.9
Decrease related to prior year tax positions	(0.9)	(2.2)	(9.3)
Increase related to current year tax positions	32.0	26.7	19.3
Decrease related to current year tax positions	(0.6)	(1.9)	(0.4)
Decreases related to settlements with taxing authorities	(0.7)	(0.1)	—
Decreases related to lapsing of statute of limitations	—	—	(5.0)
Ending balance	$ 150.4	$ 112.7	$ 88.8

We are currently under examination, or may be subject to examination, by various jurisdictions inside and outside the U.S. as well as U.S. state and municipal taxing jurisdictions for fiscal years 2006 through 2014. We are no longer subject to U.S. federal or state examination for years prior to fiscal year 2010, with the exception of one state and one city. We are no longer subject to examination in any material international markets prior to 2006.

There is a reasonable possibility that $31.2 million of the currently remaining unrecognized tax benefits may be recognized by the end of fiscal 2016 as a result of a lapse of the statute of limitations and expected consent from taxing authorities.

Note 14: Earnings per Share

As discussed in Note 1, Summary of Significant Accounting Policies, on April 9, 2015, we effected a two-for-one stock split of our $0.001 par value common stock for shareholders of record as of March 30, 2015. All share and per-share data presented in this note has been retroactively adjusted to reflect this stock split.

Calculation of net earnings per common share ("EPS") — basic and diluted *(in millions, except EPS)*:

Fiscal Year Ended	Sep 27, 2015	Sep 28, 2014	Sep 29, 2013
Net earnings attributable to Starbucks	$ 2,757.4	$ 2,068.1	$ 8.3
Weighted average common shares outstanding (for basic calculation)	1,495.9	1,506.3	1,498.5
Dilutive effect of outstanding common stock options and RSUs	17.5	20.0	26.0
Weighted average common and common equivalent shares outstanding (for diluted calculation)	1,513.4	1,526.3	1,524.5
EPS — basic	$ 1.84	$ 1.37	$ 0.01
EPS — diluted	$ 1.82	$ 1.35	$ 0.01

Potential dilutive shares consist of the incremental common shares issuable upon the exercise of outstanding stock options (both vested and non-vested) and unvested RSUs, calculated using the treasury stock method. The calculation of dilutive shares outstanding excludes out-of-the-money stock options (i.e., such options' exercise prices were greater than the average market price of our common shares for the period) because their inclusion would have been antidilutive. We had no out-of-the-money stock options as of September 27, 2015 and September 29, 2013, respectively. There were 5.3 million out-of-the-money stock options as of September 28, 2014.

Note 15: Commitments and Contingencies

Legal Proceedings

On November 12, 2013, the arbitrator in our arbitration with Kraft Foods Global, Inc. (now known as Kraft Foods Group, Inc.) ("Kraft") ordered Starbucks to pay Kraft $2,227.5 million in damages plus prejudgment interest and attorneys' fees. We estimated prejudgment interest, which included an accrual through the estimated payment date, and attorneys' fees to be approximately $556.6 million. As a result, we recorded a litigation charge of $2,784.1 million in our fiscal 2013 operating results.

In the first quarter of fiscal 2014, Starbucks paid all amounts due to Kraft under the arbitration, including prejudgment interest and attorneys' fees, and fully extinguished the litigation charge liability. Of the $2,784.1 million litigation charge accrued in the fourth quarter of fiscal 2013, $2,763.9 million was paid and the remainder was released as a litigation credit to reflect a reduction to our estimated prejudgment interest payable as a result of paying our obligation earlier than anticipated.

Starbucks is party to various other legal proceedings arising in the ordinary course of business, including, at times, certain employment litigation cases that have been certified as class or collective actions, but is not currently a party to any legal proceeding that management believes could have a material adverse effect on our consolidated financial position, results of operations or cash flows.

Note 16: Segment Reporting

Our chief executive officer and chief operating officer comprise the Company's Chief Operating Decision Maker function ("CODM"). Segment information is prepared on the same basis that our CODM manages the segments, evaluates financial results, and makes key operating decisions.

We have four reportable operating segments: 1) Americas, inclusive of the U.S., Canada, and Latin America; 2) China/Asia Pacific ("CAP"); 3) Europe, Middle East, and Africa ("EMEA") and 4) Channel Development.

Americas, CAP, and EMEA operations sell coffee and other beverages, complementary food, packaged coffees, single-serve coffee products and a focused selection of merchandise through company-operated stores and licensed stores. Our Americas segment is our most mature business and has achieved significant scale. Certain markets within our CAP and EMEA operations are still in the early stages of development and require a more extensive support organization, relative to their current levels of revenue and operating income, than our Americas operations. The Americas and EMEA segments also include certain foodservice accounts, primarily in Canada and the U.K.

Channel Development operations sell a selection of packaged coffees and single-serve products, as well as a selection of premium Tazo® teas globally. Channel Development operations also produce and sell a variety of ready-to-drink beverages, such as Frappuccino® coffee drinks, Starbucks Doubleshot® espresso drinks, Starbucks Refreshers® beverages and chilled multi-serve beverages. The U.S. foodservice business, which is included in the Channel Development segment, sells coffee and other related products to institutional foodservice companies.

Consolidated revenue mix by product type *(in millions)*:

Fiscal Year Ended	Sep 27, 2015		Sep 28, 2014		Sep 29, 2013	
Beverage	$ 11,115.4	58%	$ 9,458.4	58%	$ 8,674.7	58%
Food	3,085.3	16%	2,505.2	15%	2,189.8	15%
Packaged and single-serve coffees and teas	2,619.9	14%	2,370.0	14%	2,206.5	15%
Other[1]	2,342.1	12%	2,114.2	13%	1,795.8	12%
Total	$ 19,162.7	100%	$ 16,447.8	100%	$ 14,866.8	100%

[1] "Other" primarily consists of royalty and licensing revenues, beverage-related ingredients, ready-to-drink beverages and serveware, among other items.

In fiscal 2014, we moved ready-to-drink beverage revenues from the "Food" category to the "Other" category and combined packaged and single-serve teas, which were previously included in the "Other" category, with packaged and single-serve coffees, which are now categorized as "Packaged and single-serve coffees and teas." Additionally, we revised our discount allocation methodology to more precisely allocate sales discounts to the various revenue product categories. None of these changes had a material impact on the composition of our revenue mix by product type.

Information by geographic area (*in millions*):

Fiscal Year Ended	Sep 27, 2015	Sep 28, 2014	Sep 29, 2013
Net revenues:			
United States	$ 14,123.7	$ 12,590.6	$ 11,389.6
Other countries	5,039.0	3,857.2	3,477.2
Total	$ 19,162.7	$ 16,447.8	$ 14,866.8
Long-lived assets:			
United States	$ 5,468.1	$ 5,135.8	$ 4,641.3
Other countries	2,625.3	1,448.4	1,404.0
Total	$ 8,093.4	$ 6,584.2	$ 6,045.3

No customer accounts for 10% or more of our revenues. Revenues are shown based on the geographic location of our customers. Revenues from countries other than the U.S. consist primarily of revenues from Japan, Canada, China and the U.K., which together account for approximately 76% of net revenues from other countries for fiscal 2015.

Management evaluates the performance of its operating segments based on net revenues and operating income. The accounting policies of the operating segments are the same as those described in Note 1, Summary of Significant Accounting Policies. Operating income represents earnings before other income and expenses and income taxes. Management does not evaluate the performance of its operating segments using asset measures. The identifiable assets by segment disclosed in this note are those assets specifically identifiable within each segment and include cash and cash equivalents, net property, plant and equipment, equity and cost investments, goodwill, and other intangible assets. Assets not identified by reportable operating segment below are corporate assets and are primarily comprised of cash and cash equivalents available for general corporate purposes, investments, assets of the corporate headquarters and roasting facilities, and inventory.

The table below presents financial information for our reportable operating segments and All Other Segments for the years ended September 27, 2015, September 28, 2014, and September 29, 2013.

(in millions)	Americas	China / Asia Pacific	EMEA	Channel Development	All Other Segments	Segment Total
Fiscal 2015						
Total net revenues	$ 13,293.4	$ 2,395.9	$ 1,216.7	$ 1,730.9	$ 525.8	$ 19,162.7
Depreciation and amortization expenses	522.3	150.7	52.0	2.7	16.3	744.0
Income from equity investees	—	119.6	3.1	127.2	—	249.9
Operating income/(loss)	3,223.3	500.5	168.2	653.9	(24.8)	4,521.1
Total assets	2,726.7	2,230.5	749.1	87.3	1,785.3	7,578.9
Fiscal 2014						
Total net revenues	$ 11,980.5	$ 1,129.6	$ 1,294.8	$ 1,546.0	$ 496.9	$ 16,447.8
Depreciation and amortization expenses	469.5	46.1	59.4	1.8	15.2	592.0
Income from equity investees	—	164.0	3.7	100.6	—	268.3
Operating income/(loss)	2,809.0	372.5	119.2	557.2	(26.8)	3,831.1
Total assets	2,521.4	939.8	663.0	84.6	825.2	5,034.0
Fiscal 2013						
Total net revenues	$ 11,000.8	$ 917.0	$ 1,160.0	$ 1,398.9	$ 390.1	$ 14,866.8
Depreciation and amortization expenses	429.3	33.8	55.5	1.1	11.7	531.4
Income from equity investees	2.4	152.0	0.4	96.6	—	251.4
Operating income/(loss)	2,365.2	321.2	64.2	415.5	(34.5)	3,131.6
Total assets	2,323.4	805.0	510.6	89.2	821.1	4,549.3

The following table reconciles total segment operating income in the table above to consolidated earnings/(loss) before income taxes *(in millions)*:

Fiscal Year Ended	Sep 27, 2015	Sep 28, 2014	Sep 29, 2013
Total segment operating income	$ 4,521.1	$ 3,831.1	$ 3,131.6
Unallocated corporate operating expenses [1]	(920.1)	(750.0)	(3,457.0)
Consolidated operating income/(loss)	3,601.0	3,081.1	(325.4)
Gain resulting from acquisition of joint venture	390.6	—	—
Loss on extinguishment of debt	(61.1)	—	—
Interest income and other, net	43.0	142.7	123.6
Interest expense	(70.5)	(64.1)	(28.1)
Earnings/(loss) before income taxes	$ 3,903.0	$ 3,159.7	$ (229.9)

[1] Fiscal 2013 includes a pretax charge of $2,784.1 million resulting from the litigation charge we recorded associated with the conclusion of our arbitration with Kraft.

Note 17: Selected Quarterly Financial Information *(unaudited; in millions, except EPS)*

	First Quarter	Second Quarter	Third Quarter	Fourth Quarter	Full Year
Fiscal 2015:					
Net revenues	$ 4,803.2	$ 4,563.5	$ 4,881.2	$ 4,914.8	$ 19,162.7
Operating income	915.5	777.5	938.6	969.4	3,601.0
Net earnings attributable to Starbucks	983.1	494.9	626.7	652.5	2,757.4
EPS — diluted[1]	0.65	0.33	0.41	0.43	1.82
Fiscal 2014:					
Net revenues	$ 4,239.6	$ 3,873.8	$ 4,153.7	$ 4,180.8	$ 16,447.8
Operating income	813.5	644.1	768.5	854.9	3,081.1
Net earnings attributable to Starbucks	540.7	427.0	512.6	587.9	2,068.1
EPS — diluted[1]	0.35	0.28	0.34	0.39	1.35

[1] As discussed in Note 1, Summary of Significant Accounting Policies, on April 9, 2015, we effected a two-for-one stock split of our $0.001 par value common stock for shareholders of record as of March 30, 2015. All per-share data presented in this note has been retroactively adjusted to reflect this stock split.

Note 18: Subsequent Events

Subsequent to our fiscal year end, the European Commission has concluded that decisions by the tax authorities in the Netherlands with regards to the corporate income tax paid by one of our subsidiaries did not comply with European Union rules on state aid. Based on this decision, which covers a 7-year period from fiscal 2008 to fiscal 2014, we estimate the amount of assessed past taxes to be no more than €30 million, including interest, which equates to approximately $32 million with euro converted into U.S. dollars at a reference conversion rate of 1.075 EUR to USD. The exposure amount is not material and we are currently evaluating this decision, including any impact to our fiscal 2016 tax provisions.

REPORT OF INDEPENDENT REGISTERED PUBLIC ACCOUNTING FIRM

To the Board of Directors and Shareholders of Starbucks Corporation

Seattle, Washington

We have audited the accompanying consolidated balance sheets of Starbucks Corporation and subsidiaries (the "Company") as of September 27, 2015 and September 28, 2014, and the related consolidated statements of earnings, comprehensive income, equity, and cash flows for each of the three years in the period ended September 27, 2015. These financial statements are the responsibility of the Company's management. Our responsibility is to express an opinion on these financial statements based on our audits.

We conducted our audits in accordance with the standards of the Public Company Accounting Oversight Board (United States). Those standards require that we plan and perform the audit to obtain reasonable assurance about whether the financial statements are free of material misstatement. An audit includes examining, on a test basis, evidence supporting the amounts and disclosures in the financial statements. An audit also includes assessing the accounting principles used and significant estimates made by management, as well as evaluating the overall financial statement presentation. We believe that our audits provide a reasonable basis for our opinion.

In our opinion, such consolidated financial statements present fairly, in all material respects, the financial position of Starbucks Corporation and subsidiaries as of September 27, 2015 and September 28, 2014, and the results of their operations and their cash flows for each of the three years in the period ended September 27, 2015, in conformity with accounting principles generally accepted in the United States of America.

We have also audited, in accordance with the standards of the Public Company Accounting Oversight Board (United States), the Company's internal control over financial reporting as of September 27, 2015, based on criteria established in *Internal Control — Integrated Framework (2013)* issued by the Committee of Sponsoring Organizations of the Treadway Commission and our report dated November 12, 2015 expressed an unqualified opinion on the Company's internal control over financial reporting.

/s/ Deloitte & Touche LLP

Seattle, Washington
November 12, 2015

Item 9. *Changes in and Disagreements with Accountants on Accounting and Financial Disclosure*

Not applicable.

Item 9A. *Controls and Procedures*

REPORT OF INDEPENDENT REGISTERED PUBLIC ACCOUNTING FIRM

To the Board of Directors and Shareholders of Starbucks Corporation

Seattle, Washington

We have audited the internal control over financial reporting of Starbucks Corporation and subsidiaries (the "Company") as of September 27, 2015, based on criteria established in *Internal Control - Integrated Framework (2013)* issued by the Committee of Sponsoring Organizations of the Treadway Commission. As described in the accompanying Report of Management on Internal Control over Financial Reporting, management excluded Starbucks Coffee Japan, Ltd. ("Starbucks Japan") from its assessment of internal control over financial reporting. Starbucks Japan was acquired on October 31, 2014, and its financial statements contributed $1.6 billion, $1.1 billion, and $159.1 million to the consolidated entity's total assets, net revenues and operating income, respectively, as of and for the year ended September 27, 2015. Accordingly, our audit did not include the internal control over financial reporting at Starbucks Japan. The Company's management is responsible for maintaining effective internal control over financial reporting and for its assessment of the effectiveness of internal control over financial reporting, included in the accompanying Report of Management on Internal Control over Financial Reporting. Our responsibility is to express an opinion on the Company's internal control over financial reporting based on our audit.

We conducted our audit in accordance with the standards of the Public Company Accounting Oversight Board (United States). Those standards require that we plan and perform the audit to obtain reasonable assurance about whether effective internal control over financial reporting was maintained in all material respects. Our audit included obtaining an understanding of internal control over financial reporting, assessing the risk that a material weakness exists, testing and evaluating the design and operating effectiveness of internal control based on the assessed risk, and performing such other procedures as we considered necessary in the circumstances. We believe that our audit provides a reasonable basis for our opinion.

A company's internal control over financial reporting is a process designed by, or under the supervision of, the company's principal executive and principal financial officers, or persons performing similar functions, and effected by the company's board of directors, management, and other personnel to provide reasonable assurance regarding the reliability of financial reporting and the preparation of financial statements for external purposes in accordance with generally accepted accounting principles. A company's internal control over financial reporting includes those policies and procedures that (1) pertain to the maintenance of records that, in reasonable detail, accurately and fairly reflect the transactions and dispositions of the assets of the company; (2) provide reasonable assurance that transactions are recorded as necessary to permit preparation of financial statements in accordance with generally accepted accounting principles, and that receipts and expenditures of the company are being made only in accordance with authorizations of management and directors of the company; and (3) provide reasonable assurance regarding prevention or timely detection of unauthorized acquisition, use, or disposition of the company's assets that could have a material effect on the financial statements.

Because of the inherent limitations of internal control over financial reporting, including the possibility of collusion or improper management override of controls, material misstatements due to error or fraud may not be prevented or detected on a timely basis. Also, projections of any evaluation of the effectiveness of the internal control over financial reporting to future periods are subject to the risk that the controls may become inadequate because of changes in conditions, or that the degree of compliance with the policies or procedures may deteriorate.

In our opinion, the Company maintained, in all material respects, effective internal control over financial reporting as of September 27, 2015, based on the criteria established in *Internal Control - Integrated Framework (2013)* issued by the Committee of Sponsoring Organizations of the Treadway Commission.

We have also audited, in accordance with the standards of the Public Company Accounting Oversight Board (United States), the consolidated financial statements as of and for the fiscal year ended September 27, 2015, of the Company and our report dated November 12, 2015 expressed an unqualified opinion on those financial statements.

/s/ Deloitte & Touche LLP

Seattle, Washington
November 12, 2015

Exhibit 32

CERTIFICATIONS PURSUANT TO 18 U.S.C. SECTION 1350
AS ADOPTED PURSUANT TO SECTION 906 OF THE SARBANES-OXLEY ACT OF 2002

In connection with the Annual Report of Starbucks Corporation ("Starbucks") on Form 10-K for the fiscal year ended September 27, 2015, as filed with the Securities and Exchange Commission on November 12, 2015 (the "Report"), Howard Schultz, chairman and chief executive officer, and Scott Maw, executive vice president, chief financial officer of Starbucks, each hereby certifies, pursuant to 18 U.S.C. Section 1350, as adopted pursuant to Section 906 of the Sarbanes-Oxley Act of 2002, that, to his knowledge:

(1) the Report fully complies with the requirements of Section 13(a) or 15(d) of the Securities Exchange Act of 1934; and

(2) the information contained in the Report fairly presents, in all material respects, the financial condition and results of operations of Starbucks.

November 12, 2015

/s/ Howard Schultz

Howard Schultz

chairman and chief executive officer

November 12, 2015

/s/ Scott Maw

Scott Maw

executive vice president, chief financial officer

APPENDIX B

LIST OF THE OFFICIAL PRONOUNCEMENTS OF THE AICPA AND FASB

- **B-2** Topical Structure of the FASB Accounting Standards Codification
- **B-3** Accounting Research Bulletins (ARBs), Committee on Accounting Procedure, AICPA
- **B-3** Accounting Terminology Bulletins, Committee on Terminology, AICPA
- **B-3** Accounting Principles Board (APB) Statements, AICPA
- **B-4** Accounting Principles Board (APB) Opinions, AICPA
- **B-4** FASB Statements of Financial Accounting Standards, Financial Accounting Standards Board
- **B-10** FASB Statements of Financial Accounting Concepts, Financial Accounting Standards Board
- **B-11** FASB Interpretations, Financial Accounting Standards Board

Listed below is the topical structure of the FASB Accounting Standards Codification. On July 1, 2009, the Codification became the single authoritative source of U.S. GAAP.

Area	Topic
General Principles	105 – Generally Accepted Accounting Principles
Presentation	205 – Presentation of Financial Statements
	210 – Balance Sheet
	215 – Statement of Shareholder Equity
	220 – Comprehensive Income
	225 – Income Statement
	230 – Statement of Cash Flows
	235 – Notes to Financial Statements
	250 – Accounting Changes and Error Corrections
	255 – Changing Prices
	260 – Earnings Per Share
	270 – Interim Reporting
	272 – Limited Liability Entities
	274 – Personal Financial Statements
	275 – Risks and Uncertainties
	280 – Segment Reporting
Assets	305 – Cash and Cash Equivalents
	310 – Receivables
	32X – Investments
	330 – Inventory
	340 – Other Assets and Deferred Costs
	350 – Intangibles – Goodwill and Other
	360 – Property, Plant, and Equipment
Liabilities	405 – Liabilities
	410 – Asset Retirement and Environmental Obligations
	420 – Exit or Disposal Cost Obligations
	430 – Deferred Revenue
	440 – Commitments
	450 – Contingencies
	460 – Guarantees
	470 – Debt
	480 – Distinguishing Liabilities from Equity
Equity	505 – Equity
Revenue	605 – Revenue Recognition
	606 – Revenue from Contracts with Customers
	610 – Other Income
Expenses	705 – Cost of Sales and Services
	71X – Compensation
	720 – Other Expenses
	730 – Research and Development
	740 – Income Taxes
Broad Transactions	805 – Business Combinations
	808 – Collaborative Arrangements
	810 – Consolidation
	815 – Derivatives and Hedging
	820 – Fair Value Measurement
	825 – Financial Instruments
	830 – Foreign Currency Matters
	835 – Interest
	840 – Leases
	845 – Nonmonetary Transactions
	850 – Related Party Disclosures
	852 – Reorganizations
	855 – Subsequent Events
	860 – Transfers and Servicing
Industry	905 – Agriculture
	908 – Airlines
	91X – Contractors
	915 – Development Stage Entities

Area	Topic
Industry (Continued)	92X – Entertainment
	93X – Extractive Industries
	9XX – Financial Services
	952 – Franchisors
	954 – Health Care Entities
	958 – Not-for-Profit Entities
	96X – Plan Accounting
	97X – Real Estate
	980 – Regulated Operations
	985 – Software
	995 – U.S. Steamship Entities

Listed below are the major official pronouncements of the AICPA and the FASB that established generally accepted accounting principles in the United States prior to July 1, 2009. On that date, these pronouncements were superseded by the implementation of the FASB Accounting Standards Codification Topic 105, *Generally Accepted Accounting Principles.*

Number	Title	Date of Issuance
	Accounting Research Bulletins (ARBs), Committee on Accounting Procedure, AICPA	
43	Restatement and Revision of Accounting Research Bulletin Nos. 1–42	June 1953
	Chapter	
	1 Prior Opinions	
	2 Form of Statements	
	3 Working Capital	
	4 Inventory Pricing	
	5 Intangible Assets	
	6 Contingency Reserves	
	7 Capital Accounts	
	8 Income and Earned Surplus	
	9 Depreciation	
	10 Taxes	
	11 Government Contracts	
	12 Foreign Operations and Foreign Exchange	
	13 Compensation	
	14 Disclosure of Long-Term Leases in Financial Statements of Leases	
	15 Unamortized Discount, Issue Cost, and Redemption Premium on Bonds Refunded	
44	Declining-Balance Depreciation (Revised July 1958)	October 1954
45	Long-Term Construction-Type Contracts	October 1955
46	Discontinuance of Dating Earned Surplus	February 1956
47	Accounting for Costs of Pension Plans	September 1956
48	Business Combinations	January 1957
49	Earnings per Share	April 1958
50	Contingencies	October 1958
51	Consolidated Financial Statements	August 1959
	Accounting Terminology Bulletins, Committee on Terminology, AICPA	
1	Review and Résumé (of 8 original terminology bulletins)	August 1953
2	Proceeds, Revenue, Income, Profit, and Earnings	March 1955
3	Book Value	August 1956
4	Cost, Expense, and Loss	July 1957
	Accounting Principles Board (APB) Statements, AICPA	
1	Statement by the Accounting Principles Board	April 1962
2	Disclosure of Supplemental Financial Information by Diversified Companies	September 1967
3	Financial Statements Restated for General Price-Level Changes	June 1969
4	Basic Concepts and Accounting Principles Underlying Financial Statements of Business Enterprises	October 1970

Number	Title	Date of Issuance
	Accounting Principles Board (APB) Opinions, AICPA	
1	New Depreciation Guidelines and Rules	November 1962
2	Accounting for the "Investment Credit"	December 1962
3	The Statement of Source and Application of Funds	October 1963
4	Accounting for the "Investment Credit" (Amending No. 2)	March 1964
5	Reporting of Leases in Financial Statements of Lessee	September 1964
6	Status of Accounting Research Bulletins	October 1965
7	Accounting for Leases in Financial Statements of Lessors	May 1966
8	Accounting for the Cost of Pension Plans	November 1966
9	Reporting the Results of Operations	December 1966
10	Omnibus Opinion—1966	December 1966
11	Accounting for Income Taxes	December 1967
12	Omnibus Opinion—1967	December 1967
13	Amending Paragraph 6 of the *APB Opinion No. 9*, Application to Commercial Banks	March 1969
14	Accounting for Convertible Debt and Debt Issued with Stock Purchase Warrants	March 1969
15	Earnings per Share	May 1969
16	Business Combinations	August 1970
17	Intangible Assets	August 1970
18	The Equity Method of Accounting for Investments in Common Stock	March 1971
19	Reporting Changes in Financial Position	March 1971
20	Accounting Changes	July 1971
21	Interest on Receivables and Payables	August 1971
22	Disclosure of Accounting Policies	April 1972
23	Accounting for Income Taxes—Special Areas	April 1972
24	Accounting for Income Taxes—Investments in Common Stock Accounted for by the Equity Method	April 1972
25	Accounting for Stock Issued to Employees	October 1972
26	Early Extinguishment of Debt	October 1972
27	Accounting for Lease Transactions by Manufacturer or Dealer Lessors	November 1972
28	Interim Financial Reporting	May 1973
29	Accounting for Nonmonetary Transactions	May 1973
30	Reporting the Results of Operations—Reporting the Effects of Disposal of a Segment of a Business, and Extraordinary, Unusual and Infrequently Occurring Events and Transactions	June 1973
31	Disclosure of Lease Commitments by Lessees	June 1973
	FASB Statements of Financial Accounting Standards, Financial Accounting Standards Board	
1	Disclosure of Foreign Currency Translation Information	December 1973
2	Accounting for Research and Development Costs	October 1974
3	Reporting Accounting Changes in Interim Financial Statements (an amendment of *APB Opinion No. 28*)	December 1974
4	Reporting Gains and Losses from Extinguishment of Debt (an amendment of *APB Opinion No. 30*)	March 1975
5	Accounting for Contingencies	March 1975
6	Classification of Short-Term Obligations Expected to Be Refinanced (an amendment of *ARB No. 43*, Chapter 3A)	May 1975
7	Accounting and Reporting by Development Stage Enterprises	June 1975
8	Accounting for the Translation of Foreign Currency Transactions and Foreign Currency Financial Statements	October 1975
9	Accounting for Income Taxes—Oil and Gas Producing Companies (an amendment of *APB Opinion Nos. 11* and *23*)	October 1975
10	Extension of "Grandfather" Provisions for Business Combinations (an amendment of *APB Opinion No. 16*)	October 1975

Number	Title	Date of Issuance
	FASB Statements of Financial Accounting Standards, Financial Accounting Standards Board (Continued)	
11	Accounting for Contingencies—Transition Method (an amendment of *FASB Statement No. 5*)	December 1975
12	Accounting for Certain Marketable Securities	December 1975
13	Accounting for Leases	November 1976
14	Financial Reporting for Segments of a Business Enterprise	December 1976
15	Accounting by Debtors and Creditors for Troubled Debt Restructurings	June 1977
16	Prior Period Adjustments	June 1977
17	Accounting for Leases—Initial Direct Costs (an amendment of *FASB Statement No. 13*)	November 1977
18	Financial Reporting for Segments of a Business Enterprise Interim Financial Statements (an amendment of *FASB Statement No. 14*)	November 1977
19	Financial Accounting and Reporting by Oil and Gas Producing Companies	December 1977
20	Accounting for Forward Exchange Contracts (an amendment of *FASB Statement No. 8*)	December 1977
21	Suspension of the Reporting of Earnings per Share and Segment Information by Nonpublic Enterprises (an amendment of *APB Opinion No. 15* and *FASB Statement No. 14*)	April 1978
22	Accounting for Leases—Changes in the Provisions of Lease Agreements Resulting from Refundings of Tax-Exempt Debt (an amendment of *FASB Statement No. 13*)	June 1978
23	Inception of the Lease (an amendment of *FASB Statement No. 13*)	August 1978
24	Reporting Segment Information in Financial Statements That Are Presented in Another Enterprise's Financial Report (an amendment of *FASB Statement No. 14*)	December 1978
25	Suspension of Certain Accounting Requirements for Oil and Gas Companies (an amendment of *FASB Statement No. 19*)	February 1979
26	Profit Recognition on Sales-Type Leases of Real Estate (an amendment of *FASB Statement No. 13*)	April 1979
27	Classification of Renewals or Extensions of Existing Sales-Type or Direct Financing Leases (an amendment of *FASB Statement No. 13*)	May 1979
28	Accounting for Sales with Leasebacks (an amendment of *FASB Statement No. 13*)	May 1979
29	Determining Contingent Rentals (an amendment of *FASB Statement No. 13*)	June 1979
30	Disclosure of Information about Major Customers (an amendment of *FASB Statement No. 14*)	August 1979
31	Accounting for Tax Benefits Related to U.K. Tax Legislation Concerning Stock Relief	September 1979
32	Specialized Accounting and Reporting Principles and Practices in AICPA Statements of Position and Guides on Accounting and Auditing Matters (an amendment of *APB Opinion No. 20*)	September 1979
33	Financial Reporting and Changing Prices	September 1979
34	Capitalization of Interest Cost	October 1979
35	Accounting and Reporting by Defined Benefit Pension Plans	March 1980
36	Disclosure of Pension Information	May 1980
37	Balance Sheet Classification of Deferred Income Taxes (an amendment of *APB Opinion No. 11*)	July 1980
38	Accounting for Preacquisition Contingencies of Purchased Enterprises (an amendment of *APB Opinion No. 16*)	September 1980
39	Financial Reporting and Changing Prices: Specialized Assets—Mining and Oil and Gas (a supplement to *FASB Statement No. 33*)	October 1980

Appendix B List of the Official Pronouncements of the AICPA and FASB

Number	Title	Date of Issuance
	FASB Statements of Financial Accounting Standards, Financial Accounting Standards Board (Continued)	
40	Financial Reporting and Changing Prices: Specialized Assets—Timberlands and Growing Timber (a supplement to FASB Statement No. 33)	November 1980
41	Financial Reporting and Changing Prices: Specialized Assets—Income-Producing Real Estate (a supplement to FASB Statement No. 33)	November 1980
42	Determining Materiality for Capitalization of Interest Cost (an amendment of FASB Statement No. 34)	November 1980
43	Accounting for Compensated Absences	November 1980
44	Accounting for Intangible Assets of Motor Carriers (an amendment of Chapter 5 of ARB No. 43 and an interpretation of APB Opinion Nos. 17 and 30)	December 1980
45	Accounting for Franchise Fee Revenue	March 1981
46	Financial Reporting and Changing Prices: Motion Picture Films	March 1981
47	Disclosure of Long-Term Obligations	March 1981
48	Revenue Recognition When Right of Return Exists	June 1981
49	Accounting for Product Financing Arrangements	June 1981
50	Financial Reporting in the Record and Music Industry	November 1981
51	Financial Reporting by Cable Television Companies	November 1981
52	Foreign Currency Translation	December 1981
53	Financial Reporting by Producers and Distributors of Motion Picture Films	December 1981
54	Financial Reporting and Changing Prices: Investment Companies (an amendment of FASB Statement No. 33)	January 1982
55	Determining Whether a Convertible Security Is a Common Stock Equivalent (an amendment of APB Opinion No. 15)	February 1982
56	Designation of AICPA Guide and Statement of Position (SOP) 81-1 on Contractor Accounting and SOP 81-2 Concerning Hospital-Related Organizations as Preferable for Purposes of Applying APB Opinion 20 (an amendment of FASB Statement No. 32).	February 1982
57	Related Party Disclosures	March 1982
58	Capitalization of Interest Cost in Financial Statements That Include Investments Accounted for by the Equity Method	April 1982
59	Deferral of the Effective Date of Certain Accounting Requirements for Pension Plans of State and Local Governmental Units (an amendment of FASB Statement No. 35)	April 1982
60	Accounting and Reporting by Insurance Enterprises	June 1982
61	Accounting for Title Plant	June 1982
62	Capitalization of Interest Cost in Situations Involving Certain Tax-Exempt Borrowings and Certain Gifts and Grants	June 1982
63	Financial Reporting by Broadcasters	June 1982
64	Extinguishments of Debt Made to Satisfy Sinking-Fund Requirements (an amendment of FASB Statement No. 4)	September 1982
65	Accounting for Certain Mortgage Banking Activities	September 1982
66	Accounting for Sales of Real Estate	October 1982
67	Accounting for Costs and Initial Rental Operations of Real Estate Projects	October 1982
68	Research and Development Arrangements	October 1982
69	Disclosures about Oil- and Gas-Producing Activities	November 1982
70	Financial Reporting and Changing Prices: Foreign Currency Translation (an amendment of FASB Statement No. 33)	December 1982
71	Accounting for the Effects of Certain Types of Regulation	December 1982

Number	Title	Date of Issuance
	FASB Statements of Financial Accounting Standards, Financial Accounting Standards Board (Continued)	
72	Accounting for Certain Acquisitions of Banking or Thrift Institutions (an amendment of *APB Opinion No. 17*, an interpretation of *APB Opinion Nos. 16* and *17*, and an amendment of *FASB Statement No. 9*)	February 1983
73	Reporting a Change in Accounting for Railroad Track Structures (an amendment of *APB Opinion No. 20*)	August 1983
74	Accounting for Special Termination Benefits Paid to Employees	August 1983
75	Deferral of the Effective Date of Certain Accounting Requirements for Pension Plans of State and Local Governmental Units (an amendment of *FASB Statement No. 35*)	November 1983
76	Extinguishment of Debt (an amendment of *APB Opinion No. 26*)	November 1983
77	Reporting by Transferors for Transfers of Receivables with Recourse	December 1983
78	Classification of Obligations That Are Callable by the Creditor (an amendment of *ARB No. 43*, Chapter 3A)	December 1983
79	Elimination of Certain Disclosures for Business Combinations by Nonpublic Enterprises (an amendment of *APB Opinion No. 16*)	February 1984
80	Accounting for Futures Contracts	August 1984
81	Disclosure of Postretirement Health Care and Life Insurance Benefits	November 1984
82	Financial Reporting and Changing Prices: Elimination of Certain Disclosures (an amendment of *FAPB Statement No. 33*)	December 1984
83	Designation of AICPA Guides and Statement of Position on Accounting by Brokers and Dealers in Securities, by Employee Benefit Plans, and by Banks as Preferable for Purposes of Applying *APB Opinion No. 20*	March 1985
84	Induced Conversions of Convertible Debt (an amendment of *APB Opinion No. 26*)	March 1985
85	Yield Test for Determining Whether a Convertible Security Is a Common Stock Equivalent (an amendment of *APB Opinion No. 15*)	March 1985
86	Accounting for the Costs of Computer Software to Be Sold, Leased, or Otherwise Marketed	August 1985
87	Employers' Accounting for Pensions	December 1985
88	Employers' Accounting for Settlements and Curtailments of Defined Benefit Pension Plans and for Termination Benefits	December 1985
89	Financial Reporting and Changing Prices	December 1986
90	Regulated Enterprises—Accounting for Abandonments and Disallowances of Plant Costs (an amendment of *FASB Statement No. 71*)	December 1986
91	Accounting for Nonrefundable Fees and Costs Associated with Originating or Acquiring Loans and Initial Direct Costs of Leases	December 1986
92	Regulated Enterprises—Accounting for Phase-in Plans (an amendment of *FASB Statement No. 71*)	August 1987
93	Recognition of Depreciation by Not-for-Profit Organizations	August 1987
94	Consolidation of All Majority-Owned Subsidiaries (an amendment of *ARB No. 51*, with related amendments of *APB Opinion No. 18* and *ARB No. 43*, Chapter 12)	October 1987
95	Statement of Cash Flows	November 1987
96	Accounting for Income Taxes	December 1987
97	Accounting and Reporting by Insurance Enterprises for Certain Long-Duration Contracts and for Realized Gains and Losses from the Sale of Investments	December 1987

Number	Title	Date of Issuance
	FASB Statements of Financial Accounting Standards, Financial Accounting Standards Board (Continued)	
98	Accounting for Leases: Sale-Leaseback Transactions Involving Real Estate, Sales-Type Leases of Real Estate, Definition of the Lease Term, and Initial Direct Costs of Direct Financing Leases (an amendment of *FASB Statements No. 13, 66,* and *91* and a rescission of *FASB Statement No. 26* and *Technical Bulletin No. 79-11*)	May 1988
99	Deferral of the Effective Date of Recognition of Depreciation by Not-for-Profit Organizations (an amendment of *FASB Statement No. 93*)	September 1988
100	Accounting for Income Taxes—Deferral of the Effective Date of *FASB Statement No. 96* (an amendment of *FASB Statement No. 96*)	December 1988
101	Regulated Enterprises—Accounting for the Discontinuation of Application of *FASB Statement No. 71*	December 1988
102	Statement of Cash Flows—Exemption of Certain Enterprises and Classification of Cash Flows from Certain Securities Acquired for Resale (an amendment of *FASB Statement No. 95*)	February 1989
103	Accounting for Income Taxes—Deferral of the Effective Date of *FASB Statement No. 96* (an amendment of *FASB Statement No. 96*)	December 1989
104	Statement of Cash Flows—Net Reporting of Certain Cash Receipts and Cash Payments and Classification of Cash Flows from Hedging Transactions (an amendment of *FASB Statement No. 95*)	December 1989
105	Disclosure of Information about Financial Instruments with Off-Balance-Sheet Risk and Financial Instruments with Concentrations of Credit Risk	March 1990
106	Employers' Accounting for Postretirement Benefits Other Than Pensions	December 1990
107	Disclosure about Fair Value of Financial Instruments	December 1991
108	Accounting for Income Taxes—Deferral of the Effective Date of *FASB Statement No. 96* (an amendment of *FASB Statement No. 96*)	December 1991
109	Accounting for Income Taxes	February 1992
110	Reporting by Defined Benefit Pension Plans of Investment Contracts (an amendment of *FASB Statement No. 35*)	August 1992
111	Rescission of *FASB Statement No. 32* and Technical Corrections	November 1992
112	Employers' Accounting for Postemployment Benefits (an amendment of *FASB Statements No. 5* and *43*)	November 1992
113	Accounting and Reporting for Reinsurance of Short-Term and Long-Term Contracts	December 1992
114	Accounting by Creditors for Impairment of a Loan (an amendment of *FASB Statements No. 5* and *15*)	May 1993
115	Accounting for Certain Investments in Debt and Equity Securities	May 1993
116	Accounting for Contributions Received and Contributions Made	June 1993
117	Financial Statements of Not-for-Profit Organizations	June 1993
118	Accounting by Creditors for Impairment of a Loan—Income Recognition and Disclosures (an amendment of *FASB Statement No. 114*)	October 1994
119	Disclosure about Derivative Financial Instruments and Fair Value of Financial Instruments	October 1994
120	Accounting and Reporting by Mutual Life Insurance Enterprises and by Insurance Enterprises for Certain Long-Duration Participating Contracts (an amendment of *FASB Statements No. 60, 97,* and *113* and *Interpretation No. 40*)	January 1995

Appendix B List of the Official Pronouncements of the AICPA and FASB

Number	Title	Date of Issuance
	FASB Statements of Financial Accounting Standards, Financial Accounting Standards Board (Continued)	
121	Accounting for the Impairment of Long-Lived Assets and for Long-Lived Assets to Be Disposed Of	March 1995
122	Accounting for Mortgage Servicing Rights (an amendment of *FASB Statement No. 65*)	May 1995
123	Accounting for Stock-Based Compensation	October 1995
124	Accounting for Certain Investments Held by Not-for-Profit Organizations	November 1995
125	Accounting for Transfers and Servicing of Financial Assets and Extinguishments of Liabilities	June 1996
126	Exemption from Certain Required Disclosures about Financial Instruments for Certain Nonpublic Entities (an amendment of *FASB Statement No. 107*)	December 1996
127	Deferral of the Effective Date of Certain Provisions of *FASB Statement No. 125* (an amendment of *FASB Statement No. 125*)	December 1996
128	Earnings per Share	February 1997
129	Disclosure of Information about Capital Structure	February 1997
130	Reporting Comprehensive Income	June 1997
131	Disclosures about Segments of an Enterprise and Related Information	June 1997
132	Employers' Disclosures about Pensions and Other Postretirement Benefits (an amendment of *FASB Statements No. 87, 88, and 106*)	February 1998
133	Accounting for Derivative Instruments and Hedging Activities	June 1998
134	Accounting for Mortgage-Backed Securities Retained after the Securitization of Mortgage Loans Held for Sale by a Mortgage Banking Enterprise (an amendment of *FASB Statement No. 65*)	October 1998
135	Rescission of *FASB Statement No. 75* and Technical Corrections	February 1999
136	Transfers of Assets to a Not-for-Profit Organization or Charitable Trust That Raises or Holds Contributions for Others	June 1999
137	Accounting for Derivative Instruments and Hedging Activities—Deferral of the Effective Date of *FASB Statement No. 133* (an amendment of *FASB Statement No. 133*)	June 1999
138	Accounting for Certain Derivative Instruments and Certain Hedging Activities (an amendment of *FASB Statement No. 133*)	June 2000
139	Rescission of *FASB Statement No. 53* and amendments to *FASB Statements No. 63, 89, and 121*	June 2000
140	Accounting for Transfers and Servicing of Financial Assets and Extinguishments of Liabilities (a replacement of *FASB Statement No. 125*)	September 2000
141	Business Combinations	June 2001
142	Goodwill and Other Intangible Assets	June 2001
143	Accounting for Asset Retirement Obligations	June 2001
144	Accounting for the Impairment or Disposal of Long-Lived Assets	August 2001
145	Rescission of *FASB Statements No. 4, 44, and 64*, Amendment of *FASB Statement No. 13*, and Technical Corrections	April 2002
146	Accounting for Costs Associated with Exit or Disposal Activities	July 2002
147	Acquisitions of Certain Financial Institutions	October 2002
148	Accounting for Stock-Based Compensation-Transition and Disclosure (an amendment of *FASB Statement No. 123*)	December 2002
149	Amendment of *Statement 133* on Derivative Instruments and Hedging Activities	April 2003

Number	Title	Date of Issuance
	FASB Statements of Financial Accounting Standards, Financial Accounting Standards Board (Continued)	
150	Accounting for Certain Financial Instruments with Characteristics of Both Liabilities and Equity	May 2003
132R	Employers' Disclosures about Pensions and Other Postretirement Benefits (an amendment of *FASB Statements No. 87, 88,* and *106*)	December 2003
151	Inventory Costs (an amendment of *ARB No. 43,* Chapter 4)	November 2004
152	Accounting for Real Estate Time-Sharing Transactions (an amendment of *FASB Statements No. 66* and *67*)	December 2004
153	Exchanges of Nonmonetary Assets (an amendment of *APB Opinion No. 29*)	December 2004
123R	Share-Based Payment	December 2004
154	Accounting Changes and Error Corrections (a replacement of *APB Opinion No. 20* and *FASB Statement No. 3*)	May 2005
155	Accounting for Certain Hybrid Financial Instruments (an amendment of *FASB Statements No. 133* and *140*)	February 2006
156	Accounting for Servicing of Financial Assets (an amendment of *FASB Statement No. 140*)	March 2006
157	Fair Value Measurements	September 2006
158	Employers' Accounting for Defined Benefit Pension and Other Postretirement Plans (an amendment of *FASB Statements No. 87, 88, 106,* and *132R*)	September 2006
159	The Fair Value Option for Financial Assets and Financial Liabilities (including an amendment of *FASB Statement No. 115*)	February 2007
141R	Business Combinations	December 2007
160	Noncontrolling Interests in Consolidated Financial Statements (an amendment of *ARB No. 51*)	December 2007
161	Disclosures about Derivative Instruments and Hedging Activities (an amendment of *FASB Statement No. 133*)	March 2008
162	The Hierarchy of Generally Accepted Accounting Principles	May 2008
163	Accounting for Financial Guarantee Insurance Contracts (an interpretation of *FASB Statement No. 60*)	May 2008
164	Not-for-Profit Entities: Mergers and Acquisitions	April 2009
165	Subsequent Events	May 2009
166	Accounting for Transfers of Financial Assets	June 2009
167	Amendments to *FASB Interpretation No. 46(R)*	June 2009
168	The FASB Accounting Standards Codification and the Hierarchy of Generally Accepted Accounting Principles	June 2009
	FASB Statements of Financial Accounting Concepts, Financial Accounting Standards Board	
1	Objectives of Financial Reporting by Business Enterprises	November 1978
2	Qualitative Characteristics of Accounting Information	May 1980
3	Elements of Financial Statements of Business Enterprises	December 1980
4	Objectives of Financial Reporting by Nonbusiness Organizations	December 1980
5	Recognition and Measurement in Financial Statements of Business Enterprises	December 1984
6	Elements of Financial Statements (a replacement of *FASB Concepts Statement No. 3,* incorporating an amendment of *FASB Concepts Statement No. 2*)	December 1985
7	Using Cash Flow Information and Present Value in Accounting Measurements	February 2000
8	Conceptual Framework for Financial Reporting—Chapter 1, *The Objective of General Purpose Financial Reporting,* and Chapter 3, *Qualitative Characteristics of Useful Financial Information* (a replacement of *FASB Concepts Statements No. 1* and *No. 2*)	September 2010

Number	Title	Date of Issuance
	FASB Interpretations, Financial Accounting Standards Board (Concluded)	
1	Accounting Changes Related to the Cost of Inventory (an interpretation of *APB Opinion No. 20*)	June 1974
2	Imputing Interest on Debt Arrangements Made under the Federal Bankruptcy Act (an interpretation of *APB Opinion No. 21*)	June 1974
3	Accounting for the Cost of Pension Plans Subject to the Employee Retirement Income Security Act of 1974 (an interpretation of *APB Opinion No. 8*)	December 1974
4	Applicability of *FASB Statement No. 2* to Business Combinations Accounted for by the Purchase Method	February 1975
5	Applicability of *FASB Statement No. 2* to Development Stage Enterprises	February 1975
6	Applicability of *FASB Statement No. 2* to Computer Software	February 1975
7	Applying *FASB Statement No. 7* in Financial Statements of Established Operating Enterprises	October 1975
8	Classification of a Short-Term Obligation Repaid Prior to Being Replaced by a Long-Term Security (an interpretation of *FASB Statement No. 6*)	January 1976
9	Applying *APB Opinion Nos. 16* and *17* When a Savings and Loan Association or a Similar Institution Is Acquired in a Business Combination Accounted for by the Purchase Method	February 1976
10	Application of *FASB Statement No. 12* to Personal Financial Statements	September 1976
11	Changes in Market Value after the Balance Sheet Date (an interpretation of *FASB Statement No. 12*)	September 1976
12	Accounting for Previously Established Allowance Accounts (an interpretation of *FASB Statement No. 12*)	September 1976
13	Consolidation of a Parent and Its Subsidiaries Having Different Balance Sheet Dates (an interpretation of *FASB Statement No. 12*)	September 1976
14	Reasonable Estimation of the Amount of a Loss (an interpretation of *FASB Statement No. 5*)	September 1976
15	Translation of Unamortized Policy Acquisition Costs by a Stock Life Insurance Company (an interpretation of *FASB Statement No. 8*)	September 1976
16	Clarification of Definitions and Accounting for Marketable Equity Securities That Become Nonmarketable (an interpretation of *FASB Statement No. 12*)	February 1977
17	Applying the Lower of Cost or Market Rule in Translated Financial Statements (an interpretation of *FASB Statement No. 8*)	February 1977
18	Accounting for Income Taxes in Interim Periods (an interpretation of *APB Opinion No. 28*)	March 1977
19	Lessee Guarantee of the Residual Value of Leased Property (an interpretation of *FASB Statement No. 13*)	October 1977
20	Reporting Accounting Changes under AICPA Statements of Position (an interpretation of *APB Opinion No. 20*)	November 1977
21	Accounting for Leases in a Business Combination (an interpretation of *FASB Statement No. 13*)	April 1978
22	Applicability of Indefinite Reversal Criteria to Timing Differences (an interpretation of *APB Opinion Nos. 11* and *23*)	April 1978
23	Leases & Certain Property Owned by a Governmental Unit or Authority (an interpretation of *FASB Statement No. 13*)	August 1978
24	Lease Involving Only Part of a Building (an interpretation of *FASB Statement No. 13*)	September 1978
25	Accounting for an Unused Investment Tax Credit (an interpretation of *APB Opinion Nos. 2, 4, 11,* and *16*)	September 1978

Number	Title	Date of Issuance
FASB Interpretations, Financial Accounting Standards Board (Concluded)		
26	Accounting for Purchase of a Leased Asset by the Lessee during the Term of the Lease (an interpretation of FASB Statement No. 13)	September 1978
27	Accounting for a Loss on a Sublease (an interpretation of FASB Statement No. 13)	November 1978
28	Accounting for Stock Appreciation Rights and Other Variable Stock Option or Award Plans (an interpretation of APB Opinion Nos. 15 and 25)	December 1978
29	Reporting Tax Benefits Realized on Disposition of Investments in Certain Subsidiaries and Other Investees (an interpretation of APB Opinion Nos. 23 and 24)	February 1979
30	Accounting for Involuntary Conversions of Nonmonetary Assets to Monetary Assets (an interpretation of APB Opinion No. 29)	September 1979
31	Treatment of Stock Compensation Plans in EPS Computations (an interpretation of APB Opinion No. 15 and a modification of FASB Interpretation No. 28)	February 1980
32	Application of Percentage Limitations in Recognizing Investment Tax Credit (an interpretation of APB Opinion Nos. 2, 4, and 11)	March 1980
33	Applying FASB Statement No. 34 to Oil and Gas Producing Operations Accounted for by the Full Cost Method (an interpretation of FASB Statement No. 34)	August 1980
34	Disclosure of Indirect Guarantees of Indebtedness of Others (an interpretation of FASB Statement No. 5)	March 1981
35	Criteria for Applying the Equity Method of Accounting for Investments in Common Stock (an interpretation of APB Opinion No. 18)	May 1981
36	Accounting for Exploratory Wells in Progress at the End of a Period (an interpretation of FASB Statement No. 19)	October 1981
37	Accounting for Translation Adjustments Upon Sale of Part of an Investment in a Foreign Entity (an interpretation of FASB Statement No. 52)	July 1983
38	Determining the Measurement Date for Stock Option, Purchase, and Award Plans Involving Junior Stock (an interpretation of APB Opinion No. 25)	August 1984
39	Offsetting of Amounts Related to Certain Contracts (an interpretation of APB Opinion No. 10 and FASB Statement No. 105)	March 1992
40	Applicability of Generally Accepted Accounting Principles to Mutual Life Insurance and Other Enterprises (an interpretation of FASB Statements No. 12, 60, 97, and 113)	April 1993
41	Offsetting of Amounts Related to Certain Repurchase and Reverse Repurchase Agreements (an interpretation of APB Opinion No. 10 and a modification of FASB Interpretation No. 39)	December 1994
42	Accounting for Transfers of Assets in Which a Not-for-Profit Organization Is Granted Variance Power (an interpretation of FASB Statement No. 116)	September 1996
43	Real Estate Sales (an interpretation of FASB Statement No. 66)	June 1999
44	Accounting for Certain Transactions Involving Stock Compensation (an interpretation of APB Opinion No. 25)	March 2000
45	Guarantor's Accounting and Disclosure Requirements for Guarantees, Including Indirect Guarantees of Indebtedness of Others	November 2002
46R	Consolidation of Variable Interest Entities (an interpretation of ARB No. 51)	December 2003
47	Accounting for Conditional Asset Retirement Obligations (an interpretation of FASB Statement No. 143)	March 2005
48	Accounting for Uncertainty in Income Taxes (an interpretation of FASB Statement No. 109)	June 2006

APPENDIX C

LIST OF THE OFFICIAL PRONOUNCEMENTS OF THE IASB

C-2 International Financial Reporting Standards (IFRS), IASB

C-2 International Accounting Standards (IAS), IASC

C-3 Interpretations Issued by International Financial Reporting Interpretations Committee (IFRIC) and the Standards Interpretation Committee (SIC)

Appendix C List of the Official Pronouncements of the IASB

Listed below are the major official pronouncements of the International Accounting Standards Board (IASB) and the International Accounting Standards Committee (IASC) that have established international generally accepted accounting principles, or had a significant impact upon the establishment of these principles. These pronouncements are typically referred to as International Financial Reporting Standards (IFRS). Also listed are the chapter numbers in which the related topics are discussed.

Number		Title	Chapter Reference
		Framework for the Preparation and Presentation of Financial Statements	Chapter 2
		International Financial Reporting Standards, IASB	
IFRS	1	First-Time Adoption of International Financial Reporting Standards	
IFRS	2	Share-Based Payment	Chapter 15
IFRS	3	Business Combinations	Chapter 12
IFRS	4	Insurance Contracts	
IFRS	5	Non-Current Assets Held for Sale and Discontinued Operations	Chapter 5
IFRS	6	Exploration for and Evaluation of Mineral Resources	Chapters 10, 11
IFRS	7	Financial Instruments: Disclosures	Chapters 6, 13, 14
IFRS	8	Operating Segments	Chapter 5
IFRS	9	Financial Instruments	Chapters 6, 13, 14
IFRS	10	Consolidated Financial Statements	Chapter 13
IFRS	11	Joint Arrangements	Chapter 13
IFRS	12	Disclosure of Interests in Other Entities	Chapter 13
IFRS	13	Fair Value Measurements	Chapter 4
IFRS	14	Regulatory Deferral Accounts	
IFRS	15	Revenue from Contracts with Customers	Chapters 5, 17
IFRS	16	Leases	Chapter 20
		International Accounting Standards, IASC	
IAS	1	Presentation of Financial Statements	Chapters 4, 5, 15, 16
IAS	2	Inventories	Chapters 7, 8
IAS	3	Consolidated Financial Statements*	
IAS	4	Depreciation Accounting*	
IAS	5	Information to Be Disclosed in Financial Statements*	
IAS	6	Accounting Responses to Changing Prices*	
IAS	7	Statement of Cash Flows	Chapter 21
IAS	8	Accounting Policies, Changes in Accounting Estimates and Errors	Chapter 22
IAS	9	Accounting for Research and Development Activities*	
IAS	10	Events After the Reporting Period	Chapter 4
IAS	11	Construction Contracts	Chapter 17
IAS	12	Income Taxes	Chapter 18
IAS	13	Presentation of Current Assets and Current Liabilities*	
IAS	14	Segment Reporting*	
IAS	15	Information Reflecting the Effects of Changing Prices*	
IAS	16	Property, Plant, and Equipment	Chapter 10
IAS	17	Leases	Chapter 20
IAS	18	Revenue*	
IAS	19	Employee Benefits	Chapter 19
IAS	20	Accounting for Government Grants and Disclosure of Government Assistance	
IAS	21	The Effects of Changes in Foreign Exchange Rates	

Number		Title	Chapter Reference
		International Accounting Standards, IASC (Continued)	
IAS	22	Business Combinations*	
IAS	23	Borrowing Costs	Chapter 10
IAS	24	Related Party Disclosures	Chapter 4
IAS	25	Accounting for Investments*	
IAS	26	Accounting and Reporting by Retirement Benefit Plans	Chapter 19
IAS	27	Separate Financial Statements	
IAS	28	Investments in Associates and Joint Ventures	
IAS	29	Financial Reporting in Hyper-Inflationary Economies	
IAS	30	Disclosures in the Financial Statements of Banks and Similar Financial Institutions*	
IAS	31	Interests in Joint Ventures*	
IAS	32	Financial Instruments: Presentation	Chapters 13, 15, 16
IAS	33	Earnings per Share	Chapters 5, 16
IAS	34	Interim Financial Reporting	Chapter 5
IAS	35	Discontinuing Operations*	
IAS	36	Impairment of Assets	Chapters 11, 12
IAS	37	Provisions, Contingent Liabilities, and Contingent Assets	Chapter 9
IAS	38	Intangible Assets	Chapter 12
IAS	39	Financial Instruments: Recognition and Measurement*	
IAS	40	Investment Property	
IAS	41	Agriculture	

*Statements have been either superseded or withdrawn.

Listed below are the interpretations of IAS and IFRS developed by the International Financial Reporting Interpretations Committee (IFRIC). IFRIC replaced the former Standing Interpretations Committee (SIC) in March 2002. Interpretations are part of the IASB's authoritative literature, and therefore, financial statements may not be described as complying with International Financial Reporting Standards unless they comply with all the requirements of each applicable Standard and each applicable Interpretation.

Number		Title	Reference
		Final Interpretations Issued by IFRIC	
IFRIC	1	Changes in Existing Decommissioning, Restoration, and Similar Liabilities	IAS 37
IFRIC	2	Members' Shares in Co-operative Entities and Similar Instruments	IAS 32
IFRIC	3	Emission Rights (withdrawn)	
IFRIC	4	Determining Whether an Arrangement Contains a Lease	IAS 17
IFRIC	5	Rights to Interests Arising from Decommissioning, Restoration, and Environmental Rehabilitation Funds	IAS 8, IAS 27, IAS 28, IAS 31, IAS 37, IAS 39, SIC 12
IFRIC	6	Liabilities Arising from Participating in a Specific Market—Waste Electrical and Electronic Equipment	IAS 37
IFRIC	7	Applying the Restatement Approach under IAS 29 Financial Reporting in Hyperinflationary Economies	IAS 29
IFRIC	8	Scope of IFRS 2	IFRS 2

Number		Title	Reference
Final Interpretations Issued by IFRIC (Continued)			
IFRIC	9	Reassessment of Embedded Derivatives	IAS 39
IFRIC	10	Interim Financial Reporting and Impairment	IAS 34
IFRIC	11	IFRS 2: Group and Treasury Share Transactions	IAS 8, IAS 32, IFRS 2
IFRIC	12	Service Concession Agreements	IFRS 1, IFRS 7, IAS 8, IAS 11, IAS 16, IAS 16, IAS 18, IAS 20, IAS 23, IAS 32, IAS 36, IAS 37, IAS 38, IAS 39, IFRIC 4, SIC 29, Framework for the Preparation and Presentation of Financial Statements
IFRIC	13	Customer Loyalty Programmes	IAS 18, IAS 37, IAS 38
IFRIC	14	IAS 19—The Limit on a Defined Benefit Asset, Minimum Funding Requirements and their Interaction	IAS 19
IFRIC	15	Agreements for the Construction of Real Estate	IAS 11, IAS 18
IFRIC	16	Hedges of a Net Investment in a Foreign Operation	IAS 39
IFRIC	17	Distributions of Non-cash Assets to Owners	IAS 1, IAS 27, IAS 37
IFRIC	18	Transfers of Assets from Customers	IAS 18
IFRIC	19	Extinguishing Financial Liabilities with Equity Instruments	IFRS 2, IFRS 3, IAS 1, IAS 32, IAS 39
IFRIC	20	Stripping Costs in the Production Phase of a Surface Mine	IAS 1, IAS 2, IAS 16, IAS 38
IFRIC	21	Levies	IAS 1, IAS 8, IAS 12, IAS 20, IAS 24, IAS 34, IAS 37, IFRIC 6

Number		Title	Reference
Final Interpretations Issued by SIC (that have not been superseded)			
SIC	7	Introduction of the Euro	IAS 8, IAS 10, IAS 21
SIC	10	Government Assistance—No Specific Relation to Operating Activities	IAS 20
SIC	15	Operating Leases—Incentives	IAS 17
SIC	25	Income Taxes—Changes in the Tax Status of an Enterprise or its Shareholders	IAS 12
SIC	27	Evaluating the Substance of Transactions in the Legal Form of a Lease	IAS 1, IAS 17, IAS 18
SIC	29	Disclosure—Service Concession Arrangements	IAS 1
SIC	32	Intangible Assets—Website Costs	IAS 38

APPENDIX D

BRIEF GUIDE TO KEY DIFFERENCES BETWEEN IFRS AND U.S. GAAP BY CHAPTER

Below are brief summaries of the major differences between International Financial Reporting Standards (IFRS) and U.S. generally accepted accounting principles (GAAP) for the topics discussed in each chapter of the book. In addition, we include brief descriptions of the applications of IFRS to various transactions in each chapter. For your convenience, the page numbers on which IFRS-related content can be found are given in parentheses.

For a more complete discussion, see the coverage of IFRS in each chapter, which is highlighted with a globe icon. We also provide various questions, exercises, problems, and cases that incorporate IFRS at the end of each chapter (also identified with a globe icon).

Chapter 1: The Demand for and Supply of Financial Accounting Information (pp. 1-17 to 1-20)

- The role of the International Accounting Standards Board (IASB) in establishing International Financial Reporting Standards (IFRS) is discussed.
- The demand for international convergence of accounting standards is driven by investors' and creditors' needs for high-quality, internationally comparable financial information that is useful for decision-making in global capital markets. The convergence efforts of the FASB, SEC, and IASB are discussed.

Chapter 2: Financial Reporting: Its Conceptual Framework (pp. 2-6 to 2-9, 2-11 to 2-16)

- The FASB and IASB worked closely together to develop a common Conceptual Framework that will help standard-setters achieve the goal of uniform, consistent, high-quality financial reporting standards.
- The primary objective of financial reporting according to the FASB and the IASB is to provide financial information about the reporting entity that is useful to existing and potential investors, lenders, and other creditors in making decisions about providing resources to the entity.
- The FASB and IASB jointly established the qualitative characteristics of decision-useful information, consisting of:
  - fundamental characteristics: relevance and faithful representation
  - enhancing characteristics: comparability, verifiability, timeliness, understandability

Chapter 3: Review of a Company's Accounting System (pp. 3-2 to 3-8 and 3-15)

- Whether companies use IFRS or U.S. GAAP, accounting systems are based on similar concepts and principles. Basic components of accounting systems include the accounting equation which serves as the framework of the system, source documents that are used to generate accounting information, records used to organize and store accounting information, and financial statements which are the outputs of the accounting system.
- Both U.S. GAAP and IFRS require the accrual method of accounting.

IFRS Application: Comparative balance sheets for **LVMH Group (Moet Hennessy – Louis Vuitton)** (pp. 4-46 to 4-47)

Chapter 4: The Balance Sheet and the Statement of Shareholders' Equity (pp. 4-4 to 4-13, 4-45 to 4-47)

- The financial statements required by the IASB are similar to those required under U.S. GAAP. They include a balance sheet, income statement, statement of comprehensive income, statement of shareholders' equity, and statement of cash flows, as well as related notes and other explanatory material.
- Definitions of the elements of the balance sheet (assets, liabilities, and shareholders' equity) are similar between U.S. GAAP and IFRS.

- IFRS and U.S. GAAP both used mixed attribute measurement models to measure and report the elements of the balance sheet.
- On the balance sheet, companies using IFRS often present classifications of assets, liabilities and shareholders' equity in a different ordering than under U.S. GAAP, as follows:
  - noncurrent assets followed by current assets
  - capital and reserves (shareholders' equity) before liabilities
  - noncurrent liabilities followed by current liabilities
- IFRS present "reserves" within shareholders' equity on the balance sheet. Reserves may result from upward revaluations of property and investments, as well as currency translation differences.
- In the notes to the financial statements, IFRS require disclosures similar to U.S. GAAP. In addition, IFRS require disclosure of the measurement basis used for revaluations.

Chapter 5: The Income Statement and the Statement of Cash Flows (pp. 5-5 and 5-31 to 5-34)

- Under IFRS, companies commonly measure and report two levels of income: net income and comprehensive income.
- Simililar to U.S. GAAP, IFRS establish the definitions of various elements (revenues, expenses, gains, and losses) of net income and the principles that companies must use to measure and report income.
- IFRS do not prescribe either a single-step or multiple-step format for the income statement.
- Terminology differences may exist. For example, under IFRS, some companies use the term *turnover* to refer to *sales*.
- IFRS require expenses to be classified by their nature or function.
- IFRS require the adjustment of depreciation expense if property has been revalued upward.
- IFRS allow alternative performance measures (other than net income) to be presented on the income statement.
- U.S. GAAP and IFRS are similar in what qualifies as a discontinued operation. In addition, the presentation of discontinued operations is similar under both IFRS and U.S. GAAP.
- The measurement and presentation of earnings per share under IFRS is similar to U.S. GAAP.

IFRS Applications: Comparative income sheets for **LVMH Group** (**Moet Hennessy – Louis Vuitton**) (pp. 5-31 to 5-32) and **Nestlé** (p. 5-33)

Chapter 6: Cash and Receivables (pp. 6-31 to 6-34)

- IFRS classify most receivables in a category termed *loans and receivables*, which is not defined by U.S. GAAP. In some instances, IFRS will allow receivables to be classified as *available-for-sale* securities, which is not allowed under U.S. GAAP.
- While both IFRS and U.S. GAAP have a fair value option, IFRS are more restrictive regarding when the fair value option can be applied.
- When financial assets are transferred, U.S. GAAP focuses on whether control has been surrendered in determining whether the transfer is accounted for as a secured borrowing or a sale. Under IFRS, the derecognition of the financial asset under IFRS is based on whether the seller has transferred substantially all the risks and rewards of ownership, with control as a secondary test.

IFRS Application: Comparative accounting for a nonrecourse transfer of a financial asset (p. 6-33 to 6-34)

Chapter 7: Inventories: Cost Measurement and Flow Assumptions (p. 7-29)

- IFRS do not allow the use of the LIFO cost flow assumption.
- IFRS require the same cost flow assumption be used for all inventories that have a similar nature and use. No such requirement exists under U.S. GAAP.

IFRS Application: Application of the lower of cost or market rule (p. 8-10)

Chapter 8: Inventories: Special Valuation Issues (pp. 8-9 to 8-10)

- In applying the lower of cost or market rule to value inventory:
  - IFRS define market value as net realizable value regardless of the inventory method used, thereby eliminating the need to use a ceiling and a floor constraint as specified under U.S. GAAP (for companies that use the LIFO or retail inventory method).
  - IFRS allow the reversal of a write-down of inventory (but not above its original cost) which is recognized in income.

IFRS Application: Comparative accounting for a nonrecourse transfer of a financial asset (p. 9-25)

Chapter 9: Current Liabilities and Contingent Obligations (pp. 9-24 to 9-25)

- IFRS refers to a liability that is uncertain as to timing or amount and is recognized in the financial statements as a provision. Therefore, the term provision under IFRS is equivalent to the term contingency under U.S. GAAP.
- IFRS define "probable" as "more likely than not" to occur, which is a lower recognition threshold than under U.S. GAAP.
- IFRS require the disclosure of gain contingencies in the notes to the financial statements if an inflow of economic resources is probable.
- IFRS requires a provision to be measured at its settlement price on the balance sheet date using present value techniques whenever the effect on the measurement of the liability is material.
- If a range of estimates exists and no amount in the range is a better estimate than any other amount in the range, IFRS require that the mid-point of the range be used to measure the liability.

IFRS Applications: Disclosure by LVMH (p. 10-12), Journal entries for revaluation model (p. 10-12), Capitalization of interest (pp. 10-23 to 10-24)

Chapter 10: Property, Plant, and Equipment: Acquisition and Subsequent Investments (pp. 10-11 to 10-12, 10-23 to 10-24 and 10-26)

- IFRS allow a company to subsequently value its property, plant, and equipment using either a cost model or a revaluation model.
- Under the revaluation model, a company may write up its property, plant, and equipment to fair value.
  - An increase in fair value is recognized in other comprehensive income and accumulated in shareholders' equity as a revaluation surplus.
  - A decrease in fair value of the asset first reduces any previously recognized revaluation surplus. Any remaining decrease is recognized as an expense.
- With regard to self-constructed assets:
  - IFRS allows for the capitalization of the total amount of borrowing costs of loans obtained specifically for the purpose of constructing a qualifying asset.
  - Any interest revenue from the temporary investment of amounts borrowed specifically for construction is offset against interest costs eligible for capitalization.
- The cost of relocating or reorganizing property, plant, and equipment must be expensed.

IFRS Applications: Component depreciation (p. 11-17); Calculation and journal entries related to impairments (pp. 11-28 to 11-29); Disposal of property, plant, and equipment (p. 11-31)

Chapter 11: Depreciation, Depletion, Impairment, and Disposal (pp. 11-16 to 11-17, 11-28 to 11-29, and 11-31)

- IFRS require that the estimated useful lives and residual values of the assets and the depreciation method be reviewed at least once a year.
- When an operating asset is made up of individual components that are significant with respect to the total cost of the item, IFRS require that the initial cost of an operating asset be allocated to the significant components of the asset and the components be separately depreciated. This is called component depreciation.

- If a company has written up the value of its property, plant, and equipment, the revalued amount is used to compute subsequent depreciation expense.
- IFRS require that companies disclose the accumulated depreciation for each class of property, plant, and equipment, not just the total amount.
- IFRS require a company to annually assess whether indicators of impairment exist.
- With regard to impairments of property, plant, and equipment, there is no recoverability test under IFRS. Instead, if the impairment indicators exist, a company determines if an impairment exists by using the higher of the asset's fair value (less costs to sell) or value-in-use.
- IFRS computes an impairment loss as the difference between the asset's book value and its *recoverable amount* (the higher of the asset's fair value minus costs to sell or value in use).
- Under IFRS, an impairment loss may be reported in other comprehensive income if it reverses a previously recognized upward revaluation of the asset.
- IFRS allow an impairment loss to be reversed if the value is recovered.
- For disposals in which the item of property, plant, and equipment has been revalued upward, the revaluation surplus should be transferred out of Accumulated Other Comprehensive Income and to Retained Earnings. Under no circumstances can this revaluation surplus be transferred to income.

Chapter 12: Intangibles (pp. 12-22 to 12-24)

IFRS Application: Capitalization, amortization, and revaluation of intangible asset (pp. 12-23 to 12-24)

- In the research and development phase of internally generated intangible assets, IFRS allow costs incurred in the development phase to be capitalized if the company can demonstrate technical and economic feasibility.
- IFRS allow intangibles to be revalued upwards to fair value, with a corresponding increase in an account called *Revaluation Surplus*, which is included in shareholders' equity as a component of Accumulated Other Comprehensive Income.
- For intangible assets other than goodwill, IFRS use a one-step approach to determine if an impairment loss exists in which the impairment is calculated as the difference between the asset's carrying value and the higher of the asset's fair value (minus costs to sell) or value in use.
- For goodwill, IFRS calculate the impairment loss as the difference between the carrying amount of the cash-generating unit, including any goodwill, and the recoverable amount of the cash generating unit.
- For all intangible assets other than goodwill, IFRS allow an impairment loss related to an intangible asset to be reversed if the value is recovered.

Chapter 13: Investments and Long-Term Receivables (p. 13-26)

- IFRS divides investments into three categories—amortized cost, fair value through other comprehensive income (FVOCI), and fair value through profit and loss (FVPL). For marketable debt securities, this classification is based on the company's business model for managing financial assets and the characteristics of the contractual cash flows of the financial asset. All equity securities are classified as FVPL, unless the company does not hold the security for trading and has made an election to classify it as FVOCI.
- While both U.S. GAAP and IFRS have a fair value option, IFRS only allow this option if reporting changes in fair value though profit and loss would eliminate a measurement or recognition inconsistency (sometimes called an *accounting mismatch*) that would arise from measured assets and liabilities on different measurement bases.
- IFRS allow for the reversal of impairment losses with the amount of the reversal recognized in income.
- IFRS refer to an *equity method investee* as an *associate*.

- IFRS do not address whether an investor's interest that is represented by something other than an equity instrument but that is similar in substance to an equity instrument gives rise to significant influence over the investee.
- IFRS define joint venture arrangements, and account for joint ventures by either the equity method or proportionate consolidation.

IFRS Application: Issuance of bonds and recognition of interest (p. 14-27)

Chapter 14: Financing Liabilities: Bonds and Long-Term Notes Payable (p. 14-27)

- IFRS require the use of the effective interest rate method of amortization of discounts and premiums.
- IFRS do not record premiums and discounts in separate accounts but, instead, disclose bonds payable at their net amount.
- IFRS contain a general principle that an instrument is classified as a financial liability when it contains an obligation to transfer resources, regardless of the legal form of the instrument.
- IFRS require a company that issues a compound financial instrument containing both liability and equity components to report each component separately on its balance sheet.

IFRS Application: Modification of a share option plan (p. 15-26)

Chapter 15: Contributed Capital (pp. 15-16 and 15-25 to 15-26)

- Terminology differences may exist. For example:
  - *Shareholders' equity* is normally referred to as *capital and reserves.*
  - *Capital stock* is generally called either *issued capital* or *share capital.*
  - *Additional paid-in capital* is often referred to as *share premium.*
  - *Retained earnings* is normally referred to as a *reserve account.*
- Under IFRS, a company may have a revaluation surplus (or reserve) account if it has revalued its property, plant, and equipment or intangible assets upward to fair value.
- Share-based payment plans classified by U.S. GAAP as noncompensatory would be considered compensatory under IFRS.
- If share options vest ratably or in installments, IFRS require each installment to be treated as an individual arrangement.
- Under IFRS, no reduction in compensation cost is recognized if a share-based compensation plan is modified and the fair value of the modified plan is less than the fair value of the original plan.

IFRS Application: Earnings per share (pp. 16-36 to 16-37)

Chapter 16: Retained Earnings and Earnings Per Share (pp. 16-19 and 16-36 to 16-37)

- IFRS permit the reporting of a Revaluation Surplus (or Revaluation Reserve) within shareholders' equity.
- IFRS require the statement of changes in shareholders' equity be presented as a primary financial statement.
- Many of the disclosures that IFRS require for shareholders' capital are similar to those under U.S. GAAP.
- When applying the treasury stock method for potentially dilutive share options, IFRS do not require a company to include any unrecognized compensation cost in the assumed proceeds.
- IFRS only require the inclusion in diluted earnings per share of contingently convertible debt securities that convert when a company's stock price reaches a certain level if the target stock price had been reached at the financial statement date.
- For contracts that may be settled by the issuance of shares or payment of cash, IFRS require the if-converted method to be used.

- Because IFRS do not allow extraordinary items, there is no EPS disclosure for extraordinary items.
- IFRS allow the presentation of non-GAAP EPS amounts in the notes to the financial statements.

Chapter 17: Advanced Issues in Revenue Recognition (pp. 17-2, 17-13, and 17-16)

- The IASB and the FASB have issued a joint standard that provides a comprehensive, principles-based revenue recognition model that specifies how and when companies should recognize revenue. Thus, U.S. GAAP and IFRS are substantially converged in this area.
- In determining if a company is acting as a principle or an agent, IFRS provides one additional indicator beyond that specified under U.S. GAAP that a company may be acting as an agent – the company is not exposed to any credit risk for the amount receivable from the customer in exchange for the goods or services.
- In assessing the constraint on variable consideration, IFRS states that the variable consideration must be included in the transaction price to the extent that it is "highly probable" that a significant reversal will not occur. While U.S. GAAP uses the term "probable", both the FASB and IASB believe the interpretation of these terms will be similar.

Chapter 18: Accounting for Income Taxes (pp. 18-36 to 18-38)

IFRS Application: Comparative journal entries related to operating loss carryforward (pp. 18-37 to 18-38)

- IFRS allow a company to recognize a deferred tax asset when it is probable that it will have sufficient future taxable income against which to utilize the deferred tax asset.
- The recognition threshold for deferred tax assets is defined as "probable" under IFRS. However, IFRS do not specify a definition of "probable" with regard to deferred taxes.
- Because IFRS allow the upward revaluation of certain assets to fair value, this results in the recognition of a deferred tax amount that is reported in shareholders' equity.
- Under IFRS, a company's measurement of deferred tax assets and liabilities is based on enacted tax rates or substantially enacted tax rates (as well as the tax laws of the country in which it is located).
- IFRS provide no specific guidance on the recognition of deferred tax liabilities related to uncertain tax positions.
- IFRS require that the tax effects of any equity adjustments (e.g., asset revaluations) be reported directly in equity.

Chapter 19: Accounting for Postretirement Benefits (pp. 19-33 to 19-34)

IFRS Application: Journal entries related to pension expense and the calculation of the projected benefit obligation and the fair value of the pension plan assets (p. 19-34)

- IFRS require that all changes in the projected benefit obligation and the plan assets in the current period, in either pension expense or other comprehensive income.
- Under IFRS, pension expense has two components: service cost and net interest.
- The difference between pension expense and the amount funded would require an adjustment to either the accrued pension liability (if underfunded) or the prepaid pension asset (if overfunded).
- Any changes in the projected benefit obligation resulting from changes in estimates or assumptions and changes in the plan assets due to the difference in expected and actual returns are considered remeasurements and are immediately recognized as a component of other comprehensive income. In addition, the remeasurement amount increases or decreases the accrued pension liability or prepaid pension asset, as appropriate.
- Unanticipated changes resulting from changes in experience and assumptions will be recorded in other comprehensive income.
- Changes in the projected benefit obligation resulting from plan amendments are recognized immediately in pension expense through the service cost component.

Chapter 20: Accounting for Leases (pp. 20-4)

- IFRS focus more on the *substance* of a lease agreement rather than the *form*. For this reason, IFRS are generally less detailed and are considered more principles-based than U.S. GAAP.
- Under IFRS, a lease is classified as either a finance lease or an operating lease.
- IFRS require a lease to be capitalized as a finance lease when substantially all of the risk and rewards of ownership are transferred, as demonstrated by several examples or indicators. These indicators are:
  - lease term is for the *major part* of the economic life of the asset
  - at the inception of the lease, the present value of the minimum lease payments amounts to at least *substantially all* of the fair value of the leased asset
  - if the lessee is entitled to cancel the lease but the contract requires the lessee to assume the lessor's losses associated with the cancellation
  - if any gains or losses from fluctuations in the fair value of the residual value are rebated to the lessee
  - lessee has the ability to continue to lease for an additional period at a rent that is substantially lower than market rent
- Lease disclosures are less extensive under IFRS compared to U.S. GAAP.

Chapter 21: The Statement of Cash Flows (p. 21-16)

- If a company uses the indirect method, IFRS do not require a company using the direct method to reconcile its net income to its operating cash flows.
- When using the indirect method, IFRS do not specify the particular income line item that must begin the operating activities section.
- A company is required to report as an investing cash outflow the cash paid for any development costs (that are part of its R&D) that it capitalized as an intangible asset.
- Dividends and interest paid are allowed to be reported as either an operating cash outflow or a financing cash outflow.
- Dividends and interest received are allowed to be reported as either an operating cash inflow or an investing cash inflow.
- Bank overdrafts are reported as a financing cash inflow.
- Payments of income taxes identified with financing or investing transactions are allowed to be reported as financing or investing cash outflows.
- A company is allowed to report its cash flow per share.
- Companies are allowed more freedom in netting cash receipts and payments.
- The application of IFRS permits recognition of several types of noncash transactions that affect only balance sheet accounts (e.g., the revaluation of property, plant, and equipment and intangibles as well as reversals of inventory write-downs and impairment losses related to notes receivable).

Chapter 22: Accounting for Changes and Errors (p. 22-22)

- With regard to error correction, IFRS allow an exception to restating previously issued financial statements. When restatement for all periods is impracticable, the error can be corrected by restating the financial statements for the earliest period practicable.
- IFRS do not address when the indirect effects of a change in accounting principle should be reported nor the disclosures required.
- Relative to U.S. GAAP, IFRS require less extensive disclosures for accounting changes and error corrections.

INDEX

Page numbers in italics indicate references to figures and tables.

A

Abercrombie & Fitch, inventory disclosure, *8-8*
Accelerated Cost Recovery System (ACRS), 11-33
Accenture, company market value/intangible asset (relationship), 12-1
Accounting
    assumptions, importance, 2-16–2-22
    changes, 22-12
        description, *22-9*
        international dimension, 22-22
        reporting process, 22-3–22-4
        types, 22-3–22-4
    cycle, 3-8–3-9
        illustrating, *3-9–3-12*
    double-entry accounting, 2-3
    equation, *3-3*, 3-3–3-4
        business activities, impact, *3-4*, 3-4–*3-5*
        double-entry system, relationship, *3-6*
    errors, reporting method, 22-3–22-4
    estimates, 3-19–3-21
        accumulated depreciation, 3-20
        depreciation expense, 3-20
    estimates, changes, 22-3
        accounting process, 22-12–22-14
        company accounting, GAAP requirement, 22-13
        principle, change (impact), 22-14
    importance, 1-33–1-35
    information
        flow, *3-8*
        stakeholder demand, factors, 1-6–1-7
        usefulness, qualities, 2-11–2-16
    period, sale example, 5-24
    policies, summary, 4-26–4-27
    principles, 2-3
    principles, changes, 22-3, 22-5
        accounting process, 22-4–22-12
        direct/indirect effects, 22-11
        effects, disclosure, *22-9–22-10*
        estimates, changes (contrast), 22-13–22-14
        retrospective adjustment, impracticability, 22-11–22-12
    profession, ethics/integrity, 1-34
    records, maintenance, 8-14
    system
        accounting information flow, *3-8*
        components, 3-2–3-8
Accounting Principles Board (APB), 1-11
Accounting Research Bulletins (ARBs), 1-11
Accounting standards, 2-3
    demand, factors, 1-8–1-9
    international convergence, 1-18–1-19
    SEC authority, 1-10
Accounting Standards Codification, 2-4
Accounting Standards Update, 1-16–1-17
Accounting Standards Updates, 2-4
Accounting Standard Update (ASU), FASB adoption, 5-23
Accounts, 3-5–3-7
    accounts previously written off, collection, 6-17–6-18
    balance, 3-7
    chart, 3-5
    contra accounts, 3-7
    payable turnover, 4-43
        ratio, 4-43
    permanent accounts, 3-7
    temporary accounts (periodic accounts), 3-7
Accounts payable (trade accounts payable), 9-8, 9-32
Accounts receivable, 4-16
    aging, 6-15–6-17
        example, 6-15–6-16
    assigning, 6-21
    cash, obtaining, 6-20
    control account, example, *3-34*
    disclosure, example, *6-31*
    financing
        agreements, disclosure, 6-26–6-27
        company accounting process, 6-20–6-27
    pledging, 6-21
    recording process, 6-8–6-12
    sale, 6-23–6-24
        financial components approach, 6-25
        recording, 6-24–6-26
    sales/cash flows, importance, 6-18–6-19
    transfers
        accounting, *6-21*
        disclosure, *6-26*
    turnover, 4-42–4-43
        ratio, 4-42
Accounts receivable conversion (ARC), 6-6
Accretion expense, 10-9, 11-23
Accrual accounting, 3-15, 3-35
    usage, 5-5
Accrual-basis accounting, cash-basis accounting (conversion adjustments), *3-36*
Accrual basis, conversion, 21-14
Accruals, 3-15, 3-18–3-19
    accrued expenses, 3-18–3-19
    cash flows, relationship, *21-10*
    long-term accruals, 4-20
Accrued expenses, 3-18–3-19, 4-19
    adjusting entries, effects, *3-18*
Accrued income taxes, 3-19
    example, 3-19
Accrued interest, example, 3-18
Accrued interest income, example
Accrued liabilities, 9-15
    items, 9-32
Accrued postretirement benefit cost, 19-44
Accrued/Prepaid Pension Cost, 19-11
Accrued revenues, 3-19
    adjusting entries, effects, *3-19*
Accrued salaries, example, 3-18
Accumulated benefit obligation, 19-2, 19-10
Accumulated depreciation, 3-20
    example, 3-20
    journal entry, 11-9
    reduction, 10-25–10-26
Accumulated other comprehensive income (AOCI), 3-3, 4-24, 5-29
    dividends, 16-16
    section, capital structure element, 15-3
Accumulated other comprehensive loss, 4-24
Accumulated postretirement benefit obligation (APBO), 19-42
Acquisition
    cost (historical cost), 4-8–4-9, 10-5
        definition, 11-32
        purchased intangible asset capitalization, 12-3
    economic resource characteristic, 4-5
Activity methods (use methods), 11-4, 11-8–11-9
    units-of-production method, 11-8
Activity ratios (operating capability ratios) (efficiency ratios), 4-41–4-44
Actual returns, expected returns (differences), 19-23–19-25
Actuarial assumptions, 19-3
Actuarial funding method, 19-3, 19-10–19-11
    basis, 19-36
Actuaries, definition, 19-4
Additional capital, 15-8
Additional markup, 8-15
Additional paid-in capital, 15-8
    information, 15-43
Additions, 10-25
Adjusted historical cost, 4-8–4-9
Adjusted present value, 4-9–4-10
Adjusted trial balance, 21-39
    example, *3-23e–3-24e*
    preparation, 3-23
Adjusting entries
    accounting estimates, 3-19–3-21
    accruals, 3-18–3-19
    deferrals, 3-15–3-18
    effects, *3-15*, *3-17*, *3-18*, *3-19*, *3-20*
    example, 3-16, *3-16*, 3-17–3-18
    framework, *3-22e*
    periodic inventory, 3-21–3-22
    preparation process, 3-15–3-22
Adjustments, listing, 21-26
AFLAC, policy acquisition costs, 12-15
Agents, 1-6
    performance obligation, definition, 17-14
Aging analysis, *6-16*
Aging method, usage, 6-17
Alcon, USA (Nestlé ownership interests disposal), 5-33
Allowable tax deductions, *18-17*
Allowance method, 6-13–6-18
    usage, 8-7
Alternative inventory systems, journal entries, *7-8*
American Express
    accounts receivable financing, 6-20
    credit card sales, 6-25
American Institute of Certified Public Accountants (AICPA)
    Code of Professional Conduct, principles, *1-35*
    survey, 1-2
American International Group (AIG), restatement (2005), 22-16
Amortization, 4-18
    bonds
        acquisition (between interest dates), 13-9
        premiums/discounts, 13-6–13-9
    computation, example, *14-10*
    definition, 11-2, 12-4
    effective interest method, 14-10–14-11
    fraction, computation, *19-38*
    intangible assets, 12-4–12-6

I-1

schedule, effective interest method, *13-7*
straight-line method, 14-10
Analyses, example, *3-10–3-11*
Annual cash flows amount, determination, M-14
Annual deferred taxes, example, *18-26*
Annual depreciation expense, 3-20
Annual earnings (change), cumulative abnormal returns (association), *1-33*
Annual rate, M-4
Annual report, 3-7
Annuities
    defining, M-11
    ordinary annuity, M-11
Annuity due, M-11
    future value
        diagram, *M-15*
        example, M-15
    future value, computation process, M-15–M-16
        table approach, M-15–M-16
    present value
        diagram, *M-21, M-23*
        example, M-20
Annuity due, present value computation process, M-20–M-23
    application, M-23
    formula approach, M-20–M-22
    table approach, M-22
Antidilutive convertible security, 16-31
AOCI. *See* Accumulated other comprehensive income
APB. *See* Accounting Principles Board
APBO. *See* Accumulated postretirement benefit obligation
Apple, Inc.
    contingent liabilities, disclosure, 9-26
    dividend payment, 16-1
    investment disclosures, *13-31–13-32*
    loss contingency disclosures, *9-26–9-26*
    profitability, problems, 8-1–8-2
    software development costs, capitalization, 12-17
    stock buybacks, 15-2
Apple, Inc., contingency example, *4-28–4-29*
Applicable constraint, existence, 17-16
    assessment, 17-17–17-18
Appropriations (restrictions), 16-14
ARBs. *See* Accounting Research Bulletins
ARC. *See* Accounts receivable conversion
Arrangements, 3-5
Articles of incorporation, 15-5
Artistic-related intangible assets, 12-15
Artistic works, identifiable intangible asset, 12-13
Assets, 1-24
    acquisition, donation (usage), 10-10–10-11
    book value, deferred tax liability (relationship), *18-11*
    characteristics, 10-3
    classification, conceptual guidelines, 4-21
    cost, 11-2, 11-3
        MACRS depreciation percentage, 11-35
    current assets, 3-25, 4-16–4-17
    debt-to-assets ratio, 4-39
    decrease, 21-8
    defining, 3-3, 4-4–4-5
    depreciable assets, disclosure process, 11-18
    exchange, 14-38–14-39
        example, 14-39
        modification of terms, combination, 14-39
    expected life, 10-3
    expenditure, *5-11*
    fair value, example, 15-13
    fixed assets, 4-17–4-18

held for sale, impairment, 11-26
holding/use, impairment, 11-24–11-26
homogeneous classes, development guidelines, 4-21
impairment, 11-23
    conceptual evaluation, 11-26–11-27
increase, 21-8
information, 5-45
    example, *11-4*
intangible assets, 4-5, 4-18–4-19
monetary assets (financial assets), 4-5
new asset, capitalization, 10-26
noncurrent assets, 3-25
nonmonetary assets (nonfinancial assets), 4-5
nontangible assets, 4-5
operations, 10-3
other assets, 4-19
quick assets, 4-40
retirement obligations, 10-8–10-9
    depreciation/accretion, 11-22–11-23
    example, 10-8
seller performance, impact, 17-22
tangibility, 10-3
tangible assets, 4-5
transfer, legal requirement (absence), 9-3
Asset test, 5-44
Assigning, 6-20
Assignment
    agreement, example, *6-22*
    example, 6-22–6-23
Assumptions, 22-12–22-13
Assurance Opinion, 1-32
Assurance-type warranties, 9-27–9-27
    example, 9-28
ASU. *See* Accounting Standard Update
At a discount, 14-5
At a premium, 14-5
At par, 14-5
AT&T
    10-K information, 10-7–10-8
    annual report, 14-12
    gains/losses, expensing, 19-10
    service contract, 17-19
Attribution period (recognition period), 19-44, *19-44*
Audit Opinion, 1-32
Authorized capital stock, 15-6
Available-for-sale category, transfer, 13-19
    examples, 13-20, 13-21
Available-for-sale distribution, 16-8
Available-for-sale investment, purchase/sale (example), 21-36
Available-for-sale securities, 13-3
    changes, 21-21
    company disclosure, 13-29–13-20
    dividend income, recording, 13-14–13-15
    impairments, 13-21–13-22
    initial cost, recording, 13-14
    interest, recording, 13-14–13-15
    investments
        accounting, 13-14
        example, *13-14*
        measurement/reporting process, 13-14–13-19
        report, GAAP requirement, 21-35–21-36
    purchases/sales/maturities, cash flows, 13-30
    sales, realized gains/losses, 13-16–13-17
    unrealized holding gains/losses, recognition, 13-15–13-16
Average collection period, 6-18
Average cost, 7-14, 7-18–7-19
    usage, 8-3, 8-16
Average days in inventory, 7-34–7-35
Avoidable interest, computation, 10-19

B

Bad debt expense
    allowance, 3-20–3-21
    example, 3-21
Bad debts
    accounts previously written off, collection, 6-17–6-18
    accounts receivable, aging, 6-15–6-17
    credit sales, percentage, 6-14
    estimated bad debts, accrual failure (example), 22-24–22-25
    estimation, *6-13*
    outstanding accounts receivable, percentage, 6-14–6-15
    uncollectible accounts, writing off, 6-17
Balance sheet (statement of financial position), 4-1
    account, creation, 3-31
    assets, 1-24
    change, 3-4–3-5
    classification/presentation, differences, 4-45–4-47
    disclosures, 4-26–4-32
    elements
        measurement process, 4-7–4-14
        recognition, 4-4–4-7
    errors, impact, 22-19–22-21
    examples, *3-26, 3-37, 4-15–4-16*
    information
        analysis process, 4-32–4-45
    information, usage, 4-1
    items, classification/reporting process, 4-14–4-25
    liabilities, 1-24
    presentation, 12-11, 18-30
        differences, *4-46–4-47*
    purpose, 4-2–4-4
    shareholders' equity, 1-24–1-25
        section, example, *16-16*
    usage, 1-22–1-25, 3-25–3-26
Bank
    adjusting entries, *6-38*
    charges, 6-36
        identification, 6-37
    deposits, 6-36
        identification, 6-37
    journal entries, usage, 6-37
    overdrafts, 6-3
    reconciliation, 6-35–6-38
        completion, 6-37
        example, 6-37, *6-38*
        preparation, procedures, 6-36–6-37
Bankers Trust, derivative contracts lawsuits, 13-38
Bank of America
    financial liabilities, fair value, *14-17–14-18*
Bank of America, core deposit intangibles (gross value), 12-15
Bargain purchase, 12-22
Bargain purchase option, *20-7*
    example, 20-20
    inclusion, absence, 20-40–20-41
    presence, 20-39–20-40
    provision, absence (example), 20-15–20-17
Bargain renewal option, *20-7*
Barings Bank, bankruptcy, 13-38
Barnes & Noble, restatement (disclosure), *22-16–22-19*
Basic earnings per share, 5-26–5-27
    computation
        example, *16-25*
        process, 16-20–16-26
    earnings per common share, 16-21
    examples, 5-27, 16-21, 16-24
    reporting, example, *16-25*

Best Buy, extended warranty/service contract (purchase option), 9-29
Betterments (improvements), 10-25
Bill and hold sale, 7-11
Black and Decker, Inc., convertible preferred equity units (sale), 15-12
Black-Scholes-Merton option pricing model, 15-19
BMW, foreign corporation status, 15-4
Boeing
   long-term construction contracts, 17-26
   plane production, 7-3
      contract/program, duration (usage), 9-4
Bonds, 14-1
   acquisitions (between interest dates), amortization, 13-9
   certificate, definition, 14-3
   characteristics, 14-3–14-4, *14-4*
   conversion
      book value method, 14-23
      company recording, GAAP methods, 14-23
      example, 14-23
      market value method, 14-23
   convertible bonds, 14-22–14-28
   definition, 14-3
   discounts
      amortization, 13-6–13-9
      amortization schedule, effective interest method, *14-13*
      effective interest method, example, 14-10–14-11
      straight line example, 14-14
   equity characteristics, accounting process, 14-20–14-28
   fair value option, 14-17–14-18
   indenture, definition, 14-3
   induced conversions, 14-23–14-24
      example, 14-24
   interest
      accrual, examples, 14-15–14-16
      expense, effective interest method, *14-13*
      schedules, effective interest method, 14-12
   issuance
      detachable stock warrants, usage, 14-20–14-21
      detachable warrants, usage, 14-23
      example, *14-9*
      interest payment dates, relationship, 14-8–14-9
      process, 14-4–14-5
   issued at a discount, example, 14-6, 14-8
   issued at a premium, example, 14-6, 14-8
   issued at par, example, 14-5, 14-7
   premiums
      amortization, 13-6–13-9
      amortization schedule, effective interest method, *14-13*
      effective interest method, example, 14-11
      straight line example, 14-14–14-15
   retired at maturity, 14-19
   retired prior to maturity, 14-19–14-20
   retirement, 21-33–21-34
      example, 21-34
      retirement prior to maturity, example, 14-19
   straight-line method, 14-14–14-15
   types, *14-4*
   yield, contract rates (contrast), *14-7*
   zero-coupon bonds (deep-discount bonds), *14-4*, 14-16

Bonds payable
   changes, 21-30
   characteristics, 14-3–14-5
   issuance
      recording example, 14-7–14-8
      recording process, 14-7–14-9
      issue price, computation, 14-5–14-7
Bonus computation, example, 9-20–9-21
Bonus obligations, 9-20
Bookkeeping, costs, 7-28
Book value (carrying value), 14-10
   method, 14-23, 15-35
Borrower, incremental interest rate (usage), 13-33
Brief history (conceptual framework), 2-5–2-6
British Petroleum (BP), oil/gas properties (value), 11-31
Buildings
   changes, 21-29–21-30
   location/tracking, 20-1
   recorded cost, 10-6
Business activities, 1-4–1-6
   impact, *3-4*, 3-4–3-5
Business cash controls, 6-5–6-7
Buyer inventory, determination, 7-10
Buying, leasing (contrast), 20-6–20-7

C

Callable bonds, *14-4*
Callable preferred stock, 15-37
CAP. *See* Committee on Accounting Procedure
Capital
   additional capital, 15-8
   additional paid-in capital, 15-8
   expenditures, 10-2, 10-24
   issued capital, 15-16
   legal capital, 15-7–15-9
   share capital, 15-16
Capitalization. *See* Interest capitalization
   criteria, 20-2
   new asset, 10-26
   question, 10-1
Capitalized interest
   construction loan, examples, *10-20*, *10-21*
   example, *10-22*
   multiple accounting periods, 10-21–10-22
      example, 10-22
Capital lease
   definition, 20-2
   discount rate, 20-13
   executory costs, 20-13
   leased asset, amortization, 20-14
   lessee
      accounting, 20-12–20-19
      contingent rental payments, 20-13–20-14
      disclosure requirements, *20-22*
   next year's payments, present value, 20-17
   obligation, classification, 20-17–20-19
   present value, change, 20-17
Capital maintenance concept, 5-4
   example, 5-4
Capital One, credit card sales, 6-25
Capital stock, 15-5–15-6
   authorization, 15-10
   authorized capital stock, 15-6
   cash, issuance, 15-10–15-11
   information, 15-43
   issuance, accounting process, 15-10–15-17
   issued capital stock, 15-7
   no-par capital stock, 15-7
   outstanding capital stock, 15-7
   reacquisition, 15-41
   stock issuance costs, 15-11

   subscribed capital stock, 15-7
   subscriptions, 15-11–15-12
   terminology, 15-6–15-7
Capital structure, 14-1
   complex capital structure, 16-21
   defining, process, 15-5–15-10
   simple capital structure, 16-21
Carrefour, inventory (presence), 8-2
Carrying value (net book value), 3-20, 4-18
Cash, 4-16, 6-1, 21-4–21-5
   balance (error), effect (determination), 6-37
   bank reconciliation, 6-35–6-38
   cash-generating unit, 12-23
   classification, *6-4*
   control procedures, 6-5–6-6
   controls, business needs, 6-5–6-7
   defining, 6-3–6-5
   discounts (sales discounts), 6-9–6-11
      example, 6-9
      recording, 6-9–6-11
   dividends, 16-3–16-6, 21-31
      accounting dates, *16-5*
      dates, importance, 16-4
      declaration, 21-37
   equivalents, 4-16, 6-4, 21-4–21-5
      report, *6-5*
   inflows/outflows, 21-8
   internal controls, 6-34–6-38
   international perspective, 6-31–6-34
   issuance, 15-10–15-11
   net change, 21-6
   notes payable issuance, 14-28–14-30
      example, 14-29–14-30
   obtaining, 6-20
   payments journal, 3-35
   petty cash, 6-34–6-35
   receipts journal, 3-35
   report, *6-5*
   settlement, 14-24
   stock, combination, 14-24
Cash-basis accounting
   conversion, adjustments, *3-36*
   defining, 3-35–3-38
   example, 3-36–3-38
Cash flow hedge, 13-42–13-44
   example, *13-43*
Cash flows
   accruals, relationship, *21-10*
   amount, determination, *M-14*, *M-19*, M-23, *M-23*
   basis, accrual basis conversion, 21-14
   company cash flows (assessment), information (usage), 2-8
   computation, schedule, *21-41*
   example, *5-35*
   expected cash flows, impairment (relationship), 13-36
   importance, 6-18–6-19
   modified cash flows, *14-37*
   periodic cash flows, determination, M-19–M-20
   prediction, 5-3
   present value, *M-17*
   revenue recognition, relationship, *5-8*
   revenue timing, contrast, 5-7–5-9
   risk, 11-11
   spreadsheet, example, *21-28–21-29*, *21-43*
   statement of cash flows, 1-28
      financing section, 14-34
      information analysis process, 5-38–5-43
Cash rebates
   coupons, relationship, 9-30–9-31
   obligations, 9-29
   offering, 9-29

Caterpillar
    goods conversion, 7-3
    lease classification, 20-23–20-24
Cause/effect, association, 5-10
CECL. *See* Current expected credit losses
Ceiling, 8-3
    conceptual evaluation, 8-5–8-6
Certificates of deposit (CDs), 6-3
Change order (contract modification), 17-6
Changes, accounting, 22-1
Chart of accounts, 3-5
Check Clearing for the 21st Century Act (Check 21), 6-6
Checks
    not-sufficient funds (NSF), 6-36
Chipotle Mexican Grill, Inc., statement of cash flows, *21-22–21-23*
Cisco
    fair value example, 4-11–4-12
    present value example, 4-9–4-10
Citibank, trading assets (reporting), 13-3
Closed corporations (privately held corporations), 15-4
Closing entries
    example, *3-28*
    preparation process, 3-27–3-29
CNBC, earnings release coverage, 5-1
CNN, earnings release coverage, 5-1
Coca-Cola Company, The
    bonds, issuance, 14-3
    corporation identification, 1-9
    fair value example, 4-11
    revenue recognition, example, *5-7*
    sales, source, 1-18
    stock certificates, 15-5
    stock splits, information, 15-14
Code of Professional Conduct (CPC) (AICPA), 1-34
    principles, *1-35*
Codification. *See* Financial Accounting Standards Board
Collectability, 17-9–17-10
Commercial paper, 9-10
Commitment fees (loan origination fees), 13-34
Committee on Accounting Procedure (CAP), 1-11
Common shares
    disclosures, FASB requirements, 15-43
    potential common shares, 16-26
Common-size analysis, 4-33
    examples, *4-33, 4-34, 5-39*
    usage, 5-38–5-39
Common stock, 4-22, 15-6
    example, 4-22
    market prices, 4-31
    preferred stock, convertibility, 15-33
Company
    accounting system, review, 3-1
    accounts receivable financing, accounting process, 6-20–6-27
    agent role, indicators, *17-14*
    capital structure, 14-1
    cash flows
        assessment, information (usage), 2-8
        prediction, 5-3
    checks, comparison, 6-36–6-37
    company-wide disclosures, 5-45
    comprehensive income reporting process, 5-28–5-30
    disclosures, components, 17-26
    discount rate, usage, 19-10
    economic factors, impact (assessment), 5-3
    economic resources/claims, information (usage), 2-8–2-9
    effective tax rate, 18-17
    financial performance, assessment, 5-3
    financial statements, inventory reporting process, 7-5
    financing activities, 5-35
    financing arrangements, forms, 6-20
    future income, prediction, 5-3
    intracompany/intercompany comparisons, 4-32–4-33
    investing activities, 5-34–5-35
    liquidity, 9-2
    long-run solvency/stability, importance, 14-11–14-12
    market value, intangible assets (relationship), 12-1
    notes receivable accounting process, 6-27–6-30
    operating activities, 5-34–5-35
    operating capability, assessment, 5-3
    operating cycle, 21-21
    performance, comparison, 5-3
    positive intent and ability, 13-3
    profitability
        evaluation, 5-3
        operating capability/leverage, multiplication, 5-42
    realized gains/losses, reporting, 13-15
    records, deposits (comparison), 6-36
    return on investment (ROI)
        assessment, 5-3
        measurement, improvement, 13-18
    risk, assessment, 5-3
    share buybacks, 15-1
    stakeholders, *1-5*
    statement of cash flows
        purpose, 21-3
        reporting process, 5-34–5-38
Company inventory
    classification, 7-3–7-6
    costs determination process, 7-12–7-14
    quantity determination process, 7-9–7-12
    tracking process, 7-6–7-9
Comparability, 2-15
Comparative financial statements, 4-31–4-32
Comparative income statements (revision), FIFO (usage), *22-8*
Comparative retained earnings statements, FIFO (usage), *22-8*
Comparative weighted average shares, 16-23
Compensated absences, 9-18–9-20
    accounting, *9-19*
    vacation benefits, example, 9-19–9-20
Compensating balances, 6-3
Compensation
    cost
        estimated total, 15-21
        recognition, SARs plan (impact), *15-28*
    expense
        calculation, 15-22
        corporation recording, 15-21
        journal entry, 15-23
    liabilities, relationship, 9-15–9-21
Compensatory share option expense, example, *21-38*
Compensatory share option plans
    accounting
        fair value method, usage, 15-33
        process, 15-19–15-25
    cash flows, 21-37–21-38
    definition, 15-18
    fair value, 15-19
    fair value method, usage (FASB Exposure Draft), 15-19
    intrinsic value, 15-18–15-19
    option pricing model, 15-20–15-23
    overview, 15-18–15-19

Complex capital structure, 16-21
Component, 5-21
    depreciation, 11-17
    held for sale classification, 5-24
Composite depreciation, 11-14, 11-16
Composite methods (group methods), 11-4
Compounding, definition, M-3
Compound interest
    definition, M-4
    quarterly compound interest, computation, *M-4*
    simple interest, contrast, M-4–M-5
Comprehensive asset and liability approach
    corporation implementation, 18-6–18-7
    necessity, 18-6
Comprehensive income, 5-5
    company reporting process, 5-28–5-30
    defining, 5-28
    performance measurement/reporting, 1-27
    reduction, 19-35
    reporting alternatives, example, 5-29–5-30
    shareholders' equity/net income, relationship, *5-30*
    statement, 4-2
Comprehensive statement of cash flows, example, *21-32*
ConAgra Foods, inventory valuation above cost, *8-11*
Concepts, principles/standards/rules (differences), 2-3–2-5
Concepts Statement No. 8, 2-9
Concept Statements. *See* Statement of Financial Accounting Concepts
Conceptual evaluation, 5-47
Conceptual Framework, 2-1, 2-2–2-6
    brief history, 2-5–2-6
    current status, 2-5–2-6
    financial reporting model, defining, 2-22–2-23
    projects, 2-5
Condensed financial information, example, *21-19, 21-24–21-26*
Confirmatory value, 2-12
Consideration, amount, 17-15
Consigned goods, 7-9
Consignment, 7-9
Consignor/consignee, 7-9
Consolidated financial statements, 13-28–13-29
    notes, example, 10-12
    preparation, principles, 13-29
Consolidation, 13-4
Construction
    contract amounts, example, *17-28*
    funds, interest capitalization, 10-17
    incremental funds, actual interest (capitalization), 10-17
    interest capitalization, avoidance, 10-17
    interest, impact, 10-17–10-24
    loan, examples, *10-20, 10-21*
    recording, journal entries, *17-29–17-30*
Construction in progress, 4-18, 17-27
Constructive obligation, 17-10
Contingency
    example, *4-28–4-29*
    financial statement presentation process, 9-32–9-34
    GAAP definition, 9-22
    gain contingencies, 9-31
    loss contingencies, 4-27–4-29
Contingent issuances, 16-34
Contingent losses, example, *4-30*
Contingent obligations, 4-6, 9-1
    accounting process, 9-22–9-31
    examination, 9-24–9-25

Contingent rental payments (lessee)
    capital lease, 20-13–20-14
    operating lease, 20-12
Continuing operations
    discontinued operations, income separation, *5-23*
    income, corporation report, 16-32
    income tax expense, 5-18–5-19
    loss, corporation report, 16-32
    pretax income, 5-18
Contra account, 3-7
Contract modifications (change order), 17-6–17-9, *17-7*
    cumulative catch-up method, 17-9
    prospective method, 17-8–17-9
    seller interpretation, 17-6
Contract performance obligations
    examples, *17-10*
    identification, 5-6
        process, 17-10–17-15
    transaction price, allocation, 5-7
Contract rate (stated rate/face rate/nominal rate), 14-3
    bond yields, contrast, *14-7*
Contracts, 4-6
    amendment, 17-6
    amounts, example, *17-28*
    assets, 17-25
    collectability, 17-9–17-10
    combination, 17-6
    contract-based intangible assets, 12-15
    cost, 17-24–17-25
    definition, 17-5
    identifiable intangible asset, 12-13
    identification
        issues, 17-5–17-10
        process, 17-5–17-10
    liability, 17-25
    licensing, 17-12–17-13
    loss expectation, revenues/expenses calculation (example), *17-33–17-34*
    overall loss, example, 17-33
    performance obligation, transaction price allocation process, 17-19–17-21
    principal-agent contract considerations, 17-14–17-15
    revenue standard coverage, absence, 17-4
    separately identifiable promise, 17-11
    separation, contract modification (impact), 17-7–17-8
    termination rights, 17-5–17-6
    upfront payments, 17-11–17-12
    wholly unperformed contract, definition, 17-5
Contributed capital, 3-3, 4-7, 4-22–4-23
    example, *15-44*
    reduction, 16-12
    section
        accounts combination, 15-3
        structuring process, 15-43–15-45
    shareholders' equity, example, *15-44*
    stock buybacks, 15-1
Contributory plan, 19-3
Control
    account, 3-34
    economic resource characteristic, 4-5
    ownership, separation, 1-6–1-7, *1-7*
Conventional retail method, 8-16
Conversion, 14-20
    induced conversions, 14-23–14-24
        example, 14-24
    price, reduction, 14-23
    ratios, 16-34
    recording, 14-22–14-23
Convertible bonds, 14-22–14-28

cash settled convertible bonds, *14-26*
company issuance, motivation factors, 14-22
company sale, 14-22
conversion, recording, 14-22–14-23
equity component recognition, requirement, 14-24–14-25
example, *14-4*
issuance, recording, 14-22
Convertible preferred stock, 15-35
Convertible securities, 16-29–16-31
    antidilutive convertible security, 16-31
    if-converted method, usage, 16-29–16-30
Cook, Tim, 15-2
Copyright, definition, 12-15
Corporate assets, distribution (absence), 16-9
Corporate charter, 15-5
Corporations
    capital stock, par value, 15-7
    capital structure, defining (process), 15-5–15-10
    classification process, 15-4
    closed corporations (privately held corporations), 15-4
    definition, 15-4
    domestic corporations, 15-4
    foreign corporations, 15-4
    formation process, 15-4–15-5
    income tax expense, pretax income (matching), 18-27
    liquidation, preference, 15-38
    net income, measurement, 5-5
    open corporations (publicly traded corporations), 15-4
    organization process, 15-4–15-5
    public corporations, 15-4
    securities, issuance, 15-12
    treasury stock, acquisition, 15-38
Corridor amortization
    minimum, 19-10
    net gain/loss, 19-30–19-32
Corridor approach, 19-9
Corridor, definition, 19-9–19-10
Cost
    constraint, 2-15–2-16
    incremental cost, 17-24
    indexes, 7-30–7-31
    method, 15-38–15-41
Cost allocation methods, 11-2, 11-4
    defining, 11-4–11-9
Cost determination, 10-5–10-8
    example, 10-6
Cost flow
    FIFO cost flow relationships, *7-16*
    relationships, 7-15
Cost flow assumptions, 7-14–7-22
    alternatives, holding gains (relationship), *7-23*
    FIFO cost assumption
        periodic inventory system, *7-17*
        perpetual inventory system, *7-17*
    inventory cost flow assumptions, alternatives (consequences), 7-22–7-30
    specific identification inventory cost assumption, 7-15–7-16
Cost of goods available for sale, 3-21, 5-15, 7-4
Cost of goods sold, 3-21, 5-15
    example, *5-16*
    model, 7-5
Cost recovery
    acceleration, 11-34
    methods, 11-34
Cost-to-cost method, 17-23
    example, 17-24
Cost-to-retail ratio calculations, alternative, *8-16*
Counterbalancing errors, 22-20

Coupons, 9-29
    cash rebates, relationship, 9-30–9-31
Coverage ratios, 5-41
    example, 5-41
    interest coverage ratio, 5-41
CPC. *See* Code of Professional Conduct
Credit, 3-5
    balance
        cumulative net unrealized holding gains representation, 13-15
        subtraction, 6-16
    line of credit, establishment, 6-25
Credit cards
    holders, line of credit (establishment), 6-25
    sales, 6-25–6-26
Credit lines, 9-10
Creditors, 1-6
    accounting process, 14-40–14-42
    information, usage, 2-9–2-11
    obligations callable, 9-12
Credit sales, percentage, 6-14
Cross-sectional analysis, 4-33
Cumulative abnormal returns, annual earnings change (association), *1-33*
Cumulative catch-up method (contract modification), 17-9
Cumulative net unrealized holdings gains, 13-15
Cumulative preferred stock, 15-34
Current assets, 3-25
    changes, 21-27
        accounting, 21-44, 21-45
    types, 4-16–4-17
Current expected credit losses (CECL)
    impairment model, FASB consideration, 13-22
Current income taxes, determination, *18-9*
    steps, application, 18-15
Current liabilities, 3-25, 4-19
    accounting process, amounts determination (operating activities usage), 9-14–9-22
    changes, 21-27
        accounting, 21-44, 21-45
    classification, 9-4, 9-6
    contingent obligations, *9-1*
    defining, 9-4–9-7
    disclosure, example, *9-33–9-34*
    financial statement presentation process, 9-32–9-34
    types, *9-6*
    valuation process, 9-7
Current period, losses (example), 17-33
Current ratio, 4-40
Current replacement cost, 4-12–4-13
    example, 4-13
Current status (conceptual framework), 2-5–2-6
Current taxes, recording/reporting process, 18-9–18-16
Current values, historical values (combination), 4-8
Current-year journal entry, preparation, 22-7
Customers
    contract, identification, 5-6
        process, 17-5–17-10
    customer-related intangible assets, 12-14–12-15
    definition, 17-5
    identifiable intangible asset, 12-13
    payment, consideration, 17-18–17-19
Cypress Semiconductor Corporation, dividend payment source, 16-12

D

Data, comparability, 4-33
Date of payment (dividends), 16-4, 16-5

Date of record (dividends), 16-4
Days in operating cycle, 4-44
    example, 4-44
Dealer, profit (loss), *20-8*, 20-31
Debenture bonds, *14-4*
Debit, 3-5
    change, 13-15
Debt
    disclosure (Nike), *14-36–14-37*
    instrument, fair value option, 14-17
    issuance costs, 14-16–14-17
        example, 14-17
    long-term debt, current maturities, 4-19
    restructuring agreement, *14-37*
    retirement, fund accumulation, M-14
    security
        definition, 13-2
        impairment (other than temporary), 13-21
    short-term debt, 4-19
    terms, modification, 14-36
    troubled debt restructurings, 14-35–14-42
    voting rights, absence, 14-2
Debt financing
    cost of capital, comparison, 14-2
    financial leverage opportunity, 14-3
    funds source, 14-2
    income tax advantage, 14-2
Debtor
    accounting process, 14-36–14-40
    gain recognition
        absence, example, 14-36–14-38
        example, 14-38
Debt-to-assets ratio, 4-39
    definition, 14-12
Debt-to-equity ratio, 4-39
Decision making
    external decision making, information sources (usage), *2-23*
    information, usage, 2-8–2-9
Decision-useful financial information, qualitative characteristics, *2-12*
Decision usefulness, 2-12–2-14
    cost constraint, 2-15–2-16
    faithful representation, 2-13–2-14
    relevance, 2-12–2-13
        faithful representation, relationship, 2-14
    understandability, 2-15
Declaration date, 16-4
Declining-balance depreciation methods, example, *11-7*
Declining-balance depreciation rate, 11-6
Declining-balance method, 11-6–11-8
Deductions, accounting (example), 9-17
Defeasance, 14-20
Deferrals, *3-15–3-18*
    deferred revenues, 3-17–3-18, 4-19
    prepaid expenses, 3-15–3-15
Deferred annuity, present value (diagram), *M-26*
Deferred assets, schedule, *18-30*
Deferred income taxes, determination, *18-9*
    steps, application, 18-15
Deferred liabilities, schedule, *18-30*
Deferred ordinary annuity
    present value
        converted table factor, diagram, *M-25*
        diagram, *M-24*
        example, M-24
    present value computation process, M-24–M-26
        application, M-25–M-26
Deferred payments (future payments), 10-9–10-10

Deferred revenue (unearned revenue), 3-17–3-18, 4-19
    adjusting entries
        effects, *3-17*
        example, 3-17–3-18
    defining, 9-15
    items, 9-32
Deferred tax asset, 18-4, 18-7
    accounting, international dimension, 18-36–18-38
    creation, temporary differences (usage), 18-5–18-6
    liability book value, relationship, *18-14*
    single future deductible amount, example, 18-14
    valuation allowance, 18-8
        example, 18-15
Deferred taxes
    annual deferred taxes, example', *18-26*
    change, 21-30–21-31
    information, *18-25*
    recording/reporting process, 18-9–18-16
Deferred tax liability, 18-4, 18-7
    accounting, international dimension, 18-36–18-38
    asset book value, relationship, *18-11*
    creation, temporary differences (usage), *18-5*
    multiple tax rates, example, 18-13–18-14
    schedule, *18-12*
    single future taxable amount, example, 18-10–18-11, 18-13–18-14
Deferred tax schedules, depreciation (relationship), *18-13*
Deficit, definition, 16-2
Defined benefit pension plan
    accounting
        demonstration, 19-19–19-32
        international dimension, 19-33–19-34
    disclosures, 19-13
    information, disclosure (example), 19-26–19-27
Defined benefit plan, 19-3
    company accounting process, 19-7
    funded status, 19-11–19-13
Defined contribution plan, 19-3
    accounting, 19-5–19-6
    example, 19-6
    disclosure, example, *19-6*
Deloitte & Touche LLP report, 1-32
Depletion, 4-18, 11-1
    definition, 11-2, 11-31
    recording process, 11-31–11-33
        examples, 11-32–11-33
    unit depletion rate, calculation, 11-32
Deposits
    deposits in transit, 6-36
    refundable deposits, 9-12–9-13
Depreciable assets, disclosure
    example, *11-18*
    process, 11-18
Depreciable assets, sale, 21-33
Depreciable cost, 3-20
    depreciation base, 11-4–11-5
Depreciation, 4-18, 11-1, 20-14
    accumulated depreciation, 3-20
    alternative methods, effect, *22-14*
    base (depreciable cost), 11-4–11-5
    calculation, income tax purposes, 11-33–11-36
    changes/corrections, 11-21–11-22
    component depreciation, 11-17
    composite depreciation, 11-14, 11-16
    deferred tax schedules, relationship, *18-13*
    definition, 11-2
    effect, *11-11*

expense, 3-20
    calculation, 11-7, 11-30
    example, 3-20
    journal entry, 11-9
    factors, 11-2–11-4
    group depreciation, 11-14–11-15
    international dimension, 11-16–11-17
    issues, 11-19–11-23
    partial period depreciation, 11-19–11-12
    recording, 11-9
    straight-line depreciation, 3-20
Depreciation methods
    additional methods, 11-14–11-17
    alternatives, effect, *11-10*
    change, 11-22
    conceptual evaluation, 11-10–11-13
    factors, 11-11–11-13
    financial statement effects, 11-10–11-11
    selection, *11-12*
DEPS. *See* Diluted earnings per share
Derivative financial instruments (derivatives), 4-27, 13-37–13-44
    definition, 13-37
Detachable stock warrants, usage, 14-20–14-21
Detachable warrants, 15-15
    dual rights, 15-36
    usage, 14-23
Development, definition, 12-7
Diluted earnings per share (DEPS), 5-27
    company reporting, timing, 16-26–16-37
    computation, 16-26–16-27
        example, *16-33–16-34*
    convertible security, impact, 16-30
        computation, *16-30–16-31*
    final diluted earnings per share, computation, 16-31
    issues, 16-32–16-33
    reporting, example, *16-33–16-34*
    tentative diluted earnings per share, computation, 16-31, *16-31*
Direct effects, 22-11
Direct financing capital lease, 20-3, 20-24
Direct financing lease, 20-2
    changes, 20-41
    guaranteed residual value/payments, absence (example), 20-26–20-29
    initial direct costs, involvement, 20-31
    lessor, 20-25–20-30
    renewal, 20-41–20-42
    unguaranteed residual value/payments, example, 20-29–20-30
Direct method, 5-37–5-38, 21-10–21-14
    examples, 5-37, 21-13–21-14
    usage, 8-7, 21-39–21-46
Direct write-off method, 6-13, 6-18–6-19
Disaggregated financial information, example, 5-45–5-46
Disclosures, 5-26, 5-27, 11-25, 16-34
    company-wide disclosures, 5-45
Discontinued operation
    continuing operations, income separation, *5-23*
    defining, 5-21
    determination, 5-23
    example, *5-22*
    interim financial statements, 5-49
    operating income/loss, 5-23–5-24
    results, reporting process, 5-21–5-26
Discounting, definition, M-3
Discount period, 6-29
Discount rate, 19-3, 20-13
    usage, 19-10
Discounts
    accounting, example, 13-8–13-9
    amortization, 13-6–13-9

effective interest method, *13-8*
    process, 14-10–14-18
    changes, 21-30
Discover, Sam's Club acceptance, 6-25
Disney, bonds issuance, 14-3
Disposal, 11-1
    accounting process, 11-29–11-31
    example, 11-29–11-30
Dividends, 3-3, 4-31
    accounting process, 16-2–16-3
    accumulated other comprehensive income (AOCI), 16-16
    accumulation, 15-33
    cash dividends, 16-3–16-6
    date of payment, 16-4, 16-5
    date of record, 16-4
    declaration date, 16-4
    declaration/payment, example, 16-5
    distribution, *16-6*
        financial status, 16-3
        legal requirements, 16-3
        requirements, 16-3
    ex-dividend date, 16-4
    income, recording
        available-for-sale securities, 13-14–13-15
        trading securities, 13-11–13-12
    liquidation, 16-12
    preferred stock, preference, 15-33, 15-34
    property dividends, 16-7–16-8
    scrip dividends, 16-8
    stock dividends, 16-9–16-12
    stock splits, 16-12
    types, 16-3–16-13
    yield, importance, 16-24
Dividends payable, 9-12, 21-21
    accounts, liability, 16-11
Dollar-value LIFO
    application, 7-31–7-33
    data, *7-32*
    example, *7-32*
    inventory calculations, *7-32*
    method, 7-30–7-33
    retail inventory method, 8-23
    retail method, 8-21
Dollar-value retail method, 8-21–8-23
    examples, 8-21–8-23
Domestic corporations, 15-4
Donated asset, GAAP requirements, 10-10–10-11
Double-declining-balance
    partial period depreciation, *11-20*
Double-declining-balance method, 11-6–11-7
Double-entry accounting, 3-1
    system, 3-6
Double-entry system, accounting equation (relationship), *3-6*
Double-extension method, 7-30–7-31
Dual rights, 15-36
Dun & Bradstreet, 4-33

E

Earned capital, 4-7, 4-23–4-24
    accounts, 1-25
Earnings
    ethical dilemma, example, 7-25
    importance, 5-1
    management, 5-42–5-43, 7-24–7-25
        example, 7-25
        LIFO, usage, *7-25*
    quality, 5-42
Earnings per common share (basic earnings per share), 16-2
Earnings per share (EPS), 16-1, 16-20

components, 16-24–16-26
computation
    flowchart, *16-27*
    international dimension, 16-36–16-37
    process, 5-26–5-28, 16-20–16-26
considerations, 16-34
contingent issuances, 16-34
conversion ratios, 16-34
denominator calculations, 16-21–16-24
diluted earnings per share, 5-27
    company reporting, timing, 16-27–16-37
disclosures, 16-34
    example, 16-35, *16-35*
importance, 16-24
interim financial statements, 5-50
numerator calculations, 16-21
reporting process, 5-26–5-28
weighted average shares, 16-22
Economic factors, impact (assessment), 5-3
Economic resource, characteristics, 4-4–4-5
EDGAR. *See* Electronic Data Gathering Analysis and Retrieval System
Effective interest method (interest method), 13-7
    example, *13-7*
    usage, 14-10–14-11
        example, 14-10–14-11
Effective interest rate, 9-10
Effective rate (yield), 14-4–14-5
Effective tax rate, 18-1, 18-17
Efficiency ratios (operating capability ratios) (activity ratios), 4-41–4-44
Efforts-expended method, 17-23
EFT. *See* Electronic funds transfer
EITF. *See* Emerging Issues Task Force
Electronic Data Gathering Analysis and Retrieval System (EDGAR), 1-10
Electronic funds transfer (EFT), 6-6
Electronic payments, 6-6–6-7
Emerging Issues Task Force (EITF), 1-11
Employee Retirement Income Security Act of 1974 (ERISA), 19-37, 19-39
Employees
    discounts, 8-20
    payments, 21-11
    service, pension plan amount (attribution), 19-36–19-37
    withholdings, payroll taxes (relationship), 9-16–9-17
Employee stock purchase plan (ESPP), 15-17
Encore Capital Group, cash settled convertible bonds, *14-26*
Ending inventory, error (example), 22-23–22-24
Enhancing characteristics, 2-14–2-16
    comparability, 2-15
    timeliness, 2-15
    verifiability, 2-15
Enron, financial statement misrepresentation, 1-32
Entry recording, process, 3-9–3-12
EPBO. *See* Expected postretirement benefit obligation
Equipment
    exchange, example, 13-33–13-34
    leased equipment, change, 21-30
    lease, involvement, 20-41
    leasing, example, 20-15–20-17
    term, usage, 10-6–10-7
Equitable and constructive liabilities, 9-3
Equity
    accounts, changes, 15-3
    characteristics, 14-20–14-28
    debt financing, cost of capital (comparison), 14-2
    debt-to-equity ratio, 4-39
    defining, 4-6–4-7

exchange, 14-38–14-39
    combination, modification of terms (usage), 14-39, 14-41
    example, 14-39
securities, 13-2
    categorization, 13-4
    investments, FASB requirements, 13-18
shareholder's equity, 1-24–1-25, 4-6–4-7, 4-21–4-22
Equity method
    application/usage, 13-23, 13-24
    change, 13-27
        example, journal entries (usage), *13-28*
    example, 13-24–13-25
    investments, 13-4, 21-37
        company disclosures, 13-30
Errors
    accounting, 22-1
    analysis, 22-19–22-21
        framework, 22-21
    classification, 22-20
    correction, 11-22, 22-21–22-25
        accounting process, 22-15–22-25
        framework, 22-21
        summary, example, *22-25*
    counterbalancing errors, 22-20
    definition, 22-3
    noncounterbalancing errors, 22-20
ESPP. *See* Employee stock purchase plan
Estimated bad debts, accrual failure (example), 22-24–22-25
Estimates, 3-15, 22-12–22-13
    accounting estimates, 3-19–3-21
    adjusting entries, effects, *3-20*
    change, 11-21–11-22
Ethical dilemmas, 1-34
Events, 3-5
    subsequent events, 4-29–4-31
Ex-dividend date, 16-4
Executory contracts, 4-6
Executory costs, *20-7*, 20-13
Exercise price (strike price), 15-14
Expected cash flows, impairment (relationship), *13-36*
Expected postretirement benefit obligation (EPBO), 19-42
Expected returns
    actual returns, differences, 19-23–19-25
    assessment, external users (information usage), 2-8
Expected value approach, 17-16
Expenditures. *See* Pre-acquisition expenditures
Expenses, 5-10–5-11
    accretion expense, 10-9
    calculation, *17-33–17-34*
    cause/effect, association, 5-10
    defining, 3-4
    expenditure, *5-11*
    immediate recognition, 5-11
    noncash expenses, 21-27
    operating expenses, 5-16
    recognition, 5-10
    systematic/rational allocation, 5-10
Exploration costs, definition, 11-32
External decision making, information sources (usage), *2-23*
ExxonMobil Corporation
    income reduction, 7-23
    stock repurchase, 15-1

F

Facebook, Internet domain name, 12-14
Face rate (contract rate/stated rate/nominal rate), 14-3

Face value (par value)
    multiplication, 14-8
    price, 14-6–14-7
Face value (par value), definition, 14-3
Facilities, rearrangement costs, 10-26
Factoring, 6-20, 6-23
    agreement, example, *6-23*
FAF. *See* Financial Accounting Foundation
Fair value, 4-10–4-12, 15-19
    determination, inputs (distinction), 4-11
    disclosures, 4-12
    examples, 4-11–4-12
    financial instruments risk, relationship, 4-27
    gains/losses, examples, 13-40, 13-41–13-42
    measurement process, 4-10–4-11
    option, 4-10, 13-5, 14-17–14-18
        value, calculation, 15-20
    reporting, 6-30
Fair value hedge, 13-38–13-42
    example, *13-39*
    GAAP requirements, 13-39
    interest-rate swap, equivalence (example), 13-39–13-40
Fair value through other comprehensive income (FVOCI), 13-26
Fair value through profit and loss (FVPL), 13-26
Faithful representation, 2-13–2-14
    relevance, relationship, 2-14
FASB. *See* Financial Accounting Standards Board
Federal Deposit Insurance Corporation (FDIC), public corporation status, 15-4
Federal hospital insurance benefits, 9-16
Federal Insurance Contribution Act (F.I.C.A.) taxes, 9-16
Federal National Mortgage Association (FNMA) (**Fannie Mae**)
    restatement (2004), 22-16
    results restatement, 13-38
Federal Unemployment Tax Act (F.U.T.A.), 9-17
F.I.C.A. *See* Federal Insurance Contribution Act
Fidelity Investments (asset management company), 19-2
FIFO. *See* First-in, first-out
Final diluted earnings per share, computation, 16-31
Financial Accounting and Reporting, conceptual framework projects, *2-5*
Financial Accounting Foundation (FAF), 1-11
Financial accounting information
    demand, 1-3
    necessity, reasons, 1-4–1-8
    supply, 1-3, 1-9–1-10
Financial Accounting Standards Board (FASB), 1-10, 1-11–1-12
    accounting standards codification, 1-12–1-17
        web page, *1-14*
    accounting standards, IASB accounting standards (convergence), 1-18–1-19
    codification, 1-13–1-16
        levels, 1-14–1-15
        search process, example, *1-17*
        topics, hierarchical relationships, 1-15
        usage, 1-15–1-16
    conceptual framework, 2-2–2-6
        standard-setting process, relationship, 2-4
    Emerging Issues Task Force (EITF), 1-11
    operating procedures, 1-16, 1-16–1-17
    process, 1-16–1-17
    pronouncements, 1-12–1-13
        historical types, 1-13
    Statement of Financial Accounting (SFA) Concepts No. 5, 16-15

Statement of Financial Accounting (SFA) Concepts No. 6, 4-25, 15-2, 18-7
    structure, 1-11, *1-12*
Financial analysis, flowchart, *4-32*
Financial assets (monetary assets), 4-5
    transfer, recording (GAAP requirements), 6-20, 6-32
Financial components approach, 6-25
Financial data, 4-31
Financial flexibility, 6-2, 16-3
    defining, 9-5
    implications, 9-32
    indication, 13-4
    ratios, risk (relationship), 4-38
Financial instruments
    definition, 13-37
    fair value option, 4-10
    risk, fair value (relationship), 4-27
Financial leverage, 4-39, 14-1
    opportunity, 14-3
Financial performance, assessment, 5-3
Financial position
    changes, 4-3
    measurement, balance sheet (usage), 1-22–1-25
    report, 4-2
    statement of financial position, 1-22
Financial reporting, 1-6
    conceptual framework, 2-1
        projects, *2-5*
    decision making, information (usage), 2-8–2-9
    defining, 1-21–1-32
    determination, differences (causes), *18-3*
    economic consequences, 1-33–1-35
    liability, derecognizing, 14-18
    model, defining, 2-22–2-23
    objectives, 2-6–2-11, *2-7*
    present value techniques, usage, M-27–M-28
    SEC authority, 1-10
Financial restatements, number, 22-2
Financial statements, 1-21–1-32, 3-7–3-8
    accounting principle change, effects disclosure (impact), *22-9–22-10*
    adjustment, 22-6, 22-7
    analysis ratios, 4-35
    articulation, *4-3*
    comparative financial statements, 4-31–4-32
    contingencies, presentation process, 9-32–9-34
    current liabilities, presentation process, 9-32–9-34
    disclosures, 18-31
    effect, 8-25, 11-10–11-11
    income tax items, presentation/disclosure process, 18-30–18-34
    independent auditors' attestations, 1-32
    information, importance, 1-30–1-32
    inventory, company reporting process, 7-5
    investment disclosure process, 13-29–13-33
    management discussion and analysis (MD&A), 1-30
    managers' attestations, 1-32
    notes, 1-30
    preparation
        process, 3-23–3-27
        worksheet, usage process, 3-29–3-31
    reporting, 9-4, *17-31–17-323*
    results, report, 8-4
    retrospective adjustment, 22-7
    users, statement of cash flows information (impact), 21-6–21-7
Financial tax depreciation schedule, *18-12*

Financial Times, The (earnings release coverage), 5-1
Financing activities, 1-4, 21-4, 21-6
    adjustment, 21-21
    cash flows, *5-35*
    company financing activities, 5-35
    components, 5-35
    definition, 21-4
    items, 5-17
    performance measurement/reporting, 1-27
    spreadsheet entries, 21-27
    statement of cash flows, 1-28
Financing arrangements, forms, 6-20
Finished goods, 4-16
    inventory, 7-3
First-in, first-out (FIFO), 7-14, 7-16–7-18
    cost flow
        assumption (periodic inventory system), *7-17*
        assumption (perpetual inventory system), *7-17*
        relationships, *7-16*
    examples, 7-16, 7-17
    LIFO change, 22-8
    ratio, 8-16
    usage, 8-3
Fixed assets, 4-17–4-18, 10-3
    turnover, 4-44
Fixed compensatory share option plan, example, *15-22*
Fixed share option plan, example, 15-21–15-22
Floor, conceptual evaluation, 8-5–8-6
Flow of inventory costs, 7-3, *7-4*
FOB. *See* Free-on-board (FOB)
Ford Motor Company
    inventory, inclusion, 7-2
    land purchase, 10-5
    lease classification, 20-23–20-24
    operating losses/operating loss carryforwards, 18-19–18-20
Ford Motor Credit Company (Ford Credit), accounts receivable financing, 6-20
Foreign corporations, 15-4
Foreign currency exchange rates, changes, 21-39
Form 8-K, 1-10
Form 10-K, 1-10
Form 10-Q, 1-10
Form 20-F, 1-10, 1-19
401k plans, 19-6
Fractional shares, 16-12
Franchises, definition, 12-15
Free-on-board (FOB)
    destination, 7-9
    shipping point, 7-9, 9-8
Freight charges, 8-19
Full-cost method, 10-27
Fully participating preferred stock, 15-35
Funded status, definition, 19-11
Funds
    investments, 13-36–13-37
    long-term funds, accounting, 13-37
    plant expansion funds, 13-36
    sinking funds, 6-3, 13-36
    stock redemption funds, 13-36
F.U.T.A. *See* Federal Unemployment Tax Act
Future deductible amount, 18-18, 18-21
Future event occurrence (likelihood), company categorization (GAAP requirement), 9-23
Future income, prediction, 5-3
Future payments (deferred payments), 10-9–10-10
Future taxable amounts, 18-6, 18-11
    difference, 18-18
Future tax deductible amounts, 18-6

Future value
    calculations, summary', M-26, *M-27*
    company usage, M-3
    factors, table, *M-7*
    ordinary annuity computation process, M-12–M-15
    single sum computation process, M-5–M-9
FVOCI. *See* Fair value through other comprehensive income
FVPL. *See* Fair value through profit and loss

G

Gain contingencies, 9-31
Gain/loss. *See* Pension plans
Gain/loss on sale, 5-24–5-25
Gains, 5-11–5-12
    contingencies, 4-27–4-29
    defining, 3-4
    nonrecurring gains/losses, 5-17–5-18
    trading, 13-18
    unusual gains/losses, 5-17–5-18
General Electric
    bonds issuance, 14-3
    effective tax rates, reduction, 18-1
    long-term construction contracts, 17-26
General Electric Capital Services (GECS), accounts receivable financing, 6-20
General journal entries
    example, *3-11–3-12*
    recording process, 3-9–3-12
General ledger
    example, *3-13*
    posting process, 3-13–3-14
Generally accepted accounting principles (GAAP), 1-8
    authority, 1-12
    balance sheet classification/presentation, differences, 4-45–4-47
    basis/objectives, 2-3
    codification search process, example, *1-15*
    IFRS, reporting income similarities/differences, 5-30–5-34
    requirement, 8-2
    sources, 1-11
    three-tiered hierarchy, 4-11
    usage, 10-18
General Mills
    current liabilities, disclosure, *9-33–9-34*
    inventory disclosure, 7-35
    inventory values/methods, disclosures (example), *7-35–7-36*
    price/earnings ratio, 16-24
GlaxoSmithKline, R&D expenditures, 12-8–12-9
Global Crossing, financial statement misrepresentation, 1-32
Goldman Sachs, 5-2
Goods
    consigned goods, 7-9
    exchange, 14-31–14-32
    physical flow, 7-28
    transit, 7-9
Goods-in-process inventory (work-in-process inventory), 7-3
Goodwill, 4-19
    definition, 12-7
    impairment, 12-20–12-22
        example, 12-21–12-22
        indications, 12-21
    internally developed goodwill, 12-19
    purchased goodwill, 12-19–12-20
    purchase, example, 12-20
Google, Inc.
    corporation identification, 1-9

    cumulative foreign earnings, 18-2
    discontinued operations, 5-22
    earnings per share disclosure, 5-27
    fair value example, 4-11–4-12
    intangible assets, 12-2
        increase, 12-1
    operation, tax laws/rates, 18-1
    purchased customer relationships, assets (net value), 12-15
    R&D disclosure, 12-8
Grant date, 15-18
Gross price method, 6-10
    application, *8-13*
    conceptual evaluation, 7-14
    evaluation, 8-13–8-14
    examples, 6-10–6-11, *6-11*, *8-13*
    usage, 7-13, 8-12–8-14
        situations, 8-12
Gross profit margin, 5-38
Gross profit recognition, revenue recognition, *17-28*
Gross receivable, definition, 20-25
Gross sales revenues (gross revenues), 5-15
Group depreciation, 11-14–11-15
    example, 11-14
    journal entries, *11-15*
Group methods (composite methods), 11-4
Guaranteed residual value, 20-34
    example, *20-8*
    impact, 20-20–20-21
Guarantees, 14-32–14-33

H

Hedge
    cash flow hedge, 13-42–13-44
    definition, 13-38
    fair value hedge, 13-38–13-42
Held for sale, 5-24
Held-to-maturity category, transfer, 13-19
    examples, 3-20, 13-21
Held-to-maturity investment, sale (prior to maturity), 13-9–13-10
Held-to-maturity securities, 13-3
    bond premiums/discounts, amortization, 13-6–13-9
    company disclosure, 13-30
    company reporting, 13-4
    impairments, 13-21–13-22
    initial cost, recording, 13-6
    interest income, recognition, 13-6–13-9
    investments, measurement/reporting process, 13-6–13-10
    long-term investment, 21-36
Historical cost (acquisition cost), 4-8–4-9, 10-3
    examples, 4-8–4-9
Historical values
    current values, combination, 4-8
    reflection, 4-8
Holding gains, alternative cost flow assumptions (relationship), 7-23
Home Depot, retail inventory method (usage), 8-14
Honeywell
    corridor, expenses, 19-10
    pension disclosures, *19-14–19-18*
HSBC, scrip dividend programs, 16-8
Hyatt Hotels, sale-leaseback transactions, 20-35–20-36

I

Identifiable intangible assets, 12-3, 12-13–12-18
    categories, 12-13
If-converted method, usage, 16-29–16-30

IFRS. *See* International Financial Reporting Standards
Immediate recognition, 5-11
Impairments, 11-1. *See also* Assets
    accounting
        concerns, 11-27
        flowchart, *11-27*
        process. *See* Property, plant, and equipment.
    available-for-sale securities, 13-21–13-22
    current expected credit losses (CECL) impairment model, FASB consideration, 13-22
    defining, 12-4
    existence, examples, 12-21
    expected cash flows, relationship, *13-35*
    goodwill, 12-20–12-22
    held-to-maturity securities, 13-21–13-22
    intangible assets, 12-4–12-6
    investments (accounting process), 13-19–13-22
    losses (Radio Shack), 11-2
    loss, example, 11-25
    other than temporary impairment, 13-21
    quantitative impairment test, 12-21
    test, *11-25*
Implicit interest rate, *20-8*, 20-13
Improvements (betterments), 10-25
Imputed interest rate, 14-29
Income
    components, understanding, 5-3
    comprehensive income, performance measurement/reporting, 1-27
    continuing operations source, 5-19
    defining, 5-4–5-5
    interim income taxes, computation, *5-49*
    measurement, 7-22–7-30
    net income, performance measurement/reporting, 1-27
    other comprehensive income (OCI), 3-3, 13-43
    pretax income, 5-18
    reinvested income, 16-2
    reporting formats, 5-13–5-15
    reporting, GAAP/IFRS similarities/differences, 5-30–5-34
    summary, 3-27–3-28
Income from continuing operations, corporation report, 16-32
Income statement, 1-25–1-27, 4-2
    amounts, conversion (adjustments), *21-12*
    comparative income statements (revision), FIFO (usage), *22-8*
    components, 5-12–5-21
    comprehensive income, 1-27
    discontinued operations results, reporting process, 5-21–5-26
    elements, 5-6–5-12
    errors, impact, 22-19–22-21
    examples, *3-24*, *3-37*, *18-29*
    financial statement effect, 8-25
    financing activities, 1-27
    information analysis process, 5-38–5-43
    investing activities, 1-27
    multiple-step income statement, *5-14*
    net income, 1-27
    operating activities, 1-25, 1-27
    purposes, 5-2–5-4
    reporting, GAAP (usage), 18-2
    single-step income statement, *5-13*
    summarization, 3-7
    usage, 3-24–3-25
Income taxes, 9-21–9-22
    accounting, 18-1
        issues, 18-3–18-4

calculation, adjustments, *21-35*
depreciation schedule, *18-12*
disclosure, 18-31
effects, 7-23
expense, 5-18–5-19
    schedule, *18-28*
expense, financial reporting determination differences (causes), 18-3
global tax strategy, 18-1
interim financial statements, 5-48–5-49
interperiod income tax allocation, issues, 18-4–18-8
items, presentation/disclosure process, 18-30–18-34
laws/rates, changes, 18-15–18-16
operating loss carrybacks/carryforwards, 18-3
payable/receivable, *18-24*
payment, 21-11, 21-34–21-35
    tax reporting differences, causes, *18-3*
permanent differences, 18-3
rate, 18-7–18-8
temporary differences, 18-1, 18-3
Incremental borrowing rate, *20-8*, 20-13
Incremental costs, 17-24
Incremental funds, actual interest (capitalization), 10-17
Incremental interest rate, usage, 13-33
Incremental overhead, inclusion, 10-16–10-17
Incurred (liability characteristic), 4-6
Independent auditors, attestations, 1-32
Independent audits, 1-8
    demand, factors, 1-7–1-8
Indirect effects, 22-11
Indirect method, 5-35, 21-14–21-15
    example, 21-15
Individual Retirement Accounts (IRAs), 19-6
Induced conversions, 14-23–14-24
    example, 14-24
Information
    analysis process, 5-38–5-43
    asymmetry problems, 1-7
    condensed financial information, example, *21-19*, *21-24–21-26*
    disclosure, 22-6
    enhancing characteristics, 2-14–2-16
    qualitative characteristics, 2-11, *2-12*
    reporting, 5-45–5-46
    selection, example, *22-6–22-7*
    sources, usage, *2-23*
    usefulness, 2-9–2-11
Initial cost
    available-for sale securities, recording, 13-14
    held-to-maturity securities, recording, 13-6
    trading securities, recording, 13-11
Initial direct costs, *20-8*
    involvement, 20-31, 20-34
Initial indirect costs, involvement, 20-25
In-process R&D (IPR&D), 12-10
Input methods, 17-23
Intangible assets, 4-5, 4-18–4-19
    accounting, *12-4*
        process, 12-3–12-7
    amortization, 12-4–12-7
    artistic-related intangible assets, 12-15
    classification, *12-4*
    company review, GAAP requirement, 12-5
    contract-based intangible assets, 12-15
    customer-related intangible assets, 12-14–12-15
    disclosure
        example, *12-11–12-13*
        process, 12-11–12-13
    finite life, 12-4–12-6
    finite useful lives, 4-18

growth, World Bank estimate, 12-1
identifiable intangible assets, 12-3, 12-13–12-18
impairment, 12-4–12-7
increase (Google), 12-1
indefinite life, 12-6–12-7
    impairment test, 12-6
indefinite useful lives, 4-18–4-19
initial valuation, 12-3–12-4
internally developed intangible assets, expensing, 12-3
international dimension, 12-22–12-24
marketing-related intangible assets, 12-14
market value, relationship (Accenture study), 12-1
physical/financial nature, absence, 12-2
purchased intangible assets, capitalization, 12-3
technology-based intangible assets, 12-16–12-18
unidentifiable intangible assets, 12-3
useful life, estimation, 12-5
value, 12-1
Intangible development costs, definition, 11-32
Intel
    effective tax rates, reduction, 18-1
    land purchase, 10-5
Intercompany comparisons, 4-32–4-33
Interest
    avoidable interest
        capitalization, 10-19
        computation, 10-19
    capitalized interest, construction loan (example), 10-20
    computation, example, *14-10*
    cost, 19-7–19-8, 19-43
        calculation, 19-8
        GAAP perspective, 10-17
    expense
        computation, 14-10
        schedule, *14-37*
        summary, *20-17*
    income
        effective interest method, *13-7*
    income, recognition, 13-6–13-9
    method (effective interest method), 13-7
    payment, 21-11, 21-34
        calculation, adjustments, *21-35*
    payment dates, bonds issuance, 14-8–14-9
        example, *14-9*
    recording
        available-for-sale securities, 13-14–13-15
        trading securities, 13-11–13-12
    representation, M-3
    revenue earned, summary, *20-28*, *20-30*
    schedules, effective interest method, 14-12
Interest-bearing note, 9-8–9-9
Interest-bearing notes payable, 9-8
Interest capitalization, 10-17
    amount, determination, 10-18
    asset qualification, 10-18
    avoidance, 10-17
    GAAP, usage, 10-18
    impact, 10-22–10-23
    period, defining, 10-18
    procedures, 10-19–10-21
Interest coverage ratio, 5-41
Interest rate
    determination, 10-19, *M-8*, *M-11*
    implicit interest rate, *20-8*, 20-13
    imputed interest rate, 14-29
    unstated interest rate, finding (example), M-8, M-10–M-11
Interest rate per period, defining, M-6

Interest-rate swap
    definition, 13-38
    example, *13-39*, *13-43*
    fair value hedge, equivalence (example), 13-39–13-40
    payment, example, 13-42
Interim financial reports, 5-47–5-50
Interim financial statements, 5-47
    accounting changes, 22-12
    example, 5-49
Interim income taxes, computation, *5-49*
Interim reporting, 5-43
Interim statements
    LIFO usage, 7-35
    quarterly statements, 3-7
Internal control systems, 6-5
Internally developed goodwill, 12-19
Internally developed intangible assets, 12-3, 12-4
    expensing, 12-3
Internal Revenue Code (IRC), taxable income determination, 18-3
International Accounting Standards Board (IASB), 1-10, 1-17–1-21
    accounting standards, FASB accounting standards (convergence), 1-18–1-19
International convergence, 1-18–1-19
    problems, 1-20
International Financial Reporting Standards (IFRS), 1-8, 1-17–1-21
    balance sheet classification/presentation, differences, 4-45–4-47
    GAAP, reporting income similarities/differences, 5-30–5-34
    three-tiered hierarchy, 4-11
Internet domain name, usage, 12-14
Interperiod income tax allocation
    conceptual issues, 18-6–18-8
    current/deferred taxes, recording/reporting process, 18-9–18-16
    issues, 18-4–18-8
Interperiod tax allocation, 5-18
Intracompany comparisons, 4-32–4-33
Intraperiod income tax allocation
    example, 18-27–18-28
    impact, process, 18-27–18-29
Intraperiod tax allocation, 5-18–5-19
    example, *5-19*
Intrinsic value, 15-18–15-19
    method, 15-18
Inventories, 4-16–4-17
    accounting, 7-29
    alternative systems, journal entries, *7-8*
    company classification, 7-3–7-6
    company tracking process, 7-6–7-9
    cost, example, 8-4
    cost flow assumptions
        alternatives, consequences, 7-22–7-30
        comparison, 7-21–7-22
        effects, *7-21*
        management selection considerations, 7-26–7-30
        usage, *7-26*
    cost measurement, 7-1
    costs
        company determination process, 7-12–7-14
        flow, 7-3, *7-4*
    defining, 7-2
    determination, *7-11*
    disclosure, 7-35
    ending inventory, error (example), 22-23–22-24
    errors, effects, 8-24–8-25
        example, *8-24*

estimation process
    gross profit method, usage, 8-12–8-14
    retail inventory method, usage, 8-14–8-21
financial statements, company reporting process, 7-5
finished goods inventory, 7-3
flow assumptions, 7-1
flow of inventory costs, 7-3, *7-4*
inflows/outflows, example, *7-15*
inventory to market, reduction (recording), *8-26*
management/control, importance, 7-7
methods
    alternatives, relative use, *7-33*
    company disclosure process, 7-33–7-36
periodic inventory system, 3-21, 7-6–7-7
    comparison, 7-8
perpetual inventory system, 3-9, 7-6
    comparison, 7-8
pools, 7-31
purchases, error (example), 22-24
quantities, company determination process, 7-9–7-12
raw materials inventory, 7-3
reduction, recording, 8-7–8-8
reporting, 7-29
shrinkage, 8-20
specific identification inventory cost assumption, 7-15–7-16
spoilage, 8-20
turnover, 42
    financial ratio usage, 7-34
    ratio, 4-442
valuation, 7-26
    issues, 8-1
valuation above cost, process, 8-11
values, company disclosure process, 7-33–7-36
work in process inventories, 4-16
work-in-process inventory (goods-in-process inventory), 7-3
Investing activities, 1-4, 21-6
    adjustment, 21-21
    cash flows, *5-35*
    company investing activities, 5-34–5-35
    components, 5-35
    definition, 21-3–21-4
    items, 5-17
    performance measurement/reporting, 1-27
    spreadsheet entries, 21-27
    Starbuck's, 1-24
    statement of cash flows, 1-28
InvestinginBonds.com, bond price, 14-6
Investments, 13-1
    accounting, 13-33–13-37
        example, *13-5*
        international dimension, 13-26
    classification process, 13-3–13-5
    consolidated financial statements, 13-28–13-29
    equity method, change, 13-27
        example, *13-28*
    equity method investments, 13-4
    financial statement disclosure process, 13-29–13-33
    impairments
        accounting process, 13-19–13-22
        determination, 13-21
        expected cash flows, relationship, *13-35*
    income, investor adjustments, 13-24
    interest income, effective interest method (examples), *13-7*, *13-8*

investments between categories, transfers, 13-19–13-21
    issues, 13-27–13-29
    life insurance, cash surrender value, 13-36
    loans
        fees/origination costs, 13-34
        impairment, 13-34–13-36
    long-term investments, 4-17, 21-35–21-37
    majority active investment, 13-4
    marketable securities, 4-16
    minority active investment, 13-4
    minority passive investment, 13-3
    other than temporary impairments, 13-27
    reporting process, 13-3–13-5
    securities (bonds) distribution, 16-7–16-8
    short-term investments, 4-16, 21-35–21-37
    transfers, accounting process, 13-19–13-22
Investment securities, 13-2
Investors, 1-5–1-6
    information, usage, 2-9–2-11
IPR&D. *See* In-process R&D
Issued capital stock, 15-7, 15-16
Issuer, yield, 14-6
Items
    classification/reporting process. *See* Balance sheet.
    financing/investing activities, 5-17
    prepaid items, 4-17

J
JetBlue Airways, historical cost example, 4-9
John Deere, lease classification, 20-23–20-24
Johnson and Johnson, R&D expenditures, 12-8–12-9
Journal entry, 3-9
    alternative inventory systems usage, *7-8*
    bank usage, 6-37
    information, posting, 3-13
    preparation, 22-5–22-6

K
Kimberly-Clark Corporation, long-term liabilities (example), *4-20–4-21*
Kimpton Hotels, fair value example, *4-12*
Kraft
    legal dispute settlement, 9-2
    Starbucks distribution agreement termination, *4-30–4-31*, 5-16
Kroger, agreements, 7-2

L
Land
    building, combination (leases), 20-39–20-40
    changes, 21-28–21-29
    improvements, 10-6
    leases, 20-39
    recorded cost, 10-5
    value, 20-40–20-41
Last-in, first-out (LIFO), 7-14, 7-19–7-21
    bookkeeping, costs, 7-28
    change, 22-8
    conceptual issues, 7-28
    conformity rule, 7-23
    contracting considerations, 7-28
    cost flow assumption (periodic inventory system), *7-20*
    cost flow assumption (perpetual inventory system), *7-20*
    cost flow relationships, 7-19
    dollar-value LIFO method, 7-30–7-33
    examples, 7-19–7-20
    goods, physical flow, 7-28

    importance, 7-34–7-35
    layers, liquidation, 7-24
    liquidation, 7-30
        profit, 7-24
    ratio, 8-16
    record keeping, 7-30
    reserve, 7-34
    stock price effects, 7-28
    tax considerations, 7-28
    technological change, 7-30
    usage, 7-35, 8-3
    valuation allowance, 7-34
LCM. *See* Lower of cost or market
Leased asset
    amortization, 20-14
    estimated economic life, *20-7*
    estimated residual value, *20-7*
    fair value, *20-7*
Leased equipment, change, 21-30
Leased property, lessee depreciation, 20-14
Leasehold improvements, 4-18, 10-9
Leases
    accounting, 20-1
        future, 20-9–20-11
        international dimension, 20-4
        process, 20-11–20-21
    agreement, terms/provision (examples), *20-11, 20-15, 20-26, 20-29, 20-32, 20-36*
    capitalization criteria, *20-3*
        application, *20-32*
    capital lease
        accounting, capitalization criteria, 20-2
        definition, 20-2
    cash flows
        lessee presentation process, 20-22–20-23
        lessor presentation process, 20-34–20-35
    classification, 20-10
        application, examples, *20-15, 20-27*
        process, 20-2–20-3
        real property, involvement, *20-38–20-39*
    definition, 20-10
    disclosure requirements, 20-22
    gross investment, *20-8*
    implicit interest rate, *20-8*
    inception, *20-8*
    interest expense, summary, *20-17, 20-18*
    lessee disclosure process, 20-22–20-23
    lessor accounting/reporting process, 20-23–20-34
    lessor disclosure process, 20-34–20-35
    minimum lease payments, *20-8*
        components, 20-2
    obligation
        example, *20-23*
        reduction, 20-14–20-17
    operating lease, 20-2, 20-3
    payments
        example, 20-18–20-19
        summary, *20-17, 20-18, 20-28, 20-30*
    provisions, changes, 20-35–20-42
    real estate leases, 20-38–20-41
    receivable, *20-8*
    renewal, impact, 20-41
    reporting process, 20-11–20-21
    specialized issues, 20-35–20-42
    term, *20-8*
    transaction, initial direct costs (GAAP analysis), 20-31
Leasing
    advantages, 20-4–20-8
    buying, contrast (example), 20-6–20-7

financial reporting issues, 20-5
financing issues, 20-5
lessee advantages/disadvantages, 20-5–20-7
risk reduction issues, 20-5
strategic issues, 20-5
tax issues, 20-5
terms, *20-7–20-8*
understanding, 20-7–20-8
Legal capital, 15-7–15-9
Legal liabilities, 9-3, 9-13
LEGO Group, The (closed corporation status), 15-4
Lenders, information (usage), 2-9–2-11
Lessee
    accounting, 20-39–20-40
        example, *20-10–20-11*
    capitalization issues, 20-20–20-21
    classification criteria, application, *20-12*
    contingent rental payments, 20-12
    definition, 20-2
    disclosure requirements (operating leases/capital leases), *20-22*
    guaranteed residual value, impact, 20-20–20-21
    incremental borrowing rate, *20-8*
    lease accounting/reporting process, 20-11/20-21
    lease capitalization criteria, *20-3*
    lease cash flows, presentation process, 20-22–20-23
    lease disclosure process, 20-22–20-23
    leasing advantages/disadvantages, 20-5–20-7
    statement of cash flows presentation, 20-22
Lessor
    accounting, 20-40
        example, *20-11*
    definition, 20-2
    disclosure requirements, 20-35, *20-35*
    lease cash flows presentation process, 20-34–20-35
    lease disclosure process, 20-34–20-35
    leasing advantages/disadvantages, 20-7
    operating lease accounting, 20-24–20-25
    statement of cash flow presentation, 20-34–20-35
Leverage, 4-39, 14-1
    financial leverage, 4-39, 14-1
    operating profitability/leverage, multiplication, 5-42
Liabilities, 1-24, 4-5–4-6
    book value, deferred tax asset (relationship), *18-14*
    characteristics, 4-6
    classification, conceptual guidelines, 4-21
    compensation, relationship, 9-15–9-21
    current liabilities, 3-25, 4-19
    decrease, 21-8
    defining, 3-3, 9-3–9-4
    extinguishment, accounting process, 14-18–14-20
    financing, 14-1
        international dimension, 14-27
    homogeneous classes, development guidelines, 4-21
    identification, 9-4
    increase, 21-8
    long-term liabilities, 4-20–4-21
    noncurrent liabilities, 3-25
    other liabilities, 4-20
Licensed store revenues, 17-12–17-13
Licensees, 1-22
Licensing, 17-12–17-13
    examples, 17-13
Lien, 9-13

Life expectancy, increase, 19-2
Life insurance, cash surrender value, 13-36
LIFO. *See* Last-in, first-out
Limited legal liability, 15-4
Line of credit, establishment, 6-25
Link-chain method, 7-31
Liquidation, preference, 15-38
Liquidity, 4-39–4-41
    characteristics, 9-32
    defining, 6-2, 9-5
    importance, 9-5–9-6
Litigation, 9-26
Loans
    defeasance, 14-20
    fees/origination costs, 13-34
    impairment, 13-34
        example, 13-35–13-36
    interest payment, example, 13-40, 13-41
    origination fees (commitment fees), 13-34
London Interbank Offered Rate (LIBOR) rate, setting, 13-40
Long-term accruals, 4-20
Long-term assets (retirement), funds (usage), 13-36
Long-term contracts, 17-26–17-27
    accounting methods, 17-26, 17-27–17-35
    losses, example, 17-32–17-33
    revenue recognition, examples, 17-27–17-29
Long-term debt
    currently maturing portion, 9-10–9-12
    current maturities, 4-19
    example, *4-20–4-21*
Long-term financing instruments, 4-20
Long-term financing liabilities, company issuance (reasons), 14-2–14-3
Long-term funds, accounting, 13-37
Long-term investments, 4-17, 21-35–21-37
Long-term liabilities, 4-20–4-21
    disclosure, 14-33–14-35
    retirement, funds usage, 13-36
Long-term notes payable, 14-1
    accounting process, 14-28–14-33
    arrangement, economics (GAAP recognition), 14-28
Long-term notes receivable, 13-33–13-36
Long-term receivables, 13-1
Loss contingencies, 4-27–4-29
    defining, 9-22–9-27
    recognition/disclosure, *4-28*
    reporting, *9-24*
Losses, 5-11–5-12
    defining, 3-4
    measurement, 11-24, 12-5
    nonrecurring gains/losses, 5-17–5-18
    recognition, 20-36
    recording/reporting, 11-24
    unusual gains/losses, 5-17–5-18
Loss from continuing operations, corporation report, 16-32
Lower of average cost or market, 8-16
Lower of cost or market (LCM)
    application, 8-4–8-6
        examples, *8-4, 8-5*
        periodic inventory system, 8-25–8-27
    calculations, information, *8-5*
    conceptual evaluation, 8-9–8-10
    implementation, approaches, 8-6, *8-7*
    reporting, 8-8–8-9
    rule, 8-2–8-11
Lump-sum purchase, 10-9
LVMH
    financial statements, usage, 1-3
    liabilities/equity, *15-16*
    property, plant, and equipment (item revaluation), 10-11–10-12

LVMH Group
    balance sheet presentation, differences, *4-46–4-47*
    consolidated income statements, 5-31
    consolidated statements of comprehensive gains/losses, 5-32

M

Machine disposal, example, 11-29–11-30
MACRS. *See* Modified Accelerated Cost Recovery System
Maintenance
    costs, 11-11
    expenditures, 10-26
Majority active investment, 1-34
Management
    flexibility, GAAP allowance, 11-26
    inventory cost flow assumption, selection considerations, 7-26–7-30
    performance, evaluation, 5-3
Management discussion and analysis (MD&A), 1-30
Managers, attestations, 1-32
Mandated tax life, 11-34
Manufacturer, profit (loss), *20-8*, 20-31
Marginal tax rate, 18-7
Markdown, 8-15
    cancellation, 8-15
    net markdown, 8-15
Marketable investments, accounting (summary), *13-17*
Marketable securities, 13-2
    investments, 4-16
Marketing, identifiable intangible asset, 12-13
Marketing-related intangible assets, 12-14
Market, inventory reduction (recording), 8-7–8-8
Market-related value, 19-11
Market value
    constraints, computation, *8-3*
    cost, comparison, 8-4
    determination, 8-3, 8-4
    method, 14-23
Marks & Spencer, inventory (presence), 8-2
Markup, 8-15
    cancellation, 8-15
    net additional markup, 8-15
Mars, Incorporate (closed corporation status), 15-4
MasterCard
    accounts receivable financing, 6-20
    credit card sales, 6-25
    Sam's Club acceptance, 6-25
Materiality, 2-12–2-13
Maturity date, definition, 14-3
McDonald's Corporation
    customer experiences, differentiation, 1-22
    franchise agreement, 12-15
    impairment/disposal disclosures, *11-30*
    sales, source, 1-18
MD&A. *See* Management discussion and analysis
Medicare benefits, 9-16
Memorandum entry, example, 15-22
Merchandise inventory, 7-3
Merck, intangible assets
    disclosure, *12-11–12-13*
    internal development costs, 12-3
mFoundry, app development (Starbucks payment), 12-14
Microsoft
    corporation identification, 1-9
    effective tax rates, reduction, 18-1
    enterprise resource planning software platform, licensing, 17-13
    intangible assets, amounts/useful lives, 12-14

Minimum lease payments, 20-8
    components, 20-2
    undiscounted minimum lease payments, 20-25
Minority active investment, 13-4
    accounting
        equity method, usage, 13-23
        procedures, 13-24–13-25
        process, 13-23–13-29
    company disclosures, 13-30
    equity method, application, 13-24
    influence, determination, 13-23
Minority passive investment, 13-3
Mixed attribute measurement model, 4-7–4-8
Modified Accelerated Cost Recovery System (MACRS), 11-33
    depreciation, usage, 18-11
    example, 11-34–11-35
    principles, 11-34–11-36
Modified cash basis method, 9-28–9-29
Modified cash flows, *14-37*
Monetary assets (financial assets), 4-5
Moody's, 4-33
Morgan Stanley, 5-2
Mortgage bonds, *14-4*
Most likely amount approach, 17-16
Moving average cost flow assumption (perpetual inventory system), *7-19*
Moving average method, 7-18
Moving costs, 10-28
Multiemployer plan (pension plans), 19-39
Multiple-step formats, 5-13–5-15
Multiple-step income statement, *5-14*

N

Natural resources
    cost, company determination, 11-31–11-32
    depletion, 4-18
Navistar Financial Corporation, accounts receivable financing, 6-20
NBC, Olympic games broadcast rights (cost), 12-15
Nearest whole month convention, 11-19–11-20
Nearest whole year convention, 11-20
Nestlé
    corporation identification, 1-9
    financial statements, usage, 1-3
    receivables disclosures, *6-32–6-33*
Nestlé Group, consolidated income statement, *5-33*
Net additional markup, 8-15
Net book value (carrying value), 3-20, 4-18
Net cash flow, net income conversion (adjustments), *21-17*
Netflix, present value example, 4-9–4-10
Net income, 5-5
    adjustments, 21-14
    noncontrolling interests, impact, 5-19–5-20
    performance measurement/reporting, 1-27
    realized gains/losses, company reporting, 13-15
    shareholders' equity/comprehensive income, relationship, *5-30*
    usage, 21-26
Net markdown, 8-15
Net periodic pension cost, 19-7
Net postretirement benefit expense, 19-42–19-44
    interest cost, 19-43
    net gain/loss, amortization, 19-43–19-44
    plan assets, expected return, 19-43
    prior service cost, amortization, 19-43
    service cost, 19-42–19-43
Net price method, 6-9–6-10
    conceptual evaluation, 7-14
    examples, 6-10–6-11, *6-11*
    usage, 7-13
Net profit margin, 5-38
Net realizable value (NRV), 4-13–4-14
    ceiling, 8-3
    examples, 4-13
    reporting, 6-9
Net sales revenues (net revenues), 5-15
Net share settlement, 14-24
New asset, capitalization, 10-26
Nike
    annual report, 9-5
    common shares, number (existence), 15-6
    current liabilities, 9-7
    debt disclosure, *14-36–14-37*
    FIFO change, justification, 22-5
    price/earnings ratio, 16-20
Nominal rate (contract rate/stated rate/face rate), 14-3
Nonavoidable (liability characteristic), 4-6
Noncancelable lease term, 20-8
Noncash consideration, 17-18
Noncash expenses, 21-27
Noncash investing activities, 21-4
Noncash items, 21-6
    classification, example, *6-4*
Noncash payments, number/value (distribution), *6-6*
Noncompensatory share purchase plans, company accounting process, 15-17
Noncontributory plan, 19-4
Noncontrolling interests, 4-7, 4-24–4-25, 16-17
    examples, 4-25
Noncounterbalancing errors, 22-20
Noncurrent accounts, changes, 21-26–21-27
Noncurrent assets, 3-25
Noncurrent liabilities, 3-25
Nondeductible financial accounting expenses, *18-17*
Non-interest-bearing note, 9-9–9-10
    example, 10-10
Non-interest-bearing notes payable, 9-8
Nonmonetary assets (nonfinancial assets), 4-5
    acquisition, cost, 10-13
    exchanges, 10-14
        accounting process, 10-13–10-16
        example, 10-13
Nonmonetary exchange, 10-13, 15-13
    example, 10-15
    fair value (usage), general rule (exception), 10-15
Nonqualified pension plans, 19-4
Nonreciprocal transfer, 10-10
Nonrecurring gains/losses, 5-17–5-18
Nontaxable financial accounting revenues, 18-17
Nontrade receivables, 6-7
Noodles & Company, lease obligations, *20-23*
No-par capital stock, 15-7
No-par stock, 15-7
North America Coffee Partnership, PepsiCo (joint venture), 13-1–13-2
Norwalk Agreement, 1-19
Notes
    company receipt, 13-33
    financial statements, 1-30
    receivable, 4-16
Notes payable, 9-8–9-10, 9-32
    cash, exchange, 14-30–14-31
    goods, exchange, 14-31–14-32
    guarantees, 14-32–14-33
    issuance, 14-28–14-30
    long-term notes payable, 14-1
    property, exchange, 14-31–14-32
    rights/privileges, exchange, 14-30–14-31
    services, exchange, 14-31–14-32
Notes receivable, 6-7
    company accounting process, 6-27–6-30
    equipment, exchange, 13-33–13-34
    fair value reporting, 6-30
    long-term notes receivable, 13-33–13-37
    sale, example, 6-29
    sales/assignments, 6-28–6-29
    short-term interest-bearing notes receivable, 6-27
    short-term non-interest-bearing notes receivable, 6-28
Notional amount, definition, 13-38
Not-sufficient funds (NSF), 6-36
Novartis, Nestlé ownership interests sale, 5-33
NRV. *See* Net realizable value
NSF. *See* Not-sufficient funds

O

O.A.S.D.I. *See* Old-Age, Survivor, and Disability Insurance
Obligation
    accumulated benefit obligation, 19-2, 19-10
    bonus obligations, 9-20
    callable by the creditor, 9-12
    constructive obligation, 17-10
    contingent obligations, 4-6, 9-1
    involvement, 9-3
    pension obligation, 19-10
    performance obligations, 17-10–17-15
    projected benefit obligation, 19-3
    vested benefit obligation, 19-3, 19-10
OCI. *See* Other comprehensive income
Off-balance-sheet financing, 20-5
Office Depot, accounts receivable transfer (disclosure), *6-26*
Oil and gas properties, 10-27–10-28
Old-Age, Survivor, and Disability Insurance (O.A.S.D.I.) benefits, 9-16
One-half year convention, 11-21
    partial period depreciation, *11-21*
OPEBs. *See* Other postemployment benefits
Open corporations (publicly traded corporations), 15-4
Operating activities, 1-4–1-5, 21-5–21-6
    adjustment, 21-20
    amounts determination, 9-14–9-22
    cash flows, *5-35*
        direct method, 21-10–21-14
        indirect method, 21-14–21-15
        reporting process, 21-9–21-17
    company operating activities, 5-34–5-35
    current assets/liabilities, relationship, 21-26
    definition, 21-3
    direct method, 5-37–5-38
    indirect method, 5-35
    net cash flows, net income conversion adjustments, *21-17*
    performance measurement/reporting, 1-25, 1-27
    section, preparation
        direct method, usage, 21-39–21-46
        spreadsheet method, usage, 21-42–21-46
    spreadsheet entries, 21-27
    Starbuck's, 1-24
    statement of cash flows, 1-28
Operating capability, 16-3
    assessment, 5-3
    profitability/leverage, multiplication, 5-42
    ratios (efficiency ratios) (activity ratios), 4-41–4-44
Operating cash flows
    diagram, 21-11–21-14
    direct method, example, *21-42*

income statement amounts, conversion adjustments, 21-12
operating cash flow to total liabilities ratio, 21-7
ratio, 21-7
Operating cash inflows, 21-10–21-11, 21-41
Operating cash outflows, 21-11, 21-41–21-42
Operating cycle, 4-16, 4-41
days in operating cycle, 4-44
Operating expenditures, 10-24
Operating expenses, 5-16
example, *5-17*
interim financial statements, 5-48
Operating income (loss), 5-17
discontinued operation, 5-23–5-24
Operating lease, 20-2, 20-3, 20-23
example, 20-24–20-25
initial indirect costs, involvement, 20-25
lessee
accounting, example, 20-11–20-12
contingent rental payments, 20-12
disclosure requirements, *20-22*
lessor accounting, 20-24–20-25
Operating loss carryback
conceptual issue, 18-20
definition, 18-19
example, 18-21–18-22
refund, *18-21*
Operating loss carrybacks/carryforwards, 18-3
accounting process, 18-19–18-27
conceptual issues, 18-20–18-27
flowchart, *18-20*
Operating loss carryforward
conceptual issue, 18-20–18-21
definition, 18-19
example, *18-22–18-23*
Operating margin, 5-38
Operating payments, 21-11
Opportunity cost, argument, 16-9
OPRBs. *See* Other postretirement benefits
Option pricing model, 15-20–15-23
usage, 15-22
Option value (fair value)
calculation, 15-20
increase, factors, 15-20
Orange County (California), derivative contracts losses, 13-38
Ordinary annuity, M-11
future value
cash flows amount, determination, *M-14*
diagram, *M-12*
present value
determination, solving, M-16–M-17
diagram, *M-16*, *M-19*
Ordinary annuity, future value computation process, M-12–M-15
applications, M-14
formula approach, M-12–M-13
table approach, M-13
Ordinary annuity, present value computation process, M-16–M-20
applications, M-19–M-20
formula approach, M-17–M-18
table approach, M-18–M-19
Ordinary loss, changes, 21-29–21-30
Other assets, 4-19
Other comprehensive income (OCI), 3-3, 13-43
Other current liabilities, 9-32
Other liabilities, 4-20
Other operating income items, 5-16
Other postemployment benefits (OPEBs), 19-40
Other postretirement benefits (OPRBs), 19-40
accounting
example, 19-45–19-47

principles, 19-42
conceptual overview, 19-41–19-42
disclosure, 19-45–19-47
GAAP requirement, 19-45
expense, computation, 19-43
liability, 19-44
pension plans, similarities/differences, 19-41–19-42
plan, funding (absence), 19-43
Other than temporary impairment, 13-21, 13-27
Output methods, 17-23
Outstanding accounts receivable, percentage, 6-14–6-15
Outstanding capital stock, 15-7
Outstanding checks, 6-35–6-36
Overall materiality test, 5-44
Overhead costs, 10-16–10-17
Ownership
control, separation, 1-6–1-7, *1-7*
transfer, absence (example), *20-15*
Owners, investments/distributions, 4-25

P

Paid-in capital, 4-22
accounts, 1-25
additional paid-in capital, 15-8
example, 4-22
Panera Bread
annual report data, 11-12–11-13
depreciable assets, disclosure, *11-18*
Panera Bread, inventory
disclosures, 7-27
turnover ratios (computation), 7-7
values/methods, disclosure, *7-27*
Parent company, 4-24
Parking transaction, 7-11
Partial billings account, 17-27
Partially participating preferred stock, 15-35
Partial period depreciation, 11-19–11-21
double-declining-balance, *11-20*
one-half year convention, *11-21*
straight-line, *11-19*
sum-of-the-years'-digits, *11-20*
Participating preferred stock, 15-34–15-35, 16-5–16-6
example, 16-6
Partnerships, creation, 7-2
Par value, 15-7
capital, excess, 15-8
face value, definition, 14-3
method (stated value method), 15-39
paid-in capital, excess, 15-8
par value per share increase, reverse stock split (usage), 15-13
stated value, 4-22, 15-7
stock, 15-7
Past employment, vacation pay (earning), 9-18
Patent, definition, 12-16
Payables, 4-19
Payments, control, 6-6
Payroll taxes
accounting, example, 9-17
employee withholdings, relationship, 9-16–9-17
example, *9-16*
Pension assets, 19-10–19-14
valuation, market-related value (usage), 19-11
Pension Benefit Guaranty Corporation (PBGC), 19-39
Pension expense
components, 19-7–19-10
definition, 19-7
interest cost, 19-7–19-8

pension funding, equivalence (example), 19-19–19-21
plan assets, return, 19-8–19-10
prior service cost amortization, inclusion (example), 19-27–19-30
service cost, 19-7
Pension funding, pension expense (inequality), 19-21–19-23
Pension obligation, 19-10
discount rate, usage, 19-10
Pension plans, 19-1
accounting
conceptual issues, 19-35–19-37
differences, 19-43–19-44
issues, 19-35–19-40
accumulated benefit obligation, 19-2
assets
actual return, 19-2, 19-8
expected return, 19-3, 19-7, 19-8, 19-43
presentation, 19-36
characteristics, 19-2–19-5
company accounting process, 19-5–19-18
contributions, actuarial funding method basis, 19-36
defined benefit plan, 19-3
defined contribution plan, 19-3
definition, 19-2
disclosure, 19-26–19-32
employee service amount, 19-36–19-37
expected returns, actual returns (differences), 19-23–19-25
funded status, 19-11
gain/loss, 19-3, 19-7, 19-9
adjustment, example, 19-12
information, *19-19*
legislation, 19-39
liabilities, conceptual issue, 19-36–19-37
multiemployer plan, 19-39
net gain/loss, amortization (computation), *19-30*
net gain/loss, corridor
amortization, 19-30–19-32
computation, *19-30*
net periodic pension cost, 19-7
nonqualified pension plans, 19-4
other postretirement benefits (OPRBs), similarities/differences, 19-41–19-42
prior service cost, 19-3
conceptual issue, 19-35
prior service cost amortization, 19-7, 19-9
calculation (technical issue), 19-37–19-39
years-of-future-service method, *19-39*
projected benefit obligation, 19-3, 19-10
qualified pension plans, advantages, 19-4
relationships (employees/company/asset management company), *19-5*
reporting issues, 19-37
retirees, amount payable, 19-37
service cost, 19-3
settlements/curtailments, 19-39
spreadsheet, 19-32, *19-32*
statement of cash flow disclosures, reporting issue, 19-37
technical issues, 19-37–19-40
termination liability, 19-37
terms, 19-2–19-3
types, 19-3–19-5
vested benefit obligation, 19-3
vested benefits
amount, 19-37
reporting issue, 19-37
Pension Protection Act of 2006, 19-37

PepsiCo
   historical cost example, 4-9
   North America Coffee Partnership, joint venture, 13-1–13-2
Performance
   comparison, 4-3
   measurement/reporting, 1-25–1-27
Performance-based compensatory share option plan, example, 15-25
Performance-based plan, 15-27
Performance-based share option plans (variable-term share option plans), 15-23–15-24
Performance obligations
   entity satisfaction, 5-7
   examples, *17-10*
   identification, 5-6
   identification process, 17-10–17-15
   satisfaction, 17-27
      criteria, 17-22
      revenue recognition methods, 17-23–17-24
   transaction price, allocation, 5-7
   process, 17-19–17-21
Period costs, 7-13
Periodic accounts (temporary accounts), 3-7
Periodic cash flows, determination, M-19–M-20
Periodic inventory, 3-15, 3-21–3-22
   example, 3-21
Periodic inventory system, 3-21, 7-6–7-7, *7-17*
   LIFO cost flow assumption, *7-20*
   lower of cost or market, application, 8-25–8-26
   perpetual inventory system, comparison, 7-8
   weighted average cost flow assumption, *7-18*
Periodic system, inventory to market reduction (recording), *8-26*
Period service cost, calculation, 19-8
Permanent accounts, 3-7
Permanent differences, 18-3
   accounting process, 18-16–18-19
   definition, 18-16
   example, 18-17–18-18
   existence, 21-38
   types, *18-17*
Perpetual inventory system, 3-9, 7-6
   FIF cost flow assumption, *7-17*
   LIFO cost flow assumption, *7-20*
   moving average cost flow assumption, *7-19*
   periodic inventory system, comparison, 7-8
Petty cash, 6-34–6-35
   example, 6-35
   system, design/operation, 6-34–6-35
Pfizer, stock repurchase, 15-1
Pixar, stock certificates, 15-5
Plan assets. *See* Pension plans
Plant assets, 10-3
Plant expansion funds, 13-36
Pledging, 6-20
Political environment, standard setting, 1-20–1-21
Post-closing trial balance, 3-28–3-29, 21-39
Postdated checks, 6-3
Posting, 3-13
Postretirement benefits
   accounting, 19-1
      process, 19-40–19-47
   accrued postretirement benefit cost, 19-44
   accumulated postretirement benefit obligation (APBO), 19-42
   attribution period (recognition period), 19-44, *19-44*
   expected postretirement benefit obligation (EPBO), 19-42
   net postretirement benefit expense, 19-42–19-44
Postretirement healthcare benefits, accrual, *19-46*
Potential common shares, 16-26
Pre-acquisition expenditures, accounting process, 10-24–10-25
Predictive value, 2-12
Preemptive rights, 15-5
Preferred shares, disclosures (FASB requirements), 15-43
Preferred stock, 4-23, 15-6
   callability, 15-33
   callable preferred stock, 15-37
   calling, example, 15-37
   change, 21-30
   characteristics, specification, 15-33
   conversion, example, 15-35
   convertible preferred stock, 15-35
   cumulative preferred stock, 15-34
   description, characteristics, 15-33–15-38
   dividends, preference, 15-33, 15-34
   dual rights, 15-36
   issuance, example, 15-36
   liquidation, preference, 15-38
   mandatory redemption, 15-33
   participating preferred stock, 15-34–15-35, 16-5–16-6
      example, 16-6
   redeemable preferred stock, 15-37–15-38
   retirement, funds usage, 13-36
   stock warrants, inclusion, 15-36–15-37
   voting rights, 15-38
Premiums, 9-29–9-30
   accounting, example, 13-7–13-8
   amortization
      process, 14-10–14-18
      schedule, effective interest method (example), *13-7*
   costs, association (GAAP requirements), 9-29–9-30
   example, 9-30
Prepaid expenses, 3-15–3-16
   adjusting entries
      effects, *3-15*
      example, 3-16
   omission, example, 22-23
Prepaid items, 4-17
Present value, 4-9–4-10
   calculations, summary, *M-26*, *M-27*
   company usage, M-3
   example, 4-9–4-10
   single sum computation process, M-9–M-11
   techniques, M-27–M-28
Present value of a deferred ordinary annuity ($PV_{deferred}$), M-24. *See also* Deferred ordinary annuity
Present value of an annuity due (PV_D), M-20. *See also* Annuity due
Present value of an ordinary annuity (PV_O), M-16. *See also* Ordinary annuity
Pretax financial income, 18-3
Pretax income, 5-18
Price/earnings ratio, 16-20
   importance, 16-24
Price indexes (Weston Company), *8-22*
Principal-agent contract considerations, 17-14–17-15
Principal, performance obligation, 17-14
Principals, 1-6
Principles, concepts/standards/rules (differences), 2-3–2-5
Prior period adjustments (restatements), 22-15
   accounting process, 16-13–16-14
      example, 16-13
   issues, 22-16

Prior service cost, 19-3
   adjustment, example, 19-12
   amortization, 19-7, 19-9, 19-43
      example, 19-38–19-39
      inclusion, example, 19-27–19-30
      years-of-future-service method, *19-39*
   conceptual issue, 19-35
   prospective accounting, 19-35
Privately held corporations (closed corporations), 15-4
Privileges, exchange, 14-30–14-31
Probable, event occurrence categorization, 9-23
Probable future economic benefit (economic resource characteristic), 4-4
Procter & Gamble, derivative contracts (impact), 13-38
Product
   costs, 7-12
   defining, 1-21–1-32
   financing arrangements, 7-9, 7-11
Profitability, evaluation, 5-3
   return on shareholders' equity (ROE), usage, 15-8–15-9
Profit margin, 8-3
Profit margin analysis, 5-38–5-39
   example, *5-39*
Profit test, 5-44
Projected benefit obligation, 19-3, 19-10
   definition, 19-7–19-8
Promised good/service, distinctiveness, 17-11
Property, cost/carrying value, 20-25
Property dividends, 16-7–16-8
   available-for-sale security distribution, 16-8
   investment securities (bonds) distribution, 16-7–16-8
Property exchange, 14-31–14-32
   example, 14-32
Property, plant, and equipment, 4-17–4-18
   acquisition, 10-1
      accounting process, 10-5–10-13
   characteristics, 10-3–10-5
   company recording, 10-3
      GAAP requirements, 10-3–10-4
   company review, GAAP requirement, 11-24
   disclosure, example, *10-4*
   disposal
      accounting process, 11-29–11-31
      international dimensions, 11-31
   impairment
      international dimensions, 11-28–11-29
   impairment, accounting process, 11-23–11-29
   importance, 10-7–10-8
   investments, 10-1
   revaluation, IFRS application, 10-12
   valuation, 10-11–10-12
Property taxes, 9-13–9-14
   example, 9-13
Prospective method (contract modification), 17-8–17-9, 22-3
   advantage, 22-4
Proxy statement, 1-10
Public corporations, 15-4
Publicly traded corporations (open corporations), 15-4
Publix Super Markets, inventory assumption, 7-27
Pulte Homes, net realizable value example, 4-13
Pulte Homes, operating tax carrybacks (impact), 18-19
Purchase
   allowance, 3-9, 8-20
   bargain purchase, 12-22
   discounts, 3-10, 7-13–7-14, 8-19
      accounting, alternative methods, *7-13*

lump-sum purchase, 10-9
    obligations, 7-11–7-12
        example, 7-12
    prices, increase, 7-21
    return, 3-9, 8-20
Purchased goodwill, 12-19–12-20
Purchased identifiable intangible assets, 12-3
Purchased intangible assets, capitalization, 12-3
Purchased unidentifiable intangible assets, 12-3
Purchaser, yield, 14-6
Purchases journal, 3-35
PV$_O$. *See* Present value of an ordinary annuity

Q

Qualcomm, mobile phone technology development/patents, 12-16
Qualified pension plans, advantages, 19-4
Quantitative impairment test, 12-21
Quarterly compound interest, computation, M-4
Quarterly statements (interim statements), 3-7
Quick assets, 4-40
Quick ratio, 4-40–4-41
Qwest Communications, financial statement misrepresentation, 1-32

R

Radio Shack, impairment losses, 11-2
Rate of change analysis, 4-33–4-35
    example, *5-40*
    usage, 5-39–5-40
Rate of return, depreciation (effect), *11-11*
Ratio analysis, 4-35
    usage, 5-40–5-42
Rational allocation, 5-10
Rational, term (meaning), 11-4
Raw materials, 4-16
    inventory, 7-3
Real estate leases, 20-38–20-41
    involvement, 20-41
Realized gains/losses, company reporting
    available-for-sale securities, 13-16–13-17
    trading securities, 13-15
Reasonably probable, event occurrence categorization, 9-23
Receipts, control, 6-5–6-6
Receivables, 4-16, 6-1
    classification, 6-32
    definition, 17-25
    disclosure process, 6-30–6-34
    fair value option, 6-32
    IFRS application, 6-33–6-34
    international perspective, 6-31–6-34
    long-term receivables, 13-1
    nontrade receivables, 6-7
    sale, 6-20
    trade receivables, 6-7
    turnover
        calculation, 6-19
        ratio, 6-18
    types, 6-7–6-8
Reclamation costs (restoration costs), definition, 11-32
Recognition
    differences, 9-25
    period (attribution period), 19-44, *19-44*
    process, 4-4
Reconciliations, 5-45
    net change, 21-6
Recourse, usage, 6-20
Recoverability test, 11-24, 12-5
Redeemable preferred stock, 15-37–15-38
Refinancing intention, 9-11

Refundable deposits, 9-12–9-13
    example, 9-13
Registrar, 15-5
Reinvested income, 16-2
Related party transactions, 4-31
Relevance, 2-12–2-13
    faithful representation, relationship, 2-14
Remote, event occurrence categorization, 9-23
Remote loss contingencies, 9-23–9-24
Renewal (replacement), 10-25
Repairs
    costs, 11-11
    expenditures, 10-26
Replacement (renewal), 10-25
Replacement cost, 8-3
Reportable segments, 5-44
    disaggregated financial information, example, 5-45–5-46
Reporting entity, changes, 22-3
    accounting process, 22-15
Reporting unit, 12-21
Research and development (R&D)
    activities
        elements, 12-9
        inclusion/exclusion, example, *12-7–12-8*
    company expensing, GAAP requirement, 12-9
    costs, accounting process, 12-7–12-11
    example, 12-10
    in-process R&D (IPR&D), 12-10
Research, definition, 12-7
Residual value (salvage value), 3-20, 11-2, 11-3
    consideration, absence, 11-34–11-35
    elimination, 11-34
    guarantee, lease renewal (impact), 20-41
Restatements (prior period adjustments)
    accounting process, 16-13–16-14
    issues, 22-16
Restoration costs (reclamation costs), definition, 11-32
Restricted share awards, 15-18
Restricted share unit plans (RSUs), 15-26–15-28
    example, *15-32*
Restrictions (appropriations), 16-14
Restructuring agreements, disclosure, 14-39–14-40
Retail average cost, example, 8-18–8-19
Retail FIFO, example, 8-17
Retail inventory method
    application, 8-16–8-19
    average cost, example, *8-18*
    conceptual evaluation, 8-20
    disclosure, 8-20–8-21
    example, 8-15
    FIFO, *8-17*
    LIFO, example, *8-18*
    lower of average cost or market, *8-19*
    requirements, 8-14
    terminology, 8-15–8-16
    usage, 8-3, 8-14–8-21
Retail LIFO, example, 8-18
Retail lower of average cost or market, example, 8-19
Retail method, adjustments, 8-19–8-20
Retail value, example, 8-17
Retained earnings, 3-3, 4-23–4-24, 16-1
    comparative retained earnings statements, FIFO (usage), *22-8*
    elements, 16-2
    example, 4-24
    net income, impact, 5-20
    reconciliation, *5-20*
    reduction/decrease, 16-12, 19-35

    restrictions (appropriations), 16-14
    section, dividends report, 15-3
    statement of retained earnings, 5-20, 16-16–16-17
        example, *16-17*
Retirees, pension plan amount payment, 19-37
Retirement benefits, accounting opportunity, 19-1
Retrospective adjustment
    example, 22-6–22-9
    impracticability, 22-11–22-12
Retrospective adjustment method, 22-3, 22-5–22-9
    disadvantages, 22-4
Return on assets, 4-36, 4-37–4-38
    examples, *4-37*, 4-37–4-38
Return on common equity, 4-36, 4-38
    decomposition, 5-41–5-42
    example, *4-37*
Return on investment (ROI), 4-36–4-38
    assessment, 5-3
Return on shareholders' equity (ROE), importance, 15-8–15-9
Return rate, depreciation (effect), *11-11*
Revenue recognition, 5-6–5-7, 6-8–6-9
    asset-liability approach, 17-3
    cash flows, relationship, 5-8
    company timing, 17-2–17-5
    disclosures, 17-25–17-26
        requirements, 17-25–17-26
    examples, 5-7, 5-9–5-10
    input methods, 17-23
    types, 17-23
    issues, 17-1
    methods, 17-23–17-24
    model, steps, 17-3–17-5, *17-4*
    output methods, 17-23
    point in time recognition, 17-35
    presentation, 17-25
    revenue recognition over time, 17-33–17-35
    timing, 17-21–17-25
        examples, 17-23
Revenues
    accrual, failure (example), 22-23
    calculation, *17-33–17-34*
    defining, 3-4
    FASB definition, 17-3
    income statement element, 5-6–5-9
    interim financial reports, 5-47–5-48
    timing, cash flows (contrast), 5-6–5-8
    valuation, 6-8–6-9
Revenue test, 5-44
Reverse stock split, usage, 15-13
Reversing entries
    alternative procedures, 3-32
    example, 3-32, *3-33*
    purpose, 3-31–3-34
Rights, exchange, 14-30–14-31
Risk
    assessment, 5-3
    financial flexibility ratios, relationship, 4-38
ROE. *See* Return on shareholders' equity
Royal Caribbean
    cash/cash equivalents, reports, 6-4, *6-5*
    cash flow
        information, *6-2*
        reliance, 6-1
    quarterly revenues (2013), *6-2*
Royal Dutch Shell, scrip dividend programs, 16-8
RSUs. *See* Restricted share unit plans
Rules, 2-4
    principles/concepts/standards, differences, 2-3–2-5

S

Saks, retail inventory method (usage), 8-14
Sale
    bill and hold sale, 7-11
    gain/loss, 5-24–5-25
    later accounting period, 5-24–5-25
        example, 5-25
    sale without recourse, 6-24
    sale with recourse, 6-24–6-25
        example, 6-25
Sale-leaseback transactions, 20-35–20-37
    purchaser-lessor accounting, 20-36
    seller-lessee accounting, 20-36
        example, 20-36–20-37
Sale of depreciable asset, 21-33
Sales
    allowances, 6-11–6-12
        example, 6-11–6-12
    journal, 3-35
    return, 6-11–6-12
        example, 6-11–6-12
    revenue, 5-15
    sales tax, inclusion (example), 9-21
Sales discounts (cash discounts), 6-9–6-11
    accounting
        gross price method, *6-11*
        net price method, *6-11*
    example, 6-9
    recording, 6-9–6-11
Sales tax, 9-21
    sales, separation (example), 9-21
Sales-type capital lease, 20-3, 20-23
Sales-type lease, 20-2
    changes, 20-41
    example, 20-31–20-33
    initial direct costs, involvement, 20-34
    lessor, 20-31–20-33
    renewal, 20-41–20-42
Salvage value (residual value), 3-20, 11-2, 11-3
    consideration, absence, 11-34–11-36
    elimination, 11-34
Sam's Club, credit cards (acceptance/restriction), 6-25
Sarbanes-Oxley Act of 2002, 1-32, 6-5
SARs. *See* Share appreciation rights
Schering-Plough, Merck acquisition, 12-3
Scrip dividends, 16-8
Secured borrowing, 6-20, 6-21–6-23
Securities
    available-for-securities, 13-3
    convertible securities, 16-29–16-31
    debt security, 13-2
    equity security, 13-2
    held-to-maturity securities, 13-3
    investment securities, 13-2
    investments, summary/conceptual discussion, 13-17–13-19
    marketable securities, 4-16, 13-2
    trading securities, 13-3
Securities and Exchange Commission (SEC)
    authority, 1-10
    international convergence, 1-19–1-20
    reporting requirements, 1-10
    role, 1-9–1-10
Securities, issuance, 10-10
Securitizations, 6-20, 6-23, 6-24
Segment manager, 5-44
Segment reporting, 5-43–5-47
    example, *5-46*
    reportable segments, 5-44
Self-constructed assets
    cost
        incremental overhead, inclusion, 10-16–10-17
        cost, determination, 10-16–10-24

        example, *10-21*
        international dimension, 10-23–10-24
        overhead portion, allocation, 10-16
Seller
    inventory, determination, *7-11*
    performance, customer benefit, 17-22
Separately identifiable promise, 17-11
Serial bonds, *14-4*
Service cost, 19-3, 19-42–19-43
    definition, 19-7
Service life (useful life), 11-2, 11-3
    limitation, factors, 11-3
Services, exchange, 14-31–14-32
Service-type warranties, 9-27, 9-29
Share appreciation rights (SARs), 15-18, 15-26, 15-28–15-30
    accounting, 15-28
        example, 15-29–15-30
    annual compensation expense, *15-29*
    usage, *15-28*
Share-based compensation plans
    accounting, 15-20
    conceptual evaluation, 15-33
    cost, company recognition, 15-21
    defining, 15-18–15-33
    disclosures, 15-30
        example, *15-30–15-32*
Share-based payment plans, international dimension, 15-25–15-26
Share capital, 15-16
Shareholders (stockholders)
    definition, 15-4
    rights, 15-5–15-6
Shareholders' equity, 1-24–1-25, 4-6–4-7, 4-21–4-22
    Accumulated Other Comprehensive Income, 15-3
    categories, 4-7
    changes, 16-17
        company reporting process, 16-15–16-19
    Contributed Capital section, 15-3
    decrease, 21-8
    defining, 3-3
    increase, 21-8
    information, 15-2–15-3
    international dimension, 15-16, 16-19
    net income/comprehensive income, relationship, *5-30*
    noncontrolling interest, 16-17
    Retained Earnings section, 15-3
    statement, example, *16-2*
    treasury stock, relationship, *15-41*
Share options, 16-27–16-29
    example, 16-29
    received, recorded value, 15-23
    vesting, 15-21
Shares, change (treasury stock method), *16-28*
Share warrants, 16-27–16-29
Short-term debt, 4-19
    refinancing expectation, 9-11–9-12
        example, 9-11
    repayment/replacement, 9-12
Short-term financing techniques, 9-10
Short-term interest-bearing notes receivable, 6-27–6-28
Short-term investments, 4-16, 21-35–21-37
Short-term non-interest-bearing notes receivable, 6-28
Short-term notes receivable/payable, 21-21
Sick pay, 9-18
Simple capital structure, 16-21
Simple interest
    compound interest, contrast, M-4–M-5
    definition, M-4

Simple statement of cash flows, *21-20*
Single future deductible amount, example, 18-14
Single future taxable amount, example, 18-10–18-11
Single-step formats, 5-13–5-15
Single-step income statement, *5-13*
Single sum, future value computation process, M-5–M-9
    application, M-7–M-9
    calculation, M-6
    diagram, *M-5*
        interest rate determination, *M-8*
    formula approach, M-6–M-7
    idea, M-5–M-6
    table approach, M-7
Single sum, present value computation process, M-9–M-11
    application, M-10–M-11
    diagram, *M-9*
        interest rate determination, *M-11*
    formula approach, M-9–M-10
    idea, M-9
    table approach, M-9–M-10
Sinking funds, 6-3, 13-36
Slide, occurrence, 3-14
Social security taxes, 9-16
Software development costs, 12-16–12-18
    accounting, *12-17*
    internal use, 12-18
Solely payments of principal and interest (SPPI), 13-26
Solvency, indication, 13-4
Sony, goods conversion, 7-3
Source documents, 3-5
Southwest Airlines, sale-leaseback transactions, 20-35–20-36
Special journals, 3-35
    usage process, 3-9, 3-34
Specific identification
    inventory cost assumption, 7-15–7-16
    usage, 8-3
SPPI. *See* Solely payments of principal and interest
Spreadsheet (worksheet), 3-29–3-31
    completion, 21-26–21-31, 21-44–21-45
    entries, 21-27
    final entry, preparation, 21-31, 21-45
    preparation, 21-26, 21-43–21-44
Spreadsheet method, 21-18
    comprehensive example, 21-24
    direct method, 21-42–21-45
    steps, 21-24–21-32
    usage, 21-23–21-32
Stadium construction, recording (journal entries), *17-29–17-30*
Stakeholders
    company stakeholders, 1-5
    identification, 1-5–1-6
Stand-alone price, estimation methods, *17-20*
Standard and Poor's, 4-33
Standard and Poor's 500 (S&P500), share buybacks, 15-1
Standard-setting process, FASB Conceptual Framework (relationship), *2-4*
Standards, principles/concepts/rules (differences), 2-3–2-5
Starbuck's Corporation
    accounts payable turnover, computation, 4-43
    accounts receivable turnover, computation, 4-43
    accumulated other comprehensive income (AOCI), example, 4-24
    annual report data, 11-12–11-13
    asset retirement obligations, 10-8

assets, 1-24
    building, 10-16
balance sheet, 3-15, 3-17, 3-18, 4-6
    analysis, common-size analysis (usage), 4-33
    information, example, 4-35
    time value of money concepts, M-2
brand name
    resource, 4-5
    value, 12-2
brand value, increase, 12-19
business, 1-22
cash flow statement, 21-1
    examination, 21-5
commercial paper program, 9-10
common stock, price level, 4-22
consolidated balance sheets, *1-23*
    common-size analysis, *4-34*
    rate of change analyses, example, *4-36*
consolidated statement of cash flows, *1-29*
consolidated statement of comprehensive income, *1-26*
consolidated statement of earnings, *1-26*
consolidated statement of equity, *1-31*
consolidated statements of earnings, *5-27–5-28*
contingent loss example, *4-30*
contributed capital, *15-44*
current liabilities, 9-1, 21-7
current replacement cost example, 4-13
customer experience, improvement, 12-14
days in operating cycle, 4-44
debt ratios, example, *4-39*
deferred revenue, reporting, 9-15
defined contribution disclosure, *19-6*
disclosure, 5-27, 18-31
domestic company status, 15-4
earnings-based interest coverage ratio, 5-41
earnings before income taxes, 5-19
earnings per share disclosures, *16-35*
employee stock purchase plan (ESPP), description, 15-17
equipment reports, 10-6
Experience, 1-22
facilities, 20-1
fair value example, 4-12
FIFO, adoption, 22-5
financial analysis firms, tracking, 5-2
financial statements, 1-3, 3-2
    analysis, liquidity ratios, *4-40*
    analysis, operating capability ratios, *4-41–4-42*
    analysis, return on investment ratios, *4-37*
    analysis, risk and financial flexibility ratios, *4-38*
    notes, 4-27
financing cash payments, 21-4
finished goods inventory, 7-3
franchise, absence, 12-15
historical cost example, 4-8–4-9
identifiable intangible assets, 12-3
income statement
    common-size analysis, *5-39*
    operating expenses, categories, 5-16
    preparation, 5-14
    profit margin analysis, *5-39*
    rate of change analysis, *5-40*
    total net revenues, 515
income taxes, analysis, *18-31–18-33*
independent auditor statement, 1-32
indirect method, usage, 21-14
inventory
    composition, *7-2*
    cost flow assumption, change, 22-3

inclusion, 7-2
    report, 7-1
    turnover, 4-42
    turnover ratios, computation, 7-7
investing activities, 1-24
    focus, 21-4
investments, 13-1
    trading securities classification, 13-3
leasehold improvements, 10-7
liabilities, 1-24
licensing agreements, 17-12
logo, registered trademark, 12-2
net income, generation (examples), 4-37, 4-38
noncontrolling interests, example, 4-25
operating activities, 1-24
    cash provision, 21-3
operating cash flow to total liabilities ratio, 21-7
operating income, litigation charges, 5-16
operating leases, 20-12
organization, 15-4
performance obligation, 17-10
    satisfaction, 17-22
purchase commitments, 7-11
quarterly dividend, declaration, 16-4
rate of return for common equity shareholders, generation, 5-42
raw materials inventory, 7-3
real assets, compound rate of change (computation), 4-35
retail store locations, 20-1
revenue recognition, 5-8, 17-1
    example, *5-9–5-10*
revenue sources, 16-1
sales commission award, 17-24
sales tax, liability (recording), 9-21
service life, measurement, 11-3
share-based compensation plans, disclosure, *15-30–15-32*
share-based compensation programs, 15-18
shareholders' equity, changes, *16-18–16-19*
Starbucks Experience, 12-2, 12-19
Starbucks Mobile App for iPhone, usage, 12-14
statement of cash flows, 5-36
statement of shareholder's equity, example, 4-26
stock splits, 15-13
Stored Value Card Liability, 5-8
stored value cards, 4-19
subsequent event example, *4-30*
total assets
    example, 4-34–4-35
    report, 4-1
total contributed capital example, 4-23
total interest costs, 10-23
total net earnings, 5-20
total revenues, generation, 4-44
uncertain tax position disclosure, *18-35–18-36*
Start-up activities, expensing (GAAP requirement), 12-10
Start-up costs, 12-120
Stated interest rate, example, 10-9
Stated rate (contract rate/face rate/nominal rate), 14-3
Stated value (par value), 4-22, 15-7
    method (par value method), 15-38
Statement of cash flows, 1-28, 4-2, 21-1
    classifications, usage, 21-3–21-5
    company reporting process, 5-34–5-38
    completion, 5-36–5-37
    comprehensive statement of cash flows, example, *21-32*

    content, 21-5–21-6
    direct method, example, *21-46*
    disclosures, 19-37
    examples, *3-26–3-27, 5-36, 21-5, 21-22–21-23*
    financing activities, 1-28
    information
        analysis process, 5-38–5-43
        importance, 21-7
        provision, 21-2–21-9
        usage, 21-6–21-7
    international dimension, 21-16
    investing activities, 1-28
    lessee presentation, 20-22
    operating activities, 1-28
    overview/uses, 5-34
    preparation, 21-31, 21-45
    preparation process
        spreadsheet method, usage, 21-23–21-32
        visual inspection method, usage, 21-18–21-23
    presentation, 21-5–21-6
    reporting, 5-34–5-37
        process, 21-2–21-9
    simple statement of cash flows, example, *21-20*
    special items, accounting process, 21-33–21-39
    summarization, 3-7
    usage, 3-26
Statement of comprehensive income, example, 5-29
Statement of financial position (balance sheet), 1-22
    purpose, 4-3
Statement of retained earnings, 5-20, 16-16–16-17
    example, *16-17*
Statement of shareholders' equity (statement of changes in shareholders' equity), 1-28, 1-30, 4-1, 4-2
    defining, 4-25–4-26
    example, *4-26*
    information, 3-7
    usage/example, *3-25*, *3-25*
Statements of Financial Accounting Concepts (Concept Statements), 2-3
Statutory tax rate, 18-1, 18-17
Stock
    buybacks, 15-1
    cash, combination, 14-24
    certificate
        definition, 15-5
        illustration, *15-6*
    combined sales, 15-12
    common stock, 4-22, 15-6
    fair value, example, 15-13
    issuance costs, 15-11
    nonmonetary issuance, 15-13
    no-par stock, 15-7
    original issuances, 15-41
    par value, 15-41
    preferred stock, 4-23, 15-6
    redemption funds, 13-37
    reissuance, 15-41
    rights, 14-20
    splits, 15-13–15-14, 16-12, 16-22–16-24
        examples, 15-14, 16-23
        reverse stock split, usage, 15-13
    subscriptions, 15-11–15-12
        contract, example, 15-11–15-11
    Treasury stock, 4-23, 15-7
    warrants, 14-20, 15-14–15-15
        attachment, 15-33

detachable stock warrants, usage, 14-20–14-21
inclusion, 15-36–15-37
Stock dividends, 16-9–16-12, 16-22–16-24
accounting, flowchart, *16-10*
conceptual issues, 16-9
declaration/issuance, 21-31
examples, 16-11–16-12, 16-23
fractional shares, 16-12
GAAP, usage/requirements, 16-10
ordinary distribution, 16-9
Stockholders (shareholders), definition, 15-4
Straight-line depreciation, 3-20
example, *11-5*
expense, calculation, 11-5
Straight-line method, 11-5–11-6, 14-10, 14-14–14-15
Straight-line partial period depreciation, *11-19*
Strike price (exercise price), 15-14
Subscribed capital stock, 15-7
Subscription contract, example, 15-11–15-12
Subsequent events, 4-29–4-31
example, *4-30*
Subsidiary company, 4-24
Subsidiary ledgers
example, *3-34*
usage process, 3-34
Substitution, 10-25
Successful-efforts method, 10-27
Summarized interim financial data, preparation/disclosure, 5-50
Sum-of-the-years'-digits method, 11-6
partial period depreciation, *11-20*
SunTrust Bank
fair value example, 4-11
loan portfolio, monetary asset representation, 4-13
net realizable value example, 4-13
Suppliers, payments, 21-11
Supporting documents, 3-5
Swap derivative liability/loss, existence, 13-41
Systematic allocation, 5-10
Systematic, term (meaning), 11-4

T

T-account format, usage, 3-5–3-6
Tangible assets, 4-5
Target
agreements, 7-2
inventory, presence, 8-2
land purchase, 10-5
retail inventory method, usage, 8-14
Taxable income
amount, 18-3
computation, example, *18-18*
entries, 18-9–18-15
examples, 18-10–18-11
Taxes
benefit, 18-34
depreciation schedules, *18-12*
effective tax rate, 18-1
income taxes, 9-21–9-22
intraperiod income tax allocation, impact (process), 18-27–18-29
marginal tax rate, 18-7
position, 1834
return, reporting (IRC usage), 18-2
statutory tax rate, 18-1
temporary differences, 18-1
uncertain tax positions, accounting issues, 18-34–18-35
Teavana, Starbucks acquisition, 12-2, 13-1, 22-3
Technological feasibility, 12-17

Technology
identifiable intangible assets, 12-13
technology-based intangible assets, 12-16–12-18
Temporary accounts (periodic accounts), 3-7
Temporary differences, 18-1, 18-3
definition, 18-4
example, 18-17–18-18
impact, *18-5–18-6*
measurement, 18-7–18-8
Tentative diluted earnings per share, computation, 16-31, *16-31*
Termination liability, 19-37
Termination rights (contracts), 17-5–17-6
Terms, modification, 14-36
equity/asset exchange, combination, 14-39
Tiffany and Company, sale-leaseback transactions, 20-35–20-36
Tiffany's, inventory turns, 7-7
Time-based methods, 11-4, 11-5–11-8
Time-based plan, 15-27
Time-based restricted share plan, example, 15-27–15-28
Timeliness, 2-15
Time-series analysis, 4-32–4-33
Times-interest-earned ratio, definition, 14-12
Time value of money, 17-15–17-16
defining, M-3–M-5
Timing differences, 18-4
Total asset turnover, 4-44
Total contributed capital, 4-23
Toyota Corporation
corporation identification, 1-9
goods conversion, 7-3
sales, source, 1-18
Toys 'R' Us, revenues (seasonal variations), 5-47–5-48
Trade accounts payable (accounts payable), 9-8
Trade discounts, 6-9
Trademark (trade name), definition, 12-14
Trade receivables, 6-7
accounting, overview, 6-8, *6-8*
Trading categories, transfers, 13-19
Trading securities, 13-3
company disclosure, 13-29
initial cost, recording, 13-11
interest/dividend income, recording, 13-11–13-12
investments
classification, 13-30
company reporting, 13-4
example, *13-11*
measurement/reporting process, 13-10–13-13
sales, realized gains/losses, 13-13
short-term investments, 21-37
Trading securities
unrealized holding gains/losses, recognition, 13-12–13-13
Transaction price
allocation, 5-7
allocation process, 17-19–17-21
changes, 17-21
circumstances, change (example), 17-21
definition, 17-15
determination, 5-6–5-7
process, 17-15–17-19
noncash consideration, 17-18
stand-alone price, estimation methods, *17-20*
time value of money, 17-15–17-16
variable consideration, 17-16–17-18
Transactions, 3-5
example, *3-10–3-11*
parking transaction, 7-11
related party transactions, 4-31

Transfer (liability characteristic), 4-6
Transfer agent, 15-5
Transfers
investments (accounting process), 13-19–13-22
investments between categories, 13-19–13-21
Transposition, 3-14
Travel advances, 6-3
Treasury stock, 4-23, 15-7
accounting process, 15-38–15-43
balance sheet presentation, 15-40
corporation acquisition, reasons, 15-38
cost method, 15-39–15-41
example, 15-39
journal entries, *15-40*
defining, 15-38–15-43
handling, shareholder best interest, 15-39
method, 16-28
example, *16-28*
steps, 16-28–16-29
par value method, 15-39, 15-41–15-42
example, 15-42
journal entries, *15-42*
reissuance, 15-41
retirement, cost method (usage), 15-41
shareholders' equity, relationship, *15-41*
Trial balance, 3-14
Troubled debt restructurings, 14-35–14-42
accounting, conceptual evaluation, 14-42
agreements, disclosure, 14-39–14-40
creditor accounting, *14-42*
process, 14-40–14-42
creditor journal entries, 14-41
debtor accounting process, 14-37–14-40
terms, modification, 14-36, 14-40–14-41

U

Unasserted claims, 9-26
Uncertain tax positions
accounting issues, 18-34–18-35
disclosure, example, *18-35–18-36*
example, 18-35
Uncertainty, obligating event (relationship), 9-23
Uncollectible accounts, allowance, 3-20–3-21
Uncollectible accounts receivable
allowance method, 6-13–6-18
direct write-off method, 6-18–6-19
estimation process, 6-12–6-19
Uncollectible amounts, writing off, 6-17
Under Armour
annual report, 9-5
price/earnings ratios, 16-20
Undiscounted minimum lease payments, 20-25
Unearned revenue (deferred revenue), 3-17–3-18, 4-19
defining, 9-15
items, 9-32
omission, example, 22-22
Unfiled lawsuits, 9-26
Unguaranteed residual value, 20-34
example, *20-8*
Unidentifiable intangible assets, 12-3
accounting process, 12-19–12-24
Unit
cash-generating unit, 12-23
depletion rate, calculation, 11-32
reporting unit, 12-21
United Technologies, long-term construction contracts, 17-26
Units-of-production method (activity methods), 11-8–11-9
Units, relationship (illustration), *7-15*

Unrealized holding gains/losses
    available-for-sale securities, 13-15–13-16
    cumulative net unrealized holding gains, 13-15
    trading securities
        definition, 13-12
        recognition, 13-12–13-13
Unstated interest rate, finding (example), M-8, M-10–M-11
Unusual gains/losses, 5-17–5-18
Upfront initiation fees, example, 17-12
Upfront payments, 17-11–17-12
Useful life (service life), 11-2, 11-3
Use methods (activity methods), 11-4
Use tax, 9-21

V

Vacation benefits, example, 9-19–9-20
Vacation pay
    accrual, making, 9-18–9-19
    earning, 9-18
Vacation time, 9-18
Valuation allowance, 18-8
    deferred tax asset, relationship (example), 18-15
    example, 18-22–18-23
Vanguard (asset management company), 19-2
Variable consideration, 17-16–17-18
    amounts, determination, 17-16–17-17
    applicable constraint, existence (assessment), 17-17–17-18
Variable-term share option plans (performance-based share option plans), 15-23–15-24
Verifiability, 2-15
Verizon Communications
    annual report, 14-12
    capital expenditures, 10-2
    gains/losses, expensing, 19-10
    property, plant, and equipment (asset size), 10-1
        disclosure, *10-4*

service contract, 17-19
    10-K information, 10-7–10-8
Vested benefit obligation, 19-3, 19-10
Vested, term (usage), 15-21
VF Corporation, accounts receivable disclosure, 6-30, *6-31*
VISA
    accounts receivable financing, 6-20
    credit card sales, 6-25
Visual inspection, direct method, 21-40–21-42
Visual inspection method
    definition, 21-18
    examples, 21-18–21-20, 21-40–21-41
    steps, 21-18
    usage, 21-18–21-23
Vodafone Group plc, foreign corporation status, 15-4
Volkswagen, domestic company/foreign corporation, 15-4
Voluntary deductions, *9-16*
Voluntary payroll deductions, 9-17
Voting rights, 15-5, 15-38
    absence, 14-2, 15-33

W

Wall Street Journal, The (earnings release coverage), 5-1
Wal-Mart
    agreements, 7-2
    goods production, absence, 7-3
    inventory, presence, 8-2
    retail inventory method
        disclosure, *8-20–8-21*
        usage, 8-14
Warranties, types, 9-27
Warrants
    detachable warrants, 14-23, 15-15, 15-36
    exercise, example, 15-36
    share warrants, 16-27–16-29
Warranty obligations, 9-27–9-27
Weighted average accumulated expenditures, 10-19

borrowed amount, example, 10-19–10-21
Weighted average cost flow assumption (periodic inventory system), *7-18*
Weighted average method, 7-18
Weighted average shares, 16-22, *16-22*
    comparative weighted average shares, *16-23*
Wells Fargo, bonds issuance, 14-4
Weston Company
    cost and retail values, *8-22*
    dollar-value LIFO retail inventory method, *8-23*
    price indexes, *8-22*
Wholly unperformed contract, definition, 17-5
Withholdings, accounting (example), 9-17
Working capital, 4-39
Work in process inventories, 4-16
Work-in-process inventory (goods-in-process inventory), 7-3
    account, increase, 11-9
Worksheet (spreadsheet)
    example, *3-30*
    usage process, 3-29–3-31
World Bank, intangible assets growth estimate, 12-1
Write-down, recording, 11-25

Y

Yahoo!, earnings release coverage, 5-1
Yahoo! Finance, bond price (quote), 14-6
Years-of-future-service method, *19-39*
Yield (effective rate), 14-4–14-5

Z

Zero-coupon bonds (deep-discount bonds), 14-16
    example, *14-4*